Europe

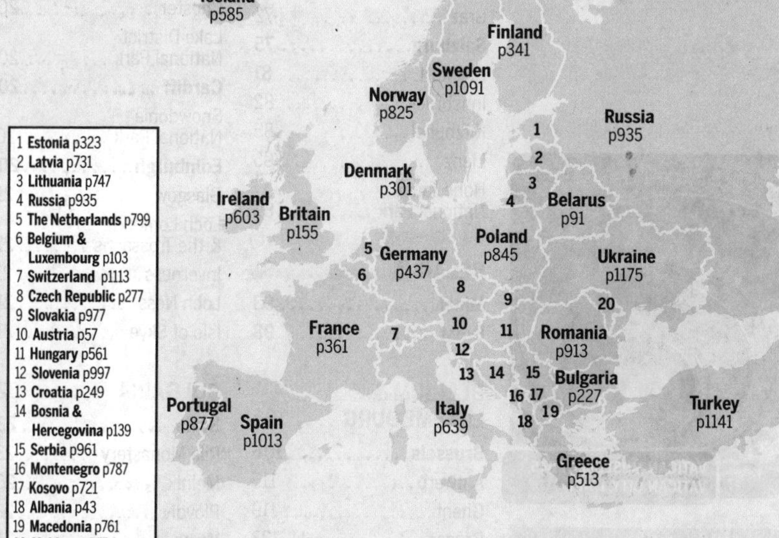

THIS EDITION WRITTEN AND RESEARCHED BY

Alexis Averbuck, Carolyn Bain, Mark Baker, Kerry Christiani, Marc Di Duca, Peter Dragicevich, Mark Elliott, Steve Fallon, Emilie Filou, Duncan Garwood, Anthony Ham, Catherine Le Nevez, Jessica Lee, Tom Masters, Anja Mutić, Sally O'Brien, Becky Ohlsen, Simon Richmond, Andrea Schulte-Peevers, Tamara Sheward, Helena Smith, Andy Symington, Luke Waterson and Neil Wilson

PLAN YOUR TRIP

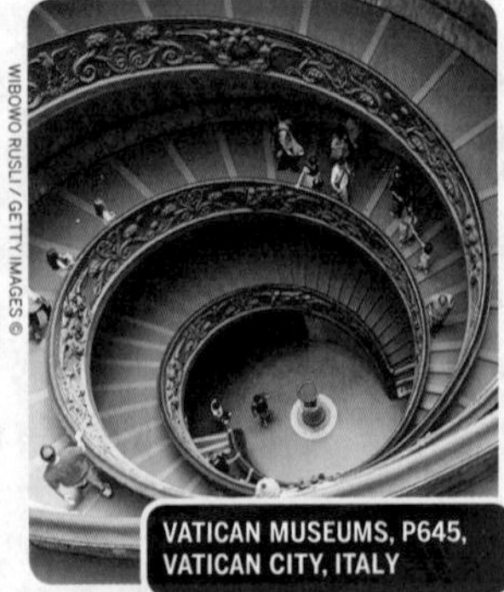
WIBOWO RUSLI / GETTY IMAGES ©

VATICAN MUSEUMS, P645, VATICAN CITY, ITALY

WIBOWO RUSLI / GETTY IMAGES ©

ARC DE TRIOMPHE, P369, PARIS, FRANCE

ON THE ROAD

Contents

ON THE ROAD

Contents

SURVIVAL GUIDE

Welcome to Europe

There simply is no way to tour Europe and not be awestruck by its scenic beauty, epic history and dazzling artistic and culinary diversity.

Cultural Heritage

Europe's almost unmanageable wealth of attractions is its biggest single draw: the birthplace of democracy in Athens, the Renaissance art of Florence, the graceful canals of Venice, the Napoleonic splendour of Paris, and the multilayered historical and cultural canvas of London. Less obvious, but no less impressive attractions include Moorish palaces in Andalucía, the remains of one of the Seven Wonders of the World in Turkey, the majesty of meticulously restored Imperial palaces in Russia's former capital St Petersburg and the ongoing project of Gaudí's La Sagrada Família in Barcelona.

Glorious Scenery

There's breathtaking natural scenery: rugged Scottish Highlands with glens and lochs; Norway's fabulous fjords, seemingly chipped to jagged perfection by giants; the vine-raked valleys of the Loire; and Cappadocia's fairy-tale landscape. If you're looking for beaches, a circuit of the Mediterranean's northern coast reveals one gem after another. Or strike out to lesser known, yet beautiful coastal regions such as the Baltic and Black Seas. Mountain lovers should head to the Alps: they march across central Europe taking in France, Switzerland, Austria, northern Italy and tiny Liechtenstein.

Raise a Glass

Europe has some of the best nightlife in the world. Globally famous DJs keep the party going in London, Berlin and Paris, all of which also offer top-class entertainment, especially theatre and live music. Other key locations for high-energy nightlife include Moscow, Belgrade, Budapest and Madrid, while those hankering for something more cosy can add Dublin's pubs or Vienna's cafes to their itinerary. Continue to party on the continent's streets at a multiplicity of festivals and celebrations, from city parades attended by hundreds of thousands to intimate concerts in an ancient ampitheatre.

Magnificent Menus

Once you've ticked off the great museums, panoramic vistas and energetic nightlife, what's left? A chance to indulge in a culinary adventure to beat all others, that's what! Who wouldn't want to snack on pizza in Naples, souvlaki in Santorini or even haggis in Scotland? But did you also know that Britain has some of the best Indian restaurants in the world; that Turkey's doner kebab is a key part of contemporary German food culture; and that in the Netherlands you can gorge on an Indonesian rijsttafel (rice table)? Once again Europe's diversity and global reach is its trump card.

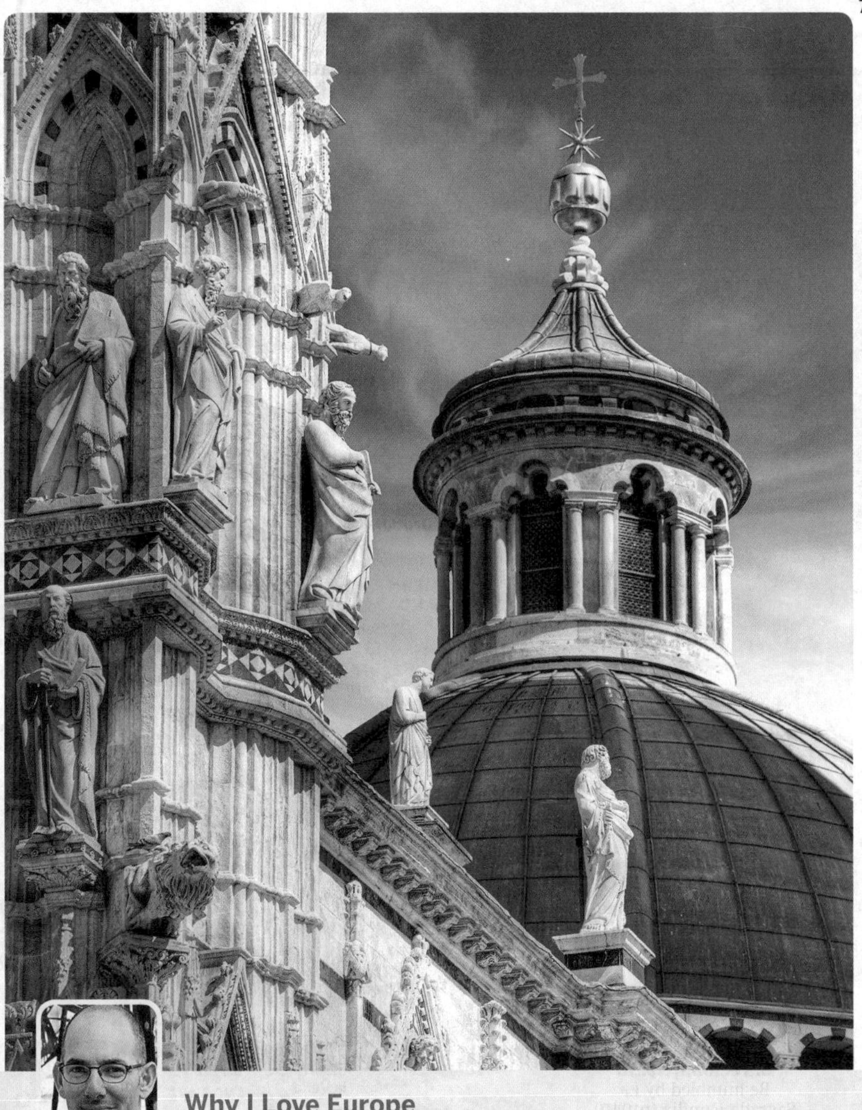

Why I Love Europe

By Simon Richmond, Writer

You're likely to feel a little overwhelmed, but once you dive into Europe, these fears will be replaced by wonder and fascination – plus something, perhaps, unexpected: a sense of connection. Very few, if any places in the world, remain untouched by European history, culture and influence. As continents go, Europe's broad variety and excellent transport infrastructure – be it air or roads, or the old standby of the Grand Tour, rail – is hard to beat and is sure to push you on to new experiences and unexpected discoveries.

For more about our writers, see page 1248

Above: Dome and facade, Siena Duomo (p694), Italy

Europe

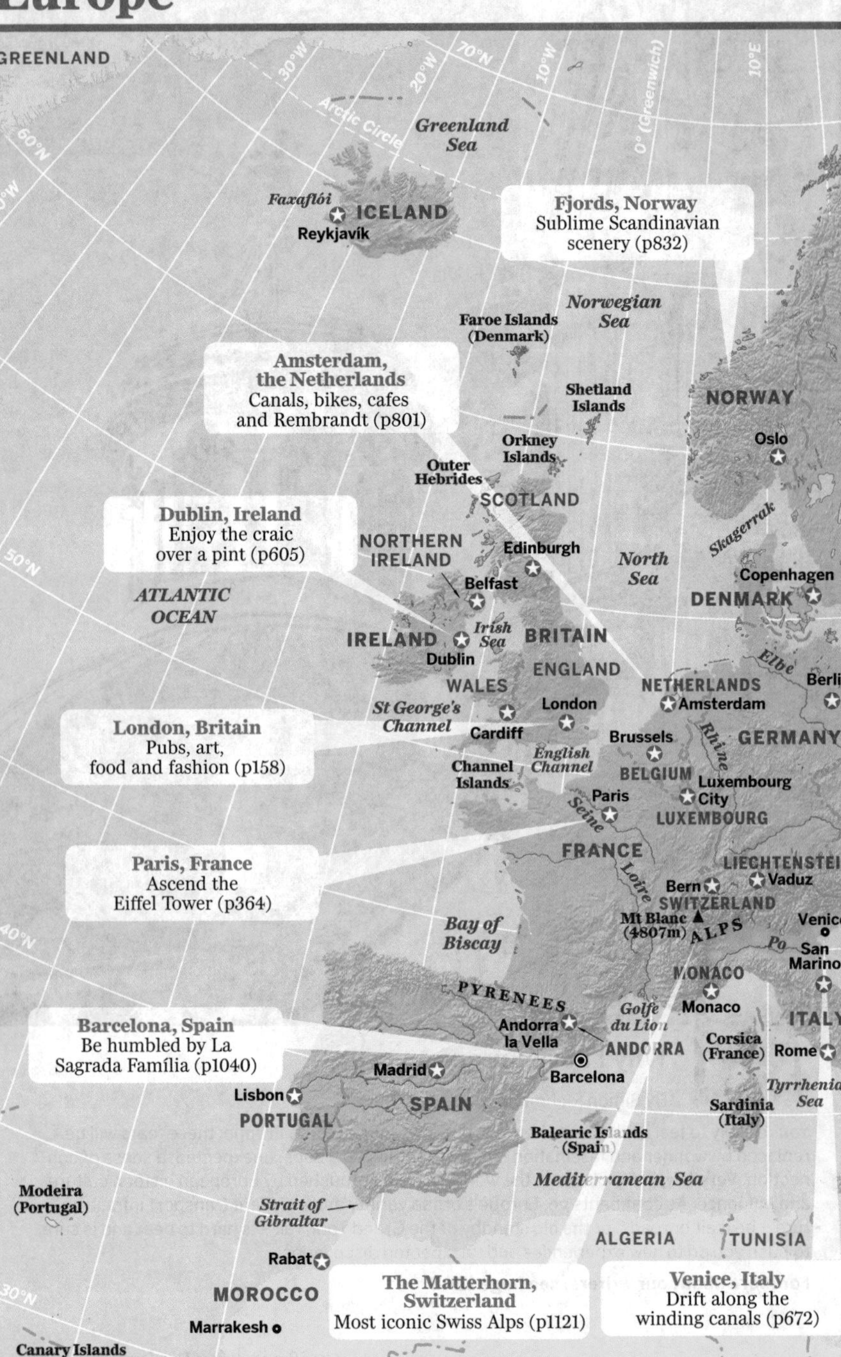

GREENLAND
Greenland Sea
Arctic Circle
Faxaflói
ICELAND
Reykjavík
Fjords, Norway
Sublime Scandinavian scenery (p832)
Norwegian Sea
Faroe Islands (Denmark)
Amsterdam, the Netherlands
Canals, bikes, cafes and Rembrandt (p801)
Shetland Islands
NORWAY
Oslo
Orkney Islands
Outer Hebrides
SCOTLAND
Dublin, Ireland
Enjoy the craic over a pint (p605)
NORTHERN IRELAND
Edinburgh
North Sea
Skagerrak
Copenhagen
DENMARK
ATLANTIC OCEAN
Belfast
IRELAND
Dublin
Irish Sea
BRITAIN
ENGLAND
WALES
Elbe
NETHERLANDS
Amsterdam
Berlin
London, Britain
Pubs, art, food and fashion (p158)
St George's Channel
Cardiff
London
Brussels
Rhine
GERMANY
English Channel
Channel Islands
BELGIUM
Luxembourg City
Paris
Seine
LUXEMBOURG
Paris, France
Ascend the Eiffel Tower (p364)
FRANCE
Loire
LIECHTENSTEIN
Vaduz
Bern
SWITZERLAND
Mt Blanc (4807m)
ALPS
Venice
Bay of Biscay
Po
San Marino
MONACO
Monaco
PYRENEES
Golfe du Lion
Andorra la Vella
ANDORRA
ITALY
Barcelona, Spain
Be humbled by La Sagrada Família (p1040)
Corsica (France)
Rome
Barcelona
Madrid
Lisbon
SPAIN
PORTUGAL
Tyrrhenian Sea
Sardinia (Italy)
Balearic Islands (Spain)
Mediterranean Sea
Modeira (Portugal)
Strait of Gibraltar
ALGERIA
TUNISIA
Rabat
MOROCCO
The Matterhorn, Switzerland
Most iconic Swiss Alps (p1121)
Venice, Italy
Drift along the winding canals (p672)
Marrakesh
Canary Islands (Spain)

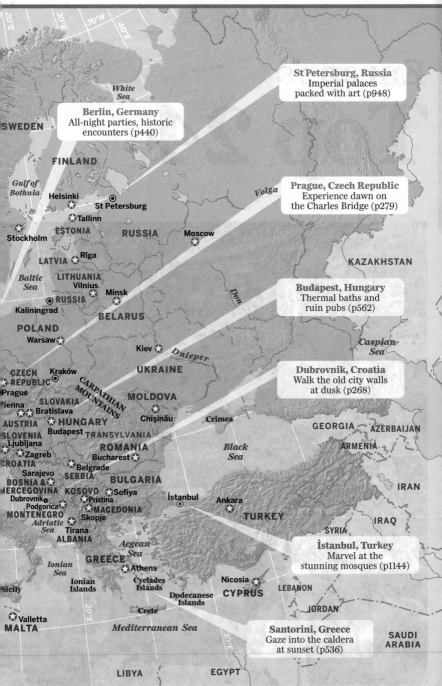

St Petersburg, Russia
Imperial palaces packed with art (p948)

Berlin, Germany
All-night parties, historic encounters (p440)

Prague, Czech Republic
Experience dawn on the Charles Bridge (p279)

Budapest, Hungary
Thermal baths and ruin pubs (p562)

Dubrovnik, Croatia
Walk the old city walls at dusk (p268)

İstanbul, Turkey
Marvel at the stunning mosques (p1144)

Santorini, Greece
Gaze into the caldera at sunset (p536)

20°E
30°E
70°N
40°E
White Sea
SWEDEN
FINLAND
Gulf of Bothnia
Helsinki
St Petersburg
Volga
Tallinn
ESTONIA
Stockholm
RUSSIA
Moscow
Rīga
LATVIA
KAZAKHSTAN
Baltic Sea
LITHUANIA
Vilnius
Minsk
Don
RUSSIA
Kaliningrad
BELARUS
POLAND
Warsaw
Caspian Sea
Kiev
Dnieper
CZECH REPUBLIC
Kraków
UKRAINE
Prague
CARPATHIAN MOUNTAINS
MOLDOVA
Vienna
SLOVAKIA
Bratislava
Chişinău
Crimea
AUSTRIA
HUNGARY
GEORGIA
AZERBAIJAN
SLOVENIA
Budapest
TRANSYLVANIA
Ljubljana
ROMANIA
ARMENIA
Zagreb
Black Sea
CROATIA
Bucharest
Belgrade
Sarajevo
SERBIA
BULGARIA
BOSNIA & HERCEGOVINA
IRAN
KOSOVO
Sofiya
Dubrovnik
Pristina
İstanbul
Ankara
Podgorica
MACEDONIA
MONTENEGRO
Skopje
TURKEY
Adriatic Sea
IRAQ
Tirana
SYRIA
ALBANIA
Aegean Sea
GREECE
Ionian Sea
Athens
Nicosia
Ionian Islands
Cyclades Islands
Sicily
LEBANON
Dodecanese Islands
CYPRUS
Crete
JORDAN
Valletta
MALTA
Mediterranean Sea
SAUDI ARABIA
LIBYA
EGYPT

Europe's Top 24

London's Nightlife, Britain

1 Can you hear that, music lovers? That's London (p158) calling – from the numerous theatres, concert halls, nightclubs, pubs and even tube stations, where on any given night hundreds, if not thousands, of performers are taking to the stage. Search for your own iconic London experience, whether it's the Proms at the Royal Albert Hall, an East End singalong around a clunky pub piano, a theatre performance in the West End, a superstar DJ set at Fabric or a floppy-fringed guitar band at a Hoxton boozer. BBC Proms, Royal Albert Hall, London

Eiffel Tower, France

2 Seven million people visit the Eiffel Tower in Paris (p364) annually and most agree that each visit is unique. From an evening ascent amid twinkling lights to lunch in the company of a staggering city panorama, there are 101 ways to 'do' it. Pedal beneath it, skip the lift and hike up, buy a crêpe from a stand or a key ring from the street, snap yourself in front of it, visit at night or – our favourite – experience the odd special occasion when all 324m of it glows a different colour.

CHRISTER FREDRIKSSON / GETTY IMAGES ©

2

HANS-PETER MERTEN / GETTY IMAGES ©

HOLGER LEUE / GETTY IMAGES ©

JOHN FREEMAN / GETTY IMAGES ©

Venice, Italy

3 There's something magical about Venice (p672) on a sunny winter's day. With far fewer tourists around and the light sharp and clear, it's the perfect time to lap up the city's unique and magical atmosphere. Ditch your map and wander the shadowy backstreets of Dorsoduro while imagining secret assignations and whispered conspiracies at every turn. Then visit two of Venice's top galleries, the Gallerie dell'Accademia and the Collezione Peggy Guggenheim, which houses works by many of the giants of 20th-century art. Grand Canal

Remembering the Berlin Wall, Germany

4 Even after 25 years, the sheer magnitude and disbelief that the Berlin Wall (p444) really cut through this city doesn't sink in. But the best way to examine its role in Berlin is to make your way – on foot or by bike – along the Berlin Wall Trail. Passing the Brandenburg Gate, analysing graffiti at the East Side Gallery or learning about its history at the Documentation Centre: the path brings it all into context. It's heartbreaking, hopeful and sombre, but integral in trying to understand Germany's capital. 'Uhrmenschen der computer' by César Olhagaray

MARIUSZ KLUZNIAK / GETTY IMAGES ©

VINCENZO LOMBARDO / GETTY IMAGES ©

Santorini, Greece

5 On first view, startling Santorini (p536) grabs your attention and doesn't let it go. The submerged caldera, surrounded by lava-layered cliffs topped by villages that look like a sprinkling of icing sugar, is one of nature's great wonders, best experienced by a walk along the clifftops from the main town of Fira to the northern village of Oia. The precariousness and impermanence of the place is breathtaking. Recover from your efforts with Santorini's ice-cold Yellow Donkey beer in Oia as you wait for its famed picture-perfect sunset.

St Petersburg, Russia

6 Marvelling at how many masterpieces there are in the Hermitage; window-shopping and people-watching along Nevsky Prospekt; gliding down canals past the grand facades of palaces and golden-domed churches; enjoying a ballet at the beautiful Mariinsky Theatre; having a banquet fit for a tsar then dancing till dawn at a dive bar in a crumbling ruin – Russia's imperial capital (p948) is a visual stunner and hedonist's delight, best visited at the height of summer when the White Nights see the city party around the clock. State Hermitage Museum

BRIAN LAWRENCE / GETTY IMAGES ©

JEAN-PIERRE LESCOURRET / GETTY IMAGES ©

Fjords, Norway

7 The drama of Norway's fjords (p832) is difficult to overstate. They cut deep into the Norwegian interior, adding texture and depth to the map of northwestern Scandinavia. Rock walls plunge from high, green meadows into water-filled canyons shadowed by pretty villages. Sognefjorden, more than 200km long, and Hardangerfjord are Norway's most extensive fjord networks, but the quiet, precipitous beauty of Nærøyfjorden (part of Sognefjorden), Lysefjord and – king of fjords – Geirangerfjord, are candidates for Scandinavia's most beautiful corner. Sognefjorden

Kraków, Poland

8 Poland's former royal capital (p853) never disappoints. It's hard to pinpoint why it's so special, but there's a satisfying aura of history radiating from the sloping stone buttresses of the medieval buildings in the Old Town that makes its streets seem, well, just right. Add the extremes of a spectacular castle and the low-key oh-so-cool bar scene within the tiny worn buildings of the Kazimierz backstreets, and it's a city you want to seriously get to know. Old Town

Dubrovnik's City Walls, Croatia

9 Get up close and personal with the city by walking Dubrovnik's spectacular city walls (p268), as history is unfurled from the battlements. No visit is complete without a leisurely walk along these ramparts, the finest in the world and Dubrovnik's main claim to fame. Built between the 13th and 16th centuries, they are still remarkably intact today, and the vistas over the terracotta rooftops and the Adriatic Sea are sublime, especially at dusk when the sundown makes the hues dramatic and the panoramas unforgettable.

LATITUDE STOCK - FRANK FELL / GETTY IMAGES ©

Prague, Czech Republic

10 Prague's big attractions – Prague Castle and Old Town Square – are highlights of the Czech capital (p279), but for a more insightful look at life two decades after the Velvet Revolution, head to local neighbourhoods around the centre. Working class Žižkov and energetic Smíchov are crammed with pubs, while elegant tree-lined Vinohrady features a diverse menu of cosmopolitan restaurants. Prague showcases many forms of art, from iconic works from the last century to more recent but equally challenging pieces. Prague Castle

SIGFRID LÓPEZ / GETTY IMAGES ©

The Matterhorn, Switzerland

11 It graces Toblerone packages and evokes stereotypical *Heidi* scenes, but nothing prepares you for the allure of the Matterhorn (p1121). As soon as you arrive at the timber-chalet-filled village of Zermatt this mighty mountain looms above you, mesmerising you with its chiselled, majestic peak. Gaze at it from a tranquil sidewalk cafe, hike in its shadow along the tangle of alpine paths above town with cowbells clinking in the distance, or pause to admire its sheer size from a ski slope.

Budapest, Hungary

12 Straddling the romantic Danube River, with Buda Hills to the west and the start of the Great Plain to the east, Budapest (p562) is perhaps the most beautiful city in Eastern Europe. Parks brim with attractions, the architecture is stunning and museums are filled with treasures. And with pleasure boats sailing the scenic Danube Bend, thermal baths belching steam and a nightlife throbbing till dawn most nights, it's easy to see why the Hungarian capital is one of the continent's most delightful and fun cities to visit. Széchenyi Baths

11

CLAUDE-OLIVIER MARTI / GETTY IMAGES ©

12

MAREMAGNUM / GETTY IMAGES ©

VISIONS OF OUR LAND / GETTY IMAGES ©

RICHARD I'ANSON / GETTY IMAGES ©

ALAN COPSON / GETTY IMAGES ©

Barcelona's La Sagrada Família, Spain

13 One of Spain's top sights, La Sagrada Família (p1040), modernist brainchild of Antoni Gaudí, remains a work in progress more than 80 years after its creator's death. Fanciful and profound, inspired by nature and barely restrained by a Gothic style, Barcelona's quirky temple soars skyward. The improbable angles and departures from architectural convention will have you shaking your head in disbelief, but the detail of the decorative flourishes on the Passion and Nativity facades are worth studying for hours.

Dublin, Ireland

14 Ireland's capital city (p605) can boast all the attractions and distractions of a major international metropolis, but manages to retain the friendliness, intimacy and atmosphere of a small town. Whether wandering the leafy Georgian terraces of St Stephen's Green or experiencing the past at Kilmainham Gaol, you're never far from a friendly pub where the beer is grand and the craic is flowing. And, of course, there's the chance to sink a pint of the black stuff at that fountainhead of froth, the original Guinness brewery.

Bay of Kotor, Montenegro

15 There's a sense of secrecy and mystery to the Bay of Kotor (p789). Grey mountain walls rise steeply from steely blue waters, getting higher and higher as you progress through their folds to the hidden reaches of the inner bay. Here, ancient stone settlements hug the shoreline, with Kotor's old alleyways concealed in its innermost reaches behind hefty stone walls. Talk about drama! But you wouldn't expect anything else of the Balkans, where life is exuberantly Mediterranean and lived full of passion on these ancient streets.

16

TIBOR BOGNAR / GETTY IMAGES ©

17

MATTEO COLOMBO / GETTY IMAGES ©

Imperial Vienna, Austria

16 Imagine what you could do with unlimited riches and Austria's top architects at your hands for 640 years: you have the Vienna (p60) of the Habsburgs. The graceful Hofburg whisks you back to the age of empires as you marvel at the treasury's imperial crowns, the equine ballet of the Spanische Hofreitschule (Spanish Riding School) and Empress Elisabeth's chandelier-lit apartments. The palace is rivalled in grandeur only by Schloss Schönbrunn and also the baroque Schloss Belvedere, both set in exquisite landscaped gardens.Hofburg

Granada's Alhambra, Spain

17 The palace complex of the Alhambra (p1076) is close to architectural perfection, perhaps the most refined example of Islamic art anywhere in the world and an enduring symbol of 800 years of Moorish rule in what was known as Al-Andalus. From afar, the Alhambra's red fortress towers dominate the Granada skyline, set against a backdrop of the Sierra Nevada's snowcapped peaks. Up close, its perfectly proportioned Generalife gardens complement the exquisite detail of the Palacio Nazariés. Put simply, this is Spain's most beautiful monument.

JEROEN P - IWILLBEHOMESOON.COM / GETTY IMAGES ©

LESHIY / GETTY IMAGES ©

Amsterdam's Canals, The Netherlands

18 To say Amsterdammers love the water is an understatement. Sure, the city (p801) made its first fortune in maritime trade, but that's ancient history. You can stroll next to the canals and check out some of the thousands of houseboats. Or, better still, go for a ride. From boat level you'll see a whole new set of architectural details, such as the ornamentations bedecking the bridges. And when you pass the canalside cafe terraces, you can just look up and wave.

Tallinn, Estonia

19 The Estonian capital (p325) is famous for its two-tiered chocolate-box Old Town of intertwining alleys, picturesque courtyards and rooftop views from medieval turrets. But be sure to step outside the Old Town walls and experience Tallinn's other treasures: Tallinn's stylish restaurants plating up fashionable New Nordic cuisine, its buzzing Scandinavian-influenced design community, its ever-growing number of museums – such as KUMU, the city's award-winning modern-art repository – or its progressive contemporary architecture.

20

DANIN TULIC / GETTY IMAGES ©

21

XU JIAN / GETTY IMAGES ©

22

VEGA / GETTY IMAGES ©

Mostar, Bosnia & Hercegovina

20 If the 1993 bombardment of Mostar's iconic 16th-century stone bridge underlined the pointlessness of Yugoslavia's brutal civil war, its painstaking reconstruction has proved symbolic of a peaceful new era. Although parts of Mostar (p149) are still dotted with bombed-out buildings, the town continues to dust itself off. Its charming Ottoman quarter has been especially convincingly rebuilt and is once again a delightful patchwork of stone mosques, souvenir peddlers and inviting cafes. Today it's tourists rather than militias that besiege the place.

Ancient Rome, Italy

21 Rome's famous seven hills (actually, there are nine) offer some superb vantage points of the delights of the city (p641). From here you may spot iconic sites including the Palatino, a gorgeous green expanse of evocative ruins, towering umbrella pines and unforgettable views over the Roman Forum; the Colosseum, perhaps the most thrilling of Rome's ancient sites; and the Pantheon, Rome's best-preserved monument. As you walk the paths around this ancient city, you can almost sense the ghosts in the air. Colosseum

Athens, Greece

22 Magnificent ruins are scattered across the mainland and islands of Greece, but it's in its capital, Athens (p514), that the greatest and most iconic of those monuments still stands. High on a rocky outcrop overlooking the city, the Acropolis epitomises the glory of ancient Greece with its graceful Parthenon, decorative Erechtheion and 17,000-seat Theatre of Dionysos. Other impressive ruins litter this resilient, vibrant city, including the mammoth Temple of Olympian Zeus, two Agoras (marketplaces – one Greek, one Roman) and first-rate museums. Parthenon

İstanbul, Turkey

23 Straddling Europe and Asia, İstanbul's resumé includes stints as the capital of the Byzantine and Ottoman Empires. The historical highlights cluster in Sultanahmet – the Aya Sofya, Blue Mosque, Topkapı Palace and Grand Bazaar. After marvelling at their ancient domes and glittering interiors, it's time to experience the vibrant contemporary life of this huge metropolis (p1144). Cross the Galata Bridge, passing ferries and fish-kebab stands, to Beyoğlu, where the nightlife thrives from chic rooftop bars to rowdy taverns. Aya Sofya

Lisbon's Alfama, Portugal

24 The Alfama (p879), with its labyrinthine alleyways, hidden courtyards and curving, shadow-filled lanes, is a magical place to lose all sense of direction and delve into the soul of the city. On the journey, you'll pass breadbox-sized grocers, brilliantly tiled buildings and cosy taverns filled with easygoing chatter, with the scent of chargrilled sardines and the mournful rhythms of fado drifting in the breeze. Then you round a bend and catch sight of steeply pitched rooftops leading down to the glittering Tejo and you know you're hooked.

Need to Know

For more information, see Survival Guide (p1187).

Currency

Euro (€), Pound (£), Swiss franc (Sfr), Rouble (R)

Language

English, French, German, Italian, Spanish, Russian, Hungarian, Greek, Turkish

Visas

EU citizens don't need visas for other EU countries. Australians, Canadians, New Zealanders and Americans don't need visas for visits of less than 90 days.

Money

ATMs are common; credit and debit cards are widely accepted.

Mobile Phones

Europe uses the GSM 900 network. If you're coming from outside Europe, it's worth buying a prepaid local SIM.

Time

Britain, Ireland and Portugal (GMT), Central Europe (GMT plus one hour), Greece, Turkey and Eastern Europe (GMT plus two hours), Russia (GMT plus three hours).

When to Go?

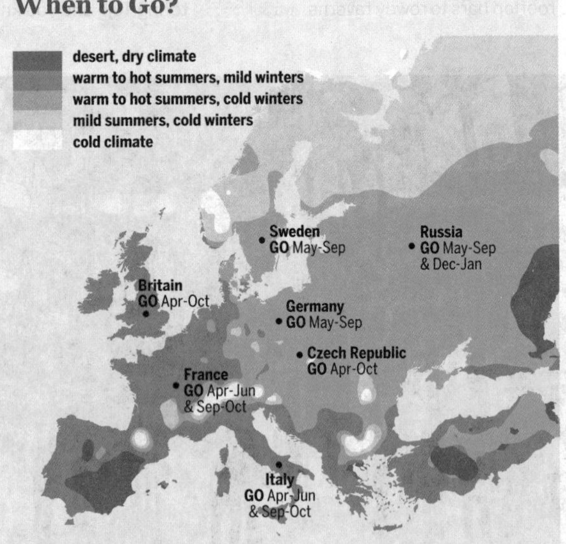

High Season (Jun–Aug)

➡ Everybody comes to Europe and all of Europe hits the road.

➡ Hotel prices and temperatures are at their highest.

➡ Expect all the major attractions to be nightmarishly busy.

Shoulder Season (Apr–May & Sep–Oct)

➡ Crowds and prices drop, except in Italy where it's still busy.

➡ Temperatures are comfortable but it can be hot in southern Europe.

➡ Overall these are the best months to travel in Europe.

Low Season (Nov–Mar)

➡ Outside ski resorts, hotels drop their prices or close down.

➡ The weather can be cold and days short, especially in northern Europe.

➡ Some places, such as resort towns, are like ghost towns.

Useful Websites

Lonely Planet (www.lonelyplanet.com/thorntree) Ask other travellers questions.

Deutsche Bahn (www.bahn.de) The best online train timetable for Europe.

Hidden Europe (www.hiddeneurope.co.uk) Fascinating magazine and online dispatches from all the continent's corners.

Couchsurfing (www.couchsurfing.org) Find a free bed and make friends in any European country.

VisitEurope (www.visiteurope.com) With information about travel in 33 member countries.

Spotted by Locals (www.spottedbylocals.com) Insider tips for cities across Europe.

What to Take

Flip-flops (thongs) For overnight train rides, in hostel bathrooms and for the beach.

Hiking boots For Europe's fantastic walks.

Ear plugs Helpful anywhere, but especially in hostels.

Anti-mosquito plugs Useful in summer, particularly in the Baltic and Scandinavia.

European plug adaptors Essential if you're coming from outside Europe.

An unlocked mobile phone For use with a local SIM card for making cheap calls.

Smart clothes So you look the part when breaking the budget.

Exchange Rates

Australia	A$1	€0.72	£0.51
Canada	C$1	€0.74	£0.53
Japan	¥100	€0.78	£0.56
NZ	NZ$1	€0.70	£0.50
US	US$1	€0.95	£0.67

For current exchange rates, see www.xe.com.

Daily Costs

Budget: Less than €60

- Dorm beds: €10–20
- Admission to museums: €5–15
- Pizza or pasta: €8–12

Midrange: €60–€200

- Double room in a small hotel: €50–100
- Short taxi trip: €10–20
- Meals in good restaurants: around €20 per person

Top end: More than €200

- Stay at iconic hotels: from €150
- Car hire: from around €30 per day
- Theatre tickets: €15–150

Accommodation

Book up to two months in advance for a July visit, or for ski resorts over Christmas and New Year.

Hotels Range from the local pub to restored castles.

B&Bs Small, family-run houses generally provide good value.

Hostels Enormous variety from backpacker palaces to real dumps.

Homestays and farmstays A great way to find out how locals really live.

Arriving in Europe

Schiphol Airport, Amsterdam (p823) Trains to the centre (20 minutes)

Heathrow Airport, London (p223) Trains (15 minutes) and Tube (one hour) to the centre

Charles de Gaulle Airport, Paris (p434) Many buses (one hour) and trains (30 minutes) to the centre

Frankfurt Airport, Frankfurt (p488) Trains (15 minutes) to the centre

Leonardo da Vinci Airport, Rome (p659) Buses (one hour) and trains (30 minutes) to the centre

Barajas Airport, Madrid (p1029) Buses (40 minutes) and Metro (15 minutes) to the centre

Getting Around

Train Europe's train network is fast and efficient, but rarely a bargain unless you book well in advance or use a rail pass wisely.

Bus Usually taken for short trips in remoter areas, though long-distance intercity buses can be very cheap.

Car You can hire a car or drive your own throughout Europe. Roads are excellent but petrol is expensive.

Ferry Boats connect Britain and Ireland with mainland Europe, Scandinavia to the Baltic countries and Germany, and Italy to the Balkans and Greece.

Plane Speed things up by flying from one end of the continent to the other.

Bicycle Slow things down on a two-wheeler, a great way to get around just about anywhere.

For much more on **getting around**, see p1198.

If You Like...

Castles & Palaces

Versailles, France The vast formal palace against which all others are measured includes the Hall of Mirrors and sumptuous gardens. (p382)

Neuschwanstein, Germany So what if it's not even 150 years old? Neuschwanstein, in the heart of the Bavarian Alps, is everybody's (including Disney's) castle fantasy. (p472)

Winter Palace, Russia Forever associated with the Russian Revolution, this golden-green baroque building is unmatched anywhere for sheer tsarist splendour. (p949)

Bran Castle, Romania Better known as Dracula's Castle, this Transylvanian beauty is straight out of a horror movie. (p922)

Alhambra, Spain This exquisite Islamic palace complex in Granada is a World Heritage–listed wonder. (p1076)

Gravensteen, Belgium The turreted stone castle of the Counts of Flanders looms over the beautiful Belgian city of Ghent. (p121)

Windsor Castle, Britain The world's largest and oldest occupied fortress is one of the British monarch's principal residences. (p187)

Topkapı Palace, Turkey Tour the opulent pavilions and jewel-filled Treasury of the former court of the Ottoman empire in İstanbul. (p1144)

Architecture

Notre Dame, France Paris' gargoyle-covered cathedral is a Gothic wonder. (p368)

Meteora, Greece Late-14th-century monasteries perch dramatically atop enormous rocky pinnacles. (p526)

La Sagrada Família, Spain Gaudí's singular work in progress, Barcelona's mighty cathedral defies imagination. (p1040)

Pantheon, Rome Commissioned during Augustus' reign, the portico of this ancient wonder is graced by Corinthian columns. (p646)

Grand Place, Belgium Brussels' breathtaking central square is ringed by gilded houses. (p106)

Overblaak Development, Netherlands This late-20th-century Rotterdam complex incorporates a 'forest' of 45°-tilted cube-shaped apartments. (p816)

Art Nouveau, Budapest Budapest hits its stride with art nouveau masterpieces such as the Museum of Applied Arts. (p562)

Blue Mosque, İstanbul Islamic style finds perfect form in the Blue Mosque, one of İstanbul's most recognisable buildings. (p1145)

Historic Sites

Stonehenge, Britain The UK's most iconic – and mysterious – archaeological site, dating back some 5000 years. (p189)

Pompeii, Italy Wander the streets and alleys of this great ancient city, buried by a volcanic eruption in AD 79. (p702)

Athens, Greece Ancient wonders include the Acropolis, Ancient Agora, Temple of Olympian Zeus and more. (p514)

Amsterdam's Canal Ring, Netherlands Stroll the Dutch capital's Golden Age canals lined with gabled buildings. (p801)

Moscow's Kremlin, Russia The seat of power to medieval tsars and modern rulers alike, Moscow's vast Kremlin offers incredible sights. (p937)

Dachau, Germany The first Nazi concentration camp is a harrowing introduction to WWII's horrors. (p470)

Sarajevo, Bosnia & Hercegovina Enjoy the bustling old Turkish quarter of arguably the Balkans' most charming town – and a proud survivor. (p141)

Beaches & Islands

Cyclades, Greece The names Mykonos, Santorini and Naxos all conjure up images of perfect golden beaches and the reality will not disappoint. (p530)

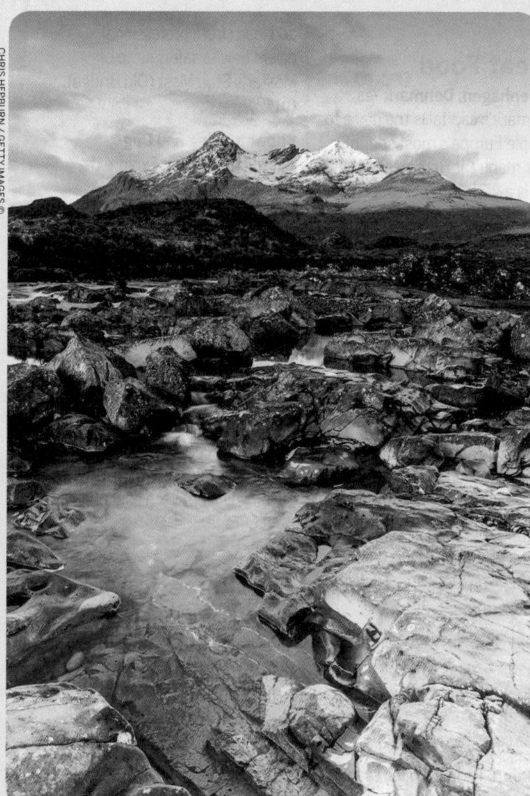

CHRIS HEPBURN / GETTY IMAGES ©

INGMAR WESEMANN / GETTY IMAGES ©

Top: Isle of Skye (p219), Scotland

Bottom: Schloss Neuschwanstein (p472), Germany

Drymades Beach, Albania The stuff of legend among backpackers, this white-sand beach remains the one to head for on Albania's rapidly developing coastline. (p52)

Menorca, Spain Beaches so beautiful you think they may be dreams, tucked away in little coves all around the sandiest and most beautiful of the Balearic Islands. (p1064)

Black Sea Coast, Bulgaria Bulgaria boasts the best beaches on the Black Sea, but we recommend avoiding the big resort towns and heading instead to smaller Sozopol. (p242)

Hvar Island, Croatia Famed for its verdancy and lilac fields, this luxurious and sunny island is the jumping-off point for the wooded Pakleni Islands. (p266)

Isle of Skye, Scotland A 50-mile-long smorgasbord of velvet moors, jagged mountains, sparkling lochs and towering sea cliffs. (p219)

Spectacular Scenery

The Alps, Switzerland There's no competition for the most stunning landscape in Europe – even its neighbours wouldn't dare suggest that theirs could rival that of beautiful Switzerland. (p1121)

Fjords, Norway From the precipitous coastline to the impossibly steep gashes that cut into the interior, Norway's fjords are simply unmissable. (p832)

Cappadocia, Turkey In the centre of Turkey, Anatolia's mountain-fringed plains give way to a land of other-worldly rock formations and underground cities – definitely one of the region's strangest landscapes. (p1167)

High Tatras, Slovakia Offering pristine snowfields, ultramarine mountain lakes, thundering waterfalls, undulating pine forests and shimmering alpine meadows. (p986)

Vatnajökull National Park, Iceland Skaftafell is the jewel in the crown of this breathtaking collection of peaks and glaciers. (p597)

Nightlife

Berlin, Germany There's nothing quite like arriving at superclub Berghain as the sun comes up, and dancing until sundown in Europe's most serious party city. (p453)

London, Britain Whether it's a quiet session down at the local pub or a full-blown night on the tiles of East London, you can be sure to have a good time in the hedonistic bars and clubs of London town. (p155)

Moscow, Russia Once famed for its 'face control' (strict door policies), Moscow is now becoming an essential stop on the clubber's world map with a slew of new democratically run bars and clubs. (p937)

Madrid, Spain Has more bars per capita than anywhere else on earth and no one goes to bed here before killing the night. (p1016)

Mykonos, Greece There are party pockets dotted throughout the Greek islands; summer revellers flock to the bars and clubs of Mykonos. (p530)

Reykjavík, Iceland Join in the *djammið*, a raucous weekend pub crawl around the Icelandic capital's vibrant cafe-bar scene. (p586)

Belgrade, Serbia The Serbian capital is one of the most vibrant places to party the night away – in summer, the Danube and Sava Rivers are clogged with *splavovi* (floating clubs). (p863)

Great Food

Copenhagen, Denmark Yes, Denmark's capital is the place to sample Europe's most sought-after menu (at Noma), and the city is awash with hotspots plating up cool New Nordic cuisine. (p310)

Naples, Italy Pizza, the peasant dish that ate the world – or the other way around – is still the best in the city of its birth: accept no imitations. (p699)

San Sebastián, Spain The Basque powerhouse boasts an impressive array of Michelin-starred restaurants. (p1054)

Lyon, France Forget Paris – the gastronomic capital of La Belle France is undoubtedly Lyon, a city that runs on pork and will have gourmands swooning. (p400)

Coastal Greece Swig on ouzo while snacking on grilled octopus; not a bad way to pack away some calories. (p530)

İstanbul, Turkey Grilled meats, kebaps and a marvellous array of meze (small dishes) can be sampled in this paradise for food lovers. (p1144)

Outdoor Fun

Bovec and Bled, Slovenia The capital of active sports in eastern Europe is tiny Slovenia, with everything from canyoning to hydrospeeding at Bovec and Bled. (p1005)

Cycling the Loire Valley, France There's a gorgeous chateau around every bend in the river in this beautiful valley. (p395)

Skiing year-round, Austria Experience Olympic-sized skiing in Innsbruck, the Alpine city ringed by famous pistes; in August, head to the glaciers for downhill action. (p82)

Bridge diving, Bosnia & Hercegovina Screw up your courage and learn from professional divers how to safely jump off Mostar's Stari Most (Old Bridge). (p149)

Snowmobiling and **Dog-Sledding, Sweden** Explore the icy wastelands of northern Sweden in the most thrilling ways possible. (p1107)

Caving, Slovakia The Slovenský Raj National Park includes one of only three aragonite caves in the world, as well as the Dobšinská Ice Cave. (p991)

Iron Curtain Cycling Route Pedal more than 9000km through 20 countries from Russia to Turkey along the old dividing line between east and west Europe.

Art Collections

Louvre, France It's not just Paris' museum, it's the world's; treasures from Europe and all over the planet in exhaustive quantity will simply dazzle you – better yet, it's free the first Sunday of each month and for some age groups. (p369)

Florence, Italy It starts with the Duomo, continues through the Uffizi Gallery and crosses the Ponte Vecchio – the entire Renaissance embodied in one city. (p684)

Hermitage, Russia Housed in the Winter Palace, this is quite simply one of the world's greatest art collections, stuffed full of treasures from Egyptian mummies to a superb cache of Picassos; free to students and on the first Thursday of the month. (p949)

Van Gogh Museum, Netherlands Despite his troubled life and struggles with poverty and madness, Van Gogh's superb creations are gloriously easy to enjoy at this Amsterdam museum. (p801)

Madrid, Spain With the Prado, Thyssen and Reina Sofía within a

JEAN-PIERRE LESCOURRET / GETTY IMAGES ©

One of Vienna's famous coffee houses

single golden mile of art, Madrid is one of Europe's premier destinations for art lovers. (p1016)

Music

Vienna's Staatsoper, Austria The premier venue in a city synonymous with opera and classical music. (p69)

Berlin, Germany Everything from the world's most acclaimed techno venue to the Berlin Philharmonic under the baton of Sir Simon Rattle can be seen in Germany's music-obsessed capital. (p453)

Irish music, Ireland The Irish love their music and it takes little – sometimes just a pint of beer – to get them singing; the West Coast hums with music pubs, especially in Galway. (p623)

Fado, Portugal The Portuguese love the melancholic and nostalgic songs of fado; hear it in Lisbon's Alfama district. (p887)

Trubači, Serbia While this wild brass music is celebrated en masse at Guča each August, ragtag *trubači* bands wander the streets of many Serbian towns year-round: if you hear a trumpet, follow that sound. (p961)

Seville, Spain Few musical forms capture the spirit of a nation quite like passionate flamenco, with this Andalucian city the heartland for Spain's best-loved musical tradition. (p961)

Cafes & Bars

Vienna's coffee houses, Austria Unchanged in decades and redolent with the air of refinement; pause for a cup served just so. (p68)

Irish pubs, Ireland Come and join the warm and gregarious crowds of locals in any pub in Ireland for a true cultural experience. (p603)

Paris' cafe society, France What's more clichéd: the practised curtness of the Parisian waiter or the studied boredom of the customer? Both are, probably, and we wouldn't miss the show for anything. (p364)

Amsterdam's tiny havens, Netherlands The Dutch call them 'brown cafes' for the former tobacco stains on the walls from legions of smokers, but they should just call them cosy, for the warm and friendly atmosphere. (p801)

Bourse cafes, Belgium Many of Brussels' most iconic cafes are within stumbling distance of the city's Bourse and are great places to sample the country's wealth of beers. (p112)

Budapest's ruin pubs, Hungary So-called 'ruin pubs' – essentially pop-up bars in abandoned buildings – are popular (and uniquely Budapest) seasonal outdoor venues in summer. (p562)

Month by Month

TOP EVENTS

Carnevale, Italy February

Glastonbury Festival, Britain June

Roskilde Festival, Denmark June

Edinburgh International Festival, Scotland August

Oktoberfest, Germany September

January

It's cold but most towns are relatively tourist free and hotel prices are rock bottom. Head to Eastern Europe's ski slopes for wallet-friendly prices, with Bosnia and Bulgaria your best bets.

Kiruna Snöfestivalen, Sweden

In the last weekend of January this Lapland snow festival (www.snofestivalen.com), based around a snow-sculpting competition, draws artists from all over Europe. There's also a husky-dog competition and a handicrafts fair.

Küstendorf Film & Music Festival, Serbia

Created and curated by Serbian director Emir Kusturica, this international indie-fest (http://kustendorf-filmandmusicfestival.org) in the town of Drvengrad, near Zlatibor in Serbia, eschews traditional red-carpet glitz for oddball inclusions vying for the 'Golden Egg' prize.

February

Carnival in all its manic glory sweeps the Catholic regions. Cold temperatures are forgotten amid masquerades, street festivals and general bacchanalia. Expect to be kissed by a stranger.

Carnaval, Netherlands

Pre-Lent is celebrated with greater vigour in Maastricht than anywhere else in northern Europe. While the rest of the Netherlands hopes the canals will freeze for ice skating, this Dutch corner cuts loose with a celebration that would have done its former Roman residents proud.

Carnevale, Italy

In the period before Ash Wednesday, Venice goes mad for masks (www.venice-carnival-italy.com). Costume balls, many with traditions centuries old, enliven the social calendar in this storied old city. Even those without a coveted invite are swept up.

Carnivals, Croatia

For colourful costumes and nonstop revelry head to Rijeka, where Carnival is the pinnacle of the year's calendar (www.rijecki-karneval.hr). Zadar and Samobor host Carnival celebrations too, with street dancing, concerts and masked balls.

Karneval/Fasching, Germany

Germany doesn't leave the pre-Lent season solely to its neighbours. Karneval is celebrated with abandon in the traditional Catholic regions including Bavaria, along the Rhine and particularly vibrantly in Cologne (www.koelnerkarneval.de/en/cologne-carnival).

March

Spring arrives in southern Europe. Further north the rest of the continent continues to freeze, though days are often bright.

Ski-Jumping World Cup, Slovenia

This exciting international competition (www.planica.si) takes place on the world's largest ski-jumping hill, in the Planica Valley at Rateče near Kranjska Gora. Held the third weekend in March, it's a must for adrenalin junkies.

St Patrick's Day, Ireland

Parades and celebrations are held on 17 March in Irish towns big and small to honour the beloved patron saint of Ireland. While elsewhere the day is a commercialised romp of green beer, in his home country it's time for a parade and celebrations with friends and family.

Budapest Spring Festival, Hungary

This two-week festival in late March is one of Europe's top classical music events (www.springfestival.hu). Concerts are held in a number of beautiful venues, including stunning churches, the opera house and the national theatre.

April

Spring arrives with a burst of colour, from the glorious bulb fields of Holland to the blooming orchards of Spain. On the most southern beaches it's time to shake the sand out of the umbrellas.

Semana Santa, Spain

There are parades of penitents and holy icons in Spain, notably Seville, during Easter week (www.semana-santa.org). Thousands of members of religious brotherhoods parade in traditional garb before thousands of spectators. Look for the pointed *capirotes* (hoods).

Settimana Santa, Italy

Italy celebrates Holy Week with processions and passion plays. By Holy Thursday Rome is thronged with the faithful and even nonbelievers are swept up by the piety of hundreds of thousands thronging the Vatican and St Peter's Basilica.

Greek Easter, Greece

The most important festival in the Greek Orthodox calendar has an emphasis on the Resurrection, so it's a celebratory event. The best part is midnight on Easter Saturday, when candles are lit and fireworks and a procession hit the streets.

Feria de Abril, Spain

Hoods off! A week-long party in Seville in late April counterbalances the religious peak of Easter (http://feriadesevilla.andalunet.com). The beautiful old squares of this gorgeous city come alive during the long, warm nights for which the nation is known.

Koningsdag (King's Day), Netherlands

The nationwide celebration on 27 April is especially fervent in Amsterdam, awash with orange costumes, fake Afros, beer, dope, leather boys, temporary roller coasters and general craziness.

May

May is usually sunny and warm and full of things to do – an excellent time to visit. It's not too hot or too crowded, though you can still expect the big destinations to feel busy.

Karneval der Kulturen, Germany

This joyous street carnival (www.karneval-berlin.de) celebrates Berlin's multicultural tapestry with parties, global nosh and a fun parade of flamboyantly costumed dancers, DJs, artists and musicians.

Beer Festival, Czech Republic

An event dear to many travellers' hearts, this Prague beer festival (www.ceskypivnifestival.cz) offers lots of food, music and – most importantly – around 70 beers from around the country from mid to late May.

Brussels Jazz Marathon, Belgium

Around-the-clock jazz performances hit Brussels during the second-last weekend in May (www.brusselsjazzmarathon.be). The saxophone is the instrument of choice for this international-flavoured city's most joyous celebration.

Queima das Fitas, Portugal

Coimbra's annual highlight is this boozy week of fado music and revelry that begins on the first Thursday in May, when students celebrate the end of the academic year.

June

The huge summer travel season hasn't started yet, but the sun has broken through the clouds and the weather is generally gorgeous across the continent.

Festa de São João, Portugal

Elaborate processions, live music on Porto's plazas and merrymaking across Portugal's second city. Squeaky plastic hammers (on sale everywhere) come out for the unusual custom of whacking one another. Everyone is fair game.

White Nights in Northern Europe

By mid-June the Baltic sun only just sinks below the horizon at night, leaving the sky a grey-white colour and encouraging locals to forget their routines and party hard. The best place to join the fun is St Petersburg, Russia, where balls, classical-music concerts and other summer events keep spirits high.

Glastonbury Festival, Britain

The town's youthful summer vibe peaks for this long weekend of music, theatre and New Age shenanigans (www.glastonburyfestivals.co.uk). It's one of England's favourite outdoor events and more than 100,000 turn up to writhe around in the grassy fields (or deep mud) at Pilton's (Worthy) Farm.

Roskilde Festival, Denmark

Northern Europe's largest music festival (www.roskilde-festival.dk) rocks Roskilde each summer. It takes place in late June but advance ticket sales are on offer in December and the festival usually sells out.

Festa de Santo António, Portugal

Feasting, drinking and dancing in Lisbon's Alfama in honour of St Anthony (12 to 13 June) top the even grander three-week Festas de Lisboa (http://festasdelisboa.com), which features processions and dozens of street parties.

Hellenic Festival, Greece

The ancient theatre at Epidavros and the Odeon of Herodes Atticus are the headline venues of Athens' annual cultural shindig (www.greekfestival.gr). The festival, which runs from mid-June to August, features music, dance, theatre and much more besides.

July

One of the busiest months for travel across Europe with outdoor cafes, beer gardens and beach clubs hopping. Expect beautiful, even steamy, weather anywhere you go.

Ultra Europe, Croatia

Held over three days in Split's Poljud Stadium (www.ultraeurope.com) this electronic music fest includes a huge beach party.

Východná, Slovakia

Slovakia's standout folk festival (www.festivalvychodna.sk) is held in a village nestled below the High Tatras.

Il Palio, Italy

Siena's great annual event is the Palio (2 July and 16 August; www.thepalio.com), a pageant culminating in a bareback horse race round Il Campo. The city is divided into 17 *contrade* (districts), of which 10 compete for the *palio* (silk banner), with emotions exploding across the city.

Paléo Festival Nyon, Switzerland

More than 250 shows and concerts are staged for this premier music festival (http://yeah.paleo.ch) held above the town of Nyon.

Sanfermines (Running of the Bulls), Spain

The Fiesta de San Fermín (Sanfermines) is the week-long nonstop festival and party in Pamplona with the daily *encierro* (running of the bulls) as its centrepiece (www.bullrunpamplona.com). Anything can happen, but it rarely ends well for the bull. Running of the Nudes (www.runningofthenudes.com), an antibullfighting event, takes place two days earlier.

Bastille Day, France

Fireworks, balls, processions, and, of course, good food and wine, for France's national day on 14 July, celebrated in every French town. Get caught up in this patriotic festival.

EXIT Festival, Serbia

Eastern Europe's most talked-about music festival (www.exitfest.org) takes place within the walls of the Petrovaradin Fortress in Serbia's second city, Novi Sad. Book early as it attracts music lovers from all over the continent with big international acts headlining.

Gentse Feesten, Belgium

Ghent is transformed into a 10-day party of music and

theatre, a highlight of which is a vast techno celebration called 10 Days Off (www.gentsefeesten.be).

Medieval Festival of the Arts, Romania

The beautiful Romanian city of Sighişoara hosts open-air concerts, parades and ceremonies, all glorifying medieval Transylvania and taking the town back to its 12th-century origins.

Bažant Pohoda, Slovakia

Slovakia's largest music festival (www.pohodafestival.sk) represents all genres of music from folk and rock to orchestral, over eight different stages. It's firmly established as one of Europe's biggest and best summer music festivals.

Amsterdam Gay Pride, Netherlands

Held at the end of July this is one of Europe's best GLBT events (www.amsterdamgaypride.nl); in 2016 it will also be the location for Euro-Pride (www.europride.com).

August

Everybody's going someplace as half of Europe shuts down to enjoy the traditional month of holiday with the other half. If it's near the beach, from Germany's Baltic to Spain's Balearics, it's mobbed and the temperatures are hot, hot, hot!

Salzburg Festival, Austria

Austria's most renowned classical-music festival (www.salzburgfestival.at) attracts international stars from late July to the end of August. That urbane person sitting by you having a glass of wine who looks like a famous cellist, probably is.

Zürich Street Parade, Switzerland

Zürich lets its hair down with an enormous techno parade (www.street-parade.ch). All thoughts of numbered accounts are forgotten as bankers, and everybody else in this otherwise staid burg, party to orgasmic, deep-base thump, thump, thump.

Notting Hill Carnival, Britain

This is Europe's largest, and London's most vibrant, outdoor carnival, where London's Caribbean community shows the city how to party (www.thenottinghillcarnival.com). Food, frolic and fun are just a part of this vast multicultural two-day celebration.

Edinburgh International Festival, Britain

Three weeks of innovative drama, comedy, dance, music and more (www.eif.co.uk). Two weeks overlap with the celebrated Fringe Festival (www.edfringe.com), which draws innovative acts from around the globe. Expect cutting-edge productions that often defy description.

Guča Trumpet Festival, Serbia

Guča's Dragačevo Trumpet Assembly (www.guca.rs) is one of the most exciting and bizarre events in all of Eastern Europe. Hundreds of thousands of revellers descend on the small Serbian town to damage their eardrums, livers and sanity in four cacophonous days of revelry.

Sziget Music Festival, Hungary

A week-long, great-value world-music festival (www.sziget.hu) held all over Budapest. Sziget features bands from around the world playing at more than 60 venues.

September

It's cooling off in every sense, from the northern countries to the romance started on a dance floor in Ibiza. Maybe the best time to visit: the weather's still good and the crowds have thinned.

Venice International Film Festival, Italy

The Mostra del Cinema di Venezia (www.labiennale.org) is Italy's top film fest and one of the world's top indie film fests. The judging here is seen as an early indication of what to look for at the next year's Oscars.

Oktoberfest, Germany

Despite its name, Germany's legendary beer-swilling party (www.oktoberfest.de) starts mid-September in Munich and finishes a week into October. Millions descend for litres of beer and carousing that has no equal. If you don't plan ahead, you'll have to sleep in Austria.

Dvořák Autumn, Czech Republic

This festival of classical music (www.kso.cz/en) honours

the work of the Czech Republic's favourite composer, Anton Dvořák. The event is held over three weeks in the spa town of Karlovy Vary.

Festes de la Mercè, Spain

Barcelona knows how to party until dawn and it outdoes itself for the Festes de la Mercè (around 24 September). The city's biggest celebration has four days of concerts, dancing, *castellers* (human-castle builders), fireworks and *correfocs* – a parade of fireworks-spitting dragons and devils.

October

Another good month to visit – almost everything is still open, while prices and visitor numbers are down. Weather can be unpredictable though, and even cold in northern Europe.

Festival at Queen's, Ireland

Belfast hosts the second-largest arts festival (www.belfastfestival.com) in the UK for three weeks in late October/early November in and around Queen's University. It's a time for the city to shed its gritty legacy, and celebrate the intellectual and the creative without excessive hype.

Wine Festival, Moldova

Wine-enriched folkloric performances in Moldova draw oenophiles and anyone wanting to profit from the 10-day visa-free regime Moldova introduces for the festival.

November

Leaves have fallen and snow is about to fall in much of Europe. Even in the temperate zones around the Med it can get chilly, rainy and blustery. Most seasonal attractions have closed for the year.

Guy Fawkes Night, Britain

Bonfires and fireworks erupt across Britain on 5 November, recalling the foiling of a plot to blow up the Houses of Parliament in the 1600s. Go to high ground in London to see glowing explosions erupt everywhere.

Iceland Airwaves, Iceland

Roll on up to Reykjavík for this great music festival featuring both Icelandic and international acts (www.icelandairwaves.is).

December

Despite freezing temperatures this is a magical time to visit Europe, with Christmas decorations brightening the dark streets. Prices remain surprisingly low provided you avoid Christmas and New Year's Eve.

Natale, Italy

Italian churches set up an intricate crib or a *presepe* (nativity scene) in the lead-up to Christmas. Some are famous, most are works of art and many date back hundreds of years and are venerated for their spiritual ties.

Christmas, Eastern Europe

Christmas is celebrated in different ways in Eastern Europe: most countries celebrate on Christmas Eve (24 December), with an evening meal and midnight Mass. In Russia, Ukraine and Belarus, Christmas falls in January, as per the Gregorian calendar.

CHRISTMAS MARKETS

In December, Christmas Markets are held across Europe, with particularly good ones in Germany, Austria, Slovakia and Czech Republic. The most famous are in Nuremberg (the Christkindlmarkt) and Vienna. Warm your hands through your mittens holding a hot mug of mulled wine and find that special (or kitsch) present. Slovak Christmas markets are regarded as some of Europe's best and a great opportunity to taste *medovina* (mead) and *lokše* (potato pancakes).

For more Christmas markets across the continent see www.christmasmarkets.com.

Itineraries

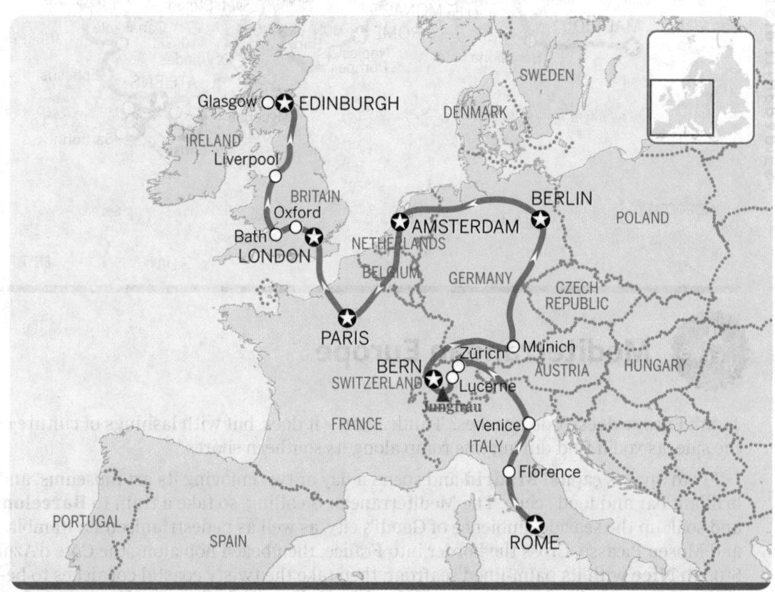

6 WEEKS First-Time Europe

This itinerary covers six iconic European countries that are essential for any first-time visitor – each is crammed with world-famous sights and unforgettable experiences.

Begin in ancient **Rome**, home to the Vatican and the Colosseum. Go north to **Florence**, a Renaissance time capsule, then glide along the canals of **Venice**. Continue to the Swiss lakeside city of **Zürich**, followed by charming **Lucerne** or **Bern**, before heading by train to the **Jungfraujoch** region to see the Alps.

Next is Germany. **Munich** is worth a stop whether it's the Oktoberfest or not, followed by hedonistic **Berlin** where you can see the remains of the wall.

Spend a couple of days in **Amsterdam** admiring works by Van Gogh and Rembrandt, as well as wandering along the canals. Move on to **Paris** to be dazzled by the Louvre, the Eiffel Tower and Versailles.

Take the Eurostar to **London**; along with great sights, enjoy superb eating, drinking and clubbing. Travel west to view Stonehenge and historic **Oxford** and **Bath**. Swing north to **Liverpool** and end your journey in Scotland, ticking off the old and new towns of **Edinburgh** and happening **Glasgow**.

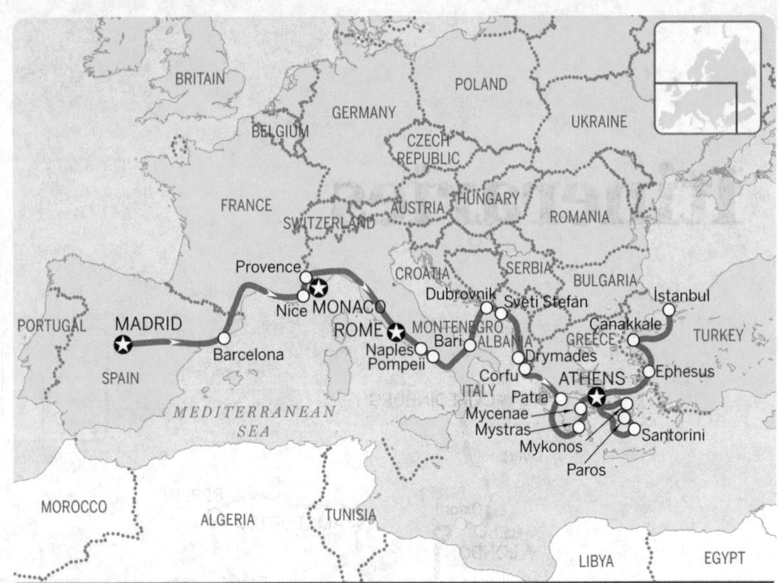

Mediterranean Europe

Think Europe doesn't do beaches? Think again – it does, but with lashings of culture on the side, as you'll find during this romp along its southern shores.

Fly to Spain's capital **Madrid** and spend a day or two enjoying its art museums, and brilliant bar and food scene. The Mediterranean is calling, so take a train to **Barcelona** and soak up the seaside ambience of Gaudí's city, as well as pedestrianised La Rambla and Museu Picasso. Cross the border into France, then beach hop along the Côte d'Azur. Stop in **Nice** with its palm-lined seafront, then take the twisty coastal corniches to beguiling **Monaco**. Spend a day or two inland in the beautiful villages of **Provence**.

Return to Nice to take the train to historic **Rome**. Continue south to energetic **Naples**, peer into ill-fated **Pompeii** and explore the stunning Amalfi Coast. Cross Italy to **Bari**, from where you head across the Adriatic by ferry to the Croatian pearl of **Dubrovnik** where you'll find marble streets, baroque buildings and spectacular city walls.

Bus it south through Montenegro and Albania – two of Europe's least-known but most-breathtaking gems. Pause at the picturesque island of **Sveti Stefan** in the former and the white crescent-shaped beaches of **Drymades** in the latter.

Greece's Ionian Islands are next and the best is **Corfu**. Sail by ferry to **Patra**, and then do a loop of the Peloponnese: catch a bus to Byzantine pin-up city **Mystras**, ancient heavyweight **Mycenae** and venerable **Athens**. Move on to Piraeus, Greece's main port, for an island-hopping expedition of the Cyclades, dreamy islands that include sophisticated **Mykonos**, laid-back **Paros** and volcanic **Santorini**. When you've had enough of Greek islands, set sail for the Turkish port Kuşadasi from lush, mountainous Samos.

Visit ancient **Ephesus**, one of the greatest surviving Graeco-Roman cities. Travel by bus north along the Aegean coast to the ruins of Troy and **Çanakkale**, the harbour town that's the base for visiting Gallipoli Peninsula. Finish up in beautiful, chaotic **İstanbul**: when you've had your fill of sightseeing, you can always relax in a *hamam* (Turkish bath).

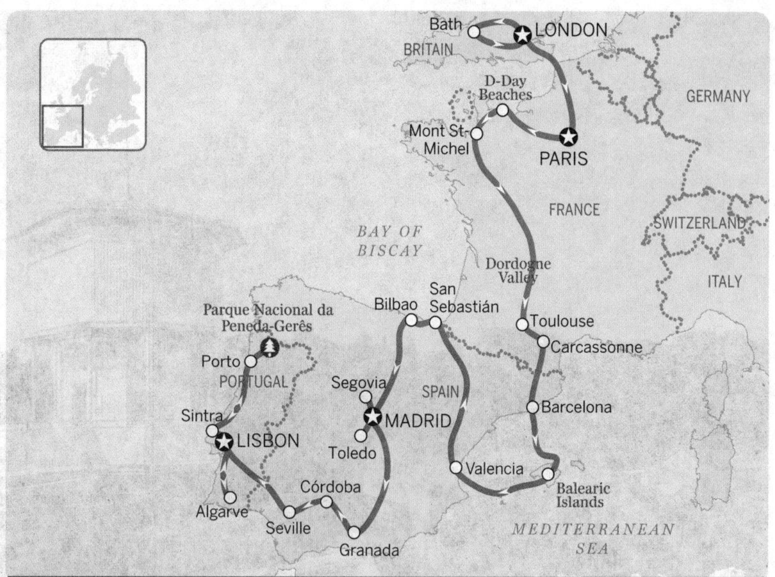

From London to the Sun

Combining the best of both worlds, this itinerary begins with urban powerhouses London and Paris, and ends with soaking up the sun in Spain and Portugal.

Enjoy several days in **London** for museums, galleries, shopping and clubbing, then take a train to **Bath** to enjoy Roman and Georgian architecture and thermal baths. Return to London to board the Eurostar to romantic **Paris**. Having dipped into the city of light's cultural sights and gourmet delights, make side trips to **D-Day Beaches** north of Bayeux and the iconic abbey of **Mont St-Michel**, which reaches for the sky from its rocky island perch.

Rail south, stopping at lively **Toulouse**. Detour to the fairytale fortified city of **Carcassonne**. Cross into Spain, pausing at supercool **Barcelona**, where you can indulge in traditional Catalan cooking as well as more avant-garde Spanish cuisine. Regular ferries sail from Barcelona to the **Balearic Islands**: relax on beaches, hike the mountains of Mallorca, or party on Ibiza. Return to mainland port **Valencia** with great nightlife and the architecturally stunning Ciudad de las Artes y las Ciencias.

Zip north to Basque seaside resort **San Sebastián**, with its delicious food scene, and then to the shimmering Museo Guggenheim in happening **Bilbao**. Turn south, making a beeline for energetic **Madrid**, for some of Europe's best galleries and bars. From here plan day trips to Moorish **Toledo** and enchanting **Segovia**.

Continue south to **Granada** to explore the exquisite Islamic fortress complex of the Alhambra. Continue your Andalusian adventures with the stunning Mezquita of **Córdoba**, before dancing the flamenco in **Seville**. Get the bus to Portugal's captivating hillside capital **Lisbon** and listen to fado in the lamplit lanes of Alfama. Sidestep to the wooded hills of **Sintra**, home to fairytale-like palaces and gardens. Further north lies Unesco World Heritage–listed **Porto**, a lovely city to explore on foot, and the **Parque Nacional da Peneda-Gerês**, where you can hike amid scenery little changed since the 12th-century founding of Portugal. Retrace your steps south to touristy **Algarve**; the coastal train journey is beautiful and there are pretty towns to stop at including Tavira and Lagos.

CULTURA TRAVEL / ATLI MAR HAFSTEINSSON / GETTY IMAGES ©

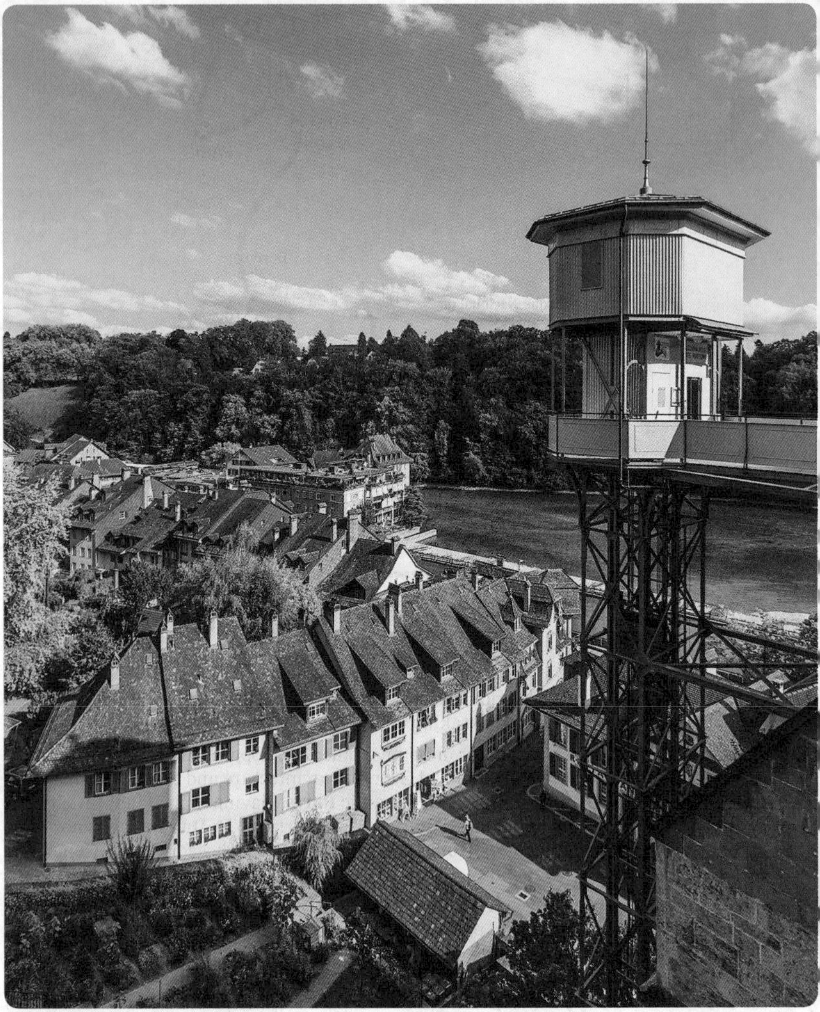

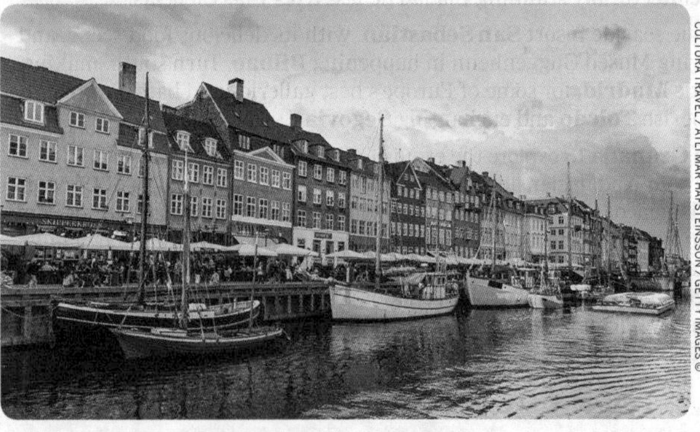

Above: Bern (p1122), Switzerland
Left: Copenhagen (p303), Denmark

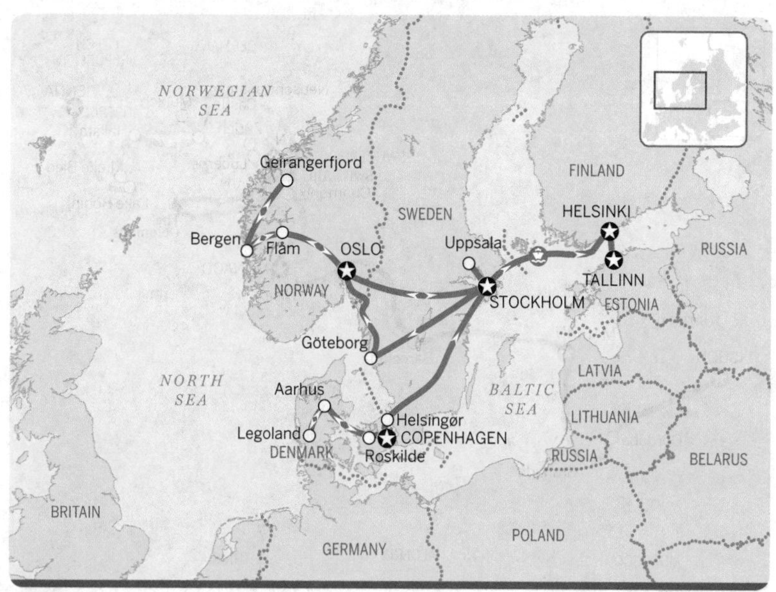

Scandinavian Highlights

Three weeks is sufficient for the classic sights of Scandinavia, though you can easily spend longer. Extra time allows detailed exploration and side trips to quieter places.

Start in Danish capital **Copenhagen**, the hipster of the Nordic block, admiring the waterfront and museums, and enjoying world-class eating options. Make day trips to the cathedral and Viking boat museum at **Roskilde**, 'Hamlet's' castle Kronborg Slot at **Helsingør**; Denmark's second but no-less-trendy city **Aarhus** where the incredible ARoS Aarhus Kunstmuseum offers nine floors of top-class art; and the country's biggest tourist attraction: **Legoland**.

Take the train to charming **Stockholm**. Sweden's capital spills across 14 islands with Gamla Stan, the oldest part, as its most beautiful. Side-trip to university town **Uppsala**, Sweden's spiritual heart, and spend the night. Creative and happening **Göteborg**, the country's second city, has interesting galleries and museums, including a great one for kids. Kids will also be thrilled by Liseberg, Scandinavia's largest amusement park. It's a 3½-hour bus ride to **Oslo**, where you can check out Munch's work in a stunning setting. Norway's capital has plenty of museums and galleries, plus the iconic Oslo Opera House, the centre of its massive waterfront redevelopment project.

From Oslo, take the long but scenic 'Norway in a Nutshell' rail day trip to **Flåm** and ride the world's steepest railway without cable or rack wheels. Continue by boat and bus along the stunning Sognefjord, Norway's deepest fjord with rock walls rising up to 1000m over the water, to **Bergen**. Admire this pretty town from a cable car and explore the quayside Bryggen district of historic buildings. From Bergen take a side trip to the mighty 20km-long emerald-green **Geirangerfjord**, a Unesco World Heritage Site and one of Scandinavia's most spectacular sights.

Return to Stockholm for a cruise circuit of the Baltic. First stop in quirky, design-diva **Helsinki**, a great base for exploring the natural wonders of Finland. Don't miss Unesco World Heritage–listed Suomenlinna, a fortress set on a tight cluster of islands connected by bridges. End your journey in picturesque **Tallinn**, the charming Estonian capital where the old town is a jumble of turrets, spires and winding streets.

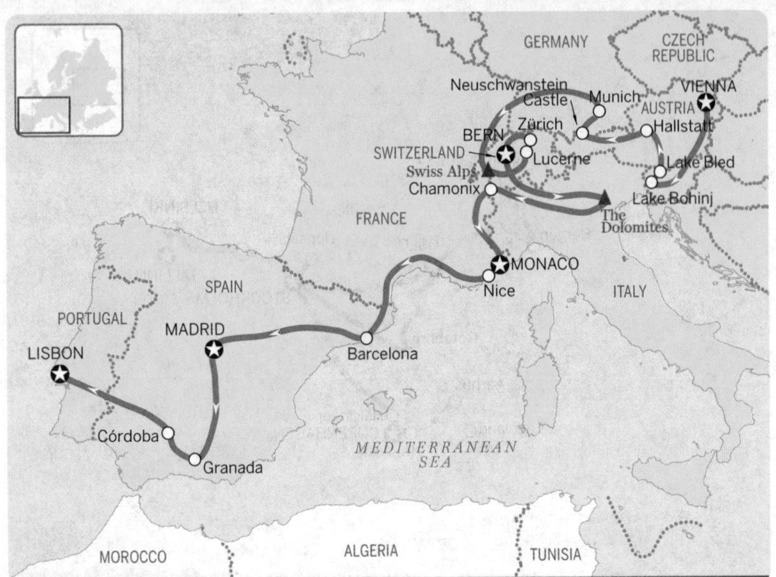

The Alps to the Iberian Peninsula

If you love gorgeous towns on the shores of brilliant-blue lakes, surrounded by soaring peaks, this itinerary is bound to please, with abundant opportunities to hike or ski.

Start with a couple of days on the Danube in elegant **Vienna** where you can tour the Habsburg palace Hofburg, world-class museums and the city's legendary coffee houses. Move on to Slovenia, pausing by emerald-green **Lake Bled** and nearby, but much less-developed, **Lake Bohinj** with the picturesque Julian Alps as the backdrop. Both locations are great for outdoor activities, offering kayaking, mountain biking and trekking.

Return to Austria for a couple of days exploring the beautiful Salzkammergut region of lakes and craggy peaks; don't miss postcard-perfect lakeside town **Hallstatt**.

Bavaria's fairytale **Neuschwanstein Castle** is next. Sample some beers in nearby **Munich**, which offers the best of traditional and contemporary Germany.

Make your way to Switzerland for a few days in the spectacular **Swiss Alps**. Visit the oft-overlooked Swiss capital of **Bern**, or sophisticated lake-side **Zürich**. Take the train to the top of Jungfrau (it's Europe's highest train station) before heading down to visit lovely **Lucerne** where candy-coloured houses are reflected in a cobalt lake.

Nip into Italy to check out the sawtooth peaks of the **Dolomites** where ski resorts abound. Head to **Chamonix** in France – a great base to explore Mont Blanc. Then it's time for coffee, wine and sun along the Côte d'Azur. Travel via **Monaco**, where you can live out James Bond fantasies at the Casino de Monte Carlo, and gorgeous **Nice**, the queen of the Riviera.

Spain's two most exciting cities, **Barcelona** and **Madrid**, beckon, packed with a wealth of sights, restaurants, bars and clubs. Head south to see the beautiful Moorish architecture of the Alhambra in **Granada** and the stunning Mezquita of **Córdoba**.

Finish in Portugal's fascinating capital **Lisbon**, with narrow cobblestone lanes, clattering bright-yellow trams and a lamplit old quarter. Make sure you sample a *pastéis de nata* (custard tart) in the waterside Belém district.

Above: Neuschwanstein Castle in Bavaria (p463), Germany

Right: Hallstatt (p81), Austria

Eastern Europe Today

Forget the stereotypes of the grim and grey 'Eastern Bloc' of the early 1990s – this half of Europe is one of the most dynamic and fast-changing places in the world.

The natural starting point is **Berlin**, once a city divided but now a veritable music, art and nightlife mecca. There's plenty of history here from the Reichstag to the Holocaust Memorial and Checkpoint Charlie.

Travel to Poland's capital **Warsaw**, a vibrant city that's survived all that history could throw at it, and beautiful **Kraków**, the amazingly preserved royal capital which miraculously was spared destruction in WWII. The centrepieces are the stunning Wawel Castle and Cathedral and the Rynek Glówny, Europe's largest medieval town square.

Next is Lithuania's capital **Vilnius**, the baroque bombshell of the Baltics with an Old Town of cobbled streets and church spires, followed by Latvia's gorgeous art nouveau **Rīga**. Round out the tour with Estonia's technophile **Tallinn**, a city that sports an impressive medieval Old Town. Head into Russia stopping first in the imperial capital of **St Petersburg**. Spend several days touring the Hermitage and other gorgeously restored palaces. Take a train to modern-day supercity **Moscow**, where the imposing Kremlin and adjacent Red Square are guaranteed to strike you with awe.

Journey into the past on a train to **Minsk** in Belarus to see how things were under communism. Continue into Ukraine and spend a few days in its bustling capital **Kyiv**, one of the former Soviet Union's more pleasant metropolises, then contrast it with Unesco World Heritage–listed **Lviv** which oozes central European charm.

Enter Romania and make a beeline for **Transylvania**. Sharpen your fangs at 'Dracula's' castle in **Bran** and enjoy the gorgeous old towns nearby. Romania's dynamic capital **Bucharest** is next, with its good museums, parks and trendy cafes.

A train zips you through the mountains to Bulgaria's loveliest town, **Veliko Târnovo**. Travel to the relaxed capital **Sofia** and then by train to Serbia's vibrant capital, **Belgrade**. Head back to Berlin via **Budapest**, where you can freshen up at the thermal baths and party at numerous pubs and bars, and romantic **Prague**, one of eastern Europe's most architecturally stunning cities.

On the Road

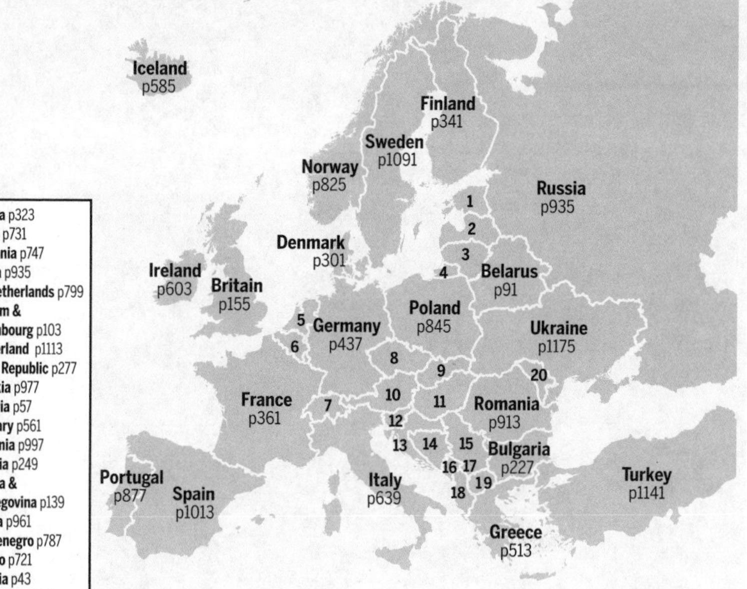

Iceland p585
Finland p341
Sweden p1091
Norway p825
Russia p935
Denmark p301
Ireland p603
Britain p155
Belarus p91
Poland p845
Germany p437
Ukraine p1175
France p361
Romania p913
Bulgaria p227
Portugal p877
Spain p1013
Italy p639
Turkey p1141
Greece p513
1
2
3
4
5
6
7
8
9
10
11
12
13
14
15
16
17
18
19
20

Albania

Includes ➡

Best Places to Eat

- Kujtimi (p54)
- Da Pucci (p47)
- Tradita G&T (p49)
- Pastarella (p47)
- Mare Nostrum (p53)

Best Places to Stay

- Tradita G&T (p49)
- Hotel Rilindja (p50)
- Trip N Hostel (p47)
- Gjirokastra Hotel (p54)
- Hotel Mangalemi (p51)

Why Go?

Albania has natural beauty in such abundance that you might wonder why it's taken a full 20 years for the country to take off as a tourist destination after the end of a particularly brutal strain of communism in 1991. So backward was Albania when it emerged blinking into the bright light of freedom that it needed two decades just to catch up with the rest of Eastern Europe. Now that it arguably has done so, Albania offers a remarkable array of unique attractions, not least due to this very isolation: ancient mountain behaviour codes, forgotten archaeological sites and villages where time seems to have stood still are all on the menu.

With its stunning mountain scenery, a thriving capital in Tirana and beaches to rival anywhere else in the Mediterranean, Albania has become the sleeper hit of the Balkans. But hurry here, as word is well and truly out.

When to Go

Tirana

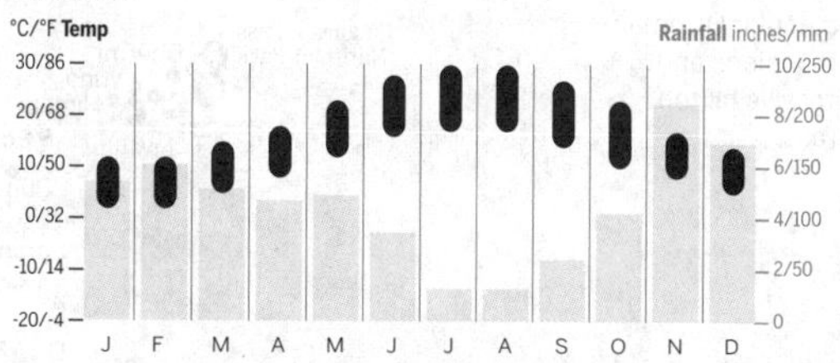

Jun Enjoy the perfect Mediterranean climate and deserted beaches.

Aug Albania's beaches may be packed, but this is a great time to explore the mountains.

Dec See features and shorts at the Tirana Film Festival, while the intrepid can snowshoe to Theth.

Albania Highlights

❶ Catch the **Lake Koman Ferry** (p50) through stunning mountain scenery, then continue to **Valbona** (p50) and trek through the 'Accursed Mountains' to **Theth** (p50).

❷ Explore the Unesco World Heritage–listed museum town of **Berat** (p50), the so-called 'city of a thousand windows'.

❸ Catch some sun at **Drymades**, (p52), just one of the many beaches on the south's dramatic Ionian Coast.

❹ Travel back in time to the ruins of **Butrint** (p53), hidden in the depths of a forest in a serene lakeside setting.

❺ Feast your eyes on the wild colour schemes and experience Blloku cafe culture in **Tirana** (p45).

❻ Take a trip to the traditional Southern Albanian mountain town of **Gjirokastra** (p54), with is spectacular Ottoman-era mansions and impressive hilltop fortress.

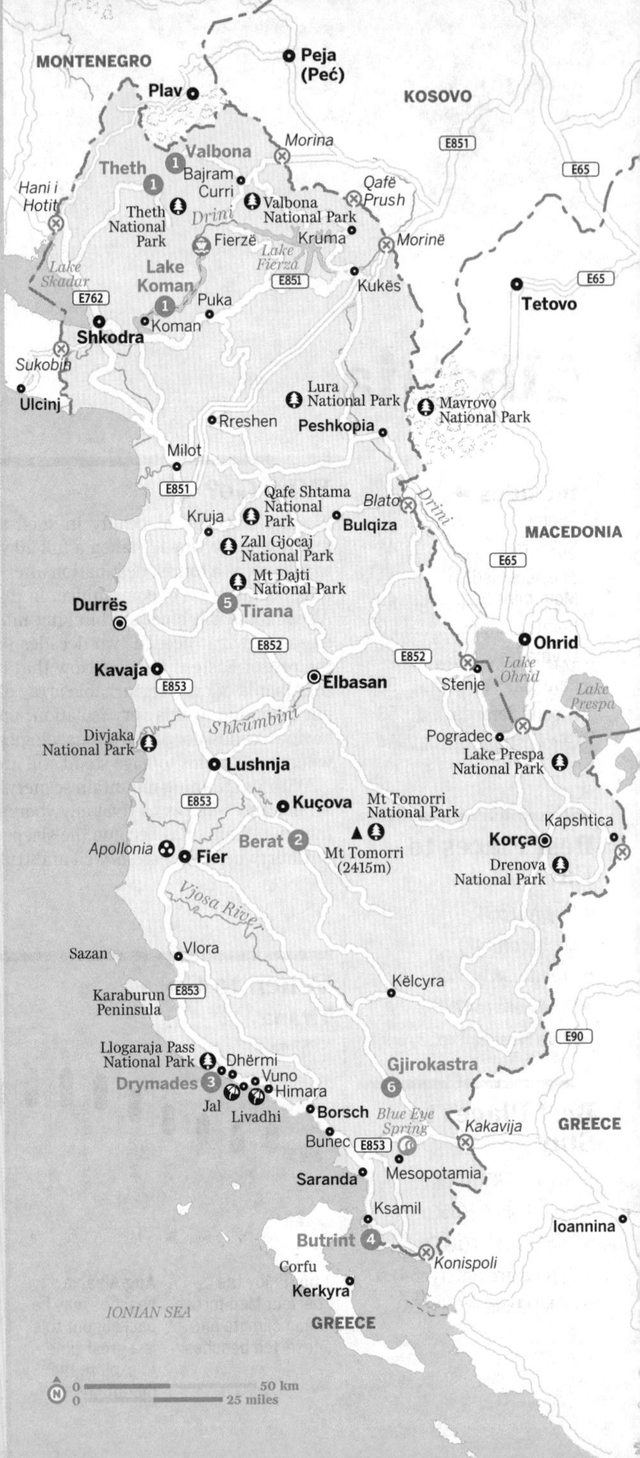

ITINERARIES

One Week

Spend a day in busy **Tirana**, checking out the various museums as well as the Blloku bars and nightclubs. On day two, make the three-hour trip to the Ottoman-era town of **Berat**. Spend a night there, before continuing down the coast for a couple of days on the beach in **Drymades**. Loop around for one last night in charming **Gjirokastra** before returning to Tirana.

Two Weeks

Follow the first week itinerary and then head north into Albania's incredible 'Accursed Mountains'. Start in **Shkodra**, from where you can get transport to **Koman** for the stunning morning ferry ride to **Fierzë**. Continue the same day to the charming mountain village of **Valbona** for a couple of nights, before trekking to **Theth** and spending your last couple of nights in the beautiful **Theth National Park**.

TIRANA

04 / POP 802,000

Lively, colourful Tirana is the beating heart of Albania, where this tiny nation's hopes and dreams coalesce into a vibrant whirl of traffic, brash consumerism and unfettered fun. Having undergone a transformation of extraordinary proportions since it awoke from its communist slumber in the early 1990s, Tirana's centre is now unrecognisable, with its buildings painted in primary colours, and public squares and pedestrianised streets a pleasure to wander.

Trendy Blloku buzzes with the well-heeled and flush hanging out in bars or zipping between boutiques, while the city's grand boulevards are lined with fascinating relics of its Ottoman, Italian and communist past – from delicate minarets to loud socialist murals. Tirana's traffic does daily battle with both itself and pedestrians in a constant scene of unmitigated chaos. Loud, crazy, colourful and dusty – Tirana is never dull.

Sights & Activities

Sheshi Skënderbej SQUARE

(Skanderbeg Sq) Skanderbeg Sq is the best place to start witnessing Tirana's daily goings-on. Until it was pulled down by an angry mob in 1991, a 10m-high bronze statue of Enver Hoxha stood here, watching over a mainly car-free square. Now only the **equestrian statue of Skanderbeg** remains.

★ **National History Museum** MUSEUM

(Muzeu Historik Kombëtar; Sheshi Skënderbej; adult/student 200/60 lekë; 10am-5pm Tue-Sat, 9am-2pm Sun) The largest museum in Albania holds many of the country's archaeological treasures and a replica of Skanderbeg's massive sword (how he held it, rode his horse and fought at the same time is a mystery). The excellent collection is almost entirely signed in English and takes you chronologically from ancient Illyria to the postcommunist era. One big highlight of the museum is a terrific exhibition of icons by Onufri, a renowned 16th-century Albanian master of colour.

★ **National Art Gallery** GALLERY

(Galeria Kombëtare e Arteve; www.gka.al; Blvd Dëshmorët e Kombit; adult/student 200/100 lekë; 10am-6pm Wed-Sun) Tracing the relatively brief history of Albanian painting from the early 19th century to the present day, this beautiful space also has temporary exhibits that are worth a look. Downstairs there's a small but interesting collection of 19th-century paintings depicting scenes from daily Albanian life, while upstairs the art takes on a political dimension with some truly fabulous examples of Albanian socialist realism.

Et'hem Bey Mosque MOSQUE

(Sheshi Skënderbej; 8am-11am) To one side of Skanderbeg Sq, the 1789–1823 Et'hem Bey Mosque was spared destruction during the atheism campaign of the late 1960s because of its status as a cultural monument. Small and elegant, it's one of the oldest buildings left in the city. Take your shoes off to look inside at the beautifully painted dome.

Palace of Culture NOTABLE BUILDING

(Pallate Kulturës; Sheshi Skënderbej) To the east of Sheshi Skënderbej is the white stone Palace of Culture, which has a theatre, shops and art galleries. Construction of the palace began as a gift from the Soviet people in 1960 and was completed in 1966, years after the 1961 Soviet–Albanian split.

Tirana

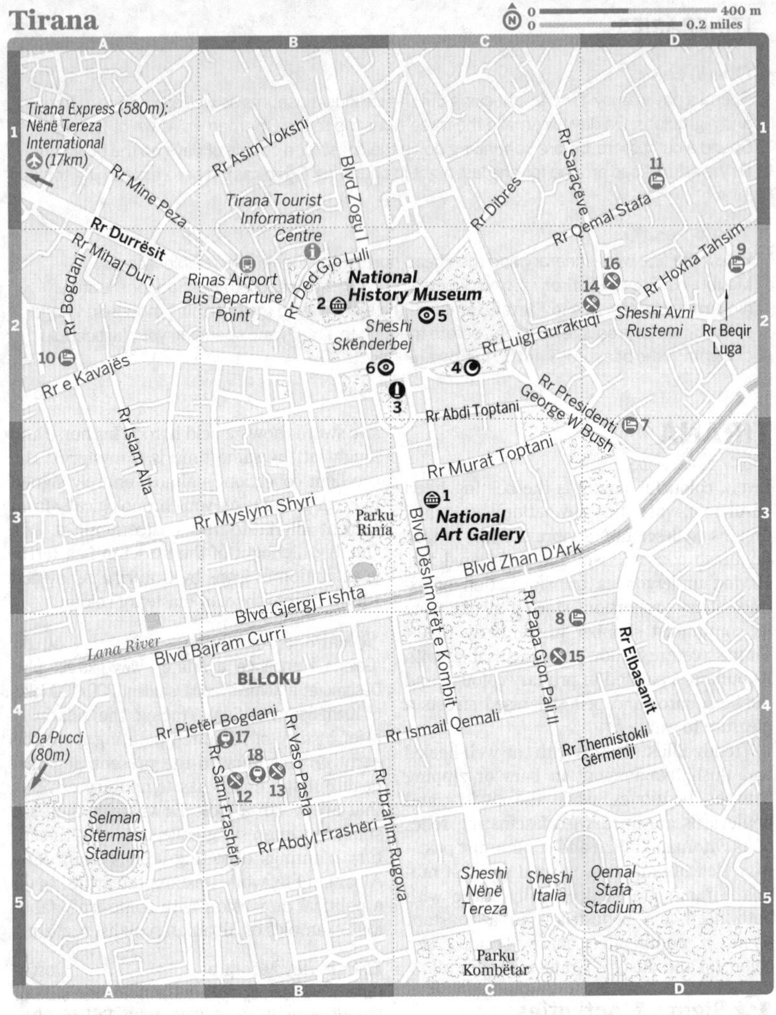

Tirana

Top Sights
1 National Art Gallery C3
2 National History Museum B2

Sights
3 Equestrian Statue of Skanderbeg C2
4 Et'hem Bey Mosque C2
5 Palace of Culture C2
6 Sheshi Skënderbej B2

Sleeping
7 Brilant Antik Hotel D3
8 Green House C4
9 Hostel Albania D2
10 Tirana Backpacker Hostel A2
11 Trip N Hostel D1

Eating
12 Era B4
13 Hola! B4
14 Oda D2
15 Pastarella C4
16 Stephen Centre D2

Drinking & Nightlife
17 Nouvelle Vague B4
18 Radio B4

Sleeping

★Trip N Hostel HOSTEL €

(068 2055 540, 068 3048 905; www.tripnhostel.com; Rr Musa Maci 1; dm/d €10/30) Tirana's coolest hostel is this recently opened place, housed in a large design-conscious house in a residential neighbourhood, with a garden out the back and a cool bar-hangout area. Dorms have handmade fixtures, curtains between beds for privacy and private lockable drawers, while there's also a roof terrace strewn with hammocks. There's a great vibe and a cool crowd as well.

★Tirana Backpacker Hostel HOSTEL €

(068 4682 353, 068 3133 451; www.tiranahostel.com; Rr e Bogdaneve 3; dm €10-11, s/d €28/35, cabin per person €14;) Albania's first ever hostel has now moved to an ever better location and remains one of the best value and most enthusiastically run places to stay in the country. Housed in a charmingly decorated house with a garden in which there are several cute cabins for those wanting something more than a dorm room, though there are also great private rooms available.

Hostel Albania HOSTEL €

(067 6748 779; www.hostel-albania.com; Rr Beqir Luga 56; dm €10-12 d €32;) Voted the best hostel in Albania in 2014, this friendly place has small four- and six-person dorms, though the basement's 14-bed dorm (€11.50) is the coolest spot in summer and dividers hide the fact that there are so many bunks down there. Zen space is in the outdoor shoes-off oriental lounge, and a filling breakfast with filter coffee is included.

★Brilant Antik Hotel HOTEL €€

(04 2251 166; www.hotelbrilant.com; Rr Jeronim de Rada 79; s/d €60/90;) This charming house-cum-hotel has plenty of character, a central location and welcoming English-speaking staff to ease you into Tirana life. Rooms are spacious, decently furnished with the odd antique, and breakfast downstairs is a veritable feast each morning.

Green House BOUTIQUE HOTEL €€€

(04 4521 015, 068 2072 262; www.greenhouse.al; Rr Jul Variboba 6; s/d €90/100;) In a cool spot in Tirana sits this modern 10-room hotel with downlit, stylish rooms that might be the city's coolest. Its sprawling downstairs terrace restaurant is a friendly expat hangout with a varied menu and a long wine list. It looks up at one of Tirana's quirkiest buildings.

Eating

Era ALBANIAN, ITALIAN €€

(04 224 3845; www.era.al; Rr Ismail Qemali; mains 400-800 lekë; 11am-midnight;) This local institution serves traditional Albanian and Italian fare in the heart of Blloku. The inventive menu includes oven-baked veal and eggs, stuffed eggplant, pizza, and pilau with chicken and pine nuts. Be warned: it's sometimes quite hard to get a seat as it's fearsomely popular, so you may have to wait. Delivery and takeaway are both available.

Oda ALBANIAN €€

(Rr Luigj Gurakuqi; mains 350-650 lekë; noon-11pm;) This tourist favourite is stuffed full of traditional Albanian arts and crafts, and while its popularity with travellers means you won't feel like you've discovered a truly authentic slice of the country, the delicious menu and pleasant atmosphere make it well worth a visit. You can choose from two brightly lit dining rooms or an atmospheric terrace.

★Da Pucci ITALIAN €€€

(069 3434 999; Rr Mustafa Qosja; mains 500-800 lekë; noon-midnight;) A surprise find in a rather out-of-the-way residential district (a short wander beyond the busy streets of Blloku) is this cosily decked out, need-to-know-about-it subterranean space that feels rather like somebody's living room. The menu, which changes daily, is brought to you on a chalkboard and waiters just about manage a basic English translation. The classic Italian home cooking is divine though. Reservations are a good idea for the evenings.

Stephen Centre CAFE €€

(Rr Hoxha Tahsim 1; mains 400-700 lekë; 8am-8pm Mon-Sat;) Looking better than ever after a 2014 refit, this Tirana classic is where to come for a great burger, fantastic Tex-Mex and enormous, great value breakfasts. Run by Christian missionaries to Albania who work with local orphans, Roma and the disabled, the Centre has no booze on the menu, but is a super friendly and relaxed hang out.

★Pastarella ITALIAN €€€

(www.pastarellarestaurant.com; Rr Mustafa Matohiti 18; mains 500-1200 lekë; 8am-midnight;) The seafood is fresh here, and forms the centre of the menu, but there's also a large range of pastas (as you'd expect), risotti and grilled meats on offer, and all are superb. There's a charming terrace to dine on, or a rather more formal inside dining room. Staff are polite and English speaking.

Hola! SPANISH €€€

(Rr Ismail Qemali; mains 600-1300 lekë; ⏲11am-11pm; 📶) The Spanish owner here was a finalist on *Masterchef Albania* who went on to found one of Tirana's most popular restaurant as a hobby, and, as the name suggests, he'll greet you at the door on most evenings. The menu here is wonderfully creative Spanish fare, ranging from delicious tapas to a splash-out paella.

Drinking

Radio BAR

(Rr Ismail Qemali 29/1; ⏲9am-1am; 📶) This place remains one of the city's coolest bars and attracts a young and alternative crowd. Set back from the street, you have to know it's here, but once inside this understated and friendly place be sure to check out the owner's collection of antique Albanian-made radios.

Nouvelle Vague BAR

(Rr Pjetër Bogdani; ⏲9am-midnight; 📶) A Blloku hotspot favoured by a cool crowd, Nouvelle Vague is one of the places to head any night of the week for a great atmosphere, full cocktail list and interesting music.

☆ Entertainment

★**Tirana Express** GALLERY, CONCERT VENUE

(www.tiranaekspres.com; Rr Dritan Hoxha) This fantastic nonprofit arts project is a unique arts space that hosts revolving temporary exhibits, concerts, installations and other events that appeal to Tirana's arty, alternative crowd. Go along and see what's on during your visit. Opening hours vary depending on what's on.

ℹ Information

Tirana Tourist Information Centre (☎04 2223 313; www.tirana.gov.al; Rr Ded Gjo Luli; ⏲9am-6pm Mon-Fri, to 2pm Sat) Friendly English-speaking staff make getting information easy at this government-run initiative just off Skanderbeg Sq.

ℹ Getting There & Around

AIR

The modern **Nënë Tereza International Airport** (Mother Teresa Airport; ☎04 2381 800; www.tirana-airport.com) is at Rinas, 17km northwest of Tirana. The Rinas Express airport bus operates an hourly (8am to 7pm) service from Rr Mine Peza a few blocks from the National History Museum for 250 lekë one way. The going taxi rate is 2000 to 2500 lekë.

BUS

Most international services depart from various parts of Blvd Zogu I, with multiple services to Skopje, Macedonia (€20, eight hours) and Pristina, Kosovo (€20, five hours) leaving from near the Tirana International Hotel, and services to Ulcinj in Montenegro (€20, four hours) leaving from in front of the Tourist Information Centre.

Services to Shkodra (300 lekë, two hours, hourly until 5pm) leave from the Zogu i Zi Roundabout at the intersection of Rr Durrësit and Rr Muhamet Gjollesha. *Furgons* (shared minibuses) to Bajram Curri (1000 lekë, 5½ hours, hourly 5am-2pm), the jumping off point for Valbona on the far side of Lake Koman, leave from here too – you'll find them outside the Logos University building.

Departures to the south leave from Rr Myhedin Llegami near the corner with Blvd Gjergj Fishta. These include services to Berat (400 lekë, three hours, every 30 min until 6pm), Saranda (1300 lekë, 6½ hours, roughly hourly 5am-midday) and Gjirokastra (1000 lekë, 6 hours, regular departures until midday, also at 2.30pm & 6.30pm). Services to Saranda will drop you off at any of the coastal villages along the way.

TAXI

Taxi stands dot the city, and taxis charge 300 to 400 lekë for a ride inside Tirana, and 500 to 600 lekë at night and to destinations outside the city centre.

NORTHERN ALBANIA

Northern Albania is a scenic wonderland where the incredible landscape of the 'Accursed Mountains' dominates and the rich and independent mountain culture strongly flavours all journeys.

Shkodra

☎022 / POP 111,000

Shkodra, the traditional centre of the Gheg cultural region, is one of the oldest cities in Europe. The ancient Rozafa Fortress has stunning views over the nearby lake, while a concerted effort to renovate the buildings in the Old Town has made wandering through Shkodra a treat for the eyes.

⊙ Sights

Rozafa Fortress CASTLE

(admission 200 lekë; ⏲10am-8pm) With spectacular views over the city and Lake Shkodra, the Rozafa Fortress is the most interesting sight in the town. Founded by the Illyrians in antiquity and rebuilt much later by the Venetians and then the Turks, the fortress takes its name from a woman named Rozafa, who was allegedly walled into the ramparts as an offering to the gods so that the construction would stand.

Marubi Permanent Photo Exhibition GALLERY
(Rr Muhamet Gjollesha; admission 100 lekë; ⏲8am-4pm Mon-Fri) The Marubi Permanent Photo Exhibition has fantastic photography by the Marubi 'dynasty', Albania's first and foremost photographers. It's poorly signposted: look for the sign Galeria e Arteve Shkodër, and once in the courtyard go through a further small gate and look for the sign in Albanian with the word Marubi in it.

Sleeping & Eating

Mi Casa Es Tu Casa HOSTEL €
(☎069 3812 054; www.micasaestucasa.it; Blvd Skenderbeu; dm/d/apt €12/30/40; @ 📶) Shkodra's best established hostel is run by the helpful, English-speaking Alba, and has a great location in the centre of town, opposite the Millenium Cinema. There's a proper hostel vibe with lots of space, bright colour schemes and a garden where you can also pitch a tent. Bike hire is available for €5 and the dorms are bright and clean.

★ **Tradita G&T** BOUTIQUE HOTEL €€
(☎068 2086 056, 022-240 537; www.traditagt.com; Rr Edith Durham 4; s/d/tr €35/50/55; P 📶) By far the best choice in town, this innovative, well-managed guesthouse is a delight. Housed in a painstakingly restored 17th-century mansion that once belonged to a famous Shkodran writer, the Tradita heaves with Albanian arts and crafts and has traditional yet very comfortable rooms with terracotta-roofed bathrooms and locally woven bed linen.

Information

The **Tourist Information Centre** (☎022 240 242; Sheshi Nënë Tereza; ⏲9am-4pm Mon-Fri 10am-noon Sat & Sun) at the intersection of Bul Skënderbeg and Rr Kolë Idromeno is run as a public-private partnership and has helpful, English-speaking staff on hand to answer your questions.

Getting There & Away

BUS

There are hourly *furgons* (400 lekë) and buses (300 lekë) to Tirana (two hours, 6am to 5pm), which depart from outside Radio Shkodra near Hotel Rozafa. There are three daily buses to Ulcinj in Montenegro that leave at 9am, 2.15pm and 4pm (€5, two hours) from outside the Tourist Information Centre. Catch the 6.30am bus to Lake Koman (500 lekë, two hours) in time for the wonderful ferry trip along the lake to Fierzë near Kosovo; most hotels can call ahead and get the *furgon* to pick you up on its way out of town. Several *furgons* depart daily for Theth between 6am and 7am (700 lekë, four hours) from outside Cafe Rusi.

TAXI

It costs between €40 and €50 for the trip from Shkodra to Ulcinj in Montenegro, depending on your haggling skills.

The Accursed Mountains

The 'Accursed Mountains' (Bjeshkët e Namuna) offer some of Albania's most impressive scenery and have exploded in recent years as a popular backpacker destination. The reason that most people come here is to do the popular hike between Valbona and Theth, which takes roughly five to six hours.

BUNKER LOVE

On the hillsides, beaches and generally most surfaces in Albania, you will notice small concrete domes (often in groups of three) with rectangular slits. Meet the bunkers: Enver Hoxha's concrete legacy, built from 1950 to 1985. Weighing in at 5 tonnes of concrete and iron, these little mushrooms are almost impossible to destroy. They were built to repel an invasion and can resist full tank assault – a fact proved by their chief engineer, who vouched for his creation's strength by standing inside one while it was bombarded by a tank. The shell-shocked engineer emerged unscathed, and tens of thousands were built. Today, some are creatively painted, one houses a tattoo artist, and some even house makeshift hostels.

In late 2014, a private bunker built for Hoxha himself was opened for the first time just outside Tirana. Built 100m below ground and designed to withstand a nuclear attack, the bunker is to open in 2015 as a museum and exhibition space.

DON'T MISS

THE LAKE KOMAN FERRY

One of Albania's undisputed highlights is this superb three-hour ferry ride across vast Lake Koman, connecting the towns of Koman and Fierzë.

The best way to experience the journey is to make a three-day, two-night loop beginning and ending in Shkodra, and taking in Koman, Fierzë, Valbona and Theth. To do this, arrange to have the morning 6.30am *furgon* (shared minibus) from Shkodra to Koman (500 lekë, two hours) pick you up at your hotel, which will get you to the departure point for the boats by 8.30am. There are two ferries daily in the summer months – both leave from Koman at 9am and arrive in Fierzë around 1pm.

On arrival in Fierzë the boats are met by *furgons* that will take you to either Bajram Curri (200 lekë) or to Valboa (400 lekë). There's no real reason to stay in Bajram Curri though, unless you plan to head to Kosovo. Hikers will want to head straight for Valbona, where you can stay for a night or two before doing the stunning day hike to Theth. After the hike you can stay for another night or two in Theth before taking a *furgon* back to Shkodra.

Valbona

Most travellers just spend a night here before trekking to Theth, though there are a wealth of other excellent hikes to do in the area – ask for guides or information at Hotel Rilindja, or check out the excellent www.journeytovalbona.com website, a DIY-kit for the entire area.

Sleeping & Eating

★ **Hotel Rilindja** GUESTHOUSE €€

(☎067 3014 637; www.journeytovalbona.com; Quku i Valbonës; per tent €6, dm per person €12, r s/d/t €30/40/50) Pioneering tourism in Valbona since 2005, the Albanian-American run Rilindja is hugely popular with travellers who love the comfortable accommodation and excellent food. The simple five rooms in the atmospheric farmhouse share a bathroom, except for one that has private facilities. The new Rezidenca up the road offers a far more upscale experience with ensuite singles, doubles and triples.

Getting There & Away

Valbona can be reached from Shkodra via the Lake Koman Ferry, and a connecting *furgon* from Fierzë (400 lekë, 1 hour). Alterrnatively it can be reached by *furgon* from Bajram Curri (200 lekë, 45 minutes).

Theth

This unique mountain village has traditional houses, an imposing church and a riverside setting dominated by a rare surviving example of a lock-in tower, where in the past locals under a blood feud could retreat to safety.

Sleeping & Eating

★ **Guesthouse Rupa** GUESTHOUSE €€

(☎068 2003 393, 022-244 077; rorupaog@yahoo.com; r per person full board €23) This wonderful option is run by the formidable Roza, who speaks good English and is a great source of information about the area. There are only five rooms, but rarely for Theth, all have private facilities. The excellent meals are taken communally around a big table, so there's a very sociable vibe.

Getting There & Around

The daily *furgon* (1000 lekë) leaves from Shkodra at 7am and will pick you up from your hotel if your hotel owner calls ahead for you. It returns between 1 and 2pm, arriving late afternoon in Shkodra.

CENTRAL ALBANIA

Berat

☎032 / POP 71,000

Berat weaves its own very special magic, and is easily a highlight of visiting Albania. Its most striking feature is the collection of white Ottoman houses climbing up the hill to its castle, earning it the title of 'town of a thousand windows' and helping it join Gjirokastra on the list of Unesco World Heritage sites in 2008. Its rugged mountain setting is particularly evocative when the clouds swirl around the tops of the minarets, or break up to show the icy top of Mt Tomorri. Berat today is now a big centre for tourism in Albania, though it has managed to retain its easy-going charm and friendly atmosphere. Don't miss it.

Sights

★Kalaja CASTLE
(admission 100 lekë; 24hr) The neighbourhood inside the castle's walls still lives and breathes; if you walk around this busy, ancient neighbourhood for long enough you'll invariably stumble into someone's courtyard thinking it's a church or ruin (no one seems to mind, though). In spring and summer the fragrance of camomile is in the air (and underfoot), and wildflowers burst from every gap between the stones.

★Onufri Museum GALLERY
(admission 200 lekë; 9am-1pm & 4-7pm Tue-Sat, to 2pm Sun May-Sep, to 4pm Tue-Sun Oct-Apr) Kala was traditionally a Christian neighbourhood, but fewer than a dozen of the 20 churches remain. The quarter's biggest church, **Church of the Dormition of St Mary** (Kisha Fjetja e Shën Mërisë), is the site of the Onufri Museum. The church itself dates from 1797 and was built on the foundations of a 10th-century church. Onufri's spectacular 16th-century artworks are displayed on the ground level along with a beautifully gilded iconostasis.

Ethnographic Museum MUSEUM
(admission 200 lekë; 9am-1pm & 4-7pm Tue-Sat, to 2pm Sun May-Sep, to 4pm Tue-Sun Oct-Apr) Down from the castle, this museum is in an 18th-century Ottoman house that's as interesting as the exhibits. The ground floor has displays of traditional clothes and the tools used by silversmiths and weavers, while the upper storey has kitchens, bedrooms and guest rooms decked out in traditional style.

Mangalem Quarter NEIGHBOURHOOD
Down in the traditionally Muslim Mangalem quarter, there are three grand mosques. The 16th-century **Sultan's Mosque** (Xhamia e Mbretit) is one of the oldest in Albania. The **Helveti teqe** behind the mosque has a beautiful carved ceiling and was specially designed with acoustic holes to improve the quality of sound during meetings. The Helveti, like the Bektashi, are a dervish order, or brotherhood, of Muslim mystics.

Sleeping & Eating

Berat Backpackers HOSTEL €
(069 7854 219; www.beratbackpackers.com; Gorica; tent/dm/r €6/12/30; mid Mar-Nov; @ wi-fi) This transformed traditional house in the Gorica quarter (across the river from Mangalem) houses one of Albania's friendliest and best-run hostels. The vine-clad establishment contains a basement bar, alfresco drinking area and a cheery, relaxed atmosphere that money can't buy. There are two airy dorms with original ceilings, and one excellent-value double room that shares the bathroom facilities with the dorms.

There's also a shaded camping area on the terrace and cheap laundry available.

★Hotel Mangalemi HOTEL €€
(068 2323 238; www.mangalemihotel.com; Rr Mihail Komneno; s/d from €30/40; P ❄ @ wi-fi) A true highlight of Berat is this gorgeous place inside two sprawling Ottoman houses where all the rooms are beautifully furnished in traditional Berati style and balconies give superb views. Its terrace restaurant (mains 400 lekë to 600 lekë; reserve in the evening) is the best place to eat in town and has great Albanian food with bonus views of Mt Tomorri.

It's on the left side of the cobblestone road leading to the castle.

Hotel Muzaka HOTEL €€
(231 999; www.hotel-muzaka.com; Gorica; s/d from €50/65; P ❄ wi-fi) This gorgeous Gorica hotel is a careful restoration of an old stone mansion on the riverfront, just over the footbridge from the centre of town. Wooden floorboards, gorgeous bathrooms and beautifully chosen pieces of furniture in the 10 spacious rooms make this a good option for those looking for some style as well as tradition in their accommodation.

There's also a pleasant restaurant here, open to the public for lunch and dinner (mains 400 lekë to 800 lekë).

White House ITALIAN €€
(Rr Antipatrea; mains 300-600 lekë; 8am-11pm) On the main road that runs north of the river, this place has a superb roof terrace with sweeping views over Berat, and serves up a mean pizza to boot. There's also a classier dining room downstairs with air-conditioning, perfect for a blowout meal.

Getting There & Away

Buses and *furgons* run between Tirana and Berat (400 lekë, three hours, half-hourly until 3pm). Services arrive in and depart from Sheshi Teodor Muzaka next to the Lead Mosque in the centre of town. There are also buses to Vlora (300 lekë, 2 hours, hourly until 2pm), Durrës (300 lekë, 2 hours, six per day) and Saranda (1200 lekë, six hours, two daily at 8am and 2pm), one of which goes via Gjirokastra (800 lekë, four hours, 8am).

SOUTHERN COAST

With rough mountains falling headfirst into bright blue seas, the coastal drive between Vlora and Saranda is easily one of the most spectacular in Eastern Europe and shouldn't missed by any visitor to Albania. While beaches can be jam-packed in August, there's plenty of space, peace and happy-to-see-you faces in the low season.

Drymades

As you zigzag down the mountain from the Llogaraja Pass National Park, the white crescent-shape beaches and azure waters lure you from below. The first beach before the alluvial fan is Palasa, and it's one of the best, and least developed beaches around, perfect for chilling out for a night or two if you have a tent. The next beach along is Drymades beach. To get here leave for main road for Dhërmi, then take the first right (signposted for the Turtle Club) and you'll reach the rocky white beach in 20 mins via the sealed road that twists through olive groves.

Sleeping

★ Sea Turtle CAMPGROUND €

(☎069 4016 057; Drymades; per person incl half-board from 1000 lekë; ⏲Jun-Sep; 📶) This great little set-up is run by two brothers. Each summer they turn the family orange orchard into a vibrant tent city, and the price includes the tent (with mattresses, sheets and pillows), breakfast and a family-cooked dinner (served up in true camp style). Hot showers are under the shade of old fig trees, or it's a short walk to the beach.

Saranda

☎0852 / POP 37,700

Saranda has grown rapidly in the past decade; skeletal high-rises crowd around its horseshoe shape and hundreds more are being built in the outlying region. Saranda is bustling in summer – buses are crowded with people carrying swimming gear and the weather means it's almost obligatory to go for a swim. A daily stream of Corfu holidaymakers take the 45-minute ferry trip to Albania, add the Albanian stamp to their passports and hit Butrint or the Blue Eye Spring before heading back.

Sleeping

SR Backpackers HOSTEL €

(☎069 4345 426; www.backpackerssr.hostel.com; Rr Mitat Hoxha 10; dm from €12; @📶) The hostel with the most central location in Saranda, this is also the cheapest option. Housed in an apartment and hosted by the gregarious English-speaking Tomi, the 14 beds here are spread over three dorms, each with its own balcony. There's one shared bathroom, a communal kitchen and a friendly atmosphere.

Hotel Porto Eda HOTEL €€

(www.portoeda.com; Rr Jonianët; r €55; P❄📶) Referencing the temporary name given to Saranda during the fascist occupation, this hotel is nevertheless a charming place and

THE ALBANIAN RIVIERA

The Albanian Riviera was a revelation a decade or so ago, when travellers began to discover the last virgin stretch of the Mediterranean coast in Europe. Since then, things have become significantly less pristine, with overdevelopment blighting many of the once charming coastal villages. But worry not: while Dhërmi and Himara may be well and truly swarming, there are still spots to kick back and enjoy the empty beaches the region was once so famous for.

One such place is **Vuno**, a tiny hillside village above picturesque Jal Beach. Each summer Vuno's primary school is filled with blow-up beds and it becomes **Shkolla Hostel** (☎068 4063 835; www.tiranahostel.com; Vuno; tent/dm €4/7; ⏲late Jun-Sep). What it lacks in infrastructure and privacy it makes up for with its goat-bell soundtrack and evening campfire. From Vuno, walk over the bridge and follow the rocky path to your right past the cemetery. It's a challenging 40-minute signed walk through olive groves to picturesque **Jal**, or a 5km walk along the main beach road.

Jal has two beaches; one has free camping while the other has a camping ground set back from the sea (including tent 2000 lekë). Fresh seafood is bountiful in Jal and there are plenty of beachside restaurants in summer.

about as central as you can get, overlooking the bay. The 24 rooms are comfortably and stylishly laid out, all with balconies and sea-views, and the welcome is warm. From September to June rooms cost just €45.

Eating

Gërthëla SEAFOOD €€

(Rr Jonianët; mains 300-1000 lekë; ⏲11am-midnight; 📶) One of Saranda's original restaurants, 'the crab' is a long-standing taverna that only has fish and seafood on the menu, and locals will tell you with certainty that it offers the best prepared versions of either available in town. The charming glass-fronted dining room is full of traditional knickknacks and there's a big wine selection to boot.

★**Mare Nostrum** INTERNATIONAL €€€

(Rr Jonianët; mains 700-1200 lekë; ⏲7am-midnight Mar-Dec) This sleek new restaurant immediately feels different to the others along the seafront: here there's elegant decor that wouldn't look out of place in a major European capital, the buzz of a smart in-the-know crowd and an imaginative menu that combines the seafood and fish you'll find everywhere else with dishes such as Indonesian chicken curry and burgers.

Information

Saranda's tiny but excellent **ZIT information centre** (☎069 324 3304; Rr Skënderbeu; ⏲9am-9pm Jul-Aug, to 4pm Mon-Fri Sep-Jun) provides information about transport and local sights and is staffed by friendly and helpful English speaking staff.

Getting There & Away

The ZIT information centre opposite the synagogue ruins has up-to-date bus timetables.

BUS

Most buses leave just uphill from the ruins on Rr Vangjel Pando, right in the centre of town. Buses to Tirana (1300 lekë, eight hours) go inland via Gjirokastra (30 lekë) and leave at 7am, 8.30am, 10.30am, 2pm, and 10pm. The 5.30am Tirana bus takes the coastal route (1300 lekë, eight hours).

In addition to the Tirana buses, there are buses to Gjirokastra's new town (300 lekë, 1½ hours) at 11.30am and 1pm – they all pass the turn-off to the Blue Eye Spring. Buses to Himara (400 lekë, two hours) leave around four times a day.

FERRY

Finikas (☎085-226 057, 067 2022 004; www.finikas-lines.com; Rr Mithat Hoxha) at the port sells hydrofoil tickets for Corfu (Jul-Aug/Sep-Jun €24/19, 45 minutes) with a daily departure at 9am, 10.30am and 4pm in the summer months. See the website for timings, which vary year round. From Corfu there are three ferries per day in summer: 9am, 1pm and 6.30pm. Note that Greek time is one hour ahead of Albanian time.

TAXI

Taxis wait for customers at the bus stop and opposite Central Park on Rr Skënderbeu. A taxi to the Greek border at Kakavija costs 4000 lekë.

Around Saranda

Butrint

The ancient ruins of **Butrint** (www.butrint.al; admission 700 lekë; ⏲8am-dusk), 18km south of Saranda, are renowned for their size, beauty and tranquillity. They're in a fantastic natural setting and are part of a 29-sq-km national park. Set aside at least two hours to explore this fascinating place.

Although the site was inhabited long before, Greeks from Corfu settled on the hill in Butrint (Buthrotum) in the 6th century BC. Within a century Butrint had become a fortified trading city with an acropolis. The lower town began to develop in the 3rd century BC, and many large stone buildings had already been built by the time the Romans took over in 167 BC. Butrint's prosperity continued throughout the Roman period, and the Byzantines made it an ecclesiastical centre. The city then went into a long decline and was abandoned until 1927, when Italian archaeologists arrived. These days Lord Rothschild's UK-based Butrint Foundation helps maintain the site.

As you enter the site the path leads to the right, to Butrint's 3rd-century-BC Greek theatre, secluded in the forest below the acropolis. Also in use during the Roman period, the theatre could seat about 2500 people. Close by are the small public baths, where geometric mosaics are buried under a layer of mesh and sand to protect them from the elements.

Getting There & Away

The municipal bus from Saranda to Butrint costs 50 lekë and leaves hourly from 8.30am to 5.30pm, and then comes back from Butrint hourly on the hour.

EASTERN ALBANIA

Gjirokastra

084 / POP 43,000

Defined by its castle, roads paved with chunky limestone and shale, imposing slate-roofed houses and views out to the Drina Valley, Gjirokastra is an intriguing hillside town described beautifully by Albania's most famous literary export and locally born author, Ismail Kadare (b 1936), in *Chronicle in Stone*. There has been a settlement here for 2500 years, though these days it's the 600 'monumental' Ottoman-era houses in town that attract visitors.

Sights

★Gjirokastra Castle CASTLE

(admission 200 lekë; 9am-7pm) Gjirokastra's eerie hilltop castle is one of the biggest in the Balkans and easily the town's best sight, most definitely worth the steep walk up from the Old Town. Inside there's an eerie collection of armoury, two good museums, a shot-down US Air Force jet and a hilariously hard-to-use audiotour that is included in your entry fee.

★Zekate House HISTORIC BUILDING

(admission 200 lekë; 9am-6pm) This incredible three-storey house dates from 1811 and has twin towers and a double-arched facade. It's fascinating to nose around the almost totally unchanged interiors of an Ottoman-era home, especially the upstairs galleries, which are the most impressive. The owners live next door and collect the payments; to get here, follow the signs past the Hotel Kalemi and keep zigzagging up the hill.

Sleeping

Kotoni B&B B&B €

(084-263 526, 069 2366 846; www.kotonihouse.com; Rr Bashkim Kokona 8; s/d from €25/30; P ❄ 🛜) Hosts Haxhi and Vita look after you in true Albanian style here: they love Gjirokastra and are happy to pass on information, as well as pack picnics for guests' day trips. The fact that these rooms are 220 years old makes up for their small size, while the astonishing views and friendly cats further sweeten the deal.

★Gjirokastra Hotel HOTEL €€

(068 4099 669, 084-265 982; Rr. Sheazi Çomo; s/d €25/35, ste €40; ❄ 🛜) A great option that combines modern facilities with traditional touches, this lovely family-run hotel inside a 300-year-old house has rooms that boast huge balconies and beautifully carved wooden ceilings. The suite is gorgeous, with a long Ottoman style sofa, original wooden doors and ceiling and magnificent stone walls.

Hotel Kalemi HOTEL €€

(084-263 724, 068 2234 373; www.hotelkalemi.tripod.com; Lagjia Palorto ; r €40; P ❄ @ 🛜) This delightful, large Ottoman-style house has spacious rooms adorned with carved ceilings, antique furnishings and large communal areas, including a broad verandah with Drina Valley views. Some rooms even have fireplaces, though bathrooms can be on the cramped side. Breakfast (juice, tea, a boiled egg and bread with delicious fig jam) is an all-local affair.

Eating

★Kujtimi ALBANIAN €€

(mains 200-800 lekë; 11am-11pm) This wonderfully laid-back outdoor restaurant, run by the Dumi family is an excellent choice. Try the delicious *trofte* (fried trout; 400 lekë), the *midhje* (fried mussels; 350 lekë) and *qifqi* (rice balls fried in herbs and egg, a local speciality). The terrace here is the perfect place to absorb the charms of the Old Town with a glass of local wine.

Taverna Kuka TRADITIONAL €€

(Rr Astrit Karagjozi; mains 300-800 lekë; 11am-midnight; 🛜) Just beyond Gjirokastra's old mosque, this largely outdoor terrace restaurant has a wonderful location and a menu full of delicious traditional Albanian cooking including *qofte* (meatballs), Saranda mussels, pork pancetta and grilled lamb.

Getting There & Away

Buses stop at the ad hoc bus station just after the Eida petrol station on the new town's main road. Services include Tirana (1200 lekë, seven hours, every 1-2 hours until 5pm), Saranda (300 lekë, one hour, hourly) and Berat (1000 lekë, four hours, 9.15am & 3.45pm). A taxi between the Old Town and the bus station is 200 lekë.

SURVIVAL GUIDE

Directory A–Z

BUSINESS HOURS

Banks 9am to 3.30pm Monday to Friday

Cafes & Bars 8am to midnight

EATING PRICE RANGES

The following price categories for the cost of a main course are used in the listings in this chapter.

€ less than 200 lekë

€€ 200 lekë to 500 lekë

€€€ more than 500 lekë

Offices 8am to 5pm Monday to Friday
Restaurants 8am to midnight
Shops 8am to 7pm; siesta time can be any time between noon and 4pm

INTERNET ACCESS

Free wi-fi is ubiquitous in all but the most basic hotels. In larger towns many restaurants also offer free access.

INTERNET RESOURCES

Albania (www.albania.al)
Balkanology (www.balkanology.com/albania)
Journey to Valbona (www.journeytovalbona.com)

MONEY

The lekë is the official currency, though the euro is widely accepted; you'll get a better deal for things in general if you use lekë. Albanian lekë can't be exchanged outside the country, so exchange or spend them before you leave.

Credit cards are accepted only in the larger hotels, shops and travel agencies, and few of these are outside Tirana.

POST

The postal system is fairly rudimentary – there are no postcodes, for example – and it certainly does not enjoy a reputation for efficiency.

PUBLIC HOLIDAYS

New Year's Day 1 January
Summer Day 16 March
Nevruz 23 March
Catholic Easter March or April
Orthodox Easter March or April
May Day 1 May
Mother Teresa Day 19 October
Independence Day 28 November
Liberation Day 29 November
Christmas Day 25 December

TELEPHONE

Albania's country phone code is ☎355. Mobile numbers begin with ☎06. To call an Albanian mobile number from abroad, dial +355 then either ☎67, ☎68 or ☎69 (ie drop the 0 before the 6).

VISAS

Visas are not required for citizens of EU countries or nationals of Australia, Canada, New Zealand, Japan, South Korea, Norway, South Africa or the USA. Travellers from other countries should check www.mfa.gov.al.

Getting There & Away

Albania has good connections in all directions: daily buses go to Kosovo, Montenegro, Macedonia and Greece. The southern seaport of Saranda is a short boat trip from Greece's Corfu, while in summer ferries also connect Himara and Vlora to Corfu. Durrës has regular ferries to Italy.

AIR

Nënë Tereza International Airport (p48) is 17km northwest of Tirana and is a modern, well-run terminal. There are no domestic flights within Albania. The following airlines fly to and from Albania:

Adria Airways (www.adria.si)
Air One (www.flyairone.it)
Alitalia (www.alitalia.com)
Austrian Airlines (www.austrian.com)
British Airways (www.britishairways.com)
Lufthansa (www.lufthansa.com)
Olympic Air (www.olympicair.com)
Pegasus Airlines (www.flypgs.com)
Turkish Airlines (www.turkishairlines.com)

LAND

Border Crossings

There are no passenger trains into Albania, so your border-crossing options are buses, *furgons*, taxis or walking to a border and picking up transport on the other side.

COUNTRY FACTS

Area 28,748 sq km

Capital Tirana

Country Code ☎355

Currency lekë

Emergency ambulance ☎127, fire ☎128, police ☎129

Language Albanian

Money ATMs in most towns

Population 2.77 million

Visas Nearly all visitors can travel visa free to Albania

SLEEPING PRICE RANGES

The following price categories for the cost of a double room in high season are used in the listings in this chapter.

€ less than €30

€€ €30 to €80

€€€ more than €80

Montenegro The main crossings link Shkodra to Ulcinj (Muriqan) and to Podgorica (Hani i Hotit).

Kosovo The closest border crossing to the Koman Ferry terminal is Morina, and further south is Qafë Prush. Near Kukës use Morinë for the highway to Tirana.

Macedonia Use Blato to get to Debar, Qafë e Thanës or Sveti Naum, each to one side of Pogradec, for accessing Ohrid.

Greece The main border crossing to and from Greece is Kakavija on the road from Athens to Tirana. It's about half an hour from Gjirokastra and 250km west of Tirana, and can take up to three hours to pass through during summer. Kapshtica (near Korça) also gets long lines in summer. Konispoli is near Butrint in Albania's south.

Bus

From Tirana, regular buses head to Pristina, Kosovo; to Skopje in Macedonia; to Ulcinj in Montenegro; and to Athens and Thessaloniki in Greece. *Furgons* and buses leave Shkodra for Montenegro, and buses head to Kosovo from Durrës. Buses travel to Greece from Albanian towns on the southern coast as well as from Tirana.

Car & Motorcycle

To enter Albania with you own vehicle you'll need a Green Card (proof of third-party insurance, issued by your insurer); check that your insurance covers Albania.

SEA

Two or three boats per day ply the route between Saranda and Corfu, in Greece, and there are plenty of ferry companies making the journey to Italy from Vlora and Durrës, as well as additional ferries from Vlora to Corfu in the summer.

Getting Around

BICYCLE

Cycling in Albania is tough but certainly feasible. Expect lousy road conditions including open drains, some abysmal driving from fellow road users and roads that barely qualify for the title. Organised groups head north for mountain biking, and cyclists are even spotted cycling the long and tough Korça–Gjirokastra road. Shkodra, Durrës and Tirana are towns where you'll see locals embracing the bike, and Tirana even has bike lanes and its own bike-sharing scheme.

BUS

Bus and *furgon* are the main form of public transport in Albania. Fares are low, and you either pay the conductor on board or when you hop off, which can be anywhere along the route.

Municipal buses operate in Tirana, Durrës, Shkodra and Vlora, and trips cost 30 lekë.

CAR & MOTORCYCLE

Car Hire

There are lots of car-hire companies operating out of Tirana, including all the major international agencies. Hiring a small car costs as little as €35 per day.

Road Rules

Drinking and driving is forbidden, and there is zero tolerance for blood-alcohol readings. Both motorcyclists and passengers must wear helmets. Speed limits are as low as 30km/h in built-up areas and 35km/h on the edges, and there are plenty of traffic police monitoring the roads. Keep your car's papers with you, as police are active checkers.

HITCHING

Though never entirely safe, hitchhiking is quite a common way for travellers to get around – though it's rare to see locals doing it.

TRAIN

Albanians prefer bus and *furgon* travel, and when you see the speed and the state of the (barely) existing trains, you'll know why.

ESSENTIAL FOOD & DRINK

In coastal areas the calamari, mussels and fish will knock your socks off, while high-altitude areas such as Llogaraja have roast lamb worth climbing a mountain for.

- **Byrek** Pastry with cheese or meat.
- **Fergesë** Baked peppers, egg and cheese, and occasionally meat.
- **Midhje** Wild or farmed mussels, often served fried.
- **Paçë koke** Sheep's head soup, usually served for breakfast.
- **Qofta** Flat or cylindrical minced-meat rissoles.
- **Sufllaqë** Doner kebab.
- **Tavë** Meat baked with cheese and egg.

Austria

Includes ➡

Why Go?

For such a small country, Austria has made it big. This is, after all, the land where Mozart was born, Strauss taught the world to waltz and Julie Andrews grabbed the spotlight with her twirling entrance in *The Sound of Music*. This is where the Habsburgs built their 600-year empire, and where past glories still shine in the resplendent baroque palaces and chandelier-lit coffee houses of Vienna, Innsbruck and Salzburg. This is a perfectionist of a country and whatever it does – mountains, classical music, new media, castles, cake, you name it – it does exceedingly well.

Beyond its grandiose cities, Austria's allure lies outdoors. And whether you're schussing down the legendary slopes of Kitzbühel, climbing high in the Alps of Tyrol or pedalling along the banks of the sprightly Danube, you'll find the kind of inspiring landscapes that no well-orchestrated symphony, camera lens or singing nun could ever quite do justice to.

Best Places to Eat

- ➡ Mini (p67)
- ➡ Tian (p67)
- ➡ Der Steirer (p74)
- ➡ Esszimmer (p79)
- ➡ Chez Nico (p83)

Best Places to Stay

- ➡ Pension Sacher (p66)
- ➡ Schlossberg Hotel (p73)
- ➡ Haus Ballwein (p78)
- ➡ Hotel Weisses Kreuz (p83)
- ➡ Hotel Edelweiss (p85)

When to Go

Vienna

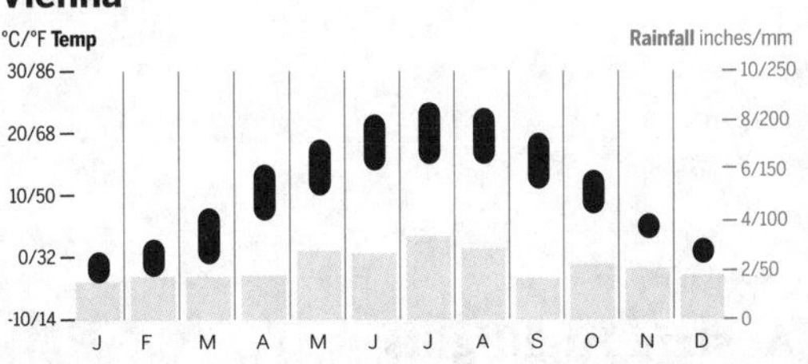

Jul & Aug Alpine hiking in Tyrol, lake swimming in Salzkammergut and lots of summer festivals.

Sep & Oct New wine in vineyards near Vienna, golden forest strolls and few crowds.

Dec & Jan Christmas markets, skiing in the Alps and Vienna waltzing into the New Year.

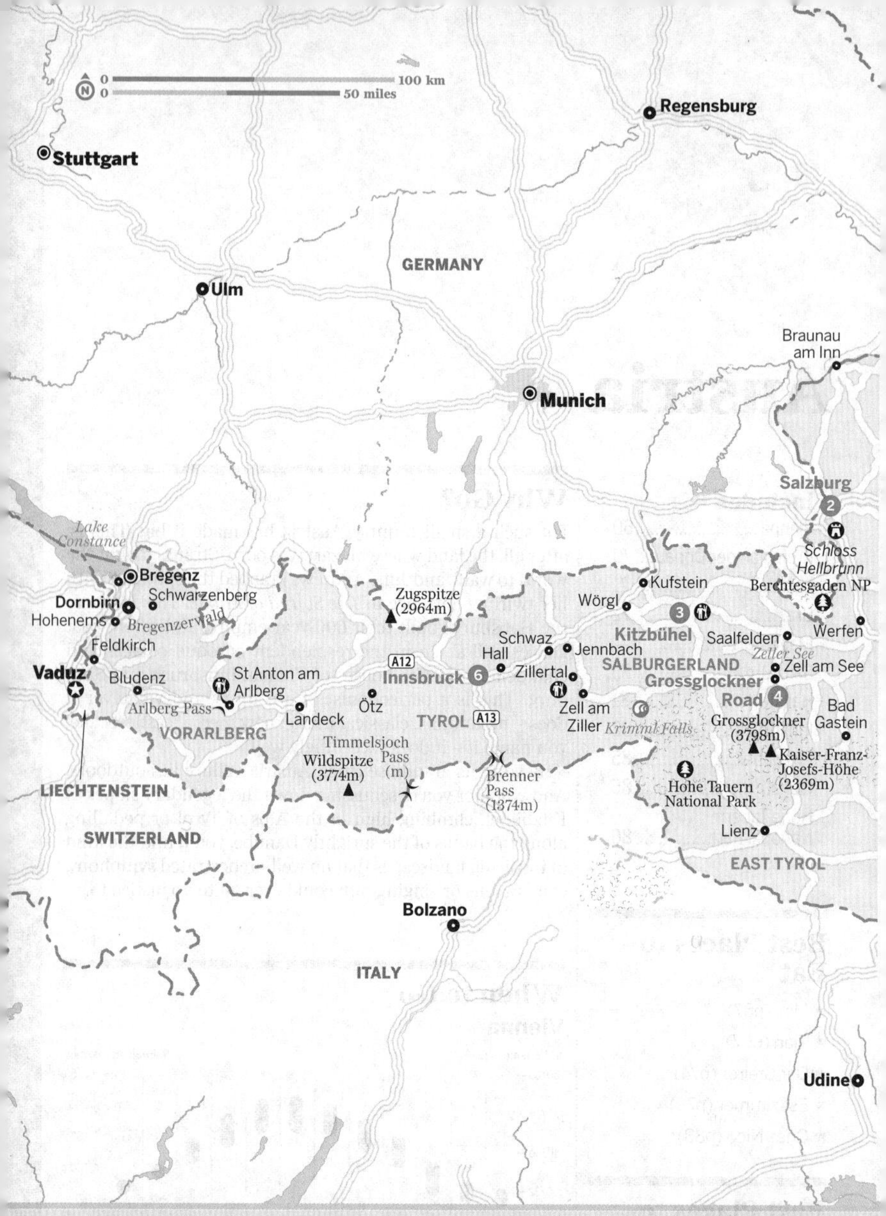

0 100 km
0 50 miles
Regensburg
Stuttgart
GERMANY
Ulm
Braunau am Inn
Munich
Salzburg
2
Schloss Hellbrunn
Lake Constance
Bregenz
Dornbirn
Schwarzenberg
Hohenems
Bregenzerwald
Zugspitze (2964m)
Kufstein
Berchtesgaden NP
Wörgl
3
Kitzbühel
Saalfelden
Werfen
Schwaz
Jennbach
Hall
Zeller See
Zell am See
SALBURGERLAND
Feldkirch
Vaduz
Bludenz
St Anton am Arlberg
Arlberg Pass
A12
Innsbruck
6
Zillertal
Grossglockner Road
4
Landeck
Ötz
TYROL
A13
Zell am Ziller
Krimml Falls
Grossglockner (3798m)
Bad Gastein
Kaiser-Franz-Josefs-Höhe (2369m)
VORARLBERG
Timmelsjoch Pass (m)
Wildspitze (3774m)
Brenner Pass (1374m)
Hohe Tauern National Park
LIECHTENSTEIN
SWITZERLAND
Lienz
EAST TYROL
Bolzano
ITALY
Udine

Austria Highlights

1 Discover the opulent Habsburg palaces, coffee houses and cutting-edge galleries of **Vienna** (p60).

2 Survey the baroque cityscape of **Salzburg** (p75) from the giddy height of 900-year-old Festung Hohensalzburg.

3 Send your spirits soaring from peak to peak hiking and skiing in **Kitzbühel** (p85).

4 Buckle up for a roller-coaster ride of Alps and glaciers on the **Grossglockner Road** (p86), one of Austria's greatest drives.

5 Dive into the crystal-clear lakes of **Salzkammergut** (p80), Austria's summer playground.

6 Whiz up to the Tyrolean Alps in Zaha Hadid's space-age funicular from picture-perfect **Innsbruck** (p82).

7 Explore the romantic Wachau and technology trailblazer Linz in the **Danube Valley** (p70).

ITINERARIES

Two Days

Spend this entire time in **Vienna**, making sure to visit the Habsburg palaces and Stephansdom before cosying up in a *Kaffeehaus* (coffee house). At night, check out the pumping bar scene.

One Week

Spend two days in Vienna, plus another day exploring the **Wachau** (Danube Valley) **wine region**, a day each in **Salzburg** and **Innsbruck**, one day exploring the **Salzkammergut lakes**, and finally one day in St Anton am Arlberg or Kitzbühel hiking or skiing (depending on the season).

VIENNA

☎01 / POP 1.79 MILLION

Few cities in the world waltz so effortlessly between the present and the past like Vienna. Its splendid historical face is easily recognised: grand imperial palaces and bombastic baroque interiors, revered opera houses and magnificent squares.

But Vienna is also one of Europe's most dynamic urban spaces. A stone's throw from Hofburg (the Imperial Palace), the MuseumsQuartier houses some of the world's most provocative contemporary art behind a striking basalt facade. In the Innere Stadt (Inner City), up-to-the-minute design stores sidle up to old-world confectioners, and Austro-Asian fusion restaurants stand alongside traditional *Beisl* (small taverns). In this Vienna, it's OK to mention poetry slam and Stephansdom in one breath.

Throw in the mass of green space within the confines of the city limits and the 'blue' Danube (Donau) cutting a path east of the historical centre, and this is a capital that is distinctly Austrian.

Sights

Heading into the Innere Stadt will take you to a different age. Designated a Unesco World Heritage Site, the heart of the city is blessed with a plethora of architectural wonders that hint at Vienna's long and colourful history.

★Hofburg — PALACE

(Imperial Palace; www.hofburg-wien.at; 01, Michaelerkuppel; 🚌1A, 2A Michaelerplatz, Ⓜ Herrengasse, 🚋D, 1, 2, 71, 46, 49 Burgring) FREE Nothing symbolises the culture and heritage of Austria more than its Hofburg, home base of the Habsburgs from 1273 to 1918. The oldest section is the 13th-century **Schweizerhof** (Swiss Courtyard), named after the Swiss guards who used to protect its precincts. The Renaissance **Swiss gate** dates from 1553. The courtyard adjoins a larger courtyard, **In der Burg**, with a monument to Emperor Franz II adorning its centre. The palace now houses the Austrian president's offices and a raft of museums.

★Kaiserappartements — PALACE

(Imperial Apartments; www.hofburg-wien.at; 01, Michaelerplatz; adult/child €11.50/7, with guided tour €13.50/8; ⏲9am-5.30pm; Ⓜ Herrengasse) The Kaiserappartements (Imperial Apartments), once the official living quarters of Franz Josef I and Empress Elisabeth, are dazzling in their chandelier-lit opulence. One section, known as the **Sisi Museum**, is devoted to Austria's most beloved empress. It has a strong focus on the clothing and jewellery of Austria's monarch. Audioguides – available in 11 languages – are also included in the admission price. Admission on guided tours includes the Kaiserappartements plus the Sisi Museum.

★Kaiserliche Schatzkammer — MUSEUM

(Imperial Treasury; www.kaiserliche-schatzkammer.at; 01, Schweizerhof; adult/under 19yr €12/free; ⏲9am-5.30pm Wed-Mon; Ⓜ Herrengasse) The Schatzkammer (Imperial Treasury) contains secular and ecclesiastical treasures of priceless value and splendour – the sheer wealth of this collection of crown jewels is staggering. As you walk through the rooms you see magnificent treasures such as a golden rose, diamond-studded Turkish sabres, a 2680-carat Colombian emerald and, the highlight of the treasury, the imperial crown.

Albertina — GALLERY

(www.albertina.at; 01, Albertinaplatz 3; adult/child €11.90/free; ⏲10am-6pm Thu-Tue, to 9pm Wed; 👪; Ⓜ Karlsplatz, Stephansplatz, 🚋D, 1, 2, 71 Kärntner Ring/Oper) Once used as the Habsburg's imperial apartments for guests, the Albertina is now a repository for the greatest collection of graphic art in the world. The permanent Batliner Collection – with paintings covering the period from Monet to Picasso – and the high quality of changing exhibitions are what really make the Albertina so worthwhile visiting.

Haus der Musik MUSEUM
(www.hdm.at; 01, Seilerstätte 30; adult/child €12/5.50, with Mozarthaus Vienna €17/7; ⌚10am-10pm; 👪; Ⓜ Karlsplatz, 🚋 D, 1, 2 Kärntner Ring/Oper) The Haus der Musik is an interesting and unusual museum as it manages to explain the world of sound in an amusing and highly interactive way (in English and German) for both children and adults. Exhibits are spread over four floors and cover everything from how sound is created, through to Vienna's Philharmonic Orchestra and street noises.

Kaisergruft CHURCH
(Imperial Burial Vault; www.kaisergruft.at; 01, Neuer Markt; adult/child €5/2.50; ⌚10am-6pm; Ⓜ Stephansplatz, Karlsplatz, 🚋 D, 1, 2, 71 Kärntner Ring/Oper) The Kaisergruft beneath the **Kapuzinerkirche** (Church of the Capuchin Friars) is the final resting place of most of the Habsburg royal family, including Empress Elisabeth.

★ Stephansdom CHURCH
(St Stephan's Cathedral; www.stephanskirche.at; 01, Stephansplatz; ⌚6am-10pm Mon-Sat, from 7am Sun, main nave & Domschatz audio tours 9-11.30am & 1-5.30pm Mon-Sat, 1-5.30pm Sun; Ⓜ Stephansplatz) Vienna's Gothic masterpiece Stephansdom, or Steffl (Little Stephan) as it's nicknamed, is Vienna's pride and joy. A church has stood here since the 12th century, and reminders of this are the Romanesque **Riesentor** (Giant Gate) and **Heidentürme**. From the exterior, the first thing that will strike you is the glorious tiled **roof**, with its dazzling row of chevrons and Austrian eagle. Inside, the magnificent Gothic stone **pulpit** presides over the main nave, fashioned in 1515 by an unknown artisan.

Pestsäule MEMORIAL
(Plague Column; 01, Graben; Ⓜ Stephansplatz) Graben is dominated by the knobbly outline of this memorial, designed by Fischer von Erlach in 1693 to commemorate the 75,000 victims of the Black Death.

★ Kunsthistorisches Museum MUSEUM
(Museum of Art History, KHM; www.khm.at; 01, Maria-Theresien-Platz; adult/under 19yr incl Neue Burg museums €14/free; ⌚10am-6pm Tue-Sun, to 9pm Thu; 👪; Ⓜ Museumsquartier, Volkstheater) One of the unforgettable experiences of being in Vienna will be a visit to the Kunsthistorisches Museum, brimming with works by Europe's finest painters, sculptors and artisans. Occupying a neoclassical building as sumptuous as the art it contains, the museum takes you on a time-travel treasure hunt from Classical Rome to Egypt and the Renaissance. If time is an issue, skip straight to the **Picture Gallery**, where you'll want to dedicate at least an hour or two to Old Masters.

IMPERIAL ENTERTAINMENT

The world-famous **Vienna Boys' Choir** (Wiener Sängerknaben; www.wienersaengerknaben.at) performs on Sunday at 9.15am (late September to June) in the Burgkapelle (Royal Chapel) in the Hofburg. **Tickets** (☎533 99 27; www.hofburgkapelle.at; 01, Schweizerhof; Sun Burgkapelle performance €9-35; Ⓜ Herrengasse) should be booked around six weeks in advance. The group also performs regularly in the Musikverein.

Another throwback to the Habsburg glory days is the **Spanish Riding School** (Spanische Hofreitschule; ☎533 90 31; www.srs.at; 01, Michaelerplatz 1; performances €31-190; 🚌 1A, 2A Michaelerplatz, Ⓜ Herrengasse), where Lipizzaner stallions gracefully perform equine ballet to classical music. For **morning training** (adult/child/family €14/7/28; ⌚10am-noon Tue-Fri Feb-Jun & mid-Aug–Dec) sessions, same-day tickets are available at the nearby **visitor centre** (Michaelerplatz 1; ⌚9am-4pm; Ⓜ Herrengasse).

ℹ MORE FOR YOUR MONEY

The **Vienna Card** (48-/72-hour €18.90/21.90) gives you unlimited travel plus discounts at selected museums, attractions, cafes and shops. It's available from hotels and ticket offices.

The City of Vienna runs some 20 **municipal museums** (www.wienmuseum.at), which are included in a free booklet available at the Rathaus. Permanent exhibitions in all are free on the first Sunday of the month.

Central Vienna

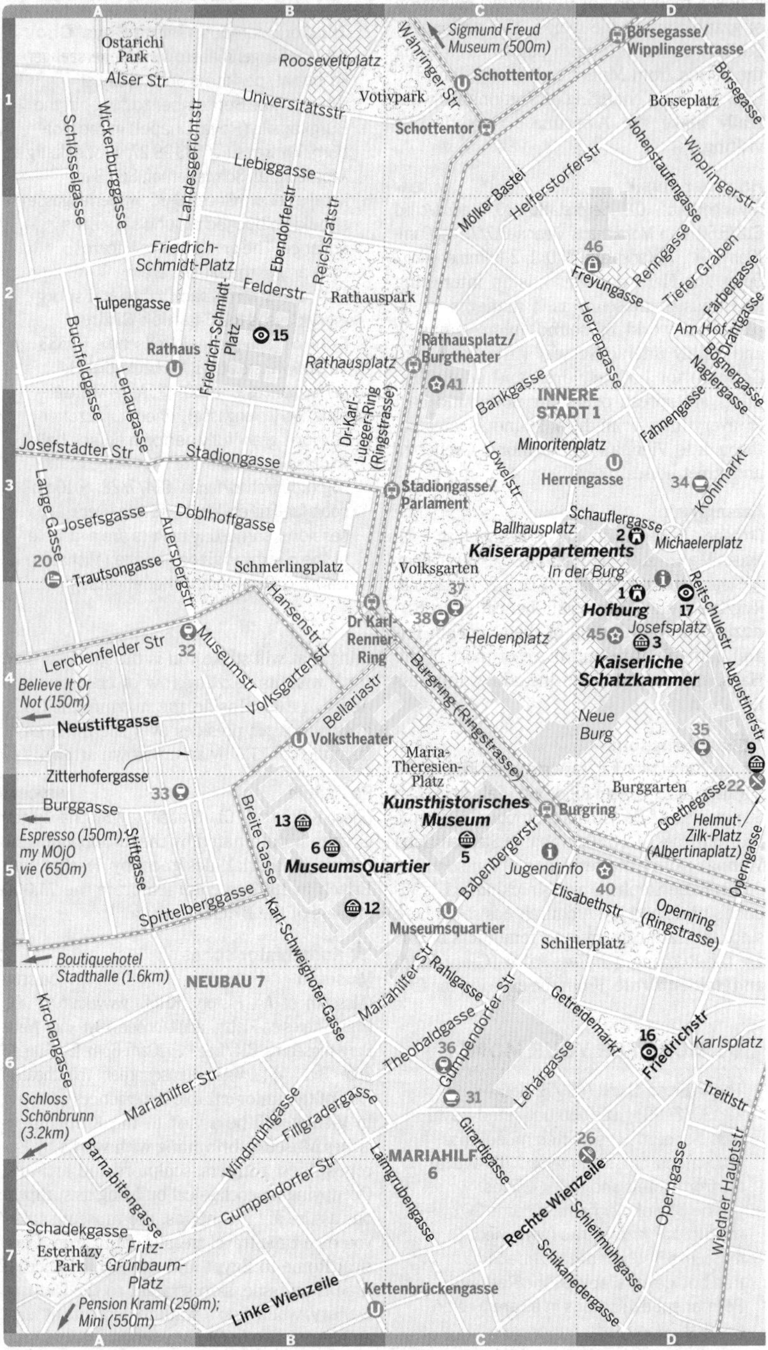

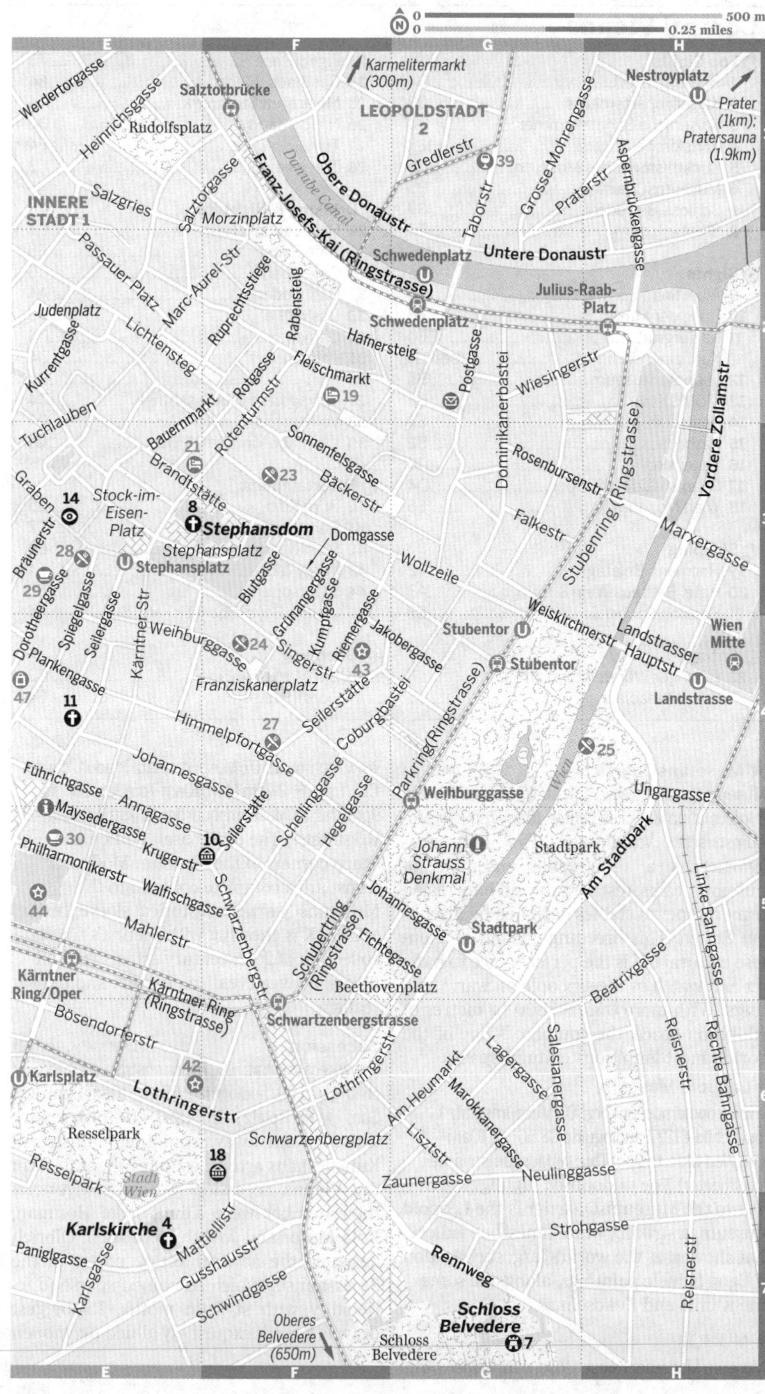
0
500 m
0
0.25 miles
Karmelitermarkt (300m)
Salztorbrücke
LEOPOLDSTADT 2
Nestroyplatz
Prater (1km); Pratersauna (1.9km)
Rudolfsplatz
INNERE STADT 1
Schwedenplatz
Julius-Raab-Platz
Stephansdom
Stephansplatz
Stubentor
Wien Mitte
Landstrasse
Weihburggasse
Johann Strauss Denkmal
Stadtpark
Kärntner Ring/Oper
Schwartzenbergstrasse
Beethovenplatz
Karlsplatz
Resselpark
Karlskirche
Schwarzenbergplatz
Oberes Belvedere (650m)
Schloss Belvedere

Central Vienna

Top Sights
- 1 Hofburg ... D4
- 2 Kaiserappartements ... D3
- 3 Kaiserliche Schatzkammer ... D4
- 4 Karlskirche ... E7
- 5 Kunsthistorisches Museum ... C5
- 6 MuseumsQuartier ... B5
- 7 Schloss Belvedere ... G7
- 8 Stephansdom ... E3

Sights
- 9 Albertina ... D4
- 10 Haus der Musik ... F5
- 11 Kaisergruft ... E4
- Kapuzinerkirche ... (see 11)
- 12 Leopold Museum ... B5
- 13 MUMOK ... B5
- 14 Pestsäule ... E3
- 15 Rathaus ... B2
- 16 Secession ... D6
- 17 Spanish Riding School ... D4
- 18 Wien Museum ... F6

Sleeping
- 19 Hollmann Beletage ... F2
- 20 Hotel Rathaus Wein & Design ... A3
- 21 Pension Sacher ... E3

Eating
- 22 Bitzinger Würstelstand am Albertinaplatz ... D5
- 23 Figlmüller ... F3
- 24 Gasthaus Pöschl ... F4
- 25 Meierei im Stadtpark ... H4
- 26 Naschmarkt ... D6
- 27 Tian ... F4
- 28 Trzesniewski ... E3

Drinking & Nightlife
- 29 Café Leopold Hawelka ... E3
- 30 Café Sacher ... E5
- 31 Café Sperl ... C6
- 32 Dachboden ... A4
- 33 Das Möbel ... A5
- 34 Demel ... D3
- 35 Palmenhaus ... D4
- 36 Phil ... C6
- 37 Volksgarten ClubDiskothek ... C4
- 38 Volksgarten Pavillon ... C4
- 39 Weinfach Vinothek & Bar ... G1

Entertainment
- 40 Burg Kino ... D5
- 41 Burgtheater ... C2
- 42 Musikverein ... E6
- 43 Porgy & Bess ... F4
- 44 Staatsoper ... E5
- 45 Vienna Boys' Choir Tickets ... D4

Shopping
- 46 Bio-Markt Freyung ... D2
- 47 Dorotheum ... E4

★ MuseumsQuartier — MUSEUM

(Museum Quarter; www.mqw.at; 07, Museumsplatz; information & ticket centre 10am-7pm; M Museumsquartier, Volkstheater) The MuseumsQuartier is a remarkable ensemble of museums, cafes, restaurants and bars inside former imperial stables designed by Fischer von Erlach. This breeding ground of Viennese cultural life is the perfect place to hang out and watch or meet people on warm evenings. With more than 60,000 sq metres of exhibition space, the complex is one of the world's most ambitious cultural spaces.

➡ Leopold Museum

(www.leopoldmuseum.org; 07, Museumsplatz 1; adult/child €12/7, audioguide €3.50; 10am-6pm Wed-Mon, to 9pm Thu; M Museumsquartier, Volkstheater) The undoubted highlight of a visit to the MuseumsQuartier is the Leopold Museum, a striking white limestone gallery that showcases the world's largest collection of Egon Schiele paintings, alongside some fine Klimts and Kokoschkas.

➡ MUMOK

(Museum Moderner Kunst, Museum of Modern Art; www.mumok.at; 07, Museumsplatz 1; adult/child €10/free; 2-7pm Mon, 10am-7pm Tue-Sun, to 9pm Thu; M Museumsquartier, Volkstheater, 49 Volkstheater) The dark basalt edifice and sharp corners of the Museum Moderner Kunst are a complete contrast to the MuseumsQuartier's historical sleeve. Inside, MUMOK is crawling with Vienna's finest collection of 20th-century art, centred on fluxus, nouveau realism, pop art and photo-realism.

Secession — LANDMARK, GALLERY

(www.secession.at; 01, Friedrichstrasse 12; adult/child €9/5.50, audioguide €3; 10am-6pm Tue-Sun; M Karlsplatz) In 1897, 19 progressive artists swam away from the mainstream Künstlerhaus artistic establishment to form the Vienna Secession *(Sezession)*. Among their number were Klimt, Josef Hoffman, Kolo Moser and Joseph M Olbrich. Olbrich designed the new exhibition centre of the Secessionists, which combined sparse functionality with stylistic motifs. Its biggest draw is Klimt's exquisitely gilded *Beethoven Frieze*.

Wien Museum MUSEUM
(www.wienmuseum.at; 04, Karlsplatz 8; adult/under 19yr €8/free, 1st Sun of month free; ⏲10am-6pm Tue-Sun; Ⓜ Karlsplatz) The Wien Museum presents a fascinating romp through Vienna's history, from Neolithic times to the mid-20th century, putting the city and its personalities in a meaningful context. Exhibits are spread over three floors, including spaces for two temporary exhibitions.

★ **Schloss Belvedere** PALACE, GALLERY
(www.belvedere.at; Oberes Belvedere adult/child €12.50/free, Unteres Belvedere €11/free, combined ticket €19/free; ⏲10am-6pm; Ⓜ Taubstummengasse, Südtiroler Platz, 🚊 D, 71 Schwarzenbergplatz) Belvedere is a masterpiece of total art and one of the world's finest baroque palaces, designed by Johann Lukas von Hildebrandt (1668–1745) for Prince Eugene of Savoy. The first of the palace's two buildings is the **Oberes Belvedere** (Upper Belvedere), showcasing Gustav Klimt's *The Kiss* (1908), the perfect embodiment of Viennese art nouveau, alongside other late-19th- to early-20th-century Austrian works. The lavish **Unteres Belvedere** (Lower Belvedere), with its richly frescoed **Marmorsaal** (Marble Hall), sits at the end of sculpture-dotted gardens.

Prater PARK
(www.wiener-prater.at; Ⓜ Praterstern) This large park encompasses meadows, woodlands, an amusement park (the **Würstelprater**) and one of the city's most visible icons, the **Riesenrad**. Built in 1897, this 65m-high Ferris wheel of *The Third Man* fame affords far-reaching views of Vienna.

Sigmund Freud Museum HOUSE, MUSEUM
(www.freud-museum.at; 09, Berggasse 19; adult/child €9/4; ⏲10am-6pm; Ⓜ Schottentor, Schottenring, 🚊 D Schlickgasse) Sigmund Freud is a bit like the telephone – once he happened, there was no going back. This is where Freud spent his most prolific years and developed his groundbreaking theories; he moved here with his family in 1891 and stayed until he was forced into exile by the Nazis in 1938.

Schloss Schönbrunn PALACE
(www.schoenbrunn.at; 13, Schönbrunne Schlossstrasse 47; Imperial Tour with audioguide adult/child €11.50/8.50, Grand Tour €14.50/9.50; ⏲8.30am-5.30pm; Ⓜ Hietzing) The Habsburgs' overwhelmingly opulent summer palace is now a Unesco World Heritage Site. Of the palace's 1441 rooms, 40 are open to the public; the Imperial Tour takes you into 26 of these.

Fountains dance in the French-style formal gardens. The gardens harbour the world's oldest zoo, the **Tiergarten**, founded in 1752; a 630m-long hedge maze; and the **Gloriette**, whose roof offers a wonderful view over the palace grounds and beyond.

Because of the popularity of the palace, tickets are stamped with a departure time and there may be a time lag, so buy your ticket straight away and then explore the gardens.

Activities

The **Donauinsel** (Danube Island) features swimming areas and paths for walking and cycling. The **Alte Donau** (Old Danube) is a landlocked arm of the Danube, a favourite of sailing and boating enthusiasts, swimmers, walkers, fisherfolk and, in winter (when it's cold enough), ice skaters.

Festivals & Events

Pick up a copy of the monthly booklet of events from the tourist office.

Opernball CULTURAL
(www.wiener-staatsoper.at; ⏲Jan/Feb) Of the 300 or so balls held in January and February, the Opernball (Opera Ball) is number one. Held in the Staatsoper, it's a supremely

SPIN OF THE RING

One of the best deals in Vienna is a self-guided tour on tram 1 or 2 of the monumental **Ringstrasse** boulevard encircling much of the Innere Stadt, which turned 150 in 2015. For the price of a single ticket you'll take in the neo-Gothic **Rathaus** (City Hall; www.wien.gv.at; 01, Rathausplatz 1; ⏲guided tours 1pm Mon, Wed & Fri; Ⓜ Rathaus, 🚊 D, 1, 2 Rathaus) FREE, the Greek Revival–style parliament, the 19th-century **Burgtheater** (National Theatre; ☎514 44 4440; www.burgtheater.at; 01, Universitätsring 2; seats €5-51, standing room €2.50, students €8; ⏲box office 9am-5pm Mon-Fri; Ⓜ Rathaus, 🚊 D, 1, 2 Rathaus) and the baroque **Karlskirche** (St Charles Church; www.karlskirche.at; Karlsplatz; adult/child €8/4; ⏲9am-5.30pm Mon-Sat, 11.30am-5.30pm Sun; Ⓜ Karlsplatz), among other sights.

lavish affair, with the men in tails and women in shining white gowns.

Wiener Festwochen ART
(www.festwochen.at; mid-May–late June) Wide-ranging program of arts from around the world.

Donauinselfest MUSIC
(https://donauinselfest.at; late Jun) FREE Held over three days on a weekend in late June, the Donauinselfest features a feast of rock, pop, folk and country performers, and attracts almost three million onlookers. Best of all, it's free!

Musikfilm Festival FILM
(http://filmfestival-rathausplatz.at; 01, Rathausplatz; Jul & Aug) Once the sun sets in July and August, the Rathausplatz is home to free screenings of operas, operettas and concerts.

Viennale Film Festival FILM
(526 59 47; www.viennale.at; late Oct-early Nov) The country's best film festival features fringe and independent films from around the world. It is held every year, with screenings at numerous locations around the city.

Christkindlmärkte CHRISTMAS MARKET
(www.christkindlmarkt.at; mid-Nov–25 Dec) Vienna's much-loved Christmas market.

Sleeping

my MOjO vie HOSTEL €
(0676-551 11 55; http://mymojovie.at; 07, Kaiserstrasse 77; dm/d/tr/q €26/56/81/104; ; Burggasse Stadthalle) An old-fashioned cage lift rattles up to these incredible backpacker digs. Everything you could wish for is here – design-focused dorms, a kitchen with free supplies, netbooks for surfing, guidebooks for browsing and even musical instruments for your own jam session.

Believe It Or Not HOSTEL €
(0676-550 00 55; www.believe-it-or-not-vienna.at; 07, Myrthengasse 10; dm €26-30; ; Volkstheater) It may seem nondescript on the face of things, but you really won't believe what a cosy, homely hostel this is. We love the dorms with mezzanine-style beds, the laid-back lounge, kitchen with free basics and laptops for guest use.

Pension Kraml PENSION €
(587 85 88; www.pensionkraml.at; 06, Brauergasse 5; s €35, d €48-78, tr €69-87, q €110-120; ; Zieglergasse) Tucked peacefully down a backstreet five minutes' walk south of Mariahilfer Strasse, this family-run pension looks back on 150 years of history and prides itself on old-school hospitality and comfort.

★ **Pension Sacher** PENSION €€
(533 32 38; www.pension-sacher.at; 01, Rothenturmstrasse 1; apt €100-152; ; Stephansplatz) Filled with chintzy knick-knacks, florals and solid wood furnishings, these super-central, spacious apartments are lovingly kept by the Sacher family of chocolate-cake fame. There's everything you need to feel right at home and the views of Stephansdom are phenomenal.

Hotel Rathaus Wein & Design BOUTIQUE HOTEL €€
(400 11 22; www.hotel-rathaus-wien.at; 08, Lange Gasse 13; s/d/tr €150/210/240; ; Rathaus, Volkstheater) Each of the open-plan, minimalist-chic rooms at this boutique hotel is dedicated to an Austrian winemaker and the minibar is stocked with premium wines from the growers themselves.

Boutiquehotel Stadthalle HOTEL €€
(982 42 72; www.hotelstadthalle.at; 15, Hackengasse 20; s €80-120, d €118-188; ; Schweglerstrasse) Welcome to Vienna's most eco-aware hotel, which has a roof fragrantly planted with lavender. Bursts of purple, pink and peach enliven rooms that blend modern with polished antiques. An organic breakfast is served in the ivy-draped courtyard garden.

Hollmann Beletage PENSION €€
(961 19 60; www.hollmann-beletage.at; 01, Köllnerhofgasse 6; d €159-229, tr €179-259, q €199-300, ste from €390; ; Schwedenplatz, 1, 2 Schwedenplatz) This minimalist establishment offers style and clean lines throughout. A terrace and lounge where you can enjoy free snacks at 2pm are bonuses, as is the small hotel cinema and the free use of an iPad.

Eating

Self-caterers can stock up at central Hofer, Billa and Spar supermarkets. Some have delis that make sandwiches to order. *Würstel Stand* (sausage stands) are great for a cheap bite on the run.

Trzesniewski SANDWICHES €
(www.trzesniewski.at; 01, Dorotheergasse 1; bread & spread €1.20; 8am-7pm Mon-Fri, 9am-5pm Sat; Stephansplatz) Possibly the finest sandwich shop in Austria, Trzesniewski has been serving spreads and breads to the entire spectrum of munchers for over 100 years.

DON'T MISS

FOOD MARKET FINDS

The sprawling **Naschmarkt** (06, Linke & Rechte Wienzeile; ⌚6am-7.30pm Mon-Fri, to 6pm Sat; Ⓜ Karlsplatz, Kettenbrückengasse) is the place to *nasch* (snack) in Vienna. Stalls are piled high with meats, fruits, vegetables, cheeses, olives, spices and wine. There are also plenty of cafes dishing up good-value lunches, along with delis and takeaway stands.

Bio-Markt Freyung (01, Freyungasse; ⌚9am-6pm Fri & Sat; Ⓜ Herrengasse, Schottentor) sells farm-fresh produce, as does the bustling **Karmelitermarkt** (02, Karmelitermarkt; ⌚6am-7.30pm Mon-Fri, to 5pm Sat; Ⓜ Taborstrasse, 🚊2 Karmeliterplatz). Head to the Saturday farmers market at the latter for brunch at one of the excellent deli-cafes.

Bitzinger Würstelstand am Albertinaplatz SAUSAGE STAND €
(01, Albertinaplatz; sausages €1.70-4.30; ⌚8am-4am; Ⓜ Karlsplatz, Stephansplatz, 🚊Kärntner Ring/Oper) Vienna has many sausage stands but this one located behind the Staatsoper is hands down one of the best.

★**Mini** FUSION €€
(☎0595-44 83; www.minirestaurant.at; 06, Marchettigasse 11; mains €16-24; ⌚11.30am-midnight; Ⓜ Pilgramgasse) A slick, vaulted interior provides the backdrop for Hungarian cuisine with a pinch of global personality at Mini. Starters like wild-boar soup warm you up nicely for bright, flavour-packed mains like swordfish in white-wine mushroom sauce. The two-course lunch is a snip at €7.90.

Meierei im Stadtpark AUSTRIAN €€
(☎713 31 68; http://steirereck.at; 03, Am Heumarkt 2a; set breakfasts €20-24, mains €11-20, 6-cheese selection €11; ⌚8am-11pm Mon-Fri, 9am-7pm Sat & Sun; 🖉; Ⓜ Stadtpark) Embedded in the greenery of the Stadtpark, the Meierei serves a bountiful breakfast until noon. It's most famous, though, for its goulash served with leek roulade (€18), and its selection of 120 types of cheese.

Gasthaus Pöschl AUSTRIAN €€
(☎513 52 88; 01, Weihburggasse 17; mains €9-18; ⌚noon-midnight; Ⓜ Stubentor) Close to pretty Franziskanerplatz, this small, wood-panelled *Beisl* brims with Viennese warmth and bonhomie. Austrian classics like *Tafelspitz* (boiled beef) and schnitzel are cooked to a T.

Figlmüller BISTRO €€
(☎512 61 77; www.figlmueller.at; 01, Wollzeile 5; mains €13-23; ⌚11am-10.30pm; 📶; Ⓜ Stephansplatz) The Viennese would simply be at a loss without Figlmüller. This famous *Beisl* has some of the biggest and best schnitzels in the business.

★**Tian** VEGETARIAN €€€
(☎890 46 65; www.tian-vienna.com; 01, Himmelpfortgasse 23; 2-/3-course lunch €26/32, 4-/8-course evening menu €81-120; ⌚noon-midnight Mon-Sat; 🖉; Ⓜ Stephansplatz, 🚊2 Weihburggasse) Stealthy charm meets urban attitude at this lounge-style, Michelin-starred restaurant that takes vegetarian cuisine to delicious heights. Lunch menus offer the best value; you can also enjoy a drink in the delightful wine bar.

Drinking & Nightlife

Pulsating bars cluster north and south of the Naschmarkt, around Spittelberg and along the Gürtel (mainly around the U6 stops of Josefstädter Strasse and Nussdorfer Strasse).

Vienna's *Heurigen*, or wine taverns, cluster in the wine-growing suburbs to the north, southwest, west and northwest of the city. Opening times are approximately from 4pm to 11pm, and wine costs around €3 per *Viertel* (250mL).

★**Dachboden** BAR
(http://25hours-hotels.com; 07, Lerchenfelder Strasse 1-3; ⌚2pm-1am Tue-Fri, noon-1am Sat, noon-10pm Sun; 📶; Ⓜ Volkstheater) Housed in the circus-themed 25hours Hotel, Dachboden has big-top views of Vienna's skyline from its decked terrace. DJs spin jazz, soul and funk on Wednesday and Friday nights.

Weinfach Vinothek & Bar WINE BAR
(www.weinfach.at; 02, Taborstrasse 11a; ⌚5-10pm Tue-Sat; 🚊2 Gredlerstrasse) This bright, modern wine store and bar extends the warmest of welcomes. The well-edited, 90-variety wine list traverses the entire Austrian spectrum and the sharing plates of local cheese and Carinthian salami are perfect for grazing. The clued-up staff arrange regular tastings and events.

Palmenhaus BAR
(www.palmenhaus.at; 01, Burggarten; ⌚11.30am-midnight Mon-Thu, 10am-1am Fri & Sat, 10am-11pm Sun; Ⓜ Karlsplatz, Museumsquartier, 🚊D, 1, 2, 71

DON'T MISS

COFFEE HOUSE CULTURE

Vienna's legendary *Kaffeehauser* (coffee houses) are wonderful places for people-watching, daydreaming, chatting and browsing the news. Most serve light meals alongside mouth-watering cakes and tortes. Expect to pay around €8 for a coffee with a slice of cake. Here are five favourites:

Café Sperl (www.cafesperl.at; 06, Gumpendorfer Strasse 11; 7am-11pm Mon-Sat, 11am-8pm Sun; ; Museumsquartier, Kettenbrückengasse) With its gorgeous *Jugendstil* (art nouveau) fittings, grand dimensions, cosy booths and unhurried air, Sperl is one of the finest coffee houses in Vienna. The must-try is Sperl Torte, an almond-and-chocolate-cream dream.

Café Leopold Hawelka (www.hawelka.at; 01, Dorotheergasse 6; 8am-1am Mon-Sat, 10am-1am Sun; Stephansplatz) Dark, moody and picture-plastered, this late-1930s coffee house was once the hang-out of artists and writers – Friedensreich Hundertwasser, Elias Canetti, Arthur Miller and Andy Warhol included.

Demel (www.demel.at; 01, Kohlmarkt 14; 9am-7pm; 1A, 2A Michaelerplatz, Herrengasse, Stephansplatz) An elegant and regal cafe within sight of the Hofburg, Demel's speciality is the Ana Demel Torte, a calorie-bomb of chocolate and nougat.

Café Sacher (www.sacher.com; 01, Philharmonikerstrasse 4; 8am-midnight; Karlsplatz, D, 1, 2, 71 Kärntner Ring/Oper) Fancy, chandelier-lit Sacher is celebrated for its Sacher Torte, a rich chocolate cake with apricot jam once favoured by Emperor Franz Josef.

Espresso (http://espresso-wien.at; 07, Burggasse 57; 7.30am-1am Mon-Fri, 10am-1am Sat & Sun; Volkstheater, 49 Siebensterngasse/Kirchengasse) For a fresh take on the coffee-house scene, stop by this retro-cool blast from the 1950s, where hipsters linger over espressos with a kick and brunch.

Burgring) Housed in a beautifully restored *Jungendstil* (art nouveau) palm house, the Palmenhaus opens onto a terrific garden terrace in summer.

Phil BAR

(www.phil.info; 06, Gumpendorfer Strasse 10-12; 5pm-1am Mon, 9am-1am Tue-Sun; Museumsquartier, Kettenbrückengasse) A retro bar, book and record store, Phil attracts a bohemian crowd happy to squat on kitsch furniture your grandma used to own. The vibe is as relaxed as can be.

Volksgarten Pavillon BAR

(www.volksgarten-pavillon.at; 01, Burgring 1; 11am-2am Apr–mid-Sep; ; Volkstheater, D, 1, 2, 71 Dr-Karl-Renner-Ring) Volksgarten Pavillon is a lovely 1950s-style pavilion with views of Heldenplatz.

Das Möbel BAR

(http://dasmoebel.at; 07, Burggasse 10; 2pm-midnight Mon-Fri, from 10am Sat & Sun; ; Volkstheater) Das Möbel wins points for its furniture, consisting entirely of one-off pieces produced by local designers – and everything is for sale.

Pratersauna CLUB

(www.pratersauna.tv; 02, Waldsteingartenstrasse 135; club 9pm-6am Wed-Sun, pool 1-9pm Fri & Sat Jun-Sep; Messe-Prater) Pool, cafe, bistro and club converge in a former sauna – these days, you'll sweat it up on the dance floor any given night.

Volksgarten ClubDiskothek CLUB

(www.volksgarten.at; 01, Burgring 1; cover from €6; 10pm-4am or later Tue & Thu-Sat; Museumsquartier, Volkstheater, D, 1, 2, 71 Dr-Karl-Renner-Ring) A hugely popular club, superbly located near the Hofburg, Volksgarten serves a clientele eager to see and be seen.

☆ Entertainment

Vienna is, and probably will be till the end of time, the European capital of opera and classical music. The line-up of music events is never-ending and even the city's buskers are often classically trained musicians.

Box offices generally open from Monday to Saturday and sell cheap (€3 to €6) standing-room tickets around an hour before performances.

For up-to-date listings, visit www.falter.at (in German).

Staatsoper OPERA
(☎514 44 7880; www.wiener-staatsoper.at; 01, Opernring 2; Ⓜ Karlsplatz, 🚋 D 1, 2 Kärntner Ring/Oper) The Staatsoper is *the* premiere opera and classical music venue in Vienna. Productions are lavish, formal affairs, where people dress up accordingly.

Musikverein CONCERT VENUE
(☎505 81 90; www.musikverein.at; 01, Bösendorferstrasse 12; seats €25-89, standing room €4-6; ⏰box office 9am-8pm Mon-Fri, to 1pm Sat; Ⓜ Karlsplatz) The opulent Musikverein holds the proud title of the best acoustics of any concert hall in Austria, which the Vienna Philharmonic Orchestra makes excellent use of.

Porgy & Bess JAZZ
(☎512 88 11; www.porgy.at; 01, Riemergasse 11; tickets around €18; ⏰concerts 7pm or 8.30pm; Ⓜ Stubentor, 🚋 2 Stubentor) Quality is the cornerstone of Porgy & Bess' continuing popularity. Its program is loaded with modern jazz acts from around the globe.

Burg Kino CINEMA
(☎587 84 06; www.burgkino.at; 01, Opernring 19; Ⓜ Museumsquartier, 🚋 D, 1, 2 Burgring) The Burg Kino shows only English-language films. It has regular screenings of *The Third Man*, Orson Welles' timeless classic set in post-WWII Vienna.

Shopping

In the alley-woven Innere Stadt, go to Kohlmarkt for designer chic, Herrengasse for antiques and Kärntnerstrasse for high-street brands. Tune into Vienna's creative pulse in the idiosyncratic boutiques and concept stores in Neubau, especially along Kirchengasse and Lindengasse.

Dorotheum ANTIQUES
(www.dorotheum.com; 01, Dorotheergasse 17; ⏰10am-6pm Mon-Fri, 9am-5pm Sat; Ⓜ Stephansplatz) The Dorotheum is among the largest auction houses in Europe. For the casual visitor it's more like a museum than an auction space, housing everything from antique toys and tableware to autographs, antique guns and, above all, lots of quality paintings.

Information

Many cafes and bars offer free wi-fi for their customers. Free public hot-spots include Rathausplatz, Naschmarkt and Prater. See www.lonelyplanet.com.au/austria/vienna for more information.

Airport Information Office (⏰7am-10pm) Full services, with maps, Vienna Card and walk-in hotel booking. Located in the Vienna International Airport arrival hall.

Allgemeines Krankenhaus (☎404 000; www.akhwien.at; 09, Währinger Gürtel 18-20) Emergency rooms available at this hospital.

Jugendinfo (Vienna Youth Information; ☎4000 84 100; www.jugendinfowien.at; 01, Babenbergerstrasse 1; ⏰2-7pm Mon-Wed, 1-6pm Thu-Sat; Ⓜ Museumsquartier, 🚋 Burgring) Jugendinfo offers various reduced-priced event tickets for 14 to 26 year olds.

Main Post Office (01, Fleischmarkt 19; ⏰7am-10pm Mon-Fri, 9am-10pm Sat & Sun; Ⓜ Schwedenplatz, 🚋 1, 2 Schwedenplatz)

Police Station (☎31 310; 01, Schottenring 7-9; Ⓜ Schottentor)

Tourist Info Wien (☎245 55; www.wien.info; 01, Albertinaplatz; ⏰9am-7pm; 📶; Ⓜ Stephansplatz, 🚋 D, 1, 2, 71 Kärntner Ring/Oper) Vienna's main tourist office, with a ticket agency, hotel booking service, free maps and every brochure under the sun.

Getting There & Away

AIR

For details on flying to Vienna, see the Getting There & Away section, p88.

BOAT

Fast hydrofoils travel eastwards to Bratislava (one way €20 to €35, 1¼ hours) daily from April to October. From May to September, they also travel twice weekly to Budapest (one way/return €109/125, 5½ hours). Bookings can be made through **DDSG Blue Danube** (☎01-58 880; www.ddsg-blue-danube.at; Handelskai 265, Vienna; Ⓜ Vorgartenstrasse).

BUS

Vienna currently has no central bus station. National Bundesbuses arrive and depart from several different locations, depending on the destination. Bus lines serving Vienna include **Eurolines** (☎0900 128 712; www.eurolines.

GETTING INTO TOWN

The fastest transport into the centre is **City Airport Train** (CAT; www.cityairporttrain.com; return adult/child €19/free; ⏰departs airport 6.06am-11.36pm, departs city 5.36am-11.06pm), which runs every 30 minutes and takes 16 minutes between the airport and Wien Mitte; book online for a €2 discount. The S-Bahn (S7) does the same journey (single €4.40) but in 25 minutes.

com; Erdbergstrasse 200; ⏲6.30am-9pm Mon-Fri; Ⓜ Erdberg).

CAR & MOTORCYCLE

The Gürtel is an outer ring road that joins up with the A22 on the north bank of the Danube and the A23 southeast of town. All the main road routes intersect with this system, including the A1 from Linz and Salzburg, and the A2 from Graz.

TRAIN

Vienna is one of central Europe's main rail hubs. **Österreichische Bundesbahn** (ÖBB; Austrian Federal Railway; www.oebb.at) is the main operator. There are direct services and connections to many European cities. Sample destinations include Budapest (€29 to €37, 2½ to 3¼ hours), Munich (€93, 4½ to five hours), Paris (€51 to €142, 11½ to 13 hours), Prague (€49, 4¼ hours) and Venice (€49 to €108, seven to 11 hours).

Vienna's main station is the Hauptbahnhof, formerly the Südbahnhof. Following a massive construction project, it became partially operational in December 2012 and is set for completion in 2015. In the meantime, some long-distance trains are being rerouted among the rest of Vienna's train stations, including the Westbahnhof and Wien Meidling. Further train stations include Franz-Josefs-Bahnhof (which handles trains to/from the Danube Valley), Wien Mitte and Wien Nord.

Getting Around

BICYCLE

Vienna's city bike scheme is called **Citybike Wien** (Vienna City Bike; www.citybikewien.at; 1st hr free, 2nd/3rd hr €1/2, per hr thereafter €4), with more than 120 bicycle stands across the city. A credit card is required to rent bikes – just swipe your card in the machine and follow the instructions (in a number of languages).

PUBLIC TRANSPORT

Vienna's unified public transport network encompasses trains, trams, buses, and underground (U-Bahn) and suburban (S-Bahn) trains. Free maps and information pamphlets are available from **Wiener Linien** (☎7909-100; www.wienerlinien.at).

All tickets must be validated at the entrance to U-Bahn stations and on buses and trams (except for weekly and monthly tickets).

Singles cost €2.20. A 24-hour ticket costs €7.60, a 48-hour ticket €13.30 and a 72-hour ticket €16.50. Weekly tickets (valid Monday to Sunday) cost €16.20.

THE DANUBE VALLEY

The stretch of Danube between Krems and Melk, known locally as the Wachau, is arguably the loveliest along the entire length of the mighty river. Both banks are dotted with ruined castles and medieval towns, and lined with terraced vineyards. Further upstream is the industrial city of Linz, Austria's avant-garde art and new technology trailblazer.

Krems an der Donau

☎02732 / POP 24,085

Sitting on the northern bank of the Danube against a backdrop of terraced vineyards, Krems marks the beginning of the Wachau. It has an attractive cobbled centre, some good restaurants and the gallery-dotted **Kunstmeile** (Art Mile; www.kunstmeile-krems.at).

Sights & Activities

Kunsthalle GALLERY

(www.kunsthalle.at; Franz-Zeller-Platz 3; admission €10; ⏲10am-5pm Tue-Sun) The flagship of Krems' Kunstmeile, an eclectic collection of galleries and museums, the Kunsthalle has a program of small but excellent changing exhibitions.

Sleeping

Arte Hotel Krems HOTEL €€

(☎71123; www.arte-hotel.at; Dr-Karl-Dorrek-Strasse 23; s/d €109/159; P 📶) This cutting-edge art hotel has 91 large, well-designed rooms with big retro prints and patterns complementing the funky '60s-style furniture.

Hotel Unter den Linden HOTEL €€

(☎82 115; www.udl.at; Schillerstrasse 5; s €67-87, d €90-118; 📶) This big, family-run hotel has knowledgeable and helpful owners, 39 bright, welcoming rooms and a convenient location in Krems itself.

ON YOUR BIKE

Many towns in the Danube Valley are part of a bike-hire network called **Nextbike** (☎02742-229 901; www.nextbike.at; per hr €1, 24hr €8). After registering using a credit card (either by calling the hotline or on the website), €1 is deducted and you can begin renting bicycles.

Information

Krems Tourismus (☎82 676; www.krems.info; Utzstrasse 1; ⏲9am-6pm Mon-Fri, 11am-6pm Sat, 11am-4pm Sun, shorter hours in winter) Helpful office well stocked with info and maps.

Getting There & Away

Frequent daily trains connect Krems with Vienna's Franz-Josefs-Bahnhof (€15.90, one hour) and Melk (€12.70, 1½ hours).

Melk

☎02752 / POP 5187

With its sparkling and majestic abbey-fortress, Melk is a highlight of any visit to the Danube Valley. Many visitors cycle here for the day – wearily pushing their bikes through the cobblestone streets.

Sights

Stift Melk MONASTERY
(Benedictine Abbey of Melk; www.stiftmelk.at; Abt Berthold Dietmayr Strasse 1; adult/child €10/5.50, with guided tour €12/7.50; ⏲9am-5.30pm May-Sep, tours 11am & 2pm Oct-Apr) Of the many abbeys in Austria, this one is the most famous. Possibly Lower Austria's finest, the monastery church dominates the complex with its twin spires and high octagonal dome. The interior is baroque gone barmy, with regiments of smirking cherubs, gilt twirls and polished faux marble. The theatrical high-altar scene, depicting St Peter and St Paul (the church's two patron saints), is by Peter Widerin. Johann Michael Rottmayr created most of the ceiling paintings, including those in the dome.

Sleeping & Eating

Restaurants and cafes with alfresco seating line the Rathausplatz.

Hotel Restaurant zur Post HOTEL €€
(☎523 45; www.post-melk.at; Linzer Strasse 1; s €65-85, d €108-125; P@) A bright and pleasant hotel in the heart of town offering 25 large, comfortable rooms in plush colours with additional touches such as brass bed lamps.

Information

The centrally located **tourist office** (☎511 60; www.stadt-melk.at; Kremser Strasse 5; ⏲9.30am-6pm Mon-Sat, to 4pm Sun Apr-Oct, 9am-5pm Mon-Thu, to 2.30pm Fri Nov-Mar) has maps and plenty of useful information.

Getting There & Away

Boats leave from the canal by Pionierstrasse, 400m north of the abbey. There are hourly trains to Vienna (€16.30, 1¼ hours).

Linz

☎0732 / POP 193,814

In Linz beginnt's (It begins in Linz) goes the Austrian saying, and it's spot on. The technology trailblazer and European Capital of Culture 2009 is blessed with a leading-edge cyber centre and world-class contemporary-art gallery.

Sights & Activities

★**Ars Electronica Center** MUSEUM
(www.aec.at; Ars Electronica Strasse 1; adult/child €8/6; ⏲9am-5pm Tue-Fri, to 9pm Thu, 10am-6pm Sat & Sun) The technology, science and digital media of the future are in the spotlight at Linz' biggest crowd-puller, the Ars Electronica Center. In the labs you can interact with robots, animate digital objects, convert your name to DNA and (virtually) travel to outer space.

Lentos GALLERY
(www.lentos.at; Ernst-Koref-Promenade 1; adult/child €8/4.50, guided tours €3; ⏲10am-6pm Tue-Sun, to 9pm Thu) Overlooking the Danube, the rectangular glass-and-steel Lentos is strikingly illuminated by night. The gallery guards one of Austria's finest modern-art collections, including works by Warhol, Schiele, Klimt, Kokoschka and Lovis Corinth, which sometimes feature in the large-scale exhibitions.

Mariendom CATHEDRAL
(Herrenstrasse 26; ⏲7.30am-7pm Mon-Sat, 8am-7.15pm Sun) Also known as the Neuer Dom, this neo-Gothic giant of a cathedral lifts your gaze to its riot of pinnacles, flying buttresses and filigree traceried windows.

Pöstlingberg VIEWPOINT
Linz spreads out beneath you atop Pöstlingberg (537m). It's a precipitous 30-minute ride aboard the narrow-gauge **Pöstlingbergbahn** (Hauptplatz; adult/child return €5.80/3; ⏲6am-10.30pm Mon-Sat, 7.30am-10.30pm Sun)

LINZ CARD

The Linz Card, giving entry to major sights and unlimited use of public transport, costs €15/25 for one/three days.

from the Hauptplatz. This gondola features in the *Guinness Book of World Records* as the world's steepest mountain railway – quite some feat for such a low-lying city!

Sleeping & Eating

Hotel am Domplatz DESIGN HOTEL €€
(☎77 30 00; www.hotelamdomplatz.at; Stifterstrasse 4; d €125-145, ste €300; ❄@📶) Sidling up to the neo-Gothic Neuer Dom, this glass-and-concrete cube reveals streamlined interiors in pristine whites and blonde wood that reveal a Nordic-style aesthetic. Wind down with a view at the rooftop spa.

k.u.k. Hofbäckerei CAFE €
(Pfarrgasse 17; coffee & cake €3-6; ⏰6.30am-6.30pm Mon-Fri, 7am-12.30pm Sat) The Empire lives on at this gloriously stuck-in-time cafe. Here Fritz Rath bakes the best Linzer Torte in town – rich, spicy and with lattice pastry that crumbles just so.

Cook INTERNATIONAL €€
(☎78 13 05; www.cook.co.at; Klammstrasse 1; mains €9.50-16; ⏰11.30am-2.30pm Mon, 11.30am-2.30pm & 6-10pm Tue-Fri) Tossing Scandinavian and Asian flavours into the same pan may seem like folly, but Cook somehow manages to pull it off. A clean-lined, crisp interior forms the backdrop for dishes such as fish soup with a generous pinch of chilli.

Information

Hotspot Linz (www.hotspotlinz.at) Free wi-fi at 120 hot spots in the city, including Ars Electronica Center and Lentos.

Tourist Information Linz (☎7070 2009; www.linz.at; Hauptplatz 1; ⏰9am-7pm Mon-Sat, 10am-7pm Sun) Brochures, accommodation listings, a free room-reservation service and a separate Upper Austria information desk can be found here. It's open shorter hours in winter.

Getting There & Around

AIR

Ryanair flies to the Blue Danube Airport (p89), 13km southwest of Linz. An hourly shuttle bus (€2.90, 20 minutes) links the airport to the main train station.

PUBLIC TRANSPORT

Single bus and tram tickets cost €2, and day passes €4.

TRAIN

Linz is halfway between Salzburg and Vienna on the main road and rail routes. Trains to Salzburg (€25.30, 1¼ hours) and Vienna (€33.60, 1½ hours) leave at least twice hourly.

THE SOUTH

Austria's two main southern states, Styria (Steiermark) and Carinthia (Kärnten), often feel worlds apart from the rest of the country, both in climate and attitude. Styria is a blissful amalgamation of genteel architecture, rolling green hills, vine-covered slopes and soaring mountains. Its capital, Graz, is one of Austria's most attractive cities. A fashion-conscious crowd heads to sun-drenched Carinthia in summer. Sidling up to Italy, the region exudes an atmosphere that's as close to Mediterranean as this staunch country gets.

Graz

☎0316 / POP 269,997

Austria's second-largest city is probably its most relaxed and, after Vienna, its liveliest for after-hours pursuits. It's an attractive place with bristling green parkland, red rooftops and a small, fast-flowing river gushing through its centre. Architecturally, it has Renaissance courtyards and provincial baroque palaces complemented by innovative modern designs. The surrounding countryside, a mixture of vineyards, mountains, forested hills and thermal springs, is within easy striking distance.

Sights

Graz is a city easily enjoyed by simply wandering aimlessly. Admission to all of the Joanneum museums with a 24-hour ticket costs €11/4 for adults/children.

★**Neue Galerie Graz** GALLERY
(www.museum-joanneum.at; Joanneumsviertel; adult/child €8/3; ⏰10am-5pm Tue-Sun; 📶; 🚋1, 3, 4, 5, 6, 7 Hauptplatz) The Neue Galerie is the crowning glory of the three museums inside the Joanneumsviertel museum complex. The stunning collection on level 0 is the highlight. Though not enormous, it showcases richly textured and colourful works by painters such as Ernst Christian Moser, Ferdinand Georg Waldmüller and Johann Nepomuk Passini. Egon Schiele is also represented here.

Kunsthaus Graz GALLERY
(www.kunsthausgraz.at; Lendkai 1; adult/child €8/3; ⏰10am-5pm Tue-Sun; 🚋1, 3, 6, 7 Südtiroler

Platz) Designed by British architects Peter Cook and Colin Fournier, this world-class contemporary-art space is a bold creation that looks something like a space-age sea slug. Exhibitions change every three to four months.

Schloss Eggenberg PALACE
(Eggenberger Allee 90; adult/child €11.50/5.50; ⌚tours 10am-4pm Tue-Sun Palm Sun-Oct; 🚊1 Schloss Eggenberg) Graz' elegant palace was created for the Eggenberg dynasty in 1625 by Giovanni Pietro de Pomis (1565–1633) at the request of Johann Ulrich (1568–1634). Admission is on a highly worthwhile guided tour during which you learn about the idiosyncrasies of each room, the stories told by the frescoes and about the Eggenberg family itself.

Murinsel BRIDGE
(🚊4, 5 Schlossplatz/Murinsel, 🚊1, 3, 6, 7 Südtiroler Platz) Murinsel is a constructed island-cum-bridge of metal and plastic in the middle of the Mur. This modern floating landmark contains a cafe, a kids' playground and a small stage.

Schlossberg VIEWPOINT
(1hr ticket for lift or funicular €2.10; 🚊4, 5 Schlossbergplatz) FREE Rising to 473m, Schlossberg is the site of the original fortress where Graz was founded and is topped by the city's most visible icon – the **Uhrenturn**. Its wooded slopes can be reached by a number of bucolic and strenuous paths, but also by lift or Schlossbergbahn funicular. Take tram 4 or 5 to Schlossplatz/Murinsel for the lift.

Landeszeughaus MUSEUM
(Styrian Armoury; www.museum-joanneum.at; Herrengasse 16; adult/child €8/3; ⌚10am-5pm Mon & Wed-Sun; 🚊1, 3, 4, 5, 6, 7 Hauptplatz) You won't need to have a passion for armour and weapons to enjoy what's on show at the Landeszeughaus. More than 30,000 pieces of glistening weaponry are housed here.

Burg CASTLE, PARK
(Hofgasse; 🚌30 Schauspielhaus, 🚊1, 3, 4, 5, 6, 7 Hauptplatz) FREE Graz' 15th-century Burg today houses government offices. At the far end of the courtyard, on the left under the arch, is an ingenious **double staircase** (1499) – the steps diverge and converge as they spiral. Adjoining it is the **Stadtpark**, the city's largest green space.

Sleeping

Hotel Daniel HOTEL €
(☎711 080; www.hoteldaniel.com; Europaplatz 1; r €64-81, breakfast €11; P ❄ @ 🛜; 🚊1, 3, 6, 7 Hauptbahnhof) The Daniel is a design hotel with slick, minimalist-style rooms. You can rent a Vespa or e-bike for €15 per day, or a Piaggio APE for €9 per hour.

★ **Schlossberg Hotel** HOTEL €€
(☎80 70-0; www.schlossberg-hotel.at; Kaiser-Franz-Josef-Kai 30; s €115-135, d €150-185, ste €210-250; P @ 🛜 🏊; 🚊4, 5 Schlossbergbahn) Central but secluded, four-star Schlossberg is blessed with a prime location at the foot of its namesake. Rooms are well sized and decorated in the style of a country inn. The rooftop terrace with views is perfect for an evening glass of wine.

Hotel zum Dom HOTEL €€
(☎82 48 00; www.domhotel.co.at; Bürgergasse 14; s €74, d €89-169, ste €189-294; P ❄ 🛜; 🚌30 Palais Trauttmansdorff/Urania, 🚊1, 3, 4, 5, 6, 7 Hauptplatz) Ceramic art crafted by a local artist lends character to graceful Hotel zum Dom, whose individually furnished rooms come either with steam/power showers or whirlpools. One suite even has a terrace whirlpool.

Eating

Aside from the following listings, there are plenty of cheap eats near Universität Graz, particularly on Halbärthgasse, Zinzendorfgasse and Harrachgasse.

Stock up for a picnic at the **farmers markets** (⌚6am-1pm Mon-Sat) on Kaiser-Josef-Platz

HUNDERTWASSER SPA

East Styria is famed for its thermal springs. Fans of Friedensreich Hundertwasser's playful architectural style won't want to miss the surreal **Rogner-Bad Blumau** (☎03383-51 00; www.blumau.com; adult/child Mon-Fri €42/23, Sat & Sun €51/28; ⌚9am-11pm), 50km east of Graz. The spa has all the characteristics of his art, including uneven floors, grass on the roof, colourful ceramics and golden spires. Overnight accommodation includes entry to the spa. Call ahead to book treatments from sound meditation to invigorating Styrian elderberry wraps.

and Lendplatz. For **fast-food stands**, head for Hauptplatz and Jakominiplatz.

★Der Steirer AUSTRIAN, TAPAS €€
(☎703 654; www.dersteirer.at; Belgiergasse 1; tapas €2, lunch menu €7.90, mains €10-22.50; ⊙11am-midnight; ; 1, 3, 6, 7 Südtiroler Platz) This Styrian neo-*Beisl* (bistro pub) and wine bar has a small but fantastic selection of local dishes, including a great goulash, and Austro-tapas if you just feel like nibbling.

Landhauskeller AUSTRIAN €€
(☎83 02 76; Schmiedgasse 9; mains €11.50-28.50; ⊙11.30am-midnight Mon-Sat; 1, 3, 4, 5, 6, 7 Hauptplatz) What started as a spit-and-sawdust pub in the 16th century has evolved into an atmospheric, medieval-style restaurant serving specialities such as its four different sorts of *Tafelspitz* (prime broiled beef).

Drinking & Nightlife

The bar scene in Graz is split between three main areas: around the university; adjacent to the Kunsthaus; and on Mehlplatz and Prokopigasse (dubbed the 'Bermuda Triangle').

La Enoteca WINE BAR
(www.laenoteca.at; Sackstrasse 14; ⊙5-11pm Mon, 11.30am-11pm Tue-Fri, 10am-11pm Sat; 1, 3, 4, 5, 6, 7 Hauptplatz) This small wine bar has an informal, relaxed atmosphere and courtyard seating, making it an ideal place to enjoy a Schilcher Sekt (sparkling rosé) with mixed antipasti.

Kulturhauskeller BAR, CLUB
(Elisabethstrasse 30; ⊙9pm-5am Tue-Sat; 7 Lichtenfelsgasse) The raunchy Kulturhauskeller is a popular student hang-out with a great cellar-pub feel and a Wednesday karaoke night.

Information

Graz Tourismus (☎80 75; www.graztourismus.at; Herrengasse 16; ⊙10am-6pm; ; 1, 3, 4, 5, 6, 7 Hauptplatz) Graz' main tourist office, with loads of free information on the city, and helpful and knowledgeable staff.

Getting There & Away

AIR

Graz airport (p89) is located 10km south of the centre and is served by carriers including **Air Berlin** (www.airberlin.com), which connects the city with Berlin.

BICYCLE

Bicycle rental is available from **Bicycle** (☎82 13 57; www.bicycle.at; Körösistrasse 5; per 24hr €10, Fri-Mon €16; ⊙7am-1pm & 2-6pm Mon-Fri).

PUBLIC TRANSPORT

Single tickets (€2.10) for buses, trams and the Schlossbergbahn are valid for one hour, but you're usually better off buying a 24-hour pass (€4.80).

TRAIN

Trains to Vienna depart hourly (€37, 2½ hours), and six daily go to Salzburg (€48.20, four hours). International train connections from Graz include Ljubljana (€30 to €40, 3½ hours) and Budapest (€51 to €73, 5½ hours).

Klagenfurt

☎0463 / POP 96,640

With its captivating location on Wörthersee and more Renaissance than baroque beauty, Klagenfurt has a distinct Mediterranean feel. Carinthia's capital makes a handy base for exploring Wörthersee's lakeside villages and elegant medieval towns to the north.

Sights & Activities

Boating and swimming are usually possible from May to September.

★Wörthersee LAKE
Owing to its thermal springs, the Wörthersee is one of the region's warmer lakes (an average 21°C in summer) and is great for swimming, lakeshore frolicking and water sports. The 50km **cycle path** around the lake is one of the 'Top 10' in Austria. In summer the tourist office cooperates with a hire company for bicycles (per day/week €11/45), which can be picked up and dropped off at points around the lake.

Europapark PARK
The green expanse and its *Strandbad* (beach) on the shores of the Wörthersee are centres for splashy fun, and especially good for kids. The park's biggest draw is **Minimundus** (www.minimundus.at; Villacher Strasse 241; adult/child €13/8; ⊙9am-7pm Mar-Sep;), a 'miniature world' with 140 replicas of the

FREE TOURS

Free guided tours depart from Klagenfurt's tourist office at 10am every Friday and Saturday.

world's architectural icons, downsized to a scale of 1:25. To get here, take bus 10, 11, 12 or 22 from Heiligengeistplatz.

Sleeping & Eating

When you check into accommodation in Klagenfurt, ask for a *Gästekarte* (guest card), entitling you to discounts.

Hotel Geyer HOTEL €€
(☎578 86; www.hotelgeyer.com; Priesterhausgasse 5; s €70-88, d €102-135, q €155-170; P 📶) Expect modern and comfortable rooms in this three-star hotel. Bonuses are the sauna and steam bath, and free use of the fitness centre around the corner.

Restaurant Maria Loretto AUSTRIAN €€
(☎24 465; Lorettoweg 54; mains €16-26; ⏲10am-midnight Wed-Mon) Situated on a headland above Wörthersee, this characterful restaurant is easily reached by foot from the *Strandbad*. It does a very good trout and some flavoursome meat dishes. Reserve for an outside table.

Information

Tourist Office (☎53 722 23; www.klagenfurt-tourismus.at; Neuer Platz 1, Rathaus; ⏲8am-6pm Mon-Fri, 10am-5pm Sat, 10am-3pm Sun) Sells Kärnten Cards and books accommodation.

Getting There & Around

AIR

Klagenfurt's airport (p89) is 3km north of town. The low-cost airline **Germanwings** (www.germanwings.com) flies to Vienna, and Berlin, Hamburg and Cologne in Germany.

BUS

Bus drivers sell single tickets (€2.10) and 24-hour passes (€4.70). Bus 40/42 shuttles between the Hauptbahnhof and the airport.

TRAIN

Two hourly direct trains run from Klagenfurt to Vienna (€52, four hours) and Salzburg (€39, 3¼ hours). Trains to Graz depart every two to three hours (€40, three hours). Trains to western Austria, Italy, Slovenia and Germany go via Villach (€6.70, 24 to 37 minutes, two to four per hour).

SALZBURG

☎0662 / POP 147,825

The joke 'If it's baroque, don't fix it' is a perfect maxim for Salzburg; the tranquil Old Town burrowed below steep hills looks much as it did when Mozart lived here 250 years ago.

A Unesco World Heritage Site, Salzburg's overwhelmingly baroque old town is entrancing both at ground level and from Hohensalzburg fortress high above. Across the fast-flowing Salzach River rests Schloss Mirabell, surrounded by gorgeous manicured gardens.

If this doesn't whet your appetite, then bypass the grandeur and head straight for kitsch-country by joining a tour of *The Sound of Music* film locations.

Sights

★Dom CATHEDRAL
(Cathedral; Domplatz; donations accepted; ⏲8am-7pm Mon-Sat, 1-7pm Sun) Gracefully crowned by a bulbous copper dome and twin spires, the Dom stands out as a masterpiece of baroque art. Bronze portals symbolising faith, hope and charity lead into the cathedral. In the nave, intricate stucco and Arsenio Mascagni's ceiling frescoes recounting the Passion of Christ guide the eye to the polychrome dome.

Dommuseum MUSEUM
(www.domquartier.at; Kapitelplatz 6; DomQuartier ticket adult/child €12/4; ⏲10am-5pm Wed-Mon) The Dommuseum is a treasure trove of sacred art. A visit whisks you past a cabinet of Renaissance curiosities crammed with crystals, coral and oddities such as armadillos and pufferfish, through rooms showcasing gem-encrusted monstrances, stained glass and altarpieces, and into the **Long Gallery**, which is graced with 17th- and 18th-century paintings, including Paul Troger's chiaroscuro *Christ and Nicodemus* (1739).

★Residenz PALACE
(www.domquartier.at; Residenzplatz 1; DomQuartier ticket adult/child €12/4; ⏲10am-5pm Wed-Mon) The crowning glory of Salzburg's new DomQuartier, the Residenz is where the prince-archbishops held court until Salzburg became part of the Habsburg Empire in the 19th century. An audio-guide tour takes in the exuberant state rooms, lavishly adorned with tapestries, stucco and frescoes by Johann Michael Rottmayr.

The 3rd floor is given over to the Residenzgalerie, where the focus is on Flemish and Dutch masters. Must-sees include Rubens' *Allegory on Emperor Charles V* and Rembrandt's chiaroscuro *Old Woman Praying*.

Salzburg

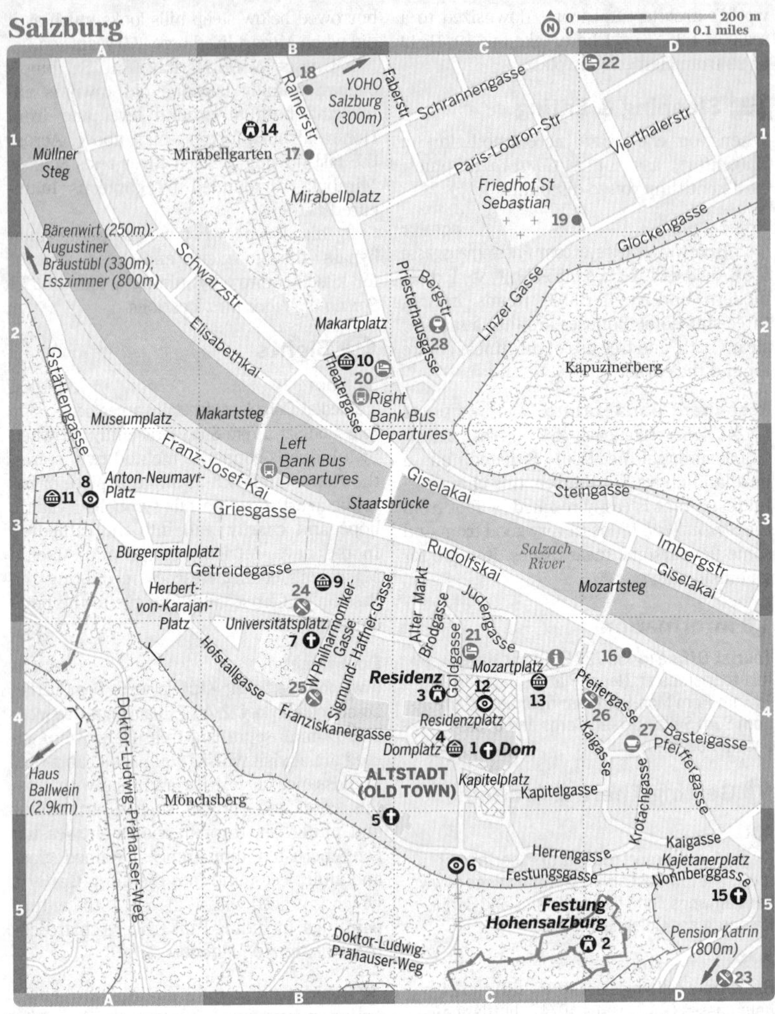

Residenzplatz SQUARE

With its horse-drawn carriages, palace and street entertainers, this stately baroque square is the Salzburg of a thousand postcards. Its centrepiece is the **Residenzbrunnen**, an enormous marble fountain ringed by four water-spouting horses and topped by a conch-shell-bearing Triton.

Salzburg Museum MUSEUM

(www.salzburgmuseum.at; Mozartplatz 1; adult/child €7/3; 9am-5pm Tue-Sun, to 8pm Thu) Housed in the baroque Neue Residenz palace, this flagship museum takes you on a fascinating romp through Salzburg past and present. Ornate rooms showcase everything from Roman excavations to prince-archbishop portraits. There are free guided tours at 6pm every Thursday.

Erzabtei St Peter CHURCH

(St Peter's Abbey; St Peter Bezirk 1-2; catacombs adult/child €2/1.50; church 8am-noon & 2.30-6.30pm, cemetery 6.30am-7pm, catacombs 10am-6pm) A Frankish missionary named Rupert founded this abbey church and monastery in around 700, making it the oldest in the German-speaking world. The cemetery is

Salzburg

Top Sights
- 1 Dom C4
- 2 Festung Hohensalzburg D5
- 3 Residenz C4

Sights
- 4 Dommuseum C4
- 5 Erzabtei St Peter B5
- 6 Festungsbahn Funicular C5
- 7 Kollegienkirche B4
- 8 Mönchsberg Lift A3
- 9 Mozarts Geburtshaus B3
- 10 Mozart-Wohnhaus B2
- 11 Museum der Moderne A3
- 12 Residenzplatz C4
- 13 Salzburg Museum C4
- 14 Schloss Mirabell B1
- 15 Stift Nonnberg D5

Activities, Courses & Tours
- 16 Bob's Special Tours D4
- 17 Fräulein Maria's Bicycle Tours B1
- 18 Salzburg Panorama Tours B1
- 19 Segway Tours C1

Sleeping
- 20 Arte Vida B2
- 21 Hotel Am Dom C4
- 22 Hotel Mozart D1

Eating
- 23 Green Garden D5
- 24 Grünmarkt B3
- 25 Triangel B4
- 26 Zwettler's D4

Drinking & Nightlife
- 27 220 Grad D4
- 28 Enoteca Settemila C2

home to the **catacombs**, cave-like chapels and crypts hewn out of the Mönchsberg cliff face.

★Festung Hohensalzburg FORT

(www.salzburg-burgen.at; Mönchsberg 34; adult/child/family €8/4.50/18.20, incl Festungsbahn funicular €11.30/6.50/26.20; 9am-7pm) Salzburg's most visible icon is this mighty 900-year-old cliff-top fortress, one of the biggest and best preserved in Europe. It's easy to spend half a day up here, roaming the ramparts for far-reaching views over the city's spires, the Salzach River and the mountains. The fortress is a steep 15-minute jaunt from the centre or a speedy ride in the glass **Festungsbahn funicular** (Festungsgasse 4).

Stift Nonnberg CHURCH

(Nonnberg Convent; Nonnberggasse 2; 7am-dusk) A short climb up the Nonnbergstiege staircase from Kaigasse or along Festungsgasse brings you to this Benedictine convent, founded 1300 years ago and made famous as *the* nunnery in *The Sound of Music*. You can visit the beautiful rib-vaulted church, but the rest of the convent is off-limits.

Kollegienkirche CHURCH

(Universitätsplatz; 8am-6pm) Johann Bernhard Fischer von Erlach's grandest baroque design is this late-17th-century university church, with a striking bowed facade. The high altar's columns symbolise the Seven Pillars of Wisdom.

Mozarts Geburtshaus MUSEUM

(Mozart's Birthplace; www.mozarteum.at; Getreidegasse 9; adult/child €10/3.50, incl Mozart-Wohnhaus €17/5; 9am-5.30pm) Wolfgang Amadeus Mozart, Salzburg's most famous son, was born in this bright-yellow townhouse in 1756 and spent the first 17 years of his life here.

Mozart-Wohnhaus MUSEUM

(Mozart's Residence; www.mozarteum.at; Makartplatz 8; adult/child €10/3.50, incl Mozarts Geburtshaus €17/5; 9am-5.30pm) Mozart's one-time residence showcases family portraits, documents and instruments. An audioguide accompanies your visit, serenading you with opera excerpts. Alongside family portraits and documents, you'll find Mozart's original fortepiano.

Museum der Moderne GALLERY

(www.museumdermoderne.at; Mönchsberg 32; adult/child €8/6; 10am-6pm Tue-Sun, to 8pm Wed) Straddling Mönchsberg's cliffs, this contemporary glass-and-marble oblong of

SALZBURG CARD

The money-saving **Salzburg Card** (1-/2-/3-day card €27/36/42) gets you entry to all of the major sights, a free river cruise, unlimited use of public transport (including cable cars) plus numerous discounts on tours and events. The card is €3 cheaper in the low season and half price for children aged 15 and under.

a gallery stands in stark contrast to the fortress. The gallery shows first-rate temporary exhibitions of 20th- and 21st-century art. There's a free guided tour of the gallery at 6.30pm every Wednesday. The **Mönchsberg Lift** (Gstättengasse 13; one way/return €2.10/3.40, incl gallery €9.70/6.80; 8am-7pm Thu-Tue, to 9pm Wed) whizzes up to the gallery year-round.

Schloss Mirabell PALACE
(Mirabellplatz 4; Marble Hall 8am-4pm Mon, Wed & Thu, 1-4pm Tue & Fri, gardens dawn-dusk) FREE Prince-Archbishop Wolf Dietrich had this splendid palace built for his mistress Salome Alt in 1606. Johann Lukas von Hildebrandt, of Schloss Belvedere fame, gave it a baroque makeover in 1721. The lavish **Marmorsaal** (Marble Hall), replete with stucco, marble and frescoes, is free to visit and provides a sublime backdrop for evening chamber concerts. For stellar fortress views, stroll the fountain-dotted gardens. *The Sound of Music* fans will naturally recognise the Pegasus statue and the steps where the von Trapps practised 'Do-Re-Mi'.

Tours

If you would rather go it alone, the tourist office has four-hour iTour audioguides (€9), which take in big-hitters such as the Residenz, Mirabellgarten and Mozartplatz.

Fräulein Maria's Bicycle Tours BICYCLE TOUR
(www.mariasbicycletours.com; Mirabellplatz 4; adult/child €30/18; 9.30am May-Sep, plus 4.30pm Jun-Aug) Belt out *The Sound of Music* faves as you pedal on one of these jolly 3½-hour bike tours, taking in film locations including the Mirabellgarten, Stift Nonnberg, Schloss Leopoldskron and Hellbrunn. No advance booking is necessary; just turn up at the meeting point on Mirabellplatz.

Salzburg Panorama Tours BUS TOUR
(87 40 29; www.panoramatours.com; Mirabellplatz; office 8am-6pm) Boasts the 'original *Sound of Music* Tour' (€40) as well as a huge range of others, including Altstadt walking tours (€15), Mozart tours (€25) and Bavarian Alps and Salzkammergut excursions (€40).

Segway Tours TOUR
(www.segway-salzburg.at; Wolf-Dietrich-Strasse 3; City/Sound of Music tour €33/60; tours 10.30am, 1pm & 3pm Apr-Oct) These guided Segway tours take in the big sights by zippy battery-powered scooter. Trundle through the city on a one-hour ride or tick off *The Sound of Music* locations on a two-hour tour.

Bob's Special Tours BUS TOUR
(84 95 11; www.bobstours.com; Rudolfskai 38; office 8.30am-5pm Mon-Fri, 1-2pm Sat & Sun) Minibus tours to *The Sound of Music* locations (€45), the Bavarian Alps (€45) and Grossglockner (€90). Prices include a free hotel pick-up for morning tours starting at 9am. Reservations essential.

Festivals & Events

Mozartwoche MUSIC
(Mozart Week; www.mozarteum.at; late Jan) World-renowned orchestras, conductors and soloists celebrate Mozart's birthday with a feast of his music.

Salzburg Festival ART
(Salzburger Festspiele; www.salzburgerfestspiele.at; late Jul-Aug) You'll need to book tickets months ahead for this venerable summer festival, running since 1920.

Sleeping

★**Haus Ballwein** GUESTHOUSE €
(82 40 29; www.haus-ballwein.at; Moosstrasse 69a; s €42-49, d €63-69, apt €98-120; P) With its bright, pine-filled rooms, mountain views, free bike hire and garden, this place is big on charm. The largest, quietest rooms face the back and have balconies and kitchenettes. It's a 10-minute trundle from the Altstadt; take bus 21 to Gsengerweg.

YOHO Salzburg HOSTEL €
(87 96 49; www.yoho.at; Paracelsusstrasse 9; dm €20-24, s €41, d €67-77; @) Free wi-fi, secure lockers, comfy bunks, plenty of cheap beer and good-value schnitzels – what more could a backpacker ask for? Except, perhaps, a merry sing along with *The Sound of Music* screened daily (yes, *every* day). The friendly crew can arrange tours, adventure sports such as rafting and canyoning, and bike hire.

Pension Katrin PENSION €€
(83 08 60; www.pensionkatrin.at; Nonntaler Hauptstrasse 49b; s €64-70, d €112-122, tr €153-168, q €172-188; P) With its flowery garden, bright and cheerful rooms and homemade goodies at breakfast, this pension is one of the homiest in Salzburg. The affable Terler family keeps everything spick and span. Take bus 5 from the Hauptbahnhof to Wäschergasse.

Hotel Am Dom BOUTIQUE HOTEL €€
(84 27 65; www.hotelamdom.at; Goldgasse 17; s €90-160, d €130-280;) Antique meets

boutique at this Altstadt hotel, where the original vaults and beams of the 800-year-old building contrast with razor-sharp design features.

Arte Vida GUESTHOUSE €€
(☎87 31 85; www.artevida.at; Dreifaltigkeitsgasse 9; s €59-129, d €86-140, apt €150-214; 📶) Arte Vida has the boho-chic feel of a Marrakesh riad, with its lantern-lit salon, communal kitchen and serene garden. Asia and Africa have provided the inspiration for the rich colours and fabrics that dress the individually designed rooms, all with DVD players and iPod docks.

Hotel Mozart HISTORIC HOTEL €€
(☎87 22 74; www.hotel-mozart.at; Franz-Josef-Strasse 27; s €95-105, d €140-155, tr €160-175; P📶) An antique-filled lobby gives way to spotless rooms with comfy beds and sizeable bathrooms at the Mozart.

Eating

Self-caterers can find picnic fixings at the **Grünmarkt** (Green Market; Universitätsplatz; ⏰7am-7pm Mon-Fri, 6am-3pm Sat).

Bärenwirt AUSTRIAN €€
(☎42 24 04; www.baerenwirt-salzburg.at; Müllner Hauptstrasse 8; mains €9.50-20; ⏰11am-11pm) Sizzling and stirring since 1663, Bärenwirt combines a woody, hunting-lodge-style interior with a river-facing terrace. Go for hearty *Bierbraten* (beer roast) with dumplings, locally caught trout or organic wild-boar bratwurst. The restaurant is 500m north of Museumplatz.

Triangel AUSTRIAN €€
(☎84 22 29; Wiener-Philharmoniker-Gasse 7; mains €10-19; ⏰noon-midnight Tue-Sat) The menu is market-fresh at this arty bistro, where the picture-clad walls pay tribute to Salzburg Festival luminaries. It does gourmet salads, a mean Hungarian goulash with organic beef, and delicious homemade ice cream.

Green Garden VEGETARIAN €€
(☎0662-841201; Nonntaler Hauptstrasse 16; mains €9.50-14.50; ⏰noon-3pm & 5.30-10pm Tue-Sat; 🖉) 🍃 The Green Garden is a breath of fresh air for vegetarians and vegans. Locavore is the word at this bright, modern cottage-style restaurant, pairing dishes like wild herb salad, saffron risotto with braised fennel and vegan fondue with organic wines in a totally relaxed setting.

Zwettler's AUSTRIAN €€
(☎84 41 99; www.zwettlers.com; Kaigasse 3; mains €9-18; ⏰4pm-2am Mon, 11.30am-2am Tue-Sat, 11.30am-midnight Sun) This gastro-pub has a lively buzz on its pavement terrace. Local grub such as schnitzel with parsley potatoes and goulash goes well with a cold, foamy Kaiser Karl wheat beer.

★Esszimmer FRENCH €€€
(☎87 08 99; www.esszimmer.com; Müllner Hauptstrasse 33; 3-course lunch €38, tasting menus €75-118; ⏰noon-2pm & 6.30-9.30pm Tue-Sat) Andreas Kaiblinger puts an innovative spin on market-driven French cuisine at Michelin-starred Esszimmer. Eye-catching art, playful backlighting and a glass floor revealing the Almkanal stream keep diners captivated, as do gastro showstoppers inspired by the seasons. Buses 7, 21 and 28 to Landeskrankenhaus stop close by.

Drinking & Nightlife

You'll find the biggest concentration of bars along both banks of the Salzach; the hippest are around Gstättengasse and Anton-Neumayr-Platz.

★Augustiner Bräustübl BREWERY
(www.augustinerbier.at; Augustinergasse 4-6; ⏰3-11pm Mon-Fri, from 2.30pm Sat & Sun) Who says monks can't enjoy themselves? Since 1621, this cheery monastery-run brewery has been serving potent homebrews in Stein tankards in the vaulted hall and beneath the chestnut trees in the 1000-seat beer garden.

Enoteca Settemila WINE BAR
(Bergstrasse 9; ⏰5-11pm Tue-Thu, from 3pm Fri & Sat) This bijou wine shop and bar brims with the enthusiasm and passion of Rafael Peil and Nina Corti. Go to sample their well-edited selection of wines, including Austrian, organic and biodynamic ones, with *taglieri* – sharing plates of cheese and *salumi* (cold cuts) from small Italian producers.

220 Grad CAFE
(Chiemseegasse 5; ⏰9am-7pm Tue-Fri, to 6pm Sat) Famous for freshly roasted coffee, this retro-chic cafe serves probably the best espresso in town and whips up superb breakfasts.

Information

Many hotels and bars offer free wi-fi, and there are several cheap internet cafes near the train station. *Bankomaten* (ATMs) are all over the place.

DOMQUARTIER

Salzburg's historic centre shines more brightly than ever since the opening of the DomQuartier in May 2014. A single ticket (adult/child €12/4) gives you access to all five sights in the complex, including the Residenz, Dommuseum and Erzabtei St Peter. For more details, visit www.domquartier.at.

Tourist Office (☎889 87 330; www.salzburg.info; Mozartplatz 5; ⊙9am-7pm) Helpful tourist office with a ticket-booking service.

Getting There & Away

AIR

Low-cost airlines including **Ryanair** (www.ryanair.com) and **easyJet** (www.easyjet.com) serve Salzburg airport (p89), 5.5km west of the city centre.

BUS

Buses depart from just outside the Hauptbahnhof on Südtiroler Platz. For bus timetables and fares, see www.svv-info.at and www.postbus.at.

TRAIN

Fast trains leave frequently for Vienna (€51, 2½ hours) via Linz (€25, 1¼ hours). There is a two-hourly express service to Klagenfurt (€39, three hours). There are hourly trains to Innsbruck (€45, two hours).

Getting Around

TO/FROM THE AIRPORT

Bus 2 runs from the Hauptbahnhof (€2.50, 19 minutes) to the airport.

BICYCLE

Top Bike (www.topbike.at; Staatsbrücke; per day €15; ⊙10am-5pm) Bicycle rental joint with half-price rental for kids. The Salzburg Card yields a 20% discount.

BUS

Bus drivers sell single (€2.50) and 24-hour (€5.50) tickets; these are cheaper when purchased in advance from machines (€1.70 and €3.40 respectively).

AROUND SALZBURG

Schloss Hellbrunn PALACE
(www.hellbrunn.at; Fürstenweg 37; adult/child/family €10.50/5/25; ⊙9am-5.30pm, to 9pm Jul & Aug; 👪) A prince-archbishop with a wicked sense of humour, Markus Sittikus built Italianate Schloss Hellbrunn as a 17th-century summer palace and an escape from his Residenz functions. The ingenious trick fountains and water-powered figures are the big draw. When the tour guides set them off, expect to get wet! Admission includes entry to the baroque palace. The rest of the sculpture-dotted gardens are free to visit. Look out for *The Sound of Music* pavilion of 'Sixteen Going on Seventeen' fame.

Bus 25 runs to Hellbrunn, 4.5km south of Salzburg, every 20 minutes from Rudolfskai in the Altstadt.

Werfen

☎06468 / POP 2963

More than 1000m above Werfen in the Tennengebirge mountains is **Eisriesenwelt** (www.eisriesenwelt.at; adult/child €11/6, incl cable car €22/12; ⊙9am-3.45pm May-Oct, to 4.45pm Jul & Aug). Billed as the world's largest accessible ice caves, this glittering ice empire is a once-seen-never-forgotten experience. Wrap up warm for subzero temperatures. Well below the caves is **Burg Hohenwerfen** (adult/child/family €11/6/26.50, incl lift €14.50/8/34.50; ⊙9am-5pm Apr-Oct; 👪), a formidable cliff-top fortress dating from 1077.

Both the ice caves and fortress can be visited as a day trip from Salzburg if you start early (tour the caves first and be at the castle by 3.15pm for the falconry show); otherwise consult the **tourist office** (☎53 88; www.werfen.at; Markt 24; ⊙9am-5pm Mon-Fri) for accommodation options.

Werfen is 45km south of Salzburg on the A10/E55 motorway. Trains run frequently to Salzburg (€8.60, 40 minutes). In summer, minibuses (return adult/child €6.50/4.90) run every 25 minutes between Eisriesenstrasse in Werfen and the car park, a 20-minute walk from the cable car to Eisriesenwelt.

SALZKAMMERGUT

A wonderland of glassy blue lakes and tall craggy peaks, Austria's Lake District is a long-time favourite holiday destination. The peaceful lakes attract visitors in droves, who come to boat, fish, swim or just laze on the shore.

Bad Ischl is the region's transport hub, but Hallstatt is its true jewel. For info visit **Salzkammergut Touristik** (☎0613-224 000; www.salzkammergut.co.at; Götzstrasse 12; ⊙9am-7pm).

The Salzkammergut Card (€4.90, available May to October) provides up to 30% discounts on sights, ferries, cable cars and some buses.

Hallstatt

☎06134 / POP 788

With pastel-hued homes, swans and towering mountains on either side of a glassy green lake, Hallstatt looks like some kind of greeting card for tranquillity. Now a Unesco World Heritage Site, Hallstatt was settled 4500 years ago and over 2000 graves have been discovered in the area, most of them dating from 1000 to 500 BC.

Sights & Activities

Salzwelten MINE

(www.salzwelten.at; funicular return plus tour adult/child/family €26/13/54, tour only €19/9.50/40; 9.30am-4.30pm late Apr–late Oct) The fascinating Salzwelten is situated high above Hallstatt on Salzberg (Salt Mountain) and is the lake's major cultural attraction. The German-English tour details how salt is formed and the history of mining, and takes visitors down into the depths on miners' slides – the largest is 60m, during which you have your photo taken.

Beinhaus CHURCH

(Bone House; Kirchenweg 40; admission €1.50; 10am-6pm May-Oct) This small charnel house contains rows of neatly stacked skulls, painted with decorative designs and the names of their former owners. Bones have been exhumed from the overcrowded graveyard since 1600, and the last skull in the collection was added in 1995.

Hallstätter See LAKE

(boat hire per hr from €11) You can hire boats and kayaks to get out on the lake, or scuba dive with the **Tauchclub Dachstein** (☎0664-88 600 481; www.dive-adventures.at; intro course from €35).

Sleeping & Eating

★**Pension Sarstein** GUESTHOUSE €

(☎82 17; Gosaumühlstrasse 83 ; d €64-80, apt €70-120;) The affable Fischer family takes pride in its little guesthouse a few minutes' walk along the lake from central Hallstatt. The old-fashioned rooms are nothing flash, but they are neat, cosy and have balconies with dreamy lake and mountain views. Family-sized apartments come with kitchenettes.

WORTH A TRIP

OBERTRAUN

Near Hallstatt, Obertraun has the intriguing **Dachstein Rieseneishöhle** (www.dachstein-salzkammergut.com; tour adult/child €14.30/8.30; core tour 9.20am-4pm May-late Oct). These caves are millions of years old and extend into the mountain for almost 80km in places.

From Obertraun it's also possible to catch a cable car to **Krippenstein** (return adult/child €28/15.50; May-Oct), where you'll find the freaky **5 Fingers viewing platform**, which protrudes over a sheer cliff face – not for sufferers of vertigo.

Restaurant zum Salzbaron EUROPEAN €€

(☎82 63; Marktplatz 104; mains €16-23; 11.30am-10pm;) One of the best gourmet acts in town, the Salzbaron is perched alongside the lake inside the Seehotel Grüner Baum and serves a seasonal pan-European menu; local trout features strongly in summer.

Information

Tourist Office (☎82 08; www.dachstein-salzkammergut.at; Seestrasse 99; 9am-5pm Mon-Fri, to 1pm Sat) Turn left from the ferry to reach this office. It stocks a free leisure map of lakeside towns, and hiking and cycling trails.

Getting There & Away

BOAT

The last ferry connection leaves Hallstatt train station at 6.50pm (€2.50, 10 minutes). Ferry excursions do the circuit of Hallstatt Lahn via Hallstatt Markt, Obersee, Untersee and Steeg return (€12, 90 minutes) three times daily from July to early September.

TRAIN

Hallstatt train station is across the lake. The boat service from there to the village coincides with train arrivals. About a dozen trains daily connect Hallstatt and Bad Ischl (€4.30, 27 minutes).

TYROL

With converging mountain ranges behind lofty pastures and tranquil meadows, Tyrol (also Tirol) captures a quintessential Alpine panoramic view. Occupying a central position is Innsbruck, the region's jewel, while in the

WORTH A TRIP

BREGENZERWALD

Only a few kilometres southeast of Bregenz, the forest-cloaked slopes, velvet-green pastures and limestone peaks of the Bregenzerwald unfold. In summer it's a glorious place to spend a few days hiking the hills and filling up on homemade cheeses in alpine dairies. Winter brings plenty of snow, and the area is noted for its downhill and cross-country skiing. The **Bregenzerwald tourist office** (☎05512-23 65; www.bregenzerwald.at; Impulszentrum 1135, Egg; ⏰9am-5pm Mon-Fri, 8am-1pm Sat) has information on the region.

northeast and southwest are superb ski resorts. In the southeast, separated somewhat from the main state since part of South Tyrol was ceded to Italy at the end of WWI, lies the protected natural landscape of the Hohe Tauern National Park, an alpine wonderland of 3000m peaks, including the country's highest, the Grossglockner (3798m).

Innsbruck

☎0512 / POP 124,579

Tyrol's capital is a sight to behold. The mountains are so close that within 25 minutes it's possible to travel from the heart of the city to over 2000m above sea level. Summer and winter outdoor activities abound, and it's understandable why some visitors only take a peek at Innsbruck proper before heading for the hills. But to do so is a shame, for Innsbruck has its own share of gems, including an authentic medieval Altstadt (Old Town), inventive architecture and vibrant student-driven nightlife.

Sights

Hofkirche CHURCH

(www.tiroler-landesmuseum.at; Universitätstrasse 2; adult/child €5/free; ⏰9am-5pm Mon-Sat, 12.30-5pm Sun) Innsbruck's pride and joy is the Gothic Hofkirche, one of Europe's finest royal court churches. It was commissioned in 1553 by Ferdinand I, who enlisted top artists of the age such as Albrecht Dürer, Alexander Colin and Peter Vischer the Elder. Top billing goes to the empty **sarcophagus of Emperor Maximilian I** (1459–1519), a masterpiece of German Renaissance sculpture, elaborately carved from black marble.

Goldenes Dachl & Museum MUSEUM

(Golden Roof; Herzog-Friedrich-Strasse 15; adult/child €4/2; ⏰10am-5pm, closed Mon Oct-Apr) Innsbruck's golden wonder is this Gothic oriel, built for Emperor Maximilian I and glittering with 2657 fire-gilt copper tiles. An audioguide whizzes you through the history in the museum; look for the grotesque tournament helmets designed to resemble the Turks of the rival Ottoman Empire.

Hofburg PALACE

(Imperial Palace; www.hofburg-innsbruck.at; Rennweg 1; adult/child €8/free; ⏰9am-5pm) Demanding attention with its imposing facade and cupolas, the Hofburg was built as a castle for Archduke Sigmund the Rich in the 15th century, expanded by Emperor Maximilian I in the 16th century and given a baroque makeover by Empress Maria Theresia in the 18th century. The centrepiece of the lavish rococo state apartments is the 31m-long **Riesensaal** (Giant's Hall).

Bergisel VIEWPOINT

(www.bergisel.info; adult/child €9.50/4.50; ⏰9am-6pm) Rising above Innsbruck like a celestial staircase, this glass-and-steel ski jump was designed by much-lauded Iraqi architect Zaha Hadid. It's 455 steps or a two-minute funicular ride to the 50m-high **viewing platform**, with a breathtaking panorama of the Nordkette range, Inntal and Innsbruck. Tram 1 trundles here from central Innsbruck.

Schloss Ambras CASTLE

(www.schlossambras-innsbruck.at; Schlosstrasse 20; adult/child/family €10/free/18; ⏰10am-5pm; 👪) Picturesquely perched on a hill and set among beautiful gardens, this Renaissance pile was acquired in 1564 by Archduke Ferdinand II, then ruler of Tyrol, who transformed it from a fortress into a palace. Don't miss the centrepiece **Spanische Saal** (Spanish Hall), the dazzling **armour collection** and the gallery's Velázquez and van Dyck originals.

CITY SAVERS

The **Innsbruck Card** allows one visit to Innsbruck's main sights/attractions, a return journey on lifts and cable cars, unlimited use of public transport including the Sightseer bus, and three-hour bike rental. It's available at the tourist office and costs €33/41/47 for 24/48/72 hours.

Stadtturm TOWER
(Herzog-Friedrich-Strasse 21; adult/child €3/1.50; ⏲10am-8pm) Climb this tower's 148 steps for 360-degree views of the city's rooftops, spires and surrounding mountains.

Activities

Anyone who loves playing in the great outdoors will be itching to head up into the Alps in Innsbruck.

Nordkettenbahnen FUNICULAR
(www.nordkette.com; one way/return to Hungerburg €4.60/7.60, Seegrube €16.50/27.50, Hafelekar €18.30/30.50; ⏲Hungerburg 7am-7.15pm Mon-Fri, 8am-7.15pm Sat & Sun, Seegrube 8.30am-5.30pm daily, Hafelekar 9am-5pm daily) Zaha Hadid's space-age funicular runs every 15 minutes, whizzing you from the Congress Centre to the slopes in no time. Walking trails head off in all directions from **Hungerburg** and **Seegrube**. For more of a challenge, there is a downhill track for mountain bikers and two fixed-rope routes *(Klettersteige)* for climbers.

Patrolled by inquisitive alpine sheep, the 2334m summit of **Hafelekar** affords tremendous views over Innsbruck to the snow-capped giants of the Austrian Alps, including 3798m Grossglockner.

Inntour ADVENTURE SPORTS
(www.inntour.com; Leopoldstrasse 4; ⏲9am-6.30pm Mon-Fri, to 5pm Sat & Sun) Based at Die Börse, Inntour arranges all manner of thrillseeking pursuits, including canyoning (€80), tandem paragliding (€105), white-water rafting (€45) and bungee jumping from the 192m Europabrücke (€140).

Sleeping

The tourist office has lists of private rooms costing between €20 and €40 per person.

Nepomuk's HOSTEL €
(☎584 118; www.nepomuks.at; Kiebachgasse 16; dm €24, d €58; 📶) Could this be backpacker heaven? Nepomuk's sure comes close, with its Altstadt location, well-stocked kitchen and high-ceilinged dorms with homely touches like CD players. The delicious breakfast in attached Cafe Munding, with homemade pastries, jam and fresh-roasted coffee, gets your day off to a grand start.

Pension Paula GUESTHOUSE €
(☎292 262; www.pensionpaula.at; Weiherburggasse 15; s €35-46, d €60-70, tr €92, q €104; P) This pension occupies an alpine chalet and has super-clean, homely rooms (most with balcony). It's up the hill towards the zoo and has great vistas across the city.

★Hotel Weisses Kreuz HISTORIC HOTEL €€
(☎594 79; www.weisseskreuz.at; Herzog-Friedrich-Strasse 31; s €39-80, d €73-149; P @ 📶) Beneath the arcades, this atmospheric Altstadt hotel has played host to guests for 500 years, including a 13-year-old Mozart. With its wood-panelled parlours, antiques and twisting staircase, the hotel oozes history with every creaking beam. Rooms are supremely comfortable, the staff are charming and breakfast is a lavish spread.

Weisses Rössl GUESTHOUSE €€
(☎583 057; www.roessl.at; Kiebachgasse 8; s €70-110, d €100-160; @ 📶) An antique rocking horse greets you at this 16th-century guesthouse. The vaulted entrance leads up to spacious rooms recently revamped with blonde wood, fresh hues and crisp white linen. The owner is a keen hunter and the restaurant (mains €10 to €18) has a meaty menu.

Eating

Markthalle MARKET €
(www.markthalle-innsbruck.at; Innrain; ⏲7am-6.30pm Mon-Fri, to 1pm Sat) Fresh-baked bread, Tyrolean cheese, organic fruit, smoked ham and salami – it's all under one roof at this riverside covered market.

Cafe Munding CAFE €
(www.munding.at; Kiebachgasse 16; cake €2-4; ⏲8am-8pm) Stop by this 200-year-old cafe for delicious cakes – try the moist chocolate raspberry Haustorte or the chocolate-marzipan Mozarttorte – and freshly roasted coffee.

★Chez Nico VEGETARIAN €€
(☎0650-451 06 24; www.chez-nico.at; Maria-Theresien-Strasse 49; 2-course lunch €14.50, 7-course menu €60; ⏲6.30-10pm Mon & Sat,

DON'T MISS

FREE GUIDED HIKES

From late May to October, Innsbruck Information (p84) arranges daily guided hikes, from sunrise walks to half-day mountain jaunts. The hikes are free with a Club Innsbruck Card, which you receive automatically when you stay overnight in Innsbruck. Pop into the tourist office to register and browse the program.

noon-2pm & 6.30-10pm Tue-Fri;) Take a petite bistro and a Parisian chef with a passion for herbs, *et voilà*, you get Chez Nico. Nicolas Curtil (Nico) cooks seasonal, all-vegetarian delights along the lines of smoked aubergine wonton and chanterelle-apricot goulash. You won't miss the meat, we swear.

Die Wilderin AUSTRIAN €€
(562 728; www.diewilderin.at; Seilergasse 5; mains €11-18; 5pm-2am Tue-Sat, 4pm-midnight Sun) Take a gastronomic walk on the wild side at this modern-day hunter-gatherer of a restaurant, where chefs take pride in local sourcing and using top-notch farm-fresh and foraged ingredients. The menu sings of the seasons, be it asparagus, game, strawberries or winter veg. The vibe is urbane and relaxed.

Himal ASIAN €€
(588 588; Universitätsstrasse 13; mains €9.50-14.50; 11.30am-2.30pm & 6-10.30pm Mon-Sat, 6-10pm Sun;) Friendly and intimate, Himal delivers vibrant, robust Nepalese flavours. Spot-on curries (some vegetarian) are mopped up with naan and washed down with mango lassis. The two-course €8.10 lunch is cracking value.

Drinking & Nightlife

Moustache BAR
(www.cafe-moustache.at; Herzog-Otto-Strasse 8; 11am-2am Tue-Sun;) Playing Spot-the-Moustache (Einstein, Charlie Chaplin and co) is the preferred pastime at this retro bolthole, with a terrace overlooking pretty Domplatz and Club Aftershave in the basement.

Hofgarten Café BAR
(www.tagnacht.at; Rennweg 6a; 7pm-4am Tue & Fri-Sat) DJ sessions and a tree-shaded beer garden are crowd-pullers at this trendy cafe-cum-bar set in the greenery of Hofgarten.

360° BAR
(Rathaus Galerien; 10am-1am Mon-Sat) Grab a cushion and drink in 360-degree views of the city and Alps from the balcony that skirts this spherical, glass-walled bar. It's a nicely chilled spot for a coffee or sundowner.

Information

Innsbruck Information (598 50; www.innsbruck.info; Burggraben 3; 9am-6pm) Main tourist office with truckloads of info on the city and surrounds, including skiing and walking.

Getting There & Away

AIR

EasyJet flies to Innsbruck Airport (p89), 4km west of the city centre.

CAR & MOTORCYCLE

Heading south by car through the Brenner Pass to Italy, you'll hit the A13 toll road (€8). Toll-free Hwy 182 follows the same route, although it is less scenic.

TRAIN

Fast trains depart at least every two hours for Bregenz (€37, 2½ hours), Salzburg (€45, two hours), Kitzbühel (€20.40, 1½ hours) and Munich (€41, 1¾ hours). There are several daily services to Lienz (€15.40, 3¾ hours).

Getting Around

Single tickets on buses and trams cost €1.80 from machines or €2 from the driver. A 24-hour ticket is €4.50. Bus F runs between the airport and Maria-Theresien-Strasse.

OTHER TOWNS WORTH A VISIT

Fancy exploring further? Here are some towns, resorts and valleys in Austria that you may want to consider for day trips or longer visits.

Zillertal Storybook Tyrol, with a steam train, snow-capped Alps and outdoor activities aplenty.

Bad Ischl Handsome spa town and a fine base for visiting the region's five lakes.

Zell am See An alpine beauty on the shores of its namesake lake. Gateway to the epic Grossglockner Road.

Eisenstadt The petite capital of Burgenland is known for its wonderful palace and famous former resident, composer Haydn.

Schladming Styrian gem in the glacial Dachstein mountains. Great for skiing, hiking, biking and white-water rafting on the Enns River.

Kitzbühel

☎05356 / POP 8211

Kitzbühel began life in the 16th century as a silver- and copper-mining town, and today preserves a charming medieval centre despite its other persona – as a fashionable and prosperous winter resort. It's renowned for the white-knuckled Hahnenkamm downhill ski race in January and the excellence of its slopes.

Activities

In winter there's first-rate intermediate skiing and freeriding on **Kitzbüheler Horn** to the north and **Hahnenkamm** to the south of town. A one-day ski pass in the peak season costs €49.

Dozens of summer **hiking trails** thread through the Kitzbühel Alps; the tourist office gives walking maps and runs free guided hikes for guests staying in town. The Flex-Ticket covering all cable cars costs €46 for three out of seven days.

Sleeping & Eating

Rates leap by up to 50% in the winter season.

Snowbunny's Hostel HOSTEL €

(☎067-6794 0233; www.snowbunnys.co.uk; Bichlstrasse 30; dm €25-45, d €80-120; @ wi-fi) This friendly, laid-back hostel is a bunny-hop from the slopes. Dorms are fine, if a tad dark; breakfast is DIY-style in the kitchen. There's a TV lounge, ski storage room and cats to stroke.

★**Hotel Edelweiss** HOTEL €€

(☎752 52; www.edelweiss-kitzbuehel.at; Marchfeldgasse 2; d incl half board €210-230; P wi-fi) Near the Hahnenkammbahn, Edelweiss oozes Tyrolean charm with its green surrounds, alpine views, sauna and cosy interiors. Your kindly hosts Klaus and Veronika let you pack up a lunch from the breakfast buffet and serve delicious five-course dinners.

Huberbräu Stüberl AUSTRIAN €€

(☎656 77; Vorderstadt 18; mains €8.50-18; 8am-midnight Mon-Sat, from 9am Sun) An old-world Tyrolean haunt with vaults and pine benches, this tavern favours substantial portions of Austrian classics, such as schnitzel, goulash and dumplings, cooked to perfection.

Information

Tourist Office (☎666 60; www.kitzbuehel.com; Hinterstadt 18; 8.30am-6pm Mon-Fri, 9am-6pm Sat, 10am-noon & 4-6pm Sun) The central tourist office has loads of info in English and a 24-hour accommodation board.

WORTH A TRIP

KRIMML FALLS

The thunderous, three-tier **Krimmler Wasserfälle** (Krimml Falls; www.wasserfaelle-krimml.at; adult/child €3/1; ticket office 8am-6pm mid-Apr–Oct) is Europe's highest waterfall at 380m, and one of Austria's most unforgettable sights. The **Wasserfallweg** (Waterfall Trail), which starts at the ticket office and weaves gently uphill through mixed forest, has numerous viewpoints with photogenic close-ups of the falls. It's about a two-hour round-trip walk.

The pretty alpine village of Krimml has a handful of places to sleep and eat – contact the **tourist office** (☎72 39; www.krimml.at; Oberkrimml 37; 8am-noon & 2-6pm Mon-Fri, 8.30-10.30am & 4.30-6.30pm Sat) for more information.

Buses run year-round from Krimml to Zell am See (€10.20, 1¼ hours, every two hours), with frequent onward train connections to Salzburg (€19.60, 1½ hours). The village is about 500m north of the waterfall, on a side turning from the B165. There are parking spaces near the falls.

Getting There & Away

Trains run frequently from Kitzbühel to Innsbruck (€20.40, 1¾ hours) and Salzburg (€29.80, 2½ hours). For Kufstein (€11, one hour), change at Wörgl.

It's quicker and cheaper to reach Lienz by bus (€15.30, two hours, every two hours) than train.

Lienz

☎04852 / POP 11,903

With the jagged Dolomites crowding its southern skyline, the capital of East Tyrol is a scenic staging point for travels through the Hohe Tauern National Park.

Sights & Activities

A €36 day pass covers skiing on the nearby **Zettersfeld** and **Hochstein** peaks. However, the area is more renowned for its 100km of cross-country trails; the town fills up for the annual Dolomitenlauf cross-country skiing race in mid-January.

Schloss Bruck CASTLE
(www.museum-schlossbruck.at; Schlossberg 1; adult/child €7.50/2.50, combined admission with Aguntum €10.50/8.50; 10am-6pm, closed Mon Sep-May) Lienz' famous medieval fortress has a museum chronicling the region's history, as well as Roman artefacts, Gothic winged altars and local costumes. The **castle tower** is used for changing exhibitions; a highlight for art enthusiasts is the **Egger-Lienz-Galerie** devoted to the emotive works of Albin Egger-Lienz.

Aguntum MUSEUM, RUINS
(www.aguntum.info; Stribach 97; adult/child €7/4, combined admission with Schloss Bruck €10.50/8.50; 9.30am-4pm May-Oct) Excavations are still under way at the Aguntum archaeological site in nearby Dölsach to piece together the jigsaw puzzle of this 2000-year-old *municipium*, which flourished as a centre of trade and commerce under Emperor Claudius. Take a stroll around the excavations, then visit the glass-walled museum to explore Lienz' Roman roots.

Sleeping & Eating

The tourist office can point you in the direction of good-value guesthouses and camping grounds.

Goldener Fisch HOTEL €€
(621 32; www.goldener-fisch.at; Kärntnerstrasse 9; s/d €65/110; P) The chestnut-tree-shaded beer garden is a big draw at this family friendly hotel. The rooms are light and modern – if not fancy – and you can wind down in the sauna and herbal steam baths.

Kirchenwirt AUSTRIAN €€
(625 00; www.kirchenwirt-lienz.at; Pfarrgasse 7; mains €9.50-29; 9am-11.30pm Sun-Thu, to 1.30am Fri & Sat) Up on a hill opposite Stadtpfarrkirche St Andrä, this is Lienz' most atmospheric restaurant. Dine on a selection of local dishes under the vaults or on the streamside terrace. The lunch special costs under €10.

Information

Tourist Office (050 212 400; www.lienzer dolomiten.net; Europaplatz 1; 8.30am-6pm Mon-Fri, 9am-noon & 2-5pm Sat, 8.30-11am Sun) Staff will help you find accommodation (even private rooms) free of charge.

Getting There & Away

There are several daily services to Innsbruck (€15.40 to €20.40, 3¼ to 4½ hours). Trains run every two hours to Salzburg (€38.90, 3½ hours). To head south by car, you must first divert west or east along Hwy 100.

Hohe Tauern National Park

Straddling Tyrol, Salzburg and Carinthia, this national park is the largest in the Alps; a 1786-sq-km wilderness of 3000m peaks, alpine meadows and waterfalls. At its heart lies **Grossglockner** (3798m), Austria's highest mountain, which towers over the 8km-long Pasterze Glacier, best seen from the outlook at **Kaiser-Franz-Josefs-Höhe** (2369m).

The 48km **Grossglockner Road** (www.grossglockner.at; Hwy 107; car/motorcycle €34.50/24.50; May-early Nov) from Bruck in Salzburgerland to Heiligenblut in Carinthia is one of Europe's greatest alpine drives. A feat of 1930s engineering, the road swings giddily around 36 switchbacks, passing jewel-coloured lakes, forested slopes and wondrous glaciers.

The major village on the Grossglockner Road is **Heiligenblut**, famous for its 15th-century pilgrimage church. Here the **tourist office** (27 00; www.heiligenblut.at; Hof 4; 9am-noon & 2-6pm Mon-Fri, 3-6pm Sat & Sun) can advise on guided ranger hikes, mountain hiking and skiing. The village also has a spick-and-span **Jugendherberge** (22 59; www.oejhv.or.at; Hof 36; dm/s/d €22/30/52; P @).

Bus 5002 runs frequently between Lienz and Heiligenblut on weekdays (€16.40, one hour), less frequently at weekends.

VORARLBERG

Vorarlberg has always been a little different. Cut off from the rest of Austria by the snow-capped Arlberg massif, this westerly region has often associated itself more with nearby Switzerland than distant Vienna, and also provides a convenient gateway to Germany and Liechtenstein.

The capital, **Bregenz**, sits prettily on the shores of Lake Constance and holds the **Bregenzer Festspiele** (Bregenz Festival; 05574-4076; www.bregenzerfestspiele.com; late Jul-late

Aug) in July/August, when opera is performed on a floating stage on the lake.

The real action here, though, is in the Arlberg region, shared by Vorarlberg and neighbouring Tyrol. Some of the country's best downhill and off-piste skiing – not to mention après-ski partying – is in **St Anton am Arlberg**, where the first ski club in the Alps was founded in 1901. The centrally located **tourist office** (05446-226 90; www.stantonamarlberg.com; Dorfstrasse 8; 8am-6pm Mon-Fri, 9am-6pm Sat, 9am-noon & 2-5pm Sun) has maps, and information on accommodation and activities.

A ski pass covering the whole Arlberg region and valid for all 85 ski lifts costs €49.50/276 for one/seven days in the high season.

Accommodation is mainly in small B&Bs. Many budget places (rates from €30 per person) are booked months in advance.

St Anton is on the main railway route between Bregenz (€20.40, 1½ hours) and Innsbruck (€21.20, 1¼ hours). It's close to the eastern entrance of the Arlberg Tunnel, the toll road connecting Vorarlberg and Tyrol (€8.50).

SURVIVAL GUIDE

Directory A–Z

ACCOMMODATION

From simple mountain huts to five-star hotels fit for kings – you'll find the lot in Austria. Tourist offices invariably keep lists and details, and some arrange bookings for free or for a nominal fee. Some useful points:

- Book ahead for the high seasons: July and August and December to April (in ski resorts).
- Some hostels and some rock-bottom digs have an *Etagendusche* (communal shower).
- In mountain resorts, high-season prices can be up to double the prices charged in the low season (May to June and October to November).

SLEEPING PRICE RANGES

Prices include a private bathroom and breakfast unless otherwise stated.

€ less than €80

€€ €80 to €200

€€€ more than €200

COUNTRY FACTS

Area 83,871 sq km

Capital Vienna

Country Code 43

Currency Euro (€)

Emergency 112

Language German

Money ATMs widely available; banks open Monday to Friday

Visas Schengen rules apply

- Some resorts issue a *Gästekarte* (guest card) when you stay overnight, offering discounts on things such as cable cars and admission.

Some useful websites include the following:

Austrian Hotelreservation (www.austrian-hotelreservation.at)

Austrian National Tourist Office (www.austria.info)

Bergfex (www.bergfex.com)

Camping in Österreich (www.campsite.at)

Accommodation Types

Alpine huts There are 236 huts in the Austrian Alps maintained by the **Österreichischer Alpenverein** (ÖAV, Austrian Alpine Club; www.alpenverein.at). Bed prices for nonmembers are from €20 in a dorm; ÖAV members pay half-price. Meals or cooking facilities are often available.

Camping Austria has some 500 camping grounds, many well equipped and scenically located. Prices can be as low as €5 per person or small tent and as high as €12. Many close in winter, so phone ahead to check. Search by region at www.camping-club.at (in German).

Hostels In Austria around 100 hostels (*Jugendherberge*) are affiliated with Hostelling International (HI). Facilities are often excellent. Four- to six-bed dorms with shower/toilet are the norm, though some places also have doubles and family rooms. See www.oejhv.or.at or www.oejhw.at for details.

Private rooms *Privatzimmer* (private rooms) are cheap (often about €50 per double). On top of this, you will find *Bauernhof* (farmhouses) in rural areas, and some *Öko-Bauernhöfe* (organic farms).

Rental accommodation *Ferienwohnungen* (self-catering apartments) are ubiquitous in Austrian mountain resorts. Contact a local tourist office for lists and prices.

ACTIVITIES

Austria is a wonderland for outdoorsy types, with much of the west given over to towering alpine peaks. Opportunities for hiking and mountaineering are boundless in Tyrol, Salzburgerland and the Hohe Tauern National Park, all of which have extensive alpine hut networks (see www.alpenverein.at). Names like St Anton, Kitzbühel and Mayrhofen fire the imagination of serious skiers, but you may find cheaper accommodation and lift passes in little-known resorts; visit www.austria.info for the lowdown.

BUSINESS HOURS

Banks 8am to 3pm Monday to Friday, to 5.30pm Thursday
Cafes 7.30am to 8pm; hours vary widely
Clubs 10pm to late
Post offices 8am to noon and 2pm to 6pm Monday to Friday, 8am to noon Saturday
Pubs 6pm to 1am
Restaurants noon to 3pm and 7pm to 11pm
Shops 9am to 6.30pm Monday to Friday, 9am to 5pm Saturday
Supermarkets 9am to 8pm Monday to Saturday

DISCOUNT CARDS

Discount Rail Cards See p90 for more information.
Student & Youth Cards International Student Identity Cards (ISIC) and European Youth Card (Euro<26; check www.euro26.org for discounts) will get you discounts at most museums, galleries and theatres. Admission is generally a little higher than the price for children.

INTERNET RESOURCES

ÖAV (www.alpenverein.at) Austrian Alpine Club
ÖBB (www.oebb.at) Austrian Federal Railways
Österreich Werbung (www.austria.info) National tourism authority

MONEY

Austria's currency is the euro. An approximate 10% tip is expected in restaurants. Pay it directly to the server; don't leave it on the table.

EATING PRICE RANGES

Price ranges in this chapter are for a two-course meal excluding drinks.

€ less than €15

€€ €15 to €30

€€€ more than €30

PUBLIC HOLIDAYS

New Year's Day (Neujahr) 1 January
Epiphany (Heilige Drei Könige) 6 January
Easter Monday (Ostermontag) March/April
Labour Day (Tag der Arbeit) 1 May
Whit Monday (Pfingstmontag) Sixth Monday after Easter
Ascension Day (Christi Himmelfahrt) Sixth Thursday after Easter
Corpus Christi (Fronleichnam) Second Thursday after Whitsunday
Assumption (Maria Himmelfahrt) 15 August
National Day (Nationalfeiertag) 26 October
All Saints' Day (Allerheiligen) 1 November
Immaculate Conception (Mariä Empfängnis) 8 December
Christmas Day (Christfest) 25 December
St Stephen's Day (Stephanitag) 26 December

TELEPHONE

- Austrian telephone numbers consist of an area code followed by the local number.
- The country code is ☎43 and the international access code is ☎00.
- The mobile network works on GSM 1800 and is compatible with GSM 900 phones. Phone shops sell prepaid SIM cards for about €10.
- Phonecards in different denominations are sold at post offices and *Tabak* (tobacconist) shops. Call centres are widespread in cities, and many internet cafes are geared for Skype calls.

TOURIST INFORMATION

Tourist offices, which are dispersed far and wide in Austria, tend to adjust their hours from one year to the next, so business hours may have changed slightly by the time you arrive.
Austrian National Tourist Office (ANTO; www.austria.info) The Austrian National Tourist Office has a number of overseas offices. There is a comprehensive listing on the ANTO website.

VISAS

Schengen visa rules apply. The Austrian Foreign Ministry website www.bmeia.gv.at lists embassies.

Getting There & Away

AIR

Among the low-cost airlines, Air Berlin flys to Graz, Innsbruck, Linz, Salzburg and Vienna, easyJet to Innsbruck, Salzburg and Vienna, and Ryanair to Linz, Salzburg and Bratislava (for Vienna).

Following are the key international airports in Austria (and neighbouring Slovakia):

Airport Bratislava (Letisko; ☎+421 2 3303 3353; www.bts.aero) Airport Letisko Bratislava is connected to Vienna International Airport and Vienna Erdberg (U3) by almost hourly buses (one way/return €7.70/14.40, 1¾ hours). Book online at www.slovaklines.sk.

Blue Danube Airport Linz (☎7221 6000; www.linz-airport.at; Flughafenstrasse 1, Hörsching) Austrian Airlines, Lufthansa, Ryanair and Air Berlin are the main airlines servicing the Blue Danube Airport, 13km southwest of the centre.

Graz Airport (☎0316-29 020; www.flughafen-graz.at) Graz airport is located 10km south of the centre and is served by carriers including Air Berlin, which connects the city with Berlin.

Innsbruck Airport (☎0512-22 525; www.innsbruck-airport.com; Fürstenweg 180) EasyJet flies to Innsbruck Airport, 4km west of the city centre.

Kärnten Airport (☎41 500; www.klagenfurt-airport.com; Flughafenstrasse 60-66) Klagenfurt's airport is 3km north of town and served by the low-cost airline germanwings.

Salzburg Airport (☎858 00; www.salzburg-airport.com; Innsbrucker Bundesstrasse 95) Salzburg airport, a 20-minute bus ride from the city centre, has regular scheduled flights to destinations all over Austria and Europe.

Vienna International Airport (☎01-7007 22 233; www.viennaairport.com) Vienna International Airport has good connections worldwide. The airport is in Schwechat, 18km southeast of Vienna.

LAND

Bus

Buses depart from Austria for as far afield as England, the Baltic countries, the Netherlands, Germany and Switzerland. But most significantly, they provide access to Eastern European cities small and large – from the likes of Sofia and Warsaw, to Banja Luka, Mostar and Sarajevo.

Services operated by **Eurolines** (www.eurolines.at) leave from Vienna and from several regional cities.

Car & Motorcycle

There are numerous entry points into Austria by road from Germany, the Czech Republic, Slovakia, Hungary, Slovenia, Italy and Switzerland. All border-crossing points are open 24 hours.

Standard European insurance and paperwork rules apply.

Train

Austria has excellent rail connections. The main services in and out of the country from the west normally pass through Bregenz, Innsbruck or Salzburg en route to Vienna. Express services to Italy go via Innsbruck or Villach; trains to Slovenia are routed through Graz.

Trains from Vienna run to many Eastern European destinations, including Bratislava, Budapest, Prague and Warsaw; there are also connections south to Italy via Klagenfurt and north to Berlin. Salzburg is within sight of the Bavarian border, and there are many trains Munich-bound and beyond from the baroque city. Innsbruck is on the main rail line from Vienna to Switzerland, and two routes also lead to Munich. Look out for the fast, comfortable RailJet services to Germany and Switzerland.

For online timetables and tickets, visit the **ÖBB** (Österreichische Bundesbahnen; Austrian Federal Railways; ☎24hr hotline 05 1717; www.oebb.at) website. SparSchiene (discounted tickets) are often available when you book online in advance and can cost as little as a third of the standard train fare.

RIVER & LAKE

Hydrofoils run to Bratislava and Budapest from Vienna; slower boats cruise the Danube between the capital and Passau. The **Danube Tourist Commission** (www.danube-river.org) has a country-by-country list of operators and agents who can book tours.

Getting Around

AIR

Austrian Airlines (www.austrian.com) The national carrier offers several flights daily between Vienna and Graz, Innsbruck, Klagenfurt, Linz and Salzburg.

BICYCLE

- All cities have at least one bike shop that doubles as a rental centre; expect to pay around €10 to €15 per day.
- Most tourist boards have brochures on cycling facilities and plenty of designated cycling routes within their region.
- You can take bicycles on any train with a bicycle symbol at the top of its timetable. For regional and long-distance trains, you'll pay an extra 10% on your ticket price. It costs €12 to take your bike on international trains.

BOAT

Services along the Danube are generally slow, scenic excursions rather than functional means of transport.

BUS

Postbus (☎24hr 05 17 17; www.postbus.at) Postbus services usually depart from outside train stations. In remote regions, there are fewer services on Saturday and often none on Sunday.

ESSENTIAL FOOD & DRINK

➡ **Make it meaty** Go for a classic Wiener schnitzel, *Tafelspitz* (boiled beef with horseradish sauce) or *Schweinebraten* (pork roast). The humble *Wurst* (sausage) comes in various guises.

➡ **On the side** Lashings of potatoes, either fried *(Pommes)*, roasted *(Bratkartoffeln)*, in a salad *(Erdapfelsalat)* or boiled in their skins *(Quellmänner)*; or try *Knödel* (dumplings) and *Nudeln* (flat egg noodles).

➡ **Kaffee und Kuchen** Coffee and cake is Austria's sweetest tradition. Must-tries: flaky apple strudel, rich, chocolatey Sacher Torte and *Kaiserschmarrn* (sweet pancakes with raisins).

➡ **Wine at the source** Jovial locals gather in rustic *Heurigen* (wine taverns) in the wine-producing east, identified by an evergreen branch above the door. Sip crisp Grüner Veltliner whites and spicy Blaufränkisch wines.

➡ **Cheese fest** Dig into gooey *Käsnudeln* (cheese noodles) in Carinthia, *Kaspressknodel* (fried cheese dumplings) in Tyrol and *Käsekrainer* (cheesy sausages) in Vienna. The hilly Bregenzerwald is studded with dairies.

CAR & MOTORCYCLE

A *Vignette* (toll sticker) is imposed on all motorways; charges for cars/motorbikes are €8.70/5 for 10 days and €25.30/12.70 for two months. *Vignette* can be purchased at border crossings, petrol stations and *Tabak* shops. There are additional tolls (usually €2.50 to €10) for some mountain tunnels.

Speed limits are 50km/h in built-up areas, 130km/h on motorways and 100km/h on other roads.

Multinational car-hire firms Avis, Budget, Europcar and Hertz all have offices in major cities. The minimum age for hiring small cars is 19 years, or 25 years for larger, 'prestige' cars. Customers must have held a driving licence for at least a year. Many contracts forbid customers to take cars outside Austria, particularly into Eastern Europe. Crash helmets are compulsory for motorcyclists.

TRAIN

Austria has a clean, efficient rail system, and if you use a discount card it's very inexpensive.

➡ Disabled passengers can use the 24-hour ☎ 05 17 17 customer number for special travel assistance; do this at least 24 hours ahead of travel (48 hours ahead for international services). Staff at stations will help with boarding and alighting.

➡ Fares quoted are for 2nd-class tickets.

➡ ÖBB (p89) is the main operator, supplemented with a handful of private lines. Tickets and timetables are available online.

➡ It's worth seeking out RailJet train services connecting Vienna, Graz, Villach, Salzburg, Innsbruck, Linz and Klagenfurt, as they travel up to 200km/h.

➡ Reservations in 2nd class within Austria cost €3.50 for most express services; recommended for travel on weekends.

Rail Passes

Depending on the amount of travelling you intend to do in Austria, rail passes can be a good deal.

Eurail Austria Pass This handy pass is available to non-EU residents; prices start at €129 for three days' unlimited 2nd-class travel within one month. See the website at www.eurail.com for all options.

Interrail Passes are for European residents and include One Country Pass Austria (three/four/six/eight days €131/154/187/219). Youths under 26 receive substantial discounts. See www.interrail.eu for all options.

Vorteilscard Reduces fares by at least 45% and is valid for a year, but not on buses. Bring a photo and your passport or ID. It costs adult/under 26 years/senior €99/19/29.

Belarus

Includes ➜

Best Places to Eat

- Grand Cafe (p96)
- Bistro de Luxe (p96)
- Food Republic (p95)
- Strawnya Talaka (p96)
- Jules Verne (p99)

Best Places to Stay

- Hotel Manastyrski (p94)
- Hermitage Hotel (p99)
- Revolucion Hostel (p93)
- Semashko (p98)

Why Go?

Eastern Europe's outcast, Belarus (Беларусь) lies at the edge of the region and seems determined to avoid integration with the rest of the continent at all costs. Taking its lead from the Soviet Union rather than the European Union, this little-visited dictatorship may seem like a strange choice for travellers, but its isolation lies at the heart of its appeal.

While the rest of Eastern Europe has charged headlong into capitalism, Belarus allows the chance to visit a Europe with minimal advertising and no litter or graffiti. Outside the monumental Stalinist capital of Minsk, Belarus offers a simple yet pleasing landscape of cornflower fields, thick forests and picturesque villages. The country also offers two excellent national parks and is home to Europe's largest mammal, the zoobr (or European bison). While travellers will always be subject to curiosity, they'll also be on the receiving end of warm hospitality and genuine welcome.

When to Go

Minsk

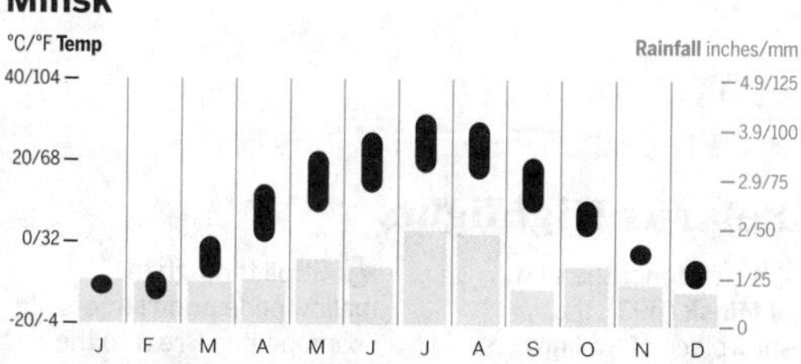

Jun–Aug Come to Belarus to escape the crowds elsewhere in Eastern Europe.

Early Jul On 6 July watch locals celebrate *Kupalye*, a fortune-telling festival with pagan roots.

Mid-Jul Join in Vitsebsk's superb Slavyansky Bazaar festival and celebrate all things Slavic.

Belarus Highlights

1 Get under the skin of **Minsk** (p93), the showpiece of Stalinist architecture and a friendly, accessible city.

2 Spot a European bison, a brown bear or a wolf at **Belavezhskaya Pushcha National Park** (p99).

3 Stroll through the mellow pedestrian streets of cosmopolitan **Brest** to the epic WWII memorial that is Brest Fortress (p98).

4 Discover the childhood home of painter Marc Chagall (p100) in **Vitsebsk**.

5 See the fairy-tale 16th-century castle (p97) that presides over the tranquil town of **Mir**.

6 Explore one of the few historical complexes to have survived WWII at **Nyasvizh**, at the gloriously restored Radziwill Palace Fortress (p97).

ITINERARIES

Three Days

Spend two days getting to know **Minsk** – its Stalinist architecture belies a lively and friendly city – before taking a day trip to **Mir** to get a feel for the lovely Belarusian countryside.

One Week

Begin with two nights in **Brest**, including a day trip to the **Belavezhskaya Pushcha National Park**, then take a train to **Minsk**, allowing yourself time for a day trip to **Mir** before continuing on to historic and charming **Vitsebsk**.

MINSK МІНСК

017 / POP 1.9 MILLION

Minsk will almost certainly surprise you. The capital of Belarus is, despite its thoroughly dreary-sounding name, a progressive and modern place quite at odds with its own reputation. Fashionable cafes, impressive restaurants and crowded nightclubs vie for your attention, while sushi bars and art galleries have taken up residence in a city centre once totally remodelled to the tastes of Stalin. Despite the strong police presence and obedient citizenry, Minsk is a thoroughly pleasant place that's not hard to become fond of.

Razed to the ground in WWII, Minsk has almost no buildings remaining from the prewar years, and there are relatively few traditional sights in the city, save two excellent museums. Instead though, there are myriad places of interest to anyone fascinated by the Soviet period and a smattering of cosmopolitan pursuits to keep you entertained come the evening.

Sights

Oktyabrskaya Pl SQUARE

(pl Kastrychnitskaya) The city's main square is referred to universally by its Russian name, Oktyabrskaya pl (October Sq; in Belarusian, it's pl Kastrychnitskaya). This is where opposition groups gather to protest against President Alexander Lukashenko from time to time, and is where the infamous 2010 presidential election protests ended in violence. The failed Denim Revolution of March 2006 was attempted here as well.

★Museum of the Great Patriotic War MUSEUM

(017-203 0792; www.warmuseum.by; pr Peremozhtsau 8; adult/student BR40,000/20,000, guided tour BR120,000; 10am-6pm Tue & Thu-Sat, 11am-7pm Wed & Sun) Housed in a garish new building after leaving its severely outdated premises on Oktyabrskaya pl, Minsk's best museum houses an excellent display detailing Belarus' suffering and heroism during the Nazi occupation. With English explanations throughout, atmospheric dioramas and a range of real tanks, airplanes and artillery from WWII, it's a big improvement on its fusty predecessor. Its section on concentration camps is particularly disturbing: an incredible 2.3 million people in Belarus were killed during the war, including 1.5 million civilians.

Belarusian State Art Museum MUSEUM

(vul Lenina 20; adult/student BR50,000/25,000; 11am-7pm Wed-Mon) This excellent state museum has been renovated and now includes a light-bathed extension out the back that features local art from the 1940s to the 1970s. Don't miss Valentin Volkov's socialist realist *Minsk on July 3, 1944* (1944–5), depicting the Red Army's arrival in the ruined city. Yudel Pen, Chagall's teacher, is well represented, including his 1914 portrait of Chagall.

Traetskae Pradmestse OLD TOWN

In lieu of any real remaining Old Town is Traetskae Pradmestse ('Trinity Suburb'), a pleasant – if tiny – re-creation of Minsk's pre-war buildings on a pretty bend of the river just a little north of the centre. It's worth strolling through for its little cafes, restaurants and shops, though the towering monoliths of modern Minsk are never very far away.

Sleeping

If you're in the city for more than a night or two, an alternative is renting an apartment. Several agencies offer this service, including **Belarus Rent** (www.belarusrent.com), **Belarus Apartment** (www.belarusapartment.com) and **Minsk4rent** (29 111 4817; www.minsk4rent.com). Rates range from €40 to €120 per night.

★Revolucion Hostel HOSTEL €

(029 614 6465; www.revolucion.by; vul Revalyutsiynaya 16; dm €9-12, d €27-35;) Right in the heart of town, this friendly and pleasingly

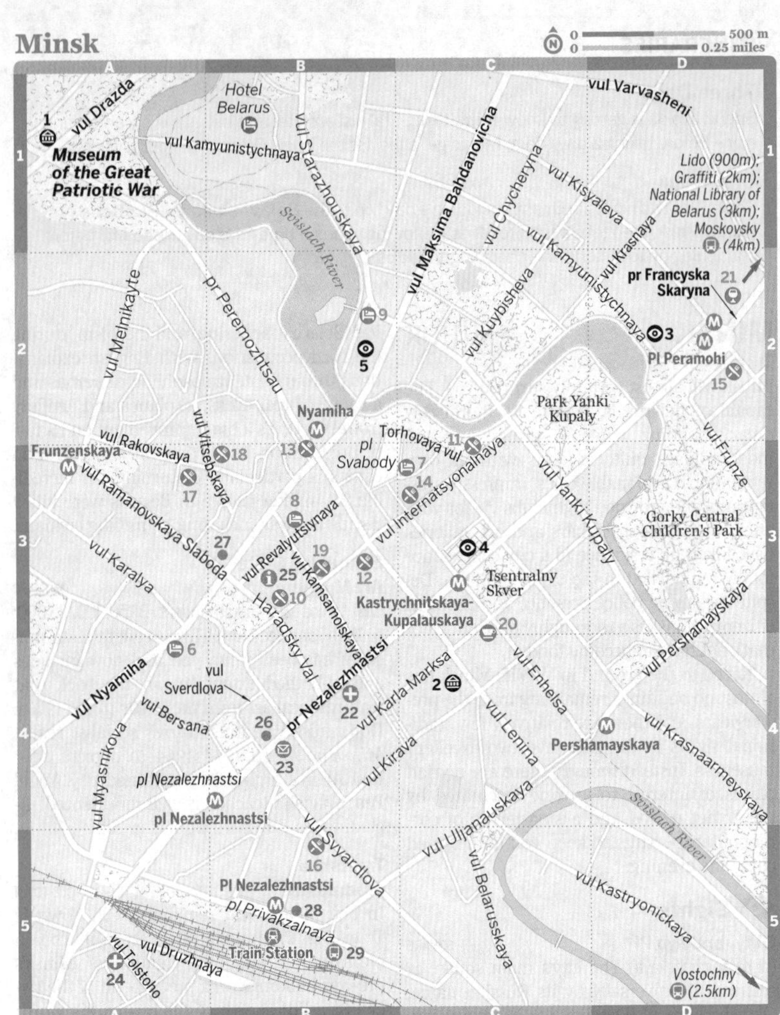

quirky hostel is festooned with photographs of various revolutionaries and even has a pet tortoise called Marseillaise. Dorms run from 4- to 12-bed, and there are a couple of double rooms as well. Extras include a roof terrace, bike hire (BR100,000 per day) and the free use of an espresso machine.

Trinity Hostel HOSTEL €
(☎029 311 2783; www.hostel-traveler.by; Starovilenskaya vul 12; dm/d €17/40; 📶) Right in the heart of Minsk, this new hostel is a great option. It's located in the Disney-esque 'Old Town', and has small dorms with 4 to 6 beds. There's a no alcohol rule, and a strict ban on making noise after 10pm, so it's not a place to come to party.

★ **Hotel Manastyrski** HISTORIC HOTEL €€€
(☎017-329 0300; www.vtroitskaya.by; vul Kirilla i Mefodya 9; s/d from €95/122; 📶) This much-needed, relatively affordable, new top-end hotel in the centre of Minsk has considerable charm and great, proactive management. Housed in the converted remains of a Benedictine monastery, the 48 rooms are smart and comfortably furnished with dark wood fittings, while the impressive corridors are decorated with frescoes (found during the renovation) and wrought iron chandeliers.

Minsk

Top Sights
1 Museum of the Great Patriotic War A1

Sights
2 Belarusian State Art Museum C4
3 Former Residence of Lee Harvey Oswald D2
4 Oktyabrskaya Pl C3
5 Traetskae Pradmestse B2

Sleeping
6 Buta Boutique Hotel A4
7 Hotel Manastyrski C3
8 Revolucion Hostel B3
9 Trinity Hostel B2

Eating
10 Bistro de Luxe B3
11 Food Republic C3
12 Grand Cafe B3
13 Gurman B3
14 Stolle C3
15 Stolle D2
16 Stolle B5
17 Stolle A3
18 Strawnya Talaka B3
19 Tapas Bar B3

Drinking & Nightlife
20 My English Granny C3
21 Ў Bar D2

Information
22 24-hour Pharmacy B4
23 Central Post Office B4
24 EcoMedservices A5
25 Minsk Tourist Information Centre B3

Transport
26 Avis B4
27 Belavia B3
Europcar .... (see 26)
28 International Train Ticket Office B5
29 Tsentralny Bus Station B5

Buta Boutique Hotel BOUTIQUE HOTEL €€
(☎029 152 2555; www.hotel-buta.by; vul Myasnikova 7; s/d from €75/80; P ❄ 📶) Minsk's first boutique hotel looks like the kind of place Louis XIV would stay had he been travelling for business; think flat-screen TVs in golden frames on the wall and lots of bling. That said, with rain showers, great views, plenty of space and quality furnishings, this is actually a good deal for the price. Location is also good, and staff are attentive and professional. Breakfast costs an extra €20.

Eating

Minsk has a decent eating scene and plenty of choice – don't believe the hype about food in Belarus; in the capital, at least, you'll eat well. Consider reserving tables at weekends.

Stolle PIE SHOP €
(www.stolle.by; vul Rakovskaya 23; pies from BR25,000; ⏲10am-11pm; 📶 📝) Stolle is a great option with delicious, freshly baked sweet and savoury pies to eat in or take away. This is the most central location of the many now open in the city and, unlike the others, there's also a full non-pie menu serving up traditional Russian and Belarusian cuisine. Other central branches include **vul Internatsyonalnaya 23** (⏲10am-10pm; 📶 📝), **vul Sverdlova 22** (⏲10am-10pm; 📶 📝) and **pr Nezalezhnastsi 38** (⏲10am-9pm; 📶 📝).

Gurman RUSSIAN €
(pr Peremozhtsau 1; mains BR20,000-100,000; ⏲8am-11pm; 📶) This Minsk institution specialises in many varieties of delicious, freshly made *pelmeni* (Russian-style ravioli stuffed with meat) and also offers a wide selection of pastas, curries and other international cuisine. The light and airy new central premises and the consistently friendly staff are other reasons to come.

★ **Food Republic** FOOD COURT €€
(www.foodrepublic.by; vul Yanki Kupaly 25; ⏲10am-midnight; 🚭 📶) This brand new restaurant complex is a real turn up for the books in dusty old Minsk: 10 different eateries and a number of food shops all under one huge industrial-style roof, with cuisine running from sushi, burgers, Italian and Turkish to a steakhouse, deli, fish restaurant and patisserie. To top it off, there's a fantastic terrace overlooking the river. This is the best place in Minsk for sheer choice and variety, and quality and service are also good.

Tapas Bar SPANISH €€
(vul Internatsyanalnaya 9/17; mains BR70,000-150,000; ⏲11am-midnight; 📶 📝) This stylish joint with olive-coloured walls, friendly service and bright dining areas serves up good tapas from a large menu. All the classics are present, as well as a range of meaty *platos calientes* (hot dishes) and excellent paella. With its good wine selection and lovely

atmosphere, it's also a great place to come for a drink in the evenings.

★Bistro de Luxe BISTRO €€€
(Haradsky Val 10; mains BR100,000-300,000; 8am-midnight Mon-Fri, 11am-midnight Sat & Sun;) Housed in a gorgeous space with chandeliers, sleek brasserie-style furnishings, a chessboard floor and aspirational toilets, Bistro de Luxe has charm and atmosphere that's hard to find elsewhere in Minsk. The food is excellent – leaning towards Italian – and service is impeccable. Breakfast served daily until midday.

Grand Cafe ITALIAN €€€
(vul Lenina 2; mains BR150,000-400,000; noon-midnight;) This classy place has great service from waiters in tuxedos, and white-linen tablecloths starched enough to cause an injury. The interesting menu is big on seasonal Italian classics, with plenty of choice and a few non-Italian variations. Alternatively, just sit at the glamorous bar and drink sensational cocktails.

Strawnya Talaka TRADITIONAL €€€
(vul Rakovskaya 18; mains BR160,000-400,000; 10am-6am) This relaxed and cosy basement place is unashamedly aimed at tourists, but it also happens to be one of the best restaurants in Minsk for an authentic local meal. Try the hare in bilberry sauce, the mushroom soup served in a loaf of bread or just a bowl of their fantastic beer snacks and the fabulous *draniki* (potato pancakes).

Drinking

★Ў Bar WINE BAR
(www.ybar.by; pr Nezalezhnastsi 37A; noon-midnight, until 2am Fri & Sat) Hidden in the courtyard of a building just off pl Peramohi, this sleek wine bar is attached to the contemporary art gallery of the same name and is the current favoured watering hole of Minsk's creative classes. There's a dazzling wine list, with a huge choice of wine by the glass, as well as delicious cakes and bar food.

My English Granny CAFE
(vul Karla Marksa 36; 9am-midnight;) This place has pulled off the incredible feat of making kitschy Victoriana look trendy in its bizarre but very cosy basement location. You'll get a good pot of tea and some gorgeous cakes here, as well as meals with a strong British bias and a great breakfast selection.

Information

INTERNET ACCESS

Free wi-fi can be had at nearly all hotels and several, but by no means all, cafes and restaurants.

MEDICAL SERVICES

24-hour Pharmacy (pr Nezalezhnastsi 16)

EcoMedservices (017-207 7474; www.ems.by; vul Tolstoho 4; 8am-9pm) The closest thing to a reliable, Western-style clinic. Dental services are offered here, too. Just south of the train station.

MONEY

ATMs can be found throughout the city and often dispense US dollars and euros as well as Belarusian roubles. Exchange bureaux dot the centre, while most banks and hotels can change euros and US dollars.

POST

Central Post Office (pr Nezalezhnastsi 10; 7am-11pm) In the centre of town.

TOURIST INFORMATION

Minsk Tourist Information Centre (017-203 3995; www.minsktourism.by; vul Revalyutsiynaya 16-24; 8.45am-1pm & 2-6pm Mon-Fri) Minsk's tourist office is central but well hidden. The entrance is in the courtyard behind building 13 on vul Revalyutsiynaya.

Getting There & Away

AIR

Flights entering and departing Belarus do so at the **Minsk-2 International Airport** (017-279 1300; www.airport.by), about 40km east of Minsk. There are daily flights to many major European cities, and Minsk remains surprisingly well connected to the rest of Europe. There are no domestic flights.

BUS

There are three main bus stations in Minsk, but most long-distance and international services leave from the Tsentralny Bus Station in the city centre.

Tsentralny Bus Station (017-227 0473; vul Bobruyskaya 6) The main bus station is next to the train station in the centre of Minsk. Buses to Mir (Novgrorodok), Vitsebsk, Brest, Hrodna and Nyasvizh depart from here, as well as international departures.

CAR

As well as outlets at the airport, both **Avis** (017-334 7990; www.avis.by) and **Europcar** (017-209 9009; www.europcar.by) can be found at Hotel Minsk (pr Nezalezhnastsi 11) .

DON'T MISS

COMRADE LEE

Just across the bridge over the Svislach River, on the west bank, is the **former residence of Lee Harvey Oswald** (vul Kamyunistychnaya 4) – it's the bottom left apartment. The alleged assassin of former US president John F Kennedy lived here for a couple of years in his early 20s. He arrived in Minsk in January 1960 after leaving the US Marines and defecting to the USSR. Once here, he truly went native: he got a job in a radio factory, married a Minsk woman, had a child – and even changed his name to Alek. But soon he returned to the United States and...you know the rest.

TRAIN

The busy and modern **Minsk train station** (☎105, 017-225 7000; Privakzalnaya pl; ⌚24hr) is pretty easy to deal with. You can buy domestic and CIS (Commonwealth of Independent States) tickets here. Downstairs is a well-signed **left luggage office** (lockers BR1000, luggage room BR2000; ⌚24hr).

You can buy tickets for non-CIS destinations at the **international train ticket office** (vul Kirova 2; ⌚8am-8pm), located across the main road in front of the train station.

Getting Around

TO/FROM THE AIRPORT

From Minsk-2 airport, a 40-minute taxi ride into town should cost around BR300,000, depending on your bargaining skills. Bus 300Э (BR6000) goes from outside the airport terminal into the city centre, via pr Nezalezhnastsi and ends at the Tsentralny Bus Station. It leaves between every 30 minutes and one hour, tapering off to every two hours during the night.

PUBLIC TRANSPORT

Minsk's metro is simple: just two lines with one transfer point at the Kastrychnitskaya-Kupalauskaya interchange on pr Nezalezhnastsi. A third line is under construction, but at present the system isn't hugely useful to travellers. It's open daily from dawn until just after midnight. One token *(zheton)* costs BR4000.

Buses, trams and trolleybuses also cost BR4000 per ride and you can buy tickets on board in most cases.

TAXI

For taxis, dial ☎035 or ☎007. Operators usually won't speak English, however. You can also hail taxis from the street.

AROUND MINSK

Nyasvizh Нясвіж

☎01770 / POP 15,000

The magical old buildings of Nyasvizh make it a great place to get in touch with Belarus' past – one that elsewhere has all too often been destroyed as the military campaigns of WWII flattened the country. This quiet but green and attractive town 120km southwest of Minsk is one of the oldest in the country, dating from the 13th century.

Sights

★**Radziwill Palace Fortress** PALACE
(adult/student BR80,000/40,000; ⌚9.30am-5.30pm) Over a causeway leading away from the town, with lovely lakes on either side, lies the beautiful Radziwill Palace Fortress (1583), the main sight in Nyasvizh. In Soviet times it was turned into a sanatorium but it has been fully restored in recent years and is looking superb.

With over 30 fully refurbished state rooms now open, a very impressive inner courtyard and clearly labelled displays, you can easily spend a couple of hours looking around.

Getting There & Away

From Minsk's Tsentralny Bus Station, there are four daily buses to and from Nyasvizh (BR63,000, 2½ hours).

Mir Мір

☎01596 / POP 2500

The charming small town of Mir, 85km southwest of Minsk, is dominated by the impossibly romantic 16th-century castle that overlooks a small lake at one end of the town. It was once owned by the powerful Radziwill princes and has been under Unesco protection since 1994.

Sights

★**Mir Castle** CASTLE
(☎01596 23 035; www.mirzamak.by/ru; adult/student BR70,000/35,000; ⌚10am-6pm) The 16th century Mir Castle rises above the town majestically and looks like something straight out of Disney. A painstaking renovation over the past decade has been completed and the place is looking simply lovely, with gorgeous grounds, impressively restored interiors and a huge display on the life and times of the Radziwills.

WORTH A TRIP

HRODNA ГРОДНА

If you're entering Belarus from northern Poland, or if you have extra time here, think about visiting Hrodna (Grodno in Russian). It was one of the few Belarusian cities that *wasn't* bombed during WWII, so it's rife with old wooden homes and, although it's a major city, it definitely has a 'big village' sort of feel to it. The city's best hotel by far is the privately run, super-friendly **Semashko** (☎0152-75 02 99; www.hotel-semashko.ru/en; vul Antonova 10; s/d incl breakfast from BR200,000/280,000; @), which you should reserve in advance due to its popularity. The room price includes use of the Oasis sauna and its small pool. Trains between Minsk and Hrodna leave five times a day (BR24,000, six hours), although *marshrutky* from Minsk's Vostochny Bus Station do the trip much faster and far more regularly (BR36,000, three hours).

Getting There & Away

From Minsk's Tsentralny Bus Station, there are buses to Navahrudak (Novogrudok in Russian) that stop in Mir (BR55,000, 2½ hours, hourly).

SOUTHERN BELARUS

Brest Брэст

☎0162 / POP 330,000

This prosperous and cosmopolitan border town looks far more to the neighbouring EU than to Minsk. It has plenty of charm and has performed a massive DIY job on itself over the past few years in preparation for its millennial celebrations in 2019.

Sights

Brest Fortress FORTRESS

(Brestskaya krepost; pr Masherava) FREE Very little remains of Brest Fortress. Certainly don't come here expecting a medieval turreted affair – this is a Soviet WWII memorial to the devastating battle that resulted when German troops advanced into the Soviet Union in the early days of Operation Barbarossa in 1941. The large complex occupies a beautiful spot at the confluence of the Bug and Mukhavets Rivers, a 20-minute walk from the town centre or a short hop on bus 17 from outside Hotel Intourist.

The fortress was built between 1838 and 1842, but by WWII it was used mainly as a barracks. The two regiments bunking here when German troops launched a surprise attack in 1941 defended the fort for an astounding month and became venerated as national legends thanks to Stalin's propaganda machine.

The Brest Fortress main entrance is its most iconic building – a huge socialist star formed from concrete. Sombre music accompanies you through the tunnel and as you leave it; on the left and past a small hill, you'll see some tanks. Straight ahead is the stone **Thirst statue**, which depicts a water-starved soldier crawling for a drink. After you cross a small bridge, to your right are the brick ruins of the **White Palace**, where the 1918 Treaty of Brest-Litovsk was signed, marking Russia's exit from WWI. Further to the right is the **Defence of Brest Fortress Museum** (adult/student BR25,000/12,500, audioguide BR20,000; ⊙9am-6pm Tue-Sun). Its extensive and dramatic exhibits demonstrate the plight of the defenders. There's also a small collection of weaponry from 18th- to 20th-century warfare, for which a separate ticket is required (BR10,000).

★ **Museum of Railway Technology** MUSEUM

(pr Masherava 2; adult/student BR15,000/10,000; ⊙8.30am-5.30pm Tue-Sun) One of Brest's most popular sights is the outdoor Museum of Railway Technology, where there's a superb collection of locomotives and carriages dating from 1903 (the *Moscow–Brest Express* with shower rooms and a very comfy main bedroom) to 1988 (far more proletarian Soviet passenger carriages). You can go inside many of them, so train enthusiasts and children tend to love it here.

Sleeping

Dream Hostel HOSTEL €

(☎033 361 0315, 0162-531 499; www.dreamhostel.by; vul Mayakaskaha 17, bldg 1, apt 5; dm €13-15;) Brest's first hostel is housed in a modern apartment building right in the middle of town. To get here go through the entrance between Tez Tour and Colombia Sportswear Company, and follow the footpath around to the right. The entry code is 5K, and it's otherwise unsigned. The hostel has three dorms with modern, clean bunks, a large TV room and kitchen.

Hotel Molodyozhnaya HOTEL €

(☎0162-216 376; www.molodezhnaya.by; vul Kamsamolskaya 6; s/d €32/42; 📶) This small and very centrally located place is a short walk from the station and has been steadily improving its facilities for the past few years. The rooms are comfortable and clean, all have private facilities and the welcome is warm. Breakfast is an extra BR70,000 per person.

★**Hermitage Hotel** HOTEL €€

(☎0162-276 000; www.hermitagehotel.by; vul Chkalova 7; s/d incl breakfast from €90/115; P❄📶) This fantastic hotel is streets ahead of even the nearest competition locally, although frankly that's not saying too much. Housed in a sensitively designed modern building, there's more than a little old-world style here, with spacious, grand and well-appointed rooms as well as impressive public areas. Multilingual staff are charming and there's good food available, including a great breakfast.

Eating & Drinking

Time's Cafe EUROPEAN €€

(vul Savetskaya 30; mains BR60,000-140,000; ⊙8.30am-11pm Mon-Fri, 11am-11pm Sat & Sun; 📶) Finally somewhere a little self-consciously cool in Brest, this friendly and smart place has a jazz-and-blues soundtrack, charming staff and a summer terrace with views onto pedestrianised vul Savetskaya. Food runs from steak in a balsamic reduction to caramelised cod with potato purée – quite different from the offerings of most places nearby. Breakfast is also served.

★**Jules Verne** FINE DINING €€

(vul Hoholya 29; mains BR100,000-170,000; ⊙noon-midnight; 📶✍) It's almost a miracle that such a great restaurant exists in Brest. Decked out like a gentleman's club and with a travel theme, this dark, atmospheric joint manages to be refined without being stuffy. It serves up cracking dishes – from mouthwatering curries and a range of French cooking to sumptuous desserts and the best coffee in town. Don't miss it.

Information

24-Hour Pharmacy (vul Hoholya 32; ⊙24 hrs)

Brest In Tourist (☎0162 225 571, 310-8304522; www.brestintourist.com; Hotel In Tourist, pr Masherava 15; ⊙9am-6pm Mon-Fri) Inside Hotel In Tourist; the English-speaking staff can arrange city tours including 'Jewish Brest' and trips to the Belavezhskaya Pushcha National Park.

Post Office (pl Lenina; ⊙8am-6pm Mon-Sat)

Getting There & Around

BUS

The **bus station** (☎114, 004; vul Mitskevicha) is in the centre of town and has left-luggage lockers and an internet cafe. There are five daily buses to Minsk (BR40,000 to BR70,000, five hours), 10 to Hrodna (BR50,000 to BR80,000, five hours) and services to Vilnius in Lithuania on Friday and Sunday (BR120,000, eight hours).

TAXI

For a taxi, call ☎061 or have your hotel call for you.

TRAIN

Trains leave for Minsk (platzkart/kupe (3rd/2nd class) BR60,000/82,000, four hours) several times daily. To get to the city from the train station, you'll have to mount a steep flight of steps from the platform; once you're up, go right on the overpass. It's a short walk, but a taxi into town should be no more than BR30,000.

Around Brest

Belavezhskaya Pushcha National Park PARK

(☎01631-56 370) A Unesco World Heritage Site some 60km north of Brest, Belavezhskaya Pushcha National Park is the oldest wildlife refuge in Europe and is the pride of Belarus. Half the park's territory lies in Poland, where it's called Białowieża National Park. Some 1300 sq km of primeval forest survives here. It's all that remains of a canopy that eight centuries ago covered northern Europe.

The area is most celebrated for its 300 or so European bison, the continent's largest land mammal. These free-range zoobr – slightly smaller than their American cousins – were driven to near extinction (the last one living in the wild was shot by a hunter in 1919) and then bred back from 52 animals that had survived in zoos.

It's entirely possible (and a great deal cheaper) to see the national park without taking a guided tour, although if you don't speak Russian you may miss some interesting commentary on trips through the woods and in the museum. From Brest take one of the six daily *marshrutky* or buses to Kamyanyuki (BR30,000, one hour 20 minutes) and walk from the village to the clearly visible reserve buildings. Once there you can walk around the park yourself, or even better, hire a bike from the museum (BR20,000 per hour). An altogether easier option is to book a day trip with Brest In Tourist.

NORTHERN BELARUS

Vitsebsk Віцебск

0212 / POP 363,000

The historic city of Vitsebsk (known universally outside Belarus by its Russian name, Vitebsk) lies a short distance from the Russian border and almost 300km from Minsk. Vitsebsk was an important centre of Jewish culture when it was one of the major cities of the 'Pale of Settlement', where Jews were allowed to live in the Russian Empire.

Sights

★Chagall Museum MUSEUM

(www.chagall.vitebsk.by; vul Punta 2; adult/student BR15,000/10,000, tours BR30,000; 11am-7pm Tue-Sun Jun-Sep, Wed-Sun Oct-May) The first museum on every itinerary should be the excellent Chagall Museum, which was established in 1992 and displays collections of Chagall lithographs (his illustrations for the Bible; 1956–60), designs to accompany Gogol's *Dead Souls* (1923–25) and graphic representations of the 12 tribes of Israel (1960).

★Marc Chagall House Museum MUSEUM

(0212-363 468; vul Pokrovskaya 11; adult/student BR15,000/10,000; 11am-7pm Tue-Sun Jun-Sep, Wed-Sun Oct-May) Across the town's river, a good 20-minute walk away from the Chagall Museum, is the Marc Chagall House Museum, where the artist lived as a child for 13 years between 1897 and 1910 – a period beautifully evoked in his autobiography, *My Life*. The simple, small house contains photographs of Chagall and his family, various possessions of theirs and some period furniture. It leads out into a garden and is very evocative of a simple Jewish-Russian childhood. Call ahead to arrange a tour of the house in English.

Festivals & Events

Slavyansky Bazaar FESTIVAL

(Slavic Bazaar; www.festival.vitebsk.by) This popular festival is held in mid-July and brings in dozens of singers and performers from Slavic countries for a week-long series of concerts. The annual event attracts tens of thousands of visitors, creating a huge party.

Sleeping

X.O. Hostel HOSTEL €

(029 718 4554, 0212-236 626; www.xostel.by; vul Suvorova 10/2; dm €8-13, d €30;) Right in the centre of the old town, Vitsebk's first hostel is a great addition to the accommodation scene, with a well-equipped kitchen, comfortable doubles and a range of dorms. The only disappointment is the mildewy smell of the bathrooms. To find it, go into the courtyard of vul Suvorova 10/2. Laundry costs BR40,000 per load.

★Hotel Eridan HOTEL €€

(0212-604 499; www.eridan-vitebsk.com; vul Savetskaya 21/17; r/ste from €60/79;) The best-value hotel in Vitsebsk is handy for the Chagall Museum and well located in the middle of the Old Town. With pleasant wooden furniture, art, antiques and old photos of Vitsebsk on the walls, there's a certain clunky post-Soviet makeover charm. Rooms are well equipped (albeit rather gaudy) and there's lots of space and light.

Eating & Drinking

Zolotoy Lev BELARUSIAN €€

(vul Suvorova 20/13; mains BR50,000-150,000; noon-midnight;) The smartest place in town is the expansive 'Golden Lion'. There's a charming interior (when the TV is off) spread over no fewer than six dining areas, a large menu offering traditional Belarusian cuisine, and a spacious outdoor area serving up *shashlyk* and beer. You'll find it on the pedestrianised main street parallel to vul Lenina.

Vitebsky Traktir INN €€

(vul Suvorova 4; mains BR40,000-100,000; noon-midnight;) This decent place has lots of charm, even if it is a little too dark for its own good. A traditional Belarusian menu is complimented by European dishes and sushi.

Getting There & Away

BUS

There are approximately hourly buses or *marshrutky* to Minsk (BR120,000 to 150,000, four to five hours). The city's bus station can be found next to the train station on vul Zamkovaya.

TRAIN

There are two or three daily trains to Minsk (BR55,000 to BR75,000, 4½ to six hours) and one to St Petersburg (BR630,000, 13 hours). There's also a daily train to both Moscow (BR595,000, 11 hours) and Brest (BR135,000, 11 hours).

SURVIVAL GUIDE

Directory A–Z

ACCOMMODATION

Rooms have private bathrooms unless otherwise indicated, but many do not include breakfast.

BUSINESS HOURS

Banks 9am to 5pm Monday to Friday

Office hours 9am to 6pm Monday to Friday

Shops 9am/10am to 9pm Monday to Saturday, to 6pm Sunday (if at all)

INSURANCE

Most visitors to Belarus are required to possess medical insurance to cover the entire period of their stay. Evidence of having purchased medical insurance with specific reference to coverage in Belarus for a minimum of €10,000 is now asked for as part of the visa application, so there's no way around this. If you have travel insurance already, ask your insurance company for a letter stating that you are covered in Belarus and for what amount. If you haven't got insurance already, you can simply buy one of the Belarus government's officially endorsed policies: check the embassy website in the country you're applying from.

INTERNET ACCESS

Internet provision is generally very good in Belarus. In major towns wireless is easy to find, and it's now totally standard in all hotels and hostels. It's also hassle free to buy a local SIM card with data at a mobile phone shop, you'll just need your passport and the address of your hotel.

INTERNET RESOURCES

Belarus Embassy in the UK (www.uk.mfa.gov.by)

Belarus Tourism (http://eng.belarustourism.by)

COUNTRY FACTS

Area 207,600 sq km

Capital Minsk

Country Code ☎375

Currency Belarusian rouble (BR)

Emergency Ambulance ☎03, Fire ☎01, Police ☎02

Language Belarusian and Russian

Money ATMs taking international cards are widely available

Population 9.46 million

Visas Needed by almost everybody

SLEEPING PRICE RANGES

The following price ranges refer to the cost of a double room:

€ less than €50

€€ €50 to €120

€€€ more than €120

MONEY

The Belarusian rouble (BR) is the national currency and the money's wide spectrum of bill denominations is overwhelming to the newcomer. Ensure you change any remaining roubles before leaving Belarus, as it's impossible to exchange the currency outside the country. ATMs and currency-exchange offices are not hard to find in Belarusian cities. Major credit cards are accepted at many of the nicer hotels, restaurants, and supermarkets in Minsk, but travellers cheques are not worth the effort.

POST

The word for post office is *pashtamt* in Belarusian, or *pochta* in Russian. You can mail important, time-sensitive items via the Express Mail Service (EMS) at most main post offices.

PUBLIC HOLIDAYS

New Year's Day 1 January

Orthodox Christmas 7 January

International Women's Day 8 March

Constitution Day 15 March

Catholic & Orthodox Easter March/April

Unity of Peoples of Russia and Belarus Day 2 April

International Labour Day (May Day) 1 May

Victory Day 9 May

Independence Day 3 July

Dzyady (Day of the Dead) 2 November

Catholic Christmas 25 December

VISAS

Nearly all visitors require a visa and arranging one before you arrive is usually essential. Belarusian visa regulations change frequently, so check the website of your nearest Belarusian embassy for the latest bureaucratic requirements.

Applications

Visa costs vary depending on the embassy you apply at and your citizenship. Americans pay more, but typically transit visas cost around €65, single-entry visas cost about €90 and to get either of those in 48 hours rather than five working days, count on paying double.

Registration

If you are staying in Belarus for more than five working days, you must have your visa officially registered. Hotels do this automatically and the service is included in the room price. They will stamp the back of your white landing card, which you keep and show to immigration agents upon departure. Note that if you're staying for fewer than five working days, there is no need to register.

Getting There & Away

Once you have your visa in your passport, the process of entering Belarus is relatively simple. Ensure you fill out one of the white migration cards in duplicate before presenting your passport to the immigration officer. Keep the half of the slip that the immigration officer returns to you, as you'll need it to leave the country.

AIR

Belarus' national airline is **Belavia** (☎ 017-220 2555; www.belavia.by; vul Nyamiha 14, Minsk), which has a good safety record and modern planes. Belavia has regular flights to London, Paris, Frankfurt, Berlin, Vienna, Rome, Milan, Barcelona, Kyiv, Istanbul, Tel Aviv, Warsaw, Prague, Rīga and many Russian cities, including Moscow and St Petersburg.

The other main airlines that fly to Minsk:

Aeroflot (www.aeroflot.com)
Air Baltic (www.airbaltic.com)
Austrian Airlines (www.aua.com)
Czech Airlines (www.csa.cz)
El Al (www.elal.co.il)
Estonian Air (www.estonian-air.ee)
Etihad Airways (www.etihad.com)
LOT Polish Airlines (www.lot.com)
Lufthansa (www.lufthansa.com)
Turkish Airlines (www.turkishairlines.com)

LAND

Belarus has good overland links to all neighbouring countries. Daily trains from Minsk serve Moscow and St Petersburg in Russia, Vilnius in Lithuania, Warsaw in Poland and Kyiv in Ukraine. Bus services, which tend to be less comfortable, connect Minsk to Moscow, St Petersburg, Kyiv, Warsaw and Vilnius; Vitsebsk to Moscow and St Petersburg; and Brest to Terespol in Poland.

Getting Around

BUS

Bus services cover much of the country and are generally a reliable, if crowded, means of transportation.

CAR & MOTORCYCLE

It's perfectly possible to hire a car in Minsk, with competition and thus standards improving in recent years. That said, there are still some pretty poor cars out there: look them over carefully and check the spare tyre before you drive off.

TRAIN

Train is a popular and scenic way to travel between the major towns of Belarus. Though the bus network is far more extensive, train travel times tend to be faster and prices are similar.

EATING PRICE RANGES

Price ranges are based on the average cost of a main course.

€ less than BR50,000

€€ BR50,000 to BR100,000

€€€ more than BR100,000

ESSENTIAL FOOD & DRINK

Belarusian cuisine rarely differs from Russian cuisine, although there are a few uniquely Belarusian dishes.

- **Belavezhskaya** A bitter herbal alcoholic drink.
- **Draniki** Potato pancakes, usually served with sour cream *(smetana)*.
- **Khaladnik** A local variation on cold borsch, a soup made from beetroot and garnished with sour cream, chopped up hard-boiled eggs and potatoes.
- **Kindziuk** A pig-stomach sausage filled with minced pork, herbs and spices.
- **Kletsky** Dumplings stuffed with mushrooms, cheese or potato.
- **Kolduni** Potato dumplings stuffed with meat.
- **Kvas** A mildly alcoholic drink made from black or rye bread and commonly sold on the streets in Belarus.
- **Manchanka** Pancakes served with a meaty gravy.

Belgium & Luxembourg

Includes ➡

Best Places to Eat

- ➡ De Stove (p126)
- ➡ De Ruyffelaer (p128)
- ➡ L'Ogenblik (p112)
- ➡ In 't Nieuwe Museum (p126)

Best Places to Stay

- ➡ Hôtel Le Dixseptième (p110)
- ➡ Hôtel Simoncini (p131)
- ➡ Auberge Aal Veinen (p134)
- ➡ B&B Dieltiens (p126)

Why Go?

Stereotypes of comic books, chips and sublime chocolates are just the start in eccentric little Belgium; its self-deprecating people have quietly spent centuries producing some of Europe's finest art and architecture. Bilingual Brussels is the dynamic yet personable EU capital, but also sports what's arguably the world's most beautiful city square. Flat, Flemish Flanders has many other alluring medieval cities, all easily linked by regular train hops. In hilly, French-speaking Wallonia, the attractions are contrastingly rural – castle villages, outdoor activities and extensive cave systems.

Independent Luxembourg, the EU's richest country, is compact and hilly with its own wealth of castle villages. The grand duchy's capital city is famed for banking but also sports a fairytale Unesco-listed historic old town. And from the brilliant beers of Belgium to the sparkling wines of Luxembourg's Moselle Valley, there's plenty to lubricate some of Europe's best dining. Welcome to the good life.

When to Go

Brussels

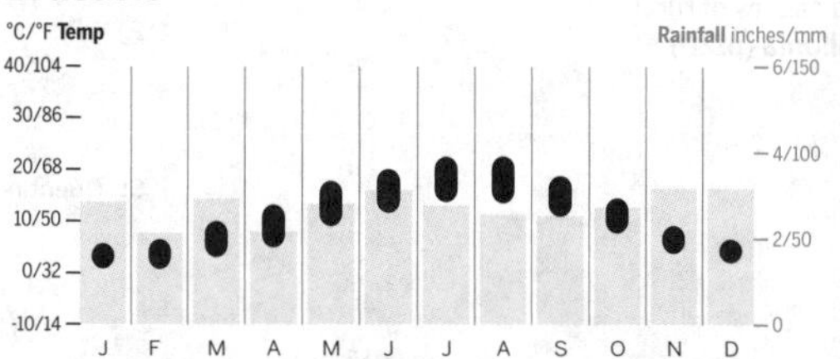

Pre-Easter weekends Belgium hosts many of Europe's weirdest carnivals, not just at Mardi Gras.

Feb & Mar Both countries symbolically burn the spirit of winter on the first weekend after Carnival.

Jul & Aug Countless festivals, hotels packed at the coast but cheaper in Brussels and Luxembourg City.

Belgium & Luxembourg Highlights

1 Come on weekdays off-season to appreciate the picture-perfect canal scenes of medieval **Bruges** (p123), without the tourist overload.

2 Be wooed by underappreciated **Ghent** (p119), one of Europe's greatest all-round discoveries.

3 Savour the 'world's most beautiful square', then seek out the remarkable cafes, chocolate shops and art nouveau survivors in **Brussels** (p106).

4 Follow fashion to hip yet historic **Antwerp** (p115).

5 Spend the weekend in Unesco-listed **Luxembourg City** (p130) then head out to the grand duchy's evocative castle villages.

6 Ponder the heartbreaking futility of WWI in Flanders' fields around meticulously rebuilt **Ypres** (p127).

7 Explore the caves and castles of rural **Wallonia** (p129).

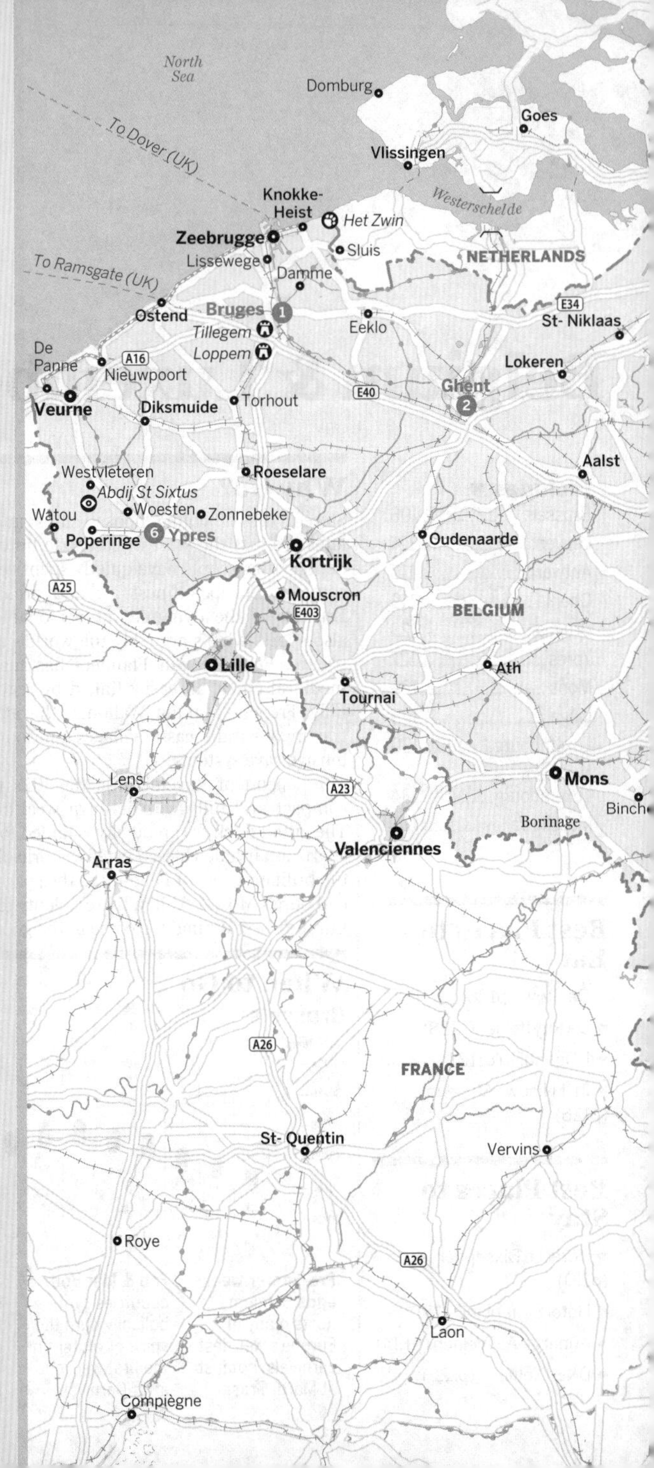

0 30 km
0 20 miles
NETHERLANDS
Tilburg
Roosendaal
Eindhoven
Venlo
A1
N1
A12
Turnhout
A21
Antwerp
4
Antwerp Airport
Herentals
Mol
Neerpelt
Roermond
Lier
Fort van Breendonk
E313
National Park Hoge Kempen
GERMANY
Mechelen
Diest
A2
Genk
Hasselt
Bokrijk Openluchtmuseum
E19
Brussels Airport
Leuven
Maastricht
3
Brussels
E313
A2
Aachen
E19
Waterloo
Louvain-la-Neuve
A3
Braine l''Alleud
Ottignies
Liège Airport
Liège
Verviers
Hautes Fagnes-Eifel Nature Park
Nivelles
Jehay
E411
Huy
Remouchamps
BELGIUM
Hautes Fagnes
Herzogenhugel
Hautes Fagnes Nature Reserve
Charleroi Airport
E42
Namur
Modave
Coo
Stavelot
Charleroi
Durbuy
Barvaux
Godinne
E25
Wallonia
7
N5
Hotton
Dinant
E421
Marloie
Houyet
Rochefort
Jemelle
La Roche-en-Ardenne
Botte de Hainaut
Lavaux-Ste-Anne
Han-sur-Lesse
Champlon
Clervaux
GERMANY
Chimay
Couvin
E46
Bastogne
Wiltz
ARDENNES
E411
Libramont
Parc Naturel de la Haute Sûre
Vianden
Diekirch
Rochehaut
E46
Ettelbrück
LUXEMBOURG
Echternach
Bouillon
Gutland
Mersch
Charleville-Mezières
Bourglinster
Grevenmacher
Arlon
Findel Airport
Orval
5
Luxembourg City
Virton
Rodange
Dudelange

ITINERARIES

Four Days

Just long enough to get a first taste of Belgium's four finest 'art cities': Bruges, Ghent, Brussels and Antwerp, all easy jump-offs or short excursions while you're train-hopping between Paris and Amsterdam. **Bruges** is the fairy-tale 'Venice of the north', **Ghent** has similar canalside charms without the tourist hordes, and **Brussels**' incomparable Grand Place is worth jumping off any train for, even if you have only a few hours to spare. Cosmopolitan **Antwerp** goes one step further, adding in fashion and diamonds. If you're overnighting make sure to hit Brussels on a weekend and Bruges on a weekday to get the best deals on accommodation.

Ten Days

Add an extra night in each of the above and consider stops in **Mechelen** and **Lier**, practising your French in **Mons** and **Tournai** on the 'back route' to France or in **Luxembourg** en route to Koblenz, Germany.

BRUSSELS

POP 1.14 MILLION

Like the country it represents, Brussels (Bruxelles, Brussel) is a surreal, multilayered place pulling several disparate identities into one enigmatic core. It subtly seduces with great art, tempting chocolate shops and classic cafes. Meanwhile a confusing architectural smorgasbord pits awesome art nouveau and 17th-century masterpieces against shabby suburbanism and the glass-faced anonymity of the EU area. Note that Brussels is officially bilingual, so all names – from streets to train stations – have both Dutch and French versions, but for simplicity we use only the French versions in this chapter.

Sights

Central Brussels

★Grand Place SQUARE

(M Gare Centrale) Brussels' incomparable central square tops any itinerary. Its splendidly spired Gothic **Hôtel de Ville** (City Hall; Pl Guillaume II) was the only building to escape bombardment by the French in 1695, quite ironic considering that it was their main target. Today the pedestrianised square's splendour is due largely to its intact **guildhalls**, rebuilt by merchant guilds after 1695 and fancifully adorned with gilded statues.

Manneken Pis MONUMENT

(cnr Rue de l'Étuve & Rue du Chêne; M Gare Centrale) From Rue Charles Buls, Brussels' most unashamedly touristy shopping street, chocolate and trinket shops lead the camera-toting hoards three blocks to the Manneken Pis. This fountain-statue of a little boy taking a leak is comically tiny and a perversely perfect national symbol for surreal Belgium. Most of the time the tiny statue's nakedness is largely hidden beneath a costume relevant to an anniversary, national day or local event: his ever-growing wardrobe is partly displayed at the **Maison du Roi** (Musée de la Ville de Bruxelles; Grand Pl; M Gare Centrale).

★Musées Royaux des Beaux-Arts GALLERY

(Royal Museums of Fine Arts; ☎02-508 32 11; www.fine-arts-museum.be; Rue de la Régence 3; adult/BrusselsCard/6-25yr €8/free/2, with Magritte Museum €13; ⏲10am-5pm Tue-Sun; M Gare Centrale, Parc) This prestigious museum incorporates the **Musée d'Art Ancien** (ancient art); the **Musée d'Art Moderne** (modern art), with works by surrealist Paul Delvaux and fauvist Rik Wouters; and the purpose-built **Musée Magritte**. The 15th-century Flemish Primitives are wonderfully represented in the Musée d'Art Ancien: there's Rogier Van der Weyden's *Pietà* with its hallucinatory dawn sky, Hans Memling's refined portraits, and the richly textured *Madonna with Saints* by the Master of the Legend of St Lucy.

★MIM MUSEUM

(Musée des Instruments de Musique; ☎02-545 01 30; www.mim.be; Rue Montagne de la Cour 2; adult/concession €12/8; ⏲9.30am-5pm Tue-Fri, 10am-5pm Sat & Sun; M Gare Centrale, Parc) Strap on a pair of headphones then step on the automated floor panels in front of the precious instruments (including world instruments and Adolphe Sax's inventions) to hear them being played. As much of a highlight as the Musical Instrument Museum itself, is its premises – the art nouveau Old England building. This former department store was built in 1899 by Paul Saintenoy and has a panoramic rooftop *café* (pub/bar) and outdoor terrace.

Palais de Justice HISTORIC BUILDING
(Place Poelaert; M Louise, 92, 94) When constructed in 1883, this gigantic domed law court was Europe's biggest building. From outside, rooftop panoramas look towards the distant Atomium and Koekelberg Basilica. A glass elevator leads down into the quirky, downmarket but gentrifying Marolles quarter.

Beyond the Centre

★**Musée Horta** MUSEUM
(02-543 04 90; www.hortamuseum.be; Rue Américaine 25; adult/child €8/4; 2-5.30pm Tue-Sun; M Horta, 91, 92) The typically austere exterior doesn't give much away, but Victor Horta's former home (designed and built 1898–1901) is an art nouveau jewel. The stairwell is the structural triumph of the house – follow the playful knots and curlicues of the banister, which become more exuberant as you ascend, ending at a tangle of swirls and glass lamps at the skylight, glazed with citrus-coloured and plain glass.

Cantillon Brewery BREWERY
(Musée Bruxellois de la Gueuze; 02-521 49 28; www.cantillon.be; Rue Gheude 56; admission €7; 9am-5pm Mon-Fri, 10am-5pm Sat; M Clemenceau) Beer lovers shouldn't miss this unique living brewery-museum. Atmospheric and family run, it's Brussels' last operating lambic brewery and still uses much of the original 19th-century equipment. After a brief explanation, visitors take a self-guided tour, including the barrel rooms where the beers mature for up to three years in chestnut wine-casks. The entry fee includes two taster-glasses of Cantillon's startlingly acidic brews.

★**Musée du Cinquantenaire** MUSEUM
(02-741 72 11; www.kmkg-mrah.be; Parc du Cinquantenaire 10; adult/child/BrusselsCard €5/free/free; 9.30am-5pm Tue-Fri, from 10am Sat & Sun; M Mérode) This astonishingly rich, global collection ranges from Ancient Egyptian sarcophagi to Meso-American masks, to icons to wooden bicycles. Decide what you want to see before coming or the sheer scope can prove overwhelming. Visually attractive spaces include the medieval stone carvings set around a neogothic cloister and the soaring Corinthian columns (convincing fibreglass props) that bring atmosphere to an original AD 420 mosaic from Roman Syria. Labelling is in French and Dutch so the English-language audioguide (€3) is worth considering.

Atomium MONUMENT, MUSEUM
(www.atomium.be; Sq de l'Atomium; adult/student/BrusselsCard €11/6/9; 10am-6pm; M Heysel, 51) The space-age Atomium looms 102m over north Brussels' suburbia resembling a steel alien from a '60s Hollywood movie. It consists of nine house-sized metallic balls linked by steel tube-columns containing escalators and lifts. The balls are arranged like a school chemistry set to represent iron atoms in their crystal lattice…except these are 165 billion times bigger. It was built as a symbol of postwar progress for the 1958 World's Fair and became an architectural icon, receiving a makeover in 2006.

Waterloo Battlefield HISTORIC SITE
(www.waterloo1815.be) A day trip from Brussels, Waterloo Battlefield (20km south) is where the course of European history changed in June 1815 with the final defeat of Napoleon. Today the rolling fields are marked by the striking cone of a grassy hill topped with a great bronze lion. You can climb it (adult/child €6/4) from the **visitor centre**, which offers a range of battle-related activities. TEC bus W from Bruxelles-Midi gets you within 800m. Don't use Waterloo train station, which is 5km away.

Tours

Brussels Bike Tours CYCLING
(0484 89 89 36; www.brusselsbiketours.com; tour incl bicycle rental adult/student €25/22; 10am Feb-Nov, 10am & 3pm Apr-Sep) Tours start from the Grand Place, taking 3½ hours including stops for beer and *frites*.

BRUSSELSCARD

The **BrusselsCard** (www.brusselscard.be; 24/48/72hr €24/36/43) allows free visits to more than 30 Brussels-area museums and free transport but you'll need to be a hyperactive museum fan to save much money. On the first Wednesday afternoon of each month many museums are free.

Central Brussels

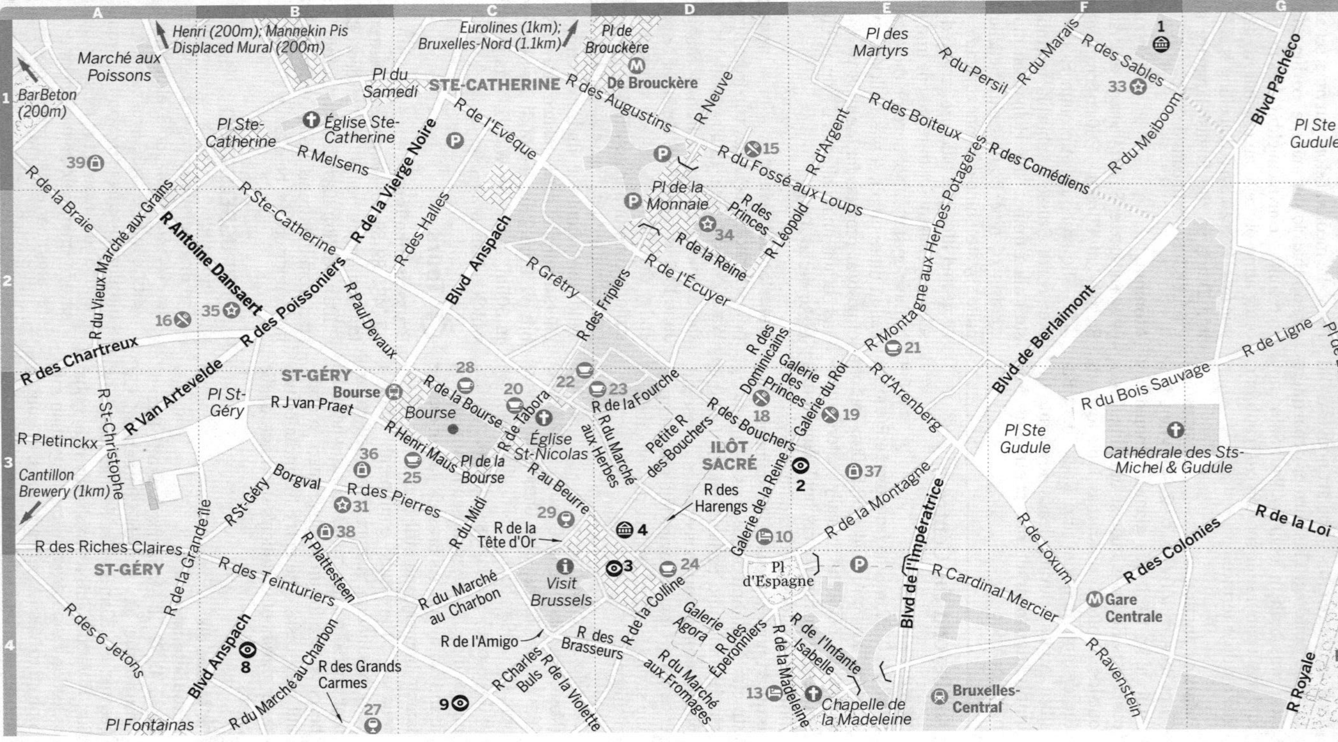

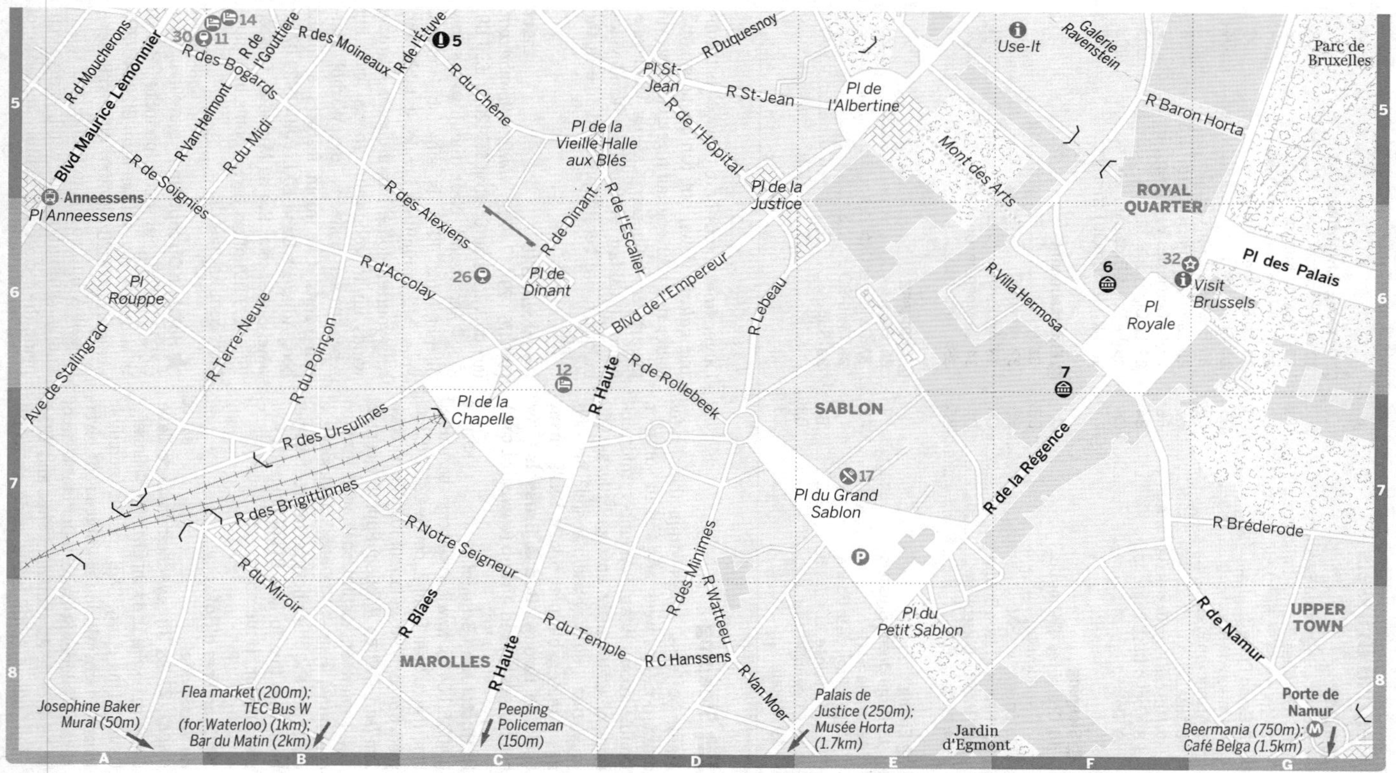
R d Moucherons
Blvd Maurice Lemonnier
R des Bogards
R de l'Gouttiere
R des Moineaux
R de l'Etuve
R du Chêne
R Duquesnoy
Pl St-Jean
R St-Jean
Pl de l'Albertine
Use-It
Galerie Ravenstein
Parc de Bruxelles
R Baron Horta
R Van Helmont
R du Midi
R de Soignies
Anneessens
Pl Anneessens
Pl de la Vieille Halle aux Blés
R de l'Hôpital
Pl de la Justice
Mont des Arts
ROYAL QUARTER
R des Alexiens
R de Dinant
R de l'Escalier
Pl des Palais
Visit Brussels
Pl Royale
R d'Accolay
Pl de Dinant
Blvd de l'Empereur
R Lebeau
R Villa Hermosa
Pl Rouppe
R Terre-Neuve
R du Poinçon
Ave de Stalingrad
R Haute
R de Rollebeek
SABLON
Pl de la Chapelle
R des Ursulines
R des Brigittinnes
Pl du Grand Sablon
R de la Régence
R Bréderode
R Notre Seigneur
R du Miroir
R Blaes
R des Minimes
R Watteeu
Pl du Petit Sablon
R de Namur
UPPER TOWN
MAROLLES
R du Temple
R C Hanssens
R Van Moer
Josephine Baker Mural (50m)
Flea market (200m); TEC Bus W (for Waterloo) (1km); Bar du Matin (2km)
Peeping Policeman (150m)
Palais de Justice (250m); Musée Horta (1.7km)
Jardin d'Egmont
Porte de Namur
Beermania (750m); Café Belga (1.5km)

Central Brussels

Sights

1 Centre Belge de la Bande Dessinée ... F1
2 Galeries St-Hubert ... E3
3 Grand Place ... D4
4 Maison du Roi ... D3
5 Manneken Pis ... C5
6 MIM ... F6
7 Musées Royaux des Beaux-Arts ... F6
8 Tibet & Duchâteau ... B4
9 Tintin ... C4

Sleeping

10 Chambres d'Hôtes du Vaudeville ... D3
11 Downtown-BXL ... B5
12 HI Hostel John Bruegel ... C6
13 Hôtel Le Dixseptième ... D4
14 La Casa-BXL ... B5

Eating

15 Belga Queen Brussels ... D1
16 Fin de Siècle ... A2
17 Le Village de la Bande Dessinée ... E7
18 L'Ogenblik ... D3
19 Mokafé ... E3

Drinking & Nightlife

20 À la Bécasse ... C3
21 À la Mort Subite ... E2
22 A l'Image de Nostre-Dame ... C3
23 Au Bon Vieux Temps ... D3
24 Chaloupe d'Or ... D4
25 Falstaff ... C3
26 La Fleur en Papier Doré ... C6
27 Le Cercle des Voyageurs ... B4
28 Le Cirio ... C3
29 Le Roy d'Espagne ... C3
30 Moeder Lambic Fontainas ... A5

Entertainment

31 AB ... B3
32 Arsène50 ... F6
33 Art Base ... F1
34 La Monnaie/De Munt ... D2
35 L'Archiduc ... B2

Shopping

36 Brüsel ... B3
37 Délices et Caprices ... E3
38 Multi-BD ... B3
39 Stijl ... A1

Sleeping

Many business hotels drop their rates dramatically at weekends and in summer. Double rooms with September midweek rates of €240 might cost as little as €69 in August – so why use a hostel? Brussels has a reasonable network of B&Bs, many bookable through **Bed & Brussels** (www.bnb-brussels.be) and **Airbnb** (www.airbnb.com).

HI Hostel John Bruegel HOSTEL €
(☎02-511 04 36; www.jeugdherbergen.be/brussel.htm; Rue du Saint Esprit 2; dm/tw €27.20/63.30, youth €24.45/57.90; ⏲lockout 10am-2pm, curfew 1am-7am; ⊖@📶; Ⓜ Louise) Superbly central but somewhat institutional with limited communal space. The attic singles are a cut above the other hostels. Internet €2 per hour, wi-fi free, lockers €1.50. There's a 10% discount for HI members.

★**Chambres d'Hôtes du Vaudeville** B&B €€
(☎0471 47 38 37; www.theatreduvaudeville.be; Galerie de la Reine 11; d from €120; 📶; 🚊Bruxelles Central) This classy B&B has an incredible location right within the gorgeous (if reverberant) Galeries St-Hubert. Delectable decor styles include African, modernist and 'Madame Loulou' (with 1920s nude sketches). Larger front rooms have clawfoot bathtubs and *galerie* views, but can be noisy with clatter that continues all night. Get keys via the art-deco-influenced Café du Vaudeville, where breakfast is included. Vaudeville's unique house beer is provided free in the minibar.

Downtown-BXL B&B €€
(☎0475 29 07 21; www.downtownbxl.com; Rue du Marché au Charbon 118-120; r €99-119; 📶; 🚊Anneessens) Near the capital's gay district, this B&B is superbly located. From the communal breakfast table and help-yourself coffee bar, a classic staircase winds up to good-value rooms featuring zebra-striped cushions and Warhol Marilyn prints. One room features a round bed. Adjacent **Casa-BXL** (☎0475 29 07 21; www.lacasabxl.com; Rue du Marché au Charbon 16; r €109-119) offers three rooms in a more Moroccan-Asian style.

★**Hôtel Le Dixseptième** BOUTIQUE HOTEL €€€
(☎02-517 17 17; www.ledixseptieme.be; Rue de la Madeleine 25; s/d/ste from €120/140/250, weekend from €120/120/200; ❄📶; 🚊Bruxelles Central) A hushed magnificence greets you in this alluring boutique hotel, partly occupying the former 17th-century residence of

the Spanish ambassador. The coffee-cream breakfast room retains original cherub reliefs. Spacious executive suites come with four-poster beds. Across a tiny enclosed courtyard-garden in the cheaper rear section, the Creuz Suite has its bathroom tucked curiously into a 14th-century vaulted basement. Lifts stop between floors so you'll need to deal with some stairs.

Eating

Fin de Siècle BELGIAN €
(Rue des Chartreux 9; mains €11.25-20; bar 4.30pm-1am, kitchen 6pm-12.30am; Bourse) From *carbonade* (beer-based hotpot) and *kriek* (cherry beer) chicken to mezzes and tandoori chicken, the food is as eclectic as the decor in this low-lit cult place. Tables are rough, music constant and ceilings purple. To quote the barman, 'there's no phone, no bookings, no sign on the door...we do everything to put people off, but they still keep coming'.

Mokafé SWEETS €
(02-511 78 70; Galerie du Roi; waffles from €3; 7.30am-11.30pm; De Brouckère) Locals get their waffles in this old-fashioned cafe under the glass arch of the Galeries-St Hubert. It's a little timeworn and dowdy inside, but wicker chairs in the beautiful arcade provide you with a view of passing shoppers.

★ **Henri** FUSION €€
(02-218 00 08; www.restohenri.be; Rue de Flandre 113; mains €15-20; noon-2pm Tue-Fri & 6-10pm Tue-Sat; Ste-Catherine) In an airy white space on this street to watch, Henri concocts tangy fusion dishes like tuna with ginger, soy and lime, artichokes with scampi, lime and olive tapenade, or Argentinean fillet steak in parsley. There's an astute wine list, and staff who know their stuff.

Le Cercle des Voyageurs BRASSERIE €€
(02-514 39 49; www.lecercledesvoyageurs.com; Rue des Grands Carmes 18; mains €15-21; 11am-midnight; ; Annessens, Bourse) Invite Phileas Fogg for coffee to this delightful bistro featuring globes, an antique-map ceiling and a travel library. If he's late, flick through an old *National Geographic* in your colonial leather chair. The global brasserie food is pretty good, and the free live music fantastic: piano jazz on Tuesdays and experimental on Thursdays. Other gigs in the cave have a small entrance fee.

Belga Queen Brussels BELGIAN €€
(02-217 21 87; www.belgaqueen.be; Rue du Fossé aux Loups 32; mains €16-25, weekday lunch €16; noon-2.30pm & 7pm-midnight; De Broukère) Belgian cuisine is given a chic, modern twist within a magnificent, if reverberant, 19th-century bank building. Classical stained-glass ceilings and marble columns are hidden behind an indecently hip oyster

COMIC-STRIP CULTURE

In Belgium, comic strips *(bande dessinée)* are revered as the 'ninth art'. Serious comic fans might enjoy Brussels' comprehensive **Centre Belge de la Bande Dessinée** (Belgian Comic Strip Centre; 02-219 19 80; www.comicscenter.net; Rue des Sables 20; adult/concession €8/6; 10am-6pm Tue-Sun; Rogier) in a distinctive Horta-designed art-nouveau building.

Comic shops include **Brüsel** (www.brusel.com; Blvd Anspach 100; 10.30am-6.30pm Mon-Sat, from noon Sun; Bourse) and **Multi-BD** (www.multibd.com; Blvd Anspach 122-124; 10.30am-7pm Mon-Sat, 12.30-6.30pm Sun; Bourse). There's even a cartoon-based cafe-restaurant, **Le Village de la Bande Dessinée** (02-523 13 23; www.comicscafe.be; Place du Grand Sablon 8; snacks from €6; 11am-11pm Tue-Sun; Louise), complete with Tintin statue and original Hergé sketches.

More than 40 cartoon murals enliven Brussels buildings; our favourites include the following:

Tibet & Duchâteau (Rue du Bon Secours 9; Bourse)

Josephine Baker Mural (Rue des Capucins 9; Porte de Hal)

Tintin (Rue de l'Étuve; Bourse)

Peeping Policeman (Rue Haute; Louise)

Mannekin Pis Displaced Mural (Rue de Flandre; Ste-Catherine)

DON'T MISS

BOURSE CAFES

Many of Brussels' most iconic cafes are within stumbling distance of the Bourse. Don't miss century-old **Falstaff** (www.lefalstaff.be; Rue Henri Maus 17; 10am-1am; Bourse) with its festival of stained-glass ceilings, or **Le Cirio** (Rue de la Bourse 18; 10am-midnight; Bourse), a sumptuous yet affordable 1866 marvel full of polished brasswork serving great-value pub meals. Three more classics are hidden up shoulder-wide alleys: the medieval yet unpretentious **A l'Image de Nostre-Dame** (off Rue du Marché aux Herbes 5; noon-midnight Mon-Fri, 3pm-1am Sat, 4-10.30pm Sun; Bourse); the 1695 Rubenseque **Au Bon Vieux Temps** (Impasse Saint Michel; 11am-midnight; Bourse), which sometimes stocks ultra-rare Westvleteren beers (€10!); and lambic specialist **À la Bécasse** (www.alabecasse.com; Rue de Tabora 11; 11am-midnight, to 1am Fri & Sat; M Gare Centrale), with its vaguely Puritanical rows of wooden tables.

counter and wide-ranging beer and cocktail bar (open noon till late). In the former bank vaults beneath, there's a cigar lounge that morphs into a nightclub after 10pm Wednesday to Saturday.

★ L'Ogenblik FRENCH €€€
(02-511 61 51; www.ogenblik.be; Galerie des Princes 1; mains €23-29, lunch €12; noon-2.30pm & 7pm-midnight; Bourse) It may be only a stone's throw from Rue des Bouchers, but this timeless bistro with its lace curtains, resident cat, marble-topped tables and magnificent wrought-iron lamp feels a world away. They've been producing French classics here for more than 30 years, and the expertise shows. Worth the price for a special meal in the heart of town.

Drinking & Nightlife

Cafe culture is one of Brussels' greatest attractions. On the Grand Place itself, 300-year-old gems, like Le Roy d'Espagne and Chaloupe d'Or are magnificent but predictably pricey. Go out of the centre a little to explore the city's new brand of laid-back hipster bars, most decorated in minimal upcycled style, and hosting DJ nights and live music events: try Café Belga, BarBeton or Bar du Matin.

★ La Fleur en Papier Doré PUB
(www.goudblommekeinpapier.be; Rue des Alexiens 53; 11am-midnight Tue-Sat, to 7pm Sun; Bruxelles Central) The nicotine-stained walls of this tiny *café*, adored by artists and locals, are covered with writings, art and scribbles by Magritte and his surrealist pals, some of which were reputedly traded for free drinks. *Ceci n'est pas un musée*, quips a sign on the door, reminding visitors to buy a drink and not just look around.

Moeder Lambic Fontainas BEER HALL
(www.moederlambic.com; Place Fontainas 8; 11am-1am Sun-Thu, to 2am Fri & Sat; Annessens, Bourse) At the last count they were serving 46 artisinal beers here, in a contemporary rather than old-world setting: walls are bare brick and hung with photos and the booths are backed with concrete. They dish up great quiches and cheese and meat platters. The mood is upbeat and the music loud.

À la Mort Subite CAFE
(02-513 13 18; www.alamortsubite.com; Rue Montagne aux Herbes Potagères 7; 11am-1am Mon-Sat, noon-midnight Sun; M Gare Centrale) An absolute classic unchanged since 1928, with lined-up wooden tables, arched mirror panels and entertainingly brusque service.

☆ Entertainment

★ L'Archiduc JAZZ
(02-512 06 52; www.archiduc.net; Rue Antoine Dansaert 6; beer/wine/cocktails €2.50/3.60/8.50; 4pm-5am; Bourse) This intimate, split-level, art-deco bar has been playing jazz since 1937. It's an unusual two-tiered circular space that can get incredibly packed but remains convivial. You might need to ring the doorbell. Saturday concerts are free (5pm), Sundays bring in international talent and admission charges vary.

La Monnaie/De Munt OPERA, THEATRE
(www.lamonnaie.be; Place de la Monnaie; M De Brouckère) Grand and glittering theatre, opera and dance venue.

Art Base LIVE MUSIC

(☎02-217 29 20; www.art-base.be; Rue des Sables 29; ⊙Fri & Sat; Ⓜ Rogier) One of the best little venues in town for music fans with eclectic tastes. Located opposite the Comic Museum, it resembles someone's living room. But the programming is first rate, and it's worth taking a punt on Greek *rebetiko*, Indian classical music, Argentinian guitar or whatever else is playing.

AB LIVE MUSIC

(Ancienne Belgique; ☎02-548 24 00; www.abconcerts.be; Blvd Anspach 110; 🚇Bourse) The AB's two auditoriums are favourite venues for mid-level international rock bands and acts such as Jools Holland and Madeleine Peyroux, plus plenty of home-grown talent. The ticket office is located on Rue des Pierres. There's a good on-site bar-restaurant that opens at 6pm (bookings essential).

Shopping

Tourist-oriented shops selling chocolate, beer, lace and Atomium baubles stretch between the Grand Place and Manneken Pis. For better chocolate shops in calmer, grander settings, peruse the resplendent **Galeries St-Hubert** (www.galeries-saint-hubert.com; off Rue du Marché aux Herbes; Ⓜ Gare Centrale) or the upmarket Sablon area, or visit the daily **flea market** (Place du Jeu-de-Balle; ⊙6am-2pm). Antwerp more than Brussels is Belgium's fashion capital, but Rue Antoine Dansaert has several cutting-edge boutiques including **Stijl** (www.stijl.be; Rue Antoine Dansaert 74; Ⓜ Ste-Catherine).

Supermarkets sell a range of Belgian beers relatively cheaply but for wider selections and the relevant glasses, try **Beermania** (www.beermania.be; Chaussée de Wavre 174; ⊙11am-9pm Mon-Sat; Ⓜ Porte de Namur) or the very personal little **Délices et Caprices** (www.the-belgian-beer-tasting-shop.be; Rue des Bouchers 68; ⊙2-8pm Thu-Mon; Ⓜ Gare Centrale).

Information

ATMs are widespread. Exchange agency rates are usually best around the Bourse. As well as the following there are info counters at Brussels Airport and Bruxelles-Midi station. For planning advice, author recommendations, traveller reviews and insider tips see www.lonelyplanet.com/belgium/brussels.

Use-It (☎02-218 39 06; www.use-it.travel/cities/detail/brussels; Galerie Ravenstein 17; ⊙10am-6.30pm Mon-Sat; 📶; Ⓜ Ste-Catherine) Meeting place for young travellers, with free coffee and tea and a list of live-music events written up by the door. They do a free alternative city tour at 2pm on Monday, with the emphasis on social history and nightlife. The printed material is first rate, with a quirky city map, a guide for wheelchair users and a beer pamphlet.

Visit Brussels (☎02-513 89 40; www.visitbrussels.be; Hôtel de Ville; ⊙9am-6pm; 🚇Bourse) Visit Brussels has stacks of city-specific information as well as handy fold-out guides (independently researched) to the best shops, restaurants and pubs in town. The Rue Royale (Rue Royale 2; ⊙9am-6pm Mon-Fri, 10am-6pm Sat-Sun; Ⓜ Parc) office is much less crowded than the Grand Place one. Here you'll also find the Arsène50 (☎02-512 57 45; www.arsene50.be; ⊙12.30-5.30pm Tue-Sat) desk, which provides great discounts for cultural events.

Getting There & Away

BUS

Eurolines (☎02-274 13 50; www.eurolines.be; Rue du Progrès 80; ⊙5.45am-8.45pm; 🚇Gare du Nord) International bus service Eurolines has buses departing from Bruxelles-Nord train station.

TRAIN

Brussels has two major stations. All main domestic trains from Brussels stop at both stations as do some Amsterdam services. Eurostar, TGV and Thalys high-speed trains stop only at Bruxelles-Midi (Brussel-Zuid). That's not in the best part of town so, on arrival, jump straight onto any local service for the four-minute hop to more conveniently central Bruxelles-Central.

Consult www.belgianrail.be for timetable information.

Getting Around

TO/FROM BRUSSELS AIRPORT

Taxi

Fares start around €40. Very bad idea in rush-hour traffic.

Train

Four per hour (5.30am to 11.50pm) costing €8.50. It takes 20 minutes to reach Bruxelles-Central, 24 minutes to Bruxelles-Midi.

TO/FROM CHARLEROI AIRPORT

Charleroi Airport is also known as Brussels-South.

Bus

L'Elan (www.voyages-lelan.be) Direct services operated by L'Elan run half-hourly to Bruxelles-Midi station (single/return

WORTH A TRIP

BRUSSELS TO ANTWERP

Direct Brussels–Antwerp trains take just over half an hour. But if you're not in a hurry consider stopping en route at a couple of other historic cities, not more than a minor diversion by train: Leuven (30 minutes) then Mechelen (22 minutes). In both towns the station is around 15 minutes' walk from the centre. And both have imaginative accommodation, including hostels, if you're too charmed to move on.

€14/23); last services to/from the airport are 8.30pm/9.25pm. It should take one hour, but allow far more time at rush hour.

Train

TEC bus A (€5, 18 minutes) links at least hourly from Charleroi Airport to Charleroi-Sud station, a 50-minute train ride from Brussels.

BICYCLE

FietsPunt/PointVelo (www.recyclo.org; Carrefour de l'Europe 2; per 1/3 days €7.50/15; 7am-7pm Mon-Fri; Bruxelles-Central) Rents long term; it's on the left as you leave Bruxelles-Central station by the Madeleine exit.

Villo! (078-05 11 10; www.en.villo.be; subscription day/week €1.60/7.65) Has 180 automated pick-up/drop-off short-term rental stands. Credit card required; read the online instructions carefully.

PUBLIC TRANSPORT

STIB/MIVB (www.stib.be) tickets are sold at metro stations, newsagents and on buses and trams. Single-/five-/10-journey tickets valid for one hour from validation cost €2.10/8/12.50 including transfers. Unlimited one/two/three-day passes cost €7/13/17. Airport buses are excluded.

FLANDERS

Leuven

POP 97,600

Lively, self-confident Leuven (Louvain in French; www.leuven.be) is Flanders' oldest university town and home to the vast **Stella Artois brewery** (www.breweryvisits.com; Vuurkruisenlaan; admission €8.50; 9am-7.30pm Tue-Sat). Its greatest attraction is a flamboyant 15th-century **Stadhuis** (Grote Markt 9; tour €4; tour 3pm) lavished with exterior statuary. Other architectural attractions are patchy due to heavy damage sustained in 20th-century wars, but the iconic **university library** has been rebuilt. Twice. **Muntstraat** is a loveable medieval alley full of restaurants and **Oude Markt** is a very lively square of wall-to-wall bars that hum till the wee hours.

The most interesting option for accommodation is the grand mansion housing **Oude Brouwerei Keyser Carel** (016 22 14 81; www.keysercarel.be; Lei 15; s/d €105/120), while homely **Leuven City Hostel** (016 84 30 33; www.leuvencityhostel.com; Ravenstraat 37; dm/d €23/54; reception 4-8pm; @) and stylish B&B **Casa Bollicine** (0497 83 97 17; www.casabollicine.be; Parijsstraat 7; s/d €120/150;) are good, relatively central accommodation choices. Directly behind the station, around 1km east, the HI Hostel **Jeugdherberg De Blauwput** (016 63 90 62; www.leuven-hostel.com; Martelarenlaan 11a; dm/d €24.60/58, youth dm/d €22.30/54.20; @) makes a good choice for those wanting to sleep near Brussels Airport, a mere 16 minutes away by train.

Mechelen

POP 82,300

Belgium's religious capital, Mechelen (Malines in French) has the **St-Romboutskathedraal** (http://sintromboutstoren.mechelen.be; Grote Markt; 8.30am-6pm) FREE, a cathedral featuring a 97m, 15th-century tower that soars above a particularly memorable central market square. There are other splendid churches on Keizerstraat where the courthouse and theatre were both once royal palaces in the days when the Low Countries were effectively run from Mechelen. Other top sights include the brilliant **Speelgoedmuseum** (015 55 70 75; www.speelgoedmuseum.be; Nekkerstraat 21; adult/child €8/5.50; 10am-5pm Tue-Sun), a toy museum, and the **Schepenhuis gallery tower** on IJzerenleen, a street of fine baroque facades leading towards the main station passing close to **Vismarkt**, the compact bar-cafe zone. There's a modern HI Hostel, the **Hostel De Zandpoort** (015 27 85 39; www.mechelen-hostel.com; Zandpoortvest 70; dm/tw €24.60/58, youth dm/tw €22.30/54.10; check-in 5-10pm; P) or try stylish **Martins Patershof** (015 46 46 46; www.martinshotels.com; Karmelietenstraat 4; from €149;), set in a 1867 Franciscan monastery.

Antwerp

POP 511,700

Cosmopolitan, confident and full of contrasts, Antwerp (Antwerpen in Dutch, Anvers in French) was one of northern Europe's foremost cities in the 17th century when it was also home to Pieter Paul Rubens, diplomat, philosopher and northern Europe's greatest baroque artist. Today it's once again in the ascendant, attracting art lovers and fashion moguls, clubbers and diamond dealers.

Sights

City Centre

Brabo Fountain STATUE

(Grote Markt) As with every great Flemish city, Antwerp's medieval heart is a classic Grote Markt (marketplace). Here the triangular, pedestrianised space features the voluptuous, baroque Brabo Fountain depicting Antwerp's hand-throwing legend. Flanked on two sides by very photogenic guildhalls, the square is dominated by an impressive Italo-Flemish Renaissance-style stadhuis (town hall), completed in 1565.

Het Steen CASTLE

(Steenplein) On a riverside knoll, Het Steen is a dinky but photogenic castle from AD 1200 occupying the site of Antwerp's original Gallo-Roman settlement. Outside is a humorous **statue of Lange Wapper**, a tall folkloric 'peeping Tom' figure showing off his codpiece to two diminutive onlookers. Directly north, the misnamed **Maritime Park** is a long, open-sided wrought-iron shed displaying a historic **barge collection**. There is nothing to see inside.

Onze-Lieve-Vrouwekathedraal CATHEDRAL

(www.dekathedraal.be; Handschoenmarkt; adult/concession €6/4; 10am-5pm Mon-Fri, to 3pm Sat, to 4pm Sun) Belgium's finest Gothic cathedral was 169 years in the making (1352–1521). Wherever you wander in Antwerp, its gracious, 123m-high spire has a habit of popping unexpectedly into view and rarely fails to jolt a gasp of awe. The sight is particularly well framed when looking up Pelgrimstraat in afternoon light.

★Museum Plantin-Moretus HISTORIC BUILDING

(www.museumplantinmoretus.be; Vrijdag Markt 22; adult/child €8/1; 10am-5pm Tue-Sun) The idea of giving a museum Unesco World Heritage status might seem odd, until you've seen this fabulous place. Once home to the world's first industrial printing works, it has been a museum since 1876. The medieval building and 1622 **courtyard garden** alone are worth the visit. Highlights include the 1640 **library**, the historic **bookshop** (room 4), and rooms 11 and 21 for their gilt leather 'wallpaper'. Then there's a priceless collection of manuscripts, tapestries and the world's oldest printing press.

Fashion District AREA

In the space of just a few streets, you'll find dozens of designer boutiques, both Belgian and international, along with a variety of streetwear, end-of-line discounters, secondhand shops and more mainstream chains. Simply stroll Nationalestraat, Lombardenvest, Huidevettersstraat and Schuttershofstraat, not missing Kammenstraat for retro labels and urban scrawl.

Rubenshuis MUSEUM

(www.rubenshuis.be; Wapper 9-11; adult/child €8/1, audio guide €2; 10am-5pm Tue-Sun) Restored along original lines, the 1611 building was built as home and studio by celebrated painter Pieter Paul Rubens. Rescued from ruins in 1937, the building is architecturally indulgent with baroque portico, rear facade and formal garden. The furniture dates from Rubens' era but was not part of the original decor. Ten Rubens canvases are displayed, including one where Eve appears to glance lustfully at Adam's fig leaf.

★Antwerpen-Centraal LANDMARK

With its neo-Gothic facade, vast main hall and splendidly proportioned dome, the 1905 Antwerpen-Centraal train station is one of the city's premier landmarks. It was rated by *Newsweek* as one of the world's five most

> **ANTWERP CARD**
>
> An **Antwerp Card** (www.visitantwerpen.be; 24/48/72hr €25/32/37) will usually save you money if you visit at least four of the city's splendid museums.

Antwerp

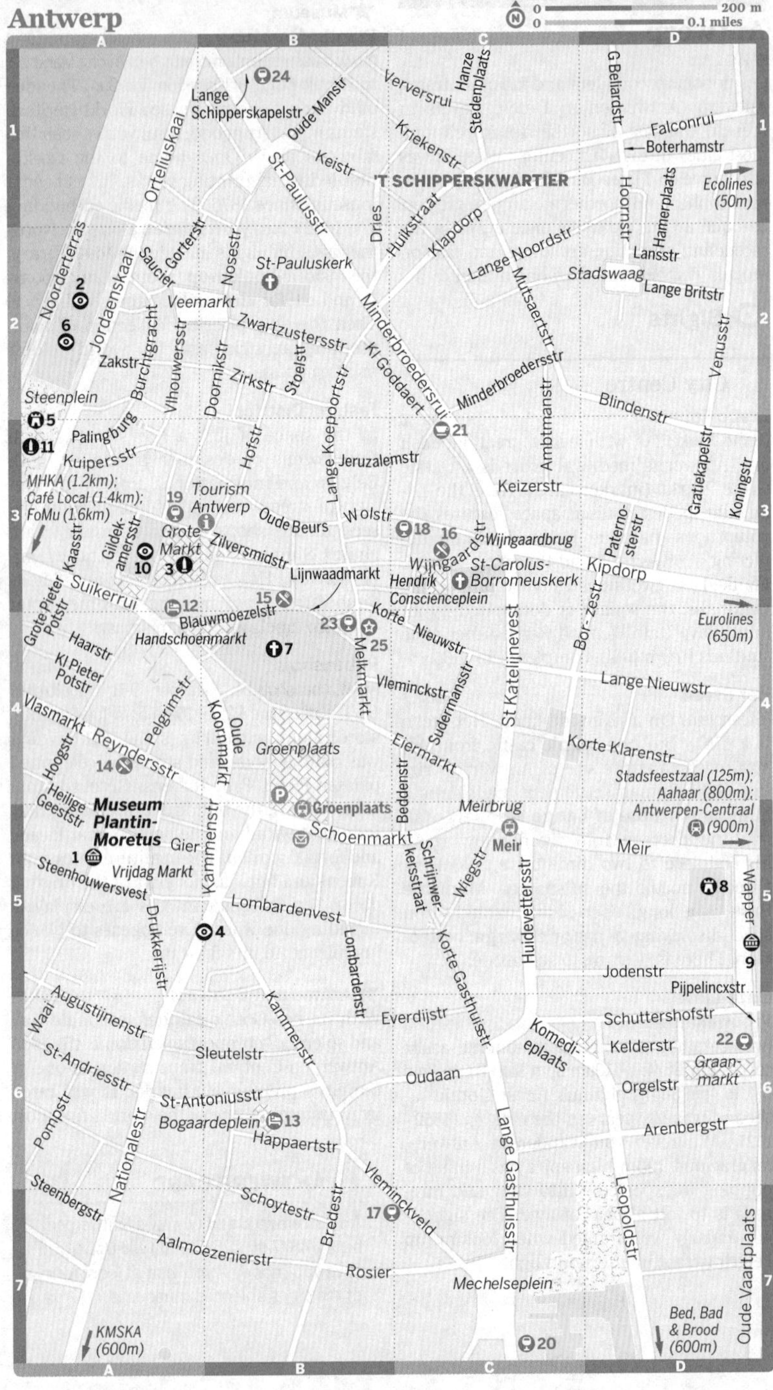

'T SCHIPPERSKWARTIER
Lange Schipperskapelstr
Oude Manstr
Verversrui
Hanze Stedenplaats
G Beliardstr
Falconrui
Boterhamstr
Kriekenstr
Keistr
St-Paulusstr
Orteliuskaai
Ecolines (50m)
Hoornstr
Hamerplaats
Dries
Huikstraat
Klapdorp
Lange Noordstr
Lansstr
Noorderterras
Gorterstr
Nosestr
St-Pauluskerk
Stadswaag
Lange Britstr
Jordaenskaai
Saucier
Veemarkt
Mutsaertstr
Zwartzustersstr
Minderbroedersrui
Venusstr
Burchtgracht
Vlhouwersstr
Doornikstr
Zakstr
Zirkstr
Stoelstr
Kl Goddaert
Minderbroedersstr
Ambtmanstr
Blindenstr
Steenplein
Palingburg
Hofstr
Lange Koepoortstr
Kuipersstr
Jeruzalemstr
Gratiekapelstr
Koningstr
MHKA (1.2km); Café Local (1.4km); FoMu (1.6km)
Tourism Antwerp
Keizerstr
Wolstr
Oude Beurs
Grote Markt
Gildekamersstr
Kaasstr
Zilversmidstr
Wijngaardstr
Wijngaardbrug
Paternosterstr
St-Carolus-Borromeuskerk
Hendrik Conscienceplein
Lijnwaadmarkt
Kipdorp
Suikerrui
Grote Pieter Potstr
Blauwmoezelstr
Handschoenmarkt
Korte Nieuwstr
Bor-zestr
Eurolines (650m)
Haarstr
Melkmarkt
Kl Pieter Potstr
Vlemincks tr
Sudermansstr
St Katelijnevest
Lange Nieuwstr
Vlasmarkt
Reyndersstr
Pelgrimstr
Oude Koornmarkt
Groenplaats
Eiermarkt
Korte Klarenstr
Hoogstr
Beddenstr
Stadsfeestzaal (125m); Aahaar (800m); Antwerpen-Centraal (900m)
Heilige Geeststr
Museum Plantin-Moretus
Groenplaats
Meirbrug
Meir
Schoenmarkt
Gier
Kammenstr
Schrijnwerkersstraat
Wiegstr
Vrijdag Markt
Steenhouwersvest
Lombardenvest
Drukkerijstr
Huidevettersstr
Wapper
Korte Gasthuisstr
Lombardenstr
Jodenstr
Pijpelincxstr
Augustijnenstr
Waai
Kammenstr
Everdijstr
Schuttershofstr
Komedieplaats
Kelderstr
Sleutelstr
St-Andriesstr
Oudaan
Graanmarkt
Orgelstr
St-Antoniusstr
Pompstr
Bogaardeplein
Arenbergstr
Happaertstr
Nationalestr
Vleminckveld
Lange Gasthuisstr
Leopoldstr
Steenbergstr
Schoytestr
Bredestr
Aalmoezenierstr
Rosier
Mechelseplein
Oude Vaartplaats
Bed, Bad & Brood (600m)
KMSKA (600m)

Antwerp

Top Sights
1 Museum Plantin-Moretus ... A5

Sights
2 Barge Collection ... A2
3 Brabo Fountain ... A3
Chocolate Line ... (see 8)
4 Fashion District ... B5
5 Het Steen ... A3
6 Maritime Park ... A2
7 Onze-Lieve-Vrouwekathedraal ... B4
8 Paleis op de Meir ... D5
9 Rubenshuis ... D5
10 Stadhuis ... A3
11 Statue of Lange Wapper ... A3

Sleeping
12 Hotel O ... A3
13 Pulcinella ... B6

Eating
14 De Groote Witte Arend ... A4
15 Kathedraalcafe ... B3
16 't Brantyser ... C3

Drinking & Nightlife
17 Bierhuis Kulminator ... B7
18 De Kat ... C3
19 Den Bengel ... A3
20 Korsåkov ... C7
21 Normo ... C3
22 Oud Arsenaal ... D6
23 Pelikaan ... B4
24 Red & Blue ... B1

Entertainment
25 De Muze ... B4

beautiful stations. It's also very practical, the multilevel platforms having had a full 21st-century makeover.

Meir

If walking from the main train station to Groenplaats, revel in the grand, statue-draped architecture of pedestrianised Meir and Leystraat. The gilt-overloaded **Stadsfeestzaal** (www.stadsfeestzaal.com; Meir 76; 9.30am-7pm Mon-Sat) is one of the world's most indulgently decorated shopping malls. Watch top-quality chocolates being made behind **Chocolate Line** (www.thechocolateline.be; 10.30am-6.30pm), a shop that fills a mural-lined room of the 1745 **Paleis op de Meir** (www.paleisopdemeir.be; Meir 50; tour €8; tour 2pm Tue-Sat).

't Zuid

Around 1km south of the Fashion District, 't Zuid is a conspicuously prosperous area dotted with century-old architecture, hip bars, fine restaurants and museums. The classic centrepiece art gallery, **KMSKA** (www.kmska.be; Leopold De Waelplaats), is closed for renovation until 2017, but there's still **MHKA** (03-238 59 60; www.muhka.be; Leuvenstraat 32; adult/child €8/1; 11am-6pm Tue-Sun, to 9pm Thu) for contemporary conceptual art, and outstanding **FoMu** (FotoMuseum; 03-242 93 00; www.fotomuseum.be; Waalsekaai 47; adult/child €8/3; 10am-5pm Tue-Sun) for photography.

Sleeping

Over 40 B&Bs can be sorted by price or map location on www.bedandbreakfast-antwerp.com, but relatively few are central.

★ **Pulcinella** HOSTEL €
(03-234 03 14; www.jeugdherbergen.be; Bogaardeplein 1; dm/tw €26.80/32.40; @ wi-fi) This giant, tailor-made HI Hostel is hard to beat for its Fashion District location and cool modernist decor. HI members save €3.

ABhostel HOSTEL €
(0473 57 01 66; www.abhostel.com; Kattenberg 110; mixed dm/tw €19/50; reception noon-3pm & 6-8pm; wi-fi) This adorable family-run hostel has lots of little added extras to make it comfy. Its inner-suburban setting is 20-minutes' walk east of Antwerpen-Centraal station, past inexpensive shops, ethnic restaurants and African wig shops. Across the street is the brilliantly unpretentious local pub **Plaza Real** (from 8pm Wed-Sun), owned by a band member of dEUS.

★ **Bed, Bad & Brood** B&B €€
(03-248 15 39; www.bbantwerp.com; Justitiestraat 43; s/d/q €75/85/135; @) In a 1910, belle-epoque-style townhouse near the vast Gerechtshof (former courthouse), BB&B has squeaky wooden floors, high ceilings, some old-fashioned furniture and a remarkable spaciousness for a B&B in this price range. Owners are assiduously keen to help. Get off trams 12 or 24 at the Gerechtshof with its verdigris statues of justice. Two-night minimum stay often applies.

Hotel O HOTEL €€

(☎03-500 89 50; www.hotelokathedral.com; Handschoenmarkt 3; r €89-129) The immediate selling point here is an unbeatable location, staring across a square at the cathedral frontage. Behind an intriguing little foyer of 1950s radios, the all-black decor is relieved by mid-sized rooms with giant Rubens prints spilling over onto the ceilings. Note that there's a second Hotel O above Nero Brasserie in Het Zuid.

Eating

For cheap, central snacks, stroll Hoogstraat, near the cathedral. For cosy if pricier options look in parallel Pelgrimstraat (with its 'secret' medieval alley, Vlaaikeusgang) or the picturesque lanes leading to Rubens' wonderful St-Carolus-Borromeuskerk. There are many more excellent options in 't Zuid, north and west of KMSKA.

't Brantyser EUROPEAN €

(☎03-233 18 33; www.brantyser.be; Hendrik Conscienceplein 7; snacks €6-12.50, mains €17-26; ⏲11.15am-10pm) The cosy, double-level Brantyser gets the antique clutter effect just right while its enviable terrace surveys one of old Antwerp's most appealing pedestrian squares. Other restaurants nearby might be more refined, but the food here is tasty and portions generous. Try the *visschotel*, a delicious melange of seafoods and fish pieces in a creamy herb sauce.

Aahaar INDIAN, VEGAN €

(www.aahaar.com; Lange Herentalsestraat 23; buffet €10; ⏲noon-3pm & 5.30-9.30pm Mon-Fri, 1-9.30pm Sat & Sun; 🌿) Unpretentious and popular little place for vegan/vegetarian Jain-Indian food including an eat-all-you-like buffet with five mains, two sweets and rice.

★De Groote Witte Arend BELGIAN €€

(☎03-233 50 33; www.degrootewittearend.be; Reyndersstraat 18; mains €13-24; ⏲10.30am-midnight, kitchen 11.30am-3pm & 5-10pm; 📶) Retaining the Tuscan stone arcade of a 15th- and 17th-century convent building, this relaxed central gem combines the joys of a good beer bar with the satisfaction of well-cooked, sensibly priced Flemish home cuisine, notably *stoemp*, *stoofvlees/carbonnades* and huge portions of rabbit in rich Westmalle sauce.

Kathedraalcafe BELGIAN €€

(Torfbrug 10; mains €14-24.50, sandwiches €8.50; ⏲noon-11pm) This ivy-clad medieval masterpiece has an astounding interior decked with angels, saints, pulpits and several deliciously sacrilegious visual jokes. Good, if pricey, sandwiches supplement the mussels, vol-au-vents and other typical local favourites. Outside dining hours, or after 11pm, come for a beer: they have St Bernardus Tripel on draught.

Drinking & Nightlife

To sound like a local, stride into a pub and ask for a *bolleke*. Don't worry, that means a 'little bowl' (ie glass) of De Koninck, the city's favourite ale. Cheap places to try it include classic *cafés* **Oud Arsenaal** (Pijpelincxstraat 4; ⏲10am-10pm Wed-Fri, 7.30am-7.30pm Sat & Sun), **De Kat** (Wolstraat 22) and the livelier **Pelikaan** (www.facebook.com/cafepelikaan; Melkmarkt 14; ⏲8.30am-3am). Mechelseplein bars including **Korsåkov** (Mechelseplein 21; snacks €3.50-5.50, Primus/Chouffe €2/2.50; ⏲10am-4am) open till very late, as do countless other great options around KMSKA in the 't Zuid area.

Den Bengel PUB

(www.cafedenengel.be; Grote Markt 5; ⏲9am-2am) Sixteenth-century guildhall pub with fabulous cathedral views from the terrace.

Bierhuis Kulminator PUB

(Vleminckveld 32; ⏲4pm-midnight Tue-Sat, from 8pm Mon) Classic beer pub boasting 700 mostly Belgian brews, including notably rare 'vintage' bottles laid down to mature for several years like fine wine.

Normo CAFE

(www.normocoffee.com; Minderbroedersrui 30; coffees €2-3.50, muffins €2; ⏲10am-7pm Mon-Fri, to 6pm Sat) Coffee is an art at Normo, from the science-project dripping station to the exposed brick walls, attractively battered tiles and bearded baristas.

Red & Blue CLUB

(www.redandblue.be; Lange Schipperskapelstraat 11; ⏲11pm-7am Thu-Sat; 🚊7) Great dance venue with decent-sized yet still intimate dance floor. It's most famous for its Saturday gay night. There's also a Thursday student night, TGIT (www.thankgoditsthursday.be), Fridays see a mixed crowd groove to house music, and some Sundays there are classic 1970s-style discos.

Café Local CLUB

(www.cafelocal.be; Waalsekaai 25; cover €7-15; 10pm-late Wed-Sun; 4) Popular, friendly 't Zuid nightclub with a Mexican trading post–themed bar-island. Wednesdays are formal (collared shirts required), Thursday student nights are free (18 to 25 year olds), Fridays are for over 40s, and Paradise Saturdays see deckchairs and palm fronds appear. On the first Sunday of each month the music takes a salsa-merengue turn.

Entertainment

For listings consult www.weekup.be/antwerp-en/week; www.zva.be in summer; and www.gratisinantwerpen.be for free events.

deSingel PERFORMING ARTS

(03-248 28 28; www.desingel.be; Desguinlei 25) Two concert halls offering a highly innovative program of classical music, international theatre and modern dance.

De Muze JAZZ

(03-226 01 26; http://jazzmuze.be; Melkmarkt 15; noon-4am) Very appealing triple-level gabled *café* with an Escher-like interior hosting great live jazz from 10pm Monday to Saturday (but not Wednesday or Thursday in summer).

Information

Tourism Antwerp (03-232 01 03; www.visitantwerpen.be; Grote Markt 13; 9am-5.45pm Mon-Sat, to 4.45pm Sun & holidays) Tourism Antwerp is a central tourist office with a branch on level zero of Antwerpen-Centraal train station.

Getting There & Away

BUS

Many regional buses (eg to Lier) leave from near Ecolines.

Ecolines (www.ecolines.net; Paardenmarkt 65) Ecolines services for Eastern Europe depart from near Antwerpen-Berchem train station, 2km southeast of Antwerpen-Centraal. The ticket agent is Euro-Maror.

Eurolines (03-233 86 62; www.eurolines.com; Van Stralenstraat 8; 9am-5.45pm Mon-Fri, to 3.15pm Sat) International Eurolines buses depart from points near Franklin Rooseveltplaats.

TRAIN

Regular services to Bruges (€14.80, 75 minutes), Brussels (€7.30, 35-49 minutes) and Ghent (€9.40, 46 minutes). High-speed service to Amsterdam.

Getting Around

Franklin Rooseveltplaats and Koningin Astridplein are hubs for the integrated network of **De Lijn** (www.delijn.be) buses and trams (some running underground metro-style).

Ghent

POP 251,100

Known as Gent in Dutch and Gand in French, Ghent is like a grittier Bruges without the crush of tourists. Nonetheless it sports photogenic canals, medieval towers, great cafes and some of Belgium's most inspired museums. Always a lively student city, Ghent goes crazy in mid-July during the 10-day **Gentse Feesten** (www.gentsefeesten.be; Jul), featuring street theatre, jazz and techno music.

Sights

Most major sights are strolling distance from Korenmarkt, the westernmost of three interlinked squares that form the heart of Ghent's historic core.

SEE MORE OF GHENT

The good-value **CityCard Gent** (www.visitgent.be; 2-/3-day ticket €30/35) provides three days' free city transport and entrance to all the sights reviewed (except boat tours) plus much more including the dynamic industrial museum, **MIAT** (Museum voor Industriële Archeologie en Textiel; www.miat.gent.be; Minnemeers 9; adult/youth €6/2; 10am-6pm Tue-Sun), the eclectic **Design Museum** (www.designmuseumgent.be; J Breydelstraat 5; adult/concession €8/6; 10am-6pm Tue-Sun) and the interactive city museum **STAM** (www.stamgent.be; Bijloke Complex; adult/concession €8/6; 10am-6pm Tue-Sun; 4). In Citadelpark near Gent-St-Pieters station, fine-art gallery **MSK** (Museum voor Schone Kunsten; 09-240 07 00; www.mskgent.be; Citadelpark; adult/youth €8/2; 10am-6pm Tue-Sun) and the cutting-edge **SMAK** (Museum of Contemporary Art; www.smak.be; Citadelpark; adult/youth €12/2, 10am-1pm Sun free; 10am-6pm Tue-Sun; 5) exhibition space are also included.

Ghent Centre

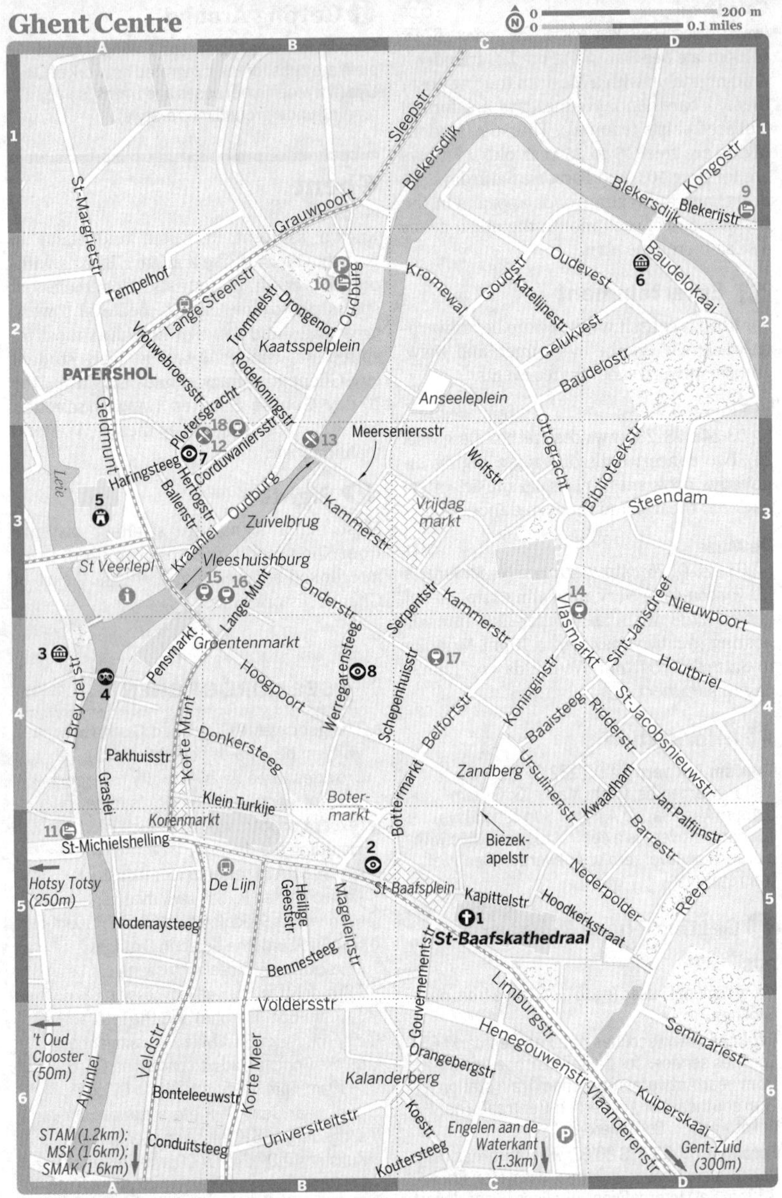

★ **St-Baafskathedraal** CHURCH
(www.sintbaafskathedraal.be; St-Baafsplein; ⌚8.30am-6pm Apr-Oct, to 5pm Nov-Mar) St-Baafs cathedral's towering interior has some fine stained glass and an unusual combination of brick vaulting with stone tracery. A €0.20 leaflet guides you round the cathedral's numerous art treasures, including a big original Rubens opposite the stairway that leads down into the partly muralled crypts. However, most visitors come to see just one magnificent work – the Van Eycks' 1432 'Flemish Primitive'

Ghent Centre

Top Sights

1 St-Baafskathedraal C5

Sights

2 Belfort B5
3 Design Museum A4
4 Grasbrug A4
5 Gravensteen A3
6 MIAT D2
7 Patershol A3
8 Werregarensteeg B4

Sleeping

9 Hostel 47 .... D1
10 Simon Says B2
11 Uppelink A5

Eating

12 Amadeus B3
13 Soup Lounge B3

Drinking & Nightlife

14 Charlatan C3
15 Het Waterhuis aan de Bierkant B3
16 Hot Club de Gand B3
17 Pink Flamingo's C4
18 Rococo B3

masterpiece, *The Adoration of the Mystic Lamb* (adult/child/audio guide €4/1.50/1).

Belfort BELFRY
(Botermarkt; adult/concession €6/2; ⌚10am-5.30pm) Ghent's soaring, Unesco-listed, 14th-century belfry is topped by a large dragon, and it's become something of a city mascot. You'll meet two previous dragon incarnations on the climb to the top (mostly by lift) but other than some bell-making exhibits the real attraction is the view. Enter through the **Lakenhalle**, Ghent's cloth hall that was left half-built in 1445 and only completed in 1903.

Werregarensteeg STREET
(www.ghentizm.be) Graffiti is positively encouraged as an art form in this tiny central alley.

Grasbrug VIEWPOINT
To admire Ghent's towers and gables at their most photogenic, stand just west of the Grasbrug bridge at dusk. It's a truly gorgeous scene, though the appealing waterfront facades of Graslei aren't as old as they look – these 'medieval' warehouses and townhouses were largely rebuilt to make Ghent look good for the 1913 World's Fair. Canal trips depart from either end of the Grasbrug and nearby Vleeshuisbrug bridges.

Gravensteen CASTLE
(www.gravensteengent.be; St-Veerleplein; adult/child €10/6; ⌚10am-6pm Apr-Oct, 9am-5pm Nov-Mar) Flanders' quintessential 12th-century stone castle comes complete with moat, turrets and arrow slits. It's all the more remarkable considering that during the 19th century the site was converted into a cotton mill. Meticulously restored since, the interior sports the odd suit of armour, a guillotine and torture devices. The relative lack of furnishings is compensated for by a hand-held 45-minute movie guide, which sets a tongue-in-cheek historical costumed drama in the rooms, prison pit and battlements.

Patershol NEIGHBOURHOOD
(www.patershol.be) Dotted with half-hidden restaurants, enchanting Patershol is a web of twisting cobbled lanes whose old-world houses were once home to leather tradesmen and to the Carmelite Fathers (Paters), hence the name. An aimless wander here is one of the city's great pleasures.

Sleeping

Ghent offers innovative accommodation in all budget ranges. Websites www.gent-accommodations.be and www.bedandbreakfast-gent.be help you gauge availability in the city's numerous appealing B&Bs.

★Engelen aan de Waterkant B&B €€
(☎09-223 08 83; www.engelenaandewaterkant.be; Ter Platen 30; s/d €120/140) Two 'angel' rooms are an opportunity for the interior-designer owner to experiment and for guests to soak up the special atmosphere in a 1900 townhouse overlooking the tree-lined canal.

Simon Says GUESTHOUSE €€
(☎09-233 03 43; www.simon-says.be; Sluizeken 8; d €110; 📶) Two fashionably styled guest rooms above an excellent coffee shop in a brightly coloured corner house with art nouveau facade.

Uppelink HOSTEL €€
(☎09-279 44 77; www.hosteluppelink.com; Sint-Michielsplein 21; dm €27.50-37.50, s €52, tw €62) Within a classic step-gabled canalside house, the show-stopping attraction at this super-central new hostel is the unbeatable view of Ghent's main towers as seen from the breakfast room and from the biggest,

cheapest dorms. Smaller rooms have little view, if any.

Hostel 47 HOSTEL €€
(☎0478 71 28 27; www.hostel47.com; Blekerijstraat 47-51; dm €26.50-29.50, d €66, tr €90; 📶) Unusually calm yet pretty central, this inviting hostel has revamped a high-ceilinged historic house with virginal white walls, spacious bunk rooms and designer fittings. Free lockers and cursory breakfast with Nespresso coffee; no bar.

Eating

Enchanting Patershol (p121) is a web of twisting cobbled lanes with old-world houses that are now interspersed with small restaurants. Others jostle for summer terrace space on Graslei's gorgeous canalside terrace. There's fast food around Korenmarkt and great-value Turkish options along Sleepstraat. Numerous vegetarian and organic choices feature on the tourist office's free Veggieplan Gent guide map. Thursday is Veggieday.

't Oud Clooster TAVERNA €
(☎09-233 78 02; www.toudclooster.be; Zwartezusterstraat 5; mains €9-18; ⏲noon-2.30pm & 6-10.30pm Mon-Fri, noon-2.30pm & 5-10.30pm Sat, 5-10.30pm Sun) Mostly candlelit at night, this atmospheric double-level 'pratcafe' is built into sections of what was long ago a nunnery, hence the sprinkling of religious statues and cherub lamp-holders. Well-priced cafe food is presented with unexpected style. Try the original curry-cream *Spaghetti Oud Clooster*.

Soup Lounge SOUP €
(www.souplounge.be; Zuivelbrug 4; small/large soup €4/5, sandwiches €2.80; ⏲10am-6pm) At this bright, central '70s-retro soup kitchen, each bowlful comes with add-your-own cheese and croutons, two rolls and a piece of fruit. Canal views are free.

Amadeus RIBS €
(☎09-225 13 85; www.amadeusspareribrestaurant.be; Plotersgracht 8/10; mains €13.75-18.75; ⏲6.30-11pm) All-you-can-eat spare ribs at four Ghent addresses, all within ancient buildings that are full of atmosphere, bustle and cheerful conversation.

Drinking & Entertainment

Try the snug **Hot Club de Gand** (www.hotclubdegand.be; Schuddevisstraatje-Groentenmarkt 15b; ⏲11.30am-late) for live jazz, gyspy or blues music, **Hotsy Totsy** (www.hotsytotsy.be; Hoogstraat 1; ⏲6pm-1am Mon-Fri, 8pm-2am Sat & Sun) for free Thursday jazz, and beautifully panelled **Rococo** (Corduwaniersstraat 5; ⏲from 10pm) for candlelit conversation. **Het Waterhuis aan de Bierkant** (www.waterhuisaandebierkant.be; Groentenmarkt 12; ⏲11am-1am) has the best beer choice including its own brews, **Pink Flamingo's** (www.pinkflamingos.be; Onderstraat 55; ⏲noon-midnight Mon-Wed, noon-3am Thu-Sat, 2pm-midnight Sun) is a retro-kitsch bar, and **Charlatan** (www.charlatan.be; Vlasmarkt 9; ⏲7pm-late Tue-Sun during term) is the place for raucous partying and eclectic live music.

Information

Ghent Tourist Office (☎09-266 56 60; www.visitgent.be; Oude Vismijn, St-Veerleplein 5; ⏲9.30am-6.30pm mid-Mar–mid-Oct, to 4.30pm mid-Oct–mid-Mar) Very helpful for free maps and accommodation bookings.

Getting There & Away

BUS

Some longer distance buses depart from **Gent-Zuid bus station** (Woodrow Wilsonplein), others from various points around Gent-St-Pieters train station.

TRAIN

Gent-Dampoort One kilometre west of the old city, this is the handiest station but only some trains stop here, including three hourly runs to Antwerp (€9.40, fast/slow 42/64 minutes) and an hourly Bruges service (€6.50, 36 minutes).

Gent-St-Pieters Located 2.5km south of the city centre, this is the main station for Brussels (€8.90, 35 minutes, twice hourly). From here there are five hourly hops to Bruges (fast/slow 24/42 minutes).

Getting Around

BICYCLE

Max Mobiel (www.max-mobiel.be; Vokselslaan 27; per day/week/month €9/25/30) Two minutes' walk south of Gent-St-Pieters station. Branch kiosk at Gent-Dampoort station.

BUS & TRAM

One-hour/all-day tickets cost €1.30/5 if purchased ahead of time from ticket machines or De Lijn offices beside **Gent-St-Pieters** (⏲7am-1.30pm & 2-7pm Mon-Fri) or in the **centre** (www.delijn.be; Cataloniestraat 4; ⏲10.15am-5pm Mon-Sat). Handy tram 1 runs from Gent-St-Pieters through the centre passing within walking distance of most major sites.

Bruges

POP 117,400

Cobblestone lanes, dreamy canals, soaring spires and whitewashed almshouses combine to make central Bruges (Brugge in Dutch) one of Europe's most picture-perfect historic cities. The only problem is that everyone knows of these charms, and the place gets mobbed.

BRUGES CITY CARD

A **Bruges City Card** (www.bruggecitycard.be; 48/72hr €46/49) gets you into numerous museums and scores you a free **canal boat tour** (adult/child €7.60/3.40; 10am-6pm Mar–mid-Nov) and discounts on bicycle rental.

Sights

The real joy of Bruges is simply wandering alongside the canals, soaking up the atmosphere. To avoid the worst crowds, explore east of pretty Jan van Eyckplein.

Markt SQUARE

The heart of ancient Bruges, the old market square is lined with pavement cafes beneath step-gabled facades. The buildings aren't always quite as medieval as they look, but together they create a fabulous scene and even the neo-Gothic **post office** is architecturally magnificent. The scene is dominated by the **Belfort**, Belgium's most famous belfry whose iconic octagonal tower is arguably better appreciated from afar than by climbing 366 claustrophobic steps to the top.

Historium MUSEUM

(www.historium.be; Markt 1; adult/child €11/5.50; 10am-6pm) An 'immersive' one-hour audio and video tour, the lavish Historium aims to take you back to medieval Bruges: you can survey the old port or watch Van Eyck paint. It's a little light on facts so for many it will be a diversion from the real sights of the city, perhaps best for entertaining kids on a rainy day.

Burg SQUARE

Bruges' 1420 **Stadhuis** (City Hall; Burg 12) is smothered in statuettes and contains a breathtaking **Gotische Zaal** (Gothic Hall; Burg; adult/concession €4/3; 9.30am-5pm), featuring dazzling polychromatic ceilings, hanging vaults and historicist murals. Tickets include entry to part of the early baroque **Brugse Vrije** (Burg 11a; 9.30am-noon & 1.30-4.30pm) next door. With its gilt highlights and golden statuettes, this palace was once the administrative centre for a large autonomous territory ruled from Bruges between 1121 and 1794.

★ **Groeningemuseum** GALLERY

(www.brugge.be; Dijver 12; adult/concession €8/6; 9.30am-5pm Tue-Sun) Bruges' most celebrated art gallery, an astonishingly rich collection whose strengths are in superb Flemish Primitive and Renaissance works, depicting the conspicuous wealth of the city with glitteringly realistic artistry. In room 2 are meditative works including Jan Van Eyck's 1436 radiant masterpiece *Madonna with Canon George Van der Paele* (1436) and the *Madonna* by the Master of the Embroidered Foliage, where the rich fabric of the Madonna's robe meets the 'real' foliage at her feet with exquisite detail.

★ **Museum St-Janshospitaal** MUSEUM

(Memlingmuseum; Mariastraat 38; adult/child €8/free; 9.30am-5pm Tue-Sun) In the restored chapel of a 12th-century hospital building with superb timber beamwork, this museum shows various torturous-looking medical implements, hospital sedan chairs and a gruesome 1679 painting of an anatomy class. But it is much better known for six masterpieces by 15th-century artist Hans Memling, including the enchanting reliquary of St Ursula. This gilded oak reliquary looks like a mini Gothic cathedral, painted with scenes from the life of St Ursula, including highly realistic Cologne cityscapes.

Brouwerij De Halve Maan BREWERY

(050 33 26 97; www.halvemaan.be; Walplein 26; 10.30am-6pm, closed mid-Jan) Founded in 1856, this is the last family *brouwerij* (brewhouse) in central Bruges. Multilingual **guided visits** (tours €7.50; 11am-4pm, to 5pm Sat), lasting 45 minutes, depart on each hour. They include a tasting but can sometimes be rather crowded. Alternatively, you can simply sip one of the excellent *Brugse Zot* (Bruges Fool, 7%) or *Straffe Hendrik* (Strong Henry, 9%) beers in the appealing brewery *café*.

Begijnhof BEGIJNHOF

(Wijngaardstraat; 6.30am-6.30pm) FREE Bruges' delightful *begijnhof* originally dates from the 13th century. Although the last *begijn*

Bruges

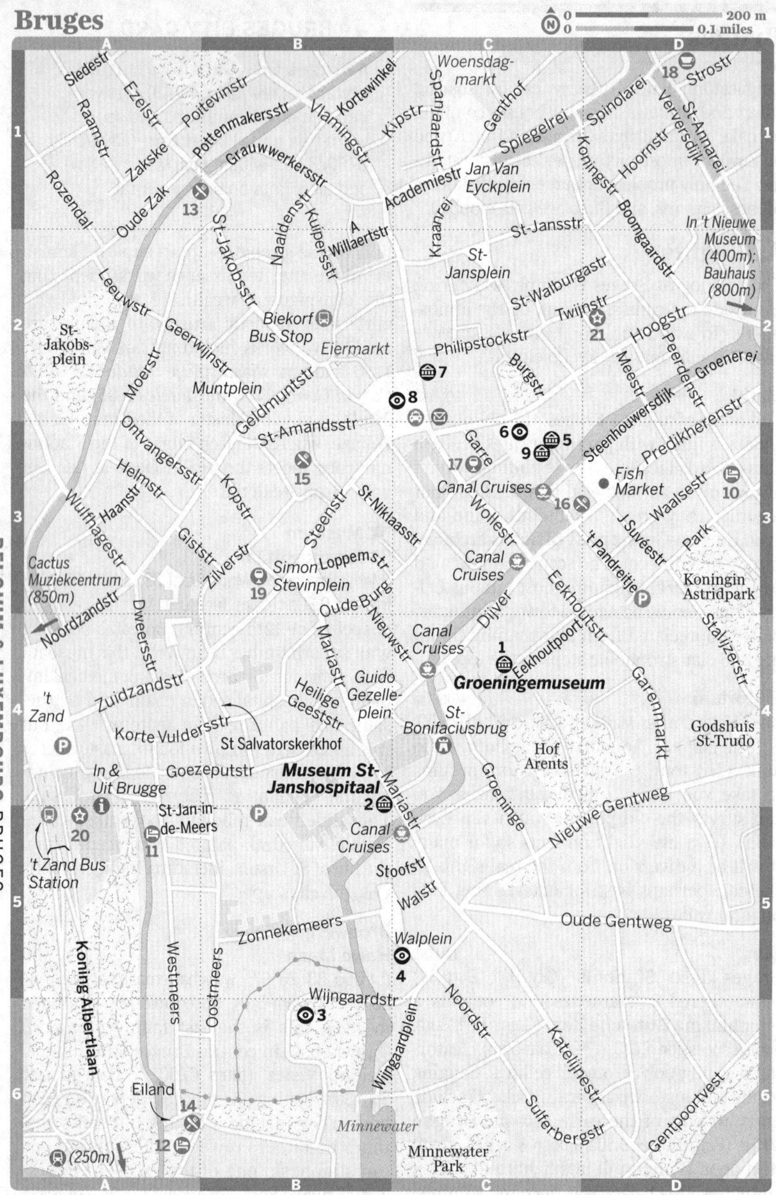

has long since passed away, today residents of the pretty, whitewashed garden complex include a convent of Benedictine nuns. Despite the hoards of summer tourists, the *begijnhof* remains a remarkably tranquil haven. In spring a carpet of daffodils adds to the quaintness of the scene. Outside the 1776 gateway bridge lies a tempting, if predictably tourist-priced, array of terraced restaurants, lace shops and waffle peddlers.

Bruges

Top Sights
1 Groeningemuseum ... C4
2 Museum St-Janshospitaal ... B4

Sights
3 Begijnhof ... B6
4 Brouwerij De Halve Maan ... C5
5 Brugse Vrije ... C3
6 Burg ... C3
Gotische Zaal ... (see 9)
7 Historium ... C2
8 Markt ... C2
9 Stadhuis ... C3

Sleeping
10 B&B Dieltiens ... D3
11 Baert B&B ... A5
12 't Keizershof ... A6

Eating
13 De Bottelier ... A1
14 De Stoepa ... A6
15 De Stove ... B3
16 Est Wijnbar ... C3

Drinking & Nightlife
17 De Garre ... C3
18 Herberg Vlissinghe ... D1
19 't Brugs Beertje ... B3

Entertainment
20 Concertgebouw ... A5
21 Retsin's Lucifernum ... D2

Tours

Quasimodo BUS
(050 37 04 70; www.quasimodo.be) Quasimodo has minibus Triple Treat tours (under/over 26 €45/55) at 9am on Monday, Wednesday and Friday from February to mid-December which visit a selection of castles plus the fascinating WWII coastal defences near Ostend. Its Flanders Fields tours (under/over 26 €45/55) at 9am Tuesday to Sunday, April to October, visits Ypres Salient.

Quasimundo BICYCLE
(050 33 07 75; www.quasimundo.eu; adult/student €28/26; Mar-Oct) Guided bicycle tours around Bruges (2½ hours, morning) or via Damme to the Dutch border (four hours, afternoon). Bike rental included. Book ahead.

Sleeping

Although there are well over 250 hotels and B&Bs, accommodation can still prove oppressively overbooked from Easter to September, over Christmas and especially at weekends, when two-night minimum stays are commonly required. In the lowest seasons (early November, late January), midrange options sometimes give big last-minute discounts. An all-night touch-screen computer outside the main tourist office displays hotel availability and contact information. The website www.brugge.be has a booking engine.

't Keizershof HOTEL €
(050 33 87 28; www.hotelkeizershof.be; Oostermeers 126; s €35-47, d €47; P) Remarkably tasteful and well kept for this price, the seven simple rooms with shared bathrooms are above a former brasserie-*café* decorated with old radios (now used as the breakfast room). Free parking.

Bauhaus HOSTEL €
(050 34 10 93; www.bauhaus.be; Langestraat 145; hostel dm/tw €16/50, hotel s/d €16/50, 2-4 person apt per weekend from €240; @) One of Belgium's most popular hang-outs for young travellers, this virtual backpacker 'village' incorporates a bustling hostel, apartments, a nightclub, internet cafe and a little chill-out room that's well hidden behind the reception and laundrette section at Langestraat 145. Simple and slightly cramped dorms are operated with key cards; hotel-section double rooms have private shower cubicles. Bike hire is also available. Take bus 6 or 16 from the train station.

★**Baert B&B** B&B €€
(050 33 05 30; www.bedandbreakfastbrugge.be; Westmeers 28; s/d €80/90) In a 1613 former stable this is one of very few places in Bruges where you'll get a private canalside terrace

WHAT'S A BEGIJNHOF?

Usually enclosed around a central garden, a *begijnhof* (*béguinage* in French) is a pretty cluster of historic houses originally built to house lay sisters. The idea originated in the 12th century when many such women were left widowed by their crusader-knight husbands. Today 14 of Flanders' historic *begijnhoven* have been declared Unesco World Heritage sites with great examples at Diest, Lier, Turnhout, Kortrijk and Bruges, which also has dozens of smaller *godshuizen* (almshouses).

(flower-decked, though not on the loveliest canal section). Floral rooms have bathrooms across the landing; bathrobes are provided. A big breakfast spread is served in a glass verandah, and extras include a welcome drink and a pack of chocolates.

★B&B Dieltiens B&B €€
(050 33 42 94; www.bedandbreakfastbruges.be; Waalsestraat 40; s €60-80, d €70-90, tr €90-100) Old and new art fills this lovingly restored classical mansion, which remains an appealingly real home run by charming musician hosts. Superbly central yet quiet. They also operate a holiday flat nearby in a 17th-century house.

Eating

Est Wijnbar TAPAS €
(050 33 38 39; www.wijnbarest.be; Braambergstraat 7; mains €9.50-12.50, tapas €3.50-9.50; 4pm-midnight Wed-Sun;) This attractive little wine bar – the building dates back to 1637 – is an especially lively spot on Sunday nights, when you can catch live jazz, blues and occasionally other musical styles from 8.30pm. It's also a pleasantly informal supper spot, with *raclette,* pasta, snacks and salads on the menu, and tasty desserts.

★De Stove BISTRO €€
(050 33 78 35; www.restaurantdestove.be; Kleine St-Amandsstraat 4; mains €19-33, menu without/with wine €48/65; noon-1.30pm Sat & Sun, 7-9pm Fri-Tue) Just 20 seats keep this gem intimate. Fish caught daily is the house speciality, but the monthly changing menu also includes the likes of wild boar fillet on oyster mushrooms. Everything, from the bread to the ice cream, is homemade. Despite perennially rave reviews, this calm, one-room, family restaurant remains friendly, reliable and inventive, without a hint of tourist tweeness.

★In 't Nieuwe Museum PUB €€
(050 33 12 22; www.nieuw-museum.com; Hooistraat 42; mains €16-22; noon-2pm & 6-10pm Thu-Tue, closed lunch Sat) So called because of the museumlike collection of brewery plaques, money boxes and other mementoes of cafe life adorning the walls, this family-owned local favourite serves five kinds of *dagschotel* (dish of the day) for lunch (€7 to €12.50), and succulent meat cooked on a 17th-century open fire in the evenings.

De Bottelier MEDITERRANEAN €€
(050 33 18 60; www.debottelier.com; St-Jakobsstraat 63; mains from €16; lunch & dinner Tue-Fri, dinner Sat) Decorated with hats and old clocks, this adorable little restaurant sits above a wine shop overlooking a delightful handkerchief of canalside garden. Pasta/veg dishes cost from €9/13.50. Diners are predominantly local. Reservations are wise.

De Stoepa BISTRO €€
(050 33 04 54; www.stoepa.be; Oostmeers 124; noon-2pm & 6pm-midnight Tue-Sat, noon-3pm & 6-11pm Sun) A gem of a place in a peaceful residential setting with a slightly hippie/Buddhist feel. Oriental statues, terracotta-coloured walls, a metal stove and wooden floors and furniture give a homey but stylish feel. Best of all though is the leafy terrace garden. Tuck into its upmarket bistro-style food.

Drinking & Nightlife

Beer-specialist cafes include **'t Brugs Beertje** (www.brugsbeertje.be; Kemelstraat 5; 4pm-midnight Mon, Thu & Sun, to 1am Fri & Sat) and alley-hidden **De Garre** (050 34 10 29; www.degarre.be; Garre 1; noon-midnight Mon-Thu, to 1am Fri & Sat) serving its own fabulous 11% Garre house brew. Old-world classic **Herberg Vlissinghe** (050 34 37 37; www.cafevlissinghe.be; Blekerstraat 2; 11am-10pm Wed & Thu, to midnight Fri & Sat, to 7pm Sun) dates from 1515. Eiermarkt, just north of Markt, has many plain but lively bars, with DJs and seemingly endless happy hours. If you're feeling brave, have a drink with a self-proclaimed vampire at the wildly eccentric **Retsin's Lucifernum** (0476 35 06 51; www.lucifernum.be; Twijnstraat 6-8; admission incl drink €6; 8-11pm Sun).

Entertainment

Concertgebouw CONCERT VENUE
(050 47 69 99; www.concertgebouw.be; 't Zand 34; tickets from €10) Bruges' stunning 21st-century concert hall is the work of architects Paul Robbrecht and Hilde Daem and takes its design cues from the city's three famous towers and red bricks. Theatre, classical music and dance are regularly staged. The tourist office is situated at street level.

Cactus Muziekcentrum LIVE MUSIC
(050 33 20 14; www.cactusmusic.be; Magdalenastraat 27) Though small, this is the city's top

venue for contemporary and world music, both live bands and international DJs. It also organises festivals including July's **Cactus Music Festival** (www.cactusfestival.be; ⌚Jul), held in the Minnewater park at the southern edge of the old city.

Information

Bruggecentraal (www.bruggecentraal.be) has events listings.

In & Uit Brugge (☎050 44 46 46; www.brugge.be; 't Zand 34; ⌚10am-6pm Mon-Sun) The tourist office is situated at street level of the big, red Concertgebouw concert hall with a branch at the train station. Standard city maps cost €0.50, comprehensive guide pamphlets €2. Excellent **Use-It guide-maps** (www.use-it.be) are free if you ask for one.

Getting There & Away

Bruges' train station is about 1.5km south of the Markt, a lovely walk via the Begijnhof.

Antwerp (€14.80, 75 minutes) Twice hourly.

Brussels (€14.10, one hour) Twice hourly.

Ghent (€6.50, fast/slow 24/42 minutes) Five hourly; two continue to more central Gent-Dampoort.

Ypres (Ieper in Dutch) Take a train to Roeselare (€5, fast/slow 22/33 minutes), then bus 94 or 95: both buses pass key WWI sites en route.

Getting Around

BICYCLE

B-Bike (☎0499 70 50 99; Zand Parking 26; per hr/day €4/12; ⌚10am-7pm Apr-Oct)

Rijwielhandel Erik Popelier (☎050 34 32 62; www.fietsenpopelier.be; Mariastraat 26; per hr/half/full day €4/8/12, tandem €10/17/25; ⌚10am-6pm) Good bicycles for adults and kids; helmets for hire, free map, no deposit.

BUS

To get from the train station to Markt, take any bus marked 'Centrum'. For the way back, buses stop at Biekorf, just northwest of Markt on Kuiperstraat.

Ypres

POP 34,900

During WWI (1914–18), historic Ypres (pronounced 'eepr'; Ieper in Dutch) was bombarded into oblivion while futile battles raged between trench networks in the surrounding poppy fields. Today, many medieval buildings have been meticulously rebuilt and the battlefields in Ypres' rolling agricultural hinterland (called the Ypres Salient) are a moving reminder of the horrors of war, with their seemingly endless graveyards and memorials.

Sights

Central Ypres

Grote Markt SQUARE

The brilliantly rebuilt **Lakenhallen**, a vast Gothic edifice originally serving as the 13th-century cloth market, dominates this very photogenic central square. It sports a 70m-high belfry, reminiscent of London's Big Ben, and hosts the gripping museum **In Flanders Fields** (www.inflandersfields.be; Lakenhallen, Grote Markt 34; adult/youth €9/4-5; ⌚10am-6pm Apr–mid-Nov, to 5pm Tue-Sun mid-Nov–Mar), a multimedia WWI experience honouring ordinary people's experiences of wartime horrors. It's very highly recommended. The ticket allows free entry to three other minor city museums.

Menin Gate MEMORIAL

(Menenpoort) A block east of Grote Markt, the famous Menin Gate is a huge stone gateway straddling the main road at the city moat. It's inscribed with the names of 54,896 'lost' British and Commonwealth WWI troops whose bodies were never found.

Ypres Salient

Many WWI sites are in rural locations that are awkward to reach without a car or tour bus. But the following are all within 600m of Ypres–Roeselare bus routes 94 and 95 (once or twice hourly weekdays, five daily weekends), so could be visited en route between Ypres and Bruges.

LAST POST

At 8pm daily, traffic through the Menin Gate is halted while buglers sound the **Last Post** (www.lastpost.be; ⌚8pm) in remembrance of the WWI dead, a moving tradition started in 1928. Every evening the scene is different, possibly accompanied by pipers, troops of cadets or maybe a military band.

Memorial Museum Passchendaele 1917 MUSEUM
(www.passchendaele.be; Ieperstraat 5; admission €7.50; ⌚10am-6pm Feb-Nov; 🚌94) In central Zonnebeke village, **Kasteel Zonnebeke** (www.zonnebeke.be) is a lake-fronted Normandy chalet-style mansion built in 1922 to replace a castle bombarded into rubble during WWI. It now hosts a tourist office, cafe and a particularly polished WWI museum charting local battle progressions with plenty of multilingual commentaries. The big attraction here is descending into its multiroom 'trench experience' with low-lit, wooden-clad subterranean bunk rooms and a soundtrack to add wartime atmosphere. Entirely indoors, explanations are much more helpful here than in 'real' trenches elsewhere.

Tyne Cot CEMETERY
(⌚24hr, visitor centre 9am-6pm Feb-Nov; 🚌94) FREE Probably the most visited Salient site, this is the world's biggest British Commonwealth war cemetery, with 11,956 graves. A huge semicircular wall commemorates another 34,857 lost-in-action soldiers whose names wouldn't fit on Ypres' Menin Gate. The name Tyne Cot was coined by Northumberland fusiliers who fancied that German bunkers on the hillside here looked like Tyneside cottages. Two such dumpy concrete bunkers sit amid the graves, with a third partly visible through the metal wreath beneath the central white Cross of Sacrifice.

Deutscher Soldatenfriedhof CEMETERY
FREE The area's main German WWI cemetery is smaller than Tyne Cot but arguably more memorable, amid oak trees and trios of squat, mossy crosses. Some 44,000 corpses were grouped together here, up to 10 per granite grave slab, and four eerie silhouette statues survey the site. Entering takes you through a black concrete 'tunnel' that clanks and hisses with distant war sounds, while four short video montages commemorate the tragedy of war. It's beyond the northern edge of Langemark on bus route 95.

Tours

Over the Top BUS
(☎0472 34 87 47; www.overthetoptours.be; Meensestraat 41; tours €40; ⌚9am-12.30pm, 1.30-5.30pm & 7.30-8.30pm) A WWI specialist bookshop towards the Menin Gate, offering twice-daily, half-day guided minibus tours of the Ypres Salient.

British Grenadier BUS
(☎057 21 46 57; www.salienttours.be; Meensestraat 5; short/long tour €30/38; ⌚9.30am-1pm, 2-6pm & 7.30-8.30pm) Two Ypres tours – the 2½-hour option takes in Hill 60, the Caterpillar Crater and the German Bayernwald trench complex, while the standard four-hour tour covers every site on the Salient.

Sleeping & Eating

Ariane Hotel HOTEL €€
(☎057 21 82 18; www.ariane.be; Slachthuisstraat 58; s/d from €89/109; P 📶) This peaceful, professionally managed, large hotel has a designer feel to the rooms and popular restaurant while wartime memorabilia dots the spacious common areas.

B&B Ter Thuyne B&B €€
(☎057 36 00 42; www.terthuyne.be; Gustave de Stuersstraat 19; d €95; @) Three comfortable rooms that are luminously bright and scrupulously clean, but not overly fashion-conscious.

★**Main Street Hotel** GUESTHOUSE €€€
(☎057 46 96 33; www.mainstreet-hotel.be; Rijselsestraat 136; d €180-260; 📶) Jumbling funky eccentricity with historical twists and luxurious comfort, this is a one-off that simply oozes character. The smallest room is designed like a mad professor's experiment, the breakfast room has a Tiffany glass ceiling…and so it goes on!

★**De Ruyffelaer** FLEMISH €€
(☎057 36 60 06; www.deruyffelaer.be; Gustave de Stuersstraat 9; mains €15-21, menus €24-33; ⌚11.30am-3.30pm Sun, 5.30-9.30pm Thu-Sun) Traditional local dishes served in an adorable, wood-panelled interior with old checkerboard floors and a brocante decor, including dried flowers, old radios and antique biscuit tins.

Information

Toerisme Ieper (☎057 23 92 20; www.ieper.be; Grote Markt 34; ⌚9am-6pm) The well-equipped tourist office is within the Lakenhallen.

Getting There & Around

BICYCLE

Hotel Ambrosia (☎057 36 63 66; www.ambrosiahotel.be; D'Hondtstraat 54; standard/electric bike per day €12/30; ⌚7.30am-7pm) Bicycle rentals.

BUS

Services pick up passengers in Grote Markt's northeast corner (check the direction carefully!). For Bruges take Roeselare-bound routes 94 or 95 then change to train.

TRAIN

Services run hourly to Ghent (€11.50, one hour) and Brussels (€17.50, 1¾ hours) via Kortrijk (€5.30, 30 minutes), where you could change for Bruges or Antwerp.

WALLONIA

Parlez-vous français? You'll need to in hilly Wallonia, Belgium's French-speaking southern half. Wallonia's cities do have their charms, though none quite manage to outshine the many Flemish 'art cities'. Wallonia's foremost attractions are mostly rural – outdoor activities, fabulous caves and ancient rural castles. This is where you'll really appreciate having your own wheels for easier access.

Mons

POP 93,100

It's fair to say that historic Mons (Bergen in Dutch) was a little slow off the starting blocks in embracing its role as European City of Culture in 2015, with many projects well behind schedule: Santiago Calatrava's train station won't open till 2018. The cube-like modern **BAM gallery** (Musée des Beaux-Arts; ☎065 40 53 24; www.bam.mons.be; Rue Neuve 8; adult/concession €8/5; ⊙hours vary) is worth a visit though, and other attractions include the 80m baroque **Beffroi** (belfry), the oversized 15th-century church of **Ste-Waudru** (www.waudru.be; Place du Chapitre; ⊙9am-6pm) and the attractive **Grand Place**. This great square comes to life on Trinity Sunday when the festivities of the **Ducasse** (www.ducasse demons) reach a raucous culmination with a George versus the dragon battle.

Dream Hotel (☎065 32 97 20; www.dreammons.be; Rue de la Grand Triperie 17; s/d €75/90; P @) offers accommodation in a quirkily decorated 19th-century chapel. For eating, tavern-style local favourite **Henri** (☎065 35 23 06; Rue d'Havré 41; ⊙noon-2.30pm & 6.30-9pm Tue-Sat, noon-2.30pm Sun & Mon) has been serving Mons dishes since 1956, while for an unforgettable dinner in 17th-century style don't miss the **Salon des Lumières** (☎0474 29 25 84; www.salondeslumieres.com; Rue du Mirroir 23; mains €16.50-20; ⊙7-10pm Wed-Sun, from 6pm winter).

WORTH A TRIP

CASTLES IN WALLONIA

By public transport you'll spend longer reaching most of Wallonia's castles than actually enjoying them. By car though, combining a handful of destinations can make for a very enjoyable day out. Wallonia's capital Namur is dominated by a massive, sober, fortified citadel, but the region has many more romantic castles including gingerbread fantasy **Château de Jehay** (www.chateaujehay.be; adult/student €5/4; ⊙2-6pm Tue-Fri, 11am-6pm Sat & Sun Apr-Sep), majestic **Château de Modave** (www.modave-castle.be; adult/youth €7.50/4; ⊙10am-5pm Tue-Sun Apr–mid-Nov; 🚻), moated fortress **Château de Lavaux-Sainte-Anne** (www.chateau-lavaux.com; adult/child €7/5; ⊙9am-5.30pm Wed-Sun, last entry 4.15pm) and crusader citadel **Château de Bouillon** (☎061 46 42 02; www.bouillon-initiative.be; Rue du Château; adult/child €7/5; ⊙10am-7pm Jul & Aug, to 5pm Mar-Jun & Sep-Nov; P 🚻).

Liège

POP 196,200

Beneath its brutally disfigured, post-industrial surface, sprawling Liège (Luik in Dutch) is a living architectural onion concealing layer upon layer of history. Fine churches abound, as befits a city that spent 800 years as the capital of an independent principality run by bishops. Proudly free-spirited citizens are disarmingly friendly and no Belgian city bubbles with more joie de vivre.

The somewhat grimy historic zone has several excellent museums. The **Grand Curtius** (www.grandcurtiusliege.be; Féronstrée 136; adult/child €9/free; ⊙10am-6pm Wed-Mon) presents a millennium's development of decorative arts, and art gallery **Musée des Beaux-Arts** (www.beauxartsliege.be; Féronstrée 86; adult/youth €5/3; ⊙10am-6pm Tue-Sun) is richly endowed, if a bit brutal architecturally.

Love it or loathe it, Liège is quirky and oddly compulsive, especially during its chaotic 15 August **festival**, held just across the river in the self-declared 'republic' of Outremeuse where there's a handy **Auberge de**

Jeunesse (☎04-344 56 89; www.lesaubergesdejeunesse.be; Rue Georges Simenon 2; dm/s/d €23/36.50/54.75; @). The most appealing central accommodation options are the cosy little **Hôtel Hors Château** (☎04-250 60 68; www.hors-chateau.be; Rue Hors Château 62; s/d/ste €78/95/125;) and the dramatic **Crowne Plaza** (☎04-222 94 94; www.crowneplazaliege.be; Mont St-Martin 9; r €109-690). For real Liègois food dine at **Le Bistrot d'en Face** (☎04-223 15 84; www.lebistrotdenface.be; Rue de la Goffe 10; mains €15-18; noon-2.30pm & 7-10.30pm Wed-Sun, closed lunch Sat) or **Amon Nanesse** (www.maisondupeket.be; Rue de l'Epée 4; meals €10.50-19.50; 10am-2am, kitchen noon-2.30pm & 6-10.30pm).

Liège's great archtectural masterpiece is its 21st-century **Guillermins train station**, shaped vaguely like a giant concrete manta-ray. That's on the Brussels–Frankfurt mainline, though Liège-Palais station is far more central.

LUXEMBOURG

Ruled by its own monarchy, the Grand Duchy of Luxembourg is famed for its banks but visually it's mostly an undulating series of pretty wooded hills dotted with castle villages. These are made accessible from the attractive capital city by excellent roads and a very well organised single-price public transport system. Luxembourg has its own language, Lëtzeburgesch, in which *moien* is the standard greeting. But most Luxembourgers also speak French and German.

Luxembourg City

POP 100,000

World Heritage–listed Luxembourg City sits high on a promontory overlooking the deep-cut valleys of the Pétrusse and Alzette Rivers. These gorges were the key to the city's defence from AD 963 when Count Sigefroi (or Siegfried) of Ardennes built a castle here. Luxembourg eventually grew to become one of Europe's strongest fortresses, earning the nickname 'Gibraltar of the North'. In 1867 the majority of the fortifications were removed as part of a treaty to reduce tensions between France and Germany, though a remarkable mass of bastion remnants and tunnels survives, providing visitors with spectacular viewpoints overlooking the old quarters of Clausen, Pfaffenthal and the Grund.

LUXEMBOURG CARD

The brilliant value **Luxembourg Card** (www.ont.lu/en/luxembourg-card; 1-/2-/3-day adult €11/19/27, family €28/48/68), marked LC in reviews, allows free admission to most of the grand duchy's main attractions and unlimited use of public transport nationwide. You can buy it from tourist offices, museums or certain hotels.

Sights

Old Town

Within the compact, mostly pedestrianised Old Town all sights are walking distance from each other. Access to the fairy-tale Grund area is easiest using a public elevator on Plateau du St-Esprit.

★Chemin de la Corniche PROMENADE

This pedestrian promenade has been hailed as 'Europe's most beautiful balcony'. It winds along the course of the 17th-century city ramparts with views across the river canyon towards the hefty fortifications of the Wenzelsmauer (Wenceslas Wall). Across Rue Sigefroi, the rampart-top walk continues along Blvd Victor Thorn to the Dräi Tier (Triple Gate) tower.

★Musée d'Histoire de la Ville de Luxembourg MUSEUM

(Luxembourg City History Museum; www.mhvl.lu; 14 Rue du St-Esprit; adult/LC €5/free; 10am-6pm Tue-Sun, to 8pm Thu) This remarkably engrossing and interactive museum hides within a series of 17th-century houses, including a former 'holiday home' of the Bishop of Orval. A lovely garden and open terrace offer great views.

Royal Palace PALACE

(17 Rue du Marché-aux-Herbes; tours €7; guided tours 4pm Mon-Sat mid-Jul & Aug) Photogenically a-twitter with little pointy turrets, this 1573 palace has been much extended over the years. It now houses the Grand Duke's office with parliament using its 1859 annexe. For a brief period in summer the palace opens for gently humorous 45-minute **guided tours**, which deal mostly with the Duke's family history. From the medieval-gothic dining room,

the palace's interior style morphs into sumptuous gilded romanticism upstairs.

MNHA MUSEUM
(Musée National d'Histoire et d'Art; www.mnha.lu; Marché-aux-Poissons; adult/LC €7/free; 10am-6pm Tue-Sun, to 8pm Thu) Startlingly modern for its Old Town setting, this unusual museum offers a fascinating if uneven coverage of art and history. It starts deep in an excavated rocky basement with exhibits of Neolithic flints then sweeps you somewhat unevenly through Gallic tomb chambers, Roman mosaics and Napoleonic medals to an excellent if relatively small art gallery. Cezanne and Picasso get a look-in while Luxembourg's Expressionist artist Joseph Kutter (1894–1941) gets a whole floor.

Cathédrale Notre Dame CHURCH
(Blvd Roosevelt; 10am-noon & 2-5.30pm) Most memorable for its distinctively elongated black spires, the 17th-century cathedral contains a tiny but highly revered Madonna-and-child idol (above the altar) and the graves of the royal family (in the crypt).

Spuerkeess MUSEUM, ARCHITECTURE
(Banque et Caisse d'Épargne de l'État; www.bcee.lu; 1 Place de Metz) FREE In a dramatic, century-old, castle-style building, Spuerkeess is the state savings bank, and hosts an intriguing **Bank Museum** (9am-5.30pm Mon-Fri) tracing 150 years of tradition and innovation in banking, from piggy banks to ATMs and bank robbers.

Kirchberg

Luxembourg's shiny-glass business district and Eurocrat 'ghetto' is across the Pont Grande-Duchesse Charlotte, the city's giant, iconic red bridge.

★**Mudam** GALLERY
(www.mudam.lu; 3 Parc Dräi Eechelen; adult/LC €7/free; 11am-8pm Wed-Fri, to 6pm Sat-Mon) Ground-breaking exhibitions of modern, installation and experiential art are hosted in this airy architectural icon designed by IM Pei. The museum's collection includes everything from photography to fashion, design and multimedia. The glass-roofed cafe makes a decent lunch/snack spot.

To find Mudam, take bus 1, 13 or 16 to 'Philharmonie', walk around the striking Philharmonie and descend past Hotel Melia. One Friday a month it's open to 10pm.

Sleeping

Luxembourg City's accommodation scene is heavy with business options but online rates are slashed at weekends and in summer.

Auberge de Jeunesse HOSTEL €
(22 68 89; luxembourg@youthhostels.lu; 2 Rue du Fort Olizy; dm/s/d €20.90/34.90/57.80, HI members €23.90/37.90/59; 9) This state-of-the-art hostel has very comfortable, sex-segregated dorms with magnetic-key entry systems. There are good-sized lockers (bring padlock), laundry facilities and masses of relaxing space including a great terrace from which to admire views to the old city. It's a short but steep walking descent from the Casemates area using a stepped path from near the 'Clausen Plateau Altmunster' bus stop.

★**Hôtel Simoncini** HOTEL €€
(22 28 44; www.hotelsimoncini.lu; 6 Rue Notre Dame; s/d Mon-Thu from €155/175, Fri-Sun €125/145;) A delightful contemporary option in the city centre, the Simoncini's foyer is a modern-art gallery and the smart, bright rooms have slight touches of retro-cool. There's free wi-fi in the lobby, and plug-in internet in rooms.

★**Hôtel Parc Beaux-Arts** BOUTIQUE HOTEL €€€
(26 86 76 1; www.parcbeauxarts.lu; 1 Rue Sigefroi; ste Mon-Thu advance/rack rates €190/400, Fri-Sun from €135;) Exuding understated luxury, this charming little hotel comprises a trio of 18th-century houses containing 10 gorgeous suites. Each features original artworks by contemporary artists, oak floors, Murano crystal lamps and a fresh rose daily. Seek out the 'secret' lounge hidden away in the original timber eaves.

Eating

Tree-shaded Place d'Armes overflows with terrace seating in summer and covers all bases from fast food to ritzy resto. Cheaper terraced places can be found on or near relatively unexotic Place de Paris, while for intimate and more original dining options, hunt out the tiny alleys and passages collectively nicknamed Ilôt Gourmand, directly behind the palace.

Anabanana VEGAN €
(www.anabanana.lu; 117 Rue de la Tour Jacob; sandwich/lunch/dinner €5/12/19; noon-2pm Tue-Fri, 7-10pm Tue-Sat;) Quaint, colourful little

Luxembourg City

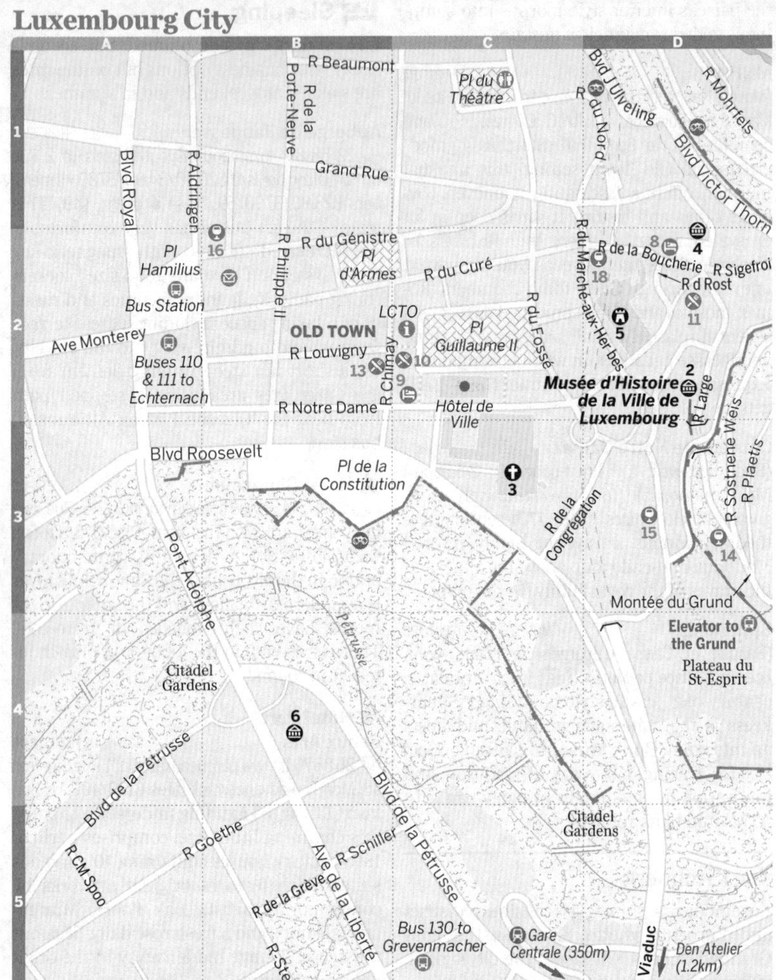

vegan-fusion restaurant with a fixed dinner choice that changes daily. Juice €4.50, no alcohol.

Bosso FRENCH, GERMAN €

(www.bosso.lu; 7 Bisserwée; mains €8.50-16; ⌚5pm-midnight Mon-Thu, from 11am Fri-Sun) In summer, the biggest attraction of this good-value Grund restaurant is the hidden courtyard garden where seating is attractively tree-shaded. Try the *flammeküeche*, wafer-thin Alsatian 'pizzas' made with sour cream instead of tomato sauce, various takes on potato rösti or just linger over a drink.

Cathy Goedert CAFE, BAKERY €

(www.cathygoedert.lu; 8 Rue Chimay; ⌚8am-6pm Tue-Sat, 9am-6pm Sun) This gleaming patisserie/boulangerie/cafe is a good option on Sunday when Luxembourg generally shuts up shop. Sumptuous cakes and pastries, plus a good variety of teas and coffees.

Á la Soupe SOUP €

(www.alasoupe.net; 9 Rue Chimay; breakfast €3.50-7, soup €4.90-7.30; ⌚9am-7.30pm Mon-Sat) Central and minimally stylish soup station serving Moroccan and detox soups, as well as classic chicken.

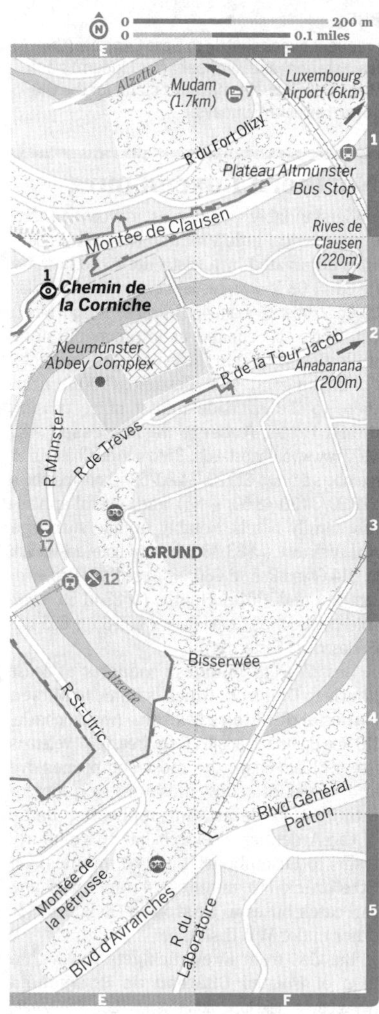

Luxembourg City

Top Sights

1 Chemin de la Corniche E2
2 Musée d'Histoire de la Ville de Luxembourg D2

Sights

Bank Museum .... (see 6)
3 Cathédrale Notre Dame C3
4 MNHA D2
5 Royal Palace D2
6 Spuerkeess B4

Sleeping

7 Auberge de Jeunesse F1
8 Hôtel Parc Beaux-Arts D2
9 Hôtel Simoncini C2

Eating

10 Á la Soupe C2
11 Am Tiirmschen D2
12 Bosso E3
13 Cathy Goedert B2

Drinking & Nightlife

14 Café des Artistes D3
15 De Gudde Wëllen D3
16 L'Interview B2
17 Liquid Café E3
18 Urban Bar D2

Am Tiirmschen LUXEMBOURG €€
(☎26 27 07 33; www.amtiirmschen.lu; 32 Rue de l'Eau, Ilôt Gourmand; mains €13-26; ⊙noon-2pm Tue-Fri, 7-10.30pm Mon-Sat) This is a great place to sample typical Luxembourg dishes, but it also serves good fish and French options in case your companions don't fancy *kniddelen* (dumplings) or smoked pork. It has a semi-successful mix of old and pseudo-old decor with heavy, bowed beams.

Drinking & Entertainment

Nearly a dozen themed bar-restaurant clubs in the **Rives de Clausen** (www.rivesdeclausen.com) form the city's liveliest youth scene. For more atmosphere, try a couple of places in Grund: either boho **Café des Artistes** (22 Montée du Grund; ⊙Tue-Sun) or tucked-away **Liquid Café** (www.liquid.lu; 17 Rue Münster; ⊙5pm-1am Mon-Fri, from 8pm Sat & Sun). Fun central cafe-bars include **Urban Bar** (www.urban.lu/urbancity.html; 2 Rue de la Boucherie; ⊙noon-late, kitchen 1-6pm), **L'Interview** (Rue Aldringen; ⊙7.30am-1am) and **De Gudde Wëllen** (www.deguddewellen.lu; 17 Rue du St-Esprit; ⊙5pm-1am Tue-Thu, 6pm-3am Fri & Sat), which has live-music nights featuring everything from drum and bass to Balkan folk. Some 700m west of Gare Centrale, factory-like **Den Atelier** (☎49 54 66; www.atelier.lu; 54 Rue de Hollerich) hosts a fine range of alternative music gigs.

Information

Bibliothèque Municipale (Municipal Library; 3 Rue Génistre; ⊙10am-7pm Tue-Fri, to 6pm Sat) Sign up (with ID) for one hour's free internet. No printing.

LCTO (Luxembourg City Tourist Office; ☎22 28 09; www.lcto.lu; Place Guillaume II; ⊙9am-6pm Mon-Sat, from 10am Sun) Free city maps, walking-tour pamphlets and event guides.

Getting There & Away

BUS

Useful international connections from beside the train station include Bitburg (bus 401, 1¼ hours) and Trier (bus 118, one hour).

TRAIN

Gare Centrale is 1km south of the old city. There are **left-luggage lockers** (Gare Centrale; per day €3; ⌚6am-9.30pm) at the far north end of platform 3; these are inaccessible at night.

There are trains to the following destinations:

Brussels (€39, two hours)

Diekirch (€2, 30 minutes) Hourly via Ettelbrück.

Liège (from €36.20, 2½ hours) Every two hours via Clervaux (one hour) and Coo (1¾ hours).

Paris (from €56, 145 minutes) By TGV.

Trier (€9-20, 50 minutes) Hourly, several continuing to Koblenz (€46.20, 130 minutes).

Getting Around

TO/FROM LUXEMBOURG AIRPORT

Luxembourg Airport (www.lux-airport.lu) is 6km east of Place d'Armes, 20 minutes by bus 16.

BICYCLE

Vélo en Ville (☎47 96 23 83; 8 Bisserwée; per half day/full day/weekend/week €12.50/20/37.50/100; ⌚10am-noon & 1-8pm Apr-Sep, 7am-3pm Mar & Oct) Mountain bikes and free cycle-routes pamphlet available; tandems cost double. Renters under 26 get 20% discounts.

Velóh (☎800 611 00; www.en.veloh.lu; subscription per week/year €1/15; ⌚24hr) Luxembourg City's short-hop bicycle-rental scheme works in a similar way to Brussels' Villo! (p114). As long as you return the bicycle within 30 minutes to any of 72 stations, each ride is free. The initial subscription is payable by bank card at one of 25 special stands.

LUXEMBOURG'S SIMPLIFIED TRANSPORT SYSTEM

Using bus, train or any combination, travel between any two points in the entire country (except border stations) costs €2/4 for two hours/one day. Buy tickets aboard buses, at train stations or in post offices.

See www.autobus.lu and www.cfl.lu for timetables.

BUS

Frequent buses shuttle to Gare Centrale (the train station) and Kirchberg (for Mudam) from Place Hamilius, the main bus stand for the Old Town. Fewer on Sundays.

Northern Luxembourg

Understandably popular as a weekend getaway, magical little **Vianden** (www.vianden-info.lu) is dominated by a vast slate-roofed **castle** (☎83 41 08 1; www.castle-vianden.lu; adult/child/LC €6/2/free; ⌚10am-4pm Nov-Feb, to 5pm Mar & Oct, to 6pm Apr-Sep) and its impregnable stone walls glow golden in the evening's floodlights. Cobbled Grand Rue descends 700m from there to the riverside tourist office passing the HI Hostel, **Auberge de Jeunesse** (☎83 41 77; www.youthhostels.lu; 3 Montée du Château; HI members dm/s/d €19.20/34.20/55.40, nonmembers €22.20/34.20/48.50; ⊖📶), and several appealing family hotels, notably unique **Auberge Aal Veinen** (☎83 43 68; www.hotel-aal-veinen.lu; 114 Grand Rue; d €80; ⌚closed mid-Dec–mid-Jan; 📶) and **Hôtel Heintz** (☎83 41 55; www.hotel-heintz.lu; 55 Grand Rue; s €55-85, d €65-110; ⌚closed Oct-Easter; 📶).

Bus 570 (18 minutes) connects at least hourly to **Diekirch**, which is home to **Musée National d'Histoire Militaire** (www.mnhm.lu; 110 Rue Bamertal; adult/LC €5/free, WWII veterans free; ⌚10am-6pm), the most comprehensive and visual of many museums commemorating 1944's devastating midwinter Battle of the Ardennes. Diekirch has twice-hourly trains to Luxembourg City (40 minutes) via **Ettelbrück** (10 minutes). From there you can catch buses to **Bastogne** (Belgium) for other major WWII sites.

Bus 545 from Ettelbrück gets you within 2km of isolated **Château de Bourscheid** (www.bourscheid.lu; adult/senior/LC €5/4/free; ⌚9.30am-6pm Apr–mid-Oct, 11am-4pm mid-Oct–Mar), Luxembourg's most evocative medieval ruined castle, and trains run north towards Liège via pretty **Clervaux**, home to a convincingly rebuilt castle that hosts the world-famous **Family of Man photography exhibition** (www.steichencollections.lu; adult/senior €6/4, under 21 free; ⌚noon-6pm Wed-Sun Mar-Jan), established in 1955 and intended as a manifesto for peace. Bus 663 (32 minutes) departs for Vianden at 8.30am, 10am, 2pm and 5pm.

Echternach

POP 5600

Echternach is home to sparse Roman excavations and Luxembourg's most important religious building, a sombre neo-Romanesque basilica rebuilt after merciless WWII bombing.

The town makes a useful base for hiking the well-signposted **Müllerthal Trails** (www.mullerthal-trail.lu) through shoulder-wide microgorges. Trail E1 (11.7km) starts from Echternach bus station, reached via pedestrianised, cafe-lined Rue de la Gare from the attractive main square. Mountain bikes (half/full day €8/15) can be rented from Echternach's modern **HI hostel** (Auberge de Jeunesse; ☎72 01 58; www.youthhostels.lu; HI members dm/s/d €21.20/36.20/53.40, nonmembers €24.20/39.20/60; ⏲reception 8-10am & 5-10pm; P), set in a lakeside country park 2km south of town. To get there head 800m southwest to the fire station (bus stop Centre de Secours on route 110 Luxembourg City–Echternach), then walk 1.2km southeast in the direction of Rodenhof (Roudenhaff). Bus 111 (55 minutes, hourly) takes an alternative route to Luxembourg City via Berdorf.

Moselle Valley

Smothering the Moselle River's steeply rising banks are the neatly clipped vineyards that produce Luxembourg's balanced rieslings, fruity rivaners and excellent *crémants* (sparkling *méthode traditionelle* wines). Taste a selection at the grand **Caves Bernard-Massard** (☎75 05 45 1; www.bernard-massard.lu; 8 Rue du Pont; tour adult/child/LC from €7/4/free; ⏲9.30am-6pm Apr-Oct) in central **Grevenmacher**, where frequent 20-minute winery tours are multilingual and spiced with humour. The Enner der Bréck bus stop outside is on bus routes 130 from Rue Heine in Luxembourg City (55 minutes, once or twice hourly).

Rentabike Miselerland (www.entente-moselle.lu/rentabike-miselerland; per day €10, LC free) bicycles can be rented from Grevenmacher's Butterfly Garden, allowing you to cycle along the riverside route via several other wineries. Return the bicycle at Remich bus station where bus 175 returns to Luxembourg City.

SURVIVAL GUIDE

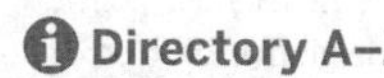

Directory A–Z

ACCOMMODATION

Tourist offices often provide free accommodation-booking assistance.

B&Bs Rooms rented in local homes *(gastenkamers/chambres d'hôtes)* can be cheap and cheerful but some offer standards equivalent to a boutique hotel (up to €160 for a double). Discounts of around €10 per room are common if you stay at least a second night.

Camping Opportunities are plentiful, especially in the Ardennes. For extensive listings see www.campingbelgique.be (Wallonia), www.camping.be (Flanders) and www.camping.lu (Luxembourg).

Holiday houses *Gîtes* are easily rented in **Wallonia** (www.gitesdewallonie.be) and **Luxembourg** (www.gites.lu), but minimum stays apply and there's a hefty 'cleaning fee' on top of quoted rates.

Hostels Typically charge around €20 to €26 for dormitory beds, somewhat less in Bruges. HI hostels (*jeugdherbergen* in Dutch, *auberges de jeunesse* in French) affiliated with **Hostelling International** (www.youthhostels.be) charge €3 less for members, and some take off €2 for under-26-year-olds. Prices usually include sheets and a basic breakfast. Always read the conditions.

Short-term apartments Bookable through sites including www.airbnb.com and www.wimdu.com.

ACTIVITIES

In mostly flat **Flanders** (www.fietsroute.org), bicycles are a popular means of everyday travel

SLEEPING PRICE RANGES

Prices include a double room with a private bathroom, except in hostels or where otherwise specified. Rates quoted are for high season, which is May to September in Bruges, Ypres and the Ardennes, but September to June in business cities. Top-end business establishments in Brussels and Luxembourg City often cut prices radically at weekends and in summer.

€ less than €60

€€ €60 to €140

€€€ more than €140

COUNTRY FACTS

Area 30,278 sq km (Belgium), 2586 sq km (Luxembourg)

Capitals Brussels (Belgium), Luxembourg City (Luxembourg)

Country Codes ☎32 (Belgium), ☎352 (Luxembourg)

Currency Euro (€)

Emergency ☎112

Languages Dutch, French, German, Lëtzeburgesch

Money ATMs are widely available; banks open Monday to Friday

Visas Schengen rules apply

and many roads have dedicated cycle lanes. In **Wallonia** (www.wallonie.be), the hilly terrain favours mountain bikes (VTT).

Canoeing and kayaking are best in the Ardennes, but don't expect rapids of any magnitude.

Local tourist offices have copious information about bicycle paths and sell regional hiking maps.

BUSINESS HOURS

Opening hours given in the text are for high season. Many tourism-based businesses reduce their hours off season.

Banks 9am to 3.30pm Monday to Friday, Saturday mornings too in Luxembourg
Brasseries 11am to midnight
Clubs 11pm to 6am Friday to Sunday
Pubs and cafes to 1am or later
Restaurants 11.30am to 2.30pm and 6.30 to 10.30pm
Shops 10am to 6pm Monday to Saturday, some close for lunch; limited opening on Sunday in Belgium
Supermarkets 9am to 8pm Monday to Saturday, some open Sundays

INTERNET RESOURCES

Belgium (www.belgiumtheplaceto.be)
Flanders (www.visitflanders.com)
Luxembourg (www.ont.lu)
Wallonia (www.wallonia.be)

MONEY

- Banks usually offer better exchange rates than exchange bureaux (*wisselkantoren* in Dutch, *bureaux de change* in French), though often only for their banking clients, especially in Luxembourg.
- ATMs are widespread, but often hidden within bank buildings.
- Tipping is not expected in restaurants or cabs: service and VAT are always included.

PUBLIC HOLIDAYS

School holidays are July and August (slightly later in Luxembourg); one week in early November; two weeks at Christmas; one week around Carnival (February/March); two weeks at Easter; and one week in May (Ascension).

Public holidays are as follows:

New Year's Day 1 January
Easter Monday March/April
Labour Day 1 May
Ascension Day Fortieth day after Easter
Whit Monday Seventh Monday after Easter
National Day (Luxembourg) 23 June
Flemish Community Festival 11 July (Flanders only)
National Day (Belgium) 21 July
Assumption 15 August
Francophone Community Festival 27 September (Wallonia only)
All Saints' Day 1 November
Armistice Day 11 November (Belgium only)
German-Speaking Community Festival 15 November (eastern cantons only)
Christmas Day 25 December

TELEPHONE

- Dial full numbers: there's no optional area code.
- The international telephone code is ☎1234 for Belgium and ☎12410 for Luxembourg.

TOURIST INFORMATION

Excellent free info-maps of each major city are given away by youth hostels or available to download from www.use-it.travel.

VISAS

Schengen visa rules apply. Embassies are listed at www.diplomatie.belgium.be/en and www.mae.lu.

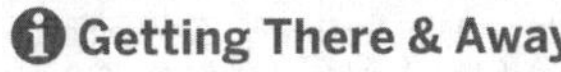

Getting There & Away

AIR

Brussels Airport (BRU; www.brusselsairport.be) is Belgium's main long-haul gateway. Budget airlines **Ryanair** (www.ryanair.com) and **WizzAir** (www.wizzair.com) use the misleadingly named Brussels–South Charleroi Airport, which is actually 55km south of Brussels, 6km north of the ragged, post-industrial city of Charleroi (an hour south of Brussels). These budget airlines offer cheap deals to numerous European destinations.

Luxembourg Airport (www.lux-airport.lu) has various European connections including **EasyJet** (www.easyjet.com) budget flights to London Gatwick.

LAND

Bus

Ecolines (p119) operates from Brussels and Antwerp to various destinations in Eastern Europe.

Eurolines (www.eurolines.eu) is a Europe-wide network. Pre-bookings are compulsory but, although nine Belgian cities are served, only Brussels, Antwerp, Ghent and Liège have ticket offices.

Useful local cross-border buses include De Panne–Dunkerque and Luxembourg City–Trier.

Car & Motorcycle

- Border crossings are not usually controlled.
- Diesel is cheaper than unleaded. Both are cheaper in Luxembourg than almost anywhere else in Western Europe.
- As in France, give way to the right.
- Motorways are toll-free, with a speed limit of 120km/h in Belgium and 130km/h in Luxembourg.

EuroStop (www.eurostop.be; per 100km €4) EuroStop matches paying hitchhikers with drivers for long-distance international rides.

EATING PRICE RANGES

Restaurant price ranges for an average main course.

€ less than €15

€€ €15 to €25

€€€ more than €25

Train

There are excellent train links with neighbouring countries.

- Amsterdam, Paris, Cologne and London are all under 2½ hours from Brussels by high-speed train. Liège, Luxembourg City and Antwerp are also on high-speed international routes. Go via Tournai to reach France by train if you want to avoid such lines and their compulsory reservations.
- For comprehensive timetables and international bookings, see www.belgianrail.be or www.cfl.lu.
- Railcards are valid on standard services but there are surcharges for high-speed lines including **Eurostar** (www.eurostar.com) to London and Lille, **Thalys** (www.thalys.com) to Amsterdam and Paris and **Fyra** (www.b-europe.com) to Amsterdam.
- **ICE** (www.db.de) runs high-speed trains that cover the route Brussels–Liège–Aachen–Cologne–Frankfurt (3¼ hours), while **TGV**

ESSENTIAL FOOD & DRINK

Belgium's famous lagers (eg Stella Artois) and white beers (Hoegaarden) are now global brands. But what has connoisseurs really drooling are the robust, rich 'abbey' beers (originally brewed in monasteries), and the 'Trappist beers' (that still are). Chimay, Rochefort, Westmalle and Orval are the best known. But for beer maniacs the one that really counts is ultra-rare Westvleteren XII.

Dining is a treat in Belgium and Luxembourg, where meals are often described as being French in quality, German in quantity. Classic, home-style dishes include the following:

- **Chicons au gratin** Endive rolled in ham and cooked in cheese/béchamel sauce.
- **Filet Américain** A blob of raw minced beef, typically topped with equally raw egg yolk.
- **Judd mat gaardebounen** Luxembourg's national dish: smoked pork-neck in a cream-based sauce with chunks of potato and broad beans.
- **Kniddelen** Dumplings.
- **Mosselen/moules** Steaming cauldrons of in-the-shell mussels, typically cooked in white wine and served with a mountain of *frites* (chips).
- **Paling in 't groen** Eel in a sorrel or spinach sauce.
- **Stoemp** Mashed veg-and-potato dish.
- **Vlaamse stoverij/carbonade flamande** Semi-sweet beer-based meat casserole.
- **Waterzooi** A cream-based chicken or fish stew.

EUROLINES BUSES FROM BELGIUM

LINE	STANDARD PRICE (€)	SUPER-PROMO PRICE (€)	DURATION (HR)	FREQUENCY
Brussels–Amsterdam	20	9	3½-4½	up to 9 daily
Brussels–Frankfurt	46	24	6	2 daily
Brussels– London	51	9	6 (day), 8½ (night)	2 daily
Bruges–London	48	9	4¼	4 weekly, daily in holidays
Brussels–Paris	34	19	4	10 daily

(www.sncf.com) links to numerous French destinations, albeit bypassing central Paris.

➡ To avoid high-speed surcharges, useful 'ordinary' cross-border services include Liège–Aachen, Tournai–Lille, Antwerp–Rosendaal (for Amsterdam) and Luxembourg–Trier.

SEA

P&O (www.poferries.com) operates a Zeebrugge–Hull route. Pedestrians cost from UK£120 one way. Fourteen hours overnight.

Getting Around

BICYCLE

Cycling is a great way to get around in flat Flanders, less so in chaotic Brussels or undulating Wallonia. The Belgian countryside is riddled with cycling routes and most tourist offices sell helpful regional cycling maps.

➡ Bike hire is available in or near most major train stations. Short-hop hire schemes are available in Brussels, Antwerp, Namur and Luxembourg City.

➡ Bikes on the train are free in Luxembourg. In Belgium it costs €5 one way (or €8 all day) on top of the rail fare. A few busy city-centre train stations don't allow bicycle transport.

BUS & TRAM

Regional buses are well coordinated with Belgium's rail network, but in rural regions you can still find that relatively short distances can involve long waits. In Brussels and Antwerp, trams that run underground are called *premetro*.

CAR & MOTORCYCLE

➡ Motorways are toll free.

➡ Speed limits are 50km/h in most towns (30km/h near schools), 70km/h to 90km/h on inter-town roads, and 120km/h on motorways in Belgium (130km/h in Luxembourg).

➡ The maximum legal blood alcohol limit is 0.05%.

➡ Car hire is available at airports and major train stations, but is usually cheaper from city-centre offices.

TAXI

Taxis must usually be pre-booked but there are ranks near main stations. Tips and taxes are always included in metered fares.

TRAIN

NMBS/SNCB (Belgian Railways; ☎02 528 28 28; www.b-rail.be) NMBS/SNCB trains are non-smoking. B-Excursions are good-value, one-day excursion fares including return rail ticket plus selected entry fees. Weekend Return Tickets valid from 7pm Friday to Sunday night cost just 20% more than a single but on weekdays a return costs twice the single price.

Bosnia & Hercegovina

Includes ➡

Best Places to Eat

- ➡ Mala Kuhinja (p146)
- ➡ Hindin Han (p151)
- ➡ Park Prinčeva (p147)

Best Places to Stay

- ➡ Muslibegović House (p151)
- ➡ Colors Inn (p145)
- ➡ Shangri-La (p151)
- ➡ Hotel Lula (p145)

Why Go?

This craggily beautiful land retains some lingering scars from the heartbreaking civil war in the 1990s. But today visitors will more likely remember Bosnia and Hercegovina (BiH) for its deep, unassuming human warmth and for the intriguing East-meets-West atmosphere born of fascinatingly blended Ottoman and Austro-Hungarian histories.

Major drawcards are the reincarnated antique centres of Sarajevo and Mostar, where rebuilt historical buildings counterpoint fashionable bars and wi-fi–equipped cafes. Fascinating Sarajevo is an architectural gem, with countless minarets amid the tile-roofed houses that rise steeply up its river flanks. Mostar is world famous for its extraordinary arc of 16th-century stone bridge, photogenically flanked by cute mill-house restaurants. The town is set at the heart of Hercegovina's sun-baked wine country, with waterfalls, a riverside sufi-house and an Ottoman fortress all nearby.

When to Go

Sarajevo

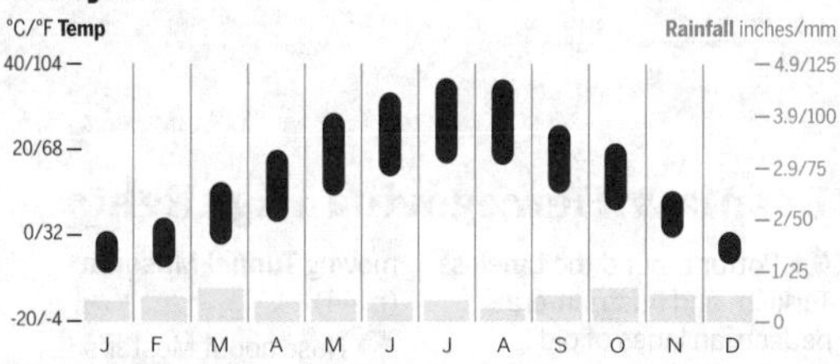

Apr–Jun & Oct Beat the heat, especially when exploring in Hercegovina from Mostar.

Jul & Aug Accommodation fills up as the cities sizzle in the summer sun.

Mid-Jan–mid-Mar Skiing gets cheaper after the New Year holidays.

Bosnia & Hercegovina Highlights

1. Potter around the timeless Turkish- and Austrian-era pedestrian lanes of old **Sarajevo** (p141).

2. Discover more about the hopes and horrors of the 1990s civil war at the intensely moving **Tunnel Museum** (p144).

3. Nose about Mostar's atmospheric Old Town, seeking ever-new angles from which to photograph young men throwing themselves off the magnificently rebuilt **Stari Most** (Old Bridge; p149).

4. Make a satisfyingly varied day trip from Mostar to **Kravice Waterfalls** (p152) and other gems of Hercegovina.

ITINERARIES

Three Days

Roam **Mostar's** Old Town and dine overlooking the famous bridge. Next day take the morning train to **Sarajevo**. Do a free walking tour to get a sense of the old town and dine with a panoramic view at Park Prinčeva. On the third day head for the History and Tunnel Museums in Sarajevo's southern suburbs.

Five Days

Extend the three day itinerary by joining a day tour ex-Mostar to visit historic **Počitelj**, quaint **Blagaj** and the impressive **Kravice** waterfalls. In Sarajevo cafe-hop around Baščaršija's *caravanserais* and extend your wanderings to the Svrzo House and the fascinating, less-visited citadel area of **Vratnik**.

SARAJEVO

☎033 / POP 419,000

The capital city's antique core has a Turkic feel, delighting visitors with narrow bazaar alleys and a plethora of 1530s Ottoman buildings. Bosnia's later annexation by Austria-Hungary is evident in surrounding groups of neo-Moorish Central European buildings, notably the recently reconstructed City Hall from which Archduke Franz Ferdinand was returning when assassinated in 1914. That shooting ultimately triggered WWI.

The city's north and south flanks are steep valley sides fuzzed with red-roofed Bosnian houses and prickled with uncountable minarets rising to green-topped mountain ridges. Westward, Sarajevo sprawls for over 10km through bland but busy Novo Sarajevo and dreary Dobrijna. Here, dismal ranks of apartment blocks remain bullet-scarred from the 1990s Yugoslav civil war, in which the capital's centuries-long history of religious harmony seemed to evaporate during almost four years of brutal siege. Many fascinating tours still focus on the civil war horrors but today the city is once again remarkably peaceful, non-threatening and photogenic.

Sights & Activities

Old Sarajevo

Baščaršija AREA

Sarajevo's bustling old quarter, Baščaršija (pronounced *bash-CHAR-shi-ya*) is a delightful warren of marble-flagged pedestrian courtyards and laneways full of Ottoman-era mosques, copper workshops, jewellery shops, *caravanserai*-cafes and inviting little restaurants. Start your explorations at the Sebilj, an 1891 ornamental gazebo-style water fountain on central 'Pigeon Sq'.

Franz Ferdinand's Assassination Spot HISTORIC SITE

(cnr Obala Kulina Bana & Zelenih Beretki) On 28 June 1914, Archduke Franz Ferdinand, heir to the Habsburg throne of Austria-Hungary, was shot by 18-year-old Gavrilo Princip. This assassination, which would be the fuse that ultimately detonated WWI, happened by an odd series of coincidences on a street corner outside what is now the Sarajevo 1878–1918 museum.

Bezistan ARCHITECTURE

(http://vakuf-gazi.ba/english/index.php/objects/ottoman-era/bezistan-tasli-han; ⊙8am-8pm Mon-Fri, 9am-2pm Sat) The 16th-century stone-vaulted covered bazaar is little more than 100m long, but squint and you could be in Istanbul. Most of the 50+ shops sell inexpensive souvenirs, scarves, cheap handbags and knock-off sunglasses.

Sarajevo City Hall ARCHITECTURE

(Vijećnica; www.nub.ba; adult/child 2KM/free; ⊙8am-5pm Mon-Fri) Storybook neo-Moorish facades make the 1898 Vijećnica Sarajevo's most beautiful Austro-Hungarian–era building. Seriously damaged during the 1990s siege, it has been laboriously restored and was reopened in 2014. As yet the only exhibits are a small collection of photos about the building's history, but it's well worth the modest entry fee to enjoy the sheer grandeur of its colourful multi-arched interior and the stained-glass ceiling.

Gazi-Husrevbey Mosque MOSQUE

(www.vakuf-gazi.ba; Sarači 18; admission 2KM; ⊙9am-noon, 2.30-3.30pm & 5-6.15pm May-Sep, closed Ramadan) Bosnia's second Ottoman governor, Gazi-Husrevbey, funded a series of splendid 16th-century buildings of which this 1531 mosque forms the greatest centrepiece.

Central Sarajevo

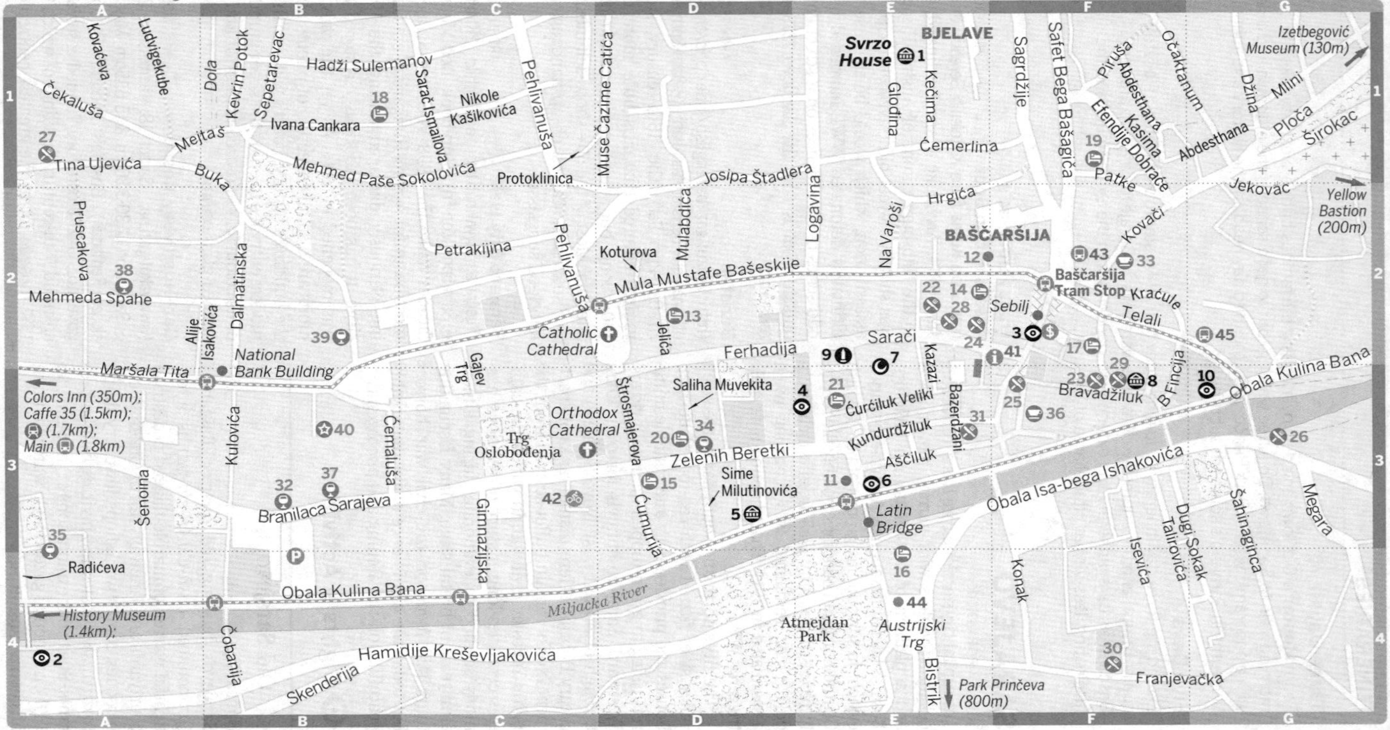

0 200 m
0 0.1 miles

Izetbegović Museum (130m)
Yellow Bastion (200m)
Colors Inn (350m); Caffe 35 (1.5km); (1.7km); Main (1.8km)
History Museum (1.4km);
Park Prinčeva (800m)

BJELAVE
BAŠČARŠIJA
Svrzo House 1
Baščaršija Tram Stop
Sebilj
National Bank Building
Catholic Cathedral
Orthodox Cathedral
Trg Oslobođenja
Gajev Trg
Latin Bridge
Atmejdan Park
Austrijski Trg
Miljacka River

Kovaćeva
Ludvigekube
Dola
Kevrin Potok
Sepetarevac
Hadži Sulemanov
Čekaluša
Mejtaš
Ivana Cankara
Sarač Ismailova
Nikole Kašikovića
Pehlivanuša
Muse Ćazime Ćatića
Protoklinica
Tina Ujevića
Buka
Mehmed Paše Sokolovića
Josipa Štadlera
Logavina
Glođina
Kečima
Ćemerlina
Sagrdžije
Safet Bega Bašagića
Piruša
Abdesthana
Kasima
Efendije Dobrače
Očaktanum
Džina
Mlini
Ploča
Širokac
Jekovac
Patke
Hrgića
Na Varoši
Kovači
Pruscakova
Petrakijina
Koturova
Mulabdića
Mula Mustafe Bašeskije
Kraćule
Telali
Mehmeda Spahe
Alije Isakovića
Dalmatinska
Jelića
Ferhadija
Sarači
Kazazi
Maršala Tita
Bravadžiluk
B Fincija
Obala Kulina Bana
Saliha Muvekita
Ćurćiluk Veliki
Kundurdžiluk
Bazerdžani
Štrosmajerova
Zelenih Beretki
Aščiluk
Kulovića
Ćemaluša
Šenoina
Branilaca Sarajeva
Sime Milutinovića
Ćumurija
Gimnazijska
Obala Isa-bega Ishakovića
Radićeva
Čobanija
Hamidije Kreševljakovića
Skenderija
Bistrik
Konak
Isevića
Dugi Sokak
Talirovića
Šahinaginca
Megara
Franjevačka

Central Sarajevo

The exterior might appear somewhat plain but there's a beautiful courtyard fountain, a 45m minaret and a splendidly proportioned interior.

Sahat Kula TOWER
(off Mudželeti Veliki) This elegant 1529 stone tower sports a half-speed 19th-century prayer-clock with Arabic numerals. It is adjusted daily so that dusk is the moment when the hands appear to show 12 o'clock.

Despića Kuća MUSEUM
(☎033-215531; http://muzejsarajeva.ba; Despićeva 2; adult/child 3/1KM, guide 5KM; ⏰10am-6pm Mon-Fri (till 4pm winter), 10am-3pm Sat) The Despića Kuća is one of the oldest surviving residential buildings in central Sarajevo, though you'd never guess so from the ho-hum facade. Inside, however, it's a house within a house, the original 1780 section retaining even the prison-style bars on stone window frames.

★ **Academy of Fine Arts Sarajevo** ARCHITECTURE
(Likovna Akademija; www.alu.unsa.ba; Obala Maka Dizdara 3) Originally built in 1899 as an evangelical church, the Gothic Revival–style Academy of Fine Arts Sarajevo has a fine facade looking like a mini version of Budapest's magnificent national parliament building. Inside the small Alu Gallery hosts occasional exhibitions.

Vratnik & Around

If you're looking for accessible but less touristed parts of the city to explore, try wandering up the (sometimes steep) lanes to the north and east of the old city centre.

★ **Svrzo House** MUSEUM
(Svrzina Kuća; ☎033-535264; http://muzejsarajeva.ba; Glođina 8; admission 3KM; ⏰10am-6pm Mon-Fri (till 4pm mid-Oct–mid-Apr), 10am-3pm Sat) An oasis of white-washed walls, cobbled courtyards and partly vine-draped dark timbers, this 18th-century house-museum is brilliantly restored and appropriately furnished, helping visitors imagine Sarajevo life in eras past.

Vratnik AREA
Built in the 1720s and reinforced in 1816, Vratnik Citadel once enclosed a whole area of the

upper city. Patchy remnants of wall fragments, military ruins and gatehouses remain. The urban area is appealingly untouristed with many small mosques and tile-roofed houses, and there are several superb viewpoints. Start a visit with a 3KM taxi hop up to the graffiti-daubed Bijela Tabija fortress ruin-viewpoint (or take buses 52 or 55 to Višegradski Kapija gatehouse) then walk back.

Yellow Bastion HISTORIC SITE
(Žuta Tabija; Jekovac bb) FREE Part-way between upper Vratnik and Kovaći Cemetery, a simple summer cafe places chairs between the trees on this overgrown former citadel bastion. Gaze out from here across the red-roofed cityscape.

Izetbegović Museum MUSEUM
(www.muzejalijaizetbegovica.ba; Ploča bb; admission 2KM; ⌚10am-6pm Mon-Fri, to 3pm Sat) Located in two 1730s stone towers linked by a section of former city wall, this two-room museum explores the background to the 1990s conflict and the role played by BiH's first president, Alija Izetbegović, in 'saving' the country.

Novo Sarajevo

For the History Museum take tram 3 and get off when you see the superb but sadly still-closed National Museum. The tram route follows Zmaja od Bosne, the city's wide east-west artery road that was dubbed 'sniper alley' during the 1990s siege because Serb gunmen in surrounding hills could pick off civilians as they tried to cross it.

History Museum MUSEUM
(☎033-226098; www.muzej.ba; Zmaja od Bosne 5; admission 5KM; ⌚9am-7pm Mon-Fri, 10am-2pm Sat & Sun, shorter hours in winter) Around half of the small but engrossing History Museum 'non-ideologically' charts the course of the 1990s conflict. Affecting personal exhibits include examples of food aid, stacks of Monopoly-style 1990s dinars and a makeshift siege-time 'home'. The exhibition's maudlin effect is emphasised by the museum building's miserable and still partly war-damaged 1970s architecture.

Butmir & Ilidža

Around 35 minutes after leaving Baščaršija, tram 3 reaches Ilidža, its western terminus. From there the very moving Tunnel Museum is some 3km southeast, around 8KM by metered taxi. Alternatively, from the tram terminus, switch to Kotorac-bound bus 32 (10 minutes). Get off at the last stop, walk across the Tilava bridge, then turn immediately left down Tuneli for 500m. The bus runs around twice hourly weekdays but only every 90 minutes on Sundays so it's often faster to walk from Ilidža. Many city tours include a Tunnel Museum visit, saving the hassle.

★**Tunnel Museum** MUSEUM
(Tunel Spasa; http://tunelspasa.ba; Tuneli bb 1; adult/student 10/5KM; ⌚9am-5pm, last entry 4.30pm, to 3.30pm Nov-Mar) The most visceral of Sarajevo's many 1990s war-experience 'attractions', this unmissable museum's centrepiece and raison d'être is a short section of the 1m wide, 1.6m high hand-dug tunnel under the airport runway which acted as the city's lifeline to the outside world during the 1992–95 siege, when Sarajevo was virtually surrounded by Serb forces.

Tours

Various companies run a range of tours in and beyond Sarajevo, many including the otherwise awkward-to-reach Tunnel Museum. Reliable operators include **Sarajevo Funky Tours** (☎062 910546; www.sarajevofunkytours.com; Besarina Čikma 5) and **Insider** (☎061 190591; www.sarajevoinsider.com; Zelenih Beretki 30; ⌚9am-6pm Mon-Fri, 9.30am-2pm Sat & Sun), which also offers a tips-only walking tour daily at 4.30pm in season starting outside its office-museum.

Festivals & Events

Sarajevo Film Festival FILM
(www.sff.ba; ⌚mid-Aug) During this globally acclaimed film fest, the whole city turns into a giant party with countless concerts and many bars opening street counters.

Sleeping

Hostels are multiplying at an incredible rate, with several great options on or near the narrow 'party street', Muvekita.

Hostel For Me HOSTEL €
(☎062 328658, 033-840135; www.hostelforme.com; 4th fl, Prote Bakovica 2; dm/breakfast €10/3; ❄📶) One of Sarajevo's best-appointed new hostels sits right within the Old Town, albeit hidden away up four flights of stairs. It's worth the climb for good-headroom bunks, huge lockers, a decent lounge area and a two-table kitchen with fine views across the Old Town roofs to the Gazi Husrevbegov Mosque.

Franz Ferdinand Hostel HOSTEL €
(033-834625; http://franzferdinandhostel.com/; Jelića 4; dm 19-27KM, d 62-82KM; 24hr;) Giant sepia photos and a floor timeline recall characters and scenes related to Sarajevo WWI history. Bunks have private powerpoints and ample headroom, and the comfortably stylish kitchen-lounge is well designed to encourage conversation between travellers.

Residence Rooms HOSTEL €
(033-200157, 061 159886; www.residencerooms.ba; 1st fl, Muvekita 1; dm 25-30KM, s/d/tr 50/80/90KM;) High ceilings and widely spaced dorm beds are complemented by a somewhat 1930s-flavoured lounge, with piano and ample seating space. The lively bars directly outside can be a blessing or a curse, depending on your party plans.

★**Hotel Lula** HOTEL €€
(033-232250; www.hotel-lula.com; Luledžina 14; s/d/tr €35/60/80;) The facade of this cute seven-room hotel is designed to harmonise with its perfect Old Town location, and there's even a mini 'cottage' in the basement dining-room area. Guest rooms are comfortably contemporary if mostly rather small; several have eaves reducing headroom. Fine value.

Villa Wien GUESTHOUSE €€
(033-972800, 062 416507; www.villa-wien.ba; Ćurčiluk Veliki 3; s/d 103/146KM; 7am-10pm;) Six well-equipped rooms come with engraved wooden furniture, kilims on parquet floors, wrought-iron bedsteads and attractive bowl-lamp chandeliers. Walls have partly exposed brick-and-timber sections and little luxuries include trouser press and a fridge pre-loaded with a few free soft drinks. There's no reception: check in at the Wiener Café downstairs before that closes (at 10.30pm).

Hotel Latinski Most HOTEL €€
(033-572660; www.hotel-latinskimost.com; Obala Isabega Isakovića 1; s/d/tr 117/158/178KM, off-season 99/138/158KM) This cosy hotel is ideal for WWI aficionados who want to survey the Franz Ferdinand assassination spot from directly across the river. Three of the smaller rooms have small balconies offering just that, and their double-glazing works remarkably well against street noise.

Hotel Safir HOTEL €€
(033-475040; www.hotelsafir.ba; Jagodića 3; s/d €50/72, off season walk-in €35/60;) For a place in this price range, the Safir goes that bit further than the competition. Off stairways featuring vibrantly colour-suffused flower photos, the eight rooms come with little mirror 'windows', big-headed showers, coffee, kettle and kitchenette (in most), free bottles of mineral water and even a little posy of flowers. Obliging 24-hour receptionists.

Hotel Michele BOUTIQUE HOTEL €€€
(033-560310; www.hotelmichele.ba; Ivana Cankara 27; s/d €55/65, apt €120-150;) Behind the exterior of an oversized contemporary townhouse, this offbeat guesthouse-hotel welcomes you into a lobby-lounge full of framed portraits and elegant fittings. Antique-effect elements are in evidence in the 12 new standard rooms, but what has drawn celebrity guests like Morgan Freeman and Kevin Spacey are the vast, indulgently furnished apartments with antique (if sometimes mismatching) furniture.

★**Colors Inn** BUSINESS HOTEL €€€
(033-276600; www.hotelcolorsinnsarajevo.com; Koševo 8; s/d from 162/212KM; P) Modernist white-grey-lime decor is given a dramatic twist with vast wall-sized black-and-white photos of 20th-century Sarajevo. The 37 comfortably fashion-conscious rooms come with

ENTITIES & AREAS

Getting your head around the divisions within Bosnia and Hercegovina (BiH) takes a bit of head-scratching. Geographically there's Bosnia in the north and Hercegovina (pronounced her-tse-GO-vina) in the south, although the term 'Bosnian' refers to anyone with BiH nationality. ('Bosniak' refers specifically to Muslim Bosnians, while simplistically put, Bosnian Croats are Catholics and Bosnian Serbs are Orthodox Christians.)

Then there are two quite different political 'entities'. Most of south and central BiH falls within the **Federation of Bosnia & Hercegovina**, which is itself subdivided into 10 cantons (five run by Bosniaks, three run by Bosnian Croats, two 'mixed'). Meanwhile, a territory comprising most of the north and arching around as far as Trebinje forms the semi-autonomous **Republik Srpska** (RS). That's predominantly Serb but certainly not in Serbia. Then there's the anomalous **Brčko District**, which falls in neither entity. Confused yet?

WORTH A TRIP

THE WORLD'S BIGGEST PYRAMID?

The otherwise forgettable leather-tanning town of Visoko, 30km northwest of Sarajevo, is overlooked by an unusually shaped hill that Semir Osmanagić, a Bosnian-American Indiana Jones–style researcher, claims is the **'World's Biggest Pyramid'** (Piramida Sunca; www.piramidasunca.ba). Osmanagić also claims that **Tunnel Ravne** (guided tour per person 10KM; ⌚9am-5.45pm Apr–mid-Nov) is a 12,000-year-old subterranean labyrinth built by the same mysterious lost culture as the pyramid.

The claims have been dismissed by the European Association of Archaeologists as a 'cruel hoax' with 'no place in the world of genuine science', but that doesn't seem to have detered visitors and volunteers.

If you want to check it out for yourself, the **Pyramid of the Sun Foundation** (☎061 994821, 033-259935; www.bosnianpyramidofthesun.com; Bravadžiluk 17; admission free, tours for 1/2/5 people 110/120/125KM; ⌚10am-10pm summer, 11am-7pm winter) organises private tours ex-Sarajevo, or you can reach Visoko independently and cheaply by taking a Sarajevo–Kakanj bus (at least hourly).

kettle, coffee and a Ferrero Rocher or three. A good buffet breakfast is laid out in a 24-hour basement dining room that's designed like a stylised birch forest. Pay 20KM extra for a substantially larger 'luxury' room.

Hotel Central HOTEL €€€
(☎033-561800; www.hotelcentral.ba; Ćumurija 8; s/d/ste 200/240/300KM; ❄📶🏊) Behind a grand Austro-Hungarian facade, most of this snazzily renovated 'hotel' is in fact an amazing three-floor gym complex with professional-standard weight rooms, saunas and a big indoor pool staffed by qualified sports training staff. The 15 huge, fashionably appointed guest rooms lead off corridors painted a lugubriously deep purple.

Eating

For inexpensive snack meals look along Bradžiluk or nearby Kundurdžiluk: **Buregdžinica Bosna** (Bravadžulik; 250g portions 2-3.50KM; ⌚7am-11pm) is excellent for cheap, fresh *burek* sold by weight. Locals argue whether **Hodžić** (Sebilj Sq; čevapi 3-6KM, kajmak 1.5KM; ⌚8am-11pm), **Mrkva** (www.mrkva.ba; Bravadžulik 15; čevapi from 3.5KM; ⌚8am-10pm) or **Željo** (Kundurdžiluk 17 & 20; ćevapi 3.5-10KM, kajmak 1.5KM; ⌚8am-10pm) serves the best *ćevapi*.

Barhana PIZZA, BOSNIAN €
(Đugalina 8; mains 5-10KM, steak 18-20KM, pizza 5-12KM, beer/rakija (fruit brandy) 2/3KM; ⌚10am-midnight, kitchen till 11.30pm) Barhana's remarkably reasonable prices pair unbeatably with its charming part-wooden cottage interior, whose centrepiece is the large brick pizza oven and open kitchen, partly masked by collections of bottles and candles.

★ **Mala Kuhinja** FUSION €€
(☎061 144741; www.malakuhinja.ba; Tina Ujevića 13; veg/chicken/beef/surprise meals 12/17/22/25KM, wine per glass/bottle 6/30KM; ⌚10am-11pm Mon-Sat, kitchen closes around 9.30pm; 📶🌱) Run by former TV celebrity chefs, the novel concept here is that staff forget menus and simply ask you what you do/don't like. Spicey? Vegan? Gluten free? No problem. And armed with this knowledge the team sets about making culinary magic in the show-kitchen. Superb.

Dveri EUROPEAN €€
(☎030-537020; www.dveri.co.ba; Prote Bakovića 12; meals 10-20KM; ⌚8am-11pm; 📶🌱) This tourist-friendly 'country cottage' eatery is densely hung with loops of garlic, corn cobs and gingham-curtained 'windows'. Classic European meat-based dishes are supplemented by inky risottos, veggie-stuffed eggplant and garlic-wine squid.

Pivnica HS INTERNATIONAL €€
(☎033-239740; www.sarajevska-pivara.com; Franjevačka 15; pasta 6-10KM, mains 10-20KM, beer from 2KM; ⌚10am-1am, kitchen 10.30am-midnight) Wild West saloon, Munich bierkeller, Las Vegas fantasy or Willy Wonka masterpiece? However you describe its decor, Pivnica HS is a vibrant place for dining on well-presented (mainly meat-based) dishes and ideal for sampling the full range of Sarajevskaya tap beers brewed next door. Try the rare unfiltered.

Morića Han BOSNIAN €€
(☎033-236119; Saraći 77; mains 8-17KM, tea/coffee 1.5/2KM; ⌚8am-11pm) Settle into cushioned wicker chairs as a single tree filters the sunlight or, at night, as lamps and lanterns glow magically between the hanging fabrics and

wooden beams of a gorgeous, historic *caravanserai* courtyard. The menu features typical Bosnian home fare including *klepe,* a vampire-slaying garlic ravioli. Cafe section but no alcohol served.

Inat Kuća BOSNIAN €€

(Spite House; ☎033-447867; www.inatkuca.ba; Velika Alifakovac 1; mains 8-15KM, steak 25KM; ⏰10am-10pm; 📶) This Sarajevo institution occupies a classic Ottoman-era house that's a veritable museum piece with central stone water-trough, a case of antique guns and fine metal-filigree lanterns. A range of Bosnian specialities are served using pewter crockery at glass-topped display tables containing traditional local jewellery.

Park Prinčeva BALKAN, EUROPEAN €€€

(☎033-222708; www.parkprinceva.ba; Iza Hidra 7; meals 16-32KM; ⏰9am-11pm; 🚌56) It's well worth the 3.50KM taxi-ride from Latinski Most to gaze out over a superb city panorama from this hillside perch, like Bono and Bill Clinton before you. From the open-sided terrace the City Hall is beautifully framed between rooftops, mosques and twinkling lights. The main chandelier-decked dining room sports a white piano, and a folk trio playing from 7.30pm.

Drinking & Entertainment

Sarajevo is chock full of appealing bars and pubs, and great cafes for coffee, cakes, ice cream and narghile (hubble-bubble) water pipes.

★ **Zlatna Ribica** BAR

(Kaptol 5; beer/wine from 4/5KM; ⏰9am-1am or later) Sedate and outwardly grand, this tiny bar is inspiringly eccentric, adding understated humour to a cosy treasure trove of antiques and kitsch, all mixed together and reflected in big art-nouveau mirrors.

Cheers PUB, PIZZA

(Muvekita 4; beer/pizza from 2.50/5.50KM; ⏰24hr) Look for the London Routemaster double-decker bus then turn the corner to find central Sarajevo's most consistently popular boozer, with music blaring and tipsy travellers bopping well after most other places have shut.

Cafe Barometar BAR

(www.facebook.com/CafeBarometar; Branilaca Sarajeva 23; ⏰8am-midnight) Like an image of HG Wells' *Time Machine,* this cafe-bar weaves together dials, pipes and wacky furniture crafted from axles, compressors and submarine parts.

Pink Houdini BAR

(www.facebook.com/JazzBluesClubPinkHoudini; Branilaca Sarajeva 31; light/dark beer 3/3.50KM; ⏰24hr) One of Sarajevo's relatively rare 24-hour drinking spots, this quirky basement jazz bar has live gigs at 10pm on Fridays and Sundays.

Dekanter WINE BAR

(☎033-263815; Radićeva 4; ⏰8am-midnight Mon-Sat, noon-midnight Sun) Sample from around 60 local and world vintages in this wine bar decorated with decanter shapes dangling from intertwined vine stems on the ceiling.

Caffe 35 BAR

(Avaz Twist Tower, 35th fl; coffee/cake/beer 2/3/4KM, sandwiches 3-5KM; ⏰8am-11pm) If you're waiting for a train, what better place to do so than admiring a full city panorama from the 35th floor cafe of 'The Balkans' Tallest Tower', just three minutes' walk away from the station.

Čajdžinica Džirlo TEAHOUSE

(www.facebook.com/CajdzinicaDzirlo; Kovači 16; tea 4.50-6KM, coffee & sherbet 3KM; ⏰8am-10pm) Minuscule but brimming with character, Džirlo offers 45 types of tea, many of them made from distinctive Bosnian herbs, served in lovely little pots.

Kuća Sevdaha CAFE

(www.artkucasevdaha.ba/en/; Halači 5; tea/coffee/sherbet from 2/2/3KM; ⏰10am-11pm) Sip Bosnian coffee, juniper sherbet, rose water or herb-tea infusions while nibbling local sweets and listening to the lilting wails of *sevdah* (traditional Bosnian music). The ancient building that surrounds the cafe's fountain courtyard is now used as a museum celebrating great 20th-century *sevdah* performers (admission 3KM, open 10am to 6pm Tuesday to Sunday).

Sloga CLUB

(www.cinemas.ba; Mehmeda Spahe 20; ⏰9pm-5am) This cavernous, club-disco-dance hall caters to an excitable, predominantly student crowd. Monday nights see Latin dance, Thursday is party night, Friday is disco and Saturday is live music. At least in principle. Modest cover charge, cheap beer.

Underground LIVE MUSIC

(www.facebook.com/undergroundclubsarajevo; Maršala Tita 56; beer 3KM; ⏰7pm-late) On Friday and Saturday nights, talented bands give classic rock songs a romping rework in this medium-sized basement venue. Concerts some Thursdays, too.

Information

Destination Sarajevo (www.sarajevo.travel) Extensive listings and information website.

Kapitals (Bascarsija 34; commission 2%, minimum 2KM; ⏲9am-11pm) Helpfully central money changers, open till late.

Sarajevo Tourism Association (www.sarajevo-tourism.com; Sarači 58; ⏲9am-8pm Mon-Fri, 10am-6pm Sat & Sun, varies seasonally.) Helpful tourist information centre.

Getting There & Away

BUS

From Sarajevo's **main bus station** (☎033-213100; www.centrotrans.com; Put Života 8; ⏲6am-10pm), beside the train station, there are frequent buses to Mostar (18KM, 2½ hours), several daily services to Zagreb and Split in Croatia, plus early-morning buses to Dubrovnik (Croatia) and Belgrade (Serbia). There are five more Belgrade services from the inconveniently distant **East Sarajevo (Lukovica) Bus Station** (Autobuska Stanica Istočno Sarajevo; ☎057-317377; www.balkanexpress-is.com; Nikole Tesle bb; ⏲6am-11.15pm), 400m beyond the western terminus stop of trolleybus 103 or bus 31E. That bus station also has buses to Podgorica and Herceg Novi in Montenegro.

TRAIN

Mostar 11KM, 2¾ hours, 6.51am and 6.57pm

Zagreb (Croatia) 61KM, nine hours via Banja Luka, 10.46am

For Budapest (Hungary) take the 12.30pm bus from Lukovica Bus Station to Belgrade (arrives 8pm) then switch to the 9.45pm overnight train from there (couchette 1960DIN ie €17, 8¼ hours).

Getting Around

TO/FROM THE AIRPORT

Taxis charge around 20KM for the 12Km drive to Baščaršija.

The nearest centre-bound bus stop is around 700m from the terminal: turn right out of the airport following black-backed 'Hotel' signs. Take the first left, shimmy right-left-right past Hotel Octagon, then turn third right at Brače Mulića 17. Before the Mercator Hypermarket (Mimar Sinana 1) cross the road and take trolleybus 103 heading back in the direction you've just come.

BICYCLE RENTAL

Gir (☎033-213687; www.gir.ba; Zelenih Berekti 14a; per hr/day/5 days city bike 3/15/25KM, mountain bike from 4/20/35KM; ⏲10am-6pm Mon-Sat, 11am-5pm Sun) Bicycle rental, sales and repairs.

PUBLIC TRANSPORT

Single-ride tickets for bus, tram or trolleybus cost 1.60KM from kiosks, 1.80KM from drivers. Tickets must be stamped once aboard.

TAXI

Paja Taxis (☎1522, 033-412555) Reliable taxi company charging on-the-metre fares (2KM plus about 1KM per kilometre).

BOSNIA & HERCEGOVINA & THE 1990S CONFLICT

Today's Bosnia & Hercegovina (BiH) remains deeply scarred by the 1990s civil war that began when post-Tito-era Yugoslavia imploded. Seen very simply, the core conflict was a territorial battle between the Bosnians, Serbs and Croats. The war that ensued is often portrayed as 'ethnic', but in fact all sides were Slavs, differing only in their (generally secularised) religious backgrounds. Indeed, many Bosniaks (Muslims), Serbs (Orthodox Christians) and Croats (Catholics) had intermarried or were friends. Yet for nearly four years a brutal and extraordinarily complex civil war raged, with atrocities committed by all sides.

Best known is the campaign of 'ethnic' cleansing in northern and eastern BiH, which aimed at creating a Serb republic. Meanwhile in Mostar, Bosnian Croats and Bosniaks traded fire across a 'front line', with Croat bombardment eventually destroying the city's world-famous Old Bridge. Sarajevo endured a long siege and, in July 1995, Dutch peacekeepers monitoring the supposedly 'safe' area of Srebrenica proved unable to prevent a Bosnian Serb force from killing an estimated 8000 Muslim men in Europe's worst mass killings since WWII. By this stage, Croats had renewed their own offensive, expelling Serbs from western BiH and the Krajina region of Croatia.

Finally two weeks of NATO air strikes in September 1995 added force to an ultimatum to end the Serbs' siege of Sarajevo and a peace conference was held in Dayton, Ohio. The resultant accords maintained BiH's pre-war external boundaries but divided the country into a complex jigsaw of semi-autonomous 'entities' and cantons to balance 'ethnic' sensibilities. This succeeded in maintaining the fragile peace but the complex political structure resulting from the war has led to bureaucratic tangles and economic stagnation.

MOSTAR

☎036 / POP 113,200

Mostar's world-famous 16th-century stone bridge is the centrepiece of its alluring, extensively restored old town where, at dusk, the lights of numerous mill-house restaurants twinkle across streamlets. Further from the centre a scattering of shattered building shells remain as moving testament to the terrible 1990s conflict that divided the city. The surrounding sun-drenched Herzegovinian countryside produces excellent wines and offers a series of tempting day-trip attractions.

Sights & Activities

Stari Most BRIDGE

The world-famous Stari Most (Old Bridge) is Mostar's indisputable visual focus. Its pale stone arch magnificently throws back the golden glow of sunset or the tasteful night-time floodlighting. The bridge's swooping stone arch was originally built between 1557 and 1566 on the orders of Suleyman the Magnificent. The current structure is a very convincing 2004 rebuild following the bridge's 1993 bombardment during the civil war. Numerous well-positioned cafes and restaurants tempt you to sit and savour the splendidly restored scene.

Bridge Diving SPECTACLE

In summer, young men leap over 20m from Stari Most's parapet. That's not a suicide attempt but a professional sport – donations are expected from spectators. Daredevil tourists can try jumping for themselves but only after paying 50KM and doing a brief training. Enquire at the Bridge-Divers' Clubhouse and listen very carefully to their advice: diving badly can prove fatal.

Crooked Bridge BRIDGE

(Kriva Ćuprija) Resembling Stari Most but in miniature, the pint-sized Crooked Bridge crosses the tiny Rabobolja creek amid a layered series of picturesque millhouse-restaurants.

Kajtaz House MUSEUM

(Gaše Ilića 21; admission 4KM; ⌚9am-7pm Apr-Oct) Hidden behind tall walls, Mostar's most historic old house was once the harem section of a larger homestead built for a 16th-century Turkish judge. Full of original artefacts, it still belongs to descendents of the original family.

Bišćevića Ćošak HOUSE

(Turkish House; Bišćevića 13; adult/student 4/3KM; ⌚8.30am-6.30pm mid-Apr–Oct, winter by tour only) Built in 1635, Bišćevića Ćošak is a one of very few traditional Turkic-styled houses to retain its original appearance. Off the small entrance courtyard, three rooms are colourfully furnished with rugs, metalwork and carved wooden furniture.

Spanski Trg AREA

Over 20 years ago Croat and Bosniak forces bombarded each other into the rubble across a 'front line' which ran along the Bulevar and Alese Šantića St. Even now, several shell-pocked skeletal buildings remain in ruins around Spanski Trg, notably the triangular nine-storey tower that was once **Ljubljanska Banka** (Kralja Zvonimira bb).

Tours

Several homestay-hostels offer well-reputed walking tours around town and/or full-day trips visiting Blagaj, Međugorje, Počitelj and the Kravice Waterfalls (around €30).

i-House Travel TOUR AGENCY

(☎063 481842, 036-580048; www.ihouse-mostar.com; Oneščukova 25; ⌚10.30am-7.30pm Mar-Dec, 10am-10pm peak season) A wide and imaginative series of small group tours (minimum two customers) including an evening vineyard wine tasting trip (four hours) and a 'Death of Yugoslavia' trip (two hours including a 'secret' base). Paragliding (€35) and rafting (€35) are also possible.

Sleeping

There are numerous small hostels, though some are dormant between November and April.

Backpackers HOSTEL €

(☎036-552408, 063 199019; www.backpackersmostar.com; Braće Felića 67; dm/d/tr €10/30/45;) With its graffiti-chic approach and music-till-late sitting area, this is Mostar's party hostel. It's above a main-street shop and currently quite small, but owner Ermin has big plans for expansion.

Hostel Nina HOSTEL €

(☎061 382743; www.hostelnina.ba; Čelebica 18; dm/d without bathroom €10/30;) This popular homestay-hostel is run by an obliging English-speaking lady whose husband, a war survivor and former bridge jumper, runs regional tours.

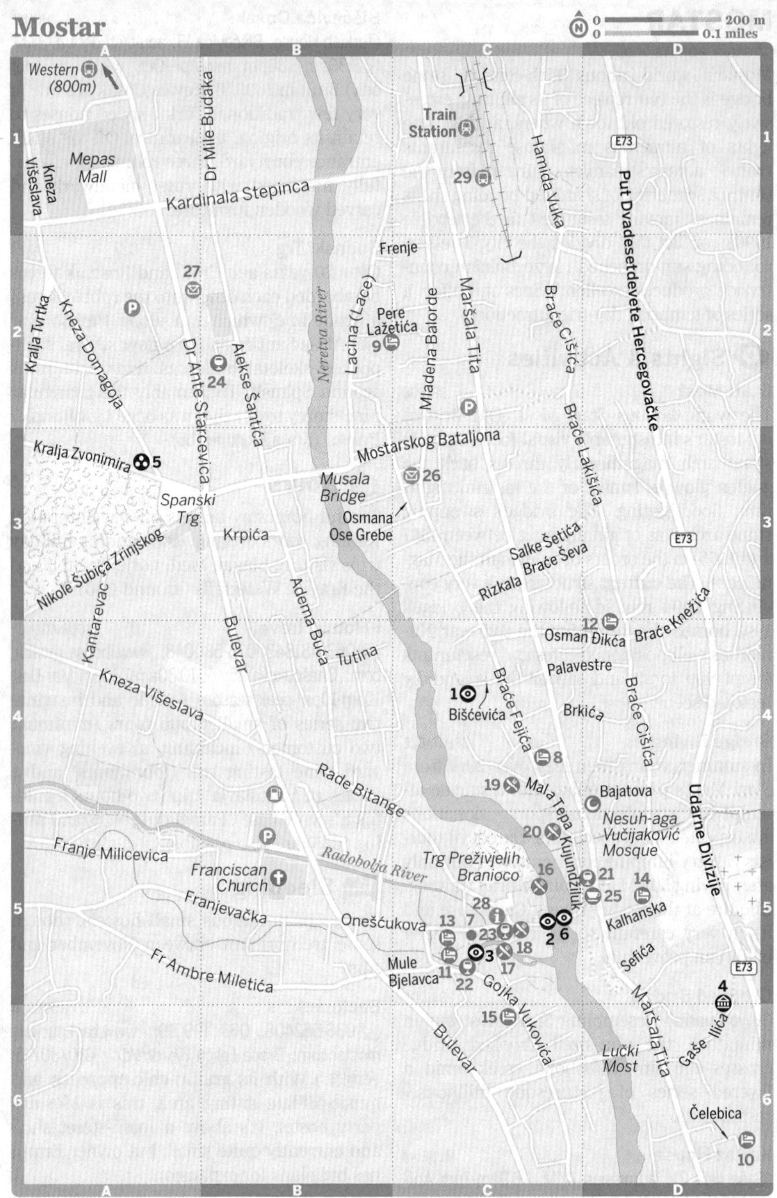

Hostel Majdas HOSTEL €
(☎061 382940; www.facebook.com/HostelMajdasMostar; Pere Lažetića 9; dm 20-23KM; ❄@📶) Mostar's cult traveller getaway, Majdas now has a garden where breakfast is served, and a loveable cat. It still offers the classic multisite around-Mostar day tours which manager-guide Bata pioneered.

Pansion Oskar GUESTHOUSE €
(☎061 823649, 036-580237; Oneščukova 33; d/tr €45/60, off-peak €35/50, s/d/tr/q without bathroom

Mostar

Sights
1 Biščevića Ćošak C4
2 Bridge Diving C5
3 Crooked Bridge C5
4 Kajtaz House D5
5 Ljubljanska Banka Tower Ruin A3
6 Stari Most C5

Activities, Courses & Tours
7 i-House Travel C5

Sleeping
8 Backpackers C4
9 Hostel Majdas B2
10 Hostel Nina D6
11 Kriva Ćuprija 1 .... C5
12 Muslibegović House D4
13 Pansion Oskar C5
14 Shangri-La D5
15 Villa Anri C6

Eating
16 Babilon C5
17 Hindin Han C5
18 Šadrvan C5
19 Tepa Vegetable Market C4
20 Urban Grill C5

Drinking & Nightlife
21 Ali Baba D5
22 Black Dog Pub C5
23 Caffe Marshall C5
24 OKC Abrašević B2
25 Terasa D5

Information
26 Bosniak Post Office C3
27 Croat Post Office A2
28 Tourist Information Centre C5

Transport
29 Main Bus Station C1

from €20/30/50/60; ❄📶) Oskar is essentially a pair of family homes above a delightful open-air garden bar-restaurant slap bang in the historic centre. Room sizes and standards vary considerably between the nine rooms.

★ **Muslibegović House** HISTORIC HOTEL €€
(☎036-551379; www.muslibegovichouse.com; Osman Đikća 41; s/d/ste €60/90/105; ⏰museum 10am-6pm mid-Apr–mid-Oct; ❄📶) In summer, tourists pay 4KM to visit this beautiful, late-17th-century Ottoman courtyard house (extended in 1871). But it's also an extremely charming boutique hotel. Room sizes and styles vary significantly, mixing excellent modern bathrooms with elements of traditional Bosnian, Turkish or even Moroccan design.

★ **Shangri-La** GUESTHOUSE €€
(☎061 169362; www.shangrila.com.ba; Kalhanska 10; d Apr–mid-Oct €41-55, s/d mid-Oct–Mar €35/39; P❄📶) Behind a pseudo-19th-century facade, eight invitingly contemporary rooms are better appointed than those of most Mostar hotels. Stari Most is three minutes' walk away past some war-ruined historic buildings, yet the location is wonderfully peaceful.

Kriva Ćuprija 1 BOUTIQUE HOTEL €€
(☎036-550953; www.hotel-mostar.ba; r 70-130KM, apt 100-180KM; ❄📶) Kriva Ćuprija 1 presents an idyllic blend of perfect Old Town location, soothing sounds of gushing streams and well-furnished rooms within a sensitively extended cluster of mill-house stone buildings.

Villa Anri HOTEL €€
(☎036-578477; www.motel-mostar.com; Braće Đukića 4; s/d/tr/q €35/40/60/80, peak season d/tr/q €70/95/115; P❄📶) The star attraction of this new four-storey hotel is the great Stari Most view from the open rooftop terrace. Two small, cosy rooms have the same views, but most other rooms are larger with modern bathrooms and an ecclectic taste in arts that ranges from tasteful to downright odd.

Eating

Cafes and restaurants with divine views of Stari Most cluster along the riverbank. Along Mala Tepa and the main central commercial street Braće Fejića you'll find supermarkets, a **vegetable market** (⏰6.30am-2pm) and several inexpensive places for *ćevapi* and other Bosnian snacks.

★ **Hindin Han** BALKAN €€
(☎036-581054; Jusovina bb; mains 7-20KM, wine per litre 15KM; ⏰11am-11pm; 📶) Hindin Han is a rebuilt historic building with several layers of summer terrace perched pleasantly above a side stream. Locals rate its food as better than most other equivalent tourist restaurants. The stuffed squid we tried (13KM) was perfectly cooked and generously garnished.

Šadrvan BALKAN €€
(Jusovina 11; mains 7-25KM; ⏰8am-11pm, closed Jan) On a vine- and tree-shaded corner where the pedestrian lane from Stari Most divides,

WORTH A TRIP

AROUND MOSTAR

Many Mostar agencies and hostels combine the following for a satisfying day trip:

Blagaj A village, whose signature sight is a half-timbered sufi-house (*tekija*) standing beside the surreally blue-green Buna River, where it gushes out of a cliff-cave.

Počitelj A steeply layered Ottoman-era fortress village that's one of BiH's most picture-perfect architectural ensembles.

Međugorje Curious for its mixture of pilgrim piety and Catholic kitsch ever since the Virgin Mary was reputedly spotted in a series of 1981 visions.

Kravice Waterfalls BiH's splendid 25m mini Niagara. Some tours give you several hours here to swim in natural pools.

this delightful tourist favourite has tables set around a trickling fountain made of old Turkish-style metalwork. Obliging costumed waiters can help explain a menu that covers all bases and takes a stab at some vegetarian options. Meat-free *đuveč* (KM8) tastes like ratatouille on rice.

Babilon BALKAN €€
(Tabhana; mains 8-20KM; 9am-10pm summer, 11am-4pm winter) The Babilon has stupendous terrace views across the river to the Old Town and Stari Most.

Urban Grill BOSNIAN €€
(Mala Tepa 26; mains 8-27KM; 8am-11pm Mon-Sat, 9am-11pm Sun) From the street level Urban Grill seems to be a slightly up-market Bosnian fast-food place. But the menu spans a great range and the big attraction is the seven-table lower terrace with unexpectedly perfect framed views of the Old Bridge.

Drinking & Nightlife

Black Dog Pub PUB
(Crooked Bridge; beer/wine from 2/4KM; 10am-late) Old Mostar's best hostelry features four specially brewed draft beers, happy hours and live acoustic music on Monday nights.

Caffe Marshall BAR
(Oneščukova bb; 8am-1am) This minuscule box bar has a ceiling draped with musical instruments and is often the latest to be active in the Old Bridge area.

Terasa CAFE
(Maršala Tita bb; coffee from 2KM; weather-dependent) Half a dozen tables on an open-air perch-terrace survey Stari Most and the Old Town towers from altogether new angles. Enter beside MUM, crossing through the little roof garden of art studio Atelje Novalić.

OKC Abrašević BAR
(036-561107; www.okcabrasevic.org; Alekse Šantića 25; coffee/beer 1/2KM; 9am-midnight) This understatedly intellectual smoky box of a bar offers Mostar's most vibrantly alternative scene and has an attached venue for off-beat gigs. It's hidden away in an unsigned courtyard on the former front line.

Ali Baba BAR
(Kujundžiluk; cocktails 10KM; 24hr Jun-Sep, 7am-7pm Oct, closed winter) Take a gaping cavern in the raw rock, add beats and colourful low lighting and hey presto, you've got this one-off party bar. A dripping tunnel leads out to a second entrance on Maršala Tita.

Information

Bosniak Post Office (Braće Fejića bb; 8am-8pm Mon-Fri, 8am-3pm Sat)

Croat Post Office (Dr Ante Starčevića bb; 7am-7pm Mon-Sat, 9am-noon Sun)

Tourist Information Centre (036-397350; Preživjelih Branioco Trg; 9am-7pm May-Sep,

COUNTRY FACTS

Area 51,129 sq km

Capital Sarajevo

Country code 387

Currency Convertible mark (KM, BAM)

Emergency ambulance 124, fire 123, police 122

Language Spoken Bosnian (Bosanski, 48%), Serbian (Српски, 37%) and Croatian (Hrvatski, 14%) are all variants of the same language.

Money Visa & MasterCard ATMs widely available

Population 3.79 million (2.37 million in the Federation, 1.33 million RS, 93,000 Brčko)

Visas Not required for most visitors (see www.mfa.ba)

closed Oct-Apr) Limited info, city tours sold (25KM).

Getting There & Around

BUS

The **main bus station** (☎036-552025; Ivana Krndelja Trg) beside the train station handles half a dozen daily services to Sarajevo, Split and Zagreb plus morning departures to Belgrade, Herceg Novi, Kotor and Vienna. For Dubrovnik there are direct buses (38KM, 4½ hours) at 7am and 10am, or you could take one of three daily buses to attractive Trebinje (21KM, four hours), from where there's a 10am bus to Dubrovnik (not Sundays). Three extra Split-bound buses use the **Western Bus Station** (☎036-348680; Autobusni Kolodvor; Vukovarska bb), 800m beyond Mepas Mall.

TRAIN

Sarajevo 11KM, 2¼ hours, 7.05am and 7.10pm
Zagreb 74.60KM, 13¼hours, 7.05am

SURVIVAL GUIDE

Directory A–Z

BUSINESS HOURS

Banks 8am to 6pm Monday to Friday, 8.30am to 1.30pm Saturday
Office hours 8am to 4pm Monday to Friday
Restaurants 11.30am to 10.30pm, varying by customer demand
Shops 8am to 6pm daily

INTERNET ACCESS

Most hotels and some cafes offer free wi-fi.

INTERNET RESOURCES

BiH Tourism (www.bhtourism.ba)
Bosnian Institute (www.bosnia.org.uk)
Office of the High Representative (www.ohr.int)

MONEY

Bosnia's convertible mark (KM or BAM), pronounced *kai-em* or *maraka*, is tied to the euro at approximately €1=1.96KM. For minor purchases, many businesses unblinkingly accept euros using a slightly customer-favourable 1:2 rate.

POST

BiH has three parallel postal organisations, each issuing their own stamps: **BH Pošta** (Federation; www.posta.ba), **Pošte Srpske** (RS; www.postesrpske.com) and **HP Post** (Croat areas, western Mostar; www.post.ba).

SLEEPING PRICE RANGES

Room prices are for high season (June to September) and assume a private bathroom and breakfast, except in hostels or where otherwise indicated.

€ less than 80KM

€€ 80KM to 190KM

€€€ more than 190KM

PUBLIC HOLIDAYS

Nationwide holidays:
New Year's Day 1 January
Independence Day 1 March
May Day 1 May
National Statehood Day 25 November

Additional holidays in the Federation:
Kurban Bajram (Islamic Feast of Sacrifice) 23 September 2015, 11 September 2016, 1 September 2017
Ramazanski Bajram (end of Ramadan) 7 July 2016, 26 June 2017, 15 June 2018
Gregorian Easter 28 March 2016, 17 April 2017, 2 April 2018
Gregorian Christmas 25 December

Additional holidays in the RS:
Orthodox Easter April/May
Orthodox Christmas 6 January

SAFE TRAVEL

Landmines and unexploded ordnance still affect 2.4% of BiH's area (see www.bhmac.org). In affected areas stick to asphalt/concrete surfaces or well-worn paths. Avoid exploring war-wrecked buildings.

VISAS

Stays of less than 90 days are visa-exempt for most European nationals, Australians, Canadians, Israelis, Japanese, Malaysians, Kiwis, Singaporians, South Koreans, Turks and US citizens. Other nationals should check www.mfa.ba for details.

EATING PRICE RANGES

The following are average costs for restaurant main courses:

€ less than 10KM

€€ 10KM to 25KM

€€€ more than 25KM

ESSENTIAL FOOD & DRINK

- **Bosanski Lonac** Slow-cooked meat-and-veg hotpot.
- **Burek** Bosnian *burek* are cylindrical or spiral lengths of filo-pastry filled with minced meat. *Sirnica* is filled instead with cheese, *krompiruša* with potato and *zeljanica* with spinach. Collectively these pies are called *pita*.
- **Ćevapi (Ćevapčići)** Minced meat formed into cylindrical pellets and served in fresh bread with melting *kajmak*.
- **Hurmastica** Syrup-soaked sponge fingers.
- **Pljeskavica** Patty-shaped *ćevapi*.
- **Kajmak** Thick semi-soured cream.
- **Klepe** Small ravioli-like triangles served in a butter-pepper drizzle with grated raw garlic.
- **Kljukuša** Potato-dough-milk dish cooked like a pie then cut into slices.
- **Ligne** Squid.
- **Pastrmka** Trout.
- **Rakija** Grappa or fruit brandy.
- **Ražnijići** Barbequed meat skewers.
- **Sogan Dolma** Slow-roasted onions filled with minced meat.
- **Sač** Traditional cooking technique using a metal hood loaded with hot charcoals.
- **Sarma** Steamed dolma-parcels of rice and minced meat wrapped in cabbage or other green leaves.
- **Tufahija** Whole stewed apple with walnut filling.
- **Uštipci** Bready fried dough-balls.

Transit through Neum (coastal BiH between Split and Dubrovnik) is possible without a Bosnian visa, assuming you have a double- or multiple-entry Croat visa.

Getting There & Away

Around a dozen airlines fly to/from Sarajevo's compact little **international airport** (Aerodrom; www.sia.ba; Kurta Šchorka 36; closed 11pm-5am).

Air Serbia (033-289 265; www.airserbia.com) connects to Banja Luka from/via Belgrade.

Mistral Air (www.mistralair.it) operates seasonal Mostar–Rome charters.

BiH cities have plenty of international bus services (notably to Belgrade, Dubrovnik, Munich, Split, Vienna and Zagreb), but the only international train is the daily Zagreb–Sarajevo–Mostar service.

Britain

Includes ➡

Best Traditional British Pubs

- ➡ Star Inn (p192)
- ➡ Bear Inn (p195)
- ➡ Old Thatch Tavern (p197)
- ➡ Blue Bell (p202)
- ➡ Café Royal Circle Bar (p212)

Best Museums

- ➡ Victoria & Albert Museum (p167)
- ➡ Ashmolean Museum (p193)
- ➡ National Railway Museum (p200)
- ➡ Kelvingrove Art Gallery & Museum (p213)
- ➡ Science Museum (p167)

Why Go?

Few places cram so much history, heritage and scenery into such a compact space as Britain. Twelve hours is all you'll need to travel from one end to the other, but you could spend a lifetime exploring – from the ancient relics of Stonehenge and Avebury, to the great medieval cathedrals of Westminster and Canterbury, and the magnificent country houses of Blenheim Palace and Castle Howard.

In fact, Britain isn't really one country at all, but three. While they haven't always been easy bedfellows, the contrasts between England, Wales and Scotland make this a rewarding place to visit. With a wealth of rolling countryside, stately cities, world-class museums and national parks to explore, Britain really is one of Europe's most unmissable destinations. And despite what you may have heard, it doesn't rain *all* the time – but even so, an umbrella and a raincoat will certainly come in handy.

When to Go

London

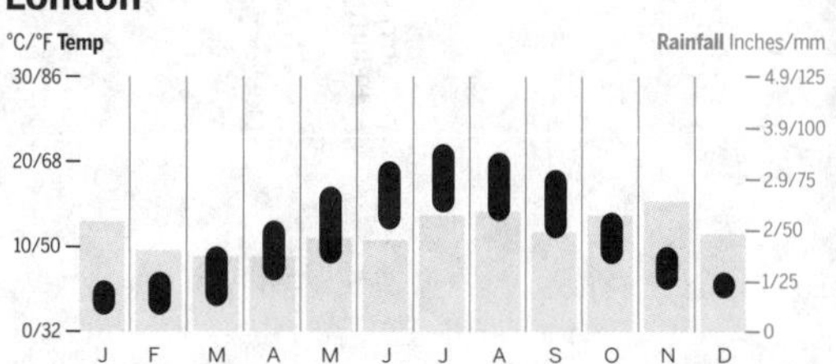

Easter–May Fewer crowds, especially in popular spots like Bath, York and Edinburgh.

Jun–Aug The weather is at its best but the coast and national parks are busy.

Mid-Sep–Oct Prices drop and the weather is often surprisingly good.

Britain Highlights

1. Explore the streets of one of the world's greatest capital cities, **London** (p158).
2. Visit Roman baths and admire grand Georgian architecture in **Bath** (p190).
3. Enjoy a Shakespeare play in the town of his birth, **Stratford-upon-Avon** (p196).
4. Marvel at the mountainous landscape of Wales' **Snowdonia National Park** (p207).
5. Delve into the history – Roman, Viking and medieval – of **York** (p200).
6. Get lost among the dreaming spires of **Oxford** (p193).
7. Step back in time wandering around the great trilithons

of **Stonehenge** (p189).

8 Join the party in Scotland's festival city, **Edinburgh** (p208).

9 Head north through the Scottish Highlands to experience the epic scenery of the **Isle of Skye** (p219).

10 Follow in the footsteps of Romantic poet William Wordsworth in the **Lake District National Park** (p204).

ITINERARIES

One Week

With just seven days, you're pretty much limited to sights in England. Spend three days seeing the sights in **London**, then head to **Oxford** for a day, followed by a day each at **Stonehenge** and historic **Bath**, before returning for a final day in London.

Two Weeks

Follow the one-week itinerary, but instead of returning to London on day seven, head north to **Stratford-upon-Avon** for everything Shakespeare. Continue north with a day in the **Lake District**, followed by two days in Scotland's capital **Edinburgh**. After a day trip to **Loch Ness**, recross the border for two days to see **York** and **Castle Howard**. Next, stop off in **Cambridge** on the way back to London.

ENGLAND

By far the biggest of the three nations that comprise Great Britain, England offers a tempting spread of classic travel experiences, from London's vibrant theatre scene and the historic colleges of Oxford, to the grand cathedrals of Canterbury and York and the mountain landscapes of the Lake District.

London

POP 7.51 MILLION

Everyone comes to London with preconceptions shaped by a multitude of books, movies, TV shows and pop songs. Whatever yours are, prepare to have them exploded by this endlessly intriguing city. Its streets are steeped in fascinating history, magnificent art, imposing architecture and popular culture. When you add a bottomless reserve of cool to this mix, it's hard not to conclude that London is one of the world's great cities, if not the greatest.

The only downside is increasing cost: London is now Europe's most expensive city for visitors, whatever their budget. But with some careful planning and a bit of common sense, you can find great bargains and freebies among the popular attractions. And many of London's greatest assets – its wonderful parks, bridges, squares and boulevards, not to mention many of its landmark museums – come completely free.

History

London first came into being as a Celtic village near a ford across the River Thames, but the city really only took off after the Roman invasion in AD 43. The Romans enclosed Londinium in walls that still find an echo in the shape of the City of London (the city's central financial district) today. Next came the Saxons, and the town they called Lundenwic prospered.

London grew in global importance throughout the medieval period, surviving devastating challenges such as the 1665 plague and the 1666 Great Fire. Many of its important landmarks such as St Paul's Cathedral were built at this time by visionary architect Christopher Wren.

By the early 1700s, Georgian London had become one of Europe's largest and richest cities. It was during the Victorian era that London really hit its stride, fuelled by vast mercantile wealth and a huge global empire.

The ravages of WWI were followed by the economic troubles of the 1920s and 1930s, but it was WWII that wrought the greatest damage: huge swathes of the city were reduced to rubble during a series of devastating bombings known as the Blitz.

During the 1960s, Swinging London became the world's undisputed cultural capital, with an explosion of provocative art, music, writing, theatre and fashion. The 1970s proved more turbulent than innovative, with widespread unrest and economic discontent, while the 1980s were marked by an economic boom in London's financial district (known as the City), which brought a forest of skyscrapers to the city's skyline.

In 2000 London got its first elected Mayor, left-wing Ken Livingstone, who served for two terms and oversaw the city's bid for the 2012 Olympics, and also dealt with the grim aftermath of the 7/7 tube bombings in 2005, when four British-born terrorists detonated bombs, killing 52 people.

Livingstone was ousted by his Eton-educated, blonde-mopped Conservative rival,

London

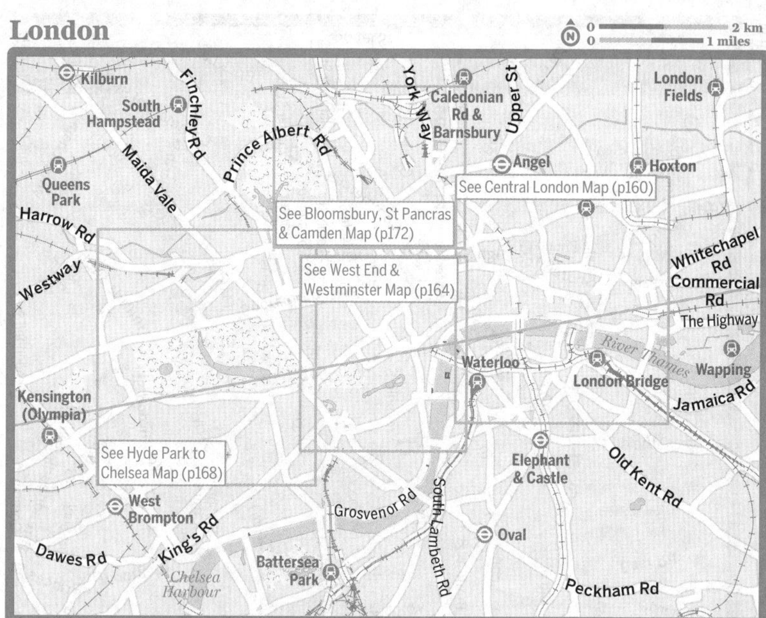

Boris Johnson, in 2008. Johnson was reelected in 2012 and oversaw the Queen's Golden Jubilee celebrations, followed by the city's hugely successful stint as Olympics host.

Sights

Westminster & St James's

★Westminster Abbey CHURCH

(Map p164; 020-7222 5152; www.westminster-abbey.org; 20 Dean's Yard, SW1; adult/child £20/9, verger tours £5; 9.30am-4.30pm Mon, Tue, Thu & Fri, to 7pm Wed, to 2.30pm Sat; Westminster) Westminster Abbey is a mixture of architectural styles, but considered the finest example of Early English Gothic (1190–1300). It's not merely a beautiful place of worship, though. The Abbey serves up the country's history cold on slabs of stone. For centuries the country's greatest have been interred here, including 17 monarchs, from Henry III (died 1272) to George II (1760).

Houses of Parliament HISTORIC BUILDING

(Map p164; www.parliament.uk; Parliament Sq, SW1; Westminster) FREE Officially called the Palace of Westminster, the Houses of Parliament's oldest part is 11th-century Westminster Hall, which is one of only a few sections that survived a catastrophic fire in 1834. Its roof, added between 1394 and 1401, is the earliest known example of a hammerbeam roof. Most of the rest of the building is a neo-Gothic confection built by Charles Barry (1795–1860) and Augustus Pugin (1812–1852).

Buckingham Palace PALACE

(Map p164; 020-7766 7300; www.royalcollection.org.uk; Buckingham Palace Rd, SW1; adult/child £20.50/11.80; 9.30am-7.30pm late Jul-Aug, to 6.30pm Sep; St James's Park, Victoria, Green Park) Built in 1703 for the Duke of Buckingham, Buckingham Palace replaced St James's Palace as the monarch's official London residence in 1837. When she's not giving her famous wave to far-flung parts of the Commonwealth, Queen Elizabeth II divides her time between here, Windsor and, in summer, Balmoral. To know if she's at home, check whether the yellow, red and blue standard is flying.

★Tate Britain GALLERY

(www.tate.org.uk; Millbank, SW1; 10am-6pm, to 10pm 1st Fri of month; Pimlico) FREE You'd think that Tate Britain might have suffered since its sexy sibling, Tate Modern, took half its collection and all of the limelight across the river. On the contrary, the venerable Tate Britain, built in 1897 by Henry Tate,

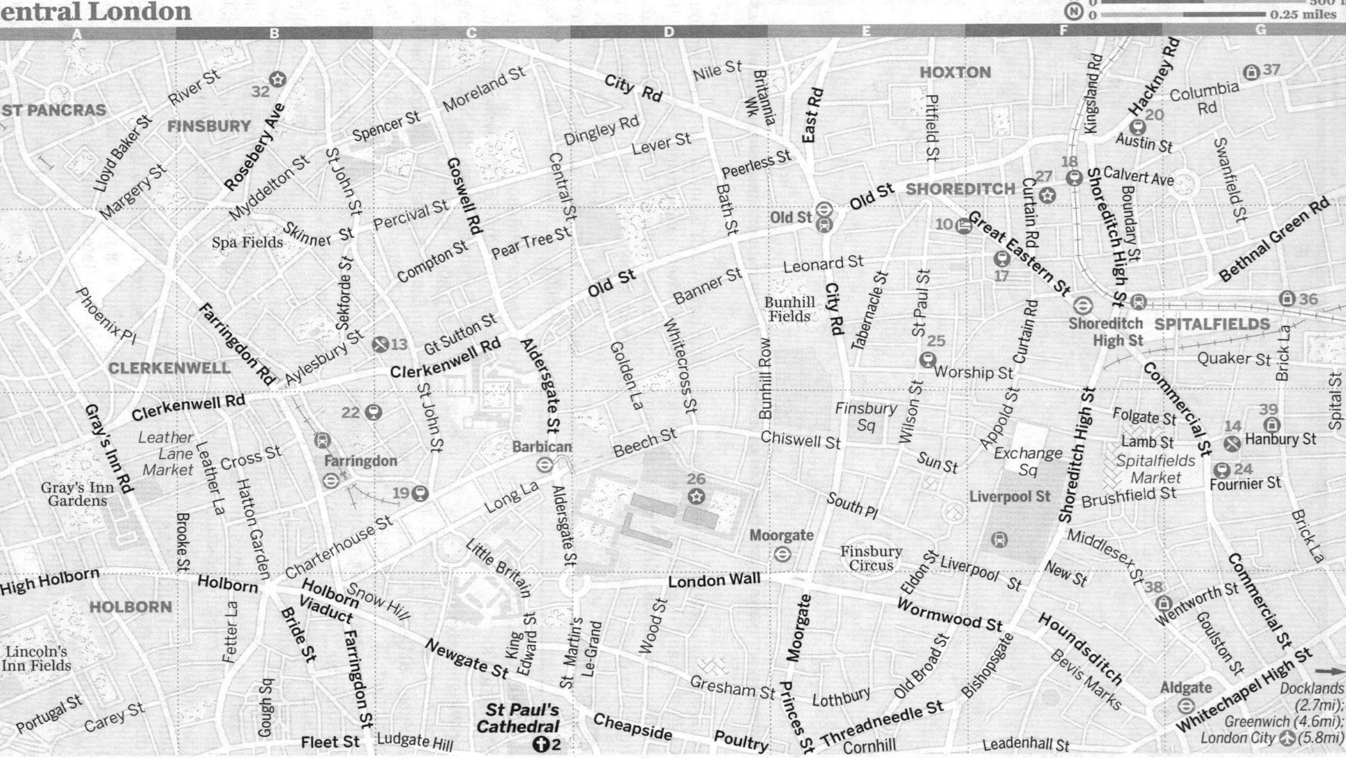
Central London
500 m
0.25 miles
ST PANCRAS
FINSBURY
CLERKENWELL
HOLBORN
HOXTON
SHOREDITCH
SPITALFIELDS
River St
Lloyd Baker St
Margery St
Rosebery Ave
Myddelton St
Spa Fields
Skinner St
St John St
Spencer St
Moreland St
Percival St
Goswell Rd
Compton St
Pear Tree St
Central St
City Rd
Dingley Rd
Lever St
Nile St
Britannia Wk
Peerless St
Bath St
East Rd
Pitfield St
Old St
Kingsland Rd
Hackney Rd
Columbia Rd
Austin St
Calvert Ave
Boundary St
Swanfield St
Curtain Rd
Shoreditch High St
Bethnal Green Rd
Great Eastern St
Leonard St
Banner St
Bunhill Fields
Tabernacle St
St Paul St
Phoenix Pl
Farringdon Rd
Sekforde St
Aylesbury St
Gt Sutton St
Clerkenwell Rd
Aldersgate St
Golden La
Whitecross St
Bunhill Row
Worship St
Quaker St
Brick La
Spital St
Commercial St
Gray's Inn Rd
Leather Lane Market
Leather La
Cross St
Hatton Garden
Farringdon
Barbican
Beech St
Chiswell St
Finsbury Sq
Wilson St
Appold St
Folgate St
Lamb St
Hanbury St
Spitalfields Market
Fournier St
Gray's Inn Gardens
Brooke St
Long La
Charterhouse St
Sun St
Exchange Sq
Liverpool St
Brushfield St
South Pl
Moorgate
Finsbury Circus
Middlesex St
High Holborn
Holborn
Holborn Viaduct
Snow Hill
Little Britain
London Wall
Eldon St
Liverpool St
New St
Wentworth St
Goulston St
Wormwood St
Houndsditch
Lincoln's Inn Fields
Fetter La
Bride St
Farringdon St
Newgate St
King Edward St
St Martin's Le-Grand
Wood St
Gresham St
Lothbury
Old Broad St
Bishopsgate
Bevis Marks
Aldgate
Whitechapel High St
Portugal St
Carey St
Gough Sq
Fleet St
Ludgate Hill
St Paul's Cathedral
Cheapside
Poultry
Princes St
Threadneedle St
Cornhill
Leadenhall St
Docklands (2.7mi); Greenwich (4.6mi); London City (5.8mi)

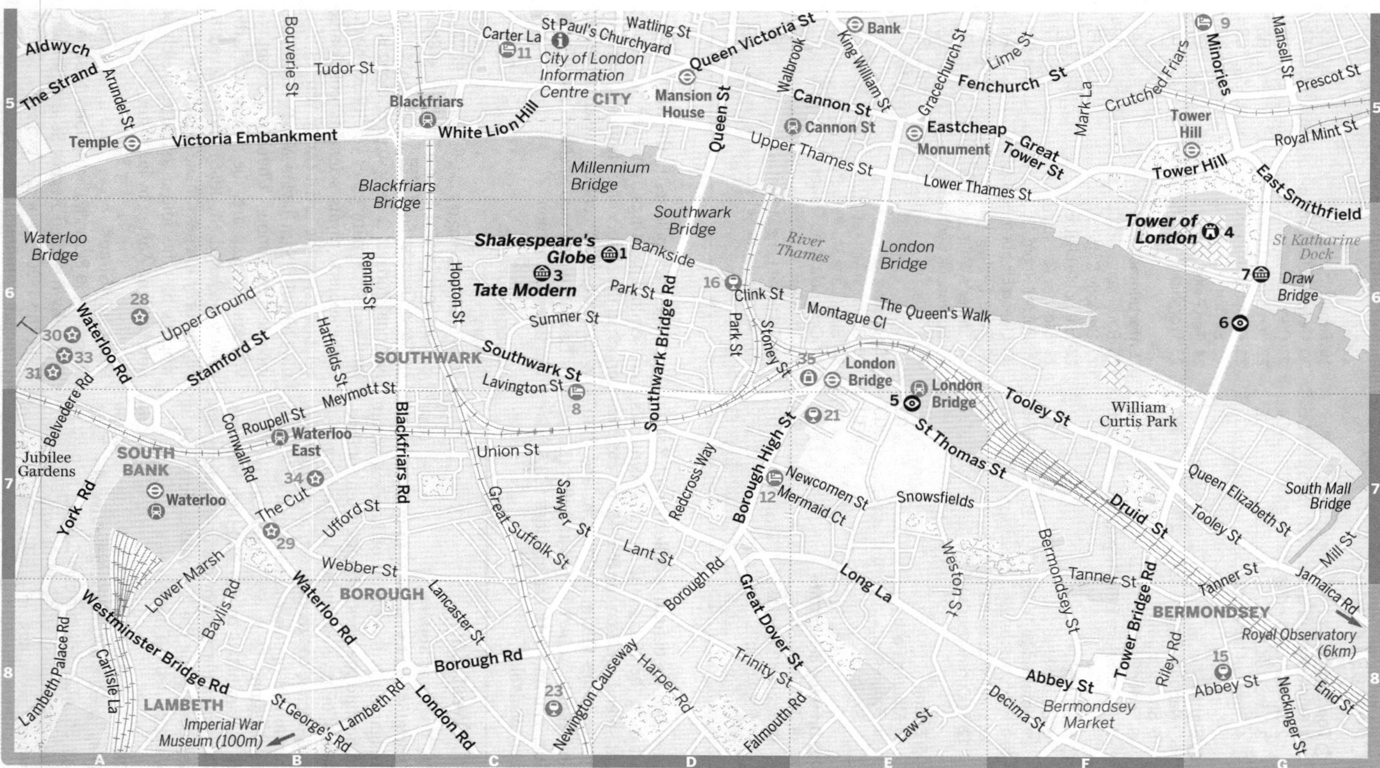
Aldwych
The Strand
Arundel St
Temple
Victoria Embankment
Bouverie St
Tudor St
Blackfriars
White Lion Hill
Carter La
11
St Paul's Churchyard
City of London Information Centre
CITY
Watling St
Queen Victoria St
Mansion House
Queen St
Walbrook
Bank
King William St
Cannon St
Cannon St
Upper Thames St
Gracechurch St
Lime St
Fenchurch St
Eastcheap
Monument
Great Tower St
Lower Thames St
Mark La
Crutched Friars
9
Minories
Tower Hill
Tower Hill
Mansell St
Prescot St
Royal Mint St
East Smithfield
Millennium Bridge
Blackfriars Bridge
Southwark Bridge
River Thames
London Bridge
Tower of London
4
St Katharine Dock
7
Draw Bridge
6
Waterloo Bridge
Shakespeare's Globe
1
Bankside
3
Tate Modern
Park St
16
Clink St
Montague Cl
The Queen's Walk
28
Upper Ground
30
33
31
Waterloo Rd
Stamford St
Hatfields St
Rennie St
Hopton St
Sumner St
SOUTHWARK
Southwark St
Southwark Bridge Rd
Park St
Stoney St
35
London Bridge
London Bridge
5
Tooley St
William Curtis Park
Belvedere Rd
Meymott St
Lavington St
8
Roupell St
Waterloo East
Cornwall Rd
Blackfriars Rd
21
St Thomas St
Jubilee Gardens
SOUTH BANK
Union St
Borough High St
Redcross Way
Newcomen St
12
Mermaid Ct
Snowsfields
Queen Elizabeth St
South Mall Bridge
York Rd
Waterloo
34
The Cut
Ufford St
Great Suffolk St
Sawyer St
Lant St
Druid St
Tooley St
Mill St
29
Webber St
Long La
Weston St
Bermondsey St
Tanner St
Tanner St
Jamaica Rd
Lower Marsh
Baylis Rd
Waterloo Rd
BOROUGH
Lancaster St
Borough Rd
Great Dover St
Tower Bridge Rd
BERMONDSEY
Riley Rd
Royal Observatory (6km)
Westminster Bridge Rd
Lambeth Palace Rd
Carlisle La
Borough Rd
Newington Causeway
Harper Rd
Trinity St
Abbey St
15
Abbey St
Enid St
LAMBETH
Imperial War Museum (100m)
St George's Rd
Lambeth Rd
London Rd
23
Falmouth Rd
Law St
Decima St
Bermondsey Market
Neckinger St
A
B
C
D
E
F
G
5
6
7
8

Central London

Top Sights

1 Shakespeare's Globe ... D6
2 St Paul's Cathedral ... C4
3 Tate Modern ... C6
4 Tower of London ... G6

Sights

National Theatre ... (see 28)
5 Shard ... E7
6 Tower Bridge ... G6
7 Tower Bridge Exhibition ... G6

Sleeping

8 Citizen M ... C7
9 Hotel Indigo Tower Hill ... G5
10 Hoxton Hotel ... E2
11 London St Paul's YHA ... C5
12 St Christopher's Village ... D7

Eating

13 Modern Pantry ... C2
14 Poppies ... G3
Skylon ... (see 31)

Drinking & Nightlife

15 40 Maltby Street ... G8
16 Anchor Bankside ... D6
17 Book Club ... F2
18 Cargo ... F1
19 Fabric ... C3
20 George & Dragon ... F1
21 George Inn ... E7
22 Jerusalem Tavern ... B3
23 Ministry of Sound ... C8
Skylon ... (see 31)
24 Ten Bells ... G3
25 Worship St Whistling Shop ... E2

Entertainment

26 Barbican ... D3
27 Comedy Cafe ... F1
28 National Theatre ... A6
29 Old Vic ... B7
Purcell Room ... (see 30)
30 Queen Elizabeth Hall ... A6
31 Royal Festival Hall ... A6
32 Sadler's Wells ... B1
33 Southbank Centre ... A6
34 Young Vic ... B7

Shopping

35 Borough Market ... E6
36 Brick Lane Market ... G2
37 Columbia Road Flower Market ... G1
38 Petticoat Lane Market ... F4
39 Sunday UpMarket ... G3

stretched its definitive collection of British art from the 16th to the late 20th centuries out splendidly. Join the free 45-minute **thematic tours** (11am, noon, 2pm and 3pm) and 15-minute **Art in Focus talks** (1.15pm Tue, Thu and Sat). Audioguides (£3.50) are also available.

West End

★Trafalgar Square SQUARE
(Map p164; Charing Cross) In many ways Trafalgar Sq is the centre of London, where rallies and marches take place, tens of thousands of revellers usher in the New Year and locals congregate for anything from communal open-air cinema and Christmas celebrations to various political protests. It is dominated by the 52m-high **Nelson's Column** and ringed by many splendid buildings, including the National Gallery and **St Martin-in-the-Fields**.

★National Gallery GALLERY
(Map p164; www.nationalgallery.org.uk; Trafalgar Sq, WC2; 10am-6pm Sat-Thu, to 9pm Fri; Charing Cross) FREE With some 2300 European paintings on display, this is one of the richest art galleries in the world. There are seminal paintings from every important epoch in the history of art from the mid-13th to the early 20th century, including works by Leonardo da Vinci, Michelangelo, Titian, Van Gogh and Renoir.

National Portrait Gallery GALLERY
(Map p164; www.npg.org.uk; St Martin's Pl, WC2; 10am-6pm Sat-Wed, to 9pm Thu & Fri; Charing Cross, Leicester Sq) FREE What makes the National Portrait Gallery so compelling is its familiarity; in many cases you'll have heard of the subject (royals, scientists, politicians, celebrities) or the artist (Andy Warhol, Annie Leibovitz, Sam Taylor-Wood). Highlights include the famous 'Chandos portrait' of William Shakespeare, the first artwork the gallery acquired (in 1856) and believed to be the only likeness made during the playwright's lifetime, and a touching sketch of novelist Jane Austen by her sister.

Piccadilly Circus SQUARE
(Map p164; Piccadilly Circus) John Nash had originally designed Regent St and Piccadilly in the 1820s to be the two most elegant

streets in town but, curbed by city planners, couldn't realise his dream to the full. He would certainly be disappointed with what Piccadilly Circus has become: swamped with visitors, flanked by flashing advertisement panels and surrounded by shops flogging tourist tat.

Madame Tussauds MUSEUM
(Map p168; ☎0870 400 3000; www.madametussauds.com/london; Marylebone Rd, NW1; adult/child £30/26; ⊙9.30am-5.30pm; ⊖Baker St) Madame Tussauds offers photo ops for days with your dream celebrity at the A-List Party (Daniel Craig, Lady Gaga, George Clooney, David and Victoria Beckham), the Bollywood gathering (Hrithik Roshan, Salman Khan) and the Royal Appointment (the Queen, Harry, William and Kate). If you're into politics, get up close and personal with Barack Obama or even London Mayor Boris Johnson.

The City

★St Paul's Cathedral CHURCH
(Map p160; www.stpauls.co.uk; St Paul's Churchyard, EC4; adult/child £16.50/7.50; ⊙8.30am-4.30pm Mon-Sat; ⊖St Paul's) Dominating the City of London with the world's second-largest church domes (and weighing in at around 65,000 tonnes), St Paul's Cathedral was designed by Christopher Wren after the Great Fire and built between 1675 and 1710. The site is ancient hallowed ground with four other cathedrals preceding Wren's English Baroque masterpiece here, the first dating from 604.

★Tower of London CASTLE
(Map p160; ☎0844 482 7777; www.hrp.org.uk/toweroflondon; Tower Hill, EC3; adult/child £22/11, audioguide £4/3; ⊙9am-5.30pm Tue-Sat, 10am-5.30pm Sun & Mon, to 4.30pm Nov-Feb; ⊖Tower Hill) The unmissable Tower of London (actually a castle of 20-odd towers) offers a window on to a gruesome and quite compelling history. This was where two kings and three queens met their death and countless others were imprisoned. Come here to see the colourful Yeoman Warders (or Beefeaters), the spectacular **Crown Jewels**, the soothsaying ravens and armour fit for a king.

Tower Bridge BRIDGE
(Map p160; ⊖Tower Hill) London was a thriving port in 1894 when elegant Tower Bridge was built. Designed to be raised to allow ships to pass, electricity has now taken over from the original steam and hydraulic engines. A lift leads up from the northern tower to the **Tower Bridge Exhibition** (Map p160; www.towerbridge.org.uk; adult/child £8/3.40; ⊙10am-6pm Apr-Sep, 9.30am-5.30pm Oct-Mar; ⊖Tower Hill), where the story of its building is recounted within the upper walkway.

DON'T MISS

BRITISH MUSEUM

The vast **British Museum** (Map p164; ☎020-7323 8000; www.britishmuseum.org; Great Russell St, WC1; ⊙10am-5.30pm Sat-Thu, to 8.30pm Fri; ⊖Russell Sq, Tottenham Court Rd) FREE isn't just the nation's largest museum, it's one of the oldest and finest anywhere in the world. Among the must-see antiquities are the **Rosetta Stone**, the key to deciphering Egyptian hieroglyphics, discovered in 1799; the controversial **Parthenon Sculptures**, stripped from the walls of the Parthenon in Athens by Lord Elgin (the British ambassador to the Ottoman Empire); and the Anglo-Saxon **Sutton Hoo relics**. The **Great Court** was restored and augmented by Norman Foster in 2000 and now has a spectacular glass-and-steel roof.

You'll need multiple visits to savour even the highlights here; take advantage of the 15 free half-hour **Eye Opener** tours between 11am and 3.45pm daily, focusing on different parts of the collection. Various multimedia iPad tours are also available (adult/child £5/3.50).

South Bank

★Tate Modern MUSEUM
(Map p160; www.tate.org.uk; Queen's Walk, SE1; ⊙10am-6pm Sun-Thu, to 10pm Fri & Sat; ; ⊖Blackfriars, Southwark or London Bridge) FREE One of London's most popular attractions, this outstanding modern and contemporary art gallery is housed in the creatively revamped **Bankside Power Station** south of the **Millennium Bridge**. A spellbinding synthesis of funky modern art and capacious industrial brick design, Tate Modern has been extraordinarily successful in bringing challenging work to the masses. A stunning extension is aiming for a 2016 completion

West End & Westminster

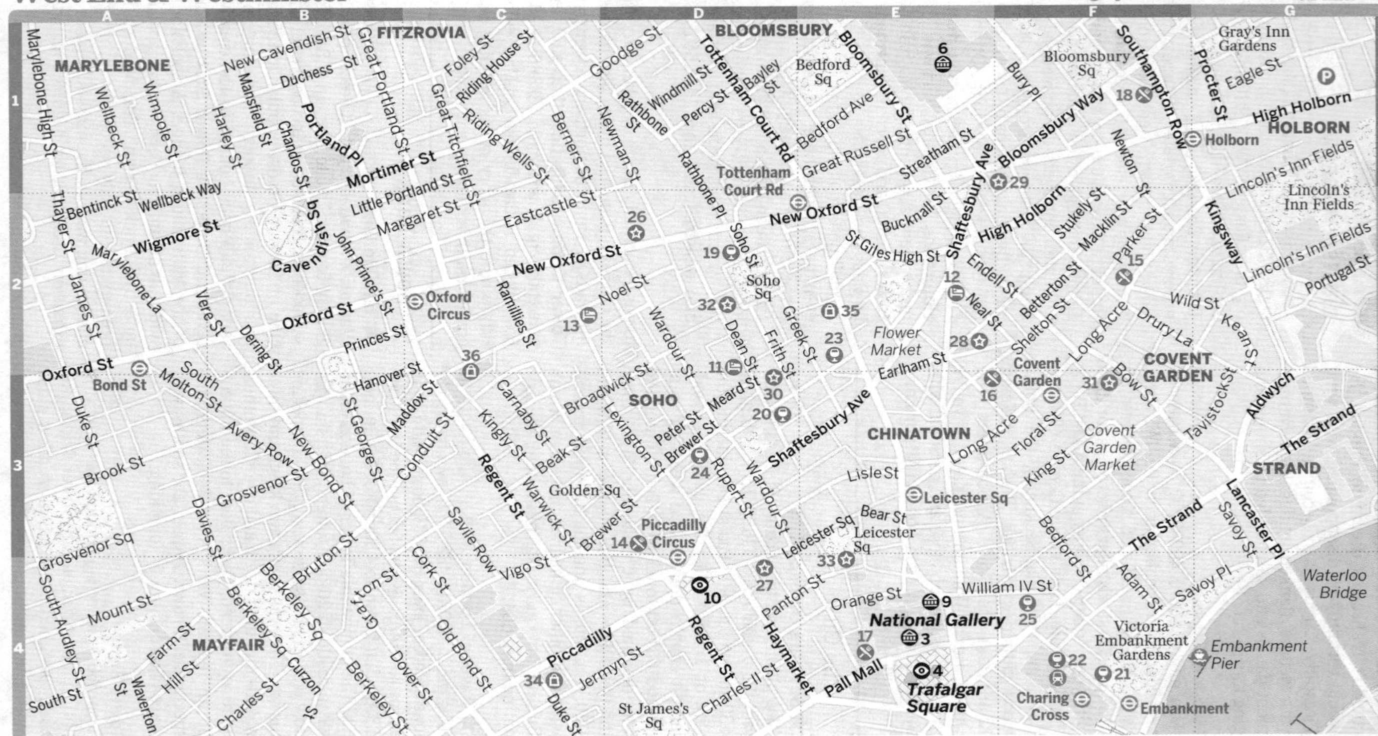

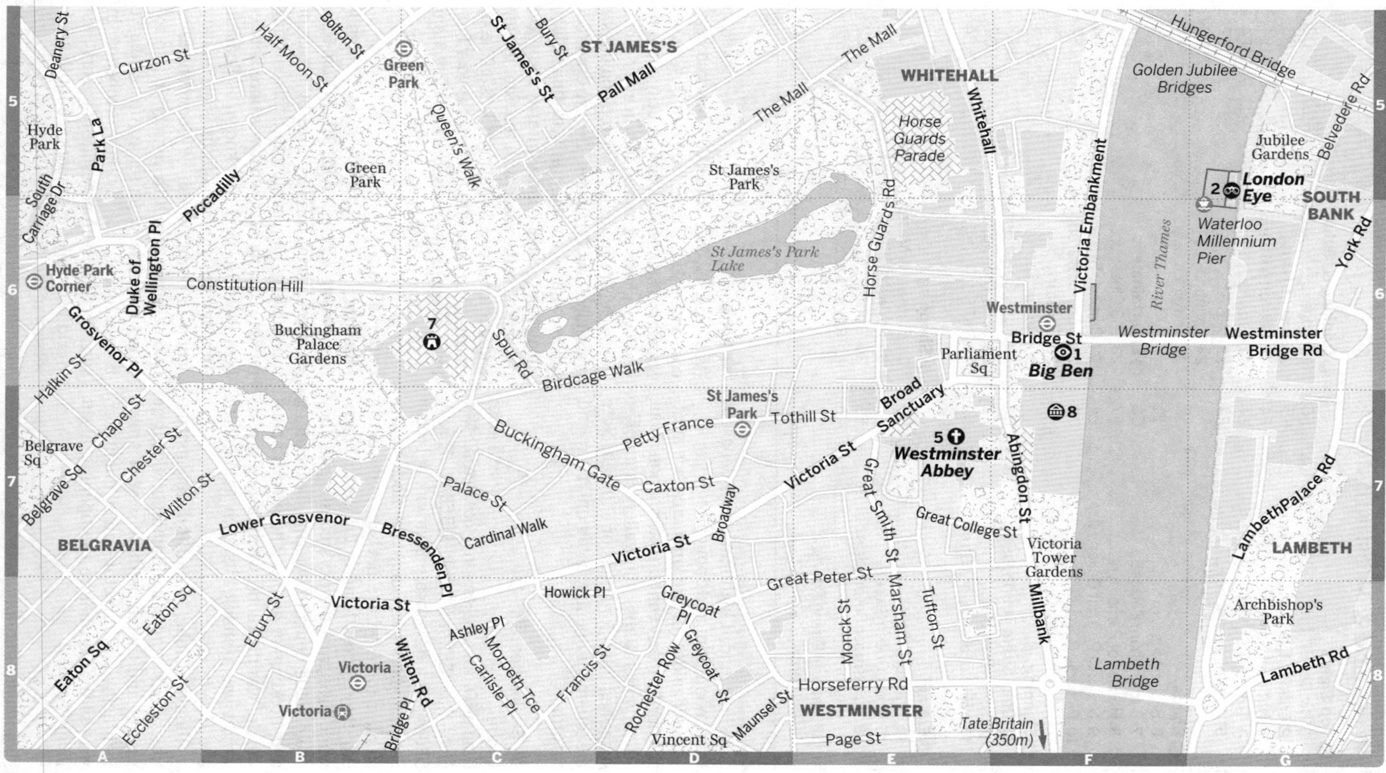
ST JAMES'S
WHITEHALL
SOUTH BANK
LAMBETH
BELGRAVIA
WESTMINSTER
Deanery St
Curzon St
Half Moon St
Bolton St
Green Park
St James's St
Bury St
Pall Mall
The Mall
Hungerford Bridge
Golden Jubilee Bridges
Belvedere Rd
Hyde Park
Park La
Queen's Walk
Green Park
St James's Park
Horse Guards Parade
Whitehall
Jubilee Gardens
2 London Eye
South Carriage Dr
Piccadilly
Duke of Wellington Pl
St James's Park Lake
Horse Guards Rd
Victoria Embankment
River Thames
Waterloo Millennium Pier
York Rd
Hyde Park Corner
Constitution Hill
Grosvenor Pl
Buckingham Palace Gardens
7
Spur Rd
Westminster
Bridge St
Westminster Bridge
Westminster Bridge Rd
Parliament Sq
1 Big Ben
Halkin St
Chapel St
Birdcage Walk
St James's Park
Tothill St
Broad Sanctuary
8
Petty France
Belgrave Sq
Chester St
Buckingham Gate
5 Westminster Abbey
Victoria St
Great Smith St
Abingdon St
Belgrave Sq
Wilton St
Palace St
Caxton St
Great College St
Lambeth Palace Rd
Lower Grosvenor
Bressenden Pl
Cardinal Walk
Broadway
Victoria St
Victoria Tower Gardens
Great Peter St
Howick Pl
Greycoat Pl
Eaton Sq
Ebury St
Victoria St
Ashley Pl
Morpeth Tce
Carlisle Pl
Monck St
Marsham St
Tufton St
Millbank
Archbishop's Park
Greycoat St
Rochester Row
Francis St
Eaton Sq
Victoria
Wilton Rd
Horseferry Rd
Lambeth Bridge
Lambeth Rd
Eccleston St
Victoria
Bridge Pl
Maunsel St
Vincent Sq
Page St
Tate Britain (350m)
A
B
C
D
E
F
G
5
6
7
8

West End & Westminster

Top Sights
1 Big Ben F6
2 London Eye G5
3 National Gallery E4
4 Trafalgar Square E4
5 Westminster Abbey E7

Sights
6 British Museum E1
7 Buckingham Palace C6
8 Houses of Parliament F7
9 National Portrait Gallery E4
10 Piccadilly Circus D4

Sleeping
11 Dean Street Townhouse D2
12 Seven Dials Hotel E2
13 YHA London Oxford Street C2

Eating
14 Brasserie Zédel D3
15 Great Queen Street F2
16 Hawksmoor Seven Dials E3
Koya .... (see 30)
17 National Dining Rooms E4
18 Orchard F1

Drinking & Nightlife
19 Edge D2
20 French House D3
21 Gordon's Wine Bar F4
22 Heaven F4
23 LAB E2
24 Spuntino D3
25 Terroirs F4

Entertainment
26 100 Club D2
27 Comedy Store D4
28 Donmar Warehouse E2
29 Popstarz F1
30 Ronnie Scott's D3
31 Royal Opera House F3
32 Soho Theatre D2
33 TKTS E4

Shopping
34 Fortnum & Mason C4
35 Foyles E2
36 Liberty C2
Ray's Jazz .... (see 35)

date. Free guided highlights tours depart at 11am, noon, 2pm and 3pm daily.

Audioguides (in five languages) are available for £4 – they contain information about 50 artworks across the gallery and offer suggested tours for adults or children. Note the late-night opening hours on Friday and Saturday.

★ Shakespeare's Globe — HISTORIC BUILDING

(Map p160; www.shakespearesglobe.com; 21 New Globe Walk, SE1; adult/child £13.50/8; 9am-5.30pm; ; Blackfriars, Southwark or London Bridge) Today's Londoners may flock to Amsterdam to misbehave, but back in the bard's day they'd cross London Bridge to Southwark. Free from the city's constraints, they could settle down to whoring, bear-baiting and heckling of actors. The most famous theatre was the Globe, where a genius playwright was penning hits such as *Macbeth* and *Hamlet*.

Today's Globe, a faithful reconstruction of oak beams, handmade bricks, lime plaster and thatch, is the vision of American actor and director Sam Wanamaker, who sadly died before the opening night in 1997.

★ London Eye — VIEWPOINT

(Map p164; 0871 781 3000; www.londoneye.com; adult/child £21/15; 10am-8pm; Waterloo) Standing 135m high in a fairly flat city, the London Eye affords views 25 miles in every direction, weather permitting. Each rotation takes a gracefully slow 30 minutes. The Eye draws 3.5 million visitors annually; at peak times (July, August and school holidays) it may seem like they are all in the queue with you. Save money and shorten queues by buying tickets online, or cough up an extra £10 to showcase your fast-track swagger. Alternatively, visit before 11am or after 3pm to avoid peak density.

Imperial War Museum — MUSEUM

(www.iwm.org.uk; Lambeth Rd, SE1; 10am-6pm; Lambeth North) FREE Fronted by a pair of intimidating 15in naval guns, this riveting museum is housed in what was once Bethlehem Royal Hospital, also known as Bedlam. Although the museum's focus is on military action involving British or Commonwealth troops during the 20th century, it also explores war in the wider sense. After extensive refurbishment, the museum reopened in summer 2014, with new state-of-the-art First World War Galleries to mark the 100th anniversary of the start of WWI.

Shard NOTABLE BUILDING
(Map p160; www.the-shard.com; 32 London Bridge St, SE1; adult/child £29.95/23.95; 10am-10pm; London Bridge) Puncturing the skies above London, the dramatic splinter-like form of the Shard has rapidly become an icon of the town. The **viewing platforms** on floors 68, 69 and 72 are open to the public and the views are, as you'd expect from a 244m vantage point, sweeping, but they come at a hefty price – book online to save £5.

As well as the viewing platform, the Shard will be home to flats, hotels and restaurants; the first three opened over the summer in 2013.

Kensington & Hyde Park

This area is called the Royal Borough of Kensington and Chelsea, and residents are certainly paid royally, earning the highest incomes in the UK (shops and restaurants will presume you do, too).

★**Victoria & Albert Museum** MUSEUM
(V&A; Map p168; www.vam.ac.uk; Cromwell Rd, SW7; 10am-5.45pm Sat-Thu, to 10pm Fri; South Kensington) FREE The Museum of Manufactures, as the V&A was known when it opened in 1852, was part of Prince Albert's legacy to the nation in the aftermath of the successful Great Exhibition of 1851, and its original aims – which still hold today – were the 'improvement of public taste in design' and 'applications of fine art to objects of utility'. It's done a fine job so far.

★**Natural History Museum** MUSEUM
(Map p168; www.nhm.ac.uk; Cromwell Rd, SW7; 10am-5.50pm; South Kensington) FREE This colossal building is infused with the irrepressible Victorian spirit of collecting, cataloguing and interpreting the natural world. The main museum building is as much a reason to visit as the world-famous collection within.

★**Science Museum** MUSEUM
(Map p168; www.sciencemuseum.org.uk; Exhibition Rd, SW7; 10am-6pm; South Kensington) FREE With seven floors of interactive and educational exhibits, this scientifically spellbinding museum will mesmerise adults and children alike, covering everything from early technology to space travel.

Hyde Park PARK
(Map p168; 5.30am-midnight; Marble Arch, Hyde Park Corner, Queensway) At 145 hectares, Hyde Park is central London's largest open space. Henry VIII expropriated it from the Church in 1536, when it became a hunting ground and later a venue for duels, executions and horse racing. The 1851 Great Exhibition was held here, and during WWII the park became an enormous potato field. These days, it's an occasional concert venue (Bruce Springsteen, the Rolling Stones, Madonna) and a full-time green space for fun and frolics, including boating on the **Serpentine**.

Hampstead & North London

With one of London's best high streets and plenty of green space, increasingly hip Marylebone is a great area to wander.

★**ZSL London Zoo** ZOO
(www.londonzoo.co.uk; Outer Circle, Regent's Park, NW1; adult/child £26/18.50; 10am-5.30pm Mar-Oct, to 4pm Nov-Feb; Camden Town) These famous zoological gardens have come a long way since being established in 1828, with massive investment making conservation, education and breeding the name of the game. Highlights include **Penguin Beach**, **Gorilla Kingdom**, **Animal Adventure** (the new childrens' zoo) and **Butterfly Paradise**. Feeding sessions or talks take place during the day. Arachnophobes can ask about the zoo's Friendly Spider Programme, designed to cure fears of all things eight-legged and hairy.

Regent's Park PARK
(www.royalparks.org.uk; 5am-dusk; Regent's Park, Baker St) The most elaborate and ordered of London's many parks, this one was created around 1820 by John Nash, who planned to use it as an estate to build palaces for the aristocracy. Although the plan never quite came off, you can get some idea of what Nash might have achieved from the buildings along the Outer Circle.

Greenwich

An extraordinary cluster of buildings has earned 'Maritime Greenwich' its place on Unesco's World Heritage list. It's also famous for straddling the hemispheres; this is the degree zero of longitude, home of the Greenwich Meridian and Greenwich Mean Time.

Hyde Park to Chelsea

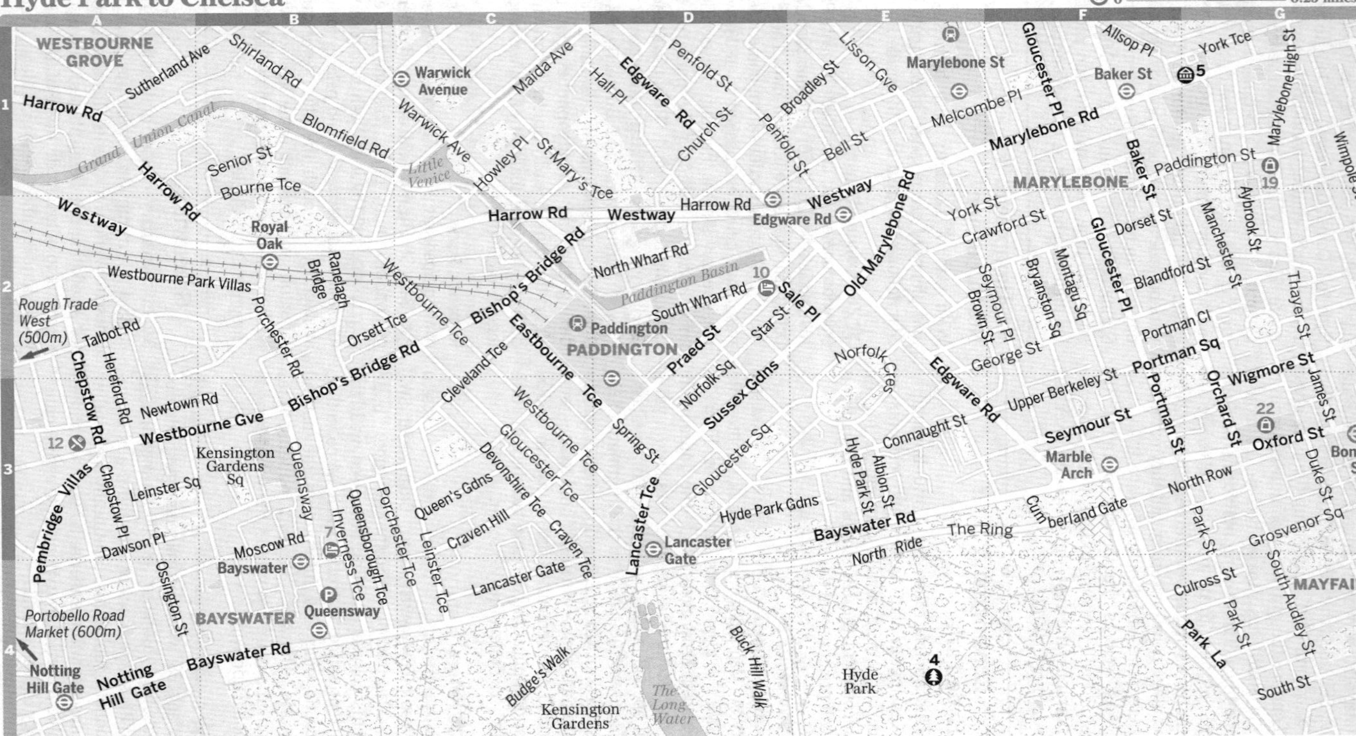

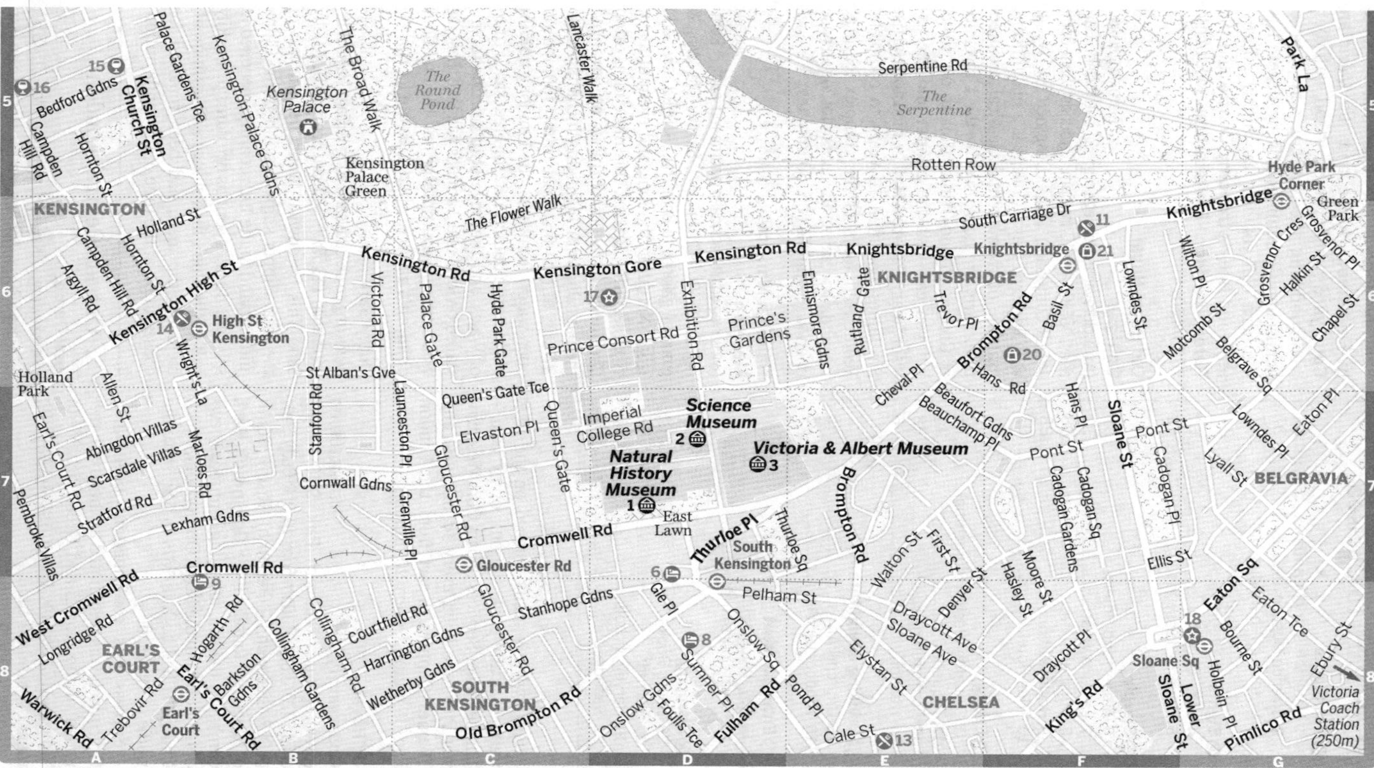

Palace Gardens Tce
Kensington Palace Gdns
The Broad Walk
The Round Pond
Lancaster Walk
Serpentine Rd
The Serpentine
Park La
15
16
Bedford Gdns
Kensington Church St
Kensington Palace
Campden Hill Rd
Hornton St
Kensington Palace Green
Rotten Row
Hyde Park Corner
Green Park
KENSINGTON
Holland St
The Flower Walk
South Carriage Dr
11
Knightsbridge
Grosvenor Cres
Grosvenor Pl
Campden Hill Rd
Hornton St
Kensington Rd
Kensington Gore
Kensington Rd
Knightsbridge
Knightsbridge
21
Wilton Pl
Halkin St
Argyll Rd
Kensington High St
Victoria Rd
Palace Gate
Hyde Park Gate
17
Exhibition Rd
Ennismore Gdns
Rutland Gate
KNIGHTSBRIDGE
Trevor Pl
Basil St
Lowndes St
Chapel St
Motcomb St
14
High St Kensington
Prince Consort Rd
Prince's Gardens
Brompton Rd
20
Belgrave Sq
Holland Park
Allen St
Wright's La
St Alban's Gve
Launceston Pl
Queen's Gate Tce
Cheval Pl
Hans Rd
Hans Pl
Sloane St
Eaton Pl
Lowndes Pl
Earl's Court Rd
Abingdon Villas
Scarsdale Villas
Marloes Rd
Stanford Rd
Elvaston Pl
Queen's Gate
Imperial College Rd
Science Museum
2
Beaufort Gdns
Beauchamp Pl
Pont St
Pont St
Victoria & Albert Museum
3
Natural History Museum
1
Cadogan Gardens
Cadogan Sq
Cadogan Pl
Lyall St
BELGRAVIA
Pembroke Villas
Stratford Rd
Cornwall Gdns
Gloucester Rd
Grenville Pl
Lexham Gdns
East Lawn
Brompton Rd
Cromwell Rd
Thurloe Pl
Thurloe Sq
South Kensington
Walton St
First St
Moore St
Hasley St
Ellis St
Cromwell Rd
Gloucester Rd
6
9
Denyer St
Eaton Sq
Eaton Tce
West Cromwell Rd
Stanhope Gdns
Gle Pl
Pelham St
Hogarth Rd
Longridge Rd
Collingham Rd
Courtfield Rd
Gloucester Rd
Onslow Sq
Draycott Ave
Sloane Ave
18
Bourne St
Ebury St
EARL'S COURT
Collingham Gardens
Harrington Gdns
8
Elystan St
Draycott Pl
Sloane Sq
Holbein Pl
Barkston Gdns
Earl's Court Rd
Wetherby Gdns
Sumner Pl
Pond Pl
Trebovir Rd
Earl's Court
SOUTH KENSINGTON
Onslow Gdns
Foulis Tce
Fulham Rd
CHELSEA
King's Rd
Lower Sloane St
Victoria Coach Station (250m)
Warwick Rd
Old Brompton Rd
Cale St
13
Pimlico Rd
A
B
C
D
E
F
G
5
6
7
8

Hyde Park to Chelsea

Top Sights
1 Natural History Museum....D7
2 Science Museum....D7
3 Victoria & Albert Museum....D7

Sights
4 Hyde Park....E4
5 Madame Tussauds....G1

Sleeping
6 Ampersand Hotel....D7
7 La Suite West....B3
8 Number Sixteen....D8
9 Rockwell....B8
10 Tune Hotel....D2

Eating
11 Dinner by Heston Blumenthal....F6
12 Taquería....A3
13 Tom's Kitchen....E8
14 Wasabi....A6

Drinking & Nightlife
15 Churchill Arms....A5
16 Windsor Castle....A5

Entertainment
17 Royal Albert Hall....D6
18 Royal Court Theatre....G8

Shopping
19 Daunt Books....G1
20 Harrods....F6
21 Harvey Nichols....F6
22 Selfridges....G3

Greenwich is easily reached on the DLR train (to Cutty Sark station), or by boat – Thames River Services depart from Westminster Pier (one hour, every 40 minutes) and Thames Clippers depart from the London Eye (35 minutes, every 20 minutes).

★ Royal Observatory HISTORIC BUILDING
(www.rmg.co.uk; Greenwich Park, SE10; adult/child £7.70/3.60; 10am-5pm; DLR Cutty Sark, DLR Greenwich, Greenwich) Rising south of Queen's House, idyllic **Greenwich Park** climbs up the hill, affording stunning views of London from the Royal Observatory, which Charles II had built in 1675 to help solve the riddle of longitude.

Success was confirmed in 1884 when Greenwich was designated as the prime meridian of the world, and Greenwich Mean Time (GMT) became the universal measurement of standard time.

In the north of the observatory is lovely **Flamsteed House** and the **Meridian Courtyard** (where you can stand with your feet straddling the western and eastern hemispheres); admission is by ticket. The southern half contains the highly informative and free **Astronomy Centre** and the **Peter Harrison Planetarium** (adult/child £6.50/4.50).

Old Royal Naval College HISTORIC BUILDING
(www.oldroyalnavalcollege.org; 2 Cutty Sark Gardens, SE10; 10am-5pm, grounds 8am-6pm; DLR Cutty Sark) FREE Designed by Wren, the Old Royal Naval College is a magnificent example of monumental classical architecture. Parts are now used by the University of Greenwich and Trinity College of Music, but you can visit the **chapel** and the extraordinary **Painted Hall**, which took artist Sir James Thornhill 19 years to complete. Yeomen-led tours of the complex leave at noon daily, taking in areas not otherwise open to the public (£6, 60 minutes).

National Maritime Museum MUSEUM
(www.rmg.co.uk/national-maritime-museum; Romney Rd, SE10; 10am-5pm, Sammy Ofer Wing & ground fl galleries to 8pm Thu; DLR Cutty Sark) FREE Narrating the long and eventful history of seafaring Britain, this museum is a top Greenwich attraction. Exhibits are arranged thematically, with highlights including **Miss Britain III** (the first boat to top 100mph on open water) from 1933, the 19m-long **golden state barge** built in 1732 for Frederick, Prince of Wales, and the huge **ship's propeller** installed on level one. Families will love these, as well as the **ship simulator** and the 2nd floor **children's gallery**, where kids can let rip.

Cutty Sark LANDMARK
(www.rmg.co.uk/cuttysark; King William Walk, SE10; adult/child £13.50/7; 10am-5pm; DLR Cutty Sark) This Greenwich landmark, the last of the great clipper ships to sail between China and England in the 19th century, reopened in spring 2012 after serious fire damage. Luckily half of the ship's furnishings and equipment, including the mast, had been removed for conservation at the time of the conflagration.

Outside Central London

Kew Gardens GARDENS
(www.kew.org; Kew Rd; adult/child £15/3.50; 10am-6.30pm Apr-Aug, earlier closing Sep-Mar;

Kew Pier, Kew Bridge, Kew Gardens) In 1759 botanists began rummaging around the world for specimens to plant in the 3-hectare Royal Botanic Gardens at Kew. They never stopped collecting, and the gardens, which have bloomed to 120 hectares, provide the most comprehensive botanical collection on earth (including the world's largest collection of orchids). Recognised as a Unesco World Heritage Site, the gardens can easily swallow a day's exploration; for those pressed for time, the Kew Explorer (adult/child £4/1) hop-on/hop-off road train takes in the main sights.

Hampton Court Palace PALACE
(www.hrp.org.uk/HamptonCourtPalace; adult/child/family £17.50/8.75/43.80; 10am-6pm Apr-Oct, to 4.30pm Nov-Mar; Hampton Court Palace, Hampton Court) Built by Cardinal Thomas Wolsey in 1514 but coaxed from him by Henry VIII just before Wolsey (as chancellor) fell from favour, Hampton Court Palace is England's largest and grandest Tudor structure. It was already one of the most sophisticated palaces in Europe when, in the 17th century, Christopher Wren designed an extension. The result is a beautiful blend of Tudor and 'restrained baroque' architecture. You could easily spend a day exploring the palace and its 24 hectares of riverside gardens.

Tours

One of the best ways to orientate yourself when you first arrive in London is with a 24-hour hop-on/hop-off pass for the double-decker bus tours. The buses loop around interconnecting routes throughout the day, providing a commentary as they go. The price includes a river cruise and three walking tours. You'll save a couple of pounds by booking online.

Original Tour BUS
(www.theoriginaltour.com; adult/child/family £29/14/86; every 20min 8.30am-5.30pm) A hop-on hop-off option with a river cruise thrown in as well as three themed walks: Changing of the Guard, Rock 'n' Roll and Jack the Ripper.

Big Bus Tours BUS
(www.bigbustours.com; adult/child/family £32/12/76; every 20min 8.30am-6pm Apr-Sep, to 5pm Oct & Mar, to 4.30pm Nov-Feb) Informative commentaries in eight languages. The ticket includes a free river cruise with City Cruises and three thematic walking tours (Royal London, Harry Potter film locations and Ghosts by Gaslight). Online booking discounts available.

BIG BEN

The Houses of Parliament's most famous feature is the clock tower known as **Big Ben** (Map p164). Strictly speaking, however, Big Ben is the tower's 13-tonne bell, named after Benjamin Hall, commissioner of works when the tower was completed in 1858.

Festivals & Events

University Boat Race SPORTS
(www.theboatrace.org) A posh-boy grudge match held annually since 1829 between the rowing crews of Oxford and Cambridge Universities (late March).

Virgin Money London Marathon SPORTS
(www.virginmoneylondonmarathon.com) Up to half a million spectators watch the whippet-thin champions and bizarrely clad amateurs take to the streets in late April.

Trooping the Colour PARADE
Celebrating the Queen's official birthday (in June), this ceremonial procession of troops, marching along the Mall for their monarch's inspection, is a pageantry overload.

Meltdown Festival MUSIC
(www.southbankcentre.co.uk) The Southbank Centre hands over the curatorial reigns to a legend of contemporary music (such as David Bowie, Morrissey or Patti Smith) to pull together a full program of concerts, talks and films in late June.

Wimbledon Lawn Tennis Championships SPORTS
(www.wimbledon.com) The world's most splendid tennis event takes place in late June.

Pride GAY & LESBIAN
(www.prideinlondon.org) The big event on the gay and lesbian calendar; a Technicolor street parade heads through the West End in late June or early July, culminating in a concert in Trafalgar Sq.

Notting Hill Carnival CARNIVAL
(www.thenottinghillcarnival.com) Every year, for three days during the last weekend of August, Notting Hill echoes to the calypso, ska, reggae and soca sounds of the Notting

Bloomsbury, St Pancras & Camden

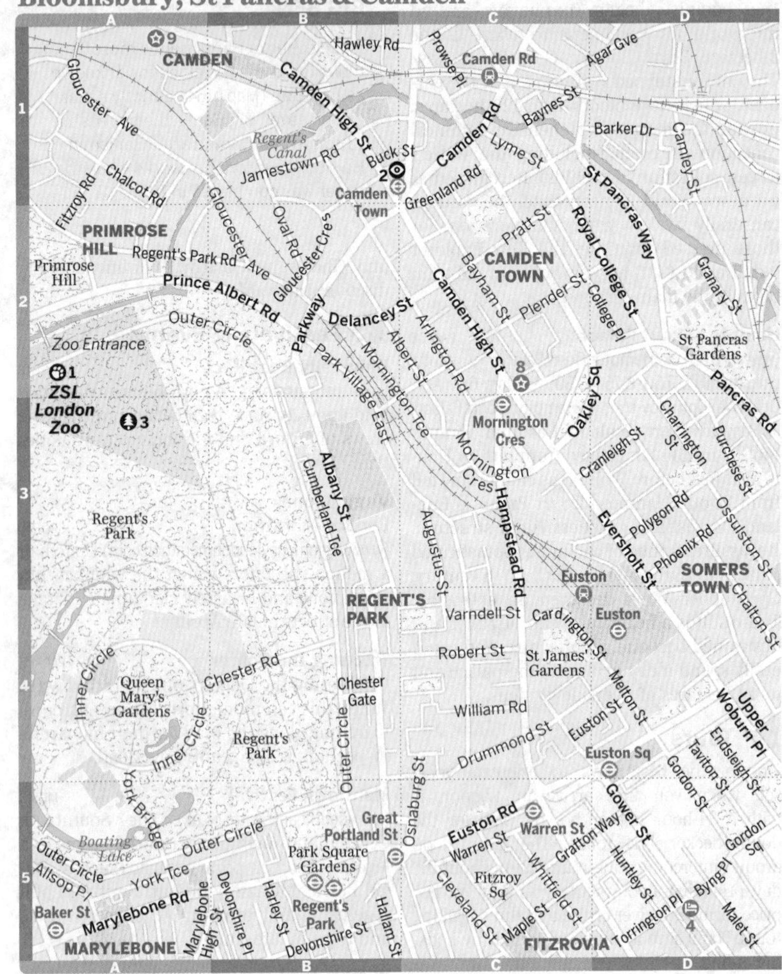

Hill Carnival. Launched in 1964 by the local Afro-Caribbean community, keen to celebrate its culture and traditions, it has grown to become Europe's largest street festival (up to one million people) and a highlight of London's annual calendar. A further undisputed attraction is the food.

Sleeping

When it comes to accommodation, London is one of the most expensive places in the world. Budget is pretty much anything below £100 per night for a double; double rooms ranging between £100 and £200 per night are considered midrange; more expensive options fall into the top-end category. Public transport is good, so you don't need to sleep at Buckingham Palace to be at the heart of things.

West End

YHA London Oxford Street HOSTEL £

(Map p164; 020-7734 1618; www.yha.org.uk; 14 Noel St, W1; dm/tw from £18/46; ; Oxford Circus) The most central of London's eight

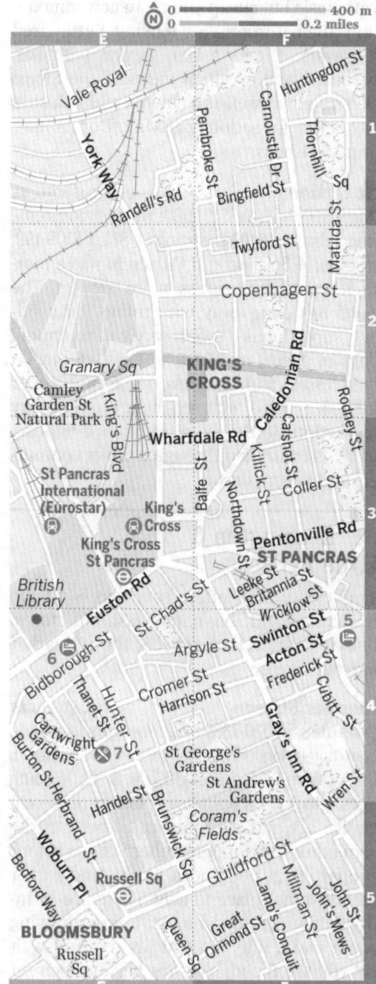

Bloomsbury, St Pancras & Camden

Top Sights
1 ZSL London Zoo A2

Sights
2 Camden Market B1
3 Regent's Park A3

Sleeping
4 Arosfa Hotel D5
5 Clink78 .... F4
6 London St Pancras YHA E4

Eating
7 North Sea Fish Restaurant E4

Entertainment
8 KOKO C2
9 Roundhouse A1

YHA hostels is also one of the most intimate, with just 104 beds and excellent shared facilities: we love the fuchsia kitchen and the bright, funky lounge. Dormitories have three and four beds and there are doubles and twins. Internet costs £1 per 20 minutes on their computers; wi-fi is £5/9 per day/week.

Clink78 HOSTEL £
(020-7183 9400; www.clinkhostels.com; 78 King's Cross Rd, WC1; dm/r from £10/25; @ wi-fi; King's Cross St Pancras) This fantastic 500-bed hostel is housed in a 19th-century magistrates courthouse where Dickens once worked as a scribe and members of the Clash made an appearance in 1978. Rooms feature pod beds (including storage space) in four- to 16-bed dormitories (there is a female aisle). There's a top kitchen with a huge dining area and a busy bar in the basement.

London St Pancras YHA HOSTEL £
(020-7388 9998; www.yha.org.uk; 79 Euston Rd, NW1; dm/r from £20/61; @ wi-fi; King's Cross St Pancras) This 185-bed hostel has modern, clean dorms sleeping four to six (nearly all with private facilities) and some private rooms. There's a good bar and cafe, although there are no self-catering facilities.

Seven Dials Hotel HOTEL ££
(Map p164; 020-7240 0823; www.sevendials hotellondon.com; 7 Monmouth St, WC2; s/d/tr/q £95/105/130/150; wi-fi; Covent Garden, Tottenham Court Rd) The Seven Dials is a clean and comfortable almost-budget option in a very central location. Half of the 18 rooms face onto charming Monmouth St; the ones at the back don't get much of a view but are quieter.

Arosfa Hotel B&B ££
(020-7636 2115; www.arosfalondon.com; 83 Gower St, WC1; s/tw/d/tr/f incl breakfast £83/128/135-155/155/185; wi-fi; Goodge St) The old Arosfa has come a long way, with Philippe Starck furniture in the lounge and a new modern look. The 17 rooms are less lavish, with cabin-like bathrooms in many of them. About half have been refurbished; they are small but remain good value. There are a

couple of family rooms; room 4 looks onto a small garden.

Dean Street Townhouse BOUTIQUE HOTEL £££
(Map p164; 020-7434 1775; www.deanstreettownhouse.com; 69-71 Dean St, W1; r £260-450; ; Tottenham Court Rd) This 39-room gem in the heart of Soho has a wonderful boudoir atmosphere with its Georgian furniture, retro black-and-white tiled bathroom floors, beautiful lighting and girly touches (Cowshed bathroom products, hairdryer *and* straighteners in every room!). 'Medium' and 'bigger' rooms have four-poster beds and antique-style bathtubs right in the room.

The City

London St Paul's YHA HOSTEL £
(Map p160; 020-7236 4965; www.yha.org.uk; 36 Carter Lane, EC4; dm £17-25, d £40-50; @; St Paul's) This 213-bed hostel, housed in a heritage-listed building, stands in the very shadow of St Paul's. Dorms have between three and 11 beds, and twins and doubles are available. There's a licensed cafeteria (breakfast £5, dinner from £6 to £8) but no kitchen, plus a lot of stairs and no lift. There's a seven-night maximum stay.

Hotel Indigo Tower Hill BOUTIQUE HOTEL ££
(Map p160; 0843 208 7007; www.hotelindigo.com/lontowerhill; 142 Minories, EC3; r weekend/weekday from £100/200; ; Aldgate) A welcome addition to the City's accommodation scene is this new branch of the US InterContinental group's boutique-hotel chain. The 46 differently styled rooms all feature four-poster beds, iPod docking stations and a 'unique scent' system that allows you to choose your own fragrance. Larger-than-life drawings and photos of the neighbourhood won't let you forget where you are.

South Bank

Immediately south of the river is good if you want to immerse yourself in workaday London and still be central.

St Christopher's Village HOSTEL £
(Map p160; 020-7939 9710; www.st-christophers.co.uk; 163 Borough High St, SE1; dm/r from £15.90/50; @; London Bridge) This 185-bed place is the flagship of a hostel chain with basic but cheap and clean accommodation (the bathrooms are looking a little tired however). There's a roof garden with bar, barbecue and excellent views of the Shard skyscraper, as well as a cinema and Belushi's bar below for serious partying. Dorms have four to 14 beds.

★ **Citizen M** BOUTIQUE HOTEL ££
(Map p160; 020-3519 1680; www.citizenm.com/london-bankside; 20 Lavington St, SE1; r £109-199; @; Southwark) If Citizen M had a motto, it would be 'less fuss, more comfort'. The hotel has done away with things it considers superfluous (room service, reception, bags of space) and instead gone all out on mattresses and bedding (heavenly super king-size beds), state-of-the-art technology (everything in the room from mood-lighting to TV is controlled through a tablet computer) and superb decor.

Kensington & Hyde Park

This classy area offers easy access to the museums and big-name fashion stores, but at a price that reflects the upmarket surroundings.

Number Sixteen HOTEL £££
(Map p168; 020-7589 5232; www.firmdalehotels.com/hotels/london/number-sixteen; 16 Sumner Pl, SW7; s from £174, d £228-360; @; South Kensington) With uplifting splashes of colour, choice art and a sophisticated-but-fun design ethos, ravishing Number Sixteen is four properties in one and a lovely (and rather labyrinthine) place to stay. There are 41 individually designed rooms, a cosy drawing room and a fully stocked library. And wait till you see the idyllic, long back garden set around a fish pond, or have breakfast in the light-filled conservatory.

Ampersand Hotel BOUTIQUE HOTEL £££
(Map p168; 020-7589 5895; www.ampersandhotel.com; 10 Harrington Rd; s & d £372; @; South Kensington) Housed in the old Norfolk Hotel building, a light, fresh and bubbly feel fills the new Ampersand, its (narrow) corridors and (stylish but smallish) rooms decorated with wallpaper designs celebrating the nearby arts and sciences of South Kensington's museums, a short stroll away. The wrapping recently off, there's a spring in its step, zest in the service and an eagerness to please.

Clerkenwell, Shoreditch & Spitalfields

★Hoxton Hotel HOTEL £

(Map p160; ☎020-7550 1000; www.hoxtonhotels.com; 81 Great Eastern St, EC2; r from £59; ❄@📶; ⊖Old St) This is hands down the best hotel deal in London. In the heart of Shoreditch, this sleek 208-room hotel aims to make its money by being full each night. You get an hour of free phone calls, free computer terminal access in the lobby, free printing and breakfast from Prêt à Manger. Rooms are small but stylish.

Notting Hill & West London

West London's Earl's Court district is lively, cosmopolitan and so popular with travelling antipodeans that it's been nicknamed Kangaroo Valley.

Tune Hotel HOTEL £

(Map p168; ☎020-7258 3140; www.tunehotels.com; 41 Praed St, W2; r £35-80; ❄@📶; ⊖Paddington) This new 137-room Malaysian-owned budget hotel offers super-duper rates for early birds who book a long way in advance. The ethos is you get the bare bones – a twin or double room, the cheapest without window – and pay for add-ons (towel, wi-fi, TV) as you see fit, giving you the chance to just put a roof over your head, if that's all you need.

Barclay House B&B ££

(☎020-7384 3390; www.barclayhouselondon.com; 21 Barclay Rd, SW6; r £110-125; @📶; ⊖Fulham Broadway) The two dapper, thoroughly modern and comfy bedrooms in this charmingly ship-shape Victorian house are a dream, from the Philippe Starck shower rooms, walnut furniture, new double-glazed sash windows and underfloor heating to the small, thoughtful details (fumble-free coat hangers, drawers packed with sewing kits and maps). The cordial, music-loving owners – bursting with tips and handy London knowledge – concoct an inclusive, homely atmosphere. Usually there is a four-night minimum stay.

Rockwell BOUTIQUE HOTEL ££

(Map p168; ☎020-7244 2000; www.therockwell.com; 181-183 Cromwell Rd, SW5; s/ste from £90/160, d £100-150; ❄@📶; ⊖Earl's Court) With an understated-cool design ethos, things are muted, dapper and more than a tad minimalist at 'budget boutique' 40-room Rockwell. Spruce and stylish, all rooms have shower, the mezzanine suite is an absolute peach and the three rooms (LG1, 2 and 3) giving on to the garden are particularly fine.

La Suite West BOUTIQUE HOTEL £££

(Map p168; ☎020-7313 8484; www.lasuitewest.com; 41-51 Inverness Tce, W2; r £179-489; ❄@📶; ⊖Bayswater) The black-and-white foyer of the Anouska Hempel–designed La Suite West – bare walls, a minimalist slit of a fireplace, an iPad for guests' use on an otherwise void white marble reception desk – presages the OCD neatness of rooms hidden away down dark corridors. The straight lines, spotless surfaces and sharp angles are accentuated by impeccable bathrooms and softened by comfortable beds and warm service.

Eating

Dining out in London has become so fashionable that you can hardly open a menu without banging into a celebrity chef. The range and quality of eating options has increased enormously over the last few decades.

West End

★Koya NOODLES £

(Map p164; www.koya.co.uk; 49 Frith St, W1; mains £7-15; ⌚noon-3pm & 5.30-10.30pm; ⊖Tottenham Court Rd, Leicester Sq) Arrive early or late if you don't want to queue at this excellent Japanese eatery. Londoners come for their fill of authentic udon noodles (served hot or cold, in soup or with a cold sauce), the efficient service and very reasonable prices.

Orchard VEGETARIAN £

(Map p164; www.orchard-kitchen.co.uk; 11 Sicilian Ave, WC1; mains £6.50-7; ⌚8am-4pm Mon-Fri; 🌶; ⊖Holborn) A boon for vegetarians in central London is this delightful retro-style cafe on a quiet pedestrian street. Mains include specialities like broccoli and Yorkshire blue cheese pie, and a sarnie (that's a sandwich to Londoners) and mug of soup is just £4.95. Desserts are unusual – try the toasted oat and currant cake with Horlicks icing.

★Brasserie Zédel FRENCH ££

(Map p164; ☎020-7734 4888; www.brasseriezedel.com; 20 Sherwood St, W1; mains £8.75-30; ⌚11.30am-midnight Mon-Sat, to 11pm Sun; 📶; ⊖Piccadilly Circus) This brasserie in the renovated art deco ballroom of a former Piccadilly hotel is the French-est eatery west of Calais. Choose from among the usual favourites, including *choucroute alsacienne* (sauerkraut with sausages and charcuterie) and duck leg confit with Puy lentils. The set menus (£8.25/11.75 for two/three courses) and *plats du jour* (£12.95) offer excellent value.

North Sea Fish Restaurant FISH & CHIPS ££
(www.northseafishrestaurant.co.uk; 7-8 Leigh St, WC1; mains £10-20; noon-2.30pm & 5.30-10.30pm Mon-Sat, 1-6pm Sun; Russell Sq) The North Sea sets out to cook fresh fish and potatoes – a simple ambition in which it succeeds admirably. Look forward to jumbo-sized plaice or halibut fillets, deep-fried or grilled, and a huge serving of chips. There's takeaway next door if you can't face the rather austere dining room.

Great Queen Street BRITISH ££
(Map p164; 020-7242 0622; 32 Great Queen St, WC2; mains £14-20; noon-2.30pm & 6-10.30pm Mon-Sat, 1-4pm Sun; Holborn) The menu at what is one of Covent Garden's best places to eat is seasonal (and changes daily), with an emphasis on quality, hearty dishes and good ingredients – there are always delicious stews, roasts and simple fish dishes. The atmosphere is lively, with a small bar downstairs. The staff are knowledgeable about the food and wine they serve and booking is essential.

National Dining Rooms BRITISH ££
(Map p164; 020-7747 2525; www.peytonandbyrne.co.uk; 1st fl, Sainsbury Wing, National Gallery, Trafalgar Sq, WC2; mains £12.50-17.50; 10am-5.30pm Sat-Thu, to 8.30pm Fri; Charing Cross) Chef Oliver Peyton's restaurant at the National Gallery styles itself as 'proudly and resolutely British', and what a great idea. The menu features an extensive and wonderful selection of British cheeses for a light lunch. For something more filling, go for the county menu, a monthly changing menu honouring regional specialities from across the British Isles.

Hawksmoor Seven Dials STEAKHOUSE £££
(Map p164; 020-7420 9390; www.thehawksmoor.com; 11 Langley St, WC2; steak £18-34, 2-/3-course express menu £24/27; noon-3pm & 5-10.30pm Mon-Sat, noon-9.30pm Sun; ; Covent Garden) Legendary among London carnivores for its mouth-watering and flavour-rich steaks from British cattle breeds, Hawksmoor's sumptuous Sunday roasts, burgers and well-executed cocktails are other showstoppers. Book ahead.

South Bank

For a feed with a local feel, head to Borough Market or Bermondsey St.

M Manze BRITISH £
(www.manze.co.uk; 87 Tower Bridge Rd, SE1; mains £2.40-6.25; 11am-2pm Mon-Thu, 10am-2.30pm Fri & Sat; Borough) Dating to 1902, M Manze (Italian roots) started off as an ice-cream seller before moving on to selling its legendary staples: pies. It's a classic operation, from the lovely tile work to the traditional working-man's menu: pie and mash, pie and liquor and you can take your eels jellied or stewed.

★ **Skylon** MODERN EUROPEAN ££
(Map p160; 020-7654 7800; www.skylon-restaurant.co.uk; 3rd fl, Royal Festival Hall, Southbank Centre, Belvedere Rd, SE1; grill mains £12.50-30, restaurant 2-/3-course meal £42/48; grill noon-11pm Mon-Sat, noon-10.30pm Sun, restaurant noon-2.30pm & 5.30-10.30pm Mon-Sat, noon-4pm Sun; ; Waterloo) Named after the defunct 1950s tower, this excellent restaurant on top of the refurbished Royal Festival Hall is divided into grill and fine-dining sections by a large **bar** (noon-1am Mon-Sat, to 10.30pm Sun; Waterloo). The decor is cutting-edge 1950s: muted colours and period chairs (trendy then, trendier now), while floor-to-ceiling windows bathe you in magnificent views of the Thames and the City.

Kensington & Hyde Park

★ **Pimlico Fresh** CAFE £
(86 Wilton Rd, SW1; mains from £4.50; 7.30am-7.30pm Mon-Fri, 9am-6pm Sat & Sun; Victoria) A wholesome choice for a healthy breakfast or lunch, this friendly two-room cafe cooks up fine homemade dishes from pies, soups, baked beans on toast and lasagne to warming bowls of porridge laced with honey, maple syrup, banana, yoghurt or sultanas, while making regular forays into creative cuisine. There's an invigorating choice of fresh fruit juices, and steaming glasses of spicy apple winter warmer fend off the cold in chillier months.

Wasabi JAPANESE £
(Map p168; www.wasabi.uk.com; Kensington Arcade, Kensington High St, W8; mains £5-8; ⌚10am-10pm Mon-Sat, 11am-9pm Sun; ⊖High St Kensington) Large, bright sit-down and takeout branch of this superb Japanese sushi and bento chain, with fantastic rice sets, noodles, rolls and salads, all good value and perfect for a fast lunch. Branches all over central London.

Tom's Kitchen MODERN EUROPEAN ££
(Map p168; ☎020-7349 0202; www.tomskitchen.co.uk; 27 Cale St, SW3; breakfast £2.50-15, mains £12.75-27; ⌚8-11.30am, noon-2.30pm & 6-10.30pm Mon-Fri, 10am-3.30pm & 6-10.30pm Sat & Sun; ⊖South Kensington) Celebrity chef Tom Aikens' restaurant serves excellent food, including award-winning breakfasts and pancakes.

★**Dinner by Heston Blumenthal** MODERN BRITISH £££
(Map p168; ☎020-7201 3833; www.dinnerbyheston.com; Mandarin Oriental Hyde Park, 66 Knightsbridge, SW1; 3-course set lunch £38, mains £28-42; ⌚noon-2.30pm & 6.30-10.30pm; 📶; ⊖Knightsbridge) Sumptuously presented Dinner is a gastronomic tour de force, taking diners on a journey through British culinary history (with inventive modern inflections). Dishes carry historical dates to convey context, while the restaurant interior is a design triumph, from the glass-walled kitchen and its overhead clock mechanism to the large windows onto the park.

Clerkenwell, Shoreditch & Spitalfields

From the hit-and-miss Bangladeshi restaurants of Brick Lane to the Vietnamese strip on Kingsland Rd, the East End's cuisine is as multicultural as its residents. Clerkenwell's hidden gems are well worth digging for; Exmouth Market is a good place to start.

Poppies FISH & CHIPS ££
(Map p160; www.poppiesfishandchips.co.uk; 6-8 Hanbury St, E1; mains £7-16; ⌚11am-11pm Mon-Thu, to 11.30pm Fri & Sat, to 10.30pm Sun; 📶; ⊖Shoreditch High St, Liverpool St) Glorious re-creation of a 1950s East End chippy, complete with waitstaff in pinnies and hairnets, and retro memorabilia. As well as the usual fishy suspects, it does jellied eels, homemade tartare sauce and mushy peas, and you can wash it all down with a glass of wine or beer. Also does a roaring takeaway trade.

WANT MORE?

For in-depth information, reviews and recommendations at your fingertips, head to the Apple App Store to purchase Lonely Planet's *London City Guide* iPhone app.

Alternatively, head to **Lonely Planet** (lonelyplanet.com/england/london) for planning advice, author recommendations, traveller reviews and insider tips.

Modern Pantry FUSION £££
(Map p160; ☎020-7553 9210; www.themodernpantry.co.uk; 47-48 St John's Sq, EC1; mains £14-21.50; ⌚noon-3pm Tue-Fri, 11am-4pm Sat & Sun, 6-10.30pm Tue-Sat; 📶; ⊖Farringdon) This three-floor Georgian town house in the heart of Clerkenwell has a cracking all-day menu, which gives almost as much pleasure to read as to eat from. Ingredients are combined sublimely into unusual dishes such as tamarind miso marinated onglet steak or panko and parmesan crusted veal escalope. The breakfasts are great, too, though sadly portions can be on the small side. Reservations recommended for the evenings.

Notting Hill & West London

Taquería MEXICAN £
(Map p168; www.taqueria.co.uk; 139-143 Westbourne Grove; tacos £5-7.50; ⌚noon-11pm Mon-Fri, 10am-11.30pm Sat, noon-10.30pm Sun; 📶; ⊖Notting Hill Gate) 🌿 You won't find fresher, limper (they're not supposed to be crispy!) tacos anywhere in London because these ones are made on the premises. It's a small casual place with a great vibe. Taquería is also a committed environmental establishment: the eggs, chicken and pork are free-range, the meat British, the fish MSC-certified and the milk and cream organic.

Ledbury FRENCH £££
(☎020-7792 9090; www.theledbury.com; 127 Ledbury Rd, W11; 4-course set lunch £50, 4-course dinner £95; ⌚noon-2pm Wed-Sun & 6.30-9.45pm daily; 📶; ⊖Westbourne Park, Notting Hill Gate) Two Michelin stars and swooningly elegant, Brett Graham's artful French restaurant attracts well-heeled diners in jeans with designer jackets. Dishes – such as roast sea bass with broccoli stem, crab and black quinoa, or saddle of roe deer with beetroot, pinot lees and

bone crisp potato – are triumphant. London gastronomes have the Ledbury on speed-dial, so reservations are crucial.

Drinking & Nightlife

As long as there's been a city, Londoners have loved to drink – and, as history shows, often immoderately. Clubland is no longer confined to the West End, with megaclubs scattered throughout the city wherever there's a venue big enough, cheap enough or quirky enough to hold them. The big nights are Friday and Saturday. Admission prices vary widely; it's often cheaper to arrive early or prebook tickets.

West End

Gordon's Wine Bar BAR

(Map p164; www.gordonswinebar.com; 47 Villiers St, WC2; ⌚11am-11pm Mon-Sat, noon-10pm Sun; ⊖Embankment) Gordon's is a victim of its own success; it is relentlessly busy and unless you arrive before the office crowd does (generally around 6pm), you can forget about getting a table. It's cavernous and dark, and the French and New World wines are heady and reasonably priced. You can nibble on bread, cheese and olives. Outside garden seating in summer.

French House BAR

(Map p164; www.frenchhousesoho.com; 49 Dean St, W1; ⌚noon-11pm Mon-Sat, noon-10.30pm Sun; ⊖Leicester Sq) French House is Soho's legendary boho boozer with a history to match: this was the meeting place of the Free French Forces during WWII, and De Gaulle is said to have drunk here often, while Dylan Thomas, Peter O'Toole and Francis Bacon all ended up on the wooden floor at least once.

Spuntino BAR

(Map p164; www.spuntino.co.uk; 61 Rupert St, W1; mains £6-10; ⌚noon-midnight Mon-Wed, to 1am Thu-Sat, to 11pm Sun; ⊖Piccadilly Circus) Speakeasy decor meets creative fusion American-Italian food at Rupert St cool customer Spuntino. Grab a seat at the bar or one of the counters at the back, but put aside time to queue (no reservations and no phone).

Terroirs WINE BAR

(Map p164; www.terroirswinebar.com; 5 William IV St, WC2; ⌚noon-11pm Mon-Sat; ⊖Charing Cross Rd) Fab two-floor spot for a pre-theatre glass or some expertly created charcuterie, with informative staff, affordable £10 lunch specials, a lively, convivial atmosphere and a breathtaking list of organic wines.

LAB COCKTAIL BAR

(Map p164; ☎020-7437 7820; www.labbaruk.com; 12 Old Compton St, W1; ⌚4pm-midnight Mon-Sat, to 10.30pm Sun; ⊖Leicester Sq, Tottenham Court Rd) A long-standing Soho favourite for almost two decades, the London Academy of Bartenders (to give it its full name) has some of the best cocktails in town. The list is the size of a small book but, fear not, if you can't make your way through it, just tell the bartenders what you feel like and they'll concoct something divine.

South Bank

★40 Maltby Street WINE BAR

(Map p160; www.40maltbystreet.com; 40 Maltby St, SE1; ⌚5.30-10pm Wed & Thu, 12.30-2pm & 5.30-10pm Fri, 11am-5pm Sat) This tunnel-like wine-bar-cum-kitchen sits under the railway arches taking trains in and out of London Bridge. It is first and foremost a wine importer focusing on organic vintages but its hospitality venture has become incredibly popular. The wine recommendations are obviously top-notch (most of them by the glass) and the food – simple, gourmet bistro fare – is spot on.

George Inn PUB

(Map p160; ☎020-7407 2056; www.nationaltrust.org.uk/george-inn; 77 Borough High St, SE1; ⌚11am-11pm; ⊖London Bridge) This magnificent old boozer is London's last surviving galleried coaching inn, dating from 1676 and mentioned in Dickens' *Little Dorrit*. It is on the site of the Tabard Inn, where the pilgrims in Chaucer's *Canterbury Tales* gathered before setting out (well lubricated, we suspect) on the road to Canterbury, Kent.

Anchor Bankside PUB

(Map p160; 34 Park St, SE1; ⌚11am-11pm Sun-Wed, to midnight Thu-Sat; ⊖London Bridge) Firmly anchored in many guidebooks (including this one) – but with good reason – this riverside boozer dates to the early 17th century (subsequently rebuilt after the Great Fire and again in the 19th century). Trips to the terrace are rewarded with superb views across the Thames but brace for a constant deluge of drinkers.

Clerkenwell, Shoreditch & Spitalfields

Jerusalem Tavern PUB

(Map p160; www.stpetersbrewery.co.uk; 55 Britton St, EC1; ⏲11am-11pm Mon-Fri; ☎; ⊖Farringdon) Starting life as one of the first London coffee houses (founded in 1703), with the 18th-century decor of occasional tile mosaics still visible, the JT is an absolute stunner, though sadly it's both massively popular and tiny, so come early to get a seat.

Book Club BAR

(Map p160; ☎020-7684 8618; www.wearetbc.com; 100 Leonard St, EC2A; ⏲8am-midnight Mon-Wed, to 2am Thu & Fri, 10am-2am Sat & Sun; ☎; ⊖Old St) This former Victorian warehouse has been transformed into an innovative temple to good times. Spacious and whitewashed with large windows upstairs and a basement bar below, it hosts a real variety of offbeat events, such as spoken word, dance lessons and life drawing, as well as a varied program of DJ nights.

Fabric CLUB

(Map p160; www.fabriclondon.com; 77a Charterhouse St, EC1; admission £8-18; ⏲10pm-6am Fri, 11pm-8am Sat, 11pm-6am Sun; ⊖Farringdon) This most impressive of superclubs is still the first stop on the London scene for many international clubbers. The crowd is hip and well dressed without overkill, and the music – electro, techno, house, drum and bass and dubstep – is as superb as you'd expect from London's top-rated club.

Ten Bells PUB

(Map p160; cnr Commercial & Fournier Sts, E1; ⏲11am-11pm Mon-Sat, noon-10.30pm Sun; ⊖Liverpool St) This landmark Victorian pub, with its large windows and beautiful tiles, is perfect for a pint after a wander round Spitalfields Market. It's famous for being one of Jack the Ripper's pick-up joints, although

GAY & LESBIAN LONDON

Generally, London's a safe place for lesbians and gays. It's rare to encounter any problem with sharing rooms or holding hands in the inner city, although it would pay to keep your wits about you at night and be conscious of your surroundings.

The West End, particularly Soho, is the visible centre of gay and lesbian London, with numerous venues clustered around Old Compton St – but many other areas have their own mini scenes.

The easiest way to find out what's going on is to pick up the free press from a venue (*Boyz, QX*); the gay section of *Time Out* (www.timeout.com/london/lgbt) is also useful. Some venues to get you started:

George & Dragon (Map p160; 2 Hackney Rd, E2; ⏲6-11pm; ⊖Old St) Once a scuzzy local pub, the George was taken over and decorated with the owner's grandma's antiques (antlers, racoon tails, old clocks), cardboard cut-outs of Cher and fairy lights, turning this one-room pub into what has remained the epicentre of the Hoxton scene for more than a decade.

Edge (Map p164; www.edgesoho.co.uk; 11 Soho Sq, W1; ⏲4pm-1am Mon-Thu, noon-to 3am Fri & Sat, 4-11.30pm Sun; ☎; ⊖Tottenham Court Rd) Overlooking Soho Sq in all its four-storey glory, the Edge is London's largest gay bar and heaves every night of the week. There are dancers, waiters in skimpy outfits, good music and a generally super-friendly vibe. There's also a straight presence, as it's so close to Oxford St. So much the better.

Heaven (Map p164; www.heavennightclub-london.com; Villiers St, WC2; ⏲11pm-5am Mon, Thu & Fri, 10pm-5am Sat; ⊖Embankment, Charing Cross) This long-standing, perennially popular gay club under the arches beneath Charing Cross station has always been host to good club nights. Monday's Popcorn (mixed dance party, all-welcome door policy) has to be one of the best weeknight's clubbing in the capital. The celebrated G-A-Y takes place here on Thursday (G-A-Y Porn Idol), Friday (G-A-Y Camp Attack) and Saturday (plain ol' G-A-Y).

Popstarz (Map p164; www.popstarz.org; The Den, 18 West Central St, WC1; ⏲10pm-4am Fri; ⊖Tottenham Court Rd) This grand dame of gay indie has been revitalised by a recent transfer to the heart of the West End. It's popular with a studenty, friendly, mixed crowd. There are three rooms of great indie pop.

these days it attracts a rather more salubrious and trendy clientele.

Worship St Whistling Shop COCKTAIL BAR

(Map p160; ☎020-7247 0015; www.whistlingshop.com; 63 Worship St, EC2; ⊙5pm-midnight Tue, to 1am Wed & Thu, to 2am Fri & Sat; ⊖Old St) A 'Victorian' drinking den that takes cocktails to a molecular level, the Whistling Shop (as Victorians called a place selling illicit booze) serves expertly crafted and highly unusual concoctions using potions conjured up in its on-site lab. Try a Panacea, Black Cat Martini or the Bosom Caresser (made with formula milk). There's an incredible array of interesting spirits, as well as a Dram Shop for a private party, and an Experience Room for the really adventurous.

Cargo CLUB

(Map p160; www.cargo-london.com; 83 Rivington St, EC2; admission free-£16; ⊙noon-1am Mon-Thu, to 3am Fri & Sat, to midnight Sun; ⊖Old St) Cargo is one of London's most eclectic clubs. Under its brick railway arches you'll find a dance-floor room, bar and outside terrace. The music policy is innovative and varied, with plenty of up-and-coming bands also on the menu. Food is available throughout the day.

Notting Hill, Bayswater & Paddington

Churchill Arms PUB

(Map p168; www.churchillarmskensington.co.uk; 119 Kensington Church St, W8; ⊙11am-11pm Mon-Wed, to midnight Thu-Sat, noon-10.30pm Sun; 📶; ⊖Notting Hill Gate) With its cascade of geraniums and Union Jack flags swaying in the breeze, the Churchill Arms is quite a sight on Kensington Church St. Renowned for its Winston memorabilia and dozens of knick-knacks on the walls, the pub is a favourite of both locals and tourists. The attached conservatory has been serving excellent Thai food for two decades (mains £6 to £10).

Windsor Castle PUB

(Map p168; www.thewindsorcastlekensington.co.uk; 114 Campden Hill Rd, W11; ⊙noon-11pm Mon-Sat, noon-10.30pm Sun; 📶; ⊖Notting Hill Gate) A classic tavern on the brow of Campden Hill Rd, this place has history, nooks and charm on tap. It's worth the search for its historic compartmentalised interior, roaring fire (in winter), delightful beer garden (in summer) and affable regulars (most always). Legend attests the bones of Thomas Paine (author of *Rights of Man*) are in the cellar.

Earl of Lonsdale PUB

(277-281 Portobello Rd, W11; ⊙noon-11pm Mon-Fri, 10am-11pm Sat, noon-10.30pm Sun; ⊖Notting Hill Gate, Ladbroke Grove) Named after the *bon vivant* founder of the AA (Automobile Association, *not* Alcoholics Anonymous), the Earl is peaceful during the day, with a mixture of old biddies and young hipsters inhabiting the reintroduced snugs. There are Samuel Smith's ales, a fantastic backroom with sofas, banquettes, open fires and a magnificent beer garden.

Greenwich & South London

Trafalgar Tavern PUB

(☎020-8858 2909; www.trafalgartavern.co.uk; 6 Park Row, SE10; ⊙noon-11pm Mon-Thu, to midnight Fri & Sat, to 10.30pm Sun; DLR Cutty Sark) Lapped by the brown waters of the Thames, this elegant tavern with big windows looking onto the river is steeped in history. Dickens apparently knocked back a few here – and used it as the setting for the wedding breakfast scene in *Our Mutual Friend* – and prime ministers Gladstone and Disraeli used to dine on the pub's celebrated whitebait.

Ministry of Sound CLUB

(Map p160; www.ministryofsound.com; 103 Gaunt St, SE1; admission £16-25; ⊙11pm-6.30am Fri & Sat; ⊖Elephant & Castle) This legendary club-cum-enormous-global-brand (four bars, four dance floors) lost some 'edge' in the early noughties but, after pumping in top DJs, the Ministry has firmly rejoined the top club ranks. Fridays is the Gallery trance night, while Saturday sessions offer the *crème de la crème* of house, electro and techno DJs.

☆ Entertainment

Theatre

London is a world capital for theatre and there's a lot more than mammoth musicals to tempt you into the West End. On performance days, you can buy half-price tickets for West End productions (cash only) from the official agency **TKTS** (Map p164; www.tkts.co.uk; Leicester Sq, WC2; ⊙10am-7pm Mon-Sat, noon-4pm Sun; ⊖Leicester Sq). The booth is the one with the clock tower; beware of touts selling dodgy tickets. For more, see www.officiallondontheatre.co.uk or www.theatremonkey.com.

National Theatre THEATRE
(Map p160; ☎020-7452 3000; www.nationaltheatre.org.uk; South Bank, SE1; ⊖Waterloo) England's flagship theatre showcases a mix of classic and contemporary plays performed by excellent casts in three theatres (Olivier, Lyttelton and Dorfman). Outstanding artistic director Nicholas Hytner (who stepped down in March 2015) oversaw a golden decade at the theatre, with landmark productions such as *War Horse*. There are also constant surprises in the program.

Royal Court Theatre THEATRE
(Map p168; ☎020-7565 5000; www.royalcourttheatre.com; Sloane Sq, SW1; ⊖Sloane Sq) Equally renowned for staging innovative new plays and old classics, the Royal Court is among London's most progressive theatres and has continued to foster major writing talent across the UK.

Tickets for concessions are £6 to £10, and £10 for everyone on Monday (four 10p standing tickets sold at the Jerwood Theatre Downstairs); tickets for under 26s are £8. Check the theatre's Facebook page for the lastest on cheap tickets.

Old Vic THEATRE
(Map p160; ☎0844 871 7628; www.oldvictheatre.com; The Cut, SE1; ⊖Waterloo) Never has there been a London theatre with a more famous artistic director. American actor Kevin Spacey took the theatrical helm in 2003, looking after this glorious theatre's program. The theatre does both new and classic plays, and its cast and directors are consistently high-profile.

Young Vic THEATRE
(Map p160; ☎020-7922 2922; www.youngvic.org; 66 The Cut, SE1; ⊖Waterloo, ⊖Southwark) This ground-breaking theatre is as much about showcasing and discovering new talent as it is about people discovering theatre. The Young Vic showcases actors, directors and plays from across the world, many of which tackle contemporary political or cultural issues such as the death penalty, racism or corruption, often blending dance and music with acting.

Donmar Warehouse THEATRE
(Map p164; ☎0844 871 7624; www.donmarwarehouse.com; 41 Earlham St, WC2; ⊖Covent Garden) The cosy Donmar Warehouse is London's 'thinking person's theatre'. The new artistic director, Josie Rourke, has staged some interesting and unusual productions such as the Restoration comedy *The Recruiting Officer*, by George Farquhar, and a restaging of Conor McPherson's *The Weir*.

Live Music

KOKO LIVE MUSIC
(www.koko.uk.com; 1a Camden High St, NW1; ⏲7-11pm Sun-Thu, to 4am Fri & Sat; ⊖Mornington Cres) Once the legendary Camden Palace, where Charlie Chaplin, the Goons and the Sex Pistols have all performed, KOKO is keeping its reputation as one of London's better gig venues. The theatre has a dance floor and decadent balconies, and attracts an indie crowd with Club NME on Friday. There are live bands almost every night of the week.

100 Club LIVE MUSIC
(Map p164; ☎020-7636 0933; www.the100club.co.uk; 100 Oxford St, W1; admission £8-20; ⏲check website for gig times; ⊖Oxford Circus, Tottenham Court Rd) This legendary London venue has always concentrated on jazz, but it's also spreading its wings to swing and rock. It once showcased Chris Barber, BB King and the Stones, and was at the centre of the punk revolution and the '90s indie scene. It hosts dancing swing gigs and local jazz musicians, as well as the occasional big name.

Roundhouse LIVE MUSIC
(www.roundhouse.org.uk; Chalk Farm Rd, NW1; ⊖Chalk Farm) The Roundhouse was once home to 1960s avant-garde theatre, then was a rock venue, then it fell into oblivion for a while before reopening a few years back. It holds great gigs and brilliant performances, from circus to stand-up comedy, poetry slam and improvisation sessions. The round shape of the building is unique and generally well used in the staging.

Ronnie Scott's JAZZ
(Map p164; ☎020-7439 0747; www.ronniescotts.co.uk; 47 Frith St, W1; ⏲7pm-3am Mon-Sat, to midnight Sun; ⊖Leicester Sq, Tottenham Court Rd) Ronnie Scott originally opened his jazz club on Gerrard St in 1959 under a Chinese gambling den. The club moved to its current location six years later and became widely known as Britain's best jazz club. Gigs are at 8.30pm (8pm Sunday) with a second one at 11.15pm Friday and Saturday, and are followed by a late show until 2am. Expect to pay between £20 and £50.

Comedy

Comedy Store COMEDY

(Map p164; ☎0844 871 7699; www.thecomedystore.co.uk; 1a Oxendon St, SW1; admission £8-23.50; ⊖Piccadilly Circus) This was one of the first (and is still one of the best) comedy clubs in London. Wednesday and Sunday night's Comedy Store Players is the most famous improvisation outfit in town, with the wonderful Josie Lawrence; on Thursdays, Fridays and Saturdays Best in Stand Up features the best on London's comedy circuit.

Comedy Cafe COMEDY

(Map p160; ☎020-7739 5706; www.comedycafe.co.uk; 68 Rivington St, EC2; admission free-£12; ⏲Wed-Sat; ⊖Old St) A major venue, the Comedy Cafe is purpose built for, well, comedy, hosting some good comedians. It can be a little too try-hard and wacky, but it's worth seeing the Wednesday night try-out spots for some wincing entertainment.

Soho Theatre COMEDY

(Map p164; ☎020-7478 0100; www.sohotheatre.com; 21 Dean St, W1; admission £10-25; ⊖Tottenham Court Rd) The Soho Theatre has developed a superb reputation for showcasing new comedy-writing talent and comedians. It's also hosted some top-notch stand-up or sketch-based comedians including Alexei Sayle and Doctor Brown. Tickets cost between £10 and £20.

Classical Music, Opera & Dance

Royal Albert Hall CONCERT VENUE

(Map p168; ☎020-7589 8212, 0845 401 5045; www.royalalberthall.com; Kensington Gore, SW7; ⊖South Kensington) This Victorian concert hall hosts classical-music, rock and other performances, but is most famously the venue for the BBC-sponsored Proms. Booking is possible, but from mid-July to mid-September Proms punters also queue for £5 standing (or 'promenading') tickets that go on sale one hour before curtain-up. Otherwise, the box office

ROLL OUT THE BARROW

London has more than 350 markets selling everything from antiques and curios to flowers and fish. Some, such as Camden and Portobello Road, are full of tourists, while others exist just for the locals.

Columbia Road Flower Market (Map p160; Columbia Rd, E2; ⏲8am-3pm Sun; ⊖Old St) A real explosion of colour and life, this weekly market sells a beautiful array of flowers, pot plants, bulbs, seeds and everything you might need for the garden. A lot of fun, even if you don't buy anything, the market gets really packed so go as early as you can, or later on, when the vendors sell off the cut flowers cheaply. It stretches from Gossett St to the Royal Oak pub.

Borough Market (Map p160; www.boroughmarket.org.uk; 8 Southwark St, SE1; ⏲11am-5pm Thu, noon-6pm Fri, 8am-5pm Sat; ⊖London Bridge) Located here in some form or another since the 13th century, 'London's Larder' has enjoyed an astonishing renaissance in the past decade. Always overflowing with food lovers, inveterate gastronomes, wide-eyed newcomers, guidebook-toting visitors and all types in between, this fantastic market has become firmly established as a sight in its own right.

Along with a section devoted to quality fresh fruit, exotic vegetables and organic meat, there's a fine-foods retail market, with the likes of home-grown honey and homemade bread plus loads of free samples. Throughout, takeaway stalls supply sizzling gourmet sausages, chorizo sandwiches and quality burgers in spades, filling the air with meaty aromas. Shoppers get queuing for cheeses at Neal's Yard Dairy, wait in line at the Monmouth Coffee Company and the Spanish deli Brindisa (www.brindisa.com), line up for takeaways at Roast, shop at butcher Ginger Pig and down pints of ale at Rake. The market simply heaves on Saturdays (get here early for the best pickings).

Camden Market (Camden High St, NW1; ⏲10am-6pm; ⊖Camden Town, Chalk Farm) Although, or perhaps because, it stopped being cutting-edge several thousand cheap leather jackets ago, Camden Market gets a whopping 10 million visitors each year and is one of London's most popular attractions. What started out as a collection of attractive craft stalls by Camden Lock on the Regent's Canal now extends most of the way from Camden Town tube station to Chalk Farm tube station.

and prepaid ticket collection counter are both through door 12 (south side of the hall).

Barbican PERFORMING ARTS
(Map p160; 020-7638 8891, 0845 121 6823; www.barbican.org.uk; Silk St, EC2; Barbican) Home to the wonderful London Symphony Orchestra and its associate orchestra, the lesser-known BBC Symphony Orchestra, the arts centre hosts scores of other leading musicians each year as well, focusing in particular on jazz, folk, world and soul artists. Dance is another strong point here.

Southbank Centre CONCERT VENUE
(Map p160; 020-7960 4200; www.southbankcentre.co.uk; Belvedere Rd, SE1; Waterloo) The Southbank Centre's overhauled **Royal Festival Hall** (Map p160; 020-7960 4242; www.southbankcentre.co.uk; admission £6-60; Waterloo) seats 3000 in a now-acoustic amphitheatre and is one of the best places for catching world and classical music artists. The sound is fantastic, the programming impeccable and there are frequent free gigs in the wonderfully expansive foyer. There are more eclectic gigs at the smaller **Queen Elizabeth Hall** (QEH; Map p160; 020-7960 4200; www.southbankcentre.co.uk; 5-11.30pm daily; Waterloo) and **Purcell Room** (Map p160), including talks and debates, dance performances, poetry readings and so forth.

Royal Opera House OPERA
(Map p164; 020-7304 4000; www.roh.org.uk; Bow St, WC2; tickets £7-250; Covent Garden) The £210 million redevelopment for the millennium gave classic opera a fantastic setting in London, and coming here for a night is a sumptuous – if pricey – affair. Although the program has been fluffed up by modern influences, the main attractions are still the opera and classical ballet – all are wonderful productions and feature world-class performers.

Sadler's Wells DANCE
(Map p160; 0844 412 4300; www.sadlerswells.com; Rosebery Ave, EC1; tickets £10-49; Angel)

Portobello Road Market (www.portobellomarket.org; Portobello Rd, W10; 8am-6.30pm Mon-Wed, Fri & Sat, to 1pm Thu; Notting Hill Gate, Ladbroke Grove) Portobello Road Market is an iconic London attraction with an eclectic mix of street food, fruit and veg, antiques, curios, collectibles, vibrant fashion and trinkets. Although the shops along Portobello Rd open daily and the fruit and veg stalls (from Elgin Cres to Talbot Rd) only close on Sunday, the busiest day by far is Saturday, when antique dealers set up shop (from Chepstow Villas to Elgin Cres).

Broadway Market (www.broadwaymarket.co.uk; London Fields, E8; 9am-5pm Sat; Bethnal Green) There's been a market down this pretty street since the late 19th century, the focus of which has these days become artisan food, arty knick-knacks, books, records and vintage clothing. A great place on a Saturday, followed by a picnic at **London Fields** (www.hackney.gov.uk; ; 55, 277, London Fields) park.

Brixton Market (www.brixtonmarket.net; Electric Ave & Granville Arcade; 8am-6pm Mon, Tue & Thu-Sat, 8am-3pm Wed; Brixton) A heady, cosmopolitan blend of silks, wigs, knock-off fashion, Halal butchers and the occasional Christian preacher on Electric Ave. Tilapia fish, pig's trotters, yams, mangoes, okra, plantains and Jamaican *bullah* cakes (gingerbread) are just some of the exotic products on sale.

Sunday UpMarket (Map p160; www.sundayupmarket.co.uk; Old Truman Brewery, Brick Lane, E1; 10am-5pm Sun; Liverpool St) Market where young designers sell wonderful clothes, music and crafts, and the excellent food hall has worldwide grub, from Ethiopian vegie dishes to Japanese delicacies. If you've got the stamina, top it all off with a browse round Spitalfields.

Brick Lane Market (Map p160; www.visitbricklane.org; Brick Lane, E1; 8am-2pm Sun; Liverpool St) Takes over a vast area with household goods, bric-a-brac, secondhand clothes and cheap fashion. You can even stop off and play carrom (similar to billiards).

Petticoat Lane Market (Map p160; Wentworth St & Middlesex St, E1; 9am-2pm Sun-Fri; Aldgate) The famous lane itself has been renamed Middlesex St. The market, however, soldiers on, selling cheap consumer items and clothes.

The theatre site dates from 1683 but was completely rebuilt in 1998; today it is the most eclectic and modern dance venue in town, with experimental dance shows of all genres and from all corners of the globe. The Lilian Baylis Studio stages smaller productions.

 Shopping

Department Stores

London's famous department stores are an attraction in themselves, even if you're not interested in buying.

Selfridges DEPARTMENT STORE
(Map p168; www.selfridges.com; 400 Oxford St, W1; ⏲9.30am-9pm Mon-Sat, 11.30am-6.15pm Sun; ⊖Bond St) Selfridges loves innovation – it's famed for its inventive window displays by international artists, gala shows and, above all, its amazing range of products. It's the trendiest of London's one-stop shops, with labels such as Boudicca, Luella Bartley, Emma Cook, Chloé and Missoni; an unparalleled food hall; and Europe's largest cosmetics department.

Fortnum & Mason DEPARTMENT STORE
(Map p164; www.fortnumandmason.com; 181 Piccadilly, W1; ⏲10am-9pm Mon-Sat, noon-6pm Sun; ⊖Piccadilly Circus) London's oldest grocery store, now into its fourth century, refuses to yield to modern times. Its staff are still dressed in old-fashioned tailcoats and it keeps its glamorous food hall supplied with hampers, cut marmalade, speciality teas and so on. Downstairs is an elegant wine bar as well as elegant kitchenware, luxury gifts and perfumes.

Liberty DEPARTMENT STORE
(Map p164; www.liberty.co.uk; Great Marlborough St, W1; ⏲10am-8pm Mon-Sat, noon-6pm Sun; ⊖Oxford Circus) An irresistible blend of contemporary styles in an old-fashioned mock-Tudor atmosphere, Liberty has a huge cosmetics department and an accessories floor, along with a breathtaking lingerie section, all at very inflated prices. A classic London souvenir is a Liberty fabric print especially in the form of a scarf.

Harrods DEPARTMENT STORE
(Map p168; www.harrods.com; 87 Brompton Rd, SW1; ⏲10am-8pm Mon-Sat, 11.30am-6pm Sun; ⊖Knightsbridge) Both garish and stylish at the same time, perennially crowded Harrods is an obligatory stop for London's tourists, from the cash strapped to the big, big spenders. The stock is astonishing and you'll swoon over the spectacular food hall.

Harvey Nichols DEPARTMENT STORE
(Map p168; www.harveynichols.com; 109-125 Knightsbridge, SW1; ⏲10am-8pm Mon-Sat, 11.30am-6pm Sun; ⊖Knightsbridge) At London's temple of high fashion, you'll find Chloé and Balenciaga bags, the city's best denim range, a massive make-up hall with exclusive lines, great jewellery and the fantastic restaurant, Fifth Floor.

Music

As befitting a global music capital, London has a wide range of music stores.

Ray's Jazz MUSIC
(Map p164; www.foyles.co.uk; 2nd fl, 107 Charing Cross Rd, WC2; ⏲9.30am-9pm Mon-Sat, 11.30am-6pm Sun; ⊖Tottenham Court Rd) Quiet and serene with friendly and helpful staff, this shop on the 2nd floor of Foyles bookshop has one of the best jazz selections in London.

Rough Trade West MUSIC
(☎020-7229 8541; www.roughtrade.com; 130 Talbot Rd, W11; ⏲10am-6.30pm Mon-Sat, 11am-5pm Sun; ⊖Ladbroke Grove) With its underground, alternative and vintage rarities, this home of the eponymous punk-music label remains a haven for vinyl junkies.

Bookshops

Foyles BOOKS
(Map p164; www.foyles.co.uk; 107 Charing Cross Rd, WC2; ⏲9.30am-9pm Mon-Sat, 11.30am-6pm Sun; ⊖Tottenham Court Rd) This is London's most legendary bookshop, where you can bet on finding even the most obscure of titles. The lovely **cafe** is on the 1st floor where you'll also find **Grant & Cutler**, the UK's largest foreign-language bookseller. Ray's Jazz is up on the 2nd floor.

Daunt Books BOOKS
(Map p168; www.dauntbooks.co.uk; 83 Marylebone High St, W1; ⏲9am-7.30pm Mon-Sat, 11am-6pm Sun; ⊖Baker St) An original Edwardian bookshop, with oak panels and gorgeous skylights, Daunt is one of London's loveliest travel bookshops. It has two floors and stocks general fiction and nonfiction titles as well.

City of London Information Centre (Map p160; www.visitthecity.co.uk; St Paul's Churchyard, EC4; ⏲9.30am-5.30pm Mon-Sat, 10am-4pm Sun; ⊖St Paul's) Tourist information, fast-track tickets to City attractions and guided walks (adult/child £6/4).

Getting There & Away

BUS & COACH

The London terminus for long-distance buses (called 'coaches' in Britain) is **Victoria Coach Station** (164 Buckingham Palace Rd, SW1; ⊖Victoria).

TRAIN

Most of London's main-line rail terminals are linked by the Circle line on the tube.

Charing Cross Canterbury

Euston Manchester, Liverpool, Carlisle, Glasgow

King's Cross Cambridge, Hull, York, Newcastle, Edinburgh, Aberdeen

Liverpool Street Stansted airport (Express), Cambridge

London Bridge Gatwick airport, Brighton

Marylebone Birmingham

Paddington Heathrow airport (Express), Oxford, Bath, Bristol, Exeter, Plymouth, Cardiff

St Pancras Gatwick and Luton airports, Brighton, Nottingham, Sheffield, Leicester, Leeds, Paris Eurostar

Victoria Gatwick airport (Express), Brighton, Canterbury

Waterloo Windsor, Winchester, Exeter, Plymouth

Getting Around

TO/FROM THE AIRPORTS

Gatwick

Main-line trains run every 15 minutes between Gatwick's South Terminal and Victoria (from £15, 37 minutes), hourly at night, or to/from St Pancras (from £10, 56 minutes) via London Bridge, City Thameslink, Blackfriars and Farringdon.

Gatwick Express (www.gatwickexpress.com; one way/return £19.90/34.90) trains run to/from Victoria every 15 minutes from 5am to 11.45pm (first/last train 3.30am/12.32am).

The **EasyBus** (www.easybus.co.uk; one way £10, return from £12) minibus service between Gatwick and Earl's Court (from 4.25am to 1am, about 1¼ hours, every 30 minutes) can cost as little as £2, depending on when you book. You're charged extra if you have more than one carry-on and one check-in bag.

Heathrow

The cheapest option from Heathrow is the Underground (tube). The Piccadilly line is accessible from every terminal (£5.70, one hour to central London, departing from Heathrow every five minutes from around 5am to 11.30pm).

Faster, and much more expensive, is the **Heathrow Express** (www.heathrowexpress.com; one way/return £21/34) train to Paddington station (15 minutes, every 15 minutes, 5.12am to 11.48pm). You can purchase tickets on board (£5 extra), from self-service machines (cash and credit cards accepted) at both stations, or online.

London City

The Docklands Light Railway (DLR) connects London City Airport to the tube network, taking 22 minutes to reach Bank station (£4.70). A black taxi costs around £30 to/from central London.

Luton

There are regular National Rail services from St Pancras (£13.90, 29 to 39 minutes) to Luton Airport Parkway station, where a shuttle bus (£1.60) will get you to the airport within 10 minutes. EasyBus minibuses head from Victoria, Earl's Court and Baker St to Luton (from £2 if booked in advance); allow 1½ hours, every 30 minutes. A taxi costs around £100 to £110.

Stansted

The **Stansted Express** (☎0845 850 0150; www.stanstedexpress.com) connects with Liverpool Street station (one way/return

OYSTER CARD

The Oyster card is a smart card on which you can store credit towards 'prepay' fares, as well as Travelcards valid for periods from a day to a year. Oyster cards are valid across the entire public transport network in London. When entering a station, simply touch your card on a reader (they have a yellow circle with the image of an Oyster card on them) and then touch again on your way out. The system will deduct the appropriate amount of credit from your card. For bus journeys, you only need to touch once upon boarding.

The benefit is that fares for Oyster card users are lower than standard ones. If you make many journeys during the day, you will never pay more than the appropriate Travelcard (peak or off peak) once the daily 'price cap' has been reached.

Oyster cards can be bought (£5 refundable deposit required) and topped up at any Underground station, travel information centre or shop displaying the Oyster logo.

To get your deposit back along with any remaining credit, simply return your Oyster card at a ticket booth.

£23.40/33.20, 46 minutes, every 15 minutes, 6am to 12.30am).

EasyBus (p185) has services between Stansted and Baker St (1¼ hours, every 20 minutes). The Airbus A6 links with Victoria Coach Station (£11, allow 1¾ hours, at least every 30 minutes).

National Express (www.nationalexpress.com) runs buses to Stansted from Liverpool St station (£9 one way, 80 minutes, every 30 minutes).

BICYCLE

Central London is mostly flat, relatively compact and the traffic moves slowly – all of which makes it surprisingly good for cyclists. It can get terribly congested though, so you'll need to keep your wits about you – and lock your bike (including both wheels) securely.

Bikes can be hired from numerous self-service docking stations through **Barclays Cycle Hire Scheme** (☎ 0845 026 3630; www.tfl.gov.uk). The hire access fee is £2 for 24 hours or £10 per week. On top of that are the ride fees: the first 30 minutes is free (making the bikes perfect for short hops), or £1/4/6/15 for one hour/90 minutes/two hours/three hours.

CAR

Don't. London was recently rated Western Europe's second-most congested city (congratulations Brussels). In addition, you'll pay £10 per day congestion charge (7am to 6pm weekdays) simply to drive into central London. If you're hiring a car to continue your trip around Britain, take the tube or train to a major airport and pick it up from there.

PUBLIC TRANSPORT

London's public transport is excellent, with tubes, trains, buses and boats getting you wherever you need to go. **TFL** (www.tfl.gov.uk), the city's public transport provider, is the glue that binds the network together. Its website has a handy journey planner and information on all services, including taxis.

Boat

Thames Clippers (www.thamesclippers.com) runs regular commuter services between Embankment, Waterloo, Blackfriars, Bankside, London Bridge, Tower, Canary Wharf, Greenwich, North Greenwich and Woolwich piers (adult/child £6/3) from 7am to midnight (from 9.30am weekends).

Bus

Buses run regularly during the day, while less frequent night buses (prefixed with the letter 'N') wheel into action when the tube stops. Single-journey bus tickets (valid for two hours) cost £2.40 (£1.40 on Oyster, capped at £4.40 per day); a weekly pass is £20.20. Buses stop on request, so clearly signal the driver with an outstretched arm.

Underground & Docklands Light Railway

The tube extends its subterranean tentacles throughout London and into the surrounding counties, with services running every few minutes from roughly 5.30am to 12.30am (7am to 11.30pm Sunday). The Docklands Light Railway (DLR) links the City to Docklands, Greenwich and London City Airport.

Lines are colour-coded (red for the Central Line, yellow for the Circle Line, black for the Northern Line and so on). It helps to know the direction you're travelling in (ie northbound or southbound, eastbound or westbound) as well as the terminus of the line you're travelling on. If you get confused, don't worry, as copies of the tube's famous map are posted everywhere, showing how the 14 different routes intersect. Be warned, however – the distances between stations on the tube map aren't remotely to scale.

Single fares cost from £2.30/4.80 with/without an Oyster card.

TAXI

London's famous black cabs are available for hire when the yellow light above the windscreen is lit. Fares are metered, with flag fall of £2.40 and the additional rate dependent on time of day, distance travelled and taxi speed. A 1-mile trip will cost between £5.60 and £8.80.

Minicabs are a cheaper alternative to black cabs and will quote trip fares in advance. Only use drivers from proper agencies; licensed minicabs aren't allowed to tout for business or pick you up off the street without a booking.

MAPS

There was a time when no Londoner would be without a pocket-sized *London A–Z* map-book. It's a great resource if you don't have a smartphone. You can buy them at newsstands and shops everywhere. For getting around the London Underground system (the tube), maps are free at underground stations.

Around London

'When you're tired of London, you're tired of life' said 18th-century Londoner Samuel Johnson. But he wasn't living in an age when too many days on the tube can leave you exhausted and grouchy. Luckily, the capital is surprisingly close to some excellent day trips; Windsor and Eton are two gems that are an easy train ride from the capital.

Windsor & Eton

POP 31,000

Dominated by the massive bulk and heavy influence of Windsor Castle, these twin towns have a rather surreal atmosphere, with the morning pomp and ceremony of the changing of the guards in Windsor and the sight of school boys dressed in formal tailcoats wandering the streets of Eton.

Sights

★Windsor Castle CASTLE, PALACE

(www.royalcollection.org.uk; Castle Hill; adult/child £19/11; ⏲9.45am-5.15pm) The largest and oldest occupied fortress in the world, Windsor Castle is a majestic vision of battlements and towers. It's used for state occasions and is one of the Queen's principal residences; if she's at home, you'll see the Royal Standard flying from the Round Tower. Join a free guided tour (every half-hour) or take a multilingual audio tour of the lavish state rooms and beautiful chapels. Note, some sections may be off-limits on any given day if they're in use.

Eton College NOTABLE BUILDING

(www.etoncollege.com) Eton is the largest and most famous public (meaning very private) school in England, and arguably the most enduring and illustrious symbol of England's class system. At the time of writing, it wasn't possible to visit the school due to building work, but check the visitors tab on its website to see whether tours have resumed.

Information

Royal Windsor Information Centre (www.windsor.gov.uk; Old Booking Hall, Windsor Royal Shopping Arcade; ⏲9.30am-5pm) Pick up a heritage walk brochure (50p).

Getting There & Away

Trains from Windsor Central station on Thames St go to London Paddington (£9.80, 27 to 43 minutes), and from Windsor Riverside station to London Waterloo (£9.80, 56 minutes). Services run half-hourly from both stations.

Canterbury

POP 43,432

Canterbury tops the charts for English cathedral cities. Many consider the World Heritage–listed cathedral that dominates its centre to be one of Europe's finest, and the town's narrow medieval alleyways, riverside gardens and ancient city walls are a joy to explore.

Sights

★Canterbury Cathedral CATHEDRAL

(www.canterbury-cathedral.org; adult/concession £10.50/9.50, tour adult/concession £5/4, audio tour adult/concession £4/3; ⏲9am-5pm Mon-Sat, 12.30-2.30pm Sun) A rich repository of more than 1400 years of Christian history, the Church of England's mother ship is a truly extraordinary place with an absorbing history. This Gothic cathedral, the highlight of the city's World Heritage Sites, is southeast England's top tourist attraction as well as a place of worship. It's also the site of English history's most famous murder: Archbishop Thomas Beckett was done in here in 1170. Allow at least two hours to do the cathedral justice.

Sleeping

Arthouse B&B B&B ££

(☎07976 725457; www.arthousebandb.com; 24 London Rd; r £75; P 📶) A night at Canterbury's most laid-back digs, housed in a 19th-century fire station, is a bit like sleeping over at a really cool art student's pad. The theme is funky and eclectic, with furniture by local designers and artwork by the instantly likeable artist owners, who have a house-studio out back.

> **WORTH A TRIP**
>
> **THE MAKING OF HARRY POTTER**
>
> Whether you're a fairweather fan or a full-on Pothead, this studio **tour** (☎0845 084 0900; www.wbstudiotour.co.uk; Studio Tour Dr, Leavesden; adult/child £31/24; ⏲9am-9.30pm) is well worth the admittedly hefty admission price. You'll need to prebook your visit for an allocated timeslot and then allow two to three hours to do the complex justice. It starts with a short film before you're ushered through giant doors into the actual set of Hogwarts' Great Hall – the first of many 'wow' moments. You'll find the studio near Watford, northwest of London – shuttle buses run from Watford Junction station.

Kipp's Independent Hostel HOSTEL £
(☎01227-786121; www.kipps-hostel.com; 40 Nunnery Fields; dm/s/d £19.50/28.50/57; @📶) Occupying a red-brick town house in a quietish residential area less than a mile from the city centre, these superb backpacker digs enjoy a homely atmosphere, clean (though cramped) dorms and rave reviews.

Eating & Drinking

Tiny Tim's Tearoom CAFE £
(34 St Margaret's St; mains £7-9; ⏰9.30am-5pm Tue-Sat, 10.30am-4pm Sun) Swish 1930s English tearoom offering hungry shoppers big breakfasts bursting with Kentish ingredients, and tiers of cakes, crumpets, cucumber sandwiches and scones plastered in clotted cream.

Goods Shed MARKET, RESTAURANT ££
(www.thegoodsshed.co.uk; Station Rd West; mains £12-20; ⏰market 9am-7pm Tue-Sat, 10am-4pm Sun, restaurant 8am-9.30pm Tue-Sat, 9am-3pm Sun) Farmers market, food hall and fabulous restaurant rolled into one, this converted warehouse by the Canterbury West train station is a hit with everyone from self-caterers to sit-down gourmets.

The chunky wooden tables sit slightly above the market hubbub but in full view of its appetite-whetting stalls, and daily specials exploit the freshest farm goodies England has to offer.

Information

Tourist Office (☎01227-378100; www.canterbury.co.uk; 18 High St; ⏰9am-5pm Mon-Wed, Fri & Sat, to 7pm Thu, 10am-5pm Sun) Located in the Beaney House of Art & Knowledge. Staff can help book accommodation, excursions and theatre tickets.

Getting There & Away

There are two train stations: Canterbury East for London Victoria and Dover; and Canterbury West for London's Charing Cross and St Pancras stations. Connections include Dover Priory (£8, 25 minutes, every 30 minutes), London St Pancras (£34, one hour, hourly) and London Victoria/Charing Cross (£28.40, 1¾ hours, two to three hourly).

Salisbury

POP 43,335

Centred on a majestic cathedral topped by the tallest spire in England, the gracious city of Salisbury has been an important provincial city for more than 1000 years.

DON'T MISS

AVEBURY

While the tour buses usually head straight to Stonehenge, prehistoric purists make for **Avebury Stone Circle**. Though it lacks the dramatic trilithons ('gateways') of its sister site across the plain, Avebury is the largest stone circle in the world and a more rewarding place to visit simply because you can get closer to the giant boulders.

A large section of Avebury village is actually inside the circle, meaning you can sleep, or at least have lunch and a pint, inside the mystic ring.

To get here, buses 5, 6 and 96 run from Salisbury (1¾ hours, hourly Monday to Saturday, five on Sunday).

Sights

★ **Salisbury Cathedral** CATHEDRAL
(☎01722-555120; www.salisburycathedral.org.uk; Cathedral Close; requested donation adult/child £6.50/3; ⏰9am-5pm Mon-Sat, noon-4pm Sun) England is endowed with countless stunning churches, but few can hold a candle to the grandeur and sheer spectacle of 13th-century Salisbury Cathedral. This early English Gothic–style structure has an elaborate exterior decorated with pointed arches and flying buttresses, and a sombre, austere interior designed to keep its congregation suitably pious. Its statuary and tombs are outstanding. Don't miss the daily tower tours and the cathedral's original, 13th-century copy of the Magna Carta. It's best experienced on a **Tower Tour** (adult/child £10/8; ⏰1-5pm daily).

★ **Salisbury Museum** MUSEUM
(☎01722-332151; www.salisburymuseum.org.uk; 65 Cathedral Close; adult/child £5/2; ⏰10am-5pm Mon-Sat, plus noon-5pm Sun Jun-Sep) The hugely important archaeological finds here include the Stonehenge Archer: the bones of a man found in the ditch surrounding the stone circle – one of the arrows found alongside probably killed him. With gold coins dating from 100 BC and a Bronze Age gold necklace, it's a powerful introduction to Wiltshire's prehistory.

Sleeping & Eating

Salisbury YHA HOSTEL £
(☎0845 371 9537; www.yha.org.uk; Milford Hill; dm/d £18/28; P @) A real gem: neat rooms in a rambling Victorian house, with a cafe-bar, laundry and dappled gardens, too.

★**St Ann's House** BOUTIQUE B&B ££
(☎01722-335657; www.stannshouse.co.uk; 32 St Ann St; s £59-64, d £89-110;) The aromas wafting from breakfast may well spur you from your room: great coffee; baked peaches with raspberry, honey and almonds; poached eggs and Parma ham. Utter elegance reigns upstairs, where well-chosen antiques, warm colours and Turkish linen ensure a supremely comfortable stay.

Cloisters PUB ££
(www.cloisterspubsalisbury.co.uk; 83 Catherine St; mains £9-13; ⊙11am-3pm & 6-9pm Mon-Fri, 11am-9pm Sat & Sun) The building dates from 1350, it's been a pub since the 1600s and today improbably warped beams reinforce an age-old vibe. It's a convivial spot for tasty beef-and-ale pie, sausage and mash or fancier foods such as an impressive lamb shank slow-braised in red wine.

Information

Tourist Office (☎01722-342860; www.visitwiltshire.co.uk; Fish Row; ⊙9am-5pm Mon-Fri, 10am-4pm Sat, 10am-2pm Sun)

Getting There & Away

BUS

National Express services include Bath (£11, 1¼ hours, one daily), Bristol (£11, 2¼ hours, one daily) and London (£17, three hours, three daily) via Heathrow. Tour buses leave Salisbury for Stonehenge regularly.

TRAIN

Trains run half-hourly from London Waterloo (£38, 1¾ hours). Hourly connections include Bath (£10, one hour), Bristol (£11, 1¼ hours) and Exeter (£25, two hours).

Stonehenge

This compelling ring of monolithic stones has been attracting a steady stream of pilgrims, poets and philosophers for the last 5000 years and is easily Britain's most iconic archaeological site.

STONE CIRCLE ACCESS VISITS

Visitors to Stonehenge normally have to stay outside the stone circle. But on **Stone Circle Access Visits** (☎0870 333 0605; www.english-heritage.org.uk; adult/child £21/12.60) you get to wander round the core of the site, getting up-close views of the bluestones and trilithons. The walks take place in the evening or early morning, so the quieter atmosphere and the slanting sunlight add to the effect. Each visit only takes 26 people; to secure a place book at least two months in advance.

The landscape around **Stonehenge** (☎0870 333 1181; www.english-heritage.org.uk; adult/child incl visitor centre £14/8.30; ⊙9am-8pm Jun-Aug, 9.30am-7pm Apr, May & Sep, 9.30am-5pm Oct-Mar) is undergoing a long-overdue revamp, which should dramatically improve the experience of those visiting when it's completed. But even before the changes, and despite the huge numbers of tourists who traipse around the perimeter, Stonehenge still manages to be a mystical, ethereal place – a haunting echo from Britain's forgotten past, and a reminder of the people who once walked the many ceremonial avenues across Salisbury Plain.

Even more intriguingly, it's still one of Britain's great archaeological mysteries: despite countless theories about what the site was used for, ranging from a sacrificial centre to a celestial timepiece, no one knows for sure what drove prehistoric Britons to expend so much time and effort on its construction.

Stonehenge now operates by timed tickets, meaning if you want guaranteed entry you have to book in advance. If you're planning a high-season visit, it's best to secure your ticket well in advance.

Getting There & Around

BUS

There is no public transport to the site. The **Stonehenge Tour** (☎0845 072 7093; www.thestonehengetour.info; adult/child £26/16) leaves Salisbury's railway and bus stations half-hourly from June to August, and hourly from September to May.

TAXI

Taxis charge £40 to go to Stonehenge from Salisbury, wait for an hour and come back.

Bath

POP 90,144

Britain is littered with beautiful cities, but precious few can hold a candle to Bath, founded on top of a network of natural hot springs. Bath's heyday was during the 18th century, when local entrepreneur Ralph Allen and the father-and-son architects John Wood the Elder and Younger, turned this sleepy backwater into the toast of Georgian society, and constructed fabulous landmarks such as the Circus and Royal Crescent.

Sights

★Roman Baths

MUSEUM

(☎01225-477785; www.romanbaths.co.uk; Abbey Churchyard; adult/child/family £13.50/8.80/38; ⌚9am-6pm, to 9pm Jul & Aug) In typically ostentatious style, the Romans constructed a complex of bathhouses above Bath's three natural hot springs, which emerge at a steady 46°C (115°F). Situated alongside a temple dedicated to the healing goddess Sulis Minerva, the baths now form one of the best-preserved ancient Roman spas in the world, encircled by 18th- and 19th-century

Bath

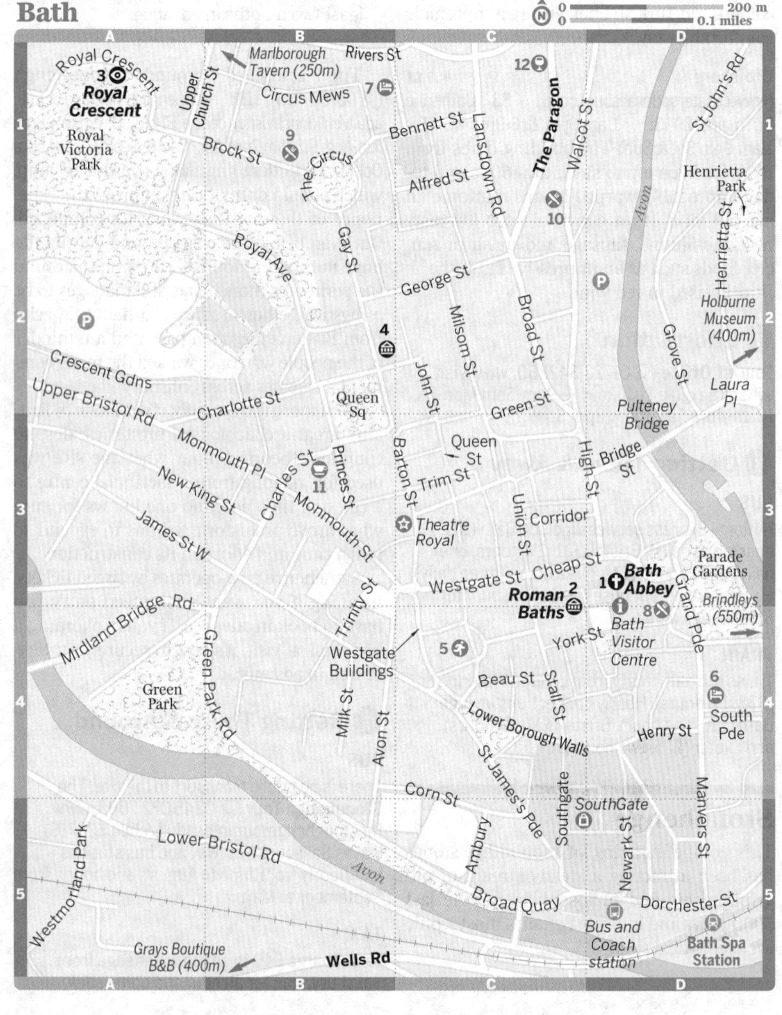

buildings. As Bath's premier attraction, the Roman Baths can get very, very busy. Avoid the worst crowds by buying tickets online, visiting early on a midweek morning, and avoiding July and August.

★ Royal Crescent HISTORIC SITE

Bath is justifiably celebrated for its glorious Georgian architecture, and it doesn't get any grander than on Royal Crescent, a semicircular terrace of majestic town houses overlooking the green sweep of Royal Victoria Park. Designed by John Wood the Younger (1728–82) and built between 1767 and 1775, the houses appear perfectly symmetrical from the outside, but the owners were allowed to tweak the interiors to their own specifications; consequently no two houses on the Crescent are quite the same.

★ Bath Abbey CHURCH

(☎01225-422462; www.bathabbey.org; requested donation £2.50; ⏲9am-6pm Mon-Sat, 1-2.30pm & 4.30-5.30pm Sun) Looming above the city centre, Bath's huge abbey church was built between 1499 and 1616, making it the last great medieval church raised in England. Its most striking feature is the west facade, where angels climb up and down stone ladders, commemorating a dream of the founder, Bishop Oliver King. **Tower tours** (towertours@bathabbey.org; adult/child £6/3; ⏲10am-5pm Apr-Aug, to 4pm Sep-Oct, 11am-4pm Jan-Mar, to 3pm Nov & Dec) leave on the hour from Monday to Friday, or every half-hour on Saturdays, but don't run on Sundays.

Bath

Top Sights

1	Bath Abbey	D3
2	Roman Baths	C3
3	Royal Crescent	A1

Sights

4	Jane Austen Centre	B2

Activities, Courses & Tours

5	Thermae Bath Spa	C4

Sleeping

6	Halcyon	D4
7	Queensberry Hotel	B1

Eating

8	Café Retro	D4
9	Circus	B1
10	Sam's Kitchen Deli	C1

Drinking & Nightlife

11	Colonna & Smalls	B3
12	Star Inn	C1

Holburne Museum GALLERY

(☎01225-388569; www.holburne.org; Great Pulteney St; ⏲10am-5pm) FREE Sir William Holburne, the 18th-century aristocrat and art fanatic, amassed a huge collection that now forms the core of the Holburne Museum, in a lavish mansion at the end of Great Pulteney St. Fresh from a three-year refit, the museum houses a roll-call of works by artists including Turner, Stubbs, William Hoare and Thomas Gainsborough, as well as 18th-century majolica and porcelain. Temporary exhibitions incur a fee.

Jane Austen Centre MUSEUM

(☎01225-443000; www.janeausten.co.uk; 40 Gay St; adult/child £8/4.50; ⏲9.45am-5.30pm) Bath is known to many as a location in Jane Austen's novels, including *Persuasion* and *Northanger Abbey*. Though Austen only lived in Bath for five years from 1801 to 1806, she remained a regular visitor, and a keen student of the city's social scene. This museum houses memorabilia relating to the writer's life in Bath, and there's a Regency tearoom that serves crumpets and cream teas in suitably frilly surroundings.

Sleeping

Bath YHA HOSTEL £

(☎0845 371 9303; www.yha.org.uk; Bathwick Hill; dm £13-20, d from £29; ⏲reception 7am-11pm; P@☎) Split across an Italianate mansion and a modern annexe, this impressive hostel is a steep climb (or a short hop on bus 18) from the city centre. The listed building means the rooms are huge, and some have period features such as cornicing and bay windows.

★ Halcyon HOTEL £££

(☎01225-444100; www.thehalcyon.com; 2/3 South Pde; d £125-145; ☎) Just what Bath needed: a smart city-centre hotel that doesn't break the bank. Situated on a terrace of townhouses off Manvers St, the Halcyon offers style on a budget: uncluttered rooms, contemporary bed linen and Philippe Starck bath fittings.

Rooms vary in size and are spread out over three floors – inconvenient as there's no lift. Self-catering apartments (£150 to £300 per night) are also available in a separate building at 15a George St.

DON'T MISS

THE THERMAE BATH SPA

Taking a dip in the Roman Baths might be off-limits, but you can still sample the city's curative waters at this fantastic modern **spa complex** (☎0844-888 0844; www.thermaebathspa.com; Bath St; ⏲9am-10pm, last entry 7.30pm), housed in a shell of local stone and plate glass. Tickets includes steam rooms, waterfall showers and a choice of two swimming pools. The showpiece attraction is the open-air rooftop pool, where you can bathe with a backdrop of Bath's cityscape – a don't-miss experience, best appreciated at dusk.

Grays Boutique B&B B&B £££
(☎01225-403020; www.graysbath.co.uk; Upper Oldfield Park; d £120-195; 📶) An elegant B&B straight out of an interiors magazine. All the rooms are individual: some with feminine flowers or polka-dot prints, others maritime stripes, but all simple and stylish (we particularly liked room 2, with its French bed and bay window). Breakfast is served in the conservatory, with eggs, milk and bacon from local farms.

The owners run a smaller but equally smart B&B on the east side of town, **Brindleys** (☎01225-310444; www.brindleysbath.co.uk; 14 Pulteney Gardens; d £110-185).

★Queensberry Hotel HOTEL £££
(☎01225-447928; www.thequeensberry.co.uk; 4 Russell St; d £115-225; P📶) The quirky Queensberry is Bath's best boutique spoil. Four Georgian town houses have been combined into one seamlessly stylish whole. Some rooms are cosy in gingham checks and country creams, others feature bright upholstery, original fireplaces and free-standing tubs. The Olive Tree Restaurant is excellent, too. Rates exclude breakfast.

Eating & Drinking

Sam's Kitchen Deli CAFE £
(☎01225-481159; www.samskitchendeli.co.uk; 61 Walcot St; lunch £8-10; ⏲8am-5pm Mon-Sat, to 10pm every 2nd Fri) Situated on Bath's hippest street, Sam's is a perfect lunch spot, with set dishes (including a daily roast) served from pans on the counter. With its dilapidated piano and reclaimed furniture, it's the epitome of a shabby-chic cafe, and very popular. There are live gigs every other Friday.

Café Retro CAFE £
(☎01225-339347; 18 York St; mains £5-11; ⏲9am-5pm Mon-Sat, 10am-5pm Sun) A poke in the eye for the corporate coffee chains. The paint job's scruffy, the crockery's ancient and none of the furniture matches, but that's all part of the charm: this is a cafe from the old school, and there's nowhere better for burgers, butties (sandwiches) or cake. Takeaways (in biodegradable containers) are available from Retro-to-Go next door.

★Circus MODERN BRITISH ££
(☎01225-466020; www.thecircuscafeandrestaurant.co.uk; 34 Brock St; mains lunch £8.30-13.50, dinner £16.50-18.50; ⏲10am-10pm Mon-Sat) Chef Ali Golden has turned this bistro into one of Bath's destination addresses. Her taste is for British dishes with a continental twist, à la Elizabeth David: rabbit, guinea-fowl, roast chicken, spring lamb, infused with herby flavours and rich sauces. It occupies the ground floor and basement of a town house near the Circus. Reservations recommended.

Marlborough Tavern GASTROPUB ££
(☎01225-423731; www.marlborough-tavern.com; 35 Marlborough Bldgs; lunch £9-13, dinner mains £13.50-21.50; ⏲noon-11pm) The queen of Bath's gastropubs, with food that's closer to a fine-dining restaurant – think duo of venison and pork tenderloin rather than bog-standard meat-and-two-veg. Chunky wooden tables and racks of wine behind the bar give it an exclusive, classy feel.

★Colonna & Smalls CAFE
(www.colonnaandsmalls.co.uk; 6 Chapel Row; ⏲8am-5.30pm Mon-Sat, 10am-4pm Sun) A connoisseur's coffeehouse. The espressos and cappuccinos are, quite simply, second to none – so if you care about your caffeine, you won't want to miss it. Proper coffee nuts can even take a barista training course.

★Star Inn PUB
(www.star-inn-bath.co.uk; 23 The Vineyards, off The Paragon; ⏲noon-11pm) Not many pubs are registered relics, but the Star is – it still has many of its 19th-century bar fittings. It's the brewery tap for Bath-based Abbey Ales;

some ales are served in traditional jugs, and you can even ask for a pinch of snuff in the 'smaller bar'.

Information

Bath Visitor Centre (☎0906 711 2000, accommodation bookings 0844 847 5256; www.visitbath.co.uk; Abbey Churchyard; ⏰9.30am-5pm Mon-Sat, 10am-4pm Sun) Sells the **Bath Visitor Card** (http://visitbath.co.uk/special-offers/bath-visitor-card; £3). The general enquiries line is charged at the premium rate of 50p per minute.

Getting There & Away

BUS

Bath's **bus and coach station** (Dorchester St; ⏰9am-5pm Mon-Sat) is near the train station. National Express coaches run directly to London (£17, 3½ hours, eight to 10 daily) via Heathrow.

TRAIN

Bath Spa station is at the end of Manvers St. Many services connect through Bristol (£7.10, 15 minutes, two or three per hour), especially to the north of England. Direct services include London Paddington/London Waterloo (£42, 1½ hours, half-hourly) and Salisbury (£16.90, one hour, hourly).

Oxford

POP 134,300

Oxford is a privileged place, one of the world's most famous university towns. The city is a wonderful place to ramble: the oldest of its 39 separate colleges dates back almost 750 years, and little has changed inside the hallowed walls since then (with the notable exception of female admissions, which only began in 1878).

Sights

Not all Oxford's colleges are open to the public. Check www.ox.ac.uk/colleges for full details.

★Ashmolean Museum — MUSEUM

(www.ashmolean.org; Beaumont St; ⏰10am-5pm Tue-Sun; 👪) FREE Britain's oldest public museum, second in repute only to London's British Museum, was established in 1683 when Elias Ashmole presented the university with the collection of curiosities amassed by the well-travelled John Tradescant, gardener to Charles I. A 2009 makeover has left the museum with new interactive features, a giant atrium, glass walls revealing galleries on different levels and a beautiful rooftop restaurant.

★Christ Church — COLLEGE

(www.chch.ox.ac.uk; St Aldate's; adult/child £8/6.50; ⏰10am-4.30pm Mon-Sat, 2-4.30pm Sun) The largest of all of Oxford's colleges and the one with the grandest quad, Christ Church is also its most popular. Its magnificent buildings, illustrious history and latter-day fame as a location for the Harry Potter films have tourists coming in droves. The college was founded in 1524 by Cardinal Thomas Wolsey, who suppressed the monastery existing on the site to acquire the funds for his lavish building project.

Magdalen College — COLLEGE

(www.magd.ox.ac.uk; High St; adult/child £5/4; ⏰1-6pm) Set amid 40 hectares of lawns, woodlands, river walks and deer park, Magdalen (*mawd*-lin), founded in 1458, is one of the wealthiest and most beautiful of Oxford's colleges. It has a reputation as an artistic college, and some of its famous students have

THE COTSWOLDS

Gorgeous villages built of honey-coloured stone, thatched cottages and atmospheric churches draw crowds of visitors to the Cotswolds. If you've ever coveted exposed beams or lusted after a cream tea in the afternoon, there's no finer place to fulfil your fantasies. This is prime tourist territory, however, and the most popular villages can be besieged by traffic in summer.

Travel by public transport requires careful planning and patience; for the most flexibility and the option of getting off the beaten track, your own car is unbeatable. Alternatively, the **Cotswolds Discoverer card** (1-/3-day bus pass £10/25, train pass £8.30/20) gives you unlimited travel on participating bus or train routes.

included writers Julian Barnes, Alan Hollinghurst, CS Lewis, John Betjeman, Seamus Heaney and Oscar Wilde, not to mention Edward VIII, TE Lawrence 'of Arabia' and Dudley Moore.

Merton College COLLEGE
(www.merton.ox.ac.uk; Merton St; admission £3; ⌚2-5pm Mon-Fri, 10am-5pm Sat & Sun) Founded in 1264, Merton is the oldest of the three original colleges and the first to adopt collegiate planning, bringing scholars and tutors together into a formal community and providing a planned residence for them. Its distinguishing architectural features include large gargoyles whose expressions suggest that they're about to throw up, and the charming 14th-century **Mob Quad** – the first of the college quads.

Bodleian Library LIBRARY
(☎01865-287400; www.bodley.ox.ac.uk; Catte St; tours £5-13; ⌚9am-5pm Mon-Sat, 11am-5pm Sun) Oxford's Bodleian Library is one of the oldest public libraries in the world and quite possibly the most impressive one you'll ever see. Casual visitors are welcome to wander around the central quad and visit the exhibition space in the foyer. For £1 you can also access the Divinity School, but the rest of the complex can only be visited on guided tours (check online or at the information desk for times; it pays to book ahead).

MESSING ABOUT ON THE RIVER

An unmissable Oxford experience, **punting** is all about sitting back and quaffing Pimms (the quintessential English summer drink) as you watch the city's glorious architecture float by. Which, of course, requires someone else to do the hard work – punting is far more difficult than it appears. If you decide to go it alone, a deposit is usually charged. Most punts hold five people including the punter. Hire them from **Magdalen Bridge Boathouse** (☎01865-202643; www.oxfordpunting.co.uk; High St; chauffered per 30min £25, self-punt per hour £20; ⌚9.30am-dusk Feb-Nov) or **Cherwell Boat House** (☎01865-515978; www.cherwellboathouse.co.uk; 50 Bardwell Rd; per hour £15-18; ⌚10am-dusk mid-Mar–mid-Oct).

Radcliffe Camera LIBRARY
(Radcliffe Sq) The Radcliffe Camera is the quintessential Oxford landmark and one of the city's most photographed buildings. The spectacular circular library/reading room, filled with natural light, was built between 1737 and 1749 in grand Palladian style, and has Britain's third-largest dome. The only way to see the interior is to join one of the extended tours (£13, 90 minutes) of the Bodleian Library.

Sleeping

Central Backpackers HOSTEL £
(☎01865-242288; www.centralbackpackers.co.uk; 13 Park End St; dm £22-28; @ 🛜) A friendly budget option located above a bar and right in the centre of town, this small hostel has basic, bright and simple rooms that sleep four to 12 people, a rooftop terrace and a small lounge with satellite TV.

★ **Oxford Coach & Horses** B&B ££
(☎01865-200017; www.oxfordcoachandhorses.co.uk; 62 St Clements St; s/d from £115/130; P 🛜) Once a coaching inn, this 18th-century building has been painted powder blue and given a fresh, modern makeover. Rooms are spacious and light-filled, and the ground floor has been converted into a large, attractive breakfast room.

Burlington House B&B ££
(☎01865-513513; www.burlington-house.co.uk; 374 Banbury Rd, Summertown; s/d from £70/97; P 🛜) Twelve big, bright and elegant rooms with patterned wallpaper and splashes of colour are available at this Victorian merchant's house. The fittings are luxurious and the bathrooms immaculate; the service is attentive; and breakfast comes complete with organic eggs and granola. It has good public transport links to town.

Remont Guesthouse B&B ££
(☎01865-311020; www.remont-oxford.co.uk; 367 Banbury Rd, Summertown; r £112-142; P @ 🛜) All modern style, subtle lighting and plush furnishings, this 25-room guesthouse has rooms decked out in cool neutrals with silky bedspreads, abstract art and huge plasma-screen TVs. There's also a sunny garden.

Eating

★ **Edamame** JAPANESE £
(www.edamame.co.uk; 15 Holywell St; mains £6-8; ⌚11.30am-2.30pm Wed-Sun, 5-8.30pm Thu-Sat) The queue out the door speaks volumes

WORTH A TRIP

GLASTONBURY

To many people, Glastonbury is synonymous with the **Glastonbury Festival of Contemporary Performing Arts** (www.glastonburyfestivals.co.uk), a majestic (and frequently mud-soaked) extravaganza of music, theatre, dance, cabaret, carnival, spirituality and general all-round weirdness that's been held on and off farmland in Pilton, just outside Glastonbury, for the last 40-something years (bar the occasional off-year to let the farm recover).

The town owes much of its spiritual fame to nearby **Glastonbury Tor** (NT; www.nationaltrust.org.uk/glastonbury-tor), a grassy hump about a mile from town, topped by the ruins of St Michael's Church. According to local legend, the tor is said to be the mythical Isle of Avalon, King Arthur's last resting place. It's also allegedly one of the world's great spiritual nodes, marking the meeting point of many mystical lines of power known as ley lines.

There is no train station in Glastonbury, but bus 376/377 runs to Wells (17 minutes, every 15 minutes) and Bristol (1½ hours, every half hour).

about the quality of food here. This tiny joint, all light wood and friendly bustle, is the best place in town for authentic Japanese cuisine. Arrive early and be prepared to wait.

★**Rickety Press** MODERN BRITISH ££
(☎01865-424581; www.thericketypress.com; 67 Cranham St; mains £13-17; ⏰noon-2.30pm & 6-9.30pm) Hidden in the backstreets of Jericho, this old corner pub serves up beautifully presented, tasty food in casual surrounds. Call in for lunch or before 7pm for a great-value express menu (two/three courses £13/15).

Door 74 MODERN BRITISH ££
(☎01865-203374; www.door74.co.uk; 74 Cowley Rd; mains £10-14; ⏰noon-3pm & 5-11pm Tue-Fri, 10am-11pm Sat, 11am-4pm Sun) This cosy little place woos its fans with a rich mix of British and Mediterranean flavours and friendly service. The menu is limited and the tables tightly packed, but the food is consistently good and weekend brunches (full English breakfast, pancakes etc) supremely filling. Book ahead.

Café Coco MEDITERRANEAN ££
(☎01865-200232; www.cafecoco.co.uk; 23 Cowley Rd; breakfast £4-10, lunch £7-12; ⏰10am-midnight Thu-Sat, 10am-5pm Sun) This Cowley Rd institution is a popular brunching destination for the hip and hungry, and is decorated with classic posters on the walls and a bald plaster-cast clown in an ice bath. The menu ranges from cooked breakfasts and waffles to pizza, salads, Mediterranean mains and pecan pie.

Drinking & Nightlife

★**Bear Inn** PUB
(www.bearoxford.co.uk; 6 Alfred St; ⏰11am-11pm; 📶) Arguably Oxford's oldest pub (there's been a pub on this site since 1242), this atmospherically creaky place requires all but the most vertically challenged to duck their heads when passing through doorways. There's a curious tie collection on the walls and ceiling (though you can no longer exchange yours for a pint), and there are usually a couple of worthy guest ales.

Eagle & Child PUB
(www.nicholsonspubs.co.uk/theeagleandchildoxford; 49 St Giles; ⏰11am-11pm; 📶) Affectionately known as the 'Bird & Baby', this atmospheric place, dating from 1650, was once the favourite haunt of authors JRR Tolkien and CS Lewis. Its wood-panelled rooms and selection of real ales still attract a mellow crowd.

Turf Tavern PUB
(www.theturftavern.co.uk; 4 Bath Pl; ⏰11am-11pm) Hidden down a narrow alleyway, this tiny medieval pub (dating from at least 1381) is one of the town's best loved; it's where US president Bill Clinton famously 'did not inhale'. Home to 11 real ales, it's always packed with a mix of students, professionals and lucky tourists who manage to find it. Plenty of outdoor seating.

Information

Tourist Office (☎01865-252200; www.visitoxfordandoxfordshire.com; 15-16 Broad St; ⏰9.30am-5pm Mon-Sat, 10am-3.30pm Sun)

DON'T MISS

BLENHEIM PALACE

One of the country's greatest stately homes, **Blenheim Palace** (www.blenheimpalace.com; adult/child £22/12, park & gardens only £13/6.50; ⌚10.30am-5.30pm daily, closed Mon & Tue Nov–mid-Feb) is a monumental baroque fantasy designed by Sir John Vanbrugh and Nicholas Hawksmoor between 1705 and 1722. Now a Unesco World Heritage Site, it's home to the 11th Duke of Marlborough. Highlights include the **Great Hall**, a vast space topped by 20m-high ceilings adorned with images of the first duke in battle; the most important public room, the opulent **Saloon**; the three **state rooms** with their plush decor and priceless china cabinets; and the magnificent 55m **Long Library**. You can also visit the **Churchill Exhibition**, dedicated to the life, work and writings of Sir Winston, who was born at Blenheim in 1874.

Blenheim Palace is near the town of Woodstock, a few miles northwest of Oxford. To get there, Stagecoach bus S3 (£3.50, 35 minutes, every half hour, hourly on Sunday) runs from George St in Oxford.

Getting There & Away

BUS

Oxford's main bus/coach station is at Gloucester Green, with frequent services to London (£14, 1¾ hours, every 15 minutes). There are also regular buses to/from Heathrow and Gatwick airports.

TRAIN

Oxford's train station has half-hourly services to London Paddington (£25, 1¼ hours) and roughly hourly trains to Birmingham (£27, 1¼ hours). Hourly services also run to Bath (£18, 1½ hours) and Bristol (£28, one to two hours), but require a change at Didcot Parkway.

Stratford-upon-Avon

POP 22,187

William Shakespeare was born in Stratford in 1564 and died here in 1616. The various buildings linked to his life form the centrepiece of a tourist attraction that verges on a cult of personality. Experiences range from the tacky (Bard-themed tearooms) to the humbling (Shakespeare's modest grave in Holy Trinity Church) and the sublime (a play by the world-famous Royal Shakespeare Company).

Sights & Activities

★Shakespeare's Birthplace HISTORIC BUILDING

(☎01789-204016; www.shakespeare.org.uk; Henley St; incl Nash's House & New Place & Halls Croft £15.90/9.50; ⌚9am-5.30pm Jul-Sep, to 5pm Oct-Jun) Start your Shakespeare quest at the house where the world's most popular playwright supposedly spent his childhood days. In fact, the jury is still out on whether this really was Shakespeare's birthplace, but devotees of the Bard have been dropping in since at least the 19th century, leaving their signatures scratched onto the windows. Set behind a modern facade, the house has restored Tudor rooms, live presentations from famous Shakespearean characters, and an engaging exhibition on Stratford's favourite son.

Anne Hathaway's Cottage HISTORIC BUILDING

(☎01789-204016; www.shakespeare.org.uk; Cottage Lane, Shottery; adult/child £9.50/5.50; ⌚9am-5pm mid-Mar–Oct) Before tying the knot with Shakespeare, Anne Hathaway lived in Shottery, a mile west of the centre of Stratford, in this delightful thatched farmhouse. As well as period furniture, it has gorgeous gardens and an orchard and arboretum, with examples of all the trees mentioned in Shakespeare's plays. A footpath (no bikes allowed) leads to Shottery from Evesham Pl.

Holy Trinity Church CHURCH

(☎01789-266316; www.stratford-upon-avon.org; Old Town; Shakespeare's grave adult/child £2/1; ⌚8.30am-6pm Mon-Sat, 12.30-5pm Sun Apr-Sep, reduced hours Oct-Mar) The final resting place of the Bard is said to be the most visited parish church in all of England. Inside are handsome 16th- and 17th-century tombs (particularly in the Clopton Chapel), some fabulous carvings on the choir stalls and, of course, the grave of William Shakespeare, with its ominous epitaph: 'cvrst be he yt moves my bones'.

Sleeping

Stratford-upon-Avon YHA HOSTEL £
(☎0845 371 9661; www.yha.org.uk; Hemmingford House, Alveston; dm/d from £19/40; P @ ☎) Set in a large 200-year-old mansion, 1.5 miles east of the town centre along Tiddington Rd, this superior hostel attracts travellers of all ages. Of its 32 rooms and dorms, 16 are en suite. There's a canteen, bar and kitchen. Buses 18 and 18A run here from Bridge St. Wi-fi is available in common areas.

Legacy Falcon HOTEL ££
(☎0844 411 9005; www.legacy-hotels.co.uk; Chapel St; d/f from £83/113; P ☎) Definitely request a room in the original 15th-century building, not the soulless modern annexe or dingy 17th-century garden house of this epicentral hotel. This way you'll get the full Tudor experience – creaky floorboards, wonky timbered walls and all. Open fires blaze in the wi-fi'd public areas; rooms have wired broadband but the best asset is the unheard-of-for-Stratford free car park.

White Sails GUESTHOUSE ££
(☎01789-550469; www.white-sails.co.uk; 85 Evesham Rd; d from £100; ❄) Plush fabrics, framed prints, brass bedsteads and shabby-chic tables and lamps set the scene at this gorgeous and intimate guesthouse on the edge of the countryside. The four individually furnished rooms come with flatscreen TVs, climate control and glamorous bathrooms.

Eating & Drinking

Sheep St is clustered with eating options, mostly aimed at theatregoers (look out for good-value pretheatre menus).

Fourteas TEAROOM £
(☎01789-293908; www.thefourteas.co.uk; 24 Sheep St; dishes £3-7, afternoon tea with/without Prosecco £17/12.50; ⏰9.30am-5pm Mon-Fri, 9am-5.30pm Sat, 11am-4pm Sun) Breaking with Stratford's Shakespearian theme, this tearoom takes the 1940s as its inspiration with beautiful old teapots, framed posters and staff in period costume. As well as premium loose-leaf teas and homemade cakes, there are hearty breakfasts, delicious sandwiches (fresh poached salmon, brie and grape), a hot dish of the day and indulgent afternoon teas.

Edward Moon's MODERN BRITISH ££
(☎01789-267069; www.edwardmoon.com; 9 Chapel St; mains £10-18; ⏰12.30-3pm & 5-10pm Mon-Fri, noon-10pm Sat & Sun) Named after a famous travelling chef who cooked up the flavours of home for the British colonial service, this snug eatery serves delicious, hearty English dishes, many livened up with herbs and spices from the East.

★**Old Thatch Tavern** PUB
(http://oldthatchtavernstratford.co.uk; Greenhill St; ⏰11.30am-11pm Mon-Sat, noon-6pm Sun; ☎) To truly appreciate Stratford's olde-worlde atmosphere, join the locals for a pint at the town's oldest pub. Built in 1470, this thatched-roofed, low-ceilinged treasure has great real ales and a gorgeous summertime courtyard.

Dirty Duck PUB
(Black Swan; Waterside; ⏰11am-11pm Mon-Sat, to 10.30pm Sun) Also called the 'Black Swan', this enchanting riverside alehouse is the only pub in England to be licensed under two names. It's a favourite thespian watering hole, with a roll-call of former regulars (Olivier, Attenborough et al) that reads like a who's who of actors.

Entertainment

★**Royal Shakespeare Company** THEATRE
(RSC; ☎0844 800 1110; www.rsc.org.uk; Waterside; tickets £10-62.50) Coming to Stratford without seeing a Shakespeare production would be like visiting Beijing and bypassing the Great Wall. The three theatre spaces run by the world-renowned Royal Shakespeare Company have witnessed performances by such legends as Lawrence Olivier, Richard Burton, Judi Dench, Helen Mirren, Ian McKellan and Patrick Stewart.

SHAKESPEARE HISTORIC HOMES

Five of the most important buildings associated with Shakespeare contain museums that form the core of the visitor experience at Stratford. All are run by the Shakespeare Birthplace Trust (www.shakespeare.org.uk).

Tickets for the three houses in town: **Shakespeare's Birthplace**, **Nash's House & New Place** and **Halls Croft** cost adult/child £15.90/9.50. If you also visit **Anne Hathaway's Cottage** and **Mary Arden's Farm**, buy a combination ticket covering all five properties (adult/child £23.90/14).

WORTH A TRIP

WARWICK

Regularly namechecked by Shakespeare, the town of Warwick is a treasure-house of medieval architecture. It is dominated by the soaring turrets of **Warwick Castle** (☎0871 265 2000; www.warwick-castle.com; castle adult/child £22.80/16.80, castle & dungeon £28.80/24, Kingdom Ticket incl castle, dungeon & exhibition £30.60/27; ⊙10am-6pm Apr-Sep, to 5pm Oct-Mar; P), founded in 1068 by William the Conqueror, and later the ancestral home of the Earls of Warwick. It's now been transformed into a major tourist attraction by the owners of Madame Tussauds, with kid-centred activities and waxworks populating the private apartments.

Stagecoach buses 16 and X18 go to Stratford-upon-Avon (£5.40, 40 minutes, half-hourly). Trains run to Birmingham (£7.50, 40 minutes, half-hourly), Stratford-upon-Avon (£5.40, 30 minutes, hourly) and London (£28.80, 1½ hours, every 20 minutes).

Stratford has two grand stages – **the Royal Shakespeare Theatre** and the **Swan Theatre** on Waterside – as well as the smaller **Courtyard Theatre** (☎0844 800 1110; www.rsc.org.uk; Southern Lane). Contact the RSC for the latest news on performance times. There are often special deals for under 25-year-olds, students and seniors, and a few tickets are held back for sale on the day of the performance, but get snapped up fast. Book well ahead.

Information

Tourist Office (☎01789-264293; www.shakespeare-country.co.uk; Bridge Foot; ⊙9am-5.30pm Mon-Sat, 10am-4pm Sun) Just west of Clopton Bridge on the corner with Bridgeway.

Getting There & Away

BUS

National Express coaches and other bus companies run from Stratford's Riverside bus station (behind the Stratford Leisure Centre on Bridgeway). Destinations include Birmingham (£8.40, one hour, twice daily), London Victoria (£17, three hours, three daily) and Oxford (£10.70, one hour, twice daily). Bus 16 runs to Warwick (£5.40, 40 minutes, half-hourly).

TRAIN

From Stratford train station, trains run to Birmingham (£7.30, 50 minutes, half-hourly) and London Marylebone (£9, two hours, up to two per hour).

Cambridge

POP 123,900

Abounding with exquisite architecture, oozing history and tradition, and renowned for its quirky rituals, Cambridge is a university town extraordinaire. The tightly packed core of ancient colleges, the picturesque 'Backs' (college gardens) leading on to the river and the leafy green meadows that surround the city give it a far more tranquil appeal than its historic rival Oxford.

Sights

Cambridge University comprises 31 colleges, though not all are open to the public. Opening hours are only a rough guide, so contact the colleges or the tourist office for more information.

★King's College Chapel CHAPEL
(☎01223-331212; www.kings.cam.ac.uk/chapel; King's Pde; adult/child £7.50/free; ⊙non-term 9.45am-4.30pm, term 9.45am-3.15pm Mon-Sat, 1.15-2.30pm Sun) In a city crammed with show-stopping buildings, this is the scene-stealer. Grandiose, 16th-century King's College Chapel is one of England's most extraordinary examples of Gothic architecture. Its inspirational, intricate 80m-long, fan-vaulted ceiling is the world's largest and soars upwards before exploding into a series of stone fireworks. This hugely atmospheric space is a fitting stage for the chapel's world-famous choir; hear it in full voice during the magnificent, free, evensong (in term time only – 5.30pm Monday to Saturday, 10.30am and 3.30pm Sunday).

★Trinity College COLLEGE
(www.trin.cam.ac.uk; Trinity St; adult/child £2/1; ⊙10am-4.30pm, closed early Apr–mid-Jun) The largest of Cambridge's colleges, Trinity offers an extraordinary Tudor gateway, an air of supreme elegance and a sweeping Great Court – the largest of its kind in the world. It also boasts the renowned and suitably musty **Wren Library** (⊙noon-2pm Mon-Fri), containing 55,000 books dated before 1820 and more than 2500 manuscripts. Works include those by Shakespeare, St Jerome,

Newton and Swift – and AA Milne's original *Winnie the Pooh;* both Milne and his son, Christopher Robin, were graduates.

The Backs PARK

Behind the Cambridge colleges' grandiose facades and stately courts, a series of gardens and parks line up beside the river. Collectively known as the Backs, the tranquil green spaces and shimmering waters offer unparalleled views of the colleges and are often the most enduring image of Cambridge for visitors. The picture-postcard snapshots of college life and graceful bridges can be seen from the riverside pathways and pedestrian bridges – or the comfort of a chauffeur-driven punt.

Fitzwilliam Museum MUSEUM

(www.fitzmuseum.cam.ac.uk; Trumpington St; donation requested; ⏲10am-5pm Tue-Sat, noon-5pm Sun) FREE Fondly dubbed 'the Fitz' by locals, this colossal neoclassical pile was one of the first public art museums in Britain, built to house the fabulous treasures that the seventh Viscount Fitzwilliam bequeathed to his old university. Expect Roman and Egyptian grave goods, artworks by many of the great masters and some more quirky collections: banknotes, literary autographs, watches and armour.

Sleeping

Cambridge YHA HOSTEL £

(☎0845 371 9728; www.yha.org.uk; 97 Tenison Rd; dm/d £21/30; @ 📶) Busy, recently renovated, popular hostel with compact dorms and good facilities near the railway station.

Cambridge Rooms B&B ££

(www.universityrooms.com/en/city/cambridge/home; s/d from £45/75) For an authentic taste of university life check into a student room in one of a range of colleges. Accommodation varies from functional singles (with shared bathroom) overlooking college courts to more modern, en suite rooms in nearby annexes. Breakfast is often in the hall (the students' dining room).

Worth House B&B ££

(☎01223-316074; www.worth-house.co.uk; 152 Chesterton Rd; s £65-75, d £65-100; P 📶) The welcome is wonderfully warm, the great-value rooms utterly delightful. Soft grey and cream meets candy-stripe reds, fancy bathrooms boast claw-footed baths and tea trays are full of treats. There's also a three-person, self-catering apartment (per week £550) two doors down.

Eating & Drinking

Fitzbillies BAKERY, CAFE £

(www.fitzbillies.com; 52 Trumpington St; cafe mains £6-16; ⏲8am-5pm Mon-Wed, 9am-9.30pm Thu-Sat, 10am-5pm Sun) Cambridge's oldest bakery has a soft, doughy place in the hearts of generations of students, thanks to its ultrasticky Chelsea buns and other sweet treats. Pick up a bag-full to take away or munch in comfort in the quaint cafe next door.

Oak BISTRO ££

(☎01223-323361; www.theoakbistro.co.uk; 6 Lensfield Rd; mains £12-20, set lunch 2/3 courses £13/16; ⏲noon-2.30pm & 6-9.30pm Mon-Sat) Truffles (white and black), olive pesto and rosemary jus are the kind of flavour intensifiers you'll find at this friendly but classy neighbourhood eatery where locally sourced duck, fish and beef come cooked just so. The set lunch is a bargain.

Chop House BRITISH ££

(www.cambscuisine.com/cambridge-chop-house; 1 Kings Pde; mains £14-20; ⏲noon-10.30pm Mon-Sat, to 9.30pm Sun) The window seats here deliver some of the best views in town – onto King's College's hallowed walls. The food is pure English establishment too: hearty steaks and chops and chips, plus a scattering of fish dishes and suet puds. Sister restaurant **St John's Chop House** (21-24 Northampton St) sits near the rear entrance to St John's College.

DON'T MISS

PUNTING ON THE BACKS

Propelling a punt along the Backs is a blissful experience – once you have the hang of it; it can also be a manic challenge to begin. If you wimp out you can always opt for a relaxing chauffeured punt.

Punt hire costs around £19 per hour, one-hour chauffeured trips of the Backs cost about £15 per person, and a return trip to Grantchester (2½ hours) will set you back around £27. Rental outfits include **Scudamore's** (www.scudamores.com; Granta Pl) and **Cambridge Chauffeur Punts** (www.punting-in-cambridge.co.uk; Silver St Bridge).

★Midsummer House MODERN BRITISH £££
(☎01223-369299; www.midsummerhouse.co.uk; Midsummer Common; 5/7/10 courses £45/75/95; ⊙noon-1.30pm Wed-Sat, 7-9pm Tue-Sat) At the region's top tables chef Daniel Clifford's double Michelin-starred creations are distinguished by depth of flavour and immense technical skill. Sample braised oxtail, coal-baked celeriac and scallops with truffle before dollops of dark chocolate, blood orange and marmalade ice cream. Wine flights start at £55.

Eagle PUB
(www.gkpubs.co.uk; Benet St; ⊙9am-11pm Mon-Sat, to 10.30pm Sun) Cambridge's most famous pub has loosened the tongues and pickled the grey cells of many an illustrious academic – among them Nobel Prize–winning scientists Crick and Watson, who discussed their research into DNA here (note the blue plaque by the door). Fifteenth-century, wood-panelled and rambling, its cosy rooms include one with WWII airmens' signatures on the ceiling. The food, served all day, is good, too.

Information

Tourist Office (☎0871 226 8006; www.visitcambridge.org; Peas Hill; ⊙10am-5pm Mon-Sat, plus 11am-3pm Sun Apr-Oct)

Getting There & Away

BUS

From Parkside there are regular **National Express** (www.nationalexpress.com) buses to London Gatwick airport (£20, 4½ hours, hourly), Heathrow airport (£17, four hours, hourly) and Oxford (£15, 3½ hours, every 30 minutes).

TRAIN

The train station is off Station Rd, which is off Hills Rd. Destinations include London Kings Cross (£18, one hour, two to four per hour) and Stansted airport (£15, 30 minutes to 1¼ hours, two per hour).

York

POP 181,100

Nowhere in northern England says 'medieval' quite like York, a city of extraordinary historical wealth that has lost little of its pre-industrial lustre. Its spider's web of narrow streets is enclosed by a magnificent circuit of 13th-century walls and the city's rich heritage is woven into virtually every brick and beam.

Sights

★York Minster CHURCH
(www.yorkminster.org; Deangate; adult/child £10/free, combined ticket incl tower £15/5; ⊙9am-5.30pm Mon-Sat, 12.45-5.30pm Sun, last admission 5pm) The remarkable York Minster is the largest medieval cathedral in all of Northern Europe, and one of the world's most beautiful Gothic buildings. Seat of the archbishop of York, primate of England, it is second in importance only to Canterbury, seat of the primate of *all* England – the separate titles were created to settle a debate over the true centre of the English church. If this is the only cathedral you visit in England, you'll still walk away satisfied.

★Jorvik Viking Centre MUSEUM
(www.jorvik-viking-centre.co.uk; Coppergate; adult/child £9.95/6.95; ⊙10am-5pm Apr-Oct, to 4pm Nov-Mar) Interactive multimedia exhibits aimed at bringing history to life often achieve exactly the opposite, but the much-hyped Jorvik manages to pull it off with aplomb. It's a smells-and-all reconstruction of the Viking settlement unearthed here during excavations in the late 1970s, brought to you courtesy of a 'time-car' monorail that transports you through 9th-century Jorvik. You can reduce time waiting in the queue by booking your tickets online and choosing the time you want to visit (£1 extra).

★City Walls ARCHAEOLOGICAL SITE
(⊙8am-dusk) FREE If the weather's good, don't miss the chance to walk the City Walls, which follow the line of the original Roman walls and give a whole new perspective on the city. Allow 1½ to two hours for the full circuit of 4.5 miles or, if you're pushed for time, the short stretch from **Bootham Bar** to **Monk Bar** is worth doing for the views of the minster.

★National Railway Museum MUSEUM
(www.nrm.org.uk; Leeman Rd; ⊙10am-6pm; P ♿) FREE While many railway museums are the sole preserve of lone men in anoraks comparing dog-eared notebooks and getting high on the smell of machine oil, coal smoke and nostalgia, this place is different. York's National Railway Museum – the biggest in the world, with more than 100 locomotives – is so well presented and crammed with fascinating stuff that it's interesting even to folk whose eyes don't mist over at

the thought of a 4-6-2 A1 Pacific class thundering into a tunnel.

Yorkshire Museum MUSEUM
(www.yorkshiremuseum.org.uk; Museum St; adult/child £7.50/free; ⊙10am-5pm) Most of York's Roman archaeology is hidden beneath the medieval city, so the recently revamped displays in the Yorkshire Museum are invaluable if you want to get an idea of what Eboracum was like. There are maps and models of Roman York, funerary monuments, mosaic floors and wall paintings, and a 4th-century bust of Emperor Constantine.

Shambles STREET
The Shambles takes its name from the Saxon word *shamel,* meaning 'slaughterhouse' – in 1862 there were 26 butcher shops on this street. Today the butchers are long gone, but this narrow cobbled lane, lined with 15th-century Tudor buildings that overhang so much they seem to meet above your head, is the most picturesque in Britain, and one of the most visited in Europe, often crammed with visitors intent on buying a tacky souvenir before rushing back to the tour bus.

Tours

Ghost Hunt of York WALKING
(www.ghosthunt.co.uk; adult/child £5/3; ⊙tours 7.30pm) The kids will just love this award-winning and highly entertaining 75-minute tour laced with authentic ghost stories. It begins at the Shambles, whatever the weather (it's never cancelled) and there's no need to book: just turn up and wait till you hear the handbell ringing…

Yorkwalk WALKING
(www.yorkwalk.co.uk; adult/child £6/5; ⊙tours 10.30am & 2.15pm Feb-Nov) Offers a series of two-hour walks on a range of themes, from the classics – Roman York, the snickelways (narrow alleys) and City Walls – to walks focused on chocolates and sweets, women in York, and the inevitable graveyard, coffin and plague tour. Walks depart from Museum Gardens Gate on Museum St; there's no need to book.

Sleeping

Despite the inflated prices of the high season, it is still tough to find a bed during midsummer.

★Fort HOSTEL £
(☎01904-620222; www.thefortyork.co.uk; 1 Little Stonegate; dm from £22, d from £68;) This new boutique hostel showcases the work of young British designers, creating affordable accommodation with a dash of character and flair. There are six- and eight-bed dorms, along with half a dozen doubles, but don't expect a peaceful retreat – the central location is in the middle of York's nightlife, and there's a lively club downstairs (earplugs are provided!).

York YHA HOSTEL £
(☎0845 371 9051; www.yha.org.uk; 42 Water End, Clifton; dm/q from £21/99; P@) Originally the Rowntree (Quaker confectioners) mansion, this handsome Victorian house makes a spacious and child-friendly youth hostel, with most of its rooms four-bed dorms. Often busy, so book early. It's about a mile northwest of the city centre; there's a riverside footpath from Lendal Bridge (poorly lit, so avoid after dark). Alternatively, take bus 2 from the train station or Museum St.

Abbeyfields B&B ££
(☎01904-636471; www.abbeyfields.co.uk; 19 Bootham Tce; s/d from £55/84;)  Expect a warm welcome and thoughtfully arranged bedrooms here, with chairs and bedside lamps for comfortable reading. Breakfasts are among the best in town, with sausage and bacon from the local butcher, freshly laid eggs from a nearby farm and the aroma of newly baked bread.

Elliotts B&B B&B ££
(☎01904-623333; www.elliottshotel.co.uk; 2 Sycamore Pl; s/d from £55/75; P@) A beautifully converted 'gentleman's residence', Elliotts leans towards the boutique end of the guesthouse market, with stylish and elegant rooms and some designer touches such as contemporary art and colourful textiles. An excellent location, both quiet and central.

YORK PASS

If you plan on visiting a lot of sights, you can save yourself some money by using a **York Pass** (www.yorkpass.com; 1/2/3 days adult £36/48/58, child £20/24/28). It grants you free access to more than 70 pay-to-visit sights in Yorkshire, including all the major attractions in York. Available at York Tourist Office, or you can buy online.

★ **Middlethorpe Hall** HOTEL £££
(☎01904-641241; www.middlethorpe.com; Bishopthorpe Rd; s/d from £139/199; P 📶) This breathtaking 17th-century country house is set in eight hectares of parkland, once the home of diarist Lady Mary Wortley Montagu. The rooms are divided between the main house, restored courtyard buildings and three cottage suites. All the rooms are beautifully decorated with original antiques and oil paintings that have been carefully selected to reflect the period.

Eating & Drinking

★ **Mannion's** CAFE, BISTRO £
(☎01904-631030; www.mannionandco.co.uk; 1 Blake St; mains £5-9; ⏲9am-5.30pm Mon-Sat, 10am-5pm Sun) Expect to queue for a table at this busy bistro (no reservations), with its maze of cosy, wood-panelled rooms and selection of daily specials. Regulars on the menu include eggs Benedict for breakfast, a chunky Yorkshire rarebit made with home-baked bread, and lunch platters of cheese and charcuterie from the attached deli. Oh, and pavlova for dessert.

Cafe No 8 CAFE, BISTRO ££
(☎01904-653074; www.cafeno8.co.uk; 8 Gillygate; 2-/3-course meal £18/22, Fri & Sat £22/27; ⏲10am-10pm; 📶 👪) A cool little place with modern artwork mimicking the Edwardian stained glass at the front, No 8 offers a day-long menu of classic bistro dishes using fresh local produce, including duck breast with blood orange and juniper, and Yorkshire pork belly with star anise, fennel and garlic. It also does breakfast daily (mains £5) and Sunday lunch (three courses £25). Booking recommended.

Parlour at Grays Court CAFE ££
(www.grayscourtyork.com; Chapter House St; mains £8-14; ⏲10am-5pm; 📶) An unexpected find in the heart of York, this 16th-century house (now a hotel) has more of a country atmosphere. Enjoy gourmet coffee and cake in the sunny garden, or indulge in a light lunch in the historic setting of the oak-panelled Jacobean gallery. The menu runs from Yorkshire rarebit to confit duck, and includes traditional afternoon tea (£18.50).

Bettys TEAROOM ££
(www.bettys.co.uk; St Helen's Sq; mains £6-14, afternoon tea £18.50; ⏲9am-9pm; 👪) Old-school afternoon tea, with white-aproned waiters, linen tablecloths and a teapot collection arranged along the walls. The house speciality is the Yorkshire Fat Rascal, a huge fruit scone smothered in melted butter, but the smoked haddock with poached egg and hollandaise sauce (seasonal) is our favourite lunch dish. No bookings – queue for a table at busy times.

★ **Blue Bell** PUB
(53 Fossgate; ⏲11am-11pm Mon-Sat, noon-10.30pm Sun) This is what a real English pub looks like – a tiny, 200-year-old wood-panelled room with a smouldering fireplace, decor untouched since 1903, a pile of ancient board games in the corner, friendly and efficient bar staff, and Timothy Taylor and Black Sheep ales on tap. Bliss, with froth on top – if you can get in (it's often full).

Information

York Tourist Office (☎01904-550099; www.visityork.org; 1 Museum St; ⏲9am-6pm Mon-Sat, 10am-5pm Sun Apr-Sep, shorter hours Oct-Mar) Visitor and transport info for all of Yorkshire, plus accommodation bookings, ticket sales and internet access.

Getting There & Away

BUS

For timetable information call **Traveline Yorkshire** (☎0871 200 2233; www.yorkshiretravel.net). All local and regional buses stop on Rougier St, about 200m northeast of the train station.

There are **National Express** (☎0871 781 8181; www.nationalexpress.com) coaches to London (£31, 5½ hours, three daily), Birmingham (£29, 3½ hours, one daily) and Newcastle (£15.20, 2¾ hours, two daily).

TRAIN

York is a major railway hub with frequent direct services to Birmingham (£45, 2¼ hours), Newcastle (£16, one hour), Leeds (£13.50, 25 minutes), London's King's Cross (£80, two hours), Manchester (£17, 1½ hours) and Scarborough (£8, 50 minutes). There are also trains to Cambridge (£65, three hours), changing at Peterborough.

Castle Howard

Stately homes may be two a penny in England, but you'll have to try hard to find one as breathtakingly stately as **Castle Howard** (www.castlehoward.co.uk; adult/child house & grounds £14/7.50, grounds only £9.50/6; ⏲house 11am-4.30pm Apr-Oct, grounds 10am-5pm Mar-Oct

& Dec, to 4pm Nov, Jan & Feb; P), a work of theatrical grandeur and audacity, and one of the world's most beautiful buildings. It's instantly recognisable from its starring role in the 1980s TV series *Brideshead Revisited* and in the 2008 film of the same name.

It's 15 miles northeast of York; **Stephenson's of Easingwold** (www.stephensonsofeasingwold.co.uk) operates a bus service (£7.50 return, 40 minutes, three times daily Monday to Saturday) from York.

Chester

Marvellous Chester is one of English history's greatest legacies. Its red-sandstone wall, which today gift-wraps a tidy collection of Tudor and Victorian buildings, was built during Roman times. The town was then called Castra Devana, and was the largest Roman fortress in Britain.

Sights

★City Walls LANDMARK
A good way to get a sense of Chester's unique character is to walk the 2-mile circuit along the walls that surround the historic centre. Originally built by the Romans around AD 70, the walls were altered substantially over the following centuries but have retained their current position since around 1200. The tourist office's *Walk Around Chester Walls* leaflet is an excellent guide.

★Rows ARCHITECTURE
Besides the City Walls, Chester's other great draw is the Rows, a series of two-level galleried arcades along the four streets that fan out in each direction from the **Central Cross**. The architecture is a handsome mix of Victorian and Tudor (original and mock) buildings that house a fantastic collection of individually owned shops.

Chester Cathedral CATHEDRAL
(☎01244-324756; www.chestercathedral.com; 12 Abbey Sq; admission £3; ⏰9am-5pm Mon-Sat, 1-4pm Sun) Originally a Benedictine abbey built on the remains of an earlier Saxon church dedicated to St Werburgh (the city's patron saint), Chester Cathedral was shut down in 1540 as part of Henry VIII's dissolution frenzy, but reconsecrated as a cathedral the following year. Although the cathedral itself was given a substantial Victorian facelift, the 12th-century cloister and its surrounding buildings are essentially unaltered and retain much of the structure from the early monastic years.

Sleeping

Chester Backpackers HOSTEL £
(☎01244-400185; www.chesterbackpackers.co.uk; 67 Boughton; dm/s/d from £16/22/34; 📶) Comfortable dorm rooms with nice pine beds in a typically Tudor white-and-black building. It's just a short walk from the city walls and there's also a pleasant garden.

★Stone Villa B&B ££
(☎01244-345014; www.stonevillachester.co.uk; 3 Stone Pl, Hoole Rd; s/d from £45/75; P📶; 🚌9) Twice winner of Chester's B&B of the Year in the last 10 years, this beautiful villa has everything you need for a memorable stay. Elegant bedrooms, a fabulous breakfast and welcoming, friendly owners all add up to one of the best lodgings in town. The property is about a mile from the city centre.

Eating

Joseph Benjamin MODERN BRITISH ££
(☎01244-344295; www.josephbenjamin.co.uk; 134-140 Northgate St; mains £13-17; ⏰9am-5pm Tue & Wed, 9am-midnight Thu-Sat, 10am-5pm Sun) A bright star in Chester's culinary firmament is this combo restaurant, bar and deli that delivers carefully prepared local produce to take out or eat in. Excellent sandwiches and gorgeous salads are the mainstay of the takeout menu, while the more formal dinner menu features fine examples of modern British cuisine.

Bar Lounge MODERN BRITISH ££
(www.barlounge.co.uk; 75 Watergate St; mains £11-18) One of the most popular spots in town is this bistro-style bar that serves up good burgers, pies and a particularly tasty beer-battered haddock and chips. There's a heated outdoor terrace for alfresco drinks.

Getting There & Away

BUS

National Express (☎08717 81 81 81; www.nationalexpress.com) coaches stop on Vicar's Lane, just opposite the tourist office. Destinations include Liverpool (£8.20, one hour, four daily), London (£23, 5½ hours, three daily) and Manchester (£7.70, 1¼ hours, three daily).

TRAIN

The train station is about a mile from the city centre. City Rail Link buses are free for people with rail tickets. Destinations include Liverpool

(£6.65, 45 minutes, hourly), London Euston (£65, 2½ hours, hourly) and Manchester (£12.60, one hour, hourly).

Lake District National Park

A dramatic landscape of ridges, lakes and peaks, including England's highest mountain, Scafell Pike (978m), the Lake District is one of Britain's most scenic corners. The awe-inspiring geography here shaped the literary personae of some of Britain's best-known poets, including William Wordsworth.

Often called simply the Lakes, the national park and surrounding area attract around 15 million visitors annually. But if you avoid summer weekends it's easy enough to miss the crush, especially if you do a bit of hiking.

There's a host of B&Bs and country-house hotels in the Lakes, plus more than 20 YHA hostels, many of which can be linked by foot if you wish to hike.

Information

Brockhole National Park Visitor Centre (015394-46601; www.lake-district.gov.uk; 10am-5pm Easter-Oct, to 4pm Nov-Easter) In a 19th-century mansion 3 miles north of Windermere on the A591, this is the Lake District's flagship tourist office, and also has a teashop, an adventure playground and gardens.

Getting There & Around

BUS

There's one daily National Express coach from London Victoria (£37, eight hours) via Lancaster and Kendal.

The main local bus operator is **Stagecoach** (www.stagecoachbus.com); you can download timetables from the website.

Bus 555 Lancaster to Keswick; stops at all the main towns including Windermere and Ambleside.

Bus 505 (Coniston Rambler) Kendal, Windermere, Ambleside and Coniston.

TRAIN

To get to the Lake District by train, you need to change at Oxenholme (on the London Euston to Glasgow line) for Kendal and Windermere, which has connections from London Euston (£99, 3½ hours), Manchester Piccadilly (£23, 1½ hours) and Glasgow (£52, 2¾ hours).

Windermere

POP 8432

Windermere – the lake and the town of the same name – has been a centre for Lakeland tourism since the first steam trains arrived in 1847. The station is still there, making this an excellent gateway.

Windermere Lake Cruises (015395-31188; www.windermere-lakecruises.co.uk; tickets from £2.70) offers scheduled boat trips across the lake from the lakeside settlement of Bowness-on-Windermere.

Sleeping

Archway B&B £

(015394-45613; www.the-archway.com; 13 College Rd, Windermere Town; d £50-86) Value is the name of the game here: this place is a no-nonsense, old-fashioned, home-away-from-home. Some of the rooms have fell views, and the breakfast is enormous, but there's no parking.

Lake District Backpackers Lodge HOSTEL £

(015394-46374; www.lakedistrictbackpackers.co.uk; High St, Windermere Town; dm/r £16/36; @) Not the fanciest hostel in the Lake District, but these Windermere digs are about the only option in town for backpackers. There are two small four-bed dorms, plus two private rooms with a double bed and a single bed above.

Boundary B&B ££

(015394-48978; www.theboundaryonline.co.uk; Lake Rd, Windermere Town; d £100-191; P) Not the cheapest sleep in Windermere, but definitely one of the swishest. Owners Steve and Helen have given this Victorian house a sleek, boutique makeover: chic decor, monochrome colours, retro furniture and all. Steve's a cricket obsessive, so all the rooms are named after famous batsmen.

Grasmere

Grasmere is a gorgeous little Lakeland village, all the more famous because of its links with Britain's leading Romantic poet, William Wordsworth.

Literary pilgrims come to **Dove Cottage** (015394-35544; www.wordsworth.org.uk; adult/child £7.50/4.50; 9.30am-5.30pm), his former home, where highlights include some fine portraits of the man himself, a cabinet containing his spectacles, and a set of scales used by his pal de Quincey to weigh out opium. At **St Oswald's Church** (Church Stile) you'll see a memorial to the poet, and in the churchyard you'll find his grave.

To cure any sombre thoughts, head for **Sarah Nelson's Gingerbread Shop** (www.grasmeregingerbread.co.uk; Church Cottage; 9.15am-5.30pm Mon-Sat, 12.30-5pm Sun) and stock up on Grasmere's famous confectionery.

Keswick

POP 5257

The main town of the north Lakes, Keswick sits beside lovely Derwent Water, a silvery curve studded by wooded islands and criss-crossed by puttering cruise boats, operated by the **Keswick Launch** (017687-72263; www.keswick-launch.co.uk; round-the-lake adult/child £9.25/4.50).

Sleeping

Keswick YHA HOSTEL £

(0845 371 9746; keswick@yha.org.uk; Station Rd; dm £13-21; @) Keswick's YHA is a beauty, lodged inside a converted woollen mill by the clattering River Rothay, and renovated thanks to the benevolence of a generous doctor. Dorms are cosy, there's an excellent cafe, and some rooms even have balconies over Fitz Park.

★**Howe Keld** B&B ££

(017687-72417; www.howekeld.co.uk; 5-7 The Heads; s £58, d £110-130; P) This gold-standard B&B pulls out all the stops: goose-down duvets, slate-floored bathrooms, chic colours and locally made furniture. The best rooms have views across Crow Park and the golf course, and the breakfast is a pick-and-mix delight. Free parking is available on the Heads if there's space.

Linnett Hill B&B ££

(017687-44518; www.linnetthillkeswick.co.uk; 4 Penrith Rd; s/d £45/80;) Much recommended by travellers, this lovingly run B&B has lots going for it: crisp white rooms, a great location near Fitz Park and keen prices that stay the same year-round. Breakfast is good too: there's a blackboard of specials to choose from, and the dining room has gingham-check tablecloths and a crackling woodburner.

DON'T MISS

HILL TOP

The cute-as-a-button farmhouse of **Hill Top** (NT; 015394-36269; www.nationaltrust.org.uk/hill-top; adult/child £9/4.50; 10.30am-4.30pm Sat-Thu mid-Feb–Oct, longer hours Jul & Aug) is a must for Beatrix Potter fans: it was her first house in the Lake District, and is also where she wrote and illustrated several of her famous tales.

The cottage is in Near Sawrey, 2 miles from Hawkshead and Ferry House. The **Cross Lakes Experience** (www.lakedistrict.gov.uk/visiting/planyourvisit/travelandtransport/crosslakes; Apr-Nov) stops en route from Ferry House to Hawkshead.

WALES

Lying to the west of England, Wales is a nation with Celtic roots, its own language and a rich historic legacy. While some areas in the south are undeniably scarred by coal mining and heavy industry, Wales boasts a landscape of wild mountains, rolling hills, rich farmland and the bustling capital city of Cardiff.

Cardiff

POP 324,800

The capital of Wales since only 1955, Cardiff has embraced its new role with vigour, emerging as one of Britain's leading urban centres in the 21st century.

Sights

Central Cardiff

★**Cardiff Castle** CASTLE

(www.cardiffcastle.com; Castle St; adult/child £12/9, incl guided tour £15/11; 9am-5pm) Cardiff Castle is, quite rightly, the city's leading attraction. There's a medieval keep at its heart, but it's the later additions that capture the imagination of many visitors: during the Victorian era extravagant mock-Gothic features were grafted onto this relic, including a clock tower and a lavish banqueting hall.

OTHER BRITISH PLACES WORTH A VISIT

Some places in Britain we recommend for day trips or longer visits:

Cornwall The southwestern tip of Britain is ringed with rugged granite seacliffs, sparkling bays, picturesque fishing villages and white sandy beaches.

Liverpool The city's waterfront is a World Heritage Site crammed with top museums including the International Slavery Museum and the Beatles Story.

Hadrian's Wall One of the country's most dramatic Roman ruins, a 2000-year-old procession of abandoned forts and towers marching across the lonely landscape of northern England.

Glen Coe Scotland's most famous glen combines those two essential qualities of Highlands landscape: dramatic scenery and deep history.

Pembrokeshire Wales' western extremity is famous for its beaches and coastal walks, as well as being home to one of Britain's finest Norman castles.

★Wales Millennium Centre ARTS CENTRE
(☎029-2063 6464; www.wmc.org.uk; Bute Pl; tours £6; ⊙tours 11am & 2.30pm) FREE The centrepiece and symbol of Cardiff Bay's regeneration is the superb Wales Millennium Centre, an architectural masterpiece of stacked Welsh slate in shades of purple, green and grey topped with an overarching bronzed steel shell. Designed by Welsh architect Jonathan Adams, it opened in 2004 as Wales' premier arts complex, housing major cultural organisations such as the Welsh National Opera, National Dance Company, National Orchestra, Literature Wales, HiJinx Theatre and Ty Cerdd (Music Centre of Wales).

Doctor Who Experience EXHIBITION
(☎0844 801 2279; www.doctorwhoexperience.com; Porth Teigr; adult/child £15/11; ⊙10am-5pm Wed-Mon, daily school holidays, last admission 3.30pm) The huge success of the reinvented classic TV series *Doctor Who*, produced by BBC Wales, has brought Cardiff to the attention of sci-fi fans worldwide. City locations have featured in many episodes, and the first two series of the spin-off *Torchwood* were also set in Cardiff Bay. Capitalising on Timelord tourism, this interactive exhibition is located right next to the BBC studios where the series is filmed – look out for the Tardis hovering outside.

Sleeping

★River House Backpackers HOSTEL £
(☎029-2039 9810; www.riverhousebackpackers.com; 59 Fitzhamon Embankment; dm/r incl breakfast from £18/42; @ 📶) Professionally run by a young brother-and-sister team and a pair of fluffy cats, the River House has a well-equipped kitchen, small garden and cosy TV lounge. The private rooms are basically small dorm rooms and share the same bathrooms. A free breakfast of cereal and toast is provided.

St David's Hotel & Spa HOTEL ££
(☎029-2045 4045; www.thestdavidshotel.com; Havannah St; r from £119; @ 📶 🏊) A glittering, glassy tower topped with a sail-like flourish, St David's epitomises Cardiff Bay's transformation from wasteland to desirable address. Almost every room has a small private balcony with a bay view. The exterior is already showing signs of wear and tear, but the rooms have been recently renovated.

Park Plaza HOTEL ££
(☎029-2011 1111; www.parkplazacardiff.com; Greyfriars Rd; r from £86; 📶 🏊) Luxurious without being remotely stuffy, the Plaza has all the five-star facilities you'd expect from an upmarket business-orientated hotel. The snug reception sets the scene, with a gas fire blazing along one wall and comfy wingback chairs. The rear rooms have leafy views over the Civic Centre.

Eating

★Coffee Barker CAFE £
(Castle Arcade; mains £4-7; ⊙8.30am-5.30pm Mon-Sat, 10.30am-4.30pm Sun; 📶 👪) Slink into an armchair, sip on a silky coffee and snack on salmon scrambled eggs or a sandwich in what is Cardiff's coolest cafe. There are plenty of magazines and toys to keep everyone amused.

Goat Major PUB £
(www.sabrain.com/goatmajor; 33 High St; pies £7.50; kitchen noon-6pm Mon-Sat, to 4pm Sun;) A solidly traditional wood-lined pub with armchairs, a fireplace and Brains Dark real ale on tap, the Goat Major's gastronomic contribution comes in the form of its selection of homemade savoury pot pies served with chips. Try the Wye Valley pie, a mixture of buttered chicken, leek, asparagus and Tintern Abbey cheese.

Conway GASTROPUB ££
(029-2022 4373; www.knifeandforkfood.co.uk; 58 Conway Rd; mains £10-15; noon-11pm;) With a sun-trap front terrace and a pleasantly laid-back vibe, this wonderful corner pub chalks up its delicious 'seasonal, fresh and local' offerings daily. Kids get their own menu, while the grownups can ponder the large selection of wines served by the glass.

Information

Cardiff Tourist Office (029-2087 3573; www.visitcardiff.com; Old Library, The Hayes; 9.30am-5.30pm Mon-Sat, 10am-4pm Sun) Cardiff's main tourist office stocks Ordnance Survey maps and Welsh books, and offers an accommodation booking service and internet access.

Getting There & Away

BUS

National Express travels to London (£19, 3½ hours), Birmingham (£27, 2¾ hours) and Bristol (£6, 1¼ hours).

TRAIN

Arriva Trains Wales (www.arrivatrainswales.co.uk) operates all train services in Wales. Direct services from Cardiff include London Paddington (£39, 2¼ hours) and Bristol (£13, 35 minutes).

WORTH A TRIP

CONWY CASTLE

On the north coast of Wales, the historic town of Conwy is utterly dominated by the Unesco-designated cultural treasure of **Conwy Castle** (Cadw; 01492-592358; www.cadw.wales.gov.uk; Castle Sq; adult/child £5.75/4.35; 9.30am-5pm; P), the most stunning of all Edward I's Welsh fortresses. Built between 1277 and 1307 on a rocky outcrop, it has commanding views across the estuary and Snowdonia National Park.

Snowdonia National Park

Snowdonia National Park (Parc Cenedlaethol Eryri; www.eryri-npa.gov.uk) was founded in 1951 (making it Wales' first national park). Around 350,000 people travel to the national park to climb, walk or take the train to the summit of Mt Snowdon, Wales' highest mountain.

Snowdon

No Snowdonia experience is complete without coming face-to-face with Snowdon (1085m). On a clear day the views stretch to Ireland and the Isle of Man. Even on a gloomy day you could find yourself above the clouds. At the top is the striking **Hafod Eryri** (10am to 20min before last train departure;) visitor centre, opened in 2009 by Prince Charles.

Six paths of varying length and difficulty lead to the summit, all taking around six hours return, or you can cheat and catch the **Snowdon Mountain Railway** (0844 493 8120; www.snowdonrailway.co.uk; return diesel adult/child £27/18, steam £35/25; 9am-5pm mid-Mar–Oct), opened in 1896 and still the UK's only public rack-and-pinion railway.

However you get to the summit, take warm, waterproof clothing, wear sturdy footwear and check the weather forecast before setting out.

Sleeping & Eating

Snowdon Ranger YHA HOSTEL £
(0800 019 1700; www.yha.org.uk; dm/tr/q £19/57/73; P @) On the A4085, 5 miles north of Beddgelert at the trailhead for the Snowdon Ranger Path, this former inn has its own adjoining lakeside beach. Accommodation is basic.

Bryn Gwynant YHA HOSTEL £
(0800 019 5465; www.yha.org.uk; Nantgwynant; dm/tw/f £19/50/73; Mar-Oct; P) Of all of the park's youth hostels, Bryn Gwynant has the most impressive building and the most idyllic setting, occupying a grand Victorian mansion looking over a lake to Snowdon – although it's certainly not flash inside. It's located 4 miles east of Beddgelert, near the start of the Watkin Path.

Getting There & Away

The **Welsh Highland Railway** (01766-516000; www.festrail.co.uk; adult/child return £35/31.50) and **Snowdon Sherpa** (0870 608 2608) buses link various places in Snowdonia with the town of Bangor, which can be reached by train from London Euston (£86, 3¼ hours, hourly).

SCOTLAND

Despite its small size, Scotland has many treasures crammed into its compact territory – big skies, lonely landscapes, spectacular wildlife, superb seafood and hospitable, down-to-earth people. From the cultural attractions of Edinburgh to the heather-clad hills of the Highlands, there's something for everyone.

Edinburgh

POP 440,000

Edinburgh is a city that just begs to be explored. From the imposing castle to the Palace of Holyroodhouse to the Royal Yacht Britannia, every corner turned reveals sudden views and unexpected vistas – green sunlit hills, a glimpse of rust-red crags, a blue flash of distant sea. But there's more to Edinburgh than sightseeing – there are top shops, world-class restaurants and bacchanalian bars to enjoy.

Sights

★Edinburgh Castle CASTLE

(www.edinburghcastle.gov.uk; adult/child incl audioguide £16/9.60; 9.30am-6pm Apr-Sep, to 5pm Oct-Mar, last admission 45min before closing; 23, 27, 41, 42) Edinburgh Castle has played a pivotal role in Scottish history, both as a royal residence – King Malcolm Canmore (r 1058–93) and Queen Margaret first made their home here in the 11th century – and as a military stronghold. The castle last saw military action in 1745; from then until the 1920s it served as the British army's main base in Scotland. Today it is one of Scotland's most atmospheric and most popular tourist attractions.

★Real Mary King's Close HISTORIC BUILDING

(0845 070 6244; www.realmarykingsclose.com; 2 Warriston's Close, High St; adult/child £12.95/7.45; 10am-9pm daily Apr-Oct, to 11pm Aug, 10am-5pm Sun-Thu, 10am-9pm Fri & Sat Nov-Mar; 23, 27, 41, 42) Edinburgh's 18th-century City Chambers were built over the sealed-off remains of Mary King's Close, and the lower levels of this medieval Old Town alley have survived almost unchanged amid the foundations for 250 years. Now open to the public, this spooky, subterranean labyrinth gives a fascinating insight into the everyday life of 17th-century Edinburgh. Costumed characters lead tours through a 16th-century town house and the plague-stricken home of a 17th-century gravedigger. Advance booking recommended.

★National Museum of Scotland MUSEUM

(www.nms.ac.uk; Chambers St; fee for special exhibitions; 10am-5pm; 2, 23, 27, 35, 41, 42, 45) FREE Broad, elegant Chambers St is dominated by the long facade of the National Museum of Scotland. Its extensive collections are spread between two buildings, one modern, one Victorian – the golden stone and striking modern architecture of the new building, opened in 1998, is one of the city's most distinctive landmarks. The five floors of the museum trace the history of Scotland from geological beginnings to the 1990s, with many imaginative and stimulating exhibits – audioguides are available in several languages.

★Royal Yacht Britannia SHIP

(www.royalyachtbritannia.co.uk; Ocean Terminal; adult/child £12.75/7.75; 9.30am-6pm Jul-Sep, to 5.30pm Apr-Jun & Oct, 10am-5pm Nov-Mar, last admission 90min before closing; ; 11, 22, 34, 35, 36) Built on Clydeside, the former Royal Yacht Britannia was the British royal family's floating holiday home during their foreign travels from the time of her launch in 1953 until her decommissioning in 1997, and is now moored permanently in front of Ocean Terminal. The tour, which you take at your own pace with an audioguide (included in admission fee and available in 20 languages), lifts the curtain on the everyday lives of the royals, and gives an intriguing insight into the Queen's private tastes.

Scottish Parliament Building NOTABLE BUILDING

(0131-348 5200; www.scottish.parliament.uk; Horse Wynd; 9am-6.30pm Tue-Thu, 10am-5.30pm

Mon, Fri & Sat in session, 10am-6pm Mon-Sat in recess; ; 35, 36) FREE The Scottish parliament building, built on the site of a former brewery, was officially opened by HM the Queen in October 2005. Designed by Catalan architect Enric Miralles (1955–2000), the ground plan of the parliament complex represents a 'flower of democracy rooted in Scottish soil' (best seen looking down from Salisbury Crags). Free, one-hour guided tours (advance booking recommended) include a visit to the Debating Chamber, a committee room, the Garden Lobby and an MSP's (Member of the Scottish Parliament) office.

Palace of Holyroodhouse PALACE

(www.royalcollection.org.uk; Horse Wynd; adult/child £11.30/6.80; 9.30am-6pm Apr-Oct, to 4.30pm Nov-Mar; ; 35, 36) This palace is the royal family's official residence in Scotland, but is more famous as the 16th-century home of the ill-fated Mary, Queen of Scots. The highlight of the tour is **Mary's Bed Chamber**, home to the unfortunate queen from 1561 to 1567. It was here that her jealous first husband, Lord Darnley, restrained the pregnant queen while his henchmen murdered her secretary – and favourite – Rizzio. A plaque in the neighbouring room marks the spot where he bled to death.

Sleeping

★Malone's Old Town Hostel HOSTEL £

(0131-226 7648; www.maloneshostel.com; 14 Forrest Rd; dm £16-25; @) No fancy decor or style credentials here, but it has got the basics right: it's clean, comfortable and friendly, and set upstairs from an Irish pub where guests get discounts on food and drink. The cherry on the cake is its superbly central location, an easy walk from the Royal Mile, the castle, the Grassmarket and Princes St.

Smart City Hostel HOSTEL £

(0131-524 1989; www.smartcityhostels.com; 50 Blackfriars St; dm £24-28, tr £99; @) A big, modern hostel, with a convivial cafe where you can buy breakfast, and mod cons such as keycard access and charging stations for mobile phones, MP3 players and laptops. Lockers in every room, a huge bar and a central location just off the Royal Mile make this a favourite among the young, party-mad crowd – don't expect a quiet night!

★Southside Guest House B&B ££

(0131-668 4422; www.southsideguesthouse.co.uk; 8 Newington Rd; s/d £75/95;) Though set in a typical Victorian terrace, the Southside transcends the traditional guesthouse category and feels more like a modern boutique hotel. Its eight stylish rooms ooze interior design, standing out from other Newington B&Bs through the clever use of bold colours and modern furniture. Breakfast is an event, with Bucks fizz (champagne mixed with orange juice) on offer to smooth the rough edges off your hangover!

B+B Edinburgh HOTEL ££

(0131-225 5084; www.bb-edinburgh.com; 3 Rothesay Tce; d/ste from £110/170;) Built in 1883 as a grand home for the proprietor of the *Scotsman* newspaper, this Victorian extravaganza of carved oak, parquet floors, stained glass and elaborate fireplaces was given a designer makeover in 2011 to create a striking contemporary hotel. Rooms on the 2nd floor are the most spacious, but the smaller top-floor rooms enjoy the finest views.

No 45 B&B ££

(0131-667 3536; www.edinburghbedbreakfast.com; 45 Gilmour Rd; s/d £70/140;) A peaceful setting, large garden and friendly owners contribute to the appeal of this Victorian terraced house, which overlooks the local bowling green. The decor is a blend of 19th and 20th century, with bold Victorian reds, pine floors and period fireplace in the lounge, a rocking horse and art nouveau lamp in the hallway, and a 1930s vibe in the three spacious bedrooms.

FESTIVAL CITY

Edinburgh boasts a frenzy of festivals throughout the year, including the world-famous **Edinburgh Festival Fringe** (0131-226 0026; www.edfringe.com), held over 3½ weeks in August. The last two weeks overlap with the first two weeks of the **Edinburgh International Festival** (0131-473 2099; www.eif.co.uk). See www.edinburghfestivals.co.uk for more.

Central Edinburgh

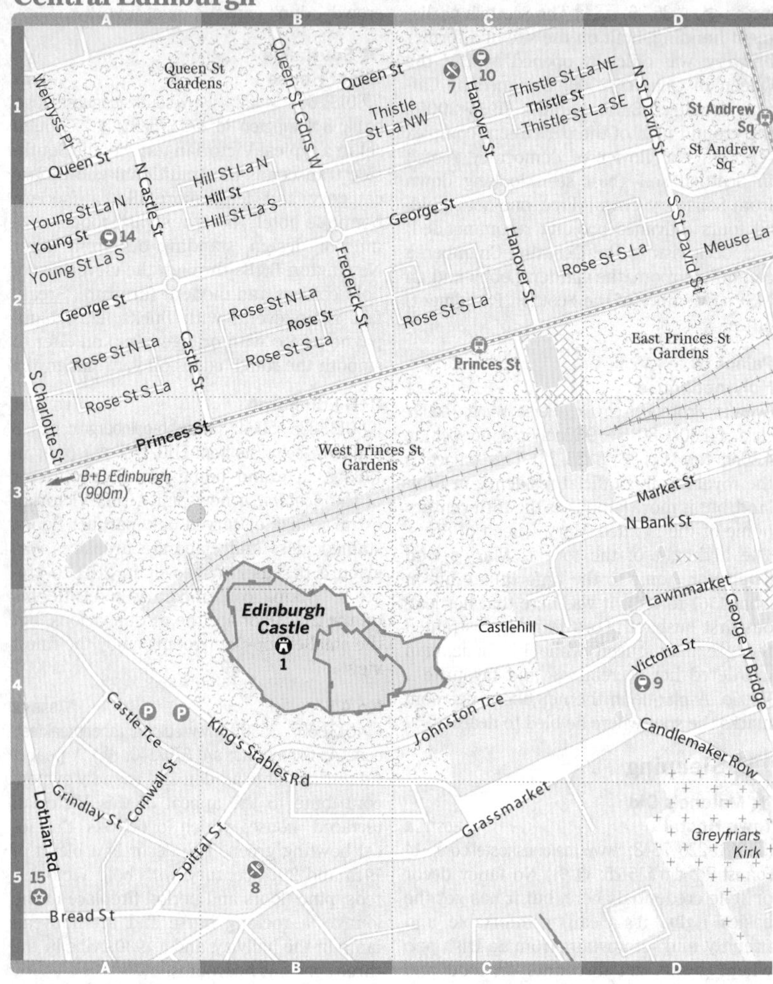

Eating

★Mums
CAFE £

(www.monstermashcafe.co.uk; 4a Forrest Rd; mains £6-9; 9am-10pm Mon-Sat, 10am-10pm Sun; 23, 27, 41, 42) This nostalgia-fuelled cafe serves up classic British comfort food that wouldn't look out of place on a 1950s menu – bacon and eggs, bangers and mash, shepherd's pie, fish and chips. But there's a twist – the food is all top-quality nosh freshly prepared from local produce, including Crombie's gourmet sausages. There's even a wine list, though we prefer the real ales and Scottish-brewed cider.

David Bann
VEGETARIAN £

(0131-556 5888; www.davidbann.com; 56-58 St Mary's St; mains £9-13; noon-10pm Mon-Fri, 11am-10pm Sat & Sun; ; 35) If you want to convince a carnivorous friend that cuisine à la veg can be as tasty and inventive as a meat-muncher's menu, take them to David Bann's stylish restaurant – dishes such as parsnip and blue cheese pudding, and

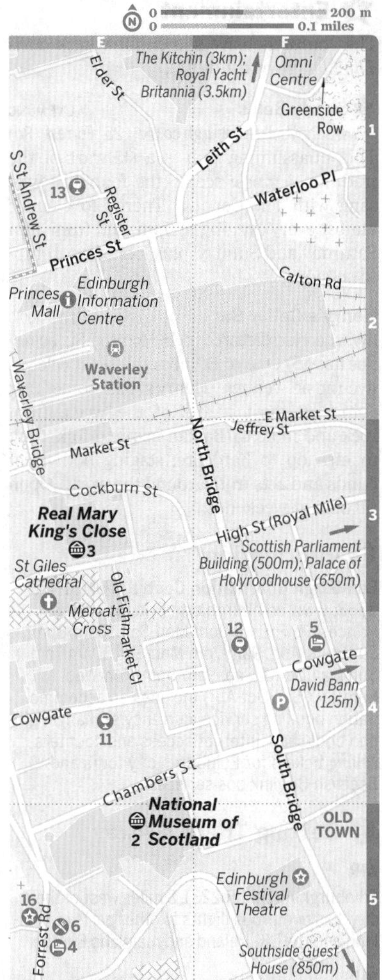

spiced aduki bean and cashew pie, are guaranteed to win converts.

★Timberyard SCOTTISH ££

(☎0131-221 1222; www.timberyard.co; 10 Lady Lawson St; mains £16-21; ⊙noon-9.30pm Tue-Sat; 📶; 🚌2, 35) 🍃 Ancient worn floorboards, cast-iron pillars, exposed joists and tables made from slabs of old mahogany create a rustic, retro atmosphere in this slow-food restaurant where the accent is on locally sourced produce from artisan growers and foragers. Typical dishes include seared

Central Edinburgh

◉ Top Sights

1 Edinburgh Castle B4
2 National Museum of Scotland E5
3 Real Mary King's Close E3

Sleeping

4 Malone's Old Town Hostel E5
5 Smart City Hostel F4

Eating

6 Mums E5
7 The Dogs C1
8 Timberyard B5

Drinking & Nightlife

9 Bow Bar D4
10 Bramble C1
11 BrewDog E4
12 Cabaret Voltaire F4
13 Café Royal Circle Bar E1
14 Oxford Bar A2

Entertainment

15 Henry's Cellar Bar A5
16 Sandy Bell's E5

scallop with apple, jerusalem artichoke and sorrel; and juniper-smoked pigeon with wild garlic flowers and beetroot.

Dogs BRITISH ££

(☎0131-220 1208; www.thedogsonline.co.uk; 110 Hanover St; mains £10-15; ⊙noon-4pm & 5-10pm; 🚌23, 27) 🍃 One of the coolest tables in town, this bistro-style place uses cheaper cuts of meat and less-well-known, more-sustainable species of fish to create hearty, no-nonsense dishes such as lamb sweetbreads on toast, baked coley with *skirlie* (fried oatmeal and onion), and devilled liver with bacon and onions.

★Kitchin SCOTTISH £££

(☎0131-555 1755; www.thekitchin.com; 78 Commercial Quay; mains £33-38, 3-course lunch £28.50; ⊙12.15-2.30pm & 6.30-10pm Tue-Thu, to 10.30pm Fri & Sat; 🖉; 🚌16, 22, 35, 36) Fresh, seasonal, locally sourced Scottish produce is the philosophy that has won a Michelin star for this elegant but unpretentious restaurant. The menu moves with the seasons, of course, so expect fresh salads in summer and game in winter, and shellfish dishes such as seared scallops with endive *tarte tatin* when there's an 'r' in the month.

Drinking & Nightlife

Bow Bar PUB

(80 West Bow; 23, 27, 41, 42) One of the city's best traditional-style pubs (it's not as old as it looks), serving a range of excellent real ales and a vast selection of malt whiskies, the Bow Bar often has standing-room only on Friday and Saturday evenings.

★Café Royal Circle Bar PUB

(www.caferoyaledinburgh.co.uk; 17 West Register St; all Princes St buses) Perhaps *the* classic Edinburgh pub, the Cafe Royal's main claims to fame are its magnificent oval bar and its Doulton tile portraits of famous Victorian inventors. Sit at the bar or claim one of the cosy leather booths beneath the stained-glass windows, and choose from the seven real ales on tap.

BrewDog BAR

(www.brewdog.com; 143 Cowgate; ; 36) The Edinburgh outpost of Scotland's self-styled 'punk brewery', BrewDog stands out among the grimy, sticky-floored dives that line the Cowgate, with its cool, industrial-chic designer look. As well as its own highly rated beers, there's a choice of four guest real ales.

Oxford Bar PUB

(www.oxfordbar.co.uk; 8 Young St; 19, 36, 37, 41, 47) The Oxford is that rarest of things: a real pub for real people, with no 'theme', no music, no frills and no pretensions. 'The Ox' has been immortalised by Ian Rankin, author of the Inspector Rebus novels, whose fictional detective is a regular here.

Bramble COCKTAIL BAR

(www.bramblebar.co.uk; 16a Queen St; 23, 27) One of those places that easily earns the title 'best-kept secret', Bramble is an unmarked cellar bar where a maze of stone and brick hideaways conceals what is arguably the city's best cocktail venue. No beer taps, no fuss, just expertly mixed drinks.

Cabaret Voltaire CLUB

(www.thecabaretvoltaire.com; 36-38 Blair St; all South Bridge buses) An atmospheric warren of stone-lined vaults houses this self-consciously 'alternative' club, which eschews huge dance floors and egotistical DJ worship in favour of a 'creative crucible' hosting an eclectic mix of DJs, live acts, comedy, theatre, visual arts and the spoken word. Well worth a look.

Entertainment

The comprehensive source for what's on is *The List* (www.list.co.uk).

★Sandy Bell's LIVE MUSIC

(www.sandybellsedinburgh.co.uk; 25 Forrest Rd) This unassuming pub is a stalwart of the traditional music scene (the founder's wife sang with The Corries). There's folk music almost every evening at 9pm, and from 3pm Saturday and Sunday, plus lots of impromptu sessions.

Henry's Cellar Bar LIVE MUSIC

(www.henryscellarbar.com; 16 Morrison St; admission free-£5) One of Edinburgh's most eclectic live-music venues, Henry's has something going on most nights of the week, from rock and indie to 'Balkan-inspired folk', funk to hip-hop to hardcore, staging both local bands and acts from around the world. Open till 3am at weekends.

Information

Edinburgh Information Centre (0131-473 3868; www.edinburgh.org; Princes Mall, 3 Princes St; 9am-9pm Mon-Sat, 10am-8pm Sun Jul & Aug, 9am-7pm Mon-Sat, 10am-7pm Sun May, Jun & Sep, 9am-5pm Mon-Wed, to 6pm Thu-Sun Oct-Apr) Includes an accommodation booking service, currency exchange, gift and bookshop, internet access and counters selling tickets for Edinburgh city tours and Scottish Citylink bus services.

Getting There & Away

AIR

Edinburgh Airport (p223), 8 miles west of the city, has numerous flights to other parts of Scotland and the UK, Ireland and mainland Europe.

BUS

Scottish Citylink (0871 266 3333; www.citylink.co.uk) buses connect Edinburgh with all of Scotland's cities and major towns, including Glasgow (£7.30, 1¼ hours, every 15 minutes), Stirling (£8, one hour, hourly) and Inverness (£30, 3½ to 4½ hours, hourly). National Express operates a direct coach service from London (£26, 10 hours, one daily).

It's also worth checking with **Megabus** (0900 160 0900; www.megabus.com) for cheap intercity bus fares from Edinburgh to London, Glasgow and Inverness.

TRAIN

The main terminus in Edinburgh is Waverley train station, in the heart of the city. Trains arriving from, and departing for, the west also stop at

Haymarket station, which is more convenient for the West End.

First ScotRail (☎ 0845 755 0033; www.scotrail.co.uk) operates a regular shuttle service between Edinburgh and Glasgow (£13.20, 50 minutes, every 15 minutes), and frequent daily services to all Scottish cities, including Stirling (£8.30, one hour, twice hourly Monday to Saturday, hourly Sunday) and Inverness (£72, 3½ hours). There are also regular trains to London Kings Cross (£85, 4½ hours, hourly) via York.

Glasgow

POP 634,680

With a population around 1½ times that of Edinburgh, and a radically different history rooted in industry and trade rather than politics and law, Glasgow stands in complete contrast to the capital. The city offers a unique blend of friendliness, energy, dry humour and urban chaos, and also boasts excellent art galleries and museums – including the famous Burrell Collection – as well as numerous good-value restaurants, countless pubs, bars and clubs, and a lively performing-arts scene.

Just 50 miles to the west of Edinburgh, Glasgow makes an easy day trip by train or bus.

Sights

Glasgow's main square in the city centre is grand **George Square**, built in the Victorian era to show off the city's wealth, and dignified by statues of notable Scots, including Robert Burns, James Watt, John Moore and Sir Walter Scott.

★Kelvingrove Art Gallery & Museum GALLERY, MUSEUM
(www.glasgowmuseums.com; Argyle St; 10am-5pm Mon-Thu & Sat, 11am-5pm Fri & Sun;) FREE A magnificent stone building, this grand Victorian cathedral of culture is a fascinating and unusual museum, with a bewildering variety of exhibits. You'll find fine art alongside stuffed animals, and Micronesian shark-tooth swords alongside a Spitfire plane, but it's not mix 'n' match: rooms are carefully and thoughtfully themed, and the collection is a manageable size. There's an excellent room of Scottish art, a room of fine French Impressionist works, and quality Renaissance paintings from Italy and Flanders.

★Burrell Collection GALLERY
(www.glasgowmuseums.com; Pollok Country Park; 10am-5pm Mon-Thu & Sat, 11am-5pm Fri & Sun) FREE One of Glasgow's top attractions was amassed by wealthy industrialist Sir William Burrell then donated to the city and is housed in an outstanding museum, in a park 3 miles south of the city centre. Burrell collected all manner of art from his teens to his death at 97, and this idiosyncratic collection of treasure includes everything from Chinese porcelain and medieval furniture to paintings by Degas and Cézanne. It's not so big as to be overwhelming, and the stamp of the collector lends an intriguing coherence.

★Riverside Museum MUSEUM
(www.glasgowmuseums.com; 100 Pointhouse Pl; 10am-5pm Mon-Thu & Sat, 11am-5pm Fri & Sun;

THE GENIUS OF CHARLES RENNIE MACKINTOSH

Charles Rennie Mackintosh (1868–1928) is to Glasgow what Gaudí is to Barcelona. A designer, architect and master of the art-nouveau style, his quirky, linear and geometric designs are seen all over Glasgow.

Many of his buildings are open to the public, though his masterpiece, the **Glasgow School of Art**, was closed after being badly damaged by fire in 2014. If you're a fan, the **Mackintosh Trail ticket** (£10), available at the tourist office or any Mackintosh building, gives you a day's free admission to all his creations, plus unlimited bus and subway travel. Highlights include the following:

Willow Tearooms (www.willowtearooms.co.uk; 217 Sauchiehall St; 9am-5pm Mon-Sat, 11am-5pm Sun;) FREE

Mackintosh House (www.hunterian.gla.ac.uk; 82 Hillhead St; 10am-5pm Tue-Sat, 11am-4pm Sun) FREE

House for an Art Lover (☎ 0141-353 4770; www.houseforanartlover.co.uk; Bellahouston Park, Dumbreck Rd; adult/child £4.50/3; 10am-4pm Mon-Wed, to 12.30pm Thu-Sun)

Glasgow

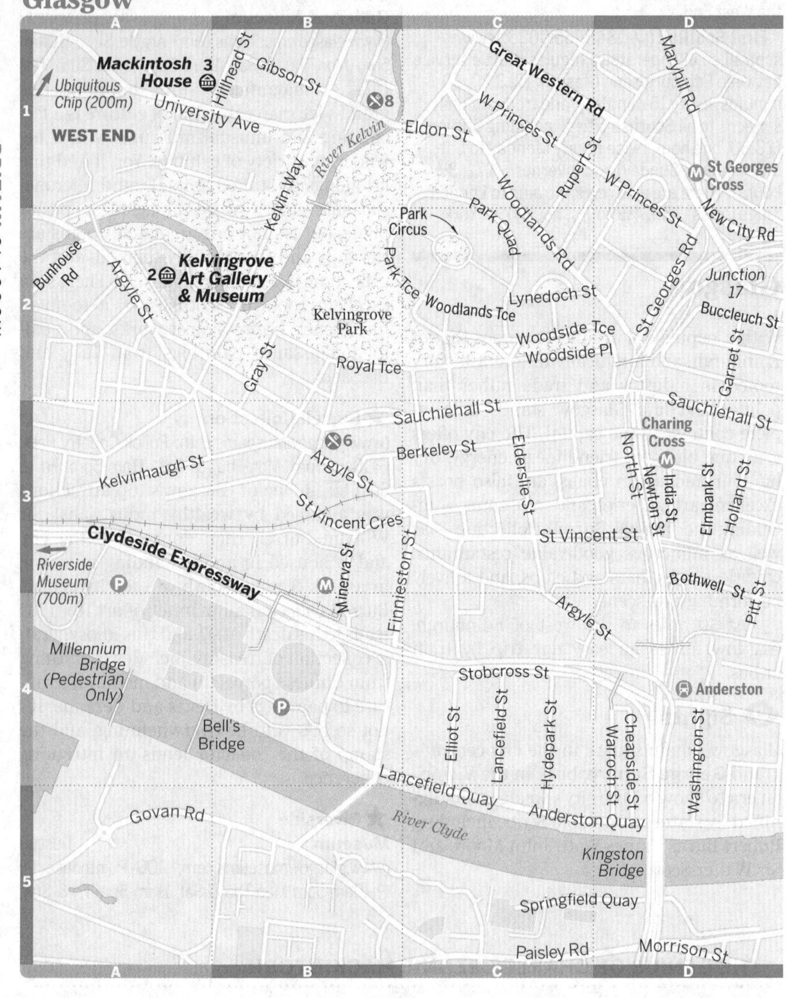

) FREE This visually impressive modern museum at Glasgow Harbour (west of the centre – get bus 100 from the north side of George Sq, or the Clyde Cruises boat service) owes its striking curved forms to British-Iraqi architect Zaha Hadid. A transport museum forms the main part of the collection, featuring a fascinating series of cars made in Scotland, plus assorted railway locos, trams, bikes (including the world's first pedal-powered bicycle from 1847) and model Clyde-built ships.

Glasgow Cathedral CHURCH

(HS; www.historic-scotland.gov.uk; Cathedral Sq; 9.30am-5.30pm Mon-Sat, 1-5pm Sun Apr-Sep, closes 4.30pm Oct-Mar) FREE Glasgow Cathedral has a rare timelessness. The dark, imposing interior conjures up medieval might and can send a shiver down the spine. It's a shining example of Gothic architecture, and, unlike nearly all Scotland's cathedrals, survived the turmoil of the Reformation mobs almost intact. Most of the current building dates from the 15th century.

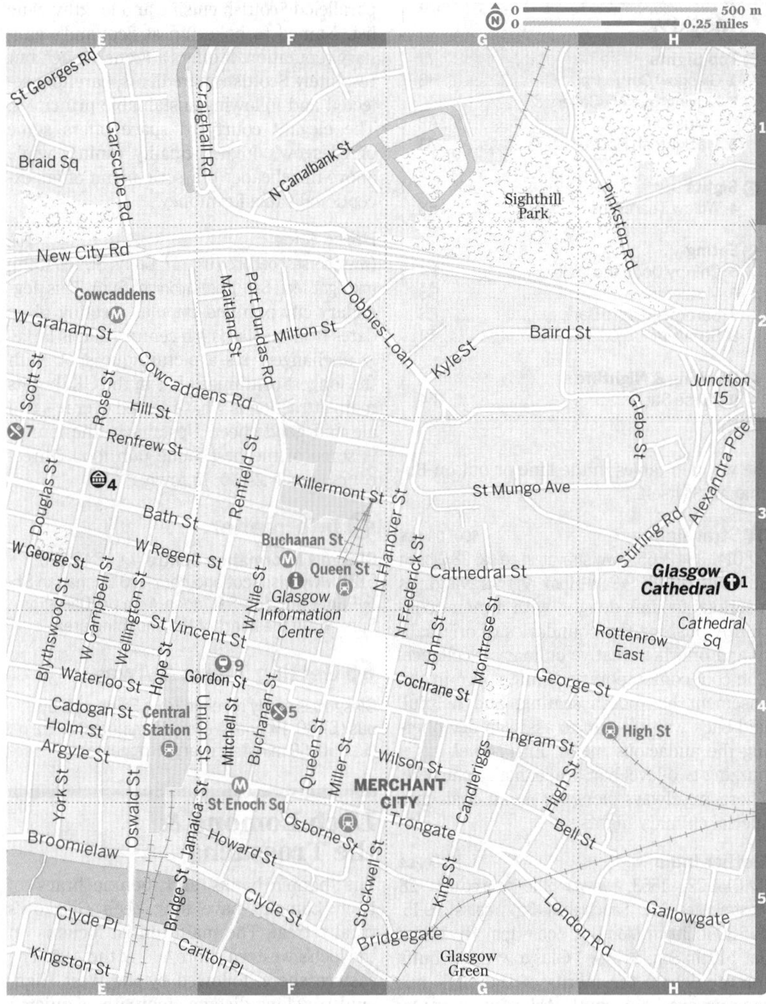

Eating & Drinking

★Saramago Café Bar

CAFE £

(www.facebook.com/saramagocafebar; 350 Sauchiehall St; light meals £3-9; food 10am-10pm Mon-Wed, 10am-11.30pm Thu-Sat, noon-11.30pm Sun;) In the airy atmosphere of the Centre for Contemporary Arts, this place does a great line in eclectic vegan fusion food, with a range of top flavour combinations from around the globe. The upstairs bar has a great deck on steep Scott St and packs out inside with a friendly hipstery crowd enjoying the eclectic DJ sets and quality tap beers.

Chippy Doon the Lane

FISH & CHIPS £

(www.thechippyglasgow.com; McCormick Lane, 84 Buchanan St; meals £6-10; noon-9.30pm;) Don't be put off by its location in a down-at-heel alleyway off the shopping precinct: this is a cut above your average chip shop. Sustainable seafood is served in a chic space, all old-time brick, metal archways and jazz. Otherwise, chow down on your takeaway at

Glasgow

Top Sights

Sights

Eating

Drinking & Nightlife

the wooden tables in the lane or out on Buchanan St itself.

★Stravaigin SCOTTISH ££
(☎0141-334 2665; www.stravaigin.co.uk; 28 Gibson St; mains £10-18; ⏲9am-11pm; 📶) Stravaigin is a serious foodie's delight, with a menu constantly pushing the boundaries of originality and offering creative culinary excellence. The cool contemporary dining space in the basement has booth seating, and helpful, laid-back waiting-staff to assist in deciphering the audacious menu. Entry-level has a buzzing two-level bar; you can also eat here. There are always plenty of menu deals and special culinary nights.

Mother India INDIAN ££
(☎0141-221 1663; www.motherindia.co.uk; 28 Westminster Tce, Sauchiehall St; mains £9-15; ⏲5.30-10.30pm Mon-Thu, noon-11pm Fri, 1-11pm Sat, 1-10pm Sun; 📶🖊👪) Glasgow curry buffs forever debate the merits of the city's numerous excellent south Asian restaurants, and Mother India features in every discussion. It may lack the trendiness of some of the up-and-comers but it's been a stalwart for years, and the quality and innovation on show is superb. The three separate dining areas are all attractive and they make an effort for kids, with a separate menu.

★Ubiquitous Chip SCOTTISH £££
(☎0141-334 5007; www.ubiquitouschip.co.uk; 12 Ashton Lane; 2-/3-course lunch £16/20, mains £23-27, brasserie mains £9-14; ⏲noon-2.30pm & 5-11pm; 📶) 🍃 The original champion of Scottish produce, this is legendary for its unparalleled Scottish cuisine and lengthy wine list. Named to poke fun at Scotland's culinary reputation, it offers a French touch but resolutely Scottish ingredients, carefully selected and following sustainable principles. The elegant courtyard space offers some of Glasgow's highest-quality dining, while above the cheaper brasserie menu offers exceptional value for money.

Horse Shoe PUB
(www.horseshoebar.co.uk; 17 Drury St; ⏲10am-midnight Mon-Sat, 11am-midnight Sun) This legendary city pub and popular meeting place dates from the late 19th century and is largely unchanged. It's a picturesque spot, with the longest continuous bar in the UK, but its main attraction is what's served over it – real ale and good cheer. Upstairs in the lounge is some of the best value pub food (three-course lunch £4.50) in town.

Information

Glasgow Information Centre (☎0845 225 5121; www.visitscotland.com; 170 Buchanan St; ⏲9am-6pm Mon-Sat, noon-4pm or 10am-5pm Sun; 📶) In the heart of the shopping area.

Getting There & Away

Glasgow is easily reached from Edinburgh by bus (£7.30, 1¼ hours, every 15 minutes) or train (£12.50, 50 minutes, every 15 minutes).

Loch Lomond & the Trossachs

The 'bonnie banks' and 'bonnie braes' of Loch Lomond have long been Glasgow's rural retreat. The main tourist focus is on the loch's western shore, along the A82. The eastern shore, followed by the West Highland Way long-distance footpath, is quieter. The region's importance was recognised when it became the heart of **Loch Lomond & the Trossachs National Park** (www.lochlomond-trossachs.org) – Scotland's first national park, created in 2002.

The nearby Trossachs is a region famous for its thickly forested hills and scenic lochs. It first gained popularity in the early 19th century when curious visitors came from across Britain, drawn by the romantic language of Walter Scott's poem *Lady of the Lake,* inspired by Loch Katrine, and his novel *Rob Roy,* about the derring-do of the region's most famous son.

The main centre for Loch Lomond boat trips is Balloch, where **Sweeney's Cruises** (☎01389-752376; www.sweeneyscruises.com; Balloch Rd, Balloch) offers a range of outings, including a one-hour cruise to Inchmurrin and back (adult/child £8.50/5, departs hourly).

Loch Katrine Cruises (☎01877-376315; www.lochkatrine.com; Trossachs Pier; 1hr cruise adult/child £13/8; ⏲Easter-Oct) runs boat trips from Trossachs Pier at the eastern tip of Loch Katrine. At 10.30am there's a departure to Stronachlachar at the other end of the loch before returning. One of these is the fabulous centenarian steamship *Sir Walter Scott*.

Sleeping & Eating

Oak Tree Inn INN ££
(☎01360-870357; www.oak-tree-inn.co.uk; Balmaha; dm/s/d £30/50/85; P) An attractive traditional inn built in slate and timber, this offers bright modern guest bedrooms for pampered hikers, super-spacious superior chambers, self-catering cottages and two four-bed bunkrooms for hardier souls. The rustic restaurant brings locals, tourists and walkers together and dishes up hearty meals that cover lots of bases (mains £9 to £12, food noon to 9pm). There's lots of outdoor seating and it brews its own beers.

★**Roman Camp Hotel** HOTEL £££
(☎01877-330003; www.romancamphotel.co.uk; Main St; s/d/superior £110/160/210; P) Callander's best hotel is centrally located but feels rural, set by the river in beautiful grounds. Endearing features include a lounge with blazing fire and a library with a tiny secret chapel. It's an old-fashioned warren of a place with four grades of room; standards are certainly luxurious, but superiors are even more appealing, with period furniture, excellent bathrooms, armchairs and fireplace.

The upmarket restaurant is open to the public. Reassuringly, the name refers not to toga parties but to a ruin in the adjacent fields.

★**Drover's Inn** PUB FOOD ££
(☎01301-704234; www.thedroversinn.co.uk; Ardlui; bar meals £8-12; ⏲11.30am-10pm Mon-Sat, 11.30am-9.30pm Sun;) This is one howff (drinking den) you shouldn't miss – a low-ceilinged place just north of Ardlui with smoke-blackened stone, barmen in kilts, and walls festooned with moth-eaten stags' heads and stuffed birds. The bar, where Rob Roy allegedly dropped by for pints, serves hearty hill-walking fuel and hosts live folk at weekends. We recommend this more as an atmospheric place to eat and drink than somewhere to stay.

★**Callander Meadows** SCOTTISH ££
(☎01877-330181; www.callandermeadows.co.uk; 24 Main St; lunch £10, mains £12-16; ⏲9am-9pm Thu-Sun;) Informal but smart, this well-loved restaurant in the centre of Callander occupies the two front rooms of a house on the main street. There's a contemporary flair for presentation and unusual flavour combinations, but a solidly British base underpins the cuisine. There's a great beer/coffee garden out the back, where you can also eat. Opens daily from June to September.

Getting There & Away

Balloch, at the southern end of Loch Lomond, can be easily reached from Glasgow by bus (£4.50, 1½ hours, at least two per hour) or train (£5.10, 45 minutes, every 30 minutes).

For exploring the Trossachs, your own transport is recommended.

Inverness

Inverness, the primary city and shopping centre of the Highlands, has a great location astride the River Ness at the northern end of the Great Glen. It's a jumping-off point for exploring northern Scotland, with the railway line from Edinburgh branching east to Elgin and Aberdeen, north to Thurso and Wick, and west to Kyle of Lochalsh (the nearest train station to the Isle of Skye). The latter route is one of Britain's great scenic rail journeys.

Sleeping

Bazpackers Backpackers Hotel HOSTEL £
(☎01463-717663; www.bazpackershostel.co.uk; 4 Culduthel Rd; dm/tw £17/44; @) This may be Inverness' smallest hostel (34 beds), but it's hugely popular. It's a friendly, quiet place – the main building has a convivial lounge centred on a wood-burning stove, and a small garden and great views (some rooms are in a separate building with no garden). The dorms and kitchen can be a bit cramped, but the showers are great.

DON'T MISS

STIRLING CASTLE

Hold Stirling and you control Scotland. This maxim has ensured that a fortress of some kind has existed here since prehistoric times. You cannot help drawing parallels with Edinburgh Castle, but many find **Stirling Castle** (HS; www.stirlingcastle.gov.uk; adult/child £14/7.50; ⌚9.30am-6pm Apr-Sep, to 5pm Oct-Mar) more atmospheric – the location, architecture, historical significance and commanding views combine to make it a grand and memorable sight.

The current castle dates from the late 14th to the 16th century, when it was a residence of the Stuart monarchs. The undisputed highlight of a visit is the fabulous, recently restored **Royal Palace**. The idea was that it should look brand new, just as when it was constructed by French masons under the orders of James V in the mid-16th century with the aim of impressing his new (also French) bride and other crowned heads of Europe. The suite of six rooms – three for the king, three for the queen – is a sumptuous riot of colour. Particularly notable are the fine fireplaces, the **Stirling Heads** – modern reproductions of painted oak discs in the ceiling of the king's audience chamber – and the fabulous series of tapestries that have been painstakingly woven over many years.

Stirling is 35 miles northwest of Edinburgh, and easily reached by train (£8.30, one hour, twice hourly Monday to Saturday, hourly Sunday).

★Trafford Bank B&B ££

(☎01463-241414; www.traffordbankguesthouse.co.uk; 96 Fairfield Rd; d £120-132; P 📶) Lots of word-of-mouth rave reviews for this elegant Victorian villa, which was once home to a bishop, just a mitre-toss from the Caledonian Canal and 10 minutes' walk west from the city centre. The luxurious rooms include fresh flowers and fruit, bathrobes and fluffy towels – ask for the Tartan Room, which has a wrought-iron king-size bed and Victorian roll-top bath.

Ardconnel House B&B ££

(☎01463-240455; www.ardconnel-inverness.co.uk; 21 Ardconnel St; r per person £35-40; 📶) The six-room Ardconnel is one of our favourites – a terraced Victorian house with comfortable en suite rooms, a dining room with crisp white table linen, and a breakfast menu that includes Vegemite for homesick antipodeans. Kids under 10 not allowed.

Eating

★Café 1 BISTRO ££

(☎01463-226200; www.cafe1.net; 75 Castle St; mains £10-24; ⌚noon-2.30pm & 5-9.30pm Mon-Fri, noon-2.30pm & 6-9.30pm Sat) Café 1 is a friendly and appealing bistro with candlelit tables amid elegant blonde-wood and wrought-iron decor. There is an international menu based on quality Scottish produce, from Aberdeen Angus steaks to crisp pan-fried sea bass and meltingly tender pork belly. The set lunch menu (two courses for £8) is served noon to 2.30pm Monday to Saturday.

Contrast Brasserie BRASSERIE ££

(☎01463-223777; www.glenmoristontownhouse.com; 20 Ness Bank; 2-course lunch £10.95, 2-course early bird £12.95, à la carte £4.95-25) Book early for what we think is one of the best-value restaurants in Inverness – a dining room that drips designer style, with smiling professional staff and truly delicious food prepared using fresh Scottish produce. The two-course lunch menu and three-course early bird menu (£16, 5pm to 6.30pm) are bargains.

Information

Inverness Tourist Office (☎01463-252401; www.visithighlands.com; Castle Wynd; internet access per 20min £1; ⌚9am-6pm Mon-Sat, 9.30am-5pm Sun Jul & Aug, 9am-5pm Mon-Sat, 10am-4pm Sun Jun, Sep & Oct, 9am-5pm Mon-Sat Apr & May) Bureau de change and accommodation booking service; also sells tickets for tours and cruises. Opening hours limited November to March.

Getting There & Away

BUS

Buses depart from **Inverness bus station** (Margaret St). Coaches from London (£45, 13 hours, one daily direct) are operated by **National Express** (☎08717 81 81 78; www.gobycoach.com); more frequent services require a change at Glasgow. Other routes include Edinburgh (£30, 3½ to 4½ hours, hourly) and Portree on the Isle of Skye (£25, 3¼ hours, three daily).

TRAIN

Trains depart from Inverness for Kyle of Lochalsh (£22, 2½ hours, four daily Monday to Saturday, two Sunday); this is one of Britain's most scenic railway lines.

There's one direct train from London each day (£100, eight to nine hours); others require a change at Edinburgh.

Loch Ness

Deep, dark and narrow, Loch Ness stretches for 23 miles between Inverness and Fort Augustus. Its bitterly cold waters have been extensively explored in search of the elusive Loch Ness monster, but most visitors see her only in cardboard cut-out form at the monster exhibitions. The village of **Drumnadrochit** is a hotbed of beastie fever, with two monster exhibitions battling it out for the tourist dollar.

Sights & Activities

Loch Ness Centre & Exhibition INTERPRETATION CENTRE
(01456-450573; www.lochness.com; adult/child £7.45/4.95; 9.30am-6pm Jul & Aug, to 5pm Easter-Jun, Sep & Oct, 10am-3.30pm Nov-Easter; P) This Nessie-themed attraction adopts a scientific approach that allows you to weigh the evidence for yourself. Exhibits include the original equipment – sonar survey vessels, miniature submarines, cameras and sediment coring tools – used in various monster hunts, as well as original photographs and film footage of sightings. You'll find out about hoaxes and optical illusions, as well as learning a lot about the ecology of Loch Ness – is there enough food in the loch to support even one 'monster', let alone a breeding population?

Urquhart Castle CASTLE
(HS; 01456-450551; adult/child £7.90/4.80; 9.30am-6pm Apr-Sep, to 5pm Oct, to 4.30pm Nov-Mar; P) Commanding a brilliant location 1.5 miles east of Drumnadrochit, with outstanding views (on a clear day), Urquhart Castle is a popular Nessie-watching hotspot. A huge visitor centre (most of which is beneath ground level) includes a video theatre (with a dramatic 'unveiling' of the castle at the end of the film) and displays of medieval items discovered in the castle.

Nessie Hunter BOAT TOUR
(01456-450395; www.lochness-cruises.com; adult/child £15/10; Easter-Oct) One-hour monster-hunting cruises, complete with sonar and underwater cameras. Cruises depart from Drumnadrochit hourly (except 1pm) from 9am to 6pm daily.

Getting There & Away

Scottish Citylink (0871 266 3333; www.citylink.co.uk) and **Stagecoach** (www.stagecoachbus.com) buses from Inverness to Fort William run along the shores of Loch Ness (six to eight daily, five on Sunday); those headed for Skye turn off at Invermoriston. There are bus stops at Drumnadrochit (£3.20, 30 minutes) and Urquhart Castle car park (£3.50, 35 minutes).

Isle of Skye

POP 9900

The Isle of Skye is the biggest of Scotland's islands (now linked to the mainland by a bridge at Kyle of Lochalsh), a 50-mile-long smorgasbord of velvet moors, jagged mountains, sparkling lochs and towering sea cliffs. It takes its name from the old Norse *sky-a,* meaning 'cloud island', a Viking reference to the often mist-enshrouded **Cuillin Hills**, Britain's most spectacular mountain range. The stunning scenery is the main attraction, including the cliffs and pinnacles of the **Old Man of Storr**, **Kilt Rock** and the **Quiraing**, but there are plenty of cosy pubs to retire to when the rain clouds close in.

Portree is the main town, with Broadford a close second; both have banks, ATMs, supermarkets and petrol stations.

Sights & Activities

Dunvegan Castle CASTLE
(01470-521206; www.dunvegancastle.com; adult/child £10/7; 10am-5.30pm Apr–mid-Oct; P) Skye's most famous historic building, and one of its most popular tourist attractions, Dunvegan Castle is the seat of the chief of Clan MacLeod. It has played host to Samuel Johnson, Sir Walter Scott and, most famously, Flora MacDonald. The oldest parts are the 14th-century keep and dungeon but most of it dates from the 17th to 19th centuries.

Skye Tours BUS TOUR
(☎01471-822716; www.skye-tours.co.uk; adult/child £35/30; ⏲Mon-Sat) Five-hour sightseeing tours of Skye in a minibus, departing from the tourist office car park in Kyle of Lochalsh (close to Kyle of Lochalsh train station).

Sleeping

Portree, the island's capital, has the largest selection of accommodation, eating places and other services.

Bayfield Backpackers HOSTEL £
(☎01478-612231; www.skyehostel.co.uk; Bayfield; dm £18; P@🛜) Clean, central and modern, this hostel provides the best backpacker accommodation in town. The owner really makes you feel welcome, and is a fount of advice on what to do and where to go in Skye.

Ben Tianavaig B&B B&B ££
(☎01478-612152; www.ben-tianavaig.co.uk; 5 Bosville Tce; r £75-88; P🛜) A warm welcome awaits from the Irish-Welsh couple that runs this appealing B&B bang in the centre of town. All four bedrooms have a view across the harbour to the hill that gives the house its name and breakfasts include free-range eggs and vegetables grown in the garden. Two-night minimum stay April to October; no credit cards.

★**Tigh an Dochais** B&B ££
(☎01471-820022; www.skyebedbreakfast.co.uk; 13 Harrapool; d £90; P) A cleverly designed modern building, Tigh an Dochais is one of Skye's best B&Bs – a little footbridge leads to the front door, which is on the 1st floor. Here you'll find the dining room (gorgeous breakfasts) and lounge offering a stunning view of sea and hills; the bedrooms (downstairs) open onto an outdoor deck with that same wonderful view.

Peinmore House B&B £££
(☎01478-612574; www.peinmorehouse.co.uk; r £135-145; P🛜) Signposted off the main road about 2 miles south of Portree, this former manse has been cleverly converted into a guesthouse that is more stylish and luxurious than most hotels. The bedrooms and bathrooms are huge (one bathroom has an armchair in it!), as is the choice of breakfast (kippers and smoked haddock on the menu), and there are panoramic views to the Old Man of Storr.

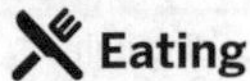

Eating

Café Arriba CAFE £
(☎01478-611830; www.cafearriba.co.uk; Quay Brae; mains £5-10; ⏲7am-6pm daily May-Sep, 8am-5pm Thu-Sat Oct-Apr; 🌶) Arriba is a funky little cafe, brightly decked out in primary colours and offering delicious flatbread melts (bacon, leek and cheese is our favourite) as well as the best choice of vegetarian grub on the island, ranging from a vegie breakfast fry-up to falafel wraps with hummus and chilli sauce. Also serves excellent coffee.

★**Harbour View Seafood Restaurant** SEAFOOD ££
(☎01478-612069; www.harbourviewskye.co.uk; 7 Bosville Tce; mains £14-19; ⏲noon-3pm & 5.30-11pm Tue-Sun) The Harbour View is Portree's most congenial place to eat. It has a homely dining room with a log fire in winter, books on the mantelpiece and bric-a-brac on the shelves. And on the table, superb Scottish seafood such as fresh Skye oysters, seafood chowder, king scallops, langoustines and lobster.

Getting There & Away

BOAT

Despite the bridge, there are still a couple of ferry links between Skye and the mainland. Ferries also operate from Uig on Skye to the Outer Hebrides.

Mallaig to Armadale (www.calmac.co.uk; per person/car £4.65/23.90) The Mallaig to Armadale ferry (30 minutes, eight daily Monday to Saturday, five to seven on Sunday) is very popular on weekends and in July and August, so book ahead if you're travelling by car.

Glenelg to Kylerhea (www.skyeferry.co.uk; car with up to four passengers £15; ⏲Easter-mid Oct) Runs a tiny vessel (six cars only) on the short Kylerhea to Glenelg crossing (five minutes, every 20 minutes). The ferry operates from 10am to 6pm daily (till 7pm June to August).

BUS

There are buses to Portree from Kyle of Lochalsh (£6.50, one hour, six daily) and Inverness (£24, 3¼ hours, three daily).

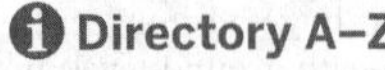

SURVIVAL GUIDE

Directory A–Z

ACCOMMODATION

Accommodation can be difficult to find during holidays (especially around Easter and New

SLEEPING PRICE RANGES

Our reviews refer to double rooms with a private bathroom, except in hostels or where otherwise specified. Quoted rates are for a double room in high season.

£ less than £60 (£100 in London)

££ £60 to £130 (£100 to £200 in London)

£££ more than £130 (£200 in London)

Year) and major events (such as the Edinburgh Festival). In summer, popular spots (York, Canterbury, Bath etc) get very crowded, so booking ahead is essential. Local tourist offices often provide an accommodation booking service for a small fee.

Hostels There are two types of hostels in Britain: those run by the **Youth Hostels Association** (www.yha.org.uk) and **Scottish Youth Hostels Association** (www.syha.org.uk), and independent hostels, most of which are listed in the **Independent Hostels Guide** (www.independenthostelguide.co.uk). The simplest hostels cost around £15 per person per night. Larger hostels with more facilities are £18 to £25. London's YHA hostels cost from £30.

B&Bs The B&B (bed and breakfast) is a great British institution. At smaller places it's pretty much a room in somebody's house; larger places may be called a 'guesthouse' (halfway between a B&B and a full hotel). Prices start from around £25 per person for a simple bedroom and shared bathroom; for around £30 to £35 per person you get a private bathroom – either down the hall or an en suite.

Hotels There's a massive choice of hotels in Britain, from small town houses to grand country mansions, from no-frills locations to boutique hideaways. At the bargain end, single/double rooms cost from £40/50. Move up the scale and you'll pay £100/150 or beyond.

Camping Campsites range from farmers' fields with a tap and basic toilet, costing from £3 per person per night, to smarter affairs with hot showers and many other facilities, charging up to £13. You usually need all your own equipment.

ACTIVITIES

Britain is a great destination for outdoor enthusiasts. Walking and cycling are the most popular activities – you can do them on a whim, and they're the perfect way to open up some beautiful corners of the country.

Cycling

Compact Britain is an excellent destination to explore by bike. Popular regions to tour include southwest England, the Yorkshire Dales, Derbyshire's Peak District, Mid-Wales and the Scottish Borders. Bike-hire outlets are widespread; rates range from £10 per day to £60 per week.

The 10,000-mile **National Cycle Network** (www.nationalcyclenetwork.org.uk) is a web of quiet roads and traffic-free tracks that pass through busy cities and remote rural areas.

Sustrans (www.sustrans.org.uk) is another useful organisation, and publishes a wide range of maps, guides and planning tools.

Walking & Hiking

Hiking is a hugely popular pastime in Britain, especially in scenic areas such as Snowdonia, the Lake District, the Yorkshire Dales and the Scottish Highlands. Various long-distance routes cross the countryside, including the **Coast to Coast** (www.thecoasttocoastwalk.info), the **Cotswold Way** (www.nationaltrail.co.uk/cotswold), the **West Highland Way** (☎ 01389-722600; www.west-highland-way.co.uk) and the **South West Coast Path** (www.southwestcoastpath.com).

The **Ramblers Association** (www.ramblers.org.uk) is the country's leading walkers' organisation.

BUSINESS HOURS

Standard opening hours:

Banks 9.30am to 4pm or 5pm Monday to Friday; main branches 9.30am to 1pm Saturday

Post Offices 9am to 5pm (5.30pm or 6pm in cities) Monday to Friday, 9am to 12.30pm Saturday (main branches to 5pm)

Pubs 11am to 11pm Sunday to Thursday, 11am to midnight or 1am Friday and Saturday

Restaurants lunch noon to 3pm, dinner 6pm to 10pm; hours vary widely

COUNTRY FACTS

Area 88,500 sq miles

Capitals London (England and the United Kingdom), Cardiff (Wales), Edinburgh (Scotland)

Country Code ☎ 44

Currency Pound sterling (£)

Emergency ☎ 999 or ☎ 112

Languages English, Welsh, Scottish Gaelic

Money ATMs are widespread; credit cards widely accepted

Population 61.4 million

Visas Schengen rules do not apply

Shops 9am to 5pm Monday to Saturday, 10am to 4pm Sunday

GAY & LESBIAN TRAVELLERS

Britain is generally a tolerant place for gays and lesbians. London, Manchester and Brighton have flourishing gay scenes, and in other sizeable cities (even some small towns) you'll find communities not entirely in the closet. That said, you'll still find pockets of homophobic hostility in some areas. Resources include the following:

Diva (www.divamag.co.uk)

Gay Times (www.gaytimes.co.uk)

London Lesbian & Gay Switchboard (www.llgs.org.uk)

INTERNET RESOURCES

Traveline (www.traveline.org.uk) Timetables and travel advice for public transport across Britain.

Visit Britain (www.visitbritain.com) Comprehensive national tourism website.

MONEY

- The currency of Britain is the pound sterling (£). Paper money (notes) comes in £5, £10, £20 and £50 denominations, although some shops don't accept £50 notes.
- ATMs, often called cash machines, are easy to find in towns and cities.
- Most banks and some post offices offer currency exchange.
- Visa and MasterCard credit and debit cards are widely accepted in Britain. Nearly everywhere uses a 'Chip and PIN' system (instead of signing).
- Smaller businesses may charge a fee for credit card use, and some take cash or cheque only.
- Tipping is not obligatory. A 10% to 15% tip is fine for restaurants, cafes, taxi drivers and pub meals; if you order drinks and food at the bar, there's no need to tip.
- Travellers cheques are rarely used.

PUBLIC HOLIDAYS

In many areas of Britain, bank holidays are just for the banks – many businesses and visitor attractions stay open.

SCOTTISH POUNDS

Scottish banks issue their own sterling banknotes. They are interchangeable with Bank of England notes, but you'll sometimes run into problems outside Scotland – shops in the south of England may refuse to accept them. They are also harder to exchange once you get outside the UK, though British banks will always exchange them.

SCHOOL HOLIDAYS

Roads get busy and hotel prices go up during school holidays.

Easter Holiday Week before and week after Easter.

Summer Holiday Third week of July to first week of September.

Christmas Holiday Mid-December to first week of January.

There are also three week-long 'half-term' school holidays – usually late February (or early March), late May and late October. These vary between Scotland, England and Wales.

New Year's Day 1 January

Easter March/April (Good Friday to Easter Monday inclusive)

May Day First Monday in May

Spring Bank Holiday Last Monday in May

Summer Bank Holiday Last Monday in August

Christmas Day 25 December

Boxing Day 26 December

SAFE TRAVEL

Britain is a remarkably safe country, but crime is not unknown in London and other cities.

- Watch out for pickpockets and hustlers in crowded areas popular with tourists, such as around Westminster Bridge in London.
- When travelling by tube, tram or urban train services at night, choose a carriage containing other people.
- Many town centres can be rowdy on Friday and Saturday nights when the pubs and clubs are emptying.
- Unlicensed minicabs – a bloke with a car earning money on the side – operate in large cities, and are worth avoiding unless you know what you're doing.

TELEPHONE

The UK uses the GSM 900/1800 network, which covers the rest of Europe, Australia and New Zealand, but isn't compatible with the North American GSM 1900. Most modern mobiles can function on both networks – but check before you leave home just in case.

Area codes in the UK do not have a standard format or length (eg Edinburgh ☎0131, London ☎020, Ambleside ☎015394). In our reviews, area codes and phone numbers have been listed together, separated by a hyphen.

Other codes include ☎0500 or ☎0800 for free calls, ☎0845 for local rates, ☎087 for

PRACTICALITIES

DVD PAL format (incompatible with NTSC and Secam).

Newspapers Tabloids include the *Sun* and *Mirror*, and *Daily Record* (in Scotland); quality 'broadsheets' include (from right to left, politically) the *Telegraph*, *Times*, *Independent* and *Guardian*.

Radio Main BBC stations and wavelengths are Radio 1 (98–99.6MHz FM), Radio 2 (88–92MHz FM), Radio 3 (90–92.2MHz FM), Radio 4 (92–94.4MHz FM) and Radio 5 Live (909 or 693AM). National commercial stations include Virgin Radio (1215Hz MW) and nonhighbrow classical specialist, Classic FM (100–102MHz FM). All are available on digital.

TV All TV in the UK is digital. Leading broadcasters include BBC, ITV and Channel 4. Satellite and cable TV providers include Sky and Virgin Media.

Weights & Measures Britain uses a mix of metric and imperial measures (eg petrol is sold by the litre but beer by the pint; mountain heights are in metres but road distances are in miles).

national rates and ☎089 or ☎09 for premium rates. Mobile phones start with ☎07 and calling them is more expensive than calling a landline. Dial ☎100 for an operator and ☎155 for an international operator as well as reverse-charge (collect) calls.

- To call outside the UK, dial ☎00, then the country code (☎1 for USA, ☎61 for Australia etc), the area code (you usually drop the initial zero) and the number.
- For directory enquiries, a host of agencies compete for your business and charge from 10p to 40p; numbers include ☎118 192, ☎118 118, ☎118 500 and ☎118 811.

TIME

Britain is on GMT/UTC. The clocks go forward for 'summer time' one hour at the end of March and go back at the end of October. The 24-hour clock is used for transport timetables.

VISAS

European Economic Area (EEA) nationals don't need a visa to visit (or work in) Britain. Citizens of Australia, Canada, New Zealand, South Africa and the USA can visit for up to six months (three months for some nationalities), but are prohibited from working. For more info see www.ukvisas.gov.uk.

Getting There & Away

AIR

London Airports

London is served by five airports; Heathrow and Gatwick are the busiest.

Gatwick (LGW; www.gatwickairport.com) Britain's number-two airport, mainly for international flights, 30 miles south of central London.

London City (LCY; www.londoncityairport.com)

London Heathrow Airport (www.heathrowairport.com) The UK's major hub welcoming flights from all over the world.

Luton (LTN; www.london-luton.co.uk) Some 35 miles north of central London, well known as a holiday-flight airport.

Stansted (STN; www.stanstedairport.com) About 35 miles northeast of central London, mainly handling charter and budget European flights.

Regional Airports

Bristol Airport (www.bristolairport.co.uk) Flights from all over Europe as well as some popular holidays destinations in North Africa and North America.

Cardiff Airport (☎01446-711111; www.cardiff-airport.com)

Edinburgh Airport (☎0844 448 8833; www.edinburghairport.com) Edinburgh Airport, 8 miles west of the city, has numerous flights to other parts of Scotland and the UK, Ireland and mainland Europe. **FlyBe/Loganair** (☎0871 700 2000; www.loganair.co.uk) operates daily flights to Inverness, Wick, Orkney, Shetland and Stornoway.

Glasgow International Airport (GLA; ☎0844 481 5555; www.glasgowairport.com) Ten miles west of the city, Glasgow International Airport handles domestic traffic and international flights.

Liverpool John Lennon Airport (☎0870 750 8484; www.liverpoolairport.com; Speke Hall Ave)

Manchester Airport (☎0161-489 3000; www.manchesterairport.co.uk) Manchester Airport, south of the city, is the largest airport outside London and is served by 13 locations throughout Britain as well as more than 50 international destinations.

ESSENTIAL FOOD & DRINK

Britain once had a reputation for bad food, but the nation has enjoyed something of a culinary revolution in the last decade or so, and you can often find fine dining based on fresh local produce.

- **Fish & chips** Long-standing favourite, best sampled in coastal towns.
- **Haggis** Scottish icon, mainly offal and oatmeal, traditionally served with 'tatties and neeps' (potatoes and turnips).
- **Sandwich** Global snack today, but an English invention from the 18th century.
- **Laverbread** Laver is a type of seaweed, mixed with oatmeal and fried to create this traditional Welsh speciality.
- **Ploughman's lunch** Bread and cheese – pub menu regular, perfect with a pint.
- **Roast beef & Yorkshire pudding** Traditional lunch on Sunday for the English.
- **Cornish pasty** Savoury pastry, southwest speciality, now available country-wide.
- **Real ale** Traditionally brewed beer, flavoured with malt and hops and served at room temperature.
- **Scotch whisky** Spirit distilled from malted and fermented barley, then aged in oak barrels for at least three years.

Newcastle International Airport (☎0871 882 1121; www.newcastleairport.com) Seven miles north of the city off the A696, the airport has direct services to many UK and European cities as well as long-haul flights to Dubai. Tour operators fly charters to the USA, Middle East and Africa.

LAND

Bus & Coach

The international network **Eurolines** (www.eurolines.com) connects a huge number of European destinations via the Channel Tunnel or ferry crossings.

Services to and from Britain are operated by **National Express** (www.nationalexpress.com).

Train

The quickest way to Europe from Britain is via the Channel Tunnel. High-speed **Eurostar** (www.eurostar.com) passenger services shuttle at least 10 times daily between London and Paris (2½ hours) or Brussels (two hours) via the Channel Tunnel. The normal one-way fare between London and Paris/Brussels costs £140 to £180; cheaper fares as low as £39 one way are possible via advance booking and by travelling off-peak.

Vehicles use the **Eurotunnel** (www.eurotunnel.com) at Folkestone in England or Calais in France. The trains run four times an hour from 6am to 10pm, then hourly. The journey takes 35 minutes. The one-way cost for a car and passengers is between £75 and £165 depending on time of day; promotional fares often bring it down to £55.

Travelling between Ireland and Britain, the main train–ferry–train route is Dublin to London, via Dun Laoghaire and Holyhead. Ferries also run between Rosslare and Fishguard or Pembroke (Wales), with train connections on either side.

SEA

Ferries sail from southern England to French ports in a couple of hours; other routes connect eastern England to the Netherlands, Germany and northern Spain, and Ireland from southwest Scotland and Wales.

The main ferry routes between Britain and mainland Europe include Dover to Calais or Boulogne (France), Harwich to Hook of Holland (Netherlands), Hull to Zeebrugge (Belgium) or Rotterdam (Netherlands), and Portsmouth to Santander or Bilbao (Spain). Routes to and from Ireland include Holyhead to Dun Laoghaire.

Competition from the Eurotunnel and budget airlines means ferry operators discount heavily

EATING PRICE RANGES

The prices we quote are for a main course at dinner unless otherwise indicated. The symbols used in each review indicate the following price ranges:

£ less than £9

££ £9 to £18

£££ more than £18

at certain times of year. The short cross-channel routes such as Dover to Calais or Boulogne can be as low as £20 for a car plus up to five passengers, although around £50 is more likely. If you're a foot passenger, or cycling, crossings can start from as little as £10 each way.

Broker sites covering all routes and options include www.ferrybooker.com and www.directferries.co.uk.

Brittany Ferries (www.brittany-ferries.com)
DFDS Seaways (www.dfds.co.uk)
Irish Ferries (www.irishferries.com)
P&O Ferries (www.poferries.com)
Stena Line (www.stenaline.com)

 Getting Around

For getting around Britain, your first choice is car or public transport. Having your own car makes the best use of time and helps reach remote places, but rental, fuel costs and parking can be expensive – so public transport is often the better way to go.

Cheapest but slowest are long-distance buses (called coaches in Britain). Trains are faster but much more expensive.

AIR

Britain's domestic air companies include **British Airways** (BA; www.britishairways.com), **Flybe/Loganair** (☎0871 700 2000; www.loganair.co.uk), **EasyJet** (EZY; www.easyjet.com) and **Ryanair** (FR; www.ryanair.com). On most shorter routes (eg London to Newcastle, or Manchester to Bristol), it's often faster to take the train once airport downtime is factored in.

BUS

Long-distance buses (coaches) nearly always offer the cheapest way to get around. Many towns have separate stations for local buses and intercity coaches; make sure you're in the right one.

National Express (www.nationalexpress.com) is England's main coach operator. North of the border, **Scottish Citylink** (www.citylink.co.uk) is the leading coach company. Tickets are cheaper if you book in advance and travel at quieter times. As a rough guide, a 200-mile trip (eg London to York) will cost around £15 to £30 if booked a few days in advance.

 **TRAVELINE**

Traveline (☎0871 200 2233; www.traveline.info) is a very useful information service covering bus, coach, taxi and train services nationwide.

Also offering cheap fares (if you're lucky, from £1) is **Megabus** (www.megabus.com), which serves about 30 destinations around Britain.

Bus Passes

National Express offers discount passes to full-time students and under-26s, called Young Persons Coachcards. They cost £10 and give 30% off standard adult fares. Also available are coachcards for people over 60, families and travellers with a disability.

For touring the country, National Express offers Brit Xplorer passes, allowing unlimited travel for seven days (£79), 14 days (£139) and 28 days (£219).

CAR & MOTORCYCLE

Most overseas driving licences are valid in Britain for up to 12 months from the date of entry.

Rental

Car rental is expensive in Britain; you'll pay from around £120 per week for the smallest model, or £250 per week for a medium-sized car (including insurance and unlimited mileage). All the major players including Avis, Hertz and Budget operate here.

Using a rental-broker site such as **UK Car Hire** (www.ukcarhire.net) or **Kayak** (www.kayak.com) can help find bargains.

It's illegal to drive a car or motorbike in Britain without (at least) third-party insurance. This is included with all rental cars.

Road Rules

The *Highway Code*, available in bookshops (or at www.gov.uk/highway-code), contains everything you need to know about Britain's road rules. The main ones to remember:

- Always drive on the left.
- Give way to your right at junctions and roundabouts.
- Always use the left-hand lane on motorways and dual carriageways, unless overtaking (passing).
- Wear seatbelts in cars and crash helmets on motorcycles.
- Don't use a mobile phone while driving.
- Don't drink and drive; the maximum blood-alcohol level allowed is 80mg/100mL (0.08%) in England and Wales, 50mg/100mL (0.05%) in Scotland.
- Yellow lines (single or double) along the edge of the road indicate parking restrictions; red lines mean no stopping whatsoever.
- Speed limits are 30mph in built-up areas, 60mph on main roads, and 70mph on motorways and dual carriageways.

TRAIN

About 20 different companies operate train services in Britain, while Network Rail operates tracks and stations. For some passengers this system can be confusing at first, but information and ticket-buying services are mostly centralised. If you have to change trains, or use two or more train operators, you still buy one ticket – valid for the whole journey. The main railcards and passes are also accepted by all train operators.

National Rail Enquiries (☎ 08457 48 49 50; www.nationalrail.co.uk) provides booking and timetable information for Britain's entire rail network.

Classes

Rail travel has two classes: 1st and standard. Travelling 1st class costs around 50% more than standard. At weekends some train operators offer 'upgrades' to first class for an extra £5 to £25 on top of your standard class fare, payable on the spot.

Costs & Reservations

The earlier you book, the cheaper it gets. You can also save if you travel 'off-peak' (ie the days and times that aren't busy). If you buy online, you can have the ticket posted (UK addresses only), or collect it from station machines on the day of travel.

There are three main fare types:

Anytime Buy anytime, travel anytime – usually the most expensive option.

Off-peak Buy anytime, travel off-peak (what is off-peak depends on the journey).

Advance Buy in advance, travel only on specific trains (usually the cheapest option).

Train Passes

If you're staying in Britain for a while, passes known as railcards (www.railcard.co.uk) are available:

16–25 Railcard For those aged 16 to 25, or a full-time UK student.

Senior Railcard For anyone over 60.

Family & Friends Railcard Covers up to four adults and four children travelling together.

Railcards cost £30 (valid for one year, available from major stations or online) and get 33% discount on most train fares, except those already heavily discounted. With the Family card, adults get 33% and children get 60% discounts, so the fee is easily repaid in a couple of journeys.

Regional Passes

Various local train passes are available covering specific areas and lines – ask at a local train station to get an idea of what's available.

National Passes

For country-wide travel, **BritRail** (www.britrail.net) passes are available for visitors from overseas. They must be bought in your country of origin (not in Britain) from a specialist travel agency. Available in seven different versions (eg England only; Scotland only; all Britain; UK and Ireland) for periods from four to 30 days.

Bulgaria

Includes ➡

Best Places to Eat

- Manastirska Magernitsa (p232)
- Mehana Chavkova House (p236)
- Han Hadji Nikoli (p241)
- Grazhdanski Klub (p238)
- Panorama (p246)

Best Places to Stay

- Red B&B (p232)
- Sofia Residence (p232)
- Hostel Old Plovdiv (p238)
- Hotel-Mehana Gurko (p241)
- Graffit Gallery Hotel (p243)

Why Go?

There's a lot to love about Bulgaria: just ask the Greeks, Romans, Byzantines and Turks, all of whom fought to claim it as their own. Billed as the oldest nation on the continent – it preceded ancient Greece by at least 1500 years – Bulgaria is rich with ancient treasure: stories abound of locals planting gardens only to have them ripped up by archaeologists after a turn of the spade unearthed priceless antiquities. The past has been preserved to remarkable effect; everything from Thracian tombs and Hellenic hoards to Roman ruins and medieval fortresses are easily accessible.

Centuries later, this Balkan beauty still beguiles, with a come-hither coastline, voluptuous mountain ranges and lush, fertile valleys laden with vines and roses. Plovdiv is the European Capital of Culture for 2019, Sofia has cool cred to rival any major metropolis, and the lively resorts of the Black Sea coast teem with modern-day pleasure pilgrims.

When to Go

Sofia

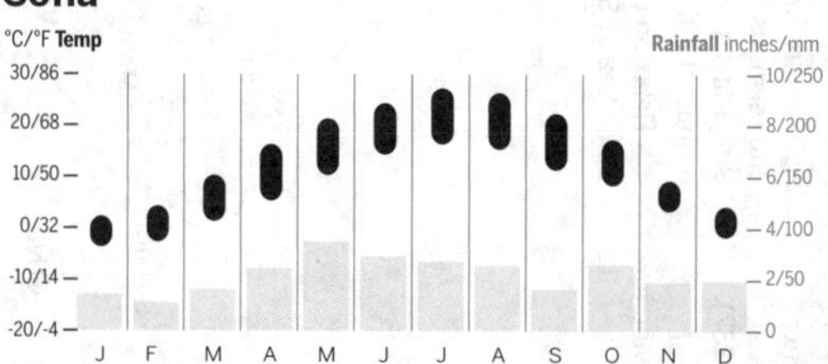

Feb Pop your cork at Melnik's Golden Grape Festival.

Jun Celebrate the sweetest harvest at Kazanlâk's Rose Festival.

Jul–Sep Spend lazy days on the Black Sea beaches and nights at Bulgaria's best clubs.

Bulgaria Highlights

1. Soak up the ancient ambience of **Plovdiv's** awesome Old Town (p237).
2. Sip a glass or two of Bulgarian vino in the wine town of **Melnik** (p235).
3. Explore the artistic and religious treasures of Bulgaria's most revered monastery at **Rila** (p235).
4. Relax on the sands of the Black Sea at **Sozopol** (p246).
5. Go clubbing, have a splash, and stroll through Primorski Park in cosmopolitan **Varna** (p243).
6. Head back in time through the National Revival houses in **Koprivshtitsa** (p239).
7. Visit the Tsars' medieval stronghold in **Veliko Târnovo** (p240).

ITINERARIES

One Week

Take a full day to hit **Sofia's** main attractions, then take the bus to **Veliko Târnovo** for a few days of sightseeing and hiking. For the rest of the week, head to **Varna** for some sea and sand, or veer south to the ancient beach towns of **Nesebâr** and **Sozopol**.

Two Weeks

Spend a few extra days in Sofia, adding in a day trip to Rila Monastery, then catch a bus to **Plovdiv** to wander the cobbled lanes of the Old Town. From there, take the mountain air in majestic Veliko Târnovo. Make for the coast, with a few nights in Varna and lively Sozopol.

SOFIA СОФИЯ

02 / POP 1.2 MILLION

Sofia (So-fia) is no Paris or Prague, but Bulgaria's capital and biggest city has a Balkan beguilement all its own. The old east-meets-west feel is still here, with a scattering of onion-domed churches, Ottoman mosques and stubborn Red Army monuments, and the city's grey, blocky architecture adds a lingering, interesting Soviet flavour to the place. Vast, leafy parks and manicured gardens offer welcome respite from the busy city streets and the ski slopes and hiking trails of mighty Mt Vitosha are right on the doorstep. With many of Bulgaria's finest museums and art galleries to explore and plenty of excellent bars, restaurants and entertainment venues, you may well end up sticking around for longer than you imagined.

Sights

Ploshtad Aleksander Nevski

★Aleksander Nevski Church CHURCH

(pl Aleksander Nevski; 7am-7pm) FREE One of *the* symbols not just of Sofia but of Bulgaria itself, this massive, awe-inspiring church was built between 1882 and 1912 in memory of the 200,000 Russian soldiers who died fighting for Bulgaria's independence during the Russo-Turkish War (1877–78).

Aleksander Nevski Crypt GALLERY

(Museum of Icons; pl Aleksander Nevski; adult/student 6/3 lv; 10am-5.30pm Tue-Sun; 1) Originally built as a final resting place for Bulgarian kings, this crypt now houses Bulgaria's biggest and best collection of icons, stretching back to the 5th century. Enter to the left of the eponymous church's main entrance.

Sveta Sofia Church CHURCH

(ul Parizh; museum adult/student 6/2 lv; 7am-7pm Apr-Oct, to 6pm Nov-Mar, museum 9am-5pm Tue-Sun; 9) Sveta Sofia Church is the capital's oldest, and gave the city its name. A newly opened subterranean **museum** houses an ancient necropolis, with 56 tombs and the remains of four other churches. Outside are the Tomb of the Unknown Soldier and an eternal flame, and the grave of Ivan Vazov, Bulgaria's most revered writer.

Sofia City Garden & Around

Royal Palace PALACE

(ul Tsar Osvoboditel; 20) Originally built as the headquarters of the Ottoman police force, it was here that Bulgaria's national hero, Vasil Levski, was tried and tortured before his public execution in 1873. After the liberation, the building was remodelled to become the official residence of Bulgaria's royal family. It houses the National Art Gallery and the Ethnographical Museum.

Ethnographical Museum MUSEUM

(Royal Palace; adult/student 3/1 lv; 10am-3.30pm Tue-Sun; 20) Displays on regional costumes, crafts and folklore are spread over two floors of the palace, and many of the rooms, with marble fireplaces, mirrors and ornate plasterwork, are worth pausing over themselves.

Archaeological Museum MUSEUM

(www.naim.bg; pl Nezavisimost; adult/student 10/2 lv; tours in English 20 lv; 10am-6pm May-Oct, to 5pm Tue-Sun Nov-Apr; 10) Housed in a former mosque built in 1496, this museum displays a wealth of Thracian, Roman and medieval artefacts. Highlights include a mosaic floor from the Church of Sveta Sofia, a 4th-century BC Thracian gold burial mask, and a magnificent bronze head, thought to represent a Thracian king.

Sveti Georgi Rotunda CHURCH

(Church of St George; www.svgeorgi-rotonda.com; bul Dondukov 2; daily services 8am, 9am & 5pm; 10) Built in the 4th century AD, this tiny

Sofia

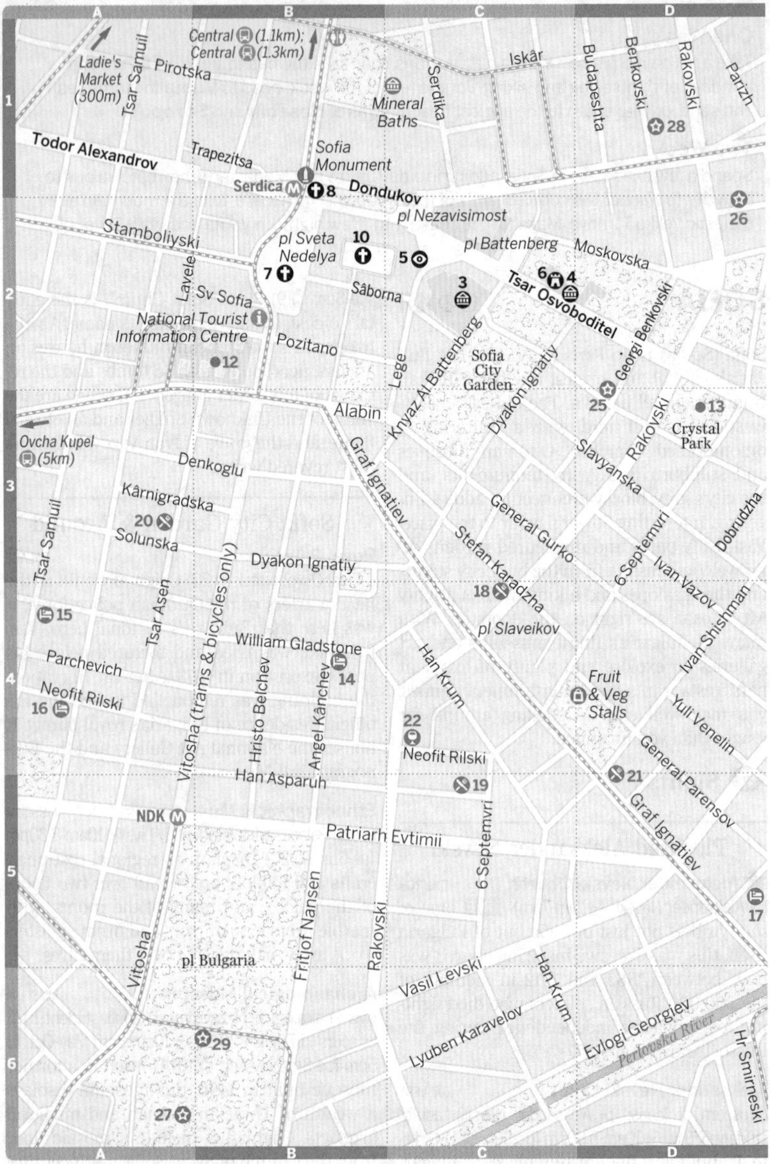

red-brick church is Sofia's oldest preserved building. The murals inside were painted between the 10th and 14th centuries. It's a busy, working church, but tourists are welcome.

President's Building NOTABLE BUILDING
(pl Nezavisimost; 🚊10) The Bulgarian president's office isn't open to the public, but the **changing of the guard** ceremony (on the hour) is a spectacle not to be missed; for the full ceremony, replete with music, weap-

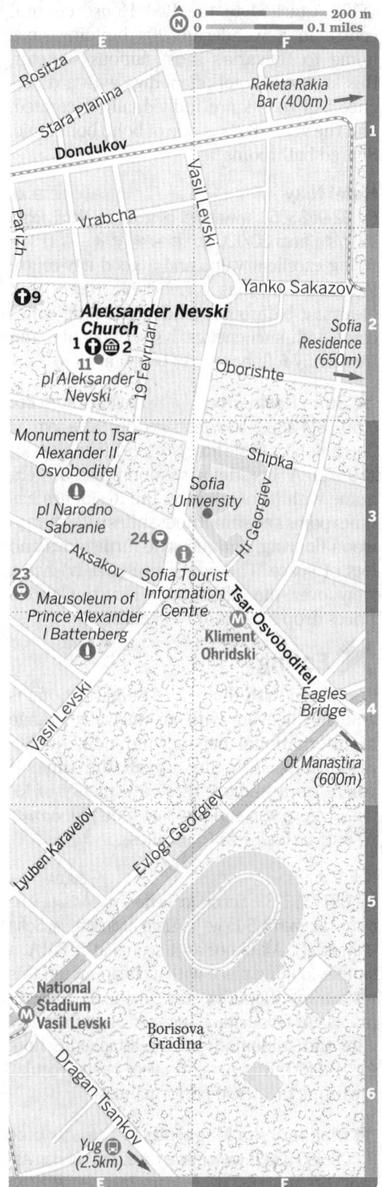

Sofia

Top Sights

1 Aleksander Nevski Church E2

Sights

2 Aleksander Nevski Crypt E2
3 Archaeological Museum C2
4 Ethnographical Museum C2
5 President's Building C2
6 Royal Palace C2
7 Sveta Nedelya Cathedral B2
8 Sveta Petka Samardzhiiska Church B1
9 Sveta Sofia Church E2
10 Sveti Georgi Rotunda B2

Activities, Courses & Tours

11 City Sighteeing Bus Tour E2
12 Free Sofia Tour B2
13 The New Sofia Pub Crawl D3

Sleeping

14 Art Hostel B4
15 Canapé Connection A4
16 Hotel Niky A4
17 Red B&B D5

Eating

18 K.E.V.A C4
19 Manastirska Magernitsa C5
20 Pastorant A3
21 The Little Things D5

Drinking & Nightlife

22 Bar Up C4
23 One More Bar E3
24 Yalta E3

Entertainment

25 Bulgaria Hall D3
26 National Opera House D2
27 National Palace of Culture A6
28 Rock It D1
29 Sofia Live Club B6

ons and all manner of pomp, be there on the first Wednesday of the month at noon.

Sveta Nedelya Cathedral CHURCH
(pl Sveta Nedelya; Ⓜ Serdika) Completed in 1863, this magnificent domed church is one of the city's major landmarks, noted for its rich, Byzantine-style murals. It was blown up by communists on 16 April 1925 in an attempt to assassinate Tsar Boris III.

Sveta Petka Samardzhiiska Church CHURCH
(bul Maria Luisa; Ⓜ Serdika) This tiny church was built during the early years of Ottoman rule (late 14th century), which explains its sunken profile and inconspicuous exterior. Inside are some 16th-century murals. It's rumoured that the Bulgarian national hero Vasil Levski is buried here.

Tours

Free Sofia Tour WALKING TOUR
(088 699 3977; www.freesofiatour.com; 11am & 6pm) FREE Explore Sofia's sights in the company of friendly and enthusiastic English-speaking young locals on this guided walk. No reservation is needed, just show up outside the Palace of Justice on bul Vitosha, at 11am or 6pm. Walks take around two hours.

New Sofia Pub Crawl TOUR
(087 761 3992; www.thenewsofiapubcrawl.com; tour 20 lv; 9pm-1am) Explore Sofia's secret haunts on this nightly knees-up. Expect lots of insights into the social side of the city (plus the odd free drink). Meet by the statue of Stefan Stambolov in Crystal Park.

City Sighteeing Bus Tour BUS TOUR
(www.citysightseeing.bg; 20 lv; hourly btwn 10am-1pm Wed-Sun) Get your bearings on this hop-on hop-off bus tour that takes in over 30 sights across Sofia. Starts on the hour at Aleksander Nevski Cathedral. Reservations required between October and March; just show up the rest of the year.

Sleeping

Accommodation in Sofia tends to be more expensive than anywhere else in Bulgaria, with prices comparable to those in Western European cities. Good-quality budget hotels are a rarity, and cheaper places that do exist are often either squalid dives or in awkward-to-reach locations; hostels are a better deal.

Art Hostel HOSTEL €
(02-987 0545; www.art-hostel.com; ul Angel Kânchev 21a; dm/s/d from 20/47/66 lv; ; 12) This bohemian hostel stands out from the crowd with its summertime art exhibitions, live music, dance performances and more. Dorms are appropriately arty and bright; private rooms are airy and welcoming. There's a great basement bar and peaceful little garden.

Canapé Connection HOSTEL €
(02-441 6373; www.canapeconnection.com; ul William Gladstone 12a; dm/s/d from 16/40/52 lv; @; 1) Run by three young travellers, Canapé is a homely place with eight- and four-bed dorms featuring wide bunks and wooden floors, as well as private rooms. Homemade *banitsa* (cheese pastry) and croissants are on the breakfast menu.

★ **Red B&B** B&B €€
(088 922 6822; www.redbandb.com; ul Lyuben Karavelov 15; s/d from 40/70 lv; @; M Vasil Levski, 10) Attached to the Red House cultural centre in a wonderful '20s building once home to Bulgaria's most famous sculptor, this six-room hotel offers digs with a difference. All rooms are individually decorated, and the general air is one of boho bonhomie. Shared bathrooms.

Hotel Niky HOTEL €€
(02-952 3058; www.hotel-niky.com; ul Neofit Rilski 16; r/ste from 80/120 lv; P; 1) Offering excellent value and a good city-centre location, Niky has comfortable rooms and gleaming bathrooms, and smart little suites come with kitchenettes. It's very popular and frequently full; be sure to book ahead.

★ **Sofia Residence** BOUTIQUE HOTEL €€€
(02-814 4888; www.residence-oborishte.com; ul Oborishte 63; s/d/ste from 176/195/215 lv; ; 9, 72) A luxurious salmon-pink '30s-era home with its own bistro, the Residence has nine rooms and sumptuous suites with cherry-wood flooring, antique-style furnishings and lots of space. The penthouse (254 lv) has a view over the Aleksander Nevski Church. Prices drop by 20% at weekends.

Eating

Compared with the rest of Bulgaria, Sofia is gourmet heaven, with an unrivalled range of international cuisine and new, quality restaurants springing up all the time. If you're on a budget, there are plenty of kiosks where you can buy fast food like *banitsa* and *palachinki* (pancakes).

K.E.V.A BULGARIAN €
(087 731 3233; School for Performing Arts, ul Rakovski 112; mains 5-15 lv; 11am-midnight; M Sofia Universitet) All is not as it seems at K.E.V.A, a simple-looking place with a cheap menu: this restaurant offers five-star cuisine at cafeteria prices. A favourite hang-out of Sofia's arty elite and students from the attached School for Performing Arts, it also hosts regular mealtime theatrical performances.

★ **Manastirska Magernitsa** BULGARIAN €€
(02-980 3883; www.magernitsa.com; ul Han Asparuh 67; mains 6-10 lv; 11am-2am; ; M NDK) This traditional *mehana* (tavern) is among the best places in Sofia to sample authentic Bulgarian cuisine. The enormous menu features recipes collected from monasteries across the country, with dishes such as 'drunken rabbit' stewed in wine as well as salads, fish, pork and game options. Portions are generous and service attentive.

The Little Things INTERNATIONAL €€
(☎088 249 0030; ul Tsar Ivan Shishman 37; mains 7-18 lv; ⊙noon-midnight; 🚎1) It's the little things – knickknacks, toys, books, flowers – that give this charming spot its name, but it's the large portions of delightful, home-style food that keep locals coming back for more. Mains includes handmade meatballs, sinful pastas and creamy fish dishes; whatever you do, try the fig cheesecake.

Pastorant ITALIAN €€€
(☎02-981 4482; www.pastorant.eu; ul Tsar Asen 16; mains 11-28 lv; ⊙noon-10.30pm; 🚭📝; Ⓜ NDK) This charming pea-green restaurant provides an intimate setting for high-quality Italian cuisine, including some inventive pasta and risotto dishes as well as traditional favourites like saltimbocca and pesto chicken.

Drinking & Nightlife

One More Bar BAR
(☎088 253 9592; ul Shishman 12; ⊙8am-2am; Ⓜ Sofia Universitet) Inside a gorgeous old house, this shabby-chic hotspot wouldn't be out of place in Melbourne or Manhattan: an extensive cocktail list, delightful summer garden and jazzy background music add to its cosmopolitan appeal.

Raketa Rakia Bar BAR
(☎02-444 6111; ul Yanko Sakazov 17; ⊙11am-midnight; 🚎11) Unsurprisingly, this rakish retro bar has a huge selection of *rakia* (fiery fermented fruit brandy) on hand; before you start working your way down the list, line your stomach with their meat-and-cream-heavy snacks and meals.

Bar Up BAR
(☎087 654 1641; ul Neofit Rilski 55; ⊙9am-midnight Mon-Thu, 9am-2am Fri-Sat, 11am-1am Sun; Ⓜ NPK) As you'd expect from a place that serves cocktails in jars and has furniture made from shipping pallets, this is a laid-back and arty place, with a regular roster of changing exhibitions to seal the deal.

Yalta CLUB
(www.yaltaclub.com; bul Tsar Osvoboditel 20; ⊙24hr; Ⓜ Sofia Universitet) Shake it with Sofia's trendy types and local and international DJ stars at this hip, hyper spot that's been going strong since 1959 (it was Bulgaria's first nightclub).

Entertainment

If you read Bulgarian, *Programata* is a comprehensive source of entertainment listings; otherwise check out its English-language website, www.programata.bg.

Live Music

Rock It LIVE MUSIC
(www.rockit.bg; ul Georgi Benkovski 14; ⊙7pm-4am Mon-Sat; Ⓜ Serdika) If you're into rock and metal, get your horns up here. This huge, two-level building shakes beneath the weight of heavy live bands, DJs and lots and lots of hair.

Sofia Live Club LIVE MUSIC
(www.sofialiveclub.com; pl Bulgaria 1; ⊙9pm-5am Wed-Sat; Ⓜ NDK) This slick venue is the city's largest live-music club. All swished up in cabaret style, it hosts local and overseas jazz, alternative, world music and rock acts.

Bulgaria Hall CLASSICAL MUSIC
(☎02-987 7656; www.sofiaphilharmonie.bg; ul Georgi Benkovski 1; ⊙ticket office 9am-8pm Mon-Fri, to 3pm Sat; 🚎9) Home of the excellent Sofia Philharmonic Orchestra.

Performing Arts

National Opera House OPERA
(☎02-987 1366; www.operasofia.bg; bul Dondukov 30, entrance on ul Vrabcha; ⊙ticket office 9am-2pm & 2.30-7pm Mon-Fri, 11am-7pm Sat, 11am-4pm Sun; 🚎9, 🚊20) Opened in 1953, this monumental edifice is the venue for grand opera and ballet performances, as well as concerts.

National Palace of Culture CONCERT VENUE
(NDK; ☎02-916 6300; www.ndk.bg; pl Bulgaria; ⊙ticket office 10am-8pm; 📶; Ⓜ NDK) The NDK (as it's usually called) has 15 halls and is the country's largest cultural complex. It maintains a regular program of events throughout the year, including film screenings, trade shows and big-name international music acts.

Shopping

Bulevard Vitosha is Sofia's main shopping street, featuring international brand-name boutiques interspersed with restaurants; the charming, rambling ul Pirotska is a central pedestrian mall lined with cheaper shops selling clothes, shoes and household goods.

Ladies' Market MARKET
(Zhenski Pazar; ul Stefan Stambolov; ⊙dawn-dusk; 🚊20) Stretching several blocks between ul Ekzarh Yosif and bul Slivnitsa, this is Sofia's biggest fresh-produce (and everything else) market. Beware pickpockets.

Ot Manastira FOOD
(From the Monastery; ☎088 775 8093; www.otmanastira.com; ul Ivan Asen II 54; ⊙10am-2pm &

3-7.30pm Mon-Fri, 10am-5.30pm Sat-Sun; Ⓜ Sofia Universitet) This small shop sells super-fresh fruit, vegetables, honey, relish and – on Fridays – fish (including caviar) all produced by the Kyustendil Monastery, 100km southwest of the city.

Information

National Tourist Information Centre (☎ 02-987 9778; www.bulgariatravel.org; ul Sveta Sofia; ⏲ 9am-5pm Mon-Fri; 🚊 5) Helpful, English-speaking staff and glossy brochures for destinations around Bulgaria.

Pirogov Hospital (☎ 02-915 4411; www.pirogov.bg; bul General Totleben 21; 🚊 4, 5) Sofia's main public hospital for emergencies.

Sofia Tourist Information Centre (☎ 02-491 8345; www.info-sofia.bg; Sofia University underpass; ⏲ 8am-8pm Mon-Fri, 10am-6pm Sat-Sun; Ⓜ Kliment Ohridski) Lots of free leaflets and maps, and helpful English-speaking staff.

Getting There & Away

AIR

Sofia Airport (☎ 02-937 2211; www.sofia-airport.bg; off bul Brussels; minibus 30) is 12km east of the city centre. The only domestic flights within Bulgaria are between Sofia and the Black Sea. **Bulgaria Air** (☎ 02-402 0400; www.air.bg; ul Ivan Vazov 2; ⏲ 8.30am-5pm Mon-Fri; 🚊 20) flies daily to Varna, with two or three daily flights between July and September; the airline also flies to Burgas.

BUS

Sofia's **central bus station** (Tsentralna Avtogara; www.centralnaavtogara.bg; bul Maria Luisa 100; 24hr; 🚊 7) is 100m south of the train station. There are dozens of counters for individual private companies, an information desk and an **OK-Supertrans taxi desk** (www.oktaxi.net; ⏲ 6am-10pm). Departures are less frequent between November and April. Frequent buses depart Sofia for Plovdiv (14 lv, 2½ hours), Veliko Târnovo (22 lv, four hours), Varna (33 lv, seven hours) and more; the easy-to-navigate www.bgrazpisanie.com has full local and international timetable and fare listings.

TRAIN

The **central train station** (bul Maria Luisa; 🚊 1, 7) is finally undergoing some much-needed renovations, scheduled to culminate in a shiny, user-friendly station in 2015. It's still operational, though travellers may find it easier to purchase tickets online (www.bdz.transportinfo.bg; you'll need to register) than battle the disruptions and typically chaotic ticket queues. Whatever you do, don't wait until the last minute to buy your tickets.

Destinations for all domestic and international services are listed on timetables in Cyrillic, but departures (for the following two hours) and arrivals (for the previous two hours) are listed in English on a large screen on the ground floor.

Sample fast train routes include Sofia to Plovdiv (12 lv, 2½ hours) and Varna (31 lv, seven hours): see www.bgrazpisanie.com (click on 'timetable') or www.bdz.bg for all domestic and international routes.

Getting Around

TO/FROM THE AIRPORT

At the time of research, Sofia Airport was linked to the city by minibus 30 (to and from pl Nezavisimost, 1.50 lv) and the slower, meandering buses 84 and 384 (from Terminals 1 and 2, respectively). These buses may be phased out once a new direct metro line – planned for completion in April 2015 – is opened.

CAR & MOTORCYCLE

Frequent public transport, cheap taxis and horrendous traffic provide little or no incentive to drive around Sofia. If you wish to explore further afield, though, renting a car is a great idea. Most majors (and cheaper local options) have offices at the airport; see www.sofia-airport.bg for a full list of companies.

PUBLIC TRANSPORT

Public transport – trams, buses, minibuses and trolleybuses, as well as the underground metro – run from 5.30am to 11pm every day.

Many buses, trams and trolleybuses are fitted with on-board ticket machines; all tickets within Sofia cost 1 lv. It's far easier and quicker, especially during peak times, to buy tickets from kiosks at stops along the route before boarding.

If you plan to use public transport frequently, buy a one-day/10-trip/one-month transit card (4/8/50 lv), valid for all lines (a monthly card just for the metro is 35 lv). All tickets must be validated by inserting them in the small machine on-board; once punched, tickets are nontransferable. Inspectors will issue on-the-spot fines (10 lv) if you don't have a ticket.

See www.sofiatraffic.bg for more information on public transport.

TAXI

By law, taxis must use meters, but those that wait around the airport, luxury hotels and within 100m of pl Sveta Nedelya will often try to negotiate an unmetered fare – which, of course, will be considerably more. All official taxis have fares per kilometre displayed in the window, and have obvious taxi signs (in English or Bulgarian) on top. **OK-Supertrans** (☎ 02-973 2121; www.oktaxi.net) or **Yellow Taxi** (☎ 02-91 119; www.yellow333.com) are reliable operators.

SOUTHERN BULGARIA

Some of Bulgaria's most precious treasures are scattered in the towns, villages and forests of the stunning south. The must-visit medieval Rila Monastery is nestled in the deep forest but easily reached by bus; tiny Melnik is awash in ancient wine; and the cobbled streets of Plovdiv, Bulgaria's second city, are lined with timeless reminders of civilisations come and gone.

The region is a scenic and craggy one; the **Rila Mountains** (www.rilanationalpark.bg) are just south of Sofia, the **Pirin Mountains** (www.pirin-np.com) rise towards the Greek border, and the Rodopi Mountains loom to the east and south of Plovdiv. There's great hiking to be had, and the south is also home to three of Bulgaria's most popular ski resorts: **Borovets**, **Bansko** and **Pamporovo**; see www.bulgariaski.com for information.

Rila Monastery

Рилски Манастир

Many Bulgarians say you haven't really been to Bulgaria until you've paid your respects to the truly heavenly, Unesco-listed **Rila Monastery** (www.rilamonastery.pmg-blg.com; ⌚7am-9pm) FREE, 120km south of Sofia. Built in 927 and heavily restored in 1469, the monastery was a stronghold of Bulgarian culture and language during Ottoman rule. Set in a magnificent forested valley ideal for hiking, the monastery is rightfully famous for its mural-plastered Nativity Church dating from the 1830s. The attached **museum** (Rila Monastery; 8 lv; ⌚8am-5pm) is home to the astonishing Rila Cross, with biblical scenes painstakingly carved in miniature. Visitors should dress modestly.

If you have time, hike up to the **Tomb of St Ivan**, the hermit founder of the monastery. The 15-minute walk begins along the road 3.7km east behind the monastery.

You can stay in simple **rooms** (☎089 687 2010; www.rilamonastery.pmg-blg.com; r 30-60 lv) at the monastery, or for something slightly more upmarket, try **Gorski Kut** (☎07054-2170; d from 50 lv; P ❄), an easy 5km away.

From Sofia's **Ovcha Kupel** (☎02-955 5362; bul Ovcha Kupel 1, also called 'Zapad', or 'West' station), one daily morning bus (12 lv, 2½ hours) goes to the monastery and returns in the afternoon. Five daily buses go to and from Rila village (4 lv). Otherwise, the **Rila Monastery Bus** (☎02-489 0883; www.rilamonasterybus.com; €25; ⌚Apr-Nov) departs Sofia at 9am, takes in the monastery and Boyana, and returns at 5pm.

Melnik Мелник

☎07437 / POP 385

Officially Bulgaria's smallest town, Melnik is one of the country's most famous wine centres. Family-run *mehanas* boast their own barrels of blood-red Melnik, the unique local varietal, which is sold in plastic jugs on the dirt streets.

Sights

The major sights here, unsurprisingly, are wineries. Melnik's wines, celebrated for more than 600 years, include the signature dark red, Shiroka Melnishka Loza; it was a favourite tipple of Winston Churchill. Shops and stands dot Melnik's cobblestone paths, with reds and whites for 3 lv to 4 lv and up.

Museum of Wine MUSEUM
(www.muzei-na-vinoto.com; ul Melnik 91; admission 5 lv; ⌚10am-7pm) Learn the history of winemaking in Melnik, ogle the 400-plus bottles of wine on display (the dirt vault is especially cool), and work your way through a tasting menu at this fun museum attached to the Hotel Bulgari. Once you find one (or four) wines that you like, fill a bottle and they'll personalise a label for you.

Mitko Manolev Winery WINERY
(Shestaka; ☎07437-2215; www.shestaka.com; admission incl tasting 2 lv; ⌚9am-dusk) For the most atmospheric adventures in *degustatsia* (wine tasting), clamber up the cobblestones to this winery, also known as Shestaka ('six-fingered'); it's named after the founder, who had an extra digit (as does his modern-day descendant Mitko). This place is basically a cellar dug into the rocks, plus a hut with tables and chairs outside. It's along the hillside trail between the Bolyaskata Kâshta ruins and the Kordopulov House. Accommodation is also available (double 35 lv).

Kordopulov House MUSEUM
(☎07437-2265; www.kordopulova-house.com; admission 3 lv; ⌚8am-8pm) Built in 1754, this four-storey former home of a prestigious wine merchant is an impressive structure. The sitting rooms have been carefully restored, and boast 19th-century murals, stained-glass windows and exquisitely carved wooden ceilings. An enormous wine cellar (tasting

WORTH A TRIP

MT VITOSHA & BOYANA

At the southern edge of Sofia, Mt Vitosha is popular for skiing and hiking at a cheaper rate than the ski resorts (it's about 30 lv for a lift ticket). The mountain is part of the 227-sq-km **Vitosha Nature Park** (www.park-vitosha.org), the oldest of its kind in Bulgaria (created in 1934). The highest point is Mt Cherni Vrâh (Black Peak; 2290m), the fourth-highest peak in Bulgaria.

Chairlifts, starting around 3km from the village of **Dragalevtsi**, run all year up to Goli Vrâh (1837m); another option is the six-person gondola at Simeonovo (Friday to Sunday only).

A trip out here could be combined with a visit to **Boyana**, home to the fabulous, Unesco-listed **Boyana Church** (www.boyanachurch.org; ul Boyansko Ezero 3; adult/student 10/1 lv, combined ticket with National Historical Museum 12 lv, guide 10 lv; ⌚9.30am-5.30pm Apr-Oct, 9am-5pm Nov-Mar; 🚌64, minibus 21), built between the 11th and 19th centuries. Its interior is adorned with colourful murals painted in 1259 that are considered among the most important examples of medieval Bulgarian art.

The decent **National Historical Museum** (www.historymuseum.org; bul Vitoshko Lale 16; adult/student 10/1 lv, combined ticket with Boyana Church 12 lv, guide 20 lv; ⌚9.30am-6pm Tue-Sun Apr-Oct, to 5.30pm Nov-Mar) is also found in Boyana. It's worth a look for the Thracian artefacts and 19th-century costumes and weapons, although many are reproductions.

Minibus 21 runs to Boyana from the city centre (hop on at bul Vasil Levski), and will drop you at the gates of the museum; it also connects the museum with the church. Alternatively, take bus 64 from Hladilnika terminal on ul Srebârna, or a taxi (about 8 to 10 lv one-way); for the museum, ask for 'Residentsia Boyana'.

available) includes 180m of illuminated labyrinthine passageways; look out for the wall full of glittering coins. The house is on the cliff face at the street's end, south of the creek: you can't miss it.

Festivals & Events

Golden Grape Festival WINE

Vino tastings, music and all manner of wine-centric wassailing. Held on the second weekend of February.

Sleeping

Most wineries offer accommodation; also look out for the 'rooms to sleep' (стаи за спане) signs in windows.

Hotel Bulgari HOTEL €

(☎7437-2215; www.hotelbulgari.net; ul Melnik 91; s/d/apt from 30/50/80 lv; 📶) This imposing building seems out of place in little old Melnik but its shiny, sleek and spacious rooms go down a treat. While the cavernous restaurant is more suitable for banquets than intimate dining, the attached wine museum is a great spot for a tipple.

★**Hotel Bolyarka** HOTEL €€

(☎07437-2383; www.melnikhotels.com; ul Melnik 34; s/d/apt incl breakfast 40/60/100 lv; P ❄ @ 📶) The spiffy Bolyarka has elegant and well-decorated rooms, and apartments with fireplaces. Sauna and massage treatments are available, but the authentic Ottoman-era hammam (Turkish bath) is for viewing only. The on-site restaurant is excellent.

Eating

All wine and no dine can make for delirious days; thankfully Melnik also excels in eateries. Try the traditional *banitsa*, a local speciality, and the mountain river trout.

★**Mehana Chavkova House** BULGARIAN €€

(☎089 350 5090; ul Melnik 112; 5-10 lv) Sit beneath the 500-year-old trees and watch Melnik meander past at this superb spot. Like many places in town, grilled meats and Bulgarian dishes are specialities (try the 'sach', a sizzling flat pan of meat and vegetables); the atmosphere and super-friendly service gives it that extra nudge above the rest.

Mehana Mencheva Kâshta BULGARIAN €€

(☎07437-2339; mains 6-11 lv; ⌚10am-11.30pm) This tiny tavern has a lovely upper porch overlooking the main street down towards the end of the village. It's popular with locals and does the full run of Bulgarian dishes.

Getting There & Away

One daily direct bus connects Melnik with Sofia (17 lv, four hours) though times vary. One daily direct bus serves Blagoevgrad (9 lv, two hours) near the border with Macedonia.

Plovdiv Пловдив

032 / POP 341,040

Awash in art galleries, bohemian cafes, museums and highbrow house museums, it's little wonder Plovdiv has been named the European Capital of Culture for 2019. A smaller, less stressful city than Sofia, pretty Plovdiv is an ideal walking city; as a lively university town, it's also on the fun frontline, with laid-back bars galore.

The past lives on in Plovdiv's atmospheric Old Town, largely restored to its mid-19th-century appearance and marked by winding cobblestone streets. Lined with historic homes, antique shops and creative salons, Plovdiv differs from 'Old Towns' in that eminent artists still live and work within its tranquil confines. The neighbourhood boasts Thracian, Roman, Byzantine and Bulgarian antiquities, most impressive being the Roman amphitheatres – the best-preserved in the Balkans and still used for performances.

Sights

Most of Plovdiv's main sights are in and around the fantastic Old Town. Its meandering cobblestone streets, overflowing with atmospheric house museums, art galleries and antique stores, are also home to welcoming nooks for eating, drinking and people-watching.

★Roman Amphitheatre HISTORIC SITE

(ul Hemus; adult/student 5/2 lv; 9am-6pm) Plovdiv's magnificent 2nd-century-AD amphitheatre, built during the reign of Emperor Trajan, was only uncovered during a freak landslide in 1972. It could hold about 6000 spectators. Now largely restored, it's one of Bulgaria's most magical venues, once again hosting large-scale special events and concerts. Visitors can admire the amphitheatre for free from several lookouts along ul Hemus, or pay admission for a scarper around.

Roman Stadium HISTORIC SITE

(www.ancient-stadium-plovdiv.eu; 9am-6pm) While the once-huge 2nd-century Roman Stadium is mostly hidden under the pedestrian mall, there are stairways from different sides allowing for at-your-leisure exploration. A new on-site 3D movie (adult/student 6/3 lv; 10 showings daily) offers an immersive experience into the stadium's glory days as a venue for gladiator matches.

Roman Odeon RUIN

Constructed between the 2nd and 5th centuries AD, the Odeon was once the seat of the city council. It now hosts occasional performances in its tiny reconstructed amphitheatre: check out the original columns. It's adjacent to the tourist information centre.

Ethnographical Museum MUSEUM

(032-626 328; www.ethnograph.info; ul Dr Chomakov 2; adult/student 5/2 lv; 9am-6pm Tue-Sun May-Oct, 9am-5pm Tue-Sun Nov-Apr) This museum houses 40,000 exhibits, including folk costumes, musical instruments, jewellery and traditional craftworks such as winemaking and beekeeping. Built in 1847, it's Plovdiv's most renowned National Revival–period home; the gorgeous garden and exquisite exterior are reasons enough to make a visit.

Church of Sveti Konstantin & Elena CHURCH

(ul Sâborna 24; 8am-7pm) This is Plovdiv's oldest church and one of its most beloved: the riotous frescoes and gilded iconostasis within belie its broody exterior. The original church – dedicated to Emperor Constantine the Great and his mother, Helena – was built in AD 337; what stands today dates to 1832.

Dzhumaya Mosque MOSQUE

(pl Dzhumaya; 6am-11pm) This, the second-oldest working mosque in Europe, was originally built in 1364, then demolished and rebuilt in the mid-15th century. With a 23m-high minaret, it was the largest of Plovdiv's more than 50 Ottoman mosques.

Tours

Free Plovdiv Tours WALKING TOUR

(www.freeplovdivtour.com; 6pm May-Sep, 2pm Oct-Apr) FREE Free two-hour-long walks taking in Plovdiv's prime attractions. Meet under the clock at the central post office in pl Tsentralen.

Sleeping

Hikers Hostel HOSTEL €

(089 676 4854; www.hikers-hostel.org; ul Sâborna 53; dm/tw from 14/50 lv; @) With a mellow, central location in the Old Town, Hikers has standard dorms and facilities, but

bonuses such as a garden lounge, hammocks and mega-friendly staff make it a worthy option. They also have off-site private rooms available; ask when booking.

9th Kilometre Complex CAMPGROUND €
(☎088 814 8174; www.9km.bg; Pazardzhiko shose; camping per person from 4 lv, caravan 6 lv, summer-only bungalow 22 lv, r renovated/unrenovated 35/30 lv; ⏲year-round; P 📶 🏊) This snazzy, family-friendly campground features a restaurant, 24-hour bar, playground and large outdoor pool. A taxi out here should cost about 12 lv. It's best to phone for bookings, rather than go through the website.

★ **Hostel Old Plovdiv** HOSTEL €€
(☎032-260 925; www.hosteloldplovdiv.com; ul Chetvarti Yanuari 3; dm/s/tw/tr/q €12/25/35/39/45; P 📶) This marvellous old building (1868) is more akin to a boutique historical hotel than a run-of-the-mill hostel. Remarkably restored by charismatic owner Hristo Giulev and his wife, this genial place – in the middle of the Old Town – is about warm welcomes and old-world charm. Every room features local antiques (from the decor to the beds themselves), and the courtyard is desperately romantic with a history all its own (Hristo will fill you in over a glass of their special iced tea).

Hotel Dafi HOTEL €€
(☎032-620 041; www.hoteldafi.com; ul Giorgi Benkovski 23; s/d/ste 49/69/120 lv; P ❄ 📶) With its mirrored tower and bland facade, the Dafi looks a bit like a small office tower from the outside, but its location in the Kapana district, comfortable rooms and astonishingly friendly staff ensure that mediocrity doesn't get a look-in. There's a good little cafe attached.

Hotel Globus HOTEL €€
(☎032-686 464; www.hotelglobus-bg.com; bul 6 Septemvri 38; d/tr/apt 69/90/120 lv; P ❄ 📶) A short walk from the Old Town and surrounded by lots of shops and cafes, the Globus has English-speaking staff and a popular restaurant attached. Rooms are sparkling; the huge, oddly windowless apartment – with over-the-top furniture, full-length heart-shaped mirror and a bear rug – must be seen to be believed.

Hotel Odeon BOUTIQUE HOTEL €€€
(☎032-622 065; www.hotelodeon.net; ul Otets Paisii 40; s/d/apt 94/117/205 lv; P ❄ 📶) Aptly named (it's across from the Roman Odeon), this restored home/hotel keeps the theme going with Roman-style columns in some rooms and an elegant old-world feel throughout. The attached restaurant has a creative and extensive vegan menu, as well as sophisticated options for carnivores.

Eating

King's Stables BULGARIAN €
(☎088 981 4255; ul Sâborna 40; mains 4-7 lv; ⏲9am-2am) The sprawling, summer-only King's Stables occupies a rolling hill ending in Roman walls. Offerings range from breakfast crepes to hearty meat dishes: be prepared to be shaken down for whatever you're eating by the trillion (clean) kittens roaming the joint. It's a lively spot, with local bands playing most nights.

Rahat Tepe GRILL €
(☎087 845 0259; ul Dr Chomakov 20; mains 4-8 lv; ⏲10am-midnight) Way up in the Old Town, the alfresco Rahat Tepe serves simple meals such as salads, beef kebabs and fried fish. Suitably rustic with great city views, it's an ideal spot for a nosh after clambering around Nebet Tepe (Nebet Hill).

★ **Grazhdanski Klub** BULGARIAN €€
(Citizens Club; ul Stoyan Chalukov 1; mains 5-12 lv; ⏲8am-1am Mon-Fri, 10am-1am Sat & Sun; 📶) A locals' favourite, this fabulous, friendly nook is just a totter down the hill from the Roman Amphitheatre. Its cool, green courtyard is a haven in hotter months. The food – mostly Bulgarian staples and sinful salads – is moreish: thankfully, portions are huge! It's attached to the endearing, free-to-enter Vazrazdane Gallery (open 10am to 6.30pm Monday to Saturday, 11am to 5pm Sunday).

Dayana GRILL €€
(☎032-623 027; ul Dondukov Korsakov 2; mains 5-9 lv; ⏲24hr; 📶) This big, popular place has a huge (and colourful) menu strong on grilled meats. Portions are fit to feed an army.

Hemingway INTERNATIONAL €€€
(☎032-267 350; www.hemingway.bg; ul Gurko 10; mains 5-22 lv; ⏲noon-1am) Papa would approve. This atmospheric spot near the Odeon comes across all 1920s Paris; it even smells like freshly baked baguettes. Seafood is a speciality, though posh takes on meaty Bulgarian classics get a good run. Unobtrusive live music provides a classy soundtrack to your meal.

Drinking & Nightlife

There are some great haunts in the Kapana district; the name means 'the trap', referring to its tight streets (north of pl Dzhumaya, between ul Rayko Daskalov to the west and bul Tsar Boris Obedinitel to the east).

★**Art Club Nylon** BAR
(088 949 6750; ul Giorgi Benkovski 8, Kapana; noon-4am Mon-Sat;) A bastion of bohemia, this damp, bare-bones but somehow wonderful place often hosts rock and indie bands playing to Plovdiv's cool kids.

Apartment 101 BAR
(ul William Gladston 8; 10am-1am Sun-Thu, to 2am Fri & Sat) A hip – but not painfully so – spot in a wonderfully ramshackle building with chill-out music and occasional live acts. The interior is op-shop chic; you'll have to be crowbarred out of the eminently hang-outable courtyard.

Petnoto CLUB
(ul Ioakim Gruev 36, Kapana; 8am-6am;) Meet the locals at this happy honkytonk, which hosts frequent music, literary, art and cinema events; it's a great place for a tipple even if nothing's on.

Club Infi CLUB
(088 828 1431; Bratya Pulievi 4, Kapana; 9pm-6am;) Packed with students, this dancey place parties until dawn...and then some.

Information

Tourist Information Centre (www.visitplovdiv.com; pl Tsentralen 1; 8.45am-noon & 12.45-6pm Mon-Fri, 10am-2pm Sat & Sun) Helpful centre near the post office providing maps and info. There's another office (ul Sâborna 22; 9am-12.30pm & 1-5.30pm Mon-Fri, 10am-2pm Sat & Sun) in the Old Town.

Getting There & Away

BUS

Plovdiv's main station is **Yug bus station** (032-626 937; bul Hristo Botev 47). Yug is diagonally opposite the train station and a 15-minute walk from the centre. Taxis cost 5 to 7 lv; local buses 7, 20 and 26 stop across the street. Frequent routes include Plovdiv to Sofia (12 lv, 2½ hours), Burgas (20 lv, five hours) and Varna (26 lv, seven hours). Check out www.bgrazpisanie.com for full destination and fare info.

The **Sever bus station** (ul Dimitar Stambolov 2), in the northern suburbs, serves destinations to the north of Plovdiv, including Veliko Târnovo (18 lv, four hours).

TRAIN

Daily direct services from the **train station** (bul Hristo Botev) include trains to Sofia (9 lv, three hours) and Burgas (14.60 lv, five hours); see www.bgrazpisanie.com or www.bdz.bg for all fares and timetables.

CENTRAL BULGARIA

The historic heart of Bulgaria beats its strongest in the country's mountainous centre. The country's past is played out in scenic settlements on both sides of the dramatic Stara Planina range; to the west, the museum village of Koprivshtitsa is renowned for its 18th- and 19th-century National Revival houses, while the lowlands town of Kazanlâk is the jumping-off point for visiting both the ancient Thracian tombs of the Valley of the Kings and the famously fragrant Valley of the Roses. The centre's hub is the magnificent Veliko Târnovo, former capital of the Bulgarian tsars; built into steep hills and bisected by a river, its medieval Tsarevets Fortress is among Europe's most spectacular citadels.

Koprivshtitsa

Копривщица

07184 / POP 2540

This romantic museum village, nestled in wooded hills between Karlovo and Sofia, is a perfectly preserved hamlet filled with Bulgarian National Revival–period architecture, cobblestone streets, and bridges that arc gently over a lovely brook. Nearly 400 buildings of architectural and historical significance are protected by government decree.

Sights

Koprivshtitsa boasts six house museums. Some are closed either on Monday or Tuesday; all keep the same hours (9.30am to 5.30pm April to October, 9am to 5pm November to March). To buy a combined ticket for all (adults/students 5/3 lv), visit the souvenir shop **Kupchinitsa**, near the tourist information centre (p240).

Oslekov House HISTORIC BUILDING
(ul Gereniloto 4; 9.30am-5.30pm Apr-Oct, 9am-5pm Nov-Mar, closed Mon) The Oslekov House (1853–6) was built by a rich merchant killed in the line of duty during the 1876 April Uprising. It's arguably the best example of Bulgarian National Revival–period architecture in Koprivshtitsa.

Kableshkov House HISTORIC BUILDING
(ul Todor Kableshkov 8; 9.30am-5.30pm Apr-Oct, 9am-5pm Nov-Mar, closed Mon) Todor Kableshkov is revered as having (probably) been the

person who fired the first shot in the 1876 uprising against the Turks. This, his glorious former home (1845), has exhibits about the April Uprising.

Sleeping & Eating

Hotel Kozlekov HOTEL €
(☎07184-3077; www.hotelkozlekov.com; ul Georgi Benkovski 8; d/studio from 50/60 lv; P @) Rustic as it gets but with amazingly modern service, this hilltop hotel is attached to a superb restaurant serving hearty Bulgarian classics. Staff speak English; some rooms have balconies.

Hotel Astra HOTEL €
(☎07184-2033; www.hotelastra.org; bul Hadzhi Nencho Palaveev 11; d/apt 50/70 lv; P) Set beautifully in a garden, the hospitable Astra is a popular place with large, well-kept rooms.

Dyado Liben BULGARIAN €€
(☎07184-2109; bul Hadzhi Nencho Palaveev 47; mains 4-9 lv; ⏲11am-midnight; 📶) This traditional restaurant housed in a huge 1852 mansion is a wonderfully atmospheric – and inexpensive – place for a hearty evening meal. It's just across the bridge leading from the main square inside the facing courtyard.

Information

There are ATMs and a post office/telephone centre in the village centre.

Tourist Information Centre (www.koprivshtitza.com; pl 20 April; ⏲10am-1pm & 2-7pm) This helpful, friendly centre in a small maroon building on the main square provides local information.

Getting There & Away

Getting to Koprivshtitsa is a bit of a challege. Being 9km north of the village, the train station requires a shuttle bus (2 lv, 15 minutes), which isn't always timed to meet incoming trains. Trains do come from Sofia (6 lv, 2½ hours, eight daily) and Burgas (19 lv, five hours, two daily). Koprivshtitsa's bus stop is more central; there are four daily buses to Sofia (13 lv, two hours) and one to Plovdiv (12 lv, two hours).

Veliko Târnovo
Велико Търново

☎062 / POP 68,780

The evocative capital of the medieval Bulgarian tsars, sublime Veliko Târnovo is dramatically set amid an amphitheatre of forested hills, divided by the ribboning Yantra River. Commanding pride of place is the magisterial Tsarevets Fortress, citadel of the Second Bulgarian Empire. It's complemented by scores of churches and other ruins, many still being unearthed. As the site of Bulgaria's most prestigious university, Veliko Târnovo also boasts a revved-up nightlife that many larger towns would envy. Top-notch city restaurants offer commanding views of the river and castle; head to the Varosha quarter and the impossibly quaint Samovodska Charshiya to grab a bite (and a bargain) in olde worlde surrounds.

Sights

★**Tsarevets Fortress** FORTRESS
(adult/student 6/2 lv, scenic elevator 2 lv; ⏲8am-7pm Apr-Oct, 9am-5pm Nov-Mar) The inescapable symbol of Veliko Târnovo, this reconstructed fortress dominates the skyline, and is one of Bulgaria's most beloved monuments. The former seat of the medieval tsars, it boasts the remains of more than 400 houses, 18 churches, the royal palace, an execution rock and more. Watch your step: there are lots of potholes, broken steps and unfenced drops. The fortress morphs into a psychedelic spectacle with a magnificent night-time sound-and-light show, held on public holidays.

Tsarevgrad Tarnov Wax Museum WAX MUSEUM
(ul Nikola Pikolo 6; adult/child 10/5 lv; ⏲9am-7pm) En route to the Fortress is this new wax museum showcasing the medieval glory days of Veliko Târnovo. Explore the well-crafted figures (everyone from kings to craftsmen get a look-in), catch an explanatory film, or get in the mood playing dress-up in period costume (5 lv).

Sarafkina Kâshta MUSEUM
(ul General Gurko 88; adult/student 6/2 lv; ⏲9am-6pm Tue-Sat) Built in 1861 by a rich Turkish moneylender, this fine five-storey National Revival–style house-museum displays antique ceramics, metalwork, woodcarvings, traditional costumes and jewellery.

Veliko Târnovo Archaeological Museum MUSEUM
(ul Ivanka Boteva 2; adult/student 6/2 lv; ⏲9am-6pm Tue-Sun) Housed in a grand old building with a courtyard full of Roman sculptures, the museum contains Roman artefacts and medieval Bulgarian exhibits including a huge mural of the tsars, plus some ancient gold from nearby neolithic settlements.

Samovodska Charshiya HISTORIC AREA
This atmospheric, cobblestoned historical quarter was Veliko Târnovo's biggest market

square in the 1880s, and remains the place to come to shop, stroll and admire the town's many National Revival–era houses.

Ulitsa Gurko HISTORIC SITE

The oldest street in Veliko Târnovo, ul Gurko is a must-stroll. Overlooking the River Yantra, its charmingly crumbling period houses – which appear to be haphazardly piled on one another – provide a million photo-ops and conversations that start with 'Imagine living here...' Sturdy shoes a must.

Sleeping

Hotel Comfort HOTEL €

(088 777 7265; www.hotelcomfortbg.com; ul P Tipografov 5; d/apt from 40/100 lv;) With jaw-dropping views of the fortress and surrounding hills, plus a stellar location just around the corner from the Samovodska Charshiya market square, this family-owned hotel is a winner. English is spoken by the amiable staff.

Hikers Hostel HOSTEL €

(0889 691 661; www.hikers-hostel.org; ul Rezervoarska 91; dm/d from 14/20 lv; @) Târnovo's most laid-back hostel, Hikers has an unassuming location high in Varosha's old quarter (a 10-minute walk from downtown). Owner Toshe Hristov does free bus/train station pick-ups and runs trips. Dorms are spartan but clean.

★ **Hotel-Mehana Gurko** HISTORIC HOTEL €€

(062-627 838; www.hotel-gurko.com; ul General Gurko 33; s/d/apt from 50/90/100 lv; @) You can't miss this gorgeous place, with riotous blooms and ye olde curios bedecking its restored 19th-century facade. Sitting pretty on Veliko Târnovo's oldest street, the Gurko is one of the best places to sleep (and eat) in town; rooms are spacious and soothing, each individually decorated and offering great views.

Old Town Apartment APARTMENT €€

(087 867 5356, 087 888 1281; ul Rakovski 4, Samovodska Charshiya; whole apt 90 lv, price drops by 10% after the 1st night;) One of the best, and best-located, digs in town, this private apartment has two balconies – one directly atop the cobblestoned Samovodska Charshiya, the other taking in a sweeping view of the entire city – a well-equipped kitchen, and a wonderful bedroom. Charming owner Tsvetelina arranges parking, baby paraphernalia and whatever else you need for a great stay.

Hotel Bolyarski HOTEL €€€

(062-613 200; www.bolyarski.com; ul Stefan Stambolov 53a; s/d incl breakfast from 70/130 lv;) The schmick Bolyarski has a phenomenal location on the bluff on ul Stambolov, with magical views of the town and river. Its modern, well-kept rooms are pitched at business travellers. Great on-site restaurant.

Eating & Drinking

Shtastlivetsa BULGARIAN €€

(062-600 656; ul Stefan Stambolov 79; mains 7-17 lv; 11am-1am;) A local institution, the 'Lucky Man' (as the impossible-to-pronounce name means in Bulgarian) has an ideal location overlooking the river's bend and a long menu of inventive meat dishes, baked-pot specials, superb pizzas and lunchtime soups – every visitor to Veliko Târnovo comes here at least once.

Hunter INTERNATIONAL €€

(088 821 0960; ul Aleksandar Stamboliyski 2; mains 5-18 lv; 8am-midnight;) As the name suggests, they do love their meat at Hunter. It's set in a pleasant garden (the woodsman's house interior is cosy in colder months) with the requisite resident cats angling for a bite of melt-in-your-mouth barbecue ribs or the ever-popular *shkembe chorba* (tripe soup). It's a mellow location for a beer or 10 as well.

★ **Han Hadji Nikoli** INTERNATIONAL €€€

(062-651 291; www.hanhadjinikoli.com; ul Rakovski 19; mains 17-30 lv;) Veliko Târnovo's finest restaurant, Han Hadji Nikoli occupies a beautifully restored 1858 building with an upstairs art gallery. High-end treats include escargots bourguignon, mussels sautéed in white wine and exquisitely prepared pork neck. A 'gourmet room' out the back has a secret menu for extreme epicures.

Tequila Bar BAR

(ul Stefan Stambolov 30; noon-3am) Overlooking the main street and around the corner from Samovodska Charshiya, Tequila Bar is a festively painted, as-fun-as-you'd-expect student bar with good cocktails and cheap beer.

Entertainment

Konstantin Kisimov Dramatic Theatre THEATRE

(062-623 526; www.teatarvtarnovo.com; ul Vasil Levski) Hosts regular international performances and Bulgarian plays.

WORTH A TRIP

TOMBS & BLOOMS: KAZANLÂK

Kazanlâk might not look like much, but this rough 'n' ready town is the perfect base for exploring two of Bulgaria's most important and iconic (if not very imaginatively named) regions: the Valley of the Roses and the Valley of the Thracian Kings.

The **Valley of the Roses** is as the name suggests; kilometres of fat, fragrant roses (the *Rosa damascena* to be precise) carefully cultivated for their delicate oils for use in everything from pricey perfumes to cooking. About 70 per cent of the world's rose oil comes from here. The annual **Rose Festival** – replete with parades, picking displays and Queen of the Roses pageant – celebrates the harvest every June. In Kazanlâk itself, the **Museum of the Roses** (☎0431-64 057; www.muzei-kazanlak.org; ul Osvobozhdenie 49; adult/child 3/1 lv; ⊙9am-5pm) gives a deeper insight into the fabulous history and many uses of the flower.

Millenniums before a single seed was sown, the Thracians, a fierce Indo-European tribe, ruled the roost. Archaeologists believe there are at least 1500 Thracian burial mounds and tombs in the vicinity; the most famous is the remarkably preserved, brightly embellished **Tomb of Kazanlâk** (Tyulbe Park; admission 20 lv; ⊙10am-5pm May-Nov, by reservation Nov-Apr), dating back to the 4th century BC. Kazanlâk also boasts a **museum** (☎0431-64 750; www.muzei-kazanlak.org; Tyulbe Park; adult/child 3/1 lv; ⊙9am-5pm May-Nov, by reservation Nov-Apr) housing a full-scaled Thracian tomb replica. More temples and tombs – including that of the great Thracian priest-king Seuthes III – are accessible via tour bus or with your own vehicle. Day trips taking in both regions can be arranged at the Kazanlâk **tourist information centre** (ul Iskra 4; ⊙8am-1pm & 2-6pm Mon-Fri).

Buses run between Kazanlâk and Sofia (20 lv, 3½ hours), Plovdiv (13 lv, two hours) and Veliko Târnovo (17 lv, 2½ hours). See www.bdz.bg for train schedules.

Melon Live Music Club LIVE MUSIC
(☎062-603 439; bul Nezavisimost 21; ⊙6pm-2am) Popular spot for live music from rock and R&B to Latin jazz. It's tucked halfway up the main street.

Shopping

Samovodska Charshiya ANTIQUES
(ul Rakovski) Veliko Târnovo's charming historic quarter is a true centre of craftsmanship, with genuine blacksmiths, potters and cutlers, among other artisans, still practising their trades here. Wander the cobblestone streets to discover bookshops and purveyors of antiques, jewellery and art housed in appealing Bulgarian National Revival houses.

Information

Hospital Stefan Cherkezov (☎062-626 841; ul Nish 1) Modern hospital with an emergency room and English-speaking doctors.

Tourist Information Centre (☎062-622 148; www.velikoturnovo.info; ul Hristo Botev 5; ⊙9am-6pm Mon-Fri, Mon-Sat Apr-Oct) English-speaking staff offering local info and advice.

Getting There & Away

BUS

Three bus stations serve Veliko Târnovo. **Zapad** (☎062-640 908; ul Nikola Gabrovski 74), about 4km southwest from the centre, is the main station. From here, buses serve Plovdiv (24 lv, four hours, at least two daily), Burgas (23 lv, four hours, three daily), Kazanlâk (10 lv, two hours, three daily) and elsewhere.

The more central **Yug bus station** (☎062-620 014; ul Hristo Botev 74) has many daily buses to Sofia (22 lv, three hours), Varna (17 lv, four hours) and Burgas (23 lv, four hours). **Etap Adress** (☎062-630 564; Hotel Etâr, ul Ivailo 2), right by the tourist information centre, also runs hourly buses to Sofia and Varna.

TRAIN

Gorna Oryakhovitsa station (☎062-826 118), 8.5km from town, and the smaller **Veliko Târnovo train station** (☎062-620 065), 1.5km west of the centre, both run frequent trains to Plovdiv (23 lv, five hours), Burgas (19 lv, five hours), Varna (14 lv, five hours) and Sofia (21 lv, five hours). The latter station may be closer, but many trains require a change at Gorna Oryakhovitsa anyway. Get there on bus 10.

BLACK SEA COAST

The Black Sea coast is the country's summer playground, attracting fun 'n' sun seekers from across Bulgaria and the world. Nicknamed 'the Red Riviera' during communism, the almost 400km-long sandy stretch is today dotted with resorts to rival Spain and Greece, though independent travellers will find plenty to explore away from the parasols and jet skis. With its rich museums and happening beachside bars, the maritime capital of Varna offers an intriguing mix of history and hedonism, while to the south, beautiful Nesebâr and Sozopol revel in their Hellenic heritage.

Varna Варна

052 / POP 335,000

Cosmopolitan Varna is by far the most interesting town on the Black Sea coast. A combination of port city, naval base and seaside resort, it's an appealing place to while away a few days, packed with history yet thoroughly modern, with an enormous park to amble around and a lengthy, white-sand beach to lounge on. In the city centre you'll find Bulgaria's largest Roman baths complex and its finest archaeological museum, as well as a dynamic cultural and restaurant scene.

Sights & Activities

Varna's main attractions are **swimming** and **strolling**; there are plenty of opportunities for both at the 8km-long **city beach**. The popular southern end has a pool complex, water slides and cafes; the central beach has thinner sand patches and is dominated by clubs. The rocky north beach is lined with restaurants; if you go further north you'll find beautiful stretches of sand plus an alfresco **thermal pool** with year-round hot water. Just in from the beach is the huge, green **Primorski Park**, dotted with cafes, statues and popcorn vendors.

Archaeological Museum MUSEUM

(www.archaeo.museumvarna.com; ul Maria Luisa 41; adult/student 10/2 lv; 10am-5pm Tue-Sun Apr-Sep, Tue-Sat Oct-Mar; 3, 9, 109) Exhibits at this vast museum, the best of its kind in Bulgaria, include 6500-year-old bangles, necklaces and earrings said to be the oldest worked gold found in the world. You'll also find Roman surgical implements, Hellenistic tombstones and touching oddments including a marble plaque listing, in Greek, the names of the city's school graduates for AD 221.

Roman Thermae RUIN

(cnr ul Han Krum & ul San Stefano; adult/student 4/2 lv; 10am-5pm Tue-Sun May-Oct, Tue-Sat Nov-Apr) The well-preserved ruins of Varna's 2nd-century-AD Roman Thermae are the largest in Bulgaria, although only a small part of the original complex still stands.

Sleeping

Flag Hostel HOSTEL €

(089 740 8115; www.varnahostel.com; ul Bratya Shkorpil 13a; dm incl breakfast 22 lv; ; 3, 9) The Flag is a long-established, sociable spot with a party atmosphere. The three dorms are basic with comfortable single beds (no bunks). Free pick-ups from the bus and train stations.

Yo Ho Hostel HOSTEL €

(088 472 9144; www.yohohostel.com; ul Ruse 23; dm/s/d/tw incl breakfast from 14/30/40/40 lv; ; 109) Shiver your timbers at this pirate-themed place, with four- and 11-bed dorm rooms and private options. Staff offer free pick-ups and can organise camping and rafting trips.

Hotel Astra HOTEL €€

(052-630 524; www.hotelastravarna.com; ul Opalchenska 9; s/d 50/60 lv; ; 9) A real bargain by Varna standards, this central, cheerful family-run hotel has 10 spacious rooms, all with terraces and basic but good-sized bathrooms.

★**Graffit Gallery Hotel** BOUTIQUE HOTEL €€€

(052-989 900; www.graffithotel.com; bul Knyaz Boris I 65; s/d from 168/185 lv; ; 9) With its own art gallery and themed rooms, this modern designer hotel is one of Varna's more colourful options. Super-efficient staff, a chic spa and gym and superb on-site dining options make this a top option if you're looking to splurge.

Grand Hotel London LUXURY HOTEL €€€

(052-664 100; www.londonhotel.bg; ul Musala 3; s/d Mon-Thu from 150/176 lv, Fri-Sun from 170/210 lv;) Varna's grandest and oldest hotel opened in 1912. Rooms are spacious and elegantly furnished, if a little chintzy; the restaurant is especially good.

Eating

★**Stariya Chinar** BULGARIAN €€

(052-949 400; ul Preslav 11; mains 7-19 lv; 8am-midnight) This is upmarket Balkan soul food at its best. Try the baked lamb, made to an old Bulgarian recipe, or the divine barbecue pork ribs; they also create some rather ornate salads. Outdoors is lovely in summer; park yourself in a traditional interior when the cooler weather strikes.

Balkanska Skara Nashentsi BULGARIAN €€
(052-630 186; ul Tsar Simeon I 27; mains 5-10lv; 11am-1am Mon-Sat, 6pm-1am Sun) This big, riotous restaurant is popular with locals for its prodigious portions of grilled meats, live music and fun atmosphere. Set menus are available.

Bistro Dragoman SEAFOOD €€
(052-621 688; ul Dragoman 43; mains 4-16 lv; 10am-11.30pm) This welcoming little place specialises in delicious takes on seafood and locally caught fish. This being the Balkans, grilled meats are also on the menu.

Drinking & Nightlife

Some of Varna's best bars exist only during the summer: head down to Kraybrezhna aleya by the beach and take your pick.

Pench's COCKTAIL BAR
(ul Dragoman 25; 2pm-2am) Want cocktails? Oh, they've got cocktails: Pench's is a two-time world record holder for having the largest number of cocktails available at a single bar. Choosing one may be the hardest decision you'll ever make. They also have a summer location by the beach at Kraybrezhna aleya.

Sundogs BAR
(088 951 3434; ul Koloni 1; 9am-midnight;) Big with expats and locals, this very friendly watering hole is a great place to make new friends, chase down excellent pub grub with a good selection of beers, or show off your smarts at the every-second-Sunday pub quiz (summer only).

4aspik CLUB
(088 911 0202; Kraybrezhna aleya; 10pm-4am) This wild summertime club specialises in Bulgarian folk-pop.

Entertainment

Varna Opera House OPERA
(052-650 555; www.operavarna.bg; pl Nezavisimost 1; ticket office 11am-1pm & 2-7pm Mon-Fri, 11am-6pm Sat) Varna's grand opera house hosts performances by the Varna Opera and Philharmonic Orchestra all year, except July and August, when some performances are staged at the Open-Air Theatre in Primorski Park.

Information

Tourist Information Centre (052-820 689; www.varnainfo.bg; pl Kiril & Metodii; 9am-7pm; 3) Plenty of free brochures and maps, and helpful multilingual staff.

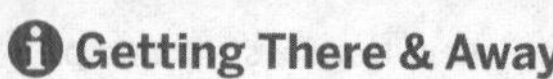

Getting There & Away

AIR

Varna's international **airport** (052-573 323; www.varna-airport.bg; 409) is 8km northwest of town. There are regular flights across Europe and to/from Sofia.

BUS

Varna's **central bus station** (bul Vladislav Varenchik 158; 148, 409) is about 2km northwest of the city centre. There are regular buses to Sofia (33 lv, seven hours), Burgas (14 lv, two hours) and all the major destinations in Bulgaria: see www.bgrazpisanie.com for fares and schedules.

TRAIN

Trains depart Varna's **train station** (052-662 3343; pl Slaveikov) for Sofia (23.60 lv, seven hours, seven daily), Plovdiv (22.20 lv, seven hours, three daily) and Veliko Târnovo (13.80 lv, four hours, one daily).

Nesebâr Несебър

0554 / POP 11,620

Postcard-pretty Nesebâr (Ne-*se*-bar) – about 40km northeast of Burgas – was settled by Greek colonists in 512 BC, though today it's more famous for its (mostly ruined) medieval churches. Though beautiful, Nesebâr is heavily commercialised, and transforms into one huge, open-air souvenir market during the high season. The Sunny Beach megaresort is 5km to the north.

Sights & Activities

All of Nesebâr's main sights are in the Old Town; around 1.5km west from there is **South Beach**, where all the usual water sports are available, including **jet-skiing** and **waterskiing**.

Archaeological Museum MUSEUM
(www.ancient-nessebar.com; ul Mesembria 2; adult/child 5/3 lv; 9am-8pm Mon-Fri, 9.30am-1.30pm & 2-7pm Sat-Sun Jul-Aug) Explore the rich history of Nesebâr – formerly Messembria – at this fine museum. Greek and Roman pottery, statues and tombstones as well as Thracian gold jewellery and ancient anchors are displayed here. There's also a collection of icons recovered from Nesebâr's numerous churches.

Sveti Stefan Church CHURCH
(ul Ribarska; adult/student 5/3 lv; 9am-7pm Mon-Fri, 9am-1pm & 1.30-6pm Sat & Sun) Built in the 11th century and reconstructed 500 years later, this is the best-preserved church in town. Its beautiful 16th- to 18th-century murals

cover virtually the entire interior. Come early, as it's popular with tour groups.

Sleeping & Eating

★**Hotel Tony** GUESTHOUSE €
(0554-42 403, 088 926 8004; ul Kraybrezhna 20; r from 40 lv; Jun-Sep;) Thanks to its low prices and excellent location overlooking the sea, the Hotel Tony books out quickly: be sure to reserve in advance. Rooms are simple but clean, and the chatty host is very helpful.

Old Nesebâr SEAFOOD €€
(0554-42 070; ul Ivan Alexander 11; mains 7-15 lv; noon-11pm) With two tiers of seating offering splendid sea views, and a menu crammed with splendid seafood dishes, this is the go-to place for a dinner (or lunch) to remember.

Getting There & Away

Nesebâr is well connected to coastal destinations by public transport; its bus station is on the small square just outside the city walls. The stop before this on the mainland is for the New Town. There are buses to Sunny Beach (1 lv, 10 minutes, every 15 minutes), Burgas (6 lv, 40 minutes, every 30 minutes), Varna (15 lv, two hours, seven daily) and Sofia (37 lv, seven hours, several daily).

Fast Ferry (www.fastferry.bg) operates a high-speed hydrofoil service to Sozopol (one way/return 27/50 lv, 30 minutes, three daily in summer, one per day on Tuesday, Wednesday, Thursday and Saturday in winter).

Burgas Бургас

056 / POP 200,270

For most visitors, the port city of Burgas (sometimes written as 'Bourgas') is no more than a transit point for the more obviously appealing resorts and historic towns further up and down the coast. If you do decide to stop over, you'll find a well-kept city with a neat, pedestrianised centre, a long, uncrowded beach and some small but interesting museums.

Burgas is also the jumping-off point for visits to **St Anastasia Island** (www.anastasia-island.com; return boat trip adult/child 9/6 lv; 10am-5.30pm summer), the only inhabited island off the Bulgarian Black Sea coast. Throughout its long history, it's served as a religious retreat, a prison and pirate bait (according to legend, a golden treasure is buried in its sands), and is today dominated by a lighthouse and a monastery, where visitors can sample various healing herb potions. It's also possible to spend the night in a monastic cell (rooms from 50 to 120 lv).

Sleeping & Eating

★**Old House Hostel** HOSTEL €
(087 984 1559; www.burgashostel.com; ul Sofroniy 2; dm/d 17/33 lv;) This charming hostel makes itself right at home in a lovely 1895 house. Dorms are airy and bright (and bunk-free!), while doubles have access to a sweet little courtyard. Right downtown and only 400m to the beach, this place is a winner.

Hotel California BOUTIQUE HOTEL €€
(056-531 000; www.burgashotel.com; ul Lyuben Karavelov 36; s/d incl breakfast 55/65 lv; P; 4) This appealing boutique hotel has large, colourful rooms and especially soft mattresses. Guests get a 20% reduction in the excellent restaurant. It's on a quiet side street about five minutes' walk west of the city centre.

★**Ethno** SEAFOOD €€
(088 787 7966; ul Aleksandrovska 49; 7-20 lv; 11am-11.30pm) This downtown restaurant does splendid things with seafood: the Black Sea mussels alone are worth a trip to Burgas. With ambient blue-and-white surrounds that recall the city's Greek heritage, the superb (English-speaking) service and a summery vibe, Ethno is classy without being uptight.

Getting There & Away

AIR

Bulgaria Air links **Burgas Airport** (056-870 248; www.bourgas-airport.com; 15), 10km northeast of town, with Sofia three times a day (April to October).

BUS

Yug bus station (pl Tsaritsa Yoanna), outside the train station at the southern end of ul Aleksandrovska, is where most travellers arrive or leave. There are regular buses to coastal destinations, including Nesebâr (6 lv, 40 minutes), Varna (14 lv, 2½ hours) and Sozopol (4.50 lv, 40 minutes). Buses also go to and from Sofia (30 lv, five to six hours) and Plovdiv (17 lv, four hours). Departures are less frequent outside summer.

TRAIN

The **train station** (ul Ivan Vazov) has ticket windows (8am to 6pm) on the right, where you can buy advance tickets for domestic and international services, while same-day tickets can be bought at the windows (24 hours) on the left. Trains run to Varna (19 lv, five to six hours, five to seven daily) and Sofia (23.60 lv, seven to eight hours, six daily).

Sozopol Созопол

☎0550 / POP 5000

With a curling peninsula of cobbled streets, sandy beaches and reminders of its ancient Greek heritage at every turn, stunning Sozopol is one of the highlights of the coast. It's not yet as crowded as Nesebâr, but its happening cultural scene, wonderful Old Town and lively street life are attracting more visitors every summer. Archaeologists, too, are drawn to Sozopol – formerly known as Apollonia – where it seems that every casual turn of a gardener's spade unearths new treasures.

Sights & Activities

Sozopol has two great beaches: **Harmani Beach** has all the good-time gear (water slides, paddle boats, beach bars), while to the north, the smaller **Town Beach** packs in the serious sun-worshippers. Stone sarcophagi – part of the ancient **Apollonia necropolis** – have been unearthed at the southern end of Harmani.

Archaeological Museum MUSEUM
(ul Han Krum 2; adult/child 8/3 lv; ⏱9am-6pm, closed Sat & Sun Oct-Apr) Housed in a drab concrete box near the port, this museum has a small but fascinating collection of local finds from its Apollonian glory days and beyond. In addition to a wealth of Hellenic treasures, the museum occasionally exhibits the skeleton of a local 'vampire', found with a stake driven through its chest.

Southern Fortress Wall & Tower Museum RUIN, MUSEUM
(ul Milet 40; museum admission 3 lv; ⏱9.30am-8pm Jul-Aug, to 5pm May & Jun, Sep & Oct) The reconstructed walls and walkways along the rocky coastline, and a 4th-century BC well that was once part of a temple to Aphrodite, are free to explore; the views are glorious. The attached museum is a bit of an anticlimax.

Festivals & Events

Apollonia Arts Festival MUSIC, ART
(www.apollonia.bg; ⏱end Aug–mid-Sep) This is the highlight of Sozopol's cultural calendar, with concerts, theatrical performances, art exhibitions, film screenings and more held across town.

Sleeping & Eating

Hotel prices drop considerably in the off-season, when visitors will have Sozopol all to themselves. Cheap eats abound along the harbourfront ul Kraybrezhna in the Old Town; more upmarket restaurants are found on ul Morski Skali.

★**Hotel Radik** HOTEL €€
(☎055-023 706; ul Republikanska 4; d/studio/apt from 68/75/95 lv; P❄📶🏊) Run by a lovely English/Bulgarian couple, the Radik is cheap, cheerful and perfectly located 100m from the Old Town and a quick stagger to the beach. Rooms have sea views and balconies; studios and apartments have good kitchenettes.

Art Hotel HOTEL €€
(☎0550-24 081; www.arthotel-sbh.com; ul Kiril & Metodii 72; d/studio Jul-Sep 70/90 lv, Oct-Jun from 50/60 lv; ❄📶) This peaceful old house, belonging to the Union of Bulgarian Artists, is within a walled courtyard towards the tip of the peninsula, away from the crowds. It has a small selection of bright, comfortable rooms with balconies, most with sea views; breakfast is served on the terraces over the sea.

★**Panorama** SEAFOOD €€
(ul Morski Skali 21; mains 8-20 lv; ⏱10am-1am) This lively place has an open terrace with fantastic views towards Sveti Ivan Island. Fresh, local fish is a mainstay of the menu. It's one of the best of many seafood spots on the street.

Getting There & Away

The small public **bus station** (ul Han Krum) is just south of the Old Town walls. Buses leave for Burgas (4.50 lv, 40 minutes) about every 30 minutes between 6am and 9pm in summer, and about once an hour in the low season. Buses run up to three times a day to Sofia (32 lv, seven hours).

Fast Ferry (☎088 580 8001; www.fastferry.bg; Fishing Harbour) runs three ferries per day

COUNTRY FACTS

Area 110,910 sq km

Capital Sofia

Country Code ☎359

Currency Lev (lv)

Emergency ☎112

Language Bulgarian

Money ATMs are everywhere

Population 7.35 million

Visas Not required for citizens of the EU, UK, USA, Canada, Australia and New Zealand for stays of less than 90 days

EATING PRICE RANGES

The following price ranges refer to a typical main course.

€ less than 5 lv

€€ 5 lv to 15 lv

€€€ more than 15 lv

to/from Nesebâr (single/return from 27/50 lv, 40 minutes) between June and September.

SURVIVAL GUIDE

 Directory A–Z

ACCOMMODATION

Sofia, Plovdiv, Veliko Târnovo, Varna and Burgas all have hostels; for cheap accommodation elsewhere, look out for signs reading 'стаи под наем' (rooms for rent). Many hotels offer discounts for longer stays or on weekends; prices may rise during summer.

FOOD

Eating out in Bulgaria is remarkably cheap, and even if you're on a tight budget, you'll have no problem eating well.

GAY & LESBIAN TRAVELLERS

Homosexuality is legal in Bulgaria, though opinion polls suggest a majority of Bulgarians have a negative opinion of it. Attitudes among younger people are slowly changing, and there are a few gay clubs and bars in Sofia and in other major cities. Useful websites include **Bulgayria** (www.gay.bg) and **Gay Bulgaria Ultimate Gay Guide** (www.gay-bulgaria.info).

INTERNET RESOURCES

Beach Bulgaria (www.beachbulgaria.com)
BG Maps (www.bgmaps.com)
Bulgaria Travel (www.bulgariatravel.org)

MONEY

The local currency is the lev (plural: leva), comprised of 100 stotinki. It is almost always abbreviated as lv. Bulgaria has no immediate plans to adopt the euro.

PUBLIC HOLIDAYS

New Year's Day 1 January
Liberation Day (National Day) 3 March
Orthodox Easter Sunday & Monday March/April; one week after Catholic/Protestant Easter
May Day 1 May
St George's Day 6 May
Cyrillic Alphabet Day 24 May
Unification Day (National Day) 6 September
Bulgarian Independence Day 22 September
National Revival Day 1 November
Christmas 25 and 26 December

TELEPHONE

To call Bulgaria from abroad, dial the international access code, add ☎359 (the country code for Bulgaria), the area code (minus the first zero) and then the number. Mobile phone numbers can be identified by the prefixes ☎087, ☎088 or ☎089.

TRAVELLERS WITH DISABILITIES

Bulgaria is not an easy destination for travellers with disabilities. Uneven and broken footpaths are common in towns and wheelchair-accessible toilets and ramps are rare outside the more expensive hotels.

VISAS

Citizens of other EU countries, as well as Australia, Canada, New Zealand, the USA and many other countries do not need a visa for stays of up to 90 days. Other nationals should contact the Bulgarian embassy in their home country for current visa requirements.

Getting There & Away

AIR

Most international visitors come and/or go via **Sofia Airport** (☎02-937 2211; www.sofia-airport.bg); there are frequent flights between Sofia and other European cities. The national carrier is **Bulgaria Air** (www.air.bg); the airport website has a full list of other carriers who service it.

LAND

Although Sofia has international bus and train connections, it's not necessary to backtrack to the capital if you're heading to, for example, Budapest, Athens or İstanbul: Plovdiv offers regular buses to all three. Heading to Belgrade by train means going through Sofia; for Skopje, you'll need to catch a bus from there, too.

Bus

Most international buses arrive in Sofia. You'll have to get off the bus at the border and walk through customs to present your passport. When travelling out of Bulgaria by bus, the cost of entry visas for the countries concerned are not included in the prices of the bus tickets.

SLEEPING PRICE RANGES

Price ranges are based on the cost of a double room with a bathroom.

€ less than 60 lv

€€ 60 lv to 120 lv (to 200 lv in Sofia)

€€€ more than 120 lv (200 lv in Sofia)

ESSENTIAL FOOD & DRINK

Fresh fruit, vegetables, dairy produce and grilled meat form the basis of Bulgarian cuisine, which is heavily influenced by Greek and Turkish cookery. Pork and chicken are the most popular meats, while tripe also features on traditional menus. You will also find recipes including duck, rabbit and venison, and fish is plentiful along the Black Sea coast.

- **Banitsa** Flaky cheese pastry, often served fresh and hot.
- **Kebabche** Thin, grilled pork sausage, a staple of every *mehana* (tavern) in the country.
- **Tarator** On a hot day there's nothing better than this delicious chilled cucumber and yoghurt soup, served with garlic, dill and crushed walnuts.
- **Beer** You're never far from a cold beer in Bulgaria. Zagorka, Kamenitza and Shumensko are the most popular nationwide brands.
- **Wine** They've been producing wine here since Thracian times and there are some excellent varieties to try.
- **Kavarma** This 'claypot meal', or meat stew, is normally made with either chicken or pork and is one of the country's most popular dishes.
- **Shkembe chorba** Traditional stomach soup is one of the more adventurous and offbeat highlights of Bulgarian cuisine.
- **Mish Mash** Summer favourite made from tomatoes, capsicum, eggs, feta and spices.
- **Shishcheta** Shish kebab consisting of chunks of chicken or pork on wooden skewers with mushrooms and peppers.
- **Musaka** Bulgarian moussaka bears more than a passing resemblance to its Greek cousin and it's a delicious staple of cheap cafeteria meals.

Car & Motorcycle

In order to drive your own car on Bulgarian roads, you will need to purchase a vignette, sold at all border crossings into Bulgaria, petrol stations and post offices. For a car, this costs 10/25 lv for one week/month.

Train

There are a number of international trains from Bulgaria, including services to Serbia, Greece and Turkey. Sofia is the main hub, although trains stop at other towns.

 Getting Around

AIR

The only scheduled domestic flights within Bulgaria are between Sofia and Varna and Sofia and Burgas. Both routes are operated by **Bulgaria Air** (www.air.bg).

BICYCLE

- Many roads are in poor condition; some major roads are always choked with traffic and bikes aren't allowed on highways.
- Many trains will carry your bike for an extra 2 lv.
- Spare parts are available in cities and major towns, but it's better to bring your own.

BUS

Buses link all cities and major towns and connect villages with the nearest transport hub. See www.bgrazpisanie.com/en/transport_companies for a comprehensive list of bus companies.

CAR & MOTORCYCLE

Bulgaria's roads are among the most dangerous in Europe and the level of fatalities each year is high. The worst time is between July and September, with drink-driving, speeding and poor road conditions contributing to accidents.

The **Union of Bulgarian Motorists** (☎02-935 7935, road assistance 02-91 146; www.uab.org; pl Positano 3, Sofia) offers 24-hour road assistance.

Road Rules

- Drive on the right.
- Drivers and passengers in the front must wear seat belts; motorcyclists must wear helmets.
- Blood-alcohol limit is 0.05%.
- Children under 12 are not allowed to sit in front.
- From November to March, headlights must be on at all times.
- Speed limits are 50km/h within towns, 90km/h on main roads and 140km/h on motor-ways.

TRAIN

Bâlgarski Dârzhavni Zheleznitsi – **Bulgarian State Railways** (BDZh; www.bdz.bg) – boasts an impressive 4278km of track across the country, linking most towns and cities. Most trains tend to be antiquated and not especially comfortable, with journey times slower than buses. On the plus side you'll have more room in a train compartment and the scenery is likely to be more rewarding. Trains are classified as *ekspresen* (express), *bârz* (fast) or *pâtnicheski* (slow passenger). Unless you absolutely thrive on train travel or want to visit a more remote town, use a fast or express train.

Croatia

Includes ➡

Best Places to Eat

- ➡ Mundoaka Street Food (p256)
- ➡ Kantinon (p260)
- ➡ Konoba Menego (p267)
- ➡ Konoba Matejuška (p264)

Best Places to Stay

- ➡ Studio Kairos (p256)
- ➡ Goli + Bosi (p264)
- ➡ Hotel Lone (p260)
- ➡ Karmen Apartments (p271)

Why Go?

If your Mediterranean fantasies feature balmy days by sapphire waters in the shade of ancient walled towns, Croatia is the place to turn them into reality.

The extraordinary Adriatic coastline, speckled with 1244 islands and strewn with historic towns, is Croatia's main attraction. The standout is Dubrovnik, its remarkable Old Town ringed by mighty defensive walls. Coastal Split showcases Diocletian's Palace, one of the world's most impressive Roman monuments, where dozens of bars, restaurants and shops thrive amid the old walls. In the heart-shaped peninsula of Istria, Rovinj is a charm-packed fishing port with narrow cobbled streets. The Adriatic isles hold much varied appeal, from glitzy Hvar Town on its namesake island to the secluded naturist coves of the Pakleni Islands just offshore.

Away from the coast, Zagreb, Croatia's lovely capital, has a booming cafe culture and art scene, while Plitvice Lakes National Park offers a verdant maze of turquoise lakes and cascading waterfalls.

When to Go

Zagreb

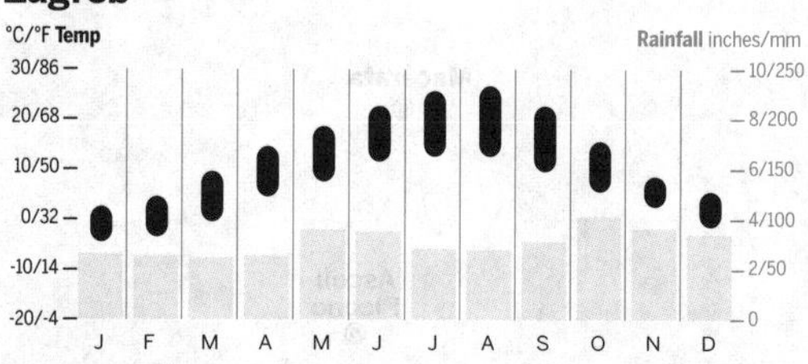

May & Sep Good weather, less tourists, full events calendar, great for hiking.

Jun Best time to visit: beautiful weather, fewer people, lower prices, the festival season kicks off.

Jul & Aug Lots of sunshine, warm sea and summer festivals; many tourists and highest prices.

Croatia Highlights

1. Gape at the Old Town wall of **Dubrovnik** (p268), which surrounds luminous marble streets and finely ornamented buildings.
2. Admire the Venetian architecture and experience the vibrant nightlife of **Hvar Town** (p267).
3. Indulge in the lively and historic delights of Diocletian's Palace in **Split** (p261).
4. Take in the remains of failed romances at the **Museum of Broken Relationships** (p252) in Zagreb.
5. Roam the steep cobbled streets and piazzas of **Rovinj** (p259), Istria's showpiece coastal town.

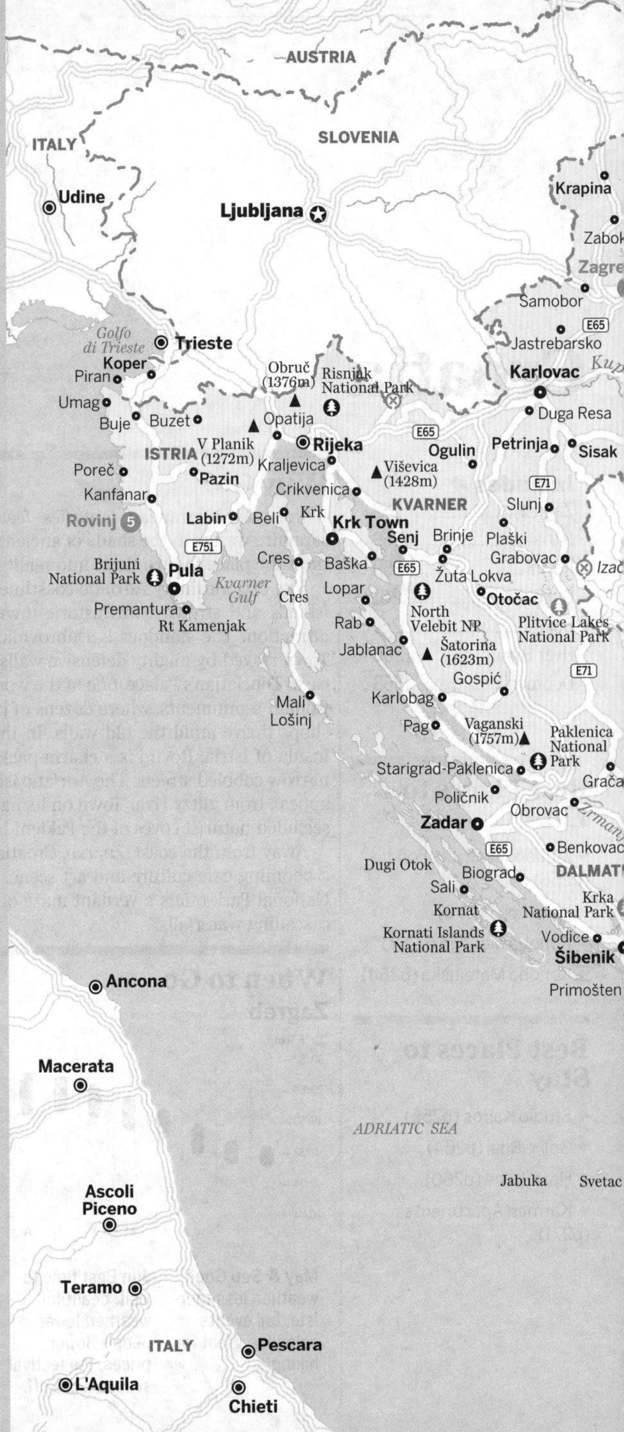

0
100 km
0
50 miles
HUNGARY
Čakovec
Goričan
Varaždin
Varaždinske
Toplice
Koprivnica
Gola
Drava
Đurđevac
A4
Križevci
Pitomača
Terezino Polje
Bjelovar
Virovitica
E661
Zagreb
Airport
Čazma
Velika
Gorica
E70
Slatina
Donji
Miholjac
Daruvar
Kapovac
(790m)
Pécs
Backi Breg
Bezdan
Beli Manastir
Kopački Rit
National Park
Osijek
Dalj
Bogojevo
Našice
Sisak
Kutina
Petrinja
Glina
Pakrac
Slavonska
Požega
Đakoračka
Breznica
E73
Borovo
Vukovar
Novi Sad
Danube
Đakovo
Vinkovci
Bačka
Palanka
Novska
Nova
Gradiška
Hrvatska
Kostajnica
Slavonski
Brod
E70
Županja
Otok
Bosanska
Dubica
Sava
Davor
Kozara
National
Park
Batrovci
Una
Sava
Brčko
Banja Luka
SERBIA
BOSNIA &
HERCEGOVINA
Knin
E71
SARAJEVO
Cikola
Sinj
Trogir
E65
3
Split
Omiš
Imotski
Gorica-
Vinjani
Donji
Supetar
Brela
Šolta
Makarska
Brač
Bol
Piva
E65
2
Stari Grad
Hvar Town
Hvar
Ploče
Metković
Metković-Doljani
Vis
Vis
Komiža
Vela
Luka
Korčula
Town
Orebić
Korčula
E65
Polače
MONTENEGRO
Pomena
Sobra
Lastovo
Mljet
National
Park
1
Dubrovnik
Ivanica
Cavtat
E65
PODGORICA
ALBANIA

ITINERARIES

Three Days

Spend a day in dynamic **Zagreb**, delving into its vibrant cafe culture and nightlife, and fascinating museums, then head down to **Rovinj** in Istria to spend a couple of days unwinding by the sea, wandering the cobbled streets and sampling the celebrated Istrian cuisine.

One Week

Start with a weekend in Zagreb, then head south to take in one of the region's best sights: the Roman ruins of Diocletian's Palace in **Split** are a living part of this exuberant seafront city. Base yourself here for two days of sightseeing, beach fun and nightlife action. Next, take the winding coastal road to **Dubrovnik**, a magnificent walled city whose beauty is bound to blow you away with the jaw-dropping sights of its Old Town.

ZAGREB

☎01 / POP 792,900

Zagreb has culture, arts, music, architecture, gastronomy and all the other things that make a quality capital city – it's no surprise that the number of visitors has risen sharply in the last couple of years. Croatia's coastal attractions aside, Zagreb has finally been discovered as a popular city-break destination in its own right.

Visually, Zagreb is a mixture of straight-laced Austro-Hungarian architecture and rough-around-the-edges socialist structures, its character a sometimes uneasy combination of the two. This mini metropolis is made for strolling the streets, drinking coffee in the permanently full cafes, popping into museums and galleries, and enjoying the theatres, concerts and cinema. It's a year-round outdoor city: in spring and summer everyone scurries to Jarun Lake in the southwest to swim, boat or dance the night away at lakeside discos, while in autumn and winter Zagrebians go skiing and hiking at nearby mountains.

Sights

As the oldest part of Zagreb, the Upper Town (Gornji Grad) offers landmark buildings and churches from the earlier centuries of Zagreb's history. The Lower Town (Donji Grad) has the city's most interesting art museums and fine examples of 19th- and 20th-century architecture.

Upper Town

Museum of Broken Relationships MUSEUM

(www.brokenships.com; Ćirilometodska 2; adult/concession 25/20KN; ⌚9am-10.30pm) Explore mementos that remain after a relationship ends at Zagreb's quirkiest museum. The innovative exhibit toured the world until it settled here in its permanent home. On display are donations from around the globe, in a string of all-white rooms with vaulted ceilings and epoxy-resin floors.

Dolac Market MARKET

(⌚6.30am-3pm Mon-Fri, to 2pm Sat, to 1pm Sun) Zagreb's colourful fruit and vegetable market is just north of Trg Bana Jelačića. Traders from all over Croatia come to sell their products at this buzzing centre of activity. Dolac has been heaving since the 1930s, when the city authorities set up a market space on the 'border' between the Upper and Lower Towns.

Cathedral of the Assumption of the Blessed Virgin Mary CATHEDRAL

(Katedrala Marijina Uznešenja; Kaptol 31; ⌚10am-5pm Mon-Sat, 1-5pm Sun) Kaptol Sq is dominated by this cathedral, formerly known as St Stephen's. Its twin spires – seemingly permanently under repair – soar over the city. Although the cathedral's original Gothic structure has been transformed many times over, the sacristy still contains a cycle of **frescoes** dating from the 13th century. An earthquake in 1880 badly damaged the cathedral; reconstruction in a neo-Gothic style began around the turn of the 20th century.

Lotrščak Tower HISTORIC BUILDING

(Kula Lotrščak; Strossmayerovo Šetalište 9; adult/concession 20/10KN; ⌚9am-9pm) This tower was built in the middle of the 13th century in order to protect the southern city gate. Climb it for a sweeping 360-degree view of the city. Near the tower is a **funicular railway** (www.zet.hr/english/funicular.aspx; ticket 4KN; ⌚6.30am-10pm), constructed in 1888, which connects the Lower and Upper Towns.

St Mark's Church CHURCH

(Crkva Svetog Marka; Trg Svetog Marka 5; ⌚mass 7.30am & 6pm Mon-Fri, 7.30am Sat, 10am, 11am & 6pm Sun) This 13th-century church is one of Zagreb's most emblematic buildings. Its colourful tiled roof, constructed in 1880, has the medieval coat of arms of Croatia, Dalmatia and Slavonia on the left side, and the emblem of Zagreb on the right. The Gothic portal, composed of 15 figures in shallow niches, was sculpted in the 14th century. The interior contains sculptures by Ivan Meštrović. You can enter the anteroom only during opening hours; the church itself is open only at Mass times.

Croatian Museum of Naïve Art MUSEUM

(Hrvatski Muzej Naivne Umjetnosti; ☎01-48 51 911; www.hmnu.org; Ćirilometodska 3; adult/concession 20/10KN; ⌚10am-6pm Tue-Fri, to 1pm Sat & Sun) If you like Croatia's naive art – a form that was highly fashionable locally and worldwide during the 1960s and 1970s and has declined somewhat since – this small museum will be a feast. It houses around 1900 paintings, drawings and some sculptures by the discipline's most important artists, such as Generalić, Mraz, Rabuzin and Smajić.

Meštrović Atelier GALLERY

(☎01-48 51 123; Mletačka 8; adult/concession 30/15KN; ⌚10am-6pm Tue-Fri, to 2pm Sat & Sun) Croatia's most recognised artist is Ivan Meštrović. This 17th-century building is his former home, where he worked and lived from 1922 to 1942; the excellent collection it houses has some 100 sculptures, drawings, lithographs and pieces of furniture from the first four decades of his artistic life. Meštrović, who also worked as an architect, designed many parts of the house himself.

City Museum MUSEUM

(Muzej Grada Zagreba; ☎01-48 51 926; www.mgz.hr; Opatička 20; adult/concession/family 30/20/50KN; ⌚10am-6pm Tue-Fri, 11am-7pm Sat, 10am-2pm Sun; 👪) Since 1907, the 17th-century Convent of St Claire has housed this historical museum, which presents the history of Zagreb through documents, artwork and crafts, as well as interactive exhibits that fascinate kids. Look for the scale model of old Gradec. Summaries of the exhibits are posted in English.

Lower Town

Trg Bana Jelačića SQUARE

Zagreb's main orientation point and its geographic heart is Trg Bana Jelačića – it's where most people arrange to meet up. If you enjoy people-watching, sit in one of the cafes and watch the tramloads of people getting out, greeting each other and dispersing among the newspaper and flower sellers.

Museum Mimara MUSEUM

(Muzej Mimara; ☎01-48 28 100; www.mimara.hr; Rooseveltov trg 5; adult/concession 40/30KN; ⌚10am-7pm Tue-Fri, to 5pm Sat, to 2pm Sun) This is the diverse private art collection – Zagreb's best – of Ante Topić Mimara, who donated over 3750 priceless objects to his native Zagreb (even though he spent much of his life in Salzburg, Austria). Housed in a neo-Renaissance former school building (1883), the collection spans a wide range of periods and regions.

Art Pavilion GALLERY

(Umjetnički Paviljon; ☎01-48 41 070; www.umjetnicki-paviljon.hr; Trg Kralja Tomislava 22; adult/concession 30/15KN; ⌚11am-7pm Tue-Sat, 10am-1pm Sun) The yellow Art Pavilion presents changing exhibitions of contemporary art. Constructed in 1897 in stunning art nouveau style, the pavilion is the only space in Zagreb that was specifically designed to host large exhibitions. In some years, the gallery shuts its doors from mid-July through August; check the website for details.

24 HOURS IN ZAGREB

Start your day with a stroll through Strossmayerov trg, Zagreb's oasis of greenery, and then walk to Trg Bana Jelačića, the city's centre. Head up to Kaptol Sq for a look at the cathedral (p252), the centre of Zagreb's religious life. While in the Upper Town, pick up some snacks at the Dolac Market (p252). Next pop into the quirky Museum of Broken Relationships (p252) and take in a view of the city from the top of Lotrščak Tower (p252) just a few steps away, then spend the evening bar crawling along Tkalčićeva.

Zagreb

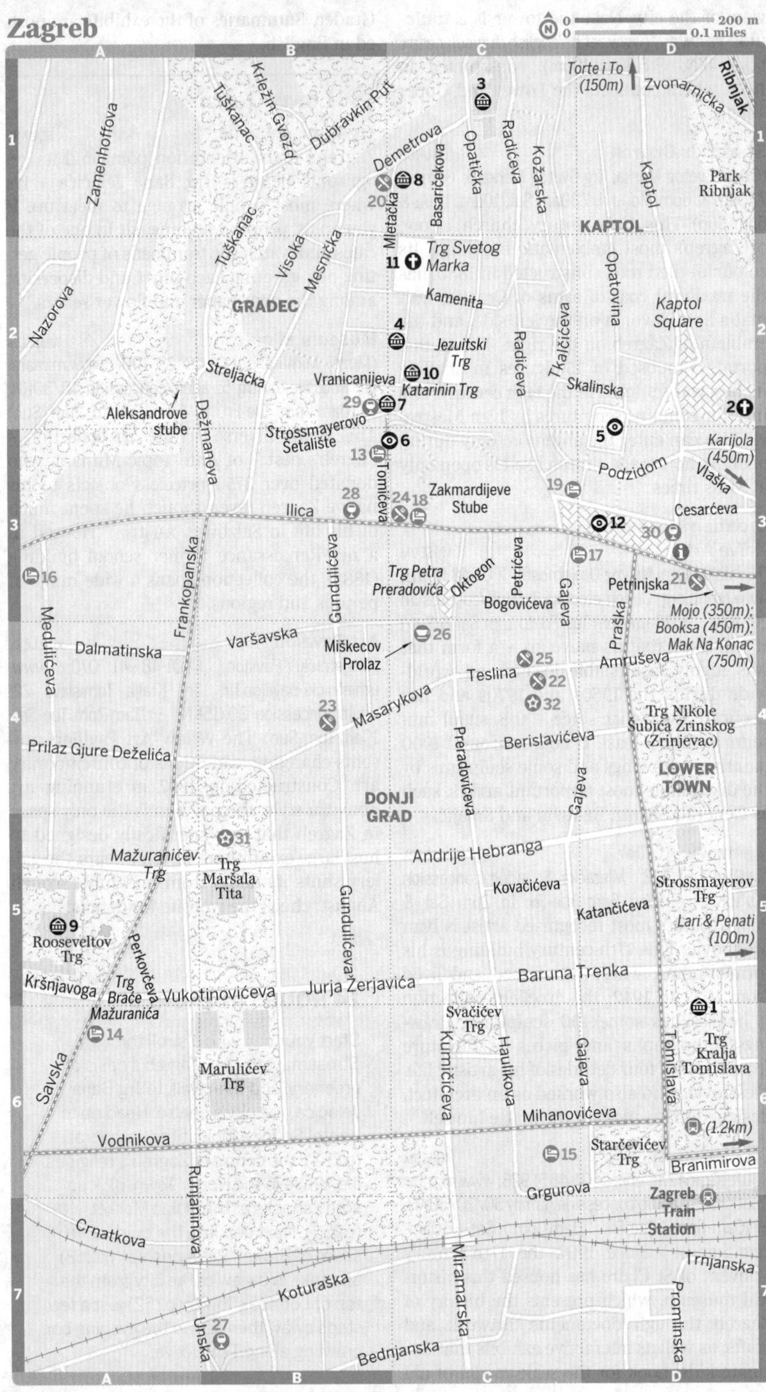
0 200 m
0 0.1 miles
Torte i To (150m)
Zvonarnička
Ribnjak
Park Ribnjak
Kaptol
KAPTOL
Tuškanac
Krležin Gvozd
Dubravkin Put
Demetrova
Zamenhoffova
Opatička
Radićeva
Kožarska
Basaričekova
Mletačka
Trg Svetog Marka
Visoka
Mesnička
GRADEC
Kamenita
Nazorova
Opatovina
Kaptol Square
Jezuitski Trg
Tkalčićeva
Streljačka
Vranicanijeva
Katarinin Trg
Skalinska
Aleksandrove stube
Strossmayerovo Šetalište
Dežmanova
Tomićeva
Podzidom
Karijola (450m)
Vlaška
Zakmardijeve Stube
Ilica
Cesarćeva
Frankopanska
Gundulićeva
Trg Petra Preradovića
Oktogon
Petrićeva
Bogovićeva
Gajeva
Petrinjska
Mojo (350m); Booksa (450m); Mak Na Konac (750m)
Medulićeva
Dalmatinska
Varšavska
Miškecov Prolaz
Praška
Amruševa
Teslina
Masarykova
Trg Nikole Šubića Zrinskog (Zrinjevac)
Prilaz Gjure Deželića
Berislavićeva
Preradovićeva
LOWER TOWN
DONJI GRAD
Mažuranićev Trg
Trg Maršala Tita
Andrije Hebranga
Kovačićeva
Strossmayerov Trg
Katančićeva
Lari & Penati (100m)
Rooseveltov Trg
Perkovčeva
Kršnjavoga
Trg Braće Mažuranića
Vukotinovićeva
Jurja Žerjavića
Baruna Trenka
Svačićev Trg
Kumičićeva
Haulikova
Trg Kralja Tomislava
Tomislava
Savska
Marulićev Trg
Mihanovićeva
(1.2km)
Vodnikova
Starčevićev Trg
Branimirova
Runjaninova
Grgurova
Zagreb Train Station
Crnatkova
Miramarska
Trnjanska
Koturaška
Promlinska
Unska
Bednjanska

Zagreb

Sights

1 Art Pavilion ... D6
2 Cathedral of the Assumption of the Blessed Virgin Mary ... D2
3 City Museum ... C1
4 Croatian Museum of Naïve Art ... C2
5 Dolac Market ... D3
6 Funicular Railway ... C3
7 Lotrščak Tower ... B2
8 Meštrović Atelier ... C1
9 Museum Mimara ... A5
10 Museum of Broken Relationships ... C2
11 St Mark's Church ... C2
12 Trg Bana Jelačića ... D3

Sleeping

13 Chillout Hostel Zagreb Downtown ... B3
14 Croatian YHA ... A6
15 Esplanade Zagreb Hotel ... C6
16 Hobo Bear Hostel ... A3
17 Hotel Dubrovnik ... D3
18 Hotel Jägerhorn ... C3
19 Main Square Apartment ... C3

Eating

20 Didov San ... B1
Le Bistro ... (see 15)
21 Mundoaka Street Food ... D3
22 Pingvin ... C4
23 Tip Top ... B4
24 Vincek ... C3
25 Vinodol ... C4
Zinfandel's ... (see 15)

Drinking & Nightlife

Basement Wine Bar ... (see 13)
26 Kino Europa ... C4
27 KSET ... B7
28 Pepermint ... B3
29 Stross ... B2
30 VIP Club ... D3

Entertainment

31 Croatian National Theatre ... B5
32 Zagrebačko Kazalište Mladih ... C4

Outside the Centre

Museum of Contemporary Art MUSEUM
(Muzej Suvremene Umjetnosti; 01-60 52 700; www.msu.hr; Avenija Dubrovnik 17; adult/concession 30/15KN; 11am-6pm Tue-Fri & Sun, to 8pm Sat) Housed in a stunning city icon designed by local star architect Igor Franić, this swanky museum displays both solo and thematic group shows by Croatian and international artists in its 17,000 sq metres. The permanent display, called *Collection in Motion,* showcases 620 edgy works by 240 artists, roughly half of whom are Croatian. There's a packed schedule of film, theatre, concerts and performance art year-round.

Tours

Funky Zagreb GUIDED TOUR
(www.funky-zagreb.com) Personalised tours that range in theme from wine tasting (340KN for 2½ to three hours) to hiking in Zagreb's surroundings (from 720KN per person for a day trip).

Blue Bike Tours BIKE TOUR
(098 18 83 344; www.zagrebbybike.com) To experience Zagreb on a bike, book one of the tours – choose between Lower Town, Upper Town or Novi Zagreb – departing daily at 10am and 2pm from Trg Bana Jelačića 15. Tours last around two hours and cost 175KN.

Sleeping

Zagreb's accommodation scene has been undergoing a noticeable change with the arrival of some of Europe's budget airlines. Hostels have mushroomed in the last few years; as of writing, there are over 30 in Zagreb, from cheap backpacker digs to more stylish hideaways. The city's business and high-end hotels are also in full flow.

Prices usually stay the same in all seasons, but be prepared for a 20% surcharge if you arrive during a festival or major event, in particular the autumn fair.

With the rise of Airbnb.com, short-term apartment rentals are becoming increasingly popular, and a good way to experience the city like a local. Recommended options include **ZIGZAG Integrated Hotel** (01-88 95 433; www.zigzag.hr; Petrinjska 9; r/apt from 450/720KN; P ❄) and **Main Square Apartment** (098 494 212; www.apartment-mainsquare.com; Trg Bana Jelačića 3; 2 people 608KN, 3-4 people 684KN; ❄).

Chillout Hostel Zagreb Downtown HOSTEL $
(01-48 49 605; www.chillout-hostel-zagreb.com; Tomićeva 5a; dm 105-125KN, s/d 300/350KN; P ❄ @) Located in the tiny pedestrian street with the funicular, this cheerful spot has no less than 170 beds just steps away from Trg Bana Jelačića. The trimmings are plentiful, and the vibe friendly. Breakfast is available.

Hobo Bear Hostel HOSTEL $

(☎01-48 46 636; www.hobobearhostel.com; Medulićeva 4; dm from 153KN, d from 436KN; ❄@📶) Inside a duplex apartment, this sparkling five-dorm hostel has exposed brick walls, hardwood floors, free lockers, a kitchen with free tea and coffee, a common room and book exchange. The three doubles are across the street. Take tram 1, 6 or 11 from Trg Bana Jelačića.

★ **Studio Kairos** B&B $$

(☎01-46 40 680; www.studio-kairos.com; Vlaška 92; s 340-420KN, d 520-620KN; ❄📶) This adorable B&B in a street-level apartment has four well-appointed rooms decked out by theme – Writers', Crafts, Music and Granny's – and there's a cosy common space where a delicious breakfast is served. The interior design is gorgeous and the friendly owners are a fountain of info. Bikes are also available for rent.

Hotel Jägerhorn HOTEL $$

(☎01-48 33 877; www.hotel-jagerhorn.hr; Ilica 14; s/d/apt 835/911/1217KN; P❄@📶) A charming, and little, recently renovated hotel that sits right underneath Lotrščak Tower (p252), the 'Hunter's Horn' has friendly service and 18 spacious, classic rooms with good views (you can gaze over leafy Gradec from the top-floor attic rooms). The downstairs terrace cafe is charming.

★ **Esplanade Zagreb Hotel** HOTEL $$$

(☎01-45 66 666; www.esplanade.hr; Mihanovićeva 1; s/d 1385/1500KN; P❄@📶) Drenched in history, this six-storey hotel was built next to the train station in 1925 to welcome the *Orient Express* crowd in grand style. It has hosted kings, artists, journalists and politicians ever since. The art-deco masterpiece is replete with walls of swirling marble, immense staircases and wood-panelled lifts.

Hotel Dubrovnik HOTEL $$$

(☎01-48 63 555; www.hotel-dubrovnik.hr; Gajeva 1; s/d from 740/885KN; P❄📶) Smack on the main square, this glass New York–wannabe is a city landmark, and the 245 well-appointed units have old-school classic style. It buzzes with business travellers who love being at the centre of the action – try to get a view of Jelačić square and watch Zagreb pass by under your window. Inquire about packages and specials.

Eating

You can pick up excellent fresh produce, cheeses and cold cuts at Dolac market (p252). The city centre's main streets, including Ilica, Teslina, Gajeva and Preradovićeva, are lined with fast-food joints and inexpensive snack bars. Note that many restaurants close in August for the summer holiday, which typically lasts anywhere from two weeks to a month.

Karijola PIZZA $

(Vlaška 63; pizzas from 42KN; ⏰11am-midnight Mon-Sat, to 11pm Sun) Locals swear by the crispy, thin-crust pizza churned out of a clay oven at this newer location of Zagreb's best pizza joint. Pizzas come with high-quality ingredients, such as smoked ham, olive oil, rich mozzarella, cherry tomatoes, rocket and shiitake mushrooms.

Tip Top SEAFOOD $

(Gundulićeva 18; mains from 40KN; ⏰7am-11pm Mon-Sat) How we love Tip Top and its waitstaff, who still sport old socialist uniforms and scowling faces that eventually turn to smiles. But we mostly love the excellent Dalmatian food. Every day has a different set menu.

Pingvin SANDWICHES $

(Teslina 7; sandwiches from 15KN; ⏰10am-4am Mon-Sat, 6pm-2am Sun) This quick-bite institution, around since 1987, offers tasty designer sandwiches and salads, which locals savour on a couple of bar stools.

Vincek BAKERY $

(Ilica 18; pastries from 6KN; ⏰8.30am-11pm Mon-Sat) This institution of a *slastičarna* (pastry shop) serves some of Zagreb's creamiest cakes. They have some serious competition, however, with **Torte i To** (Nova Ves 11, 2nd fl, Kaptol Centar; pastries from 3KN; ⏰8am-11pm Mon-Sat, 9am-11pm Sun) on the 2nd floor of Kaptol Centar, and the recently opened **Mak Na Konac** (Dukljaninova 1; pastries from 8KN; ⏰9am-9pm Mon-Sat).

★ **Mundoaka Street Food** INTERNATIONAL $$

(☎01-78 88 777; Petrinjska 2; mains from 45KN; ⏰8am-midnight Mon-Thu, to 1am Fri, 9am-1am Sat) This adorable new eatery clad in light wood, with tables outside, serves up American classics – think chicken wings and pork ribs – and a global spectrum of dishes, from Spanish tortillas to *shakshuka* eggs. Great breakfasts, muffins and cakes, all prepared by one of Zagreb's best-known chefs. Reserve ahead.

★Vinodol CROATIAN $$
(www.vinodol-zg.hr; Teslina 10; mains from 56KN; ⊙noon-11pm) The well-prepared Central European fare here is much-loved by local and overseas patrons. On warm days, eat on the covered patio (entered through an ivy-clad passageway off Teslina); the cold-weather alternative is the dining hall with vaulted stone ceilings. Highlights include the succulent lamb or veal and potatoes cooked under *peka* (domed baking lid) as well as *bukovače* (local mushrooms).

Lari & Penati MODERN CROATIAN $$
(Petrinjska 42a; mains from 60KN; ⊙noon-11pm Mon-Fri, to 5pm Sat) Small stylish bistro that serves up innovative lunch and dinner specials – they change daily according to what's market-fresh. The food is fab, the music cool and the few sidewalk tables lovely in warm weather. Closes for two weeks in August.

Didov San DALMATIAN $$
(☎01-48 51 154; www.konoba-didovsan.com; Mletačka 11; mains from 60KN; ⊙10am-midnight) This Upper Town tavern features a rustic wooden interior with ceiling beams and tables on the streetside deck. The food is based on traditional cuisine from the Neretva River delta in Dalmatia's hinterland, such as grilled frogs wrapped in prosciutto. Reserve ahead.

Zinfandel's INTERNATIONAL $$$
(☎01-45 66 644; www.esplanade.hr/cuisine/; Mihanovićeva 1; mains from 170KN; ⊙6am-11pm Mon-Sat, 6.30am-11pm Sun) The tastiest, most creative dishes in town are served with flair in the dining room of the Esplanade Zagreb Hotel (p256). For a simpler but still delicious dining experience, head to French-flavoured **Le Bistro** (www.esplanade.hr/french-chic/; Mihanovićeva 1; mains from 95KN; ⊙9am-11pm), also in the hotel – and don't miss its famous *štrukli* pastry.

Drinking & Nightlife

In the Upper Town, the chic Tkalčićeva is throbbing with bars and cafes. In the Lower Town, there's bar-lined Bogovićeva and Trg Petra Preradovića (known locally as Cvjetni trg), the most popular spot in the Lower Town for street performers and occasional bands.

One of the nicest ways to see Zagreb is to join in on the *špica* – Saturday-morning pre-lunch coffee drinking on the terraces along Bogovićeva, Preradovićeva and Tkalčićeva.

Clubs are mainly located around the Lower Town. Entry ranges from 20KN to 100KN, and things don't get lively until around midnight.

Stross BAR
(Strossmayerovo Šetalište; ⊙from 9.30pm daily Jun-Sep) A makeshift bar is set up most nights in summer at the Strossmayer promenade in the Upper Town, with cheap drinks and live music. The mixed-bag crowd, great city views and leafy ambience make it a great spot to while away your evenings.

Booksa CAFE
(www.booksa.hr; Martićeva 14d; ⊙11am-8pm Tue-Sun; 📶) Bookworms and poets, writers and performers, oddballs and artists…basically anyone creative in Zagreb comes here to chat and drink coffee, browse the library, surf with free wi-fi and hear readings at this lovely, book-themed cafe. There are English-language readings here, too; check the website. Closes for three weeks from late July.

Kino Europa CAFE, BAR
(www.kinoeuropa.hr; Varšavska 3; ⊙8.30am-midnight Mon-Thu, to 4am Fri & Sat, 11am-11pm Sun; 📶) Zagreb's oldest cinema, from the 1920s, now houses a splendid cafe, wine bar and *grapperia*. At this glass-enclosed space with an outdoor terrace, you can enjoy great coffee, over 30 types of grappa and free wi-fi. The cinema hosts film screenings and occasional dance parties.

Mojo BAR
(Martićeva 5; ⊙7am-2am Mon-Fri, 8am-2am Sat, 8am-midnight Sun) Smoky basement hang-out where live music and DJ-spun tunes are on every night. On warm nights, take your pick among 70 *rakijas* (grappas) and liqueurs and sample them on the sidewalk tables out front.

Basement Wine Bar WINE BAR
(Tomićeva 5; ⊙9am-2am Mon-Sat, 4pm-midnight Sun) A city-centre hot spot for sampling Croatian wines by the glass, this basement bar (with a few sidewalk tables) sits right by the funicular. Pair the tipple with meat and cheese platters.

VIP Club CLUB
(www.vip-club.hr; Trg Bana Jelačića 9; ⊙8pm-5am Tue-Sat, closed summer) This newcomer on the nightlife scene has quickly become a local favourite. A swank basement place on the main square, it offers a varied program, from jazz to Balkan beats. It closes in summer months.

Masters CLUB
(Ravnice bb) Zagreb's smallest club also has the most powerful sound system, the feel of a private party and top-notch local and international DJ acts spinning deep house, tech-house, dub and reggae.

Pepermint CLUB
(www.pepermint-zagreb.com; Ilica 24; ⏰10pm-5am Tue-Sat, closed Aug) Small and chic city centre club clad in white wood, with two levels and a well-to-do older crowd. Programs change weekly, ranging from vintage rockabilly and swing to soul and house.

Aquarius CLUB
(www.aquarius.hr; Aleja Matije Ljubeka bb, Jarun Lake) Past its heyday but still fun, this lake-side club has a series of rooms that open onto a huge terrace. House and techno are the standard fare but there are also hip-hop and R&B nights. During summer, Aquarius sets up shop at Zrće on Pag.

KSET CLUB
(www.kset.org; Unska 3; ⏰9am-4pm & 8pm-midnight Mon-Thu, 9am-4pm & 8pm-1am Fri, 10pm-3am Sat) Zagreb's top music venue, with everyone who's anyone performing here, from ethno to hip-hop acts. Saturday nights are dedicated to DJ music, when youngsters dance till late. You'll find gigs and events to suit most tastes.

☆ Entertainment

Zagrebačko Kazalište Mladih THEATRE
(☎01-48 72 554; www.zekaem.hr; Teslina 7; ⏰box office 10am-8pm Mon-Fri, to 2pm Sat & Sun, plus 1hr before the show) Zagreb Youth Theatre, better known as ZKM, is considered the cradle of Croatia's contemporary theatre. It hosts several festivals and many visiting troupes from around the world.

Croatian National Theatre THEATRE
(☎01-48 88 418; www.hnk.hr; Trg Maršala Tita 15; ⏰box office 10am-7pm Mon-Fri, to 1pm Sat & 1hr before the show) This neobaroque theatre, established in 1895, stages opera and ballet performances. Check out Ivan Meštrović's sculpture *The Well of Life* (1905) standing out front.

ℹ Information

There are ATMs at the bus and train stations, the airport, and at numerous locations around town. Some banks in the train and bus stations accept travellers cheques. Several cafes around town offer free wi-fi.

Atlas Travel Agency (☎01-48 07 300; www.atlas-croatia.com; Zrinjevac 17) Tours around Croatia.

KBC Rebro (☎01-23 88 888; Kišpatićeva 12; ⏰24hr) East of the city; provides emergency aid.

Main Tourist Office (☎information 0800 53 53, office 01-48 14 051; www.zagreb-tourist info.hr; Trg Bana Jelačića 11; ⏰8.30am-9pm Mon-Fri, 9am-6pm Sat & Sun Jun-Sep, 8.30am-8pm Mon-Fri, 9am-6pm Sat, 10am-4pm Sun Oct-May) Distributes free city maps and leaflets, and sells the 24- (60KN) or 72-hour (90KN) **Zagreb Card** (www.zagrebcard.fivestars.hr).

ℹ Getting There & Away

AIR

Zagreb Airport (☎01-45 62 222; www.zagreb-airport.hr) Located 17km southeast of Zagreb, this is Croatia's major airport, offering a range of international and domestic services.

BUS

Zagreb's **bus station** (☎060 313 333; www.akz.hr; Avenija M Držića 4) is 1km east of the train station. If you need to store bags, there's a **garderoba** (left luggage; bus station; per hr 5KN; ⏰24hr). Trams 2 and 6 run from the bus station to the train station. Tram 6 goes to Trg Bana Jelačića. Frequent domestic departures include: Dubrovnik (205KN to 250KN, 9½ to 11 hours, nine to 12 daily), Rovinj (150KN to 195KN, four to six hours, nine to 11 daily) and Split (115KN to 205KN, five to 8½ hours, 32 to 34 daily).

International destinations include Belgrade (220KN, six hours, five daily), Sarajevo (160KN to 210KN, seven to eight hours, four to five daily) and Vienna (225KN to 247KN, five to six hours, three daily).

TRAIN

The **train station** (☎060 333 444; www.hznet.hr; Trg Kralja Tomislava 12) is in the southern part of the city; there's a **garderoba** (train station; lockers per 24hr 15KN; ⏰24hr). It's advisable to book train tickets in advance because of limited seating.

Domestic trains head to Split (197KN to 208KN, five to seven hours, four daily). There are international departures to Belgrade (188KN, 6½ hours, daily), Ljubljana (127KN, 2½ hours, four daily), Sarajevo (238KN, eight to 9½ hours, daily) and Vienna (520KN, six to seven hours, two daily).

ℹ Getting Around

Zagreb is a fairly easy city to navigate. Traffic is bearable and the tram system efficient.

WORTH A TRIP

OTHER PLACES WORTH A VISIT

Istria Don't miss the peninsula's main city, **Pula**, with its wealth of Roman architecture. The star of the show is the remarkably well-preserved amphitheatre dating back to the 1st century. About 10km south along the indented shoreline, the **Premantura Peninsula** hides a spectacular nature park, the protected cape of Kamenjak with its lovely rolling hills, wild flowers, low Mediterranean shrubs, fruit trees and medicinal herbs, and around 30km of virgin beaches and coves.

South Dalmatia The island of **Korčula**, rich in vineyards and olive trees, is the largest island in an archipelago of 48, with plenty of opportunities for scenic drives, many quiet coves and secluded beaches, as well as Korčula Town, a striking walled town of round defensive towers, narrow stone streets and red-roofed houses that resembles a miniature Dubrovnik.

Around Dubrovnik A great excursion from Dubrovnik is the seductive island of **Mljet**, its northwestern half showcasing Mljet National Park, where the lush vegetation, pine forests and spectacular saltwater lakes are exceptionally scenic. It's an unspoiled oasis of tranquillity that, according to legend, captivated Odysseus for seven years.

TO/FROM THE AIRPORT

Bus

The Croatia Airlines bus to the airport (30KN) leaves from the bus station every half-hour or hour from about 4.30am to 8pm, and returns from the airport on the same schedule.

Taxi

Taxis cost between 110KN and 200KN.

PUBLIC TRANSPORT

Public transport (www.zet.hr) is based on an efficient network of trams, although the city centre is compact enough to make them almost unnecessary. Tram maps are posted at most stations, making the system easy to navigate.

Buy tickets at newspaper kiosks or from the driver for 10KN. Tickets can be used for transfers within 90 minutes, but only in one direction.

A *dnevna karta* (day ticket), valid on all public transport until 4am the next morning, is available for 30KN at most newspaper kiosks.

Make sure you validate your ticket when you get on the tram by inserting it in the yellow box.

TAXI

For short city rides, **Taxi Cammeo** (☎060 71 00, 1212) is typically the cheapest, the 15KN start fare includes the first two kilometres (it's 6KN for every subsequent kilometre).

ISTRIA

☎052

Continental Croatia meets the Adriatic in Istria (Istra to Croats), the heart-shaped 3600-sq-km peninsula just south of Trieste in Italy. While the bucolic interior of rolling hills and fertile plains attracts artsy visitors to its hilltop villages, rural hotels and farmhouse restaurants, the verdant indented coastline is enormously popular with the sun'n'sea set. Vast hotel complexes line much of the coast and its rocky beaches are not Croatia's best, but the facilities are wide-ranging, the sea is clean and secluded spots are still plentiful.

The coast gets flooded with tourists in summer, but you can still feel alone and undisturbed in 'Green Istria' (the interior), even in mid-August. Add acclaimed gastronomy (starring fresh seafood, prime white truffles, wild asparagus, top-rated olive oils and award-winning wines), sprinkle it with historical charm and you have a little slice of heaven.

Rovinj

POP 14,365

Rovinj (Rovigno in Italian) is coastal Istria's star attraction. While it can get overrun with tourists in summer, it remains one of the last true Mediterranean fishing ports. Wooded hills and low-rise hotels surround the old town, which is webbed with steep cobbled streets and piazzas. The 14 green islands of the Rovinj archipelago make for a pleasant afternoon away; the most popular islands are Sveta Katarina and Crveni Otok (Red Island), also known as Sveti Andrija.

The old town is contained within an egg-shaped peninsula. About 1.5km south is the

Punta Corrente Forest Park and the wooded cape of Zlatni Rt (Golden Cape), with its age-old oak and pine trees and several large hotels. There are two harbours: the northern open harbour and the small, protected harbour to the south.

Sights

★Church of St Euphemia CHURCH
(Sveta Eufemija; Petra Stankovića; ⏲10am-6pm Jun-Sep, to 4pm May, to 2pm Apr) The town's showcase, this imposing church dominates the old town from its hilltop location in the middle of the peninsula. Built in 1736, it's the largest baroque building in Istria, reflecting the period during the 18th century when Rovinj was its most populous town. Inside, look for the marble **tomb of St Euphemia** behind the right-hand altar.

Batana House MUSEUM
(Pina Budicina 2; adult/concession 10/5KN, with guide 15KN; ⏲10am-2pm & 7-11pm) On the harbour, Batana House is a museum dedicated to the *batana,* a flat-bottomed fishing boat that stands as a symbol of Rovinj's seafaring and fishing traditions. The multimedia exhibits inside the 17th-century town house have interactive displays, excellent captions and audio with *bitinada,* which are typical fishers' songs. Check out the *spacio,* the ground-floor cellar where wine was kept, tasted and sold amid much socialising (open on Tuesday and Thursday).

Grisia STREET
Lined with galleries where local artists sell their work, this cobbled street leads uphill from behind the Balbi Arch to St Euphemia. The winding narrow backstreets that spread around Grisia are an attraction in themselves. Windows, balconies, portals and squares are a pleasant confusion of styles – Gothic, Renaissance, baroque and neoclassical. Notice the unique *fumaioli* (exterior chimneys), built during the population boom when entire families lived in a single room with a fireplace.

Punta Corrente Forest Park PARK
(Zlatni Rt) Follow the waterfront on foot or by bike past Hotel Park to this verdant area, locally known as Zlatni Rt, about 1.5km south. Covered in oak and pine groves and boasting 10 species of cypress, the park was established in 1890 by Baron Hütterott, an Austrian admiral who kept a villa on Crveni Otok. You can swim off the rocks or just sit and admire the offshore islands.

Sleeping

Porton Biondi CAMPGROUND $
(☎052-813 557; www.portonbiondi.hr; Aleja Porton Biondi 1; campsites per person/tent 53/40KN; ⏲mid-Mar–Oct; 👪) This beachside campground, which sleeps 1200, is about 700m north of the old town.

Villa Baron Gautsch GUESTHOUSE $$
(☎052-840 538; www.baron-gautsch.com; IM Ronjgova 7; s/d incl breakfast 293/586KN; ❄📶) This German-owned *pansion* (guesthouse), up the leafy street leading up from Hotel Park, has 17 spick-and-span rooms, some with terraces and lovely views of the sea and the old town. Breakfast is served on the small terrace out the back. It's cash (kuna) only.

★Hotel Lone DESIGN HOTEL $$$
(☎052-632 000; www.lonehotel.com; Luje Adamovića 31; s/d 1800/2300KN; P❄@📶) Croatia's first design hotel, this 248-room powerhouse of style is a creation of Croatia's starchitects 3LHD. It rises over Lone bay like a ship dropped in the forest. Light-flooded rooms come with private terraces and five-star trimmings. Facilities include a couple of restaurants, an extensive spa and a brand-new beach club.

Eating

Male Madlene TAPAS $
(☎052-815 905; Svetog Križa 28; snacks from 30KN; ⏲11am-2pm & 7-11pm May-Sep) Adorable spot in the owner's tiny living room hanging over the sea, where she serves up creative finger food with market-fresh ingredients, based on old Italian recipes. Think tuna-filled zucchini, goat-cheese-stuffed peppers and bite-size savoury pies and cakes. A 12-snack plate for two is 100KN. Great Istrian wines by the glass. Reserve ahead, especially for evenings.

Da Sergio PIZZA $
(Grisia 11; pizzas 28-71KN; ⏲11am-3pm & 6-11pm) It's worth waiting in line to get a table at this old-fashioned two-floor pizzeria that dishes out Rovinj's best thin-crust pizza, which locals swear by. The best is Gogo, with fresh tomato and arugula (rocket) and prosciutto.

★Kantinon SEAFOOD $$
(Alda Rismonda bb; mains from 70KN; ⏲noon-11pm) Recently unveiled in its new incarnation, this top eating choice is headed up by a stellar team – one of Croatia's best chefs and an equally amazing sommelier. The food is

WORTH A TRIP

PLITVICE LAKES NATIONAL PARK

The absolute highlight of Croatia's Adriatic hinterland, this glorious expanse of forested hills and turquoise lakes is exquisitely scenic – so much so that in 1979 Unesco proclaimed the **park** (053-751 015; www.np-plitvicka-jezera.hr; adult/child Jul & Aug 180/80KN, Apr-Jun, Sep & Oct 110/55KN, Nov-Mar 55/35KN; 7am-8pm) a World Heritage Site.

Sixteen crystalline lakes tumble into each other via a series of waterfalls and cascades, while clouds of butterflies drift above. It takes upwards of six hours to explore the 18km of wooden footbridges and pathways which snake around the edges of the rumbling water on foot, but you can slice two hours off by taking advantage of the park's free boats and buses (departing every 30 minutes from April to October).

While the park is beautiful year-round, spring and autumn are the best times to visit. In spring and early summer the falls are flush with water, while in autumn the changing leaves put on a colourful display. Winter is also spectacular, although snow can limit access and the free park transport doesn't operate. If possible, avoid the peak months of July and August, when the falls reduce to a trickle, parking is problematic and the sheer volume of visitors can turn the walking tracks into a conga line.

100% Croatian, with ingredients as local and fresh as they get, and lots of seafood based on old-fashioned fishers' recipes. Don't miss their sardines *na savor*.

Monte MEDITERRANEAN **$$$**
(052-830 203; Montalbano 75; mains from 190KN; noon-2.30pm & 6.30-11pm) Rovinj's top restaurant, right below St Euphemia Church, is worth the hefty cost. Enjoy beautifully presented dishes on the elegant glassed-in terrace. Don't want to splurge? Have a pasta or risotto (from 124KN). Try the fennel ice cream. Reserve ahead in high season.

Drinking & Nightlife

Limbo CAFE, BAR
(Casale 22b; 10am-1am) Cosy cafe-bar with small candlelit tables and cushions laid out on the stairs leading to the old town's hilltop. It serves tasty snacks and good *prosecco* (sweet dessert wine).

Valentino COCKTAIL BAR
(Svetog Križa 28; 6pm-midnight) Premium cocktail prices at this high-end spot include fantastic sunset views from cushions scattered on the water's edge.

Getting There & Away

The bus station is just to the southeast of the old town, and offers a **garderoba** (per day 10KN; 6.30am-8pm). There are daily services to Zagreb (145KN to 180KN, four to five hours), Split (444KN, 11 hours) and Dubrovnik (628KN, 15 to 16 hours).

DALMATIA

Roman ruins, spectacular beaches, old fishing ports, medieval architecture and unspoilt offshore islands make a trip to Dalmatia (Dalmacija) unforgettable. Occupying the central 375km of Croatia's Adriatic coast, Dalmatia offers a matchless combination of hedonism and historical discovery. The jagged coast is speckled with lush offshore islands and dotted with historic cities.

Split

021 / POP 178,200

The second-largest city in Croatia, Split (Spalato in Italian) is a great place to see Dalmatian life as it's really lived. Always buzzing, this exuberant city has just the right balance of tradition and modernity. Step inside Diocletian's Palace (a Unesco World Heritage Site and one of the world's most impressive Roman monuments) and you'll see dozens of bars, restaurants and shops thriving amid the atmospheric old walls. To top it off, Split has a unique setting: the turquoise waters of the Adriatic backed by dramatic coastal mountains.

The Old Town is a vast open-air museum and the information signs at the important sights explain a great deal of Split's history. The seafront promenade, Obala Hrvatskog Narodnog Preporoda, better known as Riva, is the best central reference point.

Central Split

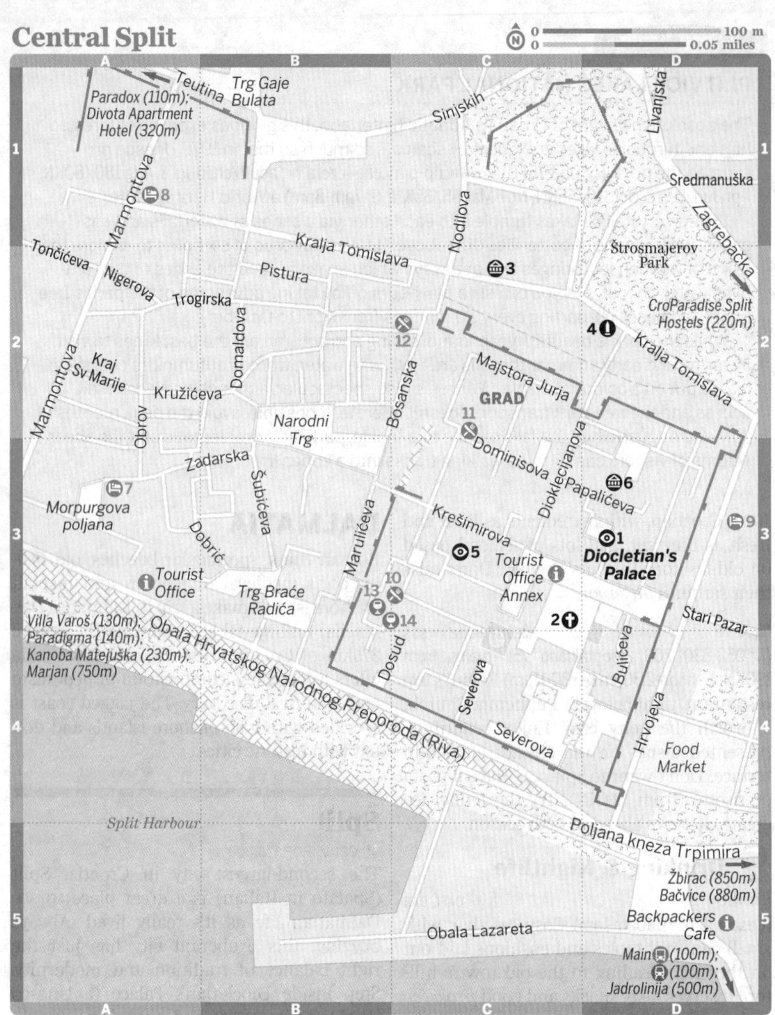

Sights

Diocletian's Palace

Facing the harbour, **Diocletian's Palace** is one of the most imposing Roman ruins in existence. Don't expect a palace though, nor a museum – this is the living heart of the city, its labyrinthine streets packed with people, bars, shops and restaurants.

It was built as a military fortress, imperial residence and fortified town, with walls reinforced by square corner towers. There are 220 buildings within the palace boundaries, which is home to about 3000 people.

Town Museum MUSEUM

(Muzej Grada Splita; www.mgst.net; Papalićeva 1; adult/concession 20/10KN; ⏲9am-9pm Tue-Fri, to 4pm Sat-Mon) Built by Juraj Dalmatinac for one of the many noblemen who lived within the palace in the Middle Ages, Papalić Palace is considered a fine example of late-Gothic style, with an elaborately carved entrance

Central Split

Top Sights
1 Diocletian's Palace D3

Sights
2 Cathedral of St Domnius C3
3 Gallery of Fine Arts..............................C2
4 Gregorius of Nin.................................D2
5 Temple of Jupiter C3
6 Town Museum D3

Sleeping
7 Goli + Bosi A3
8 Silver Central Hostel A1
9 Silver Gate..D3

Eating
10 Figa C3
11 UJE Oil Bar C2
12 Villa Spiza C2

Drinking & Nightlife
13 Fluid B3
14 Ghetto Club B3

gate that proclaimed the importance of its original inhabitants. The interior has been thoroughly restored to house this museum.

Cathedral of St Domnius CATHEDRAL
(Katedrala Svetog Duje; Duje 5; cathedral/treasury/belfry 15/15/10KN; 8am-7pm Mon-Sat, 12.30-6.30pm Sun) FREE Split's octagonal-shaped cathedral was originally built as Diocletian's mausoleum, encircled by 24 columns, that is almost completely preserved to this day. Its round domed interior has two rows of Corinthian columns and a frieze showing Emperor Diocletian and his wife. Note that admission to the cathedral also gets you free access to the Temple of Jupiter and its crypt. For 35KN, you can get a ticket that includes access to all these highlights.

Temple of Jupiter TEMPLE
(admission temple/temple & cathedral 10/35KN; 8am-7pm Mon-Sat, 12.30-6.30pm Sun) The headless sphinx in black granite guarding the entrance to the temple was imported from Egypt at the time of the temple's construction in the 5th century. Of the columns that supported a porch the temple once had, only one remains. Take a look at the barrel-vaulted ceiling and a decorative frieze on the walls. You can also pop into the crypt, which was used as a church back in the day.

Outside the Palace Walls

Gregorius of Nin MONUMENT
(Grgur Ninski) The 10th-century Croatian bishop Gregorius of Nin fought for the right to use old Croatian in liturgical services. Sculpted by Ivan Meštrović, this powerful work is one of the defining images of Split. Notice that his left big toe has been polished to a shine – it's said that rubbing the toe brings good luck and guarantees that you'll come back to Split.

Gallery of Fine Arts GALLERY
(Galerija Umjetnina Split; www.galum.hr; Kralja Tomislava 15; adult/concession 20/10KN; 11am-4pm Mon, to 7pm Tue-Fri, to 3pm Sat) In the building that once housed the city's first hospital, this gallery exhibits nearly 400 works of art spanning almost 700 years. Upstairs is the permanent collection of mainly paintings and some sculpture, a chronological journey that starts with the old masters and continues with works of modern Croatian art by the likes of Vlaho Bukovac and Ignjat Job. Temporary exhibits downstairs change every few months. The pleasant cafe has a terrace overlooking the palace.

Activities

Bačvice SWIMMING
A flourishing beach life gives Split its aura of insouciance in summer. The pebbly Bačvice is the most popular beach, awarded with a Blue Flag eco label. You'll find good **swimming**, lively ambience and *picigin* (beach-ball) games galore. There are showers and changing rooms at both ends of the beach. Bačvice is also a popular summer bar and club area for Split's younger crowd and for visitors.

Marjan WALKING TRAIL
For an afternoon away from the city buzz, Marjan (178m) is the perfect destination. Considered the lungs of the city, this hilly nature reserve offers trails through fragrant pine forests, scenic lookouts and ancient chapels.

Sleeping

Hostels have sprouted all around Split in the last couple of years. Private accommodation is still a great option; expect to pay between 300KN and 500KN for a double room; in the cheaper ones you will probably share the bathroom with the proprietor. Split has quite a few boutique hotels popping up in the old town.

CroParadise Split Hostels HOSTEL $
(☎091 444 4194; www.croparadise.com; Čulića Dvori 29; dm 200KN, s/d 250/500KN, apt from 500KN; ❄@🛜) A great collection of three hostels – Blue, Green and Pink – inside converted apartments in the neighbourhood of Manuš. The shared bar Underground (open June to September) is a starting point for pub crawls (Monday to Saturday nights). Other facilities include laundry, bike and scooter rental. Five apartments are also available.

Silver Central Hostel HOSTEL $
(☎021-490 805; www.silvercentralhostel.com; Kralja Tomislava 1; dm 190KN; ❄@🛜) In an upstairs apartment, this light-yellow-coloured boutique hostel has four dorm rooms and a pleasant lounge. It has a two-person apartment nearby (250KN to 520KN) and another hostel, **Silver Gate** (☎021-322 857; www.silvergatehostel.com; Hrvojeva 6; dm per person 180KN, d with kitchen 525KN), near the food market.

★**Goli + Bosi** HOSTEL $$
(☎021-510 999; www.gollybossy.com; Morpurgova Poljana 2; dm/s/d 240/700/800KN) Split's design hostel is the premier destination for flashpackers, with its sleek futuristic decor, hip vibe and a cool lobby cafe-bar-restaurant. For 1130KN you get the superior double (called Mala Floramy), with breakfast included and gorgeous views.

Villa Varoš GUESTHOUSE $$
(☎021-483 469; www.villavaros.hr; Miljenka Smoje 1; d/ste 586/887KN; P❄🛜) Midrangers are getting a better deal in Split nowadays, with places such as Villa Varoš around. Owned by a New Yorker Croat, Villa Varoš is central, the rooms are simple, bright and airy, and the apartment has a Jacuzzi and a small terrace.

★**Divota Apartment Hotel** HOTEL $$$
(☎091 404 1199; www.divota.hr; Plinarska 75; s/d 761/823KN; ❄🛜) Scattered across the Varoš neighbourhood in eight restored fishers' houses, Divota, owned by an artsy Swiss-Croatian, provides a retreat from the nearby palace buzz. The six contemporary rooms, nine apartments (1508KN) and a stunning three-bedroom villa (5030KN) with a courtyard come with upscale amenities, original detail and unique features, like a bedroom inside a vaulted well.

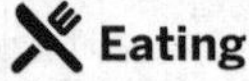

Eating

★**Villa Spiza** DALMATIAN $
(Kružićeva 3; mains from 50KN; ⊙9am-midnight Mon-Sat) Locals' favourite within the palace walls, this low-key joint offers great-quality Dalmatian mainstays that change daily – think calamari, risotto, stuffed peppers – at low prices. It's fresh home cooking served at the bar inside, or at a couple of benches outside. Service is slow but the food is prepared with care.

Figa INTERNATIONAL $
(☎021-274 491; Buvinina 1; mains from 50KN; ⊙8.30am-1am) A cool little restaurant and bar, with a funky interior and tables on the stairs outside, Figa serves nice breakfasts, seafood dishes and a wide range of salads. There's live music some nights and the kitchen stays open late. Service can be slow but comes with smiles and jokes.

Konoba Matejuška DALMATIAN $
(☎021-355 152; Tomića Stine 3; mains from 50KN; ⊙noon-midnight) Cosy, rustic tavern in an alleyway minutes from the seafront, it specialises in well-prepared seafood that also happens to be well-priced. The waitstaff are friendly. Wash down your meal with a glass of *kujunđuša,* a local white wine from Dalmatia's hinterland.

Paradigma MEDITERRANEAN $$
(☎021-645 103; Bana Josipa Jelačića 3; mains from 95KN; ⊙8am-midnight) Bringing culinary innovation to Split, this new restaurant sports modern interiors with hand-painted murals and a rooftop terrace featuring Riva views in an old building resembling a ship's bow. It's slightly hidden from the tourist scene. Highlights are its top-notch wine list and Mediterranean-inspired dishes, like olive oil *sorbetto,* sous vide steaks and *pršut* (prosciutto) powder.

UJE Oil Bar DALMATIAN $$
(Dominisova 3; mains from 70KN; ⊙9am-midnight) A restaurant and olive oil/delicatessen shop with a small selection of mains, several tapas-style dishes and olive-oil tasting options. Rustic light-wood interiors are charming, as are alfresco seats in the alley. Service can be spotty though. Their recently opened wine bar next door is set against the original stone walls of Diocletian's Palace.

Drinking & Nightlife

Žbirac CAFE
(Šetalište Petra Preradovića 1b; ⏲7am-1am Sun-Thu, to 2am Fri-Sat) This beachfront cafe is like the locals' open-air living room, a cult hang-out with great sea views, swimming day and night, *picigin* games and occasional concerts.

Ghetto Club BAR
(Dosud 10; ⏲6pm-midnight Mon-Thu, to 2am Fri-Sat) Head for Split's most bohemian and gay-friendly bar, in an intimate courtyard amid flower beds, a trickling fountain, great music and a friendly atmosphere.

Fluid BAR
(Dosud 1; ⏲8am-midnight Mon-Thu, to 1am Fri-Sat) This chic little spot is a jazzy party venue, pretty low-key and cool. Great for people-watching.

Paradox WINE BAR
(Poljana Tina Ujevića 2; ⏲9am-1am Mon-Sat, 4pm-1am Sun) Stylish wine bar with cool wine-glass chandeliers inside, alfresco tables and a great selection of well-priced Croatian wines and local cheeses to go with them.

Information

You can change money at travel agencies or the post office. There are ATMs throughout the city.

Backpackers Cafe (☎021-338 548; Kneza Domagoja bb; internet per hr 30KN; ⏲7am-8pm) Sells used books, offers luggage storage and internet access, and provides information for backpackers.

KBC Firule (☎021-556 111; Spinčićeva 1) Split's hospital.

Tourist Office (☎021-360 066; www.visitsplit.com; Hrvatskog Narodnog Preporoda 9; ⏲8am-9pm Mon-Sat, to 1pm Sun Jun-Sep) Has info on Split and sells the Split Card (35KN), which offers free and reduced prices to Split attractions and discounts on car rental, restaurants, shops and hotels. You get the card for free if you're staying in Split more than three nights.

Tourist Office Annex (☎021-345 606; www.visitsplit.com; Peristil bb; ⏲8am-9pm Mon-Sat, to 1pm Sun Jun-Sep) This tourist office annex on Peristil has shorter hours.

Turist Biro (☎021-347 100; www.turistbiro-split.hr; Hrvatskog Narodnog Preporoda 12) Its forte is private accommodation and excursions.

Getting There & Away

AIR

Split Airport (www.split-airport.hr) is 20km west of town, just 6km before Trogir. **Croatia Airlines** (☎021-895 298; www.croatiaairlines.hr; Split Airport; ⏲5.15am-8pm) operates one-hour flights to and from Zagreb several times a day and a weekly flight to Dubrovnik (summer only).

A couple of low-cost airlines fly to Split, including **Easyjet** (www.easyjet.com), **germanwings** (www.germanwings.com) and **Norwegian** (www.norwegian.com).

BOAT

Jadrolinija (☎021-338 333; www.jadrolinija.hr; Gat Sv Duje bb) handles most of the coastal ferry lines and catamarans that operate between Split and the islands.

There is also a fast passenger boat, the **Krilo** (www.krilo.hr), that goes to Hvar Town (70KN, one hour) twice daily. There's also a new connection twice weekly to Dubrovnik from mid-May through mid-October (170KN, 4½ hour).

Car ferries and passenger lines depart from separate docks; the passenger lines leave from Obala Lazareta and car ferries from Gat Sv Duje. You can buy tickets from either the main Jadrolinija office in the large ferry terminal opposite the bus station, or at one of the two stalls near the docks. You can't reserve tickets ahead of time; they're only available for purchase on the day of departure. In summer it's usually necessary to appear several hours before departure for a car ferry, and put your car in the line for boarding. There is rarely a problem or a long wait obtaining a space off-season.

BUS

Advance bus tickets with seat reservations are recommended. Most buses leave from the main **bus station** (☎060 327 777; www.ak-split.hr) beside the harbour, which has a **garderoba** (1st hr 5KN, then per hr 1.50KN; ⏲6am-10pm), to the following destinations: Dubrovnik (115KN to 137KN, 4½ hours, 15 daily), Pula (308KN to 423KN, 10 to 11 hours, three daily) and Zagreb (144KN to 175KN, seven hours, 40 daily).

Note that Split–Dubrovnik buses pass briefly through Bosnian territory, so keep your passport handy for border-crossing points.

TRAIN

There are five daily trains (89KN, six to eight hours) between Zagreb and Split **train station** (☎021-338 525; www.hznet.hr; Kneza Domagoja 9), which is just behind the bus station; two are overnight. There's a **garderoba** (per day 15KN; ⏲6am-10pm) at the station.

WORTH A TRIP

PAKLENI ISLANDS

Most visitors to Hvar Town head to the Pakleni Islands (Pakleni Otoci), which got their name, 'Hell's Islands' in Croatian, from Paklina, the resin that once coated boats and ships.

This gorgeous chain of 21 wooded isles has crystal-clean seas, hidden beaches and deserted lagoons. Taxi boats leave regularly during the high season from in front of the Arsenal to the islands of **Jerolim** and **Stipanska** (40KN, 10 to 15 minutes), which are popular naturist islands (although nudity is not mandatory). They continue on to **Ždrilca** and **Mlini** (40KN) and, further out, **Palmižana** (60KN), which has a pebble beach and the **Meneghello Place** (www.palmizana.hr), a beautiful boutique complex of villas and bungalows scattered among lush tropical gardens. Run by the artsy Meneghello family, the estate holds music recitals, and features two excellent restaurants and an art gallery. Also on Palmižana are two top restaurant-cum-hang-out spots, Toto and Laganini.

Hvar Island

☎021 / POP 10,900

Hvar is the number-one carrier of Croatia's superlatives: it's the most luxurious island, the sunniest place in the country and, along with Dubrovnik, the most popular tourist destination. Hvar is also famed for its verdancy and its lilac lavender fields.

The island's hub and busiest destination is Hvar Town. Visitors wander along the main square, explore the sights on the winding stone streets, swim on the numerous beaches or pop off to strip off to their birthday suits on the Pakleni Islands, but most of all they party at night. There are several good restaurants and a number of top hotels, as well as a couple of hostels.

The interior of the island hides abandoned ancient hamlets, towering peaks and green, largely uncharted landscapes. It's worth exploring on a day trip.

Sights & Activities

St Stephen's Square SQUARE

(Trg Svetog Stjepana) The centre of town is this rectangular square, which was formed by filling in an inlet that once stretched out from the bay. At 4500 sq metres, it's one of the largest old squares in Dalmatia. The town first developed in the 13th century to the north of the square and later spread south in the 15th century. Notice the **well** at the square's northern end, which was built in 1520 and has a wrought-iron grill dating from 1780.

Franciscan Monastery & Museum MONASTERY

(admission 25KN; ⏱9am-1pm & 5-7pm Mon-Sat) This 15th-century monastery overlooks a shady cove. The elegant **bell tower** was built in the 16th century by a well-known family of stonemasons from Korčula. The **Renaissance cloister** leads to a refectory containing lace, coins, nautical charts and valuable documents, such as an edition of *Ptolemy's Atlas,* printed in 1524.

Fortica FORTRESS

(admission 25KN; ⏱9am-9pm) Through the network of tiny streets northwest of St Stephen's Sq, climb up through a park to the citadel built on the site of a medieval castle to defend the town from the Turks. The Venetians strengthened it in 1557 and then the Austrians renovated it in the 19th century by adding barracks. Inside is a tiny collection of ancient amphorae recovered from the seabed. The view over the harbour is magnificent, and there's a lovely cafe at the top.

Tours

Secret Hvar GUIDED

(☎021-717 615; www.secrethvar.com) Don't miss the great off-road tour with Secret Hvar (600KN, with lunch in a traditional tavern), which takes in hidden beauties of the island's interior, including abandoned villages, scenic canyons, ancient stone huts, endless fields of lavender and the island's tallest peak, Sveti Nikola (626m). It also does wine tours (550KN, with snacks and samplings) and island tours (450KN).

Sleeping

Accommodation in Hvar is extremely tight in July and August; if you arrive without a booking, try the travel agencies for help. Expect to pay anywhere from 150KN to

300KN per person for a room with a private bathroom.

Helvetia Hostel HOSTEL $

(☎091 34 55 556; hajduk.hvar@gmail.com; Grge Novaka 6; dm/d 230/500KN; ❄📶) Run by a friendly islander, this hostel inside his family's old stone house just behind Riva has three dorms and two doubles. The highlight is the giant rooftop terrace where guests hang out and enjoy undisturbed views of Hvar bay and the Pakleni Islands.

Hotel Croatia HOTEL $$$

(☎021-742 400; www.hotelcroatia.net; Majerovica bb; s/d 962/1283KN; P❄@📶) Only a few steps from the sea, this medium-sized, rambling 1930s building sits among gorgeous, peaceful gardens. The rooms – with a yellow, orange and lavender colour scheme – are simple and old-fashioned. Many (pricier ones) have balconies overlooking the gardens and the sea. There's a sauna, too.

Hotel Adriana HOTEL $$$

(☎021-750 200; www.suncanihvar.com; Fabrika 28; s/d 3032/3131KN; ❄@📶) All of the bright, swanky rooms of this deluxe spa hotel overlook the sea and the medieval town. Facilities include Sensori Spa, a gorgeous rooftop pool next to the rooftop bar, a plush restaurant, 24-hour room service and more.

Eating

Konoba Menego DALMATIAN $

(☎021-742 036; www.menego.hr; Kroz Grodu 26; mains from 60KN; ⊙11.30am-2pm & 5.30pm-midnight) This rustic old house on the stairway towards Fortica is kept as simple and authentic as possible. As they say: no grill, no pizza, no Coca-Cola. The place is decked out in Hvar antiques, the staff wear traditional outfits, the service is informative and the marinated meats, cheeses and vegetables are prepared the old-fashioned Dalmatian way.

Konoba Luviji DALMATIAN $

(☎091 519 8444; Jurja Novaka 6; mains from 50KN; ⊙7pm-1am) Food brought out of the wood oven at this tavern is simple, unfussy and tasty, although portions are modestly sized. Downstairs is the *konoba* (tavern) where Dalmatian-style tapas are served, while the restaurant is upstairs on a small terrace, with old-town and harbour views.

Nonica PASTRIES, CAKES $

(☎021-718 041; Burak 23; ⊙8am-2pm & 5-11pm Mon-Sat, 8am-2pm Sun) Savour the best cakes in town at this tiny storefront cafe right behind the Arsenal. Try the old-fashioned local biscuits such as *rafioli* and *forski koloc* and the Nonica tart with choco mousse and orange peel.

Divino MEDITERRANEAN $$$

(☎021-717 541; www.divino.com.hr; Put Križa 1; mains from 130KN; ⊙10am-1am) The fabulous location and the island's best wine list are reason enough to splurge at this swank restaurant. Add innovative food (think rack of lamb with crusted pistachio) and dazzling views of the Pakleni Islands and you've got a winning formula for a special night out. Or have some sunset snacks and wine on the gorgeous terrace. Book ahead.

Drinking & Nightlife

★**Falko** BEACH BAR

(⊙8am-9pm mid-May–mid-Sep) A 3km walk from the town centre brings you to this adorable hideaway in a pine forest just above the beach. A great unpretentious alternative to the flashy spots closer to town, it serves yummy sandwiches and salads from a hut, as well as its own limoncello and *rakija*. Think low-key artsy vibe, hammocks and a local crowd.

Carpe Diem LOUNGE BAR

(www.carpe-diem-hvar.com; Riva; ⊙9am-2am) Look no further – you have arrived at the mother of Croatia's coastal clubs. From a groggy breakfast to pricey late-night cocktails, there is no time of day when this swanky place is dull. The house music spun by resident DJs is smooth, there are drinks aplenty, and the crowd is of the jet-setting kind.

Hula-Hula BEACH BAR

(www.hulahulahvar.com; ⊙9am-11pm) *The* spot to catch the sunset to the sound of techno and house music, Hula-Hula is known for its après-beach party (4pm to 9pm), where all of young trendy Hvar seems to descend for sundowner cocktails.

Kiva Bar BAR

(www.kivabarhvar.com; Fabrika bb; ⊙9pm-2am) A happening place in an alleyway just off the Riva. It's packed to the rafters most nights, with a DJ spinning old dance, pop and rock classics that really get the crowd going.

Information

Del Primi (☎091 583 7864; www.delprimi-hvar.com; Burak 23) Travel agency specialising in private accommodation. Also rents jet skis.

Hvar Adventure (☎021-717 813; www.hvar-adventure.com; Obala bb)

Luka Rent (Riva 24; per hr 10KN; ⏰9am-9pm) Internet cafe and call centre right on the Riva.

Tourist Office (☎021-741 059; www.tzhvar.hr; Trg Svetog Stjepana 42; ⏰8am-2pm & 3-9pm Jul & Aug, 8am-2pm & 3-7pm Mon-Sat, 8am-noon Sun Jun & Sep) Right on Trg Svetog Stjepana.

Getting There & Away

The local **Jadrolinija** (☎021-741 132; www.jadrolinija.hr) car ferry from Split calls at the island's main ferry port, the coastal town of Stari Grad (47KN, two hours) six times a day in summer. Jadrolinija also has three to five catamarans daily to Hvar Town (55KN to 70KN, one hour). **Krilo** (www.krilo.hr), the fast passenger boat, travels twice a day between Split and Hvar Town (70KN, one hour) in summer. You can buy tickets at **Pelegrini Tours** (☎021-742 743; www.pelegrini-hvar.hr; Riva bb).

Getting Around

Buses meet most ferries that dock at Stari Grad and go to Hvar Town (27KN, 20 minutes). There are 10 buses a day between Stari Grad and Hvar Town in summer, but services are reduced on Sunday and in the low season.

A taxi to Hvar Town costs around 275KN. **Radio Taxi Tihi** (☎098 338 824) is cheaper if there are a number of passengers to fill up the minivan.

Dubrovnik

☎020 / POP 28,500

No matter whether you are visiting Dubrovnik for the first time or if you're returning to this marvellous city, the sense of awe and beauty when you set eyes on the Stradun (the Old Town's main street) never fades. It's hard to imagine anyone becoming jaded by the marble streets and baroque buildings, or failing to be inspired by a walk along the ancient city walls that once protected a civilised, sophisticated republic for five centuries and that now look out onto the endless shimmer of the peaceful Adriatic.

Sights

All the sights are in the Old Town, which is entirely closed to cars. Looming above the city is Mt Srđ, which is connected by cable car to Dubrovnik. Pile Gate is the main entrance to the Old Town; the main street is Placa (better known as Stradun).

Old Town

★**City Walls & Forts** FORT

(Gradske Zidine; adult/child 100/30KN; ⏰9am-6.30pm Apr-Oct, 10am-3pm Nov-Mar) No visit to Dubrovnik would be complete without a walk around the spectacular city walls, the finest in the world and the city's main claim to fame. From the top, the view over the old town and the shimmering Adriatic is sublime. You can get a good handle on the extent of the shelling damage in the 1990s by gazing over the rooftops: those sporting bright new terracotta suffered damage and had to be replaced.

★**War Photo Limited** GALLERY

(☎020-322 166; www.warphotoltd.com; Antuninska 6; adult/child 40/30KN; ⏰10am-10pm daily Jun-Sep, 10am-4pm Tue-Sun May & Oct) An immensely powerful experience, this gallery features intensely compelling exhibitions curated by New Zealand photojournalist Wade Goddard, who worked in the Balkans in the 1990s. Its declared intention is to 'expose the myth of war…to let people see war as it is, raw, venal, frightening, by focusing on how war inflicts injustices on innocents and combatants alike'. There's a permanent exhibition on the upper floor devoted to the wars in Yugoslavia, but the changing exhibitions cover a multitude of conflicts.

Franciscan Monastery & Museum MONASTERY

(Muzej Franjevačkog Samostana; Placa 2; adult/child 30/15KN; ⏰9am-6pm) Within this monastery's solid stone walls is a gorgeous mid-14th-century **cloister**, a historic **pharmacy** and a small **museum** with a collection of relics and liturgical objects, including chalices, paintings, gold jewellery and pharmacy items such as laboratory gear and medical books. Artillery remains that pierced the monastery walls during the 1990s war have been saved, too.

Dominican Monastery & Museum MONASTERY
(Muzej Dominikanskog Samostana; off Sv Dominika 4; admission 30KN; ⏲9am-5pm) This imposing structure is an architectural highlight, built in a transitional Gothic-Renaissance style, and containing an impressive art collection. Constructed around the same time as the city wall fortifications in the 14th century, the stark exterior resembles a fortress more than a religious complex. The interior contains a graceful 15th-century **cloister** constructed by local artisans after the designs of the Florentine architect Maso di Bartolomeo.

Rector's Palace PALACE
(Pred Dvorom 3; admission via multimuseum pass, adult/child 80/25KN; ⏲9am-6pm May-Oct, to 4pm Nov-Apr) Built in the late 15th century for the elected rector who governed Dubrovnik, this Gothic-Renaissance palace contains the rector's office, his private chambers, public halls, administrative offices and a dungeon. During his one-month term the rector was unable to leave the building without the permission of the senate. Today the palace has been turned into the **Cultural History Museum**, with artfully restored rooms, portraits, coats of arms and coins, evoking the glorious history of Dubrovnik.

Cathedral of the Assumption CATHEDRAL
(Stolna Crkva Velike Gospe; Poljana M Držića; ⏲7.30am-6pm) Built on the site of a 7th-century basilica, Dubrovnik's original cathedral was enlarged in the 12th century, supposedly funded by a gift from England's King Richard I, the Lionheart, who was saved from a shipwreck on the nearby island of Lokrum. Soon after the first cathedral was destroyed in the 1667 earthquake, work began on this, its baroque replacement, which was finished in 1713.

Sponza Palace PALACE
(Placa bb) This superb 16th-century palace is a mixture of Gothic and Renaissance styles beginning with an exquisite Renaissance portico resting on six columns. The 1st floor has late-Gothic windows and the 2nd-floor windows are in a Renaissance style, with an alcove containing a statue of St Blaise. Sponza Palace was originally a customs house, then a mint, a state treasury and a bank.

Church of the Annunciation CHURCH
(Crkva Sv Blagovještenja; Od Puča 8; ⏲8am-7.30pm) The old town's sole Serbian Orthodox church provides an interesting contrast to the numerous Catholic churches scattered about. Dating from 1877, it suffered substantial damage during the most recent war and was only fully restored in 2009.

Synagogue SYNAGOGUE
(Sinagoga; Žudioska 5; admission 35KN; ⏲10am-8pm May-Oct, to 3pm Nov-Apr) Dating to the 15th century, this is the second-oldest synagogue (the oldest Sephardic one) in the Balkans. Inside is a museum that exhibits religious relics and documentation on the local Jewish population, including records relating to their persecution during WWII.

Orlando Column MONUMENT
(Luža Sq) Luža Sq once served as a marketplace, and this stone column – carved in 1417 and featuring the image of a medieval knight – used to be the spot where edicts, festivities and public verdicts were announced. The knight's forearm was the official linear measure of the Republic – the ell of Dubrovnik (51.1cm). Folk groups occasionally perform in the square.

East of the Old Town

★Cable Car CABLE CAR
(www.dubrovnikcablecar.com; Petra Krešimira IV bb; adult/concession return 100/50KN; ⏲9am-5pm Nov-Mar, to 8pm Apr, May & Oct, to midnight Jun-Aug, to 10pm Sep) Dubrovnik's cable car whisks you from just north of the city walls to Mt Srđ in under four minutes. Operations cease if there are high winds or a thunderstorm brewing. At the end of the line there's a stupendous perspective of the city from a lofty 405m, taking in the terracotta-tiled rooftops of the old town and the island of Lokrum, with the Adriatic and distant Elafiti Islands filling the horizon.

Dubrovnik During the Homeland War MUSEUM
(Dubrovnik u Domovinskom Ratu; adult/child 30/15KN; ⏲8am-10pm) Set inside a Napoleonic fort near the cable-car terminus, this permanent exhibition is dedicated to the siege of Dubrovnik during the 'Homeland War', as the 1990s war is dubbed in Croatia.

Dubrovnik

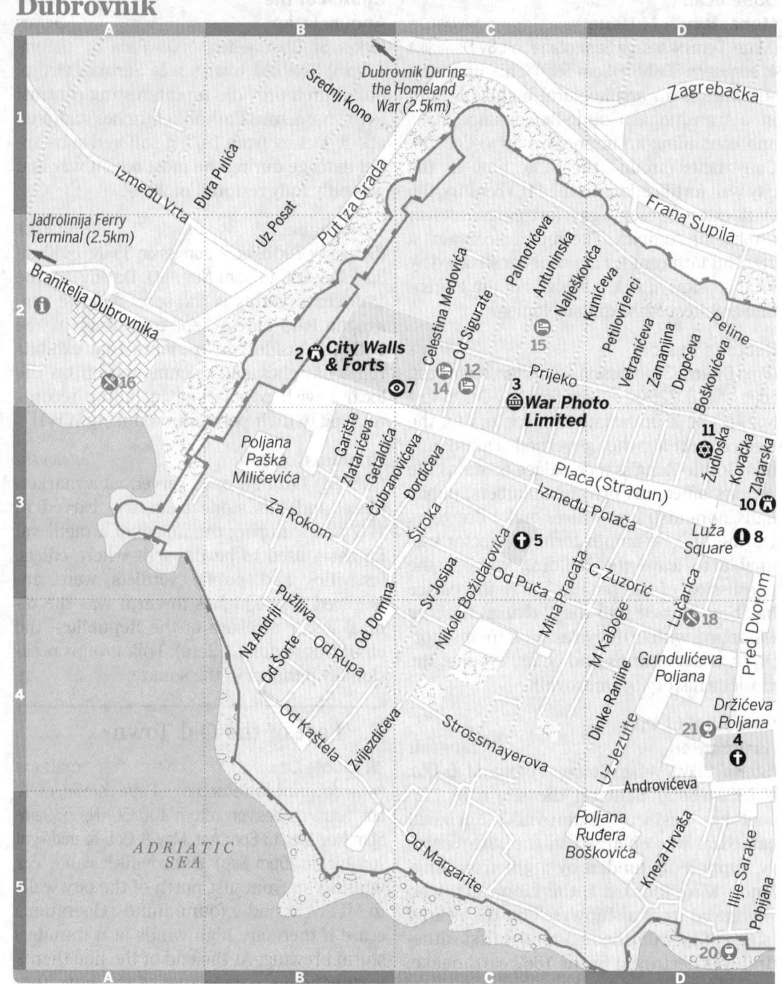

The local defenders stationed inside this fort ensured the city wasn't captured. If the displays are understandably one-sided, they still provide in-depth coverage of the events, including plenty of video footage.

The Coast

Banje Beach, around 300m east of the Ploče Gate, is the most popular city beach. A kilometre further on is **Sveti Jakov**, a good little beach that doesn't get rowdy and has showers, a bar and a restaurant. Buses 5 and 8 will get you there. **Lapad Bay** is brimming with hotel beaches that you can use without a problem; try the bay outside Hotel Kompas.

Festivals & Events

From 10 July to 25 August, the most prestigious summer festival in Croatia, the **Dubrovnik Summer Festival** (Dubrovačke ljetne Igre; 020-326 100; www.dubrovnik-festival.hr; tickets 30-350KN; Jul-Aug), presents a program of theatre, opera, concerts and dance on open-air stages throughout the city. Tickets are available online, from the festival office on Placa, and on-site one hour before the beginning of each performance.

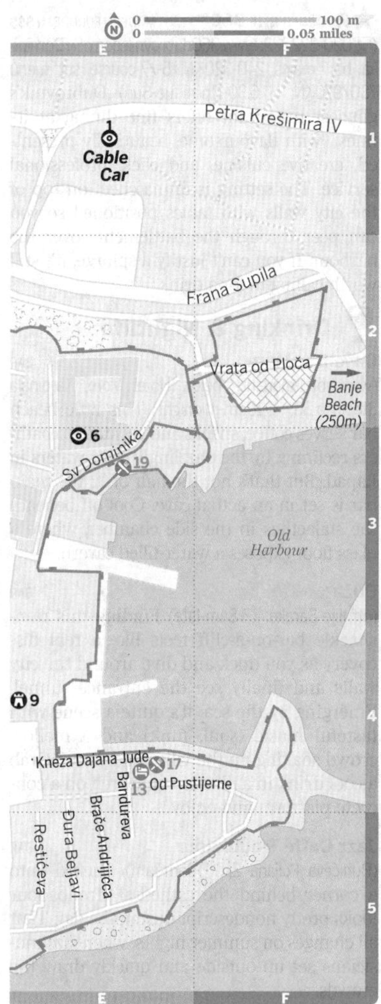

Dubrovnik

Top Sights

1	Cable Car	E1
2	City Walls & Forts	B2
3	War Photo Limited	C2

Sights

4	Cathedral of the Assumption	D4
5	Church of the Annunciation	C3
6	Dominican Monastery & Museum	E3
7	Franciscan Monastery & Museum	C2
8	Orlando Column	D3
9	Rector's Palace	E4
10	Sponza Palace	D3
11	Synagogue	D3

Sleeping

12	Hotel Stari Grad	C2
13	Karmen Apartments	E4
14	Old Town Hostel	C2
15	Rooms Vicelić	C2

Eating

16	Dubravka 1836	A2
17	Konoba Ribar	E4
18	Oliva Pizzeria	D4
19	Restaurant 360°	E3

Drinking & Nightlife

20	Buža	D5
21	Jazz Caffe Troubadour	D4

Sleeping

Dubrovnik is not a large city but accommodation is scattered all over the place; there's limited accommodation in the old town itself. Book all accommodation well in advance, especially in summer. It's the most expensive city in the country, so expect to pay more for a room here. Private accommodation is a good alternative; contact local travel agencies or the tourist office for options. In high season, expect to pay from 300KN for a double room, or from 500KN for an apartment.

Old Town

★Karmen Apartments APARTMENT $$
(☎098 619 282; www.karmendu.com; Bandureva 1; apt €95-175; ❄📶) These four inviting apartments enjoy a great location a stone's throw from Ploče harbour. All have plenty of character with art, splashes of colour, tasteful furnishings and books to browse. Apartment 2 has a little balcony while apartment 1 enjoys sublime port views. Book well ahead.

Rooms Vicelić GUESTHOUSE $$
(☎095 52 78 933; www.rooms-vicelic.com; Antuninska 10; r €90-110; ❄📶) Situated on one of the steeply stepped old town streets, this friendly, family-run place has four atmospheric stone-walled rooms with private bathrooms. Guests have use of a shared kitchenette with a microwave and a kettle.

Old Town Hostel HOSTEL $$
(☎020-322 007; www.dubrovnikoldtownhostel.com; Od Sigurate 7; dm/s/d 325/350/650KN; ⏲Mar-Nov; 📶) Converted from a historic residence – some rooms even have ceiling paintings – this centrally located hostel isn't short on charm. Dorms range from four to

six beds (including a female-only one), and there's a small kitchen. There's no air-con, only fans.

Hotel Stari Grad HOTEL $$$
(☎020-322 244; www.hotelstarigrad.com; Od Sigurate 4; s/d 1650/2100KN; ❄📶) The eight rooms at this well-located boutique hotel are smallish, but they're well presented and don't fall short on comfort. Staff are sweet and you'll enjoy the dramatic city views from the rooftop terrace. Note: there are many flights of stairs to negotiate (and no lift).

Outside the Old Town

★**Apartments Silva** GUESTHOUSE $
(☎098 244 639; silva.dubrovnik@yahoo.com; Kardinala Stepinca 62; s/d 220/440KN, apt from 440KN; ❄) Lush Mediterranean foliage lines the terraces of this lovely hillside complex, a short hop up from the beach at Lapad. The rooms are comfortable and well-priced but best of all is the spacious top-floor apartment (sleeping five). The charming host is happy to arrange free pick-ups from the bus station.

Eating

Oliva Pizzeria PIZZERIA $
(☎020-324 594; www.pizza-oliva.com; Lučarica 5; mains 40-89KN; ⊙noon-10pm) There are a few token pasta dishes on the menu, but this attractive little place is really all about pizza. And the pizza is worthy of the attention. Grab a seat on the street and tuck in.

Konoba Ribar DALMATIAN $$
(☎020-323 194; Kneza Damjana Jude bb; mains 60-120KN; ⊙10am-midnight) Serving local food the way locals like it, at more or less local prices, this little family-run eatery is a blissfully untouristy choice. They don't attempt anything fancy or clever, just big serves of traditional favourites such as risotto and stuffed squid. It's set in a little lane pressed hard up against the city walls.

Dubravka 1836 EUROPEAN $$
(☎020-426 319; www.dubravka1836.hr; Brsalje 1; mains 59-178KN; ⊙8am-11pm) Spilling on to a square right by the Pile Gate, this place is indisputably touristy. Still, it's a good spot for a light breakfast, and the locals rate the fresh fish, risotto, salads, pizza and pasta. The views are great, too.

★**Restaurant 360°** MODERN EUROPEAN $$$
(☎020-322 222; www.360dubrovnik.com; Sv Dominika bb; mains 240-320KN, 5-/7-course set menu 780/970KN; ⊙6.30-11pm Tue-Sun) Dubrovnik's glitziest restaurant offers fine dining at its finest, with flavoursome, beautifully presented, creative cuisine, and slick, professional service. The setting is unmatched, on top of the city walls with tables positioned so you can peer through the battlements over the harbour. If you can't justify a splurge, it's still worth calling in for a drink.

Drinking & Nightlife

Cave Bar More BAR
(www.hotel-more.hr; below Hotel More, Kardinala Stepinca 33; ⊙10am-midnight) This little beach bar serves coffee, snacks and cocktails to bathers reclining by the dazzlingly clear waters in Lapad. But that's not the half of it: the main bar is set in an actual cave. Cool off beneath the stalactites in the side chamber, where a glass floor exposes a water-filled cavern.

Buža BAR
(off Ilije Sarake; ⊙8am-late) Finding this ramshackle bar-on-a-cliff feels like a real discovery as you duck and dive around the city walls and finally see the entrance tunnel. Emerging by the sea, it's quite a scene with tasteful music (soul, funk) and a mellow crowd soaking up the vibes and views. Grab a cool drink in a plastic cup, perch on a concrete platform and enjoy.

Jazz Caffe Troubadour BAR
(Bunićeva Poljana 2; ⊙9am-1am) Tucked into a corner behind the cathedral, Troubadour looks pretty nondescript during the day. That all changes on summer nights, when jazz musicians set up outside and quickly draw the crowds.

Information

There are numerous ATMs in town, in Lapad and at the ferry terminal and bus station. Travel agencies and the post office will also exchange cash.

General Hospital Dubrovnik (Opća Bolnica Dubrovnik; ☎020-431 777; www.bolnica-du.hr; Dr Roka Mišetića bb; ⊙emergency department 24hr) On the southern edge of the Lapad peninsula.

Tourist Office (www.tzdubrovnik.hr) Pile (☎020-312 011; Brsalje 5; ⊙8am-9pm Jun-Sep, 8am-7pm Mon-Sat, 9am-3pm Sun Oct-May); Gruž (☎020-417 983; Obala Pape Ivana

COUNTRY FACTS

Area 56,538 sq km

Capital Zagreb

Country Code ☎385

Currency Kuna (KN)

Emergency Ambulance ☎94, police ☎92

Language Croatian

Money ATMs are available; credit cards accepted in most hotels and many restaurants

Population 4.3 million

Visas Not required for most nationalities for stays of up to 90 days

Pavla II 1; ⏲8am-9pm Jun-Sep, to 3pm Mon-Sat Oct-May); Lapad (☎020-437 460; Kralja Tomislava 7; ⏲8am-8pm Jun-Sep, to 3pm Mon-Sat Oct-May) Maps, information and advice.

ℹ Getting There & Away

AIR

Daily flights to/from Zagreb are operated by Croatia Airlines (p276). Dubrovnik Airport is served by more than a dozen other airlines from across Europe.

BOAT

The ferry terminal and the bus station are next to each other at Gruž, 3km northwest of the Old Town. A twice-weekly **Jadrolinija** (Obala Pape Ivana Pavla II 1) coastal ferry heads north to Hvar and Split.

BUS

Buses out of Dubrovnik **bus station** (☎060 305 070; Obala Pape Ivana Pavla II 44a) can be crowded, so book tickets ahead in summer. Split–Dubrovnik buses pass briefly through Bosnian territory, so keep your passport handy for border-crossing points.

All bus schedules are detailed at www.libertas-dubrovnik.hr.

ℹ Getting Around

Dubrovnik Airport (Zračna Luka Dubrovnik; www.airport-dubrovnik.hr) is in Čilipi, 19km southeast of Dubrovnik. Atlas runs the airport bus service (35KN, 30 minutes), timed around flights. Buses to Dubrovnik stop at the Pile Gate and the bus station; buses to the airport pick up from the bus station and from the bus stop near the cable car.

A taxi to the old town costs about 250KN.

SURVIVAL GUIDE

ℹ Directory A–Z

ACCOMMODATION

Private accommodation is often great-value in Croatia plus it gets you a glimpse of Croatia's own brand of hospitality. Many of the owners treat their guests like long-lost friends. Some offer the option of eating with them, which is a great way to get to know the culture.

Note that many establishments add a 30% charge for stays of less than three nights and include 'residence tax', which is around 7KN per person per day. Prices quoted in this book do not include the residence tax.

Camping

Over 500 camping grounds are scattered along the Croatian coast. Most operate from mid-April to mid-September. The exact times change from year to year, so it's wise to call in advance if you're arriving at either end of the season.

Nudist camping grounds (marked FKK) are among the best, as their secluded locations ensure peace and quiet. A good site for camping information is www.camping.hr.

Hostels

The **Croatian YHA** (☎01-48 29 294; www.hfhs.hr; Savska 5, Zagreb) operates youth hostels in Dubrovnik, Zagreb and Pula. Nonmembers pay an additional 10KN per person per day for a stamp on a welcome card; six stamps entitle you to membership. The Croatian YHA can also provide information about private youth hostels in Hvar and Zagreb.

Hotels

In August, some hotels may demand a surcharge for stays of less than three or four nights, but this is usually waived during the rest of the year, when prices drop steeply.

Breakfast is included in the prices for all hotels.

Private Rooms

The best value for money in Croatia is a private room or apartment, often within or attached to a local home – the equivalent of small private

SLEEPING PRICE RANGES

The following price categories for the cost of a double room with bathroom are used in the listings in this chapter.

€ less than 450KN

€€ 450KN to 800KN

€€€ more than 800KN

ACTIVITIES

Croatia is a great destination for outdoor activities. Cycling is tops, especially in Istria, which has more than 60 marked trails through stunning scenery. Hiking is also incredible, particularly in the national parks such as Plitvice (p261). Croatia also has some great dive sites, including many wrecks; for more info, check out the **Croatian Diving Association** (www.diving-hrs.hr). Other activities worth trying in Croatia are kayaking and rafting; Zagreb-based **Huck Finn** (www.huckfinncroatia.com) is a good contact for sea and river kayaking packages, as well as rafting. For details on rock climbing and caving, contact the **Croatian Mountaineering Association** (www.hps.hr).

guesthouses in other countries. You'll pay a 30% surcharge for stays of less than four or three nights and sometimes 50% or even 100% more for a one-night stay; it may be waived in the low season. Some will even insist on a seven-night minimum stay in the high season.

Whether you rent from an agency or rent from the owners privately, don't hesitate to bargain, especially for longer stays.

If you land in a room or apartment without a blue *sobe* or *apartmani* sign outside, the proprietor is renting to you illegally (ie not paying residence tax). They will probably be reluctant to provide their full name or phone number and you'll have absolutely no recourse in case of a problem.

BUSINESS HOURS

Hours can vary across the year.

Banks 9am to 8pm Monday to Friday, 7am to 1pm or 8am to 2pm Saturday

Bars and cafes 8am to midnight

Offices 8am to 4pm or 8.30am to 4.30pm Monday to Friday

Restaurants noon to 11pm or midnight, closed Sunday out of peak season

Shops 8am to 8pm Monday to Friday, to 2pm or 3pm Saturday

INTERNET RESOURCES

Adriatica.net (www.adriatica.net)

Croatian National Tourist Board (www.croatia.hr)

Taste of Croatia (www.tasteofcroatia.org)

MONEY

Credit Cards

Amex, MasterCard, Visa and Diners Club cards are widely accepted in large hotels, stores and many restaurants, but don't count on cards to pay for private accommodation or meals in small restaurants. You'll find ATMs accepting MasterCard, Maestro, Cirrus, Plus and Visa in most bus and train stations, airports, all major cities and most small towns.

Currency

Croatia uses the kuna (KN). Commonly circulated banknotes come in denominations of 500, 200, 100, 50, 20, 10 and five kuna. Each kuna is divided into 100 lipa. You'll find silver-coloured 50- and 20-lipa coins, and bronze-coloured 10-lipa coins.

PUBLIC HOLIDAYS

New Year's Day 1 January

Epiphany 6 January

Easter Monday March/April

Labour Day 1 May

Corpus Christi 10 June

Day of Antifascist Resistance 22 June; marks the outbreak of resistance in 1941

Statehood Day 25 June

Homeland Thanksgiving Day 5 August

Feast of the Assumption 15 August

Independence Day 8 October

All Saints' Day 1 November

Christmas 25 and 26 December

TELEPHONE

Mobile Phones

If you have an unlocked 3G phone, you can buy a SIM card for about 20KN to 50KN. You can choose from three network providers: **VIP** (www.vip.hr), **T-Mobile** (www.hrvatskitelekom.hr) and **Tele2** (www.tele2.hr).

Phone Codes

➡ To call Croatia from abroad, dial your international access code, then ☎385 (the country code for Croatia), then the area code (without the initial 0) and the local number.

EATING PRICE RANGES

Prices in this chapter are based on a main course.

€ less than 70KN

€€ 70KN to 120KN

€€€ more than 120KN

ESSENTIAL FOOD & DRINK

Croatia's cuisine reflects the varied cultures that have influenced the country over the course of its history. You'll find a sharp divide between the Italian-style cuisine along the coast and the flavours of Hungary, Austria and Turkey in the continental parts.

Istrian cuisine has been attracting international foodies in recent years for its long gastronomic tradition, fresh ingredients and unique specialities. Istria-based **Eat Istria** (www.eatistria.com) offers cooking classes and wine tours around the peninsula.

Here are a few essential food and drink items to be aware of while in Croatia:

- **Ćevapčići** Small spicy sausages of minced beef, lamb or pork.
- **Ražnjići** Small chunks of pork grilled on a skewer.
- **Burek** Pastry stuffed with ground meat, spinach or cheese.
- **Rakija** Strong Croatian brandy comes in different flavours, from plum to honey.
- **Beer** Two top types of Croatian *pivo* (beer) are Zagreb's Ožujsko and Karlovačko from Karlovac.

- To call from region to region within Croatia, start with the area code (with the initial 0); drop it when dialling within the same code.
- Phone numbers with the prefix ☎060 are either free or charged at a premium rate, so watch out for the small print. Phone numbers that begin with ☎09 are mobile phone numbers.

TOURIST INFORMATION

Croatian National Tourist Board (www.croatia.hr) is a good source of info.

VISAS

Citizens of the EU, the USA, Canada, Australia, New Zealand, Israel, Ireland, Singapore and the UK do not need a visa for stays of up to 90 days. South Africans must apply for a 90-day visa in Pretoria. Contact any Croatian embassy, consulate or travel agency abroad for information.

ℹ Getting There & Away

AIR

There are direct flights to Croatia from a number of European cities; however, there are no nonstop flights from North America to Croatia.

Major airports in Croatia include:

Dubrovnik Airport (DBV; www.airport-dubrovnik.hr) Nonstop flights from Brussels, Cologne, Frankfurt, Hanover, London (Gatwick and Stansted), Manchester, Munich, Paris, Stuttgart and many more.

Pula Airport (PUY; www.airport-pula.com) Nonstop flights from London (Gatwick and Stansted), Manchester, Oslo, Stockholm, Munich, Edinburgh, Copenhagen and more.

Split Airport (SPU; www.split-airport.hr) Nonstop flights from Berlin, Cologne, Copenhagen, Frankfurt, London, Munich, Prague, Stockholm, Rome, Venice and many more.

Zagreb Airport (ZAG; www.zagreb-airport.hr) Direct flights from all European capitals, as well as Cologne, Doha, İstanbul, Hamburg, Madrid, Munich, Moscow and Tel Aviv.

LAND

Croatia is a convenient transport hub for south-eastern Europe and the Adriatic, with border crossings with Hungary, Slovenia, Bosnia and Hercegovina (BiH), Serbia and Montenegro.

Zagreb is connected by train and/or bus to Venice, Budapest, Belgrade, Ljubljana and Sarajevo. Down south there are easy bus connections from Dubrovnik to Mostar and Sarajevo (BiH), and to Kotor (Montenegro).

From Austria, **Eurolines** (www.eurolines.com) operates buses from Vienna to several destinations in Croatia.

Bus services between Germany and Croatia are good, and fares are cheaper than the train. All buses are handled by **Deutsche Touring GmbH** (www.deutsche-touring.de); there are no Deutsche Touring offices in Croatia, but numerous travel agencies and bus stations sell its tickets.

SEA

There are a number of ferries linking Croatia with Italy, including routes from Dubrovnik to Bari, and Split to Ancona.

Blue Line (www.blueline-ferries.com)

Commodore Cruises (www.commodore-cruises.hr)

Jadrolinija (www.jadrolinija.hr)

SNAV (www.snav.com)

Venezia Lines (www.venezialines.com)

Getting Around

AIR

Croatia Airlines (☎01-66 76 555; www.croatiaairlines.hr) Croatia Airlines is the national carrier. There are daily flights between Zagreb and Dubrovnik, Osijek, Pula, Rijeka, Split and Zadar.

BOAT

Jadrolinija (p275) operates an extensive network of car ferries and catamarans along the Adriatic coast. Ferries are a lot more comfortable than buses, though somewhat more expensive.

Services operate year-round, though they are less frequent in winter. Cabins should be booked a week ahead. Deck space is usually available on all sailings.

You must buy tickets in advance at an agency or a Jadrolinija office. Tickets are not sold on board. In summer months, you need to check in two hours in advance if you bring a car.

BUS

Bus services are excellent and relatively inexpensive. There are often a number of different companies handling each route so prices can vary substantially. Luggage stowed in the baggage compartment under the bus costs extra (7KN a piece, including insurance).

At large stations, bus tickets must be purchased at the office, not from drivers. Try to book ahead to be sure of a seat, especially in the summer.

CAR & MOTORCYCLE

Croatia's motorway connecting Zagreb with Split is only a few years old and makes some routes much faster.

Car Hire

In order to rent a car you must be 21 or over, with a valid driving licence and a valid credit card.

Independent local companies are often much cheaper than the international chains, but the big companies offer one-way rentals.

Driving Licence

Any valid driving licence is sufficient to drive legally and rent a car; an international driving licence is not necessary.

The **Hrvatski Autoklub** (HAK, Croatian Auto Club; ☎01-46 40 800; www.hak.hr; Avenija Dubrovnik 44) offers help and advice. For help on the road, you can contact the nationwide **HAK road assistance** (Vučna Služba; ☎1987).

LOCAL TRANSPORT

The main form of local transport is bus. Buses in major cities such as Dubrovnik and Split run about once every 20 minutes, less on Sunday. A ride is usually around 10KN, with a small discount if you buy tickets at a *tisak* (newsstand).

Bus transport within the islands is infrequent since most people have their own cars.

TRAIN

Trains are less frequent than buses but more comfortable. For information about schedules, prices and services, contact **Croatian Railways** (Hrvatske Željeznice; ☎060 333 444; www.hznet.hr).

Zagreb is the hub for Croatia's less-than-extensive train system. No trains run along the coast and only a few coastal cities are connected with Zagreb.

Baggage is free on trains; most stations have left-luggage services, charging around 15KN a piece per day.

EU residents who hold an InterRail pass can use it in Croatia for free travel, but you're unlikely to take enough trains to justify the cost.

Czech Republic

Includes ➡

Best Places to Eat

- ➡ Sansho (p286)
- ➡ Pavillon (p295)
- ➡ Kalina (p286)
- ➡ Moritz (p297)

Best Places to Stay

- ➡ Mosaic House (p285)
- ➡ Penzión Na Hradě (p296)
- ➡ Hotel Konvice (p293)
- ➡ Savic Hotel (p285)

Why Go?

Since the fall of communism in 1989 and the opening up of Central and Eastern Europe, Prague has evolved into one of Europe's most popular travel destinations. The city offers an intact medieval core that transports you back 500 years. The 14th-century Charles Bridge, traversing two historic neighbourhoods, is one of the continent's most beautiful sights.

The city is not just about history. It's a vital urban centre with a rich array of cultural offerings. Outside the capital, castles and palaces abound – including the audacious hilltop chateau at Český Krumlov – which illuminate the stories of powerful dynasties whose influence was felt throughout Europe.

When to Go

Prague

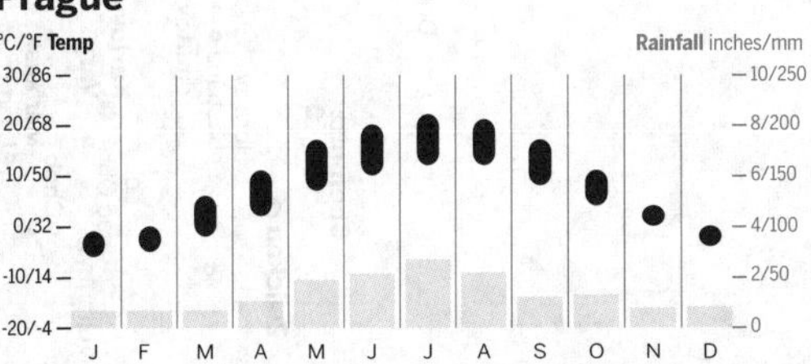

May Prague comes alive with festivals from classical music to fringe arts.

Jul Karlovy Vary shows off its arty side at the sleepy spa town's annual film festival.

Dec Prague's Christmas Market draws visitors from around the world.

Czech Republic Highlights

1. Stroll across the **Charles Bridge** (p283) in the early morning or late evening when the crowds thin out.
2. Enjoy an evening in an old-school Czech pub at **U Medvídků** (p286).
3. Join the appreciative throngs at Prague's **Astronomical Clock** (p282) at the top of the hour.
4. Repair to **Český Krumlov** (p291) to see the prettiest town in Central Europe.
5. Tour the **Pilsner Urquell Brewery** (p289) in Plzeň to see where it all started.
6. Amble through the stately town of **Olomouc** (p295), the most amazing place you've never heard of.

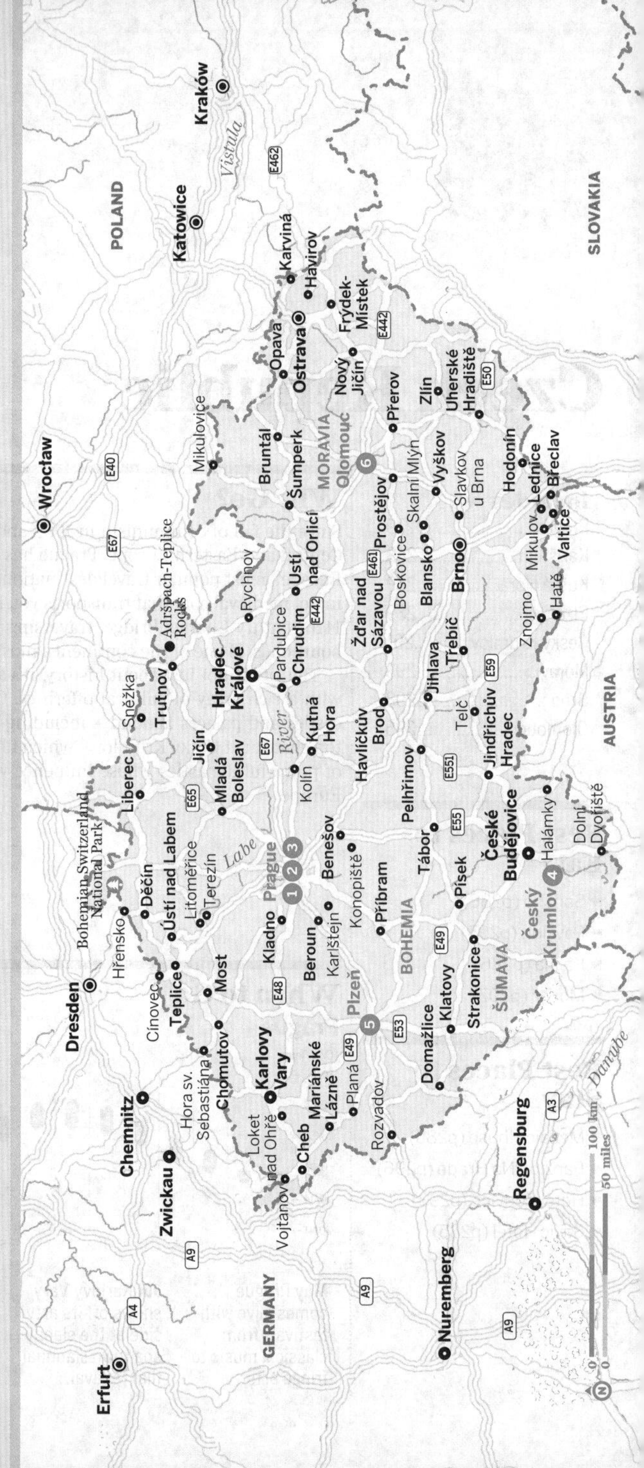

ITINERARIES

One Week

Experience the exciting combination of **Prague's** tumultuous past and energetic present. Top experiences include the grandeur of Prague Castle, Josefov's Prague Jewish Museum, and getting lost amid the bewildering labyrinth of the Old Town. Take an essential day trip to **Karlštejn**, and then head south to **Český Krumlov** for a few days of riverside R&R.

Two Weeks

Begin in **Prague** before heading west for the spa scene at **Karlovy Vary**. Balance the virtue and vice ledger with a few Bohemian brews in **Plzeň** before heading south for relaxation and rigour around **Český Krumlov**. Head east to the Renaissance grandeur of **Telč**, and to **Brno's** cosmopolitan galleries and museums. From the Moravian capital, it's just a skip to stately **Olomouc**.

PRAGUE

POP 1.24 MILLION

It's the perfect irony of Prague: you are lured here by the past, but compelled to linger by the present and the future. Fill your days with its illustrious artistic and architectural heritage – from Gothic and Renaissance to art nouveau and cubist. If Prague's seasonal legions of tourists wear you down, that's OK. Just drink a glass of the country's legendary lager, relax and rest reassured that quiet moments still exist: a private dawn on Charles Bridge, the glorious cityscape of Staré Město or getting lost in the intimate lanes of Malá Strana.

Sights

Prague nestles on the Vltava River, separating Hradčany (the Castle district) and Malá Strana (Lesser Quarter) on the west bank, from Staré Město (Old Town) and Nové Město (New Town) on the east.

Hradčany

Prague Castle CASTLE

(Pražský hrad; Map p284; ☎224 372 423; www.hrad.cz; Hradčanské náměstí; grounds free, sights adult/concession long tour 350/175Kc, short tour 250/125Kc; ⏲grounds 5am-midnight Apr-Oct, 6am-11pm Nov-Mar, gardens 10am-6pm Apr & Oct, to 7pm May & Sep, to 9pm Jun-Aug, closed Nov-Mar, historic buildings 9am-5pm Apr-Oct, to 4pm Nov-Mar; M Malostranská, 22) Prague Castle – Pražský hrad, or just *hrad* to Czechs – is Prague's most popular attraction. Looming above the Vltava's left bank, its serried ranks of spires, towers and palaces dominate the city centre like a fairy-tale fortress. Within its walls lies a varied and fascinating collection of historic buildings, museums and galleries that are home to some of the Czech Republic's greatest artistic and cultural treasures.

Old Royal Palace PALACE

(Starý královský palác; Map p284; admission with Prague Castle tour ticket; ⏲9am-5pm Apr-Oct, to 4pm Nov-Mar; 22) The Old Royal Palace is one of the oldest parts of Prague Castle, dating to 1135. It was originally used only by Czech princesses, but from the 13th to the 16th centuries it was the king's own palace. At its heart is the grand Vladislav Hall and the Bohemian Chancellery, scene of the famous Defenestration of Prague in 1618.

St Vitus Cathedral CHURCH

(Katedrála Sv Víta; Map p284; ☎257 531 622; www.katedralasvatehovita.cz; Third Courtyard, Prague Castle; admission with Prague Castle tour ticket; ⏲9am-5pm Mon-Sat, noon-5pm Sun Apr-Oct, to 4pm Nov-Mar; 22) It might appear ancient, but much of Prague's principal cathedral was completed just in time for its belated consecration in 1929. Its many treasures include the 14th-century mosaic of the Last Judgement above the Golden Gate, the baroque silver tomb of St John of Nepomuck, the ornate Chapel of St Wenceslas, and art nouveau stained glass by Alfons Mucha.

Lobkowicz Palace MUSEUM

(Lobkovický palác; Map p284; ☎233 312 925; www.lobkowicz.cz; Jiřská 3; adult/concession/family 275/200/690Kč; ⏲10am-6pm; 22) This 16th-century palace houses a private museum which includes priceless paintings, furniture and musical memorabilia. You tour with an audioguide dictated by owner

Central Prague

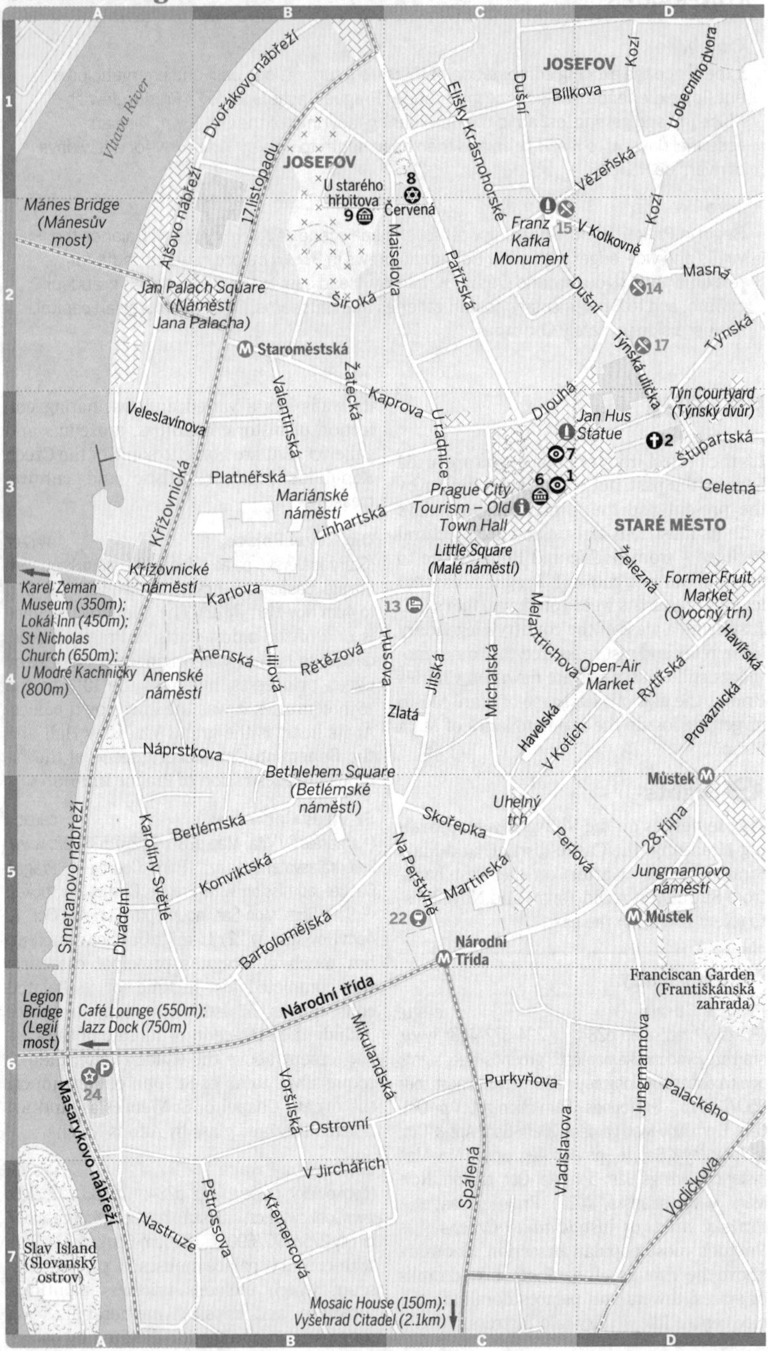

A B C D

1 2 3 4 5 6 7

JOSEFOV
Kozí
U obecního dvora
Dušní
Bílkova
Elišky Krásnohorské
Vltava River
Dvořákovo nábřeží
17 listopadu
JOSEFOV
U starého hřbitova
8
9
Červená
Vězeňská
Kozí
Franz Kafka Monument
15
V Kolkovně
Mánes Bridge (Mánesův most)
Alšovo nábřeží
Maiselova
Pařížská
Masná
Jan Palach Square (Náměstí Jana Palacha)
Široká
Dušní
14
Týnská
Staroměstská
Týnská ulička
17
Valentinská
Žatecká
Kaprova
Dlouhá
Týn Courtyard (Týnský dvůr)
Veleslavínova
U radnice
Jan Hus Statue
2
Štupartská
7
Platnéřská
6
1
Celetná
Křižovnická
Mariánské náměstí
Prague City Tourism – Old Town Hall
Linhartská
STARÉ MĚSTO
Little Square (Malé náměstí)
Křížovnické náměstí
Železná
Former Fruit Market (Ovocný trh)
Karel Zeman Museum (350m); Lokál Inn (450m); St Nicholas Church (650m); U Modré Kachničky (800m)
Karlova
13
Melantrichova
Havířská
Anenská
Řetězová
Husova
Open-Air Market
Anenské náměstí
Liliová
Jilská
Michalská
Rytířská
Zlatá
Havelská
Provaznická
V Kotcích
Náprstkova
Bethlehem Square (Betlémské náměstí)
Můstek
Uhelný trh
Skořepka
28.října
Betlémská
Perlová
Smetanovo nábřeží
Karolíny Světlé
Konviktská
Na Perštýně
Martinská
Jungmannovo náměstí
22
Můstek
Divadelní
Bartolomějská
Národní Třída
Franciscan Garden (Františkánská zahrada)
Legion Bridge (Legií most)
Café Lounge (550m); Jazz Dock (750m)
Národní třída
Mikulandská
24
Masarykovo nábřeží
Vořšilská
Purkyňova
Jungmannova
Palackého
Ostrovní
Vladislavova
V Jirchářích
Spálená
Vodičkova
Pštrossova
Křemencová
Nastruze
Slav Island (Slovanský ostrov)
Mosaic House (150m); Vyšehrad Citadel (2.1km)

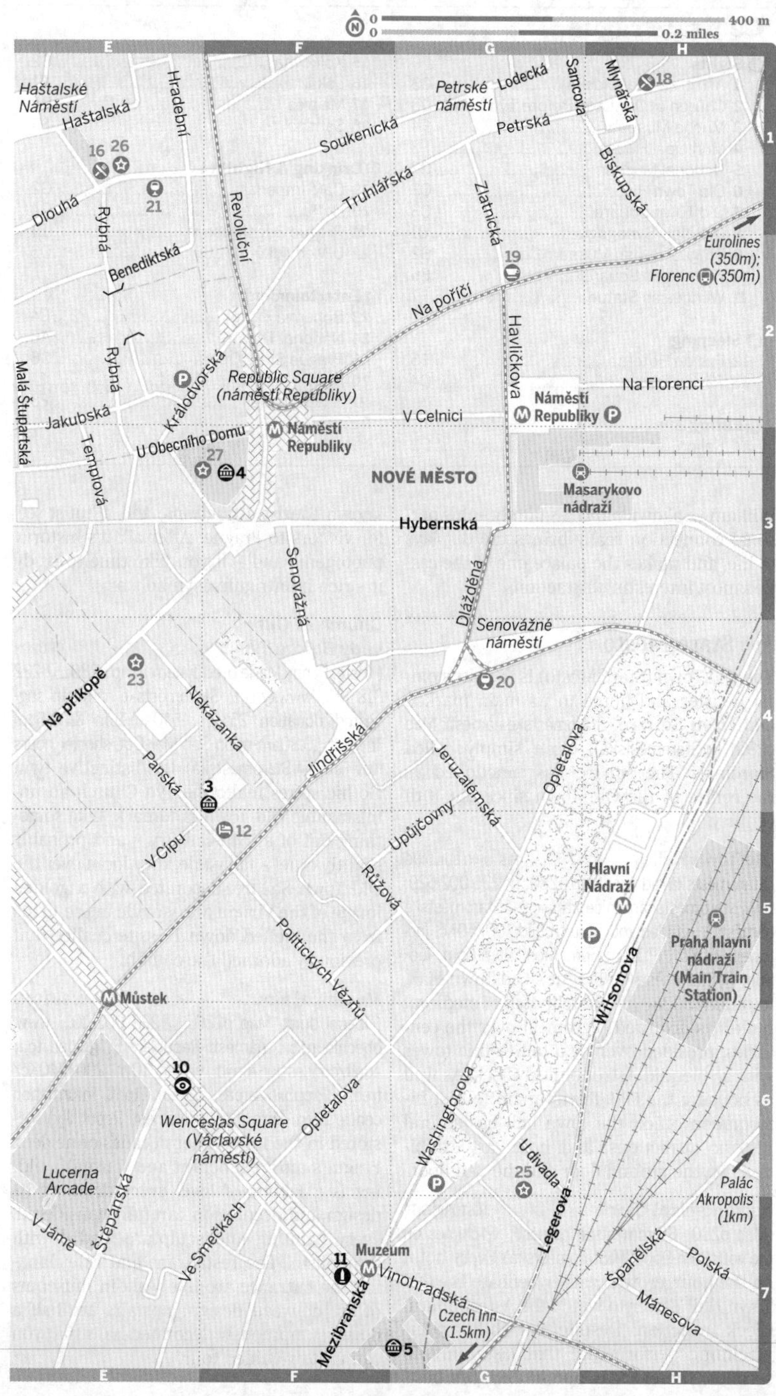

0 400 m
0 0.2 miles
Haštalské Náměstí
Haštalská
Hradební
Petrské náměstí
Lodecká
Samcova
Mlynářská
18
Petrská
Soukenická
Biskupská
16
26
21
Dlouhá
Rybná
Revoluční
Truhlářská
Zlatnická
Eurolines (350m); Florenc (350m)
Benediktská
19
Na poříčí
Havlíčkova
Rybná
Malá Štupartská
Králodvorská
Republic Square (náměstí Republiky)
Na Florenci
Náměstí Republiky
Jakubská
V Celnici
U Obecního Domu
Náměstí Republiky
Templová
27
4
NOVÉ MĚSTO
Masarykovo nádraží
Hybernská
Senovážná
Dlážděná
Senovážné náměstí
23
20
Na příkopě
Nekázanka
Jindřišská
Jeruzalémská
Opletalova
Panská
3
12
Upůjčovny
V Cípu
Hlavní Nádraží
Růžová
Politických Vězňů
Praha hlavní nádraží (Main Train Station)
Můstek
Wilsonova
10
Wenceslas Square (Václavské náměstí)
Opletalova
Washingtonova
U divadla
Lucerna Arcade
Štěpánská
25
Palác Akropolis (1km)
V Jámě
Ve Smečkách
Legerova
Španělská
Polská
Muzeum
11
Vinohradská
Mánesova
Mezibranská
Czech Inn (1.5km)
5
E
F
G
H
1
2
3
4
5
6
7

Central Prague

Sights

1	Astronomical Clock	C3
2	Church of Our Lady Before Týn	D3
3	Mucha Museum	F4
4	Municipal House	F3
5	National Museum	G7
6	Old Town Hall	C3
7	Old Town Square	C3
8	Old-New Synagogue	C1
9	Prague Jewish Museum	B2
10	Wenceslas Square	E6
11	Wenceslas Statue	F7

Sleeping

12	Fusion Hotel	F5
13	Savic Hotel	C4

Eating

14	Kalina	D2
15	Kolkovna	C2
16	Lokál	E1
17	Maitrea	D2
18	Sansho	H1

Drinking & Nightlife

19	Café Imperial	G2
20	Hoffa	G4
21	Prague Beer Museum	E1
22	U Medvídků	C5

Entertainment

23	Bohemia Ticket	E4
24	National Theatre	A6
25	Prague State Opera	G6
26	Roxy	E1
27	Smetana Hall	F3

William Lobkowicz and his family – this personal connection really brings the displays to life, and makes the palace one of the castle's most interesting attractions.

Staré Město

The Old Town (Staré Město) is the city's oldest quarter and home to its main market, **Old Town Square** (Staroměstské náměstí; Map p280; Ⓜ Staroměstská), often simply called Staromák. The square has functioned as the centre of the Old Town since the 10th century.

Old Town Hall — HISTORIC BUILDING

(Staroměstská radnice; Map p280; ☎ 236 002 629; www.staromestskaradnicepraha.cz; Staroměstské náměstí 1; guided tour adult/child 100/50Kč, incl tower 160Kč; ⏲ 11am-6pm Mon, 9am-6pm Tue-Sun; Ⓜ Staroměstská) Prague's Old Town Hall, founded in 1338, is a hotchpotch of medieval buildings acquired piecemeal over the centuries, presided over by a tall Gothic tower with a splendid Astronomical Clock. As well as housing the Old Town's main tourist information office, the town hall has several historic attractions, and hosts art exhibitions on the ground floor and the 2nd floor.

Astronomical Clock — HISTORIC SITE

(Map p280; Staroměstské náměstí; ⏲ chimes on the hour 9am-9pm; Ⓜ Staroměstská) Every hour, on the hour, crowds gather beneath the Old Town Hall Tower to watch the Astronomical Clock in action. Despite a slightly underwhelming performance that lasts only 45 seconds, the clock is one of Europe's best-known tourist attractions, and a 'must-see' for visitors to Prague. After all, it's historic, photogenic and – if you take time to study it – rich in intriguing symbolism.

Church of Our Lady Before Týn — CHURCH

(Kostel Panny Marie před Týnem; Map p280; ☎ 222 318 186; www.tyn.cz; Staroměstské náměstí; suggested donation 25Kč; ⏲ 10am-1pm & 3-5pm Tue-Sat, 10.30am-noon Sun Mar-Oct, shorter hours Nov-Feb; Ⓜ Staroměstská) Its distinctive twin Gothic spires make the Týn Church an unmistakable Old Town landmark. Like something out of a 15th-century – and probably slightly cruel – fairy tale, they loom over the Old Town Square, decorated with a golden image of the Virigin Mary made in the 1620s from the melted down Hussite chalice that previously adorned the church.

Municipal House — HISTORIC BUILDING

(Obecní dům; Map p280; ☎ 222 002 101; www.obecnidum.cz; náměstí Republiky 5; guided tour adult/concession/child under 10yr 290/240Kč/free; ⏲ public areas 7.30am-11pm, information centre 10am-8pm; 📶; Ⓜ Náměstí Republiky) Restored in the 1990s after decades of neglect, Prague's most exuberant and sensual building is a labour of love, every detail of its design and decoration carefully considered, every painting and sculpture loaded with symbolism. The restaurant and cafe flanking the entrance are like walk-in museums of art nouveau design; upstairs are half a dozen sumptuously decorated halls that you can visit by guided tour.

Malá Strana

Across the river from the Old Town are the baroque backstreets of Malá Strana (the Lesser Quarter), built in the 17th and 18th centuries by victorious Catholic clerics and noblemen on the foundations of their predecessors' Renaissance palaces.

Charles Bridge BRIDGE

(Karlův most; 24hr; 17, 18 to Karlovy lázně, 12, 20, 22 to Malostranské náměstí) FREE Strolling across Charles Bridge is everybody's favourite Prague activity. However, by 9am it's a 500m-long fairground, with an army of tourists squeezing through a gauntlet of hawkers and buskers beneath the impassive gaze of the baroque statues that line the parapets. If you want to experience the bridge at its most atmospheric, try to visit it at dawn.

St Nicholas Church CHURCH

(Kostel sv Mikuláše; 257 534 215; www.stnicholas.cz; Malostranské náměstí 38; adult/child 70/50Kč; 9am-5pm Mar-Oct, to 4pm Nov-Feb; 12, 20, 22) Malá Strana is dominated by the huge green cupola of St Nicholas Church, one of Central Europe's finest baroque buildings. (Don't confuse it with the other Church of St Nicholas on Old Town Square.) On the ceiling, Johann Kracker's 1770 *Apotheosis of St Nicholas* is Europe's largest fresco (clever trompe l'oeil technique has made the painting merge almost seamlessly with the architecture).

Karel Zeman Museum MUSEUM

(Museum of Film Special Effects; 724 341 091; www.muzeumkarlazemana.cz; Saský dvůr, Saská 3; adult/child 200/140Kč; 10am-7pm, last admission 6pm; 12, 20, 22) Bohemia-born director Karel Zeman (1910–89) was a pioneer of movie special effects whose work is little known outside the Czech Republic. This fascinating museum, established by his daughter, reveals the many tricks and techniques he perfected, and even allows visitors a bit of hands-on interaction – you can film yourself on your smartphone against painted backgrounds and 3D models.

Nové Město

Nové Město (New Town) surrounds the Old Town on all sides and was originally laid out in the 14th century. Its main public area is **Wenceslas Square** (Václavské náměstí; Map p280; M Můstek, Muzeum), lined with shops, banks and restaurants, and marked by a **statue of St Wenceslas** (sv Václav; Map p280; Václavské náměstí; M Muzeum) on horseback. The **National Museum** (Národní muzeum; Map p280; 224 497 111; www.nm.cz; Václavské náměstí 68; M Muzeum), which dominates the top of the square, is closed for long-term renovation.

PRAGUE'S JEWISH MUSEUM

The **Prague Jewish Museum** (Židovské muzeum Praha; Map p280; 222 317 191; www.jewishmuseum.cz; Reservation Centre, U starého hřbitova 3a; ordinary ticket adult/child 300/200Kč, combined ticket incl entry to Old-New Synagogue 480/320Kč; 9am-6pm Sun-Fri Apr-Oct, to 4.30pm Nov-Mar; M Staroměstská), a collection of four synagogues – the **Maisel**, **Pinkas**, **Spanish** and **Klaus** – and the former **Ceremonial Hall** and **Old Jewish Cemetery**, is one of the city's treasures. The monuments are clustered together in Josefov, a small corner of the Old Town that was home to Prague's Jews for some 800 years, before an urban-renewal project at the start of the 20th century and the Nazi occupation during WWII brought it all to an end.

The monuments cannot be visited separately but require a combined-entry ticket that is good for all of the sights and available at ticket windows throughout Josefov. A fifth synagogue, the **Old-New Synagogue** (Staronová synagóga; Map p280; www.jewishmuseum.cz; Červená 2; adult/child 200/140Kč; 9am-6pm Sun-Fri Apr-Oct, to 4.30pm Nov-Mar; 17), is still used for religious services, and requires a separate ticket or additional fee.

The museum was first established in 1906 to preserve objects from synagogues that were demolished during the slum clearance at the turn of the 20th century. The collection grew richer as a result of one of the most grotesquely ironic acts of WWII. During the Nazi occupation, the Germans took over management of the museum in order to create a 'museum of an extinct race'. To that end, they added objects from destroyed Jewish communities throughout Bohemia and Moravia.

Prague Castle

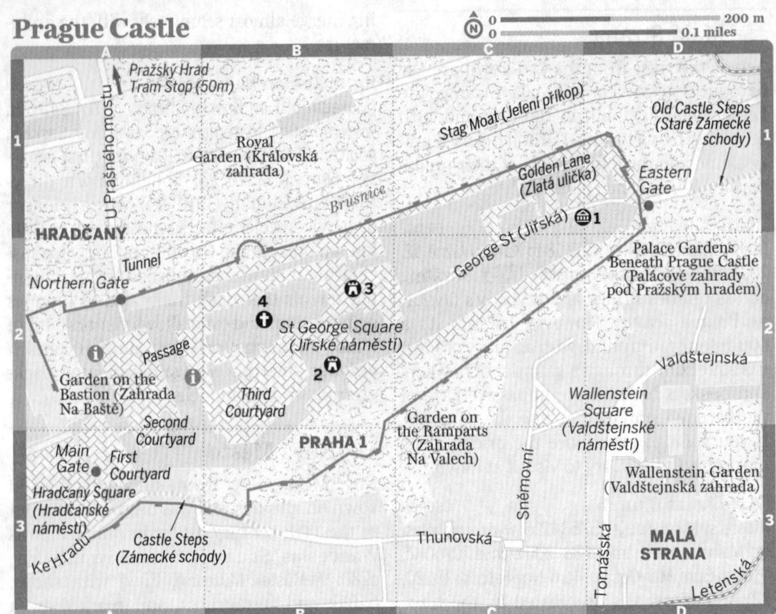

Prague Castle

Sights

1	Lobkowicz Palace	C1
2	Old Royal Palace	B2
3	Prague Castle	B2
4	St Vitus Cathedral	B2

Mucha Museum GALLERY
(Muchovo muzeum; Map p280; ☎221 451 333; www.mucha.cz; Panská 7; adult/child 240/140Kč; ⏰10am-6pm; Ⓜ Můstek) This fascinating (and busy) museum features the sensuous art nouveau posters, paintings and decorative panels of Alfons Mucha (1860–1939), as well as many sketches, photographs and other memorabilia. The exhibits include countless artworks showing Mucha's trademark Slavic maidens with flowing hair and piercing blue eyes, bearing symbolic garlands and linden boughs.

Vyšehrad Citadel FORTRESS
(☎261 225 304; www.praha-vysehrad.cz; information centre at V pevnosti 159/5b; admission to grounds free; ⏰grounds 24hr; Ⓜ Vyšehrad) FREE The Vyšehrad Citadel refers to the complex of buildings and structures atop Vyšehrad Hill that have played a role in Czech history for more than 1000 years. Although most structures date from the 18th century, the citadel is still viewed as the city's spiritual home. The sights are spread out over a wide area, with commanding views.

Festivals & Events

Prague Spring CLASSICAL MUSIC
(www.festival.cz) The Czech Republic's biggest annual cultural event, and one of Europe's most important festivals of classical music.

Prague Fringe Festival ARTS
(www.praguefringe.com) Eclectic action in late May and early June.

Christmas Market SEASONAL FESTIVAL
From 1 to 24 December in the Old Town Square.

Sleeping

Fusion Hotel HOSTEL, BOUTIQUE HOTEL €
(Map p280; ☎226 222 800; www.fusionhotels.com; Panská 9; dm from 400Kč, d/tr from 2100/2700Kč; @ 📶; 🚋3, 9, 14, 24) Billing itself as an 'affordable design hotel', Fusion certainly has style in abundance. From the revolving bar and spaceship-like UV corridor lighting, to the individually decorated bedrooms that

resemble miniature modern-art galleries, the place exudes 'cool'. You can choose from the world's most stylish backpacker dorm, private doubles, triples and family rooms, and there's a Skype booth in the lobby.

Czech Inn HOSTEL, HOTEL €
(☎267 267 600; www.czech-inn.com; Francouzská 76, Vršovice; dm 260-450Kč, s/d 1320/1540Kč, apt from 3100Kč; P ⊖ @ ≋; 🚊4, 22) The Czech Inn calls itself a hostel, but the boutique label wouldn't be out of place. Everything seems sculpted by an industrial designer, from the iron beds to the brushed-steel flooring and minimalist square sinks. It offers a variety of accommodation, from standard hostel dorm rooms to good-value private doubles (with or without private bathroom) and apartments.

★Mosaic House HOTEL, HOSTEL €€
(☎221 595 350; www.mosaichouse.com; Odborů 4; dm/tw from 370/2400Kč; ⊖ ❄ @ ≋; M Karlovo Náměstí) A blend of four-star hotel and boutique hostel, Mosaic House is a cornucopia of designer detail, from the original 1930s mosaic in the entrance hall to the silver spray-painted tree branches used as clothes racks. The backpackers dorms are kept separate from the private rooms, but have the same high-quality decor and design, as does the in-house music bar and lounge.

Lokál Inn INN €€
(☎257 014 800; www.lokalinn.cz; Míšeňská 12; d/ste 3800/4900Kč; ⊖ ≋; 🚊12, 20, 22) Polished parquet floors and painted wooden ceilings abound in this 18th-century house designed by Prague's premier baroque architect, Kilian Dientzenhofer. The eight rooms and four suites are elegant and uncluttered, and the rustic, stone-vaulted cellars house a deservedly popular pub and restaurant run by the same folk as Lokál, a popular Czech beer hall in Staré Město.

Savic Hotel HOTEL €€€
(Map p280; ☎224 248 555; www.savic.eu; Jilská 7; r from 5200Kč; ❄ @ ≋; M Můstek) From the complimentary glass of wine when you arrive to the comfy king-size beds, the Savic certainly knows how to make you feel pampered. Housed in the former monastery of St Giles, the hotel is bursting with character and full of delightful period details, including old stone fireplaces, beautiful painted timber ceilings and fragments of frescoes.

Eating

Maitrea VEGETARIAN €
(Map p280; ☎221 711 631; www.restaurace-maitrea.cz; Týnská ulička 6; mains 145-165Kč, weekday lunch 115Kč; ⏲11.30am-11.30pm Mon-Fri, noon-11.30pm Sat & Sun; ⊖ ✎; M Staroměstská) Maitrea (a Buddhist term meaning 'the future Buddha') is a beautifully designed space full of flowing curves and organic shapes, from the sensuous polished-oak furniture and fittings to the blossom-like lampshades. The menu is inventive and wholly vegetarian, with dishes such as Tex-Mex quesadillas, spicy goulash with wholemeal dumplings, and pasta with smoked tofu, spinach and parmesan.

Lokál CZECH €
(Map p280; ☎222 316 265; http://lokal-dlouha.ambi.cz; Dlouhá 33; mains 110-270Kč; ⏲11am-1am Mon-Fri, noon-1am Sat, noon-10pm Sun; 🚊5, 8, 24) Who'd have thought it possible? A classic Czech beer hall (albeit with slick modern styling); excellent *tankové pivo* (tanked Pilsner Urquell); a daily-changing menu of traditional Bohemian dishes; smiling, efficient, friendly service; and a nonsmoking area! Top restaurant chain Ambiente has turned its hand to Czech cuisine, and the result has been so successful that the place is always busy, mostly with locals.

Café Lounge CZECH €
(☎257 404 020; www.cafe-lounge.cz; Plaská 8; mains 120-390Kč; ⏲7.30am-10pm Mon-Fri, 9am-10pm Sat, 9am-5pm Sun; ⊖ ≋; 🚊6, 9, 12, 20, 22) Cosy and welcoming, Café Lounge sports an art-deco atmosphere, superb coffee, exquisite pastries and an extensive wine list. The all-day cafe menu offers freshly made salads and cornbread sandwiches, while lunch and dinner extends to dishes such as beef cheeks braised in red wine, or roast pike-perch with caraway seeds. Great breakfasts, too (served until 11am weekdays, noon on weekends).

Kolkovna CZECH €€
(Map p280; ☎224 819 701; www.vkolkovne.cz; V Kolkovně 8; mains 110-360Kč; ⏲11am-midnight; ≋; M Staroměstská) Owned and operated by the Pilsner Urquell Brewery, Kolkovna is a stylish, modern take on the traditional Prague pub, with decor by top Czech designers, and posh (but hearty) versions of classic Czech dishes such as goulash, roast duck and Moravian sparrow, as well as the Czech favourite, roast pork knuckle. All washed down with exquisite Urquell beer, of course.

★Sansho ASIAN, FUSION €€

(Map p280; 222 317 425; www.sansho.cz; Petrská 25; lunch mains 110-225Kč, 6-course dinner 850-950Kč; 11.30am-3pm & 6-11pm Tue-Thu, to 11.30pm Fri, 6-11.30pm Sat, last orders 10pm; ; 3, 8, 24) Friendly and informal best describes the atmosphere at this groundbreaking restaurant where British chef Paul Day champions Czech farmers by sourcing all his meat and vegetables locally. There's no menu – the waiter will explain what dishes are available, depending on market produce – typical dishes include curried rabbit, pork belly with watermelon salad, and 12-hour beef rendang.

Kalina FRENCH €€€

(Map p280; 222 317 715; www.kalinarestaurant.cz; Dlouhá 12; mains 330-720Kč; noon-3pm & 6-11.30pm Mon-Sat; ; 5, 8, 24) Setting a trend for taking the best of fresh Czech produce and giving it the French gourmet treatment, this smart but unfailingly friendly little restaurant offers dishes such as duck pâté with rowan berries, smoked eel with beetroot and hazelnut, and roast wild boar with red wine and juniper. The set two-course lunch menu costs 330Kč.

U Modré Kachničky CZECH €€€

(257 320 308; www.umodrekachnicky.cz; Nebovidská 6; mains 450-600Kč; noon-4pm & 6.30pm-midnight; ; 12, 20, 22) A plush and chintzy 1930s-style hunting lodge hidden away on a quiet side street, 'At the Blue Duckling' is a pleasantly old-fashioned place with quiet, candlelit nooks perfect for a romantic dinner. The menu is heavy on traditional Bohemian duck and game dishes, such as roast duck with *slivovice* (plum brandy), plum sauce and potato pancakes.

Drinking & Nightlife

Czech beers are among the world's best. The most famous brands are Plzeňský Prazdroj (Pilsner Urquell), Budvar and Prague's own Staropramen. Independent microbreweries and regional Czech beers are also becoming more popular in Prague.

U Medvídků BEER HALL

(At the Little Bear; Map p280; 224 211 916; www.umedvidku.cz; Na Perštýně 7; beer hall 11.30am-11pm, museum noon-10pm; ; M Můstek, 6, 9, 18, 22) The most micro of Prague's microbreweries, with a capacity of only 250L, U Medvídků started producing its own beer in 2005, though its trad-style beer hall has been around for many years. What it lacks in size, it makes up for in strength – the dark lager, marketed as X-Beer, is the strongest in the country, with an alcohol content of 11.8%.

Prague Beer Museum PUB

(Map p280; 732 330 912; www.praguebeermuseum.com; Dlouhá 46; noon-3am; ; 5, 8, 14) Although the name seems aimed at the tourist market, this lively and always-heaving pub is very popular with Praguers. There are no fewer than 30 Czech-produced beers on tap (plus a beer menu with tasting notes to guide you). Try a sample board – a wooden platter with five 0.15L glasses containing beers of your choice.

Café Imperial CAFE

(Map p280; 246 011 440; www.cafeimperial.cz; Na poříčí 15; 7am-11pm; ; M Náměstí Republiky) First opened in 1914, and given a complete facelift in 2007, the Imperial is a tour de force of art nouveau tiling – the walls and ceiling are covered in original ceramic tiles, mosaics, sculptured panels and bas-reliefs, with period light fittings and bronzes scattered about. The coffee is good and there are cocktails in the evening.

Hoffa COCKTAIL BAR

(Map p280; 601 359 659; www.hoffa.cz; Senovážné náměstí 22; 11am-2am Mon-Fri, 6pm-2am Sat & Sun; ; 5, 9, 26) One of Prague's first entirely smoke-free bars, Hoffa matches clean air with clean design: a long (12m long!) bar fronts a room with sleek, functional decor and a wall of windows looking out onto Senovážné náměstí's fountain of dancing sprites. Friendly staff, accomplished cocktails and good snacks – there's even homemade lemonade and iced tea at lunchtime.

★Cross Club CLUB

(736 535 010; www.crossclub.cz; Plynární 23; admission free-150Kč; cafe noon-2am, club 6pm-4am; ; M Nádraží Holešovice) An industrial club in every sense of the word: the setting in an industrial zone; the thumping music (both DJs and live acts); and the interior, an absolute must-see jumble of gadgets, shafts, cranks and pipes, many of which move and pulsate with light to the music. The program includes occasional live music, theatre performances and art happenings.

Entertainment

From dance to classical music to jazz, Prague offers plenty of entertainment options. Try the following ticket agencies to see what might be on during your visit and to snag tickets online: **Bohemia Ticket** (Map p280; ☎224 215 031; www.bohemiaticket.cz; Na příkopě 16, Nové Město; ⊙10am-7pm Mon-Fri, to 5pm Sat, to 3pm Sun) and **Ticketstream** (www.ticket-stream.cz).

Performing Arts

National Theatre OPERA, BALLET

(Národní divadlo; Map p280; ☎224 901 448; www.narodni-divadlo.cz; Národní třída 2; tickets 50-1100Kč; ⊙box offices 10am-6pm; 🚊6, 9, 18, 22) The much-loved National Theatre provides a stage for traditional opera, drama and ballet by the likes of Smetana, Shakespeare and Tchaikovsky, sharing the program alongside more modern works by composers and playwrights such as Philip Glass and John Osborne. The box offices are in the Nový síň building next door, in the Kolowrat Palace (opposite the Estates Theatre) and at the State Opera.

Prague State Opera OPERA, BALLET

(Státní opera Praha; Map p280; ☎224 901 448; www.narodni-divadlo.cz; Wilsonova 4; tickets 180-1190Kč; ⊙box office 10am-6pm; Ⓜ Muzeum) The impressive neo-rococo home of the Prague State Opera provides a glorious setting for performances of opera and ballet. An annual Verdi festival takes place here in August and September, and less conventional shows, such as Leoncavallo's rarely staged version of *La Bohème,* are also performed here.

Smetana Hall CLASSICAL MUSIC

(Smetanova síň; Map p280; ☎222 002 101; www.obecnidum.cz; náměstí Republiky 5; tickets 300-600Kč; ⊙box office 10am-6pm; Ⓜ Náměstí Republiky) The Smetana Hall, centrepiece of the stunning Municipal House (p282; Obecní dům), is the city's largest concert hall, with seating for 1200. This is the home venue of the Prague Symphony Orchestra (Symfonický orchestr hlavního města Prahy), and also stages performances of folk dance and music.

Live Music

Palác Akropolis LIVE MUSIC

(☎296 330 911; www.palacakropolis.cz; Kubelíkova 27, Žižkov; admission free-200Kč; ⊙club 7pm-5am; 📶; 🚊5, 9, 26 to Lipanska) The Akropolis is a Prague institution, a smoky, labyrinthine, sticky-floored shrine to alternative music and drama. Its various performance spaces host a smorgasbord of musical and cultural events, from DJs to string quartets to Macedonian Roma bands to local rock gods to visiting talent – Marianne Faithfull, the Flaming Lips and the Strokes have all played here.

Roxy LIVE MUSIC

(Map p280; ☎224 826 296; www.roxy.cz; Dlouhá 33; admission Fri & Sat free-300Kč; ⊙7pm-5am; 🚊5, 8, 14) Set in the ramshackle shell of an art-deco cinema, the legendary Roxy has nurtured the more independent and innovative end of Prague's club spectrum since 1987 – this is the place to see the Czech Republic's top DJs. On the 1st floor is NoD, an 'experimental space' that stages drama, dance, performance art, cinema and live music. Best nightspot in Staré Město.

Jazz Dock JAZZ

(☎774 058 838; www.jazzdock.cz; Janáčkovo nábřeží 2, Smíchov; admission 150Kč; ⊙4pm-3am; Ⓜ Anděl, 🚊7, 9, 12, 14) Most of Prague's jazz clubs are smoky cellar affairs – this riverside club is a definite step up, with clean, modern decor and a decidedly romantic view out over the Vltava. It draws some of the best local talent and occasional international acts. Go early or book to get a good table. Shows normally begin at 7pm and 10pm.

ℹ Information

The major banks are best for changing cash, but using a debit card in an ATM gives a better exchange rate. Avoid *směnárna* (private exchange booths), which advertise misleading rates and have exorbitant charges.

Na Homolce Hospital (☎257 271 111; www.homolka.cz; 5th fl, Foreign Pavilion, Roentgenova 2, Motol; 🚌167, 168 to Nemocnice Na Homolce) The best hospital in Prague, equipped and staffed to Western standards, with staff who speak English, French, German and Spanish.

Prague City Tourism – Old Town Hall (Prague Welcome; Map p280; ☎221 714 444;

WANT MORE?

For in-depth information, reviews and recommendations at your fingertips, head to the Apple App Store to purchase Lonely Planet's *Prague City Guide* and *Czech Phrasebook* iPhone apps.

Alternatively, head to www.lonelyplanet.com/czech-republic/prague for planning advice, author recommendations, traveller reviews and insider tips.

www.prague.eu; Old Town Hall, Staroměstské náměstí 5; ⌚9am-7pm; Ⓜ Staroměstská) The busiest of the Prague City Tourism branches occupies the ground floor of the Old Town Hall (enter to the left of the Astronomical Clock).

Relax Café-Bar (☎224 211 521; www.relaxcafebar.cz; Dlážděná 4; per 10min 10Kč; ⌚8am-10pm Mon-Fri, 2-10pm Sat; Wi-fi; Ⓜ Náměstí Republiky) A conveniently located internet cafe. Wi-fi is free.

Getting There & Away

There are very efficient main overland and air routes to Prague and the Czech Republic. See p298 for more details.

Getting Around

TO/FROM THE AIRPORT

To get into town from Prague airport, buy a full-price public transport ticket (32Kč) from the **Prague Public Transport Authority** (DPP; ☎296 191 817; www.dpp.cz; ⌚7am-9pm) desk in the arrivals hall and take bus 119 (20 minutes, every 10 minutes, 4am to midnight) to the end of metro line A (Dejvická), then continue by metro into the city centre (another 10 to 15 minutes; no new ticket needed).

If you're heading to the southwestern part of the city, take bus 100, which goes to the Zličín metro station (line B).

There's also an Airport Express bus (AE; 60Kč, 35 minutes, every half-hour from 5am to 10pm) that runs to Praha hlavní nádraží (Prague main train station), where you can connect to metro line C (buy ticket from driver, luggage goes free).

AAA Radio Taxi operates a 24-hour taxi service, charging from 500Kč to 650Kč depending on the destination to get to central Prague. You'll find taxi stands outside both arrivals terminals. Drivers usually speak some English and accept credit cards.

PUBLIC TRANSPORT

Prague's excellent public-transport system combines tram, metro and bus services. It's operated by the Prague Public Transport Authority (DDP), which has information desks at Prague airport (7am to 10pm) and in several metro stations, including Muzeum, Můstek, Anděl and Nádraží Holešovice. The metro operates daily from 5am to midnight.

Tickets valid on all metros, trams and buses are sold from machines at metro stations (coins only), as well as at DPP information offices and many newsstands and kiosks. Tickets can be purchased individually or as discounted day passes valid for one or three days.

A full-price individual ticket costs 32/16Kč per adult/senior aged 65 to 70 and is valid for 90 minutes of unlimited travel. For shorter journeys, buy short-term tickets that are valid for 30 minutes of unlimited travel. These cost 24/12Kč per adult/senior. One-day passes cost 110/55Kč per adult/senior; three-day passes cost 310Kč (no discount for seniors).

TAXI

Taxis are frequent and relatively inexpensive. The official rate for licensed cabs is 40Kč flagfall plus 28Kč per kilometre and 6Kč per minute while waiting. On this basis, any trip within the city centre – say, from Wenceslas Square to Malá Strana – should cost around 170Kč. A trip to the suburbs, depending on the distance, should run from around 200Kč to 400Kč, and to the airport between 500Kč and 650Kč.

The following companies offer 24-hour service and English-speaking operators:

AAA Radio Taxi (☎14014, 222 333 222; www.aaataxi.cz)

City Taxi (☎257 257 257; www.citytaxi.cz)

AROUND PRAGUE

Karlštejn

Rising above the village of Karlštejn, 30km southwest of Prague, medieval **Karlštejn Castle** (Hrad Karlštejn; ☎tour booking 311 681 617; www.hradkarlstejn.cz; adult/child Tour 1 270/180Kč, Tour 2 300/200Kč, Tour 3 150/100Kč; ⌚9am-6.30pm Jul & Aug, 9.30am-5.30pm Tue-Sun May, Jun & Sep, to 5pm Apr, to 4.30pm Oct, to 4pm Mar, reduced hours Sat & Sun only Dec-Feb) is in such good shape it wouldn't look out of place on Disneyworld's Main St. The crowds come in theme-park proportions as well, but the peaceful surrounding countryside offers views of Karlštejn's stunning exterior that rival anything you'll see on the inside.

The castle was born of a grand pedigree, originally conceived by Emperor Charles IV in the 14th century as a bastion for hiding the crown jewels. Run by an appointed burgrave, the castle was surrounded by a network of landowning knight-vassals, who came to the castle's aid whenever enemies moved against it.

Karlštejn again sheltered the Bohemian and the Holy Roman Empire crown jewels during the Hussite Wars of the 15th century, but fell into disrepair as its defences became outmoded. Considerable restoration work in the late-19th century returned the castle to its former glory.

Castle visits are by guided tour only. Some tours must be reserved in advance by phone or via the castle website.

There are three tours available: **Tour I** (50 minutes) passes through the Knight's Hall, still daubed with the coats-of-arms and names of the knight-vassals, Charles IV's Bedchamber, the Audience Hall and the Jewel House, which includes treasures from the Chapel of the Holy Cross and a replica of the St Wenceslas Crown. **Tour 2** (70 minutes, May to October only) takes in the Marian Tower, with the Church of the Virgin Mary and the Chapel of St Catherine, then moves to the Great Tower for the castle's star attraction, the exquisite Chapel of the Holy Cross. **Tour 3** (40 minutes, May to October only) visits the upper levels of the Great Tower, which provide stunning views over the surrounding countryside.

From Prague, there are frequent train departures daily from Prague's main station, *hlavní nádraží*. The journey takes 40 minutes and costs around 50Kč each way.

Kutná Hora

In the 14th century, Kutná Hora, 60km southeast of Prague, rivalled the capital in importance because of its rich deposits of silver ore. The ore ran out in 1726, leaving the medieval townscape largely unaltered. Now with several fascinating and unusual historical attractions, the Unesco World Heritage–listed town is a popular day trip from Prague.

Interestingly, most visitors come not for the silver splendour but rather to see an eerie monastery, dating from the 19th century, with an interior crafted solely from human bones. Indeed, the remarkable **Sedlec Ossuary** (Kostnice; ☎ information centre 326 551 049; www.ossuary.eu; Zámecká 127; adult/concession 90/60Kč; ⊙8am-6pm Mon-Sat, 9am-6pm Sun Apr-Sep, 9am-5pm Mar & Oct, 9am-4pm Nov-Feb), or better 'bone church', features the remains of no fewer than 40,000 people who died over the years from wars and pestilence.

Closer to the centre of Kutná Hora is the town's greatest monument: the Gothic **Cathedral of St Barbara** (Chrám sv Barbora; ☎775 363 938; www.khfarnost.cz; Barborská; adult/concession 60/40Kč; ⊙9am-6pm Apr-Oct, 10am-5pm Mon-Fri, 10am-6pm Sat & Sun Nov-Dec, 10am-4pm Jan-Mar). Rivalling Prague's St Vitus in size and magnificence, its soaring nave culminates in elegant, six-petalled ribbed vaulting, and the ambulatory chapels preserve original 15th-century frescoes. Other leading attractions include the **Hrádek** (České muzeum stříbra; ☎327 512 159; www.cms-kh.cz; Barborská 28; Tour 1 adult/concession 70/40Kč, Tour 2 120/80Kč, combined 140/90Kč; ⊙10am-6pm Jul & Aug, 9am-6pm May, Jun & Sep, 9am-5pm Apr & Oct, 10am-4pm Nov, closed Mon year-round) from the 15th century, which now houses the **Czech Silver Museum**.

Kutná Hora can be reached from Prague by either bus (68Kč, 1¾ hours) or train (101Kč, one hour). The bus station is located on the Old Town's northeastern edge, which is convenient to the central sites, but 3km from the ossuary. Kutná Hora's main train station, by contrast, is just 800m from the ossuary, but 3km from the Old Town.

BOHEMIA

The Czech Republic's western province boasts surprising variety. Český Krumlov, with its riverside setting and dramatic Renaissance castle, is in a class by itself. Big cities like Plzeň offer urban attractions like great museums and restaurants. The spa towns of western Bohemia, such as Karlovy Vary, were world famous in the 19th century and retain an old-world lustre.

Plzeň

POP 173,000

Plzeň, the regional capital of western Bohemia and the second-biggest city in Bohemia after Prague, is best known as the home of the Pilsner Urquell Brewery, but it has a handful of other interesting sights and enough good restaurants and night-time pursuits to justify an overnight stay. Most of the sights are located near the central square, but the brewery itself is about a 15-minute walk outside the city centre.

Sights

★Pilsner Urquell Brewery BREWERY

(Prazdroj; ☎377 062 888; www.prazdrojvisit.cz; U Prazdroje 7; guided tour adult/child 190/100Kč; ⊙8.30am-6pm Apr-Sep, to 5pm Oct-Mar, English tours 12.45pm, 2.15pm & 4.15pm) Plzeň's most popular attraction is the tour of the Pilsner Urquell Brewery, in operation since 1842 and arguably home to the world's best beer. Entry is by guided tour only, with three tours in English available daily. Tour highlights include a trip to the old cellars (dress warmly) and a glass of unpasteurised nectar at the end.

Brewery Museum MUSEUM
(☎377 224 955; www.prazdrojvisit.cz; Veleslavínova 6; guided tour adult/child 120/90Kč, English text 90/60Kč; ⏰10am-6pm Apr-Dec, to 5pm Jan-Mar) The Brewery Museum offers an insight into how beer was made (and drunk) in the days before Prazdroj was founded. Highlights include a mock-up of a 19th-century pub, a huge wooden beer tankard from Siberia and a collection of beer mats. All have English captions and there's a good printed English guide available.

Underground Plzeň UNDERGROUND
(Plzeňské historické podzemí; ☎377 235 574; www.plzenskepodzemi.cz; Veleslavínova 6; adult/child 100/70Kč; ⏰10am-6pm Apr-Dec, to 5pm Feb-Mar, closed Jan, English tour 1pm daily Apr-Oct) This extraordinary tour explores the passageways below the old city. The earliest were probably dug in the 14th century, perhaps for beer production or defence; the latest date from the 19th century. Of an estimated 11km that have been excavated, some 500m of tunnels are open to the public. Bring extra clothing (it's a chilly 10°C underground).

★Techmania Science Centre MUSEUM
(☎737 247 585; www.techmania.cz; cnr Borská & Břeňkova, Areál Škoda; adult/concession incl 3D planetarium 180/110Kč; ⏰8.30am-5pm Mon-Fri, 10am-6pm Sat & Sun; P Wi-Fi family-friendly; bus 15, 17) Kids will have a ball at this high-tech, interactive science centre, where they can play with infrared cameras, magnets and many other instructive and fun exhibitions. There's a 3D planetarium (included in the full-price admission) and a few full-sized historic trams and trains manufactured at the Škoda engineering works. Take the trolleybus; it's a hike from the city centre.

Sleeping

Hotel Roudna HOTEL €
(☎377 259 926; www.hotelroudna.cz; Na Roudné 13; s/d 1150/1400Kč; P @ Wi-Fi) Might very well be the city's best-value lodging. The exterior is not much to look at; but inside, rooms are well-proportioned, with high-end amenities such as flatscreen TV, minibar and desk. Breakfasts are fresh and ample. The reception is friendly. Note there's no lift. The hotel has an excellent steakhouse two doors down on the same street.

U Salzmannů PENSION €
(☎377 235 476; www.usalzmannu.com; Pražská 8; s/d 1050/1450Kč, ste 2100Kč; non-smoking Wi-Fi) This pleasant pension, right in the heart of town, sits above a very good historic pub. The standard rooms are comfortable but basic; the more luxurious double 'suites' have antique beds and small sitting rooms, as well as kitchenettes. The pub location is convenient if you overdo it; to reach your bed, just climb the stairs.

Eating

Na Parkánu CZECH €
(☎377 324 485; www.naparkanu.com; Veleslavínova 4; mains 100-200Kč; ⏰11am-11pm Mon-Thu, to 1am Fri & Sat, to 10pm Sun; Wi-Fi) Don't overlook this pleasant pub-restaurant, attached to the Brewery Museum. It may look a bit touristy, but the traditional Czech food is top rate, and the beer, naturally, could hardly be better. Try to snag a spot in the summer garden. Don't leave without trying the *nefiltrované pivo* (unfiltered beer). Reservations are an absolute must.

Aberdeen Angus Steakhouse STEAK €€
(☎725 555 631; www.angussteakhouse.cz; Pražská 23; mains 180-400Kč; ⏰11am-11pm; non-smoking Wi-Fi) For our money, this may be the best steakhouse in all of the Czech Republic. The meats hail from a nearby farm, where the livestock is raised organically. There are several cuts and sizes on offer; lunch options include a tantalising cheeseburger. The downstairs dining room is cosy; there's also a creekside terrace. Book in advance.

Information

City Information Centre (Informační centrum města Plzně; ☎378 035 330; www.icpilsen.cz; Náměstí Republiky 41; ⏰9am-7pm Apr-Sep, to 6pm Oct-Mar) Plzeň's well-stocked and -staffed tourist information office is a first port of call for visitors. Can advise on sleeping and eating options, hands out free city maps, and has a stock of brochures on what to see and do.

Getting There & Away

From Prague, eight trains (150Kč, 1½ hours) leave daily from the main station, *hlavní nádraží*. The train station is on the eastern side of town, 10 minutes' walk from nám Republiky, the Old Town Square. From Prague, the bus service to Plzeň (100Kč, one hour) is frequent (hourly), relatively fast and inexpensive.

WORTH A TRIP

A SPA STROLL THROUGH KARLOVY VARY

Karlovy Vary is the closest the Czech Republic has to a glam resort, but it is still only glam with a small 'g'. While the resort was famous across Europe in the 19th century as a health spa, these days the town attracts mostly short-term visitors, content to stroll the pretty spa area and to sip on allegedly health-restoring sulphuric compounds from ceramic, spouted drinking cups.

There are 15 mineral springs housed in or near the four main **colonnades** *(kolonády)* along the River Teplá. Each spring has its own purported medicinal properties and gushes forth at various temperatures, ranging from lukewarm to scalding hot.

The **Infocentrum** (Infocentrum Lázeňská; 355 321 176; www.karlovyvary.cz; Lázeňská 14; 9am-5pm;) has a chart of the springs and temperatures, and can advise on the various health benefits of the waters.

While frequent bus service from Prague makes this a possible day trip from Prague, there are plenty of excellent hotels for an overnight stay. **Hotel Romance Puškin** (353 222 646; www.hotelromance.cz; Tržiště 37; s/d 2450/3450Kč;) boasts a great location in the heart of the spa area and has fully renovated rooms with updated baths and comfortable beds.

Hospoda U Švejka (353 232 276; www.svejk-kv.cz; Stará Louka 10; mains 160-370Kč; 11am-11pm) is a nice choice for lunch or dinner. Though the presentation borders on kitsch, the food is actually very good and the atmosphere not unlike a classic Czech pub.

Buses are the only practical way of reaching Karlovy Vary from Prague. **Student Agency** (353 176 333; www.studentagency.cz; TG Masaryka 58/34; 9am-6pm Mon-Fri) runs frequent buses to/from Prague's Florenc bus station (from 160Kč, two hours, several daily) departing from the main bus station beside Dolní nádraží train station.

Český Krumlov

POP 14,050

Outside of Prague, Český Krumlov is arguably the Czech Republic's only other world-class sight and must-see. From a distance, the town looks like any other in the Czech countryside, but once you get closer and see the Renaissance castle towering over the undisturbed 17th-century townscape, you'll feel the appeal; this really is that fairy-tale town the tourist brochures promised. Český Krumlov is best approached as an overnight destination; it's too far for a comfortable day trip from Prague.

Sights

Český Krumlov State Castle CASTLE

(380 704 711; www.zamek-ceskykrumlov.eu; Zámek 59; adult/concession Tour 1 250/160Kč, Tour 2 240/140Kč, Theatre Tour 300/200Kč; 9am-6pm Tue-Sun Jun-Aug, to 5pm Apr, May, Sep & Oct) Český Krumlov's striking Renaissance castle, occupying a promontory high above the town, began life in the 13th century. It acquired its present appearance in the 16th to 18th centuries under the stewardship of the noble Rožmberk and Schwarzenberg families. The interiors are accessible by guided tour only, though you can stroll the grounds on your own.

Castle Museum & Tower MUSEUM, TOWER

(380 704 711; www.zamek-ceskykrumlov.eu; Zámek 59; combined entry adult/concession 130/60Kč, museum only 100/50Kč, tower only 50/30Kč; 9am-6pm Jun-Aug, to 5pm Apr & May, to 5pm Tue-Sun Sep & Oct, to 4pm Tue-Sun Jan-Mar) Located within the castle complex, this small museum and adjoining tower is an ideal option if you don't have the time or energy for a full castle tour. Through a series of rooms, the museum traces the castle's history from its origins through the present day. Climb the tower for perfect photo-op shots of the town below.

Egon Schiele Art Centrum MUSEUM

(380 704 011; www.schieleartcentrum.cz; Široká 71; adult/concession 120/70Kč; 10am-6pm Tue-Sun) This excellent private gallery houses a small retrospective of the controversial Viennese painter Egon Schiele (1890–1918), who lived in Krumlov in 1911, and raised the ire of townsfolk by hiring young girls as nude models. For this and other sins he was eventually driven away. The centre also houses interesting temporary exhibitions.

Český Krumlov

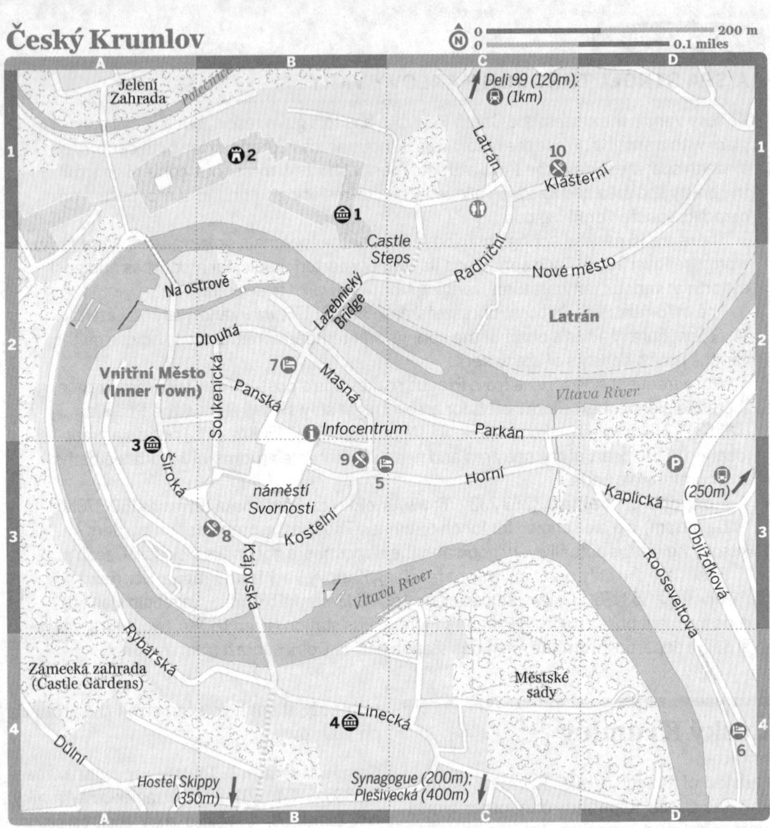

Český Krumlov

Sights
1 Castle Museum & Tower B1
2 Český Krumlov State Castle B1
3 Egon Schiele Art Centrum A3
4 Museum Fotoateliér Seidel B4

Sleeping
5 Hotel Konvice B3
6 Krumlov House D4
7 U Malého Vítka B2

Eating
8 Hospoda Na Louži B3
9 Krčma v Šatlavské B3
10 Nonna Gina C1

Museum Fotoateliér Seidel MUSEUM
(☎380 712 354; www.seidel.cz; Linecká 272; adult/concession 100/70Kč; ⊙9am-noon & 1-5pm daily Apr & Oct-Dec, Tue-Sun Jan-Mar, 9am-noon & 1-6pm daily May-Sep) This photography museum presents a moving retrospective of the work of local photographers Josef Seidel and his son František. Especially poignant are the images recording early-20th-century life in nearby villages. In the high season you should be able to join an English-language tour; if not, let the pictures tell the story.

Sleeping

★**Krumlov House** HOSTEL €
(☎380 711 935; www.krumlovhostel.com; Rooseveltova 68; dm/d/tr 300/1000/1350Kč;) Perched above the river, Krumlov House is friendly and comfortable, and has plenty of books, DVDs and local information to feed your inner wanderer. Accommodation is in six-bed en suite dorms as well as private double and triple rooms or private, self-catered apartments. The owners are English-speaking and traveller-friendly.

U Malého Vítka HOTEL €€

(380 711 925; www.vitekhotel.cz; Radniční 27; s/d 1200/1500Kč; P) We like this small hotel in the heart of the Old Town. The simple room furnishings are of high-quality, handcrafted wood, and each room is named after a traditional Czech fairy-tale character. The downstairs restaurant and cafe are very good, too.

Hotel Konvice HOTEL €€

(380 711 611; www.boehmerwaldhotels.de; Horní 144; s/d 1300/2000Kč; P) Attractive old-fashioned hotel with romantic rooms and period furnishings. Many rooms, such as No 12, have impressive wood-beamed ceilings, and all have homey architectural quirks that lend atmosphere. The service is reserved but friendly. The cook at breakfast is more than happy to whip up an egg on request (to go with the usual cold cuts and cheeses).

Eating

Nonna Gina ITALIAN €

(380 717 187; Klášterní 52; pizza 100-170Kč; 11am-10pm;) Authentic Italian flavours from the Italian Massaro family feature in this pizzeria down a quiet lane. Grab an outdoor table and pretend you're in Naples. In winter the upstairs dining room is snug and intimate.

Hospoda Na Louži CZECH €

(380 711 280; www.nalouzi.cz; Kájovská 66; mains 90-170Kč;) Nothing's changed in this wood-panelled *pivo* (beer) parlour for almost a century. Locals and tourists pack Na Louži for huge plates of Czech staples such as chicken schnitzels or roast pork and dumplings, as well as dark (and light) beer from the Eggenberg brewery. Get the fruit dumplings for dessert if you see them on the menu.

★ **Krčma v Šatlavské** CZECH €€

(380 713 344; www.satlava.cz; Horní 157; mains 180-280Kč; 11am-midnight) This medieval barbecue cellar is hugely popular with visitors, and your tablemates are much more likely to be from Austria or Asia than from the town itself. But the grilled meats – served up with gusto in a funky labyrinth illuminated by candles – are excellent and perfectly in character with Český Krumlov. Advance booking is essential.

Information

Infocentrum (380 704 622; www.ckrumlov.info; náměstí Svornosti 2; 9am-7pm Jun-Aug, to 6pm Apr, May, Sep & Oct, to 5pm Nov-Mar) One of the country's best tourist offices. Good source for transport and accommodation info, maps, internet access (per five minutes 5Kč) and audioguides (per hour 100Kč). A guide for disabled visitors is available.

Getting There & Away

From Prague (260Kč, 3½ hours), the train journey requires a change in České Budějovice. Buses are quicker and cheaper. From Prague, **Student Agency** (841 101 101; www.studentagency.cz) coaches (195Kč, three hours) leave regularly from the Na Knížecí bus station at Anděl metro station (Line B).

MORAVIA

The Czech Republic's eastern province, Moravia is yin to Bohemia's yang. If Bohemians love beer, Moravians love wine. If Bohemia is towns and cities, Moravia is rolling hills and pretty landscapes. The Moravian capital, Brno, has the museums, but the northern city of Olomouc has the captivating architecture.

Brno

POP 385,900

Among Czechs, Moravia's capital has a dull rep; a likeable place where not much actually happens. The reality, though, is different. Thousands of students ensure lively cafe and club scenes that easily rival Prague's. The museums are great, too. Brno was one of the leading centres of experimental architecture in the early 20th century, and the Unesco-protected Vila Tugendhat is considered a masterwork of functionalist design.

Sights

Špilberk Castle CASTLE

(Hrad Špilberk; 542 123 611; www.spilberk.cz; Špilberk 210/1; combined entry adult/concession 400/240Kč, casemates only 90/50Kč, tower only 50/30Kč; 9am-5pm Tue-Sun Oct-Apr, 9am-5pm daily May & Jun, 10am-6pm daily Jul-Sep) Brno's spooky hilltop castle is considered the city's most important landmark. Its history stretches back to the 13th century, when it was home to Moravian margraves and later a fortress. Under the Habsburgs in the 18th and 19th centuries, it served as a prison. Today it's home to the **Brno City Museum**, with several temporary and permanent exhibitions.

Cathedral of Sts Peter & Paul CHURCH, TOWER

(katedrála sv Petra a Pavla; www.katedrala-petrov.cz; Petrov Hill; tower adult/concession 40/30Kč; 11am-6pm Mon-Sat, from 11.45am Sun) This 14th-century cathedral atop Petrov Hill was originally built on the site of a pagan temple to Venus, and has been reconstructed many times since. The highly decorated 11m-high main altar with figures of Sts Peter and Paul was carved by Viennese sculptor Josef Leimer in 1891. You can also climb the **tower** for dramatic views.

Old Town Hall HISTORIC BUILDING

(Stará radnice; 542 427 150; www.ticbrno.cz; Radnická 8; tower adult/concession 50/30Kč; 9am-5pm) Brno's atmospheric Old Town Hall dates from the early 13th century. The tourist office is here, plus oddities including a crocodile hanging from the ceiling (known affectionately as the Brno 'dragon') and a wooden wagon wheel with a unique story. You can also climb the **tower**.

Capuchin Monastery CEMETERY

(Kapucínský klášter; www.kapucini.cz; Kapucínské náměstí; adult/concession 60/30Kč; 9am-noon & 1-4.30pm Mon-Sat, 11am-11.45am & 1-4.30pm Sun May-Sep, closed Mon mid-Feb–Apr & Oct–mid-Dec, weekends only mid-Dec–mid-Feb) One of the city's leading attractions is this ghoulish cellar **crypt** that holds the mummified remains of several city noblemen from the 18th century. Apparently the dry, well-ventilated crypt has the natural ability to turn dead bodies into mummies. Up to 150 cadavers were deposited here prior to 1784, the desiccated corpses including monks, abbots and local notables.

Labyrinth under the Cabbage Market UNDERGROUND

(Brněnské podzemí; 542 427 150; www.ticbrno.cz; Zelný trh 21; adult/concession 160/80Kč; 9am-6pm Tue-Sun) In recent years the city has opened several sections of extensive underground tunnels to the general public. This tour takes around 40 minutes to explore several cellars situated 6m to 8m below the Cabbage Market, which has served as a food market for centuries. The cellars were built for two purposes: to store goods and to hide in during wars.

★ **Vila Tugendhat** ARCHITECTURE

(Villa Tugendhat; tour booking 515 511 015; www.tugendhat.eu; Černopolni 45; adult/concession basic tour 300/180Kč, extended tour 350/210Kč; 10am-6pm Tue-Sun; 3, 5, 11 to Černopolní) Brno had a reputation in the 1920s as a centre for modern architecture in the functionalist and Bauhaus styles. Arguably the finest example is this family villa, designed by modern master Mies van der Rohe in 1930. Entry is by guided tour booked in advance by phone or email. Two tours are available: a 60-minute basic tour and 90-minute extended visit.

Sleeping

In February, April, August, September and October, Brno hosts major international trade fairs, and hotel rates increase by 40% to 100%. Book ahead if possible.

★ **Hostel Mitte** HOSTEL €

(734 622 340; www.hostelmitte.com; Panská 22; dm 500Kč, s/d 1000/1300Kč, all incl breakfast;) Set in the heart of the Old Town, this clean and stylish hostel smells and looks brand new. The rooms are named after famous Moravians (eg Milan Kundera) or famous events (Austerlitz) and decorated accordingly. There are dorms in six-bed rooms and private singles and doubles. Cute cafe on the ground floor.

Hotel Europa HOTEL €€

(515 143 100; www.hotel-europa-brno.cz; třída kpt Jaroše 27; s/d 1400/1800Kč;) Set in a quiet neighbourhood a 10-minute walk from the city centre, this self-proclaimed 'art' hotel (presumably for the wacky futuristic lobby furniture) offers clean and tastefully furnished modern rooms in a historic 19th-century building. The lobby has free wi-fi, while the rooms have cable (ethernet) connections. There is free parking out the front and in the courtyard.

Barceló Brno Palace LUXURY HOTEL €€€

(532 156 777; www.barcelo.com; Šilingrovo nám 2; r from 3600Kč;) Five-star heritage luxury comes to Brno at the Barceló Brno Palace. The lobby blends glorious 19th-century architecture with thoroughly modern touches, and the spacious rooms are both contemporary and romantic. The location on the edge of Brno's Old Town is excellent.

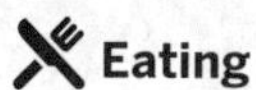

Eating

Spolek CZECH €

(☎774 814 230; www.spolek.net; Orli 22; mains 80-180Kč; ⏲9am-10pm Mon-Fri, 10am-10pm Sat & Sun;) You'll get friendly, unpretentious service at this coolly 'bohemian' (yes, we're in Moravia) haven with interesting salads and soups, and a concise but diverse wine list. Photojournalism on the walls is complemented by a funky mezzanine bookshop. It has excellent coffee, too.

Špalíček CZECH €

(☎542 211 526; Zelný trh 12; mains 80-160Kč; ⏲11am-11pm;) Brno's oldest (and maybe its 'meatiest') restaurant sits on the edge of the Cabbage Market. Ignore the irony and dig into huge Moravian meals, partnered with a local beer or something from the decent list of Moravian wines. The old-school tavern atmosphere is authentic and the daily luncheon specials are a steal.

★Pavillon INTERNATIONAL €€

(☎541 213 497; www.restaurant-pavillon.cz; Jezuitská 6; mains 250-385Kč; ⏲11am-11pm Mon-Sat, 11am-3pm Sun;) High-end dining in an elegant, airy space that recalls the city's heritage in functionalist architecture. The menu changes with the season, but usually features one vegetarian entree as well as mains with locally sourced ingredients, such as wild boar or lamb raised in the Vysočina highlands. Daily luncheon specials at 200Kč for soup, main and dessert are a steal.

Drinking

★Cafe Podnebi CAFE

(☎542 211 372; www.podnebi.cz; Údolní 5; ⏲8am-midnight Mon-Fri, from 9am Sat & Sun;) This homey, student-oriented cafe is famous citywide for its excellent hot chocolate, but it also serves very good espresso drinks. There are plenty of baked goods and sweets to snack on. In summer the garden terrace is a hidden oasis and there's a small play area for kids.

U Richarda PUB

(☎775 027 918; www.uricharda.eu; Údolní 7; ⏲11am-11pm Mon-Sat) This microbrewery is highly popular with students, who come for the great house-brewed, unpasteurised yeast beers, including a rare cherry-flavoured lager, and the good traditional Czech cooking (mains 109Kč to 149Kč). Book in advance.

Entertainment

Stará Pekárna LIVE MUSIC

(☎541 210 040; www.starapekarna.cz; Štefánikova 8; ⏲5pm-late Mon-Sat; 🚋1, 6, 7) Old and new music with blues, world beats, DJs and rock. Catch the tram to Pionýrská. Gigs usually kick off at 8pm.

Brno Philharmonic Orchestra CLASSICAL MUSIC

(Besední dům; ☎539 092 811; www.filharmonie-brno.cz; Komenského náměstí 8) The Brno Philharmonic is the city's leading orchestra for performing classical music. It conducts some 40 concerts a year, plus tours around the Czech Republic and Europe. It's particularly strong on Moravian-born, early-20th century composer Leoš Janáček. Most performances are held at Besední dům concert house. Buy tickets at the venue **box office** (⏲9am-2pm Mon & Wed, 1-6pm Tue, Thu & Fri).

Information

Tourist Information Centre (TIC Brno; ☎542 211 090; www.ticbrno.cz; Old Town Hall, Radnická 8; ⏲8am-6pm Mon-Fri, 9am-6pm Sat & Sun) Lots of great information on hand in English, including free maps. There's also a computer to check email for free.

Getting There & Away

Brno is easily reached from Prague by either bus (210Kč, 2½ hours) or train (220Kč, three hours). Bus service via the local coach service **Student Agency** (☎841 101 101; www.studentagency.cz; náměstí Svobody 17; ⏲9am-6pm Mon-Fri) is especially good. Express trains run between Brno's train station and Prague's *hlavní nádraží* every couple of hours during the day.

Olomouc

POP 100,200

Olomouc (olla-moats) is one of the Czech Republic's most underrated destinations. There's great nightlife, fuelled by a cosmopolitan student population, and a gorgeous series of central squares that would rival any European city.

Sights

Holy Trinity Column MONUMENT

(Sloup Nejsvětější Trojice; Horní náměstí) FREE The town's pride and joy is this 35m-high (115ft) baroque sculpture that dominates the square and is a popular meeting spot for

WORTH A TRIP

UNESCO HERITAGE ARCHITECTURE IN TELČ

The Unesco-protected town of Telč, perched on the border between Bohemia and Moravia, possesses one of the country's prettiest and best-preserved historic town squares.

The main attraction is the beauty of the square, **Náměstí Zachariáše z Hradce**, itself, which is lined with Renaissance burghers' houses. Most of the structures were built in the 16th century after a fire levelled the town in 1530. Famous houses include No 15, which shows the characteristic Renaissance sgraffito. The house at No 48 was given a baroque facade in the 18th century.

Telč Chateau (Zámek; ☎567 243 943; www.zamek-telc.cz; náměstí Zachariáše z Hradce 1; adult/concession route A 110/70Kč, route B 90/60Kč, combined 170/100Kč; ⏲10am-4pm Tue-Sun Apr & Oct, to 5pm May, Jun & Sep, to 6pm Jul & Aug), another Renaissance masterpiece, guards the northern end of the square. Entry is by guided tour only.

If you decide to spend the night, **Pension Steidler** (☎721 316 390; www.telc-accommodation.eu; náměstí Zachariáše z Hradce 52; s/d 500/800Kč; ⊖) offers rooms with skylights and wooden floors at a central location.

Around half-a-dozen buses make the run daily from Prague's Florenc bus station (175Kč, 2½ hours), with many connections requiring a change in Jihlava. Several daily buses run to Brno (100Kč, two hours). Check the online timetable at http://jizdnirady.idnes.cz for times.

local residents. The trinity column was built between 1716 and 1754 and is allegedly the biggest single baroque sculpture in Central Europe. In 2000 the column was awarded an inscription on Unesco's World Heritage list.

Archdiocesan Museum MUSEUM
(Arcidiecézni muzeum; ☎585 514 111; www.olmuart.cz; Václavské náměstí 3; adult/concession 70/35Kč, free Sun; ⏲10am-6pm Tue-Sun) The impressive holdings of the Archdiocesan Museum trace the history of Olomouc back 1000 years. The thoughtful layout, with helpful English signage, takes you through the original Romanesque foundations of Olomouc Castle, and highlights the cultural and artistic development of the city during the Gothic and baroque periods.

Civil Defence Shelter HISTORIC SITE
(Kryt Civilní Obrany; Bezručovy sady; admission 20Kč; ⏲tours at 10am, 1pm & 4pm Thu & Sat mid-Jun–mid-Sep) Olomouc is all about centuries-old history, but this more recent relic of the Cold War is also worth exploring on a guided tour. The shelter was built between 1953 and 1956 and was designed to shelter a lucky few from the ravages of a chemical or nuclear strike. Tours are arranged by and begin at the Olomouc Information Centre.

Sleeping

Poet's Corner HOSTEL €
(☎777 570 730; www.hostelolomouc.com; 4th fl, Sokolská 1; dm/s/d 350/700/900Kč; ⊖📶; 🚊2, 4, 6) The Australian-Czech couple who mind this friendly and exceptionally well-run hostel are a wealth of local information. There are dorms in eight-bed rooms, as well as private singles and doubles. Bicycles can be hired for 100Kč per day. In summer there's sometimes a two-night minimum stay, but Olomouc is worth it, and there's plenty of day-trip information on offer.

★ **Penzión Na Hradě** PENSION €€
(☎585 203 231; www.penzionnahrade.cz; Michalská 4; s/d 1290/1890Kč; ⊖❄📶) In terms of price/quality ratio, this is Olomouc's best deal. Worth the minor splurge if you can swing it. The location, tucked away in the shadow of St Michael's Church, is ideally central. The sleek, cool rooms have a professional design touch and there's a small garden terrace for relaxing at the back. Reserve in advance in summer.

Eating & Drinking

Drápal CZECH €
(☎585 225 818; www.restauracedrapal.cz; Havlíčkova 1; mains 110-170Kč; ⏲10am-midnight Mon-Fri, 11am-midnight Sat, 11am-11pm Sun; 📶) It's

hard to go wrong with this big historic pub on a busy corner near the town centre. The unpasteurised 12° Pilsner Urquell is arguably the best beer in Olomouc. The smallish menu is loaded with Czech classics, such as the ever-popular *Španělský ptáček* (literally 'Spanish bird'), a beef roulade stuffed with smoked sausage, parsley and a hard-boiled egg.

Moritz CZECH €€

(☎585 205 560; www.hostinec-moritz.cz; Nešverova 2; mains 120-260Kč; ⏰11am-11pm; 🚭📶) This microbrewery and restaurant is a local favourite. We reckon it's a combination of the terrific beers, good-value food, and a praise-worthy 'no smoking' policy. In summer the beer garden's the only place to be. Advance booking is a must. The location is about a 10-minute walk south of the town centre, across the busy street třída Svobody.

★Cafe 87 CAFE

(☎585 202 593; www.cafe87.cz; Denisova 47; coffee 40Kč; ⏰7.30am-9pm Mon-Fri, 8am-9pm Sat & Sun; 📶) Locals come in droves to this funky cafe beside the Olomouc Museum of Modern Art for coffee and its famous chocolate pie (45Kč). Some people still apparently prefer the dark chocolate to the white chocolate. When will they learn? It's a top spot for breakfast and toasted sandwiches, too. Seating on two floors and a rooftop terrace.

☆ Entertainment

Jazz Tibet Club LIVE MUSIC

(☎585 230 399; www.jazzclub.olomouc.com; Sokolská 48; admission free-250Kč; ⏰box office 11am-2pm) Blues, jazz and world music, including occasional international acts, feature at this popular spot, which also incorporates a good restaurant and wine bar. Buy tickets in advance at the club box office or at the Olomouc Information Centre.

ℹ Information

Olomouc Information Centre (Olomoucká Informační Služba; ☎585 513 385; www.tourism.olomouc.eu; Horní náměstí; ⏰9am-7pm) Olomouc's information centre is short on language skills, but very helpful when it comes to securing maps, brochures and tickets for events around town. It also offers regular daily sightseeing tours of the Town Hall (15Kč), and from mid-June to mid-September daily guided sightseeing tours of the city centre (50Kč).

ℹ Getting There & Away

Olomouc has fast and frequent train service to Prague (220Kč, three hours). There is also regular rail and bus service to Brno (100Kč, 1½ hours).

SURVIVAL GUIDE

ℹ Directory A–Z

ACCOMMODATION

The Czech Republic has a wide variety of accommodation options, from luxurious hotels to simple pensions and camping grounds. Prague, Brno and Český Krumlov all have decent backpacker-oriented hostels.

- In Prague hotel rates peak in spring and autumn, as well as around the Christmas and Easter holidays. Midsummer is considered 'shoulder season' and rates are about 20% lower.
- The capital is a popular destination, so be sure to book well in advance. Hotels are cheaper and less busy outside of Prague, but try to reserve ahead of arrival to get the best rate.

BUSINESS HOURS

Banks 8.30am to 4.30pm Monday to Friday
Bars 11am to midnight or later
Museums & castles Usually closed Monday year-round
Restaurants 11am to 10pm
Shops 8.30am to 6pm Monday to Friday, 8.30am to noon Saturday

GAY & LESBIAN TRAVELLERS

- Homosexuality is legal in the Czech Republic and attitudes are relatively open.

COUNTRY FACTS

Area 78,866 sq km
Capital Prague
Country Code ☎420
Currency Crown (Kč)
Emergency ☎112
Language Czech
Money ATMs all over; banks open Monday to Friday
Population 10.5 million
Visas Schengen rules apply; visas not required for most nationalities

SLEEPING PRICE RANGES

The following price ranges refer to a double room in high season:

€ less than 1600Kč

€€ 1600Kč–3700Kč

€€€ more than 3700Kč

- For online information including links to accommodation and bars see the **Prague Gay Guide** (www.prague.gayguide.net).

INTERNET RESOURCES

Czech Tourism (www.czechtourism.com)

National Bus & Train Timetable (http://jizdnirady.idnes.cz)

Prague City Tourism (www.praguecitytourism.cz)

Prague City Transport (www.dpp.cz)

Radio Prague News (www.radio.cz)

MONEY

- The best places to exchange money are banks or use your credit or debit card to withdraw money as needed from ATMs.
- Never exchange money on the street and avoid private exchange offices, especially in Prague, as they charge exorbitant commissions.
- Keep small change handy for use in public toilets and metro-ticket machines.

PUBLIC HOLIDAYS

New Year's Day 1 January

Easter Monday March/April

Labour Day 1 May

Liberation Day 8 May

Sts Cyril and Methodius Day 5 July

Jan Hus Day 6 July

Czech Statehood Day 28 September

Republic Day 28 October

Freedom and Democracy Day 17 November

Christmas 24 to 26 December

TELEPHONE

- All Czech phone numbers have nine digits. Dial all nine numbers for any call, local or long distance.
- The Czech Republic's country code is 420.
- Mobile-phone coverage (GSM 900/1800) is compatible with most European, Australian or New Zealand handsets (though generally not with North American or Japanese models).
- Purchase a Czech SIM card from any mobile-phone shop for around 500Kč (including 300Kč of calling credit).
- Local mobile numbers can be identified by prefix. Mobiles start with 601–608 or 720–779.
- Public phones operate via prepaid magnetic cards purchased at post offices or newsstands from 100Kč.

VISAS

- The Czech Republic is part of the EU's Schengen area, and citizens of most developed countries can spend up to 90 days in the country in a six-month period without a visa.

Getting There & Away

The Czech Republic is easily reached by air from key European hubs or overland by road or train from neighbouring countries. Lying along major European road and rail lines, it is a convenient hub for exploring surrounding countries. Prague has excellent rail connections to Berlin as well as Kraków, Bratislava, Budapest and Vienna.

Flights, tours and rail tickets can be booked online at www.lonelyplanet.com/travel_services.

AIR

Nearly all international flights arrive at Václav Havel Airport Prague.

Václav Havel Airport Prague (Prague Ruzyně International Airport; 220 111 888; www.prg.aero; K letišti 6, Ruzyně; ; 100, 119) Prague's main international gateway lies 17km west of the city centre. It's home to national carrier Czech Airlines and a regional hub for flights around Europe and to the Middle East (though at research time there were limited direct flights to North America). There are two main terminals: Terminal 1 handles flights outside the EU; Terminal 2 for flights within the EU.

LAND

The Czech Republic has border crossings with Germany, Poland, Slovakia and Austria. These are all EU member states within the Schengen zone, meaning there are no passport or customs checks.

Bus

- The main international terminal is Florenc bus station in Prague.

EATING PRICE RANGES

The following price ranges refer to a standard main meal:

€ less than 200Kč

€€ 200Kč–500Kč

€€€ more than 500Kč

ESSENTIAL FOOD & DRINK

➡ **Beer** Modern *pils* (light, amber-coloured lager) was invented in the city of Plzeň in the 19th century, giving Czechs bragging rights to having the best beer *(pivo)* in the world.

➡ **Dumplings** Every culture has its favourite starchy side dish; for Czechs it's *knedliky* – big bread dumplings that are perfect for mopping up gravy.

➡ **Roast Pork** Move over beef, pork *(vepřové maso)* is king here. The classic Bohemian dish, seen on menus around the country, is *vepřo-knedlo-zelo*, local slang for roast pork, bread dumplings and sauerkraut.

➡ **Braised Beef** Look out for *svíčková na smetaně* on menus. This is a satisfying slice of roast beef, served in a cream sauce, with a side of bread dumplings and a dollop of cranberry sauce.

➡ **Becherovka** A shot of this sweetish herbal liqueur from Karlovy Vary is a popular way to start (or end) a big meal.

➡ **Carp** This lowly fish *(kapr* in Czech) is given pride of place every Christmas at the centre of the family meal. *Kapr na kmíní* is fried or baked carp with caraway seed.

➡ Leading international bus carriers include Student Agency and Eurolines.

Eurolines (☎245 005 245; www.elines.cz; ÚAN Praha Florenc, Křižíkova 2110/2b; ⌚6.30am-10.30pm Mon-Fri, 6.30am-9pm Sat; 📶; Ⓜ Florenc) International bus carrier links Prague to cities around Europe. Consult the web page for a timetable and prices. Buy tickets online or at Florenc bus station.

Florenc Bus Station (ÚAN Praha Florenc; ☎900 144 444; www.florenc.cz; Křižíkova 2110/2b, Karlín; ⌚4am-midnight, information counter 6am-10pm; 📶; Ⓜ Florenc) Prague's main bus station, servicing most domestic and long-haul international routes. There's an information counter, ticket windows, a left-luggage office, and a small number of shops and restaurants. You can also usually purchase tickets directly from the driver.

Student Agency (☎bus information 841 101 101, nonstop info line 800 100 300; www.studentagency.cz; ÚAN Praha Florenc, Křižíkova 2110/2b) This modern, well-run company operates comfortable, full-service coaches to major Czech cities as well as 60 destinations around Europe. Buses usually depart from Florenc bus station, but may depart from other stations as well. Be sure to ask which station when you purchase your ticket.

Train

➡ The country's main international rail gateway is Praha hlavní nádraží (Prague main train station). The station is accessible by public transport on metro line C.

➡ There is regular rail service from Prague to and from Germany, Poland, Slovakia and Austria. Trains to/from the south and east, including from Bratislava, Vienna and Budapest, also stop at Brno's main train station.

➡ In Prague, buy train tickets at ČD Centrum, located on the lower level of the station. Credit cards are accepted. An adjoining travel agency, ČD Travel, can help work out complicated international connections.

➡ Both InterRail and Eurail passes are valid on the Czech rail network.

ČD Centrum (☎840 112 113; www.cd.cz; Praha hlavní nádraží, Wilsonova 8; ⌚3am-midnight; Ⓜ Hlavní nádraží) The main ticket office for purchasing train tickets for both domestic *(vnitrostátní jízdenky)* and international *(mezinárodní jizdenky)* destinations is located on the lower (street) level of the station. It also sells seat reservations, as well as booking couchettes and sleeping cars.

ČD Travel (☎972 241 861; www.cdtravel.cz; Praha hlavní nádraží, Wilsonova 8; ⌚9am-6pm Mon-Fri, 9am-2pm Sat Apr-Sep, 9am-5pm Mon-Fri Oct-Mar; Ⓜ Hlavní nádraží) ČD Travel is an affiliate of České dráhy (Czech Rail) and specialises in working out and booking international connections. It maintains a small office within the main ticketing area, ČD Centrum, on the lower level of Praha hlavní nádraží.

Praha hlavní nádraží (Prague main train station; ☎840 112 113; www.cd.cz; Wilsonova 8, Nové Město; Ⓜ Hlavní nádraží) Prague's main train station, handling most international and domestic arrivals and departures.

ℹ Getting Around

BUS

➡ Buses are often faster, cheaper and more convenient than trains.

➡ Many bus routes have reduced frequency (or none) on weekends.

➡ Check bus timetables and prices at http://jizdnirady.idnes.cz.

- In Prague, many (though not all) buses arrive at and depart from Florenc bus station. Be sure to double-check the correct station.
- Try to arrive at the station well ahead of departure to secure a seat. Buy tickets from the driver.

ČSAD (☎ information line 900 144 444) The national bus company links cities and smaller towns. In Prague, CŠAD buses normally arrive at and depart from Florenc bus station.

Student Agency (p299) A popular, private bus company operating convenient services between major cities.

CAR & MOTORCYCLE

- For breakdown assistance anywhere in the country, dial ☎1230.
- The minimum driving age is 18 and traffic moves on the right.
- Children aged under 12 are prohibited from sitting in the front seat.
- Drivers are required to keep their headlights on at all times.
- The legal blood-alcohol limit is zero.

TRAIN

- Czech Railways provides efficient train services to almost every part of the country.
- For an online timetable, go to http://jizdnirady.idnes.cz or www.cd.cz.

Denmark

Includes ➡

Best Places to Eat

- Schønnemann (p310)
- Höst (p310)
- Torvehallerne KBH (p310)
- Skagen waterfront (p318)
- St Pauls Apothek (p317)

Best Places to Stay

- Hotel Nimb (p309)
- Generator Hostel (p309)
- Hotel Guldsmeden (p309)
- Badepension Marienlund (p319)

Why Go?

Denmark is the bridge between Scandinavia and northern Europe. To the rest of Scandinavia, the Danes are chilled, frivolous party animals, with relatively liberal, progressive attitudes. Their culture, food, architecture and appetite for conspicuous consumption owe as much, if not more, to their German neighbours to the south than to their former colonies (Sweden, Norway and Iceland) to the north.

Packed with intriguing museums, shops, bars, nightlife and award-winning restaurants, Denmark's capital, Copenhagen, is one of the hippest, most accessible cities in Europe. And while Danish cities such as Odense and Aarhus harbour their own urbane drawcards, Denmark's other chief appeal lies in its photogenic countryside, sweeping coastline and historic sights.

When to Go

Copenhagen

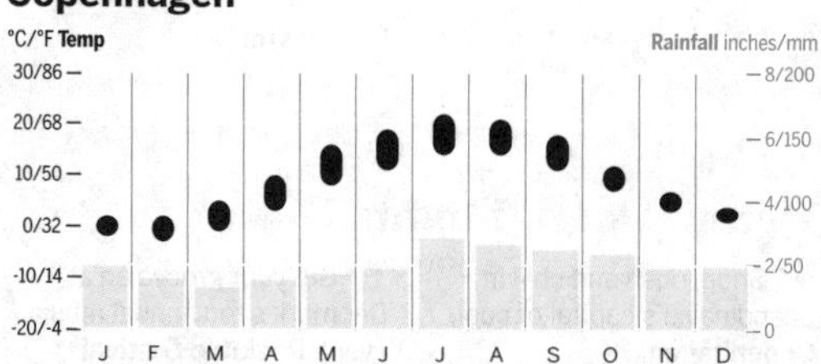

Jun & Jul Long days, buzzing beachside towns, Copenhagen Jazz and A-list rock fest Roskilde.

Sep & Oct Fewer crowds, golden landscapes and snug nights by crackling open fires.

Dec Twinkling Christmas lights, ice-skating rinks and gallons of warming *gløgg* (mulled wine).

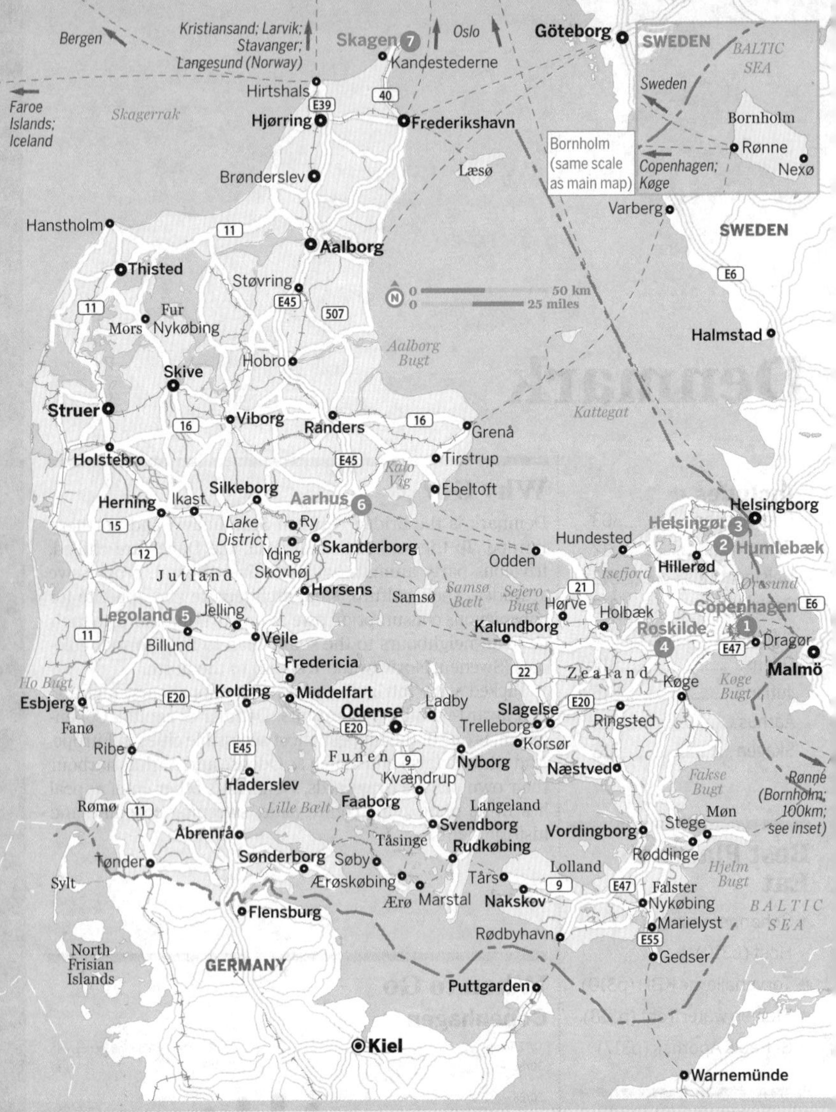

Denmark Highlights

1. Shop, nosh and chill in Scandinavia's capital of cool, **Copenhagen**.

2. Be inspired by the art and the views at the **Louisiana** (p312) in Humlebæk.

3. Snoop around **Kronborg Slot** (p313), Hamlet's epic home in Helsingør.

4. Get your groove on at Denmark's top annual music event, **Roskilde Festival** (p313).

5. Marvel at microcosmic Miniland at **Legoland** (p318) before jumping on a few rides.

6. View Aarhus rooftops through rose-coloured glass atop impressive art museum **ARoS** (p315).

7. Witness treasured artworks and clashing seas in holiday haven **Skagen** (p318).

ITINERARIES

One Week

You could comfortably spend four days in **Copenhagen** exploring the museums, hunting down Danish design and taste-testing its lauded restaurants and bars. A trip north along the coast to the magnificent modern-art museum, **Louisiana**, and then further north still to **Kronborg Slot**, before returning south via **Roskilde**, would be a great way to spend the other three days.

Two Weeks

After time in and around **Copenhagen**, head west, stopping off to see Hans Christian Andersen's birthplace in **Odense**. Continue further west to the **Jutland peninsula** for the understated hipster cool of **Aarhus** and plastic-fantastic **Legoland**, then head north to luminous **Skagen**.

COPENHAGEN

POP 1.9 MILLION

Copenhagen is the coolest kid on the Nordic block. Edgier than Stockholm and worldlier than Oslo, the Danish capital gives Scandinavia the X-factor. While this thousand-year-old harbour town has managed to retain much of its historic good looks – think copper spires and cobbled squares – the focus here is on the innovative and cutting edge. Denmark's over-achieving capital is home to a thriving design scene, its streets awash with effortlessly hip shops, cafes and bars; world-class museums and art collections; intelligent new architecture; and a galaxy of Michelin-starred restaurants.

Sights

You can walk across the city centre in an hour, and travel further with ease thanks to the cycle paths, metro, trains and buses.

Tivoli & Around

★Tivoli Gardens AMUSEMENT PARK

(www.tivoli.dk; adult/child under 8yr Dkr99/free; 11am-10pm Sun-Thu, 11am-12.30am Fri, 11am-midnight Sat early Apr-late Sep, reduced hours rest of year; ; 2A, 5A, 9A, 12, 26, 250S, 350S, S-train København H) Dating from 1843, tasteful Tivoli wins fans with its dreamy whirl of amusement rides, twinkling pavilions, carnival games and open-air stage shows. Visitors can ride the renovated, century-old **roller-coaster**, take in the famous Saturday evening **fireworks display** or just soak up the storybook atmosphere. A good tip is to go on Fridays during the summer season, when the open-air Plænen stage hosts free rock concerts from Danish bands (and the occasional international superstar) from 10pm – go early if it's a big-name act.

★Nationalmuseet MUSEUM

(National Museum; www.natmus.dk; Ny Vestergade 10; 10am-5pm Tue-Sun; ; 1A, 2A, 11A, 33, 40, 66, S-train København H) FREE For a crash course in Danish history and culture, spend an afternoon at Denmark's National Museum. It has first claims on virtually every antiquity uncovered on Danish soil, including Stone Age tools, Viking weaponry, rune stones, and medieval jewellery. Among the many highlights is a finely crafted 3500-year-old Sun Chariot, as well as bronze *lurs* (horns), some of which date back 3000 years and are still capable of blowing a tune.

Ny Carlsberg Glyptotek MUSEUM

(www.glyptoteket.dk; Dantes Plads 7, HC Andersens Blvd; adult/child Dkr75/free, Sun free; 11am-5pm Tue-Sun; ; 1A, 2A, 11A, 33, 40, 66, S-train København H) Fin de siècle architecture dallies with an eclectic mix of art at Ny Carlsberg Glyptotek. The collection is divided into two parts: Northern Europe's largest booty of antiquities, and an elegant collection of 19th-century Danish and French art. The latter includes the largest collection of Rodin sculptures outside of France, and no less than 47 Gauguin paintings. These are displayed along with works by greats like Cézanne, Van Gogh, Pissarro, Monet and Renoir.

Slotsholmen

An island separated from the city centre by a moatlike canal on three sides and the harbour on the other side, Slotsholmen is the site of Christiansborg Slot (Palace), home to Denmark's parliament.

Christiansborg Palace PALACE

(33 92 64 92; www.christiansborg.dk; Slotsholmen; 1A, 2A, 9A, 26, 40, 66, Det Kongelige Bibliotek, Christianshavn) Of Christiansborg

Central Copenhagen (København)

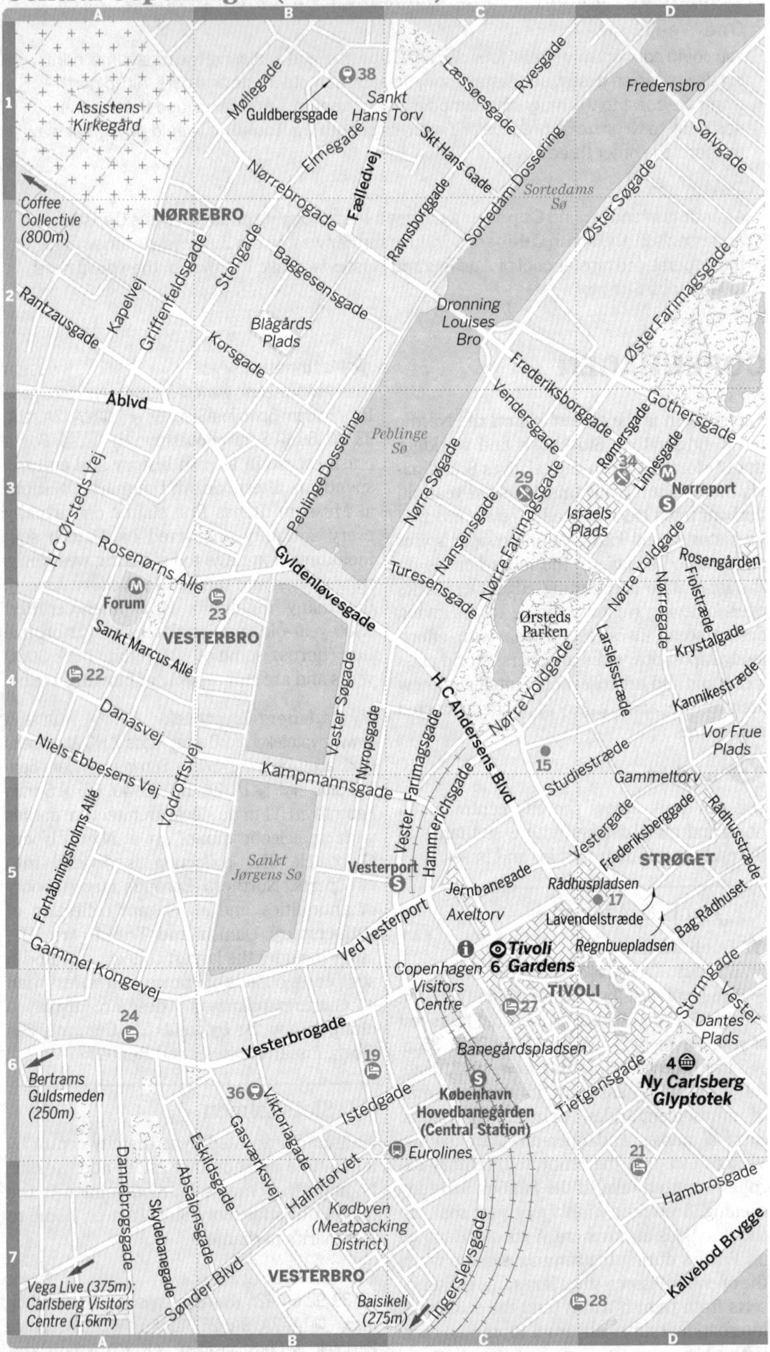

A B C D

1 2 3 4 5 6 7

Assistens Kirkegård
Coffee Collective (800m)
NØRREBRO
Møllegade
Guldbergsgade
38
Sankt Hans Torv
Elmegade
Fælledvej
Nørrebrogade
Læssøesgade
Ryesgade
Skt Hans Gade
Ravnsborggade
Sortedam Dossering
Sortedams Sø
Øster Søgade
Fredensbro
Sølvgade
Stengade
Griffenfeldsgade
Kapelvej
Rantzausgade
Baggesensgade
Blågårds Plads
Korsgade
Dronning Louises Bro
Øster Farimagsgade
Åblvd
Frederiksborggade
Vendersgade
Gothersgade
Rømersgade
Linnesgade
34
Nørreport
Peblinge Sø
Peblinge Dossering
Nørre Søgade
29
Nørre Farimagsgade
Israels Plads
H C Ørsteds Vej
Rosenørns Allé
Forum
23
Gyldenløvesgade
Turesensgade
Nansensgade
Nørre Voldgade
Rosengården
Nørregade
Fiolstræde
VESTERBRO
Sankt Marcus Allé
22
Ørsteds Parken
Larslejsstræde
Krystalgade
Kannikestræde
Vester Søgade
Nyropsgade
Vester Farimagsgade
H C Andersens Blvd
Danasvej
Niels Ebbesens Vej
Vodroffsvej
Kampmannsgade
Hammerichsgade
15
Studiestræde
Vor Frue Plads
Gammeltorv
Vestergade
Frederiksberggade
Rådhusstræde
Forhåbningsholms Allé
Sankt Jørgens Sø
Vesterport
Jernbanegade
Rådhuspladsen
17
STRØGET
Axeltorv
Lavendelstræde
Bag Rådhuset
Gammel Kongevej
Ved Vesterport
Copenhagen Visitors Centre
6 Tivoli Gardens
Regnbuepladsen
TIVOLI
27
Stormgade
Vester
Dantes Plads
24
Vesterbrogade
19
Banegårdspladsen
4 Ny Carlsberg Glyptotek
Tietgensgade
Bertrams Guldsmeden (250m)
36
Viktoriagade
Istedgade
København Hovedbanegården (Central Station)
Eurolines
Gasværksvej
Eskildsgade
Absalonsgade
Dannebrogsgade
Skydebanegade
Halmtorvet
Kødbyen (Meatpacking District)
21
Hambrosgade
Kalvebod Brygge
Ingerslevsgade
VESTERBRO
Sønder Blvd
Vega Live (375m); Carlsberg Visitors Centre (1.6km)
Baisikeli (275m)
28

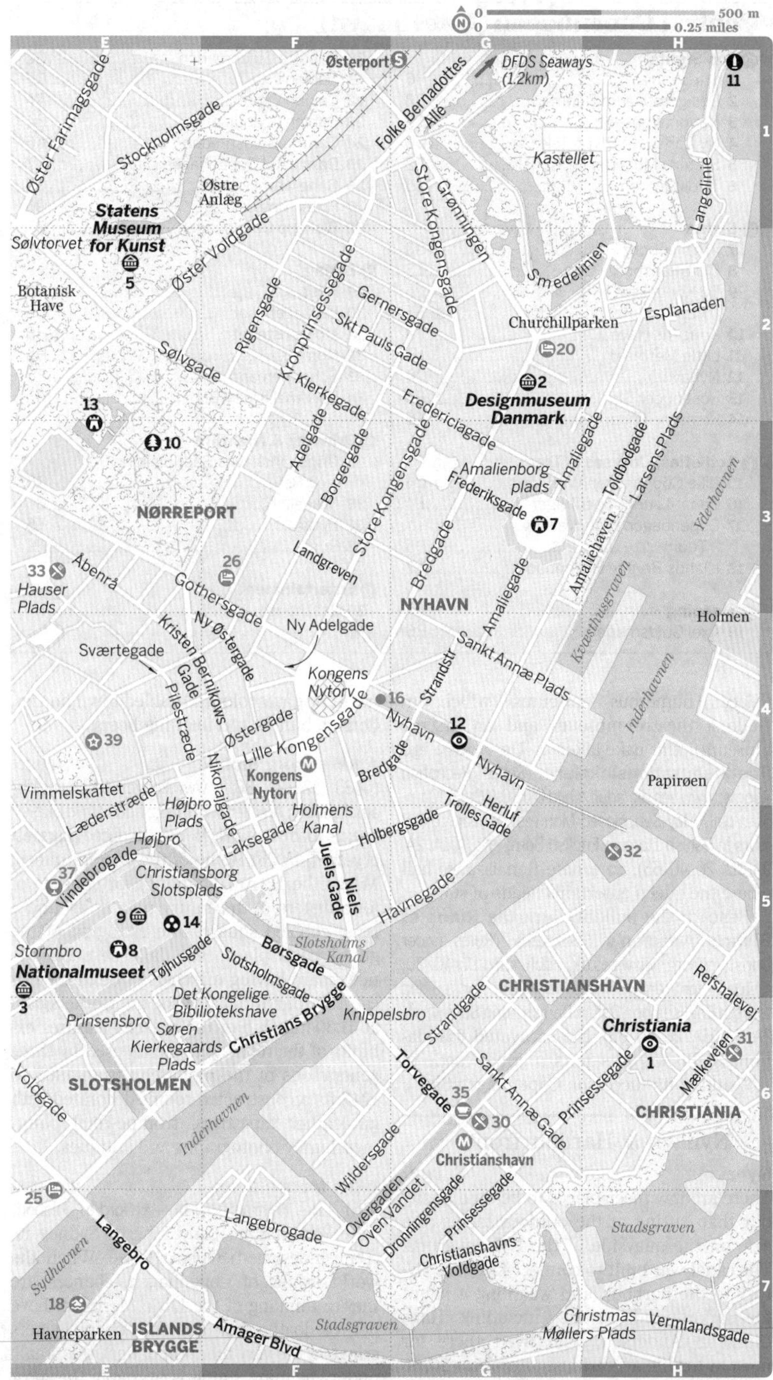

Østerport
DFDS Seaways (1.2km)
Kastellet
Statens Museum for Kunst
Designmuseum Danmark
NØRREPORT
NYHAVN
Kongens Nytorv
CHRISTIANSHAVN
Christiania
CHRISTIANIA
SLOTSHOLMEN
Nationalmuseet
ISLANDS BRYGGE
Christianshavn
Churchillparken
Amalienborg plads
Botanisk Have
Holmen
Papirøen
Havneparken
Christmas Møllers Plads

Central Copenhagen (København)

Top Sights

1	Christiania	H6
2	Designmuseum Danmark	G2
3	Nationalmuseet	E5
4	Ny Carlsberg Glyptotek	D6
5	Statens Museum for Kunst	E2
6	Tivoli Gardens	C5

Sights

7	Amalienborg Slot	G3
8	Christiansborg Palace	E5
9	De Kongelige Repræsentationslokaler	E5
10	Kongens Have	E3
11	Little Mermaid	H1
12	Nyhavn	G4
13	Rosenborg Slot	E3
14	Ruinerne under Christiansborg	E5

Activities, Courses & Tours

15	Bike Copenhagen With Mike	C4
16	Canal Tours Copenhagen	F4
17	Copenhagen Free Walking Tours	D5
18	Islands Brygge Havnebadet	E7

Sleeping

19	Axel Guldsmeden	B6
20	Babette Guldsmeden	G2
21	Cabinn City	D7
22	Cabinn Express	A4
23	Cabinn Scandinavia	B4
24	Carlton Guldsmeden	A6
25	Danhostel Copenhagen City	E7
26	Generator Hostel	F3
27	Hotel Nimb	C6
28	Wakeup Copenhagen	D7

Eating

29	Höst	C3
30	Lagkagehuset	G6
31	Morgenstedet	H6
32	Noma	H5
33	Schønnemann	E3
34	Torvehallerne KBH	D3

Drinking & Nightlife

35	Christianshavns Bådudlejning og Café	G6
36	Mikkeller	B6
37	Ruby	E5
38	Rust	B1

Entertainment

39	Jazzhouse	E4

Palace's numerous museums (which include a theatre museum and an arsenal museum), the cake-taker is **De Kongelige Repræsentationslokaler** (Royal Reception Rooms; www.ses.dk; adult/child Dkr80/40; 10am-5pm daily May-Sep, closed Mon rest of year, guided tours in Danish 11am, in English 3pm; ; 1A, 2A, 9A, 11A, 26, 40, 66), an ornate Renaissance hall where the queen entertains heads of state.

Beneath the building lurk the **Ruins of Bishop Absalon's Fortress** (Ruins under Christiansborg; www.ses.dk; adult/child Dkr40/20; 10am-5pm daily, closed Mon Oct-Apr, guided tours in English noon Sat, in Danish noon Sun; 1A, 2A, 9A, 11A, 26, 40, 66), the excavated foundations of Bishop Absalon's original castle of 1167 and of its successor, Copenhagen Slot.

Nyhavn & Harbourfront

Nyhavn CANAL

There are few nicer places to be on a sunny day than sitting at the outdoor tables of a cafe on the quayside of the Nyhavn canal. The canal was built to connect Kongens Nytorv to the harbour, and was long a haunt for sailors and writers, including Hans Christian Andersen, who lived there for most of his life at, variously, numbers 20, 18 and 67. These days Nyhavn is a tourist magnet of brightly coloured gabled town houses, herring buffets and foaming beers.

Amalienborg Slot PALACE

(33 12 21 86; www.kongernessamling.dk/amalienborg; Amalienborg Plads; adult/child Dkr90/free; 10am-4pm daily May-Oct, reduced hours rest of year; 1A, 26) Home of the current queen, Margrethe II, Amalienborg Slot consists of four austere, 18th-century palaces around a large cobbled square. The changing of the guard takes place here daily at noon, the new guard having marched through the city centre from the barracks on Gothersgade at 11.30am. One of the palaces features exhibits of the royal apartments used by three generations of the monarchy from 1863 to 1947, its reconstructed rooms decorated with gilt-leather tapestries, trompe-l'oeil paintings, family photographs and antiques.

Little Mermaid MONUMENT

(Den Lille Havfrue; 1A, Nordre Toldbod) New York has its Lady Liberty, Sydney its (Danish-designed) Opera House. When the world thinks of Copenhagen, chances are they're thinking of the Little Mermaid. Love her or loathe her (watch Copenhageners cringe at the very mention of her), this small, underwhelming statue is arguably the most photographed sight in the country, as well as the cause of countless 'is that it?' shrugs from tourists who have trudged the kilometre or so along an often windswept harbourfront to see her.

★Designmuseum Danmark MUSEUM
(www.designmuseum.dk; Bredgade 68; adult/child Dkr75/free; 11am-5pm Tue & Thu-Sun, to 9pm Wed; 1A) The 18th-century Frederiks Hospital is now the outstanding Denmark Design Museum. A must for fans of the applied arts and industrial design, its fairly extensive collection includes Danish silver and porcelain, textiles, as well as the iconic design pieces of modern innovators like Kaare Klint, Poul Henningsen and Arne Jacobsen. Also on display are ancient Chinese and Japanese ceramics, and 18th and 19th-century European decorative arts. Designmuseum Danmark lies 250m north of Marmorkirken.

Around Kongens Have

Kongens Have PARK
(King's Gardens; 6A, 11A, 42, 150S, 173E, 184, 185, 350S, Nørreport) FREE The oldest park in Copenhagen was laid out in the early 17th century by Christian IV, who used it as his vegetable patch. These days it has a little more to offer, including immaculate flower beds, romantic garden paths, and a marionette theatre with free performances during the summer season (2pm and 3pm Tuesday to Sunday). Located on the northeastern side of the park, the theatre occupies one of the neoclassical pavilions designed by Danish architect Peter Meyn.

★Statens Museum for Kunst MUSEUM
(www.smk.dk; Sølvgade 48-50; special exhibitions adult/child Dkr110/free; 10am-5pm Tue & Thu-Sun, to 8pm Wed; ; 6A, 26, 42, 173E, 184, 185) FREE Denmark's National Gallery straddles two contrasting, inter-connected buildings: a late-19th-century 'palazzo' and a sharply minimalist extension. The museum houses medieval and Renaissance works, and impressive collections of Dutch and Flemish artists including Rubens, Breughel and Rembrandt. It claims the world's finest collection of 19th-century Danish 'Golden Age' artists, among them Eckersberg, Krøyer and Hammershøi, foreign greats like Matisse and Picasso, and modern Danish heavyweights including Per Kirkeby, Richard Mortensen and Asger Jørn. Among the contemporary stars are Danish/Norwegian duo Elmgreen and Dragset, and Vietnamese-born Danish artist Danh Vo.

Rosenborg Slot CASTLE
(www.kongernessamling.dk; Øster Voldgade 4A; adult/child Dkr90/free, incl Amalienborg Palace Dkr125/free; 10am-5pm daily Jun-Aug, 10am-4pm daily May, Sep & Oct, reduced hrs rest of yr; ; 6A, 11A, 42, 150S, 173E, 184, 185, 350S, Nørreport) A 'once-upon-a-time' combo of turrets, gables and moat, the early-17th-century Rosenborg Slot was built between 1606 and 1633 by King Christian IV in Dutch Renaissance style to serve as his summer home. Today, the castle's 24 upper rooms are chronologically arranged, housing the furnishings and portraits of each monarch from Christian IV to Frederik VII. The pièce de résistance, however, is the basement Treasury, home to the dazzling crown jewels, among them Christian IV's glorious crown and the jewel-studded sword of Christian III.

Christianshavn

★Christiania NEIGHBOURHOOD
(www.christiania.org; Prinsessegade; 9A, 2A, 40, 350S, Christianshavn) Escape the capitalist crunch at Freetown Christiania, a dreadlocks-heavy commune straddling the eastern side of Christianshavn. Since its establishment by squatters in 1971, the area has drawn nonconformists from across the globe, attracted by the concept of collective business, workshops and communal living. Explore beyond the settlement's infamous 'Pusher St' – lined with shady hash and marijuana dealers – and you'll stumble upon a semi-bucolic wonderland of whimsical DIY homes,

COPENHAGEN CARD

The **Copenhagen Card** (www.copenhagencard.com; 24/48/72hr Dkr339/469/559) secures unlimited travel on buses and trains around Copenhagen and north Zealand. This covers the city's metro system, as well as suburban trains. It also gives free or discounted admission to around 70 of the region's museums and attractions. Cards can be purchased directly online and are sold at the Copenhagen Visitors Centre, Central Station, major train stations and at many hotels, campgrounds and hostels. Note, though, that several of the city's attractions are either free, or at least free one day of the week.

cosy gardens, and a handful of craft shops, eateries, beer gardens and music venues.

Outer Copenhagen

Den Blå Planet AQUARIUM

(www.denblaaplanet.dk; Jacob Fortlingsvej 1, Kastrup; adult/child 3-11yr Dkr160/95; 10am-9pm Mon, to 6pm Tue-Sun; ; 5A, Kastrup) Designed to look like a whirlpool from above, Copenhagen's new, aluminum-clad aquarium is the largest in northern Europe. The space is divided into climatic and geographic sections, the most spectacular of which is 'Ocean/Coral Reef'. Home to swarms of Technicolor tropical fish, the exhibition is also home to the centre's largest tank, a massive 4,000,000-litre showcase brimming with sharks, stingrays and other majestic creatures. If possible, visit the aquarium on a Monday evening, when it's at its quietest and most evocative.

Carlsberg Visitors Centre BREWERY

(33 27 12 82; www.visitcarlsberg.dk; Gamle Carlsberg Vej 11, Vesterbro; adult/child Dkr80/60; 10am-5pm Tue-Sun; 18, 26) Adjacent to the architecturally whimsical Carlsberg brewery, the Carlsberg Visitors Center explores the history of Danish beer from 1370 BC (yes, they carbon-dated a bog girl who was found in a peat bog caressing a jug of well-aged brew). Dioramas give the lowdown on the brewing process and en route to your final destination you'll pass antique copper vats and the stables with a dozen Jutland dray horses. The self-guided tour ends at the bar, where you can knock back two free beers.

Tours

Canal Tours Copenhagen BOAT

(32 66 00 00; www.stromma.dk; adult/child/family Dkr75/35/190; 9.30am-9pm late Jun-late Aug, reduced hours rest of year;) Canal Tours Copenhagen runs one-hour cruises of the city's canals and harbour, taking in numerous major sights, including Christiansborg Slot, Christianshavn, the Royal Library, the Opera House, Amalienborg Palace and the Little Mermaid. Embark at Nyhavn or Ved Stranden. Boats depart up to six times per hour from late June to late August, with reduced frequency the rest of the year.

Copenhagen Free Walking Tours WALKING

(www.copenhagenfreewalkingtours.dk) FREE Departing daily at 11am and 2pm from outside Rådhus (City Hall), these free, three-hour walking tours take in famous landmarks and interesting anecdotes. Tours are in English and require a minimum of five people. Free 90-minute tours of Christianshavn depart at 4pm Friday to Monday from the base of the Bishop Absalon statue on Højbro Plads.

Bike Copenhagen With Mike CYCLING

(26 39 56 88; www.bikecopenhagenwithmike.dk; Skt Peders Stræde 47; per person Dkr299) If you don't fancy walking, Bike Mike runs three-hour cycling tours of the city, departing from Skt Peders Stræde 47 in the city centre, just east of Ørstedsparken (which is southwest of Nørreport station). The tour cost includes bike and helmet rental. Seasonal options are also offered, including a Saturday evening 'Ride & Dine' tour from June to September. Cash only.

FANCY A SWIM?

Copenhagen's coolest outdoor pool complex, **Islands Brygge Havnebadet** (Islands Brygge; 7am-7pm Mon-Fri, 11am-7pm Sat & Sun Jun-Aug; ; 5A, 12, Islands Brygge) FREE, sits right in the central city's main canal. Water quality is rigorously monitored, and the lawns, BBQ facilities and eateries make it a top spot to see and be seen on a warm summer day, whether you get wet or not. Plans are underway for winter-friendly saunas and thermal baths, as well as a sixth pool.

Festivals & Events

Distortion MUSIC

(www.cphdistortion.dk) Taking place over five heady days in early June, Copenhagen Distortion celebrates the city's street life and club culture. Expect raucous block parties and top-name DJs spinning dance tracks in bars and clubs across town.

Copenhagen Jazz Festival MUSIC

(jazz.dk) Copenhagen's single largest event, and the largest jazz festival in northern Europe, hits the city over 10 days in early July. The program covers jazz in all its forms, with an impressive line-up of local and international talent.

Copenhagen Cooking FOOD

(www.copenhagencooking.dk) Scandinavia's largest food festival serves up a gut-rumbling program spanning cooking demonstrations from A-list chefs, to tastings and foodie tours of the city. Events are held in venues and restaurants across town, usually in August. A month-long winter edition takes place in February.

Sleeping

Copenhagen's slumber spots cover all bases. It's a good idea to book in advance – rooms in the most popular midrange hotels fill quickly, particularly during the convention season, typically from August to October, when prices increase significantly, too.

The Copenhagen Visitors Centre (p312) can book rooms in private homes (Dkr350/500 for singles/doubles); there is a Dkr100 booking fee if you do it via this office when you arrive, otherwise it's free online.

★Generator Hostel HOSTEL €
(www.generatorhostel.com; Adelgade 5-7; dm Dkr230-325, rm Dkr800-1070; @ wifi; bus 11A, 350S, M Kongens Nytorv) A solid choice for 'cheap chic', upbeat, design-literate Generator sits on the very edge of the city's medieval core. It's kitted out with designer furniture, slick communal areas (including a bar and outdoor terrace) and friendly, young staff. While the rooms can be a little small, all are bright and modern, with bathrooms in both private rooms and dorms.

Danhostel Copenhagen City HOSTEL €
(☎33 11 85 85; www.danhostel.dk/copenhagencity; HC Andersens Blvd 50; dm/d Dkr225/610; @ wifi; bus 1A, 2A, 12, 33, 11A, 40, 66) With interiors by design company Gubi and a cafe-bar in the lobby, this friendly, ever-popular hostel is set in a tower block overlooking the harbour just south of Tivoli Gardens (did we mention the views?). Both the dorms and private rooms are bright, light and modern, each with bathroom. Book ahead.

> **LAST-MINUTE CHEAP SLEEPS**
>
> If you arrive in Copenhagen without a hotel booking, luck may yet be on your side. The Copenhagen Visitors Centre (p311) books unfilled hotel rooms at discounted rates of up to 50%. These discounts, however, are based on supply and demand, and are not always available during busy periods.

Cabinn HOTEL €
(www.cabinn.com; s/d/tr Dkr545/675/805; @ wifi) Well managed, functional and cheap, the Cabinn chain has four hotels in Copenhagen, the most central being **Cabinn City** (☎33 46 16 16; www.cabinn.com; Mitchellsgade 14; s/d/tr Dkr545/675/805; @ wifi; bus 5A, 9A, 11A, 30, train S-train København H), just south of Tivoli. Although small and anonymous, rooms are comfortable, with cable TV, phone, free wi-fi, and private bathroom. Both **Cabinn Scandinavia** (☎35 36 11 11; www.cabinn.com; Vodroffsvej 57, Frederiksberg; s/d/tr Dkr545/675/805; bus 2A, 68, 250S, M Forum) and **Cabinn Express** (☎33 21 04 00; www.cabinn.com; Danasvej 32, Frederiksberg; s/d/tr Dkr545/675/805; @ wifi; bus 3A, 30, M Forum) are less than 2km west of Tivoli, while the newer **Cabinn Metro** (☎32 46 57 00; www.cabinn.com; Arne Jakobsens Allé 2; s/d/tr Dkr545/675/805; M Ørestad) is a short walk from Ørestad metro station, and close to the airport.

★Hotel Guldsmeden BOUTIQUE HOTEL €€
(www.hotelguldsmeden.dk) The gorgeous Guldsmeden hotels include **Bertrams** (☎70 20 81 07; Vesterbrogade 107; s/d from Dkr895/995; bus 3A, 6A), **Carlton** (☎33 22 15 00; Vesterbrogade 66; s/d from Dkr695/795; bus 6A), **Axel** (☎33 31 32 66; Helgolandsgade 7-11; s/d Dkr765/895; bus 6A, 26, train S-train København H) and newcomer **Babette** (☎33 14 15 00; Bredgade 78; s/d from Dkr795/945; wifi; bus 1A). Only the latter is not in Vesterbro, instead located between Amalienborg and Kastellet on the northern side of the city centre. All four deliver subtle, Balinese-inspired chic, with raw stone, bare wood, four-poster beds and crisp white linen.

Wakeup Copenhagen HOTEL €€
(☎44 80 00 10; www.wakeupcopenhagen.com; Carsten Niebuhrs Gade 11; rm Dkr450-1500; @ wifi; bus 11A, train S-train København H) An easy walk from Central Station and Tivoli, this is one of two Wakeup Copenhagen branches in town, well known for offering style on a budget (assuming you've booked online and in advance). The foyer is an impressive combo of concrete, glass and Arne Jacobsen chairs, while the 500-plus rooms are sharp and compact, with flat-screen TV and capsule-like showers.

★Hotel Nimb BOUTIQUE HOTEL €€€
(☎88 70 00 00; www.nimb.dk; Bernstorffsgade 5; r from Dkr2600; @ wifi; bus 2A, 5A, 9A, 12, 26, 250S, 350S, train S-train København H) Located at Tivoli, this boutique belle offers 17 individually styled rooms and suites fusing clean lines, beautiful art and antiques, luxury fabrics

and high-tech perks such as Bang & Olufsen TVs and sound systems. All rooms except three also feature a fireplace, while all bar one come with views over the amusement park. In-house perks include a savvy cocktail lounge with crackling fire.

Eating

Copenhagen's dining scene is firing. You'll find many of the coolest nosh spots in the Vesterbro neighbourhood, while bohemian Nørrebro has its fair share of cheaper, student-friendly eateries.

Torvehallerne KBH MARKET €

(www.torvehallernekbh.dk; Israels Plads; 10am-7pm Mon-Thu, to 8pm Fri, to 6pm Sat, 11am-5pm Sun) Since debuting in 2011, food market Torvehallerne KBH has become an essential stop on the Copenhagen foodie trail. A gut-rumbling ode to the fresh, the tasty and the artisanal, its beautiful stalls peddle everything from seasonal herbs and berries, to smoked meats, seafood and cheeses, smørrebrød (open sandwiches), fresh pasta, and hand-brewed coffee. You could easily spend an hour or more exploring its twin halls, chatting to the vendors and taste-testing their products. Best of all, you can enjoy some of the city's best sit-down meals here…with change to spare.

Morgenstedet VEGETARIAN €

(www.morgenstedet.dk; Langgaden; mains Dkr80-100; noon-9pm Tue-Sun; ; 2A, 9A, 40, 350S, M Christianshavn) A homely, hippy bolthole in the heart of Christiania, Morgenstedet offers but two dishes of the day, one of which is usually a soup. Choices are always vegetarian and organic, and best devoured in the bucolic bliss of the cafe garden.

Lagkagehuset BAKERY €

(32 57 36 07; www.lagkagehuset.dk; Torvegade 45; pastries from Dkr18, sandwiches Dkr50; 6am-7pm Sat-Thu, to 7.30pm Fri; ; 2A, 9A, 40, 350S, M Christianshavn) Opposite Christianshavn metro station, this is the original (and some would say best) of the Lagkagehuset bakeries. Handy for a quick bite on the go, its counters heave with luscious pastries, salubrious sandwiches, mini pizzas and heavyweight loaves of rye bread. You'll find a handful of counter seats, and free wi-fi if you insist on Instagramming your *kanelsnegle* (cinnamon roll).

★Schønnemann DANISH €€

(33 12 07 85; www.restaurantschonnemann.dk; Hauser Plads 16; smørrebrød Dkr72-178; 11.30am-5pm Mon-Sat; 6A, 11A, M Nørreport) A verified institution, Schønnemann has been lining bellies with smørrebrød and snaps since 1877. Originally a hit with farmers in town peddling their produce, the restaurant's current fan base includes revered chefs like Noma's René Redzepi. Two smørrebrød per person should suffice, with standouts including the King's Garden (potatoes with smoked mayonnaise, fried onions, chives and tomato). Make sure to order both a beer and a glass of schnapps to wash down the goodness, and always book ahead (or head in early) to avoid long lunchtime waits.

★Höst MODERN DANISH €€

(89 93 84 09; www.cofoco.dk/da/restauranter/hoest; Nørre Farimagsgade 41; mains Dkr195-215, 3-course set menu Dkr295; 5.30-9.30pm daily; 40, M Nørrebro) Höst's phenomenal popularity is a no-brainer: warm, award-winning interiors, mere-mortal prices, and New Nordic food that's equally fabulous and filling. The set menu is great value, with three smaller 'surprise dishes' thrown in, and evocative creations like salted Faroe Island scallops with corn, raw plums, pickled black trumpet mushrooms and wild garlic. The 'deluxe' wine menu is significantly better than the standard option.

★Noma MODERN DANISH €€€

(32 96 32 97; www.noma.dk; Strandgade 93; degustation menu Dkr1600; noon-4pm & 7pm-12.30am Tue-Sat; 2A, 9A, 11A, 40, 66, 350S, M Christianshavn) Noma is a Holy Grail for gastronomes across the globe. Using only Scandinavian-sourced produce such as musk ox and skyr curd, head chef René Redzepi and his team create extraordinary symphonies of flavour and texture. Tables are booked months ahead, so expect to join the waiting list. Tip: parties of four or more have a better chance of landing a table with shorter notice.

Drinking & Nightlife

Copenhagen heaves with drinking and party spots, from old-school cellar bars or bodegas, to slinky cocktail dens and cult-status clubs. On the drinking scene, the line between cafe, bar and restaurant is often blurred, with many places changing role as the day progresses. And while you can hit the dance floor most nights of the week, the club scene really revs into gear from Thursday to Saturday.

Popular drinking and clubbing hotspots include Nørrebro and Vesterbro (especially along Istedgade, west of the red-light district, and Kødbyen, closer to Central Station).

Christianshavns Bådudlejning og Café CAFE, BAR
(32 96 53 53; www.baadudlejningen.dk; Overgaden Neden Vandet 29; 9am-midnight daily Jun–mid-Aug, reduced hours rest of year, closed Oct-Mar; ; 2A, 9A, 40, 350S, Christianshavn) Right on Christianshavn's main canal, this festive, wood-decked cafe-bar is a wonderful spot for drinks by the water. It's a cosy, affable hangout, with jovial crowds, strung lights and little rowboats (available for hire) docked like bathtime toys. There's grub for the peckish, and gas heaters and tarpaulins to ward off any northern chill.

Ruby COCKTAIL BAR
(www.rby.dk; Nybrogade 10; 4pm-2am Mon-Sat, 7pm-1am Sun; 1A, 2A, 11A, 26, 40, 66) Cocktail connoisseurs raise their glasses to high-achieving Ruby. Here, hipster-geek mixologists whip-up near-flawless libations such as the Green & White (vodka, dill, white chocolate and liquorice root) and a lively crowd spill into a labyrinth of cosy, decadent rooms. For a gentlemen's club vibe, head downstairs into a world of Chesterfields, oil paintings, and wooden cabinets lined with spirits.

Mikkeller BAR
(http://mikkeller.dk; Viktoriagade 8B-C, Vesterbro; 1pm-1am Sun-Wed, to 2am Thu & Fri, noon-2am Sat; ; 6A, 26, 10, 14, S-train København H) Low-slung lights, moss-green floors and 20 brews on tap: cult-status Mikkeller flies the flag for craft beer, its rotating cast of suds including Mikkeller's own acclaimed creations and guest drops from microbreweries from around the globe. The bottled offerings are equally inspired, with cheese and snacks to soak up the foamy goodness.

Rust CLUB, LIVE MUSIC
(35 24 52 00; www.rust.dk; Guldbergsgade 8, Nørrebro; hours vary, club usually 11pm-5am Fri & Sat; 3A, 5A, 350S) A smashing place attracting one of the largest, coolest crowds in Copenhagen. Live acts focus on alternative or upcoming indie rock, hiphop or electronica, while the club churns out hiphop, dancehall and electro on Wednesdays, and house, electro and rock on Fridays and Saturdays. From 11pm, entrance is only to over 18s (Wednesday and Thursday) and over 20s (Friday and Saturday).

Coffee Collective CAFE
(coffeecollective.dk; Jægersborggade 10, Nørrebro; 7am-7pm Mon-Fri, 8am-7pm Sat & Sun; 18, 12, 66) In a city where lacklustre coffee is as common as perfect cheekbones, this micro roastery peddles the good stuff – we're talking rich, complex cups of caffeinated magic. The baristas are passionate about their beans and the cafe itself sits on creative Jægersborggade in Nørrebro. There are two other outlets, at food market Torvehallerne KBH and in Frederiksberg.

Entertainment

Copenhagen's live-music scene spans intimate jazz and blues boltholes, to mega rock venues. Further up the entertainment ladder, a string of arresting, 21st-century cultural venues, including Operaen (Copenhagen Opera House), have injected the city's cultural scene with new verve. For listings, scan www.aok.dk and www.visitcopenhagen.com.

Jazzhouse JAZZ
(33 15 47 00; www.jazzhouse.dk; Niels Hemmingsensgade 10; 11A) Copenhagen's leading jazz joint serves up top Danish and visiting talent, with music styles running the gamut from bebop to fusion jazz. Doors usually open at 7pm, with concerts starting at 8pm. On Friday and Saturday, late-night concerts (from 11pm) are also offered. Check the website for details and consider booking big-name acts in advance.

Vega Live LIVE MUSIC
(33 25 70 11; www.vega.dk; Enghavevej 40, Vesterbro; ; 3A, 10, 14) The daddy of Copenhagen's live-music and club venues, Vega hosts everyone from big-name rock, pop, blues and jazz acts to underground indie, hip hop and electro up-and-comers. Gigs take place on either the main stage (Store Vega), small stage (Lille Vega) or the revamped ground floor Ideal Bar. The venue itself is a 1950s former trade union HQ by leading Danish architect Vilhelm Lauritzen. Performance times vary; check the website.

Information

Copenhagen Visitors Centre (70 22 24 42; www.visitcopenhagen.com; Vesterbrogade 4A; 9am-6pm Mon-Sat, to 2pm Sun May, Jun & Sep, 9am-7pm Jul & Aug, 9am-4pm Mon-Fri, to 2pm Sat rest of year;) Copenhagen's excellent information centre has multilingual staff, as well as a bakery and lounge with free wi-fi and power sockets. It's the best source of information in town – free maps, masses of brochures and guides to take away, and booking services and hotel reservations available for a fee. It also sells the Copenhagen Card.

Getting There & Away

AIR

Copenhagen Airport (www.cph.dk) is Scandinavia's busiest hub, with direct connections to other destinations in Denmark, as well as in Europe, North America and Asia. It is in Kastrup, 9km southeast of the city centre.

BOAT

DFDS Seaways (☎33 42 30 10; www.dfdsseaways.com; Dampfærgevej 30) operates daily ferries to Oslo.

BUS

Long-distance buses leave from opposite the DGI-byen sports complex on Ingerslevsgade, a quick walk southwest of Central Station. Advance reservations on most international routes can be made at **Eurolines** (☎33 88 70 00; www.eurolines.dk; Halmtorvet 5).

TRAIN

Long-distance trains arrive and depart from Central Station, known officially as Københavns Hovedbanegård. A *billetautomat* (coin-operated ticket machine) is the quickest way to purchase a ticket. **DSB Billetsalg** (www.dsb.dk; ⏲7am-8pm Mon-Fri, 8am-6pm Sat & Sun) is best for reservations and for purchasing international train tickets. Alternatively, make reservations on DSB's website.

Getting Around

TO/FROM THE AIRPORT

- **DSB** (www.dsb.dk) trains link the airport with Copenhagen's Central Station (Dkr36, 14 minutes, every 12 minutes).
- The 24-hour **metro** (www.m.dk) runs every four to 20 minutes between the airport arrival terminal (station name is Lufthavnen) and the eastern side of the city centre. It doesn't stop at København H (Central Station) but is handy for Christianshavn and Nyhavn (get off at Kongens Nytorv for Nyhavn). Journey time to Kongens Nytorv is 14 minutes (Dkr36).

BICYCLE

Copenhagen's cycling culture and infrastructure is much admired. The city has around 430km of continuous, safe cycle paths, making getting around by bike a breeze. See cycleguide.dk for more.

Baisikeli (☎26 70 02 29; baisikeli.dk; Ingerslevsgade 80, Vesterbro; bicycles per 6hr/week from Dkr50/270; ⏲10am-6pm) Baisikeli is Swahili for bicycle, and the profits from this rental outlet are used to ship 1200 much-needed bikes to African communities annually. It's located beside Dybøllsbro S-train station and just south of the Kødbyen restaurant and bar precinct in Vesterbro.

BUS & TRAIN

- Buses, metro and trains use a common fare system based on zones. The basic fare of Dkr24 for up to two zones covers most city runs and allows transfers between buses and trains on a single ticket within one hour.
- If you plan on exploring sights outside the city, including Helsingør and Roskilde, you're better off buying a 24-hour ticket (all zones Dkr130) or a seven-day FlexCard (all zones Dkr590).
- The website www.rejseplanen.dk offers a handy journey planner, with transport routes, times and prices.

DON'T MISS

LOUISIANA: A MODERN ART MUST

Even if you don't have a burning passion for art, Denmark's outstanding **Louisiana** (www.louisiana.dk; Gammel Strandvej 13, Humlebæk; adult/child Dkr110/free; ⏲11am-10pm Tue-Fri, to 6pm Sat & Sun; 📶) should be high on your 'to do' list. It's a striking modernist-art mecca, sprawling across a sculpture-laced park.

The museum's permanent collection, mainly postwar paintings and graphic art, covers everything from constructivism, CoBrA movement artists and minimalist art, to abstract expressionism and pop art. Adding extra X-factor is the museum's program of fantastic temporary exhibitions.

Lousiana is in the leafy commuter town of Humlebæk, 35 minutes north of Copenhagen on the S-train's C line. For a day trip, the 24-hour transport ticket (Dkr130) is best value.

ZEALAND

Though Copenhagen is the centre of gravity for most visitors to Denmark's eastern island, there is no shortage of drawcards beyond the city limits, especially Helsingør Slot (famously known as Hamlet's castle, Elsinore) and the remarkable Viking ships of Roskilde.

Helsingør (Elsinore)

POP 46,400

Generally, visitors come to the harbour town of Helsingør, at the northeastern tip of Zealand, for one of two reasons. If they are Swedish, they come to stock up on cheap(er) booze (this is the closest point to Sweden, and ferries shuttle back and forth across the Øresund frequently). Or, more often, they come to soak up the atmosphere of Denmark's most famous and awe-inspiring castle.

Sights

Kronborg Slot CASTLE

(www.kronborg.dk; Kronborgvej; interior incl guided tour adult/child Dkr80/35; 10am-5.30pm Jun-Aug, 11am-4pm Apr-May & Sep-Oct, shorter hours rest of year; guided tours 11.30am & 1.30pm daily) The Unesco World Heritage–listed Kronborg Slot began life as Krogen, a formidable toll-house built by Danish king Erik of Pomerania in the 1420s. Expanded by Frederik II in 1585, the castle was ravaged by fire in 1629, leaving nothing but the outer walls. The tireless builder-king Christian IV rebuilt Kronborg, preserving the castle's earlier Renaissance style and adding his own baroque touches. The galleried chapel was the only part of Kronborg that escaped the flames in 1629 and gives a good impression of the castle's original appearance.

M/S Museet for Søfart MUSEUM

(Maritime Museum of Denmark; www.mfs.dk; Ny Kronborgvej 1; adult/child Dkr110/free; 10am-5pm daily Jul & Aug, 11am-5pm Tue-Sun rest of yr;) Ingeniously built in and around a dry dock beside Kronborg Slot, Denmark's subterranean Maritime Museum merits a visit as much for its design as for its enlightened, multimedia galleries. The latter explore Denmark's maritime history and culture in dynamic, contemporary ways. Alongside the usual booty of nautical instruments, sea charts and wartime objects, exhibitions explore themes as varied as the representation of sailors in popular culture, trade and exploitation in Denmark's overseas colonies, and the globe-crossing journeys of modern shipping containers.

Sleeping & Eating

Danhostel Helsingør HOSTEL €

(49 28 49 49; danhostelhelsingor.dk; Nordre Strandvej 24; dm/s/d/tr Dkr225/495/550/595; P) This 180-bed hostel is based in a coastal manor house 2km northwest of town, on a little beach looking directly across to Sweden. The run-of-the-mill dorms are in one of the smaller attached buildings. Facilities include a self-catering kitchen, small playground and outdoor ping-pong tables to keep kids amused. From Helsingør, bus 842 (Dkr24) will get you there.

Rådmand Davids Hus DANISH €

(49 26 10 43; Strandgade 70; dishes Dkr38-98; 10am-5pm Mon-Sat) What better place to gobble down Danish classics than a snug, lop-sided 17th-century house, complete with cobbled courtyard? Refuel with honest, solid staples like smørrebrød, herring, and the special 'shopping lunch', typically a generous plate of salad, salmon pâté, and slices of pork, cheese and homemade ryebread. Leave room for the Grand Marnier pancakes.

Information

Tourist Office (49 21 13 33; www.visitnordsjaelland.com; Havnepladsen 3; 10am-5pm Mon-Fri, to 2pm Sat & Sun Jul-early Aug, reduced hrs rest of yr) Opposite the train station.

Getting There & Away

Trains between Copenhagen and Helsingør run about three times hourly (Dkr108, 45 minutes). If you're day-tripping from Copenhagen, buy a 24-hour pass (Dkr130).

Roskilde

POP 47,800

Most foreigners who have heard of Roskilde know it either as the home of one of northern Europe's best music festivals, or the site of several remarkable Viking ship finds. To the Danes, however, it is a city of great royal and religious significance, as it was the capital city long before Copenhagen.

The **Roskilde Festival** (www.roskilde-festival.dk) takes place over a long weekend in early July, in fields just outside the city centre. It attracts the biggest international rock and pop names, along with 75,000 music fans, and is renowned for its relaxed, friendly atmosphere. Most visitors camp onsite.

Sights

★**Roskilde Domkirke** CATHEDRAL

(www.roskildedomkirke.dk; Domkirkepladsen; adult/child Dkr60/free; 9am-5pm Mon-Sat, 12.30-5pm Sun Apr-Sep, shorter hrs rest of yr) Not merely the crème de la crème of Danish cathedrals, this twin-towered giant is a designated Unesco World Heritage Site. Started by Bishop Absalon in 1170, the building has been rebuilt and tweaked so many times that it's now a superb showcase of 800 years' worth of Danish architecture. As the royal mausoleum, it contains the crypts of 37 Danish kings and queens – contemplating the remains of so many powerful historical figures is a moving memento mori.

★Viking Ship Museum MUSEUM
(☎46 30 02 00; www.vikingeskibsmuseet.dk; Vindeboder 12; adult/child May–mid-Oct Dkr115/free, mid-Oct–Apr Dkr80/free, boat trip excl museum Dkr90; ⏲10am-5pm late Jun–mid-Aug, to 4pm rest of year, boat trips daily mid-May–Sep) Viking fans will be wowed by the superb Viking Ship Museum, which displays five Viking ships discovered at the bottom of Roskilde Fjord. The museum is made up of two main sections – the Viking Ship Hall, where the boats themselves are kept; and Museumsø, where archaeological work takes place. There are free 45-minute guided tours in English daily at noon and 3pm from late June to the end of August, and at noon on weekends from May to late June and in September.

Danmarks Rockmuseum MUSEUM
(www.danmarksrockmuseum.dk; Rabalderstræde 1) Scheduled to open in mid-2015, the Denmark Museum of Rock Music will deliver a multisensory journey through the wild, often transgressive history of rock and roll. Interactive exhibitions will have visitors laying and remixing hits, practising various dance steps, and rocking to a virtual Roskilde Festival crowd. Check the website for opening times and pricing. From Roskilde train station, buses 202A and 212 stop 350m from the museum.

Sleeping & Eating

Danhostel Roskilde HOSTEL €
(☎46 35 21 84; www.danhostel.dk/roskilde; Vindeboder 7; dm/s/d/tr Dkr250/575/700/750; P 📶) Roskilde's modern hostel sits right next door to the Viking Ship Museum, on the waterfront. Pimped with funky black and white murals, each of the 40 large rooms has its own shower and toilet. Staff are friendly, although the mattress we slept on was frustratingly lop-sided. Cheekily, wi-fi is an extra Dkr20 per hour (Dkr100 per 24 hours).

Café Vivaldi INTERNATIONAL €€
(Stændertorvet 8; sandwiches & salads Dkr99-109, mains Dkr169-199; ⏲10am-10pm Sun-Thu, to 11pm Fri & Sat) Slap bang on the main square (cathedral views included), this faux-bistro is a good place to sit back and people-watch over abundant servings of tasty cafe grub. Edibles include soup, sandwiches, wraps, burgers and salads, as well as more substantial pasta and meat dishes. It's particularly handy on Sundays, when most of the town shuts down.

Information

Tourist Office (www.visitroskilde.com; Stændertorvet 1; ⏲10am-5pm Mon-Fri & 10am-2pm Sat Jul & Aug, reduced hr rest of yr) The local tourist office dispenses plenty of information.

Getting There & Away

Trains from Copenhagen to Roskilde are frequent (Dkr96, 25 minutes). If you're day-tripping from Copenhagen, buy a 24-hour pass (Dkr130).

FUNEN

Funen is Denmark's proverbial middle child. Lacking Zealand's capital-city pull or Jutland's geographic dominance, it's often overlooked by visitors, who perhaps make a whistle-stop visit to Hans Christian Andersen's birthplace.

Odense

POP 172,500

Currently undergoing a major revamp, Funen's millennium-old capital is a cheerful, compact city, ideal for feet and bicycles, and with enough diversions to keep you hooked for a day or two. It was here that Hans Christian Andersen entered the world, once upon a time...

Sights

★HC Andersens Hus MUSEUM
(www.museum.odense.dk; Bangs Boder 29; adult/child Dkr95/free; ⏲10am-5pm Jul & Aug, 10am-4pm Tue-Sun Sep-Jun) Lying amid the miniaturised streets of the old poor quarter (now often referred to the HCA Quarter), this museum delivers a thorough, lively telling of Andersen's extraordinary life and times. His achievements are put into an interesting historical context and leavened by some engaging audiovisual material and quirky exhibits (such as the display on his height – HCA was 25cm taller than the national average at the time).

Brandts MUSEUM
(www.brandts.dk; Brandts Torv; combined ticket adult/child Dkr90/free; ⏲10am-5pm Tue, Wed & Fri-Sun, noon-9pm Thu) The former textile mill on Brandts Passage has been beautifully converted into a sprawling art centre, with thought-provoking, well-curated changing displays (including a riveting exhibition on tattooing when we last stopped by). Note: there's free entry after 5pm Thursday.

Brandts Samling (the permanent collection) traces 250 years of Danish art, from classic to modern, and includes an impressive assemblage of international photography.

Sleeping

Cabinn Odense Hotel HOTEL €
(☎63 14 57 00; www.cabinn.com; Østre Stationsvej 7; s/d from Dkr495/625; @ 📶) Facing off with the nearby Danhostel, fighting for the budget-conscious, train-travelling custom, is this member of the popular budget-bed chain. Sure, the beds are narrow and the no-frills rooms lack charm, but at these prices it's decent value.

Danhostel Odense City HOSTEL €
(☎63 11 04 25; www.odensedanhostel.dk; Østre Stationsvej 31; dm/d from Dkr250/470; @ 📶) Perfectly placed for travellers, with the train and bus stations as neighbours and Kongens Have (a large park) directly opposite. All rooms at this large, modern hostel have bathrooms, and there's a guest kitchen, laundry and a basement TV room.

Eating & Drinking

★**Restaurant no.61** EUROPEAN €€
(☎61 69 10 35; www.no61.dk; Kongensgade 61; 2/3 courses Dkr255/295; ⏲from 5pm Tue-Sat) Winning plaudits for its embrace of classic European cooking, this cosy, farmhouse-chic bistro has a menu that changes monthly and is short, simple and seasonal. Each course presents two options: dishes plucked straight from the Funen fields might include white asparagus with truffle-infused hollandaise sauce, or a confection of strawberry, rhubarb, white chocolate and crème anglaise. Reservations recommended.

Nelle's Coffee & Wine BAR
(www.nelles.dk; Pantheonsgade; ⏲9am-10pm Mon-Thu, to midnight Fri & Sat, 9am-5.30pm Sun; 📶) Get your morning caffeine fix here (Nelle's brews the city's best coffee), then return at wine-time, to select from some 20 wines-by-the-glass (from Dkr45). Nelle's doesn't serve meals but you won't go hungry: there are morning pastries, afternoon cakes and wine-time nuts or cheese boards.

Information

Tourist Office (☎63 75 75 20; www.visitodense.com; Vestergade 2; ⏲9.30am-6pm Mon-Fri, 10am-3pm Sat, 11am-2pm Sun Jul & Aug, 10am-4.30pm Mon-Fri, to 1pm Sat Sep-Jun) Helpful, well-stocked office, in the town hall about 700m from the train station.

Getting There & Away

Odense is on the main railway line between Copenhagen (Dkr276, 1½ hours, twice hourly) and Aarhus (Dkr240, 1¾ hours, twice hourly).

JUTLAND

Denmark doesn't have a north–south divide; culturally, spiritually and to a great extent politically, it is divided into Jutland…and all the rest.

Aarhus

POP 310,800

Always the bridesmaid, never the bride, Aarhus (*oar*-hus) stands in the shadow of its bigger, brasher sibling, Copenhagen. But Denmark's affable runner-up city has hipster boutiques, bars and cafes, world-class dining and fantastic museums. Expect its stature to grow in the lead-up to 2017, when it is one of the **European Capitals of Culture** (www.aarhus2017.dk).

Sights

★**ARoS Aarhus Kunstmuseum** ART MUSEUM
(www.aros.dk; Aros Allé 2; adult/child Dkr110/free; ⏲10am-5pm Tue-Sun, to 10pm Wed; 👪) Inside the cubist, red-brick walls of Aarhus' showpiece art museum are nine floors of sweeping curves, soaring spaces and white walls, showcasing a wonderful selection of Golden Age works, Danish modernism, and an abundance of arresting and vivid contemporary art. The museum's cherry-on-top is the spectacular **Your Rainbow Panorama**, a 360-degree rooftop walkway offering technicolour views of the city through its glass panes in all shades of the rainbow.

Den Gamle By MUSEUM
(The Old Town; www.dengamleby.dk; Viborgvej 2; adult/child Dkr135/free; ⏲10am-5pm; 👪) The

Aarhus

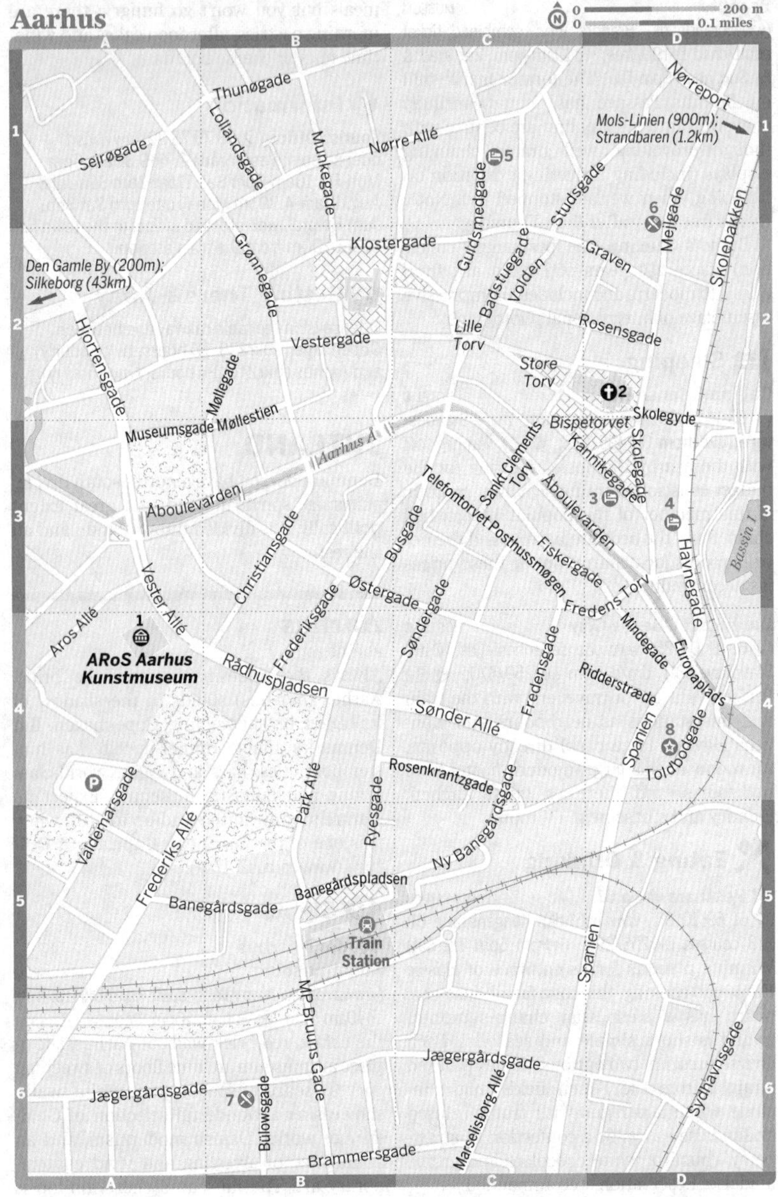

Danes' seemingly limitless enthusiasm for dressing up and re-creating history reaches its zenith at Den Gamle By. It's an engaging, picturesque open-air museum of 75 half-timbered houses brought here from all corners of Denmark and reconstructed as a provincial market town from the era of Hans Christian Andersen. Re-created neighbourhoods from 1927 and 1974 are the latest additions.

Aarhus

★**Moesgård Museum** MUSEUM
(www.moesmus.dk; Moesgård Allé; adult/child Dkr110/free; ⏲10am-5pm Tue-Sun, to 9pm Wed, open Mon Jul-Sep) Don't miss the reinvented Moesgård Museum, 10km south of the city. It reopened in October 2014 in a spectacularly designed, award-winning modern space, next door to the manor house that once accommodated its excellent prehistory exhibits. The museum's star attraction is the 2000-year-old **Grauballe Man**, whose astonishingly well-preserved body was found in 1952 in the village of Grauballe, 35km west of Aarhus.

Sleeping

CabInn Aarhus Hotel BUDGET HOTEL €
(☎86 75 70 00; www.cabinn.com; Kannikegade 14; s/d/tr from Dkr495/625/805; P@wifi) 'Best location, best price' is the CabInn chain's motto, and given that this branch doubled in size in 2014, it's clearly doing something right. The functional rooms are based on ships' cabins (hence the name) – the cheapest is *tiny*, but all come with bathroom, kettle and TV. The location is indeed top-notch. Breakfast costs Dkr70.

City Sleep-In HOTEL €
(☎86 19 20 55; www.citysleep-in.dk; Havnegade 20; dm Dkr180, d without/with bathroom Dkr450/500; @wifi) The most central hostel option has small, basic rooms – you'll be more drawn to the communal areas, such as the pretty courtyard or 1st-floor TV room. There are helpful staff, a global feel and decent amenities (lockers, kitchen, pool table, laundry).

★**Hotel Guldsmeden** BOUTIQUE HOTEL €€
(☎86 13 45 50; www.hotelguldsmeden.com; Guldsmedgade 40; d without/with bathroom from Dkr995/1395; wifi) A top pick for its excellent location, warm staff, French Colonial-style rooms with Persian rugs, pretty garden oasis and relaxed, stylish ambience. Bumper breakfasts (mainly organic) are included, as is Guldsmeden's own organic toiletries range. *Guldsmed* means both goldsmith and dragonfly in Danish – look for sweet use of the dragonfly motif in the decor.

Eating

The Latin Quarter is good for bistro-style cafes; Skolegade (and its extension, Mejlgade) delivers a handful of excellent budget options.

Oli Nico INTERNATIONAL €
(www.olinico.dk; Mejlgade 35; dishes Dkr55-125; ⏲11.30am-2pm & 5.30-9pm Mon-Fri, noon-2pm & 5.30-9pm Sat, to 9pm Sun) You may need to fight for one of the sought-after tables at Oli Nico, a small restaurant with a menu of classic dishes at astoundingly good prices (*moules frites* for Dkr60, rib-eye steak for Dkr125 – both with homemade chips!). The daily-changing three-course dinner menu (for a bargain Dkr130) may be Aarhus' best-kept food secret. No reservations; takeaway available.

★**St Pauls Apothek** MODERN SCANDINAVIAN €€
(☎86 12 08 33; www.stpaulsapothek.dk; Jægergårdsgade 76; 2/3-course menu Dkr245/295; ⏲5.30pm-midnight Tue-Thu, to 2am Fri & Sat) What was once a pharmacy is now one of Aarhus' hottest, best-value dining destinations: a Brooklyn-esque combo of hipster mixologists, vintage architectural detailing, and slinky mood lighting. The menu is small on choice but big on Nordic produce and confident food pairings – and for Dkr595, you can enjoy three courses matched with inspired, delicious cocktails. Book ahead.

Drinking & Entertainment

Aarhus is the nation's music capital, with quality music gigs in venues from dignified concert halls to beer-fuelled boltholes. For the lowdown on what's happening, click onto www.visitaarhus.com or www.aoa.dk.

Strandbaren BAR
(www.facebook.com/strandbarenaarhus; Havnebassin 7, pier 4; ⏲May-Sep) Plonk shipping containers and sand on a harbourfront spot and voila: beach bar. This chilled hang-out at Aarhus Ø (just beyond the ferry port) offers food,

DON'T MISS

LEGOLAND

Revisit your tender years at Denmark's most visited tourist attraction (beyond Copenhagen), **Legoland** (www.legoland.dk; Nordmarksvej; adult/child Dkr309/289; ⏲10am-8pm or 9pm Jul–mid-Aug, shorter hrs Apr-Jun & Sep-Oct, closed Nov-Mar; 👪). Located 1km north of the Lego company town of Billund, the sprawling theme park is a gobsmacking ode to those little plastic building blocks, with everything from giant Lego models of famous cities, landmarks and wild beasts, to re-created scenes from the Star Wars film series.

Legoland closing times vary – from 6pm to 9pm. Also worth knowing (and not well publicised) is that the park opens its gates a half-hour before the rides close, and no ticket is necessary to enter. Rides normally close one or two hours before the park itself (check the website), so with a bit of luck you could end up with 2½ hours to browse and check out Miniland for free.

In 2017 the 'experience centre' **Lego House** is set to open in Billund town itself. Featuring a bold, inspired design that resembles a stack of gigantic Lego bricks, it will incorporate exhibition areas, rooftop gardens, a cafe, a Lego store and a covered public square, and is expected to attract 250,000 visitors annually.

Billund lies in central Jutland. By train, the most common route is to disembark at Vejle and catch a bus from there (take bus 43 or 143). Buses run up to 10 times daily between Aarhus and Billund airport (Dkr160, one hour), close to the park. To plan your travel, use www.rejseplanen.dk.

drink, flirting and weather-dependent activities and events. Check hours and location on the Facebook page (harbour redevelopment may require an annual location change; opening hours are 'when the sun is shining').

Train LIVE MUSIC, CLUB
(www.train.dk; Toldbodgade 6; ⏲club from midnight Fri & Sat) Aarhus' premier club, Train is first and foremost a concert venue, with shows a couple of nights a week and some big international acts on the program. Train opens as a late-night club as well, on Friday and Saturday nights, with room for up to 1700 party-people and top-notch DJ talent. The complex also incorporates Kupé, a funky lounge club.

ℹ Information

VisitAarhus provides information online (www.visitaarhus.com), by phone (☎87 31 50 10), at summer booths and via touchscreens around town. Smartphone users can download the free VisitAarhus app.

ℹ Getting There & Away

Aarhus is well connected by train. Destinations include Copenhagen (Dkr382, three to 3½ hours, twice hourly) via Odense.

Skagen

POP 8350

With its rich art heritage, fresh seafood and photogenic neighbourhoods, Skagen (pronounced *skain*) is a delicious slice of Denmark. In the mid-19th century, artists flocked here, charmed by the radiant light's impact on the ruggedly beautiful landscape. Now tourists flock, drawn by the winning combination of busy working harbour, long sandy beaches and buzzing holiday atmosphere.

Sights

★ **Skagens Museum** MUSEUM
(www.skagensmuseum.dk; Brøndumsvej 4; adult/child Dkr90/free; ⏲10am-5pm daily May-Aug, Tue-Sun Sep-Apr) This wonderful gallery (undergoing major renovation and expansion from late 2014 into 2015) showcases the outstanding art that was produced in Skagen between 1870 and 1930.

Artists discovered Skagen's luminous light and its wind-blasted heath-and-dune landscape in the mid-19th century, and fixed eagerly on the romantic imagery of the area's fishing life that had earned the people of Skagen a hard living for centuries.

Painters such as PS Krøyer and Anna and Michael Ancher followed the contemporary fashion of painting *en plein air* (out of doors). Their work established a vivid figurative style of painting that became known internationally as the 'Skagen School'.

Grenen OUTDOORS
Appropriately enough for such a neat and ordered country, Denmark doesn't end untidily at its most northerly point, but on a neat

finger of sand just a few metres wide. You can actually paddle at its tip, where the waters of the Kattegat and Skagerrak clash, and you can put one foot in each sea – but not too far. Bathing here is forbidden because of the ferocious tidal currents.

Gammel Skagen VILLAGE, BEACH

There's a touch of Cape Cod in refined Gammel Skagen ('Old Skagen', also known as Højen), renowned for its gorgeous sunsets, upmarket hotels and well-heeled summer residents.

It was a fishing hamlet before sandstorms ravaged this windswept area and forced many of its inhabitants to move to Skagen on the more protected east coast. It's a pleasant bike ride 4km west of Skagen: head towards Frederikshavn and turn right at Højensvej, which takes you to the waterfront.

Sleeping

Danhostel Skagen HOSTEL €

(☎98 44 22 00; www.danhostelskagen.dk; Rolighedsvej 2; dm/s/d Dkr180/525/625; ⏲Mar-Nov; P ☎) Always a hive of activity, this hostel is modern, functional and spick-and-span. It's decent value, particularly for families or groups. Low-season prices drop sharply. It's 1km towards Frederikshavn from the Skagen train station (if you're coming by train, get off at Frederikshavnsvej).

★Badepension Marienlund GUESTHOUSE €€

(☎28 12 13 20; www.marienlund.dk; Fabriciusvej 8; s/d incl breakfast Dkr650/1100; ⏲Apr-Oct; P ☎) A cosy atmosphere, idyllic garden and pretty lounge and breakfast areas make Marienlund a top option. There are only 14 rooms, all light, white and simply furnished (all with bathrooms). You'll find the hotel in a peaceful residential neighbourhood west of the centre; bike hire available.

Eating

Perhaps a dozen seafood shacks line the harbour, selling fresh seafood. Prawns/shrimp *(rejer)* are the favourite order, costing around Dkr100 for a generous helping.

Information

Tourist Office (☎98 44 13 77; www.skagen-tourist.dk; Vestre Strandvej 10; ⏲9am-4pm Mon-Sat, 10am-2pm Sun late Jun-mid-Aug, shorter hrs rest of yr) In front of the harbour, with loads of info on regional sights, attractions and activities.

Getting There & Away

Trains run hourly to Frederikshavn (Dkr60, 35 minutes), where you can change for destinations further south.

The summertime (late June to mid-August) bus 99 connects Skagen with other northern towns and attractions, including Hirtshals.

SURVIVAL GUIDE

Directory A–Z

ACCOMMODATION

Camping & Cabins

- Denmark is well set up for campers, with nearly 600 campgrounds. Some are open only in the summer months. Many campgrounds offer cabins for rent.
- The per-night charge typically costs around Dkr75 for an adult, and about half that for each child. In summer some places also tack on a site charge of Dkr50 per tent/caravan; some also have a small eco tax.
- You need a camping card (Dkr110 per couple) for stays at all campgrounds. You can buy a card at the first campground you arrive at, at local tourist offices, or from the Danish Camping Board (see www.danishcampsites.dk).
- See www.danishcampsites.dk and www.dkcamp.dk.

Hostels

- Some 88 hostels make up the **Danhostel** (www.danhostel.dk) association, which is affiliated with Hostelling International (HI). Some are dedicated hostels in holiday areas, others are attached to sports centres.
- Advance reservations are advised, particularly in summer. In a few places, reception closes as early as 6pm. In most hostels the reception office is closed, and the phone not answered, between noon and 4pm.
- Typical costs are Dkr200 to Dkr275 for a dorm bed. For private rooms, expect to pay Dkr450 to Dkr720 per double, and up to Dkr100 for each additional person in larger rooms. All

SLEEPING PRICE RANGES

The following price ranges refer to a double room in high season. Unless otherwise noted, rooms have private bathroom.

€ less than Dkr700

€€ Dkr700–Dkr1500

€€€ more than Dkr1500

COUNTRY FACTS

Area 43,094 sq km

Capital Copenhagen

Country Code ☎45

Currency Krone (Dkr)

Emergency ☎112

Language Danish

Money ATMs are very common; credit cards widely accepted

Population 5.6 million

Visas Schengen visa rules apply

hostels offer family rooms. Many rooms come with bathroom.

- You'll save money with a sleep sheet or your own linen, as most hostels charge for this.
- All hostels provide breakfast costing around Dkr70.
- If you hold a valid national or international hostel card, you receive a 10% discount on rates (these can be purchased from hostels and cost Dkr70 for Danish residents, Dkr160 for foreigners). We list prices for non-cardholders.

Hotels

- Some hotels have set rates published on their websites; others have rates that fluctuate according to season and demand. Most hotel websites offer good deals, as do booking engines such as www.booking.com.
- Many business hotels offer cheaper rates on Friday and Saturday nights year-round, and during the summer peak (from about midsummer in late June until the start of the school year in early/mid-August).
- There is no hard-and-fast rule about the inclusion of breakfast in rates – many hotels include it, but for others it is optional. At budget hotels like CabInn you can purchase it for around Dkr70.

Other Accommodation

- Hundreds of places (summer cottages, innercity apartments, family-friendly houses) can be rented direct from the owner via **AirBnB** (www.airbnb.com).
- Many tourist offices book rooms in private homes for a small fee, or provide a list of local rooms on their website.

ACTIVITIES

- Denmark is well set up for outdoor activities, from walking and cycling to fishing and watersports. The **Visit Denmark** (www.visitdenmark.com) website offers great information and links.
- The best way to tour Denmark by bike is by grabbing a map and planning it yourself – a fantastic resource is the **Cyclistic** (http://cyclistic.dk/en/) website. Each county produces its own detailed 1:100,000 cycle touring maps; many of them come with booklets detailing accommodation, sights and other local information. These maps cost around Dkr129, and are available at tourist offices or online via the Danish cycling federation, **Dansk Cyklist Forbund** (shop at http://shop.dcf.dk).

BUSINESS HOURS

- Opening hours vary throughout the year. We've provided high-season opening hours; in tourist areas and establishments, hours will generally decrease in the shoulder and low seasons.
- Family-friendly attractions (museums, zoos, fun parks) in holiday hotspots generally open from June to August (possibly May to September), plus for the spring and autumn school holidays.

Banks 10am to 4pm Monday to Friday

ESSENTIAL DANISH FOOD & DRINK

- **New Nordic flavours** Sample creations inspired by the culinary movement that got everyone talking, in one of Copenhagen's hottest restaurants (book ahead).
- **Smørrebrød** Rye bread topped with anything from beef tartar to egg and shrimp, the open sandwich is Denmark's most famous culinary export.
- **Sild** Smoked, cured, pickled or fried, herring is a local staple and best washed down with generous serves of akvavit.
- **Kanelsnegle** A calorific delight, the 'cinammon snail' is a sweet, buttery pastry, sometimes laced with chocolate.
- **Akvavit** Denmark's best-loved spirit is this caraway-spiced schnapps from Aalborg, drunk straight down as a shot, followed by a chaser of *øl* (beer).
- **Lashings of beer** Carlsberg may dominate, but Denmark's battalion of microbreweries includes Mikkeller, Rise Bryggeri and Grauballe.

Bars 4pm to midnight, to 2am or later Friday and Saturday (clubs on weekends may open until 5am)

Cafes 8am to 5pm or later

Restaurants noon to 10pm (maybe earlier on weekends for brunch)

Shops 10am to 6pm Monday to Friday (possibly until 7pm on Friday), to 4pm Saturday. Some larger stores may open Sunday.

Supermarkets 8am to 8pm or to 9pm or 10pm (many with bakeries opening around 7am)

INTERNET RESOURCES

Visit Denmark (www.visitdenmark.com), Denmark's official tourism website, lists tourist offices throughout the country.

MONEY

- **ATMs** Major bank ATMs accept Visa, MasterCard and the Cirrus and Plus bank cards.
- **Credit cards** Visa and MasterCard are widely accepted. American Express and Diners Club are occasionally accepted. A surcharge of up to 3.75% is imposed on foreign credit-card transactions in some restaurants, shops and hotels.
- **Tipping** Restaurant bills and taxi fares include service charges in the quoted prices. Further tipping is not expected, although rounding up the bill is not uncommon when service has been particularly good.

PUBLIC HOLIDAYS

Banks and most businesses close on public holidays and transport schedules are commonly reduced.

New Year's Day 1 January

Maundy Thursday Thursday before Easter

Good Friday to Easter Monday March/April

Great Prayer Day Fourth Friday after Easter

Ascension Day Sixth Thursday after Easter

Whitsunday Seventh Sunday after Easter

Whitmonday Seventh Monday after Easter

Constitution Day 5 June

Christmas From noon 24 December until 26 December

New Year's Eve 31 December (from noon)

TELEPHONE

- There are no regional area codes within Denmark.
- To call Denmark from abroad: dial your country's international access code, then ☎45 (Denmark's country code), then the local number.
- To call internationally from Denmark: dial ☎00, then the country code for the country you're calling, followed by the area code and local number.
- Public payphones are elusive, but they accept coins, phonecards and credit cards. Phonecards are available from kiosks and post offices.

EATING PRICE RANGES

The following price categories for a main course are used in the listings in this chapter.

€ less than Dkr125

€€ Dkr125–Dkr250

€€€ more than Dkr250

TIME

- Denmark is one hour ahead of GMT/UTC. Clocks are moved forward one hour for daylight-saving time from late March to late October.
- Denmark uses the 24-hour clock and timetables and business hours are posted accordingly.

VISAS

- No entry visa is needed by citizens of EU and Nordic countries.
- Citizens of the USA, Canada, Australia and New Zealand don't need a visa for tourist stays of less than 90 days.
- Citizens of many African, South American, Asian and former Soviet bloc countries do require a visa. See www.nyidanmark.dk.

Getting There & Away

AIR

- The majority of international flights into Denmark land at Copenhagen Airport in Kastrup, about 9km southeast of central Copenhagen.
- A few international flights, mostly those coming from other Nordic countries or the UK, land at smaller regional airports, in Aarhus, Aalborg, Billund, Esbjerg and Sønderborg.

LAND

- Denmark's only land crossing is with Germany, although the bridge over the Øresund from Sweden functions in the same way. If travelling by road, there's a Dkr335 toll per vehicle to cross the Øresund bridge linking Copenhagen with Malmö. Trains run this route frequently (Dkr95, 35 minutes).
- **Eurolines Scandinavia** (www.eurolines.dk) offers connections to more than 500 major European cities in 26 countries. Destinations, timetables and prices are all online; advance reservations advised.
- Reliable, regular train services link Denmark to Sweden, Germany and Norway. Tickets booked online in advance can be cheaper. See www.dsb.dk for details.

SEA

- Ferry connections are possible between Denmark and Norway, Sweden, Germany, Iceland

and the Faroe Islands. The ferry link with the UK ceased in 2014.

➡ Fares on these ships vary wildly, by season and by day of the week. The highest prices tend to occur on summer weekends and the lowest on winter weekdays. Discounts are often available, including for holders of rail passes or student cards and for seniors. Bookings are advised.

Major operators and their routes are listed here.

Faroe Islands & Iceland

Smyril Line (www.smyrilline.com) Route: Hirtshals to Seyðisfjörður (Iceland) via Tórshavn (Faroe Islands).

Germany

BornholmerFærgen (www.bornholmerfaergen.dk) Route: Rønne (on Bornholm) to Sassnitz.

Scandlines (www.scandlines.com) Routes: Rødbyhavn (on Lolland) to Puttgarden; Gedser (on Falster) to Rostock.

Norway

Color Line (www.colorline.com) Routes: Hirtshals to Kristiansand; to Larvik.

DFDS Seaways (www.dfdsseaways.com) Route: Copenhagen to Oslo.

Fjordline (www.fjordline.com) Routes: Hirtshals to Kristiansand; to Bergen via Stavanger; to Langesund.

Stena Line (www.stenaline.com) Route: Frederikshavn to Oslo.

Sweden

BornholmerFærgen (www.bornholmerfaergen.dk) Route: Rønne (Bornholm) to Ystad.

Scandlines (www.scandlines.com) Route: Helsingør to Helsingborg.

Stena Line (www.stenaline.com) Routes: Frederikshavn to Gothenburg (Göteborg); Grenaa to Varberg.

NORTHERN JUTLAND FERRY PORTS

Ferries (p321) to Sweden, Norway and Iceland run from two ports at the top tip of Jutland.

➡ From **Frederikshavn**, ferries sail to Gothenburg and Oslo. Trains run between Frederikshavn and Copenhagen (Dkr445, six hours) via Odense, Aarhus and Aalborg.

➡ From **Hirtshals**, ferries connect a half-dozen Norwegian ports, and there's a weekly connection to Iceland via the Faroe Islands. To reach Hirtshals from Copenhagen (Dkr453, 5½ hours), change trains at Hjørring.

THE ESSENTIAL TRANSPORT WEBSITE

For getting around in Denmark, the essential website is www.rejseplanen.dk. It allows you to enter your start and end point, date and preferred time of travel, and will then give you the best travel option, which may involve walking or taking a bus or train. Bus routes are linked, travel times are given, and fares listed. Download the app for easy mobile access.

Getting Around

BICYCLE

➡ Cyclists here are very well catered for, with excellent cycling routes throughout the country.

➡ You'll be able to hire a bike in almost every Danish town and village. Bike-rental prices average around Dkr100/400 per day/week for something basic.

➡ Bicycles can be taken on ferries and trains for a modest fee.

BOAT

➡ Ferries link virtually all of Denmark's populated islands.

BUS

➡ Long-distance buses run a distant second to trains. Still, some cross-country bus routes work out to about 25% cheaper than trains.

➡ Popular routes include Copenhagen to Aarhus or Aalborg. A useful operator is **Abildskou** (www.abildskou.dk).

CAR & MOTORCYCLE

➡ Denmark is perfect for touring by car. Roads are in good condition and well signposted. Traffic is manageable, even in major cities such as Copenhagen (rush hours excepted).

➡ Denmark's network of ferries carries vehicles for reasonable rates. It's a good idea to make reservations, especially in summer.

TRAIN

➡ With the exception of a few short private lines, **Danske Statsbaner** (DSB; ☎70 13 14 15; www.dsb.dk) runs all Danish train services. Overall, train travel isn't expensive, in large part because distances are short.

➡ Most long-distance trains on major routes operate at least hourly during the day. In morning and evening peak times, it's advisable to make reservations (Dkr30) if travelling on the speedy InterCityLyn (ICL) and Intercity (IC) trains.

➡ There are various discounts available for students, children, seniors and groups travelling together. Good advance-purchase discounts are sometimes available – look for 'Orange' tickets.

Estonia

Includes ➡

Best Places to Eat

- Ö (p332)
- Tchaikovsky (p332)
- Leib (p331)
- Von Krahli Aed (p331)
- Altja Kõrts (p334)

Best Places to Stay

- Antonius Hotel (p336)
- Hotel Telegraaf (p331)
- Yoga Residence (p331)
- Euphoria (p331)
- Tallinn Backpackers (p330)

Why Go?

Estonia doesn't have to struggle to find a point of difference; it's completely unique. It shares a similar geography and history with Latvia and Lithuania, but it's culturally very different. Its closest ethnic and linguistic buddy is Finland, yet although they both may love to get naked together in the sauna, 50 years of Soviet rule have separated the two cultures. For the past 300 years Estonia has been linked to Russia, but the two states have as much in common as a barn swallow and a bear (their respective national symbols).

In recent decades, and with a new-found confidence, Estonia has crept from under the Soviet blanket and leapt into the arms of Europe. The love affair is mutual: Europe has fallen for the chocolate-box allure of Tallinn and its Unesco-protected Old Town, while travellers seeking something different are tapping into Estonia's captivating blend of Eastern European and Nordic appeal.

When to Go

Tallinn

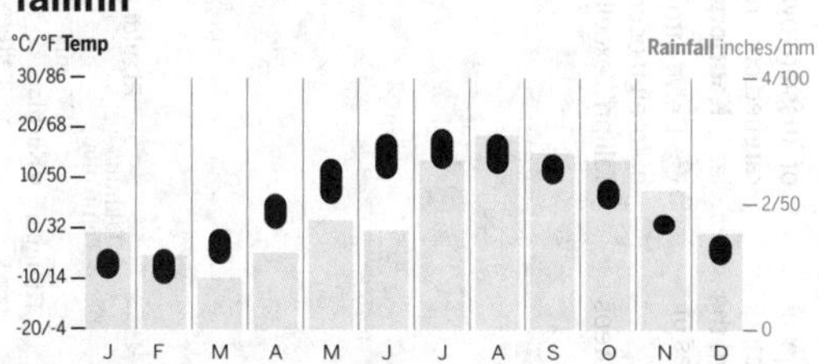

Apr & May See the country shake off winter's gloom.

Jun–Aug White nights, beach parties and loads of summer festivals.

Dec Christmas markets, mulled wine and long, cosy nights.

Estonia Highlights

1 Embark on a medieval quest for atmospheric restaurants and bars in the history-saturated lanes of Tallinn's **Old Town**.

2 Follow in the footsteps of Russian royalty within the rarefied confines of Tallinn's leafy **Kadriorg Park** (p329).

3 Delve into Estonia's history of foreign occupations in Tallinn's excellent **museums**, knowing there's the pay-off of a happy ending.

4 Stroll the broad golden sands and genteel streets of **Pärnu** (p337), Estonia's 'summer capital'.

5 Further your local education in the museums and bars of the university town of **Tartu** (p334), Estonia's second city.

6 Cycle between manor houses and discover your own slice of deserted coast in **Lahemaa National Park** (p334).

ITINERARIES

Three Days

Base yourself in **Tallinn** and spend your first day exploring all the nooks and crannies of Old Town. The following day, do what most tourists don't do – step out of Old Town. Explore Kadriorg Park for a first-rate greenery and art fix, then hit the wonderful Estonian Open-Air Museum. On your last day, hire a car or take a day tour to **Lahemaa National Park**.

One Week

Spend your first three days in Tallinn, then allow a full day to explore Lahemaa before bedding down within the national park. The following day, continue on to **Tartu** for a night or two, then finish up in **Pärnu**.

TALLINN

POP 412,000

If you're labouring under the misconception that 'former Soviet' means dull and grey, and that all tourist traps are soulless, Tallinn will delight in proving you wrong. This city has charm by the bucketload, fusing the modern and medieval to come up with a vibrant vibe all of its own. It's an intoxicating mix of church spires, glass skyscrapers, baroque palaces, appealing eateries, brooding battlements, shiny shopping malls, run-down wooden houses and cafes set on sunny squares – with a few Soviet throwbacks in the mix.

Sights & Activities

Old Town

Tallinn's medieval Old Town (Vanalinn) is without doubt the country's most fascinating locality. It's divided into Toompea (the upper town) and the lower town, which is still surrounded by much of its 2.5km defensive wall.

Toompea

According to legend, Toompea is the burial mound of Kalev, the mythical first leader of the Estonians. When Tallinn was a German town (known as Reval), this large fortified hill was the preserve of the bishop and the feudal nobility, literally looking down on the traders and lesser beings below. A couple of wonderful lookouts offer sumptuous views across the Lower Town rooftops to the sea.

St Mary's Cathedral CHURCH

(Tallinna Neitsi Maarja Piiskoplik Toomkirik; www.eelk.ee/tallinna.toom/; Toom-Kooli 6; tower adult/child €5/3; 9am-5pm daily May-Sep, 9am-3pm Tue-Sun Oct-Apr) Tallinn's cathedral (now Lutheran, originally Catholic) was founded by at least 1233, although the exterior dates mainly from the 15th century, with the tower added in 1779. This impressive, austere building was a burial ground for the rich and titled, and the whitewashed walls are decorated with the coats-of-arms of Estonia's noble families. Fit viewseekers can climb the tower.

Alexander Nevsky Cathedral CHURCH

(Lossi plats; 9am-6pm) FREE The positioning of this magnificent, onion-domed Russian Orthodox cathedral (completed in 1900), opposite the parliament buildings, was no accident: the church was one of many built in the last part of the 19th century as part of a general wave of Russification in the empire's Baltic provinces. Orthodox believers come here in droves, alongside tourists ogling the interior's striking icons and frescoes.

Toompea Castle HISTORIC BUILDING

(Lossi plats) FREE Toompea hill was topped by an early Estonian stronghold before the Danes invaded and built a castle here in 1219. Three towers have survived from the Knights of the Sword castle which replaced it, the finest of which is 14th-century Pikk Hermann (best viewed from the rear). In the 18th century the fortress underwent an extreme makeover at the hands of Russian empress Catherine the Great, converting it into the pretty-in-pink baroque palace that now houses Estonia's parliament (*riigikogu*).

Kiek in de Kök CASTLE, MUSEUM

(644 6686; www.linnamuuseum.ee; Komandandi tee 2; adult/child €4.50/2.60; 10.30am-6pm Tue-Sun) Built around 1475, this tall, stout fortress is one of Tallinn's most formidable cannon towers. Its name (amusing as it

sounds in English) is Low German for 'Peep into the Kitchen'; from the upper floors medieval voyeurs could peer into the houses below. Today it houses a branch of the City Museum, focusing mainly on the development of the town's elaborate defences.

Bastion Passages FORTRESS

(Bastionikäigud; ☎644 6686; www.linnamuuseum.ee; Komandandi tee 2; adult/child €5.80/3.20) Two-hour tours depart from Kiek in de Kök, exploring the 17th-centuring tunnels connecting the towers, built by the Swedes to help protect the city; bookings required.

Tallinn

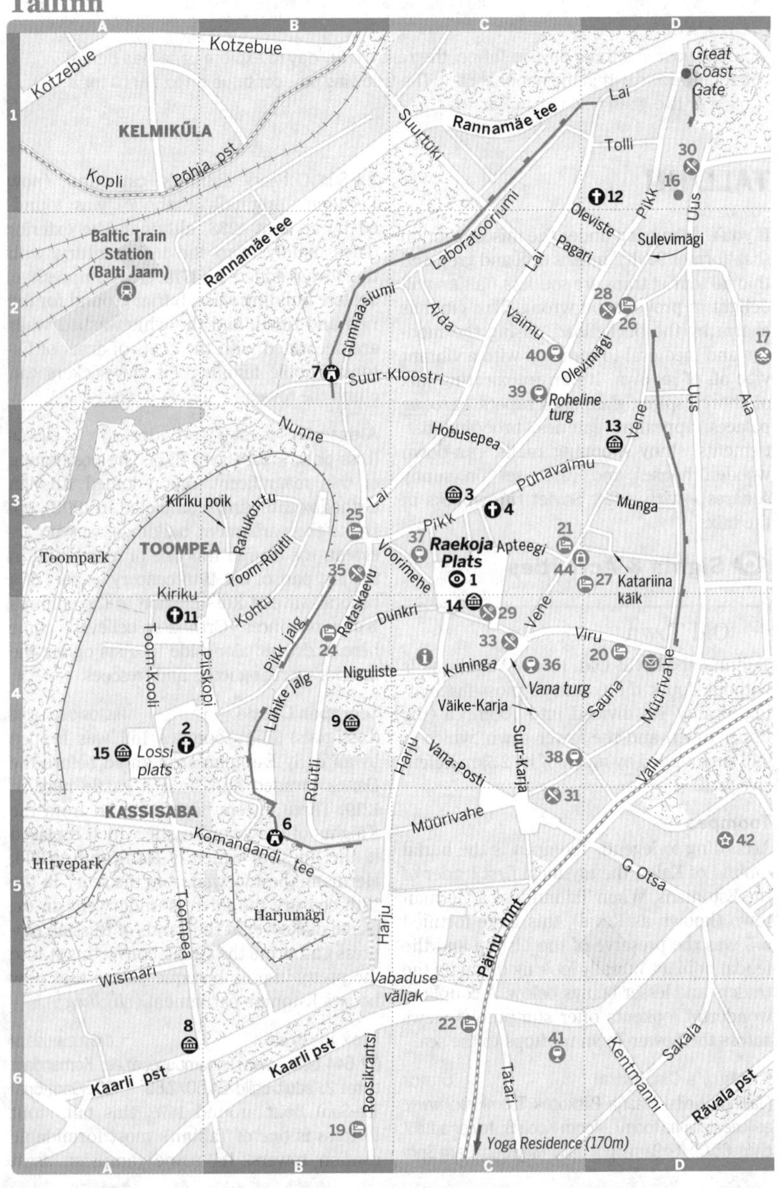

Museum of Occupations MUSEUM
(Okupatsioonide Muuseum; www.okupatsioon.ee; Toompea 8; adult/child €5/3; ⌚10am-6pm Tue-Sun) Displays illustrate the hardships and horrors of five decades of occupation, under both the Nazis (briefly) and the Soviets. The photos and artefacts are interesting but it's the videos (lengthy but enthralling) that leave the greatest impression – and the joy of a happy ending.

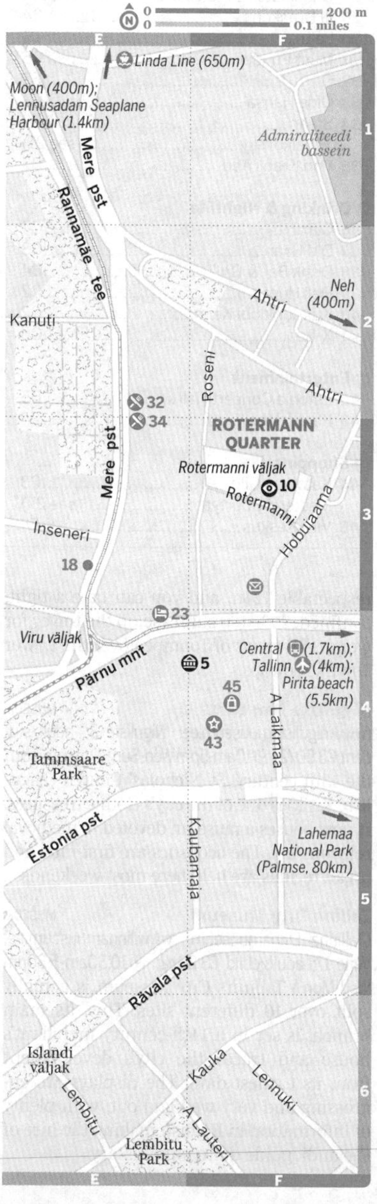

Lower Town

Picking your way along the lower town's narrow, cobbled streets is like strolling into the 15th century – not least due to the tendency of local businesses to dress their staff up in medieval garb. The most interesting street is Pikk (Long St), which starts at the Great Coast Gate and includes Tallinn's historic guild buildings.

★**Raekoja Plats** SQUARE
(Town Hall Sq) Raekoja plats has been the heart of Tallinn life since markets began here in the 11th century. It's ringed by pastel-coloured buildings from the 15th to 17th centuries, and is dominated by the Gothic town hall. Throughout summer, outdoor cafes implore you to sit and people-watch; come Christmas, a huge pine tree stands in the middle of the square. Whether bathed in sunlight or sprinkled with snow, it's always a photogenic spot.

Tallinn Town Hall HISTORIC BUILDING
(Tallinna Raekoda; ☎645 7900; www.tallinn.ee/raekoda; Raekoja plats; adult/student €5/2; ⌚10am-4pm Mon-Sat Jul-Aug, by appointment Sep-Jun) Completed in 1404, this is the only surviving Gothic town hall in northern Europe. Inside, you can visit the Trade Hall (housing a visitor book dripping in royal signatures), the Council Chamber (featuring Estonia's oldest woodcarvings, dating from 1374), the vaulted Citizens' Hall, a yellow-and-black-tiled councillor's office and a small kitchen. The steeply sloped attic has displays on the building and its restoration.

Holy Spirit Church CHURCH
(Pühavaimu Kirik; www.eelk.ee/tallinna.puhavaimu/; Pühavaimu 2; adult/child €1/50c; ⌚noon-2pm Mon-Fri, 10am-3pm Sat Jan & Feb, 10am-3pm Mon-Sat Mar, Apr & Oct-Dec, 10am-5pm Mon-Sat May-Sep) The blue-and-gold clock on the facade of this striking 13th-century Gothic Lutheran church is the oldest in Tallinn, dating from 1684. Inside there are exquisite woodcarvings and painted panels, including an altarpiece dating to 1483 and a 17th-century baroque pulpit.

Estonian History Museum MUSEUM
(Eesti Ajaloomuuseum; www.ajaloomuuseum.ee; Pikk 17; adult/child €5/3; ⌚10am-6pm, closed Wed Sep-Apr) The Estonian History Museum has filled the striking 1410 Great Guild building

Tallinn

Top Sights
1 Raekoja Plats ... C3

Sights
2 Alexander Nevsky Cathedral ... A4
Bastion Passages ... (see 6)
3 Estonian History Museum ... C3
4 Holy Spirit Church ... C3
5 Hotel Viru KGB Museum ... F4
6 Kiek in de Kök ... B5
7 Lower Town Wall ... B2
8 Museum of Occupations ... A6
9 Niguliste Museum ... B4
10 Rotermann Quarter ... F3
11 St Mary's Cathedral ... A4
12 St Olaf's Church ... D1
13 Tallinn City Museum ... D3
14 Tallinn Town Hall ... C4
15 Toompea Castle ... A4

Activities, Courses & Tours
16 City Bike ... D1
17 Kalev Spa Waterpark ... D2
18 Tallinn City Tour ... E3

Sleeping
19 Euphoria ... B6
20 Hotel Cru ... D4
21 Hotel Telegraaf ... C3
22 Hotell Palace ... C6
23 Nordic Hotel Forum ... E4
24 Old House Apartments ... B4
25 Tabinoya ... B3
26 Tallinn Backpackers ... D2
27 Villa Hortensia ... D3

Eating
28 Chedi ... D2
Chocolats de Pierre ... (see 27)
29 III Draakon ... C4
30 Leib ... D1
31 Must Puudel ... C5
32 Ö ... E2
33 Olde Hansa ... C4
34 Sfäär ... E3
Tchaikovsky ... (see 21)
35 Von Krahli Aed ... B3

Drinking & Nightlife
36 Clazz ... C4
37 DM Baar ... C3
38 Drink Bar & Grill ... C4
39 Hell Hunt ... C2
40 Kultuuriklubi Kelm ... C2
41 X-Baar ... C6

Entertainment
42 Estonia Concert Hall ... D5
43 Katusekino ... F4

Shopping
44 Katariina Gild ... C3
Masters' Courtyard ... (see 27)
45 Viru Keskus ... F4

with a series of ruminations on the Estonian psyche, presented through interactive and unusual displays. Coin collectors shouldn't miss the display in the old excise chamber, while military nuts should head downstairs. The basement also covers the history of the Great Guild itself.

Lower Town Wall FORTRESS
(Linnamüür; Gümnaasiumi 3; adult/child €1.50/75c; ⏲11am-7pm Jun-Aug, 11am-5pm Fri-Wed Apr, May, Sep & Oct, 11am-4pm Fri-Tue Nov-Mar) The most photogenic stretch of Tallinn's remaining walls connects nine towers lining the western edge of Old Town. Visitors can explore the barren nooks and crannies of three of them, with cameras at the ready for the red-rooftop views.

St Olaf's Church CHURCH
(Oleviste Kirik; www.oleviste.ee; Lai 50; tower adult/child €2/1; ⏲10am-6pm Apr-Oct) From 1549 to 1625, when its 159m steeple was struck by lightning and burnt down, this (now Baptist) church was one of the tallest buildings in the world. The current spire reaches a still respectable 124m and you can take a tight, confined, 258-step staircase up the tower for wonderful views of Toompea over the Lower Town's rooftops.

Niguliste Museum MUSEUM
(www.nigulistemuuseum.ee; Niguliste 3; adult/student €3.50/2; ⏲10am-5pm Wed-Sun) Dating from the 13th century, St Nicholas' Church (Niguliste Kirik) is one of the city's Gothic treasures. It now houses a museum devoted to medieval religious art. The acoustics are first-rate, and organ recitals are held here most weekends.

Tallinn City Museum MUSEUM
(Tallinna Linnamuuseum; www.linnamuuseum.ee; Vene 17; adult/child €3.20/2; ⏲10.30am-5.30pm Wed-Mon) Tallinn's City Museum is actually split over 10 different sites. This, its main branch, is set in a 14th-century merchant's house and traces the city's development from its earliest days. The displays are engrossing and very well laid out, with plenty of information in English making the hire of the audioguide quite unnecessary.

Kalev Spa Waterpark SWIMMING, SPA

(www.kalevspa.ee; Aia 18; 2½hr visit adult/child €12/10; 6.45am-9.30pm Mon-Fri, 8am-9.30pm Sat & Sun) For serious swimmers there's an indoor pool of Olympic proportions but there are plenty of other ways to wrinkle your skin here, including waterslides, spa pools, saunas and a kids' pool. There's also a gym, day spa and three private saunas, with the largest holding up to 20 of your closest hot-and-sweaty mates.

City Centre

Hotel Viru KGB Museum MUSEUM

(680 9300; www.viru.ee; Viru väljak 4; tour €9; daily May-Oct, Tue-Sun Nov-Apr) When the Hotel Viru was built in 1972, it was not only Estonia's first skyscraper, it was the only place for tourists to stay in Tallinn - and we mean that literally. Having all the foreigners in one place made it much easier to keep tabs on them and the locals they had contact with, which is exactly what the KGB did from their 23rd-floor spy base. The hotel offers fascinating tours of the facility; bookings essential.

Rotermann Quarter NEIGHBOURHOOD

(Rotermanni Kvartal) With impressive contemporary architecture wedged between old brick warehouses, this development has transformed a former factory complex into the city's hippest new shopping and dining precinct.

Kadriorg Park

About 2km east of Old Town (take tram 1 or 3), this beautiful park's ample acreage is Tallinn's favourite patch of green. Together with the baroque Kadriorg Palace, it was commissioned by the Russian tsar Peter the Great for his wife Catherine I soon after his conquest of Estonia (Kadriorg means Catherine's Valley in Estonian). Nowadays the oak, lilac and horse chestnut trees provide shade for strollers and picnickers, the formal pond and gardens provide a genteel backdrop for romantic promenades and wedding photos, and the children's playground is a favourite off-leash area for the city's youngsters.

Kadriorg Art Museum PALACE, GALLERY

(Kardrioru Kunstimuuseum; www.kadriorumuuseum.ee; A Weizenbergi 37; adult/child €4.80/2.80; 10am-5pm Tue & Thu-Sun, to 8pm Wed May-Sep, closed Mon & Tue Oct-Apr) Kadriorg Palace, built by Tsar Peter the Great between 1718 and 1736, now houses a branch of the Estonian Art Museum, which is devoted to Dutch, German and Italian paintings from the 16th to the 18th centuries, and Russian works from the 18th to early 20th centuries (check out the decorative porcelain with communist imagery upstairs). The building is exactly as frilly and fabulous as a palace ought to be and there's a handsome French-style flower garden at the back.

Kumu GALLERY

(www.kumu.ee; A Weizenbergi 34; all exhibitions adult/student €5.50/3.20, permanent exhibitions €4.20/2.60; 11am-6pm Tue & Thu-Sun, to 8pm Wed May-Sep, closed Mon & Tue Oct-Apr) This futuristic, Finnish-designed, seven-storey building (2006) is a spectacular structure of limestone, glass and copper, nicely integrated into the landscape. Kumu (the name is short for *kunstimuuseum* or art museum) contains the country's largest repository of Estonian art as well as constantly changing contemporary exhibits.

Pirita

Pirita's main claim to fame is that it was the base for the sailing events of the 1980 Moscow Olympics; international regattas are still held here. It's also home to Tallinn's largest and most popular **beach**.

Buses 1A, 8, 34A and 38 all run between the city centre and Pirita, with the last two continuing on to the TV Tower.

TV Tower VIEWPOINT

(Teletorn; www.teletorn.ee; Kloostrimetsa tee 58a; adult/child €8/5; 10am-7pm) Opened in time for the 1980 Olympics, this futuristic 314m tower offers brilliant views from its 22nd floor (175m). Press a button and frosted glass disks set in the floor suddenly clear, giving a view straight down. Once you're done gawping, check out the interactive displays in the space-age pods. Daredevils can try the open-air 'edge walk' (€20) or rappel their way down (€49).

Maarjamäe Palace MUSEUM

(Maarjamäe Loss; www.ajaloomuuseum.ee; Pirita tee 56; adult/child €4/2; 10am-5pm Wed-Sun) A kilometre north of Kadriorg Park, Maarjamäe is a neo-Gothic limestone manor house built in the 1870s. It's now home to the **Estonian Film Museum** and a less-visited branch of the **Estonian History Museum**, detailing the twists and turns of the 20th century.

Don't miss the Soviet sculpture graveyard at the rear of the building.

Other Neighbourhoods

★**Lennusadam**

Seaplane Harbour MUSEUM

(www.lennusadam.eu; Vesilennuki 6, Kalamaja; adult/child €10/6; ⏲10am-7pm May-Sep, Tue-Sun Oct-Apr; P) When this triple-domed hangar was completed in 1917, its reinforced-concrete shell frame construction was unique in the world. Resembling a classic Bond-villain lair, the vast space was completely restored and opened to the public in 2012 as a fascinating maritime museum, filled with interactive displays. Highlights include exploring the cramped corridors of a 1930s naval submarine, and the icebreaker and minehunter ships moored outside.

Estonian Open-Air Museum MUSEUM

(Eesti Vabaõhumuuseum; www.evm.ee; Vabaõhumuuseumi tee 12, Rocca Al Mare; adult/child May-Sep €7/3.50, Oct-Apr €5/3; ⏲10am-8pm May-Sep, to 5pm Oct-Apr) If tourists won't go to the countryside, let's bring the countryside to them. That's the modus operandi of this excellent, sprawling complex, where historic buildings have been plucked and transplanted among the tall trees. In summer the time-warping effect is highlighted by staff in period costume performing traditional activities among the wooden farmhouses and windmills.

Tours

EstAdventures WALKING, BUS

(☎53083731; www.estadventures.ee; from €15; ⏲May-Sep) Offers offbeat themed walking tours of Tallinn (Soviet, Legends, Spies, Haunted, Beer etc). Full-day excursions further afield include Lahemaa National Park and Tartu.

Tallinn Traveller Tours WALKING, CYCLING

(☎58374800; www.traveller.ee) Entertaining, good-value tours – including a free, two-hour Old Town walking tour. There are also ghost tours (€15), pub crawls (€20), bike tours (€16) and day trips as far afield as Riga (€49).

City Bike CYCLING, WALKING

(☎5111819; www.citybike.ee; Uus 33) Has a great range of Tallinn tours, by bike or on foot, as well as trips to Lahemaa National Park (€49). Two-hour cycling tours (€13 to €16) of Tallinn run year-round and include Kadriorg and Pirita.

Tallinn City Tour BUS

(☎627 9080; www.citytour.ee; 24hr-pass adult/child €19/16) Runs red double-decker buses that give you quick, easy, hop-on, hop-off access to the city's top sights. A recorded audio tour accompanies the ride. Buses leave from Mere pst, just outside Old Town.

Sleeping

Old Town

★**Tallinn Backpackers** HOSTEL €

(☎644 0298; www.tallinnbackpackers.com; Olevimägi 11; dm €12-15; @ 📶) In an ideal Old Town location, this place has a global feel and a roll-call of traveller-happy features: free wi-fi and lockers, cheap dinners, a foosball table – one dorm even has it's own sauna! There's also a regular roster of pub crawls and day trips to nearby attractions.

Tabinoya HOSTEL €

(☎632 0062; www.tabinoya.com; Nunne 1; dm/s/d from €13/30/40; @ 📶) The Baltic's first Japanese-run hostel occupies the two top floors of an old building, with dorms and a communal lounge at the top, and spacious private rooms, a kitchen and a sauna below.

Hotel Cru HOTEL €€

(☎611 7600; www.cruhotel.eu; Viru 8; s/d from €100/135; 📶) Behind its pretty powder-blue facade, this boutique 14th-century offering has richly furnished rooms with plenty of original features (timber beams and stone walls) scattered along a rabbit warren of corridors. The cheapest are a little snug.

Old House Apartments APARTMENTS €€

(☎641 1464; www.oldhouseapartments.ee; Rataskaevu 16; apt from €85; P 📶) Old House is an understatement for this wonderful 14th-century merchant's house. It's been split into eight beautifully furnished apartments (including a spacious two-bedroom one with traces of a medieval painted ceiling). There are a further 21 apartments scattered around Old Town in similar buildings, although the quality and facilities vary widely.

Villa Hortensia APARTMENTS €€

(☎5046113; www.hoov.ee; Vene 6; s/d from €45/65; 📶) Situated in the sweet, cobbled Masters'

Courtyard, Hortensia has four split-level studio apartments with kitchenettes and access to a shared communal lounge, but the two larger apartments are the real treats, with balconies and loads of character.

★ **Hotel Telegraaf** HOTEL €€€
(☎600 0600; www.telegraafhotel.com; Vene 9; s/d from €145/165; P ❄ ☎ ≋) This upmarket hotel, in a converted 19th-century former telegraph station, delivers style in spades. It boasts a spa, a pretty courtyard, an acclaimed restaurant, swanky decor and smart, efficient service.

City Centre

★ **Euphoria** HOSTEL €
(☎58373602; www.euphoria.ee; Roosikrantsi 4; dm/r from €12/40; P @ ☎) So laid-back it's almost horizontal, this hostel, just south of Old Town, is an entertaining place to stay with a palpable sense of traveller community – especially if you like hookah pipes and impromptu late-night jam sessions (pack earplugs if you don't).

★ **Yoga Residence** APARTMENTS €€
(☎5021477; http://yogaresidence.eu; Pärnu mnt 32; apt from €75; ☎) It's a strange name for what's basically a block of very modern, fresh and well-equipped apartments, a short stroll from Old Town. You can expect friendly staff, a kitchenette and, joy of joys, a washing machine. There is a second block in an older building north of Old Town.

Hotell Palace HOTEL €€
(☎680 6655; www.tallinnhotels.ee; Vabaduse Väljak 3; s/d from €115/125; ❄ @ ☎ ≋) A recent renovation has swept through this architecturally interesting 1930s hotel, leaving comfortable, tastefully furnished rooms in its wake. It's directly across the road from Freedom Sq and Old Town, and the complex includes an indoor pool, spa, sauna and small gym.

Nordic Hotel Forum HOTEL €€€
(☎622 2900; www.nordichotels.eu; Viru väljak 3; r from €135; P @ ☎ ≋) The Forum shows surprising personality for a large, business-style hotel – witness the artwork on the hotel's facade and the trees on the roof. Facilities include saunas and an indoor pool with an 8th-floor view.

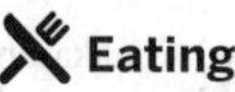

Eating

Old Town

III Draakon CAFE €
(Raekoja plats; mains €1.50-3; ⏰9am-11pm) There's bucketloads of atmosphere at this Lilliputian tavern below the Town Hall, and super-cheap elk soup, sausages and oven-hot pies. The historic setting is amped up – expect costumed wenches with a good line in tourist banter, and beer served in ceramic steins.

Must Puudel CAFE €
(Müürivahe 20; mains €6-9; ⏰9am-11pm Sun-Tue, to 2am Wed-Sat; ☎) Mismatched 1970s furniture, an eclectic soundtrack, courtyard seating, excellent coffee, cooked breakfasts (less than €5), tasty light meals, long opening hours and a name that translates as 'Black Poodle' – yep, this is Old Town's hippest cafe.

Chocolats de Pierre CAFE €
(☎641 8061; www.pierre.ee; Vene 6; snacks €3-5; ⏰8am-midnight) Nestled inside the picturesque Masters' Courtyard and offering respite from Old Town hubbub, this snug cafe is renowned for its delectable (but pricy) handmade chocolates. It also sells pastries and quiches, making it a great choice for a light breakfast or lunch.

★ **Leib** ESTONIAN €€
(☎611 9026; www.leibresto.ee; Uus 31; mains €15-17; ⏰noon-11pm) An inconspicuous gate opens onto a large lawn guarded by busts of Sean Connery and Robbie Burns. Welcome to the former home of Tallinn's Scottish club (really!), where 'simple, soulful food' is served along with homemade *leib* (bread). The slow-cooked meat and grilled fish dishes are exceptional.

★ **Von Krahli Aed** MODERN EUROPEAN €€
(☎626 9088; www.vonkrahl.ee; Rataskaevu 8; mains €6-15; ⏰noon-midnight; ✎) You'll find plenty of greenery on your plate at this rustic, plant-filled restaurant (*aed* means 'garden'). The menu embraces fresh flavours and wins fans by noting organic, gluten-, lactose- and egg-free options.

Chedi ASIAN €€
(☎646 1676; www.chedi.ee; Sulevimägi 1; mains €14-23; ⏰noon-11pm) UK-based chef Alan Yau

(of London's Michelin-starred Hakkasan and Yauatcha) consulted on the menu of sleek, sexy Chedi, and some of his trademark dishes are featured here. The modern pan-Asian food is exemplary – try the delicious crispy duck salad and the artful dumplings.

Olde Hansa ESTONIAN €€
(☎627 9020; www.oldehansa.ee; Vana turg 1; mains €10-40; ⏰10am-midnight) Amid candlelit rooms with peasant-garbed servers labouring beneath large plates of game meats, medieval-themed Olde Hansa is the place to indulge in a gluttonous feast. If it all sounds a bit cheesy, take heart – the chefs have done their research in producing historically authentic, tasty fare.

★Tchaikovsky RUSSIAN €€€
(☎600 0610; www.telegraafhotel.com; Vene 9; mains €23-26; ⏰noon-3pm & 6-11pm Mon-Fri, 1-11pm Sat & Sun) Located in a glassed-in pavilion at the heart of the Hotel Telegraaf, Tchaikovsky offers a dazzling tableau of blinged-up chandeliers, gilt frames and greenery. Service is formal and faultless, as is the classic Franco-Russian menu, all accompanied by live chamber music.

City Centre

Sfäär MODERN EUROPEAN €€
(☎56992200; www.sfaar.ee; Mere pst 6e; mains €9-16; ⏰8am-10pm Mon-Wed, to midnight Thu & Fri, 10am-midnight Sat, 10am-10pm Sun) Chic Sfäär delivers an inventive menu highlighting the best Estonian produce in a warehouse-style setting that's like something out of a Nordic design catalogue. If you just fancy a tipple, the cocktail and wine list won't disappoint.

★Ö MODERN ESTONIAN €€€
(☎661 6150; www.restoran-o.ee; Mere pst 6e; 4-/6-/8-course menu €46/59/76; ⏰6-11pm Mon-Sat) Award-winning Ö (pronounced 'er') has carved a unique space in Tallinn's culinary world, delivering inventive degustation-style menus showcasing seasonal Estonian produce. The understated dining room nicely counterbalances the theatrical cuisine.

Neh MODERN ESTONIAN €€€
(☎602 2222; www.neh.ee; Lootsi 4; mains €22-23; ⏰6pm-midnight Mon-Sat Oct, daily Nov-Feb) Taking seasonal cooking to the extreme, Neh closes completely in summer and heads to the beach – well, Pädaste Manor on Muhu island – where it runs Estonia's best restaurant. In the low season it decamps back to the city, bringing the flavours of the Baltic islands with it.

Kalamaja

Moon RUSSIAN €€
(☎631 4575; www.kohvikmoon.ee; Võrgu 3; mains €10-17; ⏰noon-11pm Mon-Sat & 1-9pm Sun Aug-Jun) Despite its location in an an unlikely lane near the water, the food here is excellent – combining Russian and broader European styles to delicious effect. Save room for dessert.

Drinking & Nightlife

★DM Baar BAR
(www.depechemode.ee; Voorimehe 4; ⏰noon-4am) If you just can't get enough of Depeche Mode, this is the bar for you. The walls are covered with all manner of memorabilia, including pictures of the actual band partying here. And the soundtrack? Do you really need to ask?

Hell Hunt PUB
(www.hellhunt.ee; Pikk 39; ⏰noon-2am; 📶) Billing itself as 'the first Estonian pub', this trusty old trooper boasts an amiable air and a huge beer selection – local and imported. Don't let the menacing-sounding name put you off – it actually means 'gentle wolf'. In summer, it spills onto the little square across the road.

Drink Bar & Grill PUB
(Väike-Karja 8; ⏰noon-11pm Mon-Thu, to 2am Fri & Sat) You know a bar means business when it calls itself Drink. This place takes its beer and cider seriously (its motto is 'no crap on tap'), and offers pub grub and long happy hours.

Kultuuriklubi Kelm BAR
(Vaimu 1; ⏰5pm-3am Mon-Thu, to 6am Fri, 7pm-6am Sat, 7pm-3am Sun) Hidden in a vaulted basement, as all good grungy rock bars should be, this hip little 'culture club' hosts art exhibitions and lots of live music.

Clazz BAR
(www.clazz.ee; Vana turg 2; ⏰6pm-midnight Mon, to 2am Tue-Thu, to 4am Fri, 2pm-4am Sat, 2pm-midnight Sun) Behind the cheesy name (a contraction of 'classy jazz') is a popular lounge bar featuring live music every night of the week (cover charge varies), ranging from jazz to soul, funk, blues and Latin.

X-Baar GAY, LESBIAN
(www.xbaar.ee; Tatari 1; ⏲4pm-1am Sun-Thu, to 3am Fri & Sat) Tallinn holds the monopoly on visible gay life in Estonia and this long-standing bar is the mainstay of the local scene. It's a relaxed kind of place, entertaining a mixed crowd of gay men and lesbians.

☆ Entertainment

Katusekino CINEMA
(www.katusekino.ee; L4 Viru Keskus, Viru Väljak 4/6; ⏲Jun-Aug) In the warmer months, an eclectic program of films (cult classics, as well as interesting new releases) plays on the rooftop of the Viru Keskus shopping centre.

Estonia Concert Hall CLASSICAL MUSIC
(Eesti Kontserdisaal; ☎614 7760; www.concert.ee; Estonia pst 4) The city's biggest classical concerts are held in this double-barrelled venue. It's Tallinn's main theatre and houses the Estonian National Opera and National Ballet.

Shopping

★Katariina Gild HANDICRAFTS
(Katariina käik; Vene 12) Lovely St Catherine's Passage (Katariina Käik) is home to several artisans' studios where you can happily browse ceramics, textiles, patchwork quilts, hats, jewellery, stained glass and beautiful leather-bound books.

Masters' Courtyard HANDICRAFTS
(Meistrite Hoov; Vene 6) Rich pickings here, with the cobbled courtyard not only home to a cosy cafe but also small stores and artisans' workshops selling quality ceramics, glass, jewellery, knitwear, woodwork and candles.

Viru Keskus SHOPPING CENTRE
(www.virukeskus.com; Viru väljak; ⏲9am-9pm) Tallinn's showpiece shopping mall is home to fashion boutiques and a great bookstore (Rahva Raamat). At the rear it connects to the upmarket Kaubamaja department store.

ℹ Information

East-Tallinn Central Hospital (Ida-Tallinna Keskhaigla; ☎620 7040; www.itk.ee; Ravi 18) Offers a full range of services, including a 24-hour emergency room.

Tallinn Tourist Information Centre (☎645 7777; www.tourism.tallinn.ee; Kullassepa 4; ⏲9am-7pm Mon-Fri, to 5pm Sat & Sun May-Aug, 9am-6pm Mon-Fri, to 3pm Sat & Sun Sep-Apr) Brochures, maps, event schedules and other info.

ℹ Getting There & Away

For international connections, see the transport information (p339) at the end of this chapter.

BUS

The **Central Bus Station** (Autobussijaam; ☎12550; Lastekodu 46) is about 2km southeast of Old Town (tram 2 or 4). During the day, buses leave at least hourly for Rakvere (from €3.50, 1½ hours), Tartu (€11, 2½ hours) and Pärnu (from €6.50, two hours). **TPilet** (www.tpilet.ee) has times and prices for all national bus services.

TRAIN

The **Central Train Station** (Balti Jaam; www.elron.ee; Toompuiestee 35) is on the northwestern edge of Old Town. Destinations include Rakvere (€5.50, three daily, 1¼ daily) and Tartu (€10, two hours, eight daily).

ℹ Getting Around

TO/FROM THE AIRPORT

- **Tallinn Airport** (Tallinna Lennujaam; ☎605 8888; www.tallinn-airport.ee; Tartu mnt 101) is 4km from the centre.
- Bus 2 runs every 20 to 30 minutes (6am to around 11pm) from the A Laikmaa stop, opposite the Tallink Hotel, next to Viru Keskus. From the airport, bus 2 will take you to the centre. Buy tickets from the driver (€1.60); journey time depends on traffic but rarely exceeds 20 minutes.
- A taxi between the airport and the city centre should cost less than €10.

PUBLIC TRANSPORT

Tallinn has an excellent network of buses, trams and trolleybuses that run from around 6am to 11pm. The major local bus station is on the basement level of Viru Keskus shopping centre, just east of Old Town. Local public transport timetables are online at www.tallinn.ee.

Public transport is free for Tallinn residents. Visitors still need to pay, either with cash (€1.60 for a single journey) or by using the e-ticketing system. Buy a plastic smartcard (€2 deposit) and top up with credit, then validate the card at the start of each journey using the orange card-readers. Fares using the e-ticketing system cost €1.10/3/5 for an hour/day/three days.

TAXI

Taxis are plentiful, but each company sets its own fare. The base fare ranges from €2 to €5, followed by 50c to €1 per kilometre. To avoid suprises, try **Krooni Takso** (☎1212; www.

kroonitakso.ee; base fare €2.50, per km 55c) or **Reval Takso** (☎1207; www.reval-takso.ee; base fare €2.30, per km 50c).

LAHEMAA NATIONAL PARK

The perfect country retreat from the capital, Lahemaa takes in a stretch of coast indented with peninsulas and bays, plus 475 sq km of pine-fresh forested hinterland. Visitors are looked after with cosy guesthouses, remote seaside campgrounds and a network of pine-scented forest trails.

Sights

★Palmse Manor HISTORIC BUILDING
(www.palmse.ee; adult/child €6/4; ⏰10am-7pm) Fully restored Palmse Manor is the showpiece of Lahemaa National Park, housing the visitor centre in its old stables. The pretty manor house (1720, rebuilt in the 1780s) is now a museum containing period furniture and clothing. Other estate buildings have also been restored and put to new use: the distillery houses a hotel, the steward's residence is a guesthouse and the farm labourers' quarters became a tavern.

Sagadi Manor & Forest Museum HISTORIC BUILDING
(☎676 7888; www.sagadi.ee; adult/child €3/2; ⏰10am-6pm May-Sep, by appointment Oct-Apr) This pretty pink-and-white baroque mansion was completed in 1753 and has been restored. The gardens are glorious (and free to visit), with the requisite lake, numerous modern sculptures, an arboretum and an endless view down a grand avenue of trees. The house ticket includes admission to the neighbouring Forest Museum, devoted to the forestry industry and the park's flora and fauna.

Sleeping & Eating

Toomarahva Turismitalu GUESTHOUSE €
(☎5050850; www.toomarahva.ee; Altja; r from €40; 📶) This farmstead comprises thatch-roofed wooden buildings and a garden full of flowers and sculptures. The converted stables contain four private rooms – two of which share bathrooms and one with kitchen facilities – or you can doss down in the hay in summer for €5. Signage is minimal – it's located opposite Swing Hill.

Sagadi Manor HOTEL, HOSTEL €€
(☎676 7888; www.sagadi.ee; Sagadi; dm €15, s/d from €60/80; @📶) Waking up within the rarefied confines of Sagadi Manor, with its gracious gardens at your disposal, is a downright lovely experience. There's a tidy 31-bed hostel in the former estate manager's house, while the hotel has fresh and comfortable rooms in the whitewashed stables block across the lawn.

★Altja Kõrts ESTONIAN €
(Altja; mains €6-9; ⏰noon-8pm) Set in a thatched, wooden building with a large terrace, this uber-rustic place serves delicious plates of traditional fare (baked pork with sauerkraut etc) to candlelit wooden tables. It's extremely atmospheric and a lot of fun.

Information

Lahemaa National Park Visitor Centre
(☎329 5555; www.lahemaa.ee; Palmse Manor; ⏰9am-6pm daily May-Oct, 9am-5pm Mon-Fri Oct-Apr) This excellent centre stocks the essential map of Lahemaa, as well as information on hiking trails, accommodation, island exploration and guiding services. It's worth starting your park visit with the free 17-minute film entitled *Lahemaa – Nature and Man*.

Getting There & Away

Hiring a car will give you the most flexibility, or you could take a tour from Tallinn. Exploring the park using public transport requires patience and time. Buses to destinations within the park leave from the town of Rakvere (connected by bus to Tallinn, Tartu and Pärnu), which is 35km southeast of Palmse. Once you've arrived in the park, bike hire is easy to arrange.

TARTU

POP 98,500

Tartu was the cradle of Estonia's 19th-century national revival and lays claim to being the nation's cultural capital. Locals talk about a special Tartu *vaim* (spirit), created by the time-stands-still feel of its wooden houses and stately buildings, and by the beauty of its parks and riverfront. It's also Estonia's premier university town, with students making up nearly one fifth of the population – guaranteeing a vibrant nightlife for a city of its size.

Sights

As the major repository of Estonia's cultural heritage, Tartu has an abundance of first-rate museums. We've listed the best of them here, but enquire at the tourist office if your interests extend to, say, farm machinery.

Old Town

Raekoja plats SQUARE

Tartu's main square is lined with grand buildings and echoes with the chink of glasses and plates in summer. The centrepiece is the late-18th-century **Town Hall**, topped by a tower and weather vane, and fronted by a statue of students kissing under a spouting umbrella.

Tartu Art Museum GALLERY

(Tartu Kunstimuuseum; www.tartmus.ee; Raekoja plats 18; adult/student €3/2; 11am-6pm Wed & Fri-Sun, to 9pm Thu) If you're leaving one of the plaza's pubs and you're not sure whether you're seeing straight, don't use this building as your guide. Foundations laid partially over an old town wall have given a pronounced lean to this, the former home of Colonel Barclay de Tolly (1761–1818) – an exiled Scot who distinguished himself in the Russian army. It now contains an engrossing gallery spread over three levels, the lowest of which is given over to temporary exhibitions.

Tartu University UNIVERSITY

(Tartu Ülikool; www.ut.ee; Ülikooli 18) Fronted by six Doric columns, the impressive main building of the university was built between 1803 and 1809. The university itself was founded in 1632 by the Swedish king Gustaf II Adolf (Gustavus Adolphus) to train Lutheran clergy and government officials. It was modelled on Uppsala University in Sweden.

University Art Museum MUSEUM

(Ülikooli Kunstimuuseum; www.kunstimuuseum.ut.ee; Ülikooli 18; adult/child €3/2; 10am-6pm Mon-Sat May-Sep, 11am-5pm Mon-Fri Oct-Apr) Within the main university building, this collection comprises mainly plaster casts of ancient Greek sculptures made in the 1860s and 1870s, along with an Egyptian mummy. The rest of the collection was evacuated to Russia in 1915 and has never returned. Admission includes entry to the graffiti-covered attic **lock-up**, where students were held in solitary confinement for various infractions.

St John's Church CHURCH

(Jaani Kirik; www.jaanikirik.ee; Jaani 5; steeple adult/child €2/1.50; 10am-6pm Tue-Sat) Dating to at least 1323, this imposing red-brick Lutheran church is unique for the rare terracotta sculptures placed in niches around its exterior and interior (look up). It lay in ruins and was left derelict following a Soviet bombing raid in 1944 and wasn't fully restored until 2005. Climb the 135 steps of the 30m steeple for a bird's-eye view of Tartu.

★Toy Museum MUSEUM

(Mänguasjamuuseum; www.mm.ee; Lutsu 8; adult/child €5/4; 11am-6pm Wed-Sun) A big hit with the under-eight crowd (and you won't see too many adults anxious to leave), this is a great place to while away a few rainy hours. Set in a late 18th-century building, this excellent museum showcases dolls, model trains, rocking horses, toy soldiers and tons of other desirables. It's all geared to be nicely interactive, with exhibits in pull-out drawers and a kids' playroom.

Toomemägi

Rising to the west of the town hall, Toomemägi (Cathedral Hill) is the original reason for Tartu's existence, functioning on and off as a stronghold from around the 5th or 6th century. It's now a tranquil park, with walking paths meandering through the trees and a pretty-as-a-picture **rotunda** which serves as a summertime cafe.

LOCAL KNOWLEDGE

STUDENT LIFE IN TARTU

The world over, students gravitate to cheap meals and booze, and in Tartu it's no different.

Genialistide Klubi (www.genklubi.ee; behind Lai 37, enter from Magasini) The Genialists' Club is an all-purpose, grungy 'subcultural establishment' that's simultaneously a bar, cafe, alternative nightclub, live-music venue, cinema, specialist Estonian CD store and, just quietly, the hippest place in Tartu.

Möku (Rüütli 18; 6pm-3am;) A popular student hangout, this tiny cellar bar spills out onto the pedestrian-only street on summer nights.

Zavood (Lai 30; 7pm-5am) This battered cellar bar attracts an alternative, down-to-earth crowd with its inexpensive drinks and lack of attitude. Student bands sometimes play here.

Tartu University Museum MUSEUM
(Tartu Ülikool Muuseum; www.muuseum.ut.ee; Lossi 25; adult/child €4/free; ⌚10am-6pm Tue-Sun May-Sep, 11am-5pm Wed-Sun Oct-Apr) Atop Toomemägi are the ruins of a Gothic cathedral, originally built by German knights in the 13th century. It was substantially rebuilt in the 15th century, despoiled during the Reformation in 1525, used as a barn, and partly rebuilt between 1804 and 1807 to house the university library, which is now a museum. Inside you'll find a reconstructed autopsy chamber and other exhibits chronicling student life.

Other Neighbourhoods

★**Science Centre AHHAA** MUSEUM
(Teaduskeskus AHHAA; www.ahhaa.ee; Sadama 1; adult/child €12/9; ⌚10am-7pm) Head under the dome for a whizz-bang series of interactive exhibits which are liable to bring out the mad scientist in kids and adults alike. Allow at least a couple of hours for button pushing, water squirting and knob twiddling. And you just haven't lived until you've set a tray of magnetised iron filings 'dancing' to Bronski Beat's *Smalltown Boy*. Upstairs there's a nightmarish collection of pickled organs and deformed foetuses courtesy of the university's medical faculty.

KGB Cells Museum MUSEUM
(KGB kongide muuseum; http://linnamuuseum.tartu.ee; Riia mnt 15b (entrance on Pepleri); adult/child €4/2; ⌚11am-4pm Tue-Sat) What do you do when a formerly nationalised building is returned to you with cells in the basement and a fearsome reputation? In this case, the family donated the basement to the Tartu City Museum, which created this sombre and highly worthwhile exhibition. Chilling in parts, the displays give a fascinating rundown on deportations, life in the Gulag camps, the Estonian resistance movement and what went on in these former KGB headquarters, known as the 'Grey House'.

Estonian National Museum MUSEUM
(Eesti Rahva Muuseum; www.erm.ee; Kuperjanovi 9; all/permanent collections €4/3; ⌚11am-6pm Tue-Sun) Focused on Estonian life and traditions, this sweet little museum's permanent displays are split into four main themes: Everyday Life, Holidays & Festivals, Regional Folk Culture and 'To be an Estonian'. There are ambitious plans afoot to create a massive new home for the museum at Raadi Manor on the outskirts of town by October 2016.

Sleeping

Terviseks HOSTEL €
(☎5655382; www.terviseksbbb.com; top floor, Raekoja plats 10; dm €15-17, s/d €22/40; @📶) In a perfect main-square location, this excellent 'backpacker's bed and breakfast' offers dorms (maximum four beds, no bunks), private rooms, a full kitchen and lots of switched-on info about the happening places in town.

★**Antonius Hotel** HOTEL €€
(☎737 0377; www.hotelantonius.ee; Ülikooli 15; s/d from €79/99; ❄📶) Sitting plumb opposite the main university building, this first-rate 18-room boutique hotel is loaded with antiques and period features. Breakfast is served in the vaulted cellar and there's a lovely summertime terrace.

Tampere Maja GUESTHOUSE €€
(☎738 6300; www.tamperemaja.ee; Jaani 4; s/d/tr/q from €48/79/99/132; P❄@📶) With strong links to the Finnish city of Tampere (Tartu's sister city), this cosy guesthouse features six warm, light-filled guest rooms in a range of sizes. Breakfast is included and each room has access to cooking facilities. And it wouldn't be Finnish if it didn't offer an authentic sauna (one to four people €13; open to non-guests).

Hotel Tartu HOTEL €€
(☎731 4300; www.tartuhotell.ee; Soola 3; s/d from €49/68; P❄📶) In a handy position across from the bus station and Tasku shopping centre, this hotel offers rooms from the Ikea school of decoration – simple but clean and contemporary. A sauna's available for hire (per hour €25).

Eating & Drinking

Crepp FRENCH €
(Rüütli 16; crepes €4.50; ⌚11am-11pm) Locals love this place. Its warm, stylish decor belies its bargain-priced crepes (of the sweet or savoury persuasion, with great combos like cherry-choc and almonds). It serves tasty salads, too.

★**Antonius** EUROPEAN €€
(☎737 0377; www.hotelantonius.ee; Ülikooli 15; mains €18-22; ⌚6-11pm) Tartu's most upmarket restaurant is within the romantic, candlelit nooks and crannies of the Antonius

Hotel's vaulted cellar, which predates the 19th-century building above it by several centuries. Expect a concise menu of meaty dishes, prepared from the finest Estonian produce.

Meat Market STEAKHOUSE €€
(☎653 3455; www.meatmarket.ee; Küütri 3; mains €13-18; ⊙noon-midnight Mon-Thu, to 2am Fri & Sat, to 9pm Sun) The name says it all, with dishes ranging from elk carpaccio to nose-to-tail Livonian beef, to smoky Azeri-style *shashlyk* (skewered meat, delivered flaming to the table). The vegie accompaniments are excellent, too. It's open late for cocktails.

La Dolce Vita ITALIAN €€
(☎740 7545; www.ladolcevita.ee; Kompanii 10; mains €7-19; ⊙11.30am-11pm) Thin-crust pizzas come straight from the wood-burning oven at this cheerful, family-friendly pizzeria. It's the real deal, with a lengthy menu of bruschetta, pizza, pasta, grills etc and classic casual decor (checked tablecloths, Fellini posters – tick).

Püssirohukelder PUB
(Lossi 28; mains €8-17; ⊙noon-2am Mon-Sat, to midnight Sun) Set in a cavernous 18th-century gunpowder cellar built into the Toomemägi hillside, this boisterous pub serves beer-accompanying snacks and meaty meals under a soaring 10m-high vaulted ceiling. There's regular live music and a large beer garden out front.

Information

Tartu Tourist Information Centre (☎744 2111; www.visittartu.com; Town Hall, Raekoja plats; ⊙9am-6pm Jun-Aug, 9am-5pm Mon-Fri, 10am-2pm Sat & Sun Sep-May) Stocks local maps and brochures, books accommodation and tour guides, and has free internet access.

Getting There & Away

BUS

From the **bus station** (☎12550; Turu 2 – enter from Soola), buses run to and from Tallinn (€11, 2½ hours, at least hourly), Rakvere (€8, 2½ hours, seven daily) and Pärnu (€11, 2¾ hours, at least hourly).

TRAIN

Tartu's beautifully restored **train station** (☎385 7123; www.elron.ee; Vaksali 6) is 1.5km southwest of the old town (at the end of Kuperjanovi street). Eight trains a day make the journey to and from Tallinn (€10, two hours).

PÄRNU

POP 40,000

Local families, young party-goers and German, Swedish and Finnish holidaymakers join together in a collective prayer for sunny weather while strolling the golden-sand beaches, sprawling parks and picturesque historic centre of Pärnu (*pair*-nu), Estonia's premier seaside resort.

The main thoroughfare of the old town is Rüütli, lined with splendid buildings dating back to the 17th century.

Sights

★Pärnu Beach BEACH
Pärnu's long, wide, golden-sand beach – sprinkled with volleyball courts, cafes and tiny changing cubicles – is easily the city's main drawcard. A curving path stretches along the sand, lined with fountains, park benches and an excellent playground. Early-20th-century buildings are strung along Ranna pst, the avenue that runs parallel to the beach. Across the road, the formal gardens of **Rannapark** are ideal for a summertime picnic.

Tallinn Gate GATE
(Tallinna Värav) The typical star shape of the 17th-century Swedish ramparts that surrounded the old town can easily be spotted on a colour map, as most of the pointy bits are now parks. The only intact section, complete with its moat, lies to the west of the centre. Where the rampart meets the western end of Kuninga, it's pierced by this tunnel-like gate that once defended the main road (it headed to the river-ferry crossing and on to Tallinn).

Activities

Tervise Paradiis Veekeskus SWIMMING, SPA
(www.terviseparadiis.ee; Side 14; adult/child 3hr €12/8, day €19/15; ⊙6.30am-10pm) At the far end of the beach, Estonia's largest water park beckons with pools, slides, tubes and other slippery fun. It's a big family-focused draw, especially when bad weather ruins beach plans. It's part of a huge resort complex. Also here are spa treatments, fitness classes and ten-pin bowling.

Hedon Spa DAY SPA
(☎449 9011; www.hedonspa.com; Ranna pst 1; ⊙9am-7pm Mon-Sat, to 2pm Sun) Built in 1927 to house Pärnu's famous mud baths, this

handsome neoclassical building has recently been fully restored and opened as a day spa. All manner of pampering treatments are offered, minus the mud.

Sleeping

In summer it's worth booking ahead; outside high season you should be able to snare a good deal (rates can be up to 50% lower).

Embrace B&B, APARTMENTS €€
(📞58873404; www.embrace.ee; Pardi 30; r from €86; P❄📶) Snuggle up in an old wooden house in a suburban street, close to the beach and water park. Rooms strike a nice balance between antique and contemporary, and there's a set of four modern self-contained apartments in a neighbouring annex.

Villa Johanna GUESTHOUSE €€
(📞443 8370; www.villa-johanna.ee; Suvituse 6; s/d/ste €50/80/100; P📶) Decorated with hanging flowerpots and planter boxes, this pretty place offers comfy pine-lined rooms on a quiet street near the beach. Some rooms have their own balconies. Not much English is spoken.

Villa Ammende HOTEL €€€
(📞447 3888; www.ammende.ee; Mere pst 7; s/d from €165/220; P📶) Luxury abounds in this refurbished 1904 art nouveau mansion, which lords it over handsomely manicured grounds. The gorgeous exterior – looking like one of the cooler Paris metro stops writ large – is matched by an elegant lobby and individually antique-furnished rooms. Rooms in the gardener's house are more affordable but lack a little of the wow factor.

Eating

Piccadilly CAFE €
(Pühavaimu 15; mains €4-7; ⌚10am-6pm Sun, to 8pm Mon-Thu, to midnight Fri & Sat) Piccadilly offers a down-tempo haven for wine-lovers and an extensive range of coffee, tea and hot choc. Savoury options include delicious salads, sandwiches and omelettes, but really it's all about the sweeties, including moreish cheesecake and handmade chocolates.

★Supelsaksad CAFE €€
(📞442 2448; www.supelsaksad.ee; Nikolai 32; mains €9-13; ⌚8am-9pm Sun & Tue-Thu, 9am-11pm Fri & Sat) Looking like it was designed by Barbara Cartland on acid (bright pink and a riot of stripes and prints), this fabulous cafe serves an appealing mix of salads, pastas and meaty mains. If you eat all your vegies, make a beeline for the bountiful cake display.

Trahter Postipoiss RUSSIAN €€
(📞446 4864; www.trahterpostipoiss.ee; Vee 12; mains €14-22; ⌚noon-11pm Sun-Thu, to 2am Fri & Sat) Housed in an 1834 postal building, this rustic tavern has excellent Russian cuisine (ranging from the simple to sophisticated), a convivial crowd and imperial portraits watching over the proceedings. The spacious courtyard opens during summer and there's live music on weekends.

Mahedik CAFE €€
(📞442 5393; www.mahedik.ee; Pühavaimu 20; breakfast €4-6, mains €7-15; ⌚9am-7pm Sun-Thu, 10am-11pm Fri & Sat) The name roughly translates as 'organic-ish', and local, seasonal fare is the focus of this cosy all-day cafe. There are cooked breakfasts, locally caught fish and a divine array of cakes.

Drinking & Nightlife

Sweet Rosie PUB
(Munga 2; ⌚11am-midnight Sun-Thu, to 2am Fri & Sat) Revellers jam into the warm, darkwood interior of this fun Irish pub for a huge beer menu, pub grub, occasional live music and a raucous good time.

Puhvet A.P.T.E.K. BAR
(www.aptek.ee; Rüütli 40; ⌚noon-midnight Sun-Thu, to 3am Fri & Sat) Drop by the old 1930s pharmacy to admire the clever restoration that has turned it into a smooth late-night haunt. Fabulous decor (including original cabinets, vials and bottles) compete for your attention with cocktails and DJs.

Club Sunset CLUB
(www.sunset.ee; Ranna pst 3; ⌚11pm-6am Fri & Sat Jun-Aug) Pärnu's biggest and most famous summertime nightclub has an outdoor beach terrace and a sleek multifloor interior with plenty of nooks for when the dance floor gets crowded. Imported DJs and bands keep things cranked until the early hours.

Information

Pärnu Tourist Information Centre (📞447 3000; www.visitparnu.com; Uus 4; ⌚9am-6pm daily Jun-Aug, 9am-5pm Mon-Fri & 10am-2pm Sat & Sun Sep-May) A very helpful centre stocking maps and brochures, and booking accommodation and rental cars for a small fee. There's a small gallery attached.

Getting There & Away

Pärnu's **bus station** (Ringi 3) is right in the centre of town, with services to/from Tallinn (from €6.50, two hours, at least hourly), Rakvere (from €8.50, 2½ hours, three daily) and Tartu (€11, 2¾ hours, at least hourly).

SURVIVAL GUIDE

Directory A–Z

ACCOMMODATION

In the budget category you'll find hostels, basic guesthouses (many with shared bathrooms) and camping grounds (generally open from mid-May to September). A dorm bed usually costs €12 to €15, and is usually a couple of euro more expensive on the weekends. Midrange options include family-run guesthouses and hotel rooms (private bathroom and breakfast generally included). At the top end there are spa resorts, historic hotels and modern tower blocks catering to the business set.

During the peak tourist season (June to August) you should try to book well in advance, particularly if you're looking for a bed in Tallinn on the weekend. There's a search engine at www.visitestonia.com for all types of accommodation.

GAY & LESBIAN TRAVELLERS

Today's Estonia is a fairly tolerant and safe home to its gay and lesbian citizens, but only Tallinn has any gay venues. Homosexuality was decriminalised in 1992 and since 2001 there has been an equal age of consent for everyone (14 years). In 2014 Estonia became the first former Soviet republic to pass a law recognising same-sex registered partnerships, coming into effect in 2016.

PUBLIC HOLIDAYS

New Year's Day 1 January
Independence Day 24 February
Good Friday March/April
Easter Sunday March/April
May Day 1 May
Pentecost Seventh Sunday after Easter; May/June

SLEEPING PRICE RANGES

The following price range codes refer to a high-season double room:

€ less than €50

€€ €50 to €140

€€€ more than €140

COUNTRY FACTS

Area 45,226 sq km

Capital Tallinn

Country Code ☎372

Currency Euro (€)

Emergency ambulance & fire ☎112, police ☎110

Language Estonian

Money ATMs all over

Visas Not required for citizens of the EU, USA, Canada, New Zealand and Australia

Victory Day (1919; Battle of Võnnu) 23 June
Jaanipäev (St John's Day; Midsummer's Day) 24 June
Day of Restoration of Independence 20 August
Christmas Eve 24 December
Christmas Day 25 December
Boxing Day 26 December

TELEPHONE

There are no area codes in Estonia. All landline numbers have seven digits; mobile numbers have seven or eight digits, beginning with ☎5.

TOURIST INFORMATION

Most major destinations have tourist offices. The national tourist board has an excellent website (www.visitestonia.com).

VISAS

EU citizens can spend unlimited time in Estonia, while citizens of Australia, Canada, Japan, New Zealand, the USA and many other countries can enter visa-free for a maximum 90-day stay over a six-month period. Travellers holding a Schengen visa do not need an additional Estonian visa. For information, see the website of the **Estonian Ministry of Foreign Affairs** (www.vm.ee).

Getting There & Away

AIR

Fourteen European airlines fly in to Tallinn Airport, including the national carrier **Estonian Air** (www.estonian-air.ee). There are also direct flights from Helsinki to Tartu Airport.

LAND

Bus

Ecolines (☎606 2217; www.ecolines.net) Seven daily buses on the Rīga–Parnu–Tallinn route (€17, four to 4¾ hours) and two on the Rīga–Tartu route (€7, four hours).

EATING PRICE RANGES

These price ranges indicate the average cost of a main course. It's common to tip up to 10% for good service.

€ less than €10

€€ €10 to €20

€€€ more than €20

Lux Express & Simple Express (☎680 0909; www.luxexpress.eu) Eleven daily buses between Tallinn and Rīga, some of which stop in Pärnu; two continue on to Vilnius. Also nine daily buses between Tallinn and St Petersburg, and four daily buses on the St Petersburg–Tartu–Rīga route.

Train

Go Rail (☎in Estonia 631 0044; www.gorail.ee) has two daily trains between Tallinn and St Petersburg (€34, 6½ hours) and an overnight between Tallinn and Moscow (from €86, 15¼ hours). There are no direct trains to Latvia; you'll need to change at Valga.

SEA

Eckerö Line (www.eckeroline.fi; Passenger Terminal A, Varasadam; adult/child/car from €19/15/19) Twice-daily car ferry from Helsinki to Tallinn (2½ hours).

Linda Line (☎699 9333; www.lindaliini.ee; Linnahall Terminal) Small, passenger-only hydrofoils travel between Helsinki and Tallinn at least two times daily from late March to late December (from €25, 1½ hours). Weather dependent.

Tallink (☎640 9808; www.tallink.com; Terminal D, Lootsi 13) Four to seven car ferries daily between Helsinki and Tallinn (passenger/vehicle from €31/26). The huge *Baltic Princess* takes 3½ hours; newer high-speed ferries take two hours. They also have an overnight ferry between Stockholm and Tallinn, via the Åland islands (passenger/vehicle from €39/62, 18 hours).

Viking Line (☎666 3966; www.vikingline.com; Terminal A, Varasadam; passenger/vehicle from €29/26) Two daily car ferries between Helsinki and Tallinn (2½ hours).

Getting Around

BUS

Buses are a good option domestically, as they're more frequent than trains and cover many destinations not serviced by the limited rail network. **TPilet** (www.tpilet.ee) has schedules and prices for all services.

TRAIN

Trains are handy for getting between Tallinn and Tartu, but services to Pärnu are extremely limited.

ESSENTIAL FOOD & DRINK

Estonian gastronomy mixes Nordic, Russian and German influences, and prizes local and seasonal produce.

- **Pork and potatoes** The traditional stodgy standbys, prepared a hundred different ways.
- **Other favourites** Include black bread, sauerkraut, black pudding, smoked meat and fish, creamy salted butter and sour cream, which is served with almost everything.
- **Desserts** On the sweet side, you'll find delicious chocolates, marzipan and cakes.
- **Seasonal** In summer, berries enter the menu in both sweet and savoury dishes, while everyone goes crazy for forest mushrooms in the autumn.
- **Favourite drinks** *Õlu* (beer) is the favourite alcoholic drink. Popular brands include Saku and A Le Coq, and aficionados should seek out the product of the local microbreweries such as Tallinn's Põhjala. Other tipples include vodka (Viru Valge and Saremaa are the best-known local brands) and Vana Tallinn, a syrupy sweet liqueur, also available in a cream version.

Finland

Includes ➡

Best Places to Eat

- Olo (p347)
- Musta Lammas (p354)
- Smor (p350)
- Hietalahden Kauppahalli (p346)

Best Places to Stay

- Lossiranta Lodge (p353)
- Dream Hostel (p351)
- Hotel Fabian (p346)

Why Go?

There's something pure, vital and exciting in the Finnish air; an invitation to get out and active year-round. How about a post-sauna dip through the ice under the majestic aurora borealis (Northern Lights), after whooshing across the snow behind a team of huskies, for an inspiring winter's day? Hiking or canoeing under the midnight sun through pine forests populated by wolves and bears isn't your typical tanning-oil summer either.

Although socially and economically in the vanguard of nations, large parts of Finland remain gloriously remote; trendsetting modern Helsinki is counterbalanced by vast forested wildernesses.

Nordic peace in lakeside cottages, summer sunshine on convivial beer terraces, avant-garde design, dark melodies and cafes with home-baking aromas are other facets of Suomi seduction. As are the independent, loyal and welcoming Finns, who do their own thing and are much the better for it.

When to Go

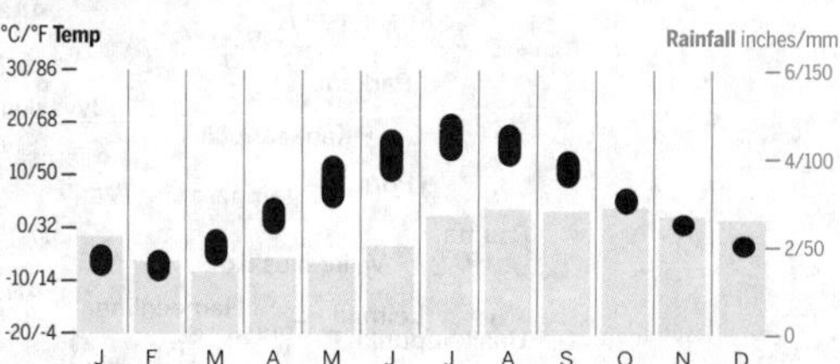

Mar & Apr There's still plenty of snow, but enough daylight to enjoy winter sports.

Jul Everlasting daylight, countless festivals and discounted accommodation.

Sep The stunning *ruska* (autumn colours) season make this prime hiking time up north.

Finland Highlights

1. Immerse yourself in harbourside **Helsinki**, creative melting pot for the latest in Finnish design and nightlife.
2. Marvel at the shimmering lakescapes of handsome **Savonlinna** (p352), and watch top-quality opera in its medieval castle.
3. Cruise Lakeland waterways, gorge on tiny fish, and sweat in the huge smoke sauna at **Kuopio** (p353).
4. Cross the Arctic Circle, hit up the awesome Arktikum museum, and visit Santa in his grotto at **Rovaniemi** (p354).
5. Learn about Sámi culture, go husky-sledding and meet reindeer at **Inari** (p356).

ITINERARIES

One Week

Helsinki demands at least a couple of days and is a good base for a day trip to **Tallinn** (Estonia) or **Porvoo**. In summer head to the **Lakeland** and explore **Savonlinna** and **Kuopio** (catch a lake ferry between them). In winter take an overnight train or budget flight to **Lapland**, visiting Santa, exploring Sámi culture and mushing with huskies. A Helsinki–Savonlinna–Kuopio–Rovaniemi–Helsinki route is a good option.

Two Weeks

Spend a few days in **Helsinki** and **Porvoo**, visit the harbour town of **Turku** and lively **Tampere**. Next stops are **Savonlinna** and **Kuopio** in the beautiful **Lakeland**. Head up to **Rovaniemi**, and perhaps as far north as the Sámi capital **Inari**. You could also fit in a summer festival, some hiking, or a quick cycling trip to **Åland**.

HELSINKI

☎09 / POP 1.1 MILLION (TOTAL URBAN AREA)

It's fitting that harbourside Helsinki, capital of a country with such watery geography, melds so graciously into the Baltic. Half the city seems liquid, and the writhings of the complex coastline include any number of bays, inlets and islands.

Though Helsinki can seem a younger sibling to other Scandinavian capitals, it's the one that went to art school, scorns pop music and works in a cutting-edge studio. The design scene here is legendary, whether you're browsing showroom brands or taking the backstreet hipster trail. The city's gourmet side is also flourishing; new gastro eateries offering locally sourced tasting menus are popping up at dizzying speed.

Sights

Kauppatori SQUARE

The heart of central Helsinki is the harbourside Kauppatori (Market Square), where cruises and ferries leave for archipelago islands. It's completely touristy these days, with reindeer souvenir stands having replaced most market stalls, but there are still some berries and flowers for sale, and adequate cheap food options.

★ Suomenlinna FORTRESS

(Sveaborg; www.suomenlinna.fi) Just a 15-minute ferry ride from the Kauppatori (market square), a visit to Suomenlinna, the 'fortress of Finland', is a Helsinki must-do. Set on a tight cluster of islands connected by bridges, the Unesco World Heritage Site was originally built by the Swedes as Sveaborg in the mid-18th century.

Tuomiokirkko CHURCH

(Lutheran Cathedral; www.helsinginseurakunnat.fi; Unioninkatu 29; ⏲9am-6pm, to midnight Jun-Aug) FREE One of CL Engel's finest creations, the chalk-white neoclassical Lutheran cathedral presides over Senaatintori. Created to serve as a reminder of God's supremacy, its high flight of stairs is now a meeting place for canoodling couples. The spartan, almost mausoleum-like interior has little ornamentation under the lofty dome – apart from an altar painting and three stern statues of Reformation heroes Luther, Melanchthon and Mikael Agricola, looking like they've just marked your theology exam and taken a dim view of your prospects.

★ Ateneum GALLERY

(www.ateneum.fi; Kaivokatu 2; adult/child €12/free; ⏲10am-6pm Tue & Fri, 9am-8pm Wed & Thu, 10am-5pm Sat & Sun) The top floor of Finland's premier art gallery is an ideal crash course in the nation's art. It houses Finnish paintings and sculptures from the 'golden age' of the late 19th century through to the 1950s, including works by Albert Edelfelt, Hugo Simberg, Helene Schjerfbeck, the Von Wright brothers and Pekka Halonen. Pride of place goes to the prolific Akseli Gallen-Kallela's triptych from the *Kalevala,* depicting Väinämöinen's pursuit of the maiden Aino. There's also a small but interesting collection of 19th- and early-20th-century foreign art.

★ Kiasma GALLERY

(www.kiasma.fi; Mannerheiminaukio 2; adult/child €10/free; ⏲10am-5pm Sun & Tue, 10am-8.30pm Wed-Fri, 10am-6pm Sat) Now just one of a series of elegant contemporary buildings in this part of town, curvaceous and quirky

Helsinki

metallic Kiasma, designed by Steven Holl and finished in 1998, is still a symbol of the city's modernisation. It exhibits an eclectic collection of Finnish and international modern art and keeps people on their toes with its striking contemporary exhibitions. The interior, with its unexpected curves and perspectives, is as invigorating as the outside.

Temppeliaukion Kirkko CHURCH

(☎09-2340 6320; www.helsinginseurakunnat.fi; Lutherinkatu 3; ⏰10am-5.45pm Mon-Sat, 11.45am-5.45pm Sun Jun-Aug, to 5pm Sep-May) The Temppeliaukio church, designed by Timo and Tuomo Suomalainen in 1969, remains one of Helsinki's foremost attractions. Hewn into solid stone, it feels close to a Finnish ideal of spirituality in nature – you could be in a rocky glade were it not for the stunning 24m-diameter roof covered in 22km of copper stripping. There are regular concerts, with great acoustics. Opening times vary depending on events, so phone or search for its Facebook page updates. There are fewer groups midweek.

Seurasaaren Ulkomuseo MUSEUM

(Seurasaari Open-Air Museum; www.seurasaari.fi; adult/child €8/2.50; ⏰11am-5pm Jun-Aug, 9am-3pm Mon-Fri, 11am-5pm Sat & Sun late May & early Sep) West of the city centre, this excellent island museum has a collection of historic wooden buildings transferred here from around Finland. There's everything from haylofts to a mansion, parsonage and church, as well as the beautiful giant rowboats used to transport churchgoing communities. Prices and hours refer to entering the buildings themselves, where guides in traditional costume demonstrate folk dancing and crafts. Otherwise, you're free to roam the picturesque wooded island, where there are several cafes.

There are guided tours in English daily at 3pm in summer. The island is also the venue for Helsinki's biggest Midsummer bonfires

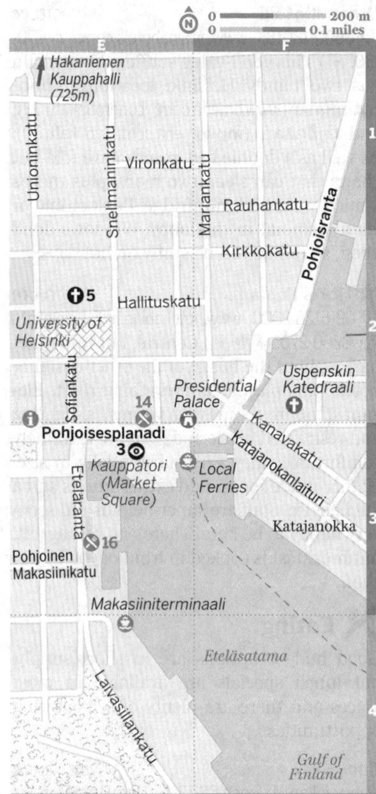

Helsinki

Top Sights

1 Ateneum D2
2 Kiasma C1

Sights

3 Kauppatori E3
4 Temppeliaukion Kirkko A1
5 Tuomiokirkko E2

Sleeping

6 Hostel Erottajanpuisto C3
7 Hotel Fabian D4
8 Hotel Finn C2
9 Hotelli Helka A2
10 Omenahotelli Lönnrotinkatu B3
11 Omenahotelli Yrjönkatu C3

Eating

12 Hietalahden Kauppahalli A4
13 Karl Fazer Café D2
14 Olo E2
15 Salve A4
16 Vanha Kauppahalli E3
17 Zucchini D3

Drinking & Nightlife

18 Bar Loose C3
19 Teerenpeli B2

Entertainment

20 Musiikkitalo B1
21 Tavastia B2

and a popular area for picnicking. From central Helsinki, take bus 24.

Activities

★Kotiharjun Sauna SAUNA
(www.kotiharjunsauna.fi; Harjutorinkatu 1; adult/child €12/6; 2-8pm Tue-Sun, sauna to 9.30pm) This traditional public wood-fired sauna in Kallio dates back to 1928. This type of place largely disappeared with the advent of shared saunas in apartment buildings, but it's a classic experience, where you can also get a scrub down and massage. There are separate saunas for men and women; bring your own towel or rent one (€3). It's a short stroll from Sörnäinen metro station. Closes Sundays June to mid-August.

Tours

There are several cruise companies departing hourly on harbour jaunts (€20 to €25) from the Kauppatori in summer.

An excellent budget tour is to do a circuit of town on **Tram 2** then **Tram 3** or vice versa; pick up the free *Sightseeing on Tram 2/3* brochure as your guide around the city.

Sleeping

Bookings are advisable year-round, as there's nearly always some event or conference on.

★Hostel Academica HOSTEL €
(09-1311 4334; www.hostelacademica.fi; Hietaniemenkatu 14; dm/s/d €28.50/63/75; Jun-Aug; P@) Finnish students live well, so in summer take advantage of this residence, a clean, busy spot packed with features (pool and sauna) and cheery staff. The modern rooms are great, and all come with bar fridges and their own bathrooms. Dorms have only two or three berths so there's no crowding. It's also environmentally sound in its design. Breakfast available. HI discount.

Hostel Erottajanpuisto HOSTEL €
(09-642 169; www.erottajanpuisto.com; Uudenmaankatu 9; dm/s/d €30/60/75; @) Helsinki's most characterful and laid-back hostel

occupies the top floor of a building in a lively street of bars and restaurants. Forget curfews, lockouts, school kids and bringing your own sleeping sheet – this is more like a guesthouse with (crowded) dormitories. Shared bathrooms are new; private rooms offer more peace and there's a great lounge and friendly folk. HI members get 10% off; breakfast is extra.

★Hotelli Helka HOTEL €€
(☎09-613 580; www.helka.fi; Pohjoinen Rautatiekatu 23; s €110-132, d €142-162; P @ 📶) One of the centre's best midrange hotels, the Helka has competent, friendly staff and excellent facilities, including free parking if you can bag one of the limited spots. Best are the rooms, which seem to smell of pine with their Artek furniture, their ice-block bedside lights and prints of rural Suomi scenes above the beds (backlit to give a moody glow).

Hotel Finn HOTEL €€
(☎09-684 4360; www.hotellifinn.fi; Kalevankatu 3B; s €59-119, d €109-199; P 📶) High in a central-city building, this friendly two-floor hotel is upbeat with helpful service and corridors darkly done out in sexy chocolate and red, with art from young Finnish photographers on the walls. Rooms all differ but are bright, with modish wallpaper and tiny bathrooms. Some are furnished with recycled materials. Rates vary widely – it can be a real bargain.

Omenahotelli HOTEL €€
(☎0600-18018; www.omenahotels.com; r €70-130; 📶) This good-value staffless hotel chain has two handy Helsinki locations: **Lönnrotinkatu** (www.omena.com; Lönnrotinkatu 13); and **Yrjönkatu** (www.omena.com; Yrjönkatu 30). As well as a double bed, rooms have fold-out chairs that can sleep two more, plus there's a microwave and minifridge. Book online or via a terminal in the lobby. Windows don't open, so rooms can be stuffy on hot days.

★Hotel Fabian HOTEL €€€
(☎09-6128 2000; www.hotelfabian.fi; Fabianinkatu 7; r €200-270; ❄ @ 📶) Central, but in a quiet part without the bustle of the other designer hotels, this place gets everything right. Elegant standard rooms with whimsical lighting and restrained modern design are extremely comfortable; they vary substantially in size. Higher-grade rooms add extra features and a kitchenette. Staff are super-helpful and seem very happy to be here. There's no restaurant, but breakfast is cooked in front of you by the chef.

Eating

Good budget options are in short supply, but lunch specials are available in most places and there are plenty of self-catering opportunities.

Zucchini VEGETARIAN €
(Fabianinkatu 4; lunch €8-12; ⏲11am-4pm Mon-Fri; 🖉) One of the city's few vegetarian cafes,

HELSINKI'S MARKET HALLS

While food stalls, fresh produce and berries can be found at the Kauppatori (Market Square), the real centre of Finnish market produce is the kauppahalli (market hall). There are three in central Helsinki, and they are fabulous places, with butchers, bakers, fishmongers and delis selling a brilliant range of traditional food. Apart from wandering around photographing the succulent range of smoked fish, they're great for self-catering, picnics and takeaway food, and all have cafes and other casual eateries.

Hakaniemen Kauppahalli (www.hakaniemenkauppahalli.fi; Hämeentie; ⏲8am-6pm Mon-Fri, to 4pm Sat; 🖉) This traditional-style Finnish food market is near the Hakaniemi metro. It's got a good range of produce and a cafe, and textile outlets upstairs. There's a summer market on the square outside.

Hietalahden Kauppahalli (www.hietalahdenkauppahalli.fi; Lönnrotinkatu 34; ⏲8am-6pm Mon-Fri, to 5pm Sat, plus 10am-4pm Sun Jun-Aug; 🖉) This renovated market at Hietalahti has a fabulous range of food stalls and eateries, including enticing cafes with upstairs seating at each end. Take tram 6.

Vanha Kauppahalli (www.vanhakauppahalli.fi; Eteläranta 1; ⏲8am-6pm Mon-Sat; 🖉) Alongside the harbour, this is Helsinki's classic market hall. Built in 1889 and recently renovated, some of it is touristy these days (reindeer kebabs?), but it's still a traditional Finnish market.

this is a top-notch lunchtime spot; queues out the door are not unusual. Piping-hot soups banish winter chills, and fresh-baked quiche on the sunny terrace out the back is a summer treat. For lunch, you can choose soup, salad or hot dishes.

Karl Fazer Café CAFE €

(www.fazer.fi; Kluuvikatu 3; light meals €6-11; 7.30am-10pm Mon-Fri, 9am-10pm Sat, 10am-6pm Sun;) This classic cafe can feel a little cavernous, but it's the flagship for the mighty chocolate empire of the same name. The cupola famously reflects sound, so locals say it's a bad place to gossip. It is ideal, however, for buying Fazer confectionery, fresh bread, salmon or shrimp sandwiches or enjoying the towering sundaes or slabs of cake. Good special-diets options.

★Kuu FINNISH €€

(09-2709 0973; www.ravintolakuu.fi; Töölönkatu 27; mains €19-30; 11.30am-midnight Mon-Fri, 2pm-midnight Sat, 2-10pm Sun) Tucked away on a corner behind the Crowne Plaza hotel on Mannerheimintie, this is an excellent choice for both traditional and modern Finnish fare. The short menu is divided between the two; innovation and classy presentation drive the contemporary dishes, while quality ingredients and exceptional flavour are keys to success throughout. Wines are very pricey, but at least there are some interesting choices.

Salve FINNISH €€

(010-766 4280; www.ravintolasalve.fi; Hietalahdenranta 11; mains €19-27; 10am-midnight Mon-Sat, 10am-11pm Sun) Down by the water in the west of town, this centenarian establishment has long been a favourite of nautical types, and has appropriately high-seas décor, with paintings of noble ships on the walls. They serve great Finnish comfort food like meatballs, fried Baltic herring and steaks in substantial quantities. The atmosphere is warm and the service kindly.

★Olo MODERN FINNISH €€€

(010-3206250; http://olo-ravintola.fi; Pohjoisesplanadi 5; lunch €53, degustations €89-137, with drinks €224-292; 11.30am-3pm Mon, 11.30am-3pm & 6pm-midnight Tue-Fri, 6pm-midnight Sat) Thought of by many as Helsinki's best restaurant, Olo occupies smart new premises in a handsome 19th-century harbourside mansion. It's at the forefront of modern-Suomi cuisine, and its memorable degustation menus incorporate both the forage ethos and a little molecular gastronomy. The shorter 'journey' turns out to be quite a long one, with numerous small culinary jewels. Book a few weeks ahead.

Drinking & Nightlife

The city centre is full of bars and clubs. For the cheapest beer in Helsinki (€3 to €4 a pint), hit working-class Kallio (near Sörnäinen metro station), north of the centre.

★Teerenpeli PUB

(www.teerenpeli.com; Olavinkatu 2; noon-2am Mon-Thu, noon-3am Fri & Sat, 3pm-midnight Sun;) Get away from the Finnish lager mainstream with this excellent pub right by Kamppi bus station. It serves very tasty ales, stouts and berry ciders from its microbrewery in Lahti, in a long, split-level place with romantic low lighting, intimate tables and an indoor smokers' patio. The highish prices keep it fairly genteel for this zone.

Bar Loose CLUB

(www.barloose.com; Annankatu 21; 4pm-2am Tue, 4pm-4am Wed-Sat, 6pm-4am Sun;) The opulent blood-red interior and comfortably cosy seating seem too stylish for a rock bar, but this is what this is, with portraits of guitar heroes lining one wall and an eclectic mix of people filling the upstairs, served by two bars. Downstairs is a club area, with live music more nights than not and DJs spinning everything from metal to mod/retro classics.

Entertainment

★Musiikkitalo CONCERT VENUE

(www.musiikkitalo.fi; Mannerheimintie 13) As cool and crisp as a gin and tonic on a glacier, this striking modern building is a great addition to central Helsinki. The interior doesn't disappoint either – the main auditorium, visible from the foyer, has stunning acoustics. There are regular classical concerts, and prices are kept low, normally around €20. The bar is a nice place to hang out for a drink.

Tavastia LIVE MUSIC

(www.tavastiaklubi.fi; Urho Kekkosenkatu 4; 8pm-1am Sun-Thu, 8pm-3am Fri, 8pm-4am Sat) One of Helsinki's legendary rock venues, this attracts both up-and-coming local acts and bigger international groups. There's a band every night of the week. Also check out what's on at Semifinal, the venue next door.

WORTH A TRIP

PORVOO

Finland's second-oldest town is an ever-popular day trip or weekender from Helsinki. Porvoo (Swedish: Borgå) officially became a town in 1380, but even before that it was an important trading post. The town's fabulous historic centre includes the famous brick-red former warehouses along the river that once stored goods bound for destinations across Europe. During the day, Old Town craft shops are bustling with visitors, but staying on a weeknight will mean you could have the place more or less to yourself. The old painted buildings are spectacular in the setting sun.

Buses depart for Porvoo from Helsinki's Kamppi bus station every 30 minutes or so (€11.80, one hour).

Shopping

Helsinki is a design epicentre, from fashion to the latest furniture and homewares. Central but touristy Esplanadi has the chic boutiques of Finnish classics. The most intriguing area to browse is nearby Punavuori, with a great retro-hipster vibe and numerous boutiques, studios and galleries to explore. A couple of hundred of these are part of **Design District Helsinki** (www.designdistrict.fi), whose invaluable map you can find at the tourist office.

Information

Internet access at public libraries is free. Large parts of the city centre have free wi-fi.

Helsinki City Tourist Office (☎09-3101 3300; www.visithelsinki.fi; Pohjoisesplanadi 19; ⌚9am-8pm Mon-Fri, 9am-6pm Sat & Sun mid-May–mid-Sep, 9am-6pm Mon-Fri, 10am-4pm Sat & Sun mid-Sep–mid-May) Busy multilingual office with a great quantity of information on the city. Also has an office at the airport (Terminal 2, Helsinki-Vantaa airport; ⌚10am-8pm May-Sep, 10am-6pm Oct-Apr).

HSL/HRT (www.hsl.fi) Public-transport information and journey planner.

Getting There & Away

AIR

There are direct flights to Helsinki-Vantaa Airport (p359), Finland's main air terminus, from many major European cities and several intercontinental ones. The airport is at Vantaa, 19km north of Helsinki.

Between them, **Finnair** (☎0600-140140; www.finnair.fi) and cheaper **FlyBe** (www.flybe.com) cover 18 Finnish cities, usually at least once per day.

BOAT

Ferries (p360) travel to Sweden (via the Åland archipelago), Estonia, Russia and Germany. There are many services, including fast ferries, to Tallinn, Estonia (p323), which is a popular day trip.

BUS

Kamppi bus station (www.matkahuolto.fi) has services departing to all of Finland. OnniBus (p359) runs budget routes to several Finnish cities from a stop outside Kiasma: book online in advance for the best prices.

TRAIN

Helsinki's **train station** (Rautatieasema; www.vr.fi) is central, linked to the metro (Rautatientori stop) and a short walk from Kamppi bus station.

The train is the fastest and cheapest way to get from Helsinki to major Finnish centres; there are also daily trains to Russia.

Getting Around

TO/FROM THE AIRPORT

Bus 615/620 (€5, 30 to 45 minutes, 5am to midnight) shuttles between Helsinki-Vantaa Airport (platform 21) and platform 3 at Rautatientori next to Helsinki's train station.

Faster Finnair buses depart from Elielinaukio platform 30 on the other side of Helsinki's train station (€6.30, 30 minutes, every 20 minutes, 5am to midnight).

There's a new airport–city rail link due to open in late 2015.

BICYCLE

With a flat inner city and well-marked cycling paths, Helsinki is ideal for cycling. Get hold of a copy of the Helsinki cycling map at the tourist office.

LOCAL TRANSPORT

HSL (www.hsl.fi) operates buses, metro, local trains, trams and the Suomenlinna ferry. A one-hour ticket (with unlimited transfers) for any transport costs €3 when purchased on board, or €2.50 (€2.20 for trams) when purchased in advance. Day or multiday tickets (per 24/48/72 hours €8/12/16) are worthwhile. Buy tickets at Rautatientori metro station, R-kioskis and the tourist office.

TURKU

☎02 / POP 182,500

Turku is Finland's oldest town and former capital, but today it's a modern maritime city, brimming with museums and boasting a robust harbourside castle and magnificent cathedral. Its heart and soul is the lovely Aurajoki, a broad ribbon spilling into the Baltic Sea harbour, lined with riverboat bars and restaurants.

Sights

★Turun Tuomiokirkko CATHEDRAL

(Turku Cathedral; ☎02-261-7100; www.turunseurakunnat.fi; cathedral free, museum adult/child €2/1; ⏲cathedral & museum 9am-8pm mid-Apr–mid-Sep, 9am-7pm mid-Sep–mid-Apr) The 'mother church' of Finland's Lutheran faith, Turku Cathedral towers over the town. Consecrated in 1300, the colossal brick Gothic building was rebuilt many times over the centuries after damaging fires.

Upstairs, a small **museum** traces the stages of the cathedral's construction, and contains medieval sculptures and religious paraphernalia.

Free **summer organ concerts** take place at 8pm Tuesday and 2pm Wednesday. English-language services are held at 4pm every Sunday (except the last of the month) year-round.

Turun Linna CASTLE

(Turku Castle; ☎02-262-0300; www.turunlinna.fi; Linnankatu 80; adult/child €9/5, guided tours €2; ⏲10am-6pm daily Jun-Aug, 10am-6pm Tue-Sun Sep-May) Founded in 1280 at the mouth of the Aurajoki, mammoth Turku Castle is easily Finland's largest. Highlights include two dungeons and sumptuous banqueting halls, as well as a fascinating **historical museum** of medieval Turku in the castle's Old Bailey. Models depict the castle's growth from a simple island fortress to a Renaissance palace. Guided tours in English run several times daily from June to August.

★Aboa Vetus & Ars Nova MUSEUM, GALLERY

(☎020-718 1640; www.aboavetusarsnova.fi; Itäinen Rantakatu 4-6; adult/child €8/5.50; ⏲11am-7pm; 👪) Art and archaeology unite here under one roof. **Aboa Vetus** (Old Turku) draws you underground to Turku's medieval streets, showcasing some of the 37,000 artefacts unearthed from the site (digs still continue). Back in the present, **Ars Nova** presents contemporary art exhibitions. The themed **Turku Biennaali** (www.turkubiennaali.fi) takes place here each summer in odd numbered years.

Opening to a grassy courtyard, the museums' cafe, Aula, hosts Sunday jazz brunches and Thursday night DJ sessions from June to August.

Festivals & Events

Ruisrock MUSIC

(www.ruisrock.fi; 1-/3-day ticket €78/128) For three days in July, Finland's oldest and largest annual rock festival – held since 1969 and attracting 100,000-strong crowds – takes over Ruissalo island.

Sleeping

Laivahostel Borea HOSTEL €

(☎040-843 6611; www.msborea.fi; Linnankatu 72; s €49, d €78-105.50, tr €102, q €124; 📶) Built in Sweden in 1960, the enormous passenger ship SS *Bore* is docked outside the Forum Marinum museum, just 500m northeast of the ferry terminal. It now contains an award-winning HI-affiliated hostel with vintage ensuite cabins. Most are squishy but if you want room to spread out, higher-priced doubles have a lounge area. Rates include a morning sauna.

★Park Hotel BOUTIQUE HOTEL €€

(☎02-273 2555; www.parkhotelturku.fi; Rauhankatu 1; s €89-124, d €115-162; @📶) Overlooking a hilly park, this art nouveau building is a genuine character, with a resident squawking parrot, Jaakko, and classical music playing in the lift (elevator). Rooms are decorated in a lovably chintzy style and equipped with minibars. Family owners and facilities such as a lounge with pool table make it the antithesis of a chain hotel.

Eating

CaféArt CAFE €

(www.cafeart.fi; Läntinen Rantakatu 5; dishes €2.20-4.80; ⏲10am-7pm Mon-Fri, 10am-5pm Sat, 11am-5pm Sun) With freshly ground coffee, prize-winning baristas, a beautifully elegant interior and artistic sensibility, there's no better place to get your caffeine-and-cake fix. In summer, the terrace spills onto the riverbank, shaded by linden trees.

★Tintå GASTROPUB €€

(☎02-230 7023; www.tinta.fi; Läntinen Rantakatu 9; lunch €8.50-13.50, pizza €12-16, mains €25-30; ⏲11am-midnight Mon, 11am-1am Tue-Thu,

WORTH A TRIP

THE ÅLAND ARCHIPELAGO

The glorious Åland archipelago is a geopolitical anomaly: the islands belong to Finland, speak Swedish, but have their own parliament, flag and stamps.

Åland is the sunniest spot in northern Europe and its sweeping white-sand beaches and flat, scenic cycling routes have great appeal. Outside the lively capital, Mariehamn, a sleepy haze hangs over the islands' tiny villages and finding your own remote beach among the 6500 skerries and islets is surprisingly easy. A lattice of bridges and free cable ferries connect the central islands, while larger car ferries run to the archipelago's outer reaches.

Several car ferries head to Åland, including those that connect Turku and Helsinki with Stockholm. Bikes are the best way to explore and are easily rented.

11am-2am Fri, noon-2am Sat, noon-10pm Sun) With a cosy exposed-brick interior, this riverside wine bar also offers weekday lunches, gourmet pizzas such as asparagus and smoked feta or prosciutto and fig, and classy mains like organic beef skewers with horseradish aioli. Grab a glass of wine and watch the world walking along the shore from the summer terrace.

★**Smor** MODERN FINNISH €€€
(☎02-536 9444; www.smor.fi; Läntinen Rantakatu 3; mains €29, 3-/6-course tasting menu €47/65, incl wine €81/130; ⏲11am-2pm & 4.30-10pm Mon-Fri, 4-10pm Sat) A vaulted cellar lit by flickering candles makes a romantic backdrop for stunning, often organic Modern Finnish cuisine: spinach waffle with quail egg and air-dried pork, roast Åland lamb with cauliflower purée and nettle sauce, or whitefish with bronze fennel. Desserts such as almond pastry with yoghurt pudding and lemon-and-thyme sorbet are equally inspired.

Drinking & Nightlife

Boat Bars BAR
Summer drinking begins on the decks of the boats lining the south bank of the river. Although most serve food, they are primarily floating beer terraces with music and shipboard socialising. If the beer prices make you wince, join locals gathering on the grassy riverbank drinking takeaway alcohol.

Information

Tourist Office (☎02-262 7444; www.visitturku.fi; Aurakatu 4; ⏲8.30am-6pm Mon-Fri, 9am-4pm Sat & Sun) Busy but helpful office with information on the entire region.

Getting There & Away

BOAT

The harbour, southwest of the city centre, has terminals for Tallink/Silja and Viking Line services to Stockholm (11 hours) via the Åland islands.

BUS

From the main **bus terminal** (www.matkahuolto.fi; Aninkaistenkatu 20) there are hourly express buses to Helsinki (€31.50, 2½ hours) and frequent services to Tampere (€25.60, 2½ hours).

TRAIN

Turku's train station is 400m northwest of the city centre; trains also stop at the ferry harbour.

Destinations include the following:

Helsinki (€34, two hours, at least hourly)
Rovaniemi (€91.40, 12 hours, four daily, usually changing in Tampere)
Tampere (€28.20, 1¾ hours, two hourly)

Getting Around

The tourist office hires bikes; ask about the scenic 250km route around the Turku archipelago.

Bus 1 runs between the harbour, kauppatori and airport (€3).

TAMPERE

☎03 / POP 217,400

Scenic Tampere, set between two vast lakes, has a down-to-earth vitality that makes it a favourite for many visitors. Through its centre churns the Tammerkoski rapids, whose grassy banks contrast with the red brick of the imposing fabric mills that once drove the city's economy. Regenerated industrial buildings now house quirky museums, enticing shops, pubs, cinemas and cafes.

Sights

★**Tuomiokirkko** CHURCH
(www.tampereenseurakunnat.fi; Tuomiokirkonkatu 3; ⏲10am-5pm May-Aug, 11am-3pm Sep-Apr) FREE An iconic example of National Romantic architecture, Tampere's cathedral dates from 1907. Hugo Simberg created the

frescoes and stained glass; you'll appreciate that they were controversial. A procession of ghostly childlike apostles holds the 'garland of life', graves and plants are tended by skeletal figures, and a wounded angel is stretchered off by two children. There's a solemn, almost mournful feel; the altarpiece, by Magnus Enckell, is a dreamlike Resurrection in similar style.

Amurin Työläismuseokortteli MUSEUM

(Amuri Museum of Workers' Housing; www.tampere.fi/amuri; Satakunnankatu 49; adult/child €7/3; ⏲10am-6pm Tue-Sun mid-May–mid-Sep) An entire block of 19th-century wooden houses, including 32 apartments, a bakery, a shoemaker, two general shops and a cafe, is preserved here. It's one of the most realistic house-museums in Finland and entertaining backstories (English translation available) give plenty of historical information.

Särkänniemi AMUSEMENT PARK

(www.sarkanniemi.fi; day pass adult/child €37/31; ⏲rides roughly 10am-7pm mid-May–Aug) This promontory amusement park complex has numerous attractions, including dozens of rides, an observation tower, art gallery, aquarium, farm zoo, planetarium and dolphinarium. Buy all-inclusive entry or pay per attraction (€10/5 per adult/child). Opening times are complex; check the website, where you can also get discounted entry. Indoor attractions stay open year-round. Take bus 20 from the train station or central square.

Tours

Trips on Tampere's magnificent lakes are extremely popular in summer. Boats for Näsijärvi leave from Mustalahti quay, while Laukontori quay serves Pyhäjärvi. Book at the tourist office.

Sleeping

★Dream Hostel HOSTEL €

(☎045-236 0517; www.dreamhostel.fi; Åkerlundinkatu 2; dm €24-29, tw/q €79/108; P @ 📶) Sparky, stylish and spacious, this is Finland's best hostel. Helpful staff, super-comfortable wide-berth dorms (unisex and female) in various sizes, a heap of facilities including bike hire, original decor and the right attitude about everything make it a real winner. It's a short walk from the train station in a quiet area.

Upstairs are compact ensuite rooms for those that want hostel atmosphere without sharing a shower.

Scandic Tampere Station HOTEL €€

(☎03-339 8000; www.scandichotels.com; Ratapihankatu 37; s/d €139/159; P ❄ @ 📶 ♿) As the name suggests, this is right by the train station. It's a sleek, beautifully designed place with a minimalist feel to the decor, based on soothing pink and mauve lighting breaking up the chic whites and blacks. Superior-plus rooms are particularly enticing, with dark-wood sauna and balcony, and don't cost a whole lot more. Facilities are modern, service excellent and prices competitive.

There are also several accessible rooms, with motorised beds.

Omenahotelli HOTEL €€

(☎0600-18018; www.omenahotels.com; Hämeenkatu 7; r €60-96; 📶 ♿) On the main drag and very handy for the train station, this receptionless hotel offers the usual comfortable rooms with twin beds, a microwave, a kettle and a fold-out couch. Rooms are great value for a family of four, for example. Book online or via the terminal at the entrance.

Eating

Tampere's speciality, *mustamakkara*, is a tasty mild blood sausage normally eaten with lingonberry jam. You can get it at the kauppahalli (market hall), a great place for cheap eats.

Tuulensuu GASTROPUB €€

(www.gastropub.net/tuulensuu; Hämeenpuisto 23; mains €17-26; ⏲11am-midnight Mon-Fri, noon-midnight Sat, 3pm-midnight Sun; 📶) The best of several Tampere gastropubs, this has a superb range of Belgian beers, good wines and a lengthy port menu. Food is lovingly prepared and features staples such as liver or schnitzel, as well as more elaborate plates like duck confit and other bistro fare inspired by Belgium and northeastern France. Even the bar snacks are gourmet: fresh-roasted almonds. Closed Sundays in summer.

Hella & Huone FRENCH, FINNISH €€€

(☎03-253 2440; www.hellajahuone.fi; Salhojankatu 48; 1/2/3/7 courses €26/40/52/76; ⏲6-11pm Tue-Sat) This smart spot serves exquisite French-influenced gourmet creations. There's a menu of seven courses: choose how many you want to have and pay accordingly. Leave room for the fine Finnish cheeses and fresh berries. There are wines matched to every course.

Drinking & Nightlife

★ **Café Europa** BAR

(www.ravintola.fi/europa; Aleksanterinkatu 29; ⌚noon-midnight Mon-Tue, noon-2am Wed-Thu, noon-3am Fri & Sat, 1pm-midnight Sun; 📶) Lavishly furnished with horsehair couches, armchairs, mirrors, chandeliers and paintings, this successfully fuses a re-creation of a 1930s-style old-Europe cafe, and is a popular meeting spot for students and anyone else who appreciates comfort, board games, Belgian and German beers, and generously proportioned sandwiches and salads. There's good summer seating out the front.

Information

Visit Tampere (☎03-56566800; www.visittampere.fi; Hämeenkatu 14B; ⌚9am-5pm Mon-Fri Sep-May, 9am-6pm Mon-Fri, 10am-3pm Sat & Sun Jun-Aug; 📶) On the main street in the centre of town. Can book activities and events.

Getting There & Away

AIR

Ryanair has daily services to several European destinations.

BUS

Regular express buses run from Helsinki (€27, 2¾ hours) and Turku (€25.60, two to three hours), and most other major towns in Finland are served from here.

TRAIN

The train station is central. Express trains run hourly to/from Helsinki (€39, 1¾ hours), and there are direct trains to Turku (€33.30, 1¾ hours) and other cities.

> **SAUNAS**
>
> For centuries the sauna has been a place to bathe, meditate, warm up and even give birth, and most Finns still use it at least once a week. Bathing is done in the nude (public saunas are nearly always sex-segregated) and Finns are quite strict about its nonsexual – even sacred – nature.
>
> Shower first. Once inside (with a temperature of 80°C to 100°C), water is thrown onto the stove using a *kauhu* (ladle), producing *löyly* (steam). A *vihta* (whisk of birch twigs and leaves) is sometimes used to lightly strike the skin, improving circulation. Cool off with a cold shower or preferably by jumping into a lake. Repeat. The sauna beer afterwards is also traditional.

LAKELAND

Most of southern Finland could be dubbed 'lakeland', but this spectacular area takes it to extremes. It often seems there's more water than land here, and what water it is: sublime, sparkling and clean, reflecting sky and forests cleanly as a mirror. It's a land that leaves an indelible impression on every visitor.

Savonlinna

☎015 / POP 27,420

One of Finland's prettiest towns, Savonlinna shimmers on a sunny day as the water ripples around its centre. It's a classic Lakeland settlement with a major attraction: perched on a rocky islet is one of Europe's most visually dramatic castles, Olavinlinna. The castle hosts July's world-famous opera festival in a spectacular setting.

Sights

★ **Olavinlinna** CASTLE

(www.olavinlinna.fi; adult/child €8/4; ⌚11am-6pm Jun–mid-Aug, 10am-4pm Mon-Fri, 11am-4pm Sat & Sun mid-Aug–mid-Dec & Jan-May) Standing immense and haughty, 15th-century Olavinlinna is one of the most spectacularly situated castles in northern Europe and, as well as being an imposing fortification, is also the stunning venue for the month-long Savonlinna Opera Festival. The castle's been heavily restored, but is still seriously impressive, not least in the way it's built directly on a rock in the middle of the lake. To visit the upper part of the interior, including the towers and chapel, you must join a guided tour (around 45 minutes).

Sleeping

Hotel beds are scarce and pricey during July's opera festival – book accommodation well in advance. Fortunately, students are out of town and their residences are converted to summer hotels and hostels.

Kesähotelli Vuorilinna SUMMER HOTEL €
(☎015-73950; www.spahotelcasino.fi; Kylpylaitoksentie; s/d €70/90, dm/hostel s €30/40; ⏲Jun-Aug; P) Set in several buildings used by students during term time, this is run by the Spahotel Casino and has an appealing location across a beautiful footbridge from the town centre. Rooms are clean and comfortable; the cheaper ones share bathroom and kitchen (no utensils) between two. Happily, dorm rates get you the same deal, and there's a HI discount.

Perhehotelli Hospitz HOTEL €€
(☎015-515 661; www.hospitz.com; Linnankatu 20; s/d €88/98; ⏲Apr-Dec; P 📶) This cosy Savonlinna classic was built in the 1930s and maintains that period's elegance. The rooms are stylish, although beds are narrow and bathrooms small; larger family rooms are available. Balconies cost a little extra. There's a pleasant terrace and orchard-garden with access to a small beach. Opera atmosphere is great with a midnight buffet, but rates rise (single/double €130/155): book eons in advance.

★**Lossiranta Lodge** BOUTIQUE GUESTHOUSE €€€
(☎044-511 2323; www.lossiranta.net; Aino Acktén Puistotie; d €160-200; P 📶) To get up close and personal with Olavinlinna Castle, this lakeside spot is the place to be: the impressive castle looms just opposite. Offering five snug little nests in an outbuilding, this is one of Finland's most charming hotels. All are very different but decorated with love and style; they come with a small kitchen (yes, that's it in the cupboard) and numerous personal touches.

Eating & Drinking

The lively lakeside kauppatori is the place for casual snacking. A *lörtsy* (turnover) is typical and comes savoury with meat *(lihalörtsy)* or sweet with apple *(omenalörtsy)* or cloudberry *(lakkalörtsy)*. Savonlinna is also famous for fried *muikku* (vendace, tiny lake fish).

★**Huvila** FINNISH €€
(☎015-555 0555; www.panimoravintolahuvila.fi; Puistokatu 4; mains €20-28; ⏲4-11pm Mon-Fri, 2-11pm Sat Jun & Aug, noon-midnight Mon-Sat, noon-10pm Sun Jul; 📶) This noble wooden building was formerly a fever hospital then asylum, but writes happier stories now as an excellent microbrewery and restaurant across the harbour from the town centre. Food focuses on fresh local ingredients with some unusual meats sometimes featuring, all expertly prepared and served. Home-brewed beers are exquisite and the terrace is a wonderful place on a sunny afternoon, with occasional live music.

Information

Savonlinna Travel (☎0600-30007; www.savonlinna.travel; Puistokatu 1; ⏲9am-4pm Mon-Fri Aug-Jun, 10am-6pm Mon-Sat, 10am-2pm Sun Jul) Tourist information including accommodation reservations, cottage booking, farmstays, opera festival tickets and tours. The Sokos Hotel Seurahuone can help with tourist information when this is closed.

Getting There & Away

In summer, boats connect Savonlinna with other Lakeland towns.

BUS

Bus services include Helsinki (€49.90, 4½ to six hours, several per day).

TRAIN

Trains from Helsinki (€65.70, 4¼ hours) require a change in Parikkala.

Kuopio

☎017 / POP 106,450

Most things a reasonable person could desire from a summery lakeside town are in Kuopio, with pleasure cruises on the azure water, spruce forests to stroll in, wooden waterside pubs, and local fish specialities to taste. And what better than a traditional smoke sauna to give necessary impetus to jump into the chilly waters?

Activities

★**Jätkänkämppä** SAUNA
(☎030 60830; www.rauhalahti.fi; adult/child €12/6; ⏲4-10pm Tue, also Thu Jun-Aug & Nov-Dec, 4-11pm Jun-Aug) This giant *savusauna* (smoke sauna) is a memorable, sociable experience that draws locals and visitors. It seats 60 and is mixed: you're given towels to wear. Bring a swimsuit for lake dipping – devoted locals and brave tourists do so even when it's covered with ice. Repeat the process several times. Then buy a beer and relax, looking over the lake in Nordic peace.

The **restaurant** (adult/child buffet plus hot plate €21/10.50; ⏲4-8pm) in the adjacent loggers' cabin serves traditional Finnish dinners when the sauna's on, with accordion

OFF THE BEATEN TRACK

THE SEAL LAKES

Easily reached from Savonlinna, the watery Linnansaari and Kolovesi National Parks are great to explore by canoe and are the habitat of a rare inland seal. See www.outdoors.fi for information on the parks, and www.saimaaholiday.net for transport, accommodation and equipment-hire services in the area.

entertainment and a lumberjack show. Buses 7 and 9 head to Rauhalahti hotel, from where it's a 600m walk, or take a summertime cruise from the harbour.

Sleeping & Eating

Hotel Atlas HOTEL €€

(020-789 6101; www.hotelatlas.fi; Haapaniemenkatu 22; s/d €130/150; P ❄ @) An historic Kuopio hotel that reopened in 2012 after complete remodelling, the Atlas is now the town's most appealing option, not least for its prime location on the kauppatori. The commodious modern rooms are of good size, with a sofa, are well soundproofed and offer perspectives over the square, or, more unusually, the interior of a department store.

Kummisetä FINNISH €€

(www.kummiseta.com; Minna Canthinkatu 44; mains €17-30; kitchen 3-9.30pm Mon-Sat) The sober brown colours of the 'Godfather' give it a traditional feel replicated on the menu, with sauces featuring fennel, berries and morel mushrooms garnishing prime cuts of beef, tender-as-young-love lamb and succulent pike-perch. Food is hearty rather than gourmet; it and the service are both excellent. In summer, eating on the spacious two-level back terrace is an absolute pleasure.

Hours change slightly every week; these are an approximation.

★ **Musta Lammas** FINNISH €€€

(017-581 0458; www.mustalammas.net; Satamakatu 4; mains €28-33, degustation menu €59; 5pm-late Mon-Sat;) One of Finland's best restaurants, the Black Sheep has a golden fleece. Set in an enchantingly romantic brick-vaulted space, it offers a short menu of delicious gourmet mains using top-quality Finnish meat and fish, with complex sauces that complement but never overpower the natural flavours. Wines include a fabulous selection of generously priced special bottles (healthy credit card required). There's also a roof terrace.

Information

Kuopio Info (0800-182-050; www.visitkuopio.fi; Apaja Shopping Centre, Kauppakatu 45; 8am-3pm Mon-Fri) Located underneath the kauppatori. Has information on regional attractions and accommodation. May open Saturdays in future.

Getting There & Away

Buses serve Helsinki (€66.30, 6½ hours) and other cities, as do trains (Helsinki €68, 4½ to five hours). In summer boats travel between Kuopio and Savonlinna.

LAPLAND

Extending hundreds of kilometres above the Arctic Circle, Lapland is Finland's true wilderness and casts a powerful spell. The midnight sun, the Sámi peoples, the aurora borealis (Northern Lights) and the wandering reindeer are all components of Lapland's magic, as is good old ho-ho-ho himself, who 'officially' resides up here.

Rovaniemi

016 / POP 60,900

A tourism boomtown, the 'official' terrestrial residence of Santa Claus is the capital of Finnish Lapland and a more-or-less obligatory northern stop. Its wonderful Arktikum museum is the perfect introduction to the mysteries of these latitudes, and Rovaniemi is a good place to organise activities from. It's also Lapland's transport hub.

Sights

★ **Arktikum** MUSEUM

(www.arktikum.fi; Pohjoisranta 4; adult/child/family €12/5/28; 9am-6pm Jun-Aug & Dec–mid-Jan, 10am-6pm Tue-Sun mid-Jan–May & Sep-Nov) With its beautifully designed glass tunnel stretching out to the Ounasjoki, this is one of Finland's best museums and well worth the admission fee if you are interested in the north. One side deals with Lapland, with information on Sámi culture and the history of Rovaniemi. The other side offers a wide-ranging display on the Arctic, with superb static and interactive displays focusing on flora and fauna, as well as on the peoples of Arctic Europe, Asia and North America.

Tours

Rovaniemi is Finnish Lapland's most popular base for winter and summer activities, offering the convenience of frequent departures and professional trips with multilingual guides. Check the tourist-office website for activities including river cruises, reindeer- and husky-sledding, rafting, snowmobiling, skiing and mountain biking.

Sleeping

Guesthouse Borealis GUESTHOUSE €
(016-342 0130; www.guesthouseborealis.com; Asemieskatu 1; s/d/tr €53/66/89;) Cordial hospitality and proximity to trains make this family-run spot a winner. Rooms are simple, bright and clean; some have a balcony. The airy dining room is the venue for breakfast, featuring Finnish porridge. Guests have use of a kitchen (and sauna for a small charge), and there are two self-contained apartments. Prices are a little higher in winter; substantially so over Christmas.

Hostel Rudolf HOSTEL €
(016-321 321; www.rudolf.fi; Koskikatu 41; dm/s/d mid-Jan–Mar €52/64/92, Apr-Nov €42/49/63, Christmas period €58/73/108;) Run by Hotel Santa Claus, where you inconveniently have to go to check-in, this staffless hostel is Rovaniemi's only one and can fill up fast. Rooms are private and good for the price, with spotless bathrooms, solid desks and bedside lamps; dorm rates get you the same deal. There's also a kitchen available but don't expect a hostel atmosphere. HI discount.

★ City Hotel HOTEL €€
(016-330 0111; www.cityhotel.fi; Pekankatu 9; s/d/superior d €129/149/177;) There's something very pleasing about this welcoming central place. It retains an intimate feel, with excellent service and plenty of extras included free of charge. Rooms are commodious and compact; they look very stylish with large windows, arty silvery objects, good beds, and plush maroon and brown fabrics. Lux rooms offer a proper double bed, while smart suites have a sauna. Cheaper in summer.

LAPLAND SEASONS

It's important to pick your time in Lapland carefully. In the far north there's no sun for 50 days of the year, and no night for 70-odd days. In June it's very muddy, and in July insects can be hard to deal with. If you're here to walk, August is great and in September the *ruska* (autumn leaves) are spectacular. There's thick snow cover from mid-October to May; December draws charter flights looking for Santa, real reindeer and guaranteed snow, but the best time for skiing and husky/reindeer/snowmobile safaris is March and April, when you get a decent amount of daylight and less-extreme temperatures.

Eating

Nili FINNISH €€
(0400-369-669; www.nili.fi; Valtakatu 20; mains €20-33; 6-11pm Mon-Sat) There's much more English than Finnish heard at this popular central restaurant, with an attractive interior and a Lapland theme. The food's tasty rather than gourmet, but uses toothsome local ingredients, with things like reindeer, lake fish, wild mushrooms and berries creating appealing northern flavours. The overpriced wine list needs work.

Drinking & Nightlife

★ Kauppayhtiö CAFE, BAR
(www.facebook.com/kauppayhtio; Valtakatu 24; 11am-8pm Mon-Thu, 11am-4am Fri & Sat;) Rovaniemi's most personable cafe, this is an oddball collection of retro curios with a coffee and gasoline theme and colourful plastic tables. All the knick-knacks are purportedly for sale here, but it's the espresso machine, charismatic outdoor lounge and stage area, salads, rolls, burgers, Wednesday-to-Sunday sushi, sundaes and bohemian Lapland crowd that keep the place ticking.

Information

Tourist Information (016-346 270; www.visitrovaniemi.fi; Maakuntakatu 29; 9am-6pm Mon-Fri, 9am-3pm Sat & Sun mid-Jun–mid-Aug & late Nov-early Jan, 9am-5pm Mon-Fri rest of year;) On the square in the middle of town. Very helpful.

Getting There & Away

AIR

Rovaniemi's airport is a major winter destination for charter flights. Finnair and Norwegian fly daily from Helsinki.

SEEING SANTA

The southernmost line at which the sun does not set on at least one day a year, the Arctic Circle (**Napapiiri** in Finnish) crosses the Sodankylä road 8km north of Rovaniemi. There's an **Arctic Circle marker** here (although the Arctic Circle can actually shift several metres daily). Surrounding the marker is **Santa Claus Village** (www.santaclausvillage.info; ⌚10am-5pm mid-Jan–May & Sep-Nov, 9am-6pm Jun-Aug, 9am-7pm Dec–mid-Jan) FREE, a touristy complex of shops, winter activities and cottage accommodation.

Santa Claus Post Office (www.santaclaus.posti.fi) here receives over half a million letters yearly from children (and adults) all over the world. Your mail sent from here will bear an official Santa stamp, and you can arrange to have it delivered at Christmas. For €7.90, you can get Santa to send a Christmas card to you.

But the top attraction for most is, of course, Santa himself, who sees visitors year-round in a rather impressive **grotto** (www.santaclauslive.com) FREE, where a huge clock mechanism (it slows the earth's rotation so that Santa can visit the whole world's children on Christmas night) eerily surrounds those queuing for an audience. The portly saint is quite a linguist, and an old hand at chatting with kids and adults alike. A private chat (around two minutes) is absolutely free, but you can't photograph the moment, and official photos of your visit start at an outrageous €25.

Bus 8 heads here from the train station, passing through the village centre (adult/child €6.60/3.80 return).

BUS

Daily connections serve just about everywhere in Lapland, including Norwegian destinations. Night buses serve Helsinki (€130.20, 12¾ hours).

TRAIN

The train between Helsinki and Rovaniemi (€84 to €102, 10 to 12 hours) is quicker and cheaper than the bus.

Inari

☎016 / POP 550

The tiny village of Inari (Sámi: Anár) is Finland's most significant Sámi centre and is *the* place to begin to learn something of their culture. The village sits on Lapland's largest lake, Inarijärvi.

Sights

★Siida MUSEUM
(www.siida.fi; adult/child €10/5; ⌚9am-8pm Jun–mid-Sep, 10am-5pm Tue-Sun mid-Sep–May) One of Finland's finest museums, Siida, a comprehensive overview of the Sámi and their environment, should not be missed. The main exhibition hall consists of a fabulous nature exhibition around the edge, detailing northern Lapland's ecology by season, with wonderful photos and information panels. In the centre of the room is detailed information on the Sámi, from their former semi-nomadic existence to modern times.

Sajos CULTURAL CENTRE
(www.sajos.fi; Siljotie; ⌚9am-5pm Mon-Fri) FREE The spectacular wood-and-glass Sámi cultural centre stands proud in the middle of town. It holds the Sámi parliament as well as a library and music archive, restaurant, exhibitions and craft shop. In summer there are tours of the building, and Sámi handicraft workshops.

Sleeping

Though small, Inari has several good lodging options.

Lomakylä Inari CAMPGROUND €
(☎016-671 108; www.saariselka.fi/lomakylainari; tent sites for 1/2/4 people €10/15/20, 2-/4-person cabins €67/79, without bathroom €40/50, cottages €85-170; P 📶) The closest cabin accommodation to town, this is 500m south of the town centre and a good option. There's a range of cabins and facilities that include a cafe. Lakeside cabins cost a little more but are worth it for the memorable sunsets. Camping and nonheated cabins are June to September only.

★Tradition Hotel Kultahovi HOTEL €€
(☎016-511 7100; www.hotelkultahovi.fi; Saarikoskentie 2; s/d €78/102, annex s/d €112/128; P @ 📶) This cosy place run by a Sámi family overlooks the Alakoski rapids and has spruce rooms, some with a great river view. The standard rooms have been recently renovated, while chambers in the annex have appealing Nordic decor, drying cupboards,

riverside balconies/terraces and (most) saunas. The restaurant (open 11am to 10.30pm) serves delicious Lappish specialities (mains €20 to €31) and has relaxing views.

Information

Tourist Office (☎020-564 7740; www.inari.fi; Inarintie 46; ⊙9am-8pm Jun–mid-Sep, 10am-5pm Tue-Sun mid-Sep–May; 📶) Located in the Siida museum. There's also a nature information point here and internet access.

Getting There & Away

Two daily buses hit Inari from Rovaniemi (€60.10, five hours) and continue to Norway.

SURVIVAL GUIDE

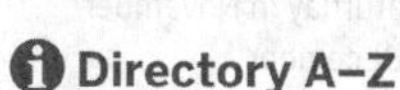

Directory A–Z

ACCOMMODATION

Solid Nordic comfort in standard rooms dominates rather than boutique accommodation.

- Most campgrounds open from June to August; sites usually cost around €14 plus €5/2 per adult/child. Most have cabins or cottages, usually excellent value; from €40 for a basic cabin to €120 for a cottage with kitchen, bathroom and sauna.
- It's worth being a member of **HI** (www.hihostels.com), as members save 10% per night at affiliated hostels.
- From June to August many student residences are made over as summer hostels and hotels.
- Hotels in Finland charge robustly. But on weekends and during the July summer holidays prices tend to drop by 40% or so. A breakfast buffet is nearly always included. Double beds are rare.
- One of Finland's joys is its plethora of cottages for rent, many in romantic lake-and-forest locations. The biggest booker is **Lomarengas** (☎030-650 2502; www.lomarengas.fi).

SLEEPING PRICE RANGES

The following price ranges refer to a double room in high season:

€ less than €70

€€ €70–€160

€€€ more than €160

COUNTRY FACTS

Area 338,145 sq km

Capital Helsinki

Country code ☎358

Currency Euro (€)

Emergency ☎112

Languages Finnish, Swedish, Sámi languages

Population 5.46 million

Visas Schengen visa rules apply

ACTIVITIES

On the Water Every waterside town has a place (frequently the campground) where you can rent a canoe, kayak or rowboat. Rental cottages often have rowboats that you can use free of charge to investigate the local lake. Rafting options range from short, Class II doddles to Class III and IV adventures, and rollicking Class V punishment.

Fishing Several permits are required of foreigners but they are very easy to arrange. See www.mmm.fi for details.

Hiking Finland has some of Europe's greatest hiking, best done from June to September, although in July mosquitoes and other biting insects can be a big problem in Lapland. Wilderness huts line the northern trails. Numerous national parks provide a well-maintained network of marked trails across the nation. Check www.outdoors.fi for more information.

Skiing The ski season runs from late November to early May and slightly longer in the north.

Dog-sledding Expeditions can range from one-hour tasters to multiday trips with overnight stays in remote forest huts.

Snowmobiling If you want to drive one, a driving licence is required.

Saunas Many hotels, hostels and campgrounds have saunas that are free with a night's stay. Large towns have public saunas.

BUSINESS HOURS

Many attractions in Finland, particularly outdoor ones, only open for a short summer season, typically mid-June to late August. Opening hours tend to shorten in winter in general.

Sample opening hours:

Alko (state alcohol store) 9am to 8pm Monday to Friday, to 6pm Saturday

Banks 9am to 4.15pm Monday to Friday

Businesses & shops 9am to 6pm Monday to Friday, to 3pm Saturday

Nightclubs 10pm to 4am Wednesday to Saturday

Pubs 11am to 1am (often later on Friday and Saturday)

Restaurants 11am to 10pm, lunch 11am to 3pm. Last orders generally an hour before closing.

INTERNET ACCESS

Public libraries Free internet terminals; there's usually a time limit. Many tourist offices have an internet terminal that you can use for free (usually 15 minutes).

Wireless internet access Very widespread; several cities have extensive networks and nearly all hotels, as well as many restaurants, cafes and bars, offer free access.

Data Very cheap. If you've got an unlocked smartphone, you can pick up a local SIM card for a few euros and charge it with a month's worth of data at a decent speed for under €20. Ask at R-Kioski shops for the latest deals.

INTERNET RESOURCES

Finnish Tourist Board (www.visitfinland.com)

MONEY

ATMs Using ATMs with a credit or debit card is by far the easiest way of getting cash.

Credit cards Widely accepted; Finns are dedicated users of plastic even to buy a cup of coffee.

Currency Euro (€). Note that one- and two-cent coins are not used in Finland.

Moneychangers Travellers cheques and cash can be exchanged at banks; in cities, independent exchange facilities such as Forex (www.forex.fi) usually offer better rates.

Tipping Service is considered to be included in bills, so there's no need to tip at all unless you want to reward exceptional service.

PUBLIC HOLIDAYS

Finland grinds to a halt twice a year: around Christmas and New Year, and during the Midsummer weekend. National public holidays:

New Year's Day 1 January

Epiphany 6 January

Good Friday March/April

Easter Sunday & Monday March/April

May Day 1 May

Ascension Day May

Whitsunday Late May or early June

Midsummer's Eve & Day Weekend in June closest to 24 June

All Saints Day First Saturday in November

Independence Day 6 December

Christmas Eve 24 December

Christmas Day 25 December

Boxing Day 26 December

TELEPHONE

➡ Public telephones basically no longer exist in Finland.

➡ The cheapest and most practical solution is to purchase a Finnish SIM card and pop it in your own phone. First make sure your phone isn't blocked from doing this by your home network.

➡ You can buy a prepaid SIM card at any R-kioski shop. You might be able to pick up a card for as little as €5, including some call credit.

ESSENTIAL FOOD & DRINK

➡ **Coffee** To fit in, eight or nine cups a day is about right, best accompanied with a *pulla* (cardamom-flavoured pastry).

➡ **Offbeat meats** Unusual meats appear on menus: reindeer is a staple up north, elk is commonly eaten, and bear is also available.

➡ **Fresh food** The kauppahalli (market hall) is where to go for a stunning array of produce. In summer, stalls at the kauppatori (market square) sell delicious fresh vegetables and fruit.

➡ **Gastro** Helsinki is the best venue for fabulous new-Suomi cuisine, with sumptuous, inventive degustation menus presenting traditional Finnish ingredients in crest-of-the-wave ways.

➡ **Alcoholic drinks** Beer is a staple, and great microbreweries are on the increase. Finns also love dissolving things in vodka; try a shot of *salmiakkikossu* (salty-liquorice flavoured) or *fisu* (Fisherman's Friend–flavoured).

➡ **Fish** Salmon is ubiquitous; tasty lake fish include arctic char, lavaret, pike-perch and scrumptious fried *muikku* (vendace).

➡ **Brunssi** Weekend *brunssi* (brunch) is all the rage in Helsinki and other cities. Book ahead for these sumptuous all-you-can-eat spreads.

EATING PRICE RANGES

The following price ranges refer to a standard main course:

€ less than €17

€€ €17–€27

€€€ more than €27

Top the credit up at the same outlets, online or at ATMs.

➡ The country code for Finland is ☎358. To dial abroad it's ☎00.

TIME

Eastern European Time (EET), an hour ahead of Sweden and Norway. In winter it's two hours ahead of UTC/GMT; from late March to late October the clocks go forward an hour.

VISAS

Schengen rules apply. Check the website www.formin.finland.fi for details.

ℹ Getting There & Away

Finland is easily accessed from Europe and beyond. There are direct flights from numerous destinations, while Baltic ferries are another good option.

AIR

Most flights to Finland land at **Helsinki-Vantaa Airport** (www.helsinki-vantaa.fi), 19km north of the capital.

Finland is easily reached by air, with direct flights to Helsinki from many European, American and Asian destinations. It's also served by budget carriers, especially Ryanair, from several European countries. Most other flights are with Finnair or Scandinavian Airlines (SAS).

LAND

There are several border crossings from northern Sweden and Norway to northern Finland, with no passport or customs formalities. Buses link northern Finland and Norway, while the shared bus station at Tornio (Finland) and Haparanda (Sweden) links the public transport systems of those countries.

There are nine main border crossings between Finland and Russia, including several in the southeast and two in Lapland. Buses and trains run from Helsinki and other cities to Russia.

SEA

Baltic ferries connect Finland with Estonia, Russia, Germany and Sweden. Book ahead in summer, at weekends and if travelling with a vehicle.

Ferry companies have detailed timetables and fares on their websites. Fares vary according to season. Main operators with their Finnish contact numbers:

Eckerö Line (☎0600-4300; www.eckeroline.fi) Finland–Sweden, Finland–Estonia.

Finnlines (☎010-343 4500; www.finnlines.com) Finland–Sweden, Finland–Germany.

Linda Line (☎0600-066 8970; www.lindaline.fi) Finland–Estonia.

St Peter Line (☎09-6187-2000; www.stpeterline.com) Finland–Russia.

Tallink/Silja Line (☎0600-15700; www.tallinksilja.com) Finland–Sweden, Finland–Estonia.

Viking Line (☎0600-41577; www.vikingline.fi) Finland–Sweden, Finland–Estonia.

ℹ Getting Around

AIR

Finnair and Flybe run a fairly comprehensive domestic service out of Helsinki.

BICYCLE

Finland is as bicycle friendly as any country you'll find, with plenty of paths and few hills. Bikes can be taken on most trains, buses and ferries. Åland is particularly good for cycling. Helmets are required by law. You can hire a bike in nearly every Finnish town.

BOAT

Lake boats were once important summer transport. These services are now largely kept on as cruises, and make a great, leisurely way to journey between towns. The most popular routes are Tampere–Hämeenlinna, Tampere–Virrat, Savonlinna–Kuopio and Lahti–Jyväskylä. The site http://lautta.net is very handy for domestic lake-boat and ferry services.

BUS

Bus is the main form of long-distance transport in Finland, with a far more comprehensive network than the train.

Ticketing is handled by **Matkahuolto** (www.matkahuolto.fi), whose excellent website has all the timetables. Matkahuolto offices work normal business hours, but you can always just buy your ticket from the driver. Prices depend on distance: the one-way fare for a 100km trip is normal/express €18.70/22.

Towns have a *linja-autoasema* (bus terminal), with local timetables displayed (*lähtevät* is departures, *saapuvat* arrivals).

Separate from the normal system, **OnniBus** (www.onnibus.com) runs a variety of budget inter-city routes in comfortable double-decker buses, best booked in advance.

OTHER PLACES WORTH VISITING

Kemi Come in winter for trips on an icebreaker and the chance to overnight in a spectacular snow castle.

Ruka This ski resort is a great year-round base for outdoor activity, with some of Finland's finest hikes and canoeing routes on the doorstep.

Joensuu Capital of Karelia, a forested region great for Orthodox festivals, trekking and wildlife-watching.

Hanko Some of Finland's loveliest coastline, and glorious old Russian villas to stay in.

Vaasa Arty town that makes a base for exploring the sunny west coast and its Swedish-influenced culture.

Jyväskylä Lively lakeside univeristy town heavily connected with Finland's most famous architect and designer Alvar Aalto.

Oulu A fine stop on the way north, this cheerful city is beautifully located on a series of linked islands.

CAR & MOTORCYCLE

Petrol is relatively expensive in Finland. Many petrol stations are unstaffed, with machines that take cards or cash. Change for cash is not given.

Hire

Car rental is expensive, but rates can work out reasonably with advance booking or with a group. A small car costs around €70/300 per day/week with 300km free per day. As ever, the cheapest deals are online.

Look out for weekend rates. These can cost little more than the rate for a single day, and you can pick up the car early afternoon on Friday and return it late Sunday or early Monday.

Car-rental franchises with offices in many Finnish cities: **Budget** (www.budget.com), **Hertz** (www.hertz.com), **Europcar** (www.europcar.com) and **Avis** (www.avis.com). One of the cheapest is **Sixt** (www.sixt.com).

Road Hazards

Wildlife Beware of elk and reindeer, which don't respect vehicles and can dash onto the road unexpectedly. This sounds comical, but elks especially constitute a deadly danger. Notify the police if there is an accident involving these animals. Reindeer are very common in Lapland; slow right down if you see one, as there will be more nearby.

Conditions Snow and ice on the roads, potentially from September to April, and as late as June in Lapland, make driving a serious undertaking. Snow chains are illegal: people use either snow tyres, which have studs, or special all-weather tyres.

Road Rules

- Finns drive on the right.
- The speed limit is 50km/h in built-up areas, from 80km/h to 100km/h on highways, and 120km/h on motorways.
- Use headlights at all times.
- Seatbelts are compulsory for all.
- Blood alcohol limit: 0.05%.
- An important feature of Finland is that there are fewer give-way signs than most countries. Traffic entering an intersection from the right has right of way. While this doesn't apply to highways or main roads, in towns cars will often nip out from the right without looking: you must give way, so be careful at smaller intersections in towns.

TRAIN

State-owned **Valtion Rautatiet** (VR; www.vr.fi) runs Finnish trains: a fast, efficient service, with prices roughly equivalent to buses on the same route.

VR's website has comprehensive timetable information. Major stations have a VR office and ticket machines; tickets can also be purchased online, where you'll also find discounted advance fares.

Fares vary slightly according to the type of train, with Pendolino the priciest. A one-way ticket for a 100km express train journey costs approximately €23 in 2nd ('eco') class. First-class ('extra') tickets cost around 35% more than a 2nd-class ticket. A return fare gives a 10% discount.

Train Passes

Eurail and InterRail offer various passes (p1204) that include train travel within Finland.

The **Eurail Scandinavia** pass gives a number of days in a two-month period, and is valid for travel in Denmark, Sweden, Norway and Finland. It costs €261 for four days, and up to €403 for 10 days. A similar but cheaper pass includes just Sweden and Finland. The **Finland Eurail Pass** costs €137/182/245 for three/five/10 days' 2nd-class travel in a one-month period within Finland.

The **InterRail Finland** pass offers travel only in Finland for three/four/six/eight days in a one-month period, costing €125/158/212/258 in 2nd class.

France

Includes ➡

Best Places to Eat

- Le Musée (p403)
- Café Saint Régis (p376)
- Restaurant Le Pim'pi (p411)
- Le Genty-Magre (p413)
- Le Café des Épices (p417)

Best Places for History

- Grotte de Lascaux (p407)
- D-Day beaches (p387)
- The Somme (p384)
- Pont du Gard (p415)
- Musée Carnavalet (p372)

Why Go?

France has so much to entice travellers – renowned gastronomy, iconic sights, splendid art heritage, a fabulous outdoors. You could sample it all in a week, but you'll invariably feel as though you've only scratched the surface of this big country.

Visiting France is certainly about seeing the big sights, but it's just as much about savouring life's little pleasures: a stroll through an elegant city square, a coffee on a sunny pavement terrace, a meal that lasts well into the afternoon or night, a scenic drive punctuated with photo stops and impromptu farm or vineyard visits. The French are big on their *art de vivre* (art of living) and you should embrace it, too.

When to Go

Paris

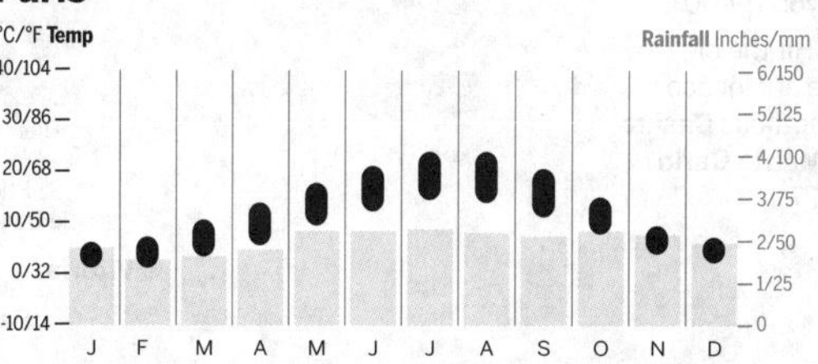

Dec–Mar Christmas markets in Alsace, snow action in the Alps and truffles in the south.

Apr–Jun France is at its springtime best, with good weather and no crowds.

Sep Cooling temperatures, abundant local produce and the *vendange* (grape harvest).

France Highlights

1. Gorge on the iconic sights and sophistication of Europe's most hopelessly romantic city, **Paris** (p364).
2. Relive the French Renaissance with extraordinary chateaux built by kings and queens in the **Loire Valley** (p395).
3. Do a Bond and swoosh down slopes in the shadow of Mont Blanc in **Chamonix** (p405).
4. Dodge tides, stroll moonlit sand and immerse yourself in legend at island abbey **Mont St-Michel** (p387).
5. Savour ancient ruins, modern art, markets, lavender and hilltop villages in slow-paced **Provence** (p415).
6. Taste bubbly in ancient *caves* (cellars) in **Épernay** (p391), the heart of Champagne.
7. Tuck into France's halest piggy-driven cuisine in a traditional *bouchon* in **Lyon** (p400).
8. Hit the big time at Monaco's sumptuous **Casino de Monte Carlo** (p427).

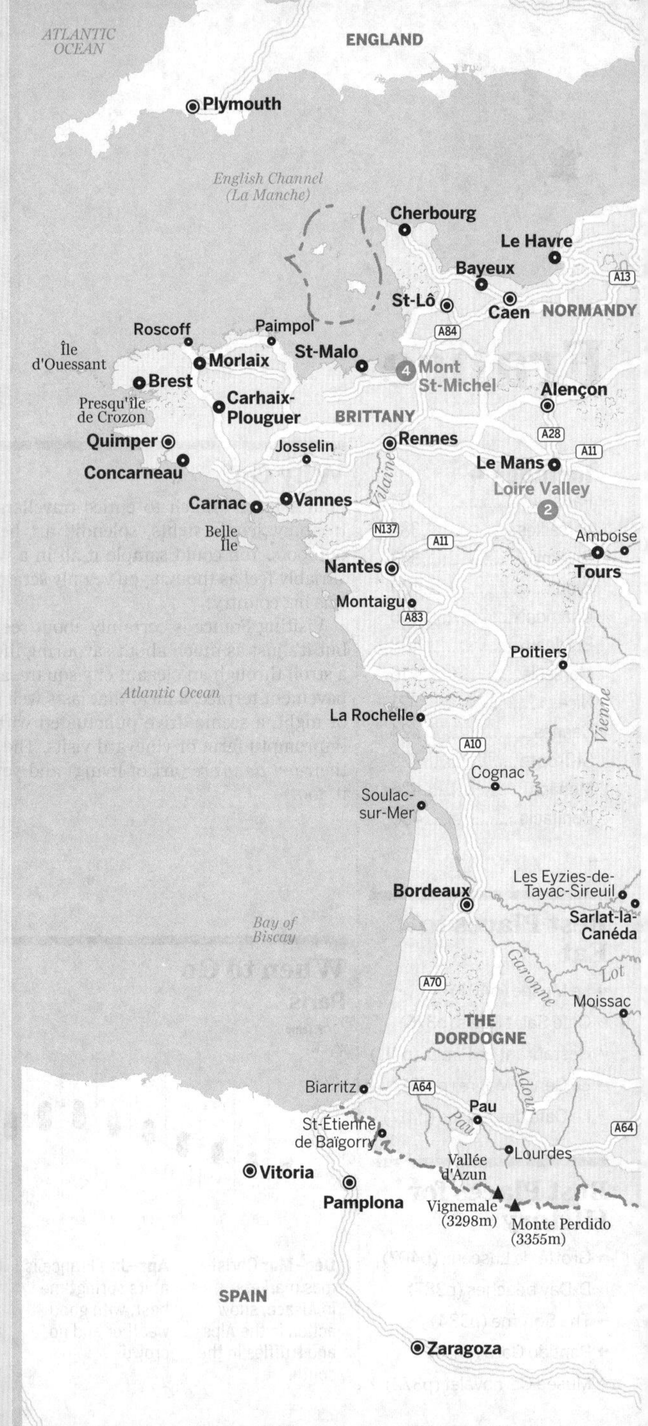

0
200 km
0
100 miles
Folkestone
Dunkirk
Calais
Boulogne-sur-Mer
BRUSSELS
NETHERLANDS
BELGIUM
Lille
Meuse
GERMANY
A28
Authie
Somme
Mainz
SOMME
LUXEMBOURG
LUXEMBOURG CITY
ouen
A1
Oise
Aisne
Reims
A4
Vernon
Marne
6
Metz
Épernay
ALSACE
Stuttgart
Versailles
1
Paris
Strasbourg
Dreux
Nancy
Seine
CHAMPAGNE
Marne
Moselle
A5
Sélestat
Chartres
Troyes
LORRAINE
Schnellenbuhl
A10
Katzenthal
A6
A31
BURGUNDY
Orléans
Saône
Auxerre
Beaugency
Chambord
Basel
LIECHTENSTEIN
Blois
Doubs
AUSTRIA
LA SOLOGNE
Dijon
Besançon
VADUZ
CÔTE D'OR
A86
BERN
Cher
Beaune
Arc-et-Senans
Loire
Arbois
Métabief
SWITZERLAND
JURA
Mont d'Or
Le Creusot
Les Rousses
Lausanne
Lake Geneva
A6
A20
A71
Les Portes du Soleil
Gueret
Chamonix
3
A72
Lyon
Annecy
Mont Blanc (4810m)
Limoges
Clermont-Ferrand
7
Rhône
Chambéry
IMOUSIN
Dordogne
St-Étienne
A48
FRENCH ALPS
ITALY
Moissac
Turenne
Drac
Puy Mary (1787m)
A49
Grenoble
Allier
Rhône
Sestriere
Valence
D921
A7
Vaison la Romaine
Cahors
Mt Lozère (1699m)
Durance
Mt Ventoux (1912m)
THE LOT
Pont du Gard
Tarn
A75
Nîmes
Avignon
Nice
8
Monaco
Ligurian Sea
Les Baux de Provence
Provence
Toulouse
Montpellier
Arles
5
Cannes
LANGUEDOC
Aix-en-Provence
A61
Marseille
St-Tropez
Carcassonne
ROUSILLON
Île Rousse
Bastia
A9
Golfe de Beauduc
Ariège
Perpignan
Calvi
ANDORRA
Monte Cinto (2706m)
ANDORRA LA VELLA
Puig Neulós
Mediterranean Sea
CORSICA
SPAIN
Ajaccio
Bonifacio
Barcelona
ITALY

ITINERARIES

One Week

Start with a couple of days exploring **Paris**, taking in the Louvre, the Eiffel Tower, Notre Dame, Montmartre and a boat trip along the Seine. Day trip to magnificent **Versailles** and then spend the rest of the week in **Normandy** to visit WWII's D-Day beaches and glorious Mont St-Michel. Or head east to **Champagne** to sample the famous bubbly and visit Reims' magnificent cathedral.

Two Weeks

With Paris and surrounds having taken up much of the first week, hop on a high-speed TGV down to **Avignon** or **Marseille** and take in the delights of Provence's Roman heritage, its beautiful hilltop villages and its famous artistic legacy. Finish your stay with a few days in **Nice**, enjoying its glittering Mediterranean landscapes and sunny cuisine. Alternatively, head southwest to elegant **Bordeaux** and its world-famous vineyards before pushing inland to the **Dordogne** with its hearty gastronomy and unique prehistoric-art heritage.

PARIS

POP 2.2 MILLION

What can be said about the sexy, sophisticated City of Lights that hasn't already been said myriad times before? Quite simply, this is one of the world's great metropolises – a trendsetter, market leader and cultural capital for over a thousand years and still going strong.

As you might expect, Paris is strewn with historic architecture, glorious galleries and cultural treasures galore. But the modern-day city is much more than just a museum piece: it's a heady hotchpotch of cultures and ideas – a place to stroll the boulevards, shop till you drop, flop riverside or simply do as the Parisians do and watch the world buzz by from a streetside cafe. Savour every moment.

Sights

Left Bank

★Eiffel Tower LANDMARK

(Map p366; ☎08 92 70 12 39; www.tour-eiffel.fr; Champ de Mars, 5 av Anatole France, 7e; lift to top adult/child €15/10.50, lift to 2nd fl €9/4.50, stairs to 2nd fl €5/3, lift 2nd fl to top €6; ⏲lifts & stairs 9am-midnight mid-Jun–Aug, lifts 9.30am-11pm, stairs 9.30am-6.30pm Sep–mid-Jun; Ⓜ Bir Hakeim or RER Champ de Mars-Tour Eiffel) No one could imagine Paris today without it. But Gustave Eiffel only constructed this elegant, 320m-tall signature spire as a temporary exhibit for the 1889 World Fair. Luckily, the art nouveau tower's popularity assured its survival. Prebook tickets online to avoid long ticket queues.

Lifts ascend to the tower's three levels; change lifts on the 2nd level for the final ascent to the top. Energetic visitors can walk as far as the 2nd level using the south pillar's 704-step stairs.

★Musée d'Orsay MUSEUM

(Map p366; www.musee-orsay.fr; 62 rue de Lille, 7e; adult/child €11/free; ⏲9.30am-6pm Tue, Wed & Fri-Sun, to 9.45pm Thu; Ⓜ Assemblée Nationale or RER Musée d'Orsay) Recently renovated to incorporate richly coloured walls and increased exhibition space, the home of France's national collection from the impressionist, postimpressionist and art nouveau movements spanning the 1840s and 1914 is the glorious former Gare d'Orsay railway station – itself an art nouveau showpiece – where a roll-call of masters and their world-famous works are on display.

Top of every visitor's must-see list is the museum's painting collections, centred on the world's largest collection of impressionist and post-impressionist art.

Musée du Quai Branly MUSEUM

(Map p366; www.quaibranly.fr; 37 quai Branly, 7e; adult/child €8.50/free; ⏲11am-7pm Tue, Wed & Sun, 11am-9pm Thu-Sat; Ⓜ Alma Marceau or RER Pont de l'Alma) No other museum in Paris so inspires travellers, armchair anthropologists and those who simply appreciate the beauty of traditional craftsmanship. A tribute to the diversity of human culture, Musée du Quai Branly presents an overview of indigenous and folk art. Its four main sections focus on Oceania, Asia, Africa and the Americas.

An impressive array of masks, carvings, weapons, jewellery and more make up the body of the rich collection, displayed in a refreshingly unique interior without rooms or high walls.

Musée Rodin GARDENS, MUSEUM

(Map p366; www.musee-rodin.fr; 79 rue de Varenne, 7e; adult/child museum incl garden €6/free, garden only €2/free; 10am-5.45pm Tue & Thu-Sun, to 8.45pm Wed; M Varenne) Sculptor, painter, sketcher, engraver and collector Auguste Rodin donated his entire collection to the French state in 1908 on the proviso that it dedicated his former workshop and showroom, the beautiful 1730 Hôtel Biron, to displaying his works. They're now installed not only in the mansion itself, but in its rose-clambered garden – one of the most peaceful places in central Paris and a wonderful spot to contemplate his famous work *The Thinker*.

Purchase tickets online to avoid queuing.

Les Catacombes CEMETERY

(Map p366; www.catacombes.paris.fr; 1 av Colonel Henri Roi-Tanguy, 14e; adult/child €8/free; 10am-8pm Tue-Sun, last admission 7pm; M Denfert Rochereau) Paris' most macabre sight is its underground tunnels lined with skulls and bones. In 1785 it was decided to rectify the hygiene problems of Paris' overflowing cemeteries by exhuming the bones and storing them in disused quarry tunnels and the Catacombes were created in 1810.

After descending 20m (via 130 narrow, dizzying spiral steps) below street level, you follow the dark, subterranean passages to reach the ossuary itself (2km in all). Exit back up 83 steps onto rue Remy Dumoncel, 14e.

Panthéon HISTORIC BUILDING

(Map p370; www.monum.fr; place du Panthéon, 5e; adult/child €7.50/free; 10am-6.30pm Apr-Sep, to 6pm Oct-Mar; M Maubert-Mutualité, Cardinal Lemoine or RER Luxembourg) Overlooking the city from its Left Bank perch, the Panthéon's stately neoclassical dome stands out as one of the most recognisable icons in the Parisian skyline. Originally a church and now a mausoleum, it has served since 1791 as the resting place of some of France's greatest thinkers, including Voltaire, Rousseau, Braille and Hugo. An architectural masterpiece, the interior is impressively vast (if slightly soulless) and certainly worth a wander. The dome is closed for renovations through 2015 (other structural work will continue through 2022).

Jardin du Luxembourg PARK

(Map p370; numerous entrances; hours vary; M St-Sulpice, Rennes or Notre Dame des Champs, or RER Luxembourg) This inner-city oasis of formal terraces, chestnut groves and lush lawns has a special place in Parisians' hearts. Napoléon dedicated the 23 gracefully laid-out hectares of the Luxembourg Gardens to the children of Paris, and many residents spent their childhood prodding 1920s wooden **sailboats** (per 30min €3; Apr-Oct) with long sticks on the octagonal **Grand Bassin** pond, watching puppets perform Punch & Judy–type shows at the **Théâtre du Luxembourg** (Map p370; www.marionnettesduluxembourg.fr; tickets €4.80; usually 3.30pm Wed, 11am & 3.30pm Sat & Sun, daily during school holidays; M Notre Dame des Champs), and riding the *carrousel* (merry-go-round) or **ponies** (Map p370).

Église St-Sulpice CHURCH

(Map p370; http://pss75.fr/saint-sulpice-paris; place St-Sulpice, 6e; 7.30am-7.30pm; M St-Sulpice) In 1646 work started on the twin-towered Church of St Sulpicius, lined inside with 21

MUSEUM DISCOUNTS & FREEBIES

If you plan on visiting a lot of museums, pick up a **Paris Museum Pass** (http://en.parismuseumpass.com; 2/4/6 days €42/56/69) or a **Paris City Passport** (www.parisinfo.com; 2/3/5 days €71/103/130), which also includes public transport and various extras. The passes get you into 60-odd venues in and around Paris, bypassing (or reducing) long ticket queues. Both passes are available from the Paris Convention & Visitors Bureau (p380).

Permanent collections at most city-run museums are free, but temporary exhibitions usually command a fee. Admission to national museums is reduced for those aged over 60 and reduced or free for those under 26, so don't buy a Paris Museum Pass or Paris City Passport if you qualify.

National museums are also free for everyone on the first Sunday of each month, except the Arc de Triomphe, Conciergerie, Musée du Louvre, Panthéon and Tours de Notre Dame, which are only free on the first Sunday of the month November to March.

Greater Paris

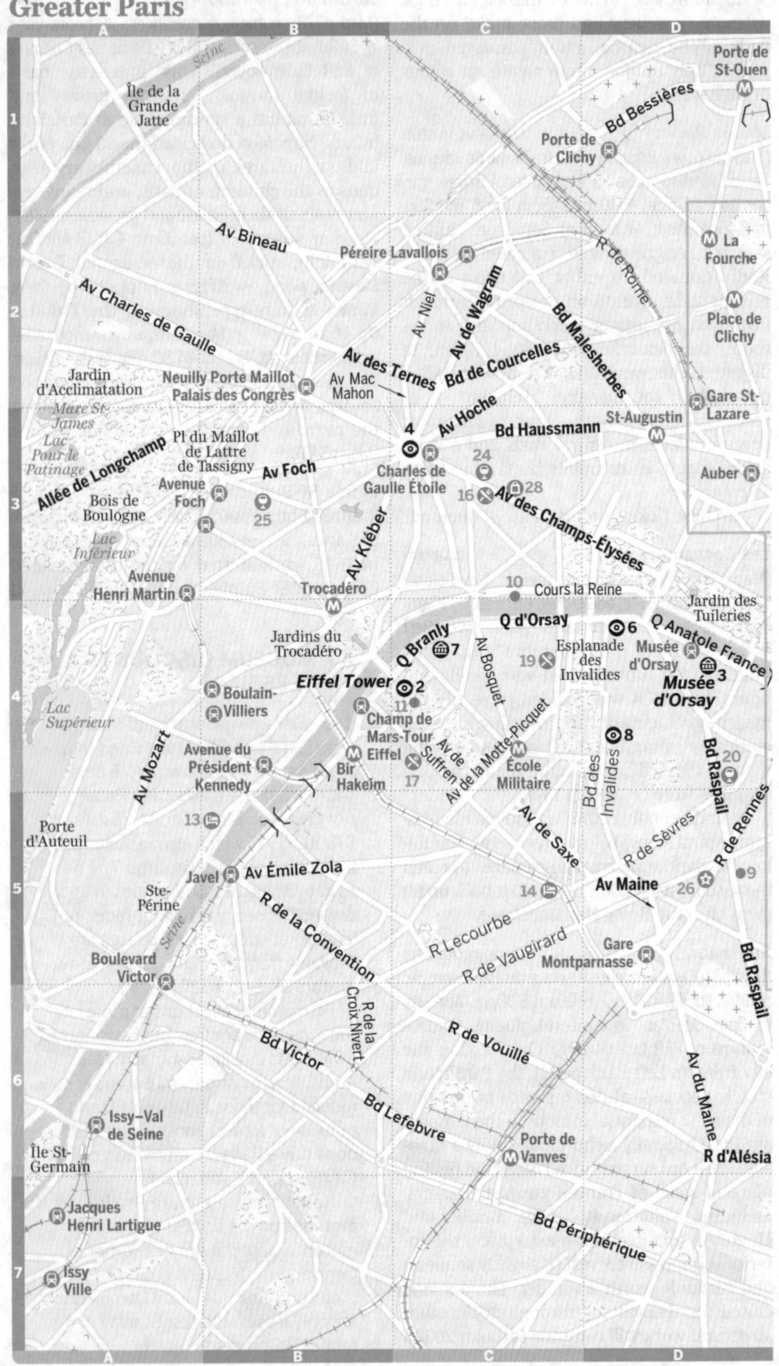

Seine
Île de la Grande Jatte
Porte de St-Ouen
Bd Bessières
Porte de Clichy
Av Bineau
Péreire Lavallois
R de Rome
La Fourche
Av Charles de Gaulle
Av Niel
Av de Wagram
Bd Malesherbes
Place de Clichy
Jardin d'Acclimatation
Neuilly Porte Maillot Palais des Congrès
Av des Ternes
Av Mac Mahon
Bd de Courcelles
Gare St-Lazare
Mare St-James
Lac Pour le Patinage
Allée de Longchamp
Pl du Maillot de Lattre de Tassigny
Av Foch
Av Hoche
Bd Haussmann
St-Augustin
Charles de Gaulle Étoile
Auber
Avenue Foch
Bois de Boulogne
Av Kléber
Av des Champs-Élysées
Lac Inférieur
Avenue Henri Martin
Trocadéro
Cours la Reine
Jardin des Tuileries
Q d'Orsay
Q Anatole France
Jardins du Trocadéro
Q Branly
Av Bosquet
Esplanade des Invalides
Musée d'Orsay
Eiffel Tower
Boulain-Villiers
Lac Supérieur
Champ de Mars-Tour Eiffel
Av de Suffren
Av de la Motte-Picquet
Av Mozart
Avenue du Président Kennedy
Bir Hakeim
École Militaire
Bd des Invalides
Bd Raspail
Porte d'Auteuil
Av de Saxe
R de Sèvres
R de Rennes
Javel
Av Émile Zola
Av Maine
Ste-Périne
R de la Convention
R Lecourbe
R de Vaugirard
Gare Montparnasse
Boulevard Victor
R de la Croix Nivert
R de Vouillé
Bd Victor
Av du Maine
Issy–Val de Seine
Bd Lefebvre
Porte de Vanves
R d'Alésia
Île St-Germain
Jacques Henri Lartigue
Bd Périphérique
Issy Ville

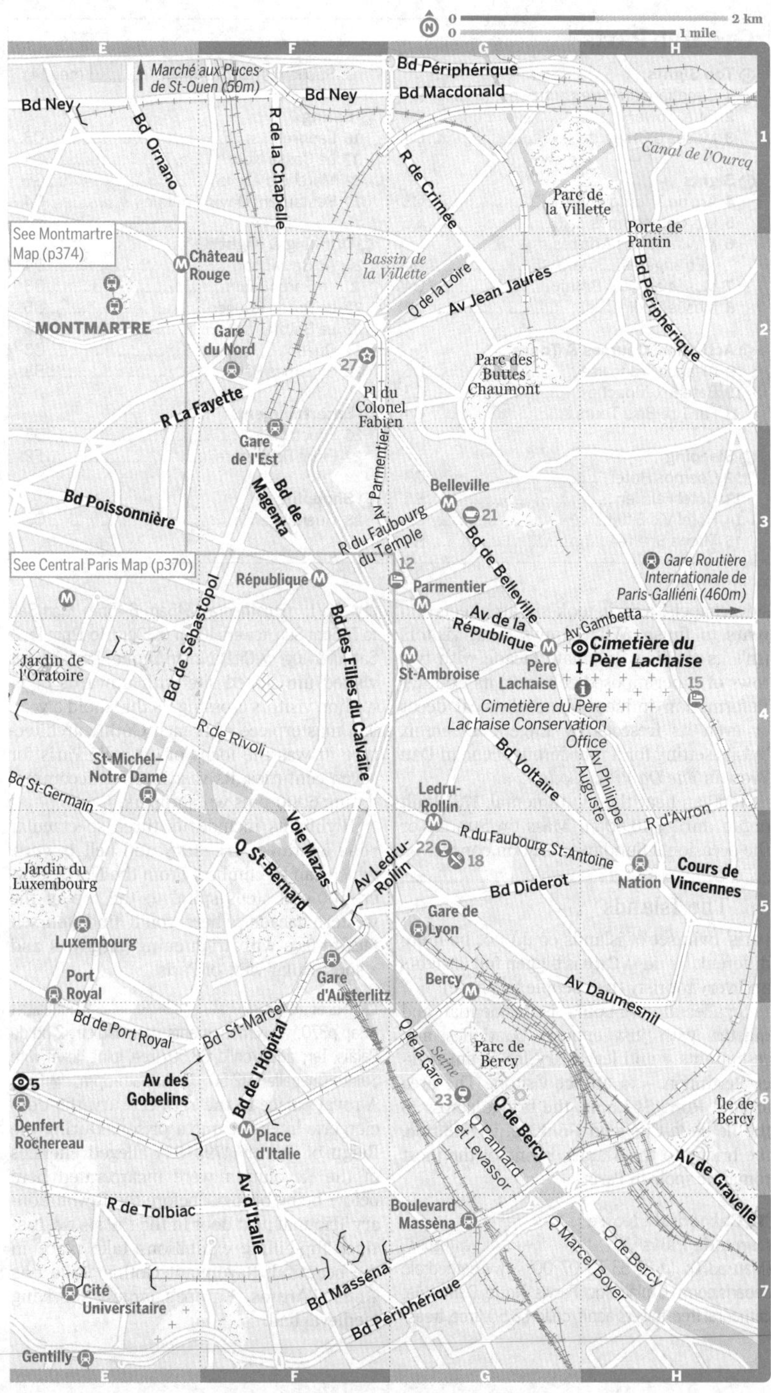

0 2 km
0 1 mile
Bd Périphérique
Marché aux Puces de St-Ouen (50m)
Bd Ney
Bd Macdonald
Bd Ornano
R de la Chapelle
R de Crimée
Canal de l'Ourcq
Parc de la Villette
See Montmartre Map (p374)
Château Rouge
Porte de Pantin
Bassin de la Villette
Q de la Loire
Av Jean Jaurès
MONTMARTRE
Gare du Nord
27
Parc des Buttes Chaumont
R La Fayette
Pl du Colonel Fabien
Gare de l'Est
Av Parmentier
Bd de Magenta
Bd Poissonnière
Belleville
21
R du Faubourg du Temple
Bd de Belleville
See Central Paris Map (p370)
12
République
Parmentier
Gare Routière Internationale de Paris-Galliéni (460m)
Bd de Sébastopol
Bd des Filles du Calvaire
Av de la République
Av Gambetta
Cimetière du Père Lachaise
1
Jardin de l'Oratoire
St-Ambroise
Père Lachaise
15
R de Rivoli
Cimetière du Père Lachaise Conservation Office
St-Michel–Notre Dame
Bd Voltaire
Av Philippe Auguste
Bd St-Germain
Ledru-Rollin
R d'Avron
Voie Mazas
Q St-Bernard
22
18
R du Faubourg St-Antoine
Nation
Cours de Vincennes
Jardin du Luxembourg
Av Ledru-Rollin
Bd Diderot
Gare de Lyon
Luxembourg
Port Royal
Gare d'Austerlitz
Bercy
Av Daumesnil
Bd de Port Royal
Bd St-Marcel
Q de la Gare
Seine
Parc de Bercy
5
Av des Gobelins
Bd de l'Hôpital
23
Île de Bercy
Denfert Rochereau
Q de Bercy
Q Panhard et Levassor
Place d'Italie
Av de Gravelle
R de Tolbiac
Av d'Italie
Boulevard Massèna
Q Marcel Boyer
Q de Bercy
Cité Universitaire
Bd Masséna
Bd Périphérique
Gentilly
FRANCE PARIS

Greater Paris

Top Sights
1 Cimetière du Père Lachaise H4
2 Eiffel Tower C4
3 Musée d'Orsay D4

Sights
4 Arc de Triomphe C3
5 Les Catacombes E6
6 Ministère des Affaires Étrangères D4
7 Musée du Quai Branly C4
8 Musée Rodin D4

Activities, Courses & Tours
9 Alliance Française D5
10 Bateaux-Mouches C3
11 Fat Tire Bike Tours C4

Sleeping
12 Cosmos Hôtel G3
13 Hôtel Félicien B5
14 Hôtel Vic Eiffel C5
15 Mama Shelter H4
Sublim Eiffel .... (see 14)

Eating
16 Ladurée C3
17 Le Casse Noix C4
18 Marché d'Aligre G5
19 Restaurant David Toutain C4

Drinking & Nightlife
20 Au Sauvignon D4
21 Le Barbouquin G3
22 Le Baron Rouge G5
23 Le Batofar G6
24 Queen C3
25 St James Paris B3

Entertainment
26 Fnac D5
27 Point Éphémère F2

Shopping
28 Guerlain C3

side chapels, and it took six architects 150 years to finish. What draws most visitors isn't its striking Italianate facade with two rows of superimposed columns, its Counter Reformation–influenced neoclassical decor or even its frescoes by Eugène Delecroix but its setting for a murderous scene in Dan Brown's *The Da Vinci Code*.

You can hear the monumental, 1781-built organ during 10.30am Mass on Sunday or the occasional Sunday-afternoon concert.

The Islands

Paris' twin set of islands could not be more different. **Île de la Cité** is bigger, full of sights and very touristy (few people live here).

Smaller **Île St-Louis** is residential and quieter, with just enough boutiques and restaurants – and legendary ice-cream maker Berthillon – to attract visitors. The area around **Pont St-Louis**, the bridge across to the Île de la Cité, and **Pont Louis-Philippe**, the bridge to the Marais, is one of the most romantic spots in Paris.

★ Cathédrale Notre Dame de Paris — CATHEDRAL

(Map p370; ☎01 53 10 07 00; www.cathedraledeparis.com; 6 place du Parvis Notre Dame, 4e; cathedral free, towers adult/child €8.50/free, treasury €2/1; ⊙cathedral 7.45am-6.45pm Mon-Sat, to 7.15pm Sun, towers 10am-6.30pm, to 11pm Fri & Sat Jul & Aug; M Cité) Notre Dame, Paris' most visited unticketed site with upwards of 14 million visitors crossing its threshold a year, is a masterpiece of French Gothic architecture. It was the focus of Catholic Paris for seven centuries, its vast interior accommodating 6000-plus worshippers.

Highlights include its three spectacular **rose windows**, **treasury** and bell **towers**, which can be climbed. From the North Tower, 400-odd steps spiral to the top of the western facade, where you'll find yourself face-to-face with frightening gargoyles and a spectacular view of Paris.

Conciergerie — MONUMENT

(Map p370; www.monuments-nationaux.fr; 2 bd du Palais, 1er; adult/child €8.50/free, joint ticket with Sainte-Chapelle €12.50; ⊙9.30am-6pm; M Cité) A royal palace in the 14th century, the Conciergerie later became a prison. During the Reign of Terror (1793–94) alleged enemies of the Revolution were incarcerated here before being brought before the Revolutionary Tribunal next door in the **Palais de Justice**. Top-billing exhibitions take place in the beautiful, Rayonnant Gothic **Salle des Gens d'Armes**, Europe's largest surviving medieval hall.

Right Bank

★Musée du Louvre MUSEUM

(Map p370; ☎01 40 20 53 17; www.louvre.fr; rue de Rivoli & quai des Tuileries, 1er; adult/child €12/free; ⏱9am-6pm Mon, Thu, Sat & Sun, to 9.45pm Wed & Fri; Ⓜ Palais Royal–Musée du Louvre) Few art galleries are as prized or daunting as the Musée du Louvre, Paris' pièce de résistance no first-time visitor to the city can resist. This is, after all, one of the world's largest and most diverse museums. Showcase to 35,000 works of art – from Mesopotamian, Egyptian and Greek antiquities to masterpieces by artists such as da Vinci, Michelangelo and Rembrandt – it would take nine months to glance at every piece, rendering advance planning essential.

★Cimetière du Père Lachaise CEMETERY

(Map p366; ☎01 43 70 70 33; www.pere-lachaise.com; 16 rue du Repos & bd de Ménilmontant, 20e; ⏱8am-6pm Mon-Fri, 8.30am-6pm Sat, 9am-6pm Sun; Ⓜ Père Lachaise or Gambetta) FREE The world's most visited cemetery, Père Lachaise, opened in 1804. Its 70,000 ornate, even ostentatious, tombs of the rich and/or famous form a verdant, 44-hectare sculpture garden. The most visited are those of 1960s rock star Jim Morrison (division 6) and Oscar Wilde (division 89). Pick up cemetery maps at the **conservation office** (Map p366; 16 rue du Repos, 20e; ⏱8.30am-12.30pm & 2-5pm Mon-Fri; Ⓜ Père Lachaise), near the main bd de Ménilmontant entrance.

Arc de Triomphe LANDMARK

(Map p366; www.monuments-nationaux.fr; place Charles de Gaulle, 8e; adult/child €9.50/free; ⏱10am-11pm Apr-Sep, to 10.30pm Oct-Mar; Ⓜ Charles de Gaulle–Étoile) If anything rivals the Eiffel Tower as the symbol of Paris, it's this magnificent 1836 monument to Napoléon's 1805 victory at Austerlitz, which he commissioned the following year. The intricately sculpted triumphal arch stands sentinel in the centre of the Étoile ('star') roundabout. From the viewing platform on top of the arch (50m up via 284 steps and well worth the climb) you can see the dozen avenues.

Centre Pompidou MUSEUM

(Map p370; ☎01 44 78 12 33; www.centrepompidou.fr; place Georges Pompidou, 4e; museum, exhibitions & panorama adult/child €13/free; ⏱11am-9pm Wed-Mon; 📶; Ⓜ Rambuteau) The Pompidou Centre has amazed and delighted visitors ever since it opened in 1977, not just for its outstanding collection of modern art – the largest in Europe – but also for its radical architectural statement. The dynamic and vibrant arts centre delights with its irresistible cocktail of galleries and cutting-edge exhibitions, hands-on workshops, dance performances, cinemas and other entertainment venues. The exterior, with its street performers and fanciful fountains (place Igor Stravinsky), is a fun place to linger.

Basilique du Sacré-Cœur BASILICA

(Map p374; www.sacre-coeur-montmartre.com; place du Parvis du Sacré-Cœur; dome adult/child €6/4, cash only; ⏱6am-10.30pm, dome 9am-7pm Apr-Sep, to 5.30pm Oct-Mar; Ⓜ Anvers) Although some may poke fun at Sacré-Cœur's unsubtle design, the view from its parvis is one of those perfect Paris postcards. More than just a basilica, Sacré-Cœur is a veritable experience, from the musicians performing on the steps to the groups of friends picnicking on the hillside park. Touristy, yes. But beneath it all, Sacré-Cœur's heart still shines gold.

Musée Picasso ART MUSEUM

(Map p370; ☎01 42 71 25 21; www.museepicassoparis.fr; 5 rue de Thorigny, 3e; admission €11; ⏱11.30am-6pm Tue-Fri, 9.30am-6pm Sat & Sun;

THE LOUVRE: TICKETS & TOURS

To best navigate the collection, opt for a self-guided **thematic trail** (1½ to three hours; download trail brochures in advance from the website) or a self-paced **multimedia guide** (€5). More formal, English-language **guided tours** depart from the Hall Napoléon, which also has free English-language maps.

The main entrance and ticket windows are covered by the 21m-high **Grande Pyramide**, a glass pyramid designed by the Chinese-born American architect IM Pei. If you don't have the Museum Pass (which gives you priority), you can avoid the longest queues (for security) outside the pyramid by entering the Louvre complex via the underground shopping centre **Carrousel du Louvre** (Map p370; www.carrouseldu-louvre.com; 99 rue de Rivoli; ⏱8am-11pm, shops 10am-8pm; 📶; Ⓜ Palais Royal–Musée du Louvre). You'll need to queue up again to buy your ticket once inside.

Central Paris

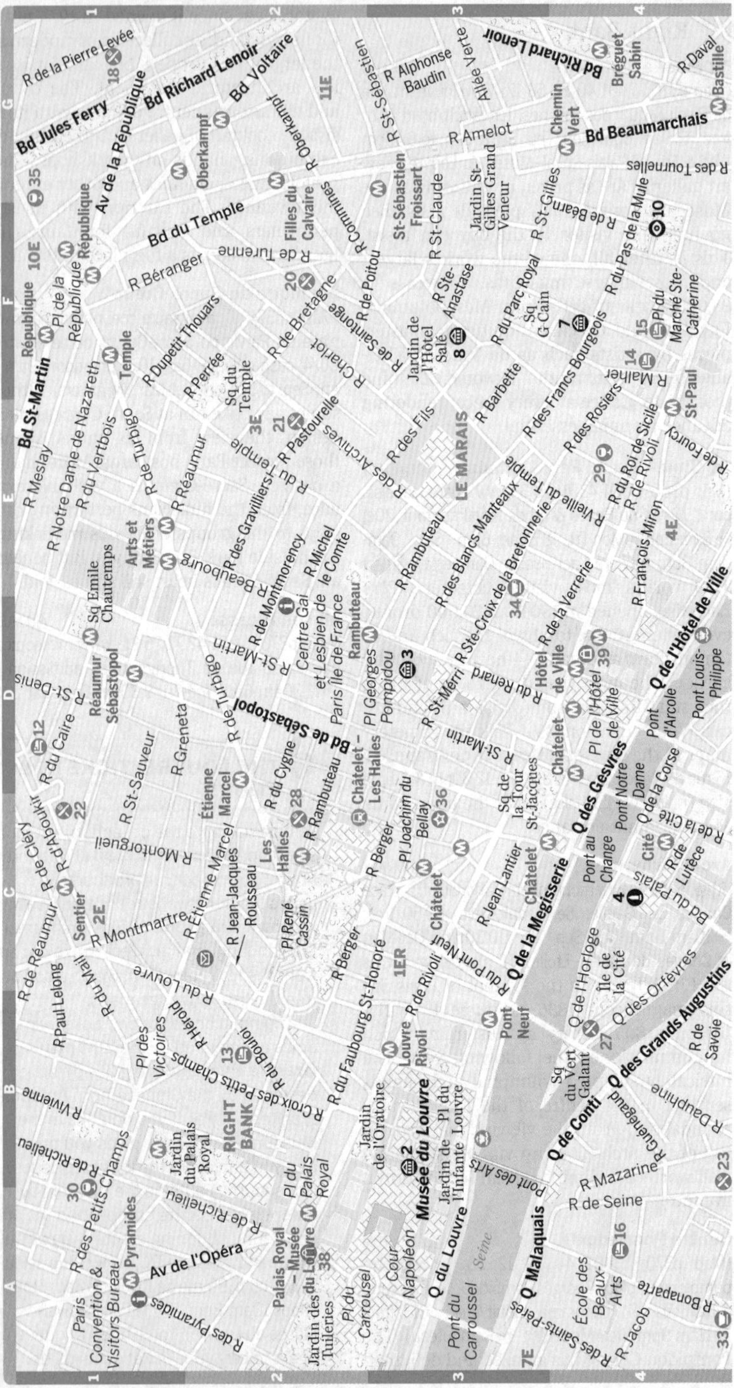

0 400 m
0 0.2 miles

A B C D E F G

1 2 3 4

Paris Convention & Visitors Bureau
Pyramides
R des Pyramides
Av de l'Opéra
R des Petits Champs
30
R de Richelieu
R Vivienne
Jardin du Palais Royal
R de Richelieu
RIGHT BANK
13
R Croix des Petits Champs
R du Bouloi
Palais Royal – Musée du Louvre
38
Pl du Palais Royal
Jardin des Tuileries
Pl du Carrousel
Cour Napoléon
2
Musée du Louvre
Jardin de l'Infante
Pl du Louvre
Jardin de l'Oratoire
Q du Louvre
Pont du Carroussel
Seine
Pont des Arts
7E
Q Malaquais
R des Saints-Pères
École des Beaux-Arts
16
R de Seine
R Mazarine
R Jacob
R Bonaparte
33
23
Q de Conti
R Guénégaud
R Dauphine
Q des Grands Augustins
R de Savoie
Sq du Vert Galant
27
Q de l'Horloge
Île de la Cité
Q des Orfèvres
Pl des Victoires
R Hérold
R du Louvre
R du Mail
R Paul Lelong
R de Réaumur
R de Cléry
R d'Aboukir
Sentier
2E
R Montmartre
22
R du Caire
12
R St-Denis
R Montorgueil
R St-Sauveur
R Étienne Marcel
R Jean-Jacques Rousseau
Pl René Cassin
R du Faubourg St-Honoré
R Berger
1ER
Louvre Rivoli
R de Rivoli
R du Pont Neuf
Pont Neuf
Q de la Megisserie
R Jean Lantier
Châtelet
4
Bd du Palais
Cité
R de Lutèce
R de la Cité
Q de la Corse
Pont au Change
Pont Notre Dame
Q des Gesvres
Pont d'Arcole
Pont Louis-Philippe
Q de l'Hôtel de Ville
Les Halles
28
R Rambuteau
Châtelet – Les Halles
R Berger
Pl Joachim du Bellay
36
Châtelet
Étienne Marcel
R Greneta
R du Cygne
Bd de Sébastopol
Réaumur Sébastopol
Sq Emile Chautemps
R de Turbigo
R St-Martin
Centre Gai et Lesbien de Paris Île de France
Pl Georges Pompidou
Rambuteau
3
R St-Merri
R St-Martin
Sq de la Tour St-Jacques
R du Renard
Hôtel de Ville
Châtelet
Pl de l'Hôtel de Ville
39
34
R de la Verrerie
R Ste-Croix de la Bretonnerie
R de Montmorency
R Beaubourg
Arts et Métiers
R des Gravilliers
R Michel le Comte
R Rambuteau
R des Blancs Manteaux
LE MARAIS
R Vieille du Temple
R François Miron
4E
R du Roi de Sicile
R de Rivoli
R des Rosiers
29
R de Fourcy
St-Paul
R Malher
14
15
Pl du Marché Ste-Catherine
R des Francs Bourgeois
R des Archives
R des Fils
R du Temple
3E
21
R Pastourelle
R Charlot
R de Saintonge
R de Bretagne
Sq du Temple
R Perrée
R Dupetit Thouars
R Réaumur
R de Turbigo
R du Vertbois
R Notre Dame de Nazareth
R Meslay
Bd St-Martin
Temple
République
Pl de la République
10E
35
République
R Béranger
Bd du Temple
R de Turenne
20
Filles du Calvaire
R Commines
R de Poitou
Jardin de l'Hôtel Salé
8
R Ste-Anastase
R St-Claude
St-Sébastien Froissart
R St-Sébastien
R Barbette
R du Parc Royal
Sq G Cain
7
R du Pas de la Mule
10
R de Béarn
R St-Gilles
Jardin St-Gilles Grand Veneur
R Amelot
R des Tournelles
Bd Beaumarchais
Chemin Vert
Bréguet Sabin
Bastille
R Daval
Bd Richard Lenoir
Allée Verte
R Alphonse Baudin
11E
R Oberkampf
Oberkampf
Bd Voltaire
Bd Richard Lenoir
Av de la République
Bd Jules Ferry
18
R de la Pierre Levée

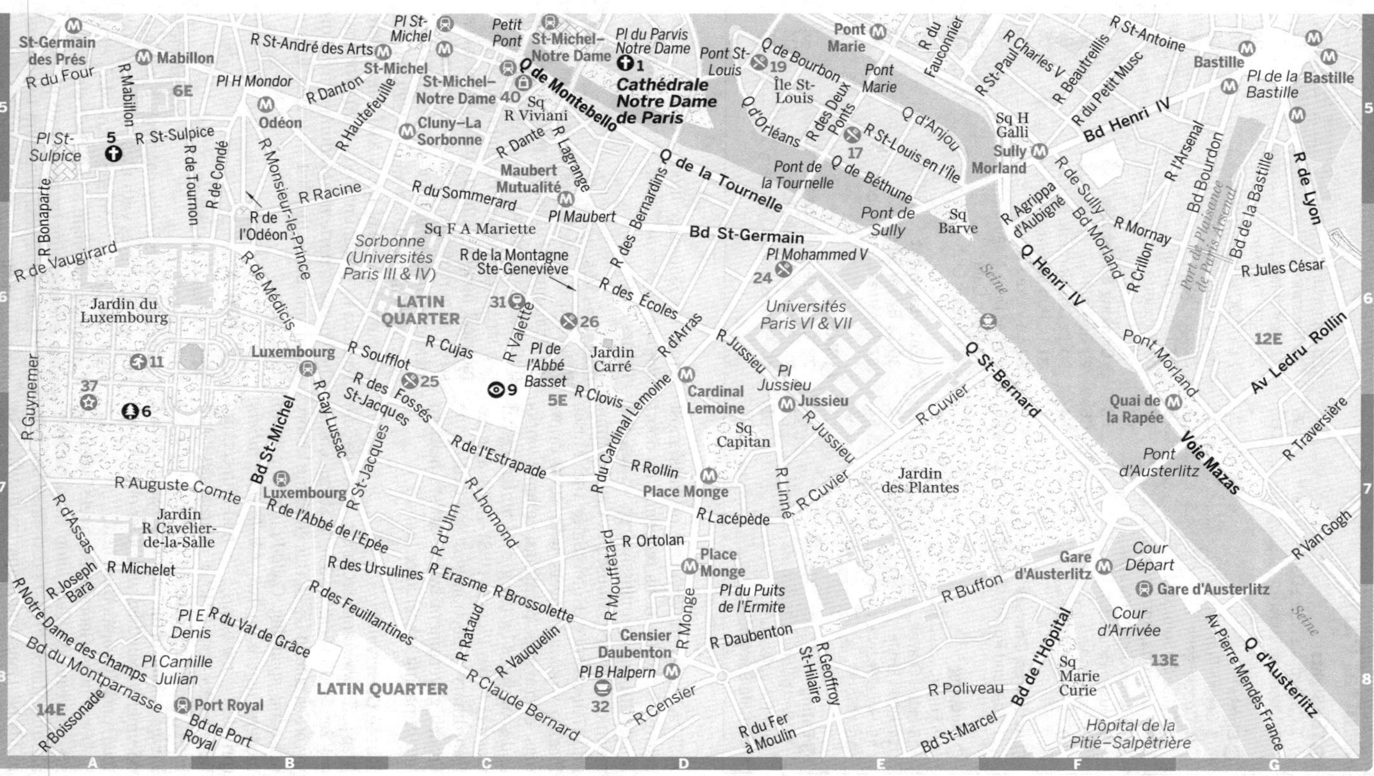
St-Germain des Prés
Mabillon
R du Four
R Mabillon
6E
Pl H Mondor
R St-André des Arts
St-Michel
Pl St-Michel
Petit Pont
St-Michel–Notre Dame
Pl du Parvis Notre Dame
1
Cathédrale Notre Dame de Paris
Q de Montebello
40
Sq R Viviani
Cluny–La Sorbonne
R Danton
R Hautefeuille
Odéon
Pl St-Sulpice
5
R St-Sulpice
R de Tournon
R de Condé
R Monsieur-le-Prince
R de l'Odéon
R Racine
R du Sommerard
R Dante
R Lagrange
Maubert Mutualité
Pl Maubert
Sq F A Mariette
R Bonaparte
R de Vaugirard
Sorbonne (Universités Paris III & IV)
R de la Montagne Ste-Geneviève
R des Bernardins
Q de la Tournelle
Bd St-Germain
Pont St-Louis
19
Q de Bourbon
Île St-Louis
Q d'Orléans
R des Deux Ponts
17
R St-Louis en l'Île
Pont de la Tournelle
Q de Béthune
Pont de Sully
Pont Marie
Q d'Anjou
R du Fauconnier
R St-Paul
R Charles V
R Beautreillis
R du Petit Musc
R St-Antoine
Bastille
Pl de la Bastille
Sq H Galli
Sully Morland
Bd Henri IV
R de Sully
R Agrippa d'Aubigné
Bd Morland
R Mornay
R Crillon
R l'Arsenal
Bd Bourdon
Port de Plaisance de Paris Arsenal
Bd de la Bastille
R de Lyon
R Jules César
Sq Barye
Q Henri IV
Seine
Pl Mohammed V
24
R de Médicis
Jardin du Luxembourg
LATIN QUARTER
31
R Valette
26
R des Écoles
R d'Arras
Universités Paris VI & VII
Luxembourg
R Soufflot
R Cujas
Pl de l'Abbé Basset
Jardin Carré
R Jussieu
Pl Jussieu
Jussieu
Cardinal Lemoine
Q St-Bernard
Pont Morland
12E
Av Ledru Rollin
11
37
6
R Guynemer
25
R des Fossés St-Jacques
9
5E
R Clovis
R du Cardinal Lemoine
Sq Capitan
R Cuvier
Quai de la Rapée
Voie Mazas
R Traversière
Bd St-Michel
R Gay Lussac
R St-Jacques
R de l'Estrapade
R Rollin
Place Monge
R Linné
Jardin des Plantes
Pont d'Austerlitz
R Auguste Comte
R de l'Abbé de l'Epée
R Lhomond
R d'Ulm
R Lacépède
R d'Assas
Jardin R Cavelier-de-la-Salle
R Ortolan
R Mouffetard
R Van Gogh
Cour Départ
Gare d'Austerlitz
R Michelet
R des Ursulines
R Erasme
R Brossolette
Pl du Puits de l'Ermite
R Buffon
R Joseph Bara
R Notre Dame des Champs
Bd du Montparnasse
Pl E Denis
R du Val de Grâce
R des Feuillantines
R Rataud
Censier Daubenton
R Monge
R Daubenton
Cour d'Arrivée
Av Pierre Mendès France
Q d'Austerlitz
Pl Camille Julian
R Vauquelin
Pl B Halpern
R Geoffroy St-Hilaire
Bd de l'Hôpital
Sq Marie Curie
13E
14E
R Boissonade
Port Royal
Bd de Port Royal
LATIN QUARTER
R Claude Bernard
32
R Censier
R du Fer à Moulin
Bd St-Marcel
R Poliveau
Hôpital de la Pitié–Salpêtrière
A
B
C
D
E
F
G
5
6
7
8

Central Paris

Top Sights
1 Cathédrale Notre Dame de Paris D5
2 Musée du Louvre B3

Sights
3 Centre Pompidou D3
4 Conciergerie C4
5 Église St-Sulpice A5
6 Jardin du Luxembourg A7
7 Musée Carnavalet F4
8 Musée Picasso F3
9 Panthéon C6
10 Place des Vosges F4

Activities, Courses & Tours
11 Shetland Ponies for Hire A6

Sleeping
12 Edgar D1
13 Hôtel Crayon B2
14 Hôtel Emile F4
15 Hôtel Jeanne d'Arc F4
16 L'Hôtel A4

Eating
17 Berthillon E5
18 Blue Valentine G1
19 Café Saint Régis D5
20 Candelaria F2
21 Dessance E2
22 Frenchie C1
23 JSFP Traiteur B4
24 L'AOC E6
25 Le Comptoir du Panthéon C6
26 Les Pipos C6
27 Les Voyelles B4
28 Pirouette C2

Drinking & Nightlife
29 3w Kafé E4
30 La Champmeslé B1
31 Le Pub St-Hilaire C6
32 Le Verre à Pied D8
33 Les Deux Magots A4
34 Open Café E3
35 Scream Club G1

Entertainment
36 Le Baiser Salé C3
37 Théâtre du Luxembourg A7

Shopping
38 Carrousel du Louvre A2
39 Paris Rendez-Vous D4
40 Shakespeare & Company C5

M St-Paul or Chemin Vert) One of Paris' most beloved art collections reopened its doors in late 2014 after a massive renovation and much controversy. Housed in the stunning, mid-17th-century Hôtel Salé, the Musée Picasso woos art lovers with 5000 drawings, engravings, paintings, ceramic works and sculptures by the *grand maître* (great master) Pablo Picasso (1881–1973). The extraordinary collection was donated to the French government by the artist's heirs in lieu of paying inheritance tax.

Musée Carnavalet MUSEUM
(Map p370; www.carnavalet.paris.fr; 23 rue de Sévigné, 3e; 10am-6pm Tue-Sun; M St-Paul, Chemin Vert or Rambuteau) FREE This engaging history museum, spanning Gallo-Roman times to modern day, is in two *hôtels particuliers* (private mansions): mid-16th-century Renaissance-style Hôtel Carnavalet and late-17th-century Hôtel Le Peletier de St-Fargeau. Some of the nation's most important documents, paintings and other objects from the French Revolution are here.

Don't miss Georges Fouquet's stunning art nouveau jewellery shop from rue Royale, and Marcel Proust's cork-lined bedroom in his bd Haussmann apartment where he wrote his 7350-page literary cycle *À la Recherche du Temps Perdu (*Remembrance of Things Past).

Place des Vosges SQUARE
(Map p370; place des Vosges, 4e; M St-Paul or Bastille) Inaugurated in 1612 as place Royale and thus Paris' oldest square, place des Vosges is a strikingly elegant ensemble of 36 symmetrical houses with ground-floor arcades, steep slate roofs and large dormer windows arranged around a leafy square with four symmetrical fountains and an 1829 copy of a mounted statue of Louis XIII. The square received its present name in 1800 to honour the Vosges *département* (administrative division) for being the first in France to pay its taxes.

Tours

★Parisien d'un jour – Paris Greeters WALKING TOUR
(www.parisgreeters.fr; by donation) See Paris through local eyes with these two- to three-hour city tours. Volunteers – knowledgeable Parisians passionate about their city in the main – lead groups (maximum six people) to their favourite spots. Minimum two weeks' notice needed.

Fat Tire Bike Tours CYCLING
(Map p366; ☎01 56 58 10 54; www.fattirebiketours.com) Day and night bike tours of the city, both in central Paris and further afield to Versailles and Monet's garden in Giverny.

Bateaux-Mouches BOAT TOUR
(Map p366; ☎01 42 25 96 10; www.bateauxmouches.com; Port de la Conférence, 8e; adult/child €13.50/5.50; ⊙Apr-Dec; MAlma Marceau) The largest river cruise company in Paris and a favourite with tour groups. Cruises (70 minutes) run regularly from 10.15am to 11pm April to September and 13 times a day between 11am and 9pm the rest of the year. Commentary is in French and English. It's located on the Right Bank, just east of the Pont de l'Alma.

Paris Walks WALKING TOUR
(☎01 48 09 21 40; www.paris-walks.com; adult/child €12/8) Long established and highly rated by our readers, Paris Walks offers two-hour thematic walking tours (art, fashion, chocolate, the French Revolution etc).

Sleeping

The Paris Convention & Visitors Bureau (p380) can find you a place to stay (no booking fee, but you need a credit card), though queues can be long in high season. To rent an apartment, try **Paris Attitude** (www.parisattitude.com).

Left Bank

Hôtel Vic Eiffel BOUTIQUE HOTEL €
(Map p366; www.hotelviceiffel.com; 92 bd Garibaldi, 15e; s/d from €99/109; ; MSèvres-Lecourbe) Outstanding value for money, this pristine hotel with chic orange and oyster-grey rooms (two are wheelchair accessible) is a short walk from the Eiffel Tower, with the metro on the doorstep. Budget-priced Classic rooms are small but perfectly functional; midrange Superior and Privilege rooms offer increased space. Friendly staff go out of their way to help.

★**Hôtel Félicien** BOUTIQUE HOTEL €€
(Map p366; ☎01 83 76 02 45; www.hotelfelicien-paris.com; 21 rue Félicien David, 16e; d €120-280; ; MMirabeau) The price-quality ratio at this chic boutique hotel, squirrelled away in a 1930s building, is outstanding. Exquisitely designed rooms feel more five-star than four, with 'White' and 'Silver' suites on the hotel's top 'Sky floor' more than satisfying their promise of indulgent cocooning. Romantics, eat your heart out.

Sublim Eiffel DESIGN HOTEL €€
(Map p366; ☎01 40 65 95 95; www.sublimeiffel.com; 94 bd Garibaldi, 15e; d from €140; ; MSèvres-Lecourbe) There's no forgetting what city you're in with the Eiffel Tower motifs in reception and rooms (along with Parisian street-map carpets and metro-tunnel-shaped bedheads) plus glittering tower views from upper-floor windows. Edgy design elements also include cobblestone staircase carpeting (there's also a lift/elevator) and, fittingly in *la ville lumière,* technicoloured in-room fibre-optic lighting. The small wellness centre/hammam offers massages.

L'Hôtel BOUTIQUE HOTEL €€€
(Map p370; ☎01 44 41 99 00; www.l-hotel.com; 13 rue des Beaux Arts, 6e; d €275-495; ; MSt-Germain des Prés) In a quiet quayside street, this award-winning hostelry is the stuff of romance, Parisian myths and urban legends. Rock- and film-star patrons fight to sleep in room 16, where Oscar Wilde died in 1900 and which is now decorated with a peacock motif, or in the art deco room 36 (which entertainer Mistinguett once stayed in), with its huge mirrored bed.

Right Bank

★**Mama Shelter** DESIGN HOTEL €
(Map p366; ☎01 43 48 48 48; www.mamashelter.com; 109 rue de Bagnolet, 20e; s/d from €79/89; ; 76, MAlexandre Dumas or Gambetta) Coaxed into its zany new incarnation by uberdesigner Philippe Starck, this former car park offers what is surely the best-value ccommodation in the city. Its 170 supercomfortable rooms feature iMacs, trademark Starck details like a chocolate-and-fuchsia colour scheme, concrete walls and even microwave ovens, while a rooftop terrace and cool pizzeria add to the hotel's street cred.

Cosmos Hôtel HOTEL €
(Map p366; ☎01 43 57 25 88; www.cosmos-hotel-paris.com; 35 rue Jean-Pierre Timbaud, 11e; s €62-75, d €68-75, tr/q €85/94; ; MRépublique) Cheap, brilliant value and just footsteps from the nightlife of rue JPT, Cosmos is a shiny star with retro style on the budget-hotel scene. It has been around for 30-odd years but, unlike most other hotels in the same price bracket, Cosmos has been treated

Montmartre

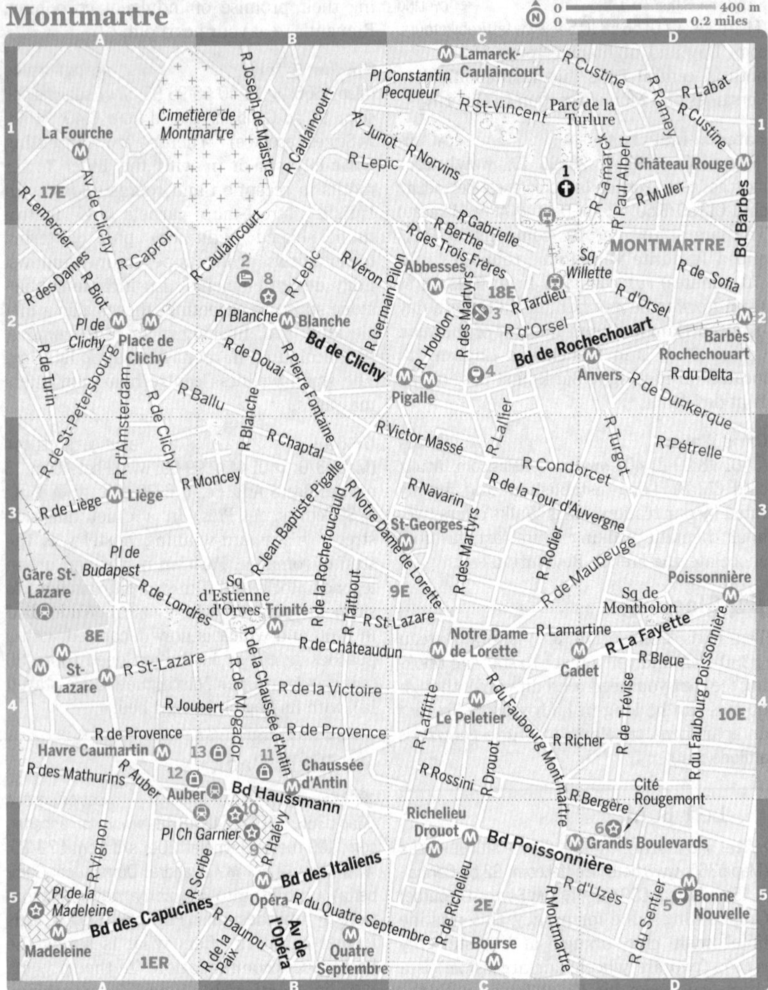

Montmartre

Sights

1 Basilique du Sacré-Cœur C1

Sleeping

2 Loft B2

Eating

3 Le Miroir C2

Drinking & Nightlife

4 La Fourmi C2
5 Le Rex Club D5

Entertainment

6 Au Limonaire D5
7 Kiosque Théâtre Madeleine A5
8 Moulin Rouge B2
9 Palais Garnier B5
10 Palais Garnier Box Office B5

Shopping

11 Galeries Lafayette B4
12 Galeries Lafayette - Home Design A4
13 Galeries Lafayette - Men's Store B4

to a thoroughly modern makeover this century. Breakfast is €8.

★Loft APARTMENT €€

(Map p374; ☎06 14 48 47 48; www.loft-paris.fr; 7 cité Véron, 18e; apt €100-270; ; M Blanche) Book months in advance to secure one of the stylish apartments in this gem, which offers an intimacy that simply cannot be replicated in a hotel. Just around the corner from the Moulin Rouge, this apartment block offers choices ranging from a two-person studio to a loft that can fit a large family or group. The owner, a culture journalist, is a great resource.

Hôtel Jeanne d'Arc HOTEL €€

(Map p370; ☎01 48 87 62 11; www.hoteljeannedarc.com; 3 rue de Jarente, 4e; s €72, d €98-120, q €250; ; M St-Paul) About the only thing wrong with this gorgeous address is everyone knows about it; book well in advance. Games to play, a painted rocking chair for tots in the bijou lounge, knick-knacks everywhere and the most extraordinary mirror in the breakfast room create a real 'family home' air in this 35-room house.

Hôtel Emile DESIGN HOTEL €€

(Map p370; ☎01 42 72 76 17; www.hotelemile.com; 2 rue Malher, 4e; s €170, d €180-230, ste €350; ; M St-Paul) Prepare to be dazzled – literally. Retro B&W, geometrically patterned carpets, curtains, wallpapers and drapes dress this chic hotel, wedged between boutiques and restaurants in the Marais. Pricier 'top floor' doubles are just that, complete with breathtaking outlook over Parisian roofs and chimney pots. Breakfast, included in the price, is on bar stools in the lobby; open the cupboard to find the 'kitchen'.

Edgar BOUTIQUE HOTEL €€

(Map p370; ☎01 40 41 05 19; www.edgarparis.com; 31 rue d'Alexandrie, 2e; d €235-295; ; M Strasbourg St-Denis) Twelve playful rooms, each decorated by a different team of artists or designers, await the lucky few who secure a reservation at this former convent/seamstress workshop. Milagros conjures up all the magic of the Far West, while Dream echoes the rich imagination of childhood with surrealist installations. Breakfast is served in the popular downstairs restaurant, and the hidden tree-shaded square is a fabulous location.

★Hôtel Molitor BOUTIQUE HOTEL €€€

(☎01 56 07 08 50; www.mltr.fr; 2 av de la porte Molitor, 16e; d from €270; ; M Michel Ange Molitor) Famed as Paris' swishest swimming pool in the 1930s (where the bikini made its first appearance, no less) and hot spot for graffiti art in the 1990s, the Molitor is one seriously mythical address. The art deco complex, built in 1929 and abandoned from 1989, has been restored to stunning effect.

Hôtel Crayon BOUTIQUE HOTEL €€€

(Map p370; ☎01 42 36 54 19; www.hotelcrayon.com; 25 rue du Bouloi, 1er; s/d €311/347; ; M Les Halles or Sentier) Line drawings by French artist Julie Gauthron bedeck walls and doors at this creative boutique hotel. The pencil *(le crayon)* is the theme, with 26 rooms sporting a different shade of each floor's chosen colour – we love the coloured-glass shower doors and the books on the bedside table that guests can swap and take home. Online deals often slash rates by more than 50%.

Eating

Left Bank

★JSFP Traiteur DELICATESSEN €

(Map p370; http://jsfp-traiteur.com; 8 rue de Buci, 6e; dishes €3.40-5.70; 9.30am-8.30pm; ; M Mabillon) Brimming with big bowls of salad, terrines, pâté and other prepared delicacies, this deli is a brilliant bet for quality Parisian 'fast food' such as quiches in a variety of flavour combinations (courgette and chive, mozzarella and basil, salmon and spinach...) to take to a nearby park, square or stretch of riverfront.

Le Comptoir du Panthéon CAFE, BRASSERIE €

(Map p370; ☎01 43 54 75 56; 5 rue Soufflot, 5e; salads €11-13, mains €12.40-15.40; 7am-1.45am; ; M Cardinal Lemoine or RER Luxembourg) Enormous, creative meal-size salads are the reason to pick this as a dining spot. Magnificently placed across from the domed Panthéon on the shady side of the street, its pavement terrace is big, busy and oh so Parisian – turn your head away from Voltaire's burial place and the Eiffel Tower pops into view.

Le Casse Noix MODERN FRENCH €€

(Map p366; ☎01 45 66 09 01; www.le-cassenoix.fr; 56 rue de la Fédération, 15e; 2-/3-course lunch menus €21/26, 3-course dinner menu €33; noon-2.30pm & 7-10.30pm Mon-Fri; M Bir Hakeim) Proving that

DON'T MISS

TOP THREE FOR SWEET TREATS

The French have something of a sweet tooth – from breakfast *viennoiseries* (sweet baked goods) to fabulous desserts, crêpes and ice creams, sweets are part and parcel of the gastronomy. Here are our top Parisian picks for a treat:

Ladurée (Map p366; www.laduree.com; 75 av des Champs-Élysées, 8e; pastries from €1.50; ⌚7.30am-11.30pm Mon-Fri, 8.30am-12.30am Sat, 8.30am-11.30pm Sun; Ⓜ George V) Its macarons are so famous they seldom need introducing.

Berthillon (Map p370; 31 rue St-Louis en l'Île, 4e; 2-/3-/4-ball cone or tub €2.50/5.50/7; ⌚10am-8pm Wed-Sun; Ⓜ Pont Marie) Berthillon is to ice cream what Château Lafite Rothschild is to wine: the Holy Grail. There are 70-odd flavours to choose from, including seasonal ones.

Dessance (Map p370; ☎01 42 77 23 62; www.dessance.fr; 74 rue des Archives, 3e; desserts à la carte €19, 4-course dessert menu €36-44; ⌚3-11pm Wed-Fri, noon-midnight Sat & Sun; 👪; Ⓜ Arts et Métiers) Incredible as it sounds, this restaurant only serves desserts – although some of the 'dishes' may surprise you.

a location footsteps from the Eiffel Tower doesn't mean compromising on quality, quantity or authenticity, 'the nutcracker' is a neighbourhood gem with a cosy retro interior, affordable prices and exceptional cuisine that changes by season and by the inspiration of owner/chef Pierre Olivier Lenormand, who has honed his skills in some of Paris' most fêted kitchens. Book ahead.

Les Pipos WINE BAR €€
(Map p370; ☎01 43 54 11 40; www.les-pipos.com; 2 rue de l'École Polytechnique, 5e; mains €13.90-26.90; ⌚8am-2am Mon-Sat; Ⓜ Maubert-Mutualité) A feast for the eyes and the senses, this *bar à vins* is above all worth a visit for its food. The bistro standards (boeuf bourguignon) and *charcuteries de terroir* (regional cold meats and sausages) are mouth-watering, as is the cheese board, which includes all the gourmet names (bleu d'Auvergne, St-Félicien, St-Marcellin). No credit cards.

L'AOC TRADITIONAL FRENCH €€
(Map p370; ☎01 43 54 22 52; www.restoaoc.com; 14 rue des Fossés St-Bernard, 5e; 2-/3-course lunch menus €21/29, mains €19-36; ⌚noon-2.30pm & 7.30-10.30pm Tue-Sat; Ⓜ Cardinal Lemoine) *'Bistrot carnivore'* is the strapline of this ingenious restaurant concocted around France's most respected culinary products. The concept is Appellation d'Origine Contrôlée (AOC), meaning everything has been reared or produced according to strict guidelines. The result? Only the best! Choose between meaty favourites (steak tartare) or the rotisserie menu, ranging from roast chicken to suckling pig.

★Restaurant David Toutain GASTRONOMIC €€€
(Map p366; ☎01 45 51 11 10; http://davidtoutain.com; 29 rue Surcouf, 7e; lunch menus €42, lunch & dinner menus €68-98; ⌚noon-2.30pm & 8-10pm Mon-Fri; Ⓜ Invalides) Prepare to be wowed: David Toutain pushes the envelope at his eponymous new restaurant with some of the most creative high-end cooking in Paris today. Mystery degustation courses include unlikely combinations such as smoked eel in green-apple and black-sesame mousse, or candied celery and truffled rice pudding with artichoke praline (stunning wine pairings available).

The Islands

★Café Saint Régis CAFE €
(Map p370; http://cafesaintregisparis.com; 6 rue Jean du Bellay, 4e; salads & mains €14.50-28; ⌚7am-2am; 📶; Ⓜ Pont Marie) Hip and historical with an effortless dose of retro vintage thrown in, Le Saint Régis – as those in the know call it – is a deliciously Parisian hangout any time of day. From pastries for breakfast to a mid-morning pancake, brasserie lunch or early evening oyster platter, Café St-Regis gets it just right. Come midnight it morphs into a late-night hot spot.

Les Voyelles MODERN FRENCH €€
(Map p370; ☎01 46 33 69 75; www.les-voyelles.com; 74 quai des Orfèvres, 4e; plat du jour €12, 2-/3-course menus €17/22.50; ⌚8am-midnight Tue-Sat; Ⓜ Pont Neuf) This new kid on the block is worth the short walk from Notre Dame. The Vowels – spot the letters casually scattered between books and beautiful objects on the shelves lining the intimate 'library' dining room – is thoroughly contemporary, with a menu ranging from finger

food to full-blown dinner to match. Its pavement terrace is Paris gold.

Right Bank

Candelaria MEXICAN €

(Map p370; www.candelariaparis.com; 52 rue Saintonge; tacos €3.20-3.75, quesadillas & tostadas €3.50, lunch menu €11.50; noon-midnight Thu-Sat, to 11pm Sun-Wed; M Filles du Calvaire) You need to know about this terribly cool taqueria to find it. Made of pure, unadulterated hipness in that brazenly nonchalant manner Paris does so well, clandestine Candelaria serves delicious homemade tacos, quesadillas and tostadas in a laid-back setting – squat at the bar in the front or lounge out back around a shared table with bar stools or at low coffee tables.

Le Miroir BISTRO €€

(Map p374; 01 46 06 50 73; http://restaurantmiroir.com; 94 rue des Martyrs, 18e; lunch menu €19.50, dinner menus €27-34; noon-2.30pm & 7.30-11pm Tue-Sat; M Abbesses) This unassuming modern bistro is smack in the middle of the Montmartre tourist trail, yet it remains a local favourite. There are lots of delightful pâtés and rillettes to start off with – guinea hen with dates, duck with mushrooms, haddock and lemon – followed by well-prepared standards like stuffed veal shoulder.

Pirouette NEOBISTRO €€

(Map p370; 01 40 26 47 81; 5 rue Mondétour, 1er; lunch menu €18, 3-/6-course dinner menu €40/60; noon-2.30pm & 7.30-10.30pm Mon-Sat; M Les Halles) In one of the best restaurants in the vicinity of the old 'belly of Paris', chef Tomy Gousset's crew is working wonders at this cool loft-like space, serving up tantalising creations ranging from seared duck, asparagus and Buddha's hand fruit to rum baba with chantilly and lime. Some unique ingredients and a new spin for French cuisine.

Blue Valentine MODERN FRENCH €€

(Map p370; 01 43 38 34 72; http://bluevalentine-restaurant.com; 13 rue de la Pierre Levée, 11e; 2-/3-course menu €29/36, 8-course tasting menu €54; noon-2.30pm & 7.30-11pm Wed-Sun, bar 7pm-2am; M République) This thoroughly modern bistro with retro decor in the increasingly gourmet 11e was a hit the moment it opened in late 2013. A hip crowd flocks here for well-crafted cocktails and Japanese chef Saito Terumitsu's exquisite dishes flavoured with edible flowers and a profusion of herbs. The menu is small – just three dishes to choose from per course – but memorable.

★**Frenchie** BISTRO €€€

(Map p370; 01 40 39 96 19; www.frenchie-restaurant.com; 5-6 rue du Nil, 2e; prix fixe menu €48; 7-11pm Mon-Fri; M Sentier) Tucked down an alley you wouldn't venture down otherwise, this bijou bistro with wooden tables and old stone walls is iconic. Frenchie is always packed and for good reason: excellent-value dishes are modern, market-driven (the menu changes daily with a choice of two dishes) and prepared with just the right dose of unpretentious creative flair by French chef Gregory Marchand.

Drinking & Nightlife

The line between bars, cafes and bistros is blurred at best. It costs more to sit at a table than to stand at the counter, more on a fancy square than a backstreet, more in the 8e than in the 18e. After 10pm many cafes charge a pricier *tarif de nuit* (night rate).

Left Bank

★**Au Sauvignon** WINE BAR

(Map p366; 80 rue des St-Pères, 7e; 8.30am-10pm Mon-Sat, to 9pm Sun; M Sèvres-Babylone) Grab a table in the evening sun at this wonderfully authentic *bar à vin* or head to the quintessential bistro interior, with an original zinc bar, tightly packed tables and hand-painted ceiling celebrating French viticultural tradition. A plate of *casse-croûtes au pain Poilâne* – toast with ham, pâté, terrine, smoked salmon, foie gras etc – is the perfect accompaniment.

★**Le Batofar** CLUB

(Map p366; www.batofar.org; opp 11 quai François Mauriac, 13e; bar 12.30pm-midnight Tue, to 6am Wed-Fri, 6pm-6am Sat; M Quai de la Gare or Bibliothèque) This much-loved, red-metal tugboat has a rooftop bar that's terrific in summer, and a respected restaurant, while the club underneath provides memorable underwater acoustics between its metal walls and portholes. Le Batofar is known for its edgy, experimental music policy and live performances, mostly electro-oriented but also incorporating hip-hop, new wave, rock, punk or jazz.

Le Verre à Pied CAFE

(Map p370; http://leverreapied.fr; 118bis rue Mouffetard, 5e; 9am-9pm Tue-Sat, 9.30am-4pm

BAR-HOPPING STREETS

Prime Parisian streets for a soirée:

Rue Vieille du Temple, 4e Marais cocktail of gay bars and chic cafes.

Rue Oberkampf, 11e Edgy urban hang outs.

Rue de Lappe, 11e Boisterous Bastille bars and clubs.

Rue de la Butte aux Cailles, 13e Village atmosphere and fun local haunts.

Rue Princesse, 6e Student and sports bars.

Sun; Ⓜ Censier Daubenton) This *café-tabac* is a pearl of a place where little has changed since 1870. Its nicotine-hued mirrored wall, moulded cornices and original bar make it part of a dying breed, but the place oozes the charm, glamour and romance of an old Paris everyone loves, including stall holders from the rue Mouffetard market who yo-yo in and out.

Les Deux Magots CAFE
(Map p370; www.lesdeuxmagots.fr; 170 bd St-Germain, 6e; ⌚7.30am-1am; Ⓜ St-Germain des Prés) If ever a cafe summed up St-Germain des Prés' early-20th-century literary scene, it's this former hang-out of anyone who was anyone. You will spend *beaucoup* to sip a coffee in a wicker chair on the terrace shaded by dark-green awnings and geraniums spilling from window boxes, but it's an undeniable piece of Parisian history.

Le Pub St-Hilaire PUB
(Map p370; 2 rue Valette, 5e; ⌚3pm-2am Mon-Thu, 3pm-4am Fri, 4pm-4am Sat, 4pm-midnight Sun; Ⓜ Maubert-Mutualité) 'Buzzing' fails to do justice to the pulsating vibe inside this student loved pub. Generous happy hours last several hours and the place is kept packed with a trio of pool tables, board games, music on two floors, hearty bar food and various gimmicks to rev up the party crowd (a metre of cocktails, 'be your own barman' etc).

Right Bank

★ St James Paris BAR
(Map p366; ☎01 44 05 81 81; www.saint-james-paris.com; 43 rue Bugeaud, 16e; drinks €15-25, Sun brunch €65; ⌚7-11pm; 📶; Ⓜ Porte Dauphine) It might be a hotel bar, but a drink at St James might well be one of your most memorable in Paris. Tucked behind a stone wall, this historic mansion opens its bar each evening to nonguests – and the setting redefines extraordinary. Winter drinks are in the library, in summer they're in the impossibly romantic garden.

★ Le Barbouquin CAFE
(Map p366; www.lebarbouquin.fr; 3 rue Ramponeau, 20e; ⌚10.30am-6pm Tue-Sat; Ⓜ Belleville) There is no lovelier spot to relax in a vintage armchair over a cup of organic tea or freshly juiced carrot-and-apple cocktail after a hectic morning at Belleville market. Secondhand books – to be borrowed, exchanged or bought – line one wall and the twinset of pavement-terrace tables outside sit on magnificently graffitied rue Dénoyez. Breakfast and weekend brunch.

Le Baron Rouge WINE BAR
(Map p366; 1 rue Théophile Roussel, 12e; ⌚10am-2pm & 5-10pm Tue-Fri, 10am-10pm Sat, 10am-4pm Sun; Ⓜ Ledru-Rollin) Just about the ultimate Parisian wine-bar experience, this place has barrels stacked against the bottle-lined walls. As unpretentious as you'll find, it's a local meeting place where everyone is welcome and it's especially busy on Sunday after the **Marché d'Aligre** (Map p366; http://marchedaligre.free.fr; rue d'Aligre, 12e; ⌚8am-1pm & 4-7.30pm Tue-Sat, 8am-1.30pm Sun; Ⓜ Ledru-Rollin) wraps up. All the usual suspects – cheese, charcuterie and oysters – will keep your belly full.

La Fourmi BAR
(Map p374; 74 rue des Martyrs, 18e; ⌚8am-1am Mon-Thu, to 3am Fri & Sat, 10am-1am Sun; Ⓜ Pigalle) A Pigalle institution, La Fourmi hits the mark with its high ceilings, long zinc bar and unpretentious vibe. Get up to speed on live music and club nights or sit down for a reasonably priced meal and drinks.

Le Rex Club CLUB
(Map p374; www.rexclub.com; 5 bd Poissonnière, 2e; ⌚midnight-7am Thu-Sat; Ⓜ Bonne Nouvelle) Attached to the art deco Grand Rex cinema, this is Paris' premier house and techno venue where some of the world's hottest DJs strut their stuff on a 70-speaker, multidiffusion sound system.

☆ Entertainment

To find out what's on, buy *Pariscope* (€0.50) or *L'Officiel des Spectacles* (€0.50; www.offi.

fr) at Parisian news kiosks. Both are published on Wednesday. The most convenient place to buy concert, performance or event tickets is megastore **Fnac** (Map p366; ☎08 92 68 36 22; www.fnactickets.com), which has numerous branches in town. If you go on the day of a performance, you can snag a half-price ticket (plus €3 commission) for ballet, theatre, opera and other performances at the discount-ticket outlet **Kiosque Théâtre Madeleine** (Map p374; opp 15 place de la Madeleine, 8e; ⊙12.30-8pm Tue-Sat, to 4pm Sun; Ⓜ Madeleine).

Moulin Rouge CABARET
(Map p374; ☎01 53 09 82 82; www.moulinrouge.fr; 82 bd de Clichy, 18e; Ⓜ Blanche) Immortalised in the posters of Toulouse-Lautrec and later on screen by Baz Luhrmann, the Moulin Rouge twinkles beneath a 1925 replica of its original red windmill. Yes, it's rife with bus-tour crowds. But from the opening bars of music to the last high kick it's a whirl of fantastical costumes, sets, choreography and sparkling wine. Booking advised.

Au Limonaire LIVE MUSIC
(Map p374; ☎01 45 23 33 33; http://limonaire.free.fr; 18 cité Bergère, 9e; ⊙6pm-2am Tue-Sat, from 7pm Sun & Mon; Ⓜ Grands Boulevards) This perfect little wine bar is one of the best places to listen to traditional French *chansons* (songs) and local singer-songwriters. Performances begin at 10pm Tuesday to Saturday and 7pm on Sunday. Entry is free; reservations are recommended if you plan on dining.

Palais Garnier OPERA
(Map p374; ☎08 92 89 90 90; www.operadeparis.fr; place de l'Opéra, 9e; Ⓜ Opéra) The city's original opera house is smaller than its Bastille counterpart, but has perfect acoustics. Due to its odd shape, some seats have limited or no visibility – book carefully. Ticket prices and conditions (including last-minute discounts) are available from the **box office** (Map p374; cnr rues Scribe & Auber; ⊙11am-6.30pm Mon-Sat).

Point Éphémère LIVE MUSIC
(Map p366; www.pointephemere.org; 200 quai de Valmy, 10e; ⊙12.30pm-2am Mon-Sat, 12.30-11pm Sun; 📶; Ⓜ Louis Blanc) This arts and music venue by the Canal St-Martin attracts an underground crowd from noon till past midnight, for drinks, meals, concerts, dance nights and even art exhibitions. At the time of writing there were three different food trucks setting up shop here three days a week after 7pm.

Le Baiser Salé LIVE MUSIC
(Map p370; www.lebaisersale.com; 58 rue des Lombards, 1er; ⊙daily; Ⓜ Châtelet) Known for its Afro and Latin jazz, and jazz fusion concerts, the Salty Kiss combines big names and unknown artists. The place has a relaxed vibe, with sets usually starting at 7.30pm or 9.30pm.

GAY & LESBIAN PARIS

The Marais (4e), especially the areas around the intersection of rue Ste-Croix de la Bretonnerie and rue des Archives, and eastwards to rue Vieille du Temple, has been Paris' main centre of gay nightlife for some three decades.

The single best source of info on gay and lesbian Paris is the **Centre Gai et Lesbien de Paris** (CGL; Map p370; ☎01 43 57 21 47; www.centrelgbtparis.org; 63 rue Beaubourg, 3e; ⊙centre & bar 3.30-8pm Mon-Fri, 1-7pm Sat, library 6-8pm Mon-Wed, 3.30-6pm Fri, 5-7pm Sat; Ⓜ Rambuteau or Arts et Métiers), with a large library and happening bar.

The following aare some top choices:

Open Café (Map p370; www.opencafe.fr; 17 rue des Archives, 4e; ⊙11am-2am; Ⓜ Hôtel de Ville) The wide terrace is prime for people-watching.

Scream Club (Map p370; www.scream-paris.com; 18 rue du Faubourg du Temple, 11e; admission €15; ⊙midnight-7am Sat; Ⓜ Belleville or Goncourt) Saturday's the night at 'Paris' biggest gay party'.

3w Kafé (Map p370; 8 rue des Écouffes, 4e; ⊙8pm-3am Wed & Thu, to 5.30am Fri & Sat; Ⓜ St-Paul) The name of this sleek spot stands for 'women with women'.

Queen (Map p366; ☎01 53 89 08 90; www.queen.fr; 102 av des Champs-Élysées, 8e; ⊙11.30pm-6.30am; Ⓜ George V) Don't miss disco night.

La Champmeslé (Map p370; www.lachampmesle.com; 4 rue Chabanais, 2e; ⊙4pm-dawn Mon-Sat; Ⓜ Pyramides) Cabaret nights, fortune telling and art exhibitions attract an older lesbian crowd.

Shopping

Guerlain PERFUME

(Map p366; ☎spa 01 45 62 11 21; www.guerlain.com; 68 av des Champs-Élysées, 8e; ⊙10.30am-8pm Mon-Sat, noon-7pm Sun; M Franklin D Roosevelt) Guerlain is Paris' most famous parfumerie, and its shop (dating from 1912) is one of the most beautiful in the city. With its shimmering mirror and marble art deco interior, it's a reminder of the former glory of the Champs-Élysées. For total indulgence, make an appointment at its decadent spa.

Paris Rendez-Vous CONCEPT STORE

(Map p370; 29 rue de Rivoli, 4e; ⊙10am-7pm Mon-Sat; M Hôtel de Ville) Only the city of Paris could be so chic as to have its own designer line of souvenirs, sold in its own ubercool concept store inside the Hôtel de Ville. Shop here for everything from clothing and homewares to Paris-themed books, toy sailing boats and signature Jardin du Luxembourg's Fermob chairs. *Quel style!*

Marché aux Puces de St-Ouen MARKET

(www.marcheauxpuces-saintouen.com; rue des Rosiers, av Michelet, rue Voltaire, rue Paul Bert & rue Jean-Henri Fabre; ⊙9am-6pm Sat, 10am-6pm Sun, 11am-5pm Mon; M Porte de Clignancourt) This vast flea market, founded in the late 19th century and said to be Europe's largest, has more than 2500 stalls grouped into a dozen *marchés* (market areas), each with its own speciality (eg Paul Bert for 17th-century furniture, Malik for clothing, Biron for Asian art). There are miles upon miles of 'freelance' stalls; come prepared to spend some time.

Shakespeare & Company BOOKS

(Map p370; www.shakespeareandcompany.com; 37 rue de la Bûcherie, 5e; ⊙10am-11pm Mon-Fri, from 11am Sat & Sun; M St-Michel) This bookshop is the stuff of legends. A kind of spell descends as you enter, weaving between nooks and crannies overflowing with new and secondhand English-language books. The original shop (12 rue l'Odéon, 6e; closed by the Nazis in 1941) was run by Sylvia Beach and became the meeting point for Hemingway's 'Lost Generation'. Readings by emerging and illustrious authors take place at 7pm most Mondays; it also hosts workshops and festivals.

Galeries Lafayette DEPARTMENT STORE

(Map p374; http://haussmann.galerieslafayette.com; 40 bd Haussmann, 9e; ⊙9.30am-8pm Mon-Sat, to 9pm Thu; M Auber or Chaussée d'Antin) *Grande dame* department store Galeries Lafayette is spread across the main store (whose magnificent stained-glass dome is over a century old), **men's store** and **homewares** store, and includes a gourmet emporium.

Catch modern art in the **gallery** (www.galeriedesgaleries.com; 1st fl; ⊙11am-7pm Tue-Sat) FREE; a **fashion show** (☎bookings 01 42 82 30 25; ⊙3pm Fri Mar-Jul & Sep-Dec by reservation); a free, windswept rooftop panorama; or take a break at one of its 19 restaurants and cafes.

Information

DANGERS & ANNOYANCES

Metro stations best avoided late at night include: Châtelet–Les Halles and its corridors; Château Rouge in Montmartre; Gare du Nord; Strasbourg St-Denis; Réaumur Sébastopol; and Montparnasse Bienvenüe.

Pickpocketing and thefts from handbags and packs is a problem wherever there are crowds (especially of tourists).

MEDICAL SERVICES

American Hospital of Paris (☎01 46 41 25 25; www.american-hospital.org; 63 bd Victor Hugo, Neuilly-sur-Seine; M Pont de Levallois) Private hospital; emergency 24-hour medical and dental care.

Hôpital Hôtel Dieu (☎01 42 34 82 34; www.aphp.fr; 1 place du Parvis Notre Dame, 4e; M Cité) One of the city's main government-run public hospitals; after 8pm use the emergency entrance on rue de la Cité.

Pharmacie Les Champs (☎01 45 62 02 41; Galerie des Champs-Élysées, 84 av des Champs-Élysées, 8e; ⊙24hr; M George V)

TOURIST INFORMATION

Paris Convention & Visitors Bureau (Office du Tourisme et des Congrès de Paris; Map p370; www.parisinfo.com; 27 rue des Pyramides, 1er; ⊙9am-7pm May-Oct, 10am-7pm Nov-Apr; M Pyramides) Main branch of the Paris Convention & Visitors Bureau, about 500m northwest of the Louvre.

Getting There & Away

AIR

There are three main airports in Paris:

Aéroport de Charles de Gaulle (p434) Most international airlines fly to CDG, 28km northeast of the centre of Paris. In French, the airport is commonly called 'Roissy'.

Aéroport d'Orly (ORY; ☎01 70 36 39 50; www.aeroportsdeparis.fr) Located 19km south of Paris but not as frequently used by international airlines.

Aéroport de Beauvais (BVA; ☎08 92 68 20 66; www.aeroportbeauvais.com) Not really in Paris at all (it's 75km north of Paris) but used by some low-cost carriers.

BUS

Gare Routière Internationale de Paris-Galliéni (☎08 92 89 90 91; 28 av du Général de Gaulle; Ⓜ Galliéni) The city's international bus terminal is in the eastern suburb of Bagnolet; it's about a 15 minute metro ride to the more central République station.

TRAIN

Paris has six major train stations serving both national and international destinations:

Gare du Nord (rue de Dunkerque, 10e; Ⓜ Gare du Nord) Trains to/from the UK, Belgium, Germany and northern France.

Gare de l'Est (bd de Strasbourg, 10e; Ⓜ Gare de l'Est) Trains to/from Germany, Switzerland and eastern areas of France.

Gare de Lyon (bd Diderot, 12e; Ⓜ Gare de Lyon) Trains to/from Provence, the Riviera, the Alps and Italy. Also serves Geneva.

Gare d'Austerlitz (bd de l'Hôpital, 13e; Ⓜ Gare d'Austerlitz) Trains to/from Spain and Portugal, and non-TGV trains to southwestern France.

Gare Montparnasse (av du Maine & bd de Vaugirard, 15e; Ⓜ Montparnasse Bienvenüe) Trains to/from western France (Brittany, Atlantic coast) and southwestern France.

Gare St-Lazare (rue St-Lazare & rue d'Amsterdam, 8e; Ⓜ St-Lazare) Trains to Normandy.

For mainline train information, check **SNCF** (www.sncf-voyages.com).

ℹ Getting Around

TO/FROM THE AIRPORTS

Getting into town is straightforward and inexpensive thanks to a fleet of public-transport options. Bus drivers sell tickets. Children aged four to 11 years pay half-price on most services.

Aéroport de Charles de Gaulle

RER B line (€9.50, approximately 50 minutes, every 10 to 15 minutes) Stops at Gare du Nord, Châtelet–Les Halles and St-Michel–Notre Dame stations in the city centre. Trains run from 5am to 11pm; there are fewer trains on weekends.

RATP bus 351 (€5.70, 60 minutes, every 30 minutes, 5.30am to 11pm) Links the airport with Place de la Nation.

Roissybus (€10.50, 45 to 60 minutes, every 15 minutes, 5.30am to 11pm) Links the airport with Opéra.

Taxi Costs €50, more at nights and weekends. Allow 40 minutes to the centre, more at rush hour.

Aéroport d'Orly

RER B and Orlyval (€10.90, 35 minutes, every four to 12 minutes, 6am to 11pm) The nearest RER station to the airport is Antony, where you connect on the dedicated Orlyval.

Air France bus 1 (€12.50, one hour, every 20 minutes, 5am to 11pm) Links the airport with Gare Montparnasse, Invalides and Arc de Triomphe.

Taxi Costs around €40, more at nights and weekends. Allow 30 minutes to the centre, more at rush hour.

Aéroport de Beauvais

The **Beauvais shuttle** (€17, 1¼ hours) links the airport with metro station Porte Maillot.

BICYCLE

The **Vélib'** (http://en.velib.paris.fr; day/week subscription €1.70/8, bike hire up to 30min/60min/90min/2hr free/€1/2/4) bike-share scheme puts 20,000-odd bikes at the disposal of Parisians and visitors to get around the city. There are around 1800 docking stations; bikes are available around the clock.

BOAT

Batobus (www.batobus.com; Port de Solférino, 7e; 1-/2-day pass €16/18; ⏲10am-9.30pm Apr-Aug, to 7pm rest of year) Batobus runs glassed-in trimarans that dock every 20 to 25 minutes at eight small piers along the Seine: Eiffel Tower, Musée d'Orsay, St-Germain des Prés, Notre Dame, Jardin des Plantes, Hôtel de Ville, Musée du Louvre and Champs-Élysées. Buy tickets online, at ferry stops or at tourist offices. You can also buy a 2-/3-day ticket covering L'Open Tour buses too for €45/49.

PUBLIC TRANSPORT

Paris' public transit system is operated by the **RATP** (www.ratp.fr).

- The same RATP tickets are valid on the metro, RER, buses, trams and Montmartre funicular. A single ticket/*carnet* of 10 costs €1.70/13.70.
- One ticket covers travel between any two metro stations (no return journeys) for 1½ hours; you can transfer between buses and between buses and trams, but not from metro to bus or vice versa.
- Keep your ticket until you exit the station or risk a fine.

Bus

- Buses run from 5.30am to 8.30pm Monday to Saturday, with certain evening lines continuing until midnight or 12.30am, when the hourly **Noctilien** (www.noctilien.fr) night buses kick in.
- Short bus rides (ie rides in one or two bus zones) cost one ticket; longer rides require two.

➡ Remember to punch single-journey tickets in the *composteur* (ticket machine) next to the driver.

Metro & RER

Paris' underground network consists of 14 numbered metro lines and the five suburban RER lines (designated by the letters A to E).

Trains usually start around 5.30am and finish sometime between 12.35am and 1.15am (2.15am Friday and Saturday).

Tourist Passes

The **Mobilis Card** allows unlimited travel for one day in two to five zones (€6.80 to €16.10) on the metro, the RER, buses, trams and suburban trains; while the **Paris Visite** 'Paris+ Suburbs+Airports' pass allows unlimited travel (including to/from airports), plus discounted entry to museums and activities, and costs €22.85/34.70/59.50 for one/two/five days.

Passes are sold at larger metro and RER stations, SNCF stations and the airports.

Travel Passes

If you're staying in Paris more than three or four days, the cheapest and easiest way to use public transport is to get a rechargeable **Navigo** (www.navigo.fr) pass.

Weekly/monthly passes beginning on a Monday/first day of the month cost €20.40/67.10. You'll also need to pay €5 for the Navigo card and provide a passport photo.

TAXI

➡ The flag fall is €2.50, plus €1 per kilometre within the city limits from 10am to 5pm Monday to Saturday (Tarif A; white light on meter).

➡ It's €1.24 per kilometre from 5pm to 10am, all day Sunday, and on public holidays (Tarif B; orange light on meter).

➡ The first piece of luggage is free; additional bags cost €1.

➡ Taxis will often refuse to take more than three passengers.

➡ You can flag taxis on the street, wait at official stands or phone/book online with **Taxis G7** (☎36 07; www.taxisg7.fr) or **Taxis Bleus** (☎01 49 36 10 10; www.taxis-bleus.com).

AROUND PARIS

Versailles

POP 88,470

Louis XIV – the Roi Soleil (Sun King) – transformed his father's hunting lodge into the monumental Château de Versailles in the mid-17th century, and it remains France's most famous, grandest palace. Situated in the prosperous, leafy and bourgeois suburb of Versailles, 28km southwest of Paris, the baroque château was the kingdom's political capital and the seat of the royal court from 1682 up until the fateful events of 1789, when revolutionaries massacred the palace guard and dragged Louis XVI and Marie Antoinette back to Paris, where they were ingloriously guillotined.

Sights

Château Versailles PALACE

(☎01 30 83 78 00; www.chateauversailles.fr; passport ticket incl estate-wide access adult/child €18/free, with musical events €25/free, palace €15/free; ⏲9am-6.30pm Tue-Sat, to 6pm Sun Apr-Oct, to 5.30pm Tue-Sun Nov-Mar; Ⓜ RER Versailles-Château–Rive Gauche) Works on the Château began in 1661 under the guidance of architect Louis Le Vau (Jules Hardouin-Mansart took over from Le Vau in the mid-1670s); painter and interior designer Charles Le Brun; and landscape artist André Le Nôtre, whose workers flattened hills, drained marshes and relocated forests to create the magnificent geometric **gardens** (except during musical events admission free; ⏲gardens 9am-8.30pm Apr-Oct, 8am-6pm Nov-Mar, park 7am-8.30pm Apr-Oct, 8am-6pm Nov-Mar).

Le Brun and his hundreds of artisans decorated every moulding, cornice, ceiling and door of the interior with the most luxurious and ostentatious of appointments: frescoes, marble, gilt and woodcarvings, many with themes and symbols drawn from Greek and Roman mythology. The opulence reaches its peak in the **Galerie des Glaces** (Hall of Mirrors), a 75m-long ballroom with 17 huge mirrors on one side and, on the other, an equal number of windows looking out over the gardens and the setting sun.

The château has undergone relatively few alterations since its construction, though almost all the interior furnishings disappeared during the Revolution and many of the rooms were rebuilt by Louis-Philippe (r 1830–48).

Getting There & Away

The easiest way to get to/from Versailles is aboard RER line C5 (€3.25, 45 minutes, every 15 minutes) from Paris' Left Bank RER stations to Versailles-Château–Rive Gauche, 700m southeast of the chateau.

VERSAILLES TIPS

Versailles is one of the country's most popular destinations, with over five million visitors annually; advance planning will make visiting more enjoyable.

- Arrive early morning and avoid Tuesday and Sunday, the busiest days.
- Prepurchase tickets on the château's website or at Fnac (p379) branches and head straight to Entrance A.
- Versailles is free on the first Sunday of every month from November to March.

Chartres

POP 40,675

The magnificent 13th-century **Cathédrale Notre Dame** (www.cathedrale-chartres.org; place de la Cathédrale; 8.30am-7.30pm daily year-round, to 10pm Tue, Fri & Sun Jun-Aug) of Chartres, crowned by two very different spires – one Gothic, the other Romanesque – rises from rich farmland 88km southwest of Paris and dominates the medieval town.

The cathedral's west, north and south entrances have superbly ornamented triple portals and its 105m-high **Clocher Vieux** (Old Bell Tower), also called the Tour Sud (South Tower), is the tallest Romanesque steeple still standing. Superb views of three-tiered flying buttresses and the 19th-century copper roof, turned green by verdigris, reward the 350-step hike up the 112m-high **Clocher Neuf** (New Bell Tower, also known as North Tower).

Inside, 172 extraordinary stained-glass windows, mainly from the 13th century, form one of the most important ensembles of medieval stained glass in the world. The three most exquisite – renowned for the depth and intensity of their tones, famously known as 'Chartres blue' – are above the west entrance and below the rose window.

Getting There & Away

Frequent SNCF trains link Paris' Gare Montparnasse (€15.60, 55 to 70 minutes) with Chartres.

Giverny

The tiny village of Giverny (pop 516), 74km northwest of Paris, was the **home of impressionist Claude Monet** (02 32 51 28 21; www.fondation-monet.com; 84 rue Claude Monet; adult/child €9.50/5, incl Musée des Impressionnismes Giverny €16.50/8; 9.30am-6pm Apr-Oct) for the last 43 years of his life. You can visit the artist's pastel-pink house and famous gardens with lily pond, Japanese bridge draped in purple wisteria, and so on. Early to late spring, daffodils, tulips, rhododendrons, wisteria and irises bloom in the flowery gardens, followed by poppies and lilies. By June, nasturtiums, roses and sweet peas are in flower, while September is the month to see dahlias, sunflowers and hollyhocks.

The nearest train station is **Vernon**, 7km west of Giverny, from where shuttle buses (€8 return, three to six daily April to October) shunt passengers to Giverny. There are around 15 trains a day from Paris Gare St-Lazare (€14.30, 50 minutes).

LILLE & THE SOMME

When it comes to culture, cuisine, beer, shopping and dramatic views of land and sea, the friendly Ch'tis (residents of France's northern tip) and their region compete with the best France has to offer. Highlights include Flemish-style Lille, the cross-Channel shopping centre of Calais, and the moving battlefields and cemeteries of WWI.

Lille

POP 232,210

Lille may be the country's most underrated major city. In recent decades, this once-grimy industrial metropolis has transformed itself – with generous government help – into a glittering and self-confident cultural and commercial hub. Highlights of the city include an attractive Old Town with a strong Flemish accent, renowned art museums, stylish shopping and a cutting-edge, student-driven nightlife.

Sights

Palais des Beaux Arts ART MUSEUM

(Fine Arts Museum; 03 20 06 78 00; www.pba-lille.fr; place de la République; adult/child €6.50/free; 2-5.30pm Mon, 10am-5.30pm Wed-Sun; M République Beaux Arts) Lille's world-renowned Fine Arts Museum displays a truly first-rate collection of 15th- to 20th-century paintings, including works by Rubens, Van Dyck and Manet. Exquisite porcelain and faience (pottery), much of it of local provenance, is on the ground floor, while in the basement you'll find classical archaeology, medieval statuary and 18th-century scale models of the fortified cities of northern France and Belgium. Information sheets in French, English and Dutch are available in each hall.

Musée d'Art Moderne, d'Art Contemporain et d'Art Brut – LaM ART MUSEUM
(☎03 20 19 68 68; www.musee-lam.fr; 1 allée du Musée, Villeneuve-d'Ascq; adult/child €7/free; ⏲10am-6pm Tue-Sun) Colourful, playful and just plain weird works of modern and contemporary art by masters such as Braque, Calder, Léger, Miró, Modigliani and Picasso are the big draw at this renowned museum and sculpture park in the Lille suburb of Villeneuve-d'Ascq, 9km east of Gare Lille-Europe. Take metro line 1 to Pont de Bois, then bus line 4 (10 minutes) to Villeneuve-d'Ascq-LaM.

Festivals & Events

★Braderie de Lille FLEA MARKET
On the first weekend in September Lille's entire city centre – 200km of footpaths – is transformed into the Braderie de Lille, billed as the world's largest flea market. It runs nonstop – yes, all night long – from 2pm on Saturday to 11pm on Sunday, when street sweepers emerge to tackle the mounds of mussel shells and old *frites* (French fries) left behind by the merrymakers.

The extravaganza – with stands selling antiques, local delicacies, handicrafts and more – dates from the Middle Ages, when Lillois servants were permitted to hawk their employers' old garments for some extra cash. Lille's tourist office can supply you with a free map of the festivities.

Sleeping & Eating

Auberge de Jeunesse HOSTEL €
(☎03 20 57 08 94; www.hifrance.org; 12 rue Malpart; dm incl breakfast €23; P@; M Mairie de Lille, République Beaux-Arts) This central former maternity hospital has 163 beds in rooms for two to eight, kitchen facilities and free parking. A few doubles have en-suite showers. Lockout is from 11am to 3pm (to 4pm Friday to Sunday).

Hotel Kanaï HOTEL €€
(☎03 20 57 14 78; www.hotelkanai.com; 10 rue de Bethune; d €75-140; @; M Rihour) In the heart of Lille's pedestrian zone, this enticing hotel offers reasonably priced rooms with a clean modern design; pick of the bunch are rooms 102 and 302, with large picture windows and plenty of natural light. All come with coffee makers, attractive tiled bathrooms, crisp linen and excellent bedding. One complaint: there's no lift.

★Meert PATISSERIE €
(☎03 20 57 07 44; www.meert.fr; 27 rue Esquermoise; waffles from €3; ⏲9.30am-9.30pm Tue-Sat, 9am-6pm Sun; M Rihour) A delightful spot for morning coffee or mid-afternoon tea, this elegant tearoom dating to 1761 is beloved for its retro decor and its *gaufres* (waffles) filled with Madagascar vanilla paste. The tearoom's 1830s-vintage chocolate shop next door has a similarly old-fashioned atmosphere.

Le Bistrot Lillois FLEMISH €
(☎03 20 14 04 15; 40 rue de Gand; mains €10-15; ⏲noon-2pm & 7.30-10pm Tue-Sat) This place owes its reputation to a menu based solidly on expertly prepared regional specialities. The highlight of the menu is *os à moëlle* (marrow bone), but other dishes worth trying include *carbonade flamande* (braised beef stewed with Flemish beer, spice bread and brown sugar) and *potjevleesch* (jellied chicken, pork, veal and rabbit).

Information

The **tourist office** (☎03 59 57 94 00; www.lilletourism.com; place Rihour; ⏲9am-6pm Mon-Sat, 10am-noon & 2-5pm Sun & holidays; M Rihour) has walking itineraries of the city (€3).

Getting There & Away

AIR

Aéroport de Lille (www.lille.aeroport.fr) is connected to all major French cities and a number of European destinations too.

TRAIN

Lille has two train stations: Gare Lille-Flandres for regional services and Paris' Gare du Nord (€35 to €61, one hour, 14 to 24 daily), and ultramodern Gare Lille-Europe for all other trains, including Eurostars to London and TGVs/Eurostars to Brussels-Nord (€19 to €30, 35 minutes, 12 daily).

The Somme

The First Battle of the Somme, a WWI Allied offensive waged in the villages and woodlands northeast of Amiens, was designed to relieve pressure on the beleaguered French troops at Verdun. On 1 July 1916, British, Commonwealth and French troops 'went over the top' in a massive assault along a 34km front. But German positions proved virtually unbreachable, and on the first day of the battle an astounding 21,392 British troops were killed and another 35,492 were wounded. Most casualties were infantrymen mown down by German machine guns. By the time the offensive was called off in mid-November, a total of 1.2 million lives had been lost on both sides. The British had advanced 12km, the French 8km.

Between 2014 and 2018, a number of events will commemorate the Centenary of WWI throughout the region – it's well worth timing your trip around them.

Sights & Activities

The battlefields and memorials are numerous and relatively scattered – joining a tour can therefore be a good option, especially if you don't have your own transport. Respected operators include **Battlefields Experience** (☎03 22 76 29 60; www.thebattleofthesomme.co.uk) and **Western Front Tours** (www.westernfronttours.com.au; ⏲mid-Mar–mid-Nov).

Historial de la Grande Guerre WAR MUSEUM
(Museum of the Great War; ☎03 22 83 14 18; www.historial.org; Château de Péronne, Péronne; adult/child incl audioguide €7.50/4; ⏲10am-6pm, closed mid-Dec–mid-Feb) The best place to begin a visit to the Somme battlefields – especially if you're interested in WWI's historical and cultural context – is the outstanding Historial de la Grande Guerre in the town of Péronne, about 60km east of Amiens. Tucked inside Péronne's massively fortified château, this award-winning museum tells the story of the war chronologically, with equal space given to the German, French and British perspectives on what happened, how and why.

Beaumont-Hamel Newfoundland Memorial WAR MEMORIAL
(☎03 22 76 70 86; www.veterans.gc.ca; Beaumont-Hamel) This evocative memorial preserves part of the Western Front in the state it was in at fighting's end. The zigzag trench system, which still fills with mud in winter, is clearly visible, as are countless shell craters and the remains of barbed-wire barriers. A path leads to an orientation table at the top of the 'Caribou mound', where a bronze caribou statue is surrounded by plants native to Newfoundland. Beaumont-Hamel is 9km north of Albert; follow the signs for 'Memorial Terreneuvien'.

WORTH A TRIP

LOUVRE-LENS

Opened with fanfare in 2012 in Lens, 35km southwest of Lille, the innovative **Louvre-Lens** (☎03 21 18 62 62; www.louvrelens.fr; 99 rue Paul Bert, Lens; ⏲10am-6pm Wed-Mon) showcases hundreds of treasures from Paris' venerable Musée du Louvre in a purpose-built, state-of-the-art exhibition space. Unlike its Parisian cousin, there's no permanent collection here. Instead, the museum's centrepiece, a 120m-long exhibition space called the **Galerie du Temps**, displays a limited but significant, ever-rotating collection of 200-plus pieces from the original Louvre, spanning that museum's full breadth and diversity of cultures and historical periods.

A second building, the glass-walled **Pavillon de Verre**, displays temporary themed exhibits. Rounding out the museum are educational facilities, an auditorium, a restaurant and a park.

Lens is accessible by regular TGV trains from Paris' Gare du Nord (€28.50 to €51, 65 to 70 minutes), as well as regional trains from Lille (from €6.80, 40 minutes).

Sleeping & Eating

★ Au Vintage B&B €
(☎06 83 03 45 26, 03 22 75 63 28; www.chambres-dhotes-albert.com; 19 rue de Corbie, Albert; d incl breakfast €65-85; P 📶) This B&B is an absolute spoil from start to finish. It occupies an elegant brick mansion with two rooms and a family suite that are furnished with taste and flair.

Our fave is Rubis, with its super-size bathroom. Evelyne and Jacky are delightful, cultured hosts who enjoy sharing their knowledge about the battlefields with their guests – in good English.

Butterworth Farm B&B €
(☎06 22 30 28 02, 03 22 74 04 47; www.butterworth-cottage.com; route de Bazentin, Pozières; d incl breakfast €65; P 📶) Beloved by Australians and Brits, this well-run venture is an excellent base. Well-tended, fresh guest

rooms are in a converted barn, the facade of which is covered with wood panels.

There's a garden, filled with flowers and herbs, for lounging in, and breakfasts are copious.

Le Tommy BRASSERIE €

(☎03 22 74 82 84; 91 route d'Albert, Pozières; mains €8-12; ⊙11am-3pm) This no-frills, slightly eccentric eatery on the main road in Pozières is ideal for a light lunch comprising a main course and dessert, or a sandwich. It also houses a small museum with WWI memorabilia and artifacts.

Information

The tourist offices in **Péronne** (☎03 22 84 42 38; www.hautesomme-tourisme.com; 16 place André Audinot, Péronne; ⊙10am-noon & 2-6pm Mon-Sat) and **Albert** (☎03 22 75 16 42; www.tourisme-paysducoquelicot.com; 6 rue Émile Zola, Albert; ⊙9am-12.30pm & 1.30-6.30pm Mon-Sat, 9am-1pm Sun) both have plenty of information in English and can help with booking tours and accommodation.

Getting There & Away

You will need your own transport to visit WWI sights. Alternatively, join a tour.

NORMANDY

Famous for cows, cider and Camembert, this largely rural region (www.normandie-tourisme.fr) is one of France's most traditional, and most visited, thanks to world-renowned sights such as the Bayeux Tapestry, the historic D-Day beaches and spectacular Mont St-Michel.

Bayeux

POP 13,350

Bayeux has become famous throughout the English-speaking world thanks to a 68m-long piece of painstakingly embroidered cloth: the 11th-century Bayeux Tapestry, whose 58 scenes vividly tell the story of the Norman invasion of England in 1066.

The town is also one of the few in Normandy to have survived WWII practically unscathed, with a centre crammed with 13th- to 18th-century buildings, wooden-framed Norman-style houses, and a spectacular Norman Gothic cathedral. It makes a great base for exploring D-Day beaches.

Sights

★Bayeux Tapestry TAPESTRY

(☎02 31 51 25 50; www.tapestry-bayeux.com; rue de Nesmond; adult/child incl audioguide €9/4; ⊙9am-6.30pm mid-Mar–mid-Nov, to 7pm May-Aug, 9.30am-12.30pm & 2-6pm mid-Nov–mid-Mar) The world's most celebrated embroidery depicts the conquest of England by William the Conqueror in 1066 from an unashamedly Norman perspective. Commissioned by Bishop Odo of Bayeux, William's half-brother, for the opening of Bayeux' cathedral in 1077, the 68.3m-long cartoon strip tells the dramatic, bloody tale with verve and vividness.

Musée d'Art et d'Histoire Baron Gérard MUSEUM

(MAHB; ☎02 31 92 14 21; www.bayeuxmuseum.com; 37 rue du Bienvenu; adult/child €7/4; ⊙9.30am-6.30pm May-Sep, 10am-12.30pm & 2-6pm Oct-Apr) Opened in 2013, this is one of France's most gorgeously presented provincial museums. The exquisite exhibits cover everything from Gallo-Roman archaeology to medieval art to paintings from the Renaissance to the 20th century, including a fine work by Gustave Caillebotte. Other highlights include impossibly delicate local lace and Bayeux-made porcelain. Housed in the former bishop's palace.

Sleeping & Eating

Les Logis du Rempart B&B €

(☎02 31 92 50 40; www.lecornu.fr; 4 rue Bourbesneur; d €60-100, tr €110-130; 📶) The three rooms of this delightful *maison de famille* ooze old-fashioned cosiness. Our favourite, the Bajocasse, has parquet floor and Toile de Jouy wallpaper. The shop downstairs is the perfect place to stock up on top-quality, homemade cider and *calvados* (apple brandy).

Hôtel d'Argouges HOTEL €€

(☎02 31 92 88 86; www.hotel-dargouges.com; 21 rue St-Patrice; d/tr/f €140/193/245; ⊙closed Dec & Jan; 🅿📶) Occupying a stately 18th-century residence with a lush little garden, this graceful hotel has 28 comfortable rooms with exposed beams, thick walls and Louis XVI–style furniture. The breakfast room, hardly changed since 1734, still has its original wood panels and parquet floors.

★ **La Reine Mathilde** PATISSERIE €
(47 rue St-Martin; cakes from €2.20; 9am-7.30pm Tue-Sun) This sumptuously decorated patisserie and *salon de thé* (tearoom), ideal for a sweet breakfast or a relaxing cup of afternoon tea, hasn't changed much since it was built in 1898.

Le Pommier NORMAN €€
(02 31 21 52 10; www.restaurantlepommier.com; 38-40 rue des Cuisiniers; lunch menus €15-18, other menus €21-39.50; noon-2pm & 7-9pm, closed Sun Nov-Feb;) At this romantic restaurant, delicious Norman classics include steamed pollock and Caen-style tripe. A vegetarian menu – a rarity in Normandy – is also available, with offerings such as soybean steak in Norman cream.

Information

The **tourist office** (02 31 51 28 28; www.bayeux-bessin-tourisme.com; pont St-Jean; 9.30am-12.30pm & 2-6pm Mon-Sat) covers both Bayeux and the surrounding region, including D-Day beaches.

Getting There & Away

Trains link Bayeux with Caen (€6.60, 20 minutes, hourly), from where there are connections to Paris' Gare St-Lazare and Rouen.

D-Day Beaches

Early on 6 June 1944, Allied troops stormed 80km of beaches north of Bayeux, code-named (from west to east) Utah, Omaha, Gold, Juno and Sword. The landings on D-Day – called *Jour J* in French – ultimately led to the liberation of Europe from Nazi occupation. For context, see www.normandiememoire.com and www.6juin1944.com.

The most brutal fighting on D-Day took place 15km northwest of Bayeux along the stretch of coastline now known as **Omaha Beach**, today a glorious stretch of fine golden sand partly lined with sand dunes and summer homes. **Circuit de la Plage d'Omaha**, a trail marked with a yellow stripe, is a self-guided tour along the beach, surveyed from a bluff above by the huge **Normandy American Cemetery & Memorial** (www.abmc.gov; Colleville-sur-Mer; 9am-6pm mid-Apr–mid-Sep, to 5pm rest of year). Featured in the opening scenes of Steven Spielberg's *Saving Private Ryan*, this is the largest American cemetery in Europe.

Caen's high-tech, hugely impressive **Mémorial – Un Musée pour la Paix** (Memorial – A Museum for Peace; 02 31 06 06 44; www.memorial-caen.fr; esplanade Général Eisenhower; adult/child €19/11.50; 9am-7pm daily mid-Feb–mid-Nov, 9.30am-6.30pm Tue-Sun mid-Nov–mid-Feb, closed 3 weeks in Jan) uses sound, lighting, film, animation and lots of exhibits to graphically explore and evoke the events of WWII, the D-Day landings and the ensuing Cold War.

Tours

Normandy Tours GUIDED TOUR
(02 31 92 10 70; www.normandy-landing-tours.com; 26 place de la Gare, Bayeux; adult/student €62/55) Offers well-regarded four- to five-hour tours of the main sites starting at 8.15am and 1.15pm on most days, as well as personally tailored trips. Based at Bayeux' Hôtel de la Gare, facing the train station.

Tours by Mémorial – Un Musée pour la Paix MINIBUS TOUR
(02 31 06 06 45; www.memorial-caen.fr; adult/child morning €64/64, afternoon €81/64; 9am & 2pm Apr-Sep, 1pm Oct-Mar, closed 3 weeks in Jan) Excellent year-round minibus tours (four to five hours), with cheaper tours in full-size buses (€39) from June to August. Rates include entry to Mémorial – Un Musée pour la Paix. Book online.

Mont St-Michel

On a rocky island opposite the coastal town of Pontorson, connected to the mainland by a narrow causeway, the sky-scraping turrets of the abbey of **Mont St-Michel** (02 33 89 80 00; www.monuments-nationaux.fr; adult/child incl guided tour €9/free; 9am-7pm, last entry 1hr before closing) provide one of France's iconic sights. The surrounding bay is notorious for its fast-rising tides: at low tide, the Mont is surrounded by bare sand for miles around; at high tide, just six hours later, the bay is submerged.

From the **tourist office** (02 33 60 14 30; www.ot-montsaintmichel.com; 9am-12.30pm & 2-6pm Sep-Jun, 9am-7pm Jul & Aug), at the base of Mont St-Michel, a cobbled street winds up to the **Église Abbatiale** (Abbey Church), incorporating elements of both Norman and Gothic architecture. Other notable sights include the arched **cloître** (cloister), the barrel-roofed **réfectoire** (dining hall), and the Gothic **Salle des Hôtes** (Guest Hall), dating from 1213. A one-hour tour is included with admission; English tours run hourly in summer, twice daily (11am and 3pm) in winter. In July and August, Monday to Saturday, there are illuminated *nocturnes* (night-time visits) with music from 7pm to midnight.

If you'd like to stay in the Mont itself, **Hôtel Du Guesclin** (☎02 33 60 14 10; www.hotelduguesclin.com; Grande Rue, Mont St-Michel; d €80-95; ⏲closed Wed night & Thu Apr-Jun & Oct–mid-Nov, hotel closed mid-Nov–Mar) is your best bet, with five of the 10 rooms offering stupendous views of the bay. Much better value and with magical views of the Mont is Vent des Grèves, a lovely B&B 1km east of La Caserne.

Getting There & Away

Transdev bus 1 links the Mont St-Michel La Caserne parking lot (2.5km from the Mont itself, which you access by free shuttle) with Pontorson (€3, 18 minutes), the nearest train station. From Pontorson, there are two to three daily trains to/from Bayeux (€23.90, 1¾ hours) and Caen (€26.10, 1¾ hours).

BRITTANY

Brittany is for explorers. Its wild, dramatic coastline, medieval towns, thick forests and the eeriest stone circles this side of Stonehenge make a trip here well worth the detour from the beaten track. This is a land of prehistoric mysticism, proud tradition and culinary wealth, where locals remain fiercely independent, where Breton culture (and cider) is celebrated and where Paris feels a very long way away indeed.

Quimper

POP 66,911

Small enough to feel like a village – with its slanted half-timbered houses and narrow cobbled streets – and large enough to buzz as the troubadour of Breton culture, Quimper (pronounced *kam-pair*) is the thriving capital of Finistère (meaning 'land's end').

Sights

Cathédrale St-Corentin CHURCH
(place St-Corentin; ⏲8.30am-noon & 1.30-6.30pm Mon-Sat, 8.30am-noon & 2-6.30pm Sun) At the centre of the city is Quimper's cathedral with its distinctive kink, said to symbolise Christ's inclined head as he was dying on the cross. Construction began in 1239 but the cathedral's dramatic twin spires weren't added until the 19th century. High on the west facade, look out for an equestrian statue of King Gradlon, the city's mythical 5th-century founder.

Musée Départemental Breton MUSEUM
(☎02 98 95 21 60; www.museedepartementalbreton.fr; 1 rue du Roi Gradlon; adult/child €5/3; ⏲9am-12.30pm & 1-5pm Tue-Sat, 2-5pm Sun) Beside the Cathédrale St-Corentin, recessed behind a magnificent stone courtyard, this superb museum showcases Breton history, furniture, costumes, crafts and archaeology, in a former bishop's palace.

Sleeping & Eating

Hôtel Manoir des Indes HOTEL €€
(☎02 98 55 48 40; www.manoir-hoteldesindes.com; 1 allée de Prad ar C'hras; s €99-125, d €158-189; P 📶 ❄) This stunning hotel conversion, located in an old manor house just a short drive from the centre of Quimper, has been restored with the globe-trotting original owner in mind. Decor is minimalist and modern, with Asian objets d'art and lots of exposed wood. It's located a five-minute drive west of Quimper, a little way north of the D100.

Crêperie du Quartier CRÊPERIE €
(☎02 98 64 29 30; 16 rue du Sallé; mains €5-9; ⏲noon-2pm Mon-Sat, 7-10pm Mon, Wed, Fri & Sat) In a town where the humble crêpe is king, this cosy stone-lined place is one of the best. Its wide-ranging menu includes a *galette* of the week and, to follow up, you can go for a crêpe stuffed with apple, caramel, ice cream, almonds and chantilly.

Information

The **tourist office** (☎02 98 53 04 05; www.quimper-tourisme.com; place de la Résistance; ⏲9am-7pm Mon-Sat, 10am-12.45pm & 3-5.45pm Sun Jul & Aug, 9.30am-12.30pm & 1.30-6.30pm Mon-Sat, 10am-12.45pm Sun Jun & Sep) has information about the wider area.

Getting There & Away

Frequent trains serve Paris' Gare Montparnasse (€55 to €65, 4¾ hours).

THE MORBIHAN MEGALITHS

Pre-dating Stonehenge by about a hundred years, **Carnac** is home to the world's greatest concentration of megalithic sites. There are more than 3000 of these upright stones scattered across the countryside between **Carnac-Ville** and **Locmariaquer** village, most of which were erected between 5000 BC and 3500 BC. No one's quite sure what purpose these sites served, or how the original builders hacked and hauled these vast granite blocks.

Because of severe erosion, the sites are usually fenced off to allow vegetation to regrow. **Guided tours** run in French year-round and in English early July to late August. Sign up at the **Maison des Mégalithes** (☎02 97 52 29 81; www.carnac.monuments-nationaux.fr; rte des Alignements; tour adult/child €6/free; ⏲9.30am-7.30pm Jul & Aug, to 5pm Sep-Apr, to 6pm May & Jun). Opposite, the largest menhir field – with no fewer than 1099 stones – is the **Alignements du Ménec**, 1km north of Carnac-Ville. From here, the D196 heads northeast for about 1.5km to the **Alignements de Kermario**. Climb the stone observation tower midway along the site to see the alignment from above. Another 500m further on are the **Alignements de Kerlescan**, while the **Tumulus St-Michel**, 400m northeast of the Carnac-Ville tourist office, dates back to at least 5000 BC.

For background, Carnac's **Musée de Préhistoire** (☎02 97 52 22 04; www.museedecarnac.fr; 10 place de la Chapelle, Carnac-Ville; adult/child €6/2.50; ⏲10am-6pm) chronicles life in and around Carnac from the Palaeolithic and Neolithic eras to the Middle Ages.

St-Malo

POP 48,800

The mast-filled port of fortified St-Malo is inextricably tied up with the deep briny blue: the town became a key harbour during the 17th and 18th centuries, functioning as a base for merchant ships and government-sanctioned privateers, and these days it's a busy cross-Channel ferry port and summertime getaway.

Sights

Walking on top of the sturdy 17th-century ramparts (1.8km) affords fine views of the old walled city known as **Intra-Muros** (Within the Walls), or Ville Close; access the ramparts from any of the city gates.

Cathédrale St-Vincent CATHEDRAL
(place Jean de Châtillon; ⏲9.30am-6pm) The city's centrepiece was constructed between the 12th and 18th centuries. During the ferocious fighting of August 1944 the cathedral was badly hit; much of its original structure (including its spire) was reduced to rubble. The cathedral was subsequently rebuilt and reconsecrated in 1971. A mosaic plaque on the floor of the nave marks the spot where Jacques Cartier received the blessing of the bishop of St-Malo before his 'voyage of discovery' to Canada in 1535.

Musée d'Histoire de St-Malo MUSEUM
(☎02 99 40 71 57; www.ville-saint-malo.fr/culture/les-musees; Château; adult/child €6/3; ⏲10am-12.30pm & 2-6pm Apr-Sep, Tue-Sun Oct-Mar) Within **Château de St-Malo**, built by the dukes of Brittany in the 15th and 16th centuries, this museum looks at the life and history of the city through nautical exhibits, model boats and marine artefacts, as well as an exhibition covering the city's cod-fishing heritage. There's also background info on the city's sons, including Cartier, Surcouf, Duguay-Trouin and the writer Chateaubriand.

Sleeping & Eating

Hôtel San Pedro HOTEL €
(☎02 99 40 88 57; www.sanpedro-hotel.com; 1 rue Ste-Anne; s €65-69, d €75-83; P ᯤ) Tucked at the back of the old city, the San Pedro has a cool, crisp, neutral-toned decor with subtle splashes of yellow paint, friendly service, great breakfast, private parking (€10) and a few bikes available for free. It features 12 rooms on four floors served by a miniature lift (forget those big suitcases!); two rooms come with sea views.

★**L'Absinthe** MODERN FRENCH €€
(☎02 99 40 26 15; www.restaurant-absinthe-cafe.fr; 1 rue de l'Orme; mains €18-24, menus €28-45; ⏲noon-2pm & 7-10pm) Hidden away in a quiet street near the covered market, this fab (and

WORTH A TRIP

CULINARY CANCALE

No day trip from St-Malo is tastier than one to **Cancale**, an idyllic Breton fishing port 14km east, famed for its offshore *parcs à huîtres* (oyster beds).

Learn all about oyster farming at the **Ferme Marine** (☎02 99 89 69 99; www.ferme-marine.com; corniche de l'Aurore; adult/child €7/3.70; ⏲guided tours in French 11am, 3pm & 5pm Jul–mid-Sep, in English 2pm), and afterwards lunch on oysters fresh from their beds at the **Marché aux Huîtres** (Pointe des Crolles; 12 oysters from €4; ⏲9am-6pm), the local oyster market atmospherically clustered around the Pointe des Crolles lighthouse.

Buses stop behind the church on place Lucidas and at Port de la Houle, next to the fish market. **Keolis St-Malo** (www.ksma.fr) has year-round services to and from St-Malo (€1.25, 30 minutes).

very French) eatery is housed in an imposing 17th-century building. Ingredients fresh from the nearby market are whipped into shape by the talented chef, Stéphane Brebel, and served in cosy surrounds. The wine list is another hit, with an all-French cast from white to red and rosé.

Information

Tourist Office (☎08 25 13 52 00; www.saint-malo-tourisme.com; esplanade St-Vincent; ⏲9am-7.30pm Mon-Sat, 10am-6pm Sun) Just outside the walls.

Getting There & Away

Brittany Ferries (www.brittany-ferries.com) sails between St-Malo and Portsmouth; **Condor Ferries** (www.condorferries.co.uk) runs to/from Poole via Jersey or Guernsey.

TGV train services go to Paris' Gare Montparnasse (€52 to €64, three hours, up to 10 daily).

CHAMPAGNE

Known in Roman times as Campania, meaning 'plain', the agricultural region of Champagne is synonymous these days with its world-famous bubbly. This multi-million-dollar industry is strictly protected under French law, ensuring that only grapes grown in designated Champagne vineyards can truly lay claim to the hallowed title. The town of Épernay, 30km south of the regional capital of Reims, is the best place to head for *dégustation* (tasting); a self-drive **Champagne Routes** (www.tourisme-en-champagne.com) wends its way through the region's most celebrated vineyards.

Reims

POP 184,652

Over the course of a millennium (from 816 to 1825), some 34 sovereigns – among them two dozen kings – began their reigns in Reims' famed cathedral. Meticulously reconstructed after WWI and again following WWII, the city – whose name is pronounced something like 'rance' and is often anglicised as Rheims – is endowed with handsome pedestrian zones, well-tended parks, lively nightlife and a state-of-the-art tramway.

Sights & Activities

The bottle-filled cellars (10°C to 12°C – bring a sweater!) of 10 Reims-area Champagne houses can be visited by a guided tour that ends, *naturellement*, with a tasting session.

★Cathédrale Notre Dame CATHEDRAL
(www.cathedrale-reims.culture.fr; place du Cardinal Luçon; tower adult/child €7.50/free, incl Palais du Tau €11/free; ⏲7.30am-7.30pm, tower tours hourly 11am-4pm Tue-Sun May-Sep) Imagine the egos and extravagance of a French royal coronation. The focal point of such bejewelled pomposity was Reims' resplendent Gothic cathedral, begun in 1211 on a site occupied by churches since the 5th century. The interior is a rainbow of stained-glass windows; the finest are the western facade's 12-petalled **great rose window**, the north transept's **rose window** and the vivid **Chagall** creations (1974) in the central axial chapel. The tourist office rents audioguides (€6) for self-paced cathedral tours.

Basilique St-Rémi BASILICA
(place du Chanoine Ladame; ⏲8am-7pm) FREE This 121m-long former Benedictine abbey church, a Unesco World Heritage Site, mixes Romanesque elements from the mid-11th century (the worn but stunning nave and transept) with early Gothic features from the latter half of the 12th century (the choir,

with a large triforium gallery and, way up top, tiny clerestory windows). Next door, **Musée St-Rémi** (53 rue Simon; adult/child €4/free; 2-6.30pm Mon-Fri, to 7pm Sat & Sun), in a 17th- and 18th-century abbey, features local Gallo-Roman archaeology, tapestries and 16th- to 19th-century military history.

Palais du Tau MUSEUM
(http://palais-tau.monuments-nationaux.fr; 2 place du Cardinal Luçon; adult/child €7.50/free, incl cathedral tower €11/free; 9.30am-12.30pm & 2-5.30pm Tue-Sun) A Unesco World Heritage Site, this former archbishop's residence, constructed in 1690, was where French princes stayed before their coronations – and where they hosted sumptuous banquets afterwards. Now a museum, it displays truly exceptional statuary, liturgical objects and tapestries from the cathedral, some in the impressive, Gothic-style Salle de Tau (Great Hall).

Mumm CHAMPAGNE HOUSE
(03 26 49 59 70; www.mumm.com; 34 rue du Champ de Mars; 1hr tours incl tasting €14-25; tours 9am-5pm daily, shorter hours & closed Sun winter) Mumm (pronounced 'moom'), the only *maison* in central Reims, was founded in 1827 and is now the world's third-largest producer (almost eight million bottles a year). Engaging and edifying one-hour tours take you through cellars filled with 25 million bottles of fine bubbly. Wheelchair accessible. Phone ahead if possible.

Taittinger CHAMPAGNE HOUSE
(03 26 85 45 35; www.taittinger.com; 9 place St-Niçaise; tours €16.50-45; 9.30am-5.30pm, shorter hours & closed Sun winter) The headquarters of Taittinger are an excellent place to come for a clear, straightforward presentation on how Champagne is actually made – there's no claptrap about 'the Champagne mystique' here. Parts of the cellars occupy 4th-century Roman stone quarries; other bits were excavated by 13th-century Benedictine monks. No need to reserve. Situated 1.5km southeast of Reims centre; take the Citadine 1 or 2 bus to the St-Niçaise or Salines stops.

Sleeping & Eating

Les Telliers B&B €€
(09 53 79 80 74; http://telliers.fr; 18 rue des Telliers; s €67-83, d €79-114, tr €115-134, q €131-155; P) Enticingly positioned down a quiet alley near the cathedral, this bijou B&B extends one of Reims' warmest *bienvenues*. The high-ceilinged rooms are big on art-deco character, handsomely decorated with ornamental fireplaces, polished oak floors and the odd antique. Breakfast costs an extra €9 and is a generous spread of pastries, fruit, fresh-pressed juice and coffee.

L'Éveil des Sens BISTRO €€
(03 26 35 16 95; www.eveildessens-reims.com; 8 rue Colbert; menus €30-38; 12.15-2pm & 7.15-10pm, closed Sun & Wed) The 'awakening of the senses' is a fitting name for this terrific bistro. Monochrome hues and white linen create a chic yet understated setting for market-fresh cuisine delivered with finesse. Nicolas Lefèvre's specialities appear deceptively simple on paper, but the flavours are profound – be it scallops with tangy Granny Smith apple or braised beef ravioli on white bean velouté.

REIMS DISCOUNTS

The great-value **Pass Reims** (€9), available at the tourist office, gives you entry to a museum of your choice and an audioguide tour of the city, plus discounts on activities such as Champagne house visits.

Information

Tourist Office (03 26 77 45 00; www.reims-tourisme.com; 2 rue Guillaume de Machault; 9am-7pm Mon-Sat, 10am-6pm Sun)

Getting There & Away

From Reims' train station, 1km northwest of the cathedral, there are services to Paris' Gare de l'Est (€36 to €44, one hour, 12 to 17 daily) and Épernay (€6.80, 30 minutes, 19 daily).

Épernay

POP 24,600

Prosperous Épernay, 25km south of Reims, is the self-proclaimed *capitale du champagne* and home to many of the world's most celebrated Champagne houses. Beneath the town's streets, some 200 million bottles of Champagne are slowly being aged, just waiting to be popped open for some fizz-fuelled celebration.

Sights & Activities

★Avenue de Champagne STREET
Épernay's handsome avenue de Champagne fizzes with *maisons de champagne*

(Champagne houses). The boulevard is lined with mansions and neoclassical villas, rebuilt after WWI. Peek through wrought-iron gates at Moët's private **Hôtel Chandon**, an early 19th-century pavilion-style residence set in landscaped gardens, which counts Wagner among its famous past guests. The haunted-looking **Château Perrier**, a red-brick mansion built in 1854 in neo-Louis XIII style, is aptly placed at number 13! The roundabout presents photo ops with its giant cork and bottle-top.

Moët & Chandon CHAMPAGNE HOUSE
(☎03 26 51 20 20; www.moet.com; 20 av de Champagne; adult incl 1/2 glasses €21/28, 10-18yr €10; ⏰tours 9.30-11.30am & 2-4.30pm, closed Sat & Sun late Jan–mid-Mar) Flying the Moët, French, European and Russian flags, this prestigious *maison* offers frequent one-hour tours that are among the region's most impressive, offering a peek at part of its 28km labyrinth of *caves* (cellars). At the shop you can pick up a 15L bottle of Brut Impérial for just €1500; a standard bottle will set you back €31.

Champagne Domi Moreau VINEYARD TOUR
(☎06 30 35 51 07, after 7pm 03 26 59 45 85; www.champagne-domimoreau.com; tours €25-30; ⏰tours 9.30am & 2.30pm except Wed & 2nd half of Aug) This company runs scenic and insightful three-hour minibus tours, in French and English, of nearby vineyards. Pick-up is across the street from the tourist office. It also organises two-hour vineyard tours by bicycle (€25). Call ahead for reservations.

Sleeping

Parva Domus B&B €€
(☎06 73 25 66 60; www.parvadomusrimaire.com; 27 av de Champagne; d €100, ste €110; 📶) Brilliantly situated on the avenue de Champagne, this vine-swathed B&B is kept spick and span by the amiable Rimaire family. Rooms have a countrified feel, with wood floors, floral fabrics and pastel colours. Sip a glass of house Champagne on the terrace or in the elegant living room.

★**La Villa Eugène** BOUTIQUE HOTEL €€€
(☎03 26 32 44 76; www.villa-eugene.com; 84 av de Champagne; d €154-333, ste €375-390; P❄📶🏊) Sitting handsomely astride the avenue de Champagne in its own grounds with an outdoor pool, La Villa Eugène is a class act. It's lodged in a beautiful 19th-century town mansion that once belonged to the Mercier family. The roomy doubles exude understated elegance, with soft, muted hues and the odd antique. Splash out more for a private terrace or four-poster.

Eating & Drinking

La Grillade Gourmande REGIONAL CUISINE €€
(☎03 26 55 44 22; www.lagrilladegourmande.com; 16 rue de Reims; menus €19-57; ⏰noon-2pm & 7.30-10pm Tue-Sat) This chic, red-walled bistro is an inviting spot to try chargrilled meats and dishes rich in texture and flavour, such as crayfish pan-fried in Champagne and lamb cooked until meltingly tender in rosemary and honey. Diners spill out onto the covered terrace in the warm months.

★**C Comme** CHAMPAGNE BAR
(www.c-comme.fr; 8 rue Gambetta; light meals €7.50-14.50, 6-glass Champagne tasting €33-39; ⏰10am-8.30pm Sun-Wed, 10am-11pm Thu, 10am-midnight Fri & Sat) The downstairs cellar has a stash of 300 different varieties of Champagne; sample them (from €5.50 a glass) in the softly lit bar-bistro upstairs. Accompany with a tasting plate of regional cheese, charcuterie and rillettes. We love the funky bottle-top tables and relaxed ambience.

Information

The **tourist office** (☎03 26 53 33 00; www.ot-epernay.fr; 7 av de Champagne; ⏰9.30am-12.30pm & 1.30-7pm Mon-Sat, 10.30am-1pm & 2-4.30pm Sun; 📶) has English brochures and maps.

Getting There & Away

The **train station** (place Mendès-France) has direct services to Reims (€6.80, 30 minutes, 19 daily) and Paris' Gare de l'Est (€23.60, 1¼ hours to 2¾ hours, 16 daily).

ALSACE & LORRAINE

Teetering on the tempestuous frontier between France and Germany, the neighbouring regions of Alsace and Lorraine are where the worlds of Gallic and Germanic culture collide. Half-timbered houses, lush vineyards and forest-clad mountains hint at Alsace's Teutonic leanings, while Lorraine is indisputably Francophile.

Strasbourg

POP 271,708

Strasbourg is the perfect overture to all that is idiosyncratic about Alsace – walking a fine tightrope between France and Germany and between a medieval past and a progressive future, it pulls off its act in inimitable Alsatian style. Roam the old town's twisting alleys lined with crooked half-timbered houses à la Grimm, feast in cosy *winstubs* (Alsatian taverns), and marvel at how a city that does Christmas markets and gingerbread so well can also be home to the glittering EU Quarter and France's second-largest student population.

Sights

★Cathédrale Notre-Dame CATHEDRAL

(place de la Cathédrale; astronomical clock adult/child €2/1.50, platform adult/child €5/2.50; ⏲7am-7pm, astronomical clock tickets sold 9.30-11am, platform 9am-7.15pm; 🚊Grand'Rue) Nothing prepares you for your first glimpse of Strasbourg's Cathédrale Notre-Dame, completed in all its Gothic grandeur in 1439. The lace-fine facade lifts the gaze little by little to flying buttresses, leering gargoyles and a 142m spire. The interior is exquisitely lit by 12th- to 14th-century **stained-glass windows**, including the western portal's jewel-like rose window. The Gothic-meets-Renaissance **astronomical clock** strikes solar noon at 12.30pm with a parade of figures portraying the different stages of life and Jesus with his apostles.

Grande Île HISTORIC QUARTER

(🚊Grand'Rue) History seeps through the twisting lanes and cafe-rimmed plazas of Grande Île, Strasbourg's Unesco World Heritage–listed island bordered by the River Ill. These streets – with their photogenic line-up of wonky, timber-framed houses in sherbet colours – are made for aimless ambling. They cower beneath the soaring magnificence of the cathedral and its sidekick, the gingerbready 15th-century **Maison Kammerzell** (rue des Hallebardes), with its ornate carvings and leaded windows. The alleys are at their most atmospheric when lantern-lit at night.

Petite France HISTORIC QUARTER

(🚊Grand'Rue) Criss-crossed by narrow lanes, canals and locks, Petite France is where artisans plied their trades in the Middle Ages. The half-timbered houses, sprouting veritable thickets of scarlet geraniums in summer, and the riverside parks attract the masses, but the area still manages to retain its Alsatian charm, especially in the early morning and late evening. Drink in views of the River Ill and the **Barrage Vauban** from the much-photographed **Ponts Couverts** (Covered Bridges) and their trio of 13th-century towers.

Sleeping & Eating

Villa Novarina DESIGN HOTEL €€

(☎03 90 41 18 28; www.villanovarina.com; 11 rue Westercamp; s €87-157, d €117-257, ste €237-537; P❄📶🏊; 🚊Droits de l'Homme) New-wave design is pitched just right at this light-flooded 1950s villa near Parc de l'Orangerie. Slick without being soulless, rooms and suites are liberally sprinkled with art and overlook gardens. Breakfast places the accent on organic, regional produce. There's a heated pool, whirlpool and spa for quiet moments. It's a 10-minute walk south of Droits de l'Homme tram stop.

★Cour du Corbeau BOUTIQUE HOTEL €€€

(☎03 90 00 26 26; www.cour-corbeau.com; 6-8 rue des Couples; r €140-175, ste €220-260; ❄📶; 🚊Porte de l'Hôpital) A 16th-century inn lovingly converted into a boutique hotel, Cour du Corbeau wins you over with its half-timbered charm and location, just steps from the river. Gathered around a courtyard, rooms blend original touches like oak parquet and Louis XV furnishings with mod cons such as flat-screen TVs.

Bistrot et Chocolat CAFE €

(www.bistrotetchocolat.net; 8 rue de la Râpe; snacks €7.50-11, brunch €12.50-26.50; ⏲11am-7pm Mon-Thu, 10am-9pm Fri-Sun; 🌿👪; 🚊Grand'Rue) Chilled bistro hailed for its solid and liquid organic chocolate (ginger is superb), day specials and weekend brunches.

★La Cuiller à Pot ALSATIAN €€

(☎03 88 35 56 30; www.lacuillerapot.com; 18b rue Finkwiller; mains €17.50-26.50; ⏲noon-2.30pm & 7-10.30pm Tue-Fri, 7-10.30pm Sat; 🚊Musée d'Art Moderne) Run by a talented husband-wife team, this little Alsatian dream of a restaurant rustles up fresh regional cuisine. Its well-edited menu goes with the seasons, but might include such dishes as fillet of beef with wild mushrooms, and homemade gnocchi and escargots in parsley jus. Quality is second to none.

Information

The **tourist office** (☎03 88 52 28 28; www.otstrasbourg.fr; 17 place de la Cathédrale; ⏰9am-7pm daily; Grand'Rue) has maps in English (€1).

Getting There & Away

AIR

Strasbourg's international **airport** (☎03 88 64 67 67; www.strasbourg.aeroport.fr) is 17km southwest of the city centre (towards Molsheim).

TRAIN

Direct services go to both European and French cities. Destinations include:

Brussels-Nord €80 to €185, 5¼ hours, three daily
Lille €96 to €140, four hours, 17 daily
Lyon €75 to €145, 4½ hours, 14 daily
Metz €26 to €42, two hours, 20 daily
Paris €75 to €134, 2¼ hours, 19 daily

DON'T MISS

GO TO MARKET

Strasbourg and Metz have excellent markets, some seasonal, others year-round institutions.

➡ **Marché Couvert** (Covered Market; place de la Cathédrale; ⏰7am-7pm Tue-Sat) Metz' Marché Couvert was once a bishop's palace. Now it's a temple to fresh local produce. This is the kind of place where you pop in for a baguette and struggle out an hour later, bags overflowing with charcuterie, ripe fruit and five sorts of *fromage*.

➡ **Marché de Noël** (www.noel.strasbourg.eu) Mulled wine, spicy *bredele* (biscuits) and a Santa-loaded children's village are all part and parcel of Strasbourg's sparkly Christmas market running from the last Saturday in November until 31 December.

Metz

POP 122,149

Straddling the confluence of the Moselle and Seille Rivers, Metz is Lorraine's graceful capital. Its Gothic marvel of a cathedral, Michelin star–studded dining scene, beautiful yellow-stone **Old Town** and regal **Quartier Impérial** (up for Unesco World Heritage status) are a joy to discover.

Sights

★Cathédrale St-Étienne CATHEDRAL
(place St-Étienne; audioguide €7, combined ticket treasury & crypt adult/child €4/2; ⏰8am-6pm, treasury & crypt 9.30am-12.30pm & 1.30-5.30pm Mon-Sat, 2-6pm Sun) The lacy golden spires of this Gothic cathedral crown Metz' skyline. Exquisitely lit by kaleidoscopic curtains of 13th- to 20th-century stained glass, the cathedral is nicknamed 'God's lantern' and its sense of height is spiritually uplifting. Notice the flamboyant **Chagall windows** in startling jewel-coloured shades of ruby, gold, sapphire, topaz and amethyst in the ambulatory, which also harbours the **treasury**. The sculpture of the **Graoully** ('grau-lee'), a dragon said to have terrified pre-Christian Metz, lurks in the 15th-century **crypt**.

Centre Pompidou-Metz GALLERY
(www.centrepompidou-metz.fr; 1 parvis des Droits de l'Homme; adult/child €7/free; ⏰11am-6pm Mon & Wed-Fri, 10am-8pm Sat, 10am-6pm Sun) Designed by Japanese architect Shigeru Ban, with a curved roof resembling a space-age Chinese hat, the architecturally innovative Centre Pompidou-Metz is the star of the city's art scene. The satellite branch of Paris' Centre Pompidou draws on Europe's largest collection of modern art to stage ambitious temporary exhibitions, such as the avant-garde works of German artist Hans Richter and the bold graphic works of American conceptual artist Sol LeWitt. The dynamic space also hosts cultural events, talks and youth projects.

Sleeping & Eating

Hôtel de la Cathédrale HISTORIC HOTEL €€
(☎03 87 75 00 02; www.hotelcathedrale-metz.fr; 25 place de Chambre; d €75-120; 📶) You can expect a friendly welcome at this classy little hotel, occupying a 17th-century town house in a prime spot right opposite the cathedral. Climb the wrought-iron staircase to your classically elegant room, with high ceilings, hardwood floors and antique trappings. Book well ahead for a cathedral view.

La Table de Pol MODERN FRENCH €€
(☎03 87 62 13 72; www.latabledepol.fr; 1/3 rue du Grand Wad; menus €17-46; ⏰noon-2pm & 7-9pm

Tue-Sat) Intimate lighting and cheek-by-jowl tables keep the mood mellow in this friendly bistro, which serves winningly fresh dishes prepared with market produce, along the lines of lamb filet mignon in a herb crust and cod filet with asparagus – all cooked to a T.

Information

The **tourist office** (03 87 55 53 76; http://tourisme.mairie-metz.fr; 2 place d'Armes; 9am-7pm Mon-Sat, 10am-5pm Sun) has free walking-tour maps.

Getting There & Away

Metz' ornate early-20th-century **train station** (place du Général de Gaulle) has a supersleek TGV linking Paris with Luxembourg. Direct trains:

Luxembourg €16.20, 45 minutes, 40 daily
Paris €60 to €75, 1½ hours, 15 daily
Strasbourg €26.40, 1½ hours, 16 daily

THE LOIRE VALLEY

One step removed from the French capital, the Loire was historically the place where princes, dukes and notable nobles established their country getaways, and the countryside is littered with some of the most extravagant architecture outside Versailles.

Blois

POP 48,393

Blois' historic château was the feudal seat of the powerful counts of Blois, and its grand halls, spiral staircases and sweeping courtyards provide a whistlestop tour through the key periods of French architecture.

Sights

★Château Royal de Blois CHÂTEAU
(02 54 90 33 33; www.chateaudeblois.fr; place du Château; adult/child €9.80/5, audioguide €4, English tours Jul & Aug free; 9am-6.30pm Apr-Sep, to 7pm Jul & Aug, shorter hours rest of year) Intended more as an architectural showpiece (look at that ornately carved facade!) than a military stronghold, Blois' château bears the creative mark of several successive French kings. It makes an excellent introduction to the châteaux of the Loire Valley, with elements of Gothic (13th century), Flamboyant Gothic (1498–1503), early Renaissance (1515–24) and classical (1630s) architecture in its four grand wings.

The most famous feature of the Renaissance wing, the royal apartments of François I and Queen Claude, is the **loggia staircase**, decorated with salamanders and curly Fs (heraldic symbols of François I).

Maison de la Magie MUSEUM
(www.maisondelamagie.fr; 1 place du Château; adult/child €9/5; 10am-12.30pm & 2-6.30pm Apr-Aug, 2-6.30pm Mon-Fri, 10am-12.30pm & 2-6.30pm Sat & Sun Sep) Opposite the château you can't miss the former home of watchmaker, inventor and conjurer Jean Eugène Robert-Houdin (1805–71), whose name was later adopted by American magician Harry Houdini. Dragons emerge roaring from the windows on the hour, while the museum inside hosts daily **magic shows**, exhibits on the history of magic, displays of optical trickery and a short historical film about Houdini.

Sleeping & Eating

Côté Loire HOTEL €
(02 54 78 07 86; www.coteloire.com; 2 place de la Grève; r €59-95;) Spotless rooms come in cheery checks, bright pastels and the odd bit of exposed brick; some have Loire views. Breakfast (€10.50) is served on a quaint interior wooden deck, and the restaurant (*menus* €21 to €31) dishes up delicious local cuisine. Find it a block off the river, southwest of Pont Jaques Gabriel.

★La Maison de Thomas B&B €€
(02 54 46 12 10; www.lamaisondethomas.fr; 12 rue Beauvoir; r incl breakfast €90;) Four spacious rooms and a friendly welcome await travellers at this beautiful B&B on a pedestrianised street halfway between the château and the cathedral. There's bike storage in the interior courtyard and a wine cellar where you can sample local vintages.

Les Banquettes Rouges FRENCH €€
(02 54 78 74 92; www.lesbanquettesrouges.com; 16 rue des Trois Marands; menus €17.50-32.50; noon-2pm & 7-10pm Tue-Sat) Handwritten slate menus and wholesome food distinguish the Red Benches: pork with chorizo and rosemary, duck with lentils, and *fondant au chocolat* to top it off.

Information

Tourist Office (☎ 02 54 90 41 41; www.bloischambord.com; 23 place du Château; ⊙9am-7pm Apr-Sep, to 5pm Oct-Mar) Helpful, and sells joint château tickets. Download the Visit Blois smartphone app.

Getting There & Away

BUS

TLC (☎ 02 54 58 55 44; www.tlcinfo.net) operates buses from Blois' train station (€2) to Chambord (line 3; 25 to 40 minutes, two Monday to Saturday) and Cheverny (line 4; 45 minutes, three Monday to Friday, one Saturday).

TRAIN

The **Blois-Chambord train station** (av Jean Laigret) is 600m uphill from Blois' château.

Amboise €7, 20 minutes, 13 daily

Paris From €28.60, 1½ to two hours, 26 daily

Tours €10.90, 40 minutes, 13 daily

Around Blois

Château de Chambord

For full-blown château splendour, you can't top **Chambord** (☎ information 02 54 50 40 00, tour & spectacle reservations 02 54 50 50 40; www.chambord.org; adult/child €11/9, parking €4; ⊙9am-6pm Apr-Sep, 10am-5pm Oct-Mar), constructed from 1519 by François I as a lavish base for hunting game in the Sologne forests but eventually used for just 42 days during the king's 32-year reign (1515–47).

The château's most famous feature is its **double-helix staircase**, attributed by some to Leonardo da Vinci, who lived in Amboise (34km southwest) from 1516 until his death three years later. The most interesting rooms are on the 1st floor, including the **king's and queen's chambers** (complete with interconnecting passages to enable late-night hijinks) and a wing devoted to the thwarted attempts of the Comte de Chambord to be crowned Henri V after the fall of the Second Empire.

Several times daily there are 1½-hour **guided tours** (€4) in English.

Chambord is 16km east of Blois and accessible by bus.

Château de Cheverny

Thought by many to be the most perfectly proportioned château of all, **Cheverny** (☎ 02 54 79 96 29; www.chateau-cheverny.fr; adult/child €9.50/6.50; ⊙9am-7pm Apr-Sep, 10am-5pm Oct-Mar) has hardly been altered since its

CHÂTEAUX TOURS

Hard-core indie travellers might balk at the idea of a tour, but don't dismiss it out of hand, especially if you don't have your own transport.

Minibus

Many private companies offer a choice of well-organised itineraries, taking in various combinations of châteaux (plus wine-tasting tours). Half-day trips cost between €23 and €36; full-day trips range from €50 to €54. Entry to the châteaux isn't included, although you'll likely get a discount on tickets. Reserve via the Tours **tourist offices** (☎ 02 47 70 37 37; www.tours-tourisme.fr; 78-82 rue Bernard Palissy; ⊙8.30am-7pm Mon-Sat, 10am-12.30pm & 2.30-5pm Sun Apr-Sep, shorter hours rest of year) or Amboise tourist office, from where most tours depart.

Bicycle

The Loire Valley is mostly flat and thus excellent cycling country.

Loire à Vélo (www.loireavelo.fr) Maintains 800km of signposted routes. Pick up a guide from tourist offices, or download route maps, audioguides and bike-hire details online.

Détours de Loire (☎ 02 47 61 22 23; www.locationdevelos.com) Has a bike-rental shop in Blois and can deliver bikes; it also allows you to collect/return bikes along the route for a small surcharge. Classic bikes cost €15/60 per day/week.

Les Châteaux à Vélo (☎ in Blois 02 54 78 62 52; www.chateauxavelo.com; per day €12-14) Has 400km of marked trails around Blois, Chambord, Cheverny and Chaumont-sur-Loire; shuttle minibus available, as well as free route maps and MP3 guides online.

construction between 1625 and 1634. Inside is a formal dining room, bridal chamber and children's playroom (complete with Napoléon III–era toys), as well as a guards' room full of pikestaffs, claymores and suits of armour.

Many priceless art works (including the *Mona Lisa*) were stashed in the château's 18th-century **Orangerie** during WWII. Near the château's gateway, the **kennels** house pedigreed French pointer/English foxhound hunting dogs still used by the owners of Cheverny; feeding time, the **Soupe des Chiens**, takes place daily at 5pm April to September.

Cheverny is 16km southeast of Blois and accessible by bus.

Amboise

POP 13,375

The childhood home of Charles VIII and the final resting place of Leonardo da Vinci, elegant Amboise, 23km northeast of Tours, is pleasantly perched along the southern bank of the Loire and overlooked by its fortified château.

Sights

Château Royal d'Amboise CHÂTEAU

(02 47 57 52 23; www.chateau-amboise.com; place Michel Debré; adult/child €10.70/7.20, with audioguide €14.70/10.20; 9am-7pm Jul & Aug, to 6pm Apr-Oct, shorter hours Nov-Mar) Elegantly tiered on a rocky escarpment above town, this easily defendable castle presented a formidable prospect to would-be attackers – but saw little military action. It was more often a weekend getaway from the official royal seat at Blois. Charles VIII (r 1483–98), born and bred here, was responsible for the château's Italianate remodelling in 1492. Today just a few of the original 15th- and 16th-century structures survive, notably the Flamboyant Gothic wing and **Chapelle St-Hubert**, the final resting place of Leonardo da Vinci. They have thrilling views to the river, town and gardens.

Le Clos Lucé HISTORIC BUILDING

(02 47 57 00 73; www.vinci-closluce.com; 2 rue du Clos Lucé; adult/child €14/9, joint family tickets reduced; 9am-8pm Jul & Aug, 9am-7pm Feb-Jun, Sep & Oct, 9am-6pm Nov & Dec, 10am-6pm Jan;) Leonardo da Vinci took up residence at this grand manor house in 1516 on the invitation of François I. An admirer of the Italian Renaissance, François named da Vinci 'first painter, engineer and king's architect'. Already 64 by the time he arrived, da Vinci spent his time sketching, tinkering and dreaming up new contraptions, scale models of which are now displayed throughout the home and its expansive **gardens**. Visitors tour rooms where da Vinci worked and the bedroom where he drew his last breath on 2 May 1519.

Sleeping & Eating

Au Charme Rabelaisien B&B €€

(02 47 57 53 84; www.au-charme-rabelaisien.com; 25 rue Rabelais; d incl breakfast €92-179; P) At this calm haven in the centre, Sylvie offers the perfect small B&B experience. Mixing modern fixtures with antique charm, three comfy rooms share a flower-filled garden, pool and free enclosed parking. The spacious Chambre Nature is delightfully secluded and only a few steps from the pool. Breakfasts are fab.

Chez Bruno BISTRO €

(02 47 57 73 49; www.bistrotchezbruno.com; 38-40 place Michel Debré; mains €8-12; lunch & dinner Tue-Sat) Uncork a host of local vintages in a lively contemporary setting just beneath the towering château. Tables of chatting visitors and locals alike dig into delicious, inexpensive regional cooking. If you're after Loire Valley wine tips, this is the place to come.

Information

The **tourist office** (02 47 57 09 28; www.amboise-valdeloire.com; quai du Général de Gaulle; 9.30am-6pm Mon-Sat, 10am-1pm & 2-5pm Sun, closed Sun Nov-Mar) offers walking tours.

Getting There & Around

From the **train station** (bd Gambetta, 1.5km north of the château), there are services to Blois (€7, 20 minutes, 13 daily) and Paris' Gare d'Austerlitz (€15, 1¾ hours, four daily).

Around Amboise

Château de Chenonceau

Spanning the languid Cher River via a series of supremely graceful arches, the castle of

Chenonceau (☎02 47 23 90 07; www.chenonceau.com; adult/child €12.50/9.50, with audioguide €17/13.50; ⏲9am-7pm Apr-Sep, shorter hours rest of year; 📶) is one of the most elegant and unusual in the Loire Valley. You can't help but be swept up in the magical architecture, the fascinating history of prominent female owners, the glorious setting and the landscaped parkland.

The château's interior is crammed with wonderful furniture and tapestries, stunning original tiled floors and a fabulous art collection including works by Tintoretto, Correggio, Rubens, Murillo, Van Dyck and Ribera. The pièce de résistance is the 60m-long window-lined **Grande Gallerie** spanning the Cher.

Make time to visit the **gardens**, too: it seems as if there's one of every kind imaginable (maze, English, vegetable, playground, flower...).

The château is located 10km southeast of Amboise. **Touraine Fil Vert** (www.tourainefilvert.com; tickets €2.20) runs two daily buses from Amboise (15 minutes, Monday to Saturday).

Château d'Azay-le-Rideau

Romantic, moat-ringed **Azay-le-Rideau** (☎02 47 45 42 04; www.azay-le-rideau.monuments-nationaux.fr/en; adult/child €8.50/free; ⏲9.30am-6pm Apr-Sep, to 7pm Jul & Aug, 10am-5.15pm Oct-Mar) is wonderfully adorned with slender turrets, geometric windows and decorative stonework, wrapped up within a shady landscaped park. Built in the 1500s on a natural island in the middle of a river, the château is one of the Loire's loveliest: Honoré de Balzac called it a 'multifaceted diamond set in the River Indre'.

Its most famous feature is its open **loggia staircase**, in the Italian style, overlooking the central courtyard and decorated with the salamanders and ermines of François I and Queen Claude.

Azay-le-Rideau is 26km southwest of Tours. The château is 2.5km from the train station, where there are eight daily services to Tours (€5.80, 30 minutes).

BURGUNDY & THE RHÔNE VALLEY

If there's one place in France where you're really going to find out what makes the nation tick, it's Burgundy. Two of the country's enduring passions – food and wine – come together in this gorgeously rural region. If you're a sucker for hearty food and the fruits of the vine, you'll be in seventh heaven.

Dijon

POP 155,900

Filled with elegant medieval and Renaissance buildings, dashing Dijon is Burgundy's capital, and the spiritual home of French mustard. Its lively Old Town is wonderful for strolling and shopping, interspersed with some snappy drinking and dining.

👁 Sights

Palais des Ducs et des États de Bourgogne PALACE

(Palace of the Dukes & States of Burgundy; place de la Libération) Once home to Burgundy's powerful dukes, this monumental palace with a neoclassical facade overlooks place de la Libération, Old Dijon's magnificent central square dating from 1686. The palace's eastern wing houses the outstanding Musée des Beaux-Arts, whose entrance is next to the **Tour de Bar**, a squat 14th-century tower that once served as a prison.

Musée des Beaux-Arts ART MUSEUM

(☎03 80 74 52 09; http://mba.dijon.fr; audioguide €4; ⏲9.30am-6pm Wed-Mon May-Oct, 10am-5pm Nov-Apr) FREE Housed in the monumental Palais des Ducs, these sprawling galleries (works of art in themselves) constitute one of France's most outstanding museums. The star attraction, reopened in September 2013 after extensive renovations, is the wood-panelled **Salle des Gardes**, which houses the ornate, carved late-medieval sepulchres of dukes John the Fearless and Philip the Bold. Other sections focus on Egyptian art, the Middle Ages in Burgundy and Europe, and six centuries of European painting, from the Renaissance to modern times.

🛏 Sleeping & Eating

Hôtel du Palais HOTEL €

(☎03 80 65 51 43; www.hoteldupalais-dijon.fr; 23 rue du Palais; s €59-79, d €65-89, q €119; ❄📶) Newly remodelled and upgraded to three-star status, this inviting hotel in a 17th-century *hôtel particulier* (private mansion) offers excellent value. The 13 rooms range from cosy, inexpensive 3rd-floor doubles tucked under the eaves to spacious, high-ceilinged family suites with

MAD ABOUT MUSTARD

If there is one pilgrimage to be made in Dijon it is to **Moutarde Maille** (03 80 30 41 02; www.maille.com; 32 rue de la Liberté; 10am-7pm Mon-Sat), the factory boutique of the company that makes Dijon's most famous mustard. The tangy odours of the sharp sauce assault your nostrils instantly upon entering and there are 36 kinds to buy, including cassis-, truffle- or celery-flavoured; sample three on tap.

Or head to **Moutarderie Fallot** (Mustard Mill; 03 80 22 10 10; www.fallot.com; 31 rue du Faubourg Bretonnière; adult/child €10/8; tasting room 9.30am-6pm Mon-Sat, tours 10am & 11.30am Mon-Sat mid-Mar–mid-Nov, plus 3.30pm & 5pm Jun-Sep, by arrangement rest of year) in neighbouring Beaune, where Burgundy's last family-run, stone-ground mustard company offers tours of its facilities and mustard museum. Reserve ahead at Beaune tourist office.

abundant natural light. The location is unbeatable, on a quiet side street five minutes' walk from supercentral place de la Libération.

Chez Léon REGIONAL CUISINE €€
(03 80 50 01 07; www.restochezleon.fr; 20 rue des Godrans; mains €17-23, lunch menus €15-19, dinner menus €25-29; noon-2pm & 7-10.30pm Tue-Sat) From bœuf bourguignon to *andouillettes* (chitterling sausages), this is the perfect primer course in hearty regional fare celebrated in a cosy and joyful atmosphere. The dining room is cluttered but there's outdoor seating in warmer months.

Information

The **tourist office** (08 92 70 05 58; www.visitdijon.com; 11 rue des Forges; 9.30am-6.30pm Mon-Sat, 10am-6pm Sun Apr-Sep, shorter hours rest of year) offers tours and maps.

Getting There & Away

BUS

Transco (03 80 11 29 29; www.cotedor.fr/cms/transco-horaires) buses stop in front of the train station; tickets (€1.50) are sold on board. Bus 44 goes to Nuits-St-Georges and Beaune.

TRAIN

Connections from Dijon's **train station** (rue du Dr Rémy) include the following:

Lyon-Part Dieu Regional train/TGV €31/36, two/1½ hours, 25 daily

Marseille TGV €89, 3½ hours, six direct daily

Paris Gare de Lyon Regional train/TGV €45/65, three/1½ hours, 25 daily

Beaune

POP 22,620

Beaune (pronounced 'bone'), 44km south of Dijon, is the unofficial capital of the Côte d'Or. This thriving town's *raison d'être* and the source of its *joie de vivre* is wine.

Sights & Activities

Beaune's amoeba-shaped old city is enclosed by **stone ramparts** sheltering wine cellars.

Hôtel-Dieu des Hospices de Beaune HISTORIC BUILDING
(www.hospices-de-beaune.com; rue de l'Hôtel-Dieu; adult/child €7/3; 9am-6.30pm) Built in 1443, this magnificent Gothic hospital (until 1971) is famously topped by stunning turrets and pitched rooftops covered in multicoloured tiles. Interior highlights include the barrel-vaulted **Grande Salle** (look for the dragons and peasant heads up on the roof beams); the mural-covered **St-Hughes Room**; an 18th-century **pharmacy** lined with flasks once filled with elixirs and powders; and the multipanelled masterpiece **Polyptych of the Last Judgement** by 15th-century Flemish painter Rogier van der Weyden, depicting Judgment Day in glorious technicolour.

Marché aux Vins WINE TASTING
(www.marcheauxvins.com; 2 rue Nicolas Rolin; 10am-7pm Apr-Oct, 10am-noon & 2-7pm Nov-Mar) Sample seven wines for €11, or 10 for €15, in the candle-lit former Église des Cordeliers and its cellars. Wandering among the vintages takes about an hour. The finest wines are at the end; look for the *premier crus* and the *grand cru* (wine of exceptional quality).

Sleeping & Eating

★ **Les Jardins de Loïs** B&B €€
(03 80 22 41 97; www.jardinsdelois.com; 8 bd Bretonnière; incl breakfast r €149, ste €180-190, apt €280-350;) An unexpected oasis in the middle of the city, this luxurious B&B

WORTH A TRIP

A TRIP BETWEEN VINES

Burgundy's most renowned vintages come from the **Côte d'Or** (Golden Hillside), a range of hills made of limestone, flint and clay that runs south from Dijon for about 60km. The northern section, the **Côte de Nuits**, stretches from Marsannay-la-Côte south to Corgoloin and produces reds known for their robust, full-bodied character. The southern section, the **Côte de Beaune**, lies between Ladoix-Serrigny and Santenay and produces great reds and whites.

Tourist offices provide brochures. The signposted **Route des Grands Crus** (www.road-of-the-fine-burgundy-wines.com) visits some of the most celebrated Côte de Nuits vineyards; mandatory tasting stops for oenophiles seeking nirvana include 16th-century **Château du Clos de Vougeot** (☎03 80 62 86 09; www.closdevougeot.fr; Vougeot; adult/child €5/2.50; ⌚9am-6.30pm Apr-Sep, 9-11.30am & 2-5.30pm Oct-Mar, closes 5pm Sat year-round, which has excellent guided tours, and **L'Imaginarium** (☎03 80 62 61 40; www.imaginarium-bourgogne.com; av du Jura, Nuits-St-Georges; adult incl basic/grand cru tasting €8/15, child €5; ⌚2-7pm Mon, 10am-7pm Tue-Sun, an entertaining wine museum in Nuits-St-Georges.

Wine & Voyages (☎03 80 61 15 15; www.wineandvoyages.com; tours from €53) and **Alter & Go** (☎06 23 37 92 04; www.alterandgo.fr; tours from €70), with an emphasis on history and winemaking methods, run minibus tours in English; reserve online or at the Dijon tourist office.

encompasses several ample rooms, including two suites and a 135-sq-metre top-floor apartment with drop-dead gorgeous views of Beaune's rooftops. The vast garden, complete with rose bushes and fruit trees, makes a dreamy place to sit and enjoy wine grown on the hotel's private *domaine*. Free parking.

Le Bacchus MODERN BURGUNDIAN €€
(☎03 80 24 07 78; 6 Faubourg Madeleine; lunch menus €14-16.50, dinner menus €26.50-33; ⌚noon-1.30pm & 7-10pm) The welcome is warm and the food exceptional at this small restaurant just outside Beaune's centre. Multilingual co-owner Anna works the tables while her partner Olivier whips up market-fresh menus that blend classic flavours (steak with Fallot mustard) with tasty surprises (gazpacho with tomato-basil ice cream). Save room for splendid desserts such as Bourbon vanilla crème brûlée, flambéed at your table.

Information

The **tourist office** (☎03 80 26 21 30; www.beaune-tourisme.fr; 6 bd Perpreuil; ⌚9am-6.30pm Mon-Sat, 9am-6pm Sun) has lots of info about nearby vineyards.

Getting There & Away

BUS

Bus 44 links Beaune with Dijon (€1.50, 1½ hours, two to seven daily), stopping at Côte d'Or villages such as Nuits-St-Georges.

TRAIN

Trains run to the following destinations:

Dijon €7.80, 25 minutes, 40 daily
Paris Gare de Lyon €75, 2¼ hours, two daily
Lyon-Part Dieu €26.50, 1¾ hours, 16 daily

Lyon

POP 499,800

Gourmets, eat your heart out: Lyon is *the* gastronomic capital of France, with a lavish table of piggy-driven dishes and delicacies to savour. The city has been a commercial, industrial and banking powerhouse for the past 500 years, and is France's third-largest city, with outstanding art museums, a dynamic nightlife, green parks and a Unesco-listed Old Town.

Sights

Vieux Lyon

Old Lyon, with its cobblestone streets and medieval and Renaissance houses below

Fourvière hill, is divided into three quarters: St-Paul (north), St-Jean (middle) and St-Georges (south). Lovely old buildings languish on **rue du Bœuf**, **rue St-Jean** and **rue des Trois Maries**.

Listen out for the chime of the **astronomical clock** of the partly Romanesque **Cathédrale St-Jean** (place St-Jean, 5e; 8.15am-7.45pm Mon-Fri, to 7pm Sat & Sun; M Vieux Lyon), striking the hour at noon, 2pm, 3pm and 4pm.

Fourvière

Over two millennia ago, the Romans built the city of Lugdunum on the slopes of Fourvière. Today, Lyon's 'hill of prayer' – topped by the **Basilique Notre Dame de Fourvière** (www.fourviere.org; place de Fourvière, 5e; rooftop tour adult/child €6/3; 8am-7pm; funicular Fourvière) and the **Tour Métallique**, an Eiffel Tower–like structure built in 1893 and used as a TV transmitter – affords spectacular views of the city. Footpaths wind uphill, but the **funicular** (place Édouard Commette, 5e; one way €1.70) is less taxing.

Presqu'île, Confluence & Croix-Rousse

Lyon's city centre lies on this 500m- to 800m-wide peninsula bounded by the rivers Rhône and Saône.

The centrepiece of main square **place des Terreaux** is a 19th-century fountain sculpted by Frédéric-Auguste Bartholdi, creator of the Statue of Liberty. The **Musée des Beaux-Arts** (www.mba-lyon.fr; 20 place des Terreaux, 1er; adult/child incl audioguide €7/free; 10am-6pm Wed, Thu & Sat-Mon, 10.30am-6pm Fri; M Hôtel de Ville) showcases France's finest collection of sculptures and paintings outside of Paris.

Lyonnais silks are showcased at the **Musée des Tissus** (www.musee-des-tissus.com; 34 rue de la Charité, 2e; adult/child €10/7.50, after 4pm €8/5.50; 10am-5.30pm Tue-Sun; M Ampère). Next door, the **Musée des Arts Décoratifs** (34 rue de la Charité, 2e; free with Musée des Tissus ticket; 10am-noon & 2-5.30pm Tue-Sun) displays 18th-century furniture, tapestries, wallpaper, ceramics and silver. Laid out in the 17th century, **place Bellecour** – one of Europe's largest public squares – is pierced by an equestrian **statue of Louis XIV**. South of here, past **Gare de Perrache**, lies **Lyon Confluence** (www.lyon-confluence.fr), the city's newest neighbourhood, where the Rhône and Saône meet. Trendy restaurants line its quays, and the ambitious **Musée des Confluences** (www.museedesconfluences.fr; 28 bd des Belges, 6e), a science-and-humanities museum inside a futuristic steel-and-glass transparent crystal, is also located here.

North of place Bellecour, the charming hilltop quarter of **Croix Rousse** is famed for its lush outdoor food market and silk-weaving tradition, illustrated by the **Maison des Canuts** (www.maisondescanuts.com; 10-12 rue d'Ivry, 4e; adult/child €6.50/3.50; 10am-6.30pm Mon-Sat, guided tours 11am & 3.30pm Mon-Sat; M Croix Rousse).

Sleeping

Auberge de Jeunesse du Vieux Lyon HOSTEL €
(04 78 15 05 50; www.fuaj.org/lyon; 41-45 montée du Chemin Neuf, 5e; dm incl breakfast €19.50-24; reception 7am-1pm, 2-8pm & 9pm-1am; @; M Vieux Lyon, funicular Minimes) Stunning city views unfold from the terrace of Lyon's HI-affiliated hostel, and from many of the (mostly six-bed) dorms. Bike parking, kitchen and laundry (wash-dry per load €4) facilities are available, and there's an on-site bar. To avoid the tiring 10-minute climb from Vieux Lyon metro station, take the funicular to Minimes station and walk downhill.

Mama Shelter HOTEL €€
(04 78 02 58 00; www.mamashelter.com/en/lyon; 13 rue Domer; r €89-149; P@; M Jean Macé) Lyon's branch of this trendy hotel chain has sleek decor, carpets splashed with calli-graffiti, firm beds, plush pillows, modernist lighting and big-screen Macs offering free in-room movies. A youthful crowd fills the long bar at the low-lit restaurant. The residential location 2km outside the centre may feel remote, but it's only three metro stops from Gare Part-Dieu and place Bellecour.

Lyon Renaissance APARTMENT €€
(04 27 89 30 58; www.lyon-renaissance.com; 3 rue des Tourelles, 5e; apt €95-115; ; M Vieux Lyon) Friendly owners Françoise and Patrick rent these two superbly situated Vieux Lyon apartments with beamed ceilings and kitchen facilities. The smaller 3rd-floor walk-up

Lyon

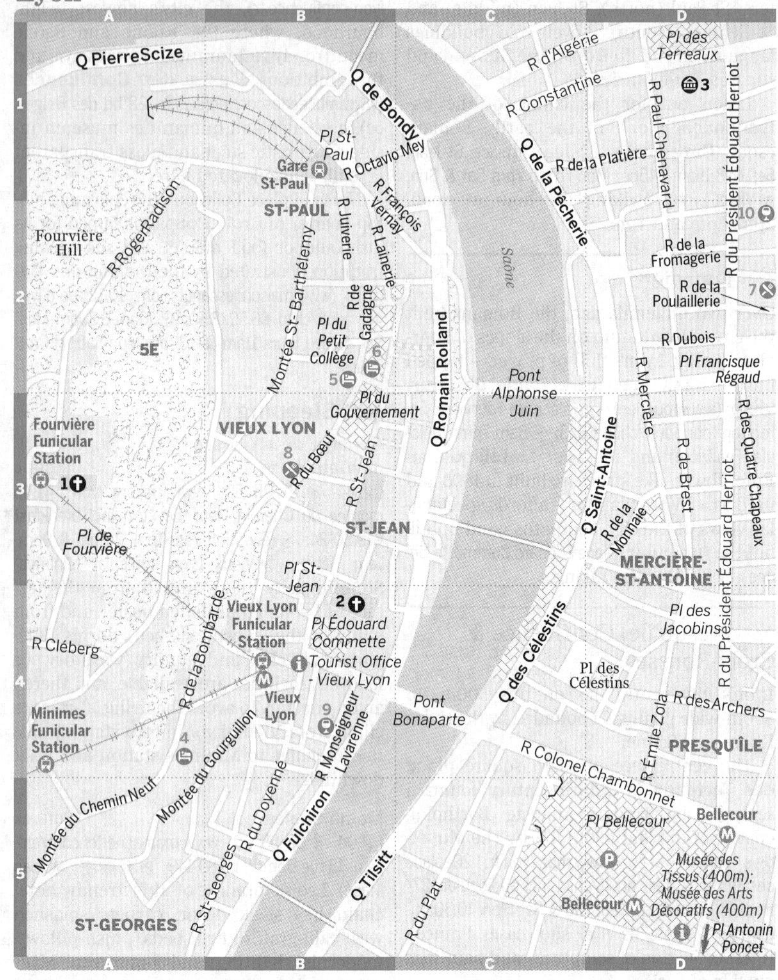

sleeps two, with windows overlooking a pretty tree-shaded square. A second unit, opposite Vieux Lyon's most famous medieval tower, has a spacious living room with ornamental fireplace and fold-out couch, plus a mezzanine with double bed.

★ **Cour des Loges** HOTEL €€€

(04 72 77 44 44; www.courdesloges.com; 2-8 rue du Bœuf, 5e; d €190-485, junior ste €340-655; ; Vieux Lyon) Four 14th- to 17th-century houses wrapped around a *traboule* (secret passage) with preserved features such as Italianate loggias make this an exquisite place to stay. Individually decorated rooms woo with designer bathroom fittings and bountiful antiques, while decadent facilities include a spa, an elegant restaurant (menus €85 to €105), swish cafe (lunch menu €17.50, mains €22 to €30) and cross-vaulted bar.

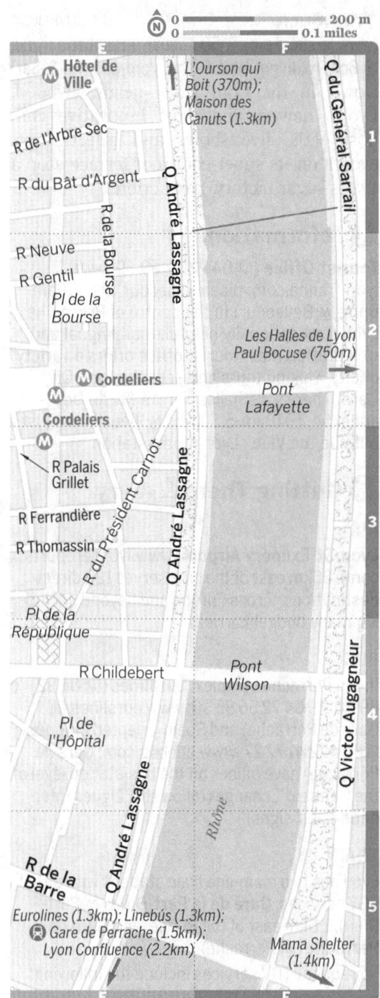

Lyon

Sights

1 Basilique Notre Dame de Fourvière A3
2 Cathédrale St-Jean B4
3 Musée des Beaux-Arts D1

Sleeping

4 Auberge de Jeunesse du Vieux Lyon A4
5 Cour des Loges B2
6 Lyon Renaissance B2

Eating

7 Le Musée D2
8 Les Adrets B3

Drinking & Nightlife

9 (L'A)Kroche B4
10 Harmonie des Vins D2

Eating

Lyon's sparkling restaurant line-up embraces all genres: French, fusion, fast and international, as well as traditional Lyonnais *bouchons* (small, friendly bistros serving local city cuisine).

★ Les Halles de Lyon Paul Bocuse MARKET €

(www.hallespaulbocuse.lyon.fr; 102 cours Lafayette, 3e; 7am-10.30pm Tue-Sat, to 4.30pm Sun; Ⓜ Part-Dieu) Lyon's famed indoor food market has nearly five dozen stalls selling countless gourmet delights. Pick up a round of runny St Marcellin from legendary cheesemonger Mère Richard, and a knobbly Jésus de Lyon from Charcuterie Sibilia. Or enjoy a sit-down lunch of local produce, especially enjoyable on Sundays when local families congregate for shellfish and white-wine brunches.

Les Adrets BOUCHON €€

(04 78 38 24 30; 30 rue du Bœuf, 5e; lunch menu €17.50, dinner menus €27-45; noon-1.30pm & 7.45-9pm Mon-Fri; Ⓜ Vieux Lyon) This atmospheric spot serves an exceptionally good-value lunch *menu* (including wine and coffee). The mix is half classic *bouchon* fare, half alternative choices such as Parma ham and truffle risotto, or duck breast with roasted pears.

★ Le Musée BOUCHON €€

(04 78 37 71 54; 2 rue des Forces; lunch/dinner menus €23/28; noon-2pm & 7.30-9.30pm Tue-Sat; Ⓜ Cordeliers) Housed in the stables of Lyon's former Hôtel de Ville, this delightful *bouchon* serves a splendid array of meat-heavy Lyonnais classics alongside veggie-centric treats such as roasted peppers with fresh goat cheese. The daily changing menu features 10 appetisers and 10 main dishes, plus five scrumptious desserts, all served on cute china plates at long family-style tables.

LYON CITY CARD

The excellent-value **Lyon City Card** (www.en.lyon-france.com/Lyon-City-Card; 1/2/3 days adult €22/32/42, child €13.50/18.50/23.50) offers free admission to every Lyon museum and a number of attractions. The card also includes unlimited city-wide transport on buses, trams, the funicular and the metro. Full-price cards are available at the tourist office, or save 10% by booking online.

L'Ourson qui Boit FUSION €€
(☎04 78 27 23 37; 23 rue Royale, 1er; lunch/dinner menus €18/28; ⏰noon-1.30pm & 7.30-9.30pm Mon, Tue & Thu-Sat; Ⓜ Croix Paquet) On the fringes of Croix Rousse, Japanese chef Akira Nishigaki puts his own splendid spin on French cuisine, with plenty of locally sourced fresh vegetables and light, clean flavours. The ever-changing menu of two daily entrées and two main dishes is complemented by good wines, attentive service and delicious desserts. Well worth reserving ahead.

Drinking & Entertainment

Cafe terraces on place des Terreaux buzz with all-hours drinkers, as do the British, Irish and other-styled pubs on nearby rue Ste-Catherine, 1er, and rue Lainerie and rue St-Jean, 5e, in Vieux Lyon.

Floating bars with DJs and live bands rock until around 3am aboard the string of *péniches* (river barges) moored along the Rhône's left bank. Scout out the section of quai Victor Augagneur between Pont Lafayette (metro Cordeliers or Guichard) and Pont de la Guillotière (metro Guillotière).

Harmonie des Vins WINE BAR
(www.harmoniedesvins.fr; 9 rue Neuve, 1er; ⏰10am-2.30pm & 6.30pm-1am Tue-Sat; 📶; Ⓜ Hôtel de Ville, Cordeliers) Find out all about French wine at this charm-laden wine bar replete with old stone walls, contemporary furnishings and tasty food.

(L'A)Kroche BAR
(www.lakroche.fr; 8 rue Monseigneur Lavarenne, 5e; ⏰4pm-1am Tue-Sat, 4-9pm Sun & Mon; Ⓜ Vieux Lyon) Hip cafe-bar with six dozen flavours of rum, daily happy hours and frequent live music with no cover charge.

★**Le Sucre** LIVE MUSIC
(www.le-sucre.eu; 50 quai Rambaud, 2e; ⏰6pm-midnight Wed & Thu, 7pm-6am Fri & Sat) Down in the Confluence neighbourhood, Lyon's newest and most innovative club hosts DJs, live shows and eclectic arts events on its super-cool roof terrace atop a 1930s sugar factory, La Sucrière.

Information

Tourist Office (☎04 72 77 69 69; www.lyon-france.com; place Bellecour, 2e; ⏰9am-6pm; Ⓜ Bellecour) In the centre of Presqu'île, Lyon's exceptionally helpful, multilingual and well-staffed main tourist office offers a variety of city walking tours and sells the Lyon City Card. There's a smaller branch (av du Doyenné, 5e; ⏰10am-5.30pm; Ⓜ Vieux Lyon) just outside the Vieux Lyon metro station.

Getting There & Away

AIR

Lyon-St-Exupéry Airport (www.lyonaeroports.com), 25km east of the city, serves 120 direct destinations across Europe and beyond, including many budget carriers.

BUS

In the Perrache complex, **Eurolines** (☎08 92 89 90 91, 04 72 56 95 30; www.eurolines.fr; Gare de Perrache) and Spain-oriented **Linebús** (☎04 72 41 72 27; www.linebus.com; Gare de Perrache) have offices on the bus-station level of the Centre d'Échange (follow the 'Lignes Internationales' signs).

TRAIN

Lyon has two main-line train stations with direct TGV services: **Gare de la Part-Dieu** (Ⓜ Part-Dieu), 1.5km east of the Rhône, and **Gare de Perrache** (Ⓜ Perrache).

Frequent TGV services include the following:

Dijon €36, 1½ hours

Marseille €52, 1¾ hours

Paris Charles de Gaulle Airport €95, two hours

Paris Gare de Lyon €73, two hours

Getting Around

Tramway **Rhônexpress** (www.rhonexpress.fr; adult/child/youth €15.70/free/13) links the airport with Part-Dieu train station in under 30 minutes.

Buses, trams, a four-line metro and two funiculars linking Vieux Lyon to Fourvière are run by **TCL** (www.tcl.fr). Public transport runs from around 5am to midnight. Tickets cost €1.70.

Time-stamp tickets on all forms of public transport or risk a fine.

Bikes are available from 200-odd bike stations thanks to **Vélo'v** (www.velov.grandlyon.com; first 30min free, next 30min €1, each subsequent 30min period €2).

THE FRENCH ALPS

Hiking, skiing, majestic panoramas – the French Alps have it all when it comes to the great outdoors. But you'll also find excellent gastronomy, good nightlife and plenty of history.

Chamonix

POP 9050 / ELEV 1037M

With the pearly white peaks of the Mont Blanc massif as a sensational backdrop, being an icon comes naturally to Chamonix. First 'discovered' by Brits William Windham and Richard Pococke in 1741, this is the mecca of mountaineering. Its knife-edge peaks, plunging slopes and massive glaciers have enthralled generations of adventurers and thrill-seekers ever since. Its après-ski scene is equally pumping.

Sights

Aiguille du Midi VIEWPOINT

A jagged finger of rock soaring above glaciers, snowfields and rocky crags, 8km from the hump of Mont Blanc, the Aiguille du Midi (3842m) is one of Chamonix' most distinctive geographical features. If you can handle the altitude, the 360-degree views of the French, Swiss and Italian Alps from the summit are (quite literally) breathtaking. Year-round, you can float in a cable car from Chamonix to the Aiguille du Midi on the vertiginous **Téléphérique de l'Aiguille du Midi** (www.compagniedumontblanc.co.uk; place de l'Aiguille du Midi; adult/child return to Aiguille du Midi €55/47, to Plan de l'Aiguille summer €29.50/25, winter €16/14; 1st ascent btwn 7.10am & 8.30am, last ascent btwn 3.30pm & 5pm).

Le Brévent VIEWPOINT

The highest peak on the western side of the Chamonix Valley, Le Brévent (2525m) has tremendous views of the Mont Blanc massif, myriad hiking trails, ledges to paraglide from and the summit restaurant **Le Panoramic**. Reach it on the **Télécabine de Planpraz** (www.compagniedumontblanc.co.uk; adult/child one way €13.20/11.20, return €16/13.60), 400m west of the tourist office, and then the **Téléphérique du Brévent** (www.compagniedumontblanc.co.uk; 29 rte Henriette d'Angeville; adult/child one way €22/18.70, return €29.50/25; mid-Dec–mid-Apr & mid-Jun–mid-Sep). Plenty of family-friendly trails begin at **Planpraz** (2000m).

Mer de Glace GLACIER

France's largest glacier, the glistening 200m-deep Mer de Glace (Sea of Ice) snakes 7km down on the northern side of Mont Blanc, moving up to 1cm an hour (about 90m a year). The **Train du Montenvers** (www.compagniedumontblanc.co.uk; adult/child one way €24/20.40, return €29.50/25; closed late Sep–mid-Oct), a picturesque, 5km-long cog railway opened in 1909, links Chamonix' Gare du Montenvers with Montenvers (1913m), from where a cable car takes you down to the glacier and the **Grotte de la Mer de Glace** (closed last half of May & late Sep–mid-Oct), an ice cave whose frozen tunnels and ice sculptures change colour like mood rings.

Activities

The ski season runs from mid-December to mid-April. Summer activities – hiking, canyoning, mountaineering etc – generally start in June and end in September. The **Compagnie des Guides de Chamonix** (04 50 53 00 88; www.chamonix-guides.com; 190 place de l'Église, Maison de la Montagne; 8.30am-noon & 2.30-7.30pm, closed Sun & Mon late Apr–mid-Jun & mid-Sep–mid-Dec) is the most famous of all the guide companies and has guides for virtually every activity, whatever the season.

Sleeping

Gîte Le Vagabond HOSTEL €

(04 50 53 15 43; www.gitevagabond.com; 365 av Ravanel-le-Rouge; dm €21, sheets €5.50, d incl breakfast €101; reception 8-10am & 4.30-10.30pm;) In a 150-year-old stage-coach inn, Chamonix' hippest bunkhouse has rooms with four to six beds and a buzzing bar with a great log fire in winter. Situated 850m southwest of Chamonix' town centre.

★ **Hôtel Richemond** HOTEL €€
(☎04 50 53 08 85; www.richemond.fr; 228 rue du Docteur Paccard; s/d/tr €75/120/153; ⌚closed mid-Apr–mid-Jun & mid-Sep–mid-Dec;) In a grand old building constructed in 1914 (and run by the same family ever since), this hotel – as friendly as it is central – has 52 spacious rooms with views of either Mont Blanc or Le Brévent; some are pleasantly old-fashioned, others recently renovated in white, black and beige, and three still have cast-iron bath-tubs. Outstanding value.

Auberge du Manoir HOTEL €€
(☎04 50 53 10 77; www.aubergedumanoir.com; 8 rte du Bouchet; s/d/tr €130/150/220; ⌚closed 2 weeks in late Apr & 2 weeks in autumn;) This beautifully converted farmhouse, ablaze with geraniums in summer, offers 18 pine-panelled rooms that are quaint but never cloying, pristine mountain views, an outdoor hot tub, a sauna and a bar whose open fire keeps things cosy. Family owned.

Eating

Papillon CAFE €
(416 rue Joseph Vallot; mains €5-8; ⌚11am-8pm Mon-Sat, 4-8pm Sun mid-Dec–early May & mid-Jun–early Oct;) A British-owned hole-in-the-wall take-out place that does great home-made curries, chilli con carne, Italian-style meatballs, noodle soup and deli-style sandwiches. Has plenty of vegie, vegan and gluten-free options.

★ **Le Cap Horn** FRENCH €€
(☎04 50 21 80 80; www.caphorn-chamonix.com; 78 rue des Moulins; lunch menu €20, other menus €29-39; ⌚noon-1.30pm or 2pm & 7-9pm or 10pm daily year-round) Housed in a gorgeous, two-storey chalet decorated with model sailboats – joint homage to the Alps and Cape Horn – this highly praised restaurant, opened in 2012, serves French and Asian-inflected dishes such as pan-seared duck breast with honey and soy sauce, fisherman's stew and, for dessert, *souffle au Grand Marnier*. Reserve for dinner Friday and Saturday in winter and summer.

Munchie FUSION €€
(☎04 50 53 45 41; www.munchie.eu; 87 rue des Moulins; mains €19-24; ⌚7pm-2am daily, closed 2 weeks May & mid-Oct–Nov) Franco-Asian fusion has been the lip-smacking mainstay of this casual, Swedish-skippered restaurant since 1997. Specialities such as steak with spicy Béarnaise sauce are presented with panache. Reservations recommended during the ski season.

Drinking & Nightlife

Nightlife rocks in Chamonix. In the centre, riverside rue des Moulins boasts a line-up of après-ski joints serving food as well as booze.

MBC MICROBREWERY
(Micro Brasserie de Chamonix; www.mbchx.com; 350 rte du Bouchet; ⌚4pm-2am Mon-Thu, 10am-2am Fri-Sun) Run by four Canadians, this trendy microbrewery is fab. Be it with their phenomenal burgers (€10 to €15), cheesecake of the week, live music (Sunday from 9.30pm) or amazing beers, MBC delivers. Busiest from 5pm to 11pm.

Chambre Neuf BAR
(272 av Michel Croz; ⌚7am-1am daily year-round;) Chamonix' most spirited après-ski party (4pm to 8pm), fuelled by a Swedish band and dancing on the tables, spills out the front door of Chambre Neuf. Wildly popular with seasonal workers.

La Terrasse BAR
(43 place Balmat; ⌚4pm-2am Mon-Fri, 1pm-2am Sat & Sun, closed May & Nov;) Overlooking Chamonix' main square and the river, this British-style pub – take the spiral staircase for the best views – serves pub grub from 4.30pm to 10.30pm and then gives itself over to music (live or DJed) and dancing. Staff are British.

Information

Tourist Office (☎04 50 53 00 24; www.chamonix.com; 85 place du Triangle de l'Amitié; ⌚9am-12.30pm & 2-6pm, longer hours winter & summer) Information on accommodation, activities, the weather and cultural events.

Getting There & Away

BUS

From **Chamonix bus station** (☎04 50 53 01 15; place de la Gare; ⌚8-11.30am & 1.15-6.15pm winter, shorter hours rest of year), next to the train station, **SAT-Mont Blanc** (☎04 50 78 05 33; www.sat-montblanc.com) operates five daily buses to/from Geneva airport (one way/return €30/50, 1½ to two hours). Advance bookings only.

TRAIN

The Mont Blanc Express narrow-gauge train trundles from St-Gervais-Le Fayet station, 23km west of Chamonix, to Martigny in Switzerland, stopping in Chamonix en route. There are nine to 12 return trips daily between Chamonix and St-Gervais (€5.50, 45 minutes). From St-Gervais-Le Fayet, there are trains to major French cities.

THE DORDOGNE

Tucked in the country's southwestern corner, the Dordogne fuses history, culture and culinary sophistication in one unforgettably scenic package. The region is best known for its sturdy *bastides* (fortified towns), clifftop châteaux and spectacular prehistoric cave paintings.

Sarlat-la-Canéda

POP 10,105

A picturesque tangle of honey-coloured buildings and medieval architecture, Sarlat-la-Canéda is incredibly scenic and perennially popular with visitors.

Sights

Part of the fun of Sarlat is getting lost in its twisting alleyways and backstreets. **Rue Jean-Jacques Rousseau** and **rue Landry** are good starting points, but for the grandest buildings and *hôtels particuliers* explore **rue des Consuls**.

Sarlat Markets MARKET

(place de la Liberté & rue de la République; ⏲8.30am-1pm Wed, 8.30am-6pm Sat) For an introductory French market experience visit Sarlat's heavily touristed Saturday market, which takes over the streets around Cathédrale St-Sacerdos. Depending on the season, delicacies include local mushrooms and duck- and goose-based products such as foie gras. Get *truffe noir* (black truffle) at the winter **Marché aux Truffes** (⏲Sat morning Dec-Feb). An atmospheric, largely organic **night market** (⏲6-10pm) operates on Thursday. Seasoned market-goers may prefer others throughout the region.

DON'T MISS

PREHISTORIC PAINTINGS

Fantastic prehistoric caves with some of the world's finest **cave art** is what makes the Vézère Valley so very special. Most of the caves are closed in winter, and get very busy in summer. Visitor numbers are strictly limited, so you'll need to reserve well ahead.

Of the valley's 175 known sites, the most famous include **Grotte de Font de Gaume** (☎05 53 06 86 00; http://eyzies.monuments-nationaux.fr; adult/child €7.50/free; ⏲guided tours 9.30am-5.30pm Sun-Fri mid-May–mid-Sep, 9.30am-12.30pm & 2-5.30pm Sun-Fri mid-Sep–mid-May), 1km northeast of Les Eyzies. About 14,000 years ago, prehistoric artists created the gallery of over 230 figures, including bison, reindeer, horses, mammoths, bears and wolves, of which 25 are on permanent display.

About 7km east of Les Eyzies, **Abri du Cap Blanc** (☎05 53 06 86 00; adult/child €7.50/free; ⏲guided tours 9.30am-5.30pm Sun-Fri mid-May–mid-Sep, 9.30am-12.30pm & 2-5.30pm Sun-Fri mid-Sep–mid-May) showcases an unusual sculpture gallery of horses, bison and deer.

Then there is **Grotte de Rouffignac** (☎05 53 05 41 71; www.grottederouffignac.fr; Rouffignac-St-Cernin-de-Reilhac; adult/child €7/4.60; ⏲9-11.30am & 2-6pm Jul & Aug, 10-11.30am & 2-5pm mid-Apr–Jun, Sep & Oct, closed Nov–mid-Apr), sometimes known as the 'Cave of 100 Mammoths' because of its painted mammoths. Access to the caves, hidden in woodland 15km north of Les Eyzies, is aboard a trundling electric train.

Star of the show goes hands down to **Grotte de Lascaux** (☎05 53 51 95 03; www.semitour.com; Montignac; adult/child €9.90/6.40, joint ticket with Le Thot €13.50/9.40; ⏲guided tours 9am-7pm Jul & Aug, 9.30am-6pm Apr-Jun, 9.30am-noon & 2-6pm Sep & Oct, shorter hours rest of year, closed Jan), 2km southeast of Montignac, featuring an astonishing menagerie including oxen, deer, horses, reindeer and mammoths, as well as an amazing 5.5m bull, the largest cave drawing ever found. The original cave was closed to the public in 1963 to prevent damage to the paintings, but the most famous sections have been meticulously recreated in a second cave nearby – a massive undertaking that required some 20 artists and took 11 years.

Cathédrale St-Sacerdos CATHEDRAL

(place du Peyrou) Once part of Sarlat's Cluniac abbey, the original abbey church was built in the 1100s, redeveloped in the early 1500s and remodelled again in the 1700s, so it's a real mix of styles. The belfry and western facade are the oldest parts of the building, while the nave, organ and interior chapels are later additions.

Sleeping & Eating

Villa des Consuls B&B €€

(05 53 31 90 05; www.villaconsuls.fr; 3 rue Jean-Jacques Rousseau; d €95-110, apt €150-190;) Despite its Renaissance exterior, the enormous rooms at Villa des Consuls are modern through and through, with shiny wood floors and sleek furnishings. Several delightful self-contained apartments dot the town, all offering the same mix of period plushness – some also have terraces overlooking the town's rooftops.

★ **Le Quatre Saisons** REGIONAL CUISINE €€

(05 53 29 48 59; www.4saisons-sarlat-perigord.com; 2 côte de Toulouse; menus from €19; 12.30-2pm & 7.30-9.30pm Thu-Mon;) A reliable local favourite, hidden in a beautiful stone house on a narrow alley leading uphill from rue de la République. The food is honest and unfussy, taking its cue from market ingredients and regional flavours. The most romantic tables have cross-town views.

Information

Tourist Office (05 53 31 45 45; www.sarlat-tourisme.com; 3 rue Tourny; 9am-7pm Mon-Sat, 10am-1pm & 2-6pm Sun May-Aug, shorter hours Sep-Apr;) Sarlat's tourist office is packed with info, but often gets overwhelmed by visitors; the website has it all.

Getting There & Away

The **train station** (av de la Gare), 1.3km south of the old city, serves Périgueux (€15.90, 1¾ hours, four daily) and Les Eyzies (€9.80, 50 minutes to 2½ hours, four daily), both via Le Buisson.

THE ATLANTIC COAST

With quiet country roads winding through vine-striped hills and wild stretches of coastal sands interspersed with misty islands, the Atlantic coast is where France gets back to nature. If you're a surf nut or beach bum, the sandy bays around Biarritz will be right up your alley, while oenophiles can sample the fruits of the vine in the high temple of French winemaking, Bordeaux.

Bordeaux

POP 236,000

The new millennium was a turning point for the city long nicknamed La Belle au Bois Dormant (Sleeping Beauty), when the mayor, ex-prime minister Alain Juppé, roused Bordeaux, pedestrianising its boulevards, restoring its neoclassical architecture and implementing a high-tech public-transport system. Today the city is a Unesco World Heritage Site and, with its merry student population and 2.5 million-odd annual tourists, scarcely sleeps at all.

Sights

The 4km-long riverfront esplanade incorporates playgrounds and bicycle paths.

Cathédrale St-André CATHEDRAL

(place Jean Moulin) Lording over the city, and a Unesco World Heritage Site prior to the city's classification, the cathedral's oldest section dates from 1096; most of what you see today was built in the 13th and 14th centuries. Exceptional masonry carvings can be seen in the north portal.

CAPC Musée d'Art Contemporain GALLERY

(rue Ferrére, Entrepôt 7; temporary exhibitions adult/child €5/2.50; 11am-6pm Tue & Thu-Sun, to 8pm Wed) Built in 1824 as a warehouse for French colonial produce like coffee, cocoa, peanuts and vanilla, the cavernous Entrepôts Lainé creates a dramatic backdrop for cutting-edge modern art at the CAPC Musée d'Art Contemporain. Entry to the permanent collection is free but there is a cover charge for any temporary exhibitions.

Musée des Beaux-Arts GALLERY

(20 cours d'Albret; 11am-6pm daily mid-Jul–mid-Aug, closed Tue rest of year) FREE The evolution of Occidental art from the Renaissance to the mid-20th century is on view at Bordeaux's Musée des Beaux-Arts, which occupies two wings of the 1770s-built Hôtel de Ville, either side of the Jardin de la Mairie (an elegant public park). The museum was established in 1801; highlights include 17th-century Flemish, Dutch and Italian paintings. Temporary exhibitions are regularly hosted at its nearby annexe, **Galerie des Beaux-Arts** (place du Colonel Raynal;

ON THE WINE TRAIL

Thirsty? The 1000-sq-km wine-growing area around the city of Bordeaux is, along with Burgundy, France's most important producer of top-quality wines. Whet your palate with Bordeaux tourist office's introductory wine-and-cheese courses (€25).

Serious students of the grape can enrol in a two-hour (€39) or two- to three-day (€390 to €690) course at the **École du Vin** (Wine School; ☎05 56 00 22 66; www.bordeaux.com) inside the **Maison du Vin de Bordeaux** (3 cours du 30 Juillet).

Bordeaux has more than 5000 estates where grapes are grown, picked and turned into wine. Smaller châteaux often accept walk-in visitors, but at many places, especially better-known ones, you have to reserve in advance. If you have your own wheels, one of the easiest to visit is **Château Lanessan** (☎05 56 58 94 80; www.lanessan.com; Cussac-Fort-Medoc; ⏰9am-noon & 2-6pm).

Favourite vine-framed villages brimming with charm and tasting/buying opportunities include medieval **St-Émilion** and port town **Pauillac**. In **Arsac-en-Médoc**, Philippe Raoux's vast glass-and-steel wine centre, **La Winery** (☎05 56 39 04 90; www.winery.fr; Rond-point des Vendangeurs, D1; ⏰10am-7pm), stuns with concerts and contemporary art exhibitions alongside tastings to determine your *signe œnologique* ('wine sign'; booking required).

Many châteaux close during October's *vendange* (grape harvest).

adult/child €5/2.50; ⏰11am-6pm daily mid-Jul–mid-Aug, closed Tue rest of year).

Sleeping

Hôtel Notre Dame HOTEL €

(☎05 56 52 88 24; 36-38 rue Notre Dame; s €53-70, d €61-79; 📶) Location is the key selling point of this good-value hotel. It's within an easy stroll of the town centre, just back from the river and in the middle of a lovely village-like neighbourhood of antique shops and relaxed cafes. It also has a wheelchair-accessible room.

Ecolodge des Chartrons B&B €€

(☎05 56 81 49 13; www.ecolodgedeschartrons.com; 23 rue Raze; s €107-205, d €119-228; 📶) Hidden away in a little side street off the quays in Bordeaux's Chartrons wine-merchant district. The owner-hosts of this *chambre d'hôte,* Veronique and Yann, have stripped back and limewashed the stone walls of an old house, scrubbed the wide floorboards and brought in recycled antique furniture to create a highly memorable place to stay.

★ **L'Hôtel Particulier** BOUTIQUE HOTEL €€€

(☎05 57 88 28 80; www.lhotel-particulier.com; 44 rue Vital-Carles; apt from €89, d from €203; 📶) When you step into this fabulous boutique hotel, with its secret courtyard garden, and find a thousand eyes staring at you from the reception walls and lampshades made only of feathers, you realise you've stumbled upon somewhere special. The rooms don't disappoint – they are highly extravagant affairs with huge fireplaces, carved ceilings, freestanding bath-tubs and quality furnishings.

There are also great value, fully equipped apartments ideal for a longer stay.

Eating

Place du Parlement, rue du Pas St-Georges, rue des Faussets and place de la Victoire are loaded with dining addresses, as is the old waterfront warehouse district around quai des Marques – great for a sunset meal or drink.

★ **Le Cheverus Café** BISTRO €

(☎05 56 48 29 73; 81-83 rue du Loup; menus from €12.50; ⏰noon-3pm & 7-9pm Mon-Sat) In a city full of neighbourhood bistros, this one, smack in the city centre, is one of the most impressive. It's friendly, cosy and chaotically busy (be prepared to wait for a table at lunchtime). The food tastes fresh and home-cooked and it dares to veer slightly away from the bistro standards of steak and chips.

Karl INTERNATIONAL €€

(☎05 56 81 01 00; place du Parlement; breakfast from €5.50; ⏰8.30am-7.30pm) Simply *the* place in town for a morning-after-the-night-before brunch. These range from light continental-style affairs to the full works with salmon, cheeses, hams and eggs. It's just as good for a snack at any time of the day and is perpetually packed with a young crowd.

SATURDAY-MORNING OYSTERS

A classic Bordeaux experience is a Saturday morning spent slurping oysters and white wine from one of the seafood stands to be found at **Marché des Capucins** (six oysters & glass of wine €6; 7am-noon Sat). Afterwards, you can peruse the stalls while shopping for the freshest ingredients for a picnic in one of the city's parks. To get there, head south down cours Pasteur and, once at place de la Victoire, turn left onto rue Élie Gintrec.

La Tupina REGIONAL CUISINE €€€
(05 56 91 56 37; www.latupina.com; 6 rue Porte de la Monnaie; menus €18-74, mains €27-45) Filled with the aroma of soup simmering inside an old *tupina* ('kettle' in Basque) over an open fire, this white-tableclothed place is feted far and wide for its seasonal southwestern French specialities such as a mini casserole of foie gras and eggs, milk-fed lamb or goose wings with potatoes and parsley.

Information

Main Tourist Office (05 56 00 66 00; www.bordeaux-tourisme.com; 12 cours du 30 Juillet; 9am-7pm Mon-Sat, 9.30am-6pm Sun) Runs an excellent range of city and regional tours. There's a small-but-helpful branch (05 56 91 64 70; 9am-noon & 1-6pm Mon-Sat, 10am-noon & 1-3pm Sun) at the train station.

Getting There & Away

AIR

Bordeaux Airport (www.bordeaux.aeroport.fr) is in Mérignac, 10km west of the city centre, with domestic and international services.

TRAIN

From Gare St-Jean, 3km from the centre, at least 16 trains daily serve Paris' Gare Montparnasse (€73, three hours).

Biarritz

POP 26,067

Edge your way south along the coast towards Spain and you arrive in stylish Biarritz, just as ritzy as its name suggests. The resort took off in the mid-19th century (Napoléon III had a rather soft spot for the place) and it still shimmers with architectural treasures from the belle époque and art deco eras. Big waves – some of Europe's best – and a beachy lifestyle are a magnet for Europe's hip surfing set.

Sights & Activities

Biarritz' *raison d'être* is its fashionable beaches, particularly central **Grande Plage** and **Plage Miramar**, lined end to end with sunbathing bodies on hot summer days. North of Pointe St-Martin, the adrenaline-pumping surfing beaches of **Anglet** (the final 't' is pronounced) continue northwards for more than 4km. Take bus 10 or 13 from the bottom of av Verdun (just near av Édouard VII).

Musée de la Mer MUSEUM
(05 59 22 75 40; www.museedelamer.com; esplanade du Rocher de la Vierge; adult/child €14/10; 9.30am-midnight Jul & Aug, 9.30am-8pm Apr-Jun, Sep & Oct, shorter hours rest of year) Housed in a wonderful art deco building, Biarritz's Musée de la Mer is seething with underwater life from the Bay of Biscay and beyond, including huge aquariums of sharks and dainty tropical reef fish, as well as exhibits on fishing recalling Biarritz's whaling past. It's the seals, though, that steal the show (feeding time, always a favourite with children, is at 10.30am and 5pm). In high season it's possible to have the place almost to yourself by visiting late at night.

Cité de l'Océan MUSEUM
(05 59 22 75 40; www.citedelocean.com; 1 av de la Plage; adult/child €11/7.30; 10am-10pm Jul & Aug, 10am-7pm Easter, Apr-Jun, Sep & Oct, shorter hours rest of year) We don't really know whether it's fair to call the Cité de l'Océan a mere 'museum'. At heart it's simply a museum of the ocean but this is entertainment, cutting-edge technology, theme park and science museum all rolled into one. During a visit you will learn all you ever wanted to know about the ocean and (sort of) ride in a submarine to watch giant squid and sperm whales do battle.

Sleeping

Auberge de Jeunesse de Biarritz HOSTEL €
(05 59 41 76 00; www.hihostels.com; 8 rue Chiquito de Cambo; dm incl sheets & breakfast €25.40; reception 9am-noon & 6-10pm, closed mid-Dec–early Jan; @ wi-fi) This popular place offers

outdoor activities including surfing. From the train station, follow the railway line westwards for 800m.

Hôtel Mirano BOUTIQUE HOTEL €€
(☎05 59 23 11 63; www.hotelmirano.fr; 11 av Pasteur; d €72-132; P ⓦ) Squiggly purple, orange and black wallpaper and oversized orange perspex light fittings are some of the rad '70s touches at this boutique retro hotel. Oh, and there's a flirty Betty Boop in the bar. The staff go above and beyond the call of duty in order to please. All up, it's one of the best deals in town.

Eating

See-and-be-seen cafes and restaurants line Biarritz' beachfront. Anglet's beaches are also becoming increasingly trendy, with cafes strung along the waterfront.

★**Restaurant le Pim'pi** FRENCH €€
(☎05 59 24 12 62; 14 av Verdun; menus €14-28, mains €17; ⊙noon-2pm Tue, noon-2pm & 7-9.30pm Wed-Sat) This is a small and resolutely old-fashioned place unfazed by all the razzmatazz around it. The daily specials are chalked up on a blackboard – most are of the classic French bistro style but are produced with such unusual skill and passion that many consider this one of the town's better places to eat.

Bistrot des Halles BASQUE €€
(☎05 59 24 21 22; 1 rue du Centre; mains €17-19; ⊙noon-2pm & 7.30-10.30pm Tue-Sat) One of a cluster of restaurants along rue du Centre that get their produce directly from the nearby covered market, this bustling place stands out from the pack by serving excellent fish and other fresh modern French market fare from the blackboard menu, in an interior adorned with old metallic advertising posters. Open daily during Easter and the summer holidays.

Drinking & Nightlife

Great bars stud rue du Port Vieux, place Clemenceau and the central food-market area.

Miremont CAFE
(☎05 59 24 01 38; www.miremont-biarritz.com; 1bis place Georges-Clemenceau; hot chocolate from €5; ⊙9am-8pm) Operating since 1880, this grande dame harks back to the time when belle-époque Biarritz was the beach resort of choice for the rich and glamorous. Today it still attracts perfectly coiffed hairdos (and that's just on the poodles) but the less chic are also welcome to come and partake of a fine selection of tea and cakes.

Ventilo Caffé BAR
(rue du Port Vieux; ⊙closed Tue Oct-Easter) Dressed up like a boudoir, this funky place continues its domination of the Biarritz young and fun bar scene.

Information

Tourist office (☎05 59 22 37 10; www.biarritz.fr; square d'Ixelles; ⊙9am-7pm Jul & Aug, shorter hours rest of year)

WORTH A TRIP

DUNE DU PILAT

This colossal sand dune (sometimes referred to as the Dune de Pyla because of its location in the resort town of Pyla-sur-Mer), 65km west of Bordeaux, stretches from the mouth of the Bassin d'Arcachon southwards for almost 3km. Already the largest in Europe, it's spreading eastwards at 4.5m a year – it has swallowed trees, a road junction and even a hotel.

The view from the top – approximately 114m above sea level – is magnificent. To the west you can see the sandy shoals at the mouth of the Bassin d'Arcachon, including the **Banc d'Arguin bird reserve** and Cap Ferret. Dense dark-green pine forests stretch from the base of the dune eastwards almost as far as the eye can see.

Take care swimming in this area: powerful currents swirl out to sea from the deceptively tranquil *baïnes* (little bays).

Although an easy day trip from Bordeaux, the area around the dune is an enjoyable place to kick back for a while. Most people camp in one of the swag of seasonal campgrounds; see www.bassin-arcachon.com.

Getting There & Away

AIR

Biarritz-Anglet-Bayonne Airport (www.biarritz.aeroport.fr), 3km southeast of Biarritz, is served by several low-cost carriers.

BUS

ATCRB (www.transports-atcrb.com) runs services down the coast to the Spanish border.

TRAIN

Biarritz-La Négresse train station, 3km south of town, is linked to the centre by bus A1.

LANGUEDOC-ROUSSILLON

Languedoc-Roussillon comes in three distinct flavours: Bas-Languedoc (Lower Languedoc), land of bullfighting, rugby and robust red wines; Haut Languedoc (Upper Languedoc), a mountainous, sparsely populated terrain made for lovers of the great outdoors; and Roussillon, to the south, snug against the rugged Pyrenees and frontier to Spanish Catalonia.

Languedoc's traditional centre, Toulouse, was shaved off when regional boundaries were redrawn almost half a century ago, but we've chosen to include it in this section.

Toulouse

POP 446,200

Elegantly set at the confluence of the Canal du Midi and the River Garonne, this vibrant southern city – nicknamed *la ville rose* (the pink city) after the distinctive hot-pink stone used in many buildings – is one of France's liveliest metropolises. Busy, buzzy and bustling with students, this riverside dame has a history stretching back more than 2000 years and has been a hub for the aerospace industry since the 1930s. With a thriving cafe and cultural scene, a wealth of impressive *hôtels particuliers* and an enormously atmospheric old quarter, France's fourth-largest city is one place you'll love to linger.

Sights & Activities

Place du Capitole SQUARE

Toulouse's magnificent main square is the city's literal and metaphorical heart, where Toulousains turn out en masse on sunny evenings to sip a coffee or an early aperitif at a pavement cafe. On the eastern side is the 128m-long facade of the **Capitole** (rue Gambetta & rue Romiguières, place du Capitole; 10am-7pm), the city hall, built in the 1750s. Inside is the **Théâtre du Capitole**, one of France's most prestigious opera venues, and the over-the-top, late-19th-century **Salle des Illustres** (Hall of the Illustrious).

To the south of the square is the city's **Vieux Quartier** (Old Quarter), a tangle of lanes and leafy squares brimming with cafes, shops and eateries.

Cité de l'Espace MUSEUM

(08 20 37 72 33; www.cite-espace.com/en; av Jean Gonord; adult €20.50-24, child €15-17.50; 10am-7pm Jul & Aug, closes at 5pm or 6pm rest of year, closed Jan) This fantastic space museum on the city's eastern outskirts explores Toulouse's interstellar industry. The hands-on exhibits include a shuttle simulator, planetarium, 3D cinema and simulated observatory, plus full-scale replicas of iconic spacecraft including the Mir Space Station and a 53m-high Ariane 5 space rocket. Multilingual audioguides allow you to explore at your own pace. To get there, catch bus 15 from allée Jean Jaurès to the last stop, from where it's a 500m walk.

Basilique St-Sernin CHURCH

(place St-Sernin; 8.30am-noon & 2-6pm Mon-Sat, 8.30am-12.30pm & 2-7.30pm Sun) With its soaring spire and unusual octagonal tower, this red-brick basilica is one of France's best-preserved Romanesque structures. Inside, the soaring nave and delicate pillars harbour the tomb of St Sernin, sheltered beneath a sumptuous canopy. The basilica was once an important stop on the Chemin de St-Jacques pilgrimage route.

Musée des Augustins MUSEUM

(www.augustins.org; 21 rue de Metz; adult/child €4/free; 10am-6pm, to 9pm Wed) Like most big French cities, Toulouse has a fabulous fine arts museum. Located within a former Augustinian monastery, it spans the centuries from the Roman era through to the early 20th century. The highlights are the French rooms, with Delacroix, Ingres and Courbet representing the 18th and 19th centuries, and works by Toulouse-Lautrec and Monet among the standouts from the 20th-century collection. Don't miss the 14th-century cloister gardens. The entrance is on rue de Metz.

Airbus Factory Tours TOUR
(☎05 34 39 42 00; www.manatour.fr/lva; tours adult/child €15.50/13) Hardcore plane-spotters can arrange a guided tour of Toulouse's massive JL Lagardère Airbus factory, 10km west of the city in Colomiers. The main factory tour includes a visit to the A380 production line; there's also a longer 'Panoramic Tour', which takes in other sections of the 700-hectare site via bus. All tours must be booked in advance online or by phone, and non-EU visitors have to book at least two days ahead. Remember to bring a passport or photo ID.

Sleeping

Hôtel La Chartreuse HOTEL €
(☎05 61 62 93 39; www.chartreusehotel.com; 4bis bd de Bonrepos; s/d/f €52/59/73) The nicest of a cluster of basic hotels that line the riverbanks near the station. It's clean, friendly and quiet, with a back garden patio for breakfast. The rooms are spartan, but the rates are dirt cheap.

★**Côté Carmes** B&B €€
(☎06 83 44 87 55; www.cote-carmes.com; 7 rue de la Dalbade; r €85-110) Elegant in the way only the French can manage, this charming B&B has three rooms straight out of an interiors catalogue. Louvre doors, parquet floors, exposed brick and upcycled furniture give it a slinky, designer feel; Chambre Paradoux is the roomiest, and has a private balcony. Breakfast is a spoil, too, with *viennoiseries*, smoothies and macaroons.

Hôtel St-Sernin BOUTIQUE HOTEL €€€
(☎05 61 21 73 08; www.hotelstsernin.com; 2 rue St-Bernard; d from €135; 📶) Parisian expats have renovated this pied-à-terre near the Basilique St-Sernin, and it has a modern, metropolitan style, with small-but-sleek rooms, the best of which have floor-to-ceiling windows overlooking the basilica.

Eating

Bd de Strasbourg, place St-Georges and place du Capitole are perfect spots for summer dining alfresco. Rue Pargaminières is the street for kebabs, burgers and other late-night student grub.

Faim des Haricots VEGETARIAN €
(☎05 61 22 49 25; www.lafaimdesharicots.fr; 3 rue du Puits Vert; menus €11-15.50; ⏲noon-3pm & 6-10pm daily; 🌿) A budget favourite, this 100% vegie restaurant serves everything *à volonté* (all you can eat). There are five courses, including a quiche, a buffet salad, a hot dish and a pudding; €15.50 buys you the lot including an aperitif and coffee.

Solilesse BISTRO €€
(☎09 83 34 03 50; www.solilesse.com; 40 rue Peyrolières; 3-course menu lunch/dinner €17.50/28.50; ⏲noon-2.30pm Wed-Sat & 8-10pm Tue-Sat) Punky chef Yohann Travostino has turned his bistro into one of the city's hottest dining addresses. He previously worked in Mexico and California, so his food blends French style with zingy west coast flavours. The industrial decor (black tables, steel, brick) echoes the modern food.

★**Le Genty-Magre** FRENCH €€€
(☎05 61 21 38 60; www.legentymagre.com; 3 rue Genty Magre; mains €16-28, menu €38; ⏲12.30-2.30pm & 8-10pm Tue-Sat) Classic French cuisine is the order of the day here, but lauded chef Romain Brard has plenty of modern tricks up his sleeve too. The dining room feels inviting, with brick walls, burnished wood and down-lights. It's arguably the best place in the city to try traditional rich dishes such as *confit de canard* or cassoulet.

Information

Tourist Office (☎05 61 11 02 22; www.toulouse-tourisme.com; square Charles de Gaulle; ⏲9am-7pm daily) In a grand building on square Charles de Gaulle.

Getting There & Away

AIR

Toulouse-Blagnac Airport (www.toulouse.aeroport.fr/en), 8km northwest of the centre, has frequent domestic and European flights. A **Navette Aéroport Flybus** (Airport Shuttle; ☎05 61 41 70 70; www.tisseo.fr) links it with town.

TRAIN

Gare Matabiau (bd Pierre Sémard), 1km northeast of the centre, is served by frequent TGVs to Bordeaux (€22 to €29, two hours) and east to Carcassonne (€14, 45 minutes to one hour).

Carcassonne

POP 49,100

Perched on a rocky hilltop and bristling with zigzag battlements, stout walls and spiky turrets, the fortified city of Carcassonne looks like something out of a children's storybook from afar. It's most people's perfect idea of a medieval castle, and it's undoubtedly an impressive spectacle – not to mention one of the Languedoc's biggest tourist draws. The **tourist office** (☎04 68 10 24 30; www.tourisme-carcassonne.fr; 28 rue de Verdun; ⌚9am-7pm daily Jul & Aug, shorter hours rest of year) can help with tours and bookings.

Sights

★La Cité FORTRESS
(⌚Porte Narbonnaise 9am-7pm Jul & Aug, to 5pm Sep-Jun) Carcassonne's rampart-ringed fortress is one of the Languedoc's most recognisable landmarks. Built on a steep spur of rock, it's been used as a defensive stronghold for nigh on 2000 years. The fortified town is encircled by two sets of battlements and 52 stone towers, topped by distinctive 'witch's hat' roofs (added by the architect Viollet-le-Duc during 19th-century restorations). The main gateway of **Porte Narbonnaise** leads into the citadel's interior, a maze of cobbled lanes and courtyards, now mostly lined by shops and restaurants.

Château Comtal CASTLE
(adult/child €8.50/free; ⌚10am-6.30pm Apr-Sep) The entrance fee lets you look around the castle itself, enjoy an 11-minute film and join an optional 30- to 40-minute guided tour of the ramparts (tours in English, July and August). Descriptive panels around the castle, in both French and English, are explicit. For more detail, invest in an audioguide (1/2 people €4.50/6).

Sleeping & Eating

La Maison Vieille B&B €€
(☎04 68 25 77 24; www.la-maison-vieille.com; 8 rue Trivalle; d €85-95; 📶) As charming a B&B as you'll find in Carcassonne. In an old mansion, the rooms are supremely tasteful: Barbecane in blues, Cité with exposed brick, Prince Noir with an in-room bath, Dame Carcas with floaty fabrics and vintage luggage. There's a walled courtyard for breakfast, and the location is ideal for Villes Haute and Basse. Rue Trivalle lies just east of the Pont Vieux.

Bloc G BISTRO €€
(☎04 68 47 58 20; www.bloc-g.com; 112 rue Barbacane; 3-course lunch €15, dinner mains €15-25; ⌚noon-2.30pm Tue-Sat, 7-10.30pm Wed-Sat) This modern diner offers far better food than most places in the citadel, for half the price. Its modern style – white walls, white chairs, white tables – is matched with modern food: a short menu of salads and *tarte salées* for lunch, and creative versions of southwest classics for supper. Great local wines by the glass, too.

Getting There & Away

There are frequent trains to Toulouse (€14, 45 minutes to one hour).

Nîmes

POP 146,500

This lively city boasts some of France's best-preserved classical buildings, including a famous Roman amphitheatre, although the city is most famous for its sartorial export, *serge de Nîmes* – better known to cowboys, clubbers and couturiers as denim.

Sights

A **Pass Nîmes Romaine** (adult/child €11.50/9), valid for three days, covers all Roman sights; buy one at the first place you visit.

★Les Arènes ROMAN SITES
(www.arenes-nimes.com; place des Arènes; adult/child €9/7; ⌚9am-8pm Jul & Aug, shorter hours rest of year) Nîmes' twin-tiered amphitheatre is the best-preserved in France. Built around 100 BC, the arena would have seated 24,000 spectators and staged gladiatorial contests and public executions, and it still provides an impressive venue for gigs, events and summer bullfights. An audioguide provides context as you explore the arena, seating areas, stairwells and corridors (rather marvellously known to Romans as *vomitories*), and afterwards you can view replicas of gladiatorial armour and original bullfighters' costumes in the museum.

Maison Carrée ROMAN SITES
(place de la Maison Carrée; adult/child €5.50/4; ⌚10am-8pm Jul & Aug, shorter hours rest of year) Constructed in gleaming limestone around AD 5, this temple was built to honour Emperor Augustus' two adopted sons. Despite the name, the Maison Carrée (Square House) is actually rectangular – to the Romans, 'square' simply meant a building with right angles. The building is beautifully preserved, complete with stately columns and triumphal steps; it's worth paying the admission to see the interior, but probably worth skipping the lame 3D film.

Festivals & Events

Féria de Pentecôte & Féria des Vendanges BULLFIGHTING

Nîmes becomes more Spanish than French during its two *férias* (bullfighting festivals): the five-day Féria de Pentecôte (Whitsuntide Festival) in June, and the three-day Féria des Vendanges on the third weekend in September. Each is marked by daily *corridas* (bullfights).

Sleeping & Eating

Auberge de Jeunesse HOSTEL €

(☎04 66 68 03 20; www.hinimes.com; 257 chemin de l'Auberge de Jeunesse, La Cigale; dm/d €16.45/38; ⏰reception 7.30am-1am) It's out in the sticks, 4km from the bus and train stations, but this hostel has lots in its favour: spacious dorms, family rooms, a garden with space for camping, and a choice of self-catering kitchen or cafe. Take bus I, direction Alès or Villeverte, and get off at the Stade stop.

Hôtel de l'Amphithéâtre HOTEL €€

(☎04 66 67 28 51; www.hoteldelamphitheatre.com; 4 rue des Arènes; s/d/f €72/92/130) Down a narrow backstreet leading away from Les Arènes, this tall town house ticks all the boxes: smart rooms with shabby-chic furniture and balconies overlooking place du Marché; a sleek palette of greys, whites and taupes; and a great buffet breakfast. It's run by an expat Cornishman and his French wife.

★**Le Cerf à Moustache** BISTRO €€

(☎09 81 83 44 33; 38 bd Victor Hugo; mains €14-35; ⏰11.45am-2pm & 7-11pm Tue-Sat) Despite its weird name, the Deer with the Moustache has quickly established itself as one of Nîmes' top bistros, with quirky decor (including reclaimed furniture and a wall full of old-book doodles), matched by chef Julien Salem's creative take on the classics. Go basic with burgers and risotto, or upmarket with crusted lamb and chunky steaks.

Information

Tourist Office (☎04 66 58 38 00; www.ot-nimes.fr; 6 rue Auguste; ⏰8.30am-8pm Mon-Fri, 9am-7pm Sat, 10am-6pm Sun Jul & Aug, shorter hours rest of year) There's also a seasonal annexe (⏰usually Jul & Aug) on esplanade Charles de Gaulle.

Getting There & Away

AIR

Ryanair is the only airline to use Nîmes' **airport** (☎04 66 70 49 49; www.nimes-aeroport.fr), 10km southeast of the city on the A54.

BUS

Edgard (www.edgard-transport.fr) runs services to Pont du Gard (40 minutes, hourly Monday to Saturday) from the bus station (next to the train station).

TRAIN

From the **train station** (bd Talabot), there are more than 12 TGVs a day to/from Paris' Gare de Lyon (€62.50 to €111, three hours). Other destinations include Avignon (€8.50, 30 minutes).

Pont du Gard

Southern France has some fine Roman sites, but for audacious engineering, nothing can top Unesco World Heritage Site **Pont du Gard** (☎04 66 37 50 99; www.pontdugard.fr; car & up to 5 passengers €18, after 8pm €10; ⏰visitor centre & museum 9am-8pm Jul & Aug, shorter hours rest of year), 21km northeast of Nîmes. This three-tiered aqueduct was once part of a 50km-long system of water channels, built around 19 BC to transport water from Uzès to Nîmes. The scale is huge: 48.8m high, 275m long and graced with 35 precision-built arches, the bridge was sturdy enough to carry up to 20,000 cubic metres of water per day. Each block was carved by hand and transported here from nearby quarries – no mean feat, considering the largest blocks weigh over 5 tonnes.

The **Musée de la Romanité** provides background on the bridge's construction, while kids can try out educational activities in the **Ludo** play area. Nearby, the 1.4km **Mémoires de Garrigue** walking trail winds upstream through typically Mediterranean scrubland, and offers some of the best bridge views.

There are large car parks on both banks of the river, about a 400m walk from the bridge.

PROVENCE

Provence conjures up images of rolling lavender fields, blue skies, gorgeous villages, wonderful food and superb wine. It certainly delivers on all those fronts, but it's not just worth visiting for its good looks – dig a little deeper and you'll also discover the multicultural metropolis of Marseille, the artistic haven of Aix-en-Provence and the old Roman city of Arles.

Marseille

POP 859,360

Marseille grows on you with its fusion of cultures, souk-like markets, millennia-old port and *corniches* (coastal roads) along rocky inlets and sun-baked beaches. Once the butt of French jokes, the *cité phocéenne* (in reference to Phocaea, the ancient Greek city located in modern-day Turkey, from where Marseille's settlers, the Massiliots, came) is looking fabulous after its facelift as the European Capital of Culture in 2013.

Sights

★Vieux Port HISTORIC QUARTER

(M Vieux Port) Ships have docked for more than 26 centuries at the city's birthplace, the colourful Old Port. The main commercial docks were transferred to the Joliette area north of here in the 1840s, but the old port remains a thriving harbour for fishing boats, pleasure yachts and tourists. The free **Cross-Port Ferry** (⏲10am-1.15pm & 2-7pm) in front of the town hall is a fun way to get out on the water, however briefly.

★Musée des Civilisations de l'Europe et de la Méditerranée MUSEUM

(MuCEM; Museum of European & Mediterranean Civilisations; ☎04 84 35 13 13; www.mucem.org; 1 esplanade du J4; Fort St-Jean free, J4 adult/child €8/5; ⏲9am-8pm Jul & Aug, 11am-7pm May, Jun, Sep & Oct, 11am-6pm Nov-Apr; 👪; M Vieux Port or Joliette) The icon of the 'new' Marseille, this stunning museum is split across two dramatically contrasting sites, linked by a vertigo-inducing foot bridge. On one side is lumbering **Fort St-Jean**, founded in the 13th century by the Knights Hospitaller of St John of Jerusalem and rebuilt by Louis XIV in the 17th century; and on the other the contemporary **J4**, a shoebox with breath-taking 'lace' skin designed by Algerian-born, Marseille-educated architect Rudi Ricciotti.

MARSEILLE CITY PASS

Buy a **City Pass** (one-/two-day €24/31) at the tourist office or www.resamarseille.com. It covers admission to museums, a city tour, unlimited public-transport travel, boat trips and so on.

Le Panier HISTORIC QUARTER

(M Vieux Port) From the Vieux Port, hike north up to this fantastic history-woven quarter, dubbed Marseille's Montmartre as much for its sloping streets as its artsy ambience. In Greek Massilia it was the site of the *agora* (marketplace), hence its name, which means 'the basket'. During WWII the quarter was dynamited and afterwards rebuilt. Today it's a mishmash of lanes hiding artisan shops, *ateliers* (workshops) and terraced houses strung with drying washing.

Basilique Notre Dame de la Garde CHURCH

(Montée de la Bonne Mère; ⏲7am-8pm Apr-Sep, 7am-7pm Oct-Mar) This opulent 19th-century Romano-Byzantine basilica occupies Marseille's highest point, La Garde (162m). Built between 1853 and 1864, it is ornamented with coloured marble, murals depicting the safe passage of sailing vessels and superb mosaics. The hilltop gives 360-degree panoramas of the city. The church's bell tower is crowned by a 9.7m-tall gilded statue of the Virgin Mary on a 12m-high pedestal. It's a 1km walk from the Vieux Port, or take bus 60 or the tourist train.

Château d'If ISLAND, CASTLE

(www.if.monuments-nationaux.fr; adult/child €5.50/free; ⏲10am-6pm May-Sep, shorter hours rest year) Immortalised in Alexandre Dumas' classic 1844 novel *Le Comte de Monte Cristo* (The Count of Monte Cristo), the 16th-century fortress-turned-prison Château d'If sits on the tiny island Île d'If, 3.5km west of the Vieux Port. Political prisoners were incarcerated here, along with hundreds of Protestants, the Revolutionary hero Mirabeau, and the Communards of 1871.

Frioul If Express (www.frioul-if-express.com; 1 quai des Belges) boats leave for Château d'If (€10.10 return, 20 minutes, around 15 daily) from the Vieux Port.

Sleeping

Hôtel Hermès DESIGN HOTEL €

(☎04 96 11 63 63; www.hotelmarseille.com; 2 rue Bonneterie; s €64, d €85-102; ❄📶; M Vieux Port) Nothing to do with the Paris design house, this excellent-value hotel has a rooftop terrace with panoramic Vieux Port views. Grab breakfast (€9) on a tray in the bright ground-floor breakfast room and ride the lift to the 5th floor for breakfast à la rooftop. Contemporary rooms have white walls and a splash of lime-green or red to complement their Scandinavian-like design.

★Hôtel Edmond Rostand DESIGN HOTEL €€
(☎04 91 37 74 95; www.hoteledmondrostand.com; 31 rue Dragon; d €90-115, tr €127-141; ; M Estrangin-Préfecture) Turn a blind eye to the grubby outside shutters of this excellent-value Logis de France hotel in the Quartier des Antiquaires. Inside, decor is a hip mix of contemporary design and vintage, with a great sofa area for lounging and 16 rooms dressed in crisp white and soothing natural hues. Some rooms overlook a tiny private garden, others the Basilique Notre Dame de la Garde.

★Au Vieux Panier B&B €€
(☎04 91 91 23 72; www.auvieuxpanier.com; 13 rue du Panier; d €100-140; M Vieux Port) The height of Le Panier shabby chic, this super-stylish *maison d'hôte* woos art lovers with original works of art. Each year artists are invited to redecorate, meaning its six rooms change annually. Staircases and corridors are like an art gallery and a drop-dead gorgeous rooftop terrace peeks across terracotta tiles to the sea on the horizon.

Eating

The Vieux Port overflows with restaurants, but choose carefully. Head to cours Julien and its surrounding streets for world cuisine.

★Café Populaire BISTRO €
(☎04 91 02 53 96; 110 rue Paradis; tapas €8-16, mains €19-23; ⊙noon-2.30pm & 8-11pm Tue-Sat; M Estrangin-Préfecture) Vintage furniture, old books on the shelves and a fine collection of glass soda bottles lend a retro air to this trendy, 1950s-styled *jazz comptoir* (counter) – a restaurant despite its name. The crowd is chic and smiling chefs in the open kitchen mesmerise with daily specials like king prawns *à la plancha* or beetroot and coriander salad.

★Le Café des Épices MODERN FRENCH €€
(☎04 91 91 22 69; www.cafedesepices.com; 4 rue du Lacydon; 2-/3-course lunch menu €25/28, dinner menu €45; ⊙noon-3pm & 6-11pm Tue-Fri, noon-3pm Sat; ; M Vieux Port) One of Marseille's best chefs, Arnaud de Grammont, infuses his cooking with a panoply of flavours: squid-ink spaghetti with sesame and perfectly cooked scallops, or coriander- and citrus-spiced potatoes topped by the catch of the day. Presentation is impeccable, the decor playful, and the colourful outdoor terrace between giant potted olive trees nothing short of superb.

Le Rhul SEAFOOD €€€
(☎04 91 52 01 77; www.lerhul.fr; 269 corniche Président John F Kennedy; bouillabaisse €53; ⊙noon-2pm & 5-9pm; 83) This long-standing classic has atmosphere (however kitschy): a 1940s seaside hotel with Mediterranean views. This is one of the most reliably consistent spots for real bouillabaisse.

Drinking & Entertainment

Options for a coffee or something stronger abound on both quays at the Vieux Port. Cafes crowd cours Honoré d'Estienne d'Orves, 1er, a large open square two blocks south of quai de Rive Neuve.

La Caravelle BAR
(34 quai du Port; ⊙7am-2am; M Vieux Port) Look up or miss this standout upstairs hideaway, styled with rich wood and leather, a zinc bar and yellowing murals. If it's sunny, snag a

WORTH A TRIP

LES CALANQUES

Marseille abuts the wild and spectacular **Parc National des Calanques** (www.calanques-parcnational.fr), a 20km stretch of high, rocky promontories, rising from brilliant-turquoise Mediterranean waters.

The sheer cliffs are occasionally interrupted by small idyllic beaches, some impossible to reach without a kayak. Amongst the most famous are the calanques of Sormiou, Port-Miou, Port-Pin and En-Vau.

October to June, the best way to see the Calanques is to hike and the best access is from the small town of Cassis. The **tourist office** (☎08 92 39 01 03; www.ot-cassis.com; quai des Moulins; ⊙9am-6.30pm Tue-Sat, 9.30am-12.30pm & 3-6pm Sun, shorter hours low season) has maps. In July and August, trails close because of fire danger: take a boat tour from Marseille or Cassis; sea kayak with **Raskas Kayak** (www.raskas-kayak.com); drive; or take a bus.

coveted spot on the port-side terrace. On Fridays, there's live jazz from 9pm to midnight.

Espace Julien LIVE MUSIC
(☎04 91 24 34 10; www.espace-julien.com; 39 cours Julien; Ⓜ Notre Dame du Mont–Cours Julien) Rock, *opérock*, alternative theatre, reggae, hip hop, Afro groove and other cutting-edge entertainment all appear on the bill; the website lists gigs.

Tourist Information

The **tourist office** (☎04 91 13 89 00; www.marseille-tourisme.com; 11 La Canebière; ⊙9am-7pm Mon-Sat, 10am-5pm Sun; Ⓜ Vieux Port) has plenty of information about the city and the Calanques.

Getting There & Away

AIR

Aéroport Marseille-Provence (p434), 25km northwest in Marignane, has numerous budget flights to various European destinations. Shuttle buses link it with the Marseille train station (€8.20, 25 minutes, every 20 minutes).

BOAT

The **passenger ferry terminal** (www.marseille-port.fr; Ⓜ Joliette) is 250m south of place de la Joliette, 1er. **SNCM** (☎08 91 70 18 01; www.sncm.fr; 61 bd des Dames; Ⓜ Joliette) boats sail to Corsica, Sardinia and North Africa.

TRAIN

From Marseille's Gare St-Charles, trains including TGVs go all over France and Europe. Services include:

Avignon €29.50, 35 minutes
Lyon €65, 1¾ hours
Nice €37, 2½ hours
Paris Gare de Lyon €113, three hours

Getting Around

Marseille has two metro lines, two tram lines and an extensive bus network, all run by **RTM** (☎04 91 91 92 10; www.rtm.fr; 6 rue des Fabres; ⊙8.30am-6pm Mon-Fri, 8.30am-noon & 1-4.30pm Sat; Ⓜ Vieux Port), where you can obtain information and transport tickets (€1.50).

Pick up a bike from 100-plus stations across the city with **Le Vélo** (www.levelo-mpm.fr).

Aix-en-Provence

POP 144,274

Aix-en-Provence is to Provence what the Left Bank is to Paris: a pocket of bohemian chic crawling with students. It's hard to believe that 'Aix' (pronounced ex) is just 25km from chaotic, exotic Marseille. The city has been a cultural centre since the Middle Ages (two of the town's most famous sons are painter Paul Cézanne and novelist Émile Zola), but for all its polish, it's still a laid-back Provençal town at heart.

Sights

A stroller's paradise, Aix's highlight is the mostly pedestrian old city, **Vieil Aix**. South of cours Mirabeau, the **Quartier Mazarin** was laid out in the 17th century, and is home to some of Aix's finest buildings.

★ **Atelier Cézanne** MUSEUM
(☎04 42 21 06 53; www.atelier-cezanne.com; 9 av Paul Cézanne; adult/child €5.50/free; ⊙10am-noon & 2-5pm) Cézanne's last studio, 1.5km north of the tourist office on a hilltop, was painstakingly preserved (and recreated: not all the tools and still-life models strewn around the room were his) as it was at the time of his death. Though the studio is inspiring, none of his works hang there. Take bus 1 or 20 to the Atelier Cézanne stop or walk the 1.5km from town.

Cours Mirabeau HISTORIC QUARTER
No avenue better epitomises Provence's most graceful city than Cours Mirabeau, a fountain-studded street sprinkled with Renaissance *hôtels particuliers* and crowned with a summertime roof of leafy plane trees. Named after the revolutionary hero Comte de Mirabeau, it was laid out in the 1640s. Cézanne and Zola hung out at **Les Deux Garçons** (53 cours Mirabeau; ⊙7am-2am), one of a clutch of busy pavement cafes.

Musée Granet MUSEUM
(www.museegranet-aixenprovence.fr; place St-Jean de Malte; adult/child €5/free; ⊙11am-7pm Tue-Sun) Housed in a 17th-century priory of the Knights of Malta, this exceptional museum is named after the Provençal painter François Marius Granet (1775–1849), who donated a large number of works. Its collections include 16th- to 20th-century Italian, Flemish and French works. Modern art reads like a who's who: Picasso, Léger, Matisse, Monet, Klee, Van Gogh and Giacometti, among others. Nine works by Cézanne are the museum's pride and joy. Excellent temporary exhibitions.

WORTH A TRIP

VAN GOGH'S ARLES

If the winding streets and colourful houses of Arles seem familiar, it's hardly surprising – Vincent van Gogh lived here for much of his life in a yellow house on place Lamartine, and the town regularly featured in his canvases. His original house was destroyed during WWII, but you can still follow in Vincent's footsteps on the evocative **Van Gogh walking circuit** – the **tourist office** (☎04 90 18 41 20; www.arlestourisme.com; esplanade Charles de Gaulle, bd des Lices; ⊙9am-6.45pm Apr-Sep, to 4.45pm Mon-Fri & 12.45pm Sun Oct-Mar; 📶) sells maps (€1). You won't see many of the artist's masterpieces in Arles, however, although the modern art gallery **Fondation Vincent Van Gogh** (☎04 90 49 94 04; www.fondation-vincentvangogh-arles.org; 33 ter rue du Docteur Fanton; adult/child €9/4; ⊙11am-7pm Tue-Sun Apr–mid-Sep, to 6pm mid-Sep–Mar) always has one on show, as well as contemporary exhibitions inspired by the Impressionist.

Two millennia ago, Arles was a major Roman settlement. The town's 20,000-seat amphitheatre, known as the **Arènes** (Amphithéâtre; adult/child incl Théâtre Antique €5.50/free; ⊙9am-8pm Jul & Aug, to 7pm May, Jun & Sep, shorter hours rest of year), is nowadays used for bullfights.

There are buses to/from Aix-en-Provence (€10.50, 1½ hours) and regular trains to/from Nîmes (€8.60, 30 minutes), Marseille (€15.30, 55 minutes) and Avignon (€7.50, 20 minutes).

Sleeping

Hôtel les Quatre Dauphins BOUTIQUE HOTEL €
(☎04 42 38 16 39; www.lesquatredauphins.fr; 54 rue Roux Alphéran; s €62-72, d €72-87; ❄📶) This sweet 13-room hotel slumbers in a former private mansion in one of the loveliest parts of town. Rooms are fresh and clean, with excellent modern bathrooms. Those with sloping, beamed ceilings in the attic are quaint but not for those who cannot pack light – the terracotta-tiled staircase is not suitcase-friendly.

★**L'Épicerie** B&B €€
(☎06 08 85 38 68; www.unechambreenville.eu; 12 rue du Cancel; d €100-130; 📶) This intimate B&B is the fabulous creation of born-and-bred Aixois lad Luc. His breakfast room recreates a 1950s grocery store, and the flowery garden out back is perfect for excellent evening dining and weekend brunch (book ahead for both). Breakfast is a veritable feast. Two rooms accommodate families of four.

Eating

★**Jacquou Le Croquant** SOUTHWEST, PROVENÇAL €
(☎04 42 27 37 19; www.jacquoulecroquant.com; 2 rue de l'Aumône Vielle; plat du jour €10.90, menus from €14; ⊙noon-3pm & 7-11pm) This veteran address, around since 1985, stands out on dozens of counts: buzzy jovial atmosphere, flowery patio garden, funky interior, early evening opening, family friendly, hearty homecooking, a menu covering all price ranges and so forth. Cuisine from south-western France is its speciality, meaning lots of duck, but the vast menu covers all bases.

Le Petit Verdot FRENCH €€
(☎04 42 27 30 12; www.lepetitverdot.fr; 7 rue d'Entrecasteaux; mains €15-25; ⊙7pm-midnight Mon-Sat) Delicious menus are designed around what's in season, and paired with excellent wines. Meats are often braised all day and vegetables are tender, stewed in delicious broths. Save room for an incandescent dessert. Lively dining occurs around tabletops made of wine crates (expect to talk to your neighbour), and the gregarious owner speaks multiple languages.

Information

The **tourist office** (☎04 42 16 11 61; www.aixenprovencetourism.com; 300 av Giuseppe Verdi; ⊙8.30am-7pm Mon-Sat, 10am-1pm & 2-6pm Sun, to 8pm Mon-Sat Jun-Sep; 📶) sells tickets for guided tours and events.

Getting There & Away

BUS

From Aix's **bus station** (☎08 91 02 40 25, 04 42 91 26 80; place Marius Bastard), a 10-minute walk southwest from La Rotonde, routes include Marseille (€5.70, 25 minutes) and Avignon (€17.40, 1¼ hours).

TRAIN

The only useful train from Aix's tiny **city centre train station** (av Victor Hugo) is to/from Marseille (€8.20, 45 minutes). Aix TGV station, 15km away and accessible by shuttle bus from the bus station (€3.70), serves most of France; Marseille (€6.20) is a mere 12 minutes away.

Avignon

POP 92,078

Hooped by 4.3km of superbly preserved stone ramparts, this graceful city is the belle of Provence's ball. Its turn as the papal seat of power has bestowed Avignon with a treasury of magnificent art and architecture, none grander than the massive medieval fortress and papal palace, the Palais des Papes. Famed for its annual performing arts festival, these days Avignon is a lively student city and an ideal spot from which to step out into the surrounding region.

Sights

Palais des Papes PALACE

(Papal Palace; www.palais-des-papes.com; place du Palais; adult/child €11/9, with Pont Saint Bénezet €13.50/10.50; 9am-8pm Jul, 9am-8.30pm Aug, shorter hours Sep-Jun) Palais des Papes, a Unesco World Heritage Site, is the world's largest Gothic palace. Built when Pope Clement V abandoned Rome in 1309, it was the papal seat for 70-odd years. The immense scale testifies to the papacy's wealth; the 3m-thick walls, portcullises and watchtowers show its insecurity.

It takes imagination to picture the former luxury of these bare, cavernous stone halls, but multimedia audioguides (€2) assist. Highlights include 14th-century chapel frescoes by Matteo Giovannetti, and the Chambre du Cerf with medieval hunting scenes.

Pont Saint Bénezet BRIDGE

(bd du Rhône; adult/child €5/4, with Palais des Papes €13.50/10.50; 9am-8pm Jul, 9am-8.30pm Aug, shorter hours Sep-Jun) Legend says Pastor Bénezet had three saintly visions urging him to build a bridge across the Rhône. Completed in 1185, the 900m-long bridge with 20 arches linked Avignon with Villeneuve-lès-Avignon. It was rebuilt several times before all but four of its spans were washed away in the 1600s. Don't be surprised if you spot someone dancing; in France, the bridge is known as Pont d'Avignon after the nursery rhyme: 'Sur le pont d'Avignon/L'on y danse, l'on y danse...' (On Avignon Bridge, all are dancing...).

Festivals & Events

Hundreds of artists take to the stage and streets during the world-famous **Festival d'Avignon** (www.festival-avignon.com; Jul) and the fringe **Festival Off** (www.avignonleoff.com), held early July to early August.

Sleeping

Hôtel Mignon HOTEL €

(04 90 82 17 30; www.hotel-mignon.com; 12 rue Joseph Vernet; s €40-60, d €65-77, tr €80-99, q €105;) Bathrooms might be tiny and the stairs up, steep and narrow, but Hôtel Mignon (literally 'Cute Hotel') remains excellent value. Its 16 rooms are clean and comfortable, and the hotel sits on Avignon's smartest shopping street. Breakfast is €7.

Le Limas B&B €€

(04 90 14 67 19; www.le-limas-avignon.com; 51 rue du Limas; s/d/tr from €130/150/250;) This chic B&B in an 18th-century town house, like something out of *Vogue Living*, is everything designers strive for when mixing old and new: state-of-the-art kitchen and minimalist white decor complementing antique fireplaces and 18th-century spiral stairs. Breakfast on the sun-drenched terrace is divine, darling.

Eating

Place de l'Horloge's touristy cafes have so-so food.

Ginette et Marcel CAFE €

(04 90 85 58 70; 27 place des Corps Saints; tartines €4-7; 11am-11pm Wed-Mon;) With tables and chairs on one of Avignon's most happening plane-tree-shaded squares, this vintage cafe styled like a 1950s grocery store is a charming spot to hang out and people-watch over a *tartine* (open-faced sandwich), tart, salad or other light dish – equally tasty for lunch or an early evening *apéro* (predinner drink). Kids adore Ginette's cherry- and violet-flavoured cordials, and Marcel's glass jars of old-fashioned sweets.

★83.Vernet MODERN FRENCH €€

(04 90 85 99 04; www.83vernet.com; 83 rue Joseph Vernet; lunch/dinner menu €19.50/€24-30; noon-3pm & 7pm-1am Mon-Sat) Forget flowery French descriptions. The menu is straightforward and to the point at this

strikingly contemporary address, magnificently at home in the 18th-century cloistered courtyard of a medieval college. Expect pan-seared scallops, squid à la plancha and beef steak in pepper sauce on the menu, and watch for weekend events that transform the lounge-style restaurant into the hippest dance floor in town.

Information

Tourist Office (04 32 74 32 74; www.avignon-tourisme.com; 41 cours Jean Jaurès; 9am-6pm Mon-Fri, to 6pm Sat, 10am-noon Sun Apr-Oct, shorter hours rest of year) Organises guided walking tours of the city, and has plenty of information on other tours and activities, including boat trips and lunch cruises on the River Rhône, and wine-tasting trips to nearby Côtes du Rhône vineyards.

Getting There & Away

BUS

The bus station is down the ramp to the right as you exit the train station. Services include Marseille (€22, 35 minutes) and Nîmes (€1.50, 1¼ hours).

TRAIN

Avignon has two stations: Gare Avignon TGV, 4km southwest in Courtine, and Gare Avignon Centre, with services to/from Arles (€7.50, 20 minutes) and Nîmes (€9.70, 30 minutes).

Some TGVs to/from Paris (€123, 3½ hours) stop at Gare Avignon Centre, but TGVs to/from Marseille (€25, 30 minutes) and Nice (€60, 3¼ hours) only use Gare Avignon TGV.

In July and August, a direct Eurostar service operates on Saturday to/from London (from €140, six hours).

THE FRENCH RIVIERA & MONACO

With its glistening seas, idyllic beaches and fabulous weather, the French Riviera (Côte d'Azur in French) screams exclusivity, extravagance and excess. It has been a favourite getaway for the European jet set since Victorian times and there is nowhere more chichi or glam in France than St-Tropez, Cannes and super-rich, sovereign Monaco.

Nice

POP 348,195

Riviera queen Nice is what good living is all about – shimmering shores, the very best of Mediterranean food, a unique historical heritage, free museums, a charming Old Town, exceptional art and alpine wilderness within an hour's drive.

Sights

★Vieux Nice HISTORIC QUARTER

(food markets 6am-1.30pm Tue-Sun) Nice's old town, a mellow-hued rabbit warren, has scarcely changed since the 1700s. Retracing its history – and therefore that of the city – is a highlight, although you don't need to be a history buff to enjoy a stroll in this atmospheric quarter. Vieux Nice is as alive and prominent today as it ever was.

Promenade des Anglais ARCHITECTURE

Palm-lined promenade des Anglais, paid for by Nice's English colony in 1822, is a fine stage for a stroll. It's particularly atmospheric in the evening, with Niçois milling about

DON'T MISS

THE CORNICHES

Some of the Riviera's most spectacular scenery stretches east between Nice and Monaco. A trio of *corniches* (coastal roads) hugs the cliffs between the two seaside cities, each higher up the hill than the last. The middle *corniche* ends in Monaco; the upper and lower continue to Menton near the French–Italian border.

Corniche Inférieure (lower) Skimming the glittering, villa-studded shoreline, this road is all about belle époque glamour, the height of which can be seen at the extravagant **Villa Ephrussi de Rothschild** (www.villa-ephrussi.com; St-Jean-Cap Ferrat; adult/child €13/10; 10am-6pm Mar-Oct, 2-6pm Nov-Feb) in St-Jean-Cap Ferrat.

Moyenne (middle) Corniche The jewel in the Riviera crown undoubtedly goes to Èze, a medieval village spectacularly located on a rocky outcrop with dazzling views of the Med.

Grande (upper) Corniche The epitomy of 'scenic drive', with sublime panoramas unfolding at every bend. Stop in La Turbie for dramatic views of Monaco.

and epic sunsets. Don't miss the magnificent facade of **Hôtel Negresco**, built in 1912, or art deco **Palais de la Méditerranée**, saved from demolition in the 1980s and now part of a 4-star palace. The promenade follows the whole Baie des Anges (4km) and has a cycle and skating lane.

Musée Matisse ART MUSEUM
(www.musee-matisse-nice.org; 164 av des Arènes de Cimiez; ⏲10am-6pm Wed-Mon) FREE Located about 2km north of the centre in the leafy quarter of Cimiez, this museum houses a fascinating assortment of works by Matisse documenting the artist's stylistic evolution, including oil paintings, drawings, sculptures, tapestries and Matisse's signature famous paper cut-outs. The permanent collection is displayed in a red-ochre 17th-century Genoese villa overlooking an olive-tree-studded park. Temporary exhibitions are hosted in the futuristic basement building. Explanations in French only.

Sleeping

Hôtel Solara HOTEL €
(☎04 93 88 09 96; www.hotelsolara.com; 7 rue de France; s/d/tr/q €65/85/120/150; ❄📶) Were it not for its fantastic location on pedestrian rue de France and the sensational terraces that half the rooms boast, we'd say the Solara was an honest-to-goodness budget-friendly choice with impeccable rooms. But with those perks (and did we mention the small fridges in each room for that evening rosé?), it is a hidden gem.

★**Nice Pebbles** SELF-CONTAINED €€
(☎04 97 20 27 30; www.nicepebbles.com; 1-/3-bedroom apt from €107/220; ❄📶) Have you ever dreamt of feeling like a real Niçois? Coming back to your designer pad in Vieux Nice, opening a bottle of ice-cold rosé and feasting on market goodies? Nice Pebbles' concept is simple: offering the quality of a 4-star boutique hotel in holiday flats. The apartments (one to three bedrooms) are gorgeous and equipped to high standards.

Nice Garden Hôtel BOUTIQUE HOTEL €€
(☎04 93 87 35 62; www.nicegardenhotel.com; 11 rue du Congrès; s/d €75/100; ❄📶) Behind heavy iron gates hides this little gem of a hotel: the nine beautifully appointed rooms, the work of the exquisite Marion, are a subtle blend of old and new and overlook a delightful garden with a glorious orange tree. Amazingly, all this charm and peacefulness is just two blocks from the promenade.

Eating

Niçois nibbles include *socca* (a thin layer of chickpea flour and olive oil batter), *salade niçoise* and *farcis* (stuffed vegetables). Restaurants in Vieux Nice are a mixed bag, so choose carefully.

★**La Rossettisserie** FRENCH €
(☎04 93 76 18 80; www.larossettisserie.com; 8 rue Mascoïnat; mains €14.50; ⏲noon-2pm & 7.30-10pm Mon-Sat) The Rossettisserie (a lovely play on the word rotisserie – roast house – and Rossetti, the name of the nearby square) only serves succulent, roast meat – beef, chicken, veal, lamb or pork. It is cooked to perfection and comes with a choice of heavenly homemade mash, ratatouille or sauté potatoes and a mixed salad. The vaulted dining room in the basement is stunning.

Chez Palmyre FRENCH €
(☎04 93 85 72 32; 5 rue Droite; menu €17; ⏲noon-1.30pm & 7-9.30pm Mon-Fri) A new chef has breathed new life into this fabulously atmospheric little restaurant, seemingly unchanged for its long life. The kitchen churns out Niçois standards with a light hand, service is sweet and the price fantastic; book ahead, even for lunch.

L'Escalinada NIÇOIS €€
(☎04 93 62 11 71; www.escalinada.fr; 22 rue Pairolière; menu €26, mains €19-25; ⏲noon-2.30pm & 7-11pm) This charming restaurant has been one of the best places in town for Niçois cuisine for the last half-century: try melt-in-your-mouth homemade gnocchi with tasty *daube* (Provençal beef stew), grilled prawns with garlic and herbs or Marsala veal stew. The staff are delightful and the welcome *kir* (white wine sweetened with blackcurrant syrup) is on the house. No credit cards.

Drinking & Entertainment

Vieux Nice's streets are stuffed with bars and cafes. There is a vibrant live-music scene.

Les Distilleries Idéales CAFE
(www.lesdistilleriesideales.fr; 24 rue de la Préfecture; ⏲9am-12.30am) Whether you're after an espresso on your way to the cours Saleya market or an *apéritif* (complete with cheese and charcuterie platters, €5.60) before trying out one of Nice's fabulous restaurants,

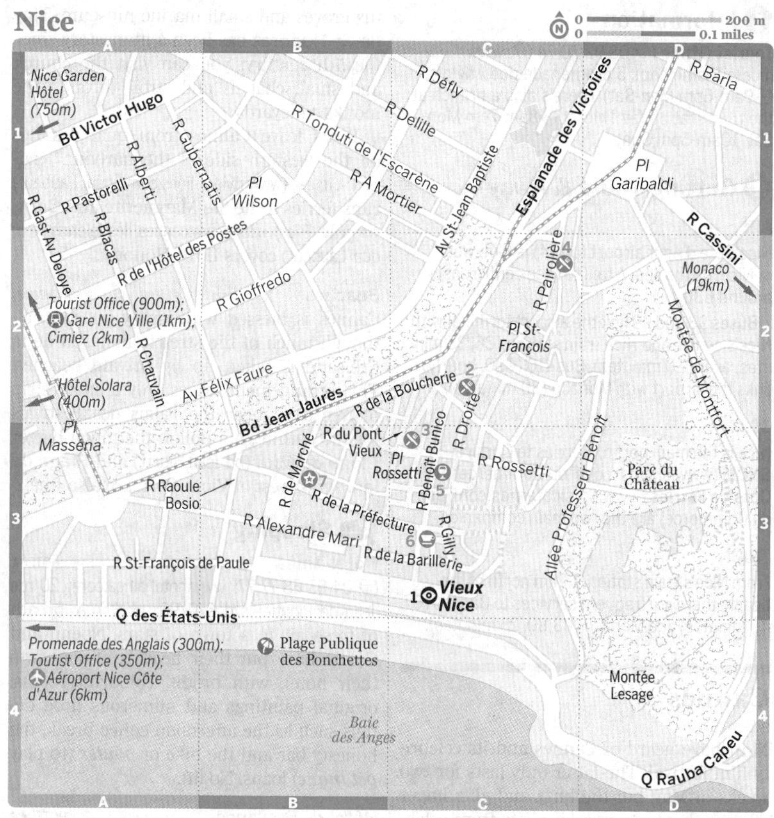

Nice

Top Sights
1 Vieux Nice C3

Eating
2 Chez Palmyre C2
3 La Rossettisserie C3
4 L'Escalinada C2

Drinking & Nightlife
5 L'Abat-Jour C3
6 Les Distilleries Idéales C3

Entertainment
7 Chez Wayne's B3

Les Distilleries is one of the most atmospheric bars in town. Tables on the small street terrace are ideal for watching the world go by. Happy hour is from 6pm to 8pm.

L'Abat-Jour BAR
(25 rue Benoît Bunico; 6.30pm-2.30am) With its vintage furniture, rotating art exhibitions and alternative music, L'Abat-Jour is all the rage with Nice's young and trendy crowd. The basement has live music or DJ sessions as the night darkens.

Chez Wayne's LIVE MUSIC
(www.waynes.fr; 15 rue de la Préfecture; 10am-2am) Raucous watering hole Chez Wayne's is a typical English pub that looks like it's been plucked out of London, Bristol or Leeds. It features excellent live bands every night and has the best atmosphere in town. The pub is also sports-mad and shows every rugby, football, Aussie Rules, tennis and cricket game worth watching.

Information

Tourist Office (☎08 92 70 74 07; www.nicetourisme.com; 5 promenade des Anglais; ⏰9am-6pm Mon-Sat) There's also a branch at the train station (av Thiers; ⏰8am-7pm Mon-Sat, 10am-5pm Sun).

Getting There & Away

AIR

Nice Côte d'Azur airport (p434) is 6km west of Nice, by the sea. A taxi to Nice centre costs around €30.

Buses 98 and 99 link the airport terminal with Nice's centre and Nice train station (€6, 35 minutes, every 20 minutes). Bus 110 (€20, hourly) links the airport with Monaco (30 minutes).

BOAT

Nice is the main port for ferries to Corsica. **SNCM** (www.sncm.fr; quai du Commerce) and **Corsica Ferries** (www.corsicaferries.com; quai du Commerce) are the two main companies.

TRAIN

From Nice's train station, 1.2km north of the beach, there are frequent services to Cannes (€7, 40 minutes) and Monaco (€3.80, 25 minutes).

Cannes

POP 73,671

Most have heard of Cannes and its celebrity film festival. The latter only lasts for two weeks in May, but the buzz and glitz linger all year thanks to regular visits from celebrities who come here to indulge in designer shopping, beaches and the palace hotels of the Riviera's glammest seafront, bd de la Croisette.

Sights & Activities

La Croisette ARCHITECTURE

The multi-starred hotels and couture shops that line the famous bd de la Croisette (aka La Croisette) may be the preserve of the rich and famous, but anyone can enjoy the palm-shaded promenade and take in the atmosphere. In fact, it's a favourite among Cannois (natives of Cannes), particularly at night when it is lit with bright colours.

Îles de Lérins ISLAND

Although just 20 minutes away by boat, these tranquil islands feel far from the madding crowd. **Île Ste-Marguerite**, where the mysterious Man in the Iron Mask was incarcerated during the late 17th century, is known for its bone-white beaches, eucalyptus groves and small marine museum. Tiny **Île St-Honorat** has been a monastery since the 5th century: you can visit the church and small chapels and stroll through the monks' vineyards.

Boats leave Cannes from quai des Îles on the western side of the harbour. **Riviera Lines** (www.riviera-lines.com; quai Laubeuf) runs ferries to Île Ste-Marguerite and **Compagnie Planaria** (www.cannes-ilesdelerins.com; quai Laubeuf) covers Île St-Honorat.

Beaches SWIMMING

Cannes is blessed with sandy beaches, although much of the stretch along bd de la Croisette is taken up by private beaches. This arrangement leaves only a small strip of free sand near the Palais des Festivals for the bathing hoi polloi; the much bigger **Plage du Midi** (bd Jean Hibert) and **Plage de la Bocca**, west of Vieux Port, are also free.

Sleeping

Hôtel Alnéa HOTEL €

(☎04 93 68 77 77; www.hotel-alnea.com; 20 rue Jean de Riouffe; s/d €70/90; ❄📶) A breath of fresh air in a town of stars, Noémi and Cédric have put their heart and soul into their hotel, with bright, colourful rooms, original paintings and numerous little details such as the afternoon coffee break, the honesty bar and the bike or *boules* (to play *pétanque*) loans. No lift.

Hôtel de Provence HOTEL €€

(☎04 93 38 44 35; www.hotel-de-provence.com; 9 rue Molière; s/d from €108/118; ❄📶) A tall town house with pale yellow walls and lavender blue shutters, the exterior of the Hôtel de Provence is true to its name. Inside, however, the design is more minimalist chic than quaint Provençal, with plenty of clean white lines. The hotel's strength is its height, with almost every room sporting a balcony or terrace.

Eating

PhilCat DELICATESSEN €

(La Pantiéro; sandwiches & salads €4.50-6; ⏰8.30am-5pm; 🖉) Don't be put off by Philipe and Catherine's unassuming prefab cabin on La Pantiéro: this is Cannes' best lunch house. Huge salads, made to order, are piled high with delicious fresh ingredients. Or if you're *really* hungry, try one of their phenomenal *pan bagna* (a moist sandwich bursting with Provençal flavours).

WORTH A TRIP

THE SCENT OF THE CÔTE D'AZUR

Mosey some 20km northwest of Cannes to inhale the sweet smell of lavender, jasmine, mimosa and orange-blossom fields. In **Grasse**, one of the world's leading perfume centres, dozens of perfumeries create essences to sell to factories (for aromatically enhanced foodstuffs and soaps) as well as to prestigious couture houses – the highly trained noses of local perfume-makers can identify 3000 scents in a single whiff.

Learn about three millennia of perfume-making at the **Musée International de la Parfumerie** (MIP; www.museesdegrasse.com; 2 bd du Jeu de Ballon; adult/child €4/free; 10.30am-5.30pm Wed-Mon;) and watch the process firsthand during a guided tour at **Fragonard perfumery** (www.fragonard.com; 20 bd Fragonard; tour free; 9am-6pm), the easiest to reach on foot. The **tourist office** (04 93 36 66 66; www.grasse.fr; place de la Buanderie; 9am-12.30pm & 2-6pm Mon-Sat;) has information on other perfumeries and field trips to local flower farms. Roses are picked mid-May to mid-June, jasmine July to late October.

Aux Bons Enfants FRENCH €€
(www.aux-bons-enfants.com; 80 rue Meynadier; menu €23, mains €16; noon-2pm & 7-10pm Tue-Sat) A people's-choice place since 1935, this informal restaurant cooks up wonderful regional dishes such as *aïoli garni* (garlic and saffron mayonnaise served with fish and vegetables), *daube* (a Provençal beef stew), and *rascasse meunière* (pan-fried rockfish), all in a convivial atmosphere. Make no plans for the afternoon after lunching here. No credit cards or reservations.

Mantel MODERN EUROPEAN €€
(04 93 39 13 10; www.restaurantmantel.com; 22 rue St-Antoine; menus €35-60; noon-2pm Fri-Mon, 7.30-10pm Thu-Tue) Discover why Noël Mantel is the hotshot of the Cannois gastronomic scene at his refined old-town restaurant. Service is stellar and the seasonal cuisine divine: try the wonderfully tender glazed veal shank in balsamic vinegar or the original poached octopus *bourride*-style. Best of all though, you get not one but two desserts from the mouth-watering dessert trolley.

Information

Tourist Office (04 92 99 84 22; www.cannes-destination.fr; Palais des Festivals, bd de la Croisette; 9am-7pm) The place to book guided tours of the city and get information on what to do and see in Cannes.

Getting There & Away

BUS

From the **bus station** (place Cornut-Gentille), buses serve Nice (€1.50, 1½ hours, every 15 minutes) and Nice airport (€20, 50 minutes, half-hourly).

TRAIN

From Cannes train station there are at least hourly services to/from Nice (€7, 40 minutes), Grasse (€4.30, 30 minutes), Monaco (€9.40, one hour) and Marseille (€32, two hours).

St-Tropez

POP 4571

In the soft autumn or winter light, it's hard to believe the pretty terracotta fishing village of St-Tropez is a stop on the Riviera celebrity circuit. It seems far removed from its glitzy siblings further up the coast, but come spring or summer, it's a different world: the population increases tenfold, prices triple and fun-seekers pile in to party till dawn, strut around the luxury-yacht-packed Vieux Port and enjoy the creature comforts of exclusive A-listers' beaches in the Baie de Pampelonne.

Sights & Activities

About 4km southeast of town is the start of **Plage de Tahiti** and its continuation, the famous **Plage de Pampelonne**, studded with St-Tropez' most legendary drinking and dining haunts.

Place des Lices SQUARE
St-Tropez's legendary and very charming central square is studded with plane trees, cafes and *pétanque* players. Simply sitting on a cafe terrace watching the world go by or jostling with the crowds at its extravaganza of a twice-weekly **market** (place des Lices; 8am-1pm Tue & Sat), jam-packed with

everything from fruit and veg to antique mirrors and flip-flops (thongs), is an integral part of the St-Tropez experience.

Musée de l'Annonciade ART MUSEUM
(place Grammont; adult/child €6/free; ⌚10am-1pm & 2-6pm Wed-Mon) In a gracefully converted 16th-century chapel, this small but famous art museum showcases an impressive collection of modern art infused with that legendary Côte d'Azur light. Pointillist Paul Signac bought a house in St-Tropez in 1892 and introduced others to the area. The museum's collection includes his *St-Tropez, Le Quai* (1899) and *St-Tropez, Coucher de Soleil au Bois de Pins* (1896).

Sleeping & Eating

Multistar campgrounds abound on the road to Plage de Pampelonne. Quai Jean Jaurès at the Vieux Port is littered with restaurants and cafes.

Hôtel Lou Cagnard HOTEL €€
(☎04 94 97 04 24; www.hotel-lou-cagnard.com; 18 av Paul Roussel; d €81-171; ⌚Mar-Oct; ❄📶) Book well ahead for this great-value courtyard charmer, shaded by lemon and fig trees, and owned by schooled hoteliers. The pretty Provençal house with lavender shutters has its very own jasmine-scented garden, strung with fairy lights at night. Bright and beautifully clean rooms are decorated with painted Provençal furniture. Five have ground-floor garden terraces. The cheapest rooms have private washbasin and stand-up bath-tub but share a toilet; most rooms have air-con.

Hôtel Le Colombier HOTEL €€
(☎04 94 97 05 31; http://lecolombierhotel.free.fr; impasse des Conquettes; d/tr from €105/235; ⌚mid-Apr–mid-Nov; ❄📶) An immaculately clean converted house, five minutes' walk from place des Lices, the Colombier's fresh, summery decor is feminine and uncluttered, with bedrooms in shades of white and vintage furniture.

★La Tarte Tropézienne CAFE, BAKERY €
(www.latartetropezienne.fr; place des Lices; mains €13-15; ⌚6.30am-7.30pm, lunch noon-3pm) This cafe-bakery is the original creator of the eponymous cake, and therefore the best place to buy St-Tropez's delicacy. But to start, choose from delicious daily specials, salads and sandwiches, which you can enjoy in the bistro inside or on the little terrace outside.

La Plage des Jumeaux SEAFOOD €€€
(☎04 94 58 21 80; www.plagedesjumeaux.com; rte de l'Épi, Pampelonne; mains €25-40; ⌚noon-3pm; 🖉👪) The top pick of St-Tropez's beach restaurants, Les Jumeaux serves beautiful seafood (including fabulous whole fish, ideal to share) and sun-bursting salads on its dreamy white-and-turquoise striped beach. Families are well catered for, with playground equipment, beach toys and a kids' menu.

Information

Tourist Office (☎08 92 68 48 28; www.sainttropeztourisme.com; quai Jean Jaurès; ⌚9.30am-1.30pm & 3-7.30pm Jul & Aug, 9.30am-12.30pm & 2-7pm Apr-Jun, Sep &Oct, to 6pm Mon-Sat Nov-Mar) Has a kiosk in Parking du Port in July and August.

Getting There & Away

From the **bus station** (☎04 94 56 25 74; av du Général de Gaulle), buses run by **VarLib** (☎04 94 24 60 00; www.varlib.fr; tickets €3) serve Ramatuelle (€3, 35 minutes) and St-Raphaël train station (€3, 1¼ hours). There are four daily buses to Toulon-Hyères airport (€3, 1½ hours).

ACCOMMODATION WARNING

Accommodation can be impossible to find, not to mention prohibitively expensive, during the Cannes Film Festival and the Monaco Grand Prix (both held in May). This applies to the coast between Menton and Cannes. July and August are busy everywhere, so book well in advance.

Monaco

POP 32,020

Squeezed into just 200 hectares, this confetti principality may be the world's second-smallest country (the Vatican is smaller), but what it lacks in size it makes up for in attitude. Glitzy, glam and screaming hedonism, Monaco is truly beguiling.

It is a sovereign state but has no border control. It has its own flag (red and white) and national holiday (19 November), and it uses the euro even though it's not part of the EU.

You can easily visit Monaco as a day trip from Nice, a short train ride away.

Sights

★Musée Océanographique de Monaco AQUARIUM
(www.oceano.mc; av St-Martin; adult/child €14/7; 10am-6pm) Stuck dramatically to the edge of a cliff since 1910, the world-renowned Musée Océanographique de Monaco, founded by Prince Albert I (1848–1922), is a stunner. Its centrepiece is its aquarium, with a 6m-deep lagoon where sharks and marine predators are separated from colourful tropical fishes by a coral reef. Upstairs, two huge colonnaded rooms retrace the history of oceanography and marine biology (and Prince Albert's contribution to the field) through photographs, old equipment, numerous specimens and interactive displays.

Le Rocher HISTORIC QUARTER
Monaco Ville, also called Le Rocher, thrusts skywards on a pistol-shaped rock. It's this strategic location overlooking the sea that became the stronghold of the Grimaldi dynasty. Built as a fortress in the 13th century, the **palace** is now the private residence of the Grimaldis. It is protected by the Carabiniers du Prince; **changing of the guard** takes place daily at 11.55am.

Jardin Exotique GARDENS
(www.jardin-exotique.mc; 62 bd du Jardin Exotique; adult/child €7.20/3.80; 9am-dusk) Home to the world's largest succulent and cactus collection, from small echinocereus to 10m-tall African candelabras, the gardens tumble down the slopes of Moneghetti through a maze of paths, stairs and bridges. Views of the principality are spectacular and the gardens are delightful. Your ticket also gets you a 35-minute **guided tour** round the **Grottes de l'Observatoire**.

Sleeping

Monaco is no budget destination when it comes to accommodation. Budget-conscious travellers should stay in nearby Nice and visit it as a day trip.

Hôtel Miramar HOTEL €€
(93 30 86 48; www.miramar.monaco-hotel.com; 1 av du Président JF Kennedy; s/d €160/185;) This modern hotel with rooftop-terrace restaurant is a great option right by the port. Seven of the 11 rooms have fabulous balconies overlooking the yachts. The hotel was entirely refurbished in 2014, giving the 1950s building a proper 21st-century make-over.

Eating

Supermarché Casino BOULANGERIE €
(17 bd Albert, 1er; pizza slices & sandwiches from €3.20; 8.30am-midnight Mon-Sat, to 9pm Sun;) It's not so much the supermarket that's worth knowing about as its excellent street-side bakery and pizzeria, which churns out freshly prepared goodies. A saviour for those keen to watch the pennies.

La Montgolfière FUSION €€
(97 98 61 59; www.lamontgolfiere.mc; 16 rue Basse; mains €14-27; noon-2pm & 7.30-9.30pm Mon, Tue & Thu-Sat) This tiny fusion wonder is an unlikely find amid the touristy jumble of Monaco's historic quarter. But what a great idea Henri and Fabienne Geraci had to breathe new life into the Rocher. The couple have spent a lot of time in Malaysia, and Henri's fusion cuisine is outstanding, as is Fabienne's welcome in their pocket-sized dining room.

Café Llorca MODERN FRENCH €€
(99 99 29 29; www.cafellorca.mc; Grimaldi Forum, 10 av Princesse Grace; menu €22, mains €15-19; noon-3pm Mon-Fri) This is Michelin-starred chef Alain Llorca's gift to lunch-goers: fabulous modern French cuisine with a fusion twist at affordable prices. The two-course lunch menu including a glass of wine is a steal. In spring/summer, make a beeline (and book) for the tables on the terrace overlooking the sea.

Drinking & Entertainment

Brasserie de Monaco MICROBREWERY
(www.brasseriedemonaco.com; 36 rte de la Piscine; noon-2am) Tourists and locals rub shoulders at Monaco's only microbrewery, which crafts rich organic ales and lager, and serves tasty (if pricey) antipasti plates. The brasserie regularly hosts live music and shows major sports events. Happy hour runs from 6.30pm to 8.30pm.

★Casino de Monte Carlo CASINO
(www.montecarlocasinos.com; place du Casino; admission Salon Europe/Salons Privés €10/20; Salon Europe 2pm-late daily, Salons Privés from 4pm Thu-Sun) Gambling – or simply watching the poker-faced gamble – in Monte Carlo's grand marble-and-gold casino is part and parcel of the Monaco experience. The building and atmosphere are an attraction in its own right and you need not play huge sums. To enter the casino, you must be at least 18.

Information

TELEPHONE

Calls between Monaco and France are international calls. Dial ☎00 followed by Monaco's country code (☎377) when calling Monaco from France or elsewhere abroad. To phone France from Monaco, dial ☎00 and France's country code (☎33).

TOURIST INFORMATION

Tourist Office (www.visitmonaco.com; 2a bd des Moulins; ⌚9am-7pm Mon-Sat, 11am-1pm Sun) Smartphone users should download the tourist office's excellent app called Monaco Travel Guide.

Getting There & Away

Monaco's **train station** (av Prince Pierre) has frequent trains to Nice (€3.80, 25 minutes), and east to Menton (€2.10, 15 minutes) and beyond into Italy. Bus 100 goes to Nice (€1.50, 45 minutes) along the Corniche Inférieure.

CORSICA

The rugged island of Corsica (Corse in French) is officially a part of France but remains fiercely proud of its own culture, history and language. It's one of the Mediterranean's most dramatic islands, with a bevy of beautiful beaches, glitzy ports and a mountainous, maquis-covered interior to explore, as well as a wild, independent spirit all of its own.

Ajaccio

POP 67,477

Ajaccio, Corsica's main metropolis, is all class and seduction. Looming over this elegant port city is the spectre of Corsica's great general: Napoléon Bonaparte was born here in 1769 and the city is dotted with statues and museums relating to him (starting with the main street in Ajaccio, cours Napoléon).

Sights & Activities

Kiosks on the quayside opposite place du Maréchal Foch sell tickets for seasonal **boat trips** around the Golfe d'Ajaccio and **Îles Sanguinaires** (adult/child €25/15), and excursions to the **Réserve Naturelle de Scandola** (adult/child €55/35).

Palais Fesch – Musée des Beaux-Arts ART MUSEUM

(www.musee-fesch.com; 50-52 rue du Cardinal Fesch; adult/child €8/5; ⌚10.30am-6pm Mon, Wed & Sat, noon-6pm Thu, Fri & Sun May-Sep, to 5pm Oct-Apr) One of the island's must-sees, this superb museum established by Napoléon's uncle has France's largest collection of Italian paintings outside the Louvre. Mostly the works of minor or anonymous 14th- to 19th-century artists, there are also canvases by Titian, Fra Bartolomeo, Veronese, Botticelli and Bellini. Look out for *La Vierge à l'Enfant Soutenu par un Ange* (Mother and Child Supported by an Angel), one of Botticelli's masterpieces. The museum also houses temporary exhibitions.

Maison Bonaparte HOUSE MUSEUM

(☎04 95 21 43 89; www.musees-nationaux-napoleoniens.org; rue St-Charles; adult/child €7/free; ⌚10.30am-12.30pm & 1.15-6pm Tue-Sun Apr-Sep, to 4.30pm Oct-Mar) Napoléon spent his first nine years in this house. Ransacked by Corsican nationalists in 1793, requisitioned by English troops from 1794 to 1796, and eventually rebuilt by Napoléon's mother, the house became a place of pilgrimage for French revolutionaries. It hosts memorabilia of the emperor and his siblings, including a glass medallion containing a lock of his hair. A comprehensive audioguide (€2) is available in several languages.

Sleeping & Eating

Hôtel Marengo HOTEL €

(☎04 95 21 43 66; www.hotel-marengo.com; 2 rue Marengo; d/tr €90/110; ⌚Apr-Oct; ❄📶) For something near to the sand, try this charmingly eccentric small hotel. Rooms have a balcony, there's a quiet flower-filled courtyard and reception is an agreeable clutter of tasteful prints and personal objects. Find it down a cul-de-sac off bd Madame Mère.

★**Hôtel Demeure Les Mouettes** BOUTIQUE HOTEL €€€

(☎04 95 50 40 40; www.hotellesmouettes.fr; 9 cours Lucien Bonaparte; d €160-340; ⌚Apr-Oct; ❄📶🏊) This peach-coloured 19th-century colonnaded mansion right on the water's edge is a dream. Views of the bay of Ajaccio from the (heated) pool and terrace are exquisite: dolphins can often be spotted very early in the morning or in the evenings. Inside, the decor is one of understated elegance and service is 4 stars.

Don Quichotte BRASSERIE €
(☎ 04 95 21 27 30; 7 rue des Halles; mains €10-18; ⏰ noon-2pm & 7-11pm Mon-Sat) Tucked behind the fish market, this inconspicuous brasserie is something of a hidden gem: the cuisine is light, fresh and generous, and an absolute bargain. Don't miss the fabulous *moules à la Corse* (Corsican-style mussels: tomato, cream, pancetta, onion, chestnut) with homemade fries – simply divine.

A Nepita BISTRO €€
(☎ 04 95 26 75 68; 4 rue San Lazaro; 2-/3-course menu €24/29; ⏰ noon-2pm Mon-Fri, 8-10pm Thu-Sat) Ajaccio's rising culinary star is winning plaudits and loyal followers for its modern French cuisine and elegant setting. It's a nice change from hearty traditional Corsican fare, although the island isn't forgotten: the menu changes daily and uses only the freshest local products, including seasonal seafood and vegetables.

Information

Tourist Office (☎ 04 95 51 53 03; www.ajaccio-tourisme.com; 3 bd du Roi Jérôme; ⏰ 8am-7pm Mon-Sat, 9am-1pm Sun; 📶)

Getting There & Away

AIR

Bus 8 (€4.50, 20 minutes) links **Aéroport d'Ajaccio Napoléon Bonaparte** (www.2a.cci.fr/Aeroport-Napoleon-Bonaparte-Ajaccio.html), 8km east, with Ajaccio's train and bus stations.

BOAT

Boats to/from Toulon, Nice and Marseille depart from Ajaccio's **Terminal Maritime et Routier** (☎ 04 95 51 55 45; quai L'Herminier).

BUS

Local bus companies have ticket kiosks inside the ferry terminal building, the arrival/departure point for buses.

TRAIN

From the **train station** (place de la Gare), services include Bastia (€21.60, four hours, five daily).

Bastia

POP 43,539

The bustling old port of Bastia has an irresistible magnetism. Allow yourself at least a day to drink in the narrow old-town alleyways of Terra Vecchia, the seething Vieux Port, the dramatic 16th-century citadel perched up high, and the compelling history museum.

Sights & Activities

Terra Vecchia HISTORIC QUARTER
A spiderweb of narrow lanes, Terra Vecchia is Bastia's heart and soul. Shady **place de l'Hôtel de Ville** hosts a lively morning market on Saturday and Sunday. One block west, baroque **Chapelle de l'Immaculée Conception** (rue des Terrasses), with its elaborately painted barrel-vaulted ceiling, briefly served as the seat of the short-lived Anglo-Corsican parliament in 1795. Further north is **Chapelle St-Roch** (rue Napoléon), with an 18th-century organ and trompe l'œil roof.

Vieux Port PORT
Bastia's Vieux Port is ringed by pastel-coloured tenements and buzzy brasseries, as well as the twin-towered **Église St-Jean Baptiste** (4 rue du Cardinal Viale Préla). The best views of the harbour are from the hillside

FRENCH TOWNS WORTH A VISIT

We couldn't possibly squeeze the whole of France into one chapter, so here are some more towns and regions worth considering for longer stays.

Alta Rocca Corsica may be an island, but its cultural heart is its mountainous hinterland.

Annecy A postcard-perfect medieval town with alpine landscapes in the background.

Arras Exceptional Flemish architecture and subterranean WWI sites.

Beaujolais An area known for its fruity red wines, and Beaujolais Nouveau (young wine drunk at just six weeks).

Cathar fortresses Travel back to the Middle Ages among Languedoc's crumbling fortresses.

Étretat Admire Mother Nature's work of art on Étretat's chalk-white cliffs.

Luberon Explore Provence's famed rolling hills and hilltop villages.

park of **Jardin Romieu**, reached via a gorgeous old stately staircase that twists uphill from the waterfront.

Terra Nova HISTORIC QUARTER
Above Jardin Romieu looms Bastia's amber-hued citadel, built from the 15th to 17th centuries as a stronghold for the city's Genoese masters. Inside, the Palais des Gouverneurs houses the **Musée de Bastia** (04 95 31 09 12; www.musee-bastia.com; place du Donjon; adult/child €5/2.50; 10am-6pm Tue-Sun Apr-Oct, shorter hours rest of year), which retraces the city's history. A few streets south, don't miss the majestic **Cathédrale Ste-Marie** (rue de l'Évêché) and nearby **Église Ste-Croix** (rue de l'Évêché), featuring gilded ceilings and a mysterious black-oak crucifix found in the sea in 1428.

Sleeping & Eating

Hôtel Central HOTEL €€
(04 95 31 69 72; www.centralhotel.fr; 3 rue Miot; s/d/apt €80/90/150;) From the vintage, black-and-white tiled floor in the entrance to the sweeping staircase and eclectic jumble of plant pots in the minuscule interior courtyard, this family-run address oozes 1940s grace. The hotel's pedigree dates to 1941 and the vintage furnishings inside the 19th-century building don't disappoint. The three apartments, with fully equipped kitchen, are great for longer stays.

★**Raugi** ICE CREAM €
(www.raugi.com; 2 rue du Chanoine Colombani; ice cream from €2; 9.30am-midnight Tue-Sat Oct-May, 9.30am-12.30pm & 2.30pm-1am Mon-Sat Jun-Sep) Going strong since 1937, Raugi is a Bastia institution. Flavours range from bog-standard raspberry, lemon and so on to Corsican chestnut, mandarin, fig, aromatic *senteur de maquis* (scent of Corsican herbal scrubland) and sweet *myrte* (myrtle). The *verrines glacées* (ice-cream desserts, €4.70) are out of this world.

Le Lavezzi MODERN FRENCH €€
(04 95 31 05 73; 8 rue St-Jean; mains €21-35, lunch menus €22) A boutique address that design-loving gourmets will love: think turquoise polished concrete floor and brightly coloured Alexander McQueen–style chairs – fabulous and funky. The real heart stealer is the twinset of 1st-floor balconies above the water with prime old-port views. Modern cuisine injects a fusion zest into classic meat and fish dishes.

Information

Tourist Office (04 95 54 20 40; www.bastia-tourisme.com; place St-Nicolas; 8am-6pm Mon-Sat, to noon Sun;) Organises guided tours of the city and has plenty of information about Cap Corse.

Getting There & Away

AIR

Aéroport Bastia-Poretta (www.bastia.aeroport.fr), 24km south, is linked by bus (€9, 35 minutes, 10 daily) with the Préfecture building in town.

BOAT

Ferry companies have information offices at **Bastia port** (www.bastia.port.fr); they are usually open for same-day ticket sales a couple of hours before sailings. Ferries sail to/from Marseille, Toulon and Nice (mainland France), and Livorno, Savona, Piombino and Genoa (Italy).

BUS & TRAIN

The **bus station** (1 rue du Nouveau Port) is north of place St-Nicolas. Additional bus stops are scattered around town. There are daily train services to Ajaccio (€21.60, four hours, five daily).

Bonifacio

POP 2994

With its glittering harbour, dramatic perch atop creamy white cliffs, and a stout citadel teetering above the cornflower-blue waters of the Bouches de Bonifacio, this dazzling port is an essential stop. Just a short hop from Sardinia, Bonifacio has a distinctly Italianate feel: sun-bleached town houses, dangling washing lines and murky chapels cram the web of alleyways of the old citadel, while, down below on the harbourside, brasseries and boat kiosks tout their wares to the droves of day trippers.

Sights

★**Citadel** HISTORIC QUARTER
(Haute Ville) Much of Bonifacio's charm comes from strolling the citadel's shady streets, several spanned by arched aqueducts designed to collect rainwater to fill the communal cistern opposite **Église Ste-Marie Majeure**. From the marina, the paved steps of **montée du Rastello** and **montée St-Roch** bring you up to the citadel's old gateway, **Porte de Gênes**, complete with an original 16th-century drawbridge.

Tours

SPMB BOAT TOUR
(☎04 95 10 97 50; www.spmbonifacio.com; Port de Bonifacio) Don't leave Bonifacio without taking a boat trip around its extraordinary coastline, where you'll get the best perspective of the town's precarious position on top of the magnificent chalky cliffs. The one-hour itinerary (adult/child €17.50/12) includes several *calanques* (deep rocky inlets), views of the Escalier du Roi d'Aragon and the **Grotte du Sdragonato** (Little Dragon Cave), a vast watery cave with a natural rooftop skylight.

Sleeping & Eating

Hôtel Le Colomba HOTEL €€
(☎04 95 73 73 44; www.hotel-bonifacio-corse.fr; rue Simon Varsi; d €112-147; Mar-Nov;) Occupying a tastefully renovated 14th-century building, this beautiful hotel is a delightful address in a picturesque (steep) street, bang in the heart of the old town. Rooms are simple and smallish, but fresh and pleasantly individual: wrought-iron bedsteads and country fabrics in some, carved bedheads and checkerboard tiles in others. Breakfast in a vaulted room is another highlight.

Kissing Pigs CORSICAN €
(☎04 95 73 56 09; 15 quai Banda del Ferro; mains €11-20) Soothingly positioned by the harbour, this widely acclaimed restaurant and wine bar serves savoury fare in a seductively cosy interior, complete with wooden fixtures and swinging sausages. It's famed for its cheese and charcuterie platters; for the indecisive, the combination *moitié-moitié* (half-half) is perfect. The Corsican wine list is another hit.

Information

Tourist Office (☎04 95 73 11 88; www.bonifacio.fr; 2 rue Fred Scamaroni; 9am-7pm mid-Apr–mid-Oct, 10am-5pm Mon-Fri mid-Oct–mid-Apr;)

Getting There & Away

AIR

A taxi into town from **Aéroport de Figari-Sud-Corse** (www.2a.cci.fr/Aeroport-Figari-Sud-Corse.html), 20km north, costs about €45.

BOAT

Sardinia's main ferry operators, **Moby** (www.moby.it) and **Saremar** (www.saremar.it), run seasonal boats between Bonifacio and Santa Teresa Gallura (Sardinia); sailing time is 50 minutes.

SURVIVAL GUIDE

Directory A–Z

ACCOMMODATION

Many tourist offices make room reservations, often for a fee of €5; many only do so if you stop by in person. In the French Alps, ski-resort tourist offices operate a central reservation service.

B&Bs

For charm, a heartfelt *bienvenue* (welcome) and home cooking, it's hard to beat a *chambre d'hôte* (B&B). Pick up lists at local tourist offices or online.

Fleurs de Soleil (www.fleursdesoleil.fr) Selective collection of 550 stylish *maisons d'hôte*, mainly in rural France.

Gîtes de France (www.gites-de-france.com) France's primary umbrella organisation for B&Bs and self-catering properties *(gîtes)*. Search by region, theme (charm, with kids, by the sea, gourmet, great garden etc), activity (fishing, wine tasting etc) or facilities (pool, dishwasher, fireplace, baby equipment etc).

Samedi Midi Éditions (www.samedimidi.com) Country, mountain, seaside… Choose your *chambre d'hôte* by location or theme (romance, golf, design, cooking courses).

Camping

- Most campgrounds open March or April to October.
- Euro-economisers should look for good-value but no-frills *campings municipaux* (municipal camping grounds).
- Accessing campgrounds without your own transport can be difficult in many areas.
- Camping in nondesignated spots (*camping sauvage*) is illegal in France.

COUNTRY FACTS

Area 551,000 sq km

Capital Paris

Country Code ☎33

Currency Euro (€)

Emergency ☎112

Language French

Money ATMs everywhere

Visas Schengen rules apply

SLEEPING PRICE RANGES

Our reviews refer to the cost of a double room with private bathroom, except in hostels or where otherwise specified. Quoted rates are for high season and exclude breakfast unless otherwise noted:

€ less than €90 (€130 in Paris)

€€ €90 to €190 (€130 to €200 in Paris)

€€€ more than €190 (€200 in Paris)

Websites with listings searchable by location and facilities include:

Camping en France (www.camping.fr)
Camping France (www.campingfrance.com)
HPA Guide (http://camping.hpaguide.com)

Hostels

Hostels range from funky to threadbare.

- A dorm bed in an *auberge de jeunesse* (youth hostel) costs €20 to €50 in Paris, and anything from €15 to €35 in the provinces; sheets are always included and often breakfast, too.
- To prevent outbreaks of bed bugs, sleeping bags are no longer permitted.
- All hostels are nonsmoking.

Hotels

- French hotels almost never include breakfast in their advertised nightly rates.
- Hotels in France are rated with one to five stars; ratings are based on objective criteria (eg size of entry hall), not service, decor or cleanliness.
- A double room has one double bed (or two singles pushed together); a room with twin beds is more expensive, as is a room with bathtub instead of shower.

ACTIVITIES

From glaciers, rivers and canyons in the Alps to porcelain-smooth cycling trails in the Dordogne and Loire Valley – not to mention 3200km of coastline stretching from Italy to Spain and from the Basque country to the Straits of Dover – France's landscapes are ripe for exhilarating outdoor escapes.

- The French countryside is criss-crossed by a staggering 120,000km of *sentiers balisés* (marked walking paths), which pass through every imaginable terrain in every region of the country. No permit is needed to hike.
- The best-known trails are the *sentiers de grande randonnée* (GR), long-distance paths marked by red-and-white-striped track indicators.
- For complete details on regional activities, courses, equipment rental, clubs, companies and organisations, contact local tourist offices.

BUSINESS HOURS

- French business hours are regulated by a maze of government regulations, including the 35-hour working week.
- The midday break is uncommon in Paris but, in general, gets longer the further south you go.
- French law requires most businesses to close Sunday; exceptions include grocery stores, *boulangeries*, florists and businesses catering to the tourist trade.
- In many places shops close on Monday.
- Many service stations open 24 hours a day and stock basic groceries.
- Restaurants generally close one or two days of the week.
- Museums tend to close on Monday or Tuesday.
- Standard hours are as follows:

Banks 9am to noon, 2 to 5pm Monday to Friday or Tuesday to Saturday

Bars 7pm to 1am Monday to Saturday

Cafes 7am or 8am to 10pm or 11pm Monday to Saturday

Club 10pm to 3am, 4am or 5am Thusday to Saturday

Post offices 8.30am or 9am to 5pm or 6pm Monday to Friday, 8am to noon Saturday

Restaurants noon to 2.30pm (or 3pm in Paris), 7pm to 11pm (or 10pm to midnight in Paris)

Shops 9am or 10am to 7pm Monday to Saturday (often closed noon to 1.30pm)

Supermarkets 8.30am to 7pm Monday to Saturday, to 12.30pm Sunday

GAY & LESBIAN TRAVELLERS

The rainbow flag flies high in France, one of Europe's most liberal countries when it comes to homosexuality.

- Paris has been a thriving gay and lesbian centre since the late 1970s.
- Bordeaux, Lille, Lyon, Toulouse and many other towns have active communities.
- Attitudes towards homosexuality tend to be more conservative in the countryside and villages.
- Same-sex marriage has been legal in France since May 2013.
- Gay Pride marches are held in major French cities from mid-May to early July.

Online, try the following websites:

France Queer Resources Directory (www.france.qrd.org) Gay and lesbian directory.

Gaipied (www.gayvox.com/guide3) Online travel guide to France, with listings by region, by Gayvox.

INTERNET RESOURCES

France 24 (www.france24.com/en/france) French news in English.

Paris by Mouth (http://parisbymouth.com) Capital dining and drinking.

Rendez-Vous en France (www.rendezvousenfrance.com) Official French government tourist office website.

Wine Travel Guides (www.winetravelguides.com) Practical guides to France's wine regions.

LANGUAGE COURSES

- All manner of French-language courses are available in Paris and provincial towns and cities; most also arrange accommodation.
- Prices and courses vary greatly; the content can often be tailored to your specific needs (for a fee).
- The website www.europa-pages.com/france lists language schools in France.

Alliance Française (Map p366; www.alliancefr.org; 101 bd Raspail, 6e, Paris; Ⓜ St-Placide) French courses (minimum one week) for all levels. *Intensif* courses meet for four hours a day five days a week; *extensif* courses involve nine hours' tuition a week.

Eurocentres (www.eurocentres.com) This affiliation of small, well-organised schools has three addresses in France: in Amboise in the charming Loire Valley, in La Rochelle and Paris.

LEGAL MATTERS

- French police have wide powers of stop-and-search and can demand proof of identity at any time.
- Foreigners must be able to prove their legal status in France (eg passport, visa, residency permit).
- French law doesn't distinguish between hard and soft drugs; penalties can be severe (including fines and jail sentences).

MONEY

Credit and debit cards are accepted almost everywhere in France.

- Some places (eg 24-hour petrol stations and some *autoroute* toll machines) only take credit cards with chips and PINs.
- In Paris and major cities, *bureaux de change* (exchange bureaus) are fast and easy, are open long hours and offer competitive exchange rates.

For lost cards, call your credit card company:

Amex (☎01 47 77 70 00)

MasterCard (☎08 00 90 13 87)

Visa (Carte Bleue; ☎08 00 90 11 79)

PUBLIC HOLIDAYS

The following *jours fériés* (public holidays) are observed in France:

New Year's Day (Jour de l'An) 1 January

Easter Sunday & Monday (Pâques & Lundi de Pâques) Late March/April

May Day (Fête du Travail) 1 May

Victoire 1945 8 May – WWII armistice

Ascension Thursday (Ascension) May – celebrated on the 40th day after Easter

Pentecost/Whit Sunday & Whit Monday (Pentecôte & Lundi de Pentecôte) Mid-May to mid-June – celebrated on the seventh Sunday after Easter

Bastille Day/National Day (Fête Nationale) 14 July – *the* national holiday

Assumption Day (Assomption) 15 August

All Saints' Day (Toussaint) 1 November

Remembrance Day (L'onze Novembre) 11 November – WWI armistice

Christmas (Noël) 25 December

TELEPHONE

Mobile Phones

- French mobile phone numbers begin with ☎06 or ☎07.
- France uses GSM 900/1800, which is compatible with the rest of Europe and Australia but not with the North American GSM 1900 or the totally different system in Japan (though some North Americans have tri-band phones that work here).
- It is usually cheaper to buy a local SIM card from a French provider such as Orange, SFR, Bouygues and Free Mobile than to use international roaming. To do this, ensure your phone is 'unlocked'.
- Recharge cards are sold at most *tabacs* (tobacconist-newsagents) and supermarkets.

Phone Codes & Useful Numbers

Calling France from abroad Dial your country's international access code, then ☎33 (France's country code), then the 10-digit local number *without* the initial zero.

Calling internationally from France Dial ☎00 (the international access code), the *indicatif* (country code), the area code (without the initial zero if there is one) and the local number.

Directory inquiries For national *service des renseignements* (directory inquiries) dial ☎11 87 12 or use the service for free online at www.118712.fr.

Emergency numbers Can be dialled from public phones without a phonecard.

VISAS

For up-to-date details on visa requirements, check the **Ministère des Affaires Étrangères** (Ministry of Foreign Affairs; Map p366; www.diplomatie.gouv.fr; 37 quai d'Orsay, 7e).

ESSENTIAL FOOD & DRINK

When you think of France it is pretty easy to start drooling over its world-renowned cuisine. Here are some taste sensations to get your mouth watering:

- **Fondue & raclette** Warming cheese dishes in the French Alps.
- **Oysters & white wine** Everywhere on the Atlantic coast, but especially in Cancale and Bordeaux.
- **Bouillabaisse** Marseille's signature hearty fish stew, eaten with croutons and *rouille* (garlic-and-chilli mayonnaise).
- **Foie gras & truffles** The Dordogne features goose and 'black diamonds' from December to March. Provence is also good for indulging in the aphrodisiacal fungi.
- **Piggy-part cuisine** Lyon is famous for its juicy *andouillette* (pig-intestine sausage), a perfect marriage with a local Côtes du Rhône red.
- **Champagne** Tasting in century-old cellars is an essential part of Champagne's bubbly experience.
- **Bordeaux & Burgundy wines** You'll find France's signature reds in every restaurant; now find out more by touring the vineyards.

Visa requirements:

- EU nationals and citizens of Iceland, Norway and Switzerland need only a passport or national identity card to enter France and stay in the country, even for stays of over 90 days. Citizens of new EU member states may be subject to various limitations on living and working in France.
- Citizens of Australia, the USA, Canada, Israel, Hong Kong, Japan, Malaysia, New Zealand, Singapore, South Korea and many Latin American countries do not need visas to visit France as tourists for up to 90 days. For longer stays of over 90 days, contact your nearest French embassy or consulate.
- Other people wishing to come to France as tourists have to apply for a Schengen Visa.
- Tourist visas cannot be changed into student visas after arrival. However, short-term visas are available for students sitting university-entrance exams in France.
- Citizens of Australia, Canada, Japan and New Zealand aged between 18 and 30 are eligible for a 12-month, multiple-entry **Working Holiday Visa** (Permis Vacances Travail).

EATING PRICE RANGES

Price ranges refer to a two-course meal.

€ less than €20

€€ €20 to €40

€€€ more than €40

Getting There & Away

AIR

International airports include the following; there are many smaller ones serving European destinations only.

Aéroport de Charles de Gaulle (CDG; www.aeroportsdeparis.fr)

Aéroport d'Orly (www.aeroportsdeparis.fr)

Aéroport Marseille-Provence (MRS; ☎ 04 42 14 14 14; www.marseille.aeroport.fr)

Aéroport Nice Côte d'Azur (http://societe.nice.aeroport.fr)

LAND

Bus

Eurolines (☎ 08 92 89 90 91; www.eurolines.eu), a grouping of 32 long-haul coach operators, links France with cities all across Europe and in Morocco and Russia. Discounts are available to people under 26 and over 60. Make advance reservations, especially in July and August.

Car & Motorcycle

A right-hand-drive vehicle brought to France from the UK or Ireland must have deflectors affixed to the headlights to avoid dazzling oncoming traffic.

Departing from the UK, **Eurotunnel Le Shuttle** (☎ in France 08 10 63 03 04, in UK 08443-35 35 35; www.eurotunnel.com) trains whisk bicycles, motorcycles, cars and coaches in 35 minutes from Folkestone through the Channel Tunnel to Coquelles, 5km southwest of Calais. Shuttles run 24 hours a day, with up to three departures an hour during peak periods. The earlier you book, the less you pay. Fares for a car, including up to nine passengers, start at €30.

Train

➡ Rail services – including a dwindling number of overnight services to/from Spain, Italy and Germany, and Eurostar services to/from the UK – link France with virtually every country in Europe.

➡ Book tickets and get train information from **Rail Europe** (www.raileurope.com). In France, ticketing is handled by **SNCF** (www.voyages-sncf.com); internet bookings are possible, but it won't post tickets outside France.

SEA

Regular ferries travel to France from the UK, Ireland and Italy.

Brittany Ferries (www.brittany-ferries.co.uk) Links between England/Ireland and Brittany and Normandy.

P&O Ferries (www.poferries.com) Ferries between England and northern France.

SNCM (www.sncm.fr) Ferries between France and Sardinia.

Getting Around

AIR

Air France (www.airfrance.com) and its subsidiaries **Hop!** (www.hop.com) and **Transavia** (www.transavia.com) control the lion's share of France's domestic airline industry.

Budget carriers offering flights within France include **EasyJet** (www.easyjet.com), **Twin Jet** (www.twinjet.net) and **Air Corsica** (www.aircorsica.com).

BUS

Buses are widely used for short-distance travel within *départements*, especially in rural areas with relatively few train lines (eg Brittany and Normandy). Unfortunately, services in some regions are infrequent and slow, in part because they were designed to get children to school rather than transport visitors around the countryside.

BICYCLE

France is a great place to cycle, and French train company SNCF does its best to make travelling with a bicycle easy; see www.velo.sncf.com for full details.

Most French cities and towns have at least one bike shop that rents out mountain bikes (VTT; around €15 a day), road bikes (VTCs) and cheaper city bikes. You have to leave ID and/or a deposit (often a credit-card slip) that you forfeit if the bike is damaged or stolen. A growing number of cities have automatic bike-rental systems.

CAR & MOTORCYCLE

A car gives you exceptional freedom and allows you to visit more remote parts of France. But it can be expensive and, in cities, parking and traffic are frequently a major headache. Motorcyclists will find France great for touring, with winding roads of good quality and lots of stunning scenery.

➡ All drivers must carry a national ID card or passport; a valid driving licence (*permis de conduire*; most foreign licences can be used in France for up to a year); car-ownership papers, known as a *carte grise* (grey card); and proof of third-party (liability) insurance.

➡ Many French motorways *(autoroutes)* are fitted with toll *(péage)* stations that charge a fee based on the distance you've travelled; factor in these costs when driving.

➡ To hire a car you'll usually need to be over 21 and in possession of a valid driving licence and a credit card. Automatic transmissions are very rare in France; you'll need to order one well in advance.

TRAIN

France's superb rail network is operated by the state-owned **SNCF** (www.sncf.com); many rural towns not on the SNCF train network are served by SNCF buses.

➡ The flagship trains on French railways are the superfast TGVs, which reach speeds in excess of 200mph and can whisk you from Paris to the Côte d'Azur in as little as three hours.

➡ Before boarding any train, you must validate *(composter)* your ticket by time-stamping it in a

CONNECTIONS

➡ High-speed trains link Paris' Gare du Nord with London's St Pancras (via the Channel Tunnel/Eurostar rail service) in just over two hours; Gare du Nord is also the point of departure for speedy trains to Brussels, Amsterdam and Cologne.

➡ Many more trains make travelling between the French capital and pretty much any city in every neighbouring country a real pleasure.

➡ Regular bus and rail links cross the French–Spanish border via the Pyrenees, and the French–Italian border via the Alps and the southern Mediterranean coast.

SNCF TRAIN FARES & DISCOUNTS

The Basics

- 1st-class travel, where available, costs 20% to 30% extra.
- Ticket prices for some trains, including most TGVs, are pricier during peak periods.
- The further in advance you reserve, the lower the fares.
- Children under four travel for free (€9 to any destination if they need a seat).
- Children aged four to 11 travel for half price.

Discount Tickets

Prem's The SNCF's most heavily discounted, use-or-lose tickets are sold online, by phone and at ticket windows/machines a maximum of 90 days and a minimum of 14 days before you travel.

Bons Plans A grab-bag of cheap options for different routes/dates, advertised online under the tab 'Dernière Minute' (Last Minute).

iDTGV Cheap tickets on advance-purchase TGV travel between about 30 cities; only sold at www.idtgv.com.

Discount Cards

Reductions of 25% to 60% are available with several discount cards (valid for one year):

Carte Jeune (€50) Available to travellers aged 12 to 27.

Carte Enfant+ (€75) For one to four adults travelling with a child aged four to 11.

Carte Sénior+ (€50) For travellers over 60.

composteur, one of those yellow posts located on the way to the platform.

Rail Passes

Residents of Europe (who do not live in France) can purchase an **InterRail One Country Pass** (www.interrailnet.com; 3/4/6/8 days €216/237/302/344, 12-25yr €147/157/199/222), which entitles its bearer to unlimited travel on SNCF trains for three to eight days over the course of a month.

For non-European residents, Rail Europe (p435) offers the **France Rail Pass** (www.francerailpass.com; 3/6/9 days over 1 month €211/301/388).

You need to really rack up the kilometres to make these passes worthwhile.

Germany

Includes ➡

Best Castles & Palaces

- Schloss Neuschwanstein (p472)
- Burg Eltz (p491)
- Wartburg (p461)
- Schloss Sanssouci (p452)

Best Iconic Sights

- Brandenburger Tor (Gate) (p441)
- Holstentor (p505)
- Kölner Dom (p492)
- Frauenkirche (p455)

Why Go?

Prepare for a roller coaster of feasts, treats and temptations as you take in Germany's soul-stirring scenery, spirit-lifting culture, old and bold architecture, big-city beauties, romantic castles and towns with half-timbered buildings.

Few countries have had as much impact on the world as Germany, which has given us the printing press, the automobile, aspirin and MP3 technology. This is the birthplace of Martin Luther, Albert Einstein and Karl Marx, of Bach, Beethoven, the Brothers Grimm and other heavyweights who have left their mark on human history.

Germany's story-book landscapes will also likely leave an even bigger imprint on your memories. There's something undeniably artistic in the way the scenery unfolds from the windswept maritime north to the off-the-charts splendour of the Alps. As much fun as it may be to rev up the engines on the autobahn, do slow down to better appreciate this complex and fascinating country.

When to Go

Berlin

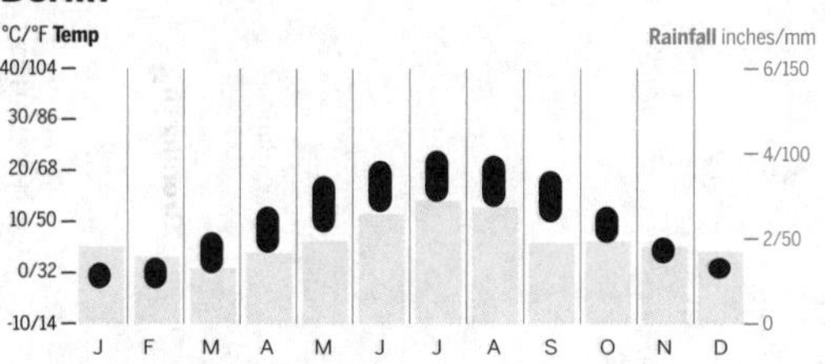

Jun–Aug Warm summers cause Germans to shed their clothes; night never seems to come.

Sep Radiant foliage and sunny skies invite outdoor pursuits, with festivals (Oktoberfest!) galore.

Dec It's icy, it's cold but lines are short and Alpine slopes and twinkly Christmas markets beckon.

Germany Highlights

1 Discover your inner party animal in **Berlin** (p440); save sleep for somewhere else as there's no time here with the clubs, museums, bars and ever-changing zeitgeist.

2 Time your journey for **Oktoberfest** (p463), Munich's bacchanal of suds, or just soak up the vibe in a beer garden.

3 Go slow in Germany's alluring small towns like **Bamberg** (p477), with winding lanes, smoked beer (!) and a lack of cliché.

4 Compare the soaring peaks of the Dom in **Cologne** (p492) with the slinky glasses of the city's famous beer.

5 Go cuckoo in the **Black Forest** (p479), discovering

0 100 km
0 50 miles

SWEDEN
DENMARK
NETHERLANDS
POLAND
North Sea
Baltic Sea
Fakse Bugt
Bornholmsgat
Langelandsbælt
Ertholmene Islands
Rügen Island
North Frisian Islands
East Frisian Islands
Frisian Islands
Waddeneilanden
Esbjerg
Kolding
Sylt
Westerland
Flensburg
Husum
Puttgarden
Kiel
Neumünster
Barth
Stralsund
Sassnitz
Binz
Greifswald
Warnemünde
Rostock
SCHLESWIG-HOLSTEIN
Cuxhaven
Elbe River
Hamburg 7
Lübeck
Wismar
Schwerin
MECKLENBURG-WESTERN POMERANIA
Neubrandenburg
Pasewalk
Szczecin
Lake Müritz
Müritz NP
Neustrelitz
Norddeich
Wilhelmshaven
Bremerhaven
Emden
Groningen
Oldenburg
Bremen
Lüneburg
Rheinsberg
BRANDENBURG
Salzwedel
Ems
LOWER SAXONY
IJssel
Celle
Stendal
Elbe
Berlin 1
Oder
Frankfurt (Oder)
Wolfsburg
Brandenburg an der Havel
Potsdam
Osnabrück
Hanover
SAXONY-ANHALT
Enschede
Hamelin
Hildesheim
Braunschweig
Magdeburg
Arnhem
Münster
Bielefeld
Bad Harzburg
Goslar
Dessau-Rosslau
Lutherstadt Wittenberg
Lübben
Cottbus
NORTH RHINE-WESTPHALIA
Paderborn
Quedlinburg
Harz Mountains
Maas
Hamm
Gelsenkirchen
Göttingen
Dortmund
Duisburg
Essen
Bochum
Kassel
Halle
Leipzig
SAXONY
Bautzen
Meissen
Görlitz
Mühlhausen
Düsseldorf
Mönchengladbach
THURINGIA
Dresden 6

its chilly crags, misty peaks and endless trails.

6 Get into the swing of **Dresden** (p455), with a creative culture beyond the restorations.

7 Cruise around one of the world's great harbours in **Hamburg** (p498), then follow the trail of the Beatles.

8 Discover the best-preserved Roman ruins north of the Alps in **Trier** (p490), a delightful wine town on the Moselle.

ITINERARIES

Three Days

Come on, that's all you got? If the answer is really yes, drive the **Romantic Road**, stopping in Rothenburg ob der Tauber and Füssen, then spend the rest of your time in **Munich**.

Five Days

Spend a couple of days in **Berlin**, head down to **Dresden** and **Nuremberg** for half a day each and wrap up your trip in **Munich**.

One Week

This gives you a little bit of time to tailor a tour beyond the highlights mentioned above. Art fans might want to build **Cologne** or **Düsseldorf** into their itinerary; romantics could consider **Heidelberg**, a Rhine cruise or a trip down the **Romantic Road**; while nature types are likely to be lured by **Garmisch-Partenkirchen**, **Berchtesgaden** or the **Black Forest**.

BERLIN

☎030 / POP 3.5 MILLION

Bismarck and Marx, Einstein and Hitler, JFK and Bowie, they've all shaped – and been shaped by – Berlin, whose richly textured history stares you in the face at every turn. You might be distracted by the trendy, edgy, gentrified streets, by the bars bleeding a laid-back cool factor, by the galleries sprouting talent and pushing the envelope, but make no mistake – reminders of the German capital's past assault you while modernity sits around the corner.

Renowned for its diversity and tolerance, its alternative culture and night-owl stamina, the best thing about Berlin is the way it reinvents itself and isn't shackled by its unique past. And the world knows this – a steady stream of Germans from other parts of the country and a league of global expatriates are flocking here to see what all the fuss is about.

Berlin

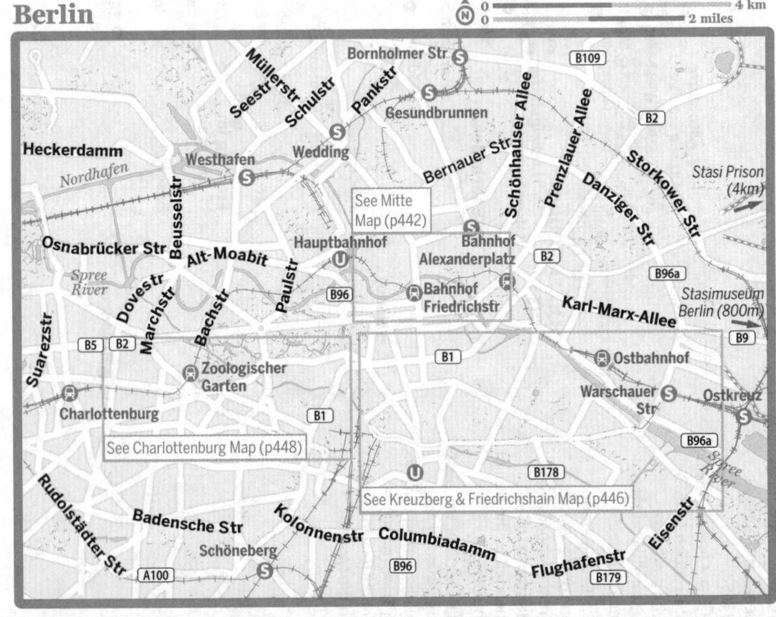

Sights

Key sights like the Reichstag, the Brandenburger Tor, Fernsehturm and Museumsinsel cluster in the historic city centre – **Mitte**. It also encompasses the maze-like historic Jewish quarter around Hackescher Markt, which now teems with fashionable boutiques, bars and restaurants. North of here, residential **Prenzlauer Berg** has a lively cafe and restaurant scene, while to the south loom the contemporary high-rises of **Potsdamer Platz**. Further south, gritty but cool **Kreuzberg** is party central, as is student-flavoured **Friedrichshain** east across the Spree River. Western Berlin's hub is **Charlottenburg**, with great shopping and a swish royal palace.

Historic Mitte

★Reichstag HISTORIC BUILDING

(Map p442; www.bundestag.de; Platz der Republik 1, Service Center: Scheidemannstrasse; lift ride 8am-midnight, last entry 11pm, Service Center 8am-8pm Apr-Oct, to 6pm Nov-Mar; 100, S Bundestag, Hauptbahnhof, Brandenburger Tor) FREE One of Berlin's most iconic buildings, the 1894 Reichstag was burned, bombed, rebuilt, buttressed by the Berlin Wall, wrapped in fabric and eventually turned into the home of Germany's parliament, the Bundestag, by Lord Norman Foster. Its most distinctive feature, the glittering glass dome, is accessible by lift (reservations mandatory, see www.bundestag.de) and affords fabulous 360-degree city views. Those without a reservation can try scoring left-over tickets in the Service Center. Bring ID.

★Brandenburger Tor & Pariser Platz LANDMARK

(Map p442; Pariser Platz; 24hr; S Brandenburger Tor, Brandenburger Tor) FREE A symbol of division during the Cold War, the landmark Brandenburg Gate now epitomises German reunification. Modelled after the Acropolis in Athens, the triumphal arch was completed in 1791 as the royal city gate and is crowned by the Quadriga sculpture – a winged goddess of victory piloting a horse-drawn chariot.

Holocaust Memorial MEMORIAL

(Memorial to the Murdered European Jews; Map p446; 030-2639 4336; www.stiftung-denkmal.de; Cora-Berliner-Strasse 1; audioguide adult/concession €4/2; field 24hr, information centre 10am-8pm Tue-Sun Apr-Sep, to 7pm Oct-Mar, last entry 45min before closing; S Brandenburger Tor, Brandenburger Tor) FREE Inaugurated in 2005, this football-field-sized memorial by American architect Peter Eisenman consists of 2711 sarcophagi-like concrete columns rising in sombre silence from undulating ground. You're free to access this maze at any point and make your individual journey through it. For context visit the subterranean **Ort der Information**; the exhibits will leave no one untouched. Audioguides are available.

Hitler's Bunker HISTORIC SITE

(Map p446; cnr In den Ministergärten & Gertrud-Kolmar-Strasse; 24hr; S Brandenburger Tor, Brandenburger Tor) Berlin was burning and Soviet tanks were advancing relentlessly when Adolf Hitler committed suicide on 30 April 1945, alongside Eva Braun, his long-time female companion, hours after their marriage. Today, a parking lot covers the site, revealing its dark history only via

BERLIN IN...

One Day

Book ahead for an early lift ride to the **Reichstag** dome, then snap a picture of the **Brandenburger Tor (Gate)** before stumbling around the **Holocaust Memorial** and admiring the contemporary architecture of **Potsdamer Platz**. Ponder Cold War madness at **Checkpoint Charlie**, then head to **Museumsinsel** to admire Queen Nefertiti and the Ishtar Gate. Finish up with a night of mirth and gaiety around **Hackescher Markt**.

Two Days

Kick off day two coming to grips with what life was like in divided Berlin at the **Gedenkstätte Berliner Mauer**. Intensify the experience at the **DDR Museum** or on a walk along the **East Side Gallery**. Spend the afternoon soaking up the urban spirit of **Kreuzberg** with its sassy shops and street art, grab dinner along the canal, drinks around Kottbusser Tor and finish up with a night of clubbing.

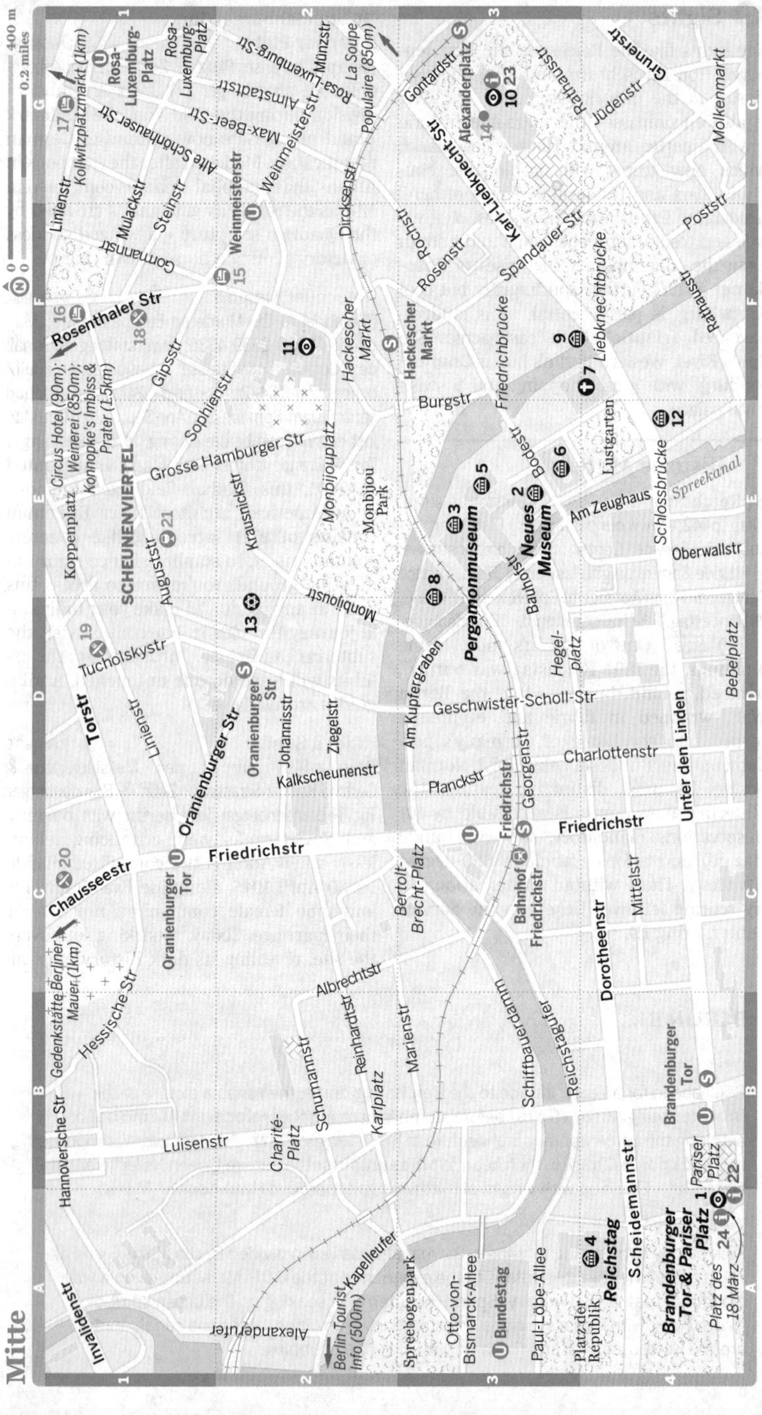

Mitte

0 — 400 m
0 — 0.2 miles

A B C D E F G
1 2 3 4

Invalidenstr
Hannoversche Str
Gedenkstätte Berliner Mauer (1km)
Hessische Str
Chausseestr
20
Torstr
Tucholskystr
19
Koppenplatz
Circus Hotel (90m); Weinerei (850m); Konnopke's Imbiss & Prater (1.5km)
Rosenthaler Str
16
18
Linienstr
17
Kollwitzplatzmarkt (1km)
Rosa-Luxemburg-Platz
SCHEUNENVIERTEL
Mulackstr
Gormannstr
Steinstr
Alte Schönhauser Str
Rosa-Luxemburg-Platz
Linienstr
Auguststr
21
Gipsstr
Sophienstr
Grosse Hamburger Str
Oranienburger Tor
Oranienburger Str
Luisenstr
Friedrichstr
15
Weinmeisterstr
Max-Beer-Str
Almstadtstr
Rosa-Luxemburg-Str
Münzstr
Oranienburger Str
13
Krausnickstr
11
Alexanderufer
Charité-Platz
Johannisstr
Schumannstr
Ziegelstr
Kalkscheunenstr
Monbijoustr
Monbijouplatz
Weinmeisterstr
Berlin Tourist Info (500m)
Kapelleufer
Reinhardtstr
Albrechtstr
Karlplatz
Monbijou Park
Hackescher Markt
Dircksenstr
La Soupe Populaire (850m)
Spreebogenpark
Marienstr
Bertolt-Brecht-Platz
Am Kupfergraben
8
Hackescher Markt
Rochstr
Gontardstr
Otto-von-Bismarck-Allee
Planckstr
Geschwister-Scholl-Str
3
Pergamonmuseum
5
Burgstr
Rosenstr
Karl-Liebknecht-Str
Alexanderplatz
14
10
23
Bundestag
Friedrichstr
Bahnhof Friedrichstr
Schiffbauerdamm
Georgenstr
Bauhofstr
Neues Museum
2
Bodestr
Friedrichbrücke
Spandauer Str
Paul-Löbe-Allee
Reichstagufer
Hegelplatz
6
9
Rathausstr
Platz der Republik
4
Reichstag
Dorotheenstr
Friedrichstr
Charlottenstr
Am Zeughaus
7
Lustgarten
Liebknechtbrücke
Jüdenstr
Scheidemannstr
Mittelstr
Schlossbrücke
12
Grunerstr
Brandenburger Tor & Pariser Platz
1
Pariser Platz
Brandenburger Tor
Unter den Linden
Oberwallstr
Spreekanal
Rathausstr
Poststr
Molkenmarkt
Platz des 18 März
24
22
Bebelplatz

Mitte

Top Sights

Sights

Activities, Courses & Tours

Sleeping

Eating

Drinking & Nightlife

Information

an information panel with a diagram of the vast bunker network, construction data and the site's post-WWII history.

Checkpoint Charlie HISTORIC SITE

(Map p446; cnr Zimmerstrasse & Friedrichstrasse; 24hr; Kochstrasse, Stadtmitte) Checkpoint Charlie was the principal gateway for foreigners and diplomats between the two Berlins from 1961 to 1990. Unfortunately, this potent symbol of the Cold War has become a tacky tourist trap, although a free open-air exhibit that illustrates milestones in Cold War history is one redeeming aspect.

Museumsinsel & Scheunenviertel

Museumsinsel (Museum Island) is Berlin's most important treasure trove, spanning 6000 years' worth of art, artefacts, sculpture and architecture from Europe and beyond. It segues into the Scheunenviertel (Barn Quarter), a compact and charismatic quarter filled with idyllic courtyards, bleeding-edge art galleries, local designer boutiques, shabby-chic bars and even a belle époque ballroom. Since reunification, the Scheunenviertel has also reprised its historic role as Berlin's main Jewish quarter.

★ **Pergamonmuseum** MUSEUM

(Map p442; 030-266 424 242; www.smb.museum; Bodestrasse 1-3; adult/concession €12/6; 10am-6pm Fri-Wed, to 8pm Thu; 100, Hackescher Markt, Friedrichstrasse) Even while undergoing renovation, the Pergamonmuseum still opens a fascinating window onto the ancient world. The palatial three-wing complex unites a rich feast of classical sculpture and monumental architecture from Greece, Rome, Babylon and the Middle East, including such famous stunners as the radiant-blue **Ishtar Gate** from Babylon, the Roman **Market Gate of Miletus** and the **Caliph's Palace** of Mshatta. Note that the namesake Pergamon Altar will be off limits until 2019.

★ **Neues Museum** MUSEUM

(New Museum; Map p442; 030-266 424 242; www.smb.museum; Bodestrasse 1-3; adult/concession €12/6; 10am-6pm Fri-Wed, to 8pm Thu; 100, 200, Hackescher Markt) David Chipperfield's reconstruction of the bombed-out Neues Museum is now the residence of Queen Nefertiti, the show-stopper of the Egyptian Museum that also features mummies, sculptures and sarcophagi. Pride of place of the Museum of Pre- and Early History in the same building goes to Trojan antiquities, a Neanderthal skull and a 3000-year-old gilded conical ceremonial hat. Museum tickets are only valid for admission during a designated half-hour time slot. Skip the queue by buying advance tickets online.

Berliner Dom CHURCH

(Berlin Cathedral; Map p442; 030-2026 9136; www.berlinerdom.de; Am Lustgarten; adult/concession/under 18yr €7/4/free; 9am-8pm Sun Apr-Sep, to 7pm Oct-Mar; 100, 200, Hackescher Markt) Pompous yet majestic, the Italian Renaissance–style former church of the royal court (1905) does triple duty as house of worship, museum and concert hall. Inside it's gilt to the hilt and outfitted with a lavish marble-and-onyx altar, a 7269-pipe Sauer organ and elaborate royal sarcophagi. Climb up the 267 steps to the gallery for glorious city views.

MORE MUSEUMSINSEL TREASURES

While the Pergamonmuseum and the Neues Museum are the highlights of Museumsinsel (Museum Island), the other three museums are no slouches in the treasure department either. Fronting the Lustgarten park the **Altes Museum** (Old Museum; Map p442; ☎030-266 424 242; www.smb.museum; Am Lustgarten; adult/concession €10/5; ⏲10am-6pm Tue, Wed & Fri-Sun, to 8pm Thu; 🚌100, 200, 🚉Friedrichstrasse, Hackescher Markt) presents Greek, Etruscan and Roman antiquities. At the northern tip of the island, the **Bodemuseum** (Map p442; ☎030-266 424 242; www.smb.museum; Am Kupfergraben/Monbijoubrücke; adult/concession €10/5; ⏲10am-6pm Tue, Wed & Fri-Sun, to 8pm Thu; 🚉Hackescher Markt) has a prized collection of European sculpture from the Middle Ages to the 18th century. Finally, there's the **Alte Nationalgalerie** (Old National Gallery; Map p442; ☎030-266 424 242; www.smb.museum; Bodestrasse 1-3; adult/concession €10/5; ⏲10am-6pm Tue, Wed & Fri-Sun, to 8pm Thu; 🚌100, 200, 🚉Hackescher Markt), one thematic focus of which is on 19th-century European painting. A combined day pass for all five museums costs €18 (concession €9).

DDR Museum MUSEUM

(GDR Museum; Map p442; ☎030-847 123 731; www.ddr-museum.de; Karl-Liebknecht-Strasse 1; adult/concession €6/4; ⏲10am-8pm Sun-Fri, to 10pm Sat; 👪; 🚌100, 200, 🚉Hackescher Markt) This interactive museum does a delightful job at pulling back the iron curtain on an extinct society. Find out that East German kids were put through collective potty training, engineers earned little more than farmers and everyone, it seems, went on nudist holidays. A highlight is a simulated ride in a Trabi.

Fernsehturm LANDMARK

(TV Tower; Map p442; ☎030-247 575 875; www.tv-turm.de; Panoramastrasse 1a; adult/child €13/8.50, Fast View ticket €19.50/11.50; ⏲9am-midnight Mar-Oct, 10am-midnight Nov-Feb; Ⓢ Alexanderplatz, 🚉Alexanderplatz) Germany's tallest structure, the 368m-high TV Tower is as iconic to Berlin as the Eiffel Tower is to Paris. On clear days, views from the panorama level at 203m are unbeatable. The upstairs Restaurant Sphere (mains €14 to €28) makes one revolution per hour. To skip the line, buy tickets online.

Hackesche Höfe HISTORIC SITE

(Map p442; ☎030-2809 8010; www.hackesche-hoefe.com; Rosenthaler Strasse 40/41, Sophienstrasse 6; 🚌M1, 🚉Hackescher Markt) FREE Thanks to its congenial mix of cafes, galleries, boutiques and entertainment venues, this attractively restored complex of eight interlinked courtyards is hugely popular with the tourist brigade. **Court I**, festooned with patterned art nouveau tiles, is the prettiest. **Court VII** leads off to the romantic **Rosenhöfe**, a single courtyard with a sunken rose garden and tendril-like balustrades.

Neue Synagoge SYNAGOGUE

(Map p442; ☎030-8802 8300; www.centrumjudaicum.de; Oranienburger Strasse 28-30; adult/concession €3.50/3, dome €2/1.50; ⏲10am-8pm Sun & Mon, to 6pm Tue-Thu, to 5pm Fri, 10am-6pm Sun & Mon Nov-Feb, 10am-2pm Fri Oct-Mar); Ⓢ Oranienburger Tor, 🚉Oranienburger Strasse) The original New Synagogue, finished in 1866 in what was then the predominantly Jewish part of the city, was Germany's largest synagogue at that time. It was destroyed in World War II and rebuilt after the Berlin Wall fell. Now this space doubles as a museum and cultural centre documenting local Jewish life.

Gedenkstätte Berliner Mauer MEMORIAL

(Berlin Wall Memorial; ☎030-467 986 666; www.berliner-mauer-gedenkstaette.de; Bernauer Strasse btwn Schwedter Strasse & Gartenstrasse; ⏲visitor center 9.30am-7pm Apr-Oct, to 6pm Nov-Mar, open-air exhibit 8am-10pm; 🚉Nordbahnhof, Bernauer Strasse, Eberswalder Strasse) FREE The central memorial site of German division extends for 1.4km along Bernauer Strasse and incorporates a section of original Wall, vestiges of the border installations and escape tunnels, a chapel and a monument. It's the only place where you can see how border fortifications developed over time. Multimedia stations, 'archaeological windows' and markers provide context and details about events that took place along here. For a great overview climb up the viewing platform at the Documentation Centre near Ackerstrasse.

Potsdamer Platz & Tiergarten

Berlin newest quarter, Potsdamer Platz was forged in the 1990s from ground once bisected by the Berlin Wall and is a showcase of contemporary architecture, with Helmut Jahn's **Sony Center** being the most eye-catching structure.

The adjacent **Kulturforum** harbours art museums and the world-famous Berliner Philharmonie. With its rambling paths and hidden beer gardens, the Tiergarten, one of Europe's largest city parks, makes for a perfect sightseeing break.

★Gemäldegalerie GALLERY

(Gallery of Paintings; Map p448; ☎030-266 424 242; www.smb.museum/gg; Matthäikirchplatz 8; adult/concession €10/5; ⏰10am-6pm Tue, Wed & Fri-Sun, to 8pm Thu; 🚌M29, M41, 200, Ⓢ Potsdamer Platz, Ⓤ Potsdamer Platz) The principal Kulturforum museum boasts one of the world's finest and most comprehensive collections of European art from the 13th to the 18th centuries. Wear comfy shoes when exploring the 72 galleries: a walk past masterpieces by Rembrandt, Dürer, Hals, Vermeer, Gainsborough and many more old masters covers almost 2km.

Topographie des Terrors MUSEUM

(Topography of Terror; Map p446; ☎030-2548 0950; www.topographie.de; Niederkirchner Strasse 8; ⏰10am-8pm, grounds until dusk or 8pm latest; 👪; Ⓢ Potsdamer Platz, Ⓤ Potsdamer Platz) FREE In the same spot where the most feared institutions of Nazi Germany (including the Gestapo headquarters and the SS central command) once stood, this compelling exhibit chronicles the stages of terror and persecution, puts a face on the perpetrators and details the impact these brutal institutions had on all of Europe. A second exhibit outside zeroes in on how life changed for Berlin and its people after the Nazis made it their capital.

Kreuzberg & Friedrichshain

Kreuzberg has a split personality: while its western section (around Bergmannstrasse) has an upmarket, genteel air, eastern Kreuzberg (around Kottbusser Tor) is a multicultural mosaic and raucous nightlife hub. You'll find more after-dark action along with some Cold War relics (including Karl-Marx-Allee, East Berlin's showcase socialist boulevard) in student-flavoured Friedrichshain across the Spree.

East Side Gallery HISTORIC SITE

(Map p446; www.eastsidegallery-berlin.de; Mühlenstrasse btwn Oberbaumbrücke & Ostbahnhof; ⏰24hr; Ⓢ Warschauer Strasse, Ⓤ Ostbahnhof, Warschauer Strasse) FREE The year was 1989. After 28 years, the Berlin Wall, that grim and grey divider of humanity, finally met its maker. Most of it was quickly dismantled along the Spree, but a 1.3km stretch became the East Side Gallery, the world's largest open-air mural collection. In more than 100 paintings, dozens of international artists translated the era's global euphoria and optimism into a mix of political statements, drug-induced musings and truly artistic visions.

Jüdisches Museum MUSEUM

(Jewish Museum; Map p446; ☎030-2599 3300; www.jmberlin.de; Lindenstrasse 9-14; adult/concession €8/3; ⏰10am-10pm Mon, to 8pm Tue-Sun, last admission 1hr before closing; Ⓢ Hallesches Tor, Kochstrasse) In a landmark building by American-Polish architect Daniel Libeskind, Berlin's Jewish Museum offers a chronicle of the trials and triumphs in 2000 years of Jewish history in Germany. The exhibit smoothly navigates through all major periods, from the Middle Ages via the Enlightenment to the community's current renaissance. Find

RECONSTRUCTION OF THE BERLIN CITY PALACE

In July 2013 construction of the Humboldt-Forum finally got underway on Schlossplatz. The facade of the humungous project will replicate the baroque Berliner Stadtschloss (Berlin City Palace), which was blown up by the East German government in 1950 and replaced 26 years later with an asbestos-riddled multipurpose hall called Palace of the Republic, which itself met the wrecking ball in 2006. The modern interior will be a forum for science, education and intercultural dialogue, and will shelter the Museum of Ethnology and the Museum of Asian Art – both currently in the outer suburb of Dahlem – as well as the Central State Library and university collections. Projected completion date is 2019. Get a sneak preview at the **Humboldt-Box** (Map p442; ☎0180-503 0707; www.humboldt-box.com; Schlossplatz; admission €2; ⏰10am-7pm; 🚌100, 200, Ⓢ Hausvogteiplatz), the oddly shaped structure next to the construction site, which also offers great views from the rooftop cafe terrace.

Kreuzberg & Friedrichshain

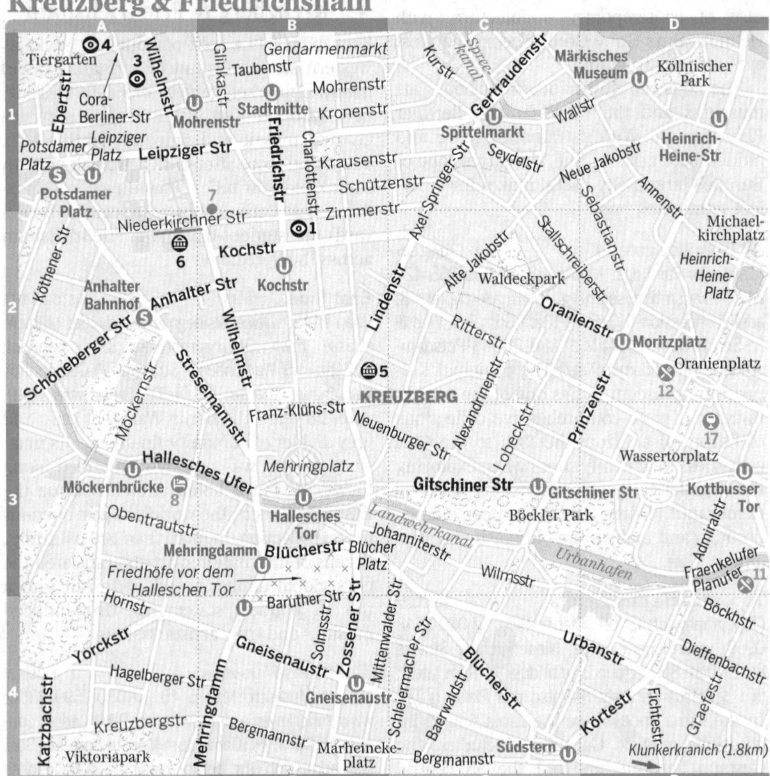

out about Jewish cultural contributions, holiday traditions, the difficult road to emancipation, and outstanding individuals such as the philosopher Moses Mendelssohn, jeans inventor Levi Strauss and the painter Felix Nussbaum.

Stasimuseum Berlin MUSEUM
(030-553 6854; www.stasimuseum.de; Haus 1, Ruschestrasse 103; adult/concession €5/4; 10am-6pm Mon-Fri, noon-6pm Sat & Sun; S Magdalenenstrasse) The former head office of the Ministry of State Security is now a museum, where you can marvel at cunningly low-tech surveillance devices (hidden in watering cans, rocks, even neckties), a prisoner transport van with teensy, lightless cells and the obsessively neat offices of Stasi chief Erich Mielke.

Stasi Prison MEMORIAL
(Gedenkstätte Hohenschönhausen; 030-9860 8230; http://en.stiftung-hsh.de; Genslerstrasse 66; adult/concession €5/2.50; German tours hourly 11am-3pm Mon-Fri Mar-Oct, 11am, 1pm & 3pm Mon-Fri Nov-Feb, hourly 10am-4pm Sat & Sun year-round, English tours 2.30pm Wed, Sat & Sun; M5 to Freienwalder Strasse) Victims of Stasi persecution often ended up in this grim remand prison, now a memorial site officially called Gedenkstätte Hohenschönhausen. Tours reveal the full extent of the terror and cruelty perpetrated upon thousands of suspected regime opponents, many utterly innocent. A new exhibit documents the history of the prison. To get here, take tram M5 from Alexanderplatz to Freienwalder Strasse, then walk 10 minutes along Freienwalder Strasse.

City West & Charlottenburg

The glittering heart of West Berlin during the Cold War, Charlottenburg has been eclipsed by historic Mitte and other eastern districts since reunification, but is now trying hard to stage a comeback with major

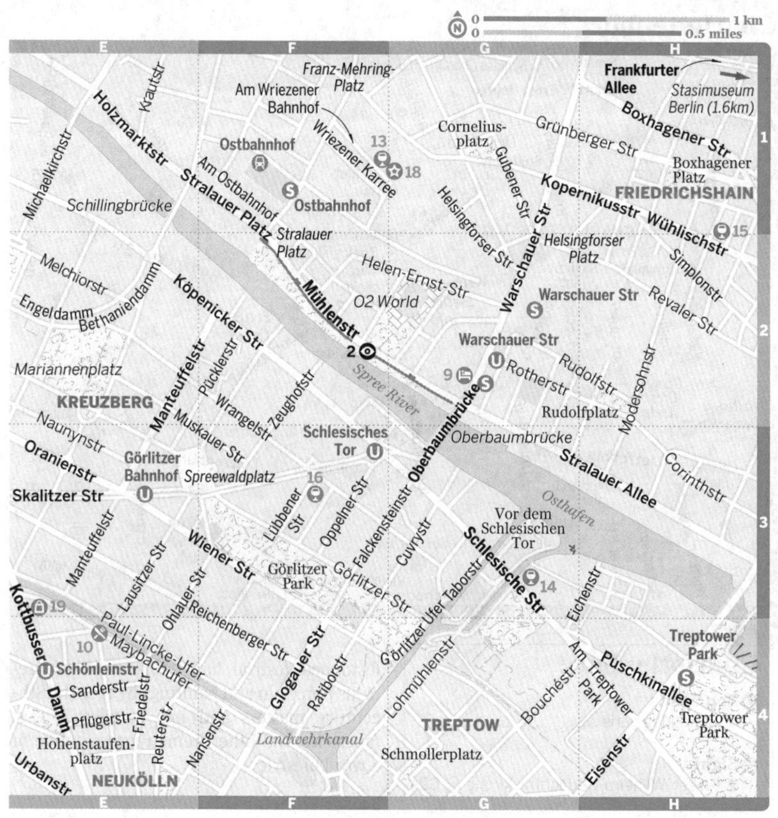

Kreuzberg & Friedrichshain

Sights

1 Checkpoint Charlie B2
2 East Side Gallery F2
3 Hitler's Bunker A1
4 Holocaust Memorial A1
5 Jüdisches Museum B2
6 Topographie des Terrors A2

Activities, Courses & Tours

7 Trabi Safari B1

Sleeping

8 Grand Hostel Berlin A3
9 Michelberger Hotel G2

Eating

10 Cafe Jacques E4
11 Defne D3
12 Max und Moritz D2

Drinking & Nightlife

13 Berghain/Panorama Bar F1
14 Club der Visionäre G3
15 Hops & Barley H1
16 Madame Claude F3
17 Würgeengel D3

Entertainment

18 Kantine am Berghain G1

Shopping

19 Türkenmarkt E3

redevelopment around Zoologischer Garten (Zoo station). Its main artery is the 3.5km-long Kurfürstendamm (Ku'damm for short), Berlin's busiest shopping strip. The main tourist attraction is the nicely restored Schloss Charlottenburg.

Charlottenburg

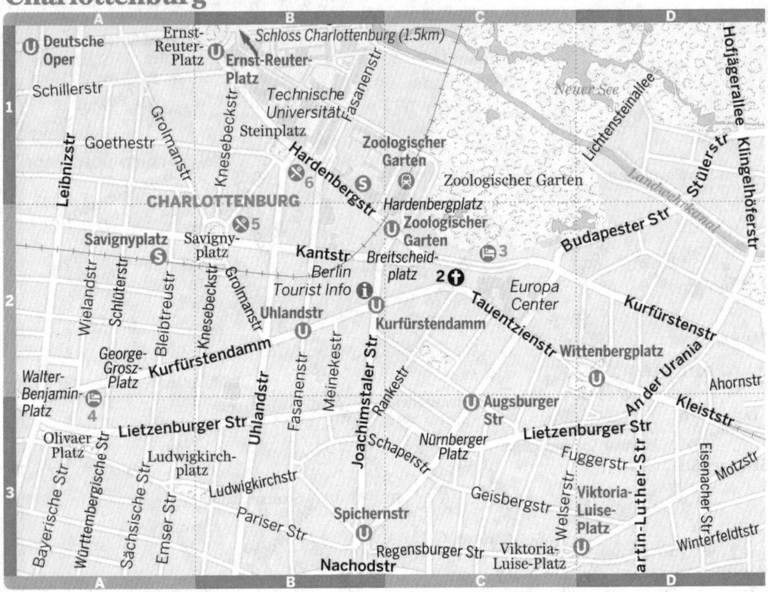

Charlottenburg

Top Sights

Sights

Sleeping

Eating

Entertainment

★ **Schloss Charlottenburg** PALACE

(030-320 910; www.spsg.de; Spandauer Damm 10-22; day pass adult/concession €15/11; hours vary by bldg; M45, 109, 309, S Richard-Wagner-Platz, Sophie-Charlotte-Platz) The grandest of Berlin's surviving royal pads consists of the main palace and three smaller buildings dotted around the lovely palace park. The Schloss palace has origins as the summer residence of Sophie Charlotte, wife of King Friedrich I, and was later enlarged by Frederick the Great. Highlights include opulently furnished private royal apartments, richly festooned festival halls, collections of precious porcelain and paintings by French 18th-century masters and lots of silver, vases, tapestries and other items representative of a royal lifestyle.

Kaiser-Wilhelm-Gedächtniskirche CHURCH

(Kaiser Wilhelm Memorial Church; Map p448; 030-218 5023; www.gedaechtniskirche.com; Breitscheidplatz; church 9am-7pm, memorial hall 10am-6pm Mon-Fri, 10am-5.30pm Sat, noon-5.30pm Sun; 100, S Zoologischer Garten, Kurfürstendamm, Zoologischer Garten) FREE The bombed-out tower of this landmark church, consecrated in 1895, serves as an antiwar memorial, standing quiet and dignified amid the roaring traffic. The adjacent octagonal hall of worship, added in 1961, has amazing midnight-blue glass walls and a giant 'floating' Jesus.

Tours

Most of the following English-language walking tours don't require reservations; just check the website for the current meeting points.

Alternative Berlin Tours WALKING

(0162 819 8264; www.alternativeberlin.com) Pay-what-you-want twice-daily subculture tours that get beneath the skin of the city,

plus a street-art workshop, an alternative pub crawl and the hardcore 'Twilight Tour'.

Berlin Walks WALKING

(☎030-301 9194; www.berlinwalks.de; adult €12-15, concession €10-12) Berlin's longest-running English-language walking tour company also does tours of Sachsenhausen Concentration Camp and Potsdam.

Fat Tire Bike Tours BICYCLE

(Map p442; ☎030-2404 7991; www.fattirebiketours.com/berlin; Panoramastrasse 1a; adult/concession €24/22; S Alexanderplatz, R Alexanderplatz) Has classic city, Nazi and Berlin Wall tours as well as a fascinating 'Raw: Berlin Exposed' tour that gets under the city's urban, subcultural skin. Tours leave from the TV Tower main entrance. E-bike tours available. Reservations recommended (and for some tours required).

Trabi Safari CAR

(Map p446; ☎030-2759 2273; www.trabi-safari.de; Zimmerstrasse 97; per person €34-60, Wall Ride €79-89; S Kochstrasse) Catch the *Good Bye, Lenin!* vibe on tours of Berlin's classic sights or the 'Wild East' with you driving or riding as a passenger in a convoy of GDR-made Trabant cars (Trabi) with live commentary (in English by prior arrangement) piped into your vehicle.

Sleeping

While hotels in Charlottenburg often have special deals, remember that staying here puts you a U-Bahn ride away from most major sights (which are in Mitte) and happening nightlife in Friedrichshain or Kreuzberg.

Historic Mitte & Scheunenviertel

Wombats City Hostel Berlin HOSTEL €

(Map p442; ☎030-8471 0820; www.wombats-hostels.com; Alte Schönhauser Strasse 2; dm/d €26/78; @ 📶; S Rosa-Luxemburg-Platz) Sociable and central, Wombats gets hostelling right. From backpack-sized in-room lockers to individual reading lamps and a guest kitchen with dishwasher, the attention to detail here is impressive. Spacious ensuite rooms are as much part of the deal as freebie linen and a welcome drink, best enjoyed with fellow party pilgrims at the 7th-floor Wombar.

★ **Circus Hotel** HOTEL €€

(☎030-2000 3939; www.circus-berlin.de; Rosenthaler Strasse 1; d €85-120; @ 📶; S Rosenthaler Platz) At our favourite budget boutique hotel, none of the mod rooms are alike, but all feature upbeat colours, thoughtful design details, sleek oak floors and quality beds. Baths have walk-in rain showers. Unexpected perks include a roof terrace with summertime yoga, bike rentals and a fabulous breakfast buffet (€9) served until 1pm. Simply good value all around.

Hotel Amano HOTEL €€

(Map p442; ☎030-809 4150; www.amanogroup.de; Auguststrasse 43; d €90-190; P ❄ @ 📶; S Rosenthaler Platz) This budget designer hotel has inviting public areas, dressed in brushed-copper walls and cocoa-hued banquettes, and efficiently styled rooms, where white furniture teams up with oak floors and natural-toned fabrics to create crisp cosiness. Space-cravers should book an apartment with kitchenette. Breakfast is €15.

Casa Camper HOTEL €€€

(Map p442; ☎030-2000 3410; www.casacamper.com; Weinmeisterstrasse 1; r/ste from €194/338; P 📶; S Weinmeisterstrasse) Catalan shoemaker Camper has translated its concept of chic yet sensible footwear into this style-pit for trend-conscious travellers. Rooms are mod if minimalist and come with day-lit bathrooms and beds that invite hitting the snooze button.

DISCOUNT CARDS

If you're on a budget, various ticket deals and passes can help you stretch your euros further.

The **Museumspass Berlin** (www.visitberlin.de; adult/concession €24/12) buys admission to the permanent exhibits of about 50 museums for three consecutive days, including big draws like the Pergamonmuseum. Sold at tourist offices and participating museums.

The **Berlin Welcome Card** (www.berlin-welcomecard.de; travel in AB zones 48/72hr €18.50/25.50, 48hr incl Potsdam & up to 3 children under 15yr €20.50, 72hr incl Museumsinsel €40.50) entitles you to unlimited public transport and up to 50% discount to 200 sights, attractions and tours for periods of two, three or five days. Sold online, at tourist offices, at U-Bahn and S-Bahn vending machines and on buses.

Minibars are eschewed for a top-floor lounge with stellar views, free breakfast and 24/7 snacks and drinks.

Kreuzberg & Friedrichshain

★Grand Hostel Berlin HOSTEL €
(Map p446; 030-2009 5450; www.grandhostel-berlin.de; Tempelhofer Ufer 14; dm from €14, d €58; @; S Möckernbrücke) Afternoon tea in the library bar? Check. Rooms with stucco-ornamented ceilings? Got 'em. Canal views? Yup. OK, the Grand Hostel may be no five-star hotel, but it is one of Berlin's most supremely comfortable and atmospheric hostels. Ensconced in a fully renovated 1870s building are private rooms and dorms with quality single beds (linen costs €3.60) and large lockers.

★Michelberger Hotel HOTEL €€
(Map p446; 030-2977 8590; www.michelbergerhotel.com; Warschauer Strasse 39; d €105-196; ; S Warschauer Strasse, Warschauer Strasse) The ultimate in creative crash pads, Michelsberger perfectly encapsulates Berlin's offbeat DIY spirit without being self-consciously cool. Rooms don't hide their factory pedigree, but are comfortable and come in sizes suitable for lovebirds, families or rock bands. Staff are friendly and clued-up, and there's a popular restaurant and live music in the lobby on some nights. Optional breakfast is €16.

City West & Charlottenburg

25hours Hotel Bikini Berlin HOTEL €€
(Map p448; 030-120 2210; www.25hours-hotels.com; Budapester Strasse 40; r from €80; @; S Zoologischer Garten, Zoologischer Garten) The 'urban jungle' theme of this hip lifestyle outpost is a reflection of its location between the city's zoo and main shopping district. Rooms are stylish, if a tad compact, with the nicer ones facing the animal park.

Hotel Askanischer Hof HOTEL €€
(Map p448; 030-881 8033; www.askanischer-hof.de; Kurfürstendamm 53; d incl breakfast €80-160; ; S Adenauerplatz) If you're after character and vintage flair, you'll find heaps of both at this 17-room jewel with a Roaring Twenties pedigree. An ornate oak door leads to a quiet oasis where no two rooms are alike, but all are filled with antiques, lace curtains, frilly chandeliers and time-worn oriental rugs. The quaint Old Berlin charms make a popular setting for fashion shoots.

Eating

Berlin is a snacker's paradise, with Turkish (your best bet), wurst (sausage), Greek, Italian and Chinese *Imbiss* (snack) stalls throughout the city. For a local snack, try a ubiquitous *Currywurst* (slivered sausage drizzled with ketchup and curry powder). Excellent farmers markets include those at **Kollwitzplatzmarkt** (Kollwitzstrasse; noon-7pm Thu, 9am-4pm Sat; S Senefelderplatz) in Prenzlauer Berg and the **Türkenmarkt** (Turkish Market; Map p446; www.tuerkenmarkt.de; Maybachufer; 11am-6.30pm Tue & Fri; S Schönleinstrasse, Kottbusser Tor) in Kreuzberg.

Historic Mitte & Scheunenviertel

Chèn Chè VIETNAMESE €€
(Map p442; www.chenche-berlin.de; Rosenthaler Strasse 13; dishes €7-11; noon-midnight; ; S Rosenthaler Platz, M1) Settle down in the charming Zen garden or beneath the hexagonal chandelier of this exotic Vietnamese teahouse and pick from the small menu of steaming *pho* (soups), curries and noodle dishes served in traditional clay pots. Exquisite tea selection and small store.

Schwarzwaldstuben GERMAN €€

(Map p442; ☎030-2809 8084; Tucholskystrasse 48; mains €7-14; ⏰9am-midnight; 🚋M1, 🚆Oranienburger Strasse) In the mood for a Hansel and Gretel moment? Then join the other 'lost kids' for satisfying southern German food amid tongue-in-cheek forest decor. Thumbs up for the *Spätzle* (mac 'n' cheese), *Maultaschen* (ravioli-like pasta) and giant schnitzel, all best washed down with a crisp Rothaus Tannenzäpfle beer, straight from the Black Forest.

Weinbar Rutz GERMAN €€€

(Map p442; ☎030-2462 8760; www.rutz-weinbar.de; Chausseestrasse 8; bar mains €16-25, 3-/4-course menu €44/54; ⏰4-11pm Tue-Sat; Ⓢ Oranienburger Tor) Below his high-concept gourmet temple, Michelin-starred Marco Müller operates a more down-to-earth wine bar where the menu has a distinct earthy and carnivorous bent. Many of the meats and sausages are sourced from Berlin and surrounds. Finish up with a Berlin cheesecake with walnuts and elderberry ice cream.

Prenzlauer Berg

Konnopke's Imbiss GERMAN €

(☎030-442 7765; www.konnopke-imbiss.de; Schönhauser Allee 44a; sausages €1.40-1.90; ⏰9am-8pm Mon-Fri, 11.30am-8pm Sat; Ⓢ Eberswalder Strasse, 🚋M1, M10) Brave the inevitable queue at this famous sausage kitchen, ensconced in the same spot below the elevated U-Bahn track since 1930, but now equipped with a heated pavilion and an English menu. The 'secret' sauce topping its classic *Currywurst* comes in a four-part heat scale from mild to wild.

La Soupe Populaire GERMAN €€

(☎030-4431 9680; www.lasoupepopulaire.de; Prenzlauer Allee 242; mains €14-21; ⏰noon-midnight Thu-Sat; Ⓢ Rosa-Luxemburg-Strasse, 🚋M2) Local top toque Tim Raue's newest gastro destination embraces the soulful goodness of German home cooking, with a best seller being his riff on *Königsberger Klopse* (veal meatballs in caper sauce). It's all served in an industrial-chic space within a defunct 19th-century brewery where patrons sit at vintage tables overlooking a gallery space showcasing changing contemporary art.

Kreuzberg

Cafe Jacques INTERNATIONAL €€

(Map p446; ☎030-694 1048; Maybachufer 14; mains €12-20; ⏰6pm-late; Ⓢ Schönleinstrasse) A favourite with off-duty chefs and local foodies, Jacques infallibly charms with flattering candlelight, arty-elegant decor, fantastic wine and uberfriendly staff. It's the perfect date spot but, quite frankly, you only have to be in love with good food to appreciate the French- and North African–inspired blackboard menu. The cold appetiser platter is big enough for sharing, fish and meat are always tops and the pasta is homemade. Reservations essential.

Max und Moritz GERMAN €€

(Map p446; ☎030-6951 5911; www.maxundmoritzberlin.de; Oranienstrasse 162; mains €9.50-17; ⏰5pm-midnight; Ⓢ Moritzplatz) The patina of yesteryear hangs over this ode-to-old-school brewpub named for the cheeky Wilhelm Busch cartoon characters. Since 1902 it has packed hungry diners and drinkers into its rustic tile-and-stucco ornamented rooms for sudsy home brews and granny-style Berlin fare. A menu favourite is the *Kutschergulasch* (goulash cooked with beer).

Defne TURKISH €€

(Map p446; ☎030-8179 7111; www.defne-restaurant.de; Planufer 92c; mains €8-20; ⏰4pm-1am Apr-Sep, 5pm-1am Oct-Mar; Ⓢ Kottbusser Tor, Schönleinstrasse) If you thought Turkish cuisine stopped at the doner kebab, canal-side Defne will teach you otherwise. The appetiser platter alone elicits intense cravings (fabulous walnut-chilli paste!), but inventive mains such as *ali nacik* (sliced lamb with puréed eggplant and yoghurt) also warrant repeat visits. Lovely summer terrace.

City West & Charlottenburg

Dicke Wirtin GERMAN €€

(Map p448; ☎030-312 4952; www.dicke-wirtin.de; Carmerstrasse 9; mains €6-16; ⏰from 11am-late; 🚆Savignyplatz) Old Berlin charm oozes from every nook and cranny of this been-here-forever pub which pours eight draught beers (including the superb Kloster Andechs) and nearly three dozen homemade schnapps varieties. Hearty local fare like roast pork, fried liver or breaded schnitzel keeps brains balanced. Bargain lunches.

Restaurant am Steinplatz GERMAN €€€

(Map p448; ☎030-312 6589; www.marriott.de; Hardenbergstrasse 12; mains €16-26; ⏰breakfast, lunch & dinner; 🚌M45, Ⓢ Ernst-Reuter-Platz, Bahnhof Zoologischer Garten, 🚆Bahnhof Zoologischer Garten) The 1920s gets a 21st-century makeover both in the kitchen and the decor at this

WORTH A TRIP

SCHLOSS & PARK SANSSOUCI

Easily reached in half an hour from central Berlin, the former royal Prussian seat of **Potsdam** lures visitors to its splendid Unesco-recognised palaces and parks dreamed up by 18th-century King Friedrich II (Frederick the Great).

Headlining the roll call of royal pads is **Schloss Sanssouci** (☎0331-969 4200; www.spsg.de; Maulbeerallee; adult/concession incl audioguide €12/8; ⏰10am-6pm Tue-Sun Apr-Oct, to 5pm Nov-Mar; 🚌650, 695), a celebrated rococo palace and the king's favourite summer retreat. Standouts on the audioguided tour include the whimsically decorated concert hall, the intimate library and the domed Marble Hall. Admission is limited and by timed ticket only; book online (http://tickets.spsg.de) to avoid wait times and/or disappointment. Tours run by the Potsdam **tourist office** (☎0331-2755 8899; www.potsdam-tourism.com; ⏰9.30am-8pm Mon-Sat, 10am-4pm Sun) guarantee entry.

Schloss Sanssouci is surrounded by a sprawling park dotted with numerous other palaces, buildings, fountains, statues and romantic corners. The one building not to be missed is the **Chinesisches Haus** (Chinese House; ☎0331-969 4200; www.spsg.de; Am Grünen Gitter; admission €2; ⏰10am-6pm Tue-Sun May-Oct; 🚌605, 606 to Schloss Charlottenhof, 🚊91 to Schloss Charlottenhof), an adorable clover-leaf-shaped pavilion decorated with exotically dressed gilded figures shown sipping tea, dancing and playing musical instruments.

Another park highlight is the **Neues Palais** (New Palace; ☎0331-969 4200; www.spsg.de; Am Neuen Palais; adult/concession incl audioguide €8/6; ⏰10am-6pm Wed-Mon Apr-Oct, to 5pm Nov-Mar; 🚌605 or 606 to Neues Palais, 🚆Potsdam Charlottenhof) at the far western end. It has built-to-impress dimensions and is filled with opulent private and representative rooms, some of which are closed for restoration.

Each building charges separate admission; a day pass to all costs €19 (concession €14).

On a nice day, it's worth exploring Potsdam's watery landscape and numerous other palaces on a **boat cruise** (☎0331-275 9210; www.schiffahrt-in-potsdam.de; Lange Brücke 6; ⏰10am-7pm Apr-Oct). The most popular one is the 90-minute *Schlösserundfahrt* (palace cruise; €13). Boats leave from docks near the Hauptbahnhof.

Regional trains leaving from Berlin-Hauptbahnhof and Zoologischer Garten need only 30 minutes to reach Potsdam Hauptbahnhof. The S-Bahn S7 from central Berlin makes the trip in about 40 minutes. You'll need an ABC ticket (€3.20) for either service.

stylish outpost. The dining room is anchored by an open kitchen where veteran chef Marcus Zimmer uses mostly regional products to execute classic Berlin recipes. Even rustic beer-hall dishes such as *Eisbein* (boiled pork knuckle) are imaginatively reinterpreted and beautifully plated.

Drinking & Nightlife

With no curfew, Berlin is a notoriously late city, where bars stay packed from dusk to dawn and beyond and some clubs don't hit their stride until 6am. Kreuzberg and Friedrichshain are currently the edgiest bar-hopping grounds, with swanky Mitte and Charlottenburg being more suited for date nights than late nights. For listings consult the biweekly city magazines *Zitty* (www.zitty.de) or *Tip* (www.tip.de), or check internet platforms such as www.residentadvisor.net.

Prater BEER GARDEN

(☎030-448 5688; www.pratergarten.de; Kastanienallee 7-9; ⏰noon-late Apr-Sep, weather permitting; S Eberswalder Strasse) This place has seen beer-soaked nights since 1837, making it Berlin's oldest beer garden. It's kept much of its traditional charm and is still perfect for guzzling a custom-brewed Prater pilsner beneath the ancient chestnut trees (self-service). Kids can romp around the small play area. In foul weather or winter, the adjacent beer hall is a fine place to sample classic Berlin dishes (mains €8 to €19).

Weinerei WINE BAR

(☎030-440 6983; www.weinerei.com; Veteranenstrasse 14; ⏰8pm-late; 📶; S Rosenthaler Platz, 🚊M1) This living-room-style wine bar works on the honour principle: you 'rent' a wine glass for €2, then help yourself to as much vino as you like and in the end decide what you want to pay. Please be fair and do not take advantage of this fantastic concept.

Madame Claude PUB

(Map p446; ☎030-8411 0859; www.madameclaude.de; Lübbener Strasse 19; ⏲from 7pm; S Schlesisches Tor, Görlitzer Bahnhof) Gravity is literally upended at this David Lynchian booze burrow where the furniture dangles from the ceiling and the moulding is on the floor. There are concerts, DJs and events every night, including eXperimondays, Wednesday's music quiz night and open-mike Sundays. The name honours a famous French prostitute – *très* apropos given the place's bordello pedigree.

Hops & Barley PUB

(Map p446; ☎030-2936 7534; Wühlischstrasse 40; ⏲from 5pm Mon-Fri, from 3pm Sat & Sun; S Warschauer Strasse, U Warschauer Strasse) Conversation flows as freely as the unfiltered pilsner, malty *Dunkel* (dark), fruity *Weizen* (wheat) and potent cider produced right at this congenial microbrewery inside a former butcher's shop. For variety, the brewmeisters produce seasonal blackboard specials such as a malty Bernstein or a robust Indian Pale Ale.

Würgeengel BAR

(Map p446; www.wuergeengel.de; Dresdener Strasse 122; ⏲from 7pm; S Kottbusser Tor) For a swish night out, point the compass to Würgeengel, a stylish art deco–style bar with lots of chandeliers and shiny black surfaces. It's always busy but especially so after the final credits roll at the adjacent Babylon cinema.

Klunkerkranich BAR

(www.klunkerkranich.de; Karl-Marx-Strasse 66; ⏲10am-midnight Mon-Sat, noon-midnight Sun, weather permitting; S Rathaus Neukölln) Open only in the warmer months, Klunkerkranich (German for 'wattled crane') is a club-garden-beach-bar combo that 'roosts' amid potted plants on the rooftop parking deck of the Neukölln Arcaden shopping mall. It's a great place for sundowners while chilling to local DJs or bands.

Berghain/Panorama Bar CLUB

(Map p446; www.berghain.de; Wriezener Bahnhof; ⏲midnight Fri-Mon morning; U Ostbahnhof) Only world-class spin masters heat up this hedonistic bass-junkie hellhole inside a labyrinthine ex-power plant. Hard-edged minimal techno dominates the ex-turbine hall (Berghain) while house dominates at Panorama Bar one floor up. Strict door, no cameras. Check the website for midweek concerts and record-release parties at the main venue and the adjacent **Kantine am Berghain** (Map p446; ☎030-2936 0210; www.berghain.de; Am Wriezener Bahnhof; ⏲hours vary; U Ostbahnhof).

Clärchens Ballhaus CLUB

(Map p442; ☎030-282 9295; www.ballhaus.de; Augustrasse 24; ⏲11am-late, dancing from 9pm or 9.30pm; 🚋M1, U Oranienburger Strasse) Yesteryear is right now at this late, great 19th-century dance hall where groovers and grannies hoof it across the parquet without even a touch of irony. There are different sounds nightly – salsa to swing, tango to disco – and a live band on Saturday.

Club der Visionäre CLUB

(Map p446; ☎030-6951 8942; www.clubdervisionaere.com; Am Flutgraben 1; ⏲from 2pm Mon-Fri, from noon Sat & Sun; S Schlesisches Tor, U Treptower Park) It's cold beer, crispy pizza and fine electro at this summertime chill and party playground in an old canal-side boatshed. Park yourself beneath the weeping willows, stake out some turf on the upstairs deck or hit the teensy dance floor. At weekends party people invade. The toilets suck.

☆ Entertainment

Berliner Philharmonie CLASSICAL MUSIC

(Map p448; ☎tickets 030-2548 8301; www.berliner-philharmoniker.de; Herbert-von-Karajan-Strasse 1; 🚌200, S Potsdamer Platz, U Potsdamer Platz) This world-famous concert hall has supreme acoustics and, thanks to Hans Scharoun's clever terraced vineyard design, not a bad

GAY & LESBIAN BERLIN

Berlin's legendary liberalism has spawned one of the world's biggest and most diverse GLBT playgrounds. The historic 'gay village' is near Nollendorfplatz in Schöneberg (Motzstrasse and Fuggerstrasse especially, get off U-Bahn station Nollendorfplatz), where the rainbow flag has proudly flown since the 1920s. The crowds skews older and leather. Current hipster central is Kreuzberg, where freewheeling party pens cluster around Mehringdamm and Oranienstrasse. Check *Siegessäule* (www.siegesaeule.de), the weekly freebie 'bible' to all things gay and lesbian in town, for the latest happenings.

WORTH A TRIP

SACHSENHAUSEN CONCENTRATION CAMP

A mere 35km north of Berlin, Sachsenhausen was built by prisoners and opened in 1936 as a prototype for other concentration camps. By 1945 some 200,000 people had passed through its sinister gates, initially mostly political opponents but later also Roma and Sinti, Jews and prisoners of war (POWs). Tens of thousands died from hunger, exhaustion, illness, exposure, medical experiments and executions. The camp became a **memorial site** (☎03301-200 200; www.stiftung-bg.de; Strasse der Nationen 22; ⌚8.30am-6pm mid-Mar–mid-Oct, to 4.30pm mid-Oct–mid-Mar, most exhibits closed Mon) FREE in 1961. A tour of the grounds, remaining buildings and exhibits will leave no one untouched.

Unless you're on a guided tour, pick up a leaflet (€0.50) or, better yet, an audioguide (€3, including leaflet) at the visitor centre to get a better grasp of this huge site. Note that although the grounds are open daily, indoor exhibits are closed on Mondays.

The S-Bahn S1 makes the trip to Oranienburg thrice hourly (€3.20, 45 minutes), from where it's a 2km signposted walk or a ride on hourly bus 804 to the camp.

seat in the house. It's the home turf of the Berliner Philharmoniker, which will be led by Sir Simon Rattle until 2018. Chamber-music concerts take place at the adjacent Kammermusiksaal.

Information

Visit Berlin (Map p442; www.visitberlin.de; Brandenburger Tor, Pariser Platz), the Berlin tourist board, operates four walk-in offices, info desks at the airports, and a **call centre** (☎030-2500 2333; ⌚9am-7pm Mon-Fri, 10am-6pm Sat, 10am-2pm Sun) with multilingual staff who field general questions and make hotel and ticket bookings. You'll find the walk-in offices at the following locations:

Brandenburger Tor (Map p442; Pariser Platz, Brandenburger Tor; ⌚9.30am-7pm Apr-Oct, to 6pm Nov-Mar; S Brandenburger Tor, U Brandenburger Tor)

Hauptbahnhof (Hauptbahnhof, Europaplatz entrance, ground fl; ⌚8am-10pm; S Hauptbahnhof, U Hauptbahnhof)

Neues Kranzler Eck (Map p448; Kurfürstendamm 22, Neues Kranzler Eck; ⌚9.30am-8pm Mon-Sat; S Kurfürstendamm)

TV Tower (Map p442; TV Tower, ground fl; ⌚10am-6pm Apr-Oct, to 4pm Nov-Mar; 🚌100, 200, S Alexanderplatz, U Alexanderplatz)

Getting There & Away

AIR

Most visitors arrive in Berlin by air. Since the opening of the new Berlin Brandenburg Airport has been delayed indefinitely, flights continue to land at the city's **Tegel** (TXL; ☎030-6091 1150; www.berlin-airport.de) and **Schönefeld** (SXF; ☎030-6091 1150; www.berlin-airport.de) airports.

BUS

Most long-haul buses arrive at the **Zentraler Omnibusbahnhof** (ZOB; ☎030-302 5361; www.iob-berlin.de; Masurenallee 4-6; S Kaiserdamm, U Messe/ICC Nord) near the trade fair grounds in far western Berlin. The U2 U-Bahn line links to the city centre. Some bus operators also stop at Alexanderplatz and other points around town.

TRAIN

Berlin has several train stations but most trains converge at the Hauptbahnhof (main train station) in the heart of the city.

Getting Around

TO/FROM THE AIRPORT

Tegel

Bus TXL bus to Alexanderplatz (€2.60, 40 minutes) via Haupbahnhof every 10 minutes. Bus X9 for Kurfürstendamm and Zoologischer Garten (Zoo station; €2.60, 20 minutes).

U-Bahn Closest U-station is Jakob-Kaiser-Platz, served by bus 109 and X9. From here, the U7 goes straight to Schöneberg and Kreuzberg (€2.60).

Schönefeld

The airport train station is about 400m from the terminals. Free shuttle buses run every 10 minutes; walking takes five to 10 minutes.

BUS TOUR ON THE CHEAP

Get a crash course in 'Berlinology' by hopping on bus 100 or 200 at Zoologischer Garten or Alexanderplatz and letting the landmarks whoosh by for the price of a standard bus ticket (€2.60, day pass €6.80). Bus 100 goes via the Tiergarten, 200 via Potsdamer Platz. Without traffic and getting off, trips take about 30 minutes.

Airport-Express Regular Deutsche Bahn regional trains, identified as RE7 and RB14 in timetables, go to central Berlin twice hourly (€3.20, 30 minutes).

S-Bahn S9 runs every 20 minutes and is handy for Friedrichshain or Prenzlauer Berg. For the Messe (trade-fair grounds), take the S45 to Südkreuz and change to the S41. Tickets cost €3.20.

PUBLIC TRANSPORT

One ticket is valid on all forms of public transport, including the U-Bahn, buses, trams and ferries. Most trips within Berlin require an AB ticket (€2.60), which is valid for two hours (interruptions and transfers allowed, but not round trips).

Tickets are available from bus drivers, vending machines at U- and S-Bahn stations (English instructions available), vending machines aboard trams and from station offices. Expect to pay cash (change given) and be sure to validate (stamp) your ticket or risk a €40 fine.

Services operate from 4am until just after midnight on weekdays, with half-hourly *Nachtbuses* (night buses) in between. At weekends the U-Bahn and S-Bahn run all night long (except the U4 and U55).

For trip planning, check the website or call the 24-hour **hotline** (☎ 030-194 49; www.bvg.de).

TAXI

You can order a **taxi** (☎ 030-20 20 20, 030-44 33 11) by phone, flag one down or pick one up at a rank. Flag fall is €3.40, then it's €1.79 per kilometre up to 7km and €1.28 for each kilometre after that. Tip about 10%. Short trips of 2km cost €4 provided you flag down a cab and request a *Kurzstrecke* before the driver has activated the meter.

CENTRAL GERMANY

Central Germany straddles the states of Thuringia and Saxony, both in the former East Germany. It takes in towns like Weimar, Eisenach and Erfurt that have been shaped by some of the biggest names in Germany history, including Goethe and Martin Luther. Further east, Dresden is a town that defines survival while Leipzig can be justifiably proud of doing its part in bringing about the downfall of East Germany. Expect this region to enlighten, inspire and, above all, surprise, you.

Dresden

☎ 0351 / POP 512,000

Proof that there is life after death, Dresden has become one of Germany's most visited cities, and for good reason. Restorations have returned its historic core to its 18th-century heyday when it was famous throughout Europe as 'Florence on the Elbe'. Scores of Italian artists, musicians, actors and master craftsmen flocked to the court of Augustus the Strong, bestowing countless masterpieces upon the city.

The devastating bombing raids in 1945 levelled most of these treasures. But Dresden is a survivor and many of the most important landmarks have since been rebuilt, including the elegant Frauenkirche. Today there's a constantly evolving arts and cultural scene and zinging pub and nightlife quarters, especially in the Outer Neustadt.

Sights

Dresden straddles the Elbe River, with the attraction-studded Altstadt (old town) in the south and the Neustadt (new town) pub and student quarter to the north.

Frauenkirche CHURCH

(www.frauenkirche-dresden.de; Neumarkt; audioguide €2.50; usually 10am-noon & 1-6pm) FREE The domed Frauenkirche – Dresden's most beloved symbol – has literally risen from the city's ashes. The original graced its skyline for two centuries before collapsing after the February 1945 bombing. After reunification a grassroots movement helped raise funds to rebuild the landmark. A spitting image of the original, it may not bear the gravitas of age but that only slightly detracts from its festive beauty inside and out. The altar, reassembled from nearly 2000 fragments, is especially striking.

Zwinger MUSEUM

(☎ 0351-4914 2000; www.skd.museum; Theaterplatz 1; adult/under 17yr €14/free; 10am-6pm Tue-Sun) The sprawling Zwinger, one of the most ravishing baroque buildings in Germany, today houses several important museums. The most important collection, the **Gemäldegalerie Alte Meister** (Old Masters Gallery), displays a roll call of such art-world darlings as Botticelli, Titian, Rubens, Vermeer and Dürer. A key work is the 500-year-old *Sistine Madonna* by Raphael. Fans of precious porcelain from Meissen and East Asia gravitate to the **Porzellansammlung**, while techno types will like the historic scientific instruments (globes, clocks, telescopes, etc) at the **Mathematisch-Physikalischer Salon**.

DON'T MISS

GRÜNES GEWÖLBE

Dresden's fortress-like Renaissance city palace was home to Saxon rulers from 1485 to 1918 and now shelters Augustus the Strong's dazzling collection of precious objects, a real-life 'Aladdin's Cave' spilling over with trinkets wrought from gold, ivory, silver, diamonds and jewels. There's so much of it that displays are spread over two separate museums: the **Historisches Grünes Gewölbe** (Historic Green Vault; 0351-4914 2000; www.skd.museum; Residenzschloss; adult/under 17yr incl audioguide €14/free; 10am-6pm Wed-Mon) and the modern **Neues Grünes Gewölbe** (New Green Vault; 0351-4914 2000; www.skd.museum; Residenzschloss; adult/under 17yr incl audioguide €14/free; 10am-6pm Wed-Mon).

If you only have time for one, make it the former, largely because objects are displayed in a series of lavishly decorated baroque-style rooms just as they were during Augustus' time. Admission is by timed ticket only and visitor numbers are limited. It's best to get advance tickets online or show up before the ticket office opens.

Don't be too disappointed, though, if you can't get into the historic chambers, for trinkets displayed in the modern New Green Vault are just as stunning.

Combination tickets to both Green Vaults cost €23 (free under age 17) and are also good for the other palace collections (coins, armour, prints and drawings) as well as the Hausmannturm (tower).

Semperoper HISTORIC BUILDING

(0351-320 7360; www.semperoper-erleben.de; Theaterplatz 2; tour adult/concession €10/6; varies) One of Germany's most famous opera houses, the Semperoper opened in 1841 and has hosted premieres of famous works by Richard Strauss, Carl Maria von Weber and Richard Wagner. Guided 45-minute tours operate almost daily (the 3pm tour is in English); exact times depend on the rehearsal and performance schedule. Buy advance tickets online to skip the queue.

Albertinum MUSEUM

(0351-4914 2000; www.skd.museum; enter from Brühlsche Terrasse or Georg-Treu-Platz 2; adult/concession/under 17yr €10/7.50/free; 10am-6pm Tue-Sun; P) After massive renovations following severe 2002 flood damage, the Renaissance-era former arsenal is now the stunning home of the **Galerie Neue Meister** (New Masters Gallery), which displays an arc of paintings by prime practitioners from the 18th to the 20th centuries – Caspar David Friedrich to Claude Monet and Gerhard Richter – in gorgeous rooms orbiting a light-filled courtyard.

Tours

NightWalk Dresden WALKING

(0172 781 5007; www.nightwalk-dresden.de; Albertplatz; tours €13; tour 9pm) Dresden is not all about baroque beauties, as you will discover on this intriguing 'behind the scenes' walking tour of its most interesting quarter, the Outer Neustadt. See fabulous street art, learn about what life was like in the former East Germany and visit fun pubs and bars. The meeting point is normally at Albertplatz but call ahead and confirm.

Grosse Stadtrundfahrt BUS

(0351-899 5650; www.stadtrundfahrt.com; Theaterplatz; day pass adult/concession €20/18; 9.30am-10pm Apr-Oct, to 8pm Nov-Mar) Narrated hop-on, hop-off tour with 22 stops, every 15 to 20 minutes, and optional short guided tours tick off all major sights.

Sleeping

Hostel Mondpalast HOSTEL €

(0351-563 4050; www.mondpalast.de; Louisenstrasse 77; dm €13-19.50, d €56, linen €2; @) Check in at the out-of-this-world bar-cafe (with cheap drinks) before being 'beamed up' to your room in the Moon Palace – each one designed to reflect a sign of the zodiac. Bonus points for the bike rentals and the well-equipped kitchen. Breakfast is €6.50.

★ **Aparthotel am Zwinger** APARTMENT €€

(0351-8990 0100; www.pension-zwinger.de; Maxstrasse 3; apt €60-112; reception 7am-10pm Mon-Fri, 9.30am-6pm Sat & Sun or by arrangement; P @) Self-caterers, families and space-cravers will appreciate these bright, functional and stylish rooms and apartments with basic kitchens. Units are spread over several buildings, but all are super central and fairly quiet. Breakfast costs €9.50.

Hotel Martha Dresden HOTEL €€

(☎0351-817 60; www.hotel-martha-dresden.de; Nieritzstrasse 11; d €113-121; 📶) Fifty rooms with big windows, wooden floors and Biedermeier-inspired furnishings combine with an attractive winter garden and a smiley welcome to make this a pleasant place to hang your hat. Breakfast costs €10. The entire hotel is wheelchair accessible. Bike rentals are available.

Eating & Drinking

The Neustadt has oodles of cafes and restaurants, especially along Königstrasse and the streets north of Albertplatz. The latter is also the centre of Dresden's nightlife. Altstadt restaurants are more tourist-geared and pricier.

Villandry MEDITERRANEAN €€

(☎0351-899 6724; www.villandry.de; Jordanstrasse 8; mains €9-22; ⏲6.30-11.30pm Mon-Sat) The folks in the kitchen here sure know how to coax maximum flavour out of even the simplest ingredients, and to turn them into super tasty Mediterranean treats for your eyes and palate. Meals are best enjoyed in the lovely courtyard.

Cafe Alte Meister INTERNATIONAL €€

(☎0351-481 0426; www.altemeister.net; Theaterplatz 1a; mains €9-20; ⏲10am-1am) If you've worked up an appetite from museum-hopping or need a break from culture overload, retreat to this elegant filling station between the Zwinger and the Semperoper for creative and seasonal bistro fare in its artsy interior or on the terrace. At night, the ambience is a bit more formal.

Raskolnikoff INTERNATIONAL €€

(☎0351-804 5706; www.raskolnikoff.de; Böhmische Strasse 34; mains €7-24; ⏲10am-2am Mon-Fri, 9am-2am Sat & Sun) An artist squat before the Wall came down, Raskolnikoff now brims with grown-up artsy-bohemian flair, especially in the sweet little garden at the back. The seasonally calibrated menu showcases the fruits of regional terroir in globally inspired dishes, and the beer is brewed locally. Upstairs are seven handsomely done-up rooms (single/double €45/62) and one studio with kitchenette (€55/72).

Twist BAR

(☎0351-795 150; Salzgasse 4; ⏲from 6pm Mon-Sat) 'Twist' is indeed the name of the game at this sky bar where classic cocktails are given – often radical – new interpretations. On the 6th floor of the Innside Hotel you'll be at eye level with the Frauenkirche dome.

Information

Tourist Office (☎0351-501 501; www.dresden.de) There are branches inside the Hauptbahnhof (Wiener Platz; ⏲8am-8pm) and Frauenkirche (Neumarkt 2; ⏲10am-7pm Mon-Fri, to 6pm Sat, to 3pm Sun). Both book rooms and tours, rent out audioguides and sell the Dresden Cards.

Getting There & Away

Dresden Airport (DRS; www.dresden-airport.de) is about 9km north of the city centre and linked by the S2 train several times hourly (€2.20, 20 minutes).

Direct train destinations include Leipzig (from €23.80, 70 to 100 minutes) and Berlin (€40, 2¼ hours). The S1 train runs to Meissen (€5.90, 35 minutes). Most trains stop at Dresden-Hauptbahnhof and at Dresden-Neustadt across the Elbe River.

Getting Around

For public transport info in Dresden, check www.dvb.de/en or call the hotline at ☎0351-8657 1011.

Leipzig

☎0341 / POP 530,500

Bustling Leipzig is an important business and transport centre, a trade-fair mecca, and – aside from Berlin – the most dynamic city in eastern Germany. Relatively low rent and throbbing nightlife are making it an attractive place to live for students and young professionals. Leipzig played a leading role in the 1989 democratic revolution and has plenty in store for history buffs keen on learning about life behind the Wall. The one-time home of Bach, Wagner and Mendelssohn, the city also looks back on a long and illustrious music tradition that continues to flourish today, as do its art and literary scenes. Another famous figure to pass through was Goethe, who set a key scene of *Faust* in the cellar of his favourite local watering hole.

Sights

Don't rush from sight to sight – wandering around Leipzig is a pleasure in itself, with many of the blocks around the central Markt criss-crossed by historic shopping arcades, including the classic **Mädlerpassage**.

WORTH A TRIP

MEISSEN

Straddling the Elbe around 25km upstream from Dresden, Meissen is the hub of European porcelain, which was first cooked up in 1710 in its imposing castle, the **Albrechtsburg** (☎03521-470 70; www.albrechtsburg-meissen.de; Domplatz 1; adult/concession incl audioguide €8/4; ⊙10am-6pm Mar-Oct, to 5pm Nov-Feb). An exhibit on the 2nd floor chronicles how it all began. Highlights of the adjacent **cathedral** (☎03521-452 490; www.dom-zu-meissen.de; Domplatz 7; adult/concession €4/2.50; ⊙9am-6pm Apr-Oct, 10am-4pm Nov-Mar) include medieval stained-glass windows and an altarpiece by Lucas Cranach the Elder. Both squat atop a ridge overlooking Meissen's cute Altstadt (old town).

Since 1863, porcelain production has taken place in a custom-built factory, about 1km south of the Altstadt. Next to it is the **Erlebniswelt Haus Meissen** (☎03521-468 208; www.meissen.com/de/meissen-besuchen/erlebniswelt-haus-meissen; Talstrasse 9; adult/concession €9/5; ⊙9am-6pm May-Oct, to 5pm Nov-Apr), a vastly popular porcelain museum where you can witness the astonishing artistry and craftsmanship that makes Meissen porcelain unique.

For details and further information about the town, stop by the **tourist office** (☎03521-419 40; www.touristinfo-meissen.de; Markt 3; ⊙10am-6pm Mon-Fri, 10am-4pm Sat & Sun Apr-Oct, 10am-5pm Mon-Fri, 10am-3pm Sat Nov, Dec, Feb & Mar).

Half-hourly S1 trains run to Meissen from Dresden's Hauptbahnhof and Neustadt train stations (€5.90, 35 minutes). For the Erlebniswelt, get off at Meissen-Triebischtal. Boats operated by **Sächsische Dampfschiffahrt** (☎03521-866 090; www.saechsische-dampfschiffahrt.de; one way/return €13.50/17.50; ⊙May-Sep) make the trip to Meissen from the Terrassenufer in Dresden in two hours. Consider going one way by boat and the other by train.

★Nikolaikirche CHURCH
(Church of St Nicholas; www.nikolaikirche-leipzig.de; Nikolaikirchhof 3; ⊙10am-6pm Mon-Sat & during services 9.30am, 11.15am & 5pm Sun) The Church of St Nicholas has Romanesque and Gothic roots but since 1797 has sported a striking neoclassical interior with palm-like pillars and cream-coloured pews. The church played a key role in the nonviolent movement that led to the downfall of the East German government. As early as 1982 it hosted 'peace prayers' every Monday at 5pm (still held today), which over time inspired and empowered local citizens to confront the injustices plaguing their country.

Zeitgeschichtliches Forum MUSEUM
(Forum of Contemporary History; ☎0341-222 00; www.hdg.de/leipzig; Grimmaische Strasse 6; ⊙9am-6pm Tue-Fri, 10am-6pm Sat & Sun) FREE This fascinating exhibit tells the political history of the German Democratic Republic (GDR) from division and dictatorship to fall-of-the-Wall ecstasy and post-Wende blues. It's essential viewing for anyone seeking to understand the late country's political power apparatus, the systematic oppression of regime critics, milestones in inter-German and international relations, and the opposition movement that led to its downfall.

Bach-Museum Leipzig MUSEUM
(☎0341-913 70; www.bachmuseumleipzig.de; Thomaskirchhof 16; adult/concession/under 16yr €8/6/free; ⊙10am-6pm Tue-Sun) This interactive museum does more than tell you about the life and accomplishments of heavyweight musician Johann Sebastian Bach. Learn how to date a Bach manuscript, listen to baroque instruments or treat your ears to any composition he ever wrote. The 'treasure room' downstairs displays rare original manuscripts.

Thomaskirche CHURCH
(☎0341-222 240; www.thomaskirche.org; Thomaskirchhof 18; tower €2; ⊙church 9am-6pm, tower 1pm, 2pm & 4.30pm Sat, 2pm & 3pm Sun Apr-Nov) The composer Johann Sebastian Bach worked in the Thomaskirche as a cantor from 1723 until his death in 1750, and his remains lie buried beneath a bronze plate in front of the altar. The Thomanerchor, once led by Bach, has been going strong since 1212 and now includes 100 boys aged eight to 18. The church tower can be climbed.

Stasi Museum MUSEUM
(☎0341-961 2443; www.runde-ecke-leipzig.de; Dittrichring 24; ⊙10am-6pm) FREE In the GDR the walls had ears, as is chillingly documented in this exhibit in the former Leipzig headquarters of the East German secret police (the

Stasi), a building known as the Runde Ecke (Round Corner). English-language audioguides aid in understanding the all-German displays on propaganda, preposterous disguises, cunning surveillance devices, recruitment (even among children), scent storage and other chilling machinations that reveal the GDR's all-out zeal when it came to controlling, manipulating and repressing its own people.

Sleeping

Motel One HOTEL €
(☎0341-337 4370; www.motel-one.de; Nikolaistrasse 23; d from €69; P ❄ ☎) The older of two Motel One outposts in Leipzig has a five-star location opposite the Nikolaikirche and also gets most other things right, from the Zeitgeist-capturing lobby-lounge to the snug but smartly designed rooms. No surprise it's often booked out. Breakfast costs €7.50.

arcona Living Bach14 HOTEL, STUDIOS €€
(☎0341-496 140; www.bach14.arcona.de; Thomaskirchhof 13/14; d from €110; ☎) In this musically themed marvel, you'll sleep sweetly in sleek rooms decorated with sound-sculpture lamps, Bach manuscript wallpaper and colours ranging from subdued olive to perky raspberry. The quietest ones are in the garden wing, while those in the historic front section have views of the famous Thomaner church.

★**Steigenberger Grandhotel Handelshof** HOTEL €€€
(☎0341-350 5810; www.steigenberger.com/Leipzig; Salzgässchen 6; r from €160; ❄ @ ☎) Behind the imposing historic facade of a 1909 municipal trading hall, this luxe lodge outclasses most of Leipzig's hotels with its super central location, charmingly efficient team and modern rooms dressed in crisp white-silver-purple colours. The stylish bilevel spa is the perfect bliss-out station.

Eating

Aside from locations listed here, another good place to head to is restaurant row on popular Muenzgasse, just south of the city centre. Take tram 10 or 11 to 'Hohe Strasse'.

Sol y Mar MEDITERRANEAN, ASIAN €€
(☎0341-961 5721; www.solymar-leipzig.de; Gottschedstrasse 4; mains €5-14; ⊙9am-late; ☎) The soft lighting, ambient sounds and sensuous interior (including padded pods for noshing in a reclining position) make this a popular place to chill and dine on feel-good food from around the Med and Asia. Weekday lunch specials from €4.90, Sunday brunch and expansive summer terrace.

★**Auerbachs Keller** GERMAN €€€
(☎0341-216 100; www.auerbachs-keller-leipzig.de; Mädlerpassage, Grimmaische Strasse 2-4; mains Keller €10-27, Weinstuben €33-35; ⊙Keller noon-11pm daily, Weinstuben 6-11pm Mon-Sat) Founded in 1525, Auerbachs Keller is one of Germany's best-known restaurants. It's cosy and touristy but the food's actually quite good and the setting memorable. There are two sections: the vaulted Grosser Keller for hearty Saxonian dishes and the four historic rooms of the Historische Weinstuben for upscale German fare. Reservations highly advised.

Max Enk MODERN GERMAN €€€
(☎0341-9999 7638; www.max-enk.de; Neumarkt 9-19; mains €20-26, 1-/2-/3-course lunch €10/12/15; ⊙noon-2pm & 6pm-1am Mon-Fri, noon-1am Sat, 11.30am-4pm Sun) People share laughs over hand-picked wines and plates of elegant comfort food kicked into high gear at this sleek outpost. The Wiener schnitzel is a reliable standby, the quality meats are grilled to perfection and the weekday multicourse lunches are a steal.

Drinking & Entertainment

Party activity centres on three main areas: the boisterous Drallewatsch pub strip, the more upmarket theatre district around Gottschedstrasse, and the mix of trendy and alt-vibe joints along Karl-Liebknecht-Strasse (aka 'Südmeile').

Moritzbastei CAFE, BAR
(☎0341-702 590; www.moritzbastei.de; Universitätsstrasse 9; ⊙10am-late Mon-Fri, from noon Sat, from 9am Sun, parties almost nightly; ☎) This legendary (sub)cultural centre in a warren of cellars of the old city fortifications keeps an all-ages crowd happy with parties, concerts, art and readings. It harbours stylish cocktail and wine bars as well as a daytime cafe (dishes €2 to €5) that serves delicious coffee along with healthy and wallet-friendly fare. Summer terrace, too.

Flowerpower PUB
(☎0341-961 3441; www.flower-power.de; Riemannstrasse 42; ⊙7pm-5am; ☎) It's party time any time at this long-running psychedelic flashback to the '60s (cool pinball machines). Admission is always free and the music tends to be older than the crowd. If you've overdone it, you can even crash upstairs for the night for €15.

Cafe Waldi CAFE, BAR
(☎0341-462 5667; www.cafewaldi.de; Peterssteinweg 10; ⊙11.30am-late Mon-Fri, 9am-late Sat & Sun) Despite its great-grandma's living room look – complete with big sofas, cuckoo clocks and mounted antlers – Waldi is an up-to-the-minute hang-out where you can eat breakfast until 4pm, fuel up on coffee and a light meal, or nurse cocktails and pints until the wee hours. On weekends, DJs rock the upstairs area with house, indie and hip hop.

ℹ Information

Tourist Office (☎0341-710 4260, room referral 0341-710 4255; www.leipzig.travel; Katharinenstrasse 8; ⊙9.30am-6pm Mon-Fri, to 4pm Sat, to 3pm Sun) Room referral, ticket sales, maps and general information. Also sells the Leipzig Card (1/3 days €9.90/19.90).

ℹ Getting There & Away

Leipzig-Halle Airport (LEJ; www.leipzig-halle-airport.de) is about 21km west of Leipzig and linked to town by half-hourly S-Bahn train (€4.30, 35 minutes).

High-speed trains frequently serve Frankfurt (€80, 3½ hours), Dresden (€28, 1¼ hours) and Berlin (€47,1¼ hours), among others.

Weimar

☎03643 / POP 65,500

Wandering around Weimar's enchanting old streets, you can sense the presence of such notables as Goethe, Schiller, Bach, Liszt and Nietzsche, who once made their home here. There are plenty of statues, plaques and museums to remind you of their legacy, along with parks and gardens to take a break from the intellectual onslaught.

Sights

★**Goethe-Nationalmuseum** MUSEUM
(☎03643-545 400; www.klassik-stiftung.de; Frauenplan 1; adult/concession/under 16yr €12/8.50/free; ⊙9am-6pm Tue-Sun Apr-Oct, to 4pm Nov-Mar) This museum has the most comprehensive and insightful exhibit about Johann Wolfgang von Goethe, who is to the Germans what Shakespeare is to the British. It incorporates his home of 50 years, left pretty much as it was upon his death in 1832. This is where Goethe worked, studied, researched and penned *Faust* and other immortal works. In a modern annex, documents and objects shed light on the man and his achievements, not only in literature but also in art, science and politics.

If you're a Goethe fan, you'll get the chills when seeing his study and the bedroom where he died, both preserved in their original state. To get the most from your visit, use the audioguide (free).

Schiller-Museum MUSEUM
(☎03643-545 400; www.klassik-stiftung.de; Schillerstrasse 12; adult/concession/under 16yr €7.50/6/free; ⊙9.30am-6pm Tue-Sun Apr-Oct, to 4pm Nov-Mar) The dramatist Friedrich von Schiller (and close friend of Goethe's) lived in Weimar from 1799 until his early death in 1805. Study up on the man, his family and life in Thuringia in a recently revamped exhibit before plunging on to the private quarters, including the study with his deathbed and the desk where he wrote *Wilhelm Tell* and other famous works.

Bauhaus Museum MUSEUM
(☎03643-545 400; www.klassik-stiftung.de; Theaterplatz 1; adult/concession/under 16yr €4.50/3/free; ⊙10am-6pm Apr-Oct, to 4pm Nov-Mar) Considering that Weimar is the 1919 birthplace of the influential Bauhaus school of art, design and architecture, this museum is a rather modest affair. A new, representative museum is expected to open in 2018.

Park an der Ilm PARK
The sprawling Park an der Ilm provides a buccolic backdrop to the town and is also home to a trio of historic houses, most notably the **Goethe Gartenhaus** (where Goethe lived from 1776 to 1782), the **Römisches Haus** (the local duke's summer retreat, with period rooms and an exhibit on the park) and the **Liszt-Haus** (where the composer resided in 1848 and again from 1869 to 1886, and wrote the *Faust Symphony*).

Sleeping

★**Casa dei Colori** B&B €€
(☎03643-489 640; www.casa-colori.de; Eisfeld 1a; d incl breakfast €95-125; P 📶) Possibly Weimar's most charming boutique *Pension* (B&B or small hotel), the Casa convincingly imports cheerfully exuberant Mediterranean flair to central Europe. The mostly good-sized rooms are dressed in bold colours and come with a small desk, a couple of comfy armchairs and a stylish bathroom.

Amalienhof HOTEL €€
(☎03643-5490; www.amalienhof-weimar.de; Amalienstrasse 2; d incl parking €97-125; P 📶) The

WORTH A TRIP

EISENACH

On the edge of the Thuringian forest, Eisenach is the birthplace of Johann Sebastian Bach, but even the town's **museum** (03691-793 40; www.bachhaus.de; Frauenplan 21; adult/concession €8.50/4.50; 10am-6pm) dedicated to the great composer plays second fiddle to its main attraction: the awe-inspiring 11th-century **Wartburg** (03691-2500; www.wartburg-eisenach.de; Auf der Wartburg 1; tour adult/concession €9/5, museum & Luther study only €5/3; tours 8.30am-5pm Apr-Oct, 9am-3.30pm Nov-Mar, English tour 1.30pm) castle.

Perched high above the town (views!), the humungous pile hosted medieval minstrel song contests and was the home of Elisabeth, a Hungarian princess later canonised for her charitable deeds. Its most famous resident, however, was **Martin Luther**, who went into hiding here in 1521 after being excommunicated and placed under papal ban. During this 10-month stay, he translated the New Testament from Greek into German, contributing enormously to the development of the written German language. His modest study is part of the guided tour. Back in town, there's an exhibit about the man and his historical impact in the **Lutherhaus** (03691-298 30; www.lutherhaus-eisenach.de; Lutherplatz 8; adult/concession €6/4; 10am-5pm, closed Mon Nov-Mar), where he lived as a schoolboy.

Arrive before 11am to avoid the worst of the crowds. From April to October, bus 10 runs hourly from 9am to 5pm from the Hauptbahnhof (central train station) to the Eselstation stop, from where it's a steep 10-minute walk up to the castle.

Regional trains run frequently to Erfurt (€11.10, 45 minutes) and Weimar (€14.40, one hour). The **tourist office** (03691-792 30; www.eisenach.de; Markt 24; 10am-6pm Mon-Fri, to 5pm Sat & Sun) can help with finding accommodation.

charms of this hotel are manifold: classy antique furnishings, richly styled rooms that point to history without burying you in it, and a late breakfast buffet for those who take their holidays seriously. It's a splendid choice.

Eating & Drinking

JoHanns Hof GERMAN €€
(03643-493 617; www.restaurant-weimar.com; Scherfgasse 1; mains €12-25, lunch special €6.50; 11.30am-2.30pm & 5-11pm Mon-Sat) JoHanns is a breezy and elegant port of call for inspired modern German cuisine and perfectly prepared choice cuts of steak, paired with a carefully curated selection of wines from the nearby Saale-Unstrut region. For a break from sightseeing, tuck into the value-priced weekday lunch specials in the cosy courtyard.

Residenz-Café INTERNATIONAL €€
(03643-594 08; www.residenz-cafe.de; Grüner Markt 4; breakfast €2.90-6.40, mains €5-12; 8am-1am;) Locally adored 'Resi' is a Viennese-style coffeehouse and a jack of all trades – everyone should find something to their taste here no matter where the hands on the clock. The 'Lovers' Breakfast' comes with sparkling wine, the cakes are delicious and the salads crisp, but perhaps the most creativity goes into the weekly specials.

Information

Tourist Office (03643-7450; www.weimar.de; Markt 10; 9.30am-7pm Mon-Sat, to 3pm Sun Apr-Oct, 9.30am-6pm Mon-Fri, to 2.30pm Sat & Sun Nov-Mar) Sells the WeimarCard (per day €14.50) for free or discounted museum admissions and travel on city buses and other benefits.

Getting There & Away

Frequent direct train connections include Erfurt (€5.30, 15 minutes), Eisenach (€15.30, one hour), Leipzig (€19.20, 1¾ hours), Dresden (€47, 2½ hours) and Berlin-Hauptbahnhof (€58, 2¼ hours). The town centre is a 20-minute walk or ride on bus 1 away.

Erfurt

0361 / POP 205,000

A little river courses through this pretty medieval pastiche of sweeping squares, time-worn alleyways, a house-lined bridge and lofty church spires. Erfurt also boasts one of Germany's oldest universities, founded by rich merchants in 1392, where Martin Luther studied philosophy before becoming a monk at the local monastery. It's a refreshingly untouristed spot and well worth exploring.

Sights

All of Erfurt's main sights cluster in the old town, about a 10-minute walk from the train station (or quick ride on tram 3, 4 or 6). The most striking panorama unfolds on the vast Domplatz where two churches – the Mariendom and the Severikirche – form a photogenic ensemble lorded over by the vast and well-preserved Petersberg citadel.

Mariendom CHURCH

(St Mary's Cathedral; ☎0361-646 1265; www.dom-erfurt.de; Domplatz; ⏲9.30am-6pm Mon-Sat, 1-6pm Sun May-Oct, to 5pm Nov-Apr) The cathedral where Martin Luther was ordained a priest has origins as a simple 8th-century chapel that grew into the stately Gothic pile you see today. Standouts in its treasure-filled interior include the stained-glass windows; the Wolfram, an 850-year-old bronze candelabrum in the shape of a man; the Gloriosa bell (1497); a Romanesque stucco Madonna; and the intricately carved choir stalls.

The steps buttressing the cathedral make for a dramatic backdrop for the popular **Domstufen-Festspiele**, a classical music festival held in July or August.

Krämerbrücke BRIDGE

(Merchants' Bridge) Flanked by cute half-timbered houses on both sides, this charming 1325 stone bridge is the only one north of the Alps that's still inhabited. To this day people live above little shops with attractive displays of chocolate and pottery, jewellery and basic souvenirs. See the bridge from above by climbing the tower of the **Ägidienkirche** (usually open 11am to 5pm) punctuating its eastern end.

Augustinerkloster CHURCH

(Augustinian Monastery; ☎0361-576 600; www.augustinerkloster.de; Augustinerstrasse 10; tour adult/concession €6/4; ⏲tours 9.30am-5pm Mon-Sat, 11am & noon Sun Apr-Oct, 9.30am-3.30pm Mon-Fri, to 2pm Sat, 11am Sun Nov-Mar) It's Luther lore galore at the very monastery where the reformer lived from 1505 to 1511, and where he was ordained as a monk and read his first Mass. You're free to roam the grounds, visit the church with its ethereal Gothic stained-glass windows and attend the prayer services. Guided tours of the monastery itself take in the cloister, a re-created Luther cell and an exhibit on Luther's life in Erfurt. You can sleep here, too. Enter on Comthurgasse.

Sleeping

Opera Hostel HOSTEL €

(☎0361-6013 1360; www.opera-hostel.de; Walkmühlstrasse 13; dm €13-20, s/d/tr €49/60/81, linen €2.50; @📶) Run with smiles and aplomb, this upmarket hostel in a historic building above a steakhouse scores big with wallet-watching global nomads. Rooms are bright and spacious, many with an extra sofa for chilling, and you can make friends in the communal kitchen and on-site lounge-bar. From the train station, take bus 51 (direction: Hochheim) to 'Alte Oper'.

Pension Rad-Hof PENSION €

(☎0361-602 7761; www.rad-hof.de; Kirchgasse 1b; d €66; @📶) The owners of this cyclist-friendly guesthouse, next to the Augustinian monastery and near the pub quarter, have gone the extra mile in renovating the building with natural materials, such as wood and mud. No two rooms are alike.

Hotel Brühlerhöhe HOTEL €€

(☎0361-241 4990; www.hotel-bruehlerhoehe-erfurt.de; Rudolfstrasse 48; d from €85; P📶) This Prussian officers' casino turned chic city hotel gets high marks for its opulent breakfast spread (€12.50) and smiley, quick-on-their-feet staff. Room are modern but cosy with chocolate brown furniture, thick carpets and sparkling baths. It's a 10-minute walk or short tram ride into the town centre.

Eating & Drinking

Pub and cafes abound in the narrow lanes of the Andreasviertel north of the Dom.

Zwiesel GERMAN €

(Michaelisstrasse 31; mains €6-9; ⏲6pm-late Mon-Thu, 3pm-late Fri-Sun) A combination of home-style food, cold beer, an epic cocktail list and an easy-going vibe has been the winning formula at Lars Schirmer's popular locals' hang-out. On colder days the art-decorated vaulted cellar beckons while in summer the action moves into the beer garden.

Henner SANDWICHES €

(☎0361-654 6691; www.henner-sandwiches.de; Weitergasse 8; dishes €3.50-8; ⏲8am-5pm Mon-Fri; 🌱) This upbeat bistro makes a great daytime pit stop for freshly made sandwiches, homemade soups and crisp salads.

Zum Wenigemarkt 13 GERMAN €€

(☎0361-642 2379; www.wenigemarkt-13.de; Wenigemarkt 13; mains €9-17; ⏲11.30am-11pm) Run by a dynamic family, this upbeat restaurant serves traditional and updated takes on Thuringian cuisine starring regionally hunted and gathered ingredients when possible. Tender salt-encrusted pork roast and trout drizzled with tangy caper white-wine sauce are both menu stars.

Information

Tourist Office (☎0361-664 00; www.erfurt-tourismus.de; Benediktsplatz 1; ⏲10am-6pm Mon-Sat, to 2pm Sun Apr-Dec, 10am-6pm Mon-Fri, to 4pm Sat, to 2pm Sun Jan-Mar) Sells the ErfurtCard (€12.90 per 48 hours), which includes a city tour, public transport and free or discounted admissions.

Getting There & Around

Fast trains leave frequently for Berlin (€61, 2¾ hours; some with change in Leipzig), Dresden (€51, 2¾ hours) and Frankfurt-am-Main (€55, 2¼ hours). Regional trains to Weimar (€5.30, 15 minutes) and Eisenach (€11.80, 45 minutes) depart at least once hourly. From Erfurt's central station, trams 3, 4 and 6 run via Anger and Fischmarkt to Domplatz.

BAVARIA

From the cloud-shredding Alps to the fertile Danube plain, Bavaria (Bayern) is a place that keeps its clichéd promises. Story-book castles bequeathed by an oddball king poke through dark forest, cowbells tinkle in flower-filled meadows, the thwack of palm on Lederhosen accompanies the clump of frothy stein on timber, and medieval walled towns go about their time-warped business.

But there's so much more than the chocolate-box idyll. Learn about Bavaria's state-of-the-art motor industry in Munich, discover its Nazi past in Nuremberg and Berchtesgaden, sip world-class wines in Würzburg or take a mind-boggling train ride up Germany's highest mountains. Destinations are often described as possessing 'something for everyone'. In Bavaria, this is no exaggeration.

Munich

☎089 / POP 1.38 MILLION

If you're looking for Alpine clichés, they're all here, but Munich also has plenty of unexpected cards down its dirndl. Folklore and age-old traditions exist side by side with sleek BMWs, designer boutiques and high-powered industry. Its museums include world-class collections of artistic masterpieces, and its music and cultural scenes are second only to Berlin's.

OKTOBERFEST

Hordes come to Munich for **Oktoberfest** (www.oktoberfest.de), running the 15 days before the first Sunday in October. Reserve accommodation well ahead and go early in the day so you can grab a seat in one of the hangar-sized beer tents spread across the Theresienwiese grounds, about 1km southwest of the Hauptbahnhof. While there is no entrance fee, those €11 1L steins of beer (called *Mass*) add up fast. Although its origins are in the marriage celebrations of Crown Prince Ludwig in 1810, there's nothing regal about this beery bacchanalia now: expect mobs, expect to meet new and drunken friends, expect decorum to vanish as night sets in and you'll have a blast.

Sights

Altstadt

★Marienplatz SQUARE

(Ⓢ Marienplatz) The heart and soul of the Altstadt, Marienplatz, is a popular gathering spot and packs a lot of personality into a compact frame. It's anchored by the Mariensäule (Mary's Column), built in 1638 to celebrate the victory over Swedish forces during the Thirty Years' War. At 11am and noon (also 5pm March to October), the square jams up with tourists craning their necks to take in the cute carillon in the Neues Rathaus (New Town Hall).

St Peterskirche CHURCH

(Church of St Peter; Rindermarkt 1; admission church free, tower adult/child €2/1; ⏲tower 9am-7pm Mon-Fri, from 10am Sat & Sun May-Oct, closes 1hr earlier Nov-Apr; Ⓢ Marienplatz, Ⓤ Marienplatz) Some 306 steps divide you from the best view of central Munich from the 92m tower of St Peterskirche, Munich's oldest church (1150). Inside awaits a virtual textbook of art through the centuries. Worth taking a closer peek at are the Gothic St-Martin-Altar, the baroque ceiling fresco by Johann Baptist Zimmermann and rococo sculptures by Ignaz Günther.

Central Munich

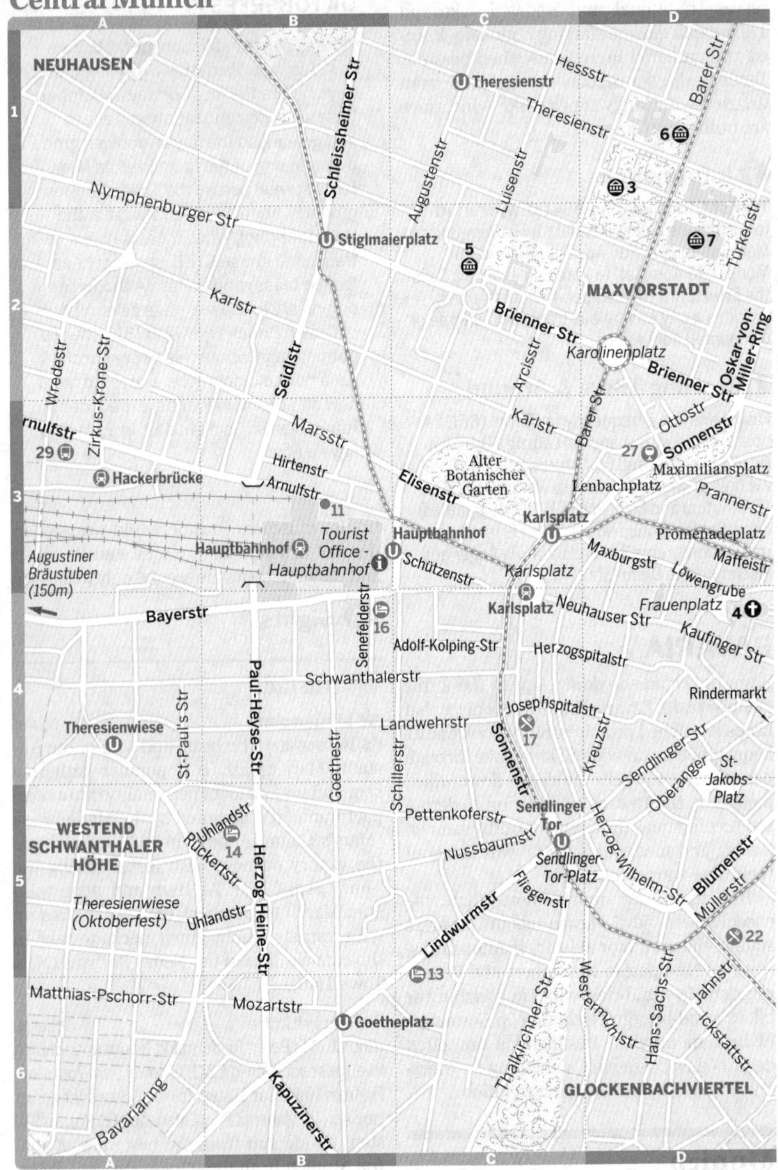

Viktualienmarkt MARKET

(⌚Mon-Fri&Sat morning; S Marienplatz, Marienplatz) Fresh fruits and vegetables, piles of artisan cheeses, tubs of exotic olives, hams and jams, chanterelles and truffles – Viktualienmarkt is a feast of flavours and one of central Europe's finest gourmet markets.

Frauenkirche CHURCH

(Church of Our Lady; ☎089-290 0820; www.muenchner-dom.de; Frauenplatz 1; ⌚7am-7pm

Central Munich

Top Sights
1 Marienplatz ... E4
2 Residenzmuseum ... E3

Sights
3 Alte Pinakothek ... D1
4 Frauenkirche ... D4
5 Lenbachhaus ... C2
6 Neue Pinakothek ... D1
7 Pinakothek der Moderne ... D2
8 Schatzkammer der Residenz ... E3
9 St Peterskirche ... E4
10 Viktualienmarkt ... E4

Activities, Courses & Tours
11 Radius Tours & Bike Rental ... B3

Sleeping
12 Flushing Meadows ... E6
13 Hotel Cocoon ... C6
14 Hotel Uhland ... B5
15 Louis Hotel ... E4
16 Wombats City Hostel Munich ... B4

Eating
17 Café Cord ... C4
18 Kochspielhaus ... E5
19 Les Deux Brasserie ... E3
20 Schmalznudel ... E4
21 Vegelangelo ... F4
22 Wirtshaus Fraunhofer ... D5
23 Wirtshaus in der Au ... F6

Drinking & Nightlife
24 Atomic Café ... E4
25 Hofbräuhaus ... E4
26 Niederlassung ... E5
27 Rote Sonne ... D3
28 Zephyr Bar ... E6

Transport
29 Zentraler Omnibusbahnhof ... A3

Sat-Wed, to 8.30pm Thu, to 6pm Fri; S Marienplatz) The landmark Frauenkirche, built between 1468 and 1488, is Munich's spiritual heart and the Mt Everest among its churches. No other building in the central city may stand taller than its onion-domed twin towers, which reach a skyscraping 99m.

Maxvorstadt, Schwabing & Englischer Garten

North of the Altstadt, Maxvorstadt is home to Munich's main university and top-drawer art museums. It segues into equally cafe-filled Schwabing, which rubs up against the vast **Englischer Garten**, one of Europe's biggest city parks and a favourite playground for locals and visitors alike.

Alte Pinakothek MUSEUM
(☎089-238 0526; www.pinakothek.de; Barer Strasse 27; adult/child €4/2, Sun €1, audioguide €4.50;

10am-8pm Tue, to 6pm Wed-Sun; Pinakotheken, Pinakotheken) Munich's main repository of old European masters is crammed with all the major players that decorated canvases between the 14th and 18th centuries. This neoclassical temple was masterminded by Leo von Klenze and is a delicacy even if you can't tell your Rembrandt from your Rubens. The collection is world famous for its exceptional quality and depth, especially when it comes to German masters. Note that some sections are closed for renovation.

Neue Pinakothek MUSEUM

(089-2380 5195; www.pinakothek.de; Barer Strasse 29; adult/child €7/5, Sun €1; 10am-6pm Thu-Mon, to 8pm Wed; Pinakotheken, Pinakotheken) The Neue Pinakothek harbours a well-respected collection of 19th- and early 20th-century paintings and sculpture, from rococo to *Jugendstil* (art nouveau). All the world-famous household names get wall space here, including crowd-pleasing French Impressionists such as Monet, Cézanne and Degas as well as Van Gogh, whose bold pigmented *Sunflowers* (1888) radiates cheer.

Pinakothek der Moderne MUSEUM

(089-2380 5360; www.pinakothek.de; Barer Strasse 40; adult/child €10/7, Sun €1; 10am-6pm Tue, Wed & Fri-Sun, to 8pm Thu; Pinakotheken, Pinakotheken) Germany's largest modern art museum unites four significant collections under a single roof: 20th-century art, applied design from the 19th century to today, a graphics collection and an architecture museum. It's housed in a spectacular building by Stephan Braunfels, whose four-storey interior centres on a vast eye-like dome from where soft natural light filters throughout blanched white galleries.

Lenbachhaus MUSEUM

(Municipal Gallery; 089-2333 2000; www.lenbachhaus.de; Luisenstrasse 33; adult/concession incl audioguide €10/5; 10am-9pm Tue, to 6pm Wed-Sun; Königsplatz, Königsplatz) Reopened to rave reviews after a four-year renovation that saw the addition of a new wing by Lord Norman Foster, this glorious gallery is once again the go-to place to admire the vibrant expressionist canvases of Kandinsky, Franz Marc, Paul Klee and other members of the ground-breaking modernist artist group called Blue Rider, founded in Munich in 1911.

NO WAVE GOODBYE

Munich is famous for beer, sausages and surfing. Yep, you read that right. Just go to the southern tip of the Englischer Garten at Prinzregentenstrasse and you'll see scores of people leaning over a bridge to cheer on wetsuit-clad daredevils as they 'hang 10' on an artificially created wave in the Eisbach creek. It's only a single wave, but it's a darn fine one.

Further Afield

Schloss Nymphenburg PALACE

(www.schloss-nymphenburg.de; adult/concession/under 18yr €6/5/free; 9am-6pm Apr–mid-Oct, 10am-4pm mid-Oct–Mar; Schloss Nymphenburg) The Bavarian royal family's summer residence and its lavish gardens sprawl around 5km northwest of the city centre. A self-guided tour kicks off in the Gallery of Beauties, where 38 portraits of attractive females chosen by an admiring King Ludwig I peer prettily from the walls. Other highlights include the Queen's Bedroom with the sleigh bed on which Ludwig II was born, and the King's Chamber resplendent with trompe l'œil ceiling frescoes.

BMW Museum MUSEUM

(089-125 016 001; www.bmw-welt.de; Am Olympiapark 2; adult/concession €8/6; museum 10am-6pm Tue-Sun, BMW Welt 9am-6pm Tue-Sun; Petuelring) The silver-bowl-shaped museum comprises seven themed 'houses' that examine the development of BMW's product line and include sections on motorcycles and motor racing. Even if you're not a petrol head, the interior design – with its curvy retro feel, futuristic bridges, squares and huge backlit wall screens – is reason enough to visit.

The museum is linked to two more architecturally stunning buildings: the BMW Headquarters (closed to the public) and the BMW-Welt showroom (admission free). Plant tours are available from 9am to 4.30pm on weekdays.

Tours

Radius Tours & Bike Rental GUIDED

(089-5502 9374; www.radiustours.com; Arnulfstrasse 3; office 8.30am-6pm Apr-Oct, to 2pm Nov-Mar) Entertaining and informative English-language tours include the donation-based city tour, a Third Reich tour and a beer-themed tour. Also does day trips to Neuschwanstein, Nuremberg and Salzburg. Rents bikes for €17 for 24 hours.

DON'T MISS

MUNICH RESIDENZ

Generations of Bavarian rulers expanded a medieval fortress into this vast and palatial compound that served as their primary residence and seat of government from 1508 to 1918. Today it's an Aladdin's cave of fanciful rooms and collections through the ages that can be seen on an audioguided tour of what is called the **Residenzmuseum** (☎089-290 671; www.residenz-muenchen.de; adult/concession/under 18yr €7/6/free; ⊙9am-6pm Apr–mid-Oct, 10am-5pm mid-Oct–Mar, last entry 1hr before closing; S Odeonsplatz). Allow at least two hours to see everything at a gallop.

Highlights include the fresco-smothered **Antiquarium** banqueting hall and the exuberantly rococo **Reiche Zimmer** (Ornate Rooms). The **Schatzkammer** (Residence Treasury; adult/concession/under 18yr with parents €7/6/free; ⊙9am-6pm Apr–mid-Oct, 10am-5pm mid-Oct–Mar, last entry 1hr before closing; S Odeonsplatz) displays a veritable banker's bonus worth of jewel-encrusted bling of yesteryear, from golden toothpicks to finely crafted swords, miniatures in ivory to gold entombed cosmetics trunks. A combined ticket for the Residenzmuseum and Schatzkammer is adult/concession €11/9.

City Bus 100 BUS
Ordinary city bus that runs from the Hauptbahnhof to the Ostbahnhof via 21 sights, including the Residenz and the Pinakothek museums.

Sleeping

Book way ahead during Oktoberfest and the busy summer. Many budget places cluster in the cheerless streets around the train station.

Wombats City Hostel Munich HOSTEL €
(☎089-5998 9180; www.wombats-hostels.com; Senefelderstrasse 1; dm €19-29, d €76; P @ 🛜; S Hauptbahnhof, 🚊 Hauptbahnhof) Munich's top hostel is a professionally run affair with a whopping 300 dorm beds plus private rooms. Dorms are painted in cheerful pastels and outfitted with wooden floors, ensuite facilities, sturdy lockers and comfy pine bunks, all in a central location near the train station. A free welcome drink awaits in the bar. Breakfast costs €3.90.

★ **Hotel Laimer Hof** HOTEL €€
(☎089-178 0380; www.laimerhof.de; Laimer Strasse 40; s/d from €65/85; P @ 🛜; 🚊 Romanplatz) Just a five-minute amble from Schloss Nymphenburg, this tranquil refuge is run by a friendly team who take time to get to know their guests. No two of the 23 rooms are alike, but all boast antique touches, oriental carpets and golden beds. Free bike rentals and coffee and tea in the lobby. Breakfast costs €10.

Hotel Uhland HOTEL €€
(☎089-543 350; www.hotel-uhland.de; Uhlandstrasse 1; s/d from €75/95; P 🛜; S Theresienwiese) The Uhland is an enduring favourite with regulars who like their hotel to feel like a home away from home. Free wi-fi and parking, a breakfast buffet with organic products, and minibar drinks that won't dent your budget are just some of the thoughtful features. Rooms have extra large waterbeds.

Flushing Meadows DESIGN HOTEL €€
(☎089-5527 9170; www.flushingmeadowshotel.com; Fraunhoferstrasse 32; studios €115-165; ⊙reception 6am-11pm; P ❄ 🛜; S Fraunhoferstrasse) Urban explorers keen on up-to-the-minute design cherish this new contender on the top two floors of a former postal office in the hip Glockenbachviertel. Each of the 11 concrete-ceilinged lofts reflects the vision of a locally known creative type, while three of the five penthouse studios have a private terrace. Breakfast costs €11.

Hotel Cocoon DESIGN HOTEL €€
(☎089-5999 3907; www.hotel-cocoon.de; Lindwurmstrasse 35; s/d from €69/89; S Sendlinger Tor, 🚊 Sendlinger Tor) Fans of retro design will strike gold in this central lifestyle hotel. Things kick off in the reception with its faux '70s veneer and dangling '60s ball chairs, and continue in the rooms. All are identical, decorated in retro oranges and greens and equipped with LCD TV, iPod dock and a 'laptop cabin'. The glass showers actually stand in the sleeping area, with only a kitschy Alpine meadow scene veiling life's vitals. Breakfast costs €9.

Louis Hotel HOTEL €€€
(☎089-411 9080; www.louis-hotel.com; Viktualienmarkt 6/Rindermarkt 2; r €159-289; S Marienplatz) An air of relaxed sophistication pervades the scene-savvy Louis, where good-sized rooms are furnished in nut and oak, natural stone

LOCAL KNOWLEDGE

BEER HALLS & BEER GARDENS

Beer drinking is not just an integral part of Munich's entertainment scene, it's a reason to visit. Following are a few options:

Augustiner Bräustuben (089-507 047; www.braeustuben.de; Landsberger Strasse 19; 10am-midnight; Holzapfelstrasse) Depending on the wind, an aroma of hops envelops you as you approach this traditional beer hall inside the actual Augustiner brewery. The Bavarian grub (mains €7.50 to €14) here is superb, especially the *Schweinshaxe* (pork knuckle). Different specials daily to boot.

Hofbräuhaus (089-290 136 100; www.hofbraeuhaus.de; Am Platzl 9; 9am-11.30pm; S Marienplatz, Kammerspiele, Marienplatz) The mothership of all beer halls is a warren of woodsy, vaulted rooms filled with beer-swilling revelers swaying to the inevitable oompah band and tucking into gut-busting Bavarian fare (mains €7.50 to €18). It's just as crazy fun as you imagined it to be. For more quiet, head to the big, flag-festooned hall upstairs.

Chinesischer Turm (089-383 8730; www.chinaturm.de; Englischer Garten 3; 10am-11pm; Chinesischer Turm, Tivolistrasse) This one's hard to ignore because of its Englischer Garten (English Garden) location and pedigree as Munich's oldest beer garden (since 1791). Camera-toting tourists and laid-back locals, picnicking families and suits sneaking a brew clomp around the wooden pagoda, serenaded by an oompah band.

and elegant tiles and equipped with the gamut of 'electronica', including iPod docks and flatscreens with Sky TV. All have small balconies facing either the courtyard or the Viktualienmarkt. Views are also terrific from the rooftop bar and restaurant. Breakfast costs €24.50.

Eating

Schmalznudel CAFE €

(Cafe Frischhut; 089-2602 3156; Prälat-Zistl-Strasse 8; pastries €1.70; 7am-6pm Mon-Fri, 5am-5pm Sat; S Marienplatz, Marienplatz) Officially called Cafe Frischhut, this little cult joint is mostly known by its nickname, *Schmalznudel*, an oily type of doughnut which is the only thing served here. Best enjoyed with a pot of steaming coffee.

Wirtshaus in der Au BAVARIAN €€

(089-448 1400; Lilienstrasse 51; mains €9-20; 5pm-midnight Mon-Fri, from 10am Sat & Sun; Deutsches Museum) This traditional Bavarian restaurant has a solid 21st-century vibe but it's the time-honoured dumpling that's the top speciality here, although carnivores might prefer the roast duck or another hearty menu item. Once a brewery, the space-rich dining room has chunky tiled floors, a lofty ceiling and a crackling fireplace in winter. When spring springs, the beer garden fills.

Wirtshaus Fraunhofer BAVARIAN €€

(089-266 460; www.fraunhofertheater.de; Fraunhoferstrasse 9; mains €7.50-19; 4pm-1am; ; Müllerstrasse) With its screechy parquet floors, stuccoed ceilings, wood panelling and virtually no trace that the last century even happened, this wonderfully characterful inn is perfect for exploring the region with a fork. The menu is a seasonally adapted checklist of southern German favourites, but also features at least a dozen vegetarian dishes.

Vegelangelo VEGETARIAN €€

(089-2880 6836; www.vegelangelo.de; Thomas-Wimmer-Ring 16; mains €10-19; noon-2pm Tue-Thu, 6pm-late Mon-Sat; ; Isartor, Isartor) Reservations are recommended at this petite vegie spot where Indian odds and ends, a piano and a small Victorian fireplace distract little from the superb meat-free cooking, all of which can be adapted to suit vegans. There's a menu-only (3/4 courses €24/30) policy Fridays and Saturdays. Cash only.

Café Cord INTERNATIONAL €€

(089-5454 0780; www.cafe-cord.tv; Sonnenstrasse 19; mains €10-20; 11am-1am Mon-Sat; S Karlsplatz, Karlsplatz, Karlsplatz) Clean-cut Cord is a good stop for a light lunch or coffee, or an ideal first stop on the club circuit. In summer the super delicious global fare (mains €10 to €20) tastes best in the romantic, twinkling courtyard.

Kochspielhaus INTERNATIONAL €€
(☎089-5480 2738; www.kochspielhaus.de; Rumfordstrasse 5; breakfast €10-16, mains €13-26; ⊙7am-8pm Sun & Mon, 6.30am-midnight Tue-Sat; Ⓢ Fraunhoferstrasse) Attached to a gourmet bakery called Backspielhaus, this modern-country-style lair accented with massive candles packages only super fresh, top-quality ingredients into clever pasta, meat and fish dishes. Also a great spot for breakfast, especially in summer when the white outdoor tables and benches beckon.

Les Deux Brasserie INTERNATIONAL €€
(☎089-710 407 373; www.lesdeux-muc.de; Maffaistrasse 3a; mains €6.50-17; ⊙noon-10pm; Ⓢ Marienplatz) Below the eponymous fine-dining restaurant, Les Deux' ground-floor brasserie is perfect for taking a tasty break without breaking the budget. Choose from such classics as mini burgers, club sandwich or Icelandic cod and chips or go for one of the more elaborate weekly specials. If the weather permits, tables spill into the courtyard.

Drinking & Nightlife

Apart from the beer halls and gardens, Munich has no shortage of lively pubs. The Glockenbachviertel, the Gärtnerplatzviertel, Maxvorstadt and Schwabing are good places to follow your ears.

Zephyr Bar COCKTAIL BAR
(www.zephyr-bar.de; Baaderstrasse 68; ⊙8pm-1am Mon-Thu, to 3am Fri & Sat; Ⓢ Fraunhoferstrasse) At one of Munich's best bars, Alex Schmaltz whips up courageous potions with unusual ingredients such as homemade cucumber-dill juice, sesame oil or banana-parsley purée. Cocktail alchemy at its finest, and a top gin selection to boot. No reservations.

Niederlassung BAR
(☎089-3260 0307; www.niederlassung.org; Buttermelcherstrasse 6; ⊙7pm-1am Tue-Thu, to 3am Fri & Sat, to midnight Sun; Ⓢ Fraunhoferstrasse, Ⓡ Isartor) From Adler Dry to Zephyr, this gin joint stocks an impressive 80 varieties of juniper juice in an unpretentious setting filled with books and sofas and humming with indie sounds. There's even a selection of different tonic waters to choose from. Happy hour from 7pm to 9pm and after midnight.

Rote Sonne CLUB
(☎089-5526 3330; www.rote-sonne.com; Maximiliansplatz 5; ⊙from 11pm Thu-Sun; Ⓠ Lenbachplatz) Named for a 1969 Munich cult movie starring It-Girl Uschi Obermaier, the Red Sun is a fiery nirvana for fans of electronic sounds. A global roster of DJs keeps the wooden dance floor packed and sweaty until the sun rises.

Atomic Café CLUB
(www.atomic.de; Neuturmstrasse 5; ⊙from 10pm Wed-Sat; Ⓠ Kammerspiele) This bastion of indie sounds with funky '60s decor is known for bookers with a knack for catching upwardly hopeful bands before their big break. Otherwise, it's party time; long-running Britwoch is the hottest Wednesday club night in town.

Information

Tourist Office (☎089-2339 6500; www.muenchen.de) Branches include Hauptbahnhof (Bahnhofplatz 2; ⊙9am-8pm Mon-Sat, 10am-6pm Sun) and Marienplatz (Marienplatz 2; ⊙10am-7pm Mon-Fri, to 5pm Sat, to 2pm Sun).

Getting There & Away

AIR

Munich Airport (MUC; www.munich-airport.de) is about 30km northeast of town and linked to the Hauptbahnhof every 10 minutes by S-Bahn (S1 and S8; €10.40, 40 minutes) and every 20 minutes by the Lufthansa Airport Bus (€10.50, 45 minutes, between 5am and 8pm).

Ryanair flies into Memmingen's **Allgäu Airport** (FMM; www.allgaeu-airport.de), 125km to the west. The Allgäu-Airport-Express travels up to seven times daily between here and Munich Hauptbahnhof (€17, €12 if bought online, 1½ hours).

BUS

Buses, including the Romantic Road Coach, depart from **Zentraler Omnibusbahnhof** (Central Bus Station, ZOB; Arnulfstrasse 21) at S-Bahn station Hackerbrücke near the main train station.

TRAIN

All services leave from the Hauptbahnhof, where **Euraide** (www.euraide.de; Desk 1, Reisezentrum, Hauptbahnhof; ⊙10am-7pm Mon-Fri Aug-Apr)

GAY & LESBIAN MUNICH

In Munich, the rainbow flag flies especially proudly along Müllerstrasse and the adjoining Glockenbachviertel. Keep an eye out for the freebie mags *Our Munich* and *Sergej*, which contain up-to-date listings and news about the community and gay-friendly establishments around town. The website **Gay Tourist Office** (www.gaytouristoffice.de) also has handy information and can book gay-friendly lodging.

WORTH A TRIP

DACHAU CONCENTRATION CAMP

About 16km northwest of central Munich, **Dachau** (Dachau Concentration Camp Memorial Site; 08131-669 970; www.kz-gedenkstaette-dachau.de; Peter-Roth-Strasse 2a, Dachau; museum admission free; 9am-5pm Tue-Sun) opened in 1933 as the first Nazi concentration camp. All in all, it 'processed' more than 200,000 inmates, killing between 30,000 and 40,000. It is now a haunting memorial that will stay long in your memory. Expect to spend two to three hours exploring the grounds and exhibits. For deeper understanding, pick up an audioguide (€3.50), join a 2½-hour tour and watch the 22-minute English-language documentary at the main museum.

From the Hauptbahnhof take the S2 to Dachau station (two-zone ticket; €5.20, 25 minutes), then catch bus 726 (direction: Saubachsiedlung) to the KZ-Gedenkstätte stop.

is a friendly English-speaking travel agency. Frequent fast and direct service include trains to Nuremberg (€55, 1¼ hours), Frankfurt (€101, 3¼ hours), Berlin (€130, six hours) and Vienna (€91.20, four hours), as well as twice-daily trains to Prague (€69.10 six hours).

Getting Around

For public transport information, consult www.mvv-muenchen.de.

Garmisch-Partenkirchen

08821 / POP 26,700

An outdoor paradise for skiers and hikers, Garmisch-Partenkirchen is blessed with a fabled setting a snowball's throw from Germany's highest peak, the 2962m-high Zugspitze. Garmisch has a more cosmopolitan feel, while Partenkirchen retains an old-world Alpine village vibe. The towns were merged for the 1936 Winter Olympics.

Sights

Zugspitze MOUNTAIN

(www.zugspitze.de; return adult/child May-Sep €51/29.50, Oct-Apr €42.50/23; train 8.15am-2.15pm) On good days, views from Germany's rooftop extend into four countries. The round trip starts in Garmisch aboard a cogwheel train (Zahnradbahn) that chugs along the mountain base to the Eibsee, an idyllic forest lake. From here, the Eibsee-Seilbahn, a super steep cable car, swings to the top at 2962m. When you're done admiring the views, the Gletscherbahn cable car brings you to the Zugspitz glacier at 2600m, from where the cogwheel train heads back to Garmisch.

The trip to the Zugspitze summit is as memorable as it is popular; beat the crowds by starting early in the day and, if possible, skip weekends altogether.

Sleeping & Eating

Reindl's Partenkirchner Hof HOTEL €€€

(08821-943 870; www.reindls.de; Bahnhofstrasse 15; d €130-230; restaurant noon-2.30pm & 6.30-11pm; P @) Though Reindl's doesn't look worthy of its five stars from the outside, this elegant, tri-winged luxury hotel is stacked with perks, a wine bar and a top-notch gourmet restaurant. Rooms are studies in folk-themed elegance and some enjoy gob-smacking mountain views.

Bräustüberl GERMAN €€

(08821-2312; www.braeustueberl-garmisch.de; Fürstenstrasse 23; mains €8.50-19) This quintessentially Bavarian tavern is the place to cosy up with some local nosh, served by dirndl-trussed waitresses, while the enormous enamel coal-burning stove revives chilled extremities. Live music on Saturdays.

Information

Tourist Office (08821-180 700; www.gapa.de; Richard-Strauss-Platz 2; 9am-6pm Mon-Sat, 10am-noon Sun) Friendly staff hand out maps, brochures and advice.

Getting There & Away

Numerous tour operators run day trips to Garmisch-Partenkirchen from Munich but there's also at least hourly direct train service (€20.10, 1¼ hour).

Berchtesgaden

08652 / POP 7600

Steeped in myth and legend, Berchtesgaden and the surrounding countryside (the Berchtesgadener Land) is almost preternaturally beautiful. Framed by six formidable mountain ranges and home to Germany's second-highest mountain, the Watzmann

(2713m), its dreamy, fir-lined valleys are filled with gurgling streams and peaceful Alpine villages. Alas, Berchtesgaden's history is also indelibly tainted by the Nazi period. The area is easily visited on a day trip from Salzburg.

Sights

Eagle's Nest HISTORIC SITE
(Kehlsteinhaus; ☎08652-2929; www.kehlsteinhaus.de; Obersalzberg; adult/child €16.10/9.30; buses 7.40am-4pm mid-May–Oct) The Eagle's Nest is a mountaintop retreat built as a 50th-birthday gift for Hitler. It took some 3000 workers only two years to carve the precipitous 6km-long mountain road, cut a 124m-long tunnel and a brass-panelled lift through the rock, and build the lodge itself (now a restaurant). It can only be reached by special shuttle bus from the Kehlsteinhaus bus station. Avoid peak hours (10am to 1pm).

On clear days, views from the top are breathtaking. If you're not driving, bus 838 makes the trip to the shuttle bus stop from the Berchtesgaden Hauptbahnhof every half hour.

At the mountain station, you'll be asked to book a spot on a return bus. Allow at least two hours to get through lines, explore the lodge and the mountaintop, and perhaps have a bite to eat. Don't panic if you miss your bus – just go back to the mountain station kiosk and rebook.

Dokumentation Obersalzberg MUSEUM
(☎08652-947 960; www.obersalzberg.de; Salzbergstrasse 41, Obersalzberg; adult/child €3/free, audioguide €2; 9am-5pm daily Apr-Oct, 10am-3pm Tue-Sun Nov-Mar, last entry 1hr before closing) In 1933 the quiet mountain village of Obersalzberg (3km from Berchtesgaden) became the second seat of Nazi power after Berlin, a dark period that's given the full historical treatment at this excellent exhibit. It documents the forced takeover of the area, the construction of the compound and the daily life of the Nazi elite. All facets of Nazi terror are dealt with, including Hitler's near-mythical appeal, his racial politics, the resistance movement, foreign policy and the death camps. A section of the underground bunker network is open for perusal. Half-hourly bus 838 from Berchtesgaden Hauptbahnhof will get you there.

Königssee LAKE
(☎08652-963 696; www.seenschifffahrt.de; Schönau; return boat adult/child €13.90/7; boats 8am-5.15pm mid-Apr–mid-Oct) Crossing the serenely picturesque, emerald green Königssee makes for some unforgettable memories and once-in-a-lifetime photo opportunities. Cradled by steep mountain walls some 5km south of Berchtesgaden, the Königssee is Germany's highest lake (603m), with drinkably pure waters shimmering into fjordlike depths. Bus 841 makes the trip out here from the Berchtesgaden Hauptbahnhof roughly every hour.

Tours

Eagle's Nest Tours TOUR
(☎08652-649 71; www.eagles-nest-tours.com; Königsseer Strasse 2; adult/child €53/35; 1.15pm mid-May–Oct) This highly reputable outfit offers a fascinating overview of Berchtesgaden's Nazi legacy.

Sleeping & Eating

Hotel Edelweiss HOTEL €€€
(☎08652-979 90; www.edelweiss-berchtesgaden.com; Maximilianstrasse 2; d €200-236) Smack dab in the town centre, the Edelweiss is Berchtesgaden's sleek new contender. The style is modern Bavarian, meaning a combination of traditional woodsy flair and such hip factors as a luxe spa, a rooftop terrace restaurant-bar with wonderful mountain views and an outdoor infinity pool. Rooms are XL-sized and most have a balcony.

HITLER'S MOUNTAIN RETREAT

Of all the German towns tainted by the Third Reich, the Berchtesgaden area carries a burden heavier than most. Hitler fell in love with the secluded Alpine village of Obersalzberg while vacationing here in the 1920s and later bought a small country home that was enlarged into an imposing residence – the Berghof.

After seizing power in 1933, the Führer established a second seat of power here and brought much of the party brass with him. They drove out the locals and turned the compound into a *Führersperrgebiet* (an off-limits area). Many important decisions, about war and peace and the Holocaust, were made here.

In the final days of WWII, British and American bombers levelled much of Obersalzberg, although the Eagle's Nest, Hitler's mountaintop eyrie, was left strangely unscathed.

DON'T MISS

SCHLOSS NEUSCHWANSTEIN

Appearing through the mountaintops like a misty mirage, **Schloss Neuschwanstein** (☎ tickets 08362-930 830; www.neuschwanstein.de; Neuschwansteinstrasse 20; adult/concession/under 18yr €12/11/free, incl Hohenschwangau €23/21/free; ⏲ 9am-6pm Apr–mid-Oct, 10am-4pm mid-Oct–Mar) was the model for Disney's *Sleeping Beauty* castle. Ludwig II planned this sugary fairy-tale pile himself, with the help of a stage designer rather than an architect. He envisioned it as a giant set on which to re-create the world of Germanic mythology, inspired by the operatic works of his friend Richard Wagner. The most impressive room is the **Sängersaal** (Minstrels' Hall), the wall frescoes depict scenes from the opera *Tannhäuser*.

Other completed sections include Ludwig's Tristan and Isolde–themed **bedroom**, dominated by a huge Gothic-style bed crowned with intricately carved cathedral-like spires; a gaudy **artificial grotto** (another allusion to *Tannhäuser*); and the Byzantine-style **Thronsaal** (Throne Room) with an incredible mosaic floor containing over two million stones. The tour ends with a 20-minute film on the castle and its creator.

For the postcard view of Neuschwanstein, walk 10 minutes up to **Marienbrücke** (Mary's Bridge).

Bräustübl BAVARIAN €€

(☎ 08652-976 724; www.braeustueberl-berchtesgaden.de; Bräuhausstrasse 13; mains €6.50-15; ⏲ 10am-1am) Past the vaulted entrance painted in Bavaria's white and blue diamonds, this cosy beer hall–beer garden is run by the local brewery. Expect a carnivorous feast with such favourite rib-stickers as pork roast and the house speciality: baked veal head (tastes better than it sounds). On Friday and Saturday, a traditional band kicks into knee-slapping action.

Information

Regional Tourist Office (☎ 08652-896 70; www.berchtesgaden.com; Königsseer Strasse 2; ⏲ 8.30am-6pm Mon-Fri, 9am-5pm Sat, 9am-3pm Sun Apr–mid-Oct, reduced hours mid-Oct–Mar) Near the train station, this office has information about the entire Berchtegaden region.

Getting There & Away

Bus 840 connects the train stations in Berchtesgaden and Salzburg twice hourly (50 minutes). Travelling from Munich by train involves a change to a bus at Freilassing (€32.80, 2½ hours).

Romantic Road

Stretching 400km from the vineyards of Würzburg to the foot of the Alps, the Romantic Road (Romantische Strasse) is by far the most popular of Germany's themed holiday routes. It passes through more than two-dozen cities and towns, most famously Rothenburg ob der Tauber.

Getting There & Around

Frankfurt and Munich are the most popular gateways for exploring the Romantic Road, especially if you decide to take the **Romantic Road Coach** (☎ 0719-126 268, 0171-653 234; www.touring-travel.eu). From April to October this special service runs one coach daily in each direction between Frankfurt and Füssen (for Neuschwanstein) via Munich; the entire trip takes around 12 hours. There's no charge for breaking the journey and continuing the next day. Note that buses get incredibly crowded in summer.

Tickets are available for the entire route or for short segments. Buy them online or from travel agents, EurAide (p469) in Munich or *Reisezentrum* offices in larger train stations.

Füssen

☎ 08362 / POP 14,900

In the foothills of the Alps, Füssen itself is a charming town, although most visitors skip it and head straight to Schloss Neuschwanstein and Hohenschwangau, the two most famous castles associated with King Ludwig II. You can see both on a long day trip from Munich, although only when spending the night, after all the day trippers have gone, will you sense a certain Alpine serenity.

Sights

The castles are about 4km outside of Füssen.

Schloss Hohenschwangau CASTLE

(☎ 08362-930 830; www.hohenschwangau.de; adult/concession/under 18yr €12/11/free, incl Neuschwanstein €23/21/free; ⏲ 8am-5.30pm Apr–mid-Oct, 9am-3.30pm mid-Oct–Mar) King Ludwig II grew up at the lovely sun-yellow Schloss

Hohenschwangau and later enjoyed spending summers here until his death in 1886. His father, Maximilian II, built this palace in a neo-Gothic style atop 12th-century ruins left by Schwangau knights. Far less showy than Neuschwanstein, Hohenschwangau has a distinctly lived-in feel where every piece of furniture is a used original. After his father died, Ludwig's main alteration was having stars, illuminated with hidden oil lamps, painted on the ceiling of his bedroom.

Sleeping & Eating

Altstadthotel Zum Hechten HOTEL €€

(08362-916 00; www.hotel-hechten.com; Ritterstrasse 6; d €94-100; P) This is one of Füssen's oldest hotels and a barrel of fun. Public areas are traditional in style while the bedrooms have a contemporary feel with beautifully patterned parquet floors, a large bed and sunny colours. The small but classy spa is great for relaxing after a day on the trail.

Restaurant Ritterstub'n GERMAN €€

(08362-7759; www.restaurant-ritterstuben.de; Ritterstrasse 4; mains €5.50-16; 11.30am-11pm Tue-Sun) This convivial pit stop has value-priced salads, snacks, lunch specials, fish, schnitzel and gluten-free dishes, and even a cute kids menu. The medieval-knight theme can be a bit grating but kids often love eating their fish sticks with their fingers or seeing mum and dad draped in a big bib.

Information

Tourist Office (08362-938 50; www.fuessen.de; Kaiser-Maximilian-Platz; 9am-6pm Mon-Fri, 10am-2pm Sat, 10am-noon Sun May-Oct, 9am-5pm Mon-Fri, 10am-2pm Sat Nov-Apr) Can help find lodging.

CASTLE TICKETS & TOURS

Both Hohenschwanstein and Neuschwanstein must be seen on guided 35-minute tours (in German or English). Timed tickets are only available from the **Ticket-Center** (08362-930 830; www.hohenschwangau.de; Alpenseestrasse 12; 8am-5.30pm Apr–mid-Oct, 9am-3.30pm mid-Oct–Mar) at the foot of the castles and may be reserved online until two days prior to your visit (recommended).

If visiting both castles on the same day, the Hohenschwangau tour is scheduled first with enough time for the steep 30- to 40-minute walk between the castles. The footsore can travel by bus or by horse drawn carriage.

Getting There & Away

Füssen is the southern terminus of the Romantic Road Coach.

Regional trains run from Munich to Füssen every two hours with onward service to the castles on bus 78 or 73 (€27.90, 2½ hours). It's possible to do this as a day trip if leaving Munich around 8am.

Rothenburg ob der Tauber

09861 / POP 11,000

With its jumble of half-timbered houses enclosed by Germany's best-preserved ramparts, Rothenburg ob der Tauber lays on the medieval cuteness with a trowel. It's an essential stop on the Romantic Road but, alas, overcrowding can detract from its charm. Visit early or late in the day (or, ideally, stay overnight) to experience this historic wonderland sans crowds.

Sights

★Jakobskirche CHURCH

(Church of St Jacob; Klingengasse 1; adult/child €2/0.50; 9am-5.30pm Mon-Sat, 10.45am-5.30pm Sun) Rothenburg's majestic 500-year-old Lutheran parish church shelters the **Heilig Blut Altar** (Sacred Blood Altar), a supremely intricate altarpiece by medieval master carver Tilman Riemenschneider (it's up the stairs behind the organ).

Rathausturm HISTORIC BUILDING

(Town Hall Tower; Marktplatz; adult/concession €2/0.50; 9.30am-12.30pm & 1-5pm daily Apr-Oct, noon-3pm Sat & Sun Jan-Mar & Nov, 10.30-2pm & 2.30-6pm daily Dec) Climb the 220 steps of the medieval town hall to the viewing platform of the Rathausturm to be rewarded with widescreen views of the Tauber.

Stadtmauer HISTORIC SITE

(Town Wall) Follow in the footsteps of sentries on a walk along Rothenburg's original 15th-century town fortifications. A 2.5km stretch of it is accessible, but even a short walk 5m to 7m above the ground delivers tremendous views over the town's red roofs.

Mittelalterliches Kriminalmuseum MUSEUM

(Medieval Crime & Punishment Museum; 09681-5359; www.kriminalmuseum.rothenburg.de; Burggasse 3-5; adult/child €5/3; 10am-6pm May-Oct, shorter hours Nov-Apr) Medieval implements of torture and punishment are on show at this gruesomely fascinating museum. Exhibits include chastity belts, masks of disgrace for gossips, a cage for cheating bakers, a neck brace for quarrelsome women and a beer-barrel pen for drunks. You can even snap a selfie of yourself in the stocks!

Sleeping & Eating

Altfränkische Weinstube HOTEL €€

(09861-6404; www.altfraenkische.de; Klosterhof 7; d €82-118;) This characterful inn has six romantic country-style rooms with exposed half-timber, bathtubs and most with four-poster or canopied beds. From 6pm onwards, the tavern serves up sound regional fare (mains €7 to €16) with a dollop of medieval cheer.

Mittermeier Restaurant & Hotel DESIGN HOTEL €€€

(09861-945 430; www.blauesau.eu; Vorm Würzburger Tor 7; d €80-200; restaurant 6-10.30pm Mon-Sat; P) You'll sleep well in this smartly designed hotel just outside the town wall. The kitchen ninjas in the vaulted cellar restaurant pair punctilious craftsmanship with top-notch ingredients, sourced regionally whenever possibly (dinner mains €22 to €38). The focus is on grills paired with creative sides and superb wines from Franconia and beyond. Breakfast costs €10.

Gasthof Butz GERMAN €

(09861-2201; Kapellenplatz 4; mains €7-15; 11.30am-2pm & 6-9pm;) For a quick goulash, schnitzel or roast pork, lug your weary legs to this locally adored, family-run inn in a former brewery. In summer two flowery beer gardens beckon. It also rents a dozen simply furnished rooms (double €36 to €75).

Information

Tourist Office (09861-404 800; www.tourismus.rothenburg.de; Marktplatz 2; 9am-6pm Mon-Fri, 10am-5pm Sat & Sun May-Oct, 9am-5pm Mon-Fri, 10am-1pm Sat Nov-Mar) Offers free internet access.

Getting There & Away

The Romantic Road Coach pauses in town for 45 minutes.

There are hourly trains to/from Steinach, a transfer point for service to Würzburg (€12.90, 1¼ hours).

Würzburg

0931 / POP 127,000

Tucked in among river valleys lined with vineyards, Würzburg beguiles long before you reach the city centre and is renowned for its art, architecture and delicate wines. Its crowning architectural glory is the Residenz, one of the finest baroque structures in Germany and a Unesco World Heritage Site.

Sights

Festung Marienberg FORTRESS

(0931-355 170; tour adult/concession €3.50/2.50; tours 11am, 2pm, 3pm & 4pm Tue-Sun, also 10am & 1pm Sat & Sun mid-Mar–Oct, 11am, 2pm & 3pm Sat & Sun Nov–mid-Mar) Enjoy panoramic city and vineyard views from this hulking fortress, the construction of which was initiated around 1200 by the local prince-bishops who governed here until 1719. Dramatically illuminated at night, the structure was only penetrated once, by Swedish troops during the Thirty Years' War, in 1631. Inside, the **Fürstenbaumuseum** (closed November to mid-March) sheds light on its former residents' pompous lifestyle, while the **Mainfränkisches Museum** presents city history and works by local late-Gothic master carver Tilmann Riemenschneider and other famous artists. The fortress is a 30-minute walk up the hill through the vineyards from the Alte Mainbrücke via the Tellsteige trail.

Dom St Kilian CHURCH

(0931-3866 2900; www.dom-wuerzburg.de; Domstrasse 40; 10am-7pm Mon-Sat, 1-6pm Sun) Würzburg's freshly renovated Romanesque cathedral has impressive dimensions, an airy feel, and precious sculpture and tombstones affixed to slender pillars. A highlight is the **Schönbornkapelle** by Balthasar Neumann.

Sleeping & Eating

Würzburg's many *Weinstuben* (wine taverns) are great for sampling the local vintages.

Hotel Zum Winzermännle HOTEL €€

(0931-541 56; www.winzermaennle.de; Domstrasse 32; s €60-80, d €90-110; P @) This family-run converted winery is a feel-good retreat in the city's pedestrianised heart. Rooms are well furnished if a little on the old-fashioned side; some among those facing the quiet courtyard have balconies. Communal areas are bright and often seasonally decorated. Breakfast costs €5.

DON'T MISS

RESIDENZ

The vast Unesco-listed **Würzburg Residenz** (www.residenz-wuerzburg.de; Balthasar-Neumann-Promenade; adult/concession/under 18yr €7.50/6.50/free; ⌚9am-6pm Apr-Oct, 10am-4.30pm Nov-Mar, 45-minute English tours 11am & 3pm, also 4.30pm Apr-Oct), built by 18th-century starchitect Balthasar Neumann as the home of the local prince-bishops, is one of Germany's most important and beautiful baroque palaces. Top billing goes to the brilliant zigzagging **staircase** lidded by what still is the world's largest fresco, a masterpiece by Giovanni Battista Tiepolo.

Most of the palace can be explored on your own. Besides the staircase, feast your eyes on the ice white stucco-adorned **Weisser Saal** (White Hall) before entering the **Kaisersaal** (Imperial Hall), canopied by yet another impressive Tiepolo fresco. Other stunners include the gilded stucco **Spiegelkabinett** (Mirror Hall), covered with a unique mirrorlike glass painted with figural, floral and animal motifs (accessible by tour only). The **Hofkirche** (Court Church) is another Neumann and Tiepolo coproduction. Its marble columns, gold leaf and profusion of angels match the Residenz in splendour and proportions.

Alte Mainmühle GERMAN €€

(☎0931-167 77; www.alte-mainmuehle.de; Mainkai 1; mains €8-23; ⌚9.30am-midnight) Tourists and locals alike cram into this old mill, accessed straight from the old bridge, to savour modern twists on Franconian classics (including delicious grilled sausages). In summer the double terrace beckons – the upper one delivers pretty views of the bridge and Marienberg Fortress. In winter retreat to the snug timber dining room.

Backöfele GERMAN €€

(☎0931-590 59; www.backoefele.de; Ursulinergasse 2; mains €7-19.50; ⌚noon-midnight Mon-Thu, to 1am Fri & Sat, to 11pm Sun) This old-timey warren has been spreading hearty Franconian food love for nearly 40 years. Find your favorite table in the cobbled courtyard or one of four historic rooms, each candlelit and uniquely furnished with local flair.

Information

Tourist Office (☎0931-372 398; www.wuerzburg.de; Marktplatz 9; ⌚10am-6pm Mon-Fri, 10am-2pm Sat Apr-Dec, 10am-2pm Sun May-Oct, 10am-5pm Mon-Fri, 10am-2pm Sat Jan-Mar) Trip planning and room reservations.

Getting There & Away

The Romantic Road Coach stops next to the Hauptbahnhof.

Frequent trains run to Bamberg (€20.10, one hour), Frankfurt (€35, 1¼ hour), Nuremberg (from €20.30, one hour) and Rothenburg ob der Tauber (via Steinach; €12.90, 1¼ hour).

Nuremberg

☎0911 / POP 510,000

Nuremberg (Nürnberg) woos visitors with its wonderfully restored medieval Altstadt, its grand castle and, in December, its magical *Christkindlmarkt* (Christmas market).

The town played a key role during the Nazi years. It was here that the fanatical party rallies were held, the boycott of Jewish businesses began and the anti-Semitic Nuremberg Laws were enacted. After WWII the city was chosen as the site of the Nuremberg Trials of Nazi war criminals.

Sights

The city centre is best explored on foot but the Nazi-related sights are a tram ride away.

Hauptmarkt SQUARE

This bustling square in the heart of the Altstadt is the site of daily markets as well as the famous *Christkindlsmarkt*. At the eastern end is the ornate Gothic **Frauenkirche** (church). Daily at noon crowds crane their necks to witness the clock's figures enact a spectacle called the *Männleinlaufen*. Rising from the square like a Gothic spire is the sculpture-festooned **Schöner Brunnen** (Beautiful Fountain). Touch the golden ring in the ornate wrought-iron gate for good luck.

Kaiserburg CASTLE

(Imperial Castle; ☎0911-244 6590; www.kaiserburg-nuernberg.de; Auf der Burg; adult/concession/under 18yr incl museum €5.50/4.50/free, tower & well €3.50/2.50/free; ⌚9am-6pm Apr-Sep, 10am-4pm

CHRISTMAS MARKETS

Beginning in late November every year, central squares across Germany are transformed into Christmas markets (*Christkindlmarkt*; also known as *Weihnachtsmärkte*). Folks stamp about between the wooden stalls, perusing seasonal trinkets (from hand-carved ornaments to plastic angels) while warming themselves with *Glühwein* (mulled, spiced red wine) and grilled sausages. Locals love'em and, not surprisingly, the markets are popular with tourists, so bundle up and carouse for hours. Markets in Nuremberg, Dresden, Cologne and Munich are especially famous.

Oct-Mar) This enormous castle complex above the Altstadt poignantly reflects Nuremberg's medieval might. Don't miss a tour of the residential wing to see the lavish Knights' and Imperial Hall, a Romanesque double chapel and an exhibit on the inner workings of the Holy Roman Empire. This segues to the **Kaiserburg Museum**, which focuses on the castle's military and building history. Elsewhere, enjoy panoramic views from the **Sinwell Tower** or peer 48m down into the **Deep Well**.

Germanisches Nationalmuseum MUSEUM
(German National Museum; ☎0911-133 10; www.gnm.de; Kartäusergasse 1; adult/concession €8/5; ⏱10am-6pm Tue & Thu-Sun, to 9pm Wed) Spanning prehistory to the early 20th century, the Germanisches Nationalmuseum is the country's most important museum of German culture. It features works by German painters and sculptors, an archaeological collection, arms and armour, musical and scientific instruments, and toys.

Memorium Nuremberg Trials MEMORIAL
(☎0911-3217 9372; www.memorium-nuremberg.de; Bärenschanzstrasse 72; adult/concession incl audioguide €5/3; ⏱10am-6pm Wed-Mon) Göring, Hess, Speer and 21 other Nazi leaders were tried for crimes against peace and humanity by the Allies in Schwurgerichtssaal 600 (Court Room 600) of this still-working courthouse. Today the room forms part of an engaging exhibit detailing the background, progression and impact of the trials using film, photographs, audiotape and even the original defendants' dock. To get here, take the U1 towards Bärenschanze and get off at Sielstrasse.

Reichsparteitagsgelände HISTORIC SITE
(Luitpoldhain; ☎0911-231 5666; www.museen-nuernberg.de; Bayernstrasse 110; grounds free, documentation centre adult/concession incl audioguide €5/3; ⏱grounds 24hr, documentation centre 9am-6pm Mon-Fri, 10am-6pm Sat & Sun) If you've ever wondered where the infamous black-and-white images of ecstatic Nazi supporters hailing their Führer were taken, it was here in Nuremberg. Much of the grounds were destroyed during Allied bombing raids, but enough remain to get a sense of the megalomania behind it, especially after visiting the excellent **Dokumentationszentrum** (Documentation Centre) served by tram 9 from the Hauptbahnhof.

Sleeping

★**Hotel Drei Raben** BOUTIQUE HOTEL €€
(☎0911-274 380; www.hoteldreiraben.de; Königstrasse 63; d from €135; P❄📶) The design of this classy charmer builds upon the legend of the three ravens perched on the building's chimney stack, who tell stories from Nuremberg lore. Art and decor in the 'mythical theme' rooms reflect a particular tale, from the life of Albrecht Dürer to the first railway.

Hotel Elch HOTEL €€
(☎0911-249 2980; www.hotel-elch.com; Irrerstrasse 9; d from €89; 📶) This snug, romantic 12-room gem of a hotel occupies a 14th-century, half-timbered house near the Kaiserburg. The antique flair is offset by contemporary art, glazed terracotta bathrooms and multihued chandeliers. The downstairs restaurant specialises in schnitzel.

Eating

Don't leave Nuremberg without trying its famous finger-sized *Nürnberger Bratwürste*.

Goldenes Posthorn GERMAN €€
(☎0911-225 153; www.die-nuernberger-bratwurst.de; Glöckleinsgasse 2, cnr Sebalder Platz; mains €7-20; ⏱11am-11pm; 🖉) Push open the heavy copper door to find a real culinary treat that has hosted royals, artists and professors (including Albrecht Dürer) since 1498. You can't go wrong sticking with the miniature local sausages, but the pork shoulder and also the house speciality – vinegar-marinated ox cheeks – are highly recommended as well.

Hexenhäusle GERMAN €€
(☎0911-4902 9095; www.hexenhaeusle-nuernberg.com; Vestnertorgraben 4; mains €7-11; ⏱11am-11pm) The half-timbered 'Witches Hut' ranks among

Nuremberg's most enchanting inns and beer gardens. Tucked next to a sturdy town gate at the foot of the castle, it serves the gamut of grilled fare and other Franconian rib-stickers with big mugs of local Zirndorfer and Tucher beer.

Information

Tourist Office (0911-233 60; www.tourismus.nuernberg.de) Both branches, at Hauptmarkt (Hauptmarkt 18; 9am-6pm Mon-Sat year-round, 10am-4pm Sun May-Oct) and in the Künstlerhaus (Königstrasse 93; 9am-7pm Mon-Sat, 10am-4pm Sun), sell the Nuremberg Card (€23) with two days of free museum entry and public transport. Staff also offer maps, info and advice.

Getting There & Away

Nuremberg **airport** (NUE; www.airport-nuernberg.de), 5km north of the city centre, is served by the U2 from Hauptbahnhof (€2.50, 12 minutes).

Rail connections from Nuremberg include Frankfurt (€55, two hours) and Munich (€55, 1½ hours).

Getting Around

For public transport information, see www.vgn.de.

Bamberg

0951 / POP 70,000

Off the major tourist routes, Bamberg is one of Germany's most delightful and authentic towns. It has a bevy of beautifully preserved historic buildings, palaces and churches in its Unesco-recognised Altstadt, a lively student population and its own style of beer.

Sights

Bamberger Dom CATHEDRAL

(www.erzbistum-bamberg.de; Domplatz; 8am-6pm Apr-Oct, to 5pm Nov-Mar) Beneath the quartet of spires, Bamberg's cathedral is packed with artistic treasures, most famously the lifesize equestrian statue of the **Bamberger Reiter** (Bamberg Horseman), whose true identity remains a mystery. It overlooks the **tomb of cathedral founders**, Emperor Heinrich II and his wife Kunigunde, splendidly carved by Tilmann Riemenschneider. The **marble tomb of Clemens II** in the west choir is the only papal burial site north of the Alps. Nearby, the **Virgin Mary altar** by Veit Stoss also warrants closer inspection.

Altes Rathaus HISTORIC BUILDING

(Old Town Hall; Obere Brücke) Like a ship in dry dock, Bamberg's 1462 Old Town Hall was built on an artifical island in the Regnitz River, allegedly because the local bishop had refused to give the town's citizens any land for its construction. Inside is a collection of precious porcelain but even more enchanting are the richly detailed frescoes adorning its facades – note the cherub's leg cheekily sticking out from its east facade.

Neue Residenz PALACE

(New Residence; 0951-519 390; www.schloesser.bayern.de; Domplatz 8; adult/child €4.50/3.50; 9am-6pm Apr-Sep, 10am-4pm Oct-Mar) This splendid episcopal palace gives you an eyeful of the lavish lifestyle of Bamberg's prince-bishops who, between 1703 and 1802, occupied its 40-odd rooms that can only be seen on guided 45-minute tours (in German). Tickets are also good for the Bavarian State Gallery, with works by Lucas Cranach the Elder and other old masters. The baroque **Rose Garden** delivers fabulous views over Bamberg's sea of red-tiled roofs.

Sleeping

Hotel Wohnbar BOUTIQUE HOTEL €

(0951-5099 8844; www.wohnbar-bamberg.de; Stangsstrasse 3; d from €59;) 'Carpe Noctem' (Seize the Night) is the motto of this charming 10-room retreat with boldly coloured, contemporary rooms near the university quarter. Those in the 'economy' category are a very tight squeeze – avoid.

Hotel Europa HOTEL €€

(0951-309 3020; www.hotel-europa-bamberg.de; Untere Königstrasse 6-8; d from €119;) This spick-and-span but unfussy affair just outside the Altstadt gets kudos for its friendliness, comfy beds and opulent breakfast, served in the winter garden or sunny courtyard. Rooms at the front are noisier but may overlook the cathedral and the red-tiled roofs of the Altstadt. Some are a bit small.

Eating & Drinking

Obere Sandstrasse near the cathedral and Austrasse near the university are both good eat and drink streets. Bamberg's unique style of beer is called *Rauchbier* (smoked beer), the distinctive flavour of which is created by drying malted barley over smouldering beechwood.

★ **Schlenkerla** GERMAN €€
(☎0951-560 60; www.schlenkerla.de; Dominikanerstrasse 6; mains €8-15; ⌚9.30am-11.30pm) Beneath wooden beams as dark as the superb *Rauchbier* poured straight from oak barrels, locals and visitors dig into scrumptious Franconian fare at this legendary flower-festooned tavern near the cathedral.

Spezial-Keller GERMAN €€
(☎0951-548 87; www.spezial-keller.de; Sternwartstrasse 8; dishes €6-13; ⌚3pm-late Tue-Fri, from noon Sat, from 10am Sun) The walk into the hills past the cathedral to this delightful beer garden is well worth it, both for the malty *Rauchbier* and the sweeping views of the Altstadt. In winter the action moves into the cosy tavern warmed by a traditional wood-burning tiled stove.

Information

Tourist Office (☎0951-297 6200; www.bamberg.info; Geyerswörthstrasse 5; ⌚9.30am-6pm Mon-Fri, to 4pm Sat, to 2.30pm Sun) Staff rent the multimedia itour Guide (four/eight hours €8.50/12) for self-guided city tours.

Getting There & Away

Getting to and from Bamberg by train usually involves a change in Würzburg.

Regensburg

☎0941 / POP 138,000

In a scene-stealing locale on the wide Danube River, Regensburg has relics of historic periods reaching back to the Romans, yet doesn't get the tourist mobs you'll find in other equally attractive German cities. Though big on the historical wow factor, today's Regensburg is a laid-back and unpretentious student town with a distinct Italianate flair.

Sights

Steinerne Brücke BRIDGE
(Stone Bridge) An incredible feat of engineering for its day, Regensburg's 900-year-old Stone Bridge was at one time the only fortified crossing of the Danube. A small historical exhibit in the southern tower traces the bridge's milestones.

Dom St Peter CHURCH
(www.bistum-regensburg.de; Domplatz; ⌚6.30am-7pm Jun-Sep, to 6pm Apr, May & Oct, to 5pm Nov-Mar) It takes a few seconds for your eyes to adjust to the dim interior of Regensburg's soaring landmark, the Dom St Peter, one of Bavaria's grandest Gothic cathedrals, with stunning kaleidoscopic stained-glass windows and an opulent, silver-sheathed main altar.

The cathedral is the home of the Domspatzen, a 1000-year-old boys choir that accompanies the 10am Sunday service (only during the school year). The Domschatzmuseum (Cathedral Treasury) brims with monstrances, tapestries and other church treasures.

Altes Rathaus HISTORIC BUILDING
(Old Town Hall; ☎0941-507 3440; Rathausplatz; adult/concession €7.50/4; ⌚English tours 3pm Apr-Oct, 2pm Nov-Mar, German tours every half hour) From 1663 to 1806, the Reichstag (imperial assembly) held its gatherings at Regensburg's old town hall, an important role commemorated by an exhibit in today's **Reichstagsmuseum**. Tours take in the lavish assembly hall and the original **torture chambers** in the cellar.

Sleeping

Elements Hotel HOTEL €€
(☎0941-3819 8600; www.hotel-elements.de; Alter Kornmarkt 3; d from €105;) Four elements, four rooms, and what rooms they are! 'Fire' blazes in plush crimson, while 'Water' is splashed with portholes and a Jacuzzi, 'Air' is playful and light and natural wood, and stone and leather reign in colonial-inspired 'Earth'. Breakfast costs €15.

Petit Hotel Orphée HOTEL €€
(☎0941-596 020; www.hotel-orphee.de; Wahlenstrasse 1; d €75-175;) Behind a humble door lies a world of genuine charm, unexpected extras and ample attention to detail. The striped floors, wrought-iron beds, original sinks and common rooms with soft cushions and well-read books give the feel of a lovingly attended home. Check-in and breakfast is nearby in the Cafe Orphée at Untere Bachgasse 8. Additional rooms are above the cafe.

Eating & Drinking

Historische Wurstkuchl GERMAN €
(☎0941-466 210; www.wurstkuchl.de; Thundorferstrasse 3; 6 sausages €8.40; ⌚8am-7pm) This titchy eatery has been serving the city's traditional finger-size sausages, grilled over beech wood and dished up with sauerkraut and sweet grainy mustard, since 1135 and lays claim to being the world's oldest sausage kitchen.

Leerer Beutel EUROPEAN €€
(☎0941-589 97; www.leerer-beutel.de; Bertoldstrasse 9; mains €12-18; ⏰6pm-1am Mon, 11am-1am Tue-Sat, 11am-3pm Sun) Subscriber to the slow-food ethos, the cavernous restaurant at the eponymous cultural centre offers an imaginatively mixed menu of Bavarian, Tyrolean and Italian dishes, served indoors or out on the car-free cobbles. From Tuesday to Friday, clued-up locals invade for the two-course lunches for €6.50.

Spitalgarten BEER GARDEN
(☎0941-847 74; www.spitalgarten.de; St Katharinenplatz 1; ⏰9am-midnight) A veritable thicket of folding chairs and slatted tables by the Danube, this is one of the best places in town for some alfresco quaffing. It claims to have brewed beer (today's Spital) here since 1350, so it probably knows what it's doing by now.

Information

Tourist Office (☎0941-507 4410; www.regensburg.de; Rathausplatz 4; ⏰9am-6pm Mon-Fri, to 4pm Sat year-round, 9.30am-4pm Sun Apr-Oct, 9.30am-2.30pm Sun Nov-Mar; 📶) In the historic Altes Rathaus. Sells tickets, tours, rooms and an audioguide for self-guided tours.

Getting There & Away

Frequent trains leave for Munich (€26.70, 1½ hours) and Nuremberg (€20.10, one hour), among others.

STUTTGART & THE BLACK FOREST

The high-tech urbanite pleasures of Stuttgart, one of the engines of the German economy, form an appealing contrast to the historic charms of Heidelberg, home to the country's oldest university and a romantic ruined castle. Beyond lies the myth-shrouded Black Forest (*Schwarzwald* in German), a pretty land of misty hills, thick forest and cute villages, with youthful and vibrant Freiburg as its only major town.

Stuttgart

☎0711 / POP 591,000

Stuttgart residents enjoy an enviable quality of life that's to no small degree rooted in its fabled car companies – Porsche and Mercedes – which show off their pedigree in two excellent museums. Hemmed in by vine-covered hills, the city has also plenty in store for fans of European art.

LOCAL KNOWLEDGE

BOHEMIAN BEANS

Stuttgart's most interesting neighbourhood is a short stroll from the city centre. The **Bohnenviertel** (Bean District) takes its name from the diet of the poor tanners, dyers and craftsmen who lived here. Today the district's cobbled lanes and gabled houses harbour idiosyncratic galleries, workshops, bookstores, wine taverns, cafes and a red-light district.

Sights

Königsstrasse, a long, pedestrianised shopping strip, links the Hauptbahnhof to the city centre. In the city centre are the Schloss and the art museums. The Mercedes-Benz Museum is about 5km northeast and the Porsche Museum 7km north of here.

Staatsgalerie Stuttgart GALLERY
(☎0711-470 400; www.staatsgalerie-stuttgart.de; Konrad-Adenauer-Strasse 30-32; permanent collection adult/concession/under 20yr €5/3/free; ⏰10am-6pm Tue, Wed & Fri-Sun, to 8pm Thu) The neoclassical-meets-contemporary Staatsgalerie bears British architect James Stirling's curvy, colourful imprint. Alongside big-name exhibitions, the gallery harbours a representative collection of European art from the 14th to the 21st centuries as well as American post-WWII avant-gardists.

Neues Schloss PALACE
(☎in Ludwigsburg 07141-182 004; www.neues-schloss-stuttgart.de; Schlossplatz; tour adult/concession €8/4) Duke Karl Eugen von Württemberg's answer to Versailles was the exuberant three-winged Neues Schloss, a baroque-neoclassical royal residence that now houses state-government ministries. A bronze statue of Emperor Wilhelm I looking dashing on his steed graces nearby **Karlsplatz**. Check the website for the tour schedule.

Mercedes-Benz Museum MUSEUM
(☎0711-1730 000; www.mercedes-benz-classic.com; Mercedesstrasse 100; adult/concession €8/4; ⏰9am-6pm Tue-Sun, last admission 5pm; 🚆S1 to Neckarpark) A futuristic swirl on the cityscape, the Mercedes-Benz Museum takes a chronological spin through the Mercedes empire. Look out for legends like the 1885 Daimler Riding Car, the world's first gasoline-powered

vehicle and the record-breaking Lightning Benz that hit 228km/h at Daytona Beach in 1909.

Porsche Museum MUSEUM
(www.porsche.com/museum; Porscheplatz 1; adult/concession €8/4; ⊙9am-6pm Tue-Sun; Ⓡ Neuwirtshaus) Like a pearly white spaceship preparing for lift-off, the barrier-free Porsche Museum is every little boy's dream. Groovy audioguides race you through the history of Porsche from its 1948 beginnings. Break to glimpse the 911 GT1 that won Le Mans in 1998.

Sleeping

Hostel Alex 30 HOSTEL €
(☎0711-838 8950; www.alex30-hostel.de; Alexanderstrasse 30; dm €25-29, d €74; P 📶) Fun-seekers on a budget should thrive at this popular hostel within walking distance of the city centre. Rooms are spotless, citrus-bright and contemporary, and the bar, sun deck and communal kitchen ideal for swapping stories with fellow travellers. Breakfast costs €8.

Der Zauberlehrling BOUTIQUE HOTEL €€€
(☎0711-237 7770; www.zauberlehrling.de; Rosenstrasse 38; s/d from €135/180; P 📶) The dreamily styled rooms at the 'Sorcerer's Apprentice' offer soothing quarters after a day on the road. Each one interprets a different theme (Mediterranean siesta, sunrise, One Thousand and One Nights) through colour, furniture and features such as canopy beds, clawfoot tubs, tatami mats or fireplaces. Breakfast costs €19.

Eating & Drinking

Stuttgart is a great place to sample Swabian specialities such as *Spätzle* (homemade noodles) and *Maultaschen* (a hearty ravioli in broth). Local wines edge out beer in popularity.

Hans-im-Glück-Platz is a hub of bars, while clubs line Theodor-Heuss-Strasse and wine taverns abound in the Bohnenviertel.

Stuttgarter Markthalle MARKET €
(Market Hall; www.markthalle-stuttgart.de; Dorotheenstrasse 4; ⊙7am-6.30pm Mon-Fri, to 5pm Sat) Self-caterers can try the Markthalle, which sells picnic fixings, and has Italian and Swabian restaurants.

Weinhaus Stetter GERMAN €€
(☎0711-240 163; www.weinhaus-stetter.de; Rosenstrasse 32; mains €4-14.50; ⊙3-11pm Mon-Fri, noon-3pm & 5.30-11pm Sat) This traditional wine tavern in the Bohnenviertel quarter serves up no-nonsense Swabian cooking, such as flavoursome *Linsen und Saiten* (lentils with sausage) and beef roast with onion, in a convivial ambience. The attached wine shop sells 650 different vintages.

Academie der Schönen Künste FRENCH €€
(☎0711-242 436; www.academie-der-schoensten-kuenste.de; Charlottenstrasse 5; mains €11-20; ⊙8am-midnight Mon-Sat, to 8pm Sun) A breakfast institution since the 1970s, the Academy has evolved into a darling French-style bistro where dishes revolve around market-fresh fare but also include such tried-and-true classics as coq au vin and *Flammekuche* (Alsatian pizza). Sit inside among bright canvases or in the charismatic couryard.

Cube INTERNATIONAL €€€
(☎0711-280 4441; www.cube-restaurant.de; Kleiner Schlossplatz 1; mains lunch €9-20, dinner €27-35; ⊙11.30am-midnight) The food is stellar but it actually plays second fiddle to the dazzling decor, refined ambience and stunning views at this glass-fronted cube atop the Kunstmuseum. Lunches are perky, fresh and international, while dinners feature more complex Pacific Rim–inspired cuisine. The lunch special for €9 is a steal.

★ **Palast der Republik** BEER GARDEN
(☎0711-226 4887; www.facebook.com/Palast Stuttgart; Friedrichstrasse 27; ⊙11am-3am; Ⓢ Friedrichsbau) The palace in question is more like a little kiosk but that's not stopping everyone from students to bankers from making this place *the* local hot spot for chilling under the trees, cold beer in hand.

Information

Tourist Office (☎0711-222 8253; www.stuttgart-tourist.de; Königstrasse 1a; ⊙9am-8pm Mon-Fri, to 6pm Sat, 11am-6pm Sun)

Getting There & Away

Stuttgart Airport (SGT; www.stuttgart-airport.com), a major hub for Germanwings, is 13km south of the city and linked to the Hauptbahnhof by S2 and S3 trains (€3.70, 30 minutes).

Trains head to all major German cities, including Frankfurt (€63, 1¼ hours) and Munich (€57, 2¼ hours).

Getting Around

For public transport information, check www.vvs.de.

Heidelberg

06221 / POP 149,000

Germany's oldest and most famous university town is renowned for its lovely Altstadt, its plethora of pubs and its evocative half-ruined castle. Millions of visitors are drawn each year to this photogenic assemblage, thereby following in the footsteps of Mark Twain, who kicked off his European travels in 1878 in Heidelberg, later recounting his bemused observations in *A Tramp Abroad.*

Sights

Heidelberg's sites cluster in the Altstadt, which starts to reveal itself only after a charm-free 15-minute walk east from the main train station or a short ride on bus 32 or 38.

★ Schloss Heidelberg CASTLE
(06221-658 880; www.schloss-heidelberg.de; adult/child incl Bergbahn €6/4, audioguide €4; grounds 24hr, castle 8am-6pm, English tours hourly 11.15am-4.15pm Mon-Fri, 10.15am-4.15pm Sat & Sun Apr-Oct, fewer tours Nov-Mar) Towering over the Altstadt, Heidelberg's ruined Renaissance castle cuts a romantic figure, especially when illuminated at night and seen across the Neckar River. Attractions include the world's largest wine cask and fabulous views. Get there either via a steep, cobbled trail in about 10 minutes or by taking the cogwheel train from Kornmarkt station (tickets include Schloss entry). After 6pm you can stroll the grounds for free.

Alte Brücke BRIDGE
(Karl-Theodor-Brücke) The 200m-long 'Old Bridge', built in 1786, connects the Altstadt with the river's right bank and the **Schlangenweg** (Snake Path), the switchbacks of which lead to the **Philosophenweg** (Philosophers' Walk). A stroll along here delivers romantic views of the town and Heidelberg Castle.

Heiliggeistkirche CHURCH
(06221-980 30; www.ekihd.de; Marktplatz; tower adult/concesssion €2/1; 11am-5pm Mon-Sat, 12.30-5pm Sun) For bird's-eye views, climb 208 stairs to the top of the tower of Heidelberg's famous 15th-century church, which was shared by Catholics and Protestants from 1706 until 1936 (it's now Protestant).

Studentenkarzer HISTORIC SITE
(Student Jail; 06221-543 554; www.uni-heidelberg.de/fakultaeten/philosophie/zegk/fpi/karzerhd.html; Augustinergasse 2; adult/concession €3/2.50; 10am-6pm daily Apr-Oct, 10am-4pm Mon-Sat Nov-Mar) From 1823 to 1914, students convicted of misdeeds such as public inebriation, loud nocturnal singing, freeing the local pigs or duelling were sent to this student jail for at least 24 hours. Judging by the inventive wall graffiti, some found their stay highly amusing.

Tours

The tourist office runs English-language **walking tours** (adult/concession €7/5; English tours 10.30am Thu-Sat Apr-Oct) of the Altstadt.

Sleeping & Eating

Steffis Hostel HOSTEL €
(06221-778 2772; www.hostelheidelberg.de; Alte Eppelheimer Strasse 50; dm €18-24, s/d without bathroom €45/56; reception 8am-10pm; P @) In a 19th-century tobacco factory near the main train station, Steffis offers bright, well-lit dorms and rooms (all with shared bathrooms), a colourful lounge that's ideal for meeting fellow travellers, a spacious kitchen and an ineffable old-school hostel vibe. Breakfast costs €3.

Perks include free wi-fi, tea, coffee and bicycles. It's situated a block north of the Hauptbahn-hof, three floors above a Lidl supermarket; access is via an industrial-size lift.

★ Arthotel Heidelberg BOUTIQUE HOTEL €€
(06221-650 060; www.arthotel.de; Grabengasse 7; d €125-200; P) This charmer is a winning blend of historic setting and sleek contemporary design. The light-flooded red and black lobby is the mere overture to the symphony of the 24 rooms. Equipped with huge bathrooms (tubs!), they're spacious and purist – except for three that sport painted ceilings from 1790. Breakfast costs €12.90.

KulturBrauerei GERMAN €€
(06221-502 980; www.heidelberger-kulturbrauerei.de; Leyergasse 6; mains €11-26.50; 7am-11pm or later) With its wood-plank floor, chairs from a Spanish monastery and black iron chandeliers, this brewpub is an atmospheric spot to tuck into regional specialities such as *Schäufele* (pork shoulder) or to quaff the house brew in the enchanting beer garden.

★ Herrenmühle Heidelberg GERMAN €€€
(06221-602 909; www.herrenmuehle-heidelberg.de; Hauptstrasse 239; mains €22-29, 3-/5-course dinner €48/69; 6-10pm Mon-Sat) A flour mill from 1690 has been turned into an elegant

and highly cultured place to enjoy upscale 'country-style' cuisine, including fish, under thick wooden beams, a candle flickering romantically at each table. Book ahead.

Information

Tourist Office (www.heidelberg-marketing.de) There are branches at Hauptbahnhof (06221-584 4444; Willy-Brandt-Platz 1; 9am-7pm Mon-Sat, 10am-6pm Sun Apr-Oct, 9am-6pm Mon-Sat Nov-Mar), right outside the main train station, and on Marktplatz (Marktplatz 10; 8am-5pm Mon-Fri, 10am-5pm Sat), in the old town. Aside from loads of helpful information both also stock a useful walking-tour map (€1.50).

Getting There & Away

There are at least hourly InterCity (IC) trains to/from Frankfurt (€22, 55 minutes) and Stuttgart (€27, 40 minutes).

Black Forest

The Black Forest (Schwarzwald) gets its name from its dark canopy of evergreens. Let winding backroads take you through misty vales, fairy-tale woodlands and villages that radiate earthy authenticity. It's not nature wild and remote, but bucolic and picturesque. And, yes, there are many, many places to buy cuckoo clocks.

Getting Around

One of Germany's most scenic roads is the Schwarzwald-Hochstrasse (B500), which meanders for 60km between Baden-Baden and Freudenstadt.

Regional trains link Alpirsbach, Schiltach, Hausach and other Black Forest villages. In Hausach, there's a connection with the Schwarzwaldbahn line which takes in Baden-Baden and Triberg.

Baden-Baden

07221 / POP 53,600

The northern gateway to the Black Forest, Baden-Baden is one of Europe's most famous spa towns whose mineral-rich waters have cured the ills of celebs from Queen Victoria to Victoria Beckham. An air of old-world luxury hangs over this beautiful town that's also home to a palatial casino.

Activities

★**Friedrichsbad** SPA

(07221-275 920; www.carasana.de; Römerplatz 1; 3hr ticket €25, incl soap-&-brush massage €37; 9am-10pm, last admission 7pm) If it's the body of Venus and the complexion of Cleopatra you desire, abandon modesty (and clothing) to wallow in thermal waters at this palatial 19th-century marble-and-mosaic-festooned spa. As Mark Twain put it, 'after 10 minutes you forget time; after 20 minutes, the world', as you slip into the regime of steaming, scrubbing, hot-cold bathing and dunking in the Roman-Irish bath.

Caracalla Spa SPA

(07221-275 940; www.carasana.de; Römerplatz 11; 2/3/4hr €15/18/21; 8am-10pm, last admission 8pm) This modern glass-fronted spa has a cluster of indoor and outdoor pools, grottoes and surge channels, making the most of the mineral-rich spring water. For those who dare to bare, saunas range from the rustic 'forest' to the roasting 95°C 'fire' variety.

Sleeping & Eating

Schweizer Hof HOTEL €€

(07221-304 60; www.schweizerhof.de; Lange Strasse 73; d €99-119) Sitting on one of Baden-Baden's smartest streets, this above-par hotel is a real find, with dapper rooms,

THE BATTLE OF THE BIRDS

Triberg being Germany's undisputed cuckoo-clock capital, it's not surprising that two giant timepieces battle for title of world's largest cuckoo clock.

The older and more charming contender calls itself the **1. Weltgrösste Kuckucksuhr** (First World's Largest Cuckoo Clock; 07722-4689; www.1weltgroesstekuckucksuhr.de; Untertalstrasse 28, Schonach; adult/concession €1.20/0.60; 9am-noon & 1-6pm) and can be found in Schonach. It kicked into gear in 1980 and took a local clockmaker three years to build by hand.

It has since been eclipsed in size by its cousin at the **Eble Uhren-Park** (07722-962 20; www.uhren-park.de; Schonachbach 27; admission €2; 9am-6pm Mon-Sat, 10am-6pm Sun), which occupies an entire house on the B33 between Triberg and Hornberg. Although undeniably bigger (and listed in the *Guinness Book of World Records*), it's more of a gimmick to lure shoppers inside a large clock shop.

chandelier-lit spaces, and a garden with sun lounges for chilling.

Rizzi INTERNATIONAL €€€
(☎07221-258 38; www.rizzi-baden-baden.de; Augustaplatz 1; mains lunch €9-24, dinner €14-52; ⏲noon-1am) A summertime favourite, this pink villa's tree-shaded patio is the place to sip excellent wines while tucking into choice steaks. Other menu faves include delicious burgers, homemade pastas and 'Rizzi-style sushi'.

Information

Branch Tourist Office (Kaiserallee 3; ⏲10am-5pm Mon-Sat, 2-5pm Sun) In the Trinkhalle. Sells events tickets.

Triberg

☎07722 / POP 4800

Cuckoo-clock capital, black forest–cake pilgrimage site and Germany's highest waterfall – Triberg is a torrent of Schwarzwald superlatives and attracts a ton of guests.

Sights

★**Triberger Wasserfälle** WATERFALL
(adult/concession/family €4/3/9.50; ⏲Mar-early Nov, 25-30 Dec) Niagara they ain't but Germany's highest waterfalls do exude their own wild romanticism. The Gutach River feeds the seven-tiered falls, which drop a total of 163m and are illuminated until 10pm.

Sleeping & Eating

Parkhotel Wehrle HISTORIC HOTEL €€€
(☎07722-860 20; www.parkhotel-wehrle.de; Gartenstrasse 24; d €155-179; P📶🏊) Hemingway once waxed lyrical about the trout he ordered at the venerable restaurant (mains €13 to €32, open 6pm to 9pm daily, noon to 2pm Sunday) that's attached to this 400-year-old hotel with integrated spa. Often with a baroque or Biedermeier touch, quarters are roomy and beautifully furnished with antiques; the best have Duravit whirlpool tubs.

Café Schäfer CAFE €
(☎07722-4465; www.cafe-schaefer-triberg.de; Hauptstrasse 33; cakes €3-4; ⏲9am-6pm Mon, Tue, Thu & Fri, 8am-6pm Sat, 11am-6pm Sun) Confectioner Claus Schäfer uses the original 1915 recipe for black forest gateau to prepare this sinful treat that layers chocolate cake (perfumed with cherry brandy), whipped cream and sour cherries and wraps it all in more cream and shaved chocolate. Trust us, it's worth the calories.

LOCAL KNOWLEDGE

SOARING ABOVE THE FOREST

Freiburg seems tiny as you drift up above the city and a tapestry of meadows and forest on the **Schauinslandbahn** (return adult/concession €12/11, one way €8.50/8; ⏲9am-5pm Oct-Jun, to 6pm Jul-Sep) to the 1284m **Schauinsland peak** (www.bergwelt-schauinsland.de). The lift provides a speedy link between Freiburg and the Black Forest highlands.

Information

Tourist Office (☎07722-866 490; www.triberg.de; Wallfahrtstrasse 4; ⏲9am-5pm Mon-Fri) Inside the Schwarzwald-Museum.

Freiburg im Breisgau

☎0761 / POP 220,300

Sitting plump at the foot of the Black Forest's wooded slopes and vineyards, Freiburg is a sunny, cheerful university town whose Altstadt is a story-book tableau of gabled town houses, cobblestone lanes and cafe-rimmed plazas. Party-loving students spice up the local nightlife and give Freiburg its relaxed air.

Sights

★**Freiburger Münster** CATHEDRAL
(Freiburg Minster; ☎0761-202 790; www.freiburger-muenster.info; Münsterplatz; tower adult/concession €2/1.50; ⏲10am-5pm Mon-Sat, 1-7.30pm Sun, tower 10am-4.45pm Mon-Sat, 1-5pm Sun) With its lacy spires, cheeky gargoyles and dizzying entrance portal, Freiburg's 11th-century minster cuts an impressive figure above the central market square. It has dazzling kaleidoscopic stained-glass windows that were mostly financed by medieval guilds, and a high altar with a masterful triptych by Dürer protege Hans Baldung Grien. The tower can be climbed.

Rathausplatz SQUARE
(Town Hall Square) Join locals relaxing in a cafe by the fountain in chestnut-shaded Rathausplatz, Freiburg's prettiest square, then pull out that camera to snap pictures of the ox-blood-red 16th-century **Altes Rathaus** (Old Town Hall) with the tourist office, the step-gabled 19th-century **Neues Rathaus** (New Town Hall) and the medieval **Martinskirche** with a modern interior.

Augustinermuseum MUSEUM

(0761-201 2531; Augustinerplatz 1; adult/concession/under 18yr €7/5/free; 10am-5pm Tue-Sun) Dip into the past as represented by artists working from the Middle Ages to the 19th century at this superb museum in a sensitively modernised monastery. The Sculpture Hall on the ground floor is especially impressive for its fine medieval sculpture and masterpieces by Renaissance artists Hans Baldung Grien and Lucas Cranach the Elder. Head upstairs for eye-level views of mounted gargoyles.

Sleeping

Black Forest Hostel HOSTEL €

(0761-881 7870; www.blackforest-hostel.de; Kartäuserstrasse 33; dm €17-27, s/d €35/58, linen €4; reception 7am-1am; @) Funky budget digs with chilled common areas, a shared kitchen, bike rental and spacey stainless-steel showers. It's a five-minute walk from the town centre.

Hotel Minerva HOTEL €€

(0761-386 490; www.minerva-freiburg.de; Poststrasse 8; d €130-165; P) All curvaceous windows and polished wood, this art nouveau charmer is five minutes' trudge from the Altstadt. The convivial rooms are painted in sunny shades and feature free wi-fi. The sauna is another plus.

Eating & Drinking

Stalls spilling over with fresh produce and flowers set up around the Freiburg Minster from Monday to Saturday between 7.30am and 1.30pm.

Markthalle FOOD HALL €

(www.markthalle-freiburg.de; Martinsgasse 235; light meals €4-8; 8am-8pm Mon-Thu, to midnight Fri & Sat) Eat your way around the world – curry to sushi, oysters to antipasti – at the food counters in this historic market hall nicknamed 'Fressgässle'.

Hausbrauerei Feierling BREWPUB €€

(0761-243 480; www.feierling.de; Gerberau 46; mains €6-12; 11am-midnight Mon-Thu, to 1am Fri & Sun;) Thumbs up for the Feierling house brew which has kept beer lovers lubricated for over a quarter century. In summer grab a table in the lovely beer garden and stave off a hangover with honest-to-goodness German classics or try one of the flavour-packed vegetarian alternatives.

LOCAL KNOWLEDGE

MEAL WITH A VIEW

Enjoy views of the city from the rooftop terrace of the self-service bistro atop the Karstadt department store at Kaiser-Joseph-Strasse 165. Bonus: free wi-fi.

Kreuzblume FRENCH, GERMAN €€€

(0761-311 94; www.hotel-kreuzblume.de; Konviktstrasse 31; 2-/3-/4-course dinner €32.50/39/47; noon-2pm Fri-Sun, 6-10pm Wed-Sun) On a flower-festooned lane, this pocket-sized restaurant with clever backlighting and a menu fizzing with bright, sunny flavours attracts a rather food-literate clientele. Each dish combines just a few hand-picked ingredients in bold and tasty ways. Service is tops.

Schlappen CAFE, PUB

(Löwenstrasse 2; 11am-1am Mon-Wed, to 2am Thu, to 3am Fri & Sat, 3pm-1am Sun) In historic digs and crammed with antiques and vintage theatre posters, this evergreen pub has made the magic happen for generations of students. Check out the skeleton in the men's toilet. Summer terrace.

Information

Tourist Office (0761-388 1880; www.freiburg.de; Rathausplatz 2-4; 8am-8pm Mon-Fri, 9.30am-5pm Sat, 10.30am-3.30pm Sun Jun-Sep, 8am-6pm Mon-Fri, 9.30am-2.30pm Sat, 10am-noon Sun Oct-May) Well stocked with 1:50,000-scale cycling maps, city maps (€1) and the useful booklet *Freiburg – Official Guide* (€4.90). Can make room bookings (€3).

Getting There & Away

Freiburg shares **EuroAirport** (BSL; www.euroairport.com) with Basel, Switzerland, and Mulhouse, France, and is served hourly by the Airport Bus (one way/return €26/42, 55 minutes).

Train connections include InterCity Express (ICE) trains to Basel (€25.20, 45 minutes) and Baden-Baden (€30, 45 minutes).

FRANKFURT & THE RHINELAND

Defined by the mighty Rhine, fine wines, medieval castles and romantic villages, Germany's heartland speaks to the imagination. Even Frankfurt, which may seem all buttoned-up business, reveals itself as a laid-back metropolis with fabulous museums and pulsating nightlife.

Frankfurt-am-Main

069 / POP 700,800

Unashamedly high-rise, Frankfurt-on-the-Main (pronounced 'mine') is a true capital of finance and business and hosts some of Europe's key trade fairs. But despite its business demeanour, Frankfurt consistently ranks high among Germany's most liveable cities thanks to its rich collection of museums, expansive parks and greenery, a lively student scene and excellent public transport.

Sights

★Römerberg SQUARE

(Kaisersaal adult/concession €2/0.50; Kaisersaal 10am-1pm & 2-5pm; Dom/Römer) The Römerberg is Frankfurt's old central square. Ornately gabled half-timbered buildings, reconstructed after WWII, give an idea of how beautiful the city's medieval core once was. Looming above it all is grand old **old town hall** *(Römer)* where scores of Holy Roman Emperors celebrated their coronations. For a who's who, visit the imposing **Kaisersaal** (Imperial Hall; enter from Limpurgerstrasse).

Kaiserdom CATHEDRAL

(Imperial/Frankfurt Cathedral; www.dom-frankfurt.de; Domplatz 14; tower adult/concession €3.50/1.50; church 9am-8pm Sat-Thu, 1-8pm Fri, tower 9am-6pm Apr-Oct, 11am-5pm Thu-Mon Nov-Mar; Dom/Römer) Dominated by an elegant Gothic **tower** (95m; can be climbed), begun in the 1400s and completed in the 1860s, Frankfurt's red sandstone cathedral is an island of calm amid the bustle of the city centre. From 1356 to 1792, the Holy Roman Emperors were elected (and, after 1562, consecrated and crowned) in the **Wahlkapelle** at the end of the right aisle (look for the modern 'skull' altar).

Museumsufer Frankfurt MUSEUM

(www.museumsufer-frankfurt.de; btwn Eiserner Steg & Friedensbrücke; S Schweizer Platz) Collectively known as the Museumsufer, more than a dozen museums line up along the south bank of the Main River. The most famous is the Städel Museum, a renowned art gallery, but fans of architecture, archaeology, applied arts, film and ethnology will also get their fill. Bus 46, which leaves from the Hauptbahnhof several times hourly, links most museums.

★Städel Museum MUSEUM

(069-605 098 117; www.staedelmuseum.de; Schaumainkai 63; adult/concession/under 12yr/family €14/12/free/24; 10am-6pm Tue, Wed, Sat & Sun, to 9pm Thur & Fri; S Schweizer Platz) Founded in 1815, this world-renowned art gallery has a truly outstanding collection of European art from the Middle Ages to today. Feast your eyes on stunning works by some of the biggest names, including Dürer, Rembrandt, Rubens, Renoir, Picasso and Cézanne. Contemporary art by such hotshots as Gerhard Richter and Francis Bacon is shown in a recently added subterranean extension lit by circular skylights.

Main Tower VIEWPOINT

(069-3650 4878; www.maintower.de; Neue Mainzer Strasse 52-58; elevator adult/child/family €6.50/4.50/17.50; 10am-9pm Sun-Thu, to 11pm Fri & Sat Apr-Oct, 10am-7pm Sun-Thu, to 9pm Fri & Sat Nov-Mar, cocktail lounge 9pm-midnight Tue-Thu, to 1am Fri & Sat; Alte Oper) Frankfurt's skyline wouldn't be the same without the Main Tower, at 200m one of the tallest and most distinctive high-rises in town. A good place to get a feel for 'Mainhattan' is 200m above street level, on the **observation platform** reached by lift in a mere 45 seconds. Be prepared for airport-type security. Closes during thunderstorms.

Sleeping

As at the stock exchange, supply and demand regulate room rates in Frankfurt. In other words, if a big trade show is in town (and it often is) prices can triple. In general, rates drop on weekends.

Frankfurt Hostel HOSTEL €

(069-247 5130; www.frankfurt-hostel.com; Kaiserstrasse 74, 3rd fl; dm €18-22, s/d from €39/49; @; Frankfurt Hauptbahnhof) Reached via a prewar marble-and-tile lobby and a mirrored lift, this lively, 200-bed hostel has a chill-out area for socialising, a small shared kitchen, wooden floors and a free breakfast buffet.

25hours Hotel by Levi's HOTEL €€

(069-256 6770; www.25hours-hotels.com; Niddastrasse 58; d weekday/weekend from €99/70, during fairs up to €390; @; Hauptbahnhof) A hit with creative types for its playful design inspired by Levi's (yes, the jeans brand) and such hip factors as a rooftop terrace, free bike and Mini rentals, and a Gibson Music Room where anyone can jam on drums and guitars. Rooms are themed by decade, from the 1930s (calm colours) to the 1980s (tiger-print walls, optical-illusion carpets). Breakfast costs €16.

Frankfurt-am-Main

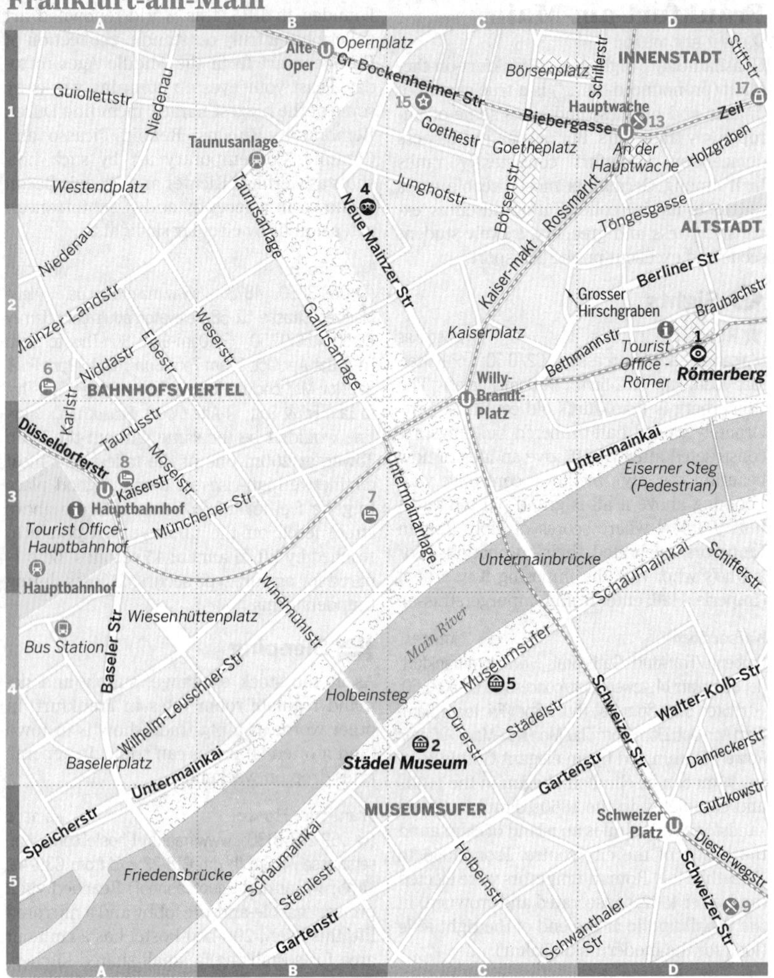

Adina Apartment Hotel HOTEL €€€

(☎069-247 4740; www.adina.eu/adina-apartment-hotel-frankfurt; Wilhelm-Leuschner-Strasse 6; studio/apt from €199/245; P❄🛜🏊; Ⓢ Willy-Brandt-Platz) Those in need of plenty of elbow room love the spacious and warmly furnished studios and apartments in this high-rise overlooking the Main River. The one- and two-bedroom units come with full kitchens, handy for self-caterers and families. Wi-fi is charged at €14.50 per 24 hours. Breakfast costs €21.

Eating & Drinking

The pedestrian strip west of Hauptwache square is nicknamed Fressgass thanks to its many (average) eateries. Cosy apple-wine taverns cluster in Alt-Sachsenhausen.

Kleinmarkthalle MARKET €

(www.kleinmarkthalle.de; Hasengasse 5; ⏰8am-6pm Mon-Fri, to 4pm Sat; Ⓢ Dom/Römer) This traditional market hall is a bustling beehive of artfully arranged stalls selling quality fruit, veg, meat, spices and delectable cheese. Feed acute tummy rumbles with delectable baked

goods, wurst (sausage) in a bun, and even sushi and tapas.

Almas TURKISH €€

(☎069-6642 6666; www.almas-restaurants.de; Wallstrasse 22; mains €11-18; ⏰5pm-midnight Tue-Thu, to 2am Fri & Sat, 10am-3pm Sun; Ⓢ Südbahnhof) With its elegantly exotic decor, Almas wouldn't look out of place in Istanbul and has a wide menu of Turkish specialities beyond the doner kebab to go with its candle-lit, linen-draped tables. Everything tastes genuine, fresh and inflected with an authentic medley of spices.

Frankfurt-am-Main

Top Sights

1 Römerberg D2
2 Städel Museum C4

Sights

3 Kaiserdom E2
4 Main Tower B1
5 Museumsufer Frankfurt C4

Sleeping

6 25hours Hotel by Levi's A2
7 Adina Apartment Hotel B3
8 Frankfurt Hostel A3

Eating

9 Adolf Wagner D5
10 Almas E4
11 Fichtekränzi F4
12 Kleinmarkthalle E1
13 Leonhard's D1
14 Metropol Cafe am Dom E2

Entertainment

15 Jazzkeller C1
16 Nachtleben E1

Shopping

17 Zeil D1

Metropol Cafe am Dom INTERNATIONAL €€

(☎069-288 287; www.metropolcafe.de; Weckmarkt 13-15; mains €6-15.80; ⏰9am-1am Tue-Sun; Ⓢ Dom/Römer) Homemade food inspired by the cuisines of the world is the name of the game at this bistro in a quiet spot next to the cathedral. It's popular with locals for its two-course lunches (€8.90), preferably enjoyed on the flowery terrace. In the evening a hipsterish crowd invades.

Leonhard's FAST FOOD €€

(☎069-219 1579; www.leonhards-restaurant.de; Zeil 116-26, 7th fl, Galeria Kaufhof; meals from €5; ⏰9.30am-9pm Mon-Sat; ✍; Ⓢ Hauptwache) High atop the Galeria Kaufhof department store, this upscale food court with outdoor terrace serves up everything from coffee and baked goods to freshly prepared fish and meat dishes.

☆ Entertainment

Jazzkeller JAZZ

(www.jazzkeller.com; Kleine Bockenheimer Strasse 18a; admission €5-25; ⏰8pm-2am Tue-Thu, 10pm-3am Fri, 9pm-2am Sat, 8pm-1am Sun; Ⓢ Alte Oper) A great jazz venue with mood, since 1952. Check out the walls for photos of jazz greats

LOCAL KNOWLEDGE

APPLE-WINE TAVERNS

Apple-wine taverns are Frankfurt's great local tradition. They serve *Ebbelwei* (Frankfurt dialect for *Apfelwein*), an alcoholic apple cider, along with local specialities like *Handkäse mit Musik* (literally, 'hand-cheese with music'). This is a round cheese soaked in oil and vinegar and topped with onions; your bowel supplies the music. Anything with *Grüne Sosse*, a sensational local herb sauce, is also a winner. **Fichtekränzi** (069-612 778; www.fichtekraenzi.de; Wallstrasse 5; dishes €2.80-14.50; 5pm-midnight; ; Lokalbahnhof) and **Adolf Wagner** (069-612 565; www.apfelwein-wagner.com; Schweizer Strasse 71; mains €8.50-13.90; 11am-midnight; ; S Südbahnhof) in Alt-Sachsenhausen are recommended.

who've played here over the years. Concerts begin at 9pm (8pm Sunday), except on DJ night (Friday) when there's dancing to Latin and funk. Hidden away in a cellar across from Goethestrasse 27.

Nachtleben CLUB

(069-206 50; www.nachtleben.net; Kurt-Schumacher-Strasse 45; 10.30am-2am Mon-Wed, to 4am Thu-Sat; S Konstablerwache) Tucked away in the southeastern corner of Konstablerwache, Nachtleben has a sedate cafe (open 7am to 2am Sunday) with a terrace on the ground floor and a basement club without 'show-me' attitude that gets bustling about 1am. Concerts showcase alt and indie bands, parties range from Britpop to techno to hip hop, depending on the night.

Shopping

Zeil MALL

(S Hauptwache) For some epic shopping, stroll along the pedestrianised Zeil, which is lined by department stores, high-street chains and malls, including the architecturally striking MyZeil. The strip is bookended by two squares called Konstablerwache and Hauptwache, both named after guardhouses of which only the one on Hauptwache survives.

Information

Tourist Office (069-2123 8800; www.frankfurt-tourismus.de) Two branches: Hauptbahnhof (Main Hall, main train station; 8am-9pm Mon-Fri, 9am-6pm Sat & Sun) and Römer (Römerberg 27; 9.30am-5.30pm Mon-Fri, to 4pm Sat & Sun; Frankfurt Hauptbahnhof), a smallish office in the central square.

Getting There & Away

AIR

Frankfurt Airport (FRA; www.frankfurt-airport.com), 12km southwest of the city centre, is Germany's busiest. S-Bahn lines S8 and S9 shuttle between the airport's regional train station (Regionalbahnhof) and the city centre (€4.35, 11 minutes) several times hourly.

Note that **Frankfurt-Hahn Airport** (HHN; www.hahn-airport.de), served by Ryanair, is actually 125km west of Frankfurt, near the Mosel Valley.

BUS

The Romantic Road Coach and long-distance buses leave from the south side of the Hauptbahnhof.

TRAIN

There are direct trains to pretty much everywhere, including Berlin (€123, four hours) and Munich (€101, 3½ hours).

Getting Around

For public transport information, go to www.rmv.de/en.

The Romantic Rhine Valley

Between Koblenz and Bingen, the Rhine cuts deeply through the Rhenish slate mountains. Nicknamed the 'Romantic Rhine', the stretch is justifiably a highlight for many Germany explorers. This is where hillsides cradle craggy cliffs and nearly vertical terraced vineyards. Idyllic villages appear around each bend, their neat half-timbered houses and church steeples seemingly plucked from the world of fairy tales. High above the river, busy with barge traffic, are the famous medieval castles, some ruined, some restored, all vestiges from a mysterious past.

Although Koblenz and Mainz are logical starting points, the area can also be explored on a long day trip from Frankfurt.

Getting There & Around

Each mode of transport on the Rhine has its own advantages and all are equally enjoyable. Try combining several.

BOAT

From about Easter to October (winter services are very limited), passenger ships run by

Köln-Düsseldorfer (KD; ☎0221-2088 318; www.k-d.com) link villages on a set timetable. You're free to get on and off as you like.

CAR

There are no bridges between Koblenz and Bingen but you can easily change banks by using a car ferry. There are five routes: Bingen–Rüdesheim, Niederheimbach–Lorch, Boppard–Filsen, Oberwesel–Kaub and St Goar–Goarshausen.

TRAIN

Villages on the Rhine's left bank (eg Bacharach and Boppard) are served hourly by local trains on the Koblenz–Mainz run. Right-bank villages such as Rüdesheim, St Goarshausen and Braubach are linked hourly to Koblenz' Hauptbahnhof and Frankfurt by the RheingauLinie train.

Bacharach

One of the prettiest of the Rhine villages, Bacharach conceals its considerable charms behind a 14th-century town wall. Beyond the thick arched gateways awaits a beautiful medieval old town graced with half-timbered town houses lining Oberstrasse, the main thoroughfare. There's no shortage of atmospheric places to eat and sample the local vintages.

For gorgeous views of village, vineyards and river, take a stroll atop the **medieval ramparts**, which are punctuated by guard towers. An especially scenic panorama unfolds from the **Postenturm** at the north end of town, from where you can also espy the filigreed ruins of the **Wernerkapelle**, a medieval chapel, and the turrets of the 12th-century hilltop **Burg Stahleck**, a castle turned **youth hostel** (☎06743-1266; www.jugendherberge.de; Burg Stahleck; s/d €27/43). Another good place to stay is the **Rhein Hotel** (☎06743-1243; www.rhein-hotel-bacharach.de; Langstrasse 50; d €78-136; P❄📶), which has 14 well-lit, soundproofed rooms with original artwork and a respected restaurant.

St Goar & St Goarshausen

These twin towns face each other across the Rhine. On the left bank, St Goar is lorded over by **Burg Rheinfels** (www.st-goar.de; adult/child €4/2; ⏲9am-6pm mid-Mar–late Oct, to 5pm until 9 Nov), one of the largest and most impressive river castles. Its labyrinthine ruins reflect the greed and ambition of the local count who built the behemoth in 1245 to levy tolls on passing ships.

Today an inexpensive ferry links St Goar with St Goarshausen and the most fabled spot along the Romantic Rhine, the **Loreley Rock**. This vertical slab of slate owes its fame to a mythical maiden whose siren songs are said to have lured sailors to their death in the river's treacherous currents.

A classy spot to spend the night is **Romantik Hotel Schloss Rheinfels** (☎06741-8020; www.schloss-rheinfels.de; d incl breakfast €130-245; P@📶🏊), right by the castle. Its three restaurants enjoy a fine reputation but there are plenty more down in the village.

Braubach

Framed by forested hillsides, vineyards and Rhine-side rose gardens, the 1300-year-old town of Braubach, on the right bank, is centred on the small, half-timbered market square. High above are the dramatic towers, turrets and crenellations of the 700-year-old **Marksburg** (☎0049-2627-536; www.marksburg.de; adult/student/6-18yr €6/5/4; ⏲10am-5pm late Mar-Oct, 11am-4pm Nov-late Mar) which – unique among the Rhine fortresses – was never destroyed. Tours (in English at 1pm and 4pm

ROMANCING THE RHINE

The Romantic Rhine Valley villages have plenty more charmers that deserve at least a quick spin. Just pick one at random and make your own discoveries. The following are some teasers:

Boppard Roman ruins and a cable car to the stunning Vierseenblick viewpoint (left bank).

Oberwesel Famous for its 3km-long medieval town wall punctuated by 16 guard towers (left bank).

Assmannhausen Relatively untouristed village known for its red wines, sweeping views and good hikes (right bank).

Rüdesheim Day-tripper-deluged but handy launch pad for the mighty Niederwalddenkmal monument and Eberbach Monastery (right bank).

from late March through early November) take in the citadel, the Gothic hall and the large kitchen, plus a grisly torture chamber.

Koblenz

Founded by the Romans, Koblenz sits at the confluence of the Rhine and Moselle Rivers, a point known as **Deutsches Eck** (German Corner) and dominated by a bombastic 19th-century statue of Kaiser Wilhelm I on horseback. On the right Rhine bank high above the Deutsches Eck – and reached by an 850m-long **Seilbahn** (Cable car; www.seilbahn-koblenz.de; return adult/child €9/4, incl fortress €11.80/5.60; ⏱10am-6pm or 7pm Apr-Oct, to 5pm Nov-Mar) – is the venerable fortress of **Festung Ehrenbreitstein** (www.diefestungehrenbreitstein.de; adult/child €6/3, incl cable car €11.80/5.60, audioguide €2; ⏱10am-6pm Apr-Oct, to 5pm Nov-Mar), one of Europe's mightiest citadels. Views are great and there's a restaurant and a regional museum inside.

Moselle Valley

Like a vine right before harvest, the Moselle hangs heavy with visitor fruit. Castles and towns with half-timbered buildings are built along the sinuous river below steep, rocky cliffs planted with vineyards. It's one of Germany's most evocative regions, with stunning views revealed at every river bend. Unlike the Romantic Rhine, it's spanned by plenty of bridges. The most scenic section unravels between Bernkastel-Kues and Cochem, 50km apart and linked by the B421.

Cochem

Easily reached by train or boat from Koblenz, Cochem is one of the most popular destinations on the Moselle thanks to its fairy-tale-like **Reichsburg** (☎02671-255; www.burg-cochem.de; Schlossstrasse 36; tours adult/concession/child €5/4.50/3; ⏱9am-5pm mid-Mar–Oct, 10am-3pm Nov & Dec, 11am, noon & 1pm Wed, Sat & Sun Jan–mid-Mar). Like many others, the 11th-century original fell victim to frenzied Frenchmen in 1689, then stood ruined for centuries until a wealthy Berliner snapped it up for a pittance in 1868 and had it restored to its current – if not always architecturally faithful – glory. The 40-minute tours (in German but English leaflet available) take in decorative rooms reflecting 1000 years' worth of tastes and styles.

The **tourist office** (☎02671-600 40; www.ferienland-cochem.de; Endertplatz 1; ⏱9am-5pm Mon-Fri Apr-Oct, 9am-1pm & 2-5pm Mon-Fri Nov-Mar, 9am-3pm Sat May–mid-Jul, 9am-5pm mid-Jul–Oct, 10am-3pm Sun Jul-Oct) has information about the entire region.

Cochem is 55km from Koblenz via the scenic B327 and B49. Regional trains shuttling between Trier (€12.90, 45 minutes) and Koblenz (€11.30, 50 minutes) stop here as well.

Beilstein

Picture-perfect Beilstein is little more than a cluster of higgledy-piggledy houses surrounded by steep vineyards. Its historic highlights include the **Marktplatz** and the ruined hilltop castle **Burg Metternich** (views!). The **Zehnthauskeller** (☎02673-900 907; www.zehnthauskeller.de; Marktplatz; ⏱11am-evening Tue-Sun) FREE houses a romantically dark, vaulted wine tavern owned by the same family that also runs two local hotels. Meals are available for €2.20 to €9. There is no tourist office.

Bus 716 goes from Cochem to Beilstein (€3.65, 20 minutes) almost hourly in season, although the approach by boat is more scenic (€12, one hour).

Bernkastel-Kues

This charming twin town straddles the Moselle about 50km downriver from Trier and is close to some of the river's most famous vineyards. Bernkastel, on the right bank, is a symphony in half-timber, stone and slate and teems with wine taverns.

Get your heart pumping by hoofing it up to **Burg Landshut**, a ruined 13th-century castle on a bluff above town. Allow 30 minutes to be rewarded with glorious valley views and a cold drink at the beer garden.

The **tourist office** (☎06531-500 190; www.bernkastel.de; Gestade 6, Bernkastel; ⏱9am-5pm Mon-Fri, 10am-5pm Sat, 10am-1pm Sun May-Oct, 9.30am-4pm Mon-Fri Nov-Apr) is in Bernkastel.

Coming from Trier, drivers should follow the B53. Using public transport involves catching the regional train to Wittlich and switching to bus 300.

Trier

☎0651 / POP 106,700

This handsome, leafy Moselle town is home to Germany's finest ensemble of Roman monuments – including thermal baths and an

WORTH A TRIP

BURG ELTZ

At the head of the beautiful Eltz Valley, **Burg Eltz** (☎02672-950 500; www.burg-eltz.de; Wierschem; tour adult/student/family €9/6.50/26; ⏰9.30am-5.30pm Apr-Oct) is one of Germany's most romantic medieval castles. Never destroyed, this vision of turrets, towers, oriels, gables and half-timber has squatted atop a rock framed by thick forest for nearly 900 years and is still owned by the original family. The decorations, furnishings, tapestries, fireplaces, paintings and armour you see during the 45-minute tour are also many hundreds of years old.

By car, you can reach Burg Eltz via Munstermaifeld. Alternatively, take a boat or train to Moselkern village and approach the castle via a lovely 5km walk (or €24 taxi ride).

amphitheatre – as well as architectural gems from later ages.

Sights

Porta Nigra GATE

(adult/student/child €3/2.10/1.50; ⏰9am-6pm Apr-Sep, to 5pm Mar & Oct, to 4pm Nov-Feb) This brooding 2nd-century city gate – blackened by time (hence the name, Latin for 'black gate') – is a marvel of engineering since it's held together by nothing but gravity and iron clamps.

Amphitheatre HISTORIC SITE

(Olewiger Strasse; adult/concession/child €3/2.10/1.50; ⏰9am-6pm Apr-Sep, to 5pm Mar & Oct, to 4pm Nov-Feb) Trier's Roman amphitheatre could accommodate 20,000 spectators for gladiator tournaments and animal fights. Beneath the arena are dungeons where prisoners sentenced to death waited next to starving beasts for the final showdown.

Kaiserthermen HISTORIC SITE

(Imperial Baths; Weberbachstrasse 41; adult/student/child €3/2.10/1.50; ⏰9am-6pm Apr-Sep, to 5pm Mar & Oct, to 4pm Nov-Feb) Get a sense of the layout of this vast Roman thermal bathing complex with its striped brick-and-stone arches from the corner lookout tower, then descend into an underground labyrinth consisting of hot- and cold-water baths, boiler rooms and heating channels.

Trierer Dom CATHEDRAL

(☎0651-979 0790; www.dominformation.de; Liebfrauenstrasse 12, cnr of Domfreihof; ⏰6.30am-6pm Apr-Oct, to 5.30pm Nov-Mar) Trier's cathedral is considered the oldest bishop's church in Germany and looms above a palace built during Roman times. Today's edifice is a study in nearly 1700 years of church architecture, with Romanesque, Gothic and baroque elements. Intriguingly, its floorplan is that of a 12-petalled flower, a symbol of the Virgin Mary.

Konstantin Basilika CHURCH

(☎0651-425 70; www.konstantin-basilika.de; Konstantinplatz 10; ⏰10am-6pm Apr-Oct, 11am-noon & 3-4pm Tue-Sat, noon-1pm Sun Jan-Mar) Constructed around AD 310 as Constantine's throne room, the brick-built basilica is now a typically austere Protestant church. With built-to-impress dimensions (67m long and 36m high), it's the largest single-room Roman structure still in existence.

Sleeping

Hotel Deutscher Hof HOTEL €€

(☎0651-977 80; www.hotel-deutscher-hof.de; Südallee 25; s/d from €60/75; P@☜) This comfortable value-priced pad a short walk south of the city centre oozes warmth and comfort in its softly lit and warmly decorated rooms. In summer there's a nice terrace for enjoying breakfast, while on colder days the sauna and steam baths beckon. Breakfast costs €8.

Hotel Villa Hügel BOUTIQUE HOTEL €€€

(☎0651-937 100; www.hotel-villa-huegel.de; Bernhardstrasse 14; d including breakfast €146-194; P@☜≈) A stylish, 33-room hillside villa where you can begin the day with sparkling wine at a lavish breakfast buffet and end it luxuriating in the 12m indoor pool and Finnish sauna. Rooms, decorated with honey-toned woods, are calming and create a sense of well-being. Served by buses 2 and 82.

Eating & Drinking

In the warm months cafes fill the old city's public squares, including the Kornmarkt. The Olewig wine district, 3km southeast of the city centre, is reached by buses 6, 16 and 81.

de Winkel PUB €

(☎0651-436 1878; www.de-winkel.de; Johannisstrasse 25; mains €6-9.50; ⏰6pm-1am Tue-Thu, to 2am Fri & Sat) Winny and Morris have presided over this locally adored watering hole for over

15 years. Join the locals for Pils and a bite, for instance the crispy chicken wings called 'Flieten' in Trier dialect.

Weinstube Kesselstadt GERMAN €€
(☎0651-411 78; www.weinstube-kesselstatt.de; Liebfrauenstrasse 10; dishes €4.50-12; ⊙10am-midnight) Sampling the local wines is a great pleasure in this charming setting, in summer on the cathedral-facing terrace. The standard menu showcases quality products from the region and is augmented by specials starring seasonal bounty like mushrooms, game or asparagus. Order at the bar.

Zum Domstein ROMAN €€
(☎0651-744 90; www.domstein.de; Hauptmarkt 5; mains €9-19, Roman dinner €17-36; ⊙8.30am-midnight) At this old-timey restaurant you can either dine like an ancient Roman or feast on more conventional German and international fare. Roman dishes are based on the recipes of a 1st-century local chef named Marcus Gavius Apicius.

Information

Tourist Office (☎0651-978 080; www.trier-info.de; ⊙9am-6pm Mon-Sat Mar-Dec, 10am-5pm Sun May-Oct, to 3pm Sun Mar, Apr, Nov & Dec, shorter hours Jan & Feb) Next to the Porta Nigra. Has excellent brochures in English and sells Moselle-area walking and cycling maps, concert tickets and boat excursions.

Getting There & Away

Frequent direct train connections include Koblenz (€22.10, 1½ to two hours), Cologne (€33, three hours) and Luxembourg (€17.30, 50 minutes).

Cologne

☎0221 / POP 1 MILLION

Cologne (Köln) offers lots of attractions, led by its famous cathedral, the filigree twin spires of which dominate the skyline. The city's museum landscape is especially strong when it comes to art but also has something in store for fans of chocolate, sports and Roman history. Its people are well known for their joie de vivre and it's easy to have a good time right along with them year-round in the beer halls of the Altstadt.

Sights

★Kölner Dom CHURCH
(Cologne Cathedral; ☎0211-1794 0200; www.koelner-dom.de; tower adult/concession/family €3/1.50/6; ⊙6am-9pm Mon-Sat May-Oct, to 7.30pm Nov-Apr, 1-3.30pm Sun year-round, tower 9am-6pm May-Sep, to 5pm Mar-Apr & Oct, to 4pm Nov-Feb) Cologne's geographical and spiritual heart – and its single-biggest tourist draw – is the magnificent Kölner Dom. With its soaring twin spires, this is the Mt Everest of cathedrals, jam-packed with art and treasures.

For an exercise fix, climb the 509 steps up the Dom's south tower to the base of the steeple that dwarfed all buildings in Europe until Gustave Eiffel built a certain tower in Paris. A good excuse to take a breather on your way up is the 24-tonne **Peter Bell** (1923), the largest free-swinging working bell in the world.

The Dom is Germany's largest cathedral and must be circled to truly appreciate its dimensions. Note how its lacy spires and flying buttresses create a sensation of lightness and fragility despite its mass and height. Soft light filters through the medieval stained-glass windows as well a much-lauded new one by contemporary artist Gerhard Richter in the transept.

The pièce de résistance among the cathedral's bevy of treasures is the **Shrine of the Three Kings** behind the main altar, a richly bejewelled and gilded sarcophagus said to hold the remains of the kings who followed the star to the stable in Bethlehem where Jesus was born. The bones were spirited out of Milan in 1164 as spoils of war by Emperor Barbarossa's chancellor and instantly turned Cologne into a major pilgrimage site.

Other highlights include the **Gero Crucifix** (970), notable for its monumental size and an emotional intensity rarely achieved in those early medieval days; the **choir stalls** from 1310, richly carved from oak; and the **altar painting** (c 1450) by Cologne artist Stephan Lochner.

★Römisch-Germanisches Museum MUSEUM
(Roman Germanic Museum; ☎0221-2212 4438; www.museenkoeln.de; Roncalliplatz 4; adult/concession €9/5; ⊙10am-5pm Tue-Sun) Sculptures and ruins displayed outside the entrance are merely the overture to a full symphony of Roman artefacts found along the Rhine. Highlights include the giant **Poblicius tomb** (AD 30–40), the magnificent 3rd-century **Dionysus mosaic**, and astonishingly well-preserved glass items. Insight into daily Roman life is gained from toys, tweezers, lamps and jewellery, the designs of which have changed surprisingly little since Roman times.

COLOGNE CARNIVAL

Ushering in Lent in late February or early March, Cologne's Carnival (Karneval) rivals Munich's Oktoberfest for exuberance, as people dress in creative costumes and party in the streets. Things kick off the Thursday before the seventh Sunday before Easter, culminate on Monday *(Rosenmontag)*, when there are televised street parades, and end on Ash Wednesday.

★ Museum Ludwig MUSEUM
(☎0221-2212 6165; www.museum-ludwig.de; Heinrich-Böll-Platz; adult/child €11/7.50, more during special exhibits; ⏲10am-6pm Tue-Sun) A mecca of 20th-century art, Museum Ludwig presents a tantalising mix of works from all major phases. Fans of German expressionism (Beckmann, Dix, Kirchner) will get their fill here as much as those with a penchant for Picasso, American pop art (Warhol, Lichtenstein) and Russian avant-garde painter Alexander Rodchenko. Rothko and Pollock are highlights of the abstract collection, while Gursky and Tillmanns are among the reasons the photography section is a must-see.

Wallraf-Richartz-Museum & Fondation Corboud MUSEUM
(☎0221-2212 1119; www.wallraf.museum; Obenmarspforten; adult/concession €13/8; ⏲10am-6pm Tue-Sun, to 9pm Thu) A famous collection of European paintings from the 13th to the 19th centuries, the Wallraf-Richartz-Museum occupies a postmodern cube designed by the late OM Ungers. Works are presented chronologically, with the oldest on the 1st floor where standouts include brilliant examples from the Cologne School, known for its distinctive use of colour. The most famous painting is Stefan Lochner's *Madonna of the Rose Bower*.

Schokoladenmuseum MUSEUM
(Chocolate Museum; ☎0221-931 8880; www.schokoladenmuseum.de; Am Schokoladenmuseum 1a; adult/concession/family €9/6.50/25; ⏲10am-6pm Tue-Fri, 11am-7pm Sat & Sun, last entry 1hr before closing) At this high-tech temple to the art of chocolate-making, exhibits on the origin of the 'elixir of the gods', as the Aztecs called it, and the cocoa-growing process are followed by a live-production factory tour and a stop at a chocolate fountain for a sample.

Tours

KD River Cruises BOAT
(☎0221-258 3011; www.k-d.com; Frankenwerft 35; adult/child €9.50/6; ⏲10.30am-5pm Apr-Oct) One of several companies offering one-hour spins taking in the splendid Altstadt panorama; other options include brunch and sunset cruises.

Sleeping

Station Hostel for Backpackers HOSTEL €
(☎0221-912 5301; www.hostel-cologne.de; Marzellenstrasse 44-56; dm €17-20, s/d from €39/55; @ Wi-Fi) Near the Hauptbahnhof, this is a hostel as hostels should be: central, convivial and economical. A lounge gives way to clean, colourful rooms sleeping one to six people. There's lots of free stuff, including linen, internet access, lockers, city maps and guest kitchen.

Stern am Rathaus HOTEL €€
(☎0221-2225 1750; www.stern-am-rathaus.de; Bürgerstrasse 6; d €105-135; Wi-Fi) This small, contemporary hotel has eight nicely spruced-up, luxuriously panelled rooms spread over three floors. It's in a quiet side street smack-dab in the Altstadt yet close to sights and plenty of restaurants. Kudos for the extra comfortable beds, the personalised service and the high-quality breakfast buffet.

Excelsior Hotel Ernst HOTEL €€€
(☎0221-2701; www.excelsiorhotelernst.com; Trankgasse 1-5; d from €230; ❄ @ Wi-Fi) Luxury is taken very seriously at this traditional hotel with a pedigree going back to 1863. Some of the plushly furnished rooms overlook the majestic Cologne cathedral. If that doesn't wow enough, perhaps a meal at the Michelin-starred restaurant will. Breakfast costs €32.

Eating & Drinking

There are plenty of beer halls and restaurants in the tourist-adored Altstadt, but for a more local vibe head to student-flavoured Zülpicher Viertel or the Belgisches Viertel, both in the city centre. Local breweries turn out a variety called *Kölsch*, which is relatively light and served in skinny 200mL glasses.

Freddy Schilling BURGERS €
(☎0221-1695 5515; www.freddyschilling.de; Kyffhäuserstrasse 34; burgers €5.50-10; ⏲noon-11pm Sun-Tue, to 11pm Fri & Sat) A wholewheat bun

Cologne

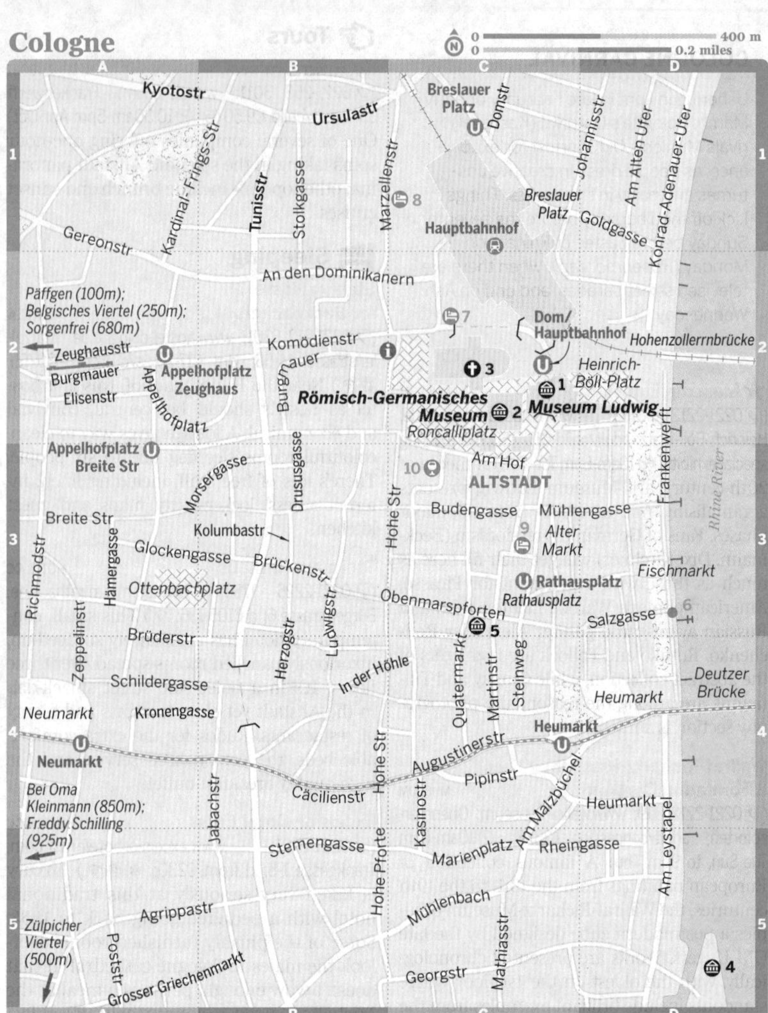

provides a solid framework for the moist patties made with beef from happy cows and drizzled with Freddy's homemade 'special' sauce. Pair it with a side of Rosi's: small butter-and-rosemary-tossed potatoes.

Bei Oma Kleinmann GERMAN €€

(☎0221-232 346; www.beiomakleinmann.de; Zülpicher Strasse 9; mains €13-21; ⏲5pm-1am Tue-Sat, to midnight Sun) Named for its long-time owner, who was still cooking almost to her last day at age 95 in 2009, this perennially booked restaurant serves a mind-boggling variety of schnitzel, made either with pork or veal and paired with homemade sauces and sides. Pull up a seat at the small wooden tables for a classic Cologne night out.

Sorgenfrei MODERN EUROPEAN €€€

(☎0221-355 7327; www.sorgenfrei-koeln.com; Antwerpener Strasse 15; mains €17-35, 2-course lunch €17, 3-/4-course dinner €35/43; ⏲noon-3pm Mon-Fri, 6pm-midnight Mon-Sat) A huge wine-by-the-glass menu is but one draw of this Belgische Viertel fine-dining treasure. Dishes are prepared with the same attention to detail yet lack of pretension found throughout this small restaurant. Hardwood floors

Cologne

Top Sights

Sights

Activities, Courses & Tours

Sleeping

Drinking & Nightlife

encourage a casual vibe that goes well with salads and simple mains at lunch and more complex creations for dinner.

★Päffgen BEER HALL
(☎0221-135 461; www.paeffgen-koelsch.de; Friesenstrasse 64-66; ⊙10am-midnight Sun-Thu, to 12.30am Fri & Sat) Busy, loud and boisterous, Päffgen has been pouring Kölsch since 1883 and hasn't lost a step since. In summer you can enjoy the refreshing brew and local specialities (€1.10 to €10.70) beneath starry skies in the beer garden.

Früh am Dom BEER HALL
(☎0221-261 3215; www.frueh-am-dom.de; Am Hof 12-14; ⊙8am-midnight) This warren of a beer hall near the Dom epitomises Cologne earthiness. Tuck into hearty meals (€2.50 to €20) sitting inside amid loads of knickknacks or on the flower-filled terrace next to a fountain. It's also known for gut-filling breakfasts (€4.30 to €9.50).

Information

Tourist Office (☎0221-346 430; www.cologne-tourism.com; Kardinal-Höffner-Platz 1; ⊙9am-8pm Mon-Sat, 10am-5pm Sun) Near the cathedral.

Getting There & Away

AIR

Köln Bonn Airport (CGN; Cologne-Bonn Airport; ☎02203-404 001; www.koeln-bonn-airport.de; Kennedystrasse) is about 18km southeast of the city centre and connected to the Hauptbahnhof by the S-Bahn S13 train every 20 minutes (€2.80, 15 minutes).

TRAIN

Services to and from Cologne are fast and frequent in all directions. A sampling: Berlin (€117, 4¼ hours), Frankfurt (€71, 1¼ hours), Düsseldorf (€11.30, 30 minutes), Bonn (€7.70, 30 minutes) and Aachen (€16.80, one hour). ICE trains leave for Brussels to connect with the Eurostar for London or Paris.

Getting Around

For public transport information, see www.vrs.de.

Düsseldorf

☎0211 / POP 596,000

Düsseldorf dazzles with boundary-pushing architecture, zinging nightlife and an art scene to rival many a metropolis. It's a posh and modern city whose economy is dominated by banking, advertising, fashion and telecommunications. However, a couple of hours of partying in the boisterous pubs of the Altstadt, the historical quarter along the Rhine, is all you need to realise that locals have no problem letting their hair down once they slip out of those Boss jackets.

Sights

K20 Grabbeplatz MUSEUM
(☎0211-838 1130; www.kunstsammlung.de; Grabbeplatz 5; adult/child €12/9.50; ⊙10am-6pm Tue-Fri, 11am-6pm Sat & Sun) A collection that spans the arc of 20th-century artistic vision gives the K20 an enviable edge in the art world. It encompasses major works by Picasso, Matisse and Mondrian and more than 100 paintings and drawings by Paul Klee. Americans represented include Jackson Pollock, Andy Warhol and Jasper John. Düsseldorf's own Joseph Beuys has a major presence as well.

K21 Ständehaus MUSEUM
(☎0211-838 1630; www.kunstsammlung.de; Ständehausstrasse 1; adult/child €12/9.50; ⊙10am-6pm Tue-Fri, 11am-6pm Sat & Sun) A stately 19th-century parliament building forms a fabulous dichotomy to the cutting-edge art of the K21, a collection showcasing only works created after the 1980s. Large-scale film and video installations and groups of works share space with site-specific rooms by an international cast of artists including Andreas Gursky, Candida Höfer, Bill Viola and Nam June Paik.

WORTH A TRIP

BONN

South of Cologne on the Rhine River, Bonn served as West Germany's capital from 1949 until 1990. For visitors, the birthplace of Ludwig van Beethoven has plenty in store, not least the great composer's birth house, a string of top-rated museums and the lovely riverside setting.

The **Beethoven-Haus** (☎0228-981 7525; www.beethoven-haus-bonn.de; Bonngasse 24-26; adult/concession €6/4.50; ⏲10am-6pm Apr-Oct, 10am-5pm Mon-Sat, 11am-5pm Sun Nov-Mar), where the composer was born in 1770, is big on memorabilia concerning his life and music. A highlight is his last piano, which was outfitted with an amplified sounding board to accommodate his deafness. Tickets are also good for an adjacent interactive Beethoven-themed 3D multimedia show.

Bonn's most stellar museums line up neatly on Museumsmeile (Museum Mile) in the heart of the former government quarter along Willy-Brandt-Allee just south of the city centre (take U-Bahn lines 16, 63 and 66). A top contender is the **Kunstmuseum Bonn** (Bonn Art Museum; ☎0228-776 260; www.kunstmuseum-bonn.de; Friedrich-Ebert-Allee 2; adult/concession €7/3.50; ⏲11am-6pm Tue & Thu-Sun, to 9pm Wed), which presents 20th-century art, including a standout collection of works by August Macke and other Rhenish expressionists. History buffs gravitate to the **Haus der Geschichte** (Museum of History; ☎0228-916 50; www.hdg.de; Willy-Brandt-Allee 14; ⏲9am-7pm Tue-Fri, 10am-6pm Sat & Sun) FREE for an engaging romp through Germany's post-WWII history.

The **tourist office** (☎0228-775 000; www.bonn.de; Windeckstrasse 1; ⏲10am-6pm Mon-Fri, to 4pm Sat, to 2pm Sun) is just off Münsterplatz and a three-minute walk, along Poststrasse, from the Hauptbahnhof (central train station).

The U-Bahn lines 16 and 18 (€7.70, one hour) and regional trains (€7.70, 30 minutes) link Cologne and Bonn several times hourly.

Medienhafen ARCHITECTURE

(Am Handelshafen) This once-dead old harbour area has been reborn as the Medienhafen, an increasingly hip quarter filled with architecture, restaurants, bars, hotels and clubs. Once-crumbling warehouses have turned into high-tech office buildings and now rub shoulders with bold new structures designed by celebrated international architects, including Frank Gehry.

Sleeping

Backpackers-Düsseldorf HOSTEL €

(☎0211-302 0848; www.backpackers-duesseldorf.de; Fürstenwall 180; dm incl small breakfast €18-24, linen €2; P @) Düsseldorf's cute indie hostel sleeps 60 in clean four- to 10-bed dorms outfitted with individual backpack-sized lockers.

Max Hotel Garni HOTEL €€

(☎0211-386 800; www.max-hotelgarni.de; Adersstrasse 65; s/d/tr €75/90/110; @) Upbeat, contemporary and run with personal flair, this charmer is a favourite Düsseldorf bargain. The 11 rooms are good sized and decked out in bright hues and warm woods. Rates include coffee, tea, soft drinks and a regional public transport pass, but breakfast costs €7.50. The reception isn't always staffed, so call ahead to arrange an arrival time.

Sir & Lady Astor HOTEL €€

(☎0211-173 370; www.sir-astor.de; Kurfürstenstrasse 18 & 23; s/d from €75/80; @) Never mind the ho-hum setting on a residential street near the Hauptbahnhof: this unique twin boutique hotel brims with class, originality and charm. Check-in is at Sir Astor, furnished in 'Scotland-meets-Africa' style, while Lady Astor across the street goes more for French floral sumptuousness. With a huge fan base and only 21 rooms in total, book early.

Eating & Drinking

The local beverage of choice is *Altbier*, a dark and semisweet beer typical of Düsseldorf.

★**Brauerei im Füchschen** GERMAN €€

(☎0211-137 470; www.fuechschen.de; Ratinger Strasse 28; snacks €1.80-6.90, mains €8.50-15.30; ⏲9am-1am Mon-Thu, to 2am Fri & Sat, to midnight Sun) Boisterous, packed and drenched with local colour – the 'Little Fox' in the Altstadt is all you expect a Rhenish beer hall to be. The kitchen makes a mean *Schweinshaxe* (roast pork leg). The high-ceilinged interior echoes with the mirthful roar of people enjoying their meals. This is one of the best *Altbier* breweries in town.

Sila Thai THAI €€€

(☎0211-860 4427; www.sila-thai.com; Bahnstrasse 76; mains €17-25; ⏰noon-3pm & 6pm-1am) Even simple curries become culinary poetry at this Thai gourmet temple with its fairy-tale setting of carved wood, rich fabrics and imported sculpture. Like a trip to Thailand without the passport. Reservations advised.

★ **Zum Uerige** BEER HALL

(☎0211-866 990; www.uerige.de; Berger Strasse 1; ⏰10am-midnight) This cavernous brewpub is the quintessential Düsseldorf haunt to try the city's typical *Altbier*. The suds flow so quickly from giant copper vats that the waitstaff – called *Köbes* – simply carry huge trays of brew and plonk down a glass whenever they spy an empty. Even on a cold day, there are groups all over the street outside.

Information

Tourist Office (☎0211-1720 2844; www.duesseldorf-tourismus.de) There are two tourist offices, the main one at the Hauptbahnhof (Immermannstrasse 65b; ⏰9.30am-7pm Mon-Fri, to 5pm Sat) and another in the Altstadt (cnr Marktstrasse & Rheinstrasse; ⏰10am-6pm), the historic centre.

Getting There & Away

Düsseldorf International Airport (DUS; www.dus-int.de) is linked to the city centre by the S-Bahn line 1 (€2.50, 10 minutes).

Regional trains travel to Cologne (€11.30, 30 minutes), Bonn (€16.80, one hour) and Aachen (€20.70, 1½ hours). Fast ICE train links include Berlin (€111, 4¼ hours), Hamburg (€82, 3½ hours) and Frankfurt (€82, 1½ hours).

Getting Around

For public transport information, go to www.vrr.de.

Aachen

☎0241 / POP 236,000

A spa town with a hopping student population and tremendous amounts of character, Aachen is most famous for its ancient cathedral. It makes for an excellent day trip from Cologne or Düsseldorf or a worthy overnight stop.

Sights

★ **Aachener Dom** CHURCH

(☎0241-447 090; www.aachendom.de; Münsterplatz; tours adult/concession €4/3; ⏰7am-7pm Apr-Dec, to 6pm Jan-Mar, tours 11am-5.30pm Mon-Fri, 1-5pm Sat & Sun, 2pm tour in English) It's impossible to overestimate the significance of Aachen's magnificent cathedral. The burial place of Charlemagne, it's where more than 30 German kings were crowned and where pilgrims have flocked since the 12th century. Before entering the church, stop by the new **Dom Visitors Centre** (☎0241-4770 9127; Klosterplatz 2; ⏰10am-1pm Mon, to 5pm Tue-Sun Jan-Mar, 10am-1pm Mon, to 6pm Tue-Sun Apr-Dec) for info and tickets for tours and the cathedral treasury.

The oldest and most impressive section is Charlemagne's palace chapel, the **Pfalzkapelle**. Completed in 800 (the year of the emperor's coronation), it's an octagonal dome encircled by a 16-sided ambulatory supported by antique Italian pillars. The colossal brass chandelier was a gift from Emperor Friedrich Barbarossa during whose reign Charlemagne was canonised in 1165.

Pilgrims have poured into Aachen ever since, drawn as much by the cult surrounding Charlemagne as by four prized relics, including the loincloth purportedly worn by Jesus at his crucifixion. To accommodate these floods of the faithful, a Gothic **choir** was docked to the chapel in 1414 and filled with such priceless 11th-century treasures as the **pala d'oro** (a gold-plated altar-front) and the jewel-encrusted gilded copper **pulpit**. At the far end is the gilded **shrine of Charlemagne** that has held the emperor's remains since 1215. In front, the equally fanciful **shrine of St Mary** shelters the four relics.

Unless you join a guided tour, you'll barely catch a glimpse of Charlemagne's white marble **throne** in the upstairs gallery. It served as the coronation throne of those 30 German kings between 936 and 1531. The tours themselves are fascinating for the level of detail they reveal about the church.

Rathaus HISTORIC BUILDING

(Town Hall; ☎0241-432 7310; Markt; adult/concession incl audioguide €5/3; ⏰10am-6pm) Fifty life-size statues of German rulers, including 30 kings crowned in town between 936 and 1531 AD, adorn the facade of Aachen's splendid Gothic town hall. It was built in the 14th century atop the foundations of Charlemagne's palace, of which only the eastern tower, the **Granusturm**, survives. Inside, the undisputed highlight is the **Krönungssaal** (coronation hall) with its epic 19th-century **frescoes** and replicas of the **imperial insignia**: a crown, orb and sword (the originals are in Vienna).

Domschatzkammer MUSEUM
(Cathedral Treasury; ☎0241-4770 9127; adult/child €5/4; ⏰10am-1pm Mon, to 5pm Tue-Sun Jan-Mar, 10am-1pm Mon, to 6pm Tue-Sun Apr-Dec) The cathedral treasury is a veritable mother lode of gold, silver and jewels. Items of particular importance include a silver and golden bust of Charlemagne, a 10th-century bejewelled processional cross known as the **Lotharkreuz** and a 1000-year-old relief-decorated **ivory situla** (a pail for holy water).

Tours

Old Town Guided Tour WALKING TOUR
(adult/child €8/4; ⏰11am Sat Apr-Dec) The tourist office runs 90-minute English-language walking tours.

Sleeping & Eating

Aachen's students have their own 'Latin Quarter' along Pontstrasse northeast of the Markt.

Hotel Drei Könige HOTEL €€
(☎0241-483 93; www.h3k-aachen.de; Büchel 5; s €90-130, d €120-160, apt €130-240; ⏰reception staffed 7am-11pm; 📶) The radiant Mediterranean decor is an instant mood enhancer at this family-run favourite with its doesn't-get-more-central location. Some rooms are a tad twee but the two-room apartment sleeps up to four. Breakfast, on the 4th floor, comes with dreamy views over the rooftops and the cathedral.

Aquis Grana City Hotel HOTEL €€
(☎0241-4430; www.hotel-aquis-grana.de; Büchel 32; d €85-165; P📶) The best quarters at this gracious hotel have terrace and balcony views of the town hall. But even in the most modest of the 98 rooms, you couldn't be any closer to the heart of town. The hotel offers a full range of services, including a bar and a restaurant.

Cafe Van den Daele CAFE €
(☎0241-357 24; www.van-den-daele.de; Büchel 18; treats from €3) Leather-covered walls, tiled stoves and antiques forge the yesteryear flair of this rambling cafe institution. Come for all-day breakfast, a light lunch, divine cakes or just to pick up a bag of homemade *Printen*, Aachen's riff on traditional *Lebkuchen*.

Am Knipp GERMAN €€
(☎0241-331 68; www.amknipp.de; Bergdriesch 3; mains €9-20; ⏰5-11pm Wed-Mon) Hungry grazers have stopped by this traditional inn since 1698, and you too will have a fine time enjoying hearty German cuisine served amid a flea market's worth of knick-knacks or, if weather permits, in the big beer garden.

Information

Tourist Office (☎0241-180 2960; www.aachen-tourist.de; Friedrich-Wilhelm-Platz; ⏰9am-6pm Mon-Fri, to 4pm Sat & Sun Apr-Dec, 9am-6pm Mon-Fri, to 2pm Sat Jan-Mar, 10am-2pm Sun Easter-Dec) Maps, general information, rooms, tours, tickets and more.

Getting There & Away

Regional trains frequently head to Cologne (€16.80, 55 minutes), Düsseldorf (€20.70, 1½ hours) and beyond.

HAMBURG & THE NORTH

Germany's windswept, maritime-flavoured north is dominated by Hamburg, a metropolis shaped by water and commerce since the Middle Ages. Bremen is a fabulous stop with fairy-tale character, and not only because of the famous Brothers' Grimm fairy tale starring a certain donkey, dog, cat and rooster. Those with a sweet tooth should not miss a side trip to Lübeck, renowned for its superb marzipan.

Hamburg

☎040 / POP 1.75 MILLION

'The gateway to the world' might be a bold claim, but Germany's second-largest city and biggest port has never been shy. Hamburg has engaged in business with the world ever since it joined the Hanseatic League trading bloc back in the Middle Ages. Today this 'harbourpolis' is the nation's premier media hub and among its wealthiest cities. It's also the site of Europe's largest urban-renewal project, the HafenCity, which is efficiently transforming the old docklands into a bold new city quarter. Hamburg's maritime spirit infuses the entire city: from architecture to menus to the cry of gulls, you always know you're near the water. The city has given rise to vibrant neighbourhoods awash with multicultural eateries, as well as the gloriously seedy Reeperbahn party and red-light district.

Sights

Rathaus HISTORIC BUILDING
(☎040-428 312 064; Rathausmarkt 1; tours adult/under 14yr €4/free; ⏰tours half-hourly 10am-3pm

Mon-Fri, to 5pm Sat, to 4pm Sun, English tours depend on demand; S Rathausmarkt, Jungfernstieg) Hamburg's baroque Rathaus is one of Europe's most opulent, renowned for the Emperor's Hall and the Great Hall, with its spectacular coffered ceiling. The 40-minute tours take in only a fraction of this beehive of 647 rooms.

North of here, you can wander through the Alsterarkaden, the Renaissance-style arcades sheltering shops and cafes alongside a canal.

★Hamburger Kunsthalle MUSEUM

(☎040-428 131 200; www.hamburger-kunsthalle.de; Glockengiesserwall; adult/concession €12/6; ⊙10am-6pm Tue, Wed & Fri-Sun, to 9pm Thu; S Hauptbahnhof) One of Germany's most prestigious art collections, the Kunsthalle displays works from the Middle Ages to today in two buildings. In the original brick one from 1869 you can admire old masters (Rembrandt, Ruisdael), 19th-century Romantics (Friedrich, Runge) and classical modernist works (Beckmann, Munch). A stark white concrete cube – the Galerie der Gegenwart – showcases mostly German artists working since the 1960s, including Neo Rauch, Jenny Holzer, Candida Höfer and Reinhard Mucha.

Chilehaus HISTORIC BUILDING

(☎040-349 194 247; www.chilehaus.de; Fischertwiete 2; S Messberg) Looking like a giant ocean liner in dry dock, the brown-brick Chilehaus is a leading example of German expressionist architecture. It was designed by Fritz Höger in 1924 for a merchant who derived his wealth from trading with Chile.

St Michaelis CHURCH

(Church of St Michael; ☎040-376 780; www.st-michaelis.de; tower adult/6-15yr €5/3.50, crypt €4/2.50, combo ticket €7/4; ⊙10am-8pm May-Oct, to 6pm Nov-Apr, last admission 30min before closing; 🚌Stadthausbrücke) 'Der Michel', as it is affectionately called, is one of Hamburg's most recognisable landmarks and northern Germany's largest Protestant baroque church. Ascending the **tower** (by steps or lift) rewards visitors with great panoramas across the city and canals. The **crypt** has an engaging multimedia exhibit on the city's history.

★Speicherstadt NEIGHBOURHOOD

(Am Sandtorkai; ⊙24hr; S Rödingsmarkt, Messberg) The seven-storey red-brick warehouses lining the Speicherstadt archipelago are a famous Hamburg symbol and the largest continuous warehouse complex in the world, recognised by Unesco as a World Heritage Site. Its distinctive architecture is best appreciated on a leisurely wander or a ride on a flat tour boat (called *Barkasse*). Many buildings contain shops, cafes and small museums.

LOCAL KNOWLEDGE

CRUISING ON THE CHEAP

This maritime city offers a bewildering array of boat trips, but there's no need to fork over €18 for a cruise to see the port. Instead, hop on one of the public ferries for the price of a standard public transport ticket (€3). The handiest line is ferry 62, which leaves from Landungsbrücken (pier 3) and travels west to Finkenwerder. Get off at the **Dockland** station to climb to the roof of this stunning office building shaped like a parallelogram for views of the container terminal, then continue to Neumühlen/Oevelgönne to look at old ships in the **museum harbour** and relax on the sandy Elbe beach with a beer from Strandperle (p503).

Miniatur Wunderland MUSEUM

(☎040-300 6800; www.miniatur-wunderland.de; Kehrwieder 2; adult/under 16yr €12/6; ⊙9.30am-6pm Mon, Wed, Thu, to 7pm Fri, to 9pm Tue, 8am-9pm Sat, 8.30am-8pm Sun; S Messberg) Even the worst cynics are quickly transformed into fans of this vast miniature world. When you see an A380 plane swoop out of the sky and land at the fully functional model of Hamburg's airport you can't help but gasp and say some variation of OMG! In busy times prepurchase your ticket online to skip the queues.

HafenCity NEIGHBOURHOOD

(☎040-3690 1799; www.hafencity.com; Info-Center, Am Sandtorkai 30; ⊙InfoCenter 10am-6pm Tue-Sun; S Baumwall, Überseequartier) HafenCity is a vast new city quarter taking shape east of the harbour. When fully completed, it's expected to be home to 12,000 people and offer work space for 40,000. It's a showcase of modern architecture with the biggest eye-catcher being the Elbphilharmonie, a vast concert hall jutting into the harbour atop a protected tea-and-cocoa warehouse. After many delays, it's expected to open in 2017. For the low-down, visit the HafenCity InfoCenter, which also runs free guided tours.

Hamburg

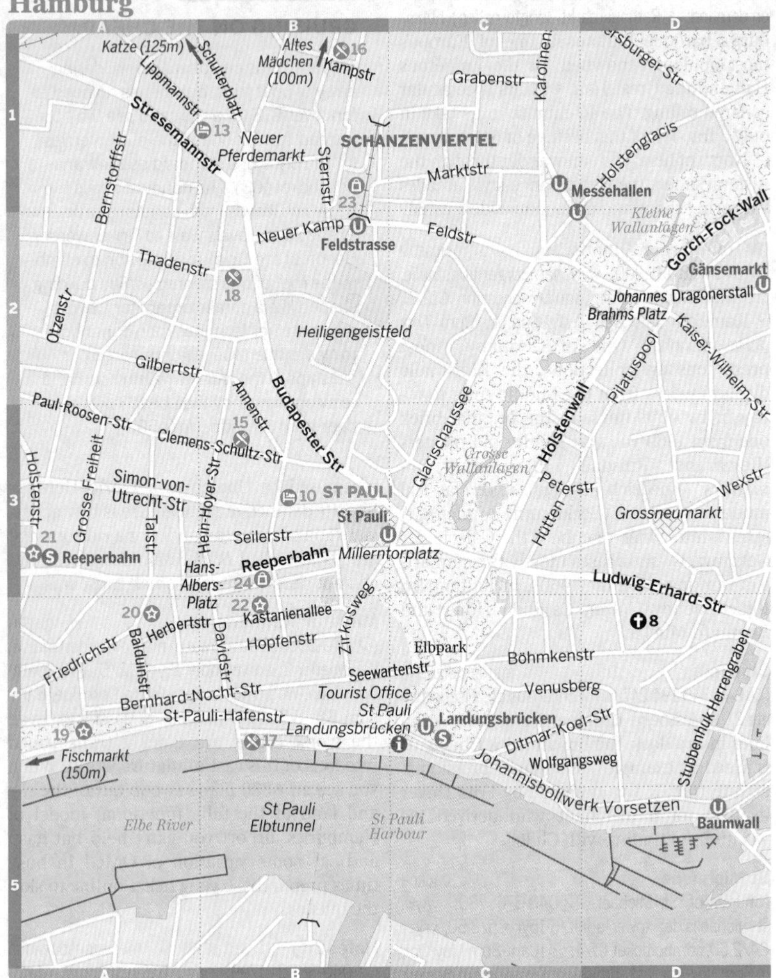

Fischmarkt MARKET

(Grosse Elbstrasse 9; 5-9.30am Sun Apr-Oct, 7-9.30am Sun Nov-Mar; 112 to Fischmarkt, Reeperbahn) Here's the perfect excuse to stay up all Saturday night. Every Sunday in the wee hours, some 70,000 locals and visitors descend upon the famous Fischmarkt in St Pauli. The market has been running since 1703, and its undisputed stars are the boisterous *Marktschreier* (market criers) who hawk their wares at full volume. Live bands also entertainingly crank out cover versions of ancient German pop songs in the adjoining Fischauktionshalle (Fish Auction Hall).

Auswanderermuseum BallinStadt MUSEUM

(Emigration Museum; 040-3197 9160; www.ballinstadt.de; Veddeler Bogen 2; adult/concession/5-12yr €12.50/10/7; 10am-6pm Apr-Oct, 10am-4.30pm Nov-Mar; Veddel) Sort of a bookend for New York's Ellis Island, Hamburg's excellent emigration museum in the original halls looks at the conditions that drove about 5 million people to leave Germany for the US and South America in search of better lives from 1850 until the 1930s. Multilingual displays address the hardships endured before and during the voyage and

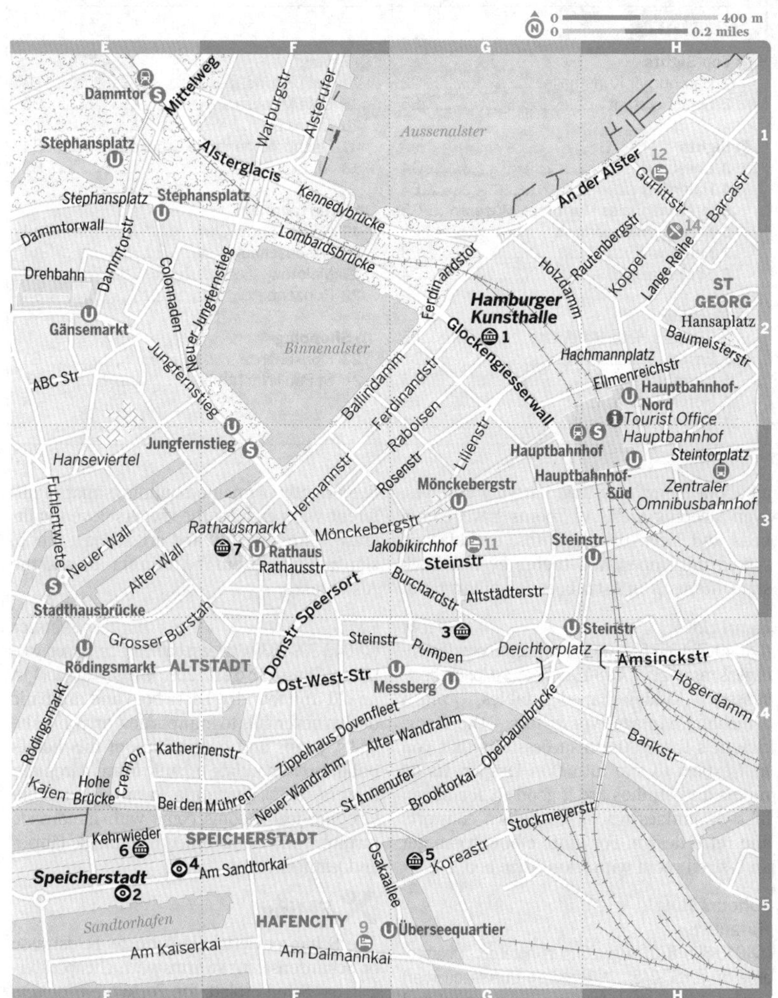

upon arrival in the New World. Although about 4km east of the city centre, Ballinstadt is easily reached by S-Bahn line S3.

Internationales Maritimes Museum MUSEUM

(☎040-3009 3300; www.internationales-maritimes-museum.de; Koreastrasse 1; adult/concession €12/8.50; ⏲10am-6pm Tue, Wed & Fri-Sun, to 8pm Thu; S Messberg) Hamburg's maritime past – and future – is fully explored in this excellent private museum that sprawls over 10 floors of a revamped brick shipping warehouse. Considered the world's largest private collection of maritime treasures, it includes a mind-numbing 26,000 model ships, 50,000 construction plans, 5000 illustrations, 2000 films, 1.5 million photographs and much more.

Sleeping

Superbude St Pauli HOTEL, HOSTEL €

(☎040-807 915 820; www.superbude.de; Juliusstrasse 1-7; dm/d from €16/60; @ ; S Sternschanze, Sternschanze, Holstenstrasse) The young and forever-young mix and mingle without a shred of prejudice at this rocking design hotel-hostel combo that's

Hamburg

Top Sights

1 Hamburger Kunsthalle ... G2
2 Speicherstadt ... E5

Sights

3 Chilehaus ... G4
4 HafenCity ... E5
5 Internationales Maritimes Museum ... G5
6 Miniatur Wunderland ... E5
7 Rathaus ... F3
8 St Michaelis ... D4

Sleeping

9 25hours Hotel HafenCity ... F5
10 East ... B3
11 Henri Hotel ... G3
12 Hotel Wedina ... H1
13 Superbude St Pauli ... B1

Eating

14 Café Koppel ... H1
15 Café Mimosa ... B3
16 Erikas Eck ... B1
17 Fischbrötchenbude Brücke 10 ... B4
18 Nil ... B2

Entertainment

19 Golden Pudel Club ... A4
20 Hasenschaukel ... A4
21 Molotow ... A3
22 Prinzenbar ... B4

Shopping

23 Flohschanze ... B1
24 St Pauli Nachtmarkt ... B3

all about living, laughing, partying and, yes, even sleeping well. All rooms have comfy beds and sleek private baths, breakfast is served until noon and there's even a 'rock star suite' with an Astra beer as a pillow treat.

Henri Hotel HOTEL €€
(040-554 357 557; www.henri-hotel.com; Bugenhagenstrasse 21; r €98-138; ; S Mönckebergstrasse) Kidney-shaped tables, plush armchairs, vintage typewriters – the Henri channels the 1950s so successfully that you half expect to run into Don Draper. Its 65 rooms and studios are a good fit for urban lifestyle junkies who like modern comforts and retro design. For more elbow room get an L-sized room with a king-size bed.

25hours Hotel HafenCity HOTEL €€
(040-855 870; www.25hours-hotel.de; Überseeallee 5; r €97-245; P; S Überseequartier) Funky decor, an infectious irreverence and postmodern vintage flair make this pad a top choice among global nomads. Sporting maritime flourishes, the decor channels an old-timey seaman's club in the lobby, the excellent restaurant and the 170 cabin-style rooms. Enjoy views of the emerging HafenCity neighbourhood from the rooftop sauna. Breakfast costs €14.

★**Hotel Wedina** HOTEL €€
(040-280 8900; www.hotelwedina.de; Gurlittstrasse 23; d €125-245; P@; S Hauptbahnhof) Margaret Atwood, Jonathan Franzen and Martin Walser are among the literary greats who've stayed at this loveable lair and left behind signed books. Rooms spread over five brightly pigmented buildings that in different ways express the owners' love for literature, architecture and art. It's just a hop, skip and jump from the train station and the Alster lakes.

East HOTEL €€
(040-309 933; www.east-hamburg.de; Simon-von-Utrecht-Strasse 31; d €113-209; ; S St Pauli) In an old iron foundry, East's bold and dramatic design never fails to impress new arrivals. The walls, lamps and huge pillars of this hotel's public areas emulate organic forms (droplets, flowers, trees), giving it a warm, rich and enveloping feel. Rooms come with handmade furniture and are accented with tactile fabrics and leather.

Eating

The Schanzenviertel (U-Bahn to Feldstrasse or Schanzenstern) swarms with cheap eateries; try Schulterblatt for Portuguese outlets or Susannenstrasse for Asian and Turkish. St Georg's Lange Reihe (U-Bahn to Hauptbahnhof) offers many characterful eating spots to suit every budget. Fish restaurants around the Landungsbrücken tend to be overrated and touristy.

★**Fischbrötchenbude Brücke 10** FISH €
(040-6504 6899; www.bruecke-10.de; Landungsbrücken, Pier 10; sandwiches €2.50-7.50; 10am-10pm Mon-Sat, 9am-10pm Sat; S Landungsbrücken, Landungsbrücken) There are a gazillion fish-sandwich vendors in Hamburg, but we're going to stick our neck out and say that this vibrant, clean and contemporary outpost

LOCAL KNOWLEDGE

TOP THREE HAMBURG MARKETS

St Pauli Nachtmarkt (Spielbudenplatz; 4-10pm Wed; S St Pauli) This after-dark farmers and gourmet market with colourful bounty and fun snack stands lures locals and visitors to the heart of St Pauli.

Flohschanze (Neuer Kamp 30; 8am-4pm Sat; S Feldstrasse) Hamburg's best flea market is nirvana for thrifty trinket hunters and vintage junkies, with hundreds of vendors holding forth outdoors in the hip Karolinenviertel.

Isemarkt (www.isemarkt.com; btwn U-Bahn stations Hoheluft & Eppendorfer Baum; 8.30am-2pm Tue & Fri; S Eppendorfer Baum, Hoheluft) Winding for over 1km beneath the elevated U-Bahn tracks, the twice-weekly Isemarkt in Eppendorf is literally the longest farmers market in Germany with some 200 vendors offering quality anything.

makes the best. Try a classic *Bismarck* (pickled herring) or *Matjes* (brined) or treat yourself to a bulging shrimp sandwich.

Café Mimosa CAFE €
(040-3202 7989; www.cafemimosa.de; Clemens-Schultz-Strasse 87; mains €3.50-12; 10am-7pm Tue-Sun; S St Pauli) This gem of a neighbourhood cafe is the go-to place for warm brioches, some of the yummiest cakes in town plus daily changing lunch specials. Sit inside among theatrical flourishes or grab a sidewalk table.

Café Koppel VEGETARIAN €
(www.cafe-koppel.de; Lange Reihe 66; mains €5-10; ; S Hauptbahnhof) Set back from busy Lange Reihe, with a garden in summer, this vegie cafe is a refined oasis, where you can hear the tinkling of spoons in coffee cups midmorning on the mezzanine floor. The menu could be an ad for the fertile fields of northern Germany as there are baked goods, salads, soups and much more made with fresh seasonal ingredients.

Altes Mädchen MODERN GERMAN €€
(040-800 077 750; www.altes-maedchen.com; Lagerstrasse 28b; mains €9-22; from noon Mon-Sat, from 10am Sun; S Sternschanze) The lofty red-brick halls of a 19th-century animal market have been upcycled into a hip culinary destination that includes a coffee roastery, a celebrity-chef restaurant, and this tarted-up brewpub with a central bar, in-house bakery and beer garden.

Erikas Eck GERMAN €€
(040-433 545; www.erikas-eck.de; Sternstrasse 98; mains €6-18; 5pm-2pm; Sternschanze) This pit-stop institution originally fed hungry workers from the nearby abattoir (today the central meat market) and now serves wallet-friendly but waist-expanding portions of schnitzel and other trad German fare to a motley crowd of clubbers, cabbies and cops 21 hours a day.

Nil INTERNATIONAL €€€
(040-439 7823; www.restaurant-nil.de; Neuer Pferdemarkt 5; mains €15.50-24; 6-10.30pm Wed-Mon; S Feldstrasse) Despite the name, this contempo tri-level restaurant doesn't do Egyptian fare but proffers a varied and inspired slow-food menu steered by the seasons and whatever regional suppliers have in store. Flavour pairings can be adventurous (scallops with kohlrabi) but usually produce tantalising results.

Drinking & Entertainment

Partying in Hamburg concentrates on the Schanzenviertel and St Pauli, a few streets further south. Most people start the night in the former, then move on to the clubs and bars of the latter around midnight. Online sources: www.szene-hamburg.de and www.neu.clubkombinat.de.

Katze BAR
(040-5577 5910; Schulterblatt 88; 3pm-midnight Mon-Thu, 6pm-3am Fri, 1pm-3am Sat, 3pm-midnight Sun; S Sternschanze) Small and sleek, this 'kitty' (Katze means 'cat') gets the crowd purring for well-priced cocktails (best caipirinhas in town) and great music (there's dancing on weekends). It's one of the most popular among the watering holes on this main Schanzenviertel booze strip.

Strandperle BAR
(040-880 1112; www.strandperle-hamburg.de; Oevelgönne 60; 10am-11pm Mon-Fri, 9am-11pm Sat & Sun May-Sep, weather permitting, shorter hours otherwise; 112) The mother of Hamburg's beach bars is a must for primo beer, burgers and people-watching. All ages and classes

LOCAL KNOWLEDGE

ST PAULI & THE REEPERBAHN

No discussion of Hamburg is complete without mentioning St Pauli, home to one of Europe's most (in)famous red-light districts. Sex shops, table-dance bars and strip clubs still line its main drag, the Reeperbahn, and side streets, but the popularity of prostitution has declined dramatically in the internet age. Today St Pauli is Hamburg's main nightlife district, drawing people of all ages and walks of life to live-music and dance clubs, chic bars and theatres.

In fact, street walkers are not even allowed to hit the pavement before 8pm and then are confined to certain areas, the most notorious being the gated Herbertstrasse (no women, and no men under 18 years allowed). Nearby, the cops of the Davidwache police station keep an eye on the lurid surrounds. A short walk west is the side street called Grosse Freiheit, where the Beatles cut their teeth at the Indra Club (No 64) and the Kaiserkeller (No 36). Both are vastly different venues today, but there's a small monument to the Fab Four in a courtyard behind No 35.

gather and mingle, especially at sunset, right on the Elbe as huge freighters glide past and you wiggle your toes in the sand. Get there by taking ferry 62 from Landungsbrücken or bus 112 from Altona station to Neumühlen/Oevelgönne.

★Golden Pudel Club LIVE MUSIC
(☎040-3197 9930; www.pudel.com; St-Pauli-Fischmarkt 27; ⏲nightly; Ⓤ Reeperbahn) In a 19th-century bootleggers' jail, this tiny bar-club is run by members of the legendary ex-punk band Die Goldenen Zitronen and is an essential stop on the St Pauli party circuit. Night after night it gets packed to the rafters for its countercultural vibe, quality bands and DJs, and relaxed crowd.

Molotow LIVE MUSIC
(☎040-430 1110; www.molotowclub.com; Holstenstrasse 5; Ⓤ Reeperbahn) The legendary indie club still rocks on as hot 'n heavy as ever after moving to new digs after its Reeperbahn location was torn down in 2013.

Prinzenbar CONCERT VENUE
(Kastanienallee 20; Ⓢ St Pauli, Ⓤ Reeperbahn) With its cheeky cherubs, stucco flourishes and wrought-iron galleries, this intimate club has chapel looks but is in fact a former cinema that now hosts stylish electro parties, concerts, queer parties and indie nights in the heart of St Pauli.

Hasenschaukel LIVE MUSIC
(☎040-1801 2721; www.hasenschaukel.de; Silbersackstrasse 17; ⏲from 9pm Tue-Sun; Ⓤ Reeperbahn) The booking policy at this unhurried pocket-size club with plush decor skews towards lo-fi indie-folk-rock and usually features pre-stardom international artists along with DJ sets. Grab a vegan midnight snack if the vintage doll lamps get too trippy after a few beers.

ℹ Information

Tourist Office (www.hamburg-tourism.de) Branches include Hauptbahnhof (Kirchenallee exit; ⏲9am-7pm Mon-Sat, 10am-6pm Sun; Ⓢ Hauptbahnhof, Ⓤ Hauptbahnhof) and St Pauli Landungsbrücken (btwn piers 4 & 5; ⏲9am-6pm Sun-Wed, to 7pm Thu-Sat; Ⓢ Landungsbrücken); note this latter branch doesn't make hotel bookings.

ℹ Getting There & Away

AIR

Hamburg Airport (HAM; www.airport.de) is linked to the city centre every 10 minutes by the S-Bahn line S1 (€3, 25 minutes). A taxi takes about a half hour and cost around €25.

BUS

The **Zentraler Omnibusbahnhof** (ZOB, Central Bus Station; ☎040-247 576; www.zob-hamburg.de; Adenauerallee 78), southeast of the Hauptbahnhof, has many domestic and international departures by Euroline, Flixbus and many other operators.

TRAIN

Hamburg is a major train hub with four mainline train stations: the Hauptbahnhof, Dammtor, Altona and Harburg. Frequent trains serve Lübeck (€13.70, 45 minutes), Bremen (from €28, 55 minutes), Berlin-Hauptbahnhof (€78, 1¾ hours), Copenhagen (€85.40, 4¾ hours) and many other cities.

Getting Around

For public transport information, go to www.hvv.de. The city is divided into zones. Fare zone A covers the city centre, inner suburbs and airport.

Lübeck

0451 / POP 214,000

Compact and charming Lübeck makes for a great day trip from Hamburg. Looking like a pair of witches' hats, the pointed towers of its landmark Holstentor (Holsten Gate) form the gateway to its historic centre that sits on an island embraced by the arms of the Trave River. The Unesco-recognised web of cobbled lanes flanked by gabled merchants' homes and spired churches is an enduring reminder of Lübeck's role as the one-time capital of the medieval Hanseatic League trading power. Today it enjoys fame as Germany's marzipan capital.

Sights

A good place to start a wander around Lübeck's old town is from the Holsten Gate. Hüxstrasse is lined by pleasant boutiques and cafes. For a breath of seaside air, take a short train ride to the Baltic port and resort of Travemünde.

★Holstentor LANDMARK

(Holsten Gate) Built in 1464 Lübeck's charming red-brick city gate is a national icon. Its pointed slate-covered towers, linked by a stepped gable, have graced postcards, paintings and posters, and the old 50 Deutschmark note. Its crooked appearance is the result of an insufficient foundation that caused the south tower to sag until the movement could be halted in the 1930s. The museum inside sheds light on the history of the gate and on Lübeck's medieval mercantile glory days.

Marienkirche CHURCH

(St Mary's Church; 0451-397 700; Marienkirchhof; adult/concession €2/1.50; 10am-6pm Apr-Sep, to 5pm Oct, to 4pm Tue-Sun Nov-Mar) This fine Gothic church boasts the world's highest brick-vaulted roof and was the model for dozens of churches in northern Germany. Crane your neck to take in the painted cross-vaulted ceilings supported by slender, ribbed pillars. Also note the astronomical clock in the north aisle next to modern glass windows inspired by a medieval Dance of Death mural destroyed in WWII. Another bombing raid brought down the church's bells, which have been left where they fell in 1942.

Petrikirche CHURCH

(Church of St Peter; 0451-397 730; www.st-petri-luebeck.de; Petrikirchhof 1; tower adult/child €3/2; 9am-9pm Apr-Sep, 10am-7pm Oct-Mar) Thanks to a lift, even the fitness-phobic get to enjoy panoramic views from the 50m-high platform in the tower of the 13th-century Petrikirche. No longer an active parish, the starkly whitewashed interior hosts exhibits and events.

Sleeping

Hotel an der Marienkirche HOTEL €

(0451-799 410; www.hotel-an-der-marienkirche.de; Schüsselbuden 4; d from €89;) After a recent renovation, this small, good-value hotel exudes cheery, contemporary Scandinavian flair and is equipped with top-quality latex mattresses and crispy linen. One of the 18 rooms even has a view of the namesake church.

Hotel Lindenhof HOTEL €€

(0451-872 100; www.lindenhof-luebeck.de; Lindenstrasse 1a; d from €94; P@) Most of the 66 rooms at this family-run hotel in a quiet side street won't hold a ton of luggage, but the opulent breakfast buffet, friendly service and little extras (such as free biscuits and newspapers) propel the Lindenhof into a superior league.

Eating

Schiffergesellschaft GERMAN €€

(0451-767 76; www.schiffergesellschaft.com; Breite Strasse 2; mains €10-25) In the historic seafarer's guild hall, Lübeck's cutest – if not

DON'T MISS

SWEET TEMPTATIONS

Niederegger (0451-530 1126; www.niederegger.de; Breite Strasse 89; 9am-7pm Mon-Fri, 9am-6pm Sat, 10am-6pm Sun) is Lübeck's mecca for marzipan, which has been made locally for centuries. The shop's elaborate displays are a feast for the eyes, and there's even a museum where you'll learn that marzipan was considered medicine in the Middle Ages. The on-site cafe serves sandwiches and salads alongside sweet treats.

OFF THE BEATEN TRACK

ANNE FRANK & BERGEN-BELSEN

The Nazi-built camp at **Bergen-Belsen** (Bergen-Belsen Memorial Site; ☎05051-475 90; www.bergen-belsen.de; Anne-Frank-Platz, Lohheide; ⊙documentation centre 10am-6pm Apr-Sep, 10am-5pm Oct-Mar, grounds until dusk) FREE began its existence in 1940 as a prisoner of war (POW) camp, but became a concentration camp after being taken over by the *Schutzstaffel* (SS) in 1943, initially to imprison Jews as hostages in exchange for German POWs held abroad. In all, 70,000 prisoners perished here, most famously Anne Frank. Victims were buried in mass graves scattered across the parklike cemetery grounds. The modern **Documentation Centre** poignantly chronicles the fates of the people who passed through here – before, during and after incarceration. A small section deals with Anne Frank, and there's also a **memorial grave stone** for her and her sister, Margot, near the cemetery's Jewish Monument.

The memorial site is in the countryside about 60km northeast of Hanover and a bit complicated to reach if you don't have your own wheels. See the website for detailed driving and public transport directions.

its best – restaurant is a veritable museum. Ships' lanterns, old model ships and revolving Chinese-style silhouette lamps dangle from the beamed ceiling of this wood-lined dining room. White-aproned waitstaff deliver regional specialities to tables here or in the hidden garden out the back. Book ahead at dinnertime.

Remise CAFE €€
(☎0451-777 73; www.remise-luebeck.de; Wahmstrasse 43-45; mains €12-20; ⊙noon-late Mon-Fri, 9am-late Sat & Sun) This charming owner-run restaurant in a former roastery specialises in grass-fed beef but also does creative pastas, regional fare and salads. In fine weather, snag a table in the vine-draped courtyard. Locals invade on 2-4-1 Monday evenings.

Brauberger GERMAN €€
(☎0451-702 0606; Alfstrasse 36; snacks €1.50-5, mains €11-18; ⊙5pm-midnight Mon-Thu, to late Fri & Sat) The air is redolent of hops at this traditional German brewery. Get a stein of the sweet, cloudy house brew *(Zwickelbier)* and tuck into a sizeable schnitzel or other traditional fare.

Information

Tourist Office (☎0451-889 9700; www.luebeck-tourismus.de; Holstentorplatz 1; ⊙9am-7pm Mon-Fri, 10am-4pm Sat, 10am-3pm Sun May-Aug, slightly reduced hours otherwise) Sells the HappyDay Card (per 24/48/72 hours €11/13/16) with discounts and free public transport. Also has a cafe and internet terminals.

Getting There & Away

Ryanair and Wizzair serve **Lübeck Airport** (LBC; www.flughafen-luebeck.de).

Regional trains connect to Hamburg twice hourly (€13.50, 45 minutes).

Bremen

☎0421 / POP 548,000

It's a shame the donkey, dog, cat and rooster in Grimm's *Town Musicians of Bremen* never actually made it here – they would have fallen in love with the place. This little city is big on charm, from the fairy-tale character statue to a jaw-dropping expressionist laneway and impressive town hall. On top of that, the Weser riverside promenade is a relaxing, bistro-and-beer-garden–lined refuge and the lively student district ('Das Viertel') along Ostertorsteinweg is filled with indie boutiques, cafes, art-house cinemas and alt-flavoured cultural venues.

Sights

Bremen's key historic sights cluster around Markt and can easily be explored on foot.

★Markt SQUARE
Bremen's Unesco-recognised Markt is striking, especially because of its ornate, gabled and sculpture-festooned Rathaus (town hall; 1410). In front stands a 5.5m-high medieval statue of the knight **Roland** (1404), the symbolic protector of Bremen's civic rights and freedoms. On the town hall's western side, you'll find a sculpture of the Town Musicians of Bremen (1951).

Dom St Petri CHURCH

(St Petri Cathedral; www.stpetridom.de; Markt; tower €1, Lead Cellar adult/concession €1.40/1; ⏲10am-6pm Mon-Fri & Sun, to 2pm Sat Jun-Sep, 10am-5pm Mon-Fri, to 2pm Sat, 2-5pm Sun Oct-Mar, tower closed Nov-Easter) Bremen's protestant main church has origins in the 8th century and got its ribbed vaulting, chapels and two high towers in the 13th century. Aside from the imposing architecture, the intricately carved pulpit and the baptismal font in the western crypt deserve a closer look. For panoramic views, climb the 265 steps to the top of the south tower. A separate entrance leads to the church's **Bleikeller**, a cellar where open coffins reveal eight bodies mummified in the incredibly dry air.

Böttcherstrasse STREET

(www.boettcherstrasse.de) The charming medieval coopers' lane was transformed into a prime example of mostly expressionist architecture in the 1920s at the instigation of coffee merchant Ludwig Roselius. Its red-brick houses sport unique facades, whimsical fountains, statues and a carillon; many house artesanal shops and art museums. Its most striking feature is Bernhard Hoetger's golden **Lichtbringer** (Bringer of Light) relief that keeps an eye on the north entrance.

Schnoor NEIGHBOURHOOD

This maze of narrow, winding alleys was once the fishermen's quarter and later a red-light district. Now its doll's-house-sized cottages contain boutiques, restaurants, cafes and galleries. Though tourist-geared, there are some lovely corners to explore around here on a leisurely amble.

Sleeping

Townside Hostel Bremen HOSTEL €

(☎0421-780 15; www.townside.de; Am Dobben 62; dm €15-25, s/d €54/76; 📶) This bright, professionally run hostel is right in the middle of Bremen's nightlife quarter and handy to Werder Bremen's stadium. Breakfast costs €5.50. Take tram 10 from Hauptbahnhof to Humboldtstrasse or tram 2 or 3 to Sielwall.

Hotel Überfluss DESIGN HOTEL €€€

(☎0421-322 860; www.hotel-ueberfluss.com; Langenstrasse 72; d €139-169, ste €345; ❄📶🏊) Just metres above river level, this cutting-edge cool hotel is a good choice for design-minded urban nomads. Black, white and chrome create a sleek, postmodern vibe that extends to the rooms that feature open bathrooms and Yves Rocher products. Suites have river views and a private sauna and whirlpool – perfect for a honeymoon. Breakfast costs €12.50.

Eating & Drinking

Tourist-oriented places cluster around Markt, which is pretty dead after dark. Das Viertel has an alternative, student-flavoured feel, while the waterfront promenade, Schlachte, is pricier and more mainstream.

Engel Weincafe CAFE €

(☎0421-6964 2390; www.engelweincafe-bremen.de; Ostertorsteinweg 31; dishes €4-11; ⏲8am-1am

WORTH A TRIP

BACK TO THE ROOTS IN BREMERHAVEN

'Give me your tired, your poor, your huddled masses', invites the *State of Liberty* in New York harbour. Well, Bremerhaven is one place that most certainly did just that. More than seven million of those landing at Ellis Island departed from here between 1830 and 1974, and the **Deutsches Auswandererhaus** (German Emigration Centre; ☎0471-902 200; www.dah-bremerhaven.de; Columbusstrasse 65; adult/child 4-16yr €12.60/6.90; ⏲10am-6pm Mar-Oct, to 5pm Nov-Feb) does a superb job of chronicling and commemorating some of their stories. You relive the stages of the journey and the emigrants' travelling conditions aboard a movie-set-like steamer, clutching the biographical details of one particular traveller. Once you've 'landed', you have to go through immigration at Ellis Island and travel on to a miniature replica of New York's Grand Central Station to start your new life.

A somewhat less engaging new exhibit reverses the theme and tells the story of immigration *to* Germany since the 17th century.

Bremerhaven is some 70km north of Bremen and is served by regional train (€12, 35 minutes). From the station, take bus 502, 505, 506, 508 or 509 to 'Havenwelten' to get to the museum and the harbour with its many old vessels (including a WWII sub) and striking contemporary architecture.

WORTH A TRIP

HANOVER'S HERRENHÄUSER GÄRTEN

Proof that Hanover is not all buttoned-down business are the grandiose baroque **Royal Gardens of Herrenhausen** (☎0511-1683 4000; www.herrenhaeuser-gaerten.de; Herrenhäuser Strasse; gardens adult/concession/under 12yr €8/4/free; ⌚9am-6pm Apr-Oct, to 4.30pm Nov-Mar, grotto 9am-5.30pm Apr-Oct, to 4pm Nov-Mar), which rank among the most important historic garden landscapes in Europe. Inspired by the park at Versailles, the sprawling grounds are perfect for slowing down and smelling the roses for a couple of hours, especially on a blue-sky day.

With its fountains, neat flowerbeds, trimmed hedges and shaped lawns, the 300-year-old **Grosser Garten** (Great Garden) is the centrepiece of the experience. Don't miss the **Niki de Saint Phalle Grotto** near the northern end, which provides a magical backdrop for the whimsical statues, fountains and coloured tile by this late French artist (1930–2002). South of here, the **Grosse Fontäne** (Big Fountain; the tallest in Europe) jets water up to 80m high. In summer fountains are synchronised during the **Wasserspiele** (water games). During the **Illuminations** the gardens and fountains are atmospherically lit at night.

Across Herrenhäuser Strasse, the **Berggarten** is redolent with a mind-boggling assortment of global flora, while east of the Grosser Garten, beyond a small canal, the lake-dotted **Georgengarten** counts the **Wilhelm-Busch-Museum** (☎0511-1699 9911; www.wilhelm-busch-museum.de; Georgengarten; adult/concession €4.50/2.50; ⌚11am-6pm Tue-Sun), with its wealth of caricature by Busch, Honoré Daumier, William Hogarth and many others, among its treasures.

If you're curious about Hanover's other sights, stop by the **tourist office** (☎information 0511-1234 5111, room reservations 0511-1234 5555; www.hannover.de; Ernst-August-Platz 8; ⌚9am-6pm Mon-Fri, 10am-3pm Sat & Sun).

Mon-Fri, 10am-1am Sat & Sun;) Exuding the nostalgic vibe of a former pharmacy, this popular hang-out gets a good crowd no matter where the hands on the clock. Come for breakfast, a hot lunch special, crispy *Flammekuche* (French pizza), carpaccio or pasta, or just some cheese and a glass of wine.

Casa MEDITERRANEAN €€
(☎0421-326 430; www.casa-bremen.com; Ostertorsteinweg 59; mains €10-27; ⌚11.30am-midnight Mon-Fri, 10am-midnight Sat & Sun;) This long-standing local favourite evokes a slight Mediterranean vibe, both in its looks and through its menu, which includes salads, pastas and an inspired selection of tapas. Top marks, though, go to the lava-grill fish and meat dishes (including a signature burger), made with quality organic meats.

Luv INTERNATIONAL €€
(☎0421-165 5599; www.restaurant-luv.de; Schlachte 15-18; mains €9-37; ⌚11am-late Mon-Fri, 10am-late Sun) This upbeat bistro has a lounge-bar feel and a menu strong on salads and pasta complemented by mostly meaty mains, including a respectable lava-grill burger, a giant Wiener Schnitzel and locally caught fish. In good weather sit beneath the twinkling lights at the outdoor tables overlooking the Weser River.

Café Sand CAFE
(☎0421-556 011; www.cafe-sand.de; Strandweg 106; ⌚from noon Mon-Sat, from 10am Sun, closing hours vary) On an island in the Weser River, this beach cafe makes you feel light years away from the city. It's favoured by everyone from swimmers and tanners to families and fans of Werder Bremen football club. Get here on foot via the Wilhelm-Kaisen-Brücke (bridge) or by ferry from the Osterdeich (return €2.20, from 3pm Friday, noon Saturday, 10am Sunday until at least 6pm).

ℹ Information

Tourist Office (☎0421-308 0010; www.bremen-tourism.de) Branches include Hauptbahnhof (⌚9am-7pm Mon-Fri, 9.30am-5pm Sat & Sun), handily located at the main train station and Markt (Langenstrasse 2-4; ⌚10am-6.30pm Mon-Sat, to 4pm Sun Apr-Oct, closes at 4pm Sat Nov-Mar), a full-service tourist office with friendly staff, near Markt.

ℹ Getting There & Around

Bremen Airport (BRE; www.airport-bremen.de) is about 3.5km south of the city and served by tram 6 (€2.50, 15 minutes).

Train connections include regional trains to Bremerhaven (€12, 35 minutes), InterCity (IC) trains to Hamburg (€28, one hour) and Cologne (€67, three hours).

SURVIVAL GUIDE

Directory A–Z

ACCOMMODATION

Reservations are a good idea, especially between June and September, around major holidays, festivals, cultural events and trade shows. Local tourist offices will often go out of their way to find something in your price range.

BUSINESS HOURS

Banks 9am to 4pm Monday to Friday, often extended hours Tuesday or Thursday

Bars 6pm to 1am

Cafes 8am to 8pm

Clubs 10pm to 4am

Post offices 9am to 6pm Monday to Friday, some Saturday mornings

Restaurants 11am to 9pm or 10pm (varies widely, 3pm to 6pm break common in rural areas)

Shops 9.30am to 8pm Monday to Saturday (shorter hours in suburbs and rural areas, possible lunchtime break)

DISCOUNT CARDS

Tourist offices in many cities sell Welcome Cards entitling visitors to free or reduced admission on museums, sights and tours, plus unlimited local public transport for the period of their validity (usually 24 or 48 hours). They can be good value if you want to fit a lot in.

GAY & LESBIAN TRAVELLERS

- Germany is a magnet for *schwule* (gay) and *lesbische* (lesbian) travellers, with the rainbow flag flying especially proudly in Berlin and Cologne, and with sizeable communities in Hamburg, Frankfurt and Munich.
- Generally speaking, attitudes towards homosexuality tend to be more conservative in rural areas, among older people and in the eastern states.

INTERNET RESOURCES

Deutschland Online (www.magazine-deutschland.de)

Facts About Germany (www.tatsachen-ueber-deutschland.de)

German National Tourist Office (www.germany.travel)

Online German Course (www.deutsch-lernen.com)

SLEEPING PRICE RANGES

Unless noted, the following price ranges refer to a double room with private bathroom and breakfast in high season.

€ less than €80

€€ €80–€170

€€€ more than €170

COUNTRY FACTS

Area 356,866 sq km

Capital Berlin

Country Code ☎49

Currency Euro (€)

Emergency ☎112

Language German

Money ATMs common, cash preferred for most purchases

Population 81.1 million

Visas Schengen rules apply

LEGAL MATTERS

- Drivers need to carry their driving licence at all times. The permissible blood-alcohol limit is 0.05%; stiff fines and a confiscated licence and even jail time are possible if caught driving over the limit.
- Drinking in public is not illegal, but please be discreet about it.
- Cannabis possession is a criminal offence and punishment may range from a warning to a court appearance.

MONEY

- Cash is king in Germany, so always carry some with you and plan to pay in cash almost everywhere.
- ATMs *(Geldautomat)* linked to international networks such as Cirrus, Plus, Star and Maestro are widely available. Check with the issuer about fees.
- Credit cards are becoming more widely accepted, but it's best not to assume that you'll be able to use one – enquire first.

PUBLIC HOLIDAYS

In addition to the following nationwide holidays, individual states observe additional (usually religious) holidays.

Neujahrstag (New Year's Day) 1 January

Ostern (Easter) Good Friday, Easter Sunday and Easter Monday

Christi Himmelfahrt (Ascension Day) Forty days after Easter

Maifeiertag/Tag der Arbeit (Labour Day) 1 May

Pfingsten (Whit/Pentecost Sunday & Monday) Fifty days after Easter

Tag der Deutschen Einheit (Day of German Unity) 3 October

Weihnachtstag (Christmas Day) 25 December

Zweiter Weihnachtstag (Boxing Day) 26 December

TELEPHONE

German phone numbers consist of an area code (three to six digits) followed by the local number (three to nine digits). Mobile phones work on GSM900/1800.

Country code ☎49

International access code ☎00

Directory inquiries ☎11837 for an English-speaking operator (charged at €1.99 per minute)

Getting There & Away

AIR

Huge Frankfurt Airport (p488) is Germany's busiest, with Munich (p469) a close second and Düsseldorf (p495) getting a good share of departures as well. Airports in Berlin, Hamburg and Cologne are comparatively small.

LAND

Bus

Bus travel is becoming increasingly popular in Germany thanks to a new crop of companies offering good-value connections within Germany and beyond aboard comfortable buses with snack bars and free wi-fi. For routes, times and prices, check www.busliniensuche.de (also in English).

The largest Europewide bus network is maintained by **Eurolines** (www.eurolines.com), a consortium of national bus companies.

Car & Motorcycle

- When bringing your own vehicle to Germany, you need a valid driving licence, car registration and proof of third-party insurance. Foreign cars must display a nationality sticker unless they have official European plates. You also need to carry a warning (hazard) triangle and a first-aid kit.
- Most German cities now have environmental zones that may only be entered by vehicles (including foreign ones) displaying an *Umweltplakette* (emissions sticker). Check with your motoring association or buy one at www.umwelt-plakette.de.

Train

- Germany has an efficient railway network with excellent links to other European destinations. Ticketing is handled by **Deutsche Bahn** (☎01806 99 66 33; www.bahn.de).
- Seat reservations are a good idea for Friday and Sunday travel on long-distance trains and highly recommended during the peak summer season and around major holidays.
- Eurail and Interrail passes are valid on all German national trains.

SEA

- Germany's main ferry ports are Kiel, Lübeck and Travemünde in Schleswig-Holstein, and Rostock and Sassnitz (on Rügen Island) in Mecklenburg–Western Pomerania. All have services to Scandinavia and the Baltic states. There are no direct ferries between Germany and the UK.
- For details and tickets, go to www.ferry-booker.com or www.ferrysavers.com.

EATING PRICE RANGES

The following price categories are for the cost of a main course:

€ less than €8

€€ €8–€18

€€€ more than €18

Getting Around

Germany has an excellent and comprehensive public transport system. Regional bus services fill the gaps in areas not well served by the rail network.

AIR

Unless you're flying from one end of the country to the other, say from Berlin or Hamburg to Munich, planes are only marginally quicker than trains once you factor in the check-in and transit times.

BICYCLE

- Cycling is allowed on all roads except autobahns (motorways). Helmets are not compulsory (not even for children).
- Bicycles may be taken on most trains but require a *Fahrradkarte* (separate ticket) and a reservation if travelling on an InterCity (IC)/ EuroCity (EC) train. They are not allowed on InterCity Express (ICE) trains.
- Most towns and cities have a private bicycle-hire station, often at or near the train station. A growing number have automated bike-rental systems.

BOAT

From April to October, boats operate on set timetables along sections of the Rhine, the Elbe and the Danube.

BUS

- Domestic buses cover an extensive nationwide network.
- In some rural areas buses may be your only option for getting around without your own vehicle. The frequency of services varies from 'rarely' to 'constantly'. Commuter-geared routes offer limited or no service in the evenings and on weekends.
- In cities, buses generally converge at the *Busbahnhof* or *Zentraler Omnibus Bahnhof* (ZOB; central bus station), which is often near the Hauptbahnhof (central train station).

CAR & MOTORCYCLE

- Driving is on the right side of the road.
- With few exceptions, no tolls are charged on public roads.
- Unless posted otherwise, speed limits are 50km/h in cities, 100km/h on country roads and no limit on the autobahn.
- Cars are impractical in urban areas. Leaving your car in a central *Parkhaus* (car park) can cost €20 per day or more.
- Visitors from most countries do not need an International Driving Permit to drive in Germany; bring your licence from home.
- To hire a car, you'll usually need to be over 25 years old and in possession of a valid driving license and a major credit card. Automatic transmissions are rare and must be booked well in advance.

LOCAL TRANSPORT

- Public transport is excellent within big cities and small towns and may include buses, *Strassenbahn* (trams), S-Bahn (light rail) and U-Bahn (underground/subway trains).
- Tickets cover all forms of transit, and fares are determined by zones or time travelled, sometimes both. *Streifenkarte* (multiticket trips) and *Tageskarte* (day passes) offer better value than single-ride tickets.
- Most tickets must be validated (stamped) upon boarding.

TRAIN

- Germany's train network is almost entirely run by **Deutsche Bahn** (www.bahn.com), although there is a growing number of routes operated by private companies.
- Of the several train types, ICE trains are the fastest and most comfortable. IC trains (EC if they cross borders) are almost as fast but older and less snazzy. Regional Express (RE) and Regionalbahn (RB) trains are regional. S-Bahn are suburban trains operating in large cities and conurbations.

MILESTONES IN GERMAN HISTORY

800 Charlemagne is crowned emperor by the pope, laying the foundation for the Holy Roman Empire, which will last until 1806.

1241 Hamburg and Lübeck sign a trading agreement, creating the base for the powerful Hanseatic League that dominates politics and trade across much of Europe throughout the Middle Ages.

1455 Johannes Gutenberg invents moveable type, which for the first time allows books to be published in larger quantities.

1517 Martin Luther challenges Catholic-church practices by posting his Ninety-Five Theses and ushering in the Reformation.

1618–48 The Thirty Years' War pits Protestants against Catholics in a far-reaching, bloody war that leaves Europe's population depleted and vast regions reduced to wasteland.

1871 A united Germany is created with Prussia at its helm, Berlin as its capital and Wilhelm I as its emperor.

1914–18 WWI: Germany, Austria-Hungary and Turkey go to war against Britain, France, Italy and Russia. Germany is defeated.

1933 Hitler comes to power, ushering in 12 years of Nazi terror that culminates in WWII and the systematic annihiliation of Jews, Roma, Sinti and other people deemed 'undesirable'.

1949 Germany is divided into a democratic West Germany under the western Allies (the US, UK and France) and a socialist East Germany under the Soviet Union.

1961 The East German government erects the Berlin Wall, dividing the country into two for the next 28 years.

1989 The Berlin Wall collapses; Germany is reunited the following year.

ESSENTIAL FOOD & DRINK

As in Britain, Germany has redeemed itself gastronomically over the past decade. These days culinary offerings are often slimmed down and healthier as many chefs let the trifecta of seasonal-regional-organic ingredients steer their menus. International flavours and cooking techniques further add pizazz to tried-and-trusted specialities, while vegan and vegetarian selections are becoming commonplace. Of course, if you crave traditional comfort food, you'll still find plenty of pork, potatoes and cabbage on the menus, especially in the countryside. Here are our top-five classic German culinary treats:

➡ **Sausage** (wurst) Favourite snack food, links come in 1500 varieties, including finger-sized *Nürnbergers*, crunchy *Thüringers* and tomato-sauce-drowned *Currywurst*.

➡ **Schweinshaxe** The mother of all pork dishes, this one presents itself as entire knuckle roasted to crispy perfection.

➡ **Königsberger Klopse** A simple but elegant plate of golf-ball-sized veal meatballs in a caper-laced white sauce and served with a side of boiled potatoes and beetroot.

➡ **Bread** Get Germans talking about bread and often their eyes will water as they describe their favourite type – usually hearty and wholegrained in infinite variations.

➡ **Black forest cake** (Schwarzwälder Kirschtorte) Multilayered chocolate sponge cake, whipped cream and kirsch confection, topped with cherries and chocolate shavings.

➡ At larger stations, you can store your luggage in a *Schliessfach* (locker) or a *Gepäckaufbewahrung* (left-luggage office).

➡ Seat reservations for long-distance travel are highly recommended, especially if you're travelling on a Friday or Sunday afternoon, during holiday periods or in summer. Reservations can be made online and at ticket counters as late as 10 minutes before departure.

➡ Buy tickets online (www.bahn.de) or at stations from vending machines or *Reisezentrum* (ticket offices). Only conductors on ICE and IC/EC trains sell tickets on board at a surcharge.

Greece

Includes ➡

Best Places to Eat

- To Maridaki (p543)
- To Steki tou Yianni (p551)
- Paparouna (p529)
- Funky Gourmet (p521)
- M-Eating (p533)

Best Places to Stay

- Aroma Suites (p538)
- Casa Leone (p543)
- Marco Polo Mansion (p546)
- Amfitriti Pension (p524)
- Siorra Vittoria (p554)

Why Go?

The alluring combination of history and ravishing beauty that has made Greece (Ελλάδα) one of the most popular destinations on the planet always seems to beckon. Within easy reach of magnificent archaeological sites such as the Acropolis, Delphi, Delos and Knossos are breathtaking beaches and relaxed tavernas serving everything from ouzo to octopus. Hiking trails criss-cross Mt Olympus, the Zagorohoria and islands like Crete and Corfu.

Wanderers can island-hop to their heart's content (each island has its own character), while party types can enjoy pulsating nightlife in Greece's vibrant modern cities and on islands such as Mykonos and Santorini. Add welcoming locals with an enticing culture to the mix and it's easy to see why most visitors head home vowing to come back. Travellers to Greece inevitably end up with a favourite site they long to return to – get out there and find yours.

When to Go

Athens

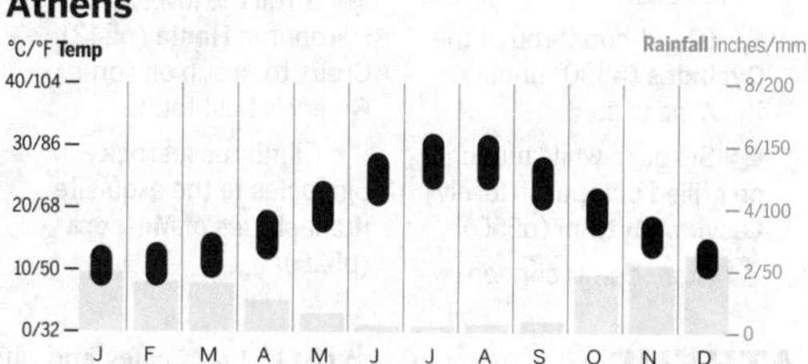

May & Jun Greece opens the shutters in time for Orthodox Easter; the best months to visit.

Jul & Aug Be prepared to battle summer crowds, high prices and soaring temperatures.

Sep & Oct The tourist season winds down; an excellent, relaxing time to head to Greece.

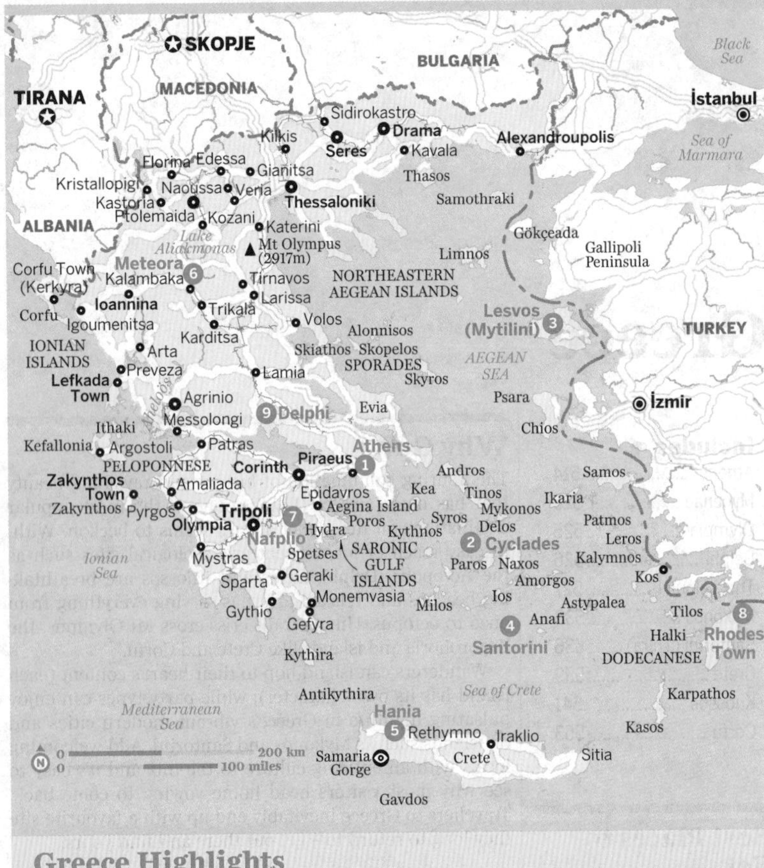

Greece Highlights

1. In **Athens** trace the ancient to the modern from the Acropolis to booming nightclubs.
2. Island-hop through the **Cyclades** (p530) under the Aegean sun.
3. Sip ouzo while munching on grilled octopus in lovely **Lesvos/Mytilini** (p550).
4. Stare dumbfounded at the dramatic volcanic caldera of incomparable **Santorini** (p536).
5. Stroll the lovely Venetian Harbour in **Hania** (p542), Crete, then sup on some of Greece's best food.
6. Climb russet rock pinnacles to the exquisite monasteries of **Meteora** (p526).
7. Use quaint **Nafplio** (p524) as a base for exploring the back roads and ruins of the Peloponnese.
8. Lose yourself within the medieval walls of the Old Town in **Rhodes Town** (p545).
9. Search for the oracle amid the dazzling ruins of **Delphi** (p526).

ATHENS ΑΘΗΝΑ

POP 3.8 MILLION

Ancient and modern, with equal measures of grunge and grace, bustling Athens is a heady mix of history and edginess. Iconic monuments mingle with first-rate museums, lively cafes and alfresco dining, and it's downright fun. With Greece's financial difficulties Athens has revealed its more restive aspect, but take the time to look beneath the surface and you'll discover a complex metropolis full of vibrant subcultures.

ITINERARIES

One Week

Explore **Athens'** museums and ancient sites on day one before spending a couple of days in the **Peloponnese** visiting Nafplio, Mycenae and Olympia; ferry to the **Cyclades** and enjoy Mykonos and spectacular Santorini.

One Month

Give yourself some more time in Athens and the Peloponnese, then visit the **Ionian Islands** for a few days. Explore the villages of Zagorohoria before travelling back to Athens via **Meteora** and **Delphi**. Take a ferry from Piraeus south to **Mykonos**, then island-hop via Santorini to **Crete**. After exploring Crete, take the ferry east to **Rhodes**, then north to **Kos**, **Samos** and **Lesvos**. Wrap up in relaxed, cosmopolitan **Thessaloniki**.

Sights

★Acropolis HISTORIC SITE

(☎210 321 0219; http://odysseus.culture.gr; adult/child/concession €12/free/6; ⏲8am-8pm Apr-Oct, to 5pm Nov-Mar; Ⓜ Akropoli) The Acropolis is the most important ancient site in the Western world. Crowned by the **Parthenon**, it stands sentinel over Athens, visible from almost everywhere within the city. Its monuments of Pentelic marble gleam white in the midday sun and gradually take on a honey hue as the sun sinks, while at night they stand brilliantly illuminated above the city. A glimpse of this magnificent sight cannot fail to exalt your spirit.

★Acropolis Museum MUSEUM

(☎210 900 0901; www.theacropolismuseum.gr; Dionysiou Areopagitou 15, Makrygianni; adult/child €5/free; ⏲8am-4pm Mon, to 8pm Tue-Sun, to 10pm Fri Apr-Oct, 9am-5pm Mon-Thu, to 10pm Fri, 9am-8pm Sat & Sun Nov-Mar; Ⓜ Akropoli) The long-awaited Acropolis Museum opened with much fanfare in 2009 in the southern foothills of the Acropolis. Ten times larger than the former on-site museum, the imposing modernist building brings together the surviving treasures of the Acropolis, including items formerly held in other museums or storage, as well as pieces returned from foreign museums. The **restaurant** has superb views (and is surprisingly good value) and there's a fine museum **shop**.

★Ancient Agora HISTORIC SITE

(☎210 321 0185; http://odysseus.culture.gr; Adrianou; adult/child €4/free, free with Acropolis pass; ⏲11am-3pm Mon, from 8am Tue-Sun; Ⓜ Monastiraki) The heart of ancient Athens was the Agora, the lively, crowded focal point of administrative, commercial, political and social activity. Socrates expounded his philosophy here, and in AD 49 St Paul came here to win converts to Christianity. The site today is a lush, refreshing respite with beautiful monuments and temples, and a fascinating **museum**.

★Roman Agora & Tower of the Winds RUIN

(☎210 324 5220; cnr Pelopida & Eolou, Monastiraki; adult/child €2/1, free with Acropolis pass; ⏲8am-3pm; Ⓜ Monastiraki) The entrance to the Roman Agora is through the well-preserved **Gate of Athena Archegetis**, which is flanked by four Doric columns. It was erected sometime during the 1st century AD and financed by Julius Caesar. The well-preserved, extraordinary **Tower of the Winds** was built in the 1st century BC by a Syrian astronomer named Andronicus.

★Temple of Olympian Zeus RUIN

(☎210 922 6330; adult/child €2/free, free with Acropolis pass; ⏲8am-8pm Apr-Oct, 8.30am-3pm Nov-Mar; Ⓜ Syntagma, Akropoli) You can't miss this striking marvel, smack in the centre of Athens. It is the largest temple in Greece and was begun in the 6th century BC by Peisistratos, but was abandoned for lack of funds. Various other leaders had stabs at completing it, but it was left to Hadrian to complete the work in AD 131. In total, it took more than 700 years to build.

★Panathenaic Stadium HISTORIC SITE

(☎210 752 2984; www.panathenaicstadium.gr; Leoforos Vasileos Konstantinou, Pangrati; adult/child €3/1.50; ⏲8am-7pm Mar-Oct, to 5pm Nov-Feb; Ⓜ Akropoli) The grand Panathenaic Stadium lies between two pine-covered hills between the neighbourhoods of Mets and Pangrati. It was originally built in the 4th century BC as a venue for the Panathenaic athletic contests. It's said that at Hadrian's inauguration in AD 120, 1000 wild animals were sacrificed in the arena. Later, the seats

Central Athens

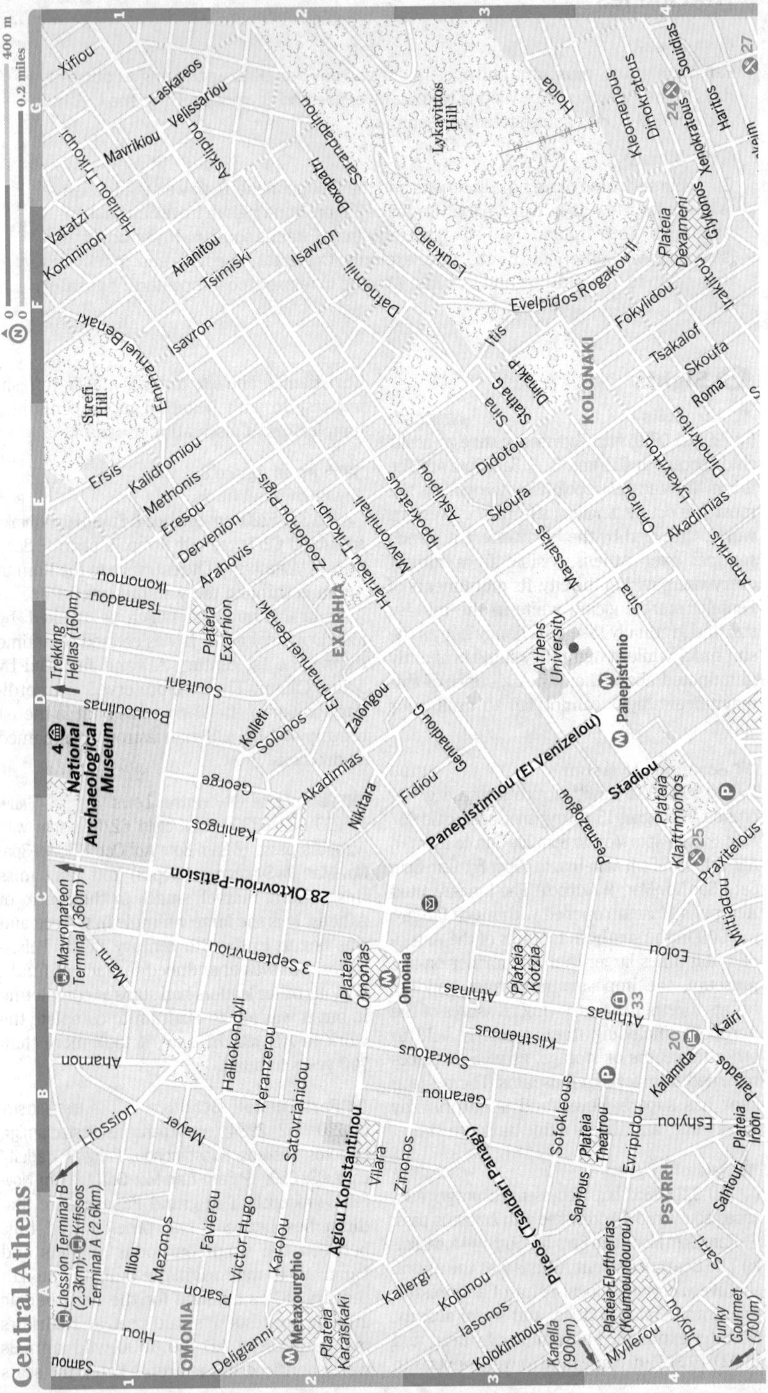

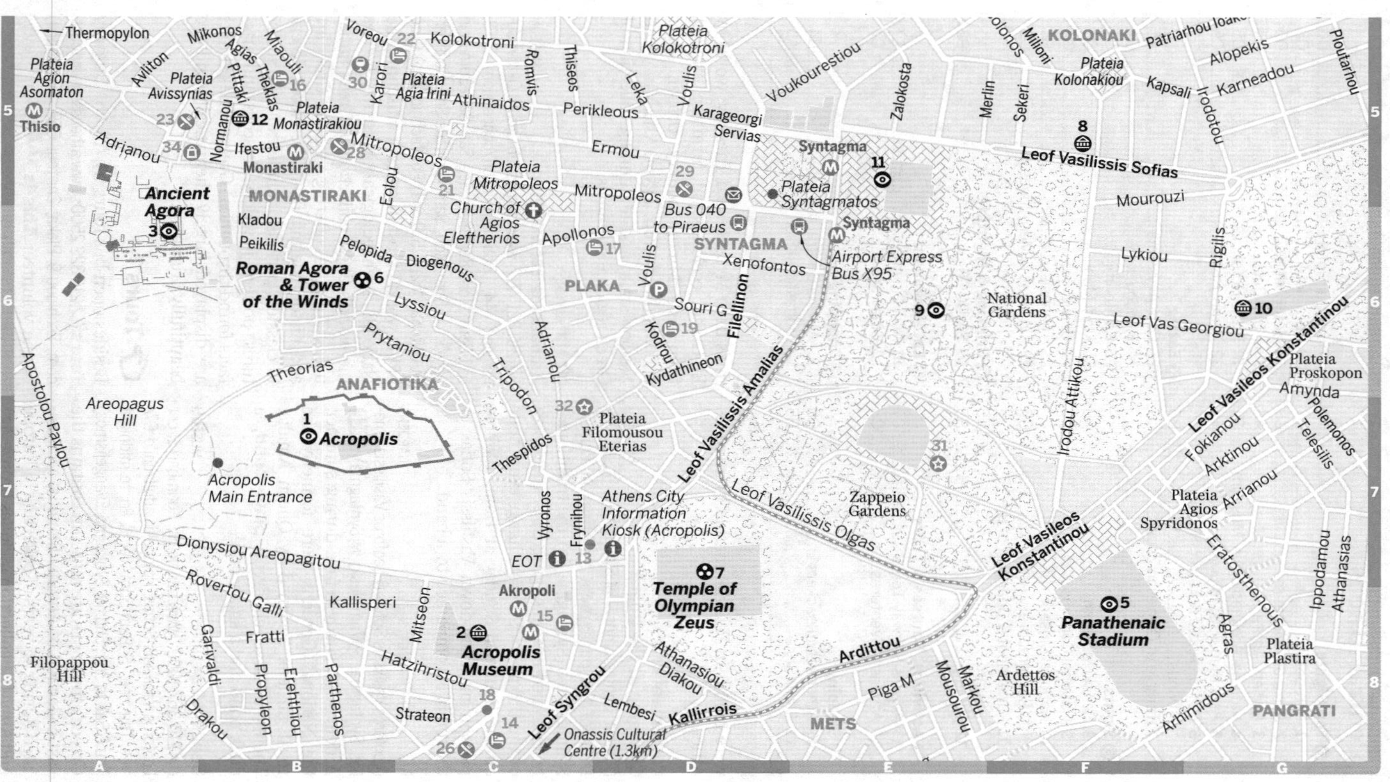
Thermopylon
Mikonos
Plateia Agion Asomaton
Thisio
Avliton
Plateia Avissynias
Agias Theklas
Pittaki
Miaouli
16
Voreou
22
30
Karori
Plateia Agia Irini
Kolokotroni
Athinaidos
Romvis
Thiseos
Plateia Kolokotroni
Leka
Perikleous
Voulis
Voukourestiou
Karageorgi Servias
Zalokosta
Merlin
Sekeri
Kolonos
Milioni
KOLONAKI
Plateia Kolonakiou
Kapsali
Patriarhou Ioakim
Alopekis
Karneadou
Irodotou
Ploutarhou
23
Normanou
12
Plateia Monastirakiou
Adrianou
34
Ifestou
Monastiraki
Mitropoleos
28
Ermou
8
Leof Vasilissis Sofias
Ancient Agora
3
MONASTIRAKI
Kladou
Peikilis
Eolou
21
Plateia Mitropoleos
Church of Agios Eleftherios
Mitropoleos
29
Plateia Syntagmatos
Syntagma
11
Mourouzi
Bus 040 to Piraeus
Apollonos
17
SYNTAGMA
Airport Express Bus X95
Lykiou
Rigilis
Pelopida
Diogenous
Roman Agora & Tower of the Winds
6
Xenofontos
PLAKA
Voulis
Souri G
Filellinon
9
National Gardens
10
Leof Vas Georgiou
Lyssiou
Prytaniou
Kodrou
19
Kydathineon
Adrianou
Leof Vasilissis Amalias
Leof Vasileos Konstantinou
Plateia Proskopon
Amynda
Theorias
ANAFIOTIKA
Tripodon
Apostolou Pavlou
Areopagus Hill
1
Acropolis
32
Plateia Filomousou Eterias
Thespidos
31
Irodou Attikou
Fokianou
Polemonos
Telesilis
Arktinou
Acropolis Main Entrance
Vyronos
Frynihou
Athens City Information Kiosk (Acropolis)
Leof Vasilissis Olgas
Zappeio Gardens
Plateia Agios Spyridonos
Arrianou
Dionysiou Areopagitou
EOT
13
7
Temple of Olympian Zeus
Leof Vasileos Konstantinou
Eratosthenous
Ippodamou
Athanasias
Rovertou Galli
Kallisperi
Mitseon
Akropoli
15
5
Panathenaic Stadium
Fratti
2
Acropolis Museum
Athanasiou Diakou
Arditou
Agras
Plateia Plastira
Filopappou Hill
Garivaldi
Propyleon
Erehthiou
Parthenos
Hatzihristou
18
Leof Syngrou
Lembesi
Piga M
Markou Mousourou
Ardettos Hill
Arhimidous
Drakou
Strateon
14
26
Kallirrois
Onassis Cultural Centre (1.3km)
METS
PANGRATI
GREECE ATHENS

Central Athens

were rebuilt in Pentelic marble by Herodes Atticus.

Parliament & Changing of the Guard BUILDING
(Plateia Syntagmatos; M Syntagma) FREE In front of the parliament building on Plateia Syntagmatos (Syntagma Sq), the traditionally costumed *evzones* (guards) of the **Tomb of the Unknown Soldier** change every hour on the hour. On Sunday at 11am, a whole platoon marches down Vasilissis Sofias to the tomb, accompanied by a band.

National Gardens GARDENS
(Leoforos Vasilissis Sofias & Leoforos Vasilissis Amalias, Syntagma; 7am-dusk; M Syntagma) FREE A delightful, shady refuge during summer, the National Gardens were formerly the royal gardens designed by Queen Amalia. There's a large children's **playground**, a duck pond and a shady **cafe**.

Benaki Museum MUSEUM
(210 367 1000; www.benaki.gr; Koumbari 1, cnr Leoforos Vasilissis Sofias, Kolonaki; adult/child €7/free, Thu free; 9am-5pm Wed & Fri, to midnight Thu & Sat, to 3pm Sun; M Syntagma, Evangelismos) Greece's finest private museum contains the vast collection of Antonis Benakis, accumulated during 35 years of collecting in Europe and Asia. The collection includes Bronze Age finds from Mycenae and Thessaly; works by El Greco; ecclesiastical furniture brought from Asia Minor; pottery, copper, silver and woodwork from Egypt, Asia Minor and Mesopotamia; and a stunning collection of Greek regional costumes.

★**National Archaeological Museum** MUSEUM
(210 821 7717; www.namuseum.gr; 28 Oktovriou-Patision 44, Exarhia; adult/concession €7/3; 1-8pm Mon, 8am-8pm Tue-Sat, 8am-3pm Sun Apr-Oct, 1-8pm Mon, 9am-4pm Tue-Sun Nov-Mar; M Viktoria, 2, 4, 5, 9 or 11 Polytechnio stop) One of the world's most important museums, the National Archaeological Museum houses the world's finest collection of Greek antiquities. Treasures offering a view of Greek art and history, dating from the Neolithic era to classical periods, include exquisite sculptures, pottery, jewellery, frescoes and artefacts found throughout Greece. The exhibits are displayed largely thematically and are beautifully presented.

Tours

Besides open-bus tours try **Athens Segway Tours** (210 322 2500; www.athenssegwaytours.com; Eschinou 9, Plaka; 2hr tour €59; M Akropoli) or the volunteer **This is My Athens** (www.

thisisathens.org). Get out of town on the cheap with **Athens: Adventures** (☎210 922 4044; www.athensadventures.gr). Hike or kayak with **Trekking Hellas** (☎210 331 0323; www.trekking.gr; Saripolou 10, Exarhia; Ⓜ Viktoria).

Festivals

Hellenic Festival PERFORMING ARTS
(www.greekfestival.gr; ⊙Jun-Sep) The ancient theatre at Epidavros and Athens' Theatre of Herodes Atticus are the headline venues of Greece's annual cultural festival featuring a top line-up of local and international music, dance and theatre.

Sleeping

Book well ahead for July and August.

★**Athens Backpackers** HOSTEL €
(☎210 922 4044; www.backpackers.gr; Makri 12, Makrygianni; dm incl breakfast €24-29, 2-/4-/6-person apt €95/125/155; ❄@🛜; Ⓜ Akropoli) The popular rooftop bar with cheap drinks and Acropolis views is a major drawcard of this modern and friendly Australian-run backpacker favourite, right near the Acropolis metro. There's a BBQ in the courtyard, a well-stocked kitchen and a busy social scene. Spotless dorms with private bathrooms and lockers have bedding, but use of towels costs €2. The same management runs well-priced modern apartments nearby.

Tempi Hotel HOTEL €
(☎210 321 3175; www.tempihotel.gr; Eolou 29, Monastiraki; d/tr €55/65, s/d without bathroom €37/47; ❄🛜; Ⓜ Monastiraki) Location and affordability are the strengths of this older, family-run place on pedestrian Eolou. Front balconies overlook Plateia Agia Irini, the scene of some of Athens' best nightlife, and side views get the Acropolis. Basic rooms have satellite TV, but bathrooms are primitive. Top-floor rooms are small and quite a hike. There is a communal kitchen.

AthenStyle HOSTEL €
(☎210 322 5010; www.athenstyle.com; Agias Theklas 10, Psyrri; dm €18-26, s/d €51/76, apt from €86; ❄@; Ⓜ Monastiraki) This bright and arty place has friendly staff, well-equipped studio apartments and hostel beds within walking distance of the Monastiraki metro, major sights and nightlife. Each dorm has lockers; some balconies have Acropolis views. Murals bedeck reception, and the cool basement lounge, with its pool table, home cinema and internet corner, holds art exhibitions. The small Acropolis-view rooftop bar hosts evening happy hours.

Hera Hotel BOUTIQUE HOTEL €€
(☎210 923 6682; www.herahotel.gr; Falirou 9, Makrygianni; d incl breakfast €120-165, ste €225; ❄@🛜; Ⓜ Akropoli) This elegant boutique hotel, a short walk from the Acropolis and Plaka, was totally rebuilt but the formal interior design is in keeping with the lovely neoclassical facade. There's lots of brass and timber, and stylish classic furnishings. The rooftop garden, restaurant and bar have spectacular views.

Plaka Hotel HOTEL €€
(☎210 322 2096; www.plakahotel.gr; Kapnikareas 7, cnr Mitropoleos, Monastiraki; d incl breakfast €125-200; ❄🛜; Ⓜ Monastiraki) It's hard to beat the Acropolis views from the rooftop garden, as well as those from top-floor rooms. Tidy rooms have light timber floors and furniture, and satellite TV, though bathrooms are on the small side. Though called the Plaka Hotel, it's actually closer to Monastiraki.

Central Hotel BUSINESS HOTEL €€
(☎210 323 4357; www.centralhotel.gr; Apollonos 21, Plaka; d/tr incl breakfast from €105/150; ❄@🛜; Ⓜ Syntagma) This stylish hotel has been tastefully decorated in light, contemporary tones. It has comfortable rooms with all the mod cons and good bathrooms. There is a lovely roof terrace with Acropolis views, a small spa and sun lounges. As its name suggests, Central Hotel is in a great location between Syntagma and Plaka.

Hotel Adonis HOTEL €€
(☎210 324 9737; www.hotel-adonis.gr; 3 Kodrou St, Plaka; s/d/tr incl breakfast €70/88/105; ❄@🛜; Ⓜ Syntagma) This comfortable pension on a quiet pedestrian street in Plaka has basic,

CHEAPER BY THE HALF-DOZEN

The €12 ticket at the Acropolis (valid for four days) includes entry to the other significant ancient sites: Ancient Agora, Roman Agora, Keramikos, Temple of Olympian Zeus and the Theatre of Dionysos.

Enter the sites free on the first Sunday of the month from November to March, and on certain holidays. Anyone aged under 18 years or with an EU student card gets in free.

CONTEMPORARY ART

Athens is not all about ancient art. For a taste of the contemporary, visit:

Taf (The Art Foundation; ☎210 323 8757; www.theartfoundation.gr; Normanou 5, Monastiraki; ⏰1pm-midnight; Ⓜ Monastiraki) Eclectic art and music gallery.

Six DOGS (☎210 321 0510; www.sixdogs.gr; Avramiotou 6, Monastiraki; Ⓜ Monastiraki) Theatre meets gallery meets live music venue.

Onassis Cultural Centre (☎213 017 8000, box office 210 900 5800; www.sgt.gr; Leoforos Syngrou 107-109, Neos Kosmos; Ⓜ Syngrou-Fix) Multimillion-euro visual and performing-arts centre.

National Museum of Contemporary Art (☎210 924 2111; www.emst.gr; Athens Conservatory, cnr Vassileos Georgiou B 17-19 & Rigillis, Kolonaki; adult/child €3/free; ⏰11am-7pm Tue, Wed & Fri-Sun, to 10pm Thu; Ⓜ Syntagma) Soon to move to its new location on Syngrou.

clean rooms with TVs. Bathrooms are small but have been excellently renovated. Take in great Acropolis views from 4th-floor rooms and the rooftop terrace where breakfast is served. No credit cards.

Hotel Cecil HOTEL €€
(☎210 321 7079; www.cecilhotel.gr; Athinas 39, Monastiraki; s/d/tr/q incl breakfast from €60/65/95/120; ❄@🛜; Ⓜ Monastiraki) This charming old hotel on busy Athinas has beautiful high, moulded ceilings, polished timber floors and an original cage-style lift. The simple rooms are tastefully furnished, but don't have fridges. Two connecting rooms with a shared bathroom are ideal for families.

Eating

Eat streets include Mitropoleos, Adrianou and Navarchou Apostoli in Monastiraki, the area around Plateia Psyrri, and Gazi, near Keramikos metro.

The fruit and vegetable **market** (Varvakios Agora; Athinas, btwn Sofokleous & Evripidou; ⏰7am-3pm Mon-Sat; Ⓜ Monastiraki, Panepistimio, Omonia) is opposite the meat market.

★**Mani Mani** GREEK €
(☎210 921 8180; www.manimani.com.gr; Falirou 10, Makrygianni; mains €9-15; ⏰2.30-11.30pm Mon-Fri, from 1pm Sat, 1-5.30pm Sun, closed Jul & Aug; Ⓜ Akropoli) Head upstairs to the relaxing, cheerful dining rooms of this delightful modern restaurant, which specialises in regional cuisine from Mani in the Peloponnese. The ravioli with Swiss chard, chervil and cheese, and the tangy Mani sausage with orange are standouts. Almost all dishes can be ordered as half portions (at half-price), allowing you to sample widely.

Oikeio MEDITERRANEAN €
(☎210 725 9216; Ploutarhou 15, Kolonaki; mains €7-13; ⏰1pm-2.30am Mon-Sat; Ⓜ Evangelismos) With excellent home-style cooking, this modern taverna lives up to its name (meaning 'homey'). It's decorated like a cosy bistro on the inside, and tables on the footpath allow people-watching without the normal Kolonaki bill. Pastas, salads and international fare are tasty, but try the *mayirefta* (ready-cooked meals) specials such as the excellent stuffed zucchini. Book ahead.

Tzitzikas & Mermingas MEZEDHES €
(☎210 324 7607; Mitropoleos 12-14, Syntagma; mezedhes €6-11; ⏰noon-11pm; Ⓜ Syntagma) Greek merchandise lines the walls of this cheery, modern *mezedhopoleio* that sits smack in the middle of central Athens. It serves a tasty range of delicious and creative mezedhes (like the honey-drizzled, bacon-wrapped cheese one) to a bustling crowd of locals.

Kalnterimi TAVERNA €
(☎210 331 0049; www.kalnterimi.gr; Plateia Agion Theodoron, cnr Skouleniou, Monastiraki; mains €6-9; ⏰noon-midnight; Ⓜ Panepistimio) Find your way behind the Church of Agii Theodori to this hidden open-air taverna offering Greek food at its most authentic. Everything is fresh cooked and delicious: you can't go wrong. Hand-painted tables spill onto the footpath along a pedestrian street and give a feeling of peace in one of the busiest parts of the city.

Filippou TAVERNA €
(☎210 721 6390; Xenokratous 19, Kolonaki; mains €8-12; ⏰noon-11pm, closed Sat night & Sun; Ⓜ Evangelismos) Why mess with what works? Filippou has been dishing out yummy Greek dishes since 1923. A chance for a little

soul cooking, with white linen, in the heart of Kolonaki.

Kanella TAVERNA €
(☎210 347 6320; Leoforos Konstantinoupoleos 70, Gazi; dishes €7-10; ⏱1.30pm-late; Ⓜ Keramikos) Homemade village-style bread, mismatched retro crockery and brown-paper tablecloths set the tone for this trendy, modern taverna serving regional Greek cuisine. Friendly staff serve daily specials such as lemon lamb with potatoes, and an excellent zucchini and avocado salad.

Thanasis SOUVLAKI €
(☎210 324 4705; Mitropoleos 69, Monastiraki; gyros €2.50; ⏱8.30am-2.30am; Ⓜ Monastiraki) In the heart of Athens' souvlaki hub, at the end of Mitropoleos, Thanasis is known for its kebabs on pitta with grilled tomato and onions.

★**Café Avyssinia** MEZEDHES €€
(☎210 321 7047; www.avissinia.gr; Kynetou 7, Monastiraki; mains €10-16; ⏱11am-1am Tue-Sat, to 7pm Sun; Ⓜ Monastiraki) Hidden away on colourful Plateia Avyssinias, in the middle of the flea market, this bohemian *mezedhopoleio* gets top marks for atmosphere, food and friendly service. It specialises in regional Greek cuisine, from warm fava to eggplants baked with tomato and cheese, and has a great selection of ouzo, *raki* (Cretan fire water) and *tsipouro* (a distilled spirit similar to ouzo but usually stronger).

★**Funky Gourmet** MEDITERRANEAN €€€
(☎210 524 2727; www.funkygourmet.com; Paramithias 3, cnr Salaminas, Keramikos; set menu from €70; ⏱7.30-11.30pm Tue-Sat; Ⓜ Metaxourgio) Noveau gastronomy meets fresh Mediterranean ingredients at this Michelin-starred restaurant. Elegant lighting, refinement and sheer joy in food make this a worthwhile stop for any foodie. The degustation menus can be paired with wines. Book ahead.

Drinking & Entertainment

Kolonaki has a mind-boggling array of cafes off Plateia Kolonakiou on Skoufa and Tsakalof. Another cafe-thick area is Adrianou, along the Ancient Agora.

Athenians know how to party. Expect people to show up after midnight. Head to Monastiraki (around Plateia Agia Irini, Plateia Karytsi or Kolokotroni), Gazi (around Voutadon and the Keramikos metro station) or Kolonaki (around Ploutarhou and Haritos or Skoufa and Omirou) and explore!

Gay bars cluster in Gazi near the railway line on Leoforos Konstantinoupoleos and Megalou Alexandrou, as well as Makrygianni, Psyrri, Metaxourghio and Exarhia. Check out www.athensinfoguide.com or www.gayguide.gr.

Although Exarhia has a bohemian bar scene, the neighbourhood has been affected recently by street demonstrations.

For events listings try: www.breathtakingathens.gr, www.elculture.gr, www.tickethour.com, www.ticketshouse.gr and www.ticketservices.gr. The Kathimerini supplement inside the *International Herald Tribune* contains event listings and a cinema guide. In summer, dance clubs move to the beachfront near Glyfada.

Shopping

Find boutiques around Syntagma, from the Attica department store past Voukourestiou and on Ermou; designer brands and cool shops in Kolonaki; and souvenirs, folk art and leather in Plaka and Monastiraki with its fun **Monastiraki Flea Market** (Adrianou, Monastiraki; ⏱daily; Ⓜ Monastiraki).

UNCERTAIN TIMES

- Due to the financial difficulties in Greece, opening hours, prices and even the existence of some establishments have fluctuated much more than usual.
- The government was running many archaeological sites on their shorter winter hours (closing around 3pm).
- With businesses associated with tourism, opening hours can always be haphazard; if trade is good, they're open, if not, they shut.
- 'High season' is usually July and August. If you turn up in 'shoulder seasons' (May and June; September and October) expect to pay significantly less. Things may be dirt cheap or closed in winter.
- If in doubt, call ahead.

WORTH A TRIP

ISLAND IN A DAY: AEGINA & HYDRA ΑΙΓΙΝΑ & ΥΔΡΑ

For islands within easy reach of Athens, head to the Saronic Gulf. **Aegina** (*eh*-yee-nah; www.aeginagreece.com), just a half hour from Piraeus is home to the impressive **Temple of Aphaia**, said to have served as a model for the construction of the Parthenon. The cat-walk queen of the Saronics, **Hydra** (ee-drah; www.hydra.gr, www.hydraislandgreece.com) is a delight, an hour and a half from Piraeus. Its picturesque horseshoe-shaped harbour town with gracious stone mansions stacked up the rocky hillsides is known as a retreat for artists, writers and celebrities. There are no motorised vehicles – apart from sanitation trucks – leading to unspoilt trails along the coast and into the mountains.

From Hydra, you can return to Piraeus, or carry on to Spetses and the Peloponnese (Metohi, Ermione and Porto Heli). Check **Hellenic Seaways** (www.hsw.gr) and **Aegina Flying Dolphins** (www.aegeanflyingdolphins.gr).

Information

DANGERS & ANNOYANCES

Crime has risen in Athens with the onset of the financial crisis. Though violent crime remains relatively rare, travellers should stay alert on the streets, especially at night.

- Streets surrounding Omonia have become markedly seedier, with an increase in prostitutes and junkies; avoid the area, especially at night.
- Watch for pickpockets on the metro and at the markets.
- When taking taxis, ask the driver to use the meter or negotiate a price in advance. Ignore stories that the hotel you've chosen is closed or full: they're angling for a commission from another hotel.
- Bar scams are commonplace, particularly in Plaka and Syntagma. Beware the over-friendly!
- With the recent financial reforms in Greece have come strikes in Athens (check http://livingingreece.gr/strikes). Picketers tend to march in Plateia Syntagmatos.

EMERGENCY

SOS Doctors (☎1016, 210 821 1888; ⏰24hr) Pay service with English-speaking doctors.

Visitor Emergency Assistance (☎112) Toll-free 24-hour service in English.

INTERNET RESOURCES

Official visitor site (www.breathtakingathens.gr)

TOURIST INFORMATION

Athens City Information Kiosk (Acropolis) (☎210 321 7116; Acropolis; ⏰9am-9pm May-Sep; Ⓜ Akropoli)

Athens City Information Kiosk (Airport) (☎210 353 0390; ⏰8am-8pm; Ⓜ Airport) Maps, transport information and all Athens info.

EOT (Greek National Tourist Organisation; ☎210 331 0347, 210 331 0716; www.visitgreece.gr; Dionysiou Areopagitou 18-20, Makrygianni; ⏰8am-8pm Mon-Fri, 10am-4pm Sat & Sun May-Sep, 9am-7pm Mon-Fri Oct-Apr; Ⓜ Akropoli) Free Athens map, transport information and *Athens & Attica* booklet.

Getting There & Away

AIR

Modern **Eleftherios Venizelos International Airport** (ATH; ☎210 353 0000; www.aia.gr) is 27km east of Athens.

BOAT

Most ferries, hydrofoils and high-speed catamarans leave from the massive port at Piraeus. Some depart from smaller ports at Rafina/Lavrio.

BUS

Athens has two main intercity **KTEL** (☎14505; www.ktel.org) bus stations: **Liossion Terminal B** (☎210 831 7153; Liossion 260, Thymarakia; Ⓜ Agios Nikolaos), 5km north of Omonia with buses to central and northern Greece (Delphi, Meteora) and **Kifissos Terminal A** (☎210 512 4910; Kifisou 100, Peristeri; Ⓜ Agios Antonios), 7km north of Omonia, with buses to Thessaloniki, the Peloponnese, Ionian Islands and western Greece. The KTEL website and tourist offices have timetables.

Buses for southern Attica (Rafina, Lavrio, Sounio) leave from the **Mavromateon Terminal** (☎210 880 8000, 210 822 5148; cnr Leoforos Alexandras & 28 Oktovriou-Patision, Pedion Areos; Ⓜ Viktoria), about 250m north of the National Archaeological Museum.

CAR & MOTORCYCLE

The airport has car rental, and Syngrou, just south of the Temple of Olympian Zeus, is dotted with car-hire firms, though driving in Athens is treacherous.

TRAIN

Intercity trains to central and northern Greece depart from the central **Larisis train station** (Stathmos Larisis; ☎14511; www.trainose.gr), about 1km northwest of Plateia Omonias (Omonia Sq), and served by the metro. For the Peloponnese, take the suburban rail to Kiato and change for other OSE services, or check for available lines at the Larisis station.

Getting Around

TO/FROM THE AIRPORT

Bus

Tickets cost €5. Twenty-four-hour services:

Piraeus Port Bus X96, 1½ hours, every 20 minutes

Plateia Syntagmatos Bus X95, 60 to 90 minutes, every 15 minutes (the Syntagma stop is on Othonos)

Terminal A (Kifissos) Bus Station Bus X93, 35 minutes, every 30 minutes

Metro

Blue line 3 links the airport to the city centre in around 40 minutes; it operates from Monastiraki from 5.50am to midnight, and from the airport from 5.30am to 11.30pm. Tickets (€8) are valid for all public transport for 70 minutes. Fare for two passengers is €14 total.

Taxi

Fixed fares are posted. Expect day/night €35/50 to the city centre, and €47/65 to Piraeus. Both trips often take at least an hour, longer with heavy traffic. Check www.athensairporttaxi.com for more info.

PUBLIC TRANSPORT

The metro, tram and bus system makes getting around central Athens and to Piraeus easy. Athens' road traffic can be horrendous. Get maps and timetables at the tourist offices or **Athens Urban Transport Organisation** (OASA; ☎185; www.oasa.gr).

Tickets good for 70 minutes (€1.20), or a 24-hour/five-day travel pass (€4/10) are valid for all forms of public transport except for airport services; the three-day tourist ticket (€20) includes airport transport. Bus/trolleybus-only tickets cannot be used on the metro.

Children under six travel free; people under 18 or over 65 pay half-fare. Buy tickets in metro stations, transport kiosks, or most *periptera* (kiosks). Validate the ticket in the machine as you board.

Bus & Trolleybus

Buses and electric trolleybuses operate every 15 minutes from 5am to midnight.

To get to Piraeus: from Syntagma and Filellinon to Akti Xaveriou catch bus 040; from the Omonia end of Athinas to Plateia Themistokleous, catch bus 049.

Metro

Trains operate from 5am to midnight (Friday and Saturday to around 2am), every three to 10 minutes. Get timetables at www.stasy.gr.

TAXI

Taxis are generally reasonable, with small surcharges for port, train and bus station pick-ups, baggage over 10kg or radio taxi. Insist on a metered rate (except for posted flat rates at the airport).

Athina 1 (☎210 921 2800)

PIRAEUS PORT — ΠΕΙΡΑΙΆΣ

Greece's main port and ferry hub fills seemingly endless quays with ships, hydrofoils and catamarans heading all over the country. All ferry companies have online timetables and booths on the quays. EOT (Greek National Tourist Organisation) in Athens has a weekly schedule, or check www.openseas.gr. Schedules are reduced in April, May and October, and are radically cut in winter, especially to smaller islands. When buying tickets, confirm the departure point – some Cyclades boats leave from Rafina or Lavrio, and Patras port serves Italy and the Ionian Islands. Igoumenitsa also serves Corfu.

The fastest and most convenient link to Athens is the metro (€1.20, 40 minutes, every 10 minutes, 5am to midnight), near the ferries. Piraeus has a station for Athens' suburban rail.

Left luggage at the metro station costs €3 per 24 hours.

The **X96** (Plateia Karaïskak; tickets €5) Piraeus–Athens Airport Express leaves from the southwestern corner of Plateia Karaïskaki. **Bus 040** goes to Syntagma in downtown Athens.

TRAIN

Suburban Rail (☎1110; www.trainose.gr) A fast suburban rail links Athens with the airport, Piraeus, the outer regions and the northern Peloponnese. It connects to the metro at Larisis, Doukissis Plakentias and Nerantziotissa stations, and goes from the airport to Kiato.

THE PELOPONNESE ΠΕΛΟΠΟΝΝΗΣΟΣ

The Peloponnese encompasses a breathtaking array of landscapes, villages and ruins, where much of Greek history has played out.

Nafplio Ναύπλιο

POP 14,200

Elegant Venetian houses and neoclassical mansions dripping with crimson bougainvillea cascade down Nafplio's hillside to the azure sea. Vibrant cafes, shops and restaurants fill winding pedestrian streets. Crenulated Palamidi Fortress perches above it all. What's not to love?

Sights

Palamidi Fortress FORT
(☎27520 28036; adult/child €4/free; ⏲8am-7.30pm May–mid-Oct, to 3pm mid-Oct–Apr) This vast and spectacular citadel stands on a 216m-high outcrop of rock with excellent views down onto the sea and surrounding land. It was built by the Venetians between 1711 and 1714, and is regarded as a masterpiece of military architecture.

Peloponnese Folklore Foundation Museum MUSEUM
(☎27520 28379; www.pli.gr; Vasileos Alexandrou 1; admission €2; ⏲9.30am-2.30pm Wed-Mon) Nafplio's award-winning museum is a beautifully arranged collection of folk costumes and household items from Nafplio's history. Established by the philanthropic owner, it's not to be missed. A lovely gift shop is on the ground floor.

Sleeping

The Old Town is *the* place to stay, but it has few budget options. Cheaper spots dot the road to Argos and Tolo.

Hotel Byron PENSION €
(☎27520 22351; www.byronhotel.gr; Platonos 2; d incl breakfast €50-70; ❄) Occupying a fine Venetian building, the Byron is a reliable favourite, with friendly management, neat rooms, iron bedsteads and period furniture.

★ **Amfitriti Pension** PENSION €€
(☎27520 96250; www.amfitriti-pension.gr; Kapodistriou 24; d incl breakfast from €60; ❄📶) Quaint antiques fill these intimate rooms in a house in the Old Town. You can also enjoy stellar views at its nearby sister hotel, **Amfitriti Belvedere**, which is chock full of brightly coloured tapestries and emits a feeling of cheery serenity.

Pension Marianna HOTEL €€
(☎27520 24256; www.pensionmarianna.gr; Potamianou 9; s incl breakfast €50, d €65-75, tr €85, q €100; P❄📶) For value and hospitality, it doesn't get better than this. The welcoming owner-hosts, the warm Zotos brothers, epitomise Greek *filoxenia* (hospitality) and serve up conviviality, travel advice and delicious breakfasts (comprising homemade produce where possible). The comfortable, squeaky-clean rooms open onto terraces where you can feast on the killer view from your hilltop position.

Eating

Nafplio's Old Town streets are loaded with standard tavernas, with best eats around Vasilissis Olgas.

Antica Gelateria di Roma GELATERIA €
(☎27520 23520; www.anticagelateria.gr; cnr Farmakopoulou & Komninou; snacks from €2; ⏲10am-11pm) The only 'true' gelato shop in Nafplio, where Italian gelati maestros Marcello, Claudia or Monica Raffo greet you with: '*Bongiorno* – this is an *Italian* gelati shop!' Only natural and local products are used and it's all made on the premises.

To Kentrikon CAFE €
(☎27520 29933; Plateia Syntagmatos; mains €4-10; ⏲8am-midnight) Relax under the shady trees on this pretty square during extensive breakfasts.

Alaloum GREEK €€
(☎27520 29883; Papanikolaou 10; mains €10-18; ⏲noon-3pm & 7pm-1am) Situated in a lovely spot overlooking a leafy square, Alaloum serves up excellent (and very generous portions of) Greek Mediterranean fare.

Information

Staikos Tours (☎27520 27950; Bouboulinas 50; ⏲9am-1pm & 3-7pm) A helpful outfit offering Avis rental cars and full travel services

DON'T MISS

ART & CULTURAL CENTRE

Nafplio's marquee arts and cultural centre, **Fougaro** (☎27520 96005; www.fougaro.gr; Asklipiou 98), opened with fanfare in 2012 in an impeccably renovated factory, which now houses an art shop, library, cafe and exhibition spaces, and holds performing-arts programs.

like occasional day-long **boat trips** (www.pegasus-cruises.gr) to Spetses, Hydra and Monemvasia.

Getting There & Away

KTEL Argolis Bus Station (☎27520 27323; www.ktel-argolidas.gr; Syngrou) has the following services:

Argos (for Peloponnese connections) €1.60, 30 minutes, half-hourly

Athens €13.10, 2½ hours, hourly (via Corinth)

Epidavros €2.90, 45 minutes, two Monday to Saturday

Mycenae €2.90, one hour, three daily

Epidavros Επιδαυρος

Spectacular World Heritage–listed **Epidavros** (☎27530 22009; admission €6; ⏲8am-8pm Apr-Oct, to 5pm Nov-Mar) was the sanctuary of Asclepius, god of medicine. Amid pine-covered hills, the magnificent **theatre** is still a venue during the Hellenic Festival, but don't miss the peaceful **Sanctuary of Asclepius**, an ancient spa and healing centre.

Go as a day trip from Nafplio (€2.90, 45 minutes, two buses Monday to Saturday).

Mycenae Μυκηνες

Although settled as early as the 6th millennium BC, **Ancient Mycenae** (☎27510 76585; adult/child €8/free; ⏲8am-6pm Apr-Oct, to 3pm Nov-Mar), pronounced mih-*kee*-nes, was at its most powerful from 1600 to 1200 BC. Mycenae's grand entrance, the **Lion Gate**, is Europe's oldest monumental sculpture.

Three buses go daily to Mycenae from Argos (€1.60, 30 minutes) and Nafplio (€2.90, one hour).

Mystras Μυστρας

Magical **Mystras** (☎23315 25363; adult/child €5/free; ⏲8.30am-7pm or 8pm Mon-Sat, to 5.30pm Sun Apr-Oct, to 3pm Nov-Mar) was once the effective capital of the Byzantine Empire. Ruins of palaces, monasteries and churches, most of them dating from between 1271 and 1460, nestle at the base of the Taÿgetos Mountains, and are surrounded by verdant olive and orange groves. Allow half a day to explore.

While only 7km from Sparta, staying in the village nearby allows you to get there early before it heats up. Enjoy exquisite views and a beautiful swimming pool at **Hotel Byzantion** (☎27310 83309; www.byzantionhotel.gr; s/d/tr €40/50/65; P ❄ @ ≋).

Camp at **Castle View** (☎27310 83303; www.castleview.gr; camp sites per adult/tent/car €6/4/4, 2-person bungalow €25; ⏲Apr-Oct; ≋), about 1km before Mystras village and set in olive trees. Buses will stop outside if you ask.

Olympia Ολυμπια

POP 1000

Tucked alongside the Kladeos River, in fertile delta country, the modern town of Olympia supports the extensive ruins of the same name. The first Olympics were staged here in 776 BC, and every four years thereafter until AD 393, when Emperor Theodosius I banned them.

Ancient Olympia (☎26240 22517; adult/child €6/free, site & museum €9/free; ⏲8am-8pm Mon-Fri, to 3pm Sat & Sun, reduced hours winter) is dominated by the immense ruined **Temple of Zeus**, to whom the games were dedicated. Don't miss the statue of **Hermes of Praxiteles**, a classical-sculpture masterpiece, at the exceptional **Archaeological Museum** (adult/child €6/free; ⏲10am-5pm Mon, 8am-8pm Tue-Sun Apr-Oct, to 3pm Nov-Mar).

Sparkling-clean **Pension Posidon** (☎26240 22567; www.pensionposidon.gr; Stefanopoulou 9; s/d/tr incl breakfast €35/45/55; ❄) and quiet, spacious **Hotel Pelops** (☎26240 22543; www.hotelpelops.gr; Varela 2; s/d/tr incl breakfast €40/50/70; ❄ @) offer the best value in the centre. Family-run **Best Western Europa** (☎26240 22650; www.hoteleuropa.gr; Drouva 1; s/d/tr incl breakfast €85/110/120; P ❄ @ ≋) above town has sweeping vistas from room balconies and the wonderful swimming pool.

Pitch your tent in the leafy grove at **Camping Diana** (☎26240 22314; www.campingdiana.gr; camp sites per adult/car/tent €8/5/6; ⏲year-round; ≋), 250m west of town.

Catch buses at the stop on the north end of town. Northbound buses go via Pyrgos (€2.30, 30 minutes), where you connect to buses for Athens, Corinth and Patra. Two buses go east from Olympia to Tripoli (€14.30, three hours) – you must reserve ahead at **KTEL Pyrgos** (26210 20600; www.ktelileias.gr). Local trains run daily to Pyrgos (€1, 30 minutes).

CENTRAL GREECE

ΚΕΝΤΡΙΚΗ ΕΛΛΑΔΑ

Central Greece's dramatic landscape of deep gorges, rugged mountains and fertile valleys is home to the magical stone pinnacle-topping monasteries of Meteora and the iconic ruins of ancient Delphi, where Alexander the Great sought advice from the Delphic oracle. Established in 1938, **Parnassos National Park** (www.en.parnassosnp.gr), to the north of Delphi, attracts naturalists, hikers (it's part of the E4 European long-distance path) and skiers.

Delphi Δελφοί

POP 2800

Modern Delphi and its adjoining ruins hang stunningly on the slopes of Mt Parnassos overlooking the shimmering Gulf of Corinth.

According to mythology, Zeus released two eagles at opposite ends of the world and they met here, thus making Delphi the centre of the world. By the 6th century BC, **Ancient Delphi** (22650 82312; www.culture.gr; site or museum adult/child €6/free, combined €9; 8am-3pm, longer hours summer) had become the Sanctuary of Apollo. Thousands of pilgrims flocked here to consult the female oracle who sat at the mouth of a fume-emitting chasm. After sacrificing a sheep or goat, pilgrims would ask a question, and a priest would translate the oracle's response into verse. Wars, voyages and business transactions were undertaken on the strength of these prophecies.

From the entrance, take the Sacred Way up to the **Temple of Apollo**, where the oracle sat. From here the path continues to the well-preserved theatre and stadium.

Opposite the main site and down the hill some 100m, don't miss the **Sanctuary of Athena** and the much-photographed **Tholos**, a 4th-century-BC columned rotunda of Pentelic marble.

In the town centre, **Rooms Pitho** (22650 82850; www.pithohotel.gr; Vasileon Pavlou & Friderikis 40a; s/d/tr incl breakfast from €40/55/65;) is friendly and quiet and **Hotel Hermes** (22650 82318; www.hermeshotel.com.gr; Vasileon Pavlou & Friderikis 27; s/d incl breakfast €45/55;) has spacious rooms sporting balconies with excellent valley views. **Hotel Apollonia** (22650 82919; www.hotelapollonia.gr; Syngrou 37-39; s/d incl breakfast €75/90;) is a bit more upmarket.

Apollon Camping (22650 82762; www.apolloncamping.gr; camp sites per person/tent €8.50/4;) is just 2km west of town, with a restaurant, pool and minimarket.

Specialities at **Taverna Vakhos** (22650 83186; www.vakhos.com; Apollonos 31; mains €6-11; noon-midnight;) include stuffed zucchini flowers and rabbit stew. Locals pack **Taverna Gargadouas** (22650 82488; Vasileon Pavlou & Friderikis; mains €7-10; noon-midnight) for grilled meats and slow-roasted lamb.

The KTEL **bus stop** (22650 82317; www.ktel-fokidas.gr; Vasileon Pavlou & Friderikis), post office and banks are all on modern Delphi's main street, Vasileon Pavlou & Friderikis. Six buses a day go to Athens Liossion Terminal B (€15.10, three hours). For Meteora/Kalambaka, take a bus to Lamia (€9.10, two hours, one daily) or Trikala (€14, 4½ hours, one daily) to transfer.

Meteora Μετέωρα

Meteora (meh-*teh*-o-rah) should be a certified Wonder of the World with its magnificent late-14th-century monasteries perched dramatically atop enormous rocky pinnacles. Try not to miss it.

Sights

While there were once monasteries on all 24 pinnacles, only six are still occupied: **Megalou Meteorou** (Grand Meteoron; 24320 22278; admission €3; 9am-5pm Wed-Mon Apr-Oct, to 4pm Thu-Mon Nov-Mar), **Varlaam** (24320 22277; admission €3; 9am-4pm Sat-Thu Apr-Oct, closed Thu Nov-Mar), **Agiou Stefanou** (24320 22279; admission €3; 9am-1.30pm & 3.30-5.30pm Tue-Sun Apr-Oct, 9.30am-1pm & 3-5pm Nov-Mar), **Agias Triados** (Holy Trinity; 24320 22220; admission €3; 9am-5pm Fri-Wed Apr-Oct, 10am-3pm Fri-Tue Nov-Mar), **Agiou Nikolaou** (Monastery of St Nikolaou Anapafsa; 24320 22375; admission €3; 9am-3.30pm Sat-Thu Apr-Oct, to 2pm Nov-Mar) and **Agias Varvaras Rousanou** (admission

€3; ⌚9am-6pm Thu-Tue Apr-Oct, to 2pm Nov-Mar). Strict dress codes apply (no bare shoulders or knees and women must wear skirts; you can borrow a long skirt at the door). Walk the footpaths between monasteries, drive the back asphalt road, or take the bus (€1.20, 20 minutes) that departs from Kalambaka and Kastraki at 9am, and returns at 1pm (12.40pm on weekends).

Meteora's stunning rocks are also a climbing paradise. Licensed mountain guide **Lazaros Botelis** (☎69480 43655, 24320 79165; meteora.guide@gmail.gr; Kastraki) shows the way.

Sleeping & Eating

The tranquil village of Kastraki, 2km from Kalambaka, is the best base for visiting.

Doupiani House PENSION €
(☎24320 75326; www.doupianihouse.com; s/d/tr incl breakfast from €45/55/65; P❄@☎) The delightful Doupiani House has the lot: spotless, tastefully decorated rooms, with balconies or garden access. Its location – just outside the village – provides a window to Meteora; it boasts one of the region's best panoramic views. There's breakfast on the terrace, birdsong and attentive hosts, Toula and Thanasis.

Vrachos Camping CAMPGROUND €
(☎24320 22293; www.campingmeteora.gr; camp sites per tent €7.50; ☒) A well-shaded campground on the Kalambaka–Kastraki road with excellent facilities.

Taverna Paradisos TAVERNA €
(☎24320 22723; mains €6.50-9; ⌚noon-3pm & 7-11pm) The traditional meals at roomy Paradisos will have you exclaiming *nostimo!* (delicious!) all the way through your dishes, thanks to local and high-quality ingredients and owner-chef Koula's magic touch. Excellent fried zucchini.

Getting There & Around

Local buses shuttle between Kalambaka and Kastraki (€1.20). Hourly buses go from Kalambaka's **KTEL bus station** (☎24320 22432; www.ktel-trikala.gr; Ikonomou) to the transport hub of Trikala (€2.30, 30 minutes), from where buses go to Ioannina (€12.50, three hours, two daily) and Athens (€29, five hours, six daily).

From Kalambaka **train station** (☎24320 22451; www.trainose.gr), trains run to Athens (regular/IC €18/29, 5½/4½ hours, both twice daily) and Thessaloniki (€15.20, four hours, one daily). You may need to change in Paleofarsalos.

MT OLYMPUS ΟΛΥΜΠΟΣ ΟΡΟΣ

Just as it did for the ancients, Greece's highest mountain, **Olympus** (www.olympusfd.gr), the cloud-covered lair of the Greek pantheon, fires the visitor's imagination today. The highest of Olympus' eight peaks is **Mytikas** (2917m), popular with trekkers, who use **Litohoro** (305m), 5km inland from the Athens–Thessaloniki highway, as their base. The main route up takes two days, with a stay overnight at one of the **refuges** (⌚May-Oct). Good protective clothing is essential, even in summer. **EOS Litohoro** (Greek Alpine Club; ☎23520 82444, 23520 84544; http://eoslitohorou.blogspot.com; ⌚9.30am-12.30pm & 6-8pm Mon-Sat Jun-Sep) has information.

NORTHERN GREECE ΒΟΡΕΙΑ ΕΛΛΑΔΑ

Northern Greece is graced with magnificent mountains, thick forests, tranquil lakes and archaeological sites. It's easy to get off the beaten track and experience aspects of Greece noticeably different to other mainland areas and the islands.

Thessaloniki Θεσσαλονικη

POP 325,182

Dodge cherry sellers in the street, smell spices in the air and enjoy waterfront breezes in Thessaloniki (thess-ah-lo-*nee*-kih), also known as Salonica. The second city of Byzantium and of modern Greece boasts countless Byzantine churches, a smattering of Roman ruins, engaging museums, shopping to rival Athens, fine restaurants and a lively cafe scene and nightlife.

Sights

Check out the seafront **White Tower** (Lefkos Pyrgos; ☎2310 267 832; www.lpth.gr; ⌚8.30am-3pm Tue-Sun) and wander *hammams* (Turkish baths), Ottoman and Roman sites including Galerius' **Rotunda** (☎2310 218 720; Plateia Agiou Georgiou; ⌚9am-5pm Tue-Sun) FREE, and churches such as the enormous, revered 5th-century **Church of Agios Dimitrios** (☎2310 270 008; Agiou Dimitriou 97; ⌚8am-10pm) with its crypt containing the relics of the city's patron saint.

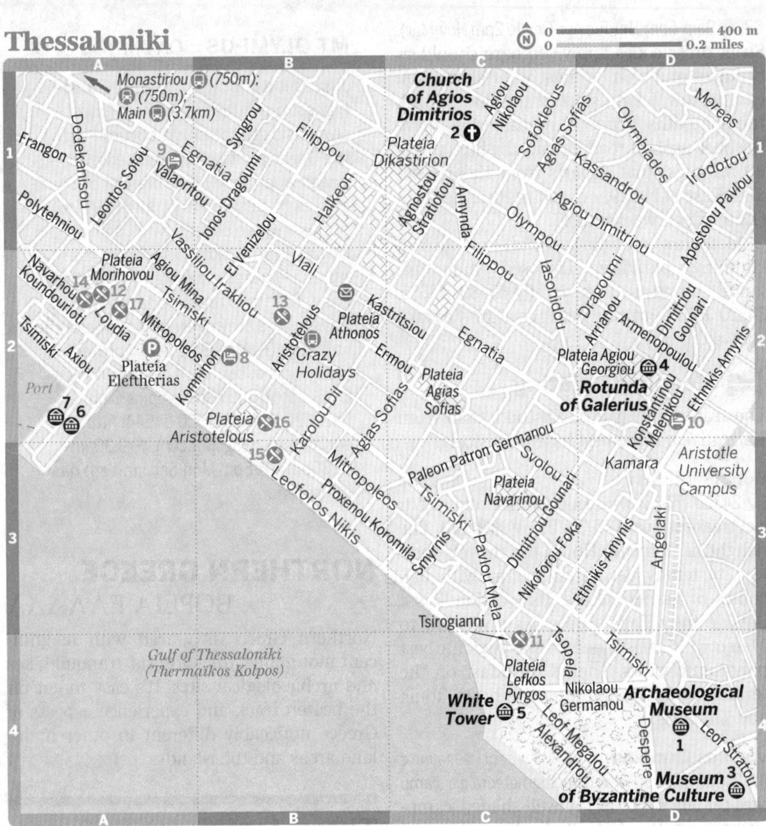

Thessaloniki

Top Sights

1	Archaeological Museum	D4
2	Church of Agios Dimitrios	C1
3	Museum of Byzantine Culture	D4
4	Rotunda of Galerius	D2
5	White Tower	C4

Sights

6	Thessaloniki Centre of Contemporary Art	A2
7	Thessaloniki Museum of Photography	A2

Sleeping

8	City Hotel	B2
9	Colors Rooms & Apartments	A1
10	Rent Rooms Thessaloniki	D2

Eating

11	Dore Zythos	C4
12	Kouzina Kioupia	A2
13	Modiano Market	B2
14	Paparouna	A2
15	To Mikraki	B3
16	Turkenlis	B2
17	Zythos	A2

The award-winning **Museum of Byzantine Culture** (☎2313 306 400; www.mbp.gr; Leof Stratou 2; adult/child €4/free, with Archaeological Museum €8; ⏰8am-8pm Apr-Oct, 9am-4pm Nov-Mar) beautifully displays splendid sculptures, mosaics, icons and other intriguing artefacts. The **Archaeological Museum** (☎2310 830 538; www.amth.gr; Manoli Andronikou 6; adult/child €6/free, with Museum of Byzantine Culture €8; ⏰8am-5pm Apr-Oct, 9am-4pm Nov-Mar) showcases prehistoric, ancient Macedonian and Hellenistic finds.

The compelling **Thessaloniki Centre of Contemporary Art** (☎2310 593 270; www.cact.

gr; Warehouse B1; adult/child €3/1.50; ⏲10am-4pm Tue-Sun, hours vary) and hip **Thessaloniki Museum of Photography** (☎2310 566 716; www.thmphoto.gr; Warehouse A, Port; adult/child €2/1; ⏲11am-7pm Tue-Sun), beside the port, are worth a look.

Sleeping

Colors Rooms & Apartments APARTMENT €
(☎2310 502 280; www.colors.com.gr; Valaoritou 21; s/d/ste €45/55/65; ❄📶) Valaoritou party people, you finally have somewhere nice to crash. These 15 sparkling-new apartments rival more expensive hotel rooms, with cool lighting, minimalist decor and mod cons including iPhone docks with radio. Four of the apartments are self-catering. A pastry breakfast (€5 extra) is brought to your room, or you can eat in the 1st-floor reception/coffee area.

Rent Rooms Thessaloniki HOSTEL €
(☎2310 204 080; www.rentrooms-thessaloniki.com; Konstantinou Melenikou 9, near Kamara; dm/s/d/tr/q incl breakfast €19/38/49/67/82; ❄📶) This well-kept Kamara-area hostel has a relaxing back-garden cafe with Rotunda views, where breakfast and drinks are served. Some dorms and rooms have mini kitchens; all have bathrooms. The friendly staff provides local info and can assist with bike rental.

City Hotel BUSINESS HOTEL €€
(☎2310 269 421; www.cityhotel.gr; Komninon 11; d/tr/ste incl breakfast from €70/90/110; ❄@📶) This sleek four-star place near Plateia Eleftherias, east of Ladadika, has handsome rooms (some wheelchair-friendly) with subdued elegance. There's a big American-style breakfast and spa centre.

Eating & Drinking

Thessaloniki is a great food town. Tavernas dot Plateia Athonos and cafes pack Leoforos Nikis, and the Ladadika quarter is tops for restaurants and bars. Head to **Modiano Market** (Vassiliou Irakliou or Ermo; ⏲7am-6pm) for fresh produce. Thessaloniki is known for its sweets: shop around!

★**Paparouna** MODERN GREEK €
(☎2310 510 852; www.paparouna.com; cnr Pangaiou 4 & Doxis; mains €5-11; ⏲10am-2am) The ever-popular Paparouna spills onto the pavement in Ladadika, sporting vibrant colours, checkerboard floor, cheerful staff and an intriguing menu that changes seasonally. Charismatic chef and owner Antonis Ladas occasionally plays Latin, soul and jazz inside.

★**Kouzina Kioupia** TAVERNA €
(☎2310 553 239; www.kouzina-kioupia.gr; Plateia Morihovou 3-5; mains €4-7; ⏲1pm-1am Mon-Sat, to 6pm Sun) Bright, friendly and spilling onto the plaza, this welcoming taverna fills with happy local families and tables full of friends. Straightforward taverna dishes are served with flare, and a good time is had by all. Occasional live music.

★**To Mikraki** TAVERNA €
(☎2310 270 517; Proxenou Koromila 2; mains €4-7.50; ⏲12.30-6pm Mon-Sat) This friendly storefront in a bastion of chic cafes offers top home-cooked Greek fare with smiling familiarity. A true neighbourhood hang-out. Look behind the counter to see the day's specials.

Zythos TAVERNA €
(Katouni 5; mains €8-12; ⏲noon-3pm & 7pm-midnight) Popular with locals, this excellent taverna with friendly staff serves up delicious standards, interesting regional specialities, good wines by the glass and beers on tap. Its second outlet is **Dore Zythos** (☎2310 279 010; Tsirogianni 7; mains €10-18; ⏲lunch & dinner), near the White Tower.

Turkenlis BAKERY €
(Aristotelous 4; sweets €1-3; ⏲8am-8pm) Renowned for *tzoureki* (sweet bread) and a mind-boggling array of sweet-scented confections.

Information

Check www.enjoythessaloniki.com for current events.

Tourist Police (☎2310 554 871; 5th fl, Dodekanisou 4; ⏲7.30am-11pm)

Getting There & Away

AIR

Makedonia International Airport (SKG; ☎2310 473 212; www.thessalonikiairport.com) is 16km southeast of the centre and served by local bus 78 (€2, one hour, from 5am to 10pm with a few night buses; www.oasth.gr). Taxis cost €25 or more (20 minutes). Olympic Air, Aegean Airlines and Astra Airlines (p558) fly throughout Greece; many airlines fly internationally.

BOAT

Weekly ferries go to, among others, Limnos (€20, eight hours), Lesvos (€30, 14 hours), Chios (€32, 19 hours) and Samos (€40, 20 hours). Check port area travel agencies such as **Karacharisis Travel & Shipping Agency** (☎2310 513 005; b_karachari@tincewind_techpath.gr; Navarhou

WORTH A TRIP

ZAGOROHORIA & VIKOS GORGE ΤΑ ΖΑΓΟΡΟΧΩΡΙΑ & ΧΑΡΑΔΡΑ ΤΟΥ ΒΙΚΟΥ

Try not to miss the spectacular **Zagori region**, with its deep gorges, abundant wildlife, dense forests and snow-capped mountains. Some 46 charming villages, famous for their grey-slate architecture, and known collectively as the Zagorohoria, are sprinkled across a large expanse of the Pindos Mountains north of Ioannina. These beautifully restored gems were once only connected by stone paths and arching footbridges, but paved roads now wind between them. Get information on walks from Ioannina's **EOS** (Greek Alpine Club; ☎ 26510 22138; www.orivatikos.gr; Smyrnis 15; ⏲ hours vary) office.

Monodendri is a popular departure point for treks through dramatic 12km-long, 900m-deep Vikos Gorge, with its sheer limestone walls. Exquisite inns with attached tavernas abound in remote (but popular) twin villages **Megalo Papingo** and **Mikro Papingo**. It's best to explore by rental car from Ioannina.

Koundourioti 8; ⏲ 8am-8.30pm) and www.openseas.gr.

BUS

The **main KTEL bus station** (☎ 2310 595 408; www.ktelmacedonia.gr; Giannitson 244), 3.7km west of the centre, services Athens (€42, 6¼ hours, 11 daily), Ioannina (€32, 4¾ hours, six daily) and other destinations. For Athens *only* you can also get on buses near the train station at **Monastiriou Bus Station** (☎ 2310 500 111; Monastiriou 69). Buses to the Halkidiki Peninsula leave from the **Halkidiki bus terminal** (☎ 2310 316 555; www.ktel-chalkidikis.gr; Karakasi 68).

KTEL serves Sofia, and small bus companies, across from the courthouse (Dikastirion), serve international destinations including Skopje, Sofia and Bucharest. Try **Simeonidis Tours** (☎ 2310 540 970; www.simeonidistours.gr; 26 Oktovriou 14; ⏲ 9am-9pm Mon-Fri, to 2pm Sat). **Crazy Holidays** (☎ 2310 241 545; www.crazy-holidays.gr; Aristotelous 10) also serves İstanbul.

TRAIN

The **train station** (☎ 2310 599 421; www.trainose.gr; Monastiriou) serves Athens (regular/IC €36/48, 6¾/5½ hours, seven/10 daily) and other domestic destinations. International trains go to Skopje and Sofia, and beyond.

CYCLADES ΚΥΚΛΑΔΕΣ

The Cyclades (kih-*klah*-dez) are Greek islands to dream about. Named after the rough *kyklos* (circle) they form around the island of Delos, they are rugged outcrops of rock in the azure Aegean, speckled with white cubist buildings and blue-domed Byzantine churches. Throw in sun-blasted golden beaches, more than a dash of hedonism and a fascinating culture, and it's easy to see why many find the Cyclades irresistible.

Mykonos Μυκονος

POP 10,190

Mykonos is the great glamour island of the Cyclades and happily flaunts its sizzling style and reputation. The high-season mix of good-time holidaymakers, cruise-ship crowds (which can reach 15,000 a day) and posturing fashionistas throngs through Mykonos Town, a traditional Cycladic maze, delighting in its authentic cubist charms and its pricey cafe-bar-shopping scene. It remains a mecca for gay travellers and the well bankrolled, but can get super-packed in high season.

Sights

The island's most popular beaches, thronged in summer, are on the southern coast. **Platys Gialos** has wall-to-wall sun lounges, while nudity is not uncommon at **Paradise Beach**, **Super Paradise**, **Elia** and more secluded **Agrari**.

Hora TOWN

(Mykonos Town) Mykonos Town is a captivating labyrinth that's home to chic boutiques and whiter-than-white houses decked with bougainvillea and geraniums, plus a handful of small museums and photogenic churches. **Little Venice**, where the sea laps up to the edge of the restaurants and bars, and Mykonos' famous hilltop **windmills** should be high on the must-see list.

Sleeping

Book well ahead in high season. Prices plummet outside of July and August, and most hotels close in winter.

Mykonos has two camping areas, both on the south coast – Paradise Beach and **Mykonos Camping** (☎22890 25915; www.mycamp.gr; Paraga Beach; camp sites per adult/child/tent €10/5/10, dm €20, bungalow per person €15-30; P 📶 🏊). Minibuses from both meet the ferries and buses go regularly into town.

Paradise Beach Camping CAMPGROUND, APARTMENT €
(☎22890 22852; www.paradisemykonos.com; camp sites per person/tent €10/5; @ 📶 🏊) There are lots of options here, including camping, beach cabins and apartments, as well as bars, a swimming pool, games etc. It is skin-to-skin mayhem in summer with a real party atmosphere.

★ **Carbonaki Hotel** BOUTIQUE HOTEL €€
(☎22890 24124; www.carbonaki.gr; 23 Panahrantou, Hora; s/d/tr/q from €120/142/180/206; ❄ 📶) This family-run boutique hotel in central Mykonos is a delightful oasis with bright, comfortable rooms, relaxing public balconies and sunny central courtyards. Chill out in the jacuzzi and small sauna. Some wheelchair access and great low-season discounts.

Manto Hotel HOTEL €€
(☎22890 22330; www.manto-mykonos.gr; Evagelistrias 1, Hora; s/d incl breakfast from €60/85; ⏲year-round; ❄ 📶) Buried in the heart of Hora, cheerful Manto is an excellent affordable option (for Mykonos), with well-kept colourful rooms, some with balconies, an inviting breakfast room and friendly owners.

Hotel Philippi PENSION €€
(☎22890 22294; www.philippihotel.com; Kalogera 25, Hora; s/d from €80/100; ⏲Apr-Oct; ❄ 📶) A verdant courtyard-garden makes this a welcome choice in the heart of Hora. Bright, clean rooms open onto a railed verandah overlooking the garden.

Fresh Hotel BOUTIQUE HOTEL €€€
(☎22890 24670; www.hotelfreshmykonos.com; Kalogera 31, Hora; d incl breakfast from €160; ⏲mid-May–Oct; ❄ @ 📶) In the heart of town with a leafy central garden, stylish breakfast room, bar and jacuzzi, rooms have wood floors and minimalist slate-and-white decor.

Eating

High prices don't necessarily reflect high quality in Mykonos Town. Cafes line the waterfront; you'll find good food and coffee drinks at **Kadena** (☎22890 29290; Hora; mains €10-20; ⏲8am-late; 📶). Souvlaki shops dot Enoplon Dynameon and Fabrika Sq (Plateia Yialos). Most places stay open late during high season.

Suisse Cafe CAFE €
(☎22890 27462; Matoyani, Hora; snacks €4-6; ⏲9am-late; 📶) Top-notch breakfasts, crêpes and people-watching.

Nautilus GREEK €€
(☎22890 27100; www.nautilus-mykonos.gr; Kalogera 6, Hora; mains €11-16; ⏲7pm-1am Mar-Nov) The whitewashed terrace spills out onto the street and Greek fusion dishes incorporate top ingredients.

To Maereio GREEK $$
(☎22890 28825; Kalogera 16, Hora; dishes €14-21; ⏲noon-3pm & 7pm-midnight) A small but

CYCLADIC CONNECTIONS

Once high season kicks in, a batch of companies run daily catamarans and ferries up and down the Cyclades. You can start from Piraeus (for Athens), Iraklio in Crete, or just about anywhere in-between.

For example, one boat heads south daily from Piraeus to Paros, Naxos, Ios and Santorini, returning along the same route. There's also a daily run from Piraeus to Syros, Tinos and Mykonos. Occasional ferries also move east–west, connecting islands laterally.

Heading north from Iraklio, another catamaran runs to Santorini, Ios, Paros, Mykonos and return.

It can all get a bit much to comprehend (the schedules are constantly changing!), so check www.openseas.gr or www.gtp.gr. Out of season, boats stop running, or go on very reduced schedules. Sometimes flying ends up being easier.

Mykonos

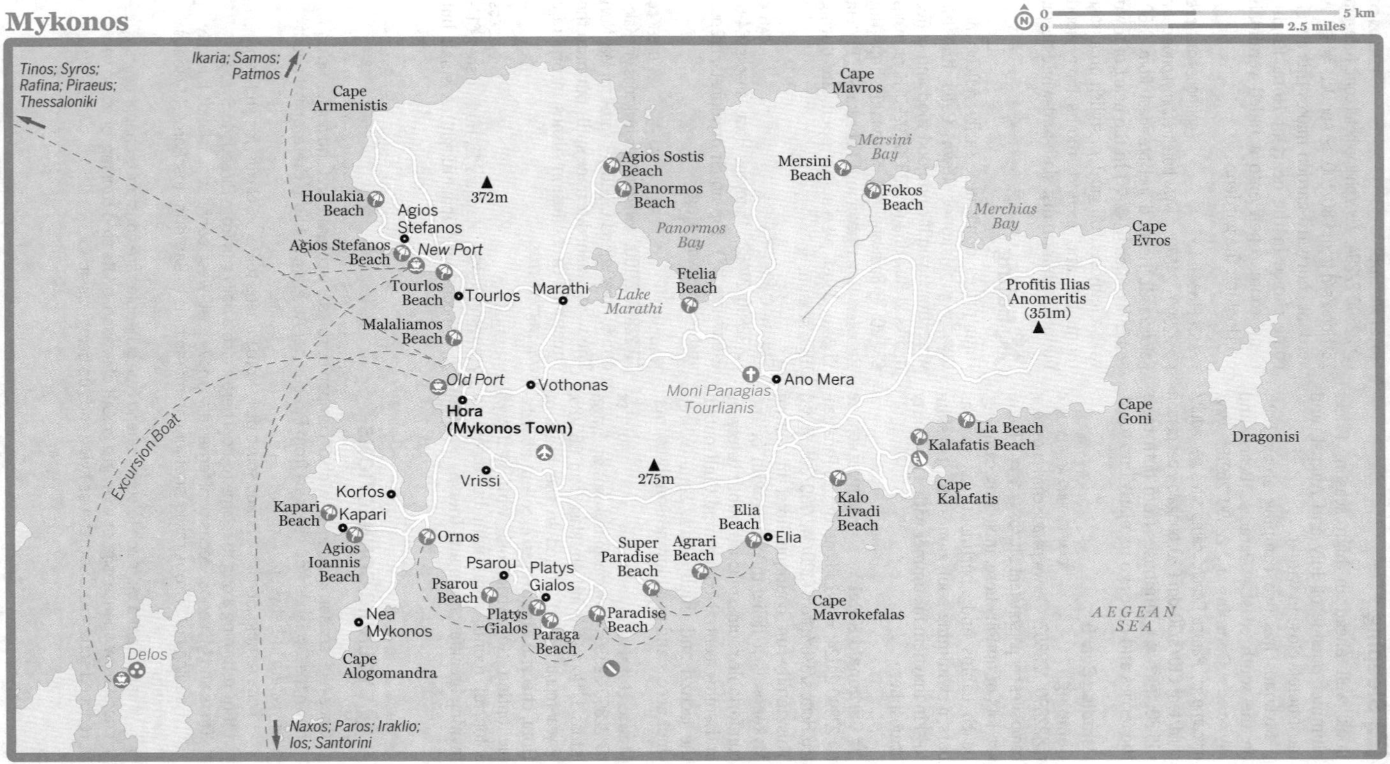

0 5 km
0 2.5 miles

Tinos; Syros; Rafina; Piraeus; Thessaloniki
Ikaria; Samos; Patmos
Cape Armenistis
Cape Mavros
Mersini Bay
Mersini Beach
Fokos Beach
Merchias Bay
Cape Evros
Agios Sostis Beach
Panormos Beach
Panormos Bay
372m
Houlakia Beach
Agios Stefanos
Agios Stefanos Beach
New Port
Tourlos Beach
Tourlos
Marathi
Lake Marathi
Ftelia Beach
Profitis Ilias Anomeritis (351m)
Malaliamos Beach
Old Port
Vothonas
Moni Panagias Tourlianis
Ano Mera
Hora (Mykonos Town)
Excursion Boat
Cape Goni
Lia Beach
Kalafatis Beach
Dragonisi
Vrissi
275m
Cape Kalafatis
Korfos
Kapari Beach
Kapari
Agios Ioannis Beach
Ornos
Elia Beach
Elia
Kalo Livadi Beach
Super Paradise Beach
Agrari Beach
Psarou
Platys Gialos
Psarou Beach
Platys Gialos
Paradise Beach
Paraga Beach
Cape Mavrokefalas
Nea Mykonos
AEGEAN SEA
Delos
Cape Alogomandra
Naxos; Paros; Iraklio; Ios; Santorini

WORTH A TRIP

DELOS

ΔΗΛΟΣ

Southwest of Mykonos, the island of **Delos** (☎22890 22259; museum & sites adult/child €5/free; ⏰8am-8pm Apr-Oct, to 3pm Nov-Mar), a Unesco World Heritage Site, is the Cyclades' archaeological jewel. Go! The mythical birthplace of twins Apollo and Artemis, splendid Ancient Delos was a shrine-turned-sacred-treasury and commercial centre. It was inhabited from the 3rd millennium BC and reached its apex of power around the 5th century BC.

Ruins include the **Sanctuary of Apollo**, containing temples dedicated to him, and the famous **Terrace of the Lions**, guarding the sacred area (the originals are in the island's museum). The **Sacred Lake** (dry since 1925) is where Leto gave birth to Apollo and Artemis, while the **Theatre Quarter** is where private houses with magnificent mosaics were built around the Theatre of Delos. The climb up Mt Kynthos (113m) is a highlight.

Take a sunhat, sunscreen and sturdy footwear. The island's cafeteria sells food and drinks. Staying overnight is forbidden.

Boats from Mykonos to Delos (€18 return, 30 minutes) go between 9am and 5pm in summer, and return between noon and 8pm. In Hora (Mykonos Town) buy tickets at the old wharf kiosk or at **Delia Travel** (☎22890 22322; www.mykonos-delia.com; Akti Kambani), **Sea & Sky** (☎22890 22853; sea-sky@otenet.gr; Akti Kambani) or Mykonos Accommodation Centre. Sometimes in summer boats go from Tinos and Naxos.

selective menu of Mykonian favourites keeps this cosy place popular.

★**M-Eating** MEDITERRANEAN €€€
(☎22890 78550; www.m-eating.gr; Kalogera 10, Hora; mains €15-26; ⏰7pm-midnight) Attentive service and relaxed luxury are the hallmarks of this creative restaurant specialising in fresh Greek products prepared with flair. Sample anything from tenderloin stuffed with Metsovo cheese to shrimp ravioli with crayfish sauce. Don't miss the Mykonian honey pie, or for beer lovers the Volcano microbrew from Santorini.

Drinking & Entertainment

Folks come to Mykonos to party. Each major beach has at least one beach bar that gets going during the day. Night action in town starts around 11pm and warms up by 1am, and revellers often relocate from Mykonos Town to **Cavo Paradiso** (☎22890 27205; www.cavoparadiso.gr; Paradise Beach) in the wee hours. Hora offers an action-packed bar hop: from cool sunset cocktails in Little Venice to sweaty trance dancing. Wherever you go, bring a bankroll (cover alone runs around €20) – the high life doesn't come cheap. Long feted as a gay travel destination, there are many gay-centric clubs and hang outs.

Information

Mykonos Accommodation Centre (☎22890 23408; www.mykonos-accommodation.com; 1st fl, Enoplon Dynameon 10, Hora) Very helpful for all things Mykonos (accommodation, guided tours, island info), including gay-related aspects. The website is loaded.

Getting There & Around

AIR

Mykonos Airport (JMK; ☎22890 22490) Daily flights connect Mykonos Airport to Athens, plus a growing number of international flights wing directly in from May to September. The airport is 3km southeast of the town centre; €1.60 by bus from the southern bus station, €9 by taxi.

BOAT

Year-round ferries serve mainland ports Piraeus (€35, 4¾ hours, one or two daily) and Rafina (sometimes quicker if you are coming directly from Athens airport), and nearby islands, Tinos and Andros. In the high season, Mykonos is well connected with all neighbouring islands, including Paros and Santorini. Hora is loaded with ticket agents.

Mykonos has two ferry quays: the Old Port, 400m north of town, where some conventional ferries and smaller fast ferries dock, and the New Port, 2km north of town, where the bigger fast ferries and some conventional ferries dock. When buying outgoing tickets, double-check which quay your ferry leaves from.

Local Boats

In summer, *caiques* (small fishing boats) from Mykonos Town and Platys Gialos putter to Paradise, Super Paradise, Agrari and Elia Beaches.

BUS

The northern bus station is near the Old Port. It serves Agios Stefanos, Elia, Kalafatis and Ano Mera. The southern bus station, on Fabrika Sq a 300m walk up from the windmills, serves the airport, Agios Ioannis, Psarou, Platys Gialos and Paradise Beach. There's also a pick-up point near the New Port.

CAR & TAXI

Car hire starts at €45 per day in high season. Scooters/quads are €20/40. Avis and Sixt are among agencies at the airport.

Taxi (☎ 22400 23700, airport 22400 22400)

Naxos Ναξος

POP 12,089

The largest of the Cyclades islands, beautiful, raw Naxos could probably survive without tourism. Green and fertile, with vast central mountains, Naxos produces olives, grapes, figs, citrus, corn and potatoes. Explore its fascinating main town, excellent beaches, remote villages and striking interior.

Naxos Town (Hora), on the west coast, is the island's capital and port.

Sights

★Kastro NEIGHBOURHOOD

(Naxos Town) Behind the waterfront, get lost in the narrow alleyways scrambling up to the spectacular hilltop 13th-century *kastro*, where the Venetian Catholics lived. You'll get super views, and there's a well-stocked **archaeological museum** (☎ 22850 22725; adult/child €3/free; ⏲ 8am-3pm Tue-Sun).

★Temple of Apollo ARCHAEOLOGICAL SITE

(The Potara) FREE From Naxos Town harbour, a causeway leads to Palatia Islet and the striking, unfinished Temple of Apollo, Naxos' most famous landmark. Simply two marble columns with a crowning lintel, it makes an arresting sight, and people gather at sunset for views back to Naxos' whitewashed houses and 13th-century *kastro* on the hilltop.

GREEK HISTORY IN A NUTSHELL

With its strategic position at the crossroads of Europe and Asia, Greece has endured a vibrant and turbulent history. During the Bronze Age (3000–1200 BC in Greece), the advanced Cycladic, Minoan and Mycenaean civilisations flourished. The Mycenaeans were swept aside in the 12th century BC by the warrior-like Dorians, who introduced Greece to the Iron Age.

By 800 BC, when Homer's *Odyssey* and *Iliad* were first written down, Greece was undergoing a cultural and military revival with the evolution of the city states, the most powerful of which were Athens and Sparta, and the development of democracy. The unified Greeks repelled the Persians twice, which was followed by an era of unparalleled growth and prosperity known as the Classical (or Golden) Age.

The Golden Age

During this period, Pericles commissioned the Parthenon, Sophocles wrote *Oedipus the King* and Socrates taught young Athenians to think. The era ended with the Peloponnesian War (431–404 BC), when the militaristic Spartans defeated the Athenians. They failed to notice the expansion of Macedonia under King Philip II, who conquered the war-weary city states.

Philip's son, Alexander the Great, marched triumphantly into Asia Minor, Egypt, Persia and parts of what are now Afghanistan and India. In 323 BC he met an untimely death at the age of 33, and his generals divided his empire between themselves.

Roman Rule & the Byzantine Empire

Roman incursions into Greece began in 205 BC. By 146 BC Greece and Macedonia had become Roman provinces. In the centuries that followed, Venetians, Franks, Normans, Slavs, Persians, Arabs and, finally, Turks, took turns chipping away at the Byzantine Empire.

The Ottoman Empire & Independence

After the end of the Byzantine Empire in 1453, when Constantinople fell to the Turks, most of Greece became part of the Ottoman Empire. The Greeks fought the War of Independence from 1821 to 1832, and in 1827 Ioannis Kapodistrias was elected the first Greek president.

DON'T MISS

KITRON-TASTING IN HALKI

The historic village of **Halki** is a top spot to try *kitron*, a liqueur unique to Naxos. While the exact recipe is top secret, visitors can taste it and stock up on supplies at **Vallindras Distillery** (☎22850 31220; ⏲10am-10pm Jul & Aug, to 6pm May, Jun, Sep & Oct) in Halki's main square. There are free tours of the old distillery's atmospheric rooms, which contain ancient jars and copper stills. *Kitron* tastings round off the trip.

★**Temple of Demeter** TEMPLE
(Dimitra's Temple; ☎22850 22725; ⏲8.30am-3pm Tue-Sun) FREE Surrounded by mountains, and gleaming in a gorgeous verdant valley sweeping to the sea, the impressive Temple of Demeter remains remarkably powerful. The ruins and reconstructions are not large, but they are historically fascinating, and the location is unparalleled – it's clear that this is a place for the worship of the goddess of the harvest. The site museum holds additional reconstructions of temple features. Signs point the way from the village of **Sangri** about 1.5km south to the site.

Beaches

The popular beach of **Agios Georgios** is just a 10-minute walk south from the main waterfront. **Agia Anna Beach**, 6km from town, and **Plaka Beach** are lined with accommodation and packed in summer. Beyond, wonderful sandy beaches continue as far south as **Pyrgaki Beach**.

Villages

A hire car or scooter will help reveal Naxos' dramatic and rugged landscape. The **Tragaea** region has tranquil villages, churches atop rocky crags and huge olive groves. Between Melanes and Kinidaros are the island's famous **marble quarries**. You'll find two ancient abandoned **kouros** (youth) statues, signposted a short walk from the road. Little **Apiranthos** settlement, perches on the slopes of **Mt Zeus** (1004m), the highest peak in the Cyclades, and has a few intermittently open **museums**. The historic village of **Halki**, one-time centre of Naxian commerce, is well worth a visit.

Lovely waterside **Apollonas** near Naxos' northern tip has a **beach**, taverna and another mysterious 10.5m **kouros** from the 7th century BC, abandoned and unfinished in an ancient marble quarry.

Sleeping

Nikos Verikokos Studios HOTEL €
(☎22850 22025; www.nikos-verikokos.com; Naxos Town; s/d/tr €40/50/60; ⏲year-round; ❄📶) Friendly Nikos maintains immaculate rooms in the heart of the old town. Some have balconies and sea views, most have little kitchenettes. Offers port pick-up with pre-arrangement.

Camping Maragas CAMPGROUND €
(☎22850 42552; www.maragascamping.gr; Agia Anna Beach; camp sites €9, d/studio from €40/60) South of Naxos Town.

Hotel Glaros BOUTIQUE HOTEL €€
(☎22850 23101; www.hotelglaros.com; Agios Georgios Beach; d €115-125, ste from €150; ⏲Apr-Oct; ❄@📶) Edgy yet homey, simple yet plush, this well-run and immaculate hotel has a seaside feel with light blues and whites and handpainted wooden furnishings. Service is efficient and thoughtful and the beach is only a few steps away. Breakfast is €7.

Eating & Drinking

Hora's waterfront is lined with eating and drinking establishments. Head into Market St in the Old Town, just down from the ferry quay, to find quality tavernas. South, only a few minutes' walk away, Main Sq is home to other excellent eateries, some of which stay open year-round.

Meze 2 SEAFOOD €
(☎22850 26401; Harbour, Naxos Town; mains €6-13; ⏲noon-midnight Apr-Oct) It would be easy to dismiss this waterfront restaurant as a tourist trap, but don't. Its Cretan and Naxian menu and fantastic service make it stand out from the bunch. The seafood is superb; try stuffed squid, grilled sardines, fisherman's *saganaki* (seafood baked with tomato sauce and feta) or mussels in ouzo and garlic. The salads are creative and filling, particularly the Naxian potato salad. Yum!

L'Osteria ITALIAN €€
(☎22850 24080; Naxos Town; mains €10-15; ⏲7pm-midnight) This authentic Italian

eatery is tucked in a small alley uphill from the harbour and beneath the *kastro* walls. Plunk yourself down in the relaxed courtyard and prepare to be gastronomically wowed. The menu changes daily with dishes like salmon lasagne and the ravioli is homemade. Need we say more?

Information

There's no official tourist information office. Try the website www.naxos-greece.net for more information.

Zas Travel (22850 23330; www.zastravel.com; Harbour, Naxos Town; 9am-9pm) Sells ferry tickets and organises accommodation, tours and car hire. Reduced hours in winter.

Getting There & Around

AIR

Naxos Airport (JNX) serves Athens daily. The airport is 3km south of town; there are no buses – a taxi costs €15, or arrange hotel pick-up.

BOAT

There are myriad high-season daily ferry and hydrofoil connections to most Cycladic islands and Crete, plus Piraeus ferries (€31, five hours) and catamarans (€48, 3¾ hours). Reduced services in winter.

BUS

Buses travel to most villages regularly in high season from in front of the **bus information office** (22850 22291; www.naxosdestinations.com; Harbour) on the port. Buy tickets at the office or its ticket machine.

CAR & MOTORCYCLE

Having your own wheels is a good idea for exploring Naxos. Car (€4 to€65) and motorcycle (€25 to €30) rentals line Hora's port and main streets.

Santorini (Thira)

Σαντορινη (Θηρα)

POP 13,500

Stunning Santorini may well have conquered a corner of your imagination before you've even set eyes on it. The startling sight of the submerged caldera almost encircled by sheer lava-layered cliffs – topped off by clifftop towns that look like a dusting of icing sugar – will grab your attention and not let it go. If you turn up in high season, though, be prepared for relentless crowds and commercialism – Santorini survives on tourism.

Sights & Activities

★Fira VILLAGE

Santorini's vibrant main town with its snaking narrow streets full of shops and restaurants perches on top of the caldera. The stunning caldera views from Fira and its neighbouring hamlet Firostefani are matched only by tiny Oia.

Museum of Prehistoric Thira MUSEUM

(22860 23217; Mitropoleos, Fira; admission €3; 8.30am-3pm Tue-Sun) On the southern edge of Fira, this museum houses extraordinary finds excavated from Akrotiri and is all the more impressive when you realise just how old they are. Most impressive is the glowing gold ibex figurine, dating from the 17th century BC and in amazingly mint condition. Also look for fossilised olive tree leaves from within the caldera from 60,000 BC.

★Oia VILLAGE

At the north of the island, the postcard-perfect village of Oia (ee-ah), famed for its sunsets, is less hectic than Fira and a must-visit. Its caldera-facing tavernas are superb spots for a meal. A path from Fira to Oia along the top of the caldera takes three to four hours to walk; otherwise take a taxi or bus. Beat the crowds in the early morning or late evening.

★Ancient Akrotiri ARCHAEOLOGICAL SITE

(22860 81366; adult/child €5/free; 8am-3pm Tue-Sun) In 1967, excavations began at the site of Akrotiri. What they uncovered was phenomenal: an ancient Minoan city buried deep beneath volcanic ash from the catastrophic eruption of 1613 BC. Today, the site retains a strong sense of place and reverent awe. Housed within a cool, protective structure, wooden walkways allow you to pass through various parts of the city.

★Santo Wines WINERY

(22860 22596; www.santowines.gr; Pyrgos; 10am-7pm) Santorini's lauded wines are its crisp, clear dry whites, such as the delectable *asyrtiko*, and the amber-coloured, unfortified dessert wine Vinsanto. At Santo Wines you can sample a range of wines and browse local products including fava beans, tomatoes, capers and preserves.

Around the Island

Santorini's known for its multihued **beaches**. The black-sand beaches of **Perissa**,

Santorini (Thira)

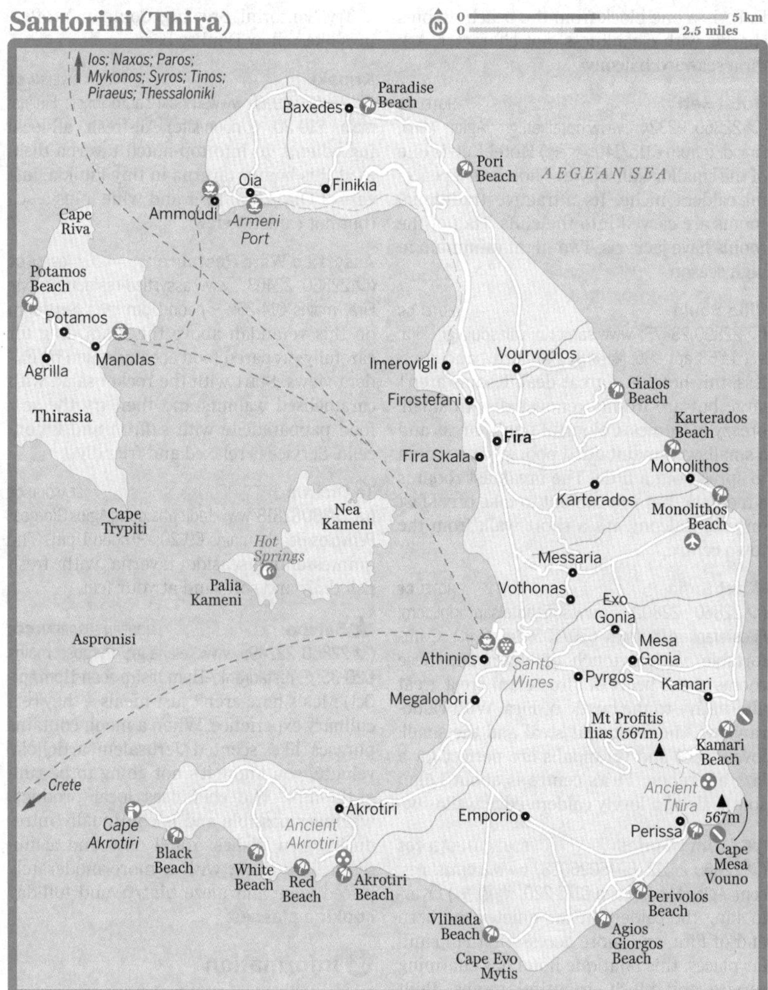

Perivolos, Agios Giorgos and **Kamari** sizzle – beach mats are essential. **Red Beach**, near Ancient Akrotiri, has impressive red cliffs and smooth, hand-sized pebbles submerged under clear water.

On a mountain between Perissa and Kamari are the atmospheric ruins of **Ancient Thira** (admission €4; ⏱8am-2.30pm Tue-Sun), first settled in the 9th century BC.

Of the volcanic islets, only **Thirasia** is inhabited. Visitors can clamber over lava on **Nea Kameni** then swim in warm springs in the sea at **Palia Kameni**. Many excursions get you there; small boats are at Fira Skala port.

Sleeping

Santorini's sleeping options are exorbitant in high season, especially anywhere with a caldera view. Many hotels offer free port and airport transfers. Check www.airbnb.com for deals.

Stelios Place HOTEL €
(☎22860 81860; www.steliosplace.com; Perissa; d/tr/q €55/70/90; P❄📶🏊) This hotel has a great position set back from the main drag

in Perissa one block from the beach. Rooms sparkle with cleanliness, not character. Ask for a seaward balcony.

Hotel Keti HOTEL €€
(☎22860 22324; www.hotelketi.gr; Agiou Mina, Fira; d/tr from €115/140; ❄📶) Hotel Keti is one of the smaller 'sunset view' hotels in a peaceful caldera niche. Its attractive traditional rooms are carved into the cliffs. Half of the rooms have jacuzzis. Two-night minimum in high season.

Villa Soula HOTEL €€
(☎22860 23473; www.santorini-villasoula.gr; Fira; s & d €68, apt €95; ❄📶🏊) Cheerful and spotless, this hotel is a great deal. Rooms aren't large but are freshly renovated with small, breezy balconies. Colourful public areas and a small, well-maintained pool give you room to spread out a little. The breakfast room is a tad dark, but you can opt to take breakfast on your balcony. It's a short walk from the town centre.

Hotel Sofia HOTEL €€
(☎22860 22802; www.sofiahotelsantorini.com; Firostefani; d/tr from €70/105; ❄📶🏊) Comfortable, with a touch of character, these rooms at the heart of Firostefani are a great alternative to the bustle of Fira. With caldera views, they're a near steal and the small, lovely pool and verandahs are perfect for a lazy afternoon. Fira's centre is about 1.5km south, along a lovely caldera-edge walkway.

★Aroma Suites BOUTIQUE HOTEL €€€
(☎22860 24112, 6945026038; www.aromasuites.com; Agiou Mina, Fira; d €175-220; ❄@📶) Overlooking the caldera at the quieter southern end of Fira, and more accessible than similar places, this boutique hotel has charming service and plush, beautiful rooms. Built into the side of the caldera, the traditional interiors are made all the more lovely with strong colour touches, canopied beds, local art, books and stereos. Balconies offer a feeling of complete seclusion.

Eating & Drinking

Overpriced, indifferent food geared towards tourists is still an unfortunate feature of summertime Fira. Prices tend to double at spots with caldera views. Cheaper eateries cluster around Fira's square. Popular bars and clubs line Erythrou Stavrou in Fira. Many diners head to Oia, legendary for its superb sunsets. Good-value tavernas line the waterfronts at Kamari and Perissa.

Try Santorini Brewing Company's offerings like Yellow Donkey beer.

Krinaki TAVERNA €€
(☎22860 71993; www.krinaki-santorini.gr; Finikia; mains €10-20; ⊙noon-late) All-fresh, all-local ingredients go into top-notch taverna dishes at this homey taverna in tiny Finikia, just east of Oia. Local beer and wine, plus a sea (but not caldera) view.

Assyrtico Wine Restaurant GREEK €€
(☎22860 22463; www.assyrtico-restaurant.com; Fira; mains €14-25; ⊙noon-11pm; 📶) Settle in on this verandah above the main drag for carefully prepared food accompanied by caldera views. Start with the rocket salad with caramelised walnuts and then try the seafood papparadelle with saffron and limoncello. Service is relaxed and friendly.

Ta Dichtia SEAFOOD €€
(☎22860 82818; www.tadichtia.com; Agios Giorgos-Perivolos Beach; mains €9-20; ⊙noon-11pm) The quintessential seaside taverna with fresh fish daily and soft sand at your feet.

★Selene MODERN EUROPEAN €€€
(☎22860 22249; www.selene.gr; Pyrgos; mains €20-35; ⊙restaurant 7-11pm, bistro noon-11pm Apr-Oct) Meals here aren't just meals – they're a culinary experience. When a menu contains phrases like 'scented Jerusalem artichoke velouté', you know it's not going to be run-of-the-mill. The chef uses local products wherever possible and is continually introducing new dishes. You'll now find a museum here along with a more moderately priced wine and meze **bistro**, and full-day **cooking classes**.

Information

There is no tourist office. Try www.santorini.net for more information.

Dakoutros Travel (☎22860 22958; www.dakoutrostravel.gr; Fira; ⊙8.30am-10pm) On the main street, just before Plateia Theotokopoulou.

Getting There & Around

AIR

Santorini Airport (JTR; ☎22860 28405; www.santoriniairport.com) Santorini Airport has daily flights to Athens, a growing number of other domestic destinations and direct international flights from throughout Europe. The airport is 5km southeast of Fira; frequent buses (€1.50) and taxis (€15) will get you there.

BOAT

The new Port of Athinios, where most ferries dock, is 10km south of Fira by road. Ferries are met by buses and taxis. The old port of Fira Skala, used by cruise ships and excursion boats, is directly below Fira and accessed by cable car (adult/child €4/2 one way), donkey (€5, up only) or by foot (588 steps).

There are daily ferries (€33.50, nine hours) and fast boats (€60, 5¼ hours) to Piraeus; daily connections in summer to Mykonos, Ios, Naxos, Paros and Iraklio; and ferries to the smaller islands in the Cyclades as well as Iraklio (Crete).

BUS

The bus station and **taxi stand** (☎22860 22555, 22860 23951) are just south of Fira's main square, Plateia Theotokopoulou. Buses go frequently to Oia, Kamari, Perissa and Akrotiri. Athinios Port buses (€2.20, 30 minutes) usually leave Fira, Kamari and Perissa one to 1½ hours before ferry departures.

CAR & MOTORCYCLE

A car (from €40 per day) or scooter is good for getting out of town. Outlets abound.

CRETE ΚΡΗΤΗ

POP 550,000

Crete is Greece's largest, most southerly island and its size, distance and independent history give it the feel of a different country. With its dramatic landscape, myriad mountain villages, unique cultural identity and some of the best food in Greece, Crete is a delight to explore.

The island is split by a spectacular chain of mountains running east to west. Major towns are on the more hospitable northern coast, while most of the southern coast is too precipitous to support large settlements. The rugged mountainous interior, dotted with caves and sliced by dramatic gorges, offers rigorous hiking and climbing. Small villages like Magarites, a potters' village near Mt Idi, offer a glimpse into traditional life.

Iraklio Ηρακλειο

POP 174,000

Iraklio (ee-*rah*-klee-oh; often spelt Heraklion), Crete's capital and economic hub, is a bustling modern city and the fifth-largest in Greece. It has a lively city centre, an excellent archaeological museum and is close to Knossos, Crete's major visitor attraction.

DON'T MISS

IRAKLIO MARKET

An Iraklio institution, just south of the Lion Fountain, narrow **Odos 1866** (1866 St) is part market, part bazaar and, despite being increasingly tourist-oriented, it's a fun place to browse and stock up on picnic supplies from fruit and vegetables, creamy cheeses and honey to succulent olives and fresh breads. Other stalls sell pungent herbs, leather goods, hats, jewellery and some souvenirs. Cap off a spree with lunch at **Giakoumis** (Theodosaki 5-8; mains €6-13; ⏰noon-11pm) or another nearby taverna (avoid those in the market itself).

Other towns are more picturesque, but in a pinch, you can stay over in Iraklio.

Iraklio's harbours face north with the landmark **Koules Venetian Fortress**. Plateia Venizelou, known for its **Lion (Morosini) Fountain**, is the heart of the city, 400m south of the old harbour up 25 Avgoustou.

Sights & Activities

★Heraklion

Archaeological Museum MUSEUM

(☎2810 279000; http://odysseus.culture.gr; Xanthoudidou 2; adult/child €6/free, incl Knossos €10; ⏰8am-8pm Apr-Oct, 11am-5pm Mon, 8am-3pm Tue-Sun Nov-Mar) This outstanding museum is one of the largest and most important in Greece. There are artefacts spanning 5500 years from neolithic to Roman times, but it's rightly most famous for its extensive Minoan collection. The beautifully restored museum makes a gleaming showcase for the artefacts, and greatly enhances any understanding of Crete's rich history. Don't skip it.

The treasure trove includes pottery, jewellery, sarcophagi, plus several famous frescoes from the sites of Knossos, Phaestos, Zakros, Malia and Agia Triada.

Cretan Adventures OUTDOORS

(☎2810 332772; www.cretanadventures.gr; 3rd fl, Evans 10) This well-regarded local company organises hiking tours, mountain biking and extreme outdoor excursions.

Sleeping

Staying in nearby Arhanes offers a chance to see Cretan wine country. Try **Arhontiko** (☎2810 881550; www.arhontikoarhanes.gr; apt

Crete

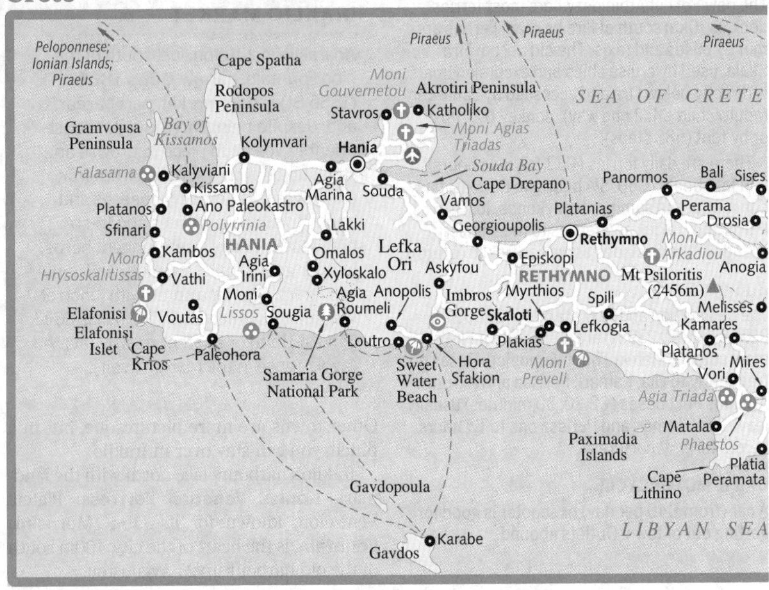

€75-95; ❄📶) with its beautifully kitted-out apartments.

Kronos Hotel HOTEL €

(☎2810 282240; www.kronoshotel.gr; Sofokli Venizelou 2; s/d €49/60; ❄@📶) After a thorough makeover this waterfront hotel pole-vaulted to the top of the budget hotel category. Rooms have double-glazed windows to block out noise, as well as balconies, phone, a tiny TV and a fridge. Some doubles have sea views (€66).

Rea Hotel HOTEL €

(☎2810 223638; www.hotelrea.gr; Kalimeraki 1, cnr Hortatson; d with/without bathroom €45/35, tr €54; ❄📶) Popular with backpackers, the family-run Rea has an easy, friendly atmosphere. Rooms all have small TVs and balconies, but some bathrooms are shared. Family rooms are available. There's a book exchange and a communal fridge.

Lato Boutique Hotel BOUTIQUE HOTEL €€

(☎2810 228103; www.lato.gr; Epimenidou 15; d incl breakfast €89-136, q from €124; P❄@📶) Iraklio goes Hollywood – with all the sass but sans attitude – at this mod boutique hotel overlooking the old harbour, easily recognised by its jazzy facade. Rooms here sport rich woods, warm reds and vinyl floors, plus custom furniture, pillow-top mattresses, a playful lighting scheme and a kettle for making coffee or tea. Back rooms overlook a modernist metal sculpture.

Eating & Drinking

Eateries, bars and cafes surround Plateia Venizelou (Lion Fountain) and the El Greco Park area. The old harbour offers seafood options.

Fyllo...Sofies CAFE €

(☎2810 284774; www.fillosofies.gr; Plateia Venizelou 33; snacks €3-7; ⏲5am-late; 📶) With a terrace spilling towards the Morosini Fountain, this been-here-forever cafe is *the* go-to place for *bougatsa*: a traditional pastry filled with cream or *myzithra* (sheep's milk cheese) and sometimes served with ice cream or sprinkled with honey and nuts.

Ippokambos SEAFOOD €

(☎2810 280240; Sofokli Venizelou 3; mains €6-13; ⏲noon-midnight Mon-Sat; 📶) Locals give this unpretentious *ouzerie* an enthusiastic thumbs up and we are only too happy to follow suit. Fish is the thing here, freshly caught, simply but expertly prepared and sold at fair prices. In summer, park yourself on the covered waterfront terrace.

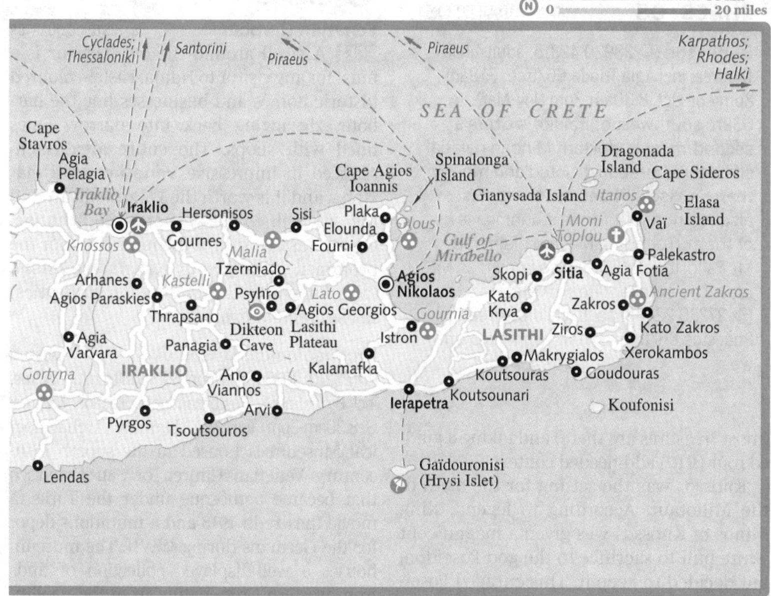

Information

Visit www.heraklion.gr for city information.

Skoutelis Travel (☎2810 280808; www.skoutelisrentacar.gr; 25 Avgoustou 24) Airline and ferry bookings, excursions around Crete and to Santorini, accommodation help and car hire.

Tourist Office (☎2810 228225; Xanthoulidou 1; ⏰9am-3pm Mon-Fri) Meagre selection of brochures and maps.

Getting There & Around

AIR

Flights from Iraklio's **Nikos Kazantzakis International Airport** (HER; ☎2810 397800; www.heraklion-airport.info) serve Athens, Thessaloniki and Rhodes plus destinations all over Europe. The airport is 5km east of town. Bus 1 travels between the airport and city centre (€1.20) every 15 minutes from 6.15am to 10.45pm.

BOAT

Daily ferries from Iraklio's **ferry port** (☎2810 244956) service Piraeus (€39, eight hours), and catamarans head to Santorini and other Cycladic islands. Ferries sail east to Rhodes (€28, 14 hours) via Agios Nikolaos, Sitia, Kasos, Karpathos and Halki. Services are reduced in winter. See www.openseas.gr.

BUS

KTEL (www.bus-service-crete-ktel.com) runs the buses on Crete. Main Bus Station A, just inland from the new harbour, serves eastern and western Crete (Agios Nikolaos, Ierapetra, Sitia, Malia, Lasithi Plateau, Hania, Rethymno and Knossos). It has useful tourist information and a left-luggage service. Bus Station B, 50m beyond the Hania Gate, serves the southern route (Phaestos, Matala and Anogia).

Knossos Κνωσσος

Crete's most famous historical attraction is the **Palace of Knossos** (☎2810 231940; adult/child €6/free, incl Heraklion Archaeological Museum €10; ⏰8am-8pm Jun-Oct, to 5pm Nov-May), 5km south of Iraklio, and the grand capital of Minoan Crete. Excavation on Knossos (k-nos-*os*) started in 1878 with Cretan archaeologist Minos Kalokerinos, and continued from 1900 to 1930 with British archaeologist Sir Arthur Evans. Today, it's hard to make sense, in the extensive restorations, of what is Evans' interpretation and what actually existed in Minoan times. But the setting is gorgeous and the ruins and re-creations impressive, incorporating an immense palace, courtyards, private apartments, baths, lively frescoes and more. Going to the Heraklion Archaeological Museum (p539) in Iraklio

PHAESTOS ΦΑΙΣΤΟΣ

Phaestos (☎28920 42315; adult/child €4/free, incl Agia Triada €6/free; ⏰8am-8pm Apr-Oct, 8.30am-3pm Nov-Mar), 63km southwest of Iraklio, is Crete's second-most important Minoan palatial site. More unreconstructed and moody than Knossos, Phaestos (fes-*tos*) is also worth a visit for its stunning views of the surrounding Mesara plain and Mt Psiloritis (2456m; also known as Mt Ida). The smaller site of **Agia Triada** (☎27230 22448; adult/child €3/free, incl Phaestos €6/free; ⏰10am-3pm) is 3km west.

(most treasures are there) and taking a guided tour (€10) add needed context.

Knossos was the setting for the myth of the Minotaur. According to legend, King Minos of Knossos was given a magnificent white bull to sacrifice to the god Poseidon, but decided to keep it. This enraged Poseidon, who punished the king by causing his wife Pasiphae to fall in love with the animal. The result of this odd union was the Minotaur – half-man and half-bull – who was imprisoned in a labyrinth beneath the king's palace at Knossos, munching on youths and maidens, before being killed by Theseus.

Buses to Knossos (€1.50, 20 minutes, three per hour) leave from Bus Station A in Iraklio.

Hania Χανια

POP 54,000

Crete's most romantic, evocative and alluring town, Hania (hahn-*yah*; often spelt Chania) is the former capital and the island's second-largest city. There is a rich mosaic of Venetian and Ottoman architecture, particularly in the area of the old harbour, which lures tourists in droves.

Modern Hania with its university retains the exoticism of a city playing with East and West and has some of the best hotels and restaurants on the island. It's an excellent base for exploring nearby idyllic beaches and a spectacular mountainous interior.

Sights

Venetian Harbour HISTORIC QUARTER

FREE A stroll around the old harbour is a must for any visitor to Hania. Pastel-coloured historic homes and businesses line the harbour, zigzagging back into narrow lanes lined with shops. The entire area is ensconced in impressive **Venetian fortifications**, and it is worth the 1.5km walk around the sea wall to the **Venetian lighthouse**. On the eastern side of the inner harbour the prominent **Mosque of Kioutsouk Hasan** (also known as the Mosque of Janissaries) houses regular exhibitions.

Archaeological Museum MUSEUM

(☎28210 90334; Halidon 30; adult/child €2/free, incl Byzantine & Postbyzantine Collection €3/free; ⏰8.30am-3pm Tue-Sun) Hania's Archaeological Museum is housed in the superb 16th-century Venetian Church of San Francisco that became a mosque under the Turks, a movie theatre in 1913 and a munitions depot for the Germans during WWII. The museum houses a well-displayed collection of finds from western Crete dating from the neolithic to the Roman eras. Artefacts from 3400 to 1200 BC include tablets with Linear A script. There is also exquisite pottery from the Geometric Age (1200–800 BC) and a case of bull figurines.

Sleeping

Hania's old harbour is loaded with great hotels that can book up, even on winter weekends; reserve ahead.

Ionas Hotel BOUTIQUE HOTEL €€

(☎28210 55090; www.ionashotel.com; cnr Sarpaki & Sorvolou; d incl breakfast €60-90; ❄📶) One of the new breed of boutique hotels in the quieter Splantzia quarter, Ionas is housed in a historic building with contemporary interior design and friendly owners. The nine rooms are kitted out with all mod cons (including a smallish jacuzzi in one), and share a terrace. Original touches include a Venetian archway in the entrance, and walls from the mid-16th century.

Palazzo Duca APARTMENT €€

(☎28210 70460; www.palazzoduca.gr; Douka 27-29; d/ste from €80/110) This reader favourite small hotel is tucked back into the streets of Hania's old harbour and has super-comfy studios and apartments with kitchenettes. Some offer port views or small balconies.

Pension Lena PENSION €€
(☎28210 86860; www.lenachania.gr; Ritsou 5; d €65; ❄📶) Run by the friendly Lena, this pension near Nea Hora beach has tastefully done rooms with an old-world feel and a scattering of antiques, though the front rooms are the most appealing. Lena also offers three independent houses.

★**Casa Leone** BOUTIQUE HOTEL €€€
(☎28210 76762; www.casa-leone.com; Parodos Theotokopoulou 18; d/ste incl breakfast from €125/160; ❄📶) This Venetian residence has been converted into a classy and romantic family-run boutique hotel. The rooms are spacious and well appointed, with balconies overlooking the harbour. There are honeymoon suites, with classic drape-canopy beds and sumptuous curtains.

Eating & Drinking

Look beyond the waterfront tourist-traps for some of the best eats on the island. The Splantzia neighbourhood is popular with discerning locals. Nightclubs dot the port, and atmospheric **Fagotto Jazz Bar** (☎28210 71877; Angelou 16; ⏰7pm-2am) has occasional live music.

★**Taverna Tamam** TAVERNA €
(☎28210 96080; Zambeliou 49; mains €7-12; ⏰noon-midnight; ✎) This excellent, convivial taverna in a converted Turkish bathhouse fills with chatting locals at tables spilling out onto the street. Meals incorporate mid-Eastern spices, and include tasty soups and a superb selection of vegetarian specialities.

★**Bougatsa tou Iordanis** CRETAN €
(☎28210 88855; Apokoronou 24; bougatsa €3) You haven't lived til you've eaten the *bougatsa* at this little storefront dedicated to the flaky, sweet-cheesy treat. It's cooked fresh in enormous slabs and carved up in front of your eyes. Pair it with a coffee and you're set for the morning.

Pallas CAFE €
(Akti Tombazi 15-17; mains €8-16; ⏰8am-midnight; 📶) For coffee and breakfast at Hania's old harbour, head to local favourite Pallas, with a 2nd-floor dining room, superb views and a brunch menu to match.

★**To Maridaki** CRETAN €€
(☎28210 08880; Daskalogianni 33; dishes €7-12; ⏰noon-midnight Mon-Sat) This modern seafood *mezedhopoleio* (mezedhes restaurant) is not to be missed. In a cheerful, bright dining room, happy visitors and locals alike tuck into impeccable, local seafood and Cretan specialities. Ingredients are fresh, the fried calamari is to die for, the house white wine is crisp and delicious, and the complimentary panna cotta to finish the meal is transcendent. What's not to love?

Information

For more information visit www.chania.gr.

Local Tourist Office (☎28210 41665; tourism@chania.gr; Milonogianni 53; ⏰9am-2pm) Modest selection at the town hall.

Tellus Travel (☎28210 91500; www.tellus-travel.gr; Halidon 108; ⏰8am-11pm) Major agency hires cars, changes money, arranges air and boat tickets, accommodation and excursions.

WORTH A TRIP

RETHYMNO & MONI ARKADIOU

Rethymno (*reth*-im-no), on the coast between Iraklio and Hania, is one of the island's architectural treasures, due to its stunning **fortress** and mix of Venetian and Turkish houses in the **old quarter**. It's worth a stop to explore the area around the old Venetian harbour, and shop in its interesting arts and crafts boutiques.

Moni Arkadiou (Arkadi Monastery; ☎28310 83136; www.arkadimonastery.gr; admission €2.50; ⏰9am-8pm Jun-Aug, shorter hour Sep-May), in the hills some 23km southeast of Rethymno, has deep significance for Cretans. A potent symbol of human resistance, it was the site of a tragic and momentous stand-off between the Turks and the Cretans in 1866, and considered a spark plug in the struggle towards freedom from Turkish occupation. Arkadiou's most impressive structure, its **Venetian church** (1587), has a striking Renaissance facade marked by eight slender Corinthian columns and topped by an ornate triple-belled tower. Its high mountain valley is beautiful, especially around sunset.

WORTH A TRIP

SOUTHWEST COAST VILLAGES

Crete's southern coastline at its western end is dotted with remote, attractive little villages that are brilliant spots to take it easy for a few days.

From Paleohora heading east are Sougia, Agia Roumeli, Loutro and Hora Sfakion. No road links the coastal resorts, but a once-daily boat from Paleohora to Sougia (€8, one hour), Agia Roumeli (€14, 1½ hours), Loutro (€15, 2½ hours) and Hora Sfakion (€16, three hours) connects the villages in summer. See www.sfakia-crete.com/sfakia-crete/ferries.html. In summer three buses daily connect Hania and Hora Sfakion (€7.60, two hours), two daily to Sougia (€7.10, 1¾ hours). If you're a keen hiker, it's also possible to walk right along this southern coast.

Paleohora This village is isolated on a peninsula with a sandy beach to the west and a pebbly beach to the east. On summer evenings the main street is closed to traffic and the tavernas move onto the road. If you're after a relaxing few days, Paleohora is a great spot to chill out. Stay at **Joanna's** (☎69785 83503, 28230 41801; www.joannas-palaiochora.com; studio €40-55; ⊙Apr-Nov; P ❄ 📶) spacious, spotless studios.

Sougia At the mouth of the **Agia Irini gorge**, Sougia (soo-yah) is a laid-back and refreshingly undeveloped spot with a wide curve of sand-and-pebble beach. The 14.5km (six hour) walk from Paleohora is popular, as is the Agia Irini gorge walk, which ends (or starts!) in Sougia. It's possible to get here by ferry, by car or on foot. Stay at **Santa Irene Apartments** (☎28230 51342; www.santa-irene.gr; apt €60-80; ⊙late Mar-early Nov; P ❄ 📶), a smart beachside complex with its own cafe.

Agia Roumeli At the mouth of the Samaria Gorge, Agia Roumeli bristles with gorge-walkers from mid-afternoon until the ferry comes to take them away. Once they are gone, this pleasant little town goes into quiet mode until the first walkers turn up in the early afternoon the following day. Right on the waterfront, **Paralia Taverna & Rooms** (☎28250 91408; www.taverna-paralia.com; Agia Roumeli; d from €30; ❄ 📶) offers excellent views, tasty Cretan cuisine, cold beer and simple, clean rooms.

Loutro This tiny village is a particularly picturesque spot, curled around the only natural harbour on the southern coast of Crete. With no vehicle access, the only way in is by boat or on foot. **Hotel Porto Loutro** (☎28250 91433; www.hotelportoloutro.com; s/d incl breakfast €50/60; ⊙mid-Mar–Oct; ❄ @) has tasteful rooms with balconies overlooking the harbour. The village beach, excellent walks, rental kayaks and boat transfers to excellent Sweetwater Beach fill peaceful days.

Hora Sfakion Renowned in Cretan history for its rebellious streak, Hora Sfakion is an amiable town. WWII history buffs know this as the place where thousands of Allied troops were evacuated by sea after the Battle of Crete. Hora Sfakion's seafront tavernas serve fresh seafood and unique *Sfakianes pites,* which look like crêpes filled with sweet or savoury local cheese. **Hotel Stavris** (☎28250 91220; www.hotel-stavris-sfakia-crete.com; s/d/tr from €28/33/38; ❄ 📶) has simple rooms and breakfast outside in its courtyard.

ℹ Getting There & Away

AIR

Hania Airport (CHQ; www.chaniaairport.com) serves Athens, Thessaloniki and seasonally cities around Europe. The airport is 14km east of town on the Akrotiri Peninsula. Taxis cost €20; buses cost €2.30.

BOAT

The port is at Souda, 9km southeast of Hania. Once-nightly **Anek** (www.anek.gr) ferries serve Piraeus (€35, nine hours). Frequent buses (€1.65) and taxis (€10) connect the town and Souda.

BUS

Frequent buses from the **main bus station** (www.bus-service-crete-ktel.com; Kydonias 73-77; left luggage per bag per day €2) run along Crete's northern coast to Iraklio (€13.80, 2¾ hours, half-hourly) and Rethymno (€6.20, one hour, half-hourly); buses run less frequently to Paleohora, Omalos and Hora Sfakion. Buses for beaches west of Hania leave from the eastern side of Plateia 1866.

Samaria Gorge

Φαραγγι Της Σαμαριας

Samaria Gorge (☎28210 45570; www.samariagorge.eu; adult/child €5/2.50; ⏲7am-sunset May-late Oct) is one of Europe's most spectacular gorges and a superb (very popular) hike. Walkers should take rugged footwear, food, drinks and sun protection for this strenuous five- to six-hour trek. You can do the walk as part of an excursion tour, or independently by taking the Omalos bus from the main bus station in Hania (€6.90, one hour) to the head of the gorge at Xyloskalo (1230m). It's a 16.7km walk (all downhill) to Agia Roumeli on the coast, from where you take a boat to Hora Sfakion (€10, 1¼ hours) and then a bus back to Hania (€7.60, 1½ hours).

You are not allowed to spend the night in the gorge, so you need to complete the walk in a day, or beat the crowds and stay over in one of the nearby villages. Other gorges, such as **Imbros** (admission €2; ⏲year-round), also make for fine walking, and are less crowded.

DODECANESE

ΔΩΔΕΚΑΝΗΣΑ

Strung out along the coast of western Turkey, the 12 main islands of the Dodecanese (*dodeca* means 12) have suffered a turbulent past of invasions and occupations that have endowed them with a fascinating diversity. Conquered successively by the Romans, the Arabs, the Knights of St John, the Turks, the Italians, then liberated from the Germans by British and Greek commandos in 1944, the Dodecanese became part of Greece in 1947. These days, tourists rule.

Rhodes Ροδος

POP 98,000

Rhodes (Rodos in Greek) is the largest island in the Dodecanese. According to mythology, the sun god Helios chose Rhodes as his bride and bestowed light, warmth and vegetation upon her. The blessing seems to have paid off, for Rhodes produces more flowers and sunny days than most Greek islands. Throw in an east coast of virtually uninterrupted sandy beaches and it's easy to understand why sun-starved northern Europeans flock here in droves. The old town is magnificent.

Rhodes Town

POP 56,000

Rhodes' capital is Rhodes Town, on the northern tip of the island. Its magnificent **Old Town**, the largest inhabited medieval town in Europe, is enclosed within massive walls and is a delight to explore. To the north is **New Town**, the commercial centre. The **town beach**, which looks out at Turkey runs around the peninsula at the northern end of New Town.

The main port, **Commercial Harbour**, is east of the Old Town, and is where the big interisland ferries dock. Northwest of here is **Mandraki Harbour**, lined with excursion boats and smaller ferries, hydrofoils and catamarans. It was the supposed site of the **Colossus of Rhodes**, a 32m-high bronze statue of Apollo built over 12 years (294–282 BC). The statue stood for a mere 65 years before being toppled by an earthquake.

Sights

A wander around Rhodes' Unesco World Heritage–listed Old Town is a must. It is reputedly the world's finest surviving example of medieval fortification, with 12m-thick

THE KNIGHTS OF ST JOHN

Island-hopping in the Dodecanese you'll quickly realise that the Knights of St John left behind a passel of castles. Originally formed as the Knights Hospitaller in Jerusalem in 1080 to provide care for poor and sick pilgrims, the knights relocated to Rhodes (via Cyprus) after the loss of Jerusalem in the First Crusade. They ousted the ruling Genoese in 1309, built a stack of castles in the Dodecanese to protect their new home, then set about irking the neighbours by committing acts of piracy against Ottoman shipping. Sultan Süleyman the Magnificent, not a man you'd want to irk, took offence and set about dislodging the knights from their strongholds. Rhodes finally capitulated in 1523 and the remaining knights relocated to Malta. They set up there as the Sovereign Military Hospitaller of Jerusalem, of Rhodes, and of Malta.

walls. A mesh of Byzantine, Turkish and Latin architecture, the Old Town is divided into the Kollakio (the Knights' Quarter, where the Knights of St John lived during medieval times), the Hora and the Jewish Quarter. The Knights' Quarter contains most of the medieval historical sights while the Hora, often referred to as the Turkish Quarter, is primarily Rhodes Town's commercial sector with shops and restaurants, thronged by tourists.

The **Knights' Quarter** is in the northern end of the Old Town. The cobbled **Avenue of the Knights** (Ippoton) is lined with magnificent medieval buildings, the most imposing of which is the **Palace of the Grand Masters** (22410 23359; admission €6; 8.30am-3pm Tue-Sun), which was restored, but never used, as a holiday home for Mussolini. From the palace, explore the **D'Amboise Gate**, the most atmospheric of the fortification gates, which takes you across the moat.

The beautiful 15th-century Knight's Hospital, closer to the seafront, now houses the excellent **Archaeological Museum** (22410 65256; Plateia Mousiou; admission €6; 8am-3pm Tue-Sun). The splendid building was restored by the Italians and has an impressive collection that includes the ethereal marble statue *Aphrodite of Rhodes*.

The pink-domed **Mosque of Süleyman**, at the top of Sokratous, was built in 1522 to commemorate the Ottoman victory against the knights, then rebuilt in 1808.

Sleeping

Mango Rooms PENSION €
(22410 24877; www.mango.gr; Plateia Dorieos 3, Old Town; d/tr €60/72;) Set in a square in Old Town, these are spotless, simple rooms with safety deposit box, fridge and bathroom. Downstairs is a restaurant and internet cafe.

LINDOS

The **Acropolis of Lindos** (22440 31258; admission €6; 8am-6pm Tue-Sun Jun-Aug, to 2.40pm Sep-May), 47km south from Rhodes Town, is an ancient city spectacularly perched atop a 116m-high rocky outcrop. Below is the town of Lindos, a tangle of streets with elaborately decorated 17th-century houses.

★ **Marco Polo Mansion** BOUTIQUE HOTEL €€
(22410 25562; www.marcopolomansion.gr; Agiou Fanouriou 40, Old Town; d incl breakfast €80-180; Apr-Oct;) We love the vivid style in this 15th-century former Ottoman official's house, with its heavy antique furniture and eastern rugs, and stained-glass windows washing the ox-blood walls in blue light. The rooms are spectacularly romantic with huge beds and tasteful furnishings. Try the split-level ex-harem bedroom. There's a top restaurant, too!

Hotel International HOTEL €€
(22410 24595; www.international-hotel.gr; 12 Kazouli St, New Town; s/d incl breakfast €50/70;) In New Town, the International is a friendly family-run operation with immaculately clean and good-value rooms only a few minutes from Rhodes' main town beach. It's a 10-minute stroll to Old Town, and prices drop by a third out of high season.

Nikos & Takis Hotel BOUTIQUE HOTEL €€€
(22410 70773; www.nikostakishotel.com; Panetiou 29; d/ste incl breakfast from €170/180; year-round;) Soaked in shades of ochre, this hilltop eyrie in the heart of the Knights' Quarter abounds in eclectic style: a melange of Moorish and high-fashion influences with frescoed arched doors, a gorgeous pebble mosaic courtyard and palace or sea views. Its eight individually designed suites are fit for royalty with four-poster beds, silk drapes, traditional wooden ceilings and tangerine-hued walls.

Service is sensational and breakfast is lavishly made to order.

Eating & Drinking

Old Rhodes is rife with tourist traps; look in the backstreets. Head further north into New Town for better value restaurants and bars.

To Meltemi TAVERNA €
(Kountourioti 8; mains €10-15; noon-6pm;) With wide sea views and just yards from the beach, this breezy taverna has a cosy, nautically themed interior, or you can dine on the semi-alfresco terrace. Staff are charming and the menu swimming in feisty salads, salted mackerel, calamari and octopus.

Pizanias TAVERNA €€
(22410 22117; Sofokleous 24; mains €8-18; noon-midnight Feb-Oct) This atmospheric little taverna tucked back into the heart of Old Town is known for its fresh seafood and

delicious fava. Dine under the trees and the night sky.

Information

For information, visit www.rodos.gr.

Tourist Information Office (EOT; ☎22410 44335; www.ando.gr/eot; cnr Makariou & Papagou; ⏱8am-2.45pm Mon-Fri) Brochures, maps, transport information and *Rodos News*, a free English-language newspaper.

Triton Holidays (☎22410 21690; www.tritondmc.gr; Plastira 9, Mandraki; ⏱9am-8pm) Air and sea travel, hire cars, accommodation and tours throughout the Dodecanese. It also sells tickets to Turkey.

Getting There & Around

AIR

Many flights daily connect Rhodes' **Diagoras Airport** (RHO; ☎22410 88700; www.rhodes-airport.org) and Athens, plus less-regular flights to Karpathos, Kastellorizo, Thessaloniki, Iraklio and Samos. International flights, budget airlines and charter flights swarm in summer. The airport is on the west coast, 16km southwest of Rhodes Town; 25 minutes and €2.20 by bus, €22 by taxi.

BOAT

Rhodes is the main port of the Dodecanese and there is a complex array of departures. Most of the daily boats to Piraeus (€59, 13 hours) sail via the Dodecanese, but some go via Karpathos, Crete and the Cyclades. In summer, catamaran services run up and down the Dodecanese daily from Rhodes to Symi or Halki, Kos, Kalymnos, Nisyros, Tilos, Patmos and Leros. Check www.openseas.gr, **Dodekanisos Seaways** (☎22410 70590; Afstralias 3) and **Blue Star Ferries** (☎21089 19800; www.bluestarferries.com). Excursion boats at the harbour also go to Symi.

To Turkey

Ferries connect Rhodes and Marmaris in Turkey (one way/return including port taxes €50/75, 50 minutes). Check www.marmarisinfo.com. For Fethiye, Turkey (one way/return including port taxes €50/75, 90 minutes) see www.alaturkaturkey.com.

BUS

Rhodes Town has two bus stations a block apart next to the New Market. The **west-side bus station** (☎22410 26300) serves the airport, Kamiros (€5, 55 minutes) and the west coast. The **east-side bus station** (☎22410 27706; www.ktelrodou.gr) serves the east coast, Lindos (€5, 1½ hours) and the inland southern villages.

BOATS TO TURKEY

Turkey is so close that it looks like you could swim there from many of the Dodecanese and Northeastern Aegean islands. Here are the boat options:

Marmaris or Fethiye from Rhodes

Bodrum from Kos

Kuşadasi (near Ephesus) from Samos

Çeşme (near İzmir) from Chios

Dikili (near Ayvalık) from Lesvos

Kos Κως

POP 19,872

Bustling Kos, only 5km from the Turkish peninsula of Bodrum, is popular with history buffs as the birthplace of Hippocrates (460–377 BC), the father of medicine. The island also attracts an entirely different crowd – hordes of sun-worshipping beach lovers from northern Europe who pack the place in summer.

Sights & Activities

Busy Kos Town has lots of **bicycle paths** and renting a bike along the pretty waterfront is great for seeing the sights. Near the Castle of the Knights is **Hippocrates Plane Tree** (Plateia Platanou, Kos Town) FREE, under which the man himself is said to have taught his pupils. The modern town is built on the vast remains of the ancient Greek one – explore the ruins!

★Asklepeion ARCHAEOLOGICAL SITE
(☎22420 28763; adult/child €4/free; ⏱8am-7.30pm Tue-Sun) On a pretty pine and olivegrove-clad hill 4km southwest of Kos Town stand the extensive ruins of the renowned healing centre that taught the principles of Hippocrates' way. Doctors and healers come from all over the world to visit.

Castle of the Knights FORTRESS
(☎22420 27927; Kos Town; admission €4; ⏱8am-2.30pm Tue-Sun) Reach the once impregnable Castle of the Knights by crossing a bridge over Finikon from **Plateia Platanou**. The castle, which had massive outer walls and an inner keep, was built in the 14th century and separated from the town by a moat (now Finikon). Damaged by an earthquake in 1495 and restored in the 16th century,

it was the knights' most stalwart defence against the encroaching Ottomans.

Ancient Agora RUIN
(Kos Town) FREE The ancient agora, with the ruins of the **Shrine of Aphrodite** and **Temple of Hercules**, is an open site south of the Castle of the Knights. A massive 3rd-century-BC stoa, with some reconstructed columns, stands on its western side.

Sleeping

Hotel Afendoulis HOTEL €
(☎22420 25321; www.afendoulishotel.com; Evripilou 1, Kos Town; s/d €30/50; ⊙Mar-Nov; ❄@📶) Peaceful Afendoulis has unfailingly friendly staff and sparkling rooms with white walls, small balconies, flat-screen TVs, hairdryers and spotless bathrooms. Downstairs there's an open breakfast room and flowery terrace with wrought-iron tables and chairs for enjoying the feast of homemade jams and marmalades.

★**Hotel Sonia** HOTEL €€
(☎22420 28798; www.hotelsonia.gr; Irodotou 9, Kos Town; s/d/tr €45/60/75; ⊙year-round; ❄📶) On a peaceful street, this pension has sparkling rooms with parquet floors, flat-screen TVs, fridges, chic bathrooms and an extra bed if you need it. There's a relaxing communal verandah with wrought-iron chairs, spacious private balconies and a decent library. Room 4 has the best sea view.

Eating & Drinking

Restaurants line the central waterfront of the old harbour in Kos Town, but backstreets harbour better value. Nightclubs dot Diakon and Nafklirou, just north of the *agora*.

H2O INTERNATIONAL €
(☎22420 47200; www.kosaktis.gr; Vasileos Georgiou 7, Kos Town; mains €10-20; ⊙11am-midnight; ❄📶🖉) The city's glitziest waterfront eatery at Kos Aktis Art Hotel is patronised by fashionistas and makes for a great stop for a healthy lunch or dinner, out on the decked terrace facing Bodrum. Choose from bruschetta, grilled veg, battered shrimp and chicken risotto, or simply plump for a sundowner mojito.

> **ISLAND SHORTCUTS**
>
> If long ferry rides eat into your holiday too much, check Aegean Airlines, Olympic Air, Astra Airlines and Sky Express (see p558) for flights. But beware baggage limits: Sky Express in particular only allows teeny bags.

Arap TURKISH €
(☎22420 28442; Platani Sq, Kos Town; mains €7-15; ⊙noon-midnight) Located in the Turkish quarter, called Platani, on the way towards the Asklepeion, this casual grill-house is tops for heaping portions of tender kebabs and delicious dips with fresh pitta. It's a bit of a dreary 2.5km walk from the centre; bike it or catch a cab.

Information

Visit www.kos.gr, www.kosinfo.gr or www.travel-to-kos.com for information.

Getting There & Around

AIR

Daily flights to Athens serve **Ippokratis Airport** (KGS; ☎22420 51229), as do flights to Rhodes and Kalymnos, and international flights and charters in summer. The airport is 28km south-west of Kos Town; buses cost €4, taxis €30.

BICYCLE

Hire bikes at the harbour to get around town.

BOAT

Kos has services to Piraeus and all islands in the Dodecanese, the Cyclades, Samos and Thessaloniki run by: **Blue Star Ferries** (☎22420 28914; Kos Town), **Anek Lines** (☎22420 28545) and **ANE Kalymnou** (☎22420 29900). Catamarans are run by Dodekanisos Seaways at the interisland ferry quay. Local passenger and car ferries run to Pothia on Kalymnos from Mastihari. For tickets, visit **Fanos Travel & Shipping** (☎22420 20035; www.kostravel.gr; 11 Akti Kountourioti, Kos Town) on the harbour.

To Turkey

In summer excursion boats depart daily for Bodrum in Turkey (€20 return, one hour).

BUS

There is a good public bus system on Kos, with the bus station on Kleopatras, near the ruins at the back of town.

NORTHEASTERN AEGEAN ISLANDS

ΤΑ ΝΗΣΙΑ ΤΟΥ ΒΟΡΕΙΟ ΑΝΑΤΟΛΙΚΟ ΑΙΓΑΙΟΥ

One of Greece's best-kept secrets, these far-flung islands are strewn across the northeastern corner of the Aegean, closer to Turkey than mainland Greece. They harbour unspoilt scenery, welcoming locals, fascinating independent cultures, and remain relatively calm even when other Greek islands are sagging with tourists at the height of summer.

Samos Σαμος

POP 32,820

A lush mountainous island only 3km from Turkey, Samos has a glorious history as the legendary birthplace of Hera, wife and sister of god-of-all-gods Zeus. Samos was an important centre of Hellenic culture, and the mathematician Pythagoras and storyteller Aesop are among its sons. The island has beaches that bake in summer, and a hinterland that is superb for hiking. Spring brings with it pink flamingos, wildflowers, and orchids that the island grows for export, while summer brings throngs of package tourists.

Vathy (Samos Town) Βαθύ Σάμος

POP 2030

Busy Vathy is an attractive working port town. Most of the action is along Themistokleous Sofouli, the main street that runs along the waterfront. The main square, Plateia Pythagorou, in the middle of the waterfront, is recognisable by its four palm trees and statue of a lion.

The first-rate **Archaeological Museum** (☎22730 27469; adult/child €3/free, Sun Nov-Mar free; ⏰8.30am-3.30pm Tue-Sun) is one of the best in the islands. **Cleomenis Hotel** (☎22730 23232; Kallistratous 33; d incl breakfast from €35) offers great, simple rooms close to the beach northeast of town. Elegant **Ino Village Hotel** (☎22730 23241; www.inovillagehotel.com; Kalami; d incl breakfast €70-145; P❄️📶🏊) in the hills north of the ferry quay has **Elea Restaurant** with terrace views over town and the harbour.

ITSA Travel (☎22730 23605; www.itsatravelsamos.gr; Themistokleous Sofouli; ⏰8am-8pm), opposite the quay, is helpful with travel inquiries, excursions, accommodation and luggage storage.

Pythagorio Πυθαγόρειο

POP 1300

Little Pythagorio, 11km south of Vathy, is where you'll disembark if you've come by boat from Patmos. It is a small, enticing town with a yacht-lined harbour and a busy, holiday atmosphere, overwhelming to some.

The 1034m-long **Evpalinos Tunnel** (☎22730 61400; Pythagorio; adult/child €4/free; ⏰8am-2pm Tue-Sun), built in the 6th century BC, was dug by political prisoners and used as an aqueduct to bring water from Mt Ampelos (1140m).

Ireon (adult/child €4/free; ⏰8.30am-3pm Tue-Sun), the legendary birthplace of the goddess Hera, is 8km west of Pythagorio. The temple at this Unesco World Heritage Site was enormous – four times the size of the Parthenon – though only one column remains.

Polyxeni Hotel (☎22730 61590; www.polyxenihotel.com; d €45-70; ❄️📶) is a fun place to stay in the heart of the waterfront action. Tavernas and bars line the waterfront.

The cordial **municipal tourist office** (☎22730 61389; deap5@otenet.gr; Lykourgou Logotheti; ⏰8am-9.30pm) is two blocks from the waterfront on the main street. The **bus stop** is two blocks further inland on the same street.

Around Samos

Samos is an island of forests, mountains, wildlife and over 30 villages, harboring excellent, cheap tavernas. The captivating villages of **Vourliotes** and **Manolates**, on the slopes of imposing **Mt Ampelos**, northwest of Vathy, are excellent walking territory and have many marked pathways.

Karlovasi, on the northwest coast, is another ferry port and interesting in its own right. Spend the night near the beach at immaculate, friendly **Hesperia Hotel Apartments** (☎22730 30706; www.hesperiahotel.gr; Karlovasi; studio/apt €50/65). The beaches south of Karlovasi, like **Potami Beach** are tops. Other choice beaches include **Tsamadou** on the north coast, **Votsalakia** in the southwest and **Psili Ammos** to the east of Pythagorio. The latter is sandy and stares straight out at Turkey, barely a couple of kilometres away. Beautiful **Bollos Beach** near Skoureika village is even more off the beaten path.

Getting There & Around

AIR

Daily flights connect Athens with Samos Airport (SMI), 4km west of Pythagorio. Several-weekly flights serve Iraklio, Rhodes, Chios and Thessaloniki. Charter flights wing in from Europe in summer.

Buses (€2) run nine times daily and taxis to Vathy/Pythagorio cost €25/6.

BOAT

Samos has two main ports: Vathy in the northeast (bigger ferries) and Pythagorio on the southeast coast (boats arriving from the south). Buses between the two take 25 minutes. Boats to Limnos, Chios and Lesvos also leave from Karlovasi. Double-check where your boat is leaving from.

A maritime hub, Samos offers daily ferries to Piraeus (€40, 12 hours), plus ferries heading north to Chios and west to the Cyclades. In summer high-speed services head south to Patmos and Kos.

To Turkey

There are daily ferries to Kuşadasi (for Ephesus) in Turkey (€35/45 one way/return, plus €10 port taxes). Day excursions are also available from April to October. Check with ITSA Travel (p549) for up-to-date details.

BUS

You can get to most of the island's villages and beaches by bus.

CAR & MOTORCYCLE

Rental cars and scooters are available all over (cars/scooters from €60/30 per day), and give you more freedom.

Lesvos (Mytilini) Λεσβος (Μυτιληνη)

POP 93,500

Lesvos, or Mytilini as it is often called, tends to do things in a big way. The third-largest of the Greek Islands after Crete and Evia, Lesvos produces half the world's ouzo and is home to over 11 million olive trees. Mountainous yet fertile, the island has world-class local cuisine, and presents excellent hiking and birdwatching opportunities, but remains refreshingly untouched in terms of tourism.

Mytilini Μυτιλήνη

POP 29,650

The capital and main port, Mytilini, is a lively student town with great eating and drinking options, plus eclectic churches and grand 19th-century mansions and museums. It is built between two harbours (north and south) with an imposing fortress on the promontory to the east. All ferries dock at the southern harbour, and most of the town's action is around this waterfront.

Sights

Check with the tourist office to see if **Teriade Museum** (☎22510 23372; www.museumteriade.gr; Varia), with its fine art collection has completed its renovations, which were ongoing at the time of research. Also ask for a complete list of the numerous local museums, including some dedicated to olive oil and ouzo.

Archaeological Museum MUSEUM
(Old Archaeological Museum; adult/child incl New Archaeological Museum €3/2; 8.30am-3pm Tue-Sun) One block north of the quay, this museum has impressive finds from neolithic to Roman times, including ceramic somersaulting female figurines and gold jewellery.

Fortress FORTRESS
(adult/child €2/free; 8.30am-2.30pm Tue-Sun) Mytilini's imposing early Byzantine fortress

SAPPHO, LESBIANS & LESVOS

Sappho, one of Greece's great ancient poets, was born on Lesvos during the 7th century BC. Most of her work was devoted to love and desire, and the objects of her affection were often female. Because of this, Sappho's name and birthplace have come to be associated with female homosexuality.

These days, Lesvos is visited by many lesbians paying homage to Sappho. The whole island is very gay-friendly, in particular the southwestern beach resort of **Skala Eresou**, which is built over ancient Eresos, where Sappho was born. The village is well set up to cater to lesbian needs and has a 'Women Together' festival held annually in September. See www.womensfestival.eu and www.sapphotravel.com for details.

was renovated in the 14th century by Genoese overlord Francisco Gatelouzo, and then the Turks enlarged it again. It's popular for a stroll and is flanked by pine forests.

Sleeping

★**Alkaios Rooms** PENSION €
(☎22510 47737, 69455 07089; www.alkaiosrooms.gr; Alkaiou 16 & 30; s/d/tr incl breakfast €35/45/55; ❄📶) This collection of 30 clean, well-kept rooms nestled discreetly in several renovated traditional buildings is Mytilini's most attractive budget option. It's a two-minute walk up from Paradosiaka Bougatsa Mytilinis on the waterfront.

Hotel Lesvion HOTEL €€
(☎22510 28177; www.lesvion.gr; Harbour; s/d/tr from €45/60/70; ❄📶) The well-positioned Lesvion, smack on the harbour, has friendly service and attractive modern rooms, some with excellent port-view balconies.

Theofilos Paradise Boutique Hotel BOUTIQUE HOTEL €€
(☎22510 43300; www.theofilosparadise.gr; Skra 7; s/d/q/ste incl breakfast from €70/95/135/120; P❄@📶≋) This smartly restored 100-year-old mansion is elegant, cheerful and good value, with modern amenities, along with a traditional *hammam* (Turkish bath). The 22 rooms are spread among three adjacent buildings surrounding a courtyard.

Eating & Drinking

Hit the streets in the bend in the harbour (Plateia Sapphou), around Ladadika, for zippy bars, cafes and creative eats.

★**To Steki tou Yianni** TAVERNA €
(☎22510 28244; Agiou Therapodos; mains €6-14; ⊙noon-3pm & 8pm-late) Head up behind the giant Agios Therapon church to this wonderful, welcoming taverna where Yianni dishes out whatever's freshest. All the produce is local, the cheeses delectable, and the fish or meat top quality. Go with the flow... this is a local hang-out, with folks arriving after 9pm. Sip a local ouzo and see what Yianni brings you.

Averoff Restaurant GREEK €
(☎22510 22180; Kountourioti, Harbour; mains €6-10; ⊙10am-10pm) No-frills eatery in the middle of the waterfront, specialising in generous *mayirefta* (ready-cooked) plates, such as chicken and potatoes, stuffed tomatoes and *briam* (oven-baked vegetable casserole).

Information

See www.lesvos.net and www.greeknet.com for information.

Tourist Office (EOT; ☎22510 42512; Aristarhou 6; ⊙9am-1pm Mon-Fri) Near the quay; offers brochures and maps.

Zoumboulis Tours (☎22510 37755; Kountourioti 69; ⊙8am-8pm) Sells ferry and plane tickets, runs boat trips to Turkey and rents rooms.

Molyvos (Mithymna) Μόλυβος (Μήθυμνα)

POP 1500

The gracious, historic town of Mithymna (known by locals as Molyvos), 62km north of Mytilini Town, winds beautifully from the picturesque **old harbour**, up through cobbled streets canopied by flowering vines to the impressive **Byzantine-Genoese Castle** (admission €2; ⊙8am-3pm Tue-Sun) on the hilltop, from which you get tremendous views out to Turkey and around the lush valleys. Ravishing to the eye, Molyvos is well worth a wander, or is a peaceful place to stay.

Eftalou hot springs (☎22530 72200; Eftalou; old common/new private bathhouse €4/5; ⊙old bathhouse 6am-9pm), 4km from town on the beach, is a superb bathhouse complex with steaming, pebbled pools. The scenery on the northern coast is extraordinary, as are its tiny villages.

Airy, friendly **Nassos Guest House** (☎22530 71432; www.nassosguesthouse.com; Arionis; d/tr without bathroom €20/35; 📶) offers shared facilities and a communal kitchen in an old Turkish house with rapturous views. **Molyvos Queen** (☎22530 71452; www.molyvos-queen.gr; apt from €60; ❄📶) has full apartments with sea or castle views.

From the bus stop, walk towards town 100m to the helpful **municipal tourist office** (☎22530 71347; www.visitmolivos.com; ⊙hours vary).

Buses to Mithymna (€6.90) take 1¾ hours from Mytilini; a rental car is a better option with so much to explore.

Around the Island

Hire a car and tour the incredible countryside. Southern Lesvos is dominated by **Mt Olympus** (968m), and grove-covered valleys. Visit wonderful mountain village **Agiasos**, with its artisan workshops making everything from handcrafted furniture to pottery. **Plomari** in the far south is the land of ouzo distilleries; tour fascinating **Varvagianni Ouzo** (☎22520 32741; ⏱9am-4pm Mon-Fri, by appointment Sat & Sun) FREE.

Western Lesvos is known for its **petrified forest** (www.petrifiedforest.gr; admission €2; ⏱9am-5pm Jul-Sep, Fri-Sun Oct-Jun), with petrified wood at least 500,000 years old, and for the gay-friendly town of **Skala Eresou**, the birthplace of Sappho (see p550). You can stay over in peaceful **Sigri**, with its broad beaches to the southwest.

Getting There & Around

AIR

Written up on flight schedules as Mytilene, Lesvos' Odysseas Airport (MJT) has daily connections with Athens and Thessaloniki. **Sky Express** (☎28102 23500; www.skyexpress.gr) flies to Iraklio, Limnos, Chios, Samos, Rhodes and Ikaria (but beware its strict baggage policy). The airport is 8km south of Mytilini town; taxis cost €10, bus €1.60.

BOAT

In summer daily fast boats leave Mytilini Town for Piraeus (€41, 11 to 13 hours) via Chios. Other ferries serve Chios, Ikaria Limnos, Thessaloniki and Samos. Check www.openseas.gr.

To Turkey

There are regular ferries each week to Dikili port (which serves Ayvalık) and to Fokias (which serves İzmir). Stop by Zoumboulis Tours (p551) for ticketing and schedules.

BUS

The long-distance bus station in Mytilini Town is beside Agia Irinis Park, near the domed church. The local bus station is opposite Plateia Sapphou, the main square.

CAR

It's worth renting a car in Lesvos to explore the vast island. There are several outlets at the airport and many in town.

SPORADES ΣΠΟΡΑΔΕΣ

Scattered to the southeast of the Pelion Peninsula, to which they were joined in prehistoric times, the 11 islands that make up the Sporades group have similarly mountainous terrain and dense vegetation, and are surrounded by scintillatingly clear seas.

The main ports for the Sporades are Volos and Agios Konstantinos on the mainland.

Skiathos Σκιαθος

POP 6150

Lush and green, Skiathos has a beach resort feel about it. Charter flights bring loads of package tourists, but the island still oozes enjoyment and is downright mellow in winter. Skiathos Town, with its quaint **old harbour**, and some excellent beaches are on the hospitable south coast.

Sights & Activities

Moni Evangelistrias (Monastery of the Annunciation; museum admission €2; ⏱10am-dusk), the most famous of the island's monasteries was a hilltop refuge for freedom fighters during the War of Independence, and the Greek flag was first raised here, in 1807.

Skiathos has superb beaches, particularly on the south coast. **Koukounaries** is popular with families, and has a wonderful protected **marshland** for water fowl. A stroll over the headland, **Big Banana Beach** is stunning, but if you want an all-over tan, head a tad further to **Little Banana Beach**, where bathing suits are a rarity. Beautiful **Lalaria** on the north coast is accessible only by boat.

At the Old Port in Skiathos Town, **boat excursions** go to nearby beaches (€10), around Skiathos Island (€25) and on full-day trips to Skopelos, Alonnisos and the Alonissos Marine Park (€35).

Sleeping

Hotel Mato HOTEL €
(☎24270 22186; www.matoskiathos.gr; 25th Martiou 30; d incl breakfast €60; ❄📶) Cosy Hotel Mato is in the centre of the picturesque pedestrianised old town, and remains open all year. Friendly proprietor Popi keeps the place spick and span and cooks fab breakfasts with farm-fresh eggs.

Hotel Bourtzi BOUTIQUE HOTEL €€€
(☎24270 21304; www.hotelbourtzi.gr; Moraitou 8; d incl breakfast from €174; P❄📶🏊) On upper Papadiamanti, the swank Bourtzi escapes much of the town noise and features high-design rooms and an inviting garden and pool. Minimum seven-night stay in summer.

Eating & Drinking

Seafood joints line Skiathos' Old Harbour, cafes and bars wrap around the whole waterfront.

MOVIES UNDER THE STARS

Summertime in Greece means open-air cinema. Athens has **Aigli Cinema** (☎210 336 9369; www.aeglizappiou.gr; Zappeio Gardens, Syntagma; Ⓜ Syntagma) and **Cine Paris** (☎210 322 0721; www.cineparis.gr; Kydathineon 22, Plaka; Ⓜ Syntagma), among others, and Skiathos boasts **Cinema Attikon** (☎69727 06305, 24720 22352; tickets €7). Catch current English-language movies under the stars, sip a beer and practise speed-reading Greek subtitles. Many other islands have similar cinemas – ask around.

Taverna-Ouzerie Kabourelia TAVERNA €
(Old Harbour; mains €4-9; ⏲noon-midnight; 📶) Poke your nose into the open kitchen to glimpse the day's catch at this popular year-round eatery at the old port, with perfect fish grills at moderate prices. Grilled octopus and *taramasalata* are just two of several standout mezedhes.

O Batis TAVERNA €
(☎24270 22288; Old Harbour; mains €4-9; ⏲noon-midnight) This popular fish taverna on the path above the old port is a local standby for reliable and well-priced fresh fish, *gavros* (marinated small fish), and fine mezedhes. Cosy atmosphere and a good selection of island wines, year-round.

Information

See www.skiathosinfo.com for information.

Getting There & Around

AIR

Skiathos Airport (JSI) is 2km northeast of Skiathos Town, and has summertime daily flights to Athens and charter flights from northern Europe. Taxis cost €6 to €15 depending on where you're headed.

BOAT

Frequent daily hydrofoils serve mainland ports Volos (€38, 1¼ hours) and Agios Konstantinos (€37, two hours), as do cheaper ferries. Hydrofoils/ferries serve Skopelos (€10/6, 20/40 minutes) and Alonnisos (€17/11, 1½/2½ hours). See **Hellenic Seaways** (☎24270 22209; www.hsw.gr) or **NEL Lines** (☎24270 22018; www.nel.gr).

Water taxis around Skiathos depart from the Old Harbour.

BUS

Crowded buses ply the south-coast road between Skiathos Town and Koukounaries (€2) every 30 minutes between 7.30am and 11pm year-round, stopping at all the beaches along the way. The bus stop is at the eastern end of the harbour.

IONIAN ISLANDS

ΤΑ ΕΠΤΑΝΗΣΑ

The idyllic cypress- and fir-covered Ionian Islands stretch down the western coast of Greece from Corfu in the north to Kythira, off the southern tip of the Peloponnese. Mountainous, with dramatic cliff-backed beaches, soft light and turquoise water, they're more Italian in feel, offering a contrasting experience to other Greek islands.

Corfu Κερκυρα

POP 101,080

Many consider Corfu, or Kerkyra (*ker*-kih-rah) in Greek, to be Greece's most beautiful island – the unfortunate consequence of which is that it's overbuilt and often overrun with crowds. Look beyond them to find its core splendour.

Corfu Town Κέρκυρα

POP 31,359

Built on a promontory and wedged between two fortresses, Corfu's **Old Town** is a tangle of narrow walking streets through gorgeous Venetian buildings. Explore the winding alleys and surprising plazas in the early morning or late afternoon to avoid the hordes of day trippers seeking souvenirs.

Sights

★**Palaio Frourio** FORTRESS
(Old Fortress; ☎26610 48310; adult/concession €4/2; ⏲8am-8pm Apr-Oct, 8.30am-3pm Nov-Mar) Constructed by the Venetians in the 15th century on the remains of a Byzantine castle and further altered by the British, this spectacular landmark offers respite from the crowds and superb views of the region. Climb to the summit of the inner outcrop, which is crowned by a lighthouse for a 360-degree panorama. The gatehouse contains a Byzantine **museum**.

WORTH A TRIP

IONIAN PLEASURES

Paxi (Πάξοι) Paxi lives up to its reputation as one of the Ionians' most idyllic and picturesque islands. At only 10km by 4km it's the smallest of the main holiday islands and makes a fine escape from Corfu's quicker-paced pleasures.

Kefallonia (Κεφαλλονιά) Tranquil cypress- and fir-covered Kefallonia, the largest Ionian island, is breathtakingly beautiful with rugged mountain ranges, rich vineyards, soaring coastal cliffs and golden beaches. It has not succumbed to package tourism to the extent that some of the other Ionian Islands have and remains low-key outside resort areas.

Ithaki (Ιθάκη) Odysseus' long-lost home in Homer's *Odyssey*, Ithaki (ancient Ithaca) remains a verdant, pristine island blessed with cypress-covered hills and beautiful turquoise coves. It's best reached from Kefallonia.

Lefkada (Λευκάδα) Lefkada has some of the best beaches in Greece, if not the world, and an easygoing way of life.

★Palace of St Michael & St George PALACE

Originally the residence of a succession of British high commissioners, this palace now houses the world-class **Museum of Asian Art** (☎26610 30443; www.matk.gr; adult/child incl audioguide €3/free, with Antivouniotissa Museum & Old Fortress €8; ⏲8.30am-3.30pm Tue-Sun), founded in 1929. Expertly curated with extensive, informative English-language placards, the collection's approximately 10,000 artefacts collected from all over Asia include priceless prehistoric bronzes, ceramics, jade figurines, coins and works of art in onyx, ivory and enamel. Additionally, the palace's **throne room** and **rotunda** are impressively adorned in period furnishings and art.

★Church of Agios Spyridon CHURCH

(Agios Spyridonos; ⏲7am-8pm) FREE The sacred relic of Corfu's beloved patron saint, St Spyridon, lies in an elaborate silver casket in the 16th-century basilica.

Antivouniotissa Museum MUSEUM

(☎26610 38313; www.antivouniotissamuseum.gr; off Arseniou; adult/child €2/1; ⏲9am-3.30pm Tue-Sun) The exquisite timber-roofed 15th-century **Church of Our Lady of Antivouniotissa** holds an outstanding collection of Byzantine and post-Byzantine icons and artefacts dating from the 13th to the 17th centuries.

Mon Repos Estate PARK

(Kanoni Peninsula; ⏲8am-7pm May-Oct, to 5pm Nov-Apr) FREE On the southern outskirts of town on the Kanoni Peninsula, an extensive wooded parkland estate surrounds an elegant neoclassical villa housing the **Museum of Palaeopolis** (☎26610 41369; www.corfu.gr; adult/concession €3/2; ⏲8am-7pm Tue-Sun May-Oct), with entertaining archaeological displays and exhibits on the history of Corfu Town. Paths lead through lush grounds to the ruins of two Doric temples; the first is truly a ruin, but the southerly **Temple of Artemis** is serenely impressive.

Sleeping

Accommodation prices fluctuate wildly depending on season; book ahead.

★Siorra Vittoria BOUTIQUE HOTEL €€

(☎26610 36300; www.siorravittoria.com; Stefanou Padova 36; s/d incl breakfast from €95/135, ste €165-190; P❄📶) Expect luxury and style at this quiet, 19th-century mansion where painstakingly restored traditional architecture and modern amenities meet. Marble bathrooms, crisp linens and genteel service make for a relaxed stay. Breakfast in the peaceful garden beneath an ancient magnolia tree. The Vittoria suite encompasses the atelier and has views to the sea.

★Bella Venezia BOUTIQUE HOTEL €€

(☎26610 46500; www.bellaveneziahotel.com; N Zambeli 4; s/d incl breakfast from €100/120; 🚭❄📶) In a neoclassical former girls' school, the Venezia has comfy rooms and an elegant ambience. Conscientious staff welcome you, and the gazebo breakfast room in the garden is delightful.

Hermes Hotel HOTEL €€

(☎26610 39268; www.hermes-hotel.gr; Markora 12; s/d/tr from €50/70/90; ❄📶) In a busy part of the new town, overlooking the market, Hermes offers simple, tidy rooms with double glazing, which are especially atmospheric in the old wing.

Eating & Drinking

Corfu has excellent restaurants. Cafes and bars line the arcaded Liston. Try Corfu Beer.

★ To Tavernaki tis Marinas TAVERNA €
(☎69816 56001; 4th Parados, Agias Sofias 1; mains €6-16; ⊙noon-midnight) Restored stone walls, smooth hardwood floors and cheerful staff lift the ambience of this taverna a cut above the rest. Check daily specials or choose anything from *mousakas* (baked layers of eggplant or zucchini, minced meat and potatoes topped with cheese sauce) or grilled sardines to steak. Accompany it all with a dram of ouzo or *tsipouro* (a spirit similar to ouzo).

Chrisomalis TAVERNA €
(☎26610 30342; N Theotoki 6; mains €8-13; ⊙noon-midnight) Smack in the heart of the old town, this ma-and-pa operation dishes out the classics. Cruise inside to choose from what's fresh.

★ La Cucina ITALIAN €€
(☎26610 45029; Guilford 17; mains €13-25; ⊙7-11pm) A long-established favourite, well-run La Cucina shines for its creative cuisine, with hand-rolled pasta dishes at the fore.

The original Guilford location is cosy warm tones and murals, while the **Moustoxidou** (☎26610 45799; cnr Guilford & Moustoxidou; ⊙7-11pm) annexe (with identical menu) is chic in glass and grey.

To Dimarchio ITALIAN, GREEK €€
(☎26610 39031; Plateia Dimarchio; mains €9-25; ⊙noon-midnight) Relax in a luxuriant rose garden on a charming square. Attentive staff serve elegant, inventive dishes, both Italian and Greek, prepared with the freshest ingredients.

Information

Tourist Police (☎26610 30265; 3rd fl, Samartzi 4) Off Plateia San Rocco.

Around the Island

To explore the island fully your own transport is best. Much of the coast just north of Corfu Town is overwhelmed with beach resorts, the south is quieter, and the west has a beautiful, if popular, coastline. The **Corfu Trail** (www.thecorfutrail.com) traverses the island north to south.

North of Corfu Town, in **Kassiopi**, **Manessis Apartments** (☎26610 34990; www.manessiskassiopi.com; Kassiopi; 4-person apt €70-100; ❄📶) offers water-view apartments.

South of Corfu Town, **Achillion Palace** (☎26610 56210; www.achillion-corfu.gr; Gastouri; adult/child €7/2, audio guide €3; ⊙8am-8pm Apr-Oct, 8.45am-4pm Nov-Mar) pulls 'em in for over-the-top royal bling. Don't miss a dinner at one of the island's best tavernas, **Klimataria** (Bellos; ☎26610 71201; mains €8-14; ⊙7pm-midnight) in nearby **Benitses**.

To gain an aerial view of the gorgeous cypress-backed bays around **Paleokastritsa**, the west coast's main resort, go to the quiet village of **Lakones**. Backpackers head to **Pelekas Beach** for low-key **Sunrock** (☎26610 94637; www.sunrockhostel.com; Pelekas Beach; dm/r per person incl breakfast & dinner €18/25; @📶), a full-board hostel. Further south, good beaches surround tiny **Agios Gordios**, which has the famous **Pink Palace** (☎26610 53103; www.thepinkpalace.com; Agios Gordios Beach; dm & r per person incl breakfast & dinner €21-50; ❄@) backpackers and is party central.

Getting There & Around

AIR

Ioannis Kapodistrias Airport (CFU; ☎26610 89600; www.corfu-airport.com) is 2km southwest of Corfu Town. **Olympic Air** (☎801 801 0101; www.olympicair.com), **Aegean Airlines** (☎26610 27100; www.aegeanair.com) and Astra Airlines (p558) fly daily to Athens and a few times weekly to Thessaloniki. **Sky Express** (☎2810 223500; www.skyexpress.gr) operates seasonal routes to other Ionian Islands and Crete (but beware its strict baggage policy). Charter planes and budget airlines fly internationally in summer. Bus 19 serves the airport (€1.50); taxis cost €7 to €10.

BOAT

Neo Limani port lies west of the Neo Frourio (New Fortress). Ferries go to Igoumenitsa (€10, 1½ hours, hourly). In summer daily ferries and hydrofoils go to Paxi, and ferries to Italy (Bari, Brindisi and Venice) also stop in Patra (€35, six hours); some stop in Kefallonia and Zakynthos. **Petrakis Lines** (Ionian Cruises; ☎26610 31649; Ethnikis Antistaseos 4, Corfu Town) goes to Saranda, Albania. Check www.openseas.gr.

BUS

Blue buses (€1.10 to €1.50) for villages near Corfu Town leave from Plateia San Rocco. Services to other destinations (around Corfu

€1.60 to €4.40) and daily buses to Athens (€45, 8½ hours) and Thessaloniki (€35, eight hours) leave from Corfu's **long-distance bus station** (☎26610 28927; www.ktelkerkyras.gr; Ioannou Theotoki, Corfu Town).

SURVIVAL GUIDE

Directory A–Z

ACCOMMODATION

Accommodation Types

Hotels Range from basic business lodging to high-end boutique extravaganzas.

Pensions and guesthouses Often include breakfast and are usually owner-operated.

Domatia Rooms for rent; owners greet ferries and buses shouting 'room!'.

Youth hostels In most major towns and on some islands.

Campgrounds Generally open April to October; standard facilities include hot showers, kitchens, restaurants and minimarkets, and often a swimming pool. Check out **Panhellenic Camping Association** (☎21036 21560; www.greececamping.gr). Wild camping is forbidden.

Mountain refuges Listed in *Greece Mountain Refuges & Ski Centres*, available free from EOT and EOS (Ellinikos Orivatikos Syndesmos, Greek Alpine Club) offices.

BUSINESS HOURS

Banks 8am to 2.30pm Monday to Thursday, 8am to 2pm Friday

Bars 8pm to late

Cafes 10am to midnight

Clubs 10pm to 4am

Post offices Rural areas 7.30am to 2pm Monday to Friday; urban offices 7.30am to 8pm Monday to Friday, 7.30am to 2pm Saturday

Restaurants 11am to 3pm and 7pm to 1am

Shops 8am to 3pm Monday, Wednesday and Saturday; 8am to 2.30pm and 5pm to 8.30pm Tuesday, Thursday and Friday (all day in summer in resorts). Sunday permitted in major tourist areas and central Athens.

CUSTOMS REGULATIONS

It is strictly forbidden to export antiquities (anything over 100 years old) without an export permit.

INTERNET ACCESS

Wi-fi is common at most sleeping and eating venues, ports, airports and some city squares.

ESSENTIAL FOOD & DRINK

Nutritious and flavourful, the food is one of the great pleasures of travelling in Greece. The country's rich culinary heritage draws from a fusion of mountain village food, island cuisine, flavours introduced by Greeks from Asia Minor, and influences from various invaders and historical trading partners. The essence of classic Greek cuisine lies in fresh, seasonal home-grown produce and generally simple, unfussy cooking that brings out the rich flavours of the Mediterranean.

➡ **Savoury appetisers** Known as mezedhes (literally, 'tastes'; meze for short), standards include tzatziki (yoghurt, cucumber and garlic), *melitzanosalata* (aubergine dip), *taramasalata* (fish-roe dip), dolmadhes (stuffed vine leaves; dolmas for short), *fasolia* (beans) and *oktapodi* (octopus).

➡ **Cheap eats** *Gyros* is pork or chicken shaved from a revolving stack of sizzling meat and wrapped in pitta bread with tomato, onion, fried potatoes and lashings of tzatziki. Souvlaki is skewered meat, usually pork.

➡ **Taverna staples** You'll find *mousaka* (layers of aubergine and mince, topped with béchamel sauce and baked) on every menu, alongside *moschari* (oven-baked veal and potatoes), *keftedhes* (meatballs), *stifado* (meat stew), *pastitsio* (baked dish of macaroni with minced meat and béchamel sauce) and *yemista* (either tomatoes or green peppers stuffed with minced meat and rice).

➡ **Sweets** Greeks are serious about their sweets, with *zaharoplasteia* (sweet shops) in even the smallest villages. Try variations on baklava (thin layers of pastry filled with honey and nuts). Or go simple: delicious Greek yogurt drizzled with honey.

➡ **Top tipples** Legendary aniseed-flavoured ouzo sipped slowly, turns a cloudy white when ice or water is added. *Raki*, the Cretan fire water, is produced from grape skins. Greek coffee, a legacy of Ottoman rule, is a favourite pastime.

COUNTRY FACTS

Area 131,944 sq km

Capital Athens

Country Code ☎30

Currency Euro (€)

Emergency ☎112

Language Greek

Money Cash is king, ATMs are common except in small villages, and credit cards only sporadically accepted.

Population 10.7 million

Visas Generally not required for stays up to 90 days. Member of Schengen Convention.

INTERNET RESOURCES

Ancient Greece (www.ancientgreece.com)
Greek Ferries (www.openseas.gr, www.greekferries.gr)
Greek National Tourist Organisation (www.gnto.gr, visitgreece.gr, www.discovergreece.com)
Greek Travel Pages (www.gtp.gr)
Virtual Greece (www.greecevirtual.gr)

MONEY

- ATMs are everywhere except small villages.
- Cash is widely used and your best bet, especially in the countryside; credit cards are not always accepted in small villages.
- Service charge is included on the bill in restaurants, but it is the custom to 'round up the bill'; same for taxis.

POST

- Tahydromia (post offices; www.elta.gr) are easily identified by their yellow sign.
- Postcards and airmail letters within the EU cost€0.60, to other destinations €0.80.

PUBLIC HOLIDAYS

New Year's Day 1 January
Epiphany 6 January
First Sunday in Lent February
Greek Independence Day 25 March
Orthodox Good Friday March/April (varies)
Orthodox Easter Sunday 12 April 2015, 1 May 2016, 16 April 2017, 8 April 2018, 28 April 2019
May Day (Protomagia) 1 May
Whit Monday (Agiou Pnevmatos) 50 days after Easter Sunday
Feast of the Assumption 15 August
Ohi Day 28 October
Christmas Day 25 December
St Stephen's Day 26 December

TELEPHONE

- Organismos Tilepikoinonion Ellados, known as OTE (o-teh), public phones abound. Phonecards are sold at OTE shops and newspaper kiosks; pressing the 'i' button brings up instructions in English.
- Mobile coverage is widespread. Visitors with GSM 900/1800 phones can make roaming calls; purchase a local SIM card, which requires a passport to register, if you're staying awhile and have an unlocked mobile.
- For directory inquiries within Greece, call ☎131; for international inquiries ☎161. Area codes are part of the 10-digit number within Greece.

TIME

Greece is in the Eastern European time zone: two hours ahead of GMT/UTC and three hours ahead on daylight-saving time (last Sunday in March through to last Sunday in October).

Getting There & Away

Regular ferry connections shuttle between Greece and the Italian ports of Ancona, Bari, Brindisi and Venice. Similarly, ferries operate between the Greek islands of Rhodes, Kos, Samos, Chios and Lesvos and the Aegean coast of Turkey.

Overland, it's possible to reach Albania, Bulgaria, the Former Yugoslav Republic of Macedonia (FYROM), Romania and Turkey from Greece. If you've got your own wheels, you can drive through border crossings with these four countries. There are train and bus connections with Greece's neighbours, but check ahead, as these have been affected by the financial crisis.

See www.seat61.com for more information on ferry travel.

SLEEPING PRICE RANGES

Accommodation is nearly always negotiable (and deeply reduced) outside peak season, especially for longer stays. Prices quoted in listings are for high season (July and August) with a private bathroom.

€ less than €60 (€80 in Athens)

€€ €60 to €150 (€80 to €150 in Athens)

€€€ more than €150

EATING PRICE RANGES

Price ranges are based on the average cost of a main dish:

€ less than €10

€€ €10 to €20

€€€ more than €20

AIR

Most visitors arrive by air, mostly into Athens. There are 17 international airports in Greece; most handle only summer charter flights to the islands.

There's a growing number of direct scheduled services into Greece by European budget airlines – **Olympic Air** (www. olympicair.com) and **Aegean Airlines** (www.aegeanair.com) also fly internationally.

LAND

Border Crossings

You can drive or ride through the following border crossings.

Albania Kakavia (60km northwest of Ioannina); Sagiada (28km north of Igoumenitsa); Mertziani (17km west of Konitsa); Krystallopigi (14km west of Kotas)

Bulgaria Promahonas (109km northeast of Thessaloniki); Ormenio (41km from Serres); Exohi (50km north of Drama)

Former Yugoslav Republic of Macedonia (FYROM) Evzoni (68km north of Thessaloniki); Niki (16km north of Florina); Doïrani (31km north of Kilkis)

Turkey Kipi (43km east of Alexandroupolis); Kastanies (139km northeast of Alexandroupolis)

Bus

Private companies and KTEL Macedonia run buses from Thessaloniki to İstanbul, Skopje and Sofia; see p530.

Albania is served by **Albatrans** (☎+355 42 259 204; www.albatrans.com.al) and **Euro Interlines** (☎+355 42251866, 210 523 4594; www.eurointerlines.com).

Bus and tour companies run buses between Greece and Sofia, Bulgaria; Budapest, Hungary; Prague, Czech Republic; and Turkey. See Simeonidis Tours (p530), **Dimidis Tours** (www. dimidistours.gr) and **Tourist Service** (www. tourist-service.com).

Train

Both international and domestic **train routes** (www.trainose.gr) have been severely curtailed due to financial problems. Check the current situation well in advance. Trains go from Thessaloniki to Bulgaria (Sofia) and FYROM (Skopje).

SEA

Check ferry routes and schedules at www.greek ferries.gr and www.openseas.gr.

If you are travelling on a rail pass, check to see if ferry travel between Italy and Greece is included. Some ferries are free, others give a discount. On some routes you will need to make reservations.

Albania

For Saranda, **Petrakis Lines** (☎26610 38690; www.ionian-cruises.com) has daily hydrofoils to Corfu (25 minutes).

Italy

Routes vary, check online.

Ancona Patra (20 hours, three daily, summer)

Bari Patra (14½ hours, daily) via Corfu (eight hours) and Kefallonia (14 hours); also to Igoumenitsa (11½ hours, daily). Some go via Zakynthos.

Brindisi Patra (15 hours, April to early October) via Igoumenitsa

Venice Patra (30 hours, up to 12 weekly, summer) via Corfu (25 hours)

Turkey

Boat services operate between Turkey's Aegean coast and the Greek Islands; see p547.

Getting Around

Greece has a comprehensive transport system and is easy to get around.

AIR

It's sometimes cheaper to fly than take the ferry, especially if you book ahead online. Domestic airlines include the following.

Aegean Airlines (☎801 112 0000; www. aegeanair.com)

Astra Airlines (☎2310 489 392; www.astra-airlines.gr) Airline based in Thessaloniki.

Hellenic Seaplanes (☎210 647 0180; www. hellenic-seaplanes.com) Charters with planned routes to the islands.

Olympic Air (☎801 801 0101; www.olympicair. com) Partly merged with Aegean.

Sky Express (☎2810 223500; www.sky express.gr) Cretan airline with flights around Greece. Beware harsh baggage restrictions.

BICYCLE

- Greece has very hilly terrain and the summer heat can be stifling. In addition, most drivers totally disregard road rules. Bicycles are carried for free on ferries.
- See www.cyclegreece.gr for bicycle tour ideas.

➡ Rental bicycles are available at most tourist centres, but are generally for pedalling around town rather than for serious riding. Prices range from €10 to €20 per day.

BOAT

For many, the idea of meandering from island to island by boat is the ultimate Greek Island dream. Beware that in high season you might find it just as stressful as rush hour back home.

Ferries come in all shapes and sizes, from state-of-the-art 'superferries' that run on the major routes, to ageing open ferries that operate local services to outlying islands. Newer high-speed ferries slash travel times, but cost more; they are often catamarans or hydrofoils.

You may have the option of 'deck class', which is the cheapest ticket, or 'cabin class' with air-con assigned seats. On larger ferries there are lounges and restaurants for everyone serving fast food or snacks.

Boat operations are highly seasonal and based on the tourist trade. Services pick up from April, and slow down by November. In winter they are reduced or cut entirely. Weather (especially wind) can result in last-minute cancellations, even in summer. If you are prone to seasickness, book seats in the centre rear of the boat, or with a window.

Be flexible. Boats seldom arrive early, but often arrive late! And some don't come at all.

Tickets can be bought at the dock, but in high season, boats are often full – plan ahead. Check www.openseas.gr or www.gtp.gr for schedules, costs and links to individual boat company websites.

The Greek Ships app for smartphones tracks ferries in real time.

BUS

Long-distance buses are operated by **KTEL** (www.ktel.org). Fares are fixed by the government and service routes can be found on the company's website or regional websites (listed in our coverage). Buses are comfortable, generally run on time, are reasonably priced and offer frequent services on major routes. Buy tickets at least an hour in advance. Buses don't have toilets

Main Ferry Routes

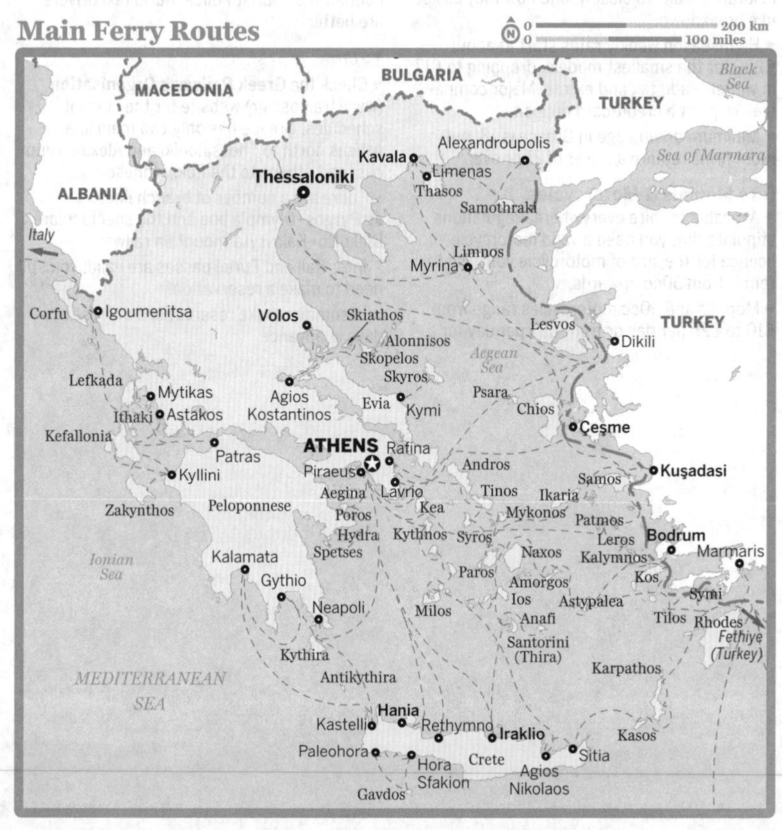

or refreshments, but stop for a break every couple of hours.

CAR & MOTORCYCLE

- A great way to explore areas in Greece that are off the beaten track, but be careful on highways – Greece has the highest road-fatality rate in Europe. The road network is decent, but freeway tolls are fairly hefty.
- Almost all islands are served by car ferries, but they are expensive; costs vary by the size of the vehicle.
- The Greek automobile club, **ELPA** (www.elpa.gr), generally offers reciprocal services to members of other national motoring associations. If your vehicle breaks down, dial ☎104.
- EU-registered vehicles are allowed free entry into Greece for six months without road taxes being due; a green card (international third-party insurance) is all that's required.

Hire Cars

- Available throughout Greece, you'll get better rates with local rental-car companies than with the big multinational outfits. Check insurance waivers closely, and how they assist in a breakdown.
- High-season weekly rates start at about €280 for the smallest models, dropping to €175 in winter – add tax and extras. Major companies request a credit-card deposit.
- Minimum driving age in Greece is 18, but most firms require a driver of 21 or over.

Hire Mopeds & Motorcycles

- Available for hire everywhere. Regulations stipulate that you need a valid motorcycle licence for the size of motorcycle you wish to rent – from 50cc upwards.
- Mopeds and 50cc motorcycles range from €10 to €25 per day or from €25 per day for a 250cc motorcycle. Outside high season, rates drop considerably.

Road Rules

- Drive on the right.
- Overtake on the left (not all Greeks do this!).
- Compulsory to wear seatbelts in the front seats, and in the back if they are fitted.
- Drink-driving laws are strict; a blood alcohol content of 0.05% incurs a fine of around €150 and over 0.08% is a criminal offence.

PUBLIC TRANSPORT

All major towns have a local bus system. Athens is the only city with a metro system.

TAXI

- Taxis are widely available and reasonably priced. Yellow city cabs are metered; rates double between midnight and 5am. Grey rural taxis do not have meters; settle on a price before you get in.
- Athens taxi drivers are gifted in their ability to make a little bit extra with every fare. If you have a complaint, note the cab number and contact the Tourist Police. Rural taxi drivers are better.

TRAIN

- Check the **Greek Railways Organisation** (www.trainose.gr) website for the current schedules. Greece has only two main lines: Athens north to Thessaloniki and Alexandroupolis, and Athens to the Peloponnese.
- There are a number of branch lines, eg Pyrgos–Olympia line and the spectacular Diakofto–Kalavryta mountain railway.
- Inter-Rail and Eurail passes are valid; you still need to make a reservation.
- In summer make reservations at least two days in advance.

Hungary

Includes ➡

Best Places to Eat

- Jókai Bisztró (p578)
- Erhardt (p573)
- Kisbuda Gyöngye (p568)
- Fő Tér (p581)

Best Places to Stay

- Hotel Palazzo Zichy (p568)
- Club Hotel Füred (p575)
- Bacchus (p576)
- Hotel Senator-Ház (p581)

Why Go?

Hungary is just the place to kick off a European adventure. Lying virtually in the centre of the continent, this land of Franz Liszt and Béla Bartók, paprika-lashed dishes, superb wines and the romantic Danube River continues to enchant visitors. The allure of Budapest, once an imperial city, is immediate at first sight, and it also boasts the hottest nightlife in the region. Other cities, too, like Pécs, the warm heart of the south, and Eger, the wine capital of the north, have much to offer travellers, as does the sprawling countryside, particularly the Great Plain, where cowboys ride and cattle roam. And where else can you laze about in an open-air thermal spa while snow patches glisten around you? That's at Hévíz at the western edge of Lake Balaton, continental Europe's largest lake and Hungary's 'inland sea', which offers innumerable opportunities for rest and recreation. In Hungary you'll find all the excitement and fun of Western Europe – at half the cost.

When to Go

Budapest

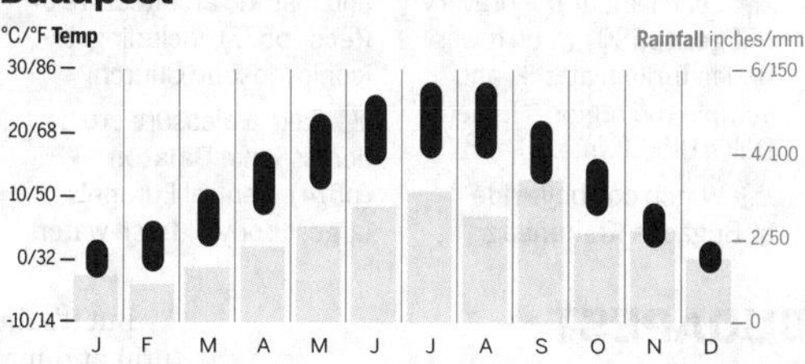

May Spring is in full swing, meaning reliable weather, cool temperatures and flowers.

Jul & Aug Sunny but often very hot; decamp to the hills or Lake Balaton (book ahead).

Sep & Oct Blue skies, mild temperatures and grape harvests – perhaps the best time to visit.

Hungary Highlights

1 Lose yourself in Europe's best nightlife – the 'ruin pubs' and 'garden clubs' of **Budapest**.

2 Learn about the bravery of **Eger** (p580) when it was under Turkish attack, and sample the region's famed Bull's Blood wine.

3 Watch cowboys ride at Bugac in **Kiskunság National Park** (p579), the heart of the Great Plain.

4 Absorb the Mediterranean-like climate and historic architecture of **Pécs** (p577), including its iconic Mosque Church.

5 Take a pleasure cruise across **Lake Balaton** (p574), Central Europe's largest body of fresh water.

6 Ease your aching muscles in the warm waters of the thermal lake in **Hévíz** (p577).

7 Mill about with artists, freethinkers and day trippers at the too-cute-for-words town of **Szentendre** (p572).

BUDAPEST

☎1 / POP 1.75 MILLION

There's no other city in Hungary like Budapest. Home to almost 20% of the national population, Hungary's capital (*főváros*; 'main city') is the nation's administrative, business and cultural centre.

But it's the beauty of Budapest – both natural and man-made – that makes it unique. Straddling a gentle curve in the Danube, the city is flanked by the Buda Hills on the west bank and the beginnings of the Great Plain to the east. Architecturally it is a gem, with enough baroque, neoclassical and art nouveau elements to satisfy everyone.

In recent years Budapest has taken on the role of the region's party town. 'Pop-up' pubs and, in the warmer months, outdoor clubs are crammed with partygoers till the wee hours.

Sights & Activities

Buda

Castle Hill (Várhegy) is Budapest's biggest tourist draw and a first port of call for any visit to the city. Here, you'll find most of Budapest's remaining medieval buildings, the Royal Palace and sweeping views of Pest across the river.

You can walk to Castle Hill up the **Király lépcső**, the 'Royal Steps' that lead northwest off Clark Ádám tér, or else take the **Sikló** (Map p564; www.bkv.hu/en/siklojegy/siklojegyek; I Szent György tér; one way/return adult 1100/1700Ft, child 650/1100Ft; 7.30am-10pm, closed 1st & 3rd Mon of month; 16, 19, 41), a funicular railway built in 1870 that ascends from Clark Ádám tér to Szent György tér near the Royal Palace.

★ Royal Palace PALACE

(Királyi Palota; Map p564; I Szent György tér; 16, 16A, 116) The massive former royal seat, razed and rebuilt at least a half-dozen times over the past seven centuries, occupies the southern end of Castle Hill. Here you'll find two important museums: the **Hungarian National Gallery** (Nemzeti Galéria; Map p564; 1-201 9082; www.mng.hu; I Szent György tér 2, Bldgs A-D; adult/concession 1400/700Ft, audio guide 800Ft; 10am-6pm Tue-Sun; 16, 16A, 116), which traces Hungarian art from the 11th century to the present day, and the **Castle Museum** (Vármúzeum; Map p564; 1-487 8800; www.btm.hu; I Szent György tér 2, Bldg E; adult/concession 1800/900Ft; 10am-6pm Tue-Sun Feb-Oct, to 4pm Nov-Mar; 16, 16A, 116, 19, 41), which looks at 2000 years of the city's life.

★ Matthias Church CHURCH

(Mátyás templom; Map p564; 1-355 5657; www.matyas-templom.hu; I Szentháromság tér 2; adult/concession 1200/800Ft; 9am-5pm Mon-Sat, 1-5pm Sun; 16, 16A, 116) The pointed spire and the colourful tiled roof make neo-Gothic Matthias Church (so named because good King Matthias Corvinus held both his weddings here) a Castle Hill landmark. Parts date back some 500 years, notably the carvings above the southern entrance, but the rest of it was designed by the architect Frigyes Schulek in 1896.

★ Fishermen's Bastion MONUMENT

(Halászbástya; Map p564; I Szentháromság tér; adult/concession 700/500Ft; 9am-11pm mid-Mar–mid-Oct; 16, 16A, 116) The bastion is a neo-Gothic folly built as a viewing platform in 1905. Its name comes from the medieval guild of fishermen responsible for defending this stretch of the castle wall.

Citadella FORT

(Map p564; www.citadella.hu; 27) FREE Built by the Habsburgs after the 1848–49 War of Independence to defend the city from further insurrection, the Citadella was obsolete by the time it was ready in 1851 and never saw battle. It is currently closed to the public.

ITINERARIES

One Week

Spend at least three days in **Budapest**, checking out the sights, museums, cafes and *kertek* (garden clubs). On your fourth day take a day trip to a Danube Bend town such as **Szentendre** or **Esztergom**. Day five can be spent getting a morning train to **Pécs** to see its lovely Turkish remains and to check out the many museums and galleries in town. If you've still got the travel bug, on day six head for **Eger**, a baroque town set in red-wine country. On your last day recuperate in one of Budapest's wonderful thermal baths.

Two Weeks

In summer make sure you spend some time exploring the towns and grassy beaches around **Lake Balaton**. **Tihany** is a rambling hillside village set on a protected peninsula, **Keszthely** is an old town with a great palace in addition to beaches, and **Hévíz** has a thermal lake. Try to see something of the **Great Plain** as well – **Szeged** is a splendid university town on the Tisza River, and **Kecskemét** a centre of Art Nouveau. Finish your trip in **Tokaj**, home of Hungary's famous sweet wine.

Buda

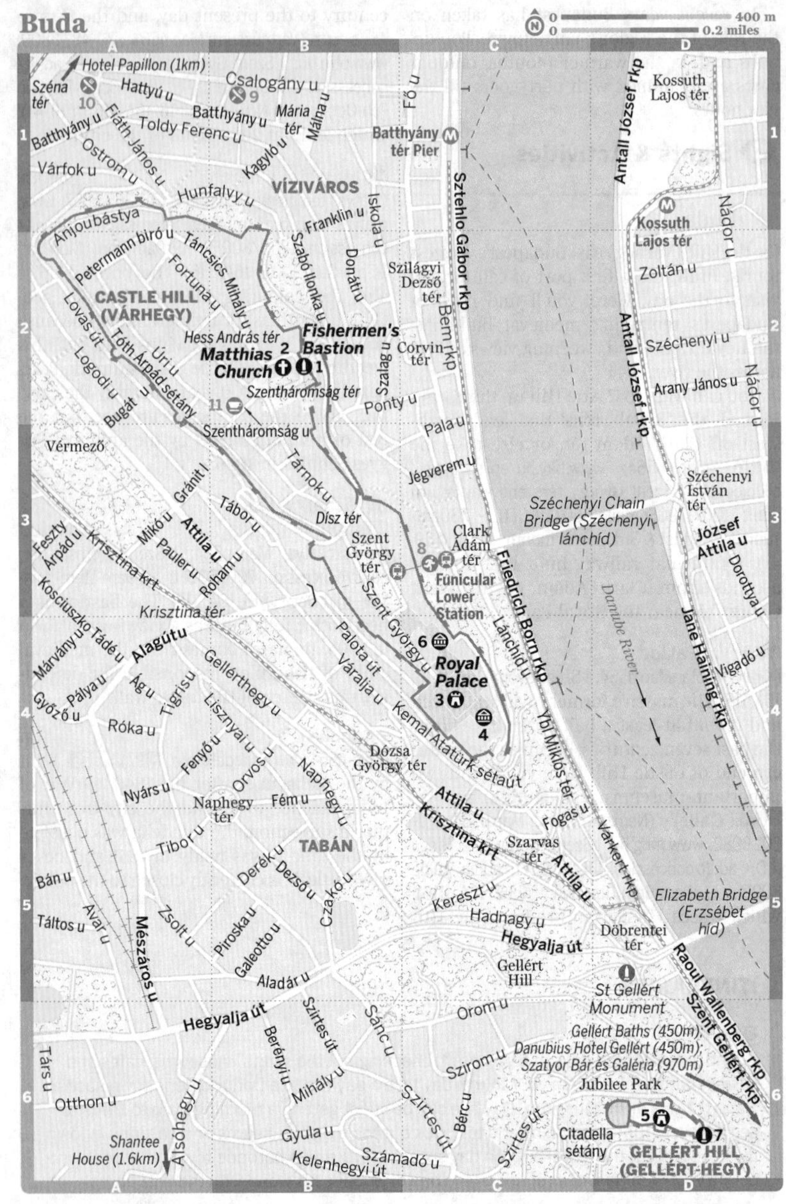

Liberty Monument MONUMENT

(Szabadság szobor; Map p564; 27) The Liberty Monument, the lovely lady with the palm frond proclaiming freedom throughout the city from atop Gellért Hill, is to the east of the Citadella. Some 14m high, she was raised in 1947 in tribute to the Soviet soldiers who died liberating Budapest in 1945.

Memento Park HISTORIC SITE

(1-424 7500; www.mementopark.hu; XXII Balatoni út 16; adult/student 1500/1000Ft; 10am-dusk;

150) Home to some 40 statues, busts and plaques of Lenin, Marx and 'heroic' workers like those that have ended up on trash heaps in other former socialist countries, Memento Park, 10km southwest of the city centre, is a mind-blowing place to visit. A direct bus (with park admission adult/child return 4900/3500Ft) departs from in front of the Le Meridien Budapest Hotel on Deák Ferenc tér at 11am year-round with an extra departure at 3pm in July and August.

★**Gellért Baths** BATHHOUSE
(Gellért Gyógyfürdő; 1-466 6166; www.gellertbath.hu; XI Kelenhegyi út 4, Danubius Hotel Gellért; weekdays/weekends incl locker 4900/5100Ft, cabin 5300/5500Ft; 6am-8pm; 7, 86, M4 Szent Gellért tér, 18, 19, 47, 49) Soaking in the art nouveau Gellért Baths, open to both men and women daily in mixed sections, has been likened to taking a bath in a cathedral. The eight thermal pools range in temperature from 26°C to 38°C.

Margaret Island

Margaret Island ISLAND
(Margit-sziget; 26) FREE Neither Buda nor Pest, 2.5km-long Margaret Island in the middle of the Danube was the domain of one religious order or another in the Middle Ages and became a public park in the mid-19th century. The island's gardens and shaded walkways are lovely places to stroll or cycle around.

Pest

★**Parliament** HISTORIC BUILDING
(Országház; Map p566; 1-441 4904; www.parlament.hu; V Kossuth Lajos tér 1-3; adult/student & EU citizen 4000/2000Ft; 8am-6pm Mon-Fri, to 4pm Sat & Sun Apr-Oct, 8am-4pm daily Nov-Mar; M2 Kossuth Lajos tér) You can visit a handful of the 691 sumptuously decorated rooms of the enormous riverfront Parliament (1902) on a guided tour and view the **Crown of St Stephen**, the nation's most important national icon.

★**Great Synagogue** SYNAGOGUE
(Nagy zsinagóga; Map p566; www.dohanystreetsynagogue.hu; VII Dohány utca 2; adult/student & child incl museum 2850/2000Ft; 10am-6pm Sun-Thu, to 4.30pm Fri Apr-Oct, reduced hours Nov-Mar; M2 Astoria) Budapest's stunning Great Synagogue (1859) is the largest Jewish house of worship in Europe. Inside, the **Hungarian Jewish Museum** (Magyar Zsidó Múzeum; Map p566; 1-343 6756; www.zsidomuzeum.hu; VII Dohány utca 2; incl in admission to Great Synagogue, call ahead for guided tours; 10am-6pm Sun-Thu, to 4pm Fri Mar-Oct, 10am-4pm Mon-Thu, to 2pm Fri Nov-Feb; M2 Astoria) contains objects relating to religious and every day life, as well as the harrowing **Holocaust Memorial Room**.

Heroes' Square SQUARE
(Hősök tere; 105, M1 Hősök tere) At the northern end of leafy Andrássy út, this huge public space holds a sprawling monument constructedin 1896 to honour the millennium of the Magyar conquest of the Carpathian Basin.

Museum of Fine Arts MUSEUM
(Szépművészeti Múzeum; www.mfab.hu; XIV Dózsa György út 41; adult/concession 1800/900Ft, temporary exhibitions 3200/1600Ft; 10am-6pm Tue-Sun; M1 Hősök tere) On the northern side of Heroes' Square, this gallery houses the nation's outstanding collection of foreign artworks in a building dating to 1906. The Old Masters collection includes seven paintings by El Greco.

City Park PARK
(Városliget; M1 Hősök tere, M1 Széchenyi fürdő) Pest's green lung, this open space covers almost a square kilometre. It has boating on a small lake in summer and ice-skating there in winter.

Central Pest

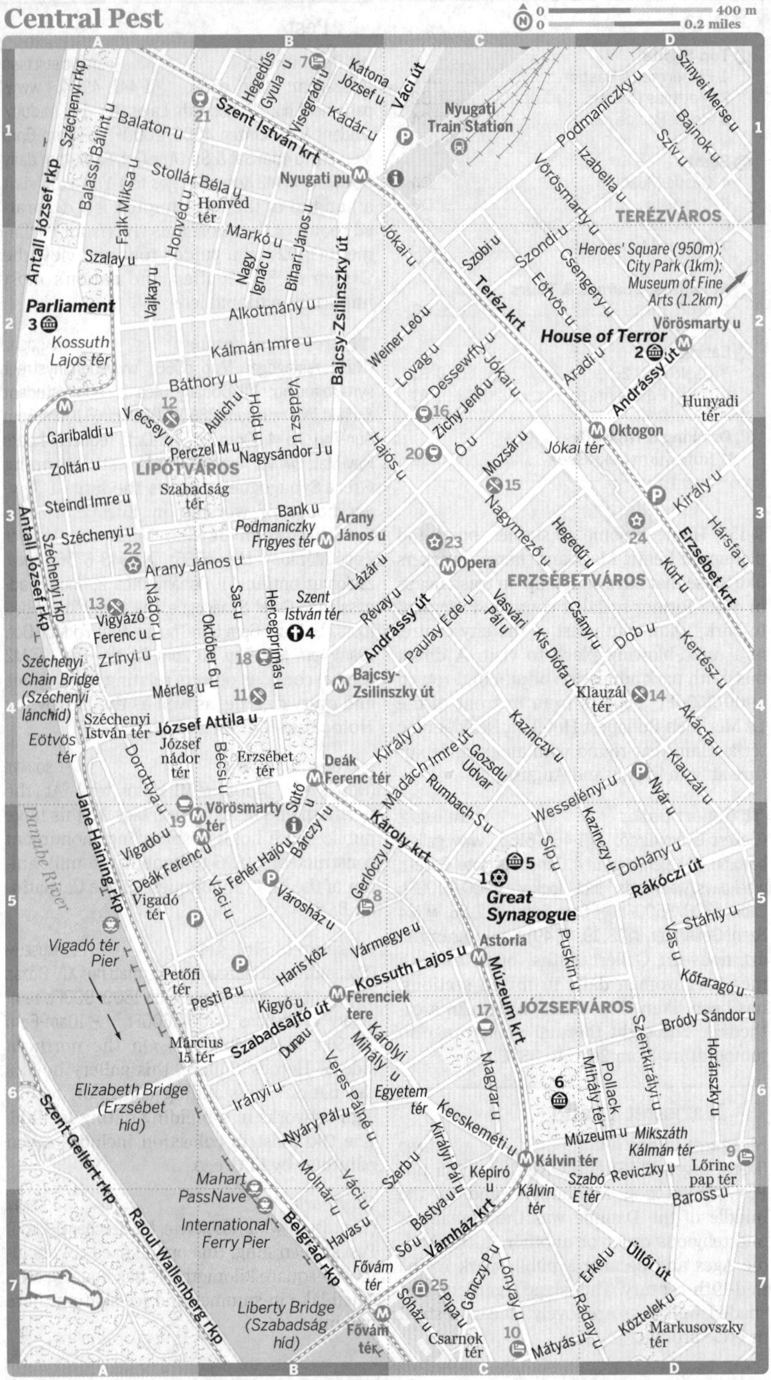

Central Pest

Top Sights
1 Great Synagogue ... C5
2 House of Terror ... D2
3 Parliament ... A2

Sights
4 Basilica of St Stephen ... B4
5 Hungarian Jewish Museum ... C5
6 Hungarian National Museum ... C6

Sleeping
7 Aventura Boutique Hostel ... B1
8 Gerlóczy Rooms deLux ... B5
9 Hotel Palazzo Zichy ... D6
10 KM Saga Guest Residence ... C7

Eating
11 Borkonyha ... B4
12 Da Mario ... A2
13 Govinda ... A3
14 Kádár ... D4
15 Pesti Disznó ... C3

Drinking & Nightlife
16 Club AlterEgo ... C2
17 Csendes ... C6
18 DiVino Borbár ... B4
19 Gerbeaud ... A4
20 Instant ... C3
21 Morrison's 2 ... B1

Entertainment
22 Aranytíz Cultural Centre ... A3
23 Hungarian State Opera House ... C3
24 Liszt Academy ... D3

Shopping
25 Nagycsarnok ... C7

★House of Terror MUSEUM
(Terror Háza; Map p566; www.terrorhaza.hu; VI Andrássy út 60; adult/concession 2000/1000Ft; 10am-6pm Tue-Sun; M1 Oktogon) The former headquarters of the dreaded secret police now houses an evocative museum that focuses on the crimes and atrocities committed by both Hungary's fascist and communist regimes.

Basilica of St Stephen CHURCH
(Szent István Bazilika; Map p566; 06 30 703 6599; www.basilica.hu; V Szent István tér; requested donation 200Ft; 9am-5pm Apr-Sep, 10am-4pm Oct-Mar; M2 Arany János utca) You can climb up to the dome at Budapest's colossal neoclassical cathedral (1905). The chapel to the left of the main altar contains the **Holy Right**, the mummified right hand of King St Stephen.

Hungarian National Museum MUSEUM
(Magyar Nemzeti Múzeum; Map p566; www.hnm.hu; VIII Múzeum körút 14-16; adult/concession 1600/800Ft; 10am-6pm Tue-Sun; 47, 49, M3/4 Kálvin tér) The Hungarian National Museum houses the nation's most important collection of historical relics – from Roman finds to coronation regalia – in an impressive neoclassical building (1847).

Széchenyi Baths BATHHOUSE
(Széchenyi Gyógyfürdő; 1-363 3210; www.szechenyibath.hu; XIV Állatkerti körút 9-11; ticket incl locker/cabin Mon-Fri 4500/5000Ft, Sat & Sun 4700/5200Ft; 6am-10pm; M1 Széchenyi fürdő) At the northern end of City Park, the immense Széchenyi Baths, open to both men and women at all times in mixed areas, counts 15 indoor and three outdoor thermal pools.

Festivals & Events

Budapest Spring Festival PERFORMING ARTS
(www.springfestival.hu) The capital's largest and most important cultural festival; in late March/early April.

Sziget Festival MUSIC
(http://szigetfestival.com) One of Europe's biggest music festivals, held in mid-August on Budapest's Óbuda Island.

Formula One Hungarian Grand Prix CAR RACING
(www.hungaroring.hu) Hungary's prime sporting event, held in late July/early August in Magyoród, 24km northeast of Budapest.

Sleeping

Buda

Shantee House HOSTEL €
(1-385 8946; www.backpackbudapest.hu; XI Takács Menyhért utca 33; beds in yurt €10, dm large/small €13/16, d €38; P@; 7, 7A, 19, 49) Budapest's first hostel has added two floors to its colourfully painted suburban 'villa' in south Buda. It's all good and the fun (and sleeping bodies in high season) still spills out into a lovely landscaped garden, with hammocks, yurt and gazebo. Two of the five doubles have private bathrooms.

Hotel Papillon HOTEL €€
(☎1-212 4750; www.hotelpapillon.hu; II Rózsahegy utca 3/b; s/d/tr €44/54/69, apt €78-90; P❄@☜≋; 🚊4, 6) One of Buda's best-kept accommodation secrets, this cosy hotel in Rózsadomb (Rose Hill) has a delightful back garden with a small swimming pool, and some of the 20 rooms have balconies. There are also four apartments available in the same building, one with a lovely roof terrace.

Danubius Hotel Gellért LUXURY HOTEL €€€
(☎1-889 5500; www.danubiusgroup.com/gellert; XI Szent Gellért tér 1; s/d/ste from €85/170/268; P❄@☜≋; Ⓜ M4 Szent Gellért tér, 🚊18, 19, 47, 49) Buda's *grande dame* is a 234-room art nouveau hotel completed in 1918. Prices depend on which way your room faces and what sort of bathroom it has. Use of the thermal baths is free for hotel guests.

Pest

Aventura Boutique Hostel HOSTEL €
(Map p566; ☎1-239 0782; www.aventurahostel.com; XIII Visegrádi utca 12; dm €9-19, d €29-56, apt €38-66; @☜; Ⓜ M3 Nyugati pályaudvar, 🚊4, 6) This very chilled hostel has four themed rooms (India, Africa, Japan and – our favourite – Space). We love the colours and fabrics, the in-house massage, and the dorms with loft sleeping for four to eight.

KM Saga Guest Residence GUESTHOUSE €
(Map p566; ☎1-217 1934; www.km-saga.hu; IX Lónyay utca 17, 3rd fl; s €30-40, d €35-55; ❄@☜; Ⓜ M4 Fővám tér) This unique place has five themed rooms, an eclectic mix of 19th-century furnishings, and hospitable, multilingual Hungarian-American owner Shandor. Two rooms share a bathroom.

Gerlóczy Rooms deLux BOUTIQUE HOTEL €€
(Map p566; ☎1-501 4000; www.gerloczy.hu; V Gerlóczy utca 1; r €80-95; ❄☜; Ⓜ M2 Astoria) A stand-out choice, Gerlóczy hits the mark with an excellent combination of good value, decor, atmosphere and professional service. Set over four floors of an 1890s building on an attractive square, the individually designed and well-proportioned rooms all have king-size beds. The winding wrought-iron staircase, domed stained-glass skylight and etched glass are wonderful touches.

★**Hotel Palazzo Zichy** HISTORIC HOTEL €€€
(Map p566; ☎1-235 4000; www.hotel-palazzo-zichy.hu; VIII Lőrinc pap tér 2; r/ste from €125/150; P⊖❄@☜; Ⓜ M3 Corvin-negyed, M3/4 Kálvin tér, 🚊4, 6) Once the sumptuous 19th-century residence of an aristocratic family, the 'palace' has been transformed into a lovely hotel, with its original features, such as wrought-iron bannisters, blending seamlessly with the ultra-modern decor. The 80 rooms, all charcoals and creams, are enlivened by red glass-topped desks, the showers are terrific, and there's a sauna and fitness room in the cellar crypt.

Eating

Buda

Nagyi Palacsintázója HUNGARIAN €
(Granny's Crepe Place; Map p564; www.nagyipali.hu; I Hattyú utca 16; pancakes 190-680Ft, set menus 1090-1190Ft; ⏲24hr; 🖉; Ⓜ M2 Széll Kálmán tér) This small eatery serves Hungarian pancakes – both savoury and sweet – round the clock and is always packed.

★**Kisbuda Gyöngye** HUNGARIAN €€
(☎1-368 6402; www.remiz.hu; III Kenyeres utca 34; mains 2780-4980Ft; ⏲noon-3pm & 7-10pm Tue-Sat; 🚌160, 260, 🚊17) Operating since the 1970s, this traditional yet very elegant Hungarian restaurant has an antique-cluttered dining room and attentive service, and manages to create a *fin-de-siècle* atmosphere. Try the excellent goose liver speciality plate with a glass of Tokaj (3980Ft), or a less complicated dish like roast duck with apples (2980Ft).

Csalogány 26 INTERNATIONAL €€€
(Map p564; ☎1-201 7892; www.csalogany26.hu; I Csalogány utca 26; mains 3600-5000Ft; ⏲noon-3pm & 7-10pm Tue-Sat; 🚌11, 39) This intimate restaurant with the unimaginative name and spartan decor turns its attention to its superb food. Try the suckling *mangalica* (a special type of Hungarian pork) with Savoy cabbage (4500Ft) or the free-range pullet with polenta (3800Ft). A three-course set lunch is a budget-pleasing 2500Ft.

Pest

The **Nagycsarnok** (Great Market; Map p566; www.piaconline.hu; IX Vámház körút 1-3; ⏲6am-5pm Mon-Fri, to 3pm Sat; Ⓜ M4 Fővám tér) is a vast historic market built of steel and glass. Head here for fruit, vegetables, deli items, fish and meat.

Kádár HUNGARIAN €
(Map p566; ☎1-321 3622; X Klauzál tér 9; mains 1250-2500Ft; ⏲11.30am-3.30pm Tue-Sat; 🚊4, 6)

Located in the heart of the Jewish district, Kádár is Budapest's most authentic *étkezde* (canteen serving simple Hungarian dishes) and attracts the hungry with its ever-changing menu.

Govinda VEGETARIAN €
(Map p566; ☎1-473 1310; www.govinda.hu; V Vigyázó Ferenc utca 4; dishes 190-990Ft; ⏰11.30am-9pm Mon-Fri, from noon Sat; ☑; 🚇15, 🚊2) This basement restaurant serves wholesome salads, soups and desserts as well as daily set-menu plates for 990/1890/2990Ft for one/two/three courses.

Da Mario ITALIAN €€
(Map p566; ☎1-301 0967; www.damario.hu; V Vécsey utca 3; mains 2000-5500Ft; ⏰11am-midnight; 🚇15, Ⓜ M2 Kossuth Lajos tér) Owned and operated by three Italian *ragazzi* (lads) from southern Italy, Da Mario can't put a foot wrong in our book. While the cold platters, soups and meat and fish mains all look good, we stick to the house-made pasta dishes (2000Ft to 3500Ft) and pizzas (1250Ft to 3000Ft) from the wood-burning stove.

Pesti Disznó HUNGARIAN €€
(Map p566; ☎1-951 4061; www.pestidiszno.hu; VI Nagymező utca 19; mains 1490-2890Ft; ⏰11am-midnight Sun-Wed, to 1am Thu-Sat; Ⓜ M1 Oktogon) Punters would be forgiven for thinking that the 'Pest Pig' was all about pork. In fact, of the dozen main courses half are poultry, fish or vegetarian. It's a wonderful space, loft-like almost, with high tables and charming, informed service. Excellent wine list.

Borkonyha HUNGARIAN €€€
(Wine Kitchen; Map p566; ☎1-266 0835; www.borkonyha.hu; V Sas utca 3; mains 3750-7150Ft; ⏰noon-midnight Mon-Sat; 🚇15, Ⓜ M1 Bajcsy-Zsilinszky út) One of four restaurants in Budapest with a Michelin star well and truly deserves the honour. Go for the signature foie gras appetiser wrapped in strudel pasty and a glass of sweet Tokaj wine. If *mangalica* (a special type of Hungarian pork) is on the menu, try it with a glass of dry Furmint. Warm and knowledgeable service.

Drinking

Buda

Ruszwurm Cukrászda CAFE
(Map p564; ☎1-375 5284; www.ruszwurm.hu; I Szentháromság utca 7; ⏰10am-7pm Mon-Fri, to 6pm Sat & Sun; 🚇6, 6A, 116) This diminutive cafe dating from 1827 is the perfect place for coffee and cakes (380Ft to 580Ft) in the Castle District.

Szatyor Bár és Galéria BAR
(Carrier Bag Bar & Gallery; ☎1-279 0290; www.szatyorbar.com; XIII Bartók Béla út 36-38; ⏰noon-1am Mon-Fri, 2pm-1am Sat & Sun; Ⓜ M4 Móricz Zsigmond körtér; 🚊18, 19, 47, 49) Sharing the same building as a popular cafe and separated by just a door, the Szatyor is funky, with cocktails, street art on the walls and a Lada driven by the poet Endre Ady.

Pest

★Instant CLUB
(Map p566; ☎06 30 830 8747; www.instant.co.hu; VI Nagymező utca 38; ⏰4pm-6am Sun-Thu, to 11am Fri & Sat; Ⓜ M1 Opera) We still love this 'ruin bar' on Pest's most vibrant nightlife strip and so do all our friends. It has six bars on three levels with underground DJs and dance parties.

Gerbeaud CAFE
(Map p566; ☎1-429 9001; www.gerbeaud.hu; V Vörösmarty tér 7; ⏰9am-9pm; Ⓜ M1 Vörösmarty tér) Founded on the northern side of Pest's busiest square in 1858, Gerbeaud has been the most fashionable meeting place for the city's elite since the 19th century. And it doesn't come cheap. Cakes start at 1950Ft.

Csendes CAFE, BAR
(Map p566; www.facebook.com/csendesvintagebar; V Ferenczy István utca 5; ⏰10am-2am Mon-Fri, from 2pm Sat, 2pm-midnight Sun; 📶; Ⓜ M2 Astoria) A quirky cafe just off the Little Ring Rd with junkyard chic decorating the walls and floor space, the 'Quietly' is just that until the regular DJ arrives and cranks up the volume.

★DiVino Borbár WINE BAR
(Map p566; ☎06 70 935 3980; www.divinoborbar.hu; V Szent István tér 3; ⏰4pm-midnight Sun-Wed, to 2am Thu-Sat; Ⓜ M1 Bajcsy-Zsilinszky út) Central and always heaving, DiVino is Budapest's most popular wine bar. Choose from 120 types of wine produced by some 30 winemakers, but be careful: those 0.1L glasses (650Ft to 2800Ft) go down quickly.

Morrison's 2 CLUB
(Map p566; ☎1-374 3329; www.morrisons.hu; V Szent István körút 11; ⏰5pm-4am; 🚊4, 6) Budapest's largest party venue, this cavernous club attracts a younger crowd with its five dance floors, half-dozen bars (including one

in a covered courtyard and one with table football). Great DJs.

Club AlterEgo GAY

(Map p566; ☎06 70 345 4302; www.alteregoclub.hu; VI Dessewffy utca 33; ⏱10pm-6am Fri & Sat; 🚊4, 6) Still Budapest's premier gay club, with the chicest crowd and the best dance vibe.

☆ Entertainment

Your best source of information in English for what's on citywide is the freebie **Budapest Funzine** (www.budapestfunzine.hu), available at hotels, bars, cinemas and wherever tourists congregate. The **Koncert Kalendárium** website, (www.muzsikalendarium.hu/), has more serious offerings: classical concerts, opera, dance and the like. You can book almost anything online from the following sites:

Jegymester (www.jegymester.hu)

Kulturinfo (www.kulturinfo.hu)

Ticket Express (www.tex.hu)

Performing Arts

Hungarian State Opera House OPERA

(Magyar Állami Operaház; Map p566; ☎box office 1-353 0170; www.opera.hu; VI Andrássy út 22; ⏱box office 11am-5pm, from 4pm Sun; Ⓜ M1 Opera) Visit the the gorgeous neo-Renaissance opera house as much to admire the incredibly rich decoration inside as to take in a performance and hear the perfect acoustics. The ballet company performs here, too.

Liszt Academy CLASSICAL MUSIC

(Liszt Zeneakadémia; Map p566; ☎1-321 0690; www.zeneakademia.hu; VI Liszt Ferenc tér 8; ⏱ticket office 11am-6pm; Ⓜ M1 Oktogon) Budapest's recently renovated premier venue for classical concerts is not just a place to hear music but also to ogle at the wonderful decorative Zsolnay porcelain and frescoes.

Aranytiz Cultural Centre TRADITIONAL MUSIC

(Aranytíz Művelődési Központ; Map p566; ☎1-354 3400; www.aranytiz.hu; V Arany János utca 10; ⏱box office 2-9pm Mon & Wed, 9am-3pm Sat; 🚌15) The Kalamajka Táncház, one of the best folk music and dance shows in town, has programs at this cultural centre from 7pm on Saturday.

🛍 Shopping

★Ecseri Piac MARKET

(www.piaconline.hu; XIX Nagykőrösi út 156; ⏱8am-4pm Mon-Fri, 5am-3pm Sat, 8am-1pm Sun; 🚌54, 84E, 89E 94E) This is one of the biggest flea markets in Central Europe, and Saturday is the best day to go. Take bus 54 from Boráros tér in Pest or express bus 84E, 89E or 94E from the Határ út stop on the M3 metro line.

ℹ Information

There are ATMs everywhere, including in the train and bus stations and at the airport. Moneychangers (particularly those along Váci utca) are best avoided.

Budapest Card (☎1-438 8080; www.budapestinfo.hu; per 24/48/72hr 4500/7500/8900Ft) Free admission to selected museums, unlimited travel on public transport, two free guided tours, and discounts for organised tours, car rental, thermal baths and selected shops and restaurants. Available at tourist offices but cheaper online.

Budapest Info (Map p566; V Sütő utca 2; ⏱8am-8pm; Ⓜ M1/M2/M3 Deák Ferenc tér) The best single source of information on Budapest.

FirstMed Centers (☎1-224 9090; www.firstmedcenters.com; I Hattyú utca 14, 5th fl; ⏱8am-8pm Mon-Fri, to 2pm Sat, urgent care 24hr; Ⓜ M2 Széll Kálmán tér) Round-the-clock emergency treatment, but expensive.

SOS Dent (☎1-269 6010, 06 30 383 3333; www.sosdent.hu; VI Király utca 14; ⏱8am-9pm) Dental practice.

Teréz Gyógyszertár (☎1-311 4439; VI Teréz körút 41; ⏱8am-8pm Mon-Fri, to 2pm Sat; Ⓜ M3 Nyugati pályaudvar) Central pharmacy.

ℹ Getting There & Away

BOAT

Mahart PassNave (Map p566; ☎1-484 4025; www.mahartpassnave.hu; V Belgrád rakpart; ⏱8am-6pm Mon-Fri; 🚊2) runs hydrofoils to Vienna from June to September, which arrive at and depart from the **International Ferry Pier** (Nemzetközi hajóállomás; Map p566; ☎1-318 1223; V Belgrád rakpart; 🚊2). See p583 for more information.

There are efficient ferry services (p572) to the towns of the Danube Bend.

BUS

Volánbusz (☎1-382 0888; www.volanbusz.hu), the national bus line, has an extensive list of destinations from Budapest. All international buses and some buses to/from western Hungary use **Népliget bus station** (☎1-219 8030; IX Üllői út 131; Ⓜ M3 Népliget). **Stadionok bus station** (☎1-219 8086; XIV Hungária körút 48-52; Ⓜ M2 Stadionok) generally serves places to the east of Budapest. Most buses to the Danube Bend arrive at and leave from the **Árpád Híd bus station** (☎1-412 2597; XIII Árbóc utca 1 ; Ⓜ M3 Árpád Híd), off XIII Róbert Károly körút, though some leave from the small suburban bus terminal next to **Újpest-Városkapu train station** (XIII Arva utca; Ⓜ M3 Újpest-Városkapu), off Váci út, which is also on the M3 blue metro line. All stations are on metro lines. If the ticket office is closed, you can buy your ticket on the bus.

CAR & MOTORCYCLE

All major international rental firms, including **Avis** (☎1-318 4240; www.avis.hu; V Arany János utca 26-28; ⏲7am-6pm Mon-Fri, 8am-2pm Sat & Sun; Ⓜ M3 Arany János utca), **Budget** (☎1-214 0420; www.budget.hu; VII Krisztina körút 41-43, Hotel Mercure Buda; ⏲8am-8pm Mon-Fri, to 6pm Sat & Sun) and **Europcar** (☎1-505 4400; www.europcar.hu; V Erzsébet tér 7-8; ⏲8am-6pm Mon & Fri, to 4.30pm Tue-Thu, to noon Sat), have offices in the city and at the airport.

TRAIN

Hungarian State Railways (MÁV) runs the country's extensive rail network. Contact the **MÁV-Start passenger service centre** (☎1-512 7921; www.mav-start.hu; V József Attila utca 16; ⏲9am-6pm Mon-Fri) for information on domestic train departures and arrivals. Its website has a useful timetable in English for planning routes.

Buy tickets at one of Budapest's three main train stations or the passenger service centre. **Keleti train station** (Eastern Train Station; VIII Kerepesi út 2-4) handles most international trains as well as domestic ones from the north and northeast. For some international destinations (eg Romania), as well as domestic ones to/from the Danube Bend and Great Plain, head for **Nyugati train station** (Western Train Station; VI Nyugati tér). For trains bound for Lake Balaton and the south, go to **Déli train station** (Southern Train Station; I Krisztina körút 37; Ⓜ M2 Déli pályaudvar). All three stations are on metro lines.

ℹ Getting Around

TO/FROM THE AIRPORT

The cheapest way to get into the city centre from Ferenc Liszt International Airport is to take city bus 200E (350Ft; on the bus 450Ft), which terminates at the Kőbánya-Kispest metro station. From there, take the M3 metro into the city centre.

The **Airport Shuttle Minibusz** (ASM; ☎1-296 8555; www.airportshuttle.hu; one way/return 3200/5500Ft) ferries passengers from the airport directly to their accommodation. Tickets are available at a clearly marked desk in the arrivals hall, though you may have to wait while the van fills up.

Taxi fares to most locations in Pest are 6000Ft and in Buda 7000Ft.

PUBLIC TRANSPORT

Public transport is run by **BKK** (Budapesti Közlekedési Központ; Centre for Budapest Transport; ☎1-258 4636; www.bkk.hu). The three underground metro lines (M1 yellow, M2 red, M3 blue) meet at Deák tér in Pest; the new green M4 links with the M2 at Keleti train station and the M3 at Kálvin tér. The HÉV suburban railway runs north from Batthyány tér in Buda to Szentendre. Travel cards are only good on the HÉV within the city limits (south of the Békásmegyer stop).

There's also an extensive network of buses, trams and trolleybuses. Public transport operates from 4.30am until 11.30pm and some 40 night buses run along main roads. Tram 6 on the Big Ring Road runs round the clock.

A single ticket for all forms of transport is 350Ft (60 minutes of uninterrupted travel on the same metro, bus, trolleybus or tram line *without* transferring/changing); a book of 10 tickets is 3000Ft. A transfer ticket (530Ft) is valid for one trip with one validated transfer/change within 90 minutes.

The three-day travel card (4150Ft) or the seven-day pass (4950Ft) make things easier, allowing unlimited travel inside the city limits. Keep your ticket or pass handy; the fine for 'riding black' is 8000Ft on the spot, or 16,000Ft if you pay later at the **BKK office** (☎1-461 6800; VII Akácfa utca 22; ⏲6am-8pm Mon-Fri, 8am-1.45pm Sat; Ⓜ M2 Blaha Lujza tér).

TAXI

Reliable companies include **Fő Taxi** (☎1-222 2222; www.fotaxi.hu) and **City Taxi** (☎1-211 1111; www.citytaxi.hu). Note that rates are higher at night and early morning.

THE DANUBE BEND

North of Budapest, the Danube breaks through the Pilis and Börzsöny Hills in a sharp bend before continuing along the Slovak border. The Roman Empire had its northern border here and medieval kings ruled Hungary from majestic palaces overlooking the river at Esztergom and Visegrád. Szentendre, once a thriving art colony, is full of museums and galleries.

ℹ Getting There & Away

BUS & TRAIN

Regular buses serve towns on the west bank of the Danube. Trains reach Szentendre and, on a separate line, Esztergom.

BOAT

The Danube is a perfect highway and regular boats ferry tourists to and from Budapest in the warmer months.

From May to September, a **Mahart PassNave** (☎1-484 4013; www.mahartpassnave.hu; Belgrád rakpart; ⏰8am-4pm Mon-Fri) ferry departs Pest's Vigadó tér at 10am (Buda's Batthány tér at 10.10am) Tuesday to Sunday bound for Szentendre (one way/return 2000/2500Ft, 1½ hours), returning at 5pm. They carry on to Visegrád (one way/return 2000/3000Ft, 3½ hours) in July and August, returning at 3.30pm. There is also an additional departure to Szentendre at 2pm (returning at 8pm) in July and August.

Hydrofoils travel to Visegrád (one way/return 4000/6000Ft, one hour) and Esztergom (one way/return 5000/7500Ft, 1½ hours) at 9.30am on Saturday and Sunday from early May to September. They return at 5pm from Esztergom and 5.30pm from Visegrád.

Szentendre

☎ 26 / POP 25,300

A a popular day-trip destination 19km north of Budapest, pretty little Szentendre (*sen-ten-dreh*) has narrow, winding streets and is a favourite with souvenir shoppers. The charming old centre around **Fő tér** (Main Square) has plentiful cafes and galleries, and there are a handful of noteworthy Serbian Orthodox churches dating from the time when Christian worshippers fled here to escape the Turkish invaders. The **Tourinform** (☎26-317 965; www.szentendreprogram.hu; Dumtsa Jenő utca 22; ⏰9am-5pm Mon-Fri, 10am-2pm Sat & Sun) office hands out maps and info about the town and region.

Just 5km to the northwest is the enormous **Hungarian Open-Air Ethnographical Museum** (Magyar Szabadtéri Néprajzi Múzeum; ☎26-502 500; www.skanzen.hu; Sztaravodai út; adult/student 1500/750Ft Apr-Oct, 1000/500Ft Nov-Mar; ⏰9am-5pm Tue-Sun Apr-Oct, 10am-4pm Sat & Sun Nov-early Dec & Feb-Mar). Walking through reassembled cottages, farms and workshops from around the country will show you what life was – and sometimes still is – like in rural Hungary. Reach it on bus 230 from bay/stop 7 at the bus station next to the train station.

The most convenient way to get to Szentendre is to take the HÉV suburban train from Buda's Batthyány tér metro station (660Ft, 40 minutes, every 10 to 20 minutes). There are efficient ferry services to Szentendre from Budapest.

Visegrád

☎ 26 / POP 1780

The spectacular vista from what remains of the 13th-century hilltop fortress in Visegrád (*vish*-eh-grahd), on a hilltop above a curve in the Danube, is what pulls visitors to this sleepy town.

After the 13th-century Mongol invasions, Hungarian kings built the mighty **Visegrád Citadel** (Visegrádi Fellegvár; ☎26-598 080; www.parkerdo.hu; Várhegy; adult/child & student 1700/850Ft; ⏰9am-5pm mid-Mar–Apr & Oct, to 6pm May-Sep, to 3pm Nov-Mar). It's a bit of a climb, but the views are well worth it. The **Royal Palace** (Királyi Palota; ☎26-597 010; www.visegradmuzeum.hu; Fő utca 29; adult/concession 1100/550Ft; ⏰9am-5pm Tue-Sun Mar-Oct, 10am-4pm Tue-Sun Nov-Feb) stands on the flood plain at the foot of the hills, closer to the centre of town. Seek information from **Visegrád Info** (☎26-597 000; www.palotahaz.hu; Dunaparti út 1; ⏰10am-6pm Apr-Oct, 10am-4pm Tue-Sun Nov-Mar).

No train line reaches Visegrád, but buses are very frequent (745Ft, 1¼ hours, hourly) to/from Budapest's Újpest-Városkapu train station, Szentendre (465Ft, 45 minutes, every 45 minutes) and Esztergom (465Ft, 45 minutes, hourly). Regular ferry services travel to Visegrád from Budapest.

Esztergom

☎ 33 / POP 28,400

It's easy to see the attraction of Esztergom – especially from a distance. The city's massive basilica, sitting high above the town and the Danube River, is an incredible sight rising magnificently from its rural setting.

But the historical significance of this town is even greater than its architectural appeal. The 2nd-century Roman emperor-to-be Marcus Aurelius wrote his famous *Meditations* while he camped here. In the 10th century, Stephen I, founder of the Hungarian state, was born here and crowned at the cathedral. From the late 10th to the mid-13th centuries Esztergom served as the Hungarian royal seat. In 1543 the Turks ravaged the town and much of it was destroyed, only to be rebuilt in the 18th and 19th centuries.

Hungary's largest church is **Esztergom Basilica** (Esztergomi Bazilika; ☎33-402 354; www.bazilika-esztergom.hu; Szent István tér 1; ⏰8am-6pm Apr-Oct, to 4pm Nov-Mar) FREE. At the southern end of the hill is the extensive **Castle Museum**

(Várműzeum; ☎33-415986; www.mnmvarmuzeuma.hu; Szent István tér 1; adult/student 1800/900Ft, courtyard only 500/250Ft, EU citizens free; ⏰10am-6pm Tue-Sun Apr-Oct, to 4pm Tue-Sun Nov-Mar), with archaeological finds from the 2nd and 3rd centuries. Below Castle Hill in the former Bishop's Palace, the **Christian Museum** (Keresztény Múzeum; ☎33-413 880; www.christianmuseum.hu; Mindszenty hercegprímás tér 2; adult/concession 900/450Ft; ⏰10am-5pm Wed-Sun Mar-Nov) contains the finest collection of medieval religious art in Hungary.

Frequent buses run to/from Budapest (930Ft, 1¼ hours), Visegrád (465Ft, 45 minutes) and Szentendre (930Ft, 1½ hours). Trains depart from Budapest's Nyugati train station (1120Ft, 1½ hours) at least hourly. Ferries travel regularly from Budapest to Esztergom (see opposite).

WESTERN HUNGARY

A visit to this region is a boon for anyone wishing to see remnants of Hungary's Roman legacy, medieval heritage and baroque splendour. Because it largely managed to avoid the Ottoman destruction of the 16th and 17th centuries, towns like Sopron retain their medieval cores; exploring their cobbled streets and hidden courtyards is a magical experience.

Sopron

☎ 99 / POP 61,250

Sopron (*showp*-ron) is an attractive border town with a history that stretches back to Roman times. It boasts some well-preserved ancient ruins and a fetching medieval square, bounded by the original town walls, that invite an hour or two of aimless meandering.

Sights

Fő tér SQUARE

(Main Square) Fő tér contains several museums, churches and monuments, including the massive **Firewatch Tower** (Tűztorony; ☎99-311 327; www.muzeum.sopron.hu; Fő tér; adult/student 1200/600Ft; ⏰10am-8pm Tue-Sun May-Sep, 10am-6pm Tue-Sun Apr & Oct, 9am-5pm Tue-Sun Nov & Dec, 10am-4pm Tue-Sun Jan-Mar), which can be climbed and houses a lovely new cafe. The 60m-high tower rises above the Old Town's northern gate and is visible from all around. In the centre of Fő tér is the 1701 **Trinity Column** (Szentháromság oszlop; Fő tér). The **Castle Wall Walk** (⏰9am-9pm Apr-Sep, to 6pm Oct-Mar) FREE takes in ruins dating from the time when Sopron was a tiny Roman outpost known as Scarbantia.

★Storno Collection MUSEUM

(Storno Gyűjtemény; %99-311 327; www.muzeum.sopron.hu; Fő tér 8; adult/senior & student 1000/500Ft; h10am-6pm Tue-Sun Apr-Oct, 9am-5pm Tue-Sun Nov & Dec, 10am-4pm Tue-Sun Jan-Mar) The Storno Collection is on the 2nd floor of **Storno House** (Storno Ház és Gyűjtemény; ☎99-311 327; www.muzeum.sopron.hu), home to the Swiss-Italian family of Ferenc Storno, chimney sweep turned art restorer, whose recarving of Romanesque and Gothic monuments throughout Transdanubia divides opinion to this day. The collection's highlights include a beautiful enclosed balcony with leaded windows and frescoes, an extensive collection of medieval weaponry, leather chairs with designs depicting the devil and dragons, and door frames made from pews taken from a nearby 15th-century church.

Sleeping

Jégverem Fogadó GUESTHOUSE €€

(☎99-510 113; www.jegverem.hu; Jégverem utca 1; s/d 7400/9800Ft; 📶) Booking ahead is essential since there are only five suite-like rooms at this 18th-century *fogadó* (inn). Even if you're not staying here, visit the terrace restaurant for enormous portions of pork, chicken and fish. And if you're wondering about the symbol of a little man with an ice pick perched on a giant cube, *jégverem* means 'ice house', which is what the place was in the 18th century.

Hotel Wollner HOTEL €€€

(☎99-524 400; www.wollner.hu; Templom utca 20; s/d/tr €75/90/110; 📶) This refined family-run hotel offers 18 spacious and tastefully decorated rooms in a 300-year-old villa in the heart of the Inner Town. It has a unique tiered garden, in which the reconstructed medieval walls of the castle can be seen, and a romantic wine cellar where you can sample some of the region's celebrated vintages.

Eating & Drinking

★Erhardt INTERNATIONAL €€€

(☎99-506 711; www.erhardts.hu; Balfi út 10; mains 2600-3900Ft; ⏰11.30am-10pm Sun-Thu, to 11pm Fri & Sat; 📝) One of the best restaurants in Sopon, with a wooden-beamed ceiling and paintings of rural scenes complementing the imaginative dishes, such as paprika catfish with oyster mushrooms, and crispy duck leg and duck breast slices. There's an extensive selection of Sopron wines to choose from (also available for purchase at its wine cellar), and the service is both informed and welcoming.

Museum Cafe CAFE
(☎06 30 667 1394; www.museumcafesopron.hu/hu; Előkapu 2-7; ⏰9am-11pm Mon-Thu, to 2am Fri & Sat, to 10pm Sun) This wonderful new venue at the foot of the Firewatch Tower has stunning views through oversized windows, cutting-edge decor, and is surrounded by a lapidary of Roman and medieval finds. And it's not just about coffee and tea here. There's also cocktails and *pálinka* (fruit-flavoured brandy) and, as blotter, sandwiches (420Ft to 880Ft) and pastries (390Ft to 690Ft).

Information

Tourinform (☎99-517 560; http://turizmus.sopron.hu; Liszt Ferenc utca 1, Ferenc Liszt Conference & Cultural Centre; ⏰9am-5pm Mon-Fri, to 1pm Sat, 9am-1pm Sun Mar-Sep only) Abundant information on Sopron and surrounds, including the local vintners.

Getting There & Away

BUS

Bus travel to/from Budapest takes forever (six hours), involves at least one transfer/change and is not recommended. There are two direct buses a day each to Keszthely (2520Ft, three hours) and to Balatonfüred (3130Ft, 4¼ hours).

TRAIN

Trains run to Budapest's Keleti train station (4525Ft, three hours, up to 12 daily). Local trains run to Wiener Neustadt/Bécsújhely (2800Ft, 40 minutes, hourly) in Austria, where you change for Vienna.

LAKE BALATON

Lake Balaton, Central Europe's largest expanse of fresh water, covers an area of 600 sq km. The main activities at this 'inland sea' are swimming, sailing and sunbathing, but the lake is also popular with cyclists lured here by more than 200km of marked bike paths that encircle the lake.

Balatonfüred

☎87 / POP 13,300

Balatonfüred (*bal*-ah-ton-fuhr-ed) is the oldest and most fashionable resort on the lake. In its glory days in the 19th century the wealthy and famous built large villas along its tree-lined streets, hoping to take advantage of the health benefits of the town's thermal waters. More recently, the lake frontage received a massive makeover and now sports the most stylish marina on Balaton. It's a great base for exploring.

Sights & Activities

Gyógy tér SQUARE
(Cure Square; Gyógy tér) This leafy square is home to the **State Hospital of Cardiology** (Állami Szívkórház; Gyógy tér 2), which put Balatonfüred on the map. In the centre you'll encounter the **Kossuth Pump House** (1853), a natural spring that dispenses slightly sulphuric, but drinkable, thermal water. If you can ignore the water's pale-yellow hue, join the locals lining up to fill their water bottles. On the northern side of the square **Balaton Pantheon** (Gyógy tér), with memorial plaques from those who took the cure here.

Public Beaches BEACH
Balatonfüred has several beaches open to the public of which **Kisfaludy Strand** (www.balatonfuredistrandok.hu; Aranyhíd sétány; adult/child 680/420Ft; ⏰8.30am-7pm mid-Jun–mid-Aug, 8am-6pm mid-May–mid-Jun & mid-Aug–mid-Sep) off Aranyhíd sétány, the eastern continuation of Tagore sétány, is the best.

Cruises CRUISE
(☎87-342 230; www.balatonihajozas.hu; ferry pier; adult/concession 1600/700Ft) One-hour pleasure cruises depart four to five times times a day from late late April to early October from the central ferry pier.

Sleeping

Hotel Blaha Lujza HOTEL €€
(☎87-581 210; www.hotelblaha.hu; Blaha Lujza utca 4; s €40-50, d €55-80; ❄📶) This small hotel is one of the loveliest places to stay in Balatonfüred. Its 22 rooms are a little compact but very comfy, and the location, seconds from the town centre and the lake, is ideal. This was the summer home of the much-loved 19th-century actress-singer Lujza Blaha from

WORTH A TRIP

TIHANY

While in Balatonfüred, don't miss the chance to visit Tihany (population 1380), a small peninsula 14km to the southwest and the place with the greatest historical significance on Lake Balaton. Activity here is centred on the tiny settlement of the same name, which is home to the celebrated **Benedictine Abbey Church** (Bencés Apátság Templom; ☎87-538-200; http://tihany.osb.hu; András tér 1; adult/child incl museum 1400/700Ft; ⏲9am-6pm May-Sep, 10am-5pm Apr & Oct, 10am-4pm Nov-Mar), filled with fantastic altars, pulpits and screens carved in the mid-18th century by an Austrian lay brother; all are baroque-rococo masterpieces in their own right. The church attracts a lot of tourists, but the peninsula itself has an isolated, almost wild feel to it. Hiking is one of Tihany's main attractions; a good map outlining the trails is available from the helpful **Tourinform** (☎87-448 804; www.tihany.hu; Kossuth Lajos utca 20; ⏲9am-7pm Mon-Fri, 10am-6pm Sat & Sun mid-Jun–mid-Sep, 10am-4pm Mon-Fri mid-Sep–mid-Jun) office just down from the church. Buses bound for Tihany depart from Balatonfüred's bus/train station (310Ft, 30 minutes) at least hourly.

1893 to 1916. Its restaurant is very popular with locals.

★Club Hotel Füred RESORT HOTEL €€€
(☎06 70 458 1242, 87-341 511; www.clubhotelfured.hu; Anna sétany 1-3; s/d €55/110, ste from €135; ❄📶🏊) This stunner of a resort hotel – right on the lake, about 1.5km from the town centre – has 43 rooms and suites in several buildings spread over 2.5 hectares of parkland and lush gardens. There's an excellent spa centre with sauna, steam room and pool, but the real delight is the private beach at the end of the garden. Stellar service, too.

Eating & Drinking

Vitorlás HUNGARIAN €€
(☎06 30 546 0940; www.vitorlasetterem.hu; Tagore sétány 1; mains 2000-3300Ft; ⏲9am-midnight) This enormous wooden villa sits right on the lake's edge at the foot of the town's pier. It's a prime spot to watch the yachts sail in and out of the harbour while munching on Hungarian cuisine and sipping local wine on the terrace. A fish dish is de rigueur here. We recommend the fiery catfish stew (3100Ft).

Karolina CAFE, BAR
(☎87-583 098; http://karolina.hu; Zákonyi Ferenc utca 4; ⏲8am-midnight daily May-Sep, noon-9pm Sun-Fri, to midnight Sat Oct-Apr) Hands-down the most popular place in town to grab a drink or a quick bite (dishes 950Ft to 2500Ft), Karolina is a sophisticated cafe-bar with live music from 8pm on weekends. The interior, with its art nouveau wall hangings and subtle lighting, has a certain decadent air about it, while the terrace area with sofas couldn't be more laid-back.

Kedves CAFE
(☎87-343 229; Blaha Lujza utca 7; ⏲8am-7pm Sun-Thu, to 10pm Fri & Sat) Join fans of Lujza Blaha and take coffee and cake (cakes 240Ft to 450Ft) at the cafe where the famous actress used to while away the hours when not in residence across the street. It's also appealing for its location, away from the madding crowds.

Information

Tourinform (☎87-580 480; www.balatonfured.info.hu; Blaha Lujza utca 5; ⏲9am-7pm Mon-Sat, 10am-4pm Sun mid-Jun–Aug, 9am-5pm Mon-Fri, to 3pm Sat Sep–mid-Jun) Well-stocked tourist office run by helpful staff.

Getting There & Around

BUS

Buses to Tihany (310Ft, 30 minutes) leave every 30 minutes or so throughout the day. Eight buses a day head for Hévíz (1490Ft, 1¾ hours) via Keszthely (1300Ft, 1½ hours). Buses and trains to Budapest (both 2520Ft, three hours) are much of a muchness, though bus departures are more frequent.

TRAIN

From April to early October, half a dozen daily ferries ply the water between Balatonfüred and Tihany (1100Ft, 30 minutes).

Keszthely

☎83 / POP 20,200

At the very western end of Lake Balaton sits Keszthely (*kest*-hey), the lake's main town and a place of grand town houses and a gentle ambience. Its small, shallow beaches are well suited to families and the lavish Festetics Palace is a must-see.

Sights & Activities

★Festetics Palace PALACE

(Festetics Kastély; ☎83-312194; www.helikonkastely.hu; Kastély utca 1; Palace & Coach Museum adult/concession 2300/1150Ft; ⏰9am-6pm Jun-Sep, 10am-5pm May, 10am-5pm Tue-Sun Oct-Apr) The glimmering white, 100-room Festetics Palace was begun in 1745; the two wings were extended out from the original building 150 years later. Some 18 rooms in the baroque south wing now contain the **Helikon Palace Museum** (Helikon Kastélymúzeum). Here too is the palace's greatest treasure, the **Helikon Library** (Helikon Könyvtár), with its 100,000 volumes and splendid carved furniture. Behind the palace in a separate building is the **Coach Museum** (Hintómúzeum; incl in admission to Festetics Palace; ⏰9am-6pm Jun-Sep, 10am-5pm May, 10am-5pm Tue-Sun Oct-Apr), which is filled with carriages and sleighs built for royalty.

Lakeside Area BEACH

The lakeside area centres on the long ferry pier. From late April to early October you can take a one-hour **pleasure cruise** (☎83-312 093; www.balatonihajozas.hu; ferry pier; ⏰adult/concession 1600/700Ft) on the lake between three and eight times daily. If you're feeling like a swim, **City Beach** (Városi Strand; adult/child 900/650Ft; ⏰8am-6pm May–mid-Sept) is just to the southwest of the ferry pier, near plenty of beer stands and food booths. Reedy **Helikon Beach** (Helikon Strand; adult/child 500/350Ft; ⏰8am-6pm May–mid-Sept) is a further 200m south.

Sleeping

★Bacchus HOTEL €€

(☎83-314 096; www.bacchushotel.hu; Erzsébet királyné útja 18; s 13,300Ft, d 16,400-21,400Ft, apt 26,000Ft; ❄📶) Bacchus' central position and immaculate rooms – each named after a grape variety – make it a popular choice with travellers and rightly so. The 26 rooms are simple but extra clean and inviting with solid wood furnishings; some even have terraces. Equally pleasing is its atmospheric cellar, which includes a lovely restaurant that includes wine tastings. Bacchus indeed.

Párizsi Udvar INN €€

(☎83-311 202; www.parizsi.huninfo.hu; Kastély utca 5; d 9400-10,500Ft, tr 11,400-13,400Ft; 📶) There's no closer accommodation to the Festetics Palace than the 'Parisian Courtyard'. Rooms are a little too big to be cosy, but they're well kept and look on to a sunny and very leafy inner courtyard (a corner of which is taken over by a daytime restaurant and beer garden).

Eating & Drinking

Margareta HUNGARIAN €

(☎83-314 882, 06 30 826 0434; www.margareta-etterem.hu/; Bercsényi Miklós utca 60; mains 1600-2500Ft; ⏰11am-10pm) Ask any local where they like to eat and one answer dominates: Margareta. It's no beauty, but the wraparound porch and hidden backyard terrace heave in the warm months, and the small interior packs them in the rest of the year. Food sticks to basic but hearty Hungarian staples. Set lunch is a snip at 990Ft.

Pelso Café CAFE

(☎06 30 222 2111, 83-315 415; Kossuth Lajos utca 38; ⏰9am-9pm Sun-Thu, to 10 pm Fri & Sat; 📶) This modern two-level cafe boasts a fantastic terrace overlooking the southern end of the main square. It does decent cakes and has a selection of teas from around the world plus the usual coffee concoctions (coffee and cake from 450Ft). But we like it best as a prime spot for an alfresco sundowner – the wine and beer list is small, but the vantage point is lovely.

Information

Tourinform (☎83-314 144; www.keszthely.hu; Kossuth Lajos utca 30; ⏰9am-7pm mid-Jun–Aug, 9am-5pm Mon-Fri, to 1pm Sat Sep–mid-Jun) An excellent source of information on Keszthely and the west Balaton area.

Getting There & Away

BUS

Buses link Keszthely with Hévíz (250Ft, 15 minutes, half-hourly), Balatonfüred (1300Ft, 1½ hours, eight daily) and Budapest (3410Ft, three hours, six daily).

TRAIN

Keszthely is on a railway branch line linking the lake's southeastern shore with Budapest (3705Ft, 3½ hours, six daily). To reach towns along Lake Balaton's northern shore, such as Balatonfüred (1640Ft, two hours) by train, you have to change at Tapolca (465Ft, 30 minutes, hourly).

WORTH A TRIP

HÉVÍZ

Hévíz (population 4685), just 8km northwest of Keszthely, is the most famous of Hungary's spa towns because of the **Gyógy-tó** (Hevíz Thermal Lake; ☎83-342 830; www.spaheviz.hu; Dr Schulhof Vilmos sétány 1; 3hr/4hr/whole day 2600/2900/3900Ft; ⏰8am-7pm Jun-Aug, 9am-6pm May & Sep, 9am-5.30pm Apr & Oct, 9am-5pm Mar & Nov-Feb) – Europe's largest 'thermal lake'. A dip into this water lily–filled lake is essential for anyone visiting the Lake Balaton region.

It's an astonishing sight: a surface of almost 4.5 hectares in the Park Wood, covered for most of the year in pink and white lotuses. The source is a spring spouting from a crater some 40m below ground that disgorges up to 80 million litres of warm water a day, renewing itself every 48 hours or so. The surface temperature averages 33°C and never drops below 22°C in winter, allowing bathing throughout the year, even when there's ice on the fir trees. Do as the locals do: rent a rubber ring (600Ft) and just float.

Buses link Hévíz with Keszthely (250Ft, 15 minutes) every half-hour.

SOUTHERN HUNGARY

Southern Hungary is a region of calm; a place to savour life at a slower pace. It's only marginally touched by tourism and touring through the countryside is like travelling back in time.

Pécs

☎72 / POP 146,600

Blessed with a mild climate, an illustrious past and a number of fine museums and monuments, Pécs (pronounced *paich*) is one of the most pleasant and interesting cities to visit in Hungary. Many travellers put it second only to Budapest on their Hungary 'must-see' list.

Sights & Activities

★Mosque Church MOSQUE
(Mecset templom; ☎72-321 976; Hunyadi János út 4; adult/concession 1000/750Ft; ⏰10am-4pm mid-Apr–mid-Oct, to noon mid-Oct–mid-Apr, shorter hours Sun) The one-time Pasha Gazi Kassim Mosque is now the **Inner Town Parish Church** (Belvárosi plébánia templom), but it's more commonly referred to as the Mosque Church. It is the largest building from the time of the Turkish occupation still standing in Hungary and the very symbol of Pécs.

Synagogue SYNAGOGUE
(Zsinagóga; Kossuth tér; adult/concession 750/500Ft; ⏰10am-5pm Sun-Fri May-Oct, 10.30am-12.30pm Sun-Fri Nov-Mar) Pécs' beautifully preserved 1869 Conservative synagogue is south of Széchenyi tér and faces renovated Kossuth tér.

Cella Septichora Visitors Centre RUIN
(Cella Septichora látogató központ; ☎72-224 755; www.pecsorokseg.hu; Janus Pannonius utca; adult/concession 1700/900Ft; ⏰10am-6pm Tue-Sun Apr-Oct, 10am-4pm Tue-Thu & Sun, to 5pm Sat & Sun Nov-Mar) This early Christian burial site illuminates a series of early Christian tombs that have been on Unesco's World Heritage list since 2000. The highlight is the so-called **Jug Mausoleum** (Korsós sírkamra; incl in admission to Cella Septichora Visitors Centre; ⏰10am-6pm Tue-Sun Apr-Oct, 10am-4pm Tue-Thu & Sun, to 5pm Sat & Sun Nov-Mar), a 4th-century Roman tomb; its name comes from a painting of a large drinking vessel with vines.

★Csontváry Museum MUSEUM
(☎72-310 544; www.jpm.hu; Janus Pannonius utca 11; adult/child 1500/750Ft; ⏰10am-6pm Tue-Sun) The Csontváry Museum shows the major works of master 19th-century symbolist painter Tivadar Kosztka Csontváry (1853–1919), whose tragic life is sometimes compared with that of his contemporary, Vincent van Gogh. Don't miss *Solitary Cedar* and *Baalbek*.

Sleeping

Hotel Főnix HOTEL €€
(☎72-311 680; www.fonixhotel.com; Hunyadi János út 2; s/d/ste 8000/13,000/14,000Ft; ❄@📶) The Főnix appears to be a hotel too large for the land it's built on and some of the 13 rooms and suites are not even big enough to swing, well, a phoenix in. Still, the welcome is always warm here and the Mosque Church is within easy reach. The suite has a large open terrace.

Corso Hotel BUSINESS HOTEL €€€

(☎72-421 900; www.corsohotel.hu; Koller utca 8; s/d/ste from 19,500/23,200/32,000Ft;) The Corso is a prime choice if you want the amenities of a business-class hotel within a 10-minute walk of the town centre. Its 81 rooms are inviting with plush carpets and velvet curtains, and all suites have their own outdoor terrace (one features a private sauna). There's a restaurant on the ground floor serving solid international and Hungarian fare.

Eating & Drinking

★ **Jókai Bisztró** HUNGARIAN €€

(☎06 20 360 7337; www.jokaibisztro.hu; Jókai tér 6; mains 1690-3390Ft; ⏲11am-midnight) Arguably the best eatery in Pécs, this charming bistro with its stylish decor and oversized lamps overlooks charming Jókai tér and a seat on the terrace in summer is hot property. The menu is short and savoury but exceptionally well constructed and seasonal; most of the produce and meat is grown and reared by the restaurant. Only downside: cavalier service.

Áfium HUNGARIAN €€

(☎72-511 434; www.afiumetterem.hu; Irgalmasok utca 2; mains 1690-3190Ft; ⏲11am-1am Mon-Sat, to midnight Sun) This homey restaurant with its delightfully retro decor will fill the needs (and stomachs) of most diners searching for Hungarian staples, but it occasionally slips across the border with such dishes as *csevap* (spicy Serbian-style meatballs of beef or pork; 1690Ft). Don't miss the 'hatted' (actually a swollen bread crust) bean soup with trotters (1190Ft). Lovely staff here.

Cooltour Café CAFE

(☎72-310 440; http://cooltourcafe.hu; Király utca 26; ⏲11am-midnight Sun-Tue, to 2am Wed & Thu, to 3am Fri & Sat) Cooltour embodies so many cool things it's hard to choose what we love best. It's a 'ruin pub', yet it's open all day, making it fine for both coffee and snacks or cocktails and mellow chit-chat. It's on the main drag, but its rear garden feels like a secret spot. Occasional live music and parties in the evening.

Information

Tourinform (☎72-213 315; www.iranypecs.hu; Széchenyi tér 7; ⏲9am-5pm Mon-Fri, 10am-3pm Sat & Sun Jun-Aug, closed Sun May, Sep & Oct, closed Sat & Sun Nov-Apr) Knowledgeable staff, copious information on Pécs and surrounds.

Getting There & Away

BUS

Eight buses a day connect Pécs with Budapest (3690Ft, 4¼ hours), eight with Szeged (3410Ft, 3¼ hours) and three with Kecskemét (3410Ft, 3½ hours).

TRAIN

Pécs is on a main rail line with Budapest's Déli train station (3950Ft, four hours, nine daily). One daily train runs from Pécs to Osijek/Eszék in Croatia (two hours), with continuing service to Sarajevo (nine hours) in Bosnia.

GREAT PLAIN

Like the outback for Australians or the Wild West for Americans, the Nagy Alföld (Great Plain) holds a romantic appeal for Hungarians. Many of these notions come as much from the collective imagination, paintings and poetry as they do from history, but there's no arguing the spellbinding potential of big-sky country. The Great Plain is home to cities of graceful architecture and rich history such as Szeged and Kecskemét.

Szeged

☎62 / POP 162,000

Szeged (*seh*-ged) is a bustling border town, with a handful of historic sights that line the embankment along the Tisza River and a clutch of sumptuous art nouveau town palaces. Importantly, it's also a big university town, which means lots of culture, lots of partying and an active festival scene that lasts throughout the year.

Sights & Activities

Dóm tér SQUARE

'Cathedral Square' contains Szeged's most important buildings and monuments and is the centre of events during the annual summer **Szeged Open-Air Festival** (☎62-541 205; www.szegediszabadteri.hu). Lording above all else is the twin-towered **Votive Church** (Fogadalmi templom; ☎62-420 157; www.szegedidom.hu; Dóm tér; ⏲6.30am-7pm Mon-Sat, from 7.30am Sun), a disproportionate brick monstrosity that was pledged after the 1879 flood but built from 1913 to 1930. Running along three sides of the square is the **National Pantheon** (Nemzeti Emlékcsarnok; ⏲24hr) FREE, with statues and reliefs of more than 100 Hungarian notables (almost 100% male).

★**New Synagogue** SYNAGOGUE
(Új Zsinagóga; ☎62-423 849; www.zsinagoga.szeged.hu; Jósika utca 10; adult/concession 500/250Ft; ⏲10am-noon & 1-5pm Sun-Fri Apr-Sep, 9am-2pm Sun-Fri Oct-Mar) The art nouveau New Synagogue, which was designed by Lipót Baumhorn in 1903, is the most beautiful Jewish house of worship in Hungary. It is still in use, though the community has dwindled from 8000 before WWII to about 50 people now. Dominating the enormous blue-and-gold interior is the cupola, decorated with stars and flowers (representing infinity and faith) and appearing to float skyward.

Reök Palace ARCHITECTURE
(Reök Palota; ☎62-541 205; www.reok.hu; Tisza Lajos körút 56; ⏲10am-6pm Tue-Sun) The Reök Palace is a mind-blowing green-and-lilac art nouveau structure built in 1907 that looks like an aquarium decoration. It's been polished up to its original lustre and now hosts regular photography and visual arts exhibitions.

Sleeping

Familia Vendégház GUESTHOUSE €€
(☎62-441 122; www.familiapanzio.hu; Szentháromság utca 71; s €27, d €35-43, tr €50; ❄📶) Families and international travellers often book up this family-run guesthouse with contemporary, if nondescript, furnishings in a great old-town building close to the train station. The two-dozen rooms have high ceilings and loads of light from tall windows. Air-conditioning costs an extra €2.

Dóm Hotel BOUTIQUE HOTEL €€€
(☎62-423 750; www.domhotel.hu; Bajza utca 6; s/d/apt from 19,900/23,900/47,000Ft; ❄@📶) A welcome addition to Szeged's top-end accomodation scene is this very smart and extremely central 16-room boutique hotel. There's a small wellness centre with Jacuzzi, sauna and massage, a popular in-house restaurant and a 21st-century underground carpark accessed by lift. But the main draw is the extremely helpful multilingual staff for whom no request is too much.

WORTH A TRIP

KECSKEMÉT

A worthwhile destination is the lovely city of Kecskemét (pop 112,000), which lies halfway between Budapest and Szeged along the main rail and road arteries. It's a surprisingly green, pedestrian-friendly place with beautiful art nouveau architecture. **Tourinform** (☎76-481 065; www.visitkecskemet.hu; Kossuth tér 1; ⏲8.30am-5.30pm Mon-Fri, 9am-1pm Sat May-Sep, 8.30-4.30pm Mon-Fri Oct-Apr) is centrally located on the main square. It can advise on sights, places to stay and outings to **Kiskunság National Park** (Kiskunsági Nemzeti Park; www.knp.hu). Kecskemét is served by bus to/from Budapest (1680Ft, 1¼ hours, half-hourly) and Szeged (1680Ft, 1¾ hours, nine daily).

Eating & Drinking

Boci Tejivó FAST FOOD €
(☎62-423 154; www.bocitejivo.hu; Zrínyi utca 2; dishes 220-890Ft; ⏲24hr; 🥗) This is a very modern take on an old-fashioned idea – the 'milk bar' so popular during socialist times. Though not vegetarian there are dozens of meatless dishes – cheese and mushroom omelettes, noodles with walnuts or poppy-seed and anything with the ever-popular *túró* (curd), especially *túrógombóc* (curd dumplings; 650Ft).

Vendéglő A Régi Hídhoz HUNGARIAN €€
(☎62-420 910; www.regihid.hu; Oskola utca 4; mains 1700-2600Ft; ⏲11.30am-11pm Sun-Thu, to midnight Fri & Sat) For an authentic meal that won't break the bank, head for 'At the Old Bridge', a traditional Hungarian restaurant with all the favourites and a great terrace just a block in from the river. It's a great place to try *Szögedi halászlé* (1700Ft), Szeged's famous fish soup.

Classic Cafe SERBIAN €€
(☎62-422 065; www.classiccafe.hu; Széchenyi tér 5; mains 2190-2700Ft; ⏲10am-midnight Mon-Sat, to 10pm Sun) This welcoming Serbian place with its lovely inner courtyard garden (fine for a quiet drink, too) serves up grills like *csevap* (spicy meatballs of beef or pork) and *pljszkavica* (meat patties).

A Cappella CAFE
(☎62-559 966; http://acappella.atw.hu/; Kárász utca 6; ⏰7am-10pm) This two-storey sidewalk cafe overlooking Klauzál tér has a generous choice of cakes (485Ft to 650Ft), ice creams and frothy coffee concoctions.

Information

Tourinform Branches include the exceptionally helpful main office (☎62-488 690; www.szegedtourism.hu; Dugonics tér 2; ⏰9am-5pm Mon-Fri, to 1pm Sat), tucked away in a courtyard near the university, and a seasonal kiosk (Széchenyi tér; ⏰8am-8pm Jun-Sep).

Getting There & Around

BUS

Buses run to Kecskemét (1680Ft, 1¾ hours, nine daily) and Pécs (3410Ft, 3¼ hours, four daily). You can also get to the Serbian city of Subotica (1200Ft, 1½ hours) up to four times a day by bus.

TRAIN

Szeged is on the main rail line to Budapest's Nyugati train station (3705Ft, 2½ hours, half-hourly); many trains also stop halfway along in Kecskemét (2375Ft, 1¼ hours).

NORTHEASTERN HUNGARY

This is the home of Hungary's two most famous wines – honey-sweet Tokaj and Eger's famed Bull's Blood – and a region of microclimates conducive to wine production. The chain of wooded hills in the northeast constitutes the foothills of the Carpathian Mountains, which stretch along the Hungarian border with Slovakia.

Eger

☎36 / POP 54,500

Filled with wonderfully preserved baroque buildings, Eger (*egg*-air) is a jewelbox of a town. Learn about the Turkish conquest and defeat at its hilltop castle, climb an original minaret, hear an organ performance at the massive basilica and, best of all, go from cellar to cellar in the Valley of Beautiful Women, tasting the celebrated Bull's Blood wine from the region where it's made.

Sights & Activities

★Eger Castle FORTRESS
(Egri Vár; ☎36-312 744; www.egrivar.hu; Vár köz 1; castle grounds adult/child 800/400Ft, incl museum 1400/700Ft; ⏰exhibits 10am-5pm Tue-Sun May-Oct, 10am-4pm Tue-Sun Nov-Apr, castle grounds 8am-8pm May-Aug, to 7pm Apr & Sep, to 6pm Mar & Oct, to 5pm Nov-Feb) Climb up cobbled Vár köz from Dózsa György tér to reach Eger Castle, erected in the 13th century after the Mongol invasion. Models and drawings in the **István Dobó Museum**, housed in the former Bishop's Palace (1470), painlessly explain the history of the castle. The **Eger Art Gallery** on the northwestern side of the courtyard has works by Canaletto and Ceruti. Beneath the castle are **casemates** *(kazamata)* hewn from solid rock, which can be visited.

Eger Basilica CHURCH
(Egri Bazilika; ☎36-420 970; www.eger-bazilika.plebania.hu; Pyrker János tér 1; requested donation adult/conession 300/100Ft; ⏰8.30am-6pm Mon-Sat, 1-6pm Sun) A highlight of the town's amazing architecture is Eger Basilica. This neoclassical monolith was designed in 1836 by József Hild, the same architect who later worked on the cathedral at Esztergom. A good time to see the place is when the ornate altars and a soaring dome create interesting acoustics for the half-hour **organ concert** (adult/child 800/500Ft; ⏰11.30am Mon-Sat, 12.30pm Sun mid-May–mid-Oct).

Minaret ISLAMIC
(☎06 70 202 4353; www.minareteger.hu; Knézich Károly utca; admission 300Ft; ⏰10am-6pm Apr-Sep, 10am-5pm Oct, 10am-3pm Sat & Sun Nov-Mar) This 40m-high minaret, topped incongruously with a cross, is one of the few reminders of the Ottoman occupation of Eger. Nonclaustrophobes will brave the 97 narrow spiral steps to the top for the awesome views.

★Valley of the Beautiful Women WINE TASTING
(Szépasszony-völgy) Wine tasting is popular in the wine cellars of this evocatively named valley. Try ruby-red Bull's Blood or any of the whites: Leányka, Olaszrizling and Hárslevelű from nearby Debrő. The choice of wine cellars can be a bit daunting so walk around and have a look yourself. The valley is a little over 1km southwest across Rte 25 and off Király utca.

★Turkish Bath
SPA

(Török Fürdő; ☎36-510 552; www.egertermal.hu; Fürdő utca 3-4; 2½hr session adult/child 2200/1500Ft; ⊙4.30-9pm Mon & Tue, 3-9pm Wed & Thu, 1-9pm Fri, 9am-9pm Sat & Sun) Nothing beats a soak and steam at this historic spa, which has a bath dating to 1617 at its core. A multimillion-forint renovation has added five pools, saunas, steam room and a hamam (Turkish bath). Various kinds of massage and treatments are also available.

Sleeping

Agria Retur Vendégház
GUESTHOUSE €

(☎36-416 650; www.returvendeghaz.hu; Knézich Károly utca 18; s/d/tr 3800/6400/9300Ft; 📶) You couldn't find sweeter hosts than the daughter and mother who own this guesthouse near the minaret. Walking up three flights of stairs, you enter a cheery communal kitchen/eating area central to four mansard rooms with fridge. Out the back is a huge garden with tables and a barbecue at your disposal.

★Hotel Senator-Ház
BOUTIQUE HOTEL €€

(Senator House Hotel; ☎36-320 466; www.senatorhaz.hu; Dobó István tér 11; s €40-48, d €53-65; ❄) Eleven warm and cosy rooms with traditional white furnishings fill the upper floors of this delightful 18th-century inn on Eger's main square. The ground floor is shared between a quality restaurant and a reception area stuffed with antiques and curios.

Dobó Vendégház
GUESTHOUSE €€

(☎36-421 407; www.dobovendeghaz.hu; Dobó István utca 19; s 9000-10,500Ft, d 13,500-15,900Ft; 📶) Tucked away along one of the old town's pedestrian streets, just below Eger Castle, this lovely little hotel has seven spic-and-span rooms, some with balconies. Check out the museum-quality Zsolnay porcelain collection in the breakfast room.

Eating & Drinking

Palacsintavár
CREPERIE €

(Pancake Castle; ☎36-413 980; www.palacsintavar.hu; Dobó István utca 9; mains 1850-2250Ft; ⊙noon-11pm Tue-Sat, to 10pm Sun) Pop art and a fascinating collection of antique cigarettes still in their packets line the walls in this eclectic eatery. Savoury *palacsinták* – pancakes, for a better word – are served with an abundance of fresh vegetables and range in flavour from Asian to Mexican. There's a large choice of sweet ones (from 1690Ft), too. Enter from Fazola Henrik utca.

★Fő Tér
HUNGARIAN €€

(Main Square; ☎36-817 482; http://fotercafe.hu; Gerl Matyas utca 2; mains 1300-3400Ft; ⊙10am-10pm) This new kid on the block facing Dobó István tér adds a bit of colour to Eger's dining scene, with its chartreuse-and-plum pop-art decor and a glassed-in terrace with a tented roof. The food is Hungarian with a contemporary taste; we loved the grilled smoked-ewe cheese with orange salad (1950Ft) and pork knuckle braised in dark beer (2000Ft).

Bikavér Borház
WINE BAR

(☎36-413 262; http://www.egrikirakat.hu/tagok-bemutatkozasa/bikaver-borhaz; Dobó István tér 10; ⊙10am-10pm) Try one or two (or three) of the region's best vintages at this central wine bar with a choice of 50-plus wines. The waiters can guide you with the right selection and supply a plate of cheese or grapes to help you cleanse your palate.

Information

Tourinform (☎36-517 715; http://www.eger.hu/hu/turizmus/tdm-tourinform; Bajcsy-Zsilinszky utca 9; ⊙8am-6pm Mon-Fri, 9am-1pm Sat & Sun Jul & Aug, 8am-5pm Mon-Fri, 9am-1pm Sat & Sun May, Jun, Sep & Oct, 8am-5pm Mon-Fri Nov-Apr) Promotes both the town and areas surrounding Eger.

Getting There & Away

BUS

From Eger, buses serve Kecskemét (3130Ft, 4½ hours, three daily) and Szeged (3950Ft, five hours, two daily). To get to Tokaj by bus, you have to go to Nyíregyháza (2520Ft, three hours,

WORTH A TRIP

TOKAJ

A worthwhile wine destination is the small village of Tokaj (population 4900), 43km northeast of Eger, which has long been celebrated for its sweet dessert wines. **Tourinform** (☎06 70 388 8870, 47-552 070; www.tokaj-turizmus.hu; Serház utca 1; ⊙9am-5pm Mon-Sat, 10am-3pm Sun Jun-Aug, 9am-4pm Mon-Fri Sep-May) is just off Rákóczi út and can help with accommodation. Travelling to/from Eger choose the train (3425Ft, two hours, hourly), though you need to change in Füzesabony. Up to seven trains a day head for Budapest (4605Ft, 2½ hours).

three daily) and catch another bus to Tokaj (650Ft, half-hour, three daily).

TRAIN

Up to eight direct trains a day head to Budapest's Keleti train station (2725Ft, two hours). You can reach Tokaj (3425Ft, two hours, hourly) with a change in Füzesabony.

SURVIVAL GUIDE

 Directory A–Z

BUSINESS HOURS

Banks 8am or 9am to 4pm or 5pm Monday to Friday

Bars Usually 11am to midnight Sunday to Thursday, to 1am or 2am on Friday and Saturday

Museums 9am or 10am to 5pm or 6pm Tuesday to Sunday

Restaurants Roughly 11am to midnight

Shops 9am or 10am to 6pm Monday to Friday, 10am to 1pm on Saturday, some to 8pm Thursday

DISCOUNT CARDS

The **Hungary Card** (www.hungarycard.hu; basic/standard/plus 2550/5800/9300Ft) offers free entry to many museums; 50% off on six return train fares and some bus and boat travel; up to 20% off selected accommodation; and 50% off the price of the Budapest Card (p570). It's available at Tourinform offices.

INTERNET RESOURCES

Hungary Museums (www.museum.hu)

Hungarian National Tourist Office (www.gotohungary.com)

COUNTRY FACTS

Area 93,030 sq km

Capital Budapest

Country Code ☎36

Currency Forint (Ft)

Emergency ambulance ☎104, emergency assistance ☎112, fire ☎105, police ☎107

Language Hungarian

Money ATMs abound

Population 9.96 million

Visas None for EU, USA, Canada, Australia and New Zealand

MEDIA

Budapest has two English-language newspapers: the weekly **Budapest Times** (www.budapesttimes.hu; 750Ft), with interesting reviews and opinion pieces, and the business-oriented biweekly **Budapest Business Journal** (www.bbjonline.hu; 1250Ft). Both are available on newsstands.

MONEY

The unit of currency is the Hungarian forint (Ft). Coins come in denominations of five, 10, 20, 50, 100 and 200Ft, and notes are denominated in 500, 1000, 2000, 5000, 10,000 and 20,000Ft. ATMs are everywhere, even in small villages. Tip waiters, hairdressers and taxi drivers approximately 10% of the total.

PUBLIC HOLIDAYS

New Year's Day 1 January

1848 Revolution Day 15 March

Easter Monday March/April

International Labour Day 1 May

Whit Monday (Pentecost) May/June

St Stephen's/Constitution Day 20 August

1956 Remembrance/Republic Day 23 October

All Saints' Day 1 November

Christmas Holidays 25 & 26 December

TELEPHONE

Hungary's country code is ☎36. To make an outgoing international call, dial ☎00 first. To dial city-to-city within the country, first dial ☎06, wait for the second dial tone and then dial the city code and phone number. You must always dial ☎06 when ringing mobile telephones. All localities in Hungary have a two-digit city code, except for Budapest, where the code is ☎1.

As with the rest of Europe, Hungarian mobile phones operate on the GSM standard network. Compatible handsets will connect automatically with local providers, but watch for high roaming fees, particularly for data downloads. A cheaper alternative is to purchase a pay-as-you-go SIM card (available at mobile-phone shops and newsagents), which will give you a temporary local number with which to make calls and send text messages.

TOURIST INFORMATION

The **Hungarian National Tourist Office** (HNTO; http://gotohungary.com) has a chain of more than 125 **Tourinform** (☎from abroad 36 1 438 80 80, within Hungary 800 36 000 000; www.tourinform.hu; ⏲8am-8pm Mon-Fri) information offices across the country. These are the best places to ask general questions and pick up brochures across the country. In the capital, you can also visit **Budapest Info** (Map p566; ☎1-438 8080; www.budapestinfo.hu).

VISAS

Citizens of virtually all European countries, as well as Australia, Canada, Israel, Japan, New Zealand and the USA, do not require visas to visit Hungary for stays of up to 90 days. Check current visa requirements on the Consular Services page of the **Ministry for Foreign Affairs** (http://konzuliszolgalat.kormany.hu/en) website.

> ### SLEEPING PRICE RANGES
>
> Price ranges for doubles with private bathrooms are categorised as follows:
>
> **€** less than 9000Ft (Budapest 15,000Ft)
>
> **€€** 9000Ft–16,5000Ft (Budapest 15,000Ft–33,500Ft)
>
> **€€€** more than 16,500Ft (Budapest 33,500Ft)
>
> Some hotels and guesthouses quote their rates in euros. In such cases, we have followed suit.

Getting There & Away

Hungary's landlocked status ensures plenty of possibilities for onward travel overland. There are direct train connections from Budapest to major cities in all of Hungary's neighbours. International buses head in all directions and in the warmer months you can take a ferry along the Danube to reach Vienna in Austria.

AIR

Ferenc Liszt International Airport (☎1-296 7000; www.bud.hu), 24km southeast of the city, has two modern terminals next to one another. Terminal 2A is served by flights from countries within the Schengen border, while other international flights and budget carriers use 2B. Among the latter serving Hungary are the following:

Air Berlin (AB; ☎06 80 017 110; www.airberlin.com; hub Cologne)

easyJet (EZY; www.easyjet.com)

Germanwings (www.germanwings.com)

Ryanair (FR; www.ryanair.com; hub London)

Wizz Air (W6; ☎06 90 181 181; www.wizzair.com; hub Katowice, Poland)

LAND

Bus

Most international buses arrive at the Népliget bus station (p570) in Budapest and most services are run by **Eurolines** (www.eurolines.com) in conjunction with its Hungarian affiliate, **Volán** (www.volan.eu). Useful international routes include buses from Budapest to Vienna in Austria, Bratislava in Slovakia, Subotica in Serbia, Rijeka in Croatia, Prague in the Czech Republic and Sofia in Bulgaria.

Car & Motorcycle

Third-party insurance is compulsory for driving in Hungary; if your car is registered in the EU, it's assumed you have it. Other motorists must show a Green Card or buy insurance at the border.

Travel on Hungarian motorways requires pre-purchase of a highway pass *(matrica)* available from petrol stations and post offices. Your licence-plate/registration number will be entered into a computer database where it can be screened by highway-mounted surveillance cameras. Prices per week are 1470/2975Ft for a motorcycle/car.

Train

Magyar Államvasutak (MÁV; ☎06 40 494 949, 1-371 9449; http://elvira.mav-start.hu/), the Hungarian State Railways, links up with international rail networks in all directions, and its schedule is available online.

EuroCity (EC) and Intercity (IC) trains require a seat reservation and payment of a supplement. Most larger train stations in Hungary have left-luggage rooms open from at least 9am to 5pm.

Some direct train connections from Budapest include Austria, Slovakia, Romania, Ukraine, Croatia, Serbia, Germany, Slovenia, Czech Republic, Poland, Switzerland, Italy, Bulgaria and Greece.

RIVER

Hydrofoils on the Danube River bound for Vienna depart Budapest at 9am on Tuesday, Thursday and Saturday, returning from Vienna at the same time on Wednesday, Friday and Sunday. Adult one-way/return fares are €99/125. Transporting a bicycle costs €25.

Getting Around

Hungary does not have any scheduled domestic flights.

BOAT

In summer there are regular passenger ferries on the Danube from Budapest to Szentendre, Visegrád and Esztergom as well as on Lake Balaton.

BUS

Domestic buses, run by the Volánbusz (p570), an association of coach operators, cover an extensive nationwide network. Timetables are posted at all stations. Some footnotes you could come across include *naponta* (daily), *hétköznap* (weekdays), *munkanapokon* (on work days), *munkaszüneti napok kivételével naponta* (daily except holidays) and *szabad és munkaszüneti*

ESSENTIAL FOOD & DRINK

Hungary enjoys perhaps the most varied and interesting cuisine in Eastern Europe. Inexpensive by Western European standards and served in huge portions, traditional Hungarian food is heavy and rich. Meat, sour cream and fat abound and the omnipresent seasoning is with paprika, which appears on restaurant tables as a condiment beside the salt and pepper. Things are lightening up though, with vegetarian, 'New Hungarian' and ethnic cuisines increasingly available.

- **Galuska** Small dumplings not unlike gnocchi that make a good accompaniment to *pörkölt*.
- **Gulyás** (goulash) Hungary's signature dish, though here it's more like a soup than a stew and made with beef, onions and tomatoes.
- **Halászlé** Highly recommended fish soup made from poached freshwater fish, tomatoes, green peppers and paprika.
- **Lángos** Street food; fried dough topped with cheese and/or *tejföl* (sour cream).
- **Palacsinta** Thin crêpes that come either *sós* (savoury) and eaten as a main course or *édes* (sweet) filled with jam, sweet cheese or chocolate sauce for dessert.
- **Pálinka** A strong brandy distilled from all kinds of fruit but especially plums and apricots.
- **Paprika** The omnipresent seasoning in Hungarian cooking, which comes in two varieties: strong *(erős)* and sweet *(édes)*.
- **Pörkölt** Paprika-infused stew; closer to what we would call goulash.
- **Savanyúság** Literally 'sourness'; anything from mildly sour-sweet cucumbers to almost acidic sauerkraut, eaten with a main course.
- **Wine** Two Hungarian wines are known internationally: the sweet dessert wine Tokaji Aszú and Egri Bikavér (Eger Bull's Blood), a full-bodied red.

napokon (on Saturday and holidays). A few large bus stations have luggage rooms, but these generally close by 6pm.

CAR & MOTORCYCLE

In general, you must be at least 21 years old and have had your driving licence for at least a year to rent a car. There is a 100% ban on alcohol when you are driving, and this rule is strictly enforced. Most cities and towns require that you pay for street parking (usually 9am to 6pm workdays) by buying temporary parking passes from machines.

LOCAL TRANSPORT

Public transport is efficient and extensive in Hungary, with bus and, in many towns, trolleybus services. Budapest, Szeged and Debrecen also have trams, and there's an extensive metro and a suburban commuter railway in Budapest. Purchase tickets at newsstands before travelling and validate them once aboard. Inspectors frequently check tickets.

EATING PRICE RANGES

Price ranges are as follows:

€ less than 2000Ft (Budapest 3000Ft)

€€ 2000Ft–3500Ft (Budapest 3000Ft–7500Ft)

€€€ more than 3500Ft (Budapest 7500Ft)

TRAIN

MÁV (☎1-444 4499; www.mav-start.hu) operates reliable train services on more than 7600km of tracks. Schedules are available online and computer information kiosks are popping up at train stations around the country.

IC trains are express trains and are the most comfortable and modern. *Gyorsvonat* (fast trains) take longer and use older cars; *személyvonat* (passenger trains) stop at every village along the way. Seat reservations *(helyjegy)* cost extra and are required on IC and some fast trains; these are indicated on the timetable by an 'R' in a box or a circle (a plain 'R' means seat reservations are available but not required).

In all stations a yellow board indicates departures *(indul)* and a white board is for arrivals *(érkezik)*. Express and fast trains are indicated in red, local trains in black.

Both **InterRail** (www.interrail.eu) and **Eurail** (www.eurail.com) passes cover Hungary.

Iceland

Includes ➡

Best Places to Eat

- ➡ Dill (p593)
- ➡ Þrír Frakkar (p592)
- ➡ Lindin (p595)
- ➡ Plássið (p598)
- ➡ Hannes Boy (p599)

Best Places to Stay

- ➡ Hótel Borg (p589)
- ➡ KEX Hostel (p589)
- ➡ Hótel Egilsen (p598)
- ➡ Ion Luxury Adventure Hotel (p595)
- ➡ Skjaldarvík (p598)

Why Go?

The energy is palpable on this magical island, where astonishing natural phenomena inspire the welcoming, creative locals and draw an increasing number of visitors in search of its untrammelled splendour. A vast volcanic laboratory, here the earth itself is restless and alive. Admire thundering waterfalls, glittering glaciers carving their way to black-sand beaches, explosive geysers, rumbling volcanoes and contorted lava fields.

In summer permanent daylight energises the already zippy inhabitants of Iceland's quaint capital, Reykjavík, with its wonderful cafe and bar scene. Fashion, design and music are woven into the city's fabric, and the museums are tops. In winter, with luck, you may see the Northern Lights shimmering across the sky. Year-round, though, adventure tours abound, getting you up close and personal with sights and sounds that will stay with you for life.

When to Go

Reykjavík

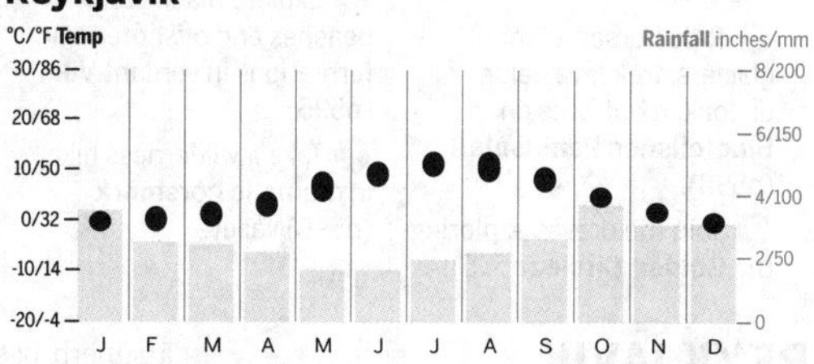

May & Jun Prime birdwatching season happily coincides with the two driest months and fewer crowds.

Aug It's full throttle in Reykjavík, the country teems with visitors and it's almost always light.

Nov–Apr The best months for Northern Lights and bare minimalism.

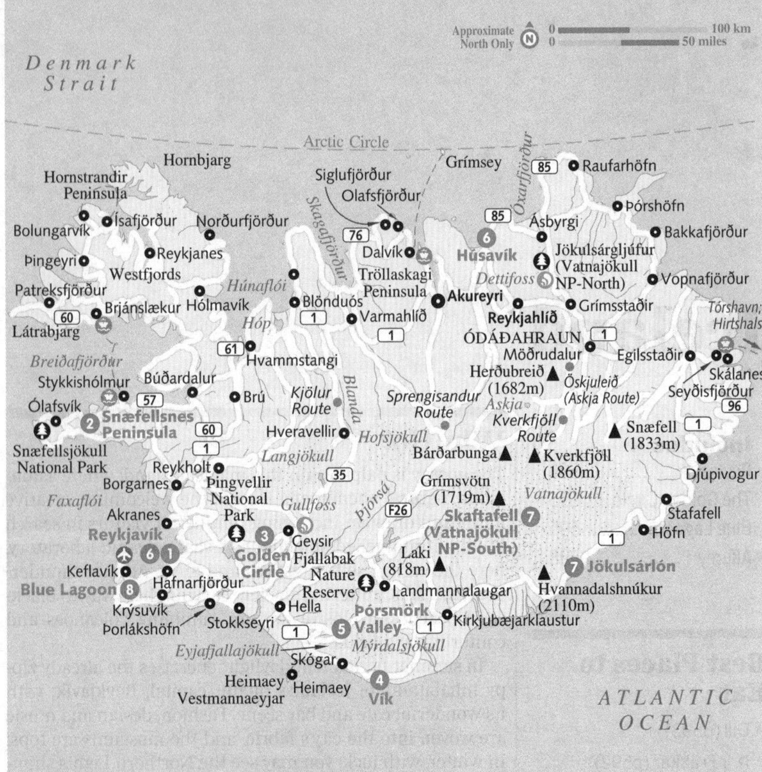

Iceland Highlights

1. Party 'til dawn on the weekend pub crawl *djammið* in lively **Reykjavík** then hit excellent museums, shops and cafes.
2. Ride horses, climb glaciers, trek lava fields, or soak in hot-pots on **Snæfellsnes Peninsula** (p598).
3. Join the droves exploring the **Golden Circle** (p595): scintillating Gullfoss waterfall, exploding geysers, and the nation's birthplace, rift valley Þingvellir.
4. Explore black-sand beaches and offshore rock formations in verdant **Vík** (p596).
5. Take a wilderness hike in dramatic **Þórsmörk** (p596) valley.
6. Go whale watching in **Húsavík** (p598) or **Reykjavík** (p588).
7. Exhaust your camera's memory card at **Skaftafell** in Vatnajökull National Park and nearby **Jökulsárlón glacial lagoon** (p597).
8. Swim through steam clouds at the world-famous **Blue Lagoon** (p595).

REYKJAVÍK

POP 121,230

The world's most northerly capital combines colourful buildings, wild nightlife and a capricious soul to brilliant effect. You'll find Viking history, captivating museums, cool music, and offbeat cafes and bars. And it's a superb base for touring Iceland's natural wonders.

Reykjavík's heart lies between Tjörnin (the Pond) and the harbour, and along Laugavegur, with nearly everything for visitors within walking distance.

Sights & Activities

★Old Reykjavík NEIGHBOURHOOD

With a series of sights and interesting historic buildings, the area dubbed Old Reykjavík is the heart of the capital, and the focal point of many historic walking tours. The area is anchored by Tjörnin, the city-centre lake, and sitting between it and Austurvöllur park to the north are the Raðhús (city hall) and Alþingi (parliament).

★National Museum MUSEUM

(Þjóðminjasafn Íslands; ☎530 2200; www.nationalmuseum.is; Suðurgata 41; adult/child Ikr1500/free, audioguide Ikr300; ⏰10am-5pm May–mid-Sep, 11am-5pm Tue-Sun mid-Sep–Apr; 🚌1, 3, 6, 12 or 14) This superb museum displays artefacts from Settlement to the modern age. Exhibits give an excellent overview of Iceland's history and culture, and the audioguide adds loads of detail. The strongest section describes the Settlement Era – including how the chieftains ruled and the introduction of Christianity – and features swords, drinking horns, silver hoards and a powerful little bronze figure of Thor. The priceless 13th-century **Valþjófsstaðir church door** is carved with the story of a knight, his faithful lion and a passel of dragons.

★Reykjavík 871±2: The Settlement Exhibition MUSEUM

(☎411 6370; www.reykjavikmuseum.is; Aðalstræti 16; adult/child Ikr1300/free; ⏰10am-5pm, English-language tour 11am Mon, Wed & Fri Jun-Aug) This fascinating archaeological ruin/museum is based around a 10th-century **Viking longhouse** unearthed here from 2001 to 2002, and the other settlement-era finds from central Reykjavík. It imaginatively combines technological wizardry and archaeology to give a glimpse into early Icelandic life.

The museum's name comes from the estimated date of the tephra layer beneath the longhouse, but don't miss the fragment of **boundary wall**, at the back of the museum that is older still (and the oldest man-made structure in Reykjavík).

★Hallgrímskirkja CHURCH

(☎510 1000; www.hallgrimskirkja.is; Skólavörðustígur; tower adult/child Ikr700/100; ⏰9am-9pm Jul & Aug, to 5pm Sep-Jun) Reykjavík's immense white-concrete church (1945–86), star of a thousand postcards, dominates the skyline, and is visible from up to 20km away. Get an unmissable view of the city by taking an elevator trip up the 74.5m-high **tower**. In contrast to the high drama outside, the Lutheran church's interior is quite plain. The most eye-catching feature is the vast 5275-pipe **organ** installed in 1992. The church's size and radical design caused controversy, and its architect, Guðjón Samúelsson (1887–1950), never saw its completion.

★Reykjavík Art Museum ART MUSEUM

(Listasafn Reykjavíkur; www.artmuseum.is; adult/child Ikr1300/free) The excellent Reykjavík Art Museum is split over three well-done sites: the large, modern downtown **Hafnarhús** (☎590 1200; Tryggvagata 17; ⏰10am-5pm Fri-Wed, to 8pm Thu) focusing on contemporary art;

ITINERARIES

Three Days

Arrive in **Reykjavík** on a weekend to catch the decadent all-night *djammið* (partying pub crawl). Sober up over brunch at Grái Kötturinn or in **Laugardalur**'s geothermal pool, admire the views from **Hallgrímskirkja**, cruise the cafes and shops near **Laugavegur**, then absorb Viking history at the National Museum or Reykjavík 871±2: The Settlement Exhibition. On day three, visit Gullfoss, Geysir and Þingvellir National Park on a **Golden Circle tour**, and soak in the **Blue Lagoon** on the way home.

Seven Days

With four more days you'll have plenty of time to head to west Iceland for **Borgarnes'** excellent Settlement Centre. Next visit **Snæfellsnes Peninsula** with its ravishing Snæfellsjökull National Park, or head inland to **Langjökull** with its ice cave, and nearby **Viðgelmir lava tube**. Explore further afield in south Iceland: **Hekla** volcano, **Skógar** with its waterfalls and hikes, **Vík** with gorgeous ocean-front landscapes, or take a super-Jeep or amphibious bus to **Þórsmörk**. **Vatnajökull National Park**, **Skaftafell** and **Jökulsárlón glacier lagoon** are worth a trip for amazing scenery and outdoor adventures. Or hop on a flight to **Akureyri** and check out the north.

Kjarvalsstaðir (☎517 1290; Flókagata, Miklatún Park; ⏱10am-5pm), in a park just east of Snorrabraut, and displaying rotating exhibits of modern art; and **Ásmundarsafn** (Ásmundur Sveinsson Museum; ☎553 2155; Sigtún; ⏱10am-5pm May-Sep, 1-5pm Oct-Apr; 🚌2, 14, 15, 17 or 19), a peaceful haven near Laugardalur for viewing sculptures by Ásmundur Sveinsson.

One ticket is good at all three sites, and if you buy after 3pm you get a 50% discount should you want a ticket the next day.

★Old Harbour NEIGHBOURHOOD

(Geirsgata) Largely a service harbour until recently, the Old Harbour has blossomed into a hot spot for tourists, with several museums, volcano and Northern Lights films and worthwhile restaurants. Whale-watching and puffin-viewing trips depart from the pier. Photo ops abound with views of fishing boats, Harpa concert hall and snowcapped mountains beyond. At the time of writing there was also a freestyle summertime children's **play area** with giant spindles and ropes, along Mýrargata.

★National Gallery of Iceland MUSEUM

(Listasafn Íslands; www.listasafn.is; Fríkirkjuvegur 7; adult/child Ikr1000/free; ⏱10am-5pm Tue-Sun Jun-Aug, 11am-5pm Sep-May) This pretty stack of marble atriums and spacious galleries overlooking Tjörnin offers ever-changing exhibits drawn from the 10,000-piece collection. The museum can only exhibit a small sample at any time; shows range from 19th- and 20th-century paintings by Iceland's favourite sons and daughters (including Jóhannes Kjarval and Nína Sæmundsson) to sculptures by Sigurjón Ólafsson and others. The museum ticket also covers entry to the **Ásgrímur Jónsson Collection** (☎515 9625; www.listasafn.is; Bergstaðastræti 74; adult/child Ikr1000/free; ⏱2-5pm Tue, Thu & Sun mid-May–mid-Sep, 2-5pm Sun mid-Sep–Nov & Feb–mid-May) and **Sigurjón Ólafsson Museum** (Listasafn Sigurjóns Ólafssonar; ☎553 2906; www.lso.is; Laugarnestangi 70; adult/child Ikr500/free; ⏱2-5pm Tue-Sun Jun–mid-Sep, 2-5pm Sat & Sun mid-Sep–Nov & Feb-May).

Volcano House FILM

(☎555 1900; www.volcanohouse.is; Tryggvagata 11; adult/child Ikr1990/500; ⏱hourly 10am-9pm) This modern theatre with a lava exhibit in the foyer screens a 55-minute pair of films about the Westman Island volcanoes and Eyjafjallajökull. They show in German once daily in summer.

Saga Museum MUSEUM

(☎511 1517; www.sagamuseum.is; Grandagarður 2; adult/child Ikr2000/800; ⏱9am-6pm) The endearingly bloodthirsty Saga Museum is where Icelandic history is brought to life by eerie silicon models and a multilanguage soundtrack with thudding axes and hair-raising screams. Don't be surprised if you see some of the characters wandering around town, as moulds were taken from Reykjavík residents (the owner's daughters are the Irish princess and the little slave gnawing a fish!).

Laugardalslaug GEOTHERMAL POOL, HOT-POT

(Sundlaugavegur 30a, Laugardalur; adult/child Ikr600/130, suit/towel rental Ikr800/550; ⏱6.30am-10pm Mon-Fri, 8am-10pm Sat & Sun; 👪) One of the largest pools in Iceland, with the best facilities: Olympic-sized indoor pool and outdoor pools, seven hot-pots, a saltwater tub, steam bath and a curling 86m water slide.

Festivals & Events

Reykjavíkers turn out in force for a day and night of art, music, dance and fireworks in mid-August on **Culture Night** (www.menningarnott.is). In November, the fab **Iceland Airwaves** (www.icelandairwaves.com) international music festival is one of the world's premier showcases for new music (Icelandic and otherwise).

Tours

Walking, bike and bus tours are the main way to take in the city. Whale-watching, puffin-spotting and sea-angling trips allow a jaunt offshore.

As lovely as the capital's sights are, though, Reykjavík is also the main hub for tours to amazing landscapes and activities around Iceland. Those without wheels, time or the desire to travel the countryside independently can use Reykjavík as a cosmopolitan base for all forms of tours from super-Jeeps and buses to horse riding, snowmobiling and heli or airplane tours. If you have time, though, head out on your own.

Elding Adventures at Sea WHALE WATCHING

(☎519 5000; www.whalewatching.is; Ægisgarður 5; ⏱harbour kiosk 8am-9pm) The city's most established and ecofriendly outfit, with an included whale exhibition and refreshments sold on board. Elding also offers angling and puffin-watching trips, combo tours, and runs the ferry to Viðey.

Reykjavík Excursions BUS
(Kynnisferðir; ☎580 5400; www.re.is; Vatnsmýrarvegur 10, BSÍ Bus Terminal) The most popular bus-tour operator (with large groups) has an enormous booklet full of summer and winter programs. Extras include horse riding, snowmobiling and themed tours tying in with festivals. Also offers 'Iceland on Your Own' bus tickets and passports for transport.

Arctic Adventures ADVENTURE TOUR
(☎562 7000; www.adventures.is; Laugavegur 11; ⊙8am-10pm) With young and enthusiastic staff, this company specialises in action-filled tours: kayaking, rafting, horse riding, quad-biking, glacier walking and so on. It has a booking office with gear shop **Fjallakofinn** (☎510 9505; www.fjallakofinn.is; Laugavegur 11; ⊙9am-7pm Mon-Fri, 10am-4pm Sat, noon-5pm Sun) in central Reykjavík.

Icelandic Mountain Guides ADVENTURE TOUR
(☎587 9999; www.mountainguides.is; Stórhöfði 33) This full-action outfit specialises in mountaineering, trekking, ice climbing and the like. It also markets itself as 'Iceland Rovers' for its super-Jeep tours.

★**Creative Iceland** CRAFT
(www.creativeiceland.is) Get involved with graphic design, cooking, arts, crafts, music… you name it. This service hooks you up with local creative people offering workshops in their art or craft.

Sleeping

Accommodation prices are for June to September; out of season, the rates drop by up to 40%.

★**KEX Hostel** HOSTEL €
(☎561 6060; www.kexhostel.is; Skúlagata 28; 4-/16-bed dm Ikr6900/3900, d with/without bathroom Ikr28,500/19,700; @🛜) An unofficial headquarters of backpackerdom and popular local gathering place, KEX is a mega-hostel with heaps of style (think retro Vaudeville meets rodeo) and sociability. Overall it's not as prim as the other hostels – and bathrooms are shared by many – but KEX is a perennial favourite for its friendly vibe and booming restaurant-bar with water views and interior courtyard.

★**Reykjavík Downtown Hostel** HOSTEL €
(☎553 8120; www.hostel.is; Vesturgata 17; 4-/10-bed dm Ikr7900/5700, d with/without bathroom Ikr23,800/20,700; @) Squeaky clean and well run, this effortlessly charming hostel gets such good reviews that it regularly lures large groups and the nonbackpacker set. Enjoy friendly service, guest kitchen and excellent rooms. Discount Ikr700 for HI members.

Salvation Army Guesthouse HOSTEL €
(☎561 3203; www.guesthouse.is; Kirkjustræti 2; dm/s/d from Ikr3500/9500/13,900; ⊙Jun-Aug; 🛜) Simple, clean rooms come in loads of sizes. Step outside and the whole of Reykjavík is at your feet. Linen Ikr900.

★**Room With A View** APARTMENT €€
(☎552 7262; www.roomwithaview.is; Laugavegur 18; apt Ikr24,400-67,940; 🛜) This ridiculously central apartment hotel offers swank studios and one- to four-bedroom apartments (that sleep 10!), decorated in luxe-Scandinavian style including kitchenettes, CD players, TVs and washing machines. They have those eponymous sea or city views, plus access to a sundeck and Jacuzzi. Each apartment varies: check online for details. The only downside is Friday and Saturday nightlife noise.

★**Grettisborg Apartments** APARTMENT €€
(☎694 7020; www.grettisborg.is; Grettisgata 53b; apt from Ikr25,500; 🛜) Like sleeping in a magazine for Scandinavian home design, these thoroughly modern studios and apartments come in 50 shades of grey (no, not like that), sporting fine furnishings and sleek built-ins.

Galtafell Guesthouse GUESTHOUSE €€
(☎551 4344; www.galtafell.com; Laufásvegur 46; d/apt incl breakfast from Ikr18,500/29,300; 🛜) In a quiet, lakeside neighbourhood within easy walking distance of the centre, the four one-bedroom apartments in this converted historic mansion contain fully equipped kitchens and cosy seating areas. Three doubles share a guest kitchen. The garden and entry spaces feel suitably lovely.

★**Hótel Borg** LUXURY HOTEL €€€
(☎551 1440; www.hotelborg.is; Pósthússtræti 9-11; d from Ikr43,600; @🛜) This historic hotel dates from 1930 and is now tricked out with super-smart beige, black and cream decor, parquet floors, leather headboards and flat-screen Bang & Olufsen TVs. The tower suite is two storeys of opulence with panoramic views. At the time of writing, a huge renovation-expansion had shuttered gourmet Borg restaurant, slated to reopen early 2015 under chef Völundur Völundarson; his bistro **Nora Magasin** is next door.

Central Reykjavík

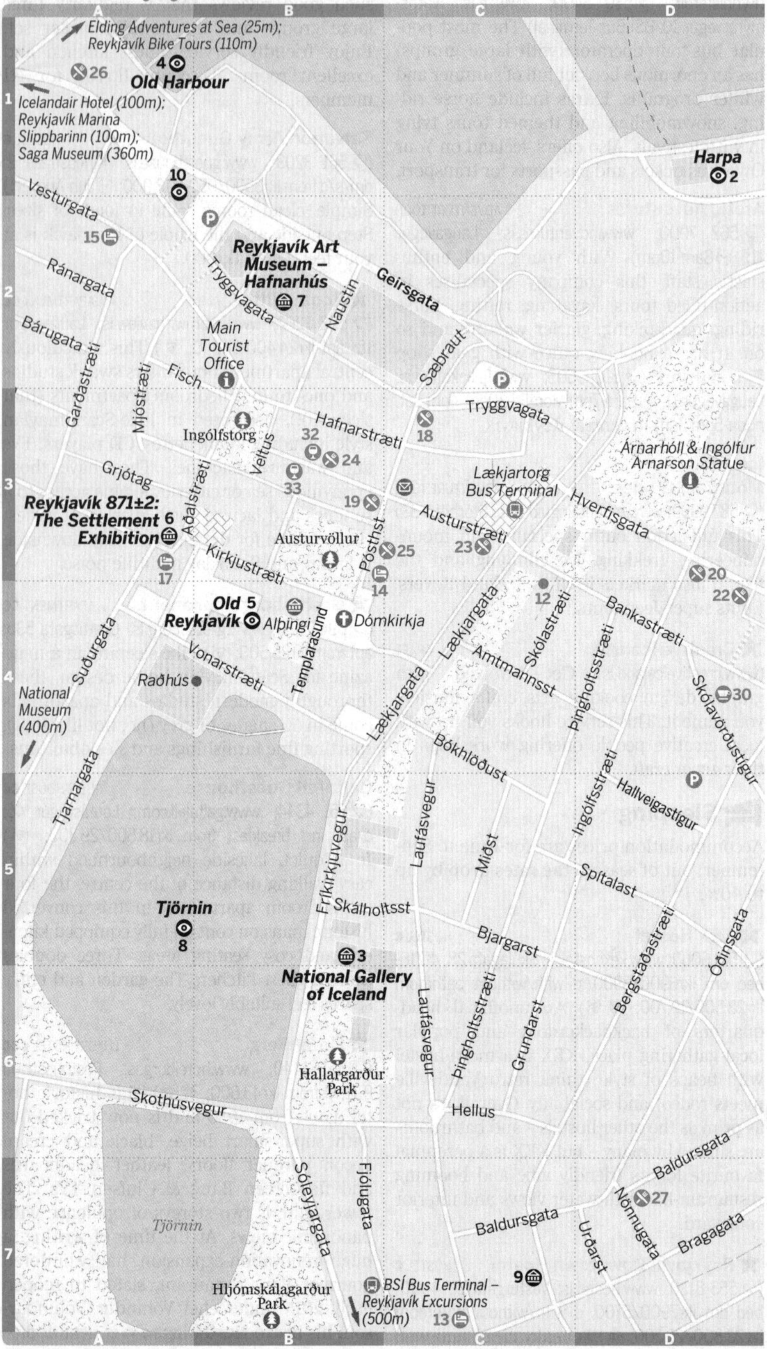

A B C D

1 2 3 4 5 6 7

Elding Adventures at Sea (25m);
Reykjavík Bike Tours (110m)

26

4 **Old Harbour**

Icelandair Hotel (100m);
Reykjavík Marina
Slippbarinn (100m);
Saga Museum (360m)

Harpa 2

10

Vesturgata

15

Ránargata

Tryggvagata

Reykjavík Art Museum – Hafnarhús 7

Naustin

Geirsgata

Bárugata

Main Tourist Office

Garðastræti

Mjóstræti

Fisch

Sæbraut

Tryggvagata

Ingólfstorg

Veltus

32

24

Hafnarstræti

18

33

Grjótag

Aðalstræti

19

Lækjartorg Bus Terminal

Árnarhóll & Ingólfur Arnarson Statue

Reykjavík 871±2: The Settlement Exhibition 6

Austurvöllur

Pósthst

Austurstræti

Hverfisgata

25

23

17

Kirkjustræti

14

12

20

22

Old Reykjavík 5

Alþingi

Dómkirkja

Templarasund

Lækjargata

Skólastræti

Bankastræti

Suðurgata

Vonarstræti

Amtmannsst

Þingholtsstræti

Raðhús

National Museum (400m)

Skólavörðustígur

30

Bókhlöðust

Ingólfsstræti

Tjarnargata

Laufásvegur

Hallveigastígur

Miðst

Fríkirkjuvegur

Spítalast

Skálholtsst

Tjörnin 8

Bjargarst

Óðinsgata

3 **National Gallery of Iceland**

Bergstaðastræti

Laufásvegur

Þingholtsstræti

Grundarst

Hallargarður Park

Skothúsvegur

Hellus

Baldursgata

Sóleyjargata

Fjólugata

27

Nönnugata

Tjörnin

Baldursgata

Urðarst

Bragagata

BSÍ Bus Terminal – Reykjavík Excursions (500m)

9

Hljómskálagarður Park

13

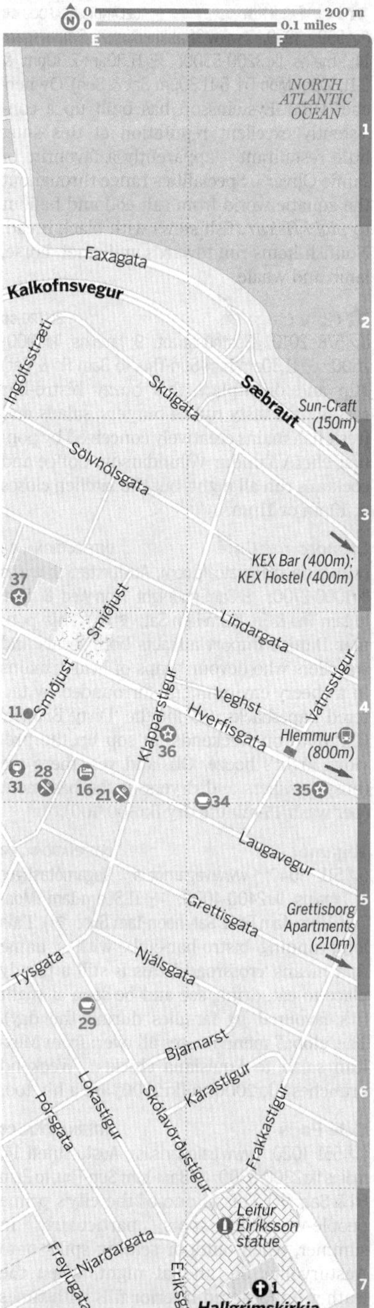

Central Reykjavík

Top Sights

1 Hallgrímskirkja F7
2 Harpa D1
3 National Gallery of Iceland B5
4 Old Harbour A1
5 Old Reykjavík B4
6 Reykjavík 871±2: The Settlement Exhibition A3
7 Reykjavík Art Museum – Hafnarhús B2
8 Tjörnin A5

Sights

9 Ásgrímur Jónsson Collection C7
10 Volcano House A1

Activities, Courses & Tours

11 Arctic Adventures E4
12 Bike Company C4

Sleeping

13 Galtafell Guesthouse C7
14 Hótel Borg B3
15 Reykjavík Downtown Hostel A2
16 Room With A View E4
17 Salvation Army Guesthouse A3

Eating

18 Bæjarins Beztu C3
19 Café Paris B3
20 Dill D3
21 Gló E4
22 Grái Kötturinn D4
23 Grillmarkaðurinn C3
24 Laundromat Café B3
25 Nora Magasin C3
26 Sægreifinn A1
27 Þrír Frakkar D7
28 Vegamót E4

Drinking & Nightlife

29 Babalú E6
30 Kaffi Mokka D4
31 Kaffibarinn E4
Kaldi .... (see 21)
32 Loftið B3
33 Micro Bar B3
34 Tiú Droppar F4

Entertainment

35 Bíó Paradís F4
36 Café Rosenberg E4
37 National Theatre E3

Shopping

Fjallakofinn .... (see 11)

★ **Icelandair Hotel Reykjavík Marina** BOUTIQUE HOTEL €€€
(☎560 8000; www.icelandairhotels.is; Mýrargata 2; d Ikr27,800-35,800; @📶) This large design hotel on the Old Harbour is adding a whole

new wing. Captivating art, cool nautical-chic design elements, up-to-the-second mod cons and clever ways to conserve space make small rooms winners overall. Attic rooms on the harbour side have excellent sea views. The lively lobby sports a live satellite feed to sights all over Iceland, and the happening **Slippbarinn** (☎560 8080; www.slippbarinn.is; Mýrargata 2; ⊙11.30am-midnight Sun-Thu, to 1am Fri & Sat).

Eating

★Gló ORGANIC, VEGETARIAN €
(☎553 1111; www.glo.is; Laugavegur 20b; mains Ikr1700-2500; ⊙11am-9pm; 📶📝) Join the cool cats in this upstairs, airy restaurant serving fresh, large daily specials loaded with Asian-influenced herbs and spices. Though not exclusively vegetarian, it's a wonderland of raw and organic foods with your choice from a broad bar of elaborate salads, from root veggies to Greek. They also have branches in **Laugardalur** (☎553 1111; Engjateigur 19; mains Ikr1700-2500; ⊙11am-9pm Mon-Fri, to 5pm Sat) and **Hafnarfjörður** (☎553 1111; www.glo.is; Strandgata 34; mains Ikr1700-2500; ⊙11am-9pm Mon-Fri, to 5pm Sat & Sun).

★Sægreifinn SEAFOOD €
(Sea Baron; ☎553 1500; www.saegreifinn.is; Geirsgata 8; mains Ikr1350-1900; ⊙11.30am-11pm) Sidle into this green harbour-side shack for the most famous lobster soup (Ikr1300) in the capital, or to choose from a fridge full of fresh fish skewers to be grilled on the spot. Though the original sea baron sold the restaurant a few years ago, the place retains a homey, laid-back feel.

Bæjarins Beztu HOT DOGS €
(www.bbp.is; Tryggvagata; hot dogs Ikr380; ⊙10am-2am Sun-Thu, to 4.30am Fri & Sat; 👪) Icelanders swear the city's best hot dogs are at this truck near the harbour (patronised by Bill Clinton and late-night bar hoppers). Use the vital sentence *Eina með öllu* ('One with everything') to get the quintessential favourite with sweet mustard, ketchup and crunchy onions.

★Grái Kötturinn CAFE €
(☎551 1544; Hverfisgata 16a; mains Ikr1000-2500; ⊙7.15am-3pm Mon-Fri, 8am-3pm Sat & Sun) Blink and you'll miss this tiny six-table cafe (a favourite of Björk's). It looks like a cross between an eccentric bookshop and an art gallery, and dishes up delicious breakfasts of toast, bagels, pancakes, or bacon and eggs served on thick, buttery slabs of freshly baked bread.

★Þrír Frakkar ICELANDIC, SEAFOOD €€
(☎552 3939; www.3frakkar.com; Baldursgata 14; mains Ikr3200-5300; ⊙11.30am-2.30pm & 6-11.30pm Mon-Fri, 6-11.30pm Sat & Sun) Owner-chef Úlfar Eysteinsson has built up a consistently excellent reputation at this snug little restaurant – apparently a favourite of Jamie Oliver's. Specialities range throughout the aquatic world from salt cod and halibut to *plokkfiskur* (fish stew) with black bread. Nonfish items run towards guillemot, horse, lamb and whale.

★Nora Magasin BISTRO €€
(☎578 2010; Pósthússtræti 9; mains Ikr1900-2500; ⊙11.30am-1am Sun-Thu, to 3am Fri & Sat) Hip and open-plan, this buzzy bistro-bar serves up a tasty run of burgers, salads and fresh fish mains creatively conceived by popular chef Völundur Völundarson. Coffee and cocktails run all night, but the kitchen closes at 10pm or 11pm.

Laundromat Café INTERNATIONAL €€
(www.thelaundromatcafe.com; Austurstæti 9; mains Ikr1000-2700; ⊙8am-midnight Mon-Wed & Sun, to 1am Thu & Fri, 10am-1am Sat; 📶👪) This popular Danish import attracts both locals and travellers who devour heaps of hearty mains in a cheery environment surrounded by tattered paperbacks. Go for the 'Dirty Brunch' (Ikr2690) on weekends, to sop up the previous night's booze. Oh, and yes, there are (busy) washers and dryers in the basement (per wash/15-minute dry Ikr500/100).

Vegamót INTERNATIONAL €€
(☎511 3040; www.vegamot.is; Vegamótastígur 4; mains Ikr2400-4000; ⊙11.30am-1am Mon-Thu, 11am-4am Fri & Sat, noon-1am Sun; 📶) This long-running bistro-bar-club, with a name that means 'crossroads', this is still a trendy place to eat, drink, see and be seen at night (it's favoured by families during the day). The 'global' menu ranges all over: from Mexican salad to Louisiana chicken. Weekend brunches (Ikr2000 to Ikr2500) are a hit, too.

Café Paris INTERNATIONAL €€
(☎551 1020; www.cafeparis.is; Austurstræti 14; mains Ikr2300-5300; ⊙8am-1am Sun-Thu, to 2am Fri & Sat; 📶) This is one of the city's prime people-watching spots, particularly in summer, when outdoor seating spills onto Austurvöllur Sq, and at night, when the leather-upholstered interior fills with tunes and tinkling wine glasses. The mediocre selection of sandwiches, salads and burgers is secondary to the scene.

★**Dill** SCANDINAVIAN €€€
(☎552 1522; www.dillrestaurant.is; Hverfisgata 12; 3-course meal from Ikr8100; ⏲7-10pm Wed-Sat) Top 'New Nordic' cuisine is the major drawcard at this elegant yet simple bistro. The focus is very much on the food – locally sourced produce served as a parade of courses. The owners are friends with the famous Noma clan, and have drawn much inspiration from the celebrated Copenhagen restaurant. Popular with locals and visitors alike, a reservation is a must.

★**Grillmarkaðurinn** FUSION €€€
(Grill Market; ☎571 7777; www.grillmarkadurinn.is; Lækargata 2a; mains Ikr4200-7200) Tippety-top dining is the order of the day here, from the moment you enter the glass atrium with the golden-globe lights to your first snazzy cocktail, and on through the meal. Service is impeccable, and locals and visitors alike rave about the food: locally sourced Icelandic ingredients prepared with culinary imagination by master chefs.

Drinking & Nightlife

Reykjavík is renowned for its weekend *djammið,* when folks buy booze from Vínbúðin (state alcohol shop), have a preparty at home, then hit the town at midnight. Many of the cool-cat cafes around town morph into bars at night. Minimum drinking age is 20.

★**Babalú** CAFE
(☎555 8845; Skólavörðustígur 22a; ⏲8am-9pm; 📶) This mellow cafe feels like the den of one of your eccentric friends. Books and board games abound and the baked goods, terraces and comfy couches are the main draw. Paninis are just OK, so fill up instead on homemade chocolate cake and apple crumble.

★**Kaffi Mokka** CAFE
(☎552 1174; www.mokka.is; Skólavörðustígur 3a; ⏲9am-6.30pm) The decor at Reykjavík's oldest coffee shop has changed little since the 1950s, and its original mosaic pillars and copper lights either look retro-cool or dead tatty, depending on your mood. The mixed clientele – from older folks to tourists to trendy artists – dig the selection of sandwiches, cakes and waffles.

★**Kaffibarinn** BAR
(www.kaffibarinn.is; Bergstaðastræti 1; ⏲2pm-1am Sun-Thu, to 4.30am Fri & Sat) This old house with the London Underground symbol over the door contains one of Reykjavík's coolest bars; it even had a starring role in the cult movie *101 Reykjavík* (2000). At weekends you'll feel like you need a famous face or a battering ram to get in. At other times it's a place for artistic types to chill with their Macs.

SMARTPHONE APPS

There's an incredible range of smartphone apps. Useful ones include **112 Iceland** app for safe travel, **Veður** (weather), and apps for bus companies such as Strætó and Reykjavík Excursions. The **Reykjavík Appy Hour** app gets special mention for listing happy hours and their prices!

★**KEX Bar** BAR
(www.kexhostel.is; Skúlagata 28; ⏲noon-11pm; 📶) Believe it or not, locals flock to this hostel bar-restaurant (mains Ikr1700 to Ikr2500) in an old cookie factory (*kex* means cookie) with broad windows facing the sea, an inner courtyard and loads of happy hipsters. The vibe is 1920s Vegas, with saloon doors, an old-school barber station, scuffed floors and happy chatter.

Tiú Droppar CAFE
(Ten Drops; ☎551 9380; Laugavegur 27; ⏲9am-1am Mon-Thu, 10am-1am Sat & Sun; 📶) Tucked in a cosy teapot-lined basement, Tiú Droppar is one of those quintessential Reykjavík cafes that serves waffles, brunches (Ikr640 to Ikr990) and sandwiches, then in the evenings morphs into a wine bar with occasional live music. It's said that the Sunday night pianist can play anything by ear.

Micro Bar BAR
(Austurstræti 6; ⏲2pm-midnight Jun-Sep, 4pm-midnight Oct-May) Boutique brews is the name of the game at this low-key spot near Austurvöllur. Bottles of beer represent a slew of brands and countries, but more importantly you'll discover 10 local draughts on tap from the island's top microbreweries: the best selection in Reykjavík. Their five-beer mini sampler costs Ikr2500; happy hour (5pm to 7pm) offers Ikr600 beers.

Loftið COCKTAIL BAR
(☎551 9400; www.loftidbar.is; Austurstræti 9, 2nd fl; ⏲2pm-1am Sun-Thu, 4pm-4am Fri & Sat) Loftið is all about high-end cocktails and good living. Dress up to join the fray at this airy upstairs lounge with a zinc-bar, retro tailor-shop-inspired decor, vintage tiles and a swank

ICELANDIC POP

Iceland produces a disproportionate number of world-class musicians. Björk (and the Sugarcubes) and Sigur Rós are Iceland's most famous musical exports. Sigur Rós' concert movie *Heima* (2007) is a must-see. New sounds surface all the time, ranging from indie-folk Of Monsters and Men, quirky troubadour Ásgeir Trausti and indie band Seabear (which produced hit acts Sin Fang and Sóley), to electronica (FM Belfast, Gus-Gus and múm). Visit www.icelandmusic.is for more info.

crowd. The well booze here is the top-shelf liquor elsewhere, and they bring in jazzy bands on Thursday nights.

Kaldi BAR
(www.kaldibar.is; Laugavegur 20b; ⏲ noon-1am Sun-Thu, to 3am Fri & Sat) Effortlessly cool with mismatched seats and teal banquettes, plus a popular smoking courtyard, Kaldi is awesome for its full range of Kaldi microbrews, not available elsewhere. Happy hour (4pm to 7pm) gets you one for Ikr650. Anyone can play the in-house piano.

☆ Entertainment

The vibrant Reykjavík live-music scene is ever-changing. There are often performances at late-night bars and cafes, and venues such as **Café Rosenberg** (☎551 2442; Klapparstígur 25-27; ⏲3pm-1am Mon-Thu, 4pm-2am Fri & Sat). Local theatres and **Harpa concert hall** (☎box office 528 5050; www.harpa.is; Austurbakki 2; ⏲box office 9am-6pm Mon-Fri, 10am-6pm Sat & Sun) bring in all of the performing arts. Reykjavík's **National Theatre** (Þjóðleikhúsið; ☎551 1200; www.leikhusid.is; Hverfisgata 19; ⏲closed Jul) stages plays, musicals and operas. Cool, central cinema **Bíó Paradís** (www.bioparadis.is; Hverfisgata 54; adult Ikr1600; 📶) screens films with English subtitles.

To see what's on, consult *Grapevine* (www.grapevine.is), *Visit Reykjavík* (www.visitreykjavik.is), *What's On in Reykjavík* (www.whatson.is/magazine), *Musik.is* (www.musik.is) or city music shops.

Shopping

Reykjavík's vibrant design culture makes for great shopping: from sleek, fish-skin purses and knitted *lopapeysur* (traditional Icelandic woollen sweaters) to unique music or lip-smacking Icelandic schnapps *brennivín*. Laugavegur is the most dense shopping street. Fashion concentrates near the Frakkastígur and Vitastígur end of Laugavegur. Skólavörðustígur is strong for arts and jewellery. Bankastræti and Austurstræti have many tourist shops.

ℹ Information

DISCOUNT CARDS

Reykjavík City Card (24/48/72hr Ikr2900/3900/4900) offers free travel on the city's Strætó buses and the ferry to Viðey; free admission to Reykjavík's municipal swimming pools and most major museums; and discounts on some tours, shops and entertainment. Get it at the tourist office, travel agencies, 10-11 supermarkets, HI hostels and some hotels.

EMERGENCY

Emergency (☎112) Ambulance, fire brigade or police.

Landspítali University Hospital (☎543 1000; www.landspitali.is; Fossvogur) Casualty department open 24/7.

MEDICAL SERVICES

Health Centre (☎585 2600; Vesturgata 7) Book in advance.

TOURIST INFORMATION

Widely distributed English-language newspaper/website *Grapevine* (www.grapevine.is) is an irreverent introduction to Reykjavík.

Main Tourist Office (Upplýsingamiðstöð Ferðamanna; ☎590 1550; www.visitreykjavik.is; Aðalstræti 2; ⏲8.30am-7pm Jun–mid-Sep, 9am-6pm Mon-Fri, to 4pm Sat, to 2pm Sun mid-Sep–May) Friendly staff and mountains of free brochures, plus maps and Strætó city bus tickets for sale. Book accommodation, tours and activities. Also one site for getting your duty-free refund.

ℹ Getting Around

BICYCLE

Hire bikes from **Reykjavík Bike Tours** (☎694 8956; www.icelandbike.com; Ægisgarður 7, Old Harbour; bike rental per 4hr from Ikr3500, tours from Ikr5500; ⏲9am-5pm Jun-Aug, reduced hours Sep-May) or **Bike Company** (☎590 8550; www.bikecompany.is; Bankastræti 2; bike rental per 5hr Ikr3500; ⏲9am-5pm Mon-Fri) for Ikr3500 per four or five hours.

BUS

Strætó (www.straeto.is) operates good buses around Reykjavík and its suburbs, as well as long-distance buses. It has online schedules and a smartphone app. Free maps such as *Welcome to Reykjavík City Map* include bus-route maps. The fare is Ikr350, with no change given. Buses run from 7am until 11pm or midnight daily (from 10am on Sunday). Services depart at 20-minute or 30-minute intervals. Limited night-bus service runs until 2am on Friday and Saturday. Buses only stop at designated bus stops, marked with a yellow letter 'S'.

TAXI

Taxis prices are high. Flagfall starts at around Ikr660. Taxis wait outside bus stations, airports and bars (on weekend nights).

BSR (☎561 0000; www.taxireykjavik.is)

Hreyfill (☎588 5522; www.hreyfill.is)

AROUND REYKJAVÍK

The Golden Circle

The Golden Circle takes in three popular attractions all within 100km of the capital: Þingvellir, Geysir and Gullfoss. It is an artificial tourist circuit (there is no valley; natural topography marks its extent) that is loved (and marketed) by thousands, and easy to see on one day-long circular drive or tour.

Þingvellir National Park (www.thingvellir.is) is inside an immense rift valley, caused by the separating North American and Eurasian tectonic plates. It's Iceland's most important historical location and a Unesco World Heritage Site: early Icelanders established the world's first democratic parliament, the Alþing, here in AD 930.

Geysir FREE, after which all spouting hot springs are named, only erupts rarely. Luckily, alongside it is the ever-reliable **Strokkur**, which spouts up to 30m approximately every five minutes. Ten kilometres east, **Gullfoss** (www.gullfoss.is) FREE is a spectacular rainbow-tinged double waterfall, which drops 32m before thundering away down a vast canyon.

Laugarvatn makes a good base for overnights and has the swanky lakeside **Fontana** (☎486 1400; www.fontana.is; adult/child/under 12yr Ikr3200/1600/free; ⏲10am-11pm Jun-Sep, 1-9pm Mon-Fri, 11am-9pm Sat & Sun Oct-May) geothermal spa.

Sleeping & Eating

★Héraðsskólinn HOSTEL, GUESTHOUSE €

(☎537 8060; www.heradsskolinn.is; dm/s/d/q without bathroom from Ikr4200/12,900/13,900/25,900; 📶) This brand-new hostel and guesthouse fills an enormous renovated historical landmark school, built in 1928 by Guðjón Samúelsson. The beautiful, lakeside building with peaked roofs offers both private rooms with shared bathrooms (some sleep up to six) and dorms, plus a spacious library/living room and a cafe (open 7am to 10pm).

Efstidalur II GUESTHOUSE €€

(☎486 1186; www.efstidalur.is; Efstidalur 2; s/d/tr incl breakfast from Ikr19,240/23,800/28,500, mains Ikr1200-5000; 📶) Located 12km northeast of Laugarvatn on a working dairy farm, Efstidalur offers wonderfully welcoming digs, tasty meals and amazing ice cream. Adorable semi-detached cottages have brilliant views of hulking Hekla and the restaurant serves beef from the farm and trout from the lake. The fun ice-cream bar scoops farm ice cream, and has windows looking into the dairy barn.

★Ion Luxury Adventure Hotel BOUTIQUE HOTEL €€€

(☎482 3415; www.ioniceland.is; Nesjavellir vid Þingvallavatn; s/d Ikr44,000/51,000; P@📶) A leader in a new breed of deluxe countryside hotels, Ion is all about local food, sustainable practices and hip, modern rooms. Its **restaurant** (www.ioniceland.is; Nesjavellir vid, Þingvallavatn; dinner mains Ikr4400-6200; ⏲11.30am-10pm) with slow-food local ingredients, bar with floor-to-ceiling plate glass windows, geothermal pool and organic spa are sumptuous. Rooms are a tad smallish, but kitted out impeccably, with fun touches like horse portraits on a wall.

★Lindin ICELANDIC €€

(☎486 1262; www.laugarvatn.is; Lindarbraut 2; restaurant mains Ikr3600-5500, bistro mains Ikr1800-4000; ⏲noon-10pm May-Sep, reduced hours Oct-Apr) Owned by Baldur, an affable, celebrated chef, Lindin is the best restaurant for miles. In a sweet little silver house, the restaurant faces the lake and is purely gourmet, with high-concept Icelandic fare featuring local or wild-caught ingredients. The casual, modern bistro serves a more informal menu from soups to an amazing reindeer burger. Book ahead for dinner in high season.

Blue Lagoon

Arguably Iceland's most famous attraction is the **Blue Lagoon** (Bláa Lónið; ☎420 8800; www.bluelagoon.com; Jun-Aug admission adult/14 & 15 year old/under 14 from €40/20/free, visitor pass (no lagoon entry) €10; ⏲9am-9pm Jun &

11-31 Aug, to 11pm Jul-10 Aug, 10am-8pm Sep-May), a milky-blue geothermal pool set in a massive black lava field, 50km southwest of Reykjavík on the Reykjanes Peninsula. The futuristic Svartsengi geothermal plant provides an other-worldly backdrop, as well as the spa's water – 70% sea water, 30% fresh water, at a perfect 38°C. Daub yourself in silica mud and loll in the hot-pots with an ice-blue cocktail. The mineral-rich waters dry hair to straw – use plenty of the provided hair conditioner.

To beat enormous crowds, go early or very late in the day, and book tickets ahead. Reykjavík Excursions (p602) buses serve the BSÍ bus terminal (or hotels and the airport on request).

SOUTH ICELAND

As you work your way east from Reykjavík, Rte 1 (the Ring Road) emerges into austere volcanic foothills punctuated by surreal steam vents and hot springs, around **Hveragerði**, then swoops through a flat, wide coastal plain, full of verdant horse farms and greenhouses, before the landscape suddenly begins to grow wonderfully jagged, after **Hella** and **Hvolsvöllur**. Hvolsvöllur's museum **Sögusetrið** (Saga Centre; ☎487 8781; www.njala.is; Hliðarvegur 14; adult/child Ikr900/free; ⏲9am-6pm mid-May–mid-Sep, 10am-5pm Sat & Sun mid-Sep–mid-May) is devoted to the dramatic events of *Njál's Saga*. Mountains thrust upwards on the inland side of the Ring Road, some of them volcanoes wreathed by mist (**Eyjafjallajökull**, site of the 2010 eruption), and the first of the awesome glaciers appears, as enormous rivers like the **Þjórsá** cut their way to the black-sand beaches rimming the Atlantic.

Throughout, roads pierce deep inland, to realms of lush waterfall-doused valleys like **Þjórsádalur** and **Fljótshlíð**, and awe-inspiring volcanoes such as **Hekla**. Two of the most renowned inland spots are **Landmannalaugar**, where vibrantly coloured rhyolite peaks meet bubbling hot springs; and **Þórsmörk**, a gorgeous, forested valley tucked away from the brutal northern elements under a series of ice caps. They are linked by the rightly famous 55km **Laugavegurinn hike**, Iceland's most popular trek (for more information, check Ferðafélag Íslands' website, www.fi.is). Since these areas lie inland on roads impassable by standard vehicles, most visitors access them on tours or amphibious buses from the southern Ring Road. Þórsmörk, one of Iceland's most popular hiking destinations, can be done as a day trip.

Skógar is the leaping-off point for Þórsmörk and boasts **Skógar Folk Museum** (Skógasafn; ☎487 8845; www.skogasafn.is; adult/child Ikr1750/free, outside structures only Ikr800; ⏲museum 9am-6pm Jun-Aug, 10am-5pm May & Sep, 11am-4pm Oct-Apr), plus nearby waterfalls **Seljalandsfoss & Gljúfurárbui** and **Skógafoss**. One of the easiest glacial tongues to reach is **Sólheimajökull**, just east of Skógar, but only climb onto the glacier accompanied by a local guide – conditions are often, and invisibly, shifting. **Vík** is surrounded by glaciers, vertiginous cliffs and black beaches such as **Reynisfjara** with the offshore rock formation **Dyrhólaey**. South of the Ring Road, the tiny fishing villages of **Stokkseyri** and **Eyrarbakki** are refreshingly local-feeling.

Churning seas lead to the **Vestmannaeyjar** archipelago offshore (sometimes called the Westman Islands), with its zippy puffins and small town **Heimaey** tucked between lava flows, explained at the excellent volcano museum **Eldheimar** (Pompeii of the North; ☎488 2000; www.eldheimar.is; Gerðisbraut 10; adult/10-18 years/child Ikr1900/1000/free; ⏲11am-6pm Jun–mid-Sep, reduced hours rest of year; 📶).

Public transport (and traffic) is solid along the Ring Road. **South Iceland Adventures** (☎770 2030; www.siadv.is) and **Southcoast Adventure** (☎867 3535; www.southadventure.is) run excellent hiking, adventure and super-Jeep tours in the region.

The popular southwest area (www.south.is) is developing quickly and infrastructure keeps improving, with family farms offering lovely guesthouses. Nevertheless, it gets very busy in high season, so advanced accommodation booking is essential.

Sleeping & Eating

For inland camping near Landmannalaugar and Þórsmörk, check **Ferðafélag Íslands** (Icelandic Touring Association; www.fi.is), which maintains the Laugavegurinn trail and huts. Þórsmörk also has private hostel-guesthouse-campground **Húsadalur** (Volcano Huts Thorsmork; ☎552 8300; www.volcanohuts.com; sites per person Ikr1600, dm/s/d & tr/cottage without bathroom Ikr6500/15,000/19,000/25,000; 📶) and Hostelling International campground **Slyppugil** (☎575 6700; www.hostel.is; sites per person Ikr1000; ⏲mid-Jun–mid-Aug). Book months ahead in high season.

Skógar & Around

★Skógar Campsite CAMPGROUND €
(sites per person Ikr1200; ⏲Jun-Aug) Great location, right by Skógafoss; the sound of falling water makes a soothing lullaby. There's a small toilet block with fresh water; pay at the hostel nearby.

★Stóra-Mörk III GUESTHOUSE, COTTAGES €€
(☎487 8903; www.storamork.com; sleeping-bag accommodation Ikr3900, d with/without bathroom Ikr16,300/11,500) About 5km beyond the cluster of traffic at the falls (Rte 249), a dirt track leads to historic Stóra-Mörk III farmhouse (mentioned, of course, in *Njál's Saga*), which offers large, homey rooms with shared facilities. The main house has some rooms with private bathrooms, a large kitchen and dining room with excellent mountain-to-sea views. Two new cottages, too.

Hótel Skógafoss HOTEL €€
(☎487 8780; www.hotelskogafoss.is; d with/without waterfall view Ikr20,000/14,900, mains Ikr1200-2300) This brand-new hotel opened in 2014 and offers simple modern rooms (half of which have views of Skógafoss) with top bathrooms. The bistro-bar (open 11am to 9.30pm June to September) is one of the best eating and drinking spots in town, with plate glass windows looking onto the falls and local beer on tap.

Country Hotel Anna COUNTRY HOTEL €€
(☎487 8950; www.hotelanna.is; Moldnúpur; s/d incl breakfast Ikr19,800/26,900, mains Ikr4200-5100; 📶) 🌿 This inn's namesake, Anna, wrote books about her world-wide voyages – and her descendants' country hotel upholds her passion for travel with seven sweetly old-fashioned rooms furnished with antiques and embroidered bedspreads. The hotel and its little restaurant (open 6pm to 8pm May to mid-September) sit at the foot of the volcano on Rte 246.

★Gamla Fjósið ICELANDIC €€
(Old Cowhouse; ☎487 7788; www.gamlafjosid.is; Hvassafell; mains Ikr1100-6500; ⏲11am-9pm Jun-Aug, reduced hours Sep-May; 📶) Built in a former cowshed that was in use until 1999, this charming eatery's focus is on farm-fresh and grass-fed meaty mains – from burgers to Volcano Soup, a spicy meat stew. The hardwood floor and low beams are cheered with polished dining tables, large wooden hutches and cheerful staff.

WORTH A TRIP

SKAFTAFELL & VATNAJÖKULL NATIONAL PARK

Skaftafell, the jewel in the crown of **Vatnajökull National Park** (www.vjp.is; www.visitvatnajokull.is), encompasses a breathtaking collection of peaks and glaciers. It's the country's favourite wilderness: 300,000 visitors per year come to marvel at thundering waterfalls, twisted birch woods, the tangled web of rivers threading across the *sandar* (sand deltas) and brilliant blue-white Vatnajökull with its myriad ice tongues. **Jökulsárlón** is a photographer's paradise, a glacial lagoon where wind and water sculpt icebergs into fantastical shapes on their way out to sea.

Icelandic Mountain Guides (IMG; ☎Reykjavík office 587 9999, Skaftafell 894 2959; www.mountainguide.is) and **Glacier Guides** (☎Reykjavík office 571 2100, Skaftafell 659 7000; www.glacierguides.is) lead glacier walks and adventure tours.

Vík & Around

★Garðar GUESTHOUSE €
(☎487 1260; http://reynisfjara-guesthouses.com; Reynisfjara; cottages Ikr12,000-17,000) Garðar, at the end of Rte 215, is a magical, view-blessed place. Friendly farmer Ragnar rents out self-contained beachside huts: one snug stone cottage sleeps two (in a bunk bed), two roomier timber cottages sleep up to four. Linen costs Ikr1000 per person.

★Vellir GUESTHOUSE €€
(Ferðaþjónustan Vellir; ☎849 9204; http://f-vellir.123.is; d with/without bathroom incl breakfast Ikr24,700/20,300, cottage from Ikr25,000; 📶) Located 1.5km down dirt Rte 219, the friendly farmstay at Vellir sits near Pétursey, a massive earthen mound that was once an island eons ago. Rooms are modern and some have sea views. There are also two cottages for rent. You can see both the ice on Mýrdalsjökull and the Atlantic Ocean on a clear day. Homecooked dinner is available by pre-order (Ikr5900).

Icelandair Hótel Vík HOTEL €€
(☎487 1480, booking 444 4000; www.icelandairhotels.com; Klettsvegur 1-5; d from Ikr24,500; 📶) This sleek, black new hotel is improbably tucked just behind the Hótel Edda, on the

eastern edge of town, near the campground. The hotels share a lobby (and have the same friendly owners), but that's where the resemblance ends. The Icelandair hotel is suitably swanky, and some rooms have views to the rear cliffs or the sea. The light, natural decor is inspired by the local environment.

Suður-Vík ICELANDIC, ASIAN €€
(☎487 1515; Suðurvíkurvegur 1; mains Ikr1750-4950; ⊙noon-10pm) The friendly ambience, from hardwood floors and interesting artwork to smiling staff, helps elevate this new restaurant beyond the competition. Food is Icelandic hearty, from heaping steak sandwiches with bacon and bearnaise sauce, to Asian (think Thai satay with rice). In a warmly lit silver building atop town. Book ahead in summer.

WEST ICELAND

Geographically close to Reykjavík yet far, far away in sentiment, west Iceland (known as Vesturland; www.west.is) is a splendid microcosm of what Iceland has to offer. Yet most tourists have missed the memo, and you're likely to have much of this wonderful region to yourself.

The long arm of **Snæfellsnes Peninsula** is a favourite for its glacier, Snæfellsjökull. The area around **Snæfellsjökull National Park** (☎436 6860; www.snaefellsjokull.is) is tops for birding, whale watching, lava field hikes and horse riding.

Inland beyond **Reykholt** you'll encounter lava tubes such as **Viðgelmir** (☎865 4060; www.fljotstunga.is; tours Ikr3000; ⊙May-Sep) and remote highland glaciers, including enormous **Langjökull** with its new **ice cave** (www.icecave.is; ⊙Mar-Oct).

Icelanders honour west Iceland for its local sagas: two of the best known, *Laxdæla Saga* and *Egil's Saga,* took place along the region's brooding waters, marked today by haunting cairns and an exceptional **Settlement Centre** (Landnámssetur Íslands; ☎437 1600; www.settlementcentre.is; Brákarbraut 13-15; 1 exhibition adult/child Ikr1900/1500, 2 exhibitions adult/child Ikr2500/1900; ⊙10am-9pm Jun-Sep, 11am-5pm Oct-May; 📶) in lively **Borgarnes**.

West Iceland offers everything from windswept beaches to historic villages and awe-inspiring terrain in one neat, little package. **Stykkishólmur** makes a great base, with its fine hotels and guesthouses such as **Hótel Egilsen** (☎554 7700; www.egilsen.is; Aðalgata 2; s/d Ikr22,000/28,500; @📶), excellent eateries such as **Plássið** (☎436 1600; www.plassid.is; Frúarstígur 1; mains Ikr1400-4200; ⊙11.30am-3pm & 6-10pm; 🌶👪), interesting museums such as **Norska Húsið** (Norwegian House; ☎433 8114; www.norskahusid.is; Hafnargata 5; admission Ikr800; ⊙noon-5pm Jun-Aug; 📶) and boats around Breiðafjörður operated by **Seatours** (Sæferðir; ☎433 2254; www.seatours.is; Smiðjustígur 3; ⊙8am-8pm mid-May–mid-Sep, 9am-5pm mid-Sep–mid-May).

NORTH ICELAND

Iceland's mammoth and magnificent north is a wonderland of moonlike lava fields, belching mudpots, epic waterfalls, snowcapped peaks and whale-filled bays. The region's top sights are variations on one theme: a grumbling, volcanically active earth.

Húsavík is Iceland's premier whale-watching destination, with up to 11 species coming to feed in summer. Go out whale and puffin spotting with **North Sailing** (☎464 7272; www.northsailing.is; Hafnarstétt 9; 3hr tour adult/child Ikr9280/4640), **Gentle Giants** (☎464 1500; www.gentlegiants.is; Hafnarstétt; 3hr tour adult/child Ikr9100/3900) or **Salka** (☎464 3999; www.salkawhalewatching.is; Garðarsbraut 6; 3hr tour adult/child Ikr8640/4000). **Siglufjörður** on the **Tröllaskagi Peninsula** offers vast vistas and rugged mountainscapes. Visit otherworldly lake **Mývatn** for its lava castles and hidden fissures. Thunderously roaring **Dettifoss** is one of Iceland's grandest waterfalls.

Akureyri

Little Akureyri, with its surprising moments of big-city living, is the best base in the north. From here you can explore by car or bus, and tour the region's highlights.

Tours

Saga Travel (☎558 888; www.sagatravel.is; Kaupvangsstræti 4) offers diverse year-round excursions and activities throughout the north.

Sleeping & Eating

Akureyri

Stay at **Sæluhús** (☎412 0800; www.saeluhus.is; Sunnutröð; studio/house Ikr23,700/42,500; 📶) with its well-equipped modern studios and houses, or **Skjaldarvík** (☎552 5200; www.skjaldarvik.is; s/d without bathroom incl breakfast

ICELANDIC SETTLEMENT & SAGAS

Rumour, myth and fantastic tales of fierce storms and barbaric dog-headed people kept most explorers away from the great northern ocean, *oceanus innavigabilis*. Irish monks who regularly sailed to the Faeroe Islands looking for seclusion were probably the first to stumble upon Iceland. It's thought that they settled around the year 700 but fled when Norsemen began to arrive in the early 9th century.

The Age of Settlement

The Age of Settlement is traditionally defined as between 870 and 930, when political strife on the Scandinavian mainland caused many to flee. Most North Atlantic Norse settlers were ordinary citizens: farmers and merchants who settled across Western Europe, marrying Britons, Westmen (Irish) and Scots.

Among Iceland's first Norse visitors was Norwegian Flóki Vilgerðarson, who uprooted his farm and headed for Snæland (archaic Viking name for Iceland) around 860. He navigated with ravens, which, after some trial and error, led him to his destination and provided his nickname, Hrafna-Flóki (Raven-Flóki). Hrafna-Flóki sailed to Vatnsfjörður on the west coast but became disenchanted with the conditions. On seeing the icebergs in the fjord he dubbed the country Ísland (Iceland) and returned to Norway. He did eventually settle in Iceland's Skagafjörður district.

According to the 12th-century *Íslendingabók* (a historical narrative of the Settlement Era), Ingólfur Arnarson fled Norway with his blood brother Hjörleifur, landing at Ingólfshöfði (southeast Iceland) in 871. He was then led to Reykjavík by a pagan ritual: he tossed his high-seat pillars (a symbol of authority) into the sea as they approached land. Wherever the gods brought the pillars ashore would be the settlers' new home. Ingólfur named Reykjavík (Smoky Bay) after the steam from its thermal springs. Hjörleifur settled near the present town of Vík, but was murdered by his slaves shortly thereafter.

Descendants of the first settlers established the world's first democratic parliament, the Alþing, in 930 at Þingvellir (Parliament Plains).

The Saga Age

The late 12th century kicked off the Saga Age, when the epic tales of the earlier 9th-to-10th-century settlement were recorded by historians and writers. These sweeping prose epics or sagas detail the family struggles, romance, vendettas and colourful characters of the Settlement Era. They are the backbone of medieval Icelandic literature and a rich source for historical understanding. Try *Egil's Saga*, the colourful adventures of a poet-warrior and grandson of a shape-shifter.

Ikr14,900/19,900; @ 🛜), a slice of guesthouse nirvana, in a farm setting 6km north of town. **Akureyri Backpackers** (☎571 9050; www.akureyribackpackers.com; Hafnarstræti 67; dm Ikr4500-5500, d without bathroom Ikr18,000; @ 🛜) offers great budget digs, and **Icelandair Hotel Akureyri** (☎518 1000; www.icelandairhotels.com; Þingvallastræti 23; d incl breakfast from Ikr28,800; @ 🛜) hits the top-end mark.

Around Akureyri

Dalvík's excellent **HI Hostel** (Vegamót; ☎865 8391, 466 1060; www.vegamot.net; Hafnarbraut 4; dm/d without bathroom Ikr4500/11,100; 🛜) and wonderful **Kaffihús Bakkabræðra** (Grundargata 1; soup & salad buffet Ikr1790; ⏰8am-11pm Mon-Fri, 10am-11pm Sat & Sun) make the sleepy village a viable option. For upmarket seafood on Tröllaskagi Peninsula don't miss **Hannes Boy** (☎461 7730; www.raudka.is; mains Ikr3290-5990; ⏰noon-2pm & 6-10pm Jun-Aug, shorter hours Sep-May) in Siglufjörður. Near Mývatn, **Vogafjós** (www.vogafjos.net; mains Ikr2550-4700; ⏰7.30am-11pm; 🛜 ✎ 👪) in Reykjahlíð serves up top local vittles and offers a nearby guesthouse.

SURVIVAL GUIDE

Directory A–Z

ACCOMMODATION

For visits between June and August travellers should book accommodation well in advance (no need to prebook campsites). All hostels and some guesthouses and hotels offer cheaper rates if guests use their own sleeping bags. There are many different room styles – we list but a few.

SLEEPING PRICE RANGES

The following price categories are based on the high-season price of a double room:

€ less than Ikr15,000 (around €100)

€€ Ikr15,000 to Ikr30,000 (€100 to €200)

€€€ more than Ikr30,000 (€200)

Generally, accommodation prices are very high compared to mainland European lodging.

Accommodation Types

Camping is allowed anywhere in Iceland, apart from on private land. In national parks and reserves you must stay in marked campsites, and most towns have designated camping areas – generally open mid-May to mid-September. The Camping Card (www.campingcard.is) can be a good deal for longer stays. Private walking clubs and Ferðafélag Íslands maintain *skálar* (mountain huts; singular *skáli*) on many popular hiking tracks – in summer, reservations are essential.

Hostelling International Iceland (www.hostel.is) administers 32 of Iceland's superb youth hostels; Akureyri and Reykjavík have private ones, too.

Gistiheimilið (guesthouses) range from private homes to purpose-built farmstays, and often have shared bathrooms. Many only open mid-May to mid-September. Check Icelandic Farm Holidays (www.farmholidays.is) for great countryside accommodation.

Hotels range from motels to boutique luxury hotels, with more being built constantly. The summer-only **Edda Hótels** (www.hoteledda.is), based in schools, often offers dorms.

ACTIVITIES

- Hiking and mountaineering is stunning all over the country, especially in national parks and nature reserves. July, August and September are the best months for walking. For details check Ferðafélag Íslands (www.fi.is).
- A vast menu of adventure tours combine ice climbing, snowmobiling, caving etc with super-Jeeps or bus tours. Most pick up from Reykjavík; see p588.
- Stables offer everything from 90-minute horse rides to multiday tours, and can combine riding with other activities, such as visiting the Golden Circle or Blue Lagoon. Some offer guesthouse accommodation. Plan on spending Ikr9000 to Ikr12,000 for a 90-minute ride.
- Hvítá river, located along the Golden Circle, is a top spot for white-water rafting and speed-boating near Reykjavík. Trips run from Reykholt, but offer Reykjavík pick-ups.
- Scuba-diving tours with Dive.is go to Þingvellir's rift waters, which have astonishing 100m visibility.
- Every town has a geothermal public pool, and natural hot-pots abound.
- Whale watching is best from mid-May to September. Boats depart from Reykjavík, although northern Húsavík is renowned for superb whale watching.
- Northern Lights tours feature in winter, and flight tours cover the whole country.

BUSINESS HOURS

Opening hours vary throughout the year (many places close outside high season); check ahead. Hours tend to be far longer June to August, and shorter September to May. Standard opening hours:

Banks 9am to 4pm Monday to Friday

Cafe-bars 10am to 1am Sunday to Thursday, 10am to between 3am and 6am Friday and Saturday

Cafes 10am to 6pm

Offices 9am to 5pm Monday to Friday

Petrol stations 8am to 10pm or 11pm

Post offices 9am to 4pm or 4.30pm Monday to Friday (to 6pm in larger towns)

Restaurants 11.30am to 2.30pm and 6pm to 9pm or 10pm

Shops 10am to 6pm Monday to Friday, to 4pm Saturday; some open Sundays in Reykjavík's major shopping strips

Supermarkets 9am to 8pm (till later in Reykjavík)

Vínbúðin (government-run alcohol stores) Variable; many outside Reykjavík only open several hours daily

CUSTOMS

For regulations, see www.customs.is.

INTERNET ACCESS

Wi-fi is common at most sleeping and eating venues. Find computers for public internet access at libraries and tourist offices.

INTERNET RESOURCES

Icelandic Tourist Board (www.visiticeland.com) With links to regional websites.

Reykjavík tourist office (www.visitreykjavik.is)

EATING PRICE RANGES

The following price categories are based on the cost of an average main course:

€ less than Ikr2000 (€13)

€€ Ikr2000 to Ikr5000 (€13 to €32)

€€€ more than Ikr5000 (€32)

MONEY

Credit cards are ubiquitous, but many transactions (such as purchasing petrol) require a PIN – get one before leaving home. ATMs take MasterCard, Visa, Cirrus, Maestro and Electron cards. VAT and service are included in marked prices. Tipping is not required. Spend over Ikr4000 in a single shop and get a 15% tax refund (see www.taxfree-worldwide.com/Iceland).

POST

Icelandic postal service (www.postur.is) is reliable. Postcards/letters to Europe cost Ikr180/310; to places outside Europe Ikr240/490.

PUBLIC HOLIDAYS

For travel during holiday periods, particularly the Commerce Day long weekend, book mountain huts and transport well in advance. The national public holidays are:

New Year's Day 1 January

Easter March or April; Maundy Thursday and Good Friday to Easter Monday (changes annually)

First Day of Summer First Thursday after 18 April

Labour Day 1 May

Ascension Day May or June (changes annually)

Whit Sunday and Whit Monday May or June (changes annually)

National Day 17 June

Commerce Day First Monday in August

Christmas 24 to 26 December

New Year's Eve 31 December

TELEPHONE

Iceland's international access code is ☎00, country code is ☎354; no area codes. For international directory assistance and reverse-charge (collect) calls, dial ☎1811. Mobile coverage is widespread. Visitors with GSM 900/1800 phones can make roaming calls. You can purchase a local SIM card (at grocery stores and petrol stations) if you're staying awhile and have an unlocked mobile.

TIME

Iceland's time zone is the same as GMT/UTC (London), but there is no daylight saving time.

COUNTRY FACTS

Area 103,000 sq km

Capital Reykjavík

Country Code ☎354

Currency Icelandic króna (Ikr)

Emergency ☎112

Languages Icelandic, English widely spoken

Money Credit cards (PIN often required at petrol pumps) and ATMs everywhere

Population 325,000

Visas Generally not required for stays up to 90 days. Member of Schengen Convention. Check Icelandic Directorate of Immigration (www.utl.is) for details.

Getting There & Away

AIR

Iceland is connected by year-round flights (including budget carriers) from **Keflavík International Airport** (KEF; www.kefairport.is), 48km southwest of Reykjavík, to a multitude of European destinations, from Norway and Sweden to France, Austria, Italy and Germany; as well as to the United States and Canada. Icelandair (www.icelandair.com) offers stopovers between the continents, and connecting flights to Akureyri in the north. Internal flights and those to Greenland and the Faroe Islands use the small **Reykjavík Domestic Airport** (REK; Reykjavíkurflugvöllur; www.reykjavikairport.is) in central Reykjavík.

To/From the Airport

Flybus (☎580 5400; www.re.is; wi-fi), **Airport Express** (☎540 1313; www.airportexpress.is; wi-fi) and discount operator **K-Express** (☎823 0099; www.kexpress.is), whose stop is off-terminal, have excellent buses connecting the airport with Reykjavík (50 minutes). Flybus offers pick-up and drop-off at many accommodations (Ikr1950 to Reykjavík, Ikr2500 to hotel), and also serves the Blue Lagoon. Buy tickets online or from ticket kiosks in the airport.

Car-hire chains are at the airport – prebooking is highly recommended. Taxis are rarely used (since they cost about Ikr15,000 to Reykjavík).

BOAT

Smyril Line (www.smyrilline.com) operates a weekly car ferry, the *Norröna*, from Hirsthals (Denmark) through Tórshavn (Faroe Islands) to Seyðisfjörður in east Iceland. Schedules vary; check online.

Getting Around

AIR

Iceland has a network of domestic flights, which locals use almost like buses. In winter a flight can be the only way to get between destinations, but winter weather plays havoc with schedules. Note that almost all domestic flights depart from the small domestic airport in Reykjavík (not Keflavík International Airport). Check Air Iceland (Flugfélag Íslands; www.airiceland.is) and Eagle Air (www.eagleair.is).

ESSENTIAL FOOD & DRINK

➡ **Traditional Icelandic dishes** These reflect a historical need to eat every scrap and make it last through winter. *Harðfiskur* (dried strips of haddock with butter), *plokkfiskur* (a hearty fish-and-potato gratin) and delicious, yoghurt-like *skyr* are tasty treats. Brave souls might try *svið* (singed sheep's head), *súrsaðir hrútspungar* (pickled ram's testicles) and *hárkarl* (fermented shark meat).

➡ **Succulent specialities** Icelandic lamb is among the tastiest on earth – sheep roam the mountains all summer, grazing on sweet grass and wild thyme. Also, superfresh fish dishes grace most menus. Reindeer meat from the eastern highlands is a high-end treat.

➡ **Whale-meat controversy** Many restaurants serve whale meat, but 75% of Icelanders never buy it. Tourists are responsible for consuming a significant proportion of these protected species. Similarly, puffins (also found on many menus) and the Greenland shark used in *hárkarl* are facing pressure. While we do not exclude restaurants that serve these meats from our listings, you can opt not to order it, or find whale-free spots at www.icewhale.is/whale-friendly-restaurants.

➡ **Favourite drinks** The traditional alcoholic brew *brennivín* is schnapps made from potatoes and caraway seeds. It's fondly known as 'black death'. Craft beers are popular: look for brews by Kaldi, Borg Brugghús and Einstök. Coffee is a national institution.

BICYCLE

Cycling is a fantastic (and increasingly popular) way to see the country's landscapes, but be prepared for harsh conditions. Most buses accept bikes. **Reykjavík Bike Tours** (www.icelandbike.com) rents touring bikes; others rent bikes for local jaunts. **Icelandic Mountain Bike Club** (http://fjallahjolaklubburinn.is) links to the annually updated *Cycling Iceland* map.

BOAT

Several year-round ferries operate major routes:

➡ Landeyjahöfn–Vestmannaeyjar (www.herjolfur.is)

➡ Stykkishólmur–Brjánslækur (www.seatours.is)

➡ Dalvík–Hrísey/Grímsey (www.saefari.is)

➡ Arskógssandur–Hrísey (www.hrisey.net)

From June to August, Bolungarvík and Ísafjörður have regular boat services to Hornstrandir (Westfjords).

BUS

➡ Iceland has an extensive network of long-distance bus routes, operated by multiple companies. Many offer bus passes. The free *Public Transport in Iceland* map has an overview of routes – look for it in tourist offices and bus terminals, especially in Reykjavík.

➡ From roughly mid-May to mid-September regularly scheduled buses serve the Ring Road, popular hiking areas of the southwest and larger Icelandic towns. The rest of the year, services range from daily to nonexistent.

➡ In summer, 4WD buses ply a few F roads (highland roads), including the Kjölur and Sprengisandur routes (inaccessible to 2WD cars).

➡ Many buses can be used as day tours (the bus spends a few hours at the final destination before returning, and may stop at various tourist destinations en route).

➡ Bus companies operate from different pick-up points. In Reykjavík, there are several bus terminals; in small towns buses usually stop at the main petrol station, but it pays to double-check.

Main bus companies:

Reykjavík Excursions (☎580 5400; www.re.is)

SBA-Norðurleið (☎550 0700; www.sba.is)

Strætó (☎540 2700; www.straeto.is)

Sterna (☎551 1166; www.sterna.is)

Trex (☎587 6000; www.trex.is; 📶)

CAR & CAMPERVAN

Renting a vehicle is expensive but extremely helpful, and gives unparalleled freedom to discover the country. Booking ahead is usually cheapest. The Ring Road is almost entirely paved, but many backcountry areas are served by dirt tracks. Note that most rental cars are not allowed on highland (F) roads. To hire a car you must be at least 20 years old (23 to 25 years for a 4WD) and hold a valid licence. Campervans offer even more independence – **Camper Iceland** (www.campericeland.is) is just one of several outfits.

HITCHING

Hitching is never entirely safe and we don't recommend it. Travellers who hitch should understand that they are taking a small but potentially serious risk. In summer hitching is possible, but you may wait a long time in rural areas.

Ireland

Includes ➡

Best Traditional Pubs

- Stag's Head (p612)
- Kyteler's Inn (p616)
- O'Connor's (p621)
- Crown Liquor Saloon (p630)
- Peadar O'Donnell's (p634)
- Crane Bar (p625)

Best Places to Eat

- Fade Street Social (p611)
- Market Lane (p618)
- Quay Street Kitchen (p625)
- Barking Dog (p630)

Why Go?

Few countries have an image so plagued by cliché. From shamrocks and *shillelaghs* (Irish fighting sticks) to leprechauns and loveable rogues, there's a plethora of platitudes to wade through before you reach the real Ireland.

But it's well worth looking beyond the tourist tat, for the Emerald Isle is one of Europe's gems, a scenic extravaganza of lakes, mountains, sea and sky. From picture-postcard County Kerry to the rugged coastline of Northern Ireland (part of the UK, distinct from the Republic of Ireland), there are countless opportunities to get outdoors and explore, whether cycling the Causeway Coast or hiking the hills of Killarney and Connemara.

There are cultural pleasures too in the land of Joyce and Yeats, U2 and the Undertones. Dublin, Cork and Belfast all have world-class art galleries and museums, while you can enjoy foot-stomping traditional music in the bars of Galway and Killarney. So push aside the shamrocks and experience the real Ireland.

When to Go

Dublin

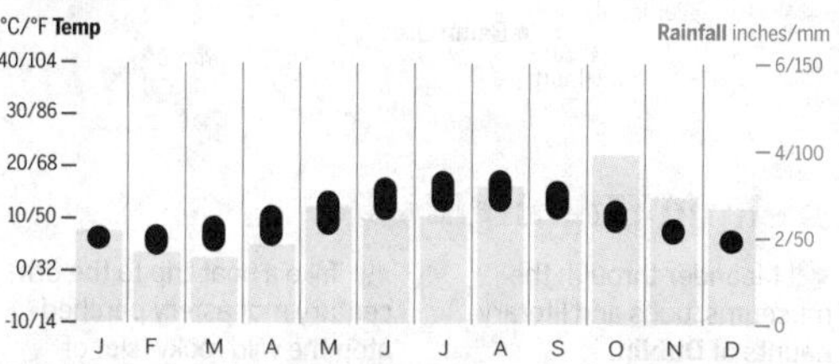

Late Mar Spring flowers everywhere, landscape is greening, St Patrick's Day festivities beckon.

Jun Best chance of dry weather, long summer evenings, Bloomsday in Dublin.

Sep & Oct Summer crowds thin, autumn colours reign, surf's up on the west coast.

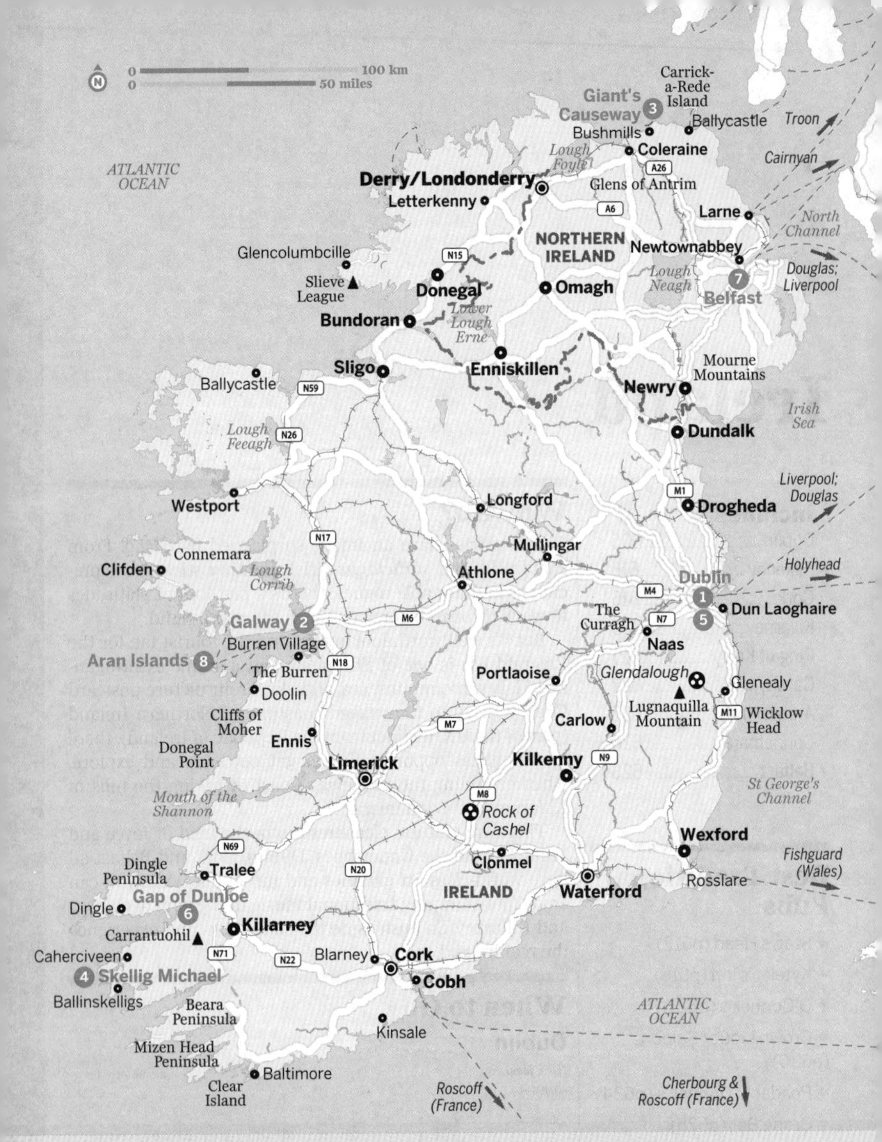

Ireland Highlights

1. Meander through the museums, pubs and literary haunts of **Dublin**.

2. Hang out in bohemian **Galway** (p623), with its hip cafes and live-music venues.

3. Hike the Causeway Coast and clamber across the **Giant's Causeway** (p632).

4. Take a boat trip to the 6th-century monastery perched atop the wild rocky islet of **Skellig Michael** (p621).

5. Sip a pint of Guinness while listening to live music in one of Dublin's **traditional pubs** (p612).

6. Cycle through the spectacular lake and mountain scenery of the **Gap of Dunloe** (p620).

7. Discover the industrial history of the city that built the world's most famous ocean liner at **Titanic Belfast** (p627).

8. Wander the wild, limestone shores of the remote and craggy **Aran Islands** (p625).

ITINERARIES

One Week

Spend a couple of days in **Dublin** ambling through the excellent national museums, and gorging yourself on Guinness and good company in Temple Bar. Get medieval in **Kilkenny** before heading on to **Cork** and discovering why they call it 'The Real Capital'. Head west for a day or two exploring the scenic **Ring of Kerry** and enchanting **Killarney**.

Two Weeks

Follow the one-week itinerary, then make your way north from Killarney to bohemian **Galway**. Using Galway as your base, explore the alluring **Aran Islands** and the hills of **Connemara**. Finally, head north to see the **Giant's Causeway** and experience the optimistic vibe in fast-changing **Belfast**.

DUBLIN

POP 1.27 MILLION

Sultry rather than sexy, Dublin exudes personality as only those who've managed to turn careworn into carefree can. The halcyon days of the Celtic Tiger (the Irish economic boom of the late 1990s), when cash cascaded like a free-flowing waterfall, have long since disappeared, and the city has once again been forced to grind out a living. But Dubliners still know how to enjoy life. They do so through their music, art and literature – things that Dubs often take for granted but, once reminded, generate immense pride.

There are world-class museums, superb restaurants and the best range of entertainment available anywhere in Ireland – and that's not including the pub, the ubiquitous centre of the city's social life and an absolute must for any visitor. And should you wish to get away from it all, the city has a handful of seaside towns at its edges that make for wonderful day trips.

Sights

Dublin's finest Georgian architecture, including its famed doorways, is found around **St Stephen's Green** (dawn-dusk; all city centre, St Stephen's Green) FREE and **Merrion Square** (dawn-dusk; 7 & 44 from city centre) FREE just south of Trinity College; both are prime picnic spots when the sun shines.

★Trinity College HISTORIC BUILDING

(01-896 1000; www.tcd.ie; College Green; 8am-10pm; all city centre) FREE This calm retreat from the bustle of contemporary Dublin is Ireland's most prestigious university, founded by Elizabeth I in 1592. Not only is it the city's most attractive historic real estate, but it's also home to one of the world's most famous – and most beautiful – books, the gloriously illuminated **Book of Kells**. There's no charge to wander around the grounds on your own, but the student-led **walking tours** (trinitytours@csc.tcd.ie; per person €5, incl Book of Kells €10; 10.15am-3.40pm Mon-Sat, to 3pm Sun mid-May–Sep, fewer midweek tours Oct-Apr), departing from the College Green entrance, are recommended.

The college was established on land confiscated from an Augustinian priory in an effort to stop the brain drain of young Protestant Dubliners, who were skipping across to Continental Europe for an education and were becoming 'infected with popery'. Trinity went on to become one of Europe's most outstanding universities, producing a host of notable graduates – how about Jonathan Swift, Oscar Wilde and Samuel Beckett at the same alumni dinner?

It remained completely Protestant until 1793, but even when the university relented and began to admit Catholics, the Church forbade it; until 1970, any Catholic who enrolled here could consider themselves excommunicated.

The campus is a masterpiece of architecture and landscaping beautifully preserved in Georgian style; the elegant Regent House entrance on College Green is guarded by statues of the writer Oliver Goldsmith (1730–74) and the orator Edmund Burke (1729–97). Through the gate, most of the buildings date from the 18th and 19th centuries, elegantly laid out around a series of interlinked squares.

The newer parts include the brutalist **Berkeley Library**, a masterpiece of modern architecture, and the 1978 **Arts & Social Science Building**, which backs onto Nassau St and provides an alternative entrance to the college. Like the Berkeley Library, it was designed by Paul Koralek; it also houses the **Douglas Hyde Gallery of Modern**

Dublin

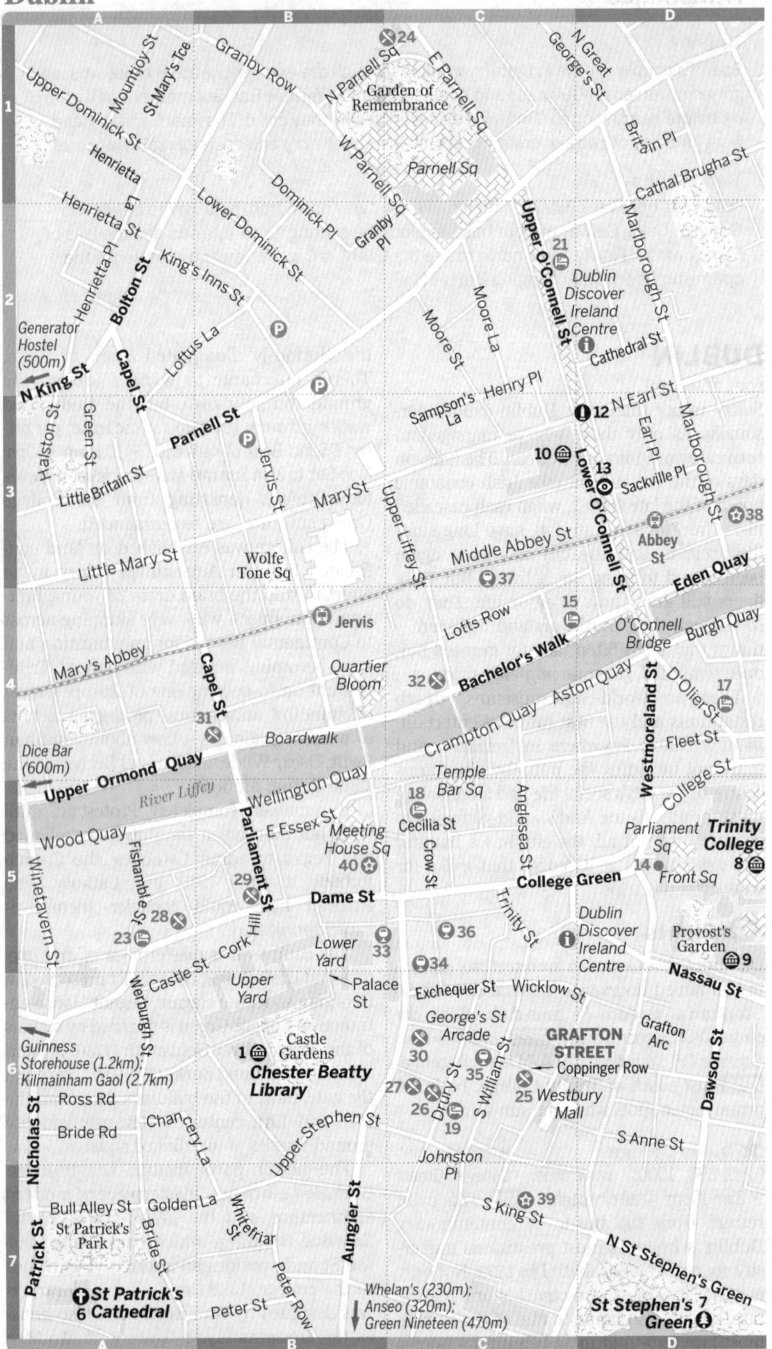
Garden of Remembrance
Parnell Sq
Upper O'Connell St
Lower O'Connell St
Dublin Discover Ireland Centre
Generator Hostel (500m)
N King St
Bolton St
Capel St
Parnell St
Mary St
Jervis St
Wolfe Tone Sq
Jervis
Middle Abbey St
Abbey St
Eden Quay
O'Connell Bridge
Bachelor's Walk
Aston Quay
Crampton Quay
Quartier Bloom
Boardwalk
Dice Bar (600m)
Upper Ormond Quay
River Liffey
Wellington Quay
Wood Quay
Temple Bar Sq
Westmoreland St
D'Olier St
College St
Trinity College
Parliament St
Dame St
College Green
Meeting House Sq
Lower Yard
Upper Yard
Castle Gardens
Chester Beatty Library
Provost's Garden
Nassau St
GRAFTON STREET
Coppinger Row
Westbury Mall
Guinness Storehouse (1.2km); Kilmainham Gaol (2.7km)
Upper Stephen St
Aungier St
St Patrick's Park
St Patrick's Cathedral
Whelan's (230m); Anseo (320m); Green Nineteen (470m)
N St Stephen's Green
St Stephen's Green

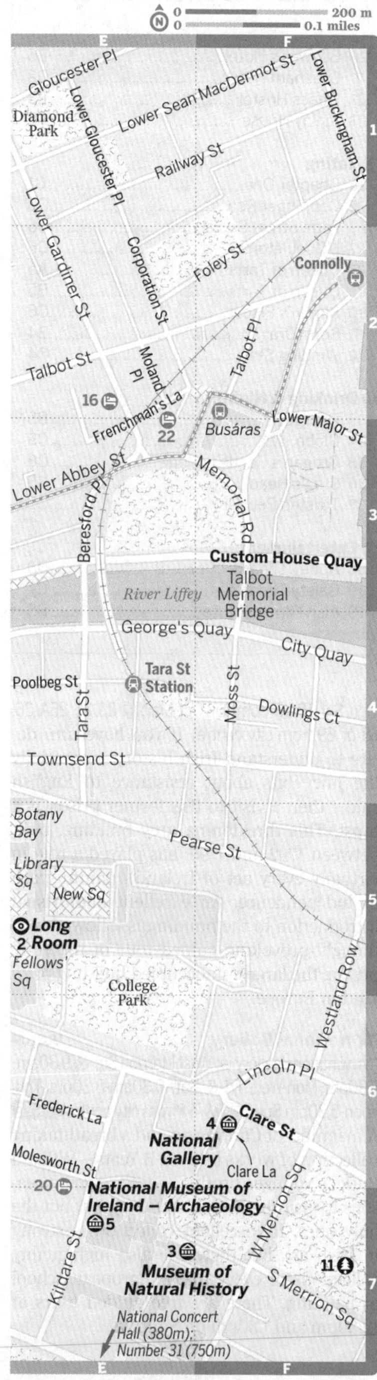

Art (www.douglashydegallery.com; Trinity College; ⏲11am-6pm Mon-Wed & Fri, to 7pm Thu, to 4.45pm Sat) FREE.

★Long Room NOTABLE BUILDING

(East Pavilion, Library Colonnades; adult/student/child €10/8/free; ⏲9.30am-5pm Mon-Sat year-round, noon-4.30pm Sun Oct-Apr, 9.30am-4.30pm Sun May-Sep; 🚌all city centre) The Old Library – built in a rather severe style by Thomas Burgh between 1712–32 – contains Trinity College's greatest treasures in its stunning, barrel-vaulted Long Room, a 65m-long temple of learning lined with gleaming bookshelves and marble busts. It houses about 250,000 of the library's oldest volumes, including the breathtaking *Book of Kells*. Other displays include a rare copy of the Proclamation of the Irish Republic, which was read by Pádraig Pearse at the beginning of the Easter Rising in 1916.

Admission includes temporary exhibitions on display in the East Pavilion.

Also here is the so-called **harp of Brian Ború**, which was definitely not in use when the army of this early Irish hero defeated the Danes at the Battle of Clontarf in 1014. It does, however, date from around 1400, making it one of the oldest harps in Ireland.

★National Museum of Ireland – Archaeology MUSEUM

(www.museum.ie; Kildare St; ⏲10am-5pm Tue-Sat, 2-5pm Sun; 🚌all city centre) FREE Among the highlights of the National Museum's archaeology branch are its superb collection of **prehistoric gold objects**; the exquisite 8th-century **Ardagh Chalice** and **Tara Brooch**, the world's finest examples of Celtic art; and ancient objects recovered from Ireland's bogs, including remarkably well-preserved human bodies. Other exhibits focus on early Christian art, the Viking period and medieval Ireland. There's a lot to see, so ask if there's a guided tour available, or buy a guidebook to help you navigate the exhibits.

★Guinness Storehouse BREWERY, MUSEUM

(www.guinness-storehouse.com; St James's Gate, South Market St; adult/student/child €18/14.50/6.50, connoisseur experience €30, discounts for online booking; ⏲9.30am-5pm Sep-Jun, to 7pm Jul & Aug; 📶; 🚌21A, 51B, 78, 78A or 123 from Fleet St, 🚊St James's) The most popular visit in town is the beer-lover's Disneyland, a multimedia bells-and-whistles homage to the country's most famous export and the city's most enduring symbol.

Dublin

Top Sights
1 Chester Beatty Library ... B6
2 Long Room ... E5
3 Museum of Natural History ... E7
4 National Gallery ... F6
5 National Museum of Ireland – Archaeology ... E7
6 St Patrick's Cathedral ... A7
7 St Stephen's Green ... D7
8 Trinity College ... D5

Sights
9 Douglas Hyde Gallery of Modern Art ... D5
10 General Post Office ... C3
11 Merrion Square ... F7
12 Monument of Light ... D3
13 O'Connell St ... D3
Trinity College & Book of Kells ... (see 2)

Activities, Courses & Tours
14 Trinity College Walking Tour ... D5

Sleeping
15 Abbey Court Hostel ... C4
16 Anchor House ... E2
17 Ashfield House ... D4
18 Barnacles ... C5
19 Brooks Hotel ... C6
20 Buswell's Hotel ... E6
21 Gresham Hotel ... C2
22 Isaacs Hostel ... E3
23 Kinlay House ... A5

Eating
24 Chapter One ... C1
25 Coppinger Row ... C6
26 Fade Street Social ... C6
27 L'Gueuleton ... C6
28 Queen of Tarts ... A5
29 Queen of Tarts ... B5
30 Simon's Place ... C6
31 Soup Dragon ... B4
32 Winding Stair ... C4

Drinking & Nightlife
33 George ... B5
34 Globe ... C5
35 Grogan's Castle Lounge ... C6
36 Stag's Head ... C5
37 Twisted Pepper ... C3

Entertainment
38 Abbey Theatre ... D3
39 Gaiety Theatre ... C7
40 Irish Film Institute ... B5

The old grain storehouse, the only part of the massive, 26-hectare St James's Gate Brewery open to the public, is a suitable cathedral in which to worship the black gold; it rises seven impressive storeys high around a stunning central atrium. At the top is the **Gravity Bar**, with panoramic views of Dublin.

★ Chester Beatty Library MUSEUM
(01-407 0750; www.cbl.ie; Dublin Castle; 10am-5pm Tue-Fri, 11am-5pm Sat, 1-5pm Sun year-round, 10am-5pm Mon May-Sep, free tours 1pm Wed, 3pm & 4pm Sun; 50, 51B, 77, 78A or 123) FREE This world-famous library, in the grounds of Dublin Castle, houses the collection of mining engineer Sir Alfred Chester Beatty (1875–1968), bequeathed to the Irish State on his death. Spread over two floors, the breathtaking collection includes more than 20,000 manuscripts, rare books, miniature paintings, clay tablets, costumes and other objects of artistic, historical and aesthetic importance, including fragments of early Christian gospels dating from AD 150–200.

★ Kilmainham Gaol MUSEUM
(www.heritageireland.com; Inchicore Rd; adult/child €6/2; 9.30am-6pm Apr-Sep, 9.30am-5.30pm Mon-Sat, 10am-6pm Sun Oct-Mar; 23, 25, 25A, 26, 68 or 69 from city centre) If you have *any* desire to understand Irish history – especially the juicy bits about resistance to English rule – then a visit to this former prison is a must. This threatening grey building, built between 1792 and 1795, has played a role in virtually every act of Ireland's painful path to independence. An excellent audiovisual introduction to the building is followed by a thought-provoking guided tour of the eerie prison, the largest unoccupied building of its kind in Europe.

★ National Gallery MUSEUM
(www.nationalgallery.ie; West Merrion Sq; 9.30am-5.30pm Mon-Wed, Fri & Sat, 9.30am-8.30pm Thu, noon-5.30pm Sun; 7 & 44 from city centre) FREE A magnificent Caravaggio and a breathtaking collection of works by Jack B Yeats – William Butler's younger brother – are the main reasons to visit the National Gallery, but not the only ones. Its excellent collection is strong in Irish art, but there are also high-quality collections of every major European school of painting. There are free guided tours at 12.30pm and 1.30pm on Sundays.

★St Patrick's Cathedral CHURCH

(www.stpatrickscathedral.ie; St Patrick's Close; adult/child €5.50/free; 9am-5pm Mon-Sat, 9-10.30am & 12.30-2.30pm Sun year-round, longer hours Mar-Oct; 50, 50A or 56A from Aston Quay, 54 or 54A from Burgh Quay) It was at this cathedral, reputedly, that St Paddy himself dunked the Irish heathens into the waters of a well, so the church that bears his name stands on one of the earliest Christian sites in the city. Although there's been a church here since the 5th century, the present building dates from 1190 or 1225 (opinions differ) and it has been altered several times, most notably in 1864 when the flying buttresses were added.

★Museum of Natural History MUSEUM

(National Museum of Ireland – Natural History; www.museum.ie; Merrion St; 10am-5pm Tue-Sat, 2-5pm Sun; 7 & 44 from city centre) FREE Dusty, weird and utterly compelling, this window into Victorian times has barely changed since Scottish explorer Dr David Livingstone opened it in 1857 (before disappearing into the African jungle). The creaky-floored interior is crammed with some two million stuffed animals, skeletons, fossils and other specimens from around the world, ranging from West African apes to pickled insects in jars. Some are free-standing, others behind glass, but everywhere you turn the animals of the 'dead zoo' are still and staring.

O'Connell St HISTORIC SITE

(24hr; all city centre) Dublin's grandest avenue is dominated by the needle-like, 120m-tall **Monument of Light**, better known as 'The Spire'. It rises from the spot once occupied by a statue of Admiral Nelson, which was blown up by the Irish Republican Army (IRA) in 1966. Nearby is the 1815 **General Post Office** (www.anpost.ie; 8am-8pm Mon-Sat; all city centre, Abbey), an important landmark of the 1916 Easter Rising, when the Irish Volunteers used it as a base for attacks against the British army.

Sleeping

Hotel rooms in Dublin aren't as expensive as they were during the Celtic Tiger years, but demand is still high and booking is highly recommended, especially if you want to stay in the city centre or within walking distance of it.

North of the Liffey

★Isaacs Hostel HOSTEL €

(01-855 6215; www.isaacs.ie; 2-5 Frenchman's Lane; dm/tw from €14/58; ; all city centre, Connolly) The north side's best hostel – hell, for atmosphere alone it's the best in town – is in a 200-year-old wine vault just around the corner from the main bus station. With summer barbecues, live music in the lounge, internet access and colourful dorms, this terrific place generates consistently good feedback from backpackers and other travellers.

★Generator Hostel HOSTEL €

(01-901 0222; www.generatorhostels.com; Smithfield Sq; dm/tw from €16/70;) This European chain brings its own brand of funky, fun design to Dublin's hostel scene, with bright colours, comfortable dorms (including women-only) and a lively social scene. Good location on a pedestrian mall next to Old Jameson Distillery.

Abbey Court Hostel HOSTEL €

(01-878 0700; www.abbey-court.com; 29 Bachelor's Walk; dm/d from €16/78; ; all cross-city) Spread over two buildings, this large, well-run hostel has 33 clean dorm beds with good storage. Its excellent facilities include a dining hall, conservatory and barbecue area. Doubles with bathroom are in the newer building where a light breakfast is provided in the adjacent cafe. Not surprisingly, this is a popular spot; reservations are advised.

Anchor House B&B €€

(01-878 6913; www.anchorhousedublin.com; 49 Lower Gardiner St; s/d €95/105; ; all city centre, Connolly) Most B&Bs in these parts offer pretty much the same stuff: TV, half-decent shower, clean linen and tea- and coffee-making facilities. The Anchor does all that, but it also has an elegance you won't find in many other B&Bs along this stretch. This lovely Georgian guesthouse, with its delicious wholesome breakfasts, comes highly recommended by readers. They're dead right.

Gresham Hotel HOTEL €€€

(01-874 6881; www.gresham-hotels.com; Upper O'Connell St; r from €145; ; all cross-city) This landmark hotel shed its traditional granny's parlour look with a major overhaul some years ago. Despite its brighter, smarter, modern appearance and a fabulous open-plan foyer, its loyal clientele – elderly groups on shopping breaks and well-heeled

Americans – continues to find it charming. Rooms are spacious and well serviced, and the location is unbeatable.

South of the Liffey

Barnacles HOSTEL €

(01-671 6277; www.barnacles.ie; 19 Lower Temple Lane; dm/tw from €17/64; P; all city centre) If you're here for a good time and not a long time, then this Temple Bar hostel is the ideal spot to meet fellow revellers; tap up the helpful and knowledgeable staff for the best places to cause mischief; and sleep off the effects of said mischief whilst being totally oblivious to the noise outside, which is constant.

Rooms are quieter at the back. Top facilities include a comfy lounge with an open fire. Linen and towels are provided. A contender for the south side's best hostel, it also has a discount deal with a nearby covered car park.

Ashfield House HOSTEL €

(01-679 7734; www.ashfieldhouse.ie; 19-20 D'Olier St; dm/tw from €14/70; @; all city centre) A stone's throw from Temple Bar and O'Connell Bridge, this modern hostel in a converted church has a selection of tidy four- and six-bed rooms, one large dorm and 25 rooms with private bathroom. It's more like a small hotel, but without the price tag. A continental-style breakfast is included – a rare beast indeed for hostels. Maximum stay is six nights.

Kinlay House HOSTEL €

(01-679 6644; www.kinlaydublin.ie; 2-12 Lord Edward St; dm/s/q from €16/26/68; all city centre) An institution among the city's hostels, this former boarding house for boys has massive, mixed 24-bed dorms, as well as smaller rooms. Its bustling location next to Christ Church Cathedral and Dublin Castle is a bonus, but some rooms suffer from noise. There are cooking facilities and a cafe, and breakfast is included. Not for the faint-hearted.

★Brooks Hotel HOTEL €€

(01-670 4000; www.sinnotthotels.com; 59-62 Drury St; r from €140; P; all cross-city, St Stephen's Green) About 120m west of Grafton St, this small, plush place has an emphasis on familial, friendly service. The decor is nouveau classic with high-veneer-panelled walls, decorative bookcases and old-fashioned sofas, while bedrooms are extremely comfortable and come fitted out in subtly coloured furnishings. The clincher though, is the king- and superking-size beds in all rooms, complete with…a pillow menu.

Buswell's Hotel HOTEL €€

(01-614 6500; www.buswells.ie; 23-27 Molesworth St; r from €141; P@; all cross-city, St Stephen's Green) This Dublin institution, open since 1882, has a long association with politicians, who wander across the road from Dáil Éireann to wet their beaks at the hotel bar. The 69 bedrooms have all been given the once-over, but have kept their Georgian charm intact.

★Number 31 GUESTHOUSE €€€

(01-676 5011; www.number31.ie; 31 Leeson Close; s/d/tr incl breakfast €240/280/320; P; all city centre) The city's most distinctive property is the former home of modernist architect Sam Stephenson, who successfully fused '60s style with 18th-century grace. Its 21 bedrooms are split between the retro coach house, with its fancy rooms, and the more elegant Georgian house, where rooms are individually furnished with tasteful French antiques and big comfortable beds.

Eating

The most concentrated restaurant area is Temple Bar but, apart from a handful of good places, the bulk of eateries offer bland, unimaginative fodder and cheap set menus for tourists. Better food and service can usually be found on either side of Grafton St, while the top-end restaurants are clustered around Merrion Sq and Fitzwilliam Sq. Fast-food chains dominate the north side, though some fine cafes and eateries are finally appearing there, too.

North of the Liffey

Soup Dragon FAST FOOD €

(www.soupdragon.com; 168 Capel St; mains €5-8; 8am-5pm Mon-Fri; all city centre, Jervis) Queues are a regular feature outside this fabulous spot that specialises in soups-on-the-go, but it also does excellent curries, stews, pies and salads. The all-day breakfast options are excellent – we especially like the mini-breakfast quiche of sausage, egg and bacon. Bowls come in three different sizes and prices include fresh bread and a piece of fruit.

★Chapter One MODERN IRISH €€€

(01-873 2266; www.chapteronerestaurant.com; 18 North Parnell Sq; 2-course lunch €29, 4-course dinner €70; 12.30-2pm Tue-Fri, 7.30-10.30pm Tue-Sat; 3, 10, 11, 13, 16, 19 or 22 from city centre) Michelin-starred Chapter One is our choice for city's best eatery. It successfully combines flawless haute cuisine with a relaxed, welcoming atmosphere that is at the heart of Irish hospitality. The food is French-inspired contemporary Irish, the menus change regularly and the service is top-notch. The three-course pre-theatre menu (€36.50) is a favourite with those heading to the Gate around the corner.

Winding Stair MODERN IRISH €€€
(☎01-873 7320; www.winding-stair.com; 40 Lower Ormond Quay; 2-course lunch €19, mains €23-27; ⌚noon-5pm & 5.30-10.30pm; 🚌all city centre) Housed within a beautiful Georgian building that was once home to the city's most beloved bookshop (the ground floor still is one), the Winding Stair's conversion to elegant restaurant has been faultless. The wonderful Irish menu – creamy fish pie, bacon and organic cabbage, steamed mussels, and Irish farmyard cheeses – coupled with an excellent wine list make for a memorable meal.

South of the Liffey

Green Nineteen IRISH €
(☎01-478 9626; www.green19.ie; 19 Lower Camden St; mains €9-14; ⌚8.30am-11pm; 📶; 🚌all city centre) 🍃 A firm favourite on Camden St's corridor of cool is this sleek hipster canteen that specialises in locally sourced, organic grub – without the fancy price tag. Braised lamb chump, corned beef, pot roast chicken and the ubiquitous burger are the meaty part of the menu, which also includes salads and vegie options. We love it.

Queen of Tarts CAFE €
(www.queenoftarts.ie; 4 Cork Hill; mains €5-10; ⌚8am-7pm Mon-Fri, 9am-7pm Sat & Sun; 🚌all city centre) Pocket-sized Queen of Tarts offers a mouth-watering array of savoury tarts, filled focaccias, fruit crumbles and brownies. There are also great healthy breakfasts and weekend brunch specials such as potato-and-chive cake with mushroom and egg, plus the coffee is splendid and the service sweet. There's a bigger version around the corner on **Cow's Lane** (www.queenoftarts.ie; 3-4 Cow's Lane; mains €5-10; ⌚8am-7pm Mon-Fri, 9am-7pm Sat & Sun; 🚌all cross-city).

Simon's Place CAFE €
(George's St Arcade, S Great George's St; sandwiches €5; ⌚8.30am-5pm Mon-Sat; ✎; 🚌all city centre) Simon hasn't had to change the menu of doorstep sandwiches and wholesome vegetarian soups since he first opened shop more than two decades ago – and why should he? His grub is as heartening and legendary as he is. It's a great place to sip a coffee and watch life go by in the old-fashioned arcade.

★ **Fade Street Social** MODERN IRISH €€
(☎01-604 0066; www.fadestreetsocial.com; Fade St; mains €19-32, tapas €5-12; ⌚12.30-2.30pm Mon-Fri, 5-10.30pm daily; 📶; 🚌all city centre) 🍃 Two eateries in one, courtesy of renowned chef Dylan McGrath: at the front, the buzzy Gastro Bar, which serves up gourmet tapas from a beautiful open kitchen. At the back, the more muted Restaurant does Irish cuts of meat – from veal to rabbit – served with homegrown, organic vegetables. Three-course lunch and early evening menu €25. Reservations suggested.

Coppinger Row MEDITERRANEAN €€
(www.coppingerrow.com; Coppinger Row; mains €17-26; ⌚noon-5.30pm & 6-11pm Mon-Sat, 12.30-4pm & 6-9pm Sun; 🚌all city centre) Virtually all of the Mediterranean basin is represented on this restaurant's ever-changing, imaginative menu. Choices include the likes of pan-fried sea bass with roast baby fennel, tomato and

FREE THRILLS

Dublin is not a cheap city, but there are plenty of attractions that won't bust your budget.

➡ Wander the grounds at **Trinity College** (College Green; college grounds free, Old Library adult/child €9/free, walking tours per person €10; ⌚9.30am-5pm Mon-Sat year-round, 9.30am-4.30pm Sun May-Sep, noon-4.30pm Sun Oct-Apr, walking tours twice per hour 10.15am-3.40pm Mon-Sat, to 3pm Sun mid-May–Sep), Dublin's oldest and most beautiful university.

➡ Discover the world's finest collection of prehistoric gold artefacts at the **National Museum of Archaeology** (p607).

➡ Explore the **Chester Beatty Library** (p608), with its collection of oriental and religious art.

➡ Gaze at Irish and European paintings at the **National Gallery** (p608).

➡ Laze at **St Stephen's Green** (p605), the city's most picturesque public park.

DUBLIN PASS

If you're planning some heavy-duty sightseeing, you'll save a packet by investing in the **Dublin Pass** (www.dublinpass.ie; adult/child 1 day €39/21, 3 day €71/42). It provides free entry to more than 30 attractions, including the Guinness Storehouse and Kilmainham Gaol, and you can also skip queues by presenting your card. It also includes free transfer to and from the airport on the Aircoach. Available from any Dublin tourist office.

olives; or rump of lamb with spiced aubergine and dried apricots. A nice touch are the filtered still and sparkling waters (€1), where 50% of the cost goes to cancer research.

L'Gueuleton FRENCH €€
(www.lgueuleton.com; 1 Fade St; mains €16-27; 12.30-3.30pm & 5.30-10pm Mon-Sat, noon-3.30pm & 5.30-9pm Sun; all city centre) Dubliners have a devil of a time pronouncing the name (which means 'a gluttonous feast' in French) and have had their patience tested with the no-reservations-get-in-line-and-wait policy, but they just can't get enough of this restaurant's robust (read: meaty and filling) take on French rustic cuisine that makes twisted tongues and sore feet a small price to pay.

Drinking & Nightlife

Temple Bar, Dublin's 'party district', is almost always packed with raucous stag (bachelor) and hen (bachelorette) parties, scantily clad girls and loud guys from Ohio wearing Guinness T-shirts. If you're just looking to get smashed and hook up with someone from another country, there's no better place in Ireland. If that's not your style, there's plenty to enjoy beyond Temple Bar. In fact, most of the best old-fashioned pubs are outside the district.

★**Stag's Head** PUB
(www.louisfitzgerald.com/stagshead; 1 Dame Ct; 10.30am-1am Mon-Sat, to midnight Sun; all city centre) The Stag's Head was built in 1770, remodelled in 1895 and thankfully not changed a bit since then. It's a superb pub, so picturesque that it often appears in films and also featured in a postage-stamp series on Irish bars. A bloody great pub, no doubt.

Grogan's Castle Lounge PUB
(www.groganspub.ie; 15 South William St; 10.30am-11.30pm Mon-Thu, 10.30am-12.30am Fri & Sat, 12.30-11pm Sun) This place is known simply as Grogan's (after the original owner), and it is a city-centre institution. It has long been a favourite haunt of Dublin's writers and painters, as well as others from the alternative bohemian set, most of whom seem to be waiting for the 'inevitable' moment when they are finally recognised as geniuses.

George GAY
(www.thegeorge.ie; 89 S Great George's St; 2-11.30pm Mon, 2pm-2.30am Tue-Fri, 12.30pm-2.30am Sat, 12.30pm-1.30am Sun) The purple mother of Dublin's gay bars is a long-standing institution, having lived through the years when it was the only place in town where the gay crowd could, well, be gay. There are other places to go, but the George remains the best, if only for tradition's sake. Shirley's legendary Sunday night bingo is as popular as ever.

Dice Bar BAR
(01-674 6710; www.thatsitdublin.com; 79 Queen St; 3pm-midnight Mon-Thu, to 1am Fri & Sat, to 11.30pm Sun; 25, 25A, 66, 67 from city centre, Museum) Co-owned by Huey from the Fun Lovin' Criminals, the Dice Bar looks like something you might find on New York's Lower East Side. Its dodgy locale, black-and-red painted interior, dripping candles and distressed seating, combined with rocking DJs most nights, make it a magnet for Dublin hipsters. It has Guinness and local craft beers.

Anseo BAR
(28 Lower Camden St; 10.30am-11.30pm Mon-Thu, 10.30am-12.30am Fri & Sat, 11am-11pm Sun; all city centre) Unpretentious, unaffected and incredibly popular, this cosy alternative bar – which is pronounced 'an-*shuh*', the Irish for 'here' – is a favourite with those who live by the credo that to try too hard is far worse than not trying at all. Wearing cool like a loose garment, the punters thrive on the mix of chat and terrific DJs.

Globe BAR
(01-671 1220; www.theglobe.ie; 11 S Great George's St; 5pm-2.30am Mon-Fri, 4pm-2.30am Sat, 4pm-1am Sun; ; all city centre) The granddaddy of the city's hipster bars, the Globe has held on to its groover status by virtue of tradition and the fact that the formula is brilliantly simple: wooden floors, plain brick walls and a no-attitude atmosphere that you just can't fake.

Twisted Pepper CLUB
(01-873 4800; www.bodytonicmusic.com/thetwistedpepper; 54 Middle Abbey St; bar 4pm-late, cafe 8.30am-6pm; all city centre, Abbey) Dublin's hippest venue comes in four parts: DJs spin great tunes in the basement; the stage is for live acts; the mezzanine is a secluded bar area above the stage; and the cafe is where you can get an Irish breakfast all day. All run by the Bodytonic crew, one of the most exciting music and production crowds in town.

Entertainment

For events, reviews and club listings, pick up a copy of the fortnightly music review *Hot Press* (www.hotpress.com), or for free cultural events, check out the weekly e-zine *Dublin Event Guide* (www.dublineventguide.com). Friday's *Irish Times* has a pull-out section called 'The Ticket' that has reviews and listings of all things arty.

Whelan's LIVE MUSIC
(01-478 0766; www.whelanslive.com; 25 Wexford St; bus 16, 122 from city centre) A Dublin institution, providing a showcase for Irish singer-songwriters and other lo-fi performers since the 1990s, Whelan's combines a traditional pub upstairs and a popular live-music venue on the ground floor. The old-fashioned ambience belies a progressive music booking policy, with a program that features many breaking new acts from rock and indie to folk and trad.

Abbey Theatre THEATRE
(01-878 7222; www.abbeytheatre.ie; Lower Abbey St; all city centre, Abbey) Ireland's renowned national theatre, founded by WB Yeats in 1904, has been reinvigorated in recent years by director Fiach MacConghaill, who has introduced lots of new blood to what was in danger of becoming a moribund corpse. The current program has a mix of Irish classics (Synge, O'Casey etc), established international names (Shepard, Mamet) and new talent (O'Rowe, Carr et al).

National Concert Hall LIVE MUSIC
(01-417 0000; www.nch.ie; Earlsfort Tce; all city centre) Ireland's premier orchestral hall hosts a variety of concerts year-round, including a series of lunchtime concerts from 1.05pm to 2pm on Tuesdays, June to August.

Gaiety Theatre THEATRE
(01-677 1717; www.gaietytheatre.com; South King St; all city centre) The Gaiety's program of plays is strictly of the fun-for-all-the-family type: West End hits, musicals, Christmas pantomimes and classic Irish plays for those simply looking to be entertained.

Irish Film Institute CINEMA
(01-679 5744; www.ifi.ie; 6 Eustace St; all city centre) The Irish Film Institute (IFI) has a couple of screens and shows classics and new art-house films, although we question some of its selections: weird and controversial can be a little tedious. The complex also has a bar, a cafe and a bookshop.

Information

All Dublin tourist offices provide walk-in services only – no phone enquiries. For tourist information by phone call 1850 230 330 from within the Republic.

Dublin Discover Ireland Centre (www.visitdublin.com; St Andrew's Church, 2 Suffolk St; 9am-5.30pm Mon-Sat, 10.30am-3pm Sun) The main tourist information centre; there's a second branch on O'Connell St (14 O'Connell St; 9am-5pm Mon-Sat).

Grafton Medical Centre (01-671 2122; www.graftonmedical.ie; 34 Grafton St; 8.30am-6pm Mon-Fri, 11am-2pm Sat) One-stop shop with male and female doctors and physiotherapists.

Hickey's Pharmacy (01-873 0427; 55 Lower O'Connell St; 8am-10pm Mon-Fri, 8.30am-10pm Sat, 10am-10pm Sun) Open till 10pm every night.

St James's Hospital (01-410 3000; www.stjames.ie; James's St) Dublin's main 24-hour accident and emergency department.

Getting There & Away

AIR

Dublin Airport (p637), about 13km north of the city centre, is Ireland's major international gateway, with direct flights from Europe, North America and Asia. Budget airlines such as Ryanair and Flybe land here.

BOAT

There are direct ferries from Holyhead in Wales to Dublin Port, 3km northeast of the city centre, and to Dun Laoghaire, 13km southeast. Boats also sail direct to Dublin Port from Liverpool and from Douglas, on the Isle of Man.

BUS

The private company **Citylink** (www.citylink.ie) has nonstop services from Dublin Airport (picking up in the city centre at Bachelor's Walk, near O'Connell Bridge) to Galway (€13, 2½ hours, hourly).

BOOK OF KELLS

The world-famous *Book of Kells*, dating from around AD 800 and thus one of the oldest books in the world, was probably produced by monks at St Colmcille's Monastery on the remote island of Iona. It contains the four gospels of the New Testament, written in Latin, as well as prefaces, summaries and other text. If it were merely words, the Book of Kells would simply be a very old book – it's the extensive and amazingly complex illustrations (the illuminations) that make it so wonderful. The superbly decorated opening initials are only part of the story, for the book has smaller illustrations between the lines.

Aircoach (www.aircoach.ie) operates a service from O'Connell St in the Dublin city centre, via Dublin Airport to Belfast.

Busáras (☎ 01-836 6111; www.buseireann.ie; Store St) pronounced buh-*saw*-ras, is Dublin's main bus station; it's just north of the Liffey.

Belfast €17, 2½ hours, hourly
Cork €15, 3¾ hours, six daily
Galway €14.50, 3¾ hours, hourly
Kilkenny €13.50, 2¼ hours, six daily
Rosslare Europort €23, four hours, five daily

TRAIN

Connolly station is north of the Liffey, with trains to Belfast, Sligo and Rosslare. Heuston station is south of the Liffey and west of the city centre, with trains for Cork, Galway, Killarney, Limerick, and most other points to the south and west. Visit www.irishrail.ie for timetables and fares.

Belfast €38, 2¼ hours, eight daily
Cork €64, 2¾ hours, hourly
Galway €36, 2¾ hours, nine daily
Killarney €67, 3¼ hours, seven daily

Getting Around

TO/FROM THE AIRPORT

Aircoach (www.aircoach.ie; one way/return €7/12) Buses every 10 to 15 minutes between 6am and midnight, hourly from midnight until 6am.

Airlink Express (☎ 01-873 4222; www.dublinbus.ie; one way/return €6/3) Bus 747 runs every 10 to 20 minutes from 5.45am to 11.30pm between the airport, central bus station (Busáras) and the Dublin Bus office on Upper O'Connell St.

Taxi There is a taxi rank directly outside the arrivals concourse. It should take about 45 minutes to get into the city centre by taxi and cost about €25, including a supplementary charge of €3 (not applied when going to the airport).

BICYCLE

Rental rates begin at around €13/70 per day/week; you'll need a €50 to €200 cash deposit and photo ID.

Dublinbikes (www.dublinbikes.ie) A pay-as-you-go service similar to London's: cyclists purchase a Smart Card (€5 for three days, €20 for one year, plus a €150 credit-card deposit) either online or at any of more than 40 stations throughout the city centre, and bike use is then free for the first 30 minutes, increasing gradually thereafter (eg €3.50 for up to three hours).

Neill's Wheels (www.rentabikedublin.com; per day/week €12.50/70) Various outlets, including Kinlay House and Isaacs Hostel.

PUBLIC TRANSPORT

Bus

Dublin Bus (www.dublinbus.ie) Local buses cost from €0.70 to €3.05 for a single journey. You must pay the exact fare when boarding; drivers don't give change. The Freedom Pass (€30) allows three days' unlimited travel on all Dublin buses including Airlink and Dublin Bus hop-on/hop-off tour buses.

Train

Dublin Area Rapid Transport (DART; ☎ 01-836 6222; www.irishrail.ie) Provides quick rail access as far north as Howth and south to Bray; Pearse and Tara St stations are handy for central Dublin. Single fares cost €2.15 to €3.05; a one-day pass costs €11.10.

Tram

Luas (www.luas.ie) Runs on two (unconnected) lines; the green line runs from the eastern side of St Stephen's Green southeast to Sandyford, and the red line runs from Tallaght to Connolly station, with stops at Heuston station, the National Museum and Busáras. Single fares range from €1.70 to €3 depending on how many zones you travel through; a one-day pass is €6.40.

TAXI

Taxis in Dublin are expensive; flag fall costs €4.10, plus €1.03 per kilometre. For taxi service, call **National Radio Cabs** (☎ 01-677 2222; www.radiocabs.ie).

Kilkenny

POP 24,400

Kilkenny (Cill Chainnigh) is the Ireland of many visitors' imaginations. Its majestic riverside castle, tangle of 17th-century passageways, rows of colourful, old-fashioned shopfronts and centuries-old pubs with traditional live music all have a timeless appeal, as does its splendid medieval cathedral. But Kilkenny is also famed for its contemporary restaurants and rich cultural life.

Sights

★Kilkenny Castle CASTLE
(www.kilkennycastle.ie; adult/child €6/2.50, audio guides €5, parkland admission free; ⏲9.30am-5pm Mar-Sep, to 4.30pm Oct-Feb, parkland daylight hours) Rising above the River Nore, Kilkenny Castle is one of Ireland's most visited heritage sites. Stronghold of the powerful Butler family, it has a history dating back to the 12th century, though much of its present look dates from the 19th century. Highlights of the guided tour include the painted roof beams of the Long Gallery and the collection of Victorian antiques. There's an excellent tearoom in the former castle kitchens, all white marble and gleaming copper.

★St Canice's Cathedral CATHEDRAL
(www.stcanicescathedral.ie; St Canice's Pl; cathedral €4, round tower €3, combined €6; ⏲9am-6pm Mon-Sat, 1-6pm Sun, shorter hours Sep-May) Ireland's second-largest medieval cathedral (after St Patrick's in Dublin), with its iconic round tower, has a long and fascinating history. Legend has it that the first monastery was built here in the 6th century by St Canice, Kilkenny's patron saint. Outside the cathedral, a 30m-high round tower rises amid ancient tombstones. It was built sometime between AD 700 and 1000 on the site of an earlier Christian cemetery; those aged over 12 can admire the view from the top.

National Craft Gallery & Kilkenny Design Centre GALLERY
(www.nationalcraftgallery.ie; Castle Yard; ⏲10am-5.30pm Tue-Sat, 11am-5.30pm Sun; 👪) Contemporary Irish crafts are showcased at these imaginative galleries, set in the former Kilkenny Castle stables that also house the shops of the Kilkenny Design Centre. Ceramics dominate, but exhibits often feature furniture, jewellery and weaving from the members of the Crafts Council of Ireland. Family days are held the second Saturday of every month with free hands-on workshops for children at 10am and 12.30pm. For additional workshops and events, check the website.

Festivals & Events

Kilkenny is rightly known as the festival capital of Ireland, with several world-class events throughout the year.

Kilkenny Arts Festival ART
(www.kilkennyarts.ie; 👪) In August the city comes alive with theatre, cinema, music, literature, visual arts, children's events and street spectacles for 10 action-packed days.

Kilkenny Rhythm & Roots MUSIC
(www.kilkennyroots.com) More than 30 pubs and other venues participate in hosting this major music festival in May, with an emphasis on country and 'old-time' American roots music.

Sleeping

Kilkenny Tourist Hostel HOSTEL €
(☎056-776 3541; www.kilkennyhostel.ie; 35 Parliament St; dm/tw from €17/42; @📶) Inside an ivy-covered 1770s Georgian town house, this cosy, 60-bed IHH hostel has a sitting room warmed by an open fireplace, and a timber- and leadlight-panelled dining room adjoining the self-catering kitchen.

Butler House BOUTIQUE HOTEL €€
(☎056-772 2828; www.butler.ie; 16 Patrick St; s/d from €90/145; P@📶) You can't stay in Kilkenny Castle, but this historic mansion is the next best thing. Once the home of the earls of Ormonde, who built the castle, today it houses a boutique hotel with aristocratic trappings including sweeping staircases, marble fireplaces, an art collection and impeccably trimmed gardens.

Celtic House B&B €€
(☎056-776 2249; www.celtic-house-bandb.com; 18 Michael St; r €70; P@📶) Artist and author Angela Byrne extends one of Ireland's warmest welcomes at her spick-and-span B&B. Some of the bright rooms have sky-lit bathrooms, others have views of the castle, and Angela's landscapes adorn many of the walls. Book ahead.

Eating

Gourmet Store SANDWICHES €
(56 High St; sandwich & coffee €5; ⌚9am-6pm Mon-Sat) In this crowded little deli, take-away sandwiches are assembled from choice imported meats and cheeses (plus a few top-notch locals).

★ **Foodworks** BISTRO, CAFE €€
(☎056-777 7696; www.foodworks.ie; 7 Parliament St; mains €8-21; ⌚noon-9.30pm Wed-Fri, noon-10pm Sat, 12.30-4.30pm Sun; 📶) The owners of this cool and casual bistro keep their own pigs and grow their own salad leaves, so it would be churlish not to try their pulled pork brioche with beetroot slaw – and you'll be glad you did. Delicious food, excellent coffee and friendly service make this a justifiably popular venue; best to book a table.

Cafe Sol MODERN IRISH €€
(☎056-776 4987; www.restaurantskilkenny.com; William St; mains lunch €10-14, 2-/3-course dinner €23/27; ⌚11am-9.30pm Mon-Thu, 11am-10pm Fri & Sat, noon-9pm Sun; 📶) Leisurely lunches stretch until 5pm at this much-loved restaurant. Local organic produce is featured in dishes that emphasise what's fresh each season. The flavours are frequently bold and have global influences. Service, albeit casual, is excellent and the whole place exudes a modern Med-bistro look.

Drinking & Nightlife

★ **Kyteler's Inn** PUB
(www.kytelersinn.com; 27 St Kieran's St; ⌚11am-midnight Sun-Thu, to 2am Fri & Sat, live music 6.30pm Mar-Oct) Dame Alice Kyteler's old house was built back in 1224 and has seen its share of history: she was charged with witchcraft in 1323. Today the rambling bar includes the orignal building, complete with vaulted ceiling and arches. There is a beer garden, courtyard and a large upstairs room for the live bands, ranging from trad to blues.

Tynan's Bridge House PUB
(St John's Bridge; ⌚10.30am-11.30pm Mon-Thu, 10.30am-12.30am Fri & Sat, 11.30am-11pm Sun) This historic 1703 Georgian pub flaunting a brilliant blue facade is the best traditional pub in town with its horseshoe bar, original tilework, regular clientele of crusty locals – and no TV! There is trad music on Wednesdays and Sundays at 9pm.

Entertainment

Watergate Theatre THEATRE
(www.watergatetheatre.com; Parliament St) The top theatre venue hosts drama, comedy and musical performances. If you're wondering why intermission lasts 18 minutes, it's so patrons can nip into **John Cleere's pub** (www.cleeres.com; 22 Parliament St; ⌚11.30am-11.30pm Mon-Thu, to 12.30am Fri & Sat, 1-11pm Sun) for a pint.

Information

Tourist Office (www.kilkennytourism.ie; Rose Inn St; ⌚9.15am-5pm Mon-Sat) Stocks excellent guides and walking maps. Located in Shee Alms House, dating from 1582 and built in local stone by benefactor Sir Richard Shee to help the poor.

Getting There & Away

BUS

Buses depart from the train station. Services include Cork (€19, three hours, two daily) and Dublin (€13.50, 2¼ hours, six daily).

TRAIN

Kilkenny train station (Dublin Rd) is east of the town centre along John St, next to the MacDonagh Junction shopping mall. Services include Dublin Heuston (€25, 1¾ hours, eight daily) and Galway (€47, 3½ hours, one daily, change at Kildare).

THE SOUTHWEST

Cork

POP 119,230

Ireland's second city is first in every important respect, at least according to the locals, who cheerfully refer to it as the 'real capital of Ireland'. The compact city centre is surrounded by interesting waterways and is chock full of great restaurants fed by arguably the best foodie scene in the country.

Sights

★ **English Market** MARKET
(www.englishmarket.ie; Princes St; ⌚9am-5.30pm Mon-Sat) It could just as easily be called the Victorian Market for its ornate vaulted ceilings and columns, but the English Market is a true gem, no matter what you name it. Scores of vendors sell some of the very best local produce, meats, cheeses and takeaway food in the region. On decent days, take your lunch to nearby **Bishop Lucey Park**, a popular alfresco eating spot.

WORTH A TRIP

ROCK OF CASHEL

The **Rock of Cashel** (www.heritageireland.com; adult/child €6/2; 9am-5.30pm mid-Mar–mid-Oct, to 7pm mid-Jun–Aug, to 4.30pm mid-Oct–mid-Mar) is one of Ireland's most spectacular archaeological sites. A prominent green hill, banded with limestone outcrops, it rises from a grassy plain on the outskirts of Cashel town and bristles with ancient fortifications. For more than 1000 years it was a symbol of power, and the seat of kings and churchmen who ruled over the region. Sturdy walls circle an enclosure that contains a complete round tower, a roofless abbey and the finest 12th-century Romanesque chapel in Ireland.

Cashel Lodge & Camping Park (062-61003; www.cashel-lodge.com; Dundrum Rd; campsite per person €10, dm/s/d €20/40/65; P) is a good place to stay, with terrific views of the Rock. Bus Éireann runs six buses daily between Cashel and Cork (€15, 1¾ hours).

Crawford Municipal Art Gallery GALLERY
(021-480 5042; www.crawfordartgallery.ie; Emmet Pl; 10am-5pm Mon-Wed, Fri & Sat, to 8pm Thu) FREE Cork's public gallery houses a small but excellent permanent collection covering the 17th century to the modern day. Highlights include works by Sir John Lavery, Jack B Yeats and Nathaniel Hone, and a room devoted to Irish women artists from 1886 to 1978 – don't miss the works by Mainie Jellet and Evie Hone.

Cork City Gaol MUSEUM
(021-430 5022; www.corkcitygaol.com; Convent Ave, Sun's Well; adult/child €8/4.50; 9.30am-5pm Apr-Oct, 10am-4pm Nov-Mar) This imposing former prison is well worth a visit, if only to get a sense of how crap life was for prisoners a century ago. An audio tour guides you around the restored cells, which feature models of suffering prisoners and sadistic-looking guards. It's very moving, bringing home the harshness of the 19th-century penal system. The most common crime was that of poverty; many of the inmates were sentenced to hard labour for stealing loaves of bread.

Sleeping

Oscar's Hostel HOSTEL €
(085 175 3458; www.oscarshostel.com; 111 Lower Glanmire Rd; dm/tw €20/44;) Pretty much brand new at the time of research, this small (32-bed) hostel is set on a busy street just 200m east of the train station and 15 minutes' walk from the city centre. Facilities are good, with a well-equipped modern kitchen, comfy common rooms and bike storage, though the bedrooms are basic.

Brú Bar & Hostel HOSTEL €
(021-455 9667; www.bruhostel.com; 57 MacCurtain St; dm/tw from €17/40; @) This buzzing hostel has its own internet cafe, with free access for guests, and a fantastic bar, popular with backpackers and locals alike. The dorms (each with a bathroom) have four to six beds and are both clean and stylish – ask for one on the upper floors to avoid bar noise. Breakfast is free.

★**Garnish House** B&B €€
(021-427 5111; www.garnish.ie; Western Rd; s/d from €89/98; P) Attention is lavished upon guests at this award-winning B&B. The legendary breakfast menu (30 choices) includes fresh fish and French toast. Typical of the touches here is the delicious porridge, which comes with creamed honey and your choice of whiskey or Baileys. Enjoy it out on the garden terrace. The 14 rooms are very comfortable; reception is open 24 hours.

★**River Lee Hotel** HOTEL €€€
(021-425 2700; www.doylecollection.com; Western Rd; r from €155; P) This modern riverside hotel brings a touch of luxury to the city centre. It has gorgeous public areas with huge sofas, a designer fireplace and a stunning five-storey glass-walled atrium, and superb service. There are well-equipped bedrooms (nice and quiet at the back, but request a corner room for extra space) and possibly the best breakfast buffet in Ireland.

Eating

Quay Co-op VEGETARIAN €
(021-431 7026; www.quaycoop.com; 24 Sullivan's Quay; mains €5-11; 8am-9pm Mon-Sat, noon-9pm Sun;) Flying the flag for alternative Cork, this place offers a range of self-service vegetarian dishes, all organic, including big breakfasts and rib-sticking soups and casseroles. It

Cork

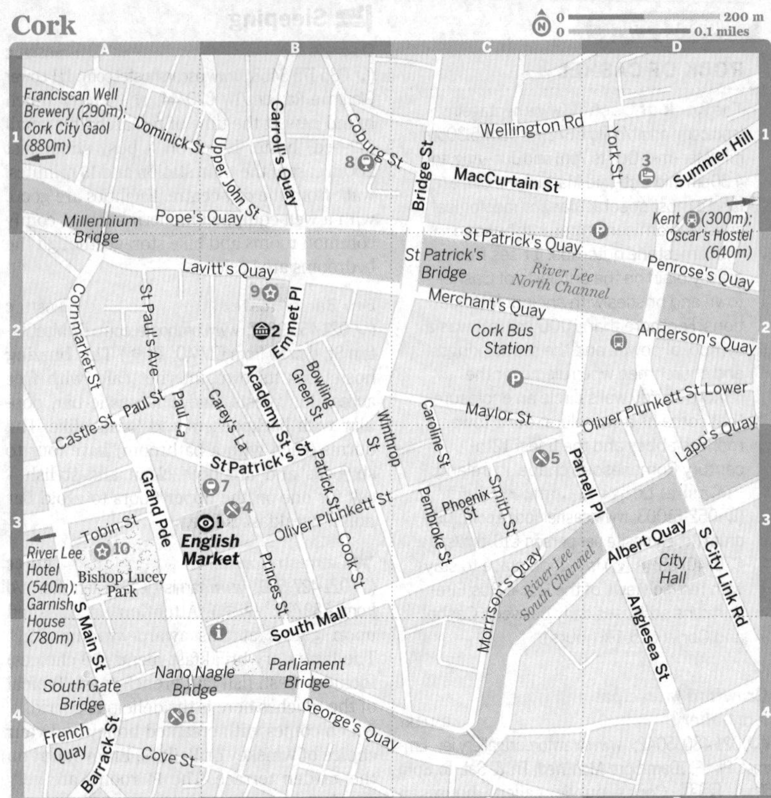

also caters for gluten-, dairy- and wheat-free needs, and is amazingly child-friendly.

★ **Market Lane** IRISH, INTERNATIONAL €€
(☎021-427 4710; www.marketlane.ie; 5 Oliver Plunkett St; mains €12-26; ⏲noon-10.30pm Mon-Sat, 1-9pm Sun; 📶👪) It's always hopping at this bright corner bistro with an open kitchen and long wooden bar. The broad menu changes often to reflect what's fresh – look out for braised pork marinated in Cork dry gin, and steaks with awesome aioli. The €10 lunch menu is a steal. No reservations; sip a drink at the bar while you wait for a table.

Farmgate Cafe CAFE, BISTRO €€
(www.farmgate.ie; English Market, Princes St, mains €6-15; ⏲8.30am-4.30pm Mon-Fri, to 5pm Sat) An unmissable experience at the heart of the English Market, the Farmgate is perched on a balcony overlooking the market below, the source of all that fresh local produce on your plate, everything from rock oysters to the lamb for an Irish stew. Up the stairs and turn left for table service, right for counter service.

🍷 Drinking & Nightlife

In Cork pubs, drink Guinness at your peril, even though Heineken now owns both of the local stout legends, Murphy's and Beamish (and closed down the latter's brewery). Cork's microbrewery, the Franciscan Well Brewery, makes quality beers, including Friar Weisse, popular in summer.

Franciscan Well Brewery PUB
(www.franciscanwellbrewery.com; 14 North Mall; ⏲3-11.30pm Mon-Thu, to 12.30am Fri & Sat, to 11pm Sun; 📶) The copper vats gleaming behind the bar give the game away: the Franciscan Well brews its own beer. The best place to enjoy it is in the enormous beer garden at the back. The pub holds regular beer festivals with other small (and often underappreciated) Irish breweries.

Cork

Top Sights

1 English Market B3

Sights

2 Crawford Municipal Art Gallery B2

Sleeping

3 Brú Bar & Hostel D1

Eating

4 Farmgate Cafe B3
5 Market Lane C3
6 Quay Co-op A4

Drinking & Nightlife

7 Mutton Lane Inn B3
8 Sin É B1

Entertainment

9 Cork Opera House B2
Half Moon Theatre ....(see 9)
10 Triskel Arts Centre A3

Sin É PUB

(www.corkheritagepubs.com; 8 Coburg St; 12.30-11.30pm Sun-Thu, to 12.30am Fri & Sat) You could easily while away an entire day at this great old place, which is everything a craic-filled pub should be – long on atmosphere and short on pretension. There's music most nights (regular sessions Tuesday at 9.30pm, Friday and Sunday at 6.30pm), much of it traditional, but with the odd surprise.

Mutton Lane Inn PUB

(www.corkheritagepubs.com; Mutton Lane; 10.30am-11.30pm Mon-Thu, 10.30am-12.30am Fri & Sat, 2-11pm Sun) Tucked down the tiniest of laneways off St Patrick's St, this inviting pub, lit by candles and fairy lights, is one of Cork's most intimate drinking holes. It's minuscule so try to get in early to bag the snug, or perch on beer kegs outside.

Entertainment

Cork's cultural life is generally of a high calibre. To see what's happening grab *WhazOn?* (www.whazon.com), a free monthly booklet available from the tourist office, newsagencies, shops, hostels and B&Bs.

Cork Opera House OPERA

(021-427 0022; www.corkoperahouse.ie; Emmet Pl; box office 10am-7pm Mon-Sat, from 6pm Sun performance nights, 10am-5.30pm Mon-Sat non-performance nights) This leading venue has been entertaining the city for more than 150 years with everything from opera and ballet to stand-up and puppet shows. Around the back, the **Half Moon Theatre** (021-427 0022; www.corkoperahouse.ie/category/genre/half-moon-theatre; Emmet Pl) presents contemporary theatre, dance, art and occasional club nights.

Triskel Arts Centre ARTS CENTRE

(021-472 2022; www.triskelart.com; Tobin St; tickets €15-20; cafe 10am-5pm Mon-Sat) Expect a varied program of live music, installation art, photography and theatre at this intimate venue. There's also a **cinema** (from 6.30pm) and a great **cafe**.

Information

Cork City Tourist Office (021-425 5100; www.corkcity.ie; Grand Pde; 9am-6pm Mon-Sat year-round, plus 10am-5pm Sun Jul & Aug) Souvenir shop and information desk. Sells Ordnance Survey maps. Stena Line ferries has a desk here.

Getting There & Around

BICYCLE

Cycle Scene (021-430 1183; www.cyclescene.ie; 396 Blarney St) has bikes for hire from €15/80 per day/week.

BOAT

Brittany Ferries (021-427 7801; www.brittanyferries.ie; 42 Grand Pde) has regular sailings from Cork to Roscoff (France). The ferry terminal is at Ringaskiddy, about 15 minutes by car southeast of the city centre along the N28.

BUS

Aircoach (01-844 7118; www.aircoach.ie) provides a direct service to Dublin city (€16) and Dublin Airport (€20) from St Patrick's Quay (three hours, hourly). **Cork bus station** (cnr Merchants Quay & Parnell Pl) is east of the city centre. Services include Dublin (€15, 3¾ hours, six daily), Kilkenny (€21, three hours, two daily) and Killarney (€27, two hours, hourly).

TRAIN

Cork's **Kent train station** (021-450 4777) is across the river. Destinations include Dublin (€64, 2¼ hours, eight daily), Galway (€57, four to six hours, seven daily, two or three changes needed) and Killarney (€28, 1½ to two hours, nine daily).

Around Cork

If you need proof of the power of a good yarn, then join the queue to get into the 15th-century **Blarney Castle** (021-438 5252;

www.blarneycastle.ie; adult/child €12/5; ⌚9am-5.30pm daily year-round, to 6pm Mon-Sat May & Sep, to 7pm Mon-Sat Jun-Aug; P), one of Ireland's most inexplicably popular tourist attractions. Tourists are here, of course, to plant their lips on the **Blarney Stone**, which supposedly gives one the gift of gab – a cliché that has entered every lexicon and tour route. Blarney is 8km northwest of Cork and buses run every half hour from Cork bus station (€7.30 return, 30 minutes).

Killarney

POP 14,200

Killarney is a well-oiled tourism machine set in a sublime landscape of lakes, forests and 1000m peaks. Its manufactured tweeness is renowned, the streets filled with tour-bus visitors shopping for soft-toy shamrocks and countless placards pointing to trad-music sessions. However, it has many charms beyond its proximity to waterfalls, woodlands, mountains and moors. In a town that's been practising the tourism game for more than 250 years, competition keeps standards high, and visitors on all budgets can expect to find superb restaurants, great pubs and good accommodation.

Sights & Activities

Most of Killarney's attractions are just outside the town. The mountain backdrop is part of **Killarney National Park** (www.killarneynationalpark.ie), which takes in beautiful Lough Leane, Muckross Lake and Upper Lake. Besides **Ross Castle** and **Muckross House**, the park also has much to explore by foot, bike or boat.

In summer the **Gap of Dunloe**, a gloriously scenic mountain pass squeezed between Purple Mountain and Carrauntuohill (at 1040m, Ireland's highest peak), is a tourist bottleneck. Rather than join the crowds taking pony-and-trap rides, **O'Connors Tours** (☎064-663 0200; www.gapofdunloetours.com; 7 High St, Killarney; ⌚Mar-Oct) can arrange a bike and boat circuit (€15; highly recommended) or bus and boat tour (€30) taking in the Gap.

Sleeping

Súgán Hostel HOSTEL €
(☎064-663 3104; www.killarneysuganhostel.com; Lewis Rd; dm €12-15, tw €38;) Behind its pub-like front, 250-year-old Súgán is an amiably eccentric hostel with an open fire in the cosy common room, low, crazy-cornered ceilings and hardwood floors. Note that it's an alcohol-free zone, which is either a good thing or a bad thing, depending on your point of view.

Fleming's White Bridge Caravan & Camping Park CAMPGROUND €
(☎086 363 0266; www.killarneycamping.com; White Bridge, Ballycasheen Rd; campsites €10-25; ⌚mid-Mar–Oct;) A lovely, sheltered, family-run campsite about 2km southeast of the town centre off the N22, Fleming's has a games room, bike hire, campers' kitchen, laundry and free trout fishing on the river that runs alongside. Your man Hillary at reception can arrange bus, bike and boat tours, if he doesn't talk the legs off you first!

★**Crystal Springs** B&B €€
(☎064-663 3272; www.crystalspringsbb.com; Ballycasheen Cross; s/d from €45/70; P) The timber deck of this wonderfully relaxing B&B overhangs the River Flesk, where trout anglers can fish for free. Rooms are richly furnished with patterned wallpapers and walnut timber; private bathrooms (most with spa baths) are huge. The glass-enclosed breakfast room also overlooks the rushing river. It's about a 15-minute stroll into town.

Kingfisher Lodge B&B €€
(☎064-663 7131; www.kingfisherlodgekillarney.com; Lewis Rd; s/d/f €70/90/120; ⌚mid-Feb–Nov; P@) Lovely back gardens are a highlight at this immaculate B&B, whose 11 rooms are done up in vivid yellows, reds and pinks. Owner Donal Carroll is a certified walking guide with a wealth of knowledge on hiking in the area.

Eating

Jam CAFE €
(☎064-663 7716; www.jam.ie; 77 Old Market Lane; mains €4-11; ⌚8am-5.30pm Mon-Sat, 10am-5.30pm Sun;) Duck down the alley to this local hideout for a changing menu of hot meals like Kerry shepherd's pie, deli items, and coffee and cake. It's all made with locally sourced produce and there are a few tables under an awning out front. There are branches in Kenmare and Cork.

Smoke House STEAK, SEAFOOD €€
(☎087 233 9611; High St; lunch mains €11-16, dinner mains €15-29; ⌚noon-10pm Mon-Fri, 9am-10pm Sat & Sun) One of Killarney's busiest restaurants, this tiled bistro was the first

establishment in Ireland to cook with a Josper (Spanish charcoal oven). Stylish salads include Norwegian king crab, and its Kerry surf 'n' turf burger – with prawns and house-made barbecue sauce – has a local following. Early bird three-course dinner is €25.

Bricín IRISH €€
(www.bricin.com; 26 High St; mains €19-26; ⏲6-9.30pm Tue-Sat) Decorated with fittings from a convent, an orphanage and a school, this Celtic deco restaurant doubles as the town museum, with Jonathan Fisher's 18th-century views of the national park taking pride of place. Try the house speciality, boxty (traditional potato pancake). Two-course dinner for €19 before 6.45pm.

Drinking & Nightlife

★O'Connor's PUB
(High St; ⏲10.30am-11pm Mon-Thu, 10.30am-12.30am Fri & Sat, 12.30-11pm Sun) This tiny traditional pub with leaded-glass doors is one of Killarney's most popular haunts. Live music plays every night; good bar food is served daily in summer. In warmer weather, the crowds spill out to the adjacent lane.

Courtney's PUB
(www.courtneysbar.com; Plunkett St; ⏲5-11.30pm Sun-Thu, 5pm-12.30am Fri, 2pm-12.30am Sat) Inconspicuous on the outside, inside this timeless pub bursts at the seams with traditional music sessions many nights year-round. This is where locals come to see their old mates perform and to kick off a night on the town.

Killarney Grand BAR, CLUB
(www.killarneygrand.com; Main St; ⏲7.30pm-2.30am Mon-Sat, to 1.30am Sun) There's traditional live music from 9pm to 11pm, bands from 11.30pm to 1.30am and a disco from 11pm at this Killarney institution. Entry is free before 11pm.

Information

Tourist Office (☎064-663 1633; www.killarney.ie; Beech Rd; ⏲9am-5pm Mon-Sat; 📶) Can handle almost any query, especially dealing with transport intricacies.

Getting There & Around

BIKE

O'Sullivan's (www.killarneyrentabike.com; Beech Rd; per day/week €15/80) offers bike rental; opposite the tourist office.

WORTH A TRIP

SKELLIG MICHAEL

Portmagee (an 80km drive west of Killarney) is the jumping-off point for an unforgettable experience: the Skellig Islands, two tiny rocks 12km off the coast. The vertiginous climb up uninhabited Skellig Michael inspires an awe that monks could have clung to life in the meagre beehive-shaped stone huts that cluster on the tiny patch of level land on top. From spring to late summer, weather permitting, boat trips run from Portmagee to Skellig Michael; the standard rate is around €50 per person, departing 10am and returning 3pm. Advance booking is essential; there are a dozen boat operators, including **Casey's** (☎066-947 2437; www.skelligislands.com; Portmagee) and **Sea Quest** (☎066-947 6214; www.skelligsrock.com).

BUS

Operating from the train station, Bus Éireann has regular services to Cork (€27, two hours, hourly), Galway via Limerick (€26, 3¾ hours, four daily) and Rosslare Harbour (€29, seven hours, three daily).

TAXI

Taxis can be found at the taxi rank on College St. A cab from the edge of town (eg Flesk campsite) into the town centre costs around €9.

TRAIN

Travelling by train to Cork (€28, 1½ to two hours, nine daily) or Dublin (€67, 3¼ hours, seven daily) sometimes involves changing at Mallow.

Ring of Kerry

The Ring of Kerry, a 179km circuit around the dramatic coastal scenery of the Iveragh Peninsula, is one of Ireland's premier tourist attractions. Most travellers tackle the ring by bus on guided day trips from Killarney, but you could spend days wandering here.

The Ring is dotted with picturesque villages (**Sneem** and **Portmagee** are worth a stop), **prehistoric sites** (ask for a guide at Killarney tourist office) and spectacular **viewpoints**, notably at Beenarourke just west of Caherdaniel, and Ladies' View (between Kenmare and Killarney). The **Ring of Skellig**, at the end of the peninsula, has

WORTH A TRIP

CLIFFS OF MOHER

Star of a million tourist brochures, the Cliffs of Moher in County Clare are one of the most popular sights in Ireland. But like many an ageing star, you have to look beyond the famous facade to appreciate its inherent attributes. In summer the site is overrun with day trippers, but there are good rewards if you're willing to walk along the clifftops for 10 minutes to escape the crowds.

The landscaped **Cliffs of Moher Visitor Centre** (www.cliffsofmoher.ie; adult/child €6/free; ⏲9am-9pm Jul-Aug, to 7pm May-Jun & Sep & Oct, (to 6pm Mar-Apr & Oct, to 5pm Nov-Feb) has exhibitions about the cliffs and their natural history. A number of bus tours leave Galway every morning for the Cliffs of Moher, including **Burren Wild Tours** (☎087 877 9565; www.burrenwalks.com; departs Galway Coach Station; adult/student €25/20; ⏲10am-5pm).

fine views of the Skellig Islands and is not as busy as the main route. You can forgo driving completely by walking part of the 200km **Kerry Way** (www.kerryway.com), which winds through the Macgillycuddy's Reeks mountains past Carrauntuohill (1040m), Ireland's highest mountain.

Sights

Kerry Bog Village Museum MUSEUM
(www.kerrybogvillage.ie; adult/child €6.50/4.50; ⏲9am-6pm) On the N70 between Killorglin and Glenbeigh, this museum recreates a 19th-century bog village, typical of the small communities that carved out a precarious living in the harsh environment of Ireland's ubiquitous peat bogs. You'll see the thatched homes of the turfcutter, blacksmith, thatcher and labourer, as well as a dairy. You can meet rare Kerry Bog ponies.

Derrynane National Historic Park HISTORIC SITE
(☎066-947 5113; www.heritageireland.ie; Derrynane; adult/child €3/1; ⏲10.30am-6pm May-Sep, 10am-5pm Wed-Sun Oct-late Nov) Derrynane House was the family home of Daniel O'Connell, the early-19th-century campaigner for Catholic emancipation. His ancestors bought the house and surrounding parkland, having grown rich on smuggling with France and Spain. It's largely furnished with O'Connell memorabilia, including the restored triumphal chariot in which he lapped Dublin after his release from prison in 1844.

Sleeping & Eating

There are plenty of hostels and B&Bs along the Ring. It's wise to book ahead, though, as some places are closed out of season and others fill up quickly.

Mannix Point Camping & Caravan Park CAMPGROUND €
(☎066-947 2806; www.campinginkerry.com; Mannix Point; backpackers per person €8.50, campervan €23; ⏲Mar-Oct; 📶) Mortimer Moriarty's award-winning coastal site has an inviting kitchen, campers' sitting room with a peat fire (no TV but regular music sessions), a barbecue area and even a birdwatching platform. And the sunsets are stunning.

★**Smuggler's Inn** INN €€
(☎066-947 4330; www.the-smugglers-inn.com; Cliff Rd; d €80-130; ⏲Apr-Oct; P📶) Across from the Waterville Golf Links at the water's edge, Smuggler's Inn is a diamond find (once you do find it: it's hard to spot if you're coming from the north). Rooms are freshly renovated – try for room 15, with a glassed-in balcony overlooking Ballinskelligs Bay.

Moorings INN €€
(☎066-947 7108; www.moorings.ie; s/d from €60/80; P📶) The Moorings is a friendly local hotel, bar and restaurant, with 16 rooms split between modern sea-view choices and simpler options, most refreshingly white. The nautical-themed **restaurant** (mains €20-25; ⏲6-10pm Tue-Sun Apr-Oct) specialises in excellent seafood, while the **Bridge Bar** (mains €10-25; ⏲food served noon-9pm) serves superb fish and chips.

Getting Around

Bus Éireann runs a once-daily Ring of Kerry bus service (No 280) from late June to late August. Buses leave Killarney at 11.30am and stop at Killorglin, Glenbeigh, Caherciveen (€16.40, 1¾ hours), Waterville, Caherdaniel and Molls Gap (€21.50), arriving back at Killarney at 4.45pm.

Travel agencies and hostels in Killarney offer daily coach tours of the Ring for about €20 to €25 year-round, lasting from 10.30am to 5pm.

THE WEST COAST

Galway

POP 75,500

Arty and bohemian, Galway (Gaillimh) is legendary around the world for its entertainment scene. Students make up a quarter of the city's population and brightly painted pubs heave with live music on any given night. Here, street life is more important than sightseeing – cafes spill out onto cobblestone streets filled with a frenzy of fiddles, banjos, guitars and Bodhráns (hand-held goatskin drums), while jugglers, painters, puppeteers and magicians in outlandish masks enchant passers-by.

Sights

★Galway City Museum MUSEUM
(www.galwaycitymuseum.ie; Spanish Pde; ⏲10am-5pm Tue-Sat year-round, noon-5pm Sun Easter-Sep) FREE This modern museum has exhibits on the city's history from 1800 to 1950, including an iconic Galway Hooker fishing boat, a collection of *currachs* (boats made from animal hides) and a controversial statue of Galway-born writer and hellraiser Pádraic Ó Conaire (1883–1928), which was previously in Eyre Sq.

★Spanish Arch HISTORIC SITE
The Spanish Arch is thought to be an extension of Galway's medieval city walls, designed to protect ships moored at the nearby quay while they unloaded goods such as wine and brandy from Spain. Today it reverberates to the beat of bongo drums, and the lawns and riverside form a gathering place for locals and visitors on a sunny day. Many watch kayakers manoeuvre over the tidal rapids of the River Corrib.

Lynch's Castle HISTORIC BUILDING
(cnr Shop & Upper Abbeygate Sts) Considered the finest town castle in Ireland, this old stone town house was built in the 14th century, though much of what you see today dates from around 1600. Stonework on the facade (the real attraction here) includes ghoulish gargoyles and the coats of arms of Henry VII, the Lynches (the most powerful of the 14 ruling Galway 'tribes') and the Fitzgeralds of Kildare.

Festivals

Galway International Arts Festival ART
(www.giaf.ie) A two-week extravaganza of art, music, theatre and comedy in mid-July.

Galway Oyster Festival FOOD, DRINK
(www.galwayoysterfest.com) Going strong for more than 50 years now, this festival draws thousands of visitors in late September.

Sleeping

★Kinlay Hostel HOSTEL €
(☎091-565 244; www.kinlayhouse.ie; Merchants Rd; dm/d €29/70; @📶) Easygoing staff, a full range of facilities and a cream-in-the-doughnut location just off Eyre Sq make this a top choice. Spanning two huge, brightly lit floors, amenities include two self-catering kitchens and two cosy TV lounges. Some rooms have bay views.

Snoozles Tourist Hostel HOSTEL €
(☎091-530 064; www.snoozleshostelgalway.ie; Forster St; dm/d €18/50; @📶) Dorms and private rooms all have bathrooms at this new hostel. It's ideal for the over-burdened as it sits near the train and bus stations. Extras include a barbecue terrace, pool table and more.

★Heron's Rest B&B €€
(☎091-539 574; www.theheronsrest.com; 16a Longwalk; s/d from €70/140; 📶) Ideally located on the banks of the Corrib, the endlessly thoughtful hosts here will give you deck chairs so you can sit outside and enjoy the scene. Other touches include holiday-friendly breakfast times (8am to 11am), decanters of port and more. Rooms, all with water views, are small and cute.

St Martins B&B B&B €€
(☎091-568 286; www.stmartins.ie; 2 Nun's Island Rd; s/d from €50/80; @📶) This beautifully kept, renovated older house right on the canal has a flower-filled garden overlooking the William O'Brien Bridge and the River Corrib. The four rooms have all the comforts and the breakfast is a few cuts above the norm (fresh-squeezed OJ). Owner Mary Sexton wins rave reviews.

Galway City

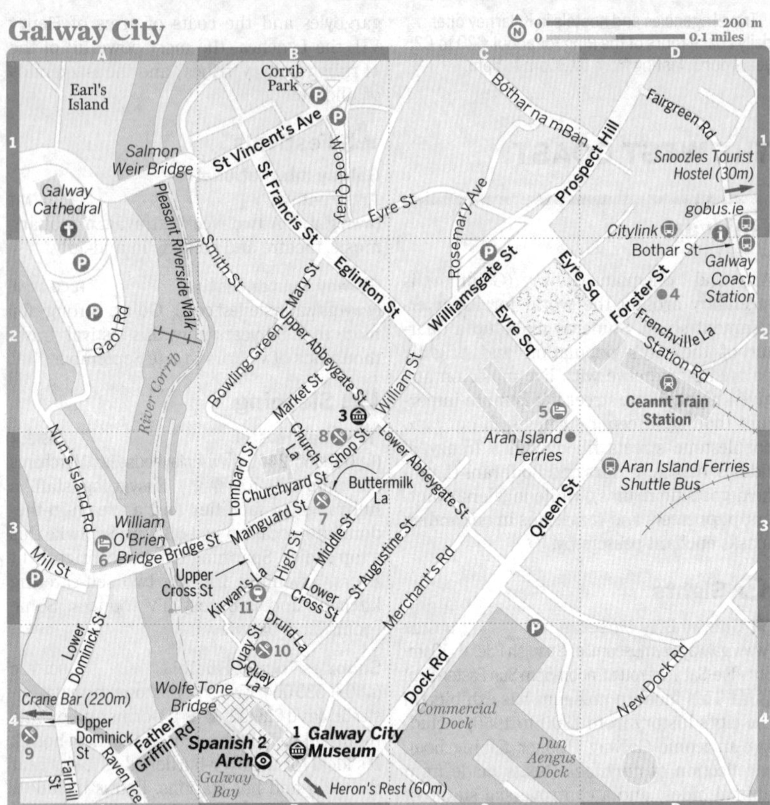

Galway City

Eating & Drinking

★McCambridge's CAFE, GROCER €

(www.mccambridges.com; 38/39 Shop St; snacks from €3, mains €7-13; ⌚cafe 9am-5.30pm Mon-Wed, 9am-10pm Thu-Sat, 10.30am-6pm Sun, grocery 9am-6pm Mon-Sat) The long-running food hall here has a superb selection of prepared salads, hot foods and other more exotic treats. Create the perfect picnic or enjoy your selections at the tables out front. The upstairs cafe is simply fabulous – modern Irish fare flavours the ever-changing menu. Creative sandwiches, salads, silky soups and savoury meals are featured.

Griffin's CAFE, BAKERY €

(www.griffinsbakery.com; Shop St; mains €4-8; ⌚8am-6pm Mon-Sat) A local institution, which, although it's been run by the Griffin family since 1876, remains as fresh as a bun hot out of the oven. The small bakery counter is laden with treats, including great scones. But the real pleasure lies upstairs in the cafe where you can choose from sandwiches, hot specials, luscious desserts and more.

★**Quay Street Kitchen** IRISH €€
(☎091-865 680; The Halls, Quay St; mains €8-18; ⏰11.45am-10.30pm; 📶 🌶) Fast and friendly service makes a great first impression at this always-busy bistro. The menu doesn't disappoint either, with a selection of steak, lamb and seafood, good vegetarian and vegan dishes, and hearty daily specials such as pork, leek and stout sausages with mashed potato and onion gravy.

★**Oscar's** SEAFOOD €€
(☎091-582 180; www.oscarsbistro.ie; Upper Dominick St; mains €15-25; ⏰6.30-9.30pm Mon-Sat, 6-9pm Sun) Galway's best seafood restaurant is just west of the tourist bustle. The long and ever-changing menu has a huge range of local specialities, from shellfish to white fish (which make some superb fish and chips). The flavours are bold, not unlike the bright red accents inside and out.

★**Séhán Ua Neáchtain** PUB
(www.tighneachtain.com; 17 Upper Cross St; ⏰noon-11.30pm Mon-Thu, noon-midnight Fri & Sat, noon-11pm Sun) Painted a bright cornflower blue, this 19th-century pub, known simply as Neáchtain's (*nock*-tans) or Naughtons, has a wraparound string of tables outside, many shaded by a large tree. It's a place where a polyglot mix of locals plop down and let the world pass them by – or stop and join them for a pint. Good lunches.

★**Crane Bar** PUB
(www.thecranebar.com; 2 Sea Rd; ⏰10.30am-11.30pm Mon-Thu, 10.30am-12.30am Fri & Sat, noon-11pm Sun) An atmospheric old pub west of the Corrib, the Crane is the best spot in Galway to catch an informal *céilidh* (session of traditional music and dancing) most nights. Talented bands play its rowdy, good-natured upstairs bar; downstairs at times it seems right out of *The Far Side*.

ℹ Information

Tourist Office (www.discoverireland.ie; Forster St; ⏰9am-5.45pm daily Easter-Sep, closed Sun Oct-Easter) Large, efficient regional information centre that can help arrange local accommodation and tours.

ℹ Getting There & Around

BICYCLE

On Yer Bike (www.onyourbikecycles.com; 40 Prospect Hill; ⏰9am-5.30pm Mon-Sat) Bike hire from €10 per day.

BUS

Bus Éireann buses depart from outside the train station. **Citylink** (www.citylink.ie; ticket office Forster St; ⏰office 9am-6pm; 📶) and **GoBus** (www.gobus.ie; Galway Coach Station; 📶) use the **coach station** (New Coach Station; Bothar St) a block northeast. Citylink has buses to Clifden (€14, 1½ hours, five daily) and Dublin (€13, 2½ hours, hourly). Bus Éireann runs buses to Killarney via Limerick (€26, 3¾ hours, four daily).

TRAIN

Trains run to and from Dublin (€36, 2¾ hours, nine daily). You can connect with other trains at Athlone.

Aran Islands

The windswept Aran Islands are one of western Ireland's major attractions. As well as their rugged beauty – they are an extension of The Burren's limestone plateau – the Irish-speaking islands have some of the country's oldest Christian and pre-Christian ruins.

There are three main islands in the group, all inhabited year-round. Most visitors head for the long and narrow (14.5km by a maximum 4km) **Inishmór** (or Inishmore). The land slopes up from the relatively sheltered northern shores of the island and plummets on the southern side into the raging Atlantic. **Inishmaan** and **Inisheer** are much smaller and receive far fewer visitors.

The **tourist office** (☎099-61263; Kilronan; ⏰10am-5pm May & Jun, 10am-5.45pm Jul & Aug, 11am-5pm Sep-Apr) operates year-round at Kilronan, the arrival point and major village of Inishmór. You can leave your luggage here and change money. Around the corner is a Spar supermarket with an ATM (many places do not accept credit cards).

Inishmór

Three spectacular forts stand guard over Inishmór, each believed to be around 2000 years old. Chief among them is **Dún Aengus** (Dún Aonghasa; www.heritageireland.ie; adult/child €3/1; ⏰9.45am-6pm Apr-Oct, 9.30am-4pm Nov-Mar, closed Mon & Tue Jan & Feb), which has three massive drystone walls that run right up to sheer drops to the ocean below.

It is protected by remarkable *chevaux de frise*, fearsome and densely packed defensive stone spikes. A small visitor centre has displays that put everything in context. A slightly strenuous 900m walkway wanders uphill to the fort itself.

Kilronan Hostel (☎099-61255; www.kilronanhostel.com; Kilronan; dm €15-30, tw €42; @) perched above Tí Joe Mac's pub, is a friendly hostel just a two-minute walk from the ferry. **Kilmurvey House** (☎099-61218; www.kilmurveyhouse.com; Kilmurvey; s/d from €55/90; ⊙Apr-Sep) offers B&B in a grand 18th-century stone mansion on the path leading to Dún Aengus.

Getting There & Away

AIR

Aer Arann Islands (☎091-593 034; www.aerarannislands.ie) Offers return flights to each of the islands several times daily (hourly in summer) for adult/child €49/27; the flights take about 10 minutes, and groups of four or more can get group rates. A connecting minibus from the Victoria Hotel in Galway costs €3 one way.

BOAT

Aran Island Ferries (www.aranislandferries.com; Galway Ticket Office, Merchant's Rd; adult/child return from €25/13; ⊙8am-5pm) The crossing can take up to one hour and is subject to cancellation in high seas. Boats leave from Rossaveal, 40km west of Galway City on the R336. Buses from Galway (adult/child €7/4) connect with the sailings; ask when you book.

Ferries to the Arans (primarily Inisheer) also operate from Doolin.

Connemara

With its shimmering black lakes, pale mountains, lonely valleys and more than the occasional rainbow, Connemara in the northwestern corner of County Galway is one of the most gorgeous corners of Ireland. It's prime hillwalking country with plenty of wild terrain, none more so than the Twelve Bens, a ridge of rugged mountains that form part of **Connemara National Park** (www.connemaranationalpark.ie; off N59; ⊙visitor centre 9am-5.30pm Mar-Oct, park 24hr) FREE.

Connemara's 'capital', **Clifden** (An Clochán), is an appealing Victorian-era country town with an oval of streets offering evocative strolls. Right in the centre of town is cheery **Clifden Town Hostel** (☎095-21076; www.clifdentownhostel.com; Market St; dm €17-22, d from €40), while the gorgeous **Dolphin Beach B&B** (☎095-21204; www.dolphinbeachhouse.com; Lower Sky Rd; s/d from €90/130, dinner €40; P) is 5km west of town.

From Galway, **Lally Tours** (☎091-562 905; www.lallytours.com; 4 Forster St; tours from adult/child €20/12) runs day-long coach tours of Connemara.

NORTHERN IRELAND

☎028 / POP 1.8 MILLION

When you cross from the Republic into Northern Ireland you notice a couple of changes: the accent is different, the road signs are in miles, and the prices are in pounds sterling. But there's no border checkpoint, no guards, not even a sign to mark the crossing point – the two countries are in a customs union, so there's no passport control and no customs declarations. All of a sudden, you're in the UK.

Dragged down for decades by the violence and uncertainty of the Troubles, Northern Ireland today is a nation rejuvenated. The 1998 Good Friday Agreement laid the groundwork for peace and raised hopes for the future, and since then this UK province has seen a huge influx of investment and redevelopment. Belfast has become a happening place with a famously wild nightlife; Derry has come into its own as a cool, artistic city; and the stunning Causeway Coast gets more and more visitors each year.

There are plenty of reminders of the Troubles – notably the 'peace lines' that divide Belfast – and the passions that have torn Northern Ireland apart over the decades still run deep. But despite occasional setbacks there is an atmosphere of determined optimism.

Belfast

POP 280,900

Once lumped with Beirut, Baghdad and Bosnia as one of the four Bs for travellers to avoid, Belfast has pulled off a remarkable transformation from bombs-and-bullets pariah to hip-hotels-and-hedonism party town. Despite the economic downturn, the city's skyline is in a constant state of flux as redevelopment continues. The old shipyards are giving way to luxury waterfront apartments in the Titanic Quarter; and Victoria Sq, Europe's biggest urban regeneration project, has added a massive city-centre shopping mall to the city's list of tourist attractions: Victorian architecture, a

BELFAST VISITOR PASS

The **Belfast Visitor Pass** (one/two/three days £6.30/10.50/14) allows unlimited travel on bus and train services in Belfast and around, and discounts on admission to Titanic Belfast and other attractions. You can buy it at airports, main train and bus stations, the Metro kiosk on Donegall Sq and the Visit Belfast Welcome Centre (p631).

glittering waterfront lined with modern art, foot-stomping music in packed-out pubs and the UK's second-biggest arts festival.

The city centre is compact, and the imposing City Hall in Donegall Sq is the central landmark. The principal shopping district is north of the square. North again, around Donegall St and St Anne's Cathedral, is the bohemian Cathedral Quarter.

South of the square, the so-called Golden Mile stretches for 1km along Great Victoria St, Shaftesbury Sq and Botanic Ave to Queen's University and the leafy suburbs of South Belfast; this area has dozens of restaurants and bars and most of the city's budget and midrange accommodation.

Sights

★Titanic Belfast EXHIBITION

(www.titanicbelfast.com; Queen's Rd; adult/child £15.50/7.25; 9am-7pm Apr & Jun-Aug, 9am-6pm May & Sep, 10am-5pm Oct-Mar) The head of the slipway where the *Titanic* was built is now occupied by the gleaming, angular edifice of Titanic Belfast, an all-singing all-dancing multimedia extravaganza that charts the history of Belfast and the creation of the world's most famous ocean liner. Cleverly designed exhibits enlivened by historic images, animated projections and soundtracks chart Belfast's rise to turn-of-the-20th-century industrial superpower, followed by a high-tech ride through a noisy, smells-and-all re-creation of the city's shipyards.

You can then explore every detail of the *Titanic's* construction, from a computer 'fly-through' from keel to bridge, to replicas of the passenger accommodation. Perhaps most poignant are the few flickering images that constitute the only film footage of the ship in existence.

★SS Nomadic HISTORIC SITE

(www.nomadicbelfast.com; Queen's Rd; adult/child £8.50/5; 10am-6pm daily Apr-Sep, to 5pm Tue-Sun Oct-Mar) The SS *Nomadic* is the only surviving vessel of the White Star Line (the shipping company that owned the *Titanic*). The little steamship once served as a tender to the giant Olympic Class ocean liners; now beautifully restored, it is home to an exhibition on the ship's history and its part in the *Titanic* story. After the one-hour guided tour that points out the original fittings, you are free to roam at will – don't miss the 1st-class toilets!

Built in Belfast in 1911, the *Nomadic* ferried 1st- and 2nd-class passengers between Cherbourg Harbour and the ocean liners that were too big to dock at the French port. On 10 April 1912 it delivered 142 1st-class passengers to the ill-fated *Titanic*. Having been requisitioned in both world wars, the ship ended up as a floating restaurant in Paris in the 1980s and '90s. In 2006 it was rescued from the breaker's yard and brought to Belfast, where it has a berth in the Hamilton Graving Dock, just northeast of the Odyssey Complex.

★Ulster Museum MUSEUM

(www.nmni.com/um; Stranmillis Rd; 10am-5pm Tue-Sun;) FREE Following a major revamp, the Ulster Museum is now one of Northern Ireland's don't-miss attractions. You could spend several hours browsing the beautifully designed displays, but if you're pressed for time don't miss the Armada Room, with artefacts retrieved from the wreck of the Spanish galleon *Girona*; Takabuti, a 2500-year-old Egyptian mummy; and the Bann Disc, a superb example of Celtic design dating from the Iron Age.

★Crown Liquor Saloon HISTORIC BUILDING

(www.nationaltrust.org.uk; 46 Great Victoria St; 11.30am-11pm Mon-Wed, 11.30am-midnight Thu-Sat, 12.30-10pm Sun) FREE There are not too many historical monuments that you can enjoy while savouring a pint of beer, but the National Trust's Crown Liquor Saloon is one of them. Belfast's most famous bar was refurbished by Patrick Flanagan in the late 19th century and displays Victorian decorative flamboyance at its best (he was looking to pull in a posh clientele from the newfangled train station and Grand Opera House across the street).

West Belfast HISTORIC SITE

Though scarred by three decades of civil unrest, the former battleground of West

Belfast

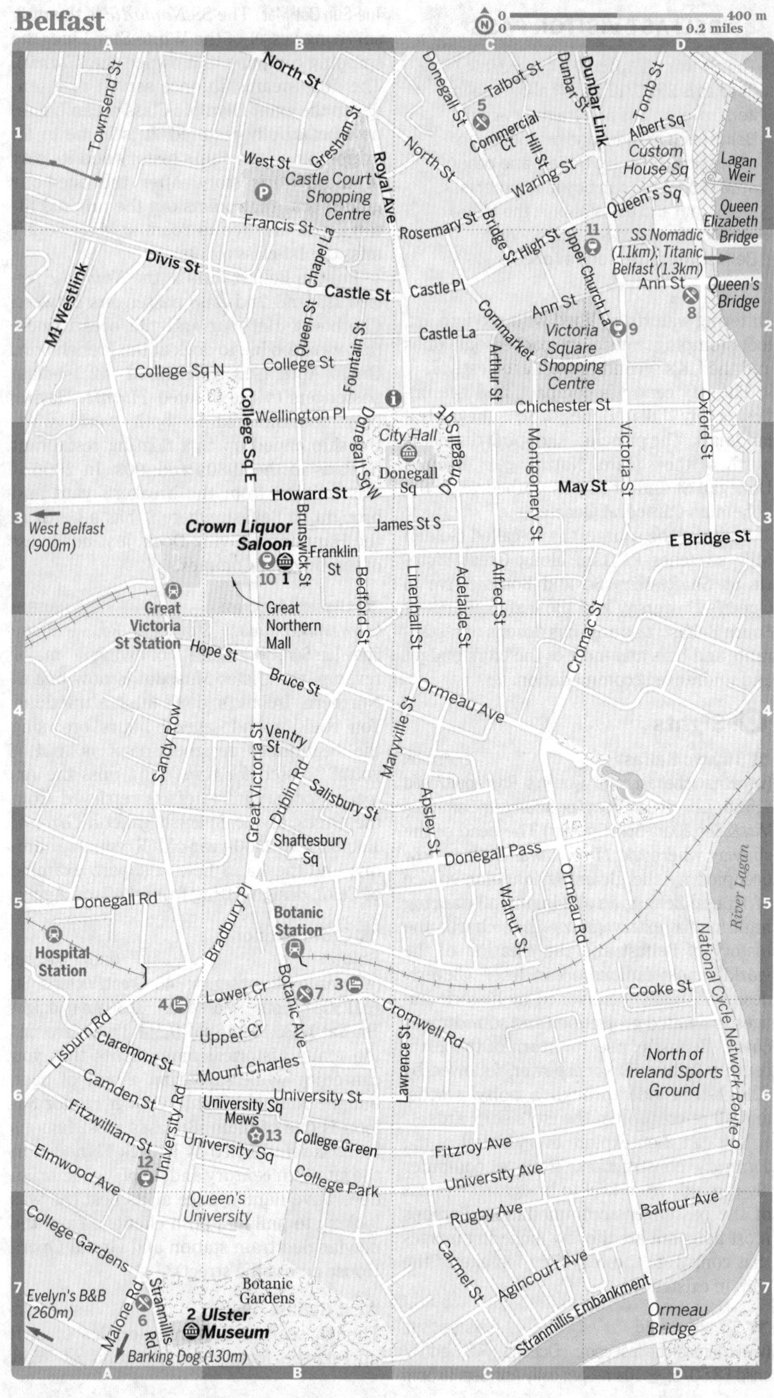
North St
Townsend St
Gresham St
Donegall St
Talbot St
Dunbar St
Dunbar Link
Tomb St
Commercial Ct
Hill St
Albert Sq
Custom House Sq
Lagan Weir
West St
Castle Court Shopping Centre
Royal Ave
North St
Waring St
Queen's Sq
Queen Elizabeth Bridge
Francis St
Rosemary St
Bridge St
High St
Upper Church La
SS Nomadic (1.1km); Titanic Belfast (1.3km)
Divis St
Chapel La
Ann St
Queen's Bridge
M1 Westlink
Castle St
Castle Pl
Cornmarket
Ann St
Queen St
Fountain St
Castle La
Victoria Square Shopping Centre
Arthur St
College Sq N
College St
College Sq E
Wellington Pl
Chichester St
Oxford St
City Hall
Donegall Sq
Donegall Sq
Donegall Sq
Montgomery St
Victoria St
Howard St
May St
West Belfast (900m)
Crown Liquor Saloon
Brunswick St
James St S
E Bridge St
Franklin St
Bedford St
Linenhall St
Adelaide St
Alfred St
Great Victoria St Station
Great Northern Mall
Cromac St
Hope St
Bruce St
Ormeau Ave
Maryville St
Sandy Row
Ventry St
Great Victoria St
Dublin Rd
Salisbury St
Apsley St
Shaftesbury Sq
Donegall Pass
Ormeau Rd
Walnut St
River Lagan
Donegall Rd
Bradbury Pl
Botanic Station
Hospital Station
Lower Cr
Botanic Ave
Cooke St
Cromwell Rd
National Cycle Network Route 9
Lisburn Rd
Claremont St
Upper Cr
Lawrence St
North of Ireland Sports Ground
Mount Charles
Camden St
University St
University Rd
University Sq Mews
Fitzwilliam St
University Sq
College Green
Fitzroy Ave
Elmwood Ave
College Park
University Ave
Queen's University
Rugby Ave
Balfour Ave
College Gardens
Carmel St
Agincourt Ave
Botanic Gardens
Evelyn's B&B (260m)
Malone Rd
Stranmillis Rd
2 Ulster Museum
Stranmillis Embankment
Ormeau Bridge
Barking Dog (130m)

Belfast

Top Sights

1 Crown Liquor Saloon....................B3
2 Ulster Museum....................A7

Sleeping

3 Tara Lodge....................B5
4 Vagabonds....................A6

Eating

5 John Hewitt Bar & Restaurant....................C1
6 Maggie May's....................A7
7 Maggie May's....................B5
8 OX....................D2

Drinking & Nightlife

9 Bittle's Bar....................D2
10 Crown Liquor Saloon....................B3
11 Muriel's Cafe-Bar....................D2
12 QUB Student Union....................A6

Entertainment

13 Queen's Film Theatre....................B6
Shine.................... (see 12)

Belfast is one of the most compelling places to visit in Northern Ireland. Falls Rd and Shankill Rd are adorned with famous **murals** expressing local political and religious passions, and divided by the infamous **Peace Line** – a 4km-long barrier that divides Catholic and Protestant districts. Take a taxi tour of the district, or pick up a map from the tourist office and explore on foot.

Festivals & Events

Féile An Phobail CULTURAL
(www.feilebelfast.com; early Aug) Said to be the largest community festival in Ireland, the Féile takes place in West Belfast over 10 days. Events include an opening carnival parade, street parties, theatre performances, concerts and historical tours of the City and Milltown cemeteries.

Festival at Queen's ART
(www.belfastfestival.com) For three weeks in late October/early November, Belfast hosts the second-largest arts festival in the UK, in and around Queen's University.

Sleeping

Many B&Bs are concentrated in the pleasant university district of South Belfast, which is well stocked with restaurants and pubs.

★ **Vagabonds** HOSTEL €
(028-9023 3017; www.vagabondsbelfast.com; 9 University Rd; dm £13-16, tw & d £40; @) Comfy bunks, lockable luggage baskets, private shower cubicles and a relaxed atmosphere are what you get at one of Belfast's best hostels, run by a couple of experienced travellers. Conveniently located close to both Queen's and the city centre.

★ **Tara Lodge** B&B €€
(028-9059 0900; www.taralodge.com; 36 Cromwell Rd; s/d from £79/89; P @) This B&B is a cut above the average, feeling more like a boutique hotel with its clean-cut, minimalist decor, friendly and efficient staff, delicious breakfasts (including porridge with Bushmills whiskey) and 24 bright and cheerful rooms. It's in a great location too, on a quiet side street just a few paces from the buzz of Botanic Ave.

★ **Old Rectory** B&B €€
(028-9066 7882; www.anoldrectory.co.uk; 148 Malone Rd; s/d £55/86; P @) A lovely Victorian villa with lots of original stained glass, this former rectory has five spacious bedrooms, a comfortable drawing room with leather sofa, and fancy breakfasts (wild-boar sausages, scrambled eggs with smoked salmon, vegie fry-ups, freshly squeezed OJ).

Evelyn's B&B B&B €€
(028-9066 5209; www.evelynsbandb.co.uk; 17 Wellington Park Tce; d from £50;) A friendly host and her even friendlier dog are the custodians of this delightful B&B, with period features including cast-iron bedsteads, a Victorian roll-top bath (the two doubles share the bathroom) and an Aga in the kitchen. Hard to find, but worth seeking out – it's on narrow Wellington Lane, leading off Wellington Park Tce (look for the purple door).

Eating

There are lots of inexpensive eating places along Botanic Ave in South Belfast, and many pubs offer good-value meals.

Maggie May's CAFE €
(www.maggiemaysbelfastcafe.co.uk; 50 Botanic Ave; mains £3-8; 8am-11pm Mon-Sat, 9am-11pm Sun;) This is a classic little cafe with cosy wooden booths, murals of old Belfast and a host of hungover students wolfing down huge Ulster fries at lunchtime. The breakfast menu runs from a vegie fry-up to French toast and maple syrup, while lunch

BELFAST CITY TOURS

Many operators, including **Harpers** (07711 757178; www.harperstaxitours.co.nr; from £30) and **Paddy Campbell's** (07990 955227; www.belfastblackcabtours.co.uk; from £30), offer guided taxi tours of West Belfast, with an even-handed account of the Troubles. They run daily for around £10 per person based on a group of three to six, or £30 total for one or two, and pick-up can be arranged.

There are a number of walking tours available, including the three-hour **Belfast Pub Crawl** (07712 603764; www.belfastcrawl.com; per person £8; 7.30pm Fri & Sat), taking in four of the city's historic pubs, and the three-hour **Titanic Tour** (07852 716655; www.titanictours-belfast.co.uk; adult/child £30/15; on demand), visiting various *Titanic* sites.

can be soup and a sandwich or beef lasagne; there's a good range of vegetarian dishes, too. BYOB.

There's a newer branch in **Stranmillis** (028-9066 8515; www.maggiemaysbelfastcafe.co.uk; 2 Malone Rd; mains £3-8; 8am-11pm Mon-Sat, 9am-11pm Sun).

John Hewitt Bar & Restaurant PUB FOOD €

(www.thejohnhewitt.com; 51 Donegall St; mains £7-9; food served noon-3pm Mon-Thu, to 5.30pm Fri & Sat;) Named for the Belfast poet and socialist, this is a modern pub with a traditional atmosphere and a well-earned reputation for excellent food. The menu changes weekly, but includes a soup of the day, inventive beef and chicken dishes, and a couple of vegetarian options. It's also a great place for a drink.

★ **Barking Dog** BISTRO €€

(028-9066 1885; www.barkingdogbelfast.com; 33-35 Malone Rd; mains £11-16; noon-3pm & 5.30-10pm Mon-Sat, noon-9pm Sun) Chunky hardwood, bare brick, candlelight and quirky design create the atmosphere of a stylishly restored farmhouse. The menu completes the feeling of cosiness and comfort with simple but sensational dishes such as the bistro's signature burger of meltingly tender beef shin wrapped in caramelised onion and horseradish cream. Superb service, too.

★ **OX** IRISH €€

(028-9031 4121; www.oxbelfast.com; 1 Oxford St; mains £16-22; noon-2.45pm & 5.45-10pm Tue-Fri, 1-2.45pm & 5.45-10pm Sat) A high-ceilinged space walled with cream-painted brick and furnished with warm golden wood creates a theatre-like ambience for the open kitchen at the back, where Michelin-trained chefs turn out some of Belfast's finest and best-value cuisine. The restaurant works with local suppliers and focuses on fine Irish beef, sustainable seafood, and seasonal vegetables and fruit. Three-course lunch/pretheatre costs £18/20.

Drinking & Nightlife

Belfast's pub scene is lively and friendly, with the older traditional pubs complemented by a rising tide of stylish designer bars.

★ **Crown Liquor Saloon** PUB

(www.nicholsonspubs.co.uk; 46 Great Victoria St; 11.30am-11pm Mon-Wed, 11.30am-midnight Thu-Sat, 12.30-10pm Sun) Belfast's most famous bar has a wonderfully ornate Victorian interior. Despite being a tourist attraction (p627), it still fills up with crowds of locals at lunchtime and in the early evening.

★ **Muriel's Cafe-Bar** BAR

(028-9033 2445; 12-14 Church Lane; 11am-1am Mon-Fri, 10am-1am Sat, 10am-midnight Sun) Hats meet harlotry (ask who Muriel was) in this delightfully snug and welcoming wee bar with retro-chic decor, old sofas and armchairs, heavy fabrics in shades of olive and dark red, gilt-framed mirrors and a cast-iron fireplace. Gin is Muriel's favourite tipple and there's a range of exotic brands to mix with your tonic. The food menu is pretty good, too.

Bittle's Bar PUB

(103 Victoria St; 11.30am-11pm Mon-Thu, 11.30am-midnight Fri & Sat, 12.30-11pm Sun) A cramped and staunchly traditional bar, Bittle's is a 19th-century triangular red-brick building decorated with gilded shamrocks. The wedge-shaped interior is covered in paintings of Ireland's literary heroes by local artist Joe O'Kane. Pride of place on the back wall is a large canvas depicting Yeats, Joyce, Behan, Beckett and Wilde. It has an excellent range of craft beers.

QUB Student Union CLUB

(www.mandelahall.com; Queen's Students Union, University Rd;) The student union has various bars and music venues hosting club nights, live bands and stand-up comedy. The monthly **Shine** (www.shine.net; admission £20; ⏲1st Sat of month) is one of the city's best club nights with resident and guest DJs pumping out harder and heavier dance music than most of Belfast's other clubs.

☆ Entertainment

The Visit Belfast Welcome Centre issues *Whatabout?*, a free monthly guide to Belfast events. Another useful guide is *The Big List* (www.thebiglist.co.uk).

Queen's Film Theatre CINEMA
(www.queensfilmtheatre.com; 20 University Sq) A two-screen art-house cinema close to the university and a major venue for the Belfast Film Festival.

Lyric Theatre THEATRE
(www.lyrictheatre.co.uk; 55 Ridgeway St) This stunning modern theatre opened to great dramatic and architectural acclaim in 2011; it is built on the site of the old Lyric Theatre, where Hollywood star Liam Neeson first trod the boards (he is now a patron).

ℹ Information

Visit Belfast Welcome Centre (☎028-9024 6609; www.visit-belfast.com; 9 Donegall Sq N; ⏲9am-5.30pm Mon-Sat, 11am-4pm Sun year-round, 9am-7pm Mon-Sat Jun-Sep; wi-fi) Provides information about the whole of Northern Ireland, and books accommodation anywhere in Ireland and Britain. Services include left luggage (not overnight), currency exchange and free wi-fi.

ℹ Getting There & Away

AIR

Belfast International Airport (p637) is 30km northwest of the city, and has flights from the UK, Europe and New York. George Best Belfast City Airport (p637) is 6km northeast of the city centre, with flights from the UK only.

BOAT

Stena Line ferries to Belfast from Cairnryan and Liverpool dock at **Victoria Terminal** (West Bank Rd), 5km north of the city centre; exit the M2 motorway at junction 1. Ferries from the Isle of Man arrive at **Albert Quay** (Corry Rd), 2km north of the centre.

Other car ferries to and from Scotland dock at Larne, 30km north of Belfast.

BUS

Europa Bus Centre, Belfast's main bus station, is behind the Europa Hotel and next door to Great Victoria St train station; it's reached via the Great Northern Mall beside the hotel. It's the main terminus for buses to Derry, Dublin and destinations in the west and south of Northern Ireland.

Ballycastle £12, two hours, three daily on weekdays, two on Saturday
Derry £12, 1¾ hours, half-hourly
Dublin £15, three hours, hourly

Aircoach (www.aircoach.ie) operates a service from Glengall St, near Europa Bus Centre, to Dublin city centre and Dublin Airport.

TRAIN

Belfast has two main train stations: Great Victoria St, next to the Europa Bus Centre, and Belfast Central, east of the city centre. If you arrive by train at Central Station, your rail ticket entitles you to a free bus ride into the city centre. A local train also connects with Great Victoria St.

Derry £11.50, 2¼ hours, seven or eight daily
Dublin £30, two hours, eight daily Monday to Saturday, five on Sunday
Larne Harbour £6.90, one hour, hourly

ℹ Getting Around

BICYCLE

Belfast Bike Tours (☎07812 114235; www.belfastbiketours.com; per person £15; ⏲10.30am & 2pm Mon, Wed, Fri & Sat Apr-Sep, Sat only Oct-Mar) hires out bikes for £15 per day. Credit-card deposit and photo ID are required.

BUS

A short trip on a city bus costs £1.40 to £2.20; a one-day ticket costs £3.70. Most local bus services depart from Donegall Sq, near the City Hall, where there's a ticket kiosk; otherwise, buy a ticket from the driver.

The Causeway Coast

Ireland isn't short of scenic coastlines, but the **Causeway Coast** between Portstewart and Ballycastle – climaxing in the spectacular rock formations of the Giant's Causeway – and the **Antrim Coast** between Ballycastle and Belfast, are as magnificent as they come.

From April to September the **Ulsterbus** (☎028-9066 6630; www.translink.co.uk) Antrim Coaster (bus 252) links Larne with Coleraine (£12, four hours, two daily) via the Glens of Antrim, Ballycastle, the Giant's Causeway, Bushmills, Portrush and Portstewart.

From Easter to September the Causeway Rambler (bus 402) links Coleraine and Carrick-a-Rede (£6, 40 minutes, seven daily) via Bushmills Distillery, the Giant's Causeway, White Park Bay and Ballintoy. The ticket allows unlimited travel in both directions for one day.

There are several hostels along the coast, including **Sheep Island View Hostel** (☎028-2076 9391; www.sheepislandview.com; 42a Main St; campsites/dm/d £6/15/40; P @), **Ballycastle Backpackers** (☎028-2076 3612; www.ballycastlebackpackers.net; 4 North St; dm/tw from £15/40; P @) and **Bushmills Youth Hostel** (☎028-2073 1222; www.hini.org.uk; 49 Main St; dm/tw from £18.50/41; closed 11am-2pm Jul & Aug, 11am-5pm Mar-Jun, Sep & Oct; @).

Sights

★Giant's Causeway LANDMARK
(www.nationaltrust.org.uk; dawn-dusk) FREE This spectacular rock formation – Northern Ireland's only Unesco World Heritage Site – is one of Ireland's most impressive and atmospheric landscape features, a vast expanse of regular, closely packed, hexagonal stone columns looking for all the world like the handiwork of giants. The phenomenon is explained in the **Giant's Causeway Visitor Experience** (☎028-2073 1855; www.giantscausewaycentre.com; adult/child £8.50/4.25; 9am-9pm Jul & Aug, to 7pm Apr-Jun & Sep, to 6pm Feb-Mar & Oct, to 5pm Nov-Jan;), a spectacular new ecofriendly building half-hidden in a hillside above the sea.

Visiting the Giant's Causeway itself is free of charge but you pay to use the car park and the visitor centre. (The admission fee is reduced by £1.50 if you arrive by bus, bike or on foot.)

From the centre it's an easy 10- to 15-minute walk downhill to the Causeway itself, but a more interesting approach is to follow the clifftop path northeast for 2km to the Chimney Tops headland, then descend the Shepherd's Steps to the Causeway. For the less mobile, a minibus shuttles from the visitors centre to the Causeway (£2 return).

★Carrick-a-Rede Rope Bridge BRIDGE
(www.nationaltrust.org.uk; Ballintoy; adult/child £5.60/2.90; 10am-7pm Jun-Aug, to 6pm Mar-May, Sep & Oct) The main attraction on the stretch of coast between Ballycastle and the Giant's Causeway is the famous (or notorious) Carrick-a-Rede Rope Bridge. The 20m-long, 1m-wide bridge of wire rope spans the chasm between the sea cliffs and the little island of Carrick-a-Rede, swaying gently 30m above the rock-strewn water. Crossing the bridge is perfectly safe, but it can be frightening if you don't have a head for heights, especially if it's breezy (in high winds the bridge is closed).

Once on the island there are good views of Rathlin Island and Fair Head to the east. The island has sustained a salmon fishery for centuries; fishermen stretch their nets out from the tip of the island to intercept the passage of salmon migrating along the coast to their home rivers. The fishermen put the bridge up every spring as they have done for the last 200 years – though it's not, of course, the original bridge.

There's a small National Trust information centre and cafe at the car park.

Derry/Londonderry

POP 107,900

Northern Ireland's second city comes as a pleasant surprise to many visitors. Derry was never the prettiest of places, and it certainly lagged behind Belfast in terms of investment and redevelopment, but in preparation for its year in the limelight as UK City of Culture 2013, the city centre was given a handsome makeover. The new **Peace Bridge**, Ebrington Sq, and the redevelopment of the waterfront and Guildhall area make the most of the city's riverside setting. And Derry's determined air of can-do optimism has made it the powerhouse of the North's cultural revival.

There's a lot of history to absorb here, from the Siege of Derry to the Battle of the Bogside – a stroll around the 17th-century city walls is a must, as is a tour of the Bogside murals. The city's lively pubs are home to a burgeoning live-music scene. But perhaps the biggest attraction is the people themselves: warm, witty and welcoming.

Derry or Londonderry? The name you use for Northern Ireland's second-largest city can be a political statement, but today most people just call it Derry, whatever their politics. The 'London' prefix was added in 1613 in recognition of the Corporation of London's role in the 'plantation' of Ulster with Protestant settlers.

In 1968 resentment at the long-running Protestant domination of the city council boiled over into a series of (Catholic-dominated) civil-rights marches. In August 1969 fighting between police and local youths in the poor Catholic Bogside district prompted the UK government to send British troops into Derry. In January 1972 'Bloody Sunday' resulted in the deaths of 13 unarmed Catholic civil-rights marchers in Derry at the hands of the British army, an event that marked the beginning of the Troubles in earnest.

Sights

★Derry's City Walls LANDMARK
(www.derryswalls.com) Completed in 1619, Derry's city walls are 8m high and 9m thick, with a circumference of about 1.5km, and are the only city walls in Ireland to survive almost intact – you can walk the parapet all the way round. Derry's nickname, the Maiden City, derives from the fact that the walls have never been breached by an invader.

★Tower Museum MUSEUM
(☎028-7137 2411; www.derrycity.gov.uk/museums; Union Hall Pl; adult/child £4/2; ⏲10am-6pm) This award-winning museum is housed in a replica 16th-century tower house. Head straight to the 5th floor for a view from the top of the tower, then work your way down through the excellent **Armada Shipwreck** exhibition, and the **Story of Derry**, where well-thought-out exhibits and audiovisuals lead you through the city's history from the founding of the monastery of St Colmcille (Columba) in the 6th century to the Battle of the Bogside in the late 1960s.

The Armada Shipwreck exhibition tells the story of *La Trinidad Valenciera* – a ship of the Spanish Armada that was wrecked at Kinnagoe Bay in Donegal in 1588. It was discovered by the City of Derry Sub-Aqua Club in 1971 and excavated by marine archaeologists. On display are bronze guns, pewter tableware and personal items – a wooden comb, an olive jar, a shoe sole – recovered from the site, along with a 2.5-tonne siege gun bearing the arms of Phillip II of Spain showing him as king of England. Allow at least two hours to do the museum justice.

★People's Gallery Murals MURALS
(Rossville St) The 12 murals that decorate the gable ends of houses along Rossville St, near Free Derry Corner, are popularly referred to as the People's Gallery. They are the work of Tom Kelly, Will Kelly and Kevin Hasson, known as 'the Bogside Artists'. The three men have spent most of their lives in the Bogside, and lived through the worst of the Troubles. They can be clearly seen from the northern part of the City Walls.

Sleeping

Derry City Independent Hostel HOSTEL €
(☎028-7128 0542; www.derry-hostel.co.uk; 12 Princes St; dm/d £16/42; @📶) Run by experienced backpackers and decorated with souvenirs from their travels around the world, this small, friendly hostel is set in a Georgian town house, just a short walk northwest of the bus station. If you've been

OTHER IRISH PLACES WORTH A VISIT

Some other places in Ireland you might like to consider for day trips or longer visits:

Dingle (65km west of Killarney) The charms of this special spot have long drawn runaways from across the world, making this port town a surprisingly cosmopolitan and creative place. There are loads of cafes, bookshops and art and craft galleries, and a friendly dolphin called Fungie who has lived in the bay for 25 years.

Glendalough (50km south of Dublin) Nestled between two lakes, haunting Glendalough (Gleann dá Loch, meaning 'Valley of the Two Lakes') is one of the most significant monastic sites in Ireland and one of the loveliest spots in the country.

Kinsale (28km south of Cork) This picturesque yachting harbour is one of the many gems that dot the coastline of County Cork, and has been labelled the gourmet capital of Ireland; it certainly contains more than its fair share of international-standard restaurants.

Slieve League (120km southwest of Derry/Londonderry) The awe-inspiring cliffs at Slieve League, rising 300m above the Atlantic Ocean, are one of Ireland's top sights. Experienced hikers can spend a day walking along the top of the cliffs via the slightly terrifying One Man's Path to Malinbeg, near Glencolumbcille.

Sligo (140km north of Galway) William Butler Yeats (1865–1939) was born in Dublin and educated in London, but his poetry is infused with the landscapes, history and folklore of his mother's native Sligo (Sligeach). He returned many times and there are plentiful reminders of his presence in this sweet, sleepy town.

here before, note that it has moved to a new location around the corner.

★**Merchant's House** B&B €€
(☎028-7126 9691; www.thesaddlershouse.com; 16 Queen St; s/d £70/75; @📶) This historic, Georgian-style town house is a gem of a B&B. It has an elegant lounge and dining room with marble fireplaces and antique furniture, TV, coffee-making facilities, homemade marmalade at breakfast and even bathrobes in the bedrooms (only one has a private bathroom). Call at **Saddler's House** (☎028-7126 9691; www.thesaddlershouse.com; 36 Great James St; s/d £75/80; @📶) first to pick up a key.

Abbey B&B B&B €€
(☎028-7127 9000; www.abbeyaccommodation.com; 4 Abbey St; s/d/f from £54/64/79; @📶) There's a warm welcome waiting at this family-run B&B just a short walk from the walled city, on the edge of the Bogside. The six rooms are stylishly decorated and include family rooms able to sleep four.

Eating

★**Primrose Cafe** CAFE €
(15 Carlisle Rd; mains £7-8; ⏲8am-5pm Mon-Sat, 11am-3pm Sun; 👪) The latest addition to Derry's cafe culture, the Primrose has prospered by sticking to the classics and doing them really well – from pancakes with maple syrup to Irish stew, and a Sunday brunch that ranges from eggs Benedict to the full Ulster fry. Even with the outdoor terrace at the back, it can be hard to find a seat.

Café del Mondo CAFE, IRISH €€
(☎028-7136 6877; www.cafedelmondo.org; Craft Village, Shipquay St; mains lunch £6-7, dinner £13-22; ⏲8.30am-6pm Mon, 8.30am-1am Tue-Sat, noon-5pm Sun, closed Sun & Mon Nov-Mar; 📶🖉) 🌿 A bohemian cafe that serves excellent fairtrade coffee as well as hearty homemade soups, artisan breads and hot lunch specials that use organic, locally sourced produce. A restaurant menu is served in the evening (best to book), offering steak, venison, seafood and a couple of vegetarian dishes.

Brown's in Town IRISH €€
(☎028-7136 2889; www.brownsrestaurant.com; 21-23 Strand Rd; mains £16-22; ⏲noon-3pm Mon-Sat, 5.30-10.30pm Tue-Sat, 5-8.30pm Sun) There's a definite art-deco feel to the decor in Brown's city centre restaurant, bringing a much-needed touch of glamour and sophistication to Derry's downtown restaurant scene. The early bird three-course dinner menu (£20, till 7.30pm Tuesday to Thursday, till 7pm Friday and Saturday) is terrific value.

Drinking & Entertainment

★**Peadar O'Donnell's** PUB
(www.peadars.com; 63 Waterloo St; ⏲11.30am-1.30am Mon-Sat, 12.30pm-12.30am Sun) A backpackers' favourite, Peadar's has traditional music sessions every night and often on weekend afternoons as well. It's done up as a typical Irish pub-cum-grocer, down to the shelves of household items, shopkeepers, scales on the counter and a museum's-worth of old bric-a-brac.

Sandino's Cafe-Bar LIVE MUSIC
(www.sandinos.com; 1 Water St; admission £3-6; ⏲11.30am-1am Mon-Sat, 1pm-midnight Sun) From the posters of Che to the Free Palestine flag to the fairtrade coffee, this relaxed cafe-bar exudes a liberal, left-wing vibe. There are live bands on Friday nights and occasionally midweek, and DJ sessions on Saturdays, plus regular theme nights and events.

Playhouse THEATRE
(www.derryplayhouse.co.uk; 5-7 Artillery St; ⏲box office 10am-5pm Mon-Fri, to 4pm Sat, plus 45min before show) Housed in beautifully restored former school buildings with an award-winning modern extension at the rear, this community arts centre stages music, dance and theatre by local and international performers.

Information

Derry Tourist Information Centre (☎028-7126 7284; www.visitderry.com; 44 Foyle St; ⏲9.30am-5pm Mon-Fri, 10am-4pm Sat & Sun year-round, longer hours Apr-Oct; 📶) Covers all of Northern Ireland and the Republic as well as Derry. It sells books and maps, and can book accommodation throughout Ireland. It has a bureau de change, bike hire and free wi-fi.

Getting There & Away

BUS

The **bus station** (☎028-7126 2261; Foyle St) is just northeast of the walled city.

Belfast £12, 1¾ hours, every 30 minutes Monday to Saturday, 11 services on Sunday

Dublin £20, four hours, every two hours daily

Airporter (☎028-7126 9996; www.airporter.co.uk; 1 Bay Rd, Culmore Rd) Runs direct from Derry to Belfast International Airport (£20, 1½ hours) and George Best Belfast City Airport (£20, two hours) hourly Monday to Friday (six or seven daily Saturday and Sunday). Buses depart from Airporter office, 1.5km north of the city centre, next to Da Vinci's Hotel.

TRAIN

Derry's train station (always referred to as Londonderry in Northern Ireland timetables) is on the eastern side of the River Foyle; a free Rail Link bus connects with the bus station.

Belfast £11.50, 2¼ hours, seven or eight daily Monday to Saturday, four on Sunday

SURVIVAL GUIDE

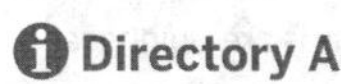

Directory A–Z

ACCOMMODATION

Hostels in Ireland can be booked solid in summer. An Óige (meaning 'youth') and Hostelling International Northern Ireland (HINI) are branches of Hostelling International (HI); An Óige has 26 hostels in the Republic, while HINI has six in the North. Other hostel associations include Independent Holiday Hostels (IHH), a cooperative group with about 120 hostels throughout the island, and the Independent Hostel Owners (IHO) association, which has more than 100 members around Ireland.

From June to September a dorm bed at most hostels costs €15 to €25 (£13 to £20), except for the more expensive hostels in Dublin, Belfast and a few other places.

Typical B&Bs cost around €35 to €45 (£25 to £40) per person a night (sharing a double room), though more luxurious B&Bs can cost upwards of €55 (£45) per person. Most B&Bs are small, so in summer they quickly fill up.

SLEEPING PRICE RANGES

Prices are listed at high-season rates (low-season rates can be 15% to 20% less), based on two people sharing a double, and include a private bathroom unless otherwise stated. Booking ahead is recommended in peak season (roughly April to October).

Republic of Ireland

€ less than €60

€€ €60 to €150

€€€ more than €150

Northern Ireland

£ less than £50

££ £50 to £120

£££ more than £120

COUNTRY FACTS

Area 84,421 sq km

Capitals Dublin (Republic of Ireland), Belfast (Northern Ireland)

Country Code Republic of Ireland ☎353, Northern Ireland ☎44

Currency Euro (€) in Republic of Ireland, pound sterling (£) in Northern Ireland

Emergency ☎112

Languages English, Irish Gaelic

Money ATMs widespread; credit cards widely accepted

Population Republic of Ireland 4.72 million, Northern Ireland 1.81 million

Visas Schengen rules do not apply

Commercial camping grounds typically charge €12 to €25 (£10 to £20) for a tent or campervan and two people. Unless otherwise indicated, prices quoted for 'campsites' are for a tent, car and two people.

The following are useful resources:

An Óige (www.anoige.ie) Hostelling International (HI)–associated national organisation with 26 hostels scattered around the Republic.

Family Homes of Ireland (www.familyhomes.ie) Lists family-run guesthouses and self-catering properties.

HINI (www.hini.org.uk) HI-associated organisation with six hostels in Northern Ireland.

Independent Holiday Hostels of Ireland (IHH; www.hostels-ireland.com) Over 100 tourist-board approved hostels throughout Ireland.

Independent Hostel Owners of Ireland (IHO; www.independenthostelsireland.com) Independent hostelling association.

ACTIVITIES

Ireland is great for outdoor activities, and tourist offices have a wide selection of information covering birdwatching, surfing (great along the west coast), scuba diving, cycling, fishing, horse riding, sailing, canoeing and many other activities.

Walking is particularly popular, although you must come prepared for wet weather. There are now well over 20 waymarked trails throughout Ireland, one of the more popular being the 200km **Kerry Way** (www.kerryway.com).

BUSINESS HOURS

Hours in both the Republic and Northern Ireland are roughly the same.

Banks 10am to 4pm Monday to Friday (to 5pm Thursday)

ESSENTIAL FOOD & DRINK

Ireland's recently acquired reputation as a gourmet destination is thoroughly deserved, with a host of chefs and producers leading a foodie revolution that has made it easy to eat well on all budgets.

- **Champ** Northern Irish dish of mashed potatoes with spring onions (scallions).
- **Colcannon** Potatoes mashed with milk, cabbage and fried onion.
- **Farl** Triangular flatbread in Northern Ireland and Donegal.
- **Irish stew** Lamb stew with potatoes, onions and thyme.
- **Soda bread** Wonderful bread – white or brown, sweet or savoury – made from very soft Irish flour and buttermilk.
- **Stout** Dark, almost black beer made with roasted barley; famous brands are Guinness in Dublin, and Murphy's and Beamish & Crawford in Cork.
- **Irish whiskey** Around 100 different types are produced by only four distilleries: Jameson, Bushmills, Cooley and recently reopened Kilbeggan.

Offices 9am to 5pm Monday to Friday

Post offices Northern Ireland 9am to 5.30pm Monday to Friday, 9am to 12.30pm Saturday; Republic 9am to 6pm Monday to Friday, 9am to 1pm Saturday. Smaller post offices may close at lunch and one day per week.

Pubs Northern Ireland 11.30am to 11pm Monday to Saturday, 12.30pm to 10pm Sunday. Pubs with late licences open until 1am Monday to Saturday and midnight Sunday; Republic 10.30am to 11.30pm Monday to Thursday, 10.30am to 12.30am Friday and Saturday, noon to 11pm Sunday. Pubs with bar extensions open to 2.30am Thursday to Saturday. All pubs close Christmas Day and Good Friday.

Restaurants Noon to 10.30pm; many close one day of the week.

Shops 9am to 5.30pm or 6pm Monday to Saturday (to 8pm on Thursday and sometimes Friday), noon to 6pm Sunday (in bigger towns only). Shops in rural towns may close at lunch and one day per week.

INTERNET RESOURCES

Failte Ireland (www.discoverireland.ie) Official tourism site

Northern Ireland Tourist Board (www.discovernorthernireland.com) Official tourism site

Entertainment Ireland (www.entertainment.ie) Countrywide entertainment listings

MONEY

The Irish Republic uses the euro (€), while Northern Ireland uses the British pound sterling (£). Banks offer the best exchange rates; exchange bureaux, open longer, have worse rates and higher commissions. Post offices generally have exchange facilities and are open on Saturday morning.

In Northern Ireland several banks issue their own Northern Irish pound notes, which are equivalent to sterling but not readily accepted in mainland Britain. Many hotels, restaurants and shops in Northern Ireland accept euros.

Tipping

Fancy hotels and restaurants usually add a 10% or 15% service charge onto bills. Simpler places usually don't add a service charge; if you decide to tip, just round up the bill (or add 10% at most). Taxi drivers do not have to be tipped, but if you do, 10% is more than generous.

PUBLIC HOLIDAYS

The main public holidays in the Republic, Northern Ireland and both:

New Year's Day 1 January

St Patrick's Day 17 March

Easter (Good Friday to Easter Monday inclusive) March/April

May Holiday First Monday in May

Christmas Day 25 December

St Stephen's Day (Boxing Day) 26 December

Northern Ireland

Spring Bank Holiday Last Monday in May

Orangemen's Day 12 July (following Monday if 12th is on the weekend)

August Bank Holiday Last Monday in August

Republic of Ireland

June Holiday First Monday in June

August Holiday First Monday in August

October Holiday Last Monday in October

TELEPHONE

The mobile- (cell-) phone network in Ireland runs on the GSM 900/1800 system compatible with the rest of Europe and Australia, but not the USA. Mobile numbers in the Republic begin with ☎085, ☎086 or ☎087 (☎07 in Northern Ireland).

A local pay-as-you-go SIM for your mobile will cost from around €10, but may work out free after the standard phone-credit refund (make sure your phone is compatible with the local provider).

To call Northern Ireland from the Republic, do not use ☎0044 as for the rest of the UK. Instead, dial ☎048 and then the local number. To dial the Republic from Northern Ireland, however, use the full international code ☎00 353, then the local number.

VISAS

If you're a European Economic Area (EEA) national, you don't need a visa to visit (or work in) either the Republic or Northern Ireland. Citizens of Australia, Canada, New Zealand, South Africa and the US can visit the Republic for up to three months, and Northern Ireland for up to six months.

There are no border controls or passport checks between the Republic of Ireland and Northern Ireland.

Getting There & Away

AIR

There are nonstop flights from Britain, Continental Europe and North America to Dublin, Shannon and Belfast International, and nonstop connections from Britain and Europe to Cork. International departure tax is normally included in the price of your ticket.

International airports in Ireland:

Belfast International Airport (BFS; ☎028-9448 4848; www.belfastairport.com) Located 30km northwest of the city; flights within/and from the UK, Europe and New York.

Dublin Airport (☎01-814 1111; www.dublinairport.com) Dublin Airport, 13km north of the centre, is Ireland's major international gateway airport, with direct flights from Europe, North America and Asia.

George Best Belfast City Airport (BHD; ☎028-9093 9093; www.belfastcityairport.com; Airport Rd) Located 6km northeast of the city centre; flights within/and from the UK.

Shannon Airport (SNN; ☎061-712 000; www.shannonairport.com; wi-fi) Has many facilities, including a free observation area for those stuck waiting. Almost everything, including ATMs and currency exchange, is on one level.

SEA

The main ferry routes between Ireland and the UK and mainland Europe:

- Belfast to Liverpool (England; 8½ hours)
- Belfast to Cairnryan (Scotland; 1¾ hours)
- Cork to Roscoff (France; 14 hours)
- Dublin to Liverpool (England; fast/slow four/8½ hours)
- Dublin and Dun Laoghaire to Holyhead (Wales; fast/slow 1½/three hours)
- Larne to Cairnryan (Scotland; 1½ hours)
- Larne to Troon (Scotland; 1½ hours; March to October only)
- Larne to Fleetwood (England; six hours)
- Rosslare to Cherbourg and Roscoff (France; 20½ hours)
- Rosslare to Fishguard and Pembroke (Wales; 3½ hours)

Competition from budget airlines has forced ferry operators to discount heavily and offer flexible fares, meaning great bargains at quiet times of the day or year. For example, the popular route across the Irish Sea between Dublin and Holyhead can cost as little as €15 (£12) for a foot passenger and €90 (£75) for a car plus up to four passengers.

A very useful online tool is www.ferrybooker.com, a single site covering all sea-ferry routes and operators out of the UK (the mainstay of sea travel to Ireland).

Main operators include the following:

Brittany Ferries (www.brittanyferries.com) Cork to Roscoff; every Saturday April to October.

Irish Ferries (www.irishferries.com) It has Dublin to Holyhead ferries (up to four per day year-round); and France to Rosslare (three times per week, mid-February to December).

Isle of Man Steam Packet Company (www.steam-packet.com) Isle of Man to Dublin and Belfast, twice weekly in summer.

P&O Irish Sea (www.poirishsea.com) Daily sailings year-round from Dublin to Liverpool, and Larne to Cairnryan. Larne to Troon runs from March to October only.

Stena Line (www.stenaline.com) Daily sailings from Holyhead to Dublin Port and Dun Laoghaire, and from Belfast to Liverpool and Cairnryan.

EATING PRICE RANGES

The following price indicators are used to indicate the cost of a main course at dinner:

Republic of Ireland

€ less than €12

€€ €12 to €25

€€€ more than €25

Northern Ireland

£ less than £12

££ £12 to £20

£££ more than £20

BUS & RAIL PASSES

There are a number of bus- or train-only and bus-and-rail passes worth considering if you plan on doing a lot of travel using public transport.

Open Road Pass (Bus) Three days' travel out of six consecutive days (€57) to 15 days out of 30 (€249) on all Bus Éireann services.

Irish Explorer (Bus & Rail) Eight days' travel out of 15 consecutive days (€245) on trains and buses within the Republic.

Irish Explorer (Rail) Five days' travel out of 15 consecutive days (€160) on trains in the Republic.

Trekker Four consecutive days' travel (€110) on all trains in the Republic.

Bus Rambler (Bus) One day's unlimited travel (£9) on Northern Ireland buses, after 9.15am, July and August only.

Sunday Day Tracker One day's unlimited travel (£7) on Northern Ireland trains, on Sundays only.

Children aged under 16 pay half-price for all these passes and for all normal tickets. Children aged under three travel for free on public transport. You can buy the above passes at most major train and bus stations in Ireland.

Discounts & Passes

Britrail Pass Has an option to add on Ireland for an extra fee, including ferry transit.

Eurail Pass Holders get a 50% discount on Irish Ferries crossings to France.

InterRail Pass Holders get a 50% discount on Irish Ferries and Stena Line services.

Getting Around

Travelling around Ireland looks simple, as the distances are short and there's a dense network of roads and railways. But in Ireland, getting from A to B seldom uses a straight line, and public transport can be expensive (particularly trains), infrequent or both. For these reasons having your own transport – either car or bicycle – can be a major advantage.

BICYCLE

Ireland's compact size, relative flatness and scenic landscapes make it an ideal cycling destination. Dodgy weather and the occasional uneven road surface are the only concerns. A good tip for cyclists in the west is that the prevailing winds make it easier to cycle from south to north.

Buses will carry bikes, but only if there's room. For trains, bear in mind:

- Intercity trains charge up to €10 per bike.
- Bikes are transported in the passenger compartment.
- Book in advance (www.irishrail.ie), as there's only room for three bikes per service.

BUS

The Republic of Ireland's national bus line, **Bus Éireann** (☎01-836 6111; www.buseireann.ie), operates services all over the Republic and into Northern Ireland. Fares are much cheaper than train fares. Return trips are usually only slightly more expensive than one-way fares, and special deals (eg same-day returns) are often available. Most intercity buses in Northern Ireland are operated by **Ulsterbus** (☎028-9066 6600; www.ulsterbus.co.uk).

CAR & MOTORCYCLE

The majority of hire companies won't rent you a car if you're under 23 and haven't had a valid driving licence for at least a year. Some companies will not hire to those aged 74 or over. Your own local licence is usually sufficient to hire a car for up to three months.

TRAIN

The Republic of Ireland's railway system, **Irish Rail** (Iarnród Éireann; ☎1850 366 222; www.irishrail.ie), has routes radiating out from Dublin, but there is no direct north–south route along the west coast. Tickets can be twice as expensive as the bus, but travel times may be dramatically reduced. Special fares are often available, and a midweek return ticket sometimes costs just a bit more than the single fare; the flip side is that fares may be significantly higher on Friday and Sunday. **Rail Users Ireland** (www.railusers.ie) can be more informative than the official website.

Northern Ireland Railways (NIR; ☎028-9089 9411; www.nirailways.co.uk; Belfast Central Station) has four lines from Belfast, one of which links up with the Republic's rail system.

Italy

Includes ➡

Best Places to Eat

- Pizzeria Gino Sorbillo (p702)
- Casa Coppelle (p655)
- Osteria Ballarò (p711)
- L'Osteria di Giovanni (p690)
- Osteria de' Poeti (p682)

Best Museums & Galleries

- Vatican Museums (p645)
- Galleria degli Uffizi (p685)
- Museo Archeologico Nazionale (p698)
- Museo e Galleria Borghese (p647)
- Gallerie dell'Accademia (p673)

Why Go?

A favourite destination since the days of the 18th-century Grand Tour, Italy may appear to hold few surprises. Its iconic monuments and masterpieces are known the world over, while cities such as Rome, Florence and Venice need no introduction.

Yet Italy is far more than the sum of its sights. Its fiercely proud regions maintain customs and culinary traditions dating back centuries, resulting in passionate festivals and delectable food at every turn. And then there are those timeless landscapes, from Tuscany's gentle hillsides to icy Alpine peaks, vertiginous coastlines and spitting southern volcanoes.

Drama is never far away in Italy and its theatrical streets and piazzas provide endless people-watching, ideally over a leisurely lunch or cool evening drink. This is, after all, the land of *dolce far niente* (sweet idleness) where simply hanging out is a pleasure and time seems to matter just that little bit less.

When to Go

Rome

°C/°F **Temp**
Rainfall inches/mm

40/104 – 30/86 – 20/68 – 10/50 – 0/32 – -10/14
6/150 – 4/100 – 2/50 – 0

J F M A M J J A S O N D

Apr & May Perfect spring weather; ideal for exploring vibrant cities and blooming countryside.

Jun & Jul Summer means beach weather and a packed festival calendar.

Oct Enjoy mild temperatures, autumn cuisine and the *vendemia* (grape harvest).

Italy Highlights

1. See awe-inspiring art and iconic monuments in **Rome**.
2. Take to the water past Gothic palaces, domed churches and crumbling piazzas in **Venice** (p672).
3. Explore the exquisite Renaissance time capsule that is **Florence** (p684).
4. Work up an appetite for the world's best pizza in the backstreets of **Naples** (p698).
5. Visit regal palaces and museums in **Turin** (p664).
6. Admire glorious Gothic architecture and renaissance art in **Siena** (p694).
7. Bask in inspiring sea views on the **Amalfi Coast** (p707).
8. Enjoy an open-air opera in one of Italy's most romantic cities, **Verona** (p670).
9. Feast on foodie delights and medieval architecture in hedonistic **Bologna** (p682).
10. Revel in drama at an ancient Greek theatre in **Syracuse** (p713).

ITINERARIES

One Week

A one-week whistle-stop tour of Italy is enough to take in the country's three most famous cities. After a couple of days exploring the unique canalscape of **Venice**, head south to **Florence**, Italy's great Renaissance city. Two days will whet your appetite for the artistic and architectural treasures that await in **Rome**.

Two Weeks

After the first week, continue south for some sea and southern passion. Spend a day dodging traffic in **Naples**, a day investigating the ruins at **Pompeii**, and a day or two admiring the **Amalfi Coast**. Then backtrack to Naples for a ferry to **Palermo** and the gastronomic delights of Sicily.

ROME

POP 2.86 MILLION

Even in this country of exquisite cities, Rome is special. Pulsating, seductive and utterly disarming, the Italian capital is an epic, monumental metropolis that will steal your heart and haunt your soul. They say a lifetime's not enough *(Roma, non basta una vita)*, but even on a short visit you'll be swept off your feet by its artistic and architectural masterpieces, its operatic piazzas, romantic corners and cobbled lanes. Yet while history reverberates all around, modern life is lived to the full – and it's this intoxicating mix of past and present, of style and urban grit that makes Rome such a compelling place.

Sights

Ancient Rome

★Colosseum RUIN

(Colosseo; Map p648; ☎06 3996 7700; www.coopculture.it; Piazza del Colosseo; adult/reduced incl Roman Forum & Palatino €12/7.50; ⏰8.30am-1hr before sunset; Ⓜ Colosseo) Rome's great gladiatorial arena is the most thrilling of the city's ancient sights. Inaugurated in AD 80, the 50,000-seat Colosseum, originally known as the Flavian Amphitheatre, was clad in travertine and covered by a huge canvas awning held aloft by 240 masts. Inside, tiered seating encircled the arena, itself built over an underground complex (the hypogeum) where animals were caged and stage sets prepared. Games involved gladiators fighting wild animals or each other.

★Palatino ARCHAEOLOGICAL SITE

(Palatine Hill; Map p648; ☎06 3996 7700; www.coopculture.it; Via di San Gregorio 30 & Via Sacra; adult/reduced incl Colosseum & Roman Forum €12/7.50; ⏰8.30am-1hr before sunset; Ⓜ Colosseo) Sandwiched between the Roman Forum and the Circo Massimo, the Palatino is an atmospheric area of towering pine trees, majestic ruins and memorable views. It was here that Romulus supposedly founded the city in 753 BC, and Rome's emperors lived in unabashed luxury. Look out for the **stadio** (stadium; Map p648), the ruins of the **Domus Flavia** (Map p648), the imperial palace, and the grandstand views over the Roman Forum from the **Orti Farnesiani** (Map p648).

★Roman Forum ARCHAEOLOGICAL SITE

(Foro Romano; Map p648; ☎06 3996 7700; www.coopculture.it; Largo della Salara Vecchia & Via Sacra; adult/reduced incl Colosseum & Palatino €12/7.50; ⏰8.30am-1hr before sunset; 🚌 Via dei Fori Imperiali) Nowadays an impressive – if rather confusing – sprawl of ruins, the Roman Forum was ancient Rome's showpiece centre, a grandiose district of temples, basilicas and vibrant public spaces. The site, which was originally an Etruscan burial ground, was first developed in the 7th century BC, growing over time to become the social, political and commercial hub of the Roman Empire. Landmark sights include the **Arco di Settimio Severo** (Arch of Septimius Severus; Map p648), the **Curia** (Map p648),

COLOSSEUM TICKETS

To avoid queues at the Colosseum, buy your ticket from the Palatino entrance (about 250m away at Via di San Gregorio 30) or at the Roman Forum (Largo della Salara Vecchia). You can also book online at www.coopculture.it (€2 booking fee).

Greater Rome

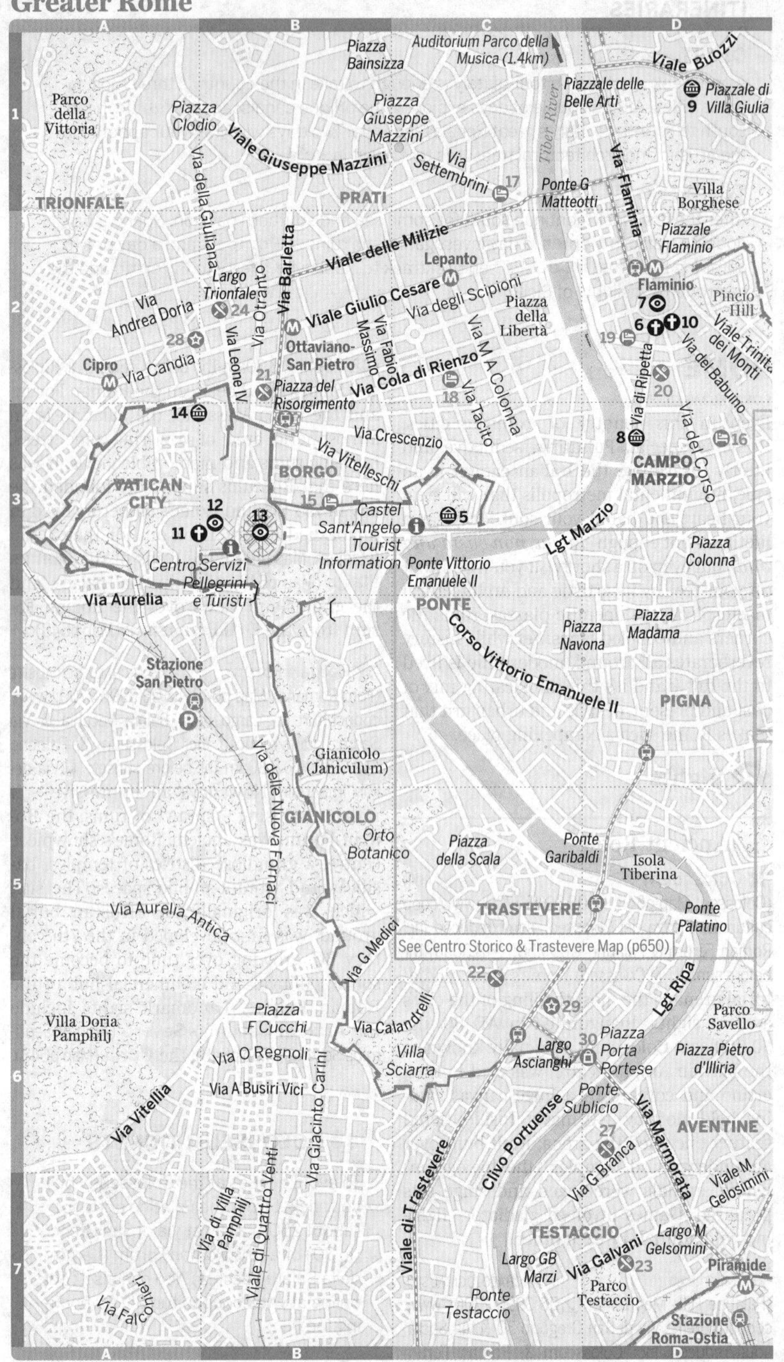

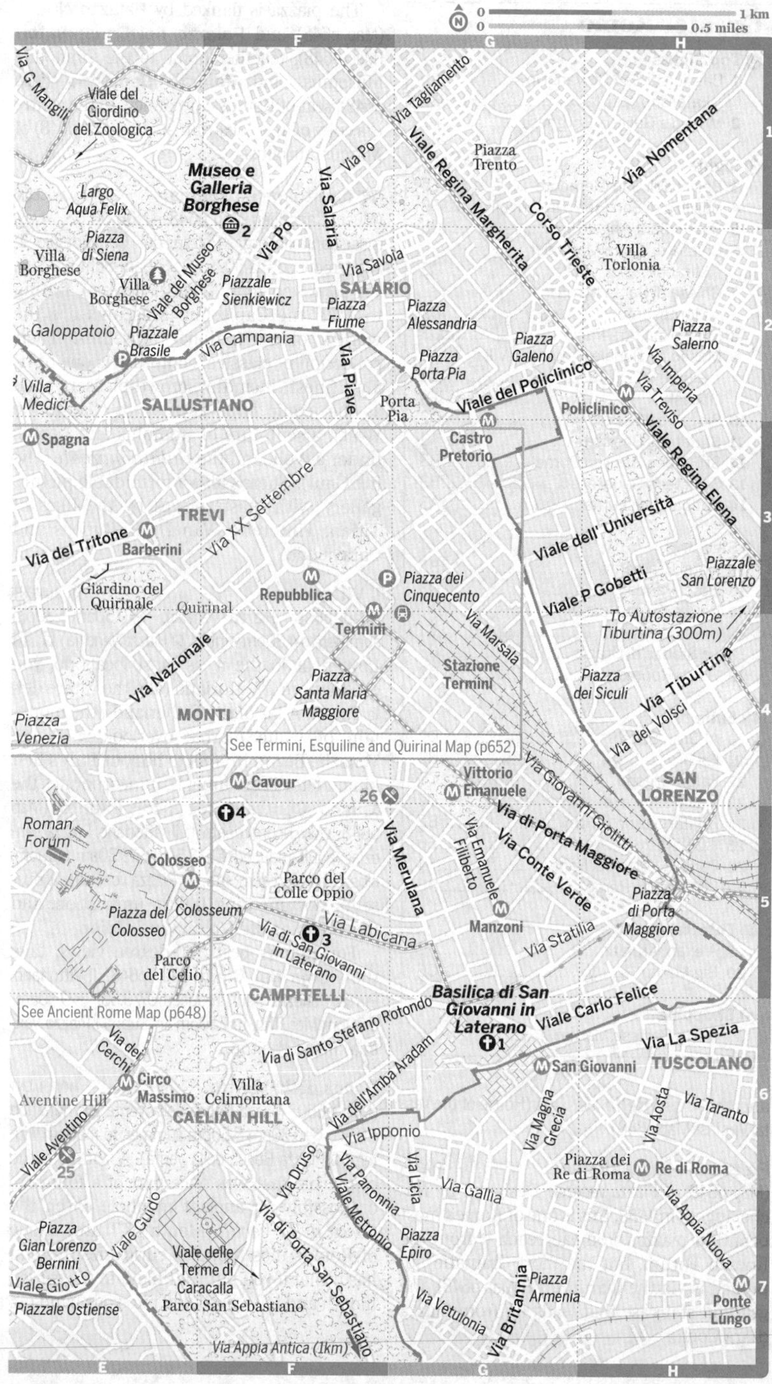

0 1 km
0 0.5 miles
Museo e Galleria Borghese
Villa Borghese
Galoppatoio
Piazzale Brasile
Via Campania
Via Po
Via Salaria
Via Piave
Viale Regina Margherita
Corso Trieste
Via Nomentana
Villa Torlonia
Piazza Trento
SALARIO
Piazza Fiume
Piazza Alessandria
Piazza Porta Pia
Porta Pia
Viale del Policlinico
Policlinico
Castro Pretorio
Viale Regina Elena
SALLUSTIANO
Spagna
TREVI
Via XX Settembre
Via del Tritone
Barberini
Giardino del Quirinale
Quirinal
Repubblica
Piazza dei Cinquecento
Termini
Via Marsala
Stazione Termini
Viale dell' Università
Viale P Gobetti
To Autostazione Tiburtina (300m)
Piazzale San Lorenzo
Via Nazionale
MONTI
Piazza Santa Maria Maggiore
Piazza Venezia
See Termini, Esquiline and Quirinal Map (p652)
Via Tiburtina
Piazza dei Siculi
Via dei Volsci
SAN LORENZO
Cavour
Vittorio Emanuele
Via Giovanni Giolitti
Via di Porta Maggiore
Via Conte Verde
Via Merulana
Roman Forum
Colosseo
Colosseum
Piazza del Colosseo
Parco del Celio
Parco del Colle Oppio
Via Labicana
Via di San Giovanni in Laterano
Manzoni
Via Statilia
Piazza di Porta Maggiore
CAMPITELLI
See Ancient Rome Map (p648)
Basilica di San Giovanni in Laterano
Viale Carlo Felice
Via di Santo Stefano Rotondo
Via dell'Amba Aradam
San Giovanni
TUSCOLANO
Via La Spezia
Circo Massimo
Villa Celimontana
CAELIAN HILL
Aventine Hill
Viale Aventino
Via Ipponio
Via Magna Grecia
Via Aosta
Via Taranto
Piazza dei Re di Roma
Re di Roma
Via Appia Nuova
Via Druso
Via Pannonia
Viale Metronio
Via Licia
Via Gallia
Piazza Epiro
Via di Porta San Sebastiano
Viale Guido
Piazza Gian Lorenzo Bernini
Viale Giotto
Piazzale Ostiense
Viale delle Terme di Caracalla
Parco San Sebastiano
Via Appia Antica (1km)
Via Vetulonia
Via Britannia
Piazza Armenia
Ponte Lungo
Via Tagliamento
Via Savoia
Via Imperia
Via Treviso
Via Emanuele Filiberto
Viale del Giordino del Zoologica
Via G Mangili
Largo Aqua Felix
Piazza di Siena
Viale del Museo Borghese
Piazzale Sienkiewicz
Villa Medici
Piazza Galeno
Piazza Salerno
Via dei Cerchi

Greater Rome

and the **Casa delle Vestali** (House of the Vestal Virgins; Map p648).

Piazza del Campidoglio PIAZZA
(Map p648; Piazza Venezia) Designed by Michelangelo in 1538, this is one of Rome's most beautiful piazzas. You can reach it from the Roman Forum, but the most dramatic approach is via the **Cordonata** (Map p648), the graceful staircase that leads up from Piazza d'Ara Coeli.

The piazza is flanked by **Palazzo Nuovo** (Map p648) and **Palazzo dei Conservatori** (Map p648), together home to the Capitoline Museums, and **Palazzo Senatorio** (Map p648), seat of Rome's city council. In the centre is a copy of an equestrian **statue** (Map p648) of Marcus Aurelius.

★**Capitoline Museums** MUSEUM
(Musei Capitolini; Map p648; 06 06 08; www.museicapitolini.org; Piazza del Campidoglio 1; adult/reduced €11.50/9.50; 9am-8pm Tue-Sun, last admission 7pm; Piazza Venezia) Dating to 1471, the Capitoline Museums are the world's oldest national museums. Their collection of classical sculpture is one of Italy's finest, including crowd-pleasers such as the iconic *Lupa capitolina* (Capitoline Wolf), a sculpture of Romulus and Remus under a wolf, and the *Galata morente* (Dying Gaul). There's also a formidable picture gallery with masterpieces by the likes of Titian, Tintoretto, Van Dyck, Rubens and Caravaggio.

Il Vittoriano MONUMENT
(Map p648; Piazza Venezia; 9.30am-5.30pm summer, to 4.30pm winter; Piazza Venezia) FREE Love it or loathe it, as most locals do, you can't ignore Il Vittoriano (aka the Altare della Patria; Altar of the Fatherland), the mountain of white marble overlooking Piazza Venezia. Begun in 1885 to honour Italy's first king, Victor Emmanuel II, it incorporates the **Museo Centrale del Risorgimento** (Map p648; www.risorgimento.it; Il Vittoriano, Piazza Venezia; adult/reduced €5/2.50; 9.30am-6.30pm, closed 1st Mon of month; Piazza Venezia), a museum documenting Italian unification, and the **Tomb of the Unknown Soldier**.

For Rome's best 360-degree views, take the **Roma dal Cielo** (Map p648; Il Vittoriano, Piazza Venezia; adult/reduced €7/3.50; 9.30am-6.30pm Mon-Thu, to 7.30pm Fri-Sun; Piazza Venezia) lift to the top.

Bocca della Verità MONUMENT
(Map p650; Piazza Bocca della Verità 18; donation €0.50; 9.30am-5.50pm summer, to 4.50pm winter; Piazza Bocca della Verità) A round piece of marble that was once part of a fountain, or possibly an ancient manhole cover, the *Bocca della Verità* (Mouth of Truth) is one of Rome's most popular curiosities. Legend has it that if you put your hand in the carved mouth and tell a lie, it will bite your hand off.

The mouth lives in the portico of the **Chiesa di Santa Maria in Cosmedin**, a beautiful medieval church.

The Vatican

The world's smallest sovereign state, the Vatican is the modern vestige of the Papal States, the papal empire that encompassed Rome and much of central Italy until Italian unification in 1861. It was formally established under the terms of the 1929 Lateran Treaty, signed by Mussolini and Pope Pius XI.

★St Peter's Basilica BASILICA
(Basilica di San Pietro; Map p642; www.vatican.va; St Peter's Sq; ⊙7am-7pm summer, to 6.30pm winter; Ⓜ Ottaviano-San Pietro) FREE In this city of outstanding churches, none can hold a candle to the Basilica di San Pietro, Italy's most spectacular cathedral. Built atop an earlier 4th-century church, it was completed in 1626 after 150 years of construction. It contains many spectacular works of art, including three of Italy's most celebrated masterpieces: Michelangelo's *Pietà*, his soaring dome, and Bernini's 29m-high baldachin over the papal altar.

Note that the basilica attracts up to 20,000 people on a busy day, so expect queues in peak periods.

St Peter's Square PIAZZA
(Piazza San Pietro; Map p642; Ⓜ Ottaviano-San Pietro) Overlooked by St Peter's Basilica, the Vatican's central square was laid out between 1656 and 1667 to a design by baroque artist Gian Lorenzo Bernini. Seen from above, it resembles a giant keyhole with two semicircular colonnades, each consisting of four rows of Doric columns, encircling a giant ellipse that straightens out to funnel believers into the basilica. The effect was deliberate – Bernini described the colonnades as representing 'the motherly arms of the church'.

★Vatican Museums MUSEUM
(Musei Vaticani; Map p642; ☎06 6988 4676; http://mv.vatican.va; Viale Vaticano; adult/reduced €16/8, free last Sun of month; ⊙9am-4pm Mon-Sat, to 12.30pm last Sun of month; Ⓜ Ottaviano-San Pietro) Founded by Pope Julius II in the early 16th century and enlarged by successive pontiffs, the Vatican Museums boast one of the world's greatest art collections. Exhibits, which are displayed along about 7km of halls and corridors, range from Egyptian mummies and Etruscan bronzes to ancient

QUEUE-JUMPING AT THE VATICAN MUSEUMS

➡ Book tickets online at http://mv.vatican.va (€4 booking fee).

➡ Time your visit: Wednesday mornings are good as everyone is at the Pope's weekly audience at St Peter's; afternoon is better than the morning; avoid Mondays, when many other museums are shut.

VATICAN MUSEUMS ITINERARY

Follow this three-hour itinerary for the museums' greatest hits:

At the top of the escalator after the entrance, head out to the **Cortile della Pigna**, a courtyard named after the Augustan-era bronze pine cone in the monumental niche. Cross the courtyard into the long corridor that is the **Museo Chiaramonti** and head left up to the **Museo Pio Clementino**, home of the Vatican's finest classical statuary. Follow through the **Cortile Ottagono** (Octagonal Courtyard) onto the **Sala Croce Greca** (Greek Cross Room) from where stairs lead up to the 1st floor.

Continue through the **Galleria dei Candelabri** (Gallery of the Candelabra), **Galleria degli Arazzi** (Tapestry Gallery) and **Galleria delle Carte Geografiche** (Map Gallery) to the **Sala di Costantino**, the first of the four **Stanze di Raffaello** (Raphael Rooms) – the others are the **Stanza d' Eliodoro**, the **Stanza della Segnatura**, home to Raphael's superlative *La Scuola di Atene* (The School of Athens), and the **Stanza dell'Incendio di Borgo**. Anywhere else these frescoed chambers would be the star attraction, but here they're the warm-up act for the museums' grand finale, the **Sistine Chapel**.

Originally built in 1484 for Pope Sixtus IV, this towering chapel boasts two of the world's most famous works of art: Michelangelo's ceiling frescoes (1508–1512) and his *Giudizio Universale* (Last Judgment; 1535–1541).

ST PETER'S BASILICA DOME

Rising imperiously over Rome's skyline, **St Peter's Basilica Dome** (Map p642; with/without lift €7/5; 8am-5.45pm summer, to 4.45pm winter; M Ottaviano-San Pietro) was Michelangelo's greatest architectural achievement. To climb it, the entrance is to the right of the basilica. You can walk the 551 steps to the top, or take a small lift halfway up and then tramp the last 320 steps. Either way, it's a steep, narrow climb that's not recommended for those who suffer from claustrophobia or vertigo. Make it to the top, though, and you're rewarded with stunning views from a lofty perch 120m above St Peter's Sq.

busts, old masters and modern paintings. Highlights include the spectacular collection of classical statuary in the Museo Pio-Clementino, a suite of frescoed rooms by Raphael, and the Michelangelo-painted Sistine Chapel.

Historic Centre

★Pantheon CHURCH
(Map p650; Piazza della Rotonda; 8.30am-7.30pm Mon-Sat, 9am-6pm Sun; Largo di Torre Argentina) FREE A striking 2000-year-old temple, now church, the Pantheon is the best preserved of Rome's ancient monuments, and one of the most influential buildings in the Western world. Built by Hadrian over Marcus Agrippa's earlier 27 BC temple, it has stood since AD 120, and although its greying, pockmarked exterior is looking its age, it's still an exhilarating experience to pass through its vast bronze doors and gaze up at the largest unreinforced concrete dome ever built.

★Piazza Navona PIAZZA
(Map p650; Corso del Rinascimento) With its ornate fountains, baroque *palazzi* (mansions) and colourful cast of street artists, hawkers and tourists, Piazza Navona is central Rome's showcase square. Built over the 1st-century Stadio di Domiziano (Domitian's Stadium), it was paved over in the 15th century and for almost 300 years hosted the city's main market. Its grand centrepiece, Bernini's **Fontana dei Quattro Fiumi** (Fountain of the Four Rivers; Map p650), is an ornate, showy work depicting personifications of the rivers Nile, Ganges, Danube and Plate.

Campo de' Fiori PIAZZA
(Map p650; Corso Vittorio Emanuele II) Noisy, colourful 'Il Campo' is a major focus of Roman life: by day it hosts a much-loved market, while at night it morphs into a raucous open-air pub. For centuries it was the site of public executions, and it was here that philosopher monk Giordano Bruno was burned at the stake for heresy in 1600. The spot is today marked by a sinister statue of the hooded monk, created by Ettore Ferrari and unveiled in 1889.

Galleria Doria Pamphilj MUSEUM
(Map p650; 06 679 73 23; www.dopart.it; Via del Corso 305; adult/reduced €11/7.50; 9am-7pm, last admission 6pm; Via del Corso) Hidden behind the grimy grey exterior of Palazzo Doria Pamphilj, this wonderful gallery boasts one of Rome's richest private art collections, with works by Raphael, Tintoretto, Brueghel, Titian, Caravaggio, Bernini and Velázquez. Masterpieces abound, but the undisputed star is Velázquez' portrait of an implacable Pope Innocent X, who grumbled that the depiction was 'too real'. Compare it with Gian Lorenzo Bernini's sculptural interpretation of the same subject.

★Trevi Fountain FOUNTAIN
(Fontana di Trevi; Map p652; Piazza di Trevi; M Barberini) The Fontana di Trevi, scene of Anita Ekberg's dip in *La Dolce Vita*, is Rome's largest and most famous fountain. A flamboyant baroque ensemble of mythical figures, wild horses and cascading rock falls, it takes up the entire side of the 17th-century Palazzo Poli.

The famous tradition is to toss a coin into the water, thus ensuring that one day you'll return to the Eternal City. On average about €3000 is thrown in every day.

Spanish Steps STAIRCASE
(Scalinata della Trinità dei Monti; Map p652; Piazza di Spagna; M Spagna) Rising from Piazza di Spagna, the Spanish Steps have been attracting visitors since the 18th century. The piazza was named after the nearby Spanish Embassy, but the staircase, designed by Italian Francesco De Sanctis and built in 1725 with French money, leads to the French **Chiesa della Trinità dei Monti** (Map p652; visite.guidate.tdm@gmail.com; Piazza Trinità dei Monti; 6.30am-8pm

Tue-Sun, tours Italian Sat 11am, French Sun/Tue 9.15/11am; Ⓜ Spagna). At the the foot of the stairs, the boat-shaped **Barcaccia** (1627) (Map p652) fountain is believed to be by Pietro Bernini (father of Gian Lorenzo Bernini).

Piazza del Popolo PIAZZA
(Map p642; Ⓜ Flaminio) This dazzling piazza was laid out in 1538 to provide a grandiose entrance to what was then Rome's main northern gateway. It has since been remodelled several times, most recently by Giuseppe Valadier in 1823.

Guarding its southern approach are Carlo Rainaldi's twin 17th-century churches, **Chiesa di Santa Maria dei Miracoli** (Map p642; Ⓜ Flaminio) and **Chiesa di Santa Maria in Montesanto** (Map p642; Ⓜ Flaminio). In the centre, the 36m-high **obelisk** (Map p642; Ⓜ Flaminio) was brought by Augustus from ancient Egypt and originally stood in Circo Massimo.

Museo dell'Ara Pacis MUSEUM
(Map p642; ☎06 06 08; http://en.arapacis.it; Lungotevere in Augusta; adult/reduced €10.50/8.50, audioguide €4; ⏱9am-7pm, last admission 6pm; Ⓜ Flaminio) The first modern construction in Rome's historic centre since WWII, Richard Meier's controversial and widely detested glass-and-marble pavilion houses the *Ara Pacis Augustae* (Altar of Peace), Augustus' great monument to peace. One of the most important works of ancient Roman sculpture, the vast marble altar – measuring 11.6m by 10.6m by 3.6m – was completed in 13 BC.

Trastevere

Trastevere is one of central Rome's most vivacious neighbourhoods, a tightly packed warren of ochre *palazzi,* ivy-clad facades and photogenic lanes. Originally working class, it's now a trendy hang-out full of bars and restaurants.

★Basilica di Santa Maria in Trastevere BASILICA
(Map p650; Piazza Santa Maria in Trastevere; ⏱7.30am-9pm; 🚌 Viale di Trastevere, 🚋 Viale di Trastevere) Nestled in a quiet corner of Trastevere's focal square, this is said to be the oldest church dedicated to the Virgin Mary in Rome. In its original form it dates to the early 3rd century, but a major 12th-century makeover saw the addition of a Romanesque bell tower and glittering facade. The portico came later, added by Carlo Fontana in 1702.

Inside, the 12th-century mosaics are the headline feature.

Villa Borghese

Accessible from Piazzale Flaminio, Pincio Hill and the top of Via Vittorio Veneto, Villa Borghese is Rome's best-known park.

★Museo e Galleria Borghese MUSEUM
(Map p642; ☎06 3 28 10; www.galleriaborghese.it; Piazzale del Museo Borghese 5; adult/reduced €11/6.50; ⏱9am-7pm Tue-Sun; 🚌 Via Pinciana) If you only have the time (or inclination) for one art gallery in Rome, make it this one. Housing what's generally considered the 'queen of all private art collections', it boasts paintings by Caravaggio, Botticelli and Raphael, as well as some spectacular sculptures by Bernini. There are highlights at every turn, but look out for Bernini's *Ratto di Proserpina* (Rape of Persephone) and Canova's *Venere vincitrice* (Conquering Venus).

To limit numbers, visitors are admitted at two-hourly intervals, so you'll need to book your ticket and get an entry time.

Museo Nazionale Etrusco di Villa Giulia MUSEUM
(Map p642; www.villagiulia.beniculturali.it; Piazzale di Villa Giulia; adult/reduced €8/4; ⏱8.30am-7.30pm Tue-Sun; 🚌 Via delle Belle Arti) Italy's finest collection of Etruscan treasures is considerately displayed in Villa Giulia, Pope Julius III's 16th-century pleasure palace, and the nearby Villa Poniatowski. Exhibits, many of which came from burial tombs in the surrounding Lazio region, range from bronze

ROMA PASS

A cumulative sightseeing and transport card, available online or from tourist information points and participating museums, the **Roma Pass** (www.romapass.it) comes in two forms:

Classic (€36; valid for three days) Provides free admission to two museums or sites, as well as reduced entry to extra sites, unlimited city transport, and discounted entry to other exhibitions and events.

48-hour (€28; valid for 48 hours) Gives free admission to one museum or site, and then as per the classic pass.

Ancient Rome

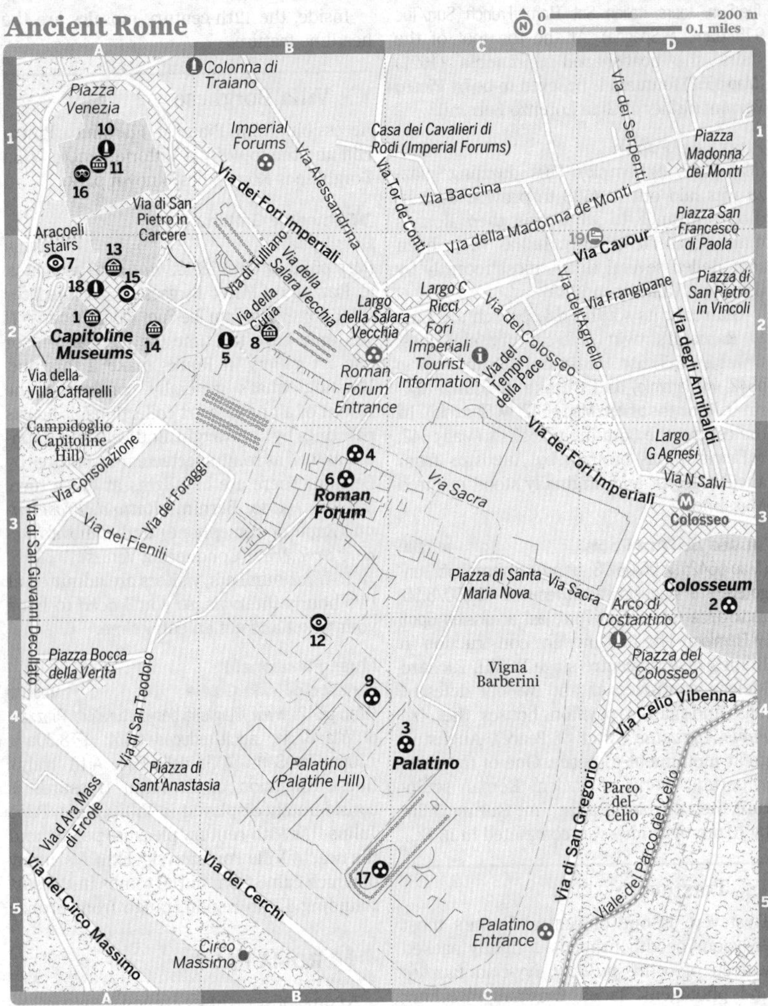

Ancient Rome

Top Sights

1	Capitoline Museums	A2
2	Colosseum	D3
3	Palatino	C4
4	Roman Forum	B3

Sights

5	Arco di Settimio Severo	B2
6	Casa delle Vestali	B3
7	Cordonata	A2
8	Curia	B2
9	Domus Flavia	B4
10	Il Vittoriano	A1
11	Museo Centrale del Risorgimento	A1
12	Orti Farnesiani	B4
	Palazzo dei Conservatori	(see 1)
13	Palazzo Nuovo	A2
14	Palazzo Senatorio	A2
15	Piazza del Campidoglio	A2
16	Roma dal Cielo	A1
17	Stadio	B5
18	Statue of Marcus Aurelius	A2

Sleeping

19	Nicolas Inn	D2

figurines and black *bucchero* tableware to temple decorations, terracotta vases and a dazzling display of sophisticated jewellery.

Must-sees include a polychrome terracotta statue of Apollo, the 6th-century BC *Sarcofago degli Sposi* (Sarcophagus of the Betrothed) and the *Euphronios Krater,* a celebrated Greek vase.

Termini & Esquiline

The largest of Rome's seven hills, the Esquiline (Esquilino) extends from the Colosseum up to Stazione Termini, Rome's main transport hub.

★Museo Nazionale Romano: Palazzo Massimo alle Terme MUSEUM

(Map p652; 06 3996 7700; www.coopculture.it; Largo di Villa Peretti 1; adult/reduced €7/3.50; 9am-7.45pm Tue-Sun; Termini) One of Rome's great unheralded museums, this is a fabulous treasure trove of classical art. The ground and 1st floors are devoted to sculpture with some breathtaking pieces – check out the *Pugile* (Boxer), a 2nd-century BC Greek bronze; the graceful 2nd-century BC *Ermafrodite dormiente* (Sleeping Hermaphrodite); and the idealised *Il discobolo* (Discus Thrower). It's the magnificent and vibrantly coloured frescoes on the 2nd floor, however, that are the real highlight.

Basilica di Santa Maria Maggiore BASILICA

(Map p652; Piazza Santa Maria Maggiore; basilica/museum/loggia/archaeological site free/€3/5/5; 7am-7pm, museum & loggia 9am-5.30pm; Piazza Santa Maria Maggiore) One of Rome's four patriarchal basilicas, this monumental 5th-century church stands on the summit of the Esquiline Hill, on the spot where snow is said to have miraculously fallen in the summer of AD 358. Much altered over the centuries, it's something of an architectural hybrid, with a 14th-century Romanesque belfry, an 18th-century baroque facade, a largely baroque interior and a series of glorious 5th-century mosaics.

Basilica di San Pietro in Vincoli BASILICA

(Map p642; Piazza di San Pietro in Vincoli 4a; 8am-12.20pm & 3-7pm summer, to 6pm winter; Cavour) Pilgrims and art lovers flock to this 5th-century basilica for two reasons: to marvel at Michelangelo's colossal *Moses* (1505) sculpture and to see the chains that supposedly bound St Peter when he was imprisoned in the Carcere Mamertino (near the Roman Forum).

Access to the church is via a flight of steps through a low arch that leads up from Via Cavour.

San Giovanni & Caelian Hill

★Basilica di San Giovanni in Laterano BASILICA

(Map p642; Piazza di San Giovanni in Laterano 4; basilica/cloister free/€5; 7am-6.30pm, cloister 9am-6pm; San Giovanni) For a thousand years this monumental cathedral was the most important church in Christendom. Commissioned by the Emperor Constantine and consecrated in AD 324, it was the first Christian basilica built in the city and, until the late 14th century, was the pope's main place of worship. It's still Rome's official cathedral and the pope's seat as the bishop of Rome.

The basilica has been revamped several times, most notably by Borromini in the 17th century, and by Alessandro Galilei, who added the vast 18th-century facade.

Basilica di San Clemente BASILICA

(Map p642; www.basilicasanclemente.com; Via di San Giovanni in Laterano; excavations adult/reduced €10/5; 9am-12.30pm & 3-6pm Mon-Sat, 12.15-6pm Sun; Via Labicana) Nowhere better illustrates the various stages of Rome's turbulent past than this fascinating multilayered church. The ground-level 12th-century basilica sits atop a 4th-century church, which, in turn, stands over a 2nd-century pagan temple and 1st-century Roman house. Beneath everything are foundations dating from the Roman Republic.

Sleeping

Ancient Rome

Nicolas Inn B&B €€

(Map p648; 06 9761 8483; www.nicolasinn.com; 1st fl, Via Cavour 295; s €95-160, d €100-180; Cavour) This sunny B&B offers a warm welcome and convenient location, a stone's throw from the Roman Forum. Run by a friendly couple, it has four big rooms, each with homely furnishings, colourful pictures and large en suite bathrooms. No children under five.

Centro Storico & Trastevere

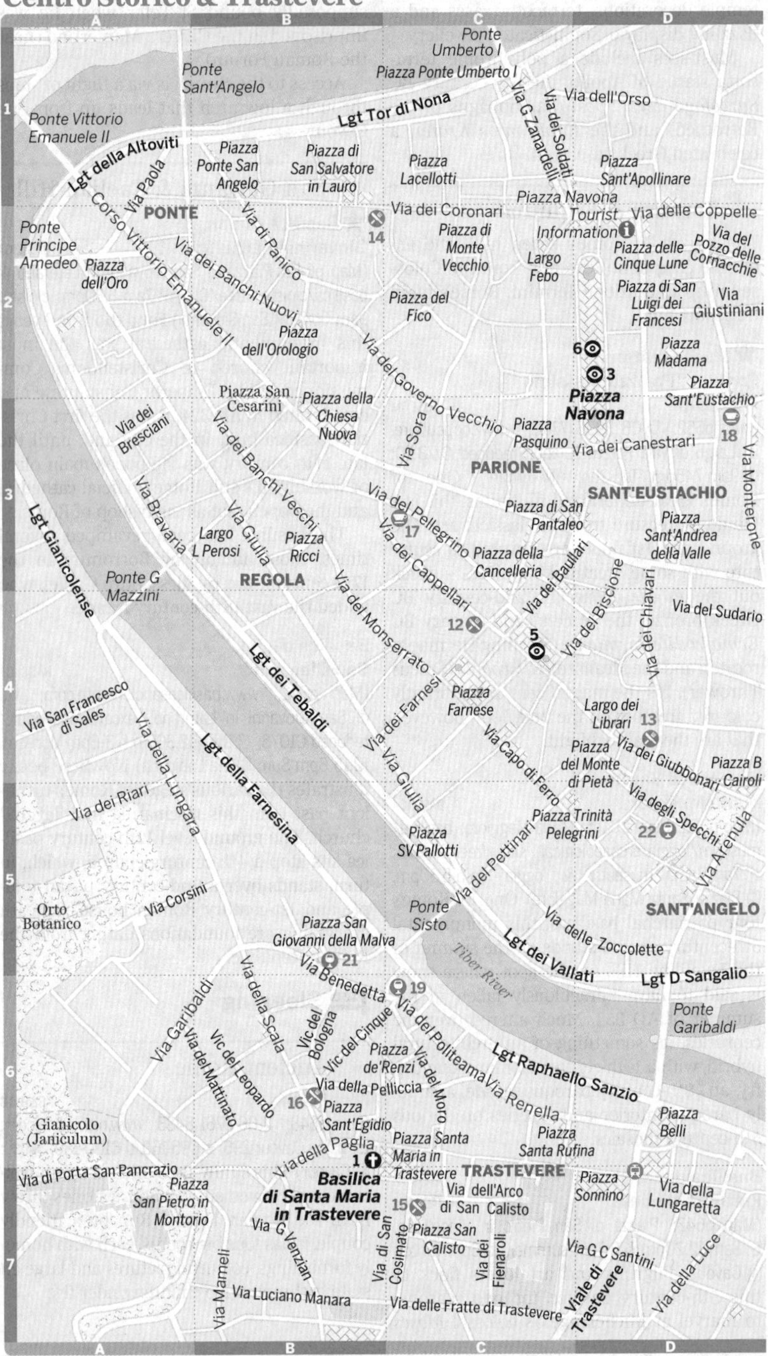

Ponte Sant'Angelo
Ponte Umberto I
Piazza Ponte Umberto I
Lgt Tor di Nona
Via G Zanardelli
Via dei Soldati
Via dell'Orso
Ponte Vittorio Emanuele II
Lgt della Altoviti
Via Paola
Piazza Ponte San Angelo
Piazza di San Salvatore in Lauro
Piazza Lacellotti
Piazza Sant'Apollinare
Piazza Navona
PONTE
Via di Panico
Via dei Coronari
14
Tourist Information
Via delle Coppelle
Ponte Principe Amedeo
Piazza dell'Oro
Corso Vittorio Emanuele II
Via dei Banchi Nuovi
Piazza di Monte Vecchio
Largo Febo
Piazza delle Cinque Lune
Via del Pozzo delle Cornacchie
Piazza del Fico
Piazza di San Luigi dei Francesi
Via Giustiniani
Piazza dell'Orologio
Via del Governo Vecchio
Piazza Madama
6
3
Piazza Navona
Piazza Sant'Eustachio
Piazza San Cesarini
Piazza della Chiesa Nuova
Via dei Bresciani
Via dei Banchi Vecchi
Via Sora
Piazza Pasquino
Via dei Canestrari
18
Via Monterone
PARIONE
SANT'EUSTACHIO
Lgt Gianicolense
Via Bravaria
Via Giulia
Largo L Perosi
Piazza Ricci
Via del Pellegrino
17
Via dei Cappellari
Piazza di San Pantaleo
Piazza Sant'Andrea della Valle
Piazza della Cancelleria
Ponte G Mazzini
REGOLA
Via del Monserrato
Via dei Baullari
Via del Biscione
Via dei Chiavari
Via del Sudario
12
5
Lgt dei Tebaldi
Via dei Farnesi
Piazza Farnese
Largo dei Librari
13
Via San Francesco di Sales
Via della Lungara
Lgt della Farnesina
Via Giulia
Via Capo di Ferro
Piazza del Monte di Pietà
Via dei Giubbonari
Piazza B Cairoli
Via dei Riari
Piazza Trinità Pelegrini
Via degli Specchi
22
Via Arenula
Piazza SV Pallotti
Via del Pettinari
Orto Botanico
Via Corsini
Ponte Sisto
SANT'ANGELO
Piazza San Giovanni della Malva
Via delle Zoccolette
Tiber River
Lgt dei Vallati
Lgt D Sangalio
21
Via Benedetta
19
Ponte Garibaldi
Via della Scala
Via Garibaldi
Via del Mattinato
Vic del Leopardo
Vic del Bologna
Vic del Cinque
Via del Politeama
Piazza de'Renzi
Via del Moro
Lgt Raphaello Sanzio
Via della Pelliccia
16
Piazza Sant'Egidio
Via Renella
Piazza Belli
Gianicolo (Janiculum)
Via della Paglia
Piazza Santa Maria in Trastevere
Piazza Santa Rufina
1
Basilica di Santa Maria in Trastevere
TRASTEVERE
Piazza Sonnino
Via della Lungaretta
Via di Porta San Pancrazio
Piazza San Pietro in Montorio
Via dell'Arco di San Calisto
15
Via G Venzian
Via di San Cosimato
Piazza San Calisto
Via dei Fienaroli
Via G C Santini
Viale di Trastevere
Via della Luce
Via Mameli
Via Luciano Manara
Via delle Fratte di Trastevere

Centro Storico & Trastevere

⊙ Top Sights

1 Basilica di Santa Maria in Trastevere B6
2 Pantheon E2
3 Piazza Navona D2

⊙ Sights

4 Bocca della Verità F7
5 Campo de' Fiori C4
6 Fontana dei Quattro Fiumi D2
7 Galleria Doria Pamphilj F3

Sleeping

8 Arco del Lauro E7
9 La Casa di Kaia E7
Maria-Rosa Guesthouse .... (see 9)

Eating

10 Armando al Pantheon E2
11 Casa Coppelle E1
12 Forno di Campo de' Fiori C4
13 Forno Roscioli D4
14 Gelateria del Teatro B2
15 Paris C7
16 Trattoria degli Amici B6

Drinking & Nightlife

17 Barnum Cafe C3
18 Caffè Sant'Eustachio D3
19 Freni e Frizioni C6
20 La Casa del Caffè Tazza d'Oro E2
21 Ma Che Siete Venuti a Fà B5
22 Open Baladin D5

The Vatican

★ Le Stanze di Orazio B&B €€

(Map p642; ☎06 3265 2474; www.lestanzediorazio.com; Via Orazio 3; r €85-125; ❄@🛜; M Lepanto) This small boutique B&B is excellent value for money. Its five bright rooms feature soothing tones and playful decor – think shimmering rainbow wallpaper, lilac accents and grey designer bathrooms. There's a small breakfast area and rooms come with kettles and tea-making kit.

Hotel Bramante HISTORIC HOTEL €€

(Map p642; ☎06 6880 6426; www.hotelbramante.com; Vicolo delle Palline 24-25; s €100-160, d €140-240, tr €175-260, q €190-300; ❄🛜; 🚌 Borgo Sant'Angelo) Nestled under the Vatican walls, the Bramante exudes country-house charm with its cosy internal courtyard, eggshell blue walls, wood-beamed ceilings and antique furniture. It's housed in the 16th-century building where architect Domenico Fontana once lived.

Termini, Esquiline and Quirinal

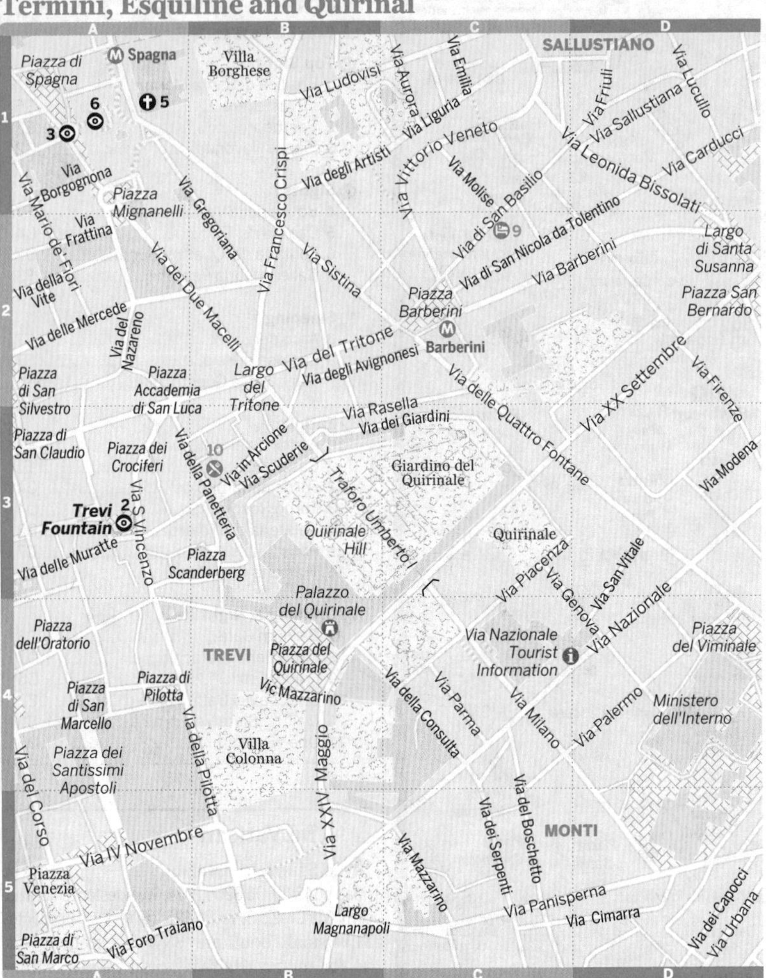

Termini, Esquiline and Quirinal

Top Sights
1 Museo Nazionale Romano: Palazzo Massimo alle Terme F3
2 Trevi Fountain A3

Sights
3 Barcaccia A1
4 Basilica di Santa Maria Maggiore F5
5 Chiesa della Trinità dei Monti A1
6 Spanish Steps A1

Sleeping
7 Beehive H2
8 Blue Hostel F5
9 Daphne Inn C2

Eating
10 San Crispino B3

Entertainment
11 Teatro dell'Opera di Roma E3

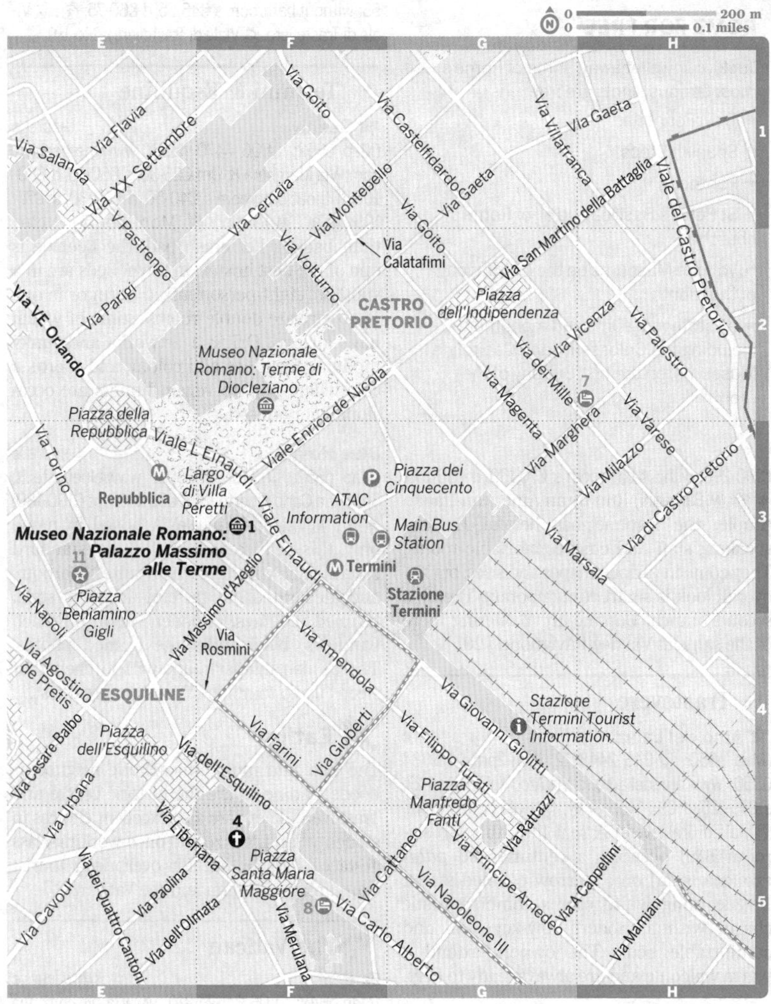

Historic Centre

Okapi Rooms HOTEL €

(Map p642; ☎06 3260 9815; www.okapirooms.it; Via della Penna 57; s €65-80, d €85-120, tr €110-140, q €120-180; ; M Flaminio) The Okapi is a smart, value-for-money choice near Piazza del Popolo. Rooms, spread over six floors of a narrow townhouse, are simple and airy with cream walls, terracotta floors and the occasional stone frieze. Some are smaller than others and several have small terraces. No breakfast.

Hotel Panda PENSION €

(Map p642; ☎06 678 01 79; www.hotelpanda.it; Via della Croce 35; s €65-80, d €85-130, tr €120-150, q €160-190; ; M Spagna) Near the Spanish Steps, in an area where a bargain is a Bulgari watch bought at the sales, the Panda flies the flag for budget accommodation. It's a friendly place with high-ceilinged rooms and simple, tasteful decor. Air-con is free in summer, but €6 in other periods.

Daphne Inn BOUTIQUE HOTEL €€

(Map p652; ☎06 8745 0086; www.daphne-rome.com; Via di San Basilio 55; s €115-180, d €130-240, ste

ROME FOR FREE

Tuck your wallet away, some of Rome's most famous sights are free:

- Trevi Fountain
- Spanish Steps
- Pantheon
- St Peter's Basilica and all of Rome's churches
- Vatican Museums on the last Sunday of the month
- All state museums and monuments, including the Colosseum and Capitoline Museums, on the first Sunday of the month

€190-290, without bathroom s €70-130, d €90-160; ; Barberini) Run by an American-Italian couple, the Daphne has helpful English-speaking staff and chic, comfortable rooms. They come in various shapes and sizes, but the overall look is smart contemporary. There's a second branch, Daphne Trevi, offering more of the same at Via degli Avignonesi 20.

Trastevere

★Arco del Lauro B&B €
(Map p650; 346 2443212, 9am-2pm 06 9784 0350; www.arcodellauro.it; Via Arco de' Tolomei 27; s €75-125, d €95-145; ; Viale di Trastevere, Viale di Trastevere) A real find, this fab six-room B&B occupies a centuries-old *palazzo* (mansion) on a narrow cobbled street. Its gleaming white rooms combine rustic charm with a modern low-key look and comfortable beds. The owners extend a warm welcome and are always ready to help.

Maria-Rosa Guesthouse B&B €
(Map p650; 338 7700067; www.maria-rosa.it; Via dei Vascellari 55; s €45-65, d €60-80, tr €95-120; ; Viale di Trastevere, Viale di Trastevere) This is a delightful B&B on the 3rd floor of a Trastevere townhouse. It's a simple affair with two guestrooms sharing a single bathroom and a small living room, but the homey decor, pot plants and books create a lovely, warm atmosphere. The owner, Sylvie, also has a further three rooms on the floor above at **La Casa di Kaia** (Map p650; 338 7700067; www.kaia-trastevere.it; Via dei Vascellari 55; without bathroom s €45-55, d €60-75; ; Viale di Trastevere, Viale di Trastevere). No lift.

Termini & Esquiline

★Beehive HOSTEL €
(Map p652; 06 4470 4553; www.the-beehive.com; Via Marghera 8; dm €25-30, s €60-70, d €80-100, without bathroom s €40-50, d €60-80, tr €75-105; ; Termini) More boutique chic than backpacker crash pad, the Beehive is one of the best hostels in town. Beds are in a spotless, eight-person mixed dorm or in one of six private double rooms, some of which have air-con. Original artworks and funky modular furniture add colour, and there's a cafe where pop-up vegan dinners are occasionally organised.

Blue Hostel HOSTEL €
(Map p652; 340 9258503; www.bluehostel.it; 3rd fl, Via Carlo Alberto 13; d €60-140, apt €100-180; ; Vittorio Emanuele) A hostel in name only, this pearl offers small, hotel-standard rooms, each with its own en suite bathroom, and decorated in tasteful low-key style: beamed ceilings, wooden floors, French windows, black-and-white framed photos. There's also an apartment, with kitchen, that sleeps up to four. No lift and no breakfast.

Eating

The best and most atmospheric neighbourhoods to dine in are the historic centre and Trastevere. There are also excellent choices in studenty San Lorenzo and once-working-class Testaccio. Watch out for overpriced tourist traps around Termini and the Vatican.

The Vatican

Fa-Bìo SANDWICHES €
(Map p642; 06 6452 5810; www.fa-bio.com; Via Germanico 43; sandwiches €5; 10am-5.30pm Mon-Fri, to 4pm Sat) Sandwiches, salads and smoothies are all prepared with speed, skill and organic ingredients at this tiny takeaway. Locals in the know come here to grab a quick lunchtime bite, and if you can squeeze in the door you'd do well to follow suit.

Hostaria Dino e Tony TRATTORIA €€
(Map p642; 06 3973 3284; Via Leone IV 60; meals €25-30; 12.30-3pm & 7-11pm, closed Sun & Aug; Ottaviano-San Pietro) An authentic old-school trattoria, Dino e Tony offers simple, no-frills

Roman cooking. Kick off with the monumental antipasto, a minor meal in its own right, before plunging into its signature *rigatoni all'amatriciana* (pasta tubes with pancetta, chilli and tomato sauce). No credit cards.

Historic Centre

★Forno Roscioli PIZZA, BAKERY €
(Map p650; Via dei Chiavari 34; pizza slices from €2, snacks from €1.50; ⏲7am-7.30pm Mon-Sat; 🚊Via Arenula) This is one of Rome's top bakeries, much loved by lunching locals who crowd here for luscious sliced pizza, prize pastries and hunger-sating *supplì* (fried rice balls). There's also a counter serving hot pastas and vegetable side dishes.

Forno di Campo de' Fiori PIZZA, BAKERY €
(Map p650; Campo de' Fiori 22; pizza slices about €3; ⏲7.30am-2.30pm & 4.45-8pm Mon-Sat; 🚌Corso Vittorio Emanuele II) This buzzing bakery on Campo de' Fiori does a roaring trade in *panini* and delicious fresh-from-the-oven *pizza al taglio* (by the slice). Aficionados swear by the *pizza bianca* ('white' pizza with olive oil, rosemary and salt), but the *panini* and *pizza rossa* ('red' pizza, with olive oil, tomato and oregano) taste plenty good, too.

★Casa Coppelle RISTORANTE €€
(Map p650; ☎06 6889 1707; www.casacoppelle.it; Piazza delle Coppelle 49; meals €35-40; ⏲12-3.30pm & 6.30-11.30pm; 🚌Corso del Rinascimento) Intimate and romantic, Casa Coppelle serves modern Italian and French-inspired food on a small piazza near the Pantheon. There's a full range of starters and pastas, but the real tours de force are the deliciously tender steaks and meat dishes. Service is quick and attentive. Book ahead.

Armando al Pantheon TRATTORIA €€
(Map p650; ☎06 6880 3034; www.armandoalpantheon.it; Salita dei Crescenzi 31; meals €40; ⏲12.30-3pm & 7-11pm Mon-Fri, 12.30-3pm Sat; 🚌Largo di Torre Argentina) A Roman institution, wood-panelled Armando is a rare find – a genuine family-run trattoria in the touristy Pantheon area. It's been on the go for more than 50 years and has served its fair share of celebs, but the focus remains fixed on traditional, earthy Roman food. Reservations recommended.

Al Gran Sasso TRATTORIA €€
(Map p642; ☎06 321 48 83; www.algransasso.com; Via di Ripetta 32; meals €35; ⏲12.30-2.30pm & 7.30-11.30pm Sun-Fri; MFlaminio) A top lunchtime spot, this is a classic, dyed-in-the-wool trattoria specialising in old-school country cooking. It's a relaxed place with a welcoming vibe, garish murals on the walls (strangely often a good sign) and tasty, value-for-money food. The fried dishes are excellent, or try one of the daily specials, chalked up on the board outside.

Trastevere

Trattoria degli Amici TRATTORIA €€
(Map p650; ☎06 580 60 33; www.trattoriadegliamici.org; Piazza Sant'Egidio 6; meals €35; ⏲12.30-3pm & 7.30-11.30pm; 🚌Viale di Trastevere, 🚊Viale di Trastevere) Boasting a prime location on a pretty piazza, this cheerful trattoria is staffed by volunteers and people with disabilities who welcome guests with a warmth not always apparent in this touristy neck of the woods. Grab a squareside table and dig into fried starters and fresh, well-prepared Italian classics.

ROME'S TOP GELATO

Fatamorgana (Map p642; Via Roma Libera 11, Piazza San Cosimato; cones & tubs from €2; ⏲noon-midnight summer, to 10.30pm winter; 🚌Viale di Trastevere, 🚊Viale di Trastevere) Creative flavours at one of Rome's new breed of gourmet gelaterie.

Il Gelato (Map p642; Viale Aventino 59; gelati €2-4.50; ⏲10am-midnight summer, 11am-9pm winter; 🚌Viale Aventino) An oupost of the gelato empire built by Rome's ice-cream king, Claudio Torcè.

Gelateria del Teatro (Map p650; Via dei Coronari 65; gelati from €2.50; ⏲11.30am-midnight; 🚌Corso del Rinascimento) Seasonal fruit and spicy chocolate flavours in the heart of the *centro storico* (historic centre).

San Crispino (Map p652; ☎06 679 39 24; Via della Panetteria 42; tubs from €2.70; ⏲11am-12.30am Mon-Thu & Sun, to 1.30am Fri & Sat; MBarberini) Near the Trevi Fountain; specialises in natural, seasonal flavours.

WORTH A TRIP

VIA APPIA ANTICA

Completed in 190 BC, the Appian Way connected Rome with Brindisi on Italy's southern Adriatic coast. It's now a much-sought-after address but it has a dark history – Spartacus and 6000 of his slave rebels were crucified here in 71 BC, and it was here that the early Christians buried their dead in the catacombs. See where at the **Catacombe di San Sebastiano** (☎06 785 03 50; www.catacombe.org; Via Appia Antica 136; adult/reduced €8/5; ⏰10am-5pm Mon-Sat, closed Dec; 🚌Via Appia Antica) or **Catacombe di San Callisto** (☎06 513 01 51; www.catacombe.roma.it; Via Appia Antica 110 & 126; adult/reduced €8/5; ⏰9am-noon & 2-5pm, closed Wed & Feb; 🚌Via Appia Antica).

To get to Via Appia Antica, take bus 660 from Colli Albani metro station (line A) or bus 118 from Piramide (line B).

Paris RISTORANTE €€€

(Map p650; ☎06 581 53 78; www.ristoranteparis.it; Piazza San Calisto 7a; meals €45-55; ⏰7.30-11pm Mon, 12.30-3pm & 7.30-11pm Tue-Sun; 🚌Viale di Trastevere, 🚋Viale di Trastevere) An old-school restaurant set in a 17th-century building with tables on a small piazza, Paris – named for its founder, not the French capital – is the best place outside the Ghetto to sample Roman-Jewish cuisine. Signature dishes include *gran fritto vegetale con baccalà* (deep-fried vegetables with salt cod) and *carciofi alla giudia* (fried artichoke).

Testaccio

Pizzeria Da Remo PIZZA €

(Map p642; ☎06 574 62 70; Piazza Santa Maria Liberatrice 44; pizzas from €5.50; ⏰7pm-1am Mon-Sat; 🚌Via Marmorata) For an authentic Roman experience, join the noisy crowds at this popular pizzeria. It's a spartan place, but the thin-crust Roman pizzas are the business, and there's a cheerful, boisterous vibe. To order, tick your choices on the sheet of paper slapped down by an overstretched waiter. Expect to queue after 8.30pm.

Flavio al Velavevodetto TRATTORIA €€

(Map p642; ☎06 574 41 94; www.ristorantevelavevodetto.it; Via di Monte Testaccio 97-99; meals €35; ⏰12.30-3pm & 7.45-11pm; 🚌Via Galvani) This welcoming eatery is the sort of place that gives Roman trattorias a good name. Housed in a rustic Pompeian-red villa, complete with covered courtyard and open-air terrace, it specialises in earthy, no-nonsense Roman food. Expect antipasti of cheeses and cured meats, huge helpings of homemade pastas, and uncomplicated meat dishes.

Termini & Esquiline

★**Panella l'Arte del Pane** BAKERY, CAFE €

(Map p642; ☎06 487 24 35; Via Merulana 54; snacks about €3.50; ⏰8am-11pm Mon-Thu, to midnight Fri & Sat, 8.30am-4pm Sun; Ⓜ Vittorio Emanuele) With a magnificent array of *pizza al taglio, arancini* (Sicilian rice balls), focaccia, fried croquettes and pastries, this smart bakery-cum-cafe is good any time of the day. The outside tables are ideal for a leisurely breakfast or chilled evening drink, or you can perch on a high stool and lunch on something from the sumptuous counter display.

Drinking & Nightlife

Much of the drinking action is in the *centro storico* (historic centre): Campo de' Fiori is popular with students and can get messy, while the area around Piazza Navona hosts a more upmarket scene. Over the river, Trastevere is another favored spot with dozens of bars and pubs.

Rome's clubbing scene is centred on Testaccio and the Ostiense area, although you'll also find places in Trastevere and the historic centre. Admission to clubs is often free, but drinks are expensive.

★**Circolo degli Artisti** CLUB

(☎06 7030 5684; www.circoloartisti.it; Via Casilina Vecchia 42; free-€15 depending on the event; ⏰depends on event; 🚌Ponte Casilino) The Circolo offers one of Rome's best nights out. Friday means Miss Loretta's disco night with '80s anthems and dance-floor classics, while Saturday sees Screamadelica unleash rock, retro and electro beats. Regular gigs are staged and, outside, there's a cool garden bar. To get here, take bus 105 from Termini.

★**Barnum Cafe** CAFE

(Map p650; www.barnumcafe.com; Via del Pellegrino 87; ⏰9am-10pm Mon, 8.30am-2am Tue-Sat; 📶; 🚌Corso Vittorio Emanuele II) A relaxed, friendly spot to check your email over a freshly squeezed orange juice or spend a pleasant hour reading a newspaper on one of the tatty old armchairs in the white bare-brick interior. Come evenings and the scene is cocktails, smooth tunes and dressed-down locals.

Caffè Sant'Eustachio CAFE
(Map p650; www.santeustachioilcaffe.it; Piazza Sant'Eustachio 82; 8.30am-1am Sun-Thu, to 1.30am Fri, to 2am Sat; Corso del Rinascimento) This small, unassuming cafe, generally three deep at the bar, is reckoned to serve the best coffee in town. Created by beating the first drops of espresso and several teaspoons of sugar into a frothy paste, then adding the rest of the coffee, it's superbly smooth and guaranteed to put some zing into your sightseeing.

Open Baladin BAR
(Map p650; www.openbaladinroma.it; Via degli Specchi 6; noon-2am; ; Via Arenula) A hip, shabby-chic lounge bar near Campo de' Fiori, Open Baladin is a leading light in Rome's thriving beer scene with more than 40 beers on tap and up to 100 bottled brews, many from artisanal microbreweries. There's also a decent food menu with *panini,* burgers and daily specials.

La Casa del Caffè Tazza d'Oro CAFE
(Map p650; www.tazzadorocoffeeshop.com; Via degli Orfani 84-86; 7am-8pm Mon-Sat, 10.30am-7.30pm Sun; Via del Corso) A busy, stand-up cafe with burnished 1940s fittings, this is one of Rome's best coffee houses. Its espresso hits the mark nicely and there's a range of delicious coffee concoctions, including a cooling *granita di caffè* (a crushed-ice coffee drink served with whipped cream).

Ma Che Siete Venuti a Fà PUB
(Map p650; www.football-pub.com; Via Benedetta 25; 11am-2am; Piazza Trilussa) Named after a football chant, which translates politely as 'What did you come here for?', this pint-sized Trastevere pub is a beer-buff's paradise, packing in a huge number of international craft beers, both bottled and on tap.

Freni e Frizioni BAR
(Map p650; 06 4549 7499; www.freniefrizioni.com; Via del Politeama 4-6; 6.30pm-2am; Piazza Trilussa) This cool Trastevere bar is housed in a former mechanic's workshop – hence its name, which means 'brakes and clutches'. It draws a young *spritz*-loving crowd that swells onto the small piazza outside to sip well-priced cocktails (from €7) and to enjoy the daily *aperitivo* (apéritif; 7pm to 10pm).

☆ Entertainment

Rome has a thriving cultural scene, with a year-round calendar of concerts, performances and festivals. A useful listings guide is *Trova Roma,* a free insert with *La Repubblica* newspaper every Thursday. Upcoming events are also listed on www.turismoroma.it and www.auditorium.com.

Auditorium Parco della Musica CONCERT VENUE
(06 8024 1281; www.auditorium.com; Viale Pietro de Coubertin 30; Viale Tiziano) Rome's main concert venue, this modernist complex combines architectural innovation with perfect acoustics. Designed by Renzo Piano, its three concert halls and 3000-seat open-air arena host everything from classical-music concerts to tango exhibitions, book readings and film screenings.

To get to the auditorium, take tram 2 from Piazzale Flaminio.

Alexanderplatz JAZZ
(Map p642; 06 3972 1867; www.alexanderplatzjazzclub.com; Via Ostia 9; 8.30pm-2am, concerts 9.45pm; M Ottaviano-San Pietro) Small and intimate, Rome's best-known jazz joint attracts top Italian and international performers and a respectful, cosmopolitan crowd. Book a table if you want to dine to the tunes.

Teatro dell'Opera di Roma OPERA
(Map p652; 06 481 70 03; www.operaroma.it; Piazza Beniamino Gigli; ballet €12-80, opera €17-160; 9am-5pm Tue-Sat, to 1.30pm Sun; M Repubblica) Rome's premier opera house boasts a plush and gilt interior, a Fascist 1920s exterior and an impressive history: it premiered Puccini's *Tosca* and Maria Callas once sang here. Opera and ballet performances are staged between September and June.

Big Mama BLUES
(Map p642; 06 581 25 51; www.bigmama.it; Vicolo di San Francesco a Ripa 18; 9pm-1.30am, shows 10.30pm, closed Jun-Sep; Viale di Trastevere, Viale di Trastevere) Head to this cramped Trastevere basement for a mellow night of Eternal City blues. A long-standing venue, it also stages jazz, funk, soul and R&B, as well as popular Italian cover bands.

WORTH A TRIP

DAY TRIPS FROM ROME

Ostia Antica

An easy train ride from Rome, Ostia Antica is one of Italy's most under appreciated archaeological sites. The ruins of ancient Rome's main seaport, the **Scavi Archeologici di Ostia Antica** (☎06 5635 0215; www.ostiaantica.beniculturali.it; Viale dei Romagnoli 717; adult/reduced €10/6; ⊙8.30am-6.15pm Tue-Sun summer, earlier closing winter), are spread out and you'll need a few hours to do them justice. Highlights include the **Terme di Nettuno** (Baths of Neptune) and steeply stacked **amphitheatre**.

To get to Ostia take the Ostia Lido train (25 minutes, half-hourly) from Stazione Porta San Paolo next to Piramide metro station. The journey is covered by standard public-transport tickets.

Tivoli

Tivoli, 30km east of Rome, is home to two Unesco-listed sites.

Five kilometres from Tivoli proper, **Villa Adriana** (☎0774 38 27 33; www.villaadriana.beniculturali.it; adult/reduced €8/4, incl temporary exhibition €11/7; ⊙9am-1hr before sunset) was Emperor Hadrian's sprawling 1st-century summer residence. One of the largest and most sumptuous villas in the Roman Empire, it was subsequently plundered for building materials, but enough remains to convey its magnificence.

Up in Tivoli's hilltop centre, the Renaissance **Villa d'Este** (☎0774 31 20 70; www.villadestetivoli.info; Piazza Trento; adult/reduced €8/4; ⊙8.30am-1hr before sunset Tue-Sun) is famous for its elaborate gardens and fountains.

Tivoli is accessible by Cotral bus (€2.30, 50 minutes, every 15 to 20 minutes) from Ponte Mammolo metro station. To get to Villa Adriana from Tivoli town centre, take CAT bus 4 or 4X (€1, 10 minutes, half-hourly) from Largo Garibaldi.

Shopping

Rome boasts the usual cast of flagship chain stores and glitzy designer outlets, but what makes shopping here fun is its legion of small, independent shops: family-run delis, small-label fashion boutiques, artisans' studios and neighbourhood markets.

Porta Portese Market MARKET
(Map p642; Piazza Porta Portese; ⊙6am-2pm Sun; 🚌Viale di Trastevere, 🚋Viale di Trastevere) To see another side of Rome, head to this mammoth flea market. With thousands of stalls selling everything from rare books and fell-off-a-lorry bikes to Peruvian shawls and MP3 players, it's crazily busy and a lot of fun. Keep your valuables safe and wear your haggling hat.

Information

DANGERS & ANNOYANCES

Rome is not a dangerous city, but petty theft can be a problem. Watch out for pickpockets around the big tourist sites, at Stazione Termini and on crowded public transport – the 64 Vatican bus is notorious.

INTERNET ACCESS

Free wi-fi is widely available in hostels, B&Bs and hotels; some also provide laptops/computers. Many bars and cafes now also offer wi-fi.

MEDICAL SERVICES

Ospedale Santo Spirito (☎06 6 83 51; Lungotevere in Sassia 1) Near the Vatican.

Pharmacy (☎06 488 00 19; Piazza dei Cinquecento 51; ⊙7am-11.30pm Mon-Fri, 8am-11.30pm Sat & Sun) There's also a pharmacy in Stazione Termini, next to platform 1, open 7.30am to 10pm daily.

TOURIST INFORMATION

For phone enquiries, the Comune di Roma runs a multilingual **tourist information line** (☎06 06 08; ⊙9am-9pm).

For information about the Vatican, contact the **Centro Servizi Pellegrini e Turisti** (Map p642; ☎06 6988 1662; St Peter's Sq; ⊙8.30am-6.15pm Mon-Sat).

There are tourist information points at **Fiumicino** (Terminal 3, International Arrivals; ⊙8am-7.30pm) and **Ciampino** (International Arrivals, baggage claim area; ⊙9am-6.30pm) airports, and at the following locations:

Castel Sant'Angelo Tourist Information (Map p642; Piazza Pia; ⊙9.30am-7.15pm)

Fori Imperiali Tourist Information (Map p648; Via dei Fori Imperiali; ⏲9.30am-7.15pm)

Piazza Navona Tourist Information (Map p650; ⏲9.30am-7pm) Near Piazza delle Cinque Lune.

Stazione Termini Tourist Information (Map p652; ⏲8am-7.45pm) In the hall adjacent to platform 24.

Trevi Fountain Tourist Information (Map p650; Via Marco Minghetti; ⏲9.30am-7pm) This tourist point is closer to Via del Corso than the fountain.

Via Nazionale Tourist Information (Map p652; Via Nazionale; ⏲9.30am-7.15pm)

USEFUL WEBSITES

060608 (www.060608.it) Comprehensive information on sights, upcoming events, transport etc.

Coop Culture (www.coopculture.it) Information and ticket booking for many major sights.

Roma Turismo (www.turismoroma.it) Rome's official tourist website, with extensive listings and up-to-date information.

ℹ Getting There & Away

AIR

Leonardo da Vinci (Fiumicino; ☎06 6 59 51; www.adr.it/fiumicino) Rome's main international airport, better known as Fiumicino, is 30km west of the city.

Ciampino (☎06 6 59 51; www.adr.it/ciampino) This smaller airport, 15km southeast of the centre, is the hub for low-cost carrier **Ryanair** (☎895 895 8989; www.ryanair.com).

BOAT

The nearest port to Rome is at Civitavecchia, about 80km to the north. Ferries sail here from Spain and Tunisia, as well as Sicily and Sardinia.

Book tickets at the Termini-based **Agenzia 365** (☎06 474 09 23; www.agenzie365.it; ⏲7am-9pm), at travel agents or online at www.traghettiweb.it. You can also buy directly at the port.

Half-hourly trains connect Civitavecchia and Roma Termini (€5 to €10, 40 minutes to 1¼ hours).

BUS

Long-distance national and international buses use the **Autostazione Tiburtina** (Piazzale Tiburtina; Ⓜ Tiburtina).

Get tickets at the Autostazione or at travel agencies.

Interbus (☎091 34 25 25; www.interbus.it) To/from Sicily.

Marozzi (☎080 579 01 11; www.marozzivt.it) To/from Sorrento, Bari and Puglia.

SENA (☎861 1991900; www.sena.it) To/from Siena, Bologna and Milan.

Sulga (☎800 099661; www.sulga.it) To/from Perugia, Assisi and Ravenna.

CAR & MOTORCYCLE

Rome is circled by the Grande Raccordo Anulare (GRA), to which all autostradas (motorways) connect, including the main A1 north–south artery, and the A12, which runs to Civitavecchia and Fiumicino airport.

Car hire is available at the airport and Stazione Termini.

TRAIN

Rome's main station is **Stazione Termini** (Piazza dei Cinquecento; Ⓜ Termini). It has regular connections to other European countries, all major Italian cities and many smaller towns.

Left luggage (Stazione Termini; 1st 5hr €6, 6-12hr per hour €0.90, 13hr & over per hour €0.40; ⏲6am-11pm) is on the lower-ground floor under platform 24.

Rome's other principal train stations are Stazione Tiburtina and Stazione Roma-Ostiense.

ℹ Getting Around

TO/FROM THE AIRPORTS

Fiumicino

The easiest way to get to/from Fiumicino is by train, but there are also bus services. The set taxi fare to the city centre is €48 (valid for up to four people with luggage).

FL1 Train (one way €8) Connects to Trastevere, Ostiense and Tiburtina stations, but not Termini. Departures from the airport every 15 minutes (hourly on Sunday and public holidays) between 5.57am and 10.42pm; from Tiburtina every 15 minutes between 5.46am and 7.31pm, then half-hourly to 10.02pm.

Leonardo Express Train (one way €14) Runs to/from Stazione Termini. Departures from the airport every 30 minutes between 6.38am and 11.08pm; from Termini between 5.50am and 10.50pm. Journey time is 30 minutes.

Ciampino

The best option from Ciampino is to take one of the regular bus services into the city centre. The set taxi fare to the city centre is €30.

SIT Bus (☎06 591 68 26; www.sitbusshuttle.com; from/to airport €4/6) Regular departures from the airport to Via Marsala outside Stazione Termini between 7.15am and 10.30pm, and from Termini between 4.30am and 9.30pm. Get tickets on the bus. Journey time is 45 minutes.

Terravision Bus (www.terravision.eu; one way €6 or €4 online) Twice-hourly departures to/from Via Marsala outside Stazione Termini. From the airport services are between 8.15am

A BRIEF HISTORY OF ITALY

Ancient Times

The Etruscans were the first major force to emerge on the Italian peninsula. By the 7th century BC they dominated central Italy, rivalled only by the Greeks from the southern colony of Magna Graecia. Both thrived until the emerging city of Rome began to flex its muscles.

Founded in the 8th century BC (legend has it by Romulus), Rome flourished, becoming a republic in 509 BC and growing to become the dominant force in the Western world. The end came for the republic when internal rivalries led to the murder of Julius Caesar in 44 BC and his great-nephew Octavian took power as Augustus, the first Roman emperor.

The empire's golden age came in the 2nd century AD, but a century later it was in decline. Diocletian split the empire into eastern and western halves, and when his successor, Constantine (the first Christian emperor), moved his court to Constantinople, Rome's days were numbered. In 476 the western empire fell to Germanic tribes.

City States & the Renaissance

The Middle Ages was a period of almost constant warfare as powerful city-states fought across central and northern Italy. Eventually Florence, Milan and Venice emerged as regional powers. Against this fractious background, art and culture thrived, culminating in an explosion of intellectual and artistic activity in 15th-century Florence – the Renaissance.

Unification

By the end of the 16th century most of Italy was in foreign hands – the Austrian Habsburgs in the north and the Spanish Bourbons in the south. Three centuries later, Napoleon's brief Italian interlude inspired the unification movement, the Risorgimento. With Count Cavour providing the political vision and Garibaldi the military muscle, the movement brought about the 1861 unification of Italy. Ten years later Rome was wrested from the papacy to become Italy's capital.

Birth of a Republic

Italy's brief Fascist interlude was a low point. Mussolini gained power in 1925 and in 1940 entered WWII on Germany's side. Defeat ensued and Il Duce was killed by partisans in April 1945. A year later, Italians voted in a national referendum to abolish the monarchy and create a constitutional republic.

The Modern Era

Italy's postwar era has been largely successful. A founding member of the European Economic Community, it survived a period of domestic terrorism in the 1970s and enjoyed sustained economic growth in the 1980s. But the 1990s heralded a period of crisis as corruption scandals rocked the nation, paving the way for billionaire media mogul Silvio Berlusconi to enter the political arena.

Recent economic crises have hit Italy hard and since Berlusconi was forced from office in 2011, successive prime ministers have struggled to cope with the country's sluggish economy. At the time of writing, centre-left PM Matteo Renzi was in the hot seat, battling to face down the increasingly militant unions and to calm social tensions.

and 12.15am; from Via Marsala between 4.30am and 9.20pm. Buy tickets at Terracafè in front of the Via Marsala bus stop. Journey time is 40 minutes.

PUBLIC TRANSPORT

Rome's public transport system includes buses, trams, metro and a suburban train network.

Tickets are valid for all forms of public transport, except for routes to Fiumicino airport. Buy tickets at *tabaccherie* (tobacconists), news-stands or vending machines; they come in various forms:

Single (BIT; €1.50) Valid for 100 minutes, but only one metro journey.

Daily (BIG; €6)

Three-day (BTI; €16.50)
Weekly (CIS; €24)

Bus

Buses and trams are run by **ATAC** (☎06 57 00 03; www.atac.roma.it).

The **main bus station** (Map p652) is on Piazza dei Cinquecento, where there's an **information booth** (Map p652; ⏰7.30am-8pm). Other important hubs are Largo di Torre Argentina and Piazza Venezia.

Buses generally run from about 5.30am until midnight, with limited services throughout the night.

Metro

Rome has two principal metro lines, A (orange) and B (blue), which cross at Termini.

Trains run between 5.30am and 11.30pm (1.30am on Friday and Saturday).

TAXI

Official licensed taxis are white with an ID number and *Roma capitale* on the sides.

Always go with the metered fare, never an arranged price (apart from the set fares to/from the airports). Official rates are posted in taxis.

You can hail a taxi, but it's often easier to phone for one or wait at a taxi rank. There are ranks at the airports, Stazione Termini, Largo di Torre Argentina, Piazza della Repubblica, the Colosseum, and Piazza del Risorgimento near the Vatican Museums.

La Capitale (☎06 49 94)
Radio Taxi (☎06 35 70; www.3570.it)
Samarcanda (☎06 55 51; www.samarcanda.it)

NORTHERN ITALY

Italy's well-heeled north is a fascinating area of historical wealth and natural diversity. Bordered by the northern Alps and boasting some of the country's most spectacular coastline, it also encompasses Italy's largest lowland area, the fertile Po Valley plain. Glacial lakes in the far north offer stunning scenery, while cities like Venice, Milan and Turin harbour artistic treasures and lively cultural scenes.

Genoa

POP 597,000

Genoa (Genova) is an absorbing city of aristocratic *palazzi*, dark, malodorous alleyways, Gothic architecture and industrial sprawl. Formerly a powerful maritime republic known as La Superba (Christopher Columbus was born here in 1451), Genoa is still an important transport hub, with ferry links to destinations across the Med and train links to the Cinque Terre.

Sights

Musei di Strada Nuova MUSEUM
(www.museidigenova.it; Via Garibaldi; combined ticket adult/reduced €9/7; ⏰9am-7pm Tue-Fri, 10am-7pm Sat & Sun) Skirting the northern edge of what was once the city limits, pedestrianised Via Garibaldi (formerly called the Strada Nuova) was planned by Galeazzo Alessi in the 16th century. It quickly became the city's most sought-after quarter, lined with the palaces of Genoa's wealthiest citizens. Three of these *palazzi* – Rosso, Bianco and Doria-Tursi – today comprise the Musei di Strada Nuova. Between them, they hold the city's finest collection of old masters.

Cattedrale di San Lorenzo CATHEDRAL
(Piazza San Lorenzo; ⏰8am-noon & 3-7pm) Genoa's zebra-striped Gothic-Romanesque cathedral owes its continued existence to the poor quality of a British WWII bomb that failed to ignite here in 1941; it still sits on the right side of the nave like an innocuous museum piece.

The cathedral, fronted by three arched portals, twisting columns and crouching lions, was first consecrated in 1118. The two bell towers and cupola were added later in the 16th century.

Sleeping & Eating

★**Hotel Cairoli** HOTEL €
(☎010 246 14 54; www.hotelcairoligenova.com; Via Cairoli 14/4; d €65-120, tr €85-130, q €90-150; ❄@🛜) For five-star service at three-star prices, book at this artful hideaway. Rooms, on the 3rd floor of a towering *palazzo*, are themed on modern artists and feature works inspired by the likes of Mondrian, Dorazio and Alexander Calder. Add in a library, chill-out area, internet point, small gym and terrace, and you have the ideal bolt-hole.

B&B Palazzo Morali B&B €
(☎010 246 70 27; www.palazzomorali.com; Piazza della Raibetta; s/d €75/85; ❄🛜) Stay in rarefied splendour at this antique-clad B&B near the Porto Antico. On the top two floors of a lofty building, its palatial rooms (some with shared

bathroom) are embellished with gold-leafed four-poster beds, gilt-framed mirrors and Genoese art.

La Cremeria delle Erbe GELATERIA €

(Piazza delle Erbe 15-17; cones from €2; ⏲11am-1am Mon-Thu & Sun, to 2am Fri & Sat) A contender for the 'best ice cream in Genoa' mantle. On agreeably shabby Piazza delle Erbe, this gelateria snares late-night diners and boozers with its array of lush, creamy flavours and generous scoops.

★**Trattoria della Raibetta** TRATTORIA €€

(☎010 246 88 77; www.trattoriadellaraibetta.it; Vico Caprettari 10-12; meals €35; ⏲noon-2.30pm & 7.30-11pm Tue-Sun) The most authentic Genoese food can be found in the family-run joints hidden in the warren of streets near the cathedral. This, a snug trattoria with a low brick-vaulted ceiling, serves regional classics such as *trofiette al pesto* alongside excellent fresh seafood.

ℹ Information

There are several tourist offices across town, including at the **airport** (☎010 601 52 47; arrivals hall; ⏲9am-6.20pm summer, to 5.50pm winter) and **Via Garibaldi** (☎010 557 29 03; www.visitgenoa.it; Via Garibaldi 12r; ⏲9am-6.20pm).

ℹ Getting There & Around

AIR

Genoa's **Cristoforo Colombo Airport** (☎010 6 01 51; www.airport.genova.it) is 6km west of the city. To get to/from it, the **Volabus** (www.amt.genova.it; one way €6) shuttle connects with Stazione Brignole and Stazione Principe. Buy tickets on board.

BOAT

Ferries sail to/from Spain, Sicily, Sardinia, Corsica and Tunisia from the **Terminal Traghetti** (Ferry Terminal; Via Milano 51), west of the city centre.

Grandi Navi Veloci (GNV; ☎010 209 45 91; www.gnv.it) Ferries to Sardinia (Porto Torres, €74) and Sicily (Palermo, €90). Also to Barcelona (Spain), Tunis (Tunisia) and Tangier (Morocco).

Moby Lines (☎199 303040; www.mobylines.it) Ferries year-round to Corsica (Bastia, €39) and Sardinia (Olbia, €73).

Tirrenia (☎89 21 23; www.tirrenia.it) To/from Sardinia (Porto Torres €60; Olbia from €41; Arbatax €91).

BUS

Buses to international and regional destinations depart from Piazza della Vittoria, south of Stazione Brignole. Book tickets at **Geotravels** (Piazza della Vittoria 57; ⏲9am-12.30pm & 3-7pm Mon-Fri, 9am-noon Sat).

Local buses are run by **AMT** (www.amt.genova.it). Tickets, which are also valid on the metro, cost €1.50.

TRAIN

Genoa has two main stations: Stazione Brignole and Stazione Principe.

From Principe Trains run to Turin (€9 to €16, two hours, at least hourly), Milan (€10.30 to €16.50, 1¾ hours, hourly), Pisa (€9 to €11, two to 3½ hours, up to 15 daily) and Rome (€25 to €48, 4½ to five hours, nine daily).

From Brignole Trains serve Riomaggiore (€7, 1½ to two hours, 18 daily) and the other Cinque Terre villages.

Cinque Terre

Liguria's eastern Riviera boasts some of Italy's most dramatic coastline, the highlight of which is the Unesco-listed **Parco Nazionale delle Cinque Terre** (Cinque Terre National Park) just west of La Spezia. Running for 18km, this awesome stretch of plunging cliffs and vine-covered hills is named after its five tiny villages: Riomaggiore, Manarola, Corniglia, Vernazza and Monterosso.

Activities

The Cinque Terre offers excellent hiking. The best known path is the 12km **Sentiero Azzurro** (Blue Trail), a one-time mule trail that links all five villages. To walk it (or any of the national park's trails) you'll need a **Cinque Terre Trekking Card** (1/2 days €7.50/14.50), or a **Cinque Terre Treno Card** (1/2 days €12/23), which also provides unlimited train travel between La Spezia and the five villages. Both cards are available at all park offices.

At the time of writing the Sentiero Azzurro was closed between Riomaggiore and Vernazza, after it sustained severe damage during heavy rainfall in 2011 and a rockfall in September 2012. Authorities hoped to have it re-opened by mid-2015, but check www.parconazionale5terre.it for the current situation.

The Sentiero Azzurro is just one of a network of footpaths and cycle trails that crisscross the park; details are available from the park offices.

If water sports are more your thing, you can hire snorkelling gear and kayaks at the **Diving Center 5 Terre** (www.5terrediving.it; Via San Giacomo) in Riomaggiore.

Information

There are park information offices at the train stations of all five villages and also at La Spezia station. They generally open 8am to 8pm daily in summer, 9am to 5pm winter.

Online information is available at www.cinqueterre.it and www.cinqueterre.com.

Getting There & Away

BOAT

Between July and September, **Golfo Paradiso** (☎0185 77 20 91; www.golfoparadiso.it) runs boats from Genoa's Porto Antico to Vernazza and Monterosso (€18 one way, €33 return).

From late March to October, the **Consorzio Marittimo Turistico 5 Terre** (☎0187 73 29 87; www.navigazionegolfodeipoeti.it) operates four daily services between La Spezia and Riomaggiore, Manarola, Vernazza and Monterosso. One-way tickets cost €12 to Riomaggiore or Manarola, €16 to Vernazza or Monterosso. Return trips are covered by a daily ticket (weekdays/weekends €25/27).

TRAIN

From Genoa Brignole, trains run to Riomaggiore (€6.80, 1½ to two hours, 18 daily), stopping at each of the villages.

From La Spezia, one to three trains an hour run up the coast between 4.30am and 11.46pm. If you're using this route and want to stop at all the villages, get the Cinque Terre Treno Card.

Monterosso

The largest and most developed of the villages, Monterosso boasts the coast's only sandy beach, as well as a wealth of eating and accommodation options.

Sleeping & Eating

★Hotel Pasquale HOTEL €€
(☎0187 81 74 77; www.hotelpasquale.it; Via Fegina 4; s €80-145, d €135-190, tr €180-250; ⊙Mar-mid-Nov; ❄☜) Offering soothing views and stylish, modern guest rooms, this friendly seafront hotel is built into Monterosso's medieval sea walls. To find it, exit the train station and go left through the tunnel towards the *centro storico*.

Ristorante Belvedere SEAFOOD €€
(☎0187 81 70 33; www.ristorante-belvedere.it; Piazza Garibaldi 38; meals €30; ⊙noon-3pm & 6.15-10.30pm Wed-Mon) With tables overlooking the beach, this unpretentious seafood restaurant is a good place to try the local bounty. Start with *penne con scampi* (pasta tubes with scampi) before diving into a rich *zuppa di pesce* (fish soup).

Vernazza

Perhaps the most attractive of the five villages, Vernazza overlooks a small, picturesque harbour.

From near the harbour, a steep, narrow staircase leads up to the **Castello Doria** (admission €1.50; ⊙10am-7pm), the oldest surviving fortification in the Cinque Terre. Dating to around 1000, it's now largely ruined except for the circular tower in the centre of the esplanade, but the castle is well worth a visit for the superb views it commands.

To spend a romantic night in Vernazza, **L'Eremo sul Mare** (☎339 268 56 17; www.eremosulmare.com; d €70-100; ❄☜) is a charming cliffside villa with just three rooms and a lovely panoramic terrace. It's a 15-minute walk from the village; follow the Sentiero Azzurro towards Corniglia.

Corniglia

Corniglia, the only village with no direct sea access, sits atop a 1000m-high rocky promontory surrounded by vineyards. To reach it from the train station, either take on the 365-step staircase or hop on a bus (€2, or free with a Cinque Terre card).

Once up in the village, you can enjoy dazzling 180-degree sea views from the **Belvedere di Santa Maria**, a heart-stopping lookout point. To find it, follow Via Fieschi through the village until you eventually reach the clifftop balcony.

Manarola

One of the busiest of the villages, Manarola tumbles down to the sea in a helter-skelter of pastel-coloured buildings, cafes, trattorias and restaurants.

Sleeping & Eating

Ostello 5 Terre HOSTEL €
(☎0187 92 00 39; www.hostel5terre.com; Via Riccobaldi 21; dm €21-24, d €55-65, f €92-132; @☜)

Manarola's hostel sits at the top of the village next to the Chiesa di San Lorenzo. Open for 11 months of the year (it closes mid-January to mid-February), it has single-sex, six-bed dorms, each with their own bathroom, and several double and family rooms.

Hotel Ca' d'Andrean HOTEL €€
(☎0187 92 00 40; www.cadandrean.it; Via Doscovolo 101; s €80-90, d €90-150; ⊙Mar–mid-Nov; ❄📶) An excellent family-run hotel in the upper part of Manarola. Rooms are big and cool, with white-grey tones and designer bathrooms, and some have private terraces. Breakfast (€7) is optional. No credit cards.

Il Porticciolo SEAFOOD €€
(☎0187 92 00 83; www.ilporticciolo5terre.it; Via Renato Birolli 92; meals €30; ⊙11.30am-11pm) One of several restaurants lining the main route down to the harbour, this is a popular spot for an alfresco seafood feast. Expect seaside bustle and a fishy menu featuring classic crowd-pleasers such as spaghetti with mussels and crispy fried squid.

Riomaggiore

The Cinque Terre's largest and easternmost village, Riomaggiore acts as the unofficial HQ.

For a taste of classic seafood and local wine, search out **Dau Cila** (☎0187 76 00 32; www.ristorantedaucila.com; Via San Giacomo 65; meals €40; ⊙8am-2am Mar-Oct), a smart restaurant-cum-wine bar perched within pebble-lobbing distance of Riomaggiore's twee harbour.

Turin

POP 902,200

With its regal *palazzi*, baroque piazzas, cafes and world-class museums, the dynamic, cultured city of Turin (Torino) is a far cry from the dour industrial centre it's often portrayed as. For centuries it was the seat of the royal Savoy family, and between 1861 and 1864, it was Italy's first post-unification capital. More recently, it hosted the 2006 Winter Olympics and was European Capital of Design in 2008.

Sights

★Mole Antonelliana LANDMARK
(Via Montebello 20; Panoramic Lift adult/reduced €7/5, incl Museo €14/11; ⊙Panoramic Lift 10am-8pm Tue-Fri & Sun, to 11pm Sat) The symbol of Turin, this 167m tower with its distinctive aluminium spire appears on the Italian two-cent coin. It was originally intended as a synagogue when construction began in 1862, but was never used as a place of worship, and nowadays houses the Museo Nazionale del Cinema.

For dazzling 360-degree views, take the **Panoramic Lift** up to the 85m-high outdoor viewing deck.

Museo Nazionale del Cinema MUSEUM
(www.museocinema.it; Via Montebello 20; adult/reduced €10/8, incl Panoramic Lift €14/11; ⊙9am-8pm Tue-Fri & Sun, to 11pm Sat) Housed in the Mole Antonelliana, this enjoyable museum takes you on a fantastic tour through cinematic history. Memorabilia on display includes Marilyn Monroe's black lace bustier, Peter O'Toole's robe from *Lawrence of Arabia* and the coffin used by Bela Lugosi's Dracula. At the heart of the museum, the vast Temple Hall is surrounded by 10 interactive 'chapels' devoted to various film genres.

Museo Egizio MUSEUM
(Egyptian Museum; www.museoegizio.it; Via Accademia delle Scienze 6; adult/reduced €7.50/3.50; ⊙8.30am-7.30pm Tue-Sun) Opened in 1824, this legendary museum in the Palazzo dell'Accademia delle Scienze houses the most important collection of Egyptian treasure outside Cairo. Two of its many highlights include a statue of Ramses II (one of the world's most important pieces of Egyptian art) and over 500 items found in 1906 in the tomb of royal architect Kha and his wife Merit (from 1400 BC).

The museum underwent a major overhaul and work was completed in 2015.

Piazza Castello PIAZZA
Turin's central square shelters a wealth of museums, theatres and cafes. Essentially baroque, it was laid out from the 14th century to serve as the seat of the Savoy dynasty. Dominating it is the part-medieval part-baroque **Palazzo Madama**, the original seat of the Italian parliament. To the north, statues of Castor and Pollux guard the entrance to **Palazzo Reale**, the royal palace built for Carlo Emanuele II in the mid-1600s.

Cattedrale di San Giovanni Battista CATHEDRAL
(Piazza San Giovanni; ⊙8am-noon & 3-7pm) Turin's 15th-century cathedral houses the famous

Shroud of Turin *(Sindone),* supposedly the cloth used to wrap the crucified Christ. A copy is on permanent display in front of the altar, while the real thing is kept in a vacuum-sealed box and rarely revealed.

Sleeping

Tomato Backpackers Hotel HOSTEL €
(☎011 020 94 00; www.tomato.to.it; Via Pellico 11; dm/s/d/tr €25/38/56/72;) This eco-friendly hostel in the trendy San Salvario area east of the train station is one of the few central places that caters to budget travellers. And it does so with style, offering pristine dorms, smart private rooms, a kitchen and a communal lounge. There's a relaxed, inclusive vibe and a long list of extras including laundry facilities and left luggage.

★**Art Hotel Boston** BOUTIQUE HOTEL €€€
(☎011 50 03 59; www.hotelbostontorino.it; Via Massena 70; s €80-150, d €110-400;) The Boston's austere classical facade gives no inkling of the artistic interiors that await inside. Public areas are filled with original works by Warhol, Lichtenstein and Aldo Mondino, while individually styled guest rooms are themed on subjects as diverse as Lavazza coffee, Ayrton Senna and Pablo Picasso.

Eating

Grom GELATERIA €
(www.grom.it; Piazza Pietro Paleocapa 1/D; cones & cups from €2.50; ⊙11am-11pm Sun-Thu, to 1am Fri & Sat summer, to midnight Fri & Sat winter) At the vanguard of the gourmet gelato trend that has spread across Italy in recent years, the Grom chain founded its first store here in 2003. Long queues testify to its success and the quality of the ice cream.

L'Hamburgheria di Eataly BURGERS €
(Piazza Solferino 16a; meals €10-15; ⊙noon-midnight) This upmarket burger bar adds a dash of style to fast-food dining with its smart brick-and-steel interior and select menu. House speciality are the gourmet burgers, all made from locally sourced Piedmontese beef, but you can also grab a hot dog or kebab, as well as an Italian craft beer to quench your thirst.

La Cantinella RISTORANTE, PIZZA €€
(☎011 819 33 11; www.lacantinella-restaurant.com; Corso Moncalieri 3/A; meals €40; ⊙7.30pm-1am) In-the-know locals flock to this intimate restaurant over the river from Piazza Vittorio Veneto. There's a full menu of pastas and pizzas, but the star performers are the steaks and spitting-hot grilled meats. Round things off with a delectably creamy chestnut mousse.

Drinking & Nightlife

Early evening is the time to make for one of the city's cafes to enjoy an *apericena*, Turin's answer to an aperitif. Order a drink (usually €5 to €10) and tuck into the sumptuous buffet included in the price. Popular precincts include Piazza Emanuele Filiberto, Piazza Savoia and Piazza Vittorio Veneto.

Information

Piazza Carlo Felice Tourist Office (☎011 53 51 81; Piazza Carlo Felice; ⊙9am-6pm) On the piazza in front of Stazione Porta Nuova.

Piazza Castello Tourist Office (☎011 53 51 81; www.turismotorino.org; Piazza Castello; ⊙9am-6pm) Central and multilingual.

Getting There & Around

From Turin's **Torino Airport** (www.turin-airport.com), 16km northwest of the city centre, airlines fly to Italy's main airports and destinations across Europe.

Sadem (www.sadem.it; one way €6.50, on bus €7.50) runs an airport shuttle (40 minutes, half-hourly) to/from Porta Nuova train station.

Trains connect with Milan (€12.20 to €24, one to two hours, up to 30 daily), Florence (€52, three hours, nine daily), Genoa (€12.20 to €19, two hours, up to 15 daily) and Rome (€72, 4¼ hours, 14 daily).

Milan

POP 1.32 MILLION

Few Italian cities polarise opinion like Milan, Italy's financial and fashion capital. Some people love the cosmopolitan, can-do atmosphere, the vibrant cultural scene and sophisticated shopping; others grumble that it's dirty, ugly and expensive. Certainly, it lacks the picture-postcard beauty of many Italian towns, but in among the urban hustle are some truly great sights: Leonardo da Vinci's *Last Supper,* the immense Duomo and La Scala opera house.

Sights

★**Duomo** CATHEDRAL
(www.duomomilano.it; Piazza del Duomo; roof terraces adult/reduced stairs €7/3.50, lift €12/6, Battistero di San Giovanni €6/4; ⊙Duomo 7am-6.40pm,

Central Milan

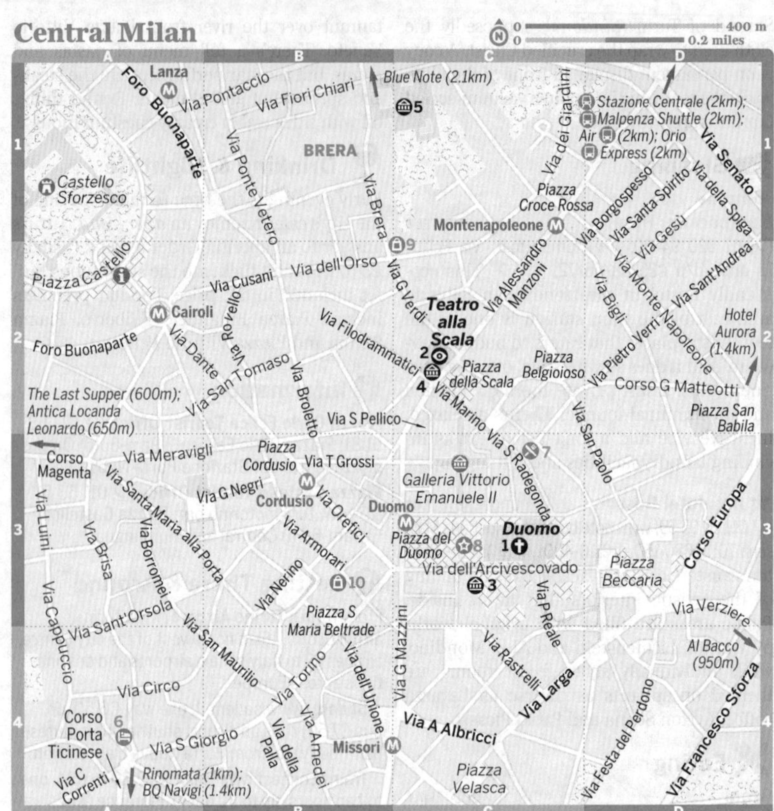

Central Milan

Top Sights

1 Duomo ... C3
2 Teatro alla Scala ... C2

Sights

3 Museo del Novecento ... C3
4 Museo Teatrale alla Scala ... C2
5 Pinacoteca di Brera ... C1

Sleeping

6 Ostello Bello ... A4

Eating

7 Luini ... C3

Entertainment

Teatro alla Scala ... (see 2)
8 Teatro alla Scala Box Office ... C3

Shopping

9 Cavalli e Nastri ... C2
10 Peck ... B3

roof terraces 9am-6.30pm, Battistero di San Giovanni 10am-6pm Tue-Sun; Ⓜ Duomo) A vision in pink Candoglia marble, Milan's extravagant Gothic cathedral aptly reflects the city's creativity and ambition. Commissioned in 1387 and finished nearly 600 years later, it boasts a pearly white facade adorned with 135 spires and 3200 statues, and a vast interior punctuated by the largest stained-glass windows in Christendom. Underground, you can see the remains of the saintly Carlo Borromeo in the crypt and explore ancient ruins in the Battistero di San Giovanni. Up top, the spired roof terraces command stunning views.

Museo del Novecento GALLERY
(☎02 8844 4061; www.museodelnovecento.org; Piazza del Duomo 12; adult/reduced €5/3; ⏱2.30-7.30pm Mon, 9.30am-7.30pm Tue, Wed, Fri & Sun, to 10.30pm Thu & Sat; Ⓜ Duomo) Overlooking Piazza del Duomo, with fabulous views of the cathedral, is Mussolini's **Arengario**, from where he would harangue huge crowds in his heyday. Now it houses Milan's museum of 20th-century art. Built around a futuristic spiral ramp (an ode to the Guggenheim), the lower floors are cramped, but the heady collection, which includes the likes of Umberto Boccioni, Campigli, de Chirico and Marinetti, more than distracts.

★**Teatro alla Scala** THEATRE
(La Scala; www.teatroallascala.org; Via Filodrammatici 2; Ⓜ Cordusio, Duomo) Giuseppe Piermarini's grand 2800-seat theatre was inaugurated in 1778 with Antonio Salieri's *Europa Riconosciuta*, replacing the previous theatre, which burnt down in a fire after a carnival gala. Costs were covered by the sale of *palchi* (private boxes), of which there are six gilt-and-crimson tiers.

In the theatre's **museum** (La Scala Museum; ☎02 8879 7473; Largo Ghiringhelli 1; admission €6; ⏱9am-12.30pm & 1.30-5.30pm), harlequin costumes and a spinet inscribed with the command 'Inexpert hand, touch me not!' hint at centuries of Milanese musical drama.

★**The Last Supper** ARTWORK
(Il Cenacolo Vinciano; ☎02 9280 0360; www.vivaticket.it; Piazza Santa Maria delle Grazie 2; adult/reduced €6.50/3.25, plus booking fee €1.50; ⏱8.15am-7pm Tue-Sun) Milan's most famous mural, Leonardo da Vinci's *The Last Supper* is hidden away on a wall of the refectory adjoining the **Basilica di Santa Maria delle Grazie**. Depicting Christ and his disciples at the dramatic moment when Christ reveals he's aware of his betrayal, it's a masterful psychological study and one of the world's most iconic images.

To see it you must book in advance or sign up for a guided city tour.

Pinacoteca di Brera GALLERY
(☎02 7226 3264; www.brera.beniculturali.it; Via Brera 28; adult/reduced €9/6; ⏱8.30am-7.15pm Tue-Thu, Sat & Sun, to 9.15pm Fri; Ⓜ Lanza) Located upstairs from the centuries-old Accademia di Belle Arti (still one of Italy's most prestigious art schools), this gallery houses Milan's most impressive collection of old masters, much of the bounty 'lifted' from Venice by Napoleon. Rembrandt, Goya and Van Dyck all have a place in the collection, but you're here to see the Italians: Titian, Tintoretto, glorious Veronese, groundbreaking Mantegna, the Bellini brothers and a Caravaggio.

Sleeping

Ostello Bello HOSTEL €
(☎02 3658 2720; www.ostellobello.com; Via Medici 4; dm €28-35, d/tr/q €98/130/160; ❄📶; 🚋Via Torino) A breath of fresh air in Milan's stiffly suited centre, this is the best hostel in town. Entrance is through its lively bar-cafe, open to nonguests, where you're welcomed with a smile and complimentary drink. Beds are in mixed dorms or spotless private rooms, and there's a kitchen, small terrace, and basement lounge equipped with guitars, board games and table football.

Hotel Aurora HOTEL €€
(☎02 204 79 60; www.hotelauroramilano.com; Corso Buenos Aires 18; s €60-135, d €80-140; ❄📶; Ⓜ Porta Venezia) Clean, quiet rooms in a strategic location await at this modest two-star hotel. The decor is business-like and fairly unforgettable, but the rates compare well with other places in town and rooms are comfortable enough. No breakfast.

Antica Locanda Leonardo HOTEL €€€
(☎02 4801 4197; www.anticalocandaleonardo.com; Corso Magenta 78; s €95-170, d €158-395; ❄@📶; Ⓜ Conciliazione) A charmer hidden in a 19th-century residence near Leonardo's *Last Supper*. Rooms exude homey comfort, from the period furniture and parquet floors to the plush drapes, while breakfast is served in the small, scented garden.

Eating & Drinking

Local specialities include *risotto alla milanese* (saffron-infused risotto cooked in bone-marrow stock) and *cotoletta alla milanese* (breaded veal cutlet).

Luini FAST FOOD €
(www.luini.it; Via Santa Radegonda 16; panzerotti €2.70; ⏱10am-3pm Mon, to 8pm Tue-Sun; Ⓜ Duomo) This historic joint is the go-to place for *panzerotti*, delicious pizza-dough parcels stuffed with a combination of mozzarella, spinach, tomato, ham or spicy salami, and then fried or baked in a wood-fired oven.

Rinomata GELATERIA €
(Ripa di Porta Ticinese; cones & tubs €2.50-4.50; ⏲noon-2am; Ⓜ Porta Genova) If dining in Navigli, skip dessert and grab an ice cream from this hole-in-the-wall gelateria. Its fabulous interior features old-fashioned fridges and glass-fronted cabinets filled with cones – and the gelato is good, too.

Al Bacco ITALIAN €€
(☎02 5412 1637; Via Marcona 1; meals €35; ⏲12.30-2.30pm & 7.30-11pm Mon-Fri, 7pm-1am Sat; 🚊Corso XXII Marzo) Search out this cosy, Slow Food–recommended restaurant east of the city centre – a block north of Corso XXII Marzo – for lovingly prepared Milanese classics. Try *tortino di riso giallo allo zafferano* (yellow rice tart with saffron) followed by *cotoletta alla milanese* (breaded veal cutlet).

BQ Navigli BAR
(Birra Artigianale di Qualità; Via Alzaia Naviglio Grande 44; ⏲6pm-2am; Ⓜ Porta Genova) This Navigli canalside bar has a fine selection of craft beers, ranging from light lagers to robust hop-heavy bitters. Soak it all up with *panini* and *piadine* (stuffed pitta breads).

☆ Entertainment

Teatro alla Scala OPERA
(☎02 8 87 91; www.teatroallascala.org; Piazza della Scala; ballet €11-127, opera €13-210; Ⓜ Duomo) La Scala's opera season runs from early December through July, but you can see theatre, ballet and concerts year-round, except for August. Tickets can be bought online or by phone up to two months before the performance, and then from the central **box office** (Galleria del Sagrato, Piazza del Duomo; ⏲noon-6pm; Ⓜ Duomo).

Blue Note JAZZ
(☎02 6901 6888; www.bluenotemilano.com; Via Borsieri 37; tickets €22-40; ⏲concerts 9pm & 11.30pm; Ⓜ Zara, Garibaldi) Top-class jazz acts from around the world perform here; get tickets by phone, online or at the door from 7.30pm. It also does a popular easy-listening Sunday brunch (€35 per adult, or €70 for two adults and two children under 12).

FOOTBALL IN MILAN

Milan is home to two of Italy's most successful *calcio* (football) teams: AC Milan and Internazionale (Inter). During the season (September to May), the two clubs play on alternate Sundays at the **Stadio Giuseppe Meazza** (Via Piccolomini 5; Ⓜ Lotto), aka the San Siro. Match tickets (from €19) are available from branches of Banca Intesa (AC Milan) and Banca Popolare di Milano (Inter).

To get to the stadium on match days, take the free shuttle bus from the Lotto (MM1) metro station.

Shopping

The Quadrilatero d'Oro (the area around Via della Spiga, Via Sant'Andrea, Via Monte Napoleone and Via Alessandro Manzoni) is the place to go for big-name designer brands. Hip younger labels can be found in Brera and Corso Magenta, while Corso Porta Ticenese and Navigli are home to Milan's street scene. Chain stores line Corso Vercelli and Corso Buenos Aires.

Peck FOOD, WINE
(☎02 802 31 61; www.peck.it; Via Spadari 9; ⏲3.30-7.30pm Mon, 9.30am-7.30pm Tue-Sat; Ⓜ Duomo) Milan's historic deli is smaller than its reputation suggests, but what it lacks in space it makes up for in variety, with a mind-boggling selection of *parmigiano reggiano* (Parmesan) and myriad other treasures: chocolates, pralines, pastries, freshly made gelato, seafood, caviar, pâtés, fruit and vegetables, truffle products, olive oils and balsamic vinegars.

Cavalli e Nastri CLOTHING
(☎02 7200 0449; www.cavallienastri.com; Via Brera 2; ⏲3.30-7.30pm Mon, 10.30am-7.30pm Tue-Sat; Ⓜ Montenapoleone) This gorgeously colourful Brera shop is known for its vintage clothes and accessories. It specialises in lovingly curated frocks, bags, jewellery and even shoes, sourced from early and mid-20th-century Italian fashion houses, and priced accordingly.

ℹ Information

Useful websites include www.turismo.milano.it and www.hellomilano.it.

24-Hour Pharmacy (☎02 669 09 35; Galleria delle Partenze, Stazione Centrale; Ⓜ Centrale FS) Located on 1st floor of the central station.

Milan Tourist Office (☎02 7740 4343; www.visitamilano.it; Piazza Castello 1; ⏲9am-6pm Mon-Fri, 9am-1.30pm & 2-6pm Sat, to 5pm Sun; Ⓜ Cairoli)

Stazione Centrale Tourist Office (☎02 7740 4318; ⏲9am-5pm Mon-Fri, to 12.30pm Sat &

Sun; Ⓜ Centrale FS) On the 2nd floor by the side of platform 21.

Getting There & Away

AIR

Linate Airport (☎ 02 23 23 23; www.milanolinate-airport.com) Located 7km east of the city centre; domestic and some European flights.

Malpensa Airport (☎ 02 23 23 23; www.milanomalpensa-airport.com) About 50km northwest of the city; northern Italy's main international airport

Orio al Serio (☎ 035 32 63 23; www.sacbo.it) Bergamo airport receives regular European flights and has direct transport links to Milan.

TRAIN

Regular trains depart Stazione Centrale for Venice (€37.50, 2½ hours), Bologna (€40, one hour), Florence (€50, 1¾ hours), Rome (€86, three hours) and other Italian and European cities.

Most regional trains also stop at Stazione Nord in Piazzale Cadorna.

Getting Around

TO/FROM THE AIRPORT

Malpensa

Malpensa Shuttle (☎ 02 5858 3185; www.malpensashuttle.it; one way €10) Coaches run to/from Piazza Luigi di Savoia next to Stazione Centrale. Departures run from the station every 20 minutes between 3.45am and 12.30am; from the airport 5am to 12.30am. Journey time 50 minutes.

Malpensa Express (☎ 02 7249 4949; www.malpensaexpress.it; one way €12) From 4.28am to 12.26am, trains run every 30 minutes between Terminal 1, Cadorna Stazione Nord (35 minutes) and Stazione Centrale (45 minutes). Passengers for Terminal 2 will need to take the free shuttle bus to/from Terminal 1.

Linate

Air Bus (www.atm-mi.it; one way €5) Half-hourly departures from Piazza Luigi di Savoia between 6am and 11pm; from the airport between 6.30am and 11.30pm. Journey time 25 minutes.

Orio al Serio

Orio Bus Express (☎ 02 3391 0794; www.autostradale.it; one way €5) This Autostradale service departs Piazza Luigi di Savoia approximately every half hour between 2.45am and 11.30pm; from Orio between 4.30am and 1am. The journey takes one hour.

PUBLIC TRANSPORT

Milan's metro, buses and trams are run by **ATM** (☎ 02 4860 7607; www.atm.it). Tickets (€1.50) are valid for one underground ride or up to 90 minutes' travel on city buses and trams. A day ticket costs €4.50. Buy them at metro stations, *tabaccherie* and newsstands.

The Lakes

Ringed by snowcapped mountains, gracious towns and landscaped gardens, the Italian lake district is an enchanting corner of the country.

Lago Maggiore

Snaking across the Swiss border, Lago Maggiore, the westernmost of the three main lakes, retains the belle époque air of its 19th-century heyday when it was a popular retreat for artists and writers.

Its headline sights are the Borromean islands, accessible from **Stresa** on the lake's western bank. **Isola Bella** is dominated by the 17th-century **Palazzo Borromeo** (☎ 0323 3 05 56; www.isoleborromee.it; adult/reduced €13/6.50, incl Isola Madre €18.50/8.50, Galleria dei Quadri €3/2; ⏰ 9am-5.30pm mid-Mar–mid-Oct), a grand baroque palace with a picture gallery (Galleria dei Quadri) and beautiful tiered gardens. Over the water, **Palazzo Madre** (☎ 0323 3 12 61; www.isoleborromee.it; adult/reduced €11/6, incl Isola Bella €18.50/8.50; ⏰ 9am-6pm mid-Mar–mid-Oct) lords it over **Isola Madre**.

In Stresa's pedestrianised centre, **Nonna Italia** (☎ 0323 93 39 22; www.nonnaitalia.net; Via Garibaldi 32; pizzas €5-8, meals €25-30) is a welcoming trattoria serving creative regional cooking. Nearby, the family-run **Hotel Fiorentina** (☎ 0323 3 02 54; www.hotelfiorentino.com; Via Bolongaro 9; s €50-60, d €80-90; ❄ 📶) has warm, modest rooms.

For further information, contact Stresa's **tourist office** (☎ 0323 3 13 08; www.stresaturismo.it; Piazza Marconi 16; ⏰ 10am-12.30pm & 3-6.30pm summer, reduced hours winter).

Getting There & Around

The easiest way to get to Stresa is by train from Milan (€8.30, one hour, up to 14 daily).

Between April and September, **Saf** (☎ 0323 55 21 72; www.safduemila.com) operates an Alibus shuttle to/from Malpensa airport (€12, one hour, six daily).

Navigazione Lago Maggiore (☎ 800 551801; www.navigazionelaghi.it) operates ferries across the lake. From Stresa, a return ticket to Isola Bella costs €6.80, to Isola Madre €10.

Lago di Como

Lago di Como, overshadowed by steep wooded hills and snowcapped peaks, is the most spectacular and least visited of the lakes. At its southwestern tip, **Como** is a prosperous town with a charming medieval centre and good ferry links.

Just over a kilometre from Como's centre, the sumptuous 18th-century **Villa Olmo** (☎031 57 61 69; www.grandimostrecomo.it; Via Cantoni 1; gardens free, villa dependent upon exhibition; ⏲villa during exhibitions 9am-12.30pm & 2-5pm Mon-Sat, gardens 7.30am-11pm summer, to 7pm winter) is a local landmark and one of the lake's many waterside villas.

For lunch head to the characterful **Osteria del Gallo** (☎031 27 25 91; www.osteriadelgallo-como.it; Via Vitani 16; meals €25-30; ⏲12.30-3pm Mon, to 9pm Tue-Sat). Also in the medieval centre, the modish **Avenue Hotel** (☎031 27 21 86; www.avenuehotel.it; Piazzole Terragni 6; d/ste from €170/220; ❄📶) offers slick four-star accommodation.

You can get more local information at the **infopoint** (www.comotourism.it; Como San Giovanni train station; 9am-5pm Wed-Mon summer, to 4.30pm winter).

ℹ Getting There & Around

Regional trains run to Como San Giovanni from Milan's Stazione Centrale and Porta Garibaldi (€4.60, one hour, hourly).

Navigazione Lago di Como (☎800 551801; www.navigazionelaghi.it) operates year-round ferries from the jetty near Piazza Cavour.

Lago di Garda

The largest and most developed of the lakes, Lago di Garda straddles the border between Lombardy and the Veneto. A good base is **Sirmione**, a picturesque village on its southern shores. Here you can investigate the **Rocca Scaligera** (Castello Scaligero; adult/reduced €4/2; ⏲8.30am-7pm Tue-Sat, to 1.30pm Sun), a medieval castle, and enjoy views over the lake's placid blue waters.

There are an inordinate number of eateries crammed into Sirmione's historic centre. One of the best is **La Fiasca** (☎030 990 61 11; www.trattorialafiasca.it; Via Santa Maria Maggiore; meals €30; ⏲noon-2.30pm & 7-10.30pm Thu-Tue), an authentic trattoria serving flavoursome lake fish.

Sirmione can be visited on a day trip from Verona, but if you want to overnight, **Hotel Marconi** (☎030 91 60 07; www.hotelmarconi.net; Via Vittorio Emanuele II 51; s €45-75, d €80-140; P❄📶) has stylishly understated rooms and relaxing lake views.

Get information from the **tourist office** (☎030 91 61 14; iat.sirmione@tiscali.it; Viale Marconi 8; ⏲9am-12.30pm & 3-6.30pm, closed Sat afternoon & Sun winter) outside the medieval walls.

ℹ Getting There & Around

Regional buses run to Sirmione from Verona (€3.50, one hour, hourly).

Navigazione Lago di Garda (☎800 551801; www.navigazionelaghi.it) operates the lake's fleet of ferries.

Verona

POP 260,000

Wander Verona's atmospheric streets and you'll understand why Shakespeare set *Romeo and Juliet* here – this is one of Italy's most beautiful and romantic cities. Known as *piccola Roma* (little Rome) for its importance in ancient times, its heyday came in the 13th and 14th centuries when it was ruled by the Della Scala (aka Scaligeri) family, who built *palazzi* and bridges, sponsored Giotto, Dante and Petrarch, oppressed their subjects and feuded with everyone else.

👁 Sights

Roman Arena RUIN

(☎045 800 32 04; www.arena.it; Piazza Brà; adult/reduced €10/7.50, incl Museo Maffeiano €11/8, or with VeronaCard €1, first Sun of month Oct-May; ⏲1.30-7.30pm Mon, 8.30am-7.30pm Tue-Sun) Verona's Roman amphitheatre, built of pink-tinged marble in the 1st century AD, survived a 12th-century earthquake to become the city's legendary open-air opera house, with seating for 30,000 people. You can visit the arena year-round, though it's at its best during the summer **opera festival**.

Casa di Giulietta MUSEUM

(Juliet's House; ☎045 803 43 03; Via Cappello 23; adult/reduced €6/4.50; ⏲1.30-7.30pm Mon, 8.30am-7.30pm Tue-Sun) Never mind that Romeo and Juliet were completely fictional characters, and that there's hardly room for two on the narrow stone balcony: romantics flock to this 14th-century house to add their lovelorn pleas to the graffiti on the courtyard gateway.

WORTH A TRIP

PADUA

Were it just for Padua's medieval centre and lively university atmosphere, the city would be a rewarding day trip from Venice. But what makes a visit so special is the **Cappella degli Scrovegni** (Scrovegni Chapel; ☎049 201 00 20; www.cappelladegliscrovegni.it; Piazza Eremitani 8; adult/reduced €13/6, night ticket €8/6, or with PadovaCard €1; ⌚9am-7pm, also 7-10pm various periods through year), home to a remarkable cycle of Giotto frescoes. Considered one of the defining masterpieces of early Renaissance art, this extraordinary work consists of 38 colourful panels, painted between 1303 and 1305, depicting episodes from the life of Christ and the Virgin Mary. Note that visits to the chapel must be booked in advance.

For information about the town's other sights, there are tourist offices at the **train station** (☎049 201 00 80; Piazza di Stazione; ⌚9am-7pm Mon-Sat, 10am-4pm Sun) and **Galleria Pedrocchi** (☎049 201 00 80; www.turismopadova.it; Vicolo Pedrocchi; ⌚9am-7pm Mon-Sat).

To fuel your wanderings, join the university crowd for a cheerful, no-nonsense lunch at **L'Anfora** (☎049 65 66 29; Via dei Soncin 13; meals €25-30; ⌚noon-3pm & 7-11pm Mon-Sat).

Trains leave for Padova from Venice (€4.05, 50 minutes) every 20 minutes or so.

Piazza delle Erbe SQUARE

Originally a Roman forum, Piazza delle Erbe is ringed with buzzing cafes and some of Verona's most sumptuous buildings, including the elegantly baroque **Palazzo Maffei**, which now houses several shops at its northern end.

Just off the piazza, the monumental arch known as the **Arco della Costa** is hung with a whale's rib. Legend holds that the rib will fall on the first just person to walk beneath it. So far, it remains intact, despite visits by popes and kings.

Piazza dei Signori SQUARE

Verona's beautiful open-air salon is ringed by a series of elegant Renaissance *palazzi*. Chief among these are the **Palazzo degli Scaligeri** (aka Palazzo Podestà), the 14th-century residence of Cangrande I Della Scala; the arched **Loggia del Consiglio**, built in the 15th century as the city council chambers; and the brick-and-tufa stone **Palazzo della Ragione**.

In the middle of the piazza is a statue of **Dante**, who was given refuge in Verona after he was exiled from Florence in 1302.

Sleeping & Eating

★Corte delle Pigne B&B €€

(☎333 7584141; www.cortedellepigne.it; Via Pigna 6a; s €60-90, d €90-130, tr & q €110-150; P ❄ 📶) In the heart of the historic centre, this three-room B&B is set around a quiet internal courtyard. It offers tasteful rooms and plenty of personal touches: a communal sweet jar, luxury toiletries, and even a Jacuzzi for one lucky couple.

Hotel Aurora HOTEL €€

(☎045 59 47 17; www.hotelaurora.biz; Piazzetta XIV Novembre 2; d €100-250, tr €130-280; ❄ 📶) This friendly three-star hotel is right in the thick of it, overlooking Piazza delle Erbe. Its light-filled rooms, some of which have piazza views, offer a mix of modern and classic decor. Breakfast can be enjoyed on the the sunny open-air terrace.

Hostaria La Vecchia Fontanina TRATTORIA €

(☎045 59 11 59; www.ristorantevecchiafontanina.com; Piazzetta Chiavica 5; meals €25; ⌚noon-2.30pm & 7-10.30pm Mon-Sat) With tables on a pint-sized piazza, cosy indoor rooms and excellent food, this historic eatery stands out from the crowd. The menu features typical Veronese dishes alongside a number of more unusual creations, such as *bigoli con ortica e ricotta affumicata* (thick spaghetti with nettles and smoked ricotta) and several heavenly desserts.

Al Pompiere TRATTORIA €€

(☎045 803 05 37; www.alpompiere.com; Vicolo Regina d'Ungheria 5; meals €45; ⌚12.40-2pm & 7.40-10.30pm Mon-Sat) The *pompiere* (firefighter's hat) is still on the wall, but the focal point at this local hot spot is the vast cheese selection and famed house-cured *salumi* (cured meats) platter. Make a meal of the starters with wine by the glass, or graduate to plates of risotto and oven-cooked pork knuckle. Reserve ahead.

Entertainment

Performances during the summer opera festival are held at the **Arena** (☎045 800 51 51; www.arena.it; box office Via Dietro Anfiteatro 6b; opera tickets €12-208; ⊙box office 9am-noon Mon-Sat & 3.15-5.45pm Mon-Fri, longer hours during opera festival).

Information

Tourist Office (☎045 806 86 80; www.tourism.verona.it; Via degli Alpini 9; ⊙9am-7pm Mon-Sat, 10am-4pm Sun) Just off Piazza Brà. Knowledgeable and helpful, with an accommodation booking desk open from 10am to 6pm Monday to Saturday.

Getting There & Around

An Aerobus (€6, 20 minutes, every 20 minutes from 5.15am to 11.35pm) links **Verona Villafranca Airport** (☎045 809 56 66; www.aeroportoverona.it), 12km outside town, with the train station. From there, buses 11, 12, 13 and 510 (90, 92, 93, 98 evenings and Sundays) run to Piazza Brà.

Trains connect with Milan (€12 to €17, one hour 20 minutes to two hours, up to three hourly), Venice (€8.50 to €18.50, 50 minutes to 2¼ hours, twice hourly) and Bologna (€10 to €18.50, 50 minutes to 1½ hours, 20 daily).

Venice

POP 264,500

Venice (Venezia) is a hauntingly beautiful city. At every turn you're assailed by unforgettable images: tiny bridges arching over limpid canals; chintzy gondolas sliding past working barges; towers and distant domes silhouetted against the watery horizon. Its celebrated sights are legion, and its labyrinthine alleyways exude a unique, almost eerie atmosphere, redolent of cloaked passions and dark secrets. Parts of the Cannaregio, Dorsoduro and Castello *sestieri* (districts) rarely see many tourists, and you can lose yourself for hours in the lanes between the Accademia and train station.

Many of the city's treasures date to its time as a powerful medieval republic known as La Serenissima.

ADMISSION DISCOUNTS

Civic Museum Pass (www.visitmuve.it, adult/reduced €24/18) Valid for single entry to 11 civic museums for six months, or just the five museums around Piazza San Marco (€16/10). Buy online or at participating museums.

Chorus Pass (www.chorusvenezia.org, adult/reduced €12/8) Covers admission to 11 churches. Buy at participating sites.

Venezia Unica City Pass (www.veneziaunica.it, adult/reduced €40/30) Combines the Civic Museum and Chorus Passes as well as providing discounted entry to other sites. Check the website for details and to purchase. Also available at HelloVenezia booths.

Sights

San Marco

★Basilica di San Marco BASILICA

(St Mark's Basilica; Map p674; ☎041 270 83 11; www.basilicasanmarco.it; Piazza San Marco; ⊙9.45am-5pm Mon-Sat, 2-5pm Sun Apr-Oct, to 4pm Sun Nov-Mar; San Marco) FREE With its tapering spires, Byzantine domes, luminous mosaics and lavish marblework, Venice's signature church is an unforgettable sight. It was originally built to house St Mark's corpse, but the first chapel burnt down in 932 and a new basilica was constructed over it in 1094. For the next 500 years it was a work in progress as successive doges added mosaics and embellishments looted from the east.

Of the many jewels inside, look out for the **Pala d'Oro** (Map p674; admission €2; ⊙9.45am-5pm Mon-Sat, 2-5pm Sun Apr-Oct, to 4pm Nov-Mar; San Marco), a stunning gold altarpiece.

Piazza San Marco PIAZZA

(Map p674; San Marco) This grand showpiece square beautifully encapsulates the splendour of Venice's past and its tourist-fuelled present. Flanked by the arcaded **Procuratie Vecchie** and **Procuratie Nuove**, it's filled for much of the day with tourists, pigeons and tour guides. To get a bird's-eye view, the Basilica di San Marco's free-standing 99m **campanile** (Bell Tower; Map p674; www.basilicasanmarco.it; Piazza San Marco; admission

€8; ⌚9am-9pm summer, to 7pm spring & autumn, 9.30am-3.45pm winter; ⛴San Marco) commands stunning 360-degree panoramas.

★**Palazzo Ducale** MUSEUM
(Ducal Palace; Map p674; ☎041 271 59 11; www.palazzoducale.visitmuve.it; Piazzetta San Marco 52; adult/reduced €17/10; ⌚8.30am-7pm Apr-Oct, to 5.30pm Nov-Mar; ⛴San Zaccaria) This grand Gothic palace was the Doge's official residence from the 9th century, and seat of the Venetian Republic's government (and prisons) for nearly seven centuries. The Doge's Apartments are on the 1st floor, but it's the lavishly decorated 2nd-floor chambers that are the real highlight. These culminate in the echoing **Sala del Maggior Consiglio** (Grand Council Hall), home to the Doge's throne and a 22m-by-7m *Paradise* painting by Tintoretto's son Domenico.

★**Ponte dei Sospiri** BRIDGE
(Map p674) One of Venice's most photographed sights, the Bridge of Sighs connects Palazzo Ducale to the 16th-century Priggione Nove (New Prisons). It's named after the sighs that condemned prisoners – including Giacomo Casanova – emitted as they were led down to the cells.

Dorsoduro

★**Gallerie dell'Accademia** GALLERY
(Map p674; ☎041 520 03 45; www.gallerieaccademia.org; Campo della Carità 1050; adult/reduced €11/8, first Sun of the month free; ⌚8.15am-2pm Mon, to 7.15pm Tue-Sun; ⛴Accademia) Venice's historic gallery traces the development of Venetian art from the 14th to 18th centuries with works by Bellini, Titian, Tintoretto, Veronese and Canaletto, among others. Housing it, the former Santa Maria della Carità convent complex

Greater Venice

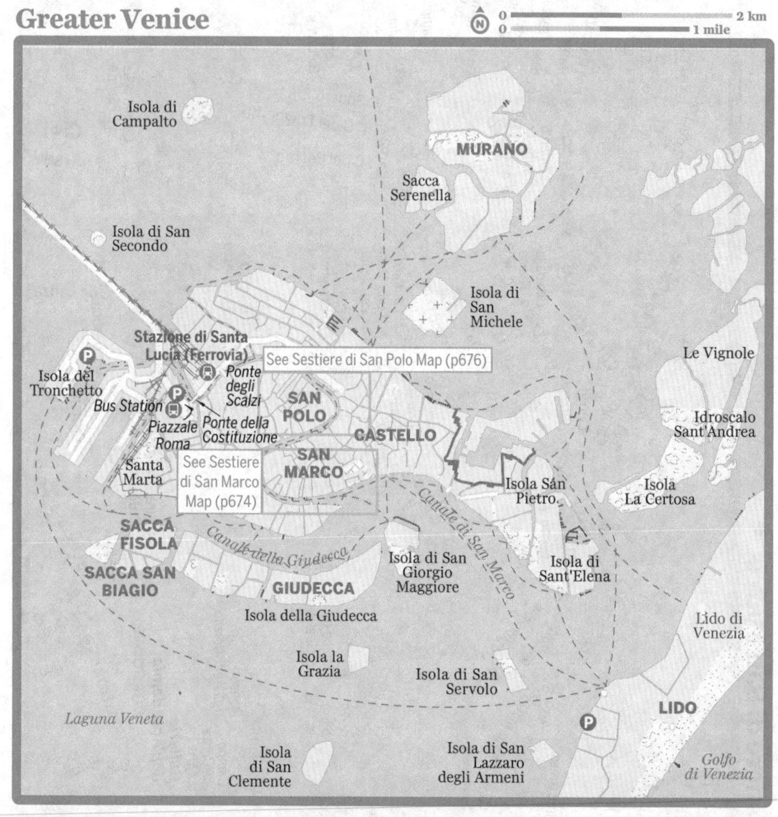

Sestiere di San Marco

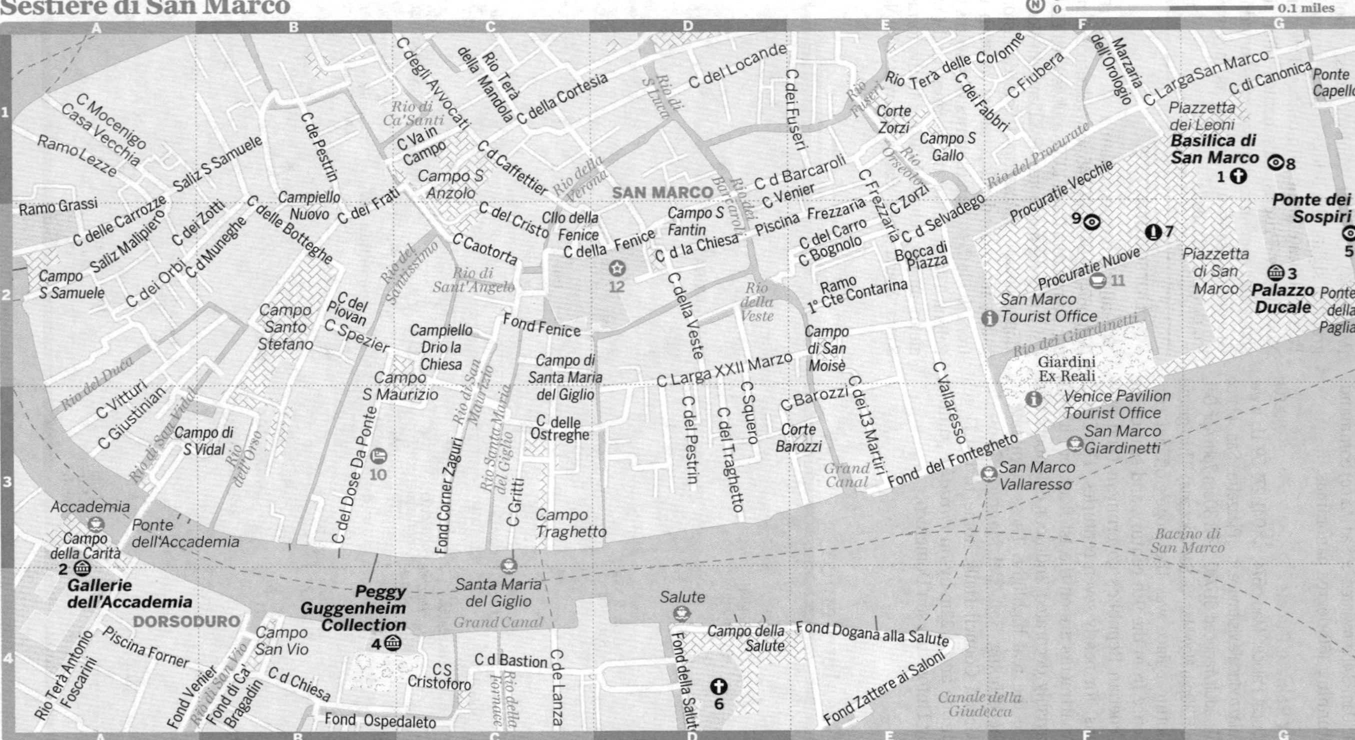
0 200 m
0 0.1 miles
N
A
B
C
D
E
F
G
1
2
3
4
C Mocenigo Casa Vecchia
Ramo Lezze
Ramo Grassi
Saliz S Samuele
C delle Carrozze
Saliz Malipiero
C dei Zotti
C d Muneghe
C dei Orbi
Campo S Samuele
C de Pestrin
Campiello Nuovo
C delle Botteghe
C dei Frati
C degli Avvocati
Rio di Ca' Santi
C Va in Campo
Rio Terà della Mandola
C della Cortesia
Campo S Anzolo
C d Caffettier
Rio della Verona
C del Cristo
Cllo della Fenice
C della Fenice
C Caotorta
Rio del Santissimo
Rio di Sant'Angelo
Campo Santo Stefano
C del Piovan
C Spezier
Campiello Drio la Chiesa
Campo S Maurizio
Rio del Duca
C Vitturi
C Giustinian
Rio di San Vidal
Campo di S Vidal
Rio dell'Orso
C del Dose Da Ponte
10
Fond Fenice
Campo di Santa Maria del Giglio
C delle Ostreghe
Rio di San Maurizio
Rio Santa Maria del Giglio
Fond Corner Zaguri
C Gritti
Campo Traghetto
Accademia
Ponte dell'Accademia
Campo della Carità
2
Gallerie dell'Accademia
DORSODURO
Piscina Forner
Rio Terà Antonio Foscarini
Fond Venier
Rio di San Vio
Fond di Ca' Bragadin
Campo San Vio
C d Chiesa
Peggy Guggenheim Collection
4
C S Cristoforo
Fond Ospedaleto
Santa Maria del Giglio
Grand Canal
C d Bastion
Rio della Fornace
C de Lanza
Salute
Fond della Salute
6
Campo della Salute
Fond Dogana alla Salute
Fond Zattere ai Saloni
Canale della Giudecca
SAN MARCO
12
Rio di S Luca
C del Locande
C dei Fuseri
Rio dei Barcaroli
C d Barcaroli
C Venier
Campo S Fantin
Piscina Frezzaria
C d la Chiesa
C della Veste
Rio della Veste
C del Carro
C Bognolo
C Frezzaria
C Zorzi
C d Selvadego
Bocca di Piazza
Ramo 1° Cte Contarina
Campo di San Moisè
C Larga XXII Marzo
C del Pestrin
C del Traghetto
C Squero
C Barozzi
Corte Barozzi
C dei 13 Martiri
Grand Canal
C Vallaresso
Fond del Fontegheto
San Marco Vallaresso
Rio Fuseri
Corte Zorzi
Rio Orseolo
Campo S Gallo
Rio Terà delle Colonne
C dei Fabbri
C Fiubera
Marzaria dell'Orologio
Rio del Procurate
Procuratie Vecchie
9
7
Procuratie Nuove
11
San Marco Tourist Office
Rio dei Giardinetti
Giardini Ex Reali
Venice Pavilion Tourist Office
San Marco Giardinetti
Bacino di San Marco
C Larga San Marco
C di Canonica
Piazzetta dei Leoni
Basilica di San Marco
8
1
Ponte dei Sospiri
5
Piazzetta di San Marco
3
Palazzo Ducale
Ponte della Paglia
Ponte Capello

Sestiere di San Marco

Top Sights

Sights

Sleeping

Drinking & Nightlife

Entertainment

maintained its serene composure for centuries until Napoleon installed his haul of Venetian art trophies here in 1807. Since then there's been nonstop visual drama inside its walls.

★Peggy Guggenheim Collection MUSEUM

(Map p674; ☎041 240 54 11; www.guggenheim-venice.it; Palazzo Venier dei Leoni 704; adult/reduced €15/9; ⏰10am-6pm Wed-Mon; Accademia) After losing her father on the *Titanic,* heiress Peggy Guggenheim became one of the great collectors of the 20th century. Her palatial canalside home, Palazzo Venier dei Leoni, showcases her stockpile of surrealist, futurist and abstract expressionist art with works by up to 200 artists, including her ex-husband Max Ernst, Jackson Pollock (among her many rumoured lovers), Picasso and Salvador Dalí.

Basilica di Santa Maria della Salute BASILICA

(La Salute; Map p674; ☎041 241 10 18; www.seminariovenezia.it; Campo della Salute 1b; admission free, sacristy adult/reduced €3/1.50; ⏰9am-noon & 3-5.30pm; Salute) Guarding the entrance to the Grand Canal, this 17th-century domed church was commissioned by Venice's plague survivors as thanks for salvation. Baldassare Longhena's uplifting design is an engineering feat that defies simple logic, and in fact the church is said to have mystical curative properties. Titian eluded the plague until age 94, leaving a legacy of masterpieces in the Salute's sacristy.

San Polo & Santa Croce

I Frari CHURCH

(Basilica di Santa Maria Gloriosa dei Frari; Campo dei Frari, San Polo 3072; adult/reduced €3/1.50; ⏰9am-6pm Mon-Sat, 1-6pm Sun; San Tomà) This soaring Italian-brick Gothic church features marquetry choir stalls, Canova's pyramid mausoleum, Bellini's achingly sweet *Madonna with Child* triptych in the sacristy and Longhena's creepy Doge Pesaro funereal monument – yet visitors are inevitably drawn to the small altarpiece. This is Titian's 1518 *Assumption,* in which a radiant red-cloaked Madonna reaches heavenward, steps onto a cloud and escapes this mortal coil. Titian himself died in 1576 and is buried here near his celebrated masterpiece.

Giudecca

Chiesa del Santissimo Redentore CHURCH

(Church of the Redeemer; Campo del SS Redentore 194; adult/reduced €3/1.50, or Chorus Pass; ⏰10am-5pm Mon-Sat; Redentore) Built to celebrate the city's deliverance from the Black Death, Palladio's *Il Redentore* was completed under Antonio da Ponte (of Rialto bridge fame) in 1592. Inside there are works by Tintoretto, Veronese and Vivarini, but the most striking is Paolo Piazza's 1619 *Gratitude of Venice for Liberation from the Plague.*

The Islands

Murano ISLAND

(4.1, 4.2) Murano has been the home of Venetian glass making since the 13th century. Tour a factory for a behind-the-scenes look at production or visit the **Museo del Vetro** (Glass Museum; ☎041 527 47 18; www.museovetro.

NAVIGATING VENICE

Venice is not an easy place to navigate and even with a map you're bound to get lost. The main area of interest lies between Santa Lucia train station (signposted as the *ferrovia*) and Piazza San Marco (St Mark's Sq). The path between the two – Venice's main drag – is a good 40- to 50-minute walk.

It also helps to know that the city is divided into six *sestieri* (districts): Cannaregio, Castello, San Marco, Dorsoduro, San Polo and Santa Croce.

Sestiere di San Polo

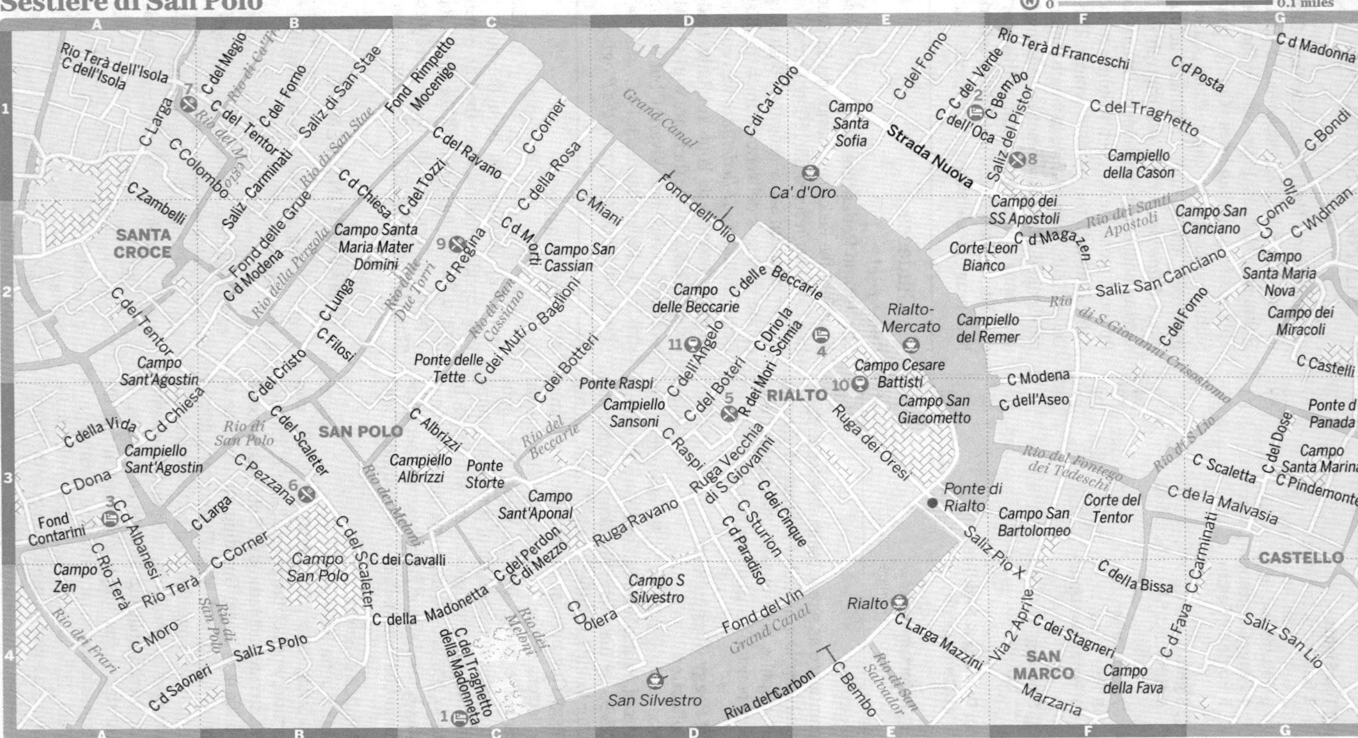

Sestiere di San Polo

Sleeping

1	Ca' Angeli	C4
2	Hotel Bernardi	E1
3	Oltre il Giardino	A3
4	Pensione Guerrato	E2

Eating

5	All'Arco	D3
6	Birraria La Corte	B3
7	Osteria La Zucca	A1
8	Trattoria da Bepi	F1
9	Vecio Fritolin	C2

Drinking & Nightlife

10	Al Mercà	E3
11	Cantina Do Spade	D2

visitmuve.it; Fondamenta Giustinian 8; adult/reduced €10/7.50; 10am-6pm Apr-Oct, to 5pm Nov-Mar; Museo) near the Museo *vaporetto* (water bus) stop. Note that at the time of writing the museum was undergoing a major overhaul.

Burano ISLAND
(12) Burano, with its cheery pastel-coloured houses, is renowned for its handmade lace. These days, however, much of the lace sold in local shops is imported.

Torcello ISLAND
(Torcello) Torcello, the republic's original island settlement, was largely abandoned due to malaria and now counts no more than 80 residents. Its mosaic-clad Byzantine cathedral, the **Basilica di Santa Maria Assunta** (041 73 01 19; Piazza Torcello; adult/reduced €5/4, incl museum €8/6, incl campanile €9; 10.30am-6pm Mar-Oct, to 5pm Nov-Feb; Torcello), is Venice's oldest.

Lido di Venezia ISLAND
(1, 2, 5.1, 5.2, 6, 8, 10, 14, N) The main draw here is the beach, but the water can be polluted and the public areas are often unkempt. Some of the beaches at the southern end of the island, such as those at Alberoni, are an exception. If you want to stay closer to the *vaporetto* stops, you'll pay about €10 to hire a chair and umbrella in the more easily accessible and cleaner areas of the beach.

Activities

Official **gondola** rates start at €80 (8am to 7pm) or €100 (7pm to 8am). Prices are per gondola for 40 minutes; maximum six people. Additional time is charged in 20-minute increments (day/night €40/50).

Festivals & Events

Carnevale CARNIVAL
(www.carnevale.venezia.it) Masquerade madness stretches over two weeks in February before Lent. Tickets to masked balls start at €140, but there's a free-flowing wine fountain to commence Carnevale, public costume parties in every *campo* (square) and a Grand Canal flotilla marking the end of festivities.

Palio delle Quattro Antiche Repubbliche Marinare CULTURAL
(Regatta of the Four Ancient Maritime Republics) The four historical maritime rivals – Pisa, Venice, Amalfi and Genoa – take turns to host this historic regatta in early June.

Venice Biennale ART
(www.labiennale.org) This major exhibition of international visual arts is held every odd-numbered year from June to November.

Festa del Redentore RELIGIOUS
(Feast of the Redeemer; www.turismovenezia.it) Walk on water across the Giudecca Canal to Il Redentore via a wobbly pontoon bridge on the third Saturday and Sunday in July, then watch the fireworks from the Zattere.

Venice International Film Festival FILM
(Mostra del Cinema di Venezia; www.labiennale.org/en/cinema) The only thing hotter than a Lido beach in August is the film festival's star-studded red carpet, usually rolled out from the last weekend in August through the first week of September.

Regata Storica CULTURAL
(www.regatastoricavenezia.it) Sixteenth-century costumes, eight-oared gondolas and ceremonial barques feature in this historical procession (usually held in September), which reenacts the arrival of the Queen of Cyprus and precedes gondola races.

Sleeping

San Marco

★ **Novecento** BOUTIQUE HOTEL €€€
(Map p674; 041 241 37 65; www.novecento.biz; Calle del Dose 2683/84; d €160-340; ; Santa Maria del Giglio) Sporting a boho-chic

look, the Novocento is a real charmer. Its nine individually designed rooms ooze style with Turkish kilim pillows, Fortuny draperies and 19th-century carved bedsteads. Outside, its garden is a lovely spot to linger over breakfast.

Dorsoduro

Hotel La Calcina HOTEL €€€

(☎041 520 64 66; www.lacalcina.com; Fondamenta Zattere ai Gesuati 780; s €100-190, d €170-370; ; Zattere) A historic waterfront landmark, this classy three-star hotel boasts a panoramic rooftop terrace, an elegant canalside restaurant, and airy, parquet-floored rooms, several facing the Giudecca Canal and Redentore church. Book ahead for rooms with views, especially No 2, where John Ruskin stayed while he wrote his classic 1876 *The Stones of Venice*.

San Polo & Santa Croce

L'Imbarcadero HOSTEL €

(☎392 341 08 61; www.hostelvenice.net; cnr Imbarcadero Riva de Biasio & Calle Zen, Santa Croce; dm €18-27; ; Riva de Biasio) A five-minute walk from the train station, this friendly hostel in Santa Croce offers spacious mixed and female-only dorms with single beds and the occasional Grand Canal view.

★**Ca' Angeli** BOUTIQUE HOTEL €€

(Map p676; ☎041 523 24 80; www.caangeli.it; Calle del Traghetto de la Madoneta 1434, San Polo; d €95-225, ste from €200; ; San Silvestro) Murano-glass chandeliers, polished parquet floors and grandstand canal views await at this refined retreat. Guestrooms are a picture, with beamed ceilings, antique carpets and big bathrooms, while the dining room, where hearty organic breakfasts are served, looks out onto the Grand Canal.

Pensione Guerrato PENSION €€

(Map p676; ☎041 528 59 27; www.pensioneguerrato.it; Calle Drio la Scimia 240a, San Polo; d/tr/q €145/165/185; ; Rialto Mercato) In a 1227 tower that was once a hostel for knights headed to the Third Crusade, smart guestrooms haven't lost their sense of history – some have frescoes or glimpses of the Grand Canal. A prime Rialto market location and helpful owners add to the package. Wi-fi in lobby. No lift.

★**Oltre il Giardino** BOUTIQUE HOTEL €€€

(Map p676; ☎041 275 00 15; www.oltreilgiardino-venezia.com; Fondamenta Contarini, San Polo 2542; d €180-250, ste €200-500; ; San Tomà) Live the dream in this garden villa, the 1920s home of Alma Mahler, the composer's widow. Hidden behind a lush walled garden, its six high-ceilinged guestrooms brim with historic charm and modern comfort, marrying precious antiques with discreet mod cons and pale ivory backdrops.

TOILETS IN VENICE

You'll find public toilets at the train station, Piazzale Roma, Accademia bridge, Campo San Bartolomeo and behind Piazza San Marco. To use them you'll need €1.50 in change (€1 at the station).

Cannaregio

Hotel Bernardi HOTEL €

(Map p676; ☎041 522 72 57; www.hotelbernardi.com; SS Apostoli Calle dell'Oca 4366; s €48-110, d €57-90, f €75-140, without bathroom s €25-32, d €45-62;) Hospitable owners, a convenient location just off the main thoroughfare and keen prices mean that the Bernardi is always heavily booked. Some of the best rooms – think timber-beamed ceilings, Murano chandeliers and gilt furniture – are in the annexe round the corner.

Giardino dei Melograni GUESTHOUSE €€

(☎041 822 61 31; www.pardesrimonim.net; Ghetto Nuovo, Cannaregio 2873/c; s €70-100, d €80-180, tr €110-210, q €140-240; ; Ferrovia Santa Lucia) Run by Venice's Jewish community, to which all proceeds go, the 'Garden of Pomegranates' is a sparkling kosher residence. It's located on the charming Campo Ghetto Nuovo just a short walk from the train station, and offers 14 bright, modern rooms.

Eating

Venetian specialities include *risi e bisi* (pea soup thickened with rice) and *sarde in saor* (fried sardines marinated in vinegar and onions). Also look out for *cicheti*, traditional Venetian bar snacks.

Dorsoduro

Grom GELATERIA €

(☎041 099 17 51; www.grom.it; Campo San Barnaba 2461; gelati €2.50-5.50; ⊙10.30am-11pm Sun-Thu,

10am-12.30am Fri & Sat, shorter hours winter; Ca' Rezzonico) One of several Grom branches across town. The consistently good gelato, made with prime, seasonal ingredients (lemons from the Amalfi Coast, pistachios from Sicily, hazelnuts from Piedmont), makes for a perfect pick-me-up.

Ristorante La Bitta RISTORANTE €€
(041 523 05 31; Calle Lunga San Barnaba 2753a; meals €35-40; 6.45-10.45pm Mon-Sat; Ca' Rezzonico) A cosy, woody restaurant near lively Campo Santa Margherita. The daily menu arrives on an artist's easel, and the hearty rustic fare looks like a still life and tastes like a carnivore's dream: steak comes snugly wrapped in bacon, veal is braised with *chiodini* mushrooms. Reservations essential. Cash only.

San Polo & Santa Croce

★All'Arco VENETIAN €
(Map p676; 041 520 56 66; Calle dell'Ochialer 436, San Polo; cicheti from €1.50; 8am-8pm Wed-Fri, to 3pm Mon, Tue & Sat; Rialto-Mercato) Search out this authentic neighbourhood *osteria* (casual tavern or eatery presided over by a host) for some of the best *cicheti* in town. Armed with ingredients from the nearby Rialto market, father-son team Francesco and Matteo serve miniature masterpieces such as poached white asparagus with seasoned pancetta, and *otrega* (butterfish) *crudo* (raw) with mint-and-olive-oil marinade.

Osteria La Zucca MODERN ITALIAN €€
(Map p676; 041 524 15 70; www.lazucca.it; Calle del Tentor 1762, Santa Croce; meals €35; 12.30-2.30pm & 7-10.30pm Mon-Sat; San Stae) With its menu of seasonal vegetarian creations and classic meat dishes, this cosy wood-panelled restaurant consistently hits the mark. Herbs and spices are used to great effect in dishes such as cinnamon-tinged pumpkin flan and lamb with dill and *pecorino* (sheep's milk cheese). The small interior can get toasty, so reserve canalside seats in summer.

Birraria La Corte RISTORANTE, PIZZA €€
(Map p676; 041 275 05 70; Campo San Polo 2168, San Polo; pizzas €7-14, meals €35; noon-3pm & 6-10.30pm; ; San Tomà) This one-time bull stable became a brewery in the 19th century to keep Venice's Austrian occupiers occupied, and beer and beef remain reliable bets. There's also pizza and much coveted piazza side seating.

Vecio Fritolin VENETIAN, SEAFOOD €€€
(Map p676; 041 522 28 81; www.veciofritolin.it; Calle della Regina 2262, Santa Croce; traditional 3-course set menu €38, meals €45; 7.30-10.30pm Tue, noon-2.30pm & 7-10.30pm Wed-Sun; San Stae) Traditionally, a *fritolin* was an eatery where diners sat at a communal table and tucked into fried fish. This is the modern equivalent, albeit smarter and more sophisticated. The menu includes meat and vegetable dishes, but the star act is the top-quality seafood, sourced daily from the nearby Rialto market.

Cannaregio

Dalla Marisa VENETIAN €€
(041 72 02 11; Fondamenta di San Giobbe 652b; set menus lunch/dinner €15/35; noon-3pm daily & 7-11pm Tue & Thu-Sat; Crea) At this Cannaregio institution, you'll be seated where there's room and have whatever Marisa's cooking, though you will be informed whether the fixed-price menu is meat- or fish-based when you book. Venetian regulars confess Marisa's *fegato alla veneziana* (Venetian calf's liver) is better than their grandmothers'. No credit cards.

Trattoria da Bepi Già "54" VENETIAN €€
(Map p676; 041 528 50 31; www.dabepi.it; Campo SS. Apostoli 4550; meals €30-40; noon-2.30pm & 7-10pm Fri-Wed; Ca' d'Oro) One of the better eateries on the touristy main drag (actually it's just a few metres off it near Santi Apostoli), this is a classic old-school trattoria with a few outside tables and a cheerfully cluttered wood-lined interior. The food is traditional Venetian with an emphasis on seafood.

★Anice Stellato VENETIAN €€€
(041 72 07 44; www.osterianicestellato.com; Fondamenta della Sensa 3272; bar snacks €13.50, meals €45-50; 10.30am-3.30pm & 6.30pm-midnight Wed-Sun; Madonna dell'Orto) Tin lamps, unadorned rustic tables and a small wooden bar set the scene for quality seafood at this excellent canalside *bacaro* (traditional Venetian *osteria*). You can munch on barside *cicheti* or go for the full à la carte menu and swoon over juicy scampi in *saor* (vinegar marinade) and grilled tuna.

Drinking & Nightlife

Cantina Do Spade BAR

(Map p676; ☎041 521 05 83; www.cantinadospade.com; Calle delle Do Spade 860, San Polo; ⏰10am-3pm & 6-10pm; 📶; 🚢Rialto) Since 1488 this cosy, brick-clad bar has kept Venice in good spirits, and the young, laid-back management extends a warm welcome to *spritz*-sipping Venetian regulars and visiting connoisseurs drinking double-malt beer and bargain Venetian cab franc. Come early for market-fresh *fritture* (batter-fried seafood).

Al Mercà WINE BAR

(Map p676; Campo Cesare Battisti 213, San Polo; ⏰10am-2.30pm & 6-9pm Mon-Thu, to 9.30pm Fri & Sat; 🚢Rialto) Discerning drinkers throng to this cupboard-sized counter on a Rialto market square to sip on top-notch *prosecco* (type of sparkling wine) and Denominazione di origine controllata (DOC; a type of trademark for a product from a specific region) wines by the glass (from €2). Arrive by 6.30pm for mini-*panini* (€1 to €2.50) and easy bar access, or mingle with crowds stretching to the Grand Canal docks.

Il Caffè Rosso CAFE

(☎041 528 79 98; Campo Santa Margherita 2963, Dorsoduro; ⏰7am-1am Mon-Sat; 📶; 🚢Ca' Rezzonico) Affectionately known as *'il rosso'*, this red-fronted cafe has been at the centre of the bar scene on Campo Santa Margherita since the late 1800s. It's at its best in the early evening, when locals snap up the sunny piazza seating to sip on inexpensive *spritzes* (a type of cocktail made with *prosecco*).

★**El Rèfolo** BAR

(www.elrefolo.it; Via Garibaldi, Castello 1580; ⏰11.30am-1am) A popular hangout in the Castello district. Like many Venetian bars, the action is centred on the street outside, particularly around 7pm when locals drop by to chat over a glass of *prosecco* (€2.50) and snack on cured meats and cheese.

Caffè Florian CAFE

(Map p136; ☎041 520 56 41; www.caffeflorian.com; Piazza San Marco 56/59; drinks €10-25; ⏰9am-midnight; 🚢San Marco) One of Venice's most famous cafes, Florian maintains rituals (if not prices) established c 1720: white-jacketed waiters serve cappuccino on silver trays, lovers canoodle in plush banquettes and the orchestra strikes up a tango as the sunset illuminates San Marco's mosaics.

Entertainment

Upcoming events are listed in the *Shows & Events* guide (€1), available at tourist offices, and at www.veneziadavivere.com.

★**Teatro La Fenice** OPERA

(Map p674; ☎041 78 65 11, theatre tours 041 78 66 75; www.teatrolafenice.it; Campo San Fantin 1965; theatre visits adult/reduced €9/6, concert/opera tickets from €15/45; ⏰tours 9.30am-6pm; 🚢Santa Maria dei Giglio) La Fenice, one of Italy's top opera houses, hosts a rich program of opera, ballet and classical music. With advance booking you can tour the theatre, but the best way to see it is with the *loggionisti* (opera buffs in the cheap top-tier seats). Get tickets at the theatre, online or through **HelloVenezia** (☎041 24 24; Piazzale Roma; ⏰7am-8pm for transport tickets, 8.30am-6.30pm for events tickets; 🚢Piazzale Roma).

Information

Airport Tourist Office (☎041 529 87 11; www.turismovenezia.it; Marco Polo Airport, arrivals hall; ⏰8.30am-7.30pm)

Ospedale Civile (☎041 529 41 11; Campo SS Giovanni e Paolo 6777; 🚢Ospedale) Venice's main hospital; for emergency care and dental treatment.

Piazzale Roma Tourist Office (☎041 529 87 11; www.turismovenezia.it; Piazzale Roma, Ground fl, multistorey car park; ⏰8.30am-2.30pm; 🚢Santa Chiara)

Police Station (Santa Croce 500; 🚢Santa Chiara)

San Marco Tourist Office (Map p674; ☎041 529 87 11; www.turismovenezia.it; Piazza San Marco 71f; ⏰8.30am-7pm; 🚢San Marco)

Station Tourist Office (☎041 529 87 11; www.turismovenezia.it; Stazione di Santa Lucia; ⏰8.30am-7pm; 🚢Ferrovia Santa Lucia)

Venice Pavilion Tourist Office (Map p674; ☎041 529 87 11; www.turismovenezia.it; Ex Giardini Reali, San Marco 30124; ⏰8.30am-7pm; 🚢San Marco)

Getting There & Away

AIR

Most flights arrive at and depart from **Marco Polo Airport** (VCE; ☎flight information 041 260 92 60; www.veniceairport.it), 12km outside Venice. Ryanair flies to/from **Treviso Airport** (TSF; ☎0422 31 51 11; www.trevisoairport.it; Via Noalese 63), about 30km away.

BOAT

Venezia Lines (☎041 882 11 01; www.venezia lines.com) operates high-speed boats to/from several ports in Croatia between mid-April and early October.

BUS

ACTV (☎ 041 24 24; www.actv.it) buses service surrounding areas. Get tickets and information at the **bus station** (Piazzale Roma).

TRAIN

Trains serve Venice's Stazione di Santa Lucia from Padua (€4.05 to €13, 50 minutes, every 10 minutes) and Verona (€7.50 to €18.50, 1¼ to 2¼ hours, half-hourly) as well as Bologna, Milan, Rome and Florence.

Direct international trains run to/from points in France, Germany, Austria and Switzerland.

Getting Around

TO/FROM THE AIRPORT

Marco Polo Airport

Alilaguna (☎ 041 240 17 01; www.alilaguna.it) operates three boat lines (approximately half-hourly) to the city centre. Tickets cost €15 to Venice, €8 to Murano.

Orange To Piazza San Marco via Rialto and the Grand Canal.

Blue Stops include Murano, the Lido, San Marco and Giudecca.

Red To Murano, the Lido and San Marco.

An **ATVO** (☎ 0421 59 46 71; www.atvo.it) shuttle bus goes to/from Piazzale Roma (one way/return €6/11, 20 minutes, half-hourly), as does ACTV bus 5 (one way/return €6/11, 25 minutes, every 15 minutes).

Treviso Airport

ATVO buses run to/from Piazzale Roma (one way/return €10/18, 70 minutes, nine daily).

BOAT

The city's main mode of public transport is the *vaporetto* (water bus). Tickets, available from ACTV booths at major *vaporetti* stops and the HelloVenezia booth on Piazzale Roma, cost €7 for a single trip, €18 for 12 hours, €20 for 24 hours, €25 for 36 hours, €30 for two days, €35 for three days and €50 for seven days. Useful routes:

1 Piazzale Roma to the train station and down the Grand Canal to San Marco and the Lido.

2 San Zaccaria (near San Marco) to the Lido via Giudecca, Piazzale Roma, the train station and Rialto.

4.1 To/from Murano via Fondamente Nove, the train station, Piazzale Roma, Redentore and San Zaccaria.

To cross the Grand Canal where there's no nearby bridge, take a *traghetto gondola* (€2 per crossing).

Trieste

POP 204,800

Italy's last city before Slovenia, Trieste merits a quick stopover. There are few must-see sights, but its imposing seafront *palazzi* lend it an impressive grandeur and the historic centre buzzes with bars and cafes. Hanging over everything is a palpable Mittel-European air, a hangover of its time an an important Austro-Hungarian port.

Sights & Activities

Piazza dell' Unità d'Italia PIAZZA

Italy's largest sea-facing piazza is a triumph of Austro-Hungarian town planning and contemporary civil pride. Flanked by the city's grandest *palazzi* (including Palazzo del Municipio), Trieste's 19th-century city hall, this vast public space is a good place for a drink or a chat, or simply for a quiet moment staring out at ships on the horizon.

No 2 Tram TOUR

(www.triestetrasporti.it; Piazza Oberdan; hourly/daily ticket €1.30/€4.30; ⊙ departures every 20min 7am-8pm) For wonderful views, jump on this vintage tram to Villa Opicina. For most of the 5km journey from Piazza Oberdan it's a regular tram, but a funicular section tackles the steep gradient as it heads up into the Carso. It's a short but significant trip – Villa Opicina was once almost entirely Slovenian-speaking and today retains a decidedly un-Italian feel.

Sleeping & Eating

★ L'Albero Nascosto BOUTIQUE HOTEL €€

(☎ 040 30 01 88; www.alberonascosto.it; Via Felice Venezian 18; s €85, d €125-145; ❄ 📶) A delightful little hotel in the middle of the old town, Nascosto is a model of discreet style. Rooms are spacious and tastefully decked out with parquet floors, original artworks, books and a vintage piece or two; most also have a small kitchen corner. Breakfasts are simple but thoughtful, with local cheeses, top-quality preserves and Illy coffee on tap.

Buffet da Siora Rosa BUFFET €

(☎ 040 30 14 60; Piazza Hortis 3; meals €25; ⊙ 8am-10pm Tue-Sat) Opened before WWII, the family-run Siora Rosa is one Trieste's traditional buffets (bar-restaurants). Sit outside or in the wonderfully retro interior and tuck into boiled pork, sauerkraut and other Germanic and Hungarian offerings, or opt for something fishly like *baccalà* (salted cod) with polenta.

Information

Tourist Office (☎040 347 83 12; www.turismofvg.it; Via dell'Orologio 1; ⊙9am-7pm Mon-Sat, to 1pm Sun)

Getting There & Around

Trains run to Trieste from Venice (€13.25 to €19, two to 3¾ hours, 25 daily). From the train station, bus 30 heads down to Piazza dell'Unità d'Italia and the seafront.

National and international buses operate from the **bus station** (☎040 42 50 20; www.autostazionetrieste.it; Via Fabio Severo 24). These include services to Croatia (Pula, Zagreb, Dubrovnik), Slovenia (Ljubljana) and further afield.

Bologna

POP 384,200

Bologna is one of Italy's great unsung destinations. Its medieval centre is an eye-catching ensemble of red-brick *palazzi*, Renaissance towers and 40km of arcaded porticoes, and there are enough sights to excite without exhausting. A university town since 1088 (Europe's oldest), it's also a prime foodie destination, home to the eponymous bolognese sauce *(ragù)* as well as tortellini, lasagne and *mortadella* (Bologna sausage).

Sights

★Basilica di San Petronio CHURCH

(Piazza Maggiore; ⊙7.45am-2pm & 3-6.30pm) Bologna's hulking Gothic basilica is the world's fifth-largest church, measuring 132m by 66m by 47m. Work began on it in 1390, but it was never finished and still today its main facade remains incomplete. Inside, look out for the huge sundial that stretches 67.7m down the eastern aisle. Designed in 1656 by Gian Cassini and Domenico Guglielmi, this was instrumental in discovering the anomalies of the Julian calendar and led to the creation of the leap year.

Torre degli Asinelli TOWER

(Piazza di Porta Ravegnana; admission €3; ⊙9am-6pm, to 5pm Oct-May) Bologna's two leaning towers are the city's main symbol. The taller of the two, the 97.6m-high Torre degli Asinelli is open to the public, though it's not advisable for the weak-kneed (there are 498 steps) or for superstitious students (local lore says if you climb it you'll never graduate). Built by the Asinelli family between 1109 and 1119, it today leans 1.3m off vertical.

Its shorter twin, the 48m-high **Torre Garisenda** is sensibly out of bounds given its drunken 3.2m tilt.

Quadrilatero AREA

To the east of Piazza Maggiore, the grid of streets around Via Clavature (Street of Locksmiths) sits on what was once Roman Bologna. Known as the Quadrilatero, this compact district is a great place for a wander with its market stalls, cafes and lavishly stocked delis.

Sleeping & Eating

Albergo delle Drapperie HOTEL €€

(☎051 22 39 55; www.albergodrapperie.com; Via delle Drapperie 5; s €64-115, d €102-160, ste €130-180; ❄📶) In the atmospheric Quadrilatero neighbourhood, the Drapperie is snugly ensconced in the upper floors of a large building. Buzz in at ground level and climb the stairs to discover 19 attractive rooms with wood-beamed ceilings, the occasional brick arch and colourful ceiling frescoes. Breakfast is €5 extra.

Hotel University Bologna HOTEL €€

(☎051 22 97 13; www.hoteluniversitybologna.com; Via Mentana 7; d €70-250; ❄📶) Student digs never felt so good. This low-key hotel offers a hospitable welcome and decent three-star rooms in the heart of the university district.

Trattoria del Rosso TRATTORIA €

(☎051 23 67 30; www.trattoriadelrosso.com; Via A Righi 30; meals €20-25; ⊙noon-midnight) The Rosso, said to be the city's oldest trattoria, is a great example of what they do so well in Bologna. A bustling, workaday eatery, it serves healthy portions of homestyle local fare at honest prices and without a frill in sight.

★Osteria de' Poeti RISTORANTE €€

(☎051 23 61 66; www.osteriadepoeti.com; Via de' Poeti 1b; meals €35-40; ⊙12.30-2.30pm & 7.30pm-3am Tue-Fri, 7.30pm-3am Sat, 12.30-2.30pm Sun) In the wine cellar of a 14th-century *palazzo*, this historic eatery is one place to get to grips with Bologna's much-lauded cuisine. Take a table by the stone fireplace and order from the selection of traditional staples such as *tortelloni al doppio burro e salvia* (homemade ravioli with butter and sage).

Information

Tourist Office (051 23 96 60; www.bolognaturismo.info; Piazza Maggiore 1e; 9am-7pm Mon-Sat, 10am-5pm Sun) Also has an office at the airport.

Getting There & Around

AIR

European and domestic flights serve **Guglielmo Marconi Airport** (051 647 96 15; www.bologna-airport.it), 8km northwest of the city.

From the airport, an Aerobus shuttle (€6, 30 minutes, every 15 to 30 minutes) connects with the train station; buy tickets on board.

BUS

Buses 25 and 30 are among several that connect the train station with the centre.

TRAIN

Bologna is a major rail hub. From the station on Piazza delle Medaglie d'Oro, there are regular high-speed trains to Milan (€33 to €40, one to two hours), Venice (€30, 1½ hours), Florence (€24, 40 minutes) and Rome (€56, 2½ hours).

Ravenna

POP 158,800

A rewarding and worthwhile day trip from Bologna, Ravenna is famous for its early Christian mosaics. These Unesco-listed treasures have been impressing visitors since the 13th century, when Dante described them in his *Divine Comedy* (much of which was written here).

Sights

Ravenna's mosaics are spread over five sites in the centre: the Basilica di San Vitale, the Mausoleo di Galla Placida, the Basilica di Sant'Appollinare Nuovo, the Museo Arcivescovile and the Battistero Neoniano. These are covered by a single ticket (€9.50, or €11.50 between March and June), available at any of the sites. The website www.ravennamosaici.it gives further information.

On the northern edge of the *centro storico* (historic centre), the sombre exterior of the 6th-century **Basilica di San Vitale** (Via Fiandrini; 9am-7pm summer, 9.30am-5pm winter) hides a dazzling interior with mosaics depicting Old Testament scenes. In the same complex, the small **Mausoleo di Galla Placidia** (Via Fiandrini; 9am-7pm summer, 9.30am-5pm winter) contains the city's oldest mosaics.

Adjoining Ravenna's unremarkable cathedral, the **Museo Arcivescovile** (Piazza Arcivescovado; 9am-7pm summer, 10am-5pm winter) boasts an exquisite 6th-century ivory throne, while next door in the **Battistero Neoniano** (Piazza del Duomo; 9am-7pm summer, 10am-5pm winter), the baptism of Christ is represented in the domed roof mosaic. To the east, the **Basilica di Sant'Apollinare Nuovo** (Via di Roma; 9am-7pm summer, 10am-5pm winter) boasts, among other

ITALIAN ART & ARCHITECTURE

Italy is littered with architectural and artistic reminders of its convoluted history. **Etruscan** tombs and **Greek** temples tell of glories long past, **Roman** amphitheatres testify to ancient bloodlust and architectural brilliance, and **Byzantine** mosaics reveal influences sweeping in from the East.

The **Renaissance** left an indelible mark, giving rise to some of Italy's greatest masterpieces: Filippo Brunelleschi's dome atop Florence's Duomo, Botticelli's *The Birth of Venus* and Michelangelo's Sistine Chapel frescoes. Contemporaries Leonardo da Vinci and Raphael further brightened the scene.

Caravaggio revolutionised the late-16th-century art world with his controversial and highly influential painting style. He worked in Rome and the south, where **baroque** art and architecture flourished in the 17th century.

In the late 18th and early 19th centuries, **neoclassicism** saw a return to sober classical lines. Its main Italian exponent was sculptor Antonio Canova.

In sharp contrast to backward-looking neoclassicism, early-20th-century **futurism** sought new ways to express the dynamism of the machine age, while Italian **rationalism** saw the development of a linear, muscular style of architecture.

Continuing in this modernist tradition are Italy's two contemporary **starchitects**: Renzo Piano, the visionary behind Rome's Auditorium, and Rome-born Massimiliano Fuksas.

things, a superb mosaic depicting a procession of martyrs headed towards Christ and his apostles.

Five kilometres southeast of the city, the apse mosaic of **Basilica di Sant'Apollinare in Classe** (Via Romea Sud; adult/reduced €5/2.50; ⌚8.30am-7.30pm Mon-Sat, 1-7.30pm Sun) is a must-see. Take bus 4 from Piazza Caduti per la Libertà.

Eating

La Gardela TRATTORIA €

(☎0544 21 71 47; Via Ponte Marino 3; meals €25; ⌚noon-2.30pm & 7-10pm Fri-Wed) Economical prices and formidable home cooking mean this bustling trattoria can be crowded, but in a pleasant, gregarious way. Professional waiters glide by with plates of Italian classics: think thin-crust pizzas, risottos, and pasta with *ragù*.

Information

Tourist Office (☎0544 3 54 04; www.turismo.ravenna.it; Via Salara 8-12; ⌚8.30am-6pm Mon-Sat, 10am-6pm Sun)

Getting There & Around

Regional trains run to/from Bologna (€7.10, 1½ hours, hourly) and destinations on the east coast.

TUSCANY & UMBRIA

Tuscany and its lesser-known neighbour, Umbria, are two of Italy's most beautiful regions. Tuscany's fabled landscape of rolling vine-covered hills dotted with cypress trees and stone villas has long been considered the embodiment of rural chic, while its historic cities and hilltop towns are home to a significant portfolio of the world's medieval and Renaissance art.

To the south, the predominantly rural region of Umbria, dubbed the 'green heart of Italy', harbours some of the country's best-preserved historic *borghi* (villages) and many important artistic, religious and architectural treasures.

Florence

POP 377,200

Visitors have rhapsodised about the beauty of Florence (Firenze) for centuries, and once here you'll appreciate why. This Renaissance time capsule is busy year-round, but even the inevitable crowds of tourists fail to diminish its lustre. A list of the city's famous sons reads like a Renaissance who's who – under 'M' alone you'll find Medici, Machiavelli and Michelangelo – and its treasure trove of galleries, museums and churches showcases a magnificent array of Renaissance art.

The city's golden age came under the Medici family between the 14th and 17th centuries. Later, it served as capital of the newly unified Italy from 1865 to 1870.

Sights

Piazza del Duomo & Around

★**Duomo** CATHEDRAL

(Cattedrale di Santa Maria del Fiore; www.operaduomo.firenze.it; Piazza del Duomo; ⌚10am-5pm Mon-Wed & Fri, to 4.30pm Thu, to 4.45pm Sat, 1.30-4.45pm Sun) FREE Florence's Duomo is the city's most iconic landmark. Capped by Filippo Brunelleschi's red-tiled **cupola** (Dome; Piazza del Duomo; incl cupola, baptistry, campanile, crypt & museum adult/reduced €10/free; ⌚8.30am-6.20pm Mon-Fri, to 5pm Sat), it's a staggering construction and its breathtaking pink, white and green marble facade and graceful *campanile* (bell tower) dominate the medieval cityscape. Sienese architect Arnolfo di Cambio began work on it 1296, but construction took almost 150 years and it wasn't consecrated until 1436. In the echoing interior, look out for frescoes by Vasari and Zuccari and up to 44 stained-glass windows.

Campanile BELL TOWER

(www.operaduomo.firenze.it; Piazza del Duomo; adult/reduced inc cathedral dome & baptistry €10/free; ⌚8.30am-7.30pm) Begun in 1334 by Giotto, the Duomo's soaring bell tower rises nearly as high as the dome. Its elaborate Gothic facade, including 16 life-size statues, was worked on by a who's who of 14th-century artists, including Giotto, Andrea Pisano, Donatello and Luca Della Robbia. Climb its 414 steps for nearly the same superb views as those from Brunelleschi's dome, but without the snaking queues.

Battistero di San Giovanni LANDMARK

(Baptistry; Piazza di San Giovanni; adult/reduced €10/free incl cupola, campanile & museum; ⌚8.15-10.15am & 11.15am-7pm Mon-Sat, 8.30am-2pm Sun &

1st Sat of month) Across from the Duomo is the 11th-century Romanesque baptistry, an octagonal striped structure of white and green marble with three sets of doors conceived as panels on which to tell the story of humanity and the Redemption. Most celebrated of all are Lorenzo Ghiberti's gilded bronze doors at the eastern entrance, known as the *Porta del Paradiso* (Gate of Paradise). What you see today, though, are copies – the originals are in the Grande Museo del Duomo.

Piazza della Signoria & Around

Piazza della Signoria PIAZZA

The hub of local life since the 13th century, this animated piazza is where Florentines flock to meet friends and chat over early-evening *aperitivi* at historic cafes. Presiding over eveything is **Palazzo Vecchio**, Florence's city hall, and the 14th-century **Loggia dei Lanzi**, an open-air gallery showcasing Renaissance sculptures, including Giambologna's *Rape of the Sabine Women* (c 1583), Benvenuto Cellini's bronze *Perseus* (1554) and Agnolo Gaddi's *Seven Virtues* (1384–89).

★ **Palazzo Vecchio** MUSEUM

(☎055 276 82 24; www.musefirenze.it; Piazza della Signoria; museum adult/reduced €10/8, tower €10/8, museum & tower €14/12, archaeology tour €2; ⏲museum 9am-midnight Mon-Wed & Fri-Sun, to 2pm Thu summer, 9am-7pm Mon-Wed & Fri-Sun, to 2pm Thu winter, tower 9am-9pm Fri-Wed, to 2pm Thu summer, 10am-5pm Fri-Wed, to 2pm Thu winter) This fortress palace, with its crenellations and 94m-high tower, was designed by Arnolfo di Cambio between 1298 and 1314 for the *signoria* (city government). From the top of the **Torre d'Arnolfo** (tower), you can revel in unforgettable rooftop views, while inside, Michelangelo's *Genio della Vittoria* (Genius of Victory) sculpture graces the **Salone dei Cinquecento**, a magnificant painted hall created for the city's 15th-century ruling Consiglio dei Cinquecento (Council of 500).

★ **Galleria degli Uffizi** GALLERY

(Uffizi Gallery; www.uffizi.firenze.it; Piazzale degli Uffizi 6; adult/reduced €8/4, incl temporary exhibition €12.50/6.25; ⏲8.15am-6.50pm Tue-Sun) Home to the world's greatest collection of Italian Renaissance art, Florence's premier gallery occupies Palazzo degli Uffizi, a handsome palace built between 1560 and 1580 to house government offices. The collection, which was bequeathed to the city by the Medici family in 1743 on condition that it never leave Florence, contains some of Italy's best-known paintings, including Piero della Francesco's profile portaits of the Duke and Duchess of Urbino and Sandro Botticelli's *La nascita di Venere* (The Birth of Venus).

BEST OF THE UFFIZI

Cut to the quick of the gallery's collection and start by getting to grips with pre-Renaissance Tuscan art in **Room 2**, home to several shimmering alterpieces by Giotto et al. Then work your way on to **Room 8** and Piero della Francesca's iconic profile portrait of the Duke and Duchess of Urbino.

More familiar images await in the **Sala di Botticelli**, including the master's great Renaissance masterpiece, *La nascita di Venere* (The Birth of Venus). Continue on to **Room 15** for a couple of works by Leonardo da Vinci and then on to **Room 35** for Michelangelo's *Doni Tondi*.

Ponte Vecchio BRIDGE

Dating to 1345, Ponte Vecchio was the only Florentine bridge to survive destruction at the hands of retreating German forces in 1944. Above the jewellers' shops on the eastern side, the **Corridoio Vasariano** is a 16th-century passageway between the Uffizi and Palazzo Pitti that runs around, rather than through, the medieval **Torre dei Mannelli** at the bridge's southern end.

★ **Museo del Bargello** MUSEUM

(www.polomuseale.firenze.it; Via del Proconsolo 4; adult/reduced €4/2; ⏲8.15am-4.50pm summer, to 1.50pm winter, closed 1st, 3rd & 5th Sun & 2nd & 4th Mon of month) It was behind the stark walls of Palazzo del Bargello, Florence's earliest public building, that the *podestà* meted out justice from the late 13th century until 1502. Today the building safeguards Italy's most comprehensive collection of Tuscan Renaissance sculpture with some of Michelangelo's best early works and a hall full of Donatello's.

Florence

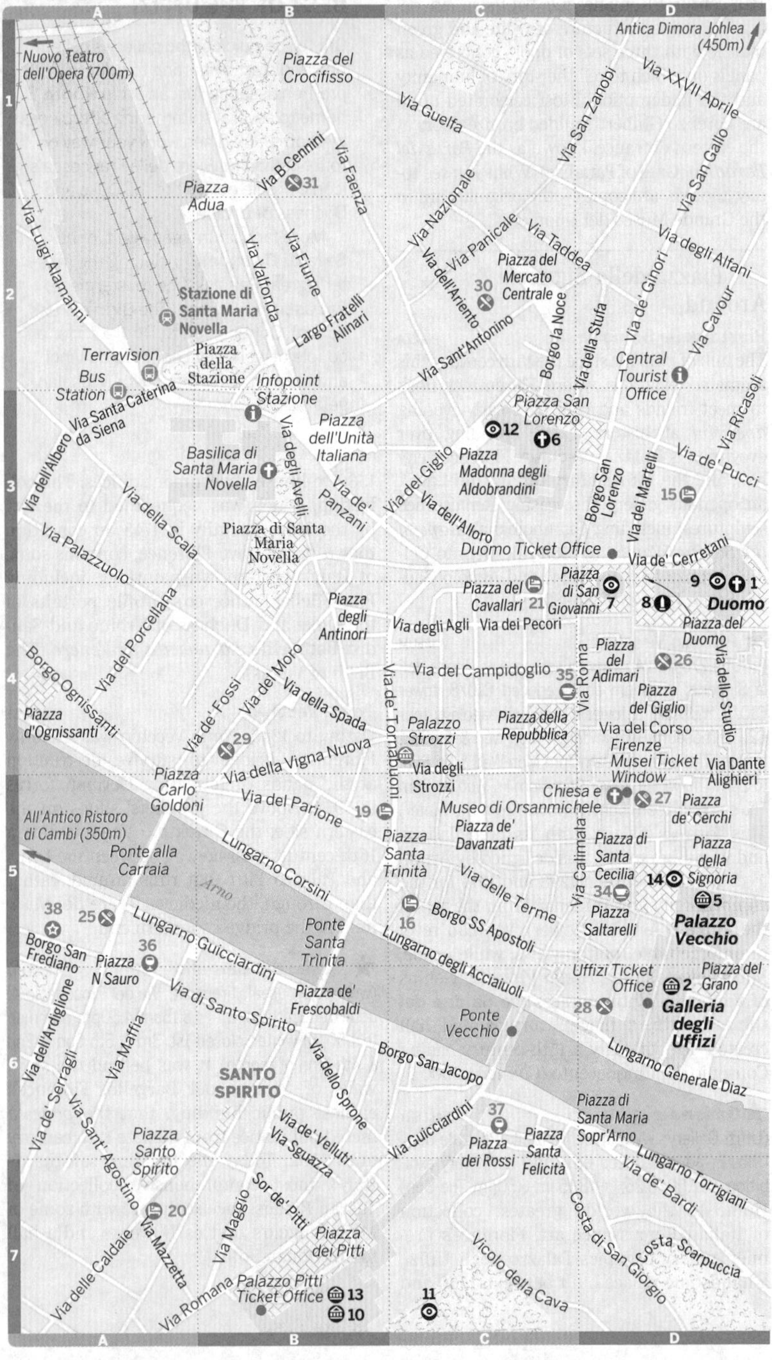

A
B
C
D
1
2
3
4
5
6
7
Nuovo Teatro dell'Opera (700m)
Piazza del Crocifisso
Antica Dimora Johlea (450m)
Via XXVII Aprile
Via Guelfa
Via San Zanobi
Via San Gallo
Via B Cennini
31
Via Faenza
Piazza Adua
Via Nazionale
Via Luigi Alamanni
Via Valfonda
Via Fiume
Via Panicale
Via Taddea
Via degli Alfani
Via dell'Ariento
Piazza del Mercato Centrale
30
Via de' Ginori
Stazione di Santa Maria Novella
Largo Fratelli Alinari
Borgo la Noce
Via Cavour
Via Sant'Antonino
Via della Stufa
Terravision
Piazza della Stazione
Bus Station
Infopoint Stazione
Central Tourist Office
Via Santa Caterina da Siena
Piazza San Lorenzo
Via Ricasoli
Piazza dell'Unità Italiana
12
6
Via dell'Albero
Via degli Avelli
Basilica di Santa Maria Novella
Via del Giglio
Piazza Madonna degli Aldobrandini
Via de' Pucci
Borgo San Lorenzo
Via dei Martelli
15
Via de' Panzani
Via della Scala
Via dell'Alloro
Piazza di Santa Maria Novella
Via Palazzuolo
Duomo Ticket Office
Via de' Cerretani
Piazza di San Giovanni
Piazza del Cavallari
21
7
8
9
1
Duomo
Piazza degli Antinori
Via degli Agli
Via dei Pecori
Piazza del Duomo
Via del Porcellana
Via Roma
Piazza del Adimari
26
Borgo Ognissanti
Via de' Tornabuoni
Via del Campidoglio
35
Via dello Studio
Via del Moro
Via della Spada
Piazza del Giglio
Piazza d'Ognissanti
Via de' Fossi
Palazzo Strozzi
Piazza della Repubblica
Via del Corso
Firenze Musei Ticket Window
29
Via della Vigna Nuova
Via degli Strozzi
Via Dante Alighieri
Piazza Carlo Goldoni
Via del Parione
Chiesa e Museo di Orsanmichele
27
Piazza de' Cerchi
All'Antico Ristoro di Cambi (350m)
19
Piazza de' Davanzati
Ponte alla Carraia
Lungarno Corsini
Piazza Santa Trinità
Via Calimala
Piazza di Santa Cecilia
Piazza della Signoria
Arno
Via delle Terme
14
34
5
38
25
16
Borgo SS Apostoli
Piazza Saltarelli
Palazzo Vecchio
Lungarno Guicciardini
Ponte Santa Trìnita
Borgo San Frediano
36
Piazza N Sauro
Lungarno degli Acciaiuoli
Uffizi Ticket Office
2
Piazza del Grano
Via di Santo Spirito
Piazza de' Frescobaldi
28
Galleria degli Uffizi
Ponte Vecchio
Via dell'Ardiglione
Via Maffia
Via dello Sprone
Borgo San Jacopo
Lungarno Generale Diaz
SANTO SPIRITO
Via de' Serragli
Via Sant'Agostino
Via de' Velluti
Via Sguazza
Via Guicciardini
37
Piazza di Santa Maria Sopr'Arno
Piazza Santo Spirito
Piazza dei Rossi
Piazza Santa Felicità
Lungarno Torrigiani
Via de' Bardi
20
Sor de' Pitti
Via Maggio
Costa di San Giorgio
Costa Scarpuccia
Via Mazzetta
Piazza dei Pitti
Vicolo della Cava
Via delle Caldaie
Via Romana
Palazzo Pitti Ticket Office
13
10
11

Florence

Top Sights

1	Duomo	D4
2	Galleria degli Uffizi	D6
3	Galleria dell'Accademia	E2
4	Museo del Bargello	E5
5	Palazzo Vecchio	D5

Sights

6	Basilica di San Lorenzo	C3
7	Battistero di San Giovanni	D4
8	Campanile	D4
9	Cupola	D4
10	Galleria Palatina	B7
11	Giardino di Boboli	C7
12	Museo delle Cappelle Medicee	C3
13	Palazzo Pitti	B7
14	Piazza della Signoria	D5

Sleeping

15	Academy Hostel	D3
16	Hotel Cestelli	C5
17	Hotel Dalí	E4
18	Hotel Morandi alla Crocetta	F2
19	Hotel Scoti	B5
20	Palazzo Guadagni Hotel	A7
21	Relais del Duomo	C4

Eating

22	Accademia Ristorante	E1
23	Del Fagioli	E6
24	Gelateria dei Neri	E6
25	Gelateria La Carraia	A5
26	Grom	D4
27	I Due Fratellini	D5
28	'Ino	D6
29	L'Osteria di Giovanni	B4
30	Mercato Centrale	C2
31	Trattoria I Due G	B1
32	Vestri	F4
33	Vivoli	E5

Drinking & Nightlife

34	Caffè Rivoire	D5
35	Gilli	C4
36	Il Santino	A5
37	Le Volpi e l'Uva	C6

Entertainment

38	La Cité	A5

San Lorenzo

Basilica di San Lorenzo BASILICA

(Piazza San Lorenzo; admission €4.50, incl Biblioteca Medicea Laurenziana €7; ⏲10am-5.30pm Mon-Sat, plus 1.30-5pm Sun winter) Considered one of the most harmonious examples of Renaissance architecture in Florence, this unfinished basilica was the Medici parish

CUT THE QUEUES

➡ Book tickets for the Uffizi and Galleria dell'Accademia, as well as several other museums, through **Firenze Musei** (Florence Museums; ☎ 055 29 48 83; www.firenzemusei.it). Note that this entails a booking fee of €4 per museum.

➡ Alternatively, the **Firenze Card** (€72, valid for 72 hours) allows you to bypass both advance booking and queues. This can be purchased online, at the Via Cavour tourist office, at Palazzo Pitti, Palazzo Vecchio or the Uffizi. Check details at www.firenzecard.it.

church and mausoleum – many members of the family are buried here. It was designed by Brunelleschi in 1425 for Cosimo the Elder, who lived nearby, and built over an earlier 4th-century church. In the solemn interior look out for Brunelleschi's austerely beautiful **Sagrestia Vecchia** (Old Sacristy) with its sculptural decoration by Donatello.

Museo delle Cappelle Medicee CHAPEL
(Medici Chapels; ☎ 055 294 883; www.polomuseale.firenze.it; Piazza Madonna degli Aldobrandini; adult/reduced €6/3; ⏰ 8.15am-1.50pm, closed 2nd & 4th Sun & 1st, 3rd & 5th Mon of month) Nowhere is Medici conceit expressed so explicitly as in their mausoleum, the Medici Chapels. Sumptuously adorned with granite, precious marble, semiprecious stones and some of Michelangelo's most beautiful sculptures, it is the burial place of 49 members of the dynasty.

San Marco

★ **Galleria dell'Accademia** GALLERY
(www.polomuseale.firenze.it; Via Ricasoli 60; adult/reduced €8/4; ⏰ 8.15am-6.50pm Tue-Sun) A lengthy queue marks the door to this gallery, built to house one of the Renaissance's most iconic masterpieces, Michelangelo's *David*. Fortunately, the world's most famous statue is worth the wait. The subtle detail of the real thing – the veins in his sinewy arms, the leg muscles, the change in expression as you move around the statue – *is* impressive.

Oltrarno

Palazzo Pitti MUSEUM
(www.polomuseale.firenze.it; Piazza dei Pitti; ⏰ 8.15am-6.50pm Tue-Sun, reduced hours winter) Commissioned by banker Luca Pitta and designed by Brunelleschi in 1457, this vast Renaissance palace was later bought by the Medici family. Over the centuries, it served as the residence of the city's rulers until the Savoys donated it to the state in 1919. Nowadays it houses several museums including the art-rich **Galleria Palatina** (incl Appartamenti Reali & Galleria d'Arte Moderna adult/reduced €8.50/4.25; ⏰ 8.15am-6.50pm Tue-Sun summer, reduced hours winter). Behind it, you can explore the palace's 17th-century gardens, the **Giardino di Boboli** (incl Museo degli Argenti, Museo delle Porcellane & Galleria del Costume adult/reduced €7/3.50; ⏰ 8.15am-7.30pm summer, reduced hours winter).

Festivals & Events

Scoppio del Carro FIREWORKS
A cart of fireworks is exploded in front of the cathedral at 11am on Easter Sunday.

Maggio Musicale Fiorentino PERFORMING ARTS
(www.operadifirenze.it) Italy's oldest arts festival features world-class performances of theatre, classical music, jazz and dance; April to June.

Festa di San Giovanni RELIGIOUS
Florence celebrates its patron saint, John, with a *calcio storico* (historic football) match on Piazza di Santa Croce and fireworks over Piazzale Michelangelo; 24 June.

Sleeping

★ **Hotel Dalí** HOTEL €
(☎ 055 234 07 06; www.hoteldali.com; Via dell'Oriuolo 17; d €90, s/d without bathroom €40/70, apt from €95; P 📶) A warm welcome from hosts Marco and Samanta awaits at this lovely small hotel. A stone's throw from the Duomo, it has 10 sunny rooms, some overlooking a leafy inner courtyard, decorated in a low-key, modern way and equipped with kettles, coffee and tea. No breakfast, but there is free parking available.

★ **Hotel Cestelli** HOTEL €
(☎ 055 21 42 13; www.hotelcestelli.com; Borgo SS Apostoli 25; d €70-100, f €80-115, without bathroom s €40-60, d €50-80; ⏰ closed 4 weeks Jan-Feb, 2-3 weeks Aug; 📶) Housed in a 12th-century *palazzo* a stiletto hop from fashionable Via

de' Tornabuoni, this intimate eight-room hotel is a gem. Rooms reveal an understated style, tastefully combining polished antiques with spangly chandeliers, vintage art and silk screens. Owners Alessio and Asumi are a mine of local information and are happy to share their knowledge. No breakfast.

Relais del Duomo B&B €
(☎055 21 01 47; www.relaisdelduomo.it; Piazza dell'Olio 2; s €40-90, d €70-130; ❄📶) Location is the prime selling point of this B&B on a quiet, traffic-free street around the corner from the Duomo. Its four elegant, pastel-coloured rooms come with parquet floors and simple, down-to-earth decor.

Academy Hostel HOSTEL €
(☎055 239 86 65; www.academyhostel.eu; Via Ricasoli 9r; dm €32-36, s/d €42/100, d without bathroom €85; ❄@📶) This classy 10-room hostel sits on the 1st floor of Baron Ricasoli's 17th-century *palazzo*. The inviting lobby area was once a theatre and 'dorms' sport maximum four or six beds, high moulded ceilings and brightly coloured lockers. No credit cards for payments under €150.

★Palazzo Guadagni Hotel HOTEL €€
(☎055 265 83 76; www.palazzoguadagni.com; Piazza Santo Spirito 9; d €150, extra bed €45; ❄📶) This delightful hotel overlooking Florence's liveliest summertime square is legendary – Zefferelli shot scenes from *Tea with Mussolini* here. Housed in an artfully revamped Renaissance palace, it has 15 spacious, tastefully styled rooms and an impossibly romantic loggia terrace with wicker chairs and predictably dreamy views.

Hotel Scoti PENSION €€
(☎055 29 21 28; www.hotelscoti.com; Via de' Tornabuoni 7; s/d/tr/q €75/130/160/185; 📶) Wedged between the designer stores on Florence's smartest shopping strip, this hidden *pensione* (small hotel) is a splendid mix of old-fashioned charm and value for money. Its 16 traditionally styled rooms are spread across the 2nd floor of a towering 16th-century *palazzo*, with some offering lovely rooftop views. The star of the show, though, is the frescoed lounge from 1780. Breakfast costs €5.

Antica Dimora Johlea B&B €€
(☎055 463 32 92; www.johanna.it; Via San Gallo 80; d €90-220; ❄@📶) A way out from the centre, this impeccable residence is a lovely retreat. There's an air of old-world elegance about the six guest rooms with their four-poster beds, creaking parquet floors, high ceilings and period furniture. Help yourself to a drink from the honesty bar and head up to the small terrace to enjoy views over to the Duomo.

Hotel Morandi alla Crocetta BOUTIQUE HOTEL €€
(☎055 234 47 47; www.hotelmorandi.it; Via Laura 50; s/d/tr/q €105/170/197/227; P❄📶) This medieval convent-turned-hotel away from the madding crowd in San Marco is a stunner. Rooms are refined and traditional in look – think antique furnishings, wood beams and oil paintings – with a quiet, old-world ambience. Pick of the bunch is frescoed room 29, the former chapel.

Eating

Classic Tuscan dishes include *ribollita*, a heavy vegetable soup, and *bistecca alla fiorentina* (Florentine steak served rare). Chianti is the local tipple.

★Mercato Centrale MARKET, FAST FOOD €
(☎055 239 97 98; www.mercatocentrale.it; Piazza del Mercato Centrale 4; dishes €7-15; ⏲10-1am, food stalls noon-3pm & 7pm-midnight; 📶) The food court concept has arrived in Florence. The 1st floor of the covered Mercato Centrale has been transformed into a vibrant food fair with a dedicated bookshop, a cookery school, wine bars and stalls selling everything from steaks and grilled burgers to smoothies, pizzas, gelato, pastries and fresh pasta. Load up and sit at the nearest free table.

'Ino SANDWICHES €
(www.inofirenze.com; Via dei Georgofili 3r-7r; panini €5-8; ⏲11.30am-4.30pm summer, noon-3.30pm Mon-Fri, 11.30am-4.30pm Sat & Sun winter) Artisanal ingredients sourced locally and mixed creatively is the secret behind this gourmet sandwich bar near the Uffizi. Create your own filling or go for a house special such as *finocchiona* (a local Tuscan salami) paired with herbed *pecorino* and pepper mustard.

I Due Fratellini SANDWICHES €
(www.iduefratellini.com; Via dei Cimatori 38r; panini €3; ⏲9am-8pm Mon-Sat) This hole-in-the-wall counter has been dishing out *panini* since 1875. Roll fillers range from ham and salsa to fishy combos such as anchovy with parsley sauce.

TOP FIVE GELATERIE

La Carraia (Piazza Nazario Sauro 25r; cones & tubs €1.50-6; ⌚11am-11pm summer, to 10pm winter) Fantastic gelateria next to Ponte Carraia.

Gelateria dei Neri (Via de' Neri 22r; cones & tubs from €1.80; ⌚9am-midnight) An old-fashioned shop serving fresh, vibrant flavours.

Gelateria Vivoli (Via dell'Isola delle Stinche 7; tubs €2-10; ⌚7.30am-midnight Tue-Sun summer, to 9pm winter) Select from the huge choice on offer and scoff it in the pretty piazza opposite.

Grom (www.grom.it; cnr Via del Campanile & Via delle Oche; cones €2.50-4.50, tubs €2.50-5.50; ⌚10am-midnight summer, to 11pm winter) Delectable flavours and organic seasonal ingredients.

Vestri (☎055 234 03 74; www.vestri.it; Borgo degli Albizi 11r; cones & tubs from €1.80; ⌚10.40am-8pm Mon-Sat) Specialises in chocolate.

Trattoria Cibrèo TUSCAN €€
(www.edizioniteatrodelsalecibreofirenze.it; Via dei Macci 122r; meals €30; ⌚12.50-2.30pm & 6.50-11pm Tue-Sat, closed Aug) Dine here and you'll instantly understand why a queue gathers outside before it opens. Once inside, revel in top-notch Tuscan cuisine: perhaps *pappa al pomodoro* (a thick soupy mash of tomato, bread and basil) followed by *polpettine di pollo e ricotta* (chicken and ricotta meatballs). No reservations, no credit cards, no coffee, and arrive early to snag a table.

Del Fagioli TUSCAN €€
(☎055 24 42 85; Corso Tintori 47r; meals €25-30; ⌚12.30-2.30pm & 7.30-10.30pm Mon-Fri, closed Aug) This cosy, woody eatery near the Basilica di Santa Croce is the archetypal Tuscan trattoria. It opened in 1966 and has been serving well-priced soups and boiled meats to throngs of appreciative local workers and residents ever since. No credit cards.

All'Antico Ristoro di' Cambi TUSCAN €€
(☎055 21 71 34; www.anticoristorodicambi.it; Via Sant'Onofrio 1r; meals €35; ⌚noon-2.30pm & 6-10.30pm Mon-Sat) Founded as a wine shop in 1950, this Oltrarno institution sticks closely to the traditional, with its long list of fine Tuscan wines, dried meats hanging from brick-vaulted ceilings and a glass case proudly displaying its highly regarded *bistecca alla fiorentina*. Meat aficionados will also enjoy the succulent *tagliata di cinta senese* (steak of Senese pork).

Accademia Ristorante TUSCAN €€
(☎055 21 73 43; www.ristoranteaccademia.it; Piazza San Marco 7r; pizzas €7-18, meals €35-40; ⌚noon-3pm & 7-11pm) Friendly staff, cheerful decor and consistently good food mean that this family-run restaurant is perennially packed. The focus is traditional regional cuisine, so expect antipasti of crostini, cured meats and cheeses, homemade pastas, meaty mains and a good selection of wood-fired pizzas.

Trattoria I Due G TUSCAN €€
(☎055 21 86 23; www.trattoriai2g.com; Via B Cennini 6r; meals €30; ⌚noon-2.30pm & 7.30-10pm Mon-Sat) Near the train station, this is a quintessential family-run trattoria specialising in earthy Tuscan cooking. Start off with a classic *parpadelle al cinghiale* (pasta ribbons with a boar-meat sauce) before getting your teeth into a tasty hunk of tender chargrilled steak.

★**L'Osteria di Giovanni** TUSCAN €€€
(☎055 28 48 97; www.osteriadigiovanni.it; Via del Moro 22; meals €50; ⌚7-10pm Mon-Fri, noon-3pm & 7-10pm Sat & Sun) It's not the decor that stands out at this smart neighbourhood eatery, it's the cuisine: sumptuous Tuscan. Imagine truffles, tender steaks and pastas such as *pici al sugo di salsiccia e cavolo nero* (thick spaghetti with a sauce of sausage and black cabbage). Throw in a complimentary glass of *prosecco* and you'll want to return time and again.

Drinking & Nightlife

★Il Santino WINE BAR

(Via Santo Spirito 60r; ⌚12.30-11pm) This pocket-sized wine bar is packed every evening. Inside, squat modern stools contrast with old brick walls, but the real action is outside, from around 9pm, when the buoyant wine-loving crowd spills onto the street.

Le Volpi e l'Uva WINE BAR

(www.levolpieluva.com; Piazza dei Rossi 1; ⌚11am-9pm Mon-Sat) This intimate spot with a marble-topped bar crowning two oak wine barrels chalks up an impressive list of Italian wines, from Tuscan Chianti's to rich Piedmontese reds and chardonnays from the Valle d'Aosta. To attain true bliss, nibble on *crostini* or Tuscan cheeses as you sip.

Caffè Rivoire CAFE

(Piazza della Signoria 4; ⌚7am-11pm Tue-Sun) Dating to 1872, this pricey number offers unbeatable people-watching on Piazza della Signoria – an ideal antidote to art overload brought on in the nearby Uffizi. Speciality of the house is its exquisite chocolate.

Gilli CAFE

(www.gilli.it; Piazza della Repubblica 39r; ⌚7.30am-1.30am) The city's grandest cafe, Gilli has been serving excellent coffee and delicious cakes since 1733. Claiming a table on the piazza is molto expensive – we prefer standing at the spacious Liberty-style bar.

Entertainment

Florence's definitive monthly listings guide, *Firenze Spettacolo* (www.firenzespettacolo.it), is sold at news-stands and has a small English-language section on the final pages.

Concerts, opera and dance are performed at the **Nuovo Teatro dell'Opera** (☎055 277 93 50; www.operadifirenze.it; Viale Fratelli Rosselli 15), also the venue for events during Maggio Musicale Fiorentino.

For live music in intimate surrounds, search out **La Cité** (www.lacitelibreria.info; Borgo San Frediano 20r; ⌚8am-2am Mon-Sat, 3pm-2am Sun; 📶).

Information

24-Hour Pharmacy (Stazione di Santa Maria Novella)

Dr Stephen Kerr: Medical Service (☎055 28 80 55, 335 8361682; www.dr-kerr.com; Piazza Mercato Nuovo 1; ⌚3-5pm Mon-Fri, or by appointment 9am-3pm Mon-Fri) Resident British doctor.

Infopoint Stazione (☎055 21 22 45; www.firenzeturismo.it; Piazza della Stazione 5; ⌚9am-7pm Mon-Sat, to 2pm Sun)

Central Tourist Office (☎055 29 08 32; www.firenzeturismo.it; Via Cavour 1r; ⌚9am-6pm Mon-Sat)

Getting There & Away

AIR

The main airport serving Florence is **Pisa International Airport** (Galileo Galilei Airport; ☎050 84 93 00; www.pisa-airport.com). There's also a small city airport 5km north of town, **Florence Airport** (Aeroport Vespucci; ☎055 306 13 00; www.aeroporto.firenze.it; Via del Termine).

BUS

The main bus station, **Autostazione Busitalia-Sita Nord** (☎800 37 37 60; Via Santa Caterina da Siena 17r; ⌚5.40am-8.40pm Mon-Sat, 6.20am-8pm Sun), is just southwest of the train station. Buses leave for Siena (€7.80, 1¼ hours, at least hourly) and San Gimignano via Poggibonsi (€6.80, 1¼ to two hours, up to 16 daily).

TRAIN

Florence's **Stazione di Santa Maria Novella** (Piazza della Stazione) is on the main Rome–Milan line. There are regular direct services to/from Pisa (€8, 45 minutes to 1½ hours), Rome (€21 to €36, 1½ to 3½ hours), Venice (€22 to €45, two hours) and Milan (€28 to €50, 1¾ to four hours).

Getting Around

TO/FROM THE AIRPORT

Terravision (www.terravision.eu; single/return €6/10) Terravision buses run to Pisa International Airport fom the bus stop outside Stazione di Santa Maria Novella on Via Luigi Alamanni. Buy tickets online, on board, or at the Terravision desk in Deanna Cafè.

Volainbus (☎800 424500; www.ataf.net; one way €6) The Volainbus shuttle runs between the bus station and Florence Airport. Departures are roughly every 20 minutes between 5.30am and 12.30am. Journey time is about 25 minutes.

PUBLIC TRANSPORT

City buses are operated by ATAF. Get tickets (€1.20 or €2 if bought on board) at *tabaccherie* and news-stands. They are valid for 90 minutes on any bus.

Pisa

POP 88,600

A handsome university city, Pisa is best known as the home of an architectural project gone terribly wrong. However, the Leaning Tower is just one of a number of noteworthy sights in its compact medieval centre.

Pisa's golden age came in the 12th and 13th centuries when it was a maritime power to rival Genoa and Venice.

LEANING TOWER VISITS

Access to the Leaning Tower is limited to 40 people at a time. To avoid disappointment, book online, or go straight to a ticket office when you arrive in Pisa to book a slot for later in the day. Visits last 30 minutes and involve a steep climb up 300-odd occasionally slippery steps. All bags must be deposited at the free left-luggage desk next to the ticket office.

Sights

★Leaning Tower — TOWER

(Torre Pendente; www.opapisa.it; Piazza dei Miracoli; admission €18; 9am-8pm summer, 10am-5pm winter) One of Italy's signature sights, the Torre Pendente truly lives up to its name, leaning a startling 3.9 degrees off the vertical. The 56m-high tower, officially the Duomo's *campanile* (bell tower), took almost 200 years to build, but was already listing when it was unveiled in 1372. Over time, the tilt, caused by a layer of weak subsoil, steadily worsened until it was finally halted by a major stabilisation project in the 1990s.

★Duomo — CATHEDRAL

(www.opapisa.it; Piazza dei Miracoli; 10am-8pm summer, 10am-12.45pm & 2-5pm winter) FREE Pisa's magnificent Romanesque Duomo was begun in 1064 and consecrated in 1118. Its striking tiered exterior, with cladding of green and cream marble bands, gives on to a vast columned interior capped by a gold wooden ceiling. The elliptical dome, the first of its kind in Europe at the time, was added in 1380.

Note that while admission is free, you'll need an entrance coupon from the ticket office or a ticket from one of the other Piazza dei Miracoli sights.

★Battistero — RELIGIOUS SITE

(Baptistry; www.opapisa.it; Piazza dei Miracoli; adult/reduced €5/3, combination ticket with Camposanto & Museo delle Sinópie adult/reduced €7/8, 2/3 sights adult/reduced €4/5; 8am-8pm summer, 10am-5pm Nov-Feb) Pisa's unusual round baptistry has one dome piled on top of another, each roofed half in lead, half in tiles, and topped by a gilt bronze John the Baptist (1395). Construction began in 1152, but it was remodelled and continued by Nicola and Giovanni Pisano more than a century later and finally completed in the 14th century. Inside, the hexagonal marble pulpit (1260) by Nicola Pisano is the highlight.

Sleeping & Eating

★Hotel Pisa Tower — HOTEL €

(050 520 00 19; www.hotelpisatower.com; Via Pisano 23; d €75-90, tr €90-100, q €110-119;) Superb value for money, a superlative location and spacious, high-ceilinged rooms – this polished newcomer is one of Pisa's best deals. Chandeliers, marble floors and old framed prints adorn the classically attired interiors, while out back, a pristine lawn adds a soothing dash of green.

Hostel Pisa Tower — HOSTEL €

(050 520 24 54; www.hostelpisatower.it; Via Piave 4; dm €20-25; @) This super friendly hostel occupies a suburban villa a couple of minutes' walk from Piazza dei Miracoli. It's a bright, cheery place with female and mixed dorms, a communal kitchen and a terrace overlooking a small back garden.

Hotel Bologna — HOTEL €€

(050 50 21 20; www.hotelbologna.pisa.it; Via Giuseppe Mazzini 57; d/tr/q €148/188/228; P) Nicely placed away from the Piazza dei Miracoli mayhem, this four-star hotel is an oasis of peace and tranquillity. Its big, bright rooms have wooden floors and colour-coordinated furnishings, and some are nicely frescoed.

Osteria La Toscana — OSTERIA €€

(050 96 90 52; Via San Frediano 10; meals €25-30; 7-11pm daily & noon-3pm Sat & Sun) This relaxed spot is one of several excellent eateries on Via San Frediano, a lively street off Piazza dei Cavalieri. Subdued lighting, bare brown walls and background jazz set the stage for ample pastas and delectable grilled meats served with a smile and quiet efficiency.

biOsteria 050 VEGETARIAN €€

(☎050 54 31 06; www.biosteria050.it; Via San Francesco 36; meals €25-30; ⏰12.30-2.30pm & 7.30-10.30pm Tue-Sat, 7.30-10.30pm Mon & Sun; ✎) Everything that Marco and Raffaele at Zero Cinquanta cook up is strictly seasonal, local and organic, with products from farms within a 50km radius of Pisa. Feast on dishes like risotto with almonds and asparagus or go for one of the excellent-value lunch specials.

Information

Check www.pisaunicaterra.it or pop into the **tourist office** (☎050 4 22 91; www.pisaunicaterra.it; Piazza Vittorio Emanuele II 16; ⏰10am-1pm & 2-4pm) in the city centre.

Getting There & Around

Pisa International Airport (www.pisa-airport.com) is linked to the city centre by the PisaMover bus (€1.30, eight minutes, every 10 minutes).

Terravision buses link the airport with Florence (one way/return €6/10, 70 minutes, 18 daily).

Frequent trains run to Lucca (€3.40, 30 minutes), Florence (€8, 45 minutes to 1¼ hours) and La Spezia (€7 to €12, 45 minutes to 1½ hours) for the Cinque Terre.

Lucca

POP 89,200

Lucca is a love-at-first-sight type of place. Hidden behind monumental Renaissance walls, its historic centre is chock-full of handsome churches, excellent restaurants and tempting *pasticcerie* (pastry shops). Founded by the Etruscans, it became a city-state in the 12th century and stayed that way for 600 years. Most of its streets and monuments date from this period.

Sights

City Wall WALL

Lucca's monumental *mura* (wall) was built around the old city in the 16th and 17th centuries and remains in almost perfect condition. Twelve metres high and 4km long, the ramparts are crowned with a tree-lined footpath that looks down on the *centro storico* and out towards the Apuane Alps. This path is a favourite location for the locals' daily *passeggiata* (traditional evening stroll).

Cattedrale di San Martino CATHEDRAL

(www.museocattedralelucca.it; Piazza San Martino; adult/reduced €3/2, with museum & Chiesa e Battistero dei SS Giovanni & Reparata €7/5; ⏰9.30am-5pm Mon-Fri, to 6pm Sat, 11.30am-5pm Sun) Lucca's predominantly Romanesque cathedral dates to the start of the 11th century. Its stunning facade was constructed in the prevailing Lucca-Pisan style and designed to accommodate the preexisting *campanile*. The reliefs over the left doorway of the portico are believed to be by Nicola Pisano, while inside, treasures include the **Volto Santo** (literally, Holy Countenance) crucifix sculpture and a wonderful 15th-century tomb in the **sacristy**.

Sleeping & Eating

★**Piccolo Hotel Puccini** HOTEL €

(☎0583 5 54 21; www.hotelpuccini.com; Via di Poggio 9; s/d €75/100; ❄📶) In an enviable central position, this welcoming three-star hotel hides behind a discreet brick exterior. Its small guestrooms reveal an attractive look with wooden floors, vintage ceiling fans and colourful, contemporary design touches.

Alla Corte degli Angeli BOUTIQUE HOTEL €€

(☎0583 46 92 04; www.allacortedegliangeli.com; Via degli Angeli 23; s/d/ste €150/250/400; ❄@📶) This boutique hotel oozes charm. Set in a 15th-century townhouse, its lovely beamed lounge gives onto 21 sunny rooms adorned with frescoed ceilings, patches of exposed brick and landscape murals. Breakfast is €10 extra.

Da Felice PIZZA €

(www.pizzeriadafelice.it; Via Buia 12; focaccias €1-3, pizza slices €1.30; ⏰11am-8.30pm Mon, 10am-8.30pm Tue-Sat) This buzzing spot behind Piazza San Michele is where the locals come for wood-fired pizza, *cecina* (salted chickpea pizza) and *castagnacci* (chestnut cakes).

La Pecora Nera TRATTORIA €€

(☎0583 46 97 38; www.lapecoraneralucca.it; Piazza San Francesco 1; pizzas €5.50-9, meals €25-30; ⏰7-11pm Wed-Fri, 11am-3pm & 7-11pm Sat & Sun) A pretty *centro storico* piazza sets the scene for alfresco dining at this laid-back trattoria. Staffed in part by young disabled people, it's a lovely spot for a pizza or dinner of earthy Tuscan fare.

WORTH A TRIP

SAN GIMIGNANO

This tiny hilltop town deep in the Tuscan countryside is a mecca for day trippers from Florence and Siena. Its nickname is the 'Medieval Manhattan', courtesy of the 14 11th-century towers that soar above its pristine *centro storico* (historic centre).

Palazzo Comunale (☎0577 99 03 12; Piazza del Duomo 2; adult/reduced €6/5; ⏲9am-6.30pm summer, 11am-5pm winter) houses San Gimignano's art gallery, the **Pinacoteca**, and tallest tower, the **Torre Grossa**.

Overlooking **Piazza del Duomo**, the **Collegiata** (Duomo, Basilica di Santa Maria Assunta; Piazza del Duomo; adult/reduced €4/2; ⏲10am-7pm Mon-Fri, to 5pm Sat, 12.30-7pm Sun summer, to 4.30pm winter), San Gimignano's Romanesque cathedral, boasts a series of superb 14th-century frescoes.

For a traditional Tuscan lunch, head to **Ristorante La Mandragola** (☎0577 94 03 77; www.locandalamandragola.it; Via Diaccetto 7; set menus €14-25, meals €35; ⏲noon-2.30pm & 7.30-9.30pm, closed Thu Nov-early Mar).

The **tourist office** (☎0577 94 00 08; www.sangimignano.com; Piazza del Duomo 1; ⏲9am-1pm & 3-7pm summer, 9am-1pm & 2-6pm winter) is on Piazza del Duomo, up Via San Giovanni from the bus stops.

Regular buses link San Gimignano with Florence (€7, 1¼ to two hours, up to 16 daily) via Poggibonsi. There are also services to/from Siena (€6, 1¼ hours, hourly).

Information

Tourist Office (☎0583 58 31 50; www.luccaitinera.it; Piazzale Verdi; ⏲9am-7pm summer, to 5pm winter) Free hotel reservations, bicycle hire and a left-luggage service.

Getting There & Away

Regional trains run to/from Florence (€7, 1½ hours, every 30 to 90 minutes) and Pisa (€8, one hour, half-hourly).

Siena

POP 54,200

Siena is one of Italy's most enchanting medieval towns. Its walled centre is a beautifully preserved warren of dark lanes punctuated with Gothic *palazzi,* and at its heart is Piazza del Campo (Il Campo), the sloping square that is the venue for the city's famous annual horse race, Il Palio.

In the Middle Ages, the city was a political and artistic force to be reckoned with, a worthy rival for its larger neighbour Florence.

Sights

★Piazza del Campo PIAZZA

This sloping piazza, popularly known as Il Campo, has been Siena's civic and social centre since being staked out by the Consiglio dei Nove (Council of Nine) in the mid-12th century. It was built on the site of a former Roman marketplace, and its pie-piece paving design is divided into nine sectors to represent the number of members of the council. At its lowest point, the graceful Gothic **Palazzo Comunale** houses the town's finest museum, the Museo Civico.

Museo Civico MUSEUM

(Palazzo Comunale, Piazza del Campo; adult/reduced €9/8; ⏲10am-7pm summer, to 6pm winter) Siena's most famous museum occupies rooms richly frescoed by artists of the Sienese school. These are unusual in that they were commissioned by the governing body of the city, rather than by the Church, and many depict secular subjects instead of the favoured religious themes of the time. The highlight is Simone Martini's celebrated *Maestà* (Virgin Mary in Majesty; 1315) in the **Sala del Mappamondo** (Hall of the World Map).

★Duomo CATHEDRAL

(www.operaduomo.siena.it; Piazza del Duomo; summer/winter €4/free, when floor displayed €7; ⏲10.30am-7pm Mon-Sat, 1.30-6pm Sun summer, 10.30am-5.30pm Mon-Sat, 1.30-5.30pm Sun winter) A triumph of Romanesque-Gothic architecture, Siena's cathedral is one of Italy's most awe-inspiring churches. According to tradition it was consecrated in 1179, but work continued on it for centuries and many of Italy's top artists contributed: Giovanni Pisano designed the intricate white, green and red marble facade; Nicola Pisano carved the elaborate pulpit; Pinturicchio painted frescoes; and Michelangelo, Donatello and Gian Lorenzo Bernini all produced sculptures. Also of note is the extraordinary inlaid floor.

Battistero di San Giovanni BAPTISTRY
(Piazza San Giovanni; admission €4; ⏲10.30am-7pm summer, to 5.30pm winter) Behind the Duomo, down a steep flight of steps, is the Baptistry, richly decorated with frescoes. At its centre is a hexagonal marble font by Jacopo della Quercia, decorated with bronze panels depicting the life of St John the Baptist by artists including Lorenzo Ghiberti *(Baptism of Christ* and *St John in Prison)* and Donatello *(The Head of John the Baptist Being Presented to Herod)*.

Museo dell'Opera del Duomo MUSEUM
(www.operaduomo.siena.it; Piazza del Duomo 8; admission €7; ⏲10.30am-7pm summer, to 5.30pm winter) The collection here showcases artworks that formerly adorned the cathedral, including 12 statues of prophets and philosophers by Giovanni Pisano that originally stood on the facade. These were designed to be viewed from ground level, which is why they look so distorted as they crane uncomfortably forward. The museum's highlight is Duccio di Buoninsegna's striking *Maestà* (1311), which was painted on both sides as a screen for the Duomo's high altar.

Festivals & Events

Il Palio PAGEANT, HORSE RACE
Dating from the Middle Ages, this spectacular annual event (held on 2 July and 16 August) includes a series of colourful pageants and a wild horse race in Piazza del Campo. Ten of Siena's 17 *contrade* (town districts) compete for the coveted *palio* (silk banner). Each *contrada* has its own traditions, symbol and colours, plus its own church and *palio* museum.

Sleeping & Eating

★Hotel Alma Domus HOTEL €
(☎0577 4 41 77; www.hotelalmadomus.it; Via Camporegio 37; s €40-52, d €60-€122, q €95-140; ❄📶) Owned by the church and still home to several Dominican nuns, this convent hotel is a lovely, peaceful oasis. Rooms, on the 3rd and 4th floors, represent excellent value for money, with a smart, modern look and pristine bathrooms. Some, for which you'll pay more, have views over to the Duomo.

Antica Residenza Cicogna B&B €
(☎0577 28 56 13; www.anticaresidenzacicogna.it; Via delle Terme 76; s €70-95, d 95-115, ste €120-155; ❄@📶) Charming host Elisa welcomes guests to her 13th-century family *palazzo*. The seven guestrooms are clean and well maintained, with painted ceilings, brick floors and the occasional patch of original fresco. There's also a tiny lounge where you can relax over complimentary Vin Santo and *cantuccini* (hard, sweet almond biscuits).

Osteria Nonna Gina TRATTORIA €
(☎0577 28 72 47; www.osterianonnagina.com; Pian dei Mantellini 2; meals €25; ⏲12.30-2.30pm & 7.30-10.30pm Tue-Sun) This cheery eatery is the picture of an old-school family-run trattoria. An oddment of accumulated clutter provides the decor as family members run between the kitchen and cosy dining room delivering steaming plates of pasta and Tuscan stews.

Morbidi DELI €
(www.morbidi.com; Via Banchi di Sopra 75; lunch buffet €12; ⏲8am-8pm Mon-Thu, to 9pm Fri & Sat) Duck under the ground-floor deli for Morbidi's excellent lunch buffet. For a mere €12 you can pick and choose from antipasti, salads, risottos, pastas and a dessert of the day. Bottled water is supplied, wine and coffee cost extra.

★Enoteca I Terzi MODERN TUSCAN €€
(☎0577 4 43 29; www.enotecaiterzi.it; Via dei Termini 7; meals €35-40; ⏲11am-1am summer, 11am-4pm & 6.30pm-midnight winter, closed Sun) Close to the Campo, this historic *enoteca* (wine bar) is a favourite with locals, who linger over working lunches, *aperitivi*, and casual dinners featuring top-notch Tuscan *salumi* (cured meats), delicate handmade pasta and wonderful wines.

Information

Tourist Office (☎0577 28 05 51; www.terresiena.it; Piazza del Duomo 1; ⏲9am-6pm daily summer, 10am-5pm Mon-Sat, to 1pm Sun winter) Opposite the Duomo. Reserves accommodation, organises car and scooter hire, and sells train tickets (commission applies). Also takes bookings for a range of day tours.

Getting There & Away

Siena Mobilità (800 922984; www.sienamobilita.it) buses run to/from Florence (€8, 1¼ hours, at least hourly), San Gimignano (€6, 1¼ hours, hourly), either direct or via Poggibonsi, and Pisa International Airport (€14, two hours, one daily).

Sena (www.sena.it) operates services to/from Rome Tiburtina (€24, three hours, nine daily), two of which continue to Fiumicino Airport; also to Milan (€36, 4½ hours, four daily), Perugia (€18, 1½ hours, two daily) and Venice (€32, 5½ hours, two daily).

Ticket offices are in the basement under the bus station on Piazza Gramsci.

Perugia

POP 166,000

With its hilltop medieval centre and international student population, Perugia is Umbria's largest and most cosmopolitan city. In July music fans inundate the city for the prestigious **Umbria Jazz festival** (www.umbriajazz.com), and in the third week of October the **Eurochocolate** (www.eurochocolate.com) festival lures chocoholics from across the globe.

Perugia has a dramatic and bloody past. In the Middle Ages, art and culture thrived: both Perugino and Raphael, his student, worked here, as powerful local dynasties fought for control of the city.

Sights

Perugia's sights are in the hilltop historic centre, concentrated on the main strip, Corso Vannucci, and Piazza IV Novembre, a handsome medieval piazza.

Cattedrale di San Lorenzo CATHEDRAL
(Piazza IV Novembre; 7.30am-noon & 3.30-6.45pm Mon-Sat, 8am-1pm & 4-7pm Sun) Overlooking Piazza IV Novembre is Perugia's stark medieval cathedral. A church has stood here since the 900s, but the version you see today was begun in 1345 from designs created by Fra Bevignate. Building continued until 1587, although the main facade was never completed. Inside you'll find dramatic late Gothic architecture, an altarpiece by Signorelli and sculptures by Duccio. The steps in front of the facade are where seemingly all of Perugia congregates; they overlook the piazza's centrepiece: the delicate pink-and-white marble **Fontana Maggiore** (Great Fountain; Piazza IV Novembre).

★**Palazzo dei Priori** PALACE
(Corso Vannucci) Flanking Corso Vannucci, this Gothic palace, constructed between the 13th and 14th centuries, is architecturally striking with its tripartite windows, ornamental portal and fortress-like crenellations. It was formerly the headquarters of the local magistracy, but now houses the city's main art gallery, the Galleria Nazionale dell'Umbria. Also of note is the **Nobile Collegio del Cambio** (Exchange Hall; www.perugiacittamuseo.it; Palazzo dei Priori, Corso Vannucci 25; admission €4.50, incl Nobile Collegio della Mercanzia €5.50; 9am-12.30pm & 2.30-5.30pm Mon-Sat, 9am-1pm Sun), Perugia's medieval money exchange, with its Perugino frescoes.

Galleria Nazionale dell'Umbria MUSEUM
(075 5866 8410; www.gallerianazionaleumbria.it; Palazzo dei Priori, Corso Vannucci 19; adult/reduced €6.50/3.25; 8.30am-7.30pm Tue-Sun) Umbria's foremost art gallery is housed in Palazzo dei Priori on the city's main strip. Its collection, one of central Italy's richest, numbers almost 3000 works, ranging from Byzantine-inspired 13th-century paintings to Gothic works by Gentile da Fabriano and Renaissance masterpieces by hometown heroes Pinturicchio and Perugino.

Sleeping & Eating

Primavera Minihotel HOTEL €
(075 572 16 57; www.primaveraminihotel.it; Via Vincioli 8; s €55-65, d €75-105, tr €95-120;) This welcoming hotel is tucked in a quiet corner of the *centro storico*. Magnificent views complement the bright rooms, decorated with period furnishings and characterful features like exposed stone, beams and wood floors. Breakfast costs €5 to €8 extra. English, French and Italian spoken.

Hotel Morlacchi PENSION €
(075 572 03 19; www.hotelmorlacchi.it; Via Tiberi 2; s €60-66, d €80-92, tr €90-115;) A friendly, old-school *pensione* near Piazza IV Novembre. The cosy, low-ceilinged rooms, spread over several floors of a 17th-century townhouse, are modest but comfortable with antiques and original artworks.

Pizzeria Mediterranea PIZZA €
(Piazza Piccinino 11/12; pizzas €4.50-12; 12.30-2.30pm & 7.30-11pm;) A classic pizzeria

WORTH A TRIP

ORVIETO

Strategically located on the main train line between Rome and Florence, this spectacularly sited hilltop town has one major drawcard: its extraordinary Gothic **Cattedrale di Orvieto** (0763 34 24 77; www.opsm.it; Piazza Duomo 26; admission €3; 9.30am-6pm Mon-Sat, 1-5.30pm Sun summer, 9.30am-1pm & 2.30-5pm Mon-Sat, 2.30-4.30pm Sun winter), built over 300 years from 1290. The facade is stunning, and the ethereally beautiful interior contains Luca Signorelli's awe-inspiring *Giudizio Universale* (The Last Judgment) fresco cycle.

For a filling meal, search out the **Trattoria del Moro Aronne** (0763 34 27 63; www.trattoriadelmoro.info; Via San Leonardo 7; meals €25-30; noon-2.30pm & 7.30-9.30pm Wed-Mon).

For information, the **tourist office** (0763 34 17 72; www.orvieto.regioneumbria.eu; Piazza Duomo 24; 8.15am-1.50pm & 4-7pm Mon-Fri, 10am-1pm & 3-6pm Sat & Sun) is opposite the cathedral.

Trains run to/from Florence (€15.40 to €19.50, 2¼ hours, hourly) and Rome (€7.50 to €13.50, 1¼ hours, hourly). From Perugia (€7 to €14.50, 1¾ to three hours, up to 13 daily), you'll need to change trains at Terontola-Cortona or Orte.

If you arrive by train, you'll need to take the **funicular** (€1.30; every 10min 7.15am-8.30pm Mon-Sat, every 15mins 8am-8.30pm Sun) up to the town centre.

with a wood-fired oven and bustling atmosphere, this popular spot does the best pizzas in town. Served bubbling hot, they come with light, Neapolitan-style bases and flavoursome toppings. Expect queues at the weekend.

Sandri CAFE, PASTICCERIA €
(Corso Vannucci 32; pastries €2.50; 7.30am-11pm) This city institution has been serving coffee and cake since 1860. Its delicately frescoed, chandelier-lit interior provides the perfect backdrop for exquisite-looking pastries, chocolates and cakes, enticingly presented in wall-to-ceiling cabinets.

Osteria a Priori OSTERIA €€
(075 572 70 98; www.osteriaapriori.it; Via dei Priori 39; meals around €30; 12.30-2.30pm & 7.30-10pm Mon-Sat) Located above an *enoteca*, this fashionable *osteria* specialises in local wines and fresh regional cuisine prepared with seasonal ingredients. Umbrian cheeses and cured meats feature alongside truffles, roast meats and autumnal mushrooms. Weekday lunch is a snip at €9. Reservations recommended.

Information

Tourist office (075 573 64 58; http://turismo.comune.perugia.it; Piazza Matteotti 18; 9am-7pm). City maps are available here. For information about what's on in town, buy a copy of *Viva Perugia* (€1) from a local newsstand.

Getting There & Around

Perugia's bus station is on Piazza dei Partigiani, from where an elevator connects with Piazza Italia in the historic centre.

Sena (861 1991900; www.sena.it) Buses serve Florence (€21, two hours, two daily) and destinations in Tuscany.

Sulga (800 099661; www.sulga.it) Buses run to/from Rome (€17, 2½ hours, four to five daily) and Fiumicino Airport (€22, 3¾ hours, two to four daily).

Umbria Mobilità (075 963 76 37; www.umbriamobilita.it) Operates buses to regional destinations, including Assisi (€4.20, 45 minutes, eight daily).

Direct trains connect with Florence (€14, 1½ to 2¼ hours, eight daily). To get to the centre from the train station, take the minimetrò (€1.50) to the Pincetto stop just below Piazza Matteotti. Alternatively, jump on bus G (€1.50, €2 on bus) to Piazza Italia or bus C to behind the Cattedrale di San Lorenzo.

Assisi

POP 28,100

The birthplace of St Francis (1182–1226), the medieval town of Assisi is a major destination for millions of pilgrims. The main sight is the Basilica di San Francesco, one of Italy's most visited churches, but the hilltop historic centre is also well worth a look.

Sights

★Basilica di San Francesco BASILICA

(www.sanfrancescoassisi.org; Piazza di San Francesco; upper church 8.30am-6.45pm, lower church & tomb 6am-6.45pm) FREE Visible for miles around, the Basilica di San Francesco is the crowning glory of Assisi's Unesco World Heritage ensemble. It's divided into an upper church, the **Basilica Superiore**, with a celebrated cycle of Giotto frescoes, and beneath, the older **Basilica Inferiore**, where you'll find frescoes by Cimabue, Pietro Lorenzetti and Simone Martini. Also here, in the Basilica's crypt, is St Francis' tomb.

Basilica di Santa Chiara BASILICA

(Piazza Santa Chiara; 6.30am-noon & 2-7pm summer, to 6pm winter) Built in a 13th-century Romanesque style, with steep ramparts and a striking pink-and-white facade, this church is dedicated to St Clare, a spiritual contemporary of St Francis and founder of the Sorelle Povere di Santa Chiara (Order of the Poor Ladies), now known as the Poor Clares. She is buried in the church's crypt, alongside the Crocifisso di San Damiano, a Byzantine cross before which St Francis was praying when he heard from God in 1205.

Sleeping & Eating

Hotel Alexander HOTEL €€

(075 81 61 90; www.hotelalexanderassisi.it; Piazza Chiesa Nuova 6; s €60-80, d €99-140;) On a small cobbled piazza by the Chiesa Nuova, the Hotel Alexander offers eight spacious rooms and a communal terrace with wonderful rooftop views. The modern decor – pale wooden floors and earthy brown tones – contrasts well with the wood-beamed ceilings and carefully preserved antiquity all around.

Trattoria da Erminio TRATTORIA €€

(075 81 25 06; www.trattoriadaerminio.it; Via Montecavallo 19; fixed-price menus €18, meals €25-30; noon-2.30pm & 7-9pm Fri-Wed) This charming backstreet trattoria is known for its grilled meats, prepared on a huge fireplace in the small dining area. In summer tables on the pretty cobbled street are hot property, and no wonder – this is old-fashioned Umbrian dining at its rustic best. You'll find it in the upper town near Piazza Matteotti.

Information

Tourist Office (075 813 86 80; www.assisi.regioneumbria.eu; Piazza del Comune 22; 9.30am-7pm daily summer, 8am-2pm & 3-6pm Mon-Fri, 9am-7pm Sat, 9am-6pm Sun winter) Stop by here for maps, leaflets and info on accommodation.

Getting There & Away

It is better to travel to Assisi by bus rather than train. Buses arrive at and depart from Piazza Matteotti in the *centro storico*.

Sulga (www.sulga.it) Buses serve Rome (€18, three hours, one daily).

Umbria Mobilità (www.umbriamobilita.it) Buses run to/from Perugia (€4, 45 minutes, eight daily).

The train station is 4km from Assisi proper in Santa Maria degli Angeli. If you arrive by train, take bus C (€1.30, €2 on board, half-hourly) to Piazza Matteotti. Regional trains run to Perugia (€2.50, 20 minutes, hourly).

SOUTHERN ITALY

A sun-bleached land of spectacular coastlines and rugged landscapes, southern Italy is a robust contrast to the more genteel north. Its stunning scenery, baroque towns and classical ruins exist alongside ugly urban sprawl and scruffy coastal development, sometimes in the space of just a few kilometres.

Yet for all its flaws, *il mezzogiorno* ('the midday sun,' as southern Italy is known) is an essential part of every Italian itinerary, offering charm, culinary good times and architectural treasures.

Naples

POP 989,100

Naples (Napoli) is dirty, noisy, dishevelled and totally exhilarating. Founded by Greek colonists, it became a thriving Roman city and was later the Bourbon capital of the Kingdom of the Two Sicilies. In the 18th century it was one of Europe's great cities, something you'll readily believe as you marvel at its profusion of baroque *palazzi*.

Sights

★Museo Archeologico Nazionale MUSEUM

(081 442 21 49; http://cir.campania.beniculturali.it/museoarcheologiconazionale; Piazza Museo Nazionale 19; adult/reduced €8/4; 9am-7.30pm

Wed-Mon; Ⓜ Museo, Piazza Cavour) Naples' premier museum showcases one of the world's finest collections of Greco-Roman artefacts. Originally a cavalry barracks and later seat of the city's university, the museum was established by the Bourbon king Charles VII in the late 18th century to house the antiquities he inherited from his mother, Elisabetta Farnese, as well as treasures looted from Pompeii and Herculaneum. Star exhibits include the celebrated *Toro Farnese* (Farnese Bull) sculpture and a series of awe-inspiring mosaics from Pompeii's Casa del Fauno.

★ Cappella Sansevero CHAPEL

(☎ 081 551 84 70; www.museosansevero.it; Via Francesco de Sanctis 19; adult/reduced €7/5; ⊙ 9.30am-6.30pm Mon & Wed-Sat, to 2pm Sun; Ⓜ Dante) It's in this Masonic-inspired baroque chapel that you'll find Giuseppe Sanmartino's incredible sculpture, *Cristo velato* (Veiled Christ), its marble veil so realistic that it's tempting to try to lift it and view Christ underneath. It's one of several artistic wonders, which also include Francesco Queirolo's sculpture *Disinganno* (Disillusion), Antonio Corradini's *Pudicizia* (Modesty) and riotously colourful frescoes by Francesco Maria Russo, the latter untouched since their creation in 1749.

Complesso Monumentale di Santa Chiara BASILICA, MONASTERY

(☎ 081 551 66 73; www.monasterodisantachiara.eu; Via Santa Chiara 49c; basilica free, Complesso Monumentale adult/reduced €6/4.50; ⊙ basilica 7.30am-1pm & 4.30-8pm, Complesso Monumentale 9.30am-5.30pm Mon-Sat, 10am-2.30pm Sun; Ⓜ Dante) Vast, Gothic and cleverly deceptive, the mighty **Basilica di Santa Chiara** stands at the heart of this tranquil monastery complex. The church was severely damaged in World War II and what you see today is actually a 20th-century re-creation of Gagliardo Primario's 14th-century original. Adjoining it are the basilica's **cloisters**, lavished with wonderfully colourful 17th-century maiolica tiles and frescoes.

★ Certosa e Museo di San Martino MONASTERY, MUSEUM

(☎ 081 229 45 10; www.polomusealenapoli.beniculturali.it; Largo San Martino 5; adult/reduced €6/3; ⊙ 8.30am-7.30pm Thu-Tue; Ⓜ Vanvitelli, funicular Montesanto Morghen) The high point (quite literally) of the Neapolitan baroque, this charterhouse-turned-museum was founded as a Carthusian monastery in the 14th century. Centred on one of Italy's finest cloisters, it has been decorated, adorned and altered over the centuries by some of Italy's finest talent, most importantly Giovanni Antonio Dosio in the 16th century and baroque master Cosimo Fanzago a century later. Nowadays, it's a superb repository of Neapolitan artistry.

Palazzo Reale di Capodimonte GALLERY

(☎ 081 749 91 11; www.polomusealenapoli.beniculturali.it; Via Miano 2; adult/reduced €7.50/3.75; ⊙ 8.30am-7.30pm Thu-Tue; 🚌 Via Capodimonte) Originally designed as a hunting lodge for Charles VII of Bourbon, this monumental palace is now home to the **Museo Nazionale di Capodimonte**, southern Italy's largest and richest art gallery. Its vast collection – much of which Charles inherited from his mother, Elisabetta Farnese, and moved here in 1759 – ranges from exquisite 12th-century altarpieces to works by Botticelli, Caravaggio, Titian and Andy Warhol.

The palace was started in 1738 and took more than a century to complete.

ARTECARDS

ArteCards (www.campaniartecard.it) offer discounted admission to museums in Naples and Campania. Get cards at participating museums, Naples Capodichino Airport, Naples' Stazione Centrale, online or by calling ☎ 800 600 601. There are several versions of the cards, of which the following two are the most useful:

Artecard Napoli (€21, valid for 3 days) Gives free entry to two sights in Naples, then discounts on others, as well as free city transport.

Artecard Campania (€32/34, valid for 3/7 days) Provides free entry to two/five sights (three-/seven-day card) across the region and discounts on others. Free public transport is covered by the three-day card, but not by the seven-day version.

Festivals & Events

Festa di San Gennaro RELIGIOUS

The faithful flock to the Duomo to witness the miraculous liquefaction of San Gennaro's

Central Naples

0 — 400 m
0 — 0.2 miles

Museo Archeologico Nazionale 2
Palazzo Reale di Capodimonte (1.9km)
Museo
Piazza Museo Nazionale
Piazza Cavour
Largo Regina Coeli
Duomo
Via Foria
Via Maria Longo
Via Santissimi Apostoli
Via d Anticaglia
Via Pisanelli
Via S Guiseppe dei Nudi
Via Tommasi
Via Broggia
Via Santa Maria di Costantinopoli
Via Francesco Saverio Correra
Via Enrico Pessina
Via della Sapienza
Via del Sole
Via Atri
Via San Paolo
Vico Giganti
Via Duomo
Via dei Tribunali
Vico Zuroli
Via della Zite
8
Piazza San Gaetano
10
Via G Maffei
Via Bellini
Vico S Domenico Soriano
Via G Brombeis
6 Piazza Bellini 13
Piazza Luigi Miraglia
Via Nilo
Via Vicaria Vecchia
Cappella Sansevero 1
Via Port'Alba
12
Dante
Piazza Dante
Via San Sebastiano
Palazzo dei Di Sangrio
Piazzetta del Nilo
Via San Biagio dei Librai
Vico S Severino
Piazza Museo Filangieri
Via Montesanto
Via Tarsia
Via Benedetto Croce
Via d'Alagno
Duomo (under construction)
Via Pellegrini
3
Via B Capasso
Piazza Nicola Amore
Via D Capitelli
Piazza del Gesù Nuovo
Via Toledo
Via Mezzocannone
Via G Paladino
Stazione Centrale (1.1km); Circumvesuviana (1.1km)
Via Pasquale Scura
Via Santa Chiara
Largo Giusso
Via Pignasecca
Via T Caravita
Piazza Monteoliveto
Largo Banchi Nuovi
Via S Liborio
Via Monteoliveto
Corso Umberto I
Piazetta Orefici
Via Formale
Piazza Carità
Via Sedile di Porto
Via Nuova Marina
Via Donnalbina
Via G Simonelli
Via C Battisti
Piazza Bovio
Via G C Cortese
Vico P Galluppi
Toledo
Via D Cerriglio
Piazza Matteotti
Università
Via Alside De Gasperi
Via Concezione a Montecalvario
Via Montecalvario
Via Bracco
Via A Diaz
Via D Fiorentini
Via Graziella
Via A Depretis
Tirrenia
Medmar
Calata Porta di Massa
Toledo
Varco Immacolatella
Via Potracarrese a Montecalvario
Via S Tommaso d'Aquino
Via F Gioia
Via S Bartolomeo
Via S Nicola alla Dogana
Via Cristoforo Colombo
Via Medina
Via S Giacomo
5 7
Via Speranzella
Via Toledo
Piazza del Municipio
Piazza Francese
Via P E Imbriani
Chiaia (under construction)
9
Municipio (under construction)
Via Santa Brigida
Vico d'Aflitto
Via Vittorio Emanuele III
Funicolare Centrale
4
Castel Nuovo
Molo Angioino
SNAV
Tirrenia
Via San Carlo
Alilauro
Piazza Trieste e Trento
14
Parco Castello
Caremar
11
Molo Beverello
Via A F Acton
Piazza del Plebiscito

Central Naples

Top Sights
1 Cappella Sansevero C2
2 Museo Archeologico Nazionale A1

Sights
3 Complesso Monumentale di Santa Chiara B3

Sleeping
4 Art Resort Galleria Umberto A6
5 Hostel of the Sun C6
6 Hotel Piazza Bellini B2
7 Romeo Hotel C6

Eating
8 Di Matteo C2
La Stanza del Gusto .... (see 6)
9 Pintauro A6
10 Pizzeria Gino Sorbillo C2

Drinking & Nightlife
11 Caffè Gambrinus A7
12 Caffè Mexico A2
13 Intra Moenia B2

Entertainment
14 Teatro San Carlo A7

blood on the Saturday before the first Sunday in May. Repeat performances take place on 19 September and 16 December.

Maggio dei Monumenti CULTURAL

A month-long cultural feast, with a bounty of concerts, performances, exhibitions, guided tours and other events across the city in May.

Sleeping

B&B Cappella Vecchia B&B €

(081 240 51 17; www.cappellavecchia11.it; Vico Santa Maria a Cappella Vecchia 11; s €50-70, d €75-100, tr €90-120; ; C24 to Piazza dei Martiri) Run by a super helpful young couple, this B&B makes a great base in the smart Chia district. It has six simple, comfy rooms with funky bathrooms, plays of colour, and Neapolitan themes, from *malocchio* (evil eye) to *spaccanapoli* (the main artery through Naples' historic centre). Breakfast is served in the spacious communal area.

Hostel of the Sun HOSTEL €

(081 420 63 93; www.hostelnapoli.com; Via G Melisurgo 15; dm €16-22, d €50-70; ; R2 to Via Depretis) The award-wining HOTS is an ultrafriendly hostel near the port. Located on the 7th floor (have €0.05 for the lift), it's a bright, sociable place with multicoloured dorms, a cute in-house bar, and pristine private rooms, with or without ensuite bathrooms.

★ **Hotel Piazza Bellini** BOUTIQUE HOTEL €€

(081 45 17 32; www.hotelpiazzabellini.com; Via Santa Maria di Costantinopoli 101; s €70-150, d €80-170; ; Dante) Only steps away from buzzing Piazza Bellini, this sharp, contemporary hotel occupies a 16th-century *palazzo*, its mint white spaces spiked with original maiolica tiles and the work of emerging artists. Rooms offer pared-back cool, with designer fittings, chic bathrooms and mirror frames drawn straight on the wall. Some also feature panoramic balconies.

Casa D'Anna GUESTHOUSE €€

(081 44 66 11; www.casadanna.it; Via Cristallini 138; s €67-102, d €95-145; ; Piazza Cavour, Museo) Everyone from artists to Parisian fashionistas adores this elegant guesthouse, lavished with antiques, books and original artwork. Its four guestrooms skillfully blend classic and contemporary design features of the highest quality, while the lush communal terrace is perfect for an alfresco tête-à-tête. Note, there's a two-night minimum stay.

Art Resort Galleria Umberto HOTEL €€

(081 497 62 81; www.artresortgalleriaumberto.it; 4th fl, Galleria Umberto I 83; r €94-193;) For a taste of Neapolitan glitz, book into this lofty four-star hotel on the upper floor of the Galleria Umberto I. Rooms are quiet and lavishly attired with frescoes, marble floors and gilt-framed paintings, as are the baroque-styled public spaces. Outside of office hours, you'll need €0.10 for the lift.

Romeo Hotel LUXURY HOTEL €€€

(081 017 50 01; www.romeohotel.it; Via Cristoforo Colombo 45; r €150-330, ste €240-650;) All A-list art, glass and steel, this top-end design hotel brings a touch of glamour to the scruffy port area. Rooms vary in size, but all are luxe and supremely comfortable, and the best offer memorable bay views. A Michelin-starred restaurant, sushi bar and fab spa add to the experience.

POMPEII & HERCULANEUM

On 24 August AD 79, Mt Vesuvius erupted, submerging the thriving port of Pompeii in lapilli (burning fragments of pumice stone) and Herculaneum in mud. Both places were quite literally buried alive, leaving thousands of people dead. The Unesco-listed ruins of both provide remarkable models of working Roman cities, complete with streets, temples, houses, baths, forums, taverns, shops and even a brothel.

Pompeii

A stark reminder of the malign forces that lie deep inside Vesuvius, the ruins of ancient **Pompeii** (081 857 53 47; www.pompeiisites.org; entrances at Porta Marina, Piazza Esedra & Piazza Anfiteatro; adult/reduced €11/5.50, incl Herculaneum €20/10; 8.30am-7.30pm summer, to 5pm winter) make for one of Europe's most compelling archaeological sites. The remains first came to light in 1594, when the architect Domenico Fontana stumbled across them while digging a canal, but systematic exploration didn't begin until 1748. Since then 44 of Pompeii's original 66 hectares have been excavated.

There's a huge amount to see at the site. Start with the **Terme Suburbane**, a public bathhouse decorated with erotic frescoes just outside **Porta Marina**, the most impressive of the city's original seven gates. Once inside the walls, continue down **Via Marina** to the grassy **foro** (forum). This was the ancient city's main piazza and is today flanked by limestone columns and what's left of the **basilica**, the 2nd-century-BC seat of the city's law courts and exchange. Opposite the basilica, the **Tempio di Apollo** is the oldest and most important of Pompeii's religious buildings, while at the forum's northern end the **Granai del Foro** (Forum Granary) stores hundreds of amphorae and a number of body casts. These were made in the 19th century by pouring plaster into the hollows left by disintegrated bodies.

A short walk away, the **Lupanare** (Brothel) pulls in the crowds with its collection of red-light frescoes. To the south, the 2nd-century-BC **Teatro Grande** is a 5000-seat theatre carved into the lava mass on which Pompeii was originally built.

Other highlights include the **Anfiteatro**, the oldest-known Roman amphitheatre in existence; the **Casa del Fauno**, Pompeii's largest private house, where many of the mosaics

Eating

Neapolitans are justifiably proud of their pizzas. There are any number of toppings but locals favour the *margherita* (tomato, basil and mozzarella) or *marinara* (tomatoes, garlic and oregano).

★ Pizzeria Gino Sorbillo PIZZA €

(081 44 66 43; www.accademiadellapizza.it; Via dei Tribunali 32; pizzas from €4; noon-1am Mon-Sat; M Dante) Day in, day out, this legendary pizzeria is besieged by hungry hordes. Once in, the frenetic atmosphere does nothing to diminish the taste of the pizzas, which are supremely good. If it's too crowded, try the 'quieter' Sorbillo a few doors away at Via dei Tribunali 38.

Di Matteo PIZZA €

(081 45 52 62; www.pizzeriadimatteo.com; Via dei Tribunali 94; snacks from €0.50, pizzas from €2.50; 9am-midnight Mon-Sat; C55 to Via Duomo) One of Naples' hard-core pizzerias, Di Matteo is fronted by a popular street-front stall that sells some of the city's best fried snacks, from *pizza fritta* (Neopolitan fried pizza) to nourishing *arancini* (stuffed rice balls). Inside, expect trademark sallow lighting, surly waitstaff and lip-smacking pizzas.

Trattoria Castel dell'Ovo SEAFOOD €€

(081 764 63 52; Via Lucculliana 28; meals €25-30; 1-3pm & 7.30pm-midnight Fri-Wed) Naples isn't all about pizza. Seafood is a citywide passion and the most atmospheric place to try it is the Borgo Marinaro. Here, fronting the marina and nestled among larger, smarter restaurants, this modest family-run trattoria serves tasty, no-nonsense fish dishes to locals and visitors alike.

now in Naples' Museo Archeologico Nazionale originated; and the **Villa dei Misteri**, home to the Dionysiac frieze, the most important fresco still on site.

To get to Pompeii, take the Circumvesuviana train to Pompeii Scavi-Villa dei Misteri (€2.90, 35 minutes from Naples; €2.20, 30 minutes from Sorrento) near the main Porta Marina entrance.

Herculaneum

Smaller and less daunting than Pompeii, **Herculaneum** (☎081 732 43 27; www.pompeiisites.org; Corso Resina 187, Ercolano; adult/reduced €11/5.50, incl Pompeii €20/10; ⏲8.30am-7.30pm summer, to 5pm winter) can reasonably be visited in a morning or afternoon.

A modest fishing port and resort for wealthy Romans, Herculaneum, like Pompeii, was destroyed by the Vesuvius eruption. But because it was much closer to the volcano, it drowned in a 16m-deep sea of mud and debris rather than in the lapilli and ash that rained down on Pompeii. This essentially fossilised the town, ensuring that even delicate items like furniture and clothing were well preserved. Excavations began after the town was rediscoverd in 1709 and continue to this day.

There are a number of fascinating houses to explore. Notable among them are the **Casa d'Argo**, a noble residence centred on a porticoed, palm-treed garden; the aristocratic **Casa di Nettuno e Anfitrite**, named after the extraordinary mosaic of Neptune in the nymphaeum (fountain and bath); and the **Casa dei Cervi**, with its marble deer, murals, and beautiful still-life paintings.

Marking the sites' southernmost tip, the 1st-century-AD **Terme Suburbane** is a wonderfully preserved baths complex with deep pools, stucco friezes and bas-reliefs looking down on marble seats and floors.

To reach Herculaneum, take the Circumvesuviana train to Ercolano (€2.20, 15 minutes from Naples; €2.20, 45 minutes from Sorrento), from where it's a 500m walk from the station; follow signs downhill to the *scavi* (ruins).

Da Michele PIZZA €

(☎081 553 92 04; www.damichele.net; Via Cesare Sersale 1; pizzas from €4; ⏲10.30am-midnight Mon-Sat) Veteran pizzeria Da Michele continues to keep things plain and simple: unadorned marble tabletops, brisk service and two types of pizza – *margherita* or *marinara*. Both are delicious. Just show up, take a ticket and wait (patiently) for your turn.

★Pintauro PASTICCERIA €

(☎348 778 16 45; Via Toledo 275; sfogliatelle €2; ⏲8am-2pm & 2.30-8pm Mon-Sat, 9am-2pm Sun Sep-May) Of Neapolitan *dolci* (sweets), the cream of the crop is the *sfogliatella,* a shell of flaky pastry stuffed with creamy, scented ricotta. This local institution has been selling *sfogliatelle* since the early 1800s, when its founder supposedly brought them to Naples from their culinary birthplace on the Amalfi Coast.

La Stanza del Gusto OSTERIA €€

(☎081 40 15 78; www.lastanzadelgusto.com; Via Costantinopoli 100; fixed-price menu €13, tasting menus €35-65; ⏲5.30pm-midnight Mon, 11am-midnight Tue-Sat; M Dante) Focused on top-quality ingredients and artisinal producers, this foodie address offers a trendy ground-floor 'cheese bar', a more-formal restaurant upstairs and a small basement deli. Frankly, the tasting menus aren't great value, but the 'cheese room' is perfect for *formaggi* (cheese), *salumi* and wine by the glass.

Drinking & Nightlife

Caffè Mexico CAFE

(Piazza Dante 86; ⏲5.30am-9pm Mon-Sat; M Dante) Naples' best (and best-loved) coffee bar – even the local cops stop by for a quick pick-me-up – is a retro-tastic combo of old-school baristas, orange espresso machine and velvety, full-flavoured *caffè*. The

OTHER SOUTHERN SPOTS WORTH A VISIT

Lecce Known as the Florence of the South; a lively university town famous for its ornate baroque architecture.

Matera A prehistoric town set on two rocky ravines, studded with primitive cave dwellings, known as *sassi*.

Aeolian Islands An archipelago of seven tiny islands off Sicily's northeastern coast. Lipari is the largest and the main hub, while Stromboli is the most dramatic, with its permanently spitting volcano.

espresso is served *zuccherato* (sweetened), so request it *amaro* if you fancy a bitter hit.

Caffè Gambrinus CAFE
(081 41 75 82; www.grancaffegambrinus.com; Via Chiaia 12; 7am-1am; R2 to Via San Carlo) Grand, chandeliered Gambrinus is Naples' oldest and most venerable cafe. Oscar Wilde knocked back a few here and Mussolini had some of the rooms shut to keep out left-wing intellectuals. Sure, the prices may be steep, but the *aperitivo* nibbles are decent and sipping a *spritz* while soaking up elegant Piazza Triesto e Trento is a moment worth savouring.

Intra Moenia CAFE
(081 29 07 20; Piazza Bellini 70; 10am-2am; ; M Dante) Despite the sloppy service, this ivy-clad literary cafe on Piazza Bellini is a good spot for chilling out. Browse limited-edition books on Neapolitan culture, pick up a vintage-style postcard, or simply sip a *prosecco* and people-watch on the piazza. Wine costs from €4 a glass and there's a range of bruschette, salads and snacks to tide off the munchies.

Entertainment

Teatro San Carlo OPERA, BALLET
(081 797 23 31; www.teatrosancarlo.it; Via San Carlo 98; box office 10am-5.30pm Mon-Sat, to 2pm Sun; R2 to Via San Carlo) One of Italy's top opera houses, the San Carlo stages a year-round program of opera, ballet and concerts. Bank on anything from €30 to €400 for opera tickets, less for ballet and concerts.

Information

Travellers should be careful about walking alone late at night near Stazione Centrale and Piazza Dante. Petty theft is also widespread so watch out for pickpockets (especially on the city's public transport) and scooter thieves.

TOURIST INFORMATION

Ospedale Loreto-Mare (081 254 21 11; Via Amerigo Vespucci; Corso Garibaldi) This hospital is on the waterfront, near the train station.

Police Station (Questura; 081 794 11 11; Via Medina 75) Has an office for foreigners. To report a stolen car, call 113.

Piazza del Gesù Nuovo (081 551 27 01; Piazza del Gesù Nuovo 7; 9am-5pm Mon-Sat, to 1pm Sun; M Dante).

Stazione Centrale (081 26 87 79; Stazione Centrale; 8.30am-8.30pm; Piazza Garibaldi).

Via San Carlo (081 40 23 94; Via San Carlo 9; 9am-5pm Mon-Sat, to 1pm Sun; R2 to Via San Carlo).

Getting There & Away

AIR

Naples Capodichino (081 789 61 11; www.gesac.it) Capodichino airport, 7km northeast of the city centre, is southern Italy's main airport. It's served by a number of major airlines and low-cost carriers, including easyJet, which operates flights to Naples from London, Paris, Berlin and several other European cities.

BOAT

Naples, the bay islands, the Amalfi Coast, Sicily and Sardinia are served by a comprehensive ferry network. Departure points:

Calata Porta di Massa Next to Molo Angioino; slow ferries to Capri, Procida and Ischia.

Molo Beverello For Sorrento, Capri, Ischia and Procida. Some services also leave from Molo Mergellina.

Molo Angioino Beside Molo Beverello; for Sicily and Sardinia

Tickets can be bought online or at Molo Beverello. For longer journeys try **Ontano Tours** (081 551 71 64; www.ontanotour.it; Molo Angioino; 8.30am-8pm Mon-Fri, to 1.30pm Sat). As a rough guide, bank on €19 for the 50-minute jet crossing to Capri, and €12.50 for the 35-minute sail to Sorrento. Services are pared back in winter and adverse sea conditions may affect schedules.

Alilauro (081 497 22 01; www.alilauro.it)

Caremar (081 551 38 82; www.caremar.it)

Medmar (☎081 333 44 11; www.medmar-group.it)
NLG (☎081 552 07 63; www.navlib.it)
Siremar (☎081 497 29 99; www.siremar.it)
SNAV (☎081 428 55 55; www.snav.it)
Tirrenia (☎892 123; www.tirrenia.it)

BUS

SITA Sud (☎089 40 51 45; www.sitasudtrasporti.it) runs buses to/from Amalfi (€4.10, two hours, up to four daily Monday through Saturday). They arrive at and depart from Varco Immacolatella on the seafront.

From the Metropark near the train station on Corso Arnaldo Lucci, **Marino** (☎080 311 23 35; www.marinobus.it) runs up to four daily buses to/from Bari (from €13, three to 3¾ hours). Get tickets from Bar Ettore at Piazza Garibaldi 95.

TRAIN

Most trains arrive at or depart from Stazione Centrale (Piazza Garinaldi) or Stazione Garibaldi underneath Stazione Centrale.

There are about 40 daily trains to Rome (€11 to €34.50, 1¼ to 2½ hours), many of which continue northwards.

Circumvesuviana (☎800 211388; www.eavsrl.it) – follow signs from the main train station – operates half-hourly trains to Sorrento (€4.10, 65 minutes) via Ercolano (€2.20, 15 minutes) for Herculaneum, and Pompeii (€2.90, 35 minutes).

Getting Around

TO/FROM THE AIRPORT

The **Alibus** (☎800 639525; www.anm.it) airport shuttle (€3, 45 minutes, every 20 minutes) runs to/from Piazza Garibaldi or Molo Beverello. Buy tickets on board.

PUBLIC TRANSPORT

You can travel around Naples by bus, metro and funicular. Journeys are covered by the Unico Napoli ticket, which comes in various forms:

Standard Valid for 90 minutes, €1.30
Daily €3.70
Weekend daily €3.10.

Note that these tickets are only valid for Naples city, they don't cover travel on the Circumvesuviana trains to Herculaneum, Pompeii and Sorrento.

Capri

POP 14,100

The most visited of the islands in the Bay of Naples, Capri deserves more than a quick day trip. Beyond the glamorous veneer of chichi cafes and designer boutiques is an island of rugged seascapes, desolate Roman ruins and a surprisingly unspoiled rural inland.

Ferries dock at Marina Grande, from where it's a short funicular ride up to Capri, the main town. A further bus ride takes you up to Anacapri.

Sights

Grotta Azzurra — CAVE

(Blue Grotto; admission €13; ⏲9am-1hr before sunset) Capri's single most famous attraction is the Grotto Azzura, a stunning sea cave illuminated by an other-worldly blue light.

The easiest way to visit is to take a tour from Marina Grande. This costs €26.50, comprising the return boat trip, a rowing boat into the cave and the cave's admission fee. Allow a good hour.

Giardini di Augusto — GARDENS

(Gardens of Augustus; admission €1; ⏲9am-1hr before sunset) Escape the crowds by seeking out these colourful gardens near the 14th-century Certosa di San Giacomo. Founded by the Emperor Augustus, they rise in a series of flowered terraces to a viewpoint offering breathtaking views over to the **Isole Faraglioni**, a group of three limestone stacks that rise vertically out of the sea.

Villa Jovis — RUIN

(Jupiter's Villa; Via Amaiuri; admission €2; ⏲9am-1pm, closed Tue 1st-15th of month, closed Sun rest of month) Some 2km east of Capri along Via Tiberio, Villa Jovis was the largest and most sumptuous of the island's 12 Roman villas and Tiberius' main Capri residence. A vast pleasure complex, now reduced to ruins, it famously pandered to the emperor's debauched tastes, and included imperial quarters and extensive bathing areas set in dense gardens and woodland.

★Seggiovia del Monte Solaro — CHAIRLIFT

(☎081 837 14 38; www.capriseggiovia.it; single/return €7.50/10; ⏲9.30am-5pm summer, to 3.30pm winter) A fast and painless way to reach Capri's highest peak, Anacapri's Seggiovia del Monte Solaro chairlift whisks you to the top of the mountain in a tranquil, beautiful ride of just 12 minutes. The views from the top are outstanding – on a clear day, you can see the entire Bay of Naples, the Amalfi Coast and the islands of Ischia and Procida.

Sleeping & Eating

Hotel Villa Eva HOTEL €€

(081 837 15 49; www.villaeva.com; Via La Fabbrica 8; d €100-160, tr €150-210, apt per person €55-70; Easter-Oct;) Nestled amid fruit and olive trees in the countryside near Anacapri, Villa Eva is an idyllic retreat, complete with swimming pool, lush gardens and sunny rooms and apartments. Stained-glass windows and vintage fireplaces add character, while the location ensures peace and quiet.

Hotel La Tosca PENSION €€

(081 837 09 89; www.latoscahotel.com; Via Dalmazio Birago 5; s €50-100, d €75-160; Apr-Oct;) Away from the glitz of Capri's town centre, this charming one-star place is hidden down a quiet back lane overlooking the Certosa di San Giacomo. The rooms are airy and comfortable, with pine furniture, light tiles, striped fabrics and large bathrooms. Several also have private terraces.

Lo Sfizio TRATTORIA, PIZZA €€

(081 837 41 28; Via Tiberio 7; pizzas €7-11, meals €30; noon-3pm & 7pm-midnight Wed-Mon Apr-Dec) On the path up to Villa Jovis, this trattoria-cum-pizzeria is ideally placed for a post sightseeing meal. It's a relaxed, down-to-earth place with a few roadside tables and a typical island menu, ranging from pizza and handmade pasta to grilled meats and baked fish.

Pulalli RISTORANTE €€

(081 837 41 08; Piazza Umberto 1; meals €35-40; noon-3pm & 7-11.30pm daily Aug, closed Tue Sep-Jul) Climb Capri's clock-tower steps to the right of the tourist office and your reward is this lofty local hang-out where fabulous wine meets a discerning selection of cheese, charcuterie, and more substantial fare such as *risotto al limone* (lemon risotto). Try for a seat on the terrace or, best of all, the coveted table on its own balcony.

Information

Information is available online at www.capritourism.com or from one of the three tourist offices: **Marina Grande** (081 837 06 34; www.capritourism.com; Quayside, Marina Grande; 9am-2pm & 3-6.50pm Mon-Sat, 9am-1pm & 2-7pm Sun), **Capri Town** (081 837 06 86; www.capritourism.com; Piazza Umberto I; 9am-7pm Mon-Sat, 9am-1pm & 2-7pm Sun) or **Anacapri** (081 837 15 24; www.capritourism.com; Via Giuseppe Orlandi 59, Anacapri; 9am-3pm).

Getting There & Around

There are year-round boats to Capri from Naples and Sorrento. Timetables and fare details are available online at www.capritourism.com.

From Naples Regular services depart from Molo Beverello. Tickets cost €19 (jetfoils), €12 (ferries).

From Sorrento Jetfoils cost €17 to €18.50, slower ferries €14.50.

On the island, buses run from Capri Town to/from Marina Grande, Anacapri and Marina Piccola. Single tickets cost €1.80 on all routes, including the funicular.

Sorrento

POP 16,700

Despite being a popular package-holiday destination, Sorrento manages to retain a laid-back southern Italian charm. There are very few sights to speak of, but there are wonderful views of Mt Vesuvius, and its small *centro storico* is an atmospheric place to explore. Sorrento's relative proximity to the Amalfi Coast, Pompeii and Capri also make it a good base for exploring the area.

Sights & Activities

You'll probably spend most of your time in the *centro storico*, a handsome area thick with souvenir stores, cafes, churches and restaurants.

Villa Comunale Park PARK

(8am-midnight summer, to 10.30pm winter) This landscaped park commands stunning views across the water to Mt Vesuvius. A popular green space to while away the sunset hours, it's a lively spot, with benches, operatic buskers and a small bar.

Bagni Regina Giovanna BEACH

Sorrento lacks a decent beach, so consider heading to Bagni Regina Giovanna, a rocky beach with clear, clean water about 2km west of town, set among the ruins of the Roman Villa Pollio Felix.

Sleeping & Eating

Casa Astarita B&B €

(081 877 49 06; www.casastarita.com; Corso Italia 67; d €70-120, tr €100-150;) Housed in a 16th-century *palazzo* on Sorrento's main strip, this charming B&B reveals a colourful, eclectic look with original vaulted ceilings, brightly painted doors and maiolica-tiled

UNICO COSTIERA

Bus travel along the Amalfi Coast is covered by the Unico Costiera travel card, available for durations of 45 minutes (€2.50), 90 minutes (€3.80), 24 hours (€7.50) and 72 hours (€18). Buy the cards from bars, *tabaccherie* (tobacconists) and SITA or Circumvesuviana ticket offices.

floors. Its six simple but well-equipped rooms surround a central parlour, where breakfast is served on a large rustic table.

Ulisse HOSTEL €
(☎081 877 47 53; www.ulissedeluxe.com; Via del Mare 22; dm €18-28, d €50-120; P❄📶) Although it calls itself a hostel, the Ulisse is about as far from a backpackers pad as a hiking boot from a stiletto. True, there are two single-sex dorms, but most rooms are plush, spacious affairs with Regency-style fabrics, marble floors and large en suite bathrooms. Breakfast is included in some rates, but costs €10 with others.

Raki GELATERIA €
(www.rakisorrento.com; Via San Cesareo 48; cones & tubs from €2; ⏲11am-late) There are numerous gelaterie in Sorrento, but this new kid on the block is making a mark with its homemade preservative-free ice cream in a number of exciting flavours. Try ricotta, walnut and honey, or vanilla and ginger, which packs a surprisingly spicy punch.

O'Puledrone SEAFOOD €€
(☎081 012 41 34; Via Marina Grande 150; meals €25-30; ⏲noon-3pm & 6.30pm-late Easter-Oct) The small harbour at Marina Grande is the place for seafood. This no-frills trattoria, run by a cooperative of local fishers, is as good a spot as any for fried fish starters, pastas and a mountainous *risotto alla pescatora* (seafood risotto).

Information

The main **tourist office** (☎081 807 40 33; www.sorrentotourism.com; Via Luigi De Maio 35; ⏲8.30am-7pm Mon-Sat summer, to 4.10pm winter) is near Piazza San Antonino, but there are also information points at the **Circumvesuviana station** (⏲10am-1pm & 3-7pm summer, to 5pm winter) and on **Piazza Tasso** (cnr Corso Italia & Via Correale; ⏲10am-1pm & 4-9pm summer, to 7pm winter).

Getting There & Away

Circumvesuviana trains run half-hourly between Sorrento and Naples (€4.10, 65 minutes) via Pompeii (€2.20, 30 minutes) and Ercolano (€2.20, 45 minutes). A daily ticket covering stops at Ercolano, Pompeii and Sorrento costs €6.30 (€3.50 on weekends).

Regular SITA buses leave from the Circumvesuviana station for the Amalfi Coast, stopping at Positano (€2.50, 40 minutes) and Amalfi (€3.80, 90 minutes).

From Marina Piccola, jetfoils (€18.50) and fast ferries (€17) sail to Capri (25 minutes, up to 16 daily).There are also summer sailings to Naples (€12.50, 35 minutes), Positano (return €32) and Amalfi (return €34).

Amalfi Coast

Stretching 50km along the southern side of the Sorrentine Peninsula, the Unesco-protected Amalfi Coast (Costiera Amalfitana) is a postcard-perfect vision of shimmering blue water fringed by vertiginous cliffs, on which whitewashed villages and terraced lemon groves cling.

Getting There & Away

SITA buses run from Sorrento to Positano (€2.50, 40 minutes) and Amalfi (€3.80, 90 minutes), and from Salerno to Amalfi (€3.80, 75 minutes).

Boat services generally run between April and October.

Alicost (☎089 87 14 83; www.alicost.it) Operates daily boats from Salerno (Molo Manfredi) to Amalfi (€8), Positano (€12) and Capri (€22).

Travelmar (☎089 87 29 50; www.travelmar.it) Has up to seven daily sailings from Salerno (Piazza Concordia) to Amalfi (€8) and Positano (€12).

Positano

POP 3950

Approaching Positano by boat, you're greeted by an unforgettable view of colourful, steeply stacked houses clinging to near-vertical green slopes. In town, the main activities are hanging out on the small beach, drinking and dining on flower-laden terraces and browsing the expensive boutiques.

The **tourist office** (☎089 87 50 67; Via del Saracino 4; ⏲9am-7pm Mon-Sat, to 2pm Sun summer, 9am-4pm Mon-Sat winter) can provide information on walking in the densely wooded Lattari Mountains.

WORTH A TRIP

RAVELLO

Elegant Ravello sits high in the clouds overlooking the coast. From Amalfi, it's a nerve-tingling half-hour bus ride (€2.50, up to three an hour), but once you've made it up, you can unwind in the ravishing gardens of **Villa Rufolo** (089 85 76 21; www.villarufolo.it; Piazza Duomo; adult/reduced €5/3; 9am-5pm) and bask in awe-inspiring views at **Villa Cimbrone** (089 85 80 72; Via Santa Chiara 26; adult/reduced €7/4; 9am-7.30pm summer, to sunset winter).

Sleeping & Eating

Pensione Maria Luisa PENSION €
(089 87 50 23; www.pensionemarialuisa.com; Via Fornillo 42; r €70-80, with sea view €95; Mar-Oct; @ wi-fi) The Maria Luisa is a friendly old-school *pensione*. Rooms feature shiny blue tiles and simple, no-frills decor; those with private balconies are well worth the extra €15 for the bay views. If you can't bag a room with a view, there's a small communal terrace offering the same sensational vistas. Breakfast is an additional €5.

Hostel Brikette HOSTEL €
(089 87 58 57; www.hostel-positano.com; Via Marconi 358; dm €24-50, d €65-145, apt €80-220; air-con wi-fi) Positano's year-round hostel is a bright, cheerful place. It has wonderful views and a range of sleeping options, from dorms to doubles and apartments. Conveniently, it also offers a daily hostelling option that allows day trippers use of the hostel's facilities, including showers, wi-fi and left luggage, for €10. Breakfast isn't included.

C'era una volta TRATTORIA, PIZZA €
(089 81 19 30; Via Marconi 127; pizzas €6, meals €25; noon-3pm & 6.30pm-late) Up in the high part of town, this authentic trattoria is a good bet for honest, down-to-earth Italian grub. Alongside regional staples, including *gnocchi alla sorrentina* (gnocchi served in a tomato and basil sauce), there's a decent selection of pizzas (to eat in or take-away) and a full menu of pastas and fail-safe mains.

Next2 RISTORANTE €€
(089 812 35 16; www.next2.it; Viale Pasitea 242; meals €45; 6.30-11.30pm) Understated elegance meets creative cuisine at this contemporary set-up. Local and organic ingredients are put to impressive use in beautifully presented dishes such as ravioli stuffed with aubergine and prawns or seabass with tomatoes and lemon-scented peas. Desserts are wickedly delicious and the alfresco sea-facing terrace is summer perfection.

Amalfi

POP 5170

Amalfi, the main hub on the coast, makes a convenient base for exploring the surrounding coastline. It's a pretty place with a tangle of narrow alleyways, stacked whitewashed houses and sun-drenched piazzas, but it can get very busy in summer as day trippers pour in to peruse its loud souvenir shops and busy eateries.

The **tourist office** (089 87 11 07; www.amalfitouristoffice.it; Corso delle Repubbliche Marinare 33; 9am-1pm & 2-6pm Mon-Sat) can provide information about sights, activities and transport.

Sights

Cattedrale di Sant'Andrea CATHEDRAL
(089 87 10 59; Piazza del Duomo; cathedral 7.30am-7.45pm, cloister 9am-7.45pm) A melange of architectural styles, Amalfi's cathedral, one of the few relics of the town's past as an 11th-century maritime superpower, makes a striking impression at the top of its sweeping flight of stairs. Between 10am and 5pm entrance is through the adjacent **Chiostro del Paradiso**, a 13th-century cloister, where you have to pay an admission fee of €3.

Grotta dello Smeraldo CAVE
(admission €5; 9.30am-4pm) Four kilometres west of Amalfi, this grotto is named after the eerie emerald colour that emanates from the water. Stalactites hang down from the 24m-high ceiling, while stalagmites grow up to 10m tall. Buses regularly pass the car park above the cave entrance (from where you take a lift or stairs down to the rowing boats). Alternatively, Coop Sant'Andrea runs boats from Amalfi (€10 return, plus cave admission). Allow 1½ hours for the return trip.

BARI

Most travellers visit Puglia's regional capital to catch a ferry. And while there's not a lot to detain you, it's worth taking an hour or so to explore Bari Vecchia (Old Bari). Here, among the labyrinthine lanes, you'll find the **Basilica di San Nicola** (www.basilicasannicola.it; Piazza San Nicola; ⌚7am-8.30pm Mon-Sat, to 10pm Sun), the impressive home to the relics of St Nicholas (aka Santa Claus).

For lunch, **Terranima** (☎080 521 97 25; www.terranima.com; Via Putignani 213/215; meals €30; ⌚11.30am-3.30pm & 6.30-10.30pm Mon-Sat, 11.30am-3.30pm Sun) serves delicious Puglian food.

Regular trains run to Bari from Rome (€39 to €43, four to six hours). Marino buses arrive from Naples (from €13, three to 3¾ hours).

Ferries sail to Greece, Croatia, Montenegro and Albania from the port, accessible by bus from the train station. Ferry companies have offices at the port, or you can get tickets at the **Morfimare** (☎080 578 98 15; www.morfimare.it; Corso de Tullio 36-40) travel agency.

Sleeping & Eating

Hotel Lidomare HOTEL €€

(☎089 87 13 32; www.lidomare.it; Largo Duchi Piccolomini 9; s/d €50/120; ❄ 📶) Family run, this old-fashioned hotel has real character. The large, luminous rooms have an air of gentility, with their appealingly haphazard decor, vintage tiles and fine antiques. Some have Jacuzzi bathtubs, others have sea views and a balcony, some have both. Breakfast is laid out, rather unusually, on top of a grand piano.

Hotel Centrale HOTEL €€

(☎089 87 26 08; www.amalfihotelcentrale.it; Largo Piccolomini 1; d €85-140; ❄ @ 📶) For the money, this is one of the best-value hotels in Amalfi. The entrance is on a tiny little piazza in the *centro storico,* but many of the small but tastefully decorated rooms overlook Piazza del Duomo. The aquamarine ceramic tiling lends it a vibrant, fresh look and the views from the rooftop terrace are magnificent.

Trattoria Il Mulino TRATTORIA, PIZZA €€

(Via delle Cartiere 36; pizzas €6-11, meals €30; ⌚11.30am-4pm & 6.30pm-midnight Tue-Sun) A TV-in-the-corner, kids-running-between-the-tables sort of place, this is about as authentic an eatery as you'll find in Amalfi. There are few surprises on the menu, just hearty, honest pastas, grilled meats and fish. For a taste of local seafood try the *scialatielli alla pescatore* (ribbon pasta with prawns, mussels, tomato and parsley).

Marina Grande SEAFOOD €€€

(☎089 87 11 29; www.ristorantemarinagrande.com; Viale Delle Regioni 4; tasting menu lunch/dinner €25/60, meals €45; ⌚noon-3pm & 6.30-11pm Tue-Sun Mar-Oct) 🍃 Run by the third generation of the same family, this beachfront restaurant serves fish so fresh it's almost flapping. It prides itself on its use of locally sourced organic produce which, in Amalfi, means high-quality seafood. Reservations recommended.

Sicily

Everything about the Mediterranean's largest island is extreme, from the beauty of its rugged landscape to its hybrid cuisine and flamboyant architecture. Over the centuries Sicily has seen off a catalogue of foreign invaders, from the Phoenicians and ancient Greeks to the Spanish Bourbons and WWII Allies. All have contributed to the island's complex and fascinating cultural landscape.

Getting There & Away

AIR

Flights from mainland Italian cities and an increasing number of European destinations serve Sicily's two main airports: Palermo's **Falcone-Borsellino Airport** (☎091 702 02 73; www.gesap.it) and Catania's **Fontanaross Airport** (☎095 723 91 11; www.aeroporto.catania.it).

BOAT

Regular car and passenger ferries cross to Sicily (Messina) from Villa San Giovanni in Calabria.

Ferries also sail from Genoa, Livorno, Civitavecchia, Naples, Salerno and Cagliari, as well as Malta and Tunisia.

Following are the major routes and the companies that operate them:

TO	DEPARTURE POINT	COMPANIES
Catania	Naples	TTT Lines
Messina	Salerno	Caronte & Tourist
Palermo	Cagliari	Tirrenia
Palermo	Civitavecchia	Grandi Navi Veloci
Palermo	Genoa	Grandi Navi Veloci
Palermo	Naples	Tirrenia, Grandi Navi Veloci
Palermo	Salerno	Grimaldi Lines

BUS

Bus services between Rome and Sicily are operated by **SAIS Trasporti** (www.saistrasporti.it) and **Segesta** (☎ 091 34 25 25; www.buscenter.it), departing from Rome Tiburtina. There are daily buses to Messina, Catania, Palermo and Syracuse.

TRAIN

Direct trains run from Rome, Naples and Reggio di Calabria to Messina and on to Palermo and Catania.

Palermo

POP 678,500

Still bearing the bruises of its WWII battering, Palermo is a compelling and chaotic city. It takes a little work, but once you've acclimatised to the congested and noisy streets you'll be rewarded with some of southern Italy's most imposing architecture, impressive art galleries, vibrant street markets and an array of tempting restaurants and cafes.

Sights

A good starting point is the **Quattro Canti**, a road junction where Palermo's four central districts converge. Nearby, **Piazza Pretoria** is dominated by the ostentatious **Fontana Pretoria**.

La Martorana CHURCH

(Chiesa di Santa Maria dell'Ammiraglio; Piazza Bellini 3; admission €2; ⏲8.30am-1pm & 3.30-5.30pm Mon-Sat, 8.30-9.45am & 11.45am-1pm Sun) On the southern side of Piazza Bellini, this luminously beautiful 12th-century church was endowed by King Roger's Syrian emir, George of Antioch, and was originally planned as a mosque. Delicate Fatimid pillars support a domed cupola depicting Christ enthroned amid his archangels. The interior is best appreciated in the morning, when sunlight illuminates magnificent Byzantine mosaics.

Chiesa Capitolare di San Cataldo CHURCH

(Piazza Bellini 3; admission €2.50; ⏲9.30am-12.30pm & 3-6pm) This 12th-century church in Arab-Norman style is one of Palermo's most striking buildings. With its dusky pink bijou domes, solid square shape, blind arcading and delicate tracery, it illustrates perfectly the synthesis of Arab and Norman architectural styles. The interior, while more austere, is still beautiful, with its inlaid floor and lovely stone-and-brickwork in the arches and domes.

Cattedrale di Palermo CATHEDRAL

(www.cattedrale.palermo.it; Corso Vittorio Emanuele; cathedral free, monumental area €7; ⏲7am-7pm Mon-Sat, 8am-1pm & 4-7pm Sun) A feast of geometric patterns, ziggurat crenulations, maiolica cupolas and blind arches, Palermo's cathedral has suffered aesthetically from multiple reworkings over the centuries, but remains a prime example of Sicily's unique Arab-Norman architectural style. The interior, while impressive in scale, is essentially a marble shell, the most interesting features of which are the royal Norman tombs (in the **Monumental Area** to the left as you enter) and **treasury**, home to Constance of Aragon's gem-encrusted 13th-century crown.

Palazzo dei Normanni PALACE

(Palazzo Reale; www.fondazionefedericosecondo.it; Piazza Indipendenza 1; adult/reduced Fri-Mon €8.50/6.50, Tue-Thu €7/5; ⏲8.15am-5.40pm Mon-Sat, to 1pm Sun) Home to Sicily's regional parliament, this venerable palace dates to the 9th century. However, it owes its current look (and name) to a major Norman makeover, during which spectacular mosaics were added to its royal apartments and magnificent chapel, the Cappella Palatina. Visits to the apartments, which are off limits from Tuesday to Thursday, take in the mosaic-lined **Sala dei Venti**, and **Sala di Ruggero II**, King Roger's 12th-century bedroom.

★Cappella Palatina CHAPEL

(Palatine Chapel; www.fondazionefedericosecondo.it; adult/reduced Fri-Mon €8.50/6.50, Tue-Thu €7/5;

⏲8.15am-5.40pm Mon-Sat, 8.15-9.45am & 11.15am-1pm Sun) This priceless jewel of a chapel, designed by Roger II in 1130, is Palermo's top tourist attraction. On the mid level of Palazzo dei Normanni's three-tiered loggia, it glitters with stunning gold mosaics, its aesthetic harmony further enhanced by the inlaid marble floors and wooden *muqarnas* ceiling, a masterpiece of Arabic-style honeycomb carving that reflects Norman Sicily's cultural complexity.

Note that queues are likely, and that you'll be refused entry if you're wearing shorts, a short skirt or a low-cut top.

★Teatro Massimo THEATRE

(☎tour reservations 091 605 35 80; www.teatromassimo.it; Piazza Giuseppe Verdi; guided tours adult/reduced €8/5; ⏲9.30am-5pm Tue-Sun) Palermo's grand neoclassical opera house took over 20 years to complete and has become one of the city's iconic landmarks. The closing scene of *The Godfather: Part III*, with its visually stunning juxtaposition of high culture, crime, drama and death, was filmed here. Guided 25-minute tours are offered in English, Spanish, French and Italian daily, except Monday.

Sleeping

★A Casa di Amici Hostel HOSTEL €

(☎091 765 46 50; www.acasadiamici.com; Via Dante 57; dm €15-23, d €46-70; ❄📶) Vibrant, friendly and full of uplifting paintings left by former guests, this funky hostel-cum-guesthouse is a great choice. Beds are in single-sex or mixed dorms, or in several imaginatively decorated rooms, each themed on a musical instrument. There's a kitchen and a yoga room, and multilingual owner Claudia provides helpful maps and advice.

B&B Panormus B&B €

(☎091 617 58 26; www.bbpanormus.com; Via Roma 72; s €45-70, d €60-83, tr €75-120; ❄📶) Keen prices, a charming host and convenient location help make this one of the city's most popular B&Bs. Its five high-ceilinged rooms, each with its own private bathroom down the passageway, are decorated in an elegant Liberty style and come with double-glazed windows and flat-screen TVs.

Butera 28 APARTMENT €€

(☎333 3165432; www.butera28.it; Via Butera 28; apt per day €60-180, per week €380-1150; ❄📶) Delightful multilingual owner Nicoletta rents 11 comfortable apartments in the 18th-century Palazzo Lanzi Tomasi, the last home of Giuseppe Tomasi di Lampedusa, author of *The Leopard*. Units range from 30 to 180 sq metres, most sleeping a family of four or more. Four apartments face the sea, most have laundry facilities and all have well-equipped kitchens.

Eating & Drinking

Three local specialities to try are *arancini, panelle* (chickpea fritters) and *cannoli* (pastry tubes filled with sweetened ricotta and candied fruit).

For an adrenalin-charged food experience, head to one of Palermo's markets: Capo on Via Sant'Agostino or Ballarò in the Albergheria quarter, off Via Maqueda.

Touring Café CAFE €

(☎091 32 27 26; Via Roma 252; arancino €1.70; ⏲6.15am-11pm Mon-Fri, to midnight Sat & Sun) Don't let the gleaming Liberty-style mirrored bar and array of picture-perfect pastries distract you. You come here for the *arancini*, great fist-sized rice balls stuffed with *ragù*, spinach or butter, and fried to a perfect golden orange.

Trattoria Il Maestro del Brodo TRATTORIA €

(☎091 32 95 23; Via Pannieri 7; meals €25; ⏲12.30-3.30pm Tue-Sun & 8-11pm Fri & Sat) This no-frills trattoria in the Vucciria offers delicious soups, an array of ultrafresh seafood, and a sensational antipasto buffet (€8) featuring a dozen-plus homemade delicacies: *sarde a beccafico* (stuffed sardines), eggplant *involtini* (rolls), smoked fish, artichokes with parsley, sun-dried tomatoes, olives and more.

★Osteria Ballarò SICILIAN €€

(☎091 791 01 84; www.osteriaballaro.it; Via Calascibetta 25; meals €35-40; ⏲12.30pm-3.15pm & 7pm-midnight) A hot new foodie address, this classy restaurant-cum-wine bar marries an atmospheric setting with fantastic island cooking. Bare stone columns, exposed-brick walls and vaulted ceilings set the stage for delicious seafood *primi*, local wines and memorable Sicilian *dolci*. Reservations recommended.

For a faster meal, you can snack on street food at the bar or take away from the hole-in-the-wall counter outside.

Kursaal Kalhesa BAR
(☎091 616 00 50; www.kursaalkalhesa.it; Foro Umberto I 21; ⌚6.30pm-1am Tue-Sun) Recently reopened after a restyling, Kursaal Kalhesa has long been a noted city nightspot. Touting itself as a restaurant, wine bar and jazz club, it draws a cool, in-the-know crowd who come to hang out over *aperitivi,* dine alfresco or catch a gig under the high vaulted ceilings – it's in a 15th-century *palazzo* on the city's massive sea walls.

Information

There are several information points across town, the most useful at the airport, **Piazza Bellini** (☎091 740 80 21; promozioneturismo@comune.palermo.it; ⌚8.30am-6.30pm Mon-Sat) and **Piazza Castelnuovo** (⌚8.30am-1pm Mon-Sat).

Ospedale Civico (☎091 666 11 11; www.ospedalecivicopa.org; Piazza Nicola Leotta) Emergency facilities.

Police Station (Questura; ☎091 21 01 11; Piazza della Vittoria 8).

Getting There & Away

National and international flights arrive at Falcone-Borsellino Airport (p709), 31km west of Palermo.

The ferry terminal is northeast of the historic centre, off Via Francesco Crispi.

The intercity bus terminal is in Piazza Cairoli, to the side of the train station. Following are the main bus companies:

Cuffaro (☎091 616 15 10; www.cuffaro.info; Via Paolo Balsamo 13) Services to Agrigento (€9, two hours, three to eight daily).

Interbus (☎091 616 79 19; www.interbus.it; Piazza Cairoli) To/from Syracuse (€13.50, 3¼ hours, three daily).

SAIS Autolinee (☎091 616 60 28; www.saisautolinee.it; Piazza Cairoli) To/from Catania (€15, 2¾ hours, 10 to 14 daily) and Messina (€26, 2¾ hours, three to six daily).

Trains serve Messina (€12 to €19.50, 2½ to 3½ hours, hourly), Agrigento (€8.50, two hours, 11 daily), Naples (€50 to €59, 9¼ hours, three daily) and Rome (€59 to €62, 11½ to 12¾ hours, four daily).

Getting Around

TO/FROM THE AIRPORT

Prestia e Comandè (☎091 58 63 51; www.prestiaecomande.it) operates a bus service from outside the train station to the airport. Buses run half-hourly between 5am and 10.30pm (11pm from the airport). Tickets for the 50-minute journey cost €6.30 and are available online or on the bus.

BUS

Walking is the best way to get around Palermo's centre, but if you want to take a bus, most stop outside or near the train station. Tickets cost €1.40 (€1.80 on board) and are valid for 90 minutes.

Taormina

POP 11,100

Spectacularly perched on a clifftop terrace overlooking the Ionian Sea and Mt Etna, this sophisticated town has attracted socialites, artists and writers ever since Greek times. Its pristine medieval core, proximity to beaches, grandstand coastal views and chic social scene make it a hugely popular summer holiday destination.

Sights & Activities

The principal pastime in Taormina is wandering the pretty hilltop streets, browsing the shops on **Corso Umberto**, the pedestrianised main strip, and eyeing up fellow holidaymakers.

For the beach, you'll need to take the **funivia** (cable car; Via Luigi Pirandello; one way €3; ⌚8.45am-1am Mon, 7.45am-1am Tue-Sun) down to Lido Mazzarò and Isola Bella.

★**Teatro Greco** RUIN
(☎094 22 32 20; Via Teatro Greco; adult/reduced €8/4; ⌚9am to 1hr before sunset) Taormina's premier sight is this perfect horseshoe-shaped theatre, suspended between sea and sky, with Mt Etna looming on the southern horizon. Built in the 3rd century BC, it's the most dramatically situated Greek theatre in the world and the second largest in Sicily (after Syracuse). In summer it's used to stage international arts and film festivals.

SAT BUS TOUR
(☎0942 2 46 53; www.satexcursions.it; Corso Umberto I 73) One of a number of agencies that organises day trips to Mt Etna (from €35), Syracuse (€45), Palermo (€55) and Agrigento (€52).

Sleeping & Eating

★**Isoco Guest House** GUESTHOUSE €
(☎0942 2 36 79; www.isoco.it; Via Salita Branco 2; r €95-120; ⌚Mar-Nov; ❄@📶) Each of the five rooms in this welcoming, gay-friendly guesthouse is dedicated to an artist, from Botticelli to graffiti pop designer Keith Har-

ing and photo legend Herb Ritts. Outside there's a garden where breakfast is served around a large table, and a roof terrace with a hot tub and stunning sea views.

Hostel Taormina HOSTEL €
(☎0942 62 55 05; www.hosteltaormina.com; Via Circonvallazione 13; dm €18-23, r €49-85; ❄📶) Friendly and laid-back, this year-round hostel occupies a house with a roof terrace commanding panoramic sea views. It's a snug, homey set-up with accommodation in three dorms, a private room and a couple of apartments. There's also a communal kitchen, a relaxed vibe and the owners go out of their way to help.

Tiramisù RISTORANTE, PIZZA €€
(☎0942 2 48 03; Via Cappuccini 1; pizzas €7-14, meals €35; ⏰12.30pm-midnight Wed-Fri, 1-3.30pm & 7.30pm-midnight Sat & Sun) Head to this stylish place near Porta Messina for excellent seafood, tasty wood-fired pizzas and traditional island dishes such as *rigatoni alla Norma,* a classic mix of pasta, aubergines, basil, tomato and ricotta. When dessert rolls around, don't miss the trademark tiramisu.

ℹ Information

Tourist Office (☎094 22 32 43; Palazzo Corvaja, Piazza Santa Caterina; ⏰8.30am-2.15pm & 3.30-6.45pm Mon-Fri, also 9am-1pm & 4-6.30pm Sat summer) Has plenty of practical information.

ℹ Getting There & Away

Taormina is best reached by bus. From the bus terminus on Via Luigi Pirandello, Interbus services leave for Messina (€4.30, 55 minutes to 1¾ hours, up to six daily), Catania (€5, 1¼ hours, six to 10 daily) and Catania's Fontanaross Airport (€8, 1½ hours, six daily).

Mt Etna

The dark silhouette of Mt Etna (3350m) broods ominously over Sicily's east coast, more or less halfway between Taormina and Catania. One of Europe's highest and most volatile volcanoes, it erupts frequently, most recently in summer 2014.

To get to Etna by public transport, take the AST bus from Catania (at 8.15am daily, also 11.20am June to September). This departs from in front of the train station (returning at 4.30pm; €6 return) and drops you at the Rifugio Sapienza (1923m), where you can pick up the **Funivia dell'Etna** (☎095 91 41 41; www.funiviaetna.com; return €30, incl bus & guide €60; ⏰9am-5.45pm summer, to 3.45pm winter) to 2500m. From there buses courier you up to the crater zone (2920m). If you want to walk, allow up to four hours for the round trip.

Gruppo Guide Alpine Etna Sud (☎095 791 47 55; www.etnaguide.com) is one of many outfits offering guided tours. Bank on around €70 to €80 for a full-day excursion.

Further Etna information is available from Catania's **tourist office** (☎095 742 55 73; www.comune.catania.it; Via Vittorio Emanuele II 172; ⏰8.15am-7.15pm Mon-Sat).

Syracuse

POP 122,300

A tumultuous past has left Syracuse (Siracusa) a beautiful baroque centre and some of Sicily's finest ancient ruins. Founded in 734 BC by Corinthian settlers, it became the dominant Greek city-state on the Mediterranean and was known as the most beautiful city in the ancient world. A devastating earthquake in 1693 destroyed most of the city's buildings, paving the way for a city-wide baroque makeover.

👁 Sights

Ortygia AREA
Connected to the modern town by bridge, Ortygia, Syracuse's historic centre, is an atmospheric warren of elaborate baroque *palazzi,* lively piazzas and busy trattorias. At its heart, the city's 7th-century **Duomo** (Piazza del Duomo; admission €2; ⏰9am-6.30pm Mon-Sat summer, to 5.30pm winter) lords it over Piazza del Duomo, one of Sicily's loveliest public spaces. The cathedral was built over a preexisting 5th-century-BC Greek temple, incorporating most of the original columns in its three-aisled structure. The sumptuous baroque facade was added in the 18th century.

Parco Archeologico della Neapolis ARCHAEOLOGICAL SITE
(☎0931 6 62 06; Viale Paradiso 14; adult/reduced €10/5, incl Museo Archeologico €13.50/7; ⏰9am-6pm) For the classicist, Syracuse's real attraction is this archaeological park, with its pearly white 5th-century-BC **Teatro Greco**. Hewn out of the rocky hillside, this 16,000-capacity amphitheatre staged the last tragedies of Aeschylus (including *The Persians*), which were first performed here in

his presence. In late spring it's brought to life with an annual season of classical theatre.

★ Museo Archeologico Paolo Orsi MUSEUM

(☎093 146 40 22; Viale Teocrito 66; adult/reduced €8/4, incl Parco Archeologico €13.50/7; ⊙9am-6pm Tue-Sat, to 1pm Sun) About 500m east of the archaeological park, this modern museum contains one of Sicily's largest and most interesting archaeological collections. Allow plenty of time to investigate the four sectors charting the area's prehistory, as well as Syracuse's development from foundation to the late Roman period.

Sleeping & Eating

★ B&B dei Viaggiatori, Viandanti e Sognatori B&B €

(☎0931 2 47 81; www.bedandbreakfastsicily.it; Via Roma 156; s €35-50, d €55-70, tr €75-80, q €90-100; ❄📶) Decorated with verve and boasting a prime Ortygia location, this relaxed B&B exudes a homey boho feel, with books and antique furniture juxtaposed against bright walls. Rooms are colourful and imaginatively decorated, while up top, the sunny roof terrace offers sweeping sea views.

B&B L'Acanto B&B €

(☎0931 44 95 55; www.bebsicily.com; Via Roma 15; s €35-50, d €55-70, tr €75-80, q €90-100; ❄📶) Set around an internal courtyard in the heart of Ortygia, L'Acanto is a popular, value-for-money B&B. Its five rooms are simply decorated and enlivened with patches of exposed stone, vintage furniture and the occasional mural.

Palazzo del Sale B&B €€

(☎093 16 59 58; www.palazzodelsale.com; Via Santa Teresa 25; d €100-120, ste €115-135; ❄📶) Housed in a historic *palazzo*, the seven rooms at this designer B&B are hot property in summer, so be sure to book ahead. All are well sized, with high ceilings, original touches and good beds. Coffee and tea are always available in the comfortable communal lounge.

★ Sicily PIZZA €

(☎392 9659949; www.sicilypizzeria.it; Via Cavour 67; pizzas €4.50-12; ⊙7.15pm-midnight Tue-Sun) Experimenting with pizzas is something you do at your peril in culinary-conservative Sicily. But that's what they do, and do well, at this funky retro-chic pizzeria. So if you're game for wood-fired pizzas topped with moreish combos like sausage, cheese, Swiss chard, pine nuts, sun-dried tomatoes and raisins, this is the place for you.

Sicilia in Tavola SICILIAN €

(☎392 4610889; Via Cavour 28; meals €25; ⊙12.30-2.30pm & 7.30-10.30pm Tue-Sun) One of a number of popular eateries on Via Cavour, this tiny trattoria enjoys a strong local reputation on the back of its homemade pasta and fresh seafood. To taste for yourself, try the *fettuccine allo scoglio* (pasta ribbons with mixed seafood). Reservations are recommended.

Information

Check out the useful website www.siracusaturismo.net.

Tourist Office (☎0800 055500; infoturismo@provsr.it; Via Roma 31; ⊙8am-8pm Mon-Sat, 9am-7pm Sun) For on-the-ground information, drop into this office in Ortygia.

Getting There & Around

Buses are a better bet than trains, serving a terminus close to the train station. Interbus runs services to/from Catania's Fontanaross Airport (€6, 1¼ hours, hourly), Catania (€6, 1½ hours, hourly) and Palermo (€13.50, 3¼ hours, three daily).

Direct trains connect with Taormina (€8.50, two hours, eight daily) and Messina (€9.50 to €15.50, 2¾ hours, seven daily).

Sd'a trasporti runs three lines of electric buses, the most useful of which is the red No 2 line, which links Ortygia with the train station and archaeological zone. Tickets, available on board, cost €0.50.

Agrigento

POP 59,000

Seen from a distance, Agrigento doesn't bode well, with rows of unsightly apartment blocks crowded onto the hillside. But behind the veneer, the city boasts a small but attractive medieval core and, down in the valley, one of Italy's greatest ancient sites, the Valley of the Temples (Valle dei Templi).

Founded around 581 BC by Greek settlers, the city was an important trading centre under the Romans and Byzantines.

For maps and information, ask at the **tourist office** (☎0922 59 31 11; www.provincia.agrigento.it; Piazzale Aldo Moro 1; ⊙9am-1pm &

2.30-7pm Mon-Fri, 9am-1pm Sat) in the Provincia building.

Sights

★Valley of the Temples ARCHAEOLOGICAL SITE
(Valle dei Templi; ☎0922 62 16 11; www.parcovalledeitempli.net; adult/reduced €10/5, incl Museo Archeologico €13.50/7; ⏲8.30am-7pm) Sicily's most enthralling archaeological site, the Parco Valle dei Templi encompasses the ruins of the ancient city of Akragas. The highlight is the stunning **Tempio della Concordia** (Temple of Concord), one of the best-preserved Greek temples in existence and one of a series built on a ridge to act as beacons for homecoming sailors.

The 13-sq-km park, 3km south of Agrigento, is split into an eastern zone, with the most spectacular temples, and, over the road, the western sector.

Sleeping & Eating

PortAtenea B&B €
(☎349 093 74 92; www.portatenea.com; Via Atenea, cnr Via C Battisti; s €39-50, d €59-75, tr €79-95; ❄📶) Conveniently located near the train and bus stations, this five-room B&B is an excellent choice. It wins plaudits for its panoramic roof terrace overlooking the Valley of the Temples, and spacious, well-appointed rooms.

Trattoria Concordia TRATTORIA €€
(☎0922 2 26 68; Via Porcello 8; meals €25-30; ⏲noon-3pm & 7-10.30pm Mon-Fri, 7-11pm Sat) This cosy side-alley eatery is a quintessential family-run trattoria. The look is rustic with rough stone walls and a low wood-beamed ceiling, and the food abundant and full of flavour. Kick off with the antipasto *rustico* (a heaving plate of frittata, sweet-and-sour aubergine, ricotta, salad, olives and more) before following with a juicy grilled steak.

Getting There & Around

The bus is the easiest way to get to and from Agrigento. Intercity buses arrive on Piazzale F Rosselli, from where it's a short walk downhill to the train station on Piazza Gugliemo Marconi, where you can catch local bus 1, 2 or 3 to the Valley of the Temples (€1.20).

Cuffaro runs buses to/from Palermo (€9, two hours, three to eight daily) and SAIS Trasporti services go to Catania (€13.50, three hours, hourly).

SURVIVAL GUIDE

Directory A–Z

ACCOMMODATION

- The bulk of Italy's accommodation is made up of *alberghi* (hotels) and *pensioni*. Other options are hostels, campgrounds, B&Bs, *agriturismi* (farm stays), mountain *rifugi* (Alpine refuges), monasteries and villa/apartment rentals.
- Prices fluctuate enormously between seasons. High-season rates apply at Easter, in summer (mid-June to August) and over the Christmas to New Year period.
- Many places in coastal resorts close between November and March.

B&Bs

- Quality varies, but the best offer comfort greater than you'd get in a similarly priced hotel room.
- Prices typically range from about €70 to €180 for a double room.

Camping

- Most Italian campgrounds are major complexes with on-site supermarkets, restaurants and sports facilities.
- In summer expect to pay up to €20 per person, and a further €25 for a tent pitch.
- Useful resources include www.campeggi.com, www.camping.it and www.italcamping.it.

Convents & Monasteries

Basic accommodation is often available in convents and monasteries. See www.monasterystays.com, a specialist online booking service.

Farm Stays

- An *agriturismo* is a good option for a country stay, although you'll usually need a car to get there.

SLEEPING PRICE RANGES

In this chapter prices quoted are for rooms with a private bathroom and, unless otherwise stated, include breakfast. The following price indicators apply (for a high-season double):

€ less than €110 (under €120 in Rome and Venice)

€€ €110–€200 (€120–€250 in Rome, €120–€220 in Venice)

€€€ more than €200 (more than €250 in Rome & €220 in Venice)

HOTEL TAX

Most Italian hotels apply a *tassa di soggiorno* (room occupancy tax) which is charged on top of your regular hotel bill. The exact amount, which varies from city to city, depends on your type of accommodation, but as a rough guide reckon on €1 to €3 per person per night in a one-star hotel, €3 to €3.50 in a B&B, €3 to €4 in a three-star hotel etc.

Prices quoted in accommodation reviews do not include the tax.

- Accommodation varies from spartan billets on working farms to palatial suites at luxury retreats.
- For listings check out www.agriturist.it or www.agriturismo.com.

Hostels

- Official HI-affiliated *ostelli per la gioventù* (youth hostels) are run by the **Italian Youth Hostel Association** (Associazione Italiana Alberghi per la Gioventù; Map p642; ☎06 487 11 52; www.aighostels.it). A valid HI card is required for these; you can get a card in your home country or directly at hostels.
- There are also many excellent private hostels offering dorms and private rooms.
- Dorm rates are typically between €15 and €30, with breakfast usually included.

Hotels & Pensioni

- A *pensione* is a small, often family-run, hotel. In cities, they are often in converted apartments.
- Hotels and *pensioni* are rated from one to five stars. As a rule, a three-star room will come with an en suite bathroom, air-con, hairdryer, minibar, safe and wi-fi.
- Many city-centre hotels offer discounts in August to lure clients from the crowded coast. Check websites for deals.

ACTIVITIES

Cycling Tourist offices can provide details on trails and guided rides. The best time is spring. Favourite areas include Tuscany, the flatlands of Emilia-Romagna, and the peaks around Lago Maggiore and Lago del Garda.

Hiking Thousands of kilometres of *sentieri* (marked trails) criss-cross the country. The hiking season is from June to September. The Italian Parks organisation (www.parks.it) lists walking trails in Italy's national parks.

Skiing Italy's ski season runs from December through to March. Prices are generally high, particularly in the top Alpine resorts – the Apennines are cheaper. A popular option is to buy a *settimana bianca* (literally 'white week') package deal, covering accommodation, food and ski passes.

BUSINESS HOURS

In reviews, the hours listed are the most commonly applied ones. Where necessary, summer/winter variations are noted. The following are the general hours for various business types:

Banks 8.30am to 1.30pm and 2.45pm to 4.30pm Monday to Friday.

Bars & Cafes 7.30am to 8pm, sometimes until 1am or 2am.

Clubs 10pm to 4am.

Museums & Galleries Generally operate summer and winter hours. Typically, summer hours apply from late March/April to October. At some places, closing time is set in relation to sunset.

Pharmacies Keep shop hours; outside of these, they open on a rotation basis – all are required to post a list of places open in the vicinity.

Post offices Major offices 8am to 7pm Monday to Friday, to 1.15pm Saturday; branch offices often close at 2pm Monday to Friday, 1pm Saturday.

Restaurants Noon to 3pm and 7.30pm to 11pm; most restaurants close one day a week.

Shops 9am to 1pm and 3.30pm to 7.30pm (or 4pm to 8pm) Monday to Saturday; in larger cities chain stores and supermarkets may stay open at lunchtime and on Sundays.

FOOD

- On the bill expect to be charged for *pane e coperto* (bread and cover charge). This is standard and is added even if you don't ask for or eat the bread.
- *Servizio* (service charge) of 10% to 15% might or might not be added; if it's not, tourists are expected to leave around 10%.
- Restaurants are nonsmoking.

GAY & LESBIAN TRAVELLERS

- Homosexuality is legal in Italy. It's well tolerated in major cities, but overt displays of affection could attract a negative response.
- Italy's main gay and lesbian organisation is **Arcigay** (☎051 1095 7241; www.arcigay.it; Via Don Minzoni 18, Bologna), based in Bologna.

INTERNET ACCESS

- Most hotels, hostels, B&Bs and *pensioni* offer free wi-fi.
- Public wi-fi is available in many large cities, but you'll generaly need an Italian mobile number to register for it.
- Internet cafes are thin on the ground. Charges are typically around €5 per hour.

- To use internet points you must present photo ID.

INTERNET RESOURCES

The following websites will whet your appetite for a trip to Italy:

Italia (www.italia.it) Mix of practical and inspirational information.

Lonely Planet (www.lonelyplanet.com/italy) Destination information, hotel booking, traveller forum and more.

Delicious Italy (www.deliciousitaly.com) Articles on Italian food and food-related news, events etc.

MONEY

ATMs Known as *bancomat*, ATMs are widespread and will accept cards displaying the appropriate sign. Visa and MasterCard are widely recognised, as are Cirrus and Maestro; American Express is less common.

EATING PRICE RANGES

The following price ranges refer to the cost of a two-course meal, glass of house wine and *coperto* (cover charge):

€ under €25

€€ €25 to €45

€€€ over €45

Credit cards Credit cards are widely accepted, although American Express less than Visa and MasterCard. Many trattorias, pizzerias and *pensioni* will only take cash, however. Don't assume museums, galleries and the like will accept credit cards. If your credit/debit card is lost, stolen or swallowed by an ATM, telephone toll free to block it: **Amex** (☎800 928391), **MasterCard** (☎800 870866) or **Visa** (☎800 819014).

ESSENTIAL FOOD & DRINK

Italian cuisine is highly regional in nature and wherever you go you'll find local specialities. That said, some staples are ubiquitous:

- **Pizza** There are two varieties: Roman, with a thin crispy base; and Neapolitan, with a higher, more doughy base. The best are always prepared in a *forno a legna* (wood-fired oven).
- **Pasta** This comes in hundreds of shapes and sizes and is served with everything from thick meat-based sauces to fresh seafood.
- **Gelato** Classic flavours include *fragola* (strawberry), *pistacchio* (pistachio), *nocciola* (hazelnut) and *stracciatella* (milk with chocolate shavings).
- **Wine** Ranges from big-name reds such as Piedmont's Barolo and Tuscany's Brunello di Montalcino to sweet Sicilian Malvasia and sparkling *prosecco* from the Veneto.
- **Caffè** Italians take their coffee seriously, drinking cappuccino only in the morning, and espressos whenever, ideally standing at a bar.

Eat Like an Italian

A full Italian meal consists of an antipasto, a *primo* (first course; pasta or rice dish), *secondo* (second/main course; usually meat or fish) with an *insalata* (salad) or *contorno* (vegetable side dish), *dolce* (dessert) and coffee. Most Italians only eat a meal this large at Sunday lunch or on a special occasion, and when eating out it's fine to mix and match and order, say, a *primo* followed by an *insalata* or *contorno*.

Italians are late diners, often not eating until after 9pm.

Where to Eat & Drink

For a full meal there are several options: **trattorias** are traditional, often family-run places serving local food and wine; **ristoranti** (restaurants) are more formal, with greater choice and smarter service; **pizzerias**, which usually open evenings only, often serve a full menu alongside pizzas.

At lunchtime **bars** and **cafes** sell *panini* (bread rolls), and many serve an evening *aperitivo* (aperitif) buffet. At an **enoteca** (wine bar) you can drink wine by the glass and snack on cheese and cured meats. Some also serve hot dishes. For a slice of pizza search out a **pizza al taglio** joint.

Tipping If *servizio* is not included, leave 10% in restaurants, a euro or two in pizzerias. It's not necessary in bars or cafes, but many people leave small change if drinking at the bar.

PUBLIC HOLIDAYS

Most Italians take their annual holiday in August. This means that many businesses and shops close down for at least part of the month, usually around Ferragosto (15 August). Easter is another busy holiday. Individual towns also have holidays to celebrate their patron saints.

Countrywide public holidays:

New Year's Day (Capodanno) 1 January
Epiphany (Epifania) 6 January
Easter Monday (Pasquetta) March/April
Liberation Day (Giorno delle Liberazione) 25 April
Labour Day (Festa del Lavoro) 1 May
Republic Day (Festa della Repubblica) 2 June
Feast of the Assumption (Ferragosto) 15 August
All Saints' Day (Ognisanti) 1 November
Feast of the Immaculate Conception (Immacolata Concezione) 8 December
Christmas Day (Natale) 25 December
Boxing Day (Festa di Santo Stefano) 26 December

SAFE TRAVEL

Italy is generally a safe country, but petty theft is prevalent. Be on your guard against pickpockets in popular tourist centres such as Rome, Florence, Venice and Naples.

TELEPHONE

- Area codes are an integral part of all Italian phone numbers and must be dialled even when calling locally.
- To call Italy from abroad, dial ☎0039 and then the area code, including the first zero.
- To call abroad from Italy, dial ☎00, then the relevant country code followed by the telephone number.
- Italian mobile phone numbers are nine or 10 digits long and start with a three-digit prefix starting with a ☎3.
- Skype is available on many hostel computers.

Mobile Phones

- Italy uses the GSM 900/1800 network, which is compatible with European and Australian devices, but not all North American cell phones.
- If you can unlock your device (check with your service provider), the cheapest way to make calls is to buy an Italian SIM card. These are available from **TIM** (www.tim.it), **Tre** (www.tre.it), **Wind** (www.wind.it) and **Vodafone** (www.vodafone.it). You'll need ID when you buy one.

VISAS

- Schengen visa rules apply for entry to Italy.
- Unless staying in a hotel/B&B/hostel etc, all foreign visitors are supposed to register with the local police within eight days of arrival.
- A *permesso di soggiorno* (permit to stay) is required by all non-EU nationals who stay in Italy longer than three months. You must apply within eight days of arriving in Italy. Check documentary requirements on www.poliziadistato.it.
- EU citizens do not require a *permesso di soggiorno*.

> **COUNTRY FACTS**
>
> **Area** 301,230 sq km
>
> **Capital** Rome
>
> **Currency** Euro (€)
>
> **Emergency** ☎112
>
> **Language** Italian
>
> **Money** ATMs widespread; credit cards widely accepted
>
> **Population** 60.78 million
>
> **Telephone** Country code ☎39, international access code ☎00
>
> **Visas** Schengen rules apply

Getting There & Away

Getting to Italy is straightforward. It is well served by international airlines and European low-cost carriers, and there are plenty of bus, train and ferry routes into the country.

Flights, tours and rail tickets can be booked online at lonelyplanet.com/bookings.

AIR

There are direct intercontinental flights to/from Rome and Milan. European flights also serve regional airports. Italy's national carrier is **Alitalia** (www.alitalia.com).

Italy's principal airports:

Leonardo da Vinci (www.adr.it/iumicino) Italy's main airport; also known as Rome Fiumicino Airport.

Rome Ciampino (www.adr.it/ciampino) Rome's second airport.

Milan Malpensa (www.milanomalpensa-airport.com) Northern Italy's principal hub.

Venice Marco Polo (www.veniceairport.it) Venice's main airport.

Pisa International (www.pisa-airport.com) Gateway for Florence and Tuscany.

MAIN INTERNATIONAL FERRY ROUTES

FROM	TO	COMPANY	MIN-MAX FARE (€)	DURATION (HR)
Ancona	Igoumenitsa	Minoan, Superfast, Anek	69-100	16½-22
Ancona	Patra	Minoan, Superfast, Anek	69-100	22-29
Ancona	Split	Jadrolinija, SNAV	48-57.50	10¾
Bari	Bar	Montenegro	50-55	9
Bari	Corfu	Superfast	78-93	9
Bari	Dubrovnik	Jadrolinija	48-57.50	10-12
Bari	Igoumenitsa	Superfast	78-93	8-12
Bari	Patra	Superfast	78-93	16
Brindisi	Igoumenitsa	Endeavor	52-83	8
Brindisi	Patra	Endeavor	56-94	14
Brindisi	Corfu	Endeavor	52-83	6½-11½
Brindisi	Kefallonia	Endeavor	56-94	12½
Civitavecchia	Barcelona	Grimaldi	45-90	20
Genoa	Barcelona	GNV	90	19½
Genoa	Tunis	GNV	111	23½
Venice	Igoumenitsa	Superfast	66-82	15
Venice	Patras	Superfast	66-82	18-21½

Naples Capodichino (www.gesac.it) Southern Italy's main airport.

Catania Fontanarossa (www.aeroporto.catania.it) Sicily's largest airport.

LAND

Bus

Eurolines (www.eurolines.it) operates buses from European destinations to many Italian cities.

Train

Milan and Venice are Italy's main international rail hubs. International trains also run to/from Rome, Genoa, Turin, Verona, Padua, Bologna, Florence and Naples. Main routes:

Milan To/from Paris, Marseille, Geneva, Zürich and Vienna.

Rome To/from Munich and Vienna.

Venice To/from Paris, Munich, Innsbruck, Salzburg and Vienna.

Voyages-sncf (☎ 0844 848 5848; http://uk.voyages-sncf.com) can provide fare information on journeys from the UK to Italy, most of which require a change at Paris. Another excellent resource is www.seat61.com.

Eurail and Inter-Rail passes are valid in Italy.

SEA

- Ferries serve Italian ports from across the Mediterranean. Timetables are seasonal, so always check ahead.
- For routes, companies and online booking try www.traghettiweb.it.
- Prices quoted in this chapter are for a one-way *poltrona* (reclinable seat).
- Holders of Eurail and Inter-Rail passes should check with the ferry company if they are entitled to a discount or free passage.
- Major ferry companies include: **Anek Lines** (www.anekitalia.com), **Endeavor Lines** (www.endeavor-lines.com), **GNV** (www.gnv.it), **Jadrolinija** (www.jadrolinija.hr), **Minoan Lines** (www.minoan.it), **Montenegro Lines** (www.montenegrolines.net), **SNAV** (www.snav.it) and **Superfast** (www.superfast.com).

ℹ Getting Around

BICYCLE

- Bikes can be taken on regional and certain international trains carrying the bike logo, but you'll need to pay a supplement (€3.50 on regional trains, €12 on international trains). Bikes can be carried free if dismantled and stored in a bike bag.
- Bikes generally incur a small supplement on ferries, typically €10 to €15.

BOAT

Navi (large ferries) sail to Sicily and Sardinia; *traghetti* (smaller ferries) and *aliscafi* (hydrofoils) cover the smaller islands.

The main embarkation points for Sardinia are Genoa, Civitavecchia and Naples; for Sicily, Naples and Villa San Giovanni in Calabria.

ADMISSION PRICES

As of July 2014, admission to state-run museums, galleries, monuments and sites is free to minors under 18. People aged between 18 and 25 are entitled to a discount. To get it, you'll need proof of your age, ideally a passport or ID card.

Admission is free to everyone on the first Sunday of each month.

Following are the major domestic ferry companies:

GNV (☎010 209 45 91; www.gnv.it) To/from Sardinia and Sicily.

Moby Lines (☎199 303040; www.moby.it) To/from Sardinia and Elba.

Sardinia Ferries (☎199 400500; www.corsica-ferries.it) To/from Sardinia.

SNAV (☎081 428 55 55; www.snav.it) To/from Aeolian Islands, Capri and Bay of Naples islands.

Tirrenia (☎892 123; www.tirrenia.it) To/from Sardinia and Sicily.

BUS

- Italy boasts an extensive and largely reliable bus network.
- Buses are not necessarily cheaper than trains, but in mountainous areas they are often the only choice.
- In larger cities, companies have ticket offices or operate through agencies, but in villages and small towns tickets are sold in bars or on the bus.
- Reservations are only necessary for high-season long-haul trips.

CAR & MOTORCYCLE

- Italy's roads are generally good, and there's an extensive network of toll autostradas (motorways).
- All EU driving licences are recognised in Italy. Holders of non-EU licences should get an International Driving Permit (IDP) through their national automobile association.
- Traffic restrictions apply in most city centres.
- To hire a car you'll require a driving licence (plus IDP if necessary) and credit card. Age restrictions vary, but generally you'll need to be 21 or over.
- If driving your own car, carry your vehicle registration certificate, driving licence and proof of third-party liability insurance cover.
- For further details, see the website of Italy's motoring organisation **Automobile Club d'Italia** (ACI; www.aci.it).
- ACI provides 24-hour roadside assistance: call ☎803 116 from a landline or Italian mobile, ☎800 116 800 from a foreign mobile.

TRAIN

Italy has an extensive rail network. Trains are relatively cheap, and many are fast and comfortable. Most services are run by **Trenitalia** (☎892021; www.trenitalia.com) but **Italo** (☎06 07 08; www.italotreno.it) also operates high-speed trains.

There are several types of train:

InterCity (IC) Trains between major cities. **Le Frecce** Fast trains: Frecciarossa, Frecciargento and Frecciabianca.

Regionale or interregionale (R) Slow local services.

Tickets

- InterCity and Frecce trains require a supplement, which is incorporated in the ticket price. If you have a standard ticket and board an InterCity you'll have to pay the difference on board.
- Frecce trains require prior reservation.
- Generally, it's cheaper to buy train tickets in Italy.
- If your ticket doesn't include a reservation with an assigned seat, you must validate it before boarding by inserting it into one of the machines dotted around stations.
- Some services offer 'ticketless' travel; book and pay for your seat on www.trenitalia.com and then communicate your booking code to the controller on board.

Kosovo

Includes ➡

Best Places to Eat

- Tiffany (p725)
- Renaissance II (p725)
- De Rada Brasserie (p725)
- Ego (p729)

Best Places to Stay

- Swiss Diamond Hotel (p725)
- Dukagjini Hotel (p727)
- Han Hostel (p723)
- Hotel Prizreni (p729)

Why Go?

Kosovo is Europe's newest country and a fascinating land at the heart of the Balkans that rewards visitors with welcoming smiles, charming mountain towns, incredible hiking opportunities and 13th-century domed Serbian monasteries just for starters. It's safe to travel here now, and indeed is one of the last corners of Europe that remains off the beaten track for travellers.

Kosovo declared independence from Serbia in 2008, and while it has been diplomatically recognised by 110 countries, there are still many nations that do not accept Kosovan independence, including Serbia. The country has been the focus of massive aid from the international community, particularly the EU and NATO, who effectively run the entity politically and keep peace between the ethnic Albanian majority and the minority Serbs. Barbs of its past are impossible to miss, however: roads are dotted with memorials to those killed in 1999, while NATO forces still guard Serbian monasteries.

When to Go

Pristina

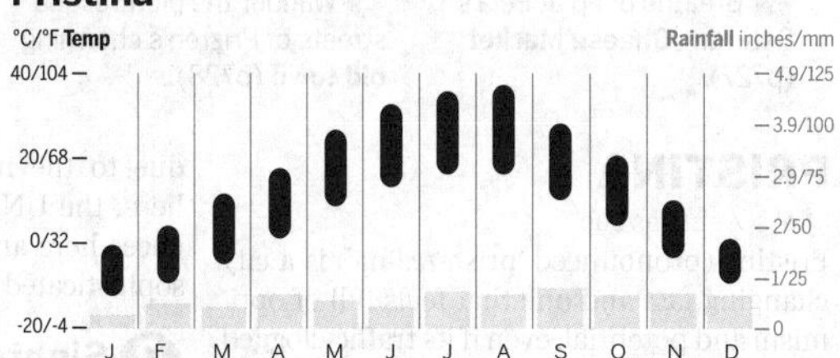

Apr Pristina International Film Festival (PriFest) brings a touch of glamour to the capital.

May–Sep You don't have to worry about high-season crowds in Kosovo!

Aug The excellent DokuFest in Prizren is Kosovo's best arts event.

Kosovo Highlights

1. See the sights in Pristina's charming **bazaar area** and discover this bustling capital.
2. Breathe deep at Peja's Saturday **Cheese Market** (p727).
3. Buy local wine and cheese at the serene 14th-century **Visoki Dečani Monastery** (p728).
4. Wander the picturesque streets of Prizren's charming **old town** (p728).
5. Trek around the **Rugova Mountains** (p727).
6. Visit Kosovo's fabulous new **Bear Sanctuary Pristina** and see rescued bears living in excellent conditions (p726).

PRISTINA

☎038 / POP 198,000

Pristina (pronounced 'prish-*tee*-na') is a city changing fast and one that feels full of optimism and potential, even if its traffic-clogged streets and mismatched architectural styles don't make it an obviously attractive place. Far more a provincial town than great city, Pristina makes for an unlikely national capital, and yet feels more cosmopolitan than the capitals of many larger Balkan nations due to the number of foreigners working here: the UN and EU both have large presences here and the city feels rich and more sophisticated as a result.

Sights

Bazaar Area

★**Ethnographic Museum** HISTORIC BUILDING
(Rr Iliaz Agushi; admission by donation; ⏰10am-5pm) This wonderful annex of the Museum

ITINERARIES

Two to Three Days

Spend a day in cool little **Pristina** and get to know Kosovo's chaotic but somehow charming capital. The next day, visit **Visoki Dečani Monastery** and then head on to **Prizren**, to see the old town's Ottoman sights and enjoy the view from the castle.

One Week

After a couple of days in the capital, and a visit to **Gračanica Monastery** and the **Bear Sanctuary**, loop to lovely **Prizren** for a night before continuing to **Peja** for monasteries and markets. Then end with a few days of hiking in the beautiful **Rugova Mountains**.

of Kosovo is housed in two beautifully preserved Ottoman houses enclosed in a large walled garden. The clued-up, super-keen English-speaking staff will give you a fascinating tour of both properties and point out the various unique pieces of clothing, weapons, jewellery and household goods on display in each. There's no better introduction to Kosovar culture to be had.

Museum of Kosovo MUSEUM
(Sheshi Adam Jashari; admission €2; ⌚10am-5pm Tue-Sat) Following a full renovation, Pristina's main museum is now open again and has displays spread over three floors.

On the ground floor you'll find an ethnological exhibit, entirely unlabelled but with some superb examples of wood carving. The 2nd floor contains a poor selection of paintings from various eras, while the top floor is an unbalanced display on the Kosovan War and the birth of the nation.

Mosques MOSQUES
Fronting the Kosovo Museum is the 15th-century **Carshi Mosque** (Agim Ramadani). Nearby, the **Sultan Mehmet Fatih Mosque** (Big Mosque; Rr Ilir Konushevci) was built by its namesake around 1461, converted to a Catholic church during the Austro-Hungarian era and refurbished again during WWII. **Jashar Pasha Mosque** (Rr Ylfete Humolli) has vibrant interiors that exemplify Turkish baroque style.

Clock Tower LANDMARK
(Sahat Kulla) This 26m-high tower dates from the 19th century and was central to the bazaar area, as it dictated when stalls should close for prayers. Following damage in the war, it now operates on electricity. The Great Hamam nearby is being renovated.

Centre

The centre of Pristina has been impressively redesigned and is now focused on the new Ibrahim Rugova Sq, the centrepiece of the city at the end of the attractively pedestrianised Bul Nenë Terezë.

National Library LIBRARY
(www.biblioteka-ks.org; Rr Agim Ramadani; ⌚7am-8pm Mon-Fri, 7am-2pm Sat) FREE Easily one of Pristina's most notable buildings, the National Library, completed in 1982 by Croatian Andrija Mutnjakovic, must be seen to be believed (think gelatinous eggs wearing armour).

National Gallery of Kosovo GALLERY
(www.galeriakombetare.com; Rr Agim Ramadani 60; ⌚10am-6pm Mon-Fri) FREE This excellent space takes a thoroughly contemporary stance on Kosovan art (don't expect to see paintings from throughout the country's history here) and is always worth a look around.

Sleeping

★Han Hostel HOSTEL €
(☎044 396 852, 044 760 792; www.hostelhan.com; Rr Fehmi Agani 2/4; dm €10-12, s/d €20/30; @🛜) Pristina's best hostel is on the 4th floor of a residential building right in the heart of town. Cobbled together from two apartments that have been joined and converted, this great space has a large communal kitchen, balconies and smart rooms with clean bathrooms. It's well set up for backpackers and run by an extremely friendly local crew.

White Tree Hostel HOSTEL €
(☎049 166 777; www.whitetreehostel.com; Rr Mujo Ulqinaku 15; dm/r €10/30; ❄🛜) Run by a well-travelled bunch of locals who took a

Pristina

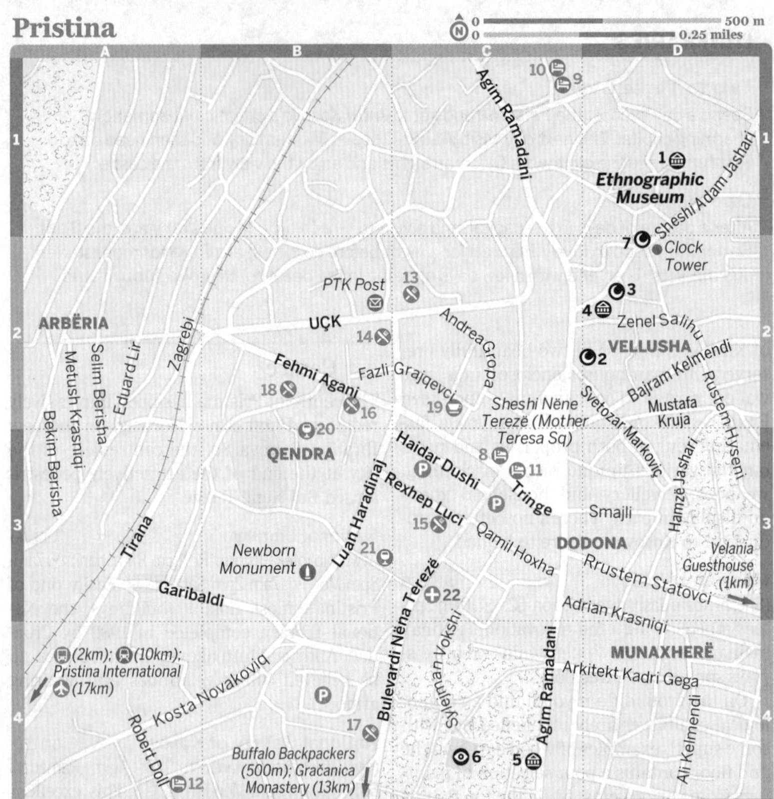

derelict house into their care, painted the tree in the courtyard white and gradually began to attract travellers with a cool backpacker vibe, this hostel has more the feel of an Albanian beach resort than a downtown Pristina bolthole. The massive 12-bed dorm has its own bathroom, there's a fully equipped kitchen and it adjoins a very chilled lounge bar, which is a perfect place to meet other travellers.

Buffalo Backpackers HOSTEL €
(045 643 261; Rr Musine Kokalari 274; dm/camping incl breakfast €10/6;) This charming dorm-only hostel has some of the cheapest and most chilled-out accommodation in the country, friendly staff and a pleasant location in a self-contained house a little south of Pristina's busy city centre.

Velania Guesthouse PENSION €
(038 531 742, 044 167 455; www.guesthouse-ks.net; Velania 4/34; dm €7, s/d/tr from €12/16/24, s/d/tr with shared bathroom from €10/14/21) This bustling guesthouse is spread over two buildings in an affluent part of town. The jovial professor who runs it loves a chat and could double as your grandfather. The hike up to it is much more fun in a taxi (€1.50) – either way consult the website first and print out the map, as it's hard to find!

Hotel Begolli HOTEL €€
(038 244 277; www.hotelbegolli.com; Rr Maliq Pashë Gjinolli 8; s/d incl breakfast €40/50, apt from €50;) While it may have gone overboard with its '90s-style furniture, Begolli is a pleasant, rather sprawling place to stay. The apartment has a Jacuzzi and a kitchen and is good value, while the normal rooms are a little on the small side, but comfy. Staff are friendly and a good breakfast is served in the ground-floor bar.

Hotel Sara HOTEL €€
(044 238 765, 038 236 203; www.hotel-sara.com; Rr Maliq Pashë Gjinolli; s/d/tr/apt incl breakfast

Pristina

Top Sights
1 Ethnographic Museum D1

Sights
2 Carshi Mosque D2
3 Jashar Pasha Mosque D2
4 Museum of Kosovo D2
5 National Gallery of Kosovo C4
6 National Library C4
7 Sultan Mehmet Fatih Mosque D2

Sleeping
8 Han Hostel C3
9 Hotel Begolli C1
10 Hotel Sara C1
11 Swiss Diamond Hotel C3
12 White Tree Hostel A4

Eating
13 De Rada Brasserie C2
14 Home Bar & Restaurant B2
15 NOMNOM C3
16 Osteria Basilico B2
17 Renaissance II B4
18 Tiffany B2

Drinking & Nightlife
19 Dit' e Nat' C2
20 Sabaja Craft Brewery B3
21 Tingle Tangle B3

Information
22 Barnatore Pharmacy C3

€30/40/50/70) In a tiny hotel-filled street by the bazaar, this 33-room hotel is rather garishly furnished in a style that suggests aspiration to boutique quality, but sadly rather misses the mark. That said, the rooms are good value at this price, and room 603 has a small balcony with great city views if you can cope with the colour scheme.

★Swiss Diamond Hotel LUXURY HOTEL €€€
(☎038 220 000; www.swissdiamondhotelprishtina.com; Sheshi Nëna Terezë; r incl breakfast from €162; P ⊖ ❄ @ ☎ ≋) This international standard five-star hotel is the choice of those who can afford it. Opened in 2012 right in the heart of the city, this place is all marble floors, obsequious staff and liveried bell boys. The rooms are lavish and the suites are immense, all decorated with expensive furnishings and many enjoying great city views.

Eating

Home Bar & Restaurant INTERNATIONAL €
(Rr Luan Haradinaj; mains €5-12; ⊙7am-11pm Mon-Sat, 11am-11pm Sun) Having been here since the dark days of 2001, this is the closest Pristina has to an expat institution, and it lives up to its name, being exceptionally cosy and friendly, with scattered curios and antiques. The menu is international and eclectic and offers exactly what most travellers will be dreaming of: spring rolls, hummus, curries, wraps, burgers and even fajitas.

★Tiffany TRADITIONAL €€
(☎038 244 040; Rr Fehmi Agani; set meal €12; ⊙9am-10pm Mon-Sat, 6-10pm Sun; ☎) The organic oral menu here (delivered by efficient, if somewhat terse, English-speaking staff) is simply dazzling: enjoy the day's grilled special, beautifully cooked seasonal vegetables drenched in olive oil, and freshly baked bread on the sun-dappled terrace. Understandably much prized by the foreign community, this brilliant place is unsigned and somewhat hidden behind a well-tended bush on Fehmi Agani.

★Renaissance II KOSOVAN €€
(☎044 118 796; Rr Xhorxh Bush; set meal €15; ⊙6pm-midnight) It's hard to imagine a less-expected find down this grotty, dark side street (look for the Green Pharmacy's neon cross and turn down here). Wooden doors open into a traditional kitchen and you'll be brought water, rakia and wine as well as a plate of sublime appetisers to enjoy as the meat course is cooked by the family's matriarch.

★De Rada Brasserie INTERNATIONAL €€
(Rr UÇK 50; mains €5-11; ⊙8am-midnight Mon-Sat; ☎) A smart and atmospheric place right in the heart of town that serves up breakfasts, lunches and early dinners to an international clientele. The menu leans towards Italian, but there's plenty of choice. Grab a table outside on the street when the weather's good.

Osteria Basilico ITALIAN €€
(Rr Fehmi Agani 29/1; mains €6-13; ⊙noon-midnight) This smart place is Pristina's most reliable Italian restaurant. There's a lovely terrace and a stylish interior where you can enjoy the wide-ranging menu, including plenty of regional classics as well as some more inventive dishes.

WORTH A TRIP

GRAČANICA MONASTERY & BEAR SANCTUARY PRISTINA

Explore beyond Pristina by heading southeast to two of the country's best sights. Dusty fingers of sunlight pierce the darkness of **Gračanica Monastery** (⌚6am-5pm) FREE, completed in 1321 by Serbian King Milutin. It's an oasis in a town that is the cultural centre of Serbs in central Kosovo. Take a Gjilan-bound bus (€0.50, 15 minutes, every 30 minutes); the monastery's on your left. Do dress respectably (that means no shorts or sleeveless tops for anyone, and head scarves for women) and you'll be very welcome to look around this historical complex and to view the gorgeous icons in the main church.

Further along the road to Gjilan is the excellent new **Bear Sanctuary Pristina** (☎045 826 072; www.vier-pfoten.org; Mramor; ⌚9am-6pm Apr-Oct, 10am-4pm Nov-Mar) FREE, in the village of Mramor. Here you can visit a number of brown bears that were rescued from cruel captivity by the charity Four Paws. All the bears here were once kept in tiny cages as mascots for restaurants, but when the keeping of bears was outlawed in Kosovo in 2010, Four Paws stepped in to care for these wonderful animals. Sadly, some of them still suffer from trauma and don't socialise well, but their excellent condition is heartening indeed. Ask to be let off any Gjilan-bound bus by the Delfina gas station at the entrance to Mramor, then follow the unsurfaced road back past the lakeside, and then follow the track around to the right.

NOMNOM INTERNATIONAL €€
(Rr Rexhep Luci 5; mains €7-14; ⌚7am-midnight) Just off the main drag, this modern two-floor bar and restaurant caters to a smart local and foreign crowd. It has a huge summer terrace, and plenty of indoor seating too. The menu offers pizza, pasta, salad, grills and burgers. Sadly, the overall style is compromised by terrible muzak.

Drinking

★Dit' e Nat' CAFE
(Rr Fazli Grajqevci 5; ⌚8am-midnight; 📶) 'Day and night', a bookshop-cafe-bar-performance space, is one of the best-kept secrets in Pristina. There's a great selection of English-language books, scrubbed wooden floorboards, strong espresso, friendly English-speaking staff and occasional live music in the evenings, including jazz. Sandwiches and a selection of cocktails are also served.

Tingle Tangle BAR
(off Rr Luan Haradinaj; ⌚9am-1am; 📶) Slip into the courtyard of a residential building in the centre of Pristina to find this unsigned boho hang-out. Tingle Tangle is owned by a much-loved local painter and the walls of this cafe-bar proudly display delightful elements of his work. A cold beer on the terrace here is a great way to start the evening amid a cool crowd.

Sabaja Craft Brewery BREWERY
(Stadioni i Prishtinës; ⌚noon-midnight) This American-Kosovar venture is Pristina's first microbrewery with several wonderful brews originating in-house, including an IPA and a Session Pale Ale. There are also various seasonal products available. To complement that, there's a relaxed vibe and a good international menu (mains €3 to €8) available.

Information

American Hospital (☎038 221 661; www.spitaliamerikan.com; Graçanicë) The best hospital in Kosovo offers American-standard health care, although not always the language skills to match. It's just outside the city in the Serbian-majority town of Graçanicë.

Barnatore Pharmacy (Bul Nëna Terezë; ⌚8am-10pm)

PTK Post (Rr UÇK; ⌚8am-10pm Mon-Sat) Post and phone services.

Getting There & Around

AIR

There is currently no public transport from **Pristina International Airport** (☎958 123; www.airportpristina.com), so you'll have to get a taxi into the city. Taxis charge €25 for the 20-minute, 18km trip to the city centre.

BUS

The **bus station** (Stacioni i Autobusëve; Rr Lidja e Pejes) is 2km southwest of the centre off Bul Bil Klinton. Taxis to the centre should cost €2. International buses from Pristina include Serbia's Belgrade (€20, 11pm daily, six hours) and Novi Pazar (€5, 10am daily, three hours); Sarajevo (Bosnia and Hercegovina) via Novi Pazar (€23, 4pm daily); Tirana, Albania (€10, daily, five hours), Skopje, Macedonia (€5, every 30 minutes from 5.30am to 5pm, 1½ hours); and Podgorica, Montenegro (€15, three daily at 5.45pm, 7pm and 7.30pm, seven hours).

TRAIN

Trains run from Pristina to Peja (€3, two daily at 8.01am and 4.41pm, two hours) and, internationally, to Skopje in Macedonia (€4, 7.22am daily, three hours).

AROUND PRISTINA

Kosovo is a small country, which can be crossed by car in any direction in around an hour. Not far in distance, but worlds away from the chaotic capital, the smaller towns of Peja and Prizren both offer a different pace and a new perspective on Kosovar life.

Peja (Peć)

039 / POP 170,000

Peja (known as Peć in Serbian) is Kosovo's third-largest city and one flanked by sites vital to Orthodox Serbians. With a Turkish-style bazaar at its heart and the dramatic but increasingly accessible Rugova Mountains all around it, it's a diverse and progressive place that's fast becoming Kosovo's tourism hub.

Sights

Patriachate of Peć MONASTERY

(044 15 07 55; 9am-6pm) This church and monastery complex are a slice of Serbian Orthodoxy that has existed here since the late 13th century. Following the war, the buildings are guarded by NATO's Kosovo Force (KFOR) and you will need to hand in your passport for the duration of your visit. From the food stands around the main square, walk along Lekë Dukagjini with the river on your left for 15 minutes until you reach the monastery walls.

Cheese Market MARKET

(8am-4pm Sat) The town's bustling bazaar makes you feel like you've turned left into İstanbul. Farmers gather here on Saturday with wooden barrels of goat's cheese, so follow your nose.

Activities

Peja has established itself as the country's tourism hub and there's an impressive number of activities on offer in the nearby Rugova Mountains, including rock climbing, mountain biking, skiing, hiking and white-water rafting.

★ **Rugova Experience** ADVENTURE TOUR

(039 432 352, 044 350 511; www.rugovaexperience.org; Mbretëreshë Teuta) This excellent, locally run company is championing the Rugova region for hikers and cultural tourists. It organises homestays in mountain villages, runs very good trekking tours, enjoys great local access and works with English-speaking guides.

Outdoor Kosovo ADVENTURE TOUR

(049 168 566; fatos64@gmail.com) An adventure tourism company that specialises in rock climbing, caving, skiing, camping, hiking and mountain biking. English is spoken.

Sleeping & Eating

★ **Dukagjini Hotel** HOTEL €€

(038 771 177; www.hoteldukagjini.com; Sheshi I Dëshmorëve 2; s/d incl breakfast €50/70;) What on earth is a hotel like this doing in Peja, you may well ask yourself as you step into the regal setting of the Dukagjini's lobby. The hotel has been totally remodelled and the entire place displays international standards you probably didn't expect in a small city in Kosovo. Rooms are large, grandly appointed and have supremely comfortable beds.

Hotel Çardak HOTEL €€

(049 801 108, 038 731 017; www.hotelcardak.com; Rr Mbretëresha Teuta 101; s/d incl breakfast €40/60;) Run by several supremely friendly brothers, this central, family-oriented place contains both a pleasant hotel with spacious and clean rooms, as well as an expansive restaurant offering up a tasty menu of pizza, pasta, risotto, steak and other meat grills (mains €3 to €8). Rooms at the front can be loud – ask for one at the back if quiet is a priority.

Kulla e Zenel Beut TRADITIONAL €€

(Rr William Walker; mains €3-9;) A charming option in the centre of town with a pleasant terrace and a cosy dining room to choose from. Excellent pizza, fresh fish, baked mussels, pasta dishes, grills and even a breakfast menu are on offer here, though service isn't particularly quick.

DON'T MISS

VISOKI DEČANI MONASTERY

This imposing whitewashed **monastery** (☎049 776 254; www.decani.org; ⏰11am-1pm & 4-6pm), 15km south of Peja, is one of Kosovo's absolute highlights. Located in an incredibly beautiful spot beneath the mountains and surrounded by a forest of pine and chestnut trees, the monastery has been here since 1327 and is today heavily guarded by KFOR. Despite frequent attacks from locals who'd like to see the Serbs leave – most recently a grenade attack in 2007 – the 25 Serbian monks living here in total isolation from the local community have stayed.

Buses go to the town of Dečani from Peja (€1, 30 minutes, every 15 minutes) on their way to Gjakovë. It's a pleasant 1km walk to the monastery from the bus stop. From the roundabout in the middle of town, take the second exit if you're coming from Peja. You'll need to surrender your passport while visiting.

Getting There & Away

BUS

The town's bus station can be found on Rr Adem Jashari, a short walk from the town centre. Frequent buses run to Pristina (€5, 90 minutes, every 20 minutes) and Prizren (€4, 80 minutes, hourly). International buses link Peja with Ulclinj (€16, 10am and 8.30pm, 10 hours) and Podgorica in Montenegro (€15, 10am, seven hours).

TRAIN

Trains depart Peja for Pristina at 5.30am and 11.10am (two hours) and depart Pristina for Peja at 7.22am and 4.41pm (two hours). The train station is in the centre of town: follow Rr Emrush Miftari away from the Hotel Dukagjini for about five minutes.

Prizren

☎029 / POP 178,000

Picturesque Prizren is Kosovo's second city and it shines with post-independence enthusiasm. If you're passing through between Albania and Pristina, the charming mosque- and church-filled old town is well worth setting aside a few hours to wander about in. It's also worth making a special journey here if you're a documentary fan: Prizren's annual Dokufest is Kosovo's leading arts event and attracts documentary makers and fans from all over the world every August.

Sights

Prizren's old town runs along both sides of the Bistrica river, and is awash with mosques and churches. It's been well restored and is a charming place to wander. The town's 15th-century **Ottoman bridge** has been superbly restored. Nearby is **Sinan Pasha Mosque** (1561), which following a full renovation is now a central landmark in Prizren. On the other side of the river to the mosque, have a peek at the architecturally refined but nonfunctioning **Gazi Mehmed Pasha Baths**.

The town's most important site is the **Orthodox Church of the Virgin of Ljeviš** (Bogorodica Ljeviška; Rr Xhemil Fluku; admission €3), a 14th-century Serbian church that was used as a mosque by the local population until 1911. After a full renovation in the 1950s, it was again largely destroyed in 1999 by the Albanian population, only to be placed back in the hands of the local Serbian community after the war. Given its location, the church is not exactly welcoming; it's surrounded by barbed wire and closed except for when visitors come to see it. You'll need to present yourself first at St George's Church, on the other side of the river, to get approval to visit from one of the few remaining Serbs in the town. This is well worth doing, however, as even though the frescoes in the church are badly damaged (the building was largely destroyed by Albanians during the war), there are some stunning, ancient wall paintings here and the entire experience is a sad and troubling example of how ethnic hatred can fracture previously peaceful societies.

There is not much of interest at the 11th-century **Kalaja** on top of the hill overlooking the old town, but the 180-degree views over Prizren from this fort are worth the walk. On the way, more barbed wire surrounds the heavily guarded **St Savior Church**, hinting at the fragility of Prizren's once-robust multiculturalism.

Sleeping & Eating

City Hostel HOSTEL €

(☎049 466 313; www.prizrencityhostel.com; Rr Iljaz Kuka 66; dm incl breakfast €11, d incl breakfast with/without bathroom €28/33; 📶) Over four

COUNTRY FACTS

Area 10,887 sq km

Capital Pristina

Country Code ☎381

Currency Euro (€)

Emergency ambulance ☎94, fire ☎93, police ☎92

Language Albanian, Serbian

Money ATMs in larger towns; banks open Monday to Friday

Population 1.82 million

Visas Kosovo is visa-free for most nationalities. All passports are stamped on arrival for a 90-day stay.

floors and a short wander from the heart of the old town, Prizren's first hostel is a great place to stay, with a friendly, international vibe and a chilled-out roof-terrace bar complete with hammocks and awesome city views. To get here follow the left bank of the river and look for Iljaz Kuka on your left.

★ **Hotel Prizreni** HOTEL €€

(☎029 225 200; www.hotelprizreni.com; Rr Shën Flori 2; s/d/tr incl breakfast €30/50/60; ❄📶) With an unbeatable location just behind the Sinan Pasha Mosque (though you may well disagree at dawn), the Prizreni is a pleasant combination of traditional and modern, with 12 stylish and contemporary rooms, great views and enthusiastic staff. There's a good restaurant downstairs (open 8am to 11pm).

★ **Ego** INTERNATIONAL €

(Sheshi Shadërvan; mains €2.50-10; ⏰8am-11pm Mon-Fri, 11am-11pm Sat & Sun; 📶) Right on Prizren's pretty main cobblestone square, this place stands out beyond the many cafes and restaurants here with its sophisticated international menu, smart decor and charming staff. Have lunch on the terrace, drinks inside or a more formal dinner in the upstairs dining room.

Ambient TRADITIONAL €

(Rr Vatrat Shqiptare; mains €3-9; ⏰8am-midnight; 📶) With by far the most charming location in Prizren beside a waterfall cascading down the cliffside by the river, and with views over the old town, this is a place to come for a romantic dinner or sundowner. The menu includes a Pasha burger, steaks, seafood and a catch of the day cooked to your specification.

ℹ Getting There & Away

Prizren is well connected to Pristina (€4, 90 minutes, every 10 to 25 minutes), Peja (€4, 90 minutes, six daily) and Albania's Tirana (€12, four hours). The bus station is on the right bank of the river, a short walk from the old town.

SURVIVAL GUIDE

ℹ Directory A–Z

ACCOMMODATION

Accommodation is booming in Kosovo, with most large towns now offering a good range of options.

BUSINESS HOURS

Reviews include opening hours only if they differ significantly from these.

Banks 8am to 5pm Monday to Friday, until 2pm Saturday

Bars 8am to 11pm (on the dot if police are cracking down)

Restaurants 8am to midnight

Shops 8am to 6pm Monday to Friday, until 3pm Saturday

INTERNET RESOURCES

Balkan Insight (www.balkaninsight.com)

Balkanology (www.balkanology.com)

In Your Pocket (www.inyourpocket.com/kosovo)

Kosovo Tourism Center (www.kosovotourismcenter.com)

UN Mission in Kosovo Online (www.unmikonline.org)

MONEY

Kosovo's currency is the euro, despite not being part of the euro zone or the EU. It's best to arrive with small denominations and euro coins are particularly useful. ATMs are common and established businesses accept credit cards.

POST

PTK post and telecommunications offices operate in Kosovo's main towns.

SLEEPING PRICE RANGES

The following price ranges are for a double room with bathroom:

€ less than €40

€€ €40 to €80

€€€ more than €80

EATING PRICE RANGES

The following price categories are for the average cost of a main course:

€ less than €5

€€ €5 to €10

€€€ more than €10

PUBLIC HOLIDAYS

New Year's Day 1 January
Independence Day 17 February
Kosovo Constitution Day 9 April
Labour Day 1 May
Europe Holiday 9 May

SAFE TRAVEL

Check government travel advisories before travelling to Kosovo. Sporadic violence occurs in North Mitrovica. Unexploded ordnance (UXO) has been cleared from roads and paths but you should seek KFOR (www.aco.nato.int/kfor.aspx) advice before venturing off beaten tracks.

VISAS

Visas are only required by some passport holders; check the **Ministry of Foreign Affairs** (www.mfa-ks.net) website for a full list of nationalities enjoying visa-free travel. This includes EU, US, Canadian, Australian and New Zealand passport holders, all of whom may stay for 90 days visa-free.

If you wish to travel between Serbia and Kosovo you'll need to enter Kosovo from Serbia first.

Getting There & Away

AIR

Pristina International Airport (☎038 5958 123; www.airportpristina.com) is 18km from the centre of Pristina. Airlines include:

Adria Airways (www.adria.si)
Air Prishtina (info.airprishtina.com)
Austrian Airlines (www.austrian.com)
Croatia Airways (www.croatiaairlines.com)
Easyjet (www.easyjet.com)
Germania (www.flygermania.de)
Germanwings (www.germanwings.com)
Kosova Airlines (www.kosovaairlines.com)
Swiss (www.swiss.com)
Turkish Airlines (www.turkishairlines.com)

LAND

Kosovo has good bus connections between Albania, Montenegro and Macedonia, with regular services from Pristina, Peja and Prizren to Tirana (Albania), Skopje (Macedonia) and Podgorica (Montenegro). There's also a train line from Pristina to Macedonia's capital, Skopje.

Border Crossings

Albania To get to Albania's Koman Ferry use the Morina border crossing west of Gjakovë. The busiest border is at Vionica, where the excellent new motorway connects to Tirana.

Macedonia Blace from Pristina and Gllobocicë from Prizren.

Montenegro The main crossing is the Kulla/Rožaje crossing on the road between Rožaje and Peja.

Serbia Due to outbreaks of violence, travellers are advised to be extra vigilant if entering Kosovo at Jarinje or Bërnjak/Banja.

Getting Around

BUS

Buses stop at distinct blue signs, but can be flagged down anywhere. Bus journeys are generally cheap, but the going can be slow on Kosovo's single-lane roads.

CAR

Serbian-plated cars have been attacked in Kosovo, and rental companies do not let cars hired in Kosovo travel to Serbia and vice versa. European Green Card vehicle insurance is not valid in the country, so you'll need to purchase vehicle insurance at the border when you enter with a car; this is a hassle-free and inexpensive procedure.

TRAIN

The train system is something of a novelty, but services connect Pristina to Peja and to Skopje in Macedonia. Locals generally take buses.

ESSENTIAL FOOD & DRINK

'Traditional' food is generally Albanian – most prominently, stewed and grilled meat and fish. *Kos* (goat's-milk yoghurt) is eaten alone or with almost anything. Turkish kebabs and *gjuveç* (baked meat and vegetables) are common.

- **Byrek** Pastry with cheese or meat.
- **Gjuveç** Baked meat and vegetables.
- **Fli** Flaky pastry pie served with honey.
- **Kos** Goat's-milk yoghurt.
- **Pershut** Dried meat.
- **Qofta** Flat or cylindrical minced-meat rissoles.
- **Tavë** Meat baked with cheese and egg.
- **Vranac** Red wine from the Rahovec region of Kosovo.

Latvia

Includes ➡

Best Places to Eat

- International (p739)
- Istaba (p739)
- 36.Line (p742)
- Vincents (p739)
- Mr Biskvīts (p743)

Best Places to Stay

- Dome Hotel (p738)
- Neiburgs (p738)
- Hotel MaMa (p741)
- Ekes Konvents (p737)
- Naughty Squirrel (p737)

Why Go?

Tucked between Estonia to the north and Lithuania to the south, Latvia is the meat of the Baltic sandwich. We're not implying that the neighbouring nations are slices of white bread, but Latvia is the savoury middle, loaded with interesting fillings. Rīga is the main ingredient and the country's cosmopolitan nexus; the Gauja Valley pines provide a thick layer of greens; onion-domed cathedrals sprout above regional towns; cheesy Euro-pop blares along coastal beaches; and the whole thing is peppered with Baltic-German, Swedish, Tsarist Russian and Soviet spice.

Travelling here is easy, language difficulties rarely arise and the simple allure of beaches, forests, castles and history-steeped streets holds plenty of appeal. Latvia may not provide the all-you-can-eat feast of other, more high-profile destinations, but it makes a tasty addition to any European menu.

When to Go

Rīga

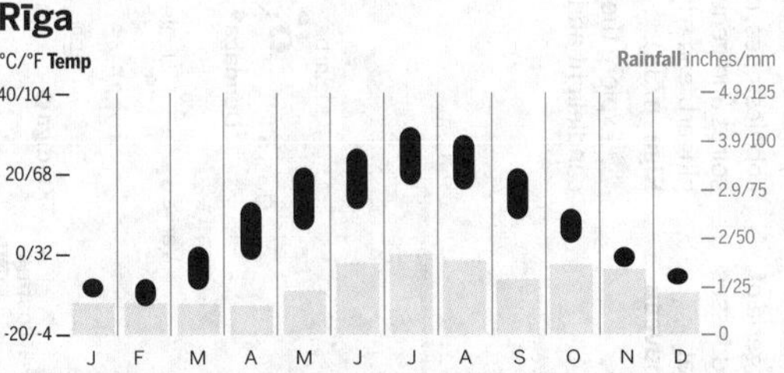

Jun–Aug Summer starts with an all-night solstice romp; then it's off to the beach.

Sep Refusing to let summer go, Rīgans sip lattes under heat lamps at alfresco cafes.

Dec Celebrate the festive season in the birthplace of the Christmas tree.

Latvia Highlights

1. Admire the menagerie of gargoyles, beasts, goddesses and twisting vines that inhabits Rīga's **art nouveau architecture** (p737).
2. Clatter along cobblestones, climb church spires and generally enjoy the gingerbread trim that is **Old Rīga** (p738).
3. Explore the castle by candlelight and then stroll the historic streets of **Cēsis** (p743).
4. Trek from castle to castle amid the forested surrounds of **Sigulda** (p742).
5. Indulge in aristocratic decadence as you wander the intricate interiors and gorgeous gardens of **Rundāle Palace** (p741).
6. Case out the castle, then laze on the long and glorious stretch of beach at **Ventspils** (p744).
7. Hobnob with Russian jet-setters in the swanky beachside spa town of **Jūrmala** (p741).

ITINERARIES

Three Days

Fill your first two days with a feast of **Rīga's** architectural eye candy and then take a day trip to opulent **Rundāle Palace**.

One Week

Spend day four lazing on the beach and coveting the gracious wooden houses of **Jūrmala**. The following morning head west to **Kuldīga** before continuing on to **Ventspils**. Spend your last days exploring **Sigulda** and **Cēsis** within the leafy confines of **Gauja National Park**.

RĪGA

POP 700,000

Rīga isn't a 'wallop you over the head with grand sights' kind of city. It's charms are much more subtle than that, coalescing around its laid-back riverside vibe, a compact historic heart and ramshackle suburbs of wooden houses. Most impressively, Rīga has the largest array of art nouveau architecture in Europe. Nightmarish gargoyles and praying goddesses adorn more than 750 buildings along the stately boulevards radiating out from the city's core.

Despite the carnage of wartime bombing, the slaughter of its large Jewish community and the subsequent decades locked behind the Iron Curtain, Rīga has entered the 21st century with a thriving cultural life and a heady cosmopolitan buzz to it.

Sights

Old Rīga (Vecrīga)

★Rīga Cathedral CATHEDRAL

(Rīgas Doms; ☎6721 3213; www.doms.lv; Doma laukums 1; admission €3; ⌚9am-5pm) Founded in 1211 as the seat of the Rīga diocese, this enormous (once Catholic, now Evangelical Lutheran) cathedral is the largest medieval church in the Baltic. The architecture is an amalgam of styles from the 13th to the 18th centuries: the eastern end, the oldest portion, has Romanesque features; the tower is 18th-century baroque; and much of the rest dates from a 15th-century Gothic rebuilding.

Rīga History & Navigation Museum MUSEUM

(Rīgas vēstures un kuģniecības muzejs; ☎6735 6676; www.rigamuz.lv; Palasta iela 4; adult/child €4.27/0.71; ⌚10am-5pm May-Sep, 11am-5pm Wed-Sun Oct-Apr) Founded in 1773, this is the oldest museum in the Baltic, situated in the old cathedral monastery. The permanent collection features artefacts from the Bronze Age all the way to WWII, ranging from lovely pre-Christian jewellery to preserved hands removed from medieval forgers. A highlight is the beautiful neoclassical Column Hall, built when Latvia was part of the Russian Empire and filled with relics from that time.

★Art Museum Rīga Bourse MUSEUM

(Mākslas muzejs Rīgas Birža; www.lnmm.lv; Doma laukums 6; adult/child €6.40/2.85; ⌚10am-6pm Tue-Thu, Sat & Sun, to 8pm Fri) Rīga's lavishly restored stock exchange building is a worthy showcase for the city's art treasures. The elaborate facade features a coterie of deities that dance between the windows, while inside, gilt chandeliers sparkle from ornately moulded ceilings. The Oriental section features beautiful Chinese and Japanese ceramics and an Egyptian mummy, but the main halls are devoted to Western art, including a Monet painting and a scaled-down cast of Rodin's *The Kiss*.

Cat House HISTORIC BUILDING

(Kaķu māja; Miestaru iela 10/12) The spooked black cats mounted on the turrets of this 1909 art nouveau–influenced building have become a symbol of Rīga. According to local legend, the building's owner was rejected from the Great Guild across the street and exacted revenge by pointing the cats' butts towards the hall. The members of the guild were outraged, and after a lengthy court battle the merchant was admitted into the club on the condition that the cats be turned in the opposite direction.

Rīga

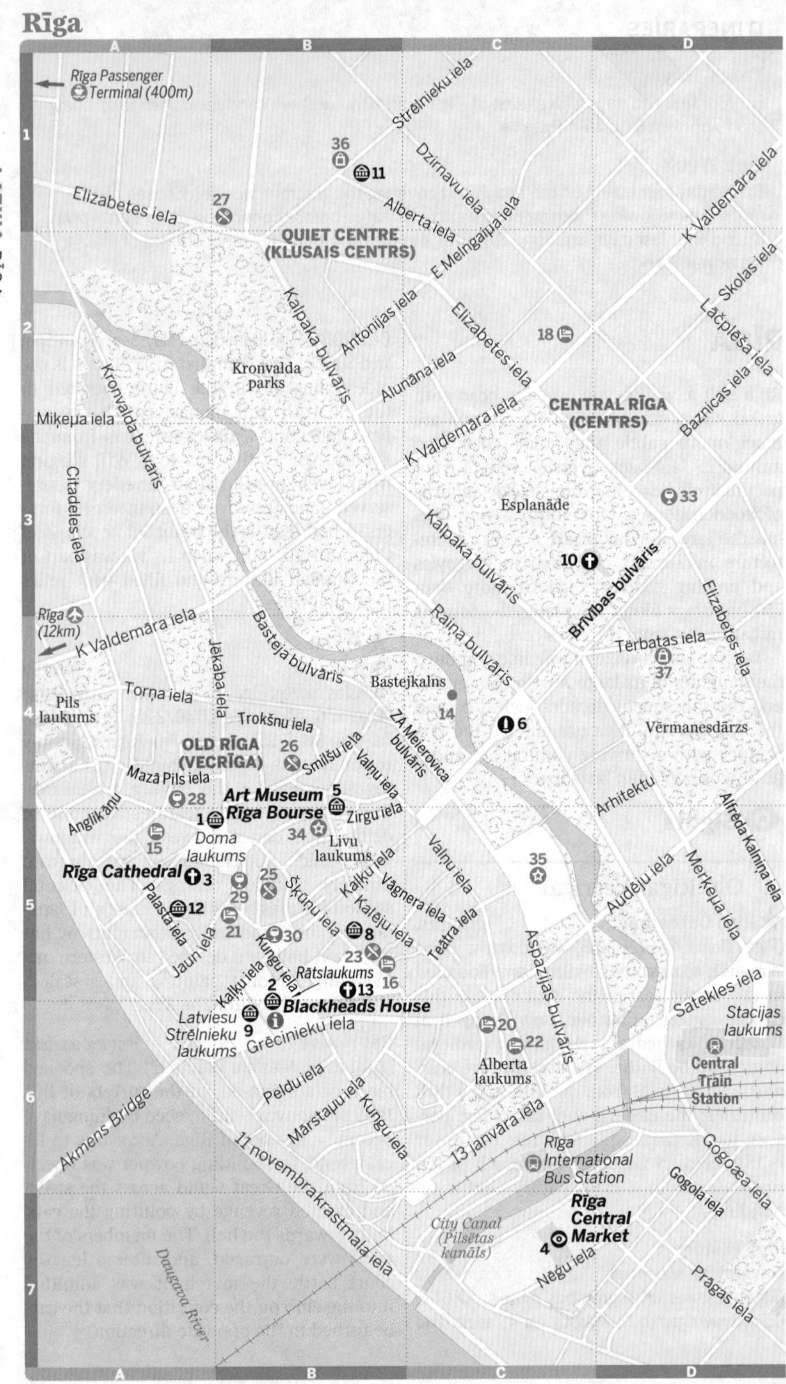

Rīga Passenger Terminal (400m)
Rīga (12km)
QUIET CENTRE (KLUSAIS CENTRS)
CENTRAL RĪGA (CENTRS)
OLD RĪGA (VECRĪGA)
Kronvalda parks
Esplanāde
Bastejkalns
Vērmanesdārzs
Pils laukums
Doma laukums
Livu laukums
Rātslaukums
Latviesu Strēlnieku laukums
Alberta laukums
Stacijas laukums
Central Train Station
Rīga International Bus Station
Rīga Central Market
City Canal (Pilsētas kanāls)
Daugava River
Akmens Bridge
Art Museum Rīga Bourse
Rīga Cathedral
Blackheads House
Strēlnieku iela
Dzirnavu iela
Alberta iela
Elizabetes iela
E Melngaiļa iela
K Valdemāra iela
Skolas iela
Lāčplēša iela
Baznicas iela
Antonijas iela
Alunāna iela
Kalpaka bulvāris
Kronvalda bulvāris
Miķeļa iela
Citadeles iela
Brīvības bulvāris
Raiņa bulvāris
Basteja bulvāris
Tērbatas iela
Jēkaba iela
Torņa iela
Trokšņu iela
Smilšu iela
Vaļņu iela
ZA Meierovica bulvāris
Mazā Pils iela
Anglikāņu
Zirgu iela
Arhitektu
Alfrēda Kalniņa iela
Merķeļa iela
Audēju iela
Palasta iela
Šķūņu iela
Kalķu iela
Vāgnera iela
Kaleju iela
Teātra iela
Aspazijas bulvāris
Jaun iela
Kungu iela
Grēcinieku iela
Satekles iela
Peldu iela
Mārstaļu iela
13 janvāra iela
11 novembra krastmala iela
Gogoļa iela
Nēģu iela
Prāgas iela

Rīga

Museum of Decorative Arts & Design MUSEUM
(Dekoratīvi lietiskās mākslas muzejs; ☎6722 7833; www.lnmm.lv; Skārņu iela 10/20; adult/child

€4.27/2.13; ⏲11am-5pm Tue & Thu-Sun, to 7pm Wed) The former St George's Church houses a museum devoted to applied art from the art nouveau period to the present, including an impressive collection of furniture, woodcuts, tapestries and ceramics. The building's foundations date back to 1207 when the Livonian Brothers of the Sword erected their castle here.

St Peter's Church CHURCH
(Sv Pētera baznīca; www.peterbaznica.riga.lv; Skārņu iela 19; adult/child €2/1, incl steeple €7/3; ⏲10am-6pm Tue-Sat, noon-6pm Sun) Forming the centrepiece of Rīga's skyline, this Gothic church is thought to be around 800 years old, making it one of the oldest medieval buildings in the Baltic. Its soaring red-brick interior is relatively unadorned, except for heraldic shields mounted on the columns. A colourful contrast is provided by the art exhibitions staged in the side aisles. At the rear of the church, a lift whisks visitors to a viewing platform 72m up the steeple.

★**Blackheads House** HISTORIC BUILDING
(Melngalvju nams; www.melngalvjunams.lv; Rātslaukums 7) At the time of writing, this fantastically ornate structure was serving as the temporary home of Latvia's president. Built in 1344 as a veritable fraternity house for the Blackheads guild of unmarried German merchants, the original house was decimated in 1941 and flattened by the Soviets seven years later. Somehow the original blueprints survived and an exact replica was completed in 2001 for Rīga's 800th birthday.

OH CHRISTMAS TREE

Rīga's Blackheads House was known for its wild parties; it was, after all, a clubhouse for unmarried merchants. On a cold Christmas Eve in 1510, a squad of bachelors, full of holiday spirit (and other spirits, so to speak), hauled a great pine tree up to their clubhouse and smothered it with flowers. At the end of the evening, they burned the tree to the ground in an impressive blaze. From then on, decorating the 'Christmas Tree' became an annual tradition, which eventually spread across the globe (the burning part never really caught on).

An octagonal commemorative plaque inlaid in cobbled Rātslaukums marks the spot where the original tree once stood.

Museum of the Occupation of Latvia MUSEUM
(Latvijas Okupācijas muzejs; ☎6721 2715; www.omf.lv; Latviešu strēlnieku laukums 1; admission by donation; ⏲11am-6pm) Inhabiting an interesting example of Soviet-era architecture on the main square, this museum carefully details Latvia's Soviet and Nazi occupations between 1940 and 1991. Some of the exhibits are extremely disturbing, including first-hand accounts of the murder of Rīga's once-substantial Jewish population, a re-creation of a gulag cell and many gruesome photographs. Allow a couple of hours to take it all in.

Central Rīga (Centrs)

Freedom Monument MONUMENT
(Brīvības bulvāris) Affectionately known as 'Milda', Rīga's Freedom Monument towers above the city between Old and Central Rīga. Paid for by public donations, the monument was designed by Kārlis Zāle and erected in 1935 where a statue of Russian ruler Peter the Great once stood.

Nativity of Christ Cathedral CATHEDRAL
(Kristus Piedzimšanas katedrāle; Brīvības bulvāris 23) With gilded cupolas peeking through the trees, this sweet little Orthodox cathedral (1883) adds a dazzling dash of Russian bling to the skyline. During the Soviet period the church was converted into a planetarium but it's since been restored to its former use.

Rīga Art Nouveau Museum MUSEUM
(Rīgas jūgendstila muzejs; www.jugendstils.riga.lv; Alberta iela 12; adult/child May-Sep €5/3.50, Oct-Apr €3.50/2.50; ⏲10am-6pm Wed-Sun) If you're curious about what lurks behind Rīga's imaginative art nouveau facades, then it's definitely worth stopping by here. Once the home of Konstantīns Pēkšēns (a local architect responsible for over 250 of the city's buildings), the interiors have been completely restored to resemble a middle-class apartment from the 1920s. Enter from Strēlnieku iela; push No 12 on the doorbell.

Moscow Suburb (Maskavas forštate)

This old part of Rīga takes its name from the main road to Moscow which runs through it. During the Nazi occupation it was the site of the Rīga Ghetto. In October 1941 the city's entire Jewish population (around 30,000 people) was crammed into the blocks east of Lāčplēša iela and enclosed by barbed wire. Later that year most of them were marched 10km to the Rumbula Forest where they were shot and buried in mass graves.

★Rīga Central Market MARKET
(Rīgas Centrāltirgus; www.centraltirgus.lv; Nēģu iela 7; ⏲8am-5pm) Haggle for your huckleberries at this vast market, housed in a series of WWI Zeppelin hangars and spilling outdoors as well. It's an essential Rīga experience, providing bountiful opportunities both for people-watching and to stock up for a picnic lunch.

Latvian Academy of Science HISTORIC BUILDING
(Latvijas Zinātņu Akadēmija; www.panoramariga.lv; Akadēmijas laukums 1; panorama €4; ⏲8am-8pm) Dubbed by local wags 'Stalin's Birthday Cake', this impressive 21-floor, 107m-high confection is Rīga's Russified Empire State Building. Construction commenced in 1951 but wasn't completed until 1961, by which time Stalin had run out of birthdays. Those with an eagle eye will spot hammers and sickles hidden in the convoluted facade. There's a wonderful viewing terrace on the 17th floor.

Tours

E.A.T. Rīga WALKING, CYCLING
(☎2246 9888; www.eatriga.lv; tours from €12) Foodies may be initially disappointed to discover that the name stands for 'Experience Alternative Tours' and the focus is on off-the-beaten-track themed walking tours (Old Rīga, Art Nouveau, Alternative Rīga, Retro Rīga). But don't fret – Rīga Food Tasting is an option. It also offers a cycling tour of Jūrmala.

Rīga By Canal BOATING
(☎2591 1523; www.kmk.lv; adult/child €18/9; ⏲10am-8pm) Enjoy a different perspective of the city aboard the 107-year-old *Darling*, a charming wooden canal cruiser that runs on 15% solar energy (the rest diesel). There are three other boats in the fleet that paddle along the same loop around the city canal and Daugava River.

DON'T MISS

ART NOUVEAU IN RĪGA

If you ask any Rīgan where to find the city's world-famous art nouveau architecture, you will always get the same answer: 'Look up!'

Rīga has the greatest number of art nouveau buildings of any city in Europe. More than 750 buildings boast this flamboyant style of decor which is also known as Jugendstil, meaning 'youth style'. It was named after Munich-based magazine, *Die Jugend*, which popularised it around the turn of the 20th century.

Rīga's art nouveau district (known more formally as the 'Quiet Centre') is anchored around **Alberta iela** (check out 2a, 4 and 13 in particular), but you'll find fine examples throughout the city. Don't miss the renovated facades of **Strēlnieku 4a** and **Elizabetes 10b** and **33**.

Sleeping

Old Rīga (Vecrīga)

★Naughty Squirrel HOSTEL €
(☎2646 1248; www.thenaughtysquirrel.com; Kalēju iela 50; dm/s/d from €16/45/55; ❄@📶) Slashes of bright paint and cartoon graffiti brighten up the city's capital of backpackerdom, which buzzes with travellers rattling the foosball table and chilling out in the TV room. Sign up for regular pub crawls, adrenaline day trips to the countryside and summer BBQs.

Rīga Old Town Hostel HOSTEL €
(☎6722 3406; www.rigaoldtownhostel.lv; Valņu iela 43; dm €11-14; ❄📶) The Aussie pub on the ground floor doubles as the hostel's hang-out space. If you can manage to lug your suitcase past the faux bookshelf door and up the twisting staircase, you'll find spacious dorms with chandeliers and plenty of sunlight.

★Ekes Konvents HOTEL €€
(☎6735 8393; www.ekeskonvents.lv; Skārņu iela 22; s/d from €60/70; 📶) Not to be confused with Konventa Sēta next door, the 600-year-old Ekes Konvents oozes wobbly medieval

WORTH A TRIP

AN ENCHANTING FOREST

If you don't have time to visit the Latvian countryside, a stop at the **Latvian Ethnographic Open-Air Museum** (Latvijas etnogrāfiskais brīvdabas muzejs; www.brivdabasmuzejs.lv; Brīvības gatve 440; adult/child May-Oct €4.27/1.42, Nov-Apr €2.13/0.71; ⏰10am-5pm) is a must. Sitting along the shores of Lake Jugla just northeast of the city limits, this stretch of forest contains more than 100 wooden buildings (churches, windmills, farmhouses etc) from each of Latvia's four cultural regions. Take bus 1 from the corner of Merķeļa iela and Tērbatas iela to the 'Brīvdabas muzejs' stop.

charm from every crooked nook and cranny. Curl up with a book in the adorable stone alcoves on the landing of each storey. Breakfast is served down the block.

★Dome Hotel HOTEL €€€
(☎6750 9010; www.domehotel.lv; Miesnieku iela 4; r from €249; 📶) It's hard to imagine that this centuries-old structure was once part of a row of butcheries. Today a gorgeous wooden staircase leads guests up to a charming assortment of uniquely decorated rooms that sport eaved ceilings, wooden panelling, upholstered furniture and picture windows with city views.

★Neiburgs HOTEL €€€
(☎6711 5522; www.neiburgs.com; Jaun iela 25/27; s/d from €152/182; ❄📶) Occupying one of Old Rīga's finest art nouveau buildings, Neiburgs blends preserved details with contemporary touches to achieve its signature boutique-chic style. Try for a room on one of the higher floors – you'll be treated to a view of a colourful clutter of gabled roofs and twisting medieval spires.

Central Rīga (Centrs)

Hotel Valdemārs HOTEL €€
(☎6733 4462; www.valdemars.lv; K Valdemāra iela 23; s/d from €56/64; ❄📶) Hidden within an art nouveau block, this Clarion Collection hotel is an excellent choice for those happy to trade fancy decor for reasonable rates. Most surprisingly, the hotel lays on breakfast, afternoon snacks and a simple dinner buffet for all guests.

Krišjānis & Ģertrūde B&B €€
(☎6750 6604; www.kg.lv; K Barona iela 39; s/d/tr incl breakfast €35/45/55; @📶) Step off the bustling intersection into this quaint, family-run B&B, adorned with still-life paintings of fruit and flowers. It's best to book ahead since there are only six cosy rooms. And pack earplugs for the traffic noise.

Hotel Bergs HOTEL €€€
(☎6777 0900; www.hotelbergs.lv; Elizabetes iela 83/85; ste from €174; P❄📶) A refurbished 19th-century building embellished with a Scandi-sleek extension, Hotel Bergs embodies the term 'luxury'. The spacious suites are lavished with high-quality monochromatic furnishings and some have kitchens. There's even a 'pillow menu', allowing guests to choose from an array of different bed pillows based on material and texture.

Eating

Old Rīga (Vecrīga)

LIDO Alus Sēta LATVIAN €
(www.lido.lv; Tirgoņu iela 6; mains around €5; 📶) The pick of the LIDO litter (Rīga's ubiquitous smorgasbord chain), Alus Sēta feels like an old Latvian brew house. It's popular with locals as well as tourists – everyone flocks here for cheap but tasty traditional fare and homemade beer. Seating spills onto the cobbled street during the warmer months.

Domini Canes EUROPEAN €€
(☎2231 4122; www.dominicanes.lv; Skārpu iela 18/20; mains €7-18; ⏰10am-10.30pm) Tables spill out onto the square at this upmarket but relaxed restaurant facing the rear of St Peter's Church. The bistro-style menu includes delicious homemade pasta dishes and plenty of fresh Latvian produce.

Uncle Vanja RUSSIAN €€
(Tēvocis Vaņa; ☎2788 6963; www.facebook.com/DjadjaVanjaRestorans; Smilšu iela 16; mains €11-21; ⏰11am-11pm) The scene opens in what looks like a comfortable 19th-century Russian home (bookshelves, tassled lamps etc). Enter stage left well-dressed serving staff bearing steaming plates of *pelmeni*, blini (pancakes), and various meat, chicken and fish dishes. Cue a lengthy vodka menu for the final act.

Le Dome Fish Restaurant SEAFOOD €€€
(☎6755 9884; www.zivjurestorans.lv; Miesnieku iela 4; mains €22-30; ⏰8am-11pm) The Dome

Hotel's restaurant quickly reminds diners that Rīga sits near a body of water that's full of delicious fish. Service is impeccable and dishes (including some meat and vegetarian options) are expertly prepared, reflecting the eclectic assortment of recipes in the modern Latvian lexicon.

Central Rīga (Centrs)

★Istaba CAFE €€

(☎6728 1141; K Barona iela 31a; mains €17; ⌚noon-11pm) Owned by local chef and TV personality Mārtiņš Sirmais, 'The Room' sits in the rafters above a gallery and occasional performance space. There's no set menu – you're subject to the cook's fancy – but expect lots of free extras (bread, dips, salad, vegies) adding up to a massive serving.

★Vincents EUROPEAN €€€

(☎6733 2634; www.restorans.lv; Elizabetes iela 19; mains €24-29; ⌚6-10pm Mon-Sat) Rīga's ritziest restaurant has served royalty and rock stars (Emperor Akihito, Prince Charles, Elton John) amid its eye-catching van Gogh–inspired decor. The head chef, Martins Ritins, is a stalwart of the Slow Food movement and crafts his ever-changing menu mainly from produce sourced directly from small-scale Latvian farmers.

Other Neighbourhoods

Although most of Rīga's best eateries are in the centre, a couple of interesting contenders have spilled to the edges.

LIDO Atpūtas Centrs LATVIAN €

(LIDO Recreation Centre; www.lido.lv; Krasta iela 76; mains around €5; ⌚11am-11pm) If Latvia and Disney World had a love child it would be this enormous log cabin dedicated to the country's coronary-inducing cuisine. Servers dressed like Baltic milkmaids bounce around as patrons hit the rows of buffets. Outside there's a kid's fun park with pony rides and ice-skating.

It's 3.5km southeast of Rīga Central Market; take tram 3, 7 or 9, get off at the 'LIDO' stop and make for the giant windmill.

★International INTERNATIONAL €€

(☎6749 1212; www.international.lv; Hospitālu iela 1; dishes €5-12; ⌚10am-midnight Mon-Fri, noon-midnight Sat & Sun; 📶) It's well worth a quick tram ride (take tram 11 and get off at Mēness iela) to this wonderful eatery for multiple small plates of yumminess. The name couldn't be more accurate, with a menu containing the likes of 'Tsar's fish soup', sushi, Thai curry and an exceptional beef Wellington.

Drinking & Nightlife

Skyline Bar COCKTAIL BAR

(www.skylinebar.lv; Elizabetes iela 55; ⌚5pm-1am Sun-Thu, 3pm-3am Fri & Sat; 📶) A must for every visitor, glitzy Skyline Bar sits on the 26th floor of the Radisson Blu Hotel Latvija. The sweeping views are the city's best (even from the toilets!), and the mix of glam spirit-sippers makes for great people-watching.

Aptieka BAR

(Pharmacy Bar; www.krogsaptieka.lv; Mazā Miesnieku iela 1; ⌚4pm-1am Sun-Wed, to 4am Thu-Sat) Antique apothecary bottles confirm the subtle-but-stylish theme at this popular drinking haunt run by a Latvian American. The music's usually excellent and it does a good line in American bar food (burgers and so on).

Egle BEER GARDEN

(www.spogulegle.lv; Kaļķu iela 1a; ⌚11am-1am) Split between a noisier half with live music most nights (everything from folk to rockabilly), and a quieter half (which generally closes early), this is the best of Old Rīga's open-air beer gardens. It shuts up shop when the weather gets really horrible.

RĪGA CHESS – KNIGHTS TO KING, THEN TSAR

Although some Latvians lament the fact that they are an ethnic minority in their own capital, others are quick to point out that Rīga was never a 'Latvian' city. Founded in 1201 by the German Bishop Albert von Buxhoevden (say that three times fast) as a bridgehead for the crusade against Europe's last remaining pagan tribes, Rīga was a stronghold for the Knights of the Sword, a member of the Hanseatic League and an important trading junction between Russia and the West. When Sweden snagged the city in 1621, it grew into the largest holding of the Swedish empire (even bigger than Stockholm). By the mid-1860s, with the Russians now as overlords, Rīga was the world's biggest timber port.

Garage WINE BAR
(www.vinabars.lv; Berga Bazārs, Elizabetes iela 83/85; ⏲10am-midnight) Apart from a semi-industrial fit-out (polished concrete floors, metal chairs) there's nothing even vaguely garagey about this chic little place. It's equal parts wine bar and cafe (the coffee's excellent), serving tapas and a limited selection of mains.

Golden GAY & LESBIAN
(www.mygoldenclub.com; Ģertrūdes iela 33/35; admission club €10; ⏲4-11pm Tue-Thu, 7pm-5am Fri, 11pm-5am Sat) The golden boy of Rīga's gay scene (admittedly that's not saying much), Golden is a friendly little place with a conservatory-like bar and a weekend-only club.

Cuba Cafe BAR
(www.cubacafe.lv; Jaun iela 15; ⏲noon-2am Sun-Tue, to 5am Wed-Sat; 📶) An authentic mojito and a table overlooking Doma laukums is just what the doctor ordered after a long day of sightseeing. On colder days, swig your caipirinha inside amid dangling Cuban flags, wobbly stained-glass lamps and the murmur of trumpet jazz.

☆ Entertainment

Latvian National Opera OPERA, BALLET
(Latvijas Nacionālajā operā; ☎6707 3777; www.opera.lv; Aspazijas bulvāris 3) With a hefty international reputation as one of the finest opera companies in all of Europe, the national opera is the pride of Latvia. It's also home to the Rīga Ballet; locally born lad Mikhail Baryshnikov got his start here.

Great Guild CLASSICAL MUSIC
(☎6722 4850; www.lnso.lv; Amatu iela 6) Home to the acclaimed Latvian National Symphony Orchestra.

🛍 Shopping

Art Nouveau Rīga SOUVENIRS
(www.artnouveauriga.lv; Strēlnieku iela 9; ⏲10am-7pm) Sells a variety of art nouveau–related souvenirs, from guidebooks and postcards to stone gargoyles and bits of stained glass.

Sakta Flower Market MARKET
(Tērbatas iela 2a; ⏲24hr) Open through the night for those post-midnight *mea culpas*, when you suspect 'Sorry I'm late, honey' just won't do the trick.

ℹ Information

ARS (☎6720 1006; www.ars-med.lv; Skolas iela 5) English-speaking doctors; 24-hour consultation available.

Tourist Information Centre (☎6730 7900; www.liveriga.com; Rātslaukums 6; ⏲10am-6pm) Dispenses tourist maps and walking-tour brochures, helps with accommodation, books day trips and sells concert tickets. It also stocks the **Rīga Card** (www.rigacard.lv; 24-/48-/72-hour card €16/20/26), which offers discounts on sights and restaurants, and free rides on public transport. Satellite offices can be found in Livu laukums (May to September only) and at the bus station.

ℹ Getting There & Away

Rīga is connected by air, bus, train and ferry to various international destinations (p746).

BUS

Buses depart from **Rīga International Bus Station** (Rīgas starptautiskā autoosta; www.autoosta.lv; Prāgas iela 1), located behind the railway embankment just beyond the south-eastern edge of Old Rīga. Destinations include Sigulda (€3, one hour, hourly), Cēsis (€4.15, two hours, hourly), Kuldīga (€6.40, 2½ to 3½ hours, 11 daily) and Ventspils (€7.55, three hours, hourly).

TRAIN

Rīga's **central train station** (Centrālā stacija; ☎6723 2135; www.pv.lv; Stacijas laukums 2) is housed in a conspicuous glass-encased shopping centre near the Central Market. Destinations include Jūrmala (€1.50, 30 minutes, half-hourly), Sigulda (€2.35, 1¼ hours, 10 daily) and Cēsis (€3.50, 1¾ hours, five daily).

ℹ Getting Around

TO/FROM THE AIRPORT

Rīga International Airport (Starptautiskā Lidosta Rīga; ☎1817; www.riga-airport.com; Mārupe District) is in Skulte, 20km west of the city centre.

The cheapest way to get to central Rīga is bus 22 (€1.20, 30 minutes), which runs every 10 to 30 minutes and stops at several points around town.

Taxis cost €12 to €15 and take about 15 minutes.

BICYCLE

Sixt Bicycle Rental (Sixt velo noma; ☎6767 6780; www.sixtbicycle.lv; per 30min/day €0.90/9) Sixt Bicycle Rental has self-hire stands conveniently positioned around Rīga and Jūrmala; simply choose your bike, call the rental service and receive the code to unlock your wheels.

PUBLIC TRANSPORT

Most of Rīga's main tourist attractions are within walking distance of one another, so you might never have to use the city's extensive network of trams, trolleybuses and buses. City transport runs daily from 5.30am to midnight. Some routes have an hourly night service. For Rīga public transport routes and schedules visit www.rigassatiksme.lv.

Tickets can be purchased in advance from the numerous Narvesen convenience stores (per trip €0.60, five-day pass €8). It costs double to buy your ticket directly from the driver (€1.20), but you can get the €0.60 fare from the automated ticket machines on board the newer trams. A trip on the 1901 heritage tram costs €1.50.

TAXI

Taxis charge around €0.70 per kilometre (usually with a surcharge between 10pm and 6am), with a flagfall of around €2.10. Insist on having the meter on before you set off. There are taxi ranks outside the bus and train stations, at the airport, and in front of a few major hotels in central Rīga, such as Radisson Blu Hotel Latvija.

AROUND RĪGA

If you're on a tight schedule, it's easy to get a taste of the Latvian countryside on day trips from Rīga. Within 75km of the capital are two national parks, the country's grandest palace and long stretches of flaxen beach.

Jūrmala

POP 55,600

The Baltic's version of the French Riviera, Jūrmala is a long string of townships with grand wooden beach houses belonging to Russian oil tycoons and their supermodel trophy wives. Even during the height of communism, Jūrmala was a place to see and be seen. On summer weekends, jet-setters and day-tripping Rīgans flock to the resort town for some serious fun in the sun.

If you don't have a car or bicycle, you're best to head straight to the townships of Majori and Dzintari, the heart of the action. A 1km-long pedestrian street, **Jomas iela**, connects the two and is considered to be Jūrmala's main drag.

WORTH A TRIP

THE BALTIC VERSAILLES

Built as a grand residence for the Duke of Courland, this magnificent palace, **Rundāle Palace** (Rundāles pils; ☎6396 2197; www.rundale.net; whole complex/house short route/garden/short route & garden €7.20/5/2.85/5.70; ⏲10am-5pm), is a monument to 18th-century aristocratic ostentatiousness, and rural Latvia's architectural highlight. It was designed by Italian baroque genius Bartolomeo Rastrelli, who is best known for the Winter Palace in St Petersburg. About 40 of the palace's 138 rooms are open to visitors, as are the wonderful formal gardens, inspired by those at Versailles.

The highway connecting Rīga to Jūrmala was known as '10 Minutes in America' during Soviet times, because locally produced films set in the USA were always filmed on this busy asphalt strip. Motorists driving the 15km into Jūrmala must pay a €2 toll per day, even if they are just passing through. Keep an eye out for the multilane self-service toll stations sitting at both ends of the resort town.

⊙ Sights

Ķemeri National Park NATIONAL PARK

(Ķemeru nacionālais parks; ☎6673 0078; www.kemerunacionalaisparks.lv) Beyond Jūrmala's stretch of celebrity summer homes lies a verdant hinterland of drowsy fishing villages, quaking bogs and thick forests. At the end of the 19th century Ķemeri was known for its curative mud and spring water, attracting visitors from as far away as Moscow.

Sleeping & Eating

★**Hotel MaMa** BOUTIQUE HOTEL €€€

(☎6776 1271; www.hotelmama.lv; Tirgonu iela 22; r from €160; 📶) The bedroom doors have thick, mattress-like padding on the interior (psycho-chic?) and the suites themselves are a veritable blizzard of white drapery. A mix of silver paint and pixie dust accents the ultramodern furnishings and amenities. If heaven had a bordello, it would probably look something like this.

★36.Line MODERN LATVIAN €€€
(☎2201 0696; www.lauris-restaurant.lv; Līnija 36; mains €12-30; ⊙11am-11pm; ☞) Popular local chef Lauris Alekseyev delivers modern twists on traditional Latvian dishes at this wonderful restaurant, occupying a slice of sand at the eastern end of Jūrmala. Enjoy the beach, then switch to casual attire for lunch or glam up for dinner. In the evening it's not uncommon to find DJs spinning beats.

Information

Tourist Information Centre (☎6714 7900; www.jurmala.lv; Lienes iela 5; ⊙9am-7pm Mon-Fri, 10am-5pm Sat, 10am-3pm Sun) Located across from Majori train station. Staff can assist with accommodation bookings and bicycle rental.

Getting There & Away

Two to three trains per hour link central Rīga to the sandy shores of Jūrmala. Disembark at Majori station (€1.50, 30 minutes) for the beach or at Ķemeri (€2.05, one hour) for the national park.

If you've got time to kill, the river boat **New Way** (☎2923 7123; www.pie-kapteina.lv; adult/child €15/10) departs from the Old Rīga riverfront at 11am daily and takes 2½ hours to reach Majori. It then leaves from Majori pier at 5pm.

Sigulda

POP 11,000

With a name that sounds like a mythical ogress, it's fitting that the gateway to **Gauja National Park** (www.gnp.gov.lv) is an enchanted little spot. Locals proudly call their pine-peppered town the 'Switzerland of Latvia', but if you're expecting a mountainous snow-capped realm, you'll be rather disappointed. Instead, Sigulda is a magical mix of scenic walking and cycling trails, extreme sports and 800-year-old castles steeped in colourful legends.

Sights

Turaida Museum Reserve CASTLE, MUSEUM
(Turaidas muzejrezervāts; ☎6797 1402; www.turaida-muzejs.lv; Turaidas iela 10; adult/child €5/1.14; ⊙10am-5pm) Turaida means 'God's Garden' in ancient Livonian, and this green knoll capped with a fairy-tale castle is certainly a heavenly place. The red-brick castle with its tall cylindrical tower was built in 1214 on the site of a Liv stronghold. A museum inside the castle's 15th-century granary offers an interesting account of the Livonian state from 1319 to 1561, and additional exhibitions can be viewed in the 42m-high Donjon Tower, and the castle's western and southern towers.

Sigulda Medieval Castle CASTLE
(Pils iela 18; adult/child €1.50/80; ⊙9am-8pm May-Sep, 9am-5pm Mon-Fri, to 8pm Sat & Sun Oct, 9am-5pm Nov-Apr) Constructed between 1207 and 1209 by the Livonian Brothers of the Sword, this castle lies mainly in picturesque ruins after being severely damaged during the Great Northern War (1700–21). Some sections have been restored and you can now walk along the front ramparts and ascend a tower at the rear where there are wonderful views over the forested Gauja Valley. See if you can spy Krimulda Manor and Turaida Castle poking through the trees.

Cable Car CABLE CAR
(☎2921 2731; Poruka iela 14; one way adult/child €4/3; ⊙10am-6.30pm Jun-Aug, to 4pm Sep-May) Save yourself some hiking time and enjoy terrific views by catching a ride on the cable car over the Gauja River. From the Sigulga side, it departs from a rocky precipice south of the bridge and heads towards Krimulda Manor.

Activities

Bobsled Track ADVENTURE SPORTS
(Bob trase; ☎6797 3813; www.bobtrase.lv; Šveices iela 13; ⊙noon-5pm Sat & Sun) Sigulda's 1200m bobsled track was built for the Soviet team. In winter you can fly down the 16-bend track at 80km/h in a five-person Vučko **soft bob** (per person €10, from October to mid-March), or book in for the real Olympian experience on the hair-raising **taxi bob** (per person €15, from November to mid-March). Summer speed fiends can ride a wheeled **summer bob** (per person €15, from May to September).

Cable Car Bungee Jump ADVENTURE SPORTS
(☎2644 0660; www.bungee.lv; Poruka iela 14; bungee jump from €30; ⊙6.30pm, 8pm & 9.30pm Wed-Sun Apr-Oct) Take your daredevil shenanigans to the next level with a 43m bungee jump from the bright-orange cable car that glides over the Gauja River. For an added thrill, jump naked.

Aerodium ADVENTURE SPORTS
(☎2838 4400; www.aerodium.lv; 2min weekday/weekend €28/32) The one-of-a-kind aerodium is a giant wind tunnel that propels participants up into the sky as though they were flying. Instructors can get about 15m high, while first-timers usually rock out at about 3m. To find the site, look for the sign along the A2 highway, 4km west of Sigulda.

Tarzāns Adventure Park ADVENTURE SPORTS
(Piedzīvojumu Parks Tarzāns; ☎2700 1187; www.tarzans.lv; Peldu iela 1; combo adult/child €32/22, toboggan €3/1.50, ropes course €17/10; ⏲10am-8pm May-Oct) Head here to swish down a toboggan track or monkey around on the 'Tarzan' ropes course. There's also a chairlift (€1), tube-sliding (€1), reverse bungy (€6), giant swing (€6), climbing wall (€1.50) and archery (€2).

Sleeping & Eating

Līvkalns B&B €€
(☎2686 4886; Pēteralas iela 3; r from €45; P❄📶) No place is more romantically rustic than this idyllic retreat next to a pond on the forest's edge. The rooms are pine-fresh and sit among a campus of adorable thatch-roof manors.

★**Mr Biskvīts** CAFE, BAKERY €
(www.mr.biskvits.lv; Ausekļa iela 9; mains €3-7; ⏲8am-9pm Mon-Sat, 9am-7pm Sun) Naughty Mr Biskvīts' candy-striped lair is filled with delicious cakes and pastries, but it's also a good spot for a cooked breakfast, a lunchtime soup or sandwich, and an evening pasta or stir-fry. The coffee's great, too.

Information

Gauja National Park Visitors Centre (☎6780 0388; www.gnp.lv; Turaida iela 2a; ⏲8.30am-8pm Apr-Oct, 8am-5pm Nov-Mar) Sells maps to the park, town and cycle routes nearby.

Sigulda Tourism Information Centre (☎6797 1335; www.tourism.sigulda.lv; Ausekļa iela 6; ⏲9am-6pm; 📶) Located within the train station, this extremely helpful centre has stacks of information about activities and accommodation.

Getting There & Around

Trains run to/from Rīga (€2.35, 1¼ hours, 10 daily) and Cēsis (€2, 45 minutes, five daily).

There are also buses to Rīga (€3, one hour, hourly) and Cēsis (€1.85, 1½ hours, daily).

Cēsis

POP 15,900

Not only is sweet little Cēsis (*tsay*-sis) one of Latvia's prettiest towns, it's also one of its oldest. Nestled within the forested confines of Gauja National Park, its cobbled lanes wend around a sturdy castle, a soaring church spire and a lazy lakeside park.

Sights

Cēsis History & Art Museum CASTLE, MUSEUM
(Cēsu Vēstures un mākslas muzejs; Pils laukums 9; whole complex/castle & garden/museum €5/3/3; ⏲10am-5pm Tue-Sun) Right from the outset when you're handed a lit candle in a glass lantern, it's clear that this isn't an ordinary museum. At its centre is **Cēsis Castle**, founded in 1209 by the Livonian Brothers of the Sword. The candle's to help you negotiate the dark spiral stair in the western tower (the views from the top over Castle Park's picturesque lake are excellent). The museum's extremely interesting displays are in the adjoining 18th-century 'new castle'.

Sleeping & Eating

Province B&B €€
(☎6412 0849; http://www.province.lv/; Niniera iela 6; r €45; P📶) This cute celery-green guesthouse pops out from the dreary Soviet-era housing nearby. The 11 rooms are simple and spotless, and there's a cafe on the ground floor. English isn't its strong point.

Vinetas un Allas Kārumlādes CAFE €
(Rīgas iela 12; snacks €3-5; ⏲9am-7pm) The sign reads 'treats for a good day', which should be enough to entice you through the doors and leave you drooling in front of the cake counter. As well as the delicious sweets on display, it serves salad and soup. It's just a shame that the coffee's not better.

Information

Cēsis Tourism Information Centre (☎6412 1815; www.tourism.cesis.lv; Pils laukums 9; ⏲10am-5pm daily May-Sep, Tue-Sun Oct-Apr) Within the Cēsis History & Art Museum building.

Getting There & Away

Four to five trains a day travel to/from Rīga (€3.50, 1¾ hours) and Sigulda (€2, 45 minutes).

There are also buses to Rīga (€4.15, two hours, hourly) and Sigulda (€1.85, 1½ hours, daily).

WESTERN LATVIA

Latvia's westernmost province, Kurzeme (Courland), offers the simple delights of beautiful beaches and a scattering of historic towns. It's hard to imagine that this low-key region once had imperial aspirations but during the 17th century, while still a semi-independent vassal of the Polish-Lithuanian Commonwealth, the Duchy of Courland had a go at colonising Tobago and the Gambia. The Great Northern War put paid to that, after which the Duchy was subsumed into the Russian Empire.

Kuldīga

POP 11,400

If Kuldīga were a tad closer to Rīga it would be crowded with day-tripping camera-clickers. Fortunately, the town is located deep in the heart of rural Kurzeme, making its quaint historic core the perfect reward for more intrepid travellers.

Kuldīga reached its peak in the 16th and early 17th centuries as one of the most important cities in the Duchy of Courland, but it was badly damaged during the Great Northern War and was never able to regain its former lustre. Today it's a favourite spot to shoot Latvian period-piece films.

There's not a lot to do here except to stroll the streets and the park in the grounds of the old castle (of which nothing much remains), admiring the sculpture garden and gazing down on pretty **Ventas Rumba**, the widest waterfall in Europe. Don't be fooled by the grandness of that title: although it stretches for 249m, it's only a couple of metres high. During spawning season salmon would have little difficulty launching themselves up and over it, giving Kuldīga the curious epithet 'city where salmon fly'.

Information

Tourist Information Centre (☎6332 2259; www.visit.kuldiga.lv; Baznīcas iela 5; ⊙9am-5pm Mon-Sat, 10am-2pm Sun May-Sep, 9am-5pm Mon-Fri Oct-Apr) Tonnes of informative brochures about the town and a souvenir shop on either side. It's located within the old town hall.

Getting There & Away

Buses run to/from Rīga (€6.40, three hours, 11 daily) and Ventspils (€6, 1¼ hours, six daily).

Ventspils

POP 36,700

Fabulous amounts of oil and shipping money have given Ventspils an economic edge over Latvia's other small cities, and although locals coddle their Užavas beer and claim that there's not much to do, tourists will find a weekend's worth of fun in the form of brilliant beaches, well-maintained parks and interactive museums.

Sights

Livionian Order Castle CASTLE, MUSEUM
(Livonijas ordeņa pils; ☎6362 2031; www.ventspilsmuzejs.lv; Jāņa iela 17; adult/child €2.10/1.10; ⊙10am-6pm Tue-Sun) This blocky building doesn't look obviously castle-like from the outside, but the 13th-century interior is home to a cutting-edge interactive local history and art museum. During Soviet rule, the castle was used as a prison and an exhibit in the stables recounts its horrors (in Latvian only). An adjacent Zen rock garden will soothe your soul afterwards.

Sleeping & Eating

Kupfernams B&B €€
(☎6362 6999; www.hotelkupfernams.lv; Kārļa iela 5; s/d €39/59; wi-fi) Our favourite spot to spend the night, this charming wooden house at the centre of Old Town has a set of cheery upstairs rooms with slanted ceilings, opening onto a communal lounge. Below, there's a cafe and a hair salon (which doubles as the reception).

Melanis Sivēns LATVIAN €€
(☎6362 2396; www.pilskrogs.lv; Jāņa iela 17; mains €6-8; ⊙noon-10pm Wed-Mon) Located in the castle's dungeon and named after a pig skeleton uncovered by archaeologists, the Black Pig is Ventspils' most atmospheric eatery. Candles flicker on wooden tables, while diners tuck into meaty mains and lashings of ale. Confirmed carnivores should consider the meat platter.

ESSENTIAL FOOD & DRINK

For centuries in Latvia, food equalled fuel, energising peasants as they worked the fields and warming their bellies during bone-chilling Baltic winters. Although it will be a few more years before globetrotters stop qualifying local restaurants as being 'good by Latvia's standards', the cuisine scene has improved by leaps and bounds over the last couple of years.

Pork, herring, boiled potatoes, sauerkraut and black bread are the traditional standbys, pepped up with dill, cottage cheese and sour cream. Other local tastes to look out for include the following:

➡ **Mushrooms** Not a sport but a national obsession, mushroom picking takes the country by storm during the first showers of autumn.

➡ **Smoked fish** Dozens of fish shacks dot the Kurzeme coast – look for the veritable smoke signals rising above the tree line.

➡ **Black Balzām** The jet-black, 45%-proof concoction is a secret recipe of more than a dozen fairy-tale ingredients including oak bark, wormwood and linden blossoms. A shot a day keeps the doctor away, so say most of Latvia's pensioners. To take the edge off, try alternating sips with some blackcurrant juice.

➡ **Alus** For such a tiny nation there's definitely no shortage of *alus* (beer) – each major town has its own brew. You can't go wrong with Užavas or Valmiermuižas.

Skroderkrogs LATVIAN €€
(☎6362 7634; Skroderu iela 6; mains €6-13; ⏲11am-10pm daily) If you're after big serves of Latvian comfort food in a pleasant local setting (candles and flowers on tables fashioned from old sewing machines), this is the place to come.

Information

Tourist Information Centre (☎6362 2263; www.visitventspils.com; Dārzu iela 6; ⏲8am-6pm Mon-Sat, 10am-4pm Sun) In the ferry terminal.

Getting There & Away

Ventspils is served by buses to/from Rīga (€7.55, three hours, hourly) and Kuldīga (€6, 1¼ hours, six daily).

SURVIVAL GUIDE

Directory A–Z

FESTIVALS & EVENTS

Check out Kultura (www.culture.lv) for a yearly listing of festivals and events across the country. At midsummer, the cities empty out as locals head to the countryside for traditional celebrations.

GAY & LESBIAN TRAVELLERS

Homosexuality was decriminalised in 1992 and an equal age of consent applies (16 years). However, negative attitudes towards gays and lesbians are the norm and violent attacks occasionally occur. Rīga has a few gay venues and in 2015 it will become the first former-Soviet city to host Europride.

INTERNET RESOURCES

Latvia Travel (www.latvia.travel)
Latvian Institute (www.latinst.lv)
Yellow Pages Directory (www.1188.lv)

PUBLIC HOLIDAYS

New Year's Day 1 January
Good Friday March or April
Easter Sunday & Monday March or April
Labour Day 1 May
Restoration of Independence Day 4 May

COUNTRY FACTS

Area 64,589 sq km

Capital Rīga

Country Code ☎371

Currency Euro (€)

Emergency ☎112

Language Latvian

Money ATMs are easy to find

Population 2 million

Visas Not required for citizens of the EU, Australia, Canada, New Zealand and the USA, among others. For further information, visit www.mfa.gov.lv.

Mothers' Day Second Sunday in May

Pentecost May or June

Līgo (Midsummer's Eve) & Jāņi (Midsummer) 23 and 24 June

National Day 18 November (if it falls on a weekend, the following Monday)

Christmas Holiday 24 to 26 December

New Year's Eve 31 December

TELEPHONE

There are no area codes in Latvia. All telephone numbers have eight digits; landlines start with ☎6 and mobile numbers with ☎2.

Getting There & Away

AIR

Fifteen European airlines fly into Rīga, including the national carrier **airBaltic** (☎9000 1100; www.airbaltic.com).

LAND

In 2007 Latvia acceded to the Schengen Agreement, which removed all border control between it and Estonia and Lithuania. Carry your travel documents with you at all times, as random border checks do occur.

Bus

Ecolines (☎6721 4512; www.ecolines.net) Routes include Rīga–Parnu–Tallinn (€17, four to 4¾ hours, seven daily), Rīga–Tartu (€7, four hours, two daily), Rīga–Vilnius (€17, four hours, seven daily), Rīga–Vilnius–Minsk (€24, eight hours, daily) and Rīga–Moscow (€60, 14 hours, daily).

Kautra/Eurolines (www.eurolines.lt) Operates buses on the Rīga–Vilnius–Warsaw–Berlin–Cologne route (€116, 29 hours).

Lux Express & Simple Express (☎6778 1350; www.luxexpress.eu) Routes include Rīga–Pärnu–Tallinn (from €13, 4½ hours, 11 daily), Rīga–Tartu–St Petersburg (from €23, 12 hours, four daily), Rīga–Vilnius (from €11, four hours, 10 daily) and Rīga–Kaliningrad (€20, eight hours, daily).

Train

International trains head from Rīga to Moscow (16 hours), St Petersburg (15 hours) and Minsk (12 hours) daily. There are no direct trains to Estonia; you'll need to change at Valka.

SEA

Stena Line (☎6362 2999; www.stenaline.nl) Car ferries head from Travemünde, Germany, to Liepāja (26 hours) and Ventspils (26 hours), and from Nynäshamn, Sweden, to Ventspils (12 hours).

Tallink Silja Line (☎6709 9700; www.tallinksilja.com; passenger/vehicle from €32/105) Overnight ferries between Rīga and Stockholm (17 hours), departing every other day.

Getting Around

BUS

- Buses are generally more frequent than trains and serve more of the country.
- Updated timetables are available at www.1188.lv and www.autoosta.lv.

CAR & MOTORCYCLE

- Driving is on the right-hand side.
- Headlights must be on at all times.
- Local car-hire companies usually allow you to drive in all three Baltic countries but not beyond.

TRAIN

- There are train services from Rīga to Jūrmala, Sigulda and Cēsis.
- Timetables are online at www.1188.lv and www.ldz.lv.

SLEEPING PRICE RANGES

Prices quoted here are for rooms with a private bathroom unless otherwise stated. We highly advise booking ahead during summer. Rates drop significantly in the colder months. The following price indicators apply for a high-season double room.

€ less than €40

€€ €40 to €80

€€€ more than €80

EATING PRICE RANGES

The following price ranges refer to a standard main course. It's common to tip up to 10% for good service.

€ less than €7

€€ €7 to €17

€€€ more than €17

Lithuania

Includes ➡

Best Places to Eat

- Leičiai (p752)
- Pilies kepyklėlė (p752)
- Senoji Kibininė (p755)
- Moksha (p756)
- Momo Grill (p758)

Best Places to Stay

- Hotel Euterpė (p757)
- Bernardinu B&B (p751)
- Miško Namas (p758)
- Litinterp Guesthouse (p757)
- Jimmy Jumps House (p751)

Why Go?

Compact Lithuania has much to offer. Those with a passion for baroque architecture, ancient castles and archaeological treasures will find plenty in the capital and beyond. There are sculpture parks and interactive museums for travellers wishing to delve into the country's traumatic recent history; modern art spaces and exhibitions to titillate those whose interests are more contemporary; and all-night clubbing in the bigger cities and on the coast for those requiring something less cerebral.

Away from the cities, the pristine beaches and giant sand dunes on the west coast are a must-see. The Hill of Crosses is an unexpected delight. Elsewhere, the country's woods and lakes come alive in summer with cyclists, berry pickers and campers.

When to Go

Vilnius

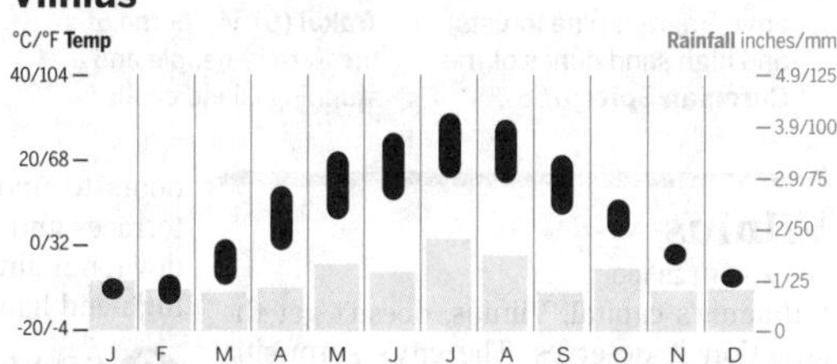

Apr Some of the world's best jazz performers are at the Kaunas International Jazz Festival.

Jun & Jul The loveliest time to explore the forests and sand dunes of the Curonian Spit.

Sep Vilnius Capital Days, a celebration of the capital with street theatre, music and fashion.

Lithuania Highlights

1. Explore beautiful baroque **Vilnius**, with its cobbled streets, church spires, bars and bistros.
2. Breathe the pure air amid fragrant pine forests and high sand dunes of the **Curonian Spit** (p758).
3. Hear the wind whistle between thousands of crosses on eerie **Hill of Crosses** (p756).
4. Wander wonderful **Trakai** (p754), home of the Karaite people and a stunning island castle.
5. Experience a taste of Lithuania's communist past at the **Grūtas sculpture park** (p754).
6. Take in the poignant WWII history of Kaunas' **Ninth Fort** (p755).

Vilnius

☎5 / POP 523,100

Lithuania's capital, Vilnius, doesn't get the attention it deserves. The city's surprising Old Town is a dazzling assemblage of baroque houses, inviting alleyways and colourful churches built around quiet courtyards. But it's no museum piece: the city's cosmopolitan heritage, enriched by Polish, Jewish and Russian influences, lends a sophisticated vibe, and thousands of students keep the energy level high. Push through big wooden doors to find lively pubs and bars, hidden terraces and romantic restaurants. Tumbledown buildings hide designer boutiques and high-end handicraft shops.

Sights

Cathedral Square & Gediminis Hill

Cathedral Square (Katedros aikštė), dominated by Vilnius Cathedral and its 57m-tall belfry, marks the centre of Vilnius and is home to

ITINERARIES

Three Days

Devote two days to exploring the baroque heart of **Vilnius**, then day trip to **Trakai** for its island castle and the homesteads of the Karaite people, stopping off at **Paneriai** on the way.

One Week

Spend four nights in **Vilnius**, with day trips to both **Trakai** and the **Grūtas Park** sculpture garden near Druskininkai. Travel cross-country to the **Hill of Crosses**, then explore some serious nature on the **Curonian Spit** for two or three days. Head back east via **Klaipėda** and **Kaunas**.

the city's most important sights. The square buzzes with local life, especially at Sunday morning Mass. Amuse yourself by hunting for the secret *stebuklas* (miracle) tile; if found, it can grant you a wish if you stand on it and turn around clockwise. It marks the spot where the 650km Tallinn–Vilnius human chain, protesting against Soviet rule, ended in 1989. The 48m-high **Gediminas Hill** rises just behind the square. The restored ruins of **Gediminas Castle** mark the spot where the city was founded in the 13th century. Scramble up (or take a handy **funicular**) for jaw-dropping views of Old Town.

Vilnius Cathedral CHURCH

(Vilniaus Arkikatedra; ☎5-261 0731; www.katedra.lt; Katedros aikštė 2; 🕐7am-7.30pm, Mass Sun 8am, 9am, 10am, 11.15am, 12.30pm, 5.30pm & 6.30pm) This national symbol occupies a spot originally used for the worship of Perkūnas, the Lithuanian thunder god; much later the Soviets turned the cathedral into a gallery. The first wooden cathedral was built here in 1387–88. **St Casimir's Chapel** at the back is the showpiece. It has a baroque cupola, coloured marble and frescoes from St Casimir's life.

★ **Palace of the Grand Dukes of Lithuania** MUSEUM

(Valdovų rumai; ☎5-212 7476; www.valdovurumai.lt; Katedros aikštė 4; adult/student €3/1.50, guided tour €20; 🕐11am-6pm Tue-Fri, 11am-4pm Sat & Sun) The palace that once marked the seat of the Lithuanian dukes has been painstakingly rebuilt and is a must for understanding Lithuanian history. The visitors' route begins on the ground floor, where traces of the old palace dating from the 16th and 17th centuries, and earlier, can still be seen, and proceeds upward through the centuries. The palace was a modern-day wonder in its day, with a vast courtyard and lively social calendar that included masked balls, banquets and jousting matches. Under the Russian occupation at the end of the 18th century, the palace was torn down and left a ruin. It reopened in 2013 after a decade-long costly restoration.

National Museum of Lithuania MUSEUM

(Lietuvos Nacionalinis Muziejus; ☎5-262 7774; www.lnm.lt; Arsenalo gatvė 1; adult/child €2/1; 🕐10am-6pm Tue-Sat) The National Museum of Lithuania, identified by a proud statue of **Mindaugas** (Arsenalo gatvė 1) – the first and only king of Lithuania – at the front, features exhibits that look at everyday Lithuanian life from the 13th century until WWII. Of particular note are some of the country's earliest coins, dating from the 14th century, as well as folk art and cross-crafting.

Gediminas Castle & Museum MUSEUM

(Gedimino Pilis ir Muziejus; ☎5-261 7453; www.lnm.lt; Gediminas Hill, Arsenalo gatvė 5; adult/child €2/1; 🕐10am-7pm May-Sep, 10am-5pm Tue-Sun Oct-Apr) Vilnius was founded on 48m-high Gediminas Hill, topped since the 13th century by the oft-rebuilt tower of ruined Gediminas Castle. For spectacular views of the Old Town, take the spiral staircase to the top of the tower, which houses the Upper Castle Museum. Exhibits include scale models of the castle in the 14th and 18th centuries and medieval arms.

Old Town

St Anne's Church CHURCH

(Šv Onos Bažnyčia; ☎8-698 17731; www.onosbaznycia.lt; Maironio gatvė 8-1; 🕐Mass 6pm Mon-Sat, 9am & 11am Sun) Arguably the most beautiful

VILNIUS CITY CARD

If you're planning to do epic amounts of sightseeing within a short period of time, the **Vilnius City Card** (☎5-250 5895; www.vilnius-tourism.lt; per 24/72hr €18/30) provides free or discounted entry to many attractions, and free transport.

Central Vilnius

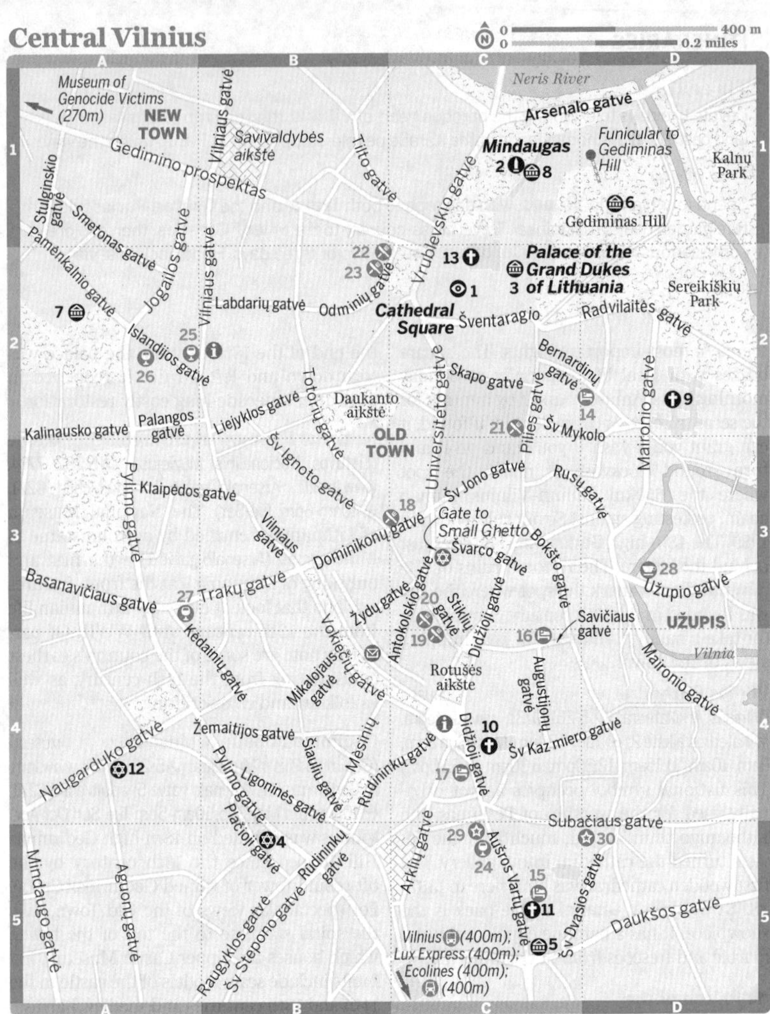

church in Vilnius is tiny, late-15th-century St Anne's Church (standing in front of the much larger **Bernardine's Church**). A graceful example of Gothic architecture, its sweeping curves and delicate pinnacles frame 33 different types of red brick. It's so fine Napoleon reputedly wanted to take it back to Paris.

St Casimir's Church CHURCH

(Šv Kazimiero Bažnyčia; ☎5-2121715; www.kazimiero.lt; Didžioji gatvė 34; ⏲7am-7pm) This striking church is the city's oldest baroque place of worship. St Casimir's dome and cross-shaped plan defined a new style for churches when the Jesuits built it between 1604 and 1615. It was destroyed and rebuilt several times over the centuries and has recently emerged from another bout of renovation.

St Teresa's Church CHURCH

(Šv Teresės Bažnyčia; ☎5-212 3513; www.ausrosvartai.lt; Aušros Vartų gatvė 14; ⏲7am-7pm) This Catholic church is baroque through and through: early baroque outside and ornate late baroque inside. Underneath its entrance is a chamber for the dead, containing examples of baroque tombs, but it is usually locked.

Gates of Dawn HISTORIC BUILDING

(Aušros Vartai; ☎5-212 3513; www.ausrosvartai.lt; Aušros Vartų 12; ⏲chapel 6am-7pm, Mass 9am,

Central Vilnius

Top Sights
1 Cathedral Square ... C2
2 Mindaugas ... C1
3 Palace of the Grand Dukes of Lithuania ... C2

Sights
4 Choral Synagogue ... B5
5 Gates of Dawn ... C5
6 Gediminas Castle & Museum ... D1
7 Holocaust Museum ... A2
8 National Museum of Lithuania ... C1
9 St Anne's Church ... D2
10 St Casimir's Church ... C4
11 St Teresa's Church ... C5
12 Tolerance Centre ... A4
13 Vilnius Cathedral ... C2

Sleeping
14 Bernardinu B&B ... D2
15 Domus Maria ... C5
16 Jimmy Jumps House ... C4
17 Radisson Blu Royal Astorija ... C4

Eating
18 Cozy ... C3
19 Leičiai ... C4
20 Lokys ... C3
21 Pilies kepyklėlė ... C2
22 Sue's Indian Raja ... B2
23 Zoe's Bar & Grill ... B2

Drinking & Nightlife
24 In Vino ... C5
25 Jackie ... A2
26 Opium ... A2
27 Pabo Latino ... A3
28 Užupio kavinė ... D3

Entertainment
29 Lithuanian National Philharmonic ... C5
30 Tamsta ... D5

10am, 5.30pm & 6.30pm Mon-Sat, 9.30am Sun) FREE The southern border of Old Town is marked by the last standing of 10 portals that were once built into the Old Town walls. This 16th-century town gate doesn't quite live up to the breathless 'Gates of Dawn' moniker, though peek inside to see Chapel of the Blessed Mary and a historic painting of the Madonna said to work miracles.

New Town & Outside Centre

★Museum of Genocide Victims MUSEUM
(Genocido Aukų Muziejus; ☎5-249 8156; www.genocid.lt/muziejus; Aukų gatvė 2a; adult/child €2/1; ⊙10am-6pm Wed-Sat, to 5pm Sun) This former headquarters of the Soviet KGB houses a museum dedicated to thousands of Lithuanians who were murdered, imprisoned or deported by the Soviet Union from WWII until the 1960s. Memorial plaques honouring those who perished tile the outside of the building. Inside, floors cover the harsh realities of Soviet occupation, including gripping personal accounts of Lithuanian deportees to Siberia.

TV Tower TOWER
(Televizijos Bokštas; ☎5-252 5333; www.telecentras.lt; Sausio 13-osios gatvė 10; adult/child €6/3; ⊙observation deck 11am-10pm; 🚌1, 3, 7, 16) It's hard to miss the 326m TV tower on the city's western horizon. This tall needle symbolises Lithuania's strength of spirit; on 13 January 1991 Soviet special forces killed some 14 people here. Lithuanian TV kept broadcasting until the troops came through the tower door. From the observation deck (190m) Vilnius is spread out before you.

Sleeping

★Jimmy Jumps House HOSTEL €
(☎8-607 88435, 5-231 3847; www.jimmyjumpshouse.com; Savičiaus gatvė 12-1; dm €11-12, r from €30; ⊖@🛜) This clean, well-run, centrally located hostel is justifiably popular among backpackers. The pine-wood bunks are modest in four- to 12-bed rooms, but extras like free walking tours, themed pub crawls and a free breakfast add up to money well spent. Offers discounts if booked directly via email. No credit cards.

★Bernardinu B&B GUESTHOUSE €€
(☎5-261 5134; www.bernardinuhouse.com; Bernardinų gatvė 5; s/d from €54/60; P❄🛜) Charming family-owned guesthouse located on one of the most picturesque lanes in the Old Town. The house dates to the 18th century, but it's been renovated and the owners have tried hard to preserve elements like old timber flooring and ceilings. Breakfast is €5 and it's brought to your door on a tray at 9am.

★Domus Maria GUESTHOUSE €€
(☎5-264 4880; www.domusmaria.lt; Aušros Vartų gatvė 12; s/d €60/80; P⊖@🛜) The guesthouse of the Vilnius archdiocese is housed in a former monastery dating to the 17th century and oozes charm. Accommodation is in the monks' chambers, but they've been given a thorough, stylish makeover. Two rooms, 207 and 307, have views of the Gates of Dawn and

are usually booked far in advance. Breakfast is served in the vaulted refectory.

Radisson Blu Royal Astorija HOTEL €€€
(☎5-212 0110; www.radissonblu.com; Didžioji gatvė 35/2; s/d/ste €180/210/360; P ⊜ @ ☎ ≋) This excellent splurge or business choice is part of a high-end chain, though the building dates from the early 20th century and exudes character. The central location, overlooking St Casimir's Church, is a plus, as are the popular wintertime Sunday brunches. Mod cons like trouser presses and safes are standard. The Superior-Class rooms got a thorough makeover in 2014.

Eating

★Pilies kepyklėlė CREPES €
(☎5-260 8992; Pilies gatvė 19; mains €3-6; ⊙9am-11pm) A standout from the crowd on Vilnius' busiest tourist street, this relaxed combination creperie-bakery mixes old-world charm with a fresh, upbeat vibe. The 9am omelette here is a must-have as are the savoury pancakes, stuffed with spinach or ham and cheese and topped with sour cream. The poppyseed cake is reputedly the best on this side of town.

★Leičiai LITHUANIAN €€
(☎5-260 9087; www.bambalyne.lt; Stiklių gatvė 4; mains €4-8; ⊙11am-midnight; ☎) This popular, earthy brew-pub and restaurant serves simple but honest Lithuanian cooking – think potato pancakes and *cepelinai* (meat-stuffed potato dumplings) at everyman prices. The beer is excellent as well, and in warm weather there's a big terrace out the back for relaxing.

Cozy INTERNATIONAL €€
(☎5-261 1137; www.cozy.lt; Dominikonų gatvė 10; mains €5-8; ⊙9am-2am Mon-Wed, to 4am Thu & Fri, 10am-4am Sat, to 2am Sun; ☎) Cozy defies easy description: is it a bar, cafe or restaurant? The food here, including several inventive salads with duck or turkey meat and more-standard mains like pork and chicken (but often given an Asian twist), is worth the trip alone. By night Cozy morphs into a welcoming drinking den, popular with students from nearby Vilnius University.

Sue's Indian Raja INDIAN €€
(☎5-266 1887; www.suesindianraja.lt; Odminių gatvė 3; mains €6-10; ✎) OK, it's strange to list an Indian restaurant as a top pick in Vilnius, but the food here is excellent and authentic. *After* you've had your fill of delicious local foods like potato pancakes and *cepelinai,* repair here to have your palate re-energised with spicy lentils, curries and vindaloo. The three-course 'business lunch', served weekdays, is a steal at €7.50.

Zoe's Bar & Grill INTERNATIONAL €€
(☎5-212 3331; www.zoesbargrill.com; Odminių gatvė 3; mains €3-8) Zoe's covers many culinary bases and does it well, with the likes of homemade meatballs and sausages, tender steaks, and spicy Thai stir-fries and soups. Dine outdoors with cathedral views or indoors and receive an impromptu cooking lesson.

★Lokys LITHUANIAN €€€
(☎5-262 9046; www.lokys.lt; Stiklių gatvė 8; mains €8.50-18) Hunt down the big wooden bear outside to find this Vilnius institution, a cellar maze going strong since 1972. Game is its mainstay, with delicacies such as beaver-meat stew with plums or quail with blackberry sauce luring the culinarily curious. Folk musicians play here on summer evenings.

Drinking & Nightlife

Užupio kavinė CAFE
(☎5-212 2138; www.uzupiokavine.lt; Užupio gatvė 2; ⊙10am-11pm; ☎) The riverside cafe here in the Bohemian neighbourhood of Užupis is the perfect spot to relax over a coffee, beer or wine. Try booking ahead on warm summer nights, as the place tends to fill up. The cosy interior is equally fun in winter. Some nights bring impromptu live entertainment.

In Vino WINE BAR
(☎5-212 1210; www.invino.lt; Aušros Vartų gatvė 7; ⊙4pm-2am Sun-Thu, to 4am Fri & Sat) Popular drinking spot in the heart of Old Town that's perfect for a girls' (or guys') night out or, if you're single and on the prowl, meeting some friendly locals. In summer sit out in the back courtyard (try to arrive early as the tables fill up fast). Though the names suggests wine, it also serves beer and cocktails.

Jackie BAR
(Vilniaus gatvė 31; ⊙6pm-2am Sun-Wed, to 3am Thu, to 5am Fri & Sat) This hopping whisky bar, specialising in American whiskeys and bourbon, gets absolutely packed most nights, so if you wish to savour your poison, go early. Or go late on the weekend if you want to catch a DJ set.

Pabo Latino CLUB
(☎5-262 1045; www.pabolatino.lt; Trakų gatvė 3/2; admission €5-8; ⊙8pm-3am Thu-Sat) This sultry-red club specialises in sweet Latino tunes and strong cocktails. Put on your dancing shoes, fortify your liver, and be prepared for a fun night out.

JEWISH VILNIUS

Over the centuries Vilnius developed into one of Europe's leading centres of Jewish life and scholarship until the community was wiped out by the occupying Nazis and their Lithuanian sympathisers during WWII. The former Jewish quarter lay in the streets west of Didžioji gatvė, including present-day Žydų gatvė (Jews St) and Gaono gatvė, named after Vilnius' most famous Jewish resident, Gaon Elijahu ben Shlomo Zalman (1720–97). The **Tolerance Centre** (5-262 9666; www.jmuseum.lt; Naugarduko gatvė 10/2; adult/child €2.40/1.20; 10am-6pm Mon-Fri, 10am-4pm Sun), a beautifully restored former Jewish theatre, houses thought-provoking displays on the history and culture of Jews in Lithuania before the Shoah (Holocaust) and occasional exhibitions. The **Holocaust Museum** (Holokausto Muziejus; 5-262 0730; www.jmuseum.lt; Pamėnkalnio gatvė 12; adult/child €2.40/1.20; 9am-5pm Mon-Thu, 9am-4pm Fri, 10am-4pm Sun), in the so-called Green House, is an unvarnished account detailing the suffering of Lithuanian Jews in an unedited display of horrific images and letters by local survivors. Vilnius' only remaining synagogue, the **Choral Synagogue** (Choralinė Sinagoga; 5-261 2523; Pilimo gatvė 39; donations welcome; 10am-2pm Mon-Fri) FREE, was built in a Moorish style in 1903 and survived because it was used as a medical store.

Opium CLUB
(8-691 41205; www.opiumclub.lt; Islandijos gatvė 4; admission €3-5; 10pm-6am Fri, 11pm-5am Sat) This compact venue – playground of the city's best DJs – is for serious clubbers. Come here and there's a good chance you'll get addicted.

☆ Entertainment

Lithuanian National Philharmonic CLASSICAL MUSIC
(Lietuvos Nacionalinė Filharmonija; 5-266 5233; www.filharmonija.lt; Aušros Vartų gatvė 5; box office 10am-7pm Tue-Sat, to noon Sun) The country's foremost go-to location for classical music, as well as festivals of popular music and other performances.

Tamsta ROCK, JAZZ
(5-212 4498; www.tamstaclub.lt; Subačiaus gatvė 11a; admission €3-5; 7pm-midnight Wed & Thu, to 2am Fri & Sat Sep-Apr) Live music by local musicians – ranging from rock to rock'n'roll to jazz. Inspired jamming some nights and the long bar gets pretty packed most evenings. Note the club shuts down during summer (June to August).

Information

Baltic-American Medical & Surgical Clinic (8-698 52655, 5-234 2020; www.bak.lt; Nemenčinės gatvė 54a; 24hr) English-speaking health care inside Vilnius University Antakalnis hospital.

Pharmacy (Gedimino Vaistinė; 5-261 0135; www.univesitetovaistine.eu; Gedimino prospektas 27; 7.30am-8pm Mon-Fri, 10am-5pm Sat, to 4pm Sun)

Vilnius Tourist Information Centre – Old Town (5-262 9660; www.vilnius-tourism.lt; Vilniaus gatvė 22; 9am-6pm;) The city's main tourist information office is a helpful repository of maps, brochures and friendly staff willing to sort out transport, accommodation and sightseeing issues.

Vilnius Tourist Information Centre – Town Hall (5-262 6470; www.vilnius-tourism.lt; Didžioji gatvė 31; 9am-12.30pm & 1.15-6pm;) Convenient branch of the official tourist office, with a wealth of glossy brochures and general information. It also arranges tour guides, books accommodation (hotel reservation fee applies) and rents bicycles.

Getting There & Away

BUS

The **bus station** (Autobusų Stotis; information 1661; www.autobusustotis.lt; Sodų gatvė 22) handles both domestic and international coach service and is situated about 1km south of Old Town, across the street from the train station. The main international bus operators include **Ecolines** (information 5-213 3300; www.ecolines.net; Geležinkelio gatvė 15; 8am-7pm Mon-Fri, 9am-5pm Sat, 9am-3pm Sun), Lux Express (p760) or one of the affiliated carriers under **Eurolines** (www.eurolines.lt).

Frequent domestic destinations include Kaunas (€6, 1½ hours, hourly), Klaipėda (€20, four to five hours, 15 daily) and Šiauliai (€15, 3¼ to five hours, more than 10 daily).

Sample international connections include Berlin (€32, 15 hours, daily), Rīga (€20, four hours, up to seven daily), Tallinn (€36, nine hours, four daily) and Warsaw (€16, eight hours, two daily).

TRAIN

From the **train station** (Geležinkelio Stotis; information 5-233 0088; www.litrail.lt; Geležinkelio gatvė 16), Vilnius is linked by rail to various international destinations, including Warsaw,

WORTH A TRIP

GRŪTAS PARK – THE GRAVEYARD OF COMMUNISM

Both entertaining and educational, **Grūtas Park** (Grūto Parkas; ☎313-55 511; www.grutoparkas.lt; Grūtas; adult/child €6/3; ⏰9am-10pm summer, to 5pm rest of year; 👪), 125km south of Vilnius, near the spa town of Druskininkai, has been an enormous hit since it opened in 2001. The sprawling grounds, built to resemble a Siberian concentration camp, feature the entire Marxist pantheon and dozens of other statuesque examples of Soviet realism, as well as assorted communist paraphernalia, exhibits on Soviet history (with a focus on the oppression of Lithuania) and loudspeakers bellowing Soviet anthems.

The statues once stood confidently in parks and squares across Lithuania, but now this is all that's left.

There are up to several buses daily between Druskininkai and Vilnius (€10, two hours), and hourly buses to/from Kaunas (€9, 2¼ hours). Ask to be let off at Grūtas village, then walk the final 1km to the park. Catch a bus back to either city from the main road.

Minsk and Moscow, though most trains run through Belarus and require a transit visa.

Frequent domestic destinations include Kaunas (€6, one to 1¾ hours, up to 17 daily), Klaipėda (€15, 4¾ hours, three daily) and Trakai (€1.60, 35 to 45 minutes, up to 10 daily).

Sample international connections include Moscow (from €90, 15 hours, three daily), Minsk (from €10, three to four hours, up to seven daily) and Warsaw (from €25, 15 hours, one daily).

Getting Around

TO/FROM THE AIRPORT

Bus 1 runs between Vilnius International Airport (p759), 5km south of the city centre, and the train station. A shuttle train service runs from the train station 17 times daily between 5.44am and 9.07pm (around €0.75). A taxi from the airport to the city centre should cost around €15.

BICYCLE

Velo-City (☎8-674 12123; www.velovilnius.lt; Aušros Vartų 7; per hr/day €3/12; ⏰9am-9pm Apr-Sep) Rents bikes and offers daily bike tours of the city. Outside high season you'll find it at Kauna gatvė 5 (open 2pm to 6pm Tuesday to Saturday).

PUBLIC TRANSPORT

Vilnius Transport (☎5-210 7050; www.vilniustransport.lt) Vilnius' public transport company operates buses and trolleybuses daily from 5am to 11pm. See the website for a (confusing) timetable. Buy individual journey tickets from the driver for €1. For longer stays, buy an electronic Vilniečio Kortelė (Vilnius Card) from news kiosks for €1.20. Using the card, a 30-minute journey costs about €0.60.

TAXI

Vilnius Veža (☎5-233 3337, 1450; www.vilniusveza.lt) Reliable radio-taxi operator. Fares are around €0.72 per kilometre.

Paneriai

During WWII the Nazis – aided by Lithuanian accomplices – murdered 100,000 people, around 70,000 of them Jews, at this site in the forest, 8km southwest of Vilnius.

From the entrance a path leads to the small **Paneriai Museum** (☎tours 662-89 575; www.jmuseum.lt; Agrastų gatvė 17; ⏰9am-5pm Sun-Thu May-Sep, by appointment Oct-Apr) FREE, with a graphic display of photographs and personal belongings of those who died here, and the grassed-over pits where the Nazis burnt the exhumed bodies of their victims.

There are hourly trains daily from Vilnius to Paneriai station (€0.60, eight to 11 minutes), from where it's a 1km walk southwest along Agrastų gatvė into the forest.

Trakai

☎528 / POP 4930

With its picturesque red-brick castle, Karaite culture, quaint wooden houses and pretty lakeside location, Trakai is a highly recommended day trip, within easy reach of the capital.

The Karaite people are named after the term *kara*, which means 'to study the scriptures' in both Hebrew and Arabic. The sect originated in Baghdad and practises strict adherence to the Torah (rejecting the rabbinic Talmud). In around 1400 the grand duke of Lithuania, Vytautas, brought about 380 Karaite families to Trakai from Crimea to serve as bodyguards. Only a dozen families remain in Trakai today and their numbers are dwindling rapidly.

Trakai's trophy piece is the fairy-tale **Trakai Castle**, occupying a small island in Lake Galvė. A footbridge links the island castle to the shore. The red-brick Gothic castle, painstakingly restored from original blueprints, dates from the late 14th century. Inside the castle, the **Trakai History Museum** (Trakų Istorijos Muziejus; 528-53 946; www.trakaimuziejus.lt; Trakai Castle; adult/senior/student & child €5.40/3.60/2.40, camera €1.20; 10am-7pm May-Sep, to 6pm Mar, Apr & Oct, to 5pm Nov-Feb) tells the story of the structure. There's a bewildering variety of objects on show – hoards of coins, weaponry and porcelain, as well as interactive displays.

You can sample *kibinai* (meat-stuffed Karaite pastries similar to empanadas or Cornish pasties) either at **Senoji Kibininė** (528-55 865; www.kibinas.lt; Karaimų gatvė 65; kibinai €2-3 each, mains €6-9; 10am-midnight) or at **Kybynlar** (8-698 06320; www.kybynlar.lt; Karaimų gatvė 29; mains €6-9; noon-9pm;).

Up to 10 trains daily (€1.60, 35 to 45 minutes) travel between Trakai and Vilnius. There are also frequent buses (€1.80, 40 minutes, twice hourly). From the bus or train station, hike about 15 minutes to find the lakes and castle.

Kaunas

37 / POP 304,000

Lithuania's second city has a compact Old Town, an entertaining array of museums and plenty of vibrant, youthful energy provided by its large student population. A good time to visit is in late April, during the **Kaunas Jazz Festival** (www.kaunasjazz.lt), when homegrown and international artists perform in venues across the city.

Sights

Old Town

The heart of Kaunas' lovely Old Town is **Rotušės Aikštė**, home of the city's former City Hall, now known as the 'Palace of Weddings', and surrounded by 15th- and 16th-century German merchants' houses.

St Francis Xavier Church & Monastery CHURCH
(8-614 49310; Rotušės aikštė 7-9; tower €1.50; tower noon-4.30pm Sat, 2-4pm Sun) The southern side of the main square, Rotušės Aikštė, is dominated by the twin-towered St Francis Xavier Church, college and Jesuit monastery complex, built between 1666 and 1720. Take a peek inside and then climb the tower for the best aerial views of Kaunas.

Sts Peter & Paul Cathedral CHURCH
(Šventų Apaštalų Petro ir Povilo Arkekatedra Bazilika; 37-324 093; Vilniaus gatvė 1; 7am-7pm Mon-Sat, 8am-7pm Sun) With its single tower, this church owes much to baroque reconstruction, especially inside, but the original 15th-century Gothic shape of its windows remains. It was probably founded by Vytautas around 1410 and now has nine altars. The **tomb of Maironis** stands outside the south wall.

New Town

Laisvės alėja, a 1.7km-long pedestrian street lined with bars, shops and restaurants, runs east from Old Town to New Town, ending at the white, neo-Byzantine **St Michael the Archangel Church**.

★**MK Čiurlionis National Art Museum** GALLERY
(MK Čiurlionio Valstybinis Dailės Muziejus; 37-229 475; www.ciurlionis.lt; Putvinskio gatvė 55; adult/child €1.80/0.90; 11am-5pm Tue-Sun) The Čiurlionis National Art Museum is Kaunas' leading museum. It has extensive collections of the romantic paintings of Mikalojus Konstantinas Čiurlionis (1875–1911), one of Lithuania's greatest artists and composers, as well as Lithuanian folk art and 16th- to 20th-century European applied art.

★**Museum of Devils** MUSEUM
(Velnių Muziejus; 37-221 587; www.ciurlionis.lt; Putvinskio gatvė 64; adult/child €1.80/0.90; 11am-5pm Tue-Sun;) Diabolical is the best word

WORTH A TRIP

A DARK CHAPTER IN KAUNAS' HISTORY'

A poignant memorial to the tens of thousands of people, mainly Jews, who were murdered by the Nazis, the excellent **Museum of the Ninth Fort** (IX Forto Muziejus; 37-377 748; www.9fortomuziejus.lt; Žemaičių plentas 73; adult/child €2.40/1.50, catacombs with guide €6; 10am-6pm Wed-Mon Apr-Oct, to 4pm Nov-Mar), 7km north of Kaunas, comprises an old WWI-era fort and the bunker-like church of the damned. Displays cover deportations of Lithuanians by the Soviets and graphic photo exhibitions track the demise of Kaunas' Jewish community.

Take bus 23 from Jonavos gatvė to the 9-ojo Forto Muziejus stop and cross under the motorway.

WORTH A TRIP

THE HILL OF CROSSES

One of Lithuania's most awe-inspiring sights is the legendary **Hill of Crosses** (Kryžių kalnas; ☎41-370 860; Jurgaičiai). The sound of the thousands of crosses – which appear to grow on the hillock – tinkling in the breeze is wonderfully eerie.

Planted here since at least the 19th century and probably much older, the crosses were bulldozed by the Soviets, but each night people crept past soldiers and barbed wire to plant more, risking their lives or freedom to express their national and spiritual fervour.

Some of the crosses are devotional, others are memorials (many for people deported to Siberia) and some are finely carved folk-art masterpieces.

The hill is 12km north of the central city of Šiauliai along Hwy A12 near the village of Jurgaičiai. From the highway, it's another 2km east from a well-marked turn-off ('Kryžių kalnas 2'). From Šiauliai, take a Joniškis-bound bus (€1.20, 10 minutes, up to seven daily) to the 'Domantai' stop and walk for 15 minutes, or grab a taxi (around €18).

Šiauliai is reachable by bus from Vilnius, Kaunas and Klaipėda. For accommodation, consult the **Tourism Information Centre** (☎41-523 110; www.siauliai.lt/tic; Vilniaus gatvė 213; ⏰9am-1pm & 2-6pm Mon-Fri, 10am-4pm Sat).

to describe the collection of 2000-odd devil statuettes in this museum, collected over the years by landscape artist Antanas Žmuidzinavičius (1876–1966). While the commentary tries to put a pseudo-intellectual sheen on things by linking the devils to Lithuanian folklore, the fun of this museum is all about the spooky masks and stories. Great for kids.

Sleeping

Apple Economy Hotel HOTEL €
(☎37-321 404; www.applehotel.lt; Valančiaus gatvė 19; s/d from €36/45; P ⊖ @ ᯤ) This simple hotel set on Old Town's edge in a quiet courtyard is a highly commendable no-frills option. The rooms are tiny, but are cheerful and done out in bright colours. The bed in our room was the most comfortable we slept on during our research in Lithuania. Some rooms have shared bathroom, while others are self-contained.

Litinterp GUESTHOUSE €
(☎37-228 718; www.litinterp.lt; Gedimino gatvė 28-7; s/d/tr €30/45/54; ⏰office 8.30am-7pm Mon-Fri, 9am-3pm Sat; P ⊖ @ ᯤ) The Litinterp empire boasts quality guesthouses in Vilnius, Klaipėda and Kaunas. There's not a lot of character here, but the rooms are cheap, clean and highly functional. The staff could not be friendlier or more knowledgeable. Call or email in advance if you plan to arrive outside office hours.

Park Inn by Radisson HOTEL €€
(☎37-306 100; www.parkinn.com/hotel-kaunas; Donelaičio gatvė 27; s/d from €80/100; P ⊖ @ ᯤ) This smart business hotel fills eight floors of a renovated building in New Town. Service is slick and professional, and rooms are standard business class, with a few added extras such as heated bathroom floors and free tea and coffee. Count on the restaurant, bar and huge conference centre on-site.

Eating

★**Moksha** INDIAN, THAI €€
(☎8-676 71649; www.moksha.lt; Vasario 16-osios gatvė 6; mains €5-8; ⏰11am-10pm; ✎) This tiny place with whitewashed brick walls and fresh flowers everywhere lures you in with exotic smells. You can expect such daily specials as lamb kofta curry or crispy duck with persimmon salad, and there are even vegan options such as lentil soup. On top of that, the service is super-friendly; a rarity in these parts.

Bernelių Užeiga – Old Town LITHUANIAN €€
(☎37-200 913; www.berneliuuzeiga.lt; Valančiaus gatvė 9; mains €5-8; ⏰11am-10pm; ✎) If it's rustic Lithuanian cuisine served by fair maidens in traditional dress that you're after, then this twinset of wooden country inns in the middle of town is for you. Another **branch** (www.berneliuuzeiga.lt; Donelaičio gatvė 11; mains €5-8; ✎) is in Donelaičio.

Drinking & Nightlife

Kavinė Kultūra CAFE
(☎8-676 25546; www.facebook.com/kavine.kultura; Donelaičio gatvė 14-16; ⏰noon-10pm Sun-Thu, noon-2am Fri & Sat; ᯤ) It calls itself a cafe, but this alternative meeting spot covers the bases from pub to cocktail bar to cosy spot to grab a cup of coffee. The clientele is skewed towards students and thinkers, and the space is a bit of fresh air for anyone looking to escape

trendier, commercial bars. Excellent bar food, salads and wings, too.

Whiskey Bar W1640 BAR
(☎37-203 984; www.viskiobaras.lt; Kurpių gatvė 29; ⏲5pm-1am Tue-Thu, 5pm-5am Fri & Sat; 📶) Tucked away down a shabby side street, this bar is a real find. Not only does it have a mind-boggling collection of whiskies (150 types, to be precise) – mostly Scotch, but also some rarer Japanese ones – the bar staff are the friendliest in town. If whisky isn't your poison, then one of its ales just might be.

Information

Tourist Office (☎37-323 436; www.visit.kaunas.lt; Laisvės alėja 36; ⏲9am-6pm Mon-Fri, 10am-3pm Sat & Sun Jun-Aug) Books accommodation, sells maps and guides, and arranges bicycle rental and guided tours of the Old Town from mid-May to September.

Getting There & Away

Kaunas' bus and train stations are located not far from each other, about 2km south of the city centre. From the bus station, frequent domestic buses leave for Klaipėda (€12, three hours, up to 16 daily) and Vilnius (€6, 1¾ hours, up to three per hour). From the train station there are several trains daily to Vilnius (€5.40, 1¼ to 1¾ hours, up to 17 daily).

Klaipėda

☎46 / POP 160,400

Klaipėda, Lithuania's main seaport, is known mainly as the gateway to the Curonian Spit, though it has a fascinating history as the East Prussian city of Memel long before it was incorporated into modern Lithuania in the 1920s. It was founded in 1252 by the Teutonic Order, who built the city's first castle, and has served as a key trading port through the centuries to modern times. It was retaken by Nazi Germany in WWII and housed a German submarine base. Though it was heavily bombed in the war, it retains a unique Prussian feel, particularly in the quiet backstreets of the historic **Old Town**.

Sights

Klaipėda Castle Museum MUSEUM
(Klaipėda Pilies Muziejus; ☎46-410 527; www.mlimuziejus.lt; Pilies gatvė 4; adult/child €1.80/0.90; ⏲10am-6pm Tue-Sat) This small museum is based inside the remains of Klaipėda's old moat-protected castle, which dates back to the 13th century. It tells the castle's story through the ages until the 19th century, when most of the structure was pulled down. You'll find fascinating photos from WWII and the immediate postwar years, when the city was rebuilt by Soviet planners.

History Museum of Lithuania Minor MUSEUM
(Mažosios Lietuvos Istorijos Muziejus; ☎46-410 524; www.mlimuziejus.lt; Didžioji Vandens gatvė 6; adult/child €1.50/0.75; ⏲10am-6pm Tue-Sat) This small museum traces the origins of 'Lithuania Minor' (Kleinlitauen), as much of the Lithuanian coastal region was referred to over the centuries as part of East Prussia. The museum includes fascinating bits of the German legacy, such as Prussian maps, labour-intensive weaving machines and traditional folk art.

Sleeping

★**Litinterp Guesthouse** B&B €
(☎46-410 644; www.litinterp.lt; Puodžių gatvė 17; s/d/tr €30/48/60, without bathroom €24/42/50; ⏲8.30am-7pm Mon-Fri, 10am-3pm Sat; P ⊖ @ 📶) This clean, quiet guesthouse gets our nod for value for money. The 19 rooms are spotless and furnished in a light pinewood that creates a fresh, contemporary look. The location is good, north of the river but within walking distance of Old Town. The breakfast (€2.90) is a letdown, just some bread, salami and cheese, but we're not complaining.

★**Hotel Euterpė** HOTEL €€
(☎46-474 703; www.euterpe.lt; Daržų gatvė 9; s/d €75/90; P ⊖ @ 📶) Our bet for the perfect small hotel is this upscale number that sides up to former German merchant houses in Old Town. Expect a warm welcome at reception and snug rooms bathed in earthy colours with a neat, minimalist look. The downstairs restaurant is excellent and there's a small terrace to enjoy your morning coffee in the open air.

Eating & Drinking

Senoji Hansa LITHUANIAN €€
(☎46-400 056; www.senojihansa.lt; Kurpių gatvė 1; mains €6-10; ⏲10am-midnight; 📶) This combination bar, restaurant and cafe sits wedged on a corner, a block down from the riverside area. It's a popular spot for lunch or dinner, with a menu consisting of meat dishes, pancakes and a very good rendition of *cepelinai*. The covered terrace is open year-round and draws a fun crowd on weekend evenings.

★Momo Grill STEAKHOUSE €€€
(☎8-693 12355; www.momogrill.lt; Liepų gatvė 20; mains €10-18; ⊙11am-10pm Tue-Sun;) This tiny, modern, minimalist steakhouse is foodie heaven and the hardest table to book in town. The small menu consists of just three cuts of beef plus grilled fish and leg of duck, and allows the chef to focus on what he does best. The austere interior of white tiles is soothing and the wine list is excellent.

Information

Tourist Office (☎46-412 186; www.klaipedainfo.lt; Turgaus gatvė 7; ⊙9am-7pm Mon-Fri, 10am-4pm Sat & Sun) Exceptionally efficient tourist office selling maps and locally published guidebooks. It arranges accommodation and English-speaking guides (around €40 per hour), can help with ferry and bus schedules to the Curonian Spit, and hires out bicycles (per hour/day €2.40/9 plus €100 deposit). It has a couple of computers for surfing (per hour €1.20).

Getting There & Away

The train and bus stations are situated near each other in the modern part of town, about 2km north of Old Town. Three daily trains run to Vilnius (€15, 4¾ hours). There's regular bus service to Vilnius (€18, four to 5½ hours, up to 14 daily) and Kaunas (€12, 2¾ to 4½ hours, up to 15 daily).

Curonian Spit

☎469 / POP 2640

This magical sliver of land, covered by pine forest, hosts some of Europe's most precious sand dunes and a menagerie of elk, deer and avian wildlife. Recognised by Unesco as a World Heritage Site, the fragile spit is divided evenly between Lithuania and Russia's Kaliningrad region, with Lithuania's half protected as **Curonian Spit National Park** (☎46-402 256; www.nerija.lt; Smiltynės gatvė 11, Smiltynė; ⊙visitors centre 9am-noon & 1-4pm Mon-Fri).

Smiltynė, where the ferries from Klaipėda dock, draws weekend crowds with the delightful aquarium and the **Lithuania Sea Museum** (Lietuvos Jūrų Muziejus; ☎46-490 754; www.juru.muziejus.lt; Smiltynė; adult/student €7.50/5; ⊙10.30am-6.30pm Tue-Sun Jun-Aug, Wed-Sun Sep, 10.30am-5.30pm Sat & Sun Oct-Dec;) inside a 19th-century fort. Further south, the village of **Juodkrantė** is awaft with the tempting smells of smoked fish (*žuvis*), while picture-perfect **Nida** is home to the unmissable 52m-high **Parnidis Dune**, with its panoramic views of the 'Lithuanian Sahara' – coastline, forest and sand extending towards Kaliningrad.

A flat **cycling trail** runs all the way from Nida to Smiltynė, passing the massive colony of grey herons and cormorants near Juodkrantė, and you stand a good chance of seeing wild boar and other wildlife along the path. Bicycles are easy to hire (around €9/12 per 12/24 hours) in Nida.

The tourist office in Klaipėda can help arrange transport and accommodation; **Miško Namas** (☎469-52 290; www.miskonamas.com; Pamario gatvė 11-2; d €75, 2-/4-person apt from €90/110; P@) and **Naglis** (☎8-699 33682; www.naglis.lt; Naglių gatvė 12; d/apt €75/100; P) are both fine choices.

Getting There & Away

To get to the spit, board a ferry at the **Old Ferry Port** (Senoji perkėla; ☎46-311 117; www.keltas.lt; Danės gatvė 1; per passenger/bicycle €0.90/free) due west of Klaipėda's Old Town (€0.90, 10 minutes, half-hourly). Vehicles must use the **New Ferry Port** (Naujoji perkėla; ☎46-311 117; www.keltas.lt; Nemuno gatvė 8; per passenger/car €0.90/12, bicycle free), 2.5km south of the passenger terminal (per car €12, at least hourly).

Buses (€4.50, one hour, at least seven times daily) run regularly between Smiltynė and Nida via Juodkrantė (€3, 15 to 20 minutes).

SURVIVAL GUIDE

Directory A–Z

ACCOMMODATION

- Book ahead in the high season for Vilnius and the Curonian Spit. High-season prices are around 30% higher than low-season prices. Prices are higher in Vilnius.
- Vilnius has numerous youth hostels. Budget accommodation is easy to find outside the capital.

BUSINESS HOURS

Banks 8am to 3pm Monday to Friday

Bars 11am to midnight Sunday to Thursday, 11am to 2am Friday and Saturday

SLEEPING PRICE RANGES

The following price ranges refer to a double room with bathroom. Breakfast is included in the price unless stated otherwise.

€ less than €45

€€ €45 to €100

€€€ more than €100

COUNTRY FACTS

Area 65,303 sq km

Capital Vilnius

Country Code ☎370

Currency Euro (€)

Emergency ☎112

Language Lithuanian

Money ATMs are everywhere

Population 2.9 million

Visas Not required for citizens of the EU, Australia, Canada, Israel, Japan, New Zealand, Switzerland or the US for stays of 90 days

Clubs 10pm to 5am Thursday to Saturday
Post offices 8am to 8pm Monday to Friday, 10am to 9pm Saturday, 10am to 5pm Sunday
Restaurants noon to 11pm; later on weekends
Shops 9am or 10am to 7pm Monday to Saturday; some open Sunday

INTERNET RESOURCES

Bus & Rail Timetable (www.stotis.lt)
In Your Pocket (www.inyourpocket.com)
Lithuania's museums (www.muziejai.lt)
Lithuania's official tourism portal (www.lithuania.travel)
Vilnius Tourism (www.vilnius-tourism.lt)

MONEY

- Lithuania adopted the euro (€) on 1 January 2015.
- Exchange money with your credit or debit card at ATMs located around the country or at major banks.
- Credit cards are widely accepted for purchases.
- Some banks still cash travellers cheques, though this is increasingly uncommon.
- Tip 10% in restaurants to reward good service.

PUBLIC HOLIDAYS

New Year's Day 1 January
Independence Day 16 February
Lithuanian Independence Restoration Day 11 March
Easter Sunday March/April
Easter Monday March/April
International Labour Day 1 May
Mothers Day First Sunday in May
Feast of St John (Midsummer) 24 June
Statehood Day 6 July
Assumption of Blessed Virgin 15 August
All Saints' Day 1 November
Christmas 25 and 26 December

TELEPHONE

- To call a landline within Lithuania, dial ☎8 followed by the city code and phone number.
- To call a mobile phone within Lithuania, dial ☎8 followed by the eight-digit number.
- To make an international call dial ☎00 before the country code.
- Prepaid SIM cards are sold by **Bitė** (www.bite.lt), **Omnitel** (www.omnitel.lt) and **Tele 2** (www.tele2.lt) for around €2.30 to €3.
- Payphones – increasingly rare given the widespread use of mobiles – only accept phonecards, sold at newspaper kiosks.

ℹ Getting There & Away

Lithuania has frequent transport links to neighbouring countries via bus, train or international ferry, though be sure to route your travel to avoid Belarus or the Russian province of Kaliningrad if you don't have a transit visa for those areas. Latvia and Poland are both members of the EU's common Schengen zone and there are no passport controls at these borders. Vilnius is the country's hub for air travel. There are a handful of direct flights from major European cities, though most routes will require a change in Warsaw or Rīga. Sweden and Germany can be reached by ferry from Klaipėda, Lithuania's international seaport.

Flights, tours and rail tickets can be booked online at www.lonelyplanet.com/travel_services.

AIR

Most international traffic to Lithuania goes through **Vilnius International Airport** (Tarptautinis Vilniaus Oro Uostas; ☎passenger information 6124 4442; www.vno.lt; Rodūnios kelias 10a; 📶; 🚌1, 2), though only a handful of major European cities, as of this writing, have direct flights.

- Many air routes include a stopover in Warsaw, Copenhagen or Rīga.
- Major carriers that service Vilnius include airBaltic, Austrian Airlines, Lufthansa, LOT and Scandinavian Airlines.

ℹ LITHUANIA'S CURRENCY

Lithuania adopted the euro on 1 January 2015. We have done our best in this chapter to convert prices to the new currency, though prices for some attractions may be slightly different than those listed here.

EATING PRICE RANGES

The following price categories refer to the average cost of a main course:

€ less than €5

€€ €5 to €12

€€€ more than €12

➡ Budget carriers include Ryanair, Wizz Air and a relatively new start-up, Air Lituanica, which began flying in 2014.

BOAT

From Klaipėda's **International Ferry Port** (☎46-395 051; www.dfdsseaways.lt; Perkėlos gatvė 10), **DFDS Seaways** (☎46-395 000; www.dfdsseaways.lt; Šaulių gatvė 19) runs passenger ferries to/from Kiel (from €80, six weekly, 22 hours) in Germany and Karlshamn, Sweden (from €75, 14 hours, daily).

BUS

The main international bus companies operating in Lithuania are **Lux Express** (☎5-233 6666; www.luxexpress.eu; Sodų 20b-1; ⏰8am-7pm Mon-Fri, 9am-7pm Sat & Sun) and **Ecolines** (☎5-213 3300; www.ecolines.net; Geležinkelio gatvė 15; ⏰8am-7pm Mon-Fri, 9am-5pm Sat, 9am-3pm Sun).

CAR & MOTORCYCLE

➡ There are no passport or customs controls if entering from Poland or Latvia.

➡ A valid entry or tranist visa is required to enter or drive through Belarus and the Russian province of Kaliningrad.

TRAIN

➡ Many international train routes, including to Warsaw and Moscow, pass through Belarus and require a transit visa.

➡ Consult the timetable at **Lithuanian Rail** (☎information 7005 5111; www.litrail.lt) for further information.

ℹ Getting Around

BICYCLE

➡ Lithuania is mostly flat and easily explored by bike.

➡ Large cities and areas popular with visitors have bike-rental and repair shops.

➡ Information about bike touring in Lithuania can be found on **BaltiCCycle** (www.balticcycle.eu).

BUS

➡ The bus network is extensive, efficient and relatively inexpensive.

➡ See **stotis.lt** (www.stotis.lt) for a national bus timetable.

CAR & MOTORCYCLE

Modern four-lane highways link Vilnius with Klaipėda (via Kaunas).

➡ Drivers must be at least 18 years old and have a valid driving licence in their country of residence.

➡ The speed limit is 50km/h in cities, 70km/h to 90km/h on two-lane highways, and 110km/h to 130km/h on motorways.

➡ The blood-alcohol limit is 0.04%.

➡ Headlights must be on day and night.

➡ International and local car-rental agencies are well represented at Vilnius International Airport. Expect to pay around €150 per week for a compact.

LOCAL TRANSPORT

➡ Lithuanian cities generally have good public transport, based on buses, trolleybuses and minibuses.

➡ A ride usually costs around €1.

TRAIN

➡ The country's efficient train network, Lithuanian Rail, links Vilnius to Kaunas, Klaipėda and Trakai, though for some journeys, including Kaunas to Klaipėda, buses are faster.

➡ The Lithuanian Rail website has a handy timetable in English.

ESSENTIAL FOOD & DRINK

➡ **Potato creations** Try the *cepelinai* (potato-dough 'zeppelin' stuffed with meat, mushrooms or cheese), *bulviniai blynai* (potato pancakes) or *žemaičių blynai* (heart-shaped mashed potato stuffed with meat and fried), or the *vedarai* (baked pig intestines stuffed with mashed potato).

➡ **Beer snacks** No drinking session is complete without a plate of smoked pigs' ears and *kepta duona* (deep-fried garlicky bread sticks).

➡ **Beetroot delight** Cold, creamy *šaltibarščiai* (beetroot soup) is a summer speciality, served with a side of fried potatoes.

➡ **Unusual meat** Sample the game, such as beaver stew or bear sausages.

➡ **Smoked fish** The Curonian Spit is famous for its smoked fish, particularly the superb *rukytas unguris* (smoked eel).

➡ **Beer and mead** Šytutys, Utenos and Kalnapilis are top beers; *midus* (mead) is a honey-tinged nobleman's drink.

Macedonia

Includes ➡

Best Places to Eat

- Stara Gradska Kuča (p766)
- Restaurant Antiko (p769)
- Letna Bavča Kaneo (p769)
- Kaj Pero (p765)
- Kebapčilnica Destan (p765)

Best Places to Stay

- Hotel Radika (p771)
- Villa Dihovo (p771)
- Sunny Lake Hostel (p769)
- Villa Jovan (p769)
- Hotel Solun (p765)

Why Go?

Macedonia (Македонија) is a small nation with a complex and fascinating history. Part Balkan, part Mediterranean and rich in Greek, Roman and Ottoman history, it offers impressive ancient sites along with buzzing modernity, managing to pack in more activity and natural beauty than would seem possible for a country its size.

Easygoing Skopje remains one of Europe's more unusual capitals, where constant urban renewal has made the city a bizarre jigsaw puzzle that never fails to surprise.

Elsewhere in the country hiking, mountain biking, wine tasting and climbing beckon, while the remote mountains conceal fascinating medieval monasteries, superb alpine trails and traditional Balkan villages. Ohrid, noted for its beaches, summer festival, sublime Byzantine churches and 34km-long lake, is the centre of the country's tourism industry, while in the winter months skiing at resorts such as Mavrovo become the main draw.

When to Go

Skopje

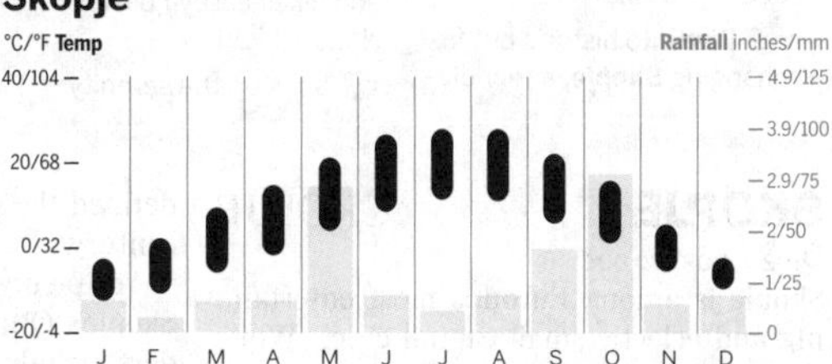

Jun–Aug Enjoy Ohrid's Summer Festival and dive into its 300m-deep lake.

Sep & Oct Partake in Skopje's Beer Fest, Jazz Festival and harvest celebrations.

Dec–Feb Ski Mavrovo and indulge in Macedonia's holiday carnivals.

Macedonia Highlights

1. Gaze out over Ohrid from the **Church of Sveti Jovan at Kaneo** (p768), immaculately set on a bluff above the lake.
2. Dive into historic but fast changing **Skopje**, a friendly, quintessentially Balkan capital.
3. Enjoy the old-world ambience of **Bitola** (p771) and hike nearby Pelister National Park.
4. Soak up the serenity at clifftop **Zrze Monastery** (p772), with sweeping views of the Pelagonian Plain and priceless Byzantine artworks.
5. Ski **Mavrovo National Park** (p770), Macedonia's premier winter resort.

SKOPJE СКОПЈЕ

02 / POP 670,000

Skopje is among Europe's most entertaining and eclectic small capital cities. While an expensive and rather kitschy government construction spree has sparked controversy in recent years, Skopje's new abundance of statuary, fountains, bridges, museums and other structures built to encourage a national identity has visitors' cameras snapping like never before and has defined the ever-changing city for the 21st century.

Yet plenty survives from earlier times – Skopje's Ottoman- and Byzantine-era wonders include the 15th-century Kameni Most (Stone Bridge), the wonderful Čaršija (old Turkish bazaar) where you can get lost for hours, Sveti Spas Church, with its ornate, hand-carved iconostasis, and Tvrdina Kale Fortress, Skopje's guardian since the 5th century.

ITINERARIES

One Week

Spend two nights in **Skopje**, marvelling at its bold new architecture, and visiting its **Čaršija** (old quarter), with historic churches, mosques, museums and an Ottoman castle. Next head southwest to Macedonia's most charming and historic town, **Ohrid**, and enjoy its spectacular lake, calling at the lush forested mountains of **Mavrovo** on the way. After two days, continue to cultured **Bitola**, the long-famed 'City of Consuls' known for its vibrant cafes and nearby **Pelister National Park**.

Two Weeks

Take your time in and around **Skopje**, **Ohrid** and **Bitola**, then add on a visit to Macedonia's famous **Zrze** monastery. Before returning to Skopje, enjoy winerey-hopping in the **Tikveš wine region**.

Sights

Ploštad Makedonija & the South Bank

Ploštad Makedonija SQUARE
(Macedonia Sq) Fronted by a Triumphal Arch, this square is the centrepiece to Skopje's audacious nation-building-through-architecture project and has massive statues dedicated to national heroes in it. The towering, central 'Warrior on a Horse' is bedecked by fountains that are illuminated at night.

Holocaust Memorial Center for the Jews of Macedonia MUSEUM
(www.holocaustfund.org; Ploštad Makedonija; 9am-7pm Tue-Fri, to 3pm Sat & Sun) FREE This moving museum commemorates the all-but-lost Sephardic Jewish culture of Macedonia through a range of photos, English-language wall texts, maps and video. The display documents the Jewish community's history in Macedonia, beginning with their expulsion from Iberia and ending in WWII, when some 98% of Macedonian Jews (7144 individuals in total) perished in the Holocaust.

Museum of the City of Skopje MUSEUM
(Mito Hadživasilev Jasmin bb; 9am-5pm Tue-Sat, to 1pm Sun) FREE Occupying the old train station building where the stone fingers of the clock remain frozen in time at 5.17am – the moment Skopje's great earthquake struck on 27 July 1963 – this museum is unsurprisingly focused on that horrific event, and the display includes video footage and photos of the immediate aftermath. It's a moving display about an event that left 1070 people dead.

Memorial House of Mother Teresa MUSEUM
(02 3290 674; www.memorialhouseofmotherteresa.org; ul Makedonija bb; 9am-8pm Mon-Fri, to 2pm Sat-Sun) FREE This extraordinarily ugly and frankly bizarre, retro-futuristic structure contains a display of memorabilia relating to the famed Catholic nun of Calcutta, born in Skopje in 1910. Look out for the Mother Teresa quotations on plaques around the city centre as well.

North Bank & Čaršija

★**Čaršija** NEIGHBOURHOOD
Čaršija is the hillside Turkish old town of Skopje and evokes the city's Ottoman past with its winding lanes filled with teahouses, mosques, craftsmen's stores, and even good nightlife. It also boasts Skopje's best historic structures and museums, and is the first place any visitor should head. Čaršija runs from the Stone Bridge to the Bit Pazar, a big, busy vegetable market purveying bric-a-brac, household goods and anything random. Expect to get pleasantly lost in its maze of narrow streets.

★**Sveti Spas Church** CHURCH
(Church of the Holy Saviour; Makarije Frčkoski 8; adult/student 120/50MKD; 9am-5pm Tue-Fri, to 3pm Sat & Sun) Partially underground (the Turks banned churches from being taller than mosques), this church dates from the 14th century and is the most historically important in the city. Its dark interior boasts a stunning wood-carved iconostasis 10m wide and 6m high, built by early-19th-century master craftsmen Makarije Frčkovski and brothers Petar and Marko Filipovski. It's rather tricky to find as its

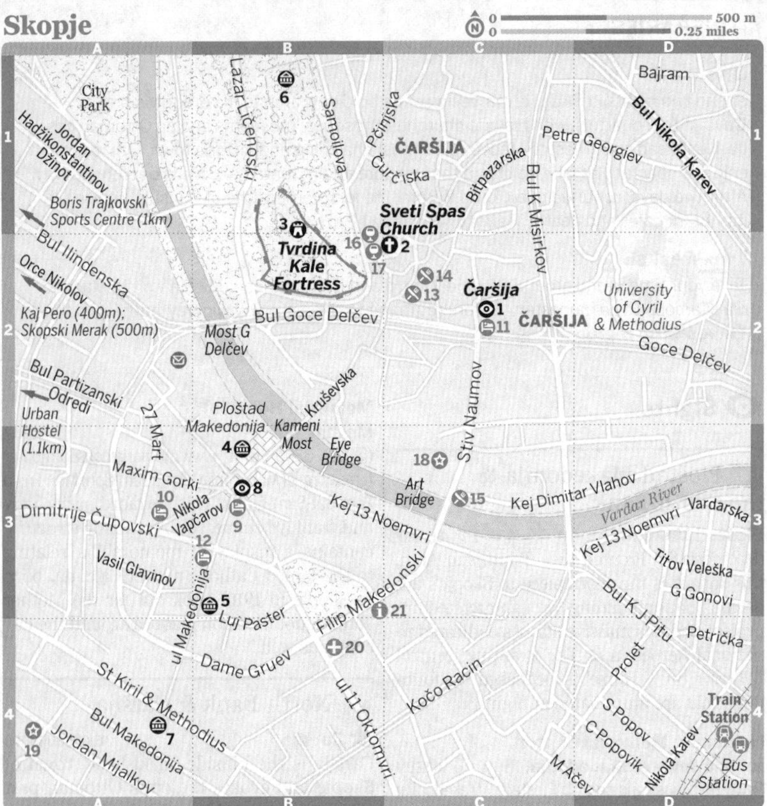

Skopje

Top Sights

1 Čaršija C2
2 Sveti Spas Church C2
3 Tvrdina Kale Fortress B1

Sights

4 Holocaust Memorial Center for the Jews of Macedonia B3
5 Memorial House of Mother Teresa B3
6 Museum of Contemporary Art B1
7 Museum of the City of Skopje A4
8 Ploštad Makedonija B3

Sleeping

9 Hotel Pelister B3
10 Hotel Solun A3
11 Hotel Super 8 .... C2
12 Rekord Hostel B3

Eating

13 Kebapčilnica Destan C2
Kebapčilnica Destan .... (see 9)
14 Pivnica An C2
Restaurant Pelister .... (see 9)
15 Stara Gradska Kuča C3

Drinking & Nightlife

16 Old Town Brewery B2
17 Vinoteka Temov B2

Entertainment

18 Macedonian National Theatre C3
19 Multimedia Center Mala Stanica A4

Information

20 City Hospital B4
21 Skopje Tourist Information Centre B3

sunken design means it doesn't really look like a church from the outside.

★ **Tvrdina Kale Fortress** FORTRESS
(daylight hours) FREE Dominating the skyline of Skopje, this *Game of Thrones*–worthy 6th-century AD Byzantine (and later, Ottoman) fortress is an easy walk up from the Čaršija and its ramparts offer great views over city and river. Inside you'll find various archaeological finds from neolithic to Ottoman times.

Museum of Contemporary Art MUSEUM
(NIMoCA; www.msuskopje.org.mk; Samoilova bb; admission 50MKD; 10am-5pm Tue-Sat, 9am-1pm Sun) Definitely a highlight of Skopje, this excellent museum is housed in an impressive building at the top of a hill with wonderful city views and an extraordinarily good collection for a city of Skopje's size. The museum was formed in the aftermath of the devastating 1963 earthquake, with artists and collections around the world donating works to form a collection that now includes works by Picasso, Léger, Hockney, Alexander Calder, Jasper Johns, Meret Oppenheim, Christo and Bridget Riley.

Sleeping

★ **Urban Hostel** HOSTEL €
(02 6142 785; www.urbanhostel.com.mk; Adolf Ciborovski 22; dm/s/d €13/24/35, apt from €46;) A short walk from the centre in the leafy Debar Maalo neighbourhood, this excellent hostel takes excellent care of its guests, with superclean rooms, comfy beds, and even some quirky extras including a fireplace and a piano. The friendly, superhelpful staff members are another highlight. It's about a 15-minute walk from the city centre.

Rekord Hostel HOSTEL €
(02 6149 954; Dimitrije Čupovski 7/1-1; dm/s/d €13/25/34;) A brand-new hostel in Skopje's heart, the Rekord is a great addition to the city's budget accommodation. There are three dorms and one private room, all of which have excellent modern beds with curtains for privacy and trunks for security. There's also a common room and a balcony, and though no kitchen, there is a fridge and a sink with plates.

Hotel Pelister BOUTIQUE HOTEL €€
(02 3239 584; www.pelisterhotel.com.mk; Ploštad Makedonija; s/d/apt from €59/69/145; @) Located above Restaurant Pelister (and you'll need to go into the restaurant to access the hotel), this place enjoys an unbeatable location on the square, overlooking the city's new architectural wonders. The five rooms are spiffy, with somewhat standard decor. Most come with a computer, while the apartment is spacious and perfect for business travellers.

Hotel Super 8 HOTEL €€
(02 3212 225; www.hotelsuper8.com.mk; Bul Krste Misirkov 57/3; s/d/tr €40/60/70;) An excellent midrange choice slap bang in the centre of town between the river and the Čaršija, this 21-room, family-run hotel has comfortable, bright and modern rooms in a modern building. There is also a communal lounge and kitchen for guests to use.

★ **Hotel Solun** HOTEL €€€
(02 3232 512; www.hotelsolun.com; Nikola Vapcarov 10; s/d from €79/99; @) Opening in 2013, the 53-room Solun is easily the best-value top-end hotel in Skopje. In a converted building in a courtyard off a street in the heart of the city, the hotel is a stylish and design-conscious place, with an enormous range of different room categories, the smallest of which are admittedly rather poky.

Eating

★ **Kebapčilnica Destan** KEBAB €
(ul 104 6; set meal 180MKD; 7am-11pm) Skopje's best beef kebabs, accompanied by seasoned grilled bread, are served at this classic Čaršija place. There's no menu; everyone gets the same thing, served gruffly by the non-English-speaking staff. But that's the charm, and the terrace is usually full – that's how good they are. There's a second, more sanitised branch on **Ploštad Makedonija** (kebabs 180MKD; 10am-11pm).

★ **Kaj Pero** MACEDONIAN €€
(Orce Nikolov 109; mains 200-600MKD; 8am-midnight;) This neighbourhood favourite has outside tables that are low lit by the street lights, giving it a great atmosphere for alfresco dining in the summer months. Inside it has a cosy, traditional feel, perfect for winter meals. The menu is focused on *skara* (meat grills), but also has an excellent local wine selection and a range of inventive nongrill dishes.

Pivnica An MACEDONIAN €€
(Kapan An; mains 300-600MKD; ⏲11am-11pm; 🗐) Housed in a *caravansarai* (inn) that is famously tricky to find (it's through an archway off the busy little square in the heart of the Čaršija where the kebab restaurants are concentrated), this place is all about Ottoman tradition in its sumptuous courtyard. The food is very good, and far superior to that served immediately outside its front door.

Skopski Merak SKARA €€
(☎02 321 2215; Debarca 51; mains 200-800MKD; 📶🗐) This hugely popular place packs both locals and visitors in with its live music on most evenings and huge menu that reads like an encyclopaedia of everything Macedonian cuisine can throw at you. It's easily one of the best *skara* places in Skopje, and as such it's worth reserving for dinner at the weekend.

Idadija SKARA €€
(Zhivko Chingo; mains 200-300MKD; ⏲noon-midnight) In Debar Maalo's *skara* corner, no-frills Idadija has been serving excellent grills for more than 80 years to punters who crowd its roadside tables. There's a relaxed vibe and great people-watching to be had.

★ **Stara Gradska Kuča** MACEDONIAN €€€
(www.starakuka.com.mk; Pajko Maalo 14; mains 300-1000MKD; ⏲10am-midnight Mon-Fri, noon-11pm Sat & Sun; 📶🗐) Housed in what the owners claim to be the oldest functioning house in Macedonia, this traditional place has a warm ambience, an excellent assortment of traditional Macedonian dishes and, sometimes, live music. It's a bit touristy, but still a snug and cosy spot with its wooden furnishings and rural village decor in the heart of Skopje.

Drinking

★ **Vinoteka Temov** BAR
(Gradište 1a; ⏲9am-midnight Mon-Thu, to 1am Fri-Sun) Skopje's best wine bar, in a restored wooden building near Sveti Spas, is refined and atmospheric. A vast wine list presents the cream of Macedonia's vineyards, available by both the glass and bottle, while live traditional and classical guitarists often play. There's also an excellent menu (mains 240MKD to 660MKD) that includes curries, burgers, kebabs and mezze.

Old Town Brewery BEER HALL
(Gradište 1; ⏲9am-1am) This beer bar can be found up a staircase from one of Čaršija's busiest pedestrian streets and is Skopje's only place for a yard of beer. The selection is good, with a range of brews made on the premises.

☆ Entertainment

Multimedia Center Mala Stanica LIVE MUSIC, ARTS
(www.nationalgallery.mk; Jordan Mijalkov 18; ⏲10am-10pm) Featuring arty, ornate decor, the National Art Gallery's cafe hosts temporary exhibitions and live music and is something of a meeting point for the city's more alternative crowd.

Information

MEDICAL SERVICES

City Hospital (☎02 3130 111; 11 Oktomvri 53; ⏲24hr)

MONEY

ATMs and *menuvačnici* (exchange offices) abound.

POST & TELEPHONE

The **main post office** (☎02 3141 141; Orce Nikolov 1; ⏲7am-7.30pm Mon-Sat, 7.30am-2.30pm Sun) is 75m northwest of Ploštad Makedonija. Others are opposite the train station, in the Gradski Trgovski Centar and in Ramstore.

TOURIST INFORMATION

Skopje Tourist Information Centre (Vasil Adzilarski bb; ⏲8.30am-4.30pm) Skopje's tourist information centre has maps available and can help with excursions and accommodation. Staff speak English.

Getting There & Away

AIR

Skopje Alexander the Great Airport (☎02 3148 333; www.airports.com.mk; Petrovec) is located 21km east of the city centre. Skopje has direct air services to many cities throughout Europe, Turkey and the Gulf. Airlines include:

Adria Airways (www.adria.si)
airberlin (www.airberlin.com)
Air Serbia (www.airserbia.com)
Austrian Airlines (www.austrian.com)
Croatia Airlines (www.croatiaairlines.hr)
Pegasus Airlines (www.flypgs.com)
Turkish Airlines (www.thy.com)
Wizz Air (www.wizzair.com)

SKOPJE 2014: A GARISH VISION?

The central district of Skopje has undergone monumental change in recent years as the Macedonian government under Prime Minister Nikola Gruevski has implemented the controversial Skopje 2014 project. The project, which began in 2010, has seen the construction of 20 new buildings and 40 new monuments in the area around the river in an attempt simultaneously to give the city a more uniform appearance and to help bolster Macedonian national pride and identity by linking the modern state to its forerunners, many of whose Macedonian credentials are in fact debatable.

Detractors bemoan the tens – if not hundreds – of millions of euros spent on the project to date, while others point out the inherently kitschiness of the plan, with its grotesquely stylised buildings, and blatantly nationalist leanings (the inclusions of Alexander the Great and Philip II of Macedon, for example, being interpreted by many as broad snubs to the Greek government, who object to Macedonia's interpretation of its ancient history).

But Skopje 2014 has at least given visitors lots of fountains, statues and other facades to photograph. Some prominent highlights include the construction of the **Art Bridge** and **Eye Bridge** over the Vadar River, both of which redefine kitschy; and the construction of the new **National Theatre**, a replica of the original building that once stood here on the riverside but was destroyed by the 1963 earthquake. Look out also for the new **Museum of Archeology** and the **Porta Macedonia**, a triumphal arch just off Skopje's main plaza.

BUS

Skopje's **bus station** (☎ 02 2466 313; www.sas.com.mk; bul Nikola Karev), with ATM, exchange office and English-language info, adjoins the train station. Bus schedules are online.

Buses to Ohrid go via Kičevo (three hours, 167km) or Bitola (four to five hours, 261km) – book ahead in summer. Most intercity buses are air-conditioned and are generally faster than trains, though more expensive.

International Buses

International services include the following:

Belgrade (1400MKD, 10 hours, eight daily)
Istanbul (1900MKD, 12 hours, three daily)
Ljubljana (3800MKD, 14 hours, one daily)
Pristina (330, two hours, 12 daily)
Sarajevo (3170MKD, 14 hours, Friday and Sunday 8pm)
Sofia (1040MKD, 5½ hours, four daily)
Thessaloniki (1300MKD, four hours, one Monday, Wednesday and Friday)
Zagreb (3200MKD, 12 hours, one daily)

TRAIN

The **train station** (Železnička Stanica; bul Jane Sandanski) serves local and international destinations. Disagreements with the Greek government have led to periodically suspended train routes with Greece, but the Skopje–Thessaloniki connection (760MKD, 4½ hours, 5.06am daily) was running at the time of research. A train serves Belgrade (1430MKD, eight hours, 8.20am & 8.10pm daily), and another reaches Pristina (330MKD, 3 hours, 4.10pm daily) in Kosovo.

Domestic Train

Local destinations include the following:

Bitola (315MKD, four hours, four daily)
Gevgelija (270MKD, 2½ hours, three daily)
Kičevo (210MKD, two hours, three daily)
Kumanovo (80MKD, 40 minutes, four daily)
Negotino (200MKD, two hours, three daily)
Prilep (250MKD, three hours, four daily)

Getting Around

TO/FROM THE AIRPORT

An airport shuttle bus, **Vardar Express** (www.vardarexpress.com), runs between the airport and the city. Buy tickets (100MKD) from the marked arrivals terminal booth. The bus leaves half-hourly or hourly, depending on passengers, and stops at several places including the bus/train station and central square. From the airport to centre, taxis cost 1200MKD.

BUS

Skopje's public city buses cost 35MKD. Private ones cost 25MKD. Both follow the same stops and numbered routes. You can buy and validate tickets on board.

TAXI

Skopje's taxis are good value, with the first kilometre costing just 40MKD, and 25MKD for subsequent kilometres. Drivers rarely speak English, but they do use their meters.

WORTH A TRIP

DAY TRIPS FROM SKOPJE

A half-hour drive, or slightly longer city bus trip, accesses tranquil **Lake Matka**. Although crowded at weekends, this idyllic spot beneath steep **Treska Canyon** is excellent, offering hiking, rock climbing, caving (€10) and ancient churches in its forested environs. On-site restaurants provide nourishment and lake views. Matka's underwater caverns are as deep, or maybe deeper, than any in Europe, at almost 218m.

Matka's traditional link with the Virgin Mary (Matka means 'womb' in Macedonian) is accentuated by grotto shrines such as **Sveta Bogorodica**. From here a steep path reaches **Sveti Spas**, **Sveta Trojca** and **Sveta Nedela** – the last, a 4km walk (around 1½ hours). These caves once sheltered ascetics and anti-Ottoman revolutionaries.

After the **Church of Sveti Nikola**, beyond the dam and across the bridge, visit the frescoed **Church of Sveti Andrej** (1389). The adjoining mountaineering hut **Matka** (☎02-3052 655) offers guides, climbing gear and accommodation.

From Skopje come by taxi (450MKD) or bus 60 along bul Partizanski Odredi (50MKD, 40 minutes, hourly).

WESTERN MACEDONIA

Ohrid Охрид

☎046 / POP 55,000

Sublime Ohrid is Macedonia's prime destination, with its atmospheric old quarter with beautiful churches along a graceful hill, topped by a medieval castle overlooking serene, 34km-long Lake Ohrid. It's undoubtedly Macedonia's most alluring attraction, especially when you factor in the nearby Galičica National Park and the further secluded beaches that dot the lake's eastern shore.

Sights

★Church of Sveti Jovan at Kaneo CHURCH

(admission 100MKD; 9am-6pm) This stunning 13th-century church is set on a cliff over the lake, and is possibly Macedonia's most photographed structure. Peer down into the azure waters and you'll see why medieval monks found spiritual inspiration here. The small church has original frescoes behind the altar.

Church of Sveta Bogorodica Perivlepta CHURCH

(Gorna Porta; admission 100MKD; 9am-1pm & 4-8pm) Just inside the Gorna Porta, this 13th-century Byzantine church, whose name translates as 'Our Lady the Most Glorious', has vivid biblical frescoes painted by Serbian masters Mihail and Eutihije and superb lake and old town views from its terrace. There's also an **icon gallery** (Gorna Porta; admission 100MKD; 9am-5pm Tue-Sun) highlighting the founders' artistic achievements.

Classical Amphitheatre AMPHITHEATRE

FREE Ohrid's impressive amphitheatre was built for theatre; the Romans later removed 10 rows to accommodate gladiators.

Car Samoil's Castle CASTLE

(admission 30MKD; 9am-7pm) The massive, turreted walls of the 10th-century castle indicate the power of the medieval Bulgarian state. Ascend the stairways to the ramparts for fantastic views over the town and lake.

Plaošnik CHURCH

(9am-6pm) FREE Down a wooded path, Plaošnik boasts the Church of Sveti Kliment i Pantelejmon. This 5th-century basilica was restored in 2002 according to its Byzantine design. The multidomed church has glass floor segments revealing the original foundations. It houses St Kliment's relics, with intricate 5th-century mosaics outside.

Sveta Sofia Cathedral CHURCH

(Car Samoil bb; adult/student 100/30MKD; 10am-7pm) Ohrid's grandest church, 11th-century Sveta Sofia, is supported by columns and decorated with elaborate, if very faded Byzantine frescoes, though they are well preserved and very vivid in the apse, still. Its superb acoustics means it's often used for concerts (300MKD). The exposed beams reveal the very real achievment constructing a church this size would have been in the 11th century.

Robev Family House National Museum MUSEUM
(Car Samoil 62; adult/student 100/50MKD; ⏲9am-2pm & 7-10pm Tue-Sun) In the heart of the old town, the 1827 National Museum is housed over several floors of the remarkably well-preserved Robev Residence. On display is everything from Greek archaeological finds, prehistoric implements and metal work to pottery, jewellery and some wonderful interiors. Across the road the Urania Residence, a further part of the museum, has an ethnographic display.

Sleeping

★ **Sunny Lake Hostel** HOSTEL €
(www.sunnylakehostel.mk/; 11 Oktombri 15; dm €10, d €20-24;) This excellent new hostel is a bustling hub for backpackers stopping off in Ohrid. There are good facilities, including a great terrace with lake views, lockers under each bed and a kitchen to cook in. The bathrooms aren't great though, and hot water isn't always available. That said, it's superbly located and a great deal for the price.

★ **Villa Jovan** HISTORIC HOTEL €
(076 377 644; vila.jovan@gmail.com; Car Samoli 44; s/d/ste €25/35/49;) There are nine rooms within this 200-year-old mansion in the heart of the Old Town, and they're charmingly rustic and full of old-world furnishings, have wooden beams and feature local art on the walls. While the rooms are definitely on the small side, the friendly English-speaking staff make you feel right at home.

Villa Lucija GUESTHOUSE €
(046 265 608; www.vilalucija.com.mk; Kosta Abraš 29; s/d/apt €20/30/50;) Lucija has Old Town ambience and lovingly decorated, breezy rooms with lake views. Breakfast is not included here, and English was nonexistent on our last visit, but it more than makes up for that with its superb location and its enviable balconies over the water.

★ **Vila Sveta Sofija** HOTEL €€
(046 254 370; www.vilasofija.com.mk; Kosta Abraš 64; s/tw/d/q €29/49/69/99;) This opulent getaway combines traditional furnishings with chic modern bathrooms in an old Ohrid mansion near Sveta Sofia. The best room is the suite, which sleeps four and has a great balcony with a lake view. Guests enjoy a private sliver of lakeside beach too, with use of umbrellas and deckchairs.

Jovanovic Guest House GUESTHOUSE €€
(070 589 218; jovanovic.guesthouse@hotmail.com; Boro Sain 5; apt from €40) This property has two apartments, both of which sleep four, set right in the middle of the Old Town. Each apartment is tastefully furnished and stuffed full of antiques. The top-floor apartment has an amazing lake view, and the owner is a professional diver who can organise diving excursions on the lake.

Eating

Ohrid has some good eating options, but plenty of mediocre places aimed at the summer tour groups as well, so choose carefully. Self-caterers should head to **Tinex supermarket** on Ohrid's main shopping street (bul Makedonski Prosvetiteli) for the best selection of foodstuffs, or buy directly from farmers at the quaint **vegetable market** (Kliment Ohridski).

Ohrid's endemic trout is endangered and (supposedly) protected from fishing – order the equally tasty mavrovska and kaliforniska varieties instead.

★ **Letna Bavča Kaneo** SEAFOOD €
(Kočo Racin 43; fish 100-200MKD; ⏲10am-midnight;) This simple 'summer terrace' on Kaneo beach is inexpensive and great. A fry-up of diminutive *plasnica* (a small fish commonly eaten fried in the Balkans), plus salad, feeds two, or try other specialities such as eel or carp. Swim in Lake Ohrid directly from the restaurant's dock and then soak up the sun while drinking a local beer – it doesn't come much better than this.

Via Scara PIZZERIA €
(www.viasacra.mk; Ilindenska 36; mains 150-300MKD; ⏲9am-midnight;) Pleasantly fusing the best of Italian and Macedonian fare, Via Scara offers up crisp and tasty pizzas as well as a good selection of Macedonian national cooking and wines. Its location is a big draw too: facing the lovely Sveta Sofia Cathedral on a cobbled street in the middle of the Old Town. Breakfast is also served, a rarity in Ohrid.

★ **Restaurant Antiko** MACEDONIAN €€
(Car Samoil 30; mains 300-650MKD) In an old Ohrid mansion in the middle of the Old Town, the famous Antiko has great traditional ambience and pricey, but good,

traditional dishes. Don't miss the excellent *tavče gravče,* a traditional Macedonian dish of beans cooked in spices and peppers, the Antiko version of which is widely held to be a classic of the genre.

Restoran Sveta Sofija MACEDONIAN €€
(Car Samoil 88; mains 300-500MKD; ⊙10am-midnight; 📶) This upscale restaurant opposite the Sveta Sofia Cathedral couldn't have a better location, and in the warmer months you can dine alfresco across the road on a little terrace. This is a great spot to try traditional fare and oenophiles will delight in being able to choose from more than 100 Macedonian wines.

Drinking & Entertainment

★ **Cuba Libre** BAR
(www.cubalibreohrid.com; Partizanska 2; ⊙10pm-4am) Perennially popular bar and nightclub. During the summer months it opens nightly and is normally standing-room-only, with DJs from all over the Balkans coming to play for the smart and up-for-it crowd.

Aquarius CAFE
(Kosta Abraš bb; ⊙10am-1am; 📶) Ohrid's original lake-terrace cafe, Aquarius remains cool for a midday coffee and is lively at night, with a cocktail menu and lake views.

Information

Sunny Land Tourism (☎070 523 227; www.sunnylandtourism.com; Car Samoil; ⊙9am-7pm) Local expert Zoran Grozdanovski can find accommodation and arrange tours and activities including mountain biking, wine tastings and boat trips on the lake.

Tourist Office (Car Samoil 38; ⊙10am-midnight) Ohrid's friendly, English-speaking tourist office in the middle of the Old Town provides general info including city maps, and can help you find accommodation and outdoor activities.

Getting There & Away

AIR

Ohrid's **St Paul the Apostle Airport** (☎046 252 820; www.airports.com.mk), 10km north, handles summertime charter flights. Take a taxi (400MKD).

BUS

From the **bus station** (7 Noemvri bb), 1.5km east of the centre, buses serve Skopje, either via Kičevo (500MKD, three hours, eight daily) or (the longer route) via Bitola (560MKD); for Bitola itself, eight daily buses run (210MKD, 1¼ hours). Buses to Struga (40MKD, 14km) leave every 15 minutes. In summer, reserve ahead for Skopje buses, or be prepared to wait. Some *kombi* (minibuses) and taxis wait at the end of Bul Makedonski Prosveiteli.

International buses serve Belgrade (via Kičevo; 1800MKD, 15 hours, one daily at 5.45am). A 7pm bus serves Sofia (1450MKD, eight hours). For Albania, take a bus to Sveti Naum (110MKD, 50 minutes, eight times a day). Cross the border and take a cab (€5, 6km) to Pogradeci. An Ohrid–Sveti Naum taxi costs 1000MKD.

Mavrovo National Park

Маврово Национален Парк

☎042

Mavrovo's ski resort is Macedonia's biggest, comprising 730 sq km of birch and pine forest, gorges, karst fields and waterfalls, plus Macedonia's highest peak, **Mt Korab** (2764m). The rarefied air and stunning vistas are great year-round.

Sights & Activities

Sveti Jovan Bigorski Monastery MONASTERY
This revered 1020 Byzantine monastery is off the Debar road. Legend attests an icon of Sveti Jovan Bigorski (St John the Baptist) miraculously appeared, and since then it's been rebuilt often – the icon occasionally reappearing, too. The impressive church also houses what is alleged to be St John's forearm.

Bigorski's awe-inspiring iconostasis was the final of just three carved by local craftsmen Makarije Frčkovski and the brothers Filipovski between 1829 and 1835. This colossal work depicting biblical scenes is enlivened with 700 tiny human and animal figures. Gazing up at this enormous, intricate masterpiece is breathtaking. Upon finishing, the carvers allegedly flung their tools into the nearby Radika River – ensuring that the secret of their artistic genius would be washed away forever.

Galičnik VILLAGE
Up a winding, tree-lined road ending in a rocky moonscape 17km southwest of Mavrovo, almost depopulated Galičnik features traditional houses along the mountainside. It's placid except for 12 and 13 July, when the **Galičnik Wedding** sees one or two lucky couples wed here. Visit, along with 3000 happy Macedonians, and enjoy eating, drinking, traditional folk dancing and music.

Sleeping & Eating

Hotel Srna SKI LODGE €

(042 388 083; www.hotelsrnamavrovo.com; s/d/apt €25/40/60;) The small Srna, 400m from Mavrovo's chairlifts and right on the shore of Lake Mavrovo, has breezy, clean rooms and is good value for this price range.

★**Hotel Radika** SPA HOTEL €€€

(042 223 300; www.radika.com.mk; s/d/apt €65/90/130; P) Just 5km from Mavrovo, this ultraposh spa hotel is perfect for pampering, with numerous massage treatments and excellent rooms. Prices fall considerably in summer, when the hotel can arrange hiking trips and rents out mountain bikes. Nondrivers should take a taxi from Gostivar (650MKD), on the Skopje-Ohrid road.

Getting There & Away

Southbound buses reach Mavrovo Anovi (2km away) en route to Debar (120MKD, seven daily), or while travelling north to Tetovo (140MKD, five daily) and Skopje (180MKD, three daily).

For Sveti Jovan Bigorski Monastery, buses transiting Debar for Ohrid or Struga will be able to drop you off.

VILLA DIHOVO

One of Macedonia's most remarkable guesthouses, **Villa Dihovo** (070 544 744, 047 293 040; www.villadihovo.com; rates negotiable;) comprises three traditionally decorated rooms in the 80-year-old home of former professional footballer Petar Cvetkovski and family. Its big flowering lawn is great for kids. The only fixed prices are for the homemade wine, beer and *rakija* (firewater); all else, room price included, is your choice.

Peter himself is a mine of information, deeply involved in the Slow Food movement, and can arrange everything from hikes to Lake Pelisterski, mountain-bike rides and an evening of wine tasting in his cellar. There's also a superb shared kitchen on the premises where guests can cook with the hosts, and a living room with an open fireplace – perfect for colder nights. Booking in advance is essential.

The village of Dihovo is just a short distance outside Bitola, and a taxi will cost between 120 MKD and 150MKD.

CENTRAL MACEDONIA

Bitola Битола

047 / POP 95,400

With elegant buildings and beautiful people, elevated Bitola (660m) has a sophistication inherited from its Ottoman days as the 'City of Consuls'. Its 18th- and 19th-century colourful town houses, Turkish mosques and cafe culture make it Macedonia's most intriguing and liveable major town.

Sights & Activities

Širok Sokak STREET

(ul Maršal Tito) Bitola's Širok Sokak is the city's most representative and stylish street, with its multicoloured facades and European honorary consulates attesting to the city's Ottoman-era sophistication. Enjoying the cafe life here as the beautiful people promenade past is an essential Bitola experience.

Church of Sveti Dimitrija CHURCH

(11 Oktomvri bb; 7am-6pm) This Orthodox church (1830) has rich frescoes, ornate lamps and a huge iconostasis.

Heraclea Lyncestis ARCHAEOLOGICAL SITE

(admission 100MKD, photos 500MKD; 9am-3pm winter, to 5pm summer) Located 1km south of Bitola (70MKD by taxi), Heraclea Lyncestis is among Macedonia's best archaeological sites. Founded by Philip II of Macedon, Heraclea became commercially significant before Romans conquered (168 BC) and its position on the Via Egnatia kept it prosperous. In the 4th century Heraclea became an episcopal seat, but it was sacked by Goths and then Slavs.

See the Roman baths, portico and amphitheatre, and the striking Early Christian basilica and episcopal palace ruins, with beautiful, well-preserved floor mosaics. They're unique in depicting endemic trees and animals. Excavations continue, so you may see newer discoveries.

WORTH A TRIP

ZRZE MONASTERY

Some 26km northwest of Prilep, towards Makedonski Brod, the 14th-century **Zrze Monastery** (Манастир Зрзе; Manastir Sveto Preobrazhenije-Zrze; 8am-5pm) FREE of the Holy Transfiguration rises like a revelation from a clifftop. The monastery's tranquil position around a spacious lawn, with views over the outstretched Pelagonian Plain, is stunning.

During Ottoman times, Zrze underwent periods of abandonment, rebuilding and plunder but remained an important spiritual centre. Its 17th-century **Church of Sts Peter and Paul** contains important frescoes and icons.

Visitors can enjoy coffee with the kind monks and a tour of the church, with its priceless frescoes and icons. While today the museum in Skopje houses Zrze's most famous icon, the Holy Mother of God Pelagonitsa (1422), a large copy remains in the church. On the adjacent hillside, excavations continue on Zrze's precursor: a 5th-century basilica.

To get to Zrze, take the road towards Makedonski Brod and turn at Ropotovo, following signs for Sv Preobraženie Manastir XIV Vek. You'll pass through three villages as the road worsens, and then you'll have a long drive through tobacco fields along a stretch of unsurfaced road, until you see the monastery on the hillside ahead of you. Near deserted Zrze village, beneath the mountain, is where you should leave your car, unless you have a 4WD vehicle. From here it's a 2km walk uphill to the monastery. There is no public transport.

Sleeping & Eating

★Chola Guest House GUESTHOUSE €
(047 224 919; www.chola.mk; Stiv Naumov 80; s/d €12/20;) Overall an excellent-value place to stay, with a quiet location in an atmospheric old mansion that has clean, well-kept rooms and colourful modern bathrooms. It's a short walk from the main drag: there is a useful map on the website, well worth consulting as the guesthouse is hard to find otherwise.

Hotel De Niro HOTEL €
(047 229 656; hotel-deniro@t-home.mk; Kiril i Metodij 5; s/d/ste from €17/34/67;) Central yet discreet with lovely old Bitola-style rooms, including a spacious apartment that sleeps four people upstairs. The owner has an art gallery, as you'll quickly see from the paintings that cover almost every centimetre of wall space. There's a good pizza-and-pasta restaurant (mains 200MKD to 450MKD) downstairs. Breakfast is €2 extra.

Hotel Milenium HOTEL €€
(047 241 001; h.milenium@t-home.mk; Maršal Tito 48; s/d/ste/apt €39/60/80/99;) Atriums with stained glass, smooth marble opulence and historic relics channel old Bitola, and the location can't be beaten. It's right on the Širok Sokak (you literally have to walk through a bustling cafe terrace to access the lobby). Rooms are enormous, with high ceilings and sparkling bathrooms, though do request a room at the back if you want peace and quiet.

El Greko PIZZA €
(071 279 848; cnr Maršal Tito & Elipda Karamandi; mains 150-350MKD; 10am-1am) This Sokak taverna and pizzeria has a great beer-hall ambience and is popular with locals. It's one of many decent places along the main street, all of which heave with locals from mid-afternoon until late in the evening.

Drinking & Entertainment

★Porta Jazz BAR
(Kiril i Metodij; 8am-1am;) There's a notably bohemian vibe at this rightly popular, funky place that's packed when live jazz and blues bands play. It's located near the Centar na Kultura, one block back from the Širok Sokak. During the day it's a very pleasant cafe where you can sip espresso on the neatly stencilled terrace.

Getting There & Away

The **bus and train stations** (Nikola Tesla) are adjacent, 1km south of the centre. Buses serve Skopje (480MKD, 3½ hours, 12 daily) via Prilep (140MKD, one hour), Kavadarci (280MKD, two hours, five daily), Strumica (460MKD, four hours, two daily) and Ohrid (210MKD, 1¼ hours, 10 daily).

For Greece, go by taxi to the border (500MKD) and then find a cab to Florina. Some Bitola cab drivers will do the whole trip for about 3000MKD.

Four daily trains serve Skopje (315MKD) via Prilep (85MKD) and Veles (170MKD).

SURVIVAL GUIDE

Directory A–Z

BUSINESS HOURS

Banks 7am to 5pm Monday to Friday

Businesses 8am to 8pm Monday to Friday, to 2pm Saturday

Cafes 10am to midnight

Post offices 6.30am to 8pm

INTERNET RESOURCES

Exploring Macedonia (www.exploringmacedonia.com)

Macedonian Information Agency (www.mia.com.mk)

Macedonian Welcome Centre (www.dmwc.org.mk)

MONEY

Macedonian denars (MKD) come in 10-, 50-, 100-, 500-, 1000- and 5000-denar notes, and one-, two-, five-, 10- and 50-denar coins. ATMs are widespread. Credit cards can often be used in larger cities, but you can't really rely on them outside Skopje.

PUBLIC HOLIDAYS

New Year's Day 1 January

Orthodox Christmas 7 January

Orthodox Easter Week March/April

Labour Day 1 May

Saints Cyril and Methodius Day 24 May

Ilinden Day 2 August

Republic Day 8 September

1941 Partisan Day 11 October

TELEPHONE

Macedonia's country code is ☎+389. Drop the initial zero in city codes and mobile prefixes (07) when calling from abroad.

VISAS

Citizens of former Yugoslav republics, Australia, Canada, the EU, Iceland, Israel, New Zealand, Norway, Switzerland, Turkey and the USA can stay for three months, visa-free. Otherwise, visa fees average from US$30 for a single-entry visa and US$60 for a multiple-entry visa. Check the Ministry of Foreign Affairs website (www.mfa.gov.mk) if unsure of your status.

COUNTRY FACTS

Area 25,713 sq km

Capital Skopje

Country Code ☎389

Currency Macedonian denar (MKD)

Emergency ambulance ☎194, fire ☎193, police ☎192

Language Macedonian, Albanian

Money ATMs are widespread in major towns

Population 2.1 million

Visas None for EU, US, Australian, Canadian or New Zealand citizens

SLEEPING PRICE RANGES

The following price indicators apply for a high-season double room:

€ less than 3000MKD/€50

€€ 3000MKD/€50 to 5000MKD/€80

€€€ more than 5000MKD/€80

Getting There & Away

Skopje's buses serve Sofia, Belgrade, Budapest, Pristina, Tirana, İstanbul, Thessaloniki and more. Trains connect Skopje to Pristina, Belgrade and Thessaloniki. The long-awaited arrival of budget airlines has improved Skopje's modest number of air connections, and it's now connected pretty well to major European cities.

AIR

Alexander the Great Airport (p766), 21km from Skopje, is Macedonia's main airport, with Ohrid's St Paul the Apostle Airport (p770) mostly only for a relatively small number of summer charters.

LAND

Bus

International routes from Macedonia generally arrive and depart from Skopje. Destinations include Belgrade, Pristina, İstanbul, Podgorica and Sofia.

Car & Motorcycle

Bringing your own vehicle into Macedonia is hassle free, though you do need a Green Card (proof of third-party insurance, issued by your insurer), endorsed for Macedonia.

Train

Macedonian Railway (www.mz.com.mk) serves Serbia,Kosovo and Greece.

EATING PRICE RANGES

The following prices are for a main meal:

€ less than 200MKD

€€ 200MKD to 350MKD

€€€ more than 350MKD

Getting Around

BICYCLE

Cycling is popular in Skopje. Traffic is light in rural areas, though mountains and reckless drivers are common.

BUS

Skopje serves most domestic destinations. Larger buses are new and air-conditioned; *kombi* (minibuses) are usually not. During summer, pre-book for Ohrid.

CAR & MOTORCYCLE

There are occasional police checkpoints; make sure you have the correct documentation. Call ☎196 for roadside assistance.

Driver's Licence

Your national driver's licence is fine, though an International Driving Permit is best.

Hire

Skopje's rental agencies include international biggies and local companies. Ohrid has many, other cities have fewer. Sedans average €60 daily, including insurance. Bring your passport, driver's licence and credit card.

Road Rules

Drive on the right. Seatbelt and headlight use is compulsory. Cars must carry replacement bulbs, two warning triangles and a first-aid kit (available at big petrol stations). Police also fine for drink driving (blood alcohol limit 0.05%). Fines are payable immediately.

TAXI

Taxis are relatively inexpensive. Skopje cabs cost 40MKD for the first kilometre, 20MKD per subsequent kilometre.

TRAIN

Major lines are Tabanovce (on the Serbian border) to Gevgelija (on the Greek border), via Kumanovo, Skopje, Veles, Negotino and Demir Kapija; and Skopje to Bitola, via Veles and Prilep. Smaller Skopje–Kičevo and Skopje–Kočani lines exist.

ESSENTIAL FOOD & DRINK

Macedonian cuisine is typically Balkan, with a combination of Mediterranean and Middle Eastern influences. There's lots of meat grills (*skara*), and plenty of fresh vegetables and herbs used in local dishes.

- **Ajvar** Sweet red-pepper sauce; accompanies meats and cheeses.
- **Šopska salata** Tomatoes, onions and cucumbers topped with flaky *sirenje* (white cheese).
- **Uviač** Rolled chicken or pork wrapped in bacon, filled with melted yellow cheese.
- **Tavče gravče** Macedonian speciality of baked beans cooked with spices, onions and herbs and served in earthenware.

Moldova

Includes ➡

Best Places to Eat

- Vatra Neamului (p779)
- Grill House (p779)
- Bastion (p779)
- Robin Pub (p779)
- Kumanyok (p784)

Best Places to Stay

- Jazz Hotel (p778)
- Hotel Russia (p784)
- Art Rustic Hotel (p777)
- Hotel Codru (p778)
- Agro Pensiunea Butuceni (p781)

Why Go?

Sandwiched between Romania and Ukraine, Moldova is as 'off the beaten track' as you can get in Europe. Attracting just a fraction of the number of visitors of neighbouring countries (12,000 to 20,000 annually in recent years), it's a natural destination for travellers who like to plant the flag and visit lands few others have gone to.

But Moldova's charms run deeper than being merely remote. The country's wines are some of the best in Europe and a fledgling wine-tourism industry, where you can tour wineries and taste the grape, has taken root. The countryside is delightfully unspoiled and the hospitality of villagers is authentic. The capital, Chişinău, is surprisingly lively, with excellent restaurants and bars. Across the Dniestr River lies the separatist Russian-speaking region of Transdniestr. It's a time-warp place, where the Soviet Union still reigns supreme and busts of Lenin line the main boulevards.

When to Go

Chişinău

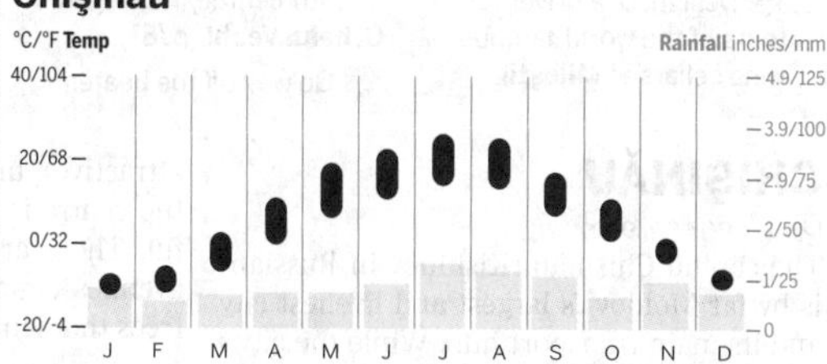

Jun Parks and restaurant terraces fill with students, and the weather is warm.

Jul High season hits its peak with hiking, wine tours and camping in full operation.

Oct The 'National Wine Day' festival takes place during the first weekend in October.

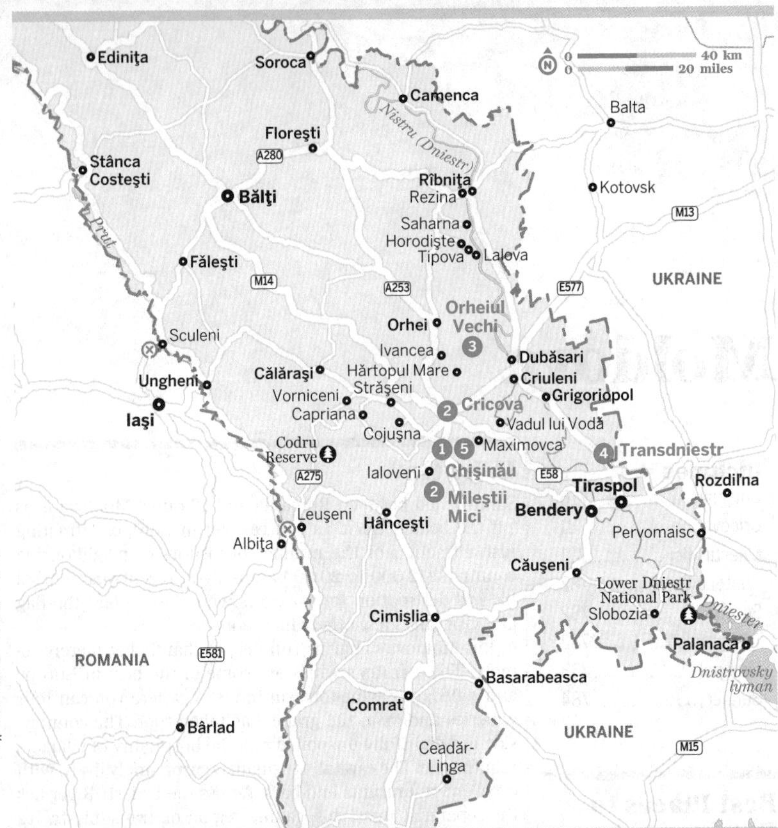

Moldova Highlights

1. Stroll the surprisingly pleasant streets and parks of the friendly capital **Chişinău** (p776).
2. Designate a driver for tours of the world-famous wine cellars at **Mileştii Mici** (p781) and **Cricova** (p781).
3. Detox at the fantastic cave monastery, burrowed by 13th-century monks, at **Orheiul Vechi** (p781).
4. Go *way* off the beaten path in the self-styled 'republic' of **Transdniestr** (p782), a surreal, living homage to the Soviet Union.
5. Gorge on the many excellent **dining options** (p779) found in Chişinău.

CHIŞINĂU

☎22 / POP 674,000

The capital Chişinău (Kishinev in Russian) is by far Moldova's largest and liveliest city and its main transport hub. While the city's origins date back six centuries to 1420, much of Chişinău (pronounced kish-i-now) was levelled in WWII and by a tragic earthquake that struck in 1940. The city was rebuilt in Soviet style from the 1950s onwards, and both the centre and outskirts are dominated by utilitarian (and frankly not very attractive) high-rise buildings. That said, the centre is surprisingly green and peaceful. There are two large parks, and main avenues cut through groves of old-growth trees that lend a serene element.

Sights

Parcul Catedralei & Grădina Publică Ştefan cel Mare şi Sfînt PARK

(Cathedral Park & Ştefan cel Mare Park; B-dul Ştefan cel Mare; 👪) These two parks diagonally oppose each other. Both are popular with

ITINERARIES

One Week

Use the capital **Chişinău** as your base and get to know this friendly and fast-changing town. Make day trips out to the stunning cave monastery at **Orheiul Vechi** and to one of the local big-name vineyards for a tour and tasting. Spend a night or two in surreal **Transdniestr** before returning to Chişinău.

Ten Days

Follow the one-week itinerary at a leisurely pace before tacking on a few smaller vineyard tours around **Chişinău**, purchasing your customs limit, and taking an overnight trip to **Soroca** to see the impressive fortress on the mighty Dniestr River.

families and canoodling teenagers on benches. Parcul Catedralei, on the northern side of B-dul Ştefan cel Mare, has two main sights: the Orthodox Cathedral and the Arc de Triomphe. Grădina Publică Ştefan cel Mare şi Sfînt is dominated by a **statue of Ştefan cel Mare** at the entrance.

Arc de Triomphe MONUMENT

(Holy Gates; Parcul Catedralei) FREE Chişinău's own Arc de Triomphe dates from the 1840s and marks the centre of the city. It was built to commemorate the victory of the Russian army over the Ottoman Empire. It's often draped with a Moldovan flag in the middle and makes for a stirring photo op.

National Archaeology & History Museum MUSEUM

(Muzeul Naţional de Istorie a Moldovei; ☎240 426; www.nationalmuseum.md; Str 31 August 1989, 121a; adult/student 10/5 lei; ⊙10am-6pm Sat-Thu;) The granddaddy of Chişinău's museums contains archaeological artefacts from the region of **Orheiul Vechi**, north of the capital, including Golden Horde coins, Soviet-era weaponry and a huge WWII diorama on the 1st floor.

Pushkin Museum MUSEUM

(☎292 685; Str Anton Pann 19; adult/student 15/5 lei; ⊙10am-4pm Tue-Sun) This is where Russia's national poet Alexander Pushkin (1799–1837) spent three years exiled between 1820 and 1823. You can view his tiny cottage, filled with original furnishings and personal items, including a portrait of his beloved Byron on his writing desk. There's also a three-room literary museum in the building facing the cottage, which documents Pushkin's dramatic life.

National Ethnographic & Nature Museum MUSEUM

(Muzeul Naţional de Etnografie şi Istorie Naturală; ☎240 056; www.muzeu.md; Str M Kogălniceanu 82; adult/child 15/10 lei, English-language tour (arrange in advance) 100 lei; ⊙10am-6pm Tue-Sun) The highlight of this massive and wonderful exhibition is a life-sized reconstruction of a dinothere (an elephantlike mammal that lived during the Pliocene epoch – 5.3 million to 1.8 million years ago) skeleton, discovered in the Rezine region in 1966. Allow at least an hour to see the museum's pop art, stuffed animals, and exhibits covering geology, botany and zoology.

Sleeping

The hotel situation in Chişinău is improving, but most new properties aim for the high end, leaving budget and midrange travellers with less to choose from. An alternative is to rent an apartment. Check out **Marisha.net** (☎06 915 57 53, 488 258; www.marisha.net; apt 500-600 lei) or **Adresa** (☎544 392; www.adresa.md; B-dul Negruzzi 1; apt 500-1800 lei), the former for cheap homestays as well as apartments.

Tapok Hostel HOSTEL €

(☎068 408 626; www.tapokhostel.com; Str Armeneasca 27a; dm 150-180 lei, r 500 lei; P) Friendly, modern youth hostel that offers accommodation in four-, six- and eight-bed dorms in a quiet location near the centre and handy to the city's best bars and restaurants. Free towels, lockers and laundry add to the charms. The four-bed dorm can be booked as a private room. Email in advance for groups or to inquire about availability.

★**Art Rustic Hotel** HOTEL €€

(☎232 593; www.art-rustic.md; Str Alexandru Hajdeu 79/1; s/d/ste 950/1100/1300 lei; P) This small boutique hotel, about 10 to 15 minutes' walk from the centre, offers excellent value. The 13 rooms are individually and imaginatively furnished (some feature

Central Chişinău

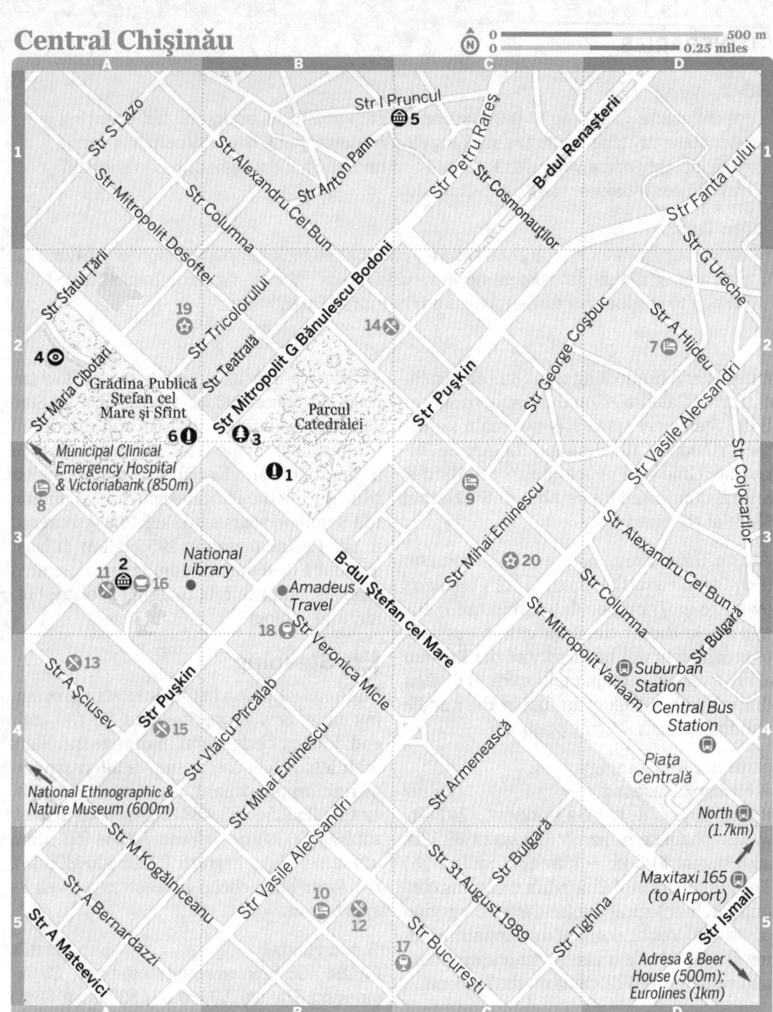

antiques). Rooms come in two classes: 'standart' and cheaper 'econom', with the latter being slightly smaller. Room 11 has a nice big terrace. Note there's no lift.

★ Jazz Hotel HOTEL €€€
(☎212 626; www.jazz-hotel.md; Str Vlaicu Pârcălab 72; s/d 1250/1800 lei; P ⊖ ❄ @ ☎) This well-run, modern hotel makes for an excellent splurge, owing chiefly to the bright, clean rooms and excellent location in the heart of the city. Drivers will enjoy free garage parking at the back. The reception is cheerful and English-speaking. The breakfast buffet offers welcome additions like smoked salmon. There's a small business centre with a computer for checking email.

★ Hotel Codru HOTEL €€€
(☎208 104; www.codru.md; Str 31 August 1989, 127; s/d incl breakfast from 1600/1800 lei; P ❄ @ ☎) Get through the ho-hum lobby and enjoy paradoxically nice rooms that become downright plush (if a bit pricey) when you reach 'luxury' classification. The central location, just across the street from the park, as well as the good balconies and immaculate bathrooms complete the package. There's also a

Central Chişinău

Sights

1 Arc de Triomphe ... B3
2 National Archaeology & History Museum ... A3
3 Parcul Catedralei & Grădina Publică Ştefan cel Mare şi Sfînt ... B2
4 Parliament House ... A2
5 Pushkin Museum ... C1
6 Statue of Ştefan cel Mare ... A2

Sleeping

7 Art Rustic Hotel ... D2
8 Hotel Codru ... A3
9 Jazz Hotel ... C3
10 Tapok Hostel ... B5

Eating

11 Bastion ... A3
12 Grill House ... B5
13 Propaganda Cafe ... A4
14 Robin Pub ... B2
15 Vatra Neamului ... A4

Drinking & Nightlife

16 Delice d'Ange ... A3
17 Dublin Irish Pub ... C5
18 Tipografia 5 ... B3

Entertainment

19 Opera & Ballet Theatre ... A2
20 Philharmonic Concert Hall ... C3

good on-site restaurant and a handy wine shop in the lobby.

Eating

Chişinău has a surprising number of good restaurants. Most are clustered in the centre in the shady neighbourhood along Str Bucureşti and Str 31 August 1989.

Propaganda Cafe INTERNATIONAL €

(☎060 096 666; Str Alexei Şciusev 70; mains 70-130 lei; ⊙11am-1am;) Highly recommended, popular student-oriented cafe that serves very good mains built around chicken, pork and beef, as well as inventive salads and desserts – all at very reasonable prices. The wine list, featuring some of Moldova's best wineries, is terrific. The playfully antique interior, done up like a 19th-century dollhouse, is worth the trip alone.

★**Vatra Neamului** MOLDOVAN €€

(☎226 839; www.vatraneamului.md; Str Bucureşti 67; mains 90-200 lei; ⊙11am-midnight;) This superb place boasts charming old-world decor and unfailingly genial staff. A long menu of imaginatively dressed-up meats – think stewed pork with polenta, baked rabbit and salmon in pastry, not to mention copious vegetarian options – may prompt repeat visits. Enter via the door on Str Puşkin.

★**Robin Pub** INTERNATIONAL €€

(☎241 127; Str Alexandru cel Bun 83; mains 90-250 lei; ⊙11am-midnight;) A friendly, affordable, local-pub feel reigns in this tastefully decorated hang-out. The menu includes omelettes, pastas and grills, including a professionally handled rib eye (150 lei), as well as a long list of desserts. Sit on the dark-leather banquettes inside or dine under the trees out front.

★**Bastion** INTERNATIONAL €€

(☎060 706 070; www.bastion.md; Str Bucureşti 68 (enter at Str 31 August 1989, 117); mains 130-200 lei; ⊙11am-midnight;) Upscale but relaxed restaurant featuring excellent grilled meats and fish, many with an Asian twist, plus a wide range of sushi dishes. Dine on white linen inside or relax on the terrace. The wine list features some of the best of local wineries such as Purcari, Chateau Vartely and Et'cetera, among others.

Beer House INTERNATIONAL €€

(☎275 627; www.beerhouse.md; B-dul Negruzzi 6/2; mains 75-250 lei; ⊙11am-11pm;) This brewery-cum-restaurant has four delicious home-brewed beers and a superb menu, warming up with chicken wings and peaking with rabbit or chicken grilled in cognac. The relaxed ambience and good service add to the charm – summer evening meals outside on the terrace are a treat.

★**Grill House** INTERNATIONAL €€€

(☎224 509; Str Armeneasca 24/2; mains 150-300 lei; ⊙11am-midnight;) It may not look like much from the street, but inside this sleek, low-lit place you'll find the best steaks in town served up by attentive staff from the glassed-in, fire-oven kitchen. Creative pasta dishes complement the array of hearty meat, seafood and fish and there's a great wine list to boot. Go down the atmospheric alley off the street.

Drinking & Nightlife

Delice d'Ange CAFE

(☎245 139; Str 31 August 117/2; ⏰9am-11pm; 📶👶) Popular central cafe offering a dazzling array of great pastries and coffee (25 lei). Sit inside or on the terrace. There's a tree, and a children's play area upstairs.

Dublin Irish Pub PUB

(☎245 855; Str Bulgară 27; ⏰10am-11pm; 📶) Very comfortable pub and restaurant with big wood-beamed ceilings and brick flooring. The drinks are on the expensive side but it's one of the few places in town where you can get a pint of Guinness and the service is very good.

Tipografia 5 LIVE MUSIC

(☎079 894 142; http://tipografia5.locals.md; Str Vlaicu Pârcălab 45; ⏰8pm-midnight Sun-Thu, 10pm-4am Fri & Sat) Alternative late-night venue for clubbing and occasional live music. The mood is student-friendly and chilled. The program tends towards indie/trendy, with some nights given over to techno and other nights to disco.

Entertainment

Opera & Ballet Theatre OPERA, BALLET

(☎box office 245 104; www.nationalopera.md; B-dul Ştefan cel Mare 152; ⏰box office 10am-1pm & 2-6pm Tue-Fri, 11am-4pm Sat & Sun) Home to the esteemed national opera and ballet company, which puts on productions from September to June.

Philharmonic Concert Hall CLASSICAL MUSIC

(☎237 262, box office 222 734; www.filarmonica.md; Str Mitropolit Varlaam 78) Moldova's National Philharmonic is based here.

Information

MEDICAL SERVICES

Municipal Clinical Emergency Hospital (☎emergency 903, info 248 435; Str Toma Ciorba 1; ⏰24hr) Has emergency services and there is a good likelihood of finding English-speaking staff.

MONEY

Victoriabank (Str 31 August 1989, 141; ⏰9am-4pm Mon-Fri)

TRAVEL AGENCIES

Amadeus Travel (Lufthansa City Center; ☎tours 211 716; www.amadeus.md; Str Puşkin 24; ⏰9am-7pm Mon-Fri) Offers a range of inland tours, including wine tours to the country's best-known vineyards such as Cricova, Cojusna, Mileştii Mici, Chateau Vartely and Purcari.

Getting There & Away

AIR

Moldova's only international airport is the modern **Chişinău International Airport** (KIV; ☎525 111; www.airport.md; Str Aeroportului 80/3), 16km southeast of the city centre. There are regular flights to many major European capitals. There are no internal flights within Moldova.

BUS

Chişinău has three bus stations: the **Central Bus Station** (Chişinău Gara; Str Mitropolit Varlaam), the **North Bus Station** (Gara de Nord; www.autogara.md) and the **Southwestern Bus Station** (Autogara Sud-vest or Gara de Sud; www.autogara.md; Şoseaua Hânceşti 143). There's also a small **Suburban Station** (Casele Suburbane). Each bus station serves different destinations (not all of them make sense geographically), so it's important to know in advance which station your bus is using.

Common bus journeys and the stations they use include Bucharest (Central Bus Station; 250 lei, 10 hours, five daily); Kyiv (North Bus Station; 280 lei, 13 hours, two daily); Moscow (North Bus Station; 800 lei, 30 hours, two daily), Orhei/Trebujeni (Suburban Station; 26 lei, 1½ hours, five daily); Soroca (North Bus Station; 70 lei, four hours, frequent); and Tiraspol (Central Bus Station; 35 lei, two hours, frequent). There's a helpful online timetable (in Romanian only) at www.autogara.md.

For long-haul international departures, **Eurolines** (☎549 813; www.eurolines.md; Aleea Garii 1; ⏰9am-6pm Mon-Fri) operates an office at the train station.

TRAIN

International trains depart from the recently renovated station, at Aleea Gării, southeast of Piaţa Negruzii.

Common train journeys from Chişinău include Bucharest (500 lei, 14 hours, daily); Tiraspol (80 lei, two hours, daily); Odesa (160 lei, five hours, daily); Moscow (900 lei, 28 to 32 hours, four to five daily); and St Petersburg (1000 lei, 40 hours, daily).

Getting Around

TO/FROM THE AIRPORT

Maxitaxi 165 departs every 20 minutes from Str Ismail, near the corner of B-dul Ştefan cel Mare for the airport (3 lei). Coming from the airport, this is the last stop. A taxi (call ☎14 222) to the centre costs from 80 lei to 100 lei.

DON'T MISS

ORHEIUL VECHI MONASTERY COMPLEX

The archaeological and ecclesiastical complex at **Orheiul Vechi** ('Old Orhei'), about 20km southeast of the modern city of Orhei (60km northeast of Chişinău), is the country's most important historical site and a place of stark natural beauty.

Occupying a remote, rocky ridge over the Răut River, the open-air complex includes ruins, fortifications, baths, caves and monasteries, ranging from the earliest days of the Dacian tribes more than 2000 years ago through the Mongol and Tatar invasions of the early Middle Ages and the time of Ştefan cel Mare, and all the way to the modern period.

Begin your visit to the region at the **Orheiul Vechi Exhibition Centre** (☎235-56 137; http://orhei.dnt.md; Trebujeni; adult/concession 10/5 lei; ⊙9am-6pm Tue-Sun), near the village of Trebujeni (along the main road just before the bridge to Butuceni). Here you'll find a small museum filled with objects recovered during archaeological digs and a helpful information centre. Exploration is done on foot; it takes about half a day to see everything.

The most impressive sight is arguably the **Cave Monastery** (Mănăstire în Peşteră; www.orhei.dnt.md; Butuceni, Orheiul Vechi; voluntary donation; ⊙8am-6pm) FREE, built inside a cliff overlooking the gently meandering river. It's marked by a small bell tower and a cross standing on the rocks. It was dug by Orthodox monks in the 13th century and remained inhabited until the 18th century. In 1996 a handful of monks returned to this secluded place of worship and are slowly restoring it. You can enter the cave via a brick archway, just below the hill from the bell tower.

The Orheiul Vechi Exhibition Centre has six pleasant rooms (600 lei) and a small restaurant, but for something more authentic, try the **Agro Pensiunea Butuceni** (☎235-56 906; www.pensiuneabutuceni.md; Butuceni; r 1000 lei;), a beautifully restored traditional guesthouse in the middle of the village of the same name.

From Chişinău, around five daily buses depart from the Suburban Station for Trebujeni (26 lei, about one hour).

BUS/MAXITAXI

Route 45 runs from Central to Southwestern Bus Station, as does maxitaxi 117 from the train station. Bus 1 goes from the train station to B-dul Ştefan cel Mare. From the city centre, trolleybuses 1, 4, 5, 8, 18 and 22 go to the train station; buses 2, 10 and 16 go to Southwestern Bus Station; and maxitaxis 176 and 191 go to North Bus Station. Tickets are sold on board for buses (2 lei) and trolleybuses (2 lei). Nippy minitaxis (3 lei, pay the driver) serve most routes in town and to many outlying villages. Maxitaxis run regularly between 6am and 10pm, with reduced service until midnight.

AROUND CHIŞINĂU

Cricova

Of Moldova's many vineyards, **Cricova** (☎tours 22-441 204; www.cricova.md; Str Ungureanu 1, Cricova; guided tours per person from 200 lei; ⊙10am-5pm Mon-Fri) is arguably the best known. Its underground wine kingdom, 15km north of Chişinău, is one of Europe's biggest. Some 60km of the 120km-long underground limestone tunnels – dating from the 15th century – are lined wall-to-wall with bottles.

The most interesting part of a tour of the winery is the wineglass-shaped cellar of collectable bottles, including some 19 bottles that once belonged to Nazi party leader Hermann Göring, a 1902 bottle of Becherovka from the Czech Republic, a 1902 bottle of Evreiesc de Paşti from Jerusalem, and pre-WWII French red wines. Legend has it that in 1966 Soviet cosmonaut Yury Gagarin entered the cellars, re-emerging (with assistance) two days later. Russian president Vladimir Putin even celebrated his 50th birthday here.

You must have private transport and advance reservations to get into Cricova or you can arrange for staff to pick you up in Chişinău.

Mileştii Mici

Similar to Cricova but bigger and possibly more impressive, the wine cellars at **Mileştii Mici** (☎tours 22-382 333; www.milestii-mici.md;

Mileştii Mici, Ialoveni; guided 40min tour per person 200 lei; tasting & lunch per person 500-900 lei; ⏲tours at 10am, 1pm, 3.30pm Mon-Fri), 20km south of Chişinău near the town of Ialoveni, stretch for something like 200km. The cellars here hold more than 2 million bottles, which makes this the world's largest wine collection, according to Guinness World Records.

Guided vehicle tours of the cellars are offered three times daily, though you'll have to book these in advance by phone or email. If you've got your own wheels, the simplest option is to drive your own car through the cellars (with a guide, and it helps to have a small car). Otherwise, you'll have to prearrange a tour through a travel agency or find someone with a car.

Chateau Cojuşna

Just 13km northwest of Chişinău, **Chateau Cojuşna vineyard** (☎22-221 630; www.migdal.md; Str Mecanizatorilor 1, Străşeni; tours 220-900 lei) in Cojuşna village in the Străşeni district, offers friendly and affordable tours, though the setting is quieter in comparison to the bigger and more popular wineries at Cricova and Mileştii Mici.

Tours lasting from one to three hours include a gift bottle, tastings and a hot meal, though you must request an English tour in advance.

Drop-ins are possible, but staff aren't always free to open the very worthwhile wine-tasting rooms, decorated in traditional style with wooden furniture carved by a local boy and his father. However, you can always buy wine (30 lei to 300 lei per bottle) from the shop.

It's possible but not easy to reach Cojuşna from Chişinău by public transport. Maxitaxis leave from Calea Eşilor. From where the maxitaxi drops you, the winery is about a 2km walk away.

Soroca

☎230 / POP 37,000

The northern city of Soroca occupies a prominent position on the Dniestr River and as such has played an outsized role in the defence of the Moldavian principality through the ages. The main attraction is the **Soroca Fortress**, part of a chain of medieval military bastions built by Moldavian princes from the 14th to the 16th centuries to defend the principality's boundaries. This fortress was founded by Ştefan cel Mare and rebuilt by his son, Petru Rareş, in 1543–45.

Sights

Soroca Fortress FORTRESS
(Cetatea Soroca; ☎30 430; Str Petru Rareş 1) This commanding structure dates from 1499 when Moldavian Prince Ştefan cel Mare built a wooden fortress here. It was given its circular shape, with five stone bastions, in the middle of the 16th century by Petru Rareş. The fortress was closed for reconstruction at the time of research.

Soroca Museum of History & Ethnography MUSEUM
(☎22 264; Str Independenţei 68; adult/student 3/2 lei; ⏲10am-1pm & 2-5pm Mon-Fri) This tiny museum is a treat; its exhibits cover archaeological finds, weapons and ethnographic displays.

Sleeping & Eating

Hotel Central HOTEL €
(☎23 456; www.soroca-hotel.com; Str Kogălniceanu 20; s/d incl breakfast 500/600 lei;) The best lodging in town is this small, partly renovated hotel in the centre. The ground-level rooms feel damp and uninviting, but the situation improves the next floor up. Room 16 is snug, clean and sports a shiny new bathroom. There's a small sauna and the terrace restaurant is good.

Nistru Hotel HOTEL €
(☎23 783; Str Alecu Russo 15; r without/with bathroom 300/400 lei) Simple, clean rooms that are fairly priced.

Getting There & Away

There are around a dozen daily buses from Chişinău's North Bus Station (four hours).

By car, Soroca is a straight shot, 150km north of Chişinău, along the M2 highway. Note that at the time of research this road was being extensively rebuilt (north of Orhei). Budget a minimum of three to four hours for the trip.

TRANSDNIESTR

POP 505,000

The self-declared republic of Transdniestr (sometimes called Transnistria, or the Pridnestrovskaya Moldavskaya Respublika, PMR, in Russian), a narrow strip of land on the eastern bank of the Dniestr River, is one of the strangest places in Eastern Europe. It's a ministate that doesn't officially exist in anyone's eyes but its own.

From the Moldovan perspective, Transdniestr is still officially part of its sovereign territory that was illegally grabbed in the early 1990s with Russian support. Officials in Transdniestr see it differently and proudly point to the territory having won its 'independence' in a bloody civil war in 1992. A bitter truce has ensued ever since.

These days, a trip to Transdniestr from Moldova is relatively easy and completely safe. Visitors will be stunned by this idiosyncratic region that still fully embraces the iconography of the Soviet period (lots of photo-worthy busts of Lenin are scattered about) as well as having its own currency, police force, army and borders.

Tiraspol

☎533 / POP 136,000

The 'capital' of Transdniestr is also, officially at least, the second-largest city in Moldova. But don't expect it to be anything like the chaotic Moldovan capital: here time seems to have stood still since the end of the Soviet Union. Eerily quiet streets, flower beds tended with military precision and old-school Soviet everything from street signs to litter-free parks named after communist grandees, Tiraspol (from the Greek, meaning 'town on the Nistru') will be one of the strangest places you'll ever visit.

Sights

Tiraspol National United Museum MUSEUM

(☎90 426; ul 25 Oktober 42; admission 25 roubles; ⏲10am-5pm Sun-Fri) The closest thing to a local history museum, it features an exhibit focusing on poet Nikolai Zelinsky, who founded the first Soviet school of chemistry. Opposite is the **Presidential Palace**, from where President Yevgeny Shevchuk rules the region. Loitering and/or photography here is likely to end in questioning and a guard-escorted trip off the property.

War Memorial MEMORIAL

(ul 25 Oktober) FREE At the western end of ul 25 Oktober stands a Soviet armoured tank from which the Transdniestran flag flies. Behind is the War Memorial with its **Tomb of the Unknown Soldier**, flanked by an eternal flame in memory of those who died on 3 March 1992 during the first outbreak of fighting. On weekends, it's covered in flowers.

Kvint Factory BRANDY FACTORY

(☎96 577; www.kvint.biz; ul Lenina 38; tours 180-900 roubles) Since 1897, Kvint has been making some of Moldova's finest brandies. Purchase a bottle of some of Europe's best-value cognac (starting at under 30 roubles) near the entrance to the plant or at one of several Kvint shops around town. Tasting tours, starting at around 180 roubles per person, must be booked in advance and normally include food.

House of Soviets NOTABLE BUILDING

(ul 25 Oktober) The House of Soviets, towering over the eastern end of ul 25 Oktober, has Lenin's angry-looking bust peering out from its prime location.

Kirov Park PARK

(ul Lenina) North along ul Lenina, towards the bus and train stations, is Kirov Park, with a statue of the Leningrad boss who was

CROSSING INTO TRANSDNIESTR

All visitors to Transdniestr are required to show a valid passport at the 'border'. The formalities are fairly straightforward and take about 15 minutes. Your passport will be scanned and used to generate a slip of paper called a 'migration card', with basic information including your name, nationality and date of birth. The migration card is free of charge and allows for a stay of up to 10 hours. You're required to keep this paper with your passport and surrender it when leaving (so don't lose it!).

The 10-hour time frame should be sufficient for most day trips and to see the main sights (or to transit the country). If you plan on staying the night, you'll have to register at the **OVIR** (☎533 55 047; ul Kotovskogo 2a (Str Cotovschi 2a); ⏲9am-noon Mon, 9am-noon & 1-4pm Tue & Thu, 1-3pm Fri) immigration office in Tiraspol. Upscale hotels will take care of the registration process for you; if you're staying in a hostel or private home, you'll need to sort this on your own in conjunction with your hosts.

assassinated in 1934, conveniently sparking mass repressions throughout the USSR.

Sleeping

You must register at OVIR (p783) in central Tiraspol if staying overnight. Marisha.net (p777) can arrange a homestay.

Tiraspol Hostel HOSTEL €
(Bottle Hotel; ☎068 571 472; www.moldovahostels.com; ul Karla Marksa 13, Ternovka (Tirnauca); dm/r 300/600 roubles;) Incredible as it seems, Tiraspol has a hostel. Run by an American expat, this converted hotel offers big dorm rooms with bath, as well as rare amenities for a hostel like pool and tennis courts. Prices include a tour. Call or email to arrange pick-up; the hostel is 3km outside of Tiraspol in an area called Ternovka.

★**Hotel Russia** HOTEL €€€
(☎38 000; www.hotelrussia.md; ul Sverdlova 69; r incl breakfast 1100 roubles;) Opening to great fanfare in 2012, this large, luxurious and smartly furnished hotel is definitely the mainstay for business people and anyone wanting comfort. Rooms come with flat-screen TVs, smart bathrooms and comfortable beds. The hotel is located on a side street just by the House of Soviets. Staff can arrange police registration.

Eating & Drinking

★**Kumanyok** UKRAINIAN €€
(☎72 034; www.kumanyok.com; ul Sverdlova 37; mains 60-140 roubles; 9am-11pm;) A second home to Transdniestr's ruling classes (as demonstrated by the rows of black Mercedes outside), this smart, traditional Ukrainian place is set in a kitsch faux-countryside home, where diners are attended to by a fleet of peasant-dressed waitresses. The menu is hearty Ukrainian fare; think dumplings, pancakes, fish, mutton and, above all, excellent, authentic borsch (red-beet soup).

Cafe Larionov INTERNATIONAL €€
(☎47 562; ul Karla Liebknechta 397; mains 70-120 roubles; 9am-11pm;) Named for Tiraspol's own avant-garde modernist painter Mikhail Larionov (1881–1964). The idea is local cuisines drawing from the cultural influences (Russian, Jewish, Moldovan) common in Larionov's time, with an emphasis on soups, stews and grilled meats. The setting is a large atrium, with a cosy terrace at the back.

Baccarat CLUB
(☎94 642; ul 25 Oktober 50; 5pm-4am) A stylish hang-out with expensive drinks and indoor/outdoor seating. Frequent karaoke nights pack the joint.

Information

Transnistria Tour (☎069 427 502; www.transnistria-tour.com) Highly recommended company that offers a full range of tours and travel services to foreign visitors. Its excellent English-language website is a great place to start planning your trip. Tours range in theme from Soviet monuments and brandy to football and ecology and start at about 300 roubles per person per day.

Getting There & Away

BUS

You can only pay for bus tickets with local currency, but there are change facilities at the combined bus and train station. Buy tickets inside the station. From Tiraspol there are eight daily buses to Odesa in Ukraine (50 roubles, three hours). Buses/maxitaxis go to Chişinău (34 roubles) nearly every half-hour from 5am to 6pm. Trolleybus 19 (2.50 roubles) and quicker maxitaxis 19 and 20 (3 roubles) cross the bridge over the Dniestr to Bendery.

TRAIN

There's a useful daily Chişinău to Odesa train, which calls at Tiraspol at 9.20am daily. Tickets to Odesa cost 100 roubles and the journey takes two hours. The train makes the return journey to Chişinău each evening, calling at Tiraspol at 7.20pm.

Bendery

☎532 / POP 93,750

Bendery (sometimes called Bender, and previously known as Tighina), on the western banks of the Dniestr River, is the greener, more aesthetically agreeable counterpart to Tiraspol. Despite civil-war bullet holes still decorating several buildings – Bendery was hardest hit by the 1992 military conflict with Moldova – the city centre is a breezy, friendly place.

The highlight is an impressive Ottoman fortress, **Bendery Fortress** (Tighina; ☎48 032; www.bendery-fortress.com; ul Kosmodemyanskoi 10; admission 50 roubles; 8am-4pm Mon-Fri, 10am-3pm Sat & Sun), located outside the centre near the Bendery–Tiraspol bridge. It was built in the 16th century and saw keen fighting between Turkish and Russian forces before it fell to Tsarist Russia permanently in the early 19th century. Until just a few years ago it was a functioning Russian army base and off limits to the public. Now you're free to amble around.

At the entrance to the city, close to the Bendery–Tiraspol bridge, is a **memorial park** dedicated to local 1992 war victims. An eternal flame burns in front of an armoured tank, from which flies the Transdniestran flag. Haunting memorials to those killed during the civil war are also scattered throughout many streets in the city centre.

SURVIVAL GUIDE

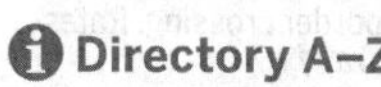

Directory A–Z

ACCOMMODATION

The accommodation situation in Chişinău is improving and the city has a number of very nice top-end hotels. The problem continues to be a lack of decent options at the midrange and budget price points. This may be one city to consider a splurge, since the difference in quality and comfort between the better hotels and cheaper options can be pronounced.

Elsewhere, most towns have small hotels that have survived from communist days and have been somewhat done up. Most hotels these days are totally nonsmoking or at least offer nonsmoking rooms.

On arriving at your hotel, you'll be asked to present your passport and fill in a short identity form.

Camping grounds *(popas turistic)* are rare. The good news is that wild camping is normally allowed unless expressly prohibited.

To supplement a lack of hotels in outlying areas, many municipalities are turning to homestays and privately run pensions. **Moldova Holiday** (www.moldovaholiday.travel) keeps an up-to-date list.

SLEEPING PRICE RANGES

The following price ranges denote one night's accommodation in a double room:

€ less than €50

€€ €50 to €120

€€€ more than €120

COUNTRY FACTS

Area 33,851 sq km

Capital Chişinău

Country Code ☎373

Currency Moldovan leu (plural lei)

Emergency ambulance ☎903, fire ☎901, police ☎902

Language Moldovan

Money ATMs abundant in Chişinău; less common in smaller cities and towns

Population 3.6 million (including Transdniestr)

Visas None for the EU, USA, Canada, Japan, Australia and New Zealand, but required for South Africa and many other countries

BUSINESS HOURS

Banks 9am to 3pm Monday to Friday

Businesses 8am to 7pm Monday to Friday, to 4pm Saturday

Museums 9am to 5pm Tuesday to Sunday

Restaurants 10am to 11pm

Shops 9am or 10am to 6pm or 7pm Monday to Saturday

MONEY

Moldova's currency is the *leu* (plural *lei*). Banknotes are denominated as 1, 5, 10, 20, 50, 100, 200, 500 and 1000 lei notes. One leu is comprised of 100 bani. Little-used coins are denominated as 1, 5, 10, 25 and 50 bani.

The easiest way to get local currency is by using your home debit or credit card through a local ATM. ATMs are scattered throughout the centre in Chişinău, but are harder to find in other towns (stock up on cash when you can). Otherwise, exchange cash at banks.

The only legal tender in Transdniestr is the Transdniestran rouble (TR). Some taxi drivers, shopkeepers and market traders will accept payment in US dollars, euros or even Moldovan lei – but generally you'll need to get your hands on roubles to buy things there. Be sure to spend all your roubles before you leave, as no one honours or exchanges this currency outside Transdniestr.

PUBLIC HOLIDAYS

New Year's Day 1 January

Orthodox Christmas 7 January

International Women's Day 8 March

Orthodox Easter April/May

Victory (1945) Day 9 May
Independence Day 27 August
National Language Day 31 August

VISAS

Citizens of EU member states, USA, Canada, Japan, Australia and New Zealand do not need visas and can stay for up to 90 days within a six-month period. South Africans and some other nationalities require an invitation from a company, organisation or individual to get a visa.

Visas can be acquired on arrival at Chişinău airport or, if arriving by bus or car from Romania, at three border points: Sculeni (north of Iaşi); Leuşeni (main Bucharest–Chişinău border); and Cahul. Visas are not issued at any other border crossings, nor when entering by train.

Check the **Ministry of Foreign Affairs** (www.mfa.gov.md) website and follow the link for Consular Affairs for the latest news on the visa situation.

EATING PRICE RANGES

The following price indicators are based on the average cost of a main course:

€ less than €5

€€ €5 to €10

€€€ more than €10

Getting There & Away

AIR

Moldova's only international airport (p780) is in Chişinău.

LAND

Moldova has decent overland links to neighbouring countries. Daily buses and trains from Chişinău head to Iaşi and Bucharest in Romania, as well as to Odesa in Ukraine. Trains also serve Moscow and St Petersburg. Buses to Odesa often avoid Transdniestr and thus the delays at the border. Trains between Chişinău and Odesa go via Tiraspol, but delays are minimal.

Bus

Moldova is well linked by bus lines to central and western Europe. While not as comfortable as the train, buses tend to be faster, though not always cheaper.

Car & Motorcyle

On arriving at the border, drivers need to show valid vehicle registration, insurance (Green Card), driving licence (US and EU licences OK) and passport. Motorists must purchase a highway sticker (vignette) to drive on Moldovan roads. Buy these at the border crossing. Rates per 7/15/30 days are €2/4/7.

Train

From Chişinău, there are four to five trains to Moscow, as well as daily service to St Petersburg and Odesa, Ukraine (via Tiraspol). There's an overnight service between Bucharest and Chişinău; at 12 to 14 hours.

Getting Around

BUS & MAXITAXI

Moldova has a comprehensive if confusing network of buses running to most towns and villages. Maxitaxis, which follow the same routes as the buses, are usually quicker and more reliable. Public transport costs 2 lei, while city maxitaxis cost 3 lei.

ESSENTIAL FOOD & DRINK

Moldovan cooking bears a strong resemblance to Romanian food across the border. The emphasis is on traditional recipes and farm-fresh ingredients rather than sophisticated preparation techniques.

- **Muşchi de vacă/porc/miel** A cutlet of beef/pork/lamb.
- **Piept de pui** The ubiquitous chicken breast.
- **Mămăligă** Cornmeal mush with a consistency between porridge and bread that accompanies many dishes.
- **Brânză** Moldova's most common cheese is a slightly salty-sour sheep's milk product that often comes grated. Put it on *mămăligă*.
- **Sarma** Cabbage-wrapped minced meat or pilau rice packages, similar to Turkish dolma or Russian *goluptsy*.
- **Wine** Look for bottles from quality local wineries like Cricova, Chateau Vartely and Purcari, among many others.

Montenegro

Includes ➡

Best Places to Eat

- ➡ Konoba Ćatovića Mlini (p794)
- ➡ Galion (p793)
- ➡ Restoran Lim (p790)
- ➡ Taste of Asia (p790)
- ➡ Juice Bar (p790)

Best Places to Stay

- ➡ Palazzo Drusko (p793)
- ➡ Palazzo Radomiri (p793)
- ➡ Hotel Astoria (p790)
- ➡ Old Town Hostel (p793)
- ➡ Hikers Den (p796)

Why Go?

Imagine a place with sapphire beaches as spectacular as Croatia's, rugged peaks as dramatic as Switzerland's, canyons nearly as deep as Colorado's, palazzi as elegant as Venice's and towns as old as Greece's. Then wrap it up in a Mediterranean climate and squish it into an area two-thirds the size of Wales, and you start to get a picture of Montenegro.

More adventurous travellers can easily sidestep the peak-season hordes on the coast by heading to the rugged mountains of the north. This is, after all, a country where wolves and bears still lurk in forgotten corners.

Montenegro, Crna Gora (Црна Гора), Black Mountain: the name itself conjures up romance and drama. There are plenty of both on offer as you explore this perfumed land, bathed in the scent of wild herbs, conifers and Mediterranean blossoms. Yes, it really is as magical as it sounds.

When to Go

Podgorica

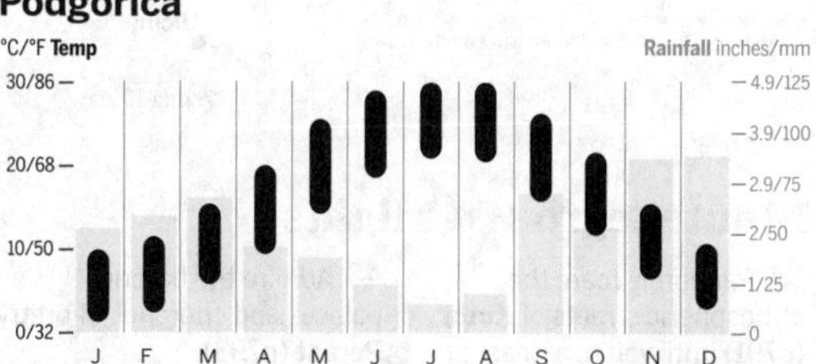

Jun Beat the peak-season rush and prices but enjoy the balmy weather.

Sep Warm water but fewer bods to share it with; shoulder season prices.

Oct The leaves turn golden, making a rich backdrop for walks in the national parks.

Montenegro Highlights

❶ Randomly roam the atmospheric streets of **Kotor** (p791) until you're at least a little lost.

❷ Drive the vertiginous route from Kotor to the Njegoš Mausoleum at the top of **Lovćen National Park** (p794).

❸ Admire the baroque palaces and churches of pretty **Perast** (p793).

❹ Seek out the spiritual at impressive cliff-clinging **Ostrog Monastery** (p796).

❺ Float through paradise, rafting between the kilometre-plus walls of the **Tara Canyon** (p796).

❻ Dive into Montenegro's history, art and culture in the old royal capital, **Cetinje** (p795).

❼ Watch the beautiful people over the rim of a coffee cup in the cobbled Old Town lanes of **Budva**.

ITINERARIES

Five Days

Basing yourself in **Kotor**, spend an afternoon in Perast and a whole day in Budva. Allow another day to explore **Lovćen National Park** and **Cetinje**.

One Week

For your final two days, head north to **Durmitor National Park**, making sure to stop at **Ostrog Monastery** on the way. Spend your time hiking, rafting and canyoning.

COASTAL MONTENEGRO

Coming from Croatia and entering the mountain-framed folds of the Bay of Kotor (Boka Kotorska), the beauty meter goes off the scale. It doesn't let up when you hit the Adriatic coast, where you'll find a charismatic set of small settlements set against clear waters and sandy beaches.

Budva Будва

☎033 / POP 13,400

The poster child of Montenegrin tourism, Budva – with its atmospheric Old Town and numerous beaches – certainly has a lot to offer. Yet the child has moved into a difficult adolescence, fuelled by rampant development that has leeched much of the charm from the place. Still, it's the buzziest place on the coast so if you're in the mood to party, this is the place to be.

Sights

Budva's best feature and star attraction is the Stari Grad (Old Town) – a mini-Dubrovnik with marbled streets and Venetian walls rising from the clear waters below. Much of it was ruined by two earthquakes in 1979 but it has since been completely rebuilt and now houses more shops, bars and restaurants than residences.

Citadela FORTRESS

(admission €2.50; ⏲9am-midnight May-Oct, to 5pm Nov-Apr) At the Stari Grad's seaward end, the old citadel offers striking views, a small museum and a library full of rare tomes and maps. It's thought to have been built on the site of the Greek acropolis, but the present incarnation dates to the 19th-century Austrian occupation. Its large terrace serves as the main stage of the annual Theatre City Festival.

Town Walls FORTRESS

(admission €1.50) A walkway about a metre wide leads around the landward walls of the Stari Grad, offering views across the rooftops and down on some beautiful hidden gardens. Admission only seems to be charged in the height of summer; at other times it's either free or locked. The entrance is near the Citadela.

Ploče Beach BEACH

(www.plazaploce.com) If the sands are getting too crowded in Budva itself, head out to this little pebbly beach at the end of a scrub-covered peninsula, 10km west of town (take the road to Kotor, turn off towards Jaz Beach and keep going). The water is crystal clear but if you prefer fresh water there are little pools set into the sunbathing terraces.

Jaz Beach BEACH

The blue waters and broad sands of Jaz Beach look spectacular when viewed from high up on the Tivat road. While it's not built up like Budva, the beach is still lined with loungers, sun umbrellas and noisy beach bars. Head down the Budva end of the beach for a little more seclusion.

Sleeping

Montenegro Freedom Hostel HOSTEL €

(☎067-523 496; montenegrofreedom@gmail.com; Cara Dušana 21; dm/tw/d €14/30/36; ❄📶) In a quieter section of the Old Town, this sociable hostel has tidy little rooms scattered between three buildings. The terraces and small courtyard are popular spots for impromptu guitar-led singalongs.

Montenegro Hostel HOSTEL €

(☎069-039 751; www.montenegrohostel.com; Vuka Karadžića 12; dm/r €12/40; ❄📶) With a right-in-the-thick-of-it Old Town location (pack earplugs), this colourful little hostel provides the perfect base for hitting the bars and beaches. Each floor has its own kitchen and bathroom, and there's a communal space at the top for fraternising.

Hotel Oliva HOTEL €€
(☎069-551 769; www.hotel-oliva.com; Velji Vinogradi bb; r €50; P ❄ 📶) Don't expect anything flashy, just a warm welcome, clean and comfortable rooms with balconies, and a nice garden studded with the olive trees that give this small hotel its name. The wi-fi doesn't extend much past the restaurant.

★**Hotel Astoria** HOTEL €€€
(☎033-451 110; www.astoriamontenegro.com; Njegoševa 4; s/d from €115/130; ❄ 📶) Water shimmers down the corridor wall as you enter this chic boutique hotel hidden in the Old Town's fortifications. The rooms are on the small side but they're beautifully furnished; the sea-view suite is spectacular.

Villa M Palace APARTMENT €€€
(☎067-402 222; www.mpalacebudva.com; Gospoština 25; apt from €110; P ❄ 📶) There's a seductive glamour to this modern block, hemmed in within a rash of new developments near the Old Town. A chandelier glistens in the lift and the walls sparkle in the darkened corridors – and that's before you even reach the luxurious one- to three-bedroom apartments.

Eating

★**Juice Bar** CAFE €
(www.juicebar.me; Vranjak 13; mains €3-10; ⏲8.30am-late) They may serve delicious juices, smoothies and shakes, but that's only part of the appeal of this cosmopolitan cafe, set on a sunny Old Town square. The crowd-pleasing menu includes light breakfasts, salads, toasted sandwiches, nachos, lasagne, cakes and muffins.

★**Restoran Lim** EUROPEAN €€
(Slovenska Obala; mains €6-19; ⏲8am-1am) Settle into one of the throne-like carved wooden chairs and feast on the likes of grilled meat and fish, homemade sausages, pizza, beef stroganoff, veal Parisienne or Weiner schnitzel. The octopus salad is excellent.

★**Taste of Asia** ASIAN €€
(☎033-455 249; Popa Jola Zeca bb; mains €10-15; ⏲noon-10pm) Spicy food is virtually non-existent in Montenegro, which makes this attractive little eatery such a welcome surprise. The menu ambles through the Orient, with dishes from Indonesia, Malaysia, Singapore and Vietnam, but lingers longest in Thailand and China.

Knez Konoba MONTENEGRIN, SEAFOOD €€
(Mitrov Ljubiše 5; mains €8-17; ⏲noon-11pm) Hidden within the Old Town's tiny lanes, this atmospheric eatery has only three outdoor tables and a handful inside. The traditional dishes are beautifully presented and often accompanied by free shots of *rakija* (fruit brandy).

Porto MONTENEGRIN, SEAFOOD €€
(☎033-451 598; www.restoranporto.com; City Marina, Šetalište bb; mains €7-18; ⏲10am-1am) From the waterfront promenade a little bridge arches over a fish pond and into this romantic restaurant where jocular bow-tie-wearing waiters flit about with plates laden with fresh seafood. The food is excellent and the wine list offers plenty of choice from around the region.

Drinking & Nightlife

Casper CAFE, BAR
(www.facebook.com/casper.budva; Petra I Petrovića bb; ⏲10am-1am Jun-Sep, 5pm-1am Oct-May; 📶) Chill out under the pine tree in this picturesque Old Town cafe-bar. DJs kick off from July, spinning everything from reggae to house. Casper hosts its own jazz festival in September.

Top Hill CLUB
(www.tophill.me; Topliški Put; events €10-25; ⏲11pm-5am Jul & Aug) The top cat of Montenegro's summer party scene attracts up to 5000 revellers to its open-air club atop Topliš Hill, offering them top-notch sound and lighting, sea views, big-name touring DJs and performances by local pop stars.

Information

Tourist Office (☎033-452 750; www.budva.travel; Njegoševa 28; ⏲9am-9pm Mon-Sat, 5-9pm Sun Jun-Aug, 8am-8pm Mon-Sat Sep-May)

Getting There & Away

The **bus station** (☎033-456 000; Popa Jola Zeca bb) has frequent services to Kotor (€3.50) and Cetinje (€3.50), and a daily bus to Žabljak (€15).

WORTH A TRIP

MORE TO EXPLORE

Herceg Novi A bustling waterfront promenade runs below a small fortified centre, with cafes and churches set on sunny squares.

Sveti Stefan Gazing down on this impossibly picturesque walled island village (now an exclusive luxury resort) provides one of the biggest 'wow' moments on the entire Adriatic coast.

Ulcinj Minarets and a hulking walled town dominate the skyline, providing a dramatic background for the holidaymakers on the beaches.

Podgorica The nation's modern capital has a buzzy cafe scene, lots of green space and some excellent galleries.

Lake Skadar National Park The Balkans' largest lake is dotted with island monasteries and provides an important sanctuary for migrating birds.

Biogradska Gora National Park Virgin forest set around a pretty lake.

Kotor Котор

☎032 / POP 13,500

Wedged between brooding mountains and a moody corner of the bay, this dramatically beautiful town combines historic grace with vibrant street life. From a distance Kotor's sturdy ancient walls are barely discernible from the mountain's grey hide but at night they're spectacularly lit, reflecting in the water to give the town a golden halo. Within those walls lie labyrinthine marbled lanes where churches, shops, bars and restaurants surprise you on hidden piazzas.

Sights & Activities

The best thing to do in Kotor is to get lost and found again in the maze of streets. You'll soon know every corner, as the town is quite small, but there are plenty of churches to pop into and many coffees to be drunk in the shady squares.

Sea Gate GATE

(Vrata od Mora) The main entrance to the town was constructed in 1555 when the town was under Venetian rule (1420–1797). Look out for the winged lion of St Mark, Venice's symbol, which is displayed prominently on the walls here and in several other spots around the town. Above the gate the date of the city's liberation from the Nazis is remembered with a communist star and a quote from Tito.

As you pass through the gate, look for the 15th-century stone relief of the Madonna and Child flanked by St Tryphon and St Bernard. Stepping through onto **Trg od Oružja** (Weapons Sq) you'll see a strange stone pyramid in front of the **clock tower** (1602); it was once used as a **pillory** to shame wayward citizens.

Town Walls FORTRESS

(admission €3; 🕒24hr, fees apply 8am-8pm May-Sep) Kotor's fortifications started to head up St John's Hill in the 9th century and by the 14th century a protective loop was completed; it was added to right up until the 19th century. The energetic can make a 1200m ascent up the fortifications via 1350 steps to a height of 260m above sea level. There are entry points near the North Gate and behind Trg od Salate; avoid the heat of the day and bring lots of water.

St Nicholas' Church CHURCH

(Crkva Sv Nikole; Trg Sv Luke) Breathe in the smell of incense and beeswax in this relatively unadorned Orthodox church (1909). The silence, the iconostasis with its silver bas-relief panels, the dark wood against bare grey walls, the filtered light through the dome and the simple stained glass conspire to create a mystical atmosphere.

St Tryphon's Cathedral CHURCH

(Katedrala Sv Tripuna; Trg Sv Tripuna; admission €2.50; 🕒8am-7pm) Kotor's most impressive building, this Catholic cathedral was consecrated in the 12th century but reconstructed after several earthquakes. When the

Kotor

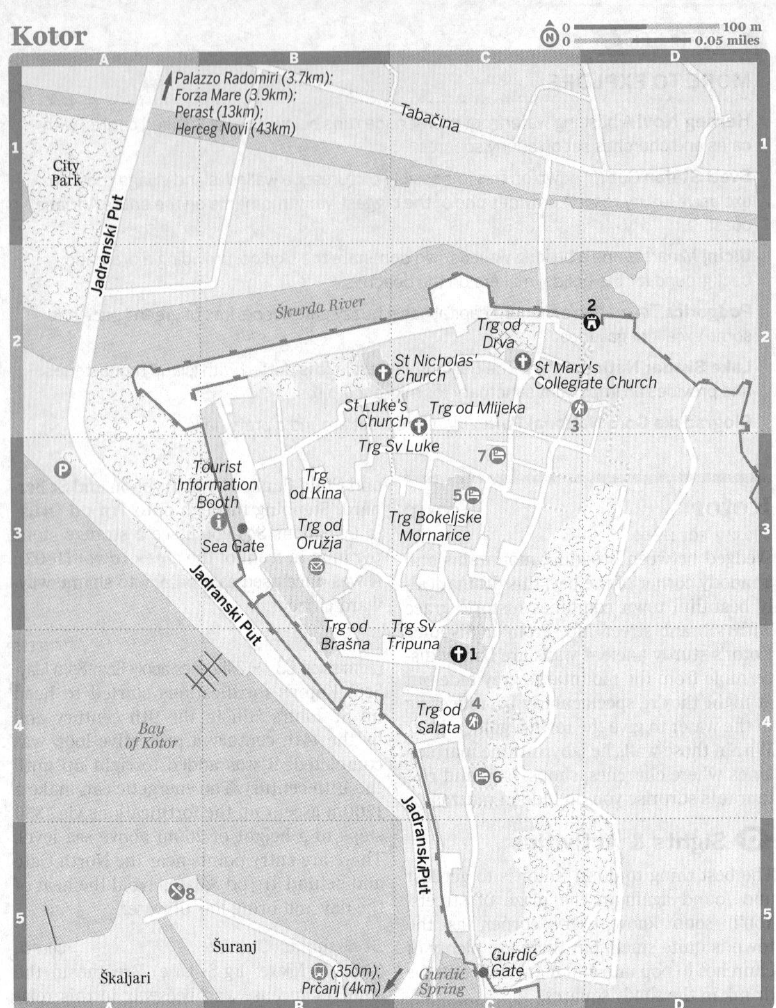

entire frontage was destroyed in 1667, the baroque bell towers were added; the left one remains unfinished. The cathedral's gently hued interior is a masterpiece of Romanesque architecture with slender Corinthian columns alternating with pillars of pink stone, thrusting upwards to support a series of vaulted roofs. Its gilded silver bas-relief altar screen is considered Kotor's most valuable treasure.

Gurdić Gate GATE

(Vrata od Gurdića) Fewer tourists make it to the south end of town, where the houses narrow into a slim corridor leading to this bastion and gate (parts of which date from the 13th century) and the drawbridge over the Gurdić spring. Without the crowds you can easily imagine yourself transported through time here.

A Day Out On Monty B SAILING

(www.montenegro4sail.com; from €79 per person) If you don't have €1000 to blow on a luxury yacht, join British expats Katie and Tim (and their two little doggies) for a sail on the 44ft ketch which doubles as their home (and kennel).

Kotor

Sights
1 St Tryphon's Cathedral......C4
2 Town Walls......D2

Activities, Courses & Tours
3 Entry to Town Walls......C2
4 Entry to Town Walls......C4

Sleeping
5 Hotel Monte Cristo......C3
6 Old Town Hostel......C4
7 Palazzo Drusko......C3

Eating
8 Galion......A5

Sleeping & Eating

Although the Stari Grad is a charming place to stay, you'd better pack earplugs. In summer the bars blast music onto the streets until 1am every night and rubbish collectors clank around at 6am. Some of the best options are just out of Kotor in quieter Dobrota. Inquire about private accommodation at the tourist information booth.

★**Old Town Hostel** HOSTEL €
(☎032-325 317; www.hostel-kotor.me; near Trg od Salata; dm €12-15, r without/with bathroom €39/44, apt €49; ❄📶) If the ghosts of the Bisanti family had any concerns when their 13th-century palazzo (palatial mansion) was converted into a hostel, they must be overjoyed now. Sympathetic renovations have brought the place to life, and the ancient stone walls now echo with the cheerful chatter of happy travellers, mixing and mingling beneath the Bisanti coat of arms.

★**Palazzo Drusko** GUESTHOUSE €€
(☎032-325 257; www.palazzodrusko.me; near Trg od Mlijeka; s/d from €49/75; ❄📶) Loaded with character and filled with antiques, this venerable 600-year-old palazzo is a memorable place to stay, right in the heart of the old town. Thoughtful extras include a guest kitchen, 3D TVs and old-fashioned radios rigged to play Montenegrin music.

Hotel Monte Cristo HOTEL €€
(☎032-322 458; www.montecristo.co.me; near Trg Bokeljske Mornarice; r/apt from €90/125; ❄📶) It's not going to win any hip design awards but this old stone place offers a cheerful welcome and clean, brightly tiled rooms in a supremely central location. There's a restaurant downstairs, so expect some noise.

★**Palazzo Radomiri** HOTEL €€€
(☎032-333 172; www.palazzoradomiri.com; Dobrota 220; s/d/ste from €110/140/200; ⏲Apr-Oct; P❄📶🏊) This honey-coloured early-18th-century palazzo on the Dobrota waterfront, 4km north of the old town, has been transformed into a first-rate boutique hotel. Some rooms are bigger and grander than others, but all 10 have sea views and luxurious furnishings. Guests can avail themselves of a small workout area, sauna, pool, private jetty, bar and restaurant.

Forza Mare HOTEL €€€
(☎032-333 500; www.forzamare.com; Kriva bb, Dobrota; r from €200; ⏲Apr-Oct; P❄📶🏊) A bridge arches over a small tiled pool before you even reach the front door of this hotel, dripping in marble, slate and a general air of over-the-top opulence. Downstairs there's a tiny private beach, an upmarket restaurant and a spa centre.

★**Galion** SEAFOOD €€€
(☎032-325 054; Šuranj bb; meals €12-23; ⏲noon-midnight) With an achingly romantic setting, extremely upmarket Galion gazes directly at the Old Town across the millionaire yachts in the marina. Fresh fish is the focus, but you'll also find steaks and pasta. It usually closes in winter.

Information

Tourist Information Booth (☎032-325 950; www.tokotor.me; outside Vrata od Mora; ⏲8am-8pm Apr-Nov, 8am-5pm Dec-Mar) Stocks free maps and brochures, and can help with contacts for private accommodation.

Getting There & Away

The **bus station** (☎032-325 809; ⏲6am-9pm) is to the south of town, just off the road leading to the Tivat tunnel. Buses head to Budva (€3.50, 40 minutes) at least hourly and to Žabljak (€13, 3½ hours) twice daily.

A taxi to Tivat airport should cost around €10.

Perast Пераст

☎032 / POP 270

Looking like a chunk of Venice that has floated down the Adriatic and anchored itself onto the Bay of Kotor, Perast hums with melancholic memories of the days when it was rich and powerful. Despite its diminutive size it boasts 16 churches and 17 formerly grand palazzi.

WORTH A TRIP

MONTENEGRO'S MOST ATMOSPHERIC EATERY

A crystalline stream flows around and under this rustic former mill, **Konoba Ćatovića Mlini** (032-373 030; www.catovicamlini.me; mains €12-25; 11am-11pm), which masquerades as a humble family-owned *konoba* but in reality is one of Montenegro's best restaurants. Watch the geese idle by as you sample the magical bread and olive oil, which appears unbidden at the table. Fish is the focus but traditional Njeguši specialities are also offered. You'll find it in the village of Morinj, in the western corner of the inner section of the Bay of Kotor.

Sights

Sveti Đorđe & Gospa od Škrpjela ISLANDS

Just offshore from Perast are two peculiarly picturesque islands. The smaller, **Sveti Đorđe** (St George), rises from a natural reef and houses a Benedictine monastery shaded by cypresses. Boats (€5 return) ferry people to its big sister, **Gospa od Škrpjela** (Our-Lady-of-the-Rocks), which was artificially created in the 15th century around a rock where an image of the Madonna was found. Every year on 22 July the locals row over with stones to continue the task.

St Nicholas' Church CHURCH

(Crkva Sv Nikole; treasury €1; 10am-6pm) This large church has never been completed, and given that it was commenced in the 17th century and the bay's Catholic community has declined markedly since then, one suspects it never will be. Its treasury contains beautifully embroidered vestments and the remains of various saints. Climb the imposing 55m bell tower for views over the bay.

Perast Museum MUSEUM

(Muzej grada Perasta; adult/child €2.50/1.50; 9am-7pm) The Bujović Palace, dating from 1694, has been lovingly preserved and converted into a museum showcasing the town's proud seafaring history. It's worth visiting for the building alone and for the wondrous photo opportunities afforded by its balcony.

Sleeping & Eating

Hotel Conte APARTMENTS €€€

(032-373 687; www.hotel-conte.com; apt €80-160;) Conte is not so much a hotel as a series of deluxe studio, one- and two-bedroom apartments in historic buildings scattered around St Nicholas' Church. The sense of age resonating from the stone walls is palpable, even with the distinctly nontraditional addition of a Jacuzzi and sauna in the flashest apartment. It's worth paying €20 extra for a sea view.

Per Astra HOTEL €€€

(032-373 608; www.perastra.me; ste €169-329; Apr-Oct; P) Located right at the top of the town (the stairs will get you fit, but they can be difficult at night), this old stone complex offers 11 suites with glitzy decor, fine views and a small pool.

Restaurant Conte SEAFOOD €€€

(032-373 687; mains €9-20; 8am-midnight;) Meals come with lashings of romance on the flower-bedecked waterside terrace of the Hotel Conte. You'll be presented with platters of whole fish to select from; the chosen one will return, cooked and silver-served, to your table.

Getting There & Away

Paid parking is available on either approach to town; car access into the town itself is restricted.

Buses stop at least hourly on the main road at the top of town. Expect to pay less than €3 for any journey within the bay between Kotor (25 minutes) and Herceg Novi (40 minutes).

CENTRAL MONTENEGRO

The heart of Montenegro – physically, spiritually and politically – is easily accessed as a day trip from the coast, but it's well deserving of a longer exploration. This really is the full Monte: soaring peaks, hidden monasteries, steep river canyons and historic towns.

Lovćen National Park Ловћен

Directly behind Kotor is Mt Lovćen (1749m), the black mountain that gave Crna Gora (Montenegro) its name (*crna/negro* means 'black' and *gora/monte* means 'mountain' in Montenegrin and Italian respectively). This locale occupies a special place in the hearts of all Montenegrins. For most of its history it represented the entire nation – a rocky island of Slavic resistance in an Ottoman sea. The old capital of Cetinje nestles in its foothills.

The national park's 6220 hectares are criss-crossed with well-marked hiking paths.

Sights & Activities

Njegoš Mausoleum MONUMENT
(Njegošev Mauzolej; admission €3; 8am-6pm) Lovćen's star attraction, this magnificent mausoleum (built 1970–74) sits at the top of its second-highest peak, Jezerski Vrh (1657m). Take the 461 steps up to the entry where two granite giantesses guard the tomb of Montenegro's greatest hero. Inside under a golden mosaic canopy a 28-tonne Petar II Petrović Njegoš rests in the wings of an eagle, carved from a single block of black granite by Croatian sculptor Ivan Meštrović.

Avanturistički Park ADVENTURE SPORTS
(069-543 156; Ivanova Korita; adult/child €18/12; 10am-6pm Jun-Aug, noon-6pm Sat & Sun May, Sep & Oct) This 2-hectare adventure park has zip lines and ropes courses of varying degrees of difficulty set among the trees near the National Park Visitor Centre.

Information

National Park Visitor Centre (www.nparkovi.me; Ivanova Korita; 9am-5pm) Offers accommodation in four-bed bungalows (€40).

Getting There & Away

If you're driving, the park can be approached from either Kotor or Cetinje (entry fee €2). Tour buses provide the only transport into the park.

Cetinje Цетиње

041 / POP 14,000

Rising from a green vale surrounded by rough, grey mountains, Cetinje is an odd mix of former capital and overgrown village where single-storey cottages and stately mansions share the same street.

Sights

A collection of four Cetinje museums and two galleries are collectively known as the National Museum of Montenegro. A joint ticket will get you into all of them (adult/child €10/5), or you can buy individual tickets.

History Museum MUSEUM
(Istorijski muzej; 041-230 310; www.mnmuseum.org; Novice Cerovića 7; adult/child €3/1.50; 9am-5pm) Housed in Cetinje's most imposing building, the former parliament (1910), this fascinating museum is well laid out, following a timeline from the Stone Age to 1955. There are few English signs but the enthusiastic staff will walk you around and give you an overview before leaving you to your own devices.

Montenegrin Art Gallery GALLERY
(Crnogorska galerija umjetnosti; www.mnmuseum.org; Novice Cerovića 7; adult/child €4/2; 9am-5pm) The national collection is split between the former parliament and a striking modern building on Cetinje's main street (mainly used for temporary exhibitions). All of Montenegro's great artists are represented, with the most famous (Milunović, Lubarda, Đurić etc) having their own separate spaces.

King Nikola Museum PALACE
(Muzej kralja Nikole; www.mnmuseum.org; Dvorski Trg; adult/child €5/2.50; 9am-5pm) Entry to this 1871 palace, home to the last sovereign of Montenegro, is by guided tour (you may need to wait for a group to form). Although looted during WWII, enough plush furnishings, stern portraits and taxidermied animals remain to capture the spirit of the court.

Njegoš Museum PALACE
(Njegošev muzej; www.mnmuseum.org; Dvorski Trg; adult/child €3/1.50; 9am-5pm) This castle-like palace was the residence of Montenegro's favourite son, prince-bishop and poet Petar II Petrović Njegoš. It was built and financed by the Russians in 1838 and housed the nation's first billiard table, hence the museum's alternative name, Biljarda.

Cetinje Monastery MONASTERY
(Cetinjski Manastir; 8am-6pm) It's a case of four times lucky for the Cetinje Monastery, having been repeatedly destroyed during Ottoman attacks and rebuilt. This sturdy incarnation dates from 1786, with its only exterior ornamentation being the capitals of columns recycled from the original building, founded in 1484.

DON'T MISS

OSTROG MONASTERY ОСТРОГ

Clinging to a cliff 900m above the Zeta valley, this gleaming white Orthodox monastery (1665) is a strangely affecting place that gives the impression that it has grown out of the very rock.

A guesthouse near the Lower Monastery offers tidy single-sex dorm rooms (€5), while in summer sleeping mats are provided for free to pilgrims in front of the Upper Monastery. There's no public transport but numerous tour buses head here from the coast.

Sleeping & Eating

Pansion 22 GUESTHOUSE €
(☎069-055 473; www.pansion22.com; Ivana Crnojevića 22; s/d €22/40; 📶) They may not be great at speaking English or answering emails, but the family who run this central guesthouse offer a warm welcome nonetheless. The rooms are simply decorated yet clean and comfortable, with views of the mountains from the top floor.

Kole MONTENEGRIN, EUROPEAN €€
(☎041-231 620; www.restaurantkole.me; Bul Crnogorskih Junaka 12; mains €3-12; ⏱7am-11pm) They serve omelettes and pasta at this snazzy modern eatery, but it's the local specialities that shine. Try the Njeguški *ražanj*, smoky spit-roasted meat stuffed with *pršut* (prosciutto) and cheese.

Information

Tourist Information (☎041-230 250; www.cetinje.travel; Novice Cerovića bb; ⏱8am-6pm Mar-Oct, to 4pm Nov-Feb)

Getting There & Away

Buses stop at Trg Golootočkih Žrtava, two blocks from the main street. There are regular services to Budva (€3.50).

Durmitor National Park Дурмитор

☎052

Magnificent scenery ratchets up to stupendous in this national park (entry €3), where ice and water have carved a dramatic landscape from the limestone. The Durmitor range has 48 peaks over 2000m, with the highest, **Bobotov Kuk**, reaching 2523m. Scattered in between are 18 glacial lakes known as *gorske oči* (mountain eyes). The largest, **Black Lake** (Crno jezero), is a pleasant 3km walk from **Žabljak**, the park's principal gateway. Slicing through the mountains at the northern edge of the national park like they were made from the local soft cheese, the **Tara River** forms a canyon that at lowest point is 1300m deep.

From December to March Durmitor is a ski resort, while in summer it's popular with hikers and rafters.

Activities

The two-day raft along the river is the country's premier outdoor attraction (May to October only). Most of the day tours from the coast traverse only the last 18km of the river – this is outside the national park and hence avoids hefty fees. This section also has the most rapids – but don't expect much in the way of white water.

Summit Travel Agency ADVENTURE TOUR
(☎052-360 082; www.summit.co.me; Njegoševa 12, Žabljak; half-/1-/2-day rafting trip €50/110/200) As well as rafting trips, this long-standing agency can arrange jeep tours, mountain-bike hire and canyoning expeditions.

Sleeping

★ **Hikers Den** HOSTEL €
(☎067-854 433; www.hostelzabljak.com; Božidara Žugića bb, Žabljak; dm €11-13, s/d €22/35; ⏱Apr-Oct; @📶) Split between three neighbouring houses, this laid-back and sociable place is by far the best hostel in the north. If you're keen on a rafting or canyoning trip, the charming hosts will happily make the arrangements.

Eko-Oaza Suza Evrope CABINS, CAMPGROUND €
(☎069-444 590; ekooazatara@gmail.com; Dobrilovina; campsites per tent/person/campervan €5/1/10, cabins €50; ⏱Apr-Oct) Consisting of four comfortable wooden cottages (each sleeping five people) and a fine stretch of lawn above the river, this magical family-run 'eco oasis' offers a genuine experience of Montenegrin hospitality. Home-cooked meals are provided on request, and rafting trips and jeep safaris can be arranged.

Hotel Soa HOTEL €€
(☎052-360 110; www.hotelsoa.com; Put Crnog Jezera bb, Žabljak; s/d/ste from €60/75/120; 📶) Rooms at this snazzy new hotel are kitted out with monsoon shower heads, Etro toiletries,

robes and slippers. Plus there's a playground, bikes for hire (per hour/day €2/10) and a restaurant.

Information

Durmitor National Park Visitor Centre (☎052-360 228; www.nparkovi.me; Jovana Cvijića bb; ⌚7am-3pm Mon-Fri) On the road to the Black Lake, this centre includes a micromuseum on the park's flora and fauna. Staff sell hiking maps and guidebooks.

Getting There & Away

The bus station is at the southern edge of Žabljak, on the Šavnik road. Bus destinations include Kotor (€13, 3½ hours, two daily) and Budva (€15, 4¾ hours, daily).

SURVIVAL GUIDE

Directory A–Z

ACCOMMODATION

Private accommodation (rooms and apartments for rent) and hotels form the bulk of the sleeping options, although there are some hostels in the more touristy areas. Camping grounds operate in summer and some of the mountainous areas have cabin accommodation in 'eco villages' or mountain huts.

In the peak summer season, some places require minimum stays (three days to a week). Many establishments on the coast close during winter. An additional tourist tax (usually less than €1 per night) is added to the rate for all accommodation types.

GAY & LESBIAN TRAVELLERS

Although homosexuality was decriminalised in 1977 and discrimination outlawed in 2010, attitudes to homosexuality remain hostile and life for gay people is extremely difficult. Many gay men resort to online connections (try www.gayromeo.com) or take their chances at a handful of cruisy beaches. Lesbians will find it even harder to access the local community.

SLEEPING PRICE RANGES

The following price indicators apply for a double room in the shoulder season (roughly June and September):

€ less than €40

€€ €40 to €100

€€€ more than €100

EATING PRICE RANGES

Tipping isn't expected, although it's common to round up to the nearest euro. The following price categories refer to a standard main course:

€ less than €7

€€ €7 to €12

€€€ more than €12

INTERNET RESOURCES

Explore Montenegro (www.exploremontenegro.com)
Montenegrin National Tourist Organisation (www.montenegro.travel)
National Parks of Montenegro (www.nparkovi.me)

PUBLIC HOLIDAYS

New Year's Day 1 and 2 January
Orthodox Christmas 6, 7 and 8 January
Orthodox Good Friday & Easter Monday Usually April/May
Labour Day 1 May
Independence Day 21 May
Statehood Day 13 July

TELEPHONE

The international access prefix is ☎00 or + from a mobile. Mobile numbers start with ☎06. Local SIM cards are easy to find.

Getting There & Away

AIR

Montenegro has two international airports – **Tivat** (TIV; ☎032-671 337; www.montenegroairports.com) and **Podgorica** (TGD; ☎020-444 244; www.montenegroairports.com) – although many visitors use Croatia's Dubrovnik Airport, which is very near the border.

Montenegro Airlines (www.montenegroairlines.com) is the national carrier.

LAND

Bus

There's a well-developed bus network linking Montenegro with major cities in the neighbouring countries, including Dubrovnik, Sarajevo, Belgrade, Priština and Shkodra.

Car & Motorcycle

Vehicles need Green Card insurance or insurance must be bought at the border.

ESSENTIAL FOOD & DRINK

Loosen your belt; you're in for a treat. By default, most Montenegrin food is local, fresh and organic, and hence very seasonal. The food on the coast is virtually indistinguishable from Dalmatian cuisine: lots of grilled seafood, garlic, olive oil and Italian dishes. Inland it's much more meaty and Serbian-influenced. The village of Njeguši in the Montenegrin heartland is famous for its *pršut* (prosciutto, air-dried ham) and cheese. Anything with Njeguški in its name is going to be a true Montenegrin dish and stuffed with these goodies.

Eating in Montenegro can be a trial for vegetarians and almost impossible for vegans. Pasta, pizza and salad are the best fallback options.

Here are some local favourites:

- **Riblja čorba** Fish soup, a staple of the coast.
- **Crni rižoto** Black risotto, coloured and flavoured with squid ink.
- **Lignje na žaru** Grilled squid, sometimes stuffed *(punjene)* with cheese and smoke-dried ham.
- **Jagnjetina ispod sača** Lamb cooked (often with potatoes) under a metal lid covered with hot coals.
- **Rakija** Domestic brandy, made from nearly anything. The local favourite is grape-based *loza.*
- **Vranac & Krstač** The most famous indigenous red and white wine varietals (respectively).

Train

At lease one train heads between Bar and Belgrade daily (€21, 17 hours); see www.zpcg.me for details.

COUNTRY FACTS

Area 13,812 sq km

Capital Podgorica

Country Code ☎382

Currency Euro (€)

Emergency ambulance ☎124, fire ☎123, police ☎122

Language Montenegrin

Money ATMs in larger towns

Population 779,000

Visas None for citizens of EU, Canada, USA, Australia, New Zealand and many other countries

SEA

Montenegro Lines (☎030-303 469; www.montenegrolines.net) operates car ferries between Bar and the Italian port of Bari.

Getting Around

BUS

The bus network is extensive and reliable. Buses are usually comfortable and air-conditioned, and are rarely full.

CAR & MOTORCYCLE

Cars drive on the right-hand side and headlights must be kept on at all times. Drivers are recommended to carry an International Driving Permit (IDP) as well as their home country's driving licence. Traffic police are everywhere, so stick to speed limits. Sadly, requests for bribes do happen (especially around the Durmitor area), so don't give the police any excuse to pull you over.

Allow more time than you'd expect for the distances involved, as the terrain will slow you down.

The major international car-hire companies have a presence in various centres.

The Netherlands

Includes ➡

Best Places to Eat

- Greetje (p807)
- De Jong (p817)
- Foodhallen (p806)
- Karaf (p820)
- Café Sjiek (p821)

Best Places to Stay

- King Kong Hostel (p817)
- Dylan (p806)
- Trash Deluxe (p821)
- Hotel New York (p817)
- Hotel de Plataan (p814)

Why Go?

Old and new intertwine in the Netherlands. The legacies of great Dutch artists Rembrandt, Vermeer and Van Gogh, beautiful 17th-century canals, windmills, tulips and quaint brown cafes lit by flickering candles coexist with ground-breaking contemporary architecture, cutting-edge fashion, homewares, design and food scenes, phenomenal nightlife and a progressive mindset.

Much of the Netherlands is famously below sea level and the pancake-flat landscape offers idyllic cycling. Locals live on bicycles and you can too. Rental outlets are ubiquitous throughout the country, which is crisscrossed with dedicated cycling paths. Allow plenty of time to revel in the magical, multifaceted capital Amsterdam, to venture further afield to charming canal-laced towns such as Leiden and Delft, and to check out Dutch cities like exquisite Maastricht, with its city walls, ancient churches and grand squares, and the pulsing port city of Rotterdam, currently undergoing an urban renaissance. It's a very big small country.

When to Go

Amsterdam

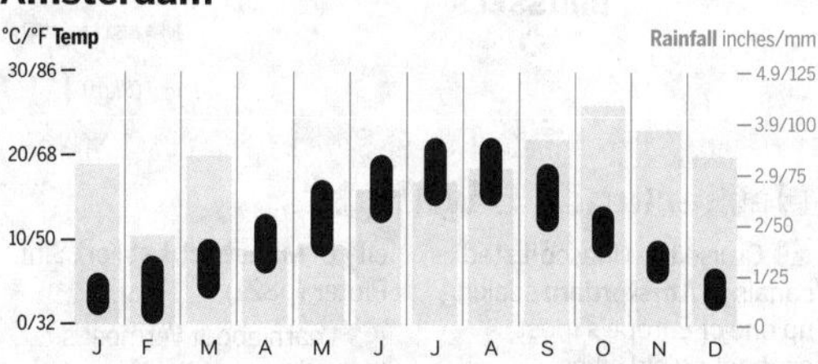

Mar–May Colour explodes as billions of bulbs bloom.

Jul Mild summer temps and long daylight hours keep you outside cycling and drinking.

Dec–Feb When the canals freeze, the Dutch passion for ice skating is on display nationwide.

Netherlands Highlights

1. Cruise the Unesco-listed canals of **Amsterdam** soaking up one of Europe's most enchanting old cities.

2. Marvel at the astonishing **Markthal Rotterdam** (p818), an architectural highlight of the Netherlands' hip-and-happening 'second city'.

3. Explore the centuries-old tunnels below the resplendent city of **Maastricht** at Fort Sint Pieter (p821).

4. Learn about Vermeer's life and work at the **Vermeer Centrum Delft** (p814).

5. Discover the tree-lined boulevards, classy museums and palatial Binnenhof buildings of **Den Haag** (p812).

6. Delve into the museums in picturesque **Leiden** (p811) and dazzling tulip displays of **Keukenhof Gardens** (p812).

7. Watch windmills twirl and meet the millers at the delightful **Zaanse Schans** (p810).

8. Follow dikes along shimmering canals or tour the tulip fields of the **Randstad** on the world's best network of cycling (p813) routes.

ITINERARIES

One Week

Spend three days canal exploring, museum hopping and cafe crawling in **Amsterdam**. Work your way through the ancient towns of the **Randstad** and the contemporary vibe of **Rotterdam**, and save a day for the grandeur of **Maastricht**.

Two Weeks

Allow four days for Amsterdam's many delights, plus a day trip to the old towns of the north, and a day or two exploring some of the region's smaller towns. Then add a day each at beautiful **Delft**, regal **Den Haag** (The Hague), student-filled **Utrecht** and buzzing **Rotterdam**. Finish off with two days in historic Maastricht.

AMSTERDAM

☎020 / POP 811,185

World Heritage–listed canals lined by gabled houses, candlelit cafes, whirring bicycles, lush parks, monumental museums, colourful markets, diverse dining, quirky shopping and legendary nightlife make the free-spirited Dutch capital one of Europe's great cities.

Amsterdam has been a liberal place since the Netherlands' Golden Age, when it was at the forefront of European art and trade. Centuries later, in the 1960s, it again led the pack – this time in the principles of tolerance, with broad-minded views on drugs and same-sex relationships taking centre stage.

Explore its many worlds-within-worlds, where nothing ever seems the same twice.

Sights

Amsterdam is compact and you can roam the city on foot, but there's also an excellent public transport network.

City Centre

Crowned by the **Royal Palace** (Koninklijk Paleis; Map p802; ☎620 40 60; www.paleisamsterdam.nl; Dam; adult/child €10/free; ⏲11am-5pm; 🚋4/9/16/24 Dam), the square that puts the 'Dam' in Amsterdam anchors the city's oldest quarter, which is also home to its infamous Red Light District.

Begijnhof HISTORIC BUILDING

(Map p802; ☎622 19 18; www.begijnhofamsterdam.nl; off Gedempte Begijnensloot; ⏲9am-5pm; 🚋1/2/5/13/17 Spui) **FREE** This enclosed former convent dates from the early 14th century. It's a surreal oasis of peace, with tiny houses and postage-stamp gardens around a well-kept courtyard. The Beguines were a Catholic order of unmarried or widowed women who cared for the elderly and lived a religious life without taking monastic vows. The last true Beguine died in 1971.

Canal Ring

Amsterdam's Canal Ring was built during the 17th-century after the seafaring port grew beyond its medieval walls, and authorities devised a ground-breaking expansion plan.

Wandering here amid architectural treasures and their reflections on the narrow waters of the Prinsengracht, Keizersgracht and Herengracht can cause days to vanish.

★ **Anne Frank Huis** MUSEUM

(☎556 71 00; www.annefrank.org; Prinsengracht 267; adult/child €9/4.50; ⏲9am-9pm, hours vary seasonally; 🚋13/14/17 Westermarkt) The Anne Frank Huis draws almost one million visitors annually (prepurchase tickets online to minimise the queues). With its reconstruction of Anne's melancholy bedroom and her actual diary – sitting alone in its glass case, filled with sunnily optimistic writing tempered by quiet despair – it's a powerful experience.

The focus of the museum is the *achterhuis* (rear house), also known as the **Secret Annexe**, a dark and airless space where the Franks and others observed complete silence during the daytime, outgrew their clothes, pasted photos of Hollywood stars on the walls and read Dickens, before being mysteriously betrayed and sent to their deaths. Opening hours vary according to the season.

Museumplein

Amsterdam's big three museums fan out around the grassy expanse of Museumplein, in the Old South neighbourhood.

★ **Van Gogh Museum** MUSEUM

(Map p804; ☎570 52 00; www.vangoghmuseum.nl; Paulus Potterstraat 7; adult/child €15/free,

Central Amsterdam

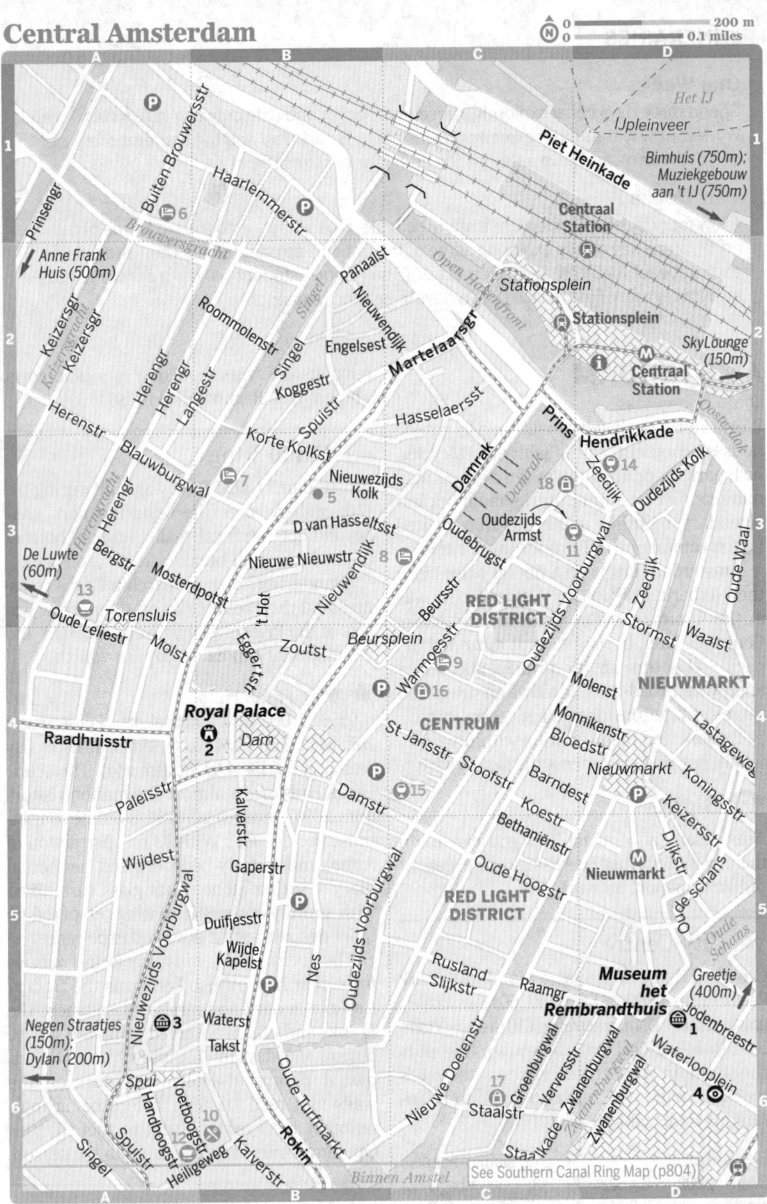

audioguide €5; ⏰9am-6pm Sat-Thu, to 10pm Fri; 📶; 🚋2/3/5/12 Van Baerlestraat) Framed by a gleaming new glass entrance hall, the world's largest Van Gogh collection offers a superb line-up of masterworks. Trace the artist's life from his tentative start through his giddy-coloured sunflower phase, and on to the black cloud that descended over him and his work. There are also paintings by contemporaries Gauguin, Toulouse-Lautrec, Monet and Bernard.

Queues can be huge; pre-booked e-tickets and discount cards expedite the process

Central Amsterdam

Top Sights

1 Museum het Rembrandthuis D6
2 Royal Palace B4

Sights

3 Begijnhof A6
4 Waterlooplein Flea Market D6

Activities, Courses & Tours

5 Yellow Bike B3

Sleeping

6 Frederic Rentabike A1
7 Hotel Brouwer B3
8 Hotel The Exchange C3
9 St Christopher's at the Winston C4

Eating

10 Vleminckx B6

Drinking & Nightlife

11 Brouwerij De Prael C3
12 Dampkring A6
13 Grey Area A3
14 In 't Aepjen D3
15 Wynand Fockink C4

Shopping

16 Condomerie Het Gulden Vlies C4
17 Droog C6
18 Kokopelli C3

with fast-track entry. Opening hours vary seasonally.

★**Rijksmuseum** MUSEUM

(National Museum; Map p804; ☎900 07 45; www.rijksmuseum.nl; Museumstraat 1; adult/child €17.50/free; ⊙9am-5pm; 🚊2/5 Hobbemastraat) The Rijksmuseum is the Netherlands' premier art trove, splashing Rembrandts, Vermeers and 7500 other masterpieces over 1.5km of galleries. To avoid the biggest crowds, come after 3pm. Or prebook tickets online, which provides fast-track entry.

The Golden Age works are the highlight. Feast your eyes on still lifes, gentlemen in ruffled collars and landscapes bathed in pale yellow light. Rembrandt's *The Night Watch* (1642) takes pride of place.

Initially titled *Company of Frans Banning Cocq* (the militia's leader), the name *The Night Watch* was bestowed years later due to a layer of grime that gave the impression it was evening. Other must-sees are the Delftware (blue-and-white pottery), intricately detailed dolls' houses and the brand-new Asian Pavilion. The sculpture-studded gardens around the exterior are free to visit.

Stedelijk Museum MUSEUM

(Map p804; ☎573 29 11; www.stedelijk.nl; Museumplein 10; adult/child €15/free, audio guide €5; ⊙10am-6pm Fri-Wed, to 10pm Thu; 📶; 🚊2/3/5/12 Van Baerlestraat) Built in 1895 to a neo-Renaissance design by AM Weissman, the Stedelijk Museum is the permanent home of the National Museum of Modern Art. Amassed by postwar curator Willem Sandberg, the modern classics here are among the world's most admired. The permanent collection includes all the blue chips of 19th- and 20th-century painting – Monet, Picasso and Chagall among them – as well as sculptures by Rodin, abstracts by Mondrian and Kandinsky, and much, much more.

Vondelpark PARK

(Map p804; www.vondelpark.nl; 🚊2/5 Hobbemastraat) FREE The lush urban idyll of the Vondelpark is one of Amsterdam's most magical places – sprawling, English-style gardens, with ponds, lawns, footbridges and winding footpaths. On a sunny day, an open-air party atmosphere ensues when tourists, lovers, cyclists, in-line skaters, pram-pushing parents, cartwheeling children, football-kicking teenagers, spliff-sharing friends and champagne-swilling picnickers all come out to play.

De Pijp

Immediately south of the Canal Ring, villagey De Pijp is dubbed Amsterdam's 'Latin Quarter'. Increasingly hip cafes, restaurants and bars spill out around its colourful street market, Albert Cuypmarkt (p808).

Heineken Experience BREWERY

(Map p804; ☎523 94 35; www.heinekenexperience.com; Stadhouderskade 78; adult/child €18/12.50; ⊙10.30am-9pm Jul & Aug, 11am-7.30pm Mon-Thu, 10.30am-9pm Fri-Sun Sep-Jun; 🚊16/24 Stadhouderskade) On the site of the company's old brewery, the crowning glory of this self-guided 'Experience' (samples aside) is a multimedia exhibit where you 'become' a beer by getting shaken up, sprayed with water and subjected to heat. True beer connoisseurs will shudder, but it's a lot of fun. Admission includes a 15-minute shuttle boat ride to the Heineken Brand Store near Rembrandtplein. Prebooking tickets online saves you €2 on the entry fee and allows you to skip the ticket queues.

Southern Canal Ring

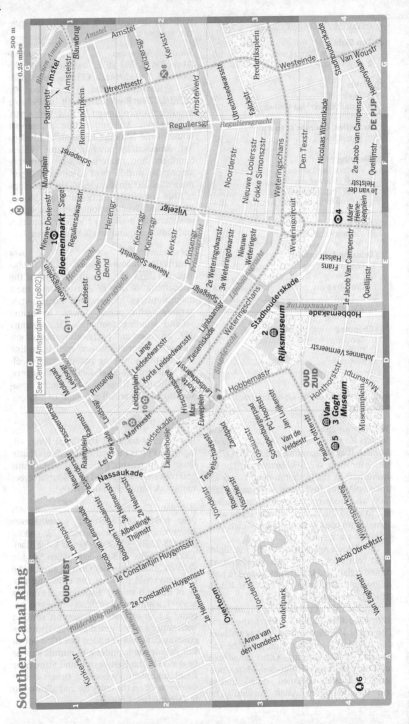

See Central Amsterdam Map (p802)

1 Bloemenmarkt
2 Rijksmuseum
3 Van Gogh Museum
4
5
6
7
8
9
10
11

OUD-WEST
OUD ZUID
DE PIJP
Golden Bend
Vondelpark
Leidsebosje
Museumplein
Leidseplein
Max Euweplein
Rembrandtplein
Muntplein
Frederiksplein
Weteringcircuit
Amstelveld
Marie Heinekenplein
Koningsplein
Raamplein
Overtoom
Nassaukade
Stadhouderskade
Vijzelgr
Herengracht
Keizersgracht
Prinsengracht
Singelgracht
Lijnbaansgracht
Leidsegracht
Reguliersgracht
Bilderdijkgracht
Jacob van Lennepkanaal
Boerenwetering
Binnen Amstel
Amstel

Southern Canal Ring

Top Sights

1	Bloemenmarkt	E1
2	Rijksmuseum	D3
3	Van Gogh Museum	C4

Sights

4	Heineken Experience	E4
5	Stedelijk Museum	C4
6	Vondelpark	A4

Activities, Courses & Tours

7	Blue Boat Company	D3

Eating

8	Tempo Doeloe	G2

Entertainment

9	Melkweg	C2
10	Uitburo	D2

Shopping

11	Young Designers United	D1

Nieuwmarkt & Plantage

The streets around the Rembrandt House are prime wandering territory, offering a vibrant mix of old Amsterdam, canals and quirky shops and cafes.

★ Museum het Rembrandthuis MUSEUM
(Rembrandt House Museum; Map p802; ☎520 04 00; www.rembrandthuis.nl; Jodenbreestraat 4; adult/child €12.50/4; ⏰10am-6pm; 🚋9/14 Waterlooplein) You almost expect to find the master himself at the Museum het Rembrandthuis, where Rembrandt van Rijn ran the Netherlands' largest painting studio, only to lose the lot when profligacy set in, enemies swooped and bankruptcy came a-knocking. The museum has scores of etchings and sketches. Ask for the free audio guide at the entrance. You can buy advance tickets online, though it's not as vital here as at some of the other big museums. There's also a mind-boggling collection of Rembrandt's possessions: seashells, weaponry, Roman busts and military helmets.

Canal Motorboats BOAT RENTAL
(☎020 422 70 07; www.canalmotorboats.com; Zandhoek 10a; 1st hr €50; ⏰9am-sunset; 🚋48 Barentszplein) This operator has small, electric aluminium boats (maximum six passengers) that are easy to drive (no boat licence required). Staff give you a map and plenty of advice, and will come and rescue you if need be. Credit-card imprint or €150 cash deposit required. Reduced rates after the first hour.

Tours

Amsterdam's **canal boats** (p810) are a relaxing way to tour the town. Avoid steamed-up glass windows by choosing boats with open seating areas, such as **Blue Boat Company** (Map p804; ☎679 13 70; www.blueboat.nl; Stadhouderskade 30; 75-minute tour adult/child €16/8.50; ⏰half-hourly 10am-6pm Mar-Oct, hourly Nov-Feb; 🚋1/2/5 Leidseplein).

Yellow Bike CYCLING
(Map p802; ☎620 69 40; www.yellowbike.nl; Nieuwezijds Kolk 29; bike rental per day €12, city/countryside tours €25/31.50; ⏰9.30am-5pm; 🚋1/2/5/13/17 Nieuwezijds Kolk) The original. Choose from city tours or the longer countryside tour through the pretty Waterland district to the north.

Sleeping

Book ahead for summer and weekends year-round. Many cheaper places cater specifically to party animals with general mayhem around the clock. Others exude refined old-world charm. Wi-fi is near universal but lifts/elevators are not.

St Christopher's at the Winston HOSTEL €€
(Map p802; ☎623 13 80; www.winston.nl; Warmoesstraat 129; dm €38-43, s €95, d €124-144; 📶; 🚋4/9/16/24/25 Dam) This place hops 24/7 with rock 'n' roll rooms and a busy club, bar, beer garden and smoking deck downstairs. En-suite dorms sleep up to eight. Most private rooms are 'art' rooms: local artists were given free rein, with super-edgy (entirely stainless steel) to questionably raunchy results. Rates include breakfast (and ear plugs!).

Hotel Brouwer HOTEL €€
(Map p802; ☎624 63 58; www.hotelbrouwer.nl; Singel 83; s €71-79, d €115-128, tr €148-178; @📶; 🚋1/2/5/13/17 Nieuwezijds Kolk) A bargain-priced (for Amsterdam) favourite, Brouwer has just eight rooms in a house dating back to 1652. Each chamber is named for a Dutch painter and furnished with simplicity, but all have canal views. There's a mix of Delft-blue tiles and early-20th-century decor, plus a tiny lift. Staff dispense friendly advice. Reserve well in advance. Cash only.

RED LIGHT DISTRICT

Just southeast of Centraal Station, on and around the parallel neon-lit canals Oudezijds Voorburgwal and Oudezijds Achterburgwal, the warren of medieval alleyways making up Amsterdam's Red Light District (locally known as De Wallen) is a carnival of vice, seething with skimpily clad prostitutes in brothel windows, raucous bars, haze-filled 'coffeeshops', strip shows, sex shows, mind-boggling museums and shops selling everything from cartoonish condoms to S&M gear and herbal highs.

The area is generally safe, but keep your wits about you and don't photograph or film prostitutes in the windows – out of respect, and to avoid having your camera flung in a canal by the women's enforcers. Seriously.

Hotel The Exchange BOUTIQUE HOTEL €€
(Map p802; ☎523 00 89; www.hoteltheexchange.com; Damrak 50; d 1-/2-/3-/4-/5-star from €93/110/128/162/196; @; 1/2/5/13/17 Nieuwezijds Kolk) The Exchange's 61 rooms have been dressed 'like models' in eye-popping style by students from the Amsterdam Fashion Institute. Anything goes, from oversized button-adorned walls to a Marie Antoinette dress tented over the bed. If you like plain decor, this isn't your place. Rooms range from small and viewless to spacious sanctums, but all have en-suite bathrooms.

Frederic Rentabike HOUSEBOAT €€
(Map p802; ☎624 55 09; www.frederic.nl; Brouwersgracht 78; houseboat from €145; ; 18/21/22 Brouwersstraat) Frederic offers nicely outfitted houseboats on the Prinsengracht, Brouwersgracht and Bloemgracht that are bona fide floating holiday homes with all mod cons. On land, the company also has various rooms and apartments in central locations. (And yes, bikes, too.)

★**Dylan** HOTEL €€€
(☎530 20 10; www.dylanamsterdam.com; Keizersgracht 384; d/ste from €350/500; @; 1/2/5 Spui) Exquisite boutique hotel the Dylan occupies an 18th-century Keizersgracht canal house ensconcing a herringbone-paved, topiary-filled inner courtyard. Bespoke furniture such as silver-leaf and mother-of-pearl drinks cabinets adorn its 40 individually decorated rooms and suites (some duplex). Its Michelin-starred Restaurant Vinkeles also hosts private chef's tables aboard its boat, the *Muze*, as it cruises the canals.

Eating

Amsterdam abounds with eateries. Superb streets for hunting include Utrechtsestraat, near Rembrandtplein; Amstelveenseweg, along the Vondelpark's western edge; and any of the little streets throughout the western canals.

★**Foodhallen** FOOD HALL €
(www.foodhallen.nl; Bellamyplein 51; most dishes €5-15; 11am-8pm Sun-Wed, to 9pm Thu-Sat; 17 Ten Katestraat) Inside the converted tram sheds housing the cultural and design complex De Hallen, this glorious international food hall has 20 stands surrounding an airy open-plan eating area. Some are offshoots of popular Amsterdam eateries, such as the Butcher (burgers) and Wild Moa Pies; look out for De Ballenbar *(bitterballen)*. It's adjacent to the lively street market Ten Katemarkt.

Vleminckx FAST FOOD €
(Map p802; Voetboogstraat 31; fries €2.10-4.10, sauces €0.60; noon-7pm Sun & Mon, 11am-7pm Tue, Wed, Fri & Sat, 11am-9pm Thu; 1/2/5 Koningsplein) This hole-in-the-wall takeaway has drawn the hordes for its monumental *frites* (French fries) since 1887. The standard is smothered in mayonnaise, though you can ask for ketchup, peanut sauce or a variety of spicy toppings.

De Luwte INTERNATIONAL €€
(☎625 85 48; www.restaurantdeluwte.nl; Leliegracht 26; mains €19.50-28.50; 6-11pm; 13/17 Westermarkt) Fabulously designed with a vertical 'living wall' garden and recycled timbers, the star of the show here is the artfully presented, Mediterranean-inspired food: slow-cooked rack of pork with risotto croquettes; cod with creamed pumpkin and truffle polenta with mushroom foam; or the house-specialty black Angus tomahawk steak for two. Great cocktails, too.

Buffet van Odette CAFE €€
(☎423 60 34; www.buffet-amsterdam.nl; Prinsengracht 598; lunch mains €7.50-15.50, dinner €14.50-20.50; kitchen 10am-10pm; ; 7/10 Spiegelgracht) Not a buffet but an airy, white-tiled, sit-down cafe with a beautiful canal-side

terrace, where Odette and Yvette show how good simple cooking can taste when you start with great ingredients and a dash of creativity. Soups, sandwiches, pastas and quiches are mostly organic, with smart little extras like pine nuts or truffle cheese.

★Greetje CONTEMPORARY DUTCH €€€
(☎779 74 50; www.restaurantgreetje.nl; Peperstraat 23-25; mains €23-27; ⏲6-10pm Sun-Fri, to 11pm Sat; 22/34/35/48 Prins Hendrikkade) Using market-fresh organic produce, Greetje resurrects and re-creates traditional Dutch recipes like beet-crusted North Sea cod, Veluwe deer stew with red cabbage and Elstar apple, or roasted Alblasserwaard pheasant with melted duck liver. A good place to start is the two-person Big Beginning, with a sampling of hot and cold starters.

Tempo Doeloe INDONESIAN €€€
(Map p804; ☎625 67 18; www.tempodoeloerestaurant.nl; Utrechtsestraat 75; mains €23.50-38.50, rijsttafel & set menus €28.50-49; ⏲6-11.30pm Mon-Sat; ; 4 Prinsengracht) Consistently ranked among Amsterdam's finest Indonesian restaurants, Tempo Doeloe's setting and service are elegant without being overdone. The same applies to the rijsttafel: a ridiculously overblown affair at many places, here it's a fine sampling of the range of flavours found in the country. Warning: dishes marked 'very hot' are indeed like napalm. The wine list is excellent.

Drinking & Nightlife

In addition to the Medieval Centre and Red Light District, party hotspots include Rembrandtplein and Leidseplein, both awash with bars, clubs, coffeeshops and pubs.

To truly experience the unique Dutch quality of *gezellig* (conviviality/cosiness), head to a history-steeped *bruin café* (brown cafe, ie pub, named for the nicotine-stained walls). Many serve food.

Around town, look out for local (often very potent) organic brews by **Brouwerij 't IJ** (www.brouwerijhetij.nl; Funenkade 7; ⏲2-8pm; 10 Hoogte Kadijk) and **Brouwerij De Prael** (Map p802; ☎408 44 69; http://deprael.nl; Oudezijds Armsteeg 26; ⏲noon-midnight Tue & Wed, to 1am Thu-Sat, to 11pm Sun; 4/9/16/24/25 Centraal Station). Both also have atmospheric pubs.

★In 't Aepjen BROWN CAFE
(Map p802; Zeedijk 1; ⏲noon-1am Mon-Thu, to 3am Fri & Sat; 4/9/16/24 Centraal Station) Candles burn even during the day at this bar based in a mid-16th-century house, which is one of two remaining wooden buildings in the city. The name allegedly comes from the bar's role in the 16th and 17th centuries as a crash pad for sailors from the Far East, who often toted *aapjes* (monkeys) with them.

Wynand Fockink TASTING HOUSE
(Map p802; www.wynand-fockink.nl; Pijlsteeg 31; ⏲3-9pm; 4/9/16/24 Dam) This small tasting house (dating from 1679) serves scores of jenever and liqueurs in an arcade behind Grand Hotel Krasnapolsky. Although there are no seats or stools, it's an intimate place to knock back a shot-glass or two. Guides give an English-language tour of the distillery every Saturday at 2pm (€17.50, reservations not required).

SkyLounge COCKTAIL BAR
(http://doubletree3.hilton.com; Oosterdoksstraat 4; ⏲11am-1am Sun-Thu, to 3am Fri & Sat; 1/2/4/5/9/14/16/24 Centraal Station) An unrivalled 360-degree panorama of Amsterdam extends from the glass-walled SkyLounge on the 11th floor of the DoubleTree Amsterdam Centraal Station hotel – and just gets better when you head out to its vast SkyTerrace, with an outdoor bar and timber decking strewn

DON'T MISS

JORDAAN

A densely populated *volksbuurt* (district for the common people) until to mid-20th century, the intimate Jordaan is now one of Amsterdam's most desirable addresses. The neighbourhood is a pastiche of modest 17th- and 18th-century merchants' houses and humble workers' homes squashed in a grid of tiny lanes peppered with bite-sized cafes and shops. There's a handful of small-scale museums (houseboat museum, tulip museum) but the real pleasure here is simply losing yourself in its charming canal-side backstreets.

GAY AMSTERDAM

Amsterdam's gay scene is one the largest in the world. Hubs include Warmoesstraat and Zeedijk in the Red Light District and Reguliersdwarsstraat in the Southern Canal Ring. **Gay Amsterdam** (www.gayamsterdam.com) lists hotels, bars, clubs and more.

with sofas. Deliberate over more than 500 different cocktails; DJs regularly hit the decks.

Air CLUB
(www.air.nl; Amstelstraat 16-24; ⏲ Thu-Sun, hours vary; 🚋 4/9/14 Rembrandtplein) One of Amsterdam's 'it' clubs, Air has an environmentally friendly design by Dutch designer Marcel Wanders including a unique tiered dance floor. Bonuses include lockers and refillable cards that preclude fussing with change at the bar. The awesome sound system attracts cutting-edge DJs spinning everything from disco to house and techno to hip hop. Dress to impress.

Coffeeshops

In the Netherlands, 'coffeeshops' are where one buys pot (marijuana).

Dampkring COFFEESHOP
(Map p802; www.dampkring-coffeeshop-amsterdam.nl; Handboogstraat 29; ⏲ 10am-1am; 📶; 🚋 1/2/5 Koningsplein) With an interior that resembles a larger-than-life lava lamp, Dampkring is a consistent Cannabis Cup winner, and known for having the most comprehensive menu in town (including details about smell, taste and effect). Its name means the ring of the earth's atmosphere where smaller items combust.

Grey Area COFFEESHOP
(Map p802; www.greyarea.nl; Oude Leliestraat 2; ⏲ noon-8pm; 🚋 1/2/5/13/14/17 Dam) Owned by a couple of laid-back American guys, this tiny shop introduced the extra-sticky, flavoursome 'Double Bubble Gum' weed to the city's smokers. Organic coffee includes free refills.

COFFEESHOP DOS & DON'TS

- ➡ Do ask at the bar for the menu of cannabis-related goods on offer, usually packaged in small bags. You can also buy ready-made joints; most shops offer rolling papers, pipes or bongs to use.
- ➡ Don't light up anywhere besides a coffeeshop without checking that it's OK to do so.
- ➡ Don't use alcohol and tobacco products – these are not permitted in coffeeshops.
- ➡ Don't ask for hard (illegal) drugs.

☆ Entertainment

Find out what's on at **I Amsterdam** (www.iamsterdam.com).

For tickets, including last-minute discounts, head to **Uitburo** (Map p804; ☎ 621 13 11; www.aub.nl; Leidseplein 26; ⏲ 10am-6pm Mon-Wed, Fri & Sat, to 9pm Thu, noon-6pm Sun; 🚋 1/2/5/7/10 Leidseplein).

Melkweg LIVE MUSIC
(Map p804; www.melkweg.nl; Lijnbaansgracht 234a; ⏲ 6pm-1am; 🚋 1/2/5/7/10 Leidseplein) In a former dairy, the nonprofit 'Milky Way' is a dazzling galaxy of diverse music. One night it's electronica, the next reggae or punk, and next heavy metal. Roots, rock and mellow singer-songwriters all get stage time, too. Check out the website for cutting-edge cinema, theatre and multimedia offerings.

Muziekgebouw aan 't IJ CONCERT VENUE
(☎ 788 20 00; www.muziekgebouw.nl; Piet Heinkade 1; tickets free-€33; ⏲ box office noon-6pm Mon-Sat & 90min before performance; 🚋 26 Muziekgebouw) Behind this multidisciplinary performing-arts venue's hi-tech exterior, the dramatically lit main hall has a flexible stage layout and great acoustics. Its jazz stage, **Bimhuis** (☎ 788 21 88; www.bimhuis.nl; Piet Heinkade 3; tickets free-€28; 🚋 26 Muziekgebouw), is more intimate. Under-30s can get €10 tickets at the box office 30 minutes before showtime, or online via http://earlybirds.muziekgebouw.nl. Everyone else should try the **Last Minute Ticket Shop** (www.lastminuteticketshop.nl) for discounts.

🛍 Shopping

The ultimate pleasure of shopping in Amsterdam is discovering some tiny shop selling something you'd find nowhere else. In the Western Canal Ring, the 'nine little streets' making up the **Negen Straatjes** (Nine Streets; www.de9straatjes.nl; 🚋 1/2/5 Spui) are dotted with them.

Markets of just about every description are scattered across the city, including Amsterdam's largest and busiest, De Pijp's **Albert Cuypmarkt** (www.albertcuypmarkt.nl; Albert Cuypstraat, btwn Ferdinand Bolstraat & Van Woustraat; ⏲ 9am-5pm Mon-Sat; 🚋 16/24 Albert Cuypstraat); the **Bloemenmarkt** (Flower Market; Map p804; Singel, btwn Muntplein & Koningsplein; ⏲ 9am-5.30pm Mon-Sat, 11am-5.30pm Sun; 🚋 1/2/5 Koningsplein), a 'floating' flower market (on pilings), with bulbs galore; and **Waterlooplein Flea Market** (Map p802; www.

waterloopleinmarkt.nl; Waterlooplein; ⌚9am-6pm Mon-Sat; 🚋9/14 Waterlooplein).

★**Droog** DESIGN, HOMEWARES
(Map p802; www.droog.com; Staalstraat 7; ⌚11am-6pm Tue-Sun; 🚋4/9/14/16/24 Muntplein) *Droog* means 'dry' in Dutch, and this slick local design house's products are strong on dry wit. You'll find all kinds of smart items you never knew you needed, like super-powerful suction cups. Also here is a gallery space, whimsical blue-and-white cafe, and fairy-tale-inspired courtyard garden that Alice in Wonderland would love, as well as a top-floor apartment (double €275 per night).

Young Designers United CLOTHING
(YDU; Map p804; www.ydu.nl; Keizersgracht 447; ⌚1-6pm Mon, 10am-6pm Tue, Wed, Fri & Sat, 10am-8pm Thu; 🚋1/2/5 Keizersgracht) Racks are rotated regularly at this affordable boutique showcasing young designers working in the Netherlands. You might spot durable basics by Agna K, minimalist knits by Andy ve Eirn, geometric dresses by Fenny Faber and soft, limited-edition knits by Mimoods. Accessorise with YDU's select range of jewellery and bags.

Condomerie Het Gulden Vlies SPECIALTY SHOP
(Map p802; condomerie.com; Warmoesstraat 141; ⌚11am-6pm Mon-Sat, 1-5pm Sun; 🚋4/9/14/16/24 Dam) Perfectly positioned for the Red Light District, this boutique sells condoms in every imaginable size, colour, flavour and design (horned devils, marijuana leaves, Delftware tiles…), along with lubricants and saucy gifts.

Kokopelli SMART SHOP
(Map p802; www.kokopelli.nl; Warmoesstraat 12; ⌚11am-10pm; 🚋4/9/16/24/25 Centraal Station) Were it not for its trade in 'magic truffles' (similar to now-outlawed psilocybin mushrooms aka magic mushrooms) you might swear this large, beautiful space was a fashionable clothing or homewares store. There's a coffee and juice bar and a chill-out lounge area overlooking Damrak.

Information

Tourist Office (VVV; Map p802; ☎702 60 00; www.iamsterdam.nl; Stationsplein 10; ⌚9am-5pm Mon-Sat, to 4pm Sun; 🚋4/9/16/24/25 Centraal Station) Maps, guides and transit passes.

I AMSTERDAM CARD

The **I Amsterdam Card** (www.iamsterdam.com; per 24/48/72hr €47/57/67) provides admission to more than 30 museums, a canal cruise, and discounts at shops, attractions and restaurants. Also includes a GVB transit pass. Available at VVV offices (tourist offices) and some hotels.

Getting There & Away

AIR

Most major airlines serve Schiphol (p823), 18km southwest of the city centre.

BUS

Eurolines connects with all major European capitals. Buses arrive at Amsterdam Duivendrecht train station, 7.5km southeast of the centre, which has an easy metro link to Centraal Station (about a 15-minute trip).

Eurolines' ticket office (www.eurolines.nl; Rokin 38a; ⌚9am-5pm Mon-Sat; 🚋4/9/14/16/24 Dam) is near the Dam.

TRAIN

Amsterdam's main train station is fabled **Centraal Station**, with extensive services to the rest of the country and major European cities.

For domestic destinations, visit the Dutch national train service, **Nederlandse Spoorwegen** (NS; www.ns.nl). **NS International** (www.nsinternational.nl) operates many international services.

Getting Around

TO/FROM THE AIRPORT

Taxi To Amsterdam from Schiphol Airport takes 25 to 45 minutes and costs about €55.

Trains To Centraal Station leave every few minutes, take 15 to 20 minutes, and cost €4/8 per single/return.

BICYCLE

Amsterdam is cycling nirvana. The city has more bicycles (881,000) than residents (811,000). About 80,000 bicycles are stolen each year, so always lock up.

Bike City (☎626 37 21; www.bikecity.nl; Bloemgracht 68-70; bike rental per day from €14; ⌚9am-6pm; 🚋13/14/17 Westermarkt) These black bikes have no advertising on them, so you can free-wheel like a local.

WORTH A TRIP

ZAANSE SCHANS

The working, inhabited village Zaanse Schans functions as an open-air **windmill gallery** (www.dezaanseschans.nl; site free, windmills adult/child €3.50/2; ⏱windmills 10am-5pm Apr-Nov, hours vary Dec-Mar) FREE on the Zaan river. Popular with tourists, its mills are completely authentic and operated with enthusiasm and love. You can explore the windmills at will, seeing the vast moving parts first-hand.

The impressive **Zaans Museum** (☎075-616 28 62; www.zaansmuseum.nl; Schansend 7; adult/child €9/5; ⏱10am-5pm; 📶) shows how wind and water were harnessed.

Trains (€3, 17 minutes, four per hour) run from Amsterdam Centraal Station (direction Alkmaar) to Koog Zaandijk, from where it's a well-signposted 1.5km walk.

BOAT

Canal Bus (☎217 05 00; www.canal.nl; Weteringschans 26; day pass adult/child €22/11; ⏱10am-6pm; 📶; 🚊1/2/5 Leidseplein) Offers a unique hop-on, hop-off service, with docks around the city near big museums and attractions.

PUBLIC TRANSPORT

Public transport in Amsterdam uses the OV-chipkaart. Rides cost €2.90 when bought on board. Unlimited-ride passes are available for one to seven days (€7.50 to €32) and are valid on trams, most buses and the metro.

GVB Information Office (www.gvb.nl; Stationsplein 10; ⏱7am-9pm Mon-Fri, 8am-9pm Sat & Sun; 🚊1/2/4/5/9/14/16/24 Centraal Station) Amsterdam's local transit authority, GVB, has an information office where you can get tickets, maps and the like. It's across the tram tracks from Centraal Station's main entrance.

TAXI

Amsterdam taxis are expensive, even over short journeys. Try **Taxicentrale Amsterdam** (TCA; ☎777 77 77; www.tcataxi.nl).

THE RANDSTAD

One of the most densely populated places on the planet, the Randstad stretches from Amsterdam to Rotterdam and is crammed with classic Dutch towns and cities such as Den Haag, Utrecht, Leiden and Delft. A cycling network links the towns amid tulip fields.

Haarlem

☎023 / POP 150,000

Just 15 minutes by train from Amsterdam, Haarlem's canals and cobblestone streets filled with gabled buildings, grand churches, museums, cosy bars, good restaurants and antique shops draw scores of day trippers.

Sights

Haarlem's centre radiates out from the **Grote Markt**. The **Town Hall** (Grote Markt 2) is worth a look, as is the cathedral, **Grote Kerk van St Bavo** (www.bavo.nl; Oude Groenmarkt 22; adult/child €2.50/1.25; ⏱10am-5pm Mon-Sat).

Frans Hals Museum GALLERY

(www.franshalsmuseum.nl; Groot Heiligland 62; adult/child €15.50/free; ⏱11am-5pm Tue-Sat, from noon Sun; 📶) A short stroll south of Grote Markt, the Frans Hals Museum is a must for anyone interested in the Dutch Masters. Kept in a poorhouse where Hals spent his final years, the collection focuses on the 17th-century Haarlem School; its pride and joy are eight group portraits of the Civic Guard that reveal Hals' exceptional attention to mood and psychological tone. Look out for works by other greats such as Pieter Brueghel the Younger and Jacob van Ruysdael.

Eating & Drinking

Restaurants line Schagchelstraat, while cafes cluster along Lange Veerstraat, and around the Grote Markt. The Saturday morning market here is one of the Netherlands' best; there's a smaller market on Monday.

De Haerlemsche Vlaamse FAST FOOD €

(Spekstraat 3; frites €2-3; ⏱11am-6.30pm Mon-Wed & Fri, to 9pm Thu, to 5pm Sat, noon-5pm Sun) Practically on the doorstep of the Grote Kerk, this miniscule *frites* (French fries) joint is a local institution. Line up for its crispy, golden fries made from fresh potatoes and one of a dozen sauces including three kinds of mayonnaise.

★ **Jopenkerk** BREWERY

(www.jopenkerk.nl; Gedempte Voldersgracht 2; ⏱brewery & cafe 10am-1am, restaurant 5.30pm-late Tue-Sat) Haarlem's most atmospheric place to drink and/or dine is this independent brewery inside a stained-glass-windowed, 1910-built church. Enjoy brews like citrusy Hopen, fruity Lente Bier or chocolatey Koyt and classic snacks (*bitterballen*, cheeses) beneath the gleaming vats, or head to the mezzanine for mains (€16.50 to €23.50) made from locally sourced, seasonal ingredients and Jopenkerk's beers, with pairings available.

Getting There & Away

Trains serve Haarlem's stunning art deco station, a 10-minute walk north of the centre. Destinations include:

Amsterdam (€4.10, 15 minutes, five to eight per hour)

Den Haag (€8.20, 35 to 40 minutes, four to six per hour)

Rotterdam (€11.90, 50 minutes, four to six per hour).

Leiden

071 / POP 122,000

Vibrant Leiden is renowned for being Rembrandt's birthplace, the home of the Netherlands' oldest university (and 20,000 students) and the place America's pilgrims raised money to lease the leaky *Mayflower* that took them to the New World in 1620. Beautiful 17th-century buildings line its canals.

Sights

The best way to experience Leiden is by strolling the historic centre, especially along the Rapenburg canal.

Pieterskerk CHURCH

(Pieterskerkhof; admission €2; 11am-6pm) Crowned by its huge steeple, Pieterskerk is often under restoration – a good thing as it has been prone to collapse since it was built in the 14th century.

The precinct here is as old Leiden as you'll get and includes the gabled old **Latin School** (Lokhorststraat 16), which – before it became a commercial building – was graced by a pupil named Rembrandt from 1616 to 1620. Across the plaza, look for the **Gravensteen** (Pieterskerkhof 6), which dates to the 13th century and was once a prison. The gallery facing the plaza was where judges watched executions.

Lakenhal MUSEUM

(www.lakenhal.nl; Oude Singel 32; adult/child €7.50/free; 10am-5pm Tue-Fri, noon-5pm Sat & Sun) Get your Rembrandt fix at the 17th-century Lakenhal, which houses the Municipal Museum, with an assortment of works by old masters, as well as period rooms and temporary exhibits. The 1st floor has been restored to the way it would have looked when Leiden was at the peak of its prosperity.

Rijksmuseum van Oudheden MUSEUM

(National Museum of Antiquities; www.rmo.nl; Rapenburg 28; adult/child €9.50/3; 10am-5pm Tue-Sun;) This museum has a world-class collection of Greek, Roman and Egyptian artefacts, the pride of which is the extraordinary **Temple of Taffeh**, a gift from former Egyptian president Anwar Sadat to the Netherlands for helping to save ancient Egyptian monuments from flood.

Sleeping & Eating

The city-centre canals and narrow old streets teem with choices. Saturday's market sprawls along Nieuwe Rijn.

Nieuw Minerva HOTEL **€€**

(512 63 58; www.nieuwminerva.nl; Boommarkt 23; s/d from €84/88; @) Located in canal-side houses dating from the 16th century, this central hotel has a mix of 40 regular (ie nothing special) and very fun themed rooms, including a room with a bed in which King Lodewijk Bonaparte (aka Louis Bonaparte) slept, the 'room of angels' – a luminous vision of white, the 'Delft blue room', and the Rembrandt room.

Oudt Leyden PANCAKES **€**

(www.oudtleyden.nl; Steenstraat 49; pancakes €8-15, mains €12.50-24.50; 11.30am-9.30pm;) Get ready to meet giant Dutch-style pancakes with creative fillings that make kids and adults alike go wide-eyed. Whether you're feeling savoury (marinated salmon, sour cream and capers), sweet (apple, raisins, almond paste, sugar and cinnamon) or simply adventurous (ginger and bacon!), this welcoming cafe hits the spot every time.

Proeverij de Dames CAFE **€€**

(www.proeverijdedames.nl; Nieuwe Rijn 37; lunch mains €7-9.50, dinner €17-20.50; 10am-10pm) Run by two women with excellent taste, this stylish canal-side cafe/wine bar opening out to a terrace has an excellent range of coffees and wines by the glass. There's a long list of small plates for nibbling, sharing or combining into a meal. House-made baked goods include double-chocolate cake and apple pie.

DON'T MISS

KEUKENHOF GARDENS

One of the Netherlands' top attractions is near Lisse, between Haarlem and Leiden. **Keukenhof** (www.keukenhof.nl; Lisse; adult/child €16/8, parking €6; 8am-7.30pm mid-Mar–mid-May, last entry 6pm;) is the world's largest bulb-flower garden, attracting nearly 800,000 visitors during a season almost as short-lived as the blooms on the millions of multicoloured tulips, daffodils and hyacinths.

Special buses link Keukenhof with Amsterdam's Schiphol airport and Leiden's Centraal Station in season; combination tickets covering entry and transport are available (adult/child €23.50/12.50). Pre-purchase tickets online to help avoid huge queues.

Information

Tourist Office (516 60 00; www.vvvleiden.nl; Stationsweg 41; 7am-7pm Mon-Fri, 10am-4pm Sat, 11am-3pm Sun) Across from the train station.

Getting There & Away

Buses leave from directly in front of Centraal Station.

Train destinations include:

Amsterdam (€8.80, 34 minutes, six per hour)
Den Haag (€3.40, 10 minutes, six per hour)
Schiphol airport (€5.70, 15 minutes, six per hour).

Den Haag

070 / POP 501,000

Flanked by wide, leafy boulevards, Den Haag (The Hague), officially known as 's-Gravenhage (Count's Hedge), is the Dutch seat of government (although Amsterdam is the capital). Embassies and various international courts of justice give the city a worldly air. Around 5km northwest, the long beach at **Scheveningen**, pronounced – if possible – as s'chay-fuhninger, is horribly overdeveloped; the hype tapers off to the south past the harbour.

Sights

★Mauritshuis MUSEUM
(www.mauritshuis.nl; Plein 29; adult/child €14/free, combined ticket with Galerij Prins Willem V €17.50; 1-6pm Mon, 10am-5pm Tue, Wed & Fri-Sun, to 8pm Thu) For a comprehensive introduction to Dutch and Flemish Art, visit the Mauritshuis, a jewel-box of a museum in an old palace and brand-new wing. Almost every work is a masterpiece, among them Vermeer's *Girl with a Pearl Earring*, Rembrandts including a wistful self-portrait from the year of his death, 1669, and *The Anatomy Lesson of Dr Nicolaes Tulp*. A five-minute walk southwest, the newly restored **Galerij Prins Willem V** (www.mauritshuis.nl; Buitenhof 35; adult/child €5/2.50, combined ticket with Mauritshuis €17.50; noon-5pm Tue-Sun) contains 150 old masters (Steen, Rubens, Potter, et al).

★Binnenhof PALACE
The Binnenhof's central courtyard (once used for executions) is surrounded by parliamentary buildings. The splendid 17th-century North Wing is still home to the Upper Chamber of the **Dutch Parliament**. The Lower Chamber formerly met in the ballroom, in the 19th-century wing; it now meets in a modern building on the south side. A highlight of the complex is the restored 13th-century **Ridderzaal** (Knights' Hall). To see the buildings you need to join a tour through visitor organisation **ProDemos** (757 02 00; www.prodemos.nl; Hofweg 1; 45-minute Ridderzaal tour €5, 90-minute government tour €10; 9.30am-5pm Mon-Sat, tours by reservation).

Afterwards, stroll around the **Hofvijver**, where the reflections of the Binnenhof and the Mauritshuis have inspired countless snapshots.

Escher in Het Paleis Museum MUSEUM
(www.escherinhetpaleis.nl; Lange Voorhout 74; adult/child €9/6.50; 11am-5pm Tue-Sun) The Lange Voorhout Palace was once Queen Emma's winter residence. Now it's home to the work of Dutch graphic artist MC Escher. The permanent exhibition features notes, letters, drafts, photos and fully mature works covering Escher's entire career, from his early realism to the later phantasmagoria. There are some imaginative displays, including a virtual reality reconstruction of Escher's impossible buildings.

Gemeentemuseum MUSEUM
(Municipal Museum; www.gemeentemuseum.nl; Stadhouderslaan 41; adult/child €17/free; 10am-5pm Tue-Sun) Admirers of De Stijl, and in particular of Piet Mondrian, mustn't miss the Berlage-designed Gemeentemuseum. It houses a large collection of works by neoplasticist

artists and others from the late 19th century, as well as extensive exhibits of applied arts, costumes and musical instruments. Take tram 17 from CS and HS to the Statenwartier stop.

Sleeping & Eating

Expats on expense accounts support a diverse and thriving cafe culture. The cobbled streets and canals off Denneweg are an excellent place to start wandering.

Corona HOTEL €€
(☎363 79 30; www.corona.nl; Buitenhof 39-42; s €90-120, d €145-175; ❄@📶) In a bullseye location by the Binnenhof, 1km southwest of Centraal Station, this well-run property occupies three 17th-century, recently renovated townhouses. The 36 rooms span a range of styles that mix classic details with modernity. On-site parking (€20) by reservation.

Zebedeüs CAFE €€
(www.zebedeus.nl; Rond de Grote Kerk 8; lunch mains €5-13.50, dinner €16.50-22.50; ⏰11am-10pm) Built right into the walls of the Grote Kerk, this organic cafe serves huge, fresh sandwiches (smoked trout, pulled pork) all day, and creative evening dishes like catfish with pancetta, duck breast with smoked garlic and caramel jus, and mushroom and lentil burgers with celeriac and mash. In fine weather, the best seats are at the chestnut-tree-shaded tables outside.

De Basiliek FRENCH, ITALIAN €€
(☎360 61 44; www.debasiliek.nl; Korte Houtstraat 4a; mains €18.50-22.50, 2-/3-course market menu €27.50/30; ⏰noon-4pm & 6-10pm Mon-Fri, 6-10pm Sat) Behind a smart facade framed by black awnings, classy De Basiliek crafts intricate dishes such as roast hare with red cabbage and figs, or duck cannoli with asparagus and truffle oil. The stellar wine list has full-bottle, half-bottle and by-the-glass options.

Shopping

Grote Markstraat is fittingly the street for large stores. Enticing boutiques line Hoogstraat, Noordeinde, Heulstraat and especially Prinsestraat.

Stanley & Livingstone BOOKS
(☎365 73 06; www.stanley-livingstone.eu; Schoolstraat 21; ⏰hours vary) Quaint travel bookshop.

Information

Tourist Office (VVV; ☎361 88 60; www.denhaag.com; Spui 68; ⏰noon-8pm Mon, 10am-8pm Tue-Fri, 10am-5pm Sat, noon-5pm Sun; 📶) On the ground floor of the public library in the landmark New Toen Hall.

Getting There & Around

A day pass for local trams costs €7.70.

Most trains use Den Haag Centraal Station (CS), but some through trains only stop at Den

THE NETHERLANDS BY BIKE

The Netherlands has more than 32,000km of dedicated bike paths (*fietspaden*), which makes it the most bike-friendly place on the planet. You can crisscross the country on the motorways of cycling: the LF routes. Standing for *landelijke fietsroutes* (long-distance routes), but virtually always simply called LF, they cover approximately 4500km. All are well marked by distinctive green-and-white signs.

The best overall maps are the widely available Falk/VVV *Fietskaart met Knooppuntennetwerk* (cycling network) maps, an easy-to-use series of 20, with keys in English, that blanket the country in 1:50,000 scale, and cost €9. Every bike lane, path and other route is shown, along with distances.

Comprehensive cycling website **Nederland Fietsland** (www.nederlandfietsland.nl) has route planners and downloadable GPS tracks, and lists every bike-rental outlet in the country.

Bike Rentals

Bicycle hire is available all over the Netherlands at hotels, independent rental outlets and train stations. Prices average around €15 per 24 hours. You'll need to show ID and leave a deposit (€50 to €150).

On Trains

You may bring your bicycle onto any train outside peak hours (6.30am to 9am and 4pm to 6.30pm Monday to Friday) as long as there is room. Bicycles require a day pass (*dagkaart fiets*; €6).

Haag HS (Holland Spoor) station just south of the centre.

Services include:

Amsterdam (€11.20, 50 minutes, up to six per hour)

Rotterdam (€4.70, 25 minutes, up to six per hour); also accessible by metro

Schiphol airport (€8.20, 30 minutes, up to six per hour)

Delft

☎015 / POP 99,737

Compact and charming, Delft makes a perfect Dutch day trip. Founded around 1100, it maintains tangible links to its romantic past despite the pressures of modernisation and tourist hordes. Many of the canal-side vistas could be scenes from the *Girl with a Pearl Earring*, the novel about Delft-born Golden Age painter Johannes Vermeer.

Sights

The **town hall** and the **Waag** on the **Grote Markt** are right out of the 17th century.

Oude Kerk CHURCH

(Old Church; www.oudeennieuwekerkdelft.nl; Heilige Geestkerkhof 25; adult/child incl Nieuwe Kerk €6.50/free; ⏲9am-6pm Apr-Oct, 11am-4pm Nov-Mar, closed Sun) The Gothic Oude Kerk, founded in 1246, is a surreal sight: its 75m-high tower leans nearly 2m from the vertical due to subsidence caused by its canal location, hence its nickname Scheve Jan ('Leaning Jan'). One of the tombs inside the church is Vermeer's.

Nieuwe Kerk CHURCH

(New Church; www.oudeennieuwekerkdelft.nl; Markt; adult/child incl Oude Kerk €6.50/free, Nieuwe Kerk tower €3.75/2.25; ⏲9am-6pm Mon-Sat Apr-Oct, hours vary Nov-Mar) Construction on Delft's Nieuwe Kerk began in 1381; it was finally completed in 1655. Amazing views extend from the 108.75m-high tower: after climbing its 376 narrow, spiralling steps you can see as far as Rotterdam and Den Haag on a clear day. It's the resting place of William of Orange (William the Silent), in a mausoleum designed by Hendrick de Keyser.

Municipal Museum het Prinsenhof MUSEUM

(http://prinsenhof-delft.nl; St Agathaplein 1; adult/child €10/5; ⏲11am-5pm, closed Mon Nov-May) Opposite the Oude Kerk, the former convent where William of Orange (William the Silent) was assassinated in 1584 (the bullet hole in the wall is preserved) is now a museum displaying various objects telling the story of the Eighty Years' War with Spain, as well as 17th-century paintings. An artist-in-residence paints interpretations of Dutch masterpieces; relax in the serene gardens.

★**Vermeer Centrum Delft** MUSEUM

(www.vermeerdelft.nl; Voldersgracht 21; adult/child €8/4; ⏲10am-5pm) As the place where Vermeer was born, lived, and worked, Delft is 'Vermeer Central' to many art-history and old-masters enthusiasts. Along with viewing life-sized images of Vermeer's oeuvre, you can tour a replica of Vermeer's studio, which reveals the way the artist approached the use of light and colour in his craft. A 'Vermeer's World' exhibit offers insight into his environment and upbringing, while temporary exhibits show how his work continues to inspire other artists.

De Candelaer STUDIO

(www.candelaer.nl; Kerkstraat 13; ⏲9.30am-6pm Mon-Sat, 11am-6pm Sun) The most central and modest Delftware outfit is de Candelaer, just off the Markt. It has five artists, a few of whom work most days. When it's quiet they'll give you a detailed tour of the manufacturing process.

Sleeping & Eating

★**Hotel de Plataan** BOUTIQUE HOTEL €€

(☎212 60 46; www.hoteldeplataan.nl; Doelenplein 9-11; s/d from €105/115; 📶) On a pretty canal-side square in the old town, this family-run gem has small but elegant standard rooms and wonderfully opulent theme rooms, including the 'Garden of Eden'; the Eastern-style 'Amber', with a Turkish massage shower; or the desert-island 'Tamarinde'. Modesty alert: many en suites are only partially screened from the room. Rates include breakfast and secure parking.

De Visbanken SEAFOOD €

(www.visbanken.nl; Camaretten 2; dishes €2-7; ⏲10am-6pm Mon, 9am-6pm Tue-Fri, 9am-5pm Sat, 10am-5pm Sun) Fish has been sold on this spot since 1342. Display cases in the old open-air pavilion entice with fresh and marinated, smoked and fried fishy treats.

Stads-Koffyhuis CAFE €

(http://stads-koffyhuis.nl; Oude Delft 133; mains €6.25-12.50; ⏲9am-7pm Mon-Fri, to 6pm Sat) The most idyllic seats at this delightful cafe are on the terrace, aboard a barge moored out front. Tuck into award-winning bread rolls, with fillings such as aged artisan Gouda with apple sauce, mustard, fresh figs and walnuts, or house-specialty pancakes, while admiring possibly the best view of the Oude Kerk, just ahead at the end of the canal.

Spijshuis de Dis CONTEMPORARY DUTCH €€
(213 17 82; www.spijshuisdedis.com; Beestenmarkt 36; mains €17-24.50; 5-10pm Tue-Sat;) Fresh fish and amazing soups served in bread bowls take centre stage at this romantic foodie haven, but meat eaters and vegetarians are well catered for, too. Creative starters include smoked, marinated mackerel on sliced apple with horseradish. Don't skip the Dutch pudding served in a wooden shoe.

Drinking & Nightlife

Locus Publicus BROWN CAFE
(www.locuspublicus.nl; Brabantse Turfmarkt 67; 11am-1am Mon-Thu, to 2am Fri & Sat, noon-1am Sun) Cosy little Locus Publicus is filled with cheery locals quaffing their way through the 175-strong beer list. There's great people-watching from the front terrace.

Information

Tourist Office (VVV; 215 40 51; www.delft.nl; Kerkstraat 3; hours vary) Sells excellent walking-tour brochures.

Getting There & Away

The area around the train station is a vast construction site while the lines are moved underground; completion is due in 2016.

Services include:

Amsterdam (€12.70, one hour, up to six per hour)
Den Haag (€2.40, 12 minutes, up to six per hour)
Rotterdam (€3.20, 12 minutes, four per hour)

Rotterdam

010 / POP 619,879

Bold new initiatives, myriad urban regeneration projects, and electrifying dining and nightlife all make Rotterdam one of the most happening cities in Europe right now. The Netherlands' exhilarating 'second city' has a diverse, multi-ethnic community, an absorbing maritime tradition centred on Europe's busiest port, and a wealth of top-class museums.

Central Rotterdam was largely levelled during WWII and spent the following decades rebuilding. It maintains a progressive, perpetual-motion approach to architecture, with an anything-goes philosophy.

Rotterdam is split by the vast Nieuwe Maas shipping channel, which is crossed by a series of tunnels and bridges, notably the dramatic Erasmusbrug. On the north side of the water, the city centre is easily strolled.

Sights & Activities

Rotterdam is a veritable open-air gallery of modern, postmodern and contemporary architecture, with mind-bending late-20th-century icons and eye-popping new additions.

Just 3km southwest of the centre, **Delfshaven**, once the official seaport for the city of Delft, survived the war and retains its historic character. Before leaving the Netherlands for America, the Pilgrims prayed for the last time at the Oude Kerk (p814); they're honoured at local brewery **Stadsbrouwerij De Pelgrim** (www.pelgrimbier.nl; Aelbrechtskolk 12; noon-midnight Wed-Sat). A reconstructed 18th-century **windmill**

MARITIME ROTTERDAM

Harbour tours, museums and exhibits bring Rotterdam's centuries-old maritime heritage to life.

Maritiem Museum Rotterdam (Maritime Museum; www.maritiemmuseum.nl; Leuvehaven 1; adult/child €8.50/4.50; 10am-5pm Tue-Sat, 11am-5pm Sun year-round, plus 10am-5pm Mon Jul & Aug) This comprehensive museum looks at the Netherlands' rich maritime traditions through an array of models that any youngster would love to take into the tub, plus interesting and explanatory displays.

Haven Museum (www.maritiemmuseum.nl; Leuvehaven 50; 10am-4pm Tue-Sat, 11am-4pm Sun) Just south of the Maritime Museum, the Haven Museum comprises all manner of old and historic ships moored in the basin. You can always wander the quays; when the visitor centre is open you can learn more about what's tied up.

Spido (www.spido.nl; Willemsplein 85; adult/child €11.25/6.90) Harbour tours lasting 75 minutes depart from the pier at Leuvehoofd near the Erasmusbrug (by Leuvehaven metro stop). There are up to 10 departures daily in July and August, fewer in the rest of the year.

Rotterdam

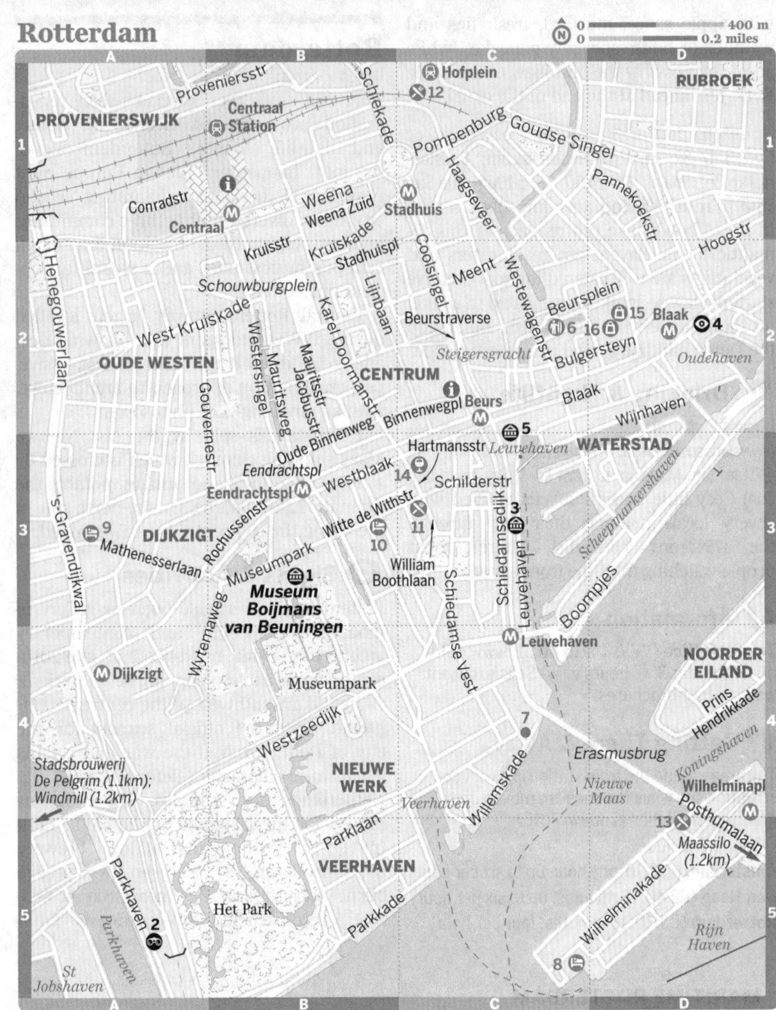

(☎010 477 9181; Voorhaven 210; ⏲1-5pm Wed, 10am-4pm Sat, hours vary) FREE overlooks the water. Take tram 4 or 8, or the metro.

★Museum Boijmans van Beuningen MUSEUM

(www.boijmans.nl; Museumpark 18-20; adult/child €15/free, Wed free; ⏲11am-5pm Tue-Sun) Among Europe's very finest museums, the Museum Boijmans van Beuningen has a permanent collection spanning all eras of Dutch and European art, including superb old masters. Among the highlights are *The Marriage Feast at Cana* by Hieronymus Bosch, the *Three Maries at the Open Sepulchre* by Van Eyck, the minutely detailed *Tower of Babel* by Pieter Brueghel the Elder, and *Portrait of Titus* and *Man in a Red Cap* by Rembrandt.

Overblaak Development NOTABLE BUILDING

Designed by Piet Blom and built from 1978 to 1984, this development near Blaak metro station is marked by its pencil-shaped tower and 'forest' of 45-degree-tilted, cube-shaped apartments on hexagonal pylons. One apartment, the **Kijk-Kubus Museum-House**

Rotterdam

(www.kubuswoning.nl; Overblaak 70; admission €3; 11am-5pm), is open to the public; the **Stayokay Rotterdam** youth hostel occupies the super-sized cube at the southern end.

Euromast VIEWPOINT
(www.euromast.nl; Parkhaven 20; adult/child from €9.25/5.90; 9.30am-10pm Apr-Sep, from 10am Oct-Mar) A 1960-built landmark, the 185m Euromast offers unparalleled 360-degree views of Rotterdam from its 100m-high observation deck. Extra diversions here include a brasserie and summertime abseiling (€52.50). The tower's two suites start from €385 including breakfast.

RiF010 SURFING
(www.rif010.nl; Steigersgracht) From early 2016, surfers, bodyboarders, stand-up paddleboarders and kayakers can take a wild 14-second ride on a naturally purified, barrelling 1.5m-high wave in an inner-city canal. Its water-level beach-house cafe provides up-close views of the action.

Sleeping

★ **King Kong Hostel** BOUTIQUE HOSTEL €
(818 87 78; www.kingkonghostel.com; Witte de Withstraat 74; dm/d/q from €22.50/75/110; @ 📶) Outdoor benches made from salvaged timbers and garden hoses by Sander Bokkinga sit outside King Kong, a design haven on Rotterdam's coolest street. Artist-designed rooms and dorms are filled with vintage and industrial furniture; fab features include hammocks, lockers equipped with device-charging points, a gourmet self-catering kitchen, roof garden and barbecue area, and Netflix.

Hotel Van Walsum HOTEL €€
(436 32 75; www.hotelvanwalsum.nl; Mathenesserlaan 199-201; s/d/tr/q from €70/85/110/125; P 📶) In a group of grand townhouses dating from 1895, but with mod-cons including a lift/elevator, this warm, welcoming family-run hotel is just 10 minutes' walk from the centre, with great public transport connections. Comfortable rooms are decorated in autumnal hues; there's a charming back garden and secure parking (per day €15). Rates include breakfast.

★ **Hotel New York** HISTORIC HOTEL €€€
(439 05 00; www.hotelnewyork.nl; Koninginnenhoofd 1; d €99-270; @ 📶) An art nouveau showpiece, the Holland-America passenger-ship line's former HQ has sweeping vistas, superb dining options including an oyster bar, a barber shop, and a water taxi ferrying guests across the Nieuwe Maas to the city centre. Rooms retain original, painstakingly restored fittings and decor; styles range from standard to timber-panelled suites in the old boardrooms with fireplaces.

Eating

Rotterdam's food scene is booming. The stunning new Markthal Rotterdam (p818) has sit-down and take-away eating options galore.

★ **De Jong** CONTEMPORARY DUTCH €€
(465 79 55; www.restaurantdejong.nl; Rampoortstraat 38; 4-course menu €40; 6-11pm Wed-Sun;) In the hip Station Hofplein complex – the former train station of the disused Hofpleinlijn railway, whose viaduct arches are being transformed into cultural and creative

spaces – adventurous chef Jim De Jong wows diners with surprise four-course menus (meat/fish or vegetarian; no à la carte) made from seasonal produce including herbs and flowers from the restaurant's garden.

Ter Marsch & Co BURGERS, STEAK €€
(www.termarschco.nl; Witte de Withstraat 70; burgers €7-12.50, mains €21-40; ⌚noon-10pm) Butcher shop-turned-bar/restaurant Ter Marsch & Co sizzles up monumental burgers (such as Scottish black Angus, pancetta and truffle mayo) and succulent steaks.

HMB INTERNATIONAL €€
(☎760 06 20; www.hmb-restaurant.nl; Holland Amerika Kade 104; mains €15-17.50, 3-course lunch menu €35, 4-/5-/6-course dinner menu €49/57/65; ⌚noon-3.30pm & 5-10pm Tue-Fri, 5-10pm Sat) On the ground floor of the glitzy 'vertical city' De Rotterdam, the Netherlands' largest building, with dazzling views of the Erasmusbrug, chic HMB serves artistically presented contemporary cuisine (veal meatballs with truffled potatoes; foie gras with eel and apple) at impressively reasonable prices. Afterwards, head to the terrace of the building's 7th-floor cocktail bar.

Bazar MIDDLE EASTERN €€
(www.bazarrotterdam.nl; Witte de Withstraat 16; mains €8.50-16; ⌚8am-11pm Mon-Thu, to midnight Fri, 9am-midnight Sat & Sun) Beneath the exotic Hotel Bazar, this lantern-lit, souq-style stalwart dishes up dolmades, couscous, hummus, felafel, kebabs, Turkish pizza, baked feta with mint and parsley, Persian lamb and more. Tables spill onto the pavement terrace.

Drinking & Nightlife

★De Witte Aap BROWN CAFE
(www.dewitteaap.nl; Witte de Withstraat 78; ⌚1pm-4am; 📶) Anchoring this artist-filled 'hood, the fabulous 'White Monkey' has live music on Wednesdays and DJs on Saturdays and is always crowded with locals. The front opens right up and a huge awning keeps inclement weather at bay.

Café LaBru BAR
(http://cafelabru.nl; Hartmansstraat 18a; ⌚2pm-1am Sun-Thu, to 2am Fri & Sat) Hard-to-find whisky, gin, rum, tequila and craft beers are on the menu at this super-cool vintage- and retro-adorned bar.

Maassilo CLUB
(www.maassilo.com; Maashaven Zuidzijde 1-2; ⌚11pm-6am Fri & Sat, hours vary Sun-Thu) Pumpin' club inside a century-old grain silo with a capacity of 6000. Check the agenda to see what party's on when.

Shopping

Brand-name shops and department stores line Lijnbaan, Beursplein and the semi-subterranean Beurstraverse. Alternative shops congregate along Meent and its surrounds, as well as Nieuwemarkt, Pannekoekstraat, Oude Binnenweg and Nieuwe Binnenweg.

★Markthal Rotterdam FOOD & DRINK
(http://markthalrotterdam.nl; Nieuwstraat; ⌚10am-8pm Mon-Thu & Sat, to 9pm Fri, noon-6pm Sun) The Netherlands' inaugural indoor food market hit headlines around the world when it opened in 2014 due to its extraordinary inverted-U-shaped design, with glass-walled apartments arcing over the foodhall's fantastical fruit- and vegetable-muralled ceiling. There's a tantalising array of produce, prepared food and drinks; shops continue downstairs, while the **Blaak** (⌚8am-5pm Tue & Sat) street market unfurls outside twice weekly.

Information

Tourist Office (☎790 01 85; www.rotterdam.info; Coolsingel 197; ⌚9.30am-6pm) Main tourist office; there's a smaller branch at the main train station (Centraal Station; ⌚9am-5.30pm).

Getting There & Away

Completed in 2014, Rotterdam's Centraal Station is an architectural stunner. There are direct services to Brussels and Paris; from late 2016, Eurostar trains linking Amsterdam with London will stop here.

Major services:

Amsterdam via Leiden (€14.80, 65 minutes, five per hour)

Amsterdam high speed (€17.10, 42 minutes, two per hour)

Schiphol airport (€11.90–€14.20, 20 to 50 minutes, five per hour)

Utrecht (€10.10, 40 minutes, four per hour)

Getting Around

Rotterdam's trams, buses and metro are operated by **RET** (www.ret.nl). Most converge in front of Centraal Station, where there's an **information booth** (⌚7am-10pm) that also sells tickets. Day passes are available for varying durations (one/two/three days €7.10/10.70/14.20). A single-ride ticket purchased from a bus driver or tram conductor costs €3.

Utrecht

030 / POP 330,772

One of the Netherlands' oldest cities, Utrecht retains a beautiful old-world city centre, ringed by unique 13th-century canal wharves below street level. Canal-side streets brim with shops, restaurants and cafes. Its spirited student community of 70,000 is the country's largest.

Utrecht's train station (the country's busiest) and adjoining, maze-like Hoog Catharijne shopping centre are being transformed by a vast construction project (www.nieuwhc.nl), due for completion in 2016.

Sights

Focus your wanderings on the **Domplein** and south along the tree-lined **Oudegracht**. The tourist office has a useful booklet covering Utrecht's myriad small museums, which feature everything from waste water to old trains.

Domtoren HISTORIC BUILDING

(Cathedral Tower; www.domtoren.nl; Domplein; tower tour adult/child €9/5; 11am-4pm) Finished in the 14th century after almost 300 years' construction, the cathedral and its tower are Utrecht's most striking medieval landmarks. In 1674 the North Sea winds reached hurricane force and blew down the cathedral's nave, leaving the tower and transept behind.

The Domtoren is 112m high, with 50 bells. It's worth the tough haul up 465 steps to the top for unbeatable city views; on a clear day you can see Amsterdam.

Centraal Museum MUSEUM

(www.centraalmuseum.nl; Nicolaaskerkhof 10; adult/child €9/4; 11am-5pm Tue-Sun;) The Centraal Museum has a wide-ranging collection. It displays applied arts dating back to the 17th century, as well as paintings by some of the Utrecht School artists and a bit of De Stijl to boot – including the world's most extensive Gerrit Rietveld collection, a dream for all minimalists. There's even a 12th-century Viking longboat that was dug out of the local mud, plus a sumptuous 17th-century dollhouse. Admission includes entry to the **Dick Bruna House** (www.centraalmuseum.nl; Nicolaaskerkhof 10; 11am-5pm Tue-Sun), the studio of author and illustrator Dick Bruna, creator of beloved cartoon rabbit Miffy (Nijntje in Dutch). Entry to the Unesco-recognised house by Utrecht architect Gerrit Rietveld, **Rietveld-Schröderhuis** (reservations 030 236 2310; www.centraalmuseum.nl; Prins Hendriklaan 50; 11am-5pm Wed-Sun), is also included.

WORTH A TRIP

OTHER DUTCH DESTINATIONS WORTH A VISIT

Other Netherlands highlights worth considering for day trips or longer visits:

Alkmaar Although touristy, its cheese ceremony (Fridays from first Friday of April to the first Friday of September) dates from the 17th century.

Deventer A sleepy Hanseatic League town with over 1000 16th- and 17th-century buildings.

Kinderdijk & Dordrecht A good day trip by fast ferry from Rotterdam is to visit Kinderdijk's Unesco-listed windmills then Dordrecht's medieval canals.

Gouda The perfect little Dutch town.

Texel Largest of the Frisian Islands, with endless walks along dune-backed beaches and excellent local seafood.

Sleeping

B&B Utrecht GUESTHOUSE €

(06 5043 4884; www.hostelutrecht.nl; Lucas Bolwerk 4; dm/s/d/tr from €19.50/57.50/65/90; @) Straddling the border between hostel and hotel, this spotless inn in an elegant old building has a communal kitchen and free breakfast, lunch and dinner ingredients. Wi-fi, scanners, printers etc are also free, along with a huge range of musical instruments and DVDs.

Mary K Hotel HOTEL €€

(230 48 88; www.marykhotel.com; Oudegracht 25; d from €120;) A bevy of Utrecht artists decorated the rooms at this ideally situated canal house. Rooms come in three basic sizes ('cosy', medium and large) but no two are alike. All make use of the original 18th-century features and you may find a timber beam running through your bathroom or a stuffed animal snoozing in the rafters.

HOLLAND OR THE NETHERLANDS?

'Holland' is a popular synonym for the Netherlands, yet it only refers to the combined provinces of Noord (North) and Zuid (South) Holland. Amsterdam is Noord-Holland's largest city; Haarlem is the provincial capital. Rotterdam is Zuid-Holland's largest city; Den Haag is its provincial capital. The rest of the country is not Holland, even if locals themselves often make the mistake.

Eating & Drinking

GYS CAFE €

(http://gysutrecht.nl; Voorstraat 77; dishes €7-10; 10am-10pm Mon-Sat;) Organic produce at this bright, airy, design-filled cafe is used in burgers (such as tofu with grilled peppers and hummus, or lamb with pumpkin and mint), sandwiches (such as tempeh with sweet potato, avocado and watercress, or smoked mackerel with beetroot mousse), soups, salads and hot dishes like eggplant schnitzel with salsa, plus tasting platters.

★ **Karaf** INTERNATIONAL €€

(233 11 04; www.restaurantkaraf.nl; Lange Nieuwstraat 71; mains €18-23.50; 5-10pm) Exquisitely presented dishes such as seabass in smoked butter, and Scottish grouse stuffed with Merquez sausage served with mulberry jus are among the reasons Karaf became an instant hit following its recent opening – along with its cool, contemporary Dutch dining room and stunning wine list.

't Oude Pothuys BROWN CAFE

(www.pothuys.nl; Oudegracht 279; 3pm-2am Mon & Tue, noon-3am Wed-Sun) In a darkened barrel-vaulted medieval cellar, this wonderfully cosy pub has nightly music, from jam sessions and emerging bands to funk and soul, jazz and blues, electro and established acts. Enjoy drinks on the canal-side pier.

Information

Tourist Office (VVV; 0900 128 87 32; www.visit-utrecht.com; Domplein 9; noon-5pm Sun & Mon, 10am-5pm Tue-Sat) Sells Domtoren tickets.

Getting There & Away

Utrecht's train station is a major connection point, including for Germany.

Key services:

Amsterdam (€7.40, 30 minutes, four per hour)

Cologne (€29-44, two hours, up to seven direct services per day)

Maastricht (€23.10, two hours, hourly)

Rotterdam (€10.10, 40 minutes, up to four per hour)

THE SOUTH

Actual hills rise on the Netherlands' southern edge, where Belgium and Germany are within range of a tossed wooden shoe. The star here is Maastricht.

Maastricht

043 / POP 121,906

In the far-flung south, the grand old city of Maastricht is well worth the journey from Amsterdam and the pearls of the Ranstad, and you can easily continue to Belgium and Germany.

Among Maastricht's 1650 listed historic buildings, look for Spanish and Roman ruins, French and Belgian architectural twists, splendid food and the cosmopolitan flair that made Maastricht the location for the signing of the namesake treaty, which created the modern EU in 1992.

It's at its most exuberant during **carnaval**, from the Friday before Shrove Tuesday until late Wednesday.

Sights

Maastricht's delights are scattered along both banks of the Maas and reward walkers.

Ringed by grand cafes, museums and churches, the large **Vrijthof** square is a focal point. Intimate **Onze Lieve Vrouweplein** is a cafe-filled square named after its church, which still attracts pilgrims. The arched stone footbridge **Sint Servaasbrug** dates from the 13th-century and links Maastricht's centre with the Wyck district.

Bonnefantenmuseum MUSEUM

(www.bonnefanten.nl; Ave Cèramique 250; adult/child €9/4.50; 11am-5pm Tue-Sun) The Bonnefantenmuseum features a 28m tower that's a local landmark. Designed by Aldo Rossi, the museum opened in 1995, and is well laid out with collections divided into departments, each on its own floor: Old Masters and medieval sculpture are on one floor, contemporary art by Limburg artists on the next, linked by a dramatic sweep of stairs. Make time for the world-class Neuteling collection of medieval art.

Sint Servaasbasiliek CHURCH
(www.sintservaas.nl; basilica free, treasury adult/child €4/free; ⏲10am-4.30pm) FREE Sint Servaasbasiliek, a pastiche of architecture dating from 1000, dominates the Vrijthof. The **Treasury** is filled with gold artwork from the 12th century. Don't miss the **shrine to St Servatius**, a Catholic diplomat who died here in 384, and be sure to duck around the back to the serene cloister **garden**.

★ **Fort Sint Pieter** FORTRESS
(☎325 21 21; www.maastrichtunderground.nl; Luikerweg 80; tour adult/child €6.20/5; ⏲English tours 12.30pm) Much of Maastricht is riddled with defensive tunnels dug into the soft sandstone over the centuries. The best place to see them is Fort Sint Pieter, now restored to its 1701 appearance. This is a really beautiful area, pastoral despite the ominous walls – the fort is an arresting sight looming over the charming hillside – and it's a fine 2km walk south of town.

Sleeping

Stayokay Maastricht HOSTEL €
(☎750 17 90; www.stayokay.com/maastricht; Maasboulevard 101; dm €21.50-37, tw €59-89; @) A vast terrace right on the Maas is the highlight of this stunner of a hostel with 199 beds in dorms and private rooms. It's 1km south of the centre in a sprawling park.

★ **Trash Deluxe** BOUTIQUE HOTEL €€
(☎852 55 00; www.trashdeluxe.nl; Boschstraat 55; d €85-115, f €200;) The name says it all. Across two historic buildings in a fabulous town-centre location (light sleepers should ask for a room at the back), this artist-designed hotel utilises recycled materials (rubber conveyor belts, industrial lighting, packing crates etc) in its ultrastylish, spacious and spotless rooms such as Glass, Metal and Concrete. Service is first rate.

Eating & Drinking

Excellent restaurants are even more common than old fortifications in Maastricht.

Bisschopsmolen BAKERY, CAFE €
(www.bisschopsmolen.nl; Stenebrug 1-3; dishes €4-8.50; ⏲9.30am-5.30pm Tue-Sat, 11am-4.30pm Sun) A working 7th-century water wheel powers a vintage flour mill that supplies its adjoining bakery. Specialties including spelt loaves and *vlaai* (seasonal fruit pies) come direct from the ovens that are on view out the back. You can dine onsite at the cafe, and, if it's not busy, self-tour the mill and see how flour's been made for eons.

★ **Café Sjiek** DUTCH €€
(www.cafesjiek.nl; St Pieterstraat 13; mains €12.50-34.50; ⏲kitchen 5pm-11pm Mon-Fri, noon-11pm Sat & Sun;) Traditional local fare at this cosy spot ranges from *zoervleis* (horse meat) with apple sauce to hearty venison stew, fresh fish and Rommedoe cheese with pear

ESSENTIAL FOOD & DRINK

- **Vlaamse frites** Iconic French fries smothered in mayonnaise or myriad other sauces.
- **Cheese** The Dutch consume almost 19kg of cheese per person per year, nearly two-thirds of which is Gouda. The tastiest hard, rich *oud* (old) varieties have strong, complex flavours.
- **Seafood** Street stalls sell seafood snacks including raw, slightly salted *haring* (herring) cut into bite-sized pieces and served with onion and pickles.
- **Indonesian** The most famous meal is a rijsttafel (rice table): an array of spicy savoury dishes such as braised beef, pork satay and ribs served with rice.
- **Kroketten** Croquettes are crumbed, deep-fried dough balls with various fillings, such as meat-filled *bitterballen*.
- **Beer** Big names like Heineken are ubiquitous; small brewers like De Drie Ringen and Gulpener are the best.
- **Jenever** Dutch gin is made from juniper berries and drunk chilled from a tulip-shaped shot glass. *Jonge* (young) jenever is smooth; strongly flavoured *oude* (old) jenever can be an acquired taste.

syrup and rye bread. It doesn't take reservations and is always busy, but you can wait at the bar. In summer there's a bevy of tables in the park across the street.

Take One BROWN CAFE
(www.takeonebiercafe.nl; Rechtstraat 28; ⏲4pm-2am Thu-Mon) Cramped and narrow from the outside, this eccentric 1930s tavern has well over 100 beers from the most obscure parts of the Benelux. It's run by a husband-and-wife team who help you select the beer most appropriate to your taste. The Bink Blonde is sweet, tangy and very good.

ℹ Information

Tourist Office (VVV; ☎325 21 21; www.vvvmaastricht.nl; Kleine Straat 1; ⏲hours vary) In the 15th-century Dinghuis; offers excellent walking-tour brochures.

ℹ Getting There & Away

Trains to Brussels and Cologne require a change in Liège.

Domestic services include:

Amsterdam (€25, 2½ hours, two per hour)
Utrecht (€23.10, two hours, two per hour)

SURVIVAL GUIDE

ℹ Directory A–Z

ACCOMMODATION

Always book accommodation ahead, especially during high season. The tourist offices operate booking services; when booking for two, make it clear whether you want two single (twin) beds or a double bed.

Many Dutch hotels have steep, perilous stairs but no lifts/elevators, although most top-end and some midrange hotels are exceptions.

Stayokay (www.stayokay.com) is the Dutch hostelling association. A youth-hostel card costs €17.50 at the hostels; nonmembers pay an extra €2.50 per night and after six nights you become a member. The usual HI discounts apply.

BUSINESS HOURS

Banks & government offices 9am to 5pm Monday to Friday
Bars and cafes 11am to 1am
Clubs Mostly 10pm to 4am
Museums Many closed Monday
Post offices 9am to 6pm Monday to Saturday
Restaurants 10am or 11am to 10pm, often with a break between 3pm and 6pm
Shops Noon to 6pm Monday, 9am to 6pm Tuesday, Wednesday, Friday and Saturday (often Sunday too in large cities), to 9pm Thursday; supermarkets to 8pm or 10pm

SLEEPING PRICE RANGES

Prices quoted include private bathrooms unless otherwise stated and are high-season rates. Breakfast is not included unless specified.

€ less than €80

€€ €80 to €160

€€€ more than €160

DISCOUNT CARDS

Museumkaart (Museum Card; www.museumkaart.nl; adult/child €55/30, plus for 1st registration €5) Free and discounted entry to some 400 museums all over the country for one year. Purchase at participating museum ticket counters or at Uitburo ticket shops.

INTERNET RESOURCES

Lonely Planet (www.lonelyplanet.com/the-netherlands)
Netherlands Board of Tourism (www.holland.com)
Windmill Database (www.molendatabase.nl)

LEGAL MATTERS

Drugs are actually illegal in the Netherlands. Possession of soft drugs up to 5g is tolerated but larger amounts can get you jailed. Hard drugs are treated as a serious crime.

Smoking is banned in all public places. In a uniquely Dutch solution, you can still smoke tobacco-free pot in coffeeshops.

MONEY

ATMs

Automatic teller machines proliferate outside banks, inside supermarkets and at train stations.

Credit Cards

Most hotels, restaurants and large stores accept major international cards. Some establishments,

TIPPING

Tipping is not essential as restaurants, hotels, bars etc include a service charge on their bills. A little extra is always welcomed though – anything from rounding up to the nearest euro to adding on 10% of the bill.

COUNTRY FACTS

Area 41,526 sq km

Capital Amsterdam

Country Code ☎31

Currency Euro (€)

Emergency ☎112

Language Dutch, English widespread

Money ATMs common, cash preferred for small purchases

Visas Schengen rules apply

however, including the Dutch railway, don't accept non-European credit cards – check first.

PUBLIC HOLIDAYS

Nieuwjaarsdag New Year's Day
Goede Vrijdag Good Friday
Eerste Paasdag Easter Sunday
Tweede Paasdag Easter Monday
Koningsdag (King's Day) 27 April
Bevrijdingsdag (Liberation Day) 5 May
Hemelvaartsdag Ascension Day
Eerste Pinksterdag Whit Sunday (Pentecost)
Tweede Pinksterdag Whit Monday
Eerste Kerstdag (Christmas Day) 25 December
Tweede Kerstdag (Boxing Day) 26 December

SAFE TRAVEL

The Netherlands is a safe country, but be sensible all the same and *always* lock your bike. Never buy drugs on the street: it's illegal and fatalities can and do occur. And don't light up joints just anywhere – stick to coffeeshops.

TELEPHONE

Country code ☎31
International access code ☎00

Getting There & Away

AIR

Huge **Schiphol airport** (AMS; www.schiphol.nl) is the Netherlands' main international airport. **Rotterdam The Hague Airport** (RTM; www.rotterdamthehagueairport.nl) and budget airline hub **Eindhoven Airport** (EIN; www.eindhovenairport.nl) are small.

LAND

Bus

European bus network **Eurolines** (www.eurolines.com) serves a dozen destinations across the Netherlands including the major cities.

Car & Motorcycle

You'll need the vehicle's registration papers, third-party insurance and an international driver's permit in addition to your domestic licence. The national auto club, **ANWB** (www.anwb.nl), has offices across the country and will provide info if you can show an auto-club card from your home country (eg AAA in the US or AA in the UK).

Train

International train connections are good. All Eurail and Inter-Rail passes are valid on the Dutch national train service, **Nederlandse Spoorwegen** (NS; www.ns.nl).

Many international services are operated by **NS International** (www.nsinternational.nl). In addition, **Thalys** (www.thalys.com) fast trains serve Brussels (where you can connect to the Eurostar) and Paris. From December 2016, direct Eurostar services will link Amsterdam, Schiphol airport and Rotterdam with London.

The high-speed line from Amsterdam (via Schiphol and Rotterdam) speeds travel times to Antwerp (1¼ hours), Brussels (two hours) and Paris (3¼ hours). German ICE high-speed trains run six direct services per day between Amsterdam and Cologne (2½ hours) via Utrecht. Many continue on to Frankfurt (four hours) via Frankfurt airport.

In peak periods, it's wise to reserve seats in advance. By tickets online at **SNCB Europe** (www.b-europe.com).

TRAIN TIPS

Be aware of the following when buying train tickets:

- Only some ticket machines accept cash, and those are coins-only, so you need a pocketful of change.
- Ticket machines that accept plastic will not work with credit and ATM cards without embedded chips (even then, not all international cards will work). The exceptions are a limited number of machines at Schiphol airport and Amsterdam Centraal.
- Ticket windows do not accept credit or ATM cards, but do accept paper euros. Queues are often long and there is a surcharge for using a ticket window.
- To buy domestic and international train tickets online with an international credit card, visit **SNCB Europe** (www.b-europe.com). You may need to print a paper copy of the ticket pdf.

SEA

Several companies operate car/passenger ferries between the Netherlands and the UK:

DFDS Seaways (www.dfdsseaways.co.uk) DFDS Seaways has overnight sailings (15 hours) between Newcastle and IJmuiden, 30km northwest of Amsterdam, linked to Amsterdam by bus (one-way €6, 40 minutes).

P&O Ferries (www.poferries.com) P&O Ferries operates an overnight ferry every evening (11¾ hours) between Hull and Europoort, 39km west of central Rotterdam. Book bus tickets (€10, 40 minutes) to/from the city when you reserve your berth.

Stena Line (www.stenaline.co.uk) Stena Line has overnight crossings between Harwich and Hoek van Holland, 31km northwest of Rotterdam, linked to central Rotterdam by train (€5.50, 30 minutes).

Getting Around

BOAT

Ferries connect the mainland with the five Frisian Islands, including Texel. Other ferries span the Westerschelde in the south of Zeeland, providing road links to the bit of the Netherlands south of here as well as to Belgium. These are popular with people using the Zeebrugge ferry terminal and run frequently year-round.

CAR & MOTORCYCLE

Hire

You must be at least 23 years of age to hire a car in the Netherlands. Outside Amsterdam, car-hire companies can be in inconvenient locations if you're arriving by train.

Road Rules

Traffic travels on the right and the minimum driving age is 18 for vehicles and 16 for motorcycles. Seat belts are required and children under 12 must ride in the back if there's room. Trams always have the right of way and, if turning right, bikes have priority.

Speed limits are generally 50km/h in built-up areas, 80km/h in the country, 100km/h on major through-roads, and 130km/h on freeways (variations are clearly indicated). Hidden speeding cameras are everywhere and they will find you through your rental car company.

LOCAL TRANSPORT

National public transport info is available in English at **9292** (www.9292ov.nl), which has an excellent smartphone app.

The universal form of transport payment in the Netherlands is the **OV-chipkaart** (www.ov-chipkaart.nl). Visitors can buy a disposable card, good for one hour, from specified vending machines in stations, at ticket windows or on board where available (correct change required). You can also buy disposable OV-chipkaarts good for unlimited use for one or more days and this is often the most convenient option, and cheaper than single-use chip cards.

Fares are also lower with refillable 'anonymous' OV-chipkaarts (€7.50 plus €3 if bought at a ticket window). These store the value of your payment and deduct the cost of trips as you use them. Purchase cards and top up at machines, newsagents or ticket windows.

When you enter *and* exit a bus, tram or train, you hold the card against a reader at the doors or station gates. The system then calculates your fare and deducts it from the card.

TRAIN

The train network is run by NS. First-class sections are barely different from 2nd-class areas, but they are less crowded. Trains are fast and frequent and serve most places of interest. Distances are short. The high-speed line between Schiphol and Rotterdam Centraal requires a 1st-/2nd-class supplement of €3/2.30. Most train stations have lockers operated by credit cards (average cost €5).

Tickets

Enkele reis One way; you can break your journey along the direct route.

Dagretour Day return; costs the same as two one-way tickets.

Dagkaart Day pass (€50.80); allows unlimited train travel throughout the country. Only good value if you're planning to spend the day on the train.

EATING PRICE RANGES

The following price categories are for the cost of a main course:

€ less than €12

€€ €12 to €25

€€€ more than €25

CONNECTIONS

Train connections to neighbouring countries are excellent. Amsterdam is linked to Cologne, Brussels and Paris by high-speed trains. From late 2016, Amsterdam and Rotterdam will have direct Eurostar services to/from London. Maastricht is right on the Belgian and German borders, with connections to Cologne and Brussels.

Norway

Includes ➡

Best Places to Eat

- Torget Fish Market (p834)
- Markveien Mat & Vinhus (p830)
- Renaa Matbaren (p836)
- Emma's Under (p841)
- Kasbah (p829)

Best Places to Stay

- The Thief (p829)
- Svinøya Rorbuer (p839)
- Hotel Park (p834)
- Westerås Gard (p837)
- Rica Ishavshotel (p841)

Why Go?

Norway is a once-in-a-lifetime destination and the essence of its appeal is remarkably simple: this is one of the most beautiful countries on earth. Impossibly steep-sided fjords cut deep gashes into the interior, grand and glorious glaciers snake down from Europe's largest ice fields, and the appeal of the Arctic is primeval. The counterpoint to so much natural beauty is found in the country's vibrant cultural life. Norwegian cities are cosmopolitan and brimful of architecture that showcases the famous Scandinavian flair for design. Yes, Norway is one of the most expensive countries on the planet, but it'll pay you back with never-to-be-forgotten experiences many times over.

When to Go

Oslo

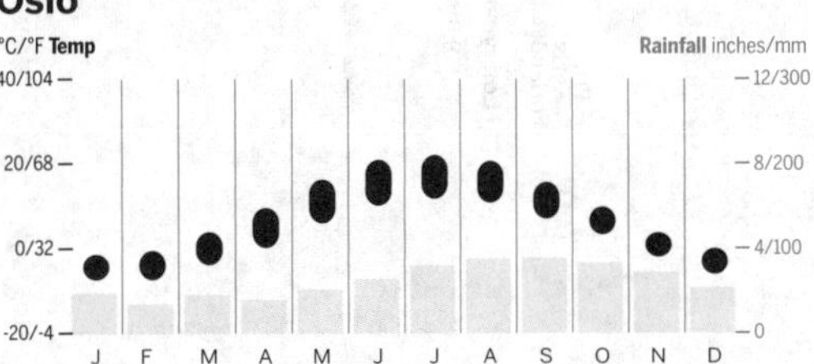

Mar There's still plenty of snow, but enough daylight to enjoy winter sports.

Jun–Aug Summers are short but intense, and the White Nights beyond the Arctic Circle magical.

Sep The stunning colours of the autumn season make this prime hiking time up north.

Norway Highlights

1. Explore Norway's No 1 fjord on the ferry from Hellesylt to **Geiranger** (p837).
2. Head for the Arctic and arguably Europe's most beautiful archipelago, the **Lofoten Islands** (p839).
3. Linger amid enchanted Bryggen buildings along the waterfront of **Bergen** (p832).
4. Hop aboard the **Oslo to Bergen railway** (p835), Norway's most spectacular rail trip.
5. Hike high above Lysefjord to Norway's most breathtaking lookout at **Pulpit Rock** (p835).
6. Journey up Norway's peerless coast from Bergen to Kirkenes aboard the **Hurtigruten coastal ferry** (p844).

7 Experience one of Norway's liveliest towns and go dog-sledding in winter at **Tromsø** (p840).

8 Enjoy the capital's cosmopolitan charms and the stunning Opera House in **Oslo** (p828).

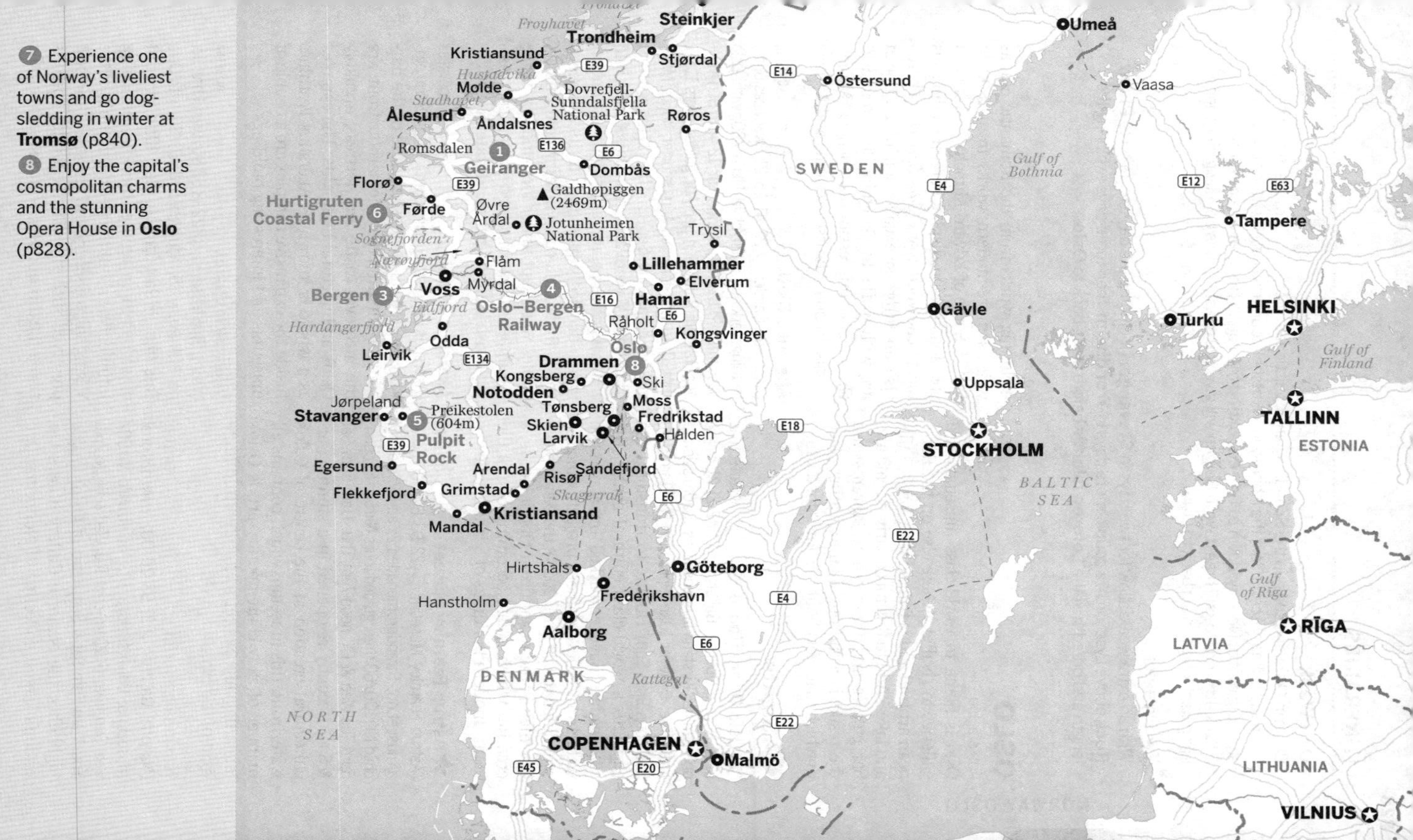

ITINERARIES

One Week

Begin in **Oslo** and soak up the Scandinavian sophistication of the city's museums, waterfront and culinary scene. Join the Norway in a Nutshell tour, travelling by train across the stunning roof of Norway, down to **Sognefjorden** then on to **Bergen** via **Gudvangen**, **Stalheim** and **Voss**. Three days in Bergen will give you a taste of this beguiling city, then jump back on the train back to Oslo.

Two Weeks

With an extra week, allow for two days in **Stavanger** (including the day excursion to **Pulpit Rock** above Lysefjord), a couple more days in **Trondheim**, then three days exploring the length and breadth of the **Lofoten Islands** before flying back to **Oslo**.

OSLO

POP 613,300

Oslo is home to world-class museums and galleries to rival anywhere else on the European art trail and is fringed with forests, hills and lakes. Add to this mix a thriving cafe and bar culture and top-notch restaurants and the result is a thoroughly intoxicating place in which to forget about the fjords for a while.

Sights

★Oslo Opera House ARCHITECTURE

(Den Norske Opera & Ballett; ☎21 42 21 21; www.operaen.no; Kirsten Flagstads plass 1; admission to foyer free; ⊙foyer 10am-9pm Mon-Fri, 11am-9pm Sat, noon-9pm Sun) Hoping to transform the city into a world-class cultural centre, the city leaders have embarked on a massive waterfront redevelopment project (which is scheduled to last until 2020), the centrepiece of which is the magnificent Opera House, a creation which is fast becoming one of the iconic modern buildings of Scandinavia.

★Astrup Fearnley Museet GALLERY

(Astrup Fearnley Museum; ☎22 93 60 60; www.afmuseet.no; Strandpromenaden 2; adult/student/child Nkr100/60/free, guided tours Nkr50; ⊙noon-5pm Tue-Wed & Fri, noon-7pm Thu, 11am-5pm Sat & Sun) Recently re-opened in a stunning architectural creation at the centre of Oslo's waterfront, this museum, which contains all manner of zany contemporary art, is Oslo's latest flagship project and the artistic highlight of the city.

Nasjonalgalleriet GALLERY

(National Gallery; ☎21 98 20 00; www.nasjonalmuseet.no; Universitetsgata 13; adult/child Nkr50/free, Sun free; ⊙10am-6pm Tue, Wed & Fri, to 7pm Thu, 11am-5pm Sat & Sun) One of Oslo's major highlights, the National Gallery houses the nation's largest collection of Norwegian art, including works from the Romantic era, as well as more-modern works from 1800 to WWII. Some of Edvard Munch's best-known creations are on display here, including his most renowned work, *The Scream*. There's also an impressive collection of European art, with works by Gauguin, Picasso and El Greco, and impressionists such as Manet, Degas, Renoir, Matisse, Cézanne and Monet.

Akershus Slott CASTLE

(Akershus Castle; ☎22 41 25 21; www.nasjonalefestningsverk.no; adult/child Nkr70/30, with Oslo pass free; ⊙10am-4pm Mon-Sat, 12-4pm Sun May-Aug, 12-5pm Sat & Sun Sep-Apr, guided tours 11am, 1pm, 3pm mid-Jun–mid-Aug, shorter hours May–mid-Jun & mid-Aug–Sep) In the 17th century, Christian IV renovated Akershus Castle into a Renaissance palace, although the front remains decidedly medieval. In its dungeons you'll find dark cubbyholes where outcast nobles were kept under lock and key, while the upper floors contained sharply contrasting lavish banquet halls and staterooms.

Akershus Festning FORTRESS

(Akershus Fortress; ⊙6am-9pm) FREE Strategically located on the eastern side of the harbour, dominating the Oslo harbourfront, are the medieval castle and fortress, arguably Oslo's architectural highlights. The complex as a whole is known as Akershus Festning. Inside the expansive complex are a couple of museums and interesting buildings.

Vikingskipshuset MUSEUM

(Viking Ship Museum; ☎22 13 52 80; www.khm.uio.no; Huk Aveny 35; adult/child Nkr60/30, with Oslo Pass free; ⊙9am-6pm May-Sep, 10am-4pm rest of year) Even in repose, there is something intimidating about the sleek, dark hulls of the Viking ships *Oseberg* and *Gokstad* – the best preserved such ships in the world. There is also a third boat at the Vikingskipshuet, the

Tune, but only a few boards and fragments remain. This museum is a must for anyone who enjoyed childhood stories of Vikings (so that's everyone).

Munchmuseet GALLERY

(Munch Museum; ☎23 49 35 00; www.munchmuseet.no; Tøyengata 53; adult/child Nkr95/40, with Oslo Pass free; ⏲10am-5pm mid-Jun–Sep, 11am-5pm Wed-Mon rest of year) Fans of Edvard Munch (1863–1944) won't want to miss the Munch Museum, which is dedicated to his life's work and has most of the pieces not contained in the National Gallery. The museum provides a comprehensive look at the artist's work, from dark *(The Sick Child)* to light *(Spring Ploughing)*. With over 1100 paintings, 4500 watercolours and 18,000 prints and sketching books bequeathed to the city by Munch himself, this is a landmark collection.

Tours

Norway in a Nutshell TOUR

(☎81 56 82 22; www.norwaynutshell.com) For the popular Norway in a Nutshell tours, book at tourist offices or at train stations. From Oslo, the typical route includes a rail trip across Hardangervidda to Myrdal, descent to along the dramatic Flåmbanen, a cruise along Nærøyfjorden to Gudvangen, a bus to Voss, a connecting train to Bergen for a short visit, then an overnight return rail trip to Oslo (including a sleeper compartment); the return tour costs Nkr2490. You can also book one-way tours to Bergen (Nkr1630).

Sleeping

★**Oslo Vandrerhjem Central** HOSTEL €

(☎23 10 08 00; www.hihostels.no/oslo.central; Kongens gate 7; from Nkr375; 📶) Slickly-run, this utterly immaculate hostel has plain and functional rooms, a big sociable lounge area, good internet access, lots of travel info and a very central location. All up, Oslo's new youth hostel is great news for budget travellers.

★**Ellingsens Pensjonat** PENSION €€

(☎22 60 03 59; www.ellingsenspensjonat.no; Holtegata 25; s/d from Nkr600/990, without bathroom s/d Nkr550/800, apt s/d Nkr700/1200; 📶) Located in a quiet, pleasant neighbourhood, this homey pension offers one of the best deals in the capital. The building dates from 1890 and many of the original features (high ceilings, rose designs) remain. Rooms are bright, airy and beautifully decorated, with fridges and kettles, and there's a small garden to lounge about in on sunny days.

Cochs Pensjonat PENSION €€

(☎23 33 24 00; www.cochspensjonat.no; Parkveien 25; s/d with kitchenette from Nkr610/840, without bathroom Nkr510/720; 📶) Opened as a guesthouse for bachelors in the 1920s, Cochs has sparsely furnished, clean rooms, some of which have kitchenettes. It's ideally located behind the Royal Palace. The rooms at the back overlooking the Slottsparken are especially spacious. There is a luggage room. The hotel offers a discounted breakfast buffet at a coffee shop around the corner from Nkr42.

★**The Thief** BOUTIQUE HOTEL €€€

(☎24 00 40 00; www.thethief.com; Landgangen 1; d from Nkr2890; 📶🏊) Part of the new waterfront development, The Thief is a world-class hotel (albeit one with a strange name) overlooking the Astrup Fearnley Museum. The hotel's decoration is inspired by the next-door art: there's moving human images in the elevators, gold knitting clocks that don't tell the time, and swish rooms with piles of cushions.

Eating

★**Kasbah** MIDDLE EASTERN €

(☎21 94 90 99; www.thekasbah.no; Kingsogate 1b; mains Nkr90-100, mezes from Nkr42; ⏲11am-1am) Graze on mezes or tuck into a more substantial lunch, including such tummy pleasers as homemade falafels and a vegie couscous soup, at this totally chilled Norwegian-run, Middle-East-flavoured restaurant bursting with colour.

Rust INTERNATIONAL €€

(☎23 62 65 05; www.rustoslo.com; Hegehaugsveien 22; tapas Nkr40-80, mains Nkr129-195; ⏲11am-1am Mon-Sat, noon-midnight Sun) On a small side street lined with cafes and restaurants, Rust is bright, colourful and 100% modern Oslo. It has plenty of outdoor seating and loads of blankets for when it gets cold. Good for a

OTHER TOWNS WORTH A VISIT

Ålesund Art deco architecture and a stunning watery location.

Røros Historic and Unesco World Heritage–listed mining village built of wood.

Lillehammer Pretty ski centre and host of the 1994 Winter Olympics.

Karasjok Spiritual capital of the Sami people in the far Arctic north.

Oslo

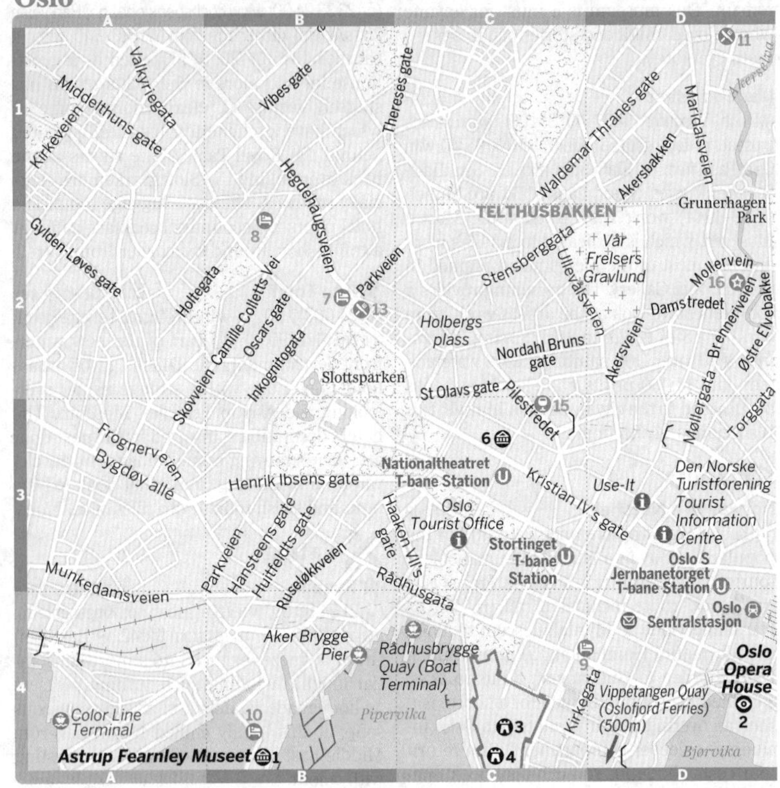

quiet cocktail, hearty salads or some creative tapas late into the night.

★Markveien Mat & Vinhus NORWEGIAN €€€
(☎22 37 22 97; Torvbakkgt 12; mains Nkr240-290, 3 courses Nkr495; ⏲4pm-1.30am Tue-Sun) With a hint of truffle oil or a dash of dill, the cooks at Markveien make Norwegian cooking unforgettable. The restaurant focuses on using local seafood and meat, as well as organic produce, to create its delectable dishes. You shouldn't miss the house specials of either lamb or crayfish.

Drinking & Entertainment

The city's best neighbourhood bar scene is along Thorvald Meyers gate and the surrounding streets in Grünerløkka. The Youngstorget area has some of the most popular places close to the city centre, while the Grønland neighbourhood has a more alternative feel.

★Fuglen COCKTAIL BAR
(www.fuglen.com; Universitetsgaten 2; ⏲7.30am-10pm Mon & Tue, 7.30am-1am Wed & Thu, 7.30am-3am Fri, 11am-3am Sat, 11am-10pm Sun) By day this is a renowned coffee bar, but by night it transforms itself into what is hands down the hippest cocktail bar in town. And if you like the retro decorations and furnishings then why not take some home with you – all the furnishings are for sale!

Bar Boca BAR
(Thorvald Meyers gate 30; ⏲noon-1am Sun-Tue, 11am-2pm Wed & Thu, 11am-3am Fri & Sat) Squeeze into what is quite possibly the smallest bar in Oslo and you'll find that you have slid back in time to the 1960s. It's retro cool and has a cocktail selection as great as its atmosphere.

★Blå JAZZ
(www.blaaoslo.no; Brenneriveien 9c; admission Nkr100-180) It would be a pity to leave Oslo without checking out Blå, which features on

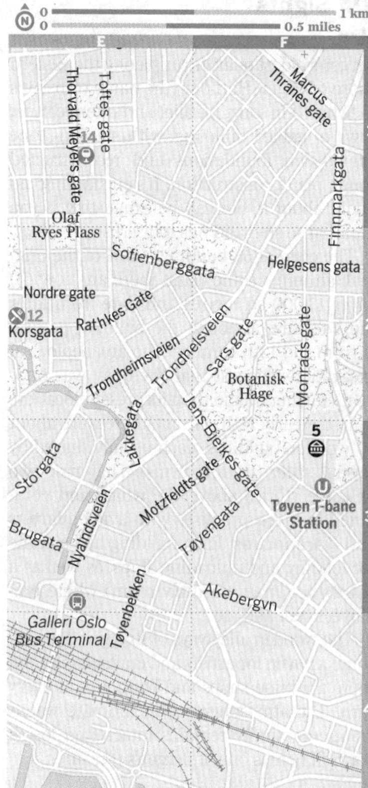

Oslo

Top Sights

1 Astrup Fearnley Museet......B4
2 Oslo Opera House......D4

Sights

3 Akershus Festning......C4
4 Akershus Slott......C4
5 Munchmuseet......F3
6 Nasjonalgalleriet......C3

Sleeping

7 Cochs Pensjonat......B2
8 Ellingsens Pensjonat......B2
9 Oslo Vandrerhjem Central......C4
10 The Thief......B4

Eating

11 Kasbah......D1
12 Markveien Mat & Vinhus......E2
13 Rust......B2

Drinking & Nightlife

14 Bar Boca......E1
15 Fuglen......C3

Entertainment

16 Blå......D2
Oslo Opera House......(see 2)

a global list of 100 great jazz clubs compiled by the savvy editors at the US jazz magazine *Down Beat*. As one editor put it, 'To get in this list means that it's quite the club'.

Oslo Opera House OPERA
(Den Norske Opera & Ballett; www.operaen.no; Kirsten Flagstads plass 1; tickets Nkr100-795; foyer 10am-11pm Mon-Fri, 11am-11pm Sat, noon-10pm Sun) Apart from being one of Norway's most impressive examples of contemporary architecture, Oslo Opera House is also the venue for world-class opera and ballet performances.

Information

Den Norske Turistforening Tourist Information Centre (DNT, Norwegian Mountain Touring Club; www.turistforeningen.no; Storget 3; 10am-5pm Mon-Wed & Fri, to 6pm Thu, to 3pm Sat) Provides information, maps and brochures on hiking in Norway and sells memberships, which include discounted rates on the use of mountain huts along the main hiking routes. You can also book some specific huts and pick up keys. It also sells hiking gear.

Oslo Tourist Office (81 53 05 55; www.visitoslo.com; Fridtjof Nansens plass 5; 9am-6pm May-Sep, to 4pm Oct-Apr) The main tourist office is located just north of the Rådhus and can provide masses of information. Look out for its useful *Oslo Guide* or the monthly *What's On in Oslo* (both are available at all tourist offices in and around the city, as well as at many sights and hotels). Sells the Oslo Pass (www.visitoslo.com/en/activities-and-attractions/oslo-pass; adult 1/2/3 days Nkr290/425/535, child & senior Nkr145/215/270).

Getting There & Away

AIR

Oslo Gardermoen International Airport (www.osl.no)

BUS

Galleri Oslo Bus Terminal (23 00 24 00; Schweigaards gate 8) Long-distance buses arrive and depart from the Galleri Oslo Bus Terminal; the train and bus stations are linked via a convenient overhead walkway for easy connections.

TRAIN

All trains arrive and depart from Oslo S in the city centre. Major destinations include Stavanger, Bergen and Trondheim.

Getting Around

TO/FROM AIRPORT

Flybussen (www.flybussen.no) Flybussen is the airport shuttle to Gardermoen International Airport, 50km north of Oslo. It departs from the bus terminal at Galleri Oslo three or four times hourly from 4.05am to 9.50pm. The trip costs Nkr120/220 one-way/return (valid one month) and takes 40 minutes.

Flytoget (www.flytoget.no) FlyToget rail services leave Asker station in the far southwest of the city for Gardermoen (Nkr190, 49 minutes) every 20 minutes between 4.18am and midnight, with departures also from the National Theatre and Oslo S.

PUBLIC TRANSPORT

Bus and tram lines lace the city. Tickets for most trips cost Nkr30/15 per adult/child if you buy them in advance (at 7-Eleven, Narvesen, Trafikanten) or Nkr50/25 if you buy them from the driver. Ticket prices are the same for the six-line Tunnelbanen (T-bane) underground.

BERGEN & THE WESTERN FJORDS

This spectacular region has truly indescribable scenery. Hardangerfjord, Sognefjord, Lysefjord and Geirangerfjord are all variants on the same theme: steep crystalline rock walls dropping with sublime force straight into the sea, often decorated with waterfalls. Bergen is an engaging and lively city with a 15th-century waterfront.

Bergen

POP 258,500

Surrounded by seven hills and fjords, Bergen is a charming city. With the Unesco World Heritage–listed Bryggen and buzzing Vågen harbour as its centrepiece, Bergen climbs the hillsides with timber-clad houses, while cable cars offer stunning views from above.

Sights

★Bryggen HISTORIC SITE

Bergen's oldest quarter runs along the eastern shore of Vågen Harbour (the name translates to 'wharf') in long, parallel and often leaning rows of gabled buildings with stacked-stone or wooden foundations and reconstructed rough-plank construction. It's enchanting, no doubt about it, but can be exhausting if you hit a cruise ship and bus tour crush.

The current 58 buildings (25% of the original, although some claim there are now 61) cover 13,000 sq metres and date from after the 1702 fire, although the building pattern is from the 12th century. The archaeological excavations suggest that the quay was once 140m further inland than its present location.

In the early 14th century, there were about 30 wooden buildings, each usually shared by several *stuer* (trading firms). They rose two or three stories above the wharf and combined business premises with living quarters and **warehouses**. Each building had a crane for loading and unloading ships, as well as a *schøtstue* (large assembly room) where employees met and ate.

The wooden alleyways of Bryggen have become a haven for artists and craftspeople, and there are bijou shops and boutiques at every turn. The atmosphere of an intimate waterfront community remains intact, and losing yourself here is one of Bergen's pleasures.

Sleeping

Citybox HOSTEL €

(☎55 31 25 00; www.citybox.no; Nygårdsgaten 31; s/d Nkr650/950, without bathroom Nkr550/750; 📶) The Citybox mini-chain began in Bergen and is one of the best of the hostel–budget hotel hybrids. Colour-splashed modern rooms make use of the original historic features and are blissfully high-ceilinged; the extra large family rooms are very generous in size and have small kitchen areas. Communal spaces,

FJORD TOURS FROM BERGEN

There are dozens of tours of the fjords from Bergen; the tourist office (p834) has a full list and you can buy tickets there or purchase them online. Most offer discounts if you have a **Bergen Card** (www.visitbergen.com/bergencard; adult/child 24hr pass Nkr200/75, 48hr Nkr260/100). For a good overview, pick up the *Round Trips – Fjord Tours & Excursions* brochure from the tourist office, which includes tours offered by a range of private companies.

Fjord Tours (☎81 56 82 22; www.fjordtours.com) has mastered the art of making the most of limited time with a series of tours into the fjords. Its popular and year-round **Norway in a Nutshell** tour is a great way to see far more than you thought possible in a single day.

Bergen

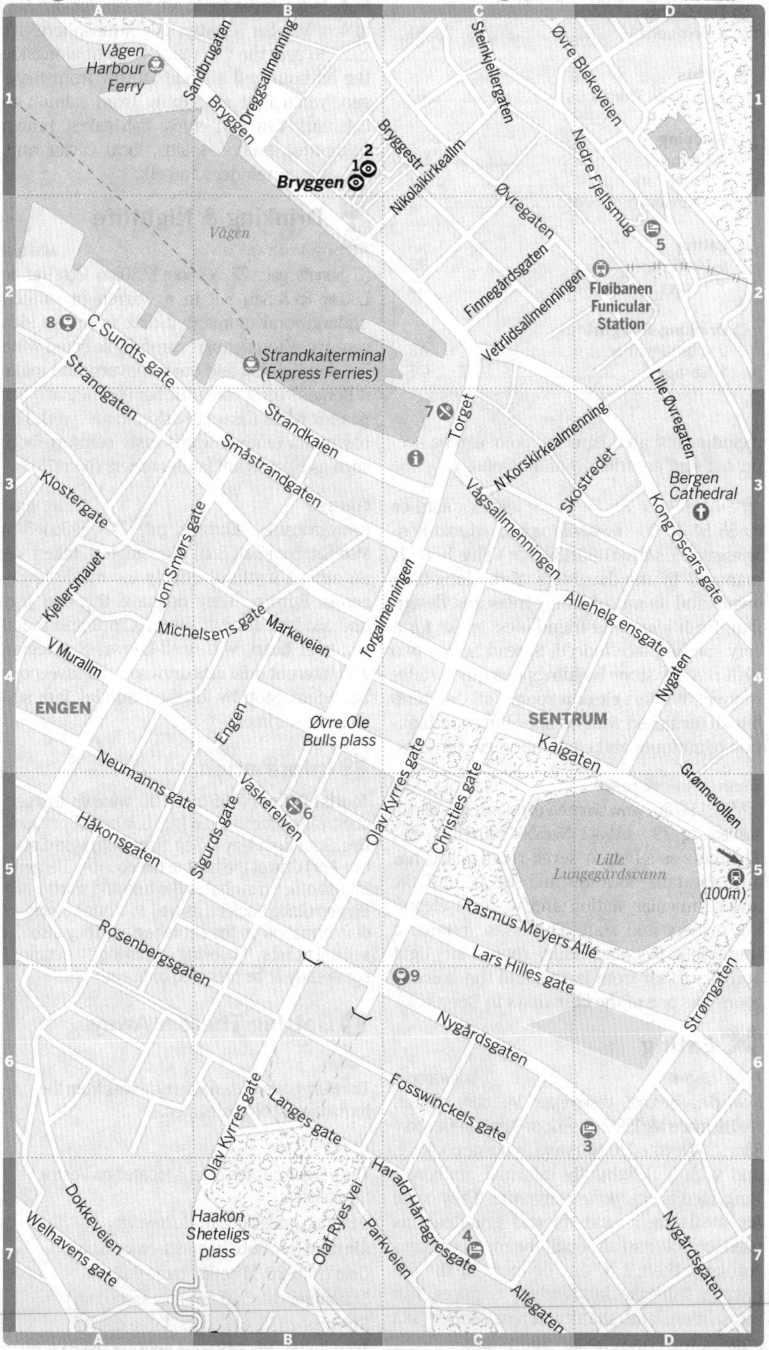

0 200 m
0 0.1 miles
A B C D
1 2 3 4 5 6 7
Vågen Harbour Ferry
Sandbrugaten
Dreggsallmenning
Bryggen
Bryggestr
Nikolaikirkeallm
Steinkjellergaten
Øvre Blekeveien
Nedre Fjellsmug
Øvregaten
Finnegårdsgaten
Vetrlidsallmenningen
Fløibanen Funicular Station
Vågen
8
C Sundts gate
Strandgaten
Strandkaiterminal (Express Ferries)
Strandkaien
7
Torget
Småstrandgaten
Klostergate
Jon Smørs gate
N Korskirkealmenning
Skostredet
Lille Øvregaten
Bergen Cathedral
Kong Oscars gate
Vågsallmenningen
Kjellersmauet
Michelsens gate
Markeveien
Torgalmenningen
Allehelg ensgate
V Murallm
ENGEN
Engen
Øvre Ole Bulls plass
SENTRUM
Nygaten
Kaigaten
Grønnevollen
Neumanns gate
Vaskerelven
6
Olav Kyrres gate
Christies gate
Håkonsgaten
Sigurds gate
Lille Lungegårdsvann
(100m)
Rasmus Meyers Allé
Lars Hilles gate
Rosenbergsgaten
9
Strømgaten
Nygårdsgaten
Fosswinckels gate
Langes gate
3
Olav Kyrres gate
Harald Hårfagresgate
Olaf Ryes vei
Parkveien
Dokkeveien
Welhavens gate
Haakon Sheteligs plass
4
Allégaten
Nygårdsgaten

Bergen

Top Sights

1 Bryggen B1

Sights

2 Bryggen Warehouses B1

Sleeping

3 Citybox D6
4 Hotel Park C7
5 Skansen Pensjonat D2

Eating

6 Pingvinen B5
7 Torget Fish Market C3

Drinking & Nightlife

8 Altona Vinbar A2
9 Garage C6

including a shared laundry room, can be hectic, but staff are friendly and helpful.

★**Hotel Park** HISTORIC HOTEL €€
(☎55 54 44 00; www.hotelpark.no; Harald Hårfagresgate 35; s/d Nkr1190/1390; 📶) This hotel is managed by the daughters of the long-time owner and its mix of family treasures, design flair, fresh ideas and friendliness make for a very special place indeed. Spread across two 19th-century stone buildings in a quiet, stately street, it offers elegant rooms, all different, but all furnished with an appealing combination of antiques and contemporary comforts.

Skansen Pensjonat GUESTHOUSE €€
(☎55 31 90 80; www.skansen-pensjonat.no; Vetrlidsalmenning 29; s/d/apt Nkr550/900/1100; 📶) This cute-as-a-button seven-room place has an unbeatable location high up behind the lower funicular station and warm, welcoming owners and staff. The house retains a traditional feel and scale, rooms are light and airy (if far from fancy), and the 'balcony room' has one of the best views in Bergen.

Eating

Pingvinen NORWEGIAN €
(www.pingvinen.no; Vaskerelven 14; daily specials Nkr119, mains Nkr159-249; ⏲1pm-3am Sun-Fri, noon-3am Sat) Devoted to Norwegian home cooking, and with a delightfully informal ambience, Pingvinen is *everyone's* favourite. They come for meals their mothers and grandparents used to cook, and although the menu changes regularly, there'll be one or more of the following: fish-cake sandwiches, reindeer, fish pie, salmon, lamb shank and *raspeballer* (aka *komle*), west-coast potato dumplings.

★**Torget Fish Market** SEAFOOD €
(www.torgetibergen.no; Torget; ⏲7am-7pm Jun-Aug, to 4pm Mon-Sat Sep-May) For atmosphere, it's hard to beat the fish market. Right alongside the harbour and a stone's throw from Bryggen, you'll find everything from salmon to calamari, fish and chips, fish cakes, prawn baguettes, seafood salads, local caviar and, sometimes, reindeer and elk.

Drinking & Nightlife

Altona Vinbar WINE BAR
(C Sundts gate 22; ⏲6pm-12.30am Mon-Thu, to 1.30am Fri & Sat) Set in a warren of vaulted underground rooms that date from the 16th century, Altona's huge, carefully selected wine list, soft lighting and quiet conversation make it Bergen's most romantic bar (particularly appealing when the weather's cold and wet). The bar menu tends towards tasty comfort food, such as Norwegian lamb burgers (Nkr175).

Garage LIVE MUSIC
(www.garage.no; Christies gate 14; ⏲3pm-3am Mon-Sat, 5pm-3am Sun) Garage has taken on an almost mythical quality for music lovers across Europe. They do have the odd jazz and acoustic act, but this is a rock and metal venue at heart, with well-known Norwegian and international acts drawn to the cavernous basement. Stop by for their Sunday jam sessions in summer.

Information

Tourist Office (☎55 55 20 00; www.visitbergen.com; Vågsallmenningen 1; ⏲8.30am-10pm Jun-Aug, 9am-8pm May & Sep, 9am-4pm Mon-Sat Oct-Apr) One of the best in the country, Bergen's tourist office distributes the free and worthwhile *Bergen Guide* booklet, as well as a huge stock of information on the entire region. They also sell rail tickets. If booking or making an enquiry, come early or be prepared to queue.

Getting There & Away

BOAT

The *Hurtigruten* coastal ferry leaves from the terminal east of Nøstegaten.

BUS

The Bergen bus terminal is located on Vestre Strømkaien.

Destinations include the following:

Ålesund (Nkr686, 10 hours, twice daily)
Oslo (Nkr680, 11 hours, three daily)
Stavanger (Nkr550, 5½ hours, six daily)
Stryn (Nkr538, 6½ hours, three daily)
Trondheim (Nkr848, 14½ hours, once daily)

WORTH A TRIP

VISITING LYSEFJORD

All along the 42km-long Lysefjord, the granite glows with an ethereal, ambient light, even on dull days. This is many visitors' favourite fjord, and there's no doubt that it has a captivating beauty. The area's most popular outing is the two-hour hike to the top of incredible Preikestolen (Pulpit Rock), 25km east of Stavanger. You can inch up to the edge of its flat top and peer 604m straight down a sheer cliff into the blue water for some intense vertigo.

Pulpit Rock by public transport

From May to mid-September, five to seven ferries a day run from Stavanger's Fiskespiren Quay to Tau, where the ferries are met by a bus, which runs between the Tau pier and the Preikestolhytta Vandrerhjem. From there, the two-hour trail leads up to Preikestolen. The last bus from Preikestolhytta to Tau leaves at 7.55pm. **Tide Reiser** (www.tidereiser.no) offers all-inclusive round-trip tickets (adult/child Nkr250/125); there are timetables online or at the tourist office. You can buy tickets at the tourist office, online or at Fiskespiren Quay.

Pulpit Rock by car

If you've got your own vehicle, you can take the car ferry (adult/child/car Nkr42/21/125, 40 minutes, up to 24 departures daily) from Stavanger's Fiskespiren Quay to Tau. From the pier in Tau, a well-signed road (Rv13) leads 19km to Preikestolhytta Vandrerhjem (take the signed turn-off after 13km). It costs Nkr70/35 per car/motorcycle to park here. The trip between Stavanger and the trailhead takes around 1½ hours.

Boat trips to Lysefjord

Two companies offer three-hour boat cruises from Stavanger to the waters below Preikestolen on Lysefjord and back.

Rødne Fjord Cruise (51 89 52 70; www.rodne.no; Skagenkaien 35-37, Stavanger; adult/senior & student/child/family Nkr450/350/280/1150; departures 10am & 2pm Sun-Fri, noon Sat Jul & Aug, noon daily May, Jun & Sep, noon Fri-Sun Oct-Apr)

Tide Reiser (51 86 87 88; www.tidereiser.no; adult/senior & student/child Nkr360/280/250; departures noon late May-late Aug, noon Sat Sep-late May)

TRAIN

The spectacular train journey between Bergen and Oslo (Nkr349 to Nkr829, 6½ to eight hours, five daily) runs through the heart of Norway. Other destinations include Voss (Nkr189, one hour, hourly) and Myrdal (Nkr286, 2¼ hours, up to nine daily) for connections to the Flåmsbana railway.

Stavanger

POP 124,940

Said by some to be the largest wooden city in Europe, Stavanger's old quarter climbs up the slopes around a pretty harbour. Stavanger is also one of Norway's liveliest urban centres and an excellent base to explore Lysefjord.

Sights

★Gamle Stavanger NEIGHBOURHOOD

Gamle (Old) Stavanger, above the western shore of the harbour, is a delight. The Old Town's cobblestone walkways pass between rows of late-18th-century whitewashed wooden houses, all immaculately kept and adorned with cheerful, well-tended flowerboxes. It well rewards an hour or two's ambling.

★Norsk Oljemuseum MUSEUM

(Oil Museum; www.norskolje.museum.no; Kjering holmen; adult/child/family Nkr100/50/250; 10am-7pm daily Jun-Aug, to 4pm Mon-Sat, to 6pm Sun Sep-May) You could spend hours in this state-of-the-art, beautifully designed museum, one of Norway's best. Focusing on oil exploration in the North Sea from discovery in 1969 until the present, it's filled with high-tech interactive displays and authentic reconstructions. Highlights include the world's largest drill bit, simulated rig working environments, documentary films on a North Sea dive crew's work day and a vast hall of amazing oil platform models.

Sleeping & Eating

★Thompsons B&B B&B €

(51 52 13 29; www.thompsonsbedandbreakfast.com; Muségata 79; s/d with shared bathroom Nkr400/500; P) Housed in a 19th-century

villa in a peaceful residential area, this four-bed B&B has a homey vibe engendered by the warm and welcoming owner, Sissel Thompson. Rooms are cosy and comfortable, and traditional Norwegian breakfast, taken around the dining table, is generous.

Comfort Hotel Square HOTEL €
(☎51 56 80 00; www.nordicchoicehotels.no; Løkkeveien 41; d from Nkr749; ❄📶) In a wavy wooden building behind Gamle Stavanger, this option from the Nordic Choice Comfort line does the hip boutique thing (exposed concrete walls, creative lighting and wall-sized photos) with chain convenience, facilities and value. Weekend rates are good value and the location is a good one.

★**Renaa Matbaren** INTERNATIONAL €€
(Breitorget 6, enter from Bakkegata; small dishes Nrk135-189, mains Nkr195-335; ⏲11am-1am Mon-Sat, 1-10pm Sun) Yes, that's a proper Tracey Emin on the far wall and an actual Anthony Gormley in the middle of the room. This perpetually bustling bistro is testament to just how cashed-up and cultured this North Sea port is. You'd be happy to be here just for the buzz, but the food is fabulous, too.

Information

Tourist Office (☎51 85 92 00; www.regionstavanger.com; Domkirkeplassen 3; ⏲9am-8pm Jun-Aug, to 4pm Mon-Fri, to 2pm Sat Sep-May) Local information and advice on Lysefjord and Preikestolen.

Getting There & Away

BUS

Most services to Oslo change at Kristiansand. Destinations include the following:

Bergen (Nkr440, 5½ hours, 13 daily)
Haugesund (Nkr220, two hours, 16 daily)
Kristiansand (Nkr390, 4½ hours, three daily)
Oslo (Nkr820, 9½ hours, three daily)

TRAIN

Most train services to Oslo change at Kristiansand. Destinations include the following:

Egersund (Nkr164, 1¼ hours, four daily)
Kristiansand (Nkr474, three hours, five daily)
Oslo (Nkr929, eight hours, up to five daily)

Sognefjorden

Sognefjorden, the world's second-longest (203km) and Norway's deepest (1308m) fjord, cuts a deep slash across the map of western Norway. In places, sheer walls rise more than 1000m above the water, while elsewhere a gentler shoreline supports farms, orchards and villages. The broad, main waterway is impressive but cruise into its narrower arms, such as the deep and lovely Nærøyfjord to Gudvangen, for idyllic views of abrupt cliff faces and cascading waterfalls. **Norled** (www.norled.no) operates a daily express boat between Bergen and both Flåm (Nkr750, 5½ hours) and Sogndal (Nkr645, 4¾ hours).

Flåm

POP 450

Scenically set at the head of Aurlandsfjorden, Flåm is a tiny village that's a jumping-off spot to explore the area. It gets a little overrun with people when a cruise ship's in port, and sees an amazing 500,000 visitors every summer.

Sights

Flåmsbana Railway SCENIC RAILWAY
(www.flaamsbana.no; adult/child one way Nkr300/150, return Nkr400/300) A 20km-long engineering wonder hauls itself up 864m of altitude gain through 20 tunnels. At a gradient of 1:18, it's the world's steepest railway that runs without cable or rack wheels. It takes a full 45 minutes to climb to Myrdal on the bleak, treeless Hardangervidda plateau, past waterfalls (there's a photo stop at awesome Kjosfossen). The railway runs year-round, with up to 10 departures daily in summer.

Sleeping & Eating

Flåm Camping & Hostel HOSTEL, CAMPGROUND €
(☎57 63 21 21; www.flaam-camping.no; car/caravan sites Nkr215/220, dm/s/tw/q Nkr300/500/865/1255, with shared bathroom Nkr230/390/650/950; ⏲Mar-Oct; 📶) Family-run and built on the site of an old family farm, there's a lot of love gone into every aspect of this operation. Rooms are spread across the lush site, each with a stylish simplicity of their own; campsites are idyllic. Located in a gorgeous spot a few minutes' walk from the station.

Fretheim Hotel HOTEL €€€
(☎57 63 63 00; www.fretheim-hotel.no; s/d Nkr1195/2190; P@📶) A haunt of fly-fishing English aristocracy in the 19th century, the vast, 122-room Fretheim, despite its size, manages to be intimate and welcoming. In the original 1870s building, 17 rooms have been restored to their historic selves, although with full modern comfort, while the American wings are straight-up contemporary luxe.

SOGNEFJORDEN BY BOAT

From Flåm, boats head out to towns around Sognefjorden. The most scenic trip from Flåm is the passenger ferry up Nærøyfjord to Gudvangen (one way/ return Nkr295/400). It leaves Flåm at 3.10pm year-round and up to five times daily between May and September. You can also hop aboard in Aurland. At Gudvangen, a connecting bus takes you to Voss, where you can pick up the train for Bergen or Oslo. The tourist office sells ferry tickets, plus the Flåm to Voss ferry-bus combination. From Flåm-Bergen there's at least one daily express boat (Nkr695, 5½ hours) via Balestrand (Nkr265, 1½ hours).

Information

Tourist Office (☎57 63 33 13; www.visitflam.com; ⊙8.30am-8pm Jun-Aug, 8.30am-4pm May & Sep) Within the train station.

Geirangerfjorden

Scattered cliffside farms, most long abandoned, still cling to the towering, near-sheer walls of twisting, 20km-long Geirangerfjord, a Unesco World Heritage Site. Waterfalls – the Seven Sisters, the Suitor, the Bridal Veil and more – sluice and tumble.

The one-hour scenic ferry trip along its length between Geiranger and Hellesylt is as much mini-cruise as means of transport – take it even if you've no particular reason to get to the other end.

Sights & Activities

Flydalsjuvet VIEWPOINT

Somewhere you've seen that classic photo, beloved of brochures, of the overhanging rock Flydalsjuvet, usually with a figure gazing down at a cruise ship in Geirangerfjord. The car park, signposted Flydalsjuvet, about 5km uphill from Geiranger on the Stryn road, offers a great view of the fjord and the green river valley, but doesn't provide the postcard view down to the last detail. For that, you'll have to drop about 150m down the hill, then descend a slippery and rather indistinct track to the edge. Your photo subject will have to scramble down gingerly and with the utmost care to the overhang about 50m further along. We advise care when walking backwards.

Coastal Odyssey KAYAKING, HIKING

(☎91 11 80 62; www.coastalodyssey.com; sea kayaks per hr/half-day/day Nkr150/450/800, kayaking hiking trips Nkr800-1250) Based at Geiranger Camping (a short walk from the ferry terminal) this recommended company is run by Canadian Jonathan Bendiksen, who learnt to kayak almost before he could walk. He rents sea kayaks and does daily hiking and canoeing trips to four of the finest destinations around the fjord.

Sleeping & Eating

★**Westerås Gard** CABIN €€

(☎93 26 44 97; www.geiranger.no/westeras; 2-bed cabins Nkr950, apt Nkr1150; ⊙May-Sep) This beautiful old working farm, 4km along the Rv63 towards Grotli, sits at the end of a narrow road dizzingly high above the bustle. Stay in one of the two farmhouse apartments, or there's five pine-clad cabins. The barn, dating to 1603, is home to a restaurant, where the owners serve dishes made with their own produce.

Brasserie Posten RESTAURANT €€

(☎70 26 13 06; www.brasserieposten.no; lunch Nkr99-124, dinner Nkr168-228; ⊙noon-11pm) A simple menu of salads, burgers, steaks, fish and pizza is elevated above the norm by a passionate local chef who sources his Heelsylt, organic dairy from Røros and makes the most of fresh herbs and vegetables. The modern Scando interior is bright and atmospheric, but the fjord-side terrace wins.

Information

Tourist Office (☎70 26 30 99; www.geiranger.no; ⊙9am-6pm mid-May–mid-Sep) Located right beside the pier.

Getting There & Away

The popular, hugely recommended run between Geiranger and Hellesylt (car with driver Nkr320, adult/child single Nkr160/79, return Nkr215/115, one hour) is quite the most spectacular scheduled ferry route in Norway. It has four to eight sailings daily from May to September (every 90 minutes until 6.30pm, June to August).

Almost as scenic is the ferry that runs twice daily between Geiranger and Valldal (adult/child single Nkr240/130, return Nkr370/190, 2¼ hours). A mini-cruise in itself, it runs from mid-June to mid-August.

NORTHERN NORWAY

With vibrant cities and some wondrous natural terrain, you'll be mighty pleased with yourself for undertaking an exploration of this huge territory that spans the Arctic Circle. An alternative to land travel is the *Hurtigruten* coastal ferry, which pulls into every sizeable port, passing some of the best coastal scenery in Scandinavia.

Trondheim

POP 182,035

Trondheim, Norway's original capital, is Norway's third-largest city after Oslo and Bergen. With its wide streets and partly pedestrianised heart, it's an attractive city with a long history. Fuelled by a large student population, it buzzes with life.

Sights

★Nidaros Domkirke CATHEDRAL

(www.nidarosdomen.no; Kongsgårdsgata; adult/child/family Nkr70/30/170, tower Nkr30; ⏲9am-7pm Mon-Fri, 9am-2pm Sat, 9am-5pm Sun mid-Jun–mid-Aug, shorter hours rest of year) Nidaros Cathedral is Scandinavia's largest medieval building. Outside, the ornately embellished, altar-like west wall has top-to-bottom statues of biblical characters and Norwegian bishops and kings, sculpted in the early 20th century. Several are copies of medieval originals, housed nowadays in the museum. Within, the cathedral is subtly lit (just see how the vibrantly coloured, modern stained-glass glows, especially in the rose window at the west end), so let your eyes attune to the gloom.

★Sverresborg Trøndelag Folkemuseum MUSEUM, ARCHITECTURE

(www.sverresborg.no; Sverresborg Allé 13; adult/child incl guided tour Nkr125/50; ⏲10am-5pm mid-May–Aug, 11am-3pm Mon-Fri, noon-4pm Sat & Sun rest of year) West of the centre, this folk museum is one of the best in Norway. The indoor exhibition, *Livsbilder* (Images of Life), displays artefacts in use over the last 150 years – from clothing to school supplies to bicycles – and has a multimedia presentation. The rest of the museum, with over 60 period buildings, is open-air, adjoining the ruins of King Sverre's castle and giving fine hilltop views of the city.

Sleeping

★Pensjonat Jarlen GUESTHOUSE €

(☎73 51 32 18; www.jarlen.no; Kongens gate 40; s/d Nkr540/690; 📶) Price, convenience and value for money are a winning combination here. After a recent overhaul, the rooms at this central spot have a contemporary look and are outstanding value, although some bathrooms could do with a fresh look. Some rooms have polished floorboards, others carpet, and most have a hot plate and fridge thrown in.

Rica Nidelven Hotel HOTEL €€

(☎73 56 80 00; www.rica.no; Havnegata 1-3; r Nkr945-1695; P@📶) A fabulous waterside location next to Solsiden and within a five-minute walk of the old part of town, this stylish hotel has attractive rooms, all 343 of them, and many have river views. The hotel won the prize for Norway's best hotel breakfast, which is reason enough to stay here.

Eating

★Ravnkloa Fish Market SEAFOOD €

(☎73 52 55 21; www.ravnkloa.no; Munkegata; snacks from Nkr45, mains Nkr150-185; ⏲10am-5pm Mon-Fri, 10am-4pm Sat) Everything looks good at this fish market that doubles as a cafe with quayside tables out front. The fish cakes are fabulous and they also do shrimp sandwiches, mussels and a fine fish soup. In addition to seafood, they sell an impressive range of cheeses and other gourmet goods.

★Baklandet Skydsstasjon NORWEGIAN €€

(☎73 92 10 44; www.skydsstation.no; Øvre Bakklandet 33; mains Nkr138-245; ⏲11am-1am Mon-Fri, noon-1am Sat & Sun) Within what began life as an 18th-century coaching inn are several cosy rooms with poky angles and listing floors. It's a hyperfriendly place where you can tuck into tasty dishes, such as its renowned fish soup ('the best in all Norway', a couple of diners assured us), or the lunchtime herring buffet (Nkr178) from Thursday to Saturday. Always leave room for a homemade cake.

Drinking

As a student town, Trondheim offers lots of through-the-night life. Solsiden (Sunnyside) is Trondheim's trendiest leisure zone. A whole wharf-side of bars and restaurants nestles beneath smart new apartment blocks, converted warehouses and now-idle cranes.

★Den Gode Nabo PUB

(www.dengodenabo.com; Øvre Bakklandet 66; ⏲4pm-1.30am Sun-Fri, 1pm-1.30am Sat) The Good Neighbour, dark and cavernous within, and nominated more than once as Norway's best pub, enjoys a prime riverside location. Indeed, part of it is on the water; reserve a table on the floating pontoon. US visitors will find Sam Adams on tap while UK ale connoisseurs can savour Bishop's Finger in the bottle.

★**Trondheim Microbryggeri** PUB
(Prinsens gate 39; ⏲5pm-midnight Mon, 3pm-2am Tue-Fri, noon-2am Sat) This splendid home-brew pub deserves a pilgrimage as reverential as anything accorded to St Olav from all committed *øl* (beer) quaffers. With up to eight of its own brews on tap and good light meals on the menu, it's a place to linger, nibble and tipple. It's down a short lane, just off Prinsens gate.

Information

Tourist Office (☎73 80 76 60; www.visittrondheim.no; Nordre gate 11; ⏲9am-6pm daily mid-Jun–mid-Aug, 9am-6pm Mon-Sat rest of year) In the heart of the city, with an accommodation booking service.

Getting There & Away

BOAT

Trondheim is a major stop on the *Hurtigruten* coastal ferry route.

BUS

The intercity bus terminal (Rutebilstasjon) adjoins Trondheim Sentralstasjon (train station, also known as Trondheim S). Nor-Way Bussekspress services run up to three times daily to Ålesund (Nkr587, seven hours, two to three daily) with one overnight bus to Bergen (Nkr848, 14½ hours).

TRAIN

There are two to four trains daily to/from Oslo (Nkr899, 6½ hours). Two head north to Bodø (Nkr1059, 9¾ hours).

Lofoten

You'll never forget your first approach to the Lofoten Islands by ferry. The islands spread their tall, craggy physique against the sky like some spiky sea dragon, and you wonder how humans eked a living in such inhospitable surroundings. The four main islands are all linked by bridges or tunnels, with buses running the entire length of the Lofoten road (E10) from Fiskebøl in the north to Å at the road's end in the southwest.

Sights & Activities

Lofoten's principal settlement, **Svolvær**, makes a pretty spot from which to base your explorations, with steep mountains rising in the background and a busy harbour. The still-active fishing village of **Henningsvær**, perched at the end of a thin promontory, is the lightest, brightest and trendiest village in the archipelago, while a spectacular 6km diversion southwards from the E10 beneath towering bare crags brings you to the cutesy village of **Nusfjord**, sprawled around its tiny, tucked-away harbour. **Å** is a very special place at what feels like the end of the world on the western tip of Lofoten. A preserved fishing village perched on forbidding rocks connected by wooden footbridges, its shoreline is lined with red-painted *rorbuer* (fishermen's huts), many of which jut into the sea.

Lofotr Viking Museum MUSEUM
(www.lofotr.no; adult/child incl guided tour mid-Jun–mid-Aug Nkr160/80, rest of year Nkr120/60; ⏲10am-7pm Jun–mid-Aug, shorter hours rest of year) In 1981 at Borg, near the centre of Vestvågøy, a farmer's plough hit the ruins of the 83m-long dwelling of a powerful Viking chieftain, the largest building of its era ever discovered in Scandinavia. The resulting Lofotr Viking Museum, 14km north of Leknes, offers a glimpse of life in Viking times. You can walk 1.5km of trails over open hilltops from the replica of the chieftain's longhouse (the main building, shaped like an upside-down boat) to the Viking-ship replica on the water.

★**Svolværgeita** HIKING, CLIMBING
You'll see it on postcards all over Lofoten – some daring soul leaping between two fingers of rock high above Svolvær. To hike up to a point just behind the two pinnacles (355m), walk northeast along the E10 towards Narvik, pass the marina, and turn left on Nyveien, then right on Blatind veg – the steep climb begins just behind the playground. The climb takes around half an hour, or an hour if you continue up to the summit of Floya. To actually climb Svolværgeita, you'll need to go with a guide – ask the tourist office for recommendations or try **Northern Alpine Guides** (☎94 24 91 10; www.alpineguides.no; Havnegata 3).

Sleeping & Eating

★**Svinøya Rorbuer** CABIN €€
(☎76 06 99 30; www.svinoya.no; Gunnar Bergs vei 2; cabins & ste Nkr1150-3200) Across a bridge on the islet of Svinøya, site of Svolvær's first settlement, are several cabins, some historic, most contemporary, and all cosy and comfortable. Reception is a veritable museum, a restored and restocked *krambua* (general store), constructed in 1828, which was Svolvær's first shop. They've properties all over the area and they're some of the best *rorbuer* in Lofoten.

★**Henningsvær Suites** APARTMENTS €€
(☎40 17 33 45; www.henningsvarsuites.no; ste Nkr1190-2500; P 📶) These stunning, spacious

suites, some of which overlook the water, are a fine option in Henningsvær. With their abundant space and light, and location, it's a great alternative to hotel accommodation.

Å Rorbuer CABIN €€
(☎76 09 11 21; www.a-rorbuer.com; d Nkr800-1100, apt Nkr1750-2000) *Rorbu* accommodation is dispersed throughout Å's historic buildings, the more expensive ones fully equipped and furnished with antiques. The newer sea house, with trim but plain rooms, has shared bathrooms, despite the hefty price.

★Fiskekrogen SEAFOOD €€€
(☎76 07 46 52; www.fiskekrogen.no; Dreyersgate 29; mains Nkr195-295, lunch dishes Nkr145-275; ⏱1-4pm & 6-11pm Sun, 6-11pm Mon-Sat Jun-Aug, shorter hours rest of year) At the end of a slipway overlooking the harbour, this dockside restaurant, a favourite of the Norwegian royal family, is Henningsvær's other culinary claim to fame. Try, in particular, the outstanding fish soup (Nkr195), but there's everything else on the menu from fish and chips to fried cod tongues. Serves whale.

Information

Tourist Office (☎76 06 98 07; www.lofoten.info; Torget; ⏱9am-10pm Mon-Fri, 9am-8pm Sat, 10am-8pm Sun mid-June–mid-Aug, shorter hours rest of year) Provides information on the entire archipelago.

Getting There & Away

BOAT

In addition to the *Hurtigruten*, the following services connect Lofoten and the mainland:

- Car ferry between Svolvær and Skutvik, on the mainland (1¾ hours)
- Car ferry between Bodø and Moskenes (three to 3½ hours)
- Foot-passenger-only express boat between Bodø and Svolvær (3¾ hours)

BUS

Buses connect all major island settlements.

Tromsø

POP 67,300

Simply put, Tromsø parties. By far the largest town in northern Norway, and administrative centre of Troms county, it's lively with an animated street scene, a respected university, the hallowed Mack Brewery – and more pubs per capita than any other Norwegian town. Its corona of snow-topped peaks provides arresting scenery, excellent summer hiking, and great winter skiing and dog-sledding.

Sights

★Arctic Cathedral CHURCH
(Ishavskatedralen; www.ishavskatedralen.no; Hans Nilsensvei 41; adult/child Nkr40/free, organ recitals Nkr70-150; ⏱9am-7pm Mon-Fri, 1-7pm Sat & Sun Jun–mid-Aug, 3-6pm Apr, May & mid-Aug–Dec, 2-6pm Feb & Mar) The 11 arching triangles of the **Arctic Cathedral** (1965), as the Tromsdalen Church is more usually called, suggest glacial crevasses and auroral curtains. The magnificent glowing stained-glass window that occupies almost the whole of the east end depicts Christ descending to earth. Look back towards the west end and the contemporary organ, a work of steely art in itself, then up high to take in the lamps of Czech crystal, hanging in space like icicles. Take bus 20 or 24.

★Polaria MUSEUM, AQUARIUM
(www.polaria.no; Hjalmar Johansens gate 12; adult/child Nkr120/60; ⏱10am-7pm mid-May–Aug, to 5pm Sep–mid-May) Daringly designed Polaria is an entertaining multimedia introduction to northern Norway and Svalbard. After an excellent 14-minute film about the latter (screened every 30 minutes), plus another about the northern lights, an Arctic walk leads to displays on shrinking sea ice, a northern lights display, aquariums of cold-water fish and – the big draw – a trio of energetic bearded seals.

★Fjellheisen CABLE CAR
(☎77 63 87 37; www.fjellheisen.no; Solliveien 12; adult/child Nkr140/60; ⏱10am-1am late May–mid-Aug, shorter hours rest of year) For a fine view of the city and midnight sun, take the cable car to the top of Mt Storsteinen (421m). There's a restaurant at the top, from where a network of hiking routes radiates. Take bus 26 and buy a combined bus and cable-car ticket (adult/child Nkr145/65).

Activities

In and around Tromsø there's a range of activities in the winter twilight, including experiencing the aurora borealis, cross-country skiing and snowshoeing, and reindeer- and dog-sledding. You can also go on showshoe safaris or try ice fishing. To whet your winter appetite, check the tourist office website.

Sleeping

Ami Hotel HOTEL €€
(☎77 62 10 00; www.amihotel.no; Skolegata 24; s/d Nkr740/910, with shared bathroom Nkr640/790; P@📶) Located beside a traffic-free road and park, this is a quiet, friendly, family-owned choice. There's a well-equipped kitchen for self-caterers and a couple of communal lounges, each with TV, internet access and free tea and coffee.

★ **Rica Ishavshotel** HOTEL €€
(☎77 66 64 00; www.rica.no/ishavshotel; Fredrik Langes gate 2; r Nkr1045-1695; @📶) Occupying a prime quayside position, this hotel is recognisable by its tall spire resembling a ship's mast. It sometimes swallows as many as five tour groups per day so summer reservations are advisable. Almost half of its attractive rooms, including many singles, have superb views of the sound, and a recent expansion and overhaul of some rooms has added to the appeal. Both guests and nonguests will enjoy its **Brasseriet** (☎77 66 64 00; mains Nkr210-375) restaurant and Skibsbroen (p841) bar.

Driv CAFE, RESTAURANT €
(www.driv.no; Tollbodgata 3; mains Nkr115-185; ⏲kitchen 11am-6pm, bar 11.30am-1.30am) This student-run converted warehouse serves meaty burgers (try its renowned Driv burger) and great salads. It organises musical and cultural events and has a disco every Saturday. In winter you can steep yourself in good company within its open-air hot tub.

★ **Emma's Under** NORWEGIAN €€
(☎77 63 77 30; www.emmas.as; Kirkegata; mains Nkr155-295; ⏲11am-10pm Mon-Fri, noon-10pm Sat) Intimate and stylish, this is one of Tromsø's most popular lunch spots, where mains include northern Norwegian staples such as reindeer fillet, lamb and stockfish. Upstairs is the more formal **Emma's Drømekjøkken** (☎77 63 77 30; Kirkegata; mains Nkr295-365; ⏲6pm-midnight Mon-Sat), a highly regarded restaurant where advance booking is essential.

Drinking & Nightlife

Tromsø enjoys a thriving nightlife, with many arguing that it's the best scene in Norway. On Friday and Saturday, most nightspots stay open to 3.30am.

★ **Skibsbroen** COCKTAIL BAR
(⏲8pm-2am Mon-Thu, 6pm-3.30am Fri & Sat) For exceptional views of the harbour, fjord and mountains beyond, take the elevator of the Rica Ishavshotel to the 4th floor. Skibsbroen (Ship's Bridge), its intimate crow's-nest bar, has friendly staff, great cocktails, and a superb panoramic view.

Blå Rock Café BAR
(Strandgata 14/16; ⏲11.30am-2am) The loudest, most raving place in town has theme evenings, almost 50 brands of beer, occasional live bands and weekend DJs. The music is rock, naturally. Every Monday hour is a happy hour.

Information

Tourist Office (☎77 61 00 00; www.visittromso.no; Kirkegata 2; ⏲9am-7pm Mon-Fri, 10am-6pm Sat & Sun mid-May–Aug, shorter hours rest of year) Produces the comprehensive *Tromsø Guide*. Has two free internet points.

Getting There & Away

AIR

Tromsø Airport (☎77 64 84 00; www.avinor.no)

Norwegian (www.norwegian.no) Norwegian flies to and from London (Gatwick), Edinburgh, Dublin and Oslo.

SAS (www.sas.no) The largest international network of Norway's carriers.

BOAT

Tromsø is a major stop on the *Hurtigruten* coastal ferry route.

BUS

The main bus terminal (sometimes called Prost neset) is on Kaigata, beside the Hurtigruten quay. There are up to three daily express buses to/from Narvik (Nkr240, 4¼ hours) and one to/from Alta (Nkr560, 6½ hours), where you can pick up a bus for Honningsvåg, and from there, on to Nordkapp.

SURVIVAL GUIDE

Directory A–Z

ACCOMMODATION

Norway offers a wide range of accommodation, from camping, hostels and pensions to international-standard hotels. You'll pay a lot more for what you get compared with other countries, but standards are high. Most hotels have wi-fi access.

Norway has more than 1000 camping grounds. Although a few complexes remain open year-round, tent and caravan sites open only from mid-May to late August. Most camping grounds also rent simple cabins with cooking facilities, where linen and blankets cost extra. Some of the more expensive cabins also have shower and toilet facilities. For a comprehensive list of Norwegian camping grounds, pick up a copy of the free *Camping* (available at some tourist offices, camping grounds and from Norsk Camping).

In Norway, reasonably priced hostels *(vandrerhjem)* offer dorm beds for the night, plus use of communal facilities that usually include a kitchen, internet access and bathrooms. A welcome recent addition to the budget end of the market are chains such as Citybox, Smarthotels and Basic Hotels. These hostel-hotel hybrids are slick and excellent value, but they're only in larger cities.

Norway's hotels are generally modern and excellent, although those with any character are pretty thin on the ground. Comfortable nationwide chain hotels are the norm and the rooms can all start to look the same after a while.

ACTIVITIES

On the water Every waterside town has a place (frequently the campsite) where you can rent a canoe, kayak or rowing boat. Geiranger is an especially fine place to take to the water with Coastal Odyssey. Rafting is common around Sjoa in Central Norway. Options range from short, Class II doddles to Class III and IV adventures, and rollicking Class V punishment.

Hiking Norway has some of Europe's best hiking, best done from June to September. Wilderness huts line the northern trails (both free shared ones and private bookable ones).

Skiing The ski season runs from late November to early May and slightly longer in the north.

Dog-sledding Expeditions can range from two-hour tasters to multiday trips with overnight stays in remote forest huts.

BUSINESS HOURS

These standard opening hours are for high season (mid-June to mid-September) and tend to decrease outside that time.

Banks 8.15am to 3pm Monday to Wednesday and Friday, 8.15am to 5pm Thursday

Central post offices 8am to 8pm Monday to Friday, 9am to 6pm Saturday; otherwise 9am to 5pm Monday to Friday, 10am to 2pm Saturday

Restaurants noon to 3pm and 6pm to 11pm

Shops 10am to 5pm Monday to Wednesday and Friday, 10am to 7pm Thursday, 10am to 2pm Saturday

Supermarkets 9am to 9pm Monday to Friday, 9am to 6pm Saturday

COUNTRY FACTS

Country Code ☎47

Currency Krone

Emergency ☎112

Language Norwegian

Money ATMs are very common, plastic taken everywhere

Population 5.15 million

Time One hour ahead of UTC/GMT (two hours ahead from late March to late October)

Visas Schengen visa rules apply

SLEEPING PRICE RANGES

The following price ranges refer to a double room with private bathroom in high season and, unless stated otherwise, include breakfast:

€ less than Nkr750

€€ Nkr750–Nkr1400

€€€ more than Nkr1400

GAY & LESBIAN TRAVELLERS

Norwegians are accepting of homosexuality, which has been legal since 1973. That said, public displays of affection are not common practice, except perhaps in some areas of Oslo. Oslo is generally the easiest place to be gay in Norway, although even here there have been occasional recent attacks on gay couples holding hands, especially in the central-eastern areas of the capital. You're most likely to encounter difficulties wherever conservative religious views predominate, whether among newly arrived Muslim immigrant communities or devoutly Lutheran communities in rural areas.

Oslo has the liveliest gay scene, and it's worth stopping by **Use-It** (☎24 14 98 20; www.use-it.no; Møllergata 3, Oslo; ⏲10am-6pm Mon-Fri, noon-5pm Sat Jul-early Aug, 11am-5pm Mon-Fri, noon-5pm Sat rest of year), where you can pick up its excellent annual *Streetwise* booklet, which has a 'Gay Guide' section.

INTERNET ACCESS

➡ Public libraries usually have at least one free internet terminal; may need to be reserved.

➡ Tourist offices often have an internet terminal that you can use (usually 15 minutes max).

➡ Wi-fi is widely available at most hotels, cafes and tourist offices, as well as some restaurants; it's generally (but not always) free. Airports have wi-fi but generally charge around Nkr60 for the first hour.

MONEY

The most convenient way to bring your money is in the form of a debit or credit card, with some extra cash for use in case of an emergency.

➡ ATMs can be found even in small villages.

- Credit cards are widely accepted; Norwegians are dedicated users of the plastic even to buy a beer or cup of coffee.
- Travellers cheques and cash can be exchanged at banks; in the big cities, independent exchange facilities usually offer better rates.
- Service is generally considered to be included in bills, so there's no need to tip at all unless you want to reward exceptional service.

PUBLIC HOLIDAYS

New Year's Day (Nyttårsdag) 1 January
Maundy Thursday (Skjærtorsdag) March/April
Good Friday (Langfredag) March/April
Easter Monday (Annen Påskedag) March/April
Labour Day (Første Mai, Arbeidetsdag) 1 May
Constitution Day (Nasjonaldag) 17 May
Ascension Day (Kristi Himmelfartsdag) May/June, 40th day after Easter
Whit Monday (Annen Pinsedag) May/June, 8th Monday after Easter
Christmas Day (Første Juledag) 25 December
Boxing Day (Annen Juledag) 26 December

TELEPHONE

- You can buy a prepaid SIM card easily. There are always deals, and you should pick up a card for as little as Nkr200, including some call credit. Top the credit up at the same outlets, online or at ATMs.
- You can also buy cut-rate phone cards that lower the cost of making international calls.
- To call abroad, dial ☎00.

Getting There & Away

Norway is well linked to other European countries by air. There are also regular bus and rail services to Norway from neighbouring Sweden and Finland (from where there are connections further afield to Europe), with less regular (and more complicated) services to/from Russia. Regular car and passenger ferries also connect southern Norwegian ports with Denmark, Sweden and Germany.

AIR

SAS (www.sas.no) The largest international network of Norway's carriers.

Norwegian (www.norwegian.com) Low-cost airline with an extensive and growing domestic and international network.

SEA

Ferry connections are possible between Norway and Denmark, Germany, Iceland, the Faroe Islands and Sweden.

Color Line (☎ in Germany 0431-7300 300, in Norway 81 00 08 11, in Sweden 0526-62000; www.colorline.com)

ESSENTIAL FOOD & DRINK

Norwegian food can be excellent. Abundant seafood, local specialities such as reindeer, and a growing trend in cutting-edge cooking are undoubtedly the highlights. The only problem (and it's a significant one) is that prices are prohibitive, meaning that a full meal in a restaurant may become something of a luxury item for all but those on expense accounts. As a result, you may end up leaving Norway pretty uninspired by its food, which is such a shame considering what's on offer.

- **Reindeer** Roast reindeer *(reinsdyrstek)* is something every nonvegetarian visitor to Norway should try at least once: best eaten rare to medium-rare.
- **Elk** Known elsewhere in the world as moose, elk *(elg)* comes in a variety of forms, including as a steak or burger.
- **Salmon** One Norwegian contribution to international cuisine that you shouldn't miss is salmon (grilled, *laks*; or smoked, *røykelaks*). An excellent salmon dish, *gravat laks* is made by marinating salmon in sugar, salt, brandy and dill, and serving it in a creamy sauce.
- **Other seafood** Common fish include cod (*torsk* or *bacalao*; often dried), boiled or fresh shrimp, herring and Arctic char (a northern river fish). Norwegians are also huge fans of *fiskesuppe*, a thin, creamy, fish-flavoured soup.
- **Meatballs** Traditional Norwegian meatballs served with mushy peas, mashed potatoes and wild-berry jam is a local, home-cooked favourite.
- **Wild berries** The most popular edible wild berries include strawberries, blackcurrants, red currants, raspberries, blueberries (huckleberries) and the lovely amber-coloured *moltebær* (cloudberries).
- **Cheeses** Norwegian cheeses have come to international attention as a result of the mild but tasty Jarlsberg. Try also the disconcertingly brown Gudbrandsdalsost made from the whey of goat's and/or cow's milk and with a slightly sweet flavour.

EATING PRICE RANGES

The following prices refer to a standard main course:

€ less than Nkr125

€€ Nkr125–Nkr200

€€€ more than Nkr200

Stena Line (☎ in Norway 02010; www.stenaline.no) Fredrikshavn to/from Oslo.

Fjord Line (☎ in Denmark 97 96 30 00, in Norway 51 46 40 99; www.fjordline.com) Hirtshals to Kristiansand, Bergen, Stavanger and Langesund (Oslo).

Getting Around

Norway has an extremely efficient public transport system and its trains, buses and ferries are often timed to link with each other, although services vary with the season. Rail lines reach as far north as Bodø (you can also reach Narvik by rail from Sweden); further north you're limited to buses and ferries. A fine alternative to land travel is the *Hurtigruten* coastal ferry, which calls in at every sizable port between Bergen and Kirkenes.

AIR

Norway has an extensive domestic network and the major Norwegian domestic routes are quite competitive, meaning that it is possible to travel for little more than the equivalent train fare.

Norwegian (www.norwegian.com) Low-cost airline with an extensive network that now includes Longyearbyen (Svalbard).

SAS (www.sas.no) Large domestic network on mainland Norway, plus flights to Longyearbyen (Svalbard).

Widerøe (www.wideroe.no) A subsidiary of SAS with smaller planes and a handful of flights to smaller regional airports.

BOAT

Norway's excellent system of ferries connects otherwise inaccessible, isolated communities with an extensive network of car ferries criss-crossing the fjords; express boats link the country's offshore islands to the mainland. Most ferries accommodate motor vehicles.

BUS

Buses on Norway's extensive long-distance bus network are comfortable and make a habit of running on time.

Lavprisekspressen (www.lavprisekspressen.no) The cheapest buses are operated by Lavprisekspressen, which sells tickets over the internet. Its buses run along the coast between Oslo and Stavanger (via Kristiansand and most towns in between) and along two north–south corridors linking Oslo with Trondheim.

Nettbuss (www.nettbuss.no) Nettbuss has a big network which includes the subsidiaries TIMEkspressen, Nettbuss Express and Bus4You (Bergen to Stavanger).

Nor-Way Bussekspress (www.nor-way.no) Nor-Way Bussekspress operates the largest network of express buses in Norway, with routes connecting most towns and cities.

CAR & MOTORCYCLE

Main highways (E16 from Oslo to Bergen and the entire E6 from Oslo to Kirkenes), are open year-round; however, often more scenic mountain roads are generally only open from June to September, snow conditions permitting. Both fuel and car rental is expensive; all the major international car-rental companies have offices throughout Norway.

Road Hazards

Older roads and mountain routes are likely to be narrow, with multiple hairpin bends and very steep gradients. On some mountain roads, caravans and campervans are forbidden or advisable only for experienced drivers, as it may be necessary to reverse in order to allow approaching traffic to pass. Watch for wandering reindeer in the far north.

TRAIN

Norwegian State Railways (Norges Statsbaner, NSB; ☎ press 9 for English 81 50 08 88; www.nsb.no) operates an excellent, though limited, system of lines connecting Oslo with Stavanger, Bergen, Åndalsnes, Trondheim, Fauske and Bodø; lines also connect Sweden with Oslo, Trondheim and Narvik. Most long-distance day trains have 1st- and 2nd-class seats and a buffet car or refreshment trolley service.

Reservations sometimes cost an additional Nkr50 and are mandatory on some long-distance routes.

THE HURTIGRUTEN

Norway's legendary **Hurtigruten coastal ferry** (☎ 81 00 30 30; www.hurtigruten.com) is a popular way to explore Norway. Each night one of 11 ferries heads north from Bergen, pulling into 35 ports on its six-day journey to Kirkenes, where it then turns around and heads back south. The return journey takes 11 days and covers 5200km. In agreeable weather (which is not guaranteed) the fjord and mountain scenery is nothing short of spectacular. On-board, meals are served in the dining room and you can buy snacks and light meals in the cafeteria.

Poland

Includes ➡

Best Places to Eat

- ➡ Restauracja Pod Norenami (p856)
- ➡ Dwie Trzecie (p851)
- ➡ Szeroka 9 (p873)
- ➡ Papierówka (p866)
- ➡ Cafe & Restaurant Steinhaus (p864)

Best Places to Stay

- ➡ Wielopole (p856)
- ➡ Castle Inn (p850)
- ➡ Hostel Mleczarnia (p864)
- ➡ Hotel Stare Miasto (p866)
- ➡ Hotel Petite Fleur (p873)

Why Go?

If they were handing out prizes for 'most eventful history', Poland would get a medal. The nation has spent centuries at the pointy end of history, grappling with war and invasion. Nothing, however, has succeeded in suppressing Poles' strong sense of nationhood and cultural identity. As a result, bustling centres like Warsaw and Kraków exude a sophisticated energy that's a heady mix of old and new.

Away from the cities, Poland is surprisingly diverse, from its northern beaches to a long chain of mountains on its southern border. In between, towns and cities are dotted with ruined castles, picturesque market squares and historic churches.

Although prices have steadily risen in the postcommunist era, Poland is still good value. As the Poles continue to reconcile their distinctive national identity with their place in Europe, it's a fascinating time to pay a visit.

When to Go

Warsaw

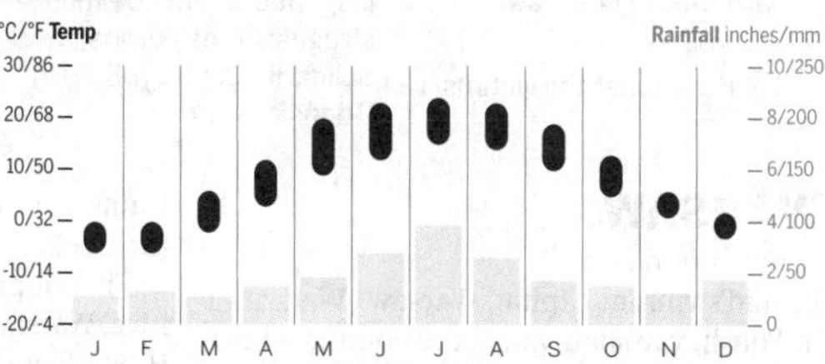

May & Jun Stately Kraków returns to life after a long winter.

Jul & Aug A brief but hot summer is good for swimming in the Baltic Sea or hiking in the mountains.

Sep & Oct Warm and sunny enough for an active city break to Warsaw.

Poland Highlights

1. Experience the beauty and history of **Kraków's** Old Town.
2. Enjoy the student-fuelled party vibe in **Wrocław** (p863).
3. Remember the victims of the Nazi German genocide at **Auschwitz-Birkenau** (p858).
4. Relive Poland's inspirational anticommunist struggle at the European Solidarity Centre (p870) in **Gdańsk**.
5. Ski or hike the Tatry mountains from **Zakopane** (p861).
6. Prepare to be dazzled by the Museum of the History of Polish Jews (p850) in **Warsaw**.

WARSAW

POP 1.73 MILLION

Poland's vibrant capital, Warsaw (Warszawa in Polish, var-shah-va), is the country's largest city and epicentre of Polish commerce and culture. It offers an abundance of museums, clubs and concert halls, as well as the widest array of eating options. It's a major transport hub, and even if you're not planning a long stay, chances are you'll change trains here or arrive at/depart from one of the city's airports.

First impressions may not be entirely positive. Warsaw was levelled during World War II by occupying German soldiers and rebuilt in the 1950s and '60s in bleak Soviet style. Modern touches added since communism fell in 1989 have softened the edges, however, and the passing decades have lent that old Soviet architecture a hip, retro gloss.

ITINERARIES

One Week

Spend a day exploring **Warsaw**, with a stroll around the Old Town and a stop at the Museum of the History of Polish Jews. Next day, head to historic **Kraków** for three days, visiting the beautiful Old Town, Wawel Castle and former Jewish district of Kazimierz. Take a day trip to **Auschwitz-Birkenau**, the former Nazi German extermination camp. Afterward, head to **Zakopane** for a day in the mountains.

Two Weeks

Follow the above itinerary, then travel to **Wrocław** for two days, taking in its graceful town square. Head north to Gothic **Toruń** for a day, then onward to **Gdańsk** for two days, exploring the museums and bars of the main town and visiting the magnificent castle at **Malbork**.

Sights

Old Town

Warsaw's Old Town looks old but dates from just around 60 years ago. It was rebuilt from the ground up after being reduced to rubble during WWII. The reconstruction, which took place between 1949 and 1963, aimed at restoring the appearance of the town in the 17th and 18th centuries. The centre is the rebuilt **Old Town Square** (Rynek Starego Miasta).

Royal Castle CASTLE

(☎22 355 5170; www.zamek-krolewski.pl; Plac Zamkowy 4; adult/concession 22/15zł; ⊙10am-4pm Tue-Sat, 11am-4pm Sun) This massive brick edifice, a copy of the original blown up by the Germans in WWII, began life as a wooden stronghold of the dukes of Mazovia in the 14th century. Its heyday came in the mid-17th century, when it became one of Europe's most splendid royal residences. It then served the tsars and, in 1918, after Poland regained independence, became the residence of the president. Today it is filled with period furniture and works of art.

Barbican FORTRESS

(ul Nowomiejska) Heading north out of the Old Town along ul Nowomiejska you'll soon see the red-brick Barbican, a semicircular defensive tower topped with a decorative Renaissance parapet. It was partially dismantled in the 19th century, but reconstructed after WWII, and is now a popular spot for buskers and art sellers.

Royal Way

This 4km historic route connects the Old Town with the modern city centre, running south from about Plac Zamkowy along elegant ul Krakowskie Przedmieście, and ul Nowy Świat all the way to busy Al Jerozolimskie.

St Anne's Church CHURCH

(ul Krakowskie Przedmieście 68) Marking the start of the Royal Way, this is arguably the most ornate church in the city. It escaped major damage during WWII, which explains why it sports an original trompe l'œil ceiling, a rococo high altar and a gorgeous organ. The facade is also baroque in style, although there are neoclassical touches here and there.

Church of the Holy Cross CHURCH

(Kościół św Krzyża; ☎22 826 8910; ul Krakowskie Przedmieście 3; ⊙10am-4pm) FREE This neighbourhood is chock-a-block with sumptuous churches, but the one most visitors will want to see is the Holy Cross, not so much for the fine baroque altarpieces that miraculously survived fighting during the Warsaw Rising, but to glimpse a small urn by the second pillar on the left side of the nave. The urn, adorned with an epitaph to Frédéric Chopin, contains what remains of the composer's heart, brought here from Paris after Chopin's death.

Chopin Museum MUSEUM

(☎booking 22 441 6251; www.chopin.museum/pl; ul Okólnik 1; adult/concession 22/13zł; ⊙11am-8pm Tue-Sun) The baroque Ostrogski Palace

Central Warsaw

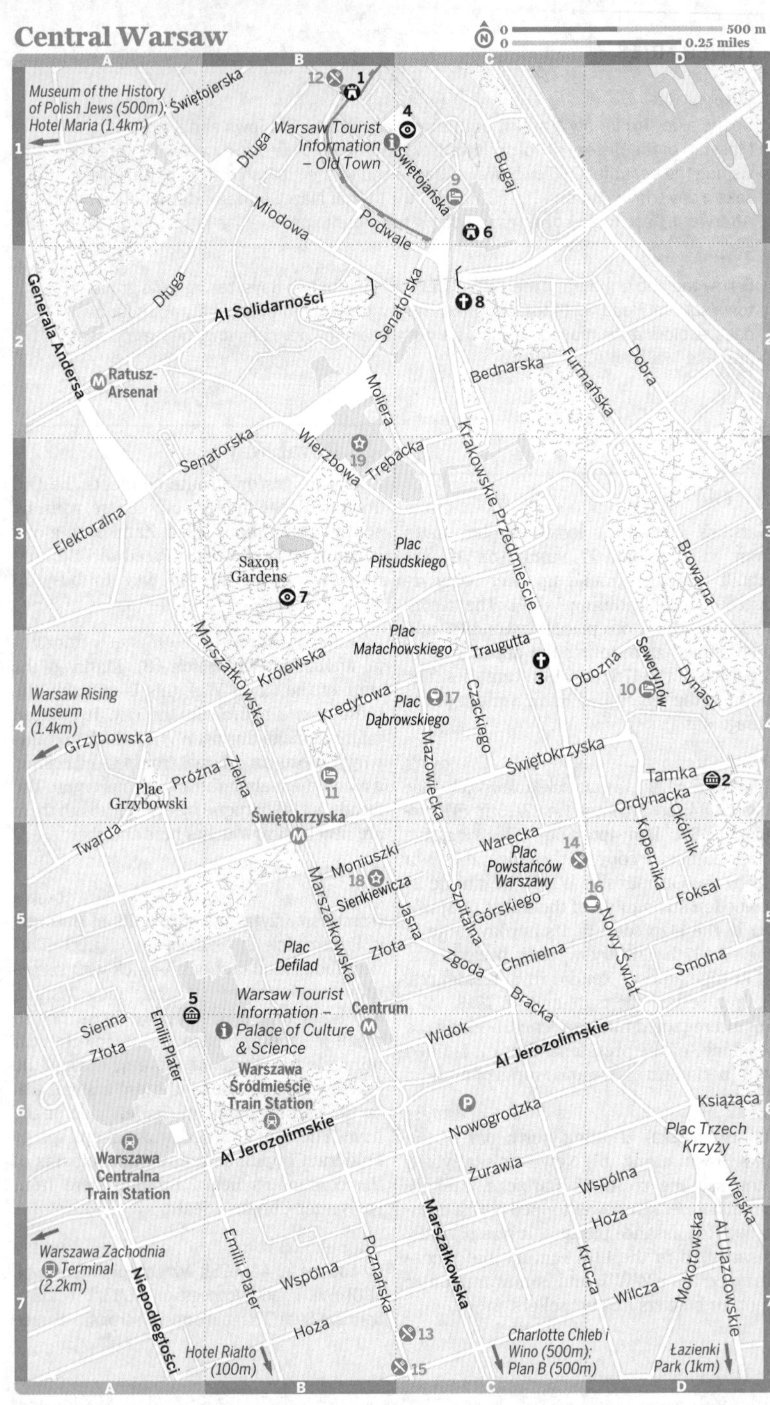
0 500 m
0 0.25 miles
Museum of the History of Polish Jews (500m); Hotel Maria (1.4km)
Świętojerska
Długa
Warsaw Tourist Information – Old Town
Świętojańska
Bugaj
Miodowa
Podwale
Generała Andersa
Długa
Al Solidarności
Senatorska
Ratusz-Arsenał
Bednarska
Furmańska
Dobra
Moliera
Senatorska
Wierzbowa
Trębacka
Krakowskie Przedmieście
Elektoralna
Plac Piłsudskiego
Saxon Gardens
Browarna
Marszałkowska
Królewska
Plac Małachowskiego
Traugutta
Obozna
Sewerynów
Dynasy
Warsaw Rising Museum (1.4km)
Kredytowa
Plac Dąbrowskiego
Czackiego
Grzybowska
Mazowiecka
Świętokrzyska
Plac Grzybowski
Próżna
Zielna
Tamka
Ordynacka
Okólnik
Świętokrzyska
Twarda
Warecka
Plac Powstańców Warszawy
Kopernika
Moniuszki
Marszałkowska
Sienkiewicza
Szpitalna
Górskiego
Foksal
Jasna
Nowy Świat
Plac Defilad
Złota
Zgoda
Chmielna
Smolna
Bracka
Warsaw Tourist Information – Palace of Culture & Science
Centrum
Sienna
Złota
Emilii Plater
Widok
Al Jerozolimskie
Warszawa Śródmieście Train Station
Nowogrodzka
Książąca
Plac Trzech Krzyży
Al Jerozolimskie
Warszawa Centralna Train Station
Żurawia
Wspólna
Wiejska
Hoża
Warszawa Zachodnia Terminal (2.2km)
Emilii Plater
Poznańska
Marszałkowska
Krucza
Mokotowska
Al Ujazdowskie
Wspólna
Wilcza
Niepodległości
Hoża
Hotel Rialto (100m)
Charlotte Chleb i Wino (500m); Plan B (500m)
Łazienki Park (1km)

Central Warsaw

is home to a high-tech, multimedia museum showcasing the work of the country's most famous composer. You're encouraged to take your time through four floors of displays, including stopping by the listening booths in the basement where you can explore Chopin's oeuvre to your heart's content. Visitation is limited each hour, so your best bet is to book your visit in advance by phone or email.

Saxon Gardens GARDENS
FREE Stretching out a couple of blocks west of ul Krakowskie Przedmieście, these magnificent gardens date from the early 18th century and were the city's first public park. Modelled on the French gardens at Versailles, the gardens are filled with chestnut trees and baroque statues (allegories of the Virtues, the Sciences and the Elements), and there's an ornamental lake overlooked by a 19th-century water tower in the form of a circular Greek temple.

City Centre & Beyond

Palace of Culture & Science HISTORIC BUILDING
(PKiN; ☎22 656 7600; www.pkin.pl; Plac Defilad 1; ⊙9am-6pm) Love it or hate it, every visitor to Warsaw should visit the iconic, Socialist-Realist PKiN. This 'gift of friendship' from the Soviet Union was built in the early 1950s, and at 231m high remains the tallest building in Poland. The structure is home to a huge congress hall, theatres, a multiplex and two museums. Take the high-speed lift to the 30th-floor (115m) **viewing terrace** (adult/concession 18/12zł; 9am to 6pm) to take it all in.

★**Warsaw Rising Museum** MUSEUM
(Muzeum Powstania Warszawskiego; ☎22 539 7905, audioguides 22 539 7941; www.1944.pl; ul Grzybowska 79; adult/concession 14/10zł, audioguide 10zł; ⊙8am-6pm Mon, Wed & Fri, 8am-8pm Thu, 10am-6pm Sat & Sun) This modern, high-tech wonder traces the history of the city's heroic but doomed uprising against the Nazi occupation in 1944 through three levels of interactive displays, photographs, film archives and personal accounts. The volume of material is overwhelming, but the museum does an excellent job of instilling visitors with a sense of the desperation residents felt in deciding whether to oppose the occupation by force, and the inevitable consequence, including the Nazis' destruction of the city in the aftermath.

Łazienki Park GARDENS
(☎22 506 0028; www.lazienki-krolewskie.pl; ul Agrykola; ⊙dawn-dusk) FREE This park – pronounced wah-*zhen*-kee – is a beautiful place of manicured greens and wild patches. Its popularity extends to families, peacocks and fans of classical music, who come for the alfresco **Chopin concerts** on Sunday afternoons at noon and 4pm from mid-May through September. Once a hunting ground attached to Ujazdów Castle, Łazienki was acquired by King Stanisław August Poniatowski in 1764 and transformed into a splendid park complete with palace, amphitheatre and various follies and other buildings.

Former Jewish District

The suburbs northwest of the Palace of Culture & Science were once predominantly inhabited by Warsaw's Jewish community.

★ **Museum of the History of Polish Jews** MUSEUM
(Polin; ☎info 22 471 0301; www.polin.pl; ul Mordechaja Anielewicza 6; adult/concession permanent exhibition 25/15zł, incl temporary exhibits 30/20zł; ⊙10am-6pm Mon, Wed-Fri & Sun, 10am-8pm Sat) This high-tech marvel of a museum, years in the planning, opened to great fanfare in 2014. The permanent exhibition traces 1000 years of Jewish history in Poland, from accounts of the earliest Jewish traders in the region through the waves of mass migration, progress and pogroms, all the way to WWII and the destruction of Europe's largest Jewish community. Take an audioguide (10zł) to get the most out of the rooms of displays, interactive maps, photos and video.

Jewish Cemetery CEMETERY
(☎22 838 2622; www.beisolam.jewish.org.pl; ul Okopowa 49/51; admission 8zł; ⊙10am-dusk Mon-Thu, 9am-1pm Fri, 11am-4pm Sun) Founded in 1806, Warsaw's main Jewish Cemetery incredibly suffered little during WWII and contains more than 150,000 tombstones, the largest collection of its kind in Europe. A notice near the entrance lists the graves of many eminent Polish Jews, including Ludwik Zamenhof, creator of the artificial international language Esperanto.

Sleeping

Apartments Apart (www.apartmentsapart.com) offers short-term apartment rentals in the Old Town and city centre.

Oki Doki Hostel HOSTEL €
(☎22 828 0122; www.okidoki.pl; Plac Dąbrowskiego 3; dm 40-90zł, s/d from 100/154zł; 📶) Oki Doki is arguably Warsaw's most popular hostel and definitely one of the best. Each of its bright, large rooms is individually named and decorated. Accommodation is in three- to eight-bed dorms, with a special three-bed dorm for women only. The owners are well travelled and know the needs of backpackers, providing a self-service laundry and bike rental. Breakfast available (15zł).

Hostel Helvetia HOSTEL €
(☎22 826 7108; www.hostel-helvetia.pl; ul Sewerynów 7; dm/r from 41/180zł; 📶) Helvetia has spick-and-span rooms, painted in warm, bright colours, with wooden floors and a good amount of space. Choose from three- to eight-bed dorms or good-value private singles and doubles. Laundry and kitchen facilities are in top order, and with a limited number of beds, it's best to book ahead in summer.

★ **Castle Inn** HOTEL €€
(☎22 887 9530; www.castleinn.eu; ul Świętojańska 2; s/d from 220/280zł; @📶) This nicely done-up 'art hotel' is housed in a 17th-century townhouse. All rooms overlook either Castle Sq or St John's Cathedral, and come in a range of playful styles. Our favourite would be No 121, 'Viktor', named for a reclusive street artist, complete with tasteful graffiti and a gorgeous castle view. Breakfast costs an extra 35zł.

Hotel Maria HOTEL €€
(☎22 838 4062; www.hotelmaria.pl; Al Jana Pawła II 71; s/d 320/380zł; P❄📶) The Maria is a rambling old house of a hotel set on three floors (no lifts, just steep wooden stairs), with friendly staff, a delightful restaurant and breakfast nook, and spacious rooms. The location is outside the centre, but convenient to the Jewish sights and just a few tram stops away from the Old Town.

Hotel Rialto BOUTIQUE HOTEL €€€
(☎22 584 8700; www.rialto.pl; ul Wilcza 73; r from 450zł; P❄@📶) This converted townhouse is a monument to early-20th-century design. Each of the 44 rooms is individually decorated in art nouveau or art deco style, with antique and reproduction furniture, period fittings and tiled or marbled baths. There are plenty of modern touches where it counts, such as flat-screen TVs, power showers, and a sauna and steam room.

Eating

Bar Mleczny Pod Barbakanem CAFETERIA €
(☎22 831 4737; ul Mostowa 27; mains 6-10zł; ⊙8am-5pm Mon-Sat; 🌿) This popular milk bar, very close to the Old Town, looks as though it hasn't changed for decades. It serves cheap, unpretentious Polish standards in a location that would be the envy of many upmarket eateries.

Beirut Hummus & Music Bar MIDDLE EASTERN €
(www.beirut.com.pl; ul Poznańska 12; mains 15-22zł; ⊙noon-1am; 📶🌿) Hip and informal, this popular place has recently expanded to add seafood (like herring or grilled calamari) to an already nice mix of hummus varieties and Middle Eastern dishes. Choose from the menu above the counter and then find

a table. There's a turntable on hand for later in the evening, when the music part of the name kicks in.

Charlotte Chleb i Wino FRENCH €€
(☎600 807 880; www.bistrocharlotte.com; Al Wyzwolenia 18, Plac Zbawiciela; mains 15-30zł; 7am-midnight Mon-Thu, to 1am Fri, 9am-1am Sat, to 10pm Sun;) Dazzling French bakery and bistro, dishing out tantalising croissants and pastries at the break of dawn, and then transitioning to big salads and crusty sandwiches through the lunch and dinner hours, and finally to wine on the terrace in the evening.

Dawne Smaki POLISH €€
(☎22 465 8320; www.dawnesmaki.pl; ul Nowy Świat 49; mains 25-50zł; noon-11pm;) Excellent, easy-to-reach place to try Polish specialties such as herring in cream, stuffed cabbage rolls, *pierogi* (dumplings) and all the rest. The interior is traditional white walls, wood and lace, without being overly hokey. Try the good-value lunch specials.

★**Dwie Trzecie** MEDITERRANEAN €€€
(☎22 623 0290; www.dwietrzecie.waw.pl; ul Wilcza 50/52; mains 30-70zł; noon-11pm;) It's worth splurging on well-turned-out dishes such as spicy pumpkin soup, flavoured with beetroot and shrimp, followed by slow-roasted veal cheeks and polenta. The interior is formal without a hint of fussiness, and the warm brick-lined walls and plank flooring lend a calming feel. The wine list is excellent, including a good choice of wine by the glass.

Drinking & Nightlife

Good places for pub crawls include along ul Mazowiecka in the centre, in Praga across the Vistula River, and the Powiśle district, near the university.

Cafe Blikle CAFE
(☎22 826 0569; www.blikle.pl; ul Nowy Świat 35; coffee from 10zł, doughnut to go from 3zł; 9am-8pm Mon-Sat, 10am-8pm Sun;) The mere fact that Blikle has survived two world wars and the pressure of communism makes it a household name. But what makes this legendary cafe truly famous is its doughnuts, for which people have been queuing up for generations. Join the back of the line and find out why.

Plan B BAR
(☎503 116 154; Al Wyzwolenia 18, Plac Zbawiciela; 11am-late) This phenomenally popular upstairs bar on Plac Zbawiciela draws a mix of students and young office workers. Find some couch space and relax to smooth beats from regular DJs. On warm summer evenings the action spills out onto the street, giving Plac Zbawiciela the feel of a summer block party.

Enklawa CLUB
(☎22 827 3151; www.enklawa.com; ul Mazowiecka 12; 10pm-4am Tue-Sat) Red and orange dominates this space with comfy plush seating, mirrored ceilings, two bars and plenty of room to dance. Check out the extensive drinks menu, hit the dance floor or observe the action from a stool on the upper balcony. Wednesday night is 'old school' night, with music from the '70s to '90s.

☆ Entertainment

Filharmonia Narodowa CLASSICAL MUSIC
(National Philharmonic; ☎switchboard 22 551 7103, tickets 22 551 7128; www.filharmonia.pl; ul Jasna 5; box office 10am-2pm & 3-7pm Mon-Fri) Home of the world-famous National Philharmonic Orchestra and Choir of Poland, founded in 1901, this venue has a concert hall (enter from ul Sienkiewicza 10) and a chamber-music hall (enter from ul Moniuszki 5), both of which stage regular concerts. The box office entrance is on ul Sienkiewicza.

Teatr Wielki OPERA
(National Opera; ☎reservations 22 826 5019; www.teatrwielki.pl; Plac Teatralny 1; box office 9am-7pm Mon-Fri, 11am-7pm Sat & Sun) This magnificent neoclassical theatre, dating from 1833 and rebuilt after WWII, is the city's main stage for opera and ballet, with a repertoire of international classics and works by Polish composers, notably Stanisław Moniuszko.

Information

Warsaw Tourist Information (www.warsawtour.pl) operates three helpful branches at various points around town: **Old Town** (Centrum Informacji Turystycznej; Stary Rynek 19/21/21a; 9am-8pm May-Sep, to 6pm Oct-Apr;), the **Palace of Culture & Science** (Plac Defilad 1, entrance from ul Emilii Plater; 8am-8pm May-Sep, to 6pm Oct-Apr;) and **Warsaw-Frédéric Chopin Airport** (Terminal A, Warsaw-Frédéric Chopin Airport, ul Żwirki i Wigury 1; 8am-8pm May-Sep, to 6pm Oct-Apr). They offer free city maps as well as advice on what to see and where to stay.

Lux Med (☎22 332 2888; www.luxmed.pl; Marriott Hotel Bldg, al Jerozolimskie 65/79;

WANT MORE?

For in-depth information, reviews and recommendations at your fingertips, head to the Apple App Store to purchase Lonely Planet's *Warsaw City Guide* and *Polish Phrasebook* iPhone apps.

Alternatively, head to www.lonelyplanet.com/poland/warsaw for planning advice, author recommendations, traveller reviews and insider tips.

7am-8pm Mon-Fri, to 4pm Sat) Private clinic with English-speaking specialist doctors and its own ambulance service; carries out laboratory tests and arranges house calls.

Verso Internet (22 635 9174; ul Freta 17; per hour 5zł; 8am-8pm Mon-Fri, 9am-5pm Sat, 10am-4pm Sun) Copy shop with internet terminals for use. Enter from ul Świętojerska.

Getting There & Away

AIR

Warsaw's main international airport, **Warsaw-Frédéric Chopin Airport** (WAW – Lotnisko Chopina w Warszawie; flight information 22 650 4220; www.lotnisko-chopina.pl; ul Żwirki i Wigury 1), 10km from the city centre, handles most flights in and out of the city. The airport's Terminal A has undergone extensive renovation. The terminal has bank ATMs, restaurants and a branch of the Warsaw Tourist Information office.

Some budget flights, including Ryanair services, use outlying **Warsaw Modlin** (801 801 880, Ryanair 703 303 033; www.modlinairport.pl; ul Generała Wiktora Thommée 1a, Nowy Dwór Mazowiecki), 35km north of the city.

BUS

Warsaw's main bus station is **Warszawa Zachodnia** (703 403 330, PKS Polonus 22 823 6200; www.pksbilety.pl; Al Jerozolimskie 144; information & tickets 6am-9pm), southwest of the centre and adjoining Warszawa Zachodnia train station. This sprawling terminal handles most (but not all) international and domestic routes. To get here from the Warszawa Centralna train station, take bus 127, 158 or 517.

Popular coach services run by **Polski Bus** (22 417 6227; www.polskibus.com) often depart from a small bus terminal near the Wilanowska metro station. Check the website for further information and give yourself plenty of time to find the bus station. Buy tickets online.

Domestic bus connections include Gdańsk (40zł, five hours, hourly), Kraków (40zł, five hours, hourly), Lublin (15zł, three hours, five daily), Toruń (25zł, three hours, five daily), Poznań (20zł, five hours, five daily) and Wrocław (30zł, five hours, five daily). Warsaw has good bus services to Berlin (80zł, 10 hours, two daily) and Prague (100zł, 11 hours, two daily).

TRAIN

Warsaw has several train stations and is connected directly to a number of international destinations. The station most travellers use is **Warszawa Centralna** (Warsaw Central; 22 391 9757; www.pkp.pl; Al Jerozolimskie 54; 24hr), but it's not always where trains start or finish so be sure to board promptly.

Regular international train services include those to Berlin (six hours, five daily), Bratislava (six hours, one daily), Budapest (10½ hours, two daily), Minsk (9½ to 12 hours, two to three daily), Moscow (18 to 21 hours, two to three daily) and Prague (8½ to 10½ hours, two daily).

Getting Around

TO/FROM THE AIRPORT

To reach the centre from Warsaw-Frédéric Chopin Airport, take commuter SKM rail service train 52 or 53. Train 52 runs to the Warszawa Zachodnia and Warszawa Śródmieście train stations, while 53 goes to Warszawa Centralna (Central Railway Station). Tickets cost 4.40zł. Bus 175 (4.40zł) terminates at Plac Piłsudskiego, about a 500m walk from the Old Town. A taxi fare between the airport and city centre is around 50zł.

From Warsaw Modlin, the easiest way to the centre is aboard the regular Modlin bus (19zł). A taxi will cost from 100zł to 130zł.

PUBLIC TRANSPORT

Warsaw has a reliable system of trams, buses and metro cars. Trams running east–west across busy Al Jerozolimskie are particularly handy.

Buy tickets from machines (have coins or small bills handy) or from news kiosks near stops. A standard ticket (4.40zł) is valid for one ride by bus, tram or metro. Day passes are available for 15zł. Be sure to validate the ticket on boarding.

TAXI

Super Taxi (196 22; www.supertaxi.pl) Reliable, inexpensive radio taxi service.

MAŁOPOLSKA

Małopolska (literally 'Lesser Poland') covers southeastern Poland from the former royal capital of Kraków to the eastern Lublin Uplands. The name does not refer to size or relative importance, but rather that

Lesser Poland was mentioned in atlases more recently (of the 15th century!) than Wielkopolska ('Greater Poland'). It's a colourful region filled with remnants of traditional life and historic cities.

Kraków

POP 756,500

Many Polish cities are centred on an attractive Old Town, but none compare to Kraków (pronounced krak-oof) for effortless beauty. As it was the royal capital of Poland until 1596 and miraculously escaped destruction in WWII, Kraków is packed with appealing historic buildings and streetscapes. One of the most important sights is Wawel Castle, from where the ancient Polish kingdom was once ruled.

South of the castle lies the former Jewish quarter of Kazimierz. Its silent synagogues are a reminder of the tragedy of WWII. These days, the quarter has been injected with new life and is home to some of the city's best bars and clubs.

Sights

Wawel Hill

South of Old Town, this prominent hilltop is crowned with the former Royal Castle and Cathedral – both enduring symbols of Poland.

★ Royal Wawel Castle CASTLE

(Zamek Królewski na Wawelu; ☎ Wawel Visitor Centre 12 422 5155; www.wawel.krakow.pl; Wawel Hill; grounds admission free, attractions priced separately; ⏰ grounds 6am-dusk) As the political and cultural heart of Poland through the 16th century, Wawel Castle is a potent symbol of national identity. It's now a museum containing five separate sections: **Crown Treasury & Armoury**; **State Rooms**; **Royal Private Apartments**; **Lost Wawel**; and **Exhibition of Oriental Art**. Each requires a separate ticket. Of the five, the State Rooms and Royal Private Apartments are most impressive. There's a limited quota of tickets, so arrive early or book in advance by phone.

Wawel Cathedral CHURCH

(☎ 12 429 9515; www.katedra-wawelska.pl; Wawel 3, Wawel Hill; cathedral free, combined entry for crypts, bell tower & museum adult/concession 12/7zł; ⏰ 9am-5pm Mon-Sat, from 12.30pm Sun) The Royal Cathedral has witnessed many coronations, funerals and entombments of Poland's monarchs and strongmen over the centuries. This is the third church on this site, consecrated in 1364. The original was founded in the 11th century by King Bolesław I Chrobry and replaced with a Romanesque construction around 1140. When that burned down in 1305, only the Crypt of St Leonard survived. Highlights include the **Holy Cross Chapel**, **Sigismund Chapel**, **Sigismund Bell**, the **Crypt of St Leonard** and **Royal Crypts**.

Old Town

This vast Rynek Główny (main square) is the focus of the Old Town and Europe's largest medieval town square (200m by 200m).

Cloth Hall HISTORIC BUILDING

(Sukiennice; www.museum.krakow.pl; Rynek Główny 1/3) FREE Dominating the middle of the square, this building was once the centre of Kraków's medieval clothing trade. It was created in the early 14th century when a roof was put over two rows of stalls, then extended into a 108m-long Gothic structure. The hall was rebuilt in Renaissance style after a fire in 1555; the arcades were added in the late 19th century.

Rynek Underground MUSEUM

(☎ 12 426 5060; www.podziemiarynku.com; Rynek Główny 1; adult/concession 19/16zł, Tue free; ⏰ 10am-8pm Mon, to 4pm Tue, to 10pm Wed-Sun) From the northern end of the Cloth Hall, enter this fascinating attraction beneath the market square. It consists of an underground route through medieval market stalls and other long-forgotten chambers. The 'Middle Ages meets 21st century' experience is enhanced by a multitude of holograms and other audiovisual wizardry. There's always a scrum at the door, so prebook an entry time at one of the tourist offices.

St Mary's Basilica CHURCH

(Basilica of the Assumption of Our Lady; ☎ 12 422 0737; www.mariacki.com; Plac Mariacki 5, Rynek Główny; adult/concession 10/5zł; ⏰ 11.30am-5.30pm Mon-Sat, 2-5.30pm Sun) Overlooking the square, this striking brick church, best known simply as St Mary's, is dominated by two towers of different heights. The first church here was built in the 1220s and following its destruction during a Tatar raid, construction of the basilica began. Tour the exquisite interior, with its remarkable Veit Stoss pentaptych, and in summer climb the **tower** for excellent

Kraków – Old Town & Wawel

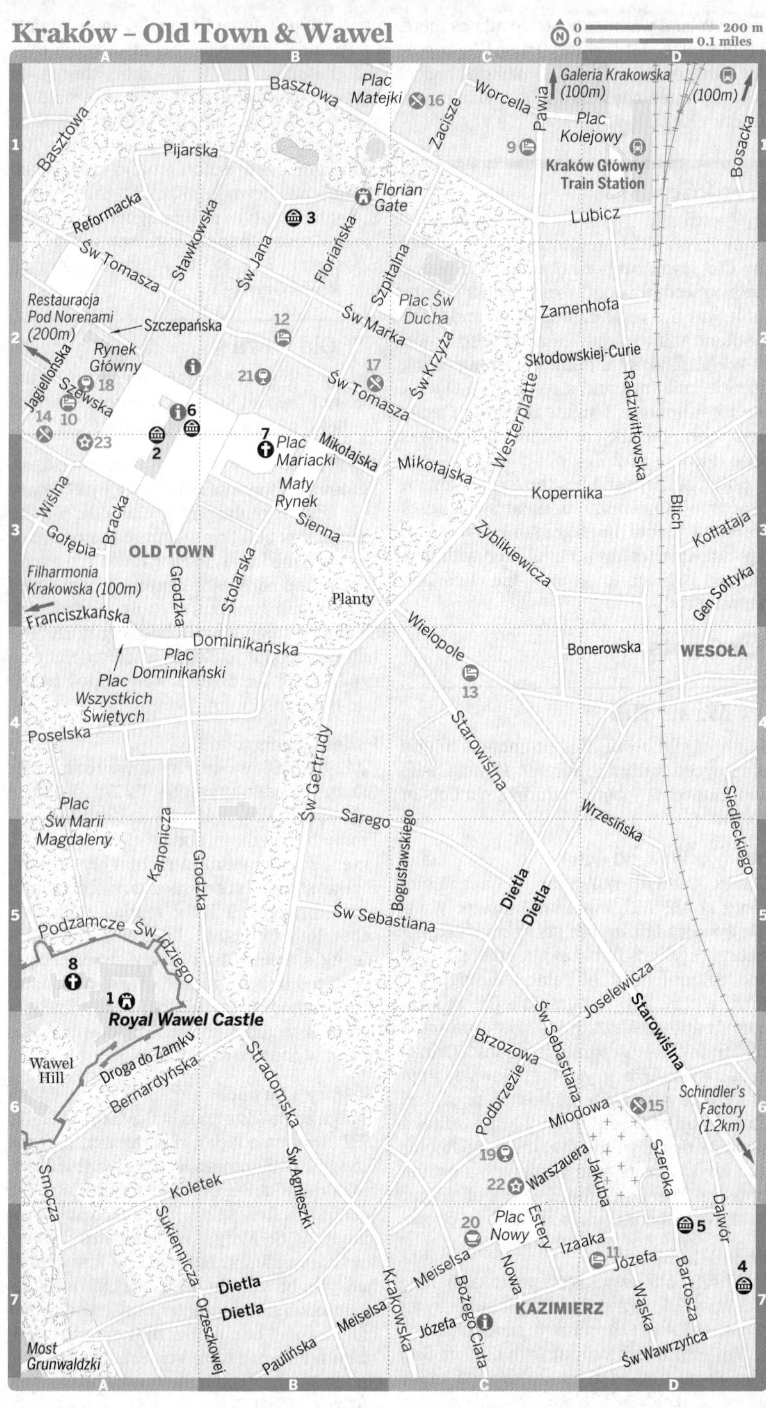

Kraków – Old Town & Wawel

Top Sights
1 Royal Wawel Castle A5

Sights
2 Cloth Hall A3
3 Czartoryski Museum B1
4 Galicia Jewish Museum D7
5 Jewish Museum D7
6 Rynek Underground A2
7 St Mary's Basilica B3
8 Wawel Cathedral A5

Sleeping
9 Greg & Tom Hostel C1
10 Hostel Flamingo A2
11 Hotel Abel D7
12 Hotel Pod Różą B2
13 Wielopole C4

Eating
14 Chimera A2
15 Dawno Temu Na Kazimierzu D6
16 Glonojad C1
17 Milkbar Tomasza B2

Drinking & Nightlife
18 Frantic A2
19 Miejsce Bar C6
20 Mleczarnia C7
21 Pauza B2

Entertainment
22 Alchemia C6
23 Baccarat Live A3

views. Don't miss the hourly *hejnał* (bugle call) from the taller tower.

Czartoryski Museum MUSEUM
(www.czartoryski.org; ul Św Jana 19) The Czartoryski Museum boasts the city's richest art collection, including Kraków's most valuable painting: Leonardo da Vinci's *Lady with an Ermine*. Among other important works is Rembrandt's *Landscape with the Good Samaritan*. Other exhibitions include Greek, Roman, Egyptian and Etruscan art as well as Turkish weaponry. At the time of research, the museum was closed for renovation but expected to reopen in 2015. During renovation, the *Lady with an Ermine* was being exhibited at Wawel Castle.

Kazimierz & Podgórze

Founded by King Kazimierz III Wielki in 1335, Kazimierz was originally an independent town and then became a Jewish district. During WWII, the Germans relocated Jews south across the Vistula River to a walled ghetto in Podgórze. They were exterminated in the nearby Płaszów Concentration Camp, as portrayed in the Steven Spielberg film *Schindler's List*. In addition to the attractions below, many synagogues are still standing and can be visited individually.

Schindler's Factory MUSEUM
(Fabryka Schindlera; ☎12 257 1017; www.mhk.pl; ul Lipowa 4; adult/concession 19/16zł, free Mon; ⏰10am-8pm Mon, 10am-4pm Tue-Sun) This impressive interactive museum covers the Nazi occupation of Kraków in WWII. It's housed in the former enamel factory of Oskar Schindler, the Nazi industrialist who famously saved the lives of members of his Jewish labour force during the Holocaust. Well-organised, innovative exhibits tell the moving story of the city from 1939 to 1945, recreating urban elements such as a tram carriage, a train station underpass and a crowded ghetto apartment within the factory walls.

Jewish Museum MUSEUM
(Old Synagogue; ☎12 422 0962; www.mhk.pl; ul Szeroka 24; adult/concession 9/7zł, free Mon; ⏰10am-2pm Mon, 9am-5pm Tue-Sun) At the southern end of ul Szeroka this museum is housed in the **Old Synagogue**, which dates to the 15th century. The prayer hall, complete with a reconstructed *bimah* (raised platform at the centre of the synagogue where the Torah is read) and the original *aron kodesh* (the niche in the eastern wall where Torah scrolls are kept), houses an exhibition of liturgical objects. Upstairs there's a photographic exhibit focusing on Jewish Kraków and the Holocaust.

Galicia Jewish Museum MUSEUM
(☎12 421 6842; www.galiciajewishmuseum.org; ul Dajwór 18; adult/concession 15/10zł; ⏰10am-6pm) This museum both commemorates Jewish victims of the Holocaust and celebrates the Jewish culture and history of the former Austro-Hungarian region of Galicia. It features an impressive photographic exhibition depicting modern-day remnants of southeastern Poland's once-thriving Jewish community, called 'Traces of Memory', along with video testimony of survivors and regular temporary exhibits.

Sleeping

Kraków is unquestionably Poland's major tourist destination, with prices to match. **AAA Kraków Apartments** (www.krakow-apartments.biz) is one of several companies offering good-value, short-term apartment rentals.

Hostel Flamingo HOSTEL €

(☎12 422 0000; www.flamingo-hostel.com; ul Szewska 4; dm 47-65zł, d 158zł; 📶) Highly rated hostel with an excellent central location, just a couple steps from the main square. Pluses – in addition to the expected amenities – include free breakfast, an in-house cafe and a cheeky attitude. Sleeping is in six- to 12-bed dorms plus a few private doubles.

Greg & Tom Hostel HOSTEL €

(☎12 422 4100; www.gregtomhostel.com; ul Pawia 12/7; dm 57zł, d from 150zł; 📶) This well-run hostel is spread over three locations, though all check-in is handled at the main branch on ul Pawia. The staff is friendly, the rooms are clean, and laundry facilities are included. On Tuesday and Saturday evenings, hot Polish meals are served.

★ **Wielopole** HOTEL €€

(☎12 422 1475; www.wielopole.pl; ul Wielopole 3; s/d 260/360zł; ❄📶) Wielopole's selection of bright, modern rooms – all of them with spotless bathrooms – is housed in a renovated block with a great courtyard on the eastern edge of the Old Town, within easy walk of Kazimierz. The breakfast spread here is impressive.

Hotel Abel HOTEL €€

(☎12 411 8736; www.abelkrakow.pl; ul Józefa 30; s/d 150/190zł; 📶) Reflecting the character of Kazimierz, this modest, good-value hotel has a distinctive personality, evident in its polished wooden staircase, arched brickwork and age-worn tiles. The rooms are clean but simply furnished. The hotel makes a good base for exploring the historic Jewish neighbourhood.

Hotel Pod Różą HOTEL €€€

(☎12 424 3300; www.podroza.hotel.com.pl; ul Floriańska 14; s 650zł, d 650-720zł; ❄@📶) A hotel that has never closed, even in the dark, dreary days of communism, 'Under the Rose' offers antiques, oriental carpets, a wonderful glassed-in courtyard restaurant and state-of-the-art facilities. Breakfast costs an extra 50zł.

> **WANT MORE?**
>
> For in-depth information, reviews and recommendations at your fingertips, head to the Apple App Store to purchase Lonely Planet's *Kraków City Guide* iPhone app.
>
> Alternatively, head to www.lonelyplanet.com/poland/malopolska/krakow for planning advice, author recommendations, traveller reviews and insider tips.

Eating

Glonojad VEGETARIAN €

(☎12 346 1677; www.glonojad.com; Plac Matejki 2; mains 10-16zł; ⏲8am-10pm; 📶🌱) Attractive modern vegetarian restaurant with a great view onto Plac Matejki, just north of the Barbican. The diverse menu has a variety of tasty dishes including samosas, curries, potato pancakes, burritos, gnocchi and soups. There's also an all-day breakfast menu, so there's no need to jump out of that hotel bed too early.

Milkbar Tomasza POLISH €

(☎12 422 1706; ul Św Tomasza 24; mains 10-20zł; ⏲8am-10pm) Cleverly modernised version of the traditional *bar mleczny* (milkbar), serving affordable dishes including breakfast in a pleasant dining area. The two-course set menu for 18zł is great value.

★ **Restauracja Pod Norenami** ASIAN, VEGETARIAN €€

(☎661 219 289; www.podnorenami.pl; ul Krupnicza 6; mains 18-30zł; ⏲10am-10pm; 📶🌱) This warm and inviting Asian-fusion restaurant is ideal for vegans and vegetarians. The menu pivots from Japanese to Thai and Vietnamese, with lots of spicy noodle and rice dishes, vegetarian sushi and many other excellent choices. Breakfast (served from 10am to noon) has Middle Eastern overtones, with hummus and pita and spicy scrambled eggs. Book in advance.

Dawno Temu Na Kazimierzu JEWISH €€

(Once upon a Time in Kazimierz; ☎12 421 2117; www.dawnotemu.nakazimierzu.pl; ul Szeroka 1; mains 20-35zł; ⏲10am-midnight) Arguably the smallest and most atmospheric of several restaurants in Kazimierz playing on the old-time Jewish theme. The traditional Polish-Jewish cooking

WORTH A TRIP

A UNESCO-PROTECTED SALT MINE

Some 14km southeast of Kraków, **Wieliczka** (12 278 7302; www.kopalnia.pl; ul Daniłowicza 10; adult/concession 79/64zł; 7.30am-7.30pm Apr-Oct, 8am-5pm Nov-Mar), pronouced vyeh-leech-kah, is famous for its deep salt mine. It's an eerie world of pits and chambers, and everything within its depths has been carved by hand from salt blocks. A section of the mine, some 22 chambers, is open to the public and it's a fascinating trip.

You visit three upper levels of the mine, from 64m to 135m below ground. Some have been made into chapels, with altarpieces and figures, others are adorned with statues and monuments – and there are even underground lakes.

Guided tours take about two hours. Wear comfortable shoes and dress warmly as the temperature in the mine is 14°C. In summer, English-language tours depart every half-hour. During the rest of the year, tours are less frequent.

Minibuses to Wieliczka (3zł) depart Kraków frequently from ul Pawia near the Galeria Krakowska shopping mall next to Kraków Główny train station.

(think of hearty variations of lamb and duck) is very good and the warm, candle-lit space, with klezmer music playing in the background, is the perfect spot to enjoy this part of Kraków.

Chimera POLISH €€€
(12 292 1212; www.chimera.com.pl; ul Św Anny 3; mains 35-60zł; 10am-10pm) Not to be confused with the salad bar of the same name, this is a Kraków classic. The vaulted cellar is the perfect setting to sample the specialty roasted lamb, goose or game meats.

Drinking & Nightlife

There are hundreds of pubs and bars in Kraków's Old Town, many housed in ancient vaulted cellars. Kazimierz also has a lively bar scene, centred around Plac Nowy.

Mleczarnia CAFE
(12 421 8532; www.mle.pl; ul Meiselsa 20; 10am-midnight; 3, 6, 8, 10) Wins the prize for best courtyard cafe. Shady trees and blooming roses make this place tops for a sunny-day drink. If it's rainy, never fear, for the cafe is warm and cosy, with crowded bookshelves and portrait-covered walls. Self service.

Miejsce Bar BAR
(600 960 876; www.miejsce.com.pl; ul Estery 1; 10am-2am;) Trendy bar that draws an eclectic mix of intellectual types, hipsters, students and generally anyone who enjoys good cocktails and a relaxed vibe. Quiet during the day; rowdier and more adventurous by night.

Pauza BAR
(12 422 4866; www.klubpauza.pl; ul Floriańska 18; 10am-2am Mon-Sat, from noon Sun; 2, 3, 4, 12, 13, 14, 15) Beloved for its alternative atmosphere, Pauza offers stiff drinks and heady conversation on the 1st floor (not to mention the occasional art exhibit and great window seats overlooking Floriańska).

Frantic CLUB
(12 423 0483; www.frantic.pl; ul Szewska 5; 10pm-4am Wed-Sat) With two dance floors, three bars, a chill-out room and top Polish and international DJs, Frantic is regularly packed out with smart young locals. There's sniffy door selection, so don't be too scruffy.

☆ Entertainment

Baccarat Live LIVE MUSIC
(605 057 234; www.baccaratlive.pl; Rynek Główny 28; 9pm-late Wed-Sat) Upmarket dance club brings in a mix of students and young professionals for live music as well as DJ and theme nights.

Alchemia LIVE MUSIC
(12 421 2200; www.alchemia.com.pl; ul Estery 5; 9am-late) This Kazimierz venue exudes a shabby-is-the-new-cool look with rough-hewn wooden benches, candlelit tables and a companionable gloom. It hosts regular live-music gigs and theatrical events through the week.

Filharmonia Krakowska CLASSICAL MUSIC
(Filharmonia im. Karola Szymanowskiego w Krakowie; reservations 12 619 8722, tickets 12 619 8733; www.filharmonia.krakow.pl; ul Zwierzyniecka 1; box office 10am-2pm & 3-7pm Tue-Fri) Home to one of the best orchestras in the country.

DON'T MISS

AUSCHWITZ-BIRKENAU

Many visitors pair a trip to Kraków with a visit to the **Auschwitz-Birkenau Museum & Memorial** (☎guides 33 844 8100; www.auschwitz.org.pl; ul Więźniów Oświęcimia 20, Oświęcim; admission free, compulsory guided tour adult/concession 25/20zł; ⊙8am-7pm Jun-Aug, 8am-6pm May & Sep, 8am-5pm Apr & Oct, 8am-4pm Mar & Nov, 8am-3pm Dec-Feb) FREE – or as it's known officially the 'Auschwitz-Birkenau: German Nazi Concentration & Extermination Camp' – in the town of Oświęcim. More than a million Jews as well large numbers of ethnic Poles and Roma were systematically murdered here by occupying Germans during WWII.

Both the main camp at Auschwitz (Auschwitz I) and a larger outlying camp at Birkenau (Auschwitz II), about 2km away, are open to the public and admission is free (though if arriving between 10am and 3pm from May to October, a guided tour is compulsory). A visit is essential to understanding the Holocaust, though the scope and nature of the crimes are horrifying and may not be suitable for children under 14.

The tour begins at the main camp, Auschwitz I, which began life as a Polish military barracks but was co-opted by the Nazis in 1940 as a death camp. Here is the infamous gate, displaying the grimly cynical message: 'Arbeit Macht Frei' (Through Work Freedom). Some 13 of 30 surviving prison blocks house museum exhibitions.

From here, the tour moves to Birkenau (Auschwitz II), where most of the killings took place. Massive and purpose-built to be efficient, the camp had more than 300 prison barracks. Here you'll find the remnants of gas chambers and crematoria.

Auschwitz-Birkenau is a workable day trip from Kraków. Most convenient are the approximately hourly buses to Oświęcim (12zł, 1½ hours), departing from the bus station in Kraków. There are also numerous minibuses to Oświęcim (10zł, 1½ hours) from the minibus stands off ul Pawia, next to Galeria Krakowska.

ℹ Information

The official tourist information office, **InfoKraków** (www.infokrakow.pl), maintains branches around town, including at the **Cloth Hall** (☎12 433 7310; Rynek Główny 1/3; ⊙9am-7pm May-Sep, 9am-5pm Oct-Apr), **Kazimierz** (☎12 422 0471; ul Józefa 7; ⊙9am-5pm), the **Old Town** (☎12 421 7787; ul Św Jana 2; ⊙9am-7pm) and the **Airport** (☎12 285 5341; John Paul II International Airport, Balice; ⊙9am-7pm).

Klub Garinet (☎12 423 2233; www.garinet.pl; ul Floriańska 18; internet per hour 4zł; ⊙9am-10pm) The pick of the crop of internet cafes near the main square.

ℹ Getting There & Away

AIR

Kraków's **John Paul II International Airport** (KRK; ☎information 12 295 5800; www.krakowairport.pl; Kapitana Mieczysława Medweckiego 1, Balice) was undergoing massive reconstruction during the time of research. Flights were operating as scheduled, but expect delays. Train service between the aiport and the centre had been temporarily suspended. If the train is not operating, public buses 292 and 208 (tickets 4zł) run to the main bus station. Taxis to the centre cost about 70zł.

The main Polish carrier LOT (p875) flies to Warsaw and other large cities. LOT subsidiary **Eurolot** (www.eurolot.com) services Gdańsk. Budget operators connect Kraków to cities in Europe.

BUS

Kraków's modern **bus station** (☎703 403 340; www.mda.malopolska.pl; ul Bosacka 18; ⊙information 7am-8pm) is conveniently located next to the main train station, Kraków Główny, on the fringe of the Old Town.

Bus travel is the best way to reach Zakopane (16zł, two hours, hourly). Modern **Polski Bus** (www.polskibus.com) coaches depart from here to Warsaw (five hours, several daily) and Wrocław (three hours, several daily); check fares and book tickets online.

TRAIN

Newly remodeled and gleaming **Kraków Główny** (Dworzec Główny; ☎information 22 391 9757; www.pkp.pl; Plac Dworcowy) train station, on the northeastern outskirts of the Old Town, handles all international trains and most domestic rail services.

Useful domestic destinations include Gdańsk (80zł, eight hours, three daily), Lublin (62zł, four hours, two daily), Poznań (80zł, eight hours, three daily), Toruń (73zł, seven hours, three daily), Warsaw (60zł to 130zł, three hours, at least hourly) and Wrocław (50zł, 5½ hours, hourly).

Popular international connections include Bratislava (7½ hours, one daily), Berlin (10 hours, one daily), Budapest (10½ hours, one daily), Lviv (7½ to 9½ hours, two daily) and Prague (10 hours, one daily).

Lublin

POP 349,000

Poland's eastern metropolis admittedly lacks the grandeur of Gdańsk or Kraków, but does have an attractive Old Town, with beautiful churches and tiny alleyways. It's a natural jumping off point for exploring southeastern Poland. Thousands of students make for a lively restaurant, bar and club scene.

Lublin plays an important role in Polish and Jewish history. It was here in 1569 that the Lublin Union was signed, uniting Poland and Lithuania to form one of the largest and most powerful entities in Europe in its day. For those interested in Jewish heritage, for centuries Lublin served as a centre of European Jewish culture. The Holocaust ended this vibrant community, and one of the most notorious Nazi extermination camps, Majdanek, lies at Lublin's doorstep.

Sights

Lublin Castle MUSEUM

(81 532 5001; www.muzeumlubelskie.pl; ul Zamkowa 9; adult/concession museum 6.50/4.50zł, chapel 6.50/4.50zł; 10am-5pm Tue-Sun) Lublin's royal castle dates from the 12th and 13th centuries, though it's been rebuilt many times over the years. It was here in 1569 where the union with Lithuania was signed. The castle is home to both the **Lublin Museum** and the surviving **Gothic Chapel of the Holy Trinity**, which dates from the 14th century. Each requires a separate entry ticket.

Historical Museum of Lublin MUSEUM

(www.muzeumlubelskie.pl; Plac Władysława Łokietka 3; adult/concession 5.50/4.50zł; 9am-4pm Wed-Sat, to 5pm Sun) Inside the **Kraków Gate** (accessed from its eastern wall), which links the Old Town to the modern city, this small museum displays documents and moving photographs of the town's history.

Cathedral of St John the Baptist CHURCH

(www.diecezja.lublin.pl; Plac Katedralny; dawn-sunset, treasury 10am-2pm & 3-5pm Tue-Sun) FREE This former Jesuit church dates from the 16th century and is the largest in Lublin. There are many impressive details to behold, including the baroque trompe l'œil frescoes (the work of Moravian artist Józef Majer) and the 17th-century altar made from a black Lebanese pear tree. The acoustic vestry (so called for its ability to project whispers) and the **treasury** *(skarbiec)*, behind the chapel, also merit attention.

Majdanek CONCENTRATION CAMP

(Państwowe Muzeum na Majdanku; 81 710 2833; www.majdanek.pl; Droga Męczenników Majdanka 67; 9am-6pm Apr-Oct, 9am-4pm Nov-Mar) FREE Four kilometres southeast of the centre is the German Nazi Majdanek extermination camp, where tens of thousands of people were murdered during WWII. Unlike other extermination camps, the Nazis went to no effort to conceal Majdanek. A 5km walk starts at the visitors centre, passes the foreboding Monument of Fight & Martyrdom, through parts of the barracks and finishes at the guarded mausoleum containing the ashes of many victims.

Old Jewish Cemetery CEMETERY

(Cmentarz żydowski; cnr ul Kalinowszczyzna & ul Sienna; by appointment) The old Jewish cemetery, established in 1541, has 30-odd readable tombstones, including the oldest Jewish tombstone in Poland in its original location. The graveyard is on a hill between ul Sienna and ul Kalinowszczyzna, about 500 metres to the east and north of the main bus terminal. It is surrounded by a high brick wall and the gate is locked. Contact the tourist office (p861) before you walk over to arrange a visit.

Tours

Underground Route WALK

(tour booking 81 534 6570; Rynek 1; adult/concession 9/7zł; 10am-4pm Tue-Fri, noon-5pm Sat & Sun) This 280m trail winds its way through connected cellars beneath the Old Town, with historical exhibitions along the way. Entry is from the neoclassical **Old Town Hall** in the centre of the pleasant Market Sq (Rynek) at approximately two-hourly intervals; check with the tourist office (p861) for exact times.

Sleeping

Hostel Lublin HOSTEL €
(792 888 632; www.hostellublin.pl; ul Lubartowska 60; dm/r 40/100zł;) The city's first modern hostel is situated within a former apartment building and contains neat, tidy dorms, a basic kitchenette and a cosy lounge. Take trolleybus 156 or 160 north from the Old Town, crossing busy Al Tysiąclecia for two stops.

Hotel Waksman HOTEL €€
(81 532 5454; www.waksman.pl; ul Grodzka 19; s/d 210/230zł, apt from 270zł;) Hotel Waksman deserves a blue ribbon for many reasons, not least of which is the atmospheric Old Town location. Each standard room (named 'yellow', 'blue', 'green' or 'red' for its decor) has individual character. The two apartments on top are special; they offer ample space for lounging or working, and views over the Old Town and castle.

Vanilla Hotel HOTEL €€
(81 536 6720; www.vanilla-hotel.pl; ul Krakowskie Przedmieście 12; s/d 330/370zł;) The name must be tongue-in-cheek. This beautiful boutique, just off the main pedestrian corso, is anything but vanilla. The rooms are filled with inspired, even bold styling, with vibrant colours, big headboards behind the beds and stylish, retro lamps and furniture. Lots of attention to detail here that continues into the stylish Jazz Age restaurant and coffee bar.

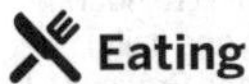

Eating

Magia INTERNATIONAL €€
(502 598 418; www.magia.lublin.pl; ul Grodzka 2; mains 20-65zł; noon-midnight;) Magia's atmosphere is eclectic; there are numerous vibes to choose from throughout the warren of dining rooms and large outdoor courtyard, with each area decorated with a touch of magic. The chef uses only fresh ingredients to create dishes ranging from tiger shrimps and snails to deer and duck, with every sort of pizza, pasta and pancake in between.

Mandragora JEWISH €€
(81 536 2020; www.mandragora.lublin.pl; Rynek 9; mains 20-60zł; noon-10pm;) There's good kitsch and there's bad kitsch, and at Mandragora, it's all good. Sure they're going for the *Fiddler on the Roof* effect with the lace tablecloths, knick-knacks and photos of old Lublin, but in the romantic Rynek locale, it works wonderfully. The food is a hearty

WORTH A TRIP

ZAMOŚĆ: POLAND'S RENAISSANCE HEART

While most Polish cities' attractions centre on their medieval heart, Zamość (zah-moshch) is pure 16th-century Renaissance. It was founded in 1580 by nobleman Jan Zamoyski and designed by an Italian architect. The splendid architecture of Zamość's Old Town escaped serious destruction in WWII and was added to Unesco's World Heritage List in 1992.

The **Rynek Wielki** (Great Market Square) is the heart of Zamość's attractive Old Town. This impressive Italianate Renaissance square (exactly 100m by 100m) is dominated by a lofty, pink town hall and surrounded by colourful, arcaded burghers' houses.

The **Museum of Zamość** (Muzeum Zamojskie; 84 638 6494; www.muzeum-zamojskie.pl; ul Ormiańska 30; adult/concession 10/5zł; 9am-5pm Tue-Sun) is based in two of the loveliest buildings on the square and houses interesting exhibits, including paintings, folk costumes and a scale model of the 16th-century town.

The city's **synagogue** (84 639 0054; www.zamosc.fodz.pl; ul Pereca 14; admission 7zł; 10am-6pm Tue-Sun) was recently reopened to the public after a long renovation. It was built around 1620 and served as the Jewish community's main house of worship until WWII, when it was shuttered by the Germans. The highlight of the exhibition is a gripping computer presentation on the history of the town's Jewish community, including its roots in Sephardic Judaism.

The helpful **tourist office** (84 639 2292; www.travel.zamosc.pl; Rynek Wielki 13; 8am-6pm Mon-Fri, 10am-5pm Sat & Sun May-Sep, 8am-5pm Mon-Fri, 9am-3pm Sat & Sun Oct-Apr) in the town hall has maps, brochures and souvenirs. Zamość makes for an easy day trip from Lublin. Buses and minibuses make the 80km trip (15zł) in around 90 minutes.

mix of Polish and Jewish, with mains like goose and duck featuring.

Drinking & Nightlife

Szklarnia CAFE

(Centrum Kultury w Lublinie; ☎81 466 6140; www.ck.lublin.pl; ul Peowiakow 12; ⏲10am-11pm Mon-Fri, noon-midnight Sat & Sun; 📶) It's not easy finding good coffee in Lublin. This sleek cafe in the recently refurbished Lublin Cultural Centre has great coffee as well as a daily selection of cakes. There's live entertainment some nights, and a nice terrace at the back in warm weather.

Złoty Osioł PUB

(☎81 532 9042; ul Grodzka 5a; ⏲3pm-midnight; 📶) Złoty Osioł offers traditional ambience and extraordinarily good-value traditional meals. There are delicious fish dishes, slightly bizarre drink selections (like hot dry wine with jelly), and daily meal sets for the indecisive. The restaurant is set in a candlelit cellar with an annexed cosy green courtyard. Folk music concerts are occasionally held here.

Information

Tourist Information Centre in Lublin (LOITiK; ☎81 532 4412; www.lublin.eu; ul Jezuicka 1/3; ⏲9am-7pm Mon-Fri, from 10am Sat & Sun May-Oct, 9am-5pm Mon-Fri, from 10am Sat & Sun Nov-Apr) Extremely helpful English-speaking staff, souvenirs for sale and lots of brochures, including handy maps of the most popular walking tours in Lublin. There's a computer on hand for short-term web-surfing.

Getting There & Away

BUS

PKS buses run from the **bus station** (☎703 402 622; ul Hutnicza 1 , cross Al Tysiąclecia), opposite the castle. From here, **Polski Bus** (www.polskibus.com) heads to Warsaw (three hours, five daily). Private minibuses run to various destinations, including Zamość (15zł, 1½ hours, hourly), from a minibus station north of the bus terminal.

TRAIN

The **train station** (Dworzec Kolejowy Lublin Główny; ☎info 19 757; www.pkp.pl; Plac Dworcowy 1) is 1.8km south of the Old Town. Useful direct train connections included to Kraków (62zł, four hours, two daily) and Warsaw (37zł, 2¾ hours, five daily).

CARPATHIAN MOUNTAINS

The Carpathians (Karpaty) stretch from the southern border with Slovakia into Ukraine, and their wooded hills and snowy mountains are a beacon for hikers, skiers and cyclists. The most popular destination here is the resort of Zakopane.

Zakopane

POP 27,485

Zakopane, 100km south of Kraków, is Poland's main alpine resort, situated at the foot of the Tatra Mountains. It's a popular jumping-off spot for trekking and mountain hikes, as well as Poland's best ski resort. The busy high street, ul Krupówki, is a jumble of tacky souvenir shops, bars and restaurants, but away from the centre, the pace slows down. This was an artists' colony in the early 20th century, and the graceful timbered villas from those days – built in what's known as the 'Zakopane style' of architecture – are still scattered around town.

Sights & Activities

Museum of Zakopane Style MUSEUM

(Willa Koliba; ☎18 201 3602; www.muzeumtatrzanskie.pl; ul Kościeliska 18; adult/concession 7/5.50zł; ⏲9am-5pm Wed-Sat, to 3pm Sun) Housed in the Villa Koliba, this was the first of several grand wooden villas designed by the noted Polish painter and architect Stanisław Witkiewicz in his 'Zakopane Style' (similar to the Arts and Crafts movement that swept the US and Britain at the turn of the 20th century). The interior has been restored to its original state, complete with the highlander furnishings and textiles, all designed for the villa.

Old Church & Cemetery CHURCH

(Stary Kościół, Pęksowy Brzyzek National Cemetery; ul Kościeliska) FREE This small, wooden church and adjoining atmospheric cemetery date from the mid-19th century. The Old Church has charming carved wooden decorations and pews, and Stations of the Cross painted on glass on the windows. Just behind, the old cemetery is certainly one of the country's most beautiful, with a number of amazing wood-carved headstones, some resembling giant chess pieces. The noted Polish painter and creator of the Zakopane Style, Stanisław Witkiewicz, is buried here beneath a modest wooden grave marker.

Morskie Oko LAKE

(admission 9zł) The most popular outing near Zakopane is to this emerald-green mountain lake, about 12km from the centre. Buses regularly depart from ul Kościuszki, across from the main bus station, for Polana Palenica (30 minutes), from where a 9km-long road continues uphill to the lake. Cars, bikes and buses are not allowed, so you'll have to walk (allow about two hours each way) or take a horse-drawn carriage to within 2km of the lake. Travel agencies organise day trips.

Mt Kasprowy Wierch Cable Car CABLE CAR

(18 201 5356; www.pkl.pl; Kuźnice; adult/concession return 58/48zł; 7.30am-4pm Jan-Mar, 7.30am-6pm Apr-Jun & Sep-Oct, 7am-9pm Jul & Aug, 9am-4pm Nov-Dec) The cable-car trip from Kuźnice (2km south of Zakopane) to the Mt Kasprowy Wierch summit (1985m) is a classic tourist experience. At the end of the ascent (20 minutes, climbing 936m), you can get off and stand with one foot in Poland and the other in Slovakia. The view from the top is spectacular (clouds permitting). The cable car normally closes for two weeks in May, and won't operate if the snow or wind conditions are dangerous.

Sleeping

Travel agencies in Zakopane can usually arrange private rooms. Expect a double to cost about 80zł in the high season in the town centre, and about 60zł for somewhere further out.

Youth Hostel Szarotka HOSTEL €

(18 201 3618; www.schroniskomlodziezowe.zakopane.org.pl; ul Nowotarska 45; dm/d 41/102zł;) This cheerful and homely place with 62 beds gets packed in the high season and is on a busy road. But it's friendly and has a kitchen and washing machine on site.

★ **Hotel Sabała** HOTEL €€€

(18 201 5092; www.sabala.zakopane.pl; ul Krupówki 11; s/d from 300/400zł;) Built in 1894 but thoroughly up to date, this striking timber hotel has a superb location overlooking the picturesque pedestrian thoroughfare. The hotel offers 51 cosy, attic-style rooms, and there's a sauna, solarium and swimming pool. The restaurant here serves both local specialties and international favourites.

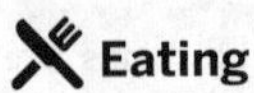

Eating

Pstrąg Górski SEAFOOD €€

(512 351 746; ul Krupówki 6a; mains 20-40zł; 10am-10pm;) This fish restaurant, done up in traditional style and overlooking a narrow stream, serves some of the freshest trout, salmon and sea fish in town. Trout is priced at 5zł and up per 100g (whole fish), bringing the price of a standard fish dinner to around 30zł, not including sides.

Stek Chałupa POLISH €€

(18 201 5918; www.stekchalupa.pl; ul Krupówki 33; mains 20-40zł; 8am-midnight;) One of the better choices on ul Krupówki. This atmospheric highlander outfit is good for grilled sausages and steaks in all their guises.

Information

Tourist Information Centre (18 201 2211; www.zakopane.pl; ul Kościuszki 17; 9am-5pm Mar-Aug, 9am-5pm Mon-Fri Sep-Feb) Small but helpful tourist office not far from the bus station has city maps and sells hiking maps. Can advise on accommodation, mountain guides and day trips.

Tatra National Park Headquarters (Tatrzański Park Narodowy; 18 202 3300; www.tpn.pl; ul Chałubińskiego 44; 9am-4pm Mon-Fri) The information office of the Tatra National Park is located in a small building near the Rondo Kuźnickie on the southern outskirts of the city. It's a good place for maps, guides and local weather and hiking information.

Getting There & Away

Though Zakopane has a small train station, the majority of visitors arrive by bus from Kraków. Coaches make the journey (16zł, two hours) every 30 to 60 minutes during the day. The leading bus company is **Szwagropol** (www.szwagropol.pl). Buy tickets bound for Kraków at Zakopane **bus station** (ul Chramcówki).

SILESIA

Silesia (Śląsk in Polish; pronounced *shlonsk*), in the far southwest of the country, is a traditional industrial and mining region with a fascinating mix of landscapes. The historic capital, Wrocław, has an enormous and beautiful town square as well as epic, student-fuelled nightlife.

Wrocław

POP 632,065

When citizens of beautiful Kraków enthusiastically encourage you to visit Wrocław (vrots-wahf), you know you're onto something good. The city's gracious Old Town is a mix of Gothic and baroque styles, and its large student population ensures a healthy number of restaurants, bars and nightclubs.

Wrocław has been traded back and forth between various domains over the centuries, but began life around 1000 AD. History buffs may know the city better as Breslau, the name it had as part of Germany until the end of WWII. When the city went over to Polish hands after the war, Wrocław was a shell of its former self. Sensitive restoration has returned the historic centre to its old beauty.

Sights

The main draw is the city's magnificent market square, the **Rynek**, dotted at the centre by the old **Town Hall** (Stary Ratusz). Note the dignified red-brick Gothic churches that are sprinkled around the centre in all directions. These statuesque beauties survived the bombardment during WWII and wear their blackened, chipped facades with pride.

Old Town

Museum of Bourgeois Art MUSEUM

(Muzeum Sztuki Mieszczańskiej; ☎71 347 1690; www.muzeum.miejskie.wroclaw.pl; Stary Ratusz; permanent exhibitions free, temporary exhibitions adult/concession 10/7zł; ⏲10am-5pm Wed-Sat, to 6pm Sun) FREE The unusual name here hides the main attraction: the Gothic interiors of the Old Town Hall. Look for the **Great Hall** (Sala Wielka) on the 1st floor, with carved decorations from the second half of the 15th century. Adjoining it is the **Princes' Room** (Sala Książęca), which was built as a chapel in the mid-14th century.

Church of St Elizabeth CHURCH

(www.kosciolgarnizon.wroclaw.pl; ul Św Elżbiety 1; tower admission 5zł; ⏲10am-7pm Mon-Sat, noon-7pm Sun, tower 9am-7pm Mon-Fri, 11am-5pm Sat, 1-5pm Sun) Just north of the Hansel and Gretel houses is this monumental Gothic brick church, with an 83m-high **tower**. You can climb the narrow stairwell with 300-plus steps to the top for a great view of Wrocław.

Church of St Mary Magdalene CHURCH

(ul Łaciarska; tower adult/concession 4/3zł; ⏲10am-6pm Mon-Sat, tower 10am-6pm Apr-Oct) One block east of the Rynek is this mighty Gothic red-brick building dating from the 14th century. Its showpiece is a copy of a Romanesque portal from around 1280 on the south wall, which originally adorned the Benedictine Abbey in Ołbin, but was moved here in 1546 after the abbey was demolished. You can climb the 72m-high **tower** and cross the so-called **Penance Footbridge**.

The original tympanum is on display in Wrocław's National Museum.

Outside the Old Town

★**Panorama of Racławice** MUSEUM

(☎71 344 1661; www.panoramaraclawicka.pl; ul Purkyniego 11; adult/concession 25/18zł; ⏲9am-5pm May-Sept, to 4pm Tue-Sun Oct-Apr) Wrocław's pride and joy is this giant painting of the battle for Polish independence fought at Racławice on 4 April 1794 between the Polish army led by Tadeusz Kościuszko and Russian troops under General Alexander Tormasov. The Poles won but it was all for naught: months later the nationwide insurrection was crushed by the tsarist army. The canvas measures 15m by 114m, and is wrapped around the internal walls of a rotunda.

National Museum MUSEUM

(☎71 372 5150; www.mnwr.art.pl; Plac Powstańców Warszawy 5; adult/concession 15/10zł; ⏲10am-5pm Tue-Sun) This treasure trove of fine art is 200m east of the Panorama of Racławice. Medieval stone sculpture is displayed on the ground floor; exhibits include the Romanesque tympanum from the portal of the Church of St Mary Magdalene, depicting the Assumption of the Virgin Mary, and 14th-century sarcophagi from the Church of SS Vincent and James. There are also collections of Silesian paintings, ceramics, silverware and furnishings from the 16th to 19th centuries.

Cathedral of St John the Baptist CHURCH

(☎71 322 2574; www.katedra.archidiecezja.wroc.pl; Plac Katedralny 18; tower adult/concession 5/4zł; ⏲10am-4pm Mon-Sat, 2-4pm Sun, tower 10am-6pm Mon-Sat) The centrepiece of Cathedral Island, this three-aisled Gothic basilica was built between 1244 and 1590. Seriously damaged during WWII, it was reconstructed in its previous Gothic form, complete with dragon guttering. For once you don't need strong legs to climb the 91m-high **tower** as there is a lift (elevator).

Sleeping

★ Hostel Mleczarnia HOSTEL €
(☎71 787 7570; www.mleczarniahostel.pl; ul Włodkowica 5; dm from 40zł, d 220zł;) This hostel on a quiet road not far from the Rynek has bags of charm, having been decorated in a deliberately old-fashioned style within a former residential building. There's a women-only dorm available, along with a kitchen and free laundry facilities. Downstairs is the excellent Mleczarnia cafe-bar.

Hostel Babel HOSTEL €
(☎71 342 0250; www.babelhostel.pl; ul Kołłątaja 16/3; dm from 45zł, d 140zł;) A tatty old staircase leads up to pleasant budget accommodation just 100m from the train station. Dorms are set in renovated apartment rooms with ornate lamps and decorative ceilings. Bathrooms are shiny clean, and guests have access to a kitchen. There's a DVD player for rainy days.

B&B Hotel Wrocław Centrum HOTEL €
(☎71 324 0980; www.hotelbb.pl; ul Ks Piotra Skargi 24-28; r 149zł;) This thrifty budget option offers plain but spotlessly clean rooms, big comfortable beds and an excellent central location, about 500m from the Rynek. Drivers will appreciate the large, protected parking lot (25zł) at the rear of the hotel. It's just under 1km from the train and bus stations.

Art Hotel HOTEL €€
(☎71 787 7400; www.arthotel.pl; ul Kiełbaśnicza 20; s/d from 280/300zł;) Elegant splurge candidate in a renovated apartment building, with tastefully restrained decor, quality fittings and gleaming bathrooms. There's a top-notch Polish-French restaurant, and a fitness room for working off any extra weight gained therein. Breakfast is an additional 50zł per person.

Eating

Bar Bazylia CAFETERIA €
(☎71 375 2065; www.bazyliabar.pl; ul Kuźnicza 42; mains 2.49zł per 100g; 8am-7pm Mon-Fri, from 7.30am Sat & Sun;) Inexpensive, bustling modern take on the classic *bar mleczny* in a curved space with huge plate-glass windows overlooking the university. The menu has Polish standards such as *bigos* (sauerkraut and meat stew) and *gołąbki* (stuffed cabbage rolls), and a decent range of salads and other vegetable dishes. Everything is priced by weight; order and pay at the till before receiving your food.

Bernard Pub-Restaurant CZECH, INTERNATIONAL €€
(☎71 344 1054; www.bernard.wroclaw.pl; Rynek 35; mains 30-60zł; 10.30am-11pm;) This lively split-level bar-restaurant was inspired by the highly respected Czech beer of the same name, and the restaurant features some Czech dishes such as rabbit and pork knee. There's also upmarket comfort food including burgers, steak and fish dishes, as well as plenty of Bernard beer. The stylish interior is conducive to a quiet evening or group outing.

★ Cafe & Restaurant Steinhaus POLISH €€€
(☎512 931 071; www.steinhaus.pl; ul Włodkowica 11; mains 40-70zł; 11am-11pm;) Old-fashioned Polish and Jewish cooking in an elegant but unfussy setting. The goose in cranberry sauce can't be topped but the grilled duck-breast comes close. Be sure to reserve on weekends as this place is justifiably popular.

Drinking & Nightlife

Mleczarnia CAFE, BAR
(☎71 788 2448; www.mle.pl; ul Włodkowica 5; 8am-4am;) Hidden away in a backstreet that was once the city's main Jewish neighbourhood, this atmospheric place is stuffed with chipped old wooden tables bearing lace doilies and candlesticks. It turns out good coffee and light meals, including breakfast. At night the cellar opens, adding another moody dimension. There's a beautiful back garden in summer.

Pub Guinness PUB
(☎71 344 6015; www.pubguinness.pl; Plac Solny 5; noon-2am;) No prizes for guessing what this pub serves. A lively, fairly authentic Irish pub, spread over three levels on a busy corner. The ground-floor bar buzzes with student and traveller groups getting together, and there's a restaurant and beer cellar as well. A good place to wind down after a hard day's sightseeing.

Jazzda CLUB

(☎607 429 602; www.jazzda.pl; Rynek 60; ⏰5pm-late Mon-Fri, noon-late Sat & Sun) Looking for a John Travolta kind of evening? This central bar and club with a lit-up, multicoloured dance floor and strobe lights will fit the bill.

Bezsenność CLUB

(☎570 669 570; www.bezsennosckub.com; ul Ruska 51, Pasaż Niepolda; ⏰7pm-late) With its alternative/rock/dance line-up and distressed decor, 'Insomnia' attracts a high-end clientele and is one of the most popular clubs in town. It's located in the Pasaż Niepolda, a group of bars, clubs and restaurants situated just off Ruska.

☆ Entertainment

Filharmonia CLASSICAL MUSIC

(☎tickets 71 792 1000; www.filharmonia.wroclaw.pl; ul Piłsudskiego 19) If you're interested in hearing classical sounds, Friday and Saturday evenings are your best bets. It's located 800m southwest of the Rynek.

ℹ Information

Intermax (☎71 794 0573; www.imx.pl; ul Psie Budy 10/11; per hour 4zł; ⏰9am-11pm) Enter from ul Kazimierza Wielkiego.

Tourist Office (☎71 344 3111; www.wroclaw-info.pl; Rynek 14; ⏰9am-9pm)

ℹ Getting There & Away

BUS

The **bus station** (Dworzec Centralny PKS; ☎71 333 0530; ul Sucha 1/11) is south of the train station and offers several daily PKS buses to Warsaw (60zł, seven hours). For most other destinations the train is a better choice, though handy **Polski Bus** (www.polskibus.com) services run from here to Warsaw (seven hours, twice daily) and Prague (five hours, twice daily).

TRAIN

Wrocław Main Train Station (Wrocław Główny; ☎71 717 3333; www.rozklad.pkp.pl; ul Piłsudskiego 105) was opened in 1857 as a lavish architectural confection. It's easily Poland's most attractive railway station and worth visiting even if you're not travelling by train. Sample destinations include Warsaw (61zł, 6½ hours, hourly), Kraków (50zł, 5½ hours, several daily), Poznań (46zł, 3½ hours, hourly) and Toruń (56zł, five hours, several daily).

WIELKOPOLSKA

Wielkopolska (Greater Poland) is the region where Poland came to life in the Middle Ages. As a result of this ancient eminence, its cities and towns are full of historic and cultural attractions. The battles of WWII later caused widespread destruction in the area, though Poznań has been since restored to its prominent economic role.

Poznań

POP 551,600

Poznań is the cultural, economic and transport hub of Wielkopolska. It's strongly associated with the early formation of the Polish kingdom at the turn of the first millennium, and Poland's first ruler, Mieszko I, is buried at Poznań Cathedral.

After the partitions of the late-18th century, Poznań fell under Prussian domination and until the re-establishment of independent Poland at the end of WWI was the German city of Posen. Much of Poznań, including the main square (Stary Rynek), was destroyed in fighting in WWII and painstakingly rebuilt in the decades after.

These days, Poznań is a vibrant university city. There's a beautiful Old Town, with a number of interesting museums and a range of lively bars, clubs and restaurants.

◉ Sights

Old Town

Town Hall HISTORIC BUILDING

(Ratusz; ☎61 856 8193; www.mnp.art.pl; Stary Rynek 1) Poznań's Renaissance Town Hall, topped with a 61m-high tower, instantly captures attention. Its graceful form replaced a 13th-century Gothic structure, which burned down in the early-16th century. Every day at noon two metal goats appear through a pair of small doors above the clock and butt their horns together 12 times, in deference to an old legend. These days, the Town Hall is home to the Historical Museum of Poznań.

Historical Museum of Poznań MUSEUM

(Muzeum Historii Miasta Poznania; ☎61 856 8000; www.mnp.art.pl; Stary Rynek 1; adult/concession 7/5zł, Sat free; ⏰9am-3pm Tue-Thu, noon-9pm Fri, 11am-6pm Sat & Sun) This museum inside the town hall displays an interesting and well-presented exhibition on the town's history, and the building's original interiors are worth the entry price on their own. The Gothic vaulted **cellars** are the only remains of the first town hall. They were initially used for trade but later became a jail.

Ostrów Tumski

The island of Ostrów Tumski, east of the main square and across the Warta River, is the place where Poznań was founded, and with it the Polish state.

Poznań Cathedral CHURCH

(Cathedral Basilica of Sts Peter & Paul; 61 852 9642; www.katedra.archpoznan.pl; ul Ostrów Tumski 17; crypt adult/concession 3.50/2.50zł; 9am-4pm) Ostrów Tumski is dominated by this monumental, double-towered cathedral. Basically Gothic with additions from later periods, most notably the baroque tops of the towers, the cathedral was damaged in 1945 and took 11 years to rebuild. The aisles and the ambulatory are ringed by a dozen chapels containing numerous tombstones. The most famous is the Golden Chapel behind the high altar, which houses the remains of the first two Polish rulers: Mieszko I and Bolesław Chrobry.

Porta Posnania Interactive Heritage Centre MUSEUM

(61 647 7634; www.bramapoznania.pl; ul Gdańska 2; adult/concession 15/9zł, audioguide 5/3zł; 9am-6pm Tue-Fri, 10am-7pm Sat & Sun;) This cutting-edge multimedia museum opened in 2014 to tell the tale of the island's eventful history and the birth of the Polish nation via interactive displays and other technological gadgetry. It's located on the island's eastern shore and is linked to the cathedral area by footbridge. The exhibitions are multilingual, but opt for an audioguide to help put everything together.

Sleeping

Poco Loco Hostel HOSTEL €

(61 883 3470; www.hostel.poco-loco.pl; ul Taczaka 23; dm 39-55zł, r 140-160zł;) Clean, well-run and central, this is one of the city's most popular hostels and for a good reason. There's dorm accommodation in four- to 10-bunk rooms plus private rooms for two to four people. There's a shared kitchen plus laundry facilities and computers. The managers are adventure travellers and pride themselves on offering good-value lodging.

Fusion Hostel HOSTEL €

(61 852 1230; www.fusionhostel.pl; ul Św Marcin 66/72; dm 50-69zł, s 119-130zł, d 195-210zł;) Hostel with a view, perched on the 7th floor of a scuffed commercial building. The decor is modern and bright, and guests have access to a lounge, a kitchen and bicycle hire. There's dorm accommodation in four- and six-bunk rooms, as well as private singles and doubles. The lift is hidden behind the security booth in the foyer.

★Hotel Stare Miasto HOTEL €€

(61 663 6242; www.hotelstaremiasto.pl; ul Rybaki 36; s/d from 224/340zł;) Stylish value-for-money hotel with a tastefully chandeliered foyer and spacious breakfast room. Rooms can be small but are clean and bright with lovely starched white sheets. Some upper rooms have skylights in place of windows.

Brovaria HOTEL €€

(61 858 6868; www.brovaria.pl; Stary Rynek 73/74; s/d from 250/290zł;) This multitalented hotel also operates as a restaurant and bar, but most impressive is its in-house boutique brewery, whose operations you can view within the building. The elegant rooms have tasteful dark timber tones, and some have views onto the Rynek.

Eating

Apetyt CAFETERIA €

(61 852 0742; ul Szkolna 4; mains 5-12zł; 9am-8pm Mon-Fri, 10am-7pm Sat, 11am-7pm Sun;) The latest-closing *bar mleczny* in town enjoys a good, central location. The Polish steam-table food is exactly what you'd expect, and none the worse for that, with *naleśniki* (crêpes) choices galore.

★Papierówka POLISH €€

(797 471 388; www.restauracjapapierowka.pl; ul Zielona 8; mains 20-40zł; 9am-10pm;) This no-frills, slow-food restaurant offers some of the best cooking in town. Order at the counter and watch a team of chefs prepare your meal in the open kitchen. There are a half-dozen daily options, reflecting what's in season. The specialty is duck, though expect a couple of pork and fish choices. The winelist is tiny but impeccable.

Ludwiku do Rondla JEWISH €€

(61 851 6638; ul Woźna 2/3; mains 26-38zł; 1-10pm) This small, cosy place, two blocks

east of the main square, specialises in both Jewish and Polish cooking – particularly where the two intertwine. Menu items are helpfully marked if an item is Polish or Jewish in origin. We started with herring in oil (Polish/Jewish) and stuffed meat roulade with buckwheat (Polish), but everything looks good.

Wiejskie Jadło POLISH €€
(☎61 853 6600; www.wiejskie-jadlo.pl; Stary Rynek 77; mains 18-51zł; ⏲10am-11pm) Compact Polish restaurant hidden a short distance back from the Rynek along ul Franciszkańska. It offers a range of filling dishes including *pierogi* (dumplings), soups, and pork in all its varied possibilities, served in a homely rustic space with flowers on the table.

Drinking & Nightlife

Proletaryat BAR
(☎61 852 4858; www.proletaryat.pl; ul Wrocławska 9; ⏲1pm-late Mon-Sat, 3pm-late Sun; 📶) Bright red communist-nostalgia bar with an array of socialist-era gear on the walls, including military insignia, portraits of Brezhnev and Marx, and the obligatory bust of Lenin in the window. Play 'spot the communist leader' while sipping a boutique beer from the Czarnków Brewery.

Atmosfera CLUB
(☎61 853 3434; www.atmosfera-klub.pl; Stary Rynek 67; ⏲6pm-late Mon-Sat; 📶) Arguably the best of several music and dance clubs located on the main square. Descend the stairs to find a large bar and dance floor. Dependable place for a very late drink, as some weekends the club stays open until 11am the next morning.

Van Diesel Music Club CLUB
(☎515 065 459; www.vandiesel.pl; Stary Rynek 88; ⏲9pm-5am Fri & Sat) Happening venue on the main square, with DJs varying their offerings between pop, house, R&B, soul and dance. Given the variety, you're sure to find a night that will get you on the dancefloor.

Entertainment

Johnny Rocker LIVE MUSIC
(☎61 850 1499; www.johnnyrocker.pl; ul Wielka 9; ⏲6pm-late) This super-smooth basement venue with a curvy bar is crammed with happy drinkers sitting cabaret-style in front of a stage that features live blues, jazz or rock acts every weekend. If the sounds are overwhelming, you can always retreat to the stylish 'red room'.

Filharmonia CLASSICAL MUSIC
(☎box office 61 853 6935; www.filharmoniapoznanska.pl; ul Św Marcin 81; ⏲box office 1-6pm) This musical institution holds concerts at least weekly by the house symphony orchestra. Poznań also has Poland's best boys' choir, the Poznańskie Słowiki (Poznań Nightingales), which can be heard here. Buy tickets at the box office or one hour before performances.

Information

Adax (☎61 850 1100; www.adaxland.poznan.pl; ul Półwiejska 28; per hr 4zł; ⏲10am-10pm Mon-Sat, from noon Sun) Near the Stary Browar shopping mall.

City Information Centre – Main Square (☎61 852 6156; www.poznan.travel; Stary Rynek 59/60; ⏲9am-8pm Mon-Sat, 10am-6pm Sun May-Sep, 10am-5pm Mon-Fri Oct-Apr) Poznań's helpful tourist information office is located conveniently on the main square. They have a wealth of information on the city and can advise on finding rooms and booking transport.

City Information Centre – Train Station (☎61 633 1016; www.poznan.travel; ul Dworcowa 2, Poznań Główny; ⏲8am-9pm Mon-Fri, 10am-5pm Sat & Sun) Branch of the Poznań tourist office located in the main train station.

Getting There & Away

BUS

The **bus station** (Dworzec PKS; ☎timetable 703 303 330; www.pks.poznan.pl; ul Stanisława Matyi 2; ⏲information 8am-7pm Mon-Sat, 10am-7pm Sun; 🚋5, 8, 11, 12, 14 to Most Dworcowy) is located near the train station and part of the Poznań City Centre transport and shopping complex. It's 1.5km southwest of the Old Town and can be reached on foot in 15 minutes, or by tram to stop 'Most Dworcowy'.

Polski Bus (www.polskibus.com) runs services to Warsaw (four hours, five daily) and Wrocław (three hours, five daily). Polski Bus coaches arrive and depart at one of two stations: the main bus station or a smaller station, Dworzec Górczyn, 3km southwest of the main station. Check the website to use the right station. Buy tickets online.

POZNAŃ CITY CARD

Poznań City Card (1 day/35 zł), available from the city information centres, provides free entry to major museums, sizable discounts at restaurants and recreational activities, and free public transport.

TRAIN

Busy **Poznań Main Train Station** (Poznań Główny; ☎61 633 1659; www.pkp.pl; ul Dworcowa 2; 🚋5, 8, 11, 12, 14 to Most Dworcowy) is 1.5km southwest of the Old Town and can be reached on foot in 15 minutes, or by tram to stop 'Most Dworcowy'.

Useful domestic train connections include to Gdańsk (60zł, 3½ hours, three daily), Kraków (80zł, eight hours, three daily), Toruń (30zł, two hours, two daily), Wrocław (60zł, 2¾ hours, five daily) and Warsaw (80zł, three hours, six daily). Poznań is a natural jumping-off spot for Berlin (150zł, three hours, six daily).

POMERANIA

Pomerania (Pomorze in Polish) is an attractive region with diverse drawcards, from beautiful beaches to architecturally pleasing cities. The historic port city of Gdańsk is situated at the region's eastern extreme, while the attractive Gothic city of Toruń lies inland.

Gdańsk

POP 460,400

The Hanseatic port of Gdańsk grew wealthy during the Middle Ages, linking inland cities with seaports around the world. That wealth is on display in the form of a bustling riverbank, mammoth red-brick churches and a gleaming central square.

Gdańsk has played an outsized role in history. The creation of the 'Free City of Danzig', at the conclusion of World War I, served as a pretext for Hitler to invade Poland at the start of WWII. The Germans fired the first shots of the war here on 1 September 1939 at the Polish garrison at Westerplatte.

In August 1980, the city became the centre of Poland's anticommunist movement with the establishment of the Solidarity trade union, led by its charismatic leader (and future Polish president), Lech Wałęsa.

Sights

Gdańsk's major sights are situated in the **Main Town** (Główne Miasto). Much of what you see, including the dazzling palaces that line the central promenade, **Long St** (ul Długa), was rebuilt from rubble after the bombardment of WWII.

A sensible approach is to walk the former **Royal Route**, starting at the **Upland Gate** (Brama Wyżynna), at the western end of Long St and the nearby **Golden Gate** (Złota Brama), a triumphal arch built in 1612. Then follow the street as it widens into Long Market (Długi Targ) to end at the majestic **Green Gate** (Brama Zielona). From here, pick up the city's evocative river walk along the embankment of the **River Motława**.

Main Town

Historical Museum of Gdańsk MUSEUM

(Town Hall; ☎58 767 9100; www.mhmg.pl; Długa 46/47; adult/concession 12/6zł; ⏰10am-1pm Tue, 10am-4pm Wed-Sat, 11am-4pm Sun) The museum is located in the historic town hall, which boasts Gdańsk's highest tower at 81.5m. The showpiece is the **Red Room** (Sala Czerwona), done up in Dutch Mannerist style from the end of the 16th century. The 2nd floor houses exhibitions related to Gdańsk's history, including photos of the destruction of 1945. From here you can enter the **tower** for great views across the city.

Amber Museum MUSEUM

(☎58 301 4733; www.mhmg.pl; Targ Węglowy 26; adult/concession 10/5zł; ⏰10am-1pm Mon, 10am-4pm Tue-Sat, 11am-4pm Sun) This museum is dedicated to all things amber and the craft of designing and creating amber jewellery. The musuem is located in the **Foregate**, a former prison and torture chamber, so in addition to amber displays, there's also some startlingly realistic displays of torture chambers. Two for one!

St Mary's Church CHURCH

(☎58 301 3982; www.bazylikamariacka.pl; ul Podkramarska 5; tower adult/concession 5/3zł; ⏰8.30am-6pm, except during services) Dominating the heart of the Main Town, St Mary's is often cited as the largest brick church in the world. Some 105m long and 66m wide at the transept, its massive squat tower climbs 78m high into the Gdańsk cityscape. Begun in 1343, St Mary's didn't reach its present proportions until 1502. Don't miss the 15th-century astronomical clock, placed in the northern transept, and the church tower (405 steps above the city).

National Maritime Museum MUSEUM

(Narodowe Muzeum Morskie w Gdańsku; ☎Maritime Cultural Centre 58 329 8700, information 58 301 8611; www.nmm.pl; ul Tokarska 21-25, entry from Motława River side; Maritime Cultural Center adult/child 8/5zł, other exhibitions priced separately; ⏰10am-4pm Tue-Sun) This is a sprawling exhibition of maritime history

Gdańsk

Gdańsk

Sights

1 Amber Museum A3
2 Historical Museum of Gdańsk C4
3 National Maritime Museum D3
4 St Mary's Church C3

Sleeping

5 3 City Hostel A2
6 Dom Aktora C2
7 Dom Zachariasza Zappio D3
8 Kamienica Gotyk C3

Eating

9 Bar Mleczny Neptun B4
10 Przystań Gdańska D2
11 Restauracja Pod Łososiem C3
12 Tawerna Mestwin C2

Drinking & Nightlife

13 Cafe Ferber B3
14 Cafe Lamus C2
15 Miasto Aniołów D4

Entertainment

16 Klub Morza Zejman D4

and Gdańsk's role through the centuries as a Baltic seaport. Headquarters is the multimillion-euro **Maritime Cultural Centre**, with a permanent interactive exhibition 'People-Ships-Ports'. Other exhibitions include the **MS Sołdek**, the first vessel to be built at the Gdańsk shipyard in the postwar years and the **Żuraw** (ul Szeroka 67/68), a 15th-century loading crane that was the biggest in its day. More displays are housed in **granaries** (ul Ołowianka 9-13) across the river.

Outside the Centre

★European Solidarity Centre MUSEUM

(Europejskie Centrum Solidarności; ☎506 195 673; www.ecs.gda.pl; Pl Solidarności 1; adult/concession 17/13zł; ⊙10am-8pm May-Sep, to 6pm Oct-Apr; 📶) This grand multimedia exhibition tracing the Polish struggle against communist rule opened in 2014 in the brand new European Solidarity Centre. Take an audioguide in English and follow a confusing if highly moving series of exhibitions through several rooms, explaining how life was in communist Poland and the key role played by the workers at the Gdańsk shipyards in creating the Solidarity trade union in 1980 and ultimately bringing down the regime in 1989.

Sleeping

★3 City Hostel HOSTEL €

(☎58 354 5454; www.3city-hostel.pl; Targ Drzewny 12/14; dm from 60zł, r 180zł; @📶) Big, modern, colourful hostel near the train station, with high ceilings, pleasant common areas, a kitchen, and a lounge with a view. Breakfast is included, plus there's computers on-hand for internet use. Reception runs round the clock.

Dom Zachariasza Zappio HOSTEL €

(☎58 322 0174; www.zappio.pl; ul Świętojańska 49; dm/s/d 60/95/170zł; 📶) Occupying a labyrinthine, chunky-beamed former merchant's house, the Zappio is so big that families with kiddies and party animals won't get in each other's way. In addition to high-ceilinged dorms sleeping up to 14, and 13 rooms of various medieval shapes and sizes, this remarkable hostel also has its own pub, bike rental, guest kitchen and 24-hour reception.

Dom Aktora HOTEL €€

(☎58 301 5901; www.domaktora.pl; ul Straganiarska 55/56; s/d 250/330zł, apt 360-570zł; P📶) The no-nonsense apartments at this former thespians' dorm are affordable and have simply equipped kitchens, making this a prime target for self-caterers. Bathrooms throughout are 21st-century conceptions but otherwise not much has changed here decor-wise since the mid-1990s. The homemade breakfast buffet is the best in town.

Kamienica Gotyk HOTEL €€

(☎58 301 8567; www.gotykhouse.eu; ul Mariacka 1; s/d 280/310zł; 📶) Wonderfully located at the St Mary's Church end of ul Mariacka, Gdańsk's oldest house is filled by this neat, clean, Gothic-themed guesthouse. The seven rooms have Gothic touches such as broken-arched doorways and hefty drapery, though most are thoroughly modern creations and bathrooms are definitely of the third millennium. There's a small Copernicus museum in the cellar and a gingerbread shop on the ground floor.

Eating

Bar Mleczny Neptun CAFETERIA €

(☎58 301 4988; www.barneptun.pl/en/; ul Długa 33/34; mains 2-16zł; ⊙7.30am-7pm Mon-Fri, 10am-7pm Sat & Sun; 📶) It's surprising just where some of Poland's communist-era milk bars have survived and this one, right on the tourist drag, is no exception. However, the Neptun is a cut above your run-of-the-mill *bar mleczny*, with potted plants, decorative tiling and free wi-fi.

★Tawerna Mestwin POLISH €€

(☎58 301 7882; ul Straganiarska 20/23; mains 20-40zl; ⊙11am-10pm Tue-Sun, to 6pm Mon; 📶) The specialty here is Kashubian regional cooking from the northwest of Poland, and dishes like potato dumplings and stuffed cabbage rolls have a pronounced homemade quality. There's usually a fish soup and fried fish as well. The interior is done out like a traditional cottage and the exposed beams and dark-green walls lend a special atmosphere.

Przystań Gdańska POLISH €€

(☎58 301 1922; ul Wartka 5; mains 17-43zł; ⊙11am-10pm) An atmospheric place to enjoy outdoor dining, with a view along the river to the Gdańsk crane. Serves Polish classics and a range of fish dishes, plus a few pizzas tossed in. The food's above average but the view from the terrace is arguably the best in the Old Town.

Restauracja Pod Łososiem POLISH €€€

(☎58 301 7652; www.podlososiem.com.pl; ul Szeroka 52/54; mains 60-85zł; ⊙noon-11pm) Founded in 1598 and famous for salmon, this is one of Gdańsk's most highly regarded restaurants. Red leather seats, brass chandeliers and a gathering of gas lamps fill out the rather sober interior, illuminated by the specialty drink here – Goldwasser. This gooey, sweet liqueur with flakes of gold was produced in its cellars from the 16th century until WWII.

Drinking & Nightlife

Cafe Lamus BAR
(☎531 194 277; ul Lawendowa 8; ⏲noon-2am; 📶) Achingly cool retro-themed bar serving a broad range of bottled beers from small local breweries. Enter from ul Straganiarska.

Cafe Ferber CAFE, BAR
(☎791 010 005; www.ferber.pl; ul Długa 77/78; ⏲9am-late; 📶) It's startling to step straight from Gdańsk's historic main street into this very modern café-bar, dominated by bright red panels, a suspended ceiling and boxy lighting. The scarlet decor contrasts with its comfy armchairs, from which you can sip coffee and cocktail creations such as the *szary kot* (grey cat). On weekends, DJs spin tunes into the wee small hours.

Miasto Aniołów CLUB
(☎58 768 5831; www.miastoaniolow.com.pl; ul Chmielna 26) The City of Angels covers all the bases – late-night revellers can hit the spacious dance floor, crash in the chill-out area, or hang around the atmospheric deck overlooking the Motława River. Nightly DJs play disco and other dance-oriented sounds.

Entertainment

State Baltic Opera Theatre OPERA
(☎58 763 4906; www.operabaltycka.pl; Al Zwycięstwa 15) Founded in 1950, Gdańsk's premier opera company resides in this opera house in the Wrzeszcz district, next to the Gdańsk Politechnika train station. Alongside the usual operatic repertoire, it stages regular ballets. Symphonic concerts are also held here.

Klub Morza Zejman LIVE MUSIC
(☎669 070 557; www.bractwozeglarzy.home.pl; Chmielna 111/113; admission 2zl; ⏲6-10pm Wed, Fri & Sat, 8pm-midnight Thu) This salty warren of crusty old sea hands on Spichlerze Island has a delightfully tumble-down feel. Most nights sailors and their wives just meet up for beers around the bar, but Thursday evenings (and occasionally other nights) bring live performances of old sea shanties (sailor songs) that simply can't be missed.

Information

Jazz 'n' Java (☎58 305 3616; ul Tkacka 17/18; per hour 6zł; ⏲10am-10pm) Internet access.

Tourist Office – Długi Targ (☎58 301 4355; www.gdansk4u.pl; Długi Targ 28/29; ⏲9am-7pm Jun-Aug, to 5pm Sep-May) Helpful, centrally located tourist information office has a free city map and loads of information on sightseeing, accommodation and transport.

WORTH A TRIP

MALBORK

Magnificent **Malbork Castle** (☎tickets 55 647 0978; www.zamek.malbork.pl; ul Starościńska 1; adult/concession 40/30zł; ⏲9am-7pm 15 Apr–15 Sep, 10am-3pm 16 Sep–14 Apr) makes a great day trip from Gdańsk. It's the largest Gothic castle in Europe and was once headquarters for the medieval Teutonic Knights. Its sinister form looms over the relatively small town and Nogat River. Trains run regularly from Gdańsk Głowny station (45 minutes). Once you get to Malbork station, turn right, cross the highway and follow ul Kościuszki to the castle. Compulsory tours come with an audio tour in English. There are places to eat at the castle and in the town.

Getting There & Away

BUS

The **bus station** (PKS Gdańsk; ☎58 302 1532; www.pks.gdansk.pl; ul 3 Maja 12) is behind the main train station. PKS buses head to Warsaw hourly (55zł, 5¾ hours), as do services of **Polski Bus** (www.polskibus.com).

TRAIN

The city's train station, **Gdańsk Główny** (Gdańsk Główny; www.pkp.pl; ul Podwale Grodzkie 1), is located on the western outskirts of the Old Town. Most long-distance trains actually start or finish at Gdynia, so make sure you get on/off quickly here.

Useful direct train connections include to Toruń (50zł, three hours, three daily), Kraków (80zł, eight hours, three daily), Poznań (30zł, 3¾ hours, three daily) and Warsaw (90zł, six hours, five daily). International destinations include Berlin (seven hours, two daily).

Toruń

POP 205,000

Toruń escaped major damage in WWII and is widely considered the best-preserved Gothic town in Poland. The city is known around the country for the quality of its gingerbread and, indeed, with its handsome, red-brick churches and elegant, intricate facades, Toruń resembles nothing more than a beautifully crafted gingerbread cookie.

WORTH A TRIP

GREAT MASURIAN LAKES

The northeastern corner of Poland features a beautiful postglacial landscape dominated by thousands of lakes. About 200km of canals connect these bodies of water, making the area a prime destination for canoeists, as well as those who love to hike, fish and mountain bike.

The towns of **Giżycko** and **Mikołajki** make good bases. Both the Giżycko **tourist office** (87 428 5265; www.gizycko.turystyka.pl; ul Wyzwolenia 2; 9am-5pm Mon-Fri, 10am-2pm Sat & Sun Apr-Oct, 9am-4pm Mon-Fri, 10am-2pm Sat Nov-Mar) and the Mikołajki **tourist office** (87 421 6850; www.mikolajki.pl; Plac Wolności 3; 10am-6pm Jun-Aug, 10am-6pm Mon-Sat May & Sep) supply useful maps for sailing and hiking, provide excursion boat schedules, and assist in finding accommodation.

Nature aside, there are some interesting fragments of history in this region. A grim reminder of the past is the **Wolf's Lair** (Wilczy Szaniec; 89 752 4429; www.wolfsschanze.pl; adult/concession 15/10zł; 8am-dusk). Located at **Gierłoż**, 8km east of Kętrzyn, this ruined complex was Hitler's wartime headquarters for his invasion of the Soviet Union. In 1944, a group of high-ranking German officers tried to assassinate Hitler here. These dramatic events were reprised in the 2008 Tom Cruise movie *Valkyrie*.

Toruń is famous as the birthplace of Nicolaus Copernicus, who revolutionised the field of astronomy in 1543 by asserting the earth travelled around the sun. He's a figure you will not be able to escape – you can even buy gingerbread men in his likeness.

Sights

The usual starting point on Toruń's Gothic trail is the **Old Town Market Square** (Rynek Staromiejski), dominated by a massive red-brick **Town Hall** and lined with finely restored houses. At the southeast corner, look for a **Statue of Copernicus**, a regular feature in holiday snaps.

Old Town Hall MUSEUM
(Ratusz Staromiejski; www.muzeum.torun.pl; Rynek Staromiejski 1; adult/concession museum 11/7zł, tower 11/7zł; museum 10am-6pm Tue-Sun May-Sep, to 4pm Tue-Sun Oct-Apr, tower 10am-8pm May-Sep, 10am-5pm Oct-Apr) The Old Town Hall dates from the 14th century and hasn't changed much since, though some Renaissance additions lent an ornamental touch to the sober Gothic structure. Today, it houses the main branch of the Toruń Regional Museum. Displays include a collection of Gothic art (painting and stained glass), a display of local 17th- and 18th-century crafts, and a gallery of Polish paintings from 1800 to the present. Climb the **tower** for a fine panoramic view of Toruń's Gothic townscape.

House of Copernicus MUSEUM
(56 660 5613; www.muzeum.torun.pl; ul Kopernika 15/17; museum adult/concession 11/8zł, audiovisual presentation 13/8zł, gingerbread exhibition 11/8zł, combined entry 22/17zł; 10am-6pm Tue-Sun May-Sep, to 4pm Tue-Sun Oct-Apr) While it's not clear if Copernicus was actually born here, this branch of the regional museum is dedicated to the famed astronomer's life and works. More engaging than the exhibitions of period furniture and writing is a short audiovisual presentation regarding Copernicus' times in Toruń, with a model of the town. A third element of the museum, titled **World of Toruń's Gingerbread**, offers insights into the arcane art of gingerbread creation.

Cathedral of SS John the Baptist & John the Evangelist CHURCH
(56 657 1480; www.katedra.diecezja.torun.pl; ul Żeglarska 16; adult/concession 3/2zł; 9am-5.30pm Mon-Sat, 2-5.30pm Sun Apr-Oct) Toruń's mammoth Gothic cathedral was begun around 1260 but only completed at the end of the 15th century. Its massive tower houses Poland's second-largest historic bell, the **Tuba Dei** (God's Trumpet). On the southern side of the tower, facing the Vistula, is a large 15th-century clock; its original face and single hand are still in working order. Check out the dent above the VIII – it's from a cannonball that struck the clock during the Swedish siege of 1703.

Gingerbread Museum MUSEUM
(Muzeum Piernika; 56 663 6617; www.muzeumpiernika.pl; ul Rabiańska 9; adult/concession 12/9.50zł; 9am-6pm) Learn about

gingerbread's history and create a spicy concoction of your own under the enlightened instruction of a mock-medieval gingerbread master. All of it takes place in a renovated 16th-century gingerbread factory.

Sleeping

Green Hostel HOSTEL €
(☎56 561 4000; www.greenhostel.eu; ul Małe Garbary 10; r from 100zł; 📶) Located up a 14th-century set of steep stairs opposite Hotel Heban, this dorm-less hostel offers 34 beds over four floors, bathrooms on each floor and 24-hour reception. Rates are not per person – you pay for the whole room and there are no singles, so this is definitely a better deal if you're travelling in a two- or moresome.

★ **Hotel Petite Fleur** HOTEL €€
(☎56 621 5100; www.petitefleur.pl; ul Piekary 25; s/d 210/270zł; 📶) One of the better midrange options in Toruń has understated rooms containing slickly polished timber furnishings and elegant prints, though the singles can be a touch space-poor. The French brick cellar restaurant is one of Toruń's better hotel eateries and the buffet breakfast is the best we had in Poland.

Hotel Pod Czarną Różą HOTEL €€
(☎56 621 9637; www.hotelczarnaroza.pl; ul Rabiańska 11; s/d 170/210zł; 📶) 'Under the Black Rose' fills out both a historic inn and a newer wing facing the river, though its interiors present a uniformly clean, up-to-date look with the odd antique reproduction. Buffet breakfast included.

Hotel Karczma Spichrz HOTEL €€
(☎56 657 1140; www.spichrz.pl; ul Mostowa 1; s/d 250/310zł, apt from 290zł; ❄📶) Wonderfully situated within a historic waterfront granary, this hotel's 19 rooms are laden with personality, featuring massive exposed beams above characterful timber furniture and contemporary bathrooms. The location by the river is within walking distance of the sights but away from the crowds. Good restaurant next door.

Eating

Bar Mleczny Pod Arkadami CAFETERIA €
(☎56 622 2428; ul Różana 1; mains 4-12zł; ⏰9am-7pm Mon-Fri, to 4pm Sat & Sun) The city centre's last remaining *bar mleczny* offers substantial Polish stodge for a fistful of złoty. The outdoor window serves up waffles, ice cream and perhaps northern Poland's best *zapiekanki* (Polish pizza).

Luizjana CAJUN €€
(☎56 692 6678; www.restauracjaluizjana.pl; ul Mostowa 10/1; mains 22-50zł; ⏰noon-10pm; 📶) Cajun or creole food is a novel concept in these parts, but one that works exceedingly well here. Enjoy mains like spicy grilled chicken served in sweet coconut sauce with rice or blackened salmon with spinach pesto in a charming, low-key cafe-like setting. Portions (especially soups) are huge and suitable for sharing. The vibe is hip without being pretentious.

★ **Szeroka 9** POLISH €€€
(☎56 622 8424; www.szeroka9.pl; ul Szeroka 9; mains 35-50zł; ⏰9am-11pm; 📶) Elegant, refined (with being fussy) dining, a short walk from the main square. The chef dabbles in traditional Polish main courses like rabbit, goose and duck, but with a contemporary flair (for example, stuffed leek and plum sauce with the goose). The service is attentive and the wine list is excellent. A perfect choice for a special meal.

Drinking & Nightlife

Kona Coast Cafe CAFE
(☎56 664 0049; www.konacoastcafe.pl; ul Chełmińska 18; ⏰9am-9pm Mon-Sat, 11am-6pm Sun; 📶) Claims to be the only cafe in town that roasts their own beans. The coffee is decent as is the homemade lemonade, chai and various cold drinks. There's also a light-meal menu.

Entertainment

Lizard King LIVE MUSIC
(☎56 621 0234; www.lizardking-torun.pl; ul Kopernika 3; ⏰7pm-late; 📶) Live-music venue with gigs ranging from local tribute bands to quite big rock acts from around Eastern and Central Europe.

Teatr Baj Pomorski PUPPETRY
(☎56 652 2424, 56 652 2029; www.bajpomorski.art.pl; ul Piernikarska 9) Puppet theatre shaped like a huge wooden cabinet, staging a variety of entertaining shows.

Information

Tourist Office (☎56 621 0930; www.torun.pl; Rynek Staromiejski 25; ⏰9am-4pm Mon & Sat, to 6pm Tue-Fri, 11am-3pm Sun; 📶) Free internet access, heaps of info and very professional staff who know their city.

Getting There & Away

BUS

The **bus station** (Dworzec Autobusowy Arriva; www.rozklady.com.pl; ul Dąbrowskiego 8-24) is a 10-minute walk north of the Old Town; from here, **Polski Bus** (www.polskibus.com) connects to Warsaw (3¾ hours, four daily) and Gdańsk (two hours, four daily). For other places, it's usually better to take the train.

TRAIN

Toruń's **main train station** (Toruń Główny; www.pkp.pl; Kujawska 1; 22, 27) is located on the opposite side of the Vistula River and linked to the Old Town by bus 22 or 27 (or a 2km walk). Useful direct train connections include those to Gdańsk (50zł, three hours, three daily), Kraków (73zł, seven hours, three daily), Poznań (30zł, two hours, two daily), Warsaw (52zł, 2¾ hours, five daily).

SURVIVAL GUIDE

Directory A–Z

ACCOMMODATION

Polish accommodation runs the gamut from youth hostels, bungalows and mountain cabins to modest hotels and pensions all the way to upmarket boutiques and business-oriented chains.

- Youth hostels are divided into 'older-style', where accommodation is offered in university dorms, and modern hostels, geared toward international backpackers. A dorm bed can cost anything from 40zł to 60zł per person per night.

COUNTRY FACTS

Area 312,679 sq km

Capital Warsaw

Country Code 48

Currency Złoty (zł)

Emergency ambulance 999, fire 998, police 997

Language Polish

Money ATMs all over; banks open Monday to Friday

Population 38.5 million

Visas Not required for citizens of the EU, US, Canada, New Zealand and Australia

SLEEPING PRICE RANGES

In this chapter, our price breakdown is based on a double room in season. Unless otherwise noted, rooms have private bathrooms and the rate includes breakfast.

€ less than 150zł

€€ 150zł to 400zł

€€€ more than 400zł

- A handy campsite resource is the website of the **Polish Federation of Camping and Caravanning** (www.pfcc.eu).
- Hotel prices vary substantially depending on the day of the week or season. In cities, expect higher rates during the week and weekend discounts. In heavily touristed areas, rates may rise over the weekend.
- Two reliable websites for arranging hotel accommodation over the internet are www.poland4u.com and www.hotelspoland.com.
- In big cities like Warsaw, Kraków and Gdańsk, private apartments are available for short-term rentals. These can offer an affordable alternative to hotels.

BUSINESS HOURS

Banks 8am to 5pm Monday to Friday, sometimes 8am to 2pm Saturday

Cafes & restaurants 11am to 11pm

Shops 10am to 6pm Monday to Friday, 10am to 2pm Saturday

Nightclubs 9pm to late

GAY & LESBIAN TRAVELLERS

- Homosexual activity is legal in Poland and overt discrimination is banned, though public attitudes are generally not supportive.
- Warsaw and Kraków are the best places to find gay-friendly bars and clubs.
- A decent, though somewhat dated, source of online information: www.gayguide.net.

INTERNET ACCESS

- Nearly all hotels and hostels offer internet, usually wi-fi.
- Many cafes, restaurants and bars offer free wi-fi for customers.
- Internet cafes are not as abundant as they once were, but normally charge around 5zł per hour.

INTERNET RESOURCES

In Your Pocket (www.inyourpocket.com)

Online train timetable (http://rozklad-pkp.pl)

Poland's official travel website (www.poland.travel)

Useful promotional website (www.polska.pl)

MONEY

- Poland's currency is the złoty (*zwo*-ti), abbreviated as zł (international currency code PLN). It's divided into 100 groszy (gr).
- *Bankomats* (ATMs) accept most international credit cards and are easily found. Private *kantors* (foreign-exchange offices) are also everywhere.
- Tipping isn't common in Poland, but feel free to leave 10% extra for waitstaff or taxi drivers if you've had good service.

PUBLIC HOLIDAYS

New Year's Day 1 January
Epiphany 6 January
Easter Sunday March/April
Easter Monday March/April
State Holiday 1 May
Constitution Day 3 May
Pentecost Sunday Seventh Sunday after Easter
Corpus Christi Ninth Thursday after Easter
Assumption Day 15 August
All Saints' Day 1 November
Independence Day 11 November
Christmas 25 and 26 December

TELEPHONE

- Polish landlines have nine digits, consisting of a two-digit area code and a seven-digit number. Mobile phone numbers have nine digits, normally starting with a 5, 6 or 7.
- To call a landline from another landline, dial ☎0 plus the area code and the seven-digit number. To call a mobile phone from a landline, dial ☎0 plus the nine-digit number.
- To call a mobile from a mobile, simply dial the number.
- To call Poland from abroad, dial the country code ☎48, then the area code plus seven-digit landline number, or the nine-digit mobile-phone number.
- The main mobile operators are Plus, Orange, T-Mobile and Play; all offer inexpensive prepaid SIM cards that come with call and data allowances.
- The cheapest way to make international calls from public telephones is via prepaid international cards, available at post offices and kiosks.

VISAS

- EU citizens do not need visas to visit Poland and can stay indefinitely.
- Citizens of Australia, Canada, Israel, New Zealand, Switzerland and the USA can stay in Poland up to 90 days without a visa.
- Other nationals should check the website of the **Ministry of Foreign Affairs** (www.msz.gov.pl).

ESSENTIAL FOOD & DRINK

- **Żurek** Hearty, sour rye soup includes sausage and hard-boiled egg.
- **Barszcz** Famous beetroot soup comes in two varieties: red (made from beetroot) and white (with wheat flour and sausage).
- **Bigos** Thick stew with sauerkraut and meat.
- **Pierogi** Flour dumplings, usually stuffed with cheese, mushrooms or meat.
- **Szarlotka** Apple cake with cream; a Polish classic.
- **Wódka** Vodka: try it plain, or ask for *myśliwska* (flavoured with juniper berries).

Getting There & Away

AIR

Warsaw-Frédéric Chopin Airport (p852) is the nation's main international gateway, while other important airports include Kraków, Gdańsk, Poznań and Wrocław.

- The national carrier **LOT** (☎call centre 801 703 703; www.lot.com) flies to major European cities and select destinations further afield.
- A vast array of budget carriers, including **Ryanair** (☎703 303 033; www.ryanair.com) and **Wizz Air** (☎703 603 993; www.wizzair.com), fly into Poland from airports across Europe, including regional airports in Britain and Ireland.

LAND

Poland is well connected to both Western and Eastern Europe by rail and bus networks.

Border Crossings

- As Poland is a member of the EU's Schengen Zone, there are no passport or customs controls if arriving from Germany, the Czech Republic, Slovakia or Lithuania.
- Expect border delays if arriving from Ukraine, Belarus or Russia's Kaliningrad province.

Bus

International buses head in all directions, including eastward to the Baltic States. From Zakopane, it's easy to hop to Slovakia via bus or minibus.

Several companies operate long-haul coach service. Two reliable operators include **Eurolines Polska** (☎146 571 777; www.eurolines.pl) and **Polski Bus** (www.polskibus.com).

Car & Motorcycle

- The minimum legal driving age is 18.
- The maximum blood-alcohol limit is 0.02%.
- All drivers are required to carry their home driving licence, along with identity card, vehicle registration and liability insurance.

Train

There are direct rail services to Berlin from Warsaw (via Poznań) and to Prague from Warsaw and Kraków. Trains also link Warsaw to Minsk in Belarus and Moscow in Russia.

SEA

Ferry services operated by **Polferries** (☎801 003 171; www.polferries.pl), **Stena Line** (☎58 660 9200; www.stenaline.pl) and **Unity Line** (www.unityline.pl) connect Poland's Baltic coast ports of Gdańsk, Gydnia and Świnoujscie to destinations in Scandinavia, including Denmark and Sweden.

Getting Around

AIR

LOT (p875) and/or its cheaper **Eurolot** (☎22 275 8740; www.eurolot.com) subsidiary fly between Warsaw, Gdańsk, Kraków, Poznań, Wrocław and Lublin.

BUS

Most buses are operated by the state bus company, PKS. It operates both ordinary buses (marked in black on timetables) and fast buses (marked in red).

- Buy tickets at bus terminals or directly from the driver.

EATING PRICE RANGES

Price ranges in this chapter are based on the average cost of a main meal.

€ less than 20zł

€€ 20zł to 40zł

€€€ more than 40zł

- Polski Bus (p876) offers modern, comfortable long-haul coach service to select large Polish cities and beyond; buy tickets from its website.

CAR

Major international car-rental companies are represented in larger cities and airports.

Avis (☎22 572 6565; www.avis.pl)

Europcar (☎22 255 5600; www.europcar.com.pl)

Hertz (☎22 500 1620; www.hertz.pl)

TRAIN

Polish State Railways (PKP; ☎information 19 757; www.pkp.pl) operates trains to nearly every tourist destination; its online timetable is helpful, providing routes, fares and intermediate stations in English.

- **EIC** (Express InterCity) and **EC** (EuroCity) trains link large cities and offer the best and fastest connections. Reservations are obligatory.
- **TLK** (Tanie Linie Kolejowe) trains tend to be as fast as EC, but are cheaper. Trains are often crowded and no reservations are taken for second class on some trains.
- **IR** (InterRegio) and **R** (Regio) are cheap and slow local trains.
- Buy tickets at station ticket windows or at special PKP passenger-service centres, located in major stations. Also buy online at the Polish State Railways (PKP) website.

Portugal

Includes ➡

Best Places to Eat

➡ Belcanto (p886)

➡ Botequim da Mouraria (p895)

➡ DOP (p905)

➡ Fangas Mercearia Bar (p900)

➡ Restaurante O Barradas (p893)

Best Places to Stay

➡ Memmo Alfama (p885)

➡ Gallery Hostel (p904)

➡ Nice Way Sintra Palace (p890)

➡ Duas Quintas (p893)

➡ Albergaria do Calvario (p895)

Why Go?

With medieval castles, frozen-in-time villages, captivating cities and golden-sand bays, the Portuguese experience can mean many things. History, terrific food and wine, lyrical scenery and all-night partying are just the beginning.

Portugal's cinematically beautiful capital, Lisbon, and its soulful northern rival, Porto, are two of Europe's most charismatic cities. Both are a joy to stroll, with gorgeous river views, rattling trams and tangled lanes hiding boutiques and vintage shops, new-wave bars, and a seductive mix of restaurants, fado (traditional Portuguese song) clubs and open-air cafes.

Beyond the cities, Portugal's landscape unfolds in all its beauty. Here, you can stay overnight in converted hilltop fortresses fronting age-old vineyards, hike amid granite peaks or explore medieval villages in the little-visited hinterland. More than 800km of coast shelters some of Europe's best beaches. You can gaze out over dramatic end-of-the-world cliffs, surf Atlantic breaks off dune-covered beaches or laze on sandy islands fronting the ocean.

When to Go

Lisbon

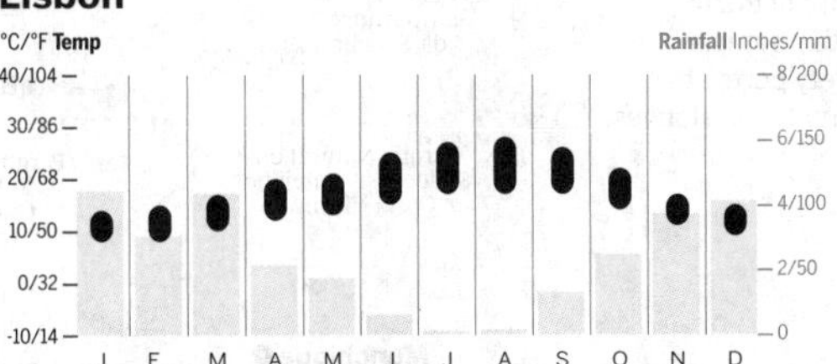

Apr & May Sunny days and wildflowers set the stage for hiking and outdoor activities.

Jun–Aug Lovely and lively, with a packed festival calendar and steamy beach days.

Late Sep & Oct Crisp mornings and sunny days; prices dip, crowds disperse.

Portugal Highlights

1. Follow the sound of fado spilling from the lamplit lanes of the **Alfama** (p887), an enchanting old-world neighbourhood in the heart of Lisbon.
2. Take in the laid-back charms of **Tavira** (p892), before hitting some of the Algarve's prettiest beaches.
3. Catch live music in a backstreet bar in **Coimbra** (p899), a festive university town with a stunning medieval centre.
4. Explore the wooded hills of **Sintra** (p889), studded with fairy-tale-like palaces, villas and gardens.
5. Conquer the trails of the ruggedly scenic **Parque Nacional da Peneda-Gerês** (p909).
6. Enjoy heady beach days in **Lagos** (p892), a surf-loving town with a vibrant drinking and dining scene.
7. Explore the Unesco World Heritage–listed centre of **Porto** (p901), sampling velvety ports at riverside wine lodges.

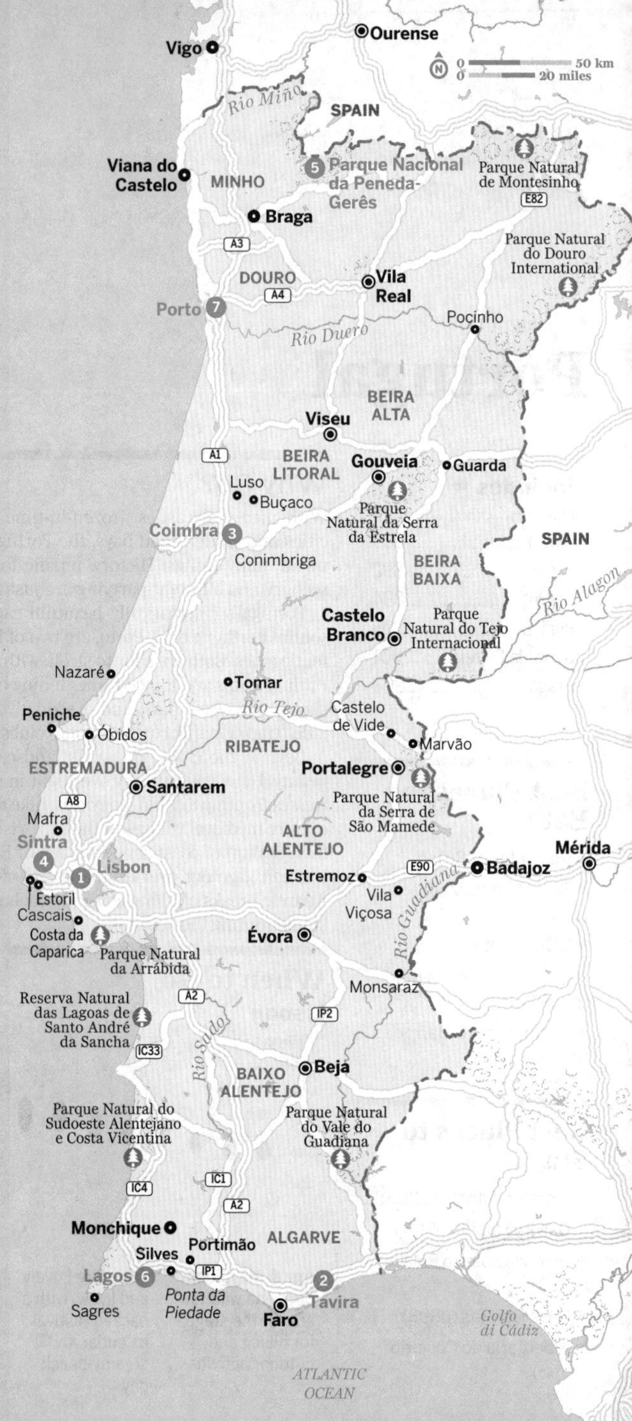

ITINERARIES

One Week

Devote three days to **Lisbon**, including a night of fado (traditional Portuguese song) in the Alfama, bar-hopping in Bairro Alto and Unesco-gazing and pastry-eating in Belém. Spend a day taking in the wooded wonderland of **Sintra**, before continuing to **Coimbra**, Portugal's own Cambridge. End your week in **Porto**, gateway to the magical wine-growing region of the Douro valley.

Two Weeks

On week two, stroll the historic lanes of **Évora** and visit the nearby megaliths. Take in the picturesque castle town of **Monsaraz** before hitting the beaches of the Algarve. Travel along the coast, visiting the pretty riverfront town of **Tavira** and the dramatic cliffs of **Sagres**. End the grand tour back in sunny **Lisbon**.

LISBON

POP 552,700

Spread across steep hillsides that overlook the Rio Tejo, Lisbon has captivated visitors for centuries. Windswept vistas at breathtaking heights reveal the city in all its beauty: Roman and Moorish ruins, white-domed cathedrals and grand plazas lined with sun-drenched cafes. The real delight of discovery, though, is delving into the narrow cobblestone lanes.

As bright-yellow trams clatter through curvy tree-lined streets, *lisboêtas* (residents of Lisbon) stroll through lamplit old quarters, much as they've done for centuries. Village-life gossip is exchanged over fresh bread and wine at tiny patio restaurants as fado singers perform in the background. In other parts of town, Lisbon reveals her youthful alter ego at stylish dining rooms and lounges, late-night street parties, riverside nightspots and boutiques selling all things classic and cutting-edge.

Just outside Lisbon, there's more to explore: enchanting woodlands, gorgeous beaches and seaside villages – all ripe for discovery.

Sights

Baixa & Alfama

Alfama is Lisbon's Moorish time capsule: a medina-like district of tangled alleys, hidden palm-shaded squares and narrow terracotta-roofed houses that tumble down to the glittering Tejo.

Castelo de São Jorge CASTLE

(http://castelodesaojorge.pt; adult/child €8.50/5; 9am-9pm Mar-Oct, 9am-6pm Nov-Feb) Towering dramatically above Lisbon, the hilltop fortifications of Castelo de São Jorge sneak into almost every snapshot. Roam its snaking ramparts and pine-shaded courtyards for superlative views over the city's red rooftops to the river.

Sé CATHEDRAL

(9am-7pm Tue-Sat, 9am-5pm Mon & Sun) FREE One of Lisbon's icons is the fortresslike *sé*, built in 1150 on the site of a mosque soon after Christians recaptured the city from the Moors.

FREE LISBOA

Aside from the **Castelo de São Jorge**, many sights in Lisbon have free entrance on Sundays from 10am to 2pm. For a free cultural fix on other days, make for Belém's **Museu Colecção Berardo** (p882) for outstanding contemporary art exhibits and the fortresslike **Sé** (cathedral), which was built on the site of a mosque in 1150. For Roman ruins, take a free tour of the **Núcleo Arqueológico** (Rua Augusta 96; 10am-6pm Mon-Sat) FREE, which contains a web of tunnels hidden under the Baixa. The **Museu de Design e da Moda** (www.mude.pt; Rua Augusta 24; 10am-6pm Tue-Sun) FREE exhibits eye-catching furniture, industrial design and couture dating to the 1930s.

Central Lisbon

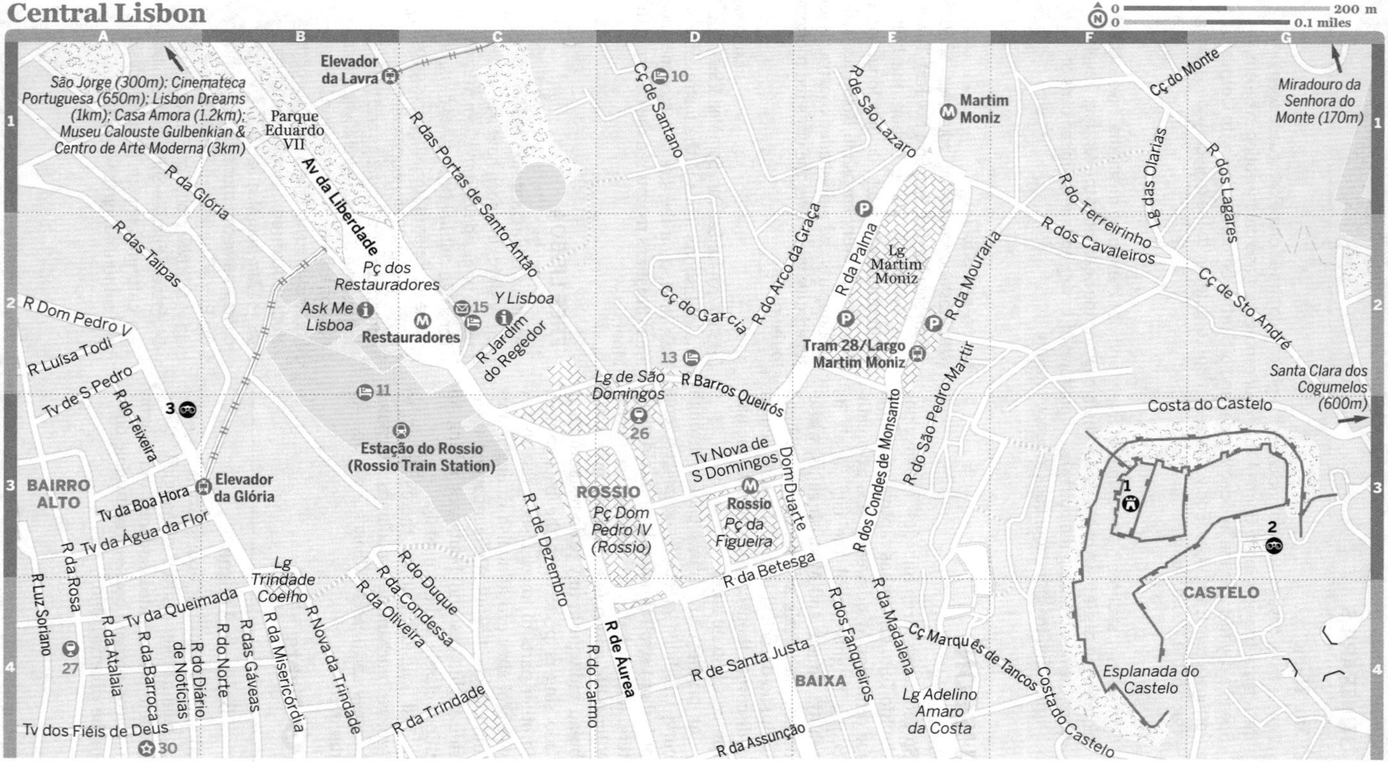

0 200 m
0 0.1 miles

São Jorge (300m); Cinemateca Portuguesa (650m); Lisbon Dreams (1km); Casa Amora (1.2km); Museu Calouste Gulbenkian & Centro de Arte Moderna (3km)
Parque Eduardo VII
Elevador da Lavra
Av da Liberdade
R das Portas de Santo Antão
R da Glória
R das Taipas
Pç dos Restauradores
Ask Me Lisboa
Restauradores
15
Y Lisboa
R Jardim do Regedor
R Dom Pedro V
R Luísa Todi
Tv de S Pedro
R do Teixeira
3
11
Estação do Rossio (Rossio Train Station)
BAIRRO ALTO
Elevador da Glória
Tv da Boa Hora
Tv da Água da Flor
R da Rosa
R Luz Soriano
27
R da Atalaia
R da Barroca
R do Diário de Notícias
R do Norte
R das Gáveas
R da Misericórdia
R Nova da Trindade
Lg Trindade Coelho
Tv da Queimada
Tv dos Fiéis de Deus
30
R da Trindade
R da Oliveira
R da Condessa
R do Duque
R 1 de Dezembro
R do Carmo
R de Áurea
ROSSIO
Pç Dom Pedro IV (Rossio)
Lg de São Domingos
26
Cç de Santano
10
Cç do Garcia
13
R Barros Queirós
R do Arco da Graça
Tv Nova de S Domingos
Dom Duarte
Rossio
Pç da Figueira
R da Betesga
R de Santa Justa
R da Assunção
BAIXA
R dos Fanqueiros
R da Madalena
R dos Condes de Monsanto
Lg Adelino Amaro da Costa
Cç Marquês de Tancos
R de São Lazaro
Martim Moniz
R da Palma
Lg Martim Moniz
Tram 28/Largo Martim Moniz
R da Mouraria
R do São Pedro Martir
R do Terreirinho
R dos Cavaleiros
Lg das Olarias
R dos Lagares
Cç do Monte
Cç de Sto André
Miradouro da Senhora do Monte (170m)
Santa Clara dos Cogumelos (600m)
Costa do Castelo
1
2
CASTELO
Esplanada do Castelo
Costa do Castelo

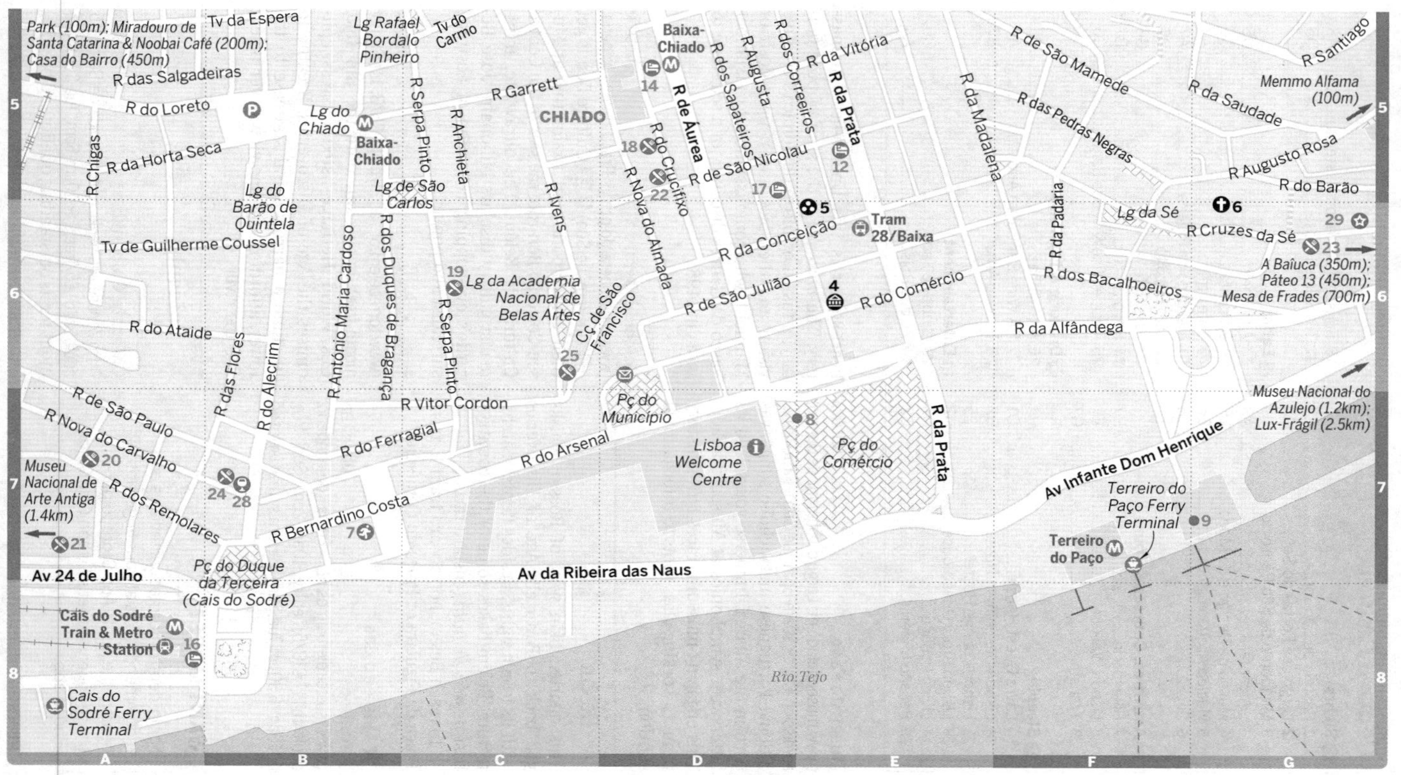
Park (100m); Miradouro de Santa Catarina & Noobai Café (200m); Casa do Bairro (450m)
Tv da Espera
R das Salgadeiras
R do Loreto
R Chigas
R da Horta Seca
Lg do Barão de Quintela
Tv de Guilherme Coussel
R do Ataide
Lg Rafael Bordalo Pinheiro
Tv do Carmo
Lg do Chiado
Baixa-Chiado
R Serpa Pinto
R Anchieta
R Garrett
CHIADO
Lg de São Carlos
R Ivens
R António Maria Cardoso
R dos Duques de Bragança
Lg da Academia Nacional de Belas Artes
Cç de São Francisco
R das Flores
R do Alecrim
R Vitor Cordon
R de São Paulo
R Nova do Carvalho
R do Ferragial
Museu Nacional de Arte Antiga (1.4km)
R dos Remolares
R Bernardino Costa
Av 24 de Julho
Pç do Duque da Terceira (Cais do Sodré)
Cais do Sodré Train & Metro Station
Cais do Sodré Ferry Terminal
R do Arsenal
Av da Ribeira das Naus
Pç do Município
Lisboa Welcome Centre
R Nova do Almada
R do Crucifixo
R de Áurea
R dos Sapateiros
R Augusta
R dos Correeiros
R da Vitória
R da Prata
R de São Nicolau
R da Conceição
Tram 28/Baixa
R de São Julião
R do Comércio
Pç do Comércio
R da Madalena
R de São Mamede
R das Pedras Negras
R da Padaria
R dos Bacalhoeiros
R da Alfândega
Lg da Sé
R Cruzes da Sé
R da Saudade
R Santiago
Memmo Alfama (100m)
R Augusto Rosa
R do Barão
A Baîuca (350m); Páteo 13 (450m); Mesa de Frades (700m)
Museu Nacional do Azulejo (1.2km); Lux-Frágil (2.5km)
Av Infante Dom Henrique
Terreiro do Paço Ferry Terminal
Terreiro do Paço
Rio Tejo

Central Lisbon

Sights

1 Castelo de São Jorge ... F3
2 Largo das Portas do Sol ... G3
3 Miradouro de São Pedro de Alcântara ... A3
4 Museu de Design e da Moda ... E6
5 Núcleo Arqueológico ... E6
6 Sé ... G6

Activities, Courses & Tours

7 Bike Iberia ... B7
8 Lisbon Walker ... E7
9 Transtejo ... G7

Sleeping

10 Lavra Guest House ... D1
11 Lisbon Destination Hostel ... B2
12 Lisbon Lounge Hostel ... E5
13 Lisbon Story Guesthouse ... D2
14 Living Lounge ... D5
15 Pensão Imperial ... C2
16 Sunset Destination Hostel ... A8
17 Travellers House ... D5

Eating

18 A Palmeira ... D5
19 Belcanto ... C6
20 Cafe Tati ... A7
21 Mercado da Ribeira ... A7
22 Oito Dezoito ... D5
23 Pois Café ... G6
24 Povo ... B7
25 Tagide Wine & Tapas Bar ... C6

Drinking & Nightlife

26 A Ginjinha ... D3
27 BA Wine Bar Bairro Alto ... A4
28 Pensão Amor ... B7

Entertainment

29 Clube de Fado ... G6
30 Zé dos Bois ... A4

Museu do Fado MUSEUM
(www.museudofado.pt; Largo do Chafariz de Dentro; admission €5; ⏲10am-6pm Tue-Sun) Fado (traditional Portuguese melancholic song) was born in the Alfama. Immerse yourself in its bittersweet symphonies at Museu do Fado. This engaging museum traces fado's history from its working-class roots to international stardom.

Belém

This quarter, 6km west of Rossio, whisks you back to Portugal's Age of Discoveries with its iconic sights. Besides heritage architecture, Belém bakes some of the country's best *pastéis de nata* (custard tarts).

To reach Belém, hop aboard tram 15 from Praça da Figueira or Praça do Comércio.

★ Mosteiro dos Jerónimos MONASTERY
(www.mosteirojeronimos.pt; Praça do Império; adult/child €10/5, entry 10am-2pm Sun free; ⏲10am-6.30pm Tue-Sun) Belém's undisputed heart-stealer is this Unesco-listed monastery. The *mosteiro* is the stuff of pure fantasy; a fusion of Diogo de Boitaca's creative vision and the spice and pepper dosh of Manuel I, who commissioned it to trumpet Vasco da Gama's discovery of a sea route to India in 1498.

Museu Colecção Berardo MUSEUM
(www.museuberardo.pt; Praça do Império; ⏲10am-7pm Tue-Sun) FREE Culture fiends get their contemporary art fix for free at Museu Colecção Berardo, the star of the Centro Cultural de Belém. The ultrawhite, minimalist gallery displays billionaire José Berardo's eye-popping collection of abstract, surrealist and pop art.

Torre de Belém TOWER
(www.torrebelem.pt; adult/child €6/3, 1st Sun of month free) Jutting out onto the Rio Tejo, this World Heritage–listed fortress epitomises the Age of Discoveries. Breathe in to climb a narrow spiral staircase to the tower, affording sublime views over Belém and the river.

WANT MORE?

For in-depth information, reviews and recommendations at your fingertips, head to the Apple App Store to purchase Lonely Planet's *Lisbon City Guide* iPhone app.

Saldanha

Museu Calouste Gulbenkian MUSEUM
(http://museu.gulbenkian.pt; Avenida de Berna 45; adult/child €5/free; ⏲10am-6pm Tue-Sun) Famous for its outstanding quality and breadth,

Museu Calouste Gulbenkian showcases an epic collection of Western and Eastern art – from Egyptian treasures to Old Master and Impressionist paintings.

Centro de Arte Moderna MUSEUM
(Modern Art Centre; www.cam.gulbenkian.pt; Rua Dr Nicaulau de Bettencourt; adult/chilld €5/free; ⌚10am-6pm Tue-Sun) Situated in a sculpture-dotted garden, the Centro de Arte Moderna reveals a stellar collection of 20th-century Portuguese and international art.

Santa Apolónia & Lapa

The museums listed here are west and east of the city centre, but are well worth visiting.

Museu Nacional do Azulejo MUSEUM
(www.museudoazulejo.pt; Rua Madre de Deus 4; adult/child €5/2.50, 1st Sun of month free; ⌚10am-6pm Tue-Sun) Housed in a sublime 16th-century convent, the museum covers the entire *azulejo* (hand-painted tile) spectrum. Star exhibits feature a 36m-long panel depicting pre-earthquake Lisbon, a Manueline cloister with weblike vaulting and exquisite blue-and-white *azulejos*, and a gold-smothered baroque chapel.

Museu Nacional de Arte Antiga MUSEUM
(Ancient Art Museum; www.museudearteantiga.pt; Rua das Janelas Verdes; adult/child €6/3, 1st Sun of month free; ⌚2-6pm Tue, 10am-6pm Wed-Sun) Set in a lemon-fronted, 17th-century palace, the Museu Nacional de Arte Antiga is Lapa's biggest draw. It presents a star-studded collection of European and Asian paintings and decorative arts.

Parque das Nações

The former Expo '98 site, this revitalised 2km-long waterfront area in the northeast equals a family fun day out, packed with public art, gardens and kid-friendly attractions.

Take the metro to **Oriente station** – a stunner designed by star Spanish architect Santiago Calatrava.

Oceanário AQUARIUM
(www.oceanario.pt; Doca dos Olivais; adult/child €14/9; ⌚10am-8pm) The closest you'll get to scuba-diving without a wetsuit, Lisbon's Oceanário is mind-blowing. No amount of hyperbole, where 8000 species splash in 7 million litres of seawater, does it justice. Huge wraparound tanks make you feel as if you are underwater, as you eyeball zebra sharks, honeycombed rays, gliding mantas and schools of neon fish.

Pavilhão do Conhecimento MUSEUM
(www.pavconhecimento.pt; Living Science Centre; adult/child €8/5; ⌚10am-6pm Tue-Fri, 11am-7pm Sat & Sun) Kids won't grumble about science at the interactive Pavilhão do Conhecimento, where they can launch hydrogen rockets, lie unhurt on a bed of nails, experience the gravity on the moon and get dizzy on a high-wire bicycle.

HEAVENLY VIEWS

Lisbon's *miradouros* (lookouts) lift spirits with their heavenly views. Some have outdoor cafes for lingering.

Largo das Portas do Sol Moorish gateway with stunning views over Alfama's rooftops.

Miradouro da Graça Pine-fringed square that's perfect for sundowners.

Miradouro da Senhora do Monte The highest lookout, with memorable castle views.

Miradouro de São Pedro de Alcântara (Rua São Pedro de Alcântara; ⌚viewpoint 24hr, cafe 10am-midnight Mon-Wed, to 2am Thu-Sun) Drinks and sweeping views on the edge of Bairro Alto.

Miradouro de Santa Catarina (Rua de Santa Catarina; ⌚24hr) FREE Youthful spot with guitar-playing rebels, artful graffiti and far-reaching views.

Tours

Lisbon Walker WALKING TOUR
(☎218 861 840; www.lisbonwalker.com; Rua dos Remédios 84; 3hr walk adult/child €15/free; ⌚10am & 2.30pm) This excellent company, with well-informed, English-speaking guides, offers themed walking tours through Lisbon, which depart from the northwest corner of Praça do Comércio.

Transtejo CRUISE
(☎210 422 417; www.transtejo.pt; Terreiro do Paço ferry terminal; adult/child €20/10; ⏲Apr-Oct) These 2½-hour river cruises are a laid-back way to enjoy Lisbon's sights with multilingual commentary.

Festivals & Events

The **Festa de Santo António** (Festival of Saint Anthony), from 12 June to 13 June, culminates the three-week **Festas de Lisboa**, with processions and dozens of street parties; it's liveliest in the Alfama.

Sleeping

Boutique hotels with river views, cosy B&Bs and palatial castle hotels – it's all in the mix in Lisbon. Book well ahead in summer.

Baixa, Rossio & Cais do Sodré

Lisbon Destination Hostel HOSTEL €
(☎213 466 457; http://destinationhostels.com; 2nd fl, Rossio Train Station; dm €23-34, d €40-80; @☎) Housed in Lisbon's loveliest train station, the stylish Lisbon Destination Hostel features a glass ceiling that lights the spacious plant-filled common area. Rooms are crisp and well kept, and there are loads of activities (bar crawls, beach day trips etc), plus facilities including a shared kitchen, game consoles and a 24-hour self-service bar. Breakfast is top notch and includes crêpes and fresh fruit.

Travellers House HOSTEL €
(☎210 115 922; www.travellershouse.com; Rua Augusta 89; dm €20-28, s €40, d €70-90; @☎) Travellers enthuse about this super-friendly hostel set in a converted 250-year-old house on Rua Augusta. As well as cosy dorms, there's a retro lounge with beanbags, an internet corner and a communal kitchen.

Sunset Destination Hostel HOSTEL €
(☎210 997 735; http://destinationhostels.com; Cais do Sodré Train Station; dm €22-28, d €32-69; @☎) This beautifully designed river-facing hostel has comfy rooms, a swanky dining room, a top-notch kitchen and a roof pool terrace with impressive river views.

Lisbon Lounge Hostel HOSTEL €
(☎213 462 061; www.lisbonloungehostel.com; Rua de São Nicolau 41; dm/d €25/64; @☎) Lisbon Lounge Hostel has artfully designed dorms, a slick lounge complete with faux moose head and a fun team. Three-course dinners, bike hire, walking tours and DJ nights are all part and parcel of these nicely chilled Baixa digs.

Lavra Guest House GUESTHOUSE €€
(☎218 820 000; www.lavra.pt; Calçada de Santano 198; d not incl breakfast €59-69; ☎) Set in a former convent that dates back two centuries, this place has stylishly set rooms with wood floors and tiny balconies. Some bathrooms are cramped. It's a short stroll from the Elevador da Lavra, or a steep climb from Largo de São Domingos.

Lisbon Story Guesthouse GUESTHOUSE €€
(☎218 879 392; www.lisbonstoryguesthouse.com; Largo de São Domingos 18; d €50-80, without bathroom €60-80; @☎) Overlooking Largo de São Domingos, Lisbon Story is a small, welcoming guesthouse with nicely maintained, light-drenched rooms, some of which sport Portuguese themes (the Tejo, tram 28, fado etc). The shoe-free lounge, with throw pillows and low tables, is a great place to chill, as is the terrace.

Pensão Imperial GUESTHOUSE €€
(☎213 420 166; Praça dos Restauradores 78; d €50-70, tr €90-100) Cheery Imperial has a terrific location in Rossio, but you'll need to grin and lug it, as there's no lift. The rooms

CYCLING THE TEJO

A **cycling/jogging path** courses along the Tejo for 7km, between Cais do Sodré and Belém. Complete with artful touches – including the poetry of Pessoa printed along parts of it – the path takes in ageing warehouses, weathered docks and open-air restaurants and nightspots.

A handy place to rent bikes is a short stroll from Cais do Sodré: **Bike Iberia** (☎213 470 347; www.bikeiberia.com; Largo Corpo Santo 5; bike hire per 2hr/day from €7.50/14; ⏲9.30am-5pm).

with high ceilings and wooden furniture are nothing flash, but some have flower-draped balconies overlooking the *praça* (town square). Bathrooms are shared, though some rooms have a shower or sink.

Alfama

Alfama Patio Hostel HOSTEL €
(☎218 883 127; http://alfama.destinationhostels.com; Rua das Escolas Gerais 3; dm €21-25, s/d €32/64; @📶) In the heart of the Alfama, this beautifully run hostel is a great place to meet other travellers, with loads of activities (from pub crawls through the Bairro Alto to day trips to the beach), plus regular barbecues on the hostel's laid-back garden-like patio. There's a stylish lounge and fantastic staff.

★Memmo Alfama BOUTIQUE HOTEL €€€
(☎210 495 660; http://memmoalfama.com; Travessa Merceeiras 27; r €150-400; ❄📶) Slip down a narrow alley to reach this gorgeous boutique newcomer to Alfama, a stunning conversion of a shoe polish factory. The rooms are an ode to whitewashed minimalism, but it's the view down to the Tejo from the roof terrace that will really blow you away.

Chiado, Bairro Alto & Príncipe Real

★Living Lounge HOSTEL €
(☎213 461 078; www.livingloungehostel.com; 2nd fl, Rua do Crucifixo 116; dm €16-20, s €35, d €60; @📶) The Living Lounge has a stylish design, attractive rooms, friendly staff and excellent amenities (full kitchen, wi-fi, bicycle hire). The nightly dinners and wide range of tours provide a fine opportunity to meet other travellers.

Casa do Bairro B&B €€
(☎914 176 969; http://shiadu.com; Beco Caldeira 1; d/tr/f €104/114/129; ❄📶) This small, welcoming guesthouse has bright rooms furnished in an attractive contemporary style, and staff have great tips on the city. Some rooms are small, and bathrooms can be rather cramped. It's hard to find (it's located on a staircase lane), so get good directions before arriving. The owners also operate four other B&Bs in Lisbon, and one in Porto.

Avenida de Liberdade, Rato & Marquês de Pombal

★Casa Amora GUESTHOUSE €€
(☎919 300 317; http://solisbon.com; Rua João Penha 13; d €105-170; ❄📶) Casa Amora has 10 beautifully designed guestrooms, with eye-catching art and iPod docks. There's a lovely garden patio where the first-rate breakfast is served. It's located in the peaceful neighbourhood of Amoreiras, a few steps from one of Lisbon's prettiest squares.

Lisbon Dreams GUESTHOUSE €€
(☎213 872 393; www.lisbondreamsguesthouse.com; Rua Rodrigo da Fonseca 29; s/d without bathroom €55/60; @📶) On a quiet street lined with jacaranda trees, Lisbon Dreams offers terrific value for its bright, modern rooms with high ceilings and excellent mattresses. The green apples are a nice touch, and there are attractive common areas to unwind in. All bathrooms are shared, but are spotlessly clean.

Eating

In addition to creative newcomers, you'll find inexpensive, traditional dining rooms home to classic Portuguese fare.

Baixa, Rossio & Cais do Sodré

A Palmeira PORTUGUESE €
(Rua do Crucifixo 69; mains €7-10; ⏲11am-9pm Mon-Fri) Popular among Baixa's lunching locals, A Palmeira dishes up good, honest Portuguese fare, from grilled fish to beef stew, in an old-fashioned tiled interior. Look for the palm on the sign.

Povo PORTUGUESE €
(Rua Nova do Carvalho 32; small plates €4-8; ⏲noon-2am Tue-Sat, 6pm-1am Sun & Mon) On bar-lined Rua Nova do Carvalho, Povo serves up tasty Portuguese comfort food in the form of *petiscos* (small plates). There's also outdoor seating and live fado nights (Thursdays are best).

Oito Dezoito PORTUGUESE €€
(☎961 330 226; www.oitodezoito.pt; Rua de São Nicolau 114; mains €12-20; ⏲noon-2am Mon-Sat) It's named after the time it takes a sunray to reach the earth, and Oito Dezoito (Eight

Eighteen) shines with its Italian-inspired cuisine. Clean lines and charcoal and cream tones create a sleek backdrop for brunch, lunch or dishes like tender roast lamb with pomegranate and chestnut sauce. Wines are available by the glass.

Alfama

Pois Café CAFE €
(www.poiscafe.com; Rua de São João da Praça 93; mains €7-10; 1-11pm Mon, 11am-11pm Tue-Sun;) Boasting a laid-back vibe, Pois Café has creative salads, sandwiches and fresh juices, plus a delicious daily special (soup and main for €9.50). Its sofas invite lazy afternoons spent reading novels and sipping coffee.

★ Santa Clara dos Cogumelos INTERNATIONAL €€
(218 870 661; www.santaclaradoscogumelos.com; Campo de Santa Clara 7; petiscos €5-8, mains €14-18; 7.30-11pm Tue-Fri, 12.30-3.30pm & 7.30-11pm Sat;) If you're a mushroom fan, this novel restaurant in the old market hall on Campo de Santa Clara is simply magic. The menu is an ode to the humble *cogumelo* (mushroom). Go for *petiscos* (tapas) like organic shiitake with garlic and coriander, mains like risotto with porcini and black trumpets, and perhaps mushroom ice cream with brownies for dessert.

Páteo 13 PORTUGUESE €€
(Calçadinha de Santo Estêvão 13; mains €8-12; 11am-11pm Tue-Sun) Follow the scent of chargrilled fish to this local favourite tucked away on a small, festively decorated plaza in the Alfama.

Chiado, Bairro Alto & Príncipe Real

Mercado da Ribeira MARKET €
(Avenida 24 de Julho; 10am-midnight Sun-Wed, 10am-2am Thu-Sat) Doing trade in fresh fruit and veg, fish and flowers since 1892, this oriental dome-topped market hall is the word on everyone's lips since *Time Out* transformed half of it into a gourmet food court in 2014. Now it's like Lisbon in microcosm, with everything from Garrafeira Nacional wines to Conserveira de Lisboa fish, Arcádia chocolate and Santini gelato.

Cafe Tati CAFE €
(213 461 279; http://cafetati.blogspot.com; Rua da Ribeira Nova 36; mains €7-8; 11am-1am Tue-Sun;) Cafe Tati has undeniable charm amid its smattering of well-lit stone-arched rooms with stencilled walls. Along with inventive *tostas* (Parma ham and raclette) and salads (goat cheese and green apple), there are appetising daily specials.

Tagide Wine & Tapas Bar FUSION €€
(213 404 010; Largo da Academia Nacional de Belas Artes 20; tapas €4-9; 12.30-3pm & 7pm-midnight Tue-Thu, 12.30-3pm & 7pm-1am Fri, 2pm-1am Sat) Not to be confused with the pricier Tagide next door, this casual, slickly modern tapas bar has pretty views to the river. Small sharing plates are imaginative and packed with flavour. Three-course lunch specials, which include a glass of wine and coffee, cost €12.50.

★ Belcanto PORTUGUESE €€€
(213 420 607; Largo de São Carlos 10; mains €42, tasting menu €90-145, 2-/3-course lunch €45/60; 12.30-3pm & 7.30-11pm Tue-Sat) Shining brighter than any other Lisbon restaurant with two Michelin stars, José Avillez' Belcanto wows diners with its well-edited, creative menu, polished service and first-rate sommelier. Signatures like sea bass with seaweed and bivalves, and rosemary-smoked beef loin with bone marrow and garlic purée elevate Portuguese to a whole new level. Reservations are essential.

Belém

Antiga Confeitaria de Belém PATISSERIE €
(Rua de Belém 86-88; pastries €1-2.50; 8am-11pm) Since 1837, this patisserie has been transporting locals to sugar-coated nirvana with heavenly *pastéis de belém*. The crisp pastry nests are filled with custard cream, baked at 200°C for that perfect golden crust, then lightly dusted with cinnamon.

Enoteca de Belém PORTUGUESE €€
(213 631 511; Travessa do Marta Pinto 10; mains €12-17; 1-11pm Tue-Sun) Tucked down a quiet lane just off Belém's main thoroughfare, this wine bar serves tasty Portuguese classics (try the octopus or the grilled Iberian

pork), matched by an excellent selection of full-bodied Douro reds and refreshing Alentejan whites.

Drinking & Nightlife

All-night street parties in Bairro Alto, sunset drinks from high-up terraces, and sumptuous art deco cafes scattered about Chiado – Lisbon has many enticing options for imbibers.

Lisbon's small gay scene is headquartered in Príncipe Real, though you'll also find a few gay bars in Bairro Alto. Lux draws both a gay and straight crowd.

Pensão Amor BAR
(www.pensaoamor.pt; Rua Nova do Carvalho 36; ⏲noon-3am Mon-Wed, noon-4am Thu-Sat) Set inside a former brothel, this cheeky bar pays homage to its passion-filled past with colourful wall murals, a library of erotic-tinged works, and a small stage where you can sometimes catch burlesque shows.

BA Wine Bar Bairro Alto WINE BAR
(Rua da Rosa 107; ⏲6-11pm Tue-Sun) One of the nicest ways to kick-start an evening is over a glass of Portuguese wine (there are 150 to choose from) and tapas at this intimate, friendly wine bar in the heart of Bairro Alto.

Noobai Café BAR
(Miradouro de Santa Catarina; ⏲noon-midnight) Great views, winning cocktails and a festive crowd make Noobai a popular draw for a sundowner.

Park BAR
(Calçada do Combro 58; ⏲1pm-2am Tue-Sat, 1-8pm Sun) If only all multi-storey car parks were like this... Climb up to the top floor, which has been transformed into one of Lisbon's hippest rooftop bars and offers sweeping views reaching right down to the Tejo.

A Ginjinha GINJINHA BAR
(Largo de Saõ Domingos 8; ⏲9am-10pm) Hipsters, old men in flat caps, office workers and tourists all meet at this microscopic *ginjinha* (cherry liqueur) bar for that moment of cherry-licking, pip-spitting pleasure.

Lux-Frágil CLUB
(www.luxfragil.com; Avenida Infante Dom Henrique, Santo Apolónia; ⏲11pm-6am Thu-Sat) Lisbon's ice-cool, must-see club, Lux hosts big-name DJs spinning electro and house. It's run by ex-Frágil maestro Marcel Reis and part-owned by John Malkovich. Grab a spot on the terrace to see the sun rise over the Tejo.

PORTUGUESE SOUL

Infused by Moorish song and the ditties of homesick sailors, bluesy, bittersweet **fado** (traditional Portuguese song) encapsulates the Lisbon psyche like nothing else. The uniquely Portuguese style was born in the Alfama, still the best place in Lisbon to hear it live. Minimum consumption charges range from €15 to €25 per person.

A Baîuca (☎218 867 284; Rua de São Miguel 20; ⏲8pm-midnight Thu-Mon) On a good night, walking into A Baîuca is like gatecrashing a family party. It's a special place with *fado vadio*, where locals take a turn and spectators hiss if anyone dares to chat during the singing.

Clube de Fado (☎218 852 704; www.clube-de-fado.com; Rua de São João da Praça 92; ⏲8pm-2am) Hosts the cream of the fado crop in vaulted, dimly lit surrounds. Big-name *fadistas* perform here alongside celebrated guitarists.

Mesa de Frades (☎917 029 436; Rua dos Remédios 139A; ⏲7pm-2am Mon-Sat) A magical place to hear fado, tiny Mesa de Frades used to be a chapel. It's tiled with exquisite *azulejos* (hand-painted tiles) and has just a handful of tables. Reserve ahead.

Entertainment

For the latest goings-on, pick up the weekly *Time Out Lisboa* (www.timeout.pt) from bookstores, or the free monthly *Follow Me Lisboa* from the tourist office.

Zé dos Bois LIVE MUSIC
(www.zedosbois.org; Rua da Barroca 59; ⏲7pm-2am) Focusing on tomorrow's performing arts and music trends, Zé dos Bois is an experimental venue with a graffitied courtyard, and an eclectic line-up of theatre, film, visual arts and live music.

Cinemas

Lisbon's cinematic standouts are the grand **São Jorge** (Avenida da Liberdade 175) and, just around the corner, **Cinemateca Portuguesa** (www.cinemateca.pt; Rua Barata Salgueiro 39); both screen offbeat, art-house, world and old films.

Sport

Lisbon's football teams are Benfica, Belenenses and Sporting. Euro 2004 led to the upgrading of the 65,000-seat **Estádio da Luz** (217 219 555; www.slbenfica.pt) and the construction of the 54,000-seat **Estádio Nacional** (214 197 212; Cruz Quebrada). State-of-the-art stadium **Estádio José de Alvalade** (Rua Prof Fernando da Fonseca) seats 54,000 and is just north of the university. Take the metro to Campo Grande.

Information

EMERGENCY

Police Station (217 654 242; Rua Capelo 13)

Tourist Police (213 421 634; Palácio Foz, Praça dos Restauradores; 24hr)

INTERNET ACCESS

Most hostels and midrange guesthouses offer wireless (usually free). Loads of cafes and restaurants also offer wi-fi – just ask for the *codigo* (access code).

Portugal Telecom (Avenida Fontes Pereira de Melo 40, Loja 4; 9am-7pm) Has rows of booths.

MEDICAL SERVICES

British Hospital (217 213 410; www.british-hospital.pt; Rua Tomás da Fonseca) English-speaking staff and English-speaking doctors.

MONEY

Cota Câmbios (Praça Dom Pedro IV 41) The best bet for changing cash or travellers cheques is a private exchange bureau like this one.

POST

Main Post Office (Praça dos Restauradores 58; 8am-10pm Mon-Fri, 9am-6pm Sat) Also has an ATM.

Post Office (Praça do Município 6) Central post office.

TOURIST INFORMATION

Ask Me Lisboa (213 463 314; www.askmelisboa.com; Palácio Foz, Praça dos Restauradores; 9am-8pm) The largest and most helpful tourist office. Can book accommodation or reserve rental cars.

Lisboa Welcome Centre (210 312 810; www.visitlisboa.com; Praça do Comércio; 9am-8pm) Main branch of Turismo de Lisboa, providing free city maps, brochures, and hotel and tour booking services. Buy the Lisboa Card here.

Y Lisboa (213 472 134; www.askmelisboa.com; Rua Jardim do Regedor 50; 10am-7pm)

USEFUL WEBSITES

Go Lisbon (www.golisbon.com) Up-to-date info on sightseeing, eating, nightlife and events.

Time Out (www.timeout.pt) Details on upcoming gigs and cultural events, interesting commentary; in Portuguese.

Visit Lisboa (www.visitlisboa.com) Lisbon's comprehensive tourism website, with the lowdown on sightseeing, transport and accommodation.

Getting There & Away

AIR

Around 6km north of the centre, **Aeroporto de Lisboa** (Lisbon Airport; 218 413 500; www.ana.pt) operates direct flights to many European cities.

BUS

Lisbon's long-distance bus terminal is **Sete Rios** (Rua das Laranjeiras), conveniently linked to both Jardim Zoológico metro station and Sete Rios train station. The big carriers, **Rede Expressos** (707 223 344; www.rede-expressos.pt) and **Eva** (707 223 344; www.eva-bus.com), run frequent services to almost every major town.

The other major terminal is **Gare do Oriente** (at Oriente metro and train station), concentrating on services to the north and to Spain. The biggest companies operating from here are **Renex** (218 956 836; www.renex.pt) and the Spanish operator **Avanza** (218 940 250; www.avanzabus.com).

TRAIN

Santa Apolónia station is the terminus for northern and central Portugal. You can catch trains from Santa Apolónia to Gare do Oriente train station, which has departures to the Algarve and international destinations. Cais do Sodré station is for Belém, Cascais and Estoril. Rossio station is the terminal for trains to Sintra via Queluz.

For fares and schedules, visit www.cp.pt.

Getting Around

TO/FROM THE AIRPORT

The **AeroBus** (www.yellowbustours.com; one way €3.50) runs every 20 minutes from 7am to 11pm, taking 30 to 45 minutes between the airport and Cais do Sodré.

A metro station on the red line gives convenient access to downtown. Change at Alameda (green line) to reach Rossio and Baixa. A taxi into town is about €15.

PUBLIC TRANSPORT

A 24-hour Bilhete Carris/Metro (€6) gives unlimited travel on all buses, trams, metros and funiculars. Pick it up from Carris kiosks and metro stations.

Bus, Tram & Funicular

Buses and trams run from 6am to 1am, with a few all-night services. Pick up a transport map from tourist offices or Carris kiosks. A single ticket costs more if you buy it on board (€2.85/1.80/3.60 for tram/bus/funicular), and much less (€1.40 per ride) if you buy a refillable Viva Viagem card (€0.50), available at Carris offices and in metro stations.

There are three funiculars: Elevador da Bica; Elevador da Glória; Elevador do Lavra.

Don't leave the city without riding tram 28 from Largo Martim Moniz through the narrow streets of the Alfama; tram 12 goes from Praça da Figueira out to Belém.

Ferry

Car, bicycle and passenger ferries leave frequently from the Cais do Sodré ferry terminal to Cacilhas (€1.20, 10 minutes). From Terreiro do Paço terminal, catamarans zip across to Montijo (€2.75, every 30 minutes) and Seixal (€2.35, every 30 minutes).

Metro

The **metro** (www.metrolisboa.pt; single/day ticket €1.40/6; ⏲6.30am-1am) is useful for hops across town and to the Parque das Nações. Buy tickets from metro ticket machines, which have English-language menus.

AROUND LISBON

Sintra

POP 26,200

Lord Byron called this hilltop town a 'glorious Eden' and, although best appreciated at dusk when the coach tours have left, it *is* a magnificent place. Less than an hour west of Lisbon, Sintra was the traditional summer retreat of Portugal's kings. Today, it's a fairytale setting of stunning palaces and manors surrounded by rolling green countryside.

Sights & Activities

Although the whole town resembles a historical theme park, there are several compulsory eye-catching sights.

★Quinta da Regaleira VILLA, GARDENS

(www.regaleira.pt; Rua Barbosa du Bocage; adult/child €6/3; ⏲10am-8pm high season, shorter hours in low season) This magical villa and gardens is a neo-Manueline extravaganza, dreamed up by Italian opera-set designer, Luigi Manini, under the orders of Brazilian coffee tycoon, António Carvalho Monteiro, aka Monteiro dos Milhões (Moneybags Monteiro). The villa is surprisingly homely inside, despite its ferociously carved fireplaces, frescoes and Venetian glass mosaics. Keep an eye out for mythological and Knights Templar symbols.

Palácio Nacional de Sintra PALACE

(www.parquesdesintra.pt; Largo Rainha Dona Amélia; adult/child €9.50/7.50; ⏲9.30am-7pm, shorter hours in low season) The star of Sintra-Vila is this palace, with its iconic twin conical chimneys and lavish interior. The whimsical interior is a mix of Moorish and Manueline styles, with arabesque courtyards, barley-twist columns and 15th- and 16th-century geometric *azulejos* (hand-painted tiles) that figure among Portugal's oldest.

Castelo dos Mouros CASTLE

(www.parquesdesintra.pt; adult/child €7.50/6; ⏲9.30am-8pm, shorter hours in low season) Soaring 412m above sea level, this mist-enshrouded ruined castle looms high above the surrounding forest. When the clouds peel away, the vistas over Sintra's palace-dotted hill and dale to the glittering Atlantic are – like the climb – breathtaking.

Palácio Nacional da Pena PALACE

(www.parquesdesintra.pt; adult/child €14/11; ⏲10am-7pm, shorter hours in low season) Rising up from a thickly wooded peak and often enshrouded in swirling mist, Palácio Nacional da Pena is a wacky confection of onion domes, Moorish keyhole gates, writhing stone snakes and crenellated towers in pinks and lemons.

Sleeping

★Nice Way

Sintra Palace HOSTEL €
(☎219 249 800; www.sintrapalace.com; Rua Sotto Mayor 22; dm €18-22, d with/without bathroom €60/50;) In a rambling mansion north of the main square, you'll find stylishly outfitted rooms, great countryside views and a lovely garden. The flickering fireplace on cold nights sweetens the deal. There's also a friendly vibe, making it a good place to meet other travellers. The fully equipped two-bedroom cottage is excellent value for families at around €75 per night.

Hotel Nova Sintra GUESTHOUSE €€
(☎219 230 220; www.novasintra.com; Largo Afonso de Albuquerque 25; s/d €75/95;) This renovated late-19th-century mansion is set above the main road. The big drawcard is the sunny terrace overlooking Sintra, where you can take breakfast. Front-facing doubles offer picturesque views, back rooms more peaceful slumber. Some rooms are rather small.

Eating

Saudade CAFE €
(Avenida Dr Miguel Bombardo 8; mains €5-7; 8.30am-8pm;) This former bakery, where Sintra's famous *queijadas* (mini cheesecakes in a crispy pastry shell) were made, has cherub-covered ceilings and a rambling interior, making it a fine spot for pastries or lighter fare (with a different soup, salad, fish- and meat-dish of the day). A gallery in the back features changing art exhibitions.

Dom Pipas PORTUGUESE €€
(Rua João de Deus 62; mains €7-13; noon-3pm & 7.30-10pm Tue-Sun) A local favourite, Dom Pipas serves up excellent Portuguese dishes, amid *azulejos* and rustic country decor. It's behind the train station (left out of the station, first left, then left again to the end).

Information

Turismo (☎219 231 157; Praça da Republica; 9.30am-6pm) Near the centre of Sintra-Vila, this helpful multilingual office has expert insight into Sintra and the surrounding areas. There's also a small train station (☎211 932 545; 10am-12.30pm & 2.30-6pm) branch, often overrun by those arriving by rail.

Getting There & Away

The Lisbon–Sintra railway terminates in Sintra, a 1km scenic walk northeast of the town's historic centre. Sintra's bus station, and another train station, are a further 1km east in the new town Portela de Sintra. Frequent shuttle buses link the historic centre with the bus station.

Train services (€2.55, 40 minutes, every 15 minutes) run between Sintra and Lisbon's Rossio station.

Getting Around

A handy bus for accessing the castle is the hop-on, hop-off Scotturb bus 434 (€5), which runs from the train station via Sintra-Vila to Castelo dos Mouros (10 minutes), Palácio da Pena (15 minutes), and back.

A taxi to Pena or Monserrate costs around €8 one way.

Cascais

POP 34,000

Cascais is a handsome seaside resort with elegant buildings, an atmospheric Old Town and a happy abundance of restaurants and bars.

Sights & Activities

Cascais' three sandy bays – **Praia da Conceição**, **Praia da Rainha** and **Praia da Ribeira** – are great for a sunbake or a tingly Atlantic dip, but attract crowds in summer.

The sea roars into the coast at **Boca do Inferno** (Hell's Mouth), 2km west of Cascais. Spectacular **Cabo da Roca**, Europe's westernmost point, is 16km from Cascais and Sintra and is served by buses from both towns.

Casa das Histórias Paula Rego GALLERY
(www.casadashistoriaspaularego.com; Avenida da República 300; adult/child €3/free; 10am-7pm Tue-Sun) FREE The Casa das Histórias Paula Rego showcases the disturbing, highly evocative paintings of one of Portugal's finest living artists.

Museu Condes de Castro Guimarães MUSEUM
(10am-5pm Tue-Sun) FREE This whimsical early-19th-century mansion complete with castle turrets and Arabic cloister sits in the grounds of the Parque Marechal Carmona.

Sleeping & Eating

Agarre o Momento GUESTHOUSE €€
(214 064 532; www.agarreomomento.com; Rua Joaquim Ereira 458; d/tr/q €60/90/120;) This welcoming guesthouse in a peaceful residential neighbourhood has bright, airy rooms plus a garden, shared kitchen and bike rental. It's a 15-minute walk (1.5km) north of the station, or a short taxi ride.

Casa Vela GUESTHOUSE €€€
(214 868 972; www.casavelahotel.com; Rua dos Bem Lembrados 17; d €135-169;) The friendly Casa Vela has earned many admirers for its bright and attractive rooms set with modern furnishings. Some rooms have a balcony overlooking the lovely gardens and pool. It's in a peaceful neighbourhood about a 10-minute walk to the old town centre.

House of Wonders CAFE €
(Largo da Misericordia 53; light meals €4-8; 10am-midnight, shorter hours in low season;) Tucked away in the old quarter, this charming Dutch-owned cafe is a traveller's delight. Aside from a warm, welcoming ambience and an artwork-filled interior, you'll find beautifully presented salads, quiches, soups and desserts.

Information

Turismo (214 822 327; www.visiteestoril.com; Rua Visconde da Luz 14; 9am-1pm & 2-7pm Mon-Sat) Sells a map of Cascais.

Getting There & Away

Trains run frequently to Cascais via Estoril (€2.15, 40 minutes) from Cais do Sodré station in Lisbon.

THE ALGARVE

It's easy to see the allure of the Algarve: breathtaking cliffs, golden sands, scalloped bays and long sandy islands. Although overdevelopment has blighted parts of the coast, head inland and you'll land solidly in lovely Portuguese countryside once again. Algarve highlights include the riverside town of Tavira, party-loving Lagos and windswept Sagres. Faro is the regional capital.

Faro

POP 65,0000

Faro is an attractive town with a palm-clad waterfront, well-maintained plazas and a small pedestrianised centre sprinkled with outdoor cafes. There are no beaches in Faro itself, though it's an easy jaunt by ferry to picturesque beaches nearby. A boat trip through the Parque Natural da Ria Formosa is another highlight.

Sights & Activities

Ilha Deserta ISLAND
Ferries go out to Ilha da Barreta (aka Ilha Deserta), a long narrow strip of sand just off the mainland.

Parque Natural da Ria Formosa NATURE RESERVE
For visits to the Ria Formosa Natural Park, sign up for a boating or birdwatching tour with the environmentally friendly outfits of **Ria Formosa** (918 720 002; www.formosamar.pt) and **Lands** (289 817 466; www.lands.pt), both in the Clube Naval in Faro's marina.

Sleeping & Eating

★ **Casa d'Alagoa** HOSTEL €
(289 813 252; www.farohostel.com; Praça Alexandre Herculano 27; dm not incl breakfast €19-25, d €70;) Housed in a renovated mansion, this welcome addition to Faro's budget scene has all the elements of today's sophisticated hostel: it's funky, laid-back and cool.

Hotel Eva HOTEL €€€
(289 001 000; www.tdhotels.pt; Avenida da República 1; s/d/ste €145/175/265;) Eva has spacious, pleasant rooms. Those facing east have balconies and views. There's a rooftop swimming pool for more marina-gazing.

Gengibre e Canela VEGETARIAN €
(289 882 424; Travessa da Mota 10; buffet €7.50; noon-3pm Mon-Sat;) Give the taste buds a break from meat and fish dishes and veg out (literally) at this Zen-like vegetarian restaurant. The buffet changes daily; there may be vegetable lasagne, *feijoada* (bean casserole) and tofu dishes.

Adega Nova PORTUGUESE €€
(☎289 813 433; www.restauranteadeganova.com; Rua Francisco Barreto 24; mains €7.50-18; ⏲11.30am-11pm) Dishing up simply grilled fish and meat, this popular place has plenty of country charm. It has a lofty beamed ceiling, rustic cooking implements on display and long, communal tables and bench seats. Service is efficient.

Information

Turismo (www.visitalgarve.pt; Rua da Misericórdia 8) This efficient, busy place offers information on Faro.

Getting There & Away

Faro airport has both domestic and international flights.

From the bus station, just west of the centre, there are at least six daily express coaches to Lisbon (€20, four hours), plus several slower services, and frequent buses to other coastal towns. There are also international buses to Madrid (€39, eight hours).

The train station is a few minutes' walk west of the bus station. Five trains run daily to Lisbon's Sete Rios station (€23.50, 3¼ hours).

Getting Around

The airport is 6km from the centre. Buses 14 and 16 (€2.20) run into town until 9pm. A taxi from the airport to the town centre costs about €12.

Tavira

POP 26,200

Set on either side of the meandering Rio Gilão, Tavira is a charming town with a hilltop castle, an old Roman bridge and a smattering of Gothic churches. The pretty sands of Ilha da Tavira are a short boat ride away.

Sights & Activities

Castelo CASTLE
FREE Tavira's ruined castle rises high and mighty above the town. Possibly dating back to Neolithic times, rebuilt by Phoenicians and later taken over by the Moors, most of what now stands is a 17th-century reconstruction. The octagonal tower offers fine views over Tavira. Note that the ramparts and steps are without railing.

Igreja da Misericórdia CHURCH
(Rua da Galeria; ⏲9am-1pm & 2-6pm Mon-Sat) FREE Built in the 1540s, this church is the Algarve's most important Renaissance monument, with a magnificent carved, arched doorway topped by statues of Nossa Senhora da Misericórdia, São Pedro and São Paulo.

Ilha da Tavira ISLAND, BEACH
An island beach connected to the mainland by a ferry at Quatro Águas. Walk the 2km or take the (summer-only) bus from the bus station.

Sleeping & Eating

Calçada Guesthouse GUESTHOUSE €€
(☎926 563 713, 927 710 771; www.calcadaguesthouse.com; Calçada de Dona Ana 12; r €85-100; ❄📶) Two British expats renovated and run this stylish, centrally located spot. It has bright, homely rooms and a gorgeous roof terrace for gazing out across Tavira's rooftops. Breakfast costs extra (€8.50), and children are welcome. Minimum-night stays sometimes apply.

Casa Simão PORTUGUESE €
(João Vaz Corte Real 10; mains €6-11; ⏲noon-3pm & 7-10pm Mon-Sat) We'll be upfront: this old-style, barn-like eatery has harsh lighting and zero romance, but that's because the delightful family owners concentrate on down-to-earth fare – they whip up great-value meals such as *javali estufado* (wild boar stew) and grills. Go for the daily specials.

Information

Turismo (☎281 322 511; www.visitalgarve.pt; Praça da República 5; ⏲9am-6pm Mon-Fri, 9am-1pm & 2-6pm Sat & Sun, to 7pm Jul & Aug) Provides local and some regional information and has accommodation listings. Changeable hours.

Getting There & Away

Some 15 trains run daily between Faro and Tavira (€3.15, 40 minutes).

Lagos

POP 31,100

In summer, the pretty fishing port of Lagos has a party vibe; its picturesque cobbled streets and pretty nearby beaches, including

Meia Praia to the east and Praia da Luz to the west, are packed with revellers and sun-seekers.

Activities

Blue Ocean DIVING
(964 665 667; www.blue-ocean-divers.de) For those who want to go diving or snorkelling. Offers a half-day discovery experience (€30), a full-day dive (€90) and a divemaster PADI scuba course (€590). It also offers kayak safaris (half-/full day €30/45, child under 12 years half price).

Kayak Adventures KAYAKING
(913 262 200; http://kayakadventureslagos.com) Has kayaking trips from Batata Beach, including snorkelling, between April and October. Trips last three hours (€25).

Sleeping

Hotel Mar Azul GUESTHOUSE €
(282 770 230; www.hotelmarazul.eu; Rua 25 de Abril 13; s €50-60, d €60-85;) This little gem is one of Lagos' best-value spots. It's a central, well-run and delightfully welcoming place, with comfortable, neat rooms, some with sea views. A simple breakfast is an added bonus.

Albergaria Marina Rio HOTEL €€€
(282 780 830; www.marinario.com; Avenida dos Descobrimentos; s €105-130, d €108-133;) Overlooking the harbour, this hotel has comfortable rooms with contemporary decor and balconies. On the downside, it faces the road and backs onto the bus station. Most rooms are twins. There's a tiny pool and roof terrace.

Eating

★A Forja PORTUGUESE €€
(282 768 588; Rua dos Ferreiros 17; mains €8-15; noon-3pm & 6.30-10pm Sun-Fri) The secret is out. This buzzing place pulls in the crowds – locals, tourists and expats – for its hearty, top-quality traditional food served in a bustling environment at great prices. Plates of the day are always reliable, as are the fish dishes.

Casinha do Petisco SEAFOOD €€
(Rua da Oliveira 51; mains €7-13; 6-11pm Mon-Sat) Blink – or be late – and you'll miss this tiny traditional gem. It's cosy and simply decorated and comes highly recommended by locals for its seafood grills and shellfish dishes.

Information

Turismo (282 763 031; www.visitalgarve.pt; Praça Gil Eanes; 9am-6pm) The very helpful staff offers excellent maps and leaflets.

Getting There & Away

Bus and train services depart frequently for other Algarve towns, and around eight times daily to Lisbon (€25.50, four hours).

Getting Around

A **bus service** (tickets €1.20-1.60; 7am-8pm Mon-Sat) provides useful connections to the beaches of Meia Praia and Luz. Rent bicycles and motorbikes from **Motorent** (282 769 716; www.motorent.pt; Rua Victor Costa e Silva; bike/motorcycle per 3 days from €21/60).

Silves

POP 11,000

The one-time capital of Moorish Algarve, Silves is a pretty town of jumbled orange rooftops scattered above the banks of the Rio Arade. Clamber around the ramparts of its fairy-tale castle for superb views.

Sleeping & Eating

★Duas Quintas RURAL INN €€
(282 449 311; www.duasquintas.com; São Estevão; d/studio €95/120;) Set among orange groves and rolling hills, this utterly charming converted farmhouse has six pleasant rooms, a living space, terraces and a pool.

★Restaurante O Barradas PORTUGUESE €€€
(282 443 308; www.obarradas.com; Palmeirinha; mains €8.50-25; 6-10pm Thu-Tue;) The star choice for foodies is this delightful converted farmhouse run by Luís and his German wife Andrea, with a romantic candlelit garden for warm-weather dining. They take pride in careful sourcing and use organic fish, meat and fruits in season. Luís is a winemaker so you can be assured of some fine wines.

Getting There & Away

Silves train station is 2km from town; trains from Lagos (€2.90, 35 minutes) stop eight times daily (from Faro, change at Tunes), to be met by local buses. Frequent trains connect Silves and Albufeira-Ferreiras (€2.45, 30 minutes).

Sagres

POP 2100

The small, elongated village of Sagres has an end-of-the-world feel with its sea-carved cliffs and empty, wind-whipped fortress high above the ocean. This coast is ideal for surfing; hire windsurfing gear at sand-dune fringed Praia do Martinhal.

Visit Europe's southwestern-most point, the **Cabo de São Vicente** (Cape St Vincent), 6km to the west. A solitary lighthouse stands on this barren cape.

Sights & Activities

Fortaleza de Sagres FORTRESS
(adult/child €3/1.50; 9.30am-8pm May-Sep, 9.30am-5.30pm Oct-Apr) Blank, hulking and forbidding, Sagres' fortress offers breathtaking views over the sheer cliffs, and all along the coast to Cabo de São Vicente. According to legend, this is where Henry the Navigator established his navigation school and primed the early Portuguese explorers.

Mar Ilimitado BOAT TOUR
(916 832 625; www.marilimitado.com; Porto da Baleeira) Mar Ilimitado, a team of marine biologists, offers a variety of 'educational' boat trips from dolphin-spotting trips (€32) to excursions up to Cabo de São Vicente (€20) and seabird watching (€40).

DiversCape DIVING
(965 559 073; www.diverscape.com; Porto da Baleeira) Diving centres are based at the port. Recommended is the PADI-certified DiversCape, which organises snorkelling expeditions (€25, two hours), plus dives of between 12m and 30m around shipwrecks.

Sagres Natura SURFING
(282 624 072; www.sagresnatura.com; Rua São Vicente) Recommended surf school. Also rents out bodyboards (€10 per day), surfboards (€15) and wetsuits (€5). The company also offers canoeing trips (€35), and bikes can be hired (€15).

Sleeping & Eating

Casa Azul B&B €
(282 624 856; www.casaazulsagres.com; Rua Dom Sebastião; d €65-125, apt €75-200;) As blue as its name suggests, Casa Azul is a popular surfer crash pad, with bright and breezy rooms decked out with splashes of bold colour. The apartments are big enough for families and come with kitchenettes and barbecue decks.

Casa do Cabo de Santa Maria GUESTHOUSE €€
(282 624 722; www.casadocabodesantamaria.com; Rua Patrão António Faústino; d €50-70, apt €70-110;) These squeaky-clean, welcoming rooms and apartments might not have sweeping views, but they are handsome and nicely furnished – excellent value (breakfast not included).

Information

Turismo (282 624 873; www.cm-viladobispo.pt; Rua Comandante Matoso; 9am-6pm, hours subject to change) Situated on a patch of green lawn, 100m east of Praça da República.

Getting There & Away

Frequent buses run daily to Sagres from Lagos (€3.80, one hour), with fewer on Sunday. One continues to Cabo de São Vicente on weekdays.

CENTRAL PORTUGAL

The vast centre of Portugal is a rugged swathe of rolling hillsides, whitewashed villages, and olive groves and cork trees. Richly historic, it is scattered with prehistoric remains and medieval castles. It's also home to one of Portugal's most architecturally rich towns, Évora, as well as several spectacular walled villages. There are fine local wines and, for the more energetic, plenty of outdoor exploring in the dramatic Beiras region.

Évora

POP 54,300

Évora is an enchanting place to delve into the past. Inside the 14th-century walls, Évora's narrow, winding lanes lead to a striking medieval cathedral, a Roman temple and a picturesque town square. These old-fashioned good looks are the backdrop to a lively student town surrounded by wineries and dramatic countryside.

Sights & Activities

Igreja de São Francisco CHURCH

(Praça 1 de Maio) FREE Évora's best-known church is a tall and huge Manueline-Gothic structure, completed around 1510 and dedicated to St Francis. Legend has it that the Portuguese navigator Gil Vicente is buried here.

Sé CATHEDRAL

(Largo do Marquês de Marialva; admission €1.50, with cloister €2.50; 9am-5pm) Guarded by a pair of rose granite towers, Évora's fortress-like medieval cathedral has fabulous cloisters and a museum jam-packed with ecclesiastical treasures.

Templo Romano RUIN

(Temple of Diana; Largo do Conde de Vila Flor) Once part of the Roman Forum, the remains of this temple dating from the 2nd or early 3rd century are a heady slice of drama right in town.

Sleeping

Hostel Namaste HOSTEL €

(266 743 014; www.hostelnamasteevora.pt; Largo Doutor Manuel Alves Branco 12; dm/s/d €17/30/45;) Maria and Carla Sofia are the kind souls who run these welcoming digs in the historic Arabic quarter. Rooms are bright, spotlessly clean and decorated with splashes of art and colour, and there's a lounge, library, kitchen and bike hire. Breakfast costs an extra €4.

★ Albergaria do Calvario BOUTIQUE HOTEL €€€

(266 745 930; www.albergariadocalvario.com; Travessa dos Lagares 3; s €98-110, d €108-120; P) Unpretentiously elegant, discreetly attentive and comfortable (but not can't-put-your-feet-up-uber-luxurious), this place has an ambience that travellers adore. The delightful staff leave no service stone unturned and breakfasts are among the region's best, with locally sourced organic produce, homemade cakes and egg dishes.

Eating

Pastelaria Conventual Pão de Rala PATISSERIE €

(Rua do Cicioso 47; pastries from €2; 7.30am-7.30pm) Out of the centre but still within the walls, this delightful spot specialises in heavenly pastries and convent cakes, all made on the premises.

★ Botequim da Mouraria PORTUGUESE €€

(266 746 775; Rua da Mouraria 16A; mains €13-16.50; noon-3pm & 6-10pm Mon-Fri, noon-3pm Sat) Poke around the old Moorish quarter to find this cosy spot serving some of Évora's finest food and wine. There are no reservations, just 12 stools at a counter.

Vinho e Noz PORTUGUESE €€

(Ramalho Orgigão 12; mains around €12; noon-10pm Mon-Sat) A delightful family runs this unpretentious place, which has professional service, a large wine list and good-quality cuisine.

Dom Joaquim PORTUGUESE €€

(266 731 105; Rua dos Penedos 6; mains €12-15; noon-3pm & 7-10.45pm Tue-Sat, noon-3pm Sun) Amid stone walls and modern artwork, Dom Joaquim serves excellent traditional cuisine including meats (game and succulent, fall-off-the-bone lamb) and seafood dishes, such as *caçao* (dogfish).

Drinking

Bookshelf CAFE

(Rua de Machede 19; 8am-8pm) A bit boho, a bit retro, this incredibly friendly cafe does a fine line in speciality teas, juices, homemade cakes and light meals.

Páteo BAR

(Rua 5 de Outubro, Beco da Espinhosa; 11am-2am;) Right in Évora's medieval heart, this bar has a pretty tree-shaded patio for nursing a glass of Alentejo wine. The food is pretty good, too.

Information

Turismo (266 777 071; www.cm-evora.pt; Praça do Giraldo 73; 9am-7pm Apr-Oct, 9am-6pm Nov-Mar) This helpful, central tourist office dishes out a great town map.

Getting There & Away

Regular trains go direct to Lisbon (€12, 80 minutes) and indirectly, via Pinhal Novo, to Faro (€26, 3¾ to 4¼ hours) and Lagos (€29, five hours). The train station is 600m south of the Jardim Público.

Monsaraz

POP 782

In a dizzy setting high above the plain, this walled village has a moody medieval feel and magnificent views. The biennial

Monsaraz Museu Aberto, held in July on even-numbered years, features exhibitions and concerts.

Housed inside a fine Gothic building beside the parish church, the **Museu de Arte Sacra** (Museum of Sacred Art; Praça Dom Nuno Álvares Pereira; adult/child €1.80/1.20; ⏲10am-6pm) contains a small collection of 14th-century wooden religious figures, 18th-century vestments and silverware.

Situated 3km north of town is the granite, 5.6m-tall **Menhir do Outeiro** FREE, one of the tallest megalithic monuments ever discovered.

A rustic, pin-drop peaceful retreat, whitewashed **St Condestável** (☎969 713 213, 266 557 181; www.condestavel-monsaraz.com; Rua Direita 4; r €60-70, ste €85; ❄📶) dates to the 17th century and offers five cool rooms with heavy carved wooden beds. Some have fine views over the plains to the lake of Alqueva.

On its hilltop perch, **Sabores de Monsaraz** (☎969 217 800; www.saboresdemonsaraz.com; Largo de S Bartolomeu; ⏲12.30-3.30pm Tue, 12.30-3.30pm & 7.30-10.30pm Wed-Sun; 👪) is a family-friendly tavern dishing up Alentejano home-cooking – meltingly tender black pork and *migas com bacalhau e coentros* (codfish with bread and coriander) and the like.

The **tourist office** (☎927 997 316; Rua Direita; ⏲10am-12.30pm & 2-5.30pm) can offer advice on accommodation.

Up to four daily buses connect Monsaraz with Reguengos de Monsaraz (€3, 35 minutes, Monday to Friday), with connections to Évora.

Peniche

POP 16,000

Popular for its nearby surfing beaches and also as a jumping-off point for Berlenga Grande, part of the beautiful Ilhas Berlengas nature reserve, the coastal city of Peniche remains a working port, giving it a slightly grittier and more 'lived-in' feel than its beach-resort neighbours. It has a walled historic centre and lovely beaches east of town.

From the bus station, it's a 10-minute walk west to the historic centre.

Sights

Fortaleza FORT

(⏲9am-12.30pm & 2-5.30pm Tue-Fri, from 10am Sat & Sun) FREE Dominating the south of the peninsula, Peniche's imposing 16th-century fortress was used in the 20th century as one of dictator Salazar's infamous jails for political prisoners.

Baleal BEACH

About 5km to the northeast of Peniche is this scenic island-village, connected to the mainland village of Casais do Baleal by a causeway. The fantastic sweep of sandy beach here offers some fine surfing. Surf schools dot the sands, as do several bar-restaurants.

Berlenga Grande ISLAND

Sitting about 10km offshore from Peniche, Berlenga Grande is a spectacular, rocky and

OTHER PORTUGUESE TOWNS WORTH A VISIT

Time not an issue? Consider tacking on a day trip or staying overnight at these Portuguese gems.

Guimarães Birthplace of Afonso Henriques, the first independent king of Portugal, this beautiful medieval town in the south of Portugal's northern Minho region is a warren of labyrinthine lanes and plazas crowned by a 1000-year-old castle.

Elvas A Unesco heritage town in the east of the Alentejo and hugging the Spanish border, with impressive star-shaped fortifications, a lovely plaza and quaint museums.

Chaves A pretty spa town straddling the mountain-fringed banks of the Rio Tâmega in Portugal's northern Trás-os-Montes region, with a well-preserved historic centre and 16-arch Roman bridge.

Batalha & Alcobaça Situated slightly inland from the Atlantic and in the heart of the country, this Estremadura duo beckon with their charming centres and two of Portugal's most stunning monasteries.

Monsanto The crowning glory of the central Beiras region is this spectacular craggy cliff-top village, perched like an eyrie above the boulder-strewn landscape.

remote island, with twisting, shocked-rock formations and gaping caverns.

Activities

Surfing

Surf camps offer week-long instruction as well as two-hour classes, plus board and wetsuit hire. Well-established names include **Baleal Surfcamp** (262 769 277; www.balealsurfcamp.com; Rua Amigos do Baleal 2; 1-/3-/5-day course €60/95/145) and **Peniche Surfcamp** (962 336 295; www.penichesurfcamp.com; Avenida do Mar 162, Casais do Baleal).

Diving

There are good diving opportunities around Peniche, and especially around Berlenga. Expect to pay about €65 to €75 for two dives (less around Peniche) with **Acuasuboeste** (918 393 444; www.acuasuboeste.com; Porto de Pesca; diving intro course €80, single dives €25-35) or **Haliotis** (262 781 160; www.haliotis.pt; Casal Ponte; single-/double-dive trip €35/75).

Sleeping

Peniche Hostel HOSTEL €
(969 008 689; www.penichehostel.com; Rua Arquitecto Paulino Montês 6; dm/d €20/50; @ wi-fi) This cosy little hostel, only steps from the tourist office and a five-minute walk from the bus station, has colourfully decorated and breezy rooms. Surfboards and bikes are available for hire, and there's an attached surf school.

Eating & Drinking

Restaurante A Sardinha SEAFOOD €
(262 781 820; Rua Vasco da Gama 81; mains €6-14; 11.30am-4pm & 6.30-10.30pm) This no-frills place on a narrow street parallel to Largo da Ribeira does a roaring trade in mains like simply grilled fish and *caldeirada* (fish stew) done well.

Java House CAFE, BAR
(Largo da Ribeira 14; 9am-3am Mon-Thu, to 4am Fri & Sat; wi-fi) The most popular joint in town, this place deals in everything from early-morning coffees to sandwiches and crêpes. The lights dim later in the evening, and DJs strut their stuff.

Getting There & Away

Peniche's **bus station** (968 903 861; Rua Dr Ernesto Moreira) is located 400m northeast of the tourist office (cross the Ponte Velha connecting the town to the isthmus). Destinations include Coimbra (€14, 2¾ hours, three daily), Leiria (€12.20, two hours, three daily), Lisbon (€8.60, 1½ hours, every one to two hours) and Óbidos (€3.15, 40 minutes, six to eight daily).

Óbidos

POP 3100

This exquisite walled village was a wedding gift from Dom Dinis to his wife Dona Isabel (beats a fondue set), and its historic centre is a delightful place to wander. Highlights include the **Igreja de Santa Maria** (Praça de Santa Maria; 9.30am-12.30pm & 2.30-7pm) FREE, with fine 17th-century *azulejos*, and views from the town walls.

From mid-July to mid-August, Óbidos hosts the **Mercado Medieval** (www.mercadomedievalobidos.pt), featuring jousting matches, wandering minstrels and abundant medieval mayhem.

Sleeping & Eating

Hostel Argonauta HOSTEL €
(262 958 088; www.hostelargonauta.com; Rua Adelaide Ribeirete 14; dm/d €25/50; wi-fi) In a pretty spot just outside the walls, this feels more like a friend's place than a hostel. Run with good cheer, it has an arty, colourful dorm with wood-stove heating and beds as well as bunks; there's also a cute double with a great view.

Petrarum Domus PORTUGUESE €€
(262 959 620; Rua Direita; mains €9-18; noon-1am Mon-Thu, to 2am Fri & Sat, to midnight Sun) Amid age-old stone walls, Petrarum serves up hearty dishes like pork with mushrooms, mixed seafood sautés and several *bacalhau* (dried salt-cod) plates.

Information

Turismo (262 959 231; www.obidos.pt; 9.30am-7.30pm) Just outside Porta da Vila, near the bus stop, with helpful multilingual staff offering town brochures and maps in four languages.

Getting There & Away

There are direct buses Monday to Friday from Lisbon (€8, 70 minutes).

Nazaré

POP 16,000

Nazaré has a bustling coastal setting with narrow cobbled lanes running down to a wide, cliff-backed beach. The town centre is jammed with seafood restaurants and bars; expect huge crowds in July and August.

Sights & Activities

The **beaches** here are superb, although swimmers should be aware of dangerous currents. Climb or take the funicular to the clifftop **Sítio**, with its cluster of fishermen's cottages and great view.

Sleeping & Eating

Many townspeople rent out rooms; doubles start at €35. Ask around near the seafront at Avenida da República.

Magic Art Hotel HOTEL €
(262 569 040; http://hotelmagic.pt; Rua Mouzinho de Albuquerque 58; s €70-85, d €75-90; P ❄) Close to the action, this breezy, newish hotel has gone for the chic modern look. Clean-lined, well-equipped white rooms with artily presented photos of old-time Nazaré contrast with appealing black slate bathrooms.

Hotel Oceano GUESTHOUSE €€
(262 561 161; www.adegaoceano.com; Avenida da República 51; d €60-85; ❄) This cordial little oceanfront place offers compact rooms, with flatscreen TV and excellent modern bathrooms. Those at the front have nice views across the beach to the cliffs and waterfront. As it's close to the action, street noise can be a problem.

★ **A Tasquinha** SEAFOOD €
(262 551 945; Rua Adrião Batalha 54; mains €6-10; noon-3pm & 7-10.30pm Tue-Sun) This exceptionally friendly family affair serves high quality seafood in a pair of snug but pretty tiled dining rooms. Expect queues on summer nights.

Information

Turismo (262 561 194; www.cm-nazare.pt; Centro Cultural da Nazaré, Avenida Manuel Remígio; 9.30am-12.30pm & 2.30-6.30pm, shorter hours in low season) On the beachfront strip, in the cultural centre in the old fish market.

Getting There & Away

Nazaré has numerous bus connections to Lisbon (€10.50, two hours).

Tomar

POP 16,000

A charming town straddling a river, Tomar has the notoriety of being home to the Knights Templar; check out their headquarters, the outstanding monastery **Convento de Cristo** (www.conventocristo.pt; Rua Castelo dos Templários; adult/child €6/free; 9am-6.30pm), a steep climb above town. Other rarities include the country's best-preserved medieval **synagogue** (Rua Dr Joaquim Jacinto 73; 10am-7pm Tue-Sun, shorter hours in low season) FREE. The town is backed by the dense greenery of the **Mata Nacional dos Sete Montes** (Seven Hills National Forest).

Sleeping & Eating

Residencial União GUESTHOUSE €
(249 323 161; www.residencialuniao.pt; Rua Serpa Pinto 94; s/d €30/50;) Tomar's most atmospheric budget choice, this once-grand town house on the main pedestrian drag features large and sprucely maintained rooms with antique furniture and fixtures.

Restaurante Tabuleiro PORTUGUESE €€
(249 312 771; Rua Serpa Pinto 140; mains €8-12; noon-3pm & 7-10pm Mon-Sat;) Located just off Tomar's main square, this family-friendly local hang-out features warm, attentive service, good traditional food and ample portions.

Information

Turismo (249 329 823; www.cm-tomar.pt; Rua Serpa Pinto; 10am-1pm & 3-7pm Apr-Sep, 9.30am-1pm & 2.30-6pm Oct-Mar) Offers a good town map and an accommodation list.

Getting There & Away

Frequent trains run to Lisbon (€9.65, two hours).

Coimbra

POP 107,000

Coimbra is a dynamic, fashionable, yet comfortably lived-in city, with a student life centred on the magnificent 13th-century university. Aesthetically eclectic, there are elegant shopping streets, ancient stone walls and backstreet alleys with hidden *tascas* (taverns) and fado bars. Coimbra was the birth and burial place of Portugal's first king, and was the country's most important city when the Moors captured Lisbon.

Sights & Activities

★ Sé Velha CATHEDRAL
(Old Cathedral; 239 825 273; Largo da Sé Velha; admission €2; 10am-6pm, closed Sun low season) Coimbra's stunning 12th-century cathedral is one of Portugal's finest examples of Romanesque architecture. The main portal and facade are exceptionally striking. Its crenellated exterior and narrow, slit-like lower windows serve as reminders of the nation's embattled early days, when the Moors were still a threat. These buildings were designed to be useful as fortresses in times of trouble.

Velha Universidade UNIVERSITY
(Old University; www.uc.pt; adult/child €9/free, incl tower €12.50/free; 9am-7.30pm mid-Mar–Oct, 9.30am-1pm & 2-5.30pm mid-Oct–mid-Mar) In every way the city's high point, the Old University consists of a series of remarkable 16th-to-18th-century buildings, all set around the vast **Patio des Escolas**, entered by way of the elegant 17th-century **Porta Férrea**, which occupies the same site as the main gate to Coimbra's Moorish stronghold. The highlight is the magnificent **library**.

Go Walks WALKING TOUR
(910 163 118; www.gowalksportugal.com; Rua do Sargento Mor 4; half-/full-day tour €25/40) Various themed walking tours – from fado to Jewish Coimbra – run by enthusiastic, knowledgeable students who speak good English (French and Spanish also bookable).

> **WORTH A TRIP**
>
> **ROMAN RUINS**
>
> **Conimbriga**, 16km south of Coimbra, is the site of the well-preserved ruins of a **Roman town** (10am-7pm), including mosaic floors, elaborate baths and trickling fountains. It's a fascinating place to explore, with a **museum** (www.conimbriga.pt; adult/child incl Roman Ruins €4.50/free; 10am-7pm) that describes the once-flourishing and later abandoned town. Frequent buses run to Condeixa, 2km from the site; there are also two direct buses from Coimbra.

O Pioneiro do Mondego KAYAKING
(239 478 385; www.opioneirodomondego.com; guided tour per person €22.50) Rents out kayaks for paddling the Mondego between Penacova and Torres de Mondego, an 18km trip.

Festivals & Events

Queima das Fitas FIESTA
(www.queimadasfitas.org) Coimbra's biggest bash is Queima das Fitas, a boozy week of fado and revelry that takes place during the first week in May when students celebrate the end of the academic year.

Sleeping

Hotel Vitória HOTEL €
(234 824 049; www.hotelvitoria.pt; Rua da Sota 9; s/d/tr €45/59/75;) This friendly family-run *residencial* has had a slick makeover. The newest rooms have a clean-line Nordic feel and lots of light. Try for a 3rd floor room for the best views of the old town or river. There's a great family room available too, and a downstairs restaurant.

Casa Pombal GUESTHOUSE €
(239 835 175; www.casapombal.com; Rua das Flores 18; d with/without bathroom €68/54; @) In a lovely old-town location, this winning, Dutch-run guesthouse squeezes tons of charm into a small space. A delicious breakfast is served in the gorgeous blue-tiled breakfast room.

Riversuites HOTEL €
(239 440 582; www.riversuiteshotel.com; Avenida João das Regras 82; d €40-52, tr €65, q €75;)

Just across the bridge from the centre, this excellent hotel has slick, modern rooms (not suites) and comforts. A decent breakfast is included, and the showers are just great.

Eating & Drinking

A colourful stop for self-caterers, the **Mercado Municipal Dom Pedro V** (Rua Olímpio Nicolau Rui Fernandes; 7am-7pm Mon-Sat) is full of lively fruit and vegetable stalls and butcher shops displaying Portuguese cuts of meat (hooves, claws and all).

Adega Paço dos Condes PORTUGUESE €
(239 825 605; Rua do Paço do Conde 1; mains €5-10; 11.30am-3pm & 6.30-11pm Mon-Sat) Usually crowded with students and Coimbra locals, this straightforward family-run grill is one of the city's best budget eateries.

★**Fangas Mercearia Bar** TAPAS €€
(934 093 636; http://fangas.pt; Rua Fernandes Tomás 45; petiscos €4-7; noon-4pm & 7pm-1am Tue-Sun;) Top-quality deli produce is used to produce delightful *petiscos* (tapas) in this bright, cheery dining room, the best place to eat in the old town. Service is slow but friendly and staff will help you choose from a delicious array of tasty platters – sausages, stuffed vegetables, conserves – and interesting wines. Book ahead as this small space always fills quickly.

Zé Manel dos Ossos TASCA €€
(Beco do Forno 12; mains €7-15; noon-3pm & 7.30-10pm Mon-Fri, noon-3pm Sat) Tucked down a nondescript alleyway, this little gem, papered with scholarly doodles and scribbled poems, serves a terrific *feijoada á leitão* (a stew of beans and suckling pig).

Restaurante Zé Neto PORTUGUESE €€
(Rua das Azeiteiras 8; mains €9-11; 9am-3pm & 7pm-midnight Mon-Sat) This marvellous family-run place specialises in homemade Portuguese standards, including *cabrito* (kid).

★**Café Santa Cruz** CAFE
(www.cafesantacruz.com; Praça 8 de Maio; 7.30am-midnight Mon-Sat) One of Portugal's most atmospheric cafes, Santa Cruz is set in a dramatically beautiful high-vaulted former chapel, with stained-glass windows, graceful stone arches, and a Ché mosaic where the altar would have been, while the terrace grants lovely views of Praça 8 de Maio.

Bar Quebra Costas BAR
(Rua Quebra Costas 45; noon-4am Mon-Fri, 2pm-4am Sat) This Coimbra classic has a sunny cobblestoned terrace, an artsy interior, friendly service, chilled-out tunes and the occasional jazz session.

Entertainment

Coimbra-style fado is more cerebral than the Lisbon variety, and its adherents are staunchly protective.

Á Capella FADO
(239 833 985; www.acapella.com.pt; Rua Corpo de Deus; admission incl one drink €10; 9pm-2am) A 14th-century chapel turned candlelit cocktail lounge, this place regularly hosts the city's most renowned fado musicians. There's a show every night at 10pm.

Information

Turismo Praça República (www.turismodecoimbra.pt; Praça da República; 9am-12.30pm & 2-6pm Mon-Fri) On the eastern side of town.

Turismo Universidade (239 834 158; www.turismodecoimbra.pt; Praça da Porta Férrea; 10am-1pm & 2-6pm Apr-Oct, shorter hours in low season) Adjacent to the Velha Universidade ticket desk, just outside the Porta Férrea.

Getting There & Away

There are frequent trains to Lisbon (€24, two to 2½ hours) and Porto (€9.50 to €17, one hour to 1¾ hours). There are also regular services to Faro and Évora via Lisbon. The main train stations are Coimbra B, 2km northwest of the centre, and central Coimbra A. Most long-distance trains call at Coimbra B. The bus station (Avenida Fernão Magalhães) is about 400m northeast of the centre.

Luso & the Buçaco Forest

POP 2000

This sylvan region harbours a lush forest of century-old trees surrounded by countryside that's dappled with heather, wildflowers and leafy ferns. There's even a fairy-tale **palace** (231 937 970; www.almeidahotels.com; Mata Nacional do Buçaco; 7-/8-course meal €35/40; lunch & dinner;) here, a 1907 neo-Manueline extravagance, where deep-pocketed visitors can dine or stay overnight. The palace lies amid the Mata Nacional do Buçaco, a forest criss-crossed with trails, dotted with crumbling chapels and graced with ponds, fountains and exotic trees. Buçaco was chosen as a retreat by 16th-century monks, and it surrounds the lovely spa town of Luso. From the centre, it's a 2km walk through forest up to the palace.

The **Maloclinic Spa** (www.maloclinictermasluso.com; Rua Álvaro Castelões; ⌚8am-1pm & 2-7pm daily high season, 9am-1pm & 2-6pm Mon-Sat low season) offers a range of soothing treatments.

Sleeping & Eating

Alegre Hotel BOUTIQUE HOTEL €€
(☎231 930 256; www.alegrehotels.com; Rua Emídio Navarro 2; s/d €45/55; P 🛜 🏊) This grand, atmospheric, pinkish-coloured 19th-century town house has large doubles with plush drapes, decorative plaster ceilings and polished period furniture. Its appeal is enhanced by an elegant entryway, formal parlour and pretty vine-draped garden with pool.

Information

Turismo (☎231 939 133; Rua Emídio Navarro 136; ⌚9.30am-1pm & 2.30-6pm) Has accommodation information, town and forest maps, internet access, and is helpful.

Getting There & Away

Buses to/from Coimbra (€3.50, 45 minutes) run four times daily each weekday and twice daily on Saturdays. Trains to/from Coimbra B station (€2.50, 25 minutes) run several times daily; it's a 15-minute walk to town from the station.

Serra da Estrela

The forested Serra da Estrela has a raw natural beauty and offers some of the country's best hiking. This is Portugal's highest mainland mountain range (1993m), and the source of its two great rivers: Rio Mondego and Rio Zêzere. The town of **Manteigas** makes a great base for hiking and exploring the area (plus skiing in winter). The **main park office** (☎275 980 060; pnse@icnf.pt; Rua 1 de Maio 2, Manteigas; ⌚9am-12.30pm & 2-5.30pm Mon-Fri) provides details of popular walks in the Parque Natural da Serra da Estrela – some of which leave from town or just outside it; additional offices are at Seia, Gouveia and Guarda.

Sleeping

Hotel Berne HOTEL €
(☎275 981 351; www.hotelberne.com; Quinta de Santo António, Manteigas; d/tr/q €65/80/105; P ❄ 🛜 🏊) Going for a Swiss feel, this lovely hotel at the bottom of town has cheerful, spotless, wood-accented rooms, many with views of Manteigas and the mountains above. There is a great restaurant and a spacious lounge.

★ **Casa das Penhas Douradas** HOTEL €€€
(☎275 981 045; www.casadaspenhasdouradas.pt; Penhas Douradas; s €120-140, d €135-160; P ❄ @ 🛜 🏊) On its mountaintop perch between Manteigas and Seia, this hotel gets everything right. The rooms all have great natural light, views, and some come with sloping ceilings or appealing terraces. An enlightened attitude to guest comfort means all sorts of welcome details, such as a heated pool, bikes and kayaks, books and DVDs, and spa and massage treatments are available.

Getting There & Around

Two regular weekday buses connect Manteigas with Guarda, from where there are onward services to Coimbra and Lisbon.

THE NORTH

Beneath the edge of Spanish Galicia, northern Portugal is a land of lush river valleys, sparkling coastline, granite peaks and virgin forests. This region is also gluttony for wine lovers: it's the home of the sprightly *vinho verde* wine (a young, slightly sparkling white or red wine) and ancient vineyards along the dramatic Rio Douro. Gateway to the north is Porto, a beguiling riverside city blending both medieval and modern attractions. Smaller towns and villages also offer cultural allure, from majestic Braga, the country's religious heart, to the seaside beauty Viana do Castelo.

Porto

POP 238,000

From across the Rio Douro at sunset, romantic Porto looks like a pop-up town, acolourful tumbledown dream with medieval relics, soaring bell towers,

Porto

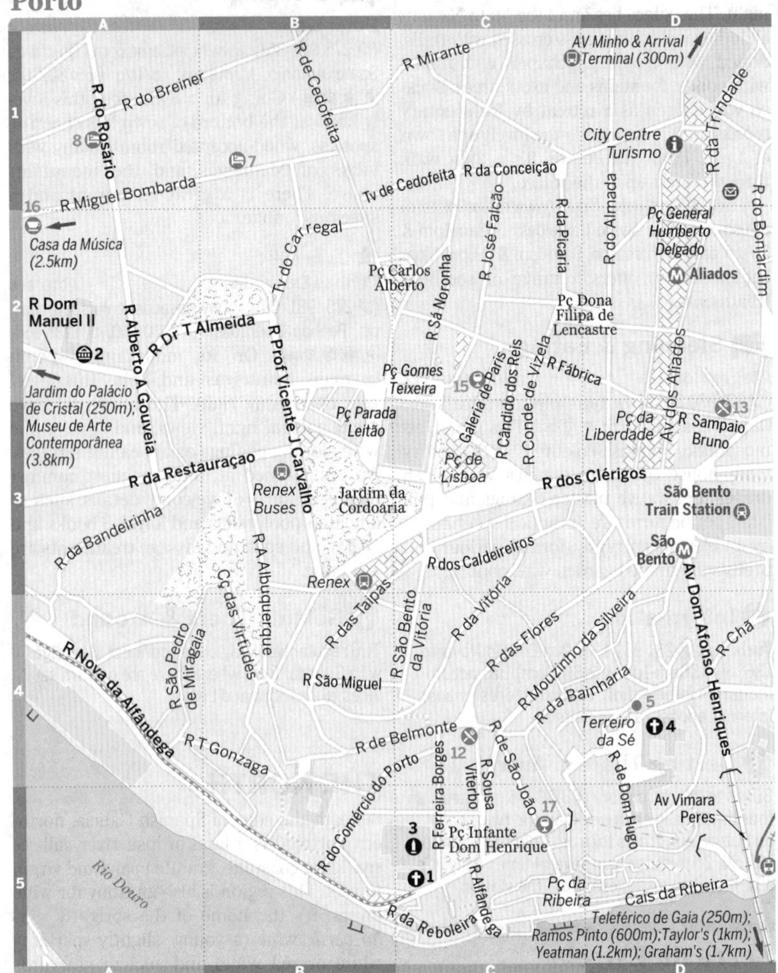

extravagant baroque churches and stately beaux-arts buildings piled on top of one another, illuminated by streaming shafts of sun. If you squint you might be able to make out the open windows, the narrow lanes and the staircases zigzagging to nowhere.

A lively walkable city with chatter in the air and a tangible sense of history, Porto's old-world riverfront district is a Unesco World Heritage Site. Across the water twinkle the neon signs of Vila Nova de Gaia, the headquarters of the major port manufacturers.

Sights & Activities

Perfect for a languid stroll, the **Ribeira** district – Porto's riverfront nucleus – is a remarkable window into the city's history. Along the riverside promenade, *barcos rabelos* (the traditional boats used to ferry port wine down the Douro) bob beneath the shadow of the photogenic Ponte de Dom Luís I.

A few kilometres west of the city centre, the seaside suburb of **Foz do Douro** is a prime destination on hot summer weekends. It has a long beach promenade and a smattering of oceanfront bars and restaurants.

★**Palácio da Bolsa** MONUMENT

(Stock Exchange; Rua Ferreira Borges; tours adult/child €7/4; ⏲9am-6.30pm Apr-Oct, 9am-12.30pm & 2-5.30pm Nov-Mar) This splendid neoclassical monument (built from 1842 to 1910) honours Porto's past and present money merchants. Just past the entrance is the glass-domed **Pátio das Nações** (Hall of Nations), where the exchange once operated. But this pales in comparison with rooms deeper inside; to visit these, join one of the half-hour guided tours, which set off every 30 minutes.

Porto

Sights

1 Igreja de São Francisco C5
2 Museu Nacional Soares dos Reis A2
3 Palácio da Bolsa C5
4 Sé D4

Activities, Courses & Tours

5 Porto Tours D4

Sleeping

6 6 Only F3
7 Gallery Hostel B1
8 ROSA ET AL Townhouse A1
9 Tattva Design Hostel E4

Eating

10 Café Majestic E2
11 Casa Guedes F3
12 DOP C4
13 Flor dos Congregados D3
14 Mercado do Bolhão E2

Drinking & Nightlife

15 Casa do Livro C2
16 Rota do Chá A2
17 Vinologia C5

Entertainment

18 Maus Hábitos F3

Sé CATHEDRAL

(Terreiro da Sé; cloisters adult/student €3/2; ⏲9am-12.30pm & 2.30-7pm Apr-Oct, to 6pm Nov-Mar) FREE From Praça da Ribeira rises a tangle of medieval alleys and stairways that eventually reach the hulking, hilltop fortress of the cathedral. Founded in the 12th century, it was largely rebuilt a century later and then extensively altered during the 18th century. However, you can still make out the church's Romanesque contours. Inside, a rose window and a 14th-century Gothic cloister remain from its early days.

Igreja de São Francisco CHURCH

(Praça Infante Dom Henrique; adult/child €3.50/1.75; ⏲9am-8pm Jul-Sep, to 7pm Mar-Jun & Oct, to 6pm Nov-Feb) Sitting on Praça Infante Dom Henrique, Igreja de São Francisco looks from the outside to be an austerely Gothic church, but inside it hides one of Portugal's most dazzling displays of baroque finery. Hardly an inch escapes unsmothered, as otherworldly cherubs and sober monks are drowned by nearly 100kg of gold leaf.

Jardim do Palácio de Cristal PARK

(Rua Dom Manuel II; 8am-9pm Apr-Sep, 8am-7pm Oct-Mar) FREE Sitting atop a bluff, this gorgeous botanical garden is one of Porto's best-loved escapes, with lawns interwoven with sun-dappled paths and dotted with fountains, sculptures, giant magnolias, camellias, cypress and olive trees. It's actually a mosaic of small gardens that open up little by little as you wander – as do the stunning views of the city and Douro River.

Museu de Arte Contemporânea MUSEUM

(www.serralves.pt; Rua Dom João de Castro 210; adult/child museums & park €8.50/free, park €4/free; 10am-7pm Tue-Fri, 10am-8pm Sat & Sun, shorter hours in winter) This arrestingly minimalist, whitewashed space was designed by the eminent Porto-based architect Álvaro Siza Vieira. Cutting-edge exhibitions are showcased in the **Casa de Serralves**, a delightful pink art deco mansion, and there's a fine permanent collection featuring works from the late 1960s to the present. Both museums are accessible on a single ticket and sit within the marvellous 18-hectare **Parque de Serralves**.

Museu Nacional Soares dos Reis MUSEUM

(www.museusoaresdosreis.pt; Rua Dom Manuel II 44; adult/child €5/free, 10am-2pm Sun free; 10am-6pm Wed-Sun, 2-6pm Tue) Porto's best art museum presents a stellar collection ranging from Neolithic carvings to Portugal's take on modernism, all housed in the formidable Palácio das Carrancas.

Teleférico de Gaia CABLE CAR

(www.gaiacablecar.com; one way/return €5/8; 10am-8pm high season, 10am-6pm low season) Don't miss a ride on the Teleférico de Gaia, an aerial gondola that provides fine views over the Douro and Porto on its short, five-minute jaunt. It runs between the southern end of the Ponte Dom Luís I and the riverside.

Taste Porto Food Tours GUIDED TOUR

(967 258 750; www.tasteportofoodtours.com; adult/child €55/40; tours 10.30am Tue-Sat, 4pm Tue-Fri) Hungry? Good. Loosen a belt notch for these superb half-day food tours, where you'll sample everything from Porto's best slow-roast pork sandwich to éclairs, fine wines, cheese and coffee.

We Hate Tourism Tours GUIDED TOUR

(913 776 598; http://wehatetourismtours.com/oporto; full-day tours around €40) If you want to sidestep tourist traps and beeline to the city's soul, WHTT is the real deal, with guides such as André buzzing with passion for Porto.

Festivals & Events

Serralves Em Festa CULTURAL

(www.serralvesemfesta.com) This huge event runs for 40 hours nonstop over one weekend in early June. Parque de Serralves hosts the main events, with concerts, avant-garde theatre and kiddie activities. Other open-air events happen all over town.

Festa de São João RELIGIOUS

(St John's Festival) Porto's biggest party. For one night in June the city erupts into music, competitions and riotous parties; this is also when merrymakers pound each other on the head with squeaky plastic mallets (you've been warned).

Noites Ritual Rock MUSIC

A weekend-long rock extravaganza in late August.

Sleeping

★ **Gallery Hostel** HOSTEL €

(224 964 313; www.gallery-hostel.com; Rua Miguel Bombarda 222; dm €22-24, d €64, tr €80;) A true travellers' hub, this hostel-gallery has clean and cosy dorms and doubles; a sunny, glass-enclosed back patio; a grassy terrace; a cinema room; a shared kitchen and a bar-music room. Throw in its free walking tours, homemade dinners on request, port wine tastings and concerts, and you'll see why it's booked up so often – reserve ahead.

Tattva Design Hostel HOSTEL €

(220 944 622; www.tattvadesignhostel.com; Rua do Cativo 26-28; dm €10-20, d €47-60, q €75-100; @) Tattva knows precisely what makes backpackers tick. The facilities are superb and the attractive rooms have thoughtful touches – big lockers, good lighting, privacy curtains, and a bathroom and balcony in every room. The open-air rooftop lounge is a great place for a sundowner. Plus it offers free walking tours.

WORTH A TRIP

THROUGH THE GRAPEVINES OF THE DOURO

Portugal's best-known river flows through the country's rural heartland. In the upper reaches, port-wine grapes are grown on steep terraced hills, punctuated by remote stone villages and, in spring, splashes of dazzling white almond blossom.

The Rio Douro is navigable right across Portugal. Highly recommended is the train journey from Porto to Pinhão (€11, 2½ hours, five daily), the last 70km clinging to the river's edge; trains continue to Pocinho (from Porto €13.50, 3¼ hours). **Porto Tours** (☎222 000 045; www.portotours.com; Calçada Pedro Pitões 15, Torre Medieval; ⏲10am-7pm), situated next to Porto's cathedral, can arrange tours, including idyllic Douro cruises.

Cyclists and drivers can choose river-hugging roads along either bank, and can visit wineries along the way (check out www.dourovalley.eu for an extensive list of wineries open to visitors). You can also stay overnight in scenic wine lodges among the vineyards.

6 Only GUESTHOUSE €€
(☎222 013 971; www.6only.pt; Rua Duque de Loulé 97; r €70-80; @) This beautifully restored guesthouse has just six rooms, all with simple but stylish details that effortlessly blend old (such as wrought-iron decorative balconies) with contemporary. There's a lounge, a Zen-like courtyard and friendly staff.

ROSA ET AL Townhouse GUESTHOUSE €€
(☎916 000 081; www.rosaetal.pt; Rua do Rosário 233; r €98-228) This gorgeously done up townhouse in the thick of Porto's art district has six suites with hardwood floors and free-standing claw-foot tubs, and a lovely garden out back. The restaurant serves delicious brunch and afternoon tea at weekends There are rotating exhibits, cooking workshops and other fun events. Breakfast costs an extra €30 per room.

Yeatman RESORT €€€
(☎220 134 200; www.the-yeatman-hotel.com; Rua do Choupelo 88; s €270-320, d €285-335, ste €615-1100) Named for one of Taylor's original founders, the Yeatman is Porto's only true five-star resort, terraced and tucked into the Gaia hillside with massive Douro and Porto views. There's a Michelin-starred chef, huge guest rooms and suites with private terrace, a decanter-shaped pool, sunken Roman baths in the fantastic Caudalie spa, and all the amenities you could desire.

Eating

★Mercado do Bolhão MARKET €
(Rua Formosa; ⏲7am-5pm Mon-Fri, to 1pm Sat) The 19th-century, wrought-iron Mercado do Bolhão does a brisk trade in fresh produce, including cheeses, olives, smoked meats, sausages, breads and more. At its lively best on Friday and Saturday mornings, the market is also sprinkled with inexpensive stalls where you can eat fish so fresh it was probably swimming in the Atlantic that morning, or sample local wines and cheeses.

Casa Guedes TASCA €
(Praça dos Poveiros 130; mains €4-9; ⏲8am-midnight Mon-Sat) Come for tasty, filling and cheap meals, or for the famous pork sandwiches, served all day.

Flor dos Congregados PORTUGUESE €€
(Travessa dos Congregados 11; mains €8-16; ⏲6.30-11pm Mon-Wed, noon-3pm & 6.30-11pm Thu-Sat) Tucked away down a narrow alley, this softly lit, family-run restaurant brims with stone-walled, wood-beamed, art-slung nooks. The frequently changing blackboard menu goes with the seasons.

Café Majestic CAFE €€
(Rua Santa Catarina 112; mains €10-18; ⏲9am-midnight) Porto's best-known tea shop is packed with prancing cherubs, opulently gilded woodwork and leather seats. The gold-braided waiters will serve you an elegant breakfast, afternoon tea or light meals – from a classic *francesinha* sandwich to salads at the healthier end of the spectrum. There's a pavement terrace.

★DOP PORTUGUESE €€€
(☎222 014 313; www.ruipaula.com; Largo de S Domingos 18; tasting menu €65; ⏲7-11pm Mon, 12.30-3pm & 7-11pm Tue-Sat) Housed in the Palácio das Artes, DOP is one of Porto's most stylish addresses, with its high ceilings and slick, monochrome interior. Much-feted chef Rui

Paula puts a creative, seasonal twist on outstanding ingredients.

Drinking & Nightlife

The bar-lined Rua Galeira de Paris and nearby streets are packed with revellers most nights. Down by the water, the open-air bar scene on Praça da Ribeira is great for drinks with a view.

Rota do Chá TEAHOUSE
(www.rotadocha.pt; Rua Miguel Bombarda 457; tea €2.50; ⏲11am-8pm Mon-Thu, noon-midnight Fri & Sat, 1-8pm Sun) This proudly bohemian cafe has a verdant but rustic back garden where students and the gallery crowd sit around low tables sampling from an enormous 300+ tea menu divided by region.

Casa do Livro LOUNGE
(Rua Galeria de Paris 85; ⏲9.30pm-4am) Vintage wallpaper, gilded mirrors and walls of books give a discreet charm to this nicely lit beer and wine bar. On weekends, DJs spin funk, soul, jazz and retro sounds in the back room.

Vinologia WINE BAR
(Rua de São João 46; ⏲4pm-midnight) This cosy wine bar is an excellent place to sample the fine quaffs of Porto, with over 200 different ports on offer. If you fall in love with a certain wine, you can usually buy a whole bottle (or even send a case home).

☆ Entertainment

★ **Casa da Música** LIVE MUSIC
(House of Music; ☎220 120 220; www.casadamusica.com; Avenida da Boavista 604) Grand and minimalist, sophisticated yet populist, Porto's music mecca is the Casa da Música, with a shoebox-style concert hall at its heart, meticulously engineered to accommodate everything from jazz duets to Beethoven's Ninth.

Maus Hábitos PERFORMING ARTS
(www.maushabitos.com; 4th fl, Rua Passos Manuel 178; ⏲noon-2am Wed & Thu, noon-4am Fri & Sat) Maus Hábitos or 'Bad Habits' is an arty, nicely chilled haunt hosting a culturally ambitious agenda. Changing exhibitions and imaginative installations adorn the walls, while live bands and DJs work the small stage.

ℹ Information

City Centre Turismo (☎223 393 472; www.visitporto.travel; Rua Clube dos Fenianos 25; ⏲9am-8pm high season, 9am-7pm low season) The main city *turismo* has a detailed city map, a transport map and the *Agenda do Porto* cultural calendar, among other printed materials.

Post Office (Praça General Humberto Delgado) Across from the main tourist office.

Santo António Hospital (☎222 077 500; www.chporto.pt; Largo Prof Abel Salazar) Has English-speaking staff.

Tourist Police (☎222 081 833; Rua Clube dos Fenianos 11; ⏲8am-2am) Multilingual station beside the main city *turismo*.

ℹ Getting There & Away

AIR

Porto's airport (p911) is connected by daily flights from Lisbon and London, and has direct links from other European cities, particularly with EasyJet and Ryanair.

BUS

Porto has many private bus companies leaving from different terminals; the main tourist office can help. In general, for Lisbon and the Algarve, the choice is **Renex** (www.renex.pt; Campo Mártires de Pátria 37) or **Rede Expressos** (☎222 006 954; www.rede-expressos.pt; Rua Alexandre Herculano 366). **Eurolines** (www.eurolines.com) runs buses to Madrid (via Guarda; €50, 10 hours) and Santiago de Compostela (via Braga; €33, five hours) in Spain.

Bus companies operate from or near Praceto Régulo Magauanha, off Rua Dr Alfredo Magalhães: **Transdev-Norte** (www.transdev.pt) goes to Braga (€6); **AV Minho** (www.avminho.pt) to Viana do Castelo (€8).

TRAIN

Porto is a northern Portugal rail hub. Most international trains, and all intercity links, start at Campanhã, 2km east of the centre.

At São Bento, you can book tickets to any other destination.

ℹ Getting Around

TO/FROM THE AIRPORT

The metro's 'violet' E line provides handy service to the airport. A one-way ride to the centre costs €1.85 and takes about 45 minutes. A daytime taxi costs €20 to €25 to/from the centre.

DON'T MISS

TASTING PORT WINE

Sitting just across the Rio Douro from Porto, **Vila Nova de Gaia** is woven into the city's fabric by stunning bridges and a shared history of port-wine making. Since the mid-18th century, port-wine bottlers and exporters have maintained their lodges here.

Today, some 30 of these lodges clamber up the river bank and most open their doors to the public for cellar tours and tastings. Among the best are **Taylor's** (223 742 800; www.taylor.pt; Rua do Choupelo 250; tour €5; 10am-6pm Mon-Fri, to 5pm Sat & Sun), **Graham's** (223 776 484; www.grahams-port.com; Rua do Agro 141; tour €5-20; 9.30am-6pm Apr-Oct, 9.30am-5.30pm Nov-Mar) and **Ramos Pinto** (223 707 000; www.ramospinto.pt; Av Ramos Pinto 400; tour & tasting €5; 10am-6pm daily May-Oct, 10am-6pm Mon-Fri Apr, 9am-5pm Mon-Fri Nov-Mar).

PUBLIC TRANSPORT

Save money on transport by purchasing a refillable **Andante Card** (€0.60), valid for transport on buses, metro, funicular and tram. You can buy them from STCP kiosks or newsagents. A 24-hour ticket for the entire public transport network, excluding trams, costs €7.

Bus

Central hubs of Porto's extensive bus system include Jardim da Cordoaria, Praça da Liberdade and São Bento station. Tickets purchased on the bus are one way €1.20/€1.85 with/without the Andante Card.

Funicular

The panoramic **Funicular dos Guindais** (one way €2; 8am-10pm, shorter hours in winter) shuttles up and down a steep incline from Avenida Gustavo Eiffel to Rua Augusto Rosa.

Metro

Porto's **metro** (www.metrodoporto.pt) currently comprises six metropolitan lines that all converge at the Trinidade stop. Tickets cost €1.20 with an Andante Card. There are also various 24-hour passes (from €4.15) available.

Tram

Porto has three antique trams that trundle around town. The most useful line, 1E, travels along the Douro towards the Foz district. A single tram ticket costs €2.50.

TAXI

To cross town, expect to pay between €5 and €8. There's a 20% surcharge at night, and an additional charge to leave city limits, which includes Vila Nova de Gaia. There are taxi ranks throughout the centre or you can call a **taxi** (225 076 400).

Viana do Castelo

POP 38,000

The jewel of the Costa Verde (Green Coast), Viana do Castelo has both an appealing medieval centre and lovely beaches just outside the city. In addition to its natural beauty, Viana do Castelo whips up some excellent seafood and hosts some magnificent traditional festivals, including the spectacular **Festa de Nossa Senhora da Agonia** in August.

Sights

The stately heart of town is **Praça da República**, with its delicate fountain and grandiose buildings, including the 16th-century **Misericórdia**, a former almshouse.

Monte de Santa Luzia HILL

There are two good reasons to visit Viana's 228m, eucalyptus-clad hill. One is the wondrous view down the coast and up the Lima valley. The other is the fabulously over-the-top, 20th-century, neo-Byzantine **Templo do Sagrado Coração de Jesus** (Temple of the Sacred Heart of Jesus; 11am-1pm & 3-8pm) FREE. You can get a little closer to heaven on its graffiti-covered roof, via a lift, followed by an elbow-scraping stairway – take the museum entrance on the ground floor.

Praia do Cabedelo BEACH

(ferry 9am-6pm) This is one of the Minho's best beaches: a 1km-long arch of blonde, powdery sand, which folds into grassy dunes backed by a grove of wind-blown pines. It's across the river from town, best reached on a five-minute ferry trip (one way/return €1.40/2.80; half-price for under-12s, free for children under six) from the pier south of Largo 5 de Outubro.

Sleeping & Eating

Ó Meu Amor GUESTHOUSE €

(258 406 513; www.omeuamor.com; Rua do Poço 19; s/d without bathroom €25/45; @) Top choice in town right in the historic centre,

this hideaway in a rambling town house full of nooks and crannies has nine adorable rooms with shared bathrooms. Guests can use the kitchen and cosy living room.

Margarida da Praça GUESTHOUSE €€
(☎258 809 630; www.margaridadapraca.com; Largo 5 de Outubro 58; s €60-75, d €78-88; @ 📶) Fantastically whimsical, this boutique inn offers thematic rooms in striking pinks, sea greens and whites, accented by stylish floral wallpaper, candelabra lanterns and lush duvets. The equally stylish lobby glows with candlelight in the evening.

Taberna do Valentim SEAFOOD €€
(Campo do Castelo; mains €9.75-12.50; ⏲12.30-3pm & 7.30-10pm Mon-Sat) This bright and buzzing seafood restaurant serves fresh grilled fish by the kilo and rich seafood stews – *arroz de tamboril* (monkfish rice) and *caldeirada* (fish stew).

O Pescador SEAFOOD €€
(☎258 826 039; Largo de São Domingos 35; mains €9.50-15.50; ⏲noon-3pm & 7-10pm Mon-Sat, noon-3pm Sun) A simple, friendly, family-run restaurant admired by locals for its good seafood and tasty lunch specials (from €6.50).

Getting There & Away

Five to 10 trains go daily to Porto (€7 to €8, 1½ hours), as well as express buses (€8, one to 1½ hours).

Braga

POP 143,000

Portugal's third-largest city boasts a fine array of churches, their splendid baroque facades looming above the old plazas and narrow lanes of the historic centre. Lively cafes, trim little boutiques and some good restaurants add to the appeal.

Sights

Sé CATHEDRAL
(www.se-braga.pt; Rua Dom Paio Mendes; ⏲8am-7pm high season, 9am-6pm low season) FREE Braga's extraordinary cathedral, the oldest in Portugal, was begun when the archdiocese was restored in 1070 and completed in the following century. It's a rambling complex made up of differing styles, and architecture buffs could spend half a day happily distinguishing the Romanesque bones from Manueline musculature and baroque frippery.

Escadaria do Bom Jesus RELIGIOUS SITE
At Bom Jesus do Monte, a hilltop pilgrimage site 5km from Braga, is an extraordinary stairway, with allegorical fountains, chapels and a superb view. City bus 2 runs frequently from Braga to the site, where you can climb the steps (pilgrims sometimes do this on their knees) or ascend by funicular railway (one way/return €1.20/2).

Sleeping

Pop Hostel HOSTEL €
(☎253 058 806; http://bragapophostel.blogspot.co.uk; Rua do Carmo 61; dm/d from €17/40; @ 📶) This small cosy hostel in a top-floor apartment is a great recent addition to Braga, with a colourfully decked lounge, a hammock on the balcony and a friendly owner who knows all the great eating and drinking spots in town. Bike hire and tours available.

★**Portuguez Inn** GUESTHOUSE €€
(☎962 130 549; www.portuguezinn.pt; Rua Dom Frei Caetano Brandão 154; per 2/4 people €96/156; P ❄ 📶) This hideaway in the historic centre bills itself as 'the world's smallest guesthouse'. Small it is, but its six levels offer a stylish micro-world that features a 1st-century Roman sewer in the basement, a cosy top-floor living room and Portuguese touches such as woollen blankets, ceramic swallows, handmade soaps and cotton dolls.

Hotel Bracara Augusta BOUTIQUE HOTEL €€
(☎253 206 260; www.bracaraaugusta.com; Avenida Central 134; s/d €79/99; P ❄ @ 📶) This stylish, grand town house offers bright, modern rooms with parquet floors, classic decor and marble bathrooms.

Eating

Anjo Verde VEGETARIAN €
(Largo da Praça Velha 21; mains €7.50-8.60; ⏲noon-3pm & 7.30-10.30pm Mon-Sat) Braga's vegetarian offering serves generous, elegantly presented plates in a lovely, airy dining room. Vegetarian lasagne, risotto and vegetable tarts are among the choices. Mains can be bland, but the spiced chocolate tart is a superstar.

Cozinha da Sé PORTUGUESE €€
(Rua Dom Frei Caetano Brandão 95; mains €10-14; ⏲lunch & dinner Wed-Sun, dinner Tue) Contemporary artwork hangs from the exposed stone walls at this intimate cheery Braga pick. Traditional standouts include baked *bacalhau* (dried salt-cod) and *açorda de marisco* (seafood stew in a bread bowl).

Information

Turismo (☎253 262 550; www.cm-braga.pt; Avenida da Liberdade 1; ⏲9am-7pm Mon-Fri, 9am-12.30pm & 2-5.30pm Sat & Sun Jun-Sep, shorter hours in low season) Braga's helpful tourist office is in an art-deco-style building facing the fountain.

Getting There & Away

Trains arrive regularly from Lisbon (€33, 3½ to 4½ hours), Coimbra (€16 to €20, 1¾ to 2½ hours) and Porto (€3.10, 50 minutes), and there are daily connections north to Viana do Castelo. Car hire is available at **AVIC** (☎253 203 910; Rua Gabriel Pereira de Castro 28; ⏲9am-7pm Mon-Fri, 9am-12.30pm Sat), with prices starting at €35 per day.

Parque Nacional da Peneda-Gerês

Spread across four impressive granite massifs, this vast park encompasses boulder-strewn peaks, precipitous valleys, gorse-clad moorlands and forests of oak and pine. It also shelters more than 100 granite villages that, in many ways, have changed little since Portugal's founding in the 12th century. For nature lovers, the stunning scenery here is unmatched in Portugal for camping, hiking and other outdoor adventures. The park's main centre is at **Vila do Gerês**, a sleepy, hot-springs village.

Activities

Hiking

There are trails and footpaths through the park, some between villages with accommodation. Leaflets detailing these are available from the park offices.

Day hikes around Vila do Gerês are popular. An adventurous option is the **old Roman road** from Mata do Albergaria (10km up-valley from Vila do Gerês), past the **Vilarinho das Furnas** reservoir to Campo do Gerês. More distant destinations include **Ermida** and **Cabril**, both with simple accommodation.

Cycling & Horse Riding

Mountain bikes can be hired in Campo do Gerês (15km northeast of Vila do Gerês) from **Equi Campo** (☎253 161 405; www.equicampo.com; ⏲9am-7pm daily Jun-Aug, 9am-7pm Sat & Sun Sep-May). Guides here also lead horse-riding trips, hikes and combination hiking/climbing/abseiling excursions.

Water Sports

Rio Caldo, 8km south of Vila do Gerês, is the base for water sports on the Caniçada Reservoir. English-run **AML** (☎253 391 779; www.aguamontanha.com; Lugar de Paredes) rents kayaks, pedal boats, rowing boats and small motorboats. It also organises kayaking trips along the Albufeira de Salamonde.

Sleeping & Eating

Vila do Gerês has plenty of *pensões* (guesthouses), but you may find vacancies are limited; many are block-booked by spa patients in summer.

Parque Campismo de Cerdeira CAMPGROUND €
(☎253 351 005; www.parquecerdeira.com; per person/tent/car €5.90/5/5, bungalow €70; ⏲year-round; P 📶 🏊) In Campo de Gêres, this place has oak-shaded sites, a laundry, a pool, a minimarket and a particularly good restaurant. The ecofriendly bungalows open onto unrivalled mountain views.

★ **Peneda Hotel** HOTEL €€
(☎251 460 040; www.penedahotel.pt; Lugar da Peneda, Arcos de Valdevez; s/d €70/75; P 📶) Once a nest for Igreja Senhora de Peneda's pilgrims, this mountain lodge features a waterfall backdrop, a gushing creek beneath and ultra-cosy rooms with blonde-wood floors, French windows and views of quaint Peneda village across the ravine. There's also a decent restaurant.

Beleza da Serra GUESTHOUSE €€
(☎253 391 457; www.bserra.com; Lugar do Bairro 25, Vilar da Veiga; d/tr €62.50/78.50; P ❄ 📶) A great base for hiking and kayaking, this friendly waterfront guesthouse overlooks the Caniçada Reservoir, 4.5km south of Vila do Gerês. It has simple, clean, comfortable rooms and a restaurant dishing up regional food.

Information

The head park office is **Adere-PG** (☎ 258 452 250; www.adere-pg.pt; Largo da Misericórdia 10; ⏰ 9am-12.30pm & 2.30-6pm Mon-Fri) in Ponte de Barca. Obtain park information and reserve cottages and other park accommodation here.

Getting There & Away

Because of the lack of transport within the park, it's good to have your own wheels. You can rent cars in Braga (p909).

SURVIVAL GUIDE

Directory A–Z

ACCOMMODATION

Portugal offers outstanding value by and large. Budget places provide some of Western Europe's cheapest digs, while you'll find atmospheric accommodation in converted castles, mansions and farmhouses.

Seasons

High season Mid-June to mid-September

Mid-season May to mid-June and mid-September to October

Low season November to April

Ecotourism & Farmstays

Turismo de Habitação (www.turihab.pt) is a private network of historic, heritage or rustic properties, ranging from 17th-century manors to quaint farmhouses or self-catering cottages. Doubles run from €60 to €120.

Pousadas

These are government-run former castles, monasteries or palaces, often in spectacular locations. For details, contact tourist offices or **Pousadas de Portugal** (www.pousadas.pt).

Guesthouses

The most common types are the *residencial* and the *pensão*, usually simple, family-owned operations. Some have cheaper rooms with shared bathrooms. Double rooms with private bathroom typically run €40 to €60.

Hostels

Portugal has a growing number of cool backpacker digs, particularly in Lisbon. Nationwide, Portugal has over 30 **pousadas da juventude** (www.pousadasjuventude.pt) within the Hostelling International (HI) system. The average price for a dorm room is about €20.

Camping

For detailed listings of camp sites nationwide, pick up the **Roteiro Campista** (www.roteiro-campista.pt), updated annually and sold at bookshops. Some of the swishest places are run by **Orbitur** (www.orbitur.pt).

SLEEPING PRICE RANGES

The following price ranges refer to a double room with private bathroom in high season. Unless otherwise stated breakfast is included in the price.

€ less than €60

€€ €60 to €120

€€€ more than €120

COUNTRY FACTS

Area 91,470 sq km

Capital Lisbon

Country Code ☎ 351

Currency Euro (€)

Emergency ☎ 112

Language Portuguese

Money ATMs are widespread; banks open Monday to Friday

Visas Schengen rules apply

BUSINESS HOURS

Opening hours vary throughout the year. We provide high-season opening hours; these hours will generally decrease in the shoulder and low seasons.

Banks 8.30am to 3pm Monday to Friday

Bars 7pm to 2am

Cafes 9am to 7pm

Malls 10am to 10pm

Nightclubs 11pm to 4am Thursday to Saturday

Post offices 8.30am to 4pm Monday to Friday

Restaurants noon to 3pm and 7pm to 10pm

Shops 9.30am to noon and 2pm to 7pm Monday to Friday, 10am to 1pm Saturday

INTERNET RESOURCES

Lonely Planet (www.lonelyplanet.com/portugal)

Portugal Tourism (www.visitportugal.com)

MONEY

There are numerous banks with ATMs located throughout Portugal. Credit cards are accepted in midrange and top-end hotels, restaurants and shops.

PUBLIC HOLIDAYS

New Year's Day 1 January

Carnaval Tuesday February/March – the day before Ash Wednesday

Good Friday March/April

Liberty Day 25 April – celebrating the 1974 revolution

Labour Day 1 May

Corpus Christi May/June – 9th Thursday after Easter

Portugal Day 10 June – also known as Camões and Communities Day

Feast of the Assumption 15 August

Republic Day 5 October – commemorating the 1910 declaration of the Portuguese Republic

All Saints' Day 1 November

Independence Day 1 December – commemorating the 1640 restoration of independence from Spain

Feast of the Immaculate Conception 8 December

Christmas Day 25 December

TELEPHONE

Portugal's country code is ☎351. There are no regional area codes. Mobile phone numbers within Portugal have nine digits and begin with ☎9.

For general information, dial ☎118, and for reverse-charge (collect) calls dial ☎120.

Phonecards are sold at post offices, newsagents and tobacconists in denominations of €5 and €10.

ESSENTIAL FOOD & DRINK

➡ **Seafood** Char-grilled *lulas* (squid), *polvo* (octopus) or *sardinhas* (sardines). Other treats: *cataplana* (seafood and sausage cooked in a copper pot), *caldeirada* (hearty fish stew) and *açorda de mariscos* (bread stew with shrimp).

➡ **Cod for all seasons** The Portuguese have dozens of ways to prepare *bacalhau* (salted cod). Try *bacalhau a brás* (grated cod fried with potatoes and eggs), *bacalhau espiritual* (cod soufflé) or *bacalhau com natas* (baked cod with cream and grated cheese).

➡ **Field & fowl** *Porco preto* (sweet 'black' pork), *leitão* (roast suckling pig), *alheira* (bread and meat sausage – formerly Kosher), *cabrito assado* (roast kid) and *arroz de pato* (duck risotto).

➡ **Drink** Port and red wines from the Douro valley, *alvarinho* and *vinho verde* (crisp, semi-sparkling wine) from the Minho and great, little-known reds from the Alentejo and the Beiras (particularly the Dão region).

➡ **Pastries** The *pastel de nata* (custard tart) is legendary, especially in Belém. Other delicacies: *travesseiros* (almond and egg pastries) and *queijadas* (mini-cheese pastries).

Getting There & Away

AIR

TAP (www.flytap.com) is Portugal's international flag carrier as well as its main domestic airline. Portugal's main airports:

Faro Airport (FAO; ☎289 800 800; www.ana.pt)

Lisbon Airport (LIS; ☎218 413 500; www.ana.pt)

Porto Airport (OPO; ☎229 432 400; www.ana.pt)

EATING PRICE RANGES

The following price ranges refer to a main course:

€ less than €10

€€ €10 to €20

€€€ more than €20

LAND

Bus

UK–Portugal and France–Portugal Eurolines services cross to Portugal via northwest Spain. Some operators:

Alsa (www.alsa.es)

Avanza (www.avanzabus.com)

Damas (www.damas-sa.es)

Eurolines (www.eurolines.com)

Eva (☎289 899 760; www.eva-bus.com)

Train

The most popular train link from Spain is on the Sud Express, operated by **Renfe** (www.renfe.com), which has a nightly sleeper service between Madrid and Lisbon.

Two other Spain–Portugal crossings are at Valença do Minho and at Caia (Caya in Spain), near Elvas.

CONNECTIONS

Travelling overland from Portugal entails a trip through Spain. Good places to cross the (invisible) border include the ferry crossing from Vila Real de Santo António in the Algarve, with onward connections to Seville. There are also links from Elvas (going across to Badajoz) and rail links from Valença do Minho in the north (heading up to Santiago de Compostela in Galicia).

Getting Around

AIR

TAP Portugal (p911) has daily Lisbon–Porto and Lisbon–Faro flights (taking less than one hour) year-round.

BICYCLE

Bicycles can be taken free on all regional and inter-regional trains as accompanied baggage. They can also go on a few suburban services on weekends. Most domestic bus lines won't accept bikes.

BUS

A host of small bus operators, most amalgamated into regional companies, run a dense network of services across the country. Among the largest companies are **Rede Expressos** (☎707 223 344; www.rede-expressos.pt), **Rodonorte** (☎259 340 710; www.rodonorte.pt) and the Algarve line Eva (p911).

Most bus-station ticket desks will give you a computer printout of fares, and services and schedules are usually posted at major stations.

Classes

Expressos Comfortable, fast buses between major cities

Rápidas Quick regional buses

Carreiras Marked CR, slow, stopping at every crossroad

CAR & MOTORCYCLE

Automobile Associations

Automóvel Clube de Portugal (ACP; ☎213 180 100; www.acp.pt) has a reciprocal arrangement with better-known foreign automobile clubs, including AA and RAC. It provides medical, legal and breakdown assistance. The 24-hour emergency help number is ☎707 509 510.

Hire

To hire a car in Portugal you must be at least 25 years old and have held your home licence for more than one year. To hire a scooter of up to 50cc you must be over 18 years old and have a valid driving licence.

Road Rules

The various speed limits for cars and motorcycles are 50km/h within cities and public centres, 90km/h on normal roads and 120km/h on motorways.

Drink-driving laws are strict in Portugal, with a maximum legal blood-alcohol level of 0.05%.

TRAIN

Caminhos de Ferro Portugueses (CP; www.cp.pt) is the statewide train network and is generally efficient.

There are four main types of long-distance service. Note that international services are marked 'IN' on timetables.

Regional (marked R on timetables) Slow trains that stop everywhere.

Interregional (IR) Reasonably fast trains.

Intercidade (IC)/**Rápido** Express trains.

Alfa Pendular Deluxe, fastest and most expensive service.

Romania

Includes ➡

Best Places to Eat

- Central Park (p924)
- Casa Bunicii (p931)
- Caru' cu Bere (p918)
- Crama Sibiul Vechi (p925)
- Bistro de l'Arte (p922)

Best Places to Stay

- Casa Georgius Krauss (p924)
- Casa Reims (p921)
- The Guest House (p922)
- Hotel Central (p927)
- Hostel Costel (p930)

Why Go?

Beautiful and beguiling, Romania's rural landscape remains relatively untouched by the country's urban evolution. It's a land of aesthetically stirring hand-ploughed fields, sheep-instigated traffic jams, and lots of homemade plum brandy.

Most visitors focus their attention on Transylvania, with its legacy of fortified Saxon towns like Braşov and Sighişoara, plus tons of stirring natural beauty. Similar in character but even more remote, the region of Maramureş offers authentic folkways and villages marked by memorable wooden churches. Across the Carpathians, the Unesco-listed painted monasteries dot southern Bucovina. The Danube Delta has more than 300 species of birds, including many rare varieties, and is an ideal spot for birdwatching.

Energetic cities such as Timişoara, Cluj-Napoca and, especially, Bucharest offer culture – both high- and low-brow – and showcase Romania as a rapidly evolving modern European country.

When to Go

Bucharest

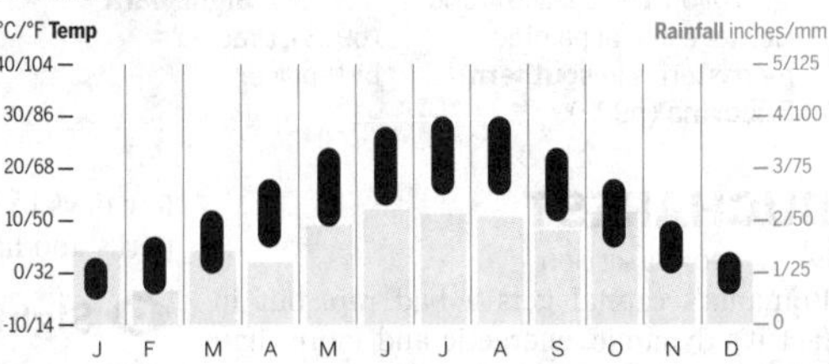

May Good for festivals, including the ever-popular Sibiu Jazz Festival.

Jun Mountain hiking starts in mid-June, while birding season gets rolling in the Danube Delta.

Sep The summer heat is gone, but sunny days are perfect for exploring big cities.

Romania Highlights

1. Ascend castles and mountains (and castles on top of mountains), using **Braşov** (p920) as a base.
2. Follow the Unesco World Heritage line of painted monasteries in **southern Bucovina** (p929).
3. Soak in **Sibiu** (p925), a beautifully restored Saxon town.
4. Explore the medieval citadel of **Sighişoara** (p923), Dracula's birthplace.
5. Row through the tributaries and the riot of nature in the **Danube Delta** (p930).
6. Enjoy the museums and cacophonous nightlife of the capital **Bucharest**.

BUCHAREST

021 / POP 1.9 MILLION

Romania's capital gets a bad rap, but in fact it's dynamic, energetic and more than a little bit funky. It's where unreconstructed communism meets unbridled capitalism; where the soporific forces of the EU meet the passions of the Balkans and Middle East. Many travellers give the city just a night or two before heading off to Transylvania but, frankly, that's not enough. Budget at least a few days to take in the museums, stroll the parks and hang out at trendy cafes.

Sights

South of the Centre

Palace of Parliament HISTORIC BUILDING
(Palatul Parlamentului/Casa Poporului; tour bookings 021-311 3611; www.cdep.ro; B-dul Naţiunile Unite; complete tour adults/students 45/23 lei,

ITINERARIES

One Week

Spend a day ambling around the **capital**, then take a train to **Braşov** – Transylvania's main event – for castles, activities and beer at streetside cafes. Spend a day in **Sighişoara**'s medieval citadel, then catch a train back to Bucharest or on to Budapest.

Two Weeks

Arrive in Bucharest by plane or **Timişoara** by train, then head into **Transylvania**, devoting a day or two each to Braşov, Sighişoara and **Sibiu**. Tour southern **Bucovina's** painted monasteries, then continue on to **Bucharest**.

standard adult/students 25/13 lei; 10am-4pm; M Izvor) The Palace of Parliament is the world's second-largest building (after the Pentagon) and former dictator Nicolae Ceauşescu's most infamous creation. Started in 1984 (and still unfinished), the building has more than 3000 rooms and covers 330,000 sq metres. Entry is by guided tour only (book in advance). Bring your passport since they check IDs. Today it houses the parliament.

Old Town & Piaţa Revoluţiei

The Old Town and Piaţa Revoluţiei mark the heart of the centre. The Old Town was the seat of power in the 15th century, but today it's a pedestrianised warren of clubs and cafes.

Piaţa Revoluţiei, just to the north, saw the heaviest fighting in the 1989 overthrow of dictator Nicolae Ceauşescu. Those days are commemorated by the **Rebirth Memorial** in the middle of the square. Nearby, the balcony of the **Central Committee of the Communist Party Building** was where he made his infamous last speech before escaping (briefly) by helicopter.

Old Princely Court RUINS
(Palatul Voievodal, Curtea Veche; Str Franceză 21-23; admission 3 lei; 10am-6pm) The Old Princely Court dates to the 15th century, when Bucharest was the capital of the Wallachian principality. The ruins are being slowly excavated but for now you can wander around some of the rooms of the former court. The **Vlad Ţepeş statue** out the front makes a good photo.

Stavropoleos Church CHURCH
(021-313 4747; www.stavropoleos.ro; Str Stavropoleos 4; 7am-8pm) The tiny and lovely Stavropoleos Church, which dates from 1724, perches a bit oddly a block over from some of Bucharest's craziest Old Town carousing. It's one church, though, that will make a lasting impression, with its courtyard filled with tombstones and an ornate wooden interior and carved wooden doors.

National History Museum MUSEUM
(Muzeul Național de Istorie a Romaniei; 021-315 8207; www.mnir.ro; Calea Victoriei 12; adult/student 27/7 lei; 10am-6pm Wed-Sun) Houses an excellent collection of maps, statues and ancient jewels, and is particularly strong on the country's ties to ancient Rome, including a replica of the 2nd-century Trajan's Column. Our favourite piece, though, is not inside the museum at all, but rather on the steps outside: a controversial (and funny) **Statue of Emperor Trajan** standing naked holding a Dacian wolf.

National Art Museum MUSEUM
(Muzeul Naţional de Artă; 021-313 3030; www.mnar.arts.ro; Calea Victoriei 49-53; admission 15 lei; 11am-7pm Wed-Sun) Housed in the 19th-century Royal Palace, this massive museum – all signed in English – houses two permanent galleries: one for National Art and the other for European Masters. The national gallery is particularly strong on ancient and medieval art, while the European gallery includes some 12,000 pieces laid out by nationality.

North of the Centre

Luxurious villas and parks line grand Şos Kiseleff, which begins at Piaţa Victoriei. The major landmark is the **Triumphal Arch** (Arcul de Triumf; Piaţa Arcul de Triumf), which stands halfway up Şos Kiseleff.

★**Grigore Antipa Natural History Museum** MUSEUM
(Muzeul de Istorie Naturală Grigore Antipa; 021-312 8826; www.antipa.ro; Şos Kiseleff 1; adult/student 20/5 lei ; 10am-8pm Wed-Sun;) One of the few attractions in Bucharest squarely aimed at kids, this natural history museum

Central Bucharest

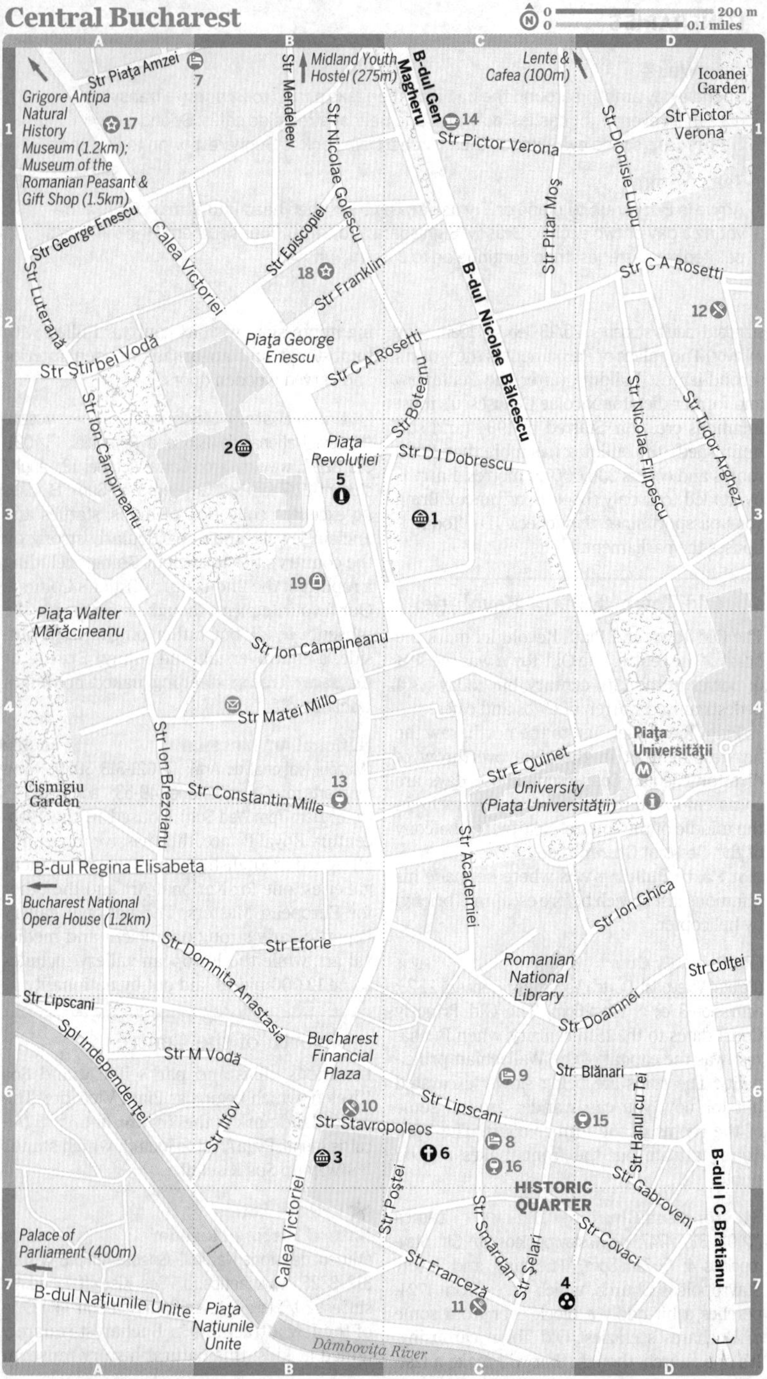

0 200 m
0 0.1 miles

A B C D
1 2 3 4 5 6 7

Str Piaţa Amzei
7
Grigore Antipa Natural History Museum (1.2km); Museum of the Romanian Peasant & Gift Shop (1.5km)
17
Str Mendeleev
Midland Youth Hostel (275m)
B-dul Gen Magheru
Lente & Cafea (100m)
Icoanei Garden
Str Pictor Verona
14
Str Nicolae Golescu
Str Pictor Verona
Str Dionisie Lupu
Str Pitar Moş
Str George Enescu
Calea Victoriei
Str Episcopiei
18
Str Franklin
B-dul Nicolae Bălcescu
Str C A Rosetti
12
Str Luterană
Piaţa George Enescu
Str Ştirbei Vodă
Str C A Rosetti
Str Boteanu
Str Nicolae Filipescu
Str Tudor Arghezi
Str Ion Câmpineanu
2
Piaţa Revoluţiei
5
Str D I Dobrescu
1
19
Piaţa Walter Mărăcineanu
Str Ion Câmpineanu
Str Matei Millo
Str Ion Brezoianu
Piaţa Universităţii
Str E Quinet
University (Piaţa Universităţii)
13
Cişmigiu Garden
Str Constantin Mille
Str Academiei
B-dul Regina Elisabeta
Bucharest National Opera House (1.2km)
Str Ion Ghica
Str Eforie
Str Domnita Anastasia
Romanian National Library
Str Colţei
Str Lipscani
Spl Independenţei
Str M Vodă
Bucharest Financial Plaza
Str Doamnei
9
Str Blănari
Str Lipscani
10
Str Stavropoleos
15
Str Ilfov
3
6
8
16
Str Hanul cu Tei
Str Poştei
Calea Victoriei
HISTORIC QUARTER
Str Gabroveni
B-dul I C Bratianu
Str Smârdan
Str Şelari
Str Covaci
Palace of Parliament (400m)
Str Franceză
4
B-dul Naţiunile Unite
Piaţa Naţiunile Unite
11
Dâmboviţa River

Central Bucharest

Sights
1 Central Committee of the Communist Party Building C3
2 National Art Museum B3
3 National History Museum B6
4 Old Princely Court C7
5 Rebirth Memorial B3
6 Stavropoleos Church C6

Sleeping
7 Hotel Amzei B1
8 Little Bucharest Old Town Hostel C6
9 Rembrandt Hotel C6

Eating
10 Caru' cu Bere B6
11 Divan C7
12 Lente & Cafea D2

Drinking & Nightlife
13 Control B4
14 Grădina Verona C1
15 La Muse D6
16 St Patrick C6

Entertainment
17 Green Hours 22 Jazz Club A1
18 Romanian Athenaeum B2

Shopping
19 Anthony Frost B3

has been thoroughly renovated and now features modern bells and whistles such as video displays, games and interactive exhibits. Much of it is signed in English.

Museum of the Romanian Peasant MUSEUM
(Muzeul Țăranului Român; ☎021-317 9661; www.muzeultaranuluiroman.ro; Şos Kiseleff 3; adult/child 8/2 lei; ⊙10am-6pm Tue-Sun) The collection of peasant bric-a-brac, costumes, icons and partially restored houses makes this one of the most popular museums in the city. There's not much English signage, but little cards in English posted in each room give a flavour of what's on offer. An 18th-century church stands in the back lot, as does a great gift shop and restaurant.

National Village Museum MUSEUM
(Muzuel Naţional al Satului; ☎021-317 9103; www.muzeul-satului.ro; Şos Kiseleff 28-30; adult/child 10/5 lei; ⊙9am-7pm Tue-Sun, to 5pm Mon;) On the shores of Herăstrău Lake, this museum is a terrific open-air collection of several dozen homesteads, churches, mills and windmills relocated from rural Romania. Built in 1936 by royal decree, it is one of Europe's oldest open-air museums and a good choice for kids to boot.

Sleeping

Hotels in Bucharest are typically aimed at businesspeople, and prices are higher here than the rest of the country. **Cert Accommodation** (☎0720-772 772; www.cert-accommodation.ro) offers good-value private apartment stays, starting at around 200 lei per night.

★Little Bucharest Old Town Hostel HOSTEL €
(☎0786-055 287; www.littlebucharest.ro; Str Smârdan 15; dm 45-60 lei, r 225 lei;) Bucharest's most central hostel is super clean, white walled and well run. Accommodation is over two floors, with dorms ranging from 6 to 12 beds. Private doubles are also available. The staff is travel-friendly and youth oriented and can advise on sightseeing and fun. The location is in the middle of Bucharest's lively Old Town.

Midland Youth Hostel HOSTEL €
(☎021-314 5323; www.themidlandhostel.com; Str Biserica Amzei 22; dm 40-60 lei;) A happening hostel, with an excellent central location not far from Piaţa Romană. Accommodation is in six-, 10- or 14-bed dorms. There's a common kitchen and free breakfast.

Rembrandt Hotel HOTEL €€
(☎021-313 9315; www.rembrandt.ro; Str Smârdan 11; tourist s/d 180/230 lei, standard s/d 260/300 lei, business s/d 350/380 lei;) It's hard to say enough good things about this place. Stylish beyond its three-star rating, this 16-room, Dutch-run hotel faces the landmark National Bank in the historic centre. Rooms come in three categories: tourist, standard and business, with the chief difference being size. All rooms have polished wooden floors, timber headboards, and DVD players. Book well in advance.

Hotel Amzei HOTEL €€€
(☎021-313 9400; www.hotelamzei.ro; Piaţa Amzei 8; s/d 450/550 lei;) This tastefully reconstructed villa just off Calea Victoriei has 22 rooms on four floors. The wrought-iron atrium in the lobby lends a refined feel. The rooms are in a more restrained contemporary style, but everything about the place says quality.

Eating

★Caru' cu Bere ROMANIAN €€

(☎021-313 7560; www.carucubere.ro; Str Stavropoleos 3-5; mains 20-45 lei; ⏲8am-midnight Sun-Thu, 8am-2am Fri & Sat; 📶) Despite a decidedly tourist-leaning atmosphere, with peasant-girl hostesses and sporadic traditional song-and-dance numbers, Bucharest's oldest beer house continues to draw in a strong local crowd. The colourful belle epoque interior and stained-glass windows dazzle, as does the classic Romanian food. Dinner reservations recommended.

Divan MIDDLE EASTERN €€

(☎021-312 3034; www.thedivan.ro; Str Franceză 46-48; mains 20-30 lei; ⏲10am-2am; 📶) Deservedly popular Turkish and Middle Eastern place, where snagging a prized terrace table will take a mix of patience and good fortune. The waiter will first bring around a tantalising selection of starters, such as hummus and babaganoush. Select a few of these and then settle back for the enormous platters of grilled meats and kebabs.

Lente & Cafea INTERNATIONAL €€

(☎021-310 7424; www.lente.ro; Str Gen Praporgescu 31; mains 25-40 lei; ⏲11.30am-1am; 📶) The *tomatina*, tomato soup served with croutons and yellow cheese, is a classic, but all the entrees are creative, filling and good value. We especially like the 'Anthos' main, which is strips of beef tenderloin flavoured with celery soy sauce and served with basmati rice. The garden terrace is a respite on a hot day.

Drinking & Nightlife

★Grădina Verona CAFE

(☎0732-003 060; Str Pictor Verona 13-15; ⏲9am-1am; 📶) A garden oasis hidden behind the Cărtureşti bookshop, serving standard-issue but excellent espresso drinks and some of the wackiest iced-tea infusions ever concocted in Romania, such as peony flower, mango and lime (it's not bad).

St Patrick PUB

(☎021-313 0336; www.stpatrick.ro; Str Smârdan 25; 📶) This popular pub gets the authentic Irish bar look down with dark woods and a green ceiling. Grab a table on busy Str Smârdan and settle back with a pint of Guinness or cider. They also do good renditions of standards such as steak and kidney pie (25 lei) and Irish breakfast (25 lei).

Control CLUB

(☎0733-927 861; www.control-club.ro; Str Constantin Mille 4; ⏲6pm-4am; 📶) This is a favourite among club-goers who like alternative, indie and garage sounds. Hosts both live acts and DJs, depending on the night.

La Muse CLUB

(☎0734-000 236; www.lamuse.ro; Str Lipscani 53; ⏲9am-3am Sun-Wed, to 6am Thu-Sat; 📶) Just about anything goes at this popular Old Town dance club. Try to arrive early, around 11pm, since it can get crowded later. La Muse draws everyone from university students to young professionals in their 20s and 30s. Everyone looks great.

Entertainment

Bucharest National Opera House OPERA

(Opera Naţională Bucureşti; ☎box office 021-310 2661; www.operanb.ro; B-dul Mihail Kogălniceanu 70-72; tickets 10-70 lei; ⏲box office 9am-1pm & 3-7pm) The city's premier venue for classical opera and ballet. Buy tickets online or at the venue box office.

Romanian Athenaeum CLASSICAL MUSIC

(Ateneul Roman; ☎box office 021-315 6875; www.fge.org.ro; Str Franklin 1-3; tickets 15-65 lei; ⏲box office noon-7pm Tue-Fri, 4-7pm Sat, 10-11am Sun) The historic Athenaeum is home to the respected George Enescu Philharmonic and offers a wide array of classical music concerts from September to May as well as a number of one-off musical shows and spectacles throughout the year. Buy tickets at the venue box office.

Green Hours 22 Jazz Club JAZZ

(☎concerts 0788-452 485; www.greenhours.ro; Calea Victoriei 120; ⏲6pm-2am) This old-school basement jazz club runs a lively program of jazz nights through the week and hosts an international jazz fest in May/June. Check the website for the schedule during your trip and try to book in advance.

Shopping

★Anthony Frost BOOKS

(☎021-311 5136; www.anthonyfrost.ro; Calea Victoriei 45; ⏲10am-8pm Mon-Fri, to 7pm Sat, to 2pm Sun) Serious readers will want to make time for arguably the best English-language bookshop in Eastern Europe. Located in a small passage next to the Creţulescu Church, this shop has a carefully chosen selection of highbrow contemporary fiction and nonfiction.

Museum of the Romanian Peasant Gift Shop FOLK CRAFTS
(www.muzeultaranuluiroman.ro; Şos Kiseleff 3; ⏲10am-6pm Tue-Sun) For beautifully made woven rugs, table runners, national Romanian costumes, ceramics and other local crafts, don't miss the excellent folk-art shop at the Museum of the Romanian Peasant; access to the shop is from the back of the museum.

Information

You'll find hundreds of bank branches and ATMs in the centre. Most banks have a currency-exchange office and can provide cash advances against credit or debit cards. Always bring your passport, since you will have to show it to change money.

Best Cafe (☎021-312 4816; www.best-cafe.ro; B-dul Mihail Kogălniceanu 19; per hr 5 lei; ⏲24hr; 📶) Internet cafe.

Bucharest Tourist Information Center (☎021-305 5500, ext 1003; http://en.seebucharest.ro; Piaţa Universităţii; ⏲10am-6pm Mon-Fri, to 2pm Sat & Sun) This small, poorly stocked tourist office is the best the city can offer visitors. While there's not much information on hand, the English-speaking staff can field basic questions, make suggestions and help locate things on a map.

Central Post Office (☎021-315 9030; www.posta-romana.ro; Str Matei Millo 10; ⏲7.30am-8pm Mon-Fri)

Emergency Clinic Hospital (☎021-599 2300, 021-9622; www.scub.ro; Calea Floreasca 8; ⏲24hr) The first port of call in any serious emergency. Arguably the city's (and country's) best emergency hospital.

Getting There & Away

AIR

All international and domestic flights use Henri Coandă International Airport (p933; often referred to by its previous name, Otopeni). Henri Coandă is 17km north of Bucharest on the road to Braşov. The airport is a modern facility, with restaurants, newsagents, currency exchange offices and ATMs.

It's also the hub for national carrier **Tarom** (☎call centre 021-204 6464, office 021-316 0220; www.tarom.ro; Spl Independenţei 17, City Centre; ⏲8.30am-7.30pm Mon-Fri, 9am-1.30pm Sat). Tarom has a comprehensive network of internal flights to major Romanian cities as well to capitals and big cities around Europe and the Middle East.

BUS

It's possible to get just about anywhere in the country by bus from Bucharest, but figuring out where your bus or maxitaxi departs from can be tricky. Bucharest has several bus stations and they don't seem to follow any discernible logic.

The best bet is to consult the websites www.autogari.ro and www.cdy.ro. Both keep up-to-date timetables and are fairly easy to manage. Another option is to ask your hotel to help with arrangements or book through a travel agency.

CAR & MOTORCYCLE

Driving in Bucharest is lunacy and you won't want to do it for more than a few minutes before you stow the car and use the metro. If you're travelling around by car and want to visit Bucharest for the day, park at a metro station on the outskirts and take the metro in.

Autonom (☎airport 0742-215 361, call centre 0721-442 266; www.autonom.com; Henri Coandă International Airport; rates per day start at around 150 lei) Reputable, locally owned car rental company offers a range of Romanian and European makes.

TRAIN

Domestic and international trains use the main station, **Gara de Nord** (☎phone reservations 021-9522; www.cfrcalatori.ro; Piaţa Gara de Nord 1; Ⓜ Gara de Nord). It's around 2km from the centre and best reached by metro. The station has restaurants, ATMs and left-luggage facilities.

Buy tickets at ticket windows. For international tickets, the private travel agency **Wasteels** (☎021-300 2730; www.triptkts.ro; Gara de Nord; ⏲10am-5pm Mon-Fri), located inside the station, can sort out complicated connections.

Sample destinations and fares from Bucharest on fast IC trains include Braşov (50 lei, three hours, several daily), Cluj-Napoca (94 lei, 10 hours, two daily), Sibiu (75 lei, six hours, two daily), Timişoara (105 lei, nine hours, two daily) and Suceava (94 lei, seven hours, one daily).

Getting Around

TO/FROM THE AIRPORT

Bus

Express bus 783 leaves every 30 to 40 minutes from the airport arrivals hall to various points in the centre, including Piaţa Victoriei and Piaţa Unirii. Buy a ticket for 7 lei from the RATB ticket booth near the stop.

Taxi

Order a taxi by touchscreen at the airport arrivals terminal. Simply choose a company and rate (all are about the same), and you'll get a ticket and number. Pay the driver. A reputable taxi to the centre should cost no more than 70 lei.

PUBLIC TRANSPORT

Bucharest's public transport system of metros, buses, trams and trolleybuses is operated by the transport authority **RATB** (Regia Autonomă de Transport Bucureşti; ☎ info 021-9391; www.ratb.ro). The system runs from 5am to approximately 11.30pm.

For buses, trams and trolleybuses, buy tickets at any RATB street kiosk, marked *'casa de bilete'*. Tickets for standard buses cost 1.30 lei per trip and are sold in two-ticket increments for 2.60 lei. Tickets for a small number of express buses, such as bus 783 which goes to the airport, cost 7 lei (good for two journeys). Punch your ticket on board or risk a spot fine.

Metro stations are identified by a large 'M'. To use the metro, buy a magnetic-strip ticket available at ticketing machines inside station entrances (have small bills handy). Tickets valid for two journeys cost 4 lei. A 10-trip ticket costs 15 lei.

TRANSYLVANIA

After a century of being name-checked in literature and cinema, the word 'Transylvania' enjoys worldwide recognition. The mere mention conjures a vivid landscape of mountains, castles, spooky moonlight and at least one well-known count with a wicked overbite. Unexplained puncture wounds notwithstanding, Transylvania is all those things and more. A melange of architecture and chic sidewalk cafes punctuate the towns of Braşov, Sighişoara and Sibiu, while the vibrant student town Cluj-Napoca has some vigorous nightlife. Bran Castle, too, is well worth the trip – even if 'Dracula' never did spend much time there.

Braşov

POP 253,200

Legend has it the Pied Piper re-emerged from Hamelin in Braşov, and indeed there's something whimsical about the city, with its fairy-tale turrets and cobbled streets. Dramatically overlooked by Mt Tâmpa, the trees sporting a russet-gold coat (and cocky Hollywood-style sign), this is a remarkably relaxed city. Wander its maze of streets, stopping for caffeine injections at bohemian cafes, and lose yourself in a beguiling coalescence of Austro-Hungarian gingerbread roofs, baroque statues, medieval spires and Soviet flat-tops.

Sights

In addition to the sights below, explore the Old Town walls and bastions that line the centre on the eastern and western flanks. Many have been restored.

Piaţa Sfatului PUBLIC SQUARE

This wide square, chock-full with cafes, was once the heart of medieval Braşov. In the centre stands the 1420 **Council House** (Casa Sfatului), topped by the **Trumpeter's Tower**, in which town councillors, known as centurions, would meet. These days at midday, traditionally costumed musicians appear from the top of the tower like figures in a Swiss clock.

Black Church CHURCH

(Biserica Neagră; ☎ 0268-511 824; www.honterusgemeinde.ro; Curtea Johannes Honterus 2; adult/child 8/5 lei; ⏲ 10am-7pm Tue-Sat, noon-7pm Sun) Braşov's main landmark, the Black Church is the largest Gothic church between Vienna and İstanbul, and is still used by German Lutherans today. Built between 1383 and 1480, it was named for its appearance after a fire in 1689. The original statues from the exterior of the apse are now inside.

Mt Tâmpa MOUNTAIN

(Telecabina Tampa; ☎ 0268-478 657; Aleea Tiberiu Brediceanu; cable car one way/return 10/16 lei; ⏲ Tue-Sun 9.30am-5pm) Towering over the city from the east, 940m Mt Tâmpa – with its Hollywood-style sign – was Braşov's original defensive wall. You can hike up (about an hour) or take a cable car to reach a small viewing platform offering stunning views over the city and the possibility of a light bite or drink at a communist-era dining room.

Sleeping

Centrum House Hostel HOSTEL €

(☎ 0727-793 169; www.hostelbrasov.eu; Str Republicii 58; dm 45 lei, r 135-360 lei; 🚭 📶) This clean and airy modern hostel, located dead centre down a passageway off Str Republicii, opened its doors in 2013 and is a great choice. The white walls, with a splash of colour here and there, give it a fresh feel. Most rooms offer various combinations of bunks and dorms (check the website). The White Room is a comfy private triple.

Braşov

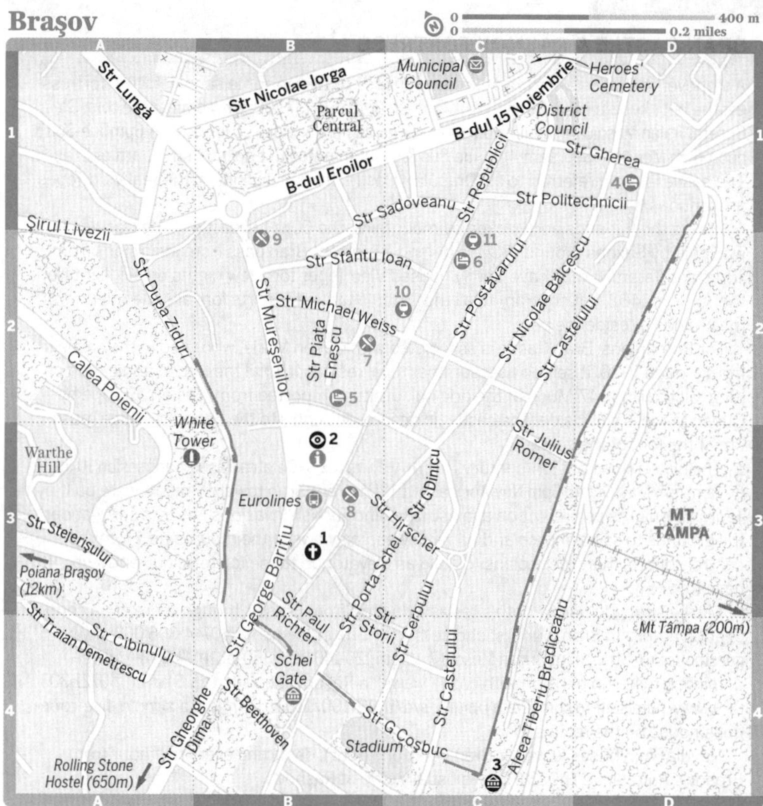

Rolling Stone Hostel HOSTEL €
(0268-513 965; www.rollingstone.ro; Str Piatra Mare 2a; dm 40 lei, r from 120 lei;) Run by helpful sisters with unlimited reserves of energy, super-friendly Stone attracts a cosmo stew of travellers. Dorms are a little crowded, save for the smaller one downstairs. The private double room (without bathroom) has couches and armoire. You'll be given a map and bags of info on arrival. Personal lockers, organised tours and basic breakfast.

★ **Casa Reims** BOUTIQUE HOTEL €€
(0368-467 325; www.casareims.ro; Str Castelului 85; s/d 200/250 lei;) High-end mum and dad boutique with glamourous touches like quality linens, flower-print spreads and hardwood floors. You'll get an enthusiastic welcome at the reception desk and a hearty home-cooked breakfast. There's a big enclosed parking lot for drivers and the pedestrian centre is five minutes away on foot. Recommended.

Braşov

Sights
- 1 Black Church ... B3
- 2 Piaţa Sfatului ... B3
- 3 Weavers' Bastion ... C4

Sleeping
- 4 Casa Reims ... D1
- 5 Casa Wagner ... B2
- 6 Centrum House Hostel ... C2

Eating
- 7 Bistro de l'Arte ... B2
- 8 Keller Steak House ... B3
- 9 Sergiana ... B2

Drinking & Nightlife
- 10 Deane's Irish Pub & Grill ... C2
- 11 Festival 39 ... C2

★ **Casa Wagner** HOTEL €€€
(0268-411 253; www.casa-wagner.com; Piaţa Sfatului 5; s/d incl breakfast 260/320 lei;)

WORTH A TRIP

BRAN CASTLE & RÂŞNOV FORTRESS

A stopover in Braşov affords an excellent chance to take in some spooky hilltop fortresses; the best known is certainly **Bran Castle** (☎0268-237 700; www.bran-castle.com; Str General Traian Moşoiu 24; adult/student 25/10 lei, camera or video 20 lei; ⌚9am-6pm Tue-Sun & noon-6pm Mon May-Sep, 9am-4pm Tue-Sun & noon-4pm Mon Oct-Apr), 30km south of Braşov. The castle is often referred to as 'Dracula's Castle', though its links to the real Vlad Ţepeş are tenuous.

Facing the flatlands and backed by mountains, the 60m-tall castle is spectacular. It was built by Saxons around 1380 to defend important Bran pass from incursions from Turks and Tatars. It may have briefly housed Vlad Ţepeş for a few nights on his flight from the Turks in 1462, but contrary to all the Dracula tat and T-shirts for sale, the ruler never maintained a residence here.

For Romanians, Bran Castle is associated with Queen Marie, who lived in the castle from around 1920. It served as a summer royal residence until the forced abdication of King Michael in 1947. Much of the original furniture imported from Western Europe by Queen Marie is still inside. The castle ticket includes entry to the open-air village museum at the foot of the castle.

The hilltop ruins of 13th-century **Râşnov Fortress** (Cetatea Râşnov; admission 10 lei; ⌚9am-7pm May-Oct, to 5pm Nov-Apr), about 12km from Bran toward Braşov, were built by Teutonic Knights as protection against Tatar and Turkish invasions. Visitors can wander the grounds to see a church and admire sweeping views of the mountains. From the central square, there were plans to build an elevator up to the fortress; currently, you'll have to hike it.

Most visitors do one or both sites as a day trip from Braşov, though there are a couple of good hotels. In Bran, our first choice is **The Guest House** (☎0744-306 062; www.guesthouse.ro; Str General Traian Moşoiu 7; r from 120-140 lei, tr 150 lei; P⊖☎♿), a welcoming, family-run pension with castle views. In Râşnov, **Pensiunea Stefi** (☎0721-303 009; www.hotelstefi-ro.com; Piaţa Unirii 5; s/d/tr 90/100/130 lei; ⊖☎) is a simple, five-room guesthouse on the main square.

Regular minibuses leave for Bran (7 lei, one hour), departing every half hour from Braşov's Autogara 2 (p923). Buses usually stop at Râşnov.

This former 15th-century German bank has been converted to a luxury boutique hotel, with 24 well-appointed rooms. Right in the heart of the city, its exposed-brick walls, tasteful furnishings, modern en suites, welcoming breakfast area and pleasant management make this an excellent choice.

Eating

★Bistro de l'Arte BISTRO €€
(☎0720-535 566; www.bistrodelarte.ro; Str Piaţa Enescu 11; mains 15-35 lei; ⌚9am-1am Mon-Sat, noon-1am Sun; ☎) Tucked down a cobbled street straight out of a folk tale, this joint has decidedly boho genes with walls dotted with local artists' work. Gazpacho soup, shrimps and tomato gratin, snails...or just a croque monsieur. Perfect for nursing a cappuccino and working on your laptop.

Sergiana ROMANIAN €€
(☎0268-419 775; http://sergianagrup.ro; Str Mureşenilor 28; mains 25-40 lei; ⌚11am-11pm) Authentically Saxon, this subterranean carnivore's heaven has two sections: the white room for 'pure' nonsmokers, and the exposed brick vaults for *fumeurs*. Choose from a menu of venison, stag, boar, pork ribs, sirloin steak, and Transylvanian sour soup with smoked gammon and tarragon (11.50 lei). A hunter's dream.

Keller Steak House STEAK €€€
(☎0268-472 278; www.kellersteakhouse.ro; Str Apollonia Hirscher 2; mains 60-90 lei; ⌚11am-11pm) One of Braşov's premier steakhouses, you can eat inside its ochre interior or tackle your sirloin outside on the terrace. Steak and Roquefort cheese, salad and boar...one thing is for certain: you won't leave here with an empty stomach.

Drinking & Nightlife

Festival 39 BAR
(☎0743-339 909; www.festival39.com; Str Republicii 62; ⌚7am-midnight) This romantic watering

hole is an art-deco dream of stained-glass ceilings, wrought-iron finery, candelabra and leather banquettes, and has a bar long enough to keep an army of barflies content. Sheer elan.

Deane's Irish Pub & Grill PUB
(☎0268-474 542; www.deanes.ro; Str Republicii 19; ⏰10am-1am Mon-Thu, 10am-3am Fri & Sat, noon-1am Sun) As if transplanted from Donegal, this subterranean Irish pub with its early-20th-century cloudy mirrored bar, shadowy booths and old-world soundtracks, is a haven for the Guinness-thirsty. Live music some nights.

Information

You'll find numerous ATMs and banks on and around Str Republicii and B-dul Eroilor.

County Hospital (☎0268-320 022; www.hospbv.ro; Calea Bucureşti 25-27; ⏰24hr) Northeast of the centre.

Internet Cafe (Str Michael Weiss 11; per hr 3 lei; ⏰24 hr)

Tourist Information Centre (☎0268-419 078; www.brasovcity.ro; Piaţa Sfatului 30; ⏰10am-6pm Mon-Fri) Easily spotted in the gold city council building in the centre of the square, the English-speaking staff offer free maps and brochures and track down hotel vacancies and train and bus times. The centre shares space with the history museum.

Getting There & Around

BUS

Maxitaxis leave every half-hour for Bucharest (30 lei, 2½ hours); about four or five maxitaxis leave for Sibiu (25 lei, 2½ hours); nine or 10 go daily to Sighişoara (25 lei, two hours). The most accessible station is **Autogara 1** (Bus Station 1; ☎0268-427 267; www.autogari.ro; B-dul Gării 1), next to the train station. Some buses, including several to Bran (7 lei, one hour), leave from **Autogara 2** (Bus Station 2; ☎0268-426 332; www.autogari.ro; Str Avram Iancu 114), 3km north of the centre.

European routes are handled by **Eurolines** (☎0268-474 008; www.eurolines.ro; Piaţa Sfatului 18; ⏰9am-8pm Mon-Fri, 10am-2pm Sat).

TRAIN

The **train station** (Gara Braşov; ☎0268-421 700; www.cfrcalatori.ro; B-dul Gării 5) is 2km northeast of the centre. Buy tickets at the station. There are ATMs and a left-luggage office. Bus 4 runs from the station to Piaţa Unirii in the centre (or walk 20 minutes).

Braşov is an important train junction and connections are good to cities around the country. Trains to Budapest also pass through here. Daily domestic train service includes hourly to Bucharest (50 lei, three hours), several to Sighişoara (41 lei, 2½ hours), two to Sibiu (50 lei, four hours) and several to Cluj-Napoca (75 lei, six hours).

Sighişoara

POP 26,400

From the moment you enter Sighişoara's fortified walls, wending your way along cobblestones to its central square, the town burns itself into your memory. It's like stepping into a kid's fairy tale, the narrow streets aglow with lustrously coloured 16th-century houses, their gingerbread roofs tumbling down to pretty cafes. Horror fans won't be disappointed either, for this Unesco-protected citadel was reputedly the birthplace of one of history's great 'monsters' – Vlad Ţepeş (The Impaler).

Sights

Most sights are clustered in the magical, medieval **Citadel** perched on a hillock and fortified with a 14th-century wall (to which 14 towers and five artillery bastions were later added).

Clock Tower MUSEUM
(Turnul cu Ceas; ☎0265-771 108; Piaţa Muzeului 1; adult/child 12/3 lei; ⏰9am-6.30pm Tue-Fri, 10am-5.30pm Sat & Sun) The symbol of the town is this magnificent medieval clock tower, built in the 14th century and expanded 200 years later. It originally housed the town council, but these days it's purely decorative. The clock and figurines were added in the 17th century. The figurines represent different medieval characters, including Peace, Justice and Law, as well as those representing Day and Night.

The tower houses a **history museum**, which affords access to the viewing platform on the upper floor. The museum is hard to follow (English signage is spotty), but there's a small exhibition on local hero and physicist Hermann Oberth. A couple floors up you can see the clock's famed figures, as well as the clanking innards of the clock behind them.

Casa Dracula HISTORIC BUILDING
(☎0265-771 596; www.casavladdracul.ro; Str Cositorarilor 5; admission 5 lei; ⏰10am-10pm) Vlad Ţepeş (aka Dracula) was reputedly born in this house in 1431 and lived here until the age of four. It's now a decent restaurant, but

for a small admission, the staff will show you Vlad's old room (and give you a little scare). Bubble-burster: the building is indeed centuries old, but has been completely rebuilt since Vlad's days.

Church on the Hill CHURCH
(Biserica din Deal; admission 3 lei; ⏲10am-6pm) A powerfully evocative late-Gothic church is situated high atop 'School Hill' (420m) and is well worth the hike to see the restored interior, with remains of frescoes dating back to the 15th century. The period altarpiece dates from 1520. Entry is via a *scara acoperită* (covered wooden stairway). Opposite the church is a historic German cemetery (open daily from 8am to 8pm).

Sleeping

Pensiune Cristina & Pavel PENSION €
(☎0744-119 211, 0744-159 667; www.pensiuneafaur.ro; Str Cojocarilor 1; dm/s/d 48/90/132 lei;) The floors are so clean at this four-room, one-dorm guesthouse, you could eat your lunch off them. En suite rooms are painted in a soothing off-white, plus there's an idyllic garden bursting with flowers. The dining/self-catering area is welcoming and, should you need it, there's a laundry service.

Burg Hostel HOSTEL €
(☎0265-778 489; www.burghostel.ro; Str Bastionului 4-6; dm 40 lei, s/d without bathroom 70/90 lei, with bathroom 80/95 lei;) Basic Burg is ubiquitously wood-walled with a number of cosy rooms – the triples have the most space. Single rooms are adequate. There's a bar downstairs, plus a pleasant courtyard to read in.

Casa Wagner HOTEL €€
(☎0265-506 014; www.casa-wagner.com; Piaţa Cetăţii 7; s/d/ste 220/260/350 lei;) This appealing 16th-century hotel has 32 rooms spread across three buildings. Think peach walls, candelabra, dark-wood furniture and tasteful rugs. The rooms in the eaves are smaller but wood-floored, cosy and very romantic for writing those Harker-esque diary entries. The ground-floor restaurant occasionally has live music in the evenings.

★ **Casa Georgius Krauss** BOUTIQUE HOTEL €€€
(☎0365-730 840; www.casakrauss.com; Str Bastionului 11; d/ste 300/450 lei;) Dazzling boutique hotel hived out of an old burgher's house at the northern end of the citadel. The lavish restoration left period details like wood-beamed ceilings, wooden floors and, in some rooms, medieval frescoes intact. The Krauss suite, no 2, with wood beams and wall paintings, is a harmonious synthesis of ancient and modern. Good in-house restaurant.

Eating

★ **Central Park** INTERNATIONAL €€
(☎0365-730 006; www.hotelcentralpark.ro; Piaţa Hermann Oberth 25; mains 25-40 lei; ⏲11am-11pm;) Even if you're not staying at the Central Park hotel, plan a meal here. Sighişoara is short on good restaurants and this is the best around. The food is a mix of Romanian and international dishes, and the carefully selected wine list offers the best domestic labels. Dress up for the lavish dining room or relax on the terrace.

Casa Dracula ROMANIAN €€
(☎0265-771 596; www.casavladdracul.ro; Str Cositorarilor 5; mains 30 lei; ⏲11am-11pm;) Despite the ghoulish Dracula bust mounted to the wall, the house where Vlad was born could have been dealt a worse blow than this atmospheric, wood-panelled restaurant. The menu scuttles from tomato soup to salmon fillet – all with Dracula-related references. With a little embellishment from you, your kids will love it.

Information

Cultural Heritage Info Centre (☎0788-115 511; www.dordeduca.ro; Piaţa Muzeului 6; ⏲10am-6pm Tue-Sun) Rents out bikes (10 lei per two hours) and offers guided tours of Sighişoara and the fortified churches as well as DVDs on the same subject. It also has maps of the city and region.

Tourist Information (☎0265-770 415; www.infosighisoara.ro; Str O Goga 8; ⏲10am-6pm Tue-Sat) Private accommodation service masquerading as a tourist information office. Can help find rooms but don't expect anything else.

Getting There & Away

BUS

Next to the train station on Str Libertăţii, the **bus station** (Autogari Sighisoara; ☎0265-771 260; www.autogari.ro; Str Libertăţii 53) sends buses around the country, including to Cluj-Napoca (30 lei, three hours) and Braşov (25 lei, two hours).

TRAIN

Sighişoara is on a main international line and has good train connections. Popular destinations include Braşov (41 lei, two hours), Bucharest (69 lei, five hours) and Cluj-Napoca (62 lei, four hours). You'll need to change trains in Mediaş to reach Sibiu (26 lei, four hours). Three daily trains go to Budapest (150 lei, 11 hours). Buy tickets at the **train station** (☎0265-771 130; www.cfr calatori.ro; Str Libertăţii 51).

Sibiu

POP 137,020

Instantly charming, with a maze of cobbled streets and baroque squares, Romania's cultural first lady has a magic all its own. Composers Franz Liszt and Johann Strauss were drawn here in the 19th century, and in 2007 Sibiu became the first Romanian city to be named an EU Capital of Culture. Most months have myriad things going on, from festivals and exhibitions to theatre and opera. There are plenty of cafes for people-watching in the three main squares.

Sights

Brukenthal Museum MUSEUM
(☎0269-217 691; www.brukenthalmuseum.ro; Piaţa Mare 5; adult/student 20/5 lei; ⊙Tue-Sun 10am-6pm) The most important art museum in this part of the country features separate galleries dedicated to European (1st floor) and Romanian (2nd floor) art. The European collection is heavy on Dutch and German painters, and features at least one masterpiece: Pieter Brueghel the Younger's *The Massacre of Innocents*. The Romanian collection is rich in portraits and landscapes.

Biserica Evanghelică CHURCH
(Evangelical Church; Piaţa Huet; closed for reconstruction) The Gothic church, built from 1300 to 1520, was closed and covered in scaffolding during our research due to long-term renovation. The work should be complete by 2016. Once the church reopens, visitors will again be able to admire the 1772 organ, featuring a staggering 6002 pipes, or climb the **church tower**.

Pharmaceutical Museum MUSEUM
(☎0269-218 191; www.brukenthalmuseum.ro; Piaţa Mică 26; adult/child 10/2.50 lei; ⊙10am-6pm Tue-Sun Apr-Oct, 10am-6pm Wed-Sun Nov-Mar) Housed in the Piaţa Mică pharmacy (opened in 1600), the Pharmaceutical Museum is a three-room collection packed with pills and powders, old microscopes and scary medical instruments. Some exhibits highlight Samuel Hahnemann, a founder of homeopathy in the 1770s.

Astra Museum of Traditional Folk Civilisation MUSEUM
(Muzeul Civilizaţiei Populare Tradiţionale Astra; ☎0269-202 447, reservations 0269-216 453; www.muzeulastra.ro; Str Pădurea Dumbrava 16-20; adult/student 15/7.50 lei; ⊙museum 10am-6pm Tue-Sun, gift shop 9am-5pm Tue-Sun) Five kilometres from the centre, this sprawling open-air museum has a dazzling 120 traditional dwellings, mills and churches brought from around the country and set among two small lakes and a tiny zoological garden. Many are signed in English, with maps showing where the structures came from. There's also a nice gift shop and restaurant with creekside bench seats.

Sleeping

Welt Hostel HOSTEL
(☎0269-700 704; www.weltkultur.ro; Str Nicolea Bălcescu 13; dm 48-53 lei; ⊖@🛜) Centrally located hostel offers Teutonically clean accommodation in four-, six- and eight-bed dorms. The choicest rooms are those toward the street; they are brighter and offer views out toward Piaţa Mare. There's a kitchen for self-caterers, as well as lockers and a friendly chill-out room. Have coffee or wine at the trendy ground-floor cafe.

The Council BOUTIQUE HOTEL €€
(☎0369-452 524; www.thecouncil.ro; Piaţa Mică 31; r standard/deluxe 220/280 lei; ⊖@🛜) Posh boutique hotel occupies a historic 14th-century townhouse that once served as the town hall. Rooms are priced as standard or deluxe, with the latter being larger and usually offering split levels, wood rafters, and better views. All of the rooms are decorated differently, so you might want to look at a few. It's dead central.

Casa Luxemburg HOTEL €€
(☎0269-216 854; www.kultours.ro; Piaţa Mică 16; s/d/tr from 260/290/350 lei; ⊖🛜) Super rooms with parquet flooring, minimal but tasteful furnishings, and well-chosen artwork. There are flat-screen TVs, armoires, bureaus and fresh-looking en suites. Overlooking the Evangelical Church and Piaţa Mică.

Eating

★**Crama Sibiul Vechi** ROMANIAN €€
(☎0269-210 461; www.sibiulvechi.ro; Str A. Papiu Ilarian 3; mains 25-30 lei; ⊙11am-10pm) Hidden in an old wine cellar with its staff dressed in traditional garb, this is the most rustically evocative restaurant in Sibiu. It's certainly the most authentic place to explore Romanian fare such as cheese croquettes, minced

WORTH A TRIP

THE WOODEN CHURCHES OF MARAMUREŞ

North of Transylvania, Maramureş is regarded as Romania's most traditional area, scattered with steepled wooden churches and villagers' homes fronted by ornately carved wooden gates.

Some of the churches date back as far as the 14th century and reflect a time when Orthodox Romanians were forbidden by their Hungarian rulers to build churches in stone. Several of the structures are now Unesco-listed heritage sites.

A good base for exploring this rural charm is the Valea Izei (Izei Valley), accessible by car or bus from **Sighetu Marmaţiei**. The valley follows the Iza River eastward from the city to the village of Ieud and beyond.

The first village, **Vadu Izei**, lies at the confluence of the Iza and Mara Rivers, 6km south of Sighetu Marmaţiei. Its museum is in the oldest house in the village (1750). From Vadu Izei, continue for 12km to **Bârsana**, dating from 1326. In 1720 it built its first church, the interior paintings of which were created by local artists Hodor Toador and Ion Plohod. The famous Orthodox **Bârsana Monastery** (Mănăstirea Bârsana) is a popular pilgrimage spot; however, the church was built only in the 1990s.

Continue south to **Rozavlea**. Its church, dedicated to the archangels Michael and Gabriel, was constructed between 1717 and 1720 in another village and moved to Rozavlea to the site of an ancient church destroyed by Tatars.

From Rozavlea, continue south to the sleepy village of **Botiza**, one of the prettiest in all of Maramureş and site of the some of the region's best homestays. Botiza's old church, built in 1694, is overshadowed by the giant new church, constructed in 1974 to serve devout Orthodox families.

Packed with wooden houses and pensioners in traditional garb, the nearby village of **Ieud** has two beautiful churches, including possibly the region's oldest wooden church.

meatballs and peasant's stew with polenta. Dimly lit, brick walled...welcome to a local treasure.

Weinkeller ROMANIAN €€
(☎0269-210 319; www.weinkeller.ro; Str Turnului 2; mains 18-30 lei; ⏰noon-midnight; 📶) Simple menu of just half-a-dozen main dishes, mixing traditional Romanian cuisine, like stuffed cabbage leaves, with Austro-Hungarian fare like *Tafelspitz* (boiled beef) and goulash. Excellent Nachbil wines pair well with the food. The snug cellar location feels just right on a cool evening.

Drinking & Nightlife

Cafe Wien CAFE
(☎0269-223 223; www.cafewien.ro; Piața Huet 4; ⏰10am-2am Mon, 9am-2am Tue-Sun; 📶) After you've strolled the lovely squares, repair here for your *kaffee und kuchen* (coffee and cake). True to its name, the Wien specialises in Old World sweets, and the view off the terrace to the lower town below is arguably the best in town.

Bohemian Flow Art & Pub BAR
(☎0269-218 388; www.bohemianflow.ro; Piaţa Mică 26; ⏰Mon-Sun 4pm-5am) Lively backstreet cellar club beneath Old Town Hostel, piping out reggae and good vibes for a young crowd.

Entertainment

Philharmonic CLASSICAL MUSIC
(☎tickets 0735-566 486; www.filarmonicasibiu.ro; Str Cetăţii 3-5; tickets 16-20 lei; ⏰box office noon-4pm Mon-Thu) Founded in 1949, this has played a key role in maintaining Sibiu's prestige as a main cultural centre of Transylvania.

Radu Stancu National Theatre THEATRE
(☎tickets 0369-101 578; www.tnrs.ro; B-dul Corneliu Coposu 2; tickets 20 lei) Plays here are usually in Romanian, with occasional productions in German through the week (check the website). It hosts the International Theatre Festival in June. Buy tickets online or at the theatre 30 minutes before performances start.

Information

ATMs are located all over the centre.

Kultours (☎0269-216 854; www.kultours.ro; Piaţa Mică 16; ⏰9am-9pm) Travel agent offering loads of city tours starting at around 40 lei as well as creative day trips and cycling tours, starting at around 90 lei. Helpful staff can hand out maps and advise on what to see and do.

Tourist Information Centre (☎0269-208 913; www.turism.sibiu.ro; Piaţa Mare 2; ⏲9am-5pm Mon-Sat, to 1pm Sun) Based at the City Hall, staff here are fantastically helpful at guiding you to make the best of the city, and cultural events, finding accommodation, and booking train and bus tickets. They also give away an excellent city map.

Getting There & Around

BUS

The **bus station** (Autogara Sibiu; www.autogari.ro; Piaţa 1 Decembrie 1918) is opposite the train station. Bus and maxitaxi services include Braşov (28 lei, 2½ hours, two daily), Bucharest (42 lei, 5½ hours, six daily), Cluj-Napoca (32 lei, 3½ hours, several daily) and Timişoara (55 lei, six hours, three daily).

TRAIN

There are five daily direct trains to Braşov (46 lei, 2½ hours), and two trains to Bucharest (75 lei, six hours) and Timişoara (75 lei, six hours). To get to/from Cluj-Napoca (54 lei, four hours), you'll usually change at Copşa Mică or Mediaş (about nine or 10 trains daily).

The **train station** (Gara Sibiu; ☎0269-211 139; www.cfrcalatori.ro; Piaţa 1 Decembrie 1918, 6) is 2km east of the centre, about 20 minutes on foot.

Cluj-Napoca

POP 305,600

Cluj-Napoca, shortened to 'Cluj' in conversation, isn't as picturesque as its Saxon neighbours, but it's famed for cafes, clubs and student life. Even outside the clubs, Cluj is one of Romania's most energised and welcoming cities.

Sights

St Michael's Church CHURCH
(Biserica Sfantul Mihail; ☎0264-592 089; Piața Unirii; ⏲9am-6pm) The vast 14th-century St Michael's Church dominates Piaţa Unirii. The neo-Gothic tower (1859) topping the Gothic hall church creates a great landmark and the church is considered to be one of the finest examples of Gothic architecture in Romania. Daily services are in Hungarian and Romanian, and evening organ concerts are often held.

The Pharmacy History Collection MUSEUM
(☎0264-595 677; Piaţa Unirii 28; adult/child 5.20/3.10 lei; ⏲10am-4pm Tue-Sun) This tiny museum near the main square can be hit or miss, depending on whether there's an English-speaking guide on hand. Tours are led by a 'pharmacist' in a white lab coat, who points like a game-show model towards (seemingly ho-hum) glass cases of ground mummy dust, medieval alchemist symbols and 18th-century aphrodisiacs.

National Art Museum MUSEUM
(☎0264-596 952; www.macluj.ro; Piaţa Unirii 30; adult/student 8/4 lei; ⏲10am-5pm Wed-Sun) Admittedly a sleepy affair, the museum houses mainly Romanian works from the 19th and 20th centuries – though there are several excellent pieces by Romanian impressionist and war painter Nicolae Grigorescu. The highlight is the setting: the baroque town palace of the noble Bánffy family, which hosted Habsburg Emperor Franz Joseph I on two occasions, in 1852 and 1887.

Fabrica de Pensule ART GALLERY
(Paintbrush Factory; ☎tours 0724-274 040; www.fabricadepensule.ro; Str Henri Barbusse 59-61; ⏲tours 4pm-8pm Mon-Fri) Cluj takes contemporary art seriously and the centre of the action is Fabrica de Pensule, a rehabilitated former paintbrush factory on the outskirts of town (4km east of Piaţa Unirii). The factory house six art galleries, including renowned painter Adrian Ghenie's Plan B. There are stages for concerts, theatre performances and happenings; check the website. Arrange free guided tours in advance by phone or email.

Sleeping

Retro Hostel HOSTEL €
(☎0264-450 452; www.retro.ro; Str Potaissa 13; dm/s/d incl breakfast from 55/100/150 lei; ⊖@🛜) Well-organised, central and with helpful staff, Retro has clean dorms and decent doubles (with TVs and shared baths). There's a pleasant cafe downstairs. Retro also lends out its bikes for free and offers a great choice of guided tours to Maramureş, the nearby Turda Salt Mine and hiking in the Apuseni Mountains.

★ **Hotel Central** HOTEL €€
(☎0264-439 959; www.hotelcentralcluj.ro; Str Victor Babeș 13; s/d/apt 260/300/390 lei; P⊖❄🛜) Midrange travellers will appreciate the value-for-money here at this modern, centrally located hotel, about 10 minutes on foot from Piaţa Unirii. On offer are sleek, air-conditioned rooms (many with separate bedroom and sitting areas). Those on the fifth floor come with roof-top terraces. Decent

breakfast and a few parking spaces out front (call ahead to reserve).

Fullton HOTEL €€

(☎0264-597 898; www.fullton.ro; Str Sextil Puşcariu 10; s 175-215 lei, d 200-240 lei;) This boutique hotel with a pea-green facade has a great location in the old town and a couple of places to park. Rooms are fragrant and fresh and have individual colour schemes, bureaus and en suites. Some, such as room 101, have four-poster beds. There's also a welcoming patio bar.

Eating

Camino INTERNATIONAL €€

(☎0749-200 117; Piaţa Muzeului 4; mains 20-30 lei; ⏲9am-midnight;) With jazz piping through its peeling arched interior decked in candelabra and threadbare rugs, this boho restaurant is perfect for solo book-reading jaunts or romantic dinner alfresco. Its homemade pasta is delicious, the salads and tapas full of zing. Breakfasts, too.

★**Bricks – (M)eating Point Restaurant** STEAKHOUSE €€€

(☎0364-730 615; www.bricksrestaurant.ro; Str Horea 2; mains 40-60 lei; ⏲11am-11pm;) Bricks has risen from the ashes of a men's drinking den to become a chi chi urban bistro. Shaded rattan chairs look out across the river, while the menu excels with plenty of grilled dishes, some vegie numbers, oriental cuisine, salads, and the best grilled rib-eye we've ever had in Romania. Excellent wine list.

Drinking & Nightlife

Cluj excels at cafes and clubs. Many of the best are clustered around a quiet square north of Piaţa Unirii called Piaţa Muzeului.

Casa Jazz BAR, LIVE MUSIC

(☎0720-944 251; Str Vasile Goldiş 2; ⏲noon-2am) With its oxblood walls ornamented with Rat Pack prints and antique trumpets, and Armstrong and Gillespie jumping on the speakers, this smoky joint is a slice of New Orleans. There are piano evenings and exhibitions, too.

Joben Bistro CAFE

(☎0720-222 800; http://joben.ro; Str Avram Iancu 29; ⏲8am-2am Mon-Thu, noon-2am Fri-Sun;) Joben Bistro is another themed cafe. This time the idea is 'steampunk'. The brick walls are artfully decorated with the flotsam of heavy industry, including cogs, levers, pulleys and clocks. The ginger-infused lemonade is a summertime winner, as is the coffee. Very good light bites, like soups and salads, on hand as well.

☆ Entertainment

National Theatre THEATRE

(Teatrul Naţional Cluj-Napoca; ☎tickets 0264-595 363; www.teatrulnationalcluj.ro; Piaţa Ştefan cel Mare 2-4; tickets from 15 lei; ⏲box office 11am-2pm & 3pm-5pm Tue-Sun) The National Theatre was designed in the 19th century by the famed Habsburg architects Fellner and Hellmer; performances are well attended. The **opera** is in the same building. Buy tickets at the nearby **box office** (Piaţa Ştefan cel Mare 14).

Flying Circus Pub CLUB

(☎0758-022 924; www.flyingcircus.ro; Str Iuliu Maniu 2; ⏲5pm-dawn;) The best of a number of student-oriented dance clubs scattered around the centre. They open at 5pm, but don't expect anything to happen until after 11pm.

Information

There are many banks and ATMs scattered around the centre.

Tourist Information Office (☎0264-452 244; www.visitcluj.ro; B-dul Eroilor 6-8; ⏲8.30am-6pm Mon-Fri, 10am-6pm Sat) Run by two proactive guys named Marius, this super-friendly office has bags of info on trekking, train and bus times, eating, accommodation and cultural sights and events.

Getting There & Around

BUS

Buses generally leave from **Autogara 2** (Autogara Beta; ☎0264-455 249; www.autogari.ro; Str Giordano Bruno 1-3), 300m northwest of the train station. Popular destinations include Braşov (60 lei, five hours, two daily), Bucharest (90 lei, eight hours, three daily) and Sibiu (34 lei, 3½ hours, eight daily).

TRAIN

Cluj has decent train connections around the country. Sample destinations include two daily direct trains to Bucharest (94 lei, 10 hours), three to Braşov (76 lei, seven hours) and two to Sighişoara (62 lei, four hours). Change at Teiuş or Mediaş for Sibiu (53 lei, five hours).

The **train station** (☎0264-592 952; www.cfrcalatori.ro; Piaţa Gării 2-3) is 1km north of the centre, a straight shot along Str Horea (10-minute walk). Buy tickets at the station or in town at the **Agenţia de Voiaj CFR** (☎0264-432 001; www.cfrcalatori.ro; Piaţa Mihai Viteazul 20;

WORTH A TRIP

PAINTED MONASTERIES OF SOUTHERN BUCOVINA

The painted monasteries of southern Bucovina are among the greatest artistic monuments of eastern Europe. In 1993 they were collectively designated a Unesco World Heritage Site.

Erected in the 15th and 16th centuries, when Moldavia was threatened by Turkish invaders, the monasteries were surrounded by strong defensive walls. Biblical stories were portrayed on the church walls in colourful pictures so that illiterate worshippers could better understand them.

The most impressive collection of monasteries is located west of Suceava. It includes the Humor, Voroneţ and Moldoviţa Monasteries.

The **Humor Monastery** (Mănăstirea Humorului; Gura Humorului; adult/student 5/2 lei; ⏲8am-7pm summer, to 4pm winter), built in 1530 and situated near the town of Gura Humorului, boasts arguably the most impressive interior frescoes.

Also not far from Gura Humorului, the **Voroneţ Monastery** (Mănăstirea Voroneţ; ☎0741-612 529; Voroneț, Gura Humorului; adult/child 5/2 lei; ⏲8am-7pm summer, to 4pm winter) is the only one to have a specific colour associated with it. 'Voroneţ Blue', a vibrant cerulean colour created from lapis lazuli and other ingredients, is prominent in its frescoes. The monastery was built in just three months and three weeks by Ştefan cel Mare following a key 1488 victory over the Turks.

Moldoviţa Monastery (Mânăstirea Moldovița; Vatra Moldoviței; adult/student 5/2 lei; ⏲8am-7pm summer, to 4pm winter) 35km northwest of the Voroneţ Monastery, occupies a fortified quadrangular enclosure with tower, gates and flowery lawns. The central painted church has been partly restored, and features impressive frescoes from 1537, although the monastery dates from 1532.

The main gateway to the monasteries is **Suceava**, which is reachable by direct train from both Bucharest (94 lei, seven hours, one daily) and Cluj-Napoca (75 lei, seven hours, four daily). By car, it's possible to see all the monasteries in a long day trip; alternatively, there are guesthouses along the way in which to stay the night.

⏲domestic tickets 8am-8pm Mon-Fri, international 8.30am-3.30pm Mon, Wed & Fri, 1-8pm Tue & Thu).

BANAT

Western Romania, with its geographic and cultural ties to neighbouring Hungary and Serbia, and historical links to the Austro-Hungarian Empire, enjoys an ethnic diversity that much of the country lacks. Timişoara, the regional hub, has a nationwide reputation as a beautiful and lively metropolis, and for a series of 'firsts'. It was the world's first city to adopt electric street lights (in 1884) and, more importantly, the first city to rise up against dictator Nicolae Ceauşescu in 1989.

Timişoara

POP 312,000

Romania's third- or fourth-largest city (depending on the source) is also one of the country's most attractive urban areas, built around a series of beautiful public squares and lavish parks and gardens. It's known as Primul Oraş Liber (First Free Town), for it was here that anti-Ceauşescu protests first exceeded the Securitate's capacity for violent suppression in 1989, eventually sending Ceauşescu and his wife to their demise.

Sights

Piaţa Unirii

Piaţa Unirii is Timişoara's most picturesque square, featuring the imposing sight of the Catholic and Serbian Orthodox **churches** facing each other.

★**Permanent Exhibition of the 1989 Revolution** MUSEUM
(☎0256-294 936; www.memorialulrevolutiei.ro; Str Popa Sapcă 3-5; admission by donation; ⏲8am-4pm Mon-Fri, 9am-1pm Sat) This work in progress is an ideal venue to brush up on the December 1989 anticommunist revolution that began in Timişoara. Displays include documentation, posters and photography from those fateful days, capped by a graphic 20-minute video

WORTH A TRIP

DANUBE DELTA

After passing through several countries and absorbing countless waterways, the Danube River empties into the Black Sea just south of the Ukrainian border.

The Danube Delta (Delta Dunării), included on Unesco's World Heritage list, is one of Romania's leading attractions. At the inland port of Tulcea, the river splits into three separate channels: the Chilia, Sulina and Sfântu Gheorghe, creating a constantly evolving 4187-sq-km wetland of marshes, floating reed islets and sandbars. There are beautiful, secluded beaches at Sulina and Sfântu Gheorghe, and the seafood, particularly the fish soup served in restaurants and pension kitchens throughout the region, is the best in Romania.

For many visitors, the main drawcard is **birdwatching**. The delta is a major migration hub for tens of thousands of birds, with the best viewing times being spring and late autumn.

Much of the delta is under the protection of the **Danube Delta Biosphere Reserve Authority** (DDBRA; ☎0240-518 924; www.ddbra.ro; Str Portului 34a; permits per day 5 lei; ⊙9am-4pm Mon-Fri), headquartered in Tulcea. All visitors to protected areas are required to purchase an entry permit at the Danube Delta Biosphere Reserve Authority office. Permits are available for a day or a week.

There is no rail service in the delta and few paved roads, meaning the primary mode of transport is by ferry. The main ferry operator is state-owned **Navrom** (☎0240-511 553; www.navromdelta.ro; Str Portului 26; ⊙ticket office 11.30am-1.30pm). It runs both traditional 'slow' ferries and faster hydrofoils from Tulcea's main port to major points in the delta.

The ferry schedule can be confusing. The helpful staff at the **Tourism Information Centre** (☎0240-519 130; www.primariatulcea.ro; Str Gării 26; ⊙8am-4pm Mon-Fri) can help piece together a journey, depending on your time and budget.

(not suitable for young children) with English subtitles. Enter from Str Oituz.

Art Museum MUSEUM
(Muzeul de Artă; ☎0256-491 592; www.muzeuldeartatm.ro; Piaţa Unirii 1; admission 10 lei; ⊙10am-6pm Tue-Sun) The museum displays a representative sample of paintings and visual arts over the centuries as well as regular, high-quality temporary exhibitions. It's housed in the baroque **Old Prefecture Palace**, built in 1754, which is worth a look inside for the graceful interiors alone.

Piaţa Victoriei

Piaţa Victoriei is a beautifully green pedestrian mall dotted with fountains and lined on both sides with shops and cafes. The square's northern end is marked by the 18th-century National Theatre & Opera House, where thousands of demonstrators gathered on 16 December 1989.

Banat History Museum MUSEUM
(Muzeul Banatului; Piaţa Huniades 1) Housed in the historic Huniades Palace, the museum was closed at the time of research for renovations expected to last until 2016. The exterior of the palace, though, is still worth a look. The origins of the building date to the 14th century and to Hungarian king Charles Robert, Prince of Anjou.

Metropolitan Cathedral CHURCH
(Catedrala Ortodoxă; www.mitropolia-banatului.ro; B-dul Regele Ferdinand I; ⊙10am-6pm) The Orthodox cathedral was built between 1936 and 1946. It's unique for its Byzantine-influenced architecture, which recalls the style of the Bucovina monasteries.

Sleeping

★**Hostel Costel** HOSTEL €
(☎0356-262 487; www.hostel-costel.ro; Str Petru Sfetca 1; dm 40-45 lei, d 135 lei; @) Run by affable staff, this charming 1920s art nouveau villa is the city's best hostel. The vibe is relaxed and congenial. There are three dorm rooms and one private double, plus ample chill rooms and a big garden. The hostel is 1km east of the centre, across the Bega Canal near the Decebal Bridge; take tram 1.

Pension Casa Leone PENSION €
(☎0256-292 621; www.casaleone.ro; B-dul Eroilor de la Tisa 67; s/d/tr 125/150/200 lei; P) This lovely seven-room pension offers exceptional service and individually decorated rooms. To

find it, take tram 8 from the train station, alight at Deliblata station and walk one block northeast to B-dul Eroilor (or call ahead to arrange transport).

★**Pensiunea Park** PENSION €€
(☎0356-264 039; www.pensiuneapark.ro; Str Remus 17; s/d/ste 170/220/250 lei; P⊖❄📶) Small, family-owned hotel in an old villa on a leafy side street, about 10 minutes' walk from Piaţa Victoriei. Lots of period touches, including beautiful chandeliers and fixtures in the hallways, though the rooms themselves are modestly furnished. There's a small terrace in the back for morning coffee and bikes to ride for free during your stay.

Eating

★**Casa Bunicii** ROMANIAN €€
(☎0356-100 870; www.casa-bunicii.ro; Str Virgil Onitiu 3; mains 20-35 lei; 👪) The names translates to 'Granny's House' and indeed this casual, family-friendly restaurant specialises in home cooking and regional specialities from the Banat. The duck soup and grilled chicken breast served in sour cherry sauce come recommended.

Casa cu Flori ROMANIAN €€
(☎0256-435 080; www.casacuflori.ro; Str Alba Iulia 1; mains 18-28 lei) One of the best-known restaurants in the city and for good reason. Excellent high-end Romanian cooking with refined service at moderate prices. In nice weather, climb three flights to the flower-lined rooftop terrace.

Drinking & Nightlife

Scârţ loc lejer CAFE
(☎0751-892 340; Str Zoe 1; ⊙10am-11pm Mon-Fri, 11am-11pm Sat, 2-11pm Sun; 📶) Old villa that's been retrofitted into a funky coffeehouse with albums pinned to the wall and chill tunes on the turntable. There are several cosy rooms in which to read and relax, but our favourite is the garden out back, with shady nooks and even hammocks for stretching out. Located about 1km south of the city centre.

La Căpiţe BEER GARDEN
(☎0720-400 333; www.lacapite.ro; B-dul Vasile Pârvan; ⊙10am-midnight Sun-Thu & 10am-4am Fri & Sat May-Oct; 📶) Shaggy riverside beer garden and alternative hangout is strategically located across the street from the university, ensuring lively crowds on warm summer evenings. Most nights bring live music or DJs. The name translates as 'haystack', and bales of hay strewn everywhere make for comfy places to sit and chill.

Aethernativ CAFE
(☎0724-012 324; Str Mărăşeşti 14; ⊙10am-1am Mon-Fri, noon-1am Sat, 5pm-1am Sun; 📶) This trendy art club, cafe and bar occupies a courtyard of a run-down building two blocks west of Piaţa Unirii and has eclectic furnishings and an alternative, student vibe. There are no signs to let you know you're here; simply find the address, push open the door and walk up a flight of stairs.

Entertainment

State Philharmonic Theatre CLASSICAL MUSIC
(Filharmonica de Stat Banatul; ☎0256-492 521; www.filarmonicabanatul.ro; B-dul CD Loga 2; ⊙box office 2-7pm Tue & Thu, 10am-2pm Mon, Wed & Fri) Classical concerts are held most evenings here. Tickets (from 40 lei) can be bought at the box office inside the theatre and one hour before performances.

National Theatre & Opera House THEATRE, OPERA
(Teatrul Naţional şi Opera Română; ☎opera 0256-201 286, theatre 0256-499 908; www.tntimisoara.com; Str Mărăşeşti 2; ⊙box office 10am-1pm, 5pm-7pm) The National Theatre & Opera House features both dramatic works and classical opera, and is highly regarded. Buy tickets (from around 40 lei) at the box office, but note that most of the dramatic works will be in Romanian.

Information

Internet Cafe (B-dul Mihai Eminescu 5; per hr 6 lei; ⊙24hr; 📶)

Timişoara County Hospital (Spitalul Clinic Judeţean de Urgenţă Timişoara; ☎0356-433 111; www.hosptm.ro; B-dul Iosif Bulbuca 10) Modern hospital, located 2km south of the centre, with 24-hour emergency service.

Tourist Information Centre (Info Centru Turistic; ☎0256-437 973; www.timisoara-info.ro; Str Alba Iulia 2) This great tourism office can assist with accommodation and trains, and provide maps and Banat regional info.

Getting There & Away

BUS

Buses and minibuses are privately operated and depart from several points around the city. Consult the website www.autogari.ro for departure points. Bus service is extensive. Sample fares include Cluj-Napoca (65 lei) and Sibiu (45 lei).

International buses leave from the **East bus station**. Main international operators include **Atlassib** (☎ call centre 0269-229 224, local office 0256-226 485; www.atlassib.ro; Str Gheorghe Lazăr 27) and **Eurolines** (☎ 0256-288 132; www.eurolines.ro; Str M Kogălniceanu 20). Belgrade-based **Gea Tours** (☎ 0316-300 257; www.geatours.rs) offers daily minibus service between Timişoara and Belgrade for one way/return 90/180 lei. Book over the website.

TRAIN

Trains depart from **Gara Timişoara-Nord** (Gara Timişoara-Nord; ☎ 0256-200 457; www.cfrcalatori.ro; Str Gării 2), the 'northern' station, west of the centre. Daily express trains include two to Bucharest (105 lei, nine hours) and two to Cluj-Napoca (75 lei, six hours).

COUNTRY FACTS

Area 237,500 sq km

Capital Bucharest

Country code ☎ 40

Currency Romanian leu

Emergency ☎ 112

Language Romanian

Money ATMs are abundant

Population 20 million

Visas Not required for citizens of the EU, USA, Canada, Australia, and New Zealand

SURVIVAL GUIDE

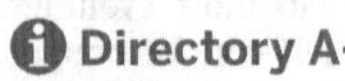

Directory A–Z

ACCOMMODATION

Romania has a wide choice of accommodation to suit most budgets, including hotels, pensions and private rooms, hostels and camping grounds. Prices are generally lower than in Western Europe.

Budget properties include hostels, camping grounds and cheaper guesthouses. Midrange accommodation includes three-star hotels and pensions. Top-end means fancy hotels, corporate chains and boutiques.

BUSINESS HOURS

Banks 9am to noon and 1pm to 5pm Monday to Friday

Clubs 8pm to 3am

Restaurants 10am to 11pm

Shops 10am to 6pm Monday to Friday, 10am to 5pm Saturday

GAY & LESBIAN TRAVELLERS

Public attitudes towards homosexuality remain relatively negative. In spite of this, Romania has made significant progress in decriminalising homosexual acts and adopting antidiscrimination laws.

- Bucharest remains the most tolerant city, though here too gay couples should refrain from open displays of affection.
- Bucharest-based **Accept Romania** (☎ 021-252 9000; www.accept-romania.ro) organises a six-day Bucharest Pride Festival in early summer.

SLEEPING PRICE RANGES

The following price categories are for the cost of a double room:

€ less than 150 lei

€€ 150 lei to 300 lei

€€€ more than 300 lei

INTERNET RESOURCES

Romanian National Tourist Office (www.romaniatourism.com)

Bucharest Life (www.bucharestlife.net)

Bus Timetable (www.autogari.ro)

Train Timetable (www.cfrcalatori.ro)

MONEY

The currency is the leu (plural: lei), noted in this guide as 'lei'. One leu is divided into 100 bani. Banknotes come in denominations of 1, 5, 10, 50, 100, 200 and 500 lei. Coins come in 50 and 10 bani.

- Romania is a member of the European Union, but the euro is not used here.
- ATMs are nearly everywhere and give 24-hour withdrawals in lei on a variety of international bank cards. Romanian ATMs require a four-digit PIN.
- The best place to exchange money is at a bank. You can also change money at a private exchange booth (*casa de schimb*), but be wary of commission charges.
- International credit and debit cards are widely accepted at hotels, restaurants and shops in cities. In rural areas, you'll need cash.

PUBLIC HOLIDAYS

New Year 1 and 2 January

Orthodox Easter Monday April/May

Labour Day 1 May

Pentecost May/June, 50 days after Easter Sunday

Assumption of Mary 15 August
Feast of St Andrew 30 November
Romanian National Day 1 December
Christmas 25 and 26 December

TELEPHONE

Romania has a modern telephone network of landlines and mobile phones. The country code is ☎40.

- All Romanian numbers have 10 digits, consisting of a ☎0, plus a city code and number. Mobile phone numbers are identified by a three-digit prefix starting with ☎7.
- Romanian mobiles use the GSM 900/1800 network, the standard throughout Europe as well as in Australia and New Zealand, but not compatible with mobile phones in North America or Japan.
- To reduce expensive roaming fees, buy a prepaid local SIM card from one of Romania's three main carriers: **Vodafone** (www.vodafone.ro), **Cosmote** (www.cosmote.ro) and **Orange** (www.orange.ro).
- Public phones require a magnetic-stripe phonecard bought at post offices and newspaper kiosks. Phonecard rates start at about 10 lei.

VISAS

Citizens of EU countries do not need visas to visit Romania and can stay indefinitely. Citizens of the USA, Canada, Australia, New Zealand, Israel, Japan and some other countries can stay for 90 days without a visa. Other nationalities check with the **Ministry of Foreign Affairs** (www.mae.ro).

Getting There & Away

AIR

Romania has good air connections to Europe and the Middle East. At the time of research there were no direct flights to Romania from North America or Southeast Asia.

Airports

The majority of international flights to Romania arrive at Bucharest's **Henri Coandă International Airport** (OTP/Otopeni; ☎021-204 1000; www.bucharestairports.ro; Şos Bucureşti-Ploieşti).

Other cities with international airports:

Cluj Avram Iancu International Airport (CLJ; ☎0264-307 500, 0264-416 702; www.airportcluj.ro; Str Traian Vuia 149-151)

Sibiu International Airport (SBZ; ☎0269-253 135; www.sibiuairport.ro; Şos Alba Iulia 73)

Timişoara Traian Vuia International Airport (TSR; ☎0256-386 089; www.aerotim.ro; Str Aeroport 2, Ghiroda)

LAND

The main train corridor to Romania from Western Europe passes through Budapest, and three trains daily make the slog down to Bucharest, via Braşov, and back. The western city of Timişoara has excellent train, bus and air connections throughout Europe. By road, the main entry points from the west are at Arad and Oradea.

Romania shares borders with five countries: Bulgaria, Hungary, Moldova, Serbia and Ukraine. It has four car-ferry crossings with Bulgaria. Highway border posts are normally open 24 hours, though smaller crossings may only be open from 8am to 8pm.

Romania is not a member of the EU's common border and customs Schengen Zone, meaning you'll have to show valid passport (and visa, if required) at the border.

Bus

Long-haul bus service remains a popular way of travelling from Romania to Western Europe, as well as to parts of southeastern Europe and Turkey. Bus travel is comparable in price to train travel, but can be faster.

Bus services to and from Western Europe are dominated by **Eurolines** (www.eurolines.ro) and **Atlassib** (☎0740-104 446, 021-420 3665; www.atlassib.ro; Soseaua Alexandriei 164). Both maintain vast networks from cities throughout Europe to destinations all around Romania. Check the websites for latest schedules and prices.

Car & Motorcycle

Ensure your documents (personal ID, car insurance and car registration) are in order before crossing into Romania.

Train

Romania is integrated into the European rail grid with decent connections to Western Europe and neighbouring countries. Trains arrive at and depart from Bucharest's main station, Gara de Nord (p919).

Budapest is the main rail gateway from Western Europe. There are three daily direct trains between Budapest and Bucharest (13 hours), with regular onward direct connections from Budapest to Prague, Munich and Vienna.

EATING PRICE RANGES

The following price categories are for the cost of a main course:

€ less than 15 lei

€€ 15 lei to 30 lei

€€€ more than 30 lei

ESSENTIAL FOOD & DRINK

Romanian food borrows heavily from its neighbours, including Turkey, Hungary and the Balkans, and is centred on pork and other meats. Farm-fresh, organically grown fruits and vegetables are in abundance, lending flavour and colour to a long list of soups and salads. Condiments typically include sour cream, garlic sauce and grated sheep's cheese, used to flavour everything from soup to the most common side dish: polenta.

- **Mămăligă** Cornmeal mush, sometimes topped with sour cream or cheese.
- **Ciorbă** Sour soup that's a mainstay of the Romanian diet.
- **Sarmale** Spiced meat wrapped in cabbage or grape leaves.
- **Covrigi** Oven-baked pretzels served warm from windows around town.
- **Ţuică** Fiery plum brandy sold in water bottles at roadside rest stops.

Getting Around

AIR

Given the poor state of the roads, flying between cities is feasible if time is a concern. The Romanian national carrier **Tarom** (☎021-204 6464; www.tarom.ro) operates a comprehensive network of domestic routes. The airline flies regularly between Bucharest and Cluj-Napoca, Iaşi, Oradea, and Timişoara.

BUS

A mix of buses and maxitaxis form the backbone of the national transport system. If you understand how the system works, you can move around easily and cheaply, but finding updated information without local help can be tough. The website www.autogari.ro is a helpful online timetable.

CAR & MOTORCYCLE

Roads are crowded and in poor condition. There are only a few stretches of motorway *(autostrada)*, meaning most travel is along two-lane national highways *(drum naţional)* or secondary roads. When calculating travel times, figure on 50km per hour.

Western-style petrol stations are plentiful. A litre of unleaded 95 octane costs about 6.20 lei. Most stations accept credit cards.

Road Rules

- Blood-alcohol limit: 0.00
- Seatbelts: compulsory
- Headlights: on day and night
- Speed limits: 90km/h on major roads, 50km/h in town

LOCAL TRANSPORT

Romanian cities have good public transportation systems. Bucharest is the only city with a metro. The method for accessing the systems is broadly similar. Purchase tickets at street kiosks marked *bilete* or *casă de bilete* before boarding and validate the ticket once aboard. For maxitaxis, buy the ticket from the driver.

Taxis

Taxis are cheap and a useful supplement to the public transport systems. Drivers are required by law to post rates on windscreens. The going rate varies but runs from 1.39 to 1.89 lei per kilometre. Any driver posting a higher fare is likely a rip-off.

TRAIN

The extensive network covers much of the country, including most of the main tourist sights. The national rail system is run by **Căile Ferate Române** (CFR | Romanian State Railways; www.cfr.ro). Romania has three types of trains that travel at different speeds. InterCity, listed as 'IC' on timetables, are the most expensive and most comfortable.

Buy tickets at station windows, specialised Agenţia de Voiaj CFR ticket offices or online at www.cfrcalatori.ro.

Russia

Includes ➡

Best Places to Eat

- ➡ Delicatessen (p943)
- ➡ Varenichnaya No 1 (p943)
- ➡ Duo Gastrobar (p953)
- ➡ Yat (p953)

Best Places to Stay

- ➡ Hotel Metropol (p943)
- ➡ Blues Hotel (p943)
- ➡ Soul Kitchen Hostel (p953)
- ➡ Rachmaninov Antique Hotel (p953)

Why Go?

Could there be a more iconic image of eastern Europe than the awe-inspiring architectural ensemble of Moscow's Red Square? The brash, exciting and oil-rich capital of Russia (Россия) is a must on any trip to the region.

St Petersburg, on the Baltic coast, is another stunner. The former imperial capital is still Russia's most beautiful and alluring city, with its grand Italianate mansions, wending canals and enormous Neva River. Also make time for Veliky Novgorod, home to an ancient stone fortress and many fresco-decorated churches. Emulating the tourist-friendly nature of its Baltic neighbours is little Kaliningrad, wedged between Poland and Lithuania on the Baltic Sea. It's a fascinating destination, combining all the best elements of its enormous mother.

Visa red tape deters many travellers from visiting – don't let it keep you from experiencing the incredible things to see and do in the European part of the world's largest country.

When to Go

Moscow

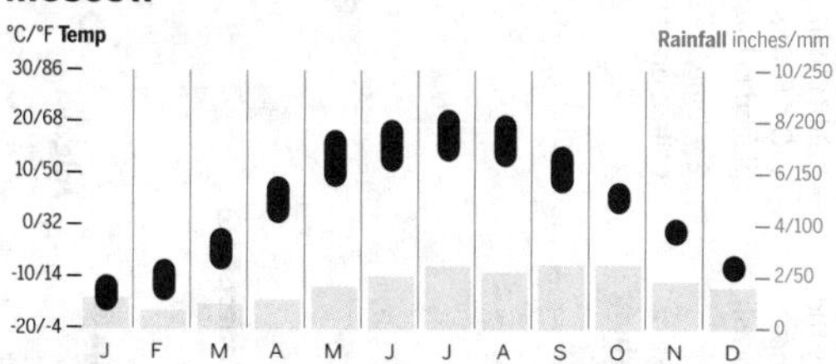

May Big military parades and a public holiday mark the end of WWII.

Jun & Jul Party during St Petersburg's White Nights, and bask on the beaches of Kaliningrad.

Dec & Jan Snow makes Moscow and St Petersburg look magical, while hotel rates drop.

Russia Highlights

1. Be awe-inspired by the massive scale and riches of **Moscow**, Russia's brash, energetic capital.
2. Take a walking, bike or boat tour of **St Petersburg** (p948), an Italianate slice of Old Europe incongruously placed in Russia.
3. Ogle the seemingly endless collection of masterpieces in St Petersburg's unrivalled **State Hermitage Museum** (p949).
4. Take a day trip out of St Petersburg to see the imperial country estates at **Petrodvorets** and **Tsarskoe Selo** (p954).
5. Trace Russia's roots back to **Veliky Novgorod** (p946) with its well-preserved kremlin and many picturesque churches.
6. Explore **Kaliningrad** (p956), once part of the Prussian empire, and home to the pristine beaches of the Kurshskaya Kosa National Park.

ITINERARIES

One Week

In **Moscow**, touring the Kremlin and Red Square will take up one day, viewing the spectacular collections at the Tretyakov, New Tretyakov and Pushkin art museums another. On day three size up the magnificent Novodevichy Convent, and the revamped Gorky Park. Take the night train to **Veliky Novgorod** and spend a day exploring its ancient kremlin and churches. The rest of the week is reserved for splendid **St Petersburg**. Wander up Nevsky pr, see Dvortsovaya pl, and spend a half-day at the Hermitage. Tour the canals and the mighty Neva River by boat. Visit Peter & Paul Fortress, the Church of the Saviour on Spilled Blood and the wonderful Russian Museum.

Two Weeks

With two extra days in Moscow, sweat it out in the luxurious Sanduny Baths or do a metro tour. In St Petersburg, spend more time in the Hermitage and other museums, and tack on an excursion to **Petrodvorets** or **Tsarskoe Selo**. Then fly to **Kaliningrad**. Admire the capital's reconstructed Gothic Cathedral and wander along the river to the excellent World Ocean Museum. Enjoy either the old Prussian charm of the spa town of **Svetlogorsk** or the sand dunes and forests of the **Kurshskaya Kosa National Park**.

Moscow Москва

495 & 499 / POP 11.5 MILLION

Intimidating in its scale, but also exciting and unforgettable, Moscow is a place that inspires extreme passion or loathing. History, power and wild capitalism hang in the air alongside an explosion of creative energy throwing up edgy art galleries and a dynamic restaurant, bar and nightlife scene.

The sturdy stone walls of the Kremlin, the apex of Russian political power and once the centre of the Orthodox Church, occupy the city's founding site on the northern bank of the Moscow River. Remains of the Soviet state, such as Lenin's Tomb, are nearby in Red Square and elsewhere in the city which radiates from the Kremlin in a series of ring roads.

Sights

The Kremlin & Red Square

Covering Borovitsky Hill on the north bank of the Moscow River, the **Kremlin** (Кремль; www.kreml.ru; adult/student R350/100; 10am-5pm Fri-Wed, ticket office 9.30am-4.30pm Fri-Wed; M Aleksandrovsky Sad) is enclosed by high walls 2.25km long, with Red Square outside the east wall. The best views of the complex are from Sofiyskaya nab across the river.

Before entering the Kremlin, deposit bags at the **left-luggage office** (per bag R60; 9am-6.30pm Fri-Wed), beneath the Kutafya Tower. The main ticket office is in the Alexandrovsky Garden. The entrance ticket covers admission to all five of the church-museums, and the Patriarch's Palace. It does not include the Armoury, the Diamond Fund Exhibition or special exhibits, which are priced separately.

From the Kutafya Tower, walk up the ramp and pass through the Kremlin walls beneath the **Trinity Gate Tower** (Троицкая надвратная башня). The lane to the right (south) passes the striking 17th-century **Poteshny Palace** (Потешный дворец), where Stalin lived. The horribly out of place glass-and-concrete **State Kremlin Palace** (Государственный Кремлевский Дворец) houses a concert and ballet auditorium, where many Western pop stars play when they are in Moscow.

Photography is not permitted inside the Armoury or any of the buildings on Sobornaya pl (Cathedral Sq).

★Armoury MUSEUM

(Оружейная палата; adult/student R700/250; 10am, noon, 2.30pm & 4.30pm; M Aleksandrovsky Sad) The Armoury dates back to 1511, when it was founded under Vasily III to manufacture and store weapons, imperial arms and regalia for the royal court. Later it also produced jewellery, icon frames and embroidery. To this day, the Armoury still contains plenty of treasures for ogling, and remains a highlight of any visit to the Kremlin. If possible, buy your time-specific ticket to the Armoury when you buy your ticket to the Kremlin.

Central Moscow

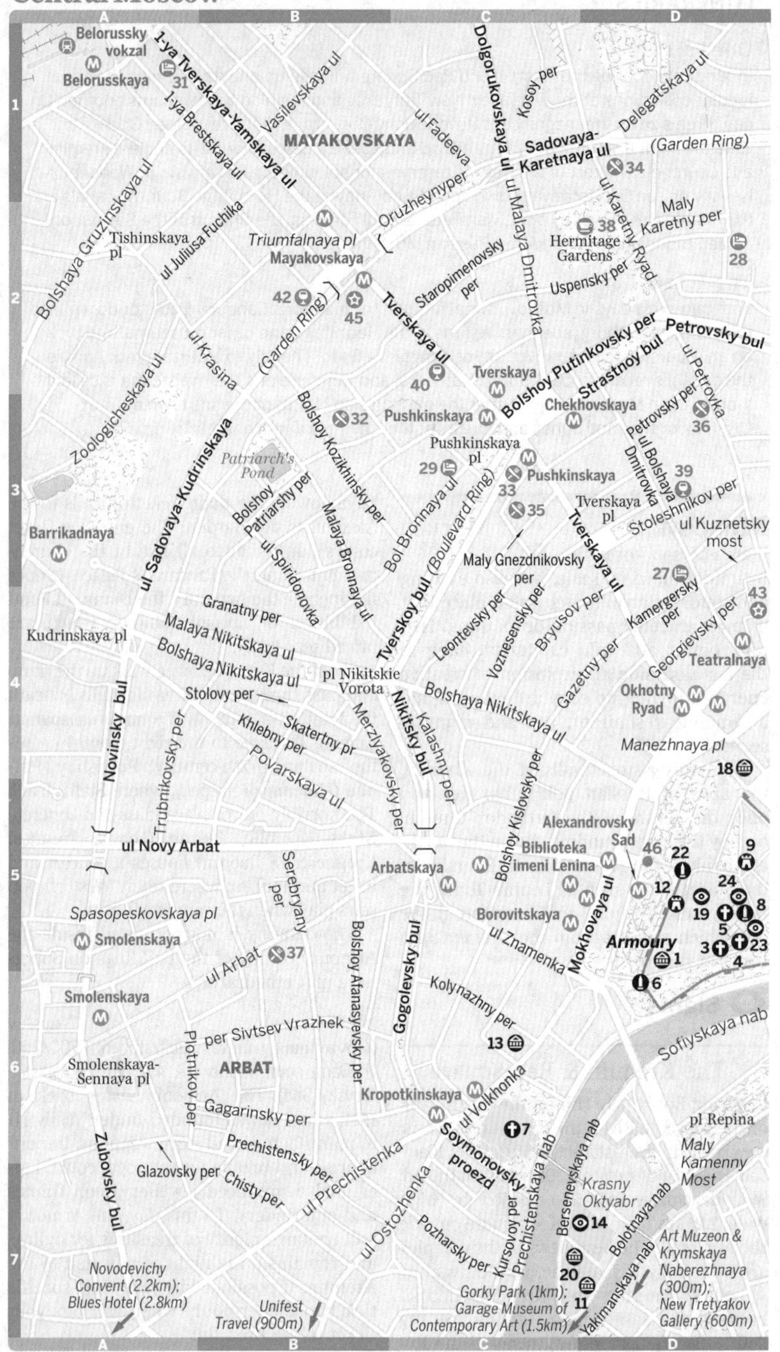

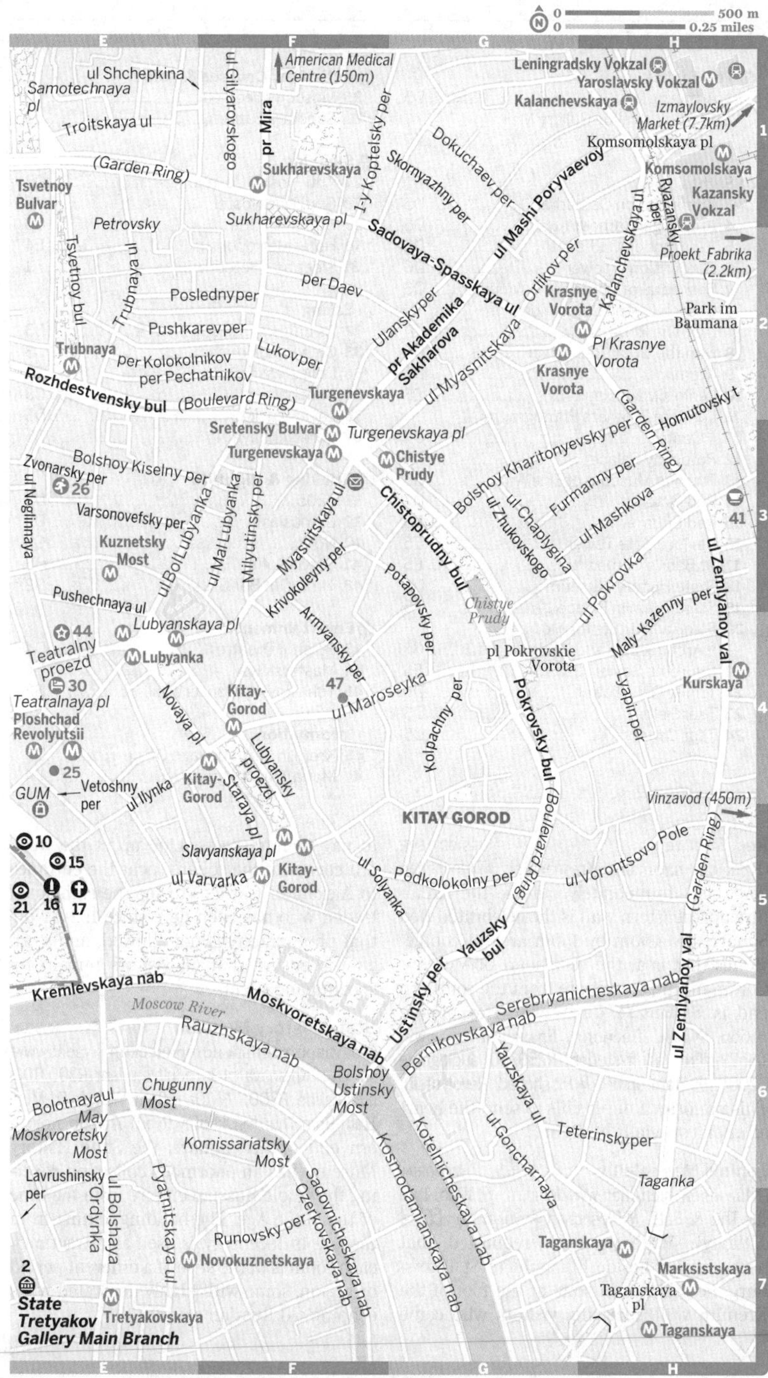
0 500 m
0 0.25 miles
E
F
G
H
1
2
3
4
5
6
7
ul Shchepkina
Samotechnaya pl
ul Gilyarovskogo
American Medical Centre (150m)
pr Mira
Troitskaya ul
(Garden Ring)
Sukharevskaya
1-y Koptelsky per
Skornyazhny per
Dokuchaev per
Leningradsky Vokzal
Yaroslavsky Vokzal
Kalanchevskaya
Izmaylovsky Market (7.7km)
Komsomolskaya pl
Komsomolskaya
Kazansky Vokzal
Ryazansky per
Kalanchevskaya ul
ul Mashi Poryvaevoy
Tsvetnoy Bulvar
Petrovsky
Sukharevskaya pl
Sadovaya-Spasskaya ul
Proekt_Fabrika (2.2km)
Tsvetnoy bul
Trubnaya ul
Posledny per
per Daev
Orlikov per
Krasnye Vorota
Park im Baumana
Pushkarev per
Ulansky per
pr Akademika Sakharova
Trubnaya
Lukov per
Pl Krasnye Vorota
per Kolokolnikov
per Pechatnikov
ul Myasnitskaya
Krasnye Vorota
Rozhdestvensky bul
(Boulevard Ring)
Turgenevskaya
(Garden Ring)
Homutovsky t
Sretensky Bulvar
Turgenevskaya pl
Turgenevskaya
Chistye Prudy
Bolshoy Kharitonyevsky per
Zvonarsky per
Bolshoy Kiselny per
26
Furmanny per
ul Neglinnaya
ul Bol Lubyanka
ul Mal Lubyanka
Milyutinsky per
Myasnitskaya ul
Chistoprudny bul
ul Zhukovskogo
ul Chaplygina
ul Mashkova
41
Varsonovefsky per
Kuznetsky Most
Krivokoleyny per
Potapovsky per
ul Zemlyanoy val
Pushechnaya ul
Chistye Prudy
ul Pokrovka
44
Lubyanskaya pl
Armyansky per
Maly Kazenny per
Teatralny proezd
Lubyanka
pl Pokrovskie Vorota
30
Kurskaya
Teatralnaya pl
Kitay-Gorod
47
ul Maroseyka
Pokrovsky bul
Lyapin per
Ploshchad Revolyutsii
Novaya pl
Kolpachny per
25
Lubyansky proezd
GUM
Vetoshny per
ul Ilynka
Kitay-Gorod
Staraya pl
(Boulevard Ring)
Vinzavod (450m)
KITAY GOROD
10
15
Slavyanskaya pl
ul Solyanka
ul Vorontsovo Pole
21
16
17
ul Varvarka
Kitay-Gorod
Podkolokolny per
(Garden Ring)
Yauzsky bul
Kremlevskaya nab
Ust'insky per
Serebryanicheskaya nab
Moscow River
Moskvoretskaya nab
Rauzhskaya nab
Bernikovskaya nab
ul Zemlyanoy val
Bolshoy Ustinsky Most
Yauzskaya ul
Bolotnaya ul
Chugunny Most
May Moskvoretsky Most
Teterinsky per
ul Goncharnaya
Komissariatsky Most
Kotelnicheskaya nab
Kosmodamianskaya nab
Lavrushinsky per
ul Bolshaya Ordynka
Pyatnitskaya ul
Sadovnicheskaya nab
Ozerkovskaya nab
Taganka
Runovsky per
Taganskaya
Novokuznetskaya
Marksistskaya
2
Taganskaya pl
State Tretyakov Gallery Main Branch
Tretyakovskaya
Taganskaya

Central Moscow

Top Sights
1 Armoury D5
2 State Tretyakov Gallery Main Branch E7

Sights
3 Annunciation Cathedral D5
4 Archangel Cathedral D5
5 Assumption Cathedral D5
6 Borovitskaya Tower D6
7 Cathedral of Christ the Saviour C6
Church Of The Deposition Of The Robe .... (see 5)
8 Ivan the Great Bell Tower D5
9 Kremlin D5
10 Lenin's Mausoleum E5
11 Lumiere Brothers Photography Centre D7
12 Poteshny Palace D5
13 Pushkin Museum of Fine Arts C6
14 Red October D7
15 Red Square E5
16 Saviour Gate Tower E5
17 St Basil's Cathedral E5
18 State History Museum D4
19 State Kremlin Palace D5
20 Strelka Institute for Media, Architecture and Design C7
21 Supreme Soviet E5
22 Trinity Gate Tower D5
23 Tsar Bell D5
24 Tsar Cannon D5

Activities, Courses & Tours
25 Moscow Free Tour E4
26 Sanduny Baths E3

Sleeping
27 Anti-Hostel Cosmic D3
28 Godzillas Hostel D2
29 Hotel de Paris C3
30 Hotel Metropol E4
31 Sleepbox Hotel A1

Eating
32 As Eat Is B3
33 Café Pushkin C3
34 Delicatessen D1
35 Khachapuri C3
36 Lavka-Lavka D3
37 Varenichnaya No 1 .... B5

Drinking & Nightlife
38 3205 .... D2
39 Enthusiast D3
40 Noor C2
41 OMG! Coffee H3
42 Time-Out Bar B2

Entertainment
43 Bolshoi Theatre D4
44 Masterskaya E4
45 Tchaikovsky Concert Hall B2

Information
46 Kremlin Left-Luggage Office D5
47 Maria Travel Agency F4

Red Square HISTORIC SITE

(Красная площадь; Krasnaya pl; Ⓜ Ploshchad Revolyutsii) Immediately outside the Kremlin's northeastern wall is the celebrated Red Square, the 400m by 150m area of cobblestones that is at the very heart of Moscow. Commanding the square from the southern end is **St Basil's Cathedral** (Покровский собор, Храм Василия Блаженного; www.saintbasil.ru; adult/student R250/50, audioguide R200; ⏲11am-5pm; Ⓜ Ploshchad Revolyutsii). This panorama never fails to send the heart aflutter, especially at night.

Lenin's Mausoleum MEMORIAL

(Мавзолей Ленина; www.lenin.ru; ⏲10am-1pm Tue-Thu & Sat; Ⓜ Ploshchad Revolyutsii) FREE Although Vladimir Ilych requested that he be buried beside his mum in St Petersburg, he still lies in state at the foot of the Kremlin wall, receiving visitors who come to pay their respects. Line up at the western corner of the square (near the entrance to Alexander Garden) to see the embalmed leader, who has been here since 1924. Note that photography is not allowed; and stern guards ensure that all visitors remain respectful and silent.

State History Museum MUSEUM

(Государственный исторический музей; www.shm.ru; Krasnaya pl 1; adult/student R300/100, audioguide R300; ⏲10am-6pm Wed & Fri-Mon, 11am-9pm Thu; Ⓜ Okhotny Ryad) At the northern end of Red Square, the State History Museum has an enormous collection covering the whole Russian empire from the time of the Stone Age. The building, dating from the late 19th century, is itself an attraction – each room is in the style of a different period or region, some with highly decorated walls echoing old Russian churches.

South of the Moscow River

★State Tretyakov Gallery Main Branch GALLERY

(Главный отдел Государственной Третьяковской галереи; www.tretyakovgallery.ru; Lavrushinsky per 10; adult/student R400/250; ⏲10am-6pm Tue, Wed, Sat & Sun, to 9pm Thu & Fri, last tickets 1hr before closing; Ⓜ Tretyakovskaya) The exotic *boyar* castle on a little lane in Zamoskvorechie contains the main branch of the State Tretyakov Gallery, housing the world's best collection of Russian icons and an outstanding collection of other prerevolutionary Russian art. Show up early to beat the queues.

New Tretyakov Gallery GALLERY

(Новая Третьяковская галерея; www.tretyakovgallery.ru/en/; ul Krymsky val 10; adult/student R400/250; ⏲10am-6pm Tue, Wed, Sat & Sun, 10am-9pm Thu & Fri, last tickets 1hr before closing; Ⓜ Park Kultury) The premier venue for 20th-century Russian art is this branch of the State Tretyakov Gallery, better known as the New Tretyakov. This place has much more than the typical socialist realist images of muscle-bound men wielding scythes, and busty women milking cows (although there's that too). The exhibits showcase avant-garde artists such as Malevich, Kandinsky, Chagall, Goncharova and Popova.

Art Muzeon & Krymskaya Naberezhnaya SCULPTURE PARK

(ul Krymsky val 10; Ⓜ Park Kultury) FREE Now fully revamped and merged with the wonderfully reconstructed Krymskaya Naberezhnaya embankment, is this motley collection of (mostly kitschy) sculpture and monuments to Soviet idols (Stalin, Sverdlov, a selection of Lenins and Brezhnevs) that were ripped from their pedestals in the post-1991 wave of anti-Soviet feeling. All of these stand in lovely gardens with boardwalks and many inviting benches.

★Gorky Park PARK

(Парк Горького; ⏲24hr; 📶👪; Ⓜ Oktyabrskaya) FREE Moscow's main escape from the city within the city is not your conventional expanse of nature preserved deep inside an urban jungle. It is not a fun fair either, though it used to be one. Its official name says it

SOBORNAYA PLOSHCHAD

On the northern side of Sobornaya pl, with five golden helmet domes and four semicircular gables facing the square, is the **Assumption Cathedral** (Успенский собор), built between 1475 and 1479. As the focal church of prerevolutionary Russia, it's the burial place of most heads of the Russian Orthodox Church from the 1320s to 1700. The iconostasis dates from 1652, but its lowest level contains some older icons, including the Virgin of Vladimir (Vladimirskaya Bogomater), an early-15th-century Rublyov-school copy of Russia's most revered image, the Vladimir Icon of the Mother of God (Ikona Vladimirskoy Bogomateri).

The delicate little single-domed church beside the west door of the Assumption Cathedral is the **Church of the Deposition of the Robe** (ерковь Ризоположения), built between 1484 and 1486 by masons from Pskov.

With its two golden domes rising above the eastern side of Sobornaya pl, the 16th-century **Ivan the Great Bell Tower** (Колокольня Ивана Великого) is the Kremlin's tallest structure. Beside the bell tower stands the **Tsar Bell** (Царь-колокол), a 202-tonne monster that cracked before it ever rang. North of the bell tower is the mammoth **Tsar Cannon** (Царь-пушка), cast in 1586 but never shot.

The 1508 **Archangel Cathedral** (Архангельский собор), at the square's southeastern corner, was for centuries the coronation, wedding and burial church of tsars. The tombs of all of Russia's rulers from the 1320s to the 1690s are here bar one (Boris Godunov, who was buried at Sergiev Posad).

Finally, the **Annunciation Cathedral** (Благовещенский собор; Blagoveshchensky sobor), at the southwest corner of Sobornaya pl and dating from 1489, contains the celebrated icons of master painter Theophanes the Greek. He probably painted the six icons at the right-hand end of the diesis row, the biggest of the six tiers of the iconostasis. Archangel Michael (the third icon from the left on the diesis row) and the adjacent St Peter are ascribed to Russian master Andrei Rublyov.

all – Maxim Gorky's Central Park of Culture & Leisure. That's exactly what it provides: culture and leisure in all shapes and forms. Designed by avant-garde architect Konstantin Melnikov as a piece of communist utopia in the 1920s, these days it showcases the enlightened transformation Moscow has undergone in the recent past.

West of the Kremlin

Pushkin Museum of Fine Arts MUSEUM

(Музей изобразительных искусств им Пушкина; www.arts-museum.ru; ul Volkhonka 12; admission each branch R200-300; ⏲10am-7pm Tue-Sun, to 9pm Thu; Ⓜ Kropotkinskaya) Moscow's premier foreign-art museum is split over three branches and shows a broad selection of European works, including masterpieces from ancient civilisations, the Italian Renaissance and the Dutch Golden Age.

Novodevichy Convent CONVENT

(Новодевичий монастырь; adult/student R300/100, photos R100; ⏲grounds 8am-8pm, museums 9am-5pm Wed-Mon; Ⓜ Sportivnaya) The Novodevichy Convent was founded in 1524 to celebrate the taking of Smolensk from Lithuania, an important step in Moscow's conquest of the old Kyivan Rus lands. The oldest and most dominant building in the grounds is the white Smolensk Cathedral, with a sumptuous interior covered in 16th-century frescoes. Novodevichy is a functioning monastery. Women are advised to cover their heads and shoulders when entering the churches, while men should wear long pants.

Cathedral of Christ the Saviour CHURCH

(Храм Христа Спасителя; ul Volkhonka 15; ⏲1-5pm Mon, 10am-5pm Tue-Sun; Ⓜ Kropotkinskaya) FREE This gargantuan cathedral was completed in 1997 – just in time to celebrate Moscow's 850th birthday. It is amazingly opulent, garishly grandiose and truly historic. The cathedral's sheer size and splendour guarantee its role as a love-it-or-hate-it landmark. Considering Stalin's plan for this site (a Palace of Soviets topped with a 100m statue of Lenin), Muscovites should at least be grateful they can admire the shiny domes of a church instead of the shiny dome of Ilyich's head.

THE BANYA

Taking a traditional Russian banya is a must. These wet saunas are a social hub and a fantastic experience for any visitor to Russia. Leave your inhibitions at home and be prepared for a beating with birch twigs (far more pleasant than it sounds). Ask at your accommodation for the nearest public banya. In Moscow, try the luxurious **Sanduny Baths** (☎495-628 4633; www.sanduny.ru; Neglinnaya ul 14; per person R1500-2300; ⏲8am-10pm; Ⓜ Kuznetsky Most) and in St Petersburg the traditional **Mytninskiye Bani** (Мытнинские бани; www.mybanya.spb.ru; Mytninskaya ul 17-19; per hr R100-200; ⏲8am-10pm Fri-Tue; Ⓜ Ploshchad Vosstaniya).

Tours

Moscow Free Tour WALKING TOUR

(☎495-222 3466; http://moscowfreetour.com; Nikolskaya ul 4/5; paid tours R950-1550) Every day, these enthusiastic ladies offer an informative, inspired two-hour guided walk around Red Square and Kitay Gorod – and it's completely free. It's so good, that (they think) you'll sign up for one of their excellent paid tours, covering the Kremlin, the Arbat and the Metro, or more thematic tours like communist Moscow or mystical Moscow.

Moscow 360 WALKING TOUR

(☎8-915-205 8360; www.moscow360.org) FREE This ambitious company offers four – count 'em, four! – different walking tours, all of which are free. They include tours of Red Square, the Cathedral of Christ the Saviour and the Metro, as well as – the most unusual – an AK-47 Tour (the tour and transport are free, but you'll pay to shoot). Tips are gratefully accepted, obviously.

Sleeping

Affordable alternatives to generally expensive hotels are the city's many hostels and rental apartments.

Godzillas Hostel HOSTEL €

(☎495-699 4223; www.godzillashostel.com; Bolshoy Karetny per 6; dm from R760, s/d R2400/2600; ❄@🛜; Ⓜ Tsvetnoy Bulvar) Tried and true, Godzillas is Moscow's best-known hostel, with dozens of beds spread out over four floors. The rooms come in various sizes, but they are all spacious and light-filled and painted in different colours. To cater to the many guests, there are bathroom facilities on each floor, three kitchens and a big living room with satellite TV.

Anti-Hostel Cosmic HOSTEL €
(☎499-390 8132; http://anti-hostel.ru; ul Bolshaya Dmitrovka 7/5 str 3; capsules from R1350; 📶; Ⓜ Teatralnaya) Occupying a converted apartment, this place marries the idea of hostel with that of capsule hotel. The location is hard to beat – Red Square is just a five-minute walk away. Capsules create a tiny, though comfortable, universe for guests to enjoy on their own. There is also a nice common area to mingle with fellow capsule-dwellers.

★**Blues Hotel** BOUTIQUE HOTEL €€
(☎495-961 1161; www.blues-hotel.ru; ul Dovatora 8; s/d from R5800/6300; 🚭❄📶; Ⓜ Sportivnaya) The location is not exactly central, but is not a disadvantage. It is steps from the red-line metro (five stops to Red Square) and a few blocks from Novodevichy, with several worthwhile restaurants in the vicinity. Considering that, this friendly, affordable boutique hotel is a gem, offering stylish, spotless rooms with king-size beds and flat-screen TVs.

Sleepbox Hotel HOTEL €€
(☎495-989 4104; www.sleepbox-hotel.ru; ul 1-ya Tverskaya-Yamskaya 27; s without bathroom from R3200, d from R4700, q from R5500; ❄📶; Ⓜ Belorusskaya) It might draw comparisons with capsule hotels, but it is actually better. Think a comfortable train compartment – it's close to what you get in this immaculately clean and unusual hotel, conveniently located for those arriving by train from Sheremetyevo airport. Common showers and toilets are very modern and clean; queues are unusual.

★**Hotel Metropol** HISTORIC HOTEL €€€
(☎499-501 7800; www.metropol-moscow.ru; Teatralny proezd 1/4; d R9930-11,400; 🚭❄@🏊; Ⓜ Teatralnaya) Nothing short of an art nouveau masterpiece, the 1907 Metropol brings an artistic, historic touch to every nook and cranny, from the spectacular exterior to the grand lobby, to the individually decorated (but small) rooms. The breakfast buffet (R2000) is ridiculously priced, but it's served under the restaurant's gorgeous stained-glass ceiling.

Hotel de Paris BOUTIQUE HOTEL €€€
(☎495-777 0052; www.hotel-deparis.ru; Bolshaya Bronnaya ul 23, bldg 3; s/d from R9000/9450; P🚭❄📶; Ⓜ Pushkinskaya) Steps from the madness of Tverskaya, this is a delightfully stylish hotel tucked into a quiet courtyard off the Boulevard Ring. Situated on the lower floors, the rooms do not get much natural light, but they feature king-size beds, Jacuzzi tubs and elegant design. Service is consistently friendly. Prices drop by 40% on weekends, offering terrific value.

Eating

★**Varenichnaya No 1** RUSSIAN €
(www.varenichnaya.ru; ul Arbat 29; mains R200-400; ⏰10am-midnight; 🚭✍📋👪; Ⓜ Arbatskaya) Retro Soviet is all the rage in Moscow, but this old-style Varenichnaya does it right, with books lining the walls, old movies on the black-and-white TV, and Cold War-era prices. The menu features tasty, filling *vareniki* and *pelmeni* (different kinds of dumplings), with sweet and savoury fillings. Bonus: an excellent housemade pickled vegie plate to make you pucker.

★**Delicatessen** INTERNATIONAL €€
(Деликатесы; www.newdeli.ru; Savodvaya-Karetnaya ul 20; mains R450-700; ⏰noon-midnight Tue-Sat; 📶📋; Ⓜ Tsvetnoy Bulvar) The affable (and chatty) owners of this place travel the world and experiment with the menu a lot, turning burgers, pizzas and pasta into artfully constructed objects of modern culinary art. The other source of joy is a cabinet filled with bottles of ripening fruity liquors, which may destroy your budget if consumed uncontrollably (a pointless warning, we know).

Khachapuri GEORGIAN €€
(☎8-985-764 3118; http://hacha.ru; Bolshoy Gnezdnikovsky per 10; khachapuri R200-350, mains R400-600; 🚭📶📋; Ⓜ Pushkinskaya) Unassuming, affordable and appetising, this urban cafe exemplifies what people love about Georgian culture: the warm hospitality and the freshly baked *khachapuri* (cheese bread). Aside from seven types of delicious *khachapuri,* there's also an array of soups, *shashlyki* (kebabs), *khinkali* (dumplings) and other Georgian favourites.

As Eat Is INTERNATIONAL €€
(Как Есть; ☎495-699 5313; www.aseatis.ru; Tryokhprudny per 11/13; mains R500-900; ⏰noon-11pm; 🚭✍📋; Ⓜ Mayakovskaya) We love the understated, eclectic interior, with its mismatched textures, appealingly packed bookshelves and vintage detailing. Even more, we love the contemporary seasonal fare, which is delightful to look at and divine to eat. It's

DON'T MISS

MOSCOW'S WHITE-HOT ART SCENE

Revamped old industrial buildings and other spaces in Moscow are where you'll find gems of Russia's super creative contemporary art scene. Apart from the following recommended spots, also see www.artguide.ru.

Garage Museum of Contemporary Art (www.garageccc.com; ul Krymsky val 9; adult/student R300/150; ⊙11am-9pm Mon-Thu; Ⓜ Oktyabrskaya) In a temporary pavilion constructed of cardboard in Gorky Park, Garage hosts exciting exhibitions by top artists.

Proekt_Fabrika (www.proektfabrika.ru; 18 Perevedenovsky per; ⊙10am-8pm Tue-Sun; Ⓜ Baumanskaya) FREE A still-functioning paper factory is the location for this nonprofit set of gallery and performance spaces enlivened by arty graffiti and creative-industry offices.

Red October (Завод Красный Октябрь; Bersenevskaya nab; Ⓜ Kropotkinskaya) FREE The red-brick buildings of this former chocolate factory now host the **Lumiere Brothers Photography Centre** (www.lumiere.ru; Bolotnaya nab 3, Bldg 1; ⊙noon-9pm Tue-Fri, to 10pm Sat & Sun) plus other galleries, cool bars and restaurants. In an adjacent building the **Strelka Institute for Media, Architecture and Design** (www.strelkainstitute.ru; bldg 5a, Bersenevskaya nab 14/5; Ⓜ Novokuznetskaya) is worth checking out for its events, bookshop and bar.

Vinzavod (Винзавод; www.winzavod.ru; 4 Syromyatnichesky per 1; Ⓜ Chkalovskaya) FREE A former wine factory has morphed into this postindustrial complex of prestigious galleries, shops, a cinema and trendy cafe.

the kind of food that would normally cost big bucks, but prices are reasonable. Extra love for the bilingual pun of a name.

Lavka-Lavka INTERNATIONAL €€
(Лавка-Лавка; ☎903-115 5033; http://restoran.lavkalavka.com/?lang=en; ul Petrovka 21 str 2; dishes R400-600; ⊙10am-midnight Sun-Thu, 10am-1am Fri-Sat; 👪; Ⓜ Teatralnaya) 🍃 Welcome to the Russian Portlandia – all the food here is organic and hails from little farms where you may rest assured all the lambs and chickens lived a very happy life before being served to you on a plate. Irony aside, this is a great place to sample local food cooked in a funky improvisational style.

Café Pushkin RUSSIAN €€€
(Кафе Пушкинъ; ☎495-739 0033; www.cafe-pushkin.ru; Tverskoy bul 26a; business lunch R750, mains R1000-2200; ⊙24hr; 🚭📶📋; Ⓜ Pushkinskaya) The tsarina of *haute-russe* dining, with an exquisite blend of Russian and French cuisines – service and food are done to perfection. The lovely 19th-century building has a different atmosphere on each floor, including a richly decorated library and a pleasant rooftop cafe.

Drinking & Nightlife

★3205 CAFE
(☎905-703 3205; www.veranda3205.ru; ul Karetny Ryad 3; ⊙11am-3am; Ⓜ Pushkinskaya) The biggest drinking/eating establishment in Hermitage Gardens, this verandah positioned at the back of the main building looks a bit like a greenhouse. In summer, tables (and patrons) spill out into the park, making it one of the city's best places for outdoor drinking. With its long bar and joyful atmosphere, the place also heaves in winter.

Enthusiast BAR
(Энтузиаст; per Stoleshnikov str 5; ⊙noon-11pm; Ⓜ Teatralnaya) Scooter enthusiast, that is. But you don't have to be one in order to enjoy this superbly laid-back bar hidden at the far end of a fancifully shaped courtyard and disguised as a spare-parts shop. On a warm day, grab a beer or cider, settle into a beach chair and let harmony descend on you.

Noor BAR
(☎499-130 6030; www.noorbar.com; ul Tverskaya 23; ⊙3pm-3am Mon-Wed, noon-6am Thu-Sun; Ⓜ Pushkinskaya) There is little to say about this misleadingly unassuming bar, apart from the fact that everything in it is close to

perfection. It has it all – prime location, convivial atmosphere, eclectic DJ music, friendly bartenders and superb drinks. Though declared 'the best' by various magazines on several occasions, it doesn't feel like they care.

Time-Out Bar COCKTAIL BAR
(www.timeoutbar.ru; 12th fl, Bolshaya Sadovaya ul 5; noon-2am Sun-Thu, noon-6am Fri & Sat; M Mayakovskaya) On the upper floors of the throwback Pekin Hotel, this trendy bar is nothing but 'now'. That includes the bartenders sporting plaid and their delicious concoctions, especially created for different times of day. The decor is pretty impressive – particularly the spectacular city skyline. Perfect place for sundowners (or sun-ups, if you last that long).

OMG! Coffee CAFE
(495-722 6954; www.omgcoffee.net; ul Staray Basmannaya 6 str 3; 8.30am-11pm Mon-Fri, 11am-11pm Sat & Sun; M Krasnye Vorota) The more Russia falls out with the US, the more Brooklyn-esque the Moscow cafe scene becomes. This smallish local is very scientific (or in their own words – psychotic) about coffee, which they buy from trusted roasting specialists and brew using seven different methods. They also serve delightful gourmet burgers and sandwiches.

☆ Entertainment

To find out what's on, see the entertainment section in Thursday's *Moscow Times*. Most theatres, including the Bolshoi, are closed between late June and early September.

★ Bolshoi Theatre BALLET, OPERA
(Большой театр; www.bolshoi.ru; Teatralnaya pl 1; tickets R200-4000; closed Jul & Aug; M Teatralnaya) An evening at the Bolshoi is still one of Moscow's most romantic and entertaining options for a night on the town. The glittering six-tier auditorium has an electric atmosphere, evoking over 235 years of premier music and dance. Both the ballet and opera companies perform a range of Russian and foreign works here. After the collapse of the Soviet Union, the Bolshoi was marred by politics, scandal and frequent turnover. Yet the show must go on – and it will.

Tchaikovsky Concert Hall CLASSICAL MUSIC
(Концертный зал имени Чайковского; 495-232 0400; www.meloman.ru; Triumfalnaya pl 4/31; tickets R300-3000; closed Jul & Aug; M Mayakovskaya) Home to the famous Moscow State Philharmonic (Moskovskaya Filharmonia), the capital's oldest symphony orchestra, Tchaikovsky Concert Hall was established in 1921. It's a huge auditorium, with seating for 1600 people. This is where you can expect to hear the Russian classics such as Stravinsky, Rachmaninov and Shostakovich, as well as other European favourites. Look out for special children's concerts.

CAFES, CLUBS & ANTI-CAFES

There's a hazy distinction between cafe, bar and nightclub in Russia's cities, with many places serving all three functions. As such, we list them all in one place.

Top clubs have strict *feis kontrol* (face control); beat by arriving early before the bouncers are posted, or by speaking English, as being a foreigner helps.

Currently popular are 'anti-cafes': 'creative spaces' where you pay by the minute and enjoy coffee, snacks and access to everything from wi-fi to computer games and musical instruments. They are great places to meet locals.

Masterskaya LIVE MUSIC
(Мастерская; www.mstrsk.ru; Teatralny proezd 3 str 3; noon-6am; ; M Lubyanka) All the best places in Moscow are tucked into far corners of courtyards, and they often have unmarked doors. Such is the case with this super-funky music venue. The eclectic, arty interior makes a cool place to chill out during the day. Evening hours give way to a diverse array of live-music acts or the occasional dance or theatre performance.

Shopping

Ul Arbat has always been a tourist attraction and is littered with souvenir shops and stalls.

GUM MALL
(ГУМ; www.gum.ru; Krasnaya pl 3; 10am-10pm; M Ploshchad Revolyutsii) The elaborate 240m facade on the northeastern side of Red Square, GUM is a bright, bustling shopping mall with hundreds of fancy stores and restaurants. With a skylight roof and three-level arcades, the spectacular interior was a revolutionary design when it was built

in the 1890s, replacing the Upper Trading Rows that previously occupied this site.

Izmaylovsky Market MARKET
(www.kremlin-izmailovo.com; Izmaylovskoye shosse 73; ⏲10am-8pm; Ⓜ Partizanskaya) This sprawling area, also known as Vernisazh market, is packed with art, handmade crafts, antiques, Soviet paraphernalia and just about anything you might want for a souvenir. You'll find Moscow's biggest original range of *matryoshki, palekh* and *khokhloma* ware, as well as less traditional woodworking crafts. There are also rugs from the Caucasus and Central Asia, pottery, linens, jewellery, fur hats, chess sets, toys, Soviet posters and much more.

METRO TOUR

For just R40 you can spend the day touring Moscow's magnificent metro stations. Many of these are marble-faced, frescoed, gilded works of art. Among our favourites are **Komsomolskaya**, a huge stuccoed hall, its ceiling covered with mosaics depicting military heroes; **Novokuznetskaya**, featuring military bas-reliefs done in sober khaki, and colourful ceiling mosaics depicting pictures of the happy life; and **Mayakovskaya**, Grand Prize winner at the 1939 World's Fair in New York.

Information

Wireless access is ubiquitous and almost always free.

36.6 (Аптека 36.6; ☎495-797 6366; www.366.ru) A chain of 24-hour pharmacies with many branches all around the city.

American Medical Centre (☎495-933 7700; www.amcenter.ru; Grokholsky per 1; ⏲24hr; Ⓜ Pr Mira) Offers 24-hour emergency service, consultations and a full range of medical specialists.

Main Post Office (Myasnitskaya ul 26; ⏲24hr; Ⓜ Chistye Prudy)

Maria Travel Agency (☎495-777 8226; www.maria-travel.com; ul Maroseyka 13; Ⓜ Kitay-Gorod) Offers visa support, apartment rental and some local tours, including the Golden Ring.

Moscow Times (www.themoscowtimes.com) Best locally published English-language newspaper, widely distributed free of charge.

Unifest Travel (☎495-234 6555; http://unifest.ru/en.html; Komsomolsky prospekt 16/2) On-the-ball travel company offers rail and air tickets, visa support and more.

Getting Around

TO/FROM THE AIRPORT

All three Moscow airports (Domodedovo, Sheremetyevo or Vnukovo) are accessible by the convenient **Aeroexpress Train** (☎8-800-700 3377; www.aeroexpress.ru; R340-400; ⏲6am-midnight) from the city centre; reduced rate is available for online purchase.

Alternatively, order an official airport taxi from the dispatcher's desk in the terminal (R2000 to R2200 to the city centre). You can save some cash by booking in advance to take advantage of the fixed rates offered by most companies (usually from R1500 to R1800 to/from any airport). Driving times vary wildly depending on traffic.

PUBLIC TRANSPORT

The **Moscow Metro** (www.mosmetro.ru) is by far the easiest, quickest and cheapest way of getting around the city. Stations are marked outside by 'M' signs. Magnetic tickets (R40) are sold at ticket booths. Save time by buying a multiple-ride ticket (five rides for R160, 11 rides for R320, 20 rides for R540). The ticket is a contactless smart card, which you must tap on the reader before going through the turnstile.

Buses, trolleybuses and trams are useful along a few radial or cross-town routes that the metro misses, and are necessary for reaching sights away from the city centre. Tickets (R40) are sold on the vehicle by a conductor.

TAXI

Unofficial taxis are still common in Moscow. Expect to pay R200 to R400 for a ride around the city centre, depending on your haggling skills.

Detskoe Taxi (Детское такси; ☎495-765 1180; www.detskoetaxi.ru; 8km for R500) 'Children's Taxi' has smoke-free cars and car seats for your children.

Taxi Blues (☎495-105 5115; www.taxi-blues.ru)

Veliky Novgorod

Великий Новгород

☎8162 / POP 219,925

Veliky Novgorod (usually shortened to Novgorod) is a proud and beautiful city, billed as the 'Birthplace of Russia'. It was here, in 862, that Prince Rurik proclaimed the modern Russian state – the Rurik dynasty went on to rule Russia for more than 750 years. Its glorious Cathedral of St Sophia is the oldest church in Russia. Straddling the

Volkhov River, this attractive, tourist-friendly destination is a popular weekend getaway for St Petersburg residents – to avoid the crowds, come during the week.

Sights

Kremlin FORTRESS

(6am-midnight) FREE On the west bank of the Volkhov River, and surrounded by a pleasant wooded park, the kremlin is one of Russia's oldest. Originally called the Detinets (and still often referred to as such), the fortification dates back to the 9th century, though it was later rebuilt with brick in the 14th century; this still stands today. The complex is worth seeing with a guide; arrange one through the tourist office. Boat tours run hourly (May to October, R300) from the Kremlin's pier and Yaroslav's Court towards Lake Ilmen: contact the tourist office to book.

★ **Cathedral of St Sophia** CHURCH

(Софийский собор; www.saintsofianovg.ortox.ru; 8am-8pm, services 10am-noon daily & 6-8pm Wed-Sun) This is the oldest church in Russia (finished in 1050) and one of the country's oldest stone buildings. It's the kremlin's focal point and you couldn't miss it if you tried – its golden dome positively *glows*. St Sophia houses many icons dating from the 14th century, but none are as important as that of Novgorod's patron saint, Our Lady of the Sign, which, the story goes, miraculously saved the city from destruction in 1170 after being struck by an arrow.

★ **Novgorod State United Museum** MUSEUM

(Новгородский государственный объединенный музей-заповедник; www.novgorodmuseum.ru; adult/student R150/100; 10am-6pm Wed-Mon, closed last Thu of the month) This must-see museum houses three strikingly comprehensive exhibitions covering the history of Veliky Novgorod, Russian woodcarving and Russian icons. The latter contains one of the world's largest collections of icons, with around 260 pieces placed in chronological order, allowing you to appreciate the progression of skills and techniques through the centuries.

Yaroslav's Court HISTORIC SITE

Across a footbridge from the kremlin are the remnants of an 18th-century market arcade. Beyond that is the market gatehouse, an array of churches sponsored by 13th- to 16th-century merchant guilds, and a 'road palace' built in the 18th century as a rest stop for Catherine the Great.

The 12th-century **Court Cathedral of St Nicholas** (Храм Николая Чудотворца; adult/student R100/60; 10am-noon & 1-6pm Wed-Sun, closed last Fri of month) is all that remains of the early palace complex of the Novgorod princes, from which Yaroslav's Court (Yaroslavovo dvorishche) gets its name. The cathedral holds church artefacts and temporary exhibitions of local interest. Downstairs you can see fragments from the church's original frescoes.

Sleeping & Eating

★ **Hotel Volkhov** HOTEL €€

(Гостиница Волхов; 8162-225 500; www.hotel-volkhov.ru; ul Predtechenskaya 24; s/d from R2150/3100; @) This centrally located, modern hotel runs like a well-oiled machine, with nicely furnished rooms, pleasant English-speaking staff, laundry service and free wi-fi. A sauna (extra fee) is available to guests. The included breakfasts (choice of Continental, Russian or 'American') are actually very good.

★ **Nice People** INTERNATIONAL €€

(Хорошие люди; 8162-730 879; www.gonicepeople.ru; ul Meretskova-Volosova 1/1; meals R380-620; 8am-midnight) By far the most appealing choice in Novgorod, this cafe-bar lives up to its name – you'll get a warm welcome from English-speaking staff, and the clientele is pretty easygoing, too. The menu includes speciality DIY salads, with a huge range of ingredients from which to choose. Other tasty treats and daily specials are written on the walls.

Getting There & Away

The train station (Новгород-на-Волхове on RZD timetables) and bus station (Автовокзал) are next to each other on Oktyabryskaya ul, 1.5km northwest of the kremlin.

Lastochka high speed trains connect with St Petersburg's Moscow Station (R400, three hours, two daily). Moscow can be reached in 4½ hours on a combination of *Lastochka* and *Sapsan* high speed trains or via a handy overnight train (*platskart/kupe* R1250/2400, eight hours) leaving at 9.20pm.

Bus services include St Petersburg (R330, four hours, 13 daily).

St Petersburg Санкт-Петербург

☎812 / POP 4.8 MILLION

Affectionately known as Piter to locals, St Petersburg is a visual delight. The Neva River and surrounding canals reflect unbroken facades of handsome 18th- and 19th-century buildings that house a spellbinding collection of cultural storehouses, culminating in the incomparable Hermitage. Home to many of Russia's greatest creative talents (Pushkin, Dostoevsky, Tchaikovsky), Piter still inspires a contemporary generation of Russians making it a liberal, hedonistic and exciting place to visit as well as a giant warehouse of culture.

The city covers many islands, some real, some created through the construction of canals. The central street is Nevsky pr, which extends some 4km from the Alexander Nevsky Monastery to the Hermitage.

Sights

General Staff Building MUSEUM

(Здание Главного штаба; www.hermitagemuseum.org; Dvortsovaya pl 6-8; admission R100; 10.30am-6pm Tue & Thu-Sun, 10.30am-9pm Wed; M Admiralteyskaya) The east wing of this magnificent building, wrapping around the south of Dvortsovaya pl and designed by Carlo Rossi in the 1820s, marries restored interiors with contemporary architecture to create a series of galleries displaying the Hermitage's amazing collection of Impressionist and post-Impressionist works. Contemporary art is here, too, often in temporary exhibitions by major artists.

Russian Museum MUSEUM

(Русский музей; www.rusmuseum.ru; Inzhenernaya ul 4; adult/student R350/150, 4-palace ticket adult/child R600/300; 10am-6pm Wed & Fri-Sun, 10am-5pm Mon, 1-9pm Thu; M Nevsky Prospekt) The handsome Mikhailovsky Palace is home to the country's biggest collection of Russian art. After the Hermitage you may feel you have had your fill of art, but try your utmost to make some time for this gem of a museum. There's also a lovely garden behind the palace.

Church on the Spilled Blood CHURCH

(Храм Спаса-на-Крови; http://cathedral.ru; Konyushennaya pl; adult/student R250/150; 10.30am-6pm Thu-Tue; M Nevsky Prospekt) This five-domed dazzler is St Petersburg's most elaborate church with a classic Russian Orthodox exterior and interior decorated with some 7000 sq metres of mosaics. Officially called the Church of the Resurrection of Christ, its far more striking colloquial name references the assassination attempt on Tsar Alexander II here in 1881.

St Isaac's Cathedral MUSEUM

(Isaakievsky Sobor; www.cathedral.ru; Isaakievskaya pl; cathedral adult/student R250/150, colonnade R150; 10.30am-6pm Thu-Tue, cathedral closed Wed, colonnade 1st & 3rd Wed; M Admiralteyskaya)

RUSSIA'S MOST FAMOUS STREET

Walking **Nevsky Prospekt** is an essential St Petersburg experience. Highlights along it incude the **Kazan Cathedral** (Казанский собор; http://kazansky-spb.ru; Kazanskaya pl 2; 8.30am-7.30pm; M Nevsky Prospekt) FREE with its curved arms reaching out towards the avenue.

Opposite is the **Singer Building** (Nevsky pr 28; M Nevsky Prospekt), a Style Moderne (art deco) beauty restored to all its splendour when it was the headquarters of the sewing-machine company; inside is the bookshop **Dom Knigi** (www.spbdk.ru; Nevsky pr 28; 9am-1am; ; M Nevsky Prospekt) and **Café Singer** (Nevsky pr 28; 9am-11pm; ; M Nevsky Prospekt), serving good food and drinks with a great view over the street.

Further along are the covered arcades of Rastrelli's historic **Bolshoy Gostiny Dvor** (Большой Гостиный Двор; http://bgd.ru; Nevsky pr 35; 10am-10pm; M Gostiny Dvor) department store, while on the corner of Sadovaya ul is the Style Moderne classic **Kupetz Eliseevs** (http://kupetzeliseevs.ru; Nevsky pr 56; 10am-10pm; ; M Gostiny Dvor) reincarnated as a luxury grocery and cafe.

An enormous **statue of Catherine the Great** stands at the centre of **Ploshchad Ostrovskogo** (Площадь Островского; M Gostiny Dvor), commonly referred to as the Catherine Gardens; at the southern end of the gardens is **Alexandrinsky Theatre** (☎812-710 4103; www.alexandrinsky.ru; pl Ostrovskogo 2; M Gostiny Dvor), where Chekhov's *The Seagull* premiered (to tepid reviews) in 1896.

DON'T MISS

STATE HERMITAGE MUSEUM

Mainly set in the magnificent Winter Palace and adjoining buildings, the **Hermitage** (Государственный Эрмитаж; www.hermitagemuseum.org; Dvortsovaya pl 2; adult/student R400/free, 1st Thu of month free, camera R200; ⊙10.30am-6pm Tue & Thu-Sun, to 9pm Wed; Ⓜ Admiralteyskaya) fully lives up to its sterling reputation. You can be absorbed by its treasures for days and still come out wanting more.

The enormous collection (over three million items, only a fraction of which are on display in around 360 rooms) almost amounts to a comprehensive history of Western European art. Viewing it demands a little planning, so choose the areas you'd like to concentrate on before you arrive. The museum consists of five connected buildings. From west to east they are:

Winter Palace Designed by Bartolomeo Rastrelli, its opulent state rooms, Great Church, Pavilion Hall and Treasure Rooms shouldn't be missed.

Small Hermitage and Old Hermitage Both were built for Catherine the Great, partly to house the art collection started by Peter the Great, which she significantly expanded. Here you'll find works by Rembrant, Da Vinci and Caravaggio.

New Hermitage Built for Nicholas II, to hold the still-growing art collection. The Old and New Hermitages are sometimes grouped together and labelled the Large Hermitage.

State Hermitage Theatre Built in the 1780s by the Giacomo Quarenghi. Concerts and ballets are still performed here.

The golden dome of St Isaac's Cathedral dominates the St Petersburg skyline. Its obscenely lavish interior is open as a museum, although services are held in the cathedral on major religious holidays. Most people bypass the museum to climb the 262 steps to the *kolonnada* (colonnade) around the drum of the dome, providing superb city views.

Peter & Paul Fortress FORTRESS

(Петропавловская крепость; www.spbmuseum.ru; grounds free, exhibitions adult R60-150, student R40-80; ⊙grounds 8.30am-8pm, exhibitions 11am-6pm Mon & Thu-Sun, 10am-5pm Tue; Ⓜ Gorkovskaya) Housing a cathedral where the Romanovs are buried, a former prison and various exhibitions, this large defensive fortress on Zayachy Island is the kernel from which St Petersburg grew into the city it is today. History buffs will love it and everyone will swoon at the panoramic views from atop the fortress walls, at the foot of which lies a sandy riverside beach, a prime spot for sunbathing.

Kunstkamera MUSEUM

(Кунсткамера; www.kunstkamera.ru; Tamozhenny per; adult/child R250/50; ⊙11am-7pm Tue-Sun; Ⓜ Admiralteyskaya) Also known as the Museum of Ethnology and Anthropology, the Kunstkamera is the city's first museum and was founded in 1714 by Peter himself. It is famous largely for its ghoulish collection of monstrosities, preserved 'freaks', two-headed mutant foetuses, deformed animals and odd body parts, all collected by Peter with the aim of educating the notoriously superstitious Russian people. While most rush to see these sad specimens, there are also very interesting exhibitions on native peoples from around the world.

Strelka LANDMARK

Among the oldest parts of Vasilyevsky Island, this eastern tip is where Peter the Great wanted his new city's administrative and intellectual centre to be. In fact, the Strelka became the focus of St Petersburg's maritime trade, symbolised by the colonnaded Customs House (now the Pushkin House). The two Rostral Columns, archetypal St Petersburg landmarks, are studded with ships' prows and four seated sculptures representing four of Russia's great rivers: the Neva, the Volga, the Dnieper and the Volkhov.

Activities

Especially during White Nights, cycling is a brilliant and economical way to get around St Petersburg's spread-out sights, restaurants and bars. Off main drags like Nevsky pr

Central St Petersburg

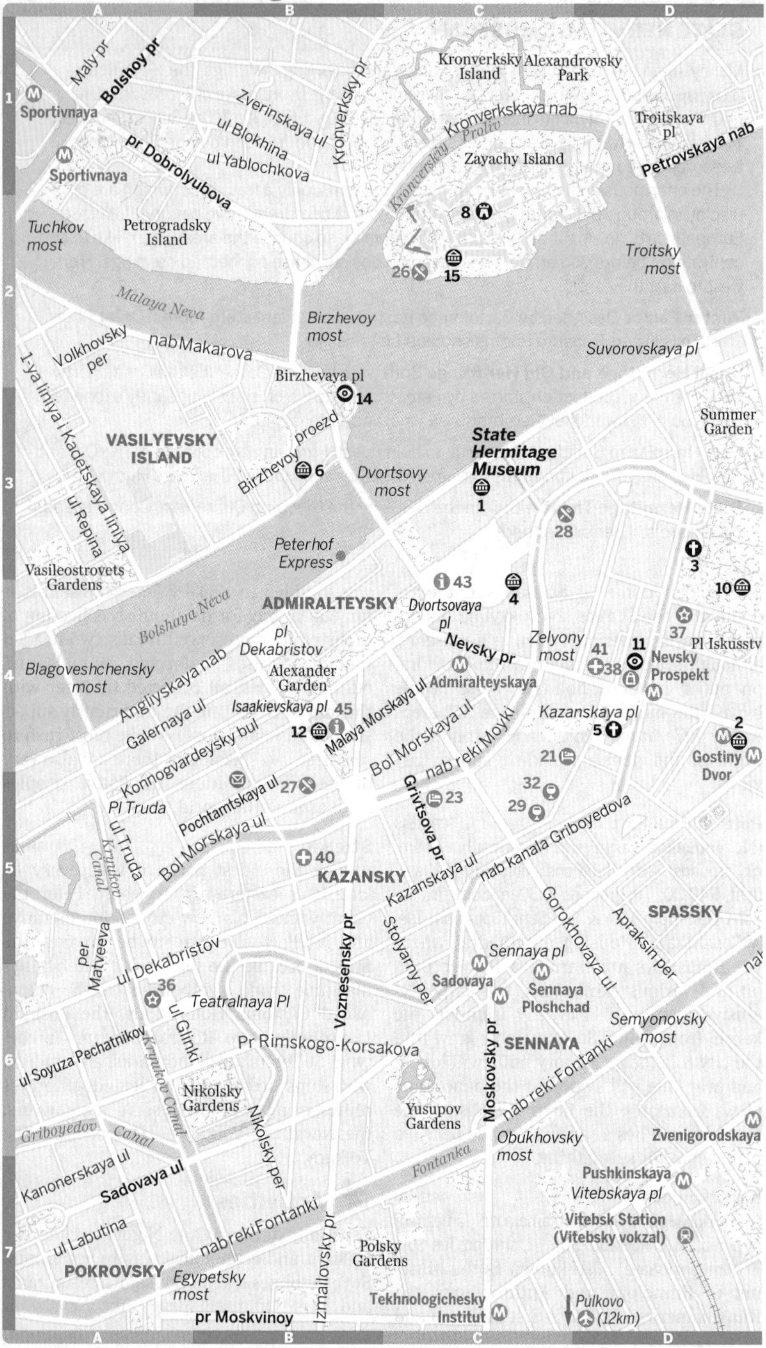

Kronverksky Island
Alexandrovsky Park
Maly pr
Bolshoy pr
Sportivnaya
Zverinskaya ul
ul Blokhina
ul Yablochkova
Kronverksky pr
Kronverkskaya nab
Kronverksky Proliv
Zayachy Island
Troitskaya pl
Petrovskaya nab
pr Dobrolyubova
Tuchkov most
Petrogradsky Island
Troitsky most
Malaya Neva
Birzhevoy most
Volkhovsky per
nab Makarova
Suvorovskaya pl
1-ya liniya i Kadetskaya liniya
Birzhevaya pl
Summer Garden
VASILYEVSKY ISLAND
Birzhevoy proezd
State Hermitage Museum
Dvortsovy most
ul Repina
Peterhof Express
Vasileostrovets Gardens
Bolshaya Neva
ADMIRALTEYSKY
Dvortsovaya pl
pl Dekabristov
Nevsky pr
Zelyony most
Pl Iskusstv
Nevsky Prospekt
Blagoveshchensky most
Angliyskaya nab
Alexander Garden
Admiralteyskaya
Galernaya ul
Isaakievskaya pl
Malaya Morskaya ul
Kazanskaya pl
Konnogvardeysky bul
Bol Morskaya ul
nab reki Moyki
Gostiny Dvor
Pl Truda
Pochtamtskaya ul
Grivtsova pr
ul Truda
Kryukov Canal
Bol Morskaya ul
nab kanala Griboyedova
KAZANSKY
Kazanskaya ul
Gorokhovaya ul
Apraksin per
SPASSKY
per Matveeva
ul Dekabristov
Voznesensky pr
Stolyarny per
Sennaya pl
Sadovaya
Sennaya Ploshchad
Teatralnaya Pl
ul Glinki
Semyonovsky most
ul Soyuza Pechatnikov
Kryukov Canal
Pr Rimskogo-Korsakova
Moskovsky pr
SENNAYA
nab reki Fontanki
Nikolsky Gardens
Nikolsky per
Yusupov Gardens
Griboyedov Canal
Obukhovsky most
Zvenigorodskaya
Fontanka
Kanonerskaya ul
Sadovaya ul
Pushkinskaya
Vitebskaya pl
Vitebsk Station (Vitebsky vokzal)
ul Labutina
nab reki Fontanki
Izmailovsky pr
Polsky Gardens
POKROVSKY
Egypetsky most
Tekhnologichesky Institut
Pulkovo (12km)
pr Moskvinoy

1 2 3 4 5 6 8 10 11 12 14 15 21 23 26 27 28 29 32 36 37 38 40 41 43 45

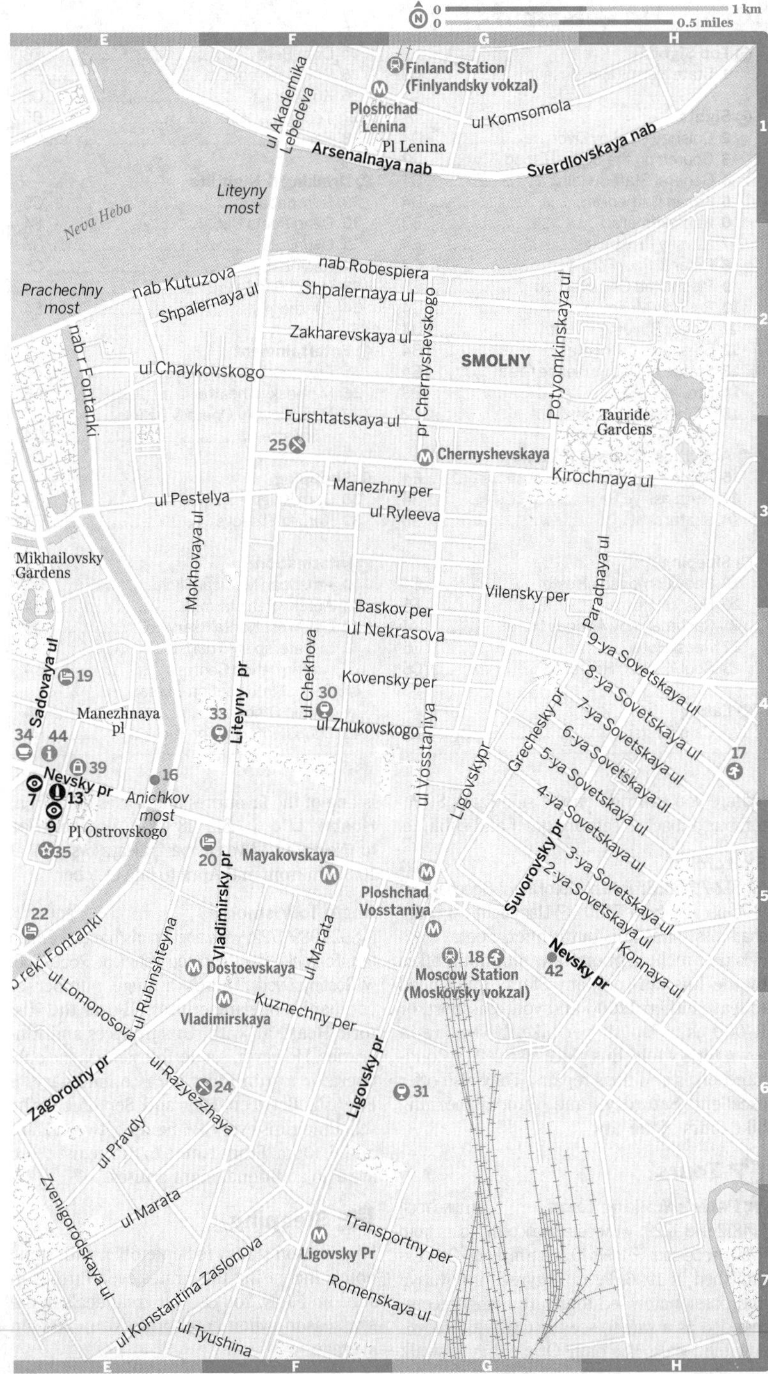
0
1 km
0
0.5 miles
E
F
G
H
Finland Station
(Finlyandsky vokzal)
Ploshchad
Lenina
Pl Lenina
ul Komsomola
ul Akademika Lebedeva
Arsenalnaya nab
Sverdlovskaya nab
Liteyny
most
Neva Нева
nab Robespiera
Prachechny
most
nab Kutuzova
Shpalernaya ul
Shpalernaya ul
Zakharevskaya ul
Potyomkinskaya ul
SMOLNY
nab r Fontanki
ul Chaykovskogo
pr Chernyshevskogo
Furshtatskaya ul
Tauride
Gardens
25
Chernyshevskaya
Kirochnaya ul
Manezhny per
ul Pestelya
ul Ryleeva
Mikhailovsky
Gardens
Mokhovaya ul
Paradnaya ul
Vilensky per
Baskov per
ul Nekrasova
9-ya Sovetskaya ul
8-ya Sovetskaya ul
Sadovaya ul
19
Kovensky per
ul Chekhova
30
Liteyny pr
7-ya Sovetskaya ul
Manezhnaya
pl
33
ul Zhukovskogo
Grechesky pr
6-ya Sovetskaya ul
34
44
Ligovskypr
17
39
5-ya Sovetskaya ul
ul Vosstaniya
Nevsky pr
16
7
13
Anichkov
most
4-ya Sovetskaya ul
9
Pl Ostrovskogo
35
20
Vladimirsky pr
Mayakovskaya
Suvorovsky pr
3-ya Sovetskaya ul
Ploshchad
Vosstaniya
2-ya Sovetskaya ul
22
nab reki Fontanki
ul Rubinshteyna
Dostoevskaya
ul Marata
18
Moscow Station
(Moskovsky vokzal)
Nevsky pr
42
Konnaya ul
ul Lomonosova
Vladimirskaya
Kuznechny per
Ligovsky pr
Zagorodny pr
ul Razyezzhaya
24
31
ul Pravdy
Zvenigorodskaya ul
ul Marata
Transportny per
Ligovsky Pr
ul Konstantina Zaslonova
Romenskaya ul
ul Tyushina
1
2
3
4
5
6
7

Central St Petersburg

Top Sights
1 State Hermitage Museum ... C3

Sights
2 Bolshoy Gostiny Dvor ... D4
3 Church on the Spilled Blood ... D3
4 General Staff Building ... C4
5 Kazan Cathedral ... D4
6 Kunstkamera ... B3
7 Nevsky Prospekt ... E4
8 Peter & Paul Fortress ... C2
9 Ploshchad Ostrovskogo ... E5
10 Russian Museum ... D4
11 Singer Building ... D4
12 St Isaac's Cathedral ... B4
13 Statue of Catherine the Great ... E4
14 Strelka ... B3
15 Trubetskoy Bastion ... C2

Activities, Courses & Tours
16 Anglo Tourismo ... E4
17 Mytninskiye Bani ... H4
18 Skatprokat ... G5

Sleeping
19 Baby Lemonade Hostel ... E4
20 Hostel Life ... F5
21 Rachmaninov Antique Hotel ... C4
22 Rossi Hotel ... E5
23 Soul Kitchen Hostel ... C5

Eating
Café Singer ... (see 11)
24 Dom Beat ... F6
25 Duo Gastrobar ... F3
26 Koryushka ... C2
27 Teplo ... B5
28 Yat ... C3

Drinking & Nightlife
29 Borodabar ... C5
30 Dead Poets Bar ... F4
31 Dyuni ... G6
32 Radiobaby ... C5
33 Union Bar & Grill ... F4
34 Ziferberg ... E4

Entertainment
35 Alexandrinsky Theatre ... E5
36 Mariinsky Theatre ... A6
37 Mikhailovsky Opera & Ballet Theatre ... D4

Shopping
38 Dom Knigi ... D4
39 Kupetz Eliseevs ... E4

Information
40 American Medical Clinic ... B5
41 Apteka Petrofarm ... D4
42 Ost-West Kontaktservice ... G5
43 St Petersburg Tourist Information Centre ... C4
44 Tourist Information Bureau Main Office ... E4
45 Tourist Information Kiosk ... B4

(where you can ride on the sidewalk), St Petersburg's backstreets are quiet and sublime.

Skatprokat CYCLING
(812-717 6838; www.skatprokat.ru; Goncharnaya ul 7; per day from R400; 11am-8pm; M Ploshchad Vosstaniya) This outfit offers rental bicycles that include brand-new mountain bikes by the Russian company Stark. You'll need to leave either R2000 and your passport, or R7000 as a deposit per bike. If you are in town for a while, this place also sells secondhand bikes and does repairs. They also offer excellent Saturday- and Sunday-morning bike tours of the city.

Tours

★ **Peter's Walking Tours** WALKING TOUR
(812-943 1229; www.peterswalk.com; tours from R750 per person; tours 10.30am mid-Apr–Oct) Established in 1996, Peter Kozyrev's innovative and passionately led tours are highly recommended as a way to see the city with knowledgable locals. The daily Original Peterswalk is one of the favourites and leaves daily from **Hostel Life** (812-318 1808; www.hostel-life.ru; Nevsky pr 47, Vosstaniya; M Mayakovskaya) at 10.30am from mid-April to late October.

Anglo Tourismo BOAT TOUR
(921-989 4722; www.anglotourismo.com; 27 nab reki Fontanki; 1hr tour adult/student R650/550; M Gostiny Dvor) There's a huge number of companies offering cruises all over the Historic Heart, all with similar prices and itineraries. However, Anglo Tourismo is the only operator to run tours with commentary in English. Between May and September the schedule runs every 1½ hours between 11am and 6.30pm. From 1 June to 31 August there are also additional night cruises.

Sleeping

High season is May to September, with some hotels increasing their rates even further in June and July. You can get great deals in the low season, when hotel prices drop 30% on average.

★ **Soul Kitchen Hostel** HOSTEL €

(8-965-816 3470; www.soulkitchenhostel.com; nab reki Moyki 62/2, apt 9, Sennaya; dm/d from R900/3600; ; M Admiralteyskaya) Soul Kitchen blends boho hipness and boutique-hotel comfort, scoring perfect 10s in many key categories: private rooms (chic), dorm beds (double-wide with privacy-protecting curtains), common areas (vast), kitchen (vast *and* beautiful) and bathrooms (downright inviting). There is also bike hire, table football, free Macs to use, free international phone calls and stunning Moyka views from a communal balcony.

Baby Lemonade Hostel HOSTEL €

(812-570 7943; www.facebook.com/pages/Baby-Lemonade-Hostel; Inzhenernaya ul 7; dm/d with shared bathroom from R790/2590, d from R3250; ; M Gostiny Dvor) The owner of Baby Lemonade is crazy about the 1960s and it shows in the pop-art, psychedelic design of this friendly, fun hostel with two pleasant, large dorms and a great kitchen and living room. However, it's worth splashing out for the boutique, hotel-worthy private rooms that are in a separate flat with great rooftop views. Breakfast included.

★ **Rachmaninov Antique Hotel** BOUTIQUE HOTEL €€

(812-327 7466; www.hotelrachmaninov.com; Kazanskaya ul 5; s/d incl breakfast from R6300/7100; ; M Nevsky Prospekt) The long-established Rachmaninov still feels like a secret place for those in the know. Perfectly located and run by friendly staff, it's pleasantly old world with hardwood floors and attractive Russian furnishings, particularly in the breakfast salon which has a grand piano.

Rossi Hotel BOUTIQUE HOTEL €€€

(812-635 6333; www.rossihotels.com; nab reki Fontanki 55; s/d/ste incl breakfast from R12,000/12,900/18,000; ; M Gostiny Dvor) Occupying a beautifully restored building on one of St Petersburg's prettiest squares, the Rossi's 53 rooms are all designed differently, but their brightness and moulded ceilings are uniform. Antique beds, super-sleek bathrooms, exposed brick walls and lots of cool designer touches create a great blend of old and new.

Eating

★ **Duo Gastrobar** FUSION €

(812-994 5443; www.duobar.ru; ul Kirochnaya 8a; mains R200-500; 1pm-midnight, to 2am Fri & Sat; ; M Chernyshevskaya) This light-bathed place, done out in wood and gorgeous glass lampshades, has really helped put this otherwise quiet area on the culinary map. Its short fusion menu excels, featuring such unlikely delights as passionfruit and gorgonzola mousse and salmon with quinoa and marscarpone. There are also more conventional choices such as risottos, pastas and salads.

★ **Yat** RUSSIAN €€

(Ять; 812-957 0023; http://eatinyat.com; nab reki Moyki 16; mains R500; 11am-11pm; ; M Admiralteyskaya) Perfectly placed for eating near to the Hermitage, this country-cottage-style restaurant has a very appealing menu of traditional dishes, which are presented with aplomb. The *shchi* (cabbage-based) soup is excellent and they offer a tempting range of flavoured vodkas. There's also a fab kids area with pet rabbits for them to feed.

Dom Beat INTERNATIONAL €€

(Дом Быта; www.dombeat.ru; ul Razyezzhaya 12; mains R300-500; ; M Ligovsky Prospekt) As if naming St Petersburg's coolest bar, lounge and restaurant after a Soviet all-purpose store and then dressing the model-gorgeous staff in tailored pastiches of factory uniforms wasn't a solid enough start, the sleek, retro-humorous interior, sumptuous menu and great atmosphere add up to make this one of the best eating choices in town.

Teplo MODERN EUROPEAN €€

(812-570 1974; www.v-teple.ru; Bolshaya Morskaya ul 45; mains R250-650; 9am-midnight; ; M Admiralteyskaya) This much-feted, eclectic and original restaurant has got it all just right. The venue itself is a lot of fun to nose around, with multiple small rooms, nooks and crannies. Service is friendly and fast (when it's not too busy) and the peppy, inventive Italian-leaning menu has something for everyone. Reservations are usually needed, so call ahead.

Koryushka RUSSIAN, GEORGIAN €€

(Корюшка; 812-917 9010; http://ginzaproject.ru/SPB/Restaurants/Korushka/About; Petropavlovskaya krepost 3, Zayachy Island; mains R500; noon-midnight; ; M Gorkovskaya) Lightly battered and fried *koryushka* (smelt) is a St Petersburg speciality every April, but you can eat the small fish year-round at this relaxed, sophisticated restaurant beside the Peter and Paul Fortress. There are plenty of other very appealing Georgian dishes on the

WORTH A TRIP

PETERHOF & TSARSKOE SELO

Several palace estates around St Petersburg, country retreats for the tsars, are now among the most spectacular sights in Russia.

Peterhof (Петергоф; also known as Petrodvorets), 29km west of the city and built for Peter the Great, is best visited for its **Grand Cascade** (ul Razvodnaya 2; ⏰10am-6pm Mon-Fri, to 8.30pm Sat, to 7pm Sun, May-early Oct) and Water Avenue, a symphony of over 140 fountains and canals located in the **Lower Park** (Нижний парк; adult/student R500/250, free Nov-Apr; ⏰9am-8pm). There are several additional palaces, villas and parks here, each of which charges its own hefty admission price.

Tsarskoe Selo (Царское Село), 25km south of the city in the town of Pushkin, is home to the baroque **Catherine Palace** (Екатерининский дворец; http://eng.tzar.ru; adult/student R400/200, audioguide R150; ⏰10am-6pm Wed-Sun, to 9pm Mon), expertly restored following its near destruction in WWII. From May to September individual visits to Catherine's Palace are limited to noon to 2pm and 4pm to 5pm, other times being reserved for tour groups.

Buses and *marshrutky* to Petrodvorets (R55, 30 minutes) run frequently from outside metro stations Avtovo and Leninsky Prospekt. From May to September, the **Peterhof Express** (adult single/return R650/1100, student single/return R450/800; ⏰10am-6pm) hydrofoil leaves from jetties behind the Hermitage and behind the Admiralty.

The easiest way to get to Tsarskoe Selo is by *marshrutka* (R35) from Moskovskaya metro station.

menu to supplement the stunning views across the Neva.

Drinking & Nightlife

★Borodabar COCKTAIL BAR

(Kazanskaya ul 11; ⏰6pm-6am; 📶; Ⓜ Nevsky Prospekt) Boroda means beard in Russian, and sure enough you'll see plenty of facial hair and tattoos in this hipster cocktail hang-out. Never mind, as the mixologists really know their stuff – we can particularly recommend their smoked old fashioned, which is infused with tobacco smoke, and their colourful (and potent) range of shots.

★Ziferberg ANTI-CAFE

(http://ziferburg.ziferblat.net; 3rd fl, Passage, Nevsky pr 48; 1st hr/thereafter per min charge R2/1, max charge R360; ⏰11am-midnight Sun-Thu, 11am-7am Fri & Sat; 📶; Ⓜ Gostiny Dvor) Occupying much of the 3rd-floor gallery of Passage is this anti-cafe with a range of quirky, boho-hipster decorated spaces, some intimate, others very social. There's an excellent range of activities to enjoy with your coffee or tea, from board games and movies to concerts by classical music students, particularly on the weekends.

Dead Poets Bar COCKTAIL BAR

(ul Zhukovskogo 12; ⏰2pm-2am; 📶; Ⓜ Mayakovskaya) This very cool place is an adult cocktail bar, with a sophisticated drinks menu and an almost unbelievable range of spirits stacked along the long bar and served up by a committed staff of mixologists. It's more of a quiet place, with low lighting, a jazz soundtrack and plenty of space to sit down.

Union Bar & Grill BAR

(Liteyny pr 55; ⏰6pm-4am Sun-Thu, until 6am Fri & Sat; 📶; Ⓜ Mayakovskaya) The Union is a glamorous and fun place, characterised by one enormous long wooden bar, low lighting and a New York feel. It's all rather adult, with a serious cocktail list and designer beers on tap. It's crazy at the weekends, but quiet during the week, and always draws a cool twenty- and thirty-something crowd.

Dyuni BAR

(Дюны; Ligovsky pr 50; ⏰4pm-midnight, to 6am Fri & Sat; 📶; Ⓜ Ploshchad Vosstaniya) What looks like a small suburban house sits rather incongruously here amid repurposed warehouses in this vast courtyard. There's a cosy indoor bar and a sand-covered outside area with table football and ping pong, which keeps the cool kids happy all night in the summer months. To find it, simply continue in a straight line from the courtyard entrance.

Radiobaby BAR, CLUB

(www.radiobaby.com; Kazanskaya ul 7; ⏰6pm-6am; Ⓜ Nevsky Prospekt) Go through the arch at Kazanskaya 5 (not 7 – that's just the street address), turn left through a second arch and you'll find this super-cool barnlike bar on your right. It's divided into several different rooms, there's a 'no techno, no house' music policy, table football, a relaxed crowd and an atmosphere of eternal hedonism. After 10pm each night the place becomes more a club than a bar.

☆ Entertainment

From July to mid-September the big theatres like the Mariinsky and the Mikhailovsky close but plenty of performances are still staged. Check the *St Petersburg Times* for comprehensive listings.

Mariinsky Theatre OPERA, BALLET
(Мариинский театр; ☎812-326 4141; www.mariinsky.ru; Teatralnaya pl 1; tickets R1000-6000; Ⓜ Sadovaya) Petersburg's most spectacular venue for ballet and opera, the Mariinsky Theatre is an attraction in its own right. Tickets can be bought online or in person, but they should be bought in advance during the summer months. The magnificent interior is the epitome of imperial grandeur, and any evening here will be an impressive experience.

Mikhailovsky Opera & Ballet Theatre OPERA, BALLET
(☎812-595 4305; www.mikhailovsky.ru; pl Iskusstv 1; tickets R300-4000; Ⓜ Nevsky Prospekt) While not quite as grand as the Mariinsky, this illustrious stage still delivers the Russian ballet or operatic experience, complete with multitiered theatre, frescoed ceiling and elaborate concerts. Pl Iskusstv (Arts Sq) is a lovely setting for this respected venue, which is home to the State Academic Opera & Ballet Company.

ℹ Information

Free wi-fi access is common across the city.

American Medical Clinic (☎812-740 2090; www.amclinic.ru; nab reki Moyki 78; ⊙24hr; Ⓜ Admiralteyskaya) One of the city's largest private clinics.

Apteka Petrofarm (Nevsky pr 22; ⊙24hr) An excellent, all-night pharmacy.

Express to Russia (☎812-570 6342; www.expresstorussia.com; Muchnoi per 2) Visas, tours, hotel bookings, tickets.

Main Post Office (Pochtamtskaya ul 9; ⊙24hr; Ⓜ Admiralteyskaya) Worth visiting for its elegant Style Moderne interior.

Ost-West Kontaktservice (☎812-327 3416; www.ostwest.com; Nevsky pr 100; ⊙10am-6pm Mon-Fri; Ⓜ Ploshchad Vosstaniya) Can find you an apartment to rent and organise tours and tickets.

St Petersburg Times (www.sptimes.ru) Published every Tuesday and Friday, when it has an indispensable listings and arts review section.

Tourist Information Bureau (☎812-310 2822; http://eng.ispb.info; Sadovaya ul 14/52; ⊙10am-7pm Mon-Fri, noon-6pm Sat; Ⓜ Gostiny Dvor) There are also branches outside the **Hermitage** (Dvortsovaya pl 12; ⊙10am-7pm; Ⓜ Admiralteyskaya), **St Isaac's Cathedral** (Isaakievskaya pl) and **Pulkovo Airport** (⊙10am-7pm Mon-Fri).

ℹ Getting Around

TO/FROM THE AIRPORT

From St Petersburg's superb new Pulkovo International Airport (p959), an official taxi to the centre should cost around R900, or you can take the bus to Moskovskaya metro station for R30, then take the metro from Moskovskaya (Line 2) all over the city for R28 – a journey of about 50 minutes all told.

PUBLIC TRANSPORT

The metro is usually the quickest way around the city. *Zhetony* (tokens) and credit-loaded cards can be bought from booths in the stations (R28).

If you are staying more than a day or two, it's worth buying a smart card (R55), which is good for multiple journeys to be used over the course of a fixed time period.

Buses, trolleybuses and *marshrutky* (fares R22 to R30) often get you closer to the sights and are especially handy to cover long distances along main avenues like Nevsky pr.

TAXI

Unofficial taxis are common. Official taxis (four-door Volga sedans with a chequerboard strip down the side and a green light in the front

MOSCOW TO ST PETERSBURG

The fastest **trains** between Moscow and St Petersburg are the *Sapsan* services (from R2600; three to four hours; six daily). There are also around 10 overnight services which can take anywhere from seven to 11 hours (*platskart/kupe* from R1000/2200). Tickets often sell out in the high months, but keep your plans flexible and you should be able to find something, even at the last minute. Many **flights** (from R2300) also connect the two cities and they rarely sell out.

WORTH A TRIP

KALININGRAD REGION КАЛИНИНГРАДСКАЯ ОБЛАСТЬ

Sandwiched by Poland and Lithuania, the Kaliningrad Region is a Russian exclave that's intimately attached to the Motherland yet also a world apart. In this 'Little Russia' – only 15,100 sq km with a population of 941,873 – you'll also find beautiful countryside, charming old Prussian seaside resorts and splendid beaches. Citizens of Japan and many European countries can visit Kaliningrad on a 72-hour visa.

The capital, **Kaliningrad** (Калининград; formely Königsberg), was once a Middle European architectural gem equal to Prague or Kraków. Precious little of this built heritage remains but there are attractive residential suburbs and remnants of the city's old fortifications that evoke the Prussian past. The most impressive building is the Gothic **Kaliningrad Cathedral** (Кафедральный собор Кёнигсберга; 4012-631 705; www.sobor-kaliningrad.ru; Kant Island; adult/student R150/130, photos R50, concerts R250-300; 10am-5pm), founded in 1333 and restored after almost being destroyed during WWII. West of the Cathedral along the river also make time for the fascinating **Museum of the World Ocean** (Музей Мирового Океана; www.world-ocean.ru/en; nab Petra Velikogo 1; adult/student R300/200, individual vessels adult/student R100/80; 10am-6pm Wed-Sun).

The best places to stay are the budget **Amigos Hostel** (Амигос Хостел; 8-911-485 2157; www.amigoshostel.ru; ul Yablonevaya Alleya 34; dm R500-550, d R1200;) and the midrange **Skipper Hotel** (Гостиница Шкипер; 4012-307 237; www.skipperhotel.ru; ul Oktyabrskaya 4a; r from R2800;) in the attractive, slightly kitsch Fish Village riverside development. There are plenty of good places to eat and drink including **Fish Club** (Рыбный клуб; ul Oktyabrskaya 4a; meals R500-1500; noon-midnight), **Zarya** (Заря; 4012-300 388; pr Mira 43; meals R200-540; 10am-3am;) and the hip apartment-cum-cafe **Kvartira** (Apartment; 4012-216 736; ul Serzhanta Koloskova 13;).

It's easy to access the region's other key sights on day trips from Kaliningrad, but if you did want to spend time away from the city, base yourself in the seaside resort of **Svetlogorsk** (Светлогорск) which is only a few hours' drive down the Baltic coast from the pine forests and Sahara-style dunes of the **Kurshskaya Kosa National Park** (Национальный парк Куршская коса; www.park-kosa.ru; admission per person/car R40/300), a Unesco World Heritage Site.

window) have meters that drivers sometimes use, though you most often pay a negotiated price.

Peterburgskoe Taksi 068 (812-324 7777, within St Petersburg just dial 068; http://taxi068.spb.ru)

Taxi Blues (812-321 8888; www.taxiblues.ru)

SURVIVAL GUIDE

Directory A–Z

ACCOMMODATION

There has been a boom in budget-friendly hostels in both Moscow and St Petersburg, and if you're on a budget you'll want to consider these – even if you typically don't 'do' hostels, most offer a few private rooms.

In hostels you're looking at R600 to R1000 for a dorm bed, and R2500 for a private room with a shared bathroom. Elsewhere hotel rooms with a bathroom start at about R3000. At the other end of the spectrum the sky is the limit, but figure on at least R10,000 for top-end accommodation in Moscow and St Petersburg (quite a bit less elsewhere).

Apartment Rental

Booking an apartment is a good way to save money on accommodation, especially for small groups. They typically cost around R4300 to

SLEEPING PRICE RANGES

The following price categories are for the cost of a double room.

€ Moscow and St Petersburg less than R3000 (rest of country less than R1500)

€€ Moscow and St Petersburg R3000 to R8000 (rest of country R1500 to R4000)

€€€ Moscow and St Petersburg more than R8000 (rest of country more than R4000)

R8600 per night. The following agencies can make bookings in Moscow and/or St Petersburg.

Enjoy Moscow (www.enjoymoscow.com; per night from US$155; 📶)

HOFA (www.hofa.ru; apartments from per night €44; 📶)

Moscow Suites (www.moscowsuites.ru; studio per night from US$199; 📶)

Ost-West Kontaktservice (p955)

BUSINESS HOURS

Restaurants and bars often stay open later than their stated hours if the establishment is full. In fact, many simply say that they work *do poslednnogo klienta* (until the last customer leaves).

Note that most museums close their ticket offices one hour (in some cases 30 minutes) before the official closing time.

Banks 9am to 6pm Monday to Friday, some open 9am to 5pm Saturday

Bars & Restaurants noon to midnight

Shops 10am to 9pm Monday to Friday, to 7pm Saturday and Sunday

INTERNET RESOURCES

Russia Made Easy (www.redtape.ru)

The Moscow Expat Site (www.expat.ru)

Visit Russia (www.visitrussia.org.uk)

Way to Russia (www.waytorussia.net)

MONEY

The Russian currency is the rouble, written as 'рубль' and abbreviated as 'руб' or 'р'. Roubles are divided into 100 almost worthless *kopeki* (kopecks). Coins come in amounts of R1, R2, R5 and R10 roubles, with banknotes in values of R10, R50, R100, R500, R1000 and R5000.

ATMs that accept all major credit and debit cards are everywhere, and most restaurants, shops and hotels in major cities gladly accept plastic. You can exchange dollars and euros (and some other currencies) at most banks; when they're closed, try the exchange counters at top-end hotels. You may need your passport. Note that crumpled or old banknotes are often refused. Many banks cash travellers cheques for a small commission.

POST

The Russian post service is **Pochta Rossia** (www.russianpost.ru). The main offices are open from 8am to 8pm or 9pm Monday to Friday, with shorter hours on Saturday and Sunday. To send a postcard or letter up to 20g anywhere in the world by air costs R26.

PUBLIC HOLIDAYS

Many businesses are closed from 1 to 7 January. Russia's main public holidays:

New Year's Day 1 January

Russian Orthodox Christmas Day 7 January

Defender of the Fatherland Day 23 February

International Women's Day 8 March

Easter Monday April

International Labour Day/Spring Festival 1 May

Victory Day 9 May

Russian Independence Day 12 June

Unity Day 4 November

SAFE TRAVEL

Travellers have nothing to fear from Russia's 'mafia' – the increasingly respectable gangster classes are not interested in such small fry. However, petty theft and pickpockets are prevalent in both Moscow and St Petersburg, so be vigilant with your belongings.

Some police officers can be bothersome, especially to dark-skinned or foreign-looking people. Other members of the police force target tourists, though reports of tourists being hassled about their documents and registration have declined. Still, you should always carry a photocopy of your passport, visa and registration stamp. If you are stopped for any reason – legitimate or illegitimate – you will surely be hassled if you don't have these.

Sadly, racism is a problem in Russia. Be vigilant on the streets around Hitler's birthday (20 April), when bands of right-wing thugs have been known to roam around spoiling for a fight with anyone who doesn't look Russian.

TELEPHONE

The international code for Russia is ☎7. The international access code from landline phones in Russia is ☎8, followed by ☎10 after the second tone, followed by the country code.

The three main mobile-phone companies, all with prepaid and 4G internet options, are

COUNTRY FACTS

Area 17,098,242 sq km

Capital Moscow

Country Code ☎7

Currency Rouble (R)

Emergency Ambulance ☎03, emergency assistance ☎112, fire ☎01, police ☎02

Language Russian

Money Plenty of ATMs, most accepting foreign cards

Population 143.8 million

Visas Required by all – apply at least a month in advance of your trip

ESSENTIAL FOOD & DRINK

Russia's rich black soil provides an abundance of grains and vegetables used in a wonderful range of breads, salads, appetisers and soups. Its waterways yield a unique range of fish and, as with any cold-climate country, there's a great love of fat-loaded dishes – Russia is no place to go on a diet!

- **Soups** For example, the lemony, meat *solyanka* or the hearty fish *ukha*.
- **Bliny** (pancakes) Served with *ikra* (caviar) or *tvorog* (cottage cheese).
- **Salads** A wide variety usually slathered in mayonnaise, including the chopped potato Olivier.
- **Pelmeni** (dumplings) Stuffed with meat and eaten with sour cream and vinegar.
- **Central Asian dishes** Try *plov* (Uzbek pilaf), *shashlyk* (kebab) or *lagman* (noodles).
- **Vodka** The quintessential Russian tipple.
- **Kvas** A refreshing, beerlike drink, or the red berry juice mix *mors*.

Beeline (www.beeline.ru), **Megafon** (www.megafon.ru) and **MTS** (www.mts.ru). Company offices are everywhere. It costs almost nothing to purchase a SIM card, but bring your passport.

Local telecom rules mean mobile calls or texts from your 'home' city or region to another city or region are more expensive – essentially long-distance calls/texts. So active callers should consider purchasing a Moscow SIM while in Moscow, and a St Petersburg SIM while in St Petersburg.

To dial another area code (mobile or land line), dial ☎8 plus 10 digits. Mobile numbers have 10 digits, always starting with ☎9 – often ☎915, ☎916 or ☎926. Mobile numbers are written in the following format: ☎8-9xx-xxx xxxx.

VISAS

Everyone needs a visa to visit Russia. For most travellers a tourist visa (single- or double-entry, valid for a maximum of 30 days) will be sufficient. If you plan to stay longer than a month, you can apply for a business visa or – if you are a US citizen – a three-year multi-entry visa.

Applying for a visa is undeniably a headache, but the process is actually quite straightforward. There are three stages: invitation, application and registration.

Invitation

To obtain a visa, everyone needs an invitation, also known as 'visa support'. Hotels and hostels will usually issue anyone staying with them an invitation voucher free or for a small fee (typically around €20 to €30). If you are not staying in a hotel or hostel, you will need to buy an invitation – this can be done through most travel agents or via specialist visa agencies, also for around €20.

Application

Invitation voucher in hand, you can then apply for a visa. Wherever in the world you are applying you can start by entering details in the online form of the Consular Department of the Russian Ministry of Foreign Affairs (https://visa.kdmid.ru/PetitionChoice.aspx).

Take care in answering the questions accurately on this form, including listing all the countries you have visited in the last 10 years and the dates of the visits – stamps in your passport will be checked against this information and if there are anomalies you will likely have to restart the process. Keep a note of the unique identity number provided for your submitted form – if you have to make changes later, you will need this to access it without having to fill in the form again from scratch.

Russian embassies in the UK and US have contracted separate agencies to process the submission of visa applications; these companies use online interfaces that direct the relevant information into the standard visa application form. In the UK, the agency is **VFS. Global** (http://ru.vfsglobal.co.uk) with offices in London and Edinburgh; in the US it's **Invisa Logistic Services** (http://ils-usa.com) with offices in Washington DC, New York, San Francisco, Houston and Seattle.

Consular offices apply different fees and slightly different application rules country by country. Avoid potential hassles by checking well in advance what these rules might be. Among the things that you will need:

- a printout of the invitation/visa support document
- a passport-sized photograph for the application form

- if you're self-employed, bank statements for the previous three months showing you have sufficient funds to cover your time in Russia.
- details of your travel insurance.

The charge for the visa will depend on the type of visa applied for and how quickly you need it.

We highly recommend applying for your visa in your home country rather than on the road.

Registration

Every visitor to Russia must have their visa registered *within seven days of arrival*, excluding weekends and public holidays. Registration is handled by your accommodating party. If staying in a homestay or rental apartment, you'll need to make arrangements with either the landlord or a friend to register you through the post office. See http://waytorussia.net/RussianVisa/Registration.html for how this can be done.

Once registered, you'll receive a registration slip. Keep this safe – that's the document that any police who stop you will ask to see. You do not need to register more than once unless you stay in additional cities for more than seven days, in which case you'll need additional registration slips.

72-Hour Visa-Free Travel

To qualify for this visa for St Petersburg, you need to enter and exit the city on a cruise or ferry such as that offered by **St Peter Line** (☎812-386 1147; www.stpeterline.com). For Kaliningrad, make arrangements in advance with locally based tour agencies.

Immigration Form

Immigration forms are produced electronically by passport control at airports. Take good care of your half of the completed form as you'll need it for registration and could face problems while travelling in Russia – and certainly will on leaving – if you can't produce it.

Getting There & Away

AIR

International flights land and take off from Moscow's three airports – **Domodedovo** (Домодедово; www.domodedovo.ru), **Sheremetyevo** (Шереметьево, SVO; ☎495-578 6565; www.svo.aero) and **Vnukovo** (Внуково; www.vnukovo.ru) – and St Petersburg's **Pulkovo** (LED; www.pulkovoairport.ru) airport. International flights to Kaliningrad's **Khrabrovo** (☎4012-610 620; www.kgd.aero) airport are rarer.

LAND

Russia has excellent train and bus connections with the rest of Europe. However, many routes connecting St Petersburg and Moscow with points east – including Kaliningrad – go through Belarus, for which you'll need a transit visa. Buses are the best way to get from St Petersburg to Tallinn. St Petersburg to Helsinki can be done by bus or train, as well as by boat.

Adjoining 13 countries, the Russian Federation has a huge number of border crossings. From Eastern Europe you are most likely to enter from Finland near Vyborg; from Estonia at Narva; from Latvia at Rēzekne; from Belarus at Krasnoye or Ezjaryshcha; and from Ukraine at Chernihiv. You can enter Kaliningrad from Lithuania and Poland at any of seven border posts.

SEA

Between early April and late September, international passenger ferries connect Stockholm, Helsinki and Tallinn with St Petersburg's **Morskoy Vokzal** (Морской вокзал; pl Morskoy Slavy 1).

Getting Around

AIR

Flying in Russia is not for the faint-hearted. Safety aside, flights can be delayed, often for hours and with little or no explanation.

That said, booking flights within Russia online is easier than ever, and domestic flights are relatively cheap. Major Russian airlines, including **Aeroflot** (www.aeroflot.com), **Rossiya** (www.rossiya-airlines.com), **S7** (www.s7.ru), **Sky Express** (www.skyexpress.ru/en), **Transaero** (www.transaero.com) and **UTAir** (www.utair.ru) have online booking, with the usual discounts for advance purchases. Otherwise, it's no problem buying a ticket at ubiquitous *aviakassa* (ticket offices) which may be able to tell you about flights that you can't easily find out about online overseas. Online agencies specialising in Russian air tickets with English interfaces include **Anywayanyday** (☎495-363 6164; www.anywayanyday.com) and **Pososhok.ru** (☎495-234 8000; www.pososhok.ru).

BUS

Buses and *marshrutky* (fixed-route vans or minibuses) are often more frequent, more

EATING PRICE RANGES

The following price categories are for the cost of a main course:

€ less than R500

€€ R500 to R1000

€€€ more than R1000

convenient and faster than trains, especially on short-distance routes. There's almost no need to reserve a seat – just arrive a good 30 minutes before the scheduled departure and buy a ticket. Prices are comparable to 3rd-class train fares.

Marshrutky are quicker than the rusty old buses and often leave when full, rather than according to a schedule. Where roads are good and villages frequent, *marshrutky* can be twice as fast as buses, and are well worth the double fare.

CAR & MOTORCYCLE

You can bring your own vehicle into Russia, but expect delays, bureaucracy and the attention of the roundly hated GAI (traffic police), who take particular delight in stopping foreign cars for document checks.

To enter Russia with a vehicle you will need a valid International Driving Permit as well as the insurance and ownership documents for your car.

As you don't really need a car to get around big cities, hiring a car comes into its own for making trips out of town where public transport may not be so good. All the major agencies have offices in Moscow and St Petersburg.

Driving is on the right-hand side, and at an intersection traffic coming from the right generally (but not always) has the right of way. The maximum legal blood-alcohol content is 0.03%, a rule that is strictly enforced.

TAXI

Russian cities have plenty of official taxis, but few people think twice about flagging down any car to request a ride. A fare is negotiated for the journey – simply state your destination and ask '*skolko?*' (how much?), and off you go. Proceed with caution if you are alone and/or it's late at night, especially if you are a woman. While exceedingly rare, violent attacks on passengers have occurred.

TRAIN

Russia's extensive train network is efficiently run by **Russian Railways** (www.eng.rzd.ru). *Prigorodny* (suburban) or short-distance trains – also known as *elektrichky* – do not require advance booking: you can buy your ticket at the *prigorodny poezd kassa* (suburban train ticket offices) at train stations.

There are a number of options on where to buy, including online from RZD. Bookings open 45 days before the date of departure. You'd be wise to buy well in advance over the busy summer months and holiday periods such as New Year and early May, when securing berths at short notice on certain trains can be difficult.

For long-distance trains, unless otherwise specified we quote 2nd-class sleeper *(kupe)* fares. Expect 1st-class (SV) fares to be double this, and 3rd class *(platskartny)* to be about 40% less. Children under five travel free if they share a berth with an adult; otherwise, children under 10 pay a reduced fare for their own berth.

You'll need your passport (or a photocopy) to buy tickets. You can buy tickets for others if you bring their passports or photocopies. Queues can be very long and move with interminable slowness. At train ticket offices (*'Zh/D kassa'*, short for *'zheleznodorozhnaya kassa'*), which are all over most cities, you can pay a surcharge of around R200 and avoid the queues. Alternatively, most travel agencies will organise the reservation and delivery of train tickets for a substantial mark-up.

Serbia

Includes ➡

Best Places to Eat

- Šešir Moj (p967)
- To Je To (p966)
- Radost Fina Kuhinjica (p967)
- Fish i Zeleniš (p972)

Best Places to Stay

- Hotel Moskva (p966)
- Hostel Bongo (p966)
- Green Studio Hostel (p965)
- Hotel Veliki (p972)

Why Go?

Warm, welcoming and a hell of a lot of fun – everything you never heard about Serbia (Србија) is true. Exuding a feisty mix of élan and *inat* (classic Serbian rebellious defiance), this country doesn't do 'mild': Belgrade is one of the world's wildest party destinations, the northern town of Novi Sad hosts the rocking EXIT festival, and even its hospitality is emphatic – expect to be greeted with *rakija* (fruit brandy) and a hearty three-kiss hello.

While political correctness is about as commonplace as a nonsmoking bar, Serbia is nevertheless a cultural crucible: the art nouveau town of Subotica revels in its proximity to Hungary, bohemian Niš echoes to the clip-clop of Roma horse carts, and minaret-studded Novi Pazar nudges some of the most sacred sites in Serbian Orthodoxy. And in the mountainous Kopaonik and Zlatibor regions, ancient traditions coexist with après-ski bling. Forget what you think you know: come and say *zdravo* (hello)…or better yet, *živeli* (cheers)!

When to Go

Belgrade

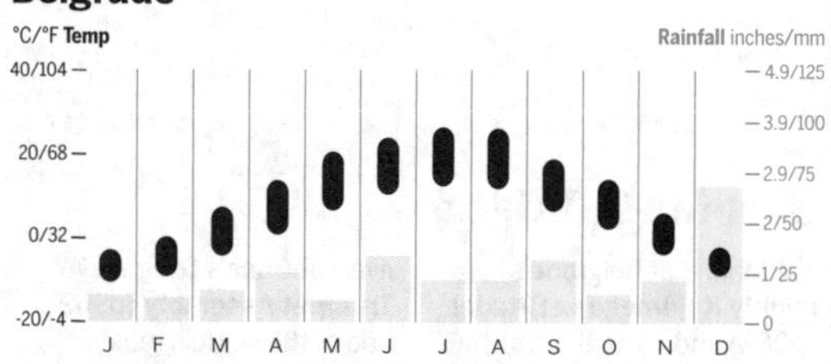

Apr Watch winter melt away with a scenic ride on the nostalgic Šargan 8 railway.

Jul & Aug Rock out at Novi Sad's EXIT, go wild at Guča and get jazzy at Nišville.

Dec–Mar Head to Zlatibor for alpine adventure.

Serbia Highlights

1 Marvel at Belgrade's mighty **Kalemegdan Citadel** (p963) and party the night away on a *splav* (river barge nightclub).

2 Witness the laid-back town of **Novi Sad** (p971) as it morphs into the state of EXIT every July.

3 Steel your eardrums (and liver) at Guča's **Dragačevo Trumpet Assembly** (p969), one of the world's most frenetic music festivals.

4 Escape reality in the fantastic village of **Drvengrad** (p971), built by director Emir Kusturica for indie drama *Life is a Miracle*.

5 Goggle at splendid surprises bursting from the Vojvodinian plains, including the art nouveau treasures of **Subotica** (p973).

6 Ponder the creepy, cryptic rock towers of **Djavolja Varoš** (p974).

7 Ski, hike or just take the mountain air in the magical villages of **Zlatibor** (p971).

ITINERARIES

One Week

Revel in three days of cultural and culinary exploration in **Belgrade**, allowing for at least one night of hitting the capital's legendary night spots. Carry on to **Novi Sad** for trips to the vineyards and monasteries of **Fruška Gora** and **Sremski Karlovci**.

Two Weeks

Follow the above itinerary then head north for the art nouveau architecture of **Subotica**, before slicing south to **Zlatibor** en route to traditional Serbian villages, the eerie **Djavolja Varoš** and the lively city of **Niš**.

BELGRADE БЕОГРАД

011 / POP 1.6 MILLION

Outspoken, adventurous, proud and audacious: Belgrade is by no means a 'pretty' capital, but its gritty exuberance makes it one of the most happening cities in Europe. It is here where the Sava River meets the Danube (Dunav), and old-world culture gives way to new-world nightlife. Grandiose coffee houses, quirky sidewalk ice-creameries and smoky dens all find rightful place along Knez Mihailova, a lively pedestrian boulevard flanked by historical buildings all the way to the ancient Kalemegdan Citadel, crown of the city. 'Belgrade' literally translates as 'White City', but Serbia's colourful capital is red hot.

Sights & Activities

★Kalemegdan Citadel FORTRESS

(Kalemegdanska tvrđava) FREE Some 115 battles have been fought over imposing, impressive Kalemegdan, and the citadel was destroyed more than 40 times throughout the centuries. Fortifications began in Celtic times, and the Romans extended it onto the flood plains during the settlement of 'Singidunum', Belgrade's Roman name. The fort's bloody history, discernible despite today's plethora of jolly cafes and funfairs, only makes Kalemegdan all the more fascinating.

Military Museum MUSEUM

(www.muzej.mod.gov.rs; Kalemegdan Citadel; adult/child 150/70DIN; 10am-5pm Tue-Sun) Tucked away in Belgrade's sprawling Kalemegdan Citadel, this museum presents the complete military history of the former Yugoslavia. Gripping displays include captured Kosovo Liberation Army weapons, bombs and missiles (courtesy of NATO), rare guns and bits of the American stealth fighter shot down in 1999. You'll find the museum through the Stambol Gate, built by the Turks in the mid-1700s and used for public executions.

National Museum MUSEUM

(Narodni Muzej; www.narodnimuzej.rs; Trg Republike 1a; adult/child 200/100DIN; 10am-5pm Tue-Wed & Fri, noon-8pm Thur & Sat, 10am-2pm Sun) Trg Republike (Republic Sq), a meeting point and outdoor exhibition space, is home to the National Museum. Lack of funding for renovations has kept it mostly shuttered for the last decade, though some exhibitions are again open to the public.

Ethnographic Museum MUSEUM

(Etnografski Muzej; www.etnografskimuzej.rs; Studentski Trg 13; adult/student 150/60DIN; 10am-5pm Tue-Sat, 9am-2pm Sun) This museum features traditional costumes, working utensils and folksy mountain-village interiors.

DON'T MISS

BELGRADE'S HISTORIC 'HOODS

Skadarska or 'Skadarlija' is Belgrade's Montmartre. This cobblestoned strip east of Trg Republike was the bohemian heartland at the turn of the 20th century; local artistes and dapper types still gather in its legion of cute restaurants and cafes.

Savamala, cool-Belgrade's destination du jour, stretches along the Sava down ul Karadjordjeva. Constructed in the 1830s for Belgrade's smart set, the neighbourhood (p968) now houses cultural centres, ramshackle, photogenic architecture, nightspots galore and a buzzing vibe.

Central Belgrade

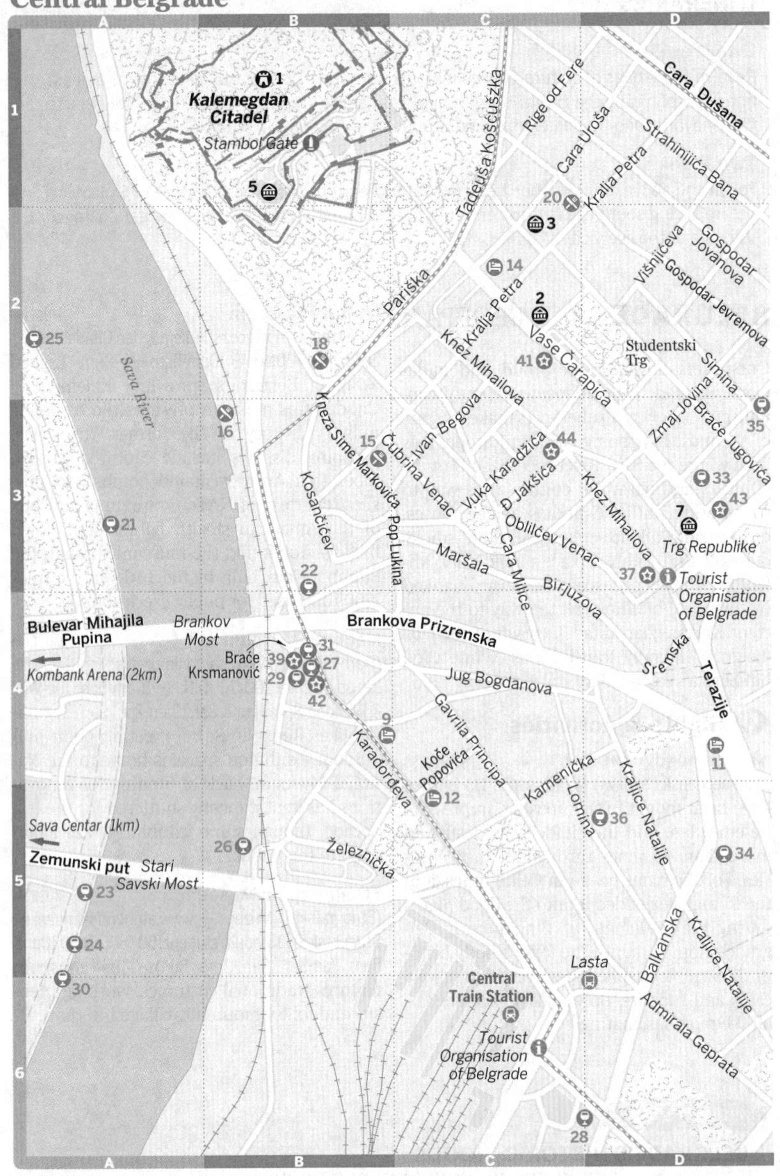

Gallery of Frescos GALLERY

(www.narodnimuzej.rs; Cara Uroša 20; admission 100DIN; ⊙10am-5pm Tue, Wed, Fri & Sat, noon-8pm Thu, 10am-2pm Sun) The gallery features replicas (and the odd original) of Byzantine Serbian church art, down to the last scratch. Unlike the sensitive originals, these frescoes can be photographed to your heart's content.

Nikola Tesla Museum MUSEUM

(www.tesla-museum.org; Krunska 51; admission incl guided tour in English 500DIN; ⊙10am-6pm Tue-Sun) Meet the man on the 100DIN note at one

of Belgrade's best museums. Tesla's ashes are kept here in a glowing, golden orb: at the time of writing, debate was raging between the museum and its supporters and the church as to whether they should be moved to hallowed ground.

Museum of Automobiles MUSEUM

(www.automuseumbgd.com; Majke Jevrosime 30; adult/child 200/80DIN; ⌚9am-7pm) A compelling collection of cars and motorcycles located in Belgrade's first public garage. Check out the '57 Caddy convertible: only 25,000km and one careful owner – President Tito.

Historical Museum of Serbia MUSEUM

(Istorijski Muzej Srbije; www.imus.org.rs; Trg Nikole Pašića 11; adult/child 200/100DIN; ⌚noon-7pm Tue-Sun) Home to an absorbing wealth of archaeological, ethnographic and military collections. It's your best bet until the National Museum reopens entirely.

Sveti Sava CHURCH

(www.hramsvetogsave.com; Svetog Save) Sveti Sava is the world's biggest Orthodox church, a fact made entirely obvious when looking at the city skyline from a distance or standing under its dome. The church is built on the site where the Turks apparently burnt relics of St Sava. Work on the church interior (frequently interrupted by wars) continues today.

Maršal Tito's Grave MONUMENT

(House of Flowers; www.mij.rs; Botićeva 6; admission incl entry to Museum of Yugoslav History 200DIN; ⌚10am-8pm Tue-Sun May-Oct, to 6pm Tue-Sun Nov-April) A visit to Tito's mausoleum is obligatory. Also on display are thousands of elaborate relay batons presented to him by young 'Pioneers', plus gifts from political leaders and the voguish set of the era. It's attached to the fascinating **Museum of Yugoslav History**. Take trolleybus 40 or 41 at the south end of Parliament on Kneza Miloša. It's the second stop after turning into Bul Mira: ask the driver to let you out at Kuća Cveća.

Ada Ciganlija BEACH

(www.adaciganlija.rs) In summertime, join the hordes of sea-starved locals (up to 250,000 a day) for sun and fun at this artificial island on the Sava. Cool down with a swim, kayak or windsurf after a leap from the 55m bungee tower. Take bus 52 or 53 from Zeleni Venac.

Sleeping

★Green Studio Hostel HOSTEL €

(☎011-218 5943; www.greenstudiohostel.com; Karađorđeva 61, 6th floor, Savamala; dm from €9, r €9-40, apt €40; ❄📶) Clean, airy and staffed by your new best friends, this sunny spot has a handy location near the bus and train stations, as well as Belgrade's main attractions. Nightly happy hours, daily activities, tons of local advice, and free *rakija*!

Central Belgrade

Top Sights
1 Kalemegdan Citadel B1

Sights
2 Ethnographic Museum C2
3 Gallery of Frescos C2
4 Historical Museum of Serbia E4
5 Military Museum B1
6 Museum of Automobiles F4
7 National Museum D3
8 Russian Church F5

Sleeping
9 Green Studio Hostel B4
10 Hostel Bongo E5
11 Hotel Moskva D4
12 Jump Inn C5
13 Soul House Apartments E3
14 YOLOstel C2

Eating
15 ? B3
Cantidna de Frida .... (see 16)
16 Comunale B3
Iguana .... (see 16)
17 Little Bay E3
18 Radost Fina Kuhinjica B2
19 Šešir Moj E3
20 Smokvica C1
Toro Latin Gastro Bar .... (see 16)

Drinking & Nightlife
21 20/44 .... A3
22 Bašta B3
23 Blaywatch A5
24 Freestyler A5
25 Hot Mess A2
Klub Beton .... (see 16)
26 Lasta B5
27 Mladost i Ludost B4
28 Mr Stefan Braun C6
29 Peron B4
30 Povetarac A6
31 Prohibicija B4
32 Radionica Bar E2
33 Rakia Bar D3
34 Samo Pivo D5
35 Tube D3
36 WATS D5

Entertainment
37 Bilet Servis D3
38 Bitef Art Cafe F3
39 Čorba Kafe B4
40 Dom Omladine E4
KC Grad .... (see 39)
41 Kolarčev University Concert Hall C2
42 Mikser House B4
43 National Theatre D3
44 Serbian Academy of Arts & Sciences C3

★ Hostel Bongo HOSTEL €
(☎011-268 5515; www.hostelbongo.com; ul Terazije 36; dm/d from €11/38; ❄☜) Guests at the modern, brightly painted Bongo can take their pick: plunge into the attractions, bars and restaurants nearby, or hide in the hostel's sweet garden terrace. Fantastic staff has oodles of hostelling experience.

YOLOstel HOSTEL €
(☎064 141 9339; www.yolostel.rs; ul Uzun Mirkova 6, Apt 6, 3rd floor; dm/d from €11/35; ❄☜) This new designer hostel enjoys an awesome location just a short stumble from Savamala. With custom-made furniture, quirky, gorgeous decor and a hip, refined air, this is not your usual backpacker flophouse.

Soul House Apartments APARTMENTS €€
(☎064 135 2255; www.soul-house.net; ul Makedonska 15; one person/two people stays from €25/35; ❄☜) These three themed apartments are located within the same building a quick amble from Trg Republike. The 'hippie suite' (€25/35) is yellow and bright, the 'modernistic studio' (€30/40) has trippy, fun furnishings, and the 'retro apartment' (€40/50) is done up Tito-era style. All have good kitchens. There's a minimum two-night stay on weekends.

Jump Inn HOTEL €€
(☎011-404 9650; www.jumpinnhotelbelgrade.com; ul Koče Popovića 2a; s/d from €60/70; P❄☜) This new design hotel, aptly located in the trendy Savamala district, has spacious, stylish rooms, all with Smart TVs, and many with Sava River and Ada Bridge views.

★ Hotel Moskva HISTORIC HOTEL €€€
(Hotel Moscow; ☎011-364 2069; www.hotelmoskva.rs; Balkanska 1; s/d/ste from €90/110/130; ❄☜) Art nouveau icon and proud symbol of the best of Belgrade, the majestic Moskva has been wowing guests, including Albert Einstein, Indira Gandhi and Alfred Hitchcock, since 1906. Laden with ye olde glamour, this is the place to write your memoirs at a big old desk.

Eating

★ To Je To BALKAN €
(bul Despota Stefana 21; mains 220-750DIN; ⏲8am-midnight) 'To je to' means 'that's it', and in this case, they're talking about meat. Piles of the stuff, grilled in all its juicy glory, make up the menu here in the forms of Sarajevo-style *ćevapi* (spicy skinless sausages), turkey kebab, sweetbreads and more. It

BETON HALA

Belgrade's bastion of banqueting is undoubtedly Beton Hala. The unglamorous name – it means 'Concrete Hall' – belies the wealth of astonishingly hip restaurants, cafes, bars and clubs that make themselves at home in the once-derelict warehouse. Beton Hall is the place to hit if you're after classy-cool nosh. We recommend:

Comunale (www.comunale.rs; Beton Hala; mains 650-1700DIN; ⏲10am-1pm) For fancy homemade pastas and a classy take on the Serbian grill.

Cantina de Frida (www.cantinadefrida.com; Beton Hala; mains 270-1300DIN; ⏲10am-3am) Tasty tapas in cool, colourful surrounds.

Iguana (www.iguana.rs; Beton Hala; mains 900-1750DIN; ⏲10am-2am) Peruse the small but smart menu to a soundtrack of live jazz.

Toro Latin Gastro Bar (www.richardsandoval.com/torobelgrade; Beton Hala; mains 400-1500DIN; ⏲10am-2am) Toro offers posh sharing plates, grilled meats galore and vegetarian and gluten-free options.

serves homemade *sarma* (stuffed cabbage rolls) on the weekends. Cheap, scrumptious and highly recommended by locals.

★Šešir Moj SERBIAN €€
(My Hat; www.restoransesirmoj.co.rs; Skadarska 21; meals 420-1300DIN; ⏲9am-1am) Roma bands tug the heartstrings while traditional dishes such as *punjena bela vešalica* (pork stuffed with *kajmak* – clotted cream) buoy the belly.

★Radost Fina Kuhinjica VEGETARIAN €€
(☎060 603 0023; Pariska 3; mains 450-1300DIN; ⏲2pm-midnight Tue-Sat, 1pm-9pm Sun; ✍) Barbecue-obsessed Serbia isn't the easiest place for vegetarians, but thanks to this cheery eatery, you'll never have to settle for eating garnish and chips again. Its ever-changing menu features curries, veg burgers, innovative pastas and meat substitutes galore, some of which are vegan. The healthy cupcakes are a delight.

? SERBIAN €€
(Znak Pitanja; www.varoskapija.rs; Kralja Petra 6; mains 550-1100DIN; ⏲9am-1am) Belgrade's oldest *kafana* has been attracting the bohemian set since 1823 with dishes such as stuffed chicken and 'lamb under the iron pan'. Its quizzical name follows a dispute with the adjacent church, which objected to the boozy tavern – originally called 'By the Cathedral' – referring to a house of god.

Smokvica CAFE €€
(www.smokvica.rs; Kralja Petra 73; meals 250-1200DIN; ⏲9am-1am; 📶) With its winsome courtyard terrace, arty crowd and with-it gourmet menu, to stumble across Smokvica ('little fig') is to forget you're in hustling, bustling Belgrade. Nibble innovative salads, gourmet tasting plates and sandwiches or just sip good coffee in an atmosphere both rare and rarified.

Little Bay EUROPEAN €€
(www.littlebay.rs; Dositejeva 9a; meals 595-1390DIN; ⏲11am-1am) Little wonder locals and visitors have long been singing the praises of this gem: it's one of the best dining experiences in Belgrade. Tuck yourself into a private opera box and let the spinach-and-feta-stuffed chicken or a traditional English roast lunch (795DIN, Sundays only) melt in your mouth.

🍷 Drinking & Nightlife

Bars

★Kafana Pavle Korčagin TAVERNA
(☎011-240 1980; Ćirila i Metodija 2a; ⏲8pm-1am) Raise a glass to Tito at this frantic, festive *kafana*. Lined with communist memorabilia and packed to the rafters with revellers this table-thumping throwback fills up nightly; reserve a table in advance.

Rakia Bar BAR
(www.rakiabar.com; Dobračina 5, Dorćol; ⏲9am-midnight Sun-Thu, to 1am Fri & Sat) An ideal spot for *rakija* rookies to get their first taste of the spirit of Serbia. English-speaking staff will guide you through the extensive drinks menu. Beware: this stuff is strong.

WATS BAR
(We Are The Shit; Lomina 5-9; ⏲6pm-1am Thur & Sat, to 2am Fri-Sat) This cheeky pre-Savamala-clubbing bar is akin to a club itself – albeit a small one – with DJs spinning and a cool crowd jostling for dancing, drinking and ogling space.

THE SAVAMALA SCENE

The once-derelict, now-dapper Savamala creative district is Belgrade's hip HQ, with bars, clubs and cultural centres that morph into achingly cool music/dance venues come sundown. Dress codes and attitudes are far more relaxed here than in other parts of the city, and in most places there appears to be an unwritten ban on turbofolk; indie, electro, funk, rock and '90s disco are the go in this part of town. And don't let the bedraggled buildings fool you; there's magic going down inside. Give these happening haunts a go:

Mikser House (www.house.mikser.rs; Karadjordjeva 46; ⏲10am-2am) Mikser House is the symbol of Savamala. Hidden in an old warehouse, it has a shop, creative workspaces, a cafe and galleries showcasing the talents of local designers; come nighttime, it morphs into a bar, restaurant and music venue hosting live acts and DJs from Serbia and around the world. Check the website for upcoming events.

KC Grad (www.gradbeograd.eu; Braće Krsmanović 4; ⏲noon-midnight Mon-Fri, 2pm-midnight Sat-Sun) Like Mikser House, this wonderful warehouse space promotes local creativity with workshops, exhibitions, a restaurant and nightly avant-garde music events.

Peron (Braće Krsmanović 12; ⏲10pm-late) Eclectic hotspot where crowds go bonkers to everything from string quartets to pounding electro.

Lasta (Hercegovačka bb, Savamalski kej; ⏲midnight-6am Thur-Sun) Belgrade's first city-side *splav* pulls in a happy crowd of hip-hop, funk, electro and disco lovers.

Mladost i Ludost (Karadjordjeva 44; ⏲9pm-5am) These two bars are within the same building; punters hepped up on old-school DJ tunes criss-cross between them at their leisure. The names mean 'youth' and 'crazy': no false advertising here!

Prohibicija BAR

(ul Karadjordjeva 36 , Savamala; ⏲9am-1am) This stylish spot is perfectly located for pre-Savamala clubbing drinks. Sip craft beers and cocktails while watching the street action out the huge windows.

Idiott BAR

(Dalmatinska 13; ⏲noon-2am) This fun little bar has long been alternative HQ in Belgrade, much loved for its '80s, punk and electro tunes, pinball machines and brilliant summer garden terrace. It's beside the Botanic Gardens.

Bašta BAR

(www.jazzbasta.com; Karadjordjeva 43, Savamala; ⏲5pm-2am) Located in an old building with a whimsical courtyard, creative cocktails and frequent live jazz, Bašta is very Savamala. Find it by clambering up the steps near Brankov Most.

Radionica Bar BAR

(Dobračina 59, Dorćol; ⏲8pm-3am weeknights, 9pm-4am Fri-Sat) 'Radionica' means 'workshop', and that's exactly what this place once was. Traces of its blue-collar past remain in its industrial-cool decor, but there's nothing rough about its hipster clientele or swish cocktail menu.

Samo Pivo BAR

(ul Balkanska 13; ⏲noon-1am) The name means 'just beer', and with seven draught beers and 50 brands of bottled beers available, it's not kidding. A great choice for when you're sick of Lav or Jelen (though of course, it has those too).

Nightclubs

Belgrade has a reputation as one of the world's top party cities, with a wild club scene limited only by imagination and hours in the day. Many clubs move to river barges in summertime.

Klub Beton NIGHTCLUB

(Beton Hala; ⏲10pm-4am) Frock up and shake your well-clad thang to sophisticated electro at this new Beton Hala nightspot.

Mr Stefan Braun NIGHTCLUB

(www.mrstefanbraun.rs; Nemanjina 4) Those who want to party like (and with) Serbian superstars will find their bliss at this 9th-storey den of decadence. Get your finest threads – and most model-like pout – on and get there before 1am to beat the queues.

Plastic NIGHTCLUB

(www.clubplastic.rs; cnr Dalmatinska & Takovska; ⏲Wed-Sat 10pm-6am Oct-May) A perennial favourite among electro-heads and booty shakers, this slick venue is frequented by top local and international DJs. The more intimate Mint Club is within Plastic. Between May and October, head to Plastic Light, the floating version of the club on the Sava River.

Tube NIGHTCLUB
(www.thetube.rs; Simina 21; ⏲11pm-6am Thu-Sat) Lovers of all music electronic will have a blast in this beautifully designed former nuclear bunker. It's a big club, but does get packed: get in early to stake yourself some space.

River Barges

According to Michael Palin, Belgrade has so many nightclubs 'they can't fit them all on land'. Indeed: the city is famous for its Sava and Danube river barge clubs, known collectively as *splavovi*. Most are open only in summer. The Sava boasts a 1.5km strip of *splavovi* on its west bank: these are the true wild-and-crazy party boats. Walk over Brankov Most or catch tram 7, 9 or 11 from the city.

Adjacent to Hotel Jugoslavija in Novi Belgrade, the 1km strip of Danube barges are a bit more sophisticated; many are restaurants that get their dancing shoes on later in the evening. Take bus 704 or 706 from Zeleni Venac and get out by Hotel Jugoslavija.

Hot Mess RIVER BARGE
(Ušće bb, Sava River; ⏲9am-3am) Hot Mess epitomises the sybaritic *splav*, with selfie-snappers posing by the on-board pool, blinding neon lights and a young, uninhibited crowd going wild to disco, house and R&B. They also do great hangover breakfasts.

Blaywatch RIVER BARGE
(www.blaywatch.com; Brodarska bb, Sava River; ⏲midnight-late) This throbbing place gets crowded and dress codes may be enforced (scruffy bad on boys, skimpy good on girls). The crowd is a mix of local 'beautiful people' and foreigners, all occupied with each other and the turbo tunes.

20/44 RIVER BARGE
(Savski kej bb, Sava River; ⏲6pm-4am) Retro, run-down and loads of fun, this alternative *splav* is named for Belgrade's map coordinates. Open year-round.

Freestyler RIVER BARGE
(www.freestyler.rs; Brodarska bb, Sava River; ⏲11pm-5am Tue-Sun) The gigantic Freestyler has been a symbol of *splav* saturnalia for years, not least for its infamous foam parties.

Povetarac RIVER BARGE
(Brodarska bb, Sava River; ⏲11pm-late, 8pm-late winter) This rusting cargo ship attracts an indie crowd. Open year-round.

Amsterdam RIVER BARGE
(www.amsterdam.rs; Kej Oslobodjenja bb, Danube River; ⏲10am-1am, until 2am Sat) Restaurant by day (and evening), polished party boat by night, with interesting cocktails, DJs and occasional live pop and folk music. It's right by the Hotel Jugoslavija.

Acapulco RIVER BARGE
(Danube River; ⏲noon-late) Blinged-up boys come here to flaunt their (new) money and she-accessories. Got a low turbofolk threshold? Start swimming.

✩ Entertainment

For concert and theatre tickets, go to **Bilet Servis** (☎0900 110 011; www.eventim.rs; Trg Republike 5; ⏲10am-8pm Mon-Fri, noon-8pm Sat). Large venues for visiting acts include **Sava Centar** (☎011-220 6060; www.savacentar.net; Milentija Popovića 9; ⏲box office 10am-8pm Mon-Fri, to 3pm Sat) and **Kombank Arena** (☎011-220 2222; www.kombankarena.rs; Bul Arsenija Čarnojevića 58; ⏲box office 10am-8pm Mon-Fri, to 3pm Sat).

MADNESS, MADE IN SERBIA

On the surface, the Dragačevo Trumpet Assembly (an annual gathering of brass musicians) sounds harmless; nerdily endearing, even. But band camp this ain't: it *is*, however, the most boisterous music festival in all of Europe, if not the world.

Known simply as 'Guča', after the western Serbian village that has hosted it each August since 1961, the four-day debauch is hedonism at its most rambunctious: tens of thousands of beer-and-brass-addled visitors dance wild *kola* (fast-paced circle dances) through the streets, gorging on spit-meat and slapping dinar on the sweaty foreheads of the (mostly Roma) *trubači* performers. The music itself is relentless and frenzy-fast; even Miles Davis confessed, 'I didn't know you could play trumpet that way.'

Sleep is a dubious proposition, but bring a tent or book ahead anyway: www.guca.rs has information on accommodation and transport.

Bitef Art Cafe LIVE MUSIC
(www.bitefartcafe.rs; Skver Mire Trailović 1; ⌚7pm-4am) There's something for everyone at this delightful hotchpotch of a cafe-club. Funk, soul and jazz get a good airing, as do rock, world music and classical. In summer, Bitef moves their stage to Kalemegdan Fortress.

Čorba Kafe LIVE MUSIC
(Braće Krsmanović 3; ⌚9am-2am Sun-Thur, til 3am Fri-Sat) This rockin' little joint has live music, from rock and metal to pop and '70s hits, almost every night of the week; it's smoky, sweaty and loud, and that's the fun of it. It's under Brankov Most.

National Theatre THEATRE
(☎011-262 0946; www.narodnopozoriste.co.rs; Trg Republike; ⌚box office 11am-3pm, 5pm until start of performance) Stages operas, dramas and ballets during winter.

Kolarčev University Concert Hall LIVE MUSIC
(☎011-263 0550; www.kolarac.rs; Studentski Trg 5; ⌚box office 10am-7.30pm) Home to the Belgrade Philharmonica.

Dom Omladine CULTURAL CENTRE
(Youth Centre; www.domomladine.org; Makedonska 22; ⌚box office 10am-10pm Mon-Sat) Hosts a range of cultural events from underground concerts to pop culture panels.

Serbian Academy of Arts & Sciences LIVE MUSIC
(☎011-234 2400; www.sanu.ac.rs; Knez Mihailova 35) Stages free concerts and exhibitions.

Information

TOURIST INFORMATION

Tourist Organisation of Belgrade (☎freecall 0800 110 011; www.tob.rs) Trg Republike 5 (☎011-263 5622; ⌚9am-7pm); Train Station (☎011-361 2732; Savski Trg 2; ⌚7am-1.30pm Mon-Sat); Nikola Tesla Airport (☎011-209 7828; ⌚9am-9.30pm) Helpful folk with a raft of brochures, city maps and all the info you could need.

WEBSITES

Belgraded (www.belgraded.com)
Belgradian (www.belgradian.com)
Lonely Planet (www.lonelyplanet.com/serbia/belgrade)

Getting There & Away

BUS

Belgrade has two adjacent bus stations, near the eastern banks of the Sava River: **BAS** (☎011-263 6299; www.bas.rs; Železnička 4) and **Lasta** (☎011-334 8555; www.lasta.rs; Železnička 2). Buses run from both to international and Serbian destinations. Sample daily routes include Belgrade to Sarajevo (2340DIN, eight hours), Ljubljana (4000DIN, 7½ hours) and Vienna

WORTH A TRIP

SREM DISTRICT СРЕМ

Fruška Gora is an 80km stretch of rolling hills where monastic life has continued since 35 monasteries were built between the 15th and 18th centuries to safeguard Serbian culture and religion from the Turks. With your own vehicle you can flit freely between the 16 remaining monasteries; otherwise, ask about tours at tourist offices in Novi Sad and Sremski Karlovci. Public transport gets you from Novi Sad to villages within the park, from where you can walk between sights. An easy outing is done with a bus from Novi Sad bound for Irig (170DIN, 40 minutes); ask to be let out at the **Novo Hopovo Monastery**. From here, walk or catch local buses to other points such as Vrdnik and Venac. Visit www.npfruskagora.co.rs for a rundown on the region; www.psdzeleznicarns.org.rs has detailed information on individual monasteries (click on 'Фрушкогорски манастири'). At the edge of Fruška Gora on the banks of the Danube is the photogenic village of **Sremski Karlovci**. Lined with stunning structures like the Orthodox cathedral (1758–62), the baroque Four Lions fountain and the Chapel of Peace at the southern end of town (where the Turks and Austrians signed the 1699 Peace Treaty), Sremski Karlovci is also at the heart of a famed wine region. Visit the **Museum of Beekeeping & Wine Cellar** (☎021-881071; www.muzejzivanovic.com; Mitropolita Stratimirovića 86) to try famous *bermet* wine, or drop in at any of the family-owned cellars around town. Buzzing during summer weekends with lively wedding parties, Sremski Karlovci also hosts a grape-harvesting festival in late September. Take frequent buses 60, 61 or 62 from Novi Sad (140DIN, 30 minutes) and visit the **tourist organisation** (☎021-882 127; www.karlovci.org.rs; Patrijarha Rajačića 1; ⌚8am-6pm Mon-Fri, 10am-6pm Sat) just off the main square.

WORTH A TRIP

ZLATIBOR

Zlatibor is a romantic region of gentle mountains, traditions and hospitality.

Quirky adventures await in the village of Mokra Gora. **Drvengrad** (Küstendorf; www.mecavnik.info; Mećavnik hill, Mokra Gora; adult/child 200/120DIN; ⏲9am-9pm) was built by Serbian director Emir Kusturica in 2002 for his film *Life is a Miracle*, and offers surreal fun and prime panoramas.

The fun of a 2½-hour journey on the twisty-turny **Šargan 8 railway** (☎bookings 031-800 125; www.serbianrailways.com; adult/child 600/300DIN; ⏲daily April-Oct, by appointment Nov-March) tourist train is its disorienting twists, turns and tunnels (all 22 of them).

Reach these sights via bus from Užice or through **Zlatibor Tours** (☎031-845 957; www.zlatibortours.com; Tržni centar, bus station; ⏲8am-10pm).

(4400DIN, 9½ hours); frequent domestic services include Subotica (800DIN, three hours), Novi Sad (520DIN, one hour), Niš (1380DIN, three hours) and Novi Pazar (1400DIN, three hours).

CAR & MOTORCYCLE

Most major car-hire companies have offices at Nikola Tesla Airport. See www.beg.aero/en for a full list.

TRAIN

The **central train station** (Savski Trg 2) has an information office on Platform 1, tourist information office, **exchange bureau** (⏲6am-10pm) and **sales counter** (⏲24hrs).

Frequent trains go to Novi Sad (288DIN, 1½ hours), Subotica (560DIN, three hours) and Niš (784DIN, four hours). See www.serbianrailways.com for timetables and fares.

Getting Around

TO/FROM THE AIRPORT

Nikola Tesla airport is 18km from Belgrade. Local bus 72 (73DIN to 150DIN, half-hourly, 5.20am to midnight from airport, 4.40am to 11.40pm from town) connects the airport with Zeleni Venac; the cheapest tickets must be purchased from news stands. A minibus also runs between the airport and the central Trg Slavija (250DIN, 5am to 3.50am from airport, 4.20am to 3.20am from the square).

Don't get swallowed up by the airport taxi shark pit: ask the tourist office in the arrivals hall to call one for you. A taxi from the airport to Knez Mihailova should be around 1800DIN.

CAR & MOTORCYCLE

Parking in Belgrade is regulated by three parking zones – red (one hour, 56DIN), yellow (two hours, 48DIN per hour) and green (three hours, 41DIN per hour). Tickets must be bought from kiosks or via SMS (in Serbian).

PUBLIC TRANSPORT

Trams and trolleybuses ply limited routes but buses chug all over town. Rechargeable BusPlus cards can be bought and topped up (73DIN per ticket) at kiosks across the city; they're 140DIN if you buy from the driver.

Tram 2 connects Kalemegdan Citadel with Trg Slavija, bus stations and the central train station.

TAXI

Move away from obvious taxi traps and flag down a distinctly labelled cruising cab, or get a local to call you one. Flagfall is 170DIN; reputable cabs should charge about 70DIN per kilometre.

VOJVODINA ВОЈВОДИНА

Home to more than 25 ethnic groups, six languages and the best of Hungarian and Serbian traditions, Vojvodina's pancake plains mask a diversity unheard of in the rest of the country. Affable capital Novi Sad hosts the eclectic EXIT festival – the largest in southeast Europe – while the hilly region of Fruška Gora keeps the noise down in hushed monasteries and ancestral vineyards. Charming Subotica, 10km from Hungary, is an oasis of art nouveau delights.

Novi Sad Нови Сад

☎021 / POP 366,860

As convivial as a *rakija* toast – and at times just as carousing – Novi Sad is a chipper town with all the spoils and none of the stress of the big smoke. Locals sprawl in pretty parks and outdoor cafes, and laneway bars along pedestrian thoroughfare Zmaj Jovina, which stretches from the town square (Trg Slobode) to Dunavska street, pack out nightly.

Sights

★**Petrovaradin Citadel** FORTRESS

(museum admission 200DIN; ⏲museum 9am-5pm Tue-Sun) Towering over the river on a

40m-high volcanic slab, this mighty citadel (*tvrđava*) is aptly nicknamed 'Gibraltar on the Danube'. Constructed with slave labour between 1692 and 1780, its dungeons have held notable prisoners including Karađorđe (leader of the first uprising against the Turks and founder of a dynasty) and Tito. Have a good gawk at the iconic clock tower: the size of the minute and hour hands are reversed so far-flung fishermen can tell the time. Within the citadel walls, a **museum** (☎021-643 3145; Petrovaradin Citadel; admission 150DIN; ⏲9am-5pm Tue-Sun) offers insight (sans English explanations) into the site's history. The museum can also arrange tours (300DIN) of Petrovaradin's creepy – but cool – underground passageways.

Museum of Vojvodina MUSEUM
(Muzej Vojvodine; www.muzejvojvodine.org.rs; Dunavska 35-7; admission 200DIN, free on Sundays; ⏲9am-7pm Tue-Fri, 10am-6pm Sat & Sun) This museum houses historical, archaeological and ethnological exhibits. Building 35 covers Vojvodinian history from Palaeolithic times to the late 19th century. Building 37 takes the story to 1945 with a harrowing emphasis on WWI and WWII.

Štrand BEACH
One of Europe's best by-the-Danube beaches.

Festivals & Events

The Petrovaradin Citadel is stormed by thousands of revellers each July during the epic **EXIT Festival** (www.exitfest.org). The first festival in 2000 lasted 100 days and galvanised a generation of younger Serbs against the Milošević regime. The festival has been attended by the likes of Chemical Brothers, Gogol Bordello and Patti Smith...and an annual tally of about 200,000 merrymakers.

Sleeping

★**Hostel Sova** HOSTEL €
(☎021-527 556; www.hostelsova.com; Ilije Ognjanovića 26; dm from €10, d €15 pp; P 📶) This cute spot is akin to a mini Novi Sad: super-friendly, attractive and given to laid-back socialising (not to mention the odd *rakija* or two). It's perched above a deceptively quiet street that's just around the corner from buzzy Zmaj Jovina and a couple of minutes' stagger from the best bars in town.

Downtown HOSTEL €
(☎021-524 818; www.hostelnovisad.com; Njegoševa 2; dm from €12, s/d €21/30; @) Super-friendly staff and an 'in the thick of it' location off Trg Slobode make this rambunctious, slightly ramshackle hostel a classic Novi Sad experience in itself.

★**Hotel Veliki** HOTEL €€
(☎021-472 3840; www.hotelvelikinovisad.com; Pašića 24; s/d €33/46, apt from €65; P ❄ 📶) Sitting atop an absolutely stupendous Vojvodinian restaurant of the same name, the Veliki ('Big') lives up to its name: some of the rooms are truly huge. Staff are delightful and the location around the corner from Zmaj Jovina is top-notch. Extra bonus: free breakfast downstairs!

Eating

Kukuriku FAST FOOD €
(Despota Stefana 5; mains 160-280DIN; ⏲8am-11pm Mon-Fri, until 1am Sat) Without a skerrick of a doubt, this hole-in-the-wall joint in the cool Chinatown district makes the freshest, tastiest *pljeskavica* in town: you will salivate over the memory of these burgers for months to come. Their homemade pizzas and other fast-food offerings are also worth loosening your belt for. They're on the right-hand corner of the unmissable cartoon-coloured building.

★**Fish i Zeleniš** MEDITERRANEAN €€
(Fish and Greens; ☎021-452 000; www.fishizelenis.com; Skerlićeva 2; mains from 680DIN; ⏲noon-midnight; 🖉) This bright, snug little nook serves up the finest vegetarian/pescatarian meals in northern Serbia. Organic, locally sourced ingredients? Ambient? Ineffably delicious? Tick, tick, tick. A three-minute walk from Zmaj Jovina.

Restoran Lipa SERBIAN €€
(www.restoranlipa.com; Svetozara Miletića 7; meals from 700DIN; ⏲9am-11pm Mon-Thur & Sun, 9am-1am Fri-Sat) This down-home eatery has been dishing up old-school ambience alongside traditional Vojvodinian fare since the 19th century. Live *tamburaši* (string-instrument serenaders) on Fridays and Saturdays.

Drinking & Nightlife

Novi Sad nightlife is far more laid-back than Belgrade's frenzy of clubs and hedonistic *splavovi*. **Laze Telečkog** (pedestrian side-street running off Zmaj Jovina) is lined with bars to suit every whim.

★**Martha's Pub** BAR
(Laze Telečkog 3; ⏲8am-3am) One of the best in a street of top bars, Martha's is a small,

smokey and stupendously sociable den famous for its divine *medovača* (honey *rakija*). Crowbar yourself inside, or get there early to nab a table outside to watch the party people of Laze Telečkog romp by.

Culture Exchange CAFE
(☎064 432 9197; www.cultureexchangeserbia.org; Jovana Subotića 21; ⊙9am-11pm; 📶) Run by a well-travelled staff of volunteers, Culture Exchange offers coffees, cakes and pretty much everything else you can imagine: free bike repairs, Serbian language classes, live music gigs, film screenings and art exhibitions. It's a top spot for pre-big-night-out drinks. There's nowhere quite like it in town (or indeed, Serbia!).

Crni Bik PUB
(Trg Mladenaca 8; ⊙10am-late) Boisterous dive bar a short stagger south of Zmaj Jovina. Friendly local eccentrics prop up the bar while eclectic bands and DJs do their thing on a small stage.

Information

Tourist Information Centre (www.turizamns.rs; Jevrejska 10; ⊙7.30am-6pm Mon-Fri, 10am-3pm Sat) Ultra-helpful with maps and English info.

Getting There & Away

The **bus station** (Bul Jaše Tomića; ⊙information counter 6am-11pm) has regular departures to Belgrade (520DIN, one hour, every 10 minutes) and Subotica (600DIN, 1½ hours), plus services to Užice (1120DIN, five hours) and Zlatibor (1300DIN, six hours). From here, four stops on bus 4 will take you to the town centre: nip down the underpass and you'll see Trg Slobode on emerging.

Frequent trains leave the **train station** (Bul Jaše Tomića 4), next door to the bus station, for Belgrade (288DIN, 1½ hours) and Subotica (384DIN, 1½ hours).

Subotica Суботица

☎024 / POP 148,000

Sugar-spun art nouveau marvels, a laid-back populace and a delicious sprinkling of Serbian and Hungarian flavours make this quaint town a worthy day trip or stopover.

Sights

Town Hall HISTORIC BUILDING
(Trg Slobode) Built in 1910, this behemoth is a curious mix of art nouveau and something Gaudí may have had a playful dab at. The council chambers – with its exquisite stained-glass windows and elaborate decor – are not to be missed.

Modern Art Gallery HISTORIC BUILDING
(www.likovnisusret.rs; Park Ferenca Rajhla 5; admission 50DIN; ⊙8am-7pm Mon-Fri, 9am-1pm Sat) This mansion was built in 1904 as an architect's design studio, and it shows. One of the most sumptuous buildings in Serbia, it's a vibrant flourish of mosaics, ceramic tiles, floral patterns and stained glass.

Sleeping

Hostel Incognito HOSTEL €
(☎062 666 674; www.hostel-subotica.com; Hugo Badalića 3; s/d/tr/apt 1000/1800/2400/7000DIN; P 📶) This basic but clean, friendly hostel is a couple of minutes' walk from all the Subotica sights. Reception is in the restaurant downstairs: call before lobbing up.

DON'T MISS

NOVI PAZAR & STUDENICA MONASTERY НОВИ ПАЗАР

Novi Pazar is the cultural centre of the Raška/Sandžak region, with a large Muslim population. Turkish coffee, cuisine and customs abound, yet some idyllic Orthodox sights are in the vicinity: this was the heartland of the Serbian medieval state.

One of the most sacred sites in Serbia, Unesco-listed **Studenica** was established in the 1190s by founder of the Serbian empire (and future saint) Stefan Nemanja and developed by his sons Vukan, Stefan and Rastko (St Sava). Active monastic life was cultivated by Sava and continues today, though this thriving little community doesn't mind visitors.

Two well-preserved churches lie within impressive white-marble walls. **Bogorodičina Crkva** (Church of Our Lady), a royal funeral church, contains Stefan's tomb. Smaller **Kraljeva Crkva** (King's Church) houses the acclaimed *Birth of the Virgin* fresco and other masterpieces.

From Novi Pazar, catch a Kraljevo-bound bus to the village of Ušće (about one hour) and hop a local bus from there, or negotiate a return taxi journey.

WORTH A TRIP

DJAVOLJA VAROŠ

Djavolja Varoš (Devil's Town) in Serbia's deep south, is a trippy cluster of 202 natural stone pyramids looming eerily over bright red, highly acidic mineral streams. According to local whispers, the towers – which teeter between 2m and 15m in height and are topped with creepy volcanic 'heads' – were formed after guests at an incestuous wedding were petrified by an offended god.

Djavolja Varoš is easily reached by car; otherwise catch a bus to Kuršumlija, and grab a taxi from there. Camping at the park isn't allowed, but there are plenty of villagers willing to take in strays. You could camp nearby, but snakes and wolves abound. It's not called Devil's Town for nothing!

Hotel Galleria HOTEL €€
(☎024-647 111; www.galleria-center.com; Matije Korvina 17; s/d 45/57€, apt/ste from 76/135€; ❄📶) These four-star rooms come over all 'gentleman's den', with warm mahogany-look fittings and beds lined with bookshelves. The hotel also houses a gigantic 'wellness centre' and several eateries. It's inside the Atrium shopping plaza.

Eating

Ravel CAFE €
(Nušićeva 2; cakes 60-200DIN; ⏲9am-10pm Mon-Sat, 11am-10pm Sun) Dainty nibbles at *gateaux* and twee tea-taking is the name of the game at this adorable art nouveau classic.

Boss Caffe INTERNATIONAL €€
(www.bosscaffe.com; Matije Korvina 7-8; mains 450-1000DIN; ⏲7am-midnight Mon-Thu, until 1am Fri-Sat, 9am-midnight Sun) The best restaurant in town has a huge menu spanning Chinese, Italian, Mexican and Serbian cuisines; somehow it pulls it off with aplomb. It's directly behind the Modern Art Gallery.

Information

Tourist Information Office (☎024-670 350; www.visitsubotica.rs; Town Hall; ⏲8am-6pm Mon-Fri, 9am-1pm Sat) Tons of friendly, English-speaking advice and info. It's also home to the Subotica Greeters, local volunteers only too thrilled to show you around their hometown (bookings essential).

Getting There & Away

From the **bus station** (www.sutrans.rs; Senćanski put 3) there are hourly services to Novi Sad (600DIN, two hours) and Belgrade (800DIN, 3½ hours). See the website for other destinations. Subotica's **train station** (Bose Milečević bb) has two trains to Szeged, Hungary (320DIN, 1¾ hours). Trains to Belgrade (560DIN, 3½ hours) stop at Novi Sad (384DIN, 1½ hours).

SOUTH SERBIA

Niš Ниш

☎018 / POP 183,000

Niš is a lively city of curious contrasts, where Roma in horse-drawn carriages trot alongside new cars, and posh cocktails are sipped in antiquated alleyways. Niš was settled in pre-Roman times and flourished during the time of local-boy-made-good Emperor Constantine (AD 280–337).

Sights

Niš Fortress FORTRESS
(Niška tvrđava; Jadranska; ⏲24hr) While its current incarnation was built by the Turks in the 18th century, there have been forts on this site since ancient Roman times. Today it's a sprawling recreational area with restaurants, cafes and market stalls. It hosts the **Nišville International Jazz Festival** (www.nisville.com) each August and **Nišomnia** (www.facebook.com/festivalnisomnia), featuring rock and electro acts, in September. The city's main pedestrian boulevard, Obrenovićeva, stretches before the citadel.

Tower of Skulls MONUMENT
(Ćele Kula; Bul Zoran Đinđić; adult/child 150/130DIN; ⏲9am-7pm Tue-Fri, to 3pm Sat-Sun) With Serbian defeat imminent at the 1809 Battle of Čegar, the Duke of Resava kamikazeed towards the Turkish defences, firing at their gunpowder stores, killing himself, 4000 of his men, and 10,000 Turks. The Turks triumphed regardless, and to deter future acts of rebellion, they beheaded, scalped and embedded in this tower the skulls of the dead Serbs. Only 58 of the initial 952 skulls remain. Contrary to Turkish intention, the tower serves as a proud monument to Serbian resistance.

Get there on any bus marked 'Niška Banja' from the stop opposite the Ambassador Hotel: ask to be let out at Ćele Kula.

Red Cross Concentration Camp MUSEUM
(Crveni Krst; Bul 12 Februar; adult/child 150/130DIN; ⌚9am-4pm Tue-Fri, 10am-3pm Sat-Sun) One of the best-preserved Nazi camps in Europe, the deceptively named Red Cross held about 30,000 Serbs, Roma, Jews and Partisans during the German occupation of Serbia (1941–45). Harrowing displays tell their stories, and those of the prisoners who attempted to flee in the biggest ever breakout from a concentration camp. A short walk north of the Niš bus station.

Sleeping

Day 'n' Night Hostel HOSTEL €
(☎064 481 5869; www.daynnighthostel.com; Božidarčeva 9; dm/s/d from €9/15/20; P ❄ 📶) This spanking new hostel is clean, bright and has a kitchen and common room on each of its two floors. Friendly English-speaking staff do their utmost to ensure you have a good stay, and can organise excursions. It's a ten-minute walk to downtown Niš.

★ **Hotel Sole** HOTEL €€
(☎018-292 432; www.hotelsole.rs; Kralja Stefana Prvovenčanog 11; s/d from €45/55 incl breakfast; P ❄ 📶) Sitting pretty right in the heart of Niš, this totally refurbished hotel has modern, super-spacious rooms and one of the best free breakfasts you'll find anywhere. Staff is top-notch.

Eating & Drinking

The cobblestoned Kopitareva (Tinkers' Alley) is chock-full of fast-paced eating and drinking options.

COUNTRY FACTS

Area 77,474 sq km

Capital Belgrade

Country Code ☎381

Currency Dinar (DIN)

Emergency Ambulance ☎94, fire ☎93, police ☎92

Language Serbian

Money ATMs are in all main and mid-sized towns

Population 7.16 million

Visas None required for citizens of the EU, UK, Australia, New Zealand, Canada and the USA

Stara Srbija SERBIAN €€
(Old Serbia; ☎018-521 902; Trg Republike 12; mains 220-1500DIN; ⌚8am-midnight) Right at home in a restored 1876 house in the centre of Niš, this atmospheric spot serves up filling, fantastic traditional southern Serbian cuisine, including baked beans with smoked meat and the divine chicken stuffed with prosciutto and *kajmak* (clotted cream).

Crazy Horse BAR
(Davidova 8; ⌚8am-2am Sat-Thu, to 4am Fri; 📶) Guinness, darts, live Irish music, Champions League on TV...in the birthplace of Constantine the Great? Crazy – like the name says – but somehow, this bar works.

Information

Tourist Organisation of Niš (☎018-250 222; www.visitnis.com; Tvrđava; ⌚7.30am-7pm

ESSENTIAL FOOD & DRINK

Serbia is famous for grilled meats; regional cuisines range from spicy Hungarian goulash in Vojvodina to Turkish kebabs in Novi Pazar. Vegetarians should try asking for '*posna hrana*' ('meatless food'); this is also suitable for vegans.

- **Kajmak** Along the lines of a salty clotted cream, this dairy delight is lashed on to everything from bread to burgers.
- **Ćevapčići** The ubiquitous skinless sausage and *pljeskavica* (spicy hamburger) make it very easy to be a carnivore in Serbia.
- **Burek** Flaky meat, cheese or vegetable pie eaten with yoghurt.
- **Karađorđeva šnicla** Similar to chicken Kiev, but with veal or pork and lashings of *kajmak* and tartar.
- **Rakija** Distilled spirit most commonly made from plums. Treat with caution: this ain't your grandpa's brandy.

Mon-Fri, 9am-1pm Sat) Helpful info within the citadel gates.

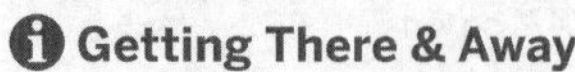

Getting There & Away

The **bus station** (Bul 12 Februar) behind the fortress has frequent services to Belgrade (1380DIN, three hours) and Brus (710DIN, 1½ hours) for Kopaonik, and three daily to Novi Pazar (1120DIN, four hours).

From the **train station** (Dimitrija Tucovića), there are seven trains to Belgrade (784DIN, 4½ hours) and two to Sofia, Badapest (730DIN, five hours).

SURVIVAL GUIDE

Directory A–Z

ACCOMMODATION

Private rooms and apartments offer superb value and can be organised through tourist offices. 'Wild' camping is possible outside national parks.

MONEY

Serbia retains the dinar (DIN); though accommodation prices are often quoted in euro, you must pay in dinar.

TELEPHONE

Local and international phonecards can be bought in post offices and tobacco kiosks. Mobile-phone SIM cards (around 200DIN) and recharge cards can be purchased at supermarkets and kiosks.

VISAS

Tourist visas for stays of less than 90 days aren't required by citizens of EU countries, most other European countries, Australia, New Zealand, Canada and the USA. **The Ministry of Foreign Affairs** (www.mfa.gov.rs/en) has full details.

Officially, all visitors must register with the police. Hotels and hostels will do this for you but if you're camping or staying in a private home, you are expected to register within 24 hours of arrival. Unofficially? This is rarely enforced, but being unable to produce registration documents upon leaving Serbia could result in a fine.

EATING PRICE RANGES

The following price categories for the cost of a main course are used in the listings in this chapter:

€ less than €6 (600DIN)

€€ €6 to €10 (600DIN to 1000DIN)

€€€ more than €10 (1000DIN)

SLEEPING PRICE RANGES

The following price categories for the cost of a high-season double room are used in the listings in this chapter:

€ less than €30 (3000DIN)

€€ €30 to €75 (3000DIN to 7000DIN)

€€€ more than €75 (7000DIN)

Getting There & Away

AIR

Belgrade's **Nikola Tesla Beograd Airport** (☎011-209 4444; www.beg.aero) handles most international flights. Serbia's national carrier is **Air Serbia** (www.airserbia.com). The airport website has a full list of Serbia-bound airlines.

LAND

Because Serbia does not acknowledge crossing points into Kosovo as international border crossings, it may not be possible to enter Serbia from Kosovo unless you first entered from Serbia. Driving Serbian-plated cars into Kosovo isn't advised, and is often not permitted by rental agencies or insurers.

Drivers need International Driving Permits. Drivers from EU countries don't need Green Card or border insurance to drive in Serbia; otherwise, border insurance costs about €107 for a car, €67 for a motorbike.

Bus services to both Western Europe and Turkey are well developed.

International rail connections leaving Serbia originate in Belgrade. For more information, visit **Serbian Railways** (www.serbianrailways.com).

Getting Around

Bus services are extensive, though outside major hubs connections can be sporadic. Reservations are only worthwhile for international buses and during festivals.

Major car-hire companies are ubiquitous. The **Automobile & Motorcycle Association of Serbia** (Auto-Moto Savez Srbije; ☎011-333 1100, roadside assist 1987; www.amss.org.rs; Ruzveltova 18) provides roadside assistance and extensive information on its website.

Serbian Railways serves Novi Sad, Subotica and Niš from Belgrade.

Bicycle paths are improving in larger cities.

Slovakia

Includes ➡

Best Places to Eat

- ➡ Traja Mušketieri (p983)
- ➡ Koliba Patria (p988)
- ➡ Republika Východu (p993)

Best Places to Stay

- ➡ Hotel Marrol's (p982)
- ➡ Grand Hotel Kempinski (p988)
- ➡ Hotel Bankov (p993)

Why Go?

Going strong over two decades as an independent state after the breakup of Czechoslovakia, Slovakia, Europe's most castellated country, is a bastion of untrammelled wildernesses, where some of the continent's densest forest coverage gives way to dramatic fortresses and craggy mountains harbouring outstanding hiking. It savours wine over beer and, in its tradition-steeped hinterland, cradles an entrancing folk culture most European nations have lost.

Slovakia's small size is possibly its biggest attraction. You can traipse woodsy waterfall-filled gorges one day and yodel from 2500m-plus peaks the next.

Dinky capital Bratislava is awash with quirky museums and backed by thick forests, but don't leave without heading east, where fortresses tower over tradition-rich medieval towns such as Levoča or Bardejov and hiking trails lace the hills. Down a *slivovica* (firewater-like plum brandy) and drink a toast for us – *nazdravie*!

When to Go

Bratislava

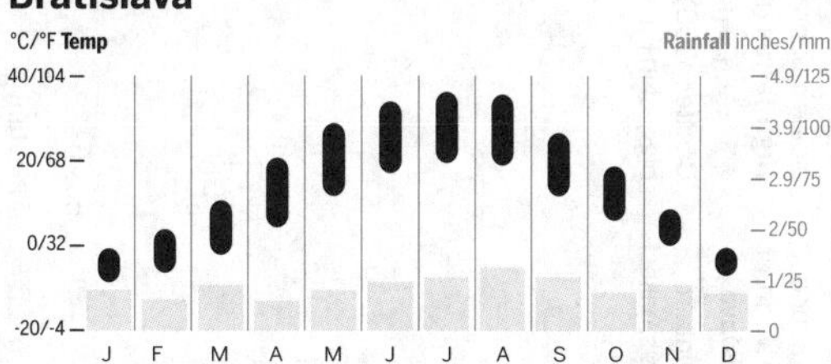

Jun & Jul Festivals abound across the country, High Tatras hiking trails are all open.

Jan & Feb Peak ski season in the mountains, but many other sights are closed.

Sep Fewer crowds but wine season means it's ripe time for alcohol-themed festivities.

Slovakia Highlights

1. Linger over drinks at one of myriad sidewalk or riverfront cafes in old town **Bratislava**.
2. Hike between mountain huts in one of Europe's smallest alpine mountain ranges, the **High Tatras** (p986).
3. Wander the ruins of **Spiš Castle** (p990), among the biggest in Europe.
4. Climb creaking ladders past crashing waterfalls in the dramatic gorges of **Slovenský Raj National Park** (p991).

ITINERARIES

Three Days

Two nights in **Bratislava** is enough to wander the old town streets and see some museums. The following day is best spent on a castle excursion, either to **Devín** or **Trenčín**. Or, better yet, spend all three days hiking in the rocky **High Tatras mountains**, staying central in the resort town of **Starý Smokovec** or in more off-beat **Ždiar** in the **Belá Tatras**.

One Week

After a day or two in **Bratislava**, venture east. Spend at least four nights around the **Tatras** so you have time to hike to a mountain hut as well as take day trips to the must-see **Spiš Castle** ruins, medieval **Levoča**, or to **Slovenský Raj National Park** for its highly rated Suchá Belá Gorge hike. For the last night or two, continue to Bardejov to marvel at its complete Renaissance town square and nearby wooden churches.

BRATISLAVA

☎02 / POP 430,000

Proximity to nature gives Slovakia's capital its strongest flavouring. The Danube wends through town, and cycle paths through its verdant flood plain begin just outside the centre. Meanwhile, erupting a 30-minute walk from the train station are the densely forested Small Carpathians; the trailer to a mountainous extent that runs countrywide, virtually unimpeded by civilisation. Then there's ski runs and vineyards to amble among.

The charming – if tiny – old town *(starý mesto)* is the place to start appreciating Bratislava. Stroll narrow pedestrian streets of pastel 18th-century buildings or sample the myriad sidewalk cafes under the watchful gaze of the city castle, harking back to medieval times. Done with the old? In with the new(er): the city boasts intriguing socialist-era architecture worth checking out and one of Eastern Europe's most spectacular modern art spaces. Contrasts like this are all part of Bratislava's allure.

History

Founded in AD 907, by the 12th century Bratislava (then called Poszony in Hungarian or Pressburg in German) was a large city in greater Hungary. King Matthias Corvinus founded a university here, Academia Istropolitana. Many of the imposing baroque palaces you see date to the reign of Austro-Hungarian empress Maria Theresa (1740–80), when the city flourished. From the 16th-century Turkish occupation of Budapest to the mid-1800s, Hungarian parliament met locally and monarchs were crowned in St Martin's Cathedral.

'Bratislava' was officially born as the second city of a Czechoslovakian state after WWI and became capital of the new nation of Slovakia in 1993.

Sights

In addition to those we recommend, there are several small museums and increasingly well-regarded galleries scattered about the old town: ask at the Bratislava Culture & Information Centre for the *Art Plan* leaflet.

★Bratislava Castle CASTLE
(www.snm.sk; grounds free, admission all exhibits adult/senior €7/4; ⊙grounds 9am-9pm, museum 10am-6pm Tue-Sun) Dominating the southwest of the old town on a hill above the Danube, the castle today is largely a 1950s reconstruction; an 1811 fire left the fortress ruined for more than a century and renovations continue. Most buildings contain administrative offices, but there is a museum of Slovakia through the ages, and lawns and ramparts provide great vantage points for city viewing.

★Museum of Jewish Culture MUSEUM
(www.snm.sk; Židovská 17; adult/child €7/2; ⊙11am-5pm Sun-Fri) The most moving of the three floors of exhibits here focuses on the large Jewish community and buildings lost during and after WWII. Black-and-white photos show the neighbourhood and synagogue before it was ploughed under.

★St Martin's Cathedral CHURCH
(Dóm sv Martina; cnr Kapitulská & Staromestská; admission €2; ⊙9-11.30am & 1-6pm Mon-Sat, 1.30-4pm Sun May-Sep, until 4pm Mon-Sat Oct-Apr) A relatively modest interior belies the elaborate history of St Martin's Cathedral: 11

Central Bratislava

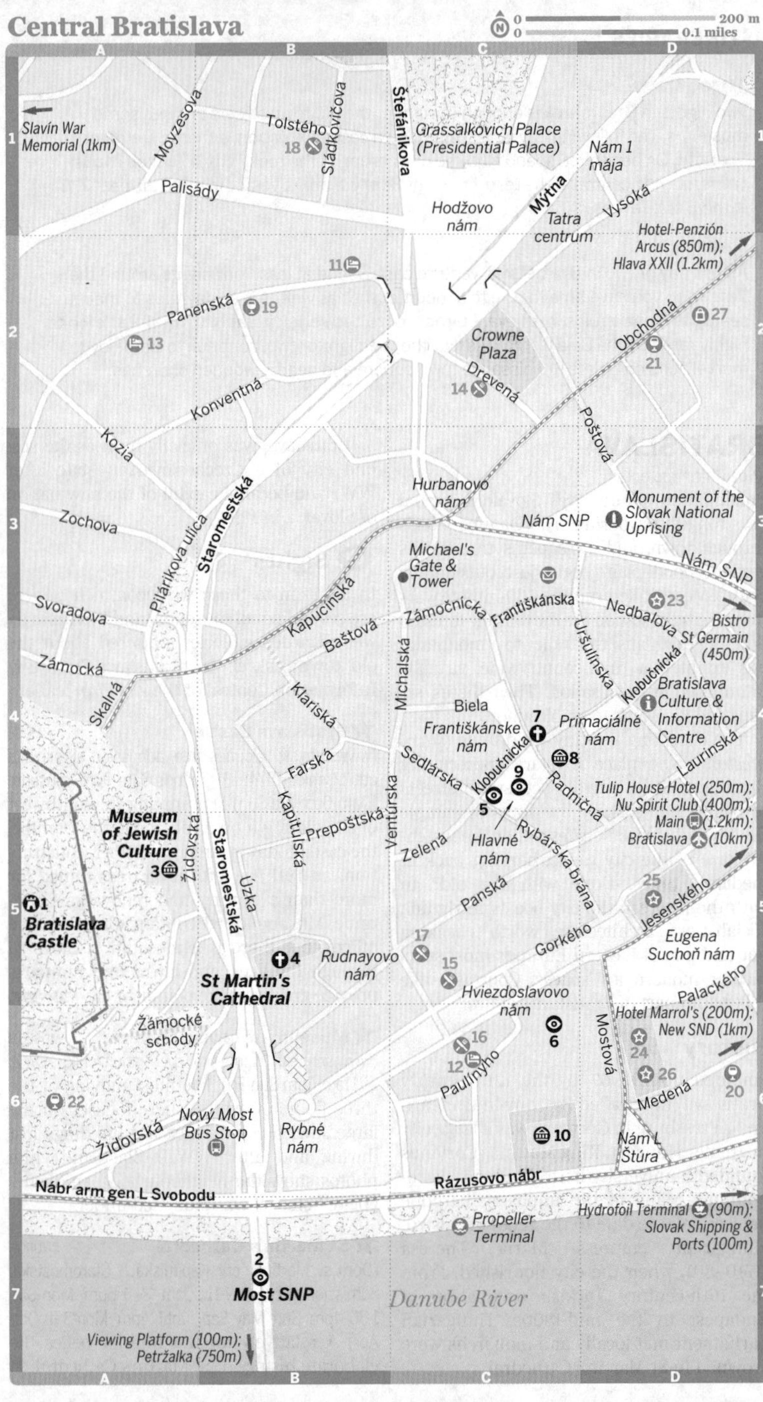

0 200 m
0 0.1 miles
Slavín War Memorial (1km)
Moyzesova
Tolstého
Sládkovičova
Štefánikova
Grassalkovich Palace (Presidential Palace)
Nám 1 mája
Palisády
Hodžovo nám
Mýtna
Tatra centrum
Vysoká
Hotel-Penzión Arcus (850m); Hlava XXII (1.2km)
Panenská
Obchodná
Crowne Plaza
Drevená
Konventná
Kozia
Poštová
Staromestská
Hurbanovo nám
Zochova
Pilárikova ulica
Nám SNP
Monument of the Slovak National Uprising
Michael's Gate & Tower
Svoradova
Kapucínska
Zámočnícka
Františkánska
Nedbalova
Bistro St Germain (450m)
Baštová
Michalská
Uršulínska
Zámocká
Skalná
Klariská
Klobučnícka
Bratislava Culture & Information Centre
Biela
Františkánske nám
Primaciálné nám
Farská
Sedlárska
Laurinská
Radničná
Tulip House Hotel (250m); Nu Spirit Club (400m); Main (1.2km); Bratislava (10km)
Museum of Jewish Culture
Židovská
Kapitulská
Prepoštská
Ventúrska
Zelená
Hlavné nám
Rybárska brána
Úzka
Panská
Jesenského
Bratislava Castle
Gorkého
Eugena Suchoň nám
St Martin's Cathedral
Rudnayovo nám
Hviezdoslavovo nám
Palackého
Zámocké schody
Mostová
Hotel Marrol's (200m); New SND (1km)
Paulínyho
Medená
Nový Most Bus Stop
Rybné nám
Nám L Štúra
Nábr arm gen L Svobodu
Rázusovo nábr
Propeller Terminal
Hydrofoil Terminal (90m); Slovak Shipping & Ports (100m)
Most SNP
Danube River
Viewing Platform (100m); Petržalka (750m)

Central Bratislava

Top Sights
1 Bratislava Castle A5
2 Most SNP B7
3 Museum of Jewish Culture A5
4 St Martin's Cathedral B5

Sights
5 Hlavné Námestie C4
6 Hviezdoslavovo Námestie C6
7 Jesuit Church C4
8 Old Town Hall C4
9 Roland's Fountain C4
10 Slovak National Gallery C6

Sleeping
11 Downtown Backpackers B2
12 Penzión Portus C6
13 Penzión Virgo A2

Eating
14 Bratislavský Meštiansky Pivovar C2
15 Café Verne C5
16 Lemon Tree C6
17 Shtoor C5
18 Traja Mušketieri B1

Drinking & Nightlife
19 Apollon Club B2
20 Nu Spirit Bar D6
21 Slovak Pub D2
22 Subclub A6

Entertainment
23 Dunaj D3
Historic SND (see 25)
24 Reduta Palace D6
25 Slovak National Theatre D5
26 Slovak Philharmonic D6

Shopping
27 Úľuv D2

Austro-Hungarian monarchs (10 kings and one queen, Maria Theresa) were crowned in this large 14th-century church. The busy motorway almost touching St Martin's follows the moat of the former city walls.

Hviezdoslavovo Námestie SQUARE
Embassies, restaurants and bars are the mainstay of the long, tree-lined plaza that anchors the pedestrian zone's southern extremity. At Hviezdoslavovo's east end, the ornate 1886 Slovak National Theatre (p983), one of the city's opera houses, steals the show. The theatre is not open for tours, but ticket prices are not prohibitive. The nearby neo-baroque 1914 **Reduta Palace** (Eugena Suchoň nám; 9am-2pm Mon, 1-7pm Tue-Fri & 1hr before concerts) houses the Slovak Philharmonic.

Hlavné Námestie SQUARE
Cafe tables outline pretty Hlavné nám (Main Sq), the site of numerous festival performances. **Roland's Fountain**, at the square's heart, is thought to have been built in 1572 as a fire hydrant of sorts. Flanking the northeast side of the square is the 1421 **Old Town Hall** (www.muzeum.bratislava.sk; adult/child €5/2; 10am-5pm Tue-Fri, 11am-6pm Sat & Sun), home to the city museum. You'll often find a musician in traditional costume playing a *fujara* on the steps of the **Jesuit Church**, on the edge of adjoining Františkánske nám.

Slovak National Gallery MUSEUM
(Slovenská Národná Galéria; 2049 6243; www.sng.sk; Rázusovo nábr 2; 10am-6pm Tue & Wed & Fri-Sun, noon-8pm Thu, closed Mon) FREE A socialist modernist building and an 18th-century palace make interesting co-hosts for the Slovak National Gallery. The nation's eclectic art collection contained here ranges from Gothic to graphic design. In 2014 the gallery experimented with free admission; they are hopeful this will still be possible in subsequent years.

Activities

Slovak Shipping & Ports BOAT TOUR
(5293 2226; www.lod.sk; Fajnorovo nábr 2) From April through September, Slovak Shipping & Ports runs 45-minute Bratislava return boat trips (adult/child €6/4.50) on the Danube. Its Devín sightseeing cruise (adult/child return €8/6) plies the waters to the castle, stops for about an hour and returns to Bratislava in 30 minutes.

Tours

Authentic Slovakia CULTURAL TOUR
(0908 308 234; www.authenticslovakia.com; per 2/4hr tour €27/43) Want to know about the Slovakia the other tours don't let on? Sign up with these guys for forays to weird socialist-era buildings and typical *krčmy* (Slovak pubs): authentic (uncensored) Slovakia.

Festivals & Events

Fjúžn CULTURAL
(www.fjuzn.sk; Apr) Dunaj (p983), an important venue for world music year-round, hosts this annual celebration of Slovak minorities and their cultures.

Cultural Summer Festival CULTURAL
(www.visit.bratislava.sk; ⏲Jun-Sep) A smorgasbord of plays and performances comes to the streets and venues around town in summer.

Bratislava Music Festival MUSIC
(www.bhsfestival.sk; ⏲Oct) One of Slovakia's best music festivals; international classical music performances take place in October.

Christmas Market SHOPPING
(⏲Nov-Dec) From late November, Hlavné and Hviezdoslavo nám fills with food and drink, crafts for sale and staged performances: very atmospheric.

Sleeping

Getting a short-term rental flat in the old town (€60 to €120 per night) is also a great way to stay central without paying hotel prices, plus you can self-cater. Family-run and friendly, the modern units of **Apartments Bratislava** (www.apartmentsbratislava.com) are our top choice. Many hostels also have kitchens.

Downtown Backpackers HOSTEL €
(☎5464 1191; www.backpackers.sk; Panenská 31; dm €17-18, tw €54; ⊖@ᯤ) The first hostel in Bratislava, Backpackers is still a boozy (you enter through a bar) bohemian classic. Red-brick walls and tapestries add character. Serves good food in the cosy downstairs restaurant.

Penzión Portus GUESTHOUSE €
(☎0911 978 026; www.portus.sk; Paulínyho 10; r incl breakfast from €40) Above an atmospheric old cellar restaurant, the modern, less-characterful rooms still represent the old town's best deal on private rooms.

Penzión Virgo GUESTHOUSE €€
(☎2092 1400; www.penzionvirgo.sk; Panenská 14; s/d/apt €61/74/85; ⊖@ᯤ) Exterior-access rooms are arranged around a courtyard; light and airy despite dark-wood floors and baroque-accent wallpaper. Sip an espresso with the breakfast buffet (€5).

Hotel-Penzión Arcus GUESTHOUSE €€
(☎5557 2522; www.hotelarcus.sk; Moskovská 5; s €54-66, d €80-100, all incl breakfast; ⊖ᯤ) Family-run place with varied rooms (some with balcony, some with courtyard views). It's 500m northeast of Tesco, via Špitalska.

★**Hotel Marrol's** BOUTIQUE HOTEL €€€
(☎5778 4600; www.hotelmarrols.sk; Tobrucká 4; d/ste incl breakfast from €152/290; ᯤ) You could imagine Kaiser Wilhelm puffing contentedly on a cigar here: no member of the aristocracy would feel out of place in these 54 sumptuous rooms and suites, or in the Jasmine spa. Considering it's a regular in 'world's best luxury hotel' lists, prices are very proletariat-friendly.

Tulip House Hotel BOUTIQUE HOTEL €€€
(☎3217 1819; www.tuliphouse.sk; Štúrova 10; ste incl breakfast €150-390; P⊖❄@ᯤ) Exquisite art nouveau property with a cafe-restaurant at street level: penthouses available, too.

Eating

The pedestrian centre is packed with overpriced samey dining options. Scour between the cracks, however, and you'll find great cafes and a few decent restaurants. Decent Slovak food isn't easy to find, but that Slovak fave, the set-lunch menu, can be a real steal.

Shtoor CAFE €
(Panská 23; light lunches €3-6; ᯤ) With its tasty, cheap, healthy lunches, Shtoor has three locations in Bratislava, but this one has the best (coffee- and cake-fuelled) atmosphere. Check out the menus: written in old-fashioned Slovak as set down by L'udovít Štúr, pioneer of Slovak literary language.

Bistro St Germain BISTRO €
(Rajská 7; mains €3-8; ⏲10am-11pm Mon-Fri, noon-11pm Sat & Sun; ᯤ) Relocated to a much bigger premise, St Germain remains a wonderfully decorated, relaxed place to gossip over homemade lemonade, cupcakes or light lunches (salads, baguettes and the like).

★**Café Verne** INTERNATIONAL €€
(Hviezdoslavovo nám 18; mains €4-11; ⏲9am-midnight) Lively, friendly, good-value dining in the old town: the Czech beers flow and everyone from expats to students wolfs down hearty no-nonsense grub, including Slovak staples and decent English breakfasts.

Hradná Hviezda FUSION €€
(☎0944 142 718; http://hradnahviezda.sk; Bratislava Castle; starters €4-7, mains €10-22; ⏲11am-11pm) Being right under Bratislava Castle, you'd think the location would signify an over-touristy low-quality joint, but this beautiful restaurant is quiet, dignified, and high end. It specialises in taking typical Slovak food and making it that little bit sexier.

Bratislavský Meštiansky Pivovar SLOVAK €€
(☎0944 512 265; www.mestianskypivovar.sk; Drevená 8; mains €5.50-19; ⏲11am-midnight Mon-Thu & Sat, to 1am Fri, to 11pm Sun; ᯤ) This stylish

microbrewery serves Bratislava's freshest beer and offers creative Slovak cooking beneath vaulted ceilings and stylised old town artwork.

Lemon Tree THAI €€€
(☎0948 109 400; www.lemontree.sk; Hviezdoslavovo nám 7; mains €7-18) Top-end Thai-Mediterranean restaurant with a 7th-floor upscale bar, Skybar, with great views. Reservations are a good idea. An €8 set menu is also offered daily.

★**Traja Mušketieri** PUB FOOD €€€
(☎5443 0019; Sládkovičova 7; mains €10-20) This way-upmarket version of a medieval tavern comes with a poetic menu. 'Treacherous Lady de Winter' is a skewered chicken stuffed with Parma ham. Courteous service; reservations recommended.

Drinking & Nightlife

From mid-April to October, sidewalk cafe tables sprout up in every corner of the pedestrian old town. Hviezdoslavovo námestie has good options. Admission prices for Bratislava's bars and clubs are usually quite low (free to €5).

Slovak Pub PUB
(Obchodná 62; ⏲10am-midnight Mon-Thu, 10am-2am Fri & Sat, noon-midnight Sun; 📶) It's touristy, but most beers are available and it serves every traditional national dish (mains €3.50 to €11) you can think of, albeit far from top quality.

Nu Spirit Bar BAR
(Medená 16; ⏲10am-2am Mon-Fri, 5pm-4am Sat & Sun) Deservedly popular cellar bar with regular live music as underground as its location: jazz, electronica, soul etc.

Nu Spirit Club CLUB
(Šafárikovo nám 7; ⏲10pm-late, closed Sun & Mon) Under the Nu Spirit umbrella, Nu Spirit Club continues the theme with big, danceable environs.

Apollon Club GAY & LESBIAN
(www.apollon-gay-club.sk; Panenská 24; ⏲6pm-3am Mon, Tue & Thu, 6pm-5am Wed, 8pm-5am Fri & Sat, 8pm-1am Sun) The gay disco in town. Tuesday is karaoke night.

Subclub CLUB
(Nábrežie arm gen L Svobodu; ⏲10pm-4am Thu-Sat) An institution in the subterranean passages under Bratislava Castle. Techno, indy, hardcore dance etc pounds out to a young crowd.

Entertainment

Check **Slovak Spectator** (http://spectator.sme.sk), the **Bratislava Culture & Information Centre** (www.bkis.sk) and **Kam do Mesta** (www.kamdomesta.sk) for the latest.

Live Music

Hlava XXII LIVE MUSIC
(Bazová 9; ⏲6pm-midnight Tue-Thu, 6pm-3am Fri & Sat) Jam sessions, blues and world beat – live. It's 1km northeast of the center, off Záhradnicka.

Performing Arts

Slovak National Theatre THEATRE
(Slovenské Národné Divadlo; SND; www.snd.sk; Hviezdoslavovo nám) The national theatre company stages quality operas (Slavic and international), ballets and dramas in two venues: the gilt decoration of the landmark **Historic SND** (www.snd.sk; Hviezdoslavovo nám, booking office cnr Jesenského & Komenského; ⏲8am-noon & 12.30-7pm Mon-Fri, 9am-1pm Sat & 1hr before shows) is a show in itself; the modern **New SND** (☎2047 2296; www.snd.sk; Pribinova 17; ⏲9am-5pm Mon- Fri) has a cafe and guaranteed English-speaking reservation line.

Slovak Philharmonic THEATRE
(www.filharm.sk; Eugena Suchoň nám; tickets €5-20; ⏲9am-2pm Mon, 1-6pm Tue-Fri & before performances) Neo-baroque 1914 Reduta Palace houses the Slovak Philharmonic: refurbishment to this grand building included adding the impressive €1.5 million organ, and there are regular acclaimed classical music concerts here.

Dunaj PERFORMING ARTS
(www.kcdunaj.sk; Nedbalova 3; ⏲4pm-late; 📶) Cultural centre hosting some of Slovakia's most interesting drama and music performances. Something is on almost nightly. Also has a bar with old town panoramas from the terrace.

Shopping

There are several crystal, craft and jewellery stores, as well as souvenir booths, around Hlavné nám. Artisan galleries and antique shops inhabit alleyways off old town streets.

Úľuv HANDICRAFTS
(www.uluv.sk; Obchodná 64) For serious folk-art shopping head to the main outlet of Úľuv, the national handicraft cooperative, where a courtyard is filled with artisans' studios. Look for *šupolienky:* expressive figures sculpted from corn husks.

SOCIALIST BRATISLAVA

The stint under socialism left its mark around town in bizarre and monumental ways.

Most SNP (New Bridge; Viedenská cesta; observation deck adult/child €6.50/3.50; ⏲10am-11pm) Colloquially called the UFO (pronounced ew-fo), this Danube-spanning bridge is a modernist marvel from 1972 with a cool viewing platform (Most SNP; admission €6.50) (sky-high admission) and, just below, a restaurant (out-of-this-world prices). The viewing platform is free if you eat in the restaurant.

Slavín War Memorial Huge memorial to the Soviets who fell in WWII, in a park of the same name which also yields great city views.

Information

Most cafes have wi-fi access; Hlavné nám and Hviezdoslavovo nám are free wi-fi zones. Bratislava has numerous banks and ATMs in the old town, with several branches on Poštova. There are also ATMs/exchange booths in the train and bus stations, and at the airport.

Bratislava Culture & Information Centre (BKIS; ☎16 186, 5441 9410; http://visit.bratislava.sk; Klobučnícká 2; ⏲9am-7pm Apr-Oct, 9am-6pm Nov-Mar) Amicable official tourist office. Brochures galore, including a small Bratislava guide.

Lonely Planet (www.lonelyplanet.com/slovakia/bratislava)

Main Police Station (☎158; Hrobákova 44) Main police station for foreigners, in Petržalka, about 3.75km south of Most SNP.

Main Post Office (Nám SNP 34-35) In a beautiful building.

Poliklinika Ruzinov (☎4827 9111; www.ruzinovskapoliklinika.sk; Ružinovská 10) Hospital with emergency services and 24-hour pharmacy.

Slovak Spectator (www.spectator.sme.sk) English-language weekly newspaper with current affairs and event listings.

Tatra Banka (Dunajská 4) English-speaking staff.

Getting There & Away

Bratislava is the main hub for trains, buses and the few planes that head in and out of the country.

AIR

Keep in mind that Vienna's much busier international airport is only 60km west.

Bratislava Airport (BTS; ☎02-3303-3353; www.bts.aero) Nine kilometres northeast of the centre. Connections to Italy, Spain, UK cities and more.

BOAT

From April to October, plying the Danube is a cruisey way to get between Bratislava and Vienna.

Slovak Shipping & Ports (☎5293 2226; www.lod.sk; Hydrofoil Terminal, Fajnorova nábr 2) Several weekly hydrofoils to Vienna and back between April and October (€18 one way, 1¾ hours). Daily runs are July and August only.

Twin City Liner (☎0903 610 716; www.twincityliner.com; Propeller Terminal, Rázusovo nábr) Up to four boats daily to Vienna (one way €20 to €35, 1½ hours) from the Hydrofoil Terminal on Fajnorova nábr 2. You can also book through the office of Flora Tours (☎5443 1023; www.floratour.sk; Kúpelná 6) on Kúpelná.

BUS

Direct destinations include cities throughout Slovakia and Europe, but the train is usually comparably priced and more convenient. The **Bratislava bus station** (Mlynské Nivy; Ⓑ Autobusová stanica, AS) is 1km east of the old town; locals call it 'Mlynské Nivy' (the street name). For schedules, see www.cp.atlas.sk.

International bus routes include those to Vienna (€7.70, 1¼ hours, 12 daily), Prague (€14, 4¾ hours, eight daily), Budapest (€10, three hours, two daily) and London (€76, 23 to 24 hours, one daily).

Eurolines (☎in Bratislava 5556 2195; www.slovaklines.sk; Bratislava bus station, Mlynské Nívy 31) Contact for most international buses.

Eurobus (☎in Košice 680 7306; www.eurobus.sk; Bratislava bus station)

Slovak Lines (www.slovaklines.sk; Bratislava bus station) Services throughout the country: outside Bratislava under the name of Slovenská Autobusová Doprava (thankfully SAD for short).

TRAIN

Rail is the main way to get around Slovakia and to neighbouring countries. Intercity (IC) and Eurocity (EC) trains are quickest. *Rychlík* (R; 'fast' trains) take slightly longer, but run more frequently and cost less. For schedules see www.cp.atlas.sk. Prices listed here are for the cheapest direct services.

Domestic trains run to Trenčin (€9.50, 1½ hours, 12 daily), Žilina (€12.50, 2½ hours, 12 daily), Poprad (€15, four hours, 12 daily) and Košice (€19, 5½ hours, 12 daily).

International trains run to Vienna (return €17.50; includes Vienna city transport, one hour, hourly), Prague (from €15 when booked through Slovak Rail website, 4¼ hours, six daily) and Budapest (€15, 2¾ hours, seven daily).

Main Train Station (Hlavná Stanica; www.slovakrail.sk; Predštanicné nám)

Getting Around

TO/FROM THE AIRPORT

- City bus 61 links Bratislava airport with the main train station (20 minutes).
- Standing taxis (over)charge about €20 to town; ask the price before you get in.
- A regular bus (€7.70) connects Vienna, Vienna airport, Bratislava bus station and Bratislava Airport.

CAR

Numerous international car-hire companies such as Hertz and Sixt have offices at Bratislava Airport.

Buchbinder (4363 7821; www.buchbinder.sk) In-town pick-up possible for a fee.

PUBLIC TRANSPORT

Bratislava has an extensive tram, bus and trolleybus network; though the old town is small, so you won't often need it. **Dopravný Podnik Bratislava** (DPB; www.dpb.sk; Hodžovo nám; 6am-7pm Mon-Fri) is the public transport company; you'll find a route map online. The office is in the underground passage beneath Hodžovo nám. Check www.imhd.zoznam.sk for city-wide schedules.

Tickets cost €0.70/0.90 for 15/60 minutes. Buy at newsstands and validate on board (or risk a legally enforceable €50 fine). Passes cost €4.50/8.30/10 for one/two/three days; buy at the DPB office, validate on board.

Important lines:

Bus 93 Main train station to Hodžovo nám then Petržalka train station.

Trolleybus 206 Bratislava bus station to Hodžovo nám.

Trolleybus 210 Bratislava bus station to Main train station.

TAXI

Standing cabs compulsively overcharge foreigners; an around-town trip should never cost above €10. To save money ask someone to help you order a taxi (not all operators speak English).

AA Euro Taxi (16 022)

Around Bratislava

Some of the best sights in Bratislava are actually way out of the city centre. The ruins of poignant **Devín Castle** (www.muzeum.bratislava.sk; adult/child €4/2; 10am-5pm Tue-Fri, to 7pm Sat & Sun May-Sep), 9km west, was once the military plaything of 9th-century warlord Prince Ratislav, with a stunning location at the confluence of the Danube and Morava rivers. Bus 29 links Devín with Bratislava's Nový Most (New Bridge) bus stop, under Most SNP. Austria is just across the river from the castle.

Heading east out of the city you'll reach **Danubiana Meulensteen Art Museum** (www.danubiana.sk; Via Danubia, Čunovo; adult/child €8/4), Slovakia's most daring contemporary art museum. Boat trips run here down the Danube from the city centre from June to October (€10/6 return, see website for details); otherwise take bus 91 from Nový Most bus stop to Čunovo and walk from the terminus (2.5km), or drive.

TATRAS MOUNTAINS

Poprad

Poprad will likely be your first experience of mountain country, being the nearest sizeable city to the High Tatras and a major regional transport hub. The delightful 16th-century neighbourhood of Spišska Sobota and a popular thermal water park may make you linger. From the adjacent train and bus stations, the central pedestrian square, Nám sv Egídia, is a five-minute walk south on Alžbetina.

Sights & Activities

Spišská Sobota NEIGHBOURHOOD

Sixteenth-century Spiš-style merchants' and artisans' houses line Spišská Sobota town square. The suburb is 1.2km northeast of Poprad's train station.

Aqua City SPA

(785 1111; www.aquacity.sk; Športová 1397; treatments €10-30; 8am-9pm) Sauna, swim, bubble and slide zones are all part of Poprad's thermal water park. The park employs admirable green initiatives; the heat and electricity derive from geothermal and solar sources.

Adventoura ADVENTURE SPORTS

(0903 641 549; www.adventoura.eu; Uherova 33) Dog sledding, hut-to-hut hikes, snowboarding...this company can organise the works. Day prices for trips around the Tatras start at about €30 per person.

Sleeping & Eating

★ **Penzión Sabato** B&B €€
(☎776 9580; www.sabato.sk; Sobotské nám 6; r incl breakfast €50-100;) Exposed stone arches, a cobblestone courtyard and open-hearth restaurant reveal this inn's 17th-century age – as do romantically decorated rooms.

★ **Vino & Tapas** INTERNATIONAL €€€
(☎0918 969 101; Sobotské nám 18; 2 courses €19; ⊙evenings Mon-Sat) It's worth splashing out on Poprad's most atmospheric restaurant. The guys here have cooked for the Queen of England, and the food's a cut above. Best phone ahead if you're set on eating here.

Information

City Information Centre (☎436 1192; www.poprad.sk; Dom Kultúry Štefániková 72, Poprad; ⊙9am-5pm Mon-Fri, 9am-noon Sat) Town info only; lists private rooms.

Getting There & Away

AIR

Poprad-Tatry International Airport (p995) is 5km west of the town centre and has a brand-new route to London four times weekly with Wizz Air.

BUS

Buses serve Levoča (€1.70, 45 minutes, hourly), Bardejov (€4.50, 2½ hours, one to two hourly) and Zakopane in Poland (€5.50, two hours, two to four daily June to October).

CAR

Pick-up around town is available by prearrangement from **Car Rental Tatran** (☎775 8157; www.autopozicovnatatry.sk).

TRAIN

Electric trains traverse the 14km or so to the High Tatras resorts. Mainline trains run directly to Bratislava (€15, four hours, hourly, four IC trains daily) and Košice (€5, 1¼ hours, hourly).

High Tatras

☎052

The High Tatras (Vysoké Tatry), the tallest range in the Carpathian Mountains, tower over most of Eastern Europe. Some 25 peaks measure above 2500m. The massif is only 25km wide and 78km long, but photo opportunities are enough to get you fantasising about a *National Geographic* career – pristine snowfields, ultramarine mountain lakes, thundering waterfalls, undulating pine forests and shimmering alpine meadows. Most of this jagged range is part of the Tatra National Park (Tanap): not that this fact has arrested considerable development on the Slovakian ski slopes.

Midmountain, three main resort towns string west to east. Štrbské Pleso is the traditional ski centre and is most crowded, with construction galore. Smokovec, 11km east, is an amalgam of the Nový (New), Starý (Old), Dolný (Lower) and Horný (Upper) settlements. Here there's still a bit of a turn-of-the-20th-century heyday feel, plus the most services. Tatranská Lomnica, 5km further, is the quaintest, quietest village. All have mountain access by cable car, funicular or chairlift. Poprad is the closest city (with mainline train station and airport), 14km south of central Starý Smokovec.

When planning your trip, keep in mind that the highest trails are closed because of snow from November to mid-June. July and August are the warmest (and most crowded) months. Hotel prices and crowds are at their lowest from October to April.

Sights & Activities

A 600km network of trails covers the alpine valleys and some peaks, with full-service mountain huts where hikers can stop for a meal or a rest along the way. Routes are colour-coded and easy to follow.

The red 65km **Tatranská Magistrála Trail** transects the High Tatras from west to east, running beneath the peaks at average elevations of 1300m to 1800m. It's connected at several points by cable car to the resort towns. Our favourite section is Skalnaté pleso to Chata pri Zelenom plese (2¼ hours).

Pick up one of the numerous detailed maps and hiking guides available at bookstores and information offices. Park regulations require you to keep to trails and refrain from picking flowers. Be aware that many trails are rocky and uneven, watch for sudden thunderstorms on ridges where there's no protection, and know that the assistance of the Mountain Rescue Service is not free.

Distances for hikes in Slovak national parks are officially given in hours rather than kilometres, so we have done the same, as per official trail estimates. Depending on the gradient and terrain in the High Tatras a reasonably fit person can expect to hike between 2km and 5km per hour.

Note that ski resorts in peak season (Christmas through January and February) command higher prices for passes. If in doubt check www.vt.sk for further information.

Smokovec Resort Towns

From Starý Smokovec a **funicular railway** (www.vt.sk; adult/child return €8/5.50; ⏲7am-7pm Jul & Aug, 8am-5pm Sep-Jun) takes you up to **Hrebienok** (1280m) where you have a great view of the **Velká Studená Valley**. From here the red **Tatranská Magistrála Trail** heads west to the lakeside **Sliezsky dom** hotel (two hours). From here, make the hike a loop by following a small green connector trail to the yellow-marked trail back to Starý Smokovec (four hours total). Following the Magistrála east for one hour brings you up to atmospheric **Zamkovského chata** hut.

Mountain climbers scale to the top of **Slavkovský štít** (2452m) via the blue trail from Starý Smokovec (seven to eight hours return). To ascend the peaks without marked hiking trails (**Gerlachovský štít** included), you must hire a guide. Contact the **Mountain Guides Society Office** (☎4422 066; www.tatraguide.sk; Starý Smokovec 38; ⏲10am-6pm Mon-Fri, noon-6pm Sat & Sun, closed weekends Oct-May).

At **Funtools** (☎0902 932 657; www.vt.sk; Hrebienok; per hour rides €5; ⏲8:30am-4:30pm Jun-Sep) you can take a fast ride down the mountain on a two-wheeled scooter, a luge-like three-wheel cart or on a four-wheel modified skateboard.

Rent mountain bikes at **Tatrasport** (www.tatry.net/tatrasport; Starý Smokovec 38; per day €12; ⏲8am-6pm), above the bus-station parking lot; www.vt.sk keeps a great list of adventurous routes (some for pros only).

Tatranská Lomnica & Around

While in the Tatras, you shouldn't miss the ride to the precipitous 2634m summit of **Lomnický štít** (bring a jacket!). From Lomnica, a large **gondola** (www.vt.sk; return adult/senior/child €14/11/1; ⏲8.30am-7pm Jul & Aug, to 4pm Sep-Jun) pauses mid-station at **Štart** before it takes you to the winter-sports area, restaurant and lake at **Skalnaté pleso**. From there you can take a smaller **cable car** (www.vt.sk; return adult/child €26/19; ⏲8.30am-5.30pm Jul & Aug, to 3.30pm Sep-Jun) right up to the giddy summit. The latter requires a time-reserved ticket. You're given 50 minutes at the top to admire the views and snack in the cafe before your return time.

Štrbské Pleso & Around

Condo and hotel development continue unabated in the village but the namesake clear-blue glacial lake *(pleso)* remains beautiful, surrounded by dark pine forest and rocky peaks. **Row boats** (per 45min €15-20; ⏲10am-6pm May-Sep) can be rented from the dock by Grand Hotel Kempinski.

One of the mountains' most popular day hikes departs from here. Follow the red-marked **Magistrála Trail** uphill from the train station on a rocky forest trail for about 1¼ hours to **Popradské pleso**, an even more idyllic lake at 1494m. The busy mountain hut there has a large, self-service restaurant. From here the Magistrála zigzags dramatically up the mountainside, then traverses east towards Sliezsky dom

There is also a year-round **chairlift** (www.parksnow.sk; return adult/child €12/9; ⏲8am-3.30pm) up to **Chata pod Soliskom**, from where it's a one-hour walk north along a red trail to the 2093m summit of **Predné Solisko**.

Park Snow (www.parksnow.sk; day-lift ticket adult/child €26/18), Štrbské Pleso's popular ski and snowboard resort, has two chairlifts, four tow lines, 12km of easy-to-moderate runs, one jump and a snow-tubing area.

Sleeping

For a full listing of Tatra lodgings, check www.tatryinfo.eu. No wild/backcountry camping is permitted: there is a camping ground near Tatranská Lomnica. For the quintessential Slovak mountain experience, you can't beat hiking from one *chata* (mountain hut; could be anything from a shack to a chalet) to the next, high up among the peaks. Food (optional meal service or restaurant) is always available. Beds fill up, so book ahead.

Smokovec Resort Towns

Look for reasonable, been-there-forever boarding houses with one-word names like 'Delta' just west of the Nový Smokovec electric train stop on the several no-name streets that run to the south.

Penzión Tatra GUESTHOUSE €
(☎0903 650 802; www.tatraski.sk; Starý Smokovec 66; s/d incl breakfast €35/50; @📶) Colourful modern rooms fill this classic 1900 alpinesque

building above the train station. It's super central. Billiard table and ski storage available.

Bilíkova Chata MOUNTAIN HUT €
(0949 579 777, 0903 691 712; www.bilikovachata.sk; s & d from €40, without bathroom €25, apt €70) Basic but beautifully located log-cabin hotel with full-service restaurant among the clouds; near Hrebienok funicular station. Big low-season discounts. Breakfast (€5) and dinner (€6) available.

Villa Siesta HOTEL €€
(478 0931; www.villasiesta.sk; Nový Smokovec 88; s/d/ste €57/87/109;) Light fills this airy, contemporary mountain villa furnished in natural hues. The full restaurant, sauna and Jacuzzi are a bonus.

Grand Hotel Starý Smokovec HOTEL €€
(290 1339; www.grandhotel.sk; Starý Smokovec 38; d €82;) More than a century of history is tied up in Starý Smokovec's *grande dame*. Rooms could use an update to the 21st century.

Tatranská Lomnica & Around

Look for private rooms (*privat* or *zimmer frei*), from €15 per person, on the back streets south and east of the train station.

★ **Zamkovského Chata** MOUNTAIN HUT €
(0905 554 471, 442 2636; www.zamka.sk; per person €15) Atmospheric wood chalet with four-bed bunk rooms and restaurant; great hike stop midway between Skalnaté Pleso and Hrebienok.

Grandhotel Praha HOTEL €€
(290 1338; www.ghpraha.sk; Tatranská Lomnica; d incl breakfast from €70;) Remember when travel was elegant and you dressed for dinner? Well, the 1899 Grandhotel's sweeping marble staircase and crystal chandeliers do. Rooms are appropriately classic and there's a snazzy spa here, high above the village.

Štrbské Pleso & Around

Horský Hotel Popradské Pleso MOUNTAIN HUT €
(0910 948 160, 0908 761 403; www.popradskepleso.com; Popradské pleso; dm €16, s/d €28/56, without bathroom €18/36) Sizeable mountain hotel with restaurant and bar. It's a one-hour rugged hike up from the village or a paved hike (same time) up from Popradské pleso train stop.

★ **Grand Hotel Kempinski** HOTEL €€€
(326 2222; www.kempinski.com/hightatras; Kupelna 6, Štrbské Pleso; d from €180-210, ste from €320;) The swankiest Tatra accommodation is the classic, villa-like Kempinski, enticing high-end travellers with evening turndown service, heated marble bathroom floors and incredible lake views. See the mountains stretch before you through two-storey glass from the luxury spa.

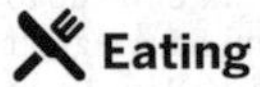

Eating

The resort towns are close enough that it's easy to sleep in one and eat in another. There's at least one grocery store per town.

Smokovec Resort Towns

Pizzeria La Montanara ITALIAN €
(Starý Smokovec 22; mains €4-8; 10am-9pm Mon-Sat, 2-10pm Sun) A local favourite, La Montanara serves good pizzas, pastas, soups and vegetables. It's above a grocery store on the eastern edge of town.

Reštaurácia Svišť SLOVAK €€
(Nový Smokovec 30; mains €5-16; 6-11pm) From hearty dumplings to beef fillet with wine reduction, this stylish Slovak restaurant does it all well – and it's surprisingly reasonable. Want to know what a typical 'Tatas plate' entails? Now's your chance! (Clue: meat).

Koliba Smokovec SLOVAK €€
(Starý Smokovec 5; mains €4-14; 3-10pm) A traditional rustic grill restaurant; some evening folk music. There's a pension, too (singles/doubles €25/40).

Štrbské Pleso & Around

★ **Koliba Patria** SLOVAK €€
(Southern lake shore, Štrbské Pleso; mains €6-15) Come here for the lovely lakeside terrace and complex meat dishes. It's certainly more refined than a typical *koliba* (rustic mountain restaurant serving Slovak sheepherder specialities).

Drinking

Tatry Pub PUB
(Tatra Komplex, Starý Smokovec; 3pm-late;) The official watering hole of the Mountain Guide Club is the liveliest place to drink, with a full schedule of dart tournaments, concerts etc.

Information

All three main resort towns have ATMs on the main street.

EMERGENCY

Mountain Rescue Service (787 7711, emergency 18 300; www.hzs.sk; Horný Smokovec 52) The main office of Slovakia.

TOURIST INFORMATION

Note that information offices do not book rooms; they hand out a brochure that lists some – not all – accommodation.

Tatra Information Office Starý Smokovec (TIK; 442 3440; www.tatry.sk/infocentrum; Starý Smokovec 23; 8am-8pm May-Sep, 8am-4pm or 6pm Oct-Apr) Largest area info office, with the most brochures.

Getting There & Around

To reach the Tatras by public transport, you first have to make it to Poprad, on the main west–east railway line between Bratislava and Košice.

From Poprad train station, a narrow-gauge electric train runs up to the resort town of Starý Smokovec. It then makes numerous stops heading west to Štrbské Pleso and east to Tatranská Lomnica; buses also run from Poprad to all three resort towns. Check schedules at www.cp.atlas.sk.

BUS

Buses run from Poprad to Starý Smokovec (€0.90, 15 minutes, half-hourly), Tatranská Lomnica (€1.30, 35 minutes, hourly) and Štrbské Pleso (€1.70, one hour, every 45 minutes).

TRAIN

From 6am until 10pm, electric trains (TEZ) run more or less hourly. Buy individual TEZ tickets at stations and block tickets (one to three) at tourist offices. Validate all on board.

The High Tatras Electric Railway has trains from Poprad up to Starý Smokovec (€1.50, 25 minutes), Tatranská Lomnica (€1.50, 40 minutes) and Štrbské Pleso (€2, 70 minutes). Other routes on this line include Štrbské Pleso–Starý Smokovec (€1.50, 40 minutes) and Štrbské Pleso–Tatranská Lomnica (€2, 70 minutes).

MULTIRESORT SKI PASSES

Park Snow and Vysoký Tatry resorts, the ski concessions in Štrbské Pleso and Tatranská Lomnica have all joined forces to offer multiday, multiresort lift passes (three-day adult/child €72/50). The **Super Slovak Ski Pass** (www.vt.sk; 10-day adult €290) covers some of the main resorts as well as other smaller ski areas around Slovakia.

EAST SLOVAKIA

Life gets, well, more laid-back the further east you venture. Somehow picturesque towns such as Levoča and Bardejov have avoided modern bustle and unfortunate 20th-century architectural decisions, while lingering over a streetfront cafe in delightful Košice is nigh-on obligatory. Meanwhile national parks beckon with untrammelled wildernesses free from those Tatras-bound tourists.

Levoča

053 / POP 14,900

So this is what Slovakia looked like in the 13th century... Unesco-listed Levoča still has its high medieval walls, surrounding old town buildings and cobblestone alleyways. At the centre of it all stands the pride of the country's religious architectural collection, the Gothic Church of St Jacob. Levoča is one of Slovakia's most important pilgrimage centres.

Sights

Church of St Jacob CHURCH
(Chrám sv Jakuba; www.chramsvjakuba.sk; Nám Majstra Pavla; adult/child €2/1; by hourly tour 11am-4pm Mon, 8.30am-4pm Tue-Sat, 1-4pm Sun) The spindles-and-spires Church of St Jacob, built in the 14th and 15th centuries, elevates your spirit with its soaring arches, precious art and rare furnishings, where the main attraction is Slovakia's tallest altar, an impressive 18m high.

Buy tickets from the cashier inside the Municipal Weights House across the street from the north door. Entry is generally on the hour. The adjacent 16th-century **cage of shame** was built to punish naughty boys and girls.

Nám Majstra Pavla SQUARE
Gothic and Renaissance eye candy abound on the main square, Nám Majstra Pavla. The private **Thurzov House** (1517), at No 7, has a characteristically frenetic Spiš Renaissance roofline. No 20 is the **Master Pavol Museum**, dedicated to the works of the city's most celebrated son. The 15th-century **Historic Town Hall** (Radnica) building, centre square, is really more interesting than the limited exhibits within.

One ticket gets you into both of the latter, as they are branches of the **Spiš Museum** (www.spisskemuzeum.com; adult/child €3.50/2.50; 9.30am-3pm Tue-Fri).

Sleeping & Eating

Hotel U Leva HOTEL €€

(☎450 2311; www.uleva.sk; Nám Majstra Pavla 24; s/d/apt €33/43/79;) Spread across two old town buildings, each of the 23 cleanly contemporary rooms is unique, and apartments come with kitchens. The fine restaurant (mains €6 to €12) combines atypical ingredients (brie, spinach) with time-honored Slovak techniques.

Information

Everything you're likely to need, banks and post office included, is on the main square. Most accommodation and restaurants have wi-fi.

Tourist Information Office (☎451 3763; http://eng.levoca.sk; Nám Majstra Pavla 58; 9am-4pm Mon-Fri year-round, plus 9am-4pm Sat & Sun May-Sep)

Getting There & Away

Levoča is on the main E50 motorway between Poprad (28km) and Košice (94km). Bus travel is the most feasible option here.

The local bus stop at Nám Štefana Kluberta is much closer to town than the bus station, which is 1km southeast of the town centre. From the bus stop, follow Košicka west two blocks and you'll hit the main square.

Frequent bus services take you to the following destinations:

Košice (€5, two hours, 12 to 14 daily)

Poprad (€1.70, 45 minutes, at least hourly) Most convenient onward mainline train connections.

Spišská Nová Ves (€0.90, 20 minutes, half-hourly) For Slovenský Raj National Park.

Spišské Podhradie (€0.90, 20 minutes, half-hourly) For Spiš Castle.

Spišské Podhradie

☎053 / POP 4000

Sprawling for four hectares above the village of Spišské Podhradie, ruined Spiš Castle is undoubtedly one of the largest in Europe. Even if you've never been, you may have seen pictures: the fortress is Slovakia's most-photographed sight. Two kilometres west, the medieval Spiš Chapter ecclesiastical settlement is also a Unesco World Heritage Site. In between, the village itself has basic services.

Sights

Spiš Castle CASTLE

(Spišský hrad; www.snm.sk; adult/child €5/3; 9am-7pm May-Sep, Oct & Nov by request) Heralding from at least as early as the 13th century, Spiš Castle and its vast complex of ruins crown a ridge above Spišské Podhradie. Its claim to fame as one of Europe's largest castle complexes will seem accurate as you explore. Be sure to ascend the central tower for spectacular panoramic views across the Spiš region, and imagine yourself as a patrolling medieval guard whilst traipsing this colossal fortress's outer walls.

Chronicles first mention the castle in 1209; it was from here that defenders allegedly repulsed the Tatars in 1241. Rulers and noble families kept adding fortifications and palaces during the 15th and 16th centuries, but by 1780 the site had already lost military significance and much was destroyed by fire. It wasn't until the 1970s that efforts were made to restore what remained. A Romanesque palace contains the very small **museum**, and the chapel adjacent to it. Night tours and medieval festivals take place some summer weekends. Get the English audio tour that brings the past into focus through story and legend.

Spiš Castle is 1km east of Spišské Podhradie, a healthy, uphill hike above the spur rail station. The easiest way to the castle by car is off the E50 highway on the east (Prešov) side.

Spiš Chapter MONASTERY

(Spišská Kapitula; adult/child €2/1) On the west side of Spišské Podhradie, you'll find still-active Spiš Chapter, a 13th-century Catholic complex encircled by a 16th-century wall. The pièce de résistance is **St Martin's Cathedral** (1273), towering above the community of quirky Gothic houses and containing some arresting 15th-century altars.

Buy tickets for the cathedral and pick up a guide from the (often-closed) information office at Spišská Kapitula 4. If you're travelling to Spiš Chapter by bus from Levoča, get off one stop (and 1km) before Spišské Podhradie, at Kapitula.

Sleeping & Eating

This is a day trip from the High Tatras or Košice.

★ **Spišsky Salaš** SLOVAK €

(☎454 1202; Levočská cesta 11; mains from €4; 10am-9pm;) Dig into lamb stew in the folksy dining room or on the covered deck, and watch the kids romp on rough-hewn play sets. The rustic log complex also has three simple rooms for rent (per person €13). It's 3km west of Spiš Chapter, on the road towards Levoča. It's a great hike from here to Spiš Chapter and Spiš Castle.

Getting There & Away

Spišské Podhradie is 15km east of Levoča and 78km northeast of Košice.

BUS

Frequent buses connect with Levoča (€0.90, 20 minutes), Poprad (€2.20, 50 minutes) and Košice (€4.25, 1½ hours).

TRAIN

An inconvenient spur railway line heads to Spišské Podhradie from Spišské Vlachy (€0.75, 15 minutes, five daily), a station on the Bratislava–Košice main line; only during summer. Check schedules at www.cp.atlas.sk.

Slovenský Raj & Around

☎053

With rumbling waterfalls, sheer gorges and dense forests, Slovenský Raj lives up to the name of 'Slovak Paradise'. A few easier trails exist, but the one-way ladder-and-chain ascents make this a national park for the passionately outdoorsy. You cling to metal rungs headed up a precipice while an icy waterfall sprays you from a metre away: pure exhilaration.

The nearest major town is uninspiring Spišská Nová Ves, 23km southeast of Poprad. Of the three trailhead resort villages, pretty Čingov, 5km west of Spišská Nová Ves, is our favourite. Podlesok (16km southwest of Poprad), has good accommodation. About 50km south, Dedinky is more of a regular village with a pub and supermarket fronting a lake.

Sights & Activities

Before you trek, pick up VKÚ's 1:25,000 Slovenský Raj hiking map (No 4) or 1:50,000 regional map (No 124). There are several good biking trails criss-crossing the national park.

Slovenský Raj National Park PARK

(www.slovenskyraj.sk; admission Jul & Aug €1, Sep-Jun free) The national park has numerous trails that include one-way *roklina* (gorge) sections and take at least half a day. Slovenský Raj is most famous for its sometimes hair-raising ladder-and-chain ascents – paths where you're clinging to a waterfall-splashed rock face on creaky metal supports.

From Čingov a green trail leads up Hornád River Gorge an hour to **Tomašovský výhľad**, a rocky outcropping and overlook that is a good short-hike destination. Or continue to the green, one-way, technically aided **Kláštorisko Gorge** trail, allowing at least eight hours for the circuit. You can also reach the Kláštorisko Gorge ascent from Podlesok (six hours). There is accommodation available at **Kláštorisko Chata**.

Another excellent alternative from Podlesok is to hike on the six- to seven-hour circuit up the dramatic, ladder and technical-assist **Suchá Belá Gorge**, then east to Kláštorisko Chata, where you'll find a reconstructed 13th-century monastery, on yellow then red trails. From there, take the blue trail down to the Hornád River; then follow the river gorge upstream to return to Podlesok.

One of the shortest, dramatic, technical-assist hikes starts at Biele Vody (15 minutes northeast of Dedinky via the red trail) and follows the green trail up **Zejmarská Gorge**. The physically fit can clamber up in 50 minutes. To get back, you can follow the green trail down to Dedinky, or there's a chairlift that works sporadically.

The best viewpoint is at Medvedia Hlava in the east of the park. Slovenský Raj's forested gorges lie in one direction, the jagged teeth of the High Tatras in the other. Access it via a 4½ hour hike from Spišská Nová Ves tourist information centre.

Dobšinská Ice Cave CAVE

(www.ssj.sk; adult/child €7/3.50; ⏲9am-4pm Tue-Sun by hourly tour, closed Oct–mid-May) The fanciful frozen formations in this Unesco-noted ice cave are more dazzling in early June than September. A 15-minute hike leads up from the settlement of Dobšinská ľadová jaskyňa to where tours begin every hour or so.

Sleeping & Eating

Many lodgings have restaurants. Several eateries and a small grocery store are available in Podlesok. The biggest supermarket is next to the bus station in Spišská Nová Ves.

Penzión Lesnica GUESTHOUSE €

(☎449 1518; www.stefani.sk; Čingov 113; s/d/apt incl breakfast €30/40/50; 📶) Nine simple, sunny-coloured rooms close to the trail fill up fast, so book ahead. The attached restaurant is one of the best local places for a Slovak repast (mains €5.50 to €15).

Grand Hotel Spiš HOTEL €

(☎449 1129; www.grandhotelspis.com; Spišské Tomášovce; s/d €26/41; P📶) Grand is a grandiose word, but services here are above par, with an agreeable mountain rusticity spreading from the public areas into the rooms. This is our favourite hotel in the park: 1km outside Čingov with good hike access.

Ranč Podlesok GUESTHOUSE €
(☎0918 407 077; www.rancpodlesok.sk; Podlesok 5; r per person from €17;) A blue park trail runs behind this stone-and-log lodge and restaurant at the park's edge. There's sand volleyball too, if you fancy it. It's 1km past the Podlesok village area.

Information

Outside Spišská Nová Ves, lodgings are the best source of information; park info booths are open July through August. Get cash before you arrive in the park; there is an ATM and exchange at Spišská Nová Ves train station. Helpful websites include www.slovenskyraj.sk.

Mountain Rescue Service (☎emergency 183 00; http://his.hzs.sk)

Tourist Information Centre (☎442 8292; en.spisskanovaves.eu; Letná 49, Spišská Nová Ves; ⏲8am-6pm Mon-Fri, 9am-1pm Sat, 2-6pm Sun) Helps with accommodation.

Getting There & Around

During low season especially, you may consider hiring a car in Košice; connections to the park can be a chore. You'll have to transfer at least once, usually in Spišská Nová Ves.

BUS

Buses travel more infrequently on weekends, most often in July and August. No buses run directly between trailhead villages. Carefully check schedules at www.cp.atlas.sk.

Buses run from Slovenský Raj's transport hub of Spišska Nová Ves to Poprad (€1.70, 40 minutes, every one to two hours). Other buses run to Levoča (€0.90, 20 minutes, hourly), Čingov (€0.60, 15 minutes, two to four direct Monday to Friday, one direct Saturday), Hrabušice (for Podlesok; €1.10, 30 minutes, nine daily Monday to Friday, four Saturday) and Dedinky (€2.50, 80 minutes, four direct Monday to Saturday).

TRAIN

Trains run from Spišska Nová Ves to Poprad (€1.50, 20 minutes, at least hourly) and Košice (€4, one hour, at least hourly). The train station is 1½ blocks east of the bus station.

Košice

☎055 / POP 240,000

East Slovakia's industrial powerhouse has cosmopolitan clout and a buoyant cultural scene plonking it firmly on Europe's city-break map, fiercely independent of Bratislava. As 2013's European Capital of Culture, Košice has accordingly initiated a new string of attractions including major arts installations in a combination of impressively revamped buildings, and eclectic events to enliven city streets.

Košice, for centuries the eastern stronghold of the Hungarian Kingdom, was always a medieval gem. New enhancements build on an arts scene already home to the paintings of Andy Warhol and one of Europe's loveliest theatres. Its vast oval-shaped *námestie* (central square) contains the largest collection of historical monuments in Slovakia, enlivened by myriad buzzing cafes and restaurants.

It's base-of-choice, too, for forays deeper into the tradition-seeped east. From here, top trips include Unesco-listed medieval Bardejov, with Slovakia's most beautiful town square, and the surrounding area's stunning wooden churches, reflecting a Carpatho-Rusyn heritage shared with neighbouring parts of Ukraine and Poland.

Sights

Hlavné Nám SQUARE
Almost all of the sights are in or around the town's long plaza-like main square, Hlavná. Landscaped flowerbeds surround the central **musical fountain**, across from the 1899 State Theatre (p993). Look for the turn-of-the-20th-century, art nouveau **Hotel Slávia** at No 63. **Shire Hall** (1779), at No 27, is where the Košice Government Program was proclaimed in 1945; today there's a minor art gallery inside.

Cathedral of St Elizabeth CHURCH
(Dóm sv Alžbety; Hlavné nám; church admission adult/child €1.50/1; ⏲1-9pm Mon, 9am-9pm Tue-Thu, 9am-8pm Fri & Sat, 1-7pm Sun) Dark, brooding 14th-century Cathedral of St Elizabeth wins the prize for the sight most likely to grace your Košice postcard home. You can't miss Europe's easternmost (and perhaps mightiest) Gothic cathedral, which dominates the square. Below the church, a **crypt** contains the tomb of Duke Ferenc Rákóczi, who was exiled to Turkey after the failed 18th-century Hungarian revolt against Austria.

Don't forget to ascend the 160 narrow, circular stone steps up the church's vertigo-inducing tower for city views. Climbing the royal staircase as the monarchs once did provides an interior perspective: note the rare interlocking flights of steps. Just to the south, the 14th-century **St Michael's Chapel** (Kaplinka sv Michala) has sporadic entry hours.

Lower Gate Underground Museum MUSEUM
(Hlavné Nám; adult/child €0.90/0.50; ⏲10am-6pm Tue-Sun May-Sep) The underground remains of

medieval Košice – lower gate, defence chambers, fortifications and waterways dating from the 13th to 15th centuries – were uncovered during construction work in 1996. Get lost in the maze-like passages of the archaeological excavations at the south end of the square.

East Slovak Museum MUSEUM
(Východoslovenské múzeum; ☎622 0309; www.vsmuzeum.sk; Hviezdoslavova 3; per exhibition €1-3; ⊙9am-5pm Tue-Sat, 9am-1pm Sun) Hidden treasure can be found at the East Slovak Museum. Workers found the secret stash of 2920 gold coins, dating from the 15th to 18th centuries, while renovating a house on Hlavná in 1935. There's a romp through various aspects of regional history, too, showcased through a former prison and a metal foundry. In the museum yard there's a relocated 1741 wooden church.

Sleeping

Penzión Slovakia GUESTHOUSE €
(☎728 9820; www.penzionslovakia.sk; Orliá 6; s/d/ste incl breakfast €45/55/65; ❄ 📶) Charming guesthouse with grill restaurant downstairs.

K2 HOSTEL €
(☎625 5948; Štúrova 32; r without bathroom from €16.50) These dowdy singles and doubles are the most centrally located budget option. Ask for a room away from the road.

★**Hotel Bankov** HISTORIC HOTEL €€
(☎632 4522 ext 4; www.hotelbankov.sk; Dolný Bankov 2; s/d from €59/74; P @ 📶 🏊) Going strong since 1869, Slovakia's oldest hotel lies 4km northwest of central Košice in a verdant location overlooking woodland. Rooms are surprisingly good value, oozing old-world charm (beams, period furniture). There's an elegant restaurant and a wellness centre, plus there's complementary taxi service for guests.

Golden Royal Hotel & Spa BOUTIQUE HOTEL €€
(☎720 1011; www.goldenroyal.sk; Vodná 8; s/d €75/90; 📶) Rooms are more modern than that classic old facade would suggest, but we love the slick furnishings. The spa goes down a treat, too. The best central option.

Eating

★**Republika Východu** INTERNATIONAL €
(Hlavné nám 31; mains €3-7; ⊙7am-10pm Mon-Thu, 7/8am-midnight Fri & Sat, 8am-10pm Sun) Proudly proclaiming independence from Western Slovakia and indeed anywhere else, Republika Východu (Republic of the East) baits you with cakes and good coffee then becalms you with its salads, pancakes and exclusively eastern takes on some of the Slovak classics. Menus are in special eastern dialect.

★**Villa Regia** INTERNATIONAL €€
(www.villaregia.sk; Dominikánske nám 3; mains €7-14; 🖉) Steaks, seafood and vegetarian dishes get artistic treatment amid a rustic old-world atmosphere. The vaulted ceilings and stone walls extend to the upstairs pension rooms.

Le Colonial INTERNATIONAL €€
(Hlavná 8; mains €8-17; ⊙11am-11pm) Get a hit of colonial plushness at this top-of-the-top-end place. The menu is rather less of an adventure, but the cooking is good.

Drinking & Entertainment

For a city this small, options are plentiful. Any sidewalk cafe on the main square is great for a drink. Check free monthly publication *Kam do Mesta* (www.kamdomesta.sk) for entertainment listings.

Caffe Trieste CAFE
(Uršulínska 2; ⊙7.30am-7.30pm) Original of the mini-chain now found in Bratislava. Knock-out espresso, in slurp-it-and-go Italian fashion.

Jazz Club CLUB
(http://jazzclub-ke.sk; Kováčska 39) DJs spin here most nights, but there are also occasional live concerts.

State Theatre THEATRE
(Štátne Divadlo Košice; ☎245 2269; www.sdke.sk; Hlavné nám 58; ⊙box office 9am-5.30pm Mon-Fri, 10am-1pm Sat) Local opera and ballet companies stage performances in this 1899 neobaroque theatre.

State Philharmonic Košice CLASSICAL MUSIC
(Štátna Filharmónia Košice, House of the Arts; ☎622 4509, 622 0763; www.sfk.sk; Moyzesova 66) Concerts take place year-round but the spring musical festival is a good time to catch performances of the city's philharmonic.

Information

Most hotels, cafes and restaurants have free wi-fi; plus catch a regularly updated list of free wi-fi spots at www.kosice.info/wifi. Lots of banks with ATMs are scattered around Hlavné nám.

City Information Centre (☎625 8888; www.visitkosice.eu; Hlavná 59; ⊙10am-6pm Mon-Fri, 10am-3pm Sat & Sun) Ask for both the free annual town guide and the colour brochure of historic sites. Guided city tours can be arranged.

Nemocnica Košice-Šaca (☎723 4313; www.nemocnicasaca.sk; Lúčna 9) Good private healthcare; 12km southwest of central Košice.

Police Station (☎158; Pribinova 6)

Getting There & Away

Check bus and train schedules at www.cp.atlas.sk.

AIR

Košice International Airport (p995) is 6km southwest of the city centre. **Czech Airlines** (www.csa.cz) has two daily flights to Bratislava (weekdays only) as well as Prague.

BUS

You can book ahead on some Ukraine-bound buses through Eurobus (p984). Getting to Poland is easier from Poprad. Destinations include Bardejov (€3.80, 1¾ hours, half-hourly), Levoča (€5, two hours, 12 to 14 daily) and Uzhhorod (Ukraine; €7, three to four hours, three daily).

CAR

Several international car-hire companies have representatives at the airport.

Buchbinder (☎683 2397; www.buchbinder.sk; Košice International Airport) Small company with good rates and gratis pick-up in the city.

TRAIN

Trains from Košice run to Bratislava (€19, five to six hours, every 1½ hours), Poprad in the High Tatras (€5, 1¼ hours, hourly) and Spišská Nová Ves for Slovenský Raj (€4, one hour, hourly). There are also trains over the border to Miskolc, Hungary (€7, 11 hours, one to two daily) and Lviv, Ukraine (€13, 11 hours, one to two daily).

Getting Around

The old town is small, so you probably can walk everywhere. Bus 23 between the airport and the train station requires a two-zone ticket (€1): buy at newsstands and validate onboard.

SURVIVAL GUIDE

Directory A–Z

ACCOMMODATION

Bratislava has more hostels and five-star hotels than midrange accommodation. Outside the capital, you'll find plenty of reasonable *penzióny* (guesthouses). Breakfast is usually available (often included) at all lodgings and wi-fi is near ubiquitous. Many lodgings offer nonsmoking rooms. Parking is only a problem in Bratislava. A recommended booking resource in the capital city is **Bratislava Hotels** (www.bratislavahotels.com).

> **SLEEPING PRICE RANGES**
>
> The below ranges are based on the price of a double room with private bathroom in high season.
>
> **€** less than €60
>
> **€€** €60–€130
>
> **€€€** more than €130

BUSINESS HOURS

Sight and attraction hours vary throughout the year; standard opening times for the tourist season (May through September) are listed below. Schedules in remoter tourist destinations vary from October to April; check ahead. Museums and other sights are usually closed on Mondays.

Banks 8am to 5pm Monday to Friday

Bars 11am to midnight Monday to Thursday, 11am to 2am Friday and Saturday, 4pm to midnight Sunday

Grocery stores 6.30am to 6pm Monday to Friday, 7am to noon Saturday

Post offices 8am to 5pm Monday to Friday, 8am to 11am Saturday

Nightclubs 4pm to 4am Wednesday to Sunday

Restaurants 10.30am to 10pm

Shops 9am to 6pm Monday to Friday, 9am to noon Saturday

INTERNET ACCESS

Wi-fi is widely available at lodgings and cafes across the country; so much so that internet cafes are becoming scarce. For the laptopless, lodgings also often have computers you can use.

INTERNET RESOURCES

Slovakia Document Store (www.panorama.sk)

Visit Bratislava (www.visit.bratislava.sk/EN/)

MONEY

- In January 2009 Slovakia's legal tender became the euro. Previously, it was the Slovak crown, or Slovenská koruna (Sk).
- Slovaks almost never tip; still, for foreigners, a 5% to 10% tip is a polite gesture for a nice meal out.

POST

Post office service is reliable (outgoing) but waits are far longer when you're expecting incoming mail from abroad. For outgoing mail, bank on five working days to other parts of Europe and seven for the US/Australia.

PUBLIC HOLIDAYS

New Year's and Independence Day 1 January

Three Kings Day 6 January

Good Friday and Easter Monday March/April

Labour Day 1 May
Victory over Fascism Day 8 May
Cyril and Methodius Day 5 July
SNP Day 29 August
Constitution Day 1 September
Our Lady of Sorrows Day 15 September
All Saint's Day 1 November
Christmas 24 to 26 December

TELEPHONE

Landline numbers can have either seven or eight digits. Mobile phone numbers (10 digits) are often used for businesses; they start with 09. When dialling from abroad, you need to drop the zero from both city area codes and mobile phone numbers. Purchase local and international phone cards at newsagents. Dial ☎00 to call out of Slovakia.

Mobile Phones

The country has GSM (900/1800MHz) and 3G UMTS networks operated by providers Orange, T-Mobile and O2.

TOURIST INFORMATION

Association of Information Centres of Slovakia (AICES; ☎44-551 4541, in Liptovský Mikuláš; www.aices.sk) Runs an extensive network of city information centres.

Slovak Tourist Board (http://slovakia.travel/en) No Slovakia-wide information office exists; it's best to go online.

VISAS

For a full list of visa requirements, see www.mzv.sk (under 'Consular Info').

- No visa is required for EU citizens.
- Visitors from Australia, New Zealand, Canada, Japan and the US do not need a visa for up to 90 days.
- Visas are required for South African nationals, among others. For the full list see www.slovak-republic.org/visa-embassies.

COUNTRY FACTS

Area 49,035 sq km

Capital Bratislava

Country Code ☎00421

Currency Euro (€)

Emergency general ☎112, fire ☎150, ambulance ☎155, police ☎158

Language Slovak

Money ATMs widely available in cities

Population 5.4 million

Visas Not required for most visitors staying less than 90 days

EATING PRICE RANGES

Restaurant review price indicators are based on the cost of a main course.

€ less than €7

€€ €7–€12

€€€ more than €12

Getting There & Away

Bratislava and Košice are the country's main entry/exit points – Poprad would be in distant third place. Flights, tours and rail tickets can be booked online at www.lonelyplanet.com/travel_services.

Entering Slovakia from the EU, indeed from most of Europe, is a breeze. Lengthy custom checks make arriving from Ukraine more tedious.

Though few airlines fly into Slovakia itself, Bratislava is just 60km from well-connected Vienna International Airport. By train from Bratislava, Budapest (three hours) and Prague (five hours) are easily reachable, as well as Vienna (one hour). Buses connect to Zakopane in Poland (two hours) from Poprad, and to Uzhhorod in Ukraine (2½ hours) via Košice.

AIR

Bratislava's intra-European airport (p984), 9km northeast of the city centre, is small. Unless you're coming from the UK, which has several direct flights, your arrival is likely to be by train. Vienna in Austria has the nearest international air hub.

Airports

Vienna International Airport (VIE; www.viennaairport.com) Austrian airport with regular buses that head the 60km east to Bratislava. Worldwide connections.

Košice International Airport (KSC; www.airportkosice.sk)

Poprad-Tatry International Airport (www.airport-poprad.sk; Na Letisko 100)

Airlines

The main airlines operating in Slovakia:

Austrian Airlines (www.aua.com) Connects Košice with Vienna.

Czech Airlines (www.csa.cz) Flies between Košice, Bratislava and Prague.

Ryanair (www.ryanair.com) Connects Bratislava with numerous destinations across the UK and Italy, coastal Spain, Dublin, Paris and Brussels.

Wizz Air (http://wizzair.com) Connects Košice and Poprad to London Luton.

LAND

Border posts between Slovakia and fellow EU Schengen member states – Czech Republic, Hungary, Poland and Austria – are nonexistent.

ESSENTIAL FOOD & DRINK

➡ **Sheep's cheese** *Bryndza* – sharp, soft and spreadable; *oštiepok* – solid and ball-shaped; *žinčina* – a traditional sheep's-whey drink (like sour milk).

➡ **Meaty moments** *Vývar* (chicken/beef broth served with *slížiky*, thin pasta strips, or liver dumplings); *kapustnica* (thick sauerkraut and meat soup, often with chorizo or mushrooms); baked duck/goose served in *lokše* (potato pancakes) and stewed cabbage.

➡ **Dumplings** Potato-based goodies in varieties such as *halušky* (mini-dumplings in cabbage or *bryndza* sauce topped with bacon) or *pirohy* (pocket-shaped dumplings stuffed with *bryndza* or smoked meat). For sweets, try *šulance* (walnut- or poppy seed–topped dumplings).

➡ **Fruit firewater** Homemade or store-bought liquor, made from berries and pitted fruits, such as *borovička* (from juniper) and *slivovica* (from plums).

You can come and go at will. This makes checks at the Ukrainian border all the more strident, as you will be entering the EU. By bus or car, expect at least one to two hours' wait.

Bus

Local buses connect Poprad and Ždiar with Poland during the summer season. Eurolines (p984) and Košice-based Eurobus (p984) handle international routes across Europe from Bratislava and heading east to Ukraine from Košice.

Car & Motorcycle

Private vehicle requirements for driving in Slovakia are registration papers, a 'green card' (proof of third-party liability insurance), nationality sticker, first-aid kit and warning triangle.

Train

See www.cp.atlas.sk for domestic and international train schedules. Direct trains connect Bratislava to Austria, the Czech Republic, Poland, Hungary and Russia; from Košice, trains connect to the Czech Republic, Poland, Ukraine and Russia. The fastest domestic trains are Intercity (IC) or Eurocity (EC). *Rychlík* (R; 'fast' trains) take slightly longer, but run more frequently and cost less. *Osobný* (Ob) trains are slowest (and cheapest).

RIVER

Danube riverboats offer an alternative way to get between Bratislava and Vienna. Vienna–Budapest boats don't stop in Bratislava.

ℹ Getting Around

AIR

Czech Airlines (p995) offers the only domestic air service: weekdays only, between Bratislava and Košice.

BICYCLE

Roads are often narrow and potholed, and in towns cobblestones and tram tracks can prove dangerous for bike riders. Bike rental is uncommon outside mountain resorts. The cost of transporting a bike by rail is usually 10% of the train ticket.

BUS

Read timetables carefully; different schedules apply for weekends and holidays (although these are still well serviced). You can find up-to-date schedules online at www.cp.atlas.sk. The main national bus companies in Slovakia are Slovenská Autobusová Doprava (SAD) and **Slovak Lines** (www.slovaklines.sk).

CAR & MOTORCYCLE

Foreign driving licences with photo ID are valid in Slovakia. *Nálepka* (toll stickers) are required on *all* green-signed motorways. Fines for not having them can be hefty. Buy at petrol stations (rental cars usually have them).

City streetside parking restrictions are eagerly enforced. Always buy a ticket from a machine, attendant or newsagent in old town centres.

Car hire is available in Bratislava and Košice primarily.

LOCAL TRANSPORT

Towns all have efficient bus systems; most villages have surprisingly good services. Bratislava and Košice have trams and trolleybuses; the High Tatras also has an efficient electric railway.

Public transport generally operates from 4.30am to 11.30pm daily.

City transport tickets are good for all local buses, trams and trolleybuses. Buy at newsstands and validate on board or risk serious fines (this is not a scam).

TRAIN

Train is the way to travel in Slovakia; most tourist destinations are off the main Bratislava–Košice line. No online reservations: ticket machines are also rare. Reserve at train station offices. Visit www.cp.atlas.sk for up-to-date schedules.

Slovak Republic Railways (ŽSR; ☎18 188; www.slovakrail.sk) Far-reaching, efficient national rail service.

Slovenia

Includes ➡

Best Places to Eat

- ➡ Špajza (p1002)
- ➡ Casa Nostromo (p1010)
- ➡ Ostarija Peglez'n (p1005)
- ➡ Skuhna (p1002)

Best Places to Stay

- ➡ Antiq Palace Hotel & Spa (p1002)
- ➡ Penzion Mayer (p1005)
- ➡ Dobra Vila (p1007)
- ➡ Max Piran (p1009)
- ➡ Hostel Tresor (p1001)

Why Go?

It's a pint-sized place, with a surface area of just over 20,000 sq km, and two million people. But 'good things come in small packages', and never was that old chestnut more appropriate than in describing Slovenia. The country has everything – from beaches, snowcapped mountains, hills awash in grape vines and wide plains blanketed in sunflowers to Gothic churches, baroque palaces and art nouveau buildings. Its incredible mixture of climates brings warm Mediterranean breezes up to the foothills of the Alps, where it can snow in summer.

The capital, Ljubljana, is a culturally rich city that values liveability and sustainability over unfettered growth. This sensitivity toward the environment also extends to rural and lesser-developed parts of the country. With more than half of its total area covered in forest, Slovenia really is one of the 'greenest' countries in the world.

When to Go

Ljubljana

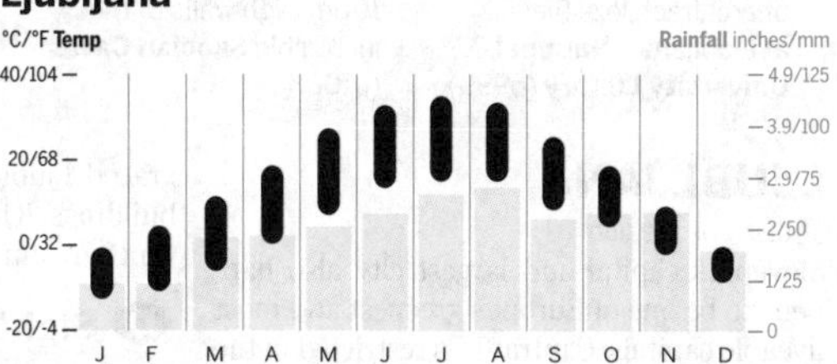

Apr–Jun Spring is a great time to be in the lowlands and the flower-carpeted valleys of the Julian Alps.

Sep This is the month for everything – still warm enough to swim and made for hiking.

Dec–Mar Everyone (and their grandma) dons their skis in this winter-sport-mad country.

Slovenia Highlights

1 Enjoy a 'flight' on the funicular up to **Ljubljana Castle**.

2 Consider the genius of architect Jože Plečnik at Ljubljana's **National & University Library** (p999).

3 Gaze on the natural perfection that is **Lake Bled** (p1005).

4 Gawk in awe at the 100m-high walls of the incredible **Škocjan Caves** (p1008).

5 Climb to the top of the country's tallest mountain, **Mt Triglav** (p1004).

6 Get lost wandering the narrow Venetian-style alleyways of **Piran** (p1009).

LJUBLJANA

☎01 / POP 283,000

Slovenia's capital and largest city also happens to be one of Europe's greenest and most liveable capitals. Car traffic is restricted in the centre, leaving the leafy banks of the emerald-green Ljubljanica River, flowing through the city's heart, free for pedestrians and cyclists. In summer, cafes set up terrace seating along the river, lending the feel of a perpetual street party. Slovenia's master of early-modern, minimalist design, Jože Plečnik, graced Ljubljana with beautiful bridges and buildings. The museums, hotels and restaurants are among the best in the country.

Sights

The easiest way to see Ljubljana is on foot. The oldest part of town, with the most important historical buildings and sights (including Ljubljana Castle), lies on the right (east) bank of the Ljubljanica River. Center, which has the lion's share of the city's museums and galleries, is on the left (west) side of the river.

ITINERARIES

Three Days

Spend a couple of days in **Ljubljana**, then head north to unwind in romantic **Bled** or **Bohinj** beside idyllic mountain lakes. Alternatively, head south to visit the caves at **Škocjan** or **Postojna**.

One Week

A full week will allow you to see all the country's top highlights. After two days in the capital head for Bled and Bohinj. Depending on the season, take a bus or drive over the hair-raising **Vršič Pass** into the valley of the vivid blue **Soča River** and take part in some adventure sports in **Bovec**. Continue south to the caves at Škocjan and Postojna and then to the sparkling Venetian port of **Piran** on the Adriatic.

★Ljubljana Castle CASTLE

(Ljubljanski Grad; ☎01-306 42 93; www.ljubljanskigrad.si; Grajska Planota 1; adult/child incl funicular & castle attractions €8/5, castle attractions only €6/3, with guided tour €10/7; ⏲9am-11pm Jun-Sep, 9am-9pm Apr, May & Oct, 10am-8pm Jan-Mar & Nov, 10am-10pm Dec) There's been a human settlement on the site of this hilltop castle since at least Celtic times, but the oldest structures these days date back 500 years and were built following an earthquake in 1511. It's free to ramble around the castle precincts, but you'll have to pay to enter the Watchtower, the Chapel of St George, to see the Slovenian history exhibition and join the costumed Time Machine tour. The fastest way to reach the castle is via the funicular from Krekov trg, which keeps the same hours as the castle.

Prešernov Trg SQUARE

The centrepiece of Ljubljana's wonderful architectural aesthetic is this marvellous square, a public space of understated elegance that not only serves as the link between the Center district and the Old Town, but as the city's favourite meeting point. The square itself is dominated by a monument to the national poet France Prešeren (1905). Immediately south of the statue is the city's architectural poster-child, the small but much celebrated Triple Bridge (Tromostovje), designed by prolific architect Jože Plečnik.

★National & University Library HISTORIC BUILDING

(Narodna in Univerzitetna Knjižnica (NUK; ☎01-200 11 10; Turjaška ulica 1; ⏲8m-8pm Mon-Fri, 9am-2pm Sat) This library is Plečnik's masterpiece, completed in 1941. To appreciate this great man's philosophy, enter through the main door (note the horse-head doorknobs) on Turjaška ulica – you'll find yourself in near darkness, entombed in black marble. As you ascend the steps, you'll emerge into a colonnade suffused with light – the light of knowledge, according to the architect's plans.

City Museum Ljubljana MUSEUM

(Mestni Muzej Ljubljana; ☎01-241 25 00; www.mgml.si; Gosposka ulica 15; adult/child €4/2.50, with special exhibits €6/4; ⏲10am-6pm Tue, Wed & Fri-Sun, to 9pm Thu) The excellent city museum focuses on Ljubljana's history, culture and politics via imaginative multimedia and interactive displays. The reconstructed Roman street that linked the eastern gates of Emona to the Ljubljanica, and the collection of well-preserved classical finds in the basement, are both worth a visit in themselves.

National Museum of Slovenia MUSEUM

(Narodni Muzej Slovenije; ☎01-241 44 00; www.nms.si; Prešernova cesta 20; adult/child €6/4, 1st Sun of month free; ⏲10am-6pm Fri-Wed, to 8pm Thu) Highlights here include the highly embossed Vače *situla*, a Celtic pail from the late 6th century BC unearthed in a town east of Ljubljana, and a Stone Age bone flute discovered near Cerkno in western Slovenia in 1995. There are also examples of Roman glass and jewellery found in 6th-century Slavic graves, along with many other historical finds. Check out the statues of the Muses and Fates relaxing on the stairway banisters.

Museum of Modern Art MUSEUM

(Moderna Galerija; ☎01-241 68 00; www.mg-lj.si; Tomšičeva ulica 14; adult/student €5/2.50; ⏲10am-6pm Tue-Sun) This museum houses the very best in Slovenian art – modern or otherwise. Keep an eye out for works by painters Tone Kralj *(Peasant Wedding)*, the expressionist France Mihelič *(The Quintet)* and the surrealist Štefan Planinc *(Primeval World series)* as well as sculptors including

Ljubljana

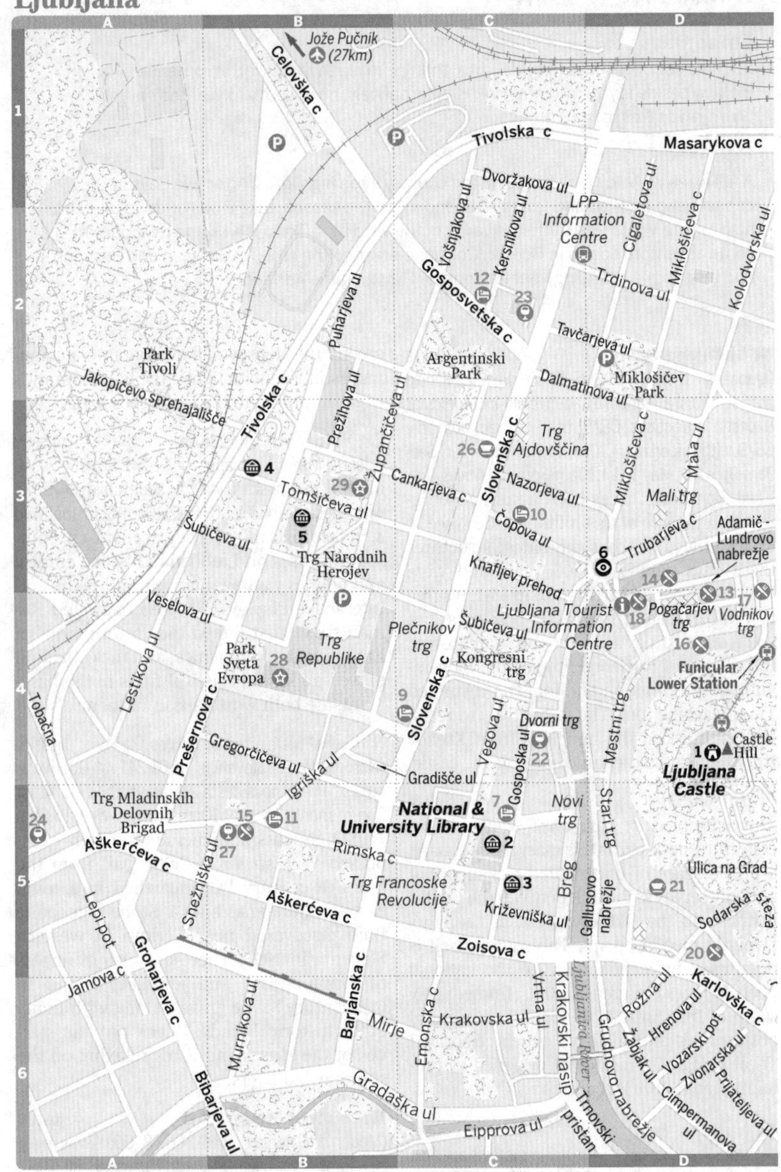

Jakob Savinšek *(Protest)*. The museum also owns works by the influential 1980s and 1990s multimedia group Neue Slowenische Kunst (NSK; *Suitcase for Spiritual Use: Baptism under Triglav*) and the artists' co-operative Irwin (*Kapital*).

Sleeping

The Ljubljana Tourist Information Centre (TIC) has details of private rooms (single/double from €30/50) and apartments (double/quad from €55/80), though only a handful are central.

Ljubljana

Top Sights
1 Ljubljana Castle D4
2 National & University Library C5

Sights
3 City Museum Ljubljana C5
4 Museum of Modern Art B3
5 National Museum of Slovenia B3
6 Prešernov Trg D3

Sleeping
7 Antiq Palace Hotel & Spa C5
8 Celica Hostel F2
9 Cubo C4
10 Hostel Tresor C3
11 Penzion Pod Lipo B5
12 Slamič B&B C2

Eating
13 Covered Market D4
14 Fish Market D3
15 Gostilna Rimska XXI B5
16 Klobasarna D4
17 Open-Air Market D4
18 Ribca D4
19 Skuhna E3
20 Špajza D5

Drinking & Nightlife
21 Cafe Kolaž D5
22 Dvorni Bar C4
23 Klub K4 .... C2
24 KMŠ Hangover A5
25 Metelkova Mesto F1
26 Nebotičnik C3
27 Žmavc B5

Entertainment
28 Cankarjev Dom B4
29 Opera Ballet Ljubljana B3

★**Hostel Tresor** HOSTEL €€
(☎01-200 90 60; www.hostel-tresor.si; Čopova ulica 38; dm €15-24, s/d €40/70; ❄@☜) This new 28-room hostel in the heart of Center is housed in a Secessionist-style former bank. The money theme continues into rooms named after currencies. Dorms have between four and 12 beds but are spacious, and beds are curtained off. The communal areas (we love the atrium) are stunning; breakfast is in the vaults.

Celica Hostel HOSTEL €€
(☎01-230 97 00; www.hostelcelica.com; Metelkova ulica 8; dm €19-27, s/d cell €58/62; @☜) This revamped former prison (1882) in Metelkova has 20 'cells', designed by different artists and architects and with original bars. There are nine rooms and apartments with three to seven beds and a packed, popular 12-bed dorm. The Celica even has its own gallery where everyone can show their work.

Slamič B&B PENSION €€
(☎01-433 82 33; www.slamic.si; Kersnikova ulica 1; s €65-75, d €95-110, ste from €135; ❄☜) It's slightly

away from the action but Slamič, a B&B above a famous cafe and teahouse, offers 17 bright rooms, some with vintage furnishings and parquet floors. Choice rooms include the ones looking on to a back garden and the one just off an enormous terrace used by the cafe.

Penzion Pod Lipo PENSION €€
(☎01-031 809 893; www.penzion-podlipo.com; Borštnikov trg 3; d/tr/q €59/75/100, ste from €125; ❄@📶) Sitting atop a famous *gostilna* (inn-like restaurant) with a 400-year-old linden tree in front, this 10-room inn offers straightforward but excellent-value accommodation in a neighbourhood filling up with bars and restaurants. We love the communal kitchen, the original hardwood floors and the east-facing terrace with deck chairs to catch the morning sun.

★Antiq Palace Hotel & Spa BOUTIQUE HOTEL €€€
(☎083 896 700, mobile 040 638 163; www.antiqpalace.com; Gosposka ulica 10 & Vegova ul 5a; s/d €180/210; ❄@📶) Among the capital's most luxurious sleeping options, the Antiq Palace occupies a 16th-century townhouse a block from the river. Accommodation is in 21 individually designed suites, some with multiple rooms and stretching to 250 sq metre in size. The list of amenities is a mile long and includes a luxurious spa and fitness centre.

Cubo BOUTIQUE HOTEL €€€
(☎01-425 60 00; www.hotelcubo.com; Slovenska cesta 15; s/d €120/140; ❄@📶) This sleek boutique hotel with 26 rooms in the centre of town boasts high-end, minimalist design. The owners have placed great emphasis on using the best construction materials – lamps formed from silkworm cocoons (would you believe?) and silver thread in the drapes. High-quality bedding and double-glazing ensure a good night's sleep.

Eating

Klobasarna FAST FOOD €
(☎051 605 017; www.klobasarna.si; Ciril-Metodov trg 15; dishes €3.50-6; ⏲10am-11pm Mon-Sat, to 3pm Sun) This hole-in-the-wall eatery in the Old Town specialising in that most Slovenian of dishes, *Kranjska klobasa*, an EU-protected fatty sausage from the city of Kranj, is almost a one-trick pony but can occasionally rustle up *jota* and *ričet*, two hearty stews, as well.

Ribca SEAFOOD €
(☎01-425 15 44; www.ribca.si; Adamič-Lundrovo nabrežje 1; dishes €4-8.50; ⏲8am-4pm Mon, 8am-9pm Tue-Sat, 11am-6pm Sun) One of the culinary joys of a visit to Ljubljana is the chance to sample inexpensive and well-prepared fish dishes. This basement seafood bar below the Plečnik Colonnade in Pogačarjev trg is one of the best for tasty fried squid, sardines and herrings. The setting is informal, though the cuisine is top notch.

★Skuhna INTERNATIONAL €
(☎041 339 978; www.skuhna.si; Trubarjeva cesta 15; mains €5-7, menu €11; ⏲11.30am-9pm Mon-Fri, noon-9pm Sat) This unique eatery is the work of two Slovenian nonprofit organisations that are helping the city's migrant community to integrate. A half-dozen chefs from countries as diverse as Egypt, Kenya and Colombia take turns cooking everyday, and the result is a cornucopia of authentic world cuisine. The choicest tables are in the kitchen.

Gostilna Rimska XXI SLOVENIAN €€
(☎01-256 56 54; http://www.r-g.si/xxi; Rimska cesta 21; mains €8.5-16; ⏲11am-11pm Mon-Fri, noon-5pm Sat) This reliable old favourite specialises in traditional Slovenian cuisine, using locally sourced ingredients and lots of home-made extras, including its own home-made beer and brandy. There's no English menu, so ask the server what looks good in the kitchen. Try the *žlikrofi* (ravioli of cheese, bacon and chives) with game sauce (€12).

★Špajza SLOVENIAN €€€
(☎01-425 30 94; www.spajza-restaurant.si; Gornji trg 28; mains €18-24; ⏲noon-11pm Mon-Sat, noon-10pm Sun) The popular 'Pantry' restaurant in the Old Town is the perfect spot for a romantic meal. The interior is decorated with rough-hewn tables and chairs, wooden floors, painted ceilings and vintage bits and pieces. The terrace in summer is a delight. The cooking is high-end Slovenian, with an emphasis on less common mains like rabbit, lamb and colt, a Slovenian speciality.

Open-Air Market MARKET
(Vodnikov trg; ⏲6am-6pm Mon-Fri, 6am-4pm Sat summer, 6am-4pm Mon-Sat winter) Self-caterers will want to head directly to Ljubljana's vast open-air market on Pogačarjev trg and Vodnikov trg, across the Triple Bridge to the southeast of Prešernov trg. Come here on Friday from 8am to 8pm from mid-March to October for **Open Kitchen** (Odprta Kuhna), a weekly food fair with home-cooked local and international specialities.

Covered Market MARKET
(Pogačarjev trg 1; 7am-4pm Mon-Fri, 7am-2pm Sat) Sells meats and cheeses.

Fish Market MARKET
(Adamič-Lundrovo nabrežje 1; 7am-4pm Mon-Fri, 7am-2pm Sat) In addition to fresh fish at the covered fish market, you'll find open-air fish stands in Vodnikov trg selling plates of fried calamari for as little as €7.

Drinking & Nightlife

Cafe Kolaž CAFE
(059 142 824; www.facebook.com/kafe.kolaz; Gornji trg 15; 9am-1am Mon-Sat, 10am-midnight Sun) One of the most chilled places to drink (and eat) in the Old Town, the gay-friendly 'Collage' picks up where the much-missed Open Cafe left off. Exhibitions, literary nights and DJ evenings, with sandwiches and canapés (€2.80 to €4.50), too.

★ **Žmavc** BAR
(01-251 03 24; Rimska cesta 21; 7.30am-1am Mon-Fri, from 10am Sat, from 6pm Sun;) Everyone's favourite louche bar in Ljubljana, this popular hang-out west of Slovenska cesta has *manga* comic-strip scenes and figures running halfway up the walls. There's a great garden terrace for summer evening drinking, but try to arrive early to snag a table. Also excellent for morning coffee.

★ **Nebotičnik** CAFE
(040 601 787; www.neboticnik.si; 12th fl, Štefanova ulica 1; 9am-1am Sun-Wed, to 3am Thu-Sat) After more than a decade in hibernation, this elegant cafe with its breathtaking terrace atop Ljubljana's famed art deco Skyscraper (1933) has reopened, and the 360-degree views are spectacular.

Dvorni Bar WINE BAR
(01-251 12 57; www.dvornibar.net; Dvorni trg 2; 8am-1am Mon-Sat, 9am-midnight Sun) This wine bar is an excellent place to taste Slovenian vintages; it stocks more than 100 varieties and has wine tastings every month (usually the 2nd Wednesday). Tapas cost €4 to €10.

KMŠ Hangover CLUB
(01-425 74 80; www.klubkms.si; Tržaška cesta 2; pub 24hr, club 10pm-6am Fri & Sat) Located in the deep recesses of a former tobacco factory complex, this studenty place stays comatose round the clock till the weekend when it turns into a raucous place with music (jungle, reggae, drum 'n' bass) and dancers all over the shop.

METELKOVA MESTO

For a scruffy antidote to trendy clubs in Ljubljana, head for **Metelkova Mesto** (Metelkova Town; www.metelkovamesto.org; Masarykova cesta 24), an ex–army garrison taken over by squatters in the 1990s and converted into a free-living commune. In this two-courtyard block, a dozen idiosyncratic bars and clubs hide behind brightly tagged doorways, coming to life generally about 7pm during the week and at 11pm at the weekend.

Klub K4 CLUB
(040 212 292; www.klubk4.org; Kersnikova ulica 4; 11pm-4am Wed, 9pm-1am Thu, 11pm-6am Fri & Sat) This evergreen venue in the basement of the Student Organisation of Ljubljana University (ŠOU) headquarters features rave-electronic music Friday and Saturday, with other styles of music on weeknights, and a popular gay and lesbian night called Klub Roza (Pink Club) usually on Sunday.

Entertainment

Ljubljana in Your Pocket (www.inyourpocket.com), which comes out every two months, is a good English-language source for what's on in the capital. Buy tickets for shows and events at the venue box office, online through Eventim (www.eventim.si), or at the Ljubljana Tourist Information Centre (p1004).

Cankarjev Dom CLASSICAL MUSIC
(01-241 71 00, box office 01-241 72 99; www.cd-cc.si; Prešernova cesta 10; box office 11am-1pm & 3-8pm Mon-Fri, 11am-1pm Sat, 1hr before performance) Ljubljana's premier cultural and conference centre has two large auditoriums (the Gallus Hall is said to have perfect acoustics) and a dozen smaller performance spaces offering a remarkable cornucopia of performance arts.

Opera Ballet Ljubljana OPERA, DANCE
(01-241 59 00, box office 01-241 59 59; www.opera.si; Župančičeva ulica 1; box office 10am-1pm & 2-6pm Mon-Fri, 10am-1pm Sat, 1hr before performance) Home to the Slovenian National Opera and Ballet companies, this historic neo-Renaissance theatre has been restored to its former glory in recent years. Enter from Cankarjeva cesta.

Information

There are ATMs at every turn, including a row of them outside the main Ljubljana Tourist Information Centre (TIC) office. At the train station you'll find a **bureau de change** (train station; ⊙8am-8pm) changing cash for no commission, but not travellers cheques.

Health Centre Ljubljana (Zdravstveni Dom Ljubljana; ☎01-472 37 00; www.zd-lj.si; Metelkova ulica 9; ⊙7.30am-7pm Mon-Fri, 8am-4pm Sat) For non-emergencies.

Ljubljana Tourist Information Centre (TIC; ☎01-306 12 15; www.visitljubljana.si; Adamič-Lundrovo nabrežje 2; ⊙8am-9pm Jun-Sep, 8am-7pm Oct-May) Knowledgeable and enthusiastic staff dispense information, maps and useful literature and help with accommodation. Maintains an excellent website.

Slovenian Tourist Information Centre (STIC; ☎01-306 45 76; www.slovenia.info; Krekov trg 10; ⊙8am-9pm Jun-Sep, 8am-7pm Mon-Fri & 9am-5pm Sat & Sun Oct-May) Good source of information for the rest of Slovenia, with free internet.

University Medical Centre Ljubljana (Univerzitetni Klinični Center Ljubljana; ☎01-522 50 50, 01-522 23 61; www.kclj.si; Zaloška cesta 2; ⊙24hr) University medical clinic with 24-hour accident and emergency service.

Getting There & Away

BUS

Buses to destinations both within Slovenia and abroad leave from the **bus station** (Avtobusna Postaja Ljubljana; ☎01-234 46 00; www.ap-ljubljana.si; Trg Osvobodilne Fronte 4; ⊙5am-11pm Mon-Sat, from 5.30am Sun) in front of the train station. Next to the ticket windows are multilingual information phones and a touch-screen computer; there's a **left luggage** (Trg OF 4; per day €2; ⊙5.30am-10.30pm Sun-Fri, 5am-10pm Sat) area at window 3. Frequent buses serve Bohinj (€8.30, two hours, hourly) via Bled (€6.50, 1¼ hours), Divača (€7.90, 1½ hours, eight daily), Piran (€12, 2½ hours, up to seven daily) and Postojna (€6, one hour, half-hourly).

TRAIN

Domestic and international trains arrive at and depart from central Ljubljana's **train station** (Železniška Postaja; ☎01-291 33 32; www.slo-zeleznice.si; Trg Osvobodilne Fronte 6; ⊙6am-10pm). Buy domestic tickets from window Nos 1 to 8, international ones from window No 9. There are **coin lockers** (Trg OF 6; per day €2-3; ⊙24hr) for left luggage on platform 1. Useful domestic destinations include Bled (€5.10, one hour, half-hourly) and Bohinjska Bistrica (€7.20, two hours, six daily) via Jesenice.

Getting Around

TO/FROM THE AIRPORT

You can reach Ljubljana's **Jože Pučnik Airport** (LJU/Aerodrom Ljubljana; ☎04-206 19 81; www.lju-airport.si/eng; Zgornji Brnik 130a, Brnik) by public bus (€4.10, 45 minutes) from stop No 28 at the bus station. These run at 5.20am and hourly from 6.10am to 8.10pm Monday to Friday; at the weekend there's a bus at 6.10am and then one every two hours from 9.10am to 7.10pm. Buy tickets from the driver.

The best of several airport-shuttle services is **GoOpti** (☎01-320 45 30; www.goopti.com), which can also transfer you to Jože Pučnik Airport (from €9, half-hour) along with some 20 other airports in the region including Venice, Vienna and Klagenfurt. Book by phone or online; rates depend on pick-up time and whether you are sharing or prefer a private transfer.

A taxi from the airport to Ljubljana will cost from €30.

BICYCLE

Ljubljana is a pleasure for cyclists, and there are bike lanes and special traffic lights everywhere. The **Bicike(lj)** (www.bicikelj.si; subscription weekly/yearly €1/€3 plus hourly rate; ⊙24hr) cycle-sharing scheme is generally geared towards residents and short rides. Instead, rent two-wheelers by the hour or day from **Ljubljana Bike** (☎01-306 45 76; www.visitljubljana.si; Krekov trg 10; per 2hr/4hr/day €2/4/8; ⊙8am-7pm Apr, May & Oct, 8am-9pm Jun-Sep) at the Slovenian Tourist Information Centre.

PUBLIC TRANSPORT

Ljubljana's city buses operate every five to 15 minutes from 5am (6am on Sunday) to around 10.30pm. A flat fare of €1.20 (good for 90 minutes of unlimited travel, including transfers) is paid with a stored-value magnetic **Urbana** (☎01-430 51 74; www.jhl.si/en/single-city-card-urbana) card, which can be purchased at newsstands, tourist offices and the **LPP Information Centre** (☎01-430 51 75; www.lpp.si; Slovenska cesta 56; ⊙7am-7pm Mon-Fri) for €2; credit can then be added (from €1 to €50).

JULIAN ALPS

The Julian Alps – named in honour of Caesar himself – form Slovenia's dramatic northwest frontier with Italy. Triglav National Park, established in 1924, includes almost all of the Alps lying within Slovenia, including triple-peaked Mt Triglav, at 2864m Slovenia's highest mountain. Along with an abundance of fauna and flora, the area offers a wide range of adventure sports.

Bled

☎04 / POP 8100

With its emerald-green lake, picture-postcard church on a tiny island, medieval castle clinging to a rocky cliff and some of the country's highest peaks as backdrops, Bled seems to have been designed by the very god of tourism. It's a small and convenient base from which to explore the mountains.

Sights

Lake Bled LAKE

(Blejsko jezero) Bled's greatest attraction is its crystal green lake, measuring just 2km by about 1.5km. Mild thermal springs warm the water to a swimmable 26°C from June through August. From the shore tiny, tear-shaped **Bled Island** (Blejski Otok; www.blejskiotok.si) beckons. There's a church and small museum on it, but the real thrill is the ride out by **gondola** (pletna; ☎041 427 155; per person return €12). The boat sets you down on the south side at the monumental South Staircase (Južno Stopnišče).

Bled Castle CASTLE, MUSEUM

(Blejski Grad; www.blejski-grad.si; Grajska cesta 25; adult/child €9/4.50; 8am-8pm Apr-Oct, 8am-6pm Nov-Mar) Perched atop a steep cliff more than 100m above the lake, Bled Castle is how most people imagine a medieval fortress to be, with towers, ramparts, moats and a terrace offering magnificent views. The castle houses a museum collection that traces the lake's history from earliest times, a chapel, a printing works and a restaurant.

Vintgar Gorge CANYON

(www.vintgar.si; adult/child €4/2; 8am-7pm late Apr-Oct) The highlight of visiting the gorge, an easy walk 4km to the northwest of the centre, is the 1600m-long wooden walkway (1893) that criss-crosses the swirling Radovna River.

Activities

Several local outfits organise a wide range of outdoor activities in and around Bled, including trekking, mountaineering, rock climbing, ski touring, cross-country skiing, mountain biking, rafting, kayaking, canyoning, caving, horse riding and paragliding.

3glav Adventures ADVENTURE SPORTS

(☎041 683 184; www.3glav-adventures.com; Ljubljanska cesta 1; 9am-7pm Apr-Oct) The number-one adventure-sport specialists in Bled for warm-weather activities from 15 April to 15 October. The most popular trip is the Emerald River Adventure (€65), an 11-hour hiking and swimming foray into Triglav National Park and along the Soča River. It also rents bikes for €15 a day.

Sleeping

Kompas has a list of private rooms and farmhouses, with prices starting at €21 per person.

Traveller's Haven HOSTEL €

(☎059 044 226, mobile 041 396 545; www.travellers-haven.si; Riklijeva cesta 1; dm/d from €19/48; @) This is arguably the nicest of several hostels clustered on a hillside on the eastern shore of the lake, about 500m north of the centre. The setting is a renovated villa, with six rooms (including one private double), a great kitchen and free laundry.

★**Penzion Mayer** PENSION €€

(☎04-576 57 40; www.mayer-sp.si; Želeška cesta 7; s/d €57/82, apt from €120; @) This flower-bedecked 12-room inn in a renovated 19th-century house is located above the lake. The larger apartment is in a lovely wooden cabin and the in-house restaurant is excellent.

Hotel Triglav Bled BOUTIQUE HOTEL €€€

(☎04-575 26 10; www.hoteltriglavbled.si; Kolodvorska cesta 33; s €89-159, d €109-179, ste from €199; @) The 22 rooms in this painstakingly restored *caravanserai* that opened in 1906 have hardwood floors and Oriental carpets and are furnished with antiques. There's an enormous sloped garden that grows the vegetables served in the terrace restaurant. It's just up from Bled Jezero train station.

Eating & Drinking

Pizzeria Rustika PIZZA €

(☎04-576 89 00; www.pizzeria-rustika.com; Riklijeva cesta 13; pizza €6-10; noon-11pm;) Conveniently located on the same hill as much of Bled's budget accommodation, Rustika serves the best pizza in town.

Slaščičarna Šmon CAFE €

(☎04-574 16 16; www.smon.si; Grajska cesta 3; 7.30am-9pm) Bled's culinary speciality is *kremna rezina* (€2.70), a layer of vanilla custard topped with whipped cream and sandwiched between two layers of flaky pastry. Šmon may not be its place of birth, but it remains the best place in which to try it.

★**Ostarija Peglez'n** SEAFOOD €€

(☎04-574 42 18; Cesta Svobode 19a; mains €9-16; noon-10.30pm) One of the better restaurants in Bled, the 'Iron Inn' has fascinating retro decor with lots of old household antiques and curios (including the eponymous iron) and serves some of the best fish dishes in town.

Pub Bled PUB
(Cesta Svobode 19a; ⏱9am-1am Sun-Thu, 9am-3am Fri & Sat) This ultra-friendly pub above the Oštarija Peglez'n restaurant has great cocktails. There's a DJ most nights.

Information

Kompas (☎04-572 75 01; www.kompas-bled.si; Bled Shopping Centre, Ljubljanska cesta 4; ⏱8am-7pm Mon-Sat, to 3pm Sun) Full-service travel agency.

Tourist Information Centre Bled (☎04-574 11 22; www.bled.si; Cesta Svobode 10; ⏱8am-9pm Mon-Sat, 9am-6pm Sun Jul & Aug, 8am-6pm Mon-Sat, 10am-4pm Sun Sep-Jun) Occupies a small office behind the lakeside Casino; rents bikes (half-/full day €8/11), does laundry (€20/16 same/next day) and has a computer for checking email.

Getting There & Around

BUS

Hourly buses run from Bled to Lake Bohinj (€3.60, 45 minutes) via Bohinjska Bistrica, with the first bus leaving around 7am and the last about 10pm. Buses depart at least hourly for Ljubljana (€6.50, 1¼ hours).

TRAIN

Bled has two train stations, though neither is close to the centre. Mainline trains to/from Ljubljana (€5.10, one hour, up to 21 daily) and Austria use Lesce-Bled station, 4km to the east of town. Trains to/from Bohinjska Bistrica (€1.85, 20 minutes, eight daily), from where you can catch a bus to Lake Bohinj, and Italy use the smaller Bled Jezero station, which is 2km west of central Bled.

Bohinj

☎04 / POP 5300

Bohinj, a larger and much less developed glacial lake 26km to the southwest of Bled, is a world apart. Triglav itself is visible from Bohinj and there are activities galore – from kayaking and mountain biking to trekking up Triglav via one of the southern approaches. **Ribčev Laz** is the main tourist hub at the lake; **Bohinjska Bistrica** (pop 1890), the area's largest centre, is 6km east of the lake and useful for its train station.

Sights & Activities

Church of St John the Baptist CHURCH
(Cerkev sv Janeza Krstnika; Ribčev Laz; ⏱10am-5pm daily Jul & Aug, 10am-5pm Sat & Sun Sep-Jun) The walls and ceilings of this picturesque church, on the northern side of the Sava Bohinjka river across the stone bridge, is covered with frescoes dating from the 14th to 16th centuries.

Savica Waterfall WATERFALL
(Slap Savica; Ukanc; adult/child €2.50/1.25; ⏱9am-6pm Jul & Aug, to 5pm Apr-Jun, Sep & Oct) This magnificent waterfall, which cuts deep into a gorge almost 80m below, is 4km from the settlement of Ukanc and can be reached by footpath from there.

Alpinsport ADVENTURE SPORTS
(☎04-572 34 86, mobile 041 596 079; www.alpinsport.si; Ribčev Laz 53; ⏱9am-8pm Jul-Sep, to 7pm Oct-Jun) Rents sporting equipment, canoes/kayaks (per hour €7/3) and bikes (per hour/day €4/13.50) and organises guided rafting, canyoning and caving trips from a kiosk near the stone bridge.

Sleeping

The tourist office can help arrange accommodation in private rooms and apartments (double €38 to €50).

Hostel Pod Voglom HOSTEL €
(☎04-572 34 61; www.hostel-podvoglom.com; Ribčev Laz 60; dm €16-18, r per person €23-27, without bath €19-22; @ 📶) This premier hostel, some 3km west of Ribčev Laz on the road to Ukanc, has 119 beds in 46 rooms in two buildings.

★**Penzion Gasperin** PENSION €€
(☎041 540 805; www.bohinj.si/gasperin; Ribčev Laz 36a; d €54-92, apt €70-120; ❄ @ 📶) This spotless chalet-style guesthouse with 24 rooms is just 350m southeast of the TIC and run by a friendly British-Slovenian couple. Most rooms have balconies.

Hotel Jezero HOTEL €€€
(☎04-572 91 00; www.bohinj.si/alpinum/jezero; Ribčev Laz 51; s €57-78, d €94-136; @ 📶 🏊) This 76-room place just opposite the lake has a lovely indoor swimming pool, two saunas and a fitness centre.

Eating

Strud'l SLOVENIAN €
(☎041 541 877; www.strudl.si; Triglavska cesta 23; mains €6-11; ⏱8am-9pm; 📶) This take on traditional farmhouse cooking is incongruously

located in the centre of Bohinska Bistrica. Try local treats such as *ričet s klobaso* (barley stew served with sausage and beans). The *hišni krožnik* (house plate) is a sampling of everything, including ham, sausage, mashed beans, sauerkraut and cooked buckwheat.

Gostilna Mihovc SLOVENIAN €
(☎051 899 111; www.gostilna-mihovc.si; Stara Fužina 118; mains €7-15; ⏲9am-11pm) This place in Stara Fužina, the next village over from Ribčev Laz, is popular for its home cooking and its home-made brandy. Try the *pasulj* (bean soup) with sausage (€6) or the grilled trout (€10). Live music at the weekend.

Information

Tourist Information Centre Ribčev Laz (TIC; ☎04-574 60 10; www.bohinj-info.com; Ribčev Laz 48; ⏲8am-8pm Mon-Sat, 8am-6pm Sun Jul & Aug, 8am-6pm Mon-Sat, 9am-3pm Sun Sep-Jun) Ask for the comprehensive new *Cycling Routes* (Kolesarske Poti) map.

Getting There & Away

BUS

Buses run regularly from Ljubljana (€8.30, two hours, hourly) to Bohinj Jezero and Ukanc – marked 'Bohinj Zlatorog' – via Bled and Bohinjska Bistrica. Around 20 buses daily go from Bled (€3.60, 45 minutes) to Bohinj Jezero (via Bohinjska Bistrica) and return, with the first bus leaving around 5am and the last about 9pm.

TRAIN

A half-dozen daily trains daily make the run to Bohinjska Bistrica from Ljubljana (€7.20, two hours), though this route requires a change in Jesenice. There are also frequent trains between Bled's small Bled Jezero station (€1.85, 20 minutes, eight daily) and Bohinjska Bistrica.

SOČA VALLEY

The Soča Valley region (Posočje) is defined by the 96km-long Soča River, coloured a deep, almost artificial cobalt blue. The valley has more than its share of historical sights, most of them related to WWI, but most visitors are here for rafting, hiking, skiing and other active sports.

Bovec

☎05 / POP 1700

Soča Valley's de facto capital, Bovec, offers plenty to adventure-sports enthusiasts. With the Julian Alps – including Mt Kanin (2587m) – above, the Soča River below and Triglav National Park all around, you could spend a week here hiking, kayaking, canyoning and mountain biking without ever doing the same thing twice.

Activities

You'll find everything you need on the compact village square, **Trg Golobarskih Žrtev**, including a half-dozen adrenaline-raising adventure-sports companies. Among the best are **Aktivni Planet** (☎031 653 417; www.aktivniplanet.si; Trg Golobarskih Žrtev 19; ⏲9am-7pm) and **Soča Rafting** (☎05-389 62 00, mobile 041 724 472; www.socarafting.si; Trg Golobarskih Žrtev 14; ⏲9am-7pm).

Rafting, kayaking and **canoeing** on the beautiful Soča River are major draws. The season lasts from April to October. Rafting trips of two to eight people over a distance of 8km to 10km (1½ hours) and cost from €37. Canoes for two are €45 for the day; single kayaks €30. A 3km **canyoning** trip, in which you descend through gorges and jump over falls near the Soča attached to a rope, costs €45.

Sleeping & Eating

Hostel Soča Rocks HOSTEL €
(☎041 317 777; http://hostelsocarocks.com; Mala Vas 120; dm €13-15, d €34-36; @📶) This new 14-room arrival sleeping 68 people is a new breed of hostel: colourful, bathed in light, spotlessly clean and with a bar that never seems to quit. Dorms sleep six people maximum and some rooms have balconies and views of Mt Kanin. Discounted activities on offer.

Martinov Hram GUESTHOUSE €€
(☎05-388 62 14; www.martinov-hram.si; Trg Golobarskih Žrtev 27; s €33-41, d €56-71; 📶) This lovely and very friendly *gostišče* (inn) near the centre has a dozen plain but adequate rooms and an excellent restaurant with an emphasis on specialities from the Bovec region.

★**Dobra Vila** BOUTIQUE HOTEL €€€
(☎05-389 64 00; www.dobra-vila-bovec.si; Mala Vas 112; d €125-165, tr €170-195; ❄@📶) This absolute stunner of an 11-room boutique hotel is housed in a one-time telephone-exchange building dating to 1932. Peppered with interesting artefacts and objets d'art, it has its own library and wine cellar, and a fabulous restaurant with set menus, a winter garden and an outdoor terrace.

Information

Tourist Information Centre Bovec (05-388 19 19; www.bovec.si; Trg Golobarskih Žrtev 8; 8.30am-8.30pm Jul & Aug, 9am-4pm Mon-Sat Sep-Jun)

Getting There & Away

There are a couple of daily buses to Ljubljana (€13.60, 3½ hours) via Kobarid and Idrija. From late June to August a service to Kranjska Gora (€6.80, 1¾ hours) via the Vršič Pass departs several times a day, continuing on to Ljubljana.

KARST & COAST

Slovenia's short coast (47km) is an area for both recreation and history; the town of Piran, famed for its Venetian Gothic architecture and picturesque narrow streets, is among the main drawcards here. En route from Ljubljana or the Soča Valley, you'll cross the Karst, a huge limestone plateau and a land of olives, ruby-red Teran wine, *pršut* (air-dried ham), old stone churches and deep subterranean caves, including those at Postojna and Škocjan.

Postojna & Škocjan Caves

05

As much of a draw as the mountains and the sea in Slovenia are two world-class but very different cave systems in the Karst area.

Sights

Postojna Cave CAVE
(Postojnska Jama; 05-700 01 00; www.postojnska-jama.eu; Jamska cesta 30; adult/child €22.90/13.70, with Predjama Castle €28.90/17.40; tours hourly 9am-5pm or 6pm May-Sep, 3 or 4 times 10am-4pm Oct-Apr) Just under 2km northwest of the town of Postojna (population 7900), Postojna Cave is one of the largest caverns in the world, and its stalagmite and stalactite formations are unequalled anywhere. It's a busy destination – visited by as many as a third of all tourists coming to Slovenia – but it's amazing how the large crowds at the entrance seem to get swallowed whole by the size of the cave.

Postojna is home to the endemic Proteus anguinus – a cute, eyeless salamander nicknamed 'the human fish' because of its skin colour. Visits of 1½ hours involve a 4km underground train ride as well as a 1.7km walk with some gradients but no steps. Dress warmly or rent a shawl as it's 8°C to 10°C down there.

Škocjan Caves CAVE
(05-708 21 10; www.park-skocjanske-jame.si; Škocjan 2; adult/child €16/7.50; tours hourly 10am-5pm Jun-Sep, 2 or 3 times 10am-3pm Oct-Apr) The quieter and more remote Škocjan Caves are 4km southeast of Divača (population 1300). A World Heritage site, this immense system is more captivating than the one at Postojna – a page right out of Jules Verne's *A Journey to the Centre of the Earth* – and for many travellers this will be the highlight of their trip to Slovenia. The temperature in the caves is constant at 12°C so bring along a light jacket or sweater. Good walking shoes, for the sometimes slippery paths, are also recommended.

You can walk to the caves from Divača in about 40 minutes; the trail is signposted. Alternatively, a van meets incoming trains (when running) or replacement buses, and ferries ticket holders to the caves up to four times a day.

Sleeping & Eating

Hotel Kras HOTEL €€
(05-700 23 00; www.hotel-kras.si; Tržaška cesta 1; s/d €71/89, apt €121;) In the heart of Postojna town a couple of kilometres southeast of the cave, this rather flash hotel offers 27 comfortable rooms with all the mod cons. If you're feeling flush, choose one of the three apartments on the top (5th) floor with enormous terraces.

Hotel Malovec HOTEL €€
(05-763 33 33; www.hotel-malovec.si; Kraška cesta 30a; s/d hotel €54/80, pension €43/54; @) This new build in the centre of Divača, some 4km northwest of the caves, has 20 modern rooms, including a large family one with balcony. There's an equal number of rooms in the Malovec's original pension right next to its popular restaurant, which serves Slovenian favourites to an appreciative local crowd.

Information

Kompas Postojna (05-721 14 80; www.kompas-postojna.si; Titov trg 2a; 8am-7pm Mon-Fri, 9am-1pm Sat Jun-Oct, 8am-6pm Mon-Fri, 9am-1pm Sat Nov-May) The best source of information in Postojna; has private rooms and changes money.

Getting There & Away

Buses from Ljubljana en route to Piran stop in Postojna (€6, one hour, half-hourly) and Divača

WORTH A TRIP

PREDJAMA CASTLE

The tiny village of Predjama (population 80), 10km northwest of Postojna, is home to the remarkable **Predjama Castle** (05-700 01 03; www.postojnska-jama.eu; Predjama 1; adult/child €9/5.40, with Postojna Cave €28.90/17.40; tours hourly 9am-7pm Jul & Aug, 9am-6pm May, Jun & Sep, 10am-5pm Apr & Oct, 10am-4pm Nov-Mar), an all-but-impregnable redoubt in the gaping mouth of a cavern halfway up a 123m cliff. Its four storeys were built piecemeal over the years since 1202, but most of what you see today is 16th century. It looks simply unconquerable.

The castle holds great features for kids of any age – a drawbridge over a raging river, holes in the ceiling of the entrance tower for pouring boiling oil on intruders, a very dank dungeon, a 16th-century chest full of treasure (unearthed in the cellar in 1991), and a hiding place at the top called Erazem's Nook. And in mid-July, the castle hosts the Erasmus Tournament, a day of medieval duelling, jousting and archery.

In summer a shuttle bus ferries joint ticket-holders from Postojna Cave to the castle hourly between 1pm and 6pm.

(€7.90, 1½ hours, eight daily). Severe ice storms in 2014 destroyed much of the track in Notranjska province; train traffic to Postojna (€5.80, one hour) and Divača (€7.70, 1¾ hours) was suspended indefinitely at the time of research, though replacement buses were in operation.

Piran

05 / POP 4700

Little Piran (Pirano in Italian) sits on the tip of a narrow peninsula, the westernmost point of Slovenian Istria. Piran Bay and Portorož (population 3000), Slovenia's largest beach resort, lie to the south. The centre of Piran's Old Town is **Tartinijev trg**, an oval-shaped, marble-paved square that was the inner harbour until it was filled in 1894.

Sights

Sergej Mašera Maritime Museum MUSEUM

(05-671 00 40; www.pomorskimuzej.si; Cankarjevo nabrežje 3; adult/child €3.50/2.10; 9am-noon & 5-9pm Tue-Sun Jul & Aug, 9am-5pm Tue-Sun Sep-Jun) Just southeast of Tartinijev trg in the lovely 19th-century Gabrielli Palace on the waterfront, this museum's focus is the sea, sailing and salt-making – three things that have been crucial to Piran's development over the centuries. The antique model ships upstairs are very fine; other rooms are filled with old figureheads and weapons, including some lethal-looking blunderbusses.

Aquarium Piran AQUARIUM

(05-673 25 72, mobile 051 602 554; www.aquariumpiran.com; Kidričevo nabrežje 4; adult/child €7/5; 9am-10pm Jun-Aug, to 9pm Apr & May, to 7pm Sep & Oct, to 5pm Nov-Mar) About 100m southwest of Tartinijev trg along the harbour, Piran's aquarium might be small, but there's a tremendous variety of sea life packed into its more than two dozen tanks.

Cathedral of St George CATHEDRAL

(Stolna Cerkev sv Jurija; Adamičeva ul 2) Piran is watched over by the hilltop Cathedral of St George, mostly dating from the 17th century. If time allows, visit the attached **Parish Museum of St George** (05-673 34 40; Adamičeva ul 2; admission €1; 9am-1pm & 5-7.30pm Tue-Fri, 9am-2pm & 5-8pm Sat, 11am-2pm & 5-8pm Sun), which contains a church plate, paintings and a lapidary in the crypt. The cathedral's free-standing **bell tower** (Zvonik; admission €2; 10am-2pm & 5-8pm) dates back to 1609 and can be climbed. The octagonal **baptistery** (1650) has imaginatively reused a 2nd-century Roman sarcophagus as a baptismal font. To the east is a reconstucted stretch of the 15th-century **town wall** complete with loopholes.

Sleeping

★Max Piran B&B €€

(05-673 34 36, mobile 041 692 928; www.maxpiran.com; Ul IX Korpusa 26; d €60-70;) Piran's most romantic accommodation has just six rooms, each bearing a woman's name rather than a number, in a delightful coral-coloured, early-18th-century townhouse.

Miracolo di Mare B&B €€

(05-921 76 60, mobile 051 445 511; www.miracolodimare.si; Tomšičeva ul 23; s €50-55, d €60-70;) A cosy B&B near the waterfront, the 'Wonder of the Sea' has a dozen charming (though smallish) rooms, some of which (like No 3 and the breakfast room) give on to the most charming raised back garden in Piran. Floors and stairs are wooden (and original) and beds metal framed.

Hotel Tartini HOTEL €€€
(☎05-671 10 00; www.hotel-tartini-piran.com; Tartinijev trg 15; s €76-92, d €102-128, ste from €140; ❄📶) This attractive, 45-room property faces Tartinijev trg and manages to catch a few sea views from the upper floors. The staff are especially friendly and helpful. For a real treat, splash out on suite No 40a; we're suckers for eyrie-like round rooms with million-euro views.

Eating

Restaurant Neptune SEAFOOD €
(☎05-673 41 11, 041 715 890; Župančičeva ul 7; mains €8-20; ⊙12pm-4pm, 6pm-10pm) It's no bad thing to be more popular with locals than tourists, and this family-run place hits all the buttons – a friendly welcome, big seafood platters and a choice of meat dishes, too.

Riva Piran SEAFOOD €€
(☎05-673 22 25; Gregorčičeva ul 46; mains €8-28; ⊙11.30am-midnight) Riva is the best waterfront seafood restaurant and is worth patronising. It has the strip's best decor, unparallelled sea views and friendly service.

★**Casa Nostromo** SEAFOOD €€
(☎030 200 000; www.piranisin.com; Tomšičeva ul 24; mains €8-22; ⊙noon-11pm) Making a big splash (as it were) on the Piran culinary scene these days is decorated chef Gradimir Dimitrić's new waterfront eatery, serving seafood and Istrian specialities.

Information

Tourist Information Centre Piran (☎05-673 44 40; www.portoroz.si; Tartinijev trg 2; ⊙9am-8pm Jul & Aug, 9am-noon & 12.30-5pm Mon-Sat, 10am-2pm Sun Sep-Jun) In the impressive Municipal Hall.

Getting There & Away

BUS

Up to seven buses a day make the run to/from Ljubljana (€12, 2½ hours, via Divača and Postojna). Some five buses go daily to Trieste (€10, 1¾ hours) in Italy, except Sundays. One bus a day heads south for Croatian Istria from late June to September, stopping at the coastal towns of Umag, Poreč and Rovinj (€10.30, 2¾ hours).

SURVIVAL GUIDE

Directory A–Z

BUSINESS HOURS

Bars Usually 11am to midnight Sunday to Thursday, to 1am or 2am on Friday and Saturday.

Banks 9am to 5pm weekdays, and (rarely) 8am to noon on Saturday.

Grocery stores 8am to 7pm weekdays, to 1pm on Saturday.

Museums 10am to 6pm Tuesday to Sunday (winter hours may be shorter).

Restaurants Generally 11am to 10pm daily.

MONEY

The official currency is the euro. Exchanging cash is simple at banks, major post offices, travel agencies and a *menjalnica* (bureau de change), although many don't accept travellers cheques. Major credit and debit cards are accepted almost everywhere, and ATMs are ubiquitous.

PUBLIC HOLIDAYS

If a holiday falls on a Sunday, then the following Monday becomes the holiday.

New Year's holidays 1 and 2 January

Prešeren Day (Slovenian Culture Day) 8 February

Easter & Easter Monday March/April

Insurrection Day 27 April

Labour Day holidays 1 and 2 May

National Day 25 June

Assumption Day 15 August

Reformation Day 31 October

All Saints Day 1 November

Christmas Day 25 December

Independence Day 26 December

COUNTRY FACTS

Area 20,273 sq km

Capital Ljubljana

Country code ☎386

Currency Euro (€)

Emergency Ambulance ☎112, fire ☎112, police ☎113

Language Slovene

Money ATMs are everywhere; banks open Monday to Friday and (rarely) Saturday morning

Population 2.06 million

Visas Not required for citizens of the EU, Australia, USA, Canada or New Zealand

ESSENTIAL FOOD & DRINK

Little Slovenia can boast an incredibly diverse cuisine, with as many as two dozen different regional styles of cooking. Here are some of the highlights:

- **Brinjevec** A very strong brandy made from fermented juniper berries (a decidedly acquired taste).
- **Gibanica** Layer cake stuffed with nuts, cheese and apple.
- **Jota** A hearty bean-and-cabbage soup.
- **Postrv** Trout, particularly the variety from the Soča River, is a real treat.
- **Potica** A kind of nut roll eaten at teatime or as a dessert.
- **Prekmurska gibanica** A rich concoction of pastry filled with poppy seeds, walnuts, apples and cheese and topped with cream.
- **Pršut** Air-dried, thinly sliced ham from the Karst region, not unlike Italian prosciutto.
- **Ričet** A rich stew of barley and beef.
- **Štruklji** Scrumptious dumplings made with curd cheese and served either savoury as a main course or sweet as a dessert.
- **Wine** Distinctively Slovenian tipples include peppery red Teran from the Karst region and Malvazija, a straw-colour white wine from the coast.
- **Žganci** The Slovenian stodge of choice – groats made from barley or corn but usually *ajda* (buckwheat).
- **Žlikrofi** Ravioli-like parcels filled with cheese, bacon and chives.

TELEPHONE

To call Slovenia from abroad, dial the international access code 386 (the country code for Slovenia), the area code (minus the initial zero) and the number. There are six area codes in Slovenia (01 to 05 and 07). To call abroad from Slovenia, dial 00 (the international access code) followed by the country and area codes and then the number. Numbers beginning with 80 in Slovenia are toll-free.

Mobile Phones

Network coverage amounts to more than 95% of the country. Mobile numbers carry the prefix 030 and 040 (SiMobil), 031, 041, 051 and 071 (Mobitel) and 070 (Tušmobil).

SIM cards with €5 credit are available for around €15 from SiMobil (www.simobil.si), Mobitel (www.mobitel.si) and Tušmobil (www.tusmobil.sil). A basic hand unit with SIM is available from vending machines at the airport and bus station for €30. Top-up scratch cards are available at post offices, newsstands and petrol stations.

All three networks have outlets throughout Slovenia, including in Ljubljana.

SLEEPING PRICE RANGES

The following price ranges refer to a double room, with ensuite toilet and bath or shower, and breakfast, unless otherwise indicated:

€ less than €50

€€ €50 to €100

€€€ more than €100

TOURIST INFORMATION

The **Slovenian Tourist Board** (Slovenska Turistična Organizacija | STO; 01-589 18 40; www.slovenia.info; Dunajska cesta 156), based in Ljubljana, is the umbrella organisation for tourist promotion in Slovenia, and produces a number of excellent brochures, pamphlets and booklets in English. In addition, the organisation oversees dozens of tourist information centres (TICs) across the country.

VISAS

Citizens of nearly all European countries, as well as Australia, Canada, Israel, Japan, New Zealand and the USA, do not require visas to visit Slovenia for stays of up to 90 days. Holders of EU and Swiss passports can enter using a national identity card.

Those who do require visas (including South Africans) can get them for up to 90 days at any Slovenian embassy or consulate – see the website of the Ministry of Foreign Affairs (www.mzz.gov.si) for a full listing. Visas cost €35 regardless of the type of visa or length of validity.

Getting There & Away

AIR

Slovenia's only international airport is Ljubljana's Jože Pučnik Airport (p1004) at Brnik, 27km north of Ljubljana. Apart from the Slovenian flag-carrier, **Adria Airways** (JP; ☎01-369 10 10, 080 13 00; www.adria-airways.com), several other airlines offer regular flights to and from Ljubljana, including budget carriers **easyJet** (☎04-206 16 77; www.easyjet.com) and **Wizz Air** (www.wizzair.com).

LAND

Bus

International bus destinations from Ljubljana include Serbia, Germany, Croatia, Bosnia & Hercegovina, Macedonia, Italy and Scandinavia. You can also catch buses to Italy and Croatia from coastal towns, including Piran.

Train

It is possible to travel to Italy, Austria, Germany, Croatia and Hungary by train; Ljubljana is the main hub, although you can hop on international trains in certain other cities. International train travel can be expensive. It is sometimes cheaper to travel as far as you can on domestic routes before crossing borders.

SEA

Piran sends catamarans to Trieste daily and to Venice at least twice a week in season.

Getting Around

BICYCLE

Cycling is a popular way of getting around. Bikes can be transported for €3.50 in the baggage compartments of some IC and regional trains. Larger buses can also carry bikes as luggage. Most towns and cities have dedicated bicycle lanes and traffic lights.

BUS

Buy your ticket at the *avtobusna postaja* (bus station) or simply pay the driver as you board. In Ljubljana you should book your seat at least a day in advance (fees: domestic €1.50, international €2.20) if you're travelling on Friday, or to destinations in the mountains or on the coast on a public holiday. Bus services are restricted on Sundays and holidays. A range of bus companies serve the country, but prices are uniform: €3.10/5.60/9.20/12.80/16.80 for 25/50/100/150/200km of travel.

CAR & MOTORCYCLE

Roads in Slovenia are generally good. Tolls are not paid separately on the motorways; instead all cars must display a *vinjeta* (road-toll sticker) on the windscreen. They cost €15/30/110 for a week/month/year for cars and €7.50/30/55 for motorbikes, and are available at petrol stations, post offices and certain newsstands and tourist information centres. These stickers will already be in place on a rental car; failure to display such a sticker risks a fine of up to €300.

Renting a car in Slovenia allows access to cheaper out-of-centre hotels and farm or village homestays. Rentals from international firms such as Avis, Budget, Europcar and Hertz vary in price; expect to pay from €40/210 a day/week, including unlimited mileage, collision damage waiver (CDW), theft protection (TP), Personal Accident Insurance (PAI) and taxes. Some smaller agencies have somewhat more competitive rates; booking on the internet is always cheaper.

Dial ☎1987 for roadside assistance.

TRAIN

Much of the country is accessible by rail, run by the national operator, **Slovenian Railways** (Slovenske Železnice, SŽ; ☎01-291 33 32; www.slo-zeleznice.si). The website has an easy-to-use timetable.

Figure on travelling at about 60km/h except on the fastest InterCity Slovenia (ICS) express trains that run at an average speed of 90km/h.

Purchase your ticket before travelling at the *železniška postaja* (train station); buying it from the conductor onboard costs an additional €2.50.

THE GREAT OUTDOORS

Slovenes have a strong attachment to nature, and most lead active, outdoor lives from an early age. As a result the choice of activities and range of facilities on offer are endless. From skiing and climbing to canyoning and cycling, Slovenia has it all and it's always affordable. The major centres are Bovec, Lake Bled and Lake Bohinj. The Slovenian Tourist Board publishes specialist brochures on skiing, hiking, cycling, golfing and horse riding, as well as one on the nation's top spas and heath resorts.

EATING PRICE RANGES

The following price ranges are an approximation for a two-course, sit-down meal for one person, with a drink. Many restaurants offer an excellent-value set menu of two or even three courses at lunch. These typically run from €5 to €10:

€ less than €15

€€ €15 to €30

€€€ more than €30

SLOVENIA GETTING THERE & AWAY

Spain

Includes ➡

Best Places to Eat

- El Celler de Can Roca (p1050)
- Simply Fosh (p1065)
- Tickets (p1046)
- Arzak (p1055)
- Mercado de San Miguel (p1024)

Best Places to Stay

- Hotel Meninas (p1020)
- Don Gregorio (p1032)
- Can Cera (p1065)
- Barceló Raval (p1044)
- Hospedería La Gran Casa Mudéjar (p1033)

Why Go?

Passionate, sophisticated and devoted to living the good life, Spain is at once a stereotype come to life and a country more diverse than you ever imagined.

Spanish landscapes stir the soul, from the jagged Pyrenees and wildly beautiful cliffs of the Atlantic northwest to charming Mediterranean coves, while astonishing architecture spans the ages at seemingly every turn. Spain's cities march to a beguiling beat, rushing headlong into the 21st century even as timeless villages serve as beautiful signposts to Old Spain. And then there's one of Europe's most celebrated (and varied) gastronomic scenes.

But, above all, Spain lives very much in the present. Perhaps you'll sense it along a crowded after-midnight street when all the world has come out to play. Or maybe that moment will come when a flamenco performer touches something deep in your soul. Whenever it happens, you'll find yourself nodding in recognition: *this* is Spain.

When to Go

Madrid

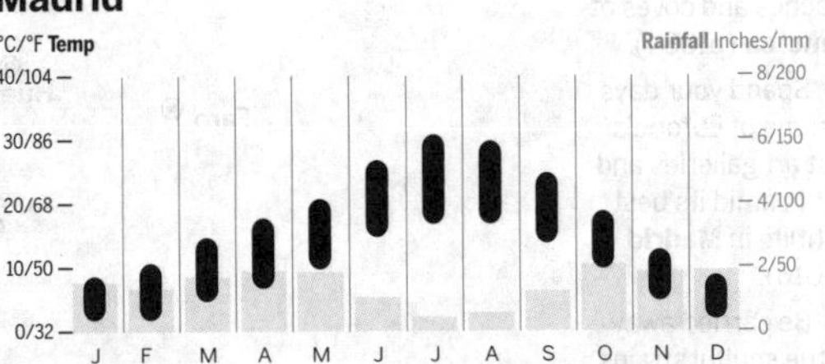

Mar & Apr Spring wildflowers, Semana Santa processions and mild southern temps.

May & Sep Mild and often balmy weather but without the crowds of high summer.

Jun–Aug Spaniards hit the coast in warm weather, but quiet corners still abound.

Spain Highlights

1 Explore the **Alhambra** (p1076), an exquisite Islamic palace complex in Granada.

2 Visit Gaudí's singular work in progress, Barcelona's **La Sagrada Família** (p1040), a cathedral that truly defies imagination.

3 Wander amid the horseshoe arches of Córdoba's **Mezquita** (p1073), close to perfection wrought in stone.

4 Eat your way through **San Sebastián** (p1055), a gourmand's paradise with an idyllic setting.

5 Join the pilgrims making their way to magnificent **Santiago de Compostela** (p1058).

6 Soak up the scent of orange blossom, admire the architecture and surrender to the party atmosphere in sunny **Seville** (p1068).

7 Discover the impossibly beautiful Mediterranean beaches and coves of **Menorca** (p1064).

8 Spend your days in some of Europe's best art galleries and nights amid its best nightlife in **Madrid** (p1016).

9 Be carried away by the soulful strains of live **flamenco** (p1027).

Bordeaux
FRANCE
Avignon
Nîmes
Montpellier
Toulouse
BASQUE COUNTRY
San Sebastián
Bilbao
Irún
NAVARRA
Golfe de Beauduc
CANTABRIA
Vitoria
PYRENEES
Perpignan
Pamplona
Miranda de Ebro
Jaca
ANDORRA LA VELLA
ANDORRA
Logroño
AP1
Figueres
Burgos
Calahorra
Huesca
CATALONIA
Girona
Fornells
Costa Brava
AP68
Lleida
Manresa
Aranda de Duero
Soria
Tossa de Mar
Zaragoza
A9
AP2
Barcelona
CASTILLA Y LEÓN
Sitges
Tarragona
ARAGÓN
A1
A23
AP7
Guadalajara
Alcalá de Henares
Teruel
Ciutadella de Menorca
Menorca
Maó
Chinchón
Cuenca
Aranjuez
Inca
A3
Mallorca
Artà
Sagunto
Manacor
Alcázar de San Juan
Palma de Mallorca
Valencia
VALENCIA
Alginet
Balearic Islands
Manzanares
Albacete
AP7
Ibiza
Denia
Valdepeñas
Benidorm
A4
Elche
Alicante
Cieza
Costa Blanca
MEDITERRANEAN SEA
MURCIA
Murcia
A7
A91
Cartagena
Guadix
Granada
Mojácar
Costa Cálida
Almería
Adra
Salobreña
Costa De Almería
ALGERIA
0 200 km
0 100 miles

ITINERARIES

One Week

Marvel at **Barcelona's** art nouveau–influenced modernista architecture and seaside style before taking the train to **San Sebastián**, with a stop in **Zaragoza** on the way. Head on to **Bilbao** for the Guggenheim Museum and end the trip living it up in **Madrid's** legendary night scene.

One Month

Fly into **Seville** and embark on a route exploring the town and picture-perfect **Ronda**, **Granada** and **Córdoba**. Take the train to **Madrid**, from where you can check out **Toledo**, **Salamanca** and **Segovia**. Make east for the coast and **Valencia**, detour northwest into the postcard-perfect villages of **Aragón** and the **Pyrenees**, then travel east into Catalonia, spending time in **Tarragona** before reaching **Barcelona**. Take a plane or boat for the **Balearic Islands**, from where you can get a flight home.

MADRID

POP 3.26 MILLION

No city on earth is more alive than Madrid, a beguiling place whose sheer energy carries a simple message: *madrileños* (people from Madrid) know how to live. Explore the old streets of the centre, relax in the plazas, soak up the culture in Madrid's excellent art museums, and spend at least one night in the city's legendary nightlife scene.

Sights & Activities

Museo del Prado — MUSEUM

(Map p1018; www.museodelprado.es; Paseo del Prado; adult/child €14/free, free 6-8pm Mon-Sat & 5-7pm Sun, audioguides €3.50, admission plus official guidebook €23; 10am-8pm Mon-Sat, 10am-7pm Sun; ; M Banco de España) Welcome to one of the world's premier art galleries. The more than 7000 paintings held in the Museo del Prado's collection (although only around 1500 are currently on display) are like a window onto the historical vagaries of the Spanish soul, at once grand and imperious in the royal paintings of Velázquez, darkly tumultuous in *Las pinturas negras* (The Black Paintings) of Goya, yet also outward-looking with sophisticated works of art from all across Europe.

Museo Thyssen-Bornemisza — MUSEUM

(Map p1022; 902 760511; www.museothyssen.org; Paseo del Prado 8; adult/concession/child €10/7/free, Mon free; 10am-7pm Tue-Sun, noon-4pm Mon; M Banco de España) The Thyssen is one of the most extraordinary private collections of predominantly European art in the world. Where the Prado or Reina Sofía enable you to study the body of work of a particular artist in depth, the Thyssen is the place to immerse yourself in a breathtaking breadth of artistic styles. Most of the big names are here, sometimes with just a single painting, but the Thyssen's gift to Madrid and the art-loving public is to have them all under one roof.

Centro de Arte Reina Sofía — MUSEUM

(Map p1022; 91 774 10 00; www.museoreinasofia.es; Calle de Santa Isabel 52; adult/concession €8/free, free Sun, 7-9pm Mon & Wed-Sat; 10am-9pm Mon, Wed, Thu & Sat, 10am-7pm Sun, closed Tue; M Atocha) Home to Picasso's *Guernica,* arguably Spain's single most famous artwork, the Centro de Arte Reina Sofía is Madrid's premier collection of contemporary art. In addition to plenty of paintings by Picasso, other major drawcards are works by Salvador Dalí (1904–89) and Joan Miró (1893–1983). The collection principally spans the 20th century up to the 1980s. The occasional non-Spaniard artist makes an appearance (including Francis Bacon's *Lying Figure;* 1966), but most of the collection is strictly peninsular.

Caixa Forum — MUSEUM, ARCHITECTURE

(Map p1022; www.fundacio.lacaixa.es; Paseo del Prado 36; 10am-8pm; M Atocha) FREE This extraordinary structure is one of Madrid's most eye-catching landmarks. Seeming to hover above the ground, this brick edifice is topped by an intriguing summit of rusted iron. On an adjacent wall is the *jardín colgante* (hanging garden), a lush vertical wall of greenery almost four storeys high. Inside there are four floors of exhibition and performance space awash in stainless steel and with soaring ceilings. The exhibitions here are always worth checking out and include photography, contemporary painting and multimedia shows.

Palacio Real PALACE

(Map p1018; ☎91 454 88 00; www.patrimonionacional.es; Calle de Bailén; adult/concession €10/5, guide/audioguide/pamphlet €7/4/1, EU citizens free last 3 hours Mon-Thu; ⊙10am-8pm Apr-Sep, to 6pm Oct-Mar; M Ópera) Spain's lavish Palacio Real is a jewel box of a palace, although it's used only occasionally for royal ceremonies; the royal family moved to the modest Palacio de la Zarzuela years ago.

When the Alcázar burned down on Christmas Day 1734, Felipe V, the first of the Bourbon kings, decided to build a palace that would dwarf all of its European counterparts. Felipe died before the palace was finished, which is perhaps why the Italianate baroque colossus has a mere 2800 rooms, just one-quarter of the original plan.

Plaza Mayor SQUARE

(Map p1022; Plaza Mayor; M Sol) Madrid's grand central square, a rare but expansive opening in the tightly packed streets of central Madrid, is one of the prettiest open spaces in Spain, a winning combination of imposing architecture, picaresque historical tales and vibrant street life coursing across its cobblestones. At once beautiful in its own right and a reference point for so many Madrid days, it also hosts the city's main tourist office (p1029), a Christmas market in December and arches leading to many laneways that lead out into the labyrinth.

★ **Parque del Buen Retiro** GARDENS

(Map p1018; ⊙6am-midnight May-Sep, to 11pm Oct-Apr; M Retiro, Príncipe de Vergara, Ibiza, Atocha) The glorious gardens of El Retiro are as beautiful as any you'll find in a European city. Littered with marble monuments, landscaped lawns, the occasional elegant building (the Palacio de Cristal is especially worth seeking out) and abundant greenery, it's quiet and contemplative during the week but comes to life on weekends. Put simply, this is one of our favourite places in Madrid.

Ermita de San Antonio de la Florida GALLERY

(Map p1018; Glorieta de San Antonio de la Florida 5; ⊙9.30am-8pm Tue-Sun, hours vary Jul & Aug; M Príncipe Pío) FREE The frescoed ceilings of the Ermita de San Antonio de la Florida

MUSEO DEL PRADO ITINERARY: ICONS OF SPANISH ART

The Museo del Prado collection can be overwhelming in scope, but if your time is limited, zero in on the museum's peerless collection of Spanish art.

Francisco José de Goya y Lucientes (Goya) is found on all three floors of the Prado, but we recommend starting at the southern end of the ground or lower level. In room 65, Goya's *El dos de mayo* and *El tres de mayo* rank among Madrid's most emblematic paintings; they bring to life the 1808 anti-French revolt and subsequent execution of insurgents in Madrid. Alongside, in rooms 67 and 68, are some of his darkest and most disturbing works, *Las pinturas negras;* they are so called in part because of the dark browns and black that dominate, but more for the distorted animalesque appearance of their characters.

There are more Goyas on the 1st floor in rooms 34 to 37. Among them are two more of Goya's best-known and most intriguing oils: *La maja vestida* and *La maja desnuda*. These portraits, in room 36, of an unknown woman, commonly believed to be the Duquesa de Alba (who may have been Goya's lover), are identical save for the lack of clothing in the latter. There are further Goyas on the top floor.

Having studied the works of Goya, turn your attention to Velázquez. Of all his works, *Las meninas* (room 12) is what most people come to see. Completed in 1656, it is more properly known as *La família de Felipe IV* (The Family of Felipe IV). The rooms surrounding *Las meninas* contain more fine works by Velázquez: watch in particular for his paintings of various members of royalty who seem to spring off the canvas – Felipe II, Felipe IV, Margarita de Austria (a younger version of whom features in *Las meninas*), El Príncipe Baltasar Carlos and Isabel de Francia – on horseback. In room 9a, seek out his masterful *La Rendición de Breda*.

Further, Bartolomé Esteban Murillo (room 17), José de Ribera (room 9), the stark figures of Francisco de Zurbarán (room 10a) and the vivid, almost surreal works of El Greco (room 8b) should all be on your itinerary.

Madrid

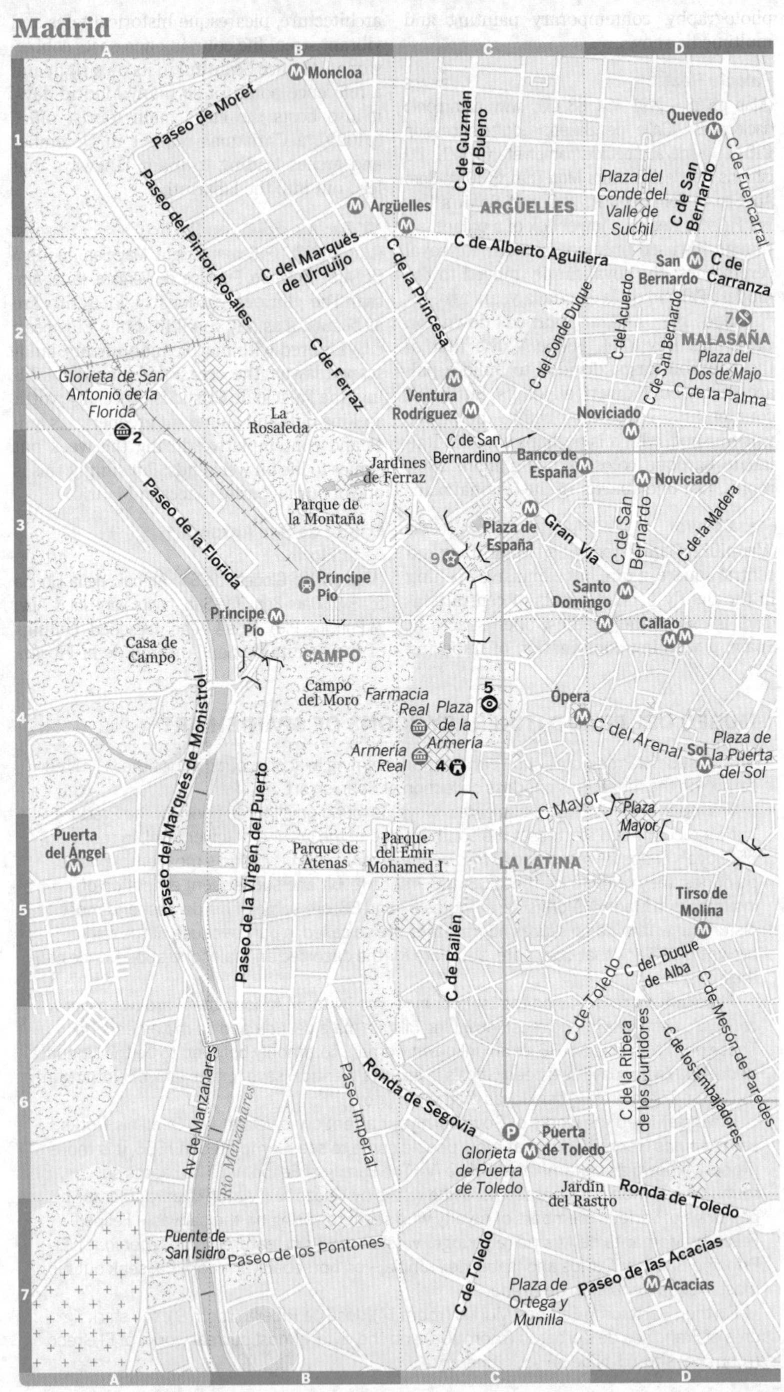

Moncloa
Paseo de Moret
C de Guzmán el Bueno
Quevedo
C de Fuencarral
Paseo del Pintor Rosales
Argüelles
ARGÜELLES
Plaza del Conde del Valle de Suchil
C de San Bernardo
C del Marqués de Urquijo
C de la Princesa
C de Alberto Aguilera
San Bernardo
C de Carranza
C de Ferraz
C del Conde Duque
C del Acuerdo
C de San Bernardo
7
MALASAÑA
Plaza del Dos de Majo
C de la Palma
Glorieta de San Antonio de la Florida
2
La Rosaleda
Ventura Rodríguez
Noviciado
C de San Bernardino
Jardines de Ferraz
Banco de España
Noviciado
Paseo de la Florida
Parque de la Montaña
Plaza de España
Gran Vía
C de San Bernardo
C de la Madera
9
Príncipe Pío
Santo Domingo
Príncipe Pío
Callao
Casa de Campo
CAMPO
Campo del Moro
Farmacia Real
Plaza de la Armería
5
Ópera
C del Arenal
Sol
Plaza de la Puerta del Sol
Armería Real
4
Paseo del Marqués de Monistrol
Paseo de la Virgen del Puerto
C Mayor
Plaza Mayor
Puerta del Ángel
Parque de Atenas
Parque del Emir Mohamed I
LA LATINA
Tirso de Molina
C de Bailén
C de Toledo
C del Duque de Alba
C de Mesón de Paredes
C de la Ribera de los Curtidores
C de los Embajadores
Av de Manzanares
Río Manzanares
Paseo Imperial
Ronda de Segovia
Puerta de Toledo
Glorieta de Puerta de Toledo
Jardín del Rastro
Ronda de Toledo
Puente de San Isidro
Paseo de los Pontones
C de Toledo
Plaza de Ortega y Munilla
Paseo de las Acacias
Acacias
SPAIN MADRID

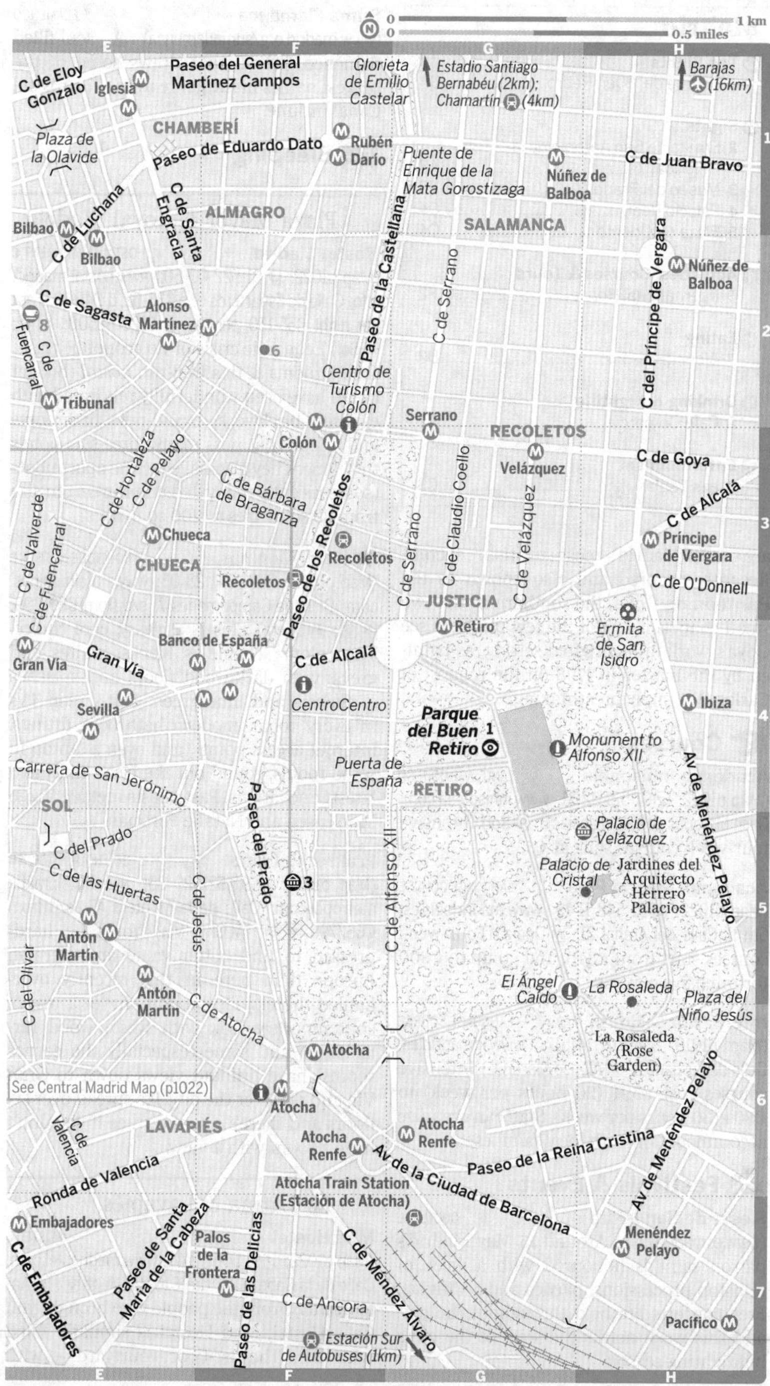

0 1 km
0 0.5 miles
C de Eloy Gonzalo
Iglesia
Paseo del General Martínez Campos
Glorieta de Emilio Castelar
Estadio Santiago Bernabéu (2km); Chamartín (4km)
Barajas (16km)
CHAMBERÍ
Plaza de la Olavide
Paseo de Eduardo Dato
Rubén Darío
Puente de Enrique de la Mata Gorostizaga
Núñez de Balboa
C de Juan Bravo
C de Luchana
C de Santa Engracia
ALMAGRO
SALAMANCA
Bilbao
Paseo de la Castellana
C de Serrano
C del Príncipe de Vergara
C de Sagasta
Alonso Martínez
C de Fuencarral
Tribunal
Centro de Turismo Colón
Serrano
RECOLETOS
Colón
Velázquez
C de Goya
C de Hortaleza
C de Pelayo
C de Bárbara de Braganza
Paseo de los Recoletos
C de Claudio Coello
C de Velázquez
C de Alcalá
Príncipe de Vergara
C de Valverde
Chueca
CHUECA
Recoletos
C de O'Donnell
JUSTICIA
Retiro
Ermita de San Isidro
Banco de España
Gran Vía
CentroCentro
Ibiza
Sevilla
Parque del Buen Retiro
Monument to Alfonso XII
Carrera de San Jerónimo
Puerta de España
RETIRO
Av de Menéndez Pelayo
SOL
Paseo del Prado
Palacio de Velázquez
C del Prado
C de las Huertas
C de Jesús
C de Alfonso XII
Palacio de Cristal
Jardines del Arquitecto Herrero Palacios
Antón Martín
C del Olivar
El Ángel Caído
La Rosaleda
Plaza del Niño Jesús
C de Atocha
La Rosaleda (Rose Garden)
Atocha
See Central Madrid Map (p1022)
LAVAPIÉS
C de Valencia
Atocha Renfe
Paseo de la Reina Cristina
Ronda de Valencia
Av de la Ciudad de Barcelona
Atocha Train Station (Estación de Atocha)
Embajadores
Paseo de Santa María de la Cabeza
Palos de la Frontera
Paseo de las Delicias
C de Méndez Álvaro
Menéndez Pelayo
C de Embajadores
C de Ancora
Pacífico
Estación Sur de Autobuses (1km)
SPAIN MADRID

Madrid

Top Sights

1 Parque del Buen Retiro G4

Sights

2 Ermita de San Antonio de la Florida A3
3 Museo del Prado F5
4 Palacio Real C4
5 Plaza de Oriente C4

Activities, Courses & Tours

6 International House F2

Eating

7 Albur D2

Drinking & Nightlife

8 Café Comercial E2

Entertainment

9 Las Tablas C3

are one of Madrid's most surprising secrets. Recently restored and also known as the **Panteón de Goya**, the southern of the two small chapels is one of the few places to see Goya's work in its original setting, as painted by the master in 1798 on the request of Carlos IV. Simply breathtaking.

Courses

Academia Inhispania LANGUAGE COURSE
(Map p1022; ☎91 521 22 31; www.inhispania.com; Calle Marqués de Valdeiglesias 3; M Sol) Intensive four-week courses start at €525.

Academia Madrid Plus LANGUAGE COURSE
(Map p1022; ☎91 548 11 16; www.madridplus.es; 6th fl, Calle del Arenal 21; M Ópera) Four-week courses start from €340, and go up to €800 for intensive courses.

International House LANGUAGE COURSE
(Map p1018; ☎902 141517; www.ihmadrid.es; Calle de Zurbano 8; M Alonso Martínez) Intensive courses cost €594 (20 hours per week) to €804 (30 hours per week). Staff can organise accommodation with local families.

Festivals & Events

Fiesta de San Isidro CULTURAL
(www.esmadrid.com) Around 15 May Madrid's patron saint is honoured with a week of nonstop processions, parties and bullfights. Free concerts are held throughout the city, and this week marks the start of the city's bullfighting season.

Suma Flamenca FLAMENCO
(www.madrid.org/sumaflamenca) A soul-filled flamenco festival that draws some of the biggest names in the genre to the Teatros del Canal in June.

Sleeping

Plaza Mayor & Royal Madrid

Hostal Madrid HOSTAL, APARTMENT €
(Map p1022; ☎91 522 00 60; www.hostal-madrid.info; Calle de Esparteros 6; s €35-62, d €45-78, d apt per night €55-150, per month €1200-2500; ❄📶; M Sol) Economic crisis or no economic crisis, the 24 rooms at this well-run *hostal* (budget hotel) have been wonderfully renovated with exposed brickwork, brand-new bathrooms and a look that puts many three-star hotels to shame. They also have terrific apartments (some recently renovated and ranging in size from 33 sq metres to 200 sq metres).

★ **Hotel Meninas** BOUTIQUE HOTEL €€
(Map p1022; ☎91 541 28 05; www.hotelmeninas.com; Calle de Campomanes 7; s/d from €89/109; ❄📶; M Ópera) This is a classy, cool choice. The colour scheme is blacks, whites and greys, with dark-wood floors and splashes of fuchsia and lime green. Flat-screen TVs in every room, modern bathroom fittings, internet access points, and even a laptop in some rooms, round out the clean lines and latest innovations. Past guests include Viggo Mortensen and Natalie Portman.

Praktik Metropol BOUTIQUE HOTEL €€
(Map p1022; ☎91 521 29 35; www.hotelpraktikmetropol.com; Calle de la Montera 47; s/d from €65/79; ❄📶; M Gran Vía) You'd be hard-pressed to find better value anywhere in Europe than here in this recently overhauled hotel. The rooms have a fresh, contemporary look with white wood furnishings, and some (especially the corner rooms) have brilliant views down to Gran Vía and out over the city. It's spread over six floors and there's a roof terrace if you don't have a room with a view.

La Latina & Lavapiés

Mad Hostel HOSTEL €
(Map p1022; ☎91 506 48 40; www.madhostel.com; Calle de la Cabeza 24; dm €16-23; ❄@📶; M Antón Martín) From the people who brought you Cat's Hostel, Mad Hostel is similarly filled with life. The 1st-floor courtyard – with

retractable roof – recreates an old Madrid *corrala* (traditional internal or communal patio) and is a wonderful place to chill, while the four- to eight-bed rooms are smallish but clean. There's a small, rooftop gym.

★**Posada del León de Oro** BOUTIQUE HOTEL €€
(Map p1022; ☎91 119 14 94; www.posadadelleondeoro.com; Calle de la Cava Baja 12; r from €121; ❄📶; Ⓜ La Latina) This rehabilitated inn has muted colour schemes and generally large rooms. There's a *corrala* in its core, and thoroughly modern rooms along one of Madrid's best-loved streets. The downstairs bar is terrific.

Sol, Santa Ana & Huertas

★**Hotel Alicia** BOUTIQUE HOTEL €€
(Map p1022; ☎91 389 60 95; www.room-matehoteles.com; Calle del Prado 2; d €100-175, ste from €200; ❄📶; Ⓜ Sol, Sevilla, Antón Martín) One of the landmark properties of the designer Room Mate chain of hotels, Hotel Alicia overlooks Plaza de Santa Ana with beautiful, spacious rooms. The style (the work of designer Pascua Ortega) is a touch more muted than in other Room Mate hotels, but the supermodern look remains intact, the downstairs bar is oh-so-cool, and the service is young and switched on.

Malasaña & Chueca

Life Hotel HOTEL €
(Map p1022; ☎91 531 42 96; www.antiguaposadadelpez.com; Calle de Pizarro 16; s/d from €39/55; ❄📶; Ⓜ Noviciado) If only all places to stay were this good. This place inhabits the shell of an historic Malasaña building, but the rooms are slick and contemporary with designer bathrooms. You're also just a few steps up the hill from Calle del Pez, one of Malasaña's most happening streets. It's an exceptionally good deal, even when prices head upwards.

★**Only You Hotel** BOUTIQUE HOTEL €€
(Map p1022; ☎91 005 22 22; www.onlyyouhotels.com; Calle de Barquillo 21; d from €157; ❄@📶; Ⓜ Chueca) This stunning new boutique hotel makes perfect use of a 19th-century Chueca mansion. The look is classy and contemporary and is the latest project by respected interior designer Lázaro Rosa Violán. Nice touches include all-day à la carte breakfasts and a portable router that you can carry with you out into the city to stay connected.

MADRID'S BEST PLAZAS

A royal palace that once had aspirations to be the Spanish Versailles. Sophisticated cafes watched over by apartments that cost the equivalent of a royal salary. The **Teatro Real** (Map p1022; ☎902 24 48 48; www.teatro-real.com; Plaza de Oriente; Ⓜ Ópera), Madrid's opera house and one of Spain's temples to high culture. Some of the finest sunset views in Madrid... Welcome to **Plaza de Oriente** (Map p1018; Ⓜ Ópera), a living, breathing monument to imperial Madrid.

On the other hand, the intimate **Plaza de la Villa** (Map p1022; Ⓜ Ópera) is one of Madrid's prettiest. Enclosed on three sides by wonderfully preserved examples of 17th-century barroco *madrileño* (Madrid-style baroque architecture – a pleasing amalgam of brick, exposed stone and wrought iron), it was the permanent seat of Madrid's city government from the Middle Ages until recent years, when Madrid's city council relocated to the grand Palacio de Cibeles on **Plaza de la Cibeles** (Map p1022; Ⓜ Banco de España).

Plaza de Santa Ana (Map p1022; Ⓜ Sevilla, Sol, Antón Martín) is a delightful confluence of elegant architecture and irresistible energy. It presides over the upper reaches of the Barrio de las Letras and this literary personality makes its presence felt with the statues of the 17th-century writers Calderón de la Barca and Federico García Lorca, and in the **Teatro Español** (Map p1022; ☎91 360 14 84; www.teatroespanol.es; Calle del Príncipe 25; Ⓜ Sevilla, Sol, Antón Martín), formerly the Teatro del Príncipe, at the plaza's eastern end. Apart from anything else, the plaza is the starting point for many a long Huertas night.

Central Madrid

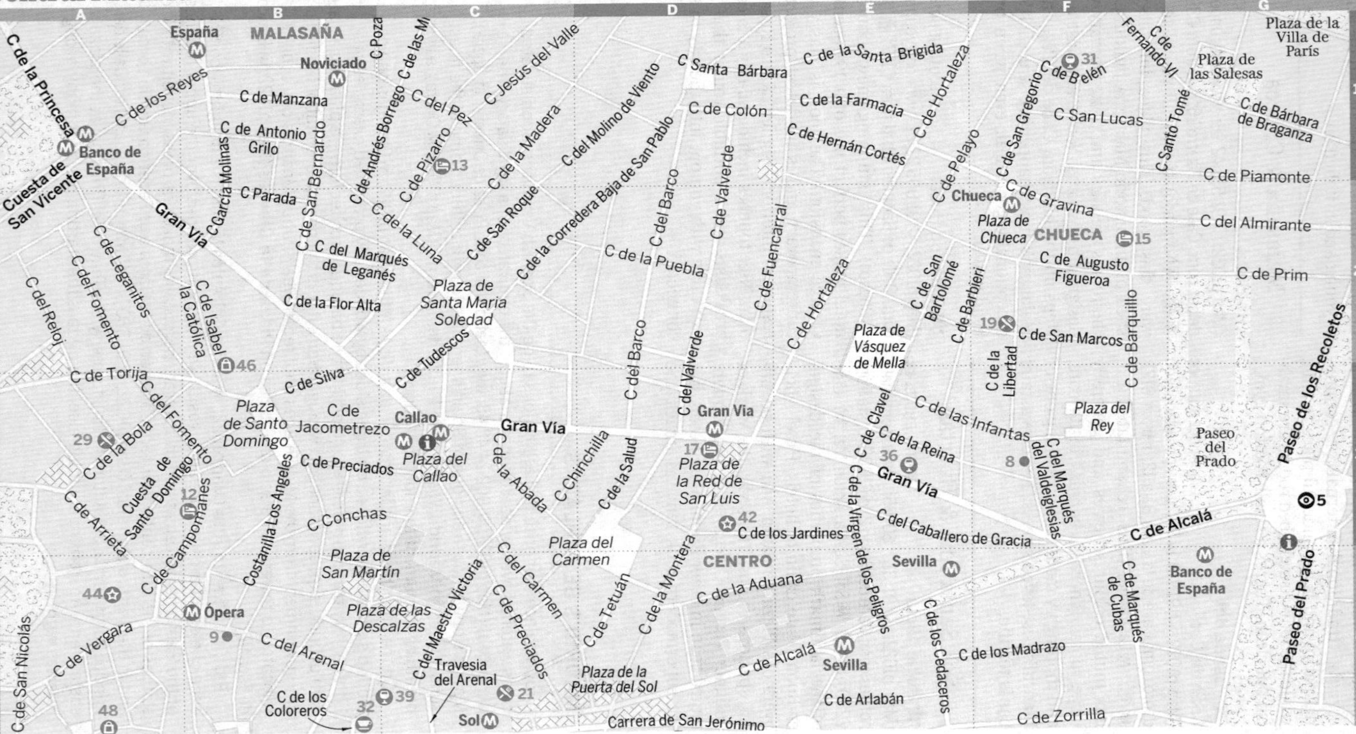

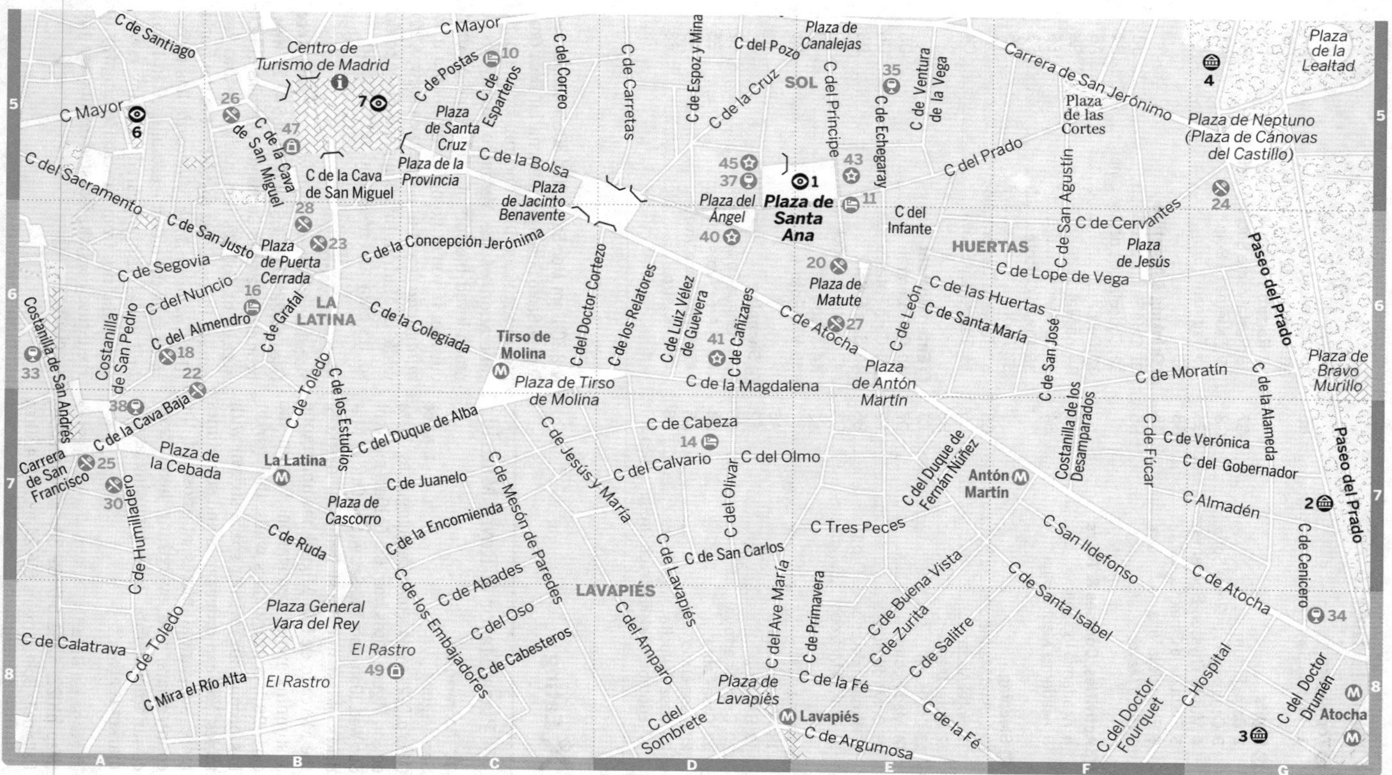

SPAIN MADRID

Central Madrid

Top Sights
1 Plaza de Santa Ana....E5

Sights
2 Caixa Forum....G7
3 Centro de Arte Reina Sofía....G8
4 Museo Thyssen-Bornemisza....G5
5 Plaza de la Cibeles....G3
6 Plaza de la Villa....A5
7 Plaza Mayor....B5

Activities, Courses & Tours
8 Academia Inhispania....F3
9 Academia Madrid Plus....B4

Sleeping
10 Hostal Madrid....C5
11 Hotel Alicia....E5
12 Hotel Meninas....B3
13 Life Hotel....C1
14 Mad Hostel....D7
15 Only You Hotel....F2
16 Posada del León de Oro....B6
17 Praktik Metropol....D3

Eating
18 Almendro 13....A6
19 Bazaar....F2
20 Casa Alberto....E6
21 Casa Labra....C4
22 Casa Lucio....A6
23 Casa Revuelta....B6
Enotaberna del León de Oro....(see 16)
24 Estado Puro....G5
25 Juana La Loca....A7
26 Mercado de San Miguel....B5
27 Ramiro's Tapas Wine Bar....E6
28 Restaurante Sobrino de Botín....B6
29 Taberna La Bola....A3
30 Txirimiri....A7

Drinking & Nightlife
31 Café Belén....F1
32 Chocolatería de San Ginés....B4
33 Delic....A6
34 Kapital....G8
35 La Venencia....E5
36 Museo Chicote....E3
37 Roof....D5
38 Taberna Tempranillo....A7
39 Teatro Joy Eslava....C4

Entertainment
40 Café Central....D6
41 Casa Patas....D6
42 Sala El Sol....D3
43 Teatro Español....E5
44 Teatro Real....A4
45 Villa Rosa....D5

Shopping
46 Antigua Casa Talavera....B2
47 El Arco Artesanía....B5
48 El Flamenco Vive....A4
49 El Rastro....B8

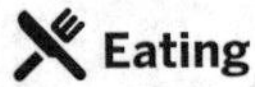

Eating

Plaza Mayor & Royal Madrid

★Mercado de San Miguel TAPAS €€
(Map p1022; www.mercadodesanmiguel.es; Plaza de San Miguel; tapas from €1; 10am-midnight Sun-Wed, 10am-2am Thu-Sat; M Sol) One of Madrid's oldest and most beautiful markets, the Mercado de San Miguel has undergone a stunning major renovation. Within the early-20th-century glass walls, the market has become an inviting space strewn with tables. You can order tapas and sometimes more substantial plates at most of the counter-bars, and everything here (from caviar to chocolate) is as tempting as the market is alive.

Taberna La Bola MADRILEÑO €€
(Map p1022; 91 547 69 30; www.labola.es; Calle de la Bola 5; mains €16-24; 1.30-4.30pm & 8.30-11pm Mon-Sat, 1.30-4.30pm Sun, closed Aug; M Santo Domingo) Taberna La Bola (going strong since 1870 and run by the sixth generation of the Verdasco family) is a much-loved bastion of traditional Madrid cuisine. If you're going to try *cocido a la madrileña* (meat-and-chickpea stew; €20) while in Madrid, this is a good place to do so. It's busy and noisy and very Madrid.

★Restaurante Sobrino de Botín CASTILIAN €€€
(Map p1022; 91 366 42 17, 91 366 42 17; www.botin.es; Calle de los Cuchilleros 17; mains €19-27; M La Latina, Sol) It's not every day that you can eat in the oldest restaurant in the world (the *Guinness Book of Records* has recognised it as the oldest – established in 1725). And it has also appeared in many novels about Madrid, from Ernest Hemingway to Frederick Forsyth. Roasted meats are the speciality.

La Latina & Lavapiés

Enotaberna del León de Oro SPANISH €€

(Map p1022; ☎91 119 14 94; www.posadadelleondeoro.com; Calle de la Cava Baja 12; mains €13-18; ⏲1-4pm & 8pm-midnight daily; Ⓜ La Latina) The stunning restoration work that brought to life the Posada del León de Oro (p1021) also bequeathed to La Latina a fine new bar-restaurant. The emphasis is on matching carefully chosen wines with

A TAPAS TOUR OF MADRID

Madrid's home of tapas is La Latina, especially along Calle de la Cava Baja and the surrounding streets.

Almendro 13 (Map p1022; ☎91 365 42 52; Calle del Almendro 13; mains €7-15; ⏲12.30-4pm & 7.30pm-midnight Sun-Thu, 12.30-5pm & 8pm-1am Fri & Sat; Ⓜ La Latina) Almendro 13 is a charming, wildly popular *taberna* (tavern) where you come for traditional Spanish tapas with an emphasis on quality rather than frilly elaborations. Cured meats, cheeses, omelettes and many variations on these themes dominate the menu – a full *racion* of the famously good *huevos rotos* (literally, 'broken eggs') served with *jamón* (ham) and thin potato slices is a meal in itself.

Juana La Loca (Map p1022; ☎91 364 05 25; Plaza de la Puerta de Moros 4; tapas from €4.50, mains €8-19; ⏲noon-1am Tue-Sun, 8pm-1am Mon; Ⓜ La Latina) Juana La Loca does a range of creative tapas with tempting options lined up along the bar, and more on the menu that they prepare to order. But we love it above all for its *tortilla de patatas* (potato and onion omelette), which is distinguished from others of its kind by the caramelised onions – simply wonderful.

Txirimiri (Map p1022; ☎91 364 11 96; www.txirimiri.es; Calle del Humilladero 6; tapas from €4; ⏲noon-4.30pm & 8.30pm-midnight, closed Aug; Ⓜ La Latina) This *pintxo* (Basque tapas) bar is a great little discovery just down from the main La Latina tapas circuit. Wonderful wines, gorgeous *pinchos* (tapas; the *tortilla de patatas* is superb) and fine risottos add up to a pretty special combination.

Casa Revuelta (Map p1022; ☎91 366 33 32; Calle de Latoneros 3; tapas from €2.60; ⏲10.30am-4pm & 7-11pm Tue-Sat, 10.30am-4pm Sun, closed Aug; Ⓜ Sol, La Latina) Casa Revuelta puts out some of Madrid's finest tapas of *bacalao* (cod) bar none – the fact that the octogenarian owner, Señor Revuelta, painstakingly extracts every fish bone in the morning and serves as a waiter in the afternoon wins the argument for us. Early on a Sunday afternoon, as the Rastro crowd gathers here, it's filled to the rafters.

Casa Labra (Map p1022; ☎91 532 14 05; www.casalabra.es; Calle de Tetuán 11; tapas from €0.90; ⏲9.30am-3.30pm & 5.30-11pm; Ⓜ Sol) Casa Labra has been going strong since 1860, an era that the decor strongly evokes. Locals love their *bacalao* and ordering it here – either as deep-fried tapas (*una tajada de bacalao* goes for €1.30) or as *una croqueta de bacalao* (€0.90 per croquette) – is a Madrid rite of initiation. As the lunchtime queues attest, they go through more than 700kg of cod every week.

Ramiro's Tapas Wine Bar (Map p1022; ☎91 843 73 47; Calle de Atocha 51; tapas from €4.50, raciones from €10; ⏲1-4.30pm & 8-11.30pm Mon-Sat, 1-4.30pm Sun; Ⓜ Antón Martín) One of the best tapas bars to open in Madrid in recent years, this fine gastrobar offers up traditional tapas with subtle but original touches. Most of the cooking comes from Castilla y León but they do exceptional things with cured meats, foie gras and prawns.

Estado Puro (Map p1022; ☎91 330 24 00; www.tapasenestadopuro.com; Plaza Neptuno (Plaza de Cánovas del Castillo) 4; tapas €2-12.50; ⏲noon-midnight Mon-Sat, to 4pm Sun; Ⓜ Banco de España, Atocha) Most places to eat along or around the Paseo del Prado are either tourist traps or upmarket temples to fine dining, but this place bucks the trend. A slick but casual tapas bar attached to the NH Paseo del Prado hotel, Estado Puro serves up fantastic tapas, many of which have their origins in Catalonia's world-famous El Bulli restaurant, such as the *tortilla española siglo XXI* (21st-century Spanish omelette, served in a glass).

creative dishes (such as baby squid with potato emulsion and rucula pesto) in a casual atmosphere. It's a winning combination.

Casa Lucio SPANISH €€

(Map p1022; ☎91 365 32 52; www.casalucio.es; Calle de la Cava Baja 35; mains €10-30; ⊙1-4pm & 8.30pm-midnight Sun-Fri, 8.30pm-midnight Sat, closed Aug; Ⓜ La Latina) Lucio has been wowing *madrileños* with his light touch, quality ingredients and home-style local cooking for ages – think roasted meats and, a Lucio speciality, eggs in abundance. There's also *rabo de toro* (bull's tail) during the Fiestas de San Isidro Labrador and plenty of *rioja* (red wine) to wash away the mere thought of it. The lunchtime *guisos del día* (stews of the day), including *cocido* on Wednesdays, are also popular.

Sol, Santa Ana & Huertas

★ Casa Alberto SPANISH, TAPAS €€

(Map p1022; ☎91 429 93 56; www.casaalberto.es; Calle de las Huertas 18; tapas from €3.25, raciones €8.50-16, mains €14-21; ⊙1.30-4pm & 8pm-midnight Tue-Sat, 1.30-4pm Sun; Ⓜ Antón Martín) One of the most atmospheric old *tabernas* of Madrid, Casa Alberto has been around since 1827. The secret to its staying power is vermouth on tap, excellent tapas at the bar and fine sit-down meals; Casa Alberto's *rabo de toro* is famous among aficionados.

Malasaña & Chueca

Bazaar CONTEMPORARY SPANISH €

(Map p1022; www.restaurantbazaar.com; Calle de la Libertad 21; mains €6.50-10; ⊙1.15-4pm & 8.30-11.30pm Sun-Wed, 1.15-4pm & 8.15pm-midnight Thu-Sat; Ⓜ Chueca) Bazaar's popularity among the well heeled and famous shows no sign of abating. Its pristine white interior design, with theatre-style lighting and wall-length windows, may draw a crowd that looks like it stepped out of the pages of *Hola!* magazine, but the food is extremely well priced and innovative and the atmosphere is casual.

Albur TAPAS, SPANISH €€

(Map p1018; ☎91 594 27 33; www.restaurantealbur.com; Calle de Manuela Malasaña 15; mains €13-18; ⊙12.30-5pm & 7.30pm-1am Mon-Thu, 12.30-5pm & 7.30pm-2am Fri, 12.30pm-2am Sat, 12.30pm-1am Sun; Ⓜ Bilbao) One of Malasaña's best deals, this place has a wildly popular tapas bar and a classy but casual restaurant out the back. Albur is known for terrific rice dishes and tapas, and has a well-chosen wine list. The restaurant waiters never seem to lose their cool, and their extremely well-priced rice dishes are the stars of the show, although in truth you could order anything here and leave well satisfied.

Drinking & Nightlife

The essence of Madrid lives in its streets and plazas, and bar-hopping is a pastime enjoyed by young and old alike. If you're after the more traditional, with tiled walls and flamenco tunes, head to Huertas. For gay-friendly drinking holes, Chueca is the place. Malasaña caters to a grungy, funky crowd, while La Latina has friendly bars that guarantee atmosphere most nights of the week. In summer, the terrace bars that pop up all over the city are unbeatable.

The bulk of Madrid bars open until 2am Sundays to Thursdays, and till 3am or 3.30am Fridays and Saturdays. Don't expect dance clubs or *discotecas* (nightclubs) to get going until after 1am at the earliest. Standard entry fee is €12, which usually includes the first drink, although megaclubs and swankier places charge a few euros more.

★ La Venencia BAR

(Map p1022; ☎91 429 73 13; Calle de Echegaray 7; ⊙1-3.30pm & 7.30pm-1.30am; Ⓜ Sol, Sevilla) La Venencia is a *barrio* (district) classic, with fine sherry from Sanlúcar and manzanilla from Jeréz poured straight from the dusty wooden barrels, accompanied by a small selection of tapas with an Andalucian bent. Otherwise, there's no music, no flashy decorations; it's all about you, your *fino* (sherry) and your friends. As one reviewer put it, it's 'a classic among classics'.

Museo Chicote COCKTAIL BAR

(Map p1022; www.museo-chicote.com; Gran Via 12; ⊙5pm-3am Mon-Thu, to 3.30am Fri & Sat; Ⓜ Gran Vía) The founder of this Madrid landmark (complete with 1930s-era interior) is said to have invented more than 100 cocktails, which the likes of Hemingway, Ava Gardner, Grace Kelly, Sophia Loren and Frank Sinatra have all enjoyed at one time or another. It's at its best after midnight, when a lounge atmosphere takes over, couples cuddle on the curved benches and some of the city's best DJs do their stuff.

Café Comercial CAFE

(Map p1018; Glorieta de Bilbao 7; 7.30am-midnight Mon-Thu, 7.30am-2am Fri, 8.30am-2am Sat, 9am-midnight Sun; ; Bilbao) This glorious old Madrid cafe proudly fights a rearguard action against progress with heavy leather seats, abundant marble and old-style waiters. It dates back to 1887 and has changed little since those days, although the clientele has broadened to include just about anyone, from writers and their laptops to old men playing chess.

Teatro Joy Eslava CLUB

(Joy Madrid; Map p1022; 91 366 37 33; www.joy-eslava.com; Calle del Arenal 11; admission €12-15; 11.30pm-6am; Sol) The only things guaranteed at this grand old Madrid dance club (housed in a 19th-century theatre) are a crowd and the fact that it'll be open (it claims to have operated every single day for the past 29 years). The music and the crowd are a mixed bag, but queues are long and invariably include locals and tourists, and even the occasional *famoso* (celebrity). Every night's a little different.

Delic BAR

(Map p1022; www.delic.es; Costanilla de San Andrés 14; 11.30am-midnight Mon-Fri, 1.30pm-midnight Sat; La Latina) We could go on for hours about this long-standing cafe-bar, but we'll reduce it to its most basic elements: nursing an exceptionally good mojito (€8) or three on a warm summer's evening at Delic's outdoor tables on one of Madrid's prettiest plazas is one of life's great pleasures. Bliss.

Taberna Tempranillo WINE BAR

(Map p1022; Calle de la Cava Baja 38; 1-3.30pm & 8pm-midnight Tue-Sun, 8pm-midnight Mon; La Latina) You could come here for the tapas, but we recommend Taberna Tempranillo primarily for its wines, of which it has a selection that puts many Spanish bars to shame, and many are sold by the glass. It's not a late-night place, but it's always packed in the early evening and on Sundays after El Rastro.

Roof COCKTAIL BAR

(Map p1022; 91 701 60 20; www.memadrid.com; Plaza de Santa Ana 14; admission €25; 9pm-1.30am Mon-Thu, 8pm-3am Fri & Sat; Antón Martín, Sol) High above the Plaza de Santa Ana, this sybaritic open-air (7th-floor) cocktail bar has terrific views over Madrid's rooftops. The high admission price announces straight away that riff-raff are not welcome and it's a place for sophisticates, with chill-out areas strewn with cushions, funky DJs and a dress policy designed to sort out the classy from the wannabes. If you suffer from vertigo, consider the equally classy **Midnight Rose** on the ground floor.

MADRID'S FAVOURITE POST-CLUBBING MUNCHIES

One of the grand icons of the Madrid night, **Chocolatería de San Ginés** (Map p1022; Pasadizo de San Ginés 5; 24hr; Sol) serves *chocolate con churros* (Spanish doughnuts with chocolate) and sees a sprinkling of tourists throughout the day, but locals pack it out in their search for sustenance on their way home from a nightclub, some time close to dawn. Only in Madrid…

Café Belén BAR

(Map p1022; Calle de Belén 5; 3.30pm-2am Sun-Thu, 3.30pm-3.30am Fri & Sat; Chueca) Café Belén is cool in all the right places – lounge and chill-out music, dim lighting, a great range of drinks (the mojitos are especially good) and a low-key crowd that's the height of casual sophistication. In short, it's one of our favourite Chueca watering holes.

Kapital CLUB

(Map p1022; 91 420 29 06; www.grupo-kapital.com; Calle de Atocha 125; admission from €18; 5.30-10.30pm & midnight-6am Fri & Sat, midnight-6am Thu & Sun; Atocha) One of the most famous megaclubs in Madrid, this seven-storey club has something for everyone: from cocktail bars and dance music to karaoke, salsa, hip hop and more chilled spaces for R&B and soul, as well as an area devoted to 'Made in Spain' music. It's such a big place that a cross-section of Madrid society (VIPs and the Real Madrid set love this place) hangs out here without ever getting in each other's way.

Entertainment

Flamenco

Las Tablas FLAMENCO

(Map p1018; 91 542 05 20; www.lastablasmadrid.com; Plaza de España 9; admission incl drink €27; 8pm & 10pm; Plaza de España) Las Tablas has a reputation for quality flamenco and reasonable prices; it could just be the best choice in town. Most nights you'll see a classic flamenco show, with plenty of throaty singing and soul-baring dancing. Antonia Moya and Marisol Navarro, leading lights in the flamenco world, are regular performers here.

Casa Patas FLAMENCO
(Map p1022; ☎91 369 04 96; www.casapatas.com; Calle de Cañizares 10; admission incl drink €34; ⊙shows 10.30pm Mon-Thu, 9pm & midnight Fri & Sat; Ⓜ Antón Martín, Tirso de Molina) One of the top flamenco stages in Madrid, this *tablao* (flamenco venue) always offers flawless quality that serves as a good introduction to the art. It's not the friendliest place in town, especially if you're only here for the show, and you're likely to be crammed in a little, but no one complains about the standard of the performances.

Villa Rosa FLAMENCO
(Map p1022; ☎91 521 36 89; www.tablaoflamencovillarosa.com; Plaza de Santa Ana 15; admission €32; ⊙11pm-6am Mon-Sat, shows 8.30pm & 10.45pm Sun-Thu, 8.30pm, 10.45pm & 12.15am Fri & Sat; Ⓜ Sol) The extraordinary tiled facade (the 1928 work of Alfonso Romero, who was responsible for the tile work in Madrid's Plaza de Toros) of this long-standing nightclub is a tourist attraction in itself; the club even appeared in the Pedro Almodóvar film *Tacones Lejanos* (High Heels; 1991). It's been going strong since 1914 and has seen many manifestations – it made its name as a flamenco venue and has recently returned to its roots with well-priced shows and meals that won't break the bank.

Jazz & Other Live Music

★Café Central JAZZ
(Map p1022; ☎91 369 41 43; www.cafecentralmadrid.com; Plaza del Ángel 10; admission €12-18; ⊙12.30pm-2.30am Sun-Thu, 12.30pm-3.30am Fri & Sat; Ⓜ Antón Martín, Sol) In 2011, the respected jazz magazine *Down Beat* included this art-deco bar on the list of the world's best jazz clubs, the only place in Spain to earn the prestigious accolade (said by some to be the jazz equivalent of earning a Michelin star) and with well over 9000 gigs under its belt, it rarely misses a beat.

★Sala El Sol LIVE MUSIC
(Map p1022; ☎91 532 64 90; www.elsolmad.com; Calle de los Jardines 3; admission incl drink €10, concert tickets €8-25; ⊙midnight-5.30am Tue-Sat Jul-Sep; Ⓜ Gran Vía) Madrid institutions don't come any more beloved than Sala El Sol. It opened in 1979, just in time for *la movida madrileña,* and quickly established itself as a leading stage for all the icons of the era, such as Nacha Pop and Alaska y los Pegamoides. *La movida* may have faded into history, but it lives on at El Sol, where the music rocks and rolls and usually resurrects the '70s and '80s, while soul and funk also get a run.

Sport

Estadio Santiago Bernabéu FOOTBALL
(☎91 398 43 00, 902 291709; www.realmadrid.com; Avenida de Concha Espina 1; tour adult/child €19/13; ⊙10am-7pm Mon-Sat, 10.30am-6.30pm Sun, except match days; Ⓜ Santiago Bernabéu) The home of **Real Madrid**, Estadio Santiago Bernabéu is a temple to football and is one of the world's great sporting arenas. For a self-guided **tour** of the stadium, buy your ticket at ticket window 10 (next to gate 7). Tickets for matches start at around €40 and can be bought online at www.realmadrid.com, while the all-important telephone number for booking tickets (which you later pick up at gate 42) is ☎902 324 324, which only works if you're calling from within Spain.

Shopping

El Rastro MARKET
(Map p1022; Calle de la Ribera de Curtidores; ⊙8am-3pm Sun; Ⓜ La Latina, Puerta de Toledo, Tirso de Molina) A Sunday morning at El Rastro is a Madrid institution. You could easily spend an entire morning inching your way down the Calle de la Ribera de Curtidores and through the maze of streets that hosts El Rastro flea market every Sunday morning. Cheap clothes, luggage, old flamenco records, even older photos of Madrid, faux designer purses, grungy T-shirts, household goods and electronics are the main fare. For every 10 pieces of junk, there's a real gem (a lost masterpiece, an Underwood typewriter) waiting to be found.

A word of warning: pickpockets love El Rastro as much as everyone else, so keep a tight hold on your belongings and don't keep valuables in easy-to-reach pockets.

Antigua Casa Talavera CERAMICS
(Map p1022; Calle de Isabel la Católica 2; ⊙10am-1.30pm & 5-8pm Mon-Fri, 10am-1.30pm Sat; Ⓜ Santo Domingo) The extraordinary tiled facade of this wonderful old shop conceals an Aladdin's cave of ceramics from all over Spain. This is not the mass-produced stuff aimed at a tourist market, but comes from the small family potters of Andalucía and

Toledo, ranging from the decorative (tiles) to the useful (plates, jugs and other kitchen items). The old couple who run the place are delightful.

El Arco Artesanía HANDICRAFTS
(Map p1022; www.artesaniaelarco.com; Plaza Mayor 9; ⌚11am-9pm; Ⓜ Sol, La Latina) This original shop in the southwestern corner of Plaza Mayor sells an outstanding array of home-made designer souvenirs, from stone and glass work to jewellery and home fittings. The papier mâché figures are gorgeous, but there's so much else here to turn your head.

El Flamenco Vive FLAMENCO
(Map p1022; www.elflamencovive.es; Calle Conde de Lemos 7; ⌚10.30am-2pm & 5-9pm Mon-Sat; Ⓜ Ópera) This temple to flamenco has it all, from guitars and songbooks to well-priced CDs, polka-dotted dancing costumes, shoes, colourful plastic jewellery and literature about flamenco. It's the sort of place that will appeal as much to curious first-timers as to serious students of the art. It also organises classes in flamenco guitar.

Information

DISCOUNT CARDS

Madrid Card (☎91 360 47 72; www.madridcard.com; 1/2/3 days adult €45/55/65, child age 6-12yr €32/38/42) If you intend to do some intensive sightseeing and travelling on public transport, the Madrid Card includes free entry to more than 50 museums in and around Madrid, free walking tours and discounts in a number of restaurants, shops, bars and car rental. The Madrid Card can be bought online (slightly cheaper), or from a list of sales outlets on the website.

EMERGENCY

Emergency (☎112)

Policía Nacional (☎091)

Servicio de Atención al Turista Extranjero (Foreign Tourist Assistance Service; ☎91 548 80 08, 91 548 85 37, 902 102112; www.esmadrid.com/satemadrid; Calle de Leganitos 19; ⌚9am-midnight; Ⓜ Plaza de España, Santo Domingo) To report thefts or other crime-related matters, your best bet is the Servicio de Atención al Turista Extranjero, which is housed in the central police station or *comisaría* (commissioner's office) of the National Police. Here you'll find specially trained officers working alongside representatives from the tourism ministry. They can also assist in cancelling credit cards, as well as contacting your embassy or your family.

MEDICAL SERVICES

Farmacia Mayor (☎91 366 46 16; Calle Mayor 13; ⌚24hr; Ⓜ Sol) Open around the clock.

Unidad Medica (Anglo American; ☎91 435 18 23; www.unidadmedica.com; Calle del Conde de Aranda 1; ⌚9am-8pm Mon-Fri, 10am-1pm Sat; Ⓜ Retiro) A private clinic with a wide range of specialisations and where all doctors speak Spanish and English, with some also speaking French and German. Each consultation costs around €125.

SAFE TRAVEL

Madrid is a generally safe city, although you should, as in most European cities, be wary of pickpockets on transport and around major tourist sights. You're most likely to fall foul of pickpockets in the most heavily touristed parts of town, notably the Plaza Mayor and surrounding streets, the Puerta del Sol, El Rastro and around the Museo del Prado. Be wary of jostling on crowded buses and the metro and, as a general rule, dark, empty streets are to be avoided; luckily, Madrid's most lively nocturnal areas are generally busy with crowds having a good time.

TOURIST INFORMATION

Centro de Turismo de Madrid (Map p1022; ☎91 588 16 36; www.esmadrid.com; Plaza Mayor 27; ⌚9.30am-8.30pm; Ⓜ Sol) Excellent city tourist office with a smaller office underneath Plaza de Colón (Map p1018; www.esmadrid.com; ⌚9.30am-8.30pm; Ⓜ Colón) and the Palacio de Cibeles (Map p1018; ⌚10am-8pm Tue-Sun; Ⓜ Plaza de España), as well as information points at Plaza de la Cibeles (Map p1022; ⌚9.30am-8.30pm; Ⓜ Banco de España), Plaza del Callao (Map p1022; Ⓜ Callao), closed for renovations at the time of writing, outside the Centro de Arte Reina Sofía (Map p1018; cnr Calle de Santa Isabel & Plaza del Emperador Carlos V; ⌚9.30am-8.30pm; Ⓜ Atocha) and at the T2 and T4 terminals at Barajas airport.

Comunidad de Madrid (www.turismomadrid.es) The regional Madrid government maintains this useful site for the entire Madrid region.

Getting There & Away

AIR

Barajas Airport (☎902 404704; www.aena.es; Ⓜ Aeropuerto T1, T2 & T3; Aeropuerto T4) Madrid's Adolfo Suarez Barajas Airport lies 15km northeast of the city and has four terminals. Terminal 4 (T4) deals mainly with flights of Iberia and its partners (eg British Airways, American Airlines and Vueling), while the remainder leave from the conjoined T1, T2 and (rarely) T3.

WORTH A TRIP

ÁVILA

Ávila's old city, just over an hour from Madrid, is surrounded by imposing city walls comprising eight monumental gates, 88 watchtowers and more than 2500 turrets. It's one of the best-preserved medieval bastions in Spain.

Murallas (adult/child under 12yr €5/free; ⏰10am-8pm Tue-Sun; 👪) Ávila's splendid 12th-century walls stretch for 2.5km atop the remains of earlier Roman and Muslim battlements and rank among the world's best-preserved medieval defensive perimeters. Two sections of the walls can be climbed – a 300m stretch that can be accessed from just inside the **Puerta del Alcázar**, and a longer 1300m stretch that runs the length of the old city's northern perimeter. The admission price includes a multilingual audioguide.

Catedral del Salvador (Plaza de la Catedral; admission €4; ⏰10am-7.30pm Mon-Fri, 10am-8pm Sat, noon-6.30pm Sun) Ávila's 12th-century cathedral is both a house of worship and an ingenious fortress: its stout granite apse forms the central bulwark in the historic city walls. The sombre Gothic-style facade conceals a magnificent interior with an exquisite early-16th-century altar frieze showing the life of Jesus, plus Renaissance-era carved choir stalls and a museum with an El Greco painting and a splendid silver monstrance by Juan de Arfe. Push the buttons to illuminate the altar and the choir stalls.

Hotel El Rastro (☎920 35 22 25; www.elrastroavila.com; Calle Cepedas; s/d €35/55; ❄📶) This atmospheric hotel occupies a former 16th-century palace with original stone, exposed brickwork and a natural earth-toned colour scheme exuding a calm understated elegance. Each room has a different form, but most have high ceilings and plenty of space. Note that the owners also run a marginally cheaper, same-name *hostal* around the corner.

Centro de Recepción de Visitantes (☎920 35 40 00, ext 790; www.avilaturismo.com; Avenida de Madrid 39; ⏰9am-8pm) Municipal tourist office.

BUS

ALSA (☎902 422242; www.alsa.es) One of the largest Spanish companies with many services throughout Spain. Most depart from Estación Sur but some buses headed north (including to Bilbao and Zaragoza, and some services to Barcelona) leave from the Intercambiador de Avenida de América with occasional services from T4 of Madrid's Barajas Airport.

Avanzabus (☎902 020052; www.avanzabus.com) Services to Extremadura (eg Cáceres), Castilla y León (eg Salamanca and Zamora) and Valencia via Cuenca, as well as Lisbon, Portugal. All leave from the Estación Sur.

Estación Sur de Autobuses (☎91 468 42 00; www.estaciondeautobuses.com; Calle de Méndez Álvaro 83; Ⓜ Méndez Álvaro) Estación Sur de Autobuses, just south of the M30 ring road, is the city's principal bus station. It serves most destinations to the south and many in other parts of the country. Most bus companies have a ticket office here, even if their buses depart from elsewhere.

TRAIN

High-speed Tren de Alta Velocidad Española (AVE) services connect Madrid with Seville (via Córdoba), Valladolid (via Segovia), Toledo, Valencia (via Cuenca), Málaga and Barcelona (via Zaragoza and Tarragona).

Estación de Chamartín (Ⓜ Chamartín) North of the city centre, Estación de Chamartín has numerous long-distance rail services, especially those to/from northern Spain. This is also where long-haul international trains arrive from Paris and Lisbon.

Puerta de Atocha (Ⓜ Atocha Renfe) The largest of Madrid's train stations is at the southern end of the city centre. The bulk of trains for Spanish destinations depart from Atocha, especially those going south.

Renfe (☎902 240202; www.renfe.es) For all train bookings.

ℹ Getting Around

TO/FROM THE AIRPORT

Bus

AeroCITY (☎91 747 75 70; www.aerocity.com; per person from €20, express service from €35 per minibus) This excellent, private minibus service takes you door-to-door between central Madrid and the airport (T1 in front of Arrivals Gate 2, T2 between gates 5 and 6, and T4 arrivals hall). It operates 24 hours and you can book by phone or online. You can reserve a seat or the entire minibus; the latter operates like a taxi.

Exprés Aeropuerto (Airport Express; www.emtmadrid.es; per person €5; 24hr;) The Exprés Aeropuerto runs between Puerta de Atocha train station and the airport. Buses run every 13 to 23 minutes from 6am to 11.30pm, and every 35 minutes throughout the rest of the night. The trip takes 40 minutes. From 11.55pm until 5.35am, departures are from the Plaza de la Cibeles, not the train station.

Metro

Line 8 of the metro (entrances in T2 and T4) runs to the Nuevos Ministerios transport interchange, which connects with lines 10 and 6. It operates from 6.05am to 2am. A one-way ticket to/from the airport costs €4.50. The journey from the airport to Nuevos Ministerios takes around 15 minutes, around 25 minutes from T4.

Taxi

There is now a fixed rate for taxis from the airport to the city centre (€30). If you're going to an airport hotel, you'll pay €20.

PUBLIC TRANSPORT

Metro (www.metromadrid.es) Madrid's modern metro is a fast, efficient and safe way to navigate Madrid, and generally easier than getting to grips with bus routes. There are numerous colour-coded lines in central Madrid and colour maps showing the metro system are available from any metro station or online.

TAXI

You can pick up a taxi at ranks throughout town or simply flag one down. Flag fall is €2.40 from 6am to 9pm Monday to Friday, €2.90 the rest of the time. Several supplementary charges, usually posted inside the taxi, apply; these include €3 from taxi ranks at train and bus stations.

CASTILLA Y LEÓN

Salamanca

POP 155,619

Whether floodlit by night or bathed in midday sun, Salamanca is a dream destination. This is a city of rare architectural splendour, awash with golden sandstone overlaid with Latin inscriptions in ochre, and with an extraordinary virtuosity of plateresque and Renaissance styles. The monumental highlights are many, with the exceptional Plaza Mayor (illuminated to stunning effect at night) an unforgettable highlight. But this is also Castilla's liveliest city, home to a massive Spanish and international student population who throng the streets at night and provide the city with youth and vitality.

Sights & Activities

★Plaza Mayor SQUARE

Built between 1729 and 1755, Salamanca's exceptional grand square is widely considered to be Spain's most beautiful central plaza. The square is particularly memorable at night when illuminated (until midnight) to magical effect. Designed by Alberto Churriguera, it's a remarkably harmonious and controlled baroque display. The medallions placed around the square bear the busts of famous figures.

Catedral Nueva & Catedral Vieja CHURCH

(www.catedralsalamanca.org) Curiously, Salamanca is home to two cathedrals: the newer and larger cathedral was built beside the old Romanesque one instead of on top of it, as was the norm. The **Catedral Nueva** (Plaza de Anaya; 9am-8pm) FREE, completed in 1733, is a late-Gothic masterpiece that took 220 years to build. Its magnificent Renaissance doorways stand out.

The largely Romanesque **Catedral Vieja** (Plaza de Anaya; admission €4.75; 10am-7.30pm) is a 12th-century temple with a stunning 15th-century altarpiece whose 53 panels depict scenes from the life of Christ and Mary, topped by a representation of the *Final Judgement*.

★Universidad Civil HISTORIC BUILDING

(Calle de los Libreros; adult/concession €4/2, Mon morning free; 9.30am-1.30pm & 4-6.30pm Mon-Sat, 10am-1.30pm Sun) The visual feast of the entrance facade is a tapestry in sandstone, bursting with images of mythical heroes, religious scenes and coats of arms.

FIND THE FROG

The facade of the Universidad Civil is an ornate mass of sculptures and carvings, and hidden among this 16th-century plateresque creation is a tiny stone frog. Legend says that those who find the frog will have good luck in studies, life and love. If you don't want any help, look away now... It's sitting on a skull on the pillar that runs up the right-hand side of the facade.

It's dominated by busts of Fernando and Isabel. Founded initially as the Estudio General in 1218, the university reached the peak of its renown in the 15th and 16th centuries. Behind the facade, the highlight of an otherwise modest collection of rooms lies upstairs: the extraordinary **university library**, the oldest university library in Europe.

Sleeping

★Hostal Concejo HOSTAL €

(☎923 21 47 37; www.hconcejo.com; Plaza de la Libertad 1; s/d €45/60; P ❄ 📶) A cut above the average *hostal*, the stylish Concejo has polished-wood floors, tasteful furnishings, light-filled rooms and a superb central location. Try and snag one of the corner rooms (like number 104) with its traditional glassed-in balcony, complete with a table, chairs and people-watching views.

Microtel Placentinos BOUTIQUE HOTEL €€

(☎923 28 15 31; www.microtelplacentinos.com; Calle de Placentinos 9; s/d incl breakfast Sun-Thu €57/73, Fri & Sat €88/100; ❄ 📶) One of Salamanca's most charming boutique hotels, Microtel Placentinos is tucked away on a quiet street and has rooms with exposed stone walls and wooden beams. The service is faultless, and the overall atmosphere is one of intimacy and discretion. All rooms have a hydromassage shower or tub and there's a summer-only outside whirpool spa.

★Don Gregorio BOUTIQUE HOTEL €€€

(☎923 21 70 15; www.hoteldongregorio.com; Calle de San Pablo 80; r/ste incl breakfast from €180/300; P ❄ 📶) A palatial hotel with part of the city's Roman Wall flanking the garden. Rooms are decorated in soothing shades of cappuccino with crisp white linens and extravagant extras, including private saunas, espresso machines and two TVs (in the suites), complimentary mini-bar, king-size beds and vast hydromassage tubs (in the standard rooms). Sumptuous antiques and medieval tapestries adorn the public areas.

Eating & Drinking

La Cocina de Toño TAPAS €€

(www.lacocinadetoño.es; Calle Gran Via 20; tapas €1.30-3.80, mains €7-20; ⏰2-4pm & 8-10pm Tue-Sat, 2-5pm Sun) This place owes its loyal following to its creative *pinchos* (snacks) and half-servings of dishes such as escalope of foie gras with roast apple and passionfruit gelatin. The restaurant serves more traditional fare as befits the decor, but the bar is one of Salamanca's gastronomic stars. Slightly removed from the old city, it draws a predominantly Spanish crowd.

Mesón Las Conchas CASTILIAN €€

(Rúa Mayor 16; mains €10-21; ⏰bar 8am-midnight, restaurant 1-4pm & 8pm-midnight; 👪) Enjoy a choice of outdoor tables, an atmospheric bar or the upstairs, wood-beamed dining area. The bar caters mainly to locals who know their *embutidos* (cured meats). For sit-down meals, there's a good mix of roasts, *platos combinados* and *raciones* (full-plate-size tapas). It serves a couple of cured meat platters (€35 for two people), and a highly rated oven-baked turbot.

★Tío Vivo MUSIC BAR

(www.tiovivosalamanca.com; Calle del Clavel 3-5; ⏰3.30pm-late) Sip drinks by flickering candlelight to a background of '80s music, enjoying the whimsical decor of carousel horses and oddball antiquities. There is live music Tuesday to Thursday from midnight, sometimes with a €5 admission.

Information

Municipal & Regional Tourist Office (☎923 21 83 42; www.turismodesalamanca.com; Plaza Mayor 14; ⏰9am-2pm & 4.30-8pm Mon-Fri, 10am-8pm Sat, 10am-2pm Sun) The Regional Tourist Office shares an office with the municipal office on Plaza Mayor. An audio city barcode guide (www.audioguiasalamanca.es) is available with the appropriate app.

Getting There & Away

The bus and train stations are a 10- and 15-minute walk, respectively, from Plaza Mayor.

BUS

Buses include the following destinations: Madrid (regular/express €16.45/24.05, 2½ to three hours, hourly), Ávila (€7.60, 1½ hours, five daily) and Segovia (€14, 2½ hours, four daily).

TRAIN

There are regular departures to Madrid's Chamartín station (€23.20, 2½ hours) via Ávila (€11.75, 1¼ hours).

Segovia

POP 56,660

Unesco World Heritage-listed Segovia has a stunning monument to Roman grandeur and a castle said to have inspired Walt Disney, and is otherwise a city of warm terracotta and sandstone hues set amid the rolling hills of Castilla.

Sights

★Acueducto ROMAN AQUEDUCT

Segovia's most recognisable symbol is El Acueducto (Roman Aqueduct), an 894m-long engineering wonder that looks like an enormous comb plunged into Segovia. First raised here by the Romans in the 1st century AD, the aqueduct was built with not a drop of mortar to hold the more than 20,000 uneven granite blocks together. It's made up of 163 arches and, at its highest point in Plaza del Azoguejo, rises 28m high.

★Alcázar CASTLE

(www.alcazardesegovia.com; Plaza de la Reina Victoria Eugenia; adult/concession/child under 6yr €5/3/free, tower €2, EU citizens free 3rd Tue of month; 10am-7pm;) Rapunzel towers, turrets topped with slate witches' hats and a *deep* moat at its base make the Alcázar a prototype fairy-tale castle, so much so that its design inspired Walt Disney's vision of Sleeping Beauty's castle. Fortified since Roman days, the site takes its name from the Arabic *al-qasr* (fortress). It was rebuilt in the 13th and 14th centuries, but the whole lot burned down in 1862. What you see today is an evocative, over-the-top reconstruction of the original.

Catedral CHURCH

(Plaza Mayor; adult/child €3/2, free 9.30am-1.15pm Sun; 9.30am-6.30pm) In the heart of town, the resplendent late-Gothic cathedral was started in 1525 and completed a mere 200 years later. The Cristo del Consuelo **chapel** houses a magnificent Romanesque doorway preserved from the original church that burned down.

Iglesia de Vera Cruz CHURCH

(Carretera de Zamarramala; admission €1.75; 10.30am-1.30pm & 4-7pm Tue-Sun Dec-Oct) This 12-sided church is one of the best preserved of its kind in Europe. Built in the early 13th century by the Knights Templar and based on Jerusalem's Church of the Holy Sepulchre, it once housed a piece of the *Vera Cruz* (True Cross), now in the nearby village church of Zamarramala (on view only at Easter).

Sleeping

Hostal Fornos HOSTAL €

(921 46 01 98; www.hostalfornos.com; Calle de la Infanta Isabel 13; s/d €41/55;) This tidy little *hostal* is a cut above most other places in this price category. It has a bright cheerful atmosphere and rooms with a fresh white-linen-and-wicker look. Some rooms are larger than others, but the value is excellent. On the downside, some readers have complained of street noise.

★Hospedería La Gran Casa Mudéjar HISTORIC HOTEL €€

(921 46 62 50; www.lacasamudejar.com; Calle de Isabel la Católica 8; r €80;) Spread over two buildings, this place has been magnificently renovated, blending genuine, 15th-century Mudéjar carved wooden ceilings in some rooms with modern amenities. In the newer wing, the rooms on the top floors have fine mountain views out over the rooftops of Segovia's old Jewish quarter. Adding to the appeal, there's a small spa and the **restaurant** comes highly recommended.

Eating

★Restaurante El Fogón Sefardí SEPHARDIC €€

(921 46 62 50; www.lacasamudejar.com; Calle de Isabel la Católica 8; mains €20-25, tapas from €2.50; 1.30-4.30pm & 5.30-11.30pm) Located within the Hospedería La Gran Casa Mudéjar, this is one of the most original places in town. Sephardic and Jewish cuisine is served either on the intimate patio or in the splendid dining hall with its original, 15th-century Mudéjar flourishes. The theme in the bar is equally diverse. Stop here for a taste of the award-winning tapas. Reservations recommended.

Casa Duque GRILL €€

(921 46 24 87; www.restauranteduque.es; Calle de Cervantes 12; mains €9-20; 12.30-4.30pm & 8.30-11.30pm) *Cochinillo asado* (roast pig) has been served at this atmospheric *mesón*

WORTH A TRIP

BURGOS & LEÓN – A TALE OF TWO CATHEDRALS

Burgos and León are cathedral towns par excellence, and both are well connected by train and bus to Madrid.

Burgos

Catedral (Plaza del Rey Fernando; adult/child under 14yr incl multilingual audioguide €6/1.50; ⌚10am-6pm) This Unesco World Heritage–listed cathedral is a masterpiece. A former modest Romanesque church, work began on a grander scale in 1221. Remarkably, within 40 years most of the French Gothic structure had been completed. You can enter the cathedral from Plaza de Santa María for free, and have access to the **Capilla del Santísimo Cristo**, with its much-revered 13th-century crucifix, and the **Capilla de Santa Tecla**, with its extraordinary ceiling. However, we recommend that you visit the cathedral in its entirety.

Hotel Norte y Londres (☎947 26 41 25; www.hotelnorteylondres.com; Plaza de Alonso Martínez 10; s/d €66/100; P@wifi) Set in a former 16th-century palace and with understated period charm, this fine hotel promises spacious rooms with antique furnishings, polished wooden floors and pretty balconies; those on the 4th floor are more modern. The bathrooms are exceptionally large, the service exceptionally efficient.

Cervecería Morito (Calle Sombrerería 27; tapas €3, raciones €5-7; ⌚12.30-3.30pm & 7-11.30pm) Cervecería Morito is the undisputed king of Burgos tapas bars and it's always crowded, deservedly so. A typical order is *alpargata* (lashings of cured ham with bread, tomato and olive oil) or the *pincho de morcilla* (small tapa of local blood sausage). The presentation is surprisingly nouvelle, especially the visual feast of salads.

Municipal Tourist office (☎947 28 88 74; www.aytoburgos.es; Plaza de Santa María; ⌚10am-8pm) Pick up its 24-hour, 48-hour and 72-hour guides to Burgos; they can also be downloaded as PDFs online.

León

Catedral (www.catedraldeleon.org; adult/concession/child under 12yr €5/4/free; ⌚8.30am-1.30pm & 4-8pm Mon-Sat, 8.30am-2.30pm & 5-8pm Sun) León's 13th-century cathedral, with its soaring towers, flying buttresses and breathtaking interior, is the city's spiritual heart. Whether spotlit by night or bathed in glorious sunshine, the cathedral, arguably Spain's premier Gothic masterpiece, exudes a glorious, almost luminous quality. The show-stopping facade has a radiant rose window, three richly sculpted doorways and two muscular towers. After going through the main entrance, lorded over by the scene of the Last Supper, an extraordinary gallery of *vidrieras* (stained-glass windows) awaits.

Panteón Real (admission €5; ⌚10am-1.30pm & 4-6.30pm Mon-Sat, 10am-1.30pm Sun) Attached to the Real Basílica de San Isidoro, Panteón Real houses the remaining sarcophagi, which rest with quiet dignity beneath a canopy of some of the finest Romanesque frescoes in Spain. Motif after colourful motif of biblical scenes drench the vaults and arches of this extraordinary hall, held aloft by marble columns with intricately carved capitals.

The pantheon also houses a small **museum** where you can admire the shrine of San Isidoro, a mummified finger of the saint (!) and other treasures.

La Posada Regia (☎987 21 31 73; www.regialeon.com; Calle de Regidores 9-11; s/d incl breakfast €55/90; ❄wifi) This place has the feel of a *casa rural* despite being in the city centre. The secret is a 14th-century building, magnificently restored (wooden beams, exposed brick and understated antique furniture), with individually styled rooms and supremely comfortable beds and bathrooms. As with anywhere in the Barri Gótic, weekend nights can be noisy.

Municipal Tourist Office (☎987 87 83 27; Plaza de San Marcelo; ⌚9.30am-2pm & 5-7.30pm) (tavern) since the 1890s. For the uninitiated, try the *menú segoviano* (€32), which includes *cochinillo,* or the *menú gastronómico* (€39). Downstairs is the informal *cueva* (cave), where you can get tapas and full-bodied *cazuelas* (stews). Reservations recommended.

Information

Centro de Recepción de Visitantes (Tourist Office; ☎921 46 67 20; www.turismodesegovia.com; Plaza del Azoguejo 1; ⏰10am-7pm Sun-Fri, 10am-8pm Sat) Segovia's main tourist office runs two-hour guided tours, departing daily at 11.15am for a minimum of four people (€13.50 per person). Reserve ahead.

Regional Tourist Office (www.segoviaturismo.es; Plaza Mayor 10; ⏰9am-8pm Sun-Thu, 9am-9pm Fri & Sat)

Getting There & Away

BUS

The bus station is just off Paseo de Ezequiel González. Buses run half-hourly to Segovia from Madrid's Paseo de la Florida bus stop (€8, 1½ hours). Buses depart to Ávila (€6, one hour, eight daily) and Salamanca (€14, 2½ hours, four daily), among other destinations.

TRAIN

There are a couple of options by train: just two normal trains run daily from Madrid to Segovia (€8, two hours), leaving you at the main train station 2.5km from the aqueduct. The faster option is the high-speed Avant (€12.50, 28 minutes), which deposits you at the newer Segovia-Guiomar station, 5km from the aqueduct.

CASTILLA-LA MANCHA

Toledo

POP 85,593

Though one of the smaller of Spain's provincial capitals, Toledo looms large in the nation's history and consciousness as a religious centre, bulwark of the Spanish church, and once-flourishing symbol of a multicultural medieval society. The old town today is a treasure chest of churches, museums, synagogues and mosques set in a labyrinth of narrow streets, plazas and inner patios in a lofty setting high above the Río Tajo. Crowded by day, Toledo changes dramatically after dark when the streets take on a moody, other-worldly air.

Sights

★Catedral CATHEDRAL

(Plaza del Ayuntamiento; adult/child €8/free; ⏰10.30am-6.30pm Mon-Sat, 2-6.30pm Sun) Toledo's cathedral reflects the city's historical significance as the heart of Catholic Spain and it's one of the most extravagant cathedrals in the country. The heavy interior, with sturdy columns dividing the space into five naves, is on a monumental scale. Every one of the numerous side chapels has artistic treasures, and other highlights include the *coro* (choir), Capilla Mayor, Transparente, *sacristía* and bell tower (for €3 extra).

Alcázar FORTRESS, MUSEUM

(Museo del Ejército; Calle Alféreces Provisionales; adult/child €5/free; ⏰11am-5pm) At the highest point in the city looms the foreboding Alcázar. Rebuilt under Franco, it has been reopened as a vast military museum. The usual displays of uniforms and medals are here, but the best part is the exhaustive historical section, with an in-depth overview of the nation's history in Spanish and English.

★Sinagoga del Tránsito SYNAGOGUE

(museosefardi.mcu.es; Calle Samuel Leví; adult/child €3/1.50, free Sat after 2pm & all day Sun, combined ticket with Museo del Greco €5; ⏰9.30am-8pm Tue-Sat Apr-Sep, to 6.30pm Tue-Sat Oct-Mar, 10am-3pm Sun) This magnificent synagogue was built in 1355 by special permission of Pedro I. The synagogue now houses the **Museo Sefardí**. The vast main prayer hall has been expertly restored and the Mudéjar decoration and intricately carved pine ceiling are striking. Exhibits provide an insight into the history of Jewish culture in Spain, and include archaeological finds, a memorial garden, costumes and ceremonial artefacts.

★Monasterio San Juan de los Reyes MONASTERY

(Calle San Juan de los Reyes 2; admission €2.50; ⏰10am-6.30pm Jun-Sep, to 5.30pm Oct-May) This imposing 15th-century Franciscan monastery and church was provocatively founded in the heart of the Jewish quarter by the Catholic monarchs Isabel and Fernando to demonstrate the supremacy of their faith. The rulers had planned to be buried here but eventually ended up in their prize conquest, Granada. The highlight is the amazing two-level cloister, a harmonious fusion of late ('flamboyant') Gothic downstairs and Mudéjar architecture upstairs, with superb statuary, arches, vaulting, elaborate pinnacles and gargoyles surrounding a lush garden with orange trees and roses.

Sleeping & Eating

Hostal Alfonso XII HOSTAL €
(☎925 25 25 09; www.hostal-alfonso12.com; Calle de Alfonso XII; s €27-40, d €35-50; ❄📶) In a great location in the *Judería* this quality *hostal* occupies an 18th-century Toledo house, meaning twisty passages and stairs, and compact rooms in curious places. It's got plenty of charm.

Casa de Cisneros BOUTIQUE HOTEL €€
(☎925 22 88 28, 925 22 88 28; www.hostal-casa-de-cisneros.com; Calle del Cardenal Cisneros; s/d €40/66; ❄📶) Right by the cathedral, this lovely 16th-century house was once the home of the cardinal and Grand Inquisitor Cisneros (often known as Ximénes). It's a top choice, with cosy, seductive rooms with original wooden beams and walls and voguish bathrooms. Archaeological works have revealed the remains of Roman baths and part of an 11th-century Moorish palace in the basement.

★ **Kumera** MODERN SPANISH €
(☎925 25 75 53; www.restaurantekumera.com; Calle Alfonso X El Sabio 2; meals €9-10, set menus €20-35; ⏲8am-2.30am Mon-Fri, 11am-2.30am Sat & Sun) With arguably the best price-quality ratio in town, this place serves up innovative takes on local traditional dishes such as *cochinito* (suckling pig), *rabo de toro* or *croquetas* (croquettes, filled with *jamón* (cured ham), squid, cod or wild mushrooms), alongside gigantic toasts and other creatively conceived dishes. The dishes with foie gras as the centrepiece are especially memorable.

La Abadía CASTILIAN, TAPAS €€
(www.abadiatoledo.com; Plaza de San Nicolás 3; raciones €4-15) In a former 16th-century palace, this atmospheric bar and restaurant has arches, niches and subtle lighting and is spread over a warren of brick-and-stone-clad rooms. The menu includes lightweight dishes and tapas, but the 'Menú de Montes de Toledo' (€19) is a fabulous collection of tastes from the nearby mountains.

Information

Main Tourist Office (☎925 25 40 30; www.toledo-turismo.com; Plaza del Ayuntamiento; ⏲10am-6pm) Within sight of the cathedral. There's another branch (Estación de Renfe; ⏲10am-3pm) at the train station.

Provincial Tourist Office (www.diputoledo.es; Subida de la Granja; ⏲8am-6pm Mon-Fri, 10am-5pm Sat, 10am-3pm Sun) At the top of the escalator.

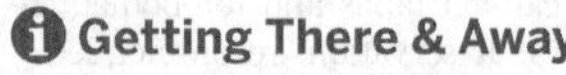

Getting There & Away

For most major destinations, you'll need to backtrack to Madrid.

BUS

From Toledo's **bus station** (Avenida de Castilla La Mancha), buses depart for Madrid's Plaza Elíptica roughly every half hour (from €5.35, one hour to 1¾ hours), some direct, some via villages. There are also services to Cuenca (€14.20, 2¼ hours).

TRAIN

From the pretty **train station** (☎902 240202; Paseo de la Rosa) high-speed AVE (Alta Velocidad Española; high-speed services) trains run every hour or so to Madrid (one way/return €12.70/20.30, 30 minutes).

CATALONIA

Barcelona

POP 1.62 MILLION

Barcelona is one of Europe's coolest cities. Despite two millennia of history, it's a forward-thinking place, always on the cutting edge of art, design and cuisine. Whether you explore its medieval palaces and plazas, admire the Modernista masterpieces, shop for designer fashions along its bustling boulevards, sample its exciting nightlife or soak up the sun on the beaches, you'll find it hard not to fall in love with this vibrant city.

As much as Barcelona is a visual feast, it will also lead you into culinary temptation. Anything from traditional Catalan cooking to the latest in avant-garde new Spanish cuisine will have your appetite in overdrive.

Sights & Activities

La Rambla

Spain's most famous boulevard, the part-pedestrianised La Rambla, explodes with life. Stretching from Plaça de Catalunya to the waterfront, it's lined with street artists, newsstands and vendors selling everything from mice to magnolias.

★Mercat de la Boqueria MARKET

(Map p1042; ☎93 318 25 84; www.boqueria.info; La Rambla 91; ⏲8am-8.30pm Mon-Sat, closed Sun; Ⓜ Liceu) Mercat de la Boqueria is possibly La Rambla's most interesting building, not so much for its Modernista-influenced design (it was actually built over a long period, from 1840 to 1914, on the site of the former St Joseph monastery), but for the action of the food market within.

Gran Teatre del Liceu ARCHITECTURE

(Map p1042; ☎93 485 99 14; www.liceubarcelona.com; La Rambla dels Caputxins 51-59; tour 20/80min €5.50/11.50; ⏲guided tour 10am, short tour 11.30am, noon, 12.30pm & 1pm; Ⓜ Liceu) If you can't catch a night at the opera, you can still have a look around one of Europe's greatest opera houses, known to locals as the Liceu. Smaller than Milan's La Scala but bigger than Venice's La Fenice, it can seat up to 2300 people in its grand horseshoe auditorium.

Barri Gòtic

You could easily spend several days or even a week exploring the Barri Gòtic, Barcelona's oldest quarter, without leaving the medieval streets. In addition to major sights, its tangle of narrow lanes and tranquil plazas conceal some of the city's most atmospheric shops, restaurants, cafes and bars.

★La Catedral CHURCH

(Map p1042; ☎93 342 82 62; www.catedralbcn.org; Plaça de la Seu; admission free, special visit €6, choir admission €2.80; ⏲8am-12.45pm & 5.15-7.30pm Mon-Sat, special visit 1-5pm Mon-Sat, 2-5pm Sun & holidays; Ⓜ Jaume I) Barcelona's central place of worship presents a magnificent image. The richly decorated main facade, laced with gargoyles and the stone intricacies you would expect of northern European Gothic, sets it quite apart from other churches in Barcelona. The facade was actually added in 1870, although the rest of the building was built between 1298 and 1460. The other facades are sparse in decoration, and the octagonal, flat-roofed towers are a clear reminder that, even here, Catalan Gothic architectural principles prevailed.

★Museu d'Història de Barcelona MUSEUM

(Map p1042; ☎93 256 21 00; www.museuhistoria.bcn.cat; Plaça del Rei; adult/child €7/free, free 1st Sun of month & 3-8pm Sun; ⏲10am-7pm Tue-Sat, 10am-8pm Sun; Ⓜ Jaume I) One of Barcelona's most fascinating museums takes you back through the centuries to the very foundations of Roman Barcino. You'll stroll over ruins of the old streets, sewers, laundries and wine- and fish-making factories that flourished here following the town's founding by Emperor Augustus around 10 BC. Equally impressive is the building itself, which was once part of the Palau Reial Major (Grand Royal Palace) on Plaça del Rei, among the key locations of medieval princely power in Barcelona.

Plaça Reial SQUARE

(Map p1042; Ⓜ Liceu) One of the most photogenic squares in Barcelona, the Plaça Reial is a delightful retreat from the traffic and pedestrian mobs on the nearby Rambla. Numerous eateries, bars and nightspots lie beneath the arcades of 19th-century neoclassical buildings, with a buzz of activity at all hours.

La Ribera

In medieval days, La Ribera was a stone's throw from the Mediterranean and the heart of Barcelona's foreign trade, with homes belonging to numerous wealthy merchants. Now it's a trendy district full of boutiques, restaurants and bars.

★Museu Picasso MUSEUM

(Map p1042; ☎93 256 30 00; www.museupicasso.bcn.cat; Carrer de Montcada 15-23; adult/child €14/free, temporary exhibitions adult/child €6.50/free, 3-8pm Sun & 1st Sun of month free; ⏲9am-7pm daily, until 9.30pm Thu; wifi; Ⓜ Jaume I) The setting alone, in five contiguous medieval stone mansions, makes the Museu Picasso unique (and worth the probable queues). The pretty courtyards, galleries and staircases preserved in the first three of these buildings are as delightful as the collection inside.

★Basílica de Santa Maria del Mar CHURCH

(Map p1042; ☎93 310 23 90; Plaça de Santa Maria del Mar; ⏲9am-1.30pm & 4.30-8.30pm, opens at 10.30am Sun; Ⓜ Jaume I) FREE At the southwest end of Passeig del Born stands the apse of Barcelona's finest Catalan Gothic church, Santa Maria del Mar (Our Lady of the Sea). Built in the 14th century with record-breaking alacrity for the time (it took just 54 years), the church is remarkable for its architectural harmony and simplicity.

Barcelona

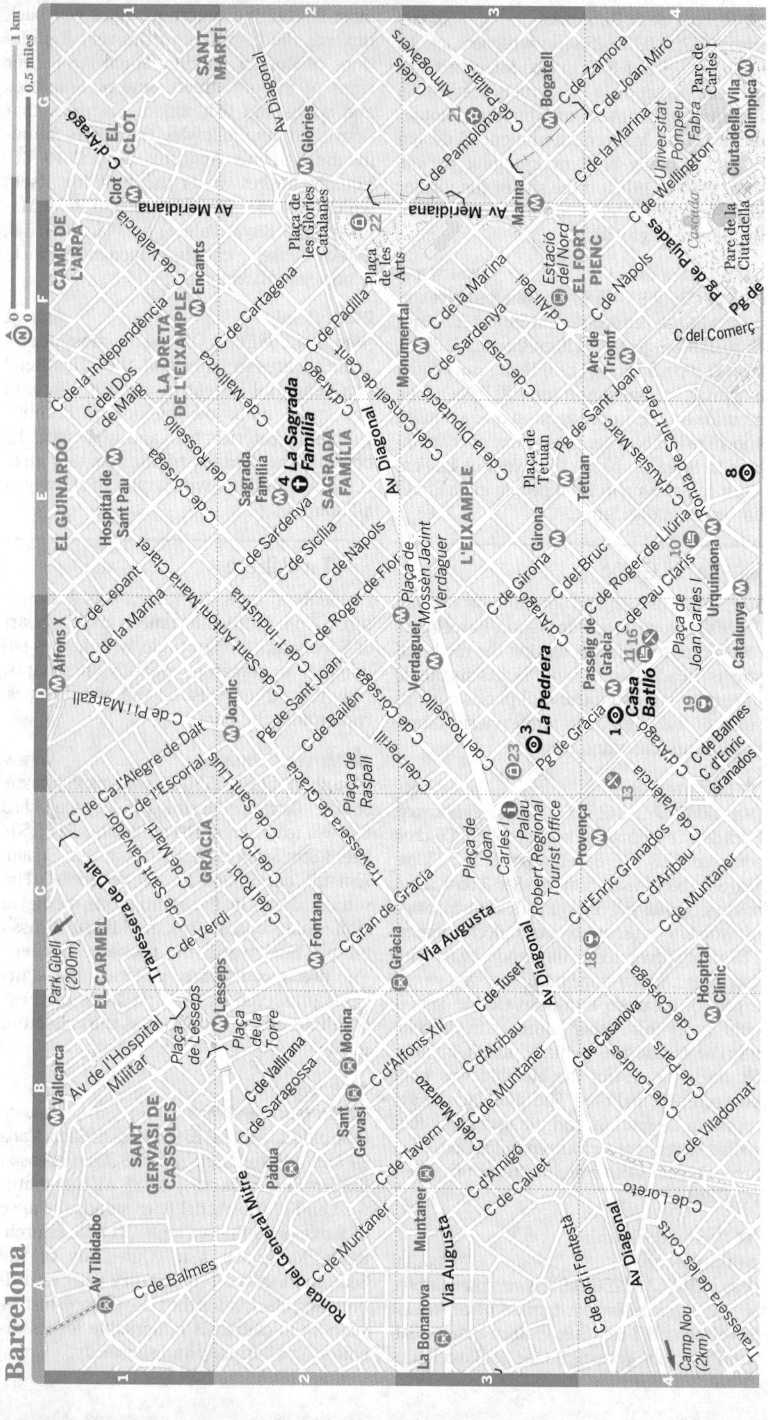

0 — 1 km
0 — 0.5 miles

A B C D E F G
1 2 3 4

Vallcarca
Park Güell (200m)
Alfons X
EL GUINARDÓ
CAMP DE L'ARPA
Av Tibidabo
EL CARMEL
Av de l'Hospital Militar
Travessera de Dalt
C de Ca l'Alegre de Dalt
C de Pi i Margall
C de Lepant
C de la Marina
Hospital de Sant Pau
C del Dos de Maig
C de la Independència
C de València
Clot
C d'Aragó
EL CLOT
SANT GERVASI DE CASSOLES
C de Balmes
Plaça de Lesseps
C de Sant Salvador
C de Martí
C de l'Escorial
C de Verdi
GRÀCIA
C de Sant Antoni Maria Claret
C de Còrsega
C del Rosselló
LA DRETA DE L'EIXAMPLE
Encants
Av Meridiana
SANT MARTÍ
Lesseps
Plaça de la Torre
Ronda del General Mitre
C de Saragossa
C de Vallirana
Pàdua
C del Robí
C de l'Or
C de Sant Lluís
Joanic
C de l'Indústria
C de Sardenya
Sagrada Família
C de Mallorca
C de Cartagena
Av Diagonal
Plaça de les Glòries Catalanes
Glòries
4 La Sagrada Família
C de Sicília
SAGRADA FAMÍLIA
C de Muntaner
Sant Gervasi
Molina
Fontana
Travessera de Gràcia
Pg de Sant Joan
C de Bailèn
C de Roger de Flor
C de Nàpols
C d'Aragó
C de Padilla
Plaça de Raspall
C de Tavern
C d'Alfons XII
Gràcia
C Gran de Gràcia
C del Perill
Av Diagonal
C del Consell de Cent
Plaça de les Arts
22
La Bonanova
Muntaner
Via Augusta
C dels Madrazo
C de Muntaner
Verdaguer
Plaça de Mossèn Jacint Verdaguer
Monumental
C dels Almogàvers
C de Pamplona
21
C d'Amigó
C de Calvet
C d'Aribau
C de Tuset
Plaça de Joan Carles I
C del Rosselló
L'EIXAMPLE
C de la Diputació
C de Sardenya
C de la Marina
C de Pallars
Palau Robert Regional Tourist Office
23
3 La Pedrera
C de Girona
Girona
Plaça de Tetuan
C de Casp
Marina
Bogatell
Av Diagonal
Pg de Gràcia
C d'Aragó
C del Bruc
Tetuan
Pg de Sant Joan
C d'Alí Bei
Estació del Nord
EL FORT PIENC
C de Zamora
C de Bori i Fontestà
18
Provença
C d'Enric Granados
13
Passeig de Gràcia
1 Casa Batlló
C de Roger de Llúria
Arc de Triomf
C de Nàpols
C de la Marina
C de Joan Miró
C de Casanova
11 16
C de Pau Claris
C d'Ausiàs Marc
Camp Nou (2km)
Travessera de les Corts
C de Loreto
C de Londres
C de París
C de Còrsega
C d'Aribau
C de València
10
Ronda de Sant Pere
Pg de Pujades
C de Wellington
Universitat Pompeu Fabra
C de Viladomat
Hospital Clínic
C de Muntaner
C d'Aragó
C de Balmes
C d'Enric Granados
19
Plaça de Joan Carles I
Urquinaona
Catalunya
8
C del Comerç
Pg de
Cascada
Parc de la Ciutadella
Ciutadella Vila Olímpica
Parc de Carles I

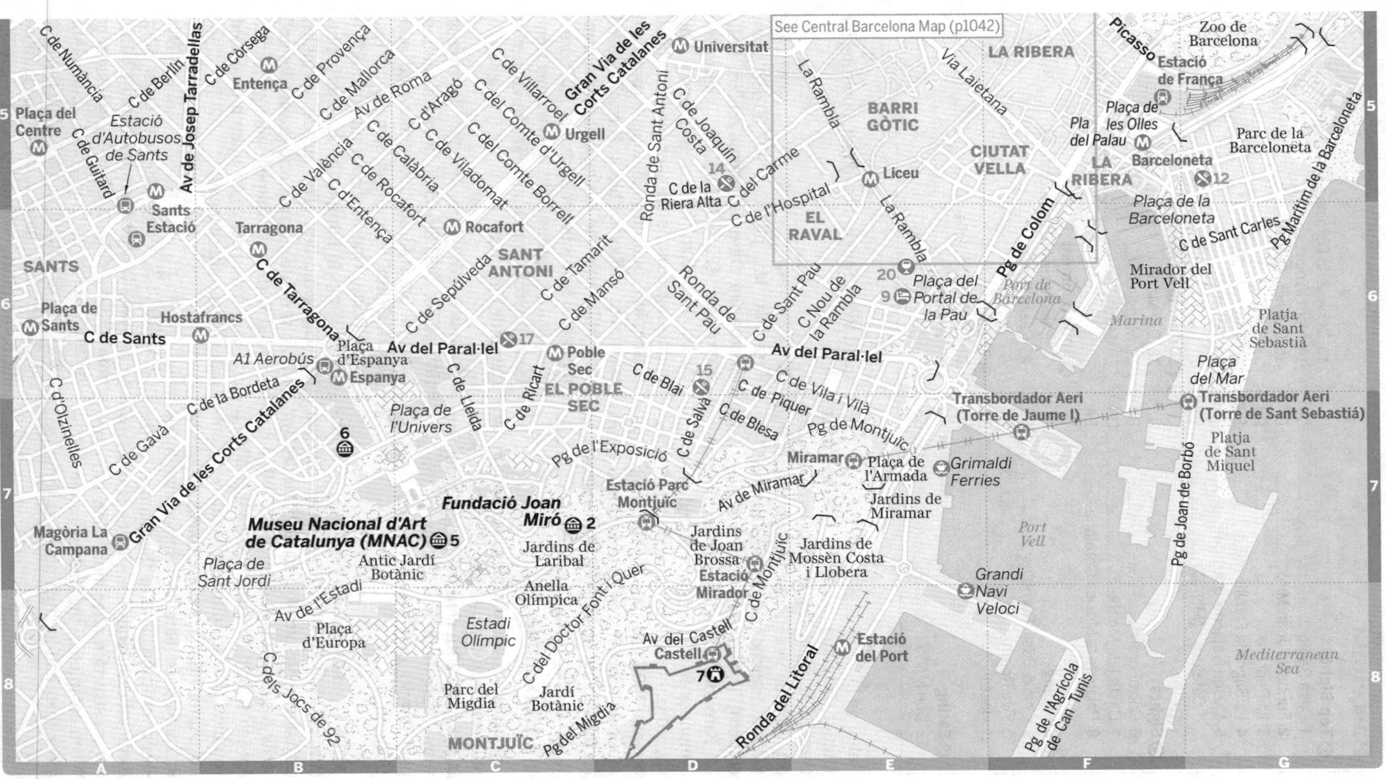

See Central Barcelona Map (p1042)
C de Numància
Plaça del Centre
C de Berlín
Estació d'Autobusos de Sants
C de Guitard
Av de Josep Tarradellas
C de Còrsega
Entença
C de Provença
C de Mallorca
Av de Roma
C d'Aragó
C de València
C de Calàbria
C de Viladomat
C de Rocafort
C d'Entença
C de Villarroel
C del Comte d'Urgell
C del Comte Borrell
Gran Via de les Corts Catalanes
Urgell
Universitat
Ronda de Sant Antoni
C de Joaquín Costa
C de la Riera Alta
C del Carme
C de l'Hospital
La Rambla
BARRI GÒTIC
CIUTAT VELLA
Via Laietana
LA RIBERA
Liceu
EL RAVAL
Picasso
Estació de França
Zoo de Barcelona
Plaça de les Olles
Pla del Palau
Barceloneta
Parc de la Barceloneta
Pg Marítim de la Barceloneta
Plaça de la Barceloneta
C de Sant Carles
Mirador del Port Vell
Sants Estació
Tarragona
Rocafort
SANTS
C de Tarragona
SANT ANTONI
C de Sepúlveda
C de Tamarit
C de Mansó
Ronda de Sant Pau
C de Sant Pau
C Nou de la Rambla
Plaça del Portal de la Pau
Pg de Colom
Port de Barcelona
Marina
Platja de Sant Sebastià
Plaça de Sants
C de Sants
Hostafrancs
Plaça d'Espanya
Espanya
A1 Aerobús
Av del Paral·lel
Poble Sec
EL POBLE SEC
C de Blai
C de Vila i Vilà
C de Piquer
Plaça del Mar
Transbordador Aeri (Torre de Jaume I)
Transbordador Aeri (Torre de Sant Sebastiá)
C d'Olzinelles
C de la Bordeta
Plaça de l'Univers
C de Lleida
C de Ricart
C de Salvà
C de Blesa
Pg de Montjuïc
Platja de Sant Miquel
C de Gavà
Gran Via de les Corts Catalanes
Pg de l'Exposició
Miramar
Plaça de l'Armada
Grimaldi Ferries
Pg de Joan de Borbó
Estació Parc Montjuïc
Av de Miramar
Jardins de Miramar
Fundació Joan Miró
Museu Nacional d'Art de Catalunya (MNAC)
Magòria La Campana
Port Vell
Plaça de Sant Jordi
Antic Jardí Botànic
Jardins de Laribal
Jardins de Joan Brossa
Estació Mirador
C de Montjuïc
Jardins de Mossèn Costa i Llobera
Anella Olímpica
C del Doctor Font i Quer
Grandi Navi Veloci
Av de l'Estadi
Plaça d'Europa
Estadi Olímpic
Av del Castell
Castell
Estació del Port
Ronda del Litoral
C dels Jocs de 92
Parc del Migdia
Jardí Botànic
Pg del Migdia
MONTJUÏC
Pg de l'Agricola de Can Tunis
Mediterranean Sea

Barcelona

Palau de la Música Catalana ARCHITECTURE
(Map p1038; ☎93 295 72 00; www.palaumusica.org; Carrer de Sant Francesc de Paula 2; adult/child €17/free; ⊙guided tours 10am-3.30pm daily; Ⓜ Urquinaona) This concert hall is a high point of Barcelona's Modernista architecture, a symphony in tile, brick, sculpted stone and stained glass. Built by Domènech i Montaner between 1905 and 1908 for the Orfeo Català musical society, it was conceived as a temple for the Catalan Renaixença (Renaissance).

L'Eixample

Modernisme, the Catalan version of art nouveau, transformed Barcelona's cityscape in the early 20th century. Most Modernista works were built in L'Eixample, the grid-plan district that was developed from the 1870s on.

★ **La Sagrada Família** CHURCH
(Map p1038; ☎93 207 30 31; www.sagradafamilia.cat; Carrer de Mallorca 401; adult/child under 11yr/senior & student €14.80/free/12.80; ⊙9am-8pm Apr-Sep, to 6pm Oct-Mar; Ⓜ Sagrada Família) If you have time for only one sightseeing outing, Antoni Gaudí's masterpiece should be it. La Sagrada Família inspires awe by its sheer verticality, and in the manner of the medieval cathedrals it emulates, it's still under construction after more than 100 years. When completed, the highest tower will be more than half as high again as those that stand today. See the boxed text, opposite, for more.

★ **La Pedrera** ARCHITECTURE
(Casa Milà; Map p1038; ☎902 202138; www.lapedrera.com; Carrer de Provença 261-265; adult/student/child €20.50/16.50/10.25; ⊙9am-8pm Mar-Oct, to 6.30pm Nov-Feb; Ⓜ Diagonal) This undulating beast is another madcap Gaudí masterpiece, built in 1905–10 as a combined apartment and office block. Formally called Casa Milà, after the businessman who commissioned it, it is better known as La Pedrera (the Quarry) because of its uneven grey stone facade, which ripples around the corner of Carrer de Provença.

★ **Casa Batlló** ARCHITECTURE
(Map p1038; ☎93 216 03 06; www.casabatllo.es; Passeig de Gràcia 43; adult/concession/child under 7yr €21.50/18.50/free; ⊙9am-9pm daily; Ⓜ Passeig de Gràcia) One of the strangest residential buildings in Europe, this is Gaudí at his hallucinogenic best. The facade, sprinkled with bits of blue, mauve and green tiles and studded with wave-shaped window frames and balconies, rises to an uneven blue-tiled roof with a solitary tower.

Park Güell PARK
(☎93 409 18 31; www.parkguell.cat; Carrer d'Olot 7; admission to central area adult/child €7/4.50; ⊙8am-9.30pm daily; 🚌24 or 32, Ⓜ Lesseps or Vallcarca) North of Gràcia and about 4km from Plaça de Catalunya, Park Güell is where Gaudí turned his hand to landscape gardening. It's a strange, enchanting place where his

DON'T MISS

LA SAGRADA FAMÍLIA HIGHLIGHTS

Roof The roof of La Sagrada Família is held up by a forest of extraordinary angled pillars. As the pillars soar towards the ceiling, they sprout a web of supporting branches, creating the effect of a forest canopy.

Nativity Facade The artistic pinnacle of the building. You can climb high up inside some of the four towers by a combination of lifts and narrow spiral staircases – a vertiginous experience.

Passion Facade The southwest Passion Facade, on the theme of Christ's last days and death, was built between 1954 and 1978 based on surviving drawings by Gaudí, with four towers and a large, sculpture-bedecked portal.

Glory Facade The Glory Facade is under construction and will, like the others, be crowned by four towers – the total of 12 representing the Twelve Apostles.

Museu Gaudí The Museu Gaudí, below ground level, includes interesting material on Gaudí's life and other works, as well as models and photos of La Sagrada Família.

Exploring La Sagrada Although essentially a building site, the completed sections and museum may be explored at leisure. Fifty-minute guided tours (€4) are offered. Alternatively, pick up an audio tour (€4), for which you need ID. Enter from Carrer de Sardenya and Carrer de la Marina. Once inside, €2.50 will get you into lifts that rise up inside towers in the Nativity and Passion Facades.

passion for natural forms really took flight – to the point where the artificial almost seems more natural than the natural.

Montjuïc

Southwest of the city centre and with views out to sea and over the city, Montjuïc serves as a Central Park of sorts and is a great place for a jog or stroll. Buses 50, 55 and 61 all head up here. A local bus, the PM (Parc de Montjuïc) line, does a circle trip from Plaça d'Espanya to the *castell* (castle or fort). Cable cars and a funicular line also access the area.

★ Museu Nacional d'Art de Catalunya (MNAC) MUSEUM

(Map p1038; ☎93 622 03 76; www.museunacional.cat; Mirador del Palau Nacional; adult/senior & child under 16yr/student €12/free/8.40, 1st Sun of month free; ⏲10am-8pm Tue-Sat, to 3pm Sun, library 10am-6pm Mon-Fri; Ⓜ Espanya) From across the city, the bombastic neobaroque silhouette of the **Palau Nacional** can be seen on the slopes of Montjuïc. Built for the 1929 World Exhibition and restored in 2005, it houses a vast collection of mostly Catalan art spanning the early Middle Ages to the early 20th century. The high point is the collection of extraordinary Romanesque frescoes.

★ Fundació Joan Miró MUSEUM

(Map p1038; ☎93 443 94 70; www.fundaciomiro-bcn.org; Parc de Montjuïc; adult/child €11/free; ⏲10am-8pm Tue-Sat, to 9.30pm Thu, to 2.30pm Sun & holidays; 🚌55, 150, funicular Paral·lel) Joan Miró, the city's best-known 20th-century artistic progeny, bequeathed this art foundation to his hometown in 1971. Its light-filled buildings, designed by close friend and architect Josep Lluís Sert (who also built Miró's Mallorca studios), are crammed with seminal works, from Miró's earliest timid sketches to paintings from his last years.

Castell de Montjuïc FORTRESS, GARDENS

(Map p1038; ☎93 256 44 45; www.bcn.cat/castelldemontjuic; Carretera de Montjuïc 66; adult/concession/child €5/3/free, Sun afternoons & 1st Sun of month free; ⏲10am-8pm; 🚌150, Telefèric de Montjuïc, Castell de Montjuïc) This forbidding *castell* dominates the southeastern heights of Montjuïc and enjoys commanding views over the Mediterranean. It dates, in its present form, from the late 17th and 18th centuries. For most of its dark history, it has been used to watch over the city and as a political prison and killing ground.

CaixaForum GALLERY

(Map p1038; ☎93 476 86 00; www.fundacio.lacaixa.es; Avinguda de Francesc Ferrer i Guàrdia 6-8; adult/student & child €4/free, 1st Sun of month free; ⏲10am-8pm Mon-Fri, to 9pm Sat & Sun;

Central Barcelona

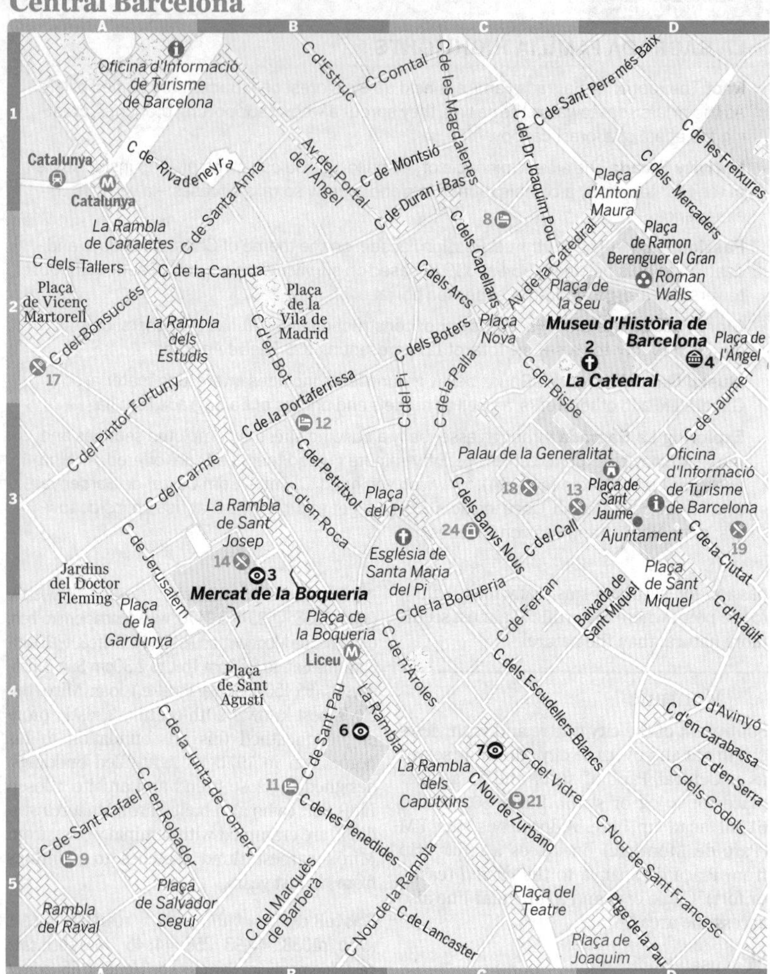

Espanya) The Caixa building society prides itself on its involvement in (and ownership of) art, in particular all that is contemporary. Its premier art expo space in Barcelona hosts part of the bank's extensive collection from around the globe. The setting is a completely renovated former factory, the Fàbrica Casaramona, an outstanding Modernista brick structure designed by Puig i Cadafalch. From 1940 to 1993 it housed the First Squadron of the police cavalry unit – 120 horses in all.

Festivals & Events

Festes de la Mercè CITY FESTIVAL

(www.bcn.cat/merce) The city's biggest party involves four days of concerts, dancing, *castellers* (human-castle builders), a fireworks display synchronised with the Montjuïc fountains, dances of giants on the Saturday, and *correfocs* – a parade of fireworks-spitting monsters and demons who run with the crowd – from all over Catalonia, on the Sunday. Held around 24 September.

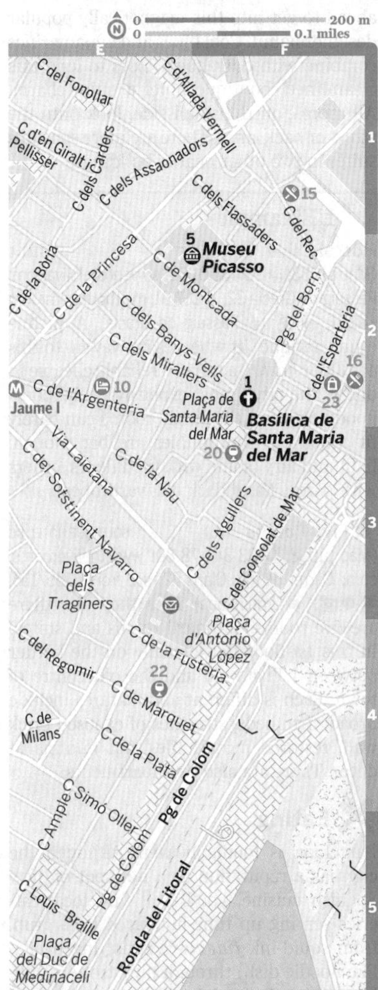

Central Barcelona

Top Sights

1 Basílica de Santa Maria del Mar F2
2 La Catedral D2
3 Mercat de la Boqueria B3
4 Museu d'Història de Barcelona D2
5 Museu Picasso E2

Sights

6 Gran Teatre del Liceu B4
7 Plaça Reial C4

Sleeping

8 Alberg Hostel Itaca C2
9 Barceló Raval A5
10 Hotel Banys Orientals E2
11 Hotel Peninsular B4
12 Vrabac B3

Eating

13 Allium C3
14 Bar Pinotxo B3
15 Bormuth F1
16 Cal Pep F2
17 Elisabets A2
18 La Vinateria del Call C3
19 Pla D3

Drinking & Nightlife

20 La Vinya del Senyor F3
21 Ocaña C5
22 Sor Rita E4

Shopping

23 Custo Barcelona F2
24 Empremtes de Catalunya C3

Día de Sant Joan MIDSUMMER

This is a colourful midsummer celebration on 24 June with bonfires, even in the squares of L'Eixample, and fireworks marking the evening that precedes this holiday.

Sleeping

Those looking for cheaper accommodation close to the action should check out the Barri Gòtic and El Raval. Some good lower-end *pensiones* are scattered about L'Eixample, as are a broad range of midrange and top-end places, most in easy striking distance of the Old Town. A growing range of options now makes it easier to stay in La Ribera and near the beaches at La Barceloneta.

La Rambla & Barri Gòtic

Alberg Hostel Itaca HOSTEL €

(Map p1042; 93 301 97 51; www.itacahostel.com; Carrer de Ripoll 21; dm €21-24, tw/d €60/70, apt €90-150; ; Jaume I) A bright, quiet hostel near the cathedral, Itaca has spacious dorms (sleeping six to 10 people) with parquet floors and spring colours, and two doubles. There's a lively vibe, and the hostel organises activities (pub crawls, flamenco concerts, free daily walking tour), making it a good option for solo travellers.

Vrabac GUESTHOUSE €€

(Map p1042; 663 494029; vrabacguesthouse.wordpress.com; Carrer de Portaferrissa 14; d €95-145, s/d without bathroom from €55/65; ; Liceu or Catalunya) In a central location just off La Rambla, Vrabac is set in a beautifully restored heritage building complete with original decorative ceilings, exposed sandstone walls and large oil paintings. Rooms vary in size and equipment – the best have elegant ceramic tile floors and sizeable balconies with private bathrooms. The cheapest are small and basic and lack a bathroom, and aren't recommended. Cash only.

El Raval

Hotel Peninsular HOTEL €

(Map p1042; 93 302 31 38; www.hotelpeninsular.net; Carrer de Sant Pau 34; s/d €57/80; Liceu) An oasis on the edge of the slightly dicey Barri Xinès, this former convent (which was connected by tunnel to the Església de Sant Agustí) has a plant-draped atrium extending its height and most of its length. The 60 rooms are simple, with tiled floors and whitewash, but mostly spacious and well kept. There are some great bargains to be had on quiet dates.

★**Barceló Raval** DESIGN HOTEL €€

(Map p1042; 93 320 14 90; www.barceloraval.com; Rambla del Raval 17-21; r from €128; Liceu) Part of the city's plans to pull the El Raval district up by the bootstraps, this oval-shaped designer hotel tower makes a 21st-century splash. The rooftop terrace offers fabulous views and the B-Lounge bar-restaurant is the toast of the town for meals and cocktails. Rooms have slick aesthetics (white with lime green or ruby-red splashes of colour), Nespresso machines and iPod docks.

Chic & Basic Ramblas DESIGN HOTEL €€

(Map p1038; 93 302 71 11; www.chicandbasicramblashotel.com; Passatge Gutenberg 7; s & d €106-116; Drassanes) The latest in the Chic & Basic chain is the most riotous to date, with quirky and colourful interiors that hit you from the second you walk in and see a vintage Seat 600 in the foyer. The rooms themselves are solid blocks of colour, and each loosely pays homage to an aspect of Barcelona life in the 1960s. All have balconies and small kitchens. Note that the name is misleading – the hotel is a couple of blocks into the Raval.

La Ribera & La Barceloneta

Hotel Banys Orientals BOUTIQUE HOTEL €€

(Map p1042; 93 268 84 60; www.hotelbanysorientals.com; Carrer de l'Argenteria 37; s €96, d €115.50-143; Jaume I) Book well ahead to get into this magnetically popular designer haunt. Cool blues and aquamarines combine with dark-hued floors to lend this clean-lined, boutique hotel a quiet charm. All rooms, on the small side, look onto the street or back lanes. There are more spacious suites in two other nearby buildings.

L'Eixample

Hostal Oliva HOSTAL €

(Map p1038; 93 488 01 62; www.hostaloliva.com; Passeig de Gràcia 32; d €51-91, r without bathroom €41-71; Passeig de Gràcia) A picturesque antique lift wheezes its way up to this 4th-floor *hostal,* a terrific, reliable cheapie in one of the city's most expensive neighbourhoods. Some of the single rooms can barely fit a bed but the doubles are big enough, light and airy (some with tiled floors, others with parquet and dark old wardrobes).

★**Five Rooms** BOUTIQUE HOTEL €€

(Map p1038; 93 342 78 80; www.thefiverooms.com; Carrer de Pau Claris 72; s/d from €155/165; Urquinaona) Like they say, there are five rooms (standard rooms and suites) in this 1st-floor flat virtually on the border between L'Eixample and the old centre of town. Each is different and features include broad, firm beds, stretches of exposed brick wall, restored mosaic tiles and minimalist decor. There are also two apartments.

Eating

Barcelona is foodie heaven. Although the city has a reputation as a hot spot of 'new Spanish cuisine', you'll still find local eateries serving up time-honoured local grub, from squid-ink *fideuà* (a satisfying paella-like noodle dish) through pigs' trotters, rabbit with snails, and *butifarra* (a tasty local sausage).

La Rambla & Barri Gòtic

Allium CATALAN, FUSION €€

(Map p1042; 93 302 30 03; Carrer del Call 17; mains €8-16; noon-4pm Mon-Tue, to 10.30pm Wed-Sat; Liceu) This inviting newcomer to Barri Gòtic serves beautifully prepared tapas dishes and changing specials (including seafood paella for one). The menu, which changes every two or threee weeks, focuses on seasonal, organic cuisine. Its bright, modern interior sets it apart from other neighbourhood options; it's also open continuously, making it a good bet for those who don't want to wait until 9pm for a meal.

La Vinateria del Call SPANISH €€
(Map p1042; ☎93 302 60 92; www.lavinateria-delcall.com; Carrer de Sant Domènec del Call 9; small plates €7-12; ⏰7.30pm-1am; Ⓜ Jaume I) In a magical setting in the former Jewish quarter, this tiny jewelbox of a restaurant serves up tasty Iberian dishes including Galician octopus, cider-cooked chorizo and the Catalan *escalivada* (roasted peppers, aubergine and onions) with anchovies. Portions are small and made for sharing, and there's a good and affordable selection of wines.

Pla FUSION €€€
(Map p1042; ☎93 412 65 52; www.elpla.cat; Carrer de la Bellafila 5; mains €18-25; ⏰7.30pm-midnight; 🌿; Ⓜ Jaume I) One of Gòtic's long-standing favourites, Pla is a stylish, romantically lit medieval dining room where the cooks churn out such temptations as oxtail braised in red wine, seared tuna with oven-roasted peppers, and polenta with seasonal mushrooms. It has a tasting menu for €38 Sunday to Thursday.

El Raval

Elisabets CATALAN €
(Map p1042; ☎93 317 58 26; Carrer d'Elisabets 2-4; mains €8-10; ⏰7.30am-11pm Mon-Thu & Sat, until 2am Fri, closed Aug; Ⓜ Catalunya) This unassuming restaurant is popular for no-nonsense local fare. The walls are dotted with old radio sets and the *menú del día* (set menu; €10.85) varies daily. If you prefer *a la carta*, try the *ragú de jabalí* (wild boar stew) and finish with *mel i mató* (a Catalan dessert made from cheese and honey). Those with a post-midnight hunger on Friday nights can probably get a meal here as late as 1am.

★ **Mam i Teca** CATALAN €€
(Map p1038; ☎93 441 33 35; Carrer de la Lluna 4; mains €9-12; ⏰1-4pm & 8pm-midnight Mon, Wed-Fri & Sun, closed Sat lunch; Ⓜ Sant Antoni) A tiny place with half a dozen tables, Mam i Teca is as much a lifestyle choice as a restaurant. Locals drop in and hang about at the bar, and diners are treated to Catalan dishes made with locally sourced products and adhering to Slow Food principles. Try, for example, cod fried in olive oil with garlic and red pepper, or pork ribs with chickpeas.

Bar Pinotxo TAPAS €€
(Map p1042; www.pinotxobar.com; Mercat de la Boqueria; mains €8-15; ⏰6am-4pm Mon-Sat; Ⓜ Liceu) Bar Pinotxo is arguably La Boqueria's, and even Barcelona's, best tapas bar. It sits among the half-dozen or so informal eateries within the market, and the popular owner, Juanito, might serve up chickpeas with a sweet sauce of pine nuts and raisins, a fantastically soft mix of potato and spinach sprinkled with coarse salt, soft baby squid with cannellini beans, or a quivering cube of caramel-sweet pork belly.

La Ribera & Waterfront

Bormuth TAPAS €
(Map p1042; ☎93 310 21 86; Carrer del Rec 31; tapas from €3.50; ⏰5pm-midnight Mon & Tue, noon-1am Wed, Thu & Sun, noon-2.30am Fri & Sat; Ⓜ Jaume I) Opened on the pedestrian Carrer del Rec in 2013, Bormuth has tapped into the vogue for old-school tapas with modern-times service and decor, and serves all the old favourites – *patatas bravas, ensaladilla* (Russian salad), tortilla – along with some less predictable and superbly prepared numbers (try the chargrilled red pepper with black pudding). The split-level dining room is never less than animated, but there's a more peaceful space with a single long table if you can assemble a group.

Can Maño SPANISH €
(Map p1038; Carrer del Baluard 12; mains €7-12; ⏰9am-4pm Tue-Sat & 8-11pm Mon-Fri; Ⓜ Barceloneta) It may look like a dive, but you'll need to be prepared to wait before being squeezed in at a packed table for a raucous night of *raciones* (posted on a board at the back) over a bottle of *turbio* – a cloudy white plonk. The seafood is abundant with first-rate squid, shrimp and fish served at rock-bottom prices.

Cal Pep TAPAS €€
(Map p1042; ☎93 310 79 61; www.calpep.com; Plaça de les Olles 8; mains €12-20; ⏰7.30-11.30pm Mon, 1-3.45pm & 7.30-11.30pm Tue-Fri, 1-3.45pm Sat, closed last 3 weeks Aug; Ⓜ Barceloneta) It's getting a foot in the door here that's the problem – there can be queues out into the square with people trying to get in. And if you want one of the five tables out the back, you'll need to call ahead. Most people are happy elbowing their way to the bar for some of the tastiest gourmet seafood tapas in town.

DON'T MISS

SEEING AN FC BARCELONA MATCH

Football in Barcelona has the aura of religion and for much of the city's population, support of FC Barcelona is an article of faith. FC Barcelona is traditionally associated with the Catalans and even Catalan nationalism.

Tickets to FC Barcelona matches are available at **Camp Nou** (☎902 189900; www.fcbarcelona.com; Carrer d'Aristides Maillol; adult/child €23/17; ⏲10am-7.30pm Mon-Sat, to 2.30pm Sun; Ⓜ Palau Reial), online (through FC Barcelona's official website), as well as through various city locations. Tourist offices sell them (the branch at Plaça de Catalunya is a centrally located option) as do FC Botiga stores. Tickets can cost anything from €35 to upwards of €250, depending on the seat and match. On match day the ticket windows open weekdays from 9am until half time, on Saturdays from 10am until half time; on Sundays they open two hours before kick off through half time.

L'Eixample & Gràcia

★ **Cerveseria Catalana** TAPAS €

(Map p1038; ☎93 216 03 68; Carrer de Mallorca 236; tapas €4-11; ⏲9.30am-1.30am; Ⓜ Passeig de Gràcia) The 'Catalan Brewery' is good for breakfast, lunch and dinner. Come for your morning coffee and croissant, or wait until lunch to enjoy choosing from the abundance of tapas and *montaditos* (tapas on a slice of bread). You can sit at the bar, on the pavement terrace or in the restaurant at the back. The variety of hot tapas, salads and other snacks draws a well-dressed crowd of locals and outsiders.

★ **Tapas 24** TAPAS €€

(Map p1038; ☎93 488 09 77; www.carlesabellan.com; Carrer de la Diputació 269; tapas €4-9; ⏲9am-midnight Mon-Sat; Ⓜ Passeig de Gràcia) Carles Abellan, master of Comerç 24 in La Ribera, runs this basement tapas haven known for its gourmet versions of old faves. Specials include the *bikini* (toasted ham and cheese sandwich – here the ham is cured and the truffle makes all the difference) and a thick black *arròs negre de sípia* (squid-ink black rice).

Montjuïc, Sants & Poble Sec

★ **Quimet i Quimet** TAPAS €€

(Map p1038; ☎93 442 31 42; Carrer del Poeta Cabanyes 25; tapas €4-11; ⏲noon-4pm & 7-10.30pm Mon-Fri, noon-4pm Sat & Sun; Ⓜ Paral·lel) Quimet i Quimet is a family-run business that has been passed down from generation to generation. There's barely space to swing a *calamar* in this bottle-lined, standing-room-only place, but it's a treat for the palate, with *montaditos* made to order. Let the folk behind the bar advise you, and order a drop of fine wine to accompany the food.

★ **Tickets** MODERN SPANISH €€€

(Map p1038; www.ticketsbar.es; Avinguda del Paral·lel 164; tapas €6-15; ⏲7-11.30pm Tue-Fri, 1.30-3.30pm & 7-11.30pm Sat, closed Aug; Ⓜ Paral·lel) This is, literally, one of the sizzling tickets in the restaurant world, a tapas bar opened by Ferran Adrià, of the legendary El Bulli, and his brother Albert. And unlike El Bulli, it's an affordable venture – if you can book a table, that is (you can only book online, and two months in advance).

Drinking & Nightlife

Barcelona clubs are spread a little more thinly than bars across the city. They tend to open from around midnight until 6am. Entry can cost from nothing to €20 (one drink usually included).

Barcelona's gay and lesbian scene is concentrated in the blocks around Carrers de Muntaner and Consell de Cent (dubbed Gayxample). Here you'll find ambience every night of the week in the bars, discos and drag clubs.

Barri Gòtic

Ocaña BAR

(Map p1042; ☎93 676 48 14; www.ocana.cat; Plaça Reial 13; ⏲5pm-2.30am Mon-Fri, from 11am Sat & Sun; Ⓜ Liceu) Named after a flamboyant artist who once lived on Plaça Reial, Ocaña is a beautifully designed space with fluted columns, stone walls, candlelit chandeliers and plush furnishings. Have a seat on the terrace and watch the passing people parade, or head downstairs to the Moorish-inspired Apotheke bar or the chic lounge a few steps away, where DJs spin for a mix of beauties and bohemians on weekend nights.

Sor Rita BAR

(Map p1042; Carrer de la Mercè 27; ⏲7pm-2.30am; Ⓜ Jaume I) A lover of all things kitsch, Sor Rita is pure eye candy, from its leopard print wallpaper to its high-heel festooned ceiling, and deliciously irreverent decorations inspired by the films of Almodóvar. It's a fun and festive scene, with special-event nights throughout the week, including tarot readings on Mondays, €5 all-you-can-eat snack buffets on Tuesdays, karaoke Wednesdays and gin specials on Thursdays.

Moog CLUB

(Map p1038; www.masimas.com/moog; Carrer de l'Arc del Teatre 3; admission €10; ⏲midnight-5am Mon-Thu & Sun, midnight-6am Fri & Sat; Ⓜ Drassanes) This fun and minuscule club is a standing favourite with the downtown crowd. In the main dance area, DJs dish out house, techno and electro, while upstairs you can groove to a nice blend of indie and occasional classic-pop throwbacks.

La Ribera

La Vinya del Senyor WINE BAR

(Map p1042; ☎93 310 33 79; www.lavinyadelsenyor.com; Plaça de Santa Maria del Mar 5; ⏲noon-1am Mon-Thu, noon-2am Fri & Sat, noon-midnight Sun; Ⓜ Jaume I) Relax on the *terrassa,* which lies in the shadow of Basílica de Santa Maria del Mar, or crowd inside at the tiny bar. The wine list is as long as *War and Peace* and there's a table upstairs for those who opt to sample by the bottle rather than the glass.

L'Eixample & Gràcia

★**Dry Martini** BAR

(Map p1038; ☎93 217 50 72; www.javierdelasmuelas.com; Carrer d'Aribau 162-166; ⏲1pm-2.30am Mon-Thu, 6pm-3am Fri & Sat; Ⓜ Diagonal) Waiters with a discreetly knowing smile will attend to your cocktail needs here. The house drink, taken at the bar or in one of the plush green leather lounges, is a safe bet. The gin and tonic comes in an enormous mug-sized glass – a couple of these and you're well on the way. Out the back is a restaurant, **Speakeasy** (Map p1038; ☎93 217 50 80; www.javierdelasmuelas.com; Carrer d'Aribau 162-166; mains €19-28; ⏲1-4pm & 8pm-midnight Mon-Fri, 8pm-midnight Sat, closed Aug; Ⓜ Diagonal).

Monvínic WINE BAR

(Map p1038; ☎932 72 61 87; www.monvinic.com; Carrer de la Diputació 249; ⏲wine bar 1.30-11pm Mon-Sat; Ⓜ Passeig de Gràcia) Proclaimed as 'possibly the best wine bar in the world' by the *Wall Street Journal,* and apparently considered unmissable by El Bulli's sommelier, Monvínic is an ode, a rhapsody even, to wine loving. The interactive wine list sits on the bar for you to browse on a digital tablet similar to an iPad and boasts more than 3000 varieties.

☆ Entertainment

Razzmatazz LIVE MUSIC

(Map p1038; ☎93 320 82 00; www.salarazzmatazz.com; Carrer de Pamplona 88; admission €12-32; ⏲midnight-3.30am Thu, to 5.30am Fri & Sat; Ⓜ Marina, Bogatell) Bands from far and wide occasionally create scenes of near hysteria in this, one of the city's classic live-music and clubbing venues. Bands can appear throughout the week (check the website), with different start times. On weekends the live music then gives way to club sounds.

★**Palau de la Música Catalana** CLASSICAL MUSIC

(Map p1038; ☎93 295 72 00; www.palaumusica.org; Carrer de Sant Francesc de Paula 2; ⏲box office 9.30am-9pm Mon-Sat; Ⓜ Urquinaona) A feast for the eyes, this Modernista confection is also the city's most traditional venue for classical and choral music, although it has a wide-ranging program, including flamenco, pop and – particularly – jazz. Just being here for a performance is an experience. Sip a preconcert tipple in the foyer, its tiled pillars all a-glitter. Head up the grand stairway to the main auditorium, a whirlpool of Modernista whimsy.

Shopping

Most mainstream fashion stores are along a shopping 'axis' that runs from Plaça de Catalunya along Passeig de Gràcia, then left (west) along Avinguda Diagonal.

The El Born area in La Ribera is awash with tiny boutiques, especially those purveying young, fun fashion. There are plenty of shops scattered throughout the Barri Gòtic (stroll Carrer d'Avinyò and Carrer de Portaferrissa). For secondhand stuff, head for El Raval, especially Carrer de la Riera Baixa.

Empremtes de Catalunya HANDICRAFTS

(Map p1042; ☎93 467 46 60; Carrer dels Banys Nous 11; ⏲10am-8pm Mon-Sat, to 2pm Sun; Ⓜ Liceu) A celebration of Catalan products, this nicely designed store is a great place to browse for unique gifts. You'll find jewellery with designs inspired by Roman iconography

WORTH A TRIP

ANDORRA

This mini-country wedged between France and Spain offers by far the best ski slopes and resort facilities in all the Pyrenees. Once the snows melt, there's an abundance of great walking, ranging from easy strolls to demanding day hikes in the principality's higher, more remote reaches. Strike out above the tight valleys and you can walk for hours, almost alone.

The only way to reach Andorra is by road from Spain or France. If driving, fill up in Andorra; fuel is substantially cheaper there. There are bus services to/from Barcelona's Estació del Nord, Barcelona's airport El Prat de Llobregat, Lleida and Toulouse (France). All bus services arrive at and leave from Andorra la Vella.

(as well as works that reference Gaudí and Barcelona's Gothic era), plus pottery, wooden toys, silk scarves, notebooks, housewares and more.

Els Encants Vells MARKET
(Fira de Bellcaire; Map p1038; ☎93 246 30 30; www.encantsbcn.com; Plaça de les Glòries Catalanes; ⏲8am-8pm Mon, Wed, Fri & Sat; Ⓜ Glòries) In a gleaming open-sided complex near Plaça de les Glòries Catalanes, the 'Old Charms' flea market is the biggest of its kind in Barcelona. Over 500 vendors ply their wares beneath massive mirror-like panels. It's all here, from antique furniture through to secondhand clothes. A lot of it is junk, but occasionally you'll stumble across a *ganga* (bargain).

Vinçon HOMEWARES
(Map p1038; ☎93 215 60 50; www.vincon.com; Passeig de Gràcia 96; ⏲10am-8.30pm Mon-Fri, 10.30am-9pm Sat; Ⓜ Diagonal) An icon of the Barcelona design scene, Vinçon has the slickest furniture and household goods (particularly lighting), both local and imported. Not surprising, really, since the building, raised in 1899, belonged to the Modernista artist Ramon Casas. Head upstairs to the furniture area – from the windows and terrace you get close side views of La Pedrera.

Custo Barcelona FASHION
(Map p1042; ☎93 268 78 93; www.custo-barcelona.com; Plaça de les Olles 7; ⏲10am-9pm Mon-Sat, noon-8pm Sun; Ⓜ Jaume I) The psychedelic decor and casual atmosphere lend this avant-garde Barcelona fashion store a youthful edge. Custo presents daring new women's and men's collections each year on the New York catwalks. The dazzling colours and cut of anything from dinner jackets to hot pants are for the uninhibited. It has five other stores around town.

Information

Purse snatching and pickpocketing are major problems, especially around Plaça de Catalunya, La Rambla and Plaça Reial.

Guàrdia Urbana (Local Police; ☎092; La Rambla 43; Ⓜ Liceu)

Mossos d'Esquadra (☎088; Carrer Nou de la Rambla 80; Ⓜ Paral.lel) Tourists who want to report thefts need to go to the Catalan police, known as the Mossos d'Esquadra.

Oficina d'Informació de Turisme de Barcelona (Map p1042; ☎93 285 38 34; www.barcelonaturisme.com; underground at Plaça de Catalunya 17-S; ⏲9.30am-9.30pm; Ⓜ Catalunya) The main Barcelona tourist information office sells walking tours, bus tours, discount cards, transport passes, tickets to shows, and can help book accommodation.There's also a branch in the ajuntament (Map p1042; ☎93 285 38 32; Carrer de la Ciutat 2; ⏲8.30am-8.30pm Mon-Fri, 9am-7pm Sat, 9am-2pm Sun & holidays; Ⓜ Jaume I), as well as in the train station and airport.

Palau Robert Regional Tourist Office (Map p1038; ☎93 238 80 91, from outside Catalonia 902 400012; www.gencat.net/probert; Passeig de Gràcia 107; ⏲10am-8pm Mon-Sat, to 2.30pm Sun; Ⓜ Diagonal) A host of material on Catalonia, audiovisual resources, a bookshop and a branch of Turisme Juvenil de Catalunya (for youth travel).

Getting There & Away

AIR

El Prat Airport (☎902 404704; www.aena.es) Barcelona's airport, El Prat de Llobregat, is 12km southwest of the city centre. Barcelona is a big international and domestic destination, with direct flights from North America as well as many European cities.

BOAT

Acciona Trasmediterránea (☎902 454645; www.trasmediterranea.es; Ⓜ Drassanes) Regular passenger and vehicular ferries to/from the Balearic Islands, operated by Acciona

Trasmediterránea, dock along both sides of the Moll de Barcelona wharf in Port Vell.

BUS

Estació del Nord (Map p1038; ☎902 260606; www.barcelonanord.cat; Carrer d'Ali Bei 80; Ⓜ Arc de Triomf) The main terminal for most domestic and international buses is the Estació del Nord. ALSA goes to Madrid (€32, eight hours, up to 16 daily), Valencia (€29, four to 4½ hours, nine to 14 daily) and many other destinations.

Estació d'Autobusos de Sants (Map p1038; Carrer de Viriat; Ⓜ Estació Sants) Eurolines (www.eurolines.es) also offers international services from Estació del Nord and Estació d'Autobusos de Sants, which is next to Estació Sants Barcelona.

TRAIN

Estació Sants (Plaça dels Països Catalans; Ⓜ Estació Sants) Virtually all trains travelling to and from destinations within Spain stop at Estació Sants. High-speed trains to Madrid via Lleida and Zaragoza take as little as two hours and 40 minutes; prices vary wildly. Other trains run to Valencia (€35 to €45, three to 4½ hours, up to 15 daily) and Burgos (from €62 to €86, 5½ to 6½ hours, four daily).

There are also international connections with French cities from the same station.

Getting Around

TO/FROM THE AIRPORT

Renfe's R2 Nord train line runs between the airport and Passeig de Gràcia (via Estació Sants) in central Barcelona (about 35 minutes). Tickets cost €4.10, unless you have a T-10 multitrip public-transport ticket.

A taxi to/from the centre, about a half-hour ride depending on traffic, costs around €30 to €35.

A1 Aerobús (Map p1038; ☎902 100104; www.aerobusbcn.com; one way/return €5.90/10.20) The A1 Aerobús runs from Terminal 1 to Plaça de Catalunya from 6.05am to 1.05am, taking 30 to 40 minutes. A2 Aerobús does the same run from Terminal 2, from 6am to 12.30am. Buy tickets on the bus.

PUBLIC TRANSPORT

Barcelona's metro system spreads its tentacles around the city in such a way that most places of interest are within a 10-minute walk of a station. Buses and suburban trains are needed only for a few destinations. A single metro, bus or suburban train ride costs €2, but a T-10 ticket, valid for 10 rides, costs €10.30.

TAXI

Taxi (☎Fonotaxi 93 300 11 00, Radiotaxi 93 303 30 33, Radiotaxi BCN 93 225 00 00) Barcelona's black-and-yellow taxis are plentiful and reasonably priced. The flag fall is €2.10.

Tarragona

POP 133,550

The eternally sunny port city of Tarragona is a fascinating mix of Mediterranean beach life, Roman history and medieval alleyways. Tarragona has a wealth of ruins, including a seaside amphitheatre and the town's medieval heart is one of the most beautifully designed in Spain, its maze of narrow cobbled streets encircled by steep walls and crowned with a splendid cathedral. A lively eating and drinking scene makes for an enticing stop.

Sights & Activities

Museu d'Història de Tarragona RUIN
(MHT; www.museutgn.com; adult/child per site €3.30/free, all sites €11.05/free; ⏲sites 9am-9pm Tue-Sat, 10am-3pm Sun Easter-Sep, 10am-7pm Tue-Sat, 10am-3pm Sun Oct-Easter) The Museu d'Història de Tarragona consists of various separate Unesco World Heritage Roman sites, as well as some other historic buildings around town. Buy a combined ticket and get exploring!

★Forùm Provincial Pretori i Circ Romans RUIN
(Plaça del Rei) This sizeable complex with two separate entrances includes part of the vaults of the **Roman circus**, where chariot races were once held, as well as the **Pretori tower** on Plaça de Rei and part of the **provincial forum**, the political heart of Tarraconensis province. The circus, 300m long, stretched from here to beyond Plaça de la Font to the west.

Passeig Arqueològic Muralles WALLS
A peaceful walk takes you around part of the perimeter of the old town between two lines of city walls; the inner ones are mainly Roman and date back to the 3rd century BC, while the outer ones were put up by the British in 1709 during the War of the Spanish Succession. Prepare to be awed by the vast gateways built by the Iberians and clamber up onto the battlements from the doorway to the right of the entrance for all-encompassing views of the city. The walk starts from the **Portal del Roser** on Avenida Catalunya.

WORTH A TRIP

GIRONA

A tight huddle of ancient arcaded houses, grand churches, climbing cobbled streets and medieval baths, all enclosed by defensive walls and a lazy river, constitute a powerful reason for visiting north Catalonia's largest city, Girona (Castilian: Gerona).

Girona-Costa Brava airport, 11km south of the centre, is Ryanair's Spanish hub. There are more than 20 trains per day to Figueres (€4.10 to €5.45, 30 minutes) and Barcelona (from €8.40, 40 minutes to 1½ hours).

Catedral (www.catedraldegirona.org; Plaça de la Catedral; adult/student incl Basílica de Sant Feliu €7/5, Sun free; ⏲10am-7.30pm Apr-Oct, 10am-6.30pm Nov-Mar) The billowing baroque facade of the cathedral towers over a flight of 86 steps rising from Plaça de la Catedral. Though the beautiful double-columned Romanesque **cloister** dates to the 12th century, most of the building is Gothic, with the second-widest nave (23m) in Christendom. The 14th-century gilt-and-silver altarpiece and canopy are memorable, as are the bishop's throne and the museum, which holds the masterly Romanesque *Tapís de la creació* (Tapestry of the Creation) and a Mozarabic illuminated *Beatus* manuscript, dating from 975.

The Call Until 1492 Girona was home to Catalonia's second-most important medieval Jewish community (after Barcelona), and its Jewish quarter, the Call, was centred on Carrer de la Força. For an idea of medieval Jewish life and culture, visit the **Museu d'Història dels Jueus de Girona**. Also known as the Centre Bonastruc Ça Porta, named after Jewish Girona's most illustrious figure, a 13th-century cabbalist philosopher and mystic, the centre – a warren of rooms and stairways around a courtyard – hosts temporary exhibitions and is a focal point for studies of Jewish Spain.

Casa Cúndaro (☎972 22 35 83; www.casacundaro.com; Pujada de la Catedral 9; s/d €88/110; ❄📶) The understated exterior of this medieval Jewish house hides five sumptuous rooms and four self-catering apartments – all combining original exposed stone walls and antique doors with modern luxuries. You couldn't wish for a more characterful base; the location right next to the cathedral is either a boon or a bane, depending on whether you enjoy the sound of church bells. Reception is at the Hotel Historic a short stroll up the hill.

El Celler de Can Roca (☎972 22 21 57; www.cellercanroca.com; Carrer Can Sunyer 48; degustation menus €150-180; ⏲1-4pm & 8.30-11pm Tue-Sat Sep-Jul) Named best restaurant in the world in 2013 by The World's 50 Best Restaurants, this place, 2km west of central Girona in a refurbished country house, is run by three brothers. The focus is 'emotional cuisine' through ever-changing takes on Catalan dishes. The style is playful and a full range of molecular gastronomy techniques is employed. The voluminous wine list arrives on a trolley. Book online 11 months in advance; if you haven't, you can join a standby list.

Tourist Office (☎972 22 65 75; www.girona.cat/turisme; Rambla de la Llibertat 1; ⏲9am-8pm Mon-Fri, 9am-2pm & 4-8pm Sat, 9am-2pm Sun) Multilingual and helpful.

★Fòrum de la Colònia RUIN

(Carrer de Lleida) The main provincial forum occupied most of what is now the old town. Further down the hill, this local plaza was occupied by a judicial basilica (where legal disputes were settled) among other buildings. Linked to the site by a footbridge is another excavated area, which includes a stretch of Roman street. The discovery of foundations of a temple to Jupiter, Juno and Minerva suggests the forum was bigger and more important than had previously been assumed.

★Museu Nacional Arqueològic de Tarragona MUSEUM

(www.mnat.cat; Plaça del Rei 5; adult/child €2.40/free; ⏲9.30am-6pm Tue-Sat, 10am-2pm Sun) This excellent museum does justice to the cultural and material wealth of Roman Tarraco. Well-laid-out exhibits include part of the Roman city walls, frescoes, sculpture and pottery. The mosaic collection traces the changing trends – from simple black-and-white designs to complex full-colour creations. A highlight is the large, almost complete *Mosaic de Peixos de la Pineda*, showing fish and sea creatures. It's open extended hours in high season.

★Catedral
CATHEDRAL

(www.catedraldetarragona.com; Plaça de la Seu; adult/child €5/3; ⏲10am-7pm Mon-Sat mid-Mar–Oct, 10am-5pm Mon-Fri, 10am-7pm Sat Nov–mid-Mar) Sitting grandly atop town, Tarragona's cathedral has both Romanesque and Gothic features, as typified by the main facade. The cloister has Gothic vaulting and Romanesque carved capitals, one of which shows rats conducting a cat's funeral...until the cat comes back to life! It's a lesson about passions seemingly lying dormant until they reveal themselves. Chambers off the cloister house the **Museu Diocesà**, with an extensive collection extending from Roman hairpins to some lovely 12th- to 14th-century polychrome woodcarvings of a breastfeeding Virgin.

Sleeping & Eating

Look for tapas bars and inexpensive cafes on the Plaça de la Font. The Moll de Pescadors (Fishermen's Wharf) is the place to go for seafood restaurants.

Hotel Plaça de la Font
HOTEL €€

(☎977 24 61 34; www.hotelpdelafont.com; Plaça de la Font 26; s/d €55/75; ❄📶) Comfortable modern rooms, with photos of Tarragona monuments above the bed, overlook a bustling terrace in a you-can't-get-more-central-than-this location, right on the popular Plaça de la Font. The ones at the front are pretty well soundproofed and have tiny balconies for people-watching.

Hotel Lauria
HOTEL €€

(☎977 23 67 12; www.hotel-lauria.com; Rambla Nova 20; s/d incl breakfast €65/77; P❄📶🏊) Right on the Rambla Nova near where it ends at a balcony overlooking the sea, this smart hotel offers great-value modern rooms with welcome splashes of colour, large bathrooms and a small swimming pool. The rooms at the back are less exposed to the noise from the Rambla.

AQ
CATALAN €€

(☎977 21 59 54; www.aq-restaurant.com; Carrer de les Coques 7; degustation €40-50; ⏲1.30-3.30pm & 8.30-11pm Tue-Sat) This is a bubbly designer haunt alongside the cathedral with stark colour contrasts (black, lemon and cream linen), slick lines and intriguing plays on traditional cooking. One of the two degustation menus is the way to go here, or try the weekday lunch *menú* for €18.

Ares
CATALAN, SPANISH €€

(www.aresrestaurant.es; Plaça del Forum; mains €11-19; ⏲1-4pm & 8.30-11.30pm Wed-Sun) Amid a riot of colourful, exuberant Modernista decor, the cordial welcome from this husband-and-wife team guarantees good eating. Some classic Catalan dishes take their place alongside quality ingredients from across Spain: Asturian cheeses, Galician seafood, Burgos black pudding. They are complemented by some recreated Roman dishes. Quality and quantity are both praiseworthy.

DALÍ'S CATALONIA

The first name that comes into your head when you lay your eyes on this red castle-like building, topped with giant eggs and stylised Oscar-like statues and studded with plaster-covered croissants, is Dalí. An entirely appropriate final resting place for the master of surrealism, the entrance to the **Teatre-Museu Dalí** (www.salvador-dali.org; Plaça de Gala i Salvador Dalí 5; admission incl Dalí Joies & Museu de l'Empordà adult/child under 9yr €12/free; ⏲9am-8pm Jul-Sep, 9.30am-6pm Tue-Sun Mar-Jun & Oct, 10.30am-6pm Tue-Sun Nov-Feb) is watched over by medieval suits of armour balancing baguettes on their heads; it has assured his immortality. 'Theatre-museum' is an apt label for this trip through the incredibly fertile imagination of one of the great showmen of the 20th century.

Port Lligat, a 1.25km walk from Cadaqués, is a tiny settlement around another lovely cove, with fishing boats pulled up on its beach. The **Casa Museu Dalí** started life as a mere fisherman's hut, was steadily altered and enlarged by Dalí, who lived here from 1930 to 1982 (apart from a dozen or so years abroad during and around the Spanish Civil War), and is now a fascinating insight into the lives of the (excuse the pun) surreal couple. We probably don't need to tell you that it's the house with a lot of little white chimneypots and two egg-shaped towers, overlooking the western end of the beach. You must book ahead.

Information

Tourist Office (☎977 25 07 95; www.tarragonaturisme.es; Carrer Major 39; ⏰10am-2pm & 3-5pm Mon-Fri, to 7pm Sat, 10am-2pm Sun) Good place for booking guided tours of the city. Opens extended hours in high season.

Getting There & Away

BUS

The **bus station** (Plaça Imperial Tarraco) is 1.5km northwest of the old town along Rambla Nova. Destinations include Barcelona (€8.70, 1½ hours, 16 daily), Lleida (€10.70, 1¾ hours, five daily) and Valencia (€21.73, three to 4½ hours, seven daily).

TRAIN

The local train station is a 10-minute walk from the old town while fast AVE trains arrive at Camp de Tarragona station, a 15-minute taxi ride from the centre. Departures include Barcelona (both normal trains and rodalies on the R14, R15 and R16 lines, €7 to €38.20, 35 minutes to 1½ hours, every 30 minutes) and Valencia (€21.70 to €38, two to 3½ hours, 19 daily).

ARAGÓN, BASQUE COUNTRY & NAVARRA

Zaragoza

POP 679,624

Zaragoza (Saragossa) is a vibrant, elegant and fascinating city. Located on the banks of the mighty Río Ebro, the residents comprise over half of Aragón's population and enjoy a lifestyle that revolves around some of the best tapas bars in the province, as well as superb shopping and a vigorous nightlife. But Zaragoza is so much more than just a good-time city: it also has a host of historical sights spanning all the great civilisations that have left their indelible mark on the Spanish soul.

Sights

★Basílica de Nuestra Señora del Pilar CHURCH
(Plaza del Pilar; lift admission €3; ⏰7am-9.30pm, lift 10am-1.30pm & 4-6.30pm Tue-Sun) FREE Brace yourself for this great baroque cavern of Catholicism. The faithful believe that it was here on 2 January AD 40 that Santiago saw the Virgin Mary descend atop a marble *pilar* (pillar). A chapel was built around the remaining pillar, followed by a series of ever-more-grandiose churches, culminating in the enormous basilica. A **lift** whisks you most of the way up the north tower from where you climb to a superb viewpoint over the domes and city.

★La Seo CATHEDRAL
(Catedral de San Salvador; Plaza de la Seo; adult/concession €4/3; ⏰10am-6pm Tue-Fri, 10am-noon & 3-6pm Sat, 10-11.30am & 2.30-6pm Sun Jun-Sep, shorter hours Oct-May) Dominating the eastern end of Plaza del Pilar, the La Seo was built between the 12th and 17th centuries and displays a fabulous spread of architectural styles from Romanesque to baroque. The cathedral stands on the site of Islamic Zaragoza's main mosque (which in turn stood upon the temple of the Roman forum). The admission price includes entry to La Seo's **Museo de Tapices** (Plaza de la Seo; ⏰10am-8.30pm Tue-Sun Jun-Sep, shorter hours Oct-May), an impressive collection of 14th- to 17th-century Flemish and French tapestries.

★Aljafería PALACE
(Calle de los Diputados; admission €3, Sun free; ⏰10am-2pm Sat-Wed, plus 4.30-8pm Mon-Wed, Fri & Sat Jul & Aug) The Aljafería is Spain's finest Islamic-era edifice outside Andalucía. Built as a pleasure palace for Zaragoza's Islamic rulers in the 11th century, it underwent its first alterations in 1118 when the city passed into Christian hands. In the 1490s the Catholic Monarchs, Fernando and Isabel, tacked on their own palace, whereafter the Aljafería fell into decay. Twentieth-century restorations brought the building back to life, and in 1987 Aragón's regional parliament was established here. Tours take place throughout the day (multilingual in July and August).

Museo Ibercaja Camón Aznar MUSEUM
(MICAZ; www.ibercaja.es; Calle de Espoz y Mina 23; ⏰10am-2.30pm & 5-9pm Tue-Sat, 10am-2.30pm Sun) FREE This collection of Spanish art through the ages is dominated by an enthralling series of etchings by Goya (on the 2nd floor), one of the premier such collections in existence. You'll also find paintings by other luminaries (including Ribera and Zurbarán), which are spread over the three storeys of this Renaissance-era mansion. There are regular temporary exhibitions.

★Museo del Foro de Caesaraugusta MUSEUM

(Plaza de la Seo 2; adult/concession/child under 8yr €3/2/free; 9am-8.30pm Tue-Sat, 10am-2pm Sun Jun-Sep, shorter hours Oct-May;) The trapezoidal building on Plaza de la Seo is the entrance to an excellent reconstruction of part of Roman Caesaraugusta's forum, now well below ground level. The remains of porticoes, shops, a great *cloaca* (sewer) system, and a limited collection of artefacts from the 1st century AD are on display. An interesting multilingual 15-minute audiovisual show breathes life into it all and culminates with a clever 'talking head' of a statue which children, in particular, will enjoy.

★Museo del Teatro de Caesaraugusta RUIN, MUSEUM

(Calle de San Jorge 12; adult/concession/child under 8yr €4/3/free; 9am-8.30pm Tue-Sat, to 1.30pm Sun;) Discovered during the excavation of a building site in 1972, the ruins of Zaragoza's Teatro Romano (Roman theatre) are the focus of this compelling museum. The theatre once seated 6000 spectators, and great efforts have been made to help visitors reconstruct the edifice's former splendour, including evening projections of a **virtual performance** (May to October) and an entertaining audiovisual production. The theatre is visible from the surrounding streets and the on-site (and excellent) cafe which may be entered separately.

Sleeping

Hotel Río Arga HOTEL €

(976 39 90 65; www.hotelrioarga.es; Calle Contamina 20; s/d €40/45;) Río Arga offers comfortable spacious rooms with easy-on-the-eye decor and large bathrooms with tubs. The private parking is a real boon given this central city location. Breakfast costs €3.75.

★Hotel Sauce BOUTIQUE HOTEL €€

(976 20 50 50; www.hotelsauce.com; Calle de Espoz y Mina 33; s €48, d €55-66;) This chic, small hotel has a great central location and overall light and airy look with white wicker, painted furniture, stripy fabrics and tasteful watercolours on the walls. The superior rooms are well worth the few euros extra. Breakfast (€8) includes homemade cakes and a much-lauded *tortilla de patatas* (potato omelette).

Sabinas APARTMENT €€

(976 20 47 10; www.sabinas.es; Calle de Alfonso I 43; d/apt €50/75;) These apartments include a contemporary-style kitchen and sitting room. The star performer is the Bayeu Attic (€120), a two-bedroom apartment with fabulous basilica views. It also has standard doubles with microwave and there's a second location at Calle Francisco Bayeu 4. Reception is at nearby Hotel Sauce.

Eating & Drinking

Zaragoza has some terrific tapas bars, with dozens of places on or close to Plaza de Santa Marta. Otherwise the narrow streets of El Tubo, north of Plaza de España, are tapas central.

Calle del Temple, southwest of Plaza del Pilar, is the spiritual home of Zaragoza's roaring nightlife. This is where the city's students head out to drink. There are more bars lined up along this street than anywhere else in Aragón.

Casa Pascualillo CONTEMPORARY TAPAS €

(Calle de la Libertad 5; tapas from €1.60, mains €5-14; noon-4pm & 7-11pm Tue-Sat, noon-4.30pm Sun) When *Metropoli,* the weekend magazine of *El Mundo* newspaper, sought out the best 50 tapas bars in Spain a few years back, it's no surprise that Casa Pascualillo made the final cut. The bar groans under the weight of enticing tapas like El Pascualillo, a 'small' *bocadillo* (filled roll) of *jamón,* oyster mushrooms and onion. There's a more formal restaurant attached.

★El Ciclón CONTEMPORARY SPANISH €€

(Plaza del Pilar 10; raciones €7-8.50, set menus €15-20; 11am-11.30pm) Opened in November 2013 by three acclaimed Spanish chefs (all with Michelin-star restaurant experience), the dishes here are superbly prepared. Choose between set menus and tapas and *raciones* such as the Canary Island favourite, *papas arrugadas* (new potatoes with a spicy coriander sauce), noodles with mussels, and artichokes with *migas* (breadcrumbs with garlic and olive oil) and cauliflower cream.

Information

Municipal Tourist Office (976 20 12 00; www.zaragozaturismo.es; Plaza del Pilar; 9am-9pm mid-Jun–mid-Oct, 10am-8pm mid-Oct–mid-Jun;) Has branch offices around town, including the train station.

Oficina de Turismo de Aragón (www.turismodearagon.com; Plaza de España; ⏲9am-2pm & 5-8pm Mon-Fri, from 10am Sat & Sun; 📶) Has plenty of brochures on the province.

Getting There & Away

AIR

Zaragoza-Sanjurjo Airport (☎976 71 23 00; www.zaragoza-airport.com) The Zaragoza-Sanjurjo airport, 8.5km west of the city, has direct Ryanair flights to/from London (Stansted), Brussels (Charleroi), Paris (Beauvais), Milan (Bergamo), Lanzarote and Seville. Iberia (www.iberia.es) and Air Europa (www.aireuropa.com) also operate a small number of domestic and international routes.

BUS

Dozens of bus lines fan out across Spain from the bus station attached to the Estación Intermodal Delicias train station.

TRAIN

Estación Intermodal Delicias (www.renfe.com; Calle Rioja 33) Zaragoza's futuristic, if rather impersonal, Estación Intermodal Delicias is connected by almost hourly high-speed AVE services to Madrid (1¼ hours) and Barcelona (from 1½ hours). There are also services to Valencia (4½ hours, three daily), Huesca (one hour), Jaca (3½ hours) and Teruel (2¼ hours).

Around Aragón

In Aragón's south, little visited **Teruel** is home to some stunning Mudéjar architecture. Nearby, **Albarracín** is one of Spain's most beautiful villages.

In the north, the Pyrenees dominate and the **Parque Nacional de Ordesa y Monte Perdido** is excellent for hiking; the pretty village of **Torla** is the gateway. South of the hamlet of **La Besurta** is the great Maladeta massif, a superb challenge for experienced climbers. This forbidding line of icy peaks, with glaciers suspended from the higher crests, culminates in **Aneto** (3404m), the highest peak in the Pyrenees. There are plenty of hiking and climbing options for all levels in these mountain parks bordering France. Another enchanting base for exploration in the region is **Aínsa**, a hilltop village of stone houses.

In Aragón's northwest, **Sos del Rey Católico** is another gorgeous stone village draped along a ridge.

San Sebastián

POP 183,300

Stylish San Sebastián (Donostia in Basque) has the air of an upscale resort, complete with an idyllic location on the shell-shaped Bahía de la Concha. The natural setting – crystalline waters, a flawless beach, green hills on all sides – is captivating. But this is one of Spain's true culinary capitals, with more Michelin stars (16) per capita than anywhere else on earth.

Sights & Activities

★Playa de la Concha BEACH

Fulfilling almost every idea of how a perfect city beach should be formed, Playa de la Concha and its westerly extension, **Playa de Ondarreta**, are easily among the best city beaches in Europe. Throughout the long summer months a fiesta atmosphere prevails, with thousands of tanned and toned bodies spread across the sands. The swimming is almost always safe.

Monte Igueldo VIEWPOINT

The views from the summit of Monte Igueldo, just west of town, will make you feel like a circling hawk staring over the vast panorama of the Bahía de la Concha and the surrounding coastline and mountains. The best way to get there is via the old-world **funicular railway** (www.monteigueldo.es; return adult/child €3.10/2.30; ⏲10am-9pm Jul, 10am-10pm Aug shorter hours rest of year) to the **Parque de Atracciones** (www.monteigueldo.es; admission €2.20; ⏲11.15am-2pm & 4-8pm Mon-Fri, until 8.30pm Sat & Sun Jul-Sep, shorter hours rest of year), a slightly tacky mini theme park at the top of the hill. Individual rides (which include roller coasters, boat rides, carousels and pony rides) cost between €1 and €2.50 extra. Trains on the funicular railway depart every 15 minutes.

San Telmo Museoa MUSEUM

(www.santelmomuseoa.com; Plaza Zuloaga 1; adult/student/child €5/3/free, Tue free; ⏲10am-8pm Tue-Sun) Both the oldest and one of the newest museums in the Basque Country, the San Telmo museum has existed since 1902 – sort of. It was actually closed for many years but after major renovation work it reopened in 2011 and is now a museum of Basque culture and society. The displays range from historical artefacts to the squiggly lines of modern art, and all the pieces reflect Basque culture and society.

Sleeping

Pensión Régil PENSION €

(☎943 42 71 43; www.pensionregil.com; Calle de Easo 9; s/d €53/59; 📶) The furnishings might be cheap and the decor a bit pink and floral for our liking, but just look at that price! You really won't get a much better deal in San Sebasián in high season. Add in that all rooms have private bathrooms, it's very close to Playa de la Concha and the young owner, Inaki, is a bit of a charmer and you can't go wrong.

★**Pensión Aida** BOUTIQUE HOTEL €€

(☎943 32 78 00; www.pensionesconencanto.com; Calle de Iztueta 9; s €62, d €84-90, studios €132-152; ❄@📶) The owners of this excellent *pensión* read the rule book on what makes a good hotel and have complied exactly. The rooms are bright and bold, full of exposed stone and everything smells fresh and clean. The communal area, stuffed with soft sofas and mountains of information, is a big plus.

Pensión Amaiur BOUTIQUE HOTEL €€

(☎943 42 96 54; www.pensionamaiur.com; Calle de 31 de Agosto 44; s €45, d €90-100; @📶) The young and friendly owners of this top-notch guesthouse, which has a prime old-town location, have really created something different here. The look of the place is 'old-granny cottage' with bright floral wallpapers and bathrooms tiled in Andalucian blue and white.

Eating & Drinking

With 16 Michelin stars (including three restaurants with the coveted three stars) and a population of 183,000, San Sebastián stands atop a pedestal as one of the culinary capitals of the planet. As if that alone weren't enough, the city is overflowing with bars – almost all of which have bar tops weighed down under a mountain of *pintxos* (Basque tapas) that almost every Spaniard will (sometimes grudgingly) tell you are the best in country.

Do what the locals do – crawls of the city centre's bars. *Pintxos* etiquette is simple. Ask for a plate and point out what *pintxos* (more like tasty mounds of food on little slices of baguette) you want. Keep the toothpicks and go back for as many as you'd like. Accompany with *txakoli,* a cloudy white wine poured like cider to create a little fizz. When you're ready to pay, hand over the plate with all the toothpicks and tell bar staff how many drinks you've had. It's an honour system that has stood the test of time. Expect to pay €2.50 to €3.50 for a *pintxo* and *txakoli*.

SPLURGE

With three shining Michelin stars, acclaimed chef Juan Mari Arzak takes some beating when it comes to *nueva cocina vasca* (Basque nouvelle cuisine) and his restaurant is, not surprisingly, considered one of the best places to eat in Spain. **Arzak** (☎+34 943 27 84 65; www.arzak.info; Avenida Alcalde José Elésegui 273; meals €189; ⏲Tue-Sat, closed Nov & late Jun) is now assisted by his daughter Elena and they never cease to innovate. Reservations, well in advance, are obligatory.

Restaurante Alberto SEAFOOD €

(☎943 42 88 84; Calle de 31 de Agosto 19; mains €12-15, menus €15; ⏲noon-4pm & 7pm-midnight Thu-Tue) A charming old seafood restaurant with a fishmonger-style window display of the day's catch. It's small and friendly and the pocket-sized dining room feels like it was once someone's living room. The food is earthy (well, OK, salty) and good, and the service swift.

★**La Fábrica** MODERN BASQUE €€

(☎943 98 05 81; Calle del Puerto 17; mains €15-20, menus from €24; ⏲1-3.30pm & 8.30-11pm Mon-Sat, 1-3.30pm Sun) The red brick interior walls and white tablecloths lend an air of class to a resturant whose modern takes on Basque classics have been making waves with San Sebastián locals over the last couple of years. At just €24, the multidish tasting menu is about the best value deal in the city.

La Cuchara de San Telmo CONTEMPORARY BASQUE €€

(www.lacucharadesantelmo.com; Calle de 31 de Agosto 28; pintxos from €2.50; ⏲7.30-11pm Tue, noon-3.30pm & 7.30-11pm Wed-Sun) This unfussy, hidden-away (and hard to find) bar offers miniature *nueva cocina vasca* (Basque nouvelle cuisine) from a supremely creative kitchen. Unlike many San Sebastián bars this one doesn't have any *pintxos* laid out on the bar top; instead you must order from the blackboard menu behind the counter.

Astelena BASQUE €€

(Calle de Iñigo 1; pintxos from €2.50; ⏲1-4.30pm & 8-11pm Tue & Thu-Sat, 1-4.30pm Wed) The *pintxos* draped across the counter in this bar, tucked into the corner of Plaza de la Constitución, stand out. Many of them are a fusion of Basque and Asian inspirations, but the best of all are perhaps the foie-gras-based treats. The great positioning means that prices are slightly elevated.

Information

Oficina de Turismo (☎943 48 11 66; www.sansebastianturismo.com; Alameda del Boulevard 8; ⏰9am-8pm Mon-Sat, 10am-7pm Sun) This friendly office offers comprehensive information on the city and the Basque Country in general.

Getting There & Away

BUS

Daily bus services leave for Bilbao (from €6.74, one hour), Bilbao Airport (€16.50, 1¼ hours), Biarritz (France; €6.75, 1¼ hours), Madrid (from €36, five hours) and Pamplona (€7.68, one hour).

TRAIN

For France you must first go to the Spanish/French border town of Irún (or sometimes trains go as far as Hendaye; Renfe from €2.65, 25 minutes), which is also served by Eusko Tren/Ferrocarril Vasco (www.euskotren.es), and change there.

Renfe Train Station (Paseo de Francia) The main Renfe train station is just across Río Urumea, on a line linking Paris to Madrid. There are several services daily to Madrid (from €47, five hours) and two to Barcelona (from €64, six hours).

Bilbao

POP 354,200

The commercial hub of the Basque Country, Bilbao (Bilbo in Basque) is best known for the magnificent Guggenheim Museum. An architectural masterpiece by Frank Gehry, the museum was the catalyst of a turnaround that saw Bilbao transformed from an industrial port city into a vibrant cultural centre. After visiting this must-see temple to modern art, spend time exploring Bilbao's Casco Viejo (Old Quarter), a grid of elegant streets dotted with shops, cafes, *pintxos* bars and several small but worthy museums.

Sights

★Museo Guggenheim — GALLERY

(www.guggenheim-bilbao.es; Avenida Abandoibarra 2; adult/student/child €13/7.50/free; ⏰10am-8pm, closed Mon Sep-Jun) Opened in September 1997, Bilbao's shimmering titanium Museo Guggenheim is one of the iconic buildings of modern architecture and it almost single-handedly lifted Bilbao out of its postindustrial depression and into the 21st century – with sensation. It boosted the city's already inspired regeneration, stimulated further development and placed Bilbao firmly in the world art and tourism spotlight.

★Museo de Bellas Artes — GALLERY

(www.museobilbao.com; Plaza del Museo 2; adult/student/child €7/5/free, free Wed; ⏰10am-8pm Wed-Mon) The Museo de Bellas Artes houses a compelling collection that includes everything from Gothic sculptures to 20th-century pop art. There are three main subcollections: classical art, with works by Murillo, Zurbarán, El Greco, Goya and van Dyck; contemporary art, featuring works by Gauguin, Francis Bacon and Anthony Caro; and Basque art, with works of the great sculptors Jorge de Oteiza and Eduardo Chillida, and strong paintings by the likes of Ignacio Zuloago and Juan de Echevarria.

Casco Viejo — OLD TOWN

The compact Casco Viejo, Bilbao's atmospheric old quarter, is full of charming streets, boisterous bars and plenty of quirky and independent shops. At the heart of the Casco are Bilbao's original seven streets, **Las Siete Calles**, which date from the 1400s.

Euskal Museoa — MUSEUM

(Museo Vasco; www.euskal-museoa.org/es/hasiera; Plaza Miguel Unamuno 4; adult/child €3/free, free Thu; ⏰10am-7pm Mon & Wed-Fri, 10am-1.30pm & 4-7pm Sat, 10am-2pm Sun) This museum is probably the most complete museum of Basque culture and history in all of Spain. The story kicks off back in the days of prehistory and from this murky period the displays bound rapidly through to the modern age.

Sleeping & Eating

The Bilbao tourism authority has a useful **reservations department** (☎902 877298; www.bilbaoreservas.com) for accommodation.

★Pensión Iturrienea Ostatua — BOUTIQUE HOTEL €€

(☎944 16 15 00; www.iturrieneaostatua.com; Calle de Santa María 14; r €50-70; 📶) Easily the most eccentric hotel in Bilbao, it's part farmyard, part old-fashioned toyshop, and a work of art in its own right. The nine rooms here

PAMPLONA & SAN FERMINES

Immortalised by Ernest Hemingway in *The Sun Also Rises*, the pre-Pyrenean city of Pamplona (Iruña in Basque) is home of the wild Sanfermines (aka Encierro or the Running of the Bulls) festival, but is also an extremely walkable city that's managed to mix the charm of old plazas and buildings with modern shops and a lively nightlife.

The Sanfermines festival is held from 6 to 14 July, when Pamplona is overrun with thrill-seekers, curious onlookers and, yes, bulls. The Encierro (Running of the Bulls) begins at 8am daily, when bulls are let loose from the Coralillos Santo Domingo. The 825m race lasts just three minutes.

Since records began in 1924, 16 people have died during Pamplona's bullrun. Many of those who run are full of bravado (and/or drink) and have little idea of what they're doing. For dedicated *encierro* news, check out www.sanfermin.com.

Animal rights groups oppose bullrunning as a cruel tradition, and the participating bulls will almost certainly all be killed in the afternoon bullfight. The PETA-organised anti-bullfighting demonstration, the Running of the Nudes, takes place two days before the first bullrun.

Tourist Office (848 42 04 20; www.turismo.navarra.es; Avenida da Roncesvalles 4; 9am-7pm Mon-Fri, 10am-2pm & 4-7pm Sat, 10am-2pm Sun) This extremely well-organised office, just opposite the statue of the bulls in the new town, has plenty of information about the city and Navarra. There are a couple of summer-only tourist info booths scattered throughout the city.

are so full of character that there'll be barely enough room for your own!

Hostal Begoña BOUTIQUE HOTEL €€
(944 23 01 34; www.hostalbegona.com; Calle de la Amistad 2; s/d from €57/66; P @ wi-fi) The owners of this outstanding place don't need voguish labels for their very stylish and individual creation. Begoña speaks for itself with colourful rooms decorated with modern artworks, all with funky tiled bathrooms and wrought-iron beds. The common areas have mountains of books, traveller information and a rack of computers for internet usage.

★ **La Viña del Ensanche** PINTXOS €
(944 15 56 15; www.lavinadelensanche.com; Calle de la Diputación 10; pintxos from €2.50, menu €30; 8.30am-11pm Mon-Fri, noon-1am Sat) Hundreds of bottles of wine line the walls of this outstanding *pintxos* bar. And when we say outstanding we mean that it could well be the best place to eat *pintxos* in all of the city.

★ **Casa Rufo** BASQUE €€
(944 43 21 72; www.casarufo.com; Hurtado de Amézaga 5; mains €10-15; 1.30-4pm & 8.30-11pm Mon-Sat) Despite the emergence of numerous glitzy restaurants that are temples to haute cuisine this resolutely old-fashioned place, with its shelves full of dusty bottles of top-quality olive oil and wine, still stands out as one of the best places to eat traditional Basque food in Bilbao.

Information

Tourist Office (www.bilbaoturismo.net) Main tourist office (944 79 57 60; Plaza Circular 1; 9am-9pm; wi-fi); airport (944 71 03 01; 9am-9pm Mon-Sat, 9am-3pm Sun); Guggenheim (Alameda Mazarredo 66; 10am-7pm daily, till 3pm Sun Sep-Jun) Bilbao's friendly tourist-office staffers are extremely helpful, well informed and, above all, enthusiastic about their city. At all offices ask for the free bimonthly *Bilbao Guía*, with its entertainment listings plus tips on restaurants, bars and nightlife. At the newly opened, state-of-the-art main tourist office there's free wi-fi access, a bank of touch-screen information computers and, best of all, some humans to help answer questions.

Getting There & Away

BUS

Regular bus services operate to/from Madrid (from €31, 4¾ hours), Barcelona (€48, seven hours), Pamplona (€15, two hours) and Santander (€6.60, 1¼ hours).

TRAIN

Two Renfe trains runs daily to Madrid (€64, six hours) and Barcelona (€65, six hours) from the Abando train station. Slow **FEVE** (www.feve.es) trains run from Concordia station next door, heading west into Cantabria and Asturias.

CANTABRIA, ASTURIAS & GALICIA

With a landscape reminiscent of parts of the British Isles, 'Green Spain' offers great walks in national parks, seafood feasts in sophisticated towns and oodles of opportunities to plunge into the ice-cold waters of the Bay of Biscay.

Santillana del Mar

Some 34km west of the regional capital, Santander, **Santillana del Mar** (www.santillanadelmar.com) is a bijou medieval village and the obvious overnight base for visiting the nearby Cueva de Altamira. Buses run three to four times a day from Santander to Santillana del Mar.

Spain's finest prehistoric art, in the **Cueva de Altamira**, 2km southwest of Santillana, was discovered in 1879. It took more than 20 years, after further discoveries of cave art in France, before scientists accepted that these wonderful paintings of bison, horses and other animals really were the handiwork of primitive people many thousands of years ago. A replica cave in the museum here now enables everyone to appreciate the inspired, 14,500-year-old paintings.

Santiago de Compostela

POP 80,000

The supposed burial place of St James (Santiago), Santiago de Compostela is a bewitching city. Christian pilgrims journeying along the Camino de Santiago often end up mute with wonder on entering its medieval centre. Fortunately, they usually regain their verbal capacities over a celebratory late-night foray into the city's lively bar scene.

Sights & Activities

★Catedral de Santiago de Compostela CATHEDRAL

(www.catedraldesantiago.es; Praza do Obradoiro; ⏲7am-8.30pm) The grand heart of Santiago, the cathedral soars above the city centre in a splendid jumble of moss-covered spires and statues. Built piecemeal over several centuries, its beauty is a mix of the original Romanesque structure (built between 1075 and 1211) and later Gothic and baroque flourishes. The tomb of Santiago beneath the main altar is a magnet for all who come to the cathedral. The artistic high point is the Pórtico de la Gloria inside the west entrance, featuring 200 masterly Romanesque sculptures.

★Museo da Catedral MUSEUM

(Colección Permanente; www.catedraldesantiago.es; Praza do Obradoiro; adult/senior, pilgrim, unemployed & student/child €6/4/free; ⏲9am-8pm Apr-Oct, 10am-8pm Nov-Mar) The Cathedral Museum spreads over four floors and includes the cathedral's large, 16th-century, Gothic/plateresque cloister. You'll see a sizeable section of Maestro Mateo's original carved stone choir (destroyed in 1604 but recently pieced back together), an impressive collection of religious art (including the *botafumeiros* – incense burners – in the 2nd-floor library), the lavishly decorated 18th-century *sala capitular* (chapter house) and, off the cloister, the Panteón de Reyes, with tombs of kings of medieval León.

Praza do Obradoiro SQUARE

Grand Praza do Obradoiro, in front of the cathedral's west facade, earned its name from the workshops set up there while the cathedral was being built. It's free of both traffic and cafes and has a unique atmosphere.

At its northern end, the Renaissance **Hostal dos Reis Católicos** (admission €3; ⏲noon-2pm & 4-6pm Sun-Fri) was built in the early 16th century by order of the Catholic Monarchs, Isabel and Fernando, as a refuge for pilgrims and a symbol of the crown's power in this ecclesiastical city. Today it shelters well-off travellers instead, as a *parador* (luxurious state-owned hotel), but its four courtyards and some other areas are open to visitors.

Colexio de Fonseca UNIVERSITY

(⏲9am-9pm Mon-Fri, 10am-8.30pm Sat) FREE Located south of Catedral de Santiago de Compostela, and in the cafe-lined Praza de Fonseca, the Colexio de Fonseca with a beautiful Renaissance courtyard and exhibition gallery was the original seat of Santiago's university (founded in 1495).

Museo das Peregrinacións e de Santiago MUSEUM

(www.mdperegrinacions.com; Praza das Praterías; adult/senior, pilgrim & student/child €2.50/1.50/free; ⏲10am-2pm & 5-8pm Tue-Sat, 11am-2pm Sun) The recently converted building on Praza das Praterías stages changing exhibitions on the themes of pilgrimage and Santiago (man and city), and affords close-up views of some of the cathedral's towers from its 3rd-floor windows. The museum's permanent collection – an extensive and interesting assemblage of art, artefacts, models and memorabilia – resides in its **original building** (www.mdperegrinacions.com; Rúa de San Miguel 4; ⌚10am-8pm Tue-Fri, 10.30am-1.30pm & 5-8pm Sat, 10.30am-1.30pm Sun) FREE 300m away, though there are plans eventually to move it to the new site.

Cathedral Rooftop Tour TOUR
(☎902 557812; www.catedraldesantiago.es; adult/senior, pilgrim, unemployed & student/child €12/10/free, combined ticket with Museo da Catedral €15/12/free; ⌚tours hourly 10am-1pm & 4-7pm, to 6pm Nov-Mar) For unforgettable bird's-eye views of the cathedral interior from its upper storeys, and of the city from the cathedral roof, take the rooftop tour, which starts in the visitor reception centre beneath the Obradoiro facade. The tours are popular, so go beforehand to book a time, or book online. One afternoon tour is usually given in English; the rest are in Spanish. Guides provide good insight into Santiago's history.

Sleeping

Meiga Backpackers HOSTEL €
(☎981 57 08 46; www.meiga-backpackers.es; Rúa dos Basquiños 67; dm incl breakfast €15; ⌚Mar-Nov; @ 📶) Clean, colourful, sociable and handily placed between the bus station and city centre, Meiga has spacious bunk dorms, a good big kitchen and lounge, and a long garden. A great choice if you're on the budget backpacking trail.

★**Hotel Costa Vella** BOUTIQUE HOTEL €€
(☎981 56 95 30; www.costavella.com; Rúa da Porta da Pena 17; s €59, d €81-97; ❄ 📶) Tranquil, thoughtfully designed rooms – some with typically Galician *galerías* (glassed-in balconies) – a friendly welcome and a lovely garden cafe make this old stone house a wonderful option, and the €6 breakfast is substantial. Even if you don't stay, it's an ideal spot for breakfast or coffee. Book ahead from May to September.

Parador Hostal dos Reis Católicos HISTORIC HOTEL €€€
(☎981 58 22 00; www.parador.es; Praza do Obradoiro 1; s/d incl breakfast from €175/190; P ❄ @ 📶) Opened in 1509 as a pilgrims' hostel, and with a claim to be the world's oldest hotel, this palatial *parador*, steps from the cathedral, is Santiago's top hotel, with regal (if rather staid) rooms. If you're not staying, stop in for a look round and coffee and cakes at the elegant cafe.

WORTH A TRIP

PICOS DE EUROPA

These jagged mountains straddling Asturias, Cantabria and northeast Castilla y León amount to some of the finest walking country in Spain. They comprise three limestone massifs (the highest peak rises 2648m). The 647-sq-km **Parque Nacional de los Picos de Europa** (www.picosdeeuropa.com) covers all three massifs and is Spain's second-biggest national park.

There are numerous places to stay and eat all over the mountains. Getting here and around by bus can be slow going but the Picos are accessible from Santander and Oviedo (the latter is easier) by bus.

Eating

O Beiro TAPAS, RACIONES €
(Rúa da Raíña 3; raciones €5-10; ⌚10am-1am Tue-Sun Mar-Dec) The house speciality is *tablas* (trays) of delectable cheeses and sausages, but there are plenty of other tapas and *raciones* at this friendly two-level wine bar. It has a terrific range of Galician wines and the fiery local grape-based liquors *orujo* and *aguardiente*.

★**O Curro da Parra** CONTEMPORARY GALICIAN €€
(www.ocurrodaparra.com; Rúa do Curro da Parra 7; mains €17-23, tapas €4-8; ⌚1.30-3.30pm & 8.30-11.30pm Tue-Sat, 1.30-3.30pm Sun) With a neat little stone-walled dining room upstairs and a narrow tapas and wine bar below, O Curro da Parra serves up a broad range of thoughtfully created, market-fresh fare. You might go for pork cheeks with apple purée and spinach – or just ask what the fish and seafood of the day are. On weekday lunchtimes there's a good-value €12 *menú mercado* (market menu).

Abastos 2.0 CONTEMPORARY GALICIAN €€
(☎981 57 61 45; www.abastosdouspuntocero.es; Rúa das Ameas 3; dishes €1-10, menú €21; ⌚noon-3pm & 8-11pm Tue-Sat) This highly original and incredibly popular marketside eatery offers new dishes concocted daily from the market's offerings. You can go for small individual items, or plates to share, or a six-item *menú* that adds up to a meal for €21. The seafood is generally fantastic, but whatever you order

you're likely to love the great tastes and delicate presentation – if you can get a seat!

Information

Oficina de Turismo de Galicia (www.turgalicia.es; Rúa do Vilar 30-32; 10am-8pm Mon-Fri, 11am-2pm & 5-7pm Sat, 11am-2pm Sun) The scoop on all things Galicia.

Oficina del Peregrino (Pilgrims' Office; 981 56 88 46; peregrinossantiago.es; Rúa do Vilar 3; 9am-9pm May-Oct, 10am-7pm Nov-Apr) People who have covered at least the last 100km of the Camino de Santiago on foot or horseback, or the last 200km by bicycle, can obtain their 'Compostela' certificate to prove it here. The website has a good deal of useful Camino info.

Turismo de Santiago (981 55 51 29; www.santiagoturismo.com; Rúa do Vilar 63; 9am-9pm, to 7pm approximately Nov-Mar) The efficient main municipal tourist office.

Getting There & Around

BUS

ALSA (902 422242; www.alsa.es) ALSA has services to Oviedo (from €30, five to seven hours), León (€30, six hours) and Madrid (€47 to €68, eight to 10 hours). ALSA also has direct daily services to Porto (€31, four hours).

Bus Station (981 54 24 16; Praza de Camilo Díaz Baliño;) The bus station is about a 20-minute walk northeast of the centre.

Castromil-Monbus (902 292900; www.monbus.es) Destinations throughout Galicia.

TRAIN

From the **train station** (981 59 18 59; Rúa do Hórreo), regional trains run up and down the coast, while a daytime Talgo and an overnight Trenhotel head to Madrid (from €50.75, 6¼ to 9½ hours).

Around Galicia

Galicia's dramatic Atlantic coastline is one of Spain's best-kept secrets, with wild and precipitous cliffs and isolated fishing villages. The lively port city of **A Coruña** has a lovely city beach and fabulous seafood (a recurring Galician theme). It's also the gateway to the stirring landscapes of the **Costa da Morte** and **Rías Altas**; the latter's highlight among many is probably **Cabo Ortegal**. Inland Galicia is also worth exploring, especially the old town of **Lugo**, surrounded by what many consider to be the world's best preserved Roman walls.

VALENCIA

POP 792,300

Spain's third-largest city is a magnificent place, content for Madrid and Barcelona to grab the headlines while it gets on with being a wonderfully liveable city with thriving cultural, eating and nightlife scenes. The star attraction is the strikingly futuristic buildings of the Ciudad de las Artes y las Ciencias, designed by local-boy-made-good Santiago Calatrava. The Barrio del Carmen also has a fistful of fabulous Modernista architecture, great museums and a large, characterful old quarter. Valencia, surrounded by the fertile fruit-and-veg farmland La Huerta, is famous as the home of rice dishes like paella, but its buzzy dining scene offers plenty more besides.

Sights & Activities

★**Ciudad de las Artes y las Ciencias** NOTABLE BUILDINGS
(City of Arts & Sciences; www.cac.es; combined ticket for Oceanogràfic, Hemisfèric & Museo de las Ciencias Príncipe Felipe adult/child €36.25/27.55) The aesthetically stunning City of Arts & Sciences occupies a massive 350,000-sq-metre swath of the old Turia riverbed. It's mostly the work of world-famous, locally born architect Santiago Calatrava. He's a controversial figure for many Valencians, who complain about the expense, and various design flaws that have necessitated major repairs. Nevertheless, if your taxes weren't involved, it's awe-inspiring stuff, and pleasingly family-oriented.

★**Oceanogràfic** AQUARIUM
(www.cac.es/oceanografic; adult/child €27.90/21; 10am-6pm Oct-Jun, 10am-8pm Jul & Sep, 10am-midnight Aug;) For most families with children this indoor-outdoor aquarium is the highlight of a visit to Valencia's City of Arts & Sciences. There are polar zones, a dolphinarium, a Red Sea aquarium, a Mediterranean seascape – and a couple of underwater tunnels, one 70m long, where the fish have the chance to gawp back at visitors. Opening hours here are approximate; check the website by date. It opens later on Saturday.

★**Catedral** CATHEDRAL
(Plaza de la Virgen; adult/child incl audioguide €5/3.50; 10am-5.30pm or 6.30pm Mon-Sat, 2-5.30pm Sun, closed Sun Nov-Feb) Valencia's cathedral was built over the mosque after the 1238 reconquest. Its low, wide, brick-vaulted

triple nave is mostly Gothic, with neoclassical side chapels. Highlights are rich Italianate frescoes above the altarpiece, a pair of Goyas in the **Chapel of San Francisco de Borja**, and...da-dah...in the flamboyant Gothic **Capilla del Santo Cáliz**, what's claimed to be the **Holy Grail**, the chalice from which Christ sipped during the Last Supper. It's a Roman-era agate cup, later modified, so at least the date is right.

Miguelete Bell Tower TOWER
(adult/child €2/1; ⏲10am-7pm or 7.30pm) Left of the main portal of the Cathedral is the entrance to the Miguelete bell tower. Clamber up the 207 steps of its spiral staircase for great 360-degree city-and-skyline views.

★**La Lonja** HISTORIC BUILDING
(Calle de la Lonja; adult/child €2/1; ⏲10am-6pm or 7pm Tue-Sat, to 3pm Sun) This splendid late-15th-century building, a Unesco World Heritage Site, was originally Valencia's silk and commodity exchange. Highlights are the colonnaded hall with its twisted Gothic pillars and the 1st-floor **Consulado del Mar** with its stunning coffered ceiling.

★**Museo de Bellas Artes** GALLERY
(San Pío V; www.museobellasartesvalencia.gva.es; Calle de San Pío V 9; ⏲10am-7pm Tue-Sun, 11am-5pm Mon) FREE Bright and spacious, the Museo de Bellas Artes ranks among Spain's best. Highlights include the grandiose Roman *Mosaic of the Nine Muses,* a collection of magnificent late-medieval altarpieces, and works by El Greco, Goya, Velázquez, Murillo and Ribalta, plus artists such as Sorolla and Pinazo of the Valencian Impressionist school.

Beaches

At the coastal end of the tram line, 3km from the centre, **Playa de las Arenas** runs north into **Playa de la Malvarrosa** and **Playa de la Patacona**, forming a wide strip of sand some 4km long. It's bordered by the **Paseo Marítimo** promenade and a string of restaurants and cafes. One block back, lively bars and discos thump out the beat in summer.

Sleeping

Pensión París HOTEL €
(☎963 52 67 66; www.pensionparis.com; Calle de Salvà 12; s €24, d €32-44; 📶) Welcoming, with spotless rooms – most with shared bathrooms, some with private facilities – this family-run option on a quiet street is the antithesis of the crowded, pack-'em-in hostel. The best of the rooms have balconies and original features from this stately old building.

Ad Hoc Monumental HOTEL €€
(☎963 91 91 40; www.adhochoteles.com; Calle Boix 4; s/d €72/84; ❄📶) Friendly Ad Hoc offers comfort and charm deep within the old quarter and also runs a splendid small restaurant (open for dinner Monday to Saturday). The late-19th-century building has been restored to its former splendour with great sensitivity, revealing original ceilings, mellow brickwork and solid wooden beams.

★**Caro Hotel** HOTEL €€€
(☎963 05 90 00; www.carohotel.com; Calle Almirante 14; r €143-214; P❄📶) Housed in a sumptuous 19th-century mansion, this sits atop some 2000 years of Valencian history, with restoration revealing a hefty hunk of the Arab wall, Roman column bases and Gothic arches. Each room is furnished in soothing dark shades, has a great king-sized bed, and varnished cement floors. Bathrooms are tops. For that very special occasion, reserve the 1st-floor grand suite, once the ballroom. Savour, too, its excellent restaurant Alma del Temple.

WORTH A TRIP

LAS FALLAS

In mid-March, Valencia hosts one of Europe's wildest street parties: **Las Fallas de San José** (www.fallas.es). For one week (12 to 19 March), the city is engulfed by an anarchic swirl of fireworks, music, festive bonfires and all-night partying. On the final night, giant *ninots* (effigies), many of political and social personages, are torched in the main plaza.

If you're not in Valencia then, see the *ninots* saved from the flames by popular vote at the **Museo Fallero** (Plaza Monteolivete 4; adult/child €2/1; ⏲10am-6pm or 7pm Tue-Sat, 10am-3pm Sun).

Eating

At weekends, locals in their hundreds head for Las Arenas, just north of the port, where a long line of restaurants overlooking the beach all serve up authentic paella in a three-course meal costing around €15.

★Carosel VALENCIAN €

(☎961 13 28 73; www.carosel.es; Calle Taula de Canvis 6; mains €7-16, menu €15; ⊙1-4pm & 9-11pm Tue-Sat, 1-4pm Sun) Jordi and his partner, Carol, run this delightful small restaurant with outdoor seating on a square. The freshest of produce from the nearby market is blended with Alicante and Valencia traditions to create salads, cocas, rices and other delicious titbits. Top value and warmly recommended.

★Delicat TAPAS, FUSION €€

(☎963 92 33 57; Calle Conde de Almodóvar 4; mains €9-14; ⊙1-4pm & 8.30-11.30pm Tue-Sat, 1-4pm Sun) At this particularly friendly, intimate option (there are only nine tables, plus the terrace in summer), Catina, up front, and her partner, Paco, on full view in the kitchen, offer an unbeatable-value, five-course menu of samplers for lunch and a range of truly innovative tapas anytime.

Lonja del Pescado FISH €€

(www.restaurantelalonjapescadovalencia.com; Calle de Eugenia Viñes 243; dishes €8-15; ⊙1-3.30pm Sat & Sun, 8-11.30pm Tue-Sun Mar-Oct, 1-3.30pm Fri-Sun, 8-11.30pm Fri & Sat Nov-Feb) One block back from the beach at Malvarrosa, this busy, informal place has plenty of atmosphere and offers unbeatable value for fresh fish. Grab an order form as you enter and fill it in at your table. The tram stops outside.

Drinking & Nightlife

The Barrio del Carmen, the university area (around Avenidas de Aragón and Blasco Ibáñez), the area around the Mercado de Abastos and, in summer, the new port area and Malvarrosa are all jumping with bars and clubs.

Café de las Horas CAFE, BAR

(www.cafedelashoras.com; Calle Conde de Almodóvar 1; ⊙10am-2am;) Offers high baroque, tapestries, music of all genres, candelabras, bouquets of fresh flowers and a long list of exotic cocktails. It does themed Sunday brunches (11am to 4pm).

Jimmy Glass MUSIC BAR

(www.jimmyglassjazz.net; Calle Baja 28; ⊙8pm-2.30am Mon-Thu, 8pm-3.30am Fri & Sat) Playing jazz from the owner's vast CD collection, Jimmy Glass also sometimes has live performances. It's just what a jazz bar should be – dim and serving jumbo measures of high-octane cocktails.

Café Museu CAFE

(Calle Museo 7; ⊙9am-11pm Mon-Thu, 9am-1.30am Fri, 11am-1.30am Sat, 11am-11pm Sun;) A real forum for bohemian souls in the Carmen district, this grungy, edgy spot has an impressive cultural program including English/Spanish conversation sessions, regular live music, theatre and more. The terrace is a popular place to knock back a few beers.

Radio City CLUB

(www.radiocityvalencia.es; Calle de Santa Teresa 19; ⊙10.30pm-3.30am Tue-Sun) Almost as much mini-cultural centre as club, Radio City, always seething, pulls in the punters with activities including cinema, flamenco and dancing to an eclectic mix. Pick up a flyer here for its younger sister, **Music Box** (Calle del Pintor Zariñena 16; ⊙midnight-7am Tue-Sat), also in the Centro Histórico, which stays open until dawn.

Information

Regional Tourist Office (☎963 98 64 22; www.comunitatvalenciana.com; Calle de la Paz 48; ⊙10am-6pm Mon-Fri, to 2pm Sat) A fount of information about the Valencia region.

Turismo Valencia Tourist Office (VLC; ☎963 15 39 31; www.turisvalencia.es; Plaza de la Reina 19; ⊙9am-7pm Mon-Sat, 10am-2pm Sun) Has several other branches around town, including Plaza del Ayuntamiento (⊙9am-7pm Mon-Sat, 10am-2pm Sun), the AVE station and airport arrivals area.

Getting There & Away

AIR

Aeropuerto de Manises (VLC; ☎902 40 47 04) Valencia's airport is 10km west of the city centre along the A3, towards Madrid.

BOAT

Acciona Trasmediterránea (☎902 45 46 45; www.trasmediterranea.es) operates car and passenger ferries to Ibiza, Mallorca and Menorca.

BUS

ALSA (www.alsa.es) Numerous buses to/from Barcelona (€29 to €35, four to five hours) and Alicante (from €20.60, 2½ hours), most passing by Benidorm.

Avanza (www.avanzabus.com) Hourly bus services to/from Madrid (€29.40, four hours).

Bus Station (☎96 346 62 66) Valencia's bus station is beside the riverbed on Avenida Menéndez Pidal. Bus 8 connects it to Plaza del Ayuntamiento.

TRAIN

From Valencia's Estación del Norte, major destinations include Alicante (€17 to €30, 1¾ hours, 11 to 13 daily) and Barcelona (€40 to €44, three to 4¼ hours, at least 14 daily). The AVE, the high-speed train, now links Madrid and Valencia, with up to 15 high-speed services daily and a journey time of around 1¾ hours.

Getting Around

Metro line 5 connects the airport, city centre and port. The high-speed tram leaves from the FGV tram station, 500m north of the cathedral, at the Pont de Fusta. This is a pleasant way to get to the beach, the paella restaurants of Las Arenas and the port.

BALEARIC ISLANDS

The Balearic Islands (Illes Balears in Catalan) adorn the glittering Mediterranean waters off Spain's eastern coastline. Beach tourism destinations *par excellence,* each of the islands has a quite distinct identity and they have managed to retain much of their individual character and beauty. All boast beaches second to none in the Med, but each offers reasons for exploring inland, too.

Check out websites like www.illesbalears.es and www.platgesdebalears.com.

Getting There & Away

AIR

In summer, charter and regular flights converge on Palma de Mallorca and Ibiza from all over Europe.

Air Berlin (www.airberlin.com)

Air Europa (www.aireuropa.com)

Iberia (www.iberia.es)

Vueling (www.vueling.com)

BOAT

Acciona Trasmediterránea (902 454645; www.trasmediterranea.es)

Baleària (902 160180; www.balearia.com)

Iscomar (902 119128; www.iscomar.com)

Compare prices and look for deals at **Direct Ferries** (www.directferries.com).

The main ferry routes to the mainland:

Ibiza (Ibiza City) To/from Barcelona (Acciona Trasmediterránea, Baleària) and Valencia (Acciona Trasmediterránea)

Ibiza (Sant Antoni) To/from Denia, Barcelona and Valencia (Baleària)

Mallorca (Palma de Mallorca) To/from Barcelona and Valencia (Acciona Trasmediterránea, Baleària) and Denia (Baleària)

Menorca (Maó) To/from Barcelona and Valencia (Acciona Trasmediterránea, Baleària)

The main interisland ferry routes:

Ibiza (Ibiza City) To/from Palma de Mallorca (Acciona Trasmediterránea and Baleària)

Mallorca (Palma de Mallorca) To/from Ibiza City (Acciona Trasmediterránea and Baleària) and Maó (Acciona Trasmediterránea and Baleària)

Mallorca (Port d'Alcúdia) To/from Ciutadella (Iscomar and Baleària)

Menorca (Ciutadella) To/from Port d'Alcúdia (Iscomar and Baleària)

Menorca (Maó) To/from Palma de Mallorca (Acciona Trasmediterránea and Baleària)

Mallorca

The sunny, warm hues of the medieval heart of Palma de Mallorca, the archipelago's capital, make a great introduction to the islands. The northwest coast, dominated by the Serra de Tramuntana mountain range, is a beautiful region of olive groves, pine forests and ochre villages, with a spectacularly rugged coastline. Most of Mallorca's best beaches are on the north and east coasts, and although many have been swallowed up by tourist developments, you can still find the occasional exception.

Palma de Mallorca

Palma de Mallorca is a graceful Mediterranean city with some world-class attractions and equally impressive culinary and nightlife scenes.

Sights & Activities

★Catedral CATHEDRAL

(La Seu; www.catedraldemallorca.org; Carrer del Palau Reial 9; adult/child €6/free; 10am-6.15pm Mon-Fri, to 2.15pm Sat) Palma's vast cathedral is the city's major architectural landmark. Aside from its sheer scale and undoubted beauty, its stunning interior features, designed by Antoni Gaudí and renowned contemporary artist Miquel Barceló, make this unlike any cathedral elsewhere in the world. The awesome structure is predominantly Gothic, apart from the main facade, which is startling, quite beautiful and completely mongrel.

WORTH A TRIP

MENORCA

Renowned for its pristine beaches and archaeological sites, tranquil Menorca was declared a Biosphere Reserve by Unesco in 1993. **Maó** absorbs most of the tourist traffic. North of Maó, a drive across a lunar landscape leads to the lighthouse at **Cap de Favàritx**. South of the cape stretch some fine sandy bays and beaches, including **Cala Presili** and **Platja d'en Tortuga**, reachable on foot.

Ciutadella, with its smaller harbour and historic buildings, has a more distinctly Spanish feel to it and is the more attractive of the island's two main towns. A narrow country road leads south of Ciutadella (follow the 'Platges' sign from the *ronda*, or ring road) and then forks twice to reach some of the island's loveliest beaches: (from west to east) **Arenal de Son Saura**, **Cala en Turqueta**, **Es Talaier**, **Cala Macarelleta** and **Cala Macarella**. As with most beaches, you'll need your own transport.

In the centre of the island, the 357m-high **Monte Toro** has great views; on a clear day you can see Mallorca. On the northern coast, the picturesque town of **Fornells** is on a large bay popular with windsurfers.

The ports in both Maó and Ciutadella are lined with bars and restaurants.

Hostal-Residencia Oasis (☎630 018008; www.hostaloasismenorca.es; Carrer de Sant Isidre 33; d €40-66, tr €56-87, q €82-103; 📶) Run by delightful friendly owners, this quiet place is close to the heart of the old quarter. Rooms, mostly with bathroom, are set beside a spacious garden courtyard. Their furnishings, though still trim, are from deep into the last century.

Tres Sants (☎971 48 22 08; www.grupelcarme.com; Carrer Sant Cristòfol 2; s €140-175, d €180-210; ❄📶🏊) Buried deep in Ciutadella's medina-like heart, Tres Sants is a slice of breezy, boho cool. The owners' attentive eye for detail shines in this beautifully converted 18th-century manor house, with frescoed walls, candlelit passageways and whitewashed rooms with nice touches like four-poster beds, sunken bathtubs and iPod docks. The subterranean pool and steam bath evokes the hotel's Roman origins.

★Palau de l'Almudaina PALACE

(Carrer del Palau Reial; adult/child €9/4, audioguide €4, guided tour €6; ⏲10am-8pm Apr-Sep, to 6pm Oct-Mar) Originally an Islamic fort, this mighty construction opposite the Catedral was converted into a residence for the Mallorcan monarchs at the end of the 13th century. The King of Spain resides here still, at least symbolically. The royal family are rarely in residence, except for the occasional ceremony, as they prefer to spend summer in the Palau Marivent (in Cala Major). At other times you can wander through a series of cavernous stone-walled rooms that have been lavishly decorated.

★Palau March MUSEUM

(Carrer del Palau Reial 18; adult/child €4.50/free; ⏲10am-6.30pm Mon-Fri, to 2pm Sat) This house, palatial by any definition, was one of several residences of the phenomenally wealthy March family. Sculptures by 20th-century greats, such as Henry Moore, Auguste Rodin, Barbara Hepworth and Eduardo Chillida, grace the outdoor terrace. Within lie many more artistic treasures from some of Spain's big names in art, such as Salvador Dalí, and Barcelona's Josep Maria Sert and Xavier Corberó, as well as an extraordinary 18th-century Neapolitan baroque *belén* (nativity scene).

★Es Baluard GALLERY

(Museu d'Art Modern i Contemporani; www.esbaluard.org; Plaça de Porta de Santa Catalina 10; adult/child €6/free, temporary exhibitions €4; ⏲10am-8pm Tue-Sat, to 3pm Sun) Built with flair and innovation into the shell of the Renaissance-era seaward walls, this contemporary art gallery is one of the finest on the island. Its temporary exhibitions are worth viewing, but the permanent collection – works by Miró, Barceló and Picasso – give the gallery its cachet.

The 21st-century concrete complex is cleverly built among the fortifications, including the partly restored remains of an 11th-century Muslim-era tower (on your right as you arrive from Carrer de Sant Pere).

★ **Museu Fundación Juan March** GALLERY
(www.march.es/arte/palma; Carrer de Sant Miquel 11; ⊙10am-6.30pm Mon-Fri, 10.30am-2pm Sat) FREE This 17th-century mansion gives an insightful overview of Spanish contemporary art. On permanent display are some 70 pieces held by the Fundación Juan March. Together they constitute a veritable who's who of mostly 20th-century artists, including Miró, Juan Gris (of cubism fame), Dalí and the sculptors Eduardo Chillida and Julio González.

Sleeping

Hostal Pons GUESTHOUSE €
(☎971 72 26 58; www.hostalpons.com; Carrer del Vi 8, Palma de Mallorca; s €30, d €60-70, tr €85;) Bang in the heart of old Palma, this is a sweet, simple family-run guesthouse. Downstairs a cat slumbers in a plant-filled patio, upstairs you'll find a book-lined lounge and rooms with rickety bedsteads and tiled floors. Cheaper rooms share communal bathrooms. The roof terrace offers peaceful respite.

Misión de San Miguel BOUTIQUE HOTEL €€
(☎971 21 48 48; www.urhotels.com; Carrer de Can Maçanet 1, Palma de Mallorca; r €75-163, ste €115-203; P@) This 32-room boutique hotel is an astounding deal with stylish designer rooms; it does the little things well with firm mattresses and rain showers, although some rooms open onto public areas and can be a tad noisy. Its restaurant, Misa Braseria, is part of the Fosh group. Service is friendly and professional.

★ **Can Cera** BOUTIQUE HOTEL €€€
(☎971 71 50 12; http://cancerahotel.com; Carrer del Convent de Sant Francesc 8, Palma de Mallorca; r €165-495;) Welcome to one of Palma's most romantic boutique bolt-holes, entered via an inner courtyard, where cobbles have been worn smooth over 700 years and a wrought-iron staircase sweeps up to guest rooms that manage the delicate act of combining history with modern design flourishes. The decor is stylish but never overblown, with high ceilings, period furnishings and richly detailed throws.

Eating

Restaurant Celler Sa Premsa SPANISH €
(☎971 72 35 29; www.cellersapremsa.com; Plaça del Bisbe Berenguer de Palou 8; mains €9-14; ⊙12.30-4pm & 7.30-11.30pm Mon-Sat) A visit to this local institution is almost obligatory. It's a cavernous tavern filled with huge old wine barrels and has walls plastered with faded bullfighting posters – you find plenty such places in the Mallorcan interior but they're a dying breed here in Palma. Mallorcan specialities dominate the menu.

Can Cera Gastro Bar MEDITERRANEAN €€
(☎971 71 50 12; www.cancerahotel.com; Carrer del Convent de Sant Francesc 8; mains €14-22, menus €18-31; ⊙1-3.30pm & 7.30-10.30pm) How enchanting: this restaurant spills out into one of Palma's loveliest inner patios at the hotel of the same name, housed in a 13th-century *palacio*. Dine by lantern light on tapas or season-focused dishes such as watermelon and tomato gazpacho and creamy rice with aioli, saffron and calamari. Note the vertical garden that attracts plenty of attention from passers-by.

★ **Simply Fosh** MODERN EUROPEAN €€€
(☎971 72 01 14; www.simplyfosh.com; Carrer de la Missió 7A; mains €23-29, menus €21.50-76; ⊙1-3.30pm & 7-10.30pm Mon-Sat) Lovingly prepared Mediterranean cooking with a novel flourish is the order of the day at this 17th-century convent refectory, one of the home kitchens of chef Marc Fosh, whose CV twinkles with Michelin stars. A slick, monochrome interior and courtyard provide the backdrop for high-quality, reasonably priced menus. The three-course lunch menu for €21.50 is a terrific deal.

Information

Consell de Mallorca Tourist Office (☎971 17 39 90; www.infomallorca.net; Plaça de la Reina 2; ⊙8am-6pm Mon-Fri, 8.30am-3pm Sat;) Covers the whole island.

Main Municipal Tourist Office (☎971 72 96 34; www.imtur.es; Casal Solleric, Passeig d'es Born 27; ⊙9am-8pm) Tourist office.

Around Palma de Mallorca

Mallorca's northwestern coast is a world away from the high-rise tourism on the other side of the island. Dominated by the Serra de Tramuntana, it's a beautiful region of olive groves, pine forests and small villages with shuttered stone buildings. There are a couple of highlights for drivers: the hair-raising road down to the small port of **Sa Calobra**, and the amazing trip along the peninsula leading to the island's northern tip, **Cap Formentor**.

Sóller is a good place to base yourself for hiking and the nearby village of **Fornalutx** is one of the prettiest on Mallorca.

From Sóller, it's a 10km walk to the beautiful hilltop village of **Deià**, where Robert Graves, poet and author of *I Claudius,* lived for most of his life. From the village, you can scramble down to the small shingle beach of **Cala de Deià**. Boasting a fine monastery and pretty streets, **Valldemossa** is further southwest down the coast.

Further east, **Pollença** and **Artà** are attractive inland towns. Nice beaches include those at **Cala Sant Vicenç**, **Cala Mondragó** and around **Cala Llombards**.

Ibiza

Ibiza (Eivissa in Catalan) is an island of extremes. Its formidable party reputation is completely justified, with some of the world's greatest clubs attracting hedonists from the world over. The interior and northeast of the island, however, are another world. Peaceful country drives, hilly green territory, a sprinkling of mostly laid-back beaches and coves, and some wonderful inland accommodation and eateries are light years from the ecstasy-fuelled madness of the clubs that dominate the west.

Ibiza City

Sights & Activities

Ibiza City's port area of **Sa Penya** is crammed with funky and trashy clothing boutiques and arty-crafty market stalls. From here, you can wander up into **D'Alt Vila**, the atmospheric old walled town.

★Ramparts HISTORIC SITE
A ramp leads from Plaça de Sa Font in Sa Penya up to the **Portal de ses Taules**, the main entrance. Above it hangs a commemorative plaque bearing Felipe II's coat of arms and an inscription recording the 1585 completion date of the fortification – seven artillery bastions joined by thick protective walls up to 22m in height.

Catedral CATHEDRAL
(Plaça de la Catedral; ⏲9.30am-1.30pm & 3-8pm) Ibiza's cathedral elegantly combines several styles: the original 14th-century structure is Catalan Gothic, but the sacristy was added in 1592 and a major baroque renovation took place in the 18th century. Inside, the **Museu Diocesà** (admission €1.50; ⏲9.30am-1.30pm Tue-Sun, closed Dec-Feb) contains centuries of religious art.

Sleeping

Many of Ibiza City's hotels and *hostales* are closed in the low season and heavily booked between April and October. Make sure you book ahead.

Vara de Rey GUESTHOUSE €€
(☎971 30 13 76; www.hibiza.com; Passeig de Vara de Rey 7; s €50-65, d €65-115, ste €115-170; ❄) Housed in a restored town mansion, this boho-flavoured guesthouse sits on the tree-lined Passeig de Vara de Rey boulevard. The look is shabby-chic in rooms with touches like chandeliers, wrought-iron bedsteads and diffused light. Suites notch up the romance with four-poster beds and D'Alt Vila views.

Hostal Parque HOTEL €€
(☎971 30 13 58; www.hostalparque.com; Plaça des Parc 4; s €60-90, d €110-190, tr €150-190, q €180-240; ❄📶) Overlooking palm-dotted Plaça des Parc, this *hostal*'s rooms have recently been spruced up with boutique touches like wood floors, contemporary art and ultra-modern bathrooms. There's a price hike for Ático (penthouse) rooms, but their roof terraces with D'Alt Vila views are something else. Street-facing rooms might be a tad noisy for light sleepers.

★Urban Spaces DESIGN HOTEL €€€
(☎871 51 71 74; http://urbanspacesibiza.com; Carrer de la Via Púnica 32; ste €200-270; ❄📶) Ira Francis-Smith is the brains behind this design newcomer with an alternative edge. Some of the world's most prolific street artists (N4T4, INKIE, JEROM, et al) have pooled their creativity in the roomy, mural-splashed suites, with clever backlighting, proper workstations and balconies with terrific views. Extras like yoga on the roof terrace and clubber-friendly breakfasts until 1pm are surefire people-pleasers.

Eating

★Comidas Bar San Juan MEDITERRANEAN €
(Carrer de Guillem de Montgrí 8; mains €4-12; ⏲1-3.30pm & 8.30-11pm Mon-Sat) More traditional than trendy, this family-run operation, with two small dining rooms, harks back to the days before Ibiza became a byword for glam. It offers outstanding value, with fish dishes and steaks for around €10. It doesn't take

reservations, so arrive early and expect to have other people at the same table as you.

S'Ametller IBIZAN €€

(☎971 31 17 80; www.restaurantsametller.com; Carrer de Pere Francès 12; menus €22-35; ⏰1-4pm & 8pm-1am Mon-Sat, 8pm-1am Sun) The 'Almond Tree' specialises in local, market-fresh cooking. The daily menu (for dessert, choose the house *flaó,* a mint-flavoured variant on cheesecake and a Balearic Islands speciality) is inventive and superb value. S'Ametller also offers cookery courses – including one that imparts the secrets of that *flaó.*

El Olivo MEDITERRANEAN €€

(☎971 30 06 80; www.elolivoibiza.org; Plaça de Vila 7; mains €19-24, tapas menu €28; ⏰7pm-1am Tue-Sun) Standing head and shoulders above most places in D'Alt Vila, this slick little bistro has plenty of pavement seating. The menu goes with the seasons in clean, bright flavours as simple as rack of lamb in a fennel-mustard crust and octopus carpaccio drizzled in Ibizan olive oil – all delivered with finesse.

Drinking & Nightlife

Sa Penya is the nightlife centre. Dozens of bars keep the port area jumping. Alternatively, various bars at Platja d'en Bossa combine sounds, sand, sea and sangria.

Much cheaper than a taxi, the **Discobus** (www.discobus.es; per person €3; ⏰midnight-6am Jun-Sep) does an all-night whirl of the major clubs, bars and hotels in Ibiza City, Platja d'en Bossa, Sant Rafel, Es Canar, Santa Eulària and Sant Antoni.

Teatro Pereira LIVE MUSIC

(www.teatropereyra.com; Carrer del Comte de Rosselló 3; ⏰8am-4am) Away from the waterfront hubbub, this time warp is all stained wood and iron girders. It was once the foyer of the long-abandoned 1893 theatre at its rear. It's often packed and offers nightly live music.

CLUBBING IN IBIZA

From late May to the end of September, the west of the island is one big, nonstop dance party from sunset to sunrise and back again. Space, Pacha and Amnesia were all in *DJ Mag*'s top 10 in 2013.

The major clubs operate nightly from around midnight to 6am from mid-May or June to early October. Theme nights, fancy-dress parties and foam parties are regular features.

Entertainment Ibiza-style doesn't come cheaply. Admission can cost anything from €20 to €65 (mixed drinks and cocktails then go for around €10 to €15).

Space (www.space-ibiza.es; Platja d'en Bossa; admission €20-75; ⏰11pm-6am) In Platja d'en Bossa, aptly named Space can pack in as many as 40 DJs and up to 8000 clubbers and is considered one of the world's best clubs. Come for the terrace, electro and parties like We Love (Sundays) and Carl Cox (Tuesdays).

Pacha (www.pacha.com; Avinguda 8 d'Agost, Ibiza City; admission €20-70; ⏰11pm-6am) Going strong since 1973, Pacha is Ibiza's original glamourpuss – a cavernous club that can hold 3000 people. The main dance floor, a sea of mirror balls, heaves to deep techno. On the terrace, tunes are more relaxing. Cherry-pick your night: David Guetta works the decks at Thursday's F*** Me I'm Famous, while hippies groove at Tuesday's Flower Power.

Amnesia (www.amnesia.es; Carretera Ibiza a San Antonio Km 5, San Rafael; admission €35-75; ⏰midnight-6am) Amnesia's sound system gives your body a massage. Beats skip from techno to trance, while the decks welcome DJ royalty like Paul Van Dyk and Sven Väth. A huge glasshouse-like terrace surrounds the central dance area. Big nights include Cocoon (Mondays), Cream (Thursdays) and foam-filled Espuma (Wednesdays and Sundays).

Privilege (www.privilegeibiza.com; San Rafael; admission €20-50; ⏰11pm-6am) Welcome to the world's biggest club. Five kilometres along the road to San Rafael, Privilege is a mind-blowing space with 20 bars, an interior pool and capacity for 10,000 clubbers. The main domed dance temple is an enormous, pulsating area, where the DJ's cabin is suspended above the pool.

Bora Bora Beach Club BAR
(www.boraboraibiza.net; ⌚noon-6am May-Sep) At Platja d'en Bossa, 4km from the old town, this is *the* place – a long beachside bar where sun and fun worshippers work off hangovers and prepare new ones. Entry's free and the ambience is chilled, with low-key club sounds wafting over the sand.

Information

Tourist Office (☎971 39 92 32; www.eivissa.es; Plaça de la Catedral; ⌚10am-2pm & 6-9pm Mon-Sat, 10am-2pm Sun) Can provide audioguides to the city; bring your passport or identity document.

Around Ibiza City

Ibiza has numerous unspoiled and relatively undeveloped beaches. **Cala de Boix**, on the northeastern coast, is the only black-sand beach on the island, while further north are the lovely beaches of **S'Aigua Blanca**.

On the north coast near Portinatx, **Cala Xarraca** is in a picturesque, secluded bay, and near Port de Sant Miquel is the attractive **Cala Benirrás**.

In the southwest, **Cala d'Hort** has a spectacular setting overlooking two rugged rock islets, Es Verda and Es Verdranell.

The best thing about rowdy **Sant Antoni**, the island's second-biggest town and north of Ibiza City, is heading to the small rock-and-sand strip on the north shore to join hundreds of others for sunset drinks at a string of chilled bars. The best known remains **Café del Mar** (www.cafedelmarmusic.com; ⌚4pm-1am), our favourite, but it's further north along the pedestrian walkway.

Check out rural accommodation at www.ibizaruralvillas.com and www.casasruralesibiza.com (in Spanish). For more standard accommodation, start at www.ibizahotelsguide.com.

Local buses (www.ibizabus.com) run to most destinations between May and October.

ANDALUCÍA

Images of Andalucía are so potent, so quintessentially Spanish that it's sometimes difficult not to feel a sense of déjà vu. It's almost as if you've already been there in your dreams: a solemn Easter parade, an ebullient spring festival, exotic nights in the Alhambra. In the stark light of day, the picture is no less compelling.

Seville

POP 703,000

A sexy, gutsy and gorgeous city, Seville is home to two of Spain's most colourful festivals, fascinating and distinctive *barrios* (the Barrio de Santa Cruz is particularly memorable), and a local population that lives life to the fullest. A fiery place (as you'll soon see in its packed and noisy tapas bars), it's also hot climate-wise – avoid July and August!

Sights

Catedral & Giralda CHURCH
(www.catedraldesevilla.es; adult/child €9/free; ⌚11am-3.30pm Mon, 11am-5pm Tue-Sat, 2.30-6pm Sun) Seville's immense cathedral, officially the biggest in the world (by volume), is awe-inspiring in its scale and sheer majesty. It stands on the site of the great 12th-century Almohad mosque, with the mosque's minaret (the Giralda) still towering beside it.

★**Alcázar** CASTLE
(www.alcazarsevilla.org; adult/child €9.50/free; ⌚9.30am-7pm Apr-Sep, 9.30am-5pm Oct-Mar) If heaven really *does* exist, then let's hope it looks a little bit like the inside of Seville's Alcázar. Built primarily in the 1300s during the so-called 'dark ages' in Europe, the architecture is anything but dark. Indeed, compared to our modern-day shopping malls and throw-away apartment blocks, it could be argued that the Alcázar marked one of history's architectural high points. Unesco agreed, making it a World Heritage Site in 1987.

Archivo de Indias MUSEUM
(Calle Santo Tomás; ⌚9.30am-4.45pm Mon-Sat, 10am-2pm Sun) FREE On the western side of Plaza del Triunfo, the Archivo de Indias is the main archive on Spain's American empire, with 80 million pages of documents dating from 1492 through to the end of the empire in the 19th century – a most effective statement of Spain's power and influence during its Golden Age. A short film inside tells the full story of the building along with some fascinating original colonial maps and documents. The building was refurbished between 2003 and 2005.

★**Hospital de los Venerables Sacerdotes** GALLERY
(☎954 56 26 96; www.focus.abengoa.es; Plaza de los Venerables 8; adult/child €5.50/2.75, Sun afternoon free; ⌚10am-2pm & 4-8pm) Once

DON'T MISS

ALCÁZAR HIGHLIGHTS

Patio del León (Lion Patio) The garrison yard of the original Alcázar (p1068). Just off here is the Sala de la Justicia (Hall of Justice), with beautiful Mudéjar plasterwork and an *artesonado* (ceiling of interlaced beams with decorative insertions). It leads on to the pretty Patio del Yeso, which is part of the 12th-century Almohad palace reconstructed in the 19th century.

Patio de la Montería The rooms surrounding this patio are filled with interesting artefacts from Seville's history.

Cuarto Real Alto The Cuarto Real Alto (Upper Royal Quarters) are open for (heavily subscribed) tours several times a day. Highlights include the 14th-century Salón de Audiencias, still the monarch's reception room, and Pedro I's bedroom, with marvellous Mudéjar tiles and plasterwork.

Palacio de Don Pedro Also called the Palacio Mudéjar, it's the single most stunning architectural feature in Seville. At the heart of the palace is the wonderful Patio de las Doncellas (Patio of the Maidens), surrounded by beautiful arches, plasterwork and tiling. The Cámara Regia (King's Quarters), on the northern side of the patio, has stunningly beautiful ceilings and wonderful plaster- and tile work. From here you can move west into the little Patio de las Muñecas (Patio of the Dolls), the heart of the palace's private quarters, featuring delicate Granada-style decoration. The Cuarto del Príncipe (Prince's Room), to its north, has a superb wooden cupola ceiling trying to re-create a starlit night sky. The spectacular Salón de Embajadores (Hall of Ambassadors), at the western end of the Patio de las Doncellas, was the throne room. On the western side of the Salón de Embajadores is the beautiful Arco de Pavones.

Salones de Carlos V Reached via a staircase at the southeastern corner of the Patio de las Doncellas, these are the much-remodelled rooms of Alfonso X's 13th-century Gothic palace.

Patio del Crucero This patio outside the Salones de Carlos V was originally the upper storey of the patio of the 12th-century Almohad palace.

Gardens From the Salones de Carlos V you can go out into the Alcázar's large and sleepy gardens, some with pools and fountains.

a residence for aged priests, this 17th-century baroque mansion guards what is perhaps Seville's most typical *sevillano* patio – it's intimate, plant embellished and spirit-reviving. The building's other highlights are its 17th-century church, with rich religious murals, and the celebrated painting *Santa Rufina* by Diego Velázquez, which was procured for a hefty €12.5 million by the on-site Centro Velázquez foundation in 2007. Other roving art exhibitions provide an excellent support act.

Museo del Baile Flamenco MUSEUM

(www.museoflamenco.com; Calle Manuel Rojas Marcos 3; adult/senior & student €10/8; ⊙10am-7pm) The brainchild of *sevillana* flamenco dancer Cristina Hoyos, this museum spread over three floors of an 18th-century palace makes a noble effort to showcase the mysterious art, although at €10 a pop it is more than a little overpriced. Exhibits include sketches, paintings, photos of erstwhile (and contemporary) flamenco greats, plus a collection of dresses and shawls.

Centro de Interpretación Judería de Sevilla MUSEUM

(☎954 04 70 89; www.juderiadesevilla.es; Calle Ximenez de Enciso; admission €6.50; ⊙10.30am-3.30pm 5-8pm Mon-Sat, 10.30am-7pm Sun) A reinterpretation of Seville's weighty Jewish history has been long overdue and what better place to start than in the city's former Jewish quarter. This new museum is encased in an old Sephardic Jewish house in the higgledy-piggledy Santa Cruz quarter, the one-time Jewish neighbourhood that never recovered from a brutal pogrom and massacre carried out in 1391. The events of the pogrom and other historical happenings are catalogued inside along with a few surviving mementos including documents, costumes and books. It's small but poignant.

Seville

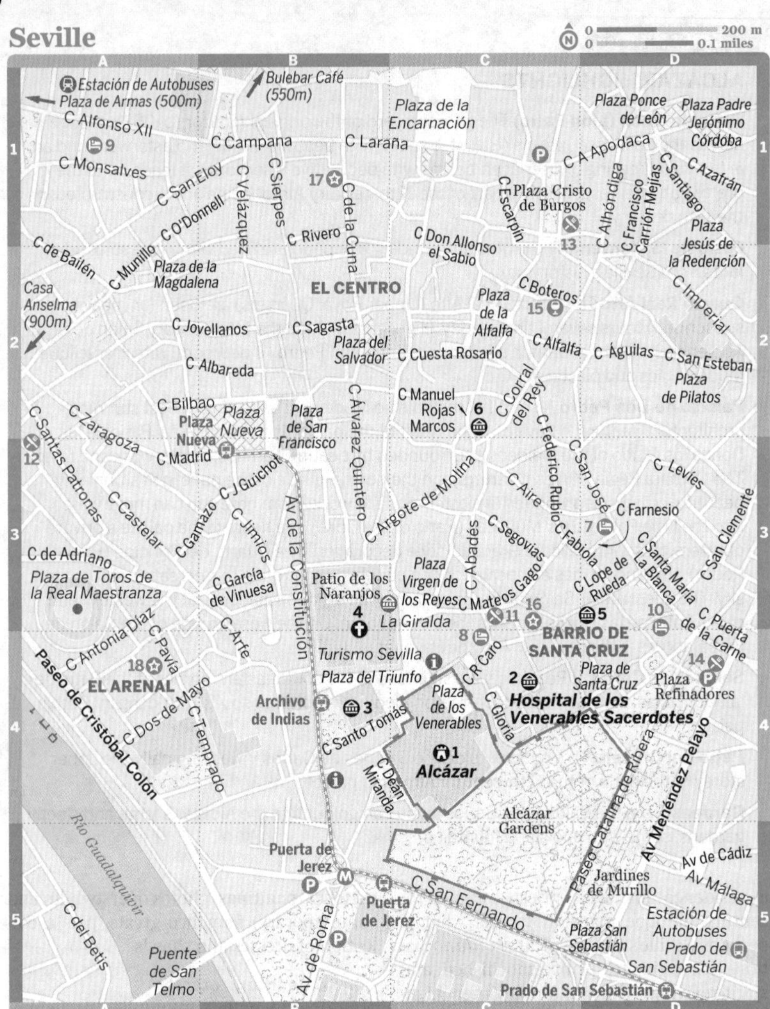

Festivals & Events

Semana Santa HOLY WEEK

(www.semana-santa.org) Every day from Palm Sunday to Easter Sunday, large, life-sized *pasos* (sculptural representations of events from Christ's Passion) are carried from Seville's churches through the streets to the cathedral, accompanied by processions that may take more than an hour to pass. The processions are organised by over 50 different *hermandades* or *cofradías* (brotherhoods, some of which include women).

Feria de Abril SPRING FAIR

The April fair, held in the second half of the month (sometimes edging into May), is the jolly counterpart to the sombre Semana Santa. The biggest and most colourful of all Andalucía's ferias is less invasive (and also less inclusive) than the Easter celebration. It takes place on El Real de la Feria, in the Los Remedios area west of the Río Guadalquivir.

Bienal de Flamenco FLAMENCO

(www.labienal.com; Sep) Most of the big names of the flamenco world participate in this major flamenco festival. Held in September in even-numbered years.

Seville

Sleeping

★ Oasis Backpackers' Hostel HOSTEL €

(☎955 26 26 96; www.oasissevilla.com; Calle Almirante Ulloa 1; dm/d incl breakfast €15/50;) It's not often you get to backpack in a palace. Seville's Oasis Backpackers', a veritable oasis in the busy city centre district, is a friendly welcoming hostel with some private room options, a cafe/bar, and a rooftop deck with a small pool.

★ Hotel Amadeus HOTEL €€

(☎954 50 14 43; www.hotelamadeussevilla.com; Calle Farnesio 6; s/d €100/114;) Just when you thought you could never find hotels with pianos in the rooms anymore, along came Hotel Amadeus. It's run by an engaging musical family in the old *judería* (Jewish quarter) where several of the astutely decorated rooms come complete with soundproofed walls and upright pianos, ensuring you don't miss out on your daily practice.

Un Patio en Santa Cruz HOTEL €€

(☎954 53 94 13; www.patiosantacruz.com; Calle Doncellas 15; s €65-85, d €65-120;) Feeling more like an art gallery than a hotel, this place has starched white walls coated in loud works of art, and strange sculptures and preserved plants. The rooms are immensely comfortable, staff are friendly, and there's a cool rooftop terrace with mosaic Moroccan tables. It's easily one of the hippest and best-value hotels in town.

★ Hotel Casa 1800 LUXURY HOTEL €€€

(☎954 56 18 00; www.hotelcasa1800sevilla.com; Calle Rodrigo Caro 6; r from €195;) Straight in at number one as Seville's favourite hotel is this newly revived Santa Cruz jewel where the word *casa* (house) is taken seriously. This really is your home away from home (albeit a posh one!), with charming staff catering for your every need. Highlights include a sweet afternoon tea buffet, plus a quartet of penthouse garden suites with Giralda views.

Eating

Bodega Santa Cruz TAPAS €

(Calle Mateos Gago; tapas €2; ⌚11.30am-midnight) Forever crowded and with a mountain of paper on the floor, this place is usually standing room only, with tapas and drinks enjoyed alfresco as you dodge the marching army of tourists squeezing through Santa Cruz's narrow streets.

Vinería San Telmo TAPAS, FUSION €€

(☎954 41 06 00; www.vineriasantelmo.com; Paseo Catalina de Ribera 4; tapas €3.50, media raciones €10; ⌚1-4.30pm & 8pm-midnight) San Telmo invented the *rascocielo* (skyscraper) tapa, an 'Empire State' of tomatoes, aubergine, goat's cheese and smoked salmon. If this and other creative nuggets such as foie gras with quail eggs and lychees, or exquisitely cooked bricks of tuna don't make you drool with expectation then you're probably dead.

★ La Brunilda TAPAS, FUSION €€

(☎954 22 04 81; Calle Galera 5; tapas €3.50-6.50; ⌚1-4pm & 8.30-11.30pm Tue-Sat, 1-4pm Sun) Seville's crown as Andalucía's tapas capital is regularly attacked by well-armed rivals from the provinces, meaning it constantly has to reinvent itself and offer up fresh competition. Enter Brunilda, a new font of fusion tapas sandwiched into an inconspicuous backstreet in the Arenal quarter where everything – including the food, staff and clientele – is pretty.

If you have unlimited appetite, try the whole menu. For those with smaller bellies, the creamy risotto is unmissable.

★**Los Coloniales** CONTEMPORARY ANDALUCIAN €€
(www.tabernacoloniales.es; cnr Calle Dormitorio & Plaza Cristo de Burgos; mains €10-12; ⏲12.30pm-12.15am) The quiet ones are always the best. It might not look like much from the outside, but take it on trust that Los Coloniales is something very special. The quality plates line up like models on a catwalk: *chorizo a la Asturiana,* a divine spicy sausage in an onion sauce served on a bed of lightly fried potato; eggplants in honey; and pork tenderloin *al whiskey* (a whisky-flavoured sauce).

Drinking & Nightlife

Bars usually open 6pm to 2am weekdays, 8pm till 3am at the weekend. Drinking and partying really get going around midnight on Friday and Saturday (daily when it's hot). In summer, dozens of open-air late-night bars *(terrazas de verano)* spring up along both banks of the river.

Plaza del Salvador is brimful of drinkers from mid-evening to 1am.

El Garlochi BAR
(Calle Boteros 4; ⏲10pm-6am) Dedicated entirely to the iconography, smells and sounds of Semana Santa, the ubercamp El Garlochi is a true marvel. A cloud of church incense hits you as you go up the stairs, and the faces of baby Jesus and the Virgin welcome you into the velvet-walled bar, decked out with more Virgins and Jesuses.

Bulebar Café BAR
(☎954 90 19 54; Alameda de Hércules 83; ⏲4pm-late) This place gets pretty *caliente* (hot) at night but is pleasantly chilled in the early evening, with friendly staff. Don't write off its spirit-reviving alfresco breakfasts that pitch earlybirds with up-all-nighters.

JAMÓN – A PRIMER

Unlike Italian prosciutto, Spanish *jamón* is a bold, deep red and well marbled with buttery fat. Like wines and olive oil, Spanish *jamón* is subject to a strict series of classifications. *Jamón serrano* refers to *jamón* made from white-coated pigs introduced to Spain in the 1950s. Once salted and semidried by the cold, dry winds of the Spanish sierra, most now go through a similar process of curing and drying in a climate-controlled shed for around a year. *Jamón serrano* accounts for approximately 90% of cured ham in Spain.

Jamón ibérico – more expensive and generally regarded as the elite of Spanish hams – comes from a black-coated pig indigenous to the Iberian Peninsula and a descendant of the wild boar. If the pig gains at least 50% of its body weight during the acorn-eating season, it can be classified as *jamón ibérico de bellota,* the most sought-after designation for *jamón*.

☆ Entertainment

Seville is arguably Spain's flamenco capital and you're most likely to catch a spontaneous atmosphere (of unpredictable quality) in one of the bars staging regular nights of flamenco with no admission fee. *Soleares,* flamenco's truest *cante jondo* (deep song), was first concocted in Triana; head here to find some of the more authentic clubs.

Tablao El Arenal FLAMENCO
(www.tablaoelarenal.com; Calle Rodo 7; admission with 1 drink €38, with dinner €72; ⏲restaurant from 7pm, shows 8pm & 10pm) Of the three places in Seville that offer flamenco dinner shows this – ask any local – is the best. A smaller seating capacity (100 compared to 600 at the Palacio Andaluz) offers greater intimacy, although, as a big venue, it still lacks the grit and – invariably – *duende* (flamenco spirit) of the *peñas* (small flamenco clubs).

Casa de la Memoria FLAMENCO
(☎954 56 06 70; www.casadelamemoria.es; Calle Cuna 6; €18; ⏲shows 7.30pm & 9pm) Neither a *tablao* nor a private *peña,* this cultural centre, recently relocated from Santa Cruz to El Centro where it is accommodated in the old stables of the Palacio de la Lebrija, offers what are, without doubt, the most intimate and authentic nightly flamenco shows in Seville.

It's perennially popular and space is limited to 100, so reserve tickets a day or so in advance by calling or visiting the venue.

Casa de la Guitarra FLAMENCO
(☎954 22 40 93; Calle Mesón del Moro 12; tickets adult/child €17/10; ⊙shows 7.30pm & 9pm) Tiny new flamenco-only venue in Santa Cruz (no food or drinks served) where a miscued step from the performing dancers would land them in the front row of the audience. Glass display cases filled with guitars of erstwhile flamenco greats adorn the walls.

Casa Anselma FLAMENCO
(Calle Pagés del Corro 49; ⊙midnight-late Mon-Sat) If you can squeeze in past the foreboding form of Anselma (a celebrated Triana flamenco dancer) at the door, you'll quickly realise that anything can happen in here. Casa Anselma is the antithesis of a tourist flamenco *tablao,* with cheek-to-jowl crowds, thick cigarette smoke, zero amplification and spontaneous outbreaks of dexterous dancing. Pure magic. (Beware: there's no sign, just a doorway embellished with *azulejos* tiles.)

Information

Tourist Office (Avenida de la Constitución 21B; ⊙9am-8pm Mon-Fri, 10am-2pm Sat & Sun, closed holidays) The staff at the Constitución office are well informed but often very busy.

Turismo Sevilla (www.turismosevilla.org; Plaza del Triunfo 1; ⊙10.30am-7pm Mon-Fri) Information on all Sevilla province.

Getting There & Away

AIR

Aeropuerto San Pablo (SVQ; www.sevilla-airport.com; ⊙24hr) Seville's airport, 7km east of the city, is Andalucía's second-busiest airport after Málaga's. Non-Spanish destinations include London, Paris, Amsterdam, Warsaw and Geneva. It is served by various budget airlines.

BUS

ALSA (www.alsa.es) Runs buses to Córdoba (€12, two hours), Granada (€23, three hours) amd Málaga (€18, 2¾ hours).

Estación de Autobuses Plaza de Armas (www.autobusesplazadearmas.es; Avenida del Cristo de la Expiración) Buses to/from the north of Sevilla province, Huelva province, Portugal and most other parts of Spain, including Madrid, leave from the main station, Estación de Autobuses Plaza de Armas. This is also the main station for Eurolines and international services to Germany, Belgium, France and beyond.

Estación de Autobuses Prado de San Sebastián (Plaza San Sebastián) Buses that do not leave from the main station, Estación de Autobuses Plaza de Armas – primarily those running inside Andalucía (except Huelva) – use the Estación de Autobuses Prado de San Sebastián. Buses from here run roughly hourly to Cádiz, Córdoba, Granada, Jerez de la Frontera, Málaga and Madrid.

TRAIN

Twenty or more superfast AVE trains, reaching speeds of 280km/h, whiz daily to/from Madrid (€76, 2½ hours). Other services include Cádiz (€16, 1¾ hours, 15 daily), Córdoba (€30, 42 minutes, more than 30 daily), Granada (€30, three hours, four daily) and Málaga (€43, two hours, 11 daily).

Estación Santa Justa (☎902 43 23 43; Avenida Kansas City) Seville's Estación Santa Justa is 1.5km northeast of the centre.

Córdoba

POP 328,000

Córdoba was once one of the most enlightened Islamic cities on earth, and enough remains to place it in the contemporary top three Andalucian draws. The centrepiece is the gigantic and exquisitely rendered Mezquita. Surrounding it is an intricate web of winding streets, geranium-sprouting flower boxes and cool intimate patios that are at their most beguiling in late spring.

Sights & Activities

★**Mezquita** MOSQUE
(☎957 47 05 12; www.mezquitadecordoba.org; Calle Cardenal Herrero; adult/child €8/4, 8.30-9.20am Mon-Sat free; ⊙8.30am-7pm Mon-Sat, 8.30-10am & 2-7pm Sun Mar-Oct, 8.30am-6pm Mon-Sat, 8.30-11.30am & 3-6pm Sun Nov-Feb) It's impossible to overemphasise the beauty of Córdoba's great mosque, with its remarkably peaceful and spacious interior. The Mezquita hints, with all its lustrous decoration, at a lavish and refined age when Muslims, Jews and Christians lived side by side and enriched their city and surroundings with a heady interaction of diverse and vibrant cultures.

Alcázar de los Reyes Cristianos CASTLE
(Castle of the Christian Monarchs; Campo Santo de Los Mártires; admission €4.50, Fri free; ⊙8.30am-8.45pm Tue-Fri, 8.30am-4.30pm Sat, 8.30am-2.30pm Sun; 👪) Built by Alfonso XI in the 14th century on the remains of Roman and Arab predecessors, the castle began life as a palace. It hosted both Fernando and Isabel, who

DON'T MISS

MEZQUITA HIGHLIGHTS

Puerta del Perdón Main entrance to the Mezquita (p1073), a 14th-century Mudéjar gateway on Calle Cardenal Herrero.

Prayer Hall Divided into 11 'naves' by lines of two-tier arches striped in red brick and white stone. Their simplicity and number give a sense of endlessness to the Mezquita.

Mihrab & Maksura The arches within and around the *maksura* (the area where the caliphs and their retinues would have prayed) are the mosque's most intricate and sophisticated, forming a forest of interwoven horseshoe shapes. The portal of the mihrab itself is a sublime crescent arch.

Patio de los Naranjos & Minaret Outside the mosque, the leafy, walled courtyard and its fountain were the site of ritual ablutions before prayer. The crowning glory of the whole complex was the minaret, which at its peak towered 48m (only 22m of the minaret still survives).

The Cathedral A 16th-century construction in the Mezquita's heart.

made their first acquaintance with Columbus here in 1486. Its terraced gardens – full of fish ponds, fountains, orange trees, flowers and topiary – are a pleasure to stroll and a joy to behold from the tower.

Centro Flamenco Fosforito MUSEUM

(☎957 48 50 39; www.centroflamencofosforito.cordoba.es; Plaza del Potro; admission €2; ⏲8.30am-7.30pm Tue-Fri, 8.30am-2.30pm Sat, 9.30am-2.30pm Sun) Possibly the best flamenco museum in Andalucía – which is saying something – this new place benefits from a fantastic location inside the ancient Posada del Potro, an inn named-checked by Cervantes in the novel, *Don Quijote de la Mancha*. Touch-screens, fantastic archive footage and arty displays meticulously explain the building blocks of flamenco and its history, along with the singers, guitarisits and dancers who defined it. You'll walk out both enthused *and* wiser.

Medina Azahara RUIN

(Madinat al-Zahra; admission €1.50, EU citizens free; ⏲10am-6.30pm Tue-Sat, to 8.30pm May-mid-Sep, to 2pm Sun) Even in the cicada-shrill heat and stillness of a summer afternoon, the Medina Azahara whispers of the power and vision of its founder, Abd ar-Rahman III. The self-proclaimed caliph began the construction of a magnificent new capital 8km west of Córdoba around 936, and took up full residence around 945. Medina Azahara was a resounding declaration of his status, a magnificent trapping of power. It was destroyed in the 11th century and just 10% of the site has been excavated.

A taxi costs €37 for the return trip, with one hour to view the site, or you can book a three-hour coach tour for €6.50 to €10 through many Córdoba hotels.

Hammam Baños Árabes BATHHOUSE

(☎957 48 47 46; cordoba.hammamalandalus.com; Calle del Corregidor Luis de la Cerda 51; bath/bath & massage €24/36; ⏲2hr sessions 10am, noon, 2pm, 4pm, 6pm, 8pm & 10pm) Follow the lead of the medieval Cordobans and dip your toe in these beautifully renovated Arab baths, where you can enjoy an aromatherapy massage, with tea, hookah and Arabic sweets in the cafe afterwards.

Sleeping

★ **Bed and Be** HOSTEL €

(☎661 420733; www.bedandbe.com; Calle Cruz Conde 22; dm/d with shared bathroom €19/60; ❄📶) Hugely engaging new accommodation thanks in part to the foresight of owner, José, who also runs free evening bike tours around the city. There's an assortment of double and dorm rooms, all superclean and as gleaming white as a *pueblo blanco*. Extra value is added with a kitchen, lounge area, roof terrace and various special events regularly organised by José.

Hotel Mezquita HOTEL €€

(☎957 47 55 85; www.hotelmezquita.com; Plaza Santa Catalina 1; s/d €42/74; ❄📶) One of the best deals in town, Hotel Mezquita stands right opposite its namesake monument, amid the bric-a-brac of the tourism zone. The 16th-century mansion has large, elegant rooms with marble floors, tall doors and balconies, some affording views of the great mosque.

Hotel Hacienda Posada de Vallina HOTEL €€

(☎957 49 87 50; www.hhposadadevallinacordoba.com; Calle del Corregidor Luís de la Cerda 83; r from €99; P ❄ @ ☎) In an enviable nook on the quiet side of the Mezquita (the building actually pre-dates it), this cleverly renovated hotel uses portraits and period furniture to enhance a plush and modern interior. There are two levels overlooking a salubrious patio and the rooms make you feel comfortable but in-period (ie medieval Córdoba). Columbus allegedly once stayed here.

Casa de los Azulejos HOTEL €€

(☎957 47 00 00; www.casadelosazulejos.com; Calle Fernando Colón 5; s/d incl breakfast from €85/107; ❄ @ ☎) Mexican and Andalucian styles converge in this stylish hotel, where the patio is all banana trees, ferns and potted palms bathed in sunlight. Colonial-style rooms feature tall antique doors, massive beds, walls in lilac and sky blue, and floors adorned with the beautiful old *azulejos* tiles that give the place its name.

Eating

Bar Santos TAPAS €

(Calle Magistral González Francés 3; tortilla €2.50; ⏲2pm-1.30am) The legendary Santos serves the best *tortilla de patatas* in town – and don't the *cordobeses* know it. Thick wedges are deftly cut from giant wheels of the stuff and customarily served with plastic forks on paper plates to take outside and gaze at the Mezquita. Don't miss it.

★Salmorejería Umami ANDALUCIAN, MODERN €€

(☎957 48 23 47; www.grupoumami.com; Calle Blanco Belmonte 6; mains €14-22; ⏲1-4pm & 8-11.30pm Mon-Sat, 1-4pm Sun) It's new, it's good and its celebrating what is probably Córdoba's most favourite dish, the locally concocted *salmonrejo,* a tomato-y version of gazpacho soup that's too thick to drink. The trick (cos there's always a trick) is that Umami does a good dozen versions of the recipe including avocado, Thai and green tea flavours. The main dishes are equally creative.

Casa Mazal JEWISH €€

(☎957 94 18 88; www.casamazal.com; Calle Tomás Conde 3; mains €12-15; ⏲12.30-4pm & 7.30-11pm) A meal here makes a fine complement to the nearby Casa de Sefarad museum, as it brings the Sephardic (Judeo-Spanish) tradition to the table. A sort of culinary diaspora, Sephardic dishes contain elements of Andalucian, Turkish, Italian and North African cuisine, with such varied items as Syrian lentil salad, honeyed eggplant fritters and *minas* (a matzo-based vegetarian lasagne) on the menu.

JEWISH CÓRDOBA

Jews were among the most dynamic and prominent citizens of Islamic Córdoba. The medieval *judería* (Jewish quarter), extending northwest from the Mezquita almost to Avenida del Gran Capitán, is today a maze of narrow streets and whitewashed buildings with flowery window boxes. Highlights include the following:

Sinagoga (Calle de los Judíos 20; ⏲9.30am-2pm & 3.30-5.30pm Tue-Sat, 9.30am-1.30pm Sun) Built in 1315, this is one of the few testaments to the Jewish presence in Andalucía, though it hasn't actually been used as a place of worship since the expulsion of Jews from Spain in 1492. It is decorated with some extravagant stuccowork that includes Hebrew inscriptions and intricate Mudéjar star and plant patterns.

Casa Andalusí (Calle de los Judíos 12; admission €2.50; ⏲10.30am-8.30pm, to 6.30pm Nov-Mar) The Casa Andalusí is a 12th-century house with a bit of an exaggerated, slightly tacky idea of Al-Andalus. It has a tinkling fountain in the patio and a variety of exhibits, mainly relating to Córdoba's medieval Muslim culture, as well as a Roman mosaic in the cellar, and a shop selling North African items.

Casa de Sefarad (www.casadesefarad.es; cnr Calle de los Judíos & Averroes; adult/reduced €4/3; ⏲11am-6pm Mon-Sat, 11am-2pm Sun) In the heart of the Judería, and once connected by underground tunnel to the Sinagoga, this small museum is devoted to the Sephardic-Judaic tradition in Spain. There is a refreshing focus on music, domestic traditions and the women intellectuals (poets, singers and thinkers) of Al-Andalus. A program of live music recitals and storytelling events runs most of the year.

Information

Municipal Tourist Office (Plaza de Judá Levi; 8.30am-2.30pm Mon-Fri)

Regional Tourist Office (Calle de Torrijos 10; 9am-7.30pm Mon-Fri, 9.30am-3pm Sat, Sun & holidays) A good source of information about Córdoba province; located inside the Palacio de Congresos y Exposiciones.

Getting There & Away

BUS

The **bus station** (957 40 40 40; www.estacionautobusescordoba.es; Glorieta de las Tres Culturas) is 1km northwest of Plaza de las Tendillas, behind the train station. Destinations include Seville (€10.36, 1¾ hours, six daily), Granada (€12.52, 2½ hours, seven daily) and Málaga (€12.75, 2¾ hours, five daily).

TRAIN

Córdoba's **train station** (957 40 02 02; Glorieta de las Tres Culturas) is on the high-speed AVE line between Madrid and Seville. Rail destinations include Seville (€10.60 to €32.10, 40 to 90 minutes, 23 or more daily), Madrid (€52 to €66.30, 1¾ to 6¼ hours, 23 or more daily), Málaga (€21 to €39.60, one to 2½ hours, nine daily) and Barcelona (€59.40 to €133, 10½ hours, four daily). For Granada (€34.30, four hours), change at Bobadilla.

Granada

ELEV 685M / POP 258,000

Granada's eight centuries as a Muslim capital are symbolised in its keynote emblem, the remarkable Alhambra, one of the most graceful architectural achievements in the Muslim world. Islam was never completely expunged here, and today it seems more present than ever in the shops, restaurants, tearooms and mosque of a growing North African community in and around the maze of the Albayzín. The tapas bars fill to bursting, while flamenco dives resound to the heart-wrenching tones of the south.

Sights & Activities

★Alhambra PALACE

(902 44 12 21; www.alhambra-tickets.es; adult/under 12yr €14/free, Generalife only €7; 8.30am-8pm 15 Mar-14 Oct, to 6pm 15 Oct-14 Mar, night visits 10-11.30pm Tue-Sat Mar-Oct, 8-9.30pm Fri & Sat Oct-Mar) The sheer red walls of the Alhambra rise from woods of cypress and elm. Inside is one of the more splendid sights of Europe, a network of lavishly decorated palaces and irrigated gardens, a World Heritage Site and the subject of scores of legends and fantasies.

★Capilla Real HISTORIC BUILDING

(www.capillarealgranada.com; Calle Oficios; admission €4; 10.15am-1.30pm & 3.30-6.30pm Mon-Sat, 11am-1.30pm & 2.30-5.30pm Sun) The Royal Chapel adjoins Granada's cathedral and is an outstanding Christian building. Catholic Monarchs Isabel and Fernando commissioned this elaborate Isabelline Gothic–style mausoleum. It was not completed until 1521; they were temporarily interred in the Convento de San Francisco.

Museo Sefardi MUSEUM

(958 22 05 78; www.museosefardidegranada.es; Placeta Berrocal 5; admission €5; 10am-2pm & 5-9pm) Expelled en masse in 1492, there are very few Sephardic Jews left living in Granada today. But this didn't stop one enterprising couple from opening up a museum to their memory in 2013, the year that the Spanish government began offering Spanish citizenship to any Sephardic Jew who could prove their Iberian ancestry. The museum is tiny,

DON'T MISS

ALHAMBRA HIGHLIGHTS

Palacios Nazaríes The central palace complex is the pinnacle of the Alhambra's design, a harmonious synthesis of space, light, shade, water and greenery that sought to conjure the gardens of paradise for the rulers who dwelt here.

Patio de los Leones (Courtyard of the Lions) Glorious, recently restored patio with exceptional rooms around the perimeter.

Palacio de Carlos V Renaissance-era circle-in-a-square ground plan. Inside, the Museo de la Alhambra has a collection of Alhambra artefacts.

Generalife From the Arabic *jinan al-'arif* (the overseer's gardens), the Generalife is a soothing arrangement of pathways, patios, pools, fountains, tall trees and, in season, flowers of every imaginable hue.

ALHAMBRA TICKETS

Up to 6600 tickets to the Alhambra are available for each day. About one-third of these are sold at the ticket office on the day, but they sell out early and you need to start queuing by 7am to be reasonably sure of getting one. It's highly advisable to book in advance (€1.40 extra per ticket).

For internet or phone bookings you need a Visa card, MasterCard or Eurocard. You receive a reference number, which you must show, along with your passport, national identity card or credit card, at the Alhambra ticket office when you pick up the ticket on the day of your visit.

The Palacios Nazaríes are open for night visits, good for atmosphere rather than detail.

Buses 30, 32 and (less directly) 34 run from near Plaza Nueva from 7am to 11pm, stopping at the ticket office and in front of the Alhambra Palace. By car, follow 'Alhambra' signs from the highway to the car park, just uphill from the ticket office.

Alhambra Advance Booking (☎902 888001, for international calls +34 958 92 60 31; www.alhambra-tickets.es) Book online or by phone.

Servicaixa (www.servicaixa.com) Buy tickets in advance from Servicaixa cash machines.

but the artefacts are interesting and they're given extra resonance spike by the vivid historical portrayal related by the owners.

Albayzín

On the hill facing the Alhambra across the Darro valley, Granada's old Muslim quarter, the Albayzín, is an open-air museum in which you can lose yourself for a whole morning. The cobblestone streets are lined with gorgeous *cármenes* (large mansions with walled gardens, from the Arabic karm for garden). It survived as the Muslim quarter for several decades after the Christian conquest in 1492.

Palacio de Dar-al-Horra PALACE
(Callejón de las Monjas) Close to the Placeta de San Miguel Bajo, off Callejón del Gallo and down a short lane, is the 15th-century Palacio de Dar-al-Horra, a romantically dishevelled mini-Alhambra that was home to the mother of Boabdil, Granada's last Muslim ruler.

Calle Calderería Nueva STREET
Linking the upper and lower parts of the Albayzín, Calle Calderería Nueva is a narrow street famous for its *teterías* (tearooms), but also a good place to shop for slippers, hookahs, jewellery and North African pottery from an eclectic cache of shops redolent of a Moroccan souk.

Colegiata del Salvador CHURCH
(Plaza del Salvador; admission €0.75; ⏲10am-1pm & 4.30-6.30pm) Plaza del Salvador, near the top of the Albayzín, is dominated by the Colegiata del Salvador, a 16th-century church on the site of the Albayzín's former main mosque, the patio of which still survives at the church's western end.

Mirador San Nicolás LOOKOUT
(Callejón de San Cecilio) Callejón de San Cecilio leads to the Mirador San Nicolás, a lookout with unbeatable views of the Alhambra and Sierra Nevada. Come back here later for sunset (you can't miss the trail then!). At any time of day take care: skilful, well-organised wallet-lifters and bag-snatchers operate here. Don't be put off; there is still a terrific atmosphere with buskers and local students intermingling with camera-touting travellers.

Sleeping

Hotel Posada del Toro BOUTIQUE HOTEL €
(☎958 22 73 33; www.posadadeltoro.com; Calle de Elvira 25; r from €54; ❄📶) A lovely small hotel with rooms set around a tranquil central patio. Walls are washed in a delectable combination of pale pistachio, peach and cream, and the rooms are similarly enticing with parquet floors, stucco detailing Alhambra-style, rustic-style furniture and small but perfectly equipped bathrooms with double sinks and hydromassage showers. The

Granada

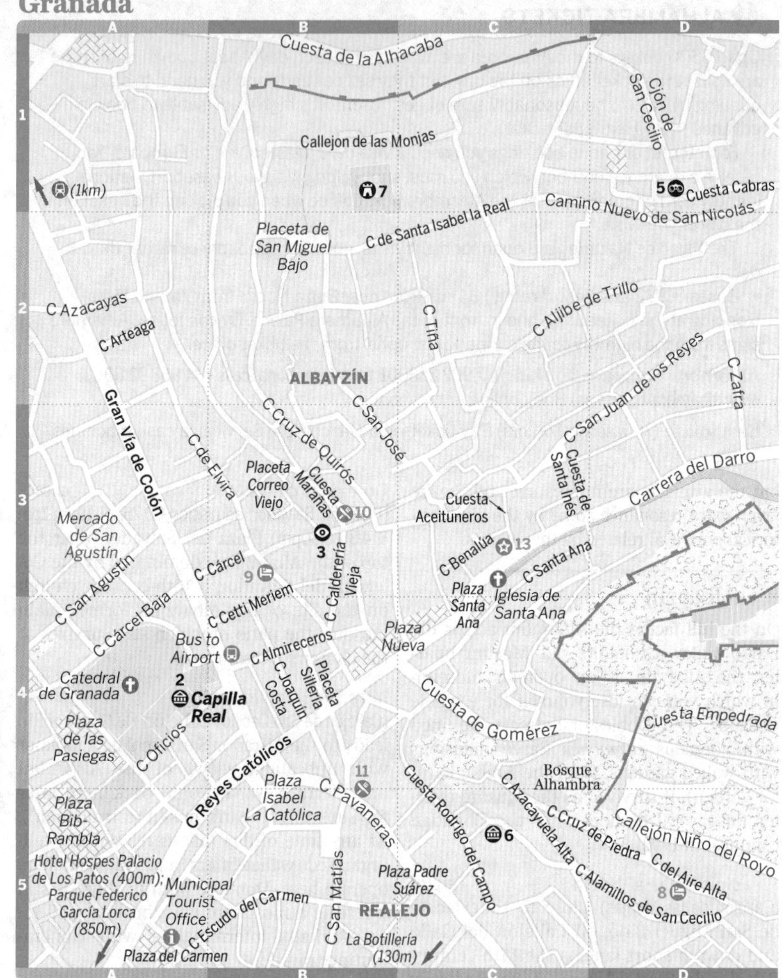

restaurant serves up Spanish dishes like Galician octopus, as well as pastas and pizza.

★Carmen de la Alcubilla del Caracol HISTORIC HOTEL €€
(☎958 21 55 51; www.alcubilladelcaracol.com; Calle del Aire Alta 12; s/d €100/120;) This exquisitely decorated place is located on the slopes of the Alhambra. Rooms are washed in pale pastel colours contrasting with cool cream and antiques. There are fabulous views and a pretty terraced garden. Ask for the room in the tower for a truly heady experience.

★Hotel Hospes Palacio de Los Patos LUXURY HOTEL €€€
(☎958 53 57 90; www.hospes.com; Solarillo de Gracia 1; r/ste €200/400; P) Put simply, the best hotel in Granada – if you can afford it – offering lucky guests sharp modernity and exemplary service in a palatial Unesco-protected building. You could write a novella about the many memorable features: the grand staircase, the postmodern chandeliers, the Arabian garden, the Roman emperor spa, the roses they leave on your bed in the afternoon.

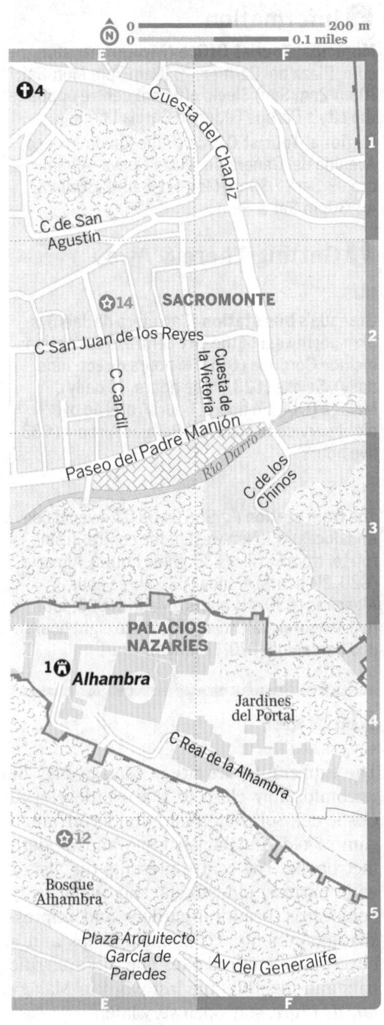

Granada

Top Sights
1 Alhambra E4
2 Capilla Real A4

Sights
3 Calle Calderería Nueva B3
4 Colegiata del Salvador E1
5 Mirador San Nicolás D1
6 Museo Sefardi C5
7 Palacio de Dar-al-Horra B1

Sleeping
8 Carmen de la Alcubilla del Caracol D5
9 Hotel Posada del Toro B3

Eating
10 Arrayanes B3
11 Carmela Restaurante B4

Entertainment
12 Casa del Arte Flamenco E5
13 Le Chien Andalou C3
14 Peña La Platería E2

Eating

Granada is one of the last bastions of that fantastic practice of free tapas with every drink, and some have an international flavour. The labyrinthine Albayzín holds a wealth of eateries tucked away in the narrow streets. Calle Calderería Nueva is a fascinating muddle of *teterías* and Arabic-influenced takeaways.

★ Arrayanes MOROCCAN €€
(958 22 84 01; www.rest-arrayanes.com; Cuesta Marañas 4; mains €15; 1.30-4.30pm & 7.30-11.30pm Sun-Fri, 1.30-4.30pm Sat;) The best Moroccan food in a city that is well known for its Moorish throwbacks? Recline on lavish patterned seating, try the rich, fruity tagine casseroles and make your decision. Note that Arrayanes does not serve alcohol.

★ La Botillería TAPAS, FUSION €€
(958 22 49 28; Calle Varela 10; mains €13-20; 1pm-1am Wed-Sun, 1-8pm Mon) Establishing a good reputation for nouveau tapas, La Botillería is just around the corner from the legendary La Tana bar, to which it has family connections. It's a more streamlined modern place than its cousin, where you can *tapear* (eat tapas) at the bar or sit down for the full monty Andalucian style. The *solomillo* (pork tenderloin) comes in a rich, wine-laden sauce.

Carmela Restaurante TAPAS, ANDALUCIAN €€
(958 22 57 94; www.restaurantecarmela.com; Calle Colcha 13; tapas €5-10; 12.30pm-midnight) Long a bastion of traditional tapas, Granada has taken a leaf out of Seville's book in this new streamlined restaurant guarded by the statue of Jewish philosopher, Yehuba ibn Tibon, at the jaws of the Realejo quarter. Best of the new breed is the made-to-order tortilla and cured ham croquettes the size of tennis balls.

ANDALUCÍA'S QUIETEST BEACHES

The coast east of Almería in eastern Andalucía is perhaps the last section of Spain's Mediterranean coast where you can have a beach to yourself. This is Spain's sunniest region – even in late March it can be warm enough to strip off and take in the rays. The best thing about the region is the wonderful coastline and semidesert scenery of the **Cabo de Gata** promontory. All along the 50km coast from El Cabo de Gata village to Agua Amarga, some of the most beautiful and empty beaches on the Mediterranean alternate with precipitous cliffs and scattered villages. The main village is laid-back **San José**, with excellent beaches nearby, such as Playa de los Genoveses and Playa de Mónsul.

☆ Entertainment

Peña La Platería FLAMENCO
(www.laplateria.org.es; Placeta de Toqueros 7) Buried in the Albayzín warren, Peña La Platería claims to be the oldest flamenco aficionados' club in Spain. It's a private affair, though, and not always open to nonmembers. Performances are usually Thursday and Saturday at 10.30pm – look presentable, and speak a little Spanish at the door, if you can.

Casa del Arte Flamenco FLAMENCO
(☎958 56 57 67; www.casadelarteflamenco.com; Cuesta de Gomérez 11; tickets €18; ⊙shows 7.30pm & 9pm) Just what Granada needed. A new small flamenco venue that is neither *tablao* nor *peña*, but something in between. The peformers are invariably top-notch; the atmosphere depends on the tourist-aficonado ration in the audience.

Le Chien Andalou FLAMENCO
(www.lechienandalou.com; Carrera del Darro 7; admission €6; ⊙shows 9.30pm & 11.30pm) This is one of Granada's most atmospheric venues to enjoy some vigorous castanet-clicking flamenco with a varied and professional line-up of musicians and dancers throughout the week. The cave-like surroundings of a renovated *aljibe* (well) create a fittingly moody setting and the whole place has a more genuine feel to it than the Sacramonte coach-tour traps. Book through the website.

ℹ Information

Municipal Tourist Office (www.granadatur.com; Plaza del Carmen; ⊙10am-7pm Mon-Sat, 10am-2pm Sun) Sleek, efficient centre opposite the city's Parque Federico García Lorca.

Regional Tourist Office (Pabellón de Acceso, Avenida del Generalife, Plaza Nueva, Alhambra; ⊙8am-7.30pm Mon-Fri, 8am-2.30pm & 4-7.30pm Sat & Sun)

ℹ Getting There & Away

BUS

Granada's **bus station** (Carretera de Jaén) is 3km northwest of the city centre. Destinations include Córdoba (€15, 2¾ hours direct, nine daily), Seville (€23, three hours, 10 daily), Málaga (€14, 1¾ hours, hourly) and an overnight service to Madrid's Barajas Airport (€33, five hours).

TRAIN

The **train station** (☎958 24 02 02; Avenida de Andaluces) is 1.5km west of the centre. Trains run to/from Seville (€30, three hours), Almería (€20, 2¼ hours), Ronda (€20, three hours), Algeciras (€30, 4½ hours), Madrid (€68, four to five hours), Valencia (€32, 7½ to eight hours) and Barcelona (€70, 12 hours).

Málaga

POP 558,000

The exuberant port city of Málaga may be uncomfortably close to the overdeveloped Costa del Sol, but it's a wonderful amalgam of old Andalucian town and modern metropolis. The centre presents the visitor with narrow, old streets and wide, leafy boulevards, beautiful gardens and impressive monuments, fashionable shops and a burgeoning cultural life. The city's terrific bars and nightlife, the last word in Málaga *joie de vivre*, stay open very late.

Sights & Activities

★**Museo Picasso Málaga** MUSEUM
(☎902 44 33 77; www.museopicassomalaga.org; Calle San Agustín 8; adult/child €7/3.50; ⊙10am-8pm Tue-Thu & Sun, to 9pm Fri & Sat) The Museo Picasso has an enviable collection of 204 works, 155 donated and 49 loaned to the museum by Christine Ruiz-Picasso (wife of Paul, Picasso's eldest son) and Bernard Ruiz-Picasso (his grandson), and includes some wonderful paintings of the family, including the heartfelt *Paulo con gorro blanco*

(Paulo with a white cap), a portrait of Picasso's eldest son painted in the 1920s.

Don't miss the Phoenician, Roman, Islamic and Renaissance archaeological remains in the museum's basement, discovered during construction works.

★Catedral de Málaga CATHEDRAL
(☎952 21 59 17; Calle Molina Lario; cathedral & museum €3.50; ⏲10am-6pm Mon-Sat, closed holidays) Málaga's cathedral was started in the 16th century when several architects set about transforming the original mosque. Of this, only the **Patio de los Naranjos** survives, a small courtyard of fragrant orange trees where the ablutions fountain used to be. The fabulous domed ceiling soars 40m into the air, while the vast colonnaded nave houses an enormous cedar-wood choir. Aisles give access to 15 chapels with gorgeous retables and a stash of 18th-century religious art.

★Alcazaba CASTLE
(Calle Alcazabilla; admission €2.10, incl Castillo de Gibralfaro €3.40; ⏲9.30am-8pm Tue-Sun Apr-Oct) No time to visit Granada's Alhambra? Then Málaga's Alcazaba can provide a taster. The entrance is next to the **Roman amphitheatre**, from where a meandering path climbs amid lush greenery: crimson bougainvillea, lofty palms, fragrant jasmine bushes and rows of orange trees. Extensively restored, this palace-fortress dates from the 11th-century Moorish period and the caliphal horseshoe arches, courtyards and bubbling fountains are evocative of this influential period in Málaga's history.

Museo de Arte Flamenco MUSEUM
(☎952 22 13 80; www.museoflamencojuanbreva.com; Calle Juan Franquelo 4; suggested donation €1; ⏲10am-2pm Tue-Sun) Fabulously laid-out over two floors in the HQ of Málaga's oldest and most prestigious *peña*, this collection of fans, costumes, posters and other flamenco paraphernalia is testimony to the city's illustrious flamenco scene.

Casa Natal de Picasso MUSEUM
(www.fundacionpicasso.malaga.eu; Plaza de la Merced 15; admission €3; ⏲9.30am-8pm) For a more intimate insight into the painter's childhood, head to the Casa Natal de Picasso, the house where Picasso was born in 1881, which now acts as a study foundation. The house has a replica 19th-century artist's studio and small quarterly exhibitions of Picasso's work. Personal memorabilia of Picasso and his family make up part of the display.

Castillo de Gibralfaro CASTLE
(admission €2.10; ⏲9am-9pm Apr-Sep, to 6pm Oct-Mar) One remnant of Málaga's Islamic past is the craggy ramparts of the Castillo de Gibralfaro, spectacularly located high on the hill overlooking the city. Built by Abd ar-Rahman I, the 8th-century Cordoban emir, and later rebuilt in the 14th century when Málaga was the main port for the emirate of Granada, the castle originally acted as a lighthouse and military barracks. Nothing much is original in the castle's interior, but the airy walkway around the ramparts affords the best views over Málaga.

★Museo Carmen Thyssen MUSEUM
(www.carmenthyssenmalaga.org; Calle Compañia 10; adult/child €6/free; ⏲10am-7.30pm Tue-Sun) One of the city's latest museums opened in 2011 in an aesthetically renovated 16th-century palace in the heart of the city's historic centre, the former old Moorish quarter of Málaga. The extensive collection concentrates on 19th-century Spanish and Andalucian art and includes paintings by some of the country's most exceptional painters, including Joaquín Sorolla y Bastida, Ignacio Zuloaga and Francisco de Zurbarán. Temporary exhibitions similarly focus on 19th-century art.

Beaches BEACHES
Sandy city beaches stretch several kilometres in each direction from the port. **Playa de la Malagueta**, handy to the city centre, has some excellent bars and restaurants close by. **Playa de Pedregalejo** and **Playa del Palo**, about 4km east of the centre, are popular and reachable by bus 11 from Paseo del Parque.

Sleeping

Hotel Carlos V HOTEL €
(☎952 21 51 20; www.hotel-carlosvmalaga.com; Calle Císter 10; s/d €36/59; P❄@) Close to the cathedral and Picasso museum, the Carlos V is enduringly popular. Renovated in 2008, bathrooms sparkle in their uniform of cream-and-white tiles. Excellent standard for the price plus helpful staff make this hotel a winner.

El Hotel del Pintor BOUTIQUE HOTEL €€
(☎952 06 09 81; www.hoteldelpintor.com; Calle Álamos 27; s/d €54/69; ❄@🛜) The red, black and white colour scheme of this friendly,

WORTH A TRIP

RONDA

Perched on an inland plateau riven by the 100m fissure of El Tajo gorge and surrounded by the beautiful Serranía de Ronda, Ronda, a two-hour drive west of Málaga, is the most dramatically sited of Andalucía's *pueblos blancos* (white villages). The **Plaza de Toros** (built 1785), considered the national home of bullfighting, is a mecca for aficionados; inside is the small but fascinating Museo Taurino. The amazing 18th-century **Puente Nuevo** (New Bridge) is an incredible engineering feat crossing the gorge to the originally Muslim Old Town (La Ciudad).

Casa del Rey Moro (House of the Moorish King; Calle Santo Domingo 17; admission €4; ⏲10am-7pm) The terraces give access to La Mina, an Islamic stairway of over 300 steps that are cut into the rock all the way down to the river at the bottom of the gorge. These steps enabled Ronda to maintain water supplies when it was under attack. It was also the point where Christian troops forced entry in 1485. The steps are not well lit and are steep and wet in places. Take care.

Enfrente Arte (☎952 87 90 88; www.enfrentearte.com; Calle Real 40, Ronda; r incl breakfast €80-90; ❄@☒) On an old cobblestoned street, Belgian-owned Enfrente offers a huge range of facilities and funky modern/oriental decor. It has a bar, pool, sauna, recreation room, flowery patio with black bamboo, film room and fantastic views out to the Sierra de las Nieves. What's more, the room price includes all drinks, to which you help yourself, and a sumptuous buffet breakfast.

Parador de Ronda (☎952 87 75 00; www.parador.es; Plaza de España; r €160-171; P❄@☎☒) Acres of shining marble and deep-cushioned furniture give this modern *parador* a certain appeal. The terrace is a wonderful place to drink in views of the gorge with your coffee or wine, especially at night.

Bodega San Francisco (www.bodegasanfrancisco.com; Calle Ruedo Alameda; raciones €6-10; ⏲1.30-5pm & 8pm-1am Wed-Mon) With three dining rooms and tables spilling out onto the narrow pedestrian street, this may well be Ronda's top tapas bar. The menu is vast and should suit the fussiest of families, even vegetarians with nine-plus salad choices. Try the *revuelto de patatas* (scrambled eggs with potatoes and peppers). House wine is good.

Municipal Tourist Office (www.turismoderonda.es; Paseo de Blas Infante; ⏲10am-7.30pm Mon-Fri, 10.15am-2pm & 3.30-6.30pm Sat, Sun & holidays) Helpful and friendly staff with a wealth of information on the town and region.

small hotel echoes the abstract artwork of *malagueño* (person from Málaga) artist Pepe Bornov, whose paintings are on permanent display throughout the public areas and rooms. Although convenient for most of the city's main sights, the rooms in the front can be noisy, especially on a Saturday night.

Eating

Most of the best eating places are sandwiched in the narrow streets between Calle Marqués de Larios and the cathedral.

El Piyayo TAPAS €

(☎952 22 90 57; www.entreplatos.es; Calle Granada 36; raciones €6-10; ⏲12.30pm-midnight) A popular traditionally tiled bar and restaurant, famed for its *pescaitos fritos* (fried fish) and typical local tapas, including wedges of crumbly Manchego cheese, the ideal accompaniment to a glass of hearty Rioja wine. The *berenjenas con miel de caña* (aubergine with molasses) are also good.

★ **El Mesón de Cervantes** TAPAS, ARGENTINIAN €€

(☎952 21 62 74; www.elmesondecervantes.com; Calle Álamos 11; mains €13-16; ⏲7pm-midnight Wed-Mon) Once a secret, then a whisper, now loud shout, Cervantes has catapulted itself into Málaga's *numero uno* restaurant among a growing number of impressed bloggers, tweeters and anyone else with taste buds and an internet connection.

It started as a humble tapas bar run by expat Argentinian, Gabriel Spatz (the original bar is still operating around the corner), but has now expanded into plush new digs with an open kitchen, fantastic family-style service and – no surprises – incredible meat dishes.

✪ Entertainment

Peña Juan Breva FLAMENCO
(Calle Juan Franquelo 4) You'll feel like a gatecrasher at someone else's party at this private *peña,* but persevere; the flamenco is *muy puro.* Watch guitarists who play like they've got 12 fingers and listen to singers who bellow forth as if their heart has been broken the previous night. There's no set schedule. Ask about dates when/if you visit the on-site Museo Arte de Flamenco.

Kelipe FLAMENCO
(☎692 829885; www.kelipe.net; Calle Pena 11; admission €20-35; ⏰shows 9pm Thu-Sat) Málaga's substantial flamenco heritage has its nexus to the northwest of Plaza de la Merced. Kelipe is a flamenco centre which puts on *muy puro* performances Thursday to Saturday; entry of €15 includes one drink and tapa – reserve ahead. Kelipe also runs intensive weekend courses in guitar and dance.

ℹ Information

Municipal Tourist Office (www.malagaturismo.com) main branch (Plaza de la Marina); Casita del Jardinero (Avenida de Cervantes 1; ⏰9am-8pm Mar-Sep, to 6pm Oct-Feb)

ℹ Getting There & Away

AIR

Málaga-Costa del Sol Airport (www.aena.es) Málaga's busy airport, the main international gateway to Andalucía, receives flights by dozens of airlines from around Europe.

BUS

Málaga's **bus station** (☎952 35 00 61; www.estabus.emtsam.es; Paseo de los Tilos) is 1km southwest of the city centre. Frequent buses go to Seville (€18, 2½ hours), Granada (€11, 1½ to two hours), Córdoba (€15, three hours) and Ronda (€9.50, 2½ hours).

TRAIN

The main station, **Málaga María Zambrano Train Station** (www.renfe.es; Explanada de la Estación), is around the corner from the bus station. The superfast AVE service runs to Madrid (€80, 2½ hours, 10 daily). Trains also go to Córdoba (€41, one hour, 18 daily) and Seville (€43, two hours, 11 daily).

EXTREMADURA

Cáceres

POP 95,925

The Ciudad Monumental (Old Town) of Cáceres is truly extraordinary. Narrow cobbled streets twist and climb among ancient stone walls lined with palaces and mansions, while the skyline is decorated with turrets, spires, gargoyles and enormous storks' nests. Protected by defensive walls, it has survived almost intact from its 16th-century heyday. At dusk or after dark, when the crowds have gone, you'll feel like you've stepped back into the Middle Ages.

◉ Sights

Concatedral de Santa María CATHEDRAL
(Plaza de Santa María; admission €1; ⏰10am-2pm & 5.30-9pm Mon-Sat, 9.30-11.50am & 5.30-7.15pm Sun) The Concatedral de Santa María, a 15th-century Gothic cathedral, creates an impressive opening scene on the Plaza de Santa María. At its southwestern corner is a modern **statue of San Pedro de Alcántara**, a 16th-century *extremeño* ascetic (his toes worn shiny by the hands and lips of the faithful). Inside, there's a magnificent carved 16th-century cedar **altarpiece**, several fine noble tombs and chapels, and a small ecclesiastical **museum**. Climb the **bell tower** for views over the old town.

★**Torre de Bujaco** TOWER
(Plaza Mayor; adult/child €2/free; ⏰10am-2pm & 5.30-8.30pm Mon-Sat, 10am-2pm Sun) As you climb up the steps to the Ciudad Monumental from the **Plaza Mayor**, turn left to climb the 12th-century Torre de Bujaco, home to an interpretative display. From the top there's a fine stork's-eye view of the Plaza Mayor.

Sleeping & Eating

★**Hotel Casa Don Fernando** BOUTIQUE HOTEL €€
(☎927 21 42 79; www.casadonfernando.com; Plaza Mayor 30; d €50-150; P ❄ 📶) The classiest midrange choice in Cáceres, this boutique hotel sits on Plaza Mayor directly opposite the Arco de la Estrella. Spread over four floors, the designer rooms and bathrooms are tastefully chic; superior rooms (€30 more than the standards) have the best plaza views (although nights can be noisy especially on

WORTH A TRIP

MOROCCO

At once African and Arab, visible from numerous points along Spain's Andalucian coast, Morocco is an exciting detour from your Western European journey. The country's attractions are endless, from the fascinating souqs and medieval architecture of Marrakesh and Fès to the Atlantic charms of Asilah and Essaouira, from the High Atlas and Rif Mountains to the soulful sand dunes of the Sahara. For further information, head to shop.lonelyplanet.com to purchase Lonely Planet's *Morocco* guide.

Casablanca and Marrakesh in particular are well-connected by air to numerous European cities, while car-and-passenger ferry services connect Tangier with Algeciras, Barcelona, Gibraltar and Tarifa, with an additional service between Nador and Almería.

weekends). Attic-style top-floor rooms are good for families.

★Restaurante Torre de Sande
FUSION €€

(☎927 21 11 47; www.torredesande.com; Calle Condes 3; set menus €25-35; ⏲1-4pm & 7pm-midnight Tue-Sat, 1-4pm Sun) Dine in the pretty courtyard on dishes like *salmorejo de cerezas del Jerte con queso de cabra* (cherry-based cold soup with goat's cheese) at this elegant gourmet restaurant in the heart of the Ciudad Monumental. More modestly, stop for a drink and a tapa at the interconnecting *tapería* (tapas bar).

Information

Main Tourist Office (☎927 01 08 34; www.turismoextremadura.com; Plaza Mayor 3; ⏲8.30am-2.30pm & 4-6pm Mon-Fri, 10am-2pm Sat & Sun) Opens later in the afternoon in summer.

Regional Tourist Office (☎927 25 55 97; www.turismocaceres.org; Palacio Carvajal, Calle Amargura 1; ⏲8am-8.45pm Mon-Fri, 10am-1.45pm & 5-7.45pm Sat, 10am-1.45pm Sun) Covers Cáceres province and city.

Getting There & Away

BUS

The **bus station** (Carretera de Sevilla; ⏲927 23 25 50) has services to Trujillo (€4.63, 40 minutes) and Mérida (€5.63, one hour).

TRAIN

Up to five trains per day run to/from Madrid (€27 to €32, four hours) and Mérida (€6, one hour).

SURVIVAL GUIDE

Directory A–Z

ACCOMMODATION

Budget options include everything from dorm-style youth hostels to family-style *pensiones* and slightly better-heeled *hostales*. At the upper end of this category you'll find rooms with air-conditioning and private bathrooms. Mid-range *hostales* and hotels are more comfortable and most offer standard hotel services. Business hotels, trendy boutique hotels and luxury hotels are usually in the top-end category.

Camping

Spain has around 1000 officially graded *campings* (camping grounds) and they vary greatly in service, cleanliness and style. They're officially rated as 1st class (1ªC), 2nd class (2ªC) or 3rd class (3ªC). Camping grounds usually charge per person, per tent and per vehicle – typically €5 to €10 for each. Many camping grounds close from around October to Easter.

Campings Online (www.campingsonline.com/espana) Booking service.

Campinguía (www.campinguia.com) Comments (mostly in Spanish) and links.

Guía Camping (www.guiacampingfecc.com) Online version of the annual *Guía Camping* (€13.60), which is available in bookshops around the country.

Hotels, Hostales & Pensiones

Most options fall into the categories of hotels (one to five stars, full amenities), *hostales* (high-end guesthouses with private bathroom; one to

COUNTRY FACTS

Area 505,370 sq km

Capital Madrid

Country Code ☎34

Currency Euro (€)

Emergency ☎112

Languages Spanish (Castilian), Catalan, Basque, Galician (Gallego)

Money ATMs everywhere

Population 47 million

Visas Schengen rules apply

three stars) or *pensiones* (guesthouses, usually with shared bathroom; one to three stars).

Paradores (☎ in Spain 902 54 79 79; www.parador.es) Among the more tempting hotels for those with a little fiscal room to manoeuvre are the 90 or so *paradores*, a state-funded chain of hotels in often stunning locations, among them towering castles and former medieval convents.

Youth Hostels

Albergues juveniles (youth hostels) are cheap places to stay, especially for lone travellers. Expect to pay from €15 to €28 per night, depending on location, age and season.

Red Española de Albergues Juveniles (REAJ, Spanish Youth Hostel Network; www.reaj.com) Spain's Hostelling International (HI) organisation, Red Española de Albergues Juveniles, has around 250 youth hostels throughout Spain. Official hostels require HI membership (you can buy a membership card at virtually all hostels) and some have curfews.

ACTIVITIES

Hiking

- Pick up Lonely Planet's *Walking in Spain* and read about some of the best treks in the country.
- Maps by Editorial Alpina are useful for hiking, especially in the Pyrenees. Buy at bookshops, sports shops and sometimes at petrol stations near hiking areas.
- GR (*Grandes Recorridos*, or long-distance) trails are indicated with red-and-white markers.

Skiing

Skiing is cheaper but less varied than in much of the rest of Europe. The season runs from December to mid-April. The best resorts are in the Pyrenees, especially in northwest Catalonia and in Aragón. The Sierra Nevada in Andalucía offers the most southerly skiing in Western Europe.

Surfing, Windsurfing & Kitesurfing

The Basque Country has good surf spots, including San Sebastián, Zarautz and the legendary left at Mundaka. Tarifa, with its long beaches and ceaseless wind, is generally considered to be the windsurfing capital of Europe. It's also a top spot for kitesurfing.

BUSINESS HOURS

Banks 8.30am to 2pm Monday to Friday; some also open 4pm to 7pm Thursday and 9am to 1pm Saturday

Central post offices 8.30am to 9.30pm Monday to Friday, 8.30am to 2pm Saturday

Nightclubs midnight or 1am to 5am or 6am

Restaurants lunch 1pm to 4pm, dinner 8.30pm to midnight or later

SLEEPING PRICE RANGES

Our reviews refer to double rooms with a private bathroom, except in hostels or where otherwise specified. Quoted rates are for high season, which is generally May to September (though this varies greatly from region to region).

€ less than €65 (€75 in Madrid & Barcelona)

€€ €65 to €140 (€75 to €200 in Madrid/Barcelona)

€€€ more than €140 (€200 in Madrid & Barcelona)

Shops 10am to 2pm and 4.30pm to 7.30pm or 5pm to 8pm Monday to Saturday; big supermarkets and department stores generally open from 10am to 10pm Monday to Saturday

GAY & LESBIAN TRAVELLERS

Homosexuality is legal in Spain. In 2005 the Socialists gave the country's conservative Catholic foundations a shake with the legalisation of same-sex marriages in Spain. Lesbians and gay men generally keep a fairly low profile, but are quite open in the cities. Madrid, Barcelona, Sitges, Torremolinos and Ibiza have particularly lively scenes.

INTERNET ACCESS

- Wi-fi is increasingly available at most hotels and in some cafes, restaurants and airports; generally (but not always) free.
- Good cybercafes are increasingly hard to find; ask at the local tourist office. Prices per hour range from €1.50 to €3.

INTERNET RESOURCES

Fiestas.net (www.fiestas.net) Festivals around the country.

Lonely Planet (www.lonelyplanet.com/spain) Destination information, hotel bookings, traveller forums and more.

Renfe (Red Nacional de los Ferrocarriles Españoles; www.renfe.com) Spain's rail network.

Tour Spain (www.tourspain.org) Culture, food and links to hotels and transport.

Turespaña (www.spain.info) Spanish tourist office's site.

LANGUAGE COURSES

Popular places to learn Spanish: Barcelona, Granada, Madrid, Salamanca and Seville.

Escuela Oficial de Idiomas (EOI; www.eeooiinet.com) The Escuela Oficial de Idiomas is a nationwide institution teaching Spanish and other local languages. On the website's opening

ESSENTIAL FOOD & DRINK

- **Paella** This signature rice dish comes in infinite varieties, although Valencia is its true home.
- **Cured meats** Wafer-thin slices of *chorizo, lomo, salchichón* and *jamón serrano* appear on most Spanish tables.
- **Tapas** These bite-sized morsels range from uncomplicated Spanish staples to pure gastronomic innovation.
- **Olive oil** Spain is the world's largest producer of olive oil.
- **Wine** Spain has the largest area of wine cultivation in the world. La Rioja and Ribera del Duero are the best-known wine-growing regions.

page, hit 'Centros' under 'Comunidad' and then 'Centros en la Red' to get to a list of schools.

MONEY

- Many credit and debit cards can be used for withdrawing money from *cajeros automáticos* (automatic teller machines) that display the relevant symbols such as Visa, MasterCard, Cirrus etc.
- Most banks will exchange major foreign currencies and offer the best rates. Ask about commissions and take your passport.
- Credit and debit cards can be used to pay for most purchases. You'll often be asked to show your passport or some other form of identification, or to type in your pin. The most widely accepted cards are Visa and MasterCard.
- Exchange offices, indicated by the word *cambio* (exchange), offer longer opening hours than banks, but worse exchange rates and higher commissions.
- In Spain, value-added tax (VAT) is known as IVA (*ee*-ba; *impuesto sobre el valor añadido*). Visitors are entitled to a refund of the 21% IVA on purchases costing more than €90.16 from any shop if they are taking them out of the EU within three months.
- Menu prices include a service charge. Most people leave some small change. Taxi drivers don't have to be tipped but a little rounding up won't go amiss.
- Travellers cheques can be changed (for a commission) at most banks and exchange offices.

PUBLIC HOLIDAYS

The two main periods when Spaniards go on holiday are Semana Santa (the week leading up to Easter Sunday) and July or August. At these times accommodation can be scarce and transport heavily booked.

There are at least 14 official holidays a year – some observed nationwide, some locally. The following are national holidays:

Año Nuevo (New Year's Day) 1 January
Viernes Santo (Good Friday) March/April
Fiesta del Trabajo (Labour Day) 1 May
La Asunción (Feast of the Assumption) 15 August
Fiesta Nacional de España (National Day) 12 October
La Inmaculada Concepción (Feast of the Immaculate Conception) 8 December
Navidad (Christmas) 25 December

Regional governments set five holidays and local councils two more. The following are common dates:

Epifanía (Epiphany) or **Día de los Reyes Magos** (Three Kings' Day) 6 January
Día de San José (St Joseph's Day) 19 March
Jueves Santo (Good Thursday) March/April. Not observed in Catalonia and Valencia.
Corpus Christi June. The Thursday after the eighth Sunday after Easter Sunday.
Día de San Juan Bautista (Feast of St John the Baptist) 24 June
Día de Santiago Apóstol (Feast of St James the Apostle) 25 July
Día de Todos los Santos (All Saints Day) 1 November
Día de la Constitución (Constitution Day) 6 December

SAFE TRAVEL

Most visitors to Spain never feel remotely threatened, but a sufficient number have unpleasant experiences to warrant an alert. The main thing to be wary of is petty theft (which may of course not seem so petty if your passport, cash, travellers cheques, credit card and camera go missing). Stay alert and you can avoid most thievery techniques. Barcelona, Madrid and Seville are the worst offenders, as are popular beaches in summer (never leave belongings unattended).

EATING PRICE RANGES

Each eating review is accompanied by one of the following symbols (the price relates to a main course).

€ less than €10

€€ €10 to €20

€€€ more than €20

TELEPHONE

Blue public payphones are common and fairly easy to use. They accept coins, phonecards and, in some cases, credit cards. Phonecards come in €6 and €12 denominations and, like postage stamps, are sold at post offices and tobacconists.

International reverse-charge (collect) calls are simple to make: dial ☎900 99, followed by the appropriate code. For example: ☎900 99 00 61 for Australia, ☎900 99 00 44 for the UK, ☎900 99 00 11 (AT&T) for the USA etc.

To speak to an English-speaking Spanish international operator, dial ☎1008 (for calls within Europe) or ☎1005 (rest of the world).

Mobile Phones

All Spanish mobile phone companies (Telefónica's MoviStar, Orange and Vodafone) offer *prepagado* (prepaid) accounts for mobiles. The SIM card costs from €10, which includes some prepaid phone time.

Mobile phone numbers in Spain start with the number ☎6.

Phone Codes

Telephone codes in Spain are an integral part of the phone number. All numbers are nine digits and you just dial that nine-digit number.

Numbers starting with ☎900 are national toll-free numbers, while those starting ☎901 to ☎905 come with varying costs; most can only be dialled from within Spain. In a similar category are numbers starting with ☎800, ☎803, ☎806 and ☎807.

TOURIST INFORMATION

Most towns and large villages of any interest have a helpful *oficina de turismo* (tourist office) where you can get maps and brochures.

Turespaña (www.spain.info) Turespaña is the country's national tourism body.

VISAS

Spain is one of 26 member countries of the Schengen Convention and Schengen visa rules apply.

Citizens or residents of EU & Schengen countries No visa required.

Citizens or residents of Australia, Canada, Israel, Japan, New Zealand and the USA No visa required for tourist visits of up to 90 days.

Other countries Check with a Spanish embassy or consulate.

To work or study in Spain A special visa may be required – contact a Spanish embassy or consulate before travel.

Getting There & Away

Flights, cars and tours can be booked online at lonelyplanet.com.

ENTERING THE COUNTRY

Immigration and customs checks usually involve a minimum of fuss, although there are exceptions. Your vehicle could be searched on arrival from Morocco; they're looking for controlled substances. Expect long delays at these borders, especially in summer.

The tiny principality of Andorra is not in the EU, so border controls (and rigorous customs checks for contraband) remain in place.

AIR

Flights from all over Europe, including numerous budget airlines, serve main Spanish airports. All of Spain's airports share the user-friendly website and flight information telephone number of **Aena** (☎902 404704; www.aena.es), the national airports authority. For more information on each airport on Aena's website, choose English and click on the drop-down menu of airports. Each airport's page has details on practical information (such as parking and public transport) and a full list of (and links to) airlines using that airport.

Madrid's Aeropuerto de Barajas is Spain's busiest (and Europe's fifth-busiest) airport. Other major airports include Barcelona's Aeroport del Prat and the airports of Palma de Mallorca, Málaga, Alicante, Girona, Valencia, Ibiza, Seville, Bilbao and Zaragoza.

LAND

Spain shares land borders with France, Portugal and Andorra.

Bus

Aside from the main cross-border routes, numerous smaller services criss-cross Spain's borders with France and Portugal. Regular buses connect Andorra with Barcelona (including winter ski buses and direct services to the airport) and other destinations in Spain (including Madrid) and France.

Avanza (☎902 020999; www.avanzabus.com) Avanza runs a Lisbon to Madrid service (€42.10, 7½ hours, two daily).

Eurolines (www.eurolines.com) Eurolines is the main operator of international bus services to Spain from most of Western Europe and Morocco. Services from France include Nice to Madrid, and Paris to Barcelona.

Train

In addition to the options listed below, two or three TGV (high-speed) trains leave from

Paris-Montparnasse for Irún, where you change to a normal train for the Basque Country and on towards Madrid.

There are plans for a high-speed rail link between Madrid and Paris. In the meantime, high-speed services travel via Barcelona.

Paris to Madrid (€198 to €228, 9¾ to 17½ hours, five daily) The slow route runs via Les Aubrais, Blois, Poitiers, Irún, Vitoria, Burgos and Valladolid. It may be quicker to take the high-speed AVE train to Barcelona and change from there.

Paris to Barcelona (from €59, 6½ hours, two daily) A recently inaugurated high-speed service runs via Valence, Nimes, Montpellier, Beziers, Narbonne, Perpignan, Figueres and Girona. High-speed services also run from Lyon (from €49, five hours) and Toulouse (from €39, three hours).

Montpellier to Lorca (€79.55, 12 to 13 hours, daily) Talgo service along the Mediterranean coast via Girona, Barcelona, Tarragona and Valencia.

Lisbon to Madrid (chair/sleeper class from €36/50, nine to 10¾ hours, daily)

Lisbon to Irún (chair/sleeper class €41/56, 14 hours, daily)

Oporto to Vigo (from €14.75, 2¼ hours, two daily)

SEA

Acciona Trasmediterránea (☎902 454645; www.trasmediterranea.es) Most Mediterranean ferry services are run by the Spanish national ferry company, Acciona Trasmediterránea.

Brittany Ferries (☎0871 244 0744; www.brittany-ferries.co.uk) Services between Spain and the UK.

Grandi Navi Veloci (Map p1038; ☎in Italy 010 209 4591; www1.gnv.it; Ⓜ Drassanes) High-speed luxury ferries between Barcelona and Genoa.

Grimaldi Ferries (Map p1038; ☎902 53 13 33, in Italy 081 496 444; www.grimaldi-lines.com; Ⓜ Drassanes) Barcelona to Civitavecchia (near Rome), Livorno (Tuscany) and Porto Torres (northwest Sardinia).

LD Lines (www.ldlines.co.uk) Gijón-Saint-Nazaire (France) and Gijón-Poole (UK).

ℹ Getting Around

Students and seniors are eligible for discounts of 30% to 50% on most types of transport within Spain.

AIR

Air Europa (www.aireuropa.com) Madrid to Ibiza, Palma de Mallorca, Vigo, Bilbao and Barcelona as well as other routes between Spanish cities.

Iberia (www.iberia.com) Spain's national airline and its subsidiary, Iberia Regional-Air Nostrum, have an extensive domestic network.

Ryanair (www.ryanair.com) Some domestic Spanish routes include Madrid to Palma de Mallorca.

Volotea (www.volotea.com) Budget airline that flies domestically and internationally. Domestic routes take in Ibiza, Palma de Mallorca, Málaga, Valencia, Vigo, Bilbao, Zaragoza and Oviedo (but not Madrid or Barcelona).

Vueling (www.vueling.com) Spanish low-cost company with loads of domestic flights within Spain, especially from Barcelona.

BOAT

Regular ferries connect the Spanish mainland with the Balearic Islands.

BUS

Spain's bus network is operated by countless independent companies and reaches into the most remote towns and villages. Many towns and cities have one main bus station where most buses arrive and depart.

It is not necessary, and often not possible, to make advance reservations for local bus journeys. It is, however, a good idea to turn up at least 30 minutes before the bus leaves to guarantee a seat. For longer trips, you can and should buy your ticket in advance.

ALSA (☎902 422242; www.alsa.es) The biggest player, this company has routes all over the country in association with various other companies.

Avanza (☎902 020999; www.avanzabus.com) Operates buses from Madrid to Extremadura, western Castilla y León and Valencia via eastern Castilla-La Mancha (eg Cuenca), often in association with other companies.

Socibus & Secorbus (☎902 229292; www.socibus.es) These two companies jointly operate services between Madrid and western Andalucía, including Cádiz, Córdoba, Huelva and Seville.

CAR & MOTORCYCLE

Spain's roads vary enormously but are generally good. Fastest are the *autopistas;* on some, you have to pay hefty tolls.

Every vehicle should display a nationality plate of its country of registration and you must always carry proof of ownership of a private vehicle.

Third-party motor insurance is required throughout Europe.

A warning triangle and a reflective jacket (to be used in case of breakdown) are compulsory.

Automobile Associations

Real Automóvil Club de España (RACE; ☑902 404545; www.race.es) The Real Automóvil Club de España is the national automobile club. They may well come to assist you in case of a breakdown, but in any event you should obtain an emergency telephone number for Spain from your own insurer.

Driving Licences

All EU member states' driving licences are recognised. Other foreign licences should be accompanied by an International Driving Permit (although in practice local licences are usually accepted). These are available from automobile clubs in your country and valid for 12 months.

Hire

To rent a car in Spain you have to have a licence, be aged 21 or over and have a credit or debit card. Rates vary widely: the best deals tend to be in major tourist areas, including airports. Prices are especially competitive in the Balearic Islands.

FERRIES TO SPAIN

A useful website for comparing routes and finding links to the relevant ferry companies is www.ferrylines.com.

From Algeria

ROUTE	DURATION	FREQUENCY
Ghazaouet to Almería	8 hr	four weekly

From France

ROUTE	DURATION	FREQUENCY
Saint-Nazaire to Gijón	15-16 hr	three weekly

From Italy

ROUTE	DURATION	FREQUENCY
Genoa to Barcelona	18 hr	three weekly
Civitavecchia (near Rome) to Barcelona	20½ hr	six to seven weekly
Livorno (Tuscany) to Barcelona	19½ hr	three weekly
Porto Torres (Sardinia) to Barcelona	12 hr	daily

From Morocco

ROUTE	DURATION	FREQUENCY
Tangier to Algeciras	90 min	up to eight daily
Tangier to Barcelona	24-35 hr	weekly
Tangier to Tarifa	35 min	up to eight daily
Nador to Almería	6 hr	up to three daily

From the UK

ROUTE	DURATION	FREQUENCY
Plymouth to Santander	20 hr	weekly
Portsmouth to Santander	24 hr	weekly
Portsmouth to Bilbao	24 hr	twice weekly
Poole to Gijón	25 hr	weekly

CONNECTIONS

Spanish airports are among Europe's best connected, while the typical overland route leads many travellers from France over the Pyrenees into Spain. Rather than taking the main road/rail route along the Mediterranean coast (or between Biarritz and San Sebastián), you could follow lesser known, pretty routes over the mountains. There's nothing to stop you carrying on to Portugal: numerous roads and the Madrid–Lisbon rail line connect the two countries.

The most obvious sea journeys lead across the Strait of Gibraltar to Morocco (p1084). The most common routes connect Algeciras or Tarifa with Tangier, from where there's plenty of transport deeper into Morocco. Car ferries also connect Barcelona with Italian ports.

There are two main rail lines to Spain from Paris, one to Madrid via the Basque Country, and another to Barcelona; both are to be upgraded to a high-speed service. The latter connects with services to the French Riviera and Switzerland.

Road Rules

- The blood-alcohol limit is 0.05%.
- The legal driving age for cars is 18. The legal driving age for motorcycles and scooters is 16 (80cc and over) or 14 (50cc and under). A licence is required.
- Motorcyclists must use headlights at all times and wear a helmet if riding a bike of 125cc or more.
- Drive on the right.
- In built-up areas, the speed limit is 50km/h (and in some cases, such as inner-city Barcelona, 30km/h), which increases to 100km/h on major roads and up to 120km/h on *autovías* and *autopistas* (toll-free and tolled dual-lane highways, respectively). Cars towing caravans are restricted to a maximum speed of 80km/h.

TRAIN

The national railway company is **Renfe** (☎902 243402; www.renfe.com). Trains are mostly modern and comfortable, and late arrivals are the exception rather than the rule. The high-speed network is in constant expansion.

Passes are valid for all long-distance Renfe trains; Inter-Rail users pay supplements on Talgo, InterCity and AVE trains. All pass-holders making reservations pay a small fee.

Among Spain's numerous types of trains:

Alaris, Altaria, Alvia, Arco and Avant Long-distance intermediate-speed services.

Cercanías For short hops and services to outlying suburbs and satellite towns in Madrid, Barcelona and 11 other cities.

Euromed Similar to the AVE trains, they connect Barcelona with Valencia and Alicante.

Regionales Trains operating within one region, usually stopping at all stations.

Talgo and Intercity Slower long-distance trains.

Tren de Alta Velocidad Española (AVE) High-speed trains that link Madrid with Barcelona, Burgos, Córdoba, Cuenca, Huesca, Lerida, Málaga, Seville, Valencia, Valladolid and Zaragoza. There are also Barcelona–Seville and Barcelona–Málaga services. In coming years Madrid–Cádiz and Madrid–Bilbao should come on line.

Trenhotel Overnight trains with sleeper berths.

Classes & Costs

- All long-distance trains have 2nd and 1st classes, known as *turista* and *preferente*, respectively. The latter is 20% to 40% more expensive.
- Fares vary enormously depending on the service (faster trains cost considerably more) and, in the case of some high-speed services such as the AVE, on the time and day of travel.
- Children aged between four and 12 years are entitled to a 40% discount; those aged under four travel for free (except on high-speed trains, for which they pay the same as those aged four to 12). Buying a return ticket often gives you a 10% to 20% discount on the return trip. Students and people up to 25 years of age with a Euro<26 Card (Carnet Joven in Spain) are entitled to 20% to 25% off most ticket prices.

Sweden

Includes ➡

Best Places to Eat

- Lisa Elmqvist (p1098)
- Thörnströms Kök (p1103)
- Camp Ripan Restaurang (p1109)
- Mrs. Brown (p1101)

Best Places to Stay

- Vandrarhem af Chapman (p1094)
- Hotel Hellsten (p1095)
- Icehotel (p1108)
- Mäster Johan Hotel (p1101)

Why Go?

As progressive and civilised as it may be, Sweden is a wild place. Its scenery ranges from barren moonscapes and impenetrable forests in the far north to sunny beaches and lush farmland further south. Its short summers and long winters mean that people cling to every last speck of summer sunshine, while in winter locals rely on candlelight and *glögg* (mulled wine) to warm their spirits. But lovers of the outdoors will thrive here in any season: winter sees skiing and dog-sledding, while the warmer months invite long hikes, swimming and sunbathing, canoeing, cycling, you name it – if it's fun and can be done outdoors, you'll find it here. For less rugged types, there's always restaurant- and nightclub-hopping and museum-perusing in cosmopolitan Stockholm, lively Göteborg and beyond.

When to Go

Stockholm

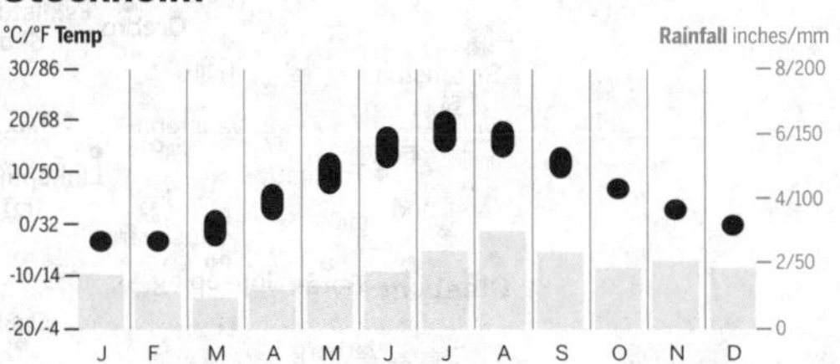

Mar There's still plenty of snow, but enough daylight to enjoy winter sports.

Jun–Aug Swedish summers are short but intense, and the White Nights beyond the Arctic Circle are magical.

Sep The stunning colours of the autumn season make this prime hiking time up north.

Sweden Highlights

❶ Hike wild reindeer-filled landscapes, explore Sami culture and sleep in the world-famous **Icehotel** (p1108) in Jukkasjärvi.

❷ Tour urban waterways, explore top-notch museums and wander the labyrinthine Old Town of **Stockholm**.

❸ Head south to **Malmö** (p1100) for edgy museums, good food and a dynamic, multicultural vibe.

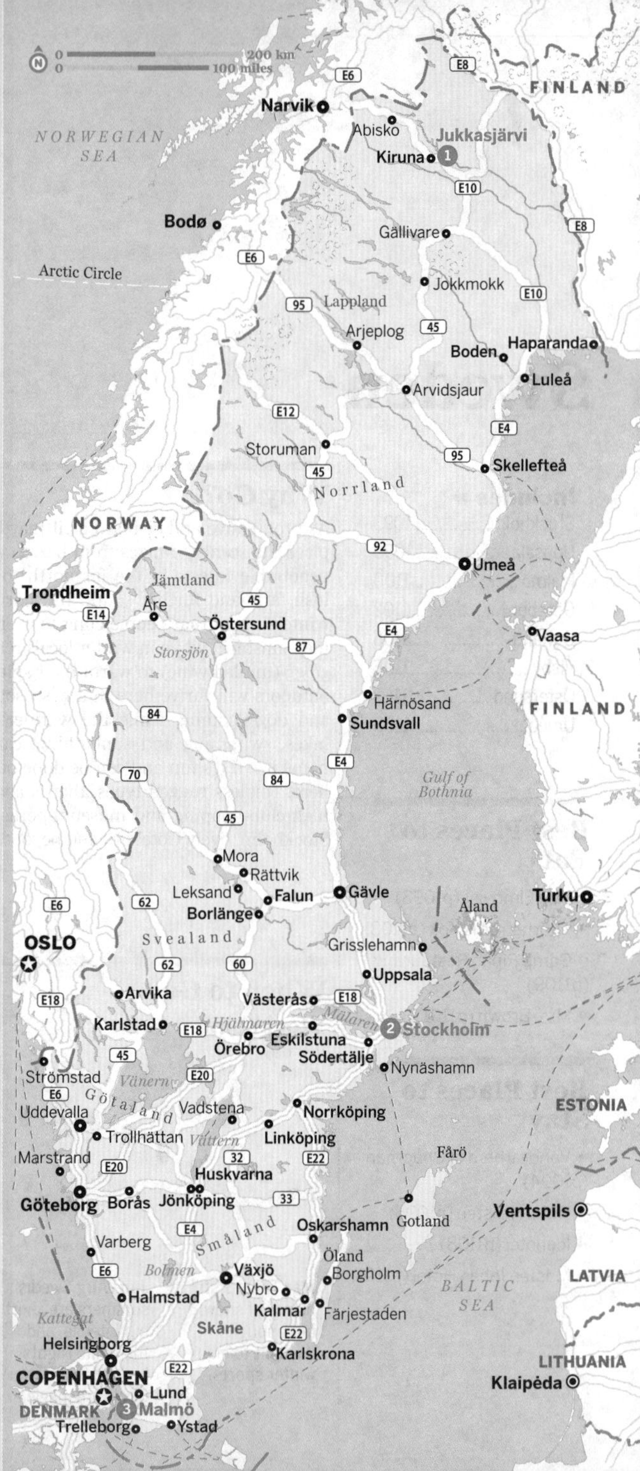

ITINERARIES

One Week

Spend three days exploring **Stockholm**, including a half-day in **Uppsala** (or, alternatively, a few hours strolling **Vaxholm** in the archipelago). Cruise over to **Göteborg** for a day or two, then continue south to the dynamic city of **Malmö**.

Two Weeks

Start as above, but from **Uppsala** go northward to **Östersund** for a day, then further up towards **Kiruna** to check out the world-famous Icehotel. Outdoorsy types will find plenty to do here, especially in winter. Looping back south, make a stop in student-heavy **Umeå**, then ferry over to **Gotland** and spend the remaining time cycling the pastoral island.

STOCKHOLM

☎08 / POP 770,890

Beautiful capital cities are no rarity in Europe, but Stockholm is near the top of the list for sheer loveliness. The saffron-and-cinnamon buildings that cover its 14 islands rise starkly out of the surrounding ice-blue water, honeyed in sunlight and frostily elegant in cold weather. The city's charms are irresistible. From its movie-set Old Town (Gamla Stan) to its ever-modern fashion sense and impeccable taste in food and design, the city acts like an immersion school in aesthetics.

Sights

Once you get over the armies of tourists wielding ice-cream cones and shopping bags, you'll discover that Gamla Stan, the oldest part of Stockholm, is also its most beautiful. The city emerged on this tiny island in the 13th century.

Kungliga Slottet PALACE

(Royal Palace; ☎08-402 61 30; www.kungahuset.se; Slottsbacken; adult/child Skr150/75, valid for 7 days; 10am-5pm mid-May–mid-Sep, closed Mon rest of year; 43, 46, 55, 59 Slottsbacken, M Gamla Stan) Kungliga Slottet was built on the ruins of Tre Kronor castle, which burned down in 1697. The north wing survived and was incorporated into the new building. Designed by court architect Nicodemus Tessin the Younger, it took 57 years to complete. Free 45-minute tours in English start at 11am and 2pm mid-May to mid-September, and at 2pm and 3pm the rest of the year. The apartments are occasionally closed for royal business; closures are noted on the website.

Nobelmuseet MUSEUM

(nobelmuseet.se; Stortorget; adult/child Skr100/70; 10am-8pm; M Gamla Stan) Nobelmuseet presents the history of the Nobel Prizes and their recipients, with a focus on the intellectual and cultural aspects of invention. It's a slick space with fascinating displays, including short films on the theme of creativity, interviews with laureates like Ernest Hemingway and Martin Luther King, and cafe chairs signed by the visiting prize recipients (flip them over to see!). The free guided tours are recommended (in English at 10.15am, 11.15am, 1pm, 3pm, 4pm and 6pm in summer).

★ **Skansen** MUSEUM

(www.skansen.se; Djurgårdsvägen; adult/child Skr160/60; 10am-10pm late Jun-Aug; 44, Djurgårdsfärjan, 7, Djurgården) The world's first open-air museum, Skansen was founded in 1891 by Artur Hazelius to give visitors an insight into how Swedes lived once upon a time. You could easily spend a day here and still not see it all (note that prices and hours vary seasonally). Around 150 traditional houses and other exhibits from across the country dot the hilltop – it's meant to be 'Sweden in miniature', complete with villages, nature, commerce and industry.

★ **Vasamuseet** MUSEUM

(www.vasamuseet.se; Galärvarvsvägen 14; adult/child Skr130/free; 8.30am-6pm; 44, Djurgårdsfärjan, 7 Nordiska museet/Vasa) A good-humoured glorification of some dodgy calculations, Vasamuseet is the custom-built home of the massive warship *Vasa*. The ship, a whopping 69m long and 48.8m tall, was the pride of the Swedish crown when it

STOCKHOLM ARCHIPELAGO

Buffering the city from the open Baltic Sea, the archipelago is a wonderland of thousands of rocky isles and little red cottages. And it's more accessible than many visitors imagine, with regular ferry services and tours.

Waxholmsbolaget (☎08-679 58 30; www.waxholmsbolaget.se; Strömkajen; single trip Skr45-130, 5-day pass Skr440, 30-day pass regular/senior Skr770/470; ⏰8am-6pm; Ⓜ Kungsträdgården), the main provider for island traffic, offers standard commuter routes and tours, as does **Strömma Kanalbolaget** (☎08-12 00 40 00; www.stromma.se; Strandvägen 8).

Vaxholm is the gateway to the archipelago (just 35km northeast of Stockholm; take bus 670 from the Tekniska Högskolan tunnelbana station). On a sunny spring day, its crooked streets and storybook houses are irresistible. It has a thriving restaurant scene and popular Christmas market.

To the south, **Utö** has sandy beaches, fairy-tale forests, abundant bird life and an excellent **bakery** (breakfast Skr80-120, lunch Skr140, sandwiches Skr40-70; ⏰8am-5pm). Tiny Gruvbryggan is the main ferry stop. Ask at the guest harbour about cycle hire. Don't miss Sweden's oldest **iron mine** (⏰24hr).

Equally charming is **Arholma** in the northern section. Once a popular resort, it has a moneyed yet agricultural feel, with green pastures, walking trails, rocky bathing spots and the delightful **Bull-August Vandrarhem** (☎0176-560 18; www.bullaugust.se; Arholma Södra Byväg 8; s/d from Skr340/575).

set off on its maiden voyage on 10 August 1628. Within minutes, the top-heavy vessel tipped and sank to the bottom of Saltsjön, along with many of the people on board. Guided tours are in English every 30 minutes in summer.

Moderna Museet MUSEUM
(☎08-52 02 35 01; www.modernamuseet.se; Exercisplan 4; adult/child Skr120/free, 6-8pm Fri free; ⏰10am-6pm Wed, Thu, Sat & Sun, to 8pm Tue & Fri, closed Mon; 🚌65, ⛴Djurgårdsfärjan) Moderna Museet is Stockholm's modern-art maverick, its permanent collection ranging from paintings and sculptures to photography, video art and installations. Highlights include work by Pablo Picasso, Salvador Dalí (*The Enigma of William Tell*), Andy Warhol, Damien Hirst and Robert Rauschenberg (*Monogram*, affectionately known as the goat in a tyre). There are important pieces by Francis Bacon, Marcel Duchamp and Matisse, as well as their Scandinavian contemporaries, and plenty of work by not yet household names.

Historiska Museet MUSEUM
(☎08-51 95 56 00; www.historiska.se; Narvavägen 13-17; adult/child Skr100/free; ⏰10am-6pm, closed Mon Sep-May; 🚌44, 56, Ⓜ Karlaplan, Östermalmstorg) The national historical collection awaits at this enthralling museum. From Iron Age skates and a Viking boat to medieval textiles and Renaissance triptychs, it spans over 10,000 years of Swedish history and culture. There's an exhibit about the medieval Battle of Gotland (1361), an excellent multimedia display on the Vikings, a room of altarpieces from the Middle Ages, a vast textile collection and a section on prehistoric culture.

Activities

Stockholm City Bikes BICYCLE RENTAL
(www.citybikes.se; 3-day/season card Skr165/300) City Bikes has around 90 self-service bicycle-hire stands across the city. Bikes can be borrowed for three-hour stretches and returned at any City Bikes stand. You'll need to purchase a bike card online or from the tourist office, a Storstockholms Lokaltrafik (SL) centre, or most hotels (see the website for a list). Rechargeable season cards are valid April to October.

Sleeping

★ **Vandrarhem af Chapman & Skeppsholmen** HOSTEL €
(☎08-463 22 66; www.stfchapman.com; Flaggmansvägen 8; dm from Skr260, r from Skr590; @; 🚌65 Skeppsholmen) The *af Chapman* is a storied vessel that has done plenty of travelling of its own. It's anchored in a superb

location, swaying gently off Skeppsholmen. Bunks are in dorms below deck. Apart from showers and toilets, all facilities are on dry land in the Skeppsholmen hostel, including a good kitchen, a laid-back common room and a TV lounge.

STF Fridhemsplan HOSTEL €
(08-653 88 00; www.fridhemsplan.se; S:t Eriksgatan 20; s/d Skr550/650, hotel s/d from Skr750/850; ; M Fridhemsplan) This modern, inviting hostel near the Fridhemsplan tunnelbana stop on Kungsholmen has nice, modern, hotel-style rooms with shared bathrooms (the hotel-standard rooms are en suite). Some rooms have windows with city views. There's a cool lounge in the lobby to hang out in, and a vast and stylish breakfast room (with a better-than-average breakfast buffet; Skr70 for hostel guests).

Hotel Anno 1647 HOTEL €€
(08-442 16 80; www.anno1647.se; Mariagränd 3; budget s/d from Skr570/740, standard s/d from Skr890/990; ; M Slussen) Just off buzzing Götgatan, this historical hotel in two beautiful buildings has labyrinthine hallways, gorgeous wooden floors and spiral staircases, affable staff, and budget as well as standard rooms – both are recommended. The latter have antique rococo wallpaper, all modern amenities and the odd chandelier. The location and reduced high-season rates make this a fantastic deal.

★ **Hotel Hellsten** HOTEL €€
(08-661 86 00; www.hellsten.se; Luntmakargatan 68; s/d from Skr1090/1490; ; M Rådmansgatan) Hip Hellsten is owned by anthropologist Per Hellsten, whose touch is evident in the rooms and common areas, which are furnished and decorated with objects from his travels and life, including Congan tribal masks and his grandmother's chandelier. Rooms are supremely comfortable and individually styled, with themes ranging from rustic Swedish to Indian exotica; some even feature original tile stoves.

Nordic 'C' Hotel HOTEL €€
(08-50 56 30 00; www.nordicchotel.com; Vasaplan 4; s/d from Skr784/824; ; M T-Centralen) A fantastic deal if you time it right and book ahead, this sister hotel to the slightly more upmarket Nordic Light has smallish but sleek rooms, great service and a cool lobby lounge area with an impressive 9000L aquarium in the foyer. The cheapest rooms are windowless and very tiny but efficiently designed and totally comfortable.

Rival Hotel HOTEL €€€
(08-54 57 89 00; www.rival.se; Mariatorget 3; s/d from Skr1895/2495; ; M Mariatorget) Owned by ABBA's Benny Andersson and overlooking leafy Mariatorget, this ravishing design hotel is a chic retro gem, complete with vintage 1940s movie theatre and art deco cocktail bar. The super-comfy rooms feature posters from great Swedish films and a teddy bear to make you feel at home. All rooms have good-size bathrooms and flat-screen TVs with Blu-ray players.

Eating

Stockholm is a city of foodies. It has more than half a dozen Michelin-starred restaurants. Its epicurean highlights don't come cheap, but you can find great value in the abundant cafes, coffee shops and vegetarian buffets.

Chokladkoppen CAFE €
(www.chokladkoppen.se; Stortorget 18; cakes Skr40-80; 9am-11pm summer, shorter hours rest of year; M Gamla Stan) Arguably Stockholm's best-loved cafe, hole-in-the-wall Chokladkoppen sits slap bang on the old town's enchanting main square. It's a gay-friendly spot, with cute waiters, a look-at-me summer terrace and yummy grub such as broccoli-and-blue-cheese pie and scrumptious cakes.

Vurma CAFE €
(www.vurma.se; Polhemsgatan 15-17; salads Skr108, sandwiches Skr60-80; 7am-7pm Mon-Fri, 8am-7pm Sat & Sun; ; M Rådhuset) Squeeze in among the locals at this friendly cafe-bakery, a reliably affordable place to get a healthy and substantial meal in an unfussy setting. The scrumptious sandwiches and salads are inspired, with ingredients like halloumi, felafel, cured salmon, avocado and greens over quinoa or pasta. The homemade bread that comes with your order is divine.

Hermitage VEGETARIAN €€
(Stora Nygatan 11; lunch/dinner & weekends Skr110/120; 11am-8pm Mon-Sat, noon-4pm Sun; ; M Gamla Stan) Herbivores love Hermitage for its simple, tasty, vegetarian buffet, easily one of the best restaurant bargains in Gamla Stan. Salad, homemade bread, tea and coffee are included in the price. Pro tip:

Stockholm

0 1 km
0 0.5 miles

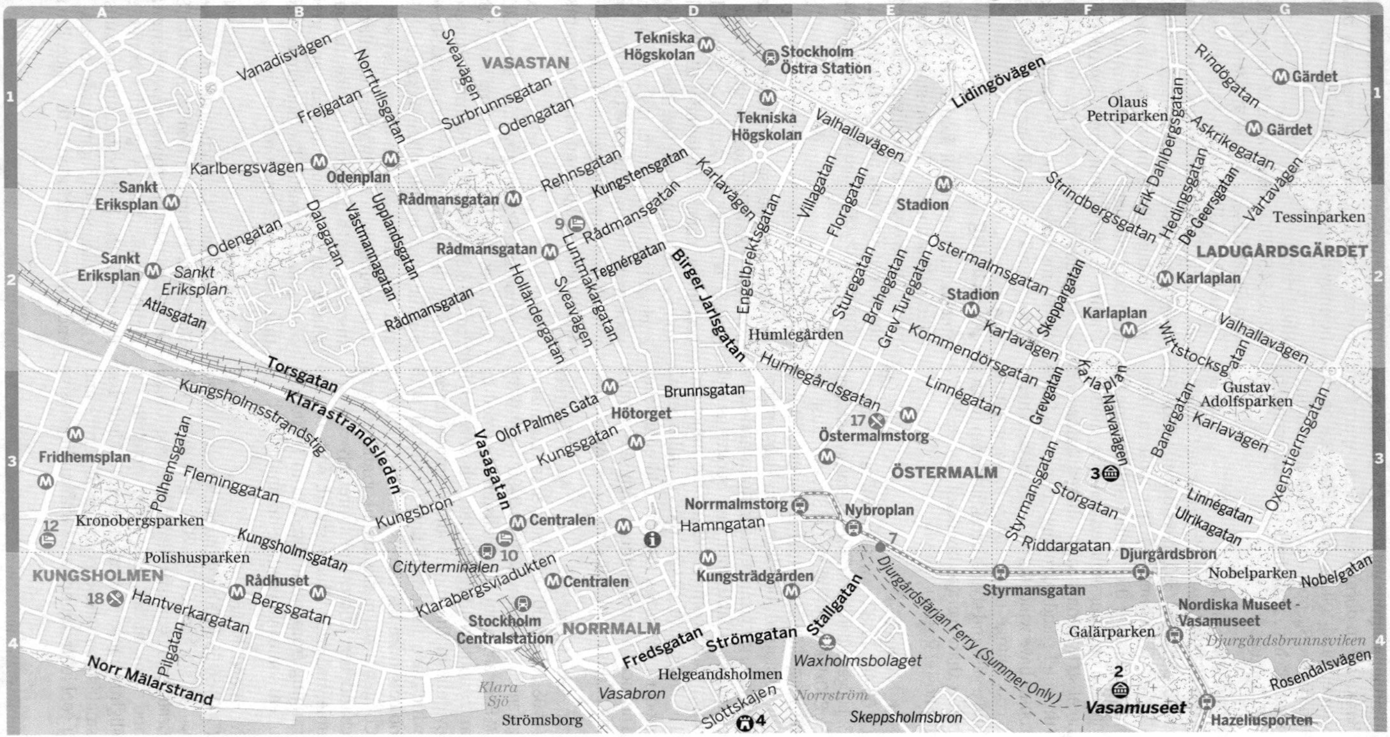

A B C D E F G
1 2 3 4

VASASTAN
Vanadisvägen
Norrtullsgatan
Sveavägen
Surbrunnsgatan
Odengatan
Frejgatan
Karlbergsvägen
Odenplan
Sankt Eriksplan
Rådmansgatan
Rehnsgatan
Kungstensgatan
Tekniska Högskolan
Stockholm Östra Station
Lidingövägen
Valhallavägen
Karlavägen
Dalagatan
Västmannagatan
Upplandsgatan
Luntmakargatan
Tegnérgatan
Birger Jarlsgatan
Engelbrektsgatan
Villagatan
Floragatan
Stadion
Strindbergsgatan
Erik Dahlbergsgatan
Hedingsgatan
De Geersgatan
Värtavägen
Askrikegatan
Rindögatan
Gärdet
Olaus Petriparken
Tessinparken
LADUGÅRDSGÄRDET
Karlaplan
Odengatan
Sankt Eriksplan
Atlasgatan
Holländergatan
Sturegatan
Brahegatan
Grev Turegatan
Östermalmsgatan
Skeppargatan
Humlegården
Kommendörsgatan
Wittstocksgatan
Gustav Adolfsparken
Torsgatan
Klarastrandsleden
Kungsholmsstrandstig
Olof Palmes Gata
Hötorget
Brunnsgatan
Humlegårdsgatan
Linnégatan
Grevgatan
Narvavägen
Banérgatan
Oxenstiernsgatan
Fridhemsplan
Polhemsgatan
Fleminggatan
Vasagatan
Kungsgatan
17 Östermalmstorg
ÖSTERMALM
Styrmansgatan
Storgatan
3
Kungsbron
Centralen
Hamngatan
Norrmalmstorg
Nybroplan
7
Riddargatan
Ulrikagatan
Djurgårdsbron
Nobelparken
Nobelgatan
12
Kronobergsparken
Kungsholmsgatan
Polishusparken
10
Cityterminalen
Klarabergsviadukten
Kungsträdgården
Stallgatan
Djurgårdsfärjan Ferry (Summer Only)
KUNGSHOLMEN
Rådhuset
18
Hantverkargatan
Bergsgatan
Stockholm Centralstation
NORRMALM
Fredsgatan
Strömgatan
Waxholmsbolaget
Nordiska Museet - Vasamuseet
Galärparken
Djurgårdsbrunnsviken
Norr Mälarstrand
Pilgatan
Helgeandsholmen
Klara Sjö
Vasabron
Norrström
Slottskajen
4
Strömsborg
Skeppsholmsbron
2
Vasamuseet
Rosendalsvägen
Hazeliusporten

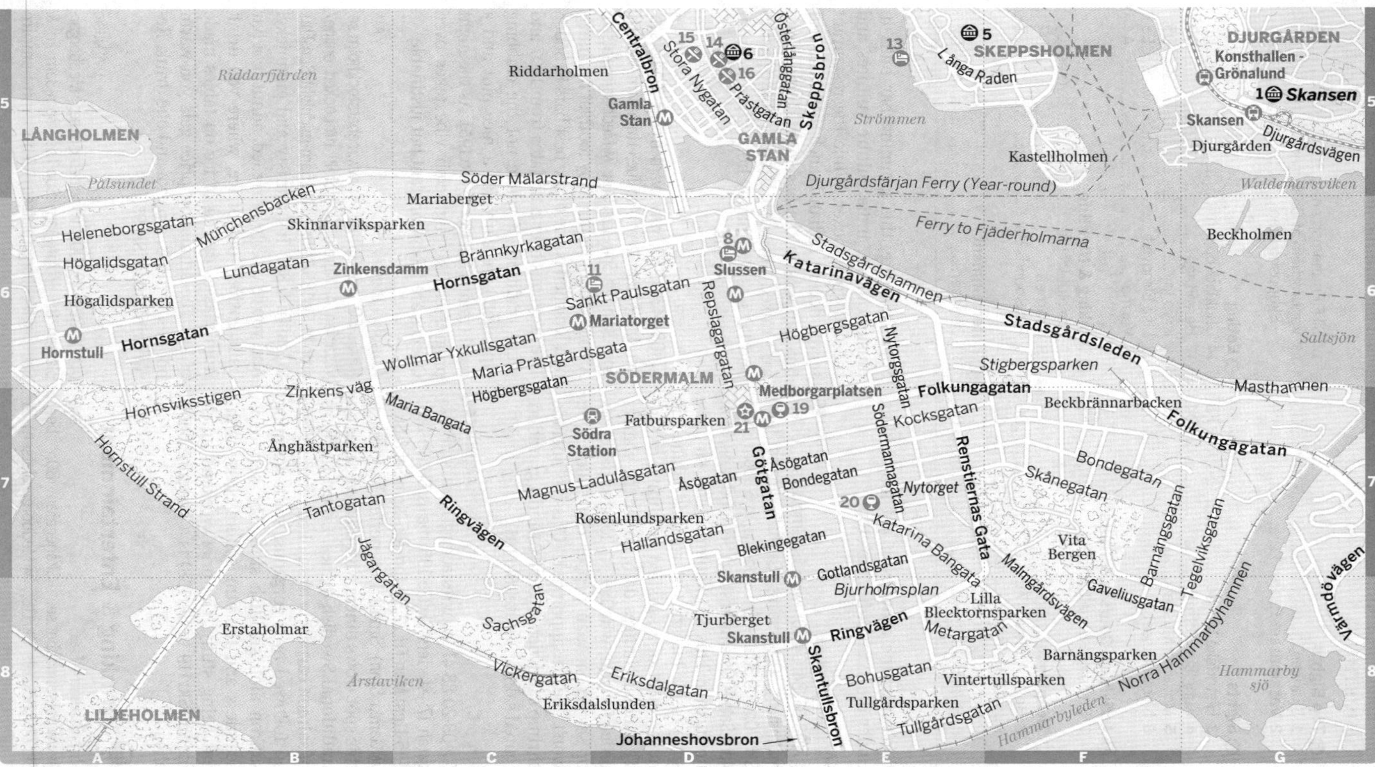
Riddarfjärden
Riddarholmen
Centralbron
15
14
6
16
Stora Nygatan
Prästgatan
Österlånggatan
Skeppsbron
13
5
Långa Raden
SKEPPSHOLMEN
DJURGÅRDEN
Konsthallen - Grönalund
1 Skansen
Gamla Stan
LÅNGHOLMEN
GAMLA STAN
Strömmen
Skansen
Djurgården
Djurgårdsvägen
Kastellholmen
Pålsundet
Söder Mälarstrand
Djurgårdsfärjan Ferry (Year-round)
Waldemarsviken
Mariaberget
Münchensbacken
Skinnarviksparken
Ferry to Fjäderholmarna
Beckholmen
Heleneborgsgatan
Brännkyrkagatan
8
Högalidsgatan
Lundagatan
Zinkensdamm
11
Slussen
Katarinavägen
Stadsgårdshamnen
Hornsgatan
Sankt Paulsgatan
Högalidsparken
Repslagargatan
Mariatorget
Stadsgårdsleden
Saltsjön
Högbergsgatan
Nytorgsgatan
Hornstull
Hornsgatan
Wollmar Yxkullsgatan
Maria Prästgårdsgata
SÖDERMALM
Stigbergsparken
Medborgarplatsen
Folkungagatan
Masthamnen
Högbergsgatan
Hornsviksstigen
Zinkens väg
Beckbrännarbacken
Maria Bangata
19
Södermannagatan
Fatbursparken
Kocksgatan
21
Folkungagatan
Södra Station
Ånghästparken
Hornstull Strand
Renstiernas Gata
Götgatan
Åsögatan
Bondegatan
Skånegatan
Magnus Ladulåsgatan
Åsögatan
Bondegatan
Nytorget
20
Tantogatan
Ringvägen
Rosenlundsparken
Katarina Bangata
Vita Bergen
Barnängsgatan
Tegelviksgatan
Hallandsgatan
Blekingegatan
Jägargatan
Skanstull
Gotlandsgatan
Malmgårdsvägen
Värmdövägen
Gaveliusgatan
Bjurholmsplan
Lilla Blecktornsparken
Sachsgatan
Erstaholmar
Tjurberget
Skanstull
Ringvägen
Metargatan
Norra Hammarbyhamnen
Barnängsparken
Vickergatan
Skantullsbron
Bohusgatan
Vintertullsparken
Hammarby sjö
Årstaviken
Eriksdalgatan
Eriksdalslunden
Tullgårdsparken
LILJEHOLMEN
Tullgårdsgatan
Hammarbyleden
Johanneshovsbron
A
B
C
D
E
F
G
5
6
7
8

Stockholm

Top Sights
1 Skansen G5
2 Vasamuseet F4

Sights
3 Historiska Museet F3
4 Kungliga Slottet D4
5 Moderna Museet E5
6 Nobelmuseet D5

Activities, Courses & Tours
7 Strömma Kanalbolaget E3

Sleeping
8 Hotel Anno 1647 D6
9 Hotel Hellsten C2
10 Nordic 'C' Hotel C3
11 Rival Hotel D6
12 STF Fridhemsplan A3
13 Vandrarhem af Chapman & Skeppsholmen E5

Eating
14 Chokladkoppen D5
15 Hermitage D5
16 Kryp In D5
17 Lisa Elmqvist E3
18 Vurma A4

Drinking & Nightlife
Absolut Icebar (see 10)
19 Kvarnen D7
20 Pet Sounds Bar E7

Entertainment
21 Debaser D7

don't miss the drawers of hot food hiding under the main buffet tabletop.

★ **Lisa Elmqvist** SEAFOOD €€
(08-55 34 04 10; www.lisaelmqvist.se; Östermalmstorg, Östermalms Saluhall; mains from Skr170; 9.30am-6pm Mon-Thu, to 6.30pm Fri, to 4pm Sat; M Östermalmstorg) Seafood fans, look no further. This Stockholm legend, suitably snug inside historic Östermalms Saluhall, is never short of a satisfied lunchtime crowd. The menu changes daily, so let the waiters order for you; whether it's lobster pancakes or seared Sichuan pepper char fillets, you won't be disappointed. Classics include shrimp sandwiches (Skr170) and a gravadlax (cured salmon) plate (Skr185).

Kryp In SWEDISH €€€
(08-20 88 41; www.restaurangkrypin.nu; Prästgatan 17; starters Skr135-195, mains Skr195-285; 5-11pm Mon-Fri, 12.30-4pm & 5-11pm Sat & Sun; M Gamla Stan) Small but perfectly formed, this spot wows diners with creative takes on traditional Swedish dishes. Expect the likes of salmon carpaccio or smoked reindeer salad followed by a gorgeous, spirit-warming saffron aioli shellfish stew. The service is seamless and the atmosphere classy without being stuffy. The brief weekend lunch menu (Skr119 to Skr158) is a bargain. Book ahead.

Drinking & Entertainment

Pet Sounds Bar BAR
(www.petsoundsbar.se; Skånegatan 80; beer Skr72, cocktails Skr118; M Medborgarplatsen) A SoFo favourite, this jamming bar pulls in music journos, indie culture vultures and the odd goth rocker. While the restaurant serves decent Italian-French grub, the real fun happens in the basement. Head down for a mixed bag of live bands, release parties and DJ sets. Hit happy hour (2pm to 6pm) for drink specials.

Kvarnen BAR
(08-643 03 80; www.kvarnen.com; Tjärhovsgatan 4; 11am-1am Mon-Tue, 11am-3am Wed-Fri, 5pm-3am Sat, 5pm-1am Sun; M Medborgarplatsen) An old-school Hammarby football fan hangout, Kvarnen is one of the best bars in Söder. The gorgeous beer hall dates from 1907 and seeps tradition; if you're not the clubbing type, get here early for a nice pint and a meal (mains Skr139 to Skr195). As the night progresses, the nightclub vibe takes over. Queues are fairly constant but justifiable.

Absolut Icebar BAR
(08-50 56 35 20; www.icebarstockholm.se; Vasaplan 4, Nordic 'C' Hotel; prebooked online/drop in Skr185/195; 11.15am-midnight Sun-Thu, to 1am Fri & Sat) It's touristy and gimmicky! And you're utterly intrigued, admit it: a bar built entirely out of ice, where you drink from glasses carved of ice on tables made of ice. The admission price gets you warm booties, mittens, a parka and one drink. Refill drinks cost Skr95.

Debaser LIVE MUSIC
(08-694 79 00; www.debaser.se; Medborgarplatsen 8; 7pm-1am Sun-Thu, 8pm-3am Fri & Sat; M Medborgarplatsen) This mini-empire

of entertainment has its flagship rock venue (Debaser Medis) on Medborgarplatsen. Emerging or bigger-name acts play most nights, while the killer club nights span anything from rock-steady to punk and electronica. (There are also a couple of restaurants around town and a location in Malmö).

Information

Stockholm Visitors Center (08-50 82 85 08; www.visitstockholm.com; Kulturhuset, Sergels Torg 3; 9am-7pm Mon-Fri, to 6pm winter, 9am-4pm Sat, 10am-4pm Sun; M T-Centralen) The main visitors centre occupies a space inside Kulturhuset on Sergels Torg.

Getting There & Away

AIR

Stockholm Arlanda (10-109 10 00; www.swedavia.se/arlanda) Stockholm's main airport, 45km north of the city centre, is reached from central Stockholm by bus and express train. Terminals two and five are for international flights; three and four are domestic; there is no terminal one.

BUS

Cityterminalen (www.cityterminalen.com; 7am-6pm) Most long-distance buses arrive and depart from Cityterminalen, which is connected to Centralstationen. The **main counter** (7am-6pm) sells tickets for several bus companies, including Flybussarna (airport coaches), Swebus Express, Svenska Buss, Eurolines and Y-Buss.

TRAIN

Stockholm is the hub for national and international train services run by SJ (Sveriges Järnväg). Ticket offices are inside **Centralstationen** (M T-Centralen).

Getting Around

TO/FROM THE AIRPORT

The **Arlanda Express** (www.arlandaexpress.com) train from Centralstationen (one-way Skr260, 20 minutes, every 15 minutes) links the city centre with Arlanda. A cheaper option is the **Flygbussarna** (www.flygbussarna.se) bus service between Arlanda and Cityterminalen (Skr99, 40 minutes, every 10 to 15 minutes).

PUBLIC TRANSPORT

Storstockholms Lokaltrafik (SL; 08-600 10 00; www.sl.se; Centralstationen, Sergels Torg; single trip Skr25-50, unlimited 24hr/72hr/7-day pass Skr115/230/300, students & seniors half-price) runs all tunnelbana (T or T-bana) metro trains, local trains and buses. Coupons, tickets and passes can be bought at T-bana stations, Pressbyrån kiosks, SL train stations and SL information offices.

UPPSALA

018 / POP 156,000

The historical and spiritual heart of the country, Uppsala has the upbeat party vibe of a university town to balance the weight of its castle, cathedral and university. Peaceful by day and lively by night, it makes an easy day trip from Stockholm, though it's worth lingering overnight to wander the deserted streets and soak up the atmosphere.

Sights

Gamla Uppsala ARCHAEOLOGICAL SITE

(www.arkeologigamlauppsala.se; 24hr; 2) FREE One of Sweden's largest and most important burial sites, Gamla Uppsala (4km north of Uppsala) contains 300 mounds from the 6th to 12th centuries. The earliest are also the three most impressive. Legend has it they contain the pre-Viking kings Aun, Egil and Adils, who appear in *Beowulf* and Icelandic historian Snorre Sturlason's *Ynglingsaga*. More recent evidence suggests the occupant of Östhögen (East Mound) was a woman, probably a female regent in her 20s or 30s.

Uppsala Slott CASTLE

(www.uppsalaslott.se; admission by guided tour only, adult/child Skr90/15; tours in English 1pm & 3pm Tue-Sun late Jun-Sep) Uppsala Slott was built by Gustav Vasa in the 1550s. It contains the state hall where kings were enthroned and Queen Kristina abdicated. It was also the scene of a brutal murder in 1567, when King Erik XIV and his guards killed Nils Sture and his two sons, Erik and Svante, after accusing them of high treason. The castle burned down in 1702 but was rebuilt and took on its present form in 1757.

Domkyrka CHURCH

(Cathedral; www.uppsaladomkyrka.se; Domkyrkoplan; 8am-6pm) FREE The Gothic Domkyrka dominates the city, just as some of those buried here, including St Erik, Gustav Vasa and the scientist Carl von Linné, dominated their country. Tours are available in English at 11am and 2pm Monday to Saturday, 4pm Sunday, in July and August.

Sleeping

STF Vandrarhem Sunnersta Herrgård HOSTEL €
(☎018-32 42 20; www.sunnerstaherrgard.se; Sunnerstavägen 24; dm Skr245, s/d incl breakfast from Skr650/770; ⊙Jan–mid-Dec; P ⊖ @ ≋ ♿; 🚌20) In a historic manor house about 6km south of the city centre, this hostel has a parklike setting at the water's edge and a good restaurant on-site. You can rent bikes (Skr50/200 per day/week) or borrow a boat, and there's free wi-fi. Hotel-standard rooms include breakfast; hostel guests can add it for Skr85.

Uppsala Vandrarhem & Hotell HOSTEL €
(☎018-24 20 08; www.uppsalavandrarhem.se; Kvarntorget 3; dm Skr190, s/d hostel Skr445/550, s/d hotel Skr750/895; P ⊖ ❄ ≋; 🚌3 Kvarntorget) This hostel, attached to Hotell Kvarntorget, is away from the action but walkable from Uppsala Central Station. Spacious rooms, some with double beds, face an enclosed courtyard that works as a breakfast room; a newly designed dividing wall has greatly reduced the resulting noise. There's a guest kitchen and laundry. Bedding is included; towels (Skr30) and breakfast (Skr69) are extra.

Best Western Hotel Svava HOTEL €€
(☎018-13 00 30; www.bestwestern.se; Bangårdsgatan 24; s/d Skr1350/1450; P ❄) Named after one of Odin's Valkyrie maidens, Hotel Svava, right opposite the train station, is a very comfortable business-style hotel with summer and weekend discounts that make it a smashing deal.

Eating

Casual dining options can be found inside **Saluhallen** (Sankt Eriks Torg; ⊙10am-6pm Mon-Thu, to 7pm Fri, to 4pm Sat, restaurants 11am-4pm Sun), an indoor market between the cathedral and the river.

Ofvandahls CAFE €
(Sysslomansgatan 3-5; cakes Skr35, snacks Skr55-75; ⊙8am-6pm Mon-Fri, 9am-5pm Sat, 11am-5pm Sun) Something of an Uppsala institution, this classy but sweet *konditori* (bakery-cafe) dates back to the 19th century and is a cut above your average coffee-and-bun shop. It's been endorsed by no less a personage than the king, and radiates old-world charm – somehow those faded red-striped awnings just get cuter every year.

Hambergs Fisk SEAFOOD €€
(www.hambergs.se; Fyristorg 8; mains Skr125-295; ⊙11.30am-10pm Tue-Sat) Let the aromas of dill and seafood tempt you into this excellent fish restaurant, in a tiny storefront facing the river. Self-caterers should check out the adjoining fresh fish counter.

Information

Tourist Office (☎018-727 48 00; www.destinationuppsala.se; Kungsgatan 59; ⊙10am-6pm Mon-Fri, to 3pm Sat, plus 11am-3pm Sun Jul & Aug) Relocated to a prime spot directly in front of the train station, this office has helpful advice, maps and brochures for the whole county.

Getting There & Away

Swebus Express runs regular direct services to Stockholm (from Skr59, 1¼ hours, hourly), which is also connected by frequent SJ trains (Skr70 to Skr110, 35 to 55 minutes one way).

SOUTHERN SWEDEN

Artists adore southern Sweden. Down here, the light is softer, the foliage brighter and the shoreline more dazzling. Sweden's southernmost county, Skåne (Scania), was Danish property until 1658 and still flaunts its differences.

Malmö

☎040 / POP 300,000

Sweden's third-largest city has a progressive, contemporary feel. Home to beautiful parks, edgy contemporary museums and some seriously good cuisine, this dynamic city has also felt more directly connected to cool Copenhagen and the rest of Europe since the opening of the Öresund bridge in 2000.

Sights

★**Malmö Museer** MUSEUM
(www.malmo.se/museer; Malmöhusvägen; adult/child Skr40/free; audioguides Skr20; ⊙10am-4pm Jun-Aug, shorter hours rest of year; ♿) Various museums with diverse themes, including handicrafts, military materiel, art and transport, are located in and around Malmöhus Slott and make up the so-called Malmö

Museer. There are gift shops and cafe-restaurants inside all the museums and plenty to keep the tots interested, including an **aquarium**. Renovated in 2014, don't miss the nocturnal hall here, wriggling with everything from bats to electric eels, plus local swimmers like cod and pike.

★Moderna Museet Malmö MUSEUM
(www.modernamuseet.se; Gasverksgatan 22; admission Skr70; ⊙11am-6pm Tue-Sun) Architects Tham & Videgård chose to make the most of the distinct 1901 Rooseum, once a power-generating turbine hall, by adding a contemporary annexe, complete with a bright, perforated orange-red facade. Venue aside, the museum's galleries are well worth visiting, with their permanent exhibition including works by such modern masters as Matisse, Dalí and Picasso.

Sleeping

STF Vandrarhem Malmö City HOSTEL €
(☎040-611 62 20; www.svenskaturistforeningen.se; Rönngatan 1; dm/d from Skr230/560; @ 📶) Don't be put off by the exterior; this is a sparkling hostel right in the city centre with a bright and airy communal kitchen and an outdoor patio. Staff are enthusiastic and helpful.

★Mäster Johan Hotel HOTEL €€€
(☎040-664 64 00; www.masterjohan.se; Mäster Johansgatan 13; r/ste from Skr1290/1790; P @ 📶) Just off Lilla Torg is one of Malmö's finest slumber spots, with spacious, elegantly understated rooms featuring beautiful oak floors, and snowy white matched with cobalt blue fabrics. Bathrooms flaunt Paloma Picasso-designed tiles, there's a sauna and gym, and the faultless breakfast buffet is served in a glass-roofed courtyard.

Eating

There's a good produce market on Möllevångstorget.

Falafel No. 1 FELAFEL €
(☎040-84 41 22; www.falafel-n1.se; Österportsgatan 2; felafel from Skr35) Malmö residents are so fond of felafel that it even features in songs by local rapper Timbuktu. Falafel No. 1 (also known as the Orient House) is a long-standing favourite, or check out the website **Everything About Falafel** (www.alltomfalafel.se) for details on other venues.

Atmosfär SWEDISH €€
(☎040-12 50 77; www.atmosfar.com; Fersensväg 4; mains from Skr125; ⊙11.30am-11pm Mon-Fri, to 2am Sat) This classy neighbourhood restaurant changes its menu regularly depending on what's in season, but you can depend on flavourful, innovative combinations like salads topped with young nasturtium leaves and veal with truffles, green peas and horseradish. The cocktails (Skr105) are similarly irresistible. Elderflower fizz, anyone?

★Mrs. Brown SWEDISH €€€
(☎040-97 22 50; www.mrsbrown.nu; Storgatan 26; mains from Skr200; ⊙noon-3.30pm & 5-10.30pm Mon-Fri, 6-10.30pm Sat; 🖉) 🌿 Demure little Mrs. Brown is the kind of neighbourhood place you dream will open up near you. The open kitchen churns out modern Scandinavian home cooking using local and organic ingredients like Greenland prawns in chilli sauce. Service is attentive but not overbearing and the dining room is decorated in a minimalist fashion that is both comforting and modish.

THE BRIDGE

The **Öresund Bridge** (www.oresundsbron.com; motorcycle/car/minibus Skr225/440/880) is the planet's longest cable-tied road and rail bridge, measuring 7.8km from Lernacken (on the Swedish side, near Malmö) to the artificial island of Peberholm (Pepper Island), south of Saltholm (Salt Island).

Local commuters pay via an electronic transmitter, while tolls for everyone else are payable by credit card, debit card or in euros, Danish or Swedish currency at the Lernacken toll booths.

Information

Tourist Office (☎040-34 12 00; www.malmotown.com; Skeppsbron 2; ⊙9am-7pm Mon-Fri, 10am-4pm Sat & Sun) Across from the Centralstationen.

Getting There & Away

BUS

Swebus Express (☎0771-21 82 18; www.swebus.se) runs two to four times daily to

WORTH A TRIP

LUND

The centrepiece of the appealing university town of Lund, just 15 minutes from Malmö by train, is the splendid Romanesque **Domkyrkan** (Kyrkogatan; 8am-6pm Mon-Fri, 9.30am-5pm Sat, to 6pm Sun) FREE, with some fantastic gargoyles over the side entrances, a giant turned to stone in the eerie crypt and an astronomical clock that sends the wooden figures whirring into action (at noon and 3pm Monday to Saturday, 1pm and 3pm on Sunday).

The town's most engaging museum, **Kulturen** (www.kulturen.com; Tegnerplatsen; adult/child Skr90/free; 10am-5pm May-Aug, noon-4pm Tue-Sat Sep-Apr;), is a huge open-air space where you can wander among birch-bark hovels, perfectly preserved cottages, churches, farms and grand 17th-century houses.

Stockholm (from Skr479, 8½ hours) and at least five daily to Göteborg (from Skr199, 3½ to four hours); at least two continue to Oslo (from Skr349, eight hours).

Svenska Buss (0771-67 67 67; www.svenskabuss.se) runs a service to Stockholm six times a week.

TRAIN

Pågatågen (local trains) operated by **Skånetrafiken** (www.skanetrafiken.se) run regularly to Helsingborg (Skr103, one hour), Lund (Skr48, 15 minutes) and other towns in Skåne.

The Malmö to Copenhagen central station train leaves every 20 minutes (Skr105, 35 minutes).

The high-speed X2000 (from Skr342, 2½ hours) and regional (from Skr235, 3¼ hours) trains run several times daily to/from Göteborg. The X2000 (from Skr750, 4½ hours, hourly) and Intercity (from Skr795, 6½ hours, infrequently) trains run between Stockholm and Malmö.

GÖTEBORG

031 / POP 549,840

Often caught in Stockholm's shadow, gregarious Göteborg (yur-te-*borry*, Gothenburg in English) packs a mighty good punch of its own. Stockholm may represent the 'big time', but many of the best and brightest ideas originate in this grassroots town.

Sights

The **Haga district**, south of the canal, is Göteborg's oldest suburb, dating back to 1648. In the 1980s and '90s, the area was thoroughly renovated and is now a cute, cobblestone maze of precious cafes and boutique shops.

★**Liseberg** AMUSEMENT PARK

(www.liseberg.se; Södra Vägen; 1-/2-day pass Skr415/595; 11am-11pm Jun–mid-Aug; ; 2, 4, 5, 6, 8, 10 Korsvägen) The attractions of Liseberg, Scandinavia's largest amusement park, are many and varied. Adrenalin blasts include the venerable wooden roller coaster Balder, its 'explosive' colleague Kanonen, where you're blasted from 0km/h to 75km/h in under two seconds, AtmosFear, Europe's tallest (116m) free-fall tower, and the park's biggest new attraction: thrilling roller coaster Helix that lets you experience weightlessness and loops the loop seven times. Softer options include carousels, fairy-tale castles, an outdoor dance floor, adventure playgrounds, and shows and concerts.

★**Mölndals Museum** MUSEUM

(031-431 34; www.museum.molndal.se; Kvarnbygatan 12; noon-6pm Tue-Sun) FREE Located in an old police station, the museum is like a vast warehouse, with a 10,000-strong booty of local nostalgia spanning a 17th-century clog to kitchen kitsch and a recreated 1930s worker's cottage. With a focus on memories and feelings, it's an evocative place where you can plunge into racks of vintage clothes, pull out hidden treasures and learn the individual items' secrets on the digital catalogue.

From Göteborg, catch a Kungsbacka-bound train to Mölndal station, then bus 752 or 756.

★**Röda Sten** GALLERY

(www.rodasten.com; Röda Sten 1; adult/under 21yr Skr40/free; noon-5pm Tue-Sun, to 7pm Wed; 3, 9 Vagnhallen Majorna) Occupying a defunct, graffitied power station beside the giant Älvsborgsbron, Röda Sten's four floors are home to such temporary exhibitions as edgy Swedish photography and cross-dressing rap videos by Danish-Filipino artist Lillibeth Cuenca Rasmussen that challenge sexuality stereotypes in Afghan society. The indie-style cafe hosts weekly live music and club nights, and offbeat one-offs like punk bike races, boxing matches and stand-up comedy. To get there, walk towards the Klippan precinct, continue under Älvsborgsbron and look for the brown-brick building.

★ **Universeum** MUSEUM
(www.universeum.se; Södra Vägen 50; adult/3-16yr Skr230/175; ⏲10am-6pm; 👪; 🚊2, 4, 5, 6, 8 Korsvägen) In what is arguably the best museum for kids in Sweden, you find yourself in the midst of a humid rainforest, complete with trickling water, tropical birds and butterflies flitting through the greenery, and tiny marmosets. On a level above, roaring dinosaurs maul each other, while next door, denizens of the deep float through the shark tunnel and venomous beauties lie coiled in the serpent tanks. In the 'technology inspired by nature' section, stick your children to the Velcro wall.

Konstmuseet GALLERY
(www.konstmuseum.goteborg.se; Götaplatsen; adult/under 25yr Skr40/free; ⏲11am-6pm Tue & Thu, to 8pm Wed, to 5pm Fri-Sun; 👪; 🚊4, 5, 7, 10 Berzeliigatan) Göteborg's premier art collection, Konstmuseet, hosts works by the French Impressionists, Rubens, Van Gogh, Rembrandt and Picasso; Scandinavian masters such as Bruno Liljefors, Edvard Munch, Anders Zorn and Carl Larsson have pride of place in the **Fürstenburg Galleries**.

Other highlights include a superb sculpture hall, the **Hasselblad Center** with its annual *New Nordic Photography* exhibition, and temporary displays of next-generation Nordic art.

The unveiling of the bronze **Poseidon** fountain out front scandalised Göteborg's strait-laced citizens, who insisted on drastic penile-reduction surgery.

Sleeping

STF Göteborg City HOSTEL €
(☎031-756 98 00; www.svenskaturistforeningen.se; Drottninggatan 63-65; s/d from Skr545/988; 📶; 🚊1, 4, 6, 9, 11 Brunnsparken) Brand new and gleaming, this large super-central hostel is all industrial chic in the cafe/dining area and lounge and plush comfort on each of its individually themed floors. All rooms are private, with en suite bathroom, thick carpeting and comfortable bed-bunks, and – rarity of rarities! – your bed linen and towels are provided for you.

Hotel Flora BOUTIQUE HOTEL €€
(☎031-13 86 16; www.hotelflora.se; Grönsakstorget 2; r from Skr840; @📶; 🚊1, 5, 6, 9, 10 Grönsakstorget) Fabulous Flora's slick, individually themed rooms flaunt black, white and a-dash-of-bright-colour interiors, designer chairs, flat-screen TVs and sparkling bathrooms, though lack of storage facilities may dismay those with extensive sartorial needs. The top-floor rooms have air-con, several rooms offer river views, and rooms overlooking the chic split-level courtyard are for night owls rather than early birds.

Dorsia Hotel BOUTIQUE HOTEL €€€
(☎031-790 10 00; www.dorsia.se; Trädgårdsgatan 6; s/d/ste from Skr1900/2500/5800; ❄@📶; 🚊3, 4, 5, 7, 10 Kungsportsplatsen) If Heaven had a bordello, it would resemble this lavish, flamboyant establishment that combines old-world decadence with cutting-edge design. Rooms delight with their heavy velvet curtains, a purple-and-crimson colour scheme and opulent beds; thick carpet in the corridors muffles your footsteps; and the fine art adorning the walls comes from the owner's own collection.

Eating

Saluhall Briggen MARKET €
(www.saluhallbriggen.se; Nordhemsgatan 28; sandwiches Skr60; ⏲9am-6pm Mon-Fri, to 3pm Sat; 🥕; 🚊1, 6, 7, 10 Prinsgatan) This covered market will have you drooling over its bounty of fresh bread, cheeses, seafood and ethnic treats. It's particularly handy for the hostel district.

Smaka SWEDISH €€
(www.smaka.se; Vasaplatsen 3; mains Skr130-225; ⏲5pm-late; 🚊1, 2, 3, 7, 10 Vasaplatsen) For top-notch Swedish *husmanskost* (traditional fare), such as the speciality meatballs with mashed potato and lingonberries, it's hard to do better than this smart yet down-to-earth restaurant-bar. Mod-Swedish options might include hake with suckling pig cheek or salmon tartar with pickled pear.

★ **Thörnströms Kök** SCANDINAVIAN €€€
(☎031-16 20 66; www.thornstromskok.com; 3 Teknologgatan; mains Skr255-285, 4-/6-/9-course menu Skr625/825/1125; ⏲6pm-1am Mon-Sat; 🚊7, 10 Kapellplatsen) Specialising in modern Scandinavian cuisine, chef Håkan shows you how he earned that Michelin star through

Göteborg

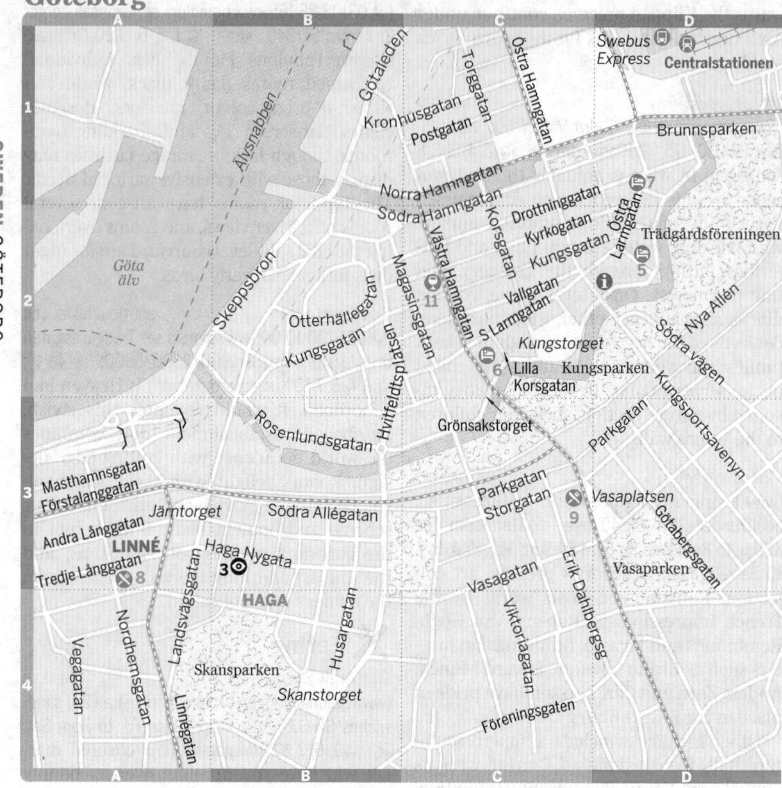

creative use of local, seasonal ingredients and flawless presentation. Feast on the likes of sweetbreads with hazelnut and cured perch with rhubarb; don't miss the remarkable milk-chocolate pudding with goat's-cheese ice cream. À la carte dishes are available if a multicourse menu overwhelms you.

Drinking

The Linné district is home to several friendly student hang-outs serving extremely cheap beer.

Barn BAR

(www.thebarn.se; Kyrkogatan 11; beer from Skr50; ⏲5pm-late Mon-Sat, from 2pm Sun; 🚊1, 3, 5, 6, 9 Domkyrkan) As the name suggests, this bar is all roughly hewn wood and copper taps, and the beer/wine/cocktail selection is guaranteed to get you merry enough to, erm, raise the barn. The burgers make fantastic stomach-liners, too.

Information

Tourist Office (☎031-368 42 00; www.goteborg.com; Kungsportsplatsen 2; ⏲9.30am-8pm) Central and busy; has a good selection of free brochures and maps.

Getting There & Away

AIR

Göteborg City Airport (www.goteborgairport.se), some 15km north of the city at Säve, is used for budget Ryanair flights to destinations including London Stansted, Glasgow and Frankfurt.

BOAT

Göteborg is a major entry point for ferries, with several car/passenger services to Denmark and Germany.

For a special view of the region, jump on a boat for an unforgettable journey along the Göta Canal. Starting in Göteborg, you'll pass through Sweden's oldest lock at Lilla Edet, opened in 1607. From there the trip crosses the great lakes

Vänern and Vättern through the rolling country of Östergötland and on to Stockholm.

BUS

Swebus Express (☎0771-21 82 18; www.swebusexpress.com) operates from the bus terminal (adjacent to the train station). Services include the following:

Malmö (Skr159, 3½ to four hours, five to eight daily)

Oslo (Skr189, 3½ hours, five to 10 daily)

Stockholm (Skr389, 6½ to seven hours, four to five daily)

TRAIN

From Centralstationen trains run to:

Copenhagen (Skr450, 3¾ hours, hourly)

Malmö (Skr195, 2½ to 3¼ hours, hourly)

Östersund (Skr820, 12 hours, daily)

Stockholm (Skr419, three to five hours, one to two hourly)

Göteborg

Top Sights
1 Liseberg F4
2 Universeum F4

Sights
3 Haga District B3
4 Konstmuseet E4

Sleeping
5 Dorsia Hotel D2
6 Hotel Flora C2
7 STF Göteborg City D1

Eating
8 Saluhall Briggen A3
9 Smaka C3
10 Thörnströms Kök E4

Drinking & Nightlife
11 Barn C2

Getting Around

Västtrafik (☎0771-41 43 00; www.vasttrafik.se) runs the city's public transport system of buses, trams and ferries. The most convenient way to travel around Göteborg is by tram. Colour-coded lines, numbered one to 13, converge near Brunnsparken (a block from Centralstationen). Holders of the **Göteborg Pass** (www.goteborg.com/en/Do/Gothenburg-City-Card/; 24/48/72hr Skr 355/495/655) travel free, including on late-night transport. Otherwise, a city transport ticket costs Skr25/19 per adult/child (Skr45 on late-night transport).

GOTLAND

Gorgeous Gotland, adrift in the Baltic, has much to brag about: a Unesco-lauded medieval capital, truffle-sprinkled woods, A-list dining hot spots, talented artisans and more hours of sunshine than anywhere else in Sweden. It's also one of the country's richest historical regions, with around 100 medieval churches and countless prehistoric sites.

Getting There & Away

Year-round car ferries between Visby and both Nynäshamn and Oskarshamn are operated by **Destination Gotland** (☎0771-22 33 00; www.destinationgotland.se). There are departures from Nynäshamn one to six times daily (about three hours). From Oskarshamn, there are one or two daily departures in either direction (three to four hours). **Gotlandsbåten** (www.gotlandsbaten.se) runs daily foot-passenger ferries (June

GOTLANDSLEDEN CYCLE PATH

Renting a bicycle and following the well-marked Gotlandsleden cycle path is one of the best ways to spend time on Gotland. It loops all around the island, mostly winding through quiet fields and forests. Hire bikes and get maps harbourside in Visby. There's an excellent hostel network along the route, with good facilities in Bunge, Lummelunda, Lärbro and Fårö.

to August) from Västervik to Visby (from Skr250, about three hours).

Getting Around

In Visby, hire bikes from Skr100 per 24 hours at **Gotlands Cykeluthyrning** (☎0498-21 41 33; www.gotlandscykeluthyrning.com; Skeppsbron 2), at the harbour. **Kollektiv Trafiken** (☎0498-21 41 12; www.gotland.se) runs buses via most villages to all corners of the island (tickets up to Skr75).

Visby

☎0498 / POP 22,590

The port town of Visby is medieval eye candy and enough to warrant a trip to Gotland all by itself. Inside its thick city walls await twisting cobbled streets, fairy-tale wooden cottages and evocative ruins. And with more restaurants per capita than any other Swedish city, it's a foodlovers' paradise.

Sights

★**Gotlands Museum** MUSEUM
(www.gotlandsmuseum.se; Strandgatan 14; adult/child Skr100/80; ⏲10am-6pm) Gotlands Museum is one of the mightiest regional museums in Sweden. While highlights include amazing 8th-century pre-Viking picture stones, human skeletons from chambered tombs and medieval wooden sculptures, the star turn is the legendary Spillings horde. At 70kg it's the world's largest booty of preserved silver treasure. Included in the ticket price is entry to the nearby **Konstmuseum** (☎0498-29 27 75; Sankt Hansgatan 21; adult/under 20yr/senior Skr50/free/40; ⏲noon-4pm Tue-Sun, closed for Midsummer), which has a small permanent collection mainly focusing on Gotland-inspired 19th- and 20th-century art, plus temporary exhibitions showcasing contemporary local artists.

Sleeping

Fängelse Vandrarhem HOSTEL €
(☎0498-20 60 50; www.visbyfangelse.se; Skeppsbron 1; dm/s/d from Skr300/400/500; 📶) This hostel offers beds year-round in the small converted cells of an old prison. It's in a handy location, between the ferry dock and the harbour restaurants, and there's an inviting terrace bar in summer. Reception is open from 9am to 2pm, so call ahead if you are arriving outside these times.

Hotel Stenugnen HOTEL €€
(☎0498-21 02 11; www.stenugnen.nu; Korsgatan 6; s/d Skr950/1250, annexe r Skr999; P 📶 👪) At this inviting small hotel, bright, whitewashed rooms are designed to make you feel as if you're sleeping in a yacht and the location is practically on top of the medieval wall. Plenty of rainy-day distractions are provided for kids and the homemade bread is just delicious. Cheaper doubles come with shared bathrooms in the annexe.

Clarion Hotel Wisby HOTEL €€€
(☎0498-25 75 00; www.clarionwisby.com; Strandgatan 6; s/d from Skr1870/2170; P @ 📶 🏊) Top of the heap in Visby is the luxurious, landmark Wisby. Medieval vaulted ceilings and sparkling candelabras contrast with funky modern furnishings. The gorgeous pool (complete with medieval pillar) occupies a converted merchant warehouse. Don't miss the 11th-century chapel, just inside the entrance.

Eating

Bakfickan SEAFOOD €€
(www.bakfickan-visby.nu; Stora Torget; lunch specials Skr95, mains Skr139-235) White-tiled walls, merrily strung lights and boisterous crowds define this foodie-loved bolt-hole, where enlightened seafood gems might include *toast skagen* (shrimps, dill and mayonnaise), pickled herrings on Gotland bread or Bakfickan's fish soup. Delicious!

Bolaget FRENCH €€
(www.gamlabolaget.se; Stora Torget 16; mains Skr179-229; ⏲1pm-2am) Take a defunct Systembolaget shop, chip the 'System' off the signage, and reinvent the space as a buzzing, French bistro-inspired hot spot. Staff members are amiable and the summertime square-side bar seating is perfect for a cool break.

Information

Tourist Office (0498-20 17 00; www.gotland.info; Donners Plats; 8am-7pm summer, to 4pm Mon-Fri, 10am-4pm Sat & Sun rest of year) The tourist office is located at Donners plats.

NORRLAND

Norrland, the northern half of Sweden, is a paradise for nature lovers who enjoy hiking, skiing and other outdoor activities; in winter the landscape is transformed by snowmobiles, dog-sleds and the eerie natural phenomena known as the aurora borealis. The north is home to the Sami people and their reindeer.

Östersund

063 / POP 44,330

This pleasant town by Storsjön lake, in whose chilly waters is said to lurk Sweden's answer to the Loch Ness monster, is an excellent activity base and gateway town for further explorations of Norrland.

Sights

★Jamtli MUSEUM

(www.jamtli.com; adult/under 18yr Skr250/free; 11am-5pm;) Jamtli, 1km north of the centre, consists of two parts. One is an open-air museum comprising painstakingly reconstructed wooden buildings, complete with enthusiastic guides wearing 19th-century period costume.

The stars of the indoor museum are the **Överhogdal Tapestries**, the oldest of their kind in Europe – Christian Viking relics from AD 1100 that feature animals, people, ships and dwellings. Another fascinating display is devoted to Storsjöodjuret, including taped interviews with those who've seen the monster, monster-catching gear and a pickled monster embryo.

LAPONIA WORLD HERITAGE AREA

The vast **Laponia World Heritage Area** (www.laponia.nu) stretches for 9400 sq km, comprising the mountains, forests and marshlands of Padjelanta, Sarek, Stora Sjöfallet and Muddus National Parks. Unusually for a World Heritage Area, it's recognised for both its cultural and its natural wealth.

Established in 1996, Laponia encompasses ancient reindeer-grazing grounds of both the Mountain and the Forest Sami, whose seven settlements and herds of around 50,000 reindeer are located here. The Sami still lead relatively traditional lives, following the reindeer during their seasonal migrations.

Sleeping

Hotel Emma HOTEL €€

(063-51 78 40; www.hotelemma.com; Prästgatan 31; s/d Skr950/1095; P) The individually styled rooms at super-central Emma nestle in crooked hallways on two floors, with homey touches like squishy armchairs and imposing ceramic stoves; some rooms have French doors facing the courtyard. The breakfast spread is a delight. Reception hours are limited, so call ahead if arriving late or early.

Hotel Jämteborg HOTEL €€

(063-51 01 01; www.jamteborg.se; Storgatan 54; hostel d/tr Skr590/840, B&B s/d/tr Skr590/690/890, hotel s/d from Skr1065/1250; P) Just imagine: you're travelling with friends but you're all on different budgets. Hotel Jämteborg comes to the rescue, with its catch-all combo of hostel beds, B&B rooms and hotel rooms in several buildings next to each other. The cheerful hotel rooms come in cream-and-crimson, defying Sweden's 'earth tones only' rule.

Information

Tourist Office (063-14 40 01; www.visitostersund.se; Rådhusgatan 44; 9am-5pm Mon-Fri, 10am-3pm Sat & Sun) The tourist office is opposite the town hall, and has free internet access.

Getting There & Away

Daily bus 45 runs north at 7.15am from Östersund to Gällivare (Skr507, 11¼ hours) via Arvidsjaur (Skr440, seven hours) and Jokkmokk (Skr507, 9½ hours) and south to Mora (Skr269, 5¼ hours, two daily).

SJ connections include two trains daily to Stockholm (Skr670, five hours) via Uppsala and up to six daily trains west to Åre (Skr181, 1¼ hours). In summer the **Inlandsbanan** (0771-53 53 53; www.inlandsbanan.se) train runs once daily north and south.

DON'T MISS

ICEHOTEL

The winter wonderland that is the **Icehotel** (☎0980-668 00; www.icehotel.com; Marnadsvägen 63; s/d/ste from Skr2300/3200/5300, cabins from Skr1900; P) in Jukkasjärvi, 18km east of Kiruna, is an international phenomenon.

The enormous hotel is built using 30,000 tonnes of snow and 4000 tonnes of ice, with international artists and designers contributing innovative ice sculptures every year.

In the ice rooms, the beds are made of compact snow and covered with reindeer skins and serious sleeping bags, guaranteed to keep you warm despite the -5°C temperature inside the rooms. Come morning, guests are revived with a hot drink and a sauna.

The attached Ice Church is popular for weddings, and the much-copied Absolut Icebar serves drinks in ice glasses.

In summer you can visit the smaller replica inside a chilled warehouse.

Umeå

☎090 / POP 115,470

With the vibrant feel of a college town (it has around 30,000 students), Umeå is a welcome outpost of urbanity in the barren north. Since the title of Culture Capital of Europe was bestowed on it in 2014, it's been strutting its stuff, showcasing northern and Sami culture.

Sights

★Västerbottens Museum MUSEUM

(www.vbm.se; Gammliavägen; ⏲10am-5pm, to 9pm Wed) FREE The star of the Gammlia museum complex, the engrossing Västerbottens Museum traces the history of the province from prehistoric times to Umeå today. Exhibitions include an enormous skis-through-the ages collection starring the world's oldest ski (5400 years old), and an exploration of Sami rock art and shaman symbols. Of the temporary exhibitions, a photographic portrayal of a single family through several decades, shot by Latvian photographer Inta Ruka, was particularly moving. Take bus 2 or 7.

Sleeping

STF Vandrarhem Umeå HOSTEL €

(☎090-771650; www.umeavandrarhem.com; Västra Esplanaden 10; dm/s/d from Skr170/300/500; @📶) This busy, efficient hostel has rooms of varying quality: try to nab a space in one of the newer rooms with beds, as opposed to the rather basic dorms with bunks. It's in a great location: a residential neighbourhood at the edge of the town centre, and the facilities (kitchen, laundry) are very handy for self-caterers. Reception hours are limited.

Stora Hotellet Umeå BOUTIQUE HOTEL €€

(☎090-77 88 70; www.storahotelletumea.se; Storgatan 46; s/d/ste from Skr1000/1150/6000; P📶) We love the muted colours and the plush, old-style furnishings that give you the impression you're adrift aboard a luxurious ship. Of the six categories of rooms, even the modest 'Superstition' presents you with luxurious queen-size bunks that real sailors could only dream of, while 'Passion' offers grander surroundings, velvet couches and his 'n' hers showers.

Eating

Vita Björn SWEDISH €€

(www.vitabjorn.se; Kajen 12; mains Skr129-285; ⏲1-9.30pm May-Sep; 🖉) Perch yourself on the sunny deck of this boat-restaurant and choose from a casual international menu of caesar salad, vegie burgers, baked salmon and beef tenderloin. For us, however, it gets no better than that simple, moreish Swedish delight – fresh grilled herring.

Rex Bar och Grill INTERNATIONAL €€€

(☎090-70 60 50; www.rexbar.com; Rädhustorget; mains Skr175-315; ⏲11am-2pm & 5-11pm Mon-Thu, 11am-2am Fri & Sat) This popular bistro has northern Swedish cuisine meeting international brasserie in a convincing explosion of flavour. Choose the northern menu (bleak roe, smoked Arctic char and reindeer steak) or opt for Iberico pork cheek or grilled courgette with morels. Alternatively, stop by for the American-style pancake-and-bacon weekend brunch. Dinner reservations on weekends recommended.

Information

Tourist Office (0090-16 16 16; www.visitumea.se; Renmarkstorget 15; 9am-7pm Mon-Fri, 10am-4pm Sat, noon-4pm Sun) Located on a central square.

Getting There & Around

Länstrafiken i Västerbotten (077-10 01 10; www.tabussen.nu)

Kiruna & Around

0980 / POP 22,940

Thousands of visitors flock to the workaday mining town of Kiruna every year to see the Icehotel in nearby Jukkasjärvi – northern Sweden's biggest attraction – and to take part in all manner of outdoor adventures: dogsledding, snowmobiling and aurora borealis tours in winter, and biking, hiking and canoeing in summer.

Sights

LKAB Iron-Ore Mine MINE

(adult/student Skr295/195) Kiruna owes its existence to the world's largest iron-ore deposit, 4km into the ground, and the action happens 914m below the surface. A visit to the depths of the LKAB iron-ore mine consists of being bussed to the InfoMine – a closed-off section of a mine tunnel, where you can hear mind-blowing stats and view jaw-droppingly large mining equipment, such as the mills used to crush ore. Tours leave daily from the tourist office between June and August.

Tours

Nutti Sami Siida CULTURAL TOUR, ADVENTURE TOUR

(0980-213 29; www.nutti.se) One of Nature's Best (an endorsement given to tour operators who have certain eco-credentials), this specialist in sustainable Sami ecotourism arranges visits to the Ráidu Sami camp to meet reindeer herders (Skr1880), take reindeer-sledding excursions (from Skr2750), northern-lights tours (Skr2700) and four-day, multi-activity Lappland tours that include dogsledding and more (Skr9450).

Kiruna Guidetur SNOW SPORTS, OUTDOORS

(0980-811 10; www.kirunaguidetur.com; Vänortsgatan 8) These popular all-rounders organise anything from overnighting in a self-made igloo, snowmobile safaris and cross-country skiing outings in winter to mountain-bike tours, rafting and quad-biking in summer.

Active Lapland SNOW SPORTS

(076-104 55 08; www.activelapland.com; Solbacksvägen 22) This experienced operator offers two-hour dog-sled rides (Skr1050), rides under the northern lights, and airport pick-ups by dog sleigh (Skr5200). It'll even let you drive your own dog-sled (Skr3200).

Sleeping

STF Vandrarhem & Hotell City HOSTEL, HOTEL €€

(0980-666 55; www.kirunahostel.com; Bergmästaregatan 7; dm/s/d from Skr250/450/500, hotel s/d/tr Skr750/850/1100; P) This catch-all hotel-and-hostel combo has a gleaming red-and-white colour scheme in its modern hotel rooms and cosy dorms. Sauna and breakfast cost extra for hostel guests, but there are handy guest kitchens.

Hotel Arctic Eden BOUTIQUE HOTEL €€

(0980-611 86; www.hotelarcticeden.se; Föraregatan 18; s/d Skr900/1200; P) At Kiruna's most luxurious lodgings, the rooms are a chic blend of Sami decor and modern technology, there's a plush spa and indoor pool, and the friendly staff can book all manner of outdoor adventures. A fine breakfast spread is served in the morning and the on-site Arctic Thai & Grill is flooded with spice-seeking customers on a daily basis.

Eating

★ **Camp Ripan Restaurang** SWEDISH €€

(www.ripan.se; Campingvägen; lunch buffet Skr100-125, dinner mains Skr245-355; 11am-2pm & 6-10pm) The unusually vegie-heavy lunch buffet is good value, but the real draw is the Sami-inspired à la carte menu featuring local, seasonal produce. We're drooling at the very thought of the reindeer steak with bacon and lingonberry sauce, pulled elk with BBQ sauce and rhubarb with licorice meringue. The restaurant's located at the local campground (of all places!).

Information

Tourist Office (☎0980-188 80; www.kirunalapland.se; Lars Janssonsgatan 17; ⊙8.30am-9pm Mon-Fri, to 6pm Sat & Sun) Inside the Folkets Hus visitor centre; has internet access and can book various tours.

Getting There & Away

AIR

Kiruna Airport (☎010-109 46 00; www.swedavia.com/kiruna), 7km east of the town, has direct flights to Stockholm.

BUS

Daily bus 91 runs to Narvik (Norway; Skr280, 2¾ hours) via Abisko (Skr175, 1¼ hours). Bus 501 goes to Jukkasjärvi (Skr40, 30 minutes, two to six daily).

TRAIN

There is a daily overnight train to Stockholm (Skr960, 17½ hours) via Uppsala (Skr960, 16¾ hours).

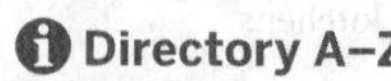

SURVIVAL GUIDE

Directory A–Z

ACCOMMODATION

At hostels, HI members save a substantial amount at affiliated places – called STF in Sweden. You'll save extra by bringing your own sleep sheet.

For info on campsites and cabins, visit www.stuga.nu.

Accommodation in Sweden is generally of a high standard.

BUSINESS HOURS

Except where indicated, we list hours for high season (mid-June to August). Expect more limited hours the rest of the year.

COUNTRY FACTS

Area 450,295 sq km

Capital Stockholm

Country Code ☎46

Emergency ☎112

Currency Krona (Skr)

Language Swedish

Money ATMs are very common, plastic taken everywhere

Population 9.72 million

Visas Schengen visa rules apply

Banks 9.30am to 3pm Monday to Friday; some city branches open to 5pm or 6pm

Bars & pubs 11am or noon to 1am or 2am

Government offices 9am to 5pm Monday to Friday

Restaurants lunch 11am to 2pm, dinner 5pm to 10pm; often closed on Sunday and/or Monday, high-end restaurants often closed for a week or two in July or August

Shops 9am to 6pm Monday to Friday, to 1pm Saturday

CHILDREN

Sweden makes it easy to travel with children, with many kid-friendly attractions and outdoor activities. Museum admission is often free for those aged under 20. Hotels will put extra beds in rooms, restaurants have family-friendly features and there are substantial transport discounts for kids.

GAY & LESBIAN TRAVELLERS

Sweden is famously liberal; since 2009 its gender-neutral marriage law has given same-sex married couples the same rights and obligations as heterosexual married couples. The national organisation for gay and lesbian rights is **Riksförbundet för Sexuellt Likaberättigande** (RFSL; ☎08-50 16 29 00; www.rfsl.se; Sveavägen 57-59).

For entertainment listings, club nights and other local information, visit www.qx.se.

INTERNET ACCESS

Most hotels and hostels have wi-fi. Free wi-fi at coffee shops is common; ask for the code when you order. Many tourist offices offer a computer terminal for visitor use (sometimes for a fee).

INTERNET RESOURCES

Lonely Planet (www.lonelyplanet.com/sweden)

Swedish Institute (www.si.se/English)

Visit Sweden (www.visitsweden.com)

MONEY

Credit and debit cards can be used almost everywhere, and ATMs are plentiful. Visa and MasterCard are standard; American Express and Discover are less widely accepted.

The default system uses cards with microchips; if your card has no chip or pin, ask the clerk to swipe it.

PUBLIC HOLIDAYS

New Year's Day 1 January

Epiphany 6 January

Good Friday March/April

Easter Sunday & Monday March/April

May Day 1 May

Ascension Day May/June

Whitsunday and/or Monday Late May or early June

Midsummer's Eve & Day Between 19 and 25 June

All Saints' Day October/November

Christmas 25 December

Boxing Day 26 December

TELEPHONE

- Public telephones are few and far between; you'll need to buy a phone card at a newsstand (Pressbyrå).
- You can buy a prepaid SIM card at newsstands or phone shops, usually for around €10, including some credit. Top up at the same outlets, online or at ATMs.
- To call abroad, dial ☎00.

TIME

Sweden is one hour ahead of UTC/GMT (two hours from late March to late October).

VISAS

Schengen visa rules apply.

Getting There & Away

AIR

Sweden's main airport is Stockholm Arlanda. Entry is straightforward; most visitors simply need to fill out and hand over a brief customs form and show their passport at immigration.

LAND

Numerous trains connect Copenhagen in Denmark to Sweden via the Öresund bridge.

SEA

Baltic and Atlantic ferries connect Sweden with eastern and northern European nations: Germany, Poland, Estonia, Latvia, Lithuania, Finland, Russia and the UK. Book ahead if travelling with a vehicle. Many ferry lines offer 50% discounts for holders of rail passes. The website www.directferries.com is useful for routes and discounted tickets.

SLEEPING PRICE RANGES

The following price ranges refer to a double in the summer season (mid-June through August); prices during the rest of the year might be twice as high:

€ less than Skr800

€€ Skr800 to Skr1600

€€€ more than Skr1600

Getting Around

BICYCLE

Bikes can be carried on many trains (though not Stockholm's tunnelbana) and most buses and ferries, but it's wise to reserve space in advance. Sweden is one of the world's most cycle-friendly destinations, with numerous places to hire bikes, cycle lanes in every city, and excellent long-distance trail networks.

BUS

Swebus Express (☎0771-21 82 18; www.swebus.se) has a large network of express buses serving the southern half of the country.

Svenska Buss (☎0771-67 67 67; www.svenskabuss.se) and **Nettbuss** (☎0771-15 15 15; www.nettbuss.se) connect many southern towns and cities with Stockholm.

Several smaller operators, including **Ybuss** (☎060-17 19 60; www.ybuss.se), have services to Östersund and Umeå.

CAR & MOTORCYCLE

If you're bringing your own car, you'll need vehicle registration documents, unlimited third-party

ESSENTIAL FOOD & DRINK

Scandinavian cuisine, once viewed as meatballs, herring and little else, is now at the forefront of modern gastronomy. New Nordic cuisine showcases local produce, blending traditional techniques and contemporary experimentation.

Swedish menu essentials:

- **Coffee** To fit in, eight or nine cups a day is about right; luckily, the region's cafes are a delight.
- **Reindeer & Game** Expect to see reindeer and other delicious game, especially up north in Sami cooking.
- **Alcohol** Beer is everywhere, and improving; but try a shot of *brännvin* (aquavit) with your pickled herring, too.
- **Fish** Salmon is ubiquitous and delicious, and smoked, cured, pickled or fried herring is fundamental. Tasty lake fish include Arctic char and pike-perch.

EATING PRICE RANGES

The following price categories refer to the average price of a main dish (entree), not including drinks:

€ less than Skr100

€€ Skr100 to Skr200

€€€ more than Skr200

liability insurance and a valid driving licence. A right-hand-drive vehicle brought from the UK or Ireland should have deflectors fitted to the headlights to avoid dazzling oncoming traffic. You must carry a reflective warning breakdown triangle.

Hire

To hire a car you have to be at least 20 (sometimes 25) years of age, with a recognised driving licence and a credit card. Avis, Hertz and Europcar have desks at Stockholm Arlanda airport and offices in most major cities. The lowest car-hire rates are generally from larger petrol stations (like Statoil and OKQ8).

TRAIN

Sweden has an extensive and reliable railway network, and trains are almost always faster than buses.

Train Passes

The Sweden Rail Pass, Eurodomino tickets and international passes, such as Inter-Rail and Eurail, are accepted on SJ services and most regional trains.

The **Eurail Scandinavia Pass** (www.eurail.com) entitles you to unlimited rail travel in Denmark, Finland, Norway and Sweden; it is valid in 2nd class only and is available for four, five, six, eight or 10 days of travel within a two-month period (prices start at youth/adult US$276/368). The X2000 trains require all rail-pass holders to pay a supplement of Skr62. The pass provides free travel on Scandlines' Helsingør to Helsingborg route and discounts on other ship routes.

CONNECTIONS

Getting to the rest of Scandinavia and further into Europe from Sweden is easy. From Stockholm there are train and bus connections to London or Berlin as well as to Denmark, Finland and Norway. Ferries are another option, with frequent connections between many Swedish ports and the rest of Europe. Airports in Stockholm and Göteborg connect Sweden with the rest of the world.

Switzerland

Includes ➡

Best Places to Eat

- Chez Vrony (p1122)
- Alpenrose (p1132)
- Grottino 1313 (p1125)
- Volkshaus Basel (p1134)

Best Places to Stay

- SYHA Basel St Alban Youth Hostel (p1133)
- Hotel Schweizerhof (p1123)
- Hotel Bahnhof (p1122)
- The Hotel (p1125)

Why Go?

What giddy romance Zermatt, St Moritz and other glitterati-encrusted names evoke. This is *Sonderfall Schweiz* ('special-case Switzerland'), a privileged neutral country set apart from others, proudly idiosyncratic, insular and unique. It's blessed with gargantuan cultural diversity: its four official languages alone speak volumes.

The Swiss don't do half measures: Zürich, their most gregarious urban centre, has cutting-edge art, legendary nightlife and one of the world's highest living standards. The national passion for sharing the great outdoors provides access (by public transport, no less!) to some of the world's most inspiring panoramic experiences.

So don't depend just on your postcard images of Bern's and Lucerne's chocolate-box architecture, the majestic Matterhorn or those pristine lakes – Switzerland is a place so outrageously beautiful it simply must be seen to be believed.

When to Go

Bern

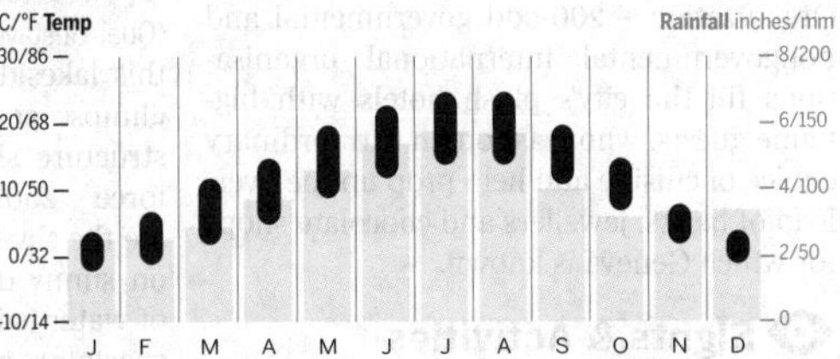

Dec–early Apr Carve through powder and eat fondue at an alpine resort.

May–Sep Hike in the shadow of the mesmerising Matterhorn and be wowed by its perfection.

Aug Celebrate Swiss National Day on 1 August and witness Swiss national pride in full force.

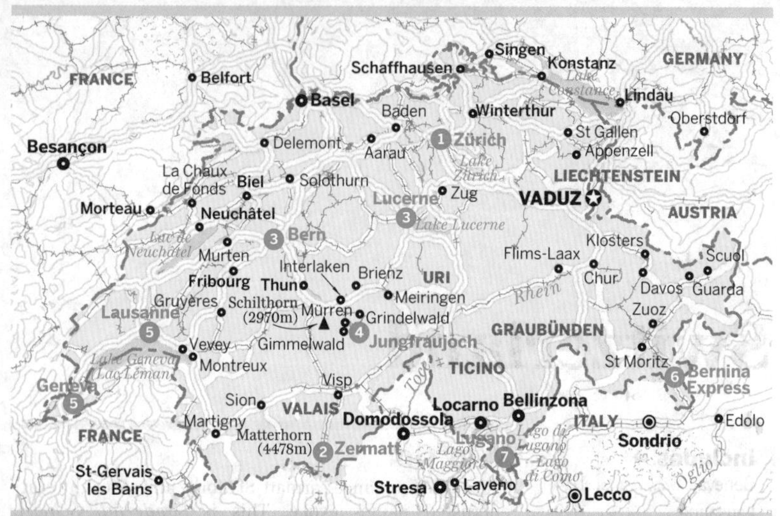

Switzerland Highlights

1. Discover zesty **Zürich** (p1129) via a daytime stroll along the city's sublime lake followed by a rollicking night out.
2. Marvel at the iconic Matterhorn and wander around the car-free alpine village of **Zermatt** (p1121).
3. Enjoy the charm of famous beauties **Bern** (p1122) and **Lucerne** (p1124): think medieval Old Town appeal, folkloric fountains and art.
4. Be wowed by the Eiger's monstrous north face on a ride to the 'top of Europe', 3471m **Jungfraujoch** (p1128).
5. Board a boat in **Geneva** for a serene Lake Geneva cruise to medieval **Lausanne** (p1118).
6. Ride one of Switzerland's iconic scenic trains, such as the **Bernina Express** (p1135).
7. Go Italian at **Lugano** (p1135), with its lovely, temperate lake setting.

GENEVA

POP 189,000

The whole world seems to be in Geneva, Switzerland's second city. The UN, the International Red Cross, the World Health Organization – 200-odd governmental and nongovernmental international organisations fill the city's plush hotels with big-name guests, who feast on an extraordinary choice of cuisine and help prop up the overload of banks, jewellers and chocolate shops for which Geneva is known.

Sights & Activities

The city centre is so compact it's easy to see many of the main sights on foot. Begin your explorations on the southern side of Lake Geneva and visit the **Jardin Anglais** (Quai du Général-Guisan) to see the **Horloge Fleurie** (Flower Clock). Crafted from 6500 flowers, the clock has ticked since 1955 and sports the world's longest second hand (2.5m).

★ Jet d'Eau FOUNTAIN

(Quai Gustave-Ador) When landing by plane, this lakeside fountain is the first dramatic glimpse you get of Geneva. The 140m-tall structure shoots up water with incredible force – 200km/h, 1360 horsepower – to create the sky-high plume, kissed by a rainbow on sunny days. At any one time, 7 tonnes of water is in the air, much of which sprays spectators on the pier beneath. Two or three times a year it is illuminated pink, blue or another colour to mark a humanitarian occasion.

ITINERARIES

One Week

Starting in vibrant **Zürich**, shop famous Bahnhofstrasse, then eat, drink and be merry. Next, head to the **Jungfrau region** to explore some kick-ass alpine scenery, whether it be by hiking or skiing. Take a pit stop in beautiful **Lucerne** before finishing up in Switzerland's delightful capital, **Bern**.

Two Weeks

As above, then head west for a French flavour in **Geneva** or lakeside **Lausanne**. Stop in **Gruyères** to dip into a cheesy fondue and overdose on meringues drowned in thick double cream. Zip to **Zermatt** or across to **St Moritz** to frolic in snow or green meadows, then loop east to taste the Italian side of Switzerland at lakeside **Lugano**.

★Cathédrale St-Pierre CATHEDRAL
(www.espace-saint-pierre.ch; Cour St-Pierre; admission free, towers adult/child Sfr5/2; ⏲9.30am-6.30pm Mon-Sat, noon-6.30pm Sun Jun-Sep, 10am-5.30pm Oct-May) FREE Begun in the 11th century, Geneva's cathedral is predominantly Gothic with an 18th-century neoclassical facade. Between 1536 and 1564 Protestant John Calvin preached here; see his seat in the north aisle. Inside the cathedral 77 steps spiral up to the attic – a fascinating glimpse at its architectural construction – from where another 40 lead to the top of the panoramic **northern** and **southern towers**.

In summer, free carillon (5pm) and organ (6pm) concerts fill the cathedral and its surrounding square with soul.

Musée International de la Croix-Rouge et du Croissant-Rouge MUSEUM
(www.micr.org; Av de la Paix 17; adult/child Sfr15/7; ⏲10am-6pm Wed-Mon Apr-Oct, 10am-5pm Nov-Mar) Compelling multimedia exhibits at Geneva's fascinating International Red Cross and Red Crescent Museum trawl through atrocities perpetuated by humanity. The litany of war and nastiness, documented in films, photos, sculptures and soundtracks, is set against the noble aims of the organisation created by Geneva businessmen and philanthropists Henri Dunant and Henri Dufour in 1864. Excellent temporary exhibitions command an additional entrance fee. Take bus 8 from Gare de Cornavin to the Appia stop.

Patek Philippe Museum WATCH MUSEUM
(☎022 807 09 10; www.patekmuseum.com; Rue des Vieux-Grenadiers 7; adult/child Sfr10/free; ⏲2-6pm Tue-Fri, 10am-6pm Sat) This elegant museum by one of Switzerland's leading luxury watchmakers displays exquisite timepieces and enamels from the 16th century to the present.

Sleeping

When checking in, ask for your free Public Transport Card, covering unlimited bus travel for the duration of your hotel stay.

Hôtel Bel' Esperance HOTEL €
(☎022 818 37 37; www.hotel-bel-esperance.ch; Rue de la Vallée 1; s/d/tr/q from Sfr110/170/210/250; ⏲reception 7am-10pm; @ 📶) This two-star hotel is extraordinary value. Rooms are quiet and cared for, those on the 1st floor share a kitchen, and there are fridges for guests to store picnic supplies – or sausages – in! Ride the lift to the 5th floor to flop on its wonderful flower-filled rooftop terrace, complete with barbecue that can be rented (Sfr8).

Hotel Edelweiss HOTEL €€
(☎022 544 51 51; www.hoteledelweissgeneva.com; Place de la Navigation 2; d Sfr160-400; ❄ @ 📶) Plunge yourself into the heart of the Swiss Alps with this Heidi-style hideout, very much the Swiss Alps *en ville* with its fireplace, wildflower-painted pine bedheads and big, cuddly St Bernard lolling over the banister. Its chalet-styled restaurant is a key address among Genevans for traditional cheese fondue.

Geneva

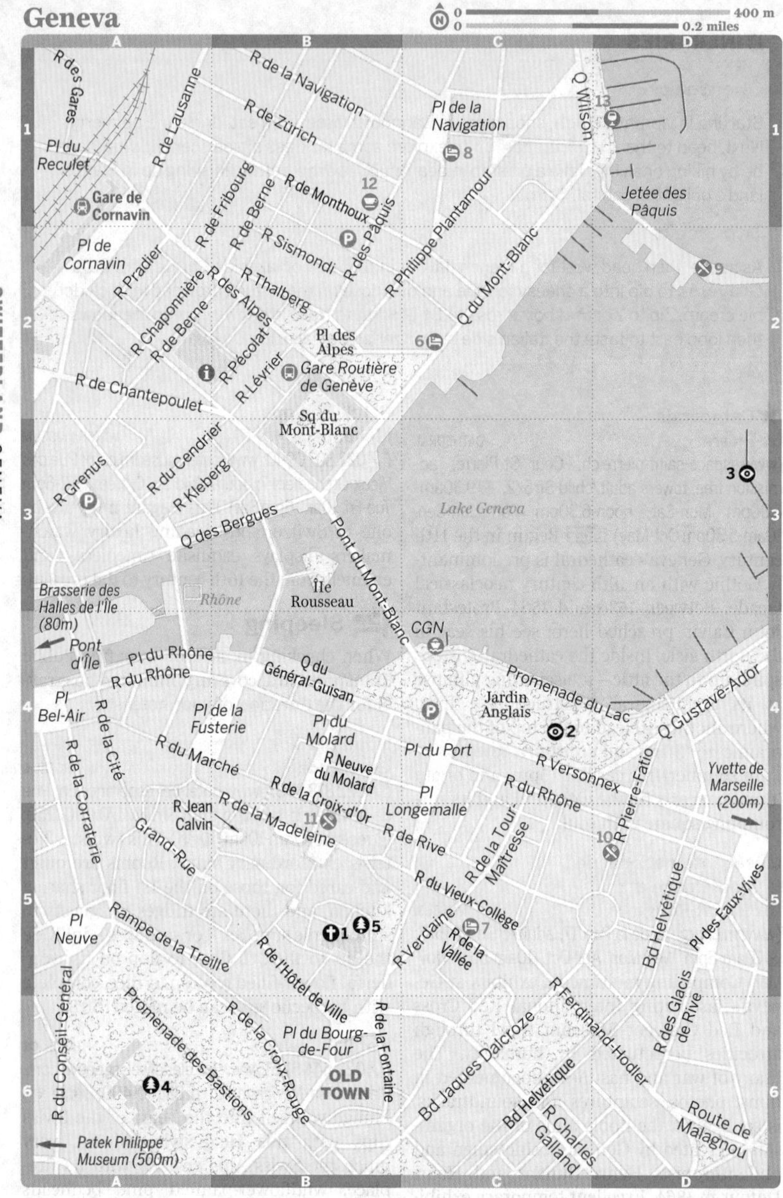

Hôtel Beau-Rivage HISTORIC HOTEL €€€
(022 716 66 66; www.beau-rivage.ch; Quai du Mont-Blanc 13; d from Sfr515; P ❄ @) Run by the Mayer family for five generations, the Beau-Rivage is a 19th-century jewel dripping in opulence.

Geneva

Sights

Sleeping

Eating

Drinking & Nightlife

Eating

Eateries crowd Place du Bourg-de-Four, Geneva's oldest square, in the lovely Old Town. Otherwise, head down the hill towards the river and Place du Molard, packed with tables and chairs for much of the year. In Pâquis, there's a tasty line-up of more affordable restaurants on Place de la Navigation.

★Buvette des Bains CAFETERIA €

(☎022 738 16 16; www.bains-des-paquis.ch; Quai du Mont-Blanc 30, Bains des Pâquis; mains Sfr14-16; ⏰7am-10.30pm) Meet Genevans at this earthy beach bar – rough and hip around the edges – at lakeside pool, Bains des Pâquis. Grab breakfast, a salad or the *plat du jour* (dish of the day), or dip into a *fondue au crémant* (Champagne fondue). Dining is self-service on trays and alfresco in summer. In summer pay Sfr2/1 per adult/child to access the canteen, inside the pub.

★Le Relais d'Entrecôte STEAKHOUSE €€

(☎022 310 60 04; www.relaisentrecote.fr; Rue Pierre Fatio 6; steak & chips Sfr42; ⏰noon-2.30pm & 7-11pm) Key vocabulary at this timeless classic where everyone eats the same dish is *à point* (medium), *bien cuit* (well done) and *saignant* (rare). It doesn't even bother with menus, just sit down, say how you like your steak cooked and wait for it to arrive – two handsome servings (!) pre-empted by a green salad and accompanied by perfectly crisp, skinny fries.

Should you have room at the end of it all, the desserts are justly raved about. No advance reservations so arrive sharp.

★Brasserie des Halles de l'Île EUROPEAN €€

(☎022 311 08 88; www.brasseriedeshallesdelile.ch; Place de l'Île 1; mains Sfr20-50; ⏰10.30am-midnight Sun & Mon, to 1am Tue-Thu, to 2am Fri & Sat) At home in Geneva's old market hall on an island, this industrial-style venue cooks up a buzzing cocktail of after-work aperitifs with music, after-dark DJs and seasonal fare of fresh vegies and regional products (look for the Appellation d'Origine Contrôllée products flagged on the menu). Arrive early to snag the best seat in the house – a superb terrace hanging over the water.

Drinking & Entertainment

Pâquis, the district in between the train station and lake, is particularly well endowed with bars. In summer the **paillote** (www.laterrasse.ch; Quai du Mont-Blanc 31; ⏰8am-midnight Apr-Sep), with wooden tables inches from the water, gets crammed.

For a dose of bohemia, head to Carouge on tram 12. This shady quarter of 17th-century houses and narrow streets has galleries, hip bars and funky shops.

Café des Arts CAFE, BAR

(Rue des Pâquis 15; ⏰11am-2am Mon-Fri, 8am-2am Sat & Sun) As much a place to drink as a daytime cafe, this Pâquis hang-out lures a local crowd with its Parisian-style terrace and artsy interior. Food-wise, think meal-size salads, designer sandwiches and a great-value lunchtime *plat du jour*.

★Yvette de Marseille BAR

(Rue Henri Blanvalet 13; ⏰5.30pm-midnight Mon & Tue, 5.30pm-1am Wed & Thu, 5.30pm-2am Fri, 6.30pm-2am Sat) No bar begs the question 'what's in the name?' more than this buzzy drinking hole. Urban and edgy, it occupies a mechanic's workshop once owned by Yvette. Note the garage door, the trap door in the floor where cars were repaired and the street number 13 (aka the departmental number of the Bouches-du-Rhône *département*, home to Marseille).

LOCAL KNOWLEDGE

PICNIC SPOTS

With mountains of fine views to pick from, Geneva is prime picnicking terrain for those reluctant to pay too much to eat. Grab a salt-studded pretzel filled with whatever you fancy (Sfr4 to Sfr6.50) from takeaway kiosk **Maison du Bretzel** (Rue de la Croix d'Or 4; pretzel Sfr4-6.50; ⏲8am-7.30pm Mon-Wed & Fri, to 9pm Thu) and head for a local picnic spot:

➡ In the contemplative shade of Henry Moore's voluptuous sculpture *Reclining Figure: Arch Leg* (1973) in the park opposite the Musée d'Art et d'Histoire.

➡ Behind the cathedral on **Terrasse Agrippa d'Abigné**, a tree-shaded park with benches, sand pit and see-saw for kids, and a fine rooftop and cathedral view.

➡ On a bench on Quai du Mont-Blanc with Mont Blanc view (sunny days only).

➡ On the world's longest bench (126m long) on chestnut tree–lined Promenade de la Treille, **Parc des Bastions**.

Chat Noir CLUB, BAR
(☎022 307 10 40; www.chatnoir.ch; Rue Vauthier 13; ⏲6pm-4am Tue-Thu, to 5am Fri & Sat) One of the busiest night spots in Carouge, the Black Cat is packed most nights thanks to its all-rounder vibe: arrive after work for an aperitif with selection of tapas to nibble on, and stay until dawn for dancing, live music and DJ sets.

Shopping

Designer shopping is wedged between Rue du Rhône and Rue de Rive; the latter has lots of chain stores. Grand-Rue in the Old Town and Carouge boast artsy boutiques.

Information

Tourist Office (☎022 909 70 00; www.geneve-tourisme.ch; Rue du Mont-Blanc 18; ⏲9am-6pm Mon-Sat, 10am-4pm Sun)

Getting There & Away

AIR

Aéroport International de Genève (p1138), 4km from town, has connections to major European cities and many others worldwide.

BOAT

CGN (Compagnie Générale de Navigation; ☎0848 811 848; www.cgn.ch) operates a web of scenic steamer services from its Jardin Anglais jetty to other villages on Lake Geneva. Many only sail May to September, including those to/from Lausanne (Sfr64, 3½ hours). Eurail and Swiss passes are valid on CGN boats or there is a one-day CGN boat pass (Sfr60).

BUS

International buses depart from the **bus station** (☎0900 320 230, 022 732 02 30; www.coach-station.com; Place Dorcière).

TRAIN

Trains run to major Swiss towns including at least every 30 minutes to/from Lausanne (Sfr21.80, 33 to 48 minutes), Bern (Sfr49, 1¾ hours) and Zürich (Sfr84, 2¾ hours).

International daily rail connections from Geneva include Paris by TGV (3¼ hours) and Milan (four hours).

Getting Around

TO/FROM THE AIRPORT

Getting from the airport is easy with regular trains into Gare de Cornavin (Sfr2.50, eight minutes). Slower bus 10 (Sfr3.50) does the same 4km trip. A metered taxi costs Sfr35 to Sfr50.

BICYCLE

Pick up a bike at Genèveroule (www.geneveroule.ch) on Place du Rhône: the first four hours are free, then it's Sfr2 per hour. Bring ID and a Sfr20 cash deposit. Find other Genèveroule stands at Bains des Pâquis, Place de l'Octroi in Carouge, and Place de Montbrillant.

PUBLIC TRANSPORT

Buses, trams, trains and boats service the city, and ticket dispensers are found at all stops. Most services are operated by **TPG** (www.tpg.ch; Rue de Montbrillant; ⏲7am-7pm Mon-Fri, 9am-6pm Sat). Typical tickets cost Sfr3.50 (one hour); a day pass is Sfr8 when purchased after 9am.

LAKE GENEVA REGION

Lausanne

POP 130,400

In a fabulous location overlooking Lake Geneva, Lausanne is an enchanting beauty with several distinct personalities: the former fishing village of Ouchy, with its lakeside bustle; the Vieille Ville (Old Town), with charming cobblestone streets and covered staircases; and Flon, a warehouse district of bars and boutiques.

Sights & Activities

★Cathédrale de Notre Dame CHURCH

(Place de la Cathédrale; ⌚9am-7pm Apr-Sep, to 5.30pm Oct-Mar) Lausanne's Gothic cathedral, Switzerland's finest, stands proudly at the heart of the Old Town. Raised in the 12th and 13th centuries on the site of earlier, humbler churches, it lacks the lightness of French Gothic buildings but is remarkable nonetheless. Pope Gregory X, in the presence of Rudolph of Habsburg (the Holy Roman Emperor) and an impressive following of European cardinals and bishops, consecrated the church in 1275.

Place de la Palud SQUARE

In the heart of the Vieille Ville, this 9th-century medieval market square – pretty as a picture – was originally bogland. For five centuries it has been home to the city government, now housed in the 17th-century **Hôtel de Ville** (town hall). A fountain pierces one end of the square, presided over by a brightly painted column topped by the allegorical figure of Justice, clutching scales and dressed in blue.

Musée Olympique MUSEUM

(☎021 621 65 11; www.olympic.org/museum; Quai d'Ouchy 1; adult/child Sfr18/10; ⌚9am-6pm May–mid-Oct daily, 10am-6pm mid-Oct–Apr Tue-Sun) Lausanne's Musée Olympique is easily the city's most lavish museum and an essential stop for sports buffs (and kids). Following a thorough revamp of its facilities, the museum reopened in 2014, with its tiered landscaped gardens and site-specific scuptural works as inviting as ever. Inside, there is a fabulous cafe with a champion lake view from its terrace, and a state-of-the-art museum recounting the Olympic story from its inception to the present day through video, interactive displays, memorabilia and temporary themed exhibitions.

Sleeping

Hotel guests get a Lausanne Transport Card providing unlimited use of public transport for the duration of their stay.

Lausanne Guest House HOSTEL €

(☎021 601 80 00; www.lausanne-guesthouse.ch; Chemin des Épinettes 4; dm from Sfr37, s/d from Sfr90/107, with shared bathroom from Sfr80/96; ⌚reception 7.30am-noon & 3-10pm; P@📶) 🍃 An attractive mansion converted into quality backpacking accommodation near the train station. Many rooms have lake views and you can hang out in the garden or terrace. Parking is Sfr11 per day, there's a 24-hour laundry and room to leave your bike. Some of the building's energy is solar.

Lhotel BOUTIQUE HOTEL €

(☎021 331 39 39; www.lhotel.ch; Place de l'Europe 6; r from Sfr130; ❄📶) This smart small hotel is ideally placed for the city's lively Flon district nightlife. Rooms are simple and startlingly white, and come with iPads; breakfast costs Sfr14. There's a fab rooftop terrace and your stay gives you access to the spa at five-star Lausanne Palace & Spa nearby for Sfr55.

Eating & Drinking

★Holy Cow BURGERS €

(www.holycow.ch; Rue Cheneau-de-Bourg 17; burger with chips & drink Sfr20; ⌚11am-10pm Mon & Tue, to 11pm Wed-Sat; 👪) A Lausanne success story, with branches in Geneva, Zürich and France, burgers (beef, chicken or vegie) feature local ingredients, creative toppings and witty names. Grab an artisanal beer, sit at a shared wooden table, and wait for your burger and fab fries to arrive in a straw basket. A second outlet can be found at **Rue des Terreaux** (Rue des Terreaux 10; burger with chips & drink Sfr20; ⌚11am-11pm Mon-Sat).

Café Romand SWISS €

(☎021 312 63 75; www.cafe-romand.ch; Place St François 2; mains Sfr16-41.50; ⌚8am-midnight

DON'T MISS

MONTREUX

This tidy lakeside town boasts Switzerland's most extraordinary castle.

Originally constructed on the shores of Lake Geneva in the 11th century, **Château de Chillon** (☎021 966 89 10; www.chillon.ch; Av de Chillon 21; adult/child Sfr12.50/6; ⏲9am-7pm Apr-Sep, 9.30am-6pm Mar & Oct, 10am-5pm Nov-Feb, last entry 1hr before close) was brought to the world's attention by Lord Byron and the world has been filing past ever since. Spend at least a couple of hours exploring its numerous courtyards, towers, dungeons and halls filled with arms, period furniture and artwork.

The castle is a lovely 45-minute lakefront walk from Montreux. Otherwise, trolley bus 1 passes every 10 minutes; better still, come on a CGN steamer from Montreux (Sfr17, 15 minutes).

Crowds throng to the legendary (and not all-jazz) **Montreux Jazz Festival** (www.montreuxjazz.com) for a fortnight in early July. Free concerts take place every day, but big-name gigs cost Sfr75 to Sfr240. Lovers of Freddie Mercury should hightail it to the **Queen Studio Experience** (www.mercuryphoenixtrust.com; Rue du Théâtre 9, Casino Barrière de Montreux; ⏲10.30am-10pm) FREE and also to the **Freddie Mercury statue** on Place du Marché.

There are frequent trains to Lausanne (Sfr12.40, 19 minutes) and other lakeside points. Make the scenic journey to Interlaken via the **GoldenPass Line** (www.goldenpass.ch; 2nd class one way Sfr57, three hours, daily; rail passes valid).

Mon-Sat) Tucked away in an unpromising looking arcade, this Lausanne legend dating to 1951 is a welcome blast from the past. Locals pour into the broad, somewhat sombre dining area filled with timber tables to revel in fondue, raclette (Sfr8.50 per serve), *cervelle au beurre noir* (brains in black butter), tripe, *pied de porc* (pork trotters) and other feisty traditional dishes.

Great Escape PUB

(☎021 312 31 94; www.the-great.ch; Rue Madeleine 18; ⏲11am-late) Everyone knows the Great Escape, a busy student pub with pub grub (great burgers) and an enviable terrace with a view over Place de la Riponne. From the aforementioned square, walk up staircase Escaliers de l'Université and turn right.

Information

The **tourist office** (☎021 613 73 21; www.lausanne-tourisme.ch; Place de la Navigation 6; ⏲9am-7pm Apr-Sep, to 6pm Oct-Mar) neighbours Ouchy metro station; there is also a **branch** (☎021 613 73 73; www.lausanne-tourisme.ch; Place de la Gare 9; ⏲9am-7pm) at the train station.

Getting There & Away

BOAT

The **CGN** (Compagnie Générale de Navigation; www.cgn.ch) steamer service runs from early April to mid-September to/from Geneva (Sfr43, 3½ hours) via Nyon. Other services lace the lake, including to Montreux (Sfr26, 1½ hours, up to six daily).

TRAIN

There are frequent trains to/from Geneva (Sfr21.80, 33 to 48 minutes) and Bern (Sfr32, 70 minutes).

Getting Around

Lausanne spans several steep hillsides, so prepare for some good walks.

Buses and trolley buses service most destinations; the vital m2 Métro line (single trip/day pass Sfr2.20/8.80) connects the lake (Ouchy) with the train station (Gare), cathedral area and Flon.

Gruyères

POP 1800

Cheese and featherweight meringues drowned in thick cream are what this dreamy village is all about. Named after the emblematic gru (crane) brandished by the medieval Counts of Gruyères, it is a riot of 15th- to 17th-century houses tumbling down a hillock. Its heart is cobbled, a castle is its crowning glory and hard AOC Gruyère (the village is Gruyères, but the 's' is dropped for the cheese) has been made for centuries in its surrounding alpine pastures.

Fondue-serving cafes line the main square.

Sights

A combined ticket covering the chateau and La Maison du Gruyère cheese dairy costs Sfr14.50 (no child combo ticket).

Château de Gruyères CASTLE

(026 921 21 02; www.chateau-gruyeres.ch; Rue du Château 8; adult/child Sfr10/3; 9am-6pm Apr-Oct, 10am-4.30pm Nov-Mar) This bewitching turreted castle, home to 19 different Counts of Gruyères who controlled the Sarine Valley from the 11th to 16th centuries, was rebuilt after a fire in 1493. Inside, view period furniture, tapestries and modern 'fantasy art' and watch a 20-minute multimedia film.

Don't miss the short footpath that weaves its way around the castle.

La Maison du Gruyère CHEESE DAIRY

(026 921 84 00; www.lamaisondugruyere.ch; Place de la Gare 3; adult/child Sfr7/3; 9am-7pm Jun-Sep, to 6pm Oct-May) The secret behind Gruyère cheese is revealed in Pringy, 1.5km from Gruyères. Cheesemaking takes place three to four times daily between 9am and 11am and 12.30pm to 2.30pm.

Getting There & Away

Gruyères can be reached by train, although the village is a 10-minute walk uphill from the train station (or you can take a free bus that meets trains).

VALAIS

This is Matterhorn country, an intoxicating land that seduces the toughest of critics with its endless panoramic vistas and breathtaking views. Switzerland's 10 highest mountains rise to the sky here, while snow fiends ski and board in one of Europe's top resorts, Zermatt.

Zermatt

POP 6000

Since the mid-19th century, Zermatt has starred among Switzerland's glitziest resorts. Today it attracts intrepid mountaineers and hikers, skiers who cruise at a snail's pace, spellbound by the scenery, and style-conscious darlings flashing designer togs in the lounge bars. But all are smitten with the **Matterhorn** (4478m), the Alps' most famous peak and an unfathomable monolith synonymous with Switzerland that you simply can't quite stop looking at.

Sights & Activities

Zermatt is **skiing** heaven, with mostly long, scenic red runs, plus a smattering of blues for ski virgins and knuckle-whitening blacks for experts. The main skiing areas in winter are **Rothorn**, **Stockhorn** and **Klein Matterhorn** – 350km of ski runs in all, with a link from Klein Matterhorn to the Italian resort of Cervinia and a **freestyle park** with half-pipe for snowboarders. **Summer skiing** (20km of runs) and **boarding** (gravity park at Plateau Rosa on the Theodul glacier) is Europe's most extensive. One-/two-day summer ski passes are Sfr82/122.

Zermatt is also excellent for **hiking**, with 400km of summer trails through some of the most incredible scenery in the Alps – the tourist office has trail maps. For Matterhorn closeups, nothing beats the highly dramatic **Matterhorn Glacier Trail** (two hours, 6.49km) from Trockener Steg to Schwarzsee; 23 information panels en route tell you everything you could possibly need to know about glaciers and glacial life.

Matterhorn Glacier Paradise CABLE CAR

(www.matterhornparadise.ch; adult/child Sfr99/49.50; 8.30am-4.20pm) Views from Zermatt's cable cars are all remarkable, but the Matterhorn Glacier Paradise is the icing on the cake. Ride Europe's highest-altitude cable car to 3883m and gawp at 14 glaciers and 38 mountain peaks over 4000m from the **Panoramic Platform** (only open in good weather). Don't miss the **Glacier Palace**, an ice palace complete with glittering ice sculptures and an ice slide to swoosh down bum first. End with some exhilarating **snow tubing** outside in the snowy surrounds.

★ **Gornergratbahn** RAILWAY
(www.gornergrat.ch; Bahnhofplatz 7; one-way adult/child Sfr42/21; ⏲7am-9.50pm) Europe's highest cogwheel railway has climbed through picture-postcard scenery to **Gornergrat** (3089m) – a 30-minute journey – since 1898. Sit on the right-hand side of the little red train to gawp at the Matterhorn. Tickets allow you to get on and off en route; there are restaurants at Riffelalp (2211m) and Riffelberg (2582m). In summer an extra train runs once a week at sunrise and sunset – the most spectacular trips of all.

Sleeping & Eating

Most places close from May to mid- (or late) June and then again from October to mid-November.

★ **Hotel Bahnhof** HOTEL €
(☎027 967 24 06; www.hotelbahnhof.com; Bahnhofstrasse; dm Sfr40-45, s/d/q from Sfr80/110/235; ⏲reception 8-11.30am & 4-7pm, closed May & Oct; 📶) Opposite the train station, these five-star budget digs have comfy beds, spotless bathrooms and family-perfect rooms for four. Dorms (Sfr5 liner obligatory) are cosy and there's a stylish lounge with armchairs to flop in and books to read. No breakfast, but feel free to prepare your own in the snazzy, open-plan kitchen.

★ **Snowboat** INTERNATIONAL €
(☎027 967 43 33; www.snowboat.ch; Vispastrasse 20; mains Sfr19-26; ⏲noon-midnight) This hybrid eating-drinking, riverside address, with marigold-yellow deckchairs sprawled across its rooftop sun terrace, is a blessing. When fondue tires, head here for barbecue-sizzled burgers (forget beef, try a lamb and goat's cheese or Indonesian chicken satay burger), super-power creative salads (the Omega 3 buster is a favourite) and great cocktails. The vibe? It's 100% fun and funky.

★ **Chez Vrony** SWISS €€
(☎027 967 25 52; www.chezvrony.ch; Findeln; breakfast Sfr28, mains Sfr23-45; ⏲9.15am-5pm Dec-Apr & mid-Jun–mid-Oct) Ride the *Sunnegga Express* to 2288m then ski down blue piste 6 or summer-hike 15 minutes to Zermatt's tastiest slope-side address in the hamlet of Findeln. Keep snug in a cream blanket or lounge on a sheepskin-cushioned chaise longue and revel in the effortless romance of this century-old farmhouse with potted Edelweiss on the tables, first-class Matterhorn views and exceptional organic cuisine.

WORTH A TRIP

GLACIER EXPRESS

You'll have a hard time avoiding the hype for the **Glacier Express** (www.glacierexpress.ch; one-way adult/child Sfr145/73), the train that links Zermatt with the eastern towns and resorts of Graubünden, including St Moritz.

Although there is some stunning scenery of glacier-cleaved valleys and soaring peaks along the route, much of the run is down in valleys, so don't expect nonstop scenic thrills. You can shorten the eight-hour duration by starting at the rail hub of Brig instead of Zermatt or by just doing the leg between St Moritz and Chur (another rail hub).

Swiss Cards cover the entire route, while Eurail and InterRail are good for about 50% of the fare.

Getting There & Around

CAR

Zermatt is car-free. Motorists have to park in Täsch (www.matterhornterminal.ch; first/subsequent day Sfr14.40/13.50) and ride the Zermatt Shuttle train (adult/child Sfr8/4, 12 minutes, every 20 minutes from 6am to 9.40pm) the last 5km to Zermatt.

TRAIN

Trains depart regularly from Brig – a major rail hub (Sfr32, 1½ hours), stopping at Visp en route. Zermatt is also the starting point of the popular *Glacier Express* to Graubünden.

BERN

POP 127,515

One of the planet's most underrated capitals, Bern is a fabulous find. With the genteel old soul of a Renaissance man and the heart of a high-flying 21st-century gal, the riverside city is both medieval and modern. The 15th-century Old Town is gorgeous enough to sweep you off your feet and make you forget the century (it's definitely worthy of its 1983 Unesco World Heritage Site status).

Sights

Bern's flag-bedecked **medieval centre** is an attraction in its own right, with 6km of covered arcades and cellar shops and bars descending from the streets. After a devastating fire in 1405, the wooden city was rebuilt in today's sandstone. The city's 11 **decorative fountains** (1545) depict historical and folkloric characters. Most are along Marktgasse as it becomes Kramgasse and Gerechtigkeitsgasse, but the most famous lies in Kornhausplatz: the **Kindlifresserbrunnen** (Ogre Fountain) of a giant snacking…on children.

★Zytglogge CLOCK TOWER
(Marktgasse) Bern's most famous Old Town sight, this ornate clock tower once formed part of the city's western gate (1191–1256). Crowds congregate to watch its revolving figures twirl at four minutes before the hour, after which the chimes begin. Tours enter the tower to see the clock mechanism from May to October; contact the tourist office for details. The clock tower supposedly helped Albert Einstein hone his special theory of relativity, developed while working as a patent clerk in Bern.

Münster CATHEDRAL
(www.bernermuenster.ch; Münsterplatz 1; tower adult/child Sfr5/2; 10am-5pm Mon-Sat, 11.30am-5pm Sun May–mid-Oct, noon-4pm Mon-Fri, 10am-5pm Sat, 11.30am-4pm Sun rest of year) Bern's 15th-century Gothic cathedral boasts Switzerland's loftiest spire (100m); climb the dizzying 344-step spiral staircase for vertiginous views. Coming down, stop by the **Upper Bells** (1356), rung at 11am, noon and 3pm daily, and the three 10-tonne **Lower Bells** (Switzerland's largest). Don't miss the main portal's **Last Judgement**, which portrays Bern's mayor going to heaven, while his Zürich counterpart is shown into hell. Afterwards, wander through the adjacent **Münsterplattform**, a bijou clifftop park with a sunny pavilion cafe.

Zentrum Paul Klee MUSEUM
(031 359 01 01; www.zpk.org; Monument im Fruchtland 3; adult/child Sfr20/7, audioguide Sfr6; 10am-5pm Tue-Sun) Bern's answer to the Guggenheim, Renzo Piano's architecturally bold 150m-long wave-like edifice houses an exhibition space that showcases rotating works from Paul Klee's prodigious and often-playful career. Interactive computer displays and audioguides help interpret the Swiss-born artist's work. Next door, the fun-packed **Kindermuseum Creaviva** (031 359 01 61; www.creaviva-zpk.org; Monument im Fruchtland 3; 10am-5pm Tue-Sun) FREE lets kids experiment with hands-on art exhibits or create original artwork with the atelier's materials during the weekend **Five Franc Studio** (www.creaviva-zpk.org/en/art-education/5-franc-studio; admission Sfr5; 10am-4.30pm Sat & Sun). Bus 12 runs from Bubenbergplatz direct to the museum.

Sleeping

Hotel Landhaus HOTEL €
(031 348 03 05; www.landhausbern.ch; Altenbergstrasse 4; dm Sfr38, s Sfr80-130, d Sfr120-180, q Sfr200-220; P @) Fronted by the river and Old Town spires, this well-run boho hotel offers a mix of stylish six-bed dorms, family rooms and doubles. Its buzzing ground-floor cafe and terrace attracts a cheery crowd. Breakfast (included with private rooms) costs Sfr8 extra for dorm-dwellers.

★Hotel Schweizerhof LUXURY HOTEL €€€
(031 326 80 80; www.schweizerhof-bern.ch; Bahnhofplatz 11; s Sfr284-640, d Sfr364-790; P @) This classy five-star offers lavish accommodation with excellent amenities and service. A hop, skip and a jump from the train station, it's geared for both business and pleasure.

Eating & Drinking

Look for interesting cafes and bistros scattered amid the arcades on Old Town streets including Zeughausgasse, Rathausgasse, Marktgasse and Kramgasse.

Altes Tramdepot SWISS €€
(031 368 14 15; www.altestramdepot.ch; Am Bärengraben; mains Sfr18-37; 11am-12.30am) At this cavernous microbrewery, Swiss specialities compete against wok-cooked stir-fries

for your affection, and the microbrews go down a treat: sample three different varieties for Sfr10.80, or four for Sfr14.50.

★Café des Pyrénées BAR
(☎031 311 30 63; www.pyri.ch; Kornhausplatz 17; ⊙9am-11.30pm Mon-Wed, to 12.30am Thu & Fri, 8am-5pm Sat) This bohemian corner joint feels like a Parisian cafe-bar. Its central location near the tram tracks makes for good people-watching.

Information

Tourist Office (☎031 328 12 12; www.bern.com; Bahnhoftplatz 10a; ⊙9am-7pm Mon-Sat, to 6pm Sun) Street-level floor of the train station. City tours, free hotel bookings, internet access. There's also a branch near the **Bear Park** (☎031 328 12 12; www.bern.com; Bärengraben; ⊙9am-6pm Jun-Sep, 10am-4pm Mar-May & Oct, 11am-4pm Nov-Feb).

Getting There & Around

Frequent trains connect to most Swiss towns, including Geneva (Sfr49, 1¾ hours), Basel (Sfr39, one hour) and Zürich (Sfr49, one hour).

Buses and trams are operated by **BernMobil** (www.bernmobil.ch); many depart from the western side of Bahnhoftplatz.

CENTRAL SWITZERLAND & BERNESE OBERLAND

These two regions should come with a health warning – caution: may cause breathlessness as the sun rises and sets over Lake Lucerne, trembling in the north face of Eiger and uncontrollable bouts of euphoria at the foot of Jungfrau.

Lucerne

POP 79,500

Recipe for a gorgeous Swiss city: take a cobalt lake ringed by mountains of myth, add a medieval Old Town and sprinkle with covered bridges, sunny plazas, candy-coloured houses and waterfront promenades. Bright, beautiful Lucerne has been Little Miss Popular since the likes of Goethe, Queen Victoria and Wagner savoured her views in the 19th century.

Sights

Your first port of call should be the medieval **Old Town**, with its ancient rampart walls and towers. Wander the cobblestone lanes and squares, pondering 15th-century buildings with painted facades and the two much-photographed covered bridges over the Reuss.

★Kapellbrücke BRIDGE
(Chapel Bridge) You haven't really been to Lucerne until you have strolled the creaky 14th-century Kapellbrücke, spanning the Reuss River in the Old Town. The octagonal water tower is original, but its gabled roof is a modern reconstruction, rebuilt after a disastrous fire in 1993. As you cross the bridge, note Heinrich Wägmann's 17th-century triangular roof panels, showing important events from Swiss history and mythology. The icon is at its most photogenic when bathed in soft golden light at dusk.

Spreuerbrücke BRIDGE
(Spreuer Bridge; btwn Kasernenplatz & Mühlenplatz) Downriver from Kapellbrücke, this 1408 structure is darker and smaller but entirely original. Lore has it that this was the only bridge where Lucerne's medieval villagers were allowed to throw *Spreu* (chaff) into the river. Here, the roof panels consist of artist Caspar Meglinger's movie-storyboard-style sequence of paintings, *The Dance of Death*, showing how the plague affected all levels of society.

★Lion Monument MONUMENT
(Löwendenkmal; Denkmalstrasse) By far the most touching of the 19th-century sights that lured so many British to Lucerne is the Lion Monument. Lukas Ahorn carved this 10m-long sculpture of a dying lion into the rock face in 1820 to commemorate Swiss soldiers who died defending King Louis XVI during the French Revolution. Mark Twain once called it the 'saddest and most moving piece of rock in the world'. For Narnia fans, it often evokes Aslan at the stone table.

Museum Sammlung Rosengart MUSEUM
(☎041 220 16 60; www.rosengart.ch; Pilatusstrasse 10; adult/student Sfr18/16; ⊙10am-6pm Apr-Oct,

WORTH A TRIP

MOUNTAIN DAY TRIPS FROM LUCERNE

Among the several (heavily marketed) day trips from Lucerne, consider the one to 2132m-high **Mt Pilatus** (www.pilatus.com). From May to October, you can reach the peak on a classic 'golden round-trip'. Board the lake steamer from Lucerne to Alpnachstad, then rise with the world's steepest cog railway to Mt Pilatus. From the summit, cable cars bring you down to Kriens via Fräkmüntegg and Krienseregg, where bus 1 takes you back to Lucerne. The return trip costs Sfr97 (less with valid Swiss, Eurail or InterRail passes).

11am-5pm Nov-Mar) Lucerne's blockbuster cultural attraction is the Sammlung Rosengart, occupying a graceful neoclassical pile. It showcases the outstanding stash of Angela Rosengart, a Swiss art dealer and close friend of Picasso. Alongside works by the great Spanish master are paintings and sketches by Cézanne, Klee, Kandinsky, Miró, Matisse and Monet. Standouts include Joan Miró's electric-blue *Dancer II* (1925) and Paul Klee's childlike *X-chen* (1938).

Verkehrshaus MUSEUM
(Swiss Museum of Transport; ☎041 370 44 44; www.verkehrshaus.ch; Lidostrasse 5; adult/child Sfr30/15; ⏲10am-6pm Apr-Oct, to 5pm Nov-Mar;) A great kid-pleaser, the fascinating interactive Verkehrshaus is deservedly Switzerland's most popular museum. Alongside space rockets, steam locomotives, bicycles and dugout canoes are hands-on activities such as flight simulators and broadcasting studios.

The museum also shelters a **planetarium** (adult/child Sfr15/9), Switzerland's largest **3D cinema** (www.filmtheater.ch; adult/child daytime Sfr18/14, evening Sfr22/19), and its newest attraction: the **Swiss Chocolate Experience** (adult/child Sfr15/9), a 20-minute ride that whirls visitors through multimedia exhibits on the origins, history, production and distribution of chocolate, from Ghana to Switzerland and beyond.

Sleeping

Backpackers Lucerne HOSTEL €
(☎041 360 04 20; www.backpackerslucerne.ch; Alpenquai 42; dm/d from Sfr33/78; ⏲reception 7-10am & 4-11pm; @) Could this be backpacker heaven? Just opposite the lake, this is a soulful place to crash with art-slung walls, bubbly staff, a well-equipped kitchen and immaculate dorms with balconies. It's a 15-minute walk southeast of the station. There's no breakfast, but guests have kitchen access.

Hotel Waldstätterhof HOTEL €€
(☎041 227 12 71; www.hotel-waldstaetterhof.ch; Zentralstrasse 4; s Sfr190, d Sfr290-315; P) Opposite the train station, this hotel with faux-Gothic exterior offers smart, modern rooms with hardwood-style floors and high ceilings, plus excellent service.

★**The Hotel** HOTEL €€€
(☎041 226 86 86; www.the-hotel.ch; Sempacherstrasse 14; s/d ste from Sfr425/455; @) This shamelessly hip hotel, bearing the imprint of architect Jean Nouvel, is all streamlined chic, with refined suites featuring stills from movie classics on the ceilings. Downstairs, Bam Bou is one of Lucerne's hippest restaurants, and the gorgeous green park across the street is a cool place to idle.

Eating & Drinking

★**Grottino 1313** ITALIAN €€
(☎041 610 13 13; www.grottino1313.ch; Industriestrasse 7; 2-course lunch menu Sfr20, 4-course dinner menu Sfr64; ⏲11am-2pm & 6-11.30pm Mon-Fri, 6-11.30pm Sat, 9am-2pm Sun) Offering a welcome escape from Lucerne's tourist throngs, this relaxed yet stylish eatery serves ever-changing 'surprise' menus featuring starters like chestnut soup with figs, creative pasta dishes, meats cooked over an open fire and scrumptious desserts. The gravel-strewn, herb-fringed front patio is lovely on a summer afternoon, while the candlelit interior exudes sheer cosiness on a winter's evening.

Wirtshaus Galliker SWISS €€
(☎041 240 10 01; Schützenstrasse 1; mains Sfr21-51; ⏲11.30am-2pm & 5-10pm Tue-Sat, closed Jul–mid-Aug) Passionately run by the

Galliker family for over four generations, this old-style, wood-panelled tavern attracts a lively bunch of regulars. Motherly waitresses dish up Lucerne soul food (rösti, *chögalipaschtetli* and the like) that is batten-the-hatches filling.

Rathaus Bräuerei BREWERY
(041 410 52 57; www.braui-luzern.ch; Unter den Egg 2; 11.30am-midnight Mon-Sat, to 11pm Sun) Sip home-brewed beer under the vaulted arches of this buzzy tavern near Kapellbrücke, or nab a pavement table and watch the river flow.

Information

Lake Lucerne Region Visitors Card (Vierwaldstättersee Gästekarte; www.luzern.com/visitors-card) Stamped by your hotel, this free card entitles visitors to discounts on various museums, sporting facilities, cable cars and lake cruises in Lucerne and the surrounding area.

Tourist Office (041 227 17 17; www.luzern.com; Zentralstrasse 5; 9am-7pm Mon-Sat, 9am-5pm Sun May-Oct, 8.30am-5.30pm Mon-Fri, 9am-5pm Sat, 9am-1pm Sun Nov-Apr) Reached from Zentralstrasse or platform 3 of the Hauptbahnhof. Offers city walking tours. Call for hotel reservations.

Getting There & Around

Frequent trains serve Interlaken Ost (Sfr31, 1¾ hours), Bern (Sfr37, one hour), Lugano (Sfr58, 2½ hours) and Zürich (Sfr24, 50 minutes).

Trains also connect Lucerne and Interlaken Ost on the stunning GoldenPass Line via Meiringen (Sfr31, two hours).

SGV (www.lakelucerne.ch) operates boats (sometimes paddle steamers) on Lake Lucerne daily. Services are extensive. Rail passes are good for free or discounted travel.

Interlaken

POP 5660

Once Interlaken made the Victorians swoon with its dreamy mountain vistas, viewed from the chandelier-lit confines of its grand hotels. Today it makes daredevils scream with its adrenalin-loaded adventures. Straddling the glittering Lakes Thun and Brienz (thus the name), and dazzled by the pearly whites of Eiger, Mönch and Jungfrau, Interlaken boasts exceptional scenery.

Sights & Activities

Switzerland is the world's second-biggest adventure-sports centre and Interlaken is its busiest hub. Sample prices are Sfr120 for rafting or canyoning, Sfr140 for hydrospeeding, Sfr130 to Sfr180 for bungee or canyon jumping, Sfr170 for tandem paragliding, Sfr180 for ice climbing, Sfr220 for hang-gliding and Sfr430 for skydiving. A half-day mountain-bike tour will set you back around Sfr25.

Harder Kulm MOUNTAIN
(www.harderkulm.ch) For far-reaching views to the 4000m giants, ride the **funicular** (adult/child return Sfr28/14; every 30min 8.10am-6.25pm late Apr-Oct, plus 7-8.30pm Jul & Aug) to 1322m Harder Kulm. Many hiking paths begin here, and the vertigo-free can enjoy the panorama from the **Zweiseensteg** (Two Lake Bridge) jutting out above the valley. The wildlife park near the valley station is home to Alpine critters, including marmots and ibex.

Sleeping

Backpackers Villa Sonnenhof HOSTEL €
(033 826 71 71; www.villa.ch; Alpenstrasse 16; dm Sfr39.50-47, s Sfr69-79, d Sfr110-148; P @) Sonnenhof is a slick combination of ultra-modern chalet and elegant art nouveau villa. Dorms are immaculate, and some have balconies with Jungfrau views. There's also a relaxed lounge, a well-equipped kitchen, a kids' playroom and a leafy garden for mountain gazing. Special family rates are available.

★**Victoria-Jungfrau Grand Hotel & Spa** LUXURY HOTEL €€€
(033 828 26 10; www.victoria-jungfrau.ch; Höheweg 41; d Sfr400-800, ste Sfr600-1000; P @) The reverent hush and impeccable service here (as well as the prices) evoke an era when only royalty and the seriously wealthy travelled. A perfect melding of well-preserved art nouveau features and modern luxury make this Interlaken's answer to Raffles – with plum views of Jungfrau, three first-class restaurants and a gorgeous spa to boot.

Eating & Drinking

Höheweg, east of Interlaken Ost train station, is lined with ethnic eateries with reasonable prices.

Sandwich Bar SANDWICHES €
(Rosenstrasse 5; snacks Sfr4-9; ⏲7.30am-7pm Mon-Fri, 8am-5pm Sat) Choose your bread and get creative with fillings like air-dried ham with sun-dried tomatoes and brie with walnuts. Or try the soups, salads, toasties and locally made ice cream.

★ **WineArt** MEDITERRANEAN €€
(☎033 823 73 74; www.wineart.ch; Jungfraustrasse 46; mains Sfr24-59, 5-course menu Sfr59; ⏲4pm-12.30am Mon-Sat) This is a delightful wine bar, lounge, restaurant and deli rolled into one. High ceilings, chandeliers and wood floors create a slick, elegant backdrop for season-driven Mediterranean food. Pair one of 600 wines with dishes as simple as buffalo mozzarella and rocket salad and corn-fed chicken with honey-glazed vegetables – quality and flavour are second to none.

ℹ Information

Tourist Office (☎033 826 53 00; www.interlakentourism.ch; Höheweg 37; ⏲8am-7pm Mon-Fri, to 5pm Sat, 10am-4pm Sun Jul & Aug, 8am-noon & 1.30-6pm Mon-Fri, 9am-noon Sat rest of year) Halfway between the stations. There's a hotel booking board outside.

ℹ Getting There & Away

There are two train stations. Interlaken West is slightly closer to the centre and is a stop for trains to Bern (Sfr27, one hour). Interlaken Ost (East) is the rail hub for all lines, including the scenic ones up into the Jungfrau region and the lovely GoldenPass Line to Lucerne (Sfr31, two hours).

Jungfrau Region

If the Bernese Oberland is Switzerland's alpine heart, the Jungfrau region is where yours will skip a beat. Presided over by glacier-encrusted monoliths Eiger, Mönch and Jungfrau (Ogre, Monk and Virgin), the scenery stirs the soul and strains the neck muscles. It's a magnet for skiers and snowboarders with its 214km of pistes, 44 lifts and much more; a one-day ski pass for either Grindelwald-Wengen or Mürren-Schilthorn costs adult/child Sfr62/31.

Come summer, hundreds of kilometres of walking trails allow you to capture the landscape from many angles, but it never looks less than astonishing.

ℹ Getting There & Around

Hourly trains (www.jungfrau.ch) depart for the Jungfrau region from Interlaken Ost station. Sit in the front half of the train for Lauterbrunnen (Sfr7.40) or the back half for Grindelwald (Sfr10.80).

From Grindelwald, trains ascend to Kleine Scheidegg (Sfr31), where you can transfer for Jungfraujoch. From Lauterbrunnen, trains ascend to Wengen (Sfr6.60) and continue to Kleine Scheidegg (Sfr23) for Jungfraujoch.

You can reach Mürren two ways from Lauterbrunnen: with a bus and cable car via Stechelberg (Sfr15) or with a cable car and train via Grütschalp (Sfr11). Do a circle trip for the full experience. Gimmelwald is reached by cable car from Stechelberg and Mürren.

Many cable cars close for servicing in April and November.

Grindelwald

POP 3760

Grindelwald's charms were discovered by skiers and hikers in the late 19th century, making it one of Switzerland's oldest resorts and the Jungfrau's largest. It has lost none of its appeal over the decades, with archetypal alpine chalets and verdant pastures set against the chiselled features of the Eiger north face.

JUNGFRAU REGION HIKING 101

There are hundreds of hikes along the hundreds of kilometres of trails in the Jungfrau region; all include some of the world's most stunning scenery. Every skill and fortitude level is accommodated and options abound. Here are two to get you started.

Grütschalp to Mürren Ride the cable car up from Lauterbrunnen and follow the trail along the railway tracks. The walk to Mürren takes about an hour and is mostly level. There are unbeatable views, alpine woods and babbling glacier-fed streams.

Männlichen to Kleine Scheidegg Reach the Männlichen lift station by cable cars from Wengen and Grindelwald. Now follow the well-marked, spectacular path down to Kleine Scheidegg. It takes about 90 minutes and you have nothing but Alps in front of you.

Activities

The **Grindelwald-First** skiing area has a mix of cruisy red and challenging black runs stretching from Oberjoch at 2486m to the village at 1050m, plus 15.5km of well-groomed cross-country ski trails. In the summer it caters to hikers with 90km of trails at about 1200m, 48km of which are open year-round.

★Kleine Scheidegg Walk HIKING

One of the region's most stunning day hikes is this 15km trek from Grindelwald Grund to Wengen via Kleine Scheidegg, which heads up through wildflower-freckled meadows to skirt below the Eiger's north face and reach Kleine Scheidegg, granting arresting views of the 'Big Three'. Allow around 5½ to six hours. The best map is the SAW 1:50,000 Interlaken (Sfr22.50).

Grindelwald Sports ADVENTURE SPORTS

(☎033 854 12 80; www.grindelwaldsports.ch; Dorfstrasse 103; ⌚8.30am-6.30pm, closed Sat & Sun in low season) Opposite the tourist office, this outfit arranges mountain climbing, ski and snowboard instruction, canyon jumping and glacier bungee jumping at the Gletscherschlucht. It also houses a cosy cafe and sells walking guides.

Sleeping

Mountain Hostel HOSTEL €

(☎033 854 38 38; www.mountainhostel.ch; Grundstrasse 58; dm Sfr37-51, d Sfr94-122; P 📶) Near Männlichen cable-car station, this is an ideal base for sports junkies, with well-kept dorms and a helpful crew. There's a beer garden, ski storage, TV lounge and mountain and e-bike rental.

★Gletschergarten HISTORIC HOTEL €€

(☎033 853 17 21; www.hotel-gletschergarten.ch; Obere Gletscherstrasse 1; s Sfr130-170, d Sfr230-300; P 📶) The sweet Breitenstein family make you feel at home in their rustic timber chalet, brimming with heirlooms from landscape paintings to snapshots of Elsbeth's grandfather who had 12 children (those were the days...). Decked out in pine and flowery fabrics, the rooms have balconies facing Unterer Gletscher at the front and Wetterhorn (best for sunset) at the back.

Wengen

POP 1300

Photogenically poised on a mountain ledge, Wengen has celestial views of the glacier-capped giant peaks' silent majesty as well as the shimmering waterfalls spilling into the Lauterbrunnen Valley below.

The village is car-free and can only be reached by train. It's a fabulous hub for **hiking** for much of the year as well as **skiing** in winter.

Hotel Bären (☎033 855 14 19; www.baeren-wengen.ch; s Sfr120-150, d Sfr160-290, tr Sfr280-380; 📶) is close to the station. Loop back under the tracks and head down the hill to this snug log chalet with bright, if compact, rooms. The affable Brunner family serves a hearty breakfast.

Jungfraujoch

Jungfraujoch (3471m) is a once-in-a-lifetime trip and there's good reason why two million people a year visit Europe's highest train station. Clear good weather is essential; check www.jungfrau.ch or call ☎033 828 79 31, and don't forget warm clothing, sunglasses and sunscreen.

From Interlaken Ost, the journey time is 2½ hours each way (Sfr197.60 return, discounts with rail passes). The last train back sets off at 5.45pm in summer and 4.45pm in winter. However, from May to October there's a cheaper Good Morning Ticket costing Sfr145 if you take the first train (which departs at 6.35am from Interlaken Ost) and leave the summit by 1pm.

Gimmelwald

POP 110

Decades ago some anonymous backpacker scribbled these words in the guestbook at the Mountain Hostel: 'If heaven isn't what it's cracked up to be, send me back to Gimmelwald'. Enough said. When the sun is out in Gimmelwald, this pipsqueak of a village will simply take your breath away. Sit outside and listen to the distant roar of avalanches on the sheer mountain faces arrayed before you.

The charming, spotless **Esther's Guest House** (☎033 855 54 88; www.esthersguesthouse.ch; Kirchstatt; s/d Sfr60/140, apt Sfr170-250; 📶) is run with love and care. For an extra

SWISS NATIONAL PARK

The Engadine's pride and joy is the Swiss National Park, easily accessed from Scuol, Zernez and S-chanf. Spanning 172 sq km, Switzerland's only national park is a nature-gone-wild swath of dolomitic peaks, shimmering glaciers, larch woodlands, pastures, waterfalls and high moors strung with topaz-blue lakes. This was the first national park to be established in the Alps, on 1 August 1914, and over 100 years later it remains true to its original conservation ethos, with the aims to protect, research and inform.

Given that nature has been left to its own devices for a century, the park is a glimpse of the Alps before the dawn of tourism. There are some 80km of well-marked hiking trails, where, with a little luck and a decent pair of binoculars, ibex, chamois, marmots and golden eagles can be sighted. The **Swiss National Park Centre** (☎081 851 41 41; www.nationalpark.ch; Zernez; exhibition adult/child Sfr7/3; ⌚8.30am-6pm Jun-Oct, 9am-noon & 2-5pm Nov-May) should be your first port of call for information on activities and accommodation. It sells an excellent 1:50,000 park map (Sfr20), which covers 21 walks through the park.

You can easily head off on your own, but you might get more out of one of the informative guided hikes run by the centre from late June to mid-October. These include wildlife-spotting treks to the Val Trupchun and high-alpine hikes to the Offenpass and Lakes of Macun. Most are in German, but many guides speak a little English. Expect to pay Sfr25 to Sfr35 per person. You should book ahead by phone.

Entry to the park and its car parks is free. Conservation is paramount here, so stick to footpaths and respect regulations prohibiting camping, littering, lighting fires, cycling, picking flowers and disturbing the animals.

Sfr15, you'll be served a delicious breakfast of homemade bread, cheese and yoghurt.

Mürren

POP 430

Arrive on a clear evening when the sun hangs low on the horizon, and you'll think you've died and gone to heaven. Car-free Mürren *is* storybook Switzerland.

Sleeping options include **Eiger Guesthouse** (☎033 856 54 60; www.eigerguesthouse.com; r Sfr110-220; 📶), by the train station, with the downstairs pub serving tasty food; and **Hotel Jungfrau** (☎033 856 64 64; www.hoteljungfrau.ch; d Sfr180-280, q apt Sfr550; 📶), overlooking the nursery slopes from its perch above Mürren. It dates to 1894 and has a beamed lounge with an open fire.

Schilthorn

There's a tremendous 360-degree panorama available from the 2970m **Schilthorn** (www.schilthorn.ch). On a clear day, you can see over 200 peaks, from Titlis to Mont Blanc and across to the German Black Forest. Note that this was the site of Blofeld's HQ in the underappreciated 1969 James Bond film *On Her Majesty's Secret Service* (as the hype endlessly reminds you).

The new **Bond World 007** (http://schilthorn.ch; admission free with cable car ticket; ⌚8am-6pm) interactive exhibition gives you the chance to pose for photos secret-agent style and relive movie moments in a helicopter and bobsled.

From Interlaken Ost, take a Sfr121.80 excursion to Lauterbrunnen, Grütschalp, Mürren and Schilthorn and return through Stechelberg to Interlaken. A return from Lauterbrunnen (via Grütschalp) and Mürren costs Sfr107, as does the return journey via the Stechelberg cable car. A return from Mürren is Sfr77.

Ask about discounts for early morning trips. There are discounts with rail passes.

ZÜRICH

POP 380,780

Zürich, Switzerland's largest city, is an enigma. A savvy financial centre with the densest public transport system in the world, it also has a gritty, postindustrial edge that always surprises and an evocative Old Town, not to mention a lovely lakeside location.

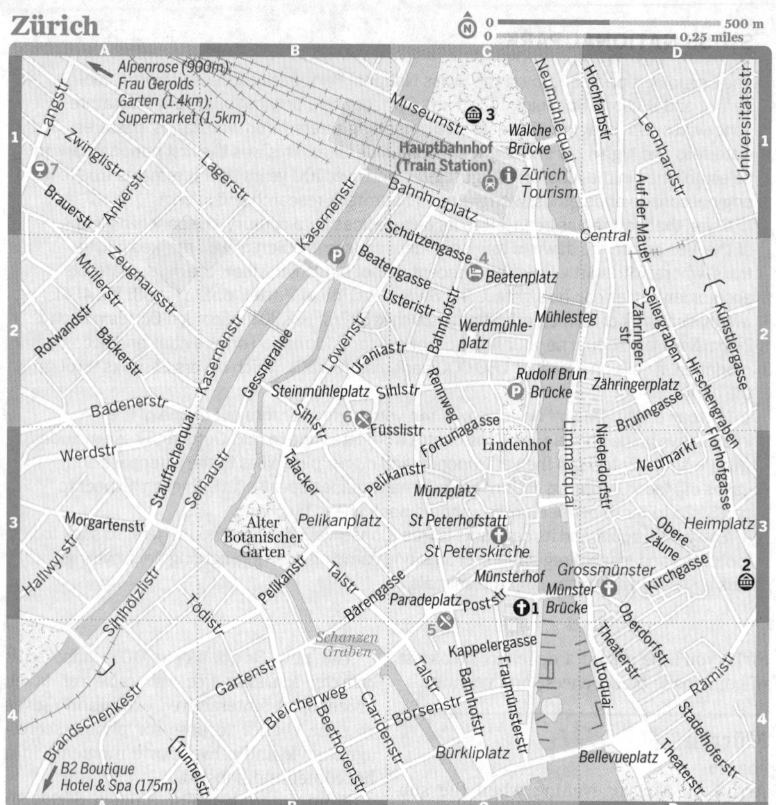

Zürich

Sights
1 Fraumünster C3
2 Kunsthaus D3
3 Schweizerisches Landesmuseum C1

Sleeping
4 Townhouse C2

Eating
5 Café Sprüngli C3
6 Haus Hiltl B2

Drinking & Nightlife
7 Longstreet Bar A1

Sights

The cobbled streets of the pedestrian Old Town line both sides of the river, while the bank vaults beneath Bahnhofstrasse, the city's most elegant shopping street, are said to be crammed with gold. On Sunday all of Zürich strolls around the lake – on a clear day you'll glimpse the Alps in the distance.

Fraumünster CHURCH
(www.fraumuenster.ch; Münsterhof; 9am-6pm Apr-Oct, 10am-4pm Nov-Mar) The 13th-century cathedral is renowned for its stunning, distinctive stained-glass windows, designed by the Russian-Jewish master Marc Chagall (1887–1985). He did a series of five windows in the choir stalls in 1971 and the rose window in the southern transept in 1978. The rose window in the northern transept was created by Augusto Giacometti in 1945.

Kunsthaus MUSEUM
(044 253 84 84; www.kunsthaus.ch; Heimplatz 1; adult/child Sfr15/free, Wed free; 10am-8pm Wed-Fri, 10am-6pm Tue, Sat & Sun) Zürich's

impressive fine arts gallery boasts a rich collection of largely European art that stretches from the Middle Ages through a mix of Old Masters to Alberto Giacometti stick figures, Monet and Van Gogh masterpieces, Rodin sculptures and other 19th- and 20th-century art. Swiss Rail and Museum Passes don't provide free admission but the ZürichCard does.

Schweizerisches Landesmuseum MUSEUM
(Swiss National Museum; www.musee-suisse.ch; Museumstrasse 2; adult/child Sfr10/free; 10am-5pm Tue, Wed & Fri-Sun, 10am-7pm Thu) Inside a purpose-built cross between a mansion and a castle sprawls this eclectic and imaginatively presented museum. The permanent collection offers an extensive tour through Swiss history, with exhibits ranging from elaborately carved and painted sleds to household and religious artefacts to a series of reconstructed historical rooms spanning six centuries. The museum remains open while undergoing a major expansion; the new archaeology section and brand-new wing are slated to open in 2016.

Sleeping

Zürich accommodation prices are fittingly high for the main city of expensive Switzerland.

★SYHA Hostel HOSTEL €
(043 399 78 00; www.youthhostel.ch/zuerich; Mutschellenstrasse 114, Wollishofen; dm Sfr43-46, s/d Sfr119/140;) A bulbous, Band-Aid-pink 1960s landmark houses this busy hostel with 24-hour reception, dining hall, sparkling modern bathrooms and dependable wi-fi in the downstairs lounge. The included breakfast features miso soup and rice alongside all the Swiss standards. It's about 20 minutes south of the Hauptbahnhof. Take tram 7 to Morgental, or the S-Bahn to Wollishofen, then walk five minutes.

Townhouse BOUTIQUE HOTEL €€
(044 200 95 95; www.townhouse.ch; Schützengasse 7; s Sfr195-395, d Sfr225-425;) With luxurious wallpapers, wallhangings, parquet floors and retro furniture, the 21 rooms in these stylish digs come in an assortment of sizes from 15 sq metres to 35 sq metres. Located close to the main train station, the hotel offers friendly service and welcoming touches including a DVD selection and iPod docking stations.

B2 Boutique Hotel & Spa BOUTIQUE HOTEL €€€
(044 567 67 67; www.b2boutiquehotels.com; Brandschenkestrasse 152; s/d from Sfr330/380;) A stone's throw from Google's European headquarters, this quirky newcomer in a renovated brewery is filled with seductive features. Topping the list are the stupendous rooftop Jacuzzi pool, the spa and the fanciful library-lounge, filled floor to ceiling with an astounding 30,000 books (bought from a local antiquarian) on 13m-high shelves. Spacious rooms sport modern decor (including the odd bean-bag chair).

From the Hauptbahnhof, take tram 13 to Enge and walk five minutes west.

Eating

Zürich has a thriving cafe culture and 2000-plus places to eat. Traditional local cuisine is very rich, as epitomised by the city's signature dish, Zürcher Geschnetzeltes (sliced veal in a creamy mushroom and white wine sauce).

★Haus Hiltl VEGETARIAN €
(044 227 70 00; hiltl.ch; Sihlstrasse 28; per 100g take-away/cafe/restaurant Sfr3.50/4.50/5.50; 6am-midnight Mon-Sat, 8am-midnight Sun;) Guinness-certified as the world's oldest vegetarian restaurant (established 1898), Hiltl proffers an astounding smorgasbord of meatless delights, from Indian and Thai curries to Mediterranean grilled vegies to salads and desserts. Browse to your heart's content, fill your plate and weigh it, then choose a seat in the informal cafe or the spiffier adjoining restaurant (economical take-away service is also available).

Café Sprüngli SWEETS €
(044 224 46 46; www.spruengli.ch; Bahnhofstrasse 21; sweets Sfr7.50-16; 7am-6.30pm Mon-Fri, 8am-6pm Sat, 9.30am-5.30pm Sun) Sit down for cakes, chocolate, coffee or ice cream at this epicentre of sweet Switzerland, in business since 1836. You can have a light lunch too, but whatever you do, don't fail to check out the heavenly chocolate shop around the corner on Paradeplatz.

WORTH A TRIP

LIECHTENSTEIN

If Liechtenstein (population 37,132) didn't exist, someone would have invented it. A tiny German-speaking mountain principality (160 sq km) governed by an iron-willed monarch in the heart of 21st-century Europe, it certainly has novelty value. Only 25km long by 12km wide (at its broadest point) – just larger than Manhattan – Liechtenstein is mostly visited by people who want a glimpse of the castle and a spurious passport stamp. Stay a little longer and you can escape into its pint-sized alpine wilderness.

Vaduz

Vaduz is a postage stamp–size city with a postcard-perfect backdrop. Crouching at the foot of forested mountains, hugging the banks of the Rhine and crowned by a turreted castle, the city has a visually stunning location.

The centre itself is curiously modern and sterile, yet just a few minutes' walk brings you to traces of the quaint village that existed just 50 years ago and quiet vineyards where the Alps seem that bit closer.

Vaduz Castle is closed to the public but is worth the climb for the vistas.

Information

Liechtenstein's international phone prefix is 423.

The **Liechtenstein Center** (www.tourismus.li) offers brochures, souvenir passport stamps (Sfr3) and the **Philatelie Liechtenstein**, which will interest stamp collectors.

Getting There & Around

The nearest train stations are in the Swiss border towns of Buchs and Sargans. From each of these towns there are frequent buses to Vaduz (Sfr7.20/9.40 from Buchs/Sargans). Buses traverse the country. Single fares (buy tickets on the bus) are Sfr2.80/3.50/4.80 for one/two/three zones. Swiss Passes are valid on all main routes.

★ Alpenrose SWISS €€

(☎044 271 39 19; alpenrose.me; Fabrikstrasse 12; mains Sfr26-42; ⏰11am-midnight Wed-Fri, 6.15-11pm Sat & Sun) With its timber-clad walls, 'No Polka Dancing' warning and multi-regional Swiss cuisine, the Alpenrose exudes cosy charm. Specialities include Ticinese risotto and *Pizokel*, a savoury kind of *Spätzli* from Graubünden – as proudly noted on the menu, they've served over 20,000kg of the stuff over the past 20 years! Save room for creamy cognac parfait and other scrumptious desserts.

Drinking & Entertainment

Options abound across town, but the bulk of the more animated drinking dens are in Züri-West, especially along Langstrasse in Kreis 4 and Hardstrasse in Kreis 5.

★ Frau Gerolds Garten BAR

(www.fraugerold.ch; Geroldstrasse 23/23a; ⏰11am-midnight Mon-Sat, noon-10pm Sun Apr-Oct, closed in bad weather; 👪) Hmm, where to start? The wine bar? The margarita bar? The gin bar? Whichever poison you choose, this wildly popular recent addition to Zürich's summertime drinking scene is pure unadulterated fun. Overhung with multicoloured streamers and sandwiched between cheery flower beds and a screeching railyard, its outdoor seating options range from picnic tables to pillow-strewn terraces to a 2nd-floor sundeck.

Longstreet Bar BAR

(☎044 241 21 72; www.longstreetbar.ch; Langstrasse 92; ⏰6pm-late Wed-Fri, 8pm-4am Sat) In the heart of the Langstrasse action, the Longstreet is a music bar with a varied roll call of DJs. Try to count the thousands of light bulbs in this purple-felt-lined one-time cabaret.

Supermarket CLUB

(☎044 440 20 05; www.supermarket.li; Geroldstrasse 17; ⏰11pm-late Thu-Sat) Looking like an innocent little house, Supermarket boasts three cosy lounge bars around the dance floor, a covered back courtyard and an interesting roster of DJs playing house and techno. Take a train from Hauptbahnhof to Hardbrücke.

Information

Zürich Tourism (☎044 215 40 00, hotel reservations 044 215 40 40; www.zuerich.com; ⏲8am-8.30pm Mon-Sat, 8.30am-6.30pm Sun)

Getting There & Away

AIR

Zürich Airport (p1138), 9km north of the centre, is Switzerland's main airport.

TRAIN

Direct trains run to Stuttgart (Sfr64, three hours), Munich (Sfr97, 4¼ hours), Innsbruck (Sfr77, 3½ hours) and other international destinations.

There are regular direct departures to most major Swiss towns, such as Lucerne (Sfr24, 45 to 50 minutes), Bern (Sfr49, one to 1¼ hours) and Basel (Sfr32, 55 minutes to 1¼ hours).

Getting Around

TO/FROM THE AIRPORT

Up to nine trains an hour run in each direction between the airport and the main train station (Sfr6.60, nine to 14 minutes).

BICYCLE

Züri Rollt (www.schweizrollt.ch) allows visitors to borrow or rent bikes from a handful of locations, including Velostation Nord across the road from the north side of the Hauptbahnhof. Bring ID and leave Sfr20 as a deposit. Rental is free if you bring the bike back on the same day and Sfr10 a day if you keep it overnight.

PUBLIC TRANSPORT

The comprehensive, unified bus, tram and S-Bahn public transit system **ZVV** (www.zvv.ch) includes boats plying the Limmat River. Short trips under five stops are Sfr2.60, typical trips are Sfr4.20. A 24-hour pass for the city centre is Sfr8.40.

NORTHERN SWITZERLAND

With business-like Basel at its heart, this region also prides itself on having the country's finest Roman ruins (at Augusta Raurica) and a gaggle of proud castles and pretty medieval villages scattered across the rolling countryside of Aargau canton.

Basel

POP 165,570

Tucked up against the French and German borders in Switzerland's northwest corner, Basel straddles the majestic Rhine. The town is home to art galleries, 30-odd museums and avant-garde architecture, and it boasts an enchanting old town centre.

Sights & Activities

Altstadt NEIGHBOURHOOD

Begin exploring Basel's delightful medieval Old Town in **Marktplatz**, dominated by the astonishingly vivid red facade of the 16th century **Rathaus**. From here, climb 400m west along Spalenberg through the former artisans' district to the 600-year-old **Spalentor** city gate, one of only three to survive the walls' demolition in 1866. Along the way, linger in captivating lanes such as Spalenberg, Heuberg and Leonhardsberg, lined by impeccably maintained, centuries-old houses.

★**Fondation Beyeler** MUSEUM

(☎061 645 97 00; www.fondationbeyeler.ch; Baselstrasse 101, Riehen; adult/child Sfr25/6; ⏲10am-6pm, to 8pm Wed) This astounding private-turned-public collection, assembled by former art dealers Hildy and Ernst Beyeler, is housed in a long, low, light-filled, open-plan building, designed by Italian architect Renzo Piano. The varied exhibits juxtapose 19th- and 20th-century works by Picasso and Rothko against sculptures by Miró and Max Ernst and tribal figures from Oceania. Take tram 6 to Riehen from Barfüsserplatz or Marktplatz.

Sleeping

Hotels are often full during Basel's trade fairs and conventions; book ahead. Guests receive a pass for free travel on public transport.

★**SYHA Basel St Alban Youth Hostel** HOSTEL €

(☎061 272 05 72; www.youthhostel.ch/basel; St Alban Kirchrain 10; dm/s/d Sfr44/122/136; 📶) Designed by Basel-based architects Buchner & Bründler, this swank modern hostel in a very pleasant neighbourhood is flanked by tree-shaded squares and a rushing creek. It's only a stone's throw from the Rhine, and 15 minutes on foot from the SBB Bahnhof (or take tram 2 to Kunstmuseum and walk five minutes downhill).

★**Hotel Krafft** HOTEL €€
(☎061 690 91 30; krafftbasel.ch; Rheingasse 12; s Sfr110-150, d Sfr175-265;) Design-savvy urbanites will love this renovated historic hotel. Sculptural modern chandeliers dangle in the creaky-floored dining room overlooking the Rhine, and minimalist Japanese-style tea bars adorn each landing of the spiral stairs.

Eating & Drinking

Head to the **Marktplatz** for a daily market and several stands selling excellent quick bites, such as local sausages and sandwiches.

★**Volkshaus Basel** BRASSERIE, BAR €€
(☎061 690 93 11; volkshaus-basel.ch; Rebgasse 12-14; mains Sfr28-56; ⏲11.30am-2pm & 6-10.30pm Mon-Fri, 11.30am-10.30pm Sat) This stylish new Herzog & de Meuron–designed venue is part resto-bar, part gallery and part performance space. For relaxed dining, head for the atmospheric beer garden, in a cobblestoned courtyard decorated with columns, vine-clad walls and light-draped rows of trees. The menu ranges from brasserie classics *(steak-frites)* to more innovative offerings (shrimp and cucumber salad with sour cream–lavender dressing). The bar is open 10am to 1am Monday to Saturday.

Information

Basel Tourismus (☎061 268 68 68; www.basel.com) SBB Bahnhof (⏲8.30am-6pm Mon-Fri, 9am-5pm Sat, to 3pm Sun & holidays); Stadtcasino (Steinenberg 14; ⏲9am-6.30pm Mon-Fri, to 5pm Sat, 10am-3pm Sun & holidays) The Stadtcasino branch organises two-hour city walking tours (adult/child Sfr18/9, in English or French upon request) starting at 2.30pm Monday to Saturday May through October, and on Saturdays the rest of the year.

Getting There & Away

AIR

The **EuroAirport** (MLH or BSL; ☎+33 3 89 90 31 11; www.euroairport.com), 5km northwest of town in France, is the main airport for Basel. It is a hub for easyJet and there are flights to major European cities.

TRAIN

Basel is a major European rail hub. The main station has TGVs to Paris (three hours) and fast ICEs to major cities in Germany.

Services within Switzerland include frequent trains to Bern (Sfr39, one hour) and Zürich (Sfr32, one hour).

Getting Around

Bus 50 links the airport and Basel's main train station (Sfr4.20, 20 minutes). Trams 8 and 11 link the station to Marktplatz (Sfr3.40, day pass Sfr9).

TICINO

Switzerland meets Italy: in Ticino the summer air is rich and hot, and peacock-proud posers propel their scooters in and out of traffic. Italian weather, Italian style. Not to mention the Italian ice cream, Italian pizza, Italian architecture and Italian language.

Locarno

POP 15,480

Italianate architecture and the northern end of Lago Maggiore, plus more hours of sunshine than anywhere else in Switzerland (2300 hours, to be precise), give this laid-back town a summer resort atmosphere.

Locarno is on the northeastern corner of Lago Maggiore, which mostly lies in Italy's Lombardy region. **Navigazione Lago Maggiore** (www.navigazionelaghi.it) operates boats across the entire lake.

Sights & Activities

Città Vecchia NEIGHBOURHOOD
Locarno's Italianate Old Town fans out from **Piazza Grande**, a photogenic ensemble of arcades and Lombard-style houses. A craft and fresh produce market takes over the square every Thursday.

★**Santuario della Madonna del Sasso** CHURCH
(⏲6.30am-6.30pm) FREE Overlooking the town, this sanctuary was built after the Virgin Mary supposedly appeared in a vision to a monk, Bartolomeo d'Ivrea, in 1480. There's a highly adorned church and several rather rough, near-life-size statue groups (including one of the Last Supper)

WORTH A TRIP

BERNINA EXPRESS

The famous **Bernina Express** (www.berninaexpress.ch; one-way Sfr84; seat reservation summer/winter Sfr14/10; ⏲ mid-May–early Dec) route (6½ hours) runs from Lugano to St Moritz, Davos and the rail hub of Chur. The four-hour route from Chur to Lugano (55 tunnels, 196 bridges) climbs high into the glaciated realms of the Alps and skirts Ticino's palm-fringed lakes. From Lugano to Tirano (in Italy), a bus is used for the scenic run along Italy's Lake Como.

The train route over the Bernina Pass between Tirano and St Moritz is one of Switzerland's most spectacular and is Unesco recognised. Some trains feature open-top cars.

in niches on the stairway. The best-known painting in the church is *La Fuga in Egitto* (Flight to Egypt), painted in 1522 by Bramantino.

A **funicular** (adult one way/return Sfr4.80/7.20, child Sfr2.20/3.60; ⏲ 8am-10pm) runs every 15 minutes from the town centre past the sanctuary to Orselina, but a more scenic, pilgrim-style approach is the 20-minute walk up the chapel-lined Via Crucis (take Via al Sasso off Via Cappuccini).

Getting There & Away

Locarno is well linked to Ticino and the rest of Switzerland via Bellinzona, or take the scenic **Centovalli Express** (www.centovalli.ch) to Brig via Domodossola in Italy.

Lugano

POP 61,840

Ticino's lush, mountain-rimmed lake isn't its only liquid asset. Lugano is also the country's third-most-important banking centre. Suits aside, it's a vivacious city, with bars and pavement cafes huddling in the spaghetti maze of steep cobblestone streets that untangle at the edge of the lake and along the flowery promenade.

Sights & Activities

The **Centro Storico** (Old Town) is a 10-minute walk downhill from the train station; take the stairs or the funicular (Sfr1.10).

Wander through the mostly porticoed lanes woven around the busy main square, **Piazza della Riforma** (which is even more lively when the Tuesday- and Friday-morning markets are held).

★Cattedrale di San Lorenzo CATHEDRAL

(St Lawrence Cathedral; Via San Lorenzo; ⏲ 6.30am-6pm) Lugano's early-16th-century cathedral conceals some fine frescoes and ornate baroque statues behind its Renaissance facade. Out front are far-reaching views over the Old Town's jumble of terracotta rooftops to the lake and mountains.

Società Navigazione del Lago di Lugano BOAT TOUR

(www.lakelugano.ch; Riva Vela 12; ⏲ Apr-late Oct) A relaxed way to see the lake's highlights is on one of these cruises, including one-hour bay tours (Sfr27.40) and three-hour morning cruises. Visit the website for timetables.

Sleeping

Many hotels close for part of the winter.

Hotel & Hostel Montarina HOTEL, HOSTEL €

(☎ 091 966 72 72; www.montarina.ch; Via Montarina 1; dm Sfr29, s Sfr82-92, d Sfr112-132; P 🛜 ≋) Occupying a pastel-pink villa dating to 1860, this hotel/hostel duo extends a heartfelt welcome. Mosaic floors, high ceilings and wrought-iron balustrades are lingering traces of old-world grandeur. There's a shared kitchen-lounge, toys to amuse the kids, a swimming pool set in palm-dotted gardens and even a tiny vineyard. Breakfast costs an extra Sfr15.

★Guesthouse Castagnola GUESTHOUSE €€

(☎ 078 632 67 47; www.gh-castagnola.com; Salita degli Olivi 2; apt Sfr120-180; P 🛜) Kristina and Mauro bend over backwards to please at their B&B, lodged in a beautifully restored 16th-century town house. Exposed stone, natural fabrics and earthy colours dominate in apartments kitted out with Nespreso coffee machines and flat-screen TVs. A generous breakfast (Sfr10 extra) is served in the courtyard. Take bus 2 to Castagnola, 2km east of the centre.

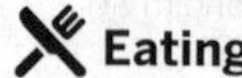

Eating

For pizza or pasta, try any of the places around Piazza della Riforma.

Bottega dei Sapori CAFE €
(Via Cattedrale 6; snacks & light meals Sfr9-14; ⏰7.30am-7.30pm Mon-Wed, to 9pm Thu-Fri, 9am-7.30pm Sat) This high-ceilinged cafe-bar does great salads, panini (for instance with air-dried beef, goat's cheese and rocket) and coffee. The tiny terrace is always packed.

★Bottegone del Vino ITALIAN €€
(☎091 922 76 89; Via Magatti 3; mains Sfr28-42; ⏰11am-11pm Mon-Sat) Favoured by the lunchtime banking brigade, this place has a season-driven menu that might include specialities such as ravioli stuffed with fine Tuscan Chianina beef. Knowledgeable waiters fuss around the tables and are only too happy to suggest the perfect Ticino tipple.

Getting There & Away

Lugano is on the main line connecting Milan to Zürich and Lucerne. Services from Lugano include Milan (Sfr17, 75 minutes), Zürich (Sfr64, 2¾ hours) and Lucerne (Sfr60, 2½ hours).

GRAUBÜNDEN

St Moritz

POP 5150

Switzerland's original winter wonderland and the cradle of alpine tourism, St Moritz (San Murezzan in Romansch) has been luring royals, celebrities and moneyed wannabes since 1864. With its shimmering aquamarine lake, emerald forests and aloof mountains, the town looks a million dollars.

Activities

With 350km of slopes, ultramodern lifts and spirit-soaring views, skiing in St Moritz is second to none, especially for confident intermediates. The general ski pass covers all the slopes.

If cross-country skiing is more your scene, you can glide across sunny plains and through snowy woods on 220km of groomed trails.

In summer the region has excellent hiking trails.

Schweizer Skischule SKIING
(☎081 830 01 01; www.skischool.ch; Via Stredas 14; ⏰8am-noon & 2-6pm Mon-Sat, 8-9am & 4-6pm Sun) The first Swiss ski school was founded in St Moritz in 1929. Today you can arrange skiing or snowboarding tuition for Sfr120/85 per day for adults/children here.

Sleeping & Eating

Jugendherberge St Moritz HOSTEL €
(☎081 836 61 11; www.youthhostel.ch/st.moritz; Via Surpunt 60; dm/s/d/q Sfr42.50/138/164/222; Wi-Fi) On the edge of the forest, this hostel has clean, quiet four-bed dorms and doubles. There's a kiosk, children's toy room, bike hire and laundrette. Bus 9 stops in front of the hostel in high season.

Chesa Spuondas HOTEL €€
(☎081 833 65 88; www.chesaspuondas.ch; Via Somplaz 47; s/d/f incl half board Sfr155/282/318; P Wi-Fi) This family hotel nestles amid meadows at the foot of forest and mountains. Rooms are in keeping with the Jugendstil villa, with high ceilings, parquet floors and the odd antique. Kids are the centre of attention here, with dedicated meal times, activities, play areas and the children's ski school a 10-minute walk away. Bus 1 from St Moritz stops nearby.

Chesa Veglia ITALIAN €€
(☎081 837 28 00; www.badruttspalace.com; Via Veglia 2; mains Sfr42-60, pizza Sfr23-36, menus Sfr45-70; ⏰noon-11.30pm) This slate-roofed, chalk-white chalet restaurant dates from 1658. The softly lit interior is all warm pine and creaking wood floors, while the terrace affords lake and mountain views. Go for pizza or regional specialities such as *Bündner Gerstensuppe* (creamy barley soup) and venison medallions with *Spätzli* (egg noodles).

Getting There & Away

Regular hourly trains make the scenic run to/from the rail hub of Chur (Sfr40, two hours).

St Moritz is also an end point on the much-hyped Glacier Express (p1122).

The Bernina Express (p1135) provides seasonal links to Lugano from St Moritz, which include the stunning Unesco-recognised train line over the Bernina Pass to Tirano in Italy.

SURVIVAL GUIDE

Directory A–Z

ACCOMMODATION

Switzerland sports traditional and creative accommodation in every price range. Many budget hotels have cheaper rooms with shared toilet and shower facilities. From there, truly, the sky is the limit. Breakfast buffets can be extensive and tasty but are not always included in room rates. Rates in cities and towns stay constant most of the year. In mountain resorts prices are seasonal (and can fall by 50% or more outside high season).

Low season Mid-September to mid-December, mid-April to mid-June

Mid-season January to mid-February, mid-June to early July, September

High season July to August, Christmas, mid-February to Easter

BUSINESS HOURS

The reviews in this guidebook won't list hours unless they differ from the hours listed here. Hours are given for the high season (April to October) and tend to decrease in the low season.

Banks 8.30am to 4.30pm Monday to Friday

Offices 8am to noon and 2pm to 5pm Monday to Friday

Restaurants noon to 2pm and 6pm to 10pm

Shops 9am to 7pm Monday to Friday (sometimes with a one- to two-hour break for lunch at noon in small towns), 9am to 6pm Saturday. In cities, there's often shopping until 9pm on Thursday or Friday. Sunday sees some souvenir shops and supermarkets at some train stations open.

SLEEPING PRICE RANGES

The following price ranges refer to a double room with a private bathroom, except in hostels or where otherwise specified. Quoted rates are for the high season and include breakfast, unless otherwise noted:

€ less than Sfr170

€€ Sfr170 to Sfr350

€€€ more than Sfr350

COUNTRY FACTS

Area 41,285 sq km

Capital Bern

Country Code ☎41

Currency Swiss franc (Sfr)

Emergency ambulance ☎144, fire ☎118, police ☎117

Languages French, German, Italian, Romansch

Money ATMs readily available

Population 8.14 million

Visas Schengen rules apply

DISCOUNT CARDS

Swiss Museum Pass (www.museumspass.ch; adult/family Sfr155/277) Regular or long-term visitors to Switzerland may want to buy this pass, which covers entry to 480 museums countrywide.

Visitors' Cards Many resorts and cities have a visitors' card *(Gästekarte)*, which provides benefits such as reduced prices for museums, pools, public transit or cable cars, plus free local public transport. Cards are issued by your accommodation.

ELECTRICITY

The electricity current is 220V, 50Hz. Swiss sockets are recessed, three holed, hexagonally shaped and incompatible with many plugs from abroad. However, they usually take the standard European two-pronged plug.

INTERNET ACCESS

Free wi-fi hot spots can be found at airports, dozens of Swiss train stations and in many hotels and cafes. Public wi-fi (provided by Swisscom) can cost Sfr5 for 30 minutes.

INTERNET RESOURCES

MySwitzerland (www.myswitzerland.com)

Swiss Info (www.swissinfo.ch)

MONEY

➡ Swiss francs are divided into 100 centimes (*Rappen* in German-speaking Switzerland). There are notes for 10, 20, 50, 100, 200 and 1000 francs, and coins for five, 10, 20 and 50 centimes, as well as for one, two and five francs. Euros are accepted by many tourism businesses.

ESSENTIAL FOOD & DRINK

- **Fondue** Switzerland's best-known dish, in which melted Emmental and Gruyère cheese are combined with white wine in a large pot and eaten with small bread chunks.
- **Raclette** Another popular artery-hardener of melted cheese served with potatoes.
- **Rösti** German Switzerland's national dish of fried shredded potatoes is served with everything.
- **Veal** Highly rated throughout the country; in Zürich, veal is thinly sliced and served in a cream sauce *(Gschnetzeltes Kalbsfleisch)*.
- **Bündnerfleisch** Dried beef, smoked and thinly sliced.
- **Chocolate** Good at any time of day and available seemingly everywhere.

- Exchange money at large train stations.
- Tipping is not necessary, given that hotels, restaurants, bars and even some taxis are legally required to include a 15% service charge in bills. You can round up the bill after a meal for good service, as locals do.

PUBLIC HOLIDAYS

New Year's Day 1 January
Easter March/April (Good Friday, Easter Sunday and Monday)
Ascension Day 40th day after Easter
Whit Sunday & Monday Seventh week after Easter
National Day 1 August
Christmas Day 25 December
St Stephen's Day 26 December

TELEPHONE

- The country code for Switzerland is ☎41. When calling Switzerland from abroad, drop the initial zero from the number; hence to call Bern, dial ☎41 31 (preceded by the overseas access code of the country you're dialling from).
- The international access code from Switzerland is ☎00. To call Britain (country code 44), start by dialling ☎00 44.
- Save money on the normal international tariff by buying a prepaid Swisscom card worth Sfr10, Sfr20, Sfr50 or Sfr100.

EATING PRICE RANGES

The following price ranges refer to the average cost of a main meal:

€ less than Sfr25

€€ Sfr25 to Sfr50

€€€ more than Sfr50

VISAS

For up-to-date details on visa requirements, go to www.eda.admin.ch.

Visas are not required for passport holders from the UK, the EU, Ireland, the USA, Canada, Australia, New Zealand, Norway and Iceland.

Getting There & Away

AIR

The main international airports:

Aéroport International de Genève (GVA; www.gva.ch) Geneva airport is 4km from the town centre.

Zürich Airport (ZRH; ☎043 816 22 11; www.zurich-airport.com) The airport is 9km north of the centre, with flights to most European capitals as well as some in Africa, Asia and North America.

LAND

Bus

Eurolines (www.eurolines.com) has buses with connections across Western Europe.

Train

Switzerland is a hub of train connections to the rest of the Continent. Zürich is the busiest international terminus, with service to all neighbouring countries. Destinations include Münich (four hours), and Vienna (eight hours), from where there are extensive onward connections to cities in Eastern Europe.

- Numerous TGV trains daily connect Paris to Geneva (three hours), Lausanne (3¾ hours), Basel (three hours) and Zürich (four hours).
- Nearly all connections from Italy pass through Milan before branching off to Zürich, Lucerne, Bern or Lausanne.
- Most connections from Germany pass through Zürich or Basel.

- Swiss Federal Railways accepts internet bookings but does not post tickets outside of Switzerland.

Getting Around

Swiss public transport is an efficient, fully integrated and comprehensive system, which incorporates trains, buses, boats and funiculars.

Marketed as the Swiss Travel System, the network has a useful website, and excellent free maps covering the country are available at train stations and tourist offices.

PASSES & DISCOUNTS

Convenient discount passes make the Swiss transport system even more appealing. For extensive travel within Switzerland, the following national travel passes generally offer better savings than Eurail or InterRail passes.

Swiss Pass This entitles the holder to unlimited travel on almost every train, boat and bus service in the country, and on trams and buses in 41 towns, plus free entry to 400-odd museums. Reductions of 50% apply on funiculars, cable cars and private railways. Different passes are available, valid between four days (Sfr272) and one month (Sfr607).

Swiss Flexi Pass This pass allows you to nominate a certain number of days – from three (Sfr260) to six (Sfr414) – during one month when you can enjoy unlimited travel.

Half-Fare Card As the name suggests, you pay only half the fare on trains with this card (Sfr120 for one month), plus you get some discounts on local-network buses, trams and cable cars.

BICYCLE

- **Rent-a-Bike** (www.rentabike.ch) allows you to rent bikes at 80 train stations in Switzerland. For an Sfr8 surcharge you can collect from one station and return to another.
- **Suisseroule** (Schweizrollt; www.schweizrollt.ch) lets you borrow a bike for free or cheaply in places like Geneva, Bern and Zürich. Bike stations are usually next to the train station or central square.
- Local tourist offices often have good cycling information.

BOAT

Ferries and steamers link towns and cities on many lakes, including Geneva, Lucerne, Lugano and Zürich.

BUS

- Yellow **post buses** (www.postbus.ch) supplement the rail network, linking towns to difficult-to-access mountain regions.
- Services are regular, and departures (usually next to train stations) are linked to train schedules.
- Swiss national travel passes are valid.
- Purchase tickets on board; some scenic routes over the Alps (eg the Lugano–St Moritz run) require reservations.

CAR

- Headlights must be on at all times, and dipped in tunnels.
- The speed limit is 50km/h in towns, 80km/h on main roads outside towns, 100km/h on single-lane freeways and 120km/h on dual-lane freeways.
- Some minor alpine passes are closed from November to May – check with the local tourist offices before setting off.

TRAIN

The Swiss rail network combines state-run and private operations. The **Swiss Federal Railway** (www.sbb.ch) is abbreviated to SBB in German, CFF in French and FFS in Italian.

- All major train stations are connected to each other by hourly departures, at least between 6am and midnight.
- Second-class seats are perfectly acceptable, but cars are often close to full. First-class carriages are more comfortable and spacious and have fewer passengers.
- Ticket vending machines accept most major credit cards from around the world.
- The SBB smartphone app is an excellent resource and can be used to store your tickets electronically.

CONNECTIONS

Landlocked between France, Germany, Austria, Liechtenstein and Italy, Switzerland is well linked, especially by train. Formalities are minimal when entering Switzerland by air, rail or road thanks to the Schengen Agreement. Fast, well-maintained roads run from Switzerland through to all bordering countries; the Alps present a natural barrier, meaning main roads generally head through tunnels to enter Switzerland. Switzerland can be reached by steamer from several lakes: from Germany, arrive via Lake Constance and from France via Lake Geneva. You can also cruise down the Rhine to Basel.

SWITZERLAND'S SCENIC TRAINS

Swiss trains, buses and boats are more than a means of getting from A to B. Stunning views invariably make the journey itself the destination. Switzerland boasts the following routes among its classic sightseeing journeys.

You're able to choose just one leg of the trip. Also, scheduled services often ply the same routes for standard fares; these are cheaper than the named trains, which often have cars with extra-large windows and require reservations.

Bernina Express (www.rhb.ch) Cuts 145km through Engadine from Chur to Tirano in 2¼ hours. May and October, continue onwards from Tirano to Lugano by bus.

Glacier Express (www.glacierexpress.ch) Famous train journey between Zermatt and St Moritz. The Brig–Zermatt alpine leg makes for pretty powerful viewing, as does the area between Disentis/Mustér and Brig.

Jungfrau Region You can spend days ogling stunning alpine scenery from the trains, cable cars and more here.

GoldenPass Line (www.goldenpass.ch) Travels between Lucerne and Montreux. The journey is in three legs, and you must change trains twice. Regular trains, without panoramic windows, work the whole route hourly.

Centovalli Express (www.centovalli.ch) An underappreciated gem of a line (two hours) that snakes along fantastic river gorges in Switzerland and Italy, from Locarno to Domodossola. Trains run through the day and it is easy to connect to Brig and beyond from Domodossola in Italy.

- Check the SBB website for cheap Supersaver tickets on major routes.
- Most stations have 24-hour lockers, usually accessible from 6am to midnight.
- Seat reservations (Sfr5) are advisable for longer journeys, particularly in the high season.

Turkey

Includes ➜

Best Places to Eat

- Antiochia (p1150)
- Hanimeli Kars Mutfağı (p1170)
- Konak Konya Mutfağı (p1167)
- Vanilla (p1164)
- Seten Restaurant (p1169)

Best Places to Stay

- Hotel Empress Zoe (p1149)
- Hideaway Hotel (p1161)
- White Garden Pansiyon (p1164)
- Koza Cave Hotel (p1168)
- Angora House Hotel (p1165)

Why Go?

Turkey walks the tightrope between Europe and Asia with ease. Its cities pack in towering minarets and spice-trading bazaars but also offer buzzing modern streetlife. Out in the countryside, this country's reputation as a bridge between continents is laid bare. Its expansive steppes and craggy mountain slopes are scattered with the remnants of once mighty empires. Lycian ruins peek from the undergrowth across the Mediterranean coast, the Roman era's pomp stretches out before you in Ephesus, while the swirling rock valleys of Cappadocia hide Byzantine monastery complexes whittled out by early Christian ascetics.

Of course, if you just want to sloth on a prime piece of beach, Turkey has you covered. But when you've brushed off the sand, this land where east meets west, and the ancient merges seamlessly with the contemporary is a fascinating mosaic of culture, history and visceral natural splendour.

When to Go

Ankara

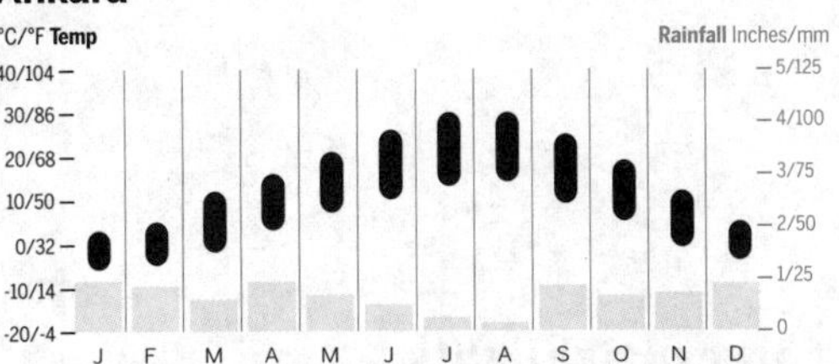

Apr & May İstanbul is a colourful kaleidoscope of tulips and it's prime hiking time on the coast.

Jun–Aug Summer temperatures sizzle and the Mediterranean resorts are in full swing.

Sep & Oct Plenty of crisp clear-sky days but the crowds have dispersed.

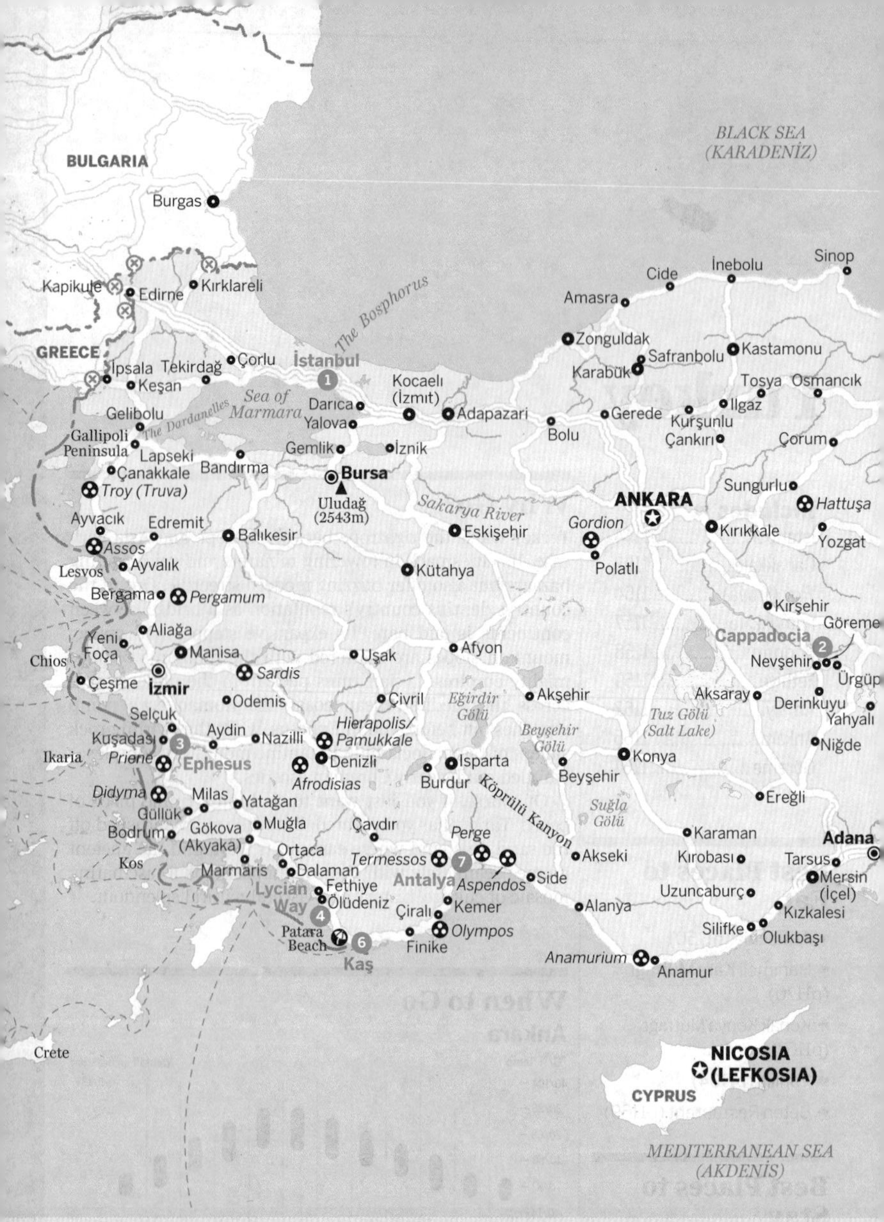

BLACK SEA
(KARADENİZ)
BULGARIA
Burgas
Kapikule
Edirne
Kırklareli
GREECE
The Bosphorus
İpsala
Tekirdağ
Çorlu
İstanbul
1
Keşan
Sea of
Marmara
The Dardanelles
Gelibolu
Gallipoli
Peninsula
Lapseki
Çanakkale
Bandırma
Darıca
Yalova
Kocaeli
(İzmit)
Adapazari
Gemlik
İznik
Bursa
Uludağ
(2543m)
Troy (Truva)
Ayvacık
Edremit
Balıkesir
Assos
Lesvos
Ayvalık
Bergama
Pergamum
Yeni
Foça
Aliağa
Chios
Manisa
Çeşme
İzmir
Sardis
Odemis
Selçuk
Kuşadası
3
Ephesus
Aydin
Nazilli
Ikaria
Priene
Didyma
Milas
Yatağan
Güllük
Bodrum
Gökova
(Akyaka)
Muğla
Kos
Marmaris
Ortaca
Dalaman
Fethiye
Ölüdeniz
Lycian
Way
4
Patara
Beach
6
Kaş
Crete
Uşak
Çivril
Hierapolis/
Pamukkale
Denizli
Afrodisias
Çavdır
Sakarya River
Eskişehir
Kütahya
Afyon
Eğirdir
Gölü
Burdur
Isparta
Köprülü Kanyon
Perge
Termessos
7
Antalya
Aspendos
Çiralı
Kemer
Olympos
Finike
Amasra
Cide
İnebolu
Sinop
Zonguldak
Safranbolu
Karabük
Kastamonu
Tosya
Osmancık
Bolu
Gerede
Ilgaz
Kurşunlu
Çankırı
Çorum
Sungurlu
ANKARA
Hattuşa
Gordion
Polatlı
Kırıkkale
Yozgat
Kırşehir
Göreme
Cappadocia
2
Nevşehir
Ürgüp
Aksaray
Derinkuyu
Yahyalı
Niğde
Akşehir
Tuz Gölü
(Salt Lake)
Beyşehir
Gölü
Beyşehir
Konya
Suğla
Gölü
Ereğli
Karaman
Adana
Akseki
Kırobası
Tarsus
Side
Mersin
(İçel)
Uzuncaburç
Alanya
Kızkalesi
Silifke
Olukbaşı
Anamurium
Anamur
NICOSIA
(LEFKOSIA)
CYPRUS
MEDITERRANEAN SEA
(AKDENİS)

Turkey Highlights

1 Ferry-hop from Europe to Asia with your camera at the ready to capture **İstanbul's** (p1144) famous minaret-studded skyline.

2 Bed down in a cave-hotel to savour modern troglodyte style amid the bizarre lunarscape of **Cappadocia** (p1167).

3 Fulfil your toga-loaded daydreams in **Ephesus** (p1156), one of the world's greatest surviving Graeco-Roman cities.

4 Explore the ruins of empires while relishing

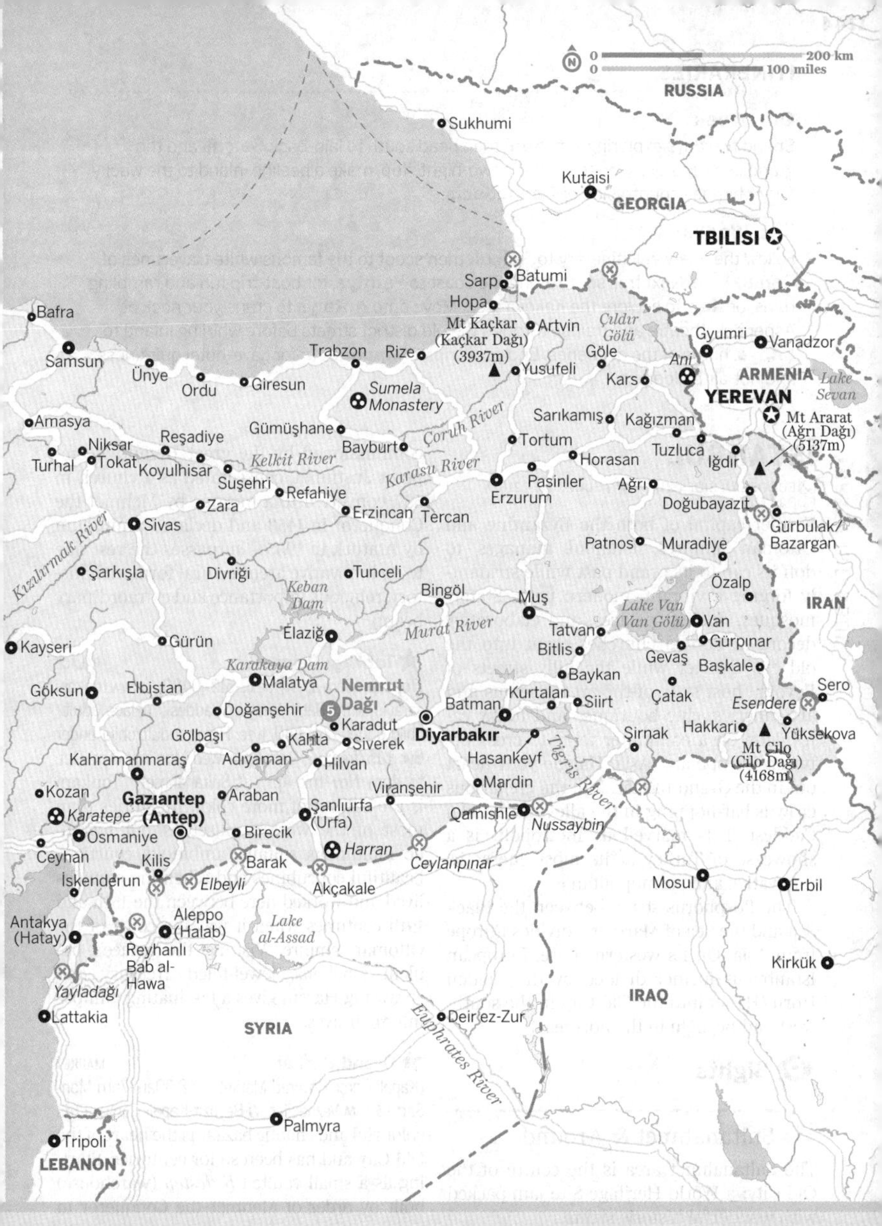

ridiculously gorgeous coastal views along the **Lycian Way** (p1160) long-distance trail.

5 Marvel at one king's egotism, amid the toppled statues on the summit of **Nemrut Dağı** (Mt Nemrut; p1169).

6 Paddle over Kekova's sunken city on a kayaking trip out of the fun activity-vortex of **Kaş** (p1161).

7 Stroll the narrow lanes between Ottoman mansions and chunks of Roman wall in the old town quarter of **Antalya** (p1162).

ITINERARIES

One Week

Spend two days exploring **İstanbul** then head south to laid-back **Selçuk** and the grandiose ruins of **Ephesus**. After a two-night stop, make a beeline inland to the wacky fairy-chimney countryside of **Cappadocia**.

Two Weeks

Follow the one-week itinerary to **Selçuk** then scoot to the famous white travertines of **Pamukkale**. Next trail south along the coast to **Fethiye**, for boat-trip fun and rambling ruins, or **Kaş**, to explore the Kekova area. Move onto **Antalya** to crane your neck at Aspendos' theatre and traipse through the old district streets before whirling inland to **Konya**, home of the dervishes. End your trip in **Cappadocia** for cave-hotel quirkiness and hot-air ballooning.

İSTANBUL

☎ EUROPEAN SIDE 0212 / ☎ ASIAN SIDE 0216 / POP 14 MILLION

Former capital of both the Byzantine and Ottoman empires, İstanbul manages to doff its cap to its grand past while stridantly forging a vibrant, modern path. Stately mosques, opulent palaces, and elaborately decorated domed churches cram into the old city quarter while the hilly streets of Beyoğlu host state-of-the-art museums and art galleries, chic boutiques and funky cafes. Hop on a commuter ferry to cross between Europe and Asia. Haggle your heart out in the Grand Bazaar. Join the gregarious crowds bar-hopping in the alleys off İstiklal Caddesi. This marvellous metropolis is a showcase of Turkey at its most energetic, innovative and cosmopolitan.

The Bosphorus strait, between the Black Sea and the Sea of Marmara, divides Europe from Asia. On its western shore, European İstanbul is further divided by the Golden Horn (Haliç) into the Old City in the southwest and Beyoğlu in the northeast.

Sights

Sultanahmet & Around

The Sultanahmet area is the centre of the Old City; a World Heritage Site jam-packed with wonderful historic sights.

★ **Aya Sofya** MUSEUM

(Hagia Sophia; ☎0212-522 1750; www.ayasofyamuzesi.gov.tr; Aya Sofya Meydanı 1; adult/child under 12yr ₺30/free; ⏲9am-6pm Tue-Sun mid-Apr–Sep, to 4pm Oct–mid-Apr; 🚊Sultanahmet) There are many important monuments in İstanbul, but this venerable structure – commissioned by the great Byzantine emperor Justinian, consecrated as a church in 537, converted to a mosque by Mehmet the Conqueror in 1453 and declared a museum by Atatürk in 1935 – surpasses the rest due to its innovative architectural form, rich history, religious importance and extraordinary beauty.

★ **Topkapı Palace** PALACE

(Topkapı Sarayı; ☎0212-512 0480; www.topkapisarayi.gov.tr; Babıhümayun Caddesi; palace adult/child under 12yr ₺30/free, Harem adult/child under 6yr ₺15/free; ⏲9am-6pm Wed-Mon mid-Apr–Oct, to 4pm Nov–mid-Apr; 🚊Sultanahmet) Topkapı is the subject of more colourful stories than most of the world's museums put together. Libidinous sultans, ambitious courtiers, beautiful concubines and scheming eunuchs lived and worked here between the 15th and 19th centuries when it was the court of the Ottoman empire. Visiting the palace's opulent pavilions, jewel-filled Treasury and sprawling Harem gives a fascinating glimpse into their lives.

★ **Grand Bazaar** MARKET

(Kapalı Çarşı, Covered Market; ⏲8.30am-7pm Mon-Sat; 🚸; Ⓜ Vezneciler, 🚊Beyazıt-Kapalı Çarşı) This colourful and chaotic bazaar is the heart of the Old City and has been so for centuries. Starting as a small vaulted *bedesten* (warehouse) built by order of Mehmet the Conqueror in

MUSEUM PASS

The **Museum Pass İstanbul** (www.muze.gov.tr/museum_pass) offers a possible ₺36 saving on entry to the Old City's major sights, and allows holders to skip admission queues.

İstanbul

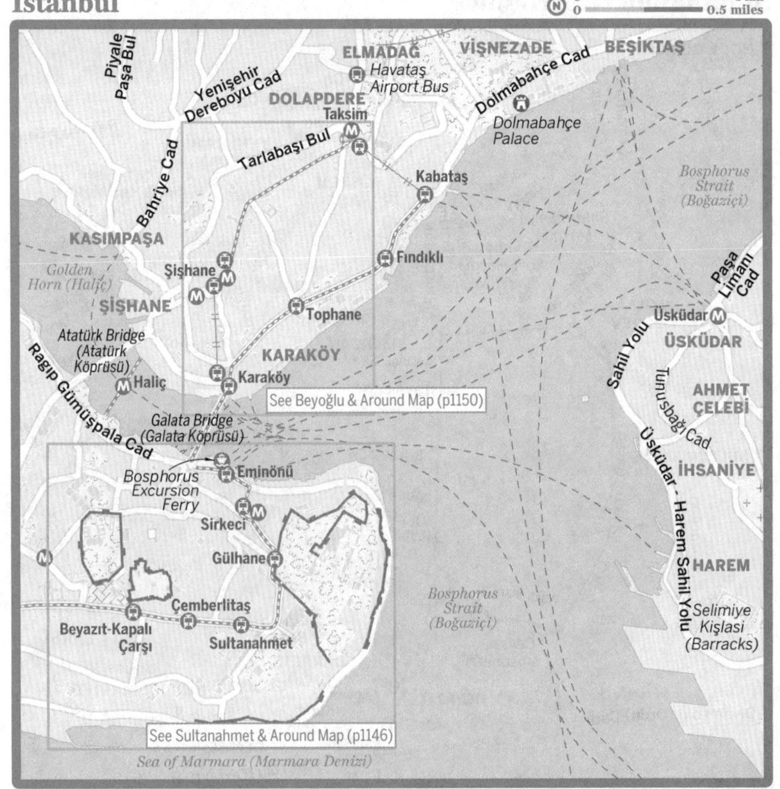

1461, it grew to cover a vast area as laneways between the *bedesten,* neighbouring shops and *hans* (caravanserais) were roofed and the market assumed the sprawling, labyrinthine form that it retains today.

Basilica Cistern CISTERN

(Yerebatan Sarnıçı; ☎0212-512 1570; www.yerebatan.com; Yerebatan Caddesi 13; admission officially ₺20 for foreigners but in reality ₺10; ⊙9am-6.30pm mid-Apr–Sep, till 5.30pm Nov–mid-Apr; Sultanahmet) This subterranean structure was commissioned by Emperor Justinian and built in 532. The largest surviving Byzantine cistern in İstanbul, it was constructed using 336 columns, many of which were salvaged from ruined temples and feature fine carved capitals. Its symmetry and sheer grandeur of conception are quite breathtaking, and its cavernous depths make a great retreat on summer days.

Blue Mosque MOSQUE

(Sultanahmet Camii; Hippodrome; ⊙closed to tourists during the 5 daily prayer times & Fri sermon; Sultanahmet) İstanbul's most photogenic building was the grand project of Sultan Ahmet I (r 1603–17), whose tomb is located on the north side of the site facing Sultanahmet Park. The mosque's wonderfully curvaceous exterior features a cascade of domes and six slender minarets. Blue İznik tiles adorn the interior and give the building its unofficial but commonly used name.

İstanbul Archaeology Museums MUSEUM

(İstanbul Arkeoloji Müzeleri; ☎0212-520 7740; www.istanbularkeoloji.gov.tr; Osman Hamdi Bey Yokuşu, Gülhane; adult/child under 12yr ₺15/free; ⊙9am-6pm Tue-Sun mid-Apr–Sep, to 4pm Oct–mid-Apr; Gülhane) This superb museum showcases archaeological and artistic treasures from the Topkapı collections. Housed

Sultanahmet & Around

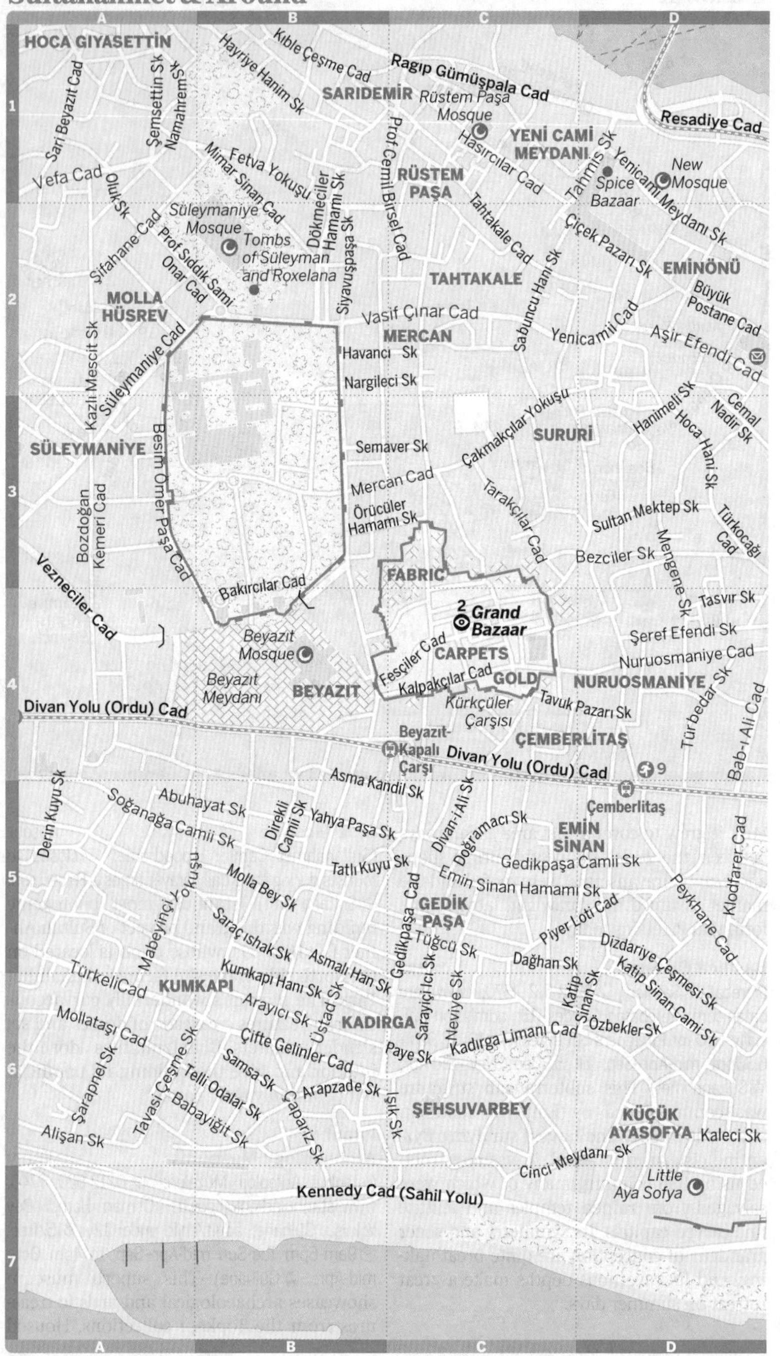

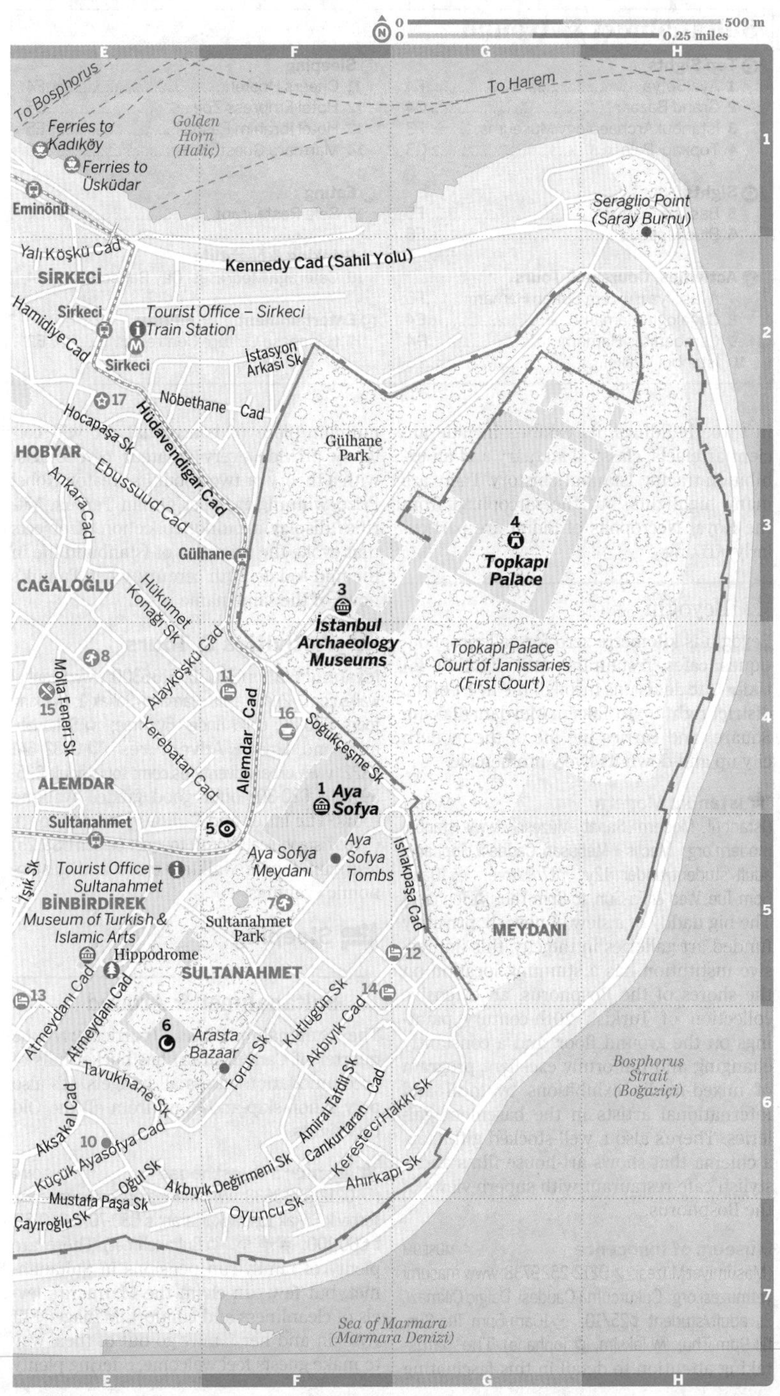

0 500 m
0 0.25 miles
E
F
G
H
To Bosphorus
To Harem
Ferries to Kadıköy
Ferries to Üsküdar
Golden Horn (Haliç)
Eminönü
Seraglio Point (Saray Burnu)
Yalı Köşkü Cad
Kennedy Cad (Sahil Yolu)
SİRKECİ
Sirkeci
Hamidiye Cad
Tourist Office – Sirkeci Train Station
Sirkeci
İstasyon Arkasi Sk
Nöbethane Cad
17
Hocapaşa Sk
Hüdavendigar Cad
HOBYAR
Ebussuud Cad
Ankara Cad
Gülhane Park
Gülhane
CAĞALOĞLU
Hükümet Konağı Sk
4
Topkapı Palace
3
İstanbul Archaeology Museums
Topkapı Palace Court of Janissaries (First Court)
8
Alayköşkü Cad
11
Molla Feneri Sk
15
Alemdar Cad
16
Soğukçeşme Sk
Yerebatan Cad
ALEMDAR
1 Aya Sofya
Sultanahmet
5
Aya Sofya Tombs
Aya Sofya Meydanı
İshakpaşa Cad
Işık Sk
Tourist Office – Sultanahmet
BİNBİRDİREK
7
Museum of Turkish & Islamic Arts
Sultanahmet Park
MEYDANI
Hippodrome
12
SULTANAHMET
13
14
Atmeydanı Cad
Atmeydanı Cad
Kutlugün Sk
Akbıyık Cad
6
Arasta Bazaar
Torun Sk
Bosphorus Strait (Boğaziçi)
Tavukhane Sk
Amiral Tafdil Sk
Cankurtaran Cad
Aksakal Cad
Keresteci Hakkı Sk
10
Küçük Ayasofya Cad
Akbıyık Değirmeni Sk
Ahırkapı Sk
Oğul Sk
Mustafa Paşa Sk
Oyuncu Sk
Çayıroğlu Sk
Sea of Marmara (Marmara Denizi)
1
2
3
4
5
6
7

Sultanahmet & Around

Top Sights
1 Aya Sofya ... F4
2 Grand Bazaar ... C4
3 İstanbul Archaeology Museums ... F3
4 Topkapı Palace ... G3

Sights
5 Basilica Cistern ... F5
6 Blue Mosque ... E6

Activities, Courses & Tours
7 Ayasofya Hürrem Sultan Hamamı ... F5
8 Cağaloğlu Hamamı ... E4
9 Çemberlitaş Hamamı ... D4
10 İstanbul Walks ... E6

Sleeping
11 Cheers Hostel ... F4
12 Hotel Empress Zoe ... G5
13 Hotel Ibrahim Pasha ... E5
14 Marmara Guesthouse ... F5

Eating
15 Sefa Restaurant ... E4

Drinking & Nightlife
16 Caferağa Medresesi Çay Bahçesi ... F4

Entertainment
17 Hocapaşa Culture Centre ... E2

in three buildings, its exhibits include ancient artefacts, classical statuary and an exhibition tracing İstanbul's history. There are many highlights, but the sarcophagi from the Royal Necropolis of Sidon are particularly striking.

Beyoğlu

Beyoğlu is kilometre zero for galleries, boutiques, cafes, restaurants and nightlife. **İstiklal Caddesi** runs through the heart of the district right up to Taksim Meydanı (Taksim Square) and carries the life of the modern city up and down its lively promenade.

★ **İstanbul Modern** GALLERY
(İstanbul Modern Sanat Müzesi; www.istanbulmodern.org; Meclis-i Mebusan Caddesi, Tophane; adult/student/under 12yr ₺17/9/free; 10am-6pm Tue, Wed & Fri-Sun, to 8pm Thu; Tophane) The big daddy of a slew of newish, privately funded art galleries in the city, this impressive institution has a stunning location on the shores of the Bosphorus, an extensive collection of Turkish 20th-century paintings on the ground floor, and a constantly changing and uniformly excellent program of mixed-media exhibitions by local and international artists in the basement galleries. There's also a well-stocked gift shop, a cinema that shows art-house films and a stylish cafe-restaurant with superb views of the Bosphorus.

Museum of Innocence MUSEUM
(Masumiyet Müzesi; 0212-252 9738; www.masumiyetmuzesi.org; Çukurcuma Caddesi, Dalgıç Çıkmazı, 2; adult/student ₺25/10; 10am-6pm Tue-Sun, till 9pm Thu; M Taksim, Tophane) The painstaking attention to detail in this fascinating museum/piece of conceptual art will certainly provide every amateur psychologist with a theory or two about its creator, Nobel Prize–winning novelist Orhan Pamuk. Vitrines display a quirky collection of objects that evoke the minutiae of İstanbullu life in the mid-to-late 20th century, when Pamuk's novel of the same name is set.

Activities & Tours

İstanbul Walks (0212-516 6300; www.istanbulwalks.com; 2nd fl, Şifa Hamamı Sokak 1; walking tours €30-80, child under 6yr free; Sultanahmet) and **Urban Adventures** (0532 641 2822; www.urbanadventures.com; tours adult €25-39, child €20-30) offer good guided walking tours. The latter and **Culinary Backstreets** (http://istanbuleats.com/; tour per person US$125) also run foodie walking tours and gastronomic evenings.

Sleeping

Sultanahmet & Around

The Sultanahmet area (particularly the quarter of Cankurtaran) has bucket-fulls of accommodation across all budgets. It's also only a hop-skip-and-jump from all the Old City sights.

★ **Marmara Guesthouse** PENSION €
(0212-638 3638; www.marmaraguesthouse.com; Terbıyık Sokak 15, Cankurtaran; s €30-70, d €40-85, f €60-100; Sultanahmet) There are plenty of family-run pensions in Sultanahmet, but few can claim the Marmara's levels of cleanliness and comfort. Manager Elif Aytekin and her family go out of their way to make guests feel welcome, offering plenty

of advice and serving a delicious breakfast on the vine-covered, sea-facing roof terrace. Rooms have comfortable beds, good bathrooms and double-glazed windows.

Cheers Hostel HOSTEL €
(☎0212-526 0200; www.cheershostel.com; Zeynep Sultan Camii Sokak 21, Cankurtaran; dm €16-22, d €60-80, tr €90-120; ❄@📶; 🚊Gülhane) The dorms here are worlds away from the impersonal barracks-like spaces in bigger hostels. Bright and airy, they feature wooden floorboards, rugs, lockers and comfortable beds; most have air-con. Bathrooms are clean and plentiful. It's a great choice in winter because the cosy rooftop bar has an open fire and a great view. Private rooms aren't as nice.

★**Hotel Empress Zoe** BOUTIQUE HOTEL €€
(☎0212-518 2504; www.emzoe.com; Akbıyık Caddesi 10, Cankurtaran; s €65-90, d €110-140, ste €160-275; ❄📶; 🚊Sultanahmet) Named after the feisty Byzantine Empress, this is one of the most impressive boutique hotels in the city. There's a range of room types but the garden suites are particularly enticing as they overlook a gorgeous flower-filled courtyard where breakfast is served in warm weather. You can enjoy an early evening drink there, or while admiring the sea view from the terrace bar.

Hotel Ibrahim Pasha BOUTIQUE HOTEL €€
(☎0212-518 0394; www.ibrahimpasha.com; Terzihane Sokak 7; r standard €100-195, deluxe €145-285; ❄@📶; 🚊Sultanahmet) This exemplary designer hotel has a great location just off the Hippodrome, a comfortable lounge with open fire, and a terrace bar with knockout views of the Blue Mosque. All of the rooms are gorgeous but some are small – opt for a deluxe one if possible. Urbane owner Mehmet Umur is a mine of information about the city.

Beyoğlu & Around

Marmara Pera HOTEL €€
(☎0212-251 4646; www.themarmarahotels.com; Meşrutiyet Caddesi 1, Tepebaşı; s €109-160, d €135-199; ❄@📶🏊; Ⓜ Şişhane, 🚊Karaköy, then funicular to Tünel) A great location in the midst of Beyoğlu's major entertainment enclave makes this high-rise modern hotel an excellent choice. Added extras include a health club, a tiny outdoor pool, a truly fabulous buffet breakfast spread and the **Mikla** (www.miklarestaurant.com; Marmara Pera Hotel, Meşrutiyet Caddesi 15, Tepebaşı; ⏱from 6pm Mon-Sat summer only; Ⓜ Şişhane, 🚊Karaköy, then funicular to Tünel) rooftop bar and restaurant. Rooms with a sea view are approximately 30% more expensive.

Witt Istanbul Hotel BOUTIQUE HOTEL €€€
(☎0212-293 1500; www.wittistanbul.com; Defterdar Yokuşu 26, Cihangir; d ste €195-385, penthouse & superior king €385-450; ❄@📶; Ⓜ Taksim, 🚊Tophane) Showcasing nearly as many designer features as an issue of *Wallpaper** magazine, this stylish apartment hotel in the trendy suburb of Cihangir has 18 suites with kitchenette, seating area, CD/DVD player, iPod dock, espresso machine, king-sized bed and huge bathroom. Penthouse and superior king suites have fabulous views. It's a short but steep climb from the Tophane tram stop.

DON'T MISS

HAMAMS: SQUEAKY-CLEAN THE TURKISH WAY

İstanbul's hamams may be pricey but it's not often you get to soap-up amid such historic finery. Our top three picks for sudsy relaxation after a long day of sightseeing:

Ayasofya Hürrem Sultan Hamamı (☎0212-517 3535; www.ayasofyahamami.com; Aya Sofya Meydanı 2; bath treatments €85-170, massages €40-75; ⏱8am-10pm; 🚊Sultanahmet)

Cağaloğlu Hamamı (☎0212-522 2424; www.cagalogluhamami.com.tr; Yerebatan Caddesi 34; bath, scrub & massage packages €50-110; ⏱8am-10pm; 🚊Sultanahmet)

Çemberlitaş Hamamı (☎0212-522 7974; www.cemberlitashamami.com; Vezir Han Caddesi 8; self-service ₺60, bath, scrub & soap massage ₺90; ⏱6am-midnight; 🚊Çemberlitaş)

Eating

İstanbul is a food-lover's paradise. Head to Beyoğlu for the cream of the city's dining scene. Check out www.istanbuleats.com for bundles of options.

Sefa Restaurant TURKISH €
(☎02-12-520 0670; www.sefarestaurant.com.tr; Nuruosmaniye Caddesi 17, Cağaloğlu; portions ₺8-14, kebaps ₺13-20; ⏱7am-5pm; 📝; 🚊Sultanahmet) This popular place near the Grand Bazaar

Beyoğlu & Around

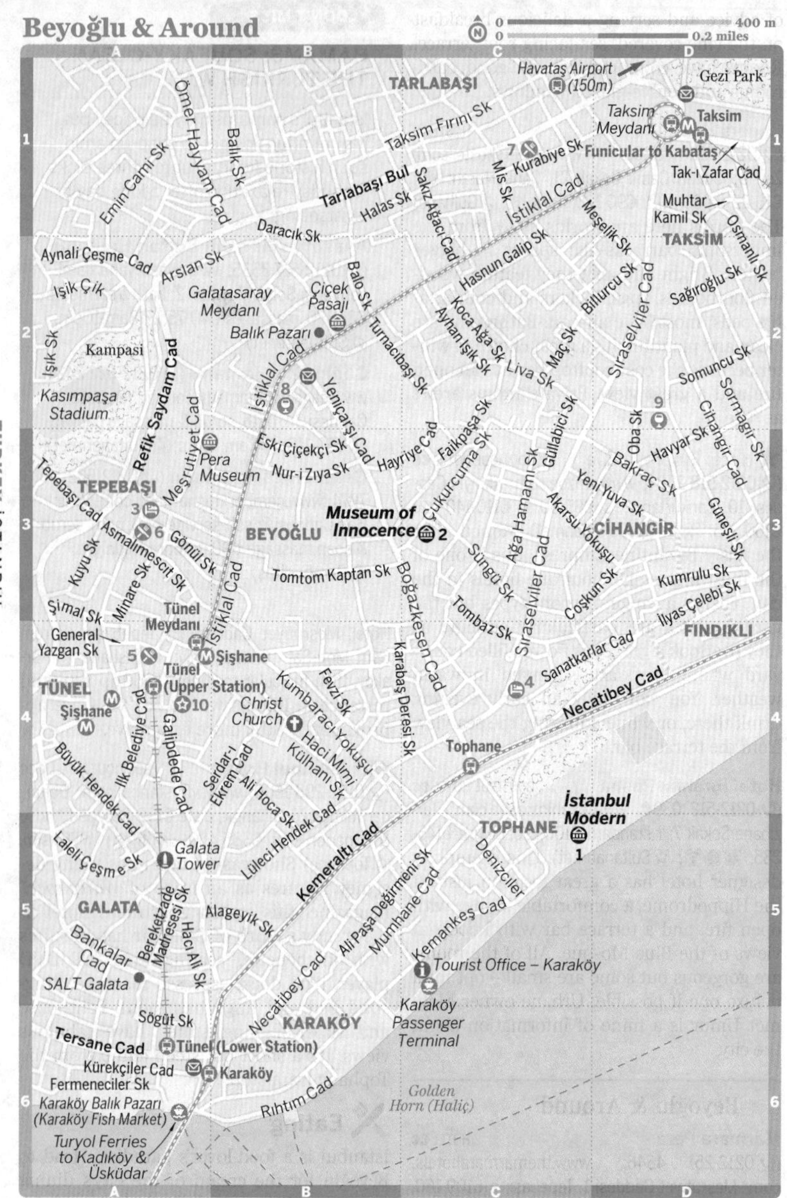

describes its cuisine as Ottoman, but what's really on offer are *hazır yemek* (ready-made dishes) and kebaps at extremely reasonable prices. You can order from an English menu or choose daily specials from the bain-marie. Try to arrive early-ish for lunch because many of the dishes run out by 1.30pm. No alcohol.

★ Antiochia ANATOLIAN €€
(☎0212-292 1100; www.antiochiaconcept.com; General Yazgan Sokak 3c, Asmalımescit; mezes

Beyoğlu & Around

Top Sights

Sleeping

Eating

Drinking & Nightlife

Entertainment

₺10-12, mains ₺18-28; lunch Mon-Fri, dinner Mon-Sat; Karaköy, then funicular to Tünel) Dishes from the southeastern city of Antakya (Hatay) are the speciality at this foodie destination. Mezes are dominated by wild thyme, pomegranate syrup, olives, walnuts and tangy home-made yoghurt, and the kebaps are equally flavoursome – try the succulent *şiş et* (grilled lamb) or *dürüm* (wrap filled with minced meat, onions and tomatoes). There's a discount at lunch.

Zübeyir Ocakbaşı KEBAPS €€
(0212-293 3951; Bekar Sokak 28; meze ₺7-9, kebaps ₺22-45; noon-1am; Kabataş, then funicular to Taksim) Every morning, the chefs at this popular *ocakbaşı* (grill house) prepare the fresh, top-quality meats to be grilled over their handsome copper-hooded barbecues that night: spicy chicken wings and Adana kebaps, flavoursome ribs, pungent liver kebaps and well-marinated lamb *şış kebaps*. Their offerings are famous throughout the city, so booking a table is essential.

★**Meze by Lemon Tree** MODERN TURKISH €€€
(0212-252 8302; www.mezze.com.tr; Meşrutiyet Caddesi 83b, Tepebaşı; mezes ₺10-30, 4-course degustation menu for 2 persons ₺160; 7-11pm; ; Şishane, Karaköy, then funicular to Tünel) Chef Gençay Üçok creates some of the most interesting – and delicious – modern Turkish food seen in the city and serves it in an intimate restaurant opposite the Pera Palace Hotel. We suggest opting for the degustation menu or sticking to the wonderful mezes here rather than ordering mains. Bookings essential.

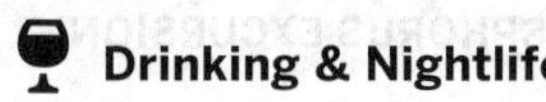

Drinking & Nightlife

Sultanahmet's bar scene is concentrated on Akbıyık Caddesi, a stone's throw from most of the accommodation. Beyoğlu is the place to go to sample the local nightlife. Nevizade and Balo Sokaks, off İstiklal Caddesi, are lined with bars.

★**360** BAR
(www.360istanbul.com; 8th fl, İstiklal Caddesi 163; noon-2am Sun-Thu, to 4am Fri & Sat; Şişhane, Karaköy, then funicular to Tünel) İstanbul's most famous bar, and deservedly so. If you can score one of the bar stools on the terrace you'll be happy indeed – the view is truly extraordinary. It morphs into a club after midnight on Friday and Saturday, when a cover charge of around ₺40 applies.

5 Kat BAR
(www.5kat.com; 5th fl, Soğancı Sokak 7, Cihangir; 5pm-1am Mon-Fri, 11am-1am Sat & Sun; Taksim, Kabataş) This İstanbul institution has been around for over two decades and is a great alternative for those who can't stomach the style overload at many of the high-profile Beyoğlu bars. In winter drinks are served in the boudoir-style bar on the 5th floor; in summer action moves to the outdoor roof terrace. Both have great Bosphorus views.

Caferağa Medresesi Çay Bahçesi TEA GARDEN
(Soğukkuyu Çıkmazı 5, off Caferiye Sokak; 8.30am-4pm; Sultanahmet) On a fine day, sipping a çay in the gorgeous courtyard of this Sinan-designed *medrese* (seminary) near Topkapı Palace is a delight. Located close to both Aya Sofya and Topkapı Palace, it's a perfect pit stop between sights. There's simple food available at lunchtime.

☆ Entertainment

Hocapaşa Culture Centre PERFORMING ARTS
(Hodjapasha Culture Centre; 0212-511 4626; www.hodjapasha.com; Hocapaşa Hamamı Sokak 3b, Sirkeci; performances adult ₺60-80, child under 12yr ₺40-50; Sirkeci) Occupying a beautifully converted 550-year-old hamam near Eminönü, this cultural centre stages a one-hour whirling dervish performance for tourists on Tuesday, Wednesday, Thursday, Saturday and Sunday evenings at 7pm, and a 1½-hour Turkish dance show on Tuesday, Thursday

DON'T MISS

THE BOSPHORUS EXCURSION BOAT

İstanbul's soul is the Bosphorus. Don't miss seeing the city's iconic skyline and riverside views from the city's real highway aboard the **Bosphorus Excursion Ferry** (Map p1145; www.ido.com.tr; Boğaz İskelesi; long tour one way/return ₺15/25, short tour ₺10; ⏲long tour 10.35am, plus 1.35pm Apr–Oct & noon summer, short tour 2.30pm Apr-Oct). Boats depart from Eminönü and stop at various points before turning around at Anadolu Kavağı. Along the way you soak up sights such as the ornate **Dolmabahçe Palace** (Dolmabahçe Sarayı; Map p1145; ☎0212-327 2626; www.millisaraylar.gov.tr; Dolmabahçe Caddesi, Beşiktaş; adult Selâmlık ₺30, Harem ₺20, joint ticket ₺40, student/child under 7yr ₺5/free; ⏲9am-3.30pm Tue-Wed & Fri-Sun Apr-Oct, to 2.30pm Nov-Mar; 🚋Kabataş then walk) and majestically modern Bosphorus Bridge, along with plenty of lavish *yalıs* (seafront mansions).

and Saturday at 9pm. Note that children under seven years are not admitted to the whirling dervish performance.

Galata Mevlevi Museum PERFORMING ARTS
(Galata Mevlevihanesi Müzesi; Galipdede Caddesi 15, Tünel; ₺40; ⏲performances 5pm Sat & Sun; 🚋Karaköy, then funicular to Tünel) The 15th-century *semahane* (whirling-dervish hall) at this *tekke* (dervish lodge) is the venue for a *sema* (ceremony) held on Saturdays and Sundays during the year. Come early (preferably days ahead) to buy your ticket.

Information

Banks, ATMs and exchange offices are widespread.

American Hospital (Amerikan Hastenesi; ☎0212-311 2000, 212-444 3777; www.americanhospitalistanbul.org/ENG; Güzelbahçe Sokak 20, Nişantaşı; ⏲24hr emergency department; Ⓜ Osmanbey)

Tourist Office – Sultanahmet (☎0212-518 8754; Hippodrome, Sultanhamet; ⏲9.30am-6pm mid-Apr–Sep, 9am-5.30pm Oct–mid-Apr; 🚋Sultanahmet)

Tourist Police (☎0212-527 4503; Yerebatan Caddesi 6) Across the street from the Basilica Cistern.

Getting There & Away

AIR

İstanbul's **Atatürk International Airport** (IST, Atatürk Havalımanı; ☎0212-463 3000; www.ataturkairport.com) is 23km west of Sultanahmet.

Sabiha Gökçen International Airport (SAW, Sabiha Gökçen Havalımanı; ☎0216-588 8888; www.sgairport.com) is 50km east, on the Asian side of the city.

BOAT

Yenikapı is the main dock for **İDO** (İDO; ☎444 4436; www.ido.com.tr) car and passenger ferries across the Sea of Marmara to Yalova, Bursa and Bandırma (from where you can catch a train to İzmir or a bus to Çanakkale).

BUS

Büyük İstanbul Otogarı (Big İstanbul Bus Station; ☎0212-658 0505; www.otogaristanbul.com), 10km northwest of Sultanahmet, is the city's main otogar (bus station) and has buses to towns and cities across the country, as well as to European destinations.

Many bus companies offer a free *servis* (shuttle bus) to/from the otogar. The metro stops here (₺4; Otogar stop) en route between Atatürk Airport and Aksaray, where you can pick up a tram to Sultanahmet.

TRAIN

Due to ongoing maintenance work, the train network in and out of İstanbul has been severely curtailed. The daily 10pm Bosfor Ekspresi between İstanbul and Bucharest via Sofia (€39 to €59 plus couchette surcharge) is still working.

A new fast train service to Ankara (₺70, 3½ hours) currently leaves, inconveniently, from Pendik Station, 20km southeast of Kadıköy on the Asian side of town.

Check **Turkish State Railways** (TCDD; www.tcdd.gov.tr) for updates.

Getting Around

Rechargable İstanbulkarts (travelcards) can be used on public transport city-wide. Purchase (₺10) and recharge them at kiosks and machines at metro and tram stops, bus terminals and ferry docks. If you're only using public transport for a few city journeys, *jetons* (single trip travel token; ₺4) can be purchased from machines at tram, metro and ferry docks.

BOAT

İstanbul's commuter ferries ply the Bosphorous between the city's European and Asian sides.

Ferries for Üsküdar and the Bosphorus leave from Eminönü dock; ferries depart from Kabataş (Adalar İskelesi dock) for the Princes' Islands.

From Karaköy, ferries depart for Kadıköy on the Asian shore.

BUS

İstanbul's efficient bus system runs between 6.30am and 11.30pm. You must have an İstanbulkart to use the buses. The major bus terminals are at Taksim Meydanı and at Beşiktaş, Kabataş, Eminönü, Kadıköy and Üsküdar.

METRO

The most useful metro service is the M1A Line connecting Aksaray with Atatürk Airport, stopping at 15 stations including the otogar (main bus station) along the way. Services leave every two to 10 minutes between 6am and midnight.

TAXI

İstanbul is full of yellow taxis, all of them with meters – insist that drivers use them. From Sultanahmet to Taksim Meydanı costs around ₺15.

TRAM & FUNICULAR

A *tramvay* (tramway) service runs from Zeytinburnu (where it connects with the M1A Metro) to Kabataş (connecting with the funicular to Taksim) via Sultanahmet, Eminönü and Karaköy (connecting with the funicular to Tünel). Trams run every five minutes from 6am to midnight.

An antique tram rattles up and down İstiklal Caddesi between Tünel funicular station and Taksim Meydanı.

The one-stop Tünel funicular between Karaköy and İstiklal Caddesi runs between 7am and 10.45pm. Another funicular runs from Kabataş (where it connects with the tram) up to the metro station at Taksim.

GETTING INTO İSTANBUL FROM THE AIRPORTS

Havataş Airport Bus (Map p1145; ☎444 2656; http://havatas.com) travels between the airports and Cumhuriyet Caddesi, just off Taksim Meydanı. Buses leave Atatürk (₺10, one hour) every 30 minutes between 4am and 1am. Its service between Sabiha Gökçen (₺13, 1½ hours) and Taksim leaves every 30 minutes between 3.30am and 1am – easily the cheapest way to get to the city from Sabiha Gökçen.

Metro From Atatürk to Zeytinburnu, where you can connect with the tram to Sultanahmet (total ₺8, one hour).

Shuttle Most hotels can book airport shuttles to/from both Atatürk (€5) and Sabiha Gökçen (€12). Check shuttle schedules at reception.

Taxi From Atatürk/Sabiha Gökçen to Sultanahmet costs around ₺45/130.

AEGEAN COAST

Turkey's Aegean coast can convincingly claim more ancient ruins per square kilometre than any other region in the world. Since time immemorial, conquerors, traders and travellers have beaten a path to the mighty monuments, and few leave disappointed.

Gallipoli (Gelibolu) Peninsula

Antipodeans and many Brits won't need an introduction to Gallipoli; it's the backbone of the 'Anzac legend', in which an Allied campaign in 1915 to knock Turkey out of WWI and open a relief route to Russia turned into one of the war's greatest fiascos. Some 130,000 men died, roughly a third from Allied forces and the rest Turkish.

Today the battlefields are part of the **Gallipoli Historical National Park** (Gelibolu Yarımadası Tarihi Milli Parkı; http://gytmp.milliparklar.gov.tr) and tens of thousands of Turks and foreigners alike come to pay their respects on pilgrimage every year. The Turkish officer responsible for the defence of Gallipoli was Mustafa Kemal (the future Atatürk); his victory is commemorated in Turkey on 18 March. On **Anzac Day** (25 April), a dawn service marks the anniversary of the Allied landings.

The easiest way to see the battlefields is with your own transport or on a tour from Çanakkale or Eceabat; try **Crowded House Tours** (☎0286-814 1565; www.crowdedhousegallipoli.com; Hüseyin Avni Sokak 4, Eceabat).

Most visitors stay in Çanakkale but **Hotel Crowded House** (☎0286-814 1565; www.crowdedhousegallipoli.com; Hüseyin Avni Sokak 4; s/d/tr €23/30/39; ❄@🛜) is a spic-and-span backpacker option if you want to sleep in Eceabat.

Çanakkale

☎0286 / POP 116,078

This sprawling harbour town has a fun and youthful vibe that would be worth visiting for even if it didn't lie across the Dardanelles from the Gallipoli Peninsula and wasn't within easy day-tripping distance to

Troy. After you've finished exploring both the modern and ancient history of the hinterland, check out this university town's hip and alternative nightlife scene in the bars and cafes that cram the cobbled lanes around the **Saat Kulesi** (clock tower), or go for a sunset stroll along the *kordon* (waterfront promenade).

Sleeping & Eating

Anzac House Hostel HOSTEL €
(☎0286-213 5969; www.anzachouse.com; Cumhuriyet Meydanı 59; dm/s/d without bathroom & excluding breakfast ₺25/45/70;) Recent years haven't been kind to Çanakkale's only backpacker hostel, with comfort and cleanliness levels plunging since the days when it was run by the Hassle Free Tours outfit. Fortunately, that crew is still based on the ground floor and was due to reclaim the lease in late 2014, promising a full renovation and improvement in services.

★**Anzac Hotel** HOTEL €€
(☎0286-217 7777; www.anzachotels.com; Saat Kulesi Meydanı 8; s €30-40, d €40-55;) An extremely professional management team ensures that this recently renovated and keenly priced hotel opposite the clock tower is well maintained and has high levels of service. Rooms are a good size, with tea- and coffee-making facilities and double-glazed windows. The convivial bar on the mezzanine shows the *Gallipoli* and *Troy* movies every night. Parking costs €2.50.

Cevahir Ev Yemekleri TURKISH €
(☎0286-213 1600; Fetvane Sokak 15; meals from ₺8; 11am-9pm) Cheap and cheerful is the motto at this popular *ev yemekleri* (eatery serving home-cooked food) close to the clock tower. Choose from bean, vegetable and meat dishes in the bain-marie. Set meals including a bowl of soup, salad and main dish with rice are available for less than ₺10. No alcohol.

★**Yalova** SEAFOOD €€€
(☎0286-217 1045; www.yalovarestaurant.com; Gümrük Sokak 7; mezes ₺6-22, mains ₺20-40) Locals have been coming here for slap-up meals since 1940. A two-storey place on the *kordon*, it serves seafood that often comes straight off the fishing boats moored out front. Head upstairs to choose from the meze and fish displays, and be sure to quaff some locally produced Suvla wine with your meal.

Getting There & Away

Regular buses go to İstanbul (₺45, six hours) and İzmir (₺40, 5¾ hours).

To Eceabat and the Gallipoli Peninsula there's an hourly ferry service (₺2.50, 25 minutes) from the harbour dock.

Troy (Truva)

Not much remains of the great city of **Troy** (☎0286-283 0536; adult/child under 12yr ₺20/free; 8am-7pm Apr-Oct, to 4.30pm Nov-Mar) and you'll have to put your imagination-hat on to envision the fateful day when the Greeks tricked the Trojans with their wooden horse. For history buffs and fans of Homer's *Iliad* though, this is one of the most important stops on the Aegean.

The site is rather confusing for non-expert eyes – audioguides (₺10) are available – but the most conspicuous features, apart from the reconstruction of the **Trojan Horse**, include the **walls** from various periods; the Graeco-Roman **Temple of Athena**; the **Roman Odeon**; and the **Bouleuterion** (Council Chamber), built around Homer's time (c 800 BC). By the time you read this the new state-of-the-art Troy archaelogical museum should be open here.

Travel agencies in Çanakkale and Eceabat offer half-day Troy tours (€25) and full-day Gallipoli battlefields and Troy excursions (around €75).

From Çanakkale, dolmuşes (minibuses) leave hourly to Troy (₺5, 35 minutes, between 9.30am and 4.30pm) from a station at the northern end of the bridge over the Sarı River.

Bergama (Pergamum)

☎0232 / POP 62,400

This workaday market town sits slap-bang below the remarkable ruins of Pergamum, site of ancient Rome's pre-eminent medical centre. During Pergamum's heyday (between Alexander the Great and the Roman domination of Asia Minor) it was one of the Middle East's richest and most powerful small kingdoms.

In town itself is the imposing remains of the **Red Hall** (Kızıl Avlu; Kınık Caddesi; admission ₺5; 8am-7pm Apr-Sep, to 5pm Oct-Mar), a 2nd-century temple dedicated to the Egyptian gods Serapis, Isis and Harpocrates. Upon the windswept hilltop, 5km from the Red Hall, and linked by a **cable car** (Bergama Akropolis Teleferik; www.facebook.com/akropolisteleferik; Akropol Caddesi; return ₺6; ⏲8am-7pm Apr-Sep, to 5pm Oct-Mar), is the **Acropolis** (Bergama Akropol; www.muze.gov.tr/akropol; Akropol Caddesi 2; admission ₺25, audioguide ₺10; ⏲8am-7pm Apr-Sep, to 5pm Oct-Mar), with its spectacular sloping theatre. The **Asclepion** (Asklepion; www.muze.gov.tr/asklepion; Prof Dr Frieldhelm Korte Caddesi 1; admission/parking ₺20/5; ⏲8am-7pm Apr-Sep, to 5pm Oct-Mar), 3km uphill from town, was Pergamum's famed medical centre. The work that famed Greek physician Galen did here in the 2nd century was the basis for Western medicine well into the 16th century.

Odyssey Guesthouse (☎0232-631 3501; www.odysseyguesthouse.com; Abacıhan Sokak 13; dm ₺25, s/d from ₺50/85, s/d without bathroom ₺40/70; ❄@📶) has superb views of the archaeological sites plus neat and tidy basic doubles.

Frequent buses run to İzmir (₺12, two hours) and there are at least two buses daily to İstanbul (₺55, 11 hours).

İzmir

☎0232 / POP 2.8 MILLION

Turkey's third-largest city is a sprawling harbourside hub with a proud history as one of the Mediterranean's cosmopolitan trading metropolises when it was known as Smyrna. Head to the ruins of the Roman **agora** (Agora Caddesi; admission ₺5; ⏲8.30am-7pm Apr-Sep, to 5.30pm Oct-Mar; 🅿) to see one of İzmir's few reminders of its grand past. Afterwards sniff out a bargain (or five) within **Kemeraltı Market** (Kemeraltı Çarşısı; ⏲8am-8pm), then soak up the city's energetic modern pulse along the *kordon* and amid the student nightlife haunts of Alsancak district.

Sleeping & Eating

Budget and midrange hotels cluster around Basmane train station.

For bundles of hip cafes and restaurants head to the area around Kıbrıs Şehitleri Caddesi in Alsancak.

Güzel İzmir Oteli HOTEL €

(☎0232-483 5069; www.guzelizmirhotel.com; 1368 Sokak 8; s/d from ₺65/80; ❄@📶) It's all change at the 'Pretty', making this budget option in Basmane even more attractive. The 30 rooms, though small, have been given a thorough facelift, there are lovely old photos of Smyrna, a sunny, sunny breakfast room and even a small fitness centre. Room 307 is larger than most and 501 gives on to the terrace.

Hotel Baylan Basmane HOTEL €€

(☎0232-483 0152; www.hotelbaylan.com; 1299 Sokak 8; s/d ₺75/120; ❄@📶) The 30-room Baylan is among Basmane's best options. The entrance via the huge car park is a little disconcerting, but inside is a spacious and attractive hotel with a welcoming terrace-cum-garden in back. All rooms have polished floorboards and large bathrooms.

★**Sakız** MODERN TURKISH €€€

(☎0232-464 1103; www.sakizalsancak.com; Şehıt Nevresbey Bulvarı 9a; mains ₺18-38, meze ₺6-16; ⏲11am-11pm Mon-Sat) Sakız, specialising in Aegean and Cretan cuisine, is the most inventive restaurant in İzmir. Its fresh meze include shrimps wrapped in filo pasty and and *köz patlıcan* (smoked aubergine with tomatoes and peppers), while some of the unusual mains are sea bass with milk thistle and haddock with Aegean herbs.

Information

Banks, ATMS and the post office can be found on and around Cumhuriyet Bulvarı, locally called İkinci (second) Kordon, a block inland from the waterfront.

Getting There & Away

BUS

Bus company ticket offices mostly cluster on Dokuz Eylül Meydanı. They usually provide a free *servis* to/from İzmir's mammoth otogar, 6.5km from the centre. Buses head to points across the country including frequent services to Bergama (₺13, two hours), Bodrum (₺27, three hours) and Selçuk (₺9, one hour).

TRAIN

Most intercity trains arrive and depart from Alsancak Garı (Train Station) including services to Ankara (₺37, 14 hours). From Basmane Garı there are seven express trains daily to Selçuk (₺6, 1½ hours).

Selçuk

☎0232 / POP 28,213

This chilled-out provincial town is just the ticket if you want to take a break from your travels for a couple of days. The monumental ruins of Ephesus sit right on

DON'T MISS

EPHESUS (EFES)

Ephesus (adult/student/parking ₺30/20/7.50; ⏲8am-7.30pm May-Oct, 8am-5pm Nov-Apr, last admission 1hr before closing) is a dazzlingly complete classical metropolis, once the capital of the Roman province of Asia Minor. A trip here is the closest you'll get to being able to conjure up daily life in the Roman age. There are a wealth of monuments to explore but don't miss:

Curetes Way Named for the demigods who helped Lena give birth to Artemis and Apollo, the Curetes Way was Ephesus' main thoroughfare, lined with statuary, great buildings, and rows of shops selling incense, silk and other goods. Walking this street is the best way to understand Ephesian daily life.

Temple of Hadrian One of Ephesus' star attractions, this ornate, Corinthian-style temple honours Trajan's successor, and originally had a wooden roof and doors. Note its main arch; supported by a central keystone, this architectural marvel remains perfectly balanced, with no need for cement or mortar. The temple's designers also covered it with intricate decorative details and patterns – Tyche, goddess of chance, adorns the first arch, while Medusa wards off evil spirits on the second.

Library of Celsus The early 2nd-century AD governor of Asia Minor, Celsus Polemaeanus, was commemorated in this magnificent library. Originally built as part of a complex, the library looks bigger than it actually is: the convex facade base heightens the central elements, while the central columns and capitals are larger than those at the ends. Facade niches hold replica statues of the Greek Virtues: Arete (Goodness), Ennoia (Thought), Episteme (Knowledge) and Sophia (Wisdom).

Great Theatre Originally built under Hellenistic King Lysimachus, the Great Theatre was reconstructed by the Romans between AD 41 and AD 117. However, they incorporated original design elements, including the ingenious shape of the *cavea* (seating area). Seating rows are pitched slightly steeper as they ascend, meaning that upper-row spectators still enjoyed good views and acoustics – useful, considering that the theatre could hold 25,000 people.

A taxi from Selçuk costs about ₺15, but it's also a pleasant 2.5km walk from town.

its doorstep, storks nest atop a preserved Roman-Byzantine aqueduct that runs right through the middle of town, and the quaint village-vibe of the centre is complemented by a scattering of interesting sights hidden down the cobblestone lanes.

Sights

Ephesus Museum MUSEUM
(Uğur Mumcu Sevgi Yolu Caddesi; admission ₺10; ⏲8.30am-6.30pm Apr-Oct, to 4.30pm Nov-Mar) This museum holds artefacts from Ephesus' Terraced Houses, including scales, jewellery and cosmetic boxes, plus coins, funerary goods and ancient statuary. The famous effigy of Phallic god Priapus, visible by pressing a button, draws giggles, and a whole room is dedicated to Eros in sculpted form. The punters also get a rise out of the multi-breasted marble Artemis statue, a very fine work indeed.

Basilica of St John RUIN, HISTORIC SITE
(St Jean Caddesi; admission incl Ayasuluk Fortress ₺10; ⏲8am-6.30pm Apr-Oct, to 4.30pm Nov-Mar) Despite a century of restoration, the once-great basilica built by Byzantine Emperor Justinian (r 527–65) is still but a skeleton of its former self. Nonetheless, it is an atmospheric site with excellent hilltop views, and the best place in the area for a sunset photo. The information panels and scale model highlight the building's original grandeur, as do the marble steps and monumental gate.

Ayasuluk Fortress CASTLE
(2013 Sokak; admission incl Basilica of St John ₺10; ⏲8am-6.30pm Apr-Oct, to 4.30pm Nov-Mar) Selçuk's crowning achievement is accessed on the same ticket as the neighbouring Basilica of St John. Excavation is ongoing and, at the time of writing, entry was by intermittent guided tours; hopefully regular

access will soon be established. The digs here, begun in 1990, have proven that there were castles on Ayasuluk Hill going back beyond the original Ephesian settlement to the neolithic age. The partially restored fortress' remains today date from Byzantine, Seljuk and Ottoman times.

Temple of Artemis RUIN
(Artemis Tapınağı; off Dr Sabrı Yayla Bulvarı; ⏲8am-7pm Apr-Oct, 8.30am-6pm Nov-Mar) FREE In an empty field on Selçuk's western extremities, this solitary reconstructed pillar is all that remains of the massive Temple of Artemis, one of the Seven Wonders of the Ancient World. At its zenith, the structure had 127 columns; today, the only way to get any sense of this grandeur is to see Didyma's better-preserved Temple of Apollo (which had 122 columns).

Sleeping & Eating

Atilla's Getaway HOSTEL, RESORT €
(☎0232-892 3847; www.atillasgetaway.com; Acarlar Köyü; dm/s/d/tw/tr €16/26/42/42/63, camping €8; ❄@📶🏊) This 'backpacker resort', named after its friendly Turkish-Australian owner, is all about relaxation, with a classically themed chill-out area gazing at the hills and a bar with pool table and nightly fires. Twice-weekly barbecues and six kinds of breakfast are offered and the volleyball court and table tennis add to the fun.

★ **Boomerang** GUESTHOUSE, HOSTEL €€
(☎0232-892 4879; www.boomerangguesthouse.com; 1047 Sokak 10; dm/s/d/tw/tr/f from €10/30/40/40/60/70; ❄📶) People do indeed keep coming back to this Turkish-Chinese operation, to spend chilled-out evenings among the trees in the stone courtyard, where the recommended bar-restaurant (mains ₺12 to ₺20) serves dishes including kebaps, Chinese food and cheesy *köfte*. Some rooms have balconies, while budget options are also available (single/double/twin/triple €20/30/30/45) along with extras such as a travel desk and bike hire.

Selçuk Köftecisi KÖFTE €€
(Şahabettin Dede Caddesi; mezes ₺8, köfte ₺12; ⏲lunch & dinner) In a modern building by the fish market, this long-running local favourite serves excellent *köfte* (meatballs), cooked to perfection and accompanied by salad, rice and fried onions. The good selection of side salads includes a spicy walnut option.

Getting There & Away

At least two buses head to İstanbul (₺80, 10 hours) daily and there are frequent services to İzmir (₺9, one hour). For Pamukkale, and destinations along the Mediterranean coast, you usually have to change buses at Denizli (₺30, three hours).

Eight trains head to İzmir (₺5.75, 1¼ hours) daily.

Pamukkale

☎0258 / POP 2630

Inland from Selçuk is one of Turkey's premier natural wonders. Pamukkale's gleaming white and wacky travertined calcite hill with its cascade of turquoise blue pools has been a tourist attraction since the classical age. On the summit, the ruins of the ancient spa resort of Hierapolis lay in testament to this area's surreal appeal.

Sights

Travertines NATURE RESERVE
(25₺; ⏲9am-7pm (summer)) The saucer-shaped travertines (or terraces, as they are also called) wind sideways down the powder-white mountain, providing stunning contrast to the clear blue sky and green plains below. To protect the unique calcite surface, guards oblige you to go barefoot, so if planning to walk down to the village via the travertines, be prepared to carry your shoes with you.

Hierapolis RUIN
The ruins of this Roman and Byzantine spa city evoke life in a bygone era, in which Greeks, Romans and Jews, pagans and Christians, and spa tourists peacefully coexisted. It became a curative centre when founded around 190 BC by Eumenes II of Pergamum, before prospering under the Romans and, even more so, the Byzantines, when large Jewish and Orthodox Christian communities comprised most of the population. Recurrent earthquakes brought disaster, and Hierapolis was finally abandoned after a 1334 tremor.

Sleeping

Beyaz Kale Pension PENSION €
(☎0258-272 2064; www.beyazkalepension.com; Oguzkaan Caddesi 4; s/d/q/f ₺60/80/130/150; ❄📶🏊) On a quiet street just outside the village centre, the cheery yellow White Castle has 10 spotless rooms on two floors, some more modern than others. The friendly lady

of the house, Hacer, serves some of the best local pension fare (dinner menu ₺20) on the relaxing rooftop terrace with travertine views. A cot is available for junior travellers.

★**Melrose House** HOTEL €€
(☎0258-272 2250; www.melrosehousehotel.com; Vali Vekfi Ertürk Caddesi 8; s €35-55, d €40-55; ❄📶🏊) The closest thing to a boutique hotel in Pamukkale, Melrose House has 17 spacious modern rooms, including a family room and suites with circular beds worthy of a Blaxploitation movie. Decor throughout mixes handmade Kütahya tiles and pillars, wallpaper and exposed stonework, and the poolside restaurant is an agreeable place to linger.

Getting There & Away

Most services to/from Pamukkale involve changing in Denizli. Bus companies should provide a free *servis* from Denizli otogar to Pamukkale's main square. Otherwise, there are frequent dolmuşes (₺5, 40 minutes) between Pamukkale and Denizli otogar.

Bodrum

☎0252 / POP 36,401

The beating heart of Turkey's holiday-resort peninsula, Bodrum hums with action during the summer months. Its natty whitewashed cottages all sporting blue trims are a postcard maker's dream while the harbour is a hive for yachties and travellers alike.

Sights

Castle of St Peter CASTLE, MUSEUM
(☎0252-316 2516; www.bodrum-museum.com; İskele Meydanı; admission ₺25, audioguide ₺10; ⊙8.30am-6.30pm, to 4.30pm winter, exhibition halls closed noon-1pm) There are splendid views from the battlements of Bodrum's magnificent castle, built by the Knights Hospitaller in the early 15th century. The castle houses the **Museum of Underwater Archaeology**, displaying the underwater archaeology treasures amassed during the building's renovation.

The Knights, based on Rhodes, built the castle during Tamerlane's Mongol invasion of Anatolia (1402), which weakened the Ottomans and gave the order an opportunity to establish this foothold in Anatolia. They used marble and stones from Mausolus' famed mausoleum and changed the city's name from Halicarnassus to Petronium (hence the Turkicised 'Bodrum').

Sleeping

★**Su Otel** BOUTIQUE HOTEL €€
(☎0252-316 6906; www.bodrumsuhotel.com; off Turgutreis Caddesi; s/d/ste from €65/95/135; ❄@📶🏊) Epitomising Bodrum's white-and-sky-blue aesthetic, the relaxing 'Water Hotel' has 25 rooms and suites around a pool glinting with silver tiles, an Ottoman restaurant and a bar scattered with red sofas. Owner Zafer's zingy artwork decorates the premises along with hand-painted İznik tiles, Ottoman candlesticks and antiques.

Antique Theatre Hotel BOUTIQUE HOTEL €€
(☎0252-316 6053; www.antiquetheatrehotel.com; Kıbrıs Şehitler Caddesi 169; r €120-140, ste €160-180; ❄📶🏊) Taking its name from the ancient theatre across the road, this opulent place enjoys great castle and sea views, and has a big outdoor pool and one of Bodrum's best hotel restaurants. Original artwork and antiques adorn the rooms, which each have an individual character and offer better value than the suites.

Eating & Drinking

The loud bars and clubs of **Bar St** (Dr Alim Bey Caddesi and Cumhuriyet Caddesi) get packed during summer nights. More refined, **Marina Yacht Club** (english.marinayachtclub.com; Neyzen Tevfik Caddesi 5) is a big, breezy waterfront nightspot.

★**Nazik Ana** TURKISH €
(Eski Hükümet Sokak 5; dishes from ₺6, kebaps ₺8-15; ⊙breakfast, lunch & dinner, closed Sun winter) This simple back-alley place offers prepared dishes hot and cold (viewable at the front counter), letting you sample different Turkish traditional dishes at shared tables. You can also order kebaps and *köfte*. It gets busy with workers at lunchtime, offering one of Bodrum's most authentic eating experiences.

Fish Market SEAFOOD €€
(off Cevat Şakir Caddesi; ⊙dinner Mon-Sat) Bodrum's fish market (sometimes called *'manavlar'* for the fruit stands at the entrance to this small network of back alleys) offers a unique sort of direct dining: you choose between myriad fresh fish and seafood on ice at fishmongers' tables and, having paid there, have them cooked at any adjoining restaurant for about ₺10.

Information

ATMs and banks congregate on Cevat Şakir Caddesi.

Tourist Office (☎0252-316 1091; Kale Meydanı; ⏲8am-6pm Mon-Fri, daily Jun-Oct)

Getting There & Away

Bodrum otogar has numerous bus services including two buses daily to Antalya (₺70, eight hours); eight services per day to İstanbul (₺90, 13 hours); and hourly buses to İzmir (₺40, 3½ hours).

Daily ferries link Bodrum with Kos in Greece (one-way/return €17/19, one hour) from April to October. There are also twice weekly ferries to Rhodes (one-way/return €50/60, 2½ hours) during July to September. For information and tickets contact the **Bodrum Ferryboat Association** (Bodrum Feribot İşletmeciliği; ☎0252-316 0882; www.bodrumferryboat.com; Kale Caddesi 22; ⏲8am-9pm May-Sep, reduced hours winter).

MEDITERRANEAN COAST

This slice of Turkey – known as the 'Turquoise Coast' – is one of the Mediterranean's most beautiful coastlines. Rugged forest-clad hills, laden with ancient ruins, fall down to a shoreline of sandy coves lapped by clear green-blue waters, all backed by craggy snow-topped mountain peaks. For hikers, sun-sloths, yachties and history-fiends this achingly gorgeous region sums up Turkey's never-ending appeal.

Fethiye

☎0252 / POP 82,000

Thanks to the 1958 earthquake, most of the ancient city of Telmessos was destroyed, but the vibrant town of Fethiye – which rose in its place – is now the hub of the western Mediterranean. Its natural harbour, in a broad bay scattered with dinky islands, is one of the finest in the region and the town's lively vibe makes it an excellent base for forays both on and off the water.

Sights & Activities

Tomb of Amyntas TOMB

(⏲8am-7pm) FREE Fethiye's most recognisable sight is the mammoth Tomb of Amyntas, an Ionic temple facade carved into the sheer rock face in 350 BC, in honour of 'Amyntas son of Hermapias'. Located south of the centre, it is best visited at sunset. Other, smaller rock tombs lie about 500m to the east.

Fethiye Museum MUSEUM

(www.lycianturkey.com/fethiye-museum.htm; 505 Sokak; admission ₺5; ⏲8am-5pm Tue-Sun) Focusing on Lycian finds from Telmessos as well as the ancient settlements of Tlos and Kaunos, this museum exhibits pottery, jewellery, small statuary and votive stones (including the important Grave Stelae and the Stelae of Promise). Its most prized significant possession, however, is the so-called Trilingual Stele from Letoön, dating from 358 BC, which was used partly to decipher the Lycian language with the help of ancient Greek and Aramaic.

BLUE VOYAGE

Fethiye is the hub of Turkey's cruising scene, and the most popular route is the 'Blue Voyage' *(Mavi Yolculuk)* to Olympos: a four-day, three-night journey on a *gület* (Turkish yacht). Boats usually call in at Ölüdeniz and Butterfly Valley and stop at Kaş, Kalkan and/or Kekova, with the final night at Gökkaya Bay opposite the eastern end of Kekova.

Depending on the season, the price is typically €165 to €250 per person including food (but water, soft drinks and alcohol are extra). Thoroughly check out your operator before signing up – shoddy companies abound selling Blue Voyage trips with bad food, crew that speak no English and added extras that never materialise. Most people that end up disappointed in their Blue Voyage have bought their trip from an agency in İstanbul. Hold off on booking your trip until you get to Fethiye. We recommend these owner-operated outfits for running a tight ship:

Ocean Yachting (☎0252-612 7798; www.bluecruise.com; Fethiye Marina; 3-night cruise per person from €225) Highly professional outfit with a swag of cruise choices.

Olympos Yachting (☎0242-892 1145; www.olymposyachting.com; Olympos; 3-night cruise from €185) Popular and recommended company based in Olympos.

DON'T MISS

WALKING THE LYCIAN WAY

Acclaimed as one of the top 10 long-distance walks in the world, Turkey's **Lycian Way** follows waymarked trails down the Mediterranean coast from Fethiye to Antalya. The route leads through pine and cedar forests in the shadow of mountains rising almost 3000m, past villages, stunning coastal views and an embarrassment of ruins at ancient Lycian cities.

Get information on walking all, or some of the sections, of the Lycian Way at www.cultureroutesinturkey.com.

12-Island Tour Excursion Boats BOAT TOUR
(per person incl lunch ₺30-35, on sailboat ₺50; ⏲10.30am-6pm mid-Apr–Oct) Many travellers sign up for the 12-Island Tour, a boat trip around Fethiye Bay. The boats usually stop at six islands and cruise by the rest. Some are booze-cruise-style tours so check you're getting what you want. Hotels and agencies sell tickets or you can negotiate a price with the boat companies around the tourist office at the marina.

Sleeping & Eating

Most accommodation is up the hill behind the marina in Karagözler or further west.

★**Yildirim Guest House** PENSION €
(☎0543 779 4732, 0252-614 4627; www.yildirimguesthouse.com; Fevzi Çakmak Caddesi 21; dm ₺25, s/d/tr ₺50/80/120; ❄☏) This shipshape hostel-pension just opposite the marina is Fethiye's top pit stop for budget travellers, with a selection of dorms (with four to six beds) and simple, spotless rooms. Well-travelled host Omer Yapıs is a mine of local information. There are free bikes for guests, free tea and coffee, and pick-ups and excursions are all easily arranged.

Villa Daffodil HOTEL €€
(☎0252-614 9595; www.villadaffodil.com; Fevzi Çakmak Caddesi 139; s €37-49, d €50-75, ste €100; ❄☏≋) This Ottoman-styled guesthouse has rooms bedecked with dark wood furnishings, old carpets and quirky details (though we're not too sure about the Ottoman-meets-Serengeti touches in some of the suites). Grab one with a sea view for the best experience. The classy pool area, at the back, is perfect for glamour-puss lounging after a long day's sightseeing.

★**Meğri Lokantasi** TURKISH €€
(☎0252-614 4047; Çarşı Caddesi 26; plates ₺6-14; ✎) Looking for us at lunchtime in Fethiye? We're usually here. Packed with locals who spill onto the streets, the Meğri offers excellent and hearty home-style cooking at very palatable prices. Mix and match your meal by choosing from the huge glass display window of vegetarian and meat dishes. It's pretty much all delicious.

Cem & Can SEAFOOD €€€
(Hal ve Pazar Yeri 67) One way to taste Fethiye's fish is to buy your own (per kilo ₺18 to ₺30) from the circle of fishmongers in the fish market, then take it to one of the restaurants opposite to have them cook it. Our favourite is Cem & Can, which charges ₺8 per head for cooking the fish, plus salad and bread.

Information

Plentiful banks and ATMs line Atatürk Caddesi, the main street. The **tourist office** (☎0252-614 1527; İskele Meydanı; ⏲8am-7pm Mon-Fri, 10am-5pm Sat & Sun) is opposite the marina.

Getting There & Away

Fethiye's otogar is 2.5km east of the centre. Buses head to Antalya (₺30, six hours) via Kaş (₺16, two hours) at least hourly.

Local dolmuşes for Ölüdeniz (₺5, 25 minutes) Kayaköy (₺4.50, 20 minutes), and surrounding villages leave from the dolmuş stop near the mosque just off Atatürk Caddesi in the centre.

Catamarans sail daily to Rhodes in Greece (one-way/return €51.50/77, 1½ hours) from Fethiye pier, opposite the tourist office.

Patara

☎0242 / POP 950

There's always plenty of room to throw down your towel on Turkey's longest uninterrupted beach. Patara has 20-odd kilometres of sandy shore to stretch out on and when sun-and-sandcastles are done for the day, the remnants of **Ancient Patara** (admission incl Patara Beach ₺5, long-stay ticket allowing 10 entries over 10 days ₺7.50; ⏲9am-7pm) sprawl along the beach access road waiting to be explored. If those ruins aren't enough, Patara is also within easy day-tripping distance to two ancient Lycian cities: **Letoön** (admission ₺8; ⏲8.30am-7pm), which has three temples with some fine mosaics, and impressive **Xanthos** (admission ₺10; ⌚9am-7pm), with a Roman theatre and Lycian pillar tombs.

All accommodation is in the postage-stamp sized village of Gelemiş, 1.5km from the beachfront. **Akay Pension** (☎0242-843 5055, 0532 410 2195; www.pataraakaypension.com; s/d/tr ₺60/90/120, apt ₺160;) and **Flower Pension** (☎0242-843 5164, 0530 511 0206; www.pataraflowerpension.com; d/tr ₺90/120, studio ₺120, apt ₺150;). Both have well-maintained rooms and balconies overlooking citrus groves.

Buses on the Fethiye–Kaş route drop you on the highway 3.5km from the village. From here dolmuşes run to the village every hour between mid-April and October.

Kaş

☎0242 / POP 7558

While other Mediterranean towns bank on their beaches for popularity, Kaş is all about adventure activities. This is Turkey's diving centre and a bundle of kayaking, hiking and boating trips are also easily organised here. It's a mellow kind of place with a squiggle of old town lanes wrapping around the small harbour, which is dominated by the craggy Greek island of Meis (Kastellorizo) just offshore.

Sights & Activities

Kaş adventure operators specialise in kayaking and boat trips to the nearby **Kekova** area with its sunken city ruins, pretty coastal scenery and charming hamlets of Üçağız and Kaleköy. Kaş is also home to Turkey's best diving opportunities and nearly all the adventure operators in town offer dive trips.

★Antiphellos Theatre RUIN
(Hastane Caddesi) FREE Antiphellos was a small settlement and the port for Phellos, the much larger Lycian town further north in the hills. The small Hellenistic theatre, 500m west of Kaş' main square, could seat some 4000 spectators and is in very good condition.

Dragoman OUTDOOR ACTIVITIES
(☎0242-836 3614; www.dragoman-turkey.com; Uzun Çarşı Sokak) Dragoman is Kaş' diving specialist, with a variety of dive packages offered (€26 for one dive, including equipment). They also organise the full gamut of outdoor activities with some interesting options other tour companies don't offer. There's sea kayaking (€25 to €50), a range of day-hike options (€26 to €40) and, for the more adventurous, coasteering (from €45).

Xanthos Travel OUTDOOR ACTIVITIES
(☎0242-836 3292; www.xanthostravel.com; İbrahim Serin Caddesi 5/A) Xanthos runs extremely popular and recommendable boat day tours in the Kekova area (€25 to €35) as well as a variety of different sea-kayaking tours that get you up close with the sunken city ruins (€30 to €45). For landlubbers there are jeep safaris (€30 to €35) and a variety of different mountain biking and trekking options.

Sleeping & Eating

Most accommodation is west and northwest of the centre along the waterfront and up the hill around the Yeni Cami (New Mosque).

Anı Pension PENSION €
(☎0533 326 4201, 0242-836 1791; www.motelani.com; Süleyman Çavuş Caddesi 12; dm ₺25, s/d ₺40/90;) The Anı leads the way for budget digs in Kaş, mostly thanks to on-the-ball host Ömer who continues to improve his pension. The decent-sized rooms all have balconies and the roof terrace is a hub where you can kick back, cool off with a beer, and swap travel stories with fellow guests.

★Hideaway Hotel HOTEL €€
(☎0532 261 0170, 0242-836 1887; www.hotelhideaway.com; Anfitiyatro Sokak; s €40, d €50-70, ste €80;) The Hideaway just keeps getting better. Run by the unstoppable Ahmet, a fount of local information, this lovely hotel has large, airy rooms (six have sea views) with a fresh white-on-white minimalist feel and gleaming modern bathrooms. There's a pool for cooling off and a chilled-out roof terrace with an honour-system bar and superb views.

Bi Lokma ANATOLIAN €€
(☎0242-836 3942; Hükümet Caddesi 2; mains ₺13-21; ⌚9am-midnight;) Also known as 'Mama's Kitchen', this place has tables meandering around a terraced garden overlooking the harbour. Sabo – the 'mama' in question – turns out great traditional Turkish soul food including excellent meze, and her famous *mantı* (Turkish ravioli; ₺13) and *börek* (filled pastry; ₺13).

Köşk ANATOLIAN €€
(☎0242-836 3857; Gürsoy Sokak 13; mains ₺14-25) In a lovely little square off a cobbled street just up from the water, Köşk occupies

a rustic, 150-year-old house with two terraces and seating in the open courtyard. Forgo the mains and feast instead on their gorgeous meze dishes, which draw from both Mediterranean and Anatolian influences. Delicious.

ℹ Getting There & Away

The otogar is along Atatürk Bulvarı, 350m north of the centre. Dolmuşes leave half-hourly to Antalya (₺24, 3½ hours) via Olympos (₺18, 2½ hours). Buses to Fethiye (₺16, 2½ hours) leave hourly.

Ferries to Meis (Kastellorizo; same-day return €25, 20 minutes) leave daily at 10am and return at 4pm. Buy tickets at the **Meis Express** (☎0242-836 1725; www.meisexpress.com) office on the harbour.

Olympos & Çıralı

☎0242

The tiny beach hamlets of Olympos and Çıralı are where you head if you're looking for days of sandy-sloth action. Olympos is an old hippy hang-out with an all-night party reputation in summer and the vine-covered ancient **Olympos ruins** (admission incl Olympos Beach ₺5, long-stay ticket allowing 10 entries over 10 days ₺7.50; ⌚9am-7.30pm) lining the dirt track to the beach.

A couple of kilometres down the beach is more sedate Çıralı, where a clutch of simple pensions sit back from the sand and life is simplified to a choice between swinging in a hammock or sunning yourself on the beach.

In the evening, trips to the famed **Chimaera** (admission ₺5), a cluster of natural flames on the slopes of Mt Olympos, is the major activity. At night the 20-odd flames are visible at sea. All Olympos accommodation run nightly tours (it's 7km from Olympos) or you can follow the signs for 2km up the hill from Çıralı.

Sleeping

Olympos' 'tree house' camps, which line the track along the valley down to the ruins, have long been the stuff of travel legend. Olympos accommodation prices are per person and include breakfast and dinner. The 'tree houses' are actually rustic, platformed bungalows. Most camps also offer bungalows with en suite.

Çıralı deals in more midrange, family-friendly, smaller pensions.

Olympos

Şaban Pansion BUNGALOW €
(☎0242-892 1265, 0507 007 6600; www.sabanpansion.com; dm ₺40, tree house ₺45, bungalow with bathroom & air-con ₺70; ❄📶) Our personal favourite, this is the place to come if you want to snooze in a hammock or on cushions in the shade of orange trees. In the words of the charming manager Meral: 'It's not a party place'. Instead it sells itself on tranquillity, space and great home cooking plus room 7 really is a tree house.

Çıralı

Hotel Canada HOTEL €€
(☎0532 431 3414, 0242-825 7233; www.canadahotel.net; d €60, 4-person bungalow €90; ❄📶🏊) This is a beautiful place offering the quintessential Çıralı experience: warmth, friendliness and housemade honey. The main house rooms are comfortable and the garden is filled with hammocks, citrus trees and 11 bungalows. Canadian Carrie and foodie husband Şaban also offer excellent set meals (€10). It's 750m from the beach; grab a free bike and pedal on down.

ℹ Getting There & Away

Buses and dolmuşes plying the Fethiye–Antalya coast road will stop near the Olympos and Çıralı junction. From there, dolmuşes (₺5) serve Olympos (9km) hourly from 8am to 8pm between May and October; and Çıralı (7km) hourly between June and September. Outside of these months, ring your guesthouse beforehand to check dolmuş times.

Antalya

☎0242 / POP 1 MILLION

The cultural capital of the Mediterranean, Antalya is a bustling modern city with a wonderfully preserved historic core. The old town quarter of Kaleiçi is a melding of Roman-Ottoman architecture that slopes downwards to a dinky harbour, with a soaring cliff edge packed with cafes and bars above, and all overlooked by the snowcapped peaks of the Beydağları (Bey Mountains). Just outside town, a clutch of dazzling ancient ruins sit on craggy slopes in easy reach for day-trippers, providing another reason to dally here.

WORTH A TRIP

ASPENDOS & PERGE

There are several magnificent Graeco-Roman ruins to explore around Antalya. Rent a car or join a tour from Antalya (from €45 per person). These are two of the best:

Aspendos (admission ₺20, parking ₺5; ⏲9am-7pm) People come in droves to this ancient site near the modern-day village of Belkıs for one reason: to view the awesome **theatre**, considered the best-preserved Roman theatre of the ancient world. It was built during Aspendos' golden age in the reign of Emperor Marcus Aurelius (AD 161–80), and used as a caravanserai by the Seljuks during the 13th century. The history of the city, though, goes all the way back to as far as the Hittite Empire (800 BC).

Perge (admission ₺20; ⏲9am-7pm) Some 17km east of Antalya and 2km north of Aksu on highway D400, Perge was one of the most important towns of ancient Pamphylia. Inside the site, walk through the massive **Roman Gate** with its four arches; to the left is the southern **nymphaeum** and well-preserved **baths**, and to the right the large square-shaped **agora**. Beyond the **Hellenistic Gate**, with its two huge towers, is the fine **colonnaded street**, where an impressive collection of columns still stands.

Sights & Activities

★Antalya Museum MUSEUM
(☎0242-236 5688; www.antalyamuzesi.gov.tr/en; Konyaaltı Caddesi 1; admission ₺20; ⏲9am-6.30pm) On no account should you miss this comprehensive museum with exhibitions covering everything from the Stone and Bronze Ages to Byzantium. The Hall of Regional Excavations exhibits finds from ancient cities in Lycia (such as Patara and Xanthos) and Pamphylia while the Hall of Gods displays beautiful and evocative statues of some 15 Olympian gods, many of them in near-perfect condition. Most of the statues, including the sublime Three Graces, were found at Perge.

★Suna & İnan Kıraç Kaleiçi Museum MUSEUM
(☎0242-243 4274; www.kaleicimuzesi.org; Kocatepe Sokak 25; adult/child ₺3/2; ⏲9am-noon & 1-6pm Thu-Tue) This small ethnography museum is housed in a lovingly restored Antalya mansion. The 2nd floor contains a series of life-size dioramas depicting some of the most important rituals and customs of Ottoman Antalya. Much more impressive is the collection of Çanakkale and Kütahya ceramics housed in the former Greek Orthodox church of Aya Yorgi (St George), just behind the main house, which has been fully restored and is worth a look in itself.

Yivli Minare HISTORIC SITE
(Fluted Minaret; Cumhuriyet Caddesi) Antalya's symbol is the Yivli Minare, a handsome and distinctive 'fluted' minaret erected by the Seljuk Sultan Aladdin Keykubad I in the early 13th century. The adjacent mosque (1373) is still in use. Within the Yivli Minare complex is the heavily restored **Mevlevi Tekke** (Whirling Dervish Monastery), which probably dates from the 13th century). Nearby to the west are two **türbe** (tombs), one from the late 14th century and the other from 1502.

Kesik Minare HISTORIC SITE
(Truncated Minaret; Hesapçı Sokak) This stump of a tower marks the ruins of a substantial building that has played a major role in Antalya's religious life over the centuries. Built originally as a 2nd-century Roman temple, it was converted into the Byzantine Church of the Virgin Mary in the 6th century and then a mosque three centuries later. It became a church again in 1361 but fire destroyed most of it in the 19th century.

Hadrian's Gate GATE
(Hadriyanüs Kapısı; Atatürk Caddesi) Commonly known as Üçkapılar (the 'Three Gates') in Antalya, the monumental Hadrian's Gate was erected for the Roman emperor's visit to Antalya in 130 AD.

Sleeping

Sabah Pansiyon PENSION €
(☎0555 365 8376, 0242-247 5345; www.sabahpansiyon.com; Hesapçı Sokak 60; dm €13, s/d/tr €25/30/45, 2-bedroom self-catering apt €100; ❄📶🏊) Our favourite budget digs in Antalya is still going strong. The Sabah has long been the first port of call for travellers

watching their kuruş, thanks to the Sabah brothers who run the place with aplomb. Rooms vary in size but all are sweet, simple and super-clean. The shaded courtyard is prime territory for meeting other travellers.

★**White Garden Pansiyon** PENSION €€
(☎0242-241 9115; www.whitegardenpansion.com; Hesapçı Geçidi 9; s/d €32/40, self-catering apt €110;) A positively delightful place to stay – full of quirky Ottoman character – the White Garden combines tidiness and class beyond its price level, with impeccable service from Metin and his staff. The building itself is a fine restoration and the courtyard is particularly charming. The breakfast here is one of the best you'll see in Turkey.

Villa Perla BOUTIQUE HOTEL €€€
(☎0242-248 4341; www.villaperla.com; Hesapçı Sokak 26; s/d €100/120;) We love this authentic Ottoman place snuggled around a courtyard complete with pool and tortoises. The seven comfortable rooms are at the top of a staircase that starts with a 12th-century stone step, the wooden ceilings are the real deal and some of the rooms have four-poster beds and folk-painted cupboards. The in-house restaurant makes excellent meze.

Eating & Drinking

For cheap eating, walk east to the **Dönerciler Çarşısı** (Market of Döner Makers; Atatürk Caddesi).

Yemenli TURKISH €€
(☎0242-247 5346; Zeytin Sokak 16; mains ₺14.50-17.50;) Tried-and-true Turkish favourites are served up at this lovely restaurant with dining either in the leafy garden courtyard or inside the charmingly renovated stone house. It's run by the same team behind the Sabah Pansiyon, so service is friendly and on-the-ball. There's a couple of excellent vegetarian options here, too.

★**Vanilla** INTERNATIONAL €€€
(☎0242-247 6013; www.vanillaantalya.com; Zafer Sokak 13; mains ₺22-40) One indicator of Antalya's rising stock is this outstanding, ultra-modern restaurant led by British chef Wayne and his Turkish wife, Emel. Banquettes, glass surfaces and cheery orange bucket chairs provide a streamlined and unfussy atmosphere, allowing you to concentrate on the menu: Mediterranean-inspired international dishes like roasted courgette and leek risotto, duck confit and chicken livers with smoked pancetta.

Castle Café CAFE
(☎0242-248 6594; Hıdırlık Sokak 48/1; ⊙8am-11pm) Our favourite place along the cliff's edge is this lively cafe and bar which attracts a good crowd of young Turks with its affordable drinks. Service can be slow but the jaw-dropping views from the terrace more than make up for it.

Information

Atatürk Caddesi is lined with banks and ATMs. The **tourist office** (☎0242-241 1747; Cumhuriyet Meydanı; ⊙8am-6pm) is just west of the Yivli Minare.

Getting There & Away

The otogar is 4km north of the centre. A tram (₺1.50) runs from here to the city centre (Ismetpaşa tram stop). From the otogar, buses whizz to destinations across the country including two overnight services to Göreme (₺50, nine hours); several daily to Konya (₺45, five hours); and frequent dolmuşes and buses to Fethiye (₺30, 7½ hours) via the coastal towns.

OTHER TURKISH TOWNS WORTH A VISIT

Amasya This picturesque clutch of Ottoman mansions stands on a riverbank beneath cliffs carved with Pontic tombs in central Anatolia.

Mardin In southeast Anatolia, minarets and honey-toned houses sit on a hillside looking over the Mesopotamian plains.

Safranbolu This World Heritage Site, northwest of Ankara, boasts Turkey's best-preserved Ottoman quarter and bristles with creaky 19th-century half-timbered houses.

Şanlıurfa One of southeast Anatolia's most fascinating towns. Walk in the footsteps of prophets in the holy Gölbaşı Park then head out of town to see the fascinating archaeological site of Göbekli Tepe.

Trabzon A vibrant Black Sea city that makes a perfect base for visiting the astounding Sumela Monastery.

CENTRAL ANATOLIA

This is the region where the whirling dervishes first swirled, Atatürk began his revolution, Alexander the Great cut the Gordion Knot, and Julius Caesar uttered his famous line, '*Veni, vidi, vici*' ('I came, I saw, I conquered'). Turkey's central plains are alive with mind-boggling history and are the best place from which to capture a sense of modern Anatolian life.

Ankara

☎0312 / POP 4.7 MILLION

İstanbullus may quip that the best view in Ankara is the train home, but the Turkish capital has more substance than its reputation as a staid administrative centre suggests. The capital established by Atatürk boasts two of the country's most important sights; the hilltop *hisar* (citadel) district is full of old-fashioned charm, and the cafe-crammed Kızılay neighbourhood is one of Turkey's hippest urban quarters.

Sights

★Museum of Anatolian Civilisations MUSEUM

(Anadolu Medeniyetleri Müzesi; ☎0312-324 3160; Gözcü Sokak 2; admission ₺15; 8.30am-6.15pm Apr-Oct, to 5pm Nov-Mar; Ⓜ Ulus) The superb Museum of Anatolian Civilisations is the perfect introduction to the complex weave of Turkey's ancient past, housing artefacts cherry-picked from just about every significant archaeological site in Anatolia.

The museum is housed in a 15th-century *bedesten*. The central room houses reliefs and statues, while the surrounding hall displays exhibits from palaeolithic, neolithic, chalcolithic, Bronze Age, Assyrian, Hittite, Phrygian, Urartian and Lydian periods. Downstairs are classical Greek and Roman artefacts and a display on Ankara's history.

Anıt Kabir MONUMENT

(Atatürk Mausoleum & Museum; www.anitkabir.org; Gençlik Caddesi; audioguide ₺10; 9am-5pm May-Oct, to 4pm Nov-Apr; Ⓜ Tandoğan) FREE The monumental mausoleum of Mustafa Kemal Atatürk (1881–1938), the founder of modern Turkey, sits high above the city with its abundance of marble and air of veneration. The tomb itself actually makes up only a small part of this fascinating complex, which consists of museums and a ceremonial courtyard. For many Turks a visit is virtually a pilgrimage, and it's not unusual to see people visibly moved. Allow at least two hours in order to visit the whole site.

Citadel NEIGHBOURHOOD

(Ankara Kalesi; Ⓜ Ulus) The imposing *hisar* is the most interesting part of Ankara to poke about in. This well-preserved quarter of thick walls and intriguing winding streets took its present shape in the 9th century AD, when the Byzantine emperor Michael II constructed the outer ramparts. The inner walls date from the 7th century.

Sleeping

The Ulus area is most convenient for the Museum of Anatolian Civilisations and citadel, but Kızılay is better for restaurants and nightlife.

Deeps Hostel HOSTEL €

(☎0312-213 6338; www.deepshostelankara.com; Ataç Sokak 46; dm/s/d without breakfast ₺30/50/75; ; Ⓜ Kızılay) At Ankara's best budget choice, friendly Şeyda, the owner of Deeps, has created a colourful, light-filled hostel with spacious dorms and rooms, and squeaky-clean, modern shared bathrooms. It's all topped off by masses of advice and information, a fully equipped kitchen and a cute communal area downstairs where you can swap your Turkish travel tales.

★Angora House Hotel HISTORIC HOTEL €€

(☎0312-309 8380; www.angorahouse.com.tr; Kale Kapısı Sokak 16; s/d €70/100; ; Ⓜ Ulus) Be utterly charmed by this restored Ottoman house, which oozes subtle elegance at every turn. The six spacious rooms are infused with loads of old-world atmosphere, featuring dark wood accents, creamy 19th-century design textiles and colourful Turkish carpets; while the walled courtyard garden is the perfect retreat from the citadel streets. Delightfully helpful staff add to the appeal.

Eating & Drinking

It's all about street stalls, hip bistros and cafe culture in Kızılay, where terraces line virtually every inch of space south of Ziya Gökalp Caddesi. Kızılay's tall, thin buildings also pack in up to five floors of nightspots.

Leman Kültür INTERNATIONAL €

(☎0312-310 8617; www.lmk.com.tr; Konur Sokak 8; mains ₺8-20; Ⓜ Kızılay) Named after a cult Turkish comic strip – and decorated accordingly – this is still the pre-party pick for a substantial feed and for spotting beautiful young educated things. The food is generally of the meatballs, burgers and grilled meats variety. Drinks are reasonably priced and the speakers crank everything from indie-electro to Türk pop.

Zenger Paşa Konağı ANATOLIAN €€
(☎0312-311 7070; www.zengerpasa.com; Doyran Sokak 13; mains ₺15-25; Ⓜ Ulus) Crammed with Ottoman ephemera, the Zenger Paşa at first looks like a deserted ethnographic museum, but climb up the rickety stairs and you'll find views of the city that are worth a visit alone. Wealthy locals love the pide (Turkish-style pizza), meze and grills, still cooked in the original Ottoman oven.

Information

The main road is Atatürk Caddesi, which connects Ulus with Kızılay and contains plenty of ATMs, banks and the post office.

Getting There & Away

BUS

From Ankara's huge **AŞTİ otogar** (Ankara Şehirlerarası Terminali İşletmesi; Mevlâna Bulvarı), buses depart to all corners of Turkey day and night. Services to İstanbul (₺19 to ₺45, six hours) leave half-hourly. The AŞTİ is at the western end of Ankara's Ankaray Metro line (fare ₺1.75), by far the easiest way to travel between the otogar and the centre.

TRAIN

Ankara Train Station (Ankara Garı; Talat Paşa Bulvarı) has high-speed trains to Konya (economy/business class ₺27.50/35, two hours, eight daily); and to Pendik, a suburb 25km east of İstanbul (₺75, 3½ hours). Slow, long-distance trains run overnight to İzmir and eastern Anatolia.

Konya

☎0332 / POP 1.1 MILLION

The home of the whirling dervish orders is both a modern economic boom town and a bastion of Seljuk culture. The centre is dotted with imposing historic monuments all topped off by the city's turquoise-domed Mevlâna Museum, one of Turkey's finest sights and most important centres of pilgrimage.

Sights

★**Mevlâna Museum** MUSEUM
(☎0332-351 1215; admission ₺5, audioguide ₺10; ⏲10am-5pm Mon, 9am-5pm Tue-Sun) For Muslims and non-Muslims alike, the main reason to come to Konya is to visit the Mevlâna Museum, the former lodge of the whirling dervishes. It's Celaleddin Rumi (later known as Mevlâna) that we have to thank for giving the world the whirling dervishes and, indirectly, the Mevlâna Museum. Calling it a mere museum, however, makes it sound dead and stale, but the truth coudn't be more different. As one of the biggest pilgrimage centres in Turkey, the museum constantly buzzes with energy.

Mevlâna Culture Centre CULTURAL CENTRE
(Whirling Dervish Performance; Aslanlı Kışla Caddesi; ⏲9pm Sat) FREE The Mevlevi worship ceremony, or *sema*, is a ritual dance representing union with God; it's what gives the dervishes their famous whirl, and appears on Unesco's third Proclamation of Masterpieces of the Oral and Intangible Heritage of Humanity. Watching a *sema* can be an evocative, romantic, unforgettable experience. There are many dervish orders worldwide that perform similar rituals, but the original Turkish version is the smoothest and purest; it's more of an elegant, trancelike dance than the raw energy seen elsewhere.

Tile Museum MUSEUM
(Karatay Medresesi Çini Müzesi; ☎0332-351 1914; Alaaddin Meydanı; admission ₺5; ⏲9am-6.40pm) Gorgeously restored, the interior central dome and walls of this former Seljuk theological school (1251) showcase some finely preserved blue-and-white Seljuk tilework. There is also an outstanding collection of ceramics on display, including exhibits of the octagonal Seljuk tiles unearthed during excavations at Kubad Abad Palace on Lake Beyşehir. Emir Celaleddin Karatay, a Seljuk general, vizier and statesman who built the *medrese*, is buried in one of the corner rooms.

Sleeping & Eating

Ulusan Otel HOTEL €
(☎0332-351 5004; Çarşi PTT Arkasi 4; s/d without bathroom ₺35/70; 📶) This is the pick of the Konya cheapies. The rooms may be totally basic, but they're bright and spotlessly clean. Shared bathrooms are immaculately kept (some rooms have private bathrooms) and the communal area is full of homely knick-knacks.

★**Derviş Otel** BOUTIQUE HOTEL €€
(☎0332-350 0842; www.dervishotel.com; Güngör Sokak 7; r €55-80; ❄📶) This airy, light-filled

200-year-old house has been converted into a rather wonderful boutique hotel. All of the seven spacious rooms have lovely soft colour schemes with local carpets covering the wooden floors, comfortable beds and modern bathrooms to boot. With enthusiastic management providing truly personal service this is a top-notch alternative to Konya's more anonymous hotels.

★ **Konak Konya Mutfağı** ANATOLIAN €€
(0332-352 8547; Piriesat Caddesi 5; mains ₺15-20; 11am-10pm) This excellent traditional restaurant is run by well-known food writer Nevin Halıcı, who puts her personal twist on Turkish classics. Grab an outside table and dine beside vine-draped pillars and a fragrant rose garden. Aubergine aficionados shouldn't miss the *sebzeli közleme* (a grill of smoked aubergine and lamb) and sweet-tooths should definitely save room to try the unusual desserts.

Somatçi ANATOLIAN €€
(0332-351 6696; www.somatci.com; Mengüc Sokak 36; mains ₺12-17; 9am-11pm) Rekindling old recipes, this exciting new restaurant uses the finest ingrediants and cooks everything with panache. Staff are happy to advise on dishes and the setting inside a carefully restored old building is spot on.

Getting There & Away

The otogar is 7km north of the centre and connected by tram. There are frequent buses to all major destinations, including Ankara (₺25, 3½ hours), İstanbul (₺68, 11½ hours) and Göreme (₺30, three hours).

Eight express trains run to/from Ankara daily (adult/child ₺27.50/13, 1¾ hours).

CAPPADOCIA

Cappadocia's cascading rock formations look like they've been plucked straight out of a fairy tale. Explore these rippling valleys, studded with cone-like rocks (called fairy chimneys), and you'll find the human history here just as fascinating as the geological wonderland. Rock-hewn churches covered in Byzantine frescoes are secreted into cliffs, the villages are honeycombed out of hillsides and vast subterranean complexes, where early Christians once hid, are tunnelled under the ground.

WORTH A TRIP

IHLARA VALLEY

A beautiful canyon full of greenery and scattered with Byzantine rock-cut churches, **Ihlara Valley** (Ihlara Vadısı; admission incl Selime Monastery ₺10; 8am-6.30pm) is an excellent spot for a ramble. A trail follows the course of the river, which flows between Selime village and its craggy **monastery** (admission incl Ihlara Valley ₺10; dawn-dusk), to Ihlara village.

Most people visit as part of a day tour which takes in the section of the gorge with the most churches. If you want to walk the entire valley – and it's definitely worth the effort – you'll need to stay overnight or have your own transport as having to change buses in both Nevşehir and Aksaray makes it tricky to do as a day trip on public transport.

In Ihlara village, **Akar Pansion** (0382-453 7018; www.ihlara-akarmotel.com; Ihlara Village; s/d/tr ₺50/100/120;) has tidy rooms and helpful management while **Star Restaurant** (0382-453 7020; www.ihlarapansion.com; Ihlara Village; mains ₺18-20;) has tasty trout meals with a great riverside setting, as well as a good camping spot.

On weekdays, six dolmuşes travel to/from Aksaray (₺5, 45 minutes) stopping at Selime, Belisırma and Ihlara village. On weekends there are fewer services.

Göreme

0384 / POP 2101

Surrounded by epic sweeps of moonscape valley, this remarkable honey-coloured village hollowed out of the hills may have long since grown beyond its farming-hamlet roots, but its charm has not diminished. Nearby, the Göreme Open-Air Museum is an all-in-one testament to Byzantine life, while if you wander out of town you'll find storybook landscapes and little-visited rock-cut churches at every turn. With its easygoing allure and stunning setting, it's no wonder Göreme continues to send travellers giddy.

DON'T MISS

CAPPADOCIA FROM ABOVE

Göreme is one of the best places in the world to go hot-air ballooning. Flight conditions are especially favourable here and seeing this remarkable landscape from above is a truly magical experience. The following Göreme-based ballooning agencies have good credentials:

Butterfly Balloons (☎0384-271 3010; www.butterflyballoons.com; Uzundere Caddesi 29)

Royal Balloon (☎0384-271 3300; www.royalballoon.com; Dutlu Sokak 9)

Sights & Activities

★Göreme Open-Air Museum MUSEUM
(Göreme Açık Hava Müzesi; ☎0384-271 2167; Müze Caddesi; admission ₺20; ⊙8am-6.30pm) One of Turkey's Unesco World Heritage Sites, the Göreme Open-Air Museum is an essential stop on any Cappadocian itinerary and deserves a two-hour visit. First an important Byzantine monastic settlement that housed some 20 monks, then a pilgrimage site from the 17th century, this splendid cluster of monastic Byzantine artistry with its rock-cut churches, chapels and monasteries is 1km uphill from Göreme's centre.

Note that the museum's highlight – the Karanlık Kilise – has an additional ₺10 entrance fee.

Güllüdere Valley PARK
The trails that loop around Güllüdere (Rose) Valley are easily accessible to all levels of walkers and provide some of the finest fairy chimney–strewn vistas in Cappadocia. As well as this, though, they hide fabulous, little-visited rock-cut churches boasting vibrant fresco fragments and intricate carvings hewn into the stone.

If you only have time to hike through one valley in Cappadocia, this is the one to choose.

Tours

Most Göreme tour companies offer two standard full-day tours referred to locally as the **Red Tour** (including visits to Göreme Open-Air Museum, Uçhisar rock castle, Paşabağı and Devrent Valleys, and Avanos), and the **Green Tour** (including a hike in Ihlara Valley and a trip to either Derinkuyu or Kaymaklı underground city).

Heritage Travel GUIDED TOUR
(☎0384-271 2687; www.turkishheritagetravel.com; Uzundere Caddesi) This highly recommended local agency specialises in tailormade Turkey packages but also runs three popular guided day tours (€60 per person) including an excellent 'Undiscovered Cappadocia' trip to Soğanlı. A range of more offbeat activities, from photography safaris (€125 per person) to cooking classes (€50 per person) and day trips to Hacıbektaş are also offered.

Yama Tours GUIDED TOUR
(☎0384-271 2508; www.yamatours.com; Müze Caddesi 2) This popular backpacker-friendly travel agency runs daily Red (regional highlights; ₺110) and Green (Ihlara Valley; ₺120) tours and can book a bag full of other Cappadocia adventures and activities for you.

Sleeping

Köse Pension HOSTEL €
(☎0384-271 2294; www.kosepension.com; Ragıp Üner Caddesi; dm ₺15, d/tr ₺100/120, s/tr without bathroom ₺30/90;) It may have no cave character, but travellers' favourite Köse is still the pick of Göreme's budget digs. Ably managed by Sabina, this friendly place provides a range of spotless rooms featuring brilliant bathrooms, bright linens and comfortable beds, more basic rooms and a spacious rooftop dorm. The swimming pool is a bonus after a long, hot hike.

Kelebek Hotel & Cave Pension HOTEL €€
(☎0384-271 2531; www.kelebekhotel.com; Yavuz Sokak 31; fairy chimney s/d €44/55, deluxe s/d €56/70, ste €85-130;) It's reassuring to know the oldie is still the goodie. Local guru Ali Yavuz leads a charming team at one of Göreme's original boutique hotels that has seen a travel industry virtually spring from beneath its stunning terrace. Exuding Anatolian inspiration at every turn, the rooms are spread over two gorgeous stone houses, each with a fairy chimney protruding skyward.

★Koza Cave Hotel BOUTIQUE HOTEL €€€
(☎0384-271 2466; www.kozacavehotel.com; Çakmaklı Sokak 49; d €80-90, ste €110-175;) Bringing a new level of eco-inspired chic to Göreme, Koza Cave is a masterclass in stylish sustainable tourism. Passionate owner Derviş spent decades living in Holland and

has incorporated Dutch eco-sensibility into every cave crevice of the 10 stunning rooms. Grey water is reused, and recycled materials and local handcrafted furniture are utilised in abundance to create sophisticated spaces. Highly recommended.

Eating

Fırın Express PIDE €

(☎0384-271 2266; Eski Belediye Yanı Sokak; pide ₺6-10;) Simply the best pide in town is found in this local haunt. The cavernous wood oven fires up meat and vegetarian options and anything doused with egg. We suggest adding an *ayran* (yoghurt drink) and a *çoban salatası* (shepherd's salad) for a delicious bargain feed.

Pumpkin Cafe ANATOLIAN €€

(☎0384-0542 808 5050; İçeridere Sokak 7; set menu ₺35; 6-11pm) With its dinky balcony decorated with whimsically carved-out pumpkins (what else), this cute-as-a-button cafe is one of the cosiest dining picks in Göreme. The daily-changing four-course set menu is a fresh feast of simple Anatolian dishes, all presented with delightful flourishes.

★Seten Restaurant MODERN TURKISH €€€

(☎271 3025; www.setenrestaurant.com; Aydınlı Sokak; mains ₺16-40;) Brimming with an artful Anatolian aesthetic, Seten is a feast for the eye as well as for the stomach. Named after the old millstones used to grind bulgur wheat, this restaurant is an education for newcomers to Turkish cuisine and a treat for well-travelled palates. Attentive service complements classic main dishes and myriad luscious and unusual meze.

Getting There & Away

AIR

Both **Kayseri Airport** (Kayseri Erkilet Havalimanı; ☎0352 337 5494; www.kayseri.dhmi.gov.tr; Kayseri Caddesi) and **Nevşehir Airport** (Nevşehir Kapadokya Havalimanı; ☎0384 421 4451; www.kapadokya.dhmi.gov.tr; Nevşehir Kapadokya Havaalanı Yolu, Gülşehir) serve central Cappadocia and have several daily flights to İstanbul.

Airport shuttle buses to Göreme from either airport must be pre-booked. All hotels can do this for you or book directly through **Helios Transfer** (☎0384 271 2257; www.heliostransfer.com; Adnan Menderes Caddesi 24/A, Göreme; per passenger to/from either airport €10).

BUS

Most long-distance buses from western Turkey terminate in Nevşehir, where a bus company free *servis* takes you on to Göreme. Make sure your ticket states your final destination, not Nevşehir. Beware of touts at Nevşehir otogar and only use the bus company's official *servis* shuttle.

The major bus companies all have offices in Göreme otogar and service destinations nationwide.

EASTERN TURKEY

Vast, remote and rugged, Eastern Anatolia is a place apart. Here you'll find spectacular archaeological sites devoid of other visitors, harshly beautiful steppe countryside, and a fascinating cultural heritage that intermingles Turkish, Kurdish, Arabic and Iranian flavours.

Be aware that a few places could be off limits to foreigners when you visit – mainly near the borders of Iraq and Syria – but the vast majority of eastern Turkey remains safe and easily accessible to independent travellers. A journey here will be the most rewarding part of your Turkish travels.

Nemrut Dağı Milli Parkı

Two thousand years ago, a meglomaniac Commagene king erected his own memorial sanctuary on **Nemrut Dağı** (Mt Nemrut; 2150m), the centrepiece of today's stunning **national park** (admission ₺8; dawn-dusk). The fallen heads of the gigantic decorative statues of gods and kings, toppled by earthquakes, form one of the country's most enduring images.

Most people arrive on a sunrise or sunset tour arranged from **Malatya** or **Kahta**, or on a tour from Cappadocia. Note that the Cappadocia tours contain an extremely long drive there and back. In Kahta the pick of the accommodation is the **Kommagene Hotel** (☎0416-725 9726, 0532 200 3856; www.kommagenehotel.com; Mustafa Kemal Caddesi 1; s/d ₺50/90;), which organises decent Nemrut Dağı tours.

The closest base is the pretty village of **Karadut**, 12km from the summit. Both **Karadut Pension** (☎0416-737 2169, 0533 616 4564; www.karadutpansiyon.net; Karadut; per person ₺40, camp site ₺10;) and **Nemrut Kervansaray Hotel** (☎0416-737 2190; www.nemrutkervansaray.com; Karadut; s/d from

€35/45; ❄🛜🏊) in Karadut can arrange pick-ups from Kahta otogar as well as transport to the summit if you don't have your own car.

Van

☎0432 / POP 353,500

Although still coping with the impact of recent earthquakes, this easygoing city has an urban buzz that differentiates it from other eastern Anatolian towns. Its setting, sitting on the southeastern shore of vast Lake Van, ringed by snowcapped mountains, is also phenomenally beautiful. Scramble up to the top of **Van Castle** (Rock of Van; admission ₺5; ⌚9am-dusk), perched on the city's edge, then take a boat trip out onto the lake to view the reliefs inside the **Akdamar Kilisesi** (Church of the Holy Cross; admission ₺5; ⌚8am-6pm), considered one of the masterworks of Armenian art.

Sleeping & Eating

Royal Berk Hotel HOTEL €€
(☎0432-215 0050; www.royalberkhotel.com; Bankası Bitişiği Sokak 5; s/d from ₺90/130) Built after the 2011 earthquakes, the Royal Berk combines spacious and very comfortable rooms with a brilliant location in a quiet laneway just metres from Van's main street. Decor stays just the right side of over-the-top, the crew at reception are easygoing and friendly, and the huge breakfast spread closely replicates what's on offer in the city's famed *kahvaltı* restaurants.

Aişe ANATOLIAN €
(Özok is Merkezi Karşi 5; mains ₺7-10; ⌚10am-4pm; 🌿) Run by an enterprising group of local women, around six different Turkish and Kurdish dishes are presented each day. Count on around ₺10 to ₺12 for a full meal including bread and soup, all best enjoyed in the restaurant's colourful outdoor patio.

Getting There & Away

There are frequent buses to Diyarbakır (₺40, seven hours) from where you can continue to Kahta (for Mt Nemrut); and to Erzurum (₺40, seven hours) from where you can continue on to Kars.

Kars

☎0474 / POP 76,700

The medieval fortress and stately, pastel-coloured Russian buildings are well worth a look, but most people come to the setting of Orhan Pamuk's novel *Snow* to visit the dramatic ruins of **Ani** (admission ₺8; ⌚8.30am-6pm May-Sep, to 3pm Oct-Apr), 45km east of the city. Formerly a Silk Road entrepôt and capital of the Armenian kingdom, Ani was deserted in 1239 after a Mongol invasion. The ghost city, with its lightning-cleaved **Church of the Redeemer**, now lies amid undulating grass overlooking the Armenian border. The site exudes an eerie ambience that is simply unforgettable.

Sleeping & Eating

Güngören Otel HOTEL €€
(☎0472-212 6767; www.gungorenhotel.com; Millet Sokak; s/d/tr ₺90/160/210; 🛜) The Güngören is a stalwart on the travelling circuit with smart rooms with flat-screen TVs and tiled bathroom. The staff speak some English, and the location on a quiet street is convenient. Some upper-floor rooms have not been renovated, so check when you book.

★**Hanimeli Kars Mutfağı** ANATOLIAN €€
(www.karshanimeli.com; Faik Bey Caddesi 156; mains ₺10-15; ⌚11am-9pm) With a rustic, country-kitchen vibe, Hanimeli specialises in homestyle cooking influenced by the broader Caucasian region. Dishes include Armemian-style *Erivan köfte* (meatballs), a silkily smooth pasta soup called *eriste aşi*, and the ravioli-like *hangel*. Roast duck is on offer, delicious Kars honey is for sale, and a refreshing local drink is *reyhane* made from purple-coloured red basil.

Getting There & Away

From the otogar, Turgutreis has a daily bus to Van at 8.30am (₺35, six hours); and there are a few daily buses to Ankara (₺50, 16 hours).

The easiest way to get to Ani is to take a taxi minibus (₺50 per person for a group of three, ₺140 for one person). This can be organised through **Celil Ersoğlu** (☎0532 226 3966; celilani@hotmail.com) or through the Kars **tourist office** (☎0432-212 1705; cnr Faik Bey and Gazi Ahmet Muhtar Paşa Caddesis; ⌚8am-5pm Mon-Fri).

TURKEY VAN

SURVIVAL GUIDE

Directory A–Z

ACCOMMODATION

Budget travellers will find backpacker hostels with dorm beds in İstanbul, along the Aegean and Mediterranean coasts, and in Cappadocia. Camping grounds are also found along the coasts and in Cappadocia. There are plentiful budget and midrange hotels and family-run pensions in tourist areas. Pensions generally represent better value.

Outside tourist areas, solo travellers of both sexes should be cautious about the cheapest hotel options. Suss out the staff and atmosphere in reception; theft and even sexual assaults have occurred in budget establishments (albeit very rarely).

The most interesting midrange and top-end options are Turkey's numerous boutique hotels, often in restored Ottoman mansions (such as in İstanbul and Antalya), and Cappadocia's cave-hotels.

BUSINESS HOURS

The working day shortens during the holy month of Ramazan (Ramadan). Friday is a normal working day in Turkey. Opening hours of tourist attractions and tourist information offices may shorten in the low season.

Bars 4pm to late

Government departments, offices and banks 8.30am to noon and 1.30pm to 5pm Monday to Friday

Information offices 8.30am to noon and 1.30pm to 5pm Monday to Friday

Nightclubs 11pm to late

Restaurants and cafes Breakfast 7.30am to 10am, lunch noon to 2.30pm, dinner 6.30pm to 10pm

Shops 9am to 6pm Monday to Friday (longer hours in tourist areas and big cities – including weekend opening)

INTERNET RESOURCES

Go Turkey (www.goturkey.com) Official Turkey tourism portal.

Lonely Planet (www.lonelyplanet.com/turkey) Info, articles, bookings and forum.

Today's Zaman (www.todayszaman.com) English-language Turkish newspaper.

Turkey From The Inside (www.turkeyfromtheinside.com) Expansive coverage of Turkish places and sights.

MONEY

- Turkish lira (₺) comes in notes of five, 10, 20, 50, 100 and 200; and coins of one, five, 10, 25 and 50 kuruş and one lira.
- Hotels and restaurants in more popular tourist destinations often quote their rates in euro.
- ATMs are widespread and dispense Turkish lira, and occasionally euros and US dollars, to Visa, MasterCard, Cirrus and Maestro card holders.
- Credit cards (Visa and MasterCard) are widely accepted by hotels, shops and restaurants, although often not by establishments outside the main tourist areas. You can also get cash advances on these cards. Amex is less commonly accepted.
- US dollars and euros are the easiest currencies to change. You'll get better rates at exchange offices than at banks.

SLEEPING PRICE RANGES

Price ranges in this book are based on the cost of a double room in high season (June to August; apart from İstanbul, where high season is April, May, September, October, Christmas and Easter) and include breakfast, en suite bathroom and taxes unless otherwise stated.

€ less than ₺90 (€90 in İstanbul)

€€ ₺90 to ₺180 (€90 to €200 in İstanbul)

€€€ more than ₺180 (€200 in İstanbul)

COUNTRY FACTS

Area 783,562 sq km

Capital Ankara

Country Code ☎90

Currency Turkish lira (₺). One Turkish lira is worth 100 kuruş

Emergency ambulance ☎112, fire ☎110, police ☎155

Language Turkish, Kurdish

Money ATMs are widespread; credit cards accepted in cities and tourist areas

Visas Tourist visas (90 days) must be purchased before travel on Turkey's electronic visa website www.evisa.gov.tr

Tipping & Bargaining

- Tipping is customary in restaurants, hotels and for services such as guided tours.
- Round up metered taxi fares to the nearest 50 kuruş.
- Leave waiters around 10% to 15% of the bill.
- Check a *servis ücreti* (service charge) hasn't been automatically added to restaurant bills.
- Hotel prices are sometimes negotiable, especially outside of peak season.
- Bargaining for souvenirs is normal in bazaars.

POST

- Turkish *postanes* (post offices) are indicated by black-on-yellow 'PTT' signs. Postcards sent abroad cost about ₺2.50.

PUBLIC HOLIDAYS

New Year's Day 1 January
National Sovereignty & Children's Day 23 April
International Workers' Day 1 May
Youth & Sports Day 19 May
Victory Day 30 August
Republic Day 28–29 October

Turkey also celebrates the main Islamic holidays, the most important of which are **Şeker Bayramı** (Sweets Holiday; 6–8 July 2016 and 26–28 June 2017), marking the end of Ramazan; and about two months later, **Kurban Bayramı** (Festival of the Sacrifice; 12–15 September 2016 and 1–4 September 2017). Due to the fact that these holidays are celebrated according to the Islamic lunar calendar, they take place around 11 days earlier every year.

SAFE TRAVEL

Turkey is in no way a dangerous country to visit, but it's always wise to be a little cautious, especially if you're travelling alone. You should watch out in particular for the following:

- In İstanbul, single men are sometimes approached and lured to a bar by new 'friends'. The victim is then made to pay an outrageous bill, regardless of what he drank. Drugging is sometimes a problem, especially for lone men. It pays to be a tad wary of who you befriend, especially when you're new to the country.
- Protests are not unheard of in major cities. Keep well away from demonstrations as tear gas and water cannons are often used.
- Although rare, sexual assaults have occurred against travellers of both sexes in hotels in central and eastern Anatolia. If a place seems leery, trust your instincts and go elsewhere.
- The 30-year conflict between the Turkish state and the PKK (Kurdistan Workers Party) ended in 2013. Peace talks subsequently stalled, and the conflict in neighbouring Syria and Iraq has complicated the situation, but both sides are committed to finding a solution. If fighting resumes, PKK attacks generally happen far from travellers' routes in remote parts of mountainous southeastern Anatolia, but check the latest situation if visiting the area.

ESSENTIAL FOOD & DRINK

Turkish food is a celebration of community and life in its home country and is made memorable by the use of seasonal ingredients, ensuring freshness and flavour.

Kebaps and *köfte* (meatballs) in all their variations are the mainstay of restaurant meals. Look out particularly for:

- **Adana kebap** Spicy *köfte* grilled on a skewer and served with onions, sumac, parsley, barbecued tomatoes and pide bread.
- **İskender kebap** Döner kebap (spit-roasted lamb slices) on fresh pide and topped with savoury tomato sauce and browned butter.
- **Tokat kebap** Lamb cubes grilled with potato, tomato, aubergine and garlic.

Meze is where Turkish cuisine really comes into its own. *Acılı ezme* (spicy tomato and onion paste), *fasulye pilaki* (white beans cooked with tomato paste and garlic), and *yaprak sarma* (vine leaves stuffed with rice, herbs and pine nuts) are just a few of the myriad meze dishes on offer.

For quick cheap eats, try pide (Turkish pizza), *lahmacun* (Arabic-style pizza), *gözleme* (savoury pancakes) and *börek* (filled pastries).

Popular non-kebap mains include *mantı* (Turkish ravioli), *saç kavurma* (stir-fried cubed meat dishes) and *güveç* (meat and vegetable stews cooked in a terracotta pot).

The national hot drink is çay, served black in tulip-shaped glasses. The Turkish liquor of choice is rakı, a fiery aniseed drink similar to Greek ouzo; do as the Turks do and cut it by half with water. *Ayran* is a refreshing yoghurt drink made by whipping up yoghurt with water and salt and is the perfect accompaniment to a kebap.

EATING PRICE RANGES

Prices in listings are based on the cost of a main course.

€ less than ₺9 (₺20 in İstanbul)

€€ ₺9 to ₺17.50 (₺20 to ₺30 in İstanbul)

€€€ more than ₺17.50 (₺30 in İstanbul)

➡ Following on from this, the border area facing Syria is currently a no-travel zone on most official travel advisory websites. Check your government's latest travel advisories for up-to-date information.

TELEPHONE

➡ Payphones require cards that can be bought at telephone centres or, for a small mark-up, at some shops.

➡ If you set up a roaming facility with your home phone provider, you should be able to connect your mobile to a network.

➡ If you buy a local SIM card and use it in your home mobile, the network detects and bars foreign phones within a month.

➡ To avoid barring, register your phone when you buy your Turkish SIM. At a certified cell phone shop, show your passport and fill in a short form declaring your phone is in Turkey. The process costs about ₺100.

VISAS

➡ Nationals of countries including Denmark, Finland, France, Germany, Israel, Italy, Japan, New Zealand, Sweden and Switzerland don't need a visa to visit Turkey for up to 90 days.

➡ Nationals of countries including Australia, Austria, Belgium, Canada, Ireland, the Netherlands, Norway, Portugal, Spain, the UK and USA need a visa, which must be purchased online at www.evisa.gov.tr before travelling.

➡ Most nationalities, including the above, are given a 90-day multiple-entry visa.

➡ In most cases, the 90-day visa stipulates 'per period 180 days'. This means you can spend three months in Turkey within a six-month period; when you leave after three months, you can't re-enter for three months.

➡ At the time of writing, the e-visa charge was US$20 for most nationalities, with a few exceptions including Australians and Canadians, who pay US$60, and South Africans, who receive it free.

➡ Your passport must be valid for at least six months from the date you enter the country.

WOMEN TRAVELLERS

Travelling in Turkey is straightforward for women, provided you follow some simple guidelines:

➡ Tailor your behaviour and dress to your surroundings. Outside of İstanbul and heavily touristed destinations, you should dress modestly.

➡ Cover your hair when visiting mosques or religious buildings.

➡ In more conservative areas (particularly out east) your contact with men should be polite and formal, not chatty and friendly or they are likely to get the wrong idea about your intentions.

➡ Very cheap hotels are not recommended for single women travellers. If a place has a bad vibe, find somewhere else.

ℹ Getting There & Away

AIR

The main international airports are in western Turkey. **Turkish Airlines** (☎0850-333 0849; www.thy.com), the national carrier, has an extensive international network.

Antalya International Airport (Antalya Havalımanı; ☎444 7423; www.aytport.com)

Dalaman International Airport (☎0252-792 5555; www.atmairport.aero/Dalaman_en/index.php)

İstanbul Atatürk International Airport (p1152)

İstanbul Sabiha Gökçen International Airport (p1152)

LAND

There are direct bus services to İstanbul from Austria, Albania, Bulgaria, Germany, Greece, Hungary, Kosovo, Macedonia, Romania and Slovenia.

The major bus companies that operate these routes are **Metro Turizm** (☎444 3455; www.metroturizm.com.tr), **Ulusoy** (p1174) and **Varan** (☎444 8999; www.varan.com.tr).

Currently the only train route operating between Europe and İstanbul is the daily Bosfor/Balkan Ekspresi to Bucharest (Romania) and Sofia (Bulgaria). See Turkish State Railways (p1174) for details.

SEA

Departure times and routes change between seasons, with fewer ferries generally running in the winter. **Ferrylines** (www.ferrylines.com) is a good starting point for information. The following is a list of ferry routes from Turkey:

Ayvalık–Lesvos, Greece Jale Tour (www.jaletour.com)

Bodrum–Kos, Greece Bodrum Ferryboat Association (www.bodrumferryboat.com); Bodrum Express Lines (www.bodrumexpresslines.com)

Bodrum–Rhodes, Greece Bodrum Ferryboat Association

Çeşme–Chios, Greece Ertürk (www.erturk.com.tr)

Datça–Rhodes, Greece Knidos Yachting (www.knidosyachting.com)

Datça–Simi, Greece Knidos Yachting

İstanbul–Illyichevsk (Odesa), Ukraine Sea Lines (www.sea-lines.net)

Kaş–Meis (Kastellorizo), Greece Meis Express (www.meisexpress.com)

Kuşadası–Samos, Greece Meander Travel (www.meandertravel.com)

Marmaris–Rhodes, Greece Yeşil Marmaris Travel & Yachting (www.yesilmarmaris.com)

Taşucu–Girne (Kyrenia), North Cyprus Akgünler Denizcilik (www.akgunler.com.tr)

Trabzon–Sochi, Russia Olympia Line (www.olympia-line.ru), Öz Star Denizcilik (Princess Victoria), Sarı Denizcilik (www.saridenizcilik.com/en); see also www.seaport-sochi.ru and www.al-port.com

Turgutreis–Kos Bodrum Ferryboat Association

 Getting Around

BUS

- Turkey's intercity bus system is as good as any you'll find, with modern, comfortable coaches crossing the country at all hours and for very reasonable prices.
- Major companies with extensive networks include **Kamil Koç** (☎444 0562; www.kamilkoc.com.tr), Metro Turizm (p1173) and **Ulusoy** (☎444 1888; www.ulusoy.com.tr).
- A town's otogar is often on the outskirts, but most bus companies provide a *servis* (free shuttle bus) to/from the centre.
- Local routes are usually operated by dolmuşes (minibuses), which might run to a timetable or set off when full.

CAR & MOTORCYCLE

- Turkey has the world's second-highest petrol prices. Petrol/diesel cost about ₺5 per litre.
- An international driving permit (IDP) is not obligatory, but handy if your driving licence is from a country likely to seem obscure to a Turkish police officer.
- You must be at least 21 years old to hire a car. Rental charges are similar to those in Europe.
- You must have third-party insurance if you are bringing your own car into the country. Buying it at the border is a straightforward process (one month €80).
- Road accidents claim about 10,000 lives each year. To survive on Turkish roads:
- Drive defensively and cautiously.
- Don't expect fellow motorists to obey traffic signs or use indicators.
- Avoid driving at night, when you won't be able to see potholes, animals, vehicles driving without lights, or vehicles stopped in the middle of the road.

TRAIN

The **Turkish State Railways** (☎444 8233; www.tcdd.gov.tr) network covers the country fairly well, with the notable exception of the coastlines. Most train journey times are notoriously long with roundabout routes, but the entire system is currently being overhauled. Check out the website **The Man In Seat Sixty-One** (www.seat61.com/turkey2) for details on Turkish train travel.

High-speed Routes

- Ankara–Konya
- Eskişehir–Konya
- İstanbul Pendik–Eskişehir–Ankara

Useful Long-haul Routes (all departing from Ankara)

- Diyarbakır via Kayseri, Sivas and Malatya
- Kars via Kayseri, Sivas and Erzurum
- Tatvan (Lake Van) via Kayseri, Sivas and Malatya

InterRail, Balkan Flexipass and Eurodomino passes are valid on the Turkish railway network, but Eurail passes are not.

Ukraine

Includes ➡

Best Places to Eat

- ➡ Spotykach (p1179)
- ➡ Masonic Restaurant (p1184)
- ➡ Arbequina (p1179)
- ➡ Dim Lehend (p1183)
- ➡ Kupol (p1183)

Best Places to Stay

- ➡ Sunflower B&B (p1179)
- ➡ Astoria (p1183)
- ➡ Hotel 7 Days (p1183)
- ➡ Dream House Hostel (p1178)

Why Go?

Big, diverse and largely undiscovered, Ukraine (Україна) is one of Europe's last genuine travel frontiers, a poor nation rich in colour-splashed tradition, off-the-map travel experiences and warm-hearted people. And with the country hitting the headlines recently for all the wrong reasons, those locals are perhaps happier than ever to see foreign visitors.

'Ukraine' means 'land on the edge', an apt title for this slab of Eurasia in many ways. This is the Slavic hinterland on Europe's periphery, just over two decades into a very troubled independence and dogged by conflict with neighbouring Russia. But it's a country whose peoples can pull together when need arises, as the recent Maidan Revolution and nationwide war effort has shown.

Most visitors head for the eclectic capital Kyiv, but architecturally rich Lviv is Ukraine's true big hope for tourism and both are well away from the conflict zones. However, while Russia continues to occupy Crimea, beach fun is off for the foreseeable future.

When to Go

Kyiv

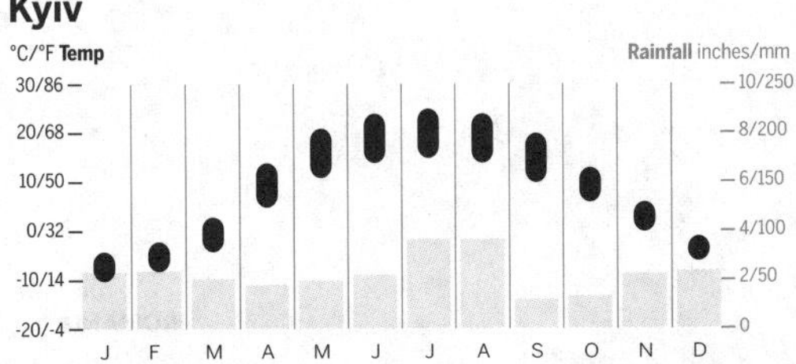

Jan Party on New Year's Eve then repent at an Orthodox Christmas service a week later.

May A great time to visit Kyiv when its countless horse chestnut trees are in blossom.

Aug Sip Ukraine's best coffee in one of Lviv's many outdoor cafes.

Ukraine Highlights

1 Inspect Kyiv's collection of mummified monks by candlelight at **Kyevo-Pecherska Lavra** (p1178).

2 Make an ascent of **Andriyivsky Uzviz** (p1178), Kyiv's most atmospheric street.

3 Do a spot of cobble-surfing in **Lviv's** (p1182) historical centre, packed with churches, museums and eccentric restaurants.

4 Take a stroll through the island town of **Kamyanets-Podilsky** (p1183) to its photogenic fortress.

Bryansk
Desna
Voronezh
RUSSIA
Kursk
E101
Seym
Chernihiv
Sumy
Desna
Kharkiv
E40
Luhansk
Kyiv
1
2
E40
Poltava
Slovyansk
Bryanka
Kramatorsk
E105
Krasny
Luch
Kostyantynivka
Horlivka
Dnipro River
Cherkasy
Kremenchutske Reservoir
Kremenchuk
E50
Donetsk
Makiyivka
Dniprodzerzhynsk
Dnipropetrovsk
E50
Kirovohrad
Zaporizhzhya
E105
Mariupol
Uman
E50
Kryvy Rih
Nikopol
E95
Berdyansk
E577
Kakhovske Reservoir
Melitopol
Pivdenny Buh
E58
Sea of Azov
Mykolaiv
Askaniya-Nova National Park
Kherson
E58
Skadovsk
Odesa
E97
E97
E105
CRIMEA
Simferopol
Bakhchysaray
Krymsky National Park
Sevastopol
Yalta
Dunaysky National Park
Danube
BLACK SEA
0
200 km
0
100 miles

ITINERARIES

Two Days

A couple of days are just enough to 'do' **Kyiv**, starting at its stellar attraction, the Kyevo-Pecherska Lavra (aka the Caves Monastery). Follow this with a hike up artsy Andriyivsky Uzviz for a taste of prewar Ukraine, before plunging into the beeswax-perfumed Byzantine interior of Unesco-listed St Sophia's Cathedral.

Five Days

Having seen the sights in Kyiv, hop aboard a slow night train to **Lviv**, Ukraine's most central European city – complete with bean-scented coffee houses, Gothic and baroque churches, and quaintly rattling trams.

Kyiv Київ

044 / POP 2.8 MILLION

Sometimes chaotic central Asia, other times quaint central Europe, Kyiv (many agree) is the former USSR's most pleasant city. A pretty spot amid the wooded hills hemming the wide River Dnipro, this eclectic capital has preserved the legacy of its former possessors, from Viking chieftains to post-Soviet dictators. Despite its starring role in the 2014 Maidan Revolution which toppled the last of those rulers, only the very centre around Maidan Nezalezhnosti bears any scars, the rest of the city untouched by the tumultuous events that put the geopolitical spotlight firmly on Ukraine.

Sights

★Kyevo-Pecherska Lavra MONASTERY

(Києво-Печерська Лавра | Caves Monastery; 044 280 3071; www.kplavra.ua; vul Lavrska 9; grounds 15uah, caves & exhibitions adult/child 50/25uah; 8am-7pm Apr-Oct, 9am-6pm Nov-Mar; M Arsenalna) Tourists and Orthodox pilgrims alike flock to the Lavra. It's easy to see why the tourists come. Set on 28 hectares of grassy hills above the Dnipro River, the monastery's tight cluster of gold-domed churches is a feast for the eyes, the hoard of Scythian gold rivals that of the Hermitage in St Petersburg, and the underground labyrinths lined with mummified monks are exotic and intriguing.

★St Sophia's Cathedral CHURCH

(pl Sofiyska; admission grounds/cathedral/bell tower 10/55/20uah; grounds 9am-7pm, cathedral 10am-6pm Thu-Tue, to 5pm Wed; M Maydan Nezalezhnosti) The interior is the most astounding aspect of Kyiv's oldest standing church, St Sophia's Cathedral. Many of the mosaics and frescoes are original, dating back to 1017–31, when the cathedral was built to celebrate Prince Yaroslav's victory in protecting Kyiv from the Pechenegs (Tribal Raiders). While equally attractive, the building's gold domes and 76m-tall wedding-cake bell tower are 18th-century baroque additions.

Andriyivsky Uzviz STREET

(M Kontraktova Pl) According to legend a man walked up the hill, erected a cross and prophesied: 'A great city will stand on this spot'. That man was the Apostle Andrew, hence the name of Kyiv's quaintest thoroughfare, a steep cobbled street that winds its way up from Kontraktova pl to vul Volodymyrska. Its vague Montparnasse feel has attracted Ukraine's wealthy, but despite gentrification it still retains an atmosphere unique for Kyiv, as well as its multiple stalls selling junk souvenirs and dubious art.

Sleeping

★Dream House Hostel HOSTEL €

(044 580 2169; www.dream-family.com; Andriyivsky uzviz 2D; dm/d from 110/390uah; M Kontraktova pl) Kyiv's most happening hostel is a gleaming 100-bed affair superbly located at the bottom of Andriyivsky uzviz. An attached cafe-bar, basement kitchen, laundry room, key cards, bike hire, tours and daily events make this a comfortable and engaging base from which to explore the capital.

Oselya BOUTIQUE HOTEL €€

(Оселя; 044 258 8281; www.oselya.in.ua; vul Kamenyariv 11; s 614uah, d from 790uah; M Lybidska) Inconveniently located around 5km south of the city centre, just to the east of Zhulyany airport, this superb seven-room family-run hotel has immaculately kept rooms in period style and receives encouraging reviews from travellers for its friendly welcome. The location feels almost rural, but you'll need to arrange a pickup from Lybidska metro station to find it, or grab a cab.

★ Sunflower B&B Hotel B&B €€€
(☎044 279 3846; www.sunflowerhotel.kiev.ua; vul Kostyolna 9/41; s/d from 850/1000uah; ; Maydan Nezalezhnosti) The name is an oxymoron – it's more B&B than hotel – but we're not complaining. The highlight is the continental breakfast delivered to your room, on request, by English-speaking staff. It's centrally located but nearly impossible to find – calling for a pickup is not a bad idea.

Eating

Kyivska Perepichka FAST FOOD €
(Київська перепічка; vul Bohdana Khmelnytskoho 3; pastry 6uah; 8.30am-9pm Mon-Sat, 10am-9pm Sun; Teatralna) A perpetually long queue moves with lightning speed towards a window where two women hand out pieces of fried dough enclosing a mouthwatering sausage. The place became a local institution long before the first 'hot dog' hit town. An essential Kyiv experience.

★ Spotykach UKRAINIAN €€
(Спотикач; ☎044 586 4095; vul Volodymyrska 16; mains 50-190uah; 11am-midnight; ; Zoloti Vorota) A tribute to the 1960s, this discreetly stylish retro-Soviet cellar will make even a hardened dissident shed a nostalgic tear. The menu is Kremlin banquet, but with a definite Ukrainian twist. *Spotykach* is vodka-based liquor made with different flavours, from blackcurrant to horseradish, and takes its name from the Russian for 'stumble' – an effect it might cause on the uninitiated.

★ Arbequina SPANISH, SEAFOOD €€
(☎044 223 9618; vul Borysa Hrinchenka; mains 80-150uah; 9am-11pm; ; Maydan Nezalezhnosti) Barcelona meets Odesa in this miniature restaurant a few steps away from Maidan. Food is mostly Spanish, but the chef successfully experiments with Black Sea fish and East European staples, which results in most unusual combinations. From Wednesday to Friday there's live Cuban or Spanish music in the evenings.

Drinking & Nightlife

Kupidon PUB
(Купідон | Cupid; vul Pushkinska 1-3/5; 10am-10pm; ; Kreshchatyk) Perhaps no longer the hotbed of nationalism it once was, Cupid is still a great Lviv-styled cellar knaypa (pub) abutting a second-hand bookshop. Well-crafted coffees and Ukrainian food are enjoyed at the jumble of table and chairs and there's plenty of reading and drawing material lying around to keep you occupied afterwards.

Kaffa COFFEE
(Каффа; prov Tarasa Shevchenka 3; 11am-10.30pm Mon, from 9am Tue-Fri, 10am-10pm Sat & Sun; Maydan Nezalezhnosti) Around for years, Kaffa still serves the most heart-pumping, rich-tasting brew in town. Coffees and teas from all over the world are served in a pot sufficient for two or three punters, in a whitewashed African-inspired interior – all ethnic masks, beads and leather.

Entertainment

Art Club 44 LIVE MUSIC
(www.club44.com.ua; vul Khreshchatyk 44B; Teatralna) Some of the best gigs and DJ nights in the city centre with everything from west Ukrainian ethno-rock to German disc spinners packing them in.

Taras Shevchenko National Opera Theatre OPERA
(☎044 235 2606; www.opera.com.ua; vul Volodymyrska 50; Zoloti Vorota) Performances at this lavish theatre (opened 1901) are grandiose affairs but tickets are cheap. True disciples of Ukrainian culture should not miss a performance of Zaporozhets za Dunaem (Zaporizhzhyans Beyond the Danube), a sort of operatic, purely Ukrainian version of Fiddler on the Roof.

Information

Almost every cafe and restaurant offers free wi-fi and there are hotspots throughout the city centre. Kyiv has no tourist office.

Central Post Office (www.ukrposhta.com; vul Khreshchatyk 22; 8am-9pm Mon-Sat, 9am-7pm Sun; Maydan Nezalezhnosti)

Lonely Planet (www.lonelyplanet.com/ukraine/kyiv)

Getting There & Away

AIR

Most international flights use Boryspil International Airport (p1186), 35km east of the city. Some domestic airlines and Wizzair use **Zhulyany airport** (☎044 585 7254; www.airport.kiev.ua), 7km southwest of the centre. There's at least one flight a day to all regional capitals and international flights serve many European cities.

Plane tickets are sold at **Kiy Avia** (www.kiyavia.com; pr Peremohy 2; 8am-9pm Mon-Fri, 8am-8pm Sat, 9am-6pm Sun; Vokzalna).

Central Kyiv

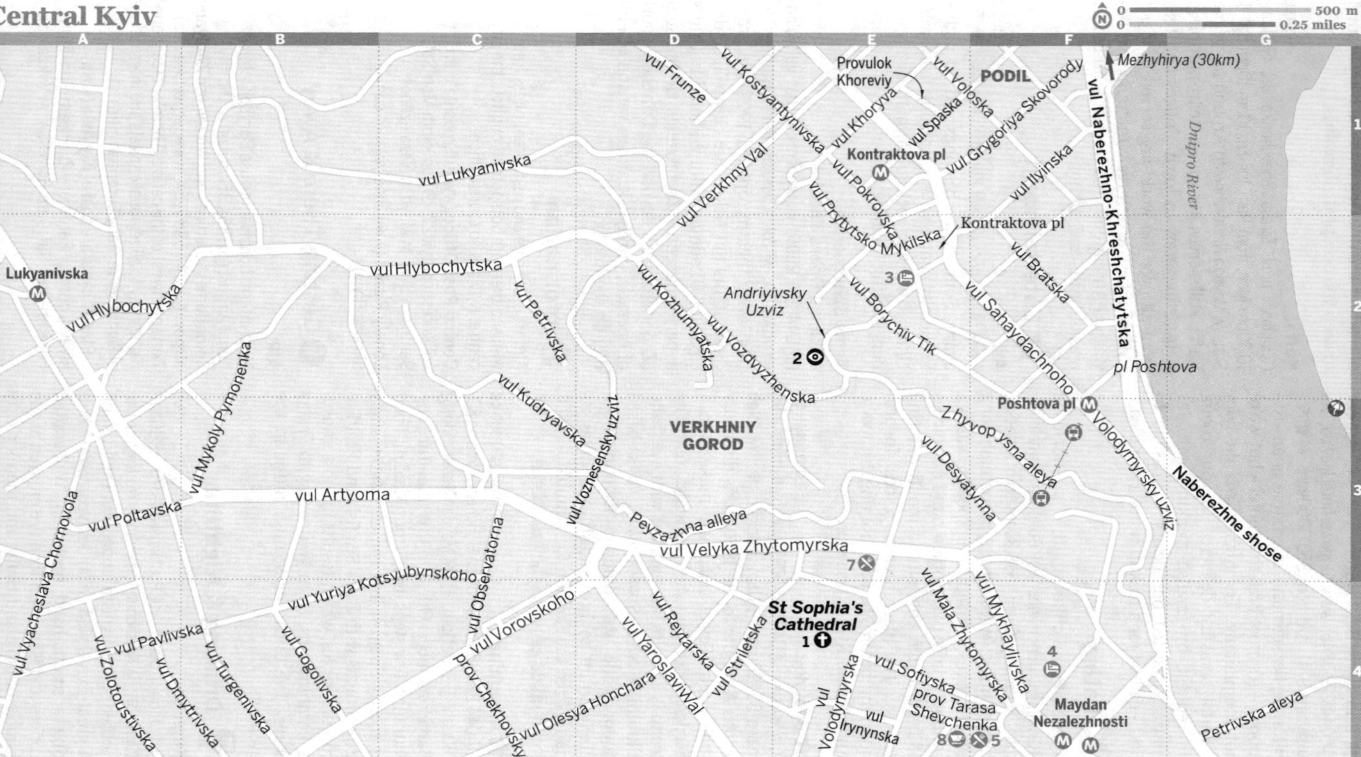

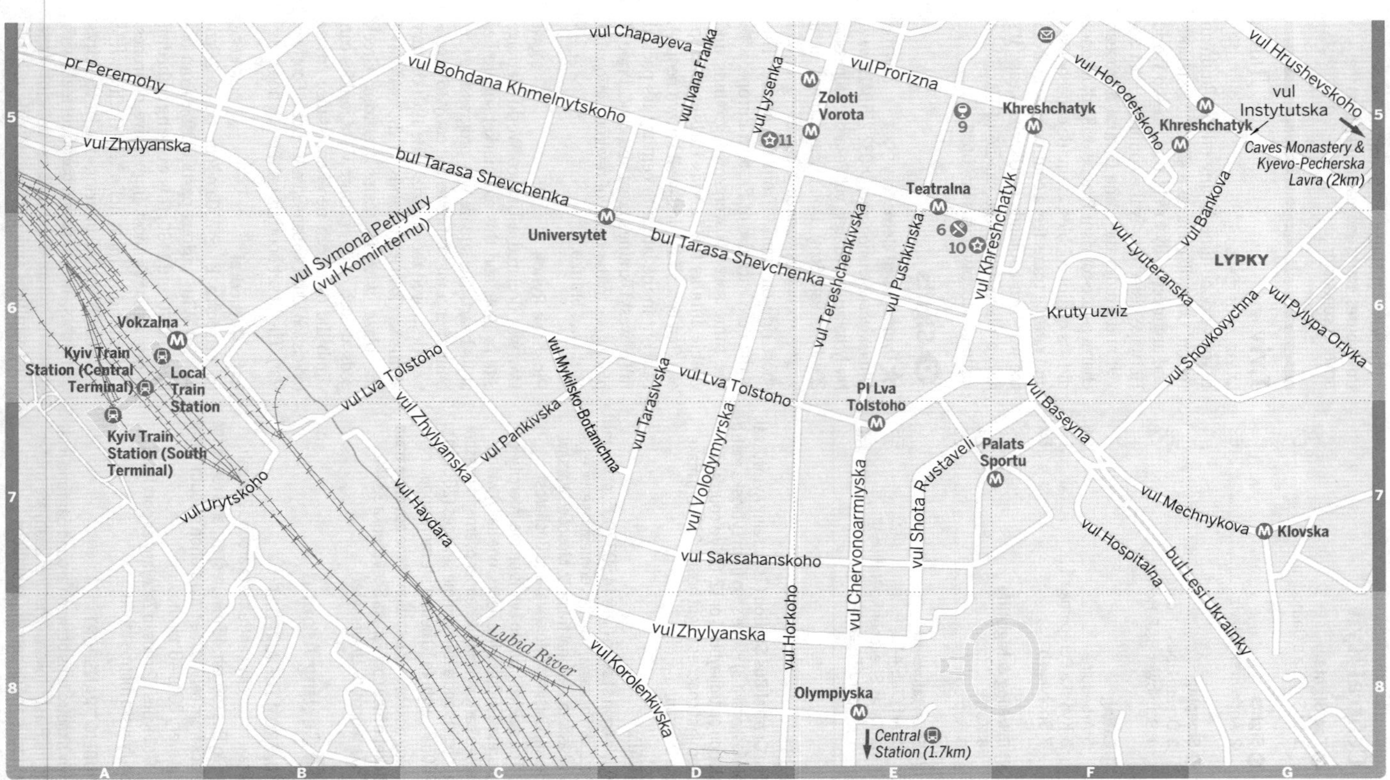

vul Chapayeva
pr Peremohy
vul Bohdana Khmelnytskoho
vul Ivana Franka
vul Lysenka
Zoloti Vorota
vul Prorizna
Khreshchatyk
vul Horodetskoho
Khreshchatyk
vul Hrushevskoho
vul Instytutska
Caves Monastery & Kyevo-Pecherska Lavra (2km)
vul Zhylyanska
bul Tarasa Shevchenka
Universytet
Teatralna
vul Bankova
vul Khreshchatyk
vul Lyuteranska
LYPKY
bul Tarasa Shevchenka
vul Tereshchenkivska
vul Pushkinska
vul Symona Petlyury (vul Kominternu)
Kruty uzviz
vul Shovkovychna
vul Pylypa Orlyka
Vokzalna
Kyiv Train Station (Central Terminal)
Local Train Station
Kyiv Train Station (South Terminal)
vul Lva Tolstoho
vul Mykilsko-Botanichna
vul Tarasivska
vul Lva Tolstoho
Pl Lva Tolstoho
vul Zhylyanska
vul Pankivska
vul Volodymyrska
vul Baseyna
Palats Sportu
vul Shota Rustaveli
vul Chervonoarmiyska
vul Urytskoho
vul Haydara
vul Mechnykova
Klovska
vul Hospitalna
vul Saksahanskoho
bul Lesi Ukrainky
vul Zhylyanska
vul Horkoho
Lybid River
vul Korolenkivska
Olympiyska
Central Station (1.7km)

Central Kyiv

Top Sights

1 St Sophia's Cathedral E4

Sights

2 Andriyivsky Uzviz E2

Sleeping

3 Dream House Hostel E2
4 Sunflower B&B Hotel F4

Eating

5 Arbequina F4
6 Kyivska Perepichka E6
7 Spotykach E3

Drinking & Nightlife

8 Kaffa E4
9 Kupidon E5

Entertainment

10 Art Club 44 ......E6
11 Taras Shevchenko National Opera Theatre D5

BUS

The **Central Bus Station** (Tsentralny Avtovokzal; pl Moskovska 3) is one stop from Lybidska metro station on trolleybus 1 or 12. Only a couple of overnight coaches (eight hours, 250uah) make the Lviv run.

TRAIN

Kyiv's **train station** (044 503 7005; pl Vokzalna 2; S Vokzalna) handles domestic services as well as international trains to Moscow, Warsaw, Berlin, Chișinău (Moldova) and Bucharest.

The quickest way to Lviv is on the Intercity+ express (260uah, five hours, one daily) which leaves early evening. Cheaper overnight passenger trains and a few daytime services (200uah to 250uah, eight to 10 hours) are more popular.

Buy tickets at the station or the **advance train ticket office** (bul Tarasa Shevchenka 38/40; 7am-9pm; S Universytet).

Getting Around

TO/FROM THE AIRPORT

A taxi to the city centre costs around 250uah.

SkyBus (50uah, 45 minutes) departs round the clock from behind the train station's South Terminal every 20 to 40 minutes.

Trolleybus 22 runs to Zhulyany airport from Shulyavska metro station.

PUBLIC TRANSPORT

Kyiv's metro runs between around 6am and midnight. Plastic tokens (*zhetony*; 2uah) are sold at windows and dispensers at stations.

Buy tickets (1.50uah to 2.50uah) for buses, trolleybuses, trams and *marshrutky* from the driver or conductor.

Lviv Львів

032 / POP 725,350

If you've done time in any other Ukrainian region, Lviv will come as a shock. Mysterious and architecturally lovely, this Unesco World Heritage–listed city is the country's least Soviet and exudes the same Central European charm as pre-tourism Prague or Kraków once did. Its quaint cobbles, aromatic coffeehouses and rattling trams feel a continent away from the war-torn badlands of Ukraine's east. It's also a place where the candle of Ukrainian national identity burns brightest.

Sights

★Lychakivske Cemetery CEMETERY

(Личаківське кладовище; 032-275 5415; www.lviv-lychakiv.ukrain.travel; vul Pekarska; admission 20uah; 9am-6pm) Don't leave town until you've seen this amazing cemetery, only a short ride on tram 7 from the centre. This is the Père Lachaise of Eastern Europe, with the same sort of overgrown grounds and Gothic aura as the famous Parisian necropolis (but containing less-well-known people). Laid out in the late 18th century, it's packed full of west Ukraine's great and good. Pride of place goes to the grave of revered nationalist poet Ivan Franko.

Ploshcha Rynok SQUARE

Lviv was declared a Unesco World Heritage Site in 1998, and this old market square lies at its heart. The square was progressively rebuilt after a major fire in the early 16th century destroyed the original. The 19th-century **Ratusha** (Town Hall) stands in the middle of the plaza, with fountains featuring Greek gods at each of its corners. Vista junkies can climb the 65m-high neo-Renaissance **tower** (admission 10uah; 9am-9pm Apr-Oct, to 6pm Nov-Mar). The ticket booth is on the 4th floor.

Latin Cathedral CATHEDRAL

(pl Katedralna 1; 7.30am-7pm, closed 2-3pm Mon-Fri) With various parts dating from between 1370 and 1480, this working cathedral is one of Lviv's most impressive churches. The exterior is most definitely Gothic while the heavily gilded interior, one of the city's highlights, has a more baroque feel, with colourfully wreathed pillars hoisting frescoed vaulting and mysterious side chapels

WORTH A TRIP

KAMYANETS-PODILSKY КАМ'ЯНЕЦЬ-ПОДІЛЬСЬКИЙ

The unique town of Kamyanets-Podilsky (K-P) stands out for its gorgeous castle backed by dramatic natural beauty. The name Kamyanets refers to the massive stone island created by a sharp bend in the river Smotrych, and the resulting verdant canyon rings a charming old town, Ukraine's best preserved.

Top billing goes to the **fortress** (adult/child 20/10uah; ⌚9am-8pm Tue-Sun, 9am-7pm Mon), one of the country's finest. The large structure is a mishmash of styles, but the overall impression is breathtaking. Scramble round the walls, turrets and dungeons then visit the fantastic museum, a nostalgic romp through the history of K-P and Ukraine over the last century.

The town's other must-see is the **Cathedral of Sts Peter & Paul** (vul Starobulvarna) in the Polish Market Sq. It features a 42m-high minaret topped by a golden statue of the Virgin Mary – K-P was where the Polish and Turkish empires collided.

As transport links are poor, you'll probably want to sleep over in K-P. The **Hotel 7 Days** (☎03849 690 69; http://7dniv.ua; vul Soborna 4; s/d from 290/480uah; ❄📶🏊) between the Old Town and the bus station has a swimming pool and 218 comfortable rooms. The most characterful place to eat is the folksy **Kafe Pid Bramoyu** (Кафе під брамою; vul Zamkova 1A; mains 15-45uah; ⌚9am-midnight), located in the 17th-century casemates, where mostly Ukrainian favourites populate the menu.

There are two or three buses per day from Lviv (130uah, seven hours) and three day buses plus several overnighters from Kyiv (200uah, seven to 11 hours). The express train from Kyiv is the quickest way to reach Kamyanets-Podilsky. It departs Kyiv at 4.48pm (108uah, seven hours) and arrives just before midnight. There's also at least one overnight sleeper service to and from Kyiv (166uah, 8½ hours).

glowing in candlelit half light. Services are in four languages including English.

Sleeping

★Old City Hostel HOSTEL €
(☎032 294 9644; www.oldcityhostel.lviv.ua; vul Beryndy 3; dm/d from 120/450uah; @📶) Occupying two floors of an elegantly fading tenement just steps from pl Rynok, this expertly run hostel with period features and views of the Shevchenko statue from the wrap-around balcony has long since established itself as the city's best. Frill-free dorms hold four to 16 beds, shower queues are unheard of, sturdy lockers keep your stuff safe and there's a well-endowed kitchen.

NTON HOTEL €€
(НТОН; ☎032 242 4959; www.hotelnton.lviv.ua; vul Shevchenka 154B; s/d from 300/420uah; ❄📶) Near the terminus of tram 7 in Lviv's western suburbs, this far-flung hotel on the road out to the Polish border may not seem too promising, but this fully renovated place is possibly Lviv's best deal. Rooms are spacious and well furnished, and contain little extras like kettles, sewing kits and hairdryers (yes, these *are* extras in Ukraine!).

★Astoria BOUTIQUE HOTEL €€€
(☎032 242 2701; www.astoriahotel.ua; vul Horodotska 15; r from 1250uah) A hotel since 1914, the Astoria was given a stylishly moody retrofit in 2013, sending it reeling back to the monochrome world of the 1930s. The seven floors are all marble and cast iron, weighty lacquered doors and hangar-style lighting. Rooms are art-deco studies in black and white and every shade in between. Breakfast is served in the superb restaurant.

Eating

★Dim Lehend UKRAINIAN €€
(Дім легенд; vul Staroyevreyska 48; mains 30-70uah; ⌚11am-2am) Dedicated to the city of Lviv, there's nothing dim about the 'House of Legends'. The five floors contain a library stuffed with Lviv-themed volumes, a room showing live webcam footage of Lviv's underground river, rooms dedicated to lions and cobblestones, and another featuring the city in sounds. The menu is limited to Ukrainian staples but coffee and desserts are excellent.

★Kupol CENTRAL EUROPEAN €€
(Купол; vul Chaykovskoho 37; mains 100-150uah; ⌚11am-9pm) One of the pretourism 'originals', this place is designed to feel like stepping

back in time – to 1938 in particular, 'the year before civilisation ended' (ie before the Soviets rolled in). The olde-worlde interior is lined with framed letters, ocean-liner ads, antique cutlery, hampers and other memorabilia, and the Polish/Austrian/Ukrainian food is tasty and served with style.

★ **Masonic Restaurant** EUROPEAN €€€
(pl Rynok 14; mains before discount 300-500uah; ⏲11am-2am) Ascend to the 2nd floor and open the door of apartment 8. You'll be accosted by an unshaven bachelor type, who eventually opens the door to reveal a fancy beamed restaurant full of Masonic symbols and portraits. Advertised as Galicia's most expensive restaurant, prices are 10 times higher than normal...so make sure you pick up a 90% discount card at Dim Lehend or Livy Bereh beforehand.

The food, by the way, is great and the beer and *kvas* (gingery, beer-like soft drink) come in crystal vases. The toilet is a candlelit Masonic throne. Ukraine's weirdest restaurant experience? Probably.

Drinking & Nightlife

Lvivska Kopalnya Kavy CAFE
(pl Rynok 10; ⏲8am-11pm; 📶) Lviv is Ukraine's undisputed coffee capital and the 'Lviv Coffee Mine' is where the stratum of arabica is excavated by the local colliers from deep beneath pl Rynok. You can tour the mine or just sample the heart-pumping end product at tables as dark as the brews inside, or out on the courtyard beneath old timber balconies.

Information

Tourist Information Centre (☎032 254 6079; www.touristinfo.lviv.ua; pl Rynok 1, Ratusha; ⏲10am-8pm Mon-Fri, to 7pm Sat, to 6pm Sun May-Sep, shorter hours Oct-Apr) Ukraine's best tourist information centre. Branches at the airport (☎067 673 9194; ⏲10am-8pm Mon-Fri, to 7pm Sat, to 6pm Sun May-Sep, shorter hours Oct-Apr) and the train station (☎032 226 2005; Ticket Hall; ⏲10am-8pm Mon-Fri, to 7pm Sat, to 6pm Sun May-Sep, shorter hours Oct-Apr).

Getting There & Away

AIR

Around 7km southwest of the centre, Lviv's **airport** (LWO; www.airport.lviv.ua) has flights to Kyiv (two daily). Book through **Kiy Avia** (☎032 255 3263; www.kiyavia.com; vul Hnyatuka 20; ⏲8am-8pm Mon-Fri, 9am-5pm Sat, 10am-3pm Sun).

There are international flights to/from Vienna, Munich, Warsaw, İstanbul, Venice, Naples, Milan and Moscow.

BUS

Take trolleybus 25 to the **main bus station** (Holovny Avtovokzal; vul Stryska) 8km south of the centre.

There are overnight services to Kyiv (210uah, nine hours, four daily) and daytime buses to Kamyanets-Podilsky (130uah, seven hours, two or three daily).

TRAIN

The quickest way to Kyiv is on the Intercity+ express (260uah, five hours, one daily) departing early morning. There are also cheaper overnight and daytime passenger trains (200uah to 250uah, eight to 10 hours).

Buy tickets from the station or city centre **train ticket office** (Залізничні квиткові каси; vul Hnatyuka 20; ⏲8am-2pm & 3-8pm Mon-Sat, to 6pm Sun).

Getting Around

From the train station, take tram 1, 6 or 9 to the centre. Trolleybus 9 goes to/from the university to the airport. Bus 48 also runs to the airport from pr Shevchenka.

SURVIVAL GUIDE

Directory A–Z

ACCOMMODATION

Ukraine has hundreds of hostels with, Lviv and Kyiv boasting tens each. There's also a bewildering array of hotel and room types from Soviet-era budget crash pads to 'six-star' overpriced luxury.

COUNTRY FACTS

Area 603,628 sq km

Capital Kyiv

Country Code ☎380

Currency Hryvnya (uah)

Emergency ☎112

Language Ukrainian, Russian

Money ATMs are common; credit cards widely accepted

Population 44.6 million

Visas Not required for EU, UK, US and Canadian citizens for stays up to 90 days

Everything in between can be hit and miss, and there are no national standards to follow.

Booking ahead isn't normally essential except around New Year. Accommodation is the single biggest expense in Ukraine, but with the virtual collapse of the hryvnya rooms are very affordable.

BUSINESS HOURS

Banks 9am to 5pm

Restaurants noon to 11pm

Shops 9am to 6pm, to 8pm or 9pm in cities

Sights 9am to 5pm or 6pm, closed at least one day a week

CUSTOMS REGULATIONS

You are allowed to bring in up to US$10,000, 1L of spirits, 2L of wine, 5L of beer, 200 cigarettes or 250g of tobacco, and gifts up to the value of €200.

GAY & LESBIAN TRAVELLERS

Ukraine is generally more tolerant of homosexuality than Russia. Homosexuality is legal, but attitudes vary across the country. Useful gay websites include www.gayua.com, www.gay.org.ua and www.gaylvov.at.ua.

INTERNET ACCESS

Most hotels offer free wi-fi and free hotspots are much more common than in Western Europe. Many restaurants and cafes have wi-fi. Internet cafes are not as common as they once were.

INTERNET RESOURCES

Brama (www.brama.com)

Infoukes (www.infoukes.com)

Ukraine.com (www.ukraine.com)

MONEY

US dollars, the euro and Russian roubles are the easiest currencies to exchange. Damaged or marked notes may not be accepted. Credit cards are increasingly accepted everywhere, however, Ukraine remains primarily a cash economy.

- Coins: one, five, 10, 25 and 50 kopecks and one hryvnya.
- Notes: one, two, five, 10, 20, 50, 100, 200 and 500 hryvnya.
- Hryvnya are virtually impossible to buy pre-departure.
- The currency saw huge devaluation in 2014.
- ATMs are common.

EATING PRICE RANGES

The following price indicators are for a main meal:

€ less than 50uah

€€ 50uah to 150uah

€€€ more than 150uah

SLEEPING PRICE RANGES

The following price indicators apply for a high-season double room:

€ less than 400uah

€€ 400uah to 800uah

€€€ more than 800uah

POST

Ukrposhta (www.ukrposhta.com) runs Ukraine's postal system. Sending a postcard or a letter up to 20g costs the equivalent of a US dollar to anywhere abroad. Mail takes about a week to Europe and around two weeks to the USA or Australia.

PUBLIC HOLIDAYS

New Year's Day 1 January

Orthodox Christmas 7 January

International Women's Day 8 March

Orthodox Easter April

Labour Day 1–2 May

Victory Day (1945) 9 May

Orthodox Pentecost June

Constitution Day 28 June

Independence Day (1991) 24 August

SAFE TRAVEL

Despite the recent conflict, western Ukraine and Kyiv remain safe. Donetsk, Luhansk and Crimea should be avoided, and care should be taken when visiting Kharkiv and Odesa.

TELEPHONE

All numbers in Ukraine start with ☎0 and there are no pre-dialling codes.

Ukraine's country code is ☎0038. To call Kyiv from overseas, dial ☎00 38 044 and the subscriber number.

To call internationally from Ukraine, dial ☎0, wait for a second tone, then dial ☎0 again, followed by the country code, city code and number.

European GSM phones work in Ukraine. Local SIM cards work out much cheaper if making several calls.

VISAS

Tourist visas for stays of less than 90 days aren't required by citizens of the EU/EEA, Canada, the USA and Japan. Australians and New Zealanders need a visa.

Getting There & Away

The majority of visitors to Ukraine fly – generally to Kyiv. Flights, tours and rail tickets can be booked online through Lonely Planet (www.lonelyplanet.com/bookings).

ESSENTIAL FOOD & DRINK

'Borshch and bread – that's our food.' With this national saying, Ukrainians admit that theirs is a cuisine of comfort, full of hearty, mild dishes designed for fierce winters rather than one of gastronomic zing. Here are some of the Ukrainian staples you are certain to find on restaurant menus:

- **Borshch** The national soup made with beetroot, pork fat and herbs.
- **Salo** Basically raw pig fat, cut into slices and eaten with bread.
- **Varenyky** Pasta pockets filled with everything from mashed potato to sour cherries.
- **Kasha** Buckwheat swimming in milk and served for breakfast.
- **Vodka** Also known as *horilka*, it accompanies every celebration and get-together – in copious amounts.

AIR

Only a couple of low-cost airlines fly to Ukraine.

Most international flights use Kyiv's main airport, **Boryspil International Airport** (☎044 393 4371; www.kbp.aero). **Lviv International Airport** (LWO; ☎032 229 8112; www.lwo.aero) also has a few international connections.

Ukraine International Airlines (PS; www.flyuia.com) is Ukraine's flag carrier.

LAND

Ukraine is well linked to its neighbours, particularly Russia and Belarus, with whom it shares the former Soviet rail system. Kyiv is connected by bus or train to Moscow, St Petersburg, Minsk, Warsaw and Budapest, as well as other Eastern European capitals. Lviv is the biggest city servicing the Polish border – it's possible to take a budget flight to Poland then cross the border to Lviv by bus or train.

Border Crossings

The Poland–Ukraine and Romania–Ukraine borders are popular smuggling routes, hence the thorough customs checks. Expect customs personnel to scrutinise your papers and search your vehicle.

Bus

Buses are slower, less frequent and less comfortable than trains for long-distance travel.

Car & Motorcycle

To bring your own vehicle into the country, you'll need your original registration papers and a 'Green Card' International Motor Insurance Certificate.

Getting Around

AIR

Flying is an expensive way of getting around. Overnight train is cheaper and more reliable.

Kiy Avia (www.kiyavia.com) has branches across the country.

BUS

Buses serve every city and small town, but are best for short trips (three hours or less). Tickets resembling shop-till receipts are sold at bus stations up to departure.

Marshrutky are minibuses that ply bus routes but stop anywhere on request. They're most common in big cities but also serve intercity routes. Fares are usually slightly higher; journey times shorter.

LOCAL TRANSPORT

Trolleybus, tram, bus and metro run in Kyiv. A ticket for one ride by bus, tram or trolleybus costs 1.50uah to 2uah. There are no return, transfer, timed or day tickets available. Tickets must be punched on board (or ripped by the conductor).

Metro barriers take plastic tokens *(zhetony)*, sold at counters inside stations.

TRAIN

For long journeys, overnight train is best. **Ukrainian Railways** (www.uz.gov.ua) features timetables and an online booking facility.

All seating classes have assigned places. Carriage *(vahon)* and bunk *(mesto)* numbers are printed on tickets.

Lyuks or SV *Spalny vahon* (SV) – 1st-class (sleeper) compartment for two people.

Kupe 2nd-class sleeper compartment for four people. Train prices quoted here are for *kupe*.

Platskart 50-bunk 3rd-class open-carriage sleeper.

C1 and C2 First/second-class on fast Intercity+ services.

Few Ukrainian Railways employees speak English; have a local write down your destination, date, time, train number etc in Cyrillic. At Kyiv train station there are dedicated windows (8 and 9) for foreigners.

Survival Guide

Directory A–Z

Accommodation

Europe offers the fullest possible range of accommodation for all budgets. In this guide we've listed reviews by budget, then author preference.

Unless otherwise stated in individual reviews or in country directories, all hotels and hostels in this book include a private bathroom and do not include breakfast.

Price Ranges

Rates are for high season. Prices often drop at other times by as much as 50%. High season in ski resorts is usually between Christmas and New Year and around the February to March winter holidays.

Each sleeping option has an indicative price category (from € to €€€) – these correspond to the price of the room relative to that country's price breakdown.

Reservations

During peak holiday periods, particularly Easter, summer and Christmas – and any time of year in popular destinations such as London, Paris and Rome – it's wise to book ahead. Most places can be reserved online. Always try to book directly with the establishment; this means you're paying just for your room, with no surcharge going to a hostel- or hotel-booking website.

B&Bs & Guesthouses

Guesthouses (pension, Gasthaus, *chambre d'hôte* etc) and B&Bs (bed and breakfasts) offer greater comfort than hostels for a marginally higher price. Most are simple affairs, normally with shared bathrooms.

In some destinations, particularly in Eastern Europe, locals wait in train stations touting rented rooms. Just be sure such accommodation isn't in a far-flung suburb that requires an expensive taxi ride to and from town. Confirm the price before agreeing to rent a room and remember that it's unwise to leave valuables in your room when you go out.

B&Bs in the UK and Ireland often aren't really budget accommodation – even the lowliest tend to have midrange prices, and there is a new generation of 'designer' B&Bs which are positively top end.

Camping

Most camping grounds are some distance from city centres; we list easily accessible camping grounds only, or include sites where it's common for travellers to bed down en masse under the stars (for example, on some Greek islands).

National tourist offices provide lists of camping grounds and camping organisations. Also see www.coolcamping.co.uk for details on prime campsites across Europe.

There will usually be a charge per tent or site, per person and per vehicle. In busy areas and in busy seasons, it's sometimes necessary to book.

Camping other than at designated grounds is difficult in Western Europe, because it's hard to find a suitably private spot.

Camping is also illegal without the permission of the local authorities (the police or local council office) or the landowner. Don't be shy about asking; you might be pleasantly surprised.

In some countries, such as Austria, the UK, France and Germany, free camping is illegal on all but private land, and in Greece it's illegal altogether but not enforced. This doesn't prevent hikers from occasionally pitching their tent, and you'll usually get away with it if you have

BOOK YOUR STAY ONLINE

For more accommodation reviews by Lonely Planet authors, check out www.lonelyplanet.com/hotels/. You'll find independent reviews, as well as recommendations on the best places to stay. Best of all, you can book online.

STAY FOR FREE

Online hospitality clubs, linking travellers with thousands of global residents who'll let you occupy their couch or spare room – and sometimes show you around town – for free, include:

Couchsurfing (www.couchsurfing.com)

Global Freeloaders (www.globalfreeloaders.com)

Hospitality Club (www.hospitalityclub.org)

5W (www.womenwelcomewomen.org.uk)

Check the rules of each organisation. Always let friends and family know where you're staying and carry your mobile phone with you.

a small tent, are discreet, stay just one or two nights, decamp during the day and don't light a fire or leave rubbish. At worst, you'll be woken by the police and asked to move on.

In Eastern Europe, free camping is more widespread.

Homestays & Farmstays

You needn't volunteer on a farm to sleep on it. In Switzerland and Germany, there's the opportunity to sleep in barns or 'hay hotels'. Farmers provide cotton undersheets (to avoid straw pricks) and woolly blankets for extra warmth, but guests need their own sleeping bag and torch. For further details, visit **Abenteuer im Stroh** (www.schlaf-im-stroh.ch) and **Hay Hotels** (www.heuhotel.de).

Hostels

There's a vast variation in hostel standards across Europe.

HI Hostels (those affiliated to Hostelling International, www.hihostels.com), usually offer the cheapest (secure) roof over your head in Europe and you don't have to be particularly young to use them. Only southern German hostels enforce a strict age limit of 26 years. That said, if you're over 26 you'll frequently pay a small surcharge (usually about €3) to stay in an official hostel.

Hostel rules vary per facility and country, but some ask that guests vacate the rooms for cleaning purposes or impose a curfew. Most offer a complimentary breakfast, although the quality of this varies.

You need to be a YHA or HI member to use HI-affiliated hostels, but nonmembers can stay by paying a few extra euros, which will be set against future membership. After sufficient nights (usually six), you automatically become a member. To join, ask at any hostel or contact your national hostelling office, which you'll find on the HI website – where you can also make online bookings.

Europe has many private hostelling organisations and hundreds of unaffiliated backpacker hostels. These have fewer rules, more self-catering kitchens and fewer large, noisy school groups. Dorms in many private hostels can be mixed sex. If you aren't happy to share mixed dorms, be sure to ask when you book.

Hotels

Hotels are usually the most expensive accommodation option, though at their lower end there is little to differentiate them from guesthouses or even hostels.

Cheap hotels around bus and train stations can be convenient for late-night or early-morning arrivals and departures, but some are also unofficial brothels or just downright sleazy. Check the room beforehand and make sure you're clear on price and what it covers.

Discounts for longer stays are usually possible and hotel owners in southern Europe *might* be open to a little bargaining if times are slack. In many countries it's common for business hotels (usually more than two stars) to slash their rates by up to 40% on Friday and Saturday nights.

University Accommodation

Some university towns rent out their student accommodation during the holiday periods. This is a popular practice in France, the UK and many Eastern European countries. University accommodation will sometimes be in single rooms (although it's more commonly in doubles or triples) and might have cooking facilities. For details ask at individual colleges or universities, at student information offices or local tourist offices.

Customs Regulations

The European Union (EU) has a two-tier customs system: one for goods bought duty-free to import to or export from the EU, and one for goods bought in another EU country where taxes and duties have already been paid.

- Entering or leaving the EU, you are allowed to carry duty-free: 200 cigarettes, 50 cigars or 250g of tobacco; 2L of still wine plus 1L of spirits over 22% alcohol or another 2L of wine (sparkling or otherwise); 50g of perfume, 250cc of eau de toilette.
- Travelling from one EU country to another, the duty-paid limits are: 800 cigarettes, 200 cigars, 1kg of tobacco, 10L of spirits, 20L of fortified wine, 90L of wine (of which not more than 60L is sparkling) and 110L of beer.
- Non-EU countries often have different regulations and many countries forbid the export of antiquities and cultural treasures.

Discount Cards

Camping Cards

The Camping Card International (CCI; www.campingcardinternational.com) is an ID that can be used instead of a passport when checking into a camping ground. Many camping grounds offer a small discount if you sign in with one and it includes third-party insurance.

Rail Passes

If you plan to visit more than a few countries, or one or two countries in-depth, you might save money with a rail pass.

Student Cards

The International Student Identity Card (www.isic.org), available for students, teachers and under-26s, offers thousands of worldwide discounts on transport, museum entry, youth hostels and even some restaurants. Apply for the cards online or via issuing offices, which include **STA Travel** (www.statravel.com).

For under-26s, there's also the **Euro<26** (www.euro26.org). Many countries have raised the age limit for this card to under 30.

Electricity

Europe generally runs on 220V, 50Hz AC, but there are exceptions. The UK runs on 230/240V AC, and some old buildings in Italy and Spain have 125V (or even 110V in Spain). The continent is moving towards a 230V standard. If your home country has a vastly different voltage you will need a transformer for delicate and important appliances.

The UK and Ireland use three-pin square plugs. Most of Europe uses the 'europlug' with two round pins. Greece, Italy and Switzerland use a third round pin in a way that the two-pin plug usually – but not always in Italy and Switzerland – fits. Buy an adaptor before leaving home; those on sale in Europe generally go the other way, but ones for visitors to Europe are also available – airports are always a good place to buy them.

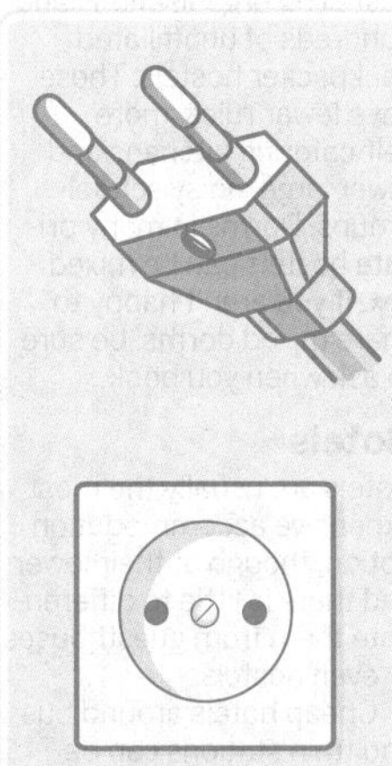

230v/50hz

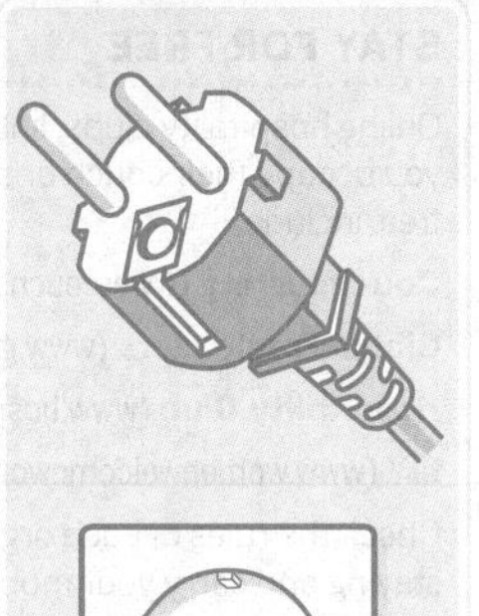

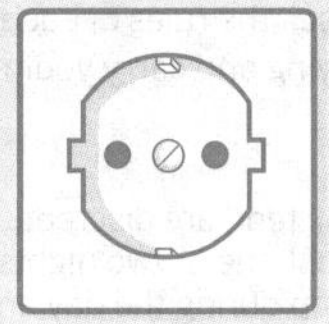

230v/50hz

230V/50Hz

Embassies & Consulates

Generally speaking, your embassy won't be much help in emergencies if the trouble you're in is remotely your own fault. Remember, you're bound by the laws of the country you're in.

In genuine emergencies you might get some assistance, but only if other channels have been exhausted. For example, if you need to get home urgently, a free ticket is exceedingly unlikely – the embassy would expect you to have insurance. If you have all your money and documents stolen, it might assist with getting a new passport, but a loan for onward travel will be out of the question.

Gay & Lesbian Travellers

Across Western Europe you'll find very liberal attitudes towards homosexuality. London, Paris, Berlin, Munich, Amsterdam, Madrid and Lisbon have thriving gay communities and pride events. The Greek islands of Mykonos and Lesvos are popular gay beach destinations. Gran Canaria and Ibiza in Spain are big centres for both gay clubbing and beach holidays.

Eastern Europe, and in particular Russia, tends to be far less progressive. Outside the big cities, attitudes become more conservative and discretion is advised, particularly in Turkey and most parts of Eastern Europe.

Health

Good health care is readily available in Western Europe and, for minor illnesses, pharmacists can give valuable advice and sell over-the-counter medication. They can also advise if you need specialised help and point you in the right direction. The standard of dental care is usually good.

While the situation in Eastern Europe has been improving since the EU accession of many countries, quality medical care is not always readily available outside major cities. Embassies, consulates and five-star hotels can usually recommend doctors or clinics.

No jabs are necessary for Europe. However, the World Health Organization (WHO) recommends that all travellers be covered for diphtheria, tetanus, measles, mumps, rubella and polio, regardless of their destination. Since most vaccines don't produce immunity until at least two weeks after they're given, visit a physician at least six weeks before departure.

Tap water is generally safe to drink in Western Europe. However, bottled water is recommended in most of Eastern Europe, and is a must in some countries, including Russia and Ukraine, where giardia can be a problem. Do not drink water from rivers or lakes as it may contain bacteria or viruses.

Condoms are widely available in Europe, however emergency contraception may not be, so take the necessary precautions.

HEALTH RESOURCES

The **World Health Organization** (www.who.int/ith/en) publishes the annually revised, free online book *International Travel and Health*. **MD Travel Health** (www.mdtravelhealth.com) provides up-to-date travel-health recommendations for every country.

It's usually a good idea to consult your government's website before departure, if one is available:

Australia (www.smartraveller.gov.au)

Canada (www.phac-aspc.gc.ca)

UK (www.gov.uk/foreign-travel-advice)

USA (www.cdc.gov/travel)

Insurance

It's foolhardy to travel without insurance to cover theft, loss and medical problems. There are a wide variety of policies, so check the small print.

Some policies specifically exclude 'dangerous activities', which can include scuba diving, motorcycling, winter sports, adventure sports or even hiking.

Check that the policy covers ambulances or an emergency flight home.

Worldwide travel insurance is available online at lonelyplanet.com/travel-insurance. You can buy, extend and claim online anytime – even if you're already on the road.

Internet Access

Internet access varies enormously across Europe. In most places, you'll be able to find wireless (wi-fi, also called WLAN in some countries), although whether it's free varies greatly.

Where the wi-fi icon (📶) appears, it means that the establishment offers free wi-fi that you can access immediately, or by asking for the access code from staff.

Access is generally straightforward, although a few tips are in order. If you can't find the @ symbol on a keyboard, try Alt Gr + 2, or Alt Gr + Q. Watch out for German and some Balkans keyboards, which reverse the Z and the Y positions. Using a French keyboard is an art unto itself.

Where necessary in relevant countries, click on the language prompt in the bottom right-hand corner of the screen or hit Ctrl + Shift to switch between the Cyrillic and Latin alphabets.

USEFUL WEB RESOURCES

Blue Flag (www.blueflag.org) Ecolabel for sustainably developed beaches and marinas.

Budget Traveller's Guide to Sleeping in Airports (www.sleepinginairports.net) Funny and useful resource for backpackers flying stand-by.

Currency Conversions (www.xe.com) Up-to-the-second exchange rates for hundreds of currencies.

Guide for Europe (www.guideforeurope.com) Has a handy hostel review page posted by visitors.

Lonely Planet (www.lonelyplanet.com/thorntree) On Lonely Planet's message board you can usually get your travel questions answered by fellow travellers in a matter of hours.

Money Saving Expert (www.moneysavingexpert.com) Excellent tips on the best UK travel insurance, mobile phones and bank cards to use abroad. The flight-checker facility shows the latest cheap flights available.

Legal Matters

You can generally purchase alcohol (beer and wine) from between 16 and 18 years of age (usually 18 for spirits), but if in doubt, ask. Although you can drive at 17 or 18, you might not be able to hire a car until you're 25.

Cigarette-smoking bans in bars and restaurants and other public places are increasingly common across Europe so ask before lighting up.

Drugs are often quite openly available in Europe, but that doesn't mean they're legal. The Netherlands is most famed for its liberal attitudes, with coffeeshops openly selling cannabis even though the drug is *not* technically legal. However, a blind eye is generally turned. The possession and purchase of small amounts (5g) of 'soft drugs' (ie marijuana and hashish) is allowed and users won't be prosecuted for smoking or carrying this amount. Don't take this relaxed attitude as an invitation to buy harder drugs; if you get caught, you'll be punished. Since 2008, magic mushrooms have been banned in the Netherlands.

In Belgium, the possession of up to 5g of cannabis is legal, but selling the drug isn't, so if you get caught at the point of sale, you could be in trouble. Switzerland has also decriminalised possession of up to 10g of marijuana.

In Portugal, the possession of *all* drugs has been decriminalised. Once again, however, selling is illegal.

Getting caught with drugs in other parts of Europe, particularly countries such as Turkey and Russia, can lead to imprisonment.

If in any doubt, err on the side of caution, and don't even think about taking drugs across international borders.

Maps

Tourist offices usually provide free but fairly basic maps.

Road atlases are essential if you're driving or cycling. Leading brands are Freytag & Berndt, Hallwag, Kümmerly + Frey, and Michelin.

Maps published by European automobile associations, such as Britain's **AA** (www.theaa.co.uk) and Germany's **ADAC** (www.adac.de), are usually excellent, and sometimes free if membership of your local association gives you reciprocal rights.

Money

The euro, used in 19 EU states as well as several other non-EU states, is made up of 100 cents. Notes come in denominations of €5, €10, €20, €50, €100, €200 and €500 euros, though any notes above €50 are rarely used on a daily basis. Coins come in 1c, 2c, 5c, 10c, 20c, 50c, €1 and €2.

Denmark, the UK and Sweden have held out against adopting the euro for political reasons, while non-EU nations, such as Albania, Belarus, Norway, Russia, Switzerland, Turkey and Ukraine, also have their own currencies.

ATMs

Across major European towns and cities international ATMs are common, but you should always have a back-up option, as there can be glitches. In some remote areas, ATMs might be scarce, too.

Much of Western Europe now uses a chip-and-pin system for added security. You will have problems if you don't have a four-digit PIN number and might have difficulties if your card doesn't have a metallic chip. Check with your bank.

Always cover the keypad when entering your PIN and make sure there are no unusual devices attached to the machine, which can copy your card's details or cause it to stick in the machine. If your card disappears and the screen goes blank before you've even entered your PIN, don't enter it – especially if a 'helpful' bystander tells you to do so. If you can't retrieve your card, call your bank's emergency number, if you can, before leaving the ATM.

Cash

It's a good idea to bring some local currency in cash, if only to cover yourself until you get to an exchange facility or find an ATM. The equivalent of €150 should usually be enough. Some extra cash in an easily exchanged currency is also a good idea, especially in Eastern Europe.

Credit Cards

Visa and MasterCard/Eurocard are more widely accepted in Europe than Amex and Diners Club; Visa (sometimes called Carte Bleue) is particularly strong in France and Spain.

There are, however, regional differences in the general acceptability of credit cards; in Germany for example, it's rare for restaurants to take credit cards. Cards are not widely accepted off the beaten track.

To reduce the risk of fraud, always keep your card in view when making transactions; for example, in restaurants that do accept cards, pay as you leave, following your card to the till. Keep transaction records and either check your statements when you return home, or check your account online while still on the road.

Letting your credit-card company know roughly where you're going lessens the chance of fraud – or of your bank cutting off the card when it sees (your) unusual spending.

Debit Cards

It's always worthwhile having a Maestro-compatible debit card, which differs from a credit card in deducting money straight from your bank account. Check with your bank or MasterCard (Maestro's parent) for compatibility.

Exchanging Money

Euros, US dollars and UK pounds are the easiest currencies to exchange. You may have trouble exchanging some lesser-known ones at small banks.

Importing or exporting some currencies is restricted or banned, so try to get rid of any local currency before you leave. Exchange your Scottish pounds before leaving the UK; nobody outside Britain will touch them.

Most airports, central train stations, big hotels and many border posts have banking facilities outside regular business hours, at times on a 24-hour basis. Post offices in Europe often perform banking tasks, tend to open longer hours and outnumber banks in remote places. While they always exchange cash, they might baulk at handling travellers cheques not in the local currency.

The best exchange rates are usually at banks. *Bureaux de change* usually – but not always – offer worse rates or charge higher commissions. Hotels and airports are almost always the worst places to change money.

International Transfers

International bank transfers are good for secure one-off movements of large amounts of money, but they might take three to five days and there will be a fee (about £25 in the UK, for example). Be sure to specify the name of the bank, plus the sort code and address of the branch where you'd like to pick up your money.

In an emergency it's quicker but more costly to have money wired via an **Amex office** (www.americanexpress.com), **Western Union** (www.westernunion.com) or **MoneyGram** (www.moneygram.com).

Taxes & Refunds

When non-EU residents spend more than a certain amount (around €75) they can usually reclaim any sales tax when leaving the country.

Making a tax-back claim is straightforward. First, make sure the shop offers duty-free sales (often a sign will be displayed reading 'Tax-Free Shopping'). When making your purchase, ask the shop attendant for a tax-refund voucher, filled in with the correct amount and the date. This can be used to claim a refund directly at international airports, or stamped at ferry ports or border crossings and mailed back for a refund.

Tipping & Bargaining

Tipping has become more complicated, with 'service charges' increasingly added to bills. In theory this means you're not obliged to tip. In practice that money often doesn't go to the server and they might make it clear they still expect a gratuity. Don't pay twice. If the service charge is optional, remove it from the bill and pay a tip. If the service charge is not optional, don't tip.

Generally, waitstaff in Western Europe tend to be paid decent wages. Bargaining isn't common in much of Europe, but is known in and around the Mediterranean. In Turkey it's virtually a way of life.

Travellers Cheques

It's become more difficult to find places that cash travellers cheques. In parts of Eastern Europe only a few banks handle them, and the process can be quite bureaucratic and costly.

That said, having a few cheques is a good back-up. If they're stolen you can claim a refund, provided you have a separate record of cheque numbers.

Amex and Thomas Cook are reliable brands of travellers cheques, while cheques in US dollars, euros or British pounds are the easiest to cash. When changing them ask about fees and commissions as well as the exchange rate.

Post

From major European centres, airmail typically takes about five days to North America and about a week to Australasian destinations, although mail from such countries as Albania or Russia is much slower.

Courier services such as DHL are best for essential deliveries.

Safe Travel

Travelling in Europe is usually very safe. The following outlines a range of general guidelines.

Discrimination

In some parts of Europe travellers of African, Arab or Asian descent may encounter discriminatory attitudes that are unrelated to them personally. In rural areas travellers whose skin colour marks them out as foreigners might experience unwanted attention.

Attitudes vary from country to country. People tend to be more accepting in cities than in the country. Race is also less of an issue in Western Europe than in parts of the former Eastern Bloc. For example, there has been a spate of racially motivated attacks in St Petersburg and other parts of Russia in recent years.

Druggings

Although rare, some drugging of travellers does occur in Europe. Travellers are especially vulnerable on trains and buses where a new 'friend' may offer you food or a drink that will knock you out, giving them time to steal your belongings.

Gassings have also been reported on a handful of overnight international trains. The best protection is to lock the door of your compartment (use your own lock if there isn't one) and to lock your bags to luggage racks, preferably with a sturdy combination cable.

If you can help it, never sleep alone in a train compartment.

Pickpockets & Thieves

Theft is definitely a problem in parts of Europe and you have to be aware of unscrupulous fellow travellers. The key is to be sensible with your possessions.

- Don't store valuables in train-station lockers or luggage-storage counters and be careful about people who offer to help you operate a locker. Also be vigilant if someone offers to carry your luggage: they might carry it away altogether.
- Don't leave valuables in your car, on train seats or in your room. When going out, don't flaunt cameras, laptops and other expensive electronic goods.
- Carry a small day pack, as shoulder bags are an open invitation for snatch-thieves. Consider using small zipper locks on your packs.
- Pickpockets are most active in dense crowds, especially in busy train stations and on public transport during peak hours. Be careful in these situations.
- Spread valuables, cash and cards around your body or in different bags.
- A money belt with your essentials (passport, cash, credit cards, airline tickets) is usually a good idea. However, so you needn't delve into it in public, carry a wallet with a day's worth of cash.
- Having your passport stolen is less of a disaster if you've recorded the number and issue date or, even better, photocopied the relevant data pages. You can also scan them and email them to yourself. If you lose your passport, notify the police immediately to get a statement and contact your nearest consulate.
- Record the serial numbers of travellers cheques and carry photocopies of your credit cards, airline tickets and other travel documents.

Scams

Most scams involve distracting you – either by kids running up to you, someone asking for directions or spilling something on you – while another person steals your wallet. Be alert in such situations.

In some countries, especially in Eastern Europe, you may encounter people claiming to be from the tourist police, the special police, the super-secret police, whatever. Unless they're wearing a uniform and have good reason for accosting you, treat their claims with suspicion.

Needless to say, never show your passport or cash to anyone on the street. Simply walk away. If someone flashes a badge, offer to accompany them to the nearest police station.

Unrest & Terrorism

Civil unrest and terrorist bombings are rare in Europe, but they do occur. Attacks by ETA (the Basque separatist group in Spain and France) and attacks by Muslim extremists in the UK, France, Denmark, Spain and Russia have all occurred in recent years. Keep an eye on the news and avoid areas where any flare-up seems likely.

Telephone

If your mobile phone is European, it's often perfectly feasible to use it on roaming throughout the Continent.

If you're coming from outside Europe, it's usually worth buying a prepaid local SIM in one European country. Even if you're not staying there long, calls across Europe will still be cheaper if they're not routed via your home country, and the prepaid card will enable you to keep a limit on your spending. In several countries you need your passport to buy a SIM card.

In order to use other SIM cards in your phone, you'll need to have your handset unlocked by your home provider. Even if your phone is locked, you can use apps such as 'whatsapp' to send free text messages internationally wherever you have wi-fi access, or Skype to make free international calls whenever you're online.

Europe uses the GSM 900 network, which also covers Australia and New Zealand, but is not compatible with the North American GSM 1900 or the totally different system in Japan and South Korea. If you have a GSM phone, check with your service provider about using it in Europe. You'll need international roaming, but this is usually free to enable.

You can call abroad from almost any phone box in Europe. Public telephones accepting phonecards (available from post offices, telephone centres, newsstands or retail outlets) are virtually the norm now; coin-operated phones are rare if not impossible to find.

Without a phonecard, you can ring from a telephone booth inside a post office or telephone centre and settle your bill at the counter. Reverse-charge (collect) calls are often possible. From many countries the Country Direct system lets you phone home by billing the long-distance carrier you use at home. These numbers can often be dialled from public phones without even inserting a phonecard.

EMERGENCY NUMBERS

The phone number ☎112 can be dialled free for emergencies in all EU states. See individual countries for country-specific emergency numbers.

Time

Europe is divided into four time zones. From west to east these are:

UTC (Britain, Ireland, Portugal) GMT (GMT+1 in summer)

CET (the majority of European countries) GMT+1 (GMT+2 in summer)

EET (Greece, Turkey, Bulgaria, Romania, Moldova, Ukraine, Belarus, Lithuania, Latvia, Estonia, Kaliningrad, Finland) GMT+2 (GMT+3 in summer)

MSK (Russia) GMT+3 (GMT+4 in summer)

At 9am in Britain it's 1am (GMT/UTC minus eight hours) on the US west coast, 4am (GMT/UTC minus five hours) on the US east coast, 10am in Paris and Prague, 11am in Athens, midday in Moscow, and 7pm (GMT/UTC plus 10 hours) in Sydney.

In most European countries, clocks are put forward one hour for daylight-saving time on the last Sunday in March, and turned back again on the last Sunday in October.

Toilets

Many public toilets require a small fee either deposited in a box or given to the attendant. Sit-down toilets are the rule in the vast majority of places. Squat toilets can still be found in rural areas, although they are definitely a dying breed.

Public-toilet provision remains changeable from city to city. If you can't find one, simply drop into a hotel or restaurant and ask to use theirs.

Tourist Information

Unless otherwise indicated, tourist offices are common and widespread, although their usefulness varies enormously from place to place.

Travellers with Disabilities

Cobbled medieval streets, 'classic' hotels, congested inner cities and underground subway systems make Europe a tricky destination for people with mobility impairments. However, the train facilities are good and some destinations boast new tram services or lifts to platforms. The following websites can help with specific details.

Accessible Europe (www.accessibleurope.com) Specialist European tours with van transport.

DisabledGo.com (www.disabledgo.com) Detailed access information to thousands of venues across the UK and Ireland.

Lonely Planet (www.lonelyplanet.com/thorntree) Share experiences on the Travellers With Disabilities branch of the Thorn Tree message board.

Mobility International Schweiz (www.mis-ch.ch) Good site (only partly in English) listing 'barrier-free' destinations in Switzerland and abroad, plus wheelchair-accessible hotels in Switzerland.

Mobility International USA (www.miusa.org) Publishes guides and advises travellers with disabilities on mobility issues.

Society for Accessible Travel & Hospitality (SATH; www.sath.org) Reams of information for travellers with disabilities.

Visas

- Citizens of the USA, Canada, Australia, New Zealand and the UK need only a valid passport to enter nearly all countries in Europe, including the entire EU.
- Belarus and Russia require a prearranged visa before arrival and even an

'invitation' from (or booking with) a tour operator or hotel. It's simpler and safer to obtain these visas before leaving home.

➡ Australians and New Zealanders need a visa for both Ukraine and Moldova.

➡ Transit visas are usually cheaper than tourist or business visas but they allow only a very short stay (one to five days) and can be difficult to extend.

➡ All visas have a 'use-by' date and you'll be refused entry afterwards. In some cases it's easier to get visas as you go along, rather than arranging them all beforehand. Carry spare passport photos (you may need from one to four every time you apply for a visa).

➡ Visas to neighbouring countries are usually issued immediately by consulates in Eastern Europe, although some may levy a hefty surcharge for 'express service'.

➡ Consulates are generally open weekday mornings (if there's both an embassy and a consulate, you want the consulate).

➡ Because regulations can change, double-check with the relevant embassy or consulate before travelling.

Volunteering

If you want to spend more time living and working in Europe, a short-term volunteer project might seem a good idea, say, teaching English in Poland or building a school in Turkey. However, most voluntary organisations levy high charges for airfares, food, lodging and recruitment (from about €250 to €800 per week), making such work impractical for most budget travellers. One exception is **WWOOF International** (www.wwoof.org) which helps link volunteers with organic farms in Germany, Slovenia, Czech Republic, Denmark, the UK, Austria and Switzerland. A small membership fee is required to join the national chapter but in exchange for your labour you'll receive free lodging and food.

For more information, Lonely Planet publishes *Volunteer: A Traveller's Guide to Making a Difference Around the World*.

Women Travellers

➡ Women may attract unwanted attention in Turkey, rural Spain and southern Italy, especially Sicily, where many men tend to engage in whistling and catcalling.

➡ Marriage is highly respected in southern Europe, and a wedding ring can help, along with talk about 'my husband'. Hitchhiking alone is not recommended anywhere.

THE SCHENGEN AREA

Twenty-six European countries are signatories to the Schengen Agreement, which has effectively dismantled internal border controls between them. They are Austria, Belgium, Czech Republic, Denmark, Estonia, Finland, France, Germany, Greece, Hungary, Iceland, Italy, Latvia, Liechtenstein, Lithuania, Luxembourg, Malta, the Netherlands, Norway, Poland, Portugal, Slovenia, Slovakia, Spain, Sweden and Switzerland.

Citizens of the US, Australia, New Zealand, Canada and the UK only need a valid passport to enter these countries. However, other nationals, including South Africans, can apply for a single visa – a Schengen visa – when travelling throughout this region.

Non-EU visitors (with or without a Schengen visa) should expect to be questioned, however perfunctorily, when first entering the region. However, later travel within the zone is much like a domestic trip, with no border controls.

If you need a Schengen visa, you must apply at the consulate or embassy of the country that's your main destination, or your point of entry. You may then stay up to a maximum of 90 days in the entire Schengen area within a six-month period. Once your visa has expired, you must leave the zone and may only re-enter after three months abroad. Shop around when choosing your point of entry, as visa prices may differ from country to country.

If you're a citizen of the US, Australia, New Zealand or Canada, you may stay visa-free a total of 90 days, during six months, within the entire Schengen region.

If you're planning a longer trip, you need to enquire directly with the relevant embassies or consulates as to whether you need a visa or visas. Your country might have bilateral agreements with individual Schengen countries allowing you to stay there longer than 90 days without a visa.

While the UK and Ireland are not part of the Schengen area, their citizens can stay indefinitely in other EU countries, only needing paperwork if they want to work long term or take up residency.

READING LIST

➡ *A Tramp Abroad* (1880; Mark Twain) Witty account of a 15-month tour by train and coach through central Europe in the 19th century.

➡ *A Time of Gifts* (1977), *Between the Woods and the Water* (1986) and *The Broken Road: Travels from Bulgaria to Mount Athos* (2013) Patrick Leigh Fermor's classic trilogy about his experiences at the age of 18 when he walked from Hoek van Holland to İstanbul in 1934.

➡ *Neither Here nor There: Travels in Europe* (1992; Bill Bryson) Twenty years after his 1970s European tour, Bryson retraces his steps with humour and acute observation.

➡ *Continental Drifter* (2000; Tim Moore) Musings on the origins of the 17th-century European Grand Tour and a modern day re-creation of it.

➡ *Rite of Passage: Tales of Backpacking 'round Europe* (2003; edited by Lisa Johnson) Stories by young travellers about conquering the Continent for the first time.

➡ Female readers have reported assaults at Turkish hotels with shared bathrooms, so women travelling to Turkey might want to consider a more expensive room with private bathroom.

➡ **Journeywoman** (www.journeywoman.com) maintains an online newsletter about solo female travels all over the world.

Work

EU citizens are allowed to work in any other EU country, but there can still be tiresome paperwork to complete. Other nationalities require special work permits that can be almost impossible to arrange, especially for temporary work. However, that doesn't prevent enterprising travellers from topping up their funds by working in the hotel or restaurant trades at beach or ski resorts, or teaching a little English – and they don't always have to do this illegally.

The UK, for example, issues special 'working holiday' visas to Commonwealth citizens who are aged between 17 and 30, valid for 12 months' work during two years (see www.ukvisas.gov.uk). Your national student-exchange organisation might be able to arrange temporary work permits to several countries.

If you have a grandparent or parent who was born in an EU country, you may have certain rights of residency or citizenship. Ask that country's embassy about dual citizenship and work permits. With citizenship, also ask about any obligations, such as military service and residency. Beware that your home country may not recognise dual citizenship.

Seasonal Work

➡ *Work Your Way Around the World* by Susan Griffith gives practical advice.

➡ Typical tourist jobs (picking grapes in France, working at a bar in Greece) often come with board and lodging, and the pay is essentially pocket money, but you'll have a good time partying with other travellers.

➡ Busking is fairly common in major European cities, but it's illegal in some parts of Switzerland and Austria. Crackdowns even occur in Belgium and Germany, where it has been tolerated in the past. Some other cities, including London, require permits and security checks. Talk to other buskers first.

EuroJobs (www.eurojobs.com) Links to hundreds of organisations looking to employ both non-Europeans (with the correct work permits) and Europeans.

Ski-jobs.co.uk (www.ski-jobs.co.uk) Mainly service jobs such as chalet hosts, bar staff and porters. Some linguistic skills required.

Natives (www.natives.co.uk) Summer and winter resort jobs, and various tips.

Picking Jobs (www.pickingjobs.com) Includes some tourism jobs.

Season Workers (www.seasonworkers.com) Best for ski-resort work and summer jobs, although it also has some childcare jobs.

Teaching English

Most schools prefer a bachelor's degree and a TEFL (Teaching English as a Foreign Language) certificate.

It is easier to find TEFL jobs in Eastern Europe than in Western Europe. The **British Council** (www.britishcouncil.org) can provide advice about training and job searches. Alternatively, try the big schools such as **Berlitz** (www.berlitz.com) and **Wall Street English** (www.wallstreetenglish.com).

Transport

GETTING THERE & AWAY

Flights, tours and rail tickets can be booked online at lonelyplanet.com/bookings/index.do.

Entering Europe

All countries require travellers to have a valid passport, preferably with at least six months between the time of departure from Europe and the passport's expiry date.

EU travellers from countries that issue national identity cards are increasingly using these to travel within the EU, although it's impossible to use these as the sole travel documents outside the EU.

Some countries require certain nationalities to buy a visa allowing entry between certain dates. Specifically, Belarus and Russia require all nationalities to obtain visas, while Australian and New Zealand travellers also need visas to enter Moldova and Ukraine. Turkey requires Australian, Canadian, South African, UK and US passport holders to buy a visa on arrival. Other nationalities may have additional requirements.

Air

Airports & Airlines

To save money, it's best to travel off-season. This means, if possible, avoid mid-June to early September, Easter, Christmas and school holidays.

Regardless of your ultimate destination, it's sometimes better to pick a recognised transport 'hub' as your initial port of entry, where high traffic volumes help keep prices down. The busiest, and therefore most obvious, hubs are London, Frankfurt, Paris and Rome. Sometimes tickets to Amsterdam, Athens, Barcelona, Berlin, İstanbul, Madrid and Vienna are worth checking out.

Long-haul airfares to Eastern Europe are rarely a bargain; you're usually better flying to a Western European hub and taking an onward budget-airline flight or train. The main hubs in Eastern Europe are Budapest, Moscow, Prague and Warsaw.

Most of the aforementioned gateway cities are also well serviced by low-cost carriers that fly to other parts of Europe.

Land

It's possible to reach Europe by various different train routes from Asia. Most common is the Trans-Siberian Railway, connecting Moscow to Siberia, the Russian Far East, Mongolia and China.

It is also possible to reach Moscow from several Central Asian states and İstanbul from Iran and Jordan. See www.seat61.com for more information about these adventurous routes.

CLIMATE CHANGE & TRAVEL

Every form of transport that relies on carbon-based fuel generates CO_2, the main cause of human-induced climate change. Modern travel is dependent on aeroplanes, which might use less fuel per kilometre per person than most cars but travel much greater distances. The altitude at which aircraft emit gases (including CO_2) and particles also contributes to their climate-change impact. Many websites offer 'carbon calculators' that allow people to estimate the carbon emissions generated by their journey and, for those who wish to do so, to offset the impact of the greenhouse gases emitted with contributions to portfolios of climate-friendly initiatives throughout the world. Lonely Planet offsets the carbon footprint of all staff and author travel.

Sea

There are numerous ferry routes between Europe and Africa, including links from Spain to Morocco, Italy and Malta to Tunisia, France to Morocco and France to Tunisia. Check out www.traghettiweb.it for comprehensive information on all Mediterranean ferries. Ferries are often filled to capacity in summer, especially to and from Tunisia, so book well in advance if you're taking a vehicle across.

Passenger freighters (typically carrying up to 12 passengers) aren't nearly as competitively priced as airlines. Journeys also take a long time. However, if you have your heart set on a transatlantic journey, **TravLtips Cruise and Freighter** (www.travltips.com) has information on freighter cruises.

GETTING AROUND

In most European countries, the train is the best option for internal transport. Check the websites of national rail systems as they often offer fare specials and national passes that are significantly cheaper than point-to-point tickets.

Air

Airlines

In recent years low-cost carriers have revolutionised European transport. Most budget airlines have a similar pricing system – namely that ticket prices rise with the number of seats sold on each flight, so book as early as possible to get a decent fare.

Some low-cost carriers (Ryanair being the prime example) have made a habit of flying to smaller, less convenient airports on the outskirts of their destination city, or even to the airports of nearby cities, so check the exact location of the departure and arrival airports before you book.

Departure and other taxes (including booking fees, checked-baggage fees and other surcharges) soon add up and are included in the final price by the end of the online booking process – usually a lot more than you were hoping to pay – but with careful choosing and advance booking you can get excellent deals.

In the face of competition from low-cost airlines, many national carriers have decided to drop their prices and/or offer special deals. Some, such as British Airways, have even adopted the low-cost model of online booking, where the customer can opt to buy just a one-way flight, or can piece together their own return journey from two one-way legs.

For a comprehensive overview of which low-cost carriers fly to or from which European cities, check out the excellent www.flycheapo.com.

Air Passes

Various travel agencies and airlines offer air passes, such as SAS's **Visit Scandinavia/Nordic Air Pass** (www.flysas.com). Check with your travel agent for current promotions.

EUROPE'S BORDER CROSSINGS

Border formalities have been relaxed in most of the EU, but still exist in all their original bureaucratic glory in the more far-flung parts of Eastern Europe.

In line with the Schengen Agreement, there are officially no passport controls at the borders between Austria, Belgium, Czech Republic, Denmark, Estonia, Finland, France, Germany, Greece, Hungary, Iceland, Italy, Hungary, Latvia, Liechtenstein, Lithuania, Luxembourg, Malta, the Netherlands, Norway, Poland, Portugal, Slovakia, Slovenia, Spain, Sweden and Switzerland. Sometimes, however, there are spot checks on trains crossing borders, so always have your passport. The UK, which is an EU country but a nonsignatory to Schengen, maintains border controls over traffic from other EU countries (except Ireland, with which it shares an open border), although there is no customs control.

Bulgaria, Croatia, Cyprus and Romania are also prospective Shengen area members – for up-to-date details see www.schengenvisainfo.com.

Most borders in Eastern Europe will be crossed via train, where border guards board the train and go through compartments checking passengers' papers. It is rare to get hit up for bribes, but occasionally in Belarus or Moldova you may face a difficulty that can only be overcome with a 'fine'. Travelling between Turkey and Bulgaria typically requires a change of trains and is subject to a lengthy border procedure.

Bicycle

Much of Europe is ideally suited to cycling. Popular cycling areas include the Belgian Ardennes, the west of Ireland, the upper reaches of the Danube in southern Germany and anywhere in the Netherlands, northern Switzerland, Denmark or the south of France. Exploring the small villages of Turkey and Eastern Europe also provides up-close access to remote areas.

A primary consideration on a cycling trip is to travel light, but you should take a few tools and spare parts, including a puncture-repair kit and an extra inner tube. Panniers are essential to balance your possessions on either side of the bike frame. Wearing a helmet is not compulsory in most countries, but is certainly sensible.

Seasoned cyclists can average 80km a day, but it depends on what you're carrying and your level of fitness.

Cyclists' Touring Club (CTC; www.ctc.org.uk) The national cycling association of the UK runs organised trips to Continental Europe.

European Cyclists' Federation (www.ecf.com) Has details of 'EuroVelo', the European cycle network of 12 pan-European cycle routes, plus tips for other tours.

SwitzerlandMobility (www.veloland.ch/en/cycling-in-switzerland.html) Details of Swiss national routes and more.

Rental & Purchase

It is easy to hire bikes throughout most of Europe. Many Western European train stations have bike-rental counters. It is sometimes possible to return the bike at a different outlet so you don't have to retrace your route. Hostels are another good place to find cheap bike hire.

There are plenty of places to buy bikes in Europe, but you'll need a specialist bicycle shop for a bike capable of withstanding a European trip. Cycling is very popular in the Netherlands and Germany, and those countries are good places to pick up a well-equipped touring bicycle.

European prices are quite high (certainly higher than in North America), however non-European residents should be able to claim back value-added tax (VAT) on the purchase.

Transporting a Bicycle

For major cycling trips, it's best to have a bike you're familiar with, so consider bringing your own rather than buying on arrival. If coming from outside Europe, ask about the airline's policy on transporting bikes before buying your ticket.

From the UK to the Continent, Eurostar (the train service through the Channel Tunnel) charges £25 to send a bike as registered luggage on its routes. You can also transport your bicycle with you on Eurotunnel through the Channel Tunnel. With a bit of tinkering and dismantling (eg removing wheels), you might be able to get your bike into a bag or sack and take it on a train as hand luggage.

Alternatively, the **European Bike Express** (www.bike-express.co.uk) is a UK-based coach service where cyclists can travel with their bicycles to various cycling destinations on the Continent.

Once on the Continent, you can put your feet up on the train if you get tired of pedalling or simply want to skip a boring section. On slower trains, bikes can usually be transported as luggage, subject to a small supplementary fee. Some cyclists have reported that Italian and French train attendants have refused bikes on slow trains, so be prepared for regulations to be interpreted differently by officious staff.

Fast trains can rarely accommodate bikes; they might need to be sent as registered luggage and may end up on a different train from the one you take. This is often the case in France and Spain.

Boat

Several different ferry companies compete on the main ferry routes, resulting in a comprehensive but complicated service. The same ferry company can have a host of different prices for the same route, depending on the time of day or year, validity of the ticket and length of your vehicle. Vehicle tickets usually include the driver and often up to five passengers free of charge.

It's worth booking ahead where possible, as there may be special reductions on off-peak crossings and advance-purchase tickets. On English Channel routes, apart from one-day or short-term excursion returns, there is little price advantage in buying a return ticket versus two singles.

Rail-pass holders are entitled to discounts or free travel on some lines. Food on ferries is often expensive (and lousy), so it's worth bringing your own. Also be aware that if you take your vehicle on board, you are usually denied access to it during the voyage.

Lake and river ferry services operate in many countries, Austria and Switzerland being just two. Some of these are very scenic.

Bus

International Buses

Often cheaper than trains, sometimes substantially so, long-distance buses also tend to be slower and less comfortable. However, in Portugal, Greece and Turkey, buses are often a better option than trains.

Europe's biggest organisation of international buses operates under the name **Eurolines** (www.eurolines.com), comprised of various national companies. A **Eurolines Pass** (www.eurolines.com/en/eurolines-pass) is offered for extensive travel, allowing passengers to visit a choice of 53 cities across Europe over 15 or 30 days. In the high season (mid-June to mid-September) the pass costs €315/405 for those aged under 26, or €375/490 for those 26 and over. It's cheaper in other periods.

Busabout (www.busabout.com) offers a 'hop-on, hop-off' service around Europe, stopping at major cities. Buses are often oversubscribed, so book each sector to avoid being stranded. It departs these cities every two days from May to the end of October.

National Buses

Domestic buses provide a viable alternative to trains in most countries. Again, they are usually slightly cheaper and somewhat slower. Buses are generally best for short hops, such as getting around cities and reaching remote villages, and they are often the only option in mountainous regions.

Reservations are rarely necessary. On many city buses you usually buy your ticket in advance from a kiosk or machine and validate it on entering the bus.

Car & Motorcycle

Travelling with your own vehicle gives flexibility and is the best way to reach remote places. However, the independence does sometimes isolate you from local life. Also, cars can be a target for theft and are often impractical in city centres, where traffic jams, parking problems and getting thoroughly lost can make it well worth ditching your vehicle and using public transport. Various car-carrying trains can help you avoid long, tiring drives.

Campervan

One popular way to tour Europe is for a group of three or four people to band together and buy or rent a campervan. London is the usual embarkation point. Look at the ads in London's free magazine **TNT** (www.tntmagazine.com) if you wish to form or join a group. *TNT* is also a good source for purchasing a van, as is **Loot** (www.loot.com).

Some secondhand dealers offer a 'buy-back' scheme for when you return from the Continent, but check the small print before signing anything and remember that if an offer seems too good to be true, it probably is. Buying and reselling privately should be more advantageous if you have time. In the UK, **DU-Insure** (www.duinsure.com) offers a campervan policy.

Fuel

- Fuel prices can vary enormously (though fuel is always more expensive than in North America or Australia).
- Unleaded petrol only is available throughout all of Europe. Diesel is usually cheaper, though the difference is marginal in Britain, Ireland and Switzerland.
- Ireland's Automobile Association maintains a webpage of European fuel prices at www.theaa.ie/AA/Motoring-Advice/Petrol-Prices.aspx.

Leasing

Leasing a vehicle involves fewer hassles than purchasing and can work out much cheaper than hiring for periods longer than 17 days. This program is limited to certain types of new cars, including Renault and Peugeot, but you save money because leasing is exempt from VAT and inclusive insurance plans are cheaper than daily insurance rates.

To lease a vehicle your permanent address must be outside the EU. In the USA, contact **Renault Eurodrive** (www.renault-eurodrive.com) for more information.

Motorcycle Touring

Europe is made for motorcycle touring, with quality winding roads, stunning scenery and an active motorcycling scene. Just make sure your wet-weather motorcycling gear is up to scratch.

- Rider and passenger crash helmets are compulsory everywhere in Europe.
- Austria, Belgium, France, Germany, Luxembourg, Portugal and Spain require that motorcyclists use headlights during the day; in other countries it is recommended.
- On ferries, motorcyclists rarely have to book ahead as they can generally be squeezed on board.
- Take note of the local custom about parking motorcycles on pavements (sidewalks). Though this is illegal in some countries, the police often turn a blind eye provided the vehicle doesn't obstruct pedestrians.

Preparations

Always carry proof of ownership of your vehicle (Vehicle Registration Document for British-registered cars). An EU driving licence is acceptable for those driving through Europe. If you have any other type of licence, you should obtain an International Driving Permit (IDP) from your motoring organisation. Check what type of licence is required in your destination prior to departure.

Third-party motor insurance is compulsory. Most UK policies automatically provide this for EU countries. Get your insurer to issue a Green Card (which may cost extra), an internationally recognised proof of insurance, and check that it lists every country you intend to visit. You'll need this in the event of an accident outside the country where the vehicle is insured.

Also ask your insurer for a European Accident Statement form, which can simplify things if worst comes to worst. Never sign statements that you can't read or understand – insist on a translation and sign it only if it's acceptable.

For non-EU countries, check the requirements with your insurer. Travellers from the UK can obtain additional advice and information from the **Association of British Insurers** (www.abi.org.uk).

Take out a European motoring assistance policy. Non-Europeans might find it cheaper to arrange international coverage with their national motoring organisation before leaving home. Ask your motoring organisation for details about the free services offered by affiliated organisations around Europe.

Every vehicle that travels across an international border should display a sticker indicating its country of registration. A warning triangle, to be used in the event of breakdown, is compulsory almost everywhere.

Some recommended accessories include a first-aid kit (compulsory in Austria, Slovenia, Croatia, Serbia, Montenegro and Greece), a spare bulb kit (compulsory in Spain), a reflective jacket for every person in the car (compulsory in France, Italy and Spain) and a fire extinguisher (compulsory in Greece and Turkey).

Residents of the UK should contact the **RAC** (www.rac.co.uk) or the **AA** (www.theaa.co.uk) for more information. Residents of the US, contact **AAA** (www.aaa.com).

Purchase

Buying a car and then selling it at the end of your European travels may work out to be a better deal than renting one, although this isn't guaranteed and you'll need to do your sums carefully.

The purchase of vehicles in some European countries is illegal for non-nationals or non-EU residents. Britain is probably the best place to buy as second-hand prices are good there. Bear in mind that British cars have steering wheels on the right-hand side. If you wish to have left-hand drive and can afford to buy a new car, prices are generally reasonable in Greece, France, Germany, Belgium, Luxembourg and the Netherlands.

Paperwork can be tricky wherever you buy, and many countries have compulsory roadworthiness checks on older vehicles.

Rental

- Renting a car is ideal for people who will need cars for 16 days or less. Anything longer, it's better to lease.
- Big international rental firms will give you reliable service and good vehicles. National or local firms can often undercut the big companies by up to 40%.
- Usually you will have the option of returning the car to a different outlet at the end of the rental period, but there's normally a charge for this and it can be very steep if it's a long way from your point of origin.
- Book early for the lowest rates and make sure you compare rates in different cities. Taxes range from 15% to 20% and surcharges apply if rented from an airport.
- If you rent a car in the EU you might not be able to take it outside the EU, and if you rent the car outside the EU, you will only be able to drive within the EU for eight days. Ask at the rental agencies for other such regulations.
- Make sure you understand what is included in the price (unlimited or paid kilometres, tax, injury insurance, collision damage waiver etc) and what your liabilities are. We recommend taking the collision damage waiver, though you can probably skip the injury insurance if you and your passengers have decent travel insurance.
- The minimum rental age is usually 21 years and sometimes 25. You'll need a credit card and to have held your licence for at least a year.
- Motorcycle and moped rental is common in some countries, such as Italy, Spain, Greece and southern France.

Road Conditions & Road Rules

- Conditions and types of roads vary across Europe. The fastest routes are generally four- or six-lane highways known locally as motorways, autoroutes, autostrade, autobahnen etc. These tend to skirt cities and plough through the countryside in straight lines, often avoiding the most scenic bits.
- Some highways incur tolls, which are often quite hefty (especially in Italy, France and Spain), but there will always be an alternative route. Motorways and other primary routes are generally in good condition.
- Road surfaces on minor routes are unreliable in some countries (eg Greece, Albania, Romania, Ireland, Russia and Ukraine), although normally they will be more than adequate.
- Except in Britain and Ireland, you should drive on the right. Vehicles brought to the Continent from any of these locales should have their headlights adjusted to avoid blinding oncoming traffic (a simple solution on older headlight lenses is to cover up a triangular section of the lens with tape). Priority is often given to traffic approaching from the right in countries that drive on the right-hand side.
- Speed limits vary from country to country. You may be surprised at the apparent disregard for traffic regulations in some places (particularly in Italy and Greece), but as a visitor it is always best to be cautious. Many driving infringements are subject to an on-the-spot fine. Always ask for a receipt.

- European drink-driving laws are particularly strict. The blood-alcohol concentration (BAC) limit when driving is usually between 0.05% and 0.08%, but in certain areas (such as Gibraltar, Bulgaria and Belarus) it can be zero.

Hitching

Hitching is never entirely safe and we cannot recommend it. Travellers who decide to hitch should understand that they are taking a small but potentially serious risk. It will be safer if they travel in pairs and let someone know where they plan to go.

- A man and woman travelling together is probably the best combination. A woman hitching on her own is taking a larger than normal risk.
- Don't try to hitch from city centres; take public transport to the suburban exit routes.
- Hitching is usually illegal on highways – stand on the slip roads or approach drivers at petrol stations and truck stops.
- Look presentable and cheerful, and make a cardboard sign indicating your intended destination in the local language.
- Never hitch where drivers can't stop in good time or without causing an obstruction.
- It is often possible to arrange a lift in advance: scan student noticeboards in colleges, or check out services such as www.carpooling.co.uk or www.drive2day.de.

HITCHING FOR CASH

In parts of Eastern Europe including Russia, Ukraine and Turkey, traditional hitchhiking is rarely practised. Instead, anyone with a car can be a taxi and it's quite usual to see locals stick their hands out (palm down) on the street, looking to hitch a lift. The difference with hitching here, however, is that you pay for the privilege. You will need to speak the local language (or at least know the numbers) to discuss your destination and negotiate a price.

Local Transport

European towns and cities have excellent local-transport systems, often encompassing trams as well as buses and metro/subway/underground-rail networks.

Most travellers will find areas of interest in European cities can be easily traversed by foot or bicycle. In Greece and Italy, travellers sometimes rent mopeds and motorcycles for scooting around a city or island.

Taxi

Taxis in Europe are metered and rates are usually high. There might also be supplements for things such as luggage, time of day, location of pick-up and any extra passengers.

Good bus, rail and underground-railway networks often render taxis unnecessary, but if you need one in a hurry, they can be found idling near train stations or outside big hotels. Lower fares make taxis more viable in some countries such as Spain, Greece, Portugal and Turkey.

Train

Comfortable, frequent and reliable, trains are *the* way to get around Europe.

- Many state railways have interactive websites publishing their timetables and fares, including www.bahn.de (Germany) and www.sbb.ch (Switzerland), which both have pages in English. **Eurail** (www.eurail.com) links to 28 European train companies.
- The very comprehensive, **The Man in Seat 61** (www.seat61.com) is a gem, while the US-based **Budget Europe Travel Service** (www.budgeteuropetravel.com) can also help with tips.
- European trains sometimes split en route to service two destinations, so even if you're on the right train, make sure you're also in the correct carriage.
- A train journey to almost every station in Europe can be booked via Voyages-sncf.com (http://uk.voyages-sncf.com/en), which also sells InterRail and other passes.

Express Trains

Eurostar (www.eurostar.com) links London's St Pancras International station, via the Channel Tunnel, with Paris' Gare du Nord (2¼ hours, up to 25 a day) and Brussels' international terminal (one hour 50 minutes, up to 12 a day). Some trains also stop at Lille and Calais in France. From December 2016, Eurostar trains will also link Amsterdam Centraal Station with London St Pancras, with stops at Schiphol airport and Rotterdam Centraal Station (and Antwerp and Brussels in Belgium), with an Amsterdam–London journey time of around four hours.

The train stations at St Pancras International, Paris, Brussels and Amsterdam are much more central than the cities' airports. So, overall, the journey takes as little time as the equivalent flight, with less hassle.

Eurostar in London also sells tickets onwards to some Continental destinations. Holders of Eurail and InterRail passes are offered discounts on some Eurostar services; check when booking.

Within Europe, express trains are identified by the symbols 'EC' (EuroCity) or 'IC' (InterCity). The French TGV, Spanish AVE and German ICE trains are even faster, reaching up to 300km/h. Supplementary fares can apply on fast trains (which you often have to pay when travelling on a rail pass), and it is a good idea (sometimes obligatory) to reserve seats at peak times and on certain lines. The same applies for branded express trains, such as the Thalys (between Paris and Brussels, Bruges, Amsterdam and Cologne), and the Eurostar Italia (between Rome and Naples, Florence, Milan and Venice).

If you don't have a seat reservation, you can still obtain a seat that doesn't have a reservation ticket attached to it. Check which destination a seat is reserved for – you might be able to sit in it until the person boards the train.

International Rail Passes

If you're covering lots of ground, you should get a rail pass. But do some price comparisons of point-to-point ticket charges and rail passes beforehand to make absolutely sure you'll break even. Also shop around for rail-pass prices as they do vary between outlets. When weighing up options, look into cheap deals that include advance-purchase reductions, one-off promotions or special circular-route tickets, particularly over the internet.

Normal point-to-point tickets are valid for two months, and you can make as many stops as you like en route; make your intentions known when purchasing and inform train conductors how far you're going before they punch your ticket.

Supplementary charges (eg for some express and overnight trains) and seat reservation fees (mandatory on some trains, a good idea on others) are not covered by rail passes. Always ask. Note that European rail passes also give reductions on Eurostar, the Channel Tunnel and on certain ferries.

Pass-holders must always carry their passport with them for identification purposes. The railways' policy is that passes cannot be replaced or refunded if lost or stolen.

NON-EUROPEAN RESIDENTS

Eurail (www.eurail.com) passes can be bought only by residents of non-European countries and should be purchased before arriving in Europe.

The most comprehensive of the various Eurail passes is the 'Global Pass' covering 28 countries. While the pass is valid on some private train lines in the region, if you plan to travel extensively in Switzerland, be warned that the many private rail networks and cable cars, especially in the Jungfrau region around Interlaken, don't give Eurail discounts. A Swiss Pass or Half-Fare Card might be an alternative or necessary addition.

The pass is valid for a set number of consecutive days or a set number of days within a period of time. Those under 26 years of age can buy a Eurail Youth pass, which only covers travel in 2nd-class compartments. Those aged 26 and over must buy the full-fare Eurail pass, which entitles you to travel 1st class.

Alternatively, there is the Select pass, which allows you to nominate four bordering countries in which you wish to travel, and then buy a pass allowing five, six, eight or 10 travel days in a two-month period. The five- and six-day passes offer an attractive price break, but for more expensive options, the continuous pass becomes better value.

Regional Passes cover two bordering countries, but you might want to ensure that they are good value given your travel plans. There are also Eurail National Passes for just one country.

Two to five people travelling together can get a Saver version of all Eurail passes for a 15% discount.

EUROPEAN RESIDENTS

InterRail (www.interrail.eu) offers passes to European residents for unlimited rail travel through 30 European and North African countries (excluding the pass-holder's country of residence). To qualify as a resident, you must have lived in a European country for six months.

While an InterRail pass will get you further than a Eurail pass along the private rail networks of Switzerland's Jungfrau region (near Interlaken), its benefits are limited. A Swiss Pass or Half-Fare Card might be a necessary addition if you plan to travel extensively in that region.

For a small fee, European residents can buy a Railplus Card, entitling the holder to a 25% discount on many (but not all) international train journeys. It is available from counters in main train stations.

National Rail Passes

National rail operators might also offer their own passes, or at least a discount card, offering substantial reductions on tickets purchased (eg the Bahn Card in Germany or the Half-Fare Card in Switzerland).

Look at individual train operator sites via http://uk.voyages-sncf.com/en/ to check. Such discount cards are usually only worth it if you're staying in the country a while and doing a lot of travelling.

Overnight Trains

There are usually two types of sleeping accommodation: dozing off upright in your seat or stretching out in a sleeper. Again, reservations are advisable, as sleeping options are allocated on a first-come, first-served basis. Couchette bunks are comfortable enough, if lacking in privacy. There are four per compartment in 1st class, six in 2nd class.

Sleepers are the most comfortable option, offering beds for one or two passengers in 1st class, or two or three passengers in 2nd class. Charges vary depending upon the journey, but they are significantly more costly than couchettes.

In the former Soviet Union, the most common options are either 2nd-class *kupeyny* compartments – which have four bunks – or the cheaper *platskartny*, which are open-plan compartments with reserved bunks. This 3rd-class equivalent is not great for those who value privacy.

Other options include the very basic bench seats in *obshchiy* (*zahalney* in Ukrainian) class and 1st-class, two-person sleeping carriages (*myagki* in Russian). In Ukrainian, this last option is known as *spalney*, but is usually abbreviated to CB in Cyrillic (pronounced *es-ve*). First class is not available on every Russian or Ukrainian train.

Security

Sensible security measures include always keeping your bags in sight (especially at stations), chaining them to luggage racks, locking compartment doors overnight and sleeping in compartments with other people. Horror stories are rare.

Language

This chapter offers basic vocabulary to help you get around Europe. Read our coloured pronunciation guides as if they were English, and you'll be understood just fine. The stressed syllables are indicated with italics. Note the use of these abbreviations: (m) for masculine, (f) for feminine, (pol) for polite and (inf) for informal.

ALBANIAN

Note that uh is pronounced as the 'a' in 'ago'. Also, ll and rr in Albanian are pronounced stronger than when they are written as single letters. Albanian is also understood in Kosovo.

Hello.	*Tungjatjeta.*	toon·dya·*tye*·ta
Goodbye.	*Mirupafshim.*	mee·roo·*paf*·sheem
Please.	*Ju lutem.*	yoo *loo*·tem
Thank you.	*Faleminderit.*	fa·le·meen·*de*·reet
Excuse me.	*Më falni.*	muh *fal*·nee
Sorry.	*Më vjen keq.*	muh vyen kech
Yes./No.	*Po./Jo.*	po/yo
Help!	*Ndihmë!*	*ndeeh*·muh
Cheers!	*Gëzuar!*	guh·*zoo*·ar

I don't understand.
Unë nuk kuptoj. — *oo*·nuh nook koop·*toy*

Do you speak English?
A flisni anglisht? — a *flees*·nee ang·*leesht*

How much is it?
Sa kushton? — sa koosh·*ton*

Where's ...?
Ku është ...? — koo *uhsh*·tuh ...

Where are the toilets?
Ku janë banjat? — koo *ya*·nuh *ba*·nyat

BULGARIAN

Note that uh is pronounced as the 'a' in 'ago' and zh as the 's' in 'pleasure'.

Hello.	Здравейте.	zdra·*vey*·te
Goodbye.	Довиждане.	do·*veezh*·da·ne
Please.	Моля.	*mol*·ya
Thank you.	Благодаря.	bla·go·dar·*ya*
Excuse me.	Извинете.	iz·vee·*ne*·te
Sorry.	Съжалявам.	suh·zhal·*ya*·vam
Yes./No.	Да./Не.	da/ne
Help!	Помощ!	*po*·mosht
Cheers!	Наздраве!	na·*zdra*·ve

I don't understand.
Не разбирам. — ne raz·*bee*·ram

Do you speak English?
Говорите ли английски? — go·*vo*·ree·te lee ang·*lees*·kee

How much is it?
Колко струва? — *kol*·ko *stroo*·va

Where's ...?
Къде се намира ...? — kuh·*de* se na·*mee*·ra ...

Where are the toilets?
Къде има тоалетни? — kuh·*de ee*·ma to·a·*let*·nee

CROATIAN & SERBIAN

Croatian and Serbian are very similar and mutually intelligible (and using them you'll also be understood in Bosnia and Hercegovina, Montenegro and parts of Kosovo). In this section the significant differences between Croatian and Serbian are indicated with (C) and (S) respectively. Note that r is rolled and zh is pronounced as the 's' in 'pleasure'.

Hello.	*Dobar dan.*	daw·ber dan
Goodbye.	*Zbogom.*	*zbo*·gom
Please.	*Molim.*	*mo*·lim
Thank you.	*Hvala.*	*hva*·la
Excuse me.	*Oprostite.*	o·*pro*·sti·te
Sorry.	*Žao mi je.*	*zha*·o mi ye
Yes./No.	*Da./Ne.*	da/ne
Help!	*Upomoć!*	*u*·po·moch
Cheers!	*Živjeli!*	*zhi*·vye·li

I don't understand.
Ja ne razumijem. ya ne ra·*zu*·mi·yem

Do you speak English?
Govorite/Govoriš li engleski? (pol/inf) *go*·vo·ri·te/*go*·vo·rish li *en*·gle·ski

How much is it?
Koliko stoji/košta? (C/S) ko·*li*·ko *sto*·yi/*kosh*·ta

Where's ...?
Gdje je ...? gdye ye ...

Where are the toilets?
Gdje se nalaze zahodi/toaleti? (C/S) gdye se *na*·la·ze *za*·ho·di/to·a·*le*·ti

CZECH

An accent mark over a vowel in written Czech indicates it's pronounced as a long sound. Note that oh is pronounced as the 'o' in 'note', uh as the 'a' in 'ago', and kh as the 'ch' in the Scottish *loch*. Also, r is rolled in Czech and the apostrophe (') indicates a slight y sound.

Hello.	*Ahoj.*	*uh*·hoy
Goodbye.	*Na shledanou.*	*nuh*·skhle·duh·noh
Please.	*Prosím.*	*pro*·seem
Thank you.	*Děkuji.*	*dye*·ku·yi
Excuse me.	*Promiňte.*	*pro*·min'·te
Sorry.	*Promiňte.*	*pro*·min'·te
Yes./No.	*Ano./Ne.*	*uh*·no/ne
Help!	*Pomoc!*	*po*·mots
Cheers!	*Na zdraví!*	nuh *zdruh*·vee

I don't understand.
Nerozumím. *ne*·ro·zu·meem

Do you speak English?
Mluvíte anglicky? *mlu*·vee·te *uhn*·glits·ki

How much is it?
Kolik to stojí? *ko*·lik to *sto*·yee

Where's ...?
Kde je ...? gde ye ...

Where are the toilets?
Kde jsou toalety? gde ysoh *to*·uh·le·ti

DANISH

All vowels in Danish can be long or short. Note that aw is pronounced as in 'saw', and ew as the 'ee' in 'see' with rounded lips.

Hello.	*Goddag.*	go·*da*
Goodbye.	*Farvel.*	faar·*vel*
Please.	*Vær så venlig.*	ver saw *ven*·lee
Thank you.	*Tak.*	taak
Excuse me.	*Undskyld mig.*	*awn*·skewl mai
Sorry.	*Undskyld.*	*awn*·skewl
Yes./No.	*Ja./Nej.*	ya/nai
Help!	*Hjælp!*	yelp
Cheers!	*Skål!*	skawl

I don't understand.
Jeg forstår ikke. yai for·*stawr i*·ke

Do you speak English?
Taler De/du engelsk? (pol/inf) *ta*·la dee/doo *eng*·elsk

How much is it?
Hvor meget koster det? vor *maa*·yet *kos*·ta dey

Where's ...?
Hvor er ...? vor ir ...

Where's the toilet?
Hvor er toilettet? vor ir toy·*le*·tet

DUTCH

It's important to distinguish between the long and short versions of each vowel sound. Note that ew is pronounced as the 'ee' in 'see' with rounded lips, oh as the 'o' in 'note', uh as the 'a' in 'ago', and kh as the 'ch' in the Scottish *loch* (harsh and throaty).

Hello.	*Dag.*	dakh
Goodbye.	*Dag.*	dakh
Please.	*Alstublieft.*	al·stew·*bleeft*
Thank you.	*Dank u.*	dangk ew
Excuse me.	*Pardon.*	par·*don*
Sorry.	*Sorry.*	*so*·ree
Yes./No.	*Ja./Nee.*	yaa/ney
Help!	*Help!*	help
Cheers!	*Proost!*	prohst

I don't understand.
Ik begrijp het niet. ik buh·*khreyp* huht neet

Do you speak English?
Spreekt u Engels? spreykt ew *eng*·uhls

How much is it?
Hoeveel kost het? hoo·*veyl* kost huht

Where's ...?
Waar is ...? waar is ...

Where are the toilets?
Waar zijn de toiletten? waar zeyn duh twa·*le*·tuhn

ESTONIAN

Double vowels in written Estonian indicate they are pronounced as long sounds. Note that air is pronounced as in 'hair'.

Hello.	*Tere.*	*te*·re
Goodbye.	*Nägemist.*	*nair*·ge·mist
Please.	*Palun.*	*pa*·lun
Thank you.	*Tänan.*	*tair*·nan
Excuse me.	*Vabandage.* (pol)	*va*·ban·da·ge
	Vabanda. (inf)	*va*·ban·da
Sorry.	*Vabandust.*	*va*·ban·dust
Yes./No.	*Jaa./Ei.*	yaa/ay
Help!	*Appi!*	*ap*·pi
Cheers!	*Terviseks!*	*tair*·vi·seks

I don't understand.
Ma ei saa aru. ma ay saa *a*·ru

Do you speak English?
Kas te räägite inglise keelt? kas te *rair*·git·te *ing*·kli·se keylt

How much is it?
Kui palju see maksab? *ku*·i *pal*·yu sey *mak*·sab

Where's ...?
Kus on ...? kus on ...

Where are the toilets?
Kus on WC? kus on *ve*·se

FINNISH

In Finnish, double consonants are held longer than their single equivalents. Note that ew is pronounced as the 'ee' in 'see' with rounded lips, and uh as the 'u' in 'run'.

Hello.	*Hei.*	hay
Goodbye.	*Näkemiin.*	*na*·ke·meen
Please.	*Ole hyvä.*	o·le *hew*·va
Thank you.	*Kiitos.*	*kee*·tos
Excuse me.	*Anteeksi.*	*uhn*·tayk·si
Sorry.	*Anteeksi.*	*uhn*·tayk·si
Yes./No.	*Kyllä./Ei.*	*kewl*·la/ay
Help!	*Apua!*	*uh*·pu·uh
Cheers!	*Kippis!*	*kip*·pis

I don't understand.
En ymmärrä. en *ewm*·mar·ra

Do you speak English?
Puhutko englantia? *pu*·hut·ko *en*·gluhn·ti·uh

How much is it?
Mitä se maksaa? *mi*·ta se *muhk*·saa

Where's ...?
Missä on ...? *mis*·sa on ...

Where are the toilets?
Missä on vessa? *mis*·sa on *ves*·suh

FRENCH

The French r sound is throaty. French also has nasal vowels (pronounced as if you're trying to force the sound through the nose), indicated here with o or u followed by an almost inaudible nasal consonant sound m, n or ng. Syllables in French words are, for the most part, equally stressed.

Hello.	*Bonjour.*	bon·zhoor
Goodbye.	*Au revoir.*	o·rer·vwa
Please.	*S'il vous plaît.*	seel voo play
Thank you.	*Merci.*	mair·see
Excuse me.	*Excusez-moi.*	ek·skew·zay·mwa
Sorry.	*Pardon.*	par·don
Yes./No.	*Oui./Non.*	wee/non
Help!	*Au secours!*	o skoor
Cheers!	*Santé!*	son·tay

I don't understand.
Je ne comprends pas. zher ner kom·pron pa

Do you speak English?
Parlez-vous anglais? par·lay·voo ong·glay

How much is it?
C'est combien? say kom·byun

Where's ...?
Où est ...? oo ay ...

Where are the toilets?
Où sont les toilettes? oo son ley twa·let

GERMAN

Note that aw is pronounced as in 'saw', ew as the 'ee' in 'see' with rounded lips, while kh and r are both throaty sounds in German.

Hello.		
(in general)	*Guten Tag.*	*goo*·ten taak
(Austria)	*Servus.*	*zer*·vus
(Switzerland)	*Grüezi.*	*grew*·e·tsi
Goodbye.	*Auf Wiedersehen.*	owf *vee*·der·zey·en
Please.	*Bitte.*	*bi*·te
Thank you.	*Danke.*	*dang*·ke
Excuse me.	*Entschuldigung.*	ent·*shul*·di·gung
Sorry.	*Entschuldigung.*	ent·*shul*·di·gung
Yes./No.	*Ja./Nein.*	yaa/nain
Help!	*Hilfe!*	*hil*·fe
Cheers!	*Prost!*	prawst

I don't understand.
Ich verstehe nicht. ikh fer·*shtey*·e nikht

Do you speak English?
Sprechen Sie Englisch? *shpre*·khen zee *eng*·lish

How much is it?
Wie viel kostet das? vee feel *kos*·tet das

Where's ...?
Wo ist ...? vaw ist ...

Where are the toilets?
Wo ist die Toilette? vo ist dee to·a·*le*·te

GREEK

Note that dh is pronounced as the 'th' in 'that', and that gh and kh are both throaty sounds, similar to the 'ch' in the Scottish *loch*.

Hello.	Γεια σου.	yia su
Goodbye.	Αντίο.	a·*di*·o
Please.	Παρακαλώ.	pa·ra·ka·*lo*
Thank you.	Ευχαριστώ.	ef·kha·ri·*sto*
Excuse me.	Με συγχωρείτε.	me sing·kho·*ri*·te
Sorry.	Συγνώμη.	si·*ghno*·mi
Yes./No.	Ναι./Οχι.	ne/*o*·hi
Help!	Βοήθεια!	vo·*i*·thia
Cheers!	Στην υγειά μας!	stin i·*yia* mas

I don't understand.
Δεν καταλαβαίνω. dhen ka·ta·la·*ve*·no

Do you speak English?
Μιλάς Αγγλικά; mi·*las* ang·gli·*ka*

How much is it?
Πόσο κάνει; *po*·so *ka*·ni

Where's ...?
Που είναι ...; pu *i*·ne ...

Where are the toilets?
Που είναι η τουαλέτα; pu *i*·ne i tu·a·*le*·ta

HUNGARIAN

A symbol over a vowel in written Hungarian indicates it's pronounced as a long sound. Double consonants should be drawn out a little longer than in English. Note that aw is pronounced as in 'law', eu as the 'u' in 'nurse', and ew as 'ee' with rounded lips. Also, r is rolled in Hungarian and the apostrophe (') indicates a slight y sound.

Hello. (to one person)
Szervusz. *ser*·vus

Hello. (to more than one person)
Szervusztok. *ser*·vus·tawk

Goodbye.	*Viszlát.*	*vis*·lat
Please.	*Kérem.* (pol) *Kérlek.* (inf)	*key*·rem *keyr*·lek
Thank you.	*Köszönöm.*	*keu*·seu·neum
Excuse me.	*Elnézést kérek.*	*el*·ney·zeysht *key*·rek
Sorry.	*Sajnálom.*	*shoy*·na·lawm
Yes.	*Igen.*	*i*·gen
No.	*Nem.*	nem
Help!	*Segítség!*	*she*·geet·sheyg

Cheers! (to one person)
Egészségedre! *e*·geys·shey·ged·re

Cheers! (to more than one person)
Egészségetekre! *e*·geys·shey·ge·tek·re

I don't understand.
Nem értem. nem *eyr*·tem

Do you speak English?
Beszél/Beszélsz angolul? (pol/inf) *be*·seyl/*be*·seyls *on*·gaw·lul

How much is it?
Mennyibe kerül? *men'*·nyi·be *ke*·rewl

Where's ...?
Hol van a ...? hawl von o ...

Where are the toilets?
Hol a vécé? hawl o *vey*·tsey

ITALIAN

The r sound in Italian is rolled and stronger than in English. Most other consonants can have a more emphatic pronounciation too (in which case they're written as double letters).

Hello.	*Buongiorno.*	bwon·*jor*·no
Goodbye.	*Arrivederci.*	a·ree·ve·*der*·chee
Please.	*Per favore.*	per fa·*vo*·re
Thank you.	*Grazie.*	*gra*·tsye
Excuse me.	*Mi scusi.* (pol) *Scusami.* (inf)	mee *skoo*·zee *skoo*·za·mee
Sorry.	*Mi dispiace.*	mee dees·*pya*·che
Yes.	*Sì.*	see
No.	*No.*	no
Help!	*Aiuto!*	ai·*yoo*·to
Cheers!	*Salute!*	sa·*loo*·te

I don't understand.
Non capisco. non ka·*pee*·sko

Do you speak English?
Parla inglese? *par*·la een·*gle*·ze

How much is it?
Quant'è? kwan·*te*

Where's ... ?
Dov'è ... ? do·*ve* ...

Where are the toilets?
Dove sono i gabinetti? *do*·ve *so*·no ee ga·bee·*ne*·tee

LATVIAN

A line over a vowel in written Latvian indicates it's pronounced as a long sound. Note that air is pronounced as in 'hair', ea as in 'ear', wa as in 'water', and dz as the 'ds' in 'adds'.

Hello.	*Sveiks.*	svayks
Goodbye.	*Atā.*	a·taa
Please.	*Lūdzu.*	*loo*·dzu
Thank you.	*Paldies.*	*pal*·deas
Excuse me.	*Atvainojiet.*	*at*·vai·nwa·yeat
Sorry.	*Piedodiet.*	*pea*·dwa·deat
Yes./No.	*Jā./Nē.*	yaa/nair
Help!	*Palīgā!*	pa·lee·gaa
Cheers!	*Priekā!*	*prea*·kaa

I don't understand.
Es nesaprotu. es *ne*·*sa*·prwa·tu

Do you speak English?
Vai Jūs runājat angliski? vai yoos ru·*naa*·yat *ang*·li·ski

How much is it?
Cik maksā? tsik mak·*saa*

Where's ...?
Kur ir ...? kur ir ...

Where are the toilets?
Kur ir tualetes? kur ir *tu*·a·le·tes

LITHUANIAN

Symbols on vowels in written Lithuanian indicate that they're pronounced as long sounds. Note that ow is pronounced as in 'how'.

Hello.	*Sveiki.*	svay·*ki*
Goodbye.	*Viso gero.*	*vi*·so *ge*·ro
Please.	*Prašau.*	pra·*show*
Thank you.	*Ačiū.*	*aa*·choo
Excuse me.	*Atleiskite.*	at·*lays*·ki·te
Sorry.	*Atsiprašau.*	at·si·pra·*show*
Yes./No.	*Taip./Ne.*	taip/ne
Help!	*Padėkit!*	pa·*dey*·kit
Cheers!	*Į sveikatą!*	ee svay·*kaa*·taa

I don't understand.
Aš nesuprantu. ash ne·su·pran·*tu*

Do you speak English?
Ar kalbate angliškai? ar *kal*·ba·te *aang*·lish·kai

How much is it?
Kiek kainuoja? keak kain·*wo*·ya

Where's ...?
Kur yra ...? kur ee·*ra* ...

Where are the toilets?
Kur yra tualetai? kur ee·*ra* tu·a·*le*·tai

MACEDONIAN

Note that r is pronounced as a rolled sound in Macedonian.

Hello.	Здраво.	*zdra*·vo
Goodbye.	До гледање.	do *gle*·da·nye
Please.	Молам.	*mo*·lam
Thank you.	Благодарам.	bla·*go*·da·ram
Excuse me.	Извинете.	iz·*vi*·ne·te
Sorry.	Простете.	*pros*·te·te
Yes./No.	Да./Не.	da/ne
Help!	Помош!	*po*·mosh
Cheers!	На здравје!	na *zdrav*·ye

I don't understand.
Јас не разбирам. yas ne *raz*·bi·ram

Do you speak English?
Зборувате ли англиски? zbo·*ru*·va·te li *an*·glis·ki

How much is it?
Колку чини тоа? *kol*·ku *chi*·ni *to*·a

Where's ...?
Каде е ...? *ka*·de e ...

Where are the toilets?
Каде се тоалетите? *ka*·de se to·a·*le*·ti·te

NORWEGIAN

In Norwegian, each vowel can be either long or short. Generally, they're long when followed by one consonant and short when followed by two or more consonants. Note that aw is pronounced as in 'law', ew as 'ee' with pursed lips, and ow as in 'how'.

Hello.	*God dag.*	go·*daag*
Goodbye.	*Ha det.*	*haa*·de
Please.	*Vær så snill.*	veyr saw snil
Thank you.	*Takk.*	tak
Excuse me.	*Unnskyld.*	*ewn*·shewl
Sorry.	*Beklager.*	bey·*klaa*·geyr
Yes./No.	*Ja./Nei.*	yaa/ney
Help!	*Hjelp!*	yelp
Cheers!	*Skål!*	skawl

I don't understand.
Jeg forstår ikke. yai fawr·*stawr* *i*·key

Do you speak English?
Snakker du engelsk? *sna*·ker doo *eyng*·elsk

How much is it?
Hvor mye koster det? vor *mew*·e kaws·ter de

Where's ...?
Hvor er ...? vor ayr ...

Where are the toilets?
Hvor er toalettene? vor eyr to·a·*le*·te·ne

POLISH

Polish vowels are generally pronounced short. Nasal vowels are pronounced as though you're trying to force the air through your nose, and are indicated with n or m following the vowel. Note also that r is rolled in Polish.

Hello.	*Cześć.*	cheshch
Goodbye.	*Do widzenia.*	do vee·*dze*·nya
Please.	*Proszę.*	*pro*·she
Thank you.	*Dziękuję.*	jyen·*koo*·ye
Excuse me.	*Przepraszam.*	pshe·*pra*·sham
Sorry.	*Przepraszam.*	pshe·*pra*·sham
Yes./No.	*Tak./Nie.*	tak/nye
Help!	*Na pomoc!*	na *po*·mots
Cheers!	*Na zdrowie!*	na *zdro*·vye

I don't understand.
Nie rozumiem. — nye ro·*zoo*·myem

Do you speak English?
Czy pan/pani mówi po angielsku? (m/f) — chi pan/*pa*·nee *moo*·vee po an·*gyel*·skoo

How much is it?
Ile to kosztuje? — ee·le to kosh·*too*·ye

Where's ...?
Gdzie jest ...? — gjye yest ...

Where are the toilets?
Gdzie są toalety? — gjye som to·*a*·*le*·ti

PORTUGUESE

Most vowel sounds in Portuguese have a nasal version (ie pronounced as if you're trying to force the sound through your nose), which is indicated in our pronunciation guides with ng after the vowel.

Hello.	*Olá.*	o·*laa*
Goodbye.	*Adeus.*	a·de·*oosh*
Please.	*Por favor.*	poor fa·*vor*
Thank you.	*Obrigado.* (m)	o·bree·*gaa*·doo
	Obrigada. (f)	o·bree·*gaa*·da
Excuse me.	*Faz favor.*	faash fa·*vor*
Sorry.	*Desculpe.*	desh·*kool*·pe
Yes./No.	*Sim./Não.*	seeng/nowng
Help!	*Socorro!*	soo·*ko*·rroo
Cheers!	*Saúde!*	sa·*oo*·de

I don't understand.
Não entendo. — nowng eng·*teng*·doo

Do you speak English?
Fala inglês? — *faa*·la eeng·*glesh*

How much is it?
Quanto custa? — *kwang*·too *koosh*·ta

Where's ...?
Onde é ...? — *ong*·de e ...

Where are the toilets?
Onde é a casa de banho? — *ong*·de e a *kaa*·za de *ba*·nyoo

ROMANIAN

Note that ew is pronounced as the 'ee' in 'see' with rounded lips, uh as the 'a' in 'ago', and zh as the 's' in 'pleasure'. The apostrophe (') indicates a very short, unstressed (almost silent) i. Moldovan is the official name of the variety of Romanian spoken in Moldova.

Hello.	*Bună ziua.*	*boo*·nuh *zee*·wa
Goodbye.	*La revedere.*	la re·ve·*de*·re
Please.	*Vă rog.*	vuh rog
Thank you.	*Mulţumesc.*	mool·tsoo·*mesk*
Excuse me.	*Scuzaţi-mă.*	skoo·*za*·tsee·muh
Sorry.	*Îmi pare rău.*	ewm' *pa*·re *ruh*·oo
Yes./No.	*Da./Nu.*	da/noo
Help!	*Ajutor!*	a·zhoo·*tor*
Cheers!	*Noroc!*	no·*rok*

I don't understand.
Eu nu înţeleg. — *ye*·oo noo ewn·tse·*leg*

Do you speak English?
Vorbiţi engleza? — vor·*beets'* en·*gle*·za

How much is it?
Cât costă? — kewt *kos*·tuh

Where's ...?
Unde este ...? — *oon*·de *yes*·te ...

Where are the toilets?
Unde este o toaletă? — oon·*de yes*·te o to·a·*le*·tuh

RUSSIAN

Note that zh is pronounced as the 's' in 'pleasure'. Also, r is rolled in Russian and the apostrophe (') indicates a slight y sound.

Hello.	Здравствуйте.	*zdrast*·vuyt·ye
Goodbye.	До свидания.	da svee·*dan*·ya
Please.	Пожалуйста.	pa·*zhal*·sta
Thank you.	Спасибо	spa·*see*·ba
Excuse me./ Sorry.	Извините, пожалуйста.	eez·vee·*neet*·ye pa·*zhal*·sta
Yes./No.	Да./Нет.	da/nyet
Help!	Помогите!	pa·ma·*gee*·tye
Cheers!	Пей до дна!	pyey da dna

I don't understand.
Я не понимаю. — ya nye pa·nee·*ma*·yu

Do you speak English?
Вы говорите по-английски? — vi ga·va·*reet*·ye pa·an·*glee*·skee

How much is it?
Сколько стоит? — *skol'*·ka *sto*·eet

Where's ...?
Где (здесь) ...? — gdye (zdyes') ...

Where are the toilets?
Где здесь туалет? — gdye zdyes' tu·al·*yet*

SLOVAK

An accent mark over a vowel in written Slovak indicates it's pronounced as a long sound. Note also that uh is pronounced as the 'a' in 'ago', and kh as the 'ch' in the Scottish *loch*. The apostrophe (') indicates a slight y sound.

Hello.	*Dobrý deň.*	*do*·bree dyen'
Goodbye.	*Do videnia.*	do *vi*·dye·ni·yuh
Please.	*Prosím.*	*pro*·seem
Thank you.	*Ďakujem*	*dyuh*·ku·yem
Excuse me.	*Prepáčte.*	*pre*·pach·tye
Sorry.	*Prepáčte.*	*pre*·pach·tye
Yes./No.	*Áno./Nie.*	a·no/*ni*·ye
Help!	*Pomoc!*	*po*·mots
Cheers!	*Nazdravie!*	*nuhz*·druh·vi·ye

I don't understand.
Nerozumiem. — *nye*·ro·zu·myem

Do you speak English?
Hovoríte po anglicky? — *ho*·vo·ree·tye po *uhng*·lits·ki

How much is it?
Koľko to stojí? — *kol'*·ko *to sto*·yee

Where's ...?
Kde je ...? — kdye ye

Where are the toilets?
Kde sú tu záchody? — kdye soo tu *za*·kho·di

SLOVENE

Note that r is pronounced as a rolled sound in Slovene.

Hello.	*Zdravo.*	*zdra*·vo
Goodbye.	*Na svidenje.*	na *svee*·den·ye
Please.	*Prosim.*	*pro*·seem
Thank you.	*Hvala.*	*hva*·la
Excuse me.	*Dovolite.*	do·vo·*lee*·te
Sorry.	*Oprostite.*	op·ros·*tee*·te
Yes./No.	*Da./Ne.*	da/ne
Help!	*Na pomoč!*	na po·*moch*
Cheers!	*Na zdravje!*	na *zdrav*·ye

I don't understand.
Ne razumem. — ne ra·*zoo*·mem

Do you speak English?
Ali govorite angleško? — a·lee go·vo·*ree*·te ang·*lesh*·ko

How much is it?
Koliko stane? — ko·lee·ko *sta*·ne

Where's ...?
Kje je ...? — kye ye ...

Where are the toilets?
Kje je stranišče? — kye ye stra·*neesh*·che

SPANISH

Note that the Spanish r is strong and rolled, th is pronounced 'with a lisp', and v is soft, pronounced almost like a 'b'.

Hello.	*Hola.*	*o*·la
Goodbye.	*Adiós.*	a·*dyos*
Please.	*Por favor.*	por fa·*vor*
Thank you.	*Gracias.*	*gra*·thyas
Excuse me.	*Perdón.*	per·*don*
Sorry.	*Lo siento.*	lo *syen*·to
Yes./No.	*Sí./No.*	see/no
Help!	*¡Socorro!*	so·*ko*·ro
Cheers!	*¡Salud!*	sa·*loo*

I don't understand.
Yo no entiendo. — yo no en·*tyen*·do

Do you speak English?
¿Habla/Hablas inglés? (pol/inf) — *a*·bla/*a*·blas een·*gles*

How much is it?
¿Cuánto cuesta? — *kwan*·to *kwes*·ta

Where's ...?
¿Dónde está ...? — *don*·de es·*ta* ...

Where are the toilets?
¿Dónde están los servicios? — *don*·de es·*tan* los ser·*vee*·thyos

SWEDISH

Swedish vowels can be short or long – generally the stressed vowels are long, except when followed by double consonants. Note that aw is pronounced as in 'saw', air as in 'hair', eu as the 'u' in 'nurse', ew as the 'ee' in 'see' with rounded lips, and oh as the 'o' in 'note'.

Hello.	*Hej.*	hey
Goodbye.	*Hej då.*	hey daw
Please.	*Tack.*	tak
Thank you.	*Tack.*	tak
Excuse me.	*Ursäkta mig.*	oor·*shek*·ta mey
Sorry.	*Förlåt.*	feur·*lawt*
Yes./No.	*Ja./Nej.*	yaa/ney
Help!	*Hjälp!*	yelp
Cheers!	*Skål!*	skawl

I don't understand.
Jag förstår inte. yaa feur·*shtawr in*·te

Do you speak English?
Talar du engelska? *taa*·lar doo *eng*·el·ska

How much is it?
Hur mycket kostar det? hoor *mew*·ke *kos*·tar de

Where's ...?
Var finns det ...? var finns de ...

Where are the toilets?
Var är toaletten? var air toh·aa·*le*·ten

TURKISH

Double vowels are pronounced twice in Turkish. Note also that eu is pronounced as the 'u' in 'nurse', ew as the 'ee' in 'see' with rounded lips, uh as the 'a' in 'ago', r is rolled and v is a little softer than in English.

Hello.	*Merhaba.*	*mer*·ha·ba
Goodbye.	*Hoşçakal.* (when leaving)	hosh·*cha*·kal
	Güle güle. (when staying)	gew·*le* gew·*le*
Please.	*Lütfen.*	*lewt*·fen
Thank you.	*Teşekkür ederim.*	te·shek·*kewr* e·*de*·reem
Excuse me.	*Bakar mısınız.*	ba·*kar* muh·suh·*nuhz*
Sorry.	*Özür dilerim.*	eu·*zewr* dee·*le*·reem
Yes./No.	*Evet./Hayır.*	e·*vet*/*ha*·yuhr
Help!	*İmdat!*	*eem*·dat
Cheers!	*Şerefe!*	she·re·*fe*

I don't understand.
Anlamıyorum. an·*la*·muh·yo·room

Do you speak English?
İngilizce konuşuyor musunuz? een·gee·*leez*·je ko·noo·*shoo*·yor moo·soo·*nooz*

How much is it?
Ne kadar? ne ka·dar

Where's ...?
... nerede? ... *ne*·re·de

Where are the toilets?
Tuvaletler nerede? too·va·let·*ler ne*·re·de

UKRAINIAN

Ukrainian vowels in unstressed syllables are generally pronounced shorter and weaker than they are in stressed syllables. Note that ow is pronounced as in 'how' and zh as the 's' in 'pleasure'. The apostrophe (') indicates a slight y sound.

Hello.	Добрий день.	*do*·bry den'
Goodbye.	До побачення.	do po·*ba*·chen·nya
Please.	Прошу.	*pro*·shu
Thank you.	Дякую.	*dya*·ku·yu
Excuse me.	Вибачте.	*vy*·bach·te
Sorry.	Перепрошую.	pe·re·*pro*·shu·yu
Yes./No.	Так./Ні.	tak/ni
Help!	Допоможіть!	do·po·mo·*zhit'*
Cheers!	Будьмо!	*bud'*·mo

I don't understand.
Я не розумію. ya ne ro·zu·*mi*·yu

Do you speak English?
Ви розмовляєте англійською мовою? vy roz·mow·*lya*·ye·te an·*hliys'*·ko·yu *mo*·vo·yu

How much is it?
Скільки це він/вона коштує? (m/f) *skil'*·ki tse vin/vo·*na* *ko*·shtu·ye

Where's ...?
Де ...? de ...

Where are the toilets?
Де туалети? de tu·a·*le*·ti

Behind the Scenes

SEND US YOUR FEEDBACK

We love to hear from travellers – your comments keep us on our toes and help make our books better. Our well-travelled team reads every word on what you loved or loathed about this book. Although we cannot reply individually to your submissions, we always guarantee that your feedback goes straight to the appropriate authors, in time for the next edition. Each person who sends us information is thanked in the next edition – the most useful submissions are rewarded with a selection of digital PDF chapters.

Visit **lonelyplanet.com/contact** to submit your updates and suggestions or to ask for help. Our award-winning website also features inspirational travel stories, news and discussions.

Note: We may edit, reproduce and incorporate your comments in Lonely Planet products such as guidebooks, websites and digital products, so let us know if you don't want your comments reproduced or your name acknowledged. For a copy of our privacy policy visit lonelyplanet.com/privacy.

OUR READERS

Many thanks to the travellers who used the last edition and wrote to us with helpful hints, useful advice and interesting anecdotes:

Andy Leerock, Balawyn Jones, Charlie Merry, Felicity Milanovic, Jukka Sutinen, Renata Buarque, Stewart Gray, Tami Vibberstoft, Tine Declerck

AUTHOR THANKS

Alexis Averbuck

For my work on Greece, honour to Alexandra Stamopoulou for always-insightful tips and overall INSPIRATION. Margarita, Kostas and Zisis, and Anthy and Costas made Athens feel like home. Cindy Camatsos generously shared Mytilini (Lesvos) secrets and John Diakostamatis the sights and adoration of Samos. My work on Iceland was a labour of love supported by many helping hands. Big thanks to Carolyn Bain, an unstintingly generous collaborator. Yva and John became inspiring family. Ryan was, as always, a peachy partner in crime.

Carolyn Bain

At Lonely Planet, my thanks to DE Gemma Graham. Big bouquets to Cristian Bonetto, my genius co-author on the full guide to Denmark. Heartfelt gratitude goes to my Danish family, the Østergaards – your warm welcomes and generosity in Skagen, Sunds and Svendborg mean the world to me. To all the Danes who rented me apartments, answered my questions, indulged my Eurovision fixation, and generally made this trip such a joy: *tusind tak*.

Mark Baker

In Lithuania, I would like to thank my friends Simona and Doug for tips on dining and drinking in Vilnius. Indraja Germanaite was kind enough to show me around beautiful Trakai and the amazing Curonian Spit. Evelina Vanclovaite introduced me to new places in Kaunas. In the Czech Republic where I live, I would like to thank my friend Katerina Pavlitova at Prague City Tourism. In Poland, friends Beata Szulęcka and Olga Brzezinska helped me to research Warsaw and Kraków. For Romania: in Timișoara, the crew at Hostel Costel. In Cluj-Napoca, photographer Crina Prida and Madalina Stanescu at the Fabrica de Pensule. In Sighișoara, dear friends Raluca and Mark Tudose. Finally, in Moldova, Diana Railean's enthusiasm for Chişinău was infectious.

Kerry Christiani

A heartfelt *obrigada* to the warm, generous, kind-natured people of Portugal, who made the road to research delightfully smooth. Big thanks in particular to designer and all-round Lisbon connoisseur Jorge Moita and SIC TV journalist Rui Pedro Reis in Lisbon. Special thanks, too, to the Porto pros, especially Cristina Azevedo and

Alexandra Santos. André at We Hate Tourism Tours and André at Taste Porto Food Tours were also stars, giving me the inside scoop on their beautiful city. A big *dankeschön* to all of the locals and super-efficient tourism professionals who made the road to research a breeze, especially the teams in Vienna, Innsbruck, Graz and Salzburg. I'd also like to thank my Vienna friends Chiara and Karin for good times and invaluable tips. Finally, thanks go to Christoph Unterkofler at Villa Trapp for taking time out to tell me the truth about one of Austria's most fascinating families.

Marc Di Duca

Huge *dyakuyu* goes to Kyiv parents-in-law Mykola and Vira for looking after sons Taras and Kirill while I was on the road. Big thanks to Markiyan in Lviv, all the staff at the Lviv tourist office and of course my wife, Tanya, for suffering my long absences from our home in Sandwich, Kent.

Peter Dragicevich

It's a special treat to be able to meet up with friends on the road. On this trip I was lucky enough to have Kaspars Zalitis and his crew show me all of their favourite haunts in their hometown of Rīga. And many thanks to Ivica Erdelja for accompanying me on the road in Montenegro.

Mark Elliott

Many thanks to Kate, Amra Begić, Miloš at Srebrenica, Jan, Boro, Branislav, Nermina, Davor at Matuško, Sanja in Banja Luka, Shoba and Leslie for the most remarkable series of coincidences, and the Aussie bridge divers (hope you survived). Endless thanks to my ever inspiring parents who, four decades ago, had the crazy idea of driving me to Bosnia in the first place.

Steve Fallon

In Hungary, my thanks to Bea Szirti and Ildikó Nagy Moran for company and suggestions. On the road, I am indebted to András Cseh (Eger), Zsuzsi Fábián (Kecskemét) and Shandor Madachy (Budapest). *Nagyon szépen köszönöm mindenkinek!* In Slovenia, *najlepša hvala* to the fab trio at the Ljubljana Tourist Board (Petra Stušek, Tatjana Radovič and Verica Leskovar) and Saša Špolar at the Slovenian Tourist Board. Along the way, hats off to Andreja Frelih and David May (Piran), Aleš Hvala (Kobarid) and Kellie and Peter Gasperin (Bohinj). It was a delight spending time with old mates Domen and Barbara Kalajžič in Bled, especially with my partner, Michael Rothschild, in tow.

Emilie Filou

Thanks to friends and family who chipped in with recommendations and joined in the research fun. Thanks also to my husband, Adolfo, for everything.

Duncan Garwood

Thanks to everyone who helped with tips and recommendations, and to the staff of Italy's tourist offices, in particular Cristina Bernasconi in Como, Manuel Testi in Ravenna, Francesca Piseddu in Milan and Michela Dibiasi in Genoa. *Grazie* also to the EDT crew in Turin; Antonello and Dora in Genoa; and Viviana in Bologna. As always, a big, heartfelt thank you to Lidia and the boys, Ben and Nick.

Anthony Ham

Special thanks to Gemma Graham, Jo Cooke, Stuart Butler, Donna Wheeler, Miles Roddis, Itziar Herrán, Francisco Palomares, Miguel Ángel Simón, Astrid Vargas and to so many Spaniards and Norwegians who were unfailingly helpful ambassadors for their country – I am deeply grateful to all of them. And it gets harder with each journey to be away from my family – to Marina, Carlota and Valentina, heartfelt thanks for enduring my absences. *Os quiero.*

Catherine Le Nevez

Hartelijk bedankt first and foremost to Julian, and to everyone throughout the Netherlands who provided insights, information and good times. *Dank u wel* in particular to Joris Rotsaert and Pamela Sturhoofd. Huge thanks too to Destination Editor Kate Morgan and all at LP. As ever, *merci encore* to my parents, brother, *belle-sœur* and *neveu*.

Jessica Lee

Big thanks to fellow authors on the *Turkey* guide: James Bainbridge, Brett Atkinson, Stuart Butler, Steve Fallon, Will Gourlay and Virginia Maxwell, and particularly to Jo Cooke. And a huge *çok teşekkürler* to Ömer Yapıs, Kazım and Ayşe Akay and Bekir Kırca, Ömer and Ahmet in Kaş, Meral and Yakup Kahveci.

Tom Masters

Thanks to Catherine Bohne, Ardi Pulaj, Dmitry Sakharov, Lena Durham, Amy Sedaris, Vesna Maric, Jan Morris, Svetlana Alliluyeva and Edith Durham, all of whom accompanied me in some form on this journey through the Balkans and Belarus.

Anja Mutić

Hvala mama, for your inspiring laughter. *Obrigada* Hoji, for being there before, during and after. A huge *hvala* to my friends in Croatia who gave me endless recommendations – this book wouldn't be the same without you. Special thanks go to Mila in Split. Finally, to the inspiring memory of my father who travels with me still.

Sally O'Brien

Thanks to Kate Morgan for the assignment, and LP authors Nicola Williams, Kerry Christiani and Gregor Clark (for fab footprints to follow), plus all the in-house staff that made this guidebook a reality.

Becky Ohlsen

Thanks to *Sweden* co-authors Anna Kaminski and Josephine Quintero for their great work, and especially to destination editor Gemma Graham; always a pleasure to work with.

Simon Richmond

Many thanks to my fellow authors and Brana at HQ; Sasha and Andrey for a lovely place to stay, the ever knowledgeable Peter Kozyrev, Chris Hamilton, Adelya Dayanova, Polina Adrianova, Dimitri Ozerkov, Vladimir Stolyarov, Yegor Churakov, Oksana, Maxim Pinigin, Alexander Kim, Maria Isserlis and Yevgenia Semenoff.

Andrea Schulte-Peevers

Big heartfelt thanks to all these wonderful people who've plied me with tips, insights, lodging and encouragement (in no particular order): Anke Gerber and Guido, Holm Friedrich, Guido Neumann, Tomas Kaiser, Andreas Gerber and Heinz, Walter Schulte, Kirsten Schmidt, Henrik Tidefjärd, Susan Paterson, Miriam Bers, Claudia Scheffler, Regine Schneider, Frank Engster, Heiner and Claudia Schuster, Renate Freiling, Silke Neumann.

Tamara Sheward

Hvala/blagodarya to the combined populations of Serbia and Bulgaria: your warm-hearted ways and inspired lunacy make it harder for me to leave the Balkans every time. Specifically, thanks and *rakija/rakia* clinks go out to the Lučić family, Dragana Eremić, Gvozden Marinković, Tsvetelina, Alexander and Tanya, Hristo, Andy, kum Ćomi, Nikola and Djordje, Gordana and Srdjan, and the brilliant Brana Vladisavljević. *Naravno, najviše se zahvaljujem mojim partnerima u kriminalu Dušanu i Maši!*

Helena Smith

Thanks to Anne and friends for all their help in Brussels first time around, and to the friendly Use-It crew.

Andy Symington

I owe a large *kiitos* to many across Finland for help on my frequent visits; thanks too to *Finland* co-author Catherine Le Nevez, destination editor Gemma Graham, my parents for constant support and to the friends who keep things ticking over at home during my frequent absences.

Luke Waterson

A hearty *ďakujem* to Erik Ševčik in Poprad – I hope one day all tour operators are as informative and helpful. Thanks go out to the myriad late-night taxi drivers, train restaurant car staff, cafe waiters and tourist information representatives that got me from A to B and helped me out when I got there. Finally, appreciative nods to the knowledgeable girls of the Human Rights League in Bratislava: how would I have discovered half the city hangouts I've listed without you?

Neil Wilson

Many thanks to all the helpful and enthusiastic staff at tourist information centres throughout Britain and Ireland, and to the many travellers I met on the road who chipped in with advice and recommendations. Thanks also to Carol Downie, and to Steven Fallon and Keith Jeffrey, Steve Hall, Russell Leaper, Brendan Bolland, Jenny Neil and Tom and Christine Duffin. Finally, many thanks to all my co-authors and to the ever-helpful and patient editors and cartographers at Lonely Planet.

ACKNOWLEDGMENTS

Climate map data adapted from Peel MC, Finlayson BL & McMahon TA (2007) 'Updated World Map of the Köppen-Geiger Climate Classification', *Hydrology and Earth System Sciences*, 11, 1633–44.

Cover photograph: Village in the Alsace region, France. Danita Delimont Stock/AWL ©

THIS BOOK

This 1st edition of Lonely Planet's *Europe* guidebook was researched and written by Alexis Averbuck, Carolyn Bain, Mark Baker, Kerry Christiani, Marc Di Duca, Peter Dragicevich, Mark Elliott, Steve Fallon, Emilie Filou, Duncan Garwood, Anthony Ham, Catherine Le Nevez, Jessica Lee, Tom Masters, Anja Mutić, Sally O'Brien, Becky Ohlsen, Simon Richmond, Andrea Schulte-Peevers, Tamara Sheward, Helena Smith, Andy Symington, Luke Waterson and Neil Wilson.

This guidebook was produced by the following:

Destination Editors Jo Cooke, Gemma Graham, Kate Morgan, James Smart, Anna Tyler, Branislava Vladisavljevic

Senior Cartographer Valentina Kremenchutskaya

Product Editors Elin Berglund, Jenna Myers, Amanda Williamson

Book Designer Wibowo Rusli

Assisting Editors Sarah Bailey, Michelle Bennett, Andrea Dobbin, Carly Hall, Kellie Langdon, Jodie Martire, Anne Mulvaney, Rosie Nicholson, Kristin Odijk, Charlotte Orr, Susan Paterson, Monique Perrin, Erin Richards, Kathryn Rowan, Kirsten Rawlings, Saralinda Turner, Jeanette Wall

Assisting Cartographer Alison Lyall

Assisting Book Designer Mazzy Prinsep

Cover Researcher Naomi Parker

Thanks to Brendan Dempsey, Ryan Evans, Anna Harris, Kate James, Elizabeth Jones, Claire Naylor, Karyn Noble, Katie O'Connell, Martine Power, Angela Tinson, Dianne Schallmeiner, Luna Soo, Gabrielle Stefanos, Lauren Wellicome, Tony Wheeler

Index

Map Pages **000**
Photo Pages 000

C

Map Pages **000**
Photo Pages **000**

Map Pages **000**
Photo Pages **000**

D

E

Map Pages **000**
Photo Pages **000**

Map Pages **000**
Photo Pages **000**

M

Map Pages **000**
Photo Pages **000**

Map Pages **000**
Photo Pages **000**

Map Pages **000**
Photo Pages 000

T

Map Pages **000**
Photo Pages **000**

Map Pages **000**
Photo Pages 000

Map Legend

Sights

- Beach
- Bird Sanctuary
- Buddhist
- Castle/Palace
- Christian
- Confucian
- Hindu
- Islamic
- Jain
- Jewish
- Monument
- Museum/Gallery/Historic Building
- Ruin
- Shinto
- Sikh
- Taoist
- Winery/Vineyard
- Zoo/Wildlife Sanctuary
- Other Sight

Activities, Courses & Tours

- Bodysurfing
- Diving
- Canoeing/Kayaking
- Course/Tour
- Sento Hot Baths/Onsen
- Skiing
- Snorkelling
- Surfing
- Swimming/Pool
- Walking
- Windsurfing
- Other Activity

Sleeping

- Sleeping
- Camping

Eating

- Eating

Drinking & Nightlife

- Drinking & Nightlife
- Cafe

Entertainment

- Entertainment

Shopping

- Shopping

Information

- Bank
- Embassy/Consulate
- Hospital/Medical
- Internet
- Police
- Post Office
- Telephone
- Toilet
- Tourist Information
- Other Information

Geographic

- Beach
- Gate
- Hut/Shelter
- Lighthouse
- Lookout
- Mountain/Volcano
- Oasis
- Park
- Pass
- Picnic Area
- Waterfall

Population

- Capital (National)
- Capital (State/Province)
- City/Large Town
- Town/Village

Transport

- Airport
- Border crossing
- Bus
- Cable car/Funicular
- Cycling
- Ferry
- Metro station
- Monorail
- Parking
- Petrol station
- S-Bahn/S-train/Subway station
- Taxi
- T-bane/Tunnelbana station
- Train station/Railway
- Tram
- Tube station
- U-Bahn/Underground station
- Other Transport

Note: Not all symbols displayed above appear on the maps in this book

Routes

- Tollway
- Freeway
- Primary
- Secondary
- Tertiary
- Lane
- Unsealed road
- Road under construction
- Plaza/Mall
- Steps
- Tunnel
- Pedestrian overpass
- Walking Tour
- Walking Tour detour
- Path/Walking Trail

Boundaries

- International
- State/Province
- Disputed
- Regional/Suburb
- Marine Park
- Cliff
- Wall

Hydrography

- River, Creek
- Intermittent River
- Canal
- Water
- Dry/Salt/Intermittent Lake
- Reef

Areas

- Airport/Runway
- Beach/Desert
- Cemetery (Christian)
- Cemetery (Other)
- Glacier
- Mudflat
- Park/Forest
- Sight (Building)
- Sportsground
- Swamp/Mangrove

Andrea Schulte-Peevers

Germany Born and raised in Germany, and educated in London and at UCLA, Andrea has travelled the distance to the moon and back in her visits to some 75 countries and now makes her home in Berlin. She's written about her native country for two decades and authored or contributed to some 80 Lonely Planet titles, including all editions of the *Germany* country guide and the *Berlin* city guide.

Tamara Sheward

Bulgaria, Serbia After years of freelance travel writing, rock'n'roll journalism and insalubrious authordom, Tamara joined Lonely Planet's ranks as the presenter of LPTV's *Roads Less Travelled: Cambodia* documentary. Since then she's stuck to covering decidedly less leech-infested destinations including Russia, Serbia and Bulgaria. Tamara is currently living in Australia's far north with her husband (whom she never would have met were it not for some late night 'researching') and daughter.

Helena Smith

Belgium, Luxembourg Helena Smith is the author of Lonely Planet's *Pocket Brussels & Bruges*, and was very glad to return to Europe's most eccentric country to work on this guide, as well as adding Luxembourg to her list of countries visited. When not travel writing, Helena writes about food and community at www.eathackney.com.

Andy Symington

Finland Andy has covered Finland for Lonely Planet several times, having first visited Helsinki many years ago more or less by accident. Walking on frozen lakes with the midday sun low in the sky made a quick and deep impression on him, even as his fingers froze in the -30°C temperatures. Since then he can't stay away, fuelled by a love of wilderness hiking, the Kalevala, huskies, saunas, Finnish mustard, moody Suomi rock and metal, but above all the Finnish people and their beautiful country.

Luke Waterson

Slovakia Luke fell in love with Slovakia and these days lives in its quirky capital, Bratislava, beside vineyards that yield some of the country's finest white wines. He's constantly planning hikes into Slovakia's forests and hills – particularly if they go via a ruined castle or a rustic *krčma* (pub). As well as writing a bunch of content about Slovakia for LP and the BBC, he also runs the quirky travel/culture blog on all things Slovak: www.englishmaninslovakia.com.

Neil Wilson

Britain, Ireland Neil was born in Scotland and, save for a few years spent abroad, has lived there most of his life; he is based near Dunkeld in Perthshire. An enduring passion for the great outdoors has inspired hillwalking, mountain-biking and sailing expeditions to every corner of Britain and Ireland. Neil has been a full-time author since 1988 and has written more than 70 guidebooks for various publishers, including Lonely Planet guides to Scotland, England and Ireland.

Catherine Le Nevez

The Netherlands Catherine's wanderlust kicked in when she first roadtripped across Europe, including the Netherlands, aged four, and she's been returning to this spirited, *gezellig* country ever since, completing her Doctorate of Creative Arts in Writing, Masters in Professional Writing, and post-grad qualifications in Editing and Publishing along the way. Catherine has worked as a freelance writer for many years and during the past decade or so she's written scores of Lonely Planet guidebooks and articles covering destinations all over Europe and beyond.

Jessica Lee

Turkey Jessica first came to Turkey in 2005 and ended up leading adventure tours across the breadth of Anatolia for four years. In 2011 she moved there to live and now calls Turkey home. As a co-author on the last two editions of Lonely Planet's *Turkey* guide she's travelled to most of Turkey's far-flung corners but especially loves the wild landscapes of the southeast, the ruin-strewn trails of the Lycian Way and the wacky rock formations of Cappadocia. She tweets @jessofarabia.

Tom Masters

Albania, Belarus, Kosovo, Macedonia Tom has been travelling in Eastern Europe since the early '90s when, as a young teenager, he travelled by train across the newly liberated 'Eastern Bloc' with his mother, an experience not unlike a Graham Greene novel. Having studied Russian, lived in St Petersburg and currently residing in the former East Berlin, Tom knows this part of the world like few others, though it constantly manages to surprise him. You can find more of his work at www.tommasters.net.

Anja Mutić

Croatia It's been more than two decades since Anja left her native Croatia. The journey took her to several countries before she made New York City her base 15 years ago. But the roots are a-calling. She's been returning to Croatia frequently for work and play, intent on discovering a new place on every visit, be it a nature park, an offbeat town or a remote island. She's happy that Croatia's beauties are appreciated worldwide but secretly longs for the time when you could head to Hvar and hear the sound of crickets instead of blasting music. Anja is online at www.everthenomad.com.

Sally O'Brien

Liechtenstein, Switzerland Since moving to Switzerland in 2007, Sally has revelled in swimming the country's lakes and rivers, snowboarding down its astounding mountains, scoffing its cheese and chocolate, and quaffing local-secret wines. Writing about this dreamy country for Lonely Planet and heading out on the road with her family to explore every last corner of her adopted home only adds to the fun.

Becky Ohlsen

Sweden A huge fan of Stockholm, Becky has spent enough time in the capital city to know where to find the no-fee public toilets but not quite enough to have absorbed any of its impressive fashion sense. Maybe next time. She also loves hiking the northern Swedish woods and stumbling over relics of the Viking age. Though raised in the mountains of Colorado, Becky has been exploring Sweden since childhood, while visiting her grandparents and other relatives.

Simon Richmond

Russia UK-born writer and photographer Simon first set foot on the continent on a family holiday to Mallorca in the 1970s. Many subsequent trips across Europe have followed with work assignments to, among other places, Portugal, Belgium, Turkey, Russia and the Baltic states. He first visited Russia in 1994, spending time in St Petersburg and Moscow and travelling by train from there to Central Asia. He's since travelled the breadth of the nation from Kamchatka in the east to Kaliningrad in the far west, stopping off at many points between. An award-winning travel writer and photographer, Simon has co-authored the last four editions of the *Russia* guide for Lonely Planet, as well as the first three editions of the *Trans-Siberian Railway* guide. Follow him on Twitter, Instagram and at www.simonrichmond.com. Simon also wrote the Plan and Survive chapters.

Marc Di Duca

Ukraine Driven by an urge to discover Eastern Europe's wilder side, Marc first hit Kyiv one dark, snow-flecked night in early 1998. Many prolonged stints, countless near misses with Kyiv's metro doors and a few too many rides in seatbelt-less Lada taxis later, he still gets excited about exploring this immense but troubled land. A busy travel writer, Marc has penned guides to Moscow, Siberia's Lake Baikal, Russia and the Trans-Siberian Railway, as well as countless other destinations around Europe.

Peter Dragicevich

Estonia, Latvia, Montenegro After a dozen years working for newspapers and magazines in both his native New Zealand and in Australia, Peter ditched the desk and hit the road. He wrote Lonely Planet's first guide to the newly independent Montenegro and has contributed to literally dozens of other Lonely Planet titles, including the *Estonia, Latvia & Lithuania* guidebook and four successive editions of *Europe on a Shoestring*.

Mark Elliott

Bosnia & Hercegovina British born travel writer Mark Elliott was only 11 when his family first dragged him to Sarajevo and stood him in the now defunct concrete footsteps of Gavrilo Princip. Fortunately no Austro-Hungarian emperors were passing at the time. He has since visited virtually every corner of BiH, supping fine Hercegovinian wines with master vintners, talking philosophy with Serb monks and Sufi mystics, and drinking more Bosnian coffee than any stomach should be subjected to.

Steve Fallon

Hungary, Slovenia Steve, who has written every edition of Lonely Planet's *Hungary* guidebook, lived in Budapest for three years in the early 1990s. From there he also researched and later wrote LP's first *Slovenia* guidebook. He maintains close contacts with both countries, returning often to Magyarország for thermal baths, Tokaj wine and *bableves* (bean soup) and to Slovenija for a glimpse of the Julian Alps in the sunshine, a dribble of *bučno olje* (pumpkinseed oil) and a dose of the dual. Find out more about Steve at www.steveslondon.com.

Emilie Filou

France Emilie was born in Paris and spent most of her childhood holidays roaming the south of France. She now lives in London, where she works as a freelance journalist specialising in development issues in Africa. She still goes to France every year for holidays and loves feasting on local market products, especially cheese and wine. See more of Emilie's work on www.emiliefilou.com; she tweets at @emiliefilou.

Duncan Garwood

Italy Duncan is a British travel writer based near Rome. Since he moved to Italy in 1997, he has travelled extensively in his adopted homeland and worked on about 30 Lonely Planet guides, including *Rome*, *Sardinia*, *Sicily* and *Italy's Best Trips*. Memories from his most recent trip include a barbecue in a Palermo street market and catching an open-air concert in Trieste's vast central piazza.

Anthony Ham

Norway, Spain Spain and Norway are two of Anthony's great loves. In 2001, Anthony (www.anthonyham.com) fell in love with Madrid on his first visit to the city. Less than a year later, he arrived on a one-way ticket, with not a word of Spanish and not knowing a single person. After ten years living in the city, he recently returned to Australia with his Spanish-born family, but he still adores his adopted country as much as the first day he arrived. And he fell in love with Norway the first time he laid eyes on her and there aren't many places in Norway he hasn't been, from Lindesnes in the south to the remote fjords of Svalbard in the far north.

OUR STORY

A beat-up old car, a few dollars in the pocket and a sense of adventure. In 1972 that's all Tony and Maureen Wheeler needed for the trip of a lifetime – across Europe and Asia overland to Australia. It took several months, and at the end – broke but inspired – they sat at their kitchen table writing and stapling together their first travel guide, *Across Asia on the Cheap*. Within a week they'd sold 1500 copies. Lonely Planet was born.

Today, Lonely Planet has offices in Franklin, London, Melbourne, Oakland, Beijing and Delhi, with more than 600 staff and writers. We share Tony's belief that 'a great guidebook should do three things: inform, educate and amuse'.

OUR WRITERS

Alexis Averbuck

Greece, Iceland Alexis lives in Hydra, Greece, takes regular reverse R&R in Athens, and makes any excuse she can to travel the isolated back roads of her adopted land. Also a self-proclaimed glacier geek, Alexis loves exploring Iceland: from surreal lava fields and sparkling fjords to ice-blue glacier tongues. A travel writer for two decades, Alexis has lived in Antarctica for a year, crossed the Pacific by sailboat and written books on her journeys through Asia and the Americas. She's also a painter. Visit www.alexisaverbuck.com.

Carolyn Bain

Denmark Melbourne-based Carolyn has been involved with Lonely Planet's *Europe on a Shoestring* title since she worked as an editor on its inaugural edition back in 1999. She has been listed as a contributing author on the eight editions since. Destinations covered over the years include Greece, Malta, Sweden and Estonia. For this book, Carolyn wrote on Denmark, a country dear to her heart, after living in the centre of it for a year as a teenager. See www.carolynbain.com.au.

Mark Baker

Czech Republic, Lithuania, Moldova, Poland, Romania Mark Baker is an independent travel writer based in Prague. He's lived in Central Europe for more than 20 years, working as a writer and editor for the *Economist*, Bloomberg and Radio Free Europe/Radio Liberty, and is an enthusiastic traveller throughout the region. He's author of several Lonely Planet guides, including *Prague & the Czech Republic*, *Estonia, Latvia & Lithuania*, *Romania & Bulgaria*, *Poland* and *Slovenia*. Tweet him @markbakerprague.

Kerry Christiani

Austria, Portugal Ever since her first post-grad trip to Austria, Kerry has seized every available chance to travel back to the country of Mozart, Maria and co. Hanging out in the cream of Vienna's coffee houses, road-testing Christmas markets and glimpsing the first snow of the season in the Alps were highlights this edition. Her love affair with Portugal began as a child hiking the cliffs of the Algarve. She's returned countless times since, and remains captivated by this country's creative spirit and beautifully melancholic soul. Kerry has authored/co-authored around two dozen travel guides, including Lonely Planet *Austria*, *Pocket Lisbon* and *Pocket Porto*. She tweets @kerrychristiani and lists her latest work at www.kerrychristiani.com.

OVER PAGE MORE WRITERS

Published by Lonely Planet Publications Pty Ltd
.BN 36 005 607 983
st edition – October 2015
SBN 978 1 74321 469 5

0 9 8 7 6 5 4 3 2 1
rinted in Singapore